522 - 08 - 19

KU-260-071

Only British Airways offers the cha-cha-chance to fly direct to seven Latin American destinations.

With at least twice-weekly flights from the UK to Rio de Janeiro, Sao Paulo, Buenos Aires, Santiago, Caracas, Bogota and Mexico City, no other airline takes you direct to more Central and South American gateways than British Airways.

For more information call 0345 222111, or tango along to your travel agent.

BRITISH AIRWAYS
The world's favourite airline

Correct at time of going to press.

Before you read this book we'd like you to know that ...

TRAILFINDERS ✈

THE TRAVEL EXPERTS

★ has some of the best-value airfares available worldwide

★ offers up to 65% *exclusive* discount on selected hotel accommodation worldwide

★ offers complete travel service including immunisation, travel insurance, map and book shop, travellers' library and Visa Shop

★ provides a comprehensive booking and information service on behalf of all the best overland adventure and expedition operators

★ is fully Government licensed and bonded

For information on Mexico, Central America or any other worldwide destination, contact us at:

42-50 Earls Court Road, London W8 6EJ
071-938 3366

56-58 Deansgate, Manchester M3 2FF
061-839 6969

48 Corn Street, Bristol BS1 1HQ
0272-299 000

254-284 Sauchiehall Street, Glasgow G2 3EH
041-353 2224

OPEN 7 DAYS A WEEK
MON - SAT 9am - 6pm, THURS 9am - 7pm & SUN 10am - 4pm

ABTA 69701   IATA   ATOL 1458

1995

MEXICO & CENTRAL AMERICAN HANDBOOK

FIFTH EDITION

Editor **Ben Box**
Assistant Editor **Sarah Cameron**
Cartographer **Sebastian Ballard**

...for a tropical Corinth arises before me
in the gleam of the sun and the fondness of the water.
Green plumes of the palm trees. Far off,
rough with antiquity, solemn with myth,
stands the stone tribe of old volcanoes
which, like all else, await their instant of infinity.
Rubén Darío *Noon*
Translated by Lysander Kemp from 'Medio Día',
Intermetzzo Tropical

2 *eoup*
4988   2404   0206
4810

TRADE & TRAVEL
Handbooks

Trade & Travel Publications Ltd
6 Riverside Court, Lower Bristol Road, Bath BA2 3DZ, England
Telephone 01225 469141 Fax 01225 469461

©Trade & Travel Publications Ltd., September 1994

ISBN 0 900751 53 3   ISSN 0965-5492

CIP DATA: A catalogue record for this book is available from the British Library

All rights reserved. No part of this publication may be reproduced, stored in a
retrieval system, or transmitted, in any form or by any means, electronic,
mechanical, photocopying, recording, or otherwise, without the prior
permission of Trade & Travel Publications Ltd.

In North America, published by

PASSPORT BOOKS
a division of *NTC Publishing Group*

4255 West Touhy Avenue
Lincolnwood (Chicago), Illinois 60646-1975, USA

ISBN 0-8442-8977-9

Library of Congress Catalog Card Number 94-66058

Passport Books and colophon are registered trademarks of NTC Publishing Group

**WARNING: While every endeavour is made to ensure that the facts
printed in this book are correct at the time of going to press, travellers
are cautioned to obtain authoritative advice from consulates, airlines,
etc, concerning current travel and visa requirements and conditions
before embarking. The publishers cannot accept legal responsibility for
errors, however caused, that are printed in this book.**

Cover illustration by Suzanne Evans

Printed and bound in Great Britain by Clays Ltd., Bungay, Suffolk

CONTENTS

4

PREFACE

As this edition goes to press, Mexico is preparing for a presidential election. The 1994 campaign has been seriously affected by the uprising of the Ejército Zapatista de Liberación Nacional in Chiapas in January and the assassination of the Partido Revolucionario Institucional candidate, Luis Donaldo Colosio, in Tijuana in March. Neither issue has been resolved. The EZLN rejected the peace accord drawn up with the government peace commissioner, who subsequently resigned. The motive for Colosio's murder has not been officially established. Because we know from the letters we receive that Chiapas is one of the most frequently-visited parts of Mexico, we hope that solutions are found rapidly, not only to ensure trouble-free tourism, but also for the benefit of the people of the region.

A climate of uncertainty also surrounds Guatemala, another popular tourist destination. Apart from a general sense of political malaise, two attacks on US women, blamed without evidence for being involved in child kidnapping, led the US State Department to issue a strict travel advisory against Guatemala. Travellers should, of course, be aware of events before embarking on a journey. However, our regular subeditor, Peter Pollard, noted in mid-1994 that tourism was being quite badly affected, especially from the USA, with fewer backpackers than usual. But, he said, with the usual precautions, travellers should not be discouraged. Except for the two instances mentioned above (whose causes are still in dispute), there is no anti-foreigner element in the problems. In over 1,500 km of car travel, the Pollard family was not stopped once by military or police and encountered no problems.

In addition, an Australian traveller, Janet Arnold, wrote in early 1994: 'Guatemala is...a very friendly country. I could not believe, for example, how we could board a bus, leave our bags up one end, sit at the other, and at the end of the four-hour journey they'd still be there...The majority of people were very eager to help us out and particularly helpful whenever I practised my Spanish.'

Responsible tourism has always been contrasted with mass tourism in terms of both effect on the environment and financial returns to local people and government. This debate has recently come to the fore in Costa Rica where the development of protected areas and nature-based tourism was formerly held up as a model for other countries to follow. Many people involved in ecotourism have expressed concern at a change in government policy aimed at attracting mass tourism projects. It is to be hoped that any attempt to develop Costa Rica as a mass tourism destination does not threaten areas already set aside for conservation and unique habitats not yet protected.

For this edition we have received considerable help from John Gibbs, resident in Mexico City, who researched the Colima region, José-Luis Juárez and Charlotte Roberts-Wray, also of Mexico City; Peter Pollard, who travelled in Guatemala in April 1994; Huw Clough and Kate Hennessy, who subedited El Salvador, Honduras, Nicaragua and Panama; John Lewis, for hotel and other information; Kevin Healey, for new details on Panama; Mathias Hock, for a thorough review of the Nicaragua chapter; and Jorge Valle-Aguiluz, for his annual update on Honduras. We are also grateful to the many travellers who have sent us corrections, suggestions and new material on the basis of their visits to the region. For transferring all this material on to disk, we should like to thank Debbie Wylde, Jo Burdall, Celia Fletcher and Lorraine Horler.

The Editor

THE EDITOR

Ben Box

A doctorate in medieval Spanish and Portugese studies provided very few job prospects for Ben Box, but a fascination for all things Latin. While studying for his degree, Ben travelled extensively in Spain and Portugal. He turned his attention to contemporary Iberian and Latin American affairs in 1980, beginning a career as a freelance writer at that time. He contributed regularly to national newspapers and learned tomes, and became editor of the first *Mexico & Central American Handbook* in 1991. During his frequent visits to the region he has travelled from the US/Mexico border to southern Chile (not all in one go) and in the Caribbean. Nevertheless, Ben recognises that there are always more places to explore. He also edits the *South American Handbook* and jointly edits the *Caribbean Islands Handbook* with Sarah Cameron. To seek diversion from a household immersed in Latin America, he plays village cricket in summer and cycles the lanes of Suffolk.

HOW TO USE THIS HANDBOOK

The Mexico and Central American Handbook is the most complete and up-to-date package of information for independent travellers on Mexico and the Central American republics currently in print. Its text is updated every year for the new edition which is published on 1 September. The text is based on the Editors' travels, contributions from national tourist authorities, notes from correspondents living in the countries we cover, detailed material and maps which Handbook users send us, and the extensive sources of information on Latin America available in London and elsewhere.

Editorial Logic Users of the Handbook will find that we employ a logical system of arrangement, which we believe is the most useful for travellers. The capital city is (with 2 exceptions, Mexico—dictated by geography, and Panama) the first place covered in detail. The territory is then divided into subsections; in Mexico, Guatemala and Costa Rica, these subsections are numbered on the country contents and map as well as in the text. In the subsections, towns appear in sequence along a route, which falls within the natural geography of the region. The routes cover the most interesting places to visit and do not necessarily constitute the shortest possible distance from A to B. Details are also given of any interesting excursions or other sights that are off the route. Travellers can therefore plan their own itineraries according to the time available, and their own special interests.

Cross Referencing and Indexing There is a complete index at the end of the book. Personalities as well as place names and sites of interest are now included. The key used is as follows: Archaeological site ▲; Beach or Marine Resort ♠; Colonial City ♣; Festival (religious or otherwise) ☆; Historical site ✳; Inland Resort ❋; Market or Traditional Shopping ✿; National Park, Natural Feature, Recommended Zoological or Botanical Garden ◆; People ▢.

To make it easier for Readers to find their way around the text, we have a comprehensive system of cross references. For ease of use, the 'see p' (page) entry has been highlighted in heavier type. On the page referred to, you will find the entry again emphasised in some form of heavier type.

Maps Three types are used:

A. Country Maps These appear at the start of each country chapter and show main access routes (not necessarily major roads in all cases), main towns, and divisions of the country as described in the text. These divisions are numbered on the map, in the country's contents list and at the text divisions in the chapter. The numbers are not recommendations as to which parts of the country are most interesting to visit, they are only for easy identification.

B. Regional Maps These give extra information on a more detailed scale and show the main physical features, towns, means of communication and points of interest.

C. City and Town Maps Generally these are detailed maps of town centres, showing means of access to bus and railway stations and airports. The main points of interest are indicated by means of a numbered key.

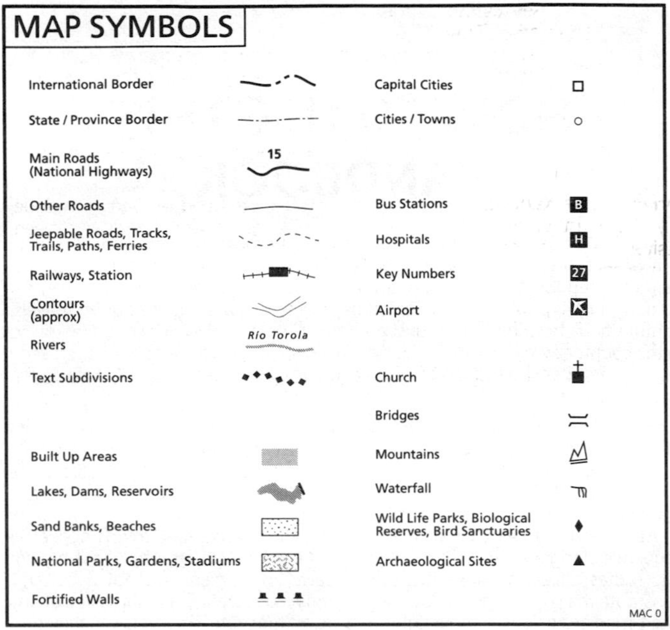
MAP SYMBOLS
International Border
State / Province Border
Main Roads (National Highways)
15
Other Roads
Jeepable Roads, Tracks, Trails, Paths, Ferries
Railways, Station
Contours (approx)
Rivers
Río Torola
Text Subdivisions
Built Up Areas
Lakes, Dams, Reservoirs
Sand Banks, Beaches
National Parks, Gardens, Stadiums
Fortified Walls
Capital Cities
Cities / Towns
Bus Stations
B
Hospitals
H
Key Numbers
27
Airport
Church
Bridges
Mountains
Waterfall
Wild Life Parks, Biological Reserves, Bird Sanctuaries
Archaeological Sites
MAC 0

Introduction and Hints This first section in the book gives information and hints that apply generally to all the countries we cover on:

- ❑ travel to and in Latin America ❑ language
- ❑ Miami ❑ photography
- ❑ money ❑ surface transport
- ❑ law enforcement ❑ hitchhiking
- ❑ security ❑ motoring and motorcycling
- ❑ responsible tourism ❑ hiking and trekking
- ❑ travelling with children ❑ cycling
- ❑ camping

Health Information This major section by Dr David Snashall of St Thomas's Hospital Medical School, London, gives details of the health risks common in Mexico and Central America, and the sensible precautions travellers should take to combat them.

Country Sections Information is set out country by country in a constant sequence as follows:

- ❑ List of contents
- ❑ Description of physical geography
  - history — people
  - economy — present form of government
- ❑ Survey of Cities, Towns and places of interest
  - things to do — things worth seeing
  - where to stay — eating out

services for visitors
❑ Information for visitors
what documents are necessary   how to get there
food   health precautions
the best time for visiting   clothing
currency regulations   other essential information

All those readers who have written with valuable updating material are listed with
thanks at the end of each chapter.

Hotels and Restaurants In large cities, lists of hotels and restaurants include
only those establishments for which positive recommendations have been
received. In smaller towns, these lists contain both the favourable
recommendations and others. In general, restaurants are grouped by
neighbourhood and by type of cuisine.

Prices Our hotel price ranges, for double rooms with taxes and service charges
but without meals unless stated, are as follows:

L+—Over US$200	**L**—US$125-$200	**A+**—US$71-125
A—US$46-70	**B**—US$31-45	**C**—US$21-30
D—US$12-20	**E**—US$7-11	**F**—US$4-6
G—Up to US$3		

Other abbreviations used in the book (apart from pp = per person; a/c = air
conditioned; rec = recommended; T = telephone; TCs = travellers' cheques; s/n
= 'sin número', no street number) should be self-explanatory.

We are also grateful to those travellers, listed below, who have sent us important information
for the 'Introduction and Hints' section which follows: Elizabeth Allison (Powys) & Sebastian
Cooper (Monmouth, Gwent), Jens Arnold (Borken, Germany), Daniel Daeniker (Zurich,
Switzerland) Andrew Dobbie (Swansea), Markus Eberl (Bonn, Germany) Lionel Ehinger
(Geneva, Switzerland), Hilary Emberton (Slough, Berks), Armin Fricke & Jasmin Troll (Berlin),
Paul Gowen (RAC, South Croyden), Mark B Gordon (Houston, Texas), Joy Hale & Derek Fess
(Columbus, Ohio), Sally & Mike Hayden (Cheltenham, Glos), Dr Jürgen Heintges
(Moeckmuehl, Germany), Peter Hennessy (Sutton, Surrey), Steve Hitov & Tillie Lacayo
(Lakeland, FL, USA), Dietlind Jochims (Asunción, Paraguay), PK (Willoughby) & Paul Whelan
(Castle Hill, Australia), Russel Lane (Salt Lake City, Utah), Thomas Meiberg (New York), Mark
Mulbacher (Lucerne, Switzerland), Carlo Muttoni (Italy), Philip Rihs (Biel, Switzerland), Mark
Schuringa (Amsterdam, Holland), Anke Schwittey (Montréal, Quebec), Helmuth Otto Stuven
& Stella Domky oer Dolby Nielsen (Copenhagen), Anton Summerer (Vienna, Austria), Francine
Winddance Twine (Colorado Springs, Co, USA) Benderoth Vitus (Hadamar) and Dirk Zeiler
(Giessen, Germany).

Óscar   613 - 27 - 43
Pilar   9036 77 6084
                    041   6804

Molino de Agua.
Vallarta y Jordán
21 957
El Dorado
Vías del sol.

Cottield £4 14 +£10 thurs
£4·44
£424 thurs
Pedro

* We specialize exclusively in travel to, from and within Latin America.

All our eggs are in one basket*

Dendn BA
£407/384

FLIGHTS ▶ We have a wide range of cut-price flight options – including one-ways, returns, 'Open Jaws' and student fares - and a host of permutations that can be tailor-made for the cost-conscious independent traveller. Ask for the PAPAGAIO magazine, our invaluable guide to the cheapest ways of getting there.

TOURS ▶ We run our own programme of 22 different escorted trips in Latin America, with guaranteed departures.
Our Central American and Mexican programme features:

GUATEMALA, MEXICO, BELIZE	23 DAYS
MEXICO	16 DAYS
COSTA RICA	11 DAYS
LA RUTA MAYA	23 DAYS
CUBA	15 DAYS

For full details, ask for an ESCORTED GROUPS brochure.

BESPOKE ▶ In addition we organise customised itineraries, including transfer and hotels, for clients who have more demands on time. Ask for our BESPOKE HOLIDAY JOURNEYS brochure.

EXPERTISE ▶ In fact amongst us all here in the office we have a range of South American travel expertise which is almost certainly unequalled anywhere in the world. We've got a good stock of relevant books and maps for sale, and insurance especially designed for travellers to developing countries.

JOURNEY LATIN AMERICA

14-16 Devonshire Road Chiswick London W4 2HD
Tel **081 747 3108** (Flights)
 081 747 8315 (Tours)
Fax **081 742 1312**

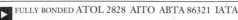

▶ FULLY BONDED ATOL 2828 AITO ABTA 86321 IATA

INTRODUCTION AND HINTS

AIR TRAVEL TO AND WITHIN THE REGION

Travel to and in Mexico and Central America All the main airlines plying to each country are given in the 'Information for Visitors' sections. Weight allowances if going direct from Europe are 20 kg for economy and business class or 30 kg for first class. If you have special baggage requirements, check with an agency about anomalies which exist on different weight allowances one way, for exmple. Many people travel to Mexico and Central America via the USA, and this usually means a luggage allowance of *2 pieces*. This varies from airline to airline, but allows you more than 20 kg. However, weight limits for internal flights are often lower; best to enquire beforehand.

Paul Davies and Leila Bayandor, of Journey Latin America, have told us:

1 It is no longer generally cheaper to fly from London rather than a point in Europe to Latin American destinations; fares vary from airline to airline, destination to destination and according to time of year. Check with an agency for the best deal for when you wish to travel.

2 Most airlines offer discounted (cheaper than official) fares of one sort or another on scheduled flights. These are not offered by the airlines direct to the public, but through agencies who specialize in this type of fare*. The very busy seasons are as follows: 7 December–15 January and July to mid-September. If you intend travelling during those times, book as far ahead as possible.

3 In the last 2 years there have been a number of charter flights to Acapulco in Mexico. The fares offered have been very cheap in low season (May) but less so at busy periods. With the

---

*In UK, these include Global Travel Club, 1 Kilnshaw, Langdon Hills, Basildon, Essex SS16 6LE (T 01268 541732); Journey Latin America, 16 Devonshire Road, Chiswick, London W4 2HD (T 0181-747 3108); Trailfinders, 48 Earl's Court Road, London W8 6EJ (T 0171-938 3366); South American Experience, 47 Causton Street, Pimlico, London SW1P 4AT (T 0171-976 5511); Steamond Ltd (flights only), 23 Eccleston Street, London SW1W 9LX (T 0171-730 8646), (for tours): 278 Batterseas Park Road, London (T 0171-738 0285); Passage to South America, 41 North End Road, West Kensington, London W14 8SZ (T 0171-602 9889); STA Travel, Priory House, 6 Wrights Lane, London W8 6TA (T 0171-938 4711). (Ed.)

promotion of Cancún as a gateway from Europe, there has been an increase in the number of scheduled flights to Mexico, at the expense of charter flights from Britain. At the same time, scheduled services from Britain have been reintroduced with British Airways' new thrice-weekly service from London to Mexico City. British Airways' flights link with Mexicana for access to the rest of the country.

4 Other fares fall into 3 groups, and are all on scheduled services:

A Excursion (return) fares with restricted validity 7-180 days (Mexico); 7-90 days (Central America). These are fixed date tickets where the dates of travel cannot be changed after issue of ticket.

B Yearly fares: these may be bought on a one-way or return basis, and usually the returns can be issued with the return date left open. You must, however, fix the route.

C Student (or Under 26) fares. Some airlines are flexible on the age limit, others strict. One way and returns available, or 'Open Jaws' (see below). NB Some student tickets carry lower priority, and should be avoided in the busy seasons (see above).

5 For people intending to travel a linear route and return from a different point from that which they entered, there are 'Open Jaws' fares, which are available on student, yearly, or excursion fares.

6 Many of these fares require a change of plane at an intermediate point, and a stopover may be permitted, or even obligatory, depending on schedules. Simply because a flight stops at a given airport does not mean you can break your journey there—the airline must have traffic rights to pick up or set down passengers between points A and B before it will be permitted. This is where dealing with a specialized agency (like Journey Latin America!) will really pay dividends. On multi-stop itineraries, the specialized agencies can often save clients hundreds of pounds.

7 Although it's a little more complicated, it's possible to sell tickets in London for travel originating in Latin America at substantially cheaper fares than those available locally. This is useful for the traveller who doesn't know where he or she will end up, or who plans to travel for more than a year. But a oneway ticket from Latin America is more expensive than a oneway in the other direction, so it's always best to buy a return.

8 Certain Central American countries impose local tax on flights originating there. Among these are Guatemala and Mexico.

9 There are several cheap French charters to Mexico and Guatemala, but no-one in the UK sells them. There are a number of 'packages' that include flights from Mexico to Cuba which can be bought locally in Mexico, or in advance from London.

Travellers starting their journey in continental Europe may try for charters at Uniclam-Voyages, 63 rue Monsieur-le Prince, 75006 Paris. Cheap flights may also be bought from Nouvelles Frontières, Paris, T (1) 41-41-58-58; Hajo Siewer Jet Tours, Martinstr 39, 57462 Olpe, Germany, T (02761) 924120; Globetrotter Travel Service, Remweg, 8001 Zürich. See also the German magazine *Reisefieber*.

10 If you buy discounted air tickets *always* check the reservation with the airline concerned to make sure the flight still exists. Also remember the IATA airlines' schedules change in March and October each year, so if you're going to be away a long time it's best to leave return flight coupons open.

In addition, it is vital to check in advance whether you are entitled to any refund or re-issued

SOUTH AMERICAN EXPERIENCE

Acknowledged experts in travel arrangements to Latin America

- Low cost airfares
- Route planning advice
- Inbound flights

- Tailor made itineraries
- Hotels – budget to luxury
- Discounts in Club & First Class

47 Causton St, Pimlico, London SW1P 4AT
Tel: 0171-976 5511 Fax: 0171-976 6908

ticket if you lose, or have stolen, a discounted air ticket.

Taca, Aviateca, Lacsa, Copa and Nica have a 'Visit Central America Programme', valid until 10 January 1995, a coupon system for flights within Central America and to the region of the USA, Mexico, South America and the Caribbean. 5-10 coupons may be purchased to cover flights divided into 5 zones; the price varies according to number of coupons and zones, ranging from US$549 to US$1,399. Aviateca and Taca also have a Maya Path fare which covers flights from US gateway cities or Mexico to Guatemala, El Salvador, Belize, Mérida or Cancún. Fares range from US$260 for 4 coupons to US$520 for 8. Details of Mexicana's Mexipass are given in Mexico, **Information for Visitors**.

Beware buying tickets from the general sales agents in Europe of minor Latin American airlines. They are sometimes incorrectly made out and therefore impossible to transfer or cash in. If you buy internal airline tickets in Latin American countries you may find cash refunds difficult to get if you change your plans: better to change your ticket for a different one. On the other hand you can save money by buying tickets in a country with a black exchange market, for local currency, for flights on its national airline. Overbooking by Latin American airlines is very common (largely due to repeated block bookings by travel agents, which everyone knows will not be used), so always reconfirm the next stage of your flight within 72 hrs of your intended departure. And it does no harm to reconfirm yet again in the last 24 hrs, just to show them you mean it, and turn up for the flight in good time (at least 2 hrs before departure).

We advise people who travel the cheap way in Latin America to pay for all transport as they go along, and not in advance. This advice does not apply to people on a tight schedule: paying as you go along may save money, but it is likely to waste your time somewhat. The one exception to this general principle is in transatlantic flights; here money is saved by booking as far as possible in one operation. International air tickets are very expensive if purchased in Latin

STEAMOND

MAKING DREAMS REALITY

As you read your way through this book, the desire to visit Latin America will take hold. Let Steamond – the acknowledged experts – take you there.
For business or pleasure, Steamond offers the discerning traveller a service second to none. Our travel experts know this exciting part of the world like the back of their hands, and specialize in creative tours and special itineraries.
Let us prepare the tour of a lifetime, just for you, and combine it with one of our special bargain-priced air fares.
For full colour brochures, air fares, tour prices and more information, just call us on the numbers below.

STEAMOND (Flights only)
23 Eccleston Street, London SW1W 9LX
Tel: 071-730 8646 Fax: 071-730 3024

STEAMOND (Tours)
278 Battersea Park Road, London SW11 3BS
Tel: 071-738 0285 Fax: 071-978 5603

 FLIGHTS • TOURS • CONFERENCES • INCENTIVES

America. If buying airline tickets routed through the USA, check that US taxes are included in the price.

The Amerbuspass covers the whole of Latin America, from Mexico City to Ushuaia, and entitles the holder to 15-20% discounts on tickets with participating operators; bookable in all Latin American capitals, Europe, Asia, Africa, Oceania, it is valid for 9,999 miles, up to 180 days. Unlimited stopovers, travel with either a confirmed or open itinerary. Contact TISA Internacional, B Irigoyen 1370, Oficina 25/26, 1138 Buenos Aires, Argentina, T 27-6591/631-1108, F 953-5508, or Av Larrazabal 493, 1408 Buenos Aires, PO Box 40 Suc 1 (B), 1401 Buenos Aires.

Travel to the USA Until July 1988 all foreigners (except Canadians) needed visas to enter the USA. Despite subsequent relaxations of visa requirements for British air travellers with round-trip tickets to the USA, it is advisable to have a visa to allow entry by land, or on airlines from South and Central America which are not 'participating carriers' on the Visa Waiver scheme. If you are thinking of travelling via the USA, or of visiting the USA after Latin America, you are strongly advised to get your visa from a US Consulate in your own country, not while travelling.

The US Department of Agriculture places restrictions on agricultural items brought to the United States from foreign countries as well as those brought to the mainland from Hawaii, Puerto Rico, and the US Virgin Islands. Prohibited items can harbour foreign animal and plant pests and diseases that could seriously damage America's crops, livestock, pets and the environment.

Because of this threat, travellers are required to list on the Customs' declaration form any meats, fruits, vegetables, plants, animals, and plant and animal products they are bringing into the country. The declaration must list all agricultural items carried in baggage, hand luggage and in vehicles coming across the border.

USDA inspectors will confiscate illegal items for destruction. Travellers who fail to declare items can be fined up to US$100 on the spot, and their exit from the airport will be delayed. Some items are permitted. Call 301-436-5908 for a copy of the helpful pamphlet, 'Travelers Tips'. The best advice is to check before purchasing an agricultural item and trying to bring it back to the United States.

Shipping There are few shipping services which carry passengers to Central America from Europe, the USA or elsewhere. Those that do are the Harrison Line, MV *Author*, which on its round trip to Felixstowe, UK, via the Caribbean and Central America, calls at ports in Venezuela and Colombia before stopping at Puerto Limón (Costa Rica). The total fare for the trip starts at £2,850 pp in a double cabin, or approximately £68 per day full board; the full round trip takes 42 days. Note that passengers buying round trips are given preference; one-way tickets are practically impossible to come by in the autumn and winter months, but can be bought in summer. Also the Horn Line sails regularly from Hamburg, Antwerp and Le Havre, via the French Antilles and Cayenne, to Moín or Santo Tomás de Castilla before returning to Europe.

The only other Central American destination is the Panama Canal through which the following passenger-carrying freight lines pass: ABC Containers, which returns from Australia and New Zealand to Liverpool via the Canal, E Coast USA, Canada and Zeebrugge; Columbus Line on round trip voyages from the USA to Australia and New Zealand; Blue Star Line between E Coast USA and Australia/New Zealand; Lykes Line from Miami/New Orleans to Colombia, Ecuador and Chile; and Egon Oldendorff from the USA. From the UK at least, confirmation of sailing times on these vessels is difficult; the same problem with one-way tickets as above applies.

Our thanks are due to John Alton of Strand Cruise and Travel Centre, Charing Cross Shopping Concourse, The Strand, London WC2N 4HZ, T 0171-836 6363, F 0171-497 0078, for the above information. Enquiries regarding passages should be made through agencies in your own country, or through Strand Cruise and Travel Centre, who also have information on occasional one-way services to the Gulf of Mexico from Europe.

Details on shipping cars are given in **Motoring**, below, and in the relevant country sections.

Warning Some countries in Latin America officially require travellers who enter their territory to have an onward or return ticket. (Look under 'Information for Visitors' sections for the countries you intend to visit.) In 1993-94 this regulation was rarely enforced by any country, although strictest tend to be Colombia and Venezuela. (In any event, it does not apply to travellers with their own vehicles.) In lieu of an onward ticket out of the country you are entering, any ticket out of another Latin American country may suffice, or proof that you have sufficient funds to buy a ticket (a credit card will do).

MIAMI

Miami is a good place for connections between Europe and Central and South America. A 5 hr transfer, whether by choice or out of necessity, may seem like a daunting prospect, but Miami airport is surprisingly user-friendly and there is quite a lot to do in the city if you have a longer stopover.

The aiport is rather like a big, horseshoe-shaped suburban shopping mall. The upper level has shops and airline check-in counters; the lower level has other services like car rentals and baggage claim. The airport is divided into a series of concourses labelled B to H.

On arrival
Immigration queues are long, and can take 30-50 mins. Heavy hand luggage is more of a nuisance than at most airports, both in the queues and because of the long walk up and down the fingers which lead to the planes. Customs is crowded, but the queue moves faster. Through booking of baggage is now possible for Miami airport; ask for a suitable label at your point of departure.

Baggage There are baggage carts in customs, but these must be left behind when you have been cleared. From this point on there are *skycaps* (tip around US$1-2 per large bag). Skycaps can also be called from the paging phones which are thick on the ground in the concourses and entrances.

There are luggage lockers at all entrances to the airport and at various other points. They cost US$1 in quarters (25 cents—look for change machines, or ask information counters). After 24 hrs, bags are taken to a storage facility next to the *lost and found* office in concourse E. The charge for storage here is US$2 per day.

For very large items there is a left luggage office (baggage service office) on the lower level of concourse G and on the second level of concourse B. Charges are US$2-6 per day, depending on the size of the item.

Filling in time
The concourses are chocabloc with snackbars, duty free shops, and gift shops selling overpriced garbage. **Note** A 6% sales tax is added to the marked price. Watch out if you are fine-tuning your US currency before departure.

The best place to pass the time and relax is probably the *Hotel MIA*, in the middle of the horseshoe on concourse E. The Lobby Lounge, open 1000-0100, is on the same floor as flight check in. The upper floors have a sundeck (free), an open air swimming pool, gym and sauna area (US$5 per day), racquetball courts (US$8 per hour), snackbar, lounge bar (the happy hour, 1700-1900, has drinks on special and complimentary snacks). There is also the *Top of The Port* restaurant, with pleasant surroundings and much better food than on the concourses (open 0700-2300; full breakfast US$7.75, lunch specials from US$8, dinner specials from US$15).

The hotel has special day rates between 0800 and 1800.

Information There are very helpful information counters in concourse E and just outside customs. They can also be contacted from any paging phone. (Counters open 0630-2230; paging phone service 24 hrs.) They will advise on ground transport, airport services, and the Miami area generally.

Nursery Mainly for changing or feeding babies, on concourse E. If locked, the information office in this concourse has a key.

Banking Barnett Bank on concourse C, Monday to Friday 0900-1600, Saturday 0900-1200. Visa and Mastercard cash advances (US$25 minimum, US$2000 maximum) on production of passport and one other piece of identification. 24-hr cashpoint on concourse outside the bank. Several foreign exchange counters, including a 24-hr one on concourse E.

Service Centre between concourses B and C has stamp machines, credit card phones, TDD phone for deaf or mute passengers, and another cashpoint.

Post Office Leave the building at the lower level of concourse B and walk a couple of metres along the airport road. Open Monday to Friday 0830-2100 and 0930-1330 on Saturday. Also sells bubble packing, padded envelopes, mailing tubes for posters etc. Express mail service in the post office is open 24 hrs.

Leaving the Airport
If you want to venture into the real world, you can use:

Rental Cars This works out at around US$30 per day for a small car. Many companies have offices on the lower level concourses. It can take an hour or more to book a car, take the company bus to its main office, fill out all the forms, and pick up a car. Leaving the car can take just as long. The information counters have a full list of companies. Some car hire firms may offer lower rates to passengers flying with certain airlines. Check in advance.

Drive Away Look for agencies, under D in the phone book, who handle cars belonging to people who have flown to their destination, but need their car driven there by someone else. It can be a quick, uncomplicated way to leave Miami if you have your passport and an international driving licence; sometimes accommodation and fuel may be included.

Buses Miami has a good bus service. Fare is US$1.25, with US$0.25 for a transfer to another route. Buses stop outside concourse E. Route 37 runs N-S every 30 mins in the day, every hour late evenings and weekends; Route 42 also runs N-S, every hour. Route J runs every 20-30 mins or every hour on Sundays to Miami Beach; Route 7 runs every 20-40 mins. Eastbound buses go downtown, westbound buses go to the Mall of the Americas and the International Mall, 2 big shopping complexes.

Routes J and 42 connect with the *Greyhound* bus terminal at Coral Gables.

Metrorail All of the airport bus routes connect with stations on the Metrorail line. This gives a quick service every 15 mins from 0600 to 2400 between downtown Miami and many suburban areas.

Metromover Metrorail tickets give a free connection to Metromover, a 1.9 mile (3 km) elevated track which whizzes round downtown Miami. The connection is at Government Center station.

Tri-Rail is another rail system which connects Miami and points N. The full journey to West Palm Beach takes 1 hr 39 mins. Connecting buses leave from outside concourse E; it is a 5 min ride to the station. Departures at 0500, 0600, 0700, 0745, 1200, 1530, 1632, 1730, 1830, 1930.

Supershuttle is a minibus running to and from the airport. You can book ahead to be picked up from a hotel or private house. The fare is US$7 for downtown, US$8 for South Miami Beach, US$13 to Fort Lauderdale airport.

Taxis are more expensive. Approximate fares are US$13 for downtown, US$18 for Miami Beach, US$42 to South Fort Lauderdale.

Hotels Rooms at the *Miami International Airport Hotel (MIA)* in the airport start at US$159 plus 12.5% tax for a double, US$104s corporate rate. Rooms are quite small but double glazing keeps out aircraft noise, very impersonal, T 1-800-327-1276 from within the USA, or 305-871-4100 from elsewhere, F 305-871-0800. Information has a good listing of downtown hotels, starting from the cheapest (*Bayman International*, Flagler Street, T 266-5098 and *Miami Springs Hotel*, 661 E Drive, T 888-8421) and ending with the most expensive (*Miami Airport Hilton*, 5101 Blue Lagoon Drive, T 262-1000, and *Marriott Hotel*, 1202 NW LeJeune Road, T 649-5000).

Information also has a separate listing of Miami Beach hotels (alphabetical, not by price). Best value in Miami Beach is the *Clay Hotel*, 1438 Washington Avenue, which has a youth hostel attached. Single rooms are US$17, hostel accommodation is less, T 305-534-2988; F 305-673-0346. *Clay Hotel* has young and friendly staff and caters for many young European tourists.

There are direct free phone lines to several hotels next to the baggage check in on lower level concourse F.

There are also reservations services which will make reservations for you. Try CRS (Toll free 1-800-683-3311), Express Reservation (Toll free 1-800-627-1356), or Room with a View (305-433-4343).

Shopping For bargains, try Flagler Street in downtown Miami, it's crowded and full of action. The suburban malls are more expensive and more relaxed: Mall of the Americas and International Mall are easiest to reach by bus.

Things to see in Miami
This guide is not the place for a full listing. The airport information office has a useful booklet, *Destination Miami*, which gives details of a wide range of cultural events.

Miami is about the nearest that the continental USA gets to a tropical environment. Many attractions are designed for visitors from the N. The Monkey Jungle, Orchid Jungle, Parrot Jungle, etc may not be that exciting if you have just seen the real thing. With half a day to spare, however, you should be able to visit any of these, or the Metrozoo, or the Seaquarium. Museums include Vizcaya, a Renaissance-style villa with formal gardens, and the Spanish Monastery in North Miami Beach, brought to America in pieces by William Randolph Hearst from Segovia in Spain, where it was first built in 1141. That, in a way, makes it the oldest building in the USA.

Miami Beach is probably the best place for a short stay. There are plenty of interesting Art Deco buildings, with restaurants and cafes along the sea front. Shops, hotels, nightclubs, etc are all within walking distance. Moreover, you can walk around at night without getting mugged. It also has the Bass Museum, with a good collection of European paintings. N of the Haulover channel is a section of beach where nude bathing is tolerated.

If you have a full day in Miami, there would be time to rent a car and drive to the *Everglades National Park*, a huge freshwater swamp with interesting wildlife and an excellent network of interpretative centres and nature trails. The nearer Florida Keys would be an alternative, but are probably not too exciting if you have just been to any of the Central American islands in the Caribbean.

Note Non-US citizens should remember that US immigration will not permit entry to the USA without an onward ticket (ie you cannot enter for the sole purpose of buying a cheap ticket to a third country). Moreover, while agencies in Miami can sell cheap tickets (eg Getaway Travel, Le Jeune Rd, Coral Gables), it is very difficult to check air tickets purchased outside the USA through a Miami agency. A recommended travel agent is Jorge Domínguez (Uruguayan) at *Bestway*, 420 Lincoln Rd, Suite 359, Miami Beach, FL 33139, T (305) 672-3035, F 672-2580.

Note also that Houston, Continental's hub, is another good place for connections to the region.

DOCUMENTATION AND SECURITY

Passports   Remember that Latin Americans, especially officials, are very document-minded. You should always carry your passport in a safe place about your person, or if not going far, leave it in the hotel safe. If staying in a country for several weeks, it is worth while registering at your Embassy or Consulate. Then, if your passport is stolen, the process of replacing it is simplified and speeded up. Keeping photocopies of essential documents, including your flight ticket, and some additional passport-sized photographs, is recommended.

Remember that it is your responsibility to ensure that your passport is stamped in and out when you cross frontiers. The absence of entry and exit stamps can cause serious difficulties: seek out the proper migration offices if the stamping process is not carried out as you cross. Also, do not lose your entry card; replacing one causes a lot of trouble, and possibly expense. Citizens of countries which oblige visitors to have a visa (eg France) can expect more delays and problems at border crossings.

If planning to study in Latin America for a long period, make every effort to get a student visa in advance.

Identity and Membership Cards   Membership cards of British, European and US motoring organizations have been found useful for discounts off hotel charges, car rentals, maps, towing charges, etc. Student cards must carry a photograph if they are to be of any use in Latin America for discounts. (If you describe yourself as a student on your tourist card you may be able to get discounts, even if you haven't a student card). Business people should carry a good supply of visiting cards, which are essential for good business relations in Latin America. Identity, membership or business cards in Spanish (or a translation) and an official letter of introduction in Spanish are also useful.

If you are in full-time education you will be entitled to an International Student Identity Card, which is distributed by student travel offices and travel agencies in 77 countries. The ISIC gives you special prices on all forms of transport (air, sea, rail etc), and access to a variety of other concessions and services. If you need to find the location of your nearest ISIC office contact: The ISIC Association, Box 9048, 1000 Copenhagen, Denmark T (+45) 33 93 93 03.

Money is best carried in US dollar travellers' cheques (denominations of US$50 and US$100 are preferable, though one does need a few of US$20) or cash. Sterling and other currencies are not recommended. Travellers' cheques are convenient but they attract thieves (though refunds can of course be arranged) and you will find that they are more difficult than dollar bills to change in small towns. Though the risk of loss is greater, many travellers take part of their funds in US dollar notes; better rates and lower commissions can usually be obtained for them. In many countries, US dollar notes are only accepted if they are in excellent condition. Low-value US dollar bills should be carried for changing into local currency if arriving in a country when banks or *casas de cambio* are closed (US$5 or US$10 bills). They are very useful for shopping: shopkeepers and exchange shops (*casas de cambio*) tend to give better exchange rates than hotels or banks (but see below). The better hotels will normally change travellers' cheques for their guests (often at a rather poor rate), but if you're travelling on the cheap it is essential to keep in funds; watch weekends and public holidays carefully and never run out of local currency. Take plenty of local currency, in small denominations, when making trips into the interior. Spread your money around your person: less chance of thieves finding it all. Don't leave cash in your shoe, it may become too damaged to exchange or use.

We recommend in general the use of American Express, Visa or Thomas Cook US$ travellers' cheques, but should point out that less commission is often charged on Citibank or Bank of America cheques, if they are cashed at Latin American branches of those banks. These cheques are always accepted by banks, even though they may not be as well known outside banks as those of American Express, Visa or Thomas Cook. It is a good idea to take 2 kinds of cheque: if large numbers of one kind have recently been forged or stolen, making people suspicious, it is unlikely to have happened simultaneously with the other kind. Several banks charge a high fixed commission for changing travellers' cheques—sometimes as much as US$5-10 a cheque—because they don't really want to be bothered. Exchange houses (*casas de cambio*) are usually much better for this service. Some establishments may ask to see the customer's record of purchase before accepting travellers' cheques. **Note** In Mexico, *casas de cambio* may be open longer hours than banks, but they do not offer better exchange rates.

There is an active (but illegal) black market in local currency in those countries that have no free exchange; it is, however, not illegal to buy currency outside the country you are about to enter, up to any limit that may be imposed. Changing money on the black market: if possible, do not do so alone. If unsure of the currency of the country you are about to enter, check rates with more than one changer at the border, or ask locals or any traveller who may be leaving that country. If changing travellers' cheques on the black market, do not sign the cheque until you have received and counted your money.

Credit cards of the Visa and Mastercard (Eurocard, Access) groups are useful, and so are American Express (Amex), Carte Blanche and Diners Club. Conceal them very carefully (*not* under the insole of a shoe, however: that may render them unusable!), and make sure you know the correct procedure if they are lost or stolen. In many countries obtaining a cash advance against a credit card is the easiest way to add to one's funds. In the area covered by this book, Mexico, Guatemala, Costa Rica and Panama have automatic telling machines (ATMs) of the Visa network which permit the withdrawal of cash. Mastercard/Cirrus ATMs can be found in all countries except Cuba. Credit card transactions are normally at an officially recognized rate of exchange (sometimes, if there are several, the least favourable one); you may find it much cheaper to pay cash and get the parallel rate. Many establishments in Latin America charge a fee of about 5% on credit card transactions (irrespective of any taxes); although forbidden by credit card company rules there is not a lot you can do about this, except get the charge itemized on the receipt and complain to the card company. For credit card security, insist that imprints are made in your presence and that any imprints incorrectly completed should be torn into tiny pieces. Also destroy the carbon papers after the form is completed (signatures can be copied from them).

NB Remember that a transfer of funds, even by telex, can take several days, and charges can be high; a recommended method is, before leaving, to find out which local bank is correspondent to your bank at home, then when you need funds, telex your own bank and ask them to telex the money to the local bank (confirming by air mail). It is possible to obtain money within hours by this method.

Whenever you leave a country, sell any local currency before leaving, because the further away you get, the less the value of a country's money. **Note** When departing by air, never forget that you have to pay airport departure tax; do not leave yourself short of money.

Americans (we are told) should know that if they run out of funds they can usually expect no help from the US Embassy or Consul other than a referral to some welfare organization. In this regard, find out before you go precisely what services and assistance your embassy or consulate can provide if you find yourself in difficulties.

Law Enforcement   Whereas in Europe and North America we are accustomed to law enforcement on a systematic basis, in general, enforcement in Latin America is achieved by periodic campaigns. The most typical is a round-up of criminals in the cities just before Christmas. In December, therefore, you may well be asked for identification at any time, and if you cannot produce it, you will be jailed. At first sight, on arrival, it may seem that you can flout the law with impunity, because everybody else is obviously doing so. If a visitor is jailed his friends should take him food every day. This is especially important for people on a diet, such as diabetics. It must also be borne in mind that in the event of a vehicle accident in which anyone is injured, all drivers involved are automatically detained until blame has been established, and this does not usually take less than 2 weeks.

Never offer a bribe unless you are fully conversant with the customs of the country. Wait until the official makes the suggestion, or offer money in some form which is apparently not bribery, eg 'In our country we have a system of on-the-spot fines (*multas de inmediato*). Is there a similar system here?' Do not assume that an official who accepts a bribe is prepared to do anything else that is illegal. You bribe him to persuade him to do his job, or to persuade him not to do it, or to do it more quickly, or more slowly. You do not bribe him to do something which is against the law. The mere suggestion would make him very upset. If an official suggests that a bribe must be paid before you can proceed on your way, be patient (assuming you have the time) and he may relent.

Security   Generally speaking, most places in Latin America are no more dangerous than any major city in Europe or North America. In provincial towns, main places of interest, on day time buses and in ordinary restaurants the visitor should be quite safe. Nevertheless, in large cities particularly, crime exists, most of which is opportunistic. If you are aware of the dangers, act confidently and use your common sense you will lessen many of the risks. The following tips, all endorsed by travellers, are meant to forewarn, but not alarm, you. Keep all documents secure; hide your main cash supply in different places or under your clothes (extra pockets sewn inside shirts and trousers, pockets closed with a zip or safety pin, moneybelts—best worn below the waist rather than at it or around the neck, neck or leg pouches, and elasticated support bandages for keeping money and cheques above the elbow or below the knee have been repeatedly recommended—the last by John Hatt in *The Tropical Traveller*). Keep cameras in bags (preferably with a chain or wire in the strap to defeat the slasher) or briefcases; take spare spectacles (eyeglasses); don't wear wrist-watches or jewellery. If you wear a shoulder-bag in a market, carry it in front of you. Backpacks are vulnerable to slashers: a good idea is to cover the pack with a sack (a plastic one will also keep out rain and dust) with maybe a layer of wire netting between, or make an inner frame of chicken wire. Use a pack which is lockable at its base.

Ignore mustard smearers and paint or shampoo sprayers, and strangers' remarks like 'what's that on your shoulder?' or 'have you seen that dirt on your shoe?'. Furthermore, don't bend over to pick up money or other items in the street. These are all ruses intended to distract your attention and make you easy for an accomplice to steal from. If someone follows you when you're in the street, let him catch up with you and 'give him the eye'. Take local advice about being out at night. If walking after dark, walk in the road, not on the pavement/sidewalk.

Be wary of 'plainclothes policemen'; insist on seeing identification and on going to the police station by main roads. Do not hand over your identification (or money—which he should not need to see anyway) until you are at the station. On no account take them directly back to your lodgings. Be even more suspicious if he seeks confirmation of his status from a passer-by. If someone tries to bribe you, insist on a receipt. If attacked, remember your assailants may well be armed, and try not to resist.

It is best, if you can trust your hotel, to leave any valuables you don't need in safe-deposit there, when sightseeing locally. Always keep an inventory of what you have deposited. If you don't trust the hotel, lock everything in your pack and secure that in your room (some people take eyelet-screws for padlocking cupboards or drawers). If you lose valuables, always report to the police and note details of the report—for insurance purposes.

When you have all your luggage with you at a bus or railway station, be especially careful: don't get into arguments with any locals if you can help it, and lock all the items together with a chain or cable if you are waiting for some time. Take a taxi between airport/bus station/railway station and hotel, if you can possibly afford it. Keep your bags with you in the taxi and pay only when you and your luggage are safely out of the vehicle. Make sure the taxi has inner door handles, in case a quick exit is needed. Avoid night buses; never arrive at night; and watch your belongings whether they are stowed inside or outside the cabin (rooftop luggage racks create extra problems, which are sometimes unavoidable—make sure your bag is waterproof). Major bus lines often issue a luggage ticket when bags are stored in the bus' hold, generally a safe system. When getting on a bus, keep your ticket handy; someone sitting in your seat may be a distraction for an accomplice to rob you while you are sorting out the problem. Finally, never accept food, drink, sweets or cigarettes from unknown fellow-travellers on buses or trains. They may be drugged, and you would wake up hours later without your belongings. In this connection, never accept a bar drink from an opened bottle (unless you can see that that bottle is in general use): always have it uncapped in front of you.

A last point: a courteous, friendly manner of speaking, including to beggars and market vendors, may avoid your being 'set up' for robbery or assault. For specific local problems, see under the individual countries in the text.

Drugs Users of drugs, even of soft ones, without medical prescription should be particularly careful, as some countries impose heavy penalties—up to 10 years' imprisonment—for even the simple possession of such substances. In this connection, the planting of drugs on travellers, by traffickers or the police, is not unknown. If offered drugs on the street, make no response at all and keep walking. Note that people who roll their own cigarettes are often suspected of carrying drugs and subjected to intensive searches. Advisable to stick to commercial brands of cigarettes—but better still not to smoke at all.

ACCOMMODATION

Hotels A cheap but not bad hotel might be US$10 a night upwards in Mexico, less in some, but not all of, the Central American countries. For the indigent, it is a good idea to ask for a boarding house—*casa de huéspedes, hospedaje, pensión, casa familial* or *residencial*, according to country; they are normally to be found in abundance near bus and railway stations and markets. Good value hotels can also be found near truckers' stops/service stations; they are usually secure. There are often great seasonal variations in hotel prices in resorts. Note that in the text the term 'with bath' usually means 'with shower and toilet', not 'with bath tub'. Remember, cheaper hotels don't always supply soap, towels and toilet paper. Useful tips: book even cheap hotels in advance by registered mail, if you receive no reply, don't worry; ask the car rental agency employees at the airport for advice when you arrive, as long as they are not busy, they may have better-value recommendations than airport tourist offices; always ask for the best room. To avoid price hikes for gringos, ask if there is a cheaper room.

Note The electric showers used in innumerable hotels may be dangerous. Before using them, check the wiring for obvious flaws and try not to touch the rose while it is producing hot water.

Youth Hostels Organizations affiliated to the Youth Hostels movement exist in Mexico, Costa Rica and Guatemala. Further information in the country sections and from the IYHA.

Meals There is a paragraph on each nation's food under 'Information for Visitors'. Most restaurants serve a daily special meal, usually at lunchtime, which is cheaper than other dishes and good. Vegetarians should be able to list all the foods they cannot eat; saying 'Soy vegetariano/a' (I'm a vegetarian) or 'no como carne' (I don't eat meat) is often not enough.

Camping There is a growing network of organized campsites, to which reference is made in the text immediately below hotel lists, under each town. If there is no organized site in town, a football pitch or gravel pit might serve. Géraldine des Cressonnières, of Linkebeek, Belgium, gives the following rules for 'wild' camping: (1) arrive in daylight; (2) ask permission to camp from the parish priest, or the fire chief, or the police, or a farmer regarding his own property; (3) never ask a group of people—especially young people; (4) never camp on a beach (because of sandflies and thieves). If you can't get information from anyone, camp in a spot where you can't be seen from the nearest inhabited place.

Gas cylinders and bottles are usually exchangeable, but if not can be recharged; specify whether you use butane or propane. Liquid fuels are readily available: for a methylated spirit-burning stove, the following fuels apply, *alcohol desnaturalizado, alcohol metílico, alcohol puro (de caña)* or *alcohol para quemar* (avoid this in Honduras as it does not burn). Ask for 95%, but 70% will suffice. In Mexico fuel is sold in supermarkets; in all countries it can be found in chemists/pharmacies.

Hammocks A hammock can be an invaluable piece of equipment, especially if travelling on the cheap. It will be of more use than a tent because many places have hammock-hooks, or you can sling a hammock between trees, etc. Bryan Crawford, of Beauly, Inverness-shire, Scotland, recommends carrying a 10m rope and some plastic sheeting. 'The rope gives a good choice of tree distances and the excess provides a hanging frame for the plastic sheeting to keep the rain off. Metal S-hooks can be very useful, especially under lorries'. Don't forget a mosquito net if travelling in insect-infected areas. Tips on buying a hammock are given in the Mérida (Yucatán) **Shopping** section. Good hammocks are also sold in Guatamala. If in any doubt about quality or size, seek advice before buying. And as Remo Bulgheroni of Killroergen (Switzerland) says: 'don't make a mess with your end strings because it makes your hammock useless and only the sellers can help you fast.'

Toilets Many hotels, restaurants and bars have inadequate water supplies. **Almost without exception, used toilet paper should not be flushed down the pan, but placed in the receptacle provided.** This applies even in quite expensive hotels. Failing to observe this custom will block the pan or drain, a considerable health risk.

Cockroaches These are ubiquitous and unpleasant, but not dangerous. Take some insecticide powder if staying in cheap hotels, trailer parks, etc; Baygon (Bayer) has been recommended. Stuff toilet paper in any holes in walls that you may suspect of being parts of cockroach runs.

ETIQUETTE AND LANGUAGE

Travellers' Appearance There is a natural prejudice in all countries against travellers who ignore personal hygiene and have a generally dirty and unkempt appearance. Most Latin Americans, if they can afford it, devote great care to their clothes and appearance; it is appreciated if visitors do likewise. How you dress is mostly how people will judge you. Buying clothing locally can help you look less like a tourist. The general prejudice previously reported against backpacks has virtually disappeared, unless carried by those whom officials identify as 'hippies'. One tip we have received; young people of informal dress and life-style may find it advantageous to procure a letter from someone in an official position testifying to their good character, on official-looking notepaper.

Some countries have laws or prejudices against the wearing by civilians of army-surplus clothing. Men wearing earrings are liable to be ridiculed in more 'macho' communities (ie in some rural areas). A medium weight shawl with some wool content is recommended for women: it can double as pillow, light blanket, bathrobe or sunscreen as required. For men, a smart jacket can be very useful.

Courtesy Remember that politeness—even a little ceremoniousness—is much appreciated. In this connection professional or business cards are useful (and have even been known to secure for their owners discount prices in hotels). Men should always remove any headgear and say 'con permiso' when entering offices, and be prepared to shake hands (this is much commoner in Latin America than in Europe or North America); always say 'Buenos días' before midday, or 'Buenas tardes' and wait for a reply before proceeding further; in a word, don't rush them! Always remember that the traveller from abroad has enjoyed greater advantages in life than most Latin American minor officials, and should be friendly and courteous in consequence. Never be impatient; do not criticize situations in public: the officials may know more English than you think and they can certainly interpret gestures and facial expressions. Be judicious about discussing politics with strangers (especially in Guatemala, Honduras, Nicaragua and El Salvador). Politeness can be a liability, however, in some situations; most Latin Americans are disorderly queuers. In Mexico, though, orderly queuing is common. On the other hand, Mexicans rarely respect punctuality. In commercial transactions (buying a meal, goods in a shop, etc) politeness should be accompanied by firmness, and always ask the price first.

Moira Chubb, from New Zealand, suggests that if you are a guest and are offered food that arouses your suspicions, the only courteous way out is to feign an allergy or a stomach ailment. If worried about the purity of ice for drinks, ask for a beer.

▼ ▼ ▼ ▼ ▼ **LEARN SPANISH** ▼ ▼ ▼ ▼ ▼

in Argentina, Chile, Costa Rica, Ecuador, El Salvador, Guatemala, Honduras, Mexico, Panama, Peru, Uruguay, and Venezuela.

- Learn Spanish the RIGHT way FAST
- For all ages and all levels
- Most programs start Mondays year round
- Private or small groups, 3-8 hours/day
- Pre-departure planning and assistance
- Comprehensive travel insurance

AmeriSpan Unlimited
THE BRIDGE BETWEEN CULTURES

Call for free information USA & Canada 1-800-879-6640 • Worldwide 215-829-0996
Fax 215-829-0418 • USA office: PO Box 40513, Philadelphia, PA 19106-0513
Guatemala office: 6a Avenida Norte #34, Antigua Guatemala, Tele./Fax 502-9-323-343

Language Without some knowledge of Spanish you can become very frustrated and feel helpless in many situations. English, or any other language, is absolutely useless off the beaten track. Some initial study, to get you up to a basic Spanish vocabulary of 500 words or so, and a pocket dictionary and phrase-book, are most strongly recommended: your pleasure will be doubled if you can talk to the locals. Not all the locals speak Spanish, of course; you will find that some Indians in the more remote highland parts of Guatemala speak only their indigenous languages, though there will usually be at least 1 person in each village who can speak Spanish.

The basic Spanish of Hispanic America is that of south-western Spain, with soft 'c's' and 'z's' pronounced as 's', and not as 'th' as in the other parts of Spain. Castilian Spanish is readily understood, but is not appreciated when spoken by non-Spaniards; try and learn the basic Latin American pronunciation. Differences in vocabulary also exist, both between peninsular Spanish and Latin American Spanish, and between the usages of the different countries. Language classes are available at low cost at a number of centres in Mexico and Central America, for instance Cuernavaca, Antigua, Quezaltenango, San José, and others. See the text for details, under **Language Courses**.

INTERNAL SURFACE TRANSPORT

Surface Transport The continent has a growing road system for motor traffic, with frequent bus services. Some bus services in Mexico and Central America are excellent. In mountainous country, however, do not expect buses to get to their destination, after long journeys, anywhere near on time. Do not turn up for a bus at the last minute; if it is full it may depart early. Tall travellers are advised to take aisle, not window seats on long journeys as this allows more leg room. When the journey takes more than 3 or 4 hrs, meal stops at country inns or bars, good and bad, are the rule. Often no announcement is made on the duration of the stop: follow the driver, if he eats, eat. See what the locals are eating—and buy likewise, or make sure you're stocked up well on food and drink at the start. For drinks, stick to bottled water or soft drinks or coffee (black). The food sold by vendors at bus stops may be all right: watch if locals are buying, though unpeeled fruit is of course reliable. (See above on **Security** in buses.)

In the few countries where trains run, they are slower than buses. They do tend, however, to provide finer scenery, and you can normally see much more wildlife than from the road—it is less disturbed by 1 or 2 trains a day than by the more frequent road traffic. Moreover, so many buses now show video films that you can't see the countryside because the curtains are drawn. Complaining loudly to the conductor that you cannot see the beautiful landscape may persuade him to

---

INSTITUTE OF LATIN AMERICAN STUDIES
University of London

The centre for graduate study of Latin America. Programmes:
    MA in Area Studies (Latin America)
    MSc in Latin American Politics
    MSc in Environmental Issues in Latin America
    MA in Latin American Literature and Culture
    PhD programmes in Economics, History, Sociology, Politics

Institute of Latin American Studies, 31 Tavistock Square, London WC1H 9HA
Tel. (071) 387 5671 Fax. (071) 388 5024

give you his seat at the front.

Hitchhiking This custom is quite common in Latin America, and travellers have reported success in virtually all countries. Neatness of appearance certainly helps. See **Information for Visitors** sections for local conditions. If trying to hitchhike away from main roads and in sparsely-populated areas, however, allow plenty of time.

Hitchhiking in Latin America is reasonably safe and straightforward for males and couples, provided one speaks some Spanish. It is a most enjoyable mode of transport—a good way to meet the local people, to improve one's languages and to learn about the country. Truck drivers in particular are often well versed in things of interest one is passing, eg crops and industries. Some trucking companies, though, do not allow their drivers to take hitchhikers.

A few general hints: in remoter parts, make enquiries first about the volume of traffic on the road. On long journeys, set out at crack of dawn, which is when trucks usually leave. They tend to go longer distances than cars.

Motoring *Binka and Robin Le Breton write*:

Preparing the Car What kind of motoring you do will depend on what kind of car you set out with. Four-wheel drive is not necessary, although it does give you greater flexibility in mountain and jungle territory. Wherever you travel you should expect from time to time to find roads that are badly maintained, damaged or closed during the wet season, and delays because of floods, landslides and huge potholes. Don't plan your schedules too tightly.

Diesel cars are much cheaper to run than petrol ones, and the fuel is easily available. Most towns can supply a mechanic of sorts, and probably parts for Bosch fuel injection equipment. Watch the mechanics like a hawk, since there's always a brisk market in spares, and some of yours may be highly desirable. That apart, they enjoy a challenge, and can fix most things, eventually.

The electronic ignition and fuel metering systems on modern emission controlled cars are allergic to humidity, heat and dust, and cannot be repaired by bush mechanics. Standard European and Japanese cars run on fuel with a higher octane rating than is commonly available in North, South or Central America, and unleaded fuel is not available, except in Mexico and Guatemala. The most easily maintained petrol engined cars, then, are the types manufactured in Latin American countries, ie pre-emission control models such as the VW Kombi with carburettors and conventional (non-electronic) ignition, or the old type Toyota Landcruisers common in Central America. Older model American cars, especially Ford or GM pickups, are easily maintained, but high fuel consumption offsets this advantage. (Francesca Pagnacco of Exeter adds: Japan has cleaned up in Mexico and Central America as far as transport goes, although Toyota has not arrived yet in Mexico—it is best to bring any little Toyota spares at the outset. Isuzu, Mitsubishi and Datsun/Nissan are present throughout the region. American makes—Ford, Chevrolet, Dodge—are mostly popular in Mexico and Costa Rica. Volkswagen is also present in the region, notably Mexico.)

Preparing the car for the journey is largely a matter of common sense: obviously any part that is not in first class condition should be replaced. It's well worth installing extra heavy-duty shock-absorbers (such as Spax or Koni) before starting out, because a long trip on rough roads in a heavily laden car will give heavy wear. Fit tubes on 'tubeless' tyres, since air plugs for tubeless tyres are hard to find, and if you bend the rim on a pothole, the tyre will not hold air. Take spare tubes, and an extra spare tyre. Although you really don't need spare plugs, fan-belts, radiator hoses or even headlamp bulbs because local equivalents can easily be found, it is wise to take plugs and a spare fanbelt for those occasions late at night or in remote areas when you might need them. You can also change the fanbelt after a stretch of long, hot driving to prevent wear. However, if your car has sophisticated electrics, spare 'black boxes' for the ignition and fuel injection are advisable, plus a spare voltage regulator or the appropriate diodes for the alternator, and elements for the fuel, air and oil filters if these are not a common type. (Some drivers take a spare alternator of the correct amps.) Dirty fuel is a frequent problem, so be prepared to change filters more often than you would at home: in a diesel car you will need to check the sediment bowl often, too. An extra in-line fuel filter is a good idea if feasible (metal canister type preferable to plastic), and for travel on dusty roads an oil bath air filter is best for a diesel car. It is wise to carry a spade, jumper cables, tow rope and an air pump. A 12 volt neon light for camping and repairs will be invaluable. Spare fuel containers should be steel and not plastic, and a siphon pipe is essential for those places where fuel is sold right out of the drum. Take a 10 litre water container for self and vehicle. Note that in some areas gas stations are few and far between. Fill up when you see one: the next one may be out of fuel. Some countries have periodic fuel conservation strategies which means you can't get any after a certain hour in the evening, and often not at weekends either.

Apart from the mechanical aspects, spare no ingenuity in making your car secure. Your model should be the Brink's armoured van: anything less secure can be broken into by the determined and skilled thief. Use heavy chain and padlocks to chain doors shut, fit security catches on windows, remove interior window winders (so that a hand reaching in from a forced vent cannot open the window). All these will help, but none is foolproof. Anything on the outside—wing mirrors, spot lamps, motifs etc—is likely to be stolen too. So are wheels if not secured by locking nuts. Try never to leave the car unattended except in a locked garage or guarded parking space. Street children will generally protect your car fiercely in exchange for a tip. Be sure to note down key numbers and carry spares of the most important ones.

Documents A 'carnet de passage' is no longer necessary in any country. Land entry procedures for all countries are simple, though time-consuming, as the car has to be checked by customs, police and agriculture officials (see, however, Mexico, **Automobiles** in **Information for Visitors**, on regulations). All you need is the registration document in the name of the driver, or, in the case of a car registered in someone else's name, a notarised letter of authorisation. Note that Costa Rica does not recognize the International Driving Licence, which is otherwise useful. In Guatemala, Honduras and Costa Rica, the car's entry is stamped into the passport so you may not leave the country even temporarily without it. A written undertaking that the vehicle will be re-exported after temporary importation is useful and may be requested in Nicaragua, Costa Rica and Panama. Most countries give a limited period of stay, but allow an extension if requested in advance. Of course, do be very careful to keep **all** the papers you are given when you enter, to produce when you leave. (An army of 'helpers' loiters at each border crossing, waiting to guide motorists to each official in the correct order, for a tip. They can be very useful, but don't give them your papers.) Bringing a car in by sea or air is much more complicated and expensive: generally you will have to hire an agent to clear it through, expensive and slow. Insurance for the vehicle against accident, damage or theft is best arranged in the country of origin, but it is getting increasingly difficult to find agencies who offer this service—American International Underwriters no longer does. In Latin American countries it is very expensive to insure against accident and theft, especially as you should take into account the value of the car increased by duties calculated in real (ie non devaluing) terms. If the car is stolen or written off, you will be required to pay very high duty on its value. A few countries (eg Costa Rica) insist on compulsory third party insurance, to be bought at the border: in other countries it's technically required, but not checked up on (again, see Mexico, **Automobiles**, for details on Sanborns and other insurers, who will insure vehicles for driving in Mexico and Central America). Get the legally required minimum cover—not expensive—as soon as you can, because if you should be involved in an accident and are uninsured, your car could be confiscated. If anyone is hurt, pick them up and go straight to the nearest police station or hospital if you are able to do so. Otherwise you may find yourself facing a hostile crowd, even if you are not to blame. Expect frequent road checks by police, military (especially Honduras, where there is a check point on entering and leaving every town), agricultural and forestry produce inspectors, and any other curious official (or guerrilla) who wants to know what a foreigner is doing driving around in his domain. Smiling simple-minded patience is the best tactic to avoid harassment by zealous, often not very well educated officials on these occasions.

From Central To South America—how to avoid the Darién Gap Shipping from Panama to mainland South America is expensive, and requires some shopping around to find the cheapest way. The shipping lines and agents, and the prices for the services from Panama and elsewhere change frequently. Current details will be found in the Panama chapter under **Shipping a Vehicle**, p 846.

Car Hire The main international car hire companies operate in all countries, but tend to be very expensive, reflecting the high costs and accident rates. Hotels and tourist agencies will tell you where to find cheaper rates, but you will need to check that you have such basics as spare wheel and toolkit and functioning lights etc. You'll probably have more fun if you drive yourself, although it's always possible to hire a car with driver—usually somebody's uncle's old banger which will almost certainly run out of fuel /break down after the first few kilometres. If you plan to do a lot of driving and will have time at the end to dispose of it, investigate the possibility of buying a second hand car locally: since hiring is so expensive it may well work out cheaper and will probably do you just as well. For visiting Mexico and beyond, investigate the cost of buying a vehicle in the USA and selling it there at the end of a round trip (do not try to sell a car illegally in Mexico or Central America).

Car Hire Insurance Check exactly what the hirer's insurance policy covers. In many cases it will only protect you against minor bumps and scrapes, not major accidents, nor 'natural' damage (eg flooding). Ask if extra cover is available. Also find out, if using a credit card, whether the card automatically includes insurance. Beware of being billed for scratches which were on the vehicle before you hired it.

Note For RV/motorhome users, a surge protector is recommended to prevent damage to electrical equipment.

Motorcycling The following advice was received from Ashley Rawlings of Bath (England): People are generally very friendly to motorcyclists and you can make many friends by returning friendship to those who show an interest in you.
   The Machine should be off road capable: my choice would be the BMW R80/100/GS for its rugged and simple design and reliable shaft drive, but a Kawasaki KLR 650s, Honda Transalp/Dominator, or the ubiquitous Yamaha XT600 Tenere would also be suitable. Buying a bike in the States and driving down works out cheaper than buying one in the UK. A road bike can go most places, an off road bike can go at the cost of greater effort.
   Preparations: Many roads in Latin America are rough. Fit heavy duty front fork springs and the best quality rebuildable shock absorber you can afford (Ohlins, White Power). Fit lockable luggage such as Krausers (reinforce luggage frames) or make some detachable aluminium panniers. Fit a tank bag and tank panniers for better weight distribution. A large capacity fuel tank (Acerbis), +300 mile/480 km range is essential if going off the beaten track. A washable air filter is a good idea (K&N), also fuel filters, fueltap rubber seals and smaller jets for high altitude Andean motoring. A good set of trails-type tyres as well as a high mudguard are useful. Get to know the bike before you go, ask the dealers in your country what goes wrong with it and arrange a link whereby you can get parts flown out to you. If riding a chain driven bike, a fully enclosed chaincase is useful. A hefty bash plate/sump guard is invaluable.
   Spares: Reduce service intervals by half if driving in severe conditions. A spare rear tyre is useful but you can buy modern tyres in most capital cities. Take oil filters, fork and shock seals, tubes, a good manual, spare cables (taped into position) a plug cap and spare plug lead. A spare electronic ignition is a good idea, try and buy a second hand one and make arrangements to have parts sent out to you. A first class tool kit is a must and if riding a bike with a chain

then a spare set of sprockets and an 'o' ring chain should be carried. Spare brake and clutch levers should also be taken as these break easily in a fall. Parts are few and far between, but mechanics are skilled at making do and can usually repair things. Castrol oil can be bought everywhere and relied upon.

Take a puncture repair kit and tyre levers. Find out about any weak spots on the bike and improve them. Get the book for international dealer coverage from your manufacturer, but don't rely on it. They frequently have few or no parts for modern, large machinery.

Clothes and Equipment: A tough waterproof jacket, comfortable strong boots, gloves and a helmet with which you can use glass goggles (Halycon) which will not scratch and wear out like a plastic visor. The best quality tent and camping gear that you can afford and a petrol stove which runs on bike fuel are helpful.

Security: Not a problem in most countries. Try not to leave a fully laden bike on its own. An Abus D or chain will keep the bike secure. A cheap alarm gives you peace of mind if you leave the bike outside a hotel at night. Most hotels will allow you to bring the bike inside. Look for hotels that have a courtyard or more secure parking and never leave luggage on the bike overnight or whilst unattended.

Documents: Passport, International Driving Licence, bike registration document are necessary. The Carnet de Passage seems only to be absolutely necessary for Ecuador but even there the Customs may allow you through in transit for a limited period.

Shipping: Bikes may be sent from Panama to Colombia by cargo flight (eg CAC). This costs approx US$150 for a 200kg bike (1994 price). You must drain the fuel and oil and remove the battery, but it is easier to disconnect and seal the overflow tube. Tape cardboard over fragile bits and insist on loading the bike yourself. The Darién Gap is impossible unless you carry the bike. It may be possible to get a ship from Colón to Turbo, but flying is just as cheap and safer. Road Knights Motorcycle Club on Allbrook Air Force Base in Panama has full information.

Border Crossings: All borders in Central America seem to work out at about US$20 per vehicle. The exceptions to this are Mexico (see **Automobiles** in Mexico **Information for Visitors**) and Panama (approx US$4.50). All borders are free on exit, or should be on most occasions. Do not try to cross borders on a Sunday or a holiday anywhere as you are charged double the rate in Central America and a charge is levied on the usually free borders in South America. I found South American customs and immigration inspectors mostly to be friendly, polite and efficient. Central America, however, was a different story and it was sometimes very difficult to find out exactly what was being paid for. If in doubt ask to see the boss and/or the rule book.

Travelling with Children We are grateful to Tim and Arlene Frost, of New Zealand, for the following notes, and to Linda and Lawrence Foster, of Wembley, and Hallam and Carole Murray, of London SW11, for additional suggestions.

People contemplating overland travel in Latin America with children should remember that a lot of time can be spent waiting for buses, trains, and especially for aeroplanes. On bus journeys, if the children are good at amusing themselves, or can readily sleep while travelling, the problems can be considerably lessened. If your child is of an early reading age, take reading material with you as it is difficult, and expensive, to find. A bag of, say 30 pieces, of Duplo or Lego can keep young children occupied for hours. Travel on trains, while not as fast or at times as comfortable as buses, allows more scope for moving about. Some trains provide tables between seats, so that games can be played. (Beware of doors left open for ventilation, especially if air-conditioning is not working—Ed.)

Food can be a problem if the children are not adaptable. It is easier to take biscuits, drinks, bread etc with you on longer trips than to rely on meal stops where the food may not be to taste. Avocados are safe, easy to eat and nutritious; they can be fed to babies as young as 6 months and most older children like them. A small immersion heater and jug for making hot drinks is invaluable, but remember that electric current varies. Try and get a dual-voltage one (110v and 220v).

Fares: On all long-distance buses you pay for each seat, and there are no half-fares if the children occupy a seat each. For shorter trips it is cheaper, if less comfortable, to seat small children on your knee. Often there are spare seats which children can occupy after tickets have been collected. In city and local excursion buses, small children generally do not pay a fare, but are not entitled to a seat when paying customers are standing. On sightseeing tours you should *always* bargain for a family rate—often children can go free. (In trains, reductions for children are general, but not universal.)

All civil airlines charge half for children under 12, but some military services don't have half-fares, or have younger age limits. Note that a child travelling free on a long excursion is not always covered by the operator's travel insurance; it is advisable to pay a small premium to arrange cover.

Hotels. In all hotels, bargain for rates. If charges are per person, always insist that 2 children will occupy 1 bed only, therefore counting as 1 tariff. If rates are per bed, the same applies. In either case you can almost always get a reduced rate at cheaper hotels. Occasionally when travelling with a child you will be refused a room in a hotel that is 'unsuitable'. (In restaurants, you can normally buy children's helpings, or divide 1 full-size helping between 2 children.)

Travel with children can bring you into closer contact with Latin American families, and generally, presents no special problems—in fact the path is often smoother for family groups. Officials tend to be more amenable where children are concerned and they are pleased if your child knows a little Spanish. Moreover, even thieves and pickpockets seem to have some of the traditional respect for families, and may leave you alone because of it! Always carry a copy of your child's birth certificate and passport-size photos.

Cycling Hallam Murray writes: Over the past decade, bicycle technology has improved in leaps and bounds. With the advent of Kevlar tyres and puncture-resistant inner tubes it is now theoretically possible to cycle from Alaska to Tierra del Fuego without so much as a single puncture. For the traveller with a zest for adventure and a limited budget there is unlikely to be a finer way to explore. At first glance a bicycle may not appear to be the most obvious vehicle for a major journey, but given ample time and reasonable energy it most certainly is the best. It can be ridden, carried by almost every form of transport from an aeroplane to a canoe, and can even be lifted across one's shoulders over short distances. On my most recent journey from Lake Titicaca to Tierra del Fuego—largely on unpaved roads, many of which would have defeated even the most robust car or truck—I was often envied by travellers using more orthodox transport, for I was able to travel at my own pace, to explore more remote regions and to meet people who are not normally in contact with tourists.

Choosing a Bicycle: The choice of bicycle depends on the type and length of expedition being undertaken and on the terrain and road surfaces likely to be encountered. Unless you are planning a journey almost exclusively on paved roads—when a high quality touring bike such as a Dawes Super Galaxy would probably suffice—I would strongly recommend a mountain bike. The good quality ones (and the cast iron rule is **never** to skimp on quality) are incredibly tough and rugged, with low gear ratios for difficult terrain, wide tyres with plenty of tread for good road-holding, cantilever brakes, and a low centre of gravity for improved stability. Expect to pay upwards of US$800 for such a machine. Although touring bikes, and to a lesser extent mountain bikes, and spares are available in the larger Latin American cities, remember that in the developing world most indigenous manufactured

Travelling Light in Central America?

Travelling Light makes an exclusive range of smart but practical cotton clothing for men and women travelling in hot countries.
We also supply high quality accessories like insect repellents, money belts, sunglasses and flight bags.

Write or ring for free mail order catalogue to

TRAVELLING LIGHT

(CAH), Morland, Penrith, Cumbria CA10 3AZ, UK. Telephone 0931 714488 goods are shoddy and rarely last. In some countries, such as Mexico, Chile and Uruguay, imported components can be found but they tend to be extremely expensive. (Shimano parts are generally the easiest to find.) Buy everything you possibly can before you leave home.

Bicycle Equipment: A small but comprehensive tool kit (to include chain rivet and crank removers, a spoke key and possibly a block remover), a spare tyre and inner tubes, a puncture repair kit with plenty of extra patches and glue, a set of brake blocks, brake and gear cables and all types of nuts and bolts, at least 12 spokes (best taped to the chain stay), a light oil for the chain, tube of waterproof grease, a pump secured by a pump lock, a Blackburn parking block (my choice for the most invaluable accessory and they are cheap and virtually weightless), a cyclometer, a loud bell, and a secure lock and chain. *Richard's Bicycle Book* makes useful reading for even the most mechanically minded.

Luggage and equipment: Strong and waterproof front and back panniers are a must. When packed these are likely to be heavy and should be carried on the strongest racks available. Poor quality racks have ruined many a journey for they take incredible strain on unpaved roads. A top bag cum rucksack (eg Carradice) makes a good addition for use on and off the bike. I used a Cannondale front bag for my maps, camera, compass, altimeter, notebook and small tape-recorder. My total luggage weighed 27 kg—on the high side, but I never felt seriously overweight. (Adrian Stöckli of Basel recommends Ortlieb luggage—front and back—which is waterproof and almost 'sandproof'.) 'Gaffa' tape is excellent for protecting vulnerable parts of panniers and for carrying out all manner of repairs. My most vital equipment included a light and waterproof tent, a 3 season sleeping bag, an Optimus petrol stove (the best I have ever used for it is light and efficient and petrol can be found almost everywhere), a plastic survival bag for storing luggage at night when camping, 4 elastic straps, 4 one-litre water bottles, Swiss Army knife, torch, candle, comprehensive medical kit, money belts, a hat and sunglasses to protect against hours of ferocious tropical sun and small presents such as postcards of home, balloons and plastic badges. A rubber mouse can do wonders for making contact with children in isolated villages.

All equipment and clothes should be packed in plastic bags to give extra protection against dust and rain. (Also protect documents etc carried close to the body from sweat.) Always take the minimum clothing. It's better to buy extra items en route when you find you need them. Naturally the choice will depend on whether you are planning a journey through tropical

Guides to Central America

The Maya Road: Eastern Mexico, Belize and lowland Guatemala – a guide for ecotourists

No frills guide to hiking in Mexico: A pocket-sized guide to 33 hikes and climbs

Getting to know Panama: Beaches, rain forest, people

Guide to Belize: Very detailed information and advice for ecotourists

Send for a catalogue of **Bradt** guides

Bradt Publications	Peribo Pty Ltd	Globe Pequot Press
41 Nortoft Rd	26 Tepko Rd	PO Box 833
Chalfont St Peter	Terrey Hills	Old Saybrook
Bucks SL9 0LA, England	NSW 2084, Australia	CT 06475, USA

Bradt

lowlands, deserts, high mountains or a combination, and whether rain is to be expected. Generally it is best to carry several layers of thin light clothes than fewer bulky, heavy ones. Always keep one set of dry clothes, including long trousers, to put on at the end of the day. I would not have parted with my incredibly light, strong, waterproof and wind resistant goretex jacket and overtrousers. I could have sold them 100 times over and in Bolivia was even offered a young mule in exchange! I took 2 pairs of training shoes and found these to be ideal for both cycling and walking.

Useful Tips: Wind, not hills is the enemy of the cyclist. Try to make the best use of the times of day when there is little; mornings tend to be best but there is no steadfast rule. Take care to avoid dehydration, by drinking regularly. In hot, dry areas with limited supplies of water, be sure to carry an ample supply. For food I carried the staples (sugar, salt, dried milk, tea, coffee, porridge oats, raisins, dried soups, etc) and supplemented these with whatever local foods I could find in the markets. Give your bicycle a thorough daily check for loose nuts or bolts or bearings. See that all parts run smoothly. A good chain should last 2,000 miles, 3,200 km or more but be sure to keep it as clean as possible—an old toothbrush is good for this—and to oil it lightly from time to time. Always camp out of sight of a road. Remember that thieves are attracted to towns and cities, so when sight-seeing, try to leave your bicycle with someone such as a café owner or a priest. Country people tend to be more honest and are usually friendly and very inquisitive. However, don't take unnecessary risks; always see that your bicycle is secure (most hotels will allow bikes to be kept in rooms). In more remote regions dogs can be vicious; carry a stick or some small stones to frighten them off. Traffic on main roads can be a nightmare; it is usually far more rewarding to keep to the smaller roads or to paths if they exist. Most towns have a bicycle shop of some description, but it is best to do your own repairs and adjustments whenever possible. In an emergency it is amazing how one can improvise with wire, string, dental floss, nuts and bolts, odd pieces of tin or 'Gaffa' tape!

The Expedition Advisory Centre, administered by the Royal Geographical Society, 1, Kensington Gore, London SW7 2AR has published a useful monograph entitled *Bicycle Expeditions*, by Paul Vickers. Published in March 1990, it is available direct from the Centre, price £6.50 (postage extra if outside the UK).

Matthias Müller of Berlin 31 adds: From Guatemala to Panama, border officials ask for a document of ownership and a frame number for your bicycle. Without these you will have a lot of trouble crossing frontiers. Ryan Flegal of Los Angeles, California, recommends attaching a rear view mirror 'so you know when to bail because cars are too close behind.' He also says that, instead of taking your own expensive bicycle from home with the attendant need for specialized tools and high risks of loss, one can buy a bike in Latin America. 'Affix a sturdy rear rack, improvise securing luggage to the bicycle, and go. Carry only a patch kit and wrench to remove the wheel, and rely on the many bike mechanics in the area to do the rest'. Also take water purification. Another cyclist, Andy Walter (Swindon UK), agrees that local mechanics, of whom there are plenty in Mexico (usually in every town), are competent and inventive. He adds that in Mexico most roads have a good gravel shoulder to cycle on; displaying a Mexican flag helps to keep the truckers patient and prompts encouragement.

Hiking and Trekking Hilary Bradt, the well-known trekker, author and publisher, writes: A network of paths and tracks covers much of Central America and is in constant use by the local people. In Guatemala, which has a large Indian population, you can walk just about anywhere, but in the more European countries, particularly Costa Rica you must usually limit yourself to the many excellent national parks with hiking trails. Most Central American countries have an Institutos Geográfico Militar which sells topographical maps, scale 1:100,000 or 1:50,000. The physical features shown on these are usually accurate; the trails and place names less so. National Parks offices also sell maps.

Hiking and backpacking should not be approached casually. Even if you only plan to be out a couple of hours you should have comfortable, safe footwear (which can cope with the wet) and a daypack to carry your sweater and waterproof (which must be more than showerproof—Ed). At high altitudes the difference in temperature between sun and shade is remarkable. The longer trips mentioned in this book require basic backpacking equipment. Essential items are: backpack with frame, sleeping bag, closed cell foam mat for insulation, stove, tent or tarpaulin, dried food (not tins), water bottle, compass. Some but not all of these things are available locally.

Hikers have little to fear from the animal kingdom apart from insects (although it's best to avoid actually stepping on a snake), and robbery and assault are very rare. You are much more of a threat to the environment than vice versa. Leave no evidence of your passing; don't litter and don't give gratuitous presents of sweets or money to rural villagers. Respect their system of reciprocity; if they give you hospitality or food, then is the time to reciprocate with presents.

Maps and Guide Books Those from the Institutos Geográficos Militares in the capitals (see above) are often the only good maps available in Latin Amercica. It is therefore wise to get as many as possible in your home country before leaving, especially if travelling by land. A recommended series of general maps is that published by International Travel Map Productions (ITM), World Wide Books and Maps, 736A Granville Street, Vancouver BC, V6Z 1G3, Canada, compiled with historical notes, by Kevin Healey. Available are South America South, North East and North West (1:4,000,000), Amazon Basin (1:4,000,000), The Galapagos Islands (1:500,000), Central America (1:1,800,000), Guatemala and El Salvador (1: 500,000), Costa Rica (1:500,000), Belize (1:350,000), Mexico (1:3,300,000), Mexico City (1:10,000), Mexico South (1:1,000,000), the Yucatán (1:1,000,000) and Baja California (1:1,000,000). Details of Bradt Publications' Backpacking Guide Series, other titles and imported maps and guides are mentioned in our country 'Information for Visitors' sections.

A very useful book, highly recommended, aimed specifically at the budget traveller is *The Tropical Traveller*, by John Hatt (Penguin Books, 3rd edition 1993).

The South American Explorers' Club is at Avenida Portugal 146 (Casilla 3714), Lima, Peru (T 31-44-80), and 1254 Toledo, Apartado 21-431, Eloy Alfaro, Quito, Ecuador (T 566-076), and 126 Indian Creek Road, Ithaca, NY 14850, USA, T (607) 277-0488. The Club publishes a quarterly magazine, *South American Explorer*, which is of great interest, and covers Central American topics. The South American Explorers Club is represented in the UK by Bradt Publications.

The Latin American Travel Advisor is a quarterly news bulletin with up-to-date detailed and reliable information on counties throughout South and Central America. The publication focuses on public safety, health, weather and natural phenomena, travel costs, the economy and politics. It includes maps, tables, and charts comparing different countries and analyzing trends. Every issue has a feature article, a detailed column about each country and a 2-page summary called *The Continent at a Glance*. Available by mail or fax. For a free sample copy contact PO Box 17-17-908, Quito, Ecuador, F 593-2-562-566, E-Mail rku@pi pro ec on Internet.

Literature This Handbook does not at present have space to contain sections on Latin American literature. Interested readers are recommended to see Jason Wilson, *Traveller's Literary Companion, South and Central America* (Brighton, UK: In Print, 1993), which has extracts from works by Latin American writers and by non-Latin Americans about the various countries and has very useful bibliographies.

GENERAL ADVICE

Responsible Tourism Mark Eckstein of David Bellamy Associates writes: Much has been written about the adverse impacts of tourism on the environment and local communities. It is usually assumed that this only applies to the more excessive end of the travel industry such as the Spanish Costas and Bali. However it now seems that travellers can have an impact at almost any density and this is especially true in areas 'off the beaten track' where local people may not be used to western conventions and lifestyles, and natural environments may be very sensitive.

Of course, tourism can have a beneficial impact and this is something to which every traveller can contribute. Many National Parks are part funded by receipts from people who travel to see exotic plants and animals, Barro Colorado (Panama) and the Cockscomb Jaguar Sanctuary (Belize) are good examples of such sites. Similarly, travellers can promote patronage and protection of valuable archaeological sites and heritages through their interest and entrance fees.

However, where visitor pressure is high and/or poorly regulated, damage can occur. This is especially so in parts of the Caribbean where some tour operators are expanding their activities with scant regard for the environment or local communities. It is also unfortunately true that many of the most popular destinations are in ecologically sensitive areas easily disturbed by extra human pressures. The desire to visit sites and communities that are off the beaten track is a driving force for many travellers. However, these are the areas that are often most sensitive to change as a result of increased pressure from visitors. Eventually the very features that tourists travel so far to see may become degraded and so we seek out new sites, discarding the old, and leaving someone else to deal with the plight of local communities and the damaged environment.

Fortunately, there are signs of a new awareness of the responsibilities that the travel industry and its clients need to endorse. For example, some tour operators fund local conservation projects and travellers are now more aware of the impact they may have on host cultures and environments. We can all contribute to the success of what is variously described as responsible, green or alternative tourism. All that is required is a little forethought and consideration. It would be impossible to identify all the possible impacts that might need to be addressed by travellers, but it is worthwhile noting the major areas in which we can all take a more responsible attitude in the countries we visit. These include, changes to natural ecosystems (air, water, land, ecology and wildlife), cultural values (beliefs and behaviour) and the built environment (sites of antiquity and archaeological significance). At an individual level, travellers can reduce their impact if greater consideration is given to their activities. Backpacking along the Maya trade routes makes for great stories, but how do local communities cope with the sudden invasive interest in their lives? Will the availability of easy tourist money and gauche behaviour affect them for the worse, possibly diluting the significance of culture and customs? Similarly, have the environmental implications of increased visitor pressure been considered? Litter and disturbance of wildlife might seem to be small issues and, on an individual scale they probably are, however multiplied several fold they become more serious (as the Inca Trail in Peru can attest).

Some of these impacts are caused by factors beyond the direct control of travellers, such as the management and operation of a hotel chain. Even here it is possible to voice concern about damaging activities and an increasing number of hotels and travel operators are taking 'green concerns' seriously, even if it is only to protect their share of the market.

Environmental Legislation Legislation is increasingly being enacted to control damage to the environment, and in some cases this can have a bearing on travellers. The establishment of National Parks may involve rules and guidelines for visitors and these should always be followed. In addition there may be local or national laws controlling behaviour and use of natural resources (especially wildlife) that are being increasingly enforced. If in doubt, ask. Finally, international legislation, principally the Convention on International Trade in Endangered Species of Wild Fauna and Flora (CITES), may affect travellers.

CITES aims to control the trade in live specimens of endangered plants and animals and also 'recognizable parts or derivatives' of protected species. Sale of Black Coral, Turtle Shells, Protected Orchids and other wildlife is strictly controlled by signatories of the convention. The full list of protected wildlife varies, so if you feel the need to purchase souvenirs and trinkets derived from wildlife, it would be prudent to check whether they are protected. CITES signatories in Central America are: Belize, Costa Rica, El Salvador, Guatemala, Honduras, Nicaragua and Panama. Mexico is not a signatory, although it does have strict laws on the import and export of wildlife. In addition, most European countries, the USA and Canada are all signatories of CITES. Importation of CITES protected species into these countries can lead to heavy fines, confiscation of goods and even imprisonment. Information on the status of legislation and protective measures can be obtained from Traffic International, UK office T (0223) 277427.

Green Travel Companies and Information The increasing awareness of the environmental impact of travel and tourism has led to a range of advice and information services as well as spawning specialist travel companies who claim to provide 'responsible travel' for clients. This is an expanding field and the veracity of claims needs to be substantiated in some cases. The following organizations and publications can provide useful information for those with an interest in pursuing responsible travel opportunities.

Organizations **Green Flag International** Aims to work with travel industry and conservation bodies to improve environments at travel destinations and also to promote conservation programmes at resort destinations. Provides a travellers guide for 'green' tourism as well as advice on destinations, T (UK-0223) 893587. **Tourism Concern** Aims to promote a greater understanding of the impact of tourism on host communities and environments; Froebel College, Roehampton Lane, London SW15 5PU, T (UK-081) 878-9053. **Centre for Responsible Tourism** CRT coordinates a North American network and advises on N American sources of information on responsible tourism. CRT, 2 Kensington Rd, San Anselmo, California, USA. **Centre for the Advancement of Responsive Travel** CART has a range of publications available as well as information on alternative holiday destinations, T (UK-0732) 352757.

Publications *The Good Tourist* by Katie Wood and Syd House (1991) published by Mandarin Paperbacks; addresses issues surrounding environmental impacts of tourism, suggests ways in which damage can be minimised, suggests a range of environmentally sensitive holidays and projects. *Independent Guide to Real Holidays Abroad*, Frank Barrett (1991), suggestions for a range of special interest holidays. Available from the Independent Newspaper (UK).

Souvenirs Remember that these can almost invariably be bought more cheaply away from the capital, though the choice may be less wide. Bargaining seems to be the general rule in most countries' street markets, but don't make a fool of yourself by bargaining over what, to you, is a small amount of money.

If British travellers have no space in their luggage, they might like to remember Tumi, the Latin American Craft Centre, who specialize in Mexican and Andean products and who produce cultural and educational videos for schools: at 23 Chalk Farm Road, London NW1 (T 071-485 4152), 8/9 New Bond Street Place, Bath (T 0225 462367), 1/2 Little Clarendon St, Oxford (T 0865-512307), Bristol, 82 Park St, and Tucan, 29 Bond St, Brighton (T 0273-26351). Tumi (Music) Ltd specializes in different rhythms of Latin America. In Edinburgh there is a Mexican shop called Azteca. There are similar shops in the USA; one good one is on the ground floor of Citicorp Center, Lexington Avenue and 53rd Street, New York.

Photography Always ask permission before photographing people. Take as much film from home as you can; it is expensive in most places, although it can be bought cheaply in the USA or in the Colón Tax Free Zone (Panama). Fuji film is usually harder to find than Kodak. Slide film is also difficult to find. Kodachrome is almost impossible to buy. Some travellers (but not all) have advised against mailing exposed films home; either take them with you, or have them developed, but not printed, once you have checked the laboratory's quality. Note that postal authorities may use less sensitive equipment for X-ray screening than the airports do. Modern controlled X-ray machines are supposed to be safe even when a slow film passes through it dozens of times, but it is worth trying to avoid X-ray as the doses are cumulative. Many airport officials will allow film to be passed outside X-ray arches; they may also hand-check a suitcase with a large quantity of film if asked politely.

Dan Buck and Anne Meadows write: A note on developing film in Latin America. Black and white is a problem. Often it is shoddily machine-processed and the negatives are ruined. Ask the store if you can see an example of their laboratory's work and if they hand-develop.

Jeremy Till and Sarah Wigglesworth suggest that exposed film can be protected in humid areas by putting it in a balloon and tying a knot. Similarly, keeping your camera in a plastic bag may reduce the effects of humidity.

Mail Postal services in most countries are not very efficient, and pilfering is frequent. All mail, especially packages, should be registered. Some travellers recommend that mail should be sent to one's Embassy (or, if a card-or cheque holder, American Express agent) rather than to the Poste Restante/General Delivery (*Lista de Correos*) department of a country's Post Office. Some Embassies and post offices, however, do not keep mail for more than a month. If there seems to be no mail at the Lista under the initial letter of your surname, ask them to look under the initial of your forename or your middle name. For the smallest risk of misunderstanding, use title, initial and surname only. (If you're a British male, and all else fails, ask them to look under 'E' for 'Esquire'!—Geoffrey van Dulken.)

Phones US travellers should know about AT&T's 'USA Direct', by which you can connect with an AT&T operator without going through a local one. It is much cheaper than operator-assisted calls and is widely available. Other countries have similar systems, eg UK, Canada; obtain details before leaving home.

Communicating by fax is a convenient way of sending messages home. Many places with public fax machines (post offices, telephone companies or shops) will receive messages as well as send.

World Band Radio Richard Robinson writes: South America has more local and community radio stations than practically anywhere else in the world; a shortwave (world band) radio offers a practical means to brush up on the language, sample popular culture and absorb some of the richly varied regional music. International broadcasters such as the BBC World Service, the Voice of America and the Quito-based Evangelical station, HCJB, keep the traveller abreast of news and events, in both English and Spanish.

Compact or miniature portables are recommended, with digital tuning and a full range of shortwave bands, as well as FM, long and medium wave. Detailed advice on radio models (£150 for a decent one) and wavelengths can be found in the annual publication, *Passport to World Band Radio* (Box 300, Penn's Park, PA 18943, USA). Details of local stations are listed in *World TV and Radio Handbook* (WRTH), PO Box 9027, 1006 AA Amsterdam, The Netherlands, US$19.95. Both of these, free wavelength guides and selected radio sets, are available from the BBC World Service Bookshop, Bush House Arcade, Bush House, Strand, London WC2B 4PH, UK, T 071-257 2576.

Travelling Alone Many points of security, dress and language have been covered already. These additional hints have mainly been supplied by women, but most apply to any single traveller. When you set out, err on the side of caution until your instincts have adjusted to the customs of a new culture. If, as a single woman, you can befriend a local woman, you will learn much more about the country you are visiting. Unless actively avoiding foreigners like yourself, don't go too far from the beaten track; there is a very definite 'gringo trail' which you can join, or follow, if seeking company. This can be helpful when seeking safe accommodation, especially if arriving after dark (which is best avoided). Remember that for a single woman a taxi at night can be as dangerous as wandering around on her own. At borders dress as smartly as possible. Travelling by train is a good way to meet locals, but buses are much easier for a person alone; on major routes your seat is often reserved and your luggage can usually be locked in the hold. It is easier for men to take the friendliness of locals at face value; women may be subject to much unwanted attention. To help minimize this, do not wear suggestive clothing and, advises Alex Rossi of Jawa Timur, Indonesia, do not flirt. By wearing a wedding ring, carrying a photograph of your 'husband' and 'children', and saying that your 'husband' is close at hand, you may dissuade an aspiring suitor. If politeness fails, and a man persists, specially mentioning sex or being obnoxious, do not feel bad about showing offence and departing. When accepting a social invitation, make sure that someone knows the address and the time you left. Ask if you can bring a friend (even if you do not intend to do so). A good rule is always to act with confidence, as though you know where you are going, even if you do not. Someone who looks lost is more likely to attract unwanted attention. Do not disclose to strangers where you are staying. (Much of this information was supplied by Alex Rossi, and by Deirdre Mortell of Carrigaline, Co Cork).

Final Hints Everybody has his/her own list. Items most often mentioned include a small portable stove (liquid fuel is more readily available than gas—though the latter is becoming more common—and you need a combination canteen to go with it), air cushions for slatted seats, inflatable travel pillow for neck support, strong shoes (and remember that footwear over 9½ English size, or 42 European size, is difficult to obtain in Latin America except Argentina and Brazil), money-belt or neck pouch; a small first-aid kit and handbook, fully waterproof top clothing, waterproof treatment for leather footwear, wax earplugs (which are impossible to find outside large cities) and airline-type eye mask to help you sleep in noisy and poorly curtained hotel rooms, rubber-thong Japanese-type sandals (flip-flops), a polyethylene sheet 2 x 1m to cover possibly infested beds and train floors and shelter your luggage, polyethylene bags of varying sizes (up to heavy duty rubbish bag size) with ties, a toilet bag you can tie round your waist, a sheet sleeping-bag and pillow-case or a separate pillow-case—in some countries they are not changed often in cheap hotels, a mosquito net (or a hammock with a fitted net), a straw hat which can be rolled or flattened and reconstituted after 15 mins soaking in water, a clothes line, a nailbrush (useful for scrubbing dirt off clothes as well as off oneself), a vacuum flask, a water bottle, a small dual-voltage immersion heater, a small dual-voltage (or battery-driven) electric fan, tea bags, a light nylon waterproof shopping bag, a universal bath- and basin-plug of the flanged type that will fit any waste-pipe (or improvise one from a sheet of thick rubber), string, velcro, electrical insulating tape, large penknife preferably with tin and bottle openers, scissors and corkscrew—the famous Swiss Army range has been repeatedly recommended (for knife sharpening, go to a butcher's shop), collapsible drinking beaker, electric motor-cycle alarm for luggage protection, a flour sack and roll of wire mesh for ditto, alarm clock or watch, candle, torch (flashlight)—especially one that will clip on to a pocket or belt, pocket mirror, small transistor radio with earphones, pocket dictionary, pocket calculator, an adaptor and flex to enable you to take power from an electric-light socket (the Edison screw type is the most commonly used), a padlock for the doors of the cheapest and most casual hotels (or for tent zip if camping), spare chain-lengths and padlock for securing luggage to bed or bus/train seat. Useful medicaments are given at the end of the 'Health Information' section (**p 46**); to these might be added some lip salve with sun protection, and pre-moistened wipes (such as 'Wet Ones'). Always carry toilet paper. Natural fabric sticking plasters, as well as being long-lasting, are much appreciated as gifts. Dental floss can be used for backpack repairs, in addition to its original purpose. **Never** carry firearms. Their possession could land you in serious trouble.

A note for **contact lens wearers**: the availability of products for the care of lenses varies from country to country (throughout Central America, but not Mexico, it is hard to find). In any country, lens solutions can be difficult to find outside major cities. Where available, it is expensive. Practice also varies as to whether it is stocked by chemists/pharmacies or opticians.

Be careful when asking directions. Women probably know more about the neighbourhood; men about more distant locations. Policemen are often helpful. However, many Latin Americans will give you the wrong answer rather than admit they do not know; this may be partly because they fear losing face, but is also because they like to please. You are more likely to get reliable information if you carefully refrain from asking leading questions.

Lastly, a good principle is to take half the clothes (trousers with plenty of pockets are very useful), and twice the money, that you think you will need.

WILL YOU HELP US?

We do all we can to get our facts right in the **MEXICO & CENTRAL AMERICAN HANDBOOK**. Each section is thoroughly revised each year, but the territory is vast and our eyes cannot be everywhere. If you have enjoyed a tour, trek, train trip, beach, museum or any other activity and would like to share it, please write with all the details. We are always pleased to hear about any restaurants, bars or hotels you have enjoyed. When writing, please give the year on the cover of your Handbook and the page number referred to. In return we will send you details of our special guidebook offer.

Thank you very much indeed for your help.

TRADE & TRAVEL
Handbooks

Write to The Editor, Mexico & Central American Handbook, Trade & Travel, 6 Riverside Court, Lower Bristol Road, Bath BA2 3DZ. England

HEALTH INFORMATION

The following information has been compiled for us by Dr David Snashall, who is presently Senior Lecturer in Occupational Health at St Thomas's Hospital Medical School in London and Chief Medical Advisor of the British Foreign and Commonwealth Office. He has travelled extensively in Central and South America, worked in Peru and in East Africa and keeps in close touch with developments in preventative and tropical medicine. We incorporate also some welcome observations on the text by Dr C J Schofield, editor of Parasitology Today.

THE TRAVELLER to Mexico and Central America is inevitably exposed to health risks not encountered in Britain or the USA, especially if he/she spends time in the tropical regions. Epidemic diseases have been largely brought under control by vaccination programmes and public sanitation but, in rural areas, the latter is rudimentary and the chances of contracting infections of various sorts are much higher than at home.

There are English-speaking doctors in most major cities. If you fall ill the best plan may be to attend the out-patient department of a local hospital or contact your Embassy representative for the name of a reputable doctor. (We give the names of hospitals and some recommended doctors in the main city sections.—Ed) Medical practices vary from those at home but remember they have particular experience in dealing with locally-occurring diseases.

Self-medication is undesirable except for minor complaints but may be forced on you by circumstances. Whatever the circumstances, be wary of medicines prescribed for you by pharmacists; many are poorly trained and unscrupulous enough to sell you potentially dangerous drugs or old stock they want to get rid of. The large number of pharmacies throughout Central America is a considerable surprise to most people, as is the range of medicines you can purchase over the counter. There is a tendency towards over-prescription of drug mixtures and in general this should be resisted. Many drugs are manufactured under licence from American or European companies so the trade names may be familiar to you. This means that you do not need to carry a whole chest of medicines, but remember that the shelf-life of some items, especially vaccines and antibiotics, is markedly reduced in tropical conditions. Buy your supplies at the better outlets where they have refrigerators, even though it is more expensive. Check the expiry date of all preparations you buy.

Immigration officials sometimes confiscate scheduled drugs (Lomotil is an example) if they are not accompanied by a doctor's prescription.

With the following precautions and advice, you should keep as healthy as usual. Make local enquiries about health risks if you are apprehensive and take the general advice of European or North American families who have lived or are living in the country.

Before you go take out medical insurance. You should have a dental check-up, obtain a spare glasses prescription, a spare oral contraceptive prescription and, if you suffer from a chronic illness (such as diabetes, high blood pressure, ear or sinus troubles, cardiopulmonary disease or a nervous disorder) arrange for a check-up with your doctor, who can at the same time provide you with a letter explaining the details of your disability, if possible in English and Spanish. Check current practice in malaria prophylaxis (prevention).

Inoculations Smallpox vaccination is no longer required anywhere in the world. A major outbreak of cholera occurred, unusually, in Peru in 1990-91. The epidemic spread subsequently to much of South America and to Central American countries including Mexico. Cholera vaccination is available but it is not very effective. Occasionally border officials may ask to see proof of such vaccination, especially if you are arriving from a South American country where the epidemic is still rife.

The following vaccinations are recommended:

Yellow fever: this is a live vaccine not to be given to children under 9 months of age or persons allergic to eggs. Immunity lasts 10 years. An international certificate of yellow fever vaccination will be given and should be kept because it is sometimes asked for.

Typhoid (monovalent): 1 dose followed by a booster in a month's time. Immunity from this course lasts 2 to 3 years. An oral preparation has been developed.

Poliomyelitis: this is a live vaccine generally given orally and a full course consists of 3 doses with a booster in tropical regions every 3 to 5 years.

Tetanus: 1 dose should be given with a booster (vital) at 6 weeks and another at 6 months, and 10-yearly boosters thereafter are recommended.

Children should, in addition, be properly protected against diphtheria, and against pertussis (whooping cough) and measles, both of which tend to be more serious infections than at home. Measles, mumps and rubella vaccine is now widely available but those teenage girls who have not had rubella (German measles) should be tested and vaccinated. Consult your doctor for advice on tuberculosis inoculation: the disease is still widespread.

Infectious Hepatitis (jaundice) is endemic throughout Mexico and Central America and seems to be frequently caught by travellers. The main symptoms are

"Is it safe to travel in Central America?"

GET SOUND ADVICE...

· From our quarterly news bulletin:
  The Latin American Travel Advisor.
· Featuring up-to-date details about public safety,
  health, weather, travel costs, the economy and politics.
· Urgent information is available by fax.
· Plus a complete selection of books, maps and videos.
· Request your free sample edition & traveller's catalogue.

...OR LET US GUIDE YOU.

· We are **professional private guides**, not travel agents,
  tour brokers or operators.
· No packages or pre-assigned groups. *You* set the pace and
  choose the style of your travels, anywhere in Latin America.
· English, French, German, Spanish and Portuguese spoken.
· Send us a brief description of your travel interests today.

LATIN AMERICAN TRAVEL CONSULTANTS

| THE LATIN AMERICAN TRAVEL ADVISOR | TRAVEL BOOKS & MAPS | PROFESSIONAL PRIVATE GUIDES |

P.O. Box 17-17-908, Quito, Ecuador. Fax: +593-2-562-566. Internet: rku@pi.pro.ec pains in the stomach, lack of appetite, lassitude, and the typical yellow colour of the skin. Medically speaking there are 2 different types, the less serious but more common is hepatitis A, for which the best protection is the careful preparation of food, the avoidance of contaminated drinking water and scrupulous attention to toilet hygiene. Human normal immunoglobulin (gamma globulin) confers considerable protection against the disease and is particularly useful in epidemics; it should be obtained from a reputable source and is certainly useful for travellers who intend to live rough: they should have a shot before leaving and have it repeated every 6 months. The dose of gamma globulin depends on the concentration of the particular preparation used, so the manufacturer's advice should be taken. A smaller dose than usual can be given if exposure is for 1 or 2 months only. At last an effective vaccination against hepatitis A has been developed and is generally available. Three shots over 6 months appear to give very good protection lasting up to 10 years.

The other, more serious, version is hepatitis B which is acquired usually by injections with unclean needles, blood transfusions, as a sexually transmitted disease and possibly by insect bites. This disease can be effectively prevented by a specific vaccination requiring 3 shots over 6 months before travelling but this is quite expensive. If you have had jaundice in the past it would be worthwhile having a blood test to see if you are immune to either of the 2 types because this might avoid the necessity for vaccination or gamma globulin.

Other vaccinations might be considered in the case of epidemics, eg meningitis. There is an effective vaccination against **rabies** which should be considered by all travellers, especially those going to remote areas and if there is a particular occupational risk, ie zoologists or veterinarians.

AIDS in Mexico and Central America is increasing in its prevalence, as in most countries, but is still largely confined to the well known high risk sections of the population, ie homosexual men, intravenous drug abusers, prostitutes and children of infected mothers. The main risk to travellers is from casual sex in the main cities, and the same precautions should be taken as when encountering any sexually transmitted disease. The AIDS virus (HIV) can be passed via unsterilized needles which have been previously used to inject an HIV positive patient, but the risk of this is very small indeed. It would however be sensible to check that needles have been properly sterilised or disposable needles used. If you wish to take your own disposable needles, be prepared to explain what they are for. The risk of receiving a blood transfusion with blood infected with the HIV virus is greater than from dirty needles because of the amount of fluid exchanged. Supplies of blood for transfusion should now be screened for HIV in all reputable hospitals so again the risk must be very small indeed. Catching the AIDS virus does not usually produce an illness in itself; the only way to be sure if you feel you have been put at risk is to have a blood test for HIV antibodies on your return to a place where there are reliable laboratory facilities. The test does not become positive for many weeks.

Common Problems, some of which will almost certainly be encountered, are:

Heat and Cold Full acclimatization to high temperatures takes about 2 weeks and during this period it is normal to feel relatively apathetic, especially if the relative humidity is high. Drink plenty of water (up to 15 litres a day are required when working physically hard in the tropics), use salt on your food and avoid extreme exertion. Tepid showers are more cooling than hot or cold ones. Large hats do not cool you down, but do prevent sunburn. Remember that, especially in the highlands, there can be a large and sudden drop in temperature between sun and shade and between night and day, so dress accordingly. Warm jackets and woollens are essential after dark at high altitude.

Altitude The highest major city in Mexico/Central America is Mexico City at 2,240m which is unlikely to cause any symptons more serious than some breathlessness and heart pounding. The following remarks therefore apply mainly to hill walkers and mountain climbers. Acute mountain sickness or *soroche* can strike from about 3,000m upwards. It is more likely to affect those who ascend rapidly (eg by plane) and those who over-exert themselves. Teenagers are particularly prone. Past experience is not always a good guide: the author, having spent years in Peru travelling constantly between sea level and very high altitude, never suffered the slightest symptoms, then was severely affected climbing Kilimanjaro in Tanzania.

On reaching heights above 3,000m, heart pounding and shortness of breath, especially on exertion, are almost universal and a normal response to the lack of oxygen in the air. *Soroche* takes a few hours or days to come on and presents with headache, lassitude, dizziness, loss of appetite, nausea and vomiting. Insomnia is common and often associated with a suffocating feeling when lying in bed. Keen observers may note their breathing tends to wax and wane at night and their face tends to be puffy in the mornings—this is all part of the syndrome. The treatment is rest, pain killers (preferably not aspirin-based) for the headache and anti-sickness pills for vomiting. Oxygen may help at very high altitudes. Various local panaceas ("Coramina glucosada', 'Effortil', 'Micoren') have their advocates.

On arrival at places over 3,000m, a few hours' rest in a chair and avoidance of alcohol, cigarettes and heavy food will go a long way towards preventing *soroche*. Should the symptoms be severe and prolonged it is best to descend to lower altitude and re-ascend slowly or in stages. If this is impossible because of shortage of time or if the likelihood of acute mountain sickness is high then the drug Acetazoleamide (Diamox) can be used as a preventative and continued during the ascent. There is good evidence of the value of this drug in the prevention of *soroche* but some people do experience funny side effects. The usual dose is 500 mg of the slow-release preparation each night, starting the night before ascending above 3,000m. (Detailed information is available from the Mountain Medicine Centre, c/o Dr Charles Clarke, Dept of Neurological Sciences, St Bartholomew's Hospital, 38 Little Britain, London EC1A 7BE—Ed)

Other problems experienced at high altitude are sunburn, excessively dry air causing skin cracking, sore eyes (it may be wise to leave your contact lenses out) and stuffy noses. It is unwise to ascend to high altitude if you are pregnant, especially in the first 3 months, or if you have any history of heart, lung or blood disease, including sickle-cell.

There is a further, albeit rare, hazard due to rapid ascent to high altitude called acute pulmonary oedema. The condition comes on quite rapidly with breathlessness, noisy breathing, cough, blueness of the lips and frothing at the mouth. Anybody developing this must be brought down as soon as possible, given oxygen and taken to hospital.

Rapid descent from high places will aggravate sinus and middle ear infections, and make bad teeth ache painfully. The same problems are sometimes experienced during descent at the end of a flight.

Despite these various hazards (mostly preventable) of high-altitude travel, many people find the environment healthier and more invigorating than at sea-level.

Intestinal Upsets Practically nobody escapes this one, so be prepared for it. Most of the time it is due to the insanitary preparation of food. Don't eat uncooked fish or vegetables, fruit with the skin on (always peel your fruit yourself), food that is exposed to flies, or salads. Tap water is rarely safe outside the major cities, especially in the rainy season, and stream water is often contaminated by communities living surprisingly high in the mountains. Filtered or bottled (make sure it is opened in your presence—Ed) water is usually available and safe. If your hotel has a central hot-water supply, this is safe to drink after cooling. (In Mexico, many hotels provide chilled drinking water.) Ice for drinks should be made from boiled water but rarely is, so stand your glass on the ice cubes rather than putting them in the drink. Dirty water should first be strained through a filter bag (available from camping shops) and then boiled or treated. Water in general can be rendered safe in the following ways: boil for 5 mins at sea level, longer at higher altitudes; or add 3 drops of household bleach (but not modern, treated bleach) to 1 pint of water and leave for 15 mins; or add 1 drop of tincture of iodine to 1 pint of water and leave for 3 mins. Commercial water-sterilizing tablets are available, for instance Sterotabs from Boots, England. (Also recommended are compact water filters, for instance Travel Well, Pre Mac (Kent) Ltd, Tunbridge Wells, or the Swiss-made Katadyn.)

Fresh, unpasteurized milk is a source of food poisoning germs, tuberculosis and brucellosis. This applies equally to ice-cream, yoghurt and cheese made from unpasteurized milk. Fresh milk can be rendered safe by heating it to 62°C for 30 mins followed by rapid cooling, or by boiling it. Matured or processed cheeses are safer than fresh varieties. Heat-treated (UHT), pasteurized or sterilized milk is becoming more available. Fruit juice should be pure, not diluted with water.

Diarrhoea – Diagnosis and treatment   Diarrhoea is usually caused by eating food which is contaminated by food poisoning germs. Drinking water is rarely the culprit. Seawater or river water is more likely to be contaminated by sewage and so swimming in such dilute effluent can also be a cause. Infection with various organisms can give rise to diarrhoea, eg viruses, bacteria (eg Escherichia coli, probably the most common cause), protozoa (amoeba), salmonella and cholera. The diarrhoea may come on suddenly or rather slowly. It may or may nor be accompanied by vomiting or by severe abdominal pain and the passage of blood or mucus when it is called dysentery. How do you know which type you have and how to treat it?

If you can time the onset of the diarrhoea to the minute (acute) then it is probably due to a virus or a bacterium and/or the onset of dysentery. The treatment, in addition to rehydration is Ciprofloxacin 500 mgs every 12 hrs. The drug is now widely available as are various similar ones.

If the diarrhoea comes on slowly or intermittently (sub-acute) then it is more likely to be protozoal ie caused by an amoeba or giardia and antibiotics will have little effect. These cases are best treated by a doctor, as is any outbreak of diarrhoea continuing for more than 3 days. Sometimes blood is passed in sub-acute amoebic dysentery and for this you should certainly seek medical help. If this is not available then the best treatment is probably Tinidazole (Fasigyn) 1 tablet 4 times a day for 3 days. If there are severe stomach cramps, the following drugs may help but are not very useful in the management of acute diarrhoea: Loperamide (Imodium, Arret) and Diphenoxylate with Atropine (Lomotil).

Any kind of diarrhoea whether or not accompanied by vomiting responds well to the replacement of water and salts taken as frequent small sips of some kind of rehydration solution. There are preparatory preparations consisting of sachets of powder which you dissolve in boiled water, or you can make your own by adding half of teaspoonful of salt (3.5 grams) and 4 tablespoonfuls of sugar (40 grams) to a litre of boiled water.

Thus the lynchpins of treatment for diarrhoea are rest, fluid and salt replacement, antibiotics such as Ciprofloxacin for the bacterial types and special diagnostic tests and medical treatment for the amoeba and giardia infections. Salmonella infections and cholera can be devastating diseases and it would be wise to get to a hospital as soon as possible if these were suspected. Fasting, peculiar diets and the consumption of large quantities of yoghurt have not been found useful in calming travellers diarrhoea or in rehabilitating inflamed bowels. Oral rehydration has on the other hand, especially in children, been a lifesaving technique and it should always be practised whatever other treatment you use. As there is some evidence that alcohol and milk might prolong diarrhoea they should probably be avoided during and immediately after an attack. Diarrhoea occurring day after day for long periods of time (chronic diarrhoea) is notoriously resistant to amateur attempts at treatment and again warrants proper diagnostic tests (most towns with reasonable-sized hospitals have laboratories for stool samples). There are ways of preventing travellers diarrhoea for short periods of time by taking antibiotics, but this is not a foolproof technique and should not be used other than in exceptional circumstances. Doxycycline is possibly the best drug. Some preventatives such as Enterovioform can have serious side effects if taken for long periods.

Paradoxically, constipation is also common, probably induced by dietary change, inadequate fluid intake in hot places and long bus journeys. Simple laxatives are useful in the short term (the Editor recommends Senokot) and bulky foods such as maize, beans and plenty of fruit are also useful.

Insects These can be a great nuisance, especially in the tropics, and some, of course, are carriers of serious diseases. The best way of keeping them away at night is to sleep off the ground with a mosquito net and to burn mosquito coils containing pyrethrum. The best way to use insecticide aerosol sprays is to spray the room thoroughly in all areas and then shut the door for a while, re-entering when the smell has dispersed. Tablets of insecticide are also available which, when placed on a heated mat plugged into a wall socket, fill the room with insecticide fumes in the same way. The best repellents contain di-ethyl-meta-toluamide (DET) or di-methyl phthalate—sold as 'Deet', 'Six-Twelve Plus', 'Off', 'Boots' Liquid Insect Repellent', 'Autan', 'Flypel'. Liquid is best for arms and face (care around eyes) and aerosol spray for clothes and ankles to deter chiggers, mites and ticks. Liquid DEET suspended in water can be used to impregnate cotton clothes and mosquito nets.

If you are bitten, itching may be relieved by baking-soda baths, anti-histamine tablets (care with alcohol or driving), corticosteroid creams (great care—never use if any hint of sepsis) or by judicious scratching. Calamine lotion and cream have limited effectiveness and antihistamine creams (eg Antihisan, May & Baker) have a tendency to cause skin allergies and are, therefore, not generally recommended.

Bites which become infected (commonly in the tropics) should be treated with a local antiseptic or antibiotic cream, such as Cetrimide BP (Savlon, ICI) as should infected scratches.

Skin infestations with body lice (crabs) and scabies are, unfortunately, easy to pick up. Use gamma benzene hexachloride for lice and benzene benzoate solution for scabies. Crotamiton cream (Eurax, Geigy) alleviates itching and also kills a number of skin parasites. Malathion lotion 5% (Prioderm) kills lice effectively, but do not use the toxic agricultural insecticide Malathion.

Ticks attach themselves usually to the lower part of the body often after walking in areas where cattle have grazed. They take a while to attach themselves strongly but do swell up as they suck your blood. The important thing is to remove them gently so that they do not inject any disease into your body and if the head part of the tick is left inside the skin it may cause a nasty allergic reaction some days later, and become infected. Don't use petrol, vaseline, lighted cigarettes etc, to remove the tick but, with a pair of tweezers, remove the beast gently by gripping it at the attached (head) end and rock it out very much the way that a tooth is extracted.

Certain tropical flies which lay their eggs under the skin of sheep and cattle also occasionally do the same thing to humans with the unpleasant result that a maggot grows under the skin and this presents as a boil or pimple. The best way of removing these is to cover the boil with oil, vaseline or nail varnish so as to stop the maggot breathing, then to squeeze it out gently the next day.

Malaria in Central America is theoretically confined to coastal and jungle zones. The disease is not common. Mosquitoes do not thrive above 2,500m so you are safe at altitude. There are different varieties of malaria, some resistant to the normal drugs. Make local enquiries if you intend to visit possibly infected zones and use one of the following prophylactic regimes. Start taking the tablets a few days before exposure and continue to take them for 6 weeks after leaving the malarial zone. Remember to give the drugs to babies and children also. Opinion varies on the precise drugs and dosage to be used for protection; all the drugs may have some side effects, and it is important to balance the risk of catching the disease against the albeit rare side effects. The increasing complexity of the subject as the malarial parasite becomes immune to the new generation of drugs has made concentration on the physical prevention of being bitten by mosquitoes more important, ie the use of long-sleeved shirts/blouses and long trousers, repellents and nets. Clothing impregnated with an insecticide, Permethrin or Deltamethrin, is now becoming available, as are wide-meshed mosquito nets impregnated with the same substance. These are lighter to carry and less claustrophobic to sleep in.

Prophylactic regimes:
Proguanil (Paludrine ICI 100 mg, 2 tablets daily) *or* Chloroquine (Avloclor; ICI, Malarivon; Wallace MFG, Nivaquine, May & Baker; Resochin, Bayer; Aralen 300 mg base (2 tablets) weekly).

Where there is a high risk of Chloroquine-resistant falciparum malaria, take Chloroquine plus Proguanil in the above-mentioned doses and carry Fansidar (Roche, also spelt Falsidar) for treatment; *or* add Paludrine 2 tablets per day to your routine Chloroquine prophylaxis.

Some authorities are recommending alternative drugs for prophylaxis, eg Mefloquin, Doxycycline. Before going to a malarial area, seek expert advice since changes worldwide in the subject are so rapid.

You can catch malaria even when sticking to the above rules, although it is unlikely. If you do develop symptoms (high fever, shivering, headache, sometimes diarrhoea) seek medical advice immediately. If this is not possible, and there is a great likelihood of malaria, the *treatment* is:

Normal types: Chloroquine, a single dose of 4 tablets (600 mg) followed by 2 tablets (300 mg) in 6 hrs and 300 mg each day following.
Falciparum type or type in doubt: Fansidar, single dose of 3 tablets. (We have been told that this drug does not combine well with alcohol, so best to avoid drinking during treatment period.)

If Falciparum type malaria is definitely diagnosed, it is wise to get to a good hospital as the treatment can be complex and the illness very serious.

Pregnant women are particularly prone to malaria and should stick to Proguanil as a prophylactic. Chloroquine may cause eye damage if taken over a long period. The safety of Fansidar has been questioned and, at the time of writing, it is not recommended for prophylaxis.

Sunburn The burning power of the tropical sun, especially at high altitude, is phenomenal. Always wear a wide-brimmed hat and use some form of suncream lotion on untanned skin. Normal temperate-zone suntan lotions (protection factor up to 7) are not much good; you need to use the types designed specifically for the tropics, or for mountaineers or skiers, with the highest protection factor. These are often not available in Central America; a reasonable substitute is zinc oxide ointment. Glare from the sun can cause conjunctivitis, so wear sunglasses. especially on tropical beaches, where high protection-factor sunscreen cream should also be used.

Snakebite If you are unlucky enough to be bitten by a venomous snake, spider, scorpion or sea creature, try (within limits) to catch the animal for identification. The reactions to be expected are: fright, swelling, pain and bruising around the bite, soreness of the regional lymph glands, nausea, vomiting and fever. If any of the following symptoms supervene, get the victim to a doctor without delay: numbness and tingling of the face, muscular spasms, convulsion, shortness of breath and haemorrhage. The tiny coral snake, with red, black and white bands, is the most dangerous, but is very timid.

Commercial snakebite and scorpion kits are available, but only useful for the specific type of snake or scorpion for which they are designed. The serum has to be given intravenously so is not much good unless you have had some practice at making injections into veins. If the bite is on a limb, immobilize the limb and apply a tight bandage between the bite and the body, releasing it for 90 seconds every 15 mins. Reassurance of the bitten person is very important because death from snakebite is very rare. Do not slash the bite area and try to suck out the poison because this sort of heroism does more harm than good. Hospitals usually hold stocks of snake bite serum. Best precaution: don't walk in snake territory with bare feet or sandals—wear proper shoes or boots.

Spiders and Scorpions These may be found in the more basic hotels. The sting of some species of Mexican scorpions can be quite dangerous. Anti-venom is available in the larger hospitals. If bitten by a spider, or stung by a scorpion, rest and take plenty of fluids, and call a doctor. Precaution: keep beds away from the walls, investigate the underside of the toilet seat and look inside shoes before putting them on in the morning.

Other Afflictions Remember that **rabies** is endemic throughout Latin America so avoid dogs that are behaving strangely, and cover your toes at night to foil the vampire bats, which also carry the disease. If you are bitten, try to have the animal captured for observation and see a doctor at once. Treatment with human diploid vaccine is now extremely effective and worth seeking out if the likelihood of having contracted rabies is high.
Dengue fever has made its appearance in southern Mexico and the lower-lying parts of Central America; also in Brazil. No treatment: you must just avoid mosquito bites.
Typhus can still occur, carried by ticks. There is usually a reaction at the site of the bite and a fever: seek medical advice.
Intestinal worms are common, and the more serious ones such as **hookworm** can be contracted from walking barefoot on infested earth or beaches. Various other tropical diseases can be caught in jungle areas, usually transmitted by biting insects; they are often related to African diseases and were probably introduced by the slave trade from Africa.
Onchocerciasis (river-blindness), carried by blackflies, is found in parts of Mexico. Cutaneous **leishmaniasis** (Espundia) is carried by sandflies and causes a sore that won't heal; wearing long trousers and long-sleeved shirts in infectious areas helps to avoid the fly. Epidemics of meningitis occur from time to time.
Dangerous animals Apart from mosquitoes, the most dangerous animals are men, be they bandits or behind steering wheels. Think carefully about violent confrontations and wear a seatbelt, if you are lucky enough to have one available to you.
Prickly heat, a very common itchy rash, is avoided by frequent washing and by wearing loose clothing. Cured by allowing skin to dry off through use of powder, and spending 2 nights in an air-conditioned hotel! **Athlete's foot** and other fungal infections are best treated with Tinaderm.

Psychological disorders First time exposure to countries where sections of the population live in extreme poverty or squalor and may even be starving can cause odd psychological reactions in visitors. So can the exceptional curiosity extended to visitors, especially women. Simply be prepared for this and try not to over-react.

When you return home   Remember to take your anti-malarial tablets for 6 weeks. If you have had attacks of diarrhoea, it is worth having a stool specimen tested in case you have picked up amoebic dysentery. If you have been living rough, a blood test may be worthwhile to detect worms and other parasites. If you have been exposed to bilharzia by swimming in lakes, etc, check by means of a blood test when you get home, but leave it for 6 weeks because the test is slow to become positive. Report any untoward symptoms to your doctor and tell the doctor exactly where you have been and, if you know, what is the likelihood of diseases to which you were exposed.

Basic supplies   The following items you may find useful to take with you from home: sunglasses (if you use clip-on sunglasses, take a spare pair – Ed), ear plugs, suntan cream, insect repellent, flea powder, mosquito net, coils or tablets, tampons, condoms, contraceptives, water sterilizing tablets, anti-malaria tablets, anti-infective ointment, dusting powder for feet, travel sickness pills, antacid tablets, anti-diarrhoea tablets, sachets of rehydration salts and a first aid kit.

Health packs containing sterile syringes, needles, gloves, etc, are available for travellers from various sources (eg Schiphol airport, Amsterdam); one such is made by Safa of Liverpool, UK. Emergency dental kits are available at leading retail outlets and dentists, made by Dental Save, 144 High St, Nailsea, Avon, BS19 1AP, UK, T 0275-810291, F 0275-858112, also available from Fiona Mahon Associates, PO Box 204, Hayes, Middx, UB4 9HN, UK, T 081-842 3141, F 081-845 7370.

Further information on health risks abroad, vaccinations, etc, may be available from a local travel clinic. If you wish to take specific drugs with you such as antibiotics, these are best prescribed by your own doctor. Beware, however, that not all doctors can be experts on the health problems of tropical countries. More detailed or more up-to-date information than local doctors can provide are available from various sources.

In the UK there are hospital departments specializing in tropical diseases in London, Liverpool, Birmingham and Glasgow and the Malaria Reference Laboratory at the London School of Hygiene and Tropical Medicine provides free advice about malaria, T 071-636 7921. In the USA the local public health services can give such information and information is available centrally from the Centres for Disease Control in Atlanta, T (404) 332 4559.

There are in addition computerized databases which can be accessed for a specific destination, up to the minute information. In the UK there is MASTA (Medical Advisory Service to Travellers Abroad), T 071-631 4408, Tx 895 3474, F 071-436 5389 and Travax (Glasgow, T 041-946 7120, extension 247).

Further information on medical problems overseas can be obtained from the book by Richard Dawood (Editor) – *Travellers Health, How to Stay Healthy Abroad*, Oxford University Press, 1992, £7.99. We strongly recommend this revised and updated edition, especially to the intrepid traveller heading for the more out of the way places. General advice is also available in the UK in 'Health Advice for Travellers' published jointly by the Department of Health and the Central Office of Information available free from your UK Travel Agent.

PRECOLUMBIAN CIVILIZATIONS

The Aztec empire which Hernán Cortés encountered in 1519 and subsequently destroyed was the third major power to have dominated what is now known as Mexico. Before it, the empires of Teotihuacan and Tula each unified what had essentially been an area of separate Indian groups. All 3, together with their neighbours such as the Maya (dealt with below) and their predecessors, belong to a more-or-less common culture called Mesoamerica. Despite the wide variety of climates and terrains that fall within Mesoamerica's boundaries, from northern Mexico to El Salvador and Honduras, the civilizations that developed there were interdependent, sharing the same agriculture (based on maize, beans and squash) and many sociological features. These included an enormous pantheon, with the god of rain and the feathered serpent hero predominant; the offering of blood to the gods, from oneself and from sacrificial victims usually taken in war; pyramid-building; a game played with a rubber ball; trade in feathers, jade and other valuable objects, possibly from as far away as the Andean region of South America; hieroglyphic writing; astronomy; an elaborate calendar.

The Mesoamerican calendar was a combination of a 260-day almanac year and the 365-day solar year. A given day in one of the years would only coincide with that in the other every 52 years, a cycle called the Calendar Round. In order to give the Calendar Round a context within a larger timescale, a starting date for both years was devised; the date chosen by the Classic Maya was equivalent to 3113 BC in Christian time. Dates measured from this point are called Long Count dates.

Historians divide Mesoamerican civilizations into 3 periods, the Pre-classic, which lasted until about AD 300, the Classic, until AD 900, and the Post-classic, from 900 until the Spanish conquest. An alternative delineation is: Olmec, Teotihuacan and Aztec, named after the dominant civilizations within each of those periods.

Who precisely the Olmecs were, where they came from and why they disappeared, is a matter of debate. It is known that they flourished from about 1400 to 400 BC, that they lived in the Mexican Gulf Coast region between Veracruz and Tabasco, and that all later civilizations have their roots ultimately in Olmec culture. They carved colossal heads, stelae (tall, flat monuments), jade figures and altars; they gave great importance to the jaguar and the serpent in their imagery; they built large ceremonial centres, such as San Lorenzo and La Venta. Possibly derived from the Olmecs and gaining importance in the first millenium BC was the centre in the Valley of Oaxaca at Monte Albán. This was a major city, with certain changes of influence, right through until the end of the Classic period. Also derived from the Olmecs was the Izapa civilization, on the Pacific border of present day Mexico and Guatemala. Here seems to have taken place the progression from the Olmec to the Maya civilization, with obvious connections in artistic style, calendar-use, ceremonial architecture and the transformation of the Izapa Long-lipped God into the Maya Long-nosed God.

Almost as much mystery surrounds the origins of Teotihuacan as those of the

Olmecs. Teotihuacan, 'the place where men become gods', was a great urban state, holding in its power most of the central highlands of Mexico. Its influence can be detected in the Maya area, Oaxaca and the civilizations on the Gulf Coast which succeeded the Olmecs. The monuments in the city itself are enormous, the planning precise; it is estimated that by the 7th century AD some 125,000 people were living in its immediate vicinity. Early evidence did not suggest that Teotihuacan's power was gained by force, but research now indicates both human sacrifice and sacred warfare. Again for reasons unknown, Teotihuacan's influence over its neighbours ended around 600 AD. Its glory coincided with that of the Classic Maya, but the latter's decline occurred some 300 years later, at which time a major change affected all Mesoamerica.

The start of the Post-classic period, between the Teotihuacan and Aztec horizons, was marked by an upsurge in militarism. In the semi-deserts to the N of the settled societies of central Mexico and Veracruz lived groups of nomadic hunters. These people, who were given the general name of Chichimecs, began to invade the central region and were quick to adopt the urban characteristics of the groups they overthrew. The Toltecs of Tula were one such invading force, rapidly building up an empire stretching from the Gulf of Mexico to the Pacific in central Mexico. Infighting by factions within the Toltecs split the rulers and probably hastened the empire's demise sometime after 1150. The exiled leader Topíltzin Quetzalcóatl (Featherd Serpent) is possibly the founder of the Maya-Toltec rule in the Yucatán (the Maya spoke of a Mexican invader named Kukulcán—Feathered Serpent). He is certainly the mythical figure the Aztec ruler, Moctezuma II, took Cortés to be, returning by sea from the E.

Another important culture which developed in the first millenium AD was the Mixtec, in western Oaxaca. They infiltrated all the territory held by the Zapotecs, who had ruled Monte Albán during the Classic period and had built many other sites in the Valley of Oaxaca, including Mitla. The Mixtecs, in alliance with the Zapotecs successfully withstood invasion by the Aztecs.

The process of transition from semi-nomadic hunter-gatherer to city and empire-builder continued with the Aztecs, who bludgeoned their way into the midst of rival city states in the vacuum left by the destruction of Tula. They rose from practically nothing to a power almost as great as Teotihuacan in about 200 years. From their base at Tenochtitlán in Lake Texcoco in the Valley of Mexico they extended through aggression their sphere of influence from the Tarascan Kingdom in the N to the Maya lands in the S. Not only did the conquered pay heavy tribute to their Aztec overlords, but they also supplied the constant flow of sacrificial victims needed to satisfy the deities, at whose head was Huitzilopochtli, the warrior god of the Sun. The speed with which the Aztecs adapted to a settled existence and fashioned a highly effective political state is remarkable. Their ability in sculpting stone, in pottery, in writing books, and in architecture (what we can gather from what the Spaniards did not destroy), was great. Surrounding all this activity was a strictly ritual existence, with ceremonies and feasts dictated by the 2 enmeshing calendars.

It is impossible to say whether the Aztec empire would have gone the way of its predecessors had not the Spaniards arrived to precipitate its collapse. Undoubtedly, the Europeans received much assistance from people who had been oppressed by the Aztecs and who wished to be rid of them. Needless to say, Cortés, with his horses and an unknown array of military equipment in relatively few hands, brought to an end in 2 years an extraordinary culture.

The best known of the pre-Conquest Indian civilizations of the present Central American area was the Maya, which is thought to have evolved in a formative period in the Pacific highlands of Guatemala and El Salvador between 1500 BC and about AD 100. After 200 years of growth it entered what is known today as its Classic period when the civilization flourished in Guatemala, Belize and Honduras, and in Chiapas, Campeche and Yucatán (Mexico).

The Maya civilization was based on independent and antagonistic city states, including Tikal, Uaxactún, Kaminaljuyú, Iximché, Zaculeu and Quiriguá in Guatemala; Copán in Honduras; Altún Ha, Caracol, Lamanai in Belize; Tazumal and San Andrés in El Salvador; and Palenque, Bonampak (both in Chiapas), Uxmal, Mayapán, Tulum and the Puuc hill cities of Sayil, Labná and Kabah (all on the Yucatán peninsula) in Mexico. Recent research has revealed that these cities, far from being the peaceful ceremonial centres as once imagined, were warring adversaries, striving to capture victims for sacrifice. Furthermore, much of the cultural activity, controlled by a theocratic minority of priests and nobles, involved blood-letting, by even the highest members of society. Royal blood was the most precious offering that could be made to the gods. This change in perception of the Maya was the result of the discovery of defended cities and of a greater understanding of the Maya's hieroglyphic writing. Although John Lloyd Stephens' prophecy that 'a key surer than that of the Rosetta stone will be discovered' has not been fulfilled, the painstaking decipherment of the glyphs has uncovered many of the secrets of Maya society (see *Breaking the Maya Code* by Michael D Coe, Thames and Hudson).

Alongside the preoccupation with blood was an artistic tradition rich in ceremony, folklore and dance. They achieved paper codices and glyphic writing, which also appears on stone monuments and their fine ceramics; they were skilful weavers and traded over wide areas, though they did not use the wheel and had no beasts of burden. The cities were all meticulously dated. Mayan art is a mathematical art: each column, figure, face, animal, frieze, stairway and temple expresses a date or a time relationship. When, for example, an ornament on the ramp of the Hieroglyphic Stairway at Copán was repeated some 15 times, it was to express that number of elapsed 'leap' years. The 75 steps stand for the number of elapsed intercalary days. The Mayan calendar was a nearer approximation to sidereal time than either the Julian or the Gregorian calendars of Europe; it was only .000069 of a day out of true in a year. They used the zero centuries in advance of the Old World, plotted the movements of the sun, moon, Venus and other planets, and conceived a cycle of more than 1,800 million days.

Their tools and weapons were flint and hard stone, obsidian and fire-hardened wood, and yet with these they hewed out and transported great monoliths over miles of difficult country, and carved them over with intricate glyphs and figures which would be difficult enough with modern chisels. Also with those tools they grew lavish crops. To support urban populations now believed to number tens of thousands, and a population density of 150 per sq km (compared with less than 1 per sq km today), an agricultural system was developed of raised fields, fertilized by fish and vegetable matter from surrounding canals.

The height of the Classic period lasted until AD 900-1000, after which time the Maya concentrated into Yucatán after a successful invasion of their other lands by non-Maya people (this is only one theory: another is that they were forced to flee after a peasants' revolt against them). They then came under the influence of the Toltecs who invaded Yucatán; Chichén Itzá is considered to be an example of a Maya city which displays a great many Toltec features. From that time their culture declined. The Toltecs, who had firm control in Yucatán in the 10th century, gradually spread their empire as far as the southern borders of Guatemala. They in turn, however, were conquered by the Aztecs, who did not penetrate into Central America.

LA RUTA MAYA AND PASEO PANTERA

INTEGRATED TOURISM AND CONSERVATION

The Ruta Maya is an ambitious project which aims to tap the tourist potential of that region of southern Mexico and Central America once dominated by the Maya. It involves the cooperation of public and private tourist bodies of Mexico, Guatemala, Belize, El Salvador and Honduras. It is one of the regions of the world with the greatest variety of tourist attractions. As well as archaeological sites, the various countries share to a greater or lesser degree modern Maya culture, national parks, beaches, lakes, volcanoes and various types of forest. There is still a long way to go before the fully-integrated tourist circuit envisaged in the *National Geographic* magazine of October 1989 comes to fruition. To date, a regional Ruta Maya headquarters has been inaugurated just outside Belize City, tour operators have been meeting regularly to plan cross-border routes, etc, and the concept has become well established.

Many archaeological sites are already popular tourist attractions, with the accompanying infrastructure (eg Tikal, Guatemala p 479; Palenque, Chichén Itzá, Mexico p 289 and p 316; Copán, Honduras p 645). Others, while thoroughly excavated, are less well-known and yet others, still under excavation, are destined to become part of the tourist route (eg Caracol, Belize p 558; Calakmul, Mexico p 347; Joya del Cerén, El Salvador p 591). As present-day knowledge of the historical Maya grows, so efforts are being made to safeguard the traditions of the Maya peoples living now, traditions which are both centuries old and enmeshed with Catholicism. In the context of the Ruta Maya, such safeguards must include the avoidance of the worst aspects of voyeuristic tourism. Both people and their environment face economic and population pressures. The expansion of natural parks, for instance the recent enlargement by 55,000 hectares of the Montes Azules biological reserve in Lacandonia to include Bonampak and Yaxchilán (Mexico p 294), have been welcomed. Parks in existence cover rainforest and cloud forest, Belize's diverse environments, including marine, the *biotopos* in Guatemala and the waterbird sanctuaries in northern Yucatán, Mexico. Of the landscapes, one can mention the chain of volcanoes extending through Mexico, Guatemala and El Salvador, associated with which are some beautiful lakes, or, offshore, the cayes and reefs of Belize.

The Ruta Maya should prove beneficial in terms of road building, flight links, hotel construction and ease of access between neighbouring countries. One major question surrounds this development, though; is there a danger that the Ruta Maya will isolate this region as a tourist 'hot spot', to the detriment of the region itself (ie as an extension of what is generally accepted to be overdevelopment at Cancún, Mexico p 322), and to the detriment of other parts of Mexico and the rest of Central America through a lack of comparable funding? It is to be hoped that this danger will not arise. Mexican tourism projects are spread over many areas in the country, taking in a wide array of archaeological heritage, both pre-conquest and colonial. Beach developments, such as Huatulco

(Mexico **see p 250**), are taking place concurrently with whatever progress is being made on the Ruta Maya. A colonial cities programme, covering 51 places, has been developed. For both Guatemala and Belize, the Ruta Maya will build on the attractions to which visitors are already drawn. While Copán, Honduras' main Maya connection may act as an enticement for people to travel to other parts of the country, El Salvador will expect the Ruta Maya to encourage the reemergence of a tourist industry after many years of civil war. Much depends upon how great a percentage of Ruta Maya tourism is concentrated in the package tour market.

The Ruta Maya is not the only project under way. **The Mundo Maya** is a sister project to the Ruta Maya in that it covers the same area, but is operated by Central American and Mexican representatives (the Ruta Maya was founded in the USA). The second is **Paseo Pantera**, also initiated in the USA, a regional wildlands conservation project, within which ecotourism will play an important part. The panther (*pantera*), found throughout all the Americas, has been adopted as the symbol of a plan to preserve the biological diversity of Central America, from Guatemala and Belize to Panama. Recognizing the importance of the isthmus as the point of interchange between wildlife in North and South America, Paseo Pantera aims to link conservation schemes, which so far (with 1 or 2 exceptions) have been undertaken by the individual countries. The project will last for 5 years, in which time it will attempt to set up a cooperative approach to 2 main problems. 1) The fragmention of forests has caused loss of flora, fauna and wildlife habitats and has threatened forest watersheds. 2) Overfishing, contamination and sedimentation have caused serious degradation of coastal and marine environments.

It is proposed that nature tourism, under the auspices of Paseo Pantera, will provide funds for the purchase and management of protected areas, promote environmental education and, with the participation of willing local communities, channel profits into economic development. There will be some overlap with the Ruta/Mundo Maya zone, for instance in the Maya Biosphere Reserve (which includes Tikal), Belize's Barrier Reef and Maya Mountains, but other key areas, such as the linking of Nicaragua's huge Bosawas rainforest reserve with Honduras' Río Plátano Reserve (p 663) and the Nicaraguan/Costa Rican Sí-A-Paz/Tortuguera (p 769) collaboration, or conservation in Bocas del Toro, Panama (p 838), will be a spur to tourism in other parts of the region.

Contacts: Wilbur Garrett, Ruta Maya Foundation, 209 Seneca Road, Great Falls, VA 22066, USA, T (703) 450-4160 (**Ruta Maya**). Dr Archie F Carr III, or Kathleen Williams, Mesoamerican and Caribbean Program, Wildlife Conservation International, 4424 NW 13th St, Suite A-2, Gainesville, FL 32609, USA, T (904) 371-1713, F (904) 375-2449 (**Paseo Pantera**). **Mundo Maya**, 7a Avenida 14-44, Zona 9, Guatemala City, Guatemala, T (502) 2-340-323, F (502) 2-340-341.

Maps in this volume which refer to areas discussed in the Ruta Maya: Mexico (p 57), Regional South (p 237) and Yucatán (p 284); Guatemala , Country Map (p 437) and El Petén and Alta Verapaz (p 478); Belize, Country Map (p 528) and Cayes Map (p 542); El Salvador, Country Map (p 574); Honduras, Western Honduras and Copán (p 643).

THE MUSIC OF THE REGION

by Nigel Gallop

Mexico

Mexican Music is particularly attractive and vibrant and a vigorous radio, film and recording industry has helped make it highly popular throughout Latin America. There can be no more representative an image of Mexico than the Mariachi musician and his *charro* costume. The Spanish conquistadores and the churchmen that followed them imposed European musical culture on the defeated natives with a heavy hand and it is this influence that remains predominant. Nobody knows what precolumbian music sounded like and even the music played today in the Indian communities is basically Spanish in origin. African slaves introduced a third ingredient, but there is no Afro-Mexican music as such and indeed there are few black Mexicans. The music brought from Europe has over the centuries acquired a highly distinctive sound and style of which every Mexican is justly proud, even if many of the young now prefer to listen to Anglo-American rock and pop, like their counterparts the world over.

There is a basic distinction between Indian and Mestizo music. The former is largely limited to the Indians' own festive rituals and dances, religious in nature and solemn in expression. The commonest instruments are flute and drum, with harp and violin also widely used. Some of the most spectacular dances are those of the Concheros (mainly urban), the Quetzales (from the Sierra de Puebla), the Voladores (flying pole—also Sierra de Puebla), the Tarascan dances from around Lake Pátzcuaro and the Yaqui deer dance (Sonora).

Mestizo music clearly has more mass appeal in what is an overwhelmingly mixed population. The basic form is the *son* (also called *huapango* in eastern areas), featuring a driving rhythm overlaid with dazzling instrumentals. Each region has its own style of *son*, such as the *son huasteco* (Northeast), *son calentano* (Michoacán/Guerrero), *chilena* (Guerrero coast), *son mariachi* (Jalisco), *jarana* (Yucatán) and *son jarocho* (Veracruz). One *son jarocho* that has achieved world status is 'La Bamba'. Instrumental backing is provided in almost all these areas by a combination of large and small guitars, with the violin as virtuoso lead in the *huasteca* and the harp in Veracruz. The *chilena* of Guerrero is said to have been introduced by Chilean seamen and miners on their way to the California gold rush, while Yucatán features a version of the Colombian *bambuco*. The *son* is a dance form for flirtation between couples, as befits a land of passionate men and women, and often involves spectacular heel-and-toe stamping by the man. Another widespread dance rhythm is the *jarabe*, including the patriotic 'Jarabe Tapatío', better known to the English-speaking world as the 'Mexican Hat Dance'. Certain regions are known for more sedate rhythms and a quite different choice of instruments. In the N, the Conjunto Norteño leads with an accordion and favours the polka as a rhythm. In Yucatán they prefer wind and brass instruments, while the Isthmus of Tehuantepec is the home of the *marimba* (xylophone), which it shares with neighbouring Guatemala.

For singing, as opposed to dancing, there are 3 extremely popular genres. First is the *corrido*, a narrative form derived from old Spanish ballads, which swept across the country with the armies of the Revolution and has remained a potent vehicle for popular expression ever since. A second is the *canción* (literally 'Song'), which gives full rein to the romantic, sentimental aspect of the Mexican character and is naturally slow and languid. 'Las Mañanitas' is a celebrated song for serenading people on their birthdays. The third form is the *ranchera*, a sort of Mexican Country and Western, associated originally with the cattle-men of the Bajío region. Featured in a whole series of Mexican films of the 1930s and 1940s, *rancheras* became known all over the Spanish-speaking world as the typical Mexican music. The film and recording industry turned a number of Mexican artists into household names throughout Latin America. The 'immortals' are Pedro Infante, Jorge Negrete, Pedro Vargas, Miguel Aceves Mejía and the Trio Los Panchos, with Agustín Lara as an equally celebrated and prolific songwriter and composer, particularly of romantic *boleros*. To all outsiders and most Mexicans however there is nothing more musically Mexican than *mariachi*, a word said to be derived from the French 'mariage', introduced at the time of Maximilian and Carlota.

Originating in the state of Jalisco, *mariachi* bands arrived in Mexico City in the 1920s and have never looked back. Trumpets now take the lead, backed by violins and guitars and the players all wear *charro* (cowboy) costume, including the characteristic hat. They play all the major musical forms and can be found almost every evening in Mexico City's Plaza Garibaldi, where they congregate to be seen, heard and, they hope, hired. This is the very soul of Mexico.

Finally, there are a number of distinguished 20th century composers who have produced symphonies and other orchestral works based on indigenous and folk themes. Carlos Chávez is the giant and his 'Sinfonía India' a particularly fine example. Other notable names are Silvestre Revueltas ('Sensemayá'), Pablo Moncayo ('Huapango'), Blas Galindo ('Sones de Mariachi') and Luis Sandi ('Yaqui Music').

Central America

Native music is at its most vigorous and flourishing at either end of the region, in Guatemala and Panama. In the intervening 4 republics its presence is more localized and indeed elusive. From Guatemala southwards a rich musical tradition based largely on the *marimba* (xylophone) as an instrument and the *son* as a song/dance genre fades fast but continues tenuously all the way down to Costa Rica, while Panama has its own very distinctive vein of traditional music, with a combination of Spanish and African elements. While the influence of Mexican music is all pervasive in the northern 5 republics, Panama is more closely linked with the Caribbean coasts of Colombia and Venezuela in its musical idioms.

Guatemala is the heartland of the *marimba*, which it shares with parts of southern Mexico. How this came about has been much debated between adherents of a native precolumbian origin and those who believe the *marimba* came from Africa with colonial slavery. Whatever its origins, it is now regarded as the national instrument in Guatemala, belonging equally to Indian and *ladino*. Among the Indians the more rustic *marimba de tecomate* with gourds as resonators is still to be found, whereas most instruments now have the box resonator. The manufacture and playing of *marimbas* has developed to the point where a number of them are now combined to form an orchestra, as with the Pans of Trinidad. Among the best known *marimba* orchestras are the Marimba Tecún Umán, Marimba Antigua and highly sophisticated Marimba Nacional de Concierto. Every village has its *marimba* players and no wedding or other secular celebration would be complete without them. The music played is generally either a fast or slow *son*, but the modern repertoire is likely to include many Mexican numbers.

Although the *marimba* is basic to the Indians as well as to the *ladinos*, the former have other instruments for their religious rituals and processions, such as the *tun* (a precolumbian drum), *tzicolaj* (flute), *chirimía* (oboe) and violin. These are the instruments that accompany the colourful vernacular dances of the 'Culebra' (snake), 'Venado' (deer) and 'Palo Volador' (flying pole), as also the 'Baile de las Canastas' and 'Rabinal Achí', 2 precolombian historical dramas that have amazingly survived the conquest and colonial period and are still performed at Chajul and Rabinal (Alta Verapaz) respectively.

El Salvador and **Honduras** are 2 countries that tend to 'hide their light under a bushel' as regards native music. It is here above all that the Mexican music industry seems to exert an overwhelming cultural influence, while the virtual absence of an Indian population may also be partly responsible, since it is so often they who maintain traditions and hold to the past, as in Guatemala. Whatever the reason, the visitor who is seeking specifically Salvadorean or Honduran native music will find little to satisfy him or her. El Salvador is an extension of 'marimba country', but in both republics popular songs and dances are often accompanied by the guitar and seem to lack a rhythm or style that can be pinpointed as specifically local. Honduras does share with Belize and Guatemala the presence of Garifuna or Black Caribs on the Caribbean coast. These descendants of Carib Indians and escaped black slaves were deported to the area from St Vincent in the late 18th century and continue to maintain a very separate identity, including their own religious observances, music and dances, profoundly African in spirit and style.

In **Nicaragua** we again find ourselves in 'marimba country' and here again the basic musical genre is the *son*, here called the 'Son Nica'. There are a number of popular dances for couples with the names of animals, like 'La Vaca' (cow), 'La Yeguita' (mare) and 'El Toro' (bull). The folklore capital of Nicaragua is the city of Masaya and the musical heart of Masaya is the Indian quarter of Monimbó. Here the *marimba* is king, but on increasingly rare occasions may be supported by the *chirimía* (oboe), *quijada de asno* (asses jaw) and *quijongo*, a single-string bow with gourd resonator. Some of the most traditional Sones are 'El Zañate', 'Los Novios' and 'La Perra Renca', while the more popular dances still to be found are 'Las Inditas', 'Las Negras', 'Los Diablitos' and 'El Torovenado', all involving masked characters. Diriamba is another centre of tradition, notable for the folk play known as 'El Güeguense', accompanied by violin, fife and drum and the dance called 'Toro Guaco'. The Caribbean coast is a totally different cultural region, home to the Miskito Indians and English speaking black people of Jamaican origin concentrated around Bluefields. The latter have a maypole dance and their music is typically Afro-Caribbean, with banjos, accordeons, guitars and of course drums as the preferred instruments.

Costa Rica is the southernmost in our string of 'marimba culture' countries. The guitar is also a popular instrument for accompanying folk dances, while the *chirimía* and *quijongo*, already encountered further N, have not yet totally died out in the Chorotega region of Guanacaste Province. This province is indeed the heartland of Costa Rican folklore and the 'Punto Guanacasteco', a heel-and-toe dance for couples, has been officially decreed to be the 'typical national dance', although it is not in fact traditional, but was composed at the turn of the century by Leandro Cabalceta Brau during a brief sojourn in gaol. There are other dances too, such as the 'Botijuela Tamborito' and 'Cambute', but it must honestly be said that they will not be found in the countryside as a tradition, but are performed on stage when outsiders need to be shown some native culture. Among the country's most popular native performers are the duet Los Talolingas, authors of

'La Guaria Morada', regarded as the 'second national anthem' and Lorenzo 'Lencho' Salazar, whose humorous songs in the vernacular style are considered quintessentially 'tico'.

Some of the republic's rapidly deculturizing Indian groups have dances of their own, like the 'Danza de los Diablitos' of the Borucas, the 'Danza del Sol' and 'Danza de la Luna' of the Chorotegas and the 'Danza de los Huesos' of the Talamancas. A curious ocarina made of beeswax, the *dru mugata* is still played by the Guaymí Indians and is said to be the only truly precolumbian instrument still to be found. The drum and flute are traditional among various groups, but the guitar and accordeon are moving in to replace them. As in the case of Nicaragua, the Caribbean coast of Costa Rica, centred on Puerto Limón, is inhabited by black people who came originally from the English speaking islands and whose music reflects this origin. The *sinkit* seems to be a strictly local rhythm, but the *calypso* is popular and the *cuadrille*, square dance and maypole dance are also found. There is too a kind of popular hymn called the *saki*. Brass, percussion and string instruments are played, as also the accordeon.

Panama is the crossroads of the Americas, where Central America meets South America and the Caribbean backs onto the Pacific. One of the smallest Latin American republics and the last to achieve independence, from Colombia, it nonetheless possesses an outstandingly rich and attractive musical culture. Albeit related to that of the Caribbean coast of Colombia and Venezuela, it is extremely distinctive. The classic Panamanian folk dances are the *tambor* or *tamborito*, *cumbia*, *punto* and *mejorana*, largely centred on the central provinces of Coclé and Veraguas and those of Herrera and Los Santos on the Azuero Peninsula. Towns that are particularly noted for their musical traditions are Los Santos, Ocú, Las Tablas, Tonosí and Chorrera. The dances are for couples and groups of couples and the rhythms are lively and graceful, the man often fanning the girl with his hat. The woman's *pollera* costume is arguably the most beautiful in Latin America and her handling of the voluminous skirt is an important element of the dance. The *tamborito* is considered to be Panama's national dance and is accompanied by 3 tall drums. The *cumbia*, which has a common origin with the better known Colombian dance of the same name, has a fast variant called the *atravesado*, while the *punto* is slower and more stately. The name *mejorana* is shared by a small native guitar, a dance, a song form and a specific tune. The commonest instruments to be found today are the tall drums that provide the basic beat, the violin, the guitar and the accordeon, with the last named rapidly becoming predominant. The *tuna* is a highly rhythmic musical procession with womens' chorus and massed hand-clapping.

Turning to song, there are 2 traditional forms, both of Spanish origin, the *copla*, sung by women and accompanying the *tamborito*, and the *mejorana*, which is a male solo preserve, with the lyrics in the form of *décimas*, a verse form used by the great Spanish poets of the Golden Age. It is accompanied by the ukulele-like guitar of the same name. Quite unique to Panama are the *salomas* and *gritos*, the former between 2 or more men. The yodelling and falsetto of the *salomas* are in fact carried over into the singing style and it is this element, more than any other, that gives Panamanian folk song its unique and instantly recognizable sound. There are other traditional masked street dances of a carnavalesque nature, such as the very African 'Congos', the 'Diablicos Sucios' (dirty little devils) and the 'Grandiablos' (big devils). In the area of the Canal there is a significant English speaking black population, similar to those in Nicaragua and Costa Rica, who also sing *calypso*, while the Guaymí Indians in the W and the Cuna and Chocó of the San Blas islands and Darién isthmus possess their own song, rituals and very attractive flute music.

MEXICO

Maps Country, 57; Regional North, 71; San Luis Potosí, 77; Querétaro, 80; Ciudad Juárez/El Paso, 85; Chihuahua, 91; Zacatecas, 100; Guanajuato, 106; Dolores Hidalgo, 111; San Miguel de Allende, 113; Mazatlán, 127; Mazatlán Orientation, 130; Puerto Vallarta, 135; Puerto Vallarta Orientation, 137; Guadalajara, 140; West Central Mexico, 150; Pátzcuaro, 158; Morelia, 162; Toluca, 167; Mexico City Orientation, 171; Mexico City, 173; Mexico City Metro, 189; Mexico City environs, 201; Puebla, 209; Southern Mexico, 213; Veracruz, 217; Taxco, 237; Acapulco, 240; Oaxaca, 254; Oaxaca environs, 261; Tapachula, 267; Tuxtla Gutiérrez, 269; San Cristóbal de las Casas, 274; Yucatán including Maya sites, 284; Palenque, 290; Mérida, 306; Valladolid, 320; Cancún Environs, 323; Cancún, 325; Isla Mujeres, 329; Isla Mujeres town, 330; Playa del Carmen, 332; Cozumel, 335; San Miguel de Cozúmel, 337; Chetumal, 344; Baja California North, 349; Tijuana, 354; Baja California South, 362; La Paz, 370.

INTRODUCTION

CORTES, asked what the country looked like, crushed a piece of parchment in his fist, released it and said: 'That is the map of Mexico.' This crumpled land is so splendid to the eye, and so exotic to the other senses, that millions, mainly from the USA, visit it each year.

Mexico is the third largest country in Latin America and the most populous

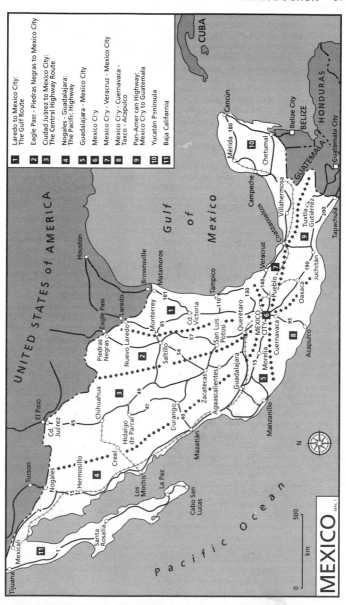

MEXICO MAC 1

1. Laredo to Mexico City:
   The Gulf Route
2. Eagle Pass - Piedras Negras to Mexico City
3. Ciudad Juárez to Mexico City:
   The Central Highway Route
4. Nogales - Guadalajara:
   The Pacific Highway
5. Guadalajara - Mexico City
6. Mexico City
7. Mexico City - Veracruz - Mexico City
8. Mexico City - Cuernavaca -
   Taxco - Acapulco
9. Pan-American Highway;
   Mexico City to Guatemala
10. Yucatán Peninsula
11. Baja California

Spanish-speaking country anywhere (84.4 million people). Its geography ranges from swamp to desert, from tropical lowland jungle to high alpine vegetation above the tree line, from thin arid soils to others so rich that they grow three crops a year. Over half the country is at an altitude of over 1,000 metres and much at over 2,000 metres; over half is arid and another 30% semi-arid. Only about 30 million hectares (16% of the total land area) can be cultivated, and of these 33% are irrigable.

Mexico has an area equal to about a quarter of the United States, with which it has a frontier of 2,400 km. The southern frontier of 885 km is with Guatemala and Belize. It has a coast line of 2,780 km on the Gulf of Mexico and the Caribbean, and of 7,360 km on the Pacific and the Gulf of California.

The structure of the land mass is extremely complicated, but may be simplified (with large reservations) as a plateau flanked by ranges of mountains roughly paralleling the coasts. The northern part of the plateau is low, arid and thinly populated; it takes up 40% of the total area of Mexico but holds only 19% of its people. From the Bolsón de Mayrán as far S as the Balsas valley, the level rises considerably; this southern section of the central plateau is crossed by a volcanic range of mountains in which the intermont basins are high and separated. The basin of Guadalajara is at 1,500 metres, the basin of México at 2,300 metres, and the basin of Toluca, W of Mexico City, is at 2,600 metres. Above the lakes and valley bottoms of this contorted middle-land rise the magnificent volcano cones of Orizaba (5,700 metres), Popocatépetl (5,452 metres), Ixtaccíhuatl (5,286 metres), Nevado de Toluca (4,583 metres), Matlalcueyetl or La Malinche (4,461 metres), and Cofre de Perote (4,282 metres). This mountainous southern end of the plateau, the heart of Mexico, has ample rainfall. Though only 14% of the area of Mexico, it holds nearly half of the country's people. Its centre, in a small high intermont basin measuring only 50 km square, is Mexico City, with 20 or so million inhabitants.

The two high ranges of mountains which rise E and W of the plateau, between it and the sea, are great barriers against communications: there are far easier routes N along the floor of the plateau to the United States than there are to either the E coast or the W. In the W there are rail and road links across the Sierra Madre Occidental from Guadalajara to the Pacific at the port of Mazatlán; both continue northward through a coastal desert to Nogales. The Sierra Madre Oriental is more kindly; in its mountain ramparts a pass inland from Tampico gives road-rail access to Monterrey, a great industrial centre, and the highland basins; and another from Veracruz leads by a fair gradient to the Valley of México.

South of the seven intermont basins in the south-central region the mountainland is still rugged but a little lower (between 1,800 and 2,400 metres), with much less rainfall. After some 560 km it falls away into the low-lying Isthmus of Tehuantepec. Population is sparse in these southern mountains and is settled on the few flat places where commercial crops can be grown. Subsistence crops are sown on incredibly steep slopes. The Pacific coast here is forbidding and its few ports of little use, though there is massive development of tourism in such places as Acapulco, Zihuatanejo, Puerto Escondido and Huatulco. Very different are the Gulf Coast and Yucatán; half this area is classed as flat, and much of it gets enough rain the year round, leading to its becoming one of the most important agricultural and cattle raising areas in the country. The Gulf Coast also provides most of Mexico's oil and sulphur. Geographically, North America may be said to come to an end in the Isthmus of Tehuantepec. S of the Isthmus the land rises again into the thinly populated highlands of Chiapas.

Climate and vegetation depend upon altitude. The *tierra caliente* takes in the coastlands and plateau lands below 750 metres. The *tierra templada*, or temperate zone is at 750 to 2,000 metres. The *tierra fría*, or cold zone, is from 2,000 metres upwards. Above the tree line at 4,000 metres are high moorlands (*páramos*).

The climate of the inland highlands is mostly mild, but with sharp changes of temperature between day and night, sunshine and shade. Generally, winter is the dry season and summer the wet season. There are only two areas where rain falls the year round: S of Tampico along the lower slopes of the Sierra Madre Oriental and across the Isthmus of Tehuantepec into Tabasco state; and along the Pacific coast of the state of Chiapas. Both areas together cover only 12% of Mexico. These wetter parts get most of their rain between June and September, when the skies are so full of clouds that the temperature is lowered: May is a hotter month than July. Apart from these favoured regions, the rest of the country suffers from a climate in which the rainy season hardly lives up to its name and the dry season almost always does.

History Of the many Indian nations in the vast territory of Mexico, the two most important before the Conquest were the Aztecs of Tenochtitlán (now Mexico City) and the Maya of Yucatán. The Aztecs, a militarist, theocratic culture, had obtained absolute control over the whole Valley of México and a loose control of some other regions. The Maya were already in decline by the time the Spaniards arrived. A brief history of these and other pre-Conquest, Mexican people is given in the introduction.

The 34-year-old Cortés disembarked near the present Veracruz with about 500 men, some horses and cannon, on 21 April 1519. They marched into the interior; their passage was not contested; they arrived at Tenochtitlán in November and were admitted into the city as guests of the reigning monarch, Moctezuma. There they remained until June of the next year, when Pedro de Alvarado, in the absence of Cortés, murdered hundreds of Indians to quell his own fear of a rising. At this treacherous act the Indians did in fact rise, and it was only by good luck that the Spanish troops, with heavy losses, were able to fight their way out of the city on the Noche Triste (the Night of Sorrows) of 30 June. Next year Cortés came back with reinforcements and besieged the city. It fell on 30 August 1521, and was utterly razed. Cortés then turned to the conquest of the rest of the country. One of the main factors in his success was his alliance with the Tlaxcalans, old rivals of the Aztecs. The fight was ruthless, and the Aztecs were soon mastered.

There followed 300 years of Spanish rule. In the early years all the main sources of gold and silver were discovered. Spanish grandees stepped into the shoes of dead Aztec lords and inherited their great estates and their wealth of savable souls with little disturbance, for Aztec and Spanish ways of holding land were not unlike: the *ejido* (or agrarian community holding lands in common), the *rancho*, or small private property worked by the owner; and that usually huge area which paid tribute to its master, the Spanish *encomienda*, soon to be converted into the *hacienda*, with its absolute title to the land and its almost feudal way of life. Within the first 50 years all the Indians in the populous southern valleys of the plateau had been christianized and harnessed to Spanish wealth-getting from mine and soil. The more scattered and less profitable Indians of the N and S had to await the coming of the missionizing Jesuits in 1571, a year behind the Inquisition. Too often, alas, the crowded Jesuit missions proved as fruitful a source of smallpox or measles as of salvation, with the unhappy result that large numbers of Indians died; their deserted communal lands were promptly filched by some neighbouring *encomendero*: a thieving of public lands by private interests which continued for 400 years.

By the end of the 16th century the Spaniards had founded most of the towns which are still important, tapped great wealth in mining, stock raising and sugar-growing, and firmly imposed their way of life and belief. Government was by a Spanish-born upper class, based on the subordination of the Indian and *mestizo* populations and a strict dependence on Spain for all things. As throughout all Hispanic America, Spain built up resistance to itself by excluding from government both Spaniards born in Mexico and the small body of educated *mestizos*.

The standard of revolt was raised in 1810 by the curate of Dolores, Miguel Hidalgo. The Grito de Dolores: 'Perish the Spaniards' ("Mueran los gachupines"), collected 80,000 armed supporters, and had it not been for Hidalgo's loss of nerve and failure to engage the Spaniards, the capital might have been captured in the first month and a government created not differing much from the royal Spanish government. But eleven years of fighting created bitter differences. A loyalist general, Agustín de Iturbide, joined the rebels and proclaimed an independent Mexico in 1821. His Plan of Iguala proposed an independent monarchy with a ruler from the Spanish royal family, but on second thoughts Iturbide proclaimed himself Emperor in 1822: a fantasy which lasted one year. A federal republic was created on 4 October 1824, with General Guadalupe Victoria as President. Conservatives stood for a highly centralized government; Liberals favoured federated sovereign states. The tussle of interests expressed itself in endemic civil war. In 1836, Texas, whose cotton-growers and cattle-ranchers had been infuriated by the abolition of slavery in 1829, rebelled against the dictator, Santa Ana, and declared its independence. It was annexed by the United States in 1845. War broke out and US troops occupied Mexico City in 1847. Next year, under the terms of the treaty of Guadalupe Hidalgo, the US acquired half Mexico's territory: all the land from Texas to California and from the Río Grande to Oregon.

A period of reform dominated by independent Mexico's great hero, the Zapotec Indian, Benito Juárez, began in 1857. The church, in alliance with the conservatives, hotly contested by civil war his liberal programme of popular education, freedom of the press and of speech, civil marriage and the separation of church and state. Juárez won, but the constant civil strife wrecked the economy, and Juárez was forced to suspend payment on the national debt. Promptly, Spain, France and Britain landed a joint force at Veracruz to protect their financial rights. The British and the Spanish soon withdrew, but the French force pushed inland and occupied Mexico City in 1863. Juárez took to guerrilla warfare against the invaders. The Archduke Maximilian of Austria became Emperor of Mexico with Napoleon III's help, but United States insistence and the gathering strength of Prussia led to the withdrawal of the French troops in 1867. Maximilian, betrayed and deserted, was captured by the Juaristas at Querétaro, tried, and shot on 19 June. Juárez resumed control and died in July 1872. He was the first Mexican leader of any note who had died naturally since 1810.

Sebastián Lerdo de Tejada, the distinguished scholar who followed him, was soon tricked out of office by General Porfirio Díaz, who ruled Mexico from 1876 to 1910. Díaz's paternal, though often ruthless, central authority did introduce a period of 35 years of peace. A superficial prosperity followed upon peace; a civil service was created, finances put on a sound basis, banditry put down, industries started, railways built, international relations improved, and foreign capital protected. But the main mass of peasants had never been so wretched; their lands were stolen from them, their personal liberties curtailed, and many were sold into forced labour on tobacco and henequen plantations from which death was the only release.

It was this open contradiction between dazzling prosperity and hideous distress which led to the upheaval of November 1910 and to Porfirio Díaz's self-exile in Paris. A new leader, Francisco Madero, who came from a landowning family in Coahuila, championed a programme of political and social reform, including the restoration of stolen lands. Madero was initially supported by revolutionary leaders such as Emiliano Zapata in Morelos, Pascual Orozco in Chihuahua and Pancho Villa in the N. During his presidency (1911-13), Madero neither satisfied his revolutionary supporters, nor pacified his reactionary enemies. After a coup in February 1913, led by General Victoriano Huerta, Madero was brutally murdered, but the great new cry, *Tierra y Libertad* (Land and Liberty) was not to be quieted until the revolution was made safe by the election of Alvaro Obregón to the Presidency in 1920. Before then, Mexico was in a state of civil war, leading first to the exile of Huerta in 1914, then the dominance of Venustiano Carranza's revolutionary faction over that of Zapata (assassinated in 1919) and Villa. Later, President Lázaro Cárdenas fulfilled some of the more important economic objectives of the revolution; it was his regime (1934-40) that brought about the division of the great estates into *ejidos* (or communal lands), irrigation, the raising of wages, the spread of education, the beginnings of industrialization, the nationalization of the oil wells and the railways. Later presidents nationalized electric power, the main airlines and parts of industry, but at the same time encouraged both Mexican and foreign (mainly US) entrepreneurs to develop the private sector. All presidents have pursued an independent and non-aligned foreign policy.

In 1946, the official party assumed the name Partido Revolucionario Institucional (PRI), since when it held a virtual monopoly over all political activity. Having comfortably won all elections against small opposition parties, in the 1980s electoral majorities were cut as opposition to dictatorship by the Party grew. Corruption and fraud were claimed to be keeping the PRI in power. The PRI candidate in 1988, Carlos Salinas de Gortari, saw his majority dramatically reduced when Cuauhtémoc Cárdenas (son of the former president), at the head of a breakaway PRI faction, stood in opposition to him. The disaffected PRI members and others subsequently formed the Partido de la Revolución Democrática (PRD), which rapidly gained support as liberalization of many of the PRI's long-held political and economic traditions became inevitable. In 1989, for the first time, a state governorship was conceded by the PRI, to the right wing party, Partido de Acción Nacional (PAN).

On New Year's Day of the election year, 1994, at the moment when the North American Free Trade Agreement (NAFTA—Mexico, USA and Canada) came into force, a guerrilla group briefly took control of several towns in Chiapas. The Ejército Zapatista de Liberación Nacional (EZLN) demanded social justice, indigenous people's rights, democracy at all levels of Mexican politics, an end to government corruption, and land reform for the peasantry. A possible PRI presidential contender, Manuel Camacho Solís, was given charge of negotiations with the EZLN and some progress was made, including the cessation of hostilities and a number of government concessions. All talks were suspended, however, following the assassination in Tijuana on 23 March of the PRI's appointed presidential candidate, Luis Donaldo Colosio. At the time of going to press, only Colosio's confessed killer, Mario Aburta Martínez, was in custody: whether he acted alone or was part of an organized plot had not been ascertained. Further disquiet was caused by the murder of the Tijuana police chief in April and, in separate incidents, the kidnapping of several prominent businessmen. These events did not instil the confidence necessary to revive a sluggish economy. To replace Colosio, President Salinas nominated Ernesto Zedillo Ponce de León, a US-trained economist and former education minister, who had not held any elected office. Zedillo's policies were expected to differ little from those of Salinas. His opponents for the presidency in elections in August 1994 were to be Cuauhtémoc Cárdenas of the PRD and Diego Fernández de Cevallos of the PAN. The government invited the UN to assist Mexican observers of the elections.

The People About 15% consider themselves white and about 29% Indian; about 55% are *mestizos*, a mixture in varying proportions of Spanish and Indian; a small percentage (mostly in the coastal zones of Veracruz, Guerrero and Chiapas) are a mixture of black and white or black and Indian or *mestizo*. Mexico also has infusions of other European peoples, Arab and Chinese. There is a national cultural prejudice in favour of the Indian rather than the Spanish element, though this does not prevent Indians from being looked down on by the more hispanic elements. There is hardly a single statue of Cortés in the whole of Mexico, but he does figure, pejoratively, in the frescoes of Diego Rivera and his contemporaries. On the other hand the two last Aztec emperors, Moctezuma and Cuauhtémoc, are national heroes.

Among the estimated 24 million Indians there are 54 groups or sub-divisions, each with its own language. The Indians are far from evenly distributed; 36% live on the Central Plateau (mostly Hidalgo, and México); 35% are along the southern Pacific coast (Oaxaca, Chiapas, Guerrero), and 23% along the Gulf coast (mostly Yucatán and Veracruz): 94% of them, that is, live in these three regions. There are also sizable concentrations in Nayarit and Durango, Michoacán, and Chihuahua, Sinoloa and Sonora. The main groups are: Pápago (Sonora); Yaqui (Sonora); Mayo (Sonora and Sinaloa); Tarahumara (Chihuahua); Huastec and Otomí in San Luis Potosí; Cora and Huichol (Nayarit); Purépecha/Tarasco (Michoacán); scattered groups of Nahua in Michoacán, Guerrero, Jalisco, Veracruz and other central states; Totonac (Veracruz); Tiapaneco (Guerrero); in Oaxaca state, Mixtec, Mixe and Zapotec; in Chiapas, Lacandón, Tzoltzil, Tzeltal, Chol and others; Maya in Campeche, Yucatán and Quintano Roo.

The issue of access to the land has always been the country's fundamental problem, and it was a despairing landless peasantry that rose in the Revolution of 1910 and swept away Porfirio Díaz and the old system of huge estates. The accomplishments of successive PRI governments have been mixed. Life for the peasant is still hard. The minimum wage barely allows a simple diet of beans, rice, and *tortillas*. The home is still, possibly, a shack with no windows, no water, no sanitation, and the peasant may still not be able to read or write, but something was done to redistribute the land in the so-called *ejido* system, which gave either communal or personal control of the land. The peasant was freed from the landowner, and his family received some basic health and educational facilities from the state. In 1992 new legislation was approved which radically overhauled the outdated agricultural sector with far-reaching political and economic consequences. Farmers now have the right to become private property owners, if two-thirds of the *ejido* votes in favour; to form joint ventures with private businessmen; and to use their land as collateral for loans. Private property owners may form joint stock companies, thereby avoiding the constitutional limits on the size of farms and helping them to raise capital. The failure of any agricultural reforms to benefit the peasants of Chiapas was one of the roots of the EZLN uprising in early 1994.

The Economy   Mexico has been an oil producer, since the 1880s and was the world's leading producer in 1921, but by 1971 had become a net importer. This position was reversed in the mid-1970s with the discovery in 1972 of major new oil reserves. Mexico is the world's fifth largest producer at 2.7m barrels a day of crude petroleum, 65% of this coming from offshore wells in the Gulf of Campeche, and 28% from onshore fields in the Chiapas-Tabasco area in the SE. Proven reserves stood at 51bn barrels in 1992 (giving 51 years until exhaustion). Natural gas production in 1991 was 38bn cu m. Mexico depends on oil and gas to generate 73% of its electricity and exports of crude oil, oil products and natural gas account for a third of exports and about 20% of government revenues.

Mexico's mineral resources are legendary. Precious metals make up about 36% of non-oil mineral output. The country is the world's leading producer of silver (although low prices have forced the closure of hundreds of mines), fluorite and arsenic, and is among the world's major producers of strontium, graphite, copper, iron ore, sulphur, mercury, lead and zinc. Mexico also produces gold,

Mexico : Fact File	
Geographic	
Land area	1,958,201 sq km
forested	22.3%
pastures	39.0%
cultivated	13.0%
Demographic	
Population (1992)	84,439,000
annual growth rate (1987-92)	1.6%
urban	71.3%
rural	28.7%
density	43.1 per sq km
Religious affiliation	
Roman Catholic	89.7%
Birth rate per 1,000 (1990)	31.2
	(world av 26.4)
Death rate per 1,000 (1990)	5.0
	(world av 9.2)
Education and Health	
Life expectancy at birth,	
male	66.5 years
female	73.1 years
Infant mortality rate	
per 1,000 live births (1988)	46.6
Physicians (1987)	1 per 600 persons
Hospital beds (1990)	
	1 per 1,298 persons
Calorie intake as %	
of FAO requirement	131%
Population age 25 and over	
with no formal schooling	13.4%
Literate males (over 15)	90.2%
Literate females (over 15)	84.8%
Economic	
GNP ('90 market prices)	US$214,500mn
GNP per capita	US$2,490
Public external	
debt (1992)	US$76,087mn
Tourism receipts (1992)	US$6,641mn
Inflation (annual av 1986-91)	56.1%
Radio	1 per 5.1 persons
Television	1 per 6.7 persons
Telephone	1 per 7.6 persons
Employment	
Population economically active (1990)	
	24,063,283
Unemployment rate	2.7%
% of labour force in	
agriculture	22.0
mining	1.1
manufacturing	18.7
construction	6.6
Military forces	175,000
Source Encyclopaedia Britannica	

molybdenum, antimony, bismuth, cadmium, selenium, tungsten, magnesium, common salt, celestite, fuller's earth and gypsum. It is estimated that although 60% of Mexico's land mass has mineral potential, only 25% is known, and only 5% explored in detail.

Agriculture has been losing importance since the beginning of the 1970s and now contributes only 9% of gdp. About 13% of the land surface is under cultivation, of which only about one-quarter is irrigated. Over half of the developed cropland lies in the interior highlands. Mexico's agricultural success is almost always related to rainfall and available water for irrigation. On average, four out of every ten years are good, while four are drought years.

Manufacturing, including oil refining and petrochemicals, contributes 23% of gdp. Mexico City is the focal point for manufacturing activity and the metropolitan area holds about 45% of the employment in manufacturing and 30% of the country's industrial establishments. The government offers tax incentives to companies relocating away from Mexico City and the other major industrial centres of Guadalajara and Monterrey; target cities are Tampico, Coatzacoalcos, Salina Cruz and Lázaro Cárdenas, while much of the manufacturing export activity takes place in the in-bond centres along the border with the USA. There are now over 2,000 *maquiladoras* (in-bond), employing about 518,000 people. Several large industrial plants have been ordered closed to control pollution in Mexico City.

Tourism is a large source of foreign exchange and the largest employer, with about a third of the workforce. About 6.7mn tourists visit Mexico every year, of whom about 85% come from the USA. The Government is actively encouraging new investment in tourism and foreign investment is being welcomed in hotel construction projects.

During 1978-81 the current account of the balance of payments registered increasing deficits because of domestic expansion and world recession. Mounting public sector deficits were covered by foreign borrowing of increasingly shorter terms until a bunching of short term maturities and a loss of foreign exchange reserves caused Mexico to declare its inability to service its debts in August 1982, thus triggering what became known as the international debt crisis. Under the guidance of an IMF programme and helped by commercial bank debt rescheduling agreements, Mexico was able to improve its position largely because of a 40% drop in imports in both 1982 and 1983. In 1986, however, the country was hit by the sharp fall in oil prices, which reduced export revenues by 28%, despite a rapid growth of 37% in non-oil exports through vigorous promotion and exchange rate depreciation policies. Several debt rescheduling and new money agreements were negotiated during the 1980s with the IMF, the World Bank and the commercial banks. Mexico managed to secure progressively easier terms, helped by the US administration's concern for geopolitical reasons, and debt growth was contained. Prepayment of private debt and debt/equity conversions even reduced the overall level of foreign debt. In 1989, Mexico negotiated the first debt reduction package with commercial banks, which was designed to cut debt servicing and restructure debt over a 30-year period supported by collateral from multinational creditors and governments. As a result of this agreement and higher oil prices during the Gulf crisis, foreign exchange reserves rose sharply and the Government was able to curb the rate of currency depreciation and reduce interest rates. Large capital inflows financed a growing trade and current account deficit caused by strong demand for imports as the economy picked up.

The economic improvement allowed President Salinas to open negotiations with the USA on a free trade agreement which, including Canada, would open up the whole of North America (NAFTA). Major economic reforms were introduced to encourage private investment, including the privatization of many state-owned industries, banks and basic public services, such as telephones, motorways, water treatment, electricity generation, railways and ports. New legislation made it easier to invest in mining (except uranium) and foreign investment was permitted in several previously restricted areas. Although Pemex is not for sale, steps have been taken to break the company up into semi-autonomous units, some of which could be opened to private capital in an attempt to improve efficiency, safety and pollution control. On 1 January 1993, the Government introduced the New Peso, equal to 1,000 old pesos. Both pesos will be legal tender until 1 January 1995. The Government's tight fiscal and monetary policies led to low inflation and a budget surplus, but at the cost of high real interest rates to attract capital from overseas to finance the massive current account deficit. Devaluation was ruled out, partly for political reasons. The combined effect of these factors raised the cost for the private sector to restructure in order to compete under impending NAFTA rules. As a result gdp growth was only 0.4%, largely owing to a 1.5% fall in manufacturing output. This in turn restricted imports, which eased Mexico's trade deficit (US$13.6bn, a 15.1% decrease against 1992).

The political unrest in the first half of 1994 threatened the stability of the peso against the dollar, so interest rates remained high to protect the currency. Swift government responses to the various crises prevented a stock market crash, but the political climate, plus higher US interest rates which raised the cost of financing the current account deficit (US$23.4bn in 1993), dampened confidence and jeopardised a rapid return to economic growth.

In May 1993, in an historic move, a constitutional amendment gave the Mexican central bank autonomy over monetary policy and independence from the Government.

Government Under the 1917 Constitution Mexico is a federal republic of 31 states and a Federal District containing the capital, Mexico City. The President, who appoints the Ministers, is elected for 6 years and can never be re-elected.

Congress consists of the 64-seat Senate, half elected every 3 years on a rotational basis, and the 500-seat Chamber of Deputies, elected every 3 years. There is universal suffrage, and one Deputy for 60,000 inhabitants.

Local Administration The States enjoy local autonomy and can levy their own taxes, and each State has its Governor, legislature and judicature. The President appoints the Chief of the Federal District.

Religion   Roman Catholicism is the principal religion, but the State is determinedly secular. Because of its identification firstly with Spain, then with the Emperor Maximilian and finally with Porfirio Díaz, the Church has been severely persecuted in the past by reform-minded administrations, and priests are still not supposed to wear ecclesiastical dress (see *The Lawless Roads* and *The Power and the Glory*, by Graham Greene). Rapprochement between State and Church was being sought in the early 1990s.

LAREDO TO MEXICO CITY: THE GULF ROUTE (1)

Sections 1 to 4 describe the four great road routes from the US border towards Mexico City. First, the Gulf Route from Laredo (by Pan-American Highway), which takes in the major industrial centre of Monterrey and the port of Tampico.

The route passes through the coastal state of Tamaulipas before entering Huastec and Otomí Indian regions and then leads to the old silver-mining centre of Pachuca. The first route to be opened was the Gulf Route: Nuevo Laredo-Mexico City: 1,226 km (760 miles). Traffic from the central and eastern parts of the United States can enter NE Mexico through four gateways along the Río Bravo; at Matamoros (see below), opposite Brownsville (which has 90% Mexican population, despite being in the USA; cheap hotel, **D** *Hotel Bienvenidos*, about 200 metres from Río Grande bridge, if you don't want to cross the border at night); at **Reynosa** (**D** *Hotel San Carlos*, on Zócalo, rec; **E** *Plaza* on main square; in McAllen, **E** *Arcade*, corner of Cedar and N 12th St, 2 blocks from Greyhound terminal, 5 from Valley Transit bus terminal) opposite McAllen; at Ciudad Miguel Alemán, opposite Roma; and at **Nuevo Laredo** (population 400,000), opposite Laredo—by far the most important of them. The roads from these places all converge upon Monterrey (a new toll road from Nuevo Laredo is the quickest route, US$41; the old route is 80 km longer). There are alternative roads from Reynosa and Matamoros which join the Nuevo Laredo-Mexico City highway at Montemorelos and Ciudad Victoria, respectively: the latter runs along the tropical Gulf coastal plain and then climbs sharply through the Sierra Madre Oriental to Ciudad Victoria, at 333 metres.

Hotels at Nuevo Laredo: **C** *Alameda*, on plaza; **C** *Dos Laredos*, Matamoros y 15 de Junio; **E** *Calderón*, with bath, hot water, fan, run down, friendly; many others. **Motels A** *Hacienda*, Prol Reforma 5530; **B** *Reforma*, Av Guerrero 822. Cheap hotel in Laredo, **D** *The Bender*. 2 trailer parks, the better of the two is E side of Route I 35, Main St exit, 10 mins from border.

Crafts Shop Centro Artesanal Nuevo Laredo, Maclovio Herrera 3030, T 2-63-99.

Train Aguila Azteca to **Mexico City** from Nuevo Laredo, US$17 2nd class, US$28 1st class, US$43 *primera especial*, daily at 1855, 24 hrs, meals on train poor, take your own food, little difference between 1st and 2nd classes (leaves Mexico City for the border at 0900). Information: Av López César de Lara y Mina, Apdo Postal 248, Nuevo Laredo, Tamps, 88000 Mexico, T (871) 280-97; or PO Box 595, Laredo, TX 78042.

Buses Buses to **Mexico City** with Estrella Blanca/Transportes del Norte 9 buses a day, 16½ hrs, US$42. Buses for **Monterrey** (4 hrs, US$10, departures every hour), **Guadalajara** (18 hrs, US$46.50, 9 a day, Transportes del Norte or Estrella Blanca), to **San Luis Potosí**, US$38,

Tampico, Morelia (17 hrs, US$43).

The Nuevo Laredo bus station is not near the border; take a bus to the border, then walk across. It is not possible to get a bus from the Laredo Greyhound terminal to the Nuevo Laredo terminal unless you have a ticket to the interior. Connecting tickets from Houston via Laredo to Monterrey are available, 14 hrs. Some buses to Laredo connect with Greyhound buses in the US.

Useful addresses in Laredo **Mexican Consulate**, Farragut and Maine, 4th light on the right after leaving Interstate 35, open 0800-1400 Mon-Fri, helpful. **Exchange** UNB charges 1% commission on TCs; IBC no commission under US$500. **Car Insurance** AAA on San Bernardo Av (exit 4 on Interstate 35); Sanborns on Santa Ursula (exit 16 on Interstate 35), a bit more expensive, open 24 hrs a day; Johnson's Mexico Insurance, Tepeyac Agent, Lafayette and Santa Ursula (59 and Interstate 35), US$2.60/day, open 24 hrs, rec. **Car Tyres**, Tire Center of Laredo Inc, 815 Park, at San Bernardo Av. **Fax** and to receive letter, TCR, Martin and Sandra Resendez, 820 Juarez, near post office, international service.

Crossing into Mexico The best way is by the Colombia Bridge: on Interstate 35, take the exit to Milo (the first exit N of the Tourist Bureau and is signed). It opened summer 1992 so there is little traffic and has friendly staff, but does involve a 40 km detour. Once in Mexico you can either go back to Nuevo Laredo, or continue to Monterrey via Ciudad Anáhuac and Lampazos. In the latter case there is no checkpoint 20 km after the border. The direct route is on San Bernardo parallel to I 35 on the W; turn W at Washington, S at Salinas, cross about 10 traffic lights and turn E to the International bridge. Do not be directed into the narrow columns: after verbal processing, go 2 miles to the full processing location at Av Cesar López de Lara 1200, opposite train station. This entails six steps, including photocopying of documents (keep copies), US$2-3, and the bureaucracy described under **Automobiles** in Information for Visitors.

If pressed for time, avoid 20 November and other national holidays as there are delays at customs owing to Mexicans visiting the USA in large numbers. Border formalities can take 2 hrs or more.

Tolls Total road toll Nuevo Laredo-Mexico City US$135.

Matamoros (470,000 people), has a bright and unforbidding museum, designed to let a prospective tourist know what he can expect in Mexico. It is well worth a visit.

Hotels C *Ritz*, Matamoros y Siete. There are 4 motels on the road to the beach, all C/B.

Craft shop **Centro Artesanal Matamoros**, Calle 5a Hurtado and Alvaro Obregón (T 2-03-84).

Buses Several lines run first-class buses to **Mexico City** in 14 hrs for US$38. Transportes del Norte to **Ciudad Victoria** for US$10.75 (4 hrs).

Rail Tamaulipeco *servicio estrella* train leaves Matamoros at 0920 for Reynosa (opposite McAllen, Texas, arrives 1125) and Monterrey (arrives 1600, US$14.45 *primera especial*).

Visas can be obtained in Brownsville from the Mexican Consulate at 940, E Washington. About 8 km outside Matamoros there is an immigration check-point; to cross this point a visa must be shown which must be signed at the bus station by an immigration official. Without this signature you will be sent back.

110 km S of Matamoros is *San Fernando*, a convenient distance from the border, especially if driving to the USA. **B** *Hotel Las Palomas*, on highway, quite good; excellent pizza place, serving more than pizza, near the *Hotel América*.

After 130 km of grey-green desert, the road from Nuevo Laredo climbs the Mamulique Pass, which it crosses at 700 metres, and then descends to Monterrey. There is a toll bypass and a free truck route around the city.

Monterrey, capital of Nuevo León state, third largest city in Mexico, 253 km S of the border and 915 km from Mexico City. Altitude: 538 metres, and evenings are cool. The city is dominated by the Cerro de la Silla from the E. Its population now approaches 3 million and is still growing in spite of its unattractive climate—too hot in summer, too cold in winter, dusty at most times—and its shortage of water. It now turns out (using cheap gas from near the Texas border and increasingly from the new gas fields in the S), over 75% of Mexico's iron and steel, and many other products accompanied by an almost permanent industrial smog. Its people are highly skilled and educated, but its architecture is drab, its layout seems unplanned and its streets are congested. In its main centre, Plaza Zaragoza, there is a pleasant 18th century Cathedral badly damaged in the war against the US in 1846-47, when it was used by Mexican troops as a powder magazine. Plaza Zaragoza, Plaza 5 de Mayo and many surrounding blocks now form the Gran Plaza, claimed to be the biggest civic square in the world; its centrepiece is the Laser Beam Tower. (There is a clean public convenience beneath the Gran Plaza, on Matamoros between Avs Zua Zua and Zaragoza, near the Neptune Fountain.) Calle Morelos is a pedestrians-only shopping centre. Its famous Instituto Tecnológico (Av Garza Sada 2501) has valuable collections of books on 16th century Mexican history, of rare books printed in Indian tongues, and 2,000 editions of Don Quixote in all languages.

Students of architecture should see the remarkable church of San José Obrero built in a working-class district by Enrique de la Mora and his team. The Monterrey Museum is in the grounds of the Cuauhtémoc Brewery, Av Universidad (beer—in small bottles—is handed out free in the gardens). The Mexican Baseball Hall of Fame is in part of the museum, as is a museum of Modern Art; open Tues-Fri 0930-1800, Sat-Sun 1030-1730. The Alfa Cultural Centre, in the Garza García suburb, has a fine planetarium and an astronomy and physics section with do-it-yourself illustrations of mechanical principles, etc. In a separate building is a Rufino Tamayo stained-glass window. Reached by special bus from W end of Alameda, hourly on the hour 1500-2000, the centre is open 1500-1920, closed Mon. The Alameda Gardens, between Avs Aremberri and Washington, on Av Pino Suárez, are a pleasant place to sit (open 1000-1700, closed Tues). The Cerro del Obispado affords good views, smog permitting. The Palace (1787) is a regional museum (open Tues-Sat 1000-1300, 1500-1800, Sun 1000-1700); it served as HQ for both Pancho Villa and Gen Zachary Taylor. Take No 1 bus which stops at the foot of the hill.

Hotels It is difficult to obtain accommodation because of the constant movement of people travelling N/S. **L** *Holiday Inn*, Av Universidad 101, T 766555, also at Av Eugenio Garza Sada 3680 S, T 762400, F 320565; **L** *Holiday Inn Crowne Plaza*, Av Constitución 300 Oriente, near Plaza Zaragoza, best, T (91-83) 19-60-00; **A+** *Ambassador*, Hidalgo y Galeana, T 422040; **A+** *Ancira*, Hidalgo y Escobedo, T 432060; **A+** *Colonial*, Escobedo y Hidalgo, T 436791; **A+** *Río*, Padre Mier 194 Poniente, T 449510; **A+** *Royal Courts* (Best Western), Av Universidad 314, T and F 762017; **C** *Yamallel*, Zaragoza 912, Nte Madero, T 753400, good; **D** *Nuevo León*, Amado Nervo 1007 Norte con Av Madero, T 741900, with bath (hot water), dark, seedy, poor value, close to bus station.

D *Estación*, Guadalupe Victoria 1450, opp train station, bath; **D** *Posada*, Juan Méndez 1515, Norte, with bath, rec. Many hotels between Colón and Reforma, 2 blocks from the bus station, nothing below US$15. **Youth Hostel**, Av Madero Oriente s/n, Parque Fundidora, CP64000, T 557360.

Motels A *El Paso Autel*, Zaragoza y Martínez, T 400690; **D** *Motel/Trailerpark Nueva Castilla*, on Highway 85 before Saltillo bypass, 12 spaces for RVs with hook-up, pool, hot showers, reasonable restaurant, clean but drab, US$17 for vehicle and 2 people; several on Nuevo Laredo highway.

Restaurant 23 eating places around the 'Zona Rosa' and Plaza Zaragoza in the heart of town. Vegetarian: *Los Girasoles* on Juan Ignacio Ramón (number not known), possibly best, *menú del día* US$2.50; *Señor Natural*, Escobedo 713, about same price; *Superbom*, Padre Mier, upstairs, *menú*, US$4.

Exchange If stuck without pesos on Sunday, the red hotel/restaurant just opposite the bus station changes TCs if you buy something in the restaurant.

British Consulate (Honorary) Mr Edward Lawrence, Privada de Tamazunchale 104, Colonia del Valle, Garza García. T (52-83) 782565/569114. **Canadian Consul**, T 443200.

Tourist Office Infotur on Gran Plaza (W side). Large city maps available at bookshops. Office by an airport on highway from Nuevo Laredo, helpful.

Railways Nuevo Regiomontano (*servicio estrella*) leaves for **Mexico City** at 1950; it leaves Mexico City at 1800, 15 hrs, (from US$79 for a sleeper, *primera especial* US$38). Tamaulipeco (*servicio estrella*) leaves at 1030 for **Reynosa** (arr 1440, US$10.60) and **Matamoros** (arr 1710, US$14.45). To **Mexico City** (US$13.25 2nd class) and the port of **Tampico** daily. Day trains are slow.

Airport Aeropuerto del Norte, 24 km from centre. Daily flights from Mexico City take 1 hr 20 mins.

Bus Terminal on Av Colón, between Calzada B Reyes and Av Pino Suárez. Monterrey-**Mexico City**, US$33, 12½ hrs. A more scenic trip is from Mexico City (northern bus terminal) to **Ciudad Valles**, 10 hrs, from where there are many connecting buses to Monterrey. To **San Luis Potosí**, US$14.80. To **Nuevo Laredo**, departures every hour, 4 hrs, US$10. To **Matamoros**, Transportes del Norte, 4 hrs, US$10. To **Chihuahua** with Transportes del Norte, 8 a day, 12 hrs, US$30. Frequent buses to **Saltillo**, but long queues for tickets. To **Guadalajara**, US$36.50. To Santiago for Cola de Caballo falls, US$1.65.

NB Motorists If driving Monterrey-Saltillo, there is nothing to indicate you are on the toll road until it is too late. The toll is US$7. Look for the old road.

In the hills around are the bathing resort of ***Topo Chico***, 6½ km to the NW; water from its hot springs is bottled and sold throughout Mexico; and 18 km away Chipinque Mesa, at 1,280 metres in the Sierra Madre, with magnificent views of the Monterrey area.

W of Monterrey, off the Saltillo road are the **García Caves** (about 10 km from Villa García, which is 40 km from Monterrey). The entrance is 800 metres up, by cable car, and inside are beautiful stalagmites and stalactites. At the foot of the cable car are a pool and recreational centre. A tour of the caves takes 1½ hrs, and it is compulsory to go in a group with a guide. You can take a bus to Villa García, but it is a dusty walk to the caves. On Sun Transportes Saltillo-Monterrey run a bus to the caves at 0900, 1000 and 1100. Otherwise, take an agency tour, eg Osetur (details from Infotur); book at *Hotel Ancira* (on Tues, US$3.50).

Leaving Monterrey, the road threads the narrow and lovely Huajuco canyon; from Santiago village a road runs to within 2 km of the Cola de Caballo, or Horsetail, Falls, in the **Cumbres de Monterrey** national park. (First-class hotel on the way, and you can get a colectivo, US$1.65, from the bus stop to the falls, and a horse, US$1.65, to take you to the top of the falls, entrance US$2.40; cost of guide US$5.) The road drops gradually into lower and warmer regions, passing through a succession of sub-tropical valleys with orange groves, banana plantations and vegetable gardens.

At ***Montemorelos***, just off the highway, 79 km S of Monterrey, a branch road from the Matamoros-Monterrey highway comes in. On 53 km is ***Linares*** (100,000 people), a fast-expanding town.

Hotels B *Escondido Court*, motel, clean, a/c, pool and restaurant, rec, 1½ km N of Linares on Route 855; **B** *Hotel Guidi*, nr the plaza.

Bus Linares to **San Luis Potosí**, US$14.80.

A most picturesque 96 km highway runs W from Linares up the lovely Santa Rosa canyon, up and over the Sierra Madre after Iturbide, turn S on top of the Sierra Madre and continue on good road through the unspoilt Sierra via La Escondida and Dr Arroyo. At San Roberto, N of Matehuala (**see p 75**) join the Highway 57 route from Eagle Pass to Mexico City.

(Km 706) ***Ciudad Victoria***, capital of Tamaulipas state, a quiet, clean, unhurried city with a shaded plaza and a tiny church perched on the top of a hill. Here Route 85 from Monterrey and Route 101 from Matamoros meet. It is often used as a stop-over. Alt: 336 metres; pop: 300,000 (state population 1990, 2,244,200).

Hotels A *Santorín* (Best Western), Cristóbal Colón Nte 349, T 128938, T 128342, a/c, TV, parking, restaurant; **B** *Sierra Gorda*, Hidalgo 990 Oriente, T 32280, garage US$0.70 a night. **D** *San Francisco*, 10 minutes walk straight from bus station, bath, hot water, clean, TV, changes dollars. *Trailer Park*, Libramiento 101-85, follow signs, good service, electricity, hot showers; owner (Rosie) has travel information, US$10 for 2 plus vehicle. Several hotels by bus station, including **E** *Central*, basic, OK, laundry facilities; in the centre, in the same range are *Bernabe* and *El Dorado*. There is also a laundromat behind the plaza.

Motels B *Los Monteros*, Plaza Hidalgo, T 20300, downtown; **B** *Panorámica*, Lomas de Santuario, T 25506.

Buses Terminal is on the outskirts. Omnibuses Blancos to Ciudad Valles (see below) for US$8.50. Bus Ciudad Victoria-Mexico City 10 hrs, US$26.65.

Excursion NE of Ciudad Victoria is Nueva Ciudad Padilla; nearby is Viejo Padilla, where Agustín de Iturbide was shot in 1824. Also nearby is Presa Vicente Guerrero, a large lake with good fishing and many tourist facilities.

SW of Ciudad Victoria, 20 km along Route 101 (direction Jamuave) is a sign to the Zona Arqueológica **El Balcón de Moctezuma**. The site consists of circular buildings and staircases, showing Huastec influence. It is similar to Chicomostoc, La Quemada and Casas Grandes and was a commerical centre with contacts with tribes in present day USA. Ask for the guide Don Gabino, who took part in the excavations, which were completed in June 1990. From the signpost to the Zona Arqueológica it's a 4 km walk, then 100m uphill (a high clearance vehicle can get within 100m and you can park at Altas Cumbres near the site). We are grateful to Helmut Zettl, Ebergassing, for this information.

After crossing the Tropic of Cancer the road enters the solid green jungle of the tropical lowlands. 137 km S of Ciudad Victoria is **Ciudad Mante** (Km 570), which is almost exactly the mid-way point between Matamoros and Mexico City and makes a convenient stop-over place. The city is, however, dirty. It has a Museo de Antropología e Historia, with objects from the Huastec culture. Best hotel is probably the **B** *Mante*, Guerrero 500 Nte, T 20990, shaded grounds at N edge of business sector; **D** *Monterrey*, Av Juárez 503, Ote, T 21512, in old section, with bath, hot water, a/c, cable TV, helpful manager speaks English, safe parking, rec, new annex at back, restaurant not so good; several hotels a few blocks S of Zócalo. 45 km N of Ciudad Mante is the village of **Gómez Farias**, an important centre for ornithological research: the highlands above the village represent the northernmost extent of several tropical vegetation formations. Many tropical bird species reach the northern limit of their range. Gómez Farias is reached by turning off the main highway, 14 km over a paved road to the town plaza. From there, an easy 2-km walk provides excellent views of bird habitats. (Jim Turner, Oak Grove, Missouri).

Monterrey trains run via Ciudad Victoria to the Caribbean port of **Tampico**, population: 560,000, definitely not a tourist attraction, reached by a fine road from Ciudad Mante, in a rich sugar-growing area, a deviation of 156 km. Tampico is on the northern bank of the Río Pánuco, not far from a large oilfield: there are storage tanks and refineries for miles along the southern bank. The summer heat, rarely above 35°C, is tempered by sea breezes, but June and July are trying. Cold northerlies blow now and again during the winter. There are two pleasant plazas, Plaza de Armas at Colón y Carranza, with squirrels in the trees, and Plaza de la Libertad, Madero y Juárez. Fishing (both sea and river) is excellent. Huge, interesting market, but watch your possessions carefully. The Playa de Miramar, a beach resort, is a tram or bus-ride from the city, but is reported dirty. If walking there, go along the breakwater (Escollera Norte) on N side of Río Pánuco, for views of the shipping and to see the monument to Mexican merchant seamen killed in World War II. The Museo de la Cultura Huasteca in Ciudad Madero, an adjacent town, is worth visiting (Instituto Tecnológico, Av 1 de Mayo y Sor Juana Inés de la Cruz—in poor condition); take a colectivo, 'Madero", from the centre of Tampico to the Zócalo in Ciudad Madero, then another to the Instituto; open 1000-1500, except Mon, small but select collection. Ciudad Madero claims to be Mexico's petroleum capital, with a huge oil refinery.

A second paved road from Tampico joins the Nuevo Laredo-México highway further S at Ciudad Valles. There are direct buses to Brownsville (Texas). A splendid new bridge was opened at the end of 1988 to replace the ferry to Villa Cuauhtémoc. Further S, the coast road, Route 180, enters Veracruz state, leading to Tuxpan, Poza Rica and Veracruz (the northern towns of that state are described on **p 227).**

Hotels A+ *Camino Real*, Av Hidalgo 2000, T 38811; **A+** *Impala*, Mirón 220 Pte, T 20990; **A+** *Inglaterra*, Mirón y Olmos; **B** *Imperial*, Aurora Sur 201, T 25678, clean, shower, fan, but noisy; **B** *Nuevo León*, Aduana N 107, T 24370, a/c, shower, clean; **B** *Tampico*, Carranza 513, T 24970; **C** *Ritz*, on Miramar beach, beautiful beach, deserted at night.

Several cheap hotels nr Plaza de la Libertad: eg *Sevilla* (always full), **E** *América*, nr market on Olmos, dirty but safe; **E** *Rex*, dirty, no hot water. All hotels downtown near market should be treated with discretion; many have a rapid turnover.

RVs can stay in the parking lot of the airport, which has rest rooms, US$15 per vehicle, noisy from traffic.

Restaurant *El Diligencias*, Héroes del Canonero Tampico 415 Oriente y Gral López de Lara, excellent seafood; *Emir*, FA Olmos between Díaz Mirón y Madero, good; for breakfast, *El Selecto*, opp market.

German Consul, 2 de Enero, 102 Sur-A, Hon Consul Dieter Schulze. Postal Address: Apdo 775, T (91-72) 129784/129817. Also deals with British affairs.

Tourist Office Plaza de Armas, above *Chantal* ice cream parlour on Calle FA Olmos, helpful.

Trains To **Monterrey** at 2115, arr 0545, with sleeper; 0745 (2nd class), arr 1850. To **San Luis Potosí** at 0630, 2nd class, arr 2020.

(Km 548) Antiguo Morelos. A road turns off W to San Luis Potosí (**see p 76**) 314 Km, and Guadalajara (**see p 138**).

(Km 476) *Ciudad Valles* (pop 320,000), on a winding river and a popular stop-over with many hotels (**A** *San Fernando*, T 20184; **A** *Valles*, T 20050, with trailer park, full hook-up, hot shower, a bit run-down, US$10 for 2 in car, both on Carretera México-Laredo). Museo Regional Huasteco, Calles Rotarios y Artes (or Peñaloza), open 1000-1200, 1400-1800, Mon-Fri, centre of archaeological and ethnographic research for the Huastec region. Omnibus Oriente to San Luis Potosí for US$6.60 (4 hrs); Mexico City 10 hrs. The road to Tampico (145 km) goes through the oil camp of El Ebano.

(Km 370) *Tamazunchale* (alt 206 metres, 150,000 people), with riotous tropical vegetation, is perhaps the most popular of all the overnight stops. (*San Antonio Hotel*; **B** *Mirador*, good, but passing traffic by night is noisy; **E** *Hotel OK*, cheapest but not rec; *Pemex Tourist Camp*, nice position, poor plumbing.) The road S of here begins a spectacular climb to the highland, winding over the rugged terrain cut by the Río Moctezuma and its tributaries. The highest point on the road is 2,502 metres. From (Km 279) Jacala there is a dizzying view into a chasm. *Zimapán* (*Posada del Rey*, fascinating but very run down, out on the highway), with a charming market place and a small old church in the plaza, is as good a place as any to stay the night. From (Km 178) *Portezuelo* a paved road runs W to Querétaro (**see p 79**), 140 Km.

In an area of 23,300 sq km N and S of (Km 169) *Ixmiquilpan*, just off the highway, 65,000 Otomí Indians 'live the bitterest and saddest life". The beautifully worked Otomí belts and bags may sometimes be bought at the Monday market, and also in the Artesanía shop in the main street almost opposite the government aid offices.

See early Indian frescoes in the main church, which is one of the 16th century battlemented Augustinian monastery-churches; the monastery is open to the public. John Streather writes: 'At sunset each day white egrets come to roost in the trees outside the church; it's worth going up on to the battlements to see them swoop down. The church of El Carmen is worth a visit too, lovely W façade and gilded altars inside. There is also a 16th century bridge over the river; beautiful

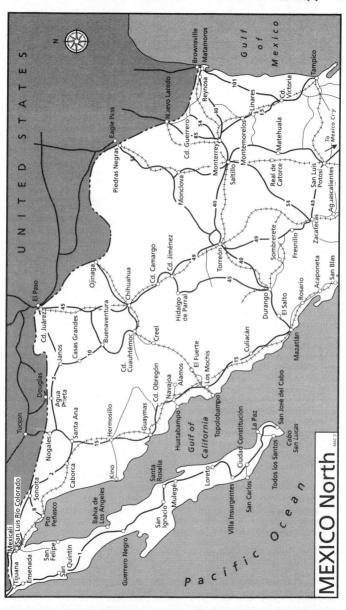

MEXICO North

walk along the ahuehuete-lined banks".

Hotels C *Hotel Diana*, rear buildings slightly dearer rooms but much cleaner, rec, safe parking.

Near Ixmiquilpan are several warm swimming pools, both natural and man-made—San Antonio, Dios Padre, Las Humedades, and near Tephé (the only warm-water bath, clean, entry US$0.40) and Tzindejé (this is about 20 mins from town). The Otomí villages of La Lagunita, La Pechuga and La Bonanza, in a beautiful valley, have no modern conveniences, but the people are charming and friendly.

The Barranca de Tolantongo, 37 km NE of Ixmiquilpan, is about 1,500m deep with a waterfall and thermal spring; at weekends there is a small eating place. Entry US$2, car parking US$2 at entrance to recreational area; camping permitted. To get there take the road towards El Cardonal, then an unpaved turn-off about 3 km before El Cardonal (there is a bus from Pachuca).

Actopán (Km 119) has another fine 16th century Augustinian church and convent (**B** *Hotel Rira*). From Actopán a 56 km branch road runs to one of Mexico's great archaeological sites: Tula, capital of the Toltecs (**see p 203**).

On the way to Tula there is an interesting cooperative village, *Cruz Azul*. Free concerts on Sun mornings at 1000 in front of main market. At (Km 85) Colonia, a road runs left for 8 km to:

Pachuca, one of the oldest silver-mining centres in Mexico and capital of Hidalgo state. Pop: 320,000 (state population 1990, 1,880,600); alt: 2,445 metres. The Aztecs mined here before the Spaniards came and the hills are honeycombed with old workings and terraced with tailings. Even today the silver output is one of the largest of any mine in the world. Although the centre is largely modern, there are a number of colonial buildings among its narrow, steep and crooked streets. These include the treasury for the royal tribute, Las Cajas Reales, Venustiano Carranza 106 (1670), now used as offices; Las Casas Coloradas (1785), on Plaza Pedro María Anaya, now the Tribunal Superior Justicia; and a former Franciscan convent (1596) on Plaza Bartolomé de Medina, 5 blocks S of the Zócalo at Arista y Hidalgo. An outstanding photographic museum is in the large cloister on the far side of the convent. The Museo Regional de Hidalgo, displaying chronological exhibits of the state's history, is known as the Centro Cultural Hidalgo (open Tues-Sun, 1000-1400, 1600-1900—may close early on Sun pm). In the complex there are a souvenir shop with reproductions of ceramic and metal anthropological items and recordings of indigenous music. Casa de las Artesanías for Hidalgo state is at the junction of Avenidas Revolución y Juárez. In the Plaza Independencia is a huge clock with four Carrara marble figures. The modern buildings include a notable theatre, the Palacio de Gobierno (which has a mural depicting ex-President Echeverría's dream of becoming Secretary-General of the UN), and the Banco de Hidalgo. The town centre is partly pedestrianized. An electric railway and a road run 10 km to the large silver-mining camp of Real (or Mineral) del Monte, picturesque and with steep streets. Collective taxis also run frequently from beside Las Cajas (US$0.40 pp).

Hotels C *De los Baños*, good, friendly and helpful, rec; **C** *Motel San Antonio*, 6 km from Pachuca on road to Mexico City (ask repeatedly for directions), spacious rooms, good value, clean, quiet, restaurant; **D** *Colonial*, Guerrero 505, central; **D** *Juárez*, Barreda 107, with bath, some rooms without windows, just before Real del Monte, in superb wooded surroundings. **E** *Grenfell*, Plaza Independencia 116, T 50277, with bath, clean, friendly, pleasant, good value (cheaper without bath, but communal toilets are filthy), bus from bus station passes the door; inexpensive hotels near the centre are hard to find.

Restaurant *Casino Español*, Matamoros 207, 2nd floor, old-time favourite. *La Blanca*, next to *Hotel de los Baños*, local dishes, rec; *El Buen Gusto*, Arista y Viaducto Nuevo Hidalgo, clean, good value *comida corrida*; *Palacio*, Av Juárez 200D, excellent breakfast, central. 'Paste' is the local survivor from Cornish miners' days; a good approximation of the real pasty, but a bit peppery! Eg at *Pastes Pachuqueños*, Arista 1023, rec.

Tourist Office In clock tower, Plaza Independencia, opposite *Hotel Grenfell*.

Transport Bus terminal is outside town; take any bus marked 'Central".

Cornish miners settled at **Real del Monte** in the 19th century; their descendants can be recognized among the people. At each entry to the town is a mural commemorating the first strike in the Americas, by silver miners in 1776. The Panteón Inglés (English cemetery) is on a wooded hill opposite the town (ask the caretaker for the key). Mineral del Chico is a beautiful little town 30 km from Pachuca in the **El Chico National Park**. The Park has many campsites and the town weekend homes for the wealthy of Mexico City. There are huge rock formations covered in pine forests; splendid walks. Bus from Pachuca bus station.

N of Pachuca via Atotonilco el Grande, where there are a chapel and convent half-way down a beautiful canyon, is the impressive **Barranca de Metztitlán** which has a wealth of different varieties of cacti, including the 'hairy old man' cactus, and a huge 17th century monastery. Farther N (difficult road) is Molango, where there is a restored convent, Nuestra Señora de Loreto. 34 km NE of Pachuca is **San Miguel Regla**, a mid-18th century *hacienda* built by the Conde de Regla, and now run as a resort, fine atmosphere, excellent service. A road continues to **Tulancingo**, on the Pachuca-Poza Rica road, Route 130. 17 km from Pachuca, and a further 4 km off Route 130 to the right is **Epazoyucan**, a village with an interesting convent of San Andrés. After Tulancingo, Route 119 branches off to the right to **Zacatlán**, famous for its apple orchards and now also producing plums, pears and cider. Its alpine surroundings include an impressive national park, **Valle de las Piedras Encimadas** (stacked rocks), camping possible. Nearby is *Posada Campestre al Final de la Senda*, a ranch with weekend accommodation, horse riding, walks, B, pp full board, T Puebla 413 821 for reservations. Some 16 km S of Zacatlán is **Chignahuapan** (about 1½ hrs from Puebla), a leading producer of *sarapes*, surrounded by several curative spas.

30 km from Tulancingo on Route 130 is *La Cabaña* restaurant, of log-cabin construction; thereafter, the road descends with many bends and slow lorries, and in winter there may be fog. At **Huachinango**, an annual flower fair is held in March; 22 km from here is **Xicotepec de Juárez** (*Mi Ranchito*, one of the nicest small hotels in Mexico; **D** *Italia*, near main square). Along the route are the villages of **Pahuatlan** and **San Pablito**, where sequined headbands are made, and paintings are done on flattened *amate* bark. The entire route from desert to jungle is 190 km, taking 5 hrs.

A 4-lane highway now runs from Pachuca to Mexico City via (Km 27) Venta de Carpio, from which a road runs E to Acolman, 12 km, and Teotihuacan, another 10 km. Neither of these places should be missed (**see p 200**); buses are available from Pachuca; get them at the tollbooth on the highway to Mexico City.

At Santa Clara, 13 km short of the Capital, the road forks. The right-hand fork (easy driving) goes direct to the City; the left fork goes through Villa Madero, where you can see the shrine of Guadalupe.

EAGLE PASS—PIEDRAS NEGRAS TO MEXICO CITY (2)

A popular route which goes through various mining centres (for silver and gemstones): Real de Catorce is now a ghost town; San Luis Potosí has many historical features, as does Querétaro, now an industrial city retaining a well-kept colonial centre.

This route, 1,328 km (825 miles), is 102 km longer than the Laredo route, but is very wide, very fast and much easier to drive. Take in enough gasoline at Monclova to cover the 205 km to Saltillo. Hotel, restaurant and camping prices have risen rapidly.

Piedras Negras, pop 150,000, altitude 220 metres, is across the Río Bravo from Eagle Pass, Texas. (Artesanía shop—Centro Artesanal Piedras Negras, Edificio la Estrella, Puerta México, T 2-10-87.) Beyond Hermanas (137 km) the highway begins to climb gradually up to the plateau country.

Rail Coahuilense *servicio estrella* train leaves for **Saltillo** at 0915 (arr 1855), US$5.75 2nd class, US$9.70 1st class, US$18.10 *primera especial*.

Monclova (243 km from border) has one of the largest steel mills in Mexico, and 250,000 people.

Then comes ***Saltillo*** (448 km; alt: 1,600 metres; population: 650,000), capital of Coahuila state (1990 pop 1,971,300), a cool, dry popular resort noted for the excellence of its *sarapes*. Its 18th century cathedral, a mixture of romanesque, churrigueresque, baroque and plateresque styles, is the best in northern Mexico and it has a grand market. Good golf, tennis, swimming. College students from the US attend the popular Summer School at the Universidad Interamericana. On Blvd Nazario Ortiz Garza, the house of the artist Juan Antonio Villarreal Ríos (Casa 1, Manzana 1, Colonia Saltillo 400, T 152707/151206—home) has an exhibition in every room of Dali-esque work, entry is free and visitors are welcome, phone first. Good views from El Cerro del Pueblo overlooking city. An 87-km road runs E to Monterrey, both toll (US$7) and *vía libre*. You turn right for Mexico City.

Festival Local *feria* in first half of August; cheap accommodation impossible to find at this time. Indian dances during 30 May and 30 August; picturesque ceremonies and bullfights during October *fiestas*. *Pastorelas*, the story of the Nativity, are performed in the neighbourhood in Christmas week.

Saltillo Hotels Several hotels a short distance from the plaza at the intersection of Allende and Aldama, the main streets. **A+** *San Jorge*, Manuel Acuña Norte 240, T 22222, F 29400; **B** *Saade*, Aldama 397, T 33400; **B** *Urdiñola*, Victoria 211, T 40940, reasonable; **C** *De Avila*, Padre Flores 211, T 37272, basic, cold water, safe motorcycle parking. **C** *Metropolí*, Allende 436, basic, with shower, a little dark but adequate, quiet. Cheaper are **D** *Hidalgo*, on Padre Flores, without bath, not worth paying for bath in room, cold water only (hot baths open to public and guests for small fee). **E** *Zamora*, Ramos Arzipe (Poniente) 552, cheap, noisy, clean, tepid water; also cheap **E** *El Conde*, Pérez Treviño y Acuña. Several hotels in front of the bus station, eg **E** *Central*, with bath, ample safe parking.

Several good **motels** in this area, eg **A+** *Camino Real*, Blvd Los Fundadores 2000, T 52525, F 53813; **A+** *Eurotel Plaza* (Best Western), 2 km N of centre, Blvd V Carranza Norte 4100, T and F 151000, parking, a/c, TV, restaurant, etc, AAA rec; **A** *Huizache*, Blvd Carranza 1746, T 28112; **A** *La Fuente*, Blvd Fundadores, T 22090.

Trailer park: turn right on road into town from Monterrey between *Hotel del Norte* and *Kentucky Fried Chicken*, hook-ups, toilets, basic.

Restaurants *Viena*, Acuña 519, rec; *Victoria*, Padre Flores 221, by *Hotel Hidalgo* has reasonable *comida*. *Café Bagdad*, Hidalgo 849 y Castillo, excellent snacks, live music or theatre at weekends. Excellent *licuados* (milkshakes) upstairs in the market. Many restaurants and bars in front of the bus station. Drinks and night-time view can be had at the *Rodeway Inn* on the N side of town.

Telephones Long-distance calls from *Café Victoria*, Padre Flores 221, near market.

Tourist Office Near crossroads of Allende and Blvd Francisco Coss in old railway station, long way from centre. Map with all useful addresses, incl hotels.

Bus Terminal is a long way from centre; minibuses to Pérez Treviño y Allende (for centre) will take luggage. Bus to **Mexico City**, 1st class, US$29.50, 11 hrs. To **Ciudad Acuña**, 2nd class, US$14.30, 8 hrs. To **Monterrey** and **Nuevo Laredo** with Transportes del Norte. For **Torreón**, all buses originate in Monterrey and tickets only sold when bus arrives; be prepared to stand.

Train Regiomontano (*servicio estrella*) calls here en route to Mexico City at 2200, and to Monterrey and Nuevo Laredo at 0545. *Primera especial* Saltillo-Mexico City, 12 hrs, US$33.65, sleepers from US$70. To Monterrey US$4.45 *primera especial*. Coahuilense (*servicio estrella*) connects with Regiomontano for Piedras Negras 0815 (7½ hrs).

From San Roberto junction (581 km from Saltillo), a 96-km road runs E over the Sierra Madre to Linares, on the Gulf Route (**see p 68**).

After about 720 km we reach **_Matehuala_**, an important road junction (there is a very helpful Chrysler agent, ask for Mike McGregor). Fiesta, 6-20 January.

Accommodation A _Motel Trailerpark Las Palmas_, on the N edge of town (Km 617), T 20001, clean, English spoken and paperbacks sold, bowling alley and miniature golf, tours to Real de Catorce (see below) arranged; _El Dorado_ nearby, T 20174, cheaper, rec; **D** _Hotel Matehuala_, near centre, colonial building, full of furniture, adequate; **E** _Alamo_, Calle Guerrero 116, clean and very pleasant rooms, rec; _María Ester_ and **E** pp _Primavera_, opp each other near centre. _Restaurant La Fontella_ in the centre, good regional food.

Bus To San Luis Potosí, with Estrella Blanca, 2½ hrs, US$6.25; **Mexico City** (US$22), **Monterrey** and **Querétaro**.

Chris and Miyuki Kerfoot write: From Saltillo to Matehuala by 2nd class bus, Estrella Blanca, 1½ hrs, US$3.75 to San Roberto, which is no more than a road junction with a Pemex petrol station, hitch to the junction of Highways 58 and 68 and catch a bus (Transportes Tamaulipas) to Matehuala (US$5, 4.50 hrs). From these junctions near Caleana to La Soledad the scenery is worthwhile, as the road winds its way up and down through wooded valleys. The final section to Matehuala passes through undulating scrub country.

56 km W of Matehuala is one of Mexico's most interesting old mining towns, **_Real de Catorce_** (altitude 2,765m), founded in 1772. This remarkable city, clustering around the sides of a valley, used to be so quiet that you can hear the river in the canyon, 1,000 metres below. It is becoming increasingly popular as a tourist destination, with new hotels being built.

To get there, turn left along the Zacatecas road through Cedral. After 27 km turn left off the paved road, on to a cobblestone one. The road passes through Potrero, a big centre for nopal cactus. Some people live in the old mine workings and old buildings. Huichol Indians are seen here occasionally. A silver mine is still being worked at Santana.

Real de Catorce is approached through Ogarrio, an old mine gallery widened (only just) to allow trucks through (US$1.65 toll to drive through). It is 2½ km long, and very eerie, with the odd tunnel leading off into the gloom on either side. There is an overtaking bay half way through. A small chapel to the Virgen de los Dolores is by the entrance. The tunnel opens out abruptly into the old city, originally called Real d'Alamos de la Purísima Concepción de los Catorce. Legend has it that 14 bandits hid in nearby caves until the silver was discovered and the town founded. Engineers came from Ireland, Germany and France. The first church was the Virgen del Guadalupe (1779), a little way out of town (beautiful ceiling paintings remain, as well as the black coffin used for the Mass of the Cuerpo Presente). Many of the images from this church were moved to the Church of San Francisco (1817), which is believed to be miraculous. The floor of the church is made of wooden panels, which can be lifted up to see the catacombs below. In a room to one side of the main altar are _retablos_, touchingly simple paintings on tin, as votive offerings to the Saint for his intercession. Next to the church is a small museum (entry US$0.10) showing mining equipment, etc, worth a visit. In the early 19th century, when the population was about 40,000, Real minted its own coins, which circulated only within the city limits (they are now collectors' items). After World War II the population fell dramatically to 400, but it has risen now to about 1,200, since silver is being worked again and tourism is growing. Guided tours are available from the Casa de la Moneda, in front of the Cathedral; they include the Palenque, an 8-sided amphitheatre built in 1863, which seated 500-600 people (this is otherwise closed to the public). In the Casa de la Moneda you can see silversmiths at work.

There is a pilgrimage here for San Francisco (whose day is 4 October), on foot from Matehuala, overnight on 3 October (take local bus from Matehuala to La Paz and join the groups of pilgrims who set out from early evening onwards; walk takes about 7 hrs, be prepared for rain). It is possible to walk from Matehuala to Real de Catorce, other than on the San Francisco pilgrimage, with the aid of the 1:50,000 map from INEGI (see **Information for Visitors, p 393**). On Good Friday, thousands of visitors gather to watch a lively passion play 'with almost real Roman soldiers and very colourful Jews and apostles".

Hotels One in the main street, very comfortable with restaurant and bar, expensive, another, **D** *Hotel Real*, in a side street, clean, nice atmosphere, friendly Italian owner, good restaurant, rec. Several other hotels, and various restaurants. Accommodation is easy to find: boys greet new arrivals and will guide motorists through the peculiar one-way system (or face a police fine). Basic rooms F pp.

Transport Many buses a day with Transportes Tamaulipas, from the corner of Calle del Guerrero and Mendiz, US$2 one-way. A taxi can be hired nearby for US$25—economic for 4 people; local buses from office 1 block N of the Zócalo. Real de Catorce can also be reached from Saltillo or San Luis Potosí by train, but schedules are awkward. Station, called Catorce, is 13 km away. Jeeps collect passengers from the station (US$16.50 per jeep) and follow a more spectacular route than the minibuses.

No fuel on sale in Real de Catorce; the Pemex Station before Cedral does not have *magna sin*, the one before Matehuala does.

Huizache (785 km) is the junction with the Guadalajara-Antiguo Morelos-Tampico highway. At 901 km we come to San Luis Potosí.

San Luis Potosí, 423 km from Mexico City, capital of its state, is the centre of a rich mining and agricultural area, which has expanded industrially in recent years. Alt: 1,880 metres; pop: 850,000 (state pop 1990, 2,002,000). Glazed, many-coloured tiles are a feature of the city: one of its shopping streets, the main plaza, and the domes of many of its churches are covered with them. It became an important centre after the discovery of the famous San Pedro silver mine in the 16th century, and a city in 1658. The **Cathedral** is on **Plaza Hidalgo**. See the churches of **San Francisco**, with its white and blue tiled dome and suspended glass boat in the transept (try and get into the magnificent sacristy); **El Carmen**, in **Plaza Morelos**, with a grand tiled dome, an intricate façade, and a fine pulpit and altar inside (the **Teatro de la Paz** is next door); the baroque **Capilla de Aránzazu**, behind San Francisco inside the regional museum (see below); the **Capilla de Loreto** with a baroque façade; **Iglesia de San Miguelito**, in the oldest part of the city; **San Agustín**, with its ornate baroque tower; and the startling modern **Templo de la Santa Cruz**, in the Industria Aviación district, designed by Enrique de la Mora. The **Palacio de Gobierno**, begun 1770, contains oil-paintings of past governors, and the colonial treasury, **Antigua Real Caja**, built 1767. Other points of interest are the pedestrian precinct in Calle Hidalgo and the **Caja del Agua** fountain (1835) in Av Juárez. **Plaza de San Francisco** is very pleasant. The modern railway station has frescoes by Fernando Leal. The **Teatro Alarcón** is by Tresguerras (see under Celaya, **p 110**). Locally made *rebozos* (the best are from Santa María del Río) are for sale in the markets. The **University** was founded in 1804. A scenic road leads to Aguascalientes airport.

Feria In the second fortnight of August.

Hotels Many between the railway station and the cathedral. **A+** *Panorama*, Av Venustiano Carranza 315, T 121777, F 124591; **A** *María Cristina*, Juan Sarabia 110, Altos, T 129408, F 186417, with swimming pool on roof, modern, clean, with restaurant, good value); **B** *Nápoles*, Juan Sarabia 120, T 128418, F 142104, rec; **D** *Jardín*, Los Bravo 530, T 123152, good, restaurant rec; **D** *Nacional*, Manuel José Othon, on the Alameda, 1 block from train station, with bath, cheaper without, basic; **D** *Progreso*, Aldama 415, T 120366, dark, rather seedy; **D** *Universidad*, Universidad 1435, between train and bus station, clean, friendly, hot showers. **E** *El Principal*, Juan Sarabia opp *María Cristina*, with bath, OK, loud TV in hall; **E** *Gran*, Bravo 235, F without bath, hot water, friendly but basic, electrics and toilets leave something to be desired. **Youth Hostel**, Diagonal Sur, on the SW side of the Glorieta Juárez, 5 min walk from central bus station, F, CP 78000, T 181617.

Note for motorists driving into the centre, parking is very difficult. There is an *estacionamiento* near the police station on Eje Vial, US$1 for first hour, US$0.65 for each subsequent hour.

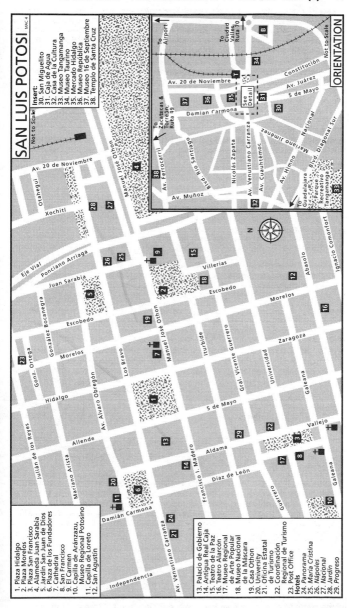

SAN LUIS POTOSI

Not to Scale

MAC-4

Insert:
30. San Miguelito
31. Caja de Agua
32. Casa de la Cultura
33. Museo Tangamanga
34. Museo Taurino
35. Mercado Hidalgo
36. Museo Republica
37. Museo 16 de Septiembre
38. Templo de Santa Cruz

ORIENTATION

To Airport
To Ciudad Valles, Ruta 70

Av. 20 de Noviembre

Constitución

Av. Juárez

5 de Mayo

Damian Carmona

To Zacatecas & Torreón, Ruta 49

Av. Ferrocarril

Blvd Río santiago

Nicolás Zapata

Av. Venustiano Carranza

Av. Cuauhtémoc

Av. Himno

Av. Muñoz

Mariano Jiménez

Nacional

Blvd Diagonal Sur

Parque Recreativo Tangamanga

To Guadalajara & Mexico City

See Detail

Not to Scale

Streets (main map)

Av. 20 de Noviembre

Otahegui

Xochitl

Eje Vial

Ponciano Arriaga

Juan Sarabia

Gonz. Ortega

González Bocanegra

Escobedo

Morelos

Hidalgo

Allende

Julián de los Reyes

Mariano Arista

Av. Alvaro Obregón

Los Bravo

Manuel José Othon

Villerias

Escobedo

Morelos

Iturbide

Gral. Vicente Guerrero

Universidad

Zaragoza

Galeana

Abasolo

Ignacio Comonfort

5 de Mayo

Aldama

Francisco I. Madero

Diaz de León

Guerrero

Galeana

Vallejo

Damián Carmona

Independencia

Av. Venustiano Carranza

N

1. Plaza Hidalgo
2. Plaza Morelos
3. Plaza San Francisco
4. Alameda Juan Sarabia
5. Jardín San Juan de Dios
6. Plaza de los Fundadores
7. Cathedral
8. San Francisco
9. El Carmen
10. Capilla de Aránzazu, Museo Regional Potosino
11. Capilla de Loreto
12. San Agustín
13. Palacio de Gobierno
14. Antigua Real Caja
15. Teatro de la Paz
16. Teatro Alarcón
17. Museo Regional de Arte Popular
18. Museo Nacional de la Máscara
19. Casa Othon
20. University
21. Oficina Estatal de Turismo
22. Coordinación Regional de Turismo
23. Post Office

Hotels
24. Panorama
25. María Cristina
26. Nápoles
27. Nacional
28. Jardín
29. Progreso

Motels All along Highway 57: **L** *Hostal del Quijote*, Km 420, T 181312, F 185105, five-star, convention facilities, 6 km S on the San Luis Potosí-Mexico City highway, one of the best in Mexico; **A** *Cactus*, T 121871; **A** *Santa Fe*, T 125109; all with pools. Also **A+** *Tuna* (Best Western), Highway 80, nr exit to Guadalajara, T 131207, F 111415, parking, pool, restaurant and bar, near University campus; **C** *Mansión Los Arcos*, a few km S of San Luis Potosí, signposted, with restaurant and safe parking.

Restaurants *Los Molinos*, in *Hostal del Quijote*, excellent well-served food; *Tokio*, Los Bravo 510, excellent *comida*. *El Girasol*, Guerrero 345, vegetarian; good cafeteria at bus station. *Café Florida*, Juan Sarabia 230; *Pacífico*, Juan Sarabia y Manuel José Othon, clean bathroom, good menu, open 24 hrs, highly rec; and many other reasonably-priced eating places at western end of Alameda Juan Sarabia. *Café Progreso*, Aldama, next to hotel of same name, good coffee, cheap food, clean toilets. **Health food** store, 5 de Mayo 325, fairly limited.

Shopping Local sweets and craftwork at Plaza del Carmen 325, Los Bravo 546 and Escobedo 1030. The famous local painter, Vicente Guerrero, lives in a modest neighbourhood at Plata 407, Colonia Morales (T 3-80-57) where he also has his studio. Markets: head N on Hidalgo and you come to Mercado Hidalgo, then Mercado República, and Mercado 16 de Septiembre. 3-storey hypermarket, *Chalita*, on Jardín San Juan de Dios between Av Alavaro Obregón and Los Bravo.

Museums **Museo Regional de Arte Popular**, open Tues-Sat 1000-1345, 1600-1745; Sun 1000-1400, Mon 1000-1500, next to San Francisco church. Nearby is **Museo Regional Potosino**, archaeological, and a collection of wrought iron work, Capilla Aránzazu on 2nd floor, open Tues-Fri 1000-1300, 1500-1800, Sat 1000-1200, Sun 1000-1300. **La Casa de la Cultura** on Av Carranza, halfway between the centre and university, is a converted mansion with frequent art displays and musical recitals, open Tues-Fri, 1000-1400, 1600-1800, Sat 1000-1400, 1800-2100. **Museo Nacional de la Máscara**, in Palacio Federal, has most complete collection of masks in the country, open Tues-Fri 1000-1400, 1600-1800, Sat-Sun 1000-1400. In Parque Tangamanga (still under development S of city) is **Museo Tangamanga** in an old hacienda, also a Planetarium, observatory and open air theatre (open 0600-1800). In Plaza España, next to the Plaza de Toros, is a **Museo Taurino** (E of Alameda on Universidad y Triana, Tues-Sat 1100-1330, 1730-1930). **Casa Othon**, Manuel José Othon 225, is the birthplace and home of the poet, open Tues-Fri 0800-1900, Sat and Sun 1000-1300; in the Palacio de Gobierno some rooms may be visited Mon-Fri 0930-1330.

Post Office Morelos y González Ortega.

Tourist Office Dirección Estatal de Turismo, Carranza 325; Coordinación Regional de Turismo, Jardín Guerrero 14 (Plaza San Francisco), both helpful.

Buses Station on outskirts of town 1½ km from centre. Bus to centre US$0.20. Flecha Amarilla to **Querétaro**, US$7, 2 hrs, US$13.25 (ETN luxury service) (88 km of 4-lane highway have been built N of Querétaro, about half the way, and 40 km have also been completed to the S of San Luis Potosí); to **San Miguel de Allende**, 2nd class, daily, with Flecha Amarilla; to **Nuevo Laredo**, US$42. To Linares, US$14.80. To Matehuala, 2½ hrs, US$6.25, with Estrella Blanca. To **Monterrey**, US$14.80. To **Mexico City**, US$6.25, 5 hrs non-stop, US$28 with ETN.

Train To **Querétaro**, US$6 1st class, US$3.35 2nd, supposed to leave at 1005 but arrives full and late from Nuevo Laredo; to **Mexico City**, 10-11 hrs, US$17.85 *primera especial*, sleepers from US$37 (6¼ hrs on Regiomontano *servicio estrella*, leaves 0345, arrives Mexico City 1000); to **San Miguel de Allende**, 3-4 hrs.

Excursions Hot springs at Ojocaliente, Balneario de Lourdes and Gogorrón. *Balneario de Lourdes* (hotel, clean, nice atmosphere, small pool, B) is S of San Luis Potosí. *Gogorrón* is clean and relaxing, with pools, hot tubs, picnic grounds and campsites. There is a restaurant. A day trip or overnight camp-out is recommended in the lightly wooded hills and meadows near the microwave station (at 2,600 metres) 40 km E of San Luis Potosí: go 35 km along the Tampico highway and continue up 5 km of cobblestone road to the station. Good views and flora.

(1,021 km from border) *San Luis De La Paz*, the junction with Route 110 leading W to three of the most attractive towns in Mexico: Dolores Hidalgo, Guanajuato, and San Miguel de Allende. (See p 105-115). No one who yields to the temptation of this detour can hope to get back to the main route for three or four days.

Near San Luis is another of Mexico's mining ghost-towns, **Pozos** (alt 2,305m), once one of the most important mining centres of Mexico. First you come to the ruins. It's very silent and a complete contrast to Real de Catorce. Many of the mining shafts still remain pristine and very deep. Drive on and you reach the town, where several workshops have prehispanic musical instruments and artefacts for show and sale, all handmade mostly in Pozos. Particularly helpful was the lady at *Cademac* (near the square, open Mon-Sat 1000-1900), who demonstrated how many of the not-so-obvious instruments worked.

Pozos was founded in 1576 when silver was discovered. Last century the population reached 80,000 but following the Revolution most of the foreign (French and Spanish) owners left and the workforce migrated to the capital. After the 1985 earthquake there, people who had lost their homes drifted back. The men now work in Querétaro and the women work at home making clothes to sell in local markets. The population has slowly risen to 2,000. The town is very quiet and the whole area was decreed a historical monument in 1982. (Francesca Pagnacco, Exeter, Devon.) There are no rooms to let.

(1,105 km) **Querétaro**, pop: 550,000; alt: 1,865 metres (can be quite cold at night); 215 km from the capital. The city was founded in 1531 and the name means 'Place of Rocks' in Tarascan. It is now an important industrial centre and capital of Querétaro state (pop 1990 1,044,200), an old and beautiful city, dotted with attractive squares. (No buses in the centre.) Hidalgo's rising in 1810 was plotted here, and it was also here that Emperor Maximilian surrendered after defeat, was tried, and was shot, on 19 June 1867, on the Cerro de las Campanas (the Hill of Bells), outside the city.

La Corregidora (Doña Josefa Ortiz de Domínguez, wife of the Corregidor, or Mayor), a member of the group of plotters for independence masquerading as a society for the study of the fine arts, was able, in 1810, to get word to Father Hidalgo that their plans for revolt had been discovered. Hidalgo immediately gave the cry (*grito*) for independence. Today, the Corregidor gives the Grito from the balcony of the **Palacio Municipal** (on Plaza Independencia) every 15 September at 1100 (it is echoed on every civic balcony thoughout Mexico on this date). La Corregidora's home may be visited.

Buildings to see: the **Santa Rosa de Viterbo** church and monastery, remodelled by Francisco Tresguerras (tours in English); his reconstruction of **Santa Clara**, one of the loveliest churches in Mexico, and that is saying much; the church and monastery of **Santa Cruz**, which served as the HQ of Maximilian and his forces (view from the bell tower); the church of **San Felipe**, now being restored for use as the Cathedral; the splendid **Palacio Federal**, once an Augustinian convent with exceptionally fine cloisters, now restored with an art gallery containing some beautiful works; the important and elegant **Museo Regional** on the main plaza, known as the Plaza de Armas or as Plaza Obregón (not all its galleries are always open) which contains much material on the revolution of 1810 and the 1864-67 period (entry US$4.35); the **Teatro de la República**, where Maximilian and his generals were tried, and where the Constitution of 1917 (still in force) was drafted; the **aqueduct**, built in 1726 and 9 km long, very impressive. Several *andadores* (pedestrian walkways) have been developed, greatly adding to the amenities of the city; prices are high here. The *andadores* replace particular roads in places—eg Av 16 de Septiembre becomes Andador de la Corregidora in the centre, and then reverts to its original name. There are local opals, amethysts and topazes for sale; remarkable mineral specimens are shaped into spheres, eggs, mushrooms, and then polished until they shine like jewels (US$10-30, cheaper than San Juan del Río, but more expensive than Taxco). Recommended is Lapidaría Querétaro, Pasteur Norte 72 (Hermanos Ramírez), for fine opals. City tour plus execution site and Juárez monument, excellent value, from J Guadalupe Velásquez 5, Jardines de Oro, Santa Cruz, T 21298, daily at 1130, US$12. On Sun,

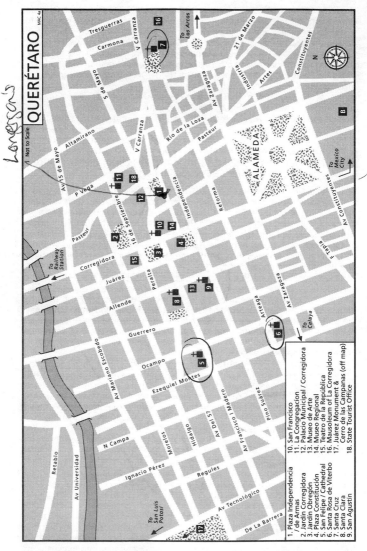

QUERÉTARO

Not to Scale

Lonossons

1. Plaza Independencia / de Armas
2. Jardín Corregidora
3. Jardín Obregón
4. Plaza Constitución
5. San Felipe / Cathedral
6. Santa Rosa de Viterbo
7. Santa Cruz
8. Santa Clara
9. San Agustín
10. La Congregación
11. Palacio Municipal / Corregidora
12. Museo de Arte
13. Museo Regional
14. Plaza Constitución
15. Teatro de la República
16. Mausoleum of La Corregidora
17. Juárez Monument & Cerro de las Campanas (off map)
18. State Tourist Office

family excursions leave the Plaza de Armas at 1000. Try local Hidalgo Pinot Noir wine.

There is a *feria agricola* from 2nd week of December until Christmas; bull fights and cock fights. On New Year's Eve there is a special market and special performances are given in the main street.

Hotels A+ *Holiday Inn*, Av 5 de Febrero y Pino Suárez, on Highway 57, T 60202, F 168902, 5-star, restaurant, bars; also 5-star, *Antigua Hacienda Galindo*, Km 5 on road to Amealco, Apartado Postal 16, T 20050, F 20100; **A+** *Mirabel*, Constituyentes 2, T 143585, good, garage, restaurant; *Casa Blanca*, 4-star, Constituyentes 69 Poniente, T 160102, F 160100; *Real de Minas*, Constituyentes 124, T 60444/60257, 4 star; *Danés*, Pino Suárez 32, T 602243; **B** *Corregidora*, Corregidora 138, T 140406, reasonable but noisy; **B** *Del Marqués*, Juárez Norte 104, T 20414, clean; **C** *Plaza*, Plaza Obregón, T 21138, airy, lovely inner patio, modernized, safe, clean, comfortable; **D** *El Cid*, Prolongación Corregidora, T 23518, more of a motel, clean, good value, close to bus station (left out of bus station and first left); **D** *Hidalgo*, near Zócalo, Madero 11 Poniente, T 20081, with bath, excellent value for two or more, not so for singles (English owner, Adrian Leece); **D** *Impala*, Zargoza y Corregidora, W of Alameda Park, T 22570, close to bus station, overpriced, dirty (don't let the new façade and lobby fool you); **D** *Posada* Pino Suárez, with bath, modern, but small, dirty rooms, poor value; **D** *San Agustín*, Pino Suárez 12, T 23919, small. **Youth Hostel**, Av del Ejército Republicano, ex-Convento de la Cruz, E, running water am only, T 143050.

Motels *Posada Campestre*, Madero y Circunvalación, T 16-27-28; **A+** *Jurica*, edge of town on road to San Luis Potosí, former *hacienda*, with gardens, squash, golf-course, opulent, T 21081; **A+** *La Mansión*, 6½ km S of town, excellent dining facilities, gorgeous grounds; **A** *Azteca*, 15 km N on road to San Luis Potosí, T 22060; **A** *Flamingo*, on Constituyentes Poniente 138, T 162093, comfortable. *Cafés in Plaza Endela*

Restaurants *Mesón Santa Rosa*, Pasteur 17, in hotel of same name, good but expensive, restored colonial building; *Fonda del Refugio*, Jardín Corregidora, pretty but food is poor; *La Corregidora*, on the other side of the street, is reportd as greatly superior. *Don Juan*, Jardín Corregidora, rec (*Pizza Piazza* at same location is not rec); *Flor de Querétaro*, on Plaza Obregón, Juárez Norte 5, good but pricey; on same square, *Manolo*, good paella; *La Cocina Mexicana*, Pino Suárez 17, opp *Hotel San Agustín*, cheap and good but rather dark, à la carte better value than *comida corrida*; *Arcangel*, Plaza Chica, pleasant setting, good food; *Le Bon Vivant*, Pino Suárez, cheap, good value, rec; *Ostionería Tampico*, Corregidora Nte 3, good cheap fish. *Bisquetes*, in arcade of old *Gran Hotel* on Zócala, good value.

Entertainment *Corral de Comedias*, Carranza 39, T 207-65, an original theatre company, colonial surroundings and suppers; *JBJ Disco*, Blvd Zona Dorada, Fracc Los Arcos. Mariachis play in the Jardín Corregidora, 16 de Septiembre y Corregidora, in the evenings. The town band plays in the Jardín Obregón on Sunday evening, lovely atmosphere.

Post Office Arteaga Poniente 5 (inadequate). DHL, International courier service, Blvd Zona Dorada 37, Fracc Los Arcos, T 1425-26 or 1452-56, open Mon-Fri 0900-1800, Sat 0900-1200.

Tourist Office State office, Pasteur 17, on Plaza Independencia at junction with Libertad; federal office Av Constituyentes Ote 102 (away from centre T 13-84-83/13-85-11).

Bus Mexico City (Terminal del Norte) frequent 1st and 2nd class buses, 2½ hrs, US$7.15, several companies, US$15.50 ETN; to **Nuevo Laredo**, US$51, to **San Miguel de Allende**, 1 hr, hourly with Flecha Amarilla, US$2.20. To **Guadalajara**; US$12 (US$22 ETN). To **San Juan del Río**, US$2, ½ hr, frequent. To **Tula** US$5. To **Guanajuato**, US$5.75, 2½ hrs. (Flecha Amarilla), 1030, 1230, 1430; to **San Luis Potosí**, Flecha Amarilla, US$7, ETN, US$13.25, 2 hrs; to **Pachuca**, US$4.50, 4½ hrs (Estrella Blanca, poor buses).

Rail The station is not far N of the centre, close to Prolongación Corregidora. Constitucionalista (*servicio estrella*) leaves **Mexico City** for Querétaro 0700 (US$10.10), arriving 3½ hrs later; returns to Mexico City at 1735 arr 2115. At Querétaro, the service divides to **San Miguel Allende** (arr 1130, very crowded) and **San Luis Potosí** (arr 1350), and **Guanajato**, via Silao, (arr 1325). To **Guadalajara** stopping train at 2342, arr 0720. División del Norte train (for Ciudad Juárez) leaves Mexico City at 0800, arrives Querétaro 1130, US$5.40 1st class; the Mexico City-Nuevo Laredo train leaves the capital at 0900, passing Querétaro 1300, 2nd class US$3.25, 1st US$5.40, *primera especial* US$8.30.

Excursions There is a Huapango dance festival on 15 April at *San Joaquín* in the Sierra de Querétaro. Interesting wood carvings may be seen at Apaseo el Grande 28 km away.

Tim Connell writes: **The Missions of Querétaro**. A little-known feature of Querétaro is the existence of eighteenth-century missions in the far NE of the state. They were founded by Fray Junípero de la Serra, who later went on to establish missions in California with names like Nuestra Señora de los Angeles and San Francisco de Asís. (He is also said to have planted a miraculous tree in the convent of the Santa Cruz in Querétaro by thrusting his staff into the ground. The tree is apparently the only one of its kind in the world to have cruciform thorns.)

All five missions have been restored, and two of them have state-run hotels nearby. (Both hotels highly recommended and inexpensive. The restaurant at Concá is not very good however.) The journey itself requires something of a head for heights in that there are said to be seven hundred curves en route. (There is a slightly shorter way, but that has over a thousand...) The road (Route 120) goes through the small market town of Ezequiel Montes (pop 5,000). 25 km beyond the town of Colón it passes within 10 km of the quite remarkable **Peñón de Bernal**, a massive rocky outcrop 350 metres high. The bends really start after Vizarrón, a local centre for marble. Much of the journey from here on is through rather arid and yet dramatic terrain with gorges and panoramic views. The high point (aptly enough) is called la Puerta del Cielo, as you can actually look down on the clouds. As the road begins to descend so the vegetation becomes more tropical and the weather gets much warmer. (Jalpan is at only 700 metres above sea level, Concá 500). There is a petrol station at **Cadeyreta** (Km 75) and Ahuacatlán (Km 166) as well as Vizarrón. There are ruins at San Joaquín (Km 138) but the road is very steep and the ruins often swathed in mist. San Joaquín is famous for the annual Huapango dance festival (see above). Cadeyreta itself is colonial in style, and has two noteworthy churches in the main square, one dedicated to St Peter, the other St Paul. The latter houses an important collection of colonial religious art. Nearby is the Casa de los Alemanes, which houses an enormous collection of cacti.

Jalpan, the first of the missions, becomes visible way below in a broad lush valley. It is the largest of the missions, which are located in valleys that spread out from here. Jalpan was the first to be founded in 1774 and has cloisters as well as the main church. Opposite is the hotel, well appointed in colonial style with swimming pool. The town itself is picturesque without being spoilt. All the churches are distinguished by the profusion of baroque carving, their superb location and the care with which they have been conserved: **Landa**, 18 km to the N, Tilaco 25 km beyond Landa to the E, and **Tancoyol** 37 km to the NW. (The roads are good apart from the last 15 km into Tilaco).

38 km further on from Jalpan is **Concá**. There is a larger hotel in its own grounds a few kilometres from the village and mission, again in colonial style with a pool fed by warm spring water. Acamaya, freshwater crayfish, is a local speciality. At the bridge of Concá nearby a hot water river flows into one with cold water. The church itself is built on a ridge, creating a dramatic skyline when viewed from below. The village is very small. Two restaurants and a general store.

It is reported to be possible to drive from Concá to San Luis Potosí, which is about 3 hrs further on. The journey to Jalpan from Querétaro takes about 6 hrs. At least three days should be allowed to see everything properly.

There is a 4-lane motorway (US$3 a car) from Irapuato past Querétaro to Mexico City. Along it (48 km from Querétaro) is **San Juan del Río** (**A+ Hotel Mansión Galindo**, T 20050, restored hacienda—apparently given by Cortés to his mistress Malinche—beautiful building; **D Hotel Layseca**, Av Juárez 9 Oriente, colonial building, large rooms, nice furniture, excellent, car parking, no restaurant; several picturesque hotels, D), near where the best fighting bulls are raised; the town is a centre for handicrafts, and also for polishing gemstones—opals and amethysts. There is one friendly and reasonable shop: La Guadalupana, 16 de Septiembre 5; others are expensive and less friendly. Several balnearios in San Juan (try Venecia, cold water, very quiet mid-week, US$1.30). A branch road runs NE from San Juan to the picturesque town of **Tequesquiapán**, with thermal baths, fine climate, water sports, weekend residences, expensive, good hotels (**A El Relox**, Morelos 8, T 30066, spa pool open to non-residents; **Maridelphi**, similar price; **Las Cavas**,

Paseo Media Luna 8, T 30804, F 30671), **Artesanías Bugambilia**, on the main square, rec. Note that town is deserted from Monday to Thursday and big reductions in hotel prices can be found. On the other hand, there is nothing other than the resort: a good cheap Mexican meal is hard to find. (Restaurant **La Chiapaneca**, Carrizal 19, centre, opposite craft market, is very good, reasonably-priced, clean). The dam near the town is worth a visit. There is a geyser, at Tecozautla, 1¼ hrs from Tequisquiapán. Between San Juan del Río and Tequesquiapán, a small track leads off the main road 4 km to the village of La Trinidad, near which lie some of the opal mines which are still in operation. Bernal, a city some 60 km from Querétaro, is a centre for clothing, blankets, wall hangings and carpets made by cottage industry, barter politely for good prices. Then at 1,167 km, Palmillas, 153 km to Mexico City.

Bus San Juan del Río-Tequesquiapán US$1, 20 mins.

Tolls Between San Juan del Río and Mexico City, 3 tolls, US$1.65, US$5 and US$5. The 3-lane vía libre is perfectly good.

The Mexico City motorway passes close to Tula and Tepozotlán (**see p 203**). There are various country clubs along the road. In the state park of El Ocotal is a Swiss-chalet style hotel with excellent restaurant, B.

CIUDAD JUAREZ TO MEXICO CITY (3)

A route of much historical interest: Chihuahua has strong links with the revolutionary and independence movements, besides being the starting point for a magnificent rail journey to the Pacific, through Tarahumara Indian country: Zacatecas is a mining centre. Aguascalientes is colonial, but of far greater colonial significance are Guanajuato and San Miguel de Allende, while Dolores Hidalgo is the birthplace of Mexican independence.

Ciudad Juárez, opposite El Paso, Texas; to Mexico City: 1,866 km; altitude 1,150 metres. Juárez and El Paso have over 1.1 million people each; the cross border industry has made Ciudad Juárez the largest maquiladora city in the world. Twin plant assembly and manufacturing operations now supersede tourism and agriculture in the city.

The Spanish conquistador Cabeza de Vaca discovered the Paso del Norte on the Camino Real. The name was retained until 1888 when Porfirio Díaz renamed the city after Benito Juárez. Today four bridges link the two cities: Santa Fe, for pedestrians, and cars leaving Mexico; Stanton Street, for pedestrians and cars leaving USA; Cordova bridge (2-way traffic); and the new Zaragosa toll bridge to the E. The Río Bravo/Grande, which divides the cities and forms the border, has been canalized and is used for irrigation upstream, so often it has little or no water.

Points of Interest In Ciudad Juárez, the **Nuestra Señora de Guadalupe de El Paso del Norte** mission was the first established in the region; the building was completed in 1668. It, and the nearby **Cathedral**, are 2 blocks W of Av Juárez on 16 de Septiembre. At the junction of Av Juárez and 16 de Septiembre is the Aduana, the former customs building, now the **Museo Histórico**. In Parque Chamizal, just across the Cordova bridge, are the **Museo de Arte Prehispánica** with exhibits from each Mexican state, **Botanic Gardens** and a memorial to Benito Juárez. Continuing S down Av Lincoln, you come to the Pronaf area with the **Museo de Arte Historia**. The University Cultural Centre and the **Fonart** artisan centre, which acts as a Mexican 'shop window"—well worth it for the uninitiated tourist. There are a number of markets, the racetrack is very popular (with dog races in spring and summer), the **Plaza Monumental de Toros** (López

Mateos y Triunfo de la República) holds bullfights between April and September, and *charreadas* (rodeos) are held at various locations. The main street is Av Juárez, on or near which are most of the souvenir shops, hotels, cheap and expensive restaurants, clubs and bars. The bars and other nightlife cater mostly for El Paso high school students who can drink at 18 in Mexico, but not till 21 in El Paso.

To the E of El Paso, the **Ysleta Mission** is the oldest in Texas (1680), built by Franciscan monks and Tigua Indians, who have a 'reservation' (more like a suburb) nearby; the Socorro mission (1681) and San Elizario Presidio (1789, rebuilt 1877-87) are in the same direction. There are a number of museums, including the **Americana Museum** in the Civic Centre (which also houses a performing arts centre, convention centre and tourist office), the **Museum of Art** at 1211 Montana and The **Fort Bliss Air Defence Museum** of the nearby Air Base. Conducted tours of El Paso (US$10—same price for Juárez) usually take in Fort Bliss, the University, the Scenic Drive and the Tigua Reservation. Very few services are open at weekends in El Paso.

Hotels A+ *Calinda Quality Inn*, Calz Hermanos Escobar 3515, T 137250; *Holiday Inn Express*, Paseo Triunfo de la República 8745, T 296000, F 296020; **B** *Impala*, Lerdo Norte 670, T 91160431/0491, clean, OK; **C** *Continental*, Lerdo Sur 112 (downtown), T 150084, clean, TV, noisy, not friendly, restaurant good; **C** *Parador Juárez*, Miguel Ahumada 615 Sur, T 159184; and many others in the upper price ranges. **F** *San Luis*, Mariscal y Morelos, 1 block S of, and behind, Cathedral, cheapest but filthy and insecure; better are **D** *Correo*, Lerdo Sur 250, just across 16 de Septiembre and **D** *Juárez*, Lerdo Norte 143, close to Stanton Street bridge.

In El Paso there are many places to stay, ranging from the *Westin Paso del Norte Hotel*, with its Tiffany glass dome, black and pink marble lobby and European chandeliers (the most expensive), T 534-3000, to the **B** *Plaza Motor Hotel*, next to Greyhound station (the original HIlton, still in good condition), quiet, and **A** *Ramada* (on Oregon, rec, T 544-3300), many motels, to the **C** *Gardner*, 311 E Franklin Ave, T 532-3661, hot water, shared bath, TV and phone in room, rooms with bath available, also serves as *Youth Hostel*, US$12 for members only.

Restaurants Many eating places either side of the border; it is reported that, in the better restaurants, meals are cheaper in El Paso. In Juárez, *Taco Cabaña* on Calle de la Peña, next to *Hotel Continental*, and *El Gordo No 2*, Francisco Madero, 1/2 block from 16 de Septiembre, are good for tacos and burritos (about US$2-3); *Florida*, Juárez 301, 2 blocks from *Hotel Impala*, clean, good food and service; plenty of Chinese restaurants.

Taxis In Juárez charge by zone, from US$2.75 to US$7.25.

Exchange In Ciudad Juárez most *cambios* are on Av Juárez and Av de las Américas; there is also a *cambio* at the bus terminal. Rates vary very little, some places charge commission on travellers' cheques; some are safer than others. The best and most convenient exchange houses are in El Paso: **Valuta Corp**, 301 Paisano Drive, buys and sells all foreign currencies, wires money transfers, open 24 hrs inc holidays, commission charged on all travellers' cheques except Amex; **Melek Corp**, 306 Paisano Drive, not open 24 hrs, otherwise offers most of the same services as Valuta but only dollars and pesos; **Loren Inc**, 1611 Paisano Drive, much the same, but rates slightly worse (if coming from US immigration, when you reach Paisano Drive/Highway 62, turn E for these places). In El Paso, banks are closed on Sat.

Consulates US, López Mateos 924, Cd Juárez, T 13-40-48. British (Honorary) Mr CR Maingot, Calle Fresno 185, Campestre Juárez, T (91-16) 75791. Mexican, 910, E San Antonio, El Paso, T 533-4082.

Tourist Offices In Ciudad Juárez, on ground floor of the Presidencia (City Hall, at Malecón y Francisco Villa), on left as you cross Santa Fe bridge, T 14-01-23; in El Paso T 534-0536. El Paso Tourist Office in Civic Centre Plaza, T 534-0686; also at airport.

Rail División del Norte (*servicio estrella*) leaves Ciudad Juárez for **Mexico City** (1,970 km), at 2200, 36 hrs, fare one way is US$26.50 2nd class, US$43.35 1st class. Reverse journey leaves at 2000 from Mexico City. The route is through Chihuahua, Torreón, Zacatecas, Aguascalientes, León, Silao (for Guanajuato), Celaya and Querétaro. At 0800, Mon, Wed and Fri and train leaves Ciudad Juárez for **La Junta** (W of Ciudad Cuauhtémoc, **see below, p 96**), via **Nuevo Casas Grandes** and **Madera**; on Tues, Thur and Sat at 0800 a train goes as far as Madera. Journey times (very approximately): 5 1/2 hrs to Nuevo Casas Grandes (240 km), 12

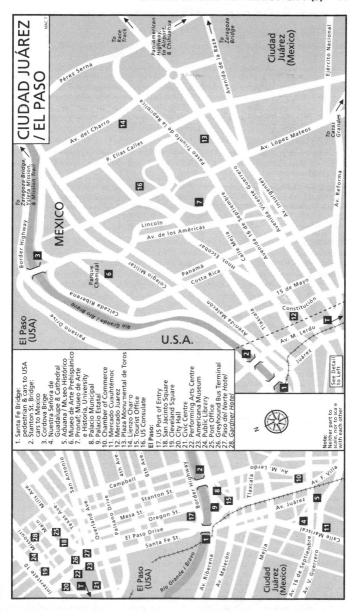

CIUDAD JUÁREZ / EL PASO

MAP 7

To Race Track

Pan-American Highway, to Airport, & Chihuahua

To Zaragoza Bridge

Ciudad Juárez (Mexico)

Ejército Nacional

Pérez Serna

Avenida de la Raza

Avenida Vicente Guerrero

Av. López Mateos

To Casas Grandes

Av. del Charro

P. Elías Calles

Paseo Triunfo de la República

Av. Reforma

To Zaragoze Bridge, Yeleta Missions, & Mission Trail

Border Highway

MEXICO

Lincoln

Av. de los Américas

Av. Insurgentes

Calle Mejía

Avenida 16 de Septiembre

Hnos. Escobar

Panamá

Costa Rica

15 de Mayo

Constitución

Parque Chamizal

Colegio Militar

Calzada Ribereña

Rio Grande / Rio Bravo

Paisano Drive

El Paso (USA)

U.S.A.

Tlaxcala

Avenida Malecón

Av. M. Lerdo

Juárez

See Detail to Left

El Paso:

- 17. US Port of Entry
- 18. San Jacinto Square
- 19. Cleveland Square
- 20. City Hall
- 21. Civic Centre
- 22. Performing Arts Centre
- 23. Americana Museum
- 24. Public Library
- 25. Post Office
- 26. Greyhound Bus Terminal
- 27. Paso del Norte Hotel
- 28. Gardner Hotel

1. Santa Fe Bridge: pedestrian & cars to USA
2. Stanton St. Bridge: cars to Mexico
3. Cordova Brige
4. Nuestra Señora de Guadalupe & Cathedral
5. Aduana / Mseo Histórico
6. Museo de Arte Prehispánico
7. Pronaf, Museo de Arte e Historia University
8. Palacio Municipal
9. Palacio Estatal
10. Chamber of Commerce
11. Mercado Cuauhtémoc
12. Mercado Juárez
13. Plaza Monumental de Toros
14. Lienzo Charo
15. Tourist Office
16. US Consulate

Note: Inner part to scale, not to scale with each other

N

San Antonio

4th Ave.

6th Ave.

Campbell

Stanton St.

Border Highway

Av. M. Lerdo

Av. F. Villa

Overland Ave.

Paisano Drive

Mesa St.

Oregon St.

Av. Juárez

El Paso Drive

Santa Fe St.

Texas Ave.

San Jacinto

Mills Ave.

Main

Missouri

Interstate 10

El Paso (USA)

Rio Grande / Rio Bravo

Av. Ribereña

Av. Malecón

Mejía

Ciudad Juárez (Mexico)

Av. 16 de Septiembre

Av. V. Guerrero

Calle Mariscal

Tlaxcala

hrs to Madera (432 km) and 14 hrs to La Junta (572 km). Station in Ciudad Juárez is a couple of blocks S of junction of Av Juárez and 16 de Septiembre. Information: T (16) 12-25-57 14-97-17 (Nacionales de México) or 545-2247 (Amtrak in El Paso).

Road Sanborns, for insurance and information, 440 Raynolds, El Paso, T (915) 779-3538, F 772-1795, open Mon-Fri 0830-1700. AAA office: 916 Mesa Avenue, El Paso.

Buses Terminal was on Paseo Triunfo de la República, at corner of Av López Mateos, but has moved some distance S of this location. From the terminal to centre or Santa Fe bridge, taxi fare is about US$10. Shuttle but to **El Paso** US$5.50, hourly, to Greyhound Terminal. From Ciudad Juárez, several bus companies run to **Chihuahua** (4 hrs, US$17.50) and on to **Mexico City** (26 hrs, US$66), via all the major cities en route, eg **Torreón** (US$27), **Zacatecas** (US$43.75, **Aguascalientes** (US$46.25), or **San Luis Potosí** (US$46.25), **Querétaro** (US$56). Services also to **Monterrey** (US$44), eg Trans del Norte, 8 a day, **Hermosillo** (US$26.50) and **Tijuana** (US$44 1st class, Caballero Azteca), **Guadalajara** (US$50), **Mazatlán** (US$53), and other Pacific coast destinations.

Express Limousine service El Paso-Los Angeles, US$40, El Paso-Albuquerque US$27; the El Paso office is just across the Juárez bridge at 6th and Oregon. Greyhound, El Paso, T 532-2365.

Airports Ciudad Juárez's airport is 19 km S of the city; flights by AeroMéxico to **Mexico City**, and, among others, **Chihuahua**, **Guadalajara**, **Monterrey** and **Mazatlán**. Aviacsa to Monterrey and Mérida. El Paso's airport is near Fort Bliss and Biggs Field military airbase with flights by American, Delta, America West Airlines and Southwest Airlines to all parts of the USA. Colectivo Ciudad Juárez airport to El Paso, or El Paso airport, US$15.50.

Crossing the border From El Paso you can get on a bus outside Gate 9 of the Greyhound terminal and pay the driver (US$1.50); as you cross the border he should stop and wait for your documents to be processed. On entry you are automatically given 30 days to stay in Mexico, unless you ask for longer. Trolley buses cross the border for short trips. Alternatively you can walk across (US$0.15 toll pp). Walking from Mexico to the USA costs US$0.55 (toll for cars leaving Mexico US$2.05). Border formalities are minimal, although you are likely to have your bags searched on entering USA on foot because most pedestrians do not carry luggage. If you cross into the USA with a view to leaving the USA by plane, as a non-US citizen you must ask for an immigration card for when you do leave; you may have problems without one. Remember, also, to have your US visa if you require one. **NB** El Paso is on Mountain Standard Time, which is 1 hr behind Central Standard Time and General Mexican Time.

There is a new border crossing at Santa Teresa, New Mexico, just W of El Paso. For trucks and southbound travellers by car, this will avoid the congestion of Ciudad Juárez.

The road is wide, mostly flat, easy to drive, and not as interesting as the Gulf and Pacific routes. From Ciudad Juárez, for some 50 km along the Río Bravo, there is an oasis which grows cotton of an exceptionally high grade. The next 160 km of the road to Mexico City are through desert; towns en route are Salamayuca (restaurant), at Km 58; *Villa Ahumada* (131 km—*Hotel Cactus*, T 4-22-50; **D** *Casa Blanca*, with bath and hot water, room heater, clean, opp train depot on main street, $\frac{1}{2}$ block S of bus terminal). At 180 Km is Moctezuma (restaurant). The road leads into grazing lands and the valley of Chihuahua. The road Chihuahua-Ciudad Juárez is being made into an *autopista*; toll 30 km N of Chihuahua, US$6.30 for cars or pick-ups (the alternative is a long 2-sides-of-a-triangle detour to avoid the toll).

This is the country of the long-haired, fleet-footed Tarahumara Indians, able, it is said, to outstrip a galloping horse and to run down birds. A few Indians can be seen in Chihuahua and Nuevo Casas Grandes, mostly women and children and most, sadly, begging. Tarahumara can be seen in much less unfortunate conditions and in greater numbers in Creel and beyond, but note that the Indians are shy, living in remote ranchos rather than the towns. 12 December is a festival for the Tarahumara.

Mexico Route 2 runs W from Ciudad Juárez, roughly parallel with the Mexico-US border. Between Juárez and Janos, at the northern end of lateral Mexico 24, is the dusty border town of **Palomas**, Chihuahua, opposite Columbus, New Mexico. The modern border facilities are open 24 hrs; Mexican auto insurance is available, but Mexican Customs is at Tres Caminos, the junction with Mexico 2,40.50 km S. Palomas itself has few contemporary attractions apart from limited duty-free shopping for liquor and pharmaceuticals, but Columbus was the site of Pancho Villa's 1916 incursion into New Mexico, which led to reprisals by the forces of American General John J Pershing. The Columbus Historical Museum (open daily from 1000 to 1600), three miles N of the border, offers exhibits on Villa's sacking and burning of Columbus.

Hotels Reasonable accommodation at **D** *Hotel Restaurant San Francisco*, also *Motel Santa Cruz Hotel Regis*. On the Columbus side, **A** *Martha's Place* (T 531-2467), an attractive bed and breakfast, and **C** *Motel Columbus*.

Camping Excellent, well-maintained sites at Pancho Villa State Park, opposite the Columbus Historical Museum, for US$7 per night, additional charge for electrical hook-up.

Buses There is no public transport on the US side, but hourly buses connect Palomas with Tres Caminos, where travellers can board buses from Juárez to Nuevo Casas Grandes (see below).

At the intersection of Mexico Route 2 and Chihuahua Route 10 to Nuevo Casas Grandes is **Janos** (*Restaurant Durango*, de facto bus station at the intersection, has good inexpensive food; several others at junction, plus **D** *Hotel Restaurant La Fuente*). The landscape between Ciudad Juárez and Nuevo Casas Grandes is quite barren and, in the winter months, it can be cold.

Near Janos are the northernmost Mennonite colonies in Mexico; numerous vendors sell Mennonite cheese, which also has a market in upscale restaurants across the border in New Mexico. The German-speaking Mennonites are very conspicuous, the men in starched overalls and the women in long dresses and leggings, their heads covered with scarves.

Northwest of Janos, via the border route of Mexico 2, are the border crossings of **Agua Prieta** (opposite Douglas, Arizona) and **Naco** (adjacent to its Arizona namesake and a short distance S of the historic, picturesque copper mining town of Bisbee). Agua Prieta (population 80,000) is growing rapidly with the proliferation of *maquiladoras* on both sides of the border. If possible, avoid crossing in late afternoon, when traffic across the border can be very congested as Mexican labourers return home from Douglas.

Agua Prieta is 162 km from Janos via Route 2, which crosses the scenic Sierra San Luís, covered by dense oak-juniper woodland, to the continental divide (elevation 1820 metres) at Puerto San Luís, the border between the states of Sonora and Chihuahua. There are outstanding views of the sprawling rangelands to the W. From Km 95 before Janos there are potholes in the highway which extend for 100 km and require close attention, but they are not disastrously bad. Southbound motorists from the United States must present their papers to Mexican customs at La Joya, a lonely outpost 70 km NW of Janos.

Information The Mexican tourist office on Calle I, left around the corner from the crossing at Agua Prieta, was abandoned without notice in December 1991, but may reopen. On the Douglas side, the Chamber of Commerce (T 364-2477) at 1125 Pan American has good information on Mexico as well as Arizona, with a wealth of maps (including Agua Prieta) and brochures. Librolandia del Centro, a bookstore, has a good selection of material on local and regional history.

Hotels Unusually for Mexican cities, Agua Prieta lacks true budget accommodation in the centre and near the border; the main alternatives are **A/B** *Motel La Hacienda*, two blocks from the border; **B** *Hotel El Greco*; **B** *Motel Ruiz*; in Naco, the only formal accommodation is **D** *Motel Colonial*, which is often full, but the manager may tolerate a night's auto camping within the motel compound. Accommodation is cheaper in Douglas, on the Arizona side:

C *Border Motel*; the venerable **B** *Gadsden Hotel*, a registered historical landmark, has been used as a location for Western films. **C** *Motel 6*. Rates are higher in Bisbee, a very popular tourist destination, but the town offers good value for money.

Camping   RV parks on the Arizona side charge about US$10 per night for vehicle, US$5 for tent camping: *Double Adobe Trailer Park* off Highway 80, *Copper Horse Shoe R V Park* on Highway 666.

Restaurants   In Agua Prieta, *El Pollo Loco*, near the plaza, for roasted chicken; in Naco, *Restaurant Juárez*. On the Douglas side, restaurant at *Hotel Gadsden* is good and reasonable, but the best selection in the area is at Bisbee, 10 miles N of Naco.

Buses   From Agua Prieta, Tres Estrellas and Transportes Norte de Sonora offer service to **Ciudad Juárez** (4 daily, US$13.25), **Chihuahua** (9 daily, US$20), **Nogales** (4 daily, US$8.25), **Tijuana** (6 daily, US$33), **Hermosillo** (8 daily, US$13.25), **Guaymas** (4 daily, US$18), **Navojoa** (3 daily, US$24.75), **Los Mochis** (4 daily, US$30), and **Mexico City** (daily, US$82.50).
   Bridgewater Transport (T 364-2233) connects Douglas with Tucson twice daily (US$30), with connections to Los Angeles (US$92, but more expensive if purchased in California).

Crossing the border   Both the Agua Prieta and Naco ports of entry are open 24 hrs. There is no public transport other than taxi to Naco, Arizona, but there are buses from Naco, Sonora, to Agua Prieta and Nogales. Mexican automobile insurance is not available in Naco, Sonora, but readily obtained at Douglas. Mexican consulate in Douglas, helpful.

Warning   Drug smuggling, auto theft, and other illegal activities are common knowledge along the south-eastern Arizona border. Watch your belongings and money closely even during 'routine' searches by US Customs officials, whose reputation has been sullied by reports of corruption in recent years. Moreover, the police in Agua Prieta have a bad reputation for stopping drivers for no good reason and trying to extract bribes on the threat of jail.

The archaeological site of **Casas Grandes**, or Paquimé, can be reached from Chihuahua, Ciudad Juárez or Agua Prieta. Nuevo Casas Grandes is a town built around the railway; it is very dusty when dry, the wind blowing clouds of dust down the streets, and when wet the main street becomes a river. There is not much to do, but there are cinemas which show US and Mexican films (don't be put off by people standing at the back, there are usually seats free).

   Casas Grandes/Paquimé was probably a trading centre, which reached its peak between 1210 and 1261 AD. The city was destroyed by fire in 1340. Its commercial influence is said to have reached as far as Colorado in the N and into southern Mexico. At its height, it had multi-storeyed buildings; the niches that held the beams for the upper floors are still visible in some buildings. A water system, also visible, carried hot water from thermal springs to the N, and acted as drainage. Most of the buildings are of a type of adobe, but some are faced with stone. One can see a ball court and various plazas among the buildings. The site is well-tended. Significant archaeological reconstruction is under way at Casas Grandes (1993). About 2 hrs is sufficient to see it all; open 1000-1700, entry US$3.50. To get there take a yellow bus from outside the furniture shop at 16 de Septiembre y Constitución Pte in Nuevo Casas Grandes, US$0.20, 15 mins. From the square in Casas Grandes village either take Calle Constitución S out of the square past the school, walk to the end of the road, cross a gulley, then straight on for a bit, turn right and you will see the site, or take Av Juárez W out of the square and turn left at the sign to Paquimé, 1 km.

Paquimé ceramics, copying the original patterns, either black on black, or beige with intricate red and grey designs, are made in the village of Mata Ortiz, 21 km from Nuevo Casas Grandes. Either take a bus from Calle Jesus Urueta, W of the railway track, at 1630 (return at 0800), US$2.40, take the train which is supposed to pass through Nuevo Casas Grandes on Tues, Thurs and Sat at 1300, arriving 1400 (return Mon, Wed, Fri 1225), or hitch.

Accommodation can only be found in Nuevo Casas Grandes: **B** *Motel Hacienda*, Av Juárez 2603, T 4-10-46/7/8/9/50, the best, sometimes has Paquimé ceramics on sale; **C** *California*, Constitución Pte 209, reasonable, takes credit cards, hot water takes a while to come through; **C** *Motel Piñón*, Juárez 605, T 4-10-66, helpful; **C** *Paquimé*, with fan and a/c, clean, large, pleasant, rec; **C** *Parque*, Av Juárez, just past main square heading N, with TV and phone; **D** *Juárez*, A Obregón 110, between bus companies, supposedly hot water, some English spoken, basic bathroom (take your key with you when you go out); *Suites Victoria*, Guadalupe Victoria, 1 block W of Constitución Pte, off 5 de Mayo.

Restaurants *Café de la Esquina*, 5 de Mayo y A Obregón, near bus offices, cheap, clean, friendly, popular; *Tacos El Brasero*, Obregón opp *Hotel Juárez*, open 24 hrs; *Dinno's Pizza*, Minerva y Constitución Ote, fair, takes credit cards, opp Ciné Variedades; *Alameda*, next to *Hotel California*, for breakfast and *comida corrida*, average; *Denni's*, Juárez y Jesús Urueta, mostly steaks, quite good, good service.

Exchange Banks on 5 de Mayo and Constitución Ote; **Casa de Cambio California** next to hotel of that name.

Long-distance Telephone at Rivera bus office, on Alvaro Obregón.

Buses All bus offices are on Alvaro Obregón. Several daily to **Ciudad Juárez**, 3 companies, 4 hrs, US$10.60; 3 companies to **Chihuahua**, 5 hrs, US$12.10; Omnibús de México to **Mexico City** once a day via El Sueco, once via Cuauhtémoc, also to **Monterrey**; Chihuahua Madera to **Cuauhtémoc** and **Madera**; Caballero Azteca to **Agua Prieta** (3 a day), **Hermosillo**, **Tijuana** and **Nogales** (once each).

Train The station, between Constitución Poniente and Oriente (as is the railway), is at 1,454 metres, 240 km from Ciudad Juárez. In theory trains call daily, except Sun, en route to Ciudad Juárez and La Junta or Madera.

From Chihuahua, the turn-off from the road to Ciudad Juárez is near El Sueco (157 km from Chihuahua, 219 from Ciudad Juárez); from here State Highway 10 to Nuevo Casas Grandes (198 km) passes through Constitución (bus stop), Flores Magón (hotel) and Buenaventura (114 km, a pleasant-looking place). About 100 km from El Sueco a brief section of 'camino sinuoso' affords views of the plains you have just crossed; from Buenaventura the road passes through different valleys, of varying degrees of fertility, the most productive being Buenaventura itself and Lagunillas. Buses from Chihuahua to Nuevo Casas Grandes go either via El Sueco or via Ciudad Cuauhtémoc (see below) and Madera (the Sierra route), which has some pleasant landscapes (if heading S from the USA, via Casas Grandes, you can continue on the Sierra route to Creel on the Chihuahua-Los Mochis railway).

Chihuahua, capital of Chihuahua state; alt: 1,420 metres; pop: 800,000 (state population 1990, 2,440,000); centre of a mining and cattle area (375 km from the border, 1,479 km from the capital). It is mostly a modern city, but has strong historical connections, especially with the Mexican Revolution. Summer temperatures often reach 40°C but be prepared for ice at night as late as November. Rain falls from July to September. The local hairless small dog has a constant body temperature of 40°C (104°F)—the world's only authentic 'hot dog". Pancho Villa operated in the country around, and once captured the city by disguising his men as peasants going to market. The **Quinta Luz** (1914), Calle 10 No 3014, where Pancho Villa lived, is now the Museo de la Revolución, with many old photographs and car in which Pancho Villa was assasinated ("looking like a Swiss cheese from all the bullet holes") well worth a visit, open 0900-1300 and 1500-1900 (US$1). There are also associations with the last days of Padre Hidalgo: the old tower of the **Capilla Real** in which he awaited his execution is now in the **Palacio Federal** (Libertad y Guerrero). The dungeon (calabozo) is quite unremarkable and the Palacio itself is very neglected. The **Palacio de Gobierno**, on the other hand, is in fine condition, with a dramatic set of murals by Aaron Piña Morales depicting Chihuahua's history. There are a number of old mansions (see **Museums** below) and the Paseo Bolívar area is pleasant. Calle Libertad is for pedestrians only from Plaza Constitución to the Palacios de Gobierno and Federal. Calle Cuarta (4a) and streets that cross it NW of Juárez are bustling with market stalls and restaurants. Worth looking at is the **Cathedral** on Plaza Constitución, begun 1717, finished 1789; its Baroque façade dates from 1738, the interior is mostly unadorned, with square columns, glass chandeliers and a carved altar piece.

Hotels A+ *Palacio del Sol*, Independencia 500 y Niños Héroes, T 166000, F 159947, smart, with Torres del Sol travel agency and Número Una car rental; **A+** *San Francisco*, Victoria 504, T 167770, *Degá* restaurant good for steaks; **A** *El Campanario*, Blvd Díaz Ordaz 1405, 2 blocks SW of Cathedral, T 154545, good rooms, clean, TV, rec; **B** *Victoria*, Juárez y Colón, T 128893, courtyard, overpriced, noisy, dingy; **C** *Balflo*, Niños Héroes 321, T 160300, modern, poor value; **C** *El Cobre*, Calle 10A y Progreso, with bathroom, hot water, TV, comfortable, *Bejarano* restaurant good, very expensive laundry; **D** *Plaza*, behind cathedral, Calle 4, No 206, T 155833, noisy, quite clean, cold shower, fair, run down; **D** *San Juan*, Victoria 823, T 128491, in old colonial house, reasonable food, water sometimes scarce, rec; **E** *Reforma*, Calle Victoria 809, T 125808, basic, friendly, noisy, rec.

D *Del Carmen*, Calle 10 No 4, T 157096, with hot water, a/c, OK; round corner, **E** *Roma*, Libertad 1015, T 127652, with hot water, run down (taxi drivers on commission bring tourists here), neither has restaurant. **E** *Posada Aida*, Calle 10, with bath and hot water (supposedly), friendly, helpful, night porter will watch cars parked outside (*Cabral* on Calle 10A is not rec, brothel); **E** *Casa de Huéspedes*, Libertad 1405, with bath, basic but clean, several others in the same street; **E** *Turista*, Juárez 817, with bath, dirty beds, clean bathroom, noisy and damp. The cheaper hotels are in Calle Juárez and its cross-streets; the cheapest are behind the cathedral.

Motels B *Mirador*, Universidad 1309, T 132205; **C** *Nieves*, Tecnológico y Ahuehuetes, T 132516.

Restaurants The smartest and best are in the "Zona Dorada", NE of the centre on Juárez, near Colón, eg: *Los Parados de Tomy Vega*, Juárez 3316, *La Calesa*, Juárez y Colón, and *La Olla*, Juárez 3331, excellent steaks. *La Parilla*, Victoria 450, rec; *El Trastevere*, opp *Hotel San Francisco*, Italian, not cheap, rec; *Mi Café*, Victoria 807, good, not cheap, friendly; *La Galatea*, Juárez y Segunda, restaurant within department store, rec, especially for breakfast; *Armando's*, Aldama y V Guerrero, for snacks, refrescos, coffee; *Ostionería de la Monja*, nr main Plaza, good seafood. *Kosmovita* for natural products (shop), at Independencia 725. Corn (maize) is sold on the streets, excellent with cheese, lime, salt and chile. The market is between Calles 2a and 6a, SE of Av Niños Heroes, small but good for fruit and vegetables.

Taxis work on a zone system. Agree price before boarding, to avoid unpleasant surprises. **Town buses** cost US$0.15, go everywhere, ask which one to take.

Museums The **Museo Regional**, in the former mansion Quinta Gameros at Bolívar 401, with interesting exhibits and extremely fine Art-Nouveau rooms: the dining room, child's room features Little Red Riding Hood scenes; bathroom, frogs playing among reeds, etc, exhibition of Paquimé ceramics, and temporary exhibitions (open Tues-Sun 0900-1300, 1600-1900, US$0.70). **Museo de Arte e Industria Populares**, Av Reforma 5 (Tarahumara art and lifestyle; shops; open Tues—Sat 0900-1300, 1600-1900, free); **Museo de Casa Juárez**, Calle Juárez y Quinta, house and office of Benito Juárez (Mon-Fri 0900-1500, 1600-1800). **Museo de Arte Sacro**, Libertad y Segunda, Mon-Fri 1400-1800. In the SE of the town near Calle Zarco are ancient aqueducts.

Exchange Banks around Plaza Constitución. *Casa de cambio Rachasa*, Independencia y Guadalupe Victoria, on Plaza, 3% commission but good rates (also at Aldama 711); *Hernández*, Aldama 410, T 162399, Mon-Fri 0900-1400, 1600-1900, Sat 0900-1500. Exchange is available in the bus terminal, but rates are slightly better downtown.

Post Office and Telecommunications Calle Libertad in the Palacio Federal. Also in Central Camionera. Credit card phone outside AeroMéxico office on Guadalupe Victoria, ½ block from Plaza Constitución (towards Carranza). Main phone office on Av Universidad.

Laundry Ocampo 1412.

Travel Agents *Wagon-Lits*, Independencia 1412, very helpful, *Guillermo Bechman*, T 3-02-53, arranges stays at cabins above Bahuichivo, nr Copper Canyon, 2 nights US$50.

Tourist Office Departamento de Comercio y Turismo, Libertad 1300 y Calle 13, 10° piso, Mon-Fri 0900-1500, T 162436.

Airport 20 km from centre on road to Ojinaga, airport buses collect passengers from hotels, fare US$1.10, also minibuses. Taxi US$16 (no other transport at night). Aeroméxico to Ciudad Juárez, Guadalajara, Hermosillo, Mexico City, Monterrey, Tijuana and Torreón, and Aerolitoral to Albuquerque, NM, El Paso, Los Mochis, La Paz.

Buses New bus terminal, 8 km from centre on way to airport, SE of town, 20 mins by bus to centre (US$0.30), or taxi US$5 (fixed price). There is an exchange office (beware shortchanging). To **Mexico City** and intermediate destinations, frequent services with several companies: Mexico City, 20 hrs, US$53; Querétaro, US$45.50; San Luis Potosí, US$36.50;

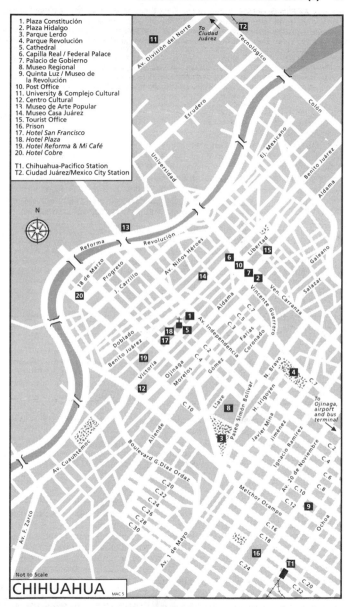

1. Plaza Constitución
2. Plaza Hidalgo
3. Parque Lerdo
4. Parque Revolución
5. Cathedral
6. Capilla Real / Federal Palace
7. Palacio de Gobierno
8. Museo Regional
9. Quinta Luz / Museo de la Revolución
10. Post Office
11. University & Complejo Cultural
12. Centro Cultural
13. Museo de Arte Popular
14. Museo Casa Juárez
15. Tourist Office
16. Prison
17. Hotel San Francisco
18. Hotel Plaza
19. Hotel Reforma & Mi Café
20. Hotel Cobre

T1. Chihuahua-Pacifico Station
T2. Ciudad Juárez/Mexico City Station

CHIHUAHUA MAC 5

Aguascalientes, US$33.50; Zacatecas, US$33, 12 hrs; Durango, US$32; Torreón, US$16.50. 2nd class bus, to **Hidalgo del Parral**, US$7, 1st class US$10.50, 2½ hrs. To **Mazatlán**, 2 companies, US$38, 19 hrs, heart-stopping view. To **Creel**, see below; to **Nuevo Casas Grandes**, see above (note that Chihuahua-Madera buses go either via El Sueco, or via the Sierra). At busy times allow several hours to buy tickets for buses going N, often full as they start elsewhere: to **Ciudad Juárez**, many buses, US$17.50. To other border points: Caballero Azteca to **Tijuana**, US$55, 3 a day, or with Tres Estrellas de Oro at 2400, 1st class express, US$50, and to **Agua Prieta**, US$20, 4 a day; also to **Hermosillo**, US$31, twice. Trans del Norte to **Nuevo Laredo** at 2030, US$36; also to **Monterrey**, US$30, and **Saltillo**, US$25 (other companies also to Monterrey). To **Guadalajara**, several, US$41, including Estrella Blanca which also goes to **Acapulco**, US$63, and **Puerto Vallarta**, US$53.

The famous Santa Eulalia mining camp is 16 km away; 8 km from town is one of the largest smelting plants in the world.

Chihuahua may also be reached from the border at **Ojinaga**, be sure to stop at the border, not the bus station 2 km further on, otherwise an easy crossing to Presidio, used infrequently by foreigners. **Hotel Parral**, cheap. Cheap meals at *Lonchería Avenida*, across from bus station; bus from Chihuahua, US$6, also daily train service. On the way to Chihuahua from Ojinaga is **Ciudad Delicias** (*Hotel Delicias*, nr market, several others of similar quality nearby—bus from Chihuahua hourly, US$3). If leaving Mexico here, make sure they stamp your papers.

Railway There are two railway stations in Chihuahua: the station for Ciudad Juárez and Mexico City is 3 km walk along Av Niños Héroes, left at Av Colón, which becomes Av Tecnológico, past the river and right along Av División Norte. If looking for a taxi, take care of your luggage. Train División del Norte to **Mexico City**, daily at 0315, 30 hrs, no food provided, soft drinks available, fares 2nd class, US$21.25, 1st class US$35.50, book in advance if you can. Train to **Zacatecas** about 16-21 hrs, US$12 (2nd class train at 1230, tickets sold 1 hr before departure). División del Norte (*servicio estrella*) for **Ciudad Juárez** leaves 0120 (5 hrs), US$8.

The station for the 631-km Chihuahua-Pacífico railway is one block behind the prison (nr Av 20 de Noviembre and Blvd Díaz Ordaz—take bus marked C Rosario, or walk up Av Independencia, then right along Paseo Bolívar or Av 20 de Noviembre); in the early morning you may have to take a taxi. Taxi fare between the 2 stations US$6.65, negotiate price. Information: Apdo Postal 46, Chihuahua, CHIH, Mexico, T (141) 2-2284/3867, or Av Central 140, piso 6, Ala 'C' 06358 Mexico DF, T (905) 547-8545/6939.

The train journey to **Los Mochis** is very spectacular and exciting on the descent to the coast beyond Creel: book seats in advance. Sit on left hand side of carriage going to Los Mochis. The *servicio estrella* leaves daily at 0700, supposedly arriving at Creel at about 1225, Divisadero at 1345 and Los Mochis at 2050, local time, but delays are common (reserved seat US$36, poor breakfast included, restaurant for other meals (not cheap); fare to Creel US$16.15); double check all details as they are subject to frequent change. There is food at 2-3 stations along the way (eg Divisadero). An ordinary train ("mixto") to Los Mochis leaves at 0800, but often late, tickets are not sold until the 1st class train has left (2nd class only, carriages are 1st Class, a/c and comfortable, most windows do not open, mixed reports on cleanliness, US$8.60; fare to Creel US$3.85, arrives 1400), reaching Divisadero at 1530 and Los Mochis at 2225. As the most interesting part of the journey is between Creel and Los Mochis it is better to travel from Los Mochis; that section of the line is described under Los Mochis. If wishing to see the best scenery, there is little point in taking the train Chihuahua- Creel- Chihuahua (on this stretch, the cheaper train is just as good as the *servicio estrella*). If planning to spend a few days in Creel, there are frequent buses Chihuahua-Creel (9 a day, 4-5 hrs direct, some much slower, US$10, paved all the way). If taking the train from Creel to the Pacific with a view to connecting with a train to the N or S buy a ticket to Sufragio (US$17.50 in *servicio estrella*, US$4.30 on ordinary train, both arrive after dark—see p 351) not Los Mochis.

The railway (and road) from Chihuahua crosses the Sierra of the Tarahumara Indians, who call themselves the Raramuri ("those who run fast"), and were originally cave-dwellers and nomads. They now work as day-labourers in the logging stations and have settled around the mission churches built by the Spanish in the 17th century.

Creel (pop 5,000), at 2,356 metres (very cold in winter) is the commercial centre of the Tarahumara region, an important timber centre and tourist resort, colourful and pleasant. Creel is easily reached by car from El Paso or Arizona. On the central square, just below the railway, are two churches (one of which broadcasts classical music in the evening), the Presidencia Municipal containing the post office (second door inside on right), the Banco Serfín and the Misión Tarahumara, which sells maps of the region (US$3.10 for topographical sheets, US$1.35 for simpler ones), description of the train ride and other good buys (such as excellent photographs of Indians). The Misión acts as a quasi-tourist office. There are several souvenir shops selling Tarahumara weavings, musical instruments, pine-needle baskets, etc. Also on sale are books such as *The National Parks of NW Mexico* (also obtainable from R Fisher, PO Box 40092, Tucson, Arizona 85717) and *Mexico's Copper Canyon Country*, Fayhee (Cordillera Press, PO Box 3699, Evergreen, CO 80439, T 303-670 3010).

Hotels A *Motel Parador La Montaña*, Av López Mateos 41, T 560075 (full board available), will exchange foreign currency at reasonable rates (horses can be hired here, US$5 and a tip for guides—2 hrs are necessary to get anywhere; spectacular countryside); on same street: *Cabañas Berlis* at No 31; **A** *Motel Cascada Inn*, with restaurant and, opposite, *Tarahumara*, T 600252. Motels *Parador* and *Cascada* have live music most evenings. **D** *Korachi*, in cabin, E in room, opp railway, neither helpful nor clean; **D** *Nuevo*, other side of railway from station, meals overpriced, but nice and clean, some inside rooms dark; **E** pp *Posada de Creel*, 1½ blocks S of station on opposite side of the tracks, T (91-145) 60142, Apdo Postal 7, remodelled building, very clean, rooms with bath a little more expensive, hot water, helpful, English-speaking managers, coffee served from 0630, rec; **E** *Chávez*, by railway. **F** pp *Casa de Huéspedes Margarita*, López Mateos 11, T 6-00-45, no sign, between the two churches on corner of square, cheapest in dormitory rising to **A**, double with bath, good communal meals, very popular meeting place (book in advance in high season), Margarita's reps meet arriving passengers, quite pushy, organizes tours (see below), horses can be hired (US$2.50/hr with guide, lazy horses), highly rec (if full, Margarita's sister will put you up for E with dinner and breakfast, enjoyable). **D/E** *Pension Creel*, Av López Mateos 61, on the main street about 1 km from the plaza and railway station, T (52145) 60071, F (52145) 60200, breakfast included, shared bath, kitchen and living room, cabins with kitchen for rent (same price), tourist information, mountain bikes for hire and tours organized. A few km out of town is **A** *Cabaña de las Barrancas de Urique*, with 3 meals, with minibus service to and from station. 7 km out, on lake, Jan Milburn runs *Tarahumara Indian Park*, shared or individual cabins. About 40 mins drive from station is **L** pp *Copper Canyon Sierra Lodge* (Apdo 3, 33200 Creel, Chihuahua, full board, US reservation, 1100 Owendale Drive, Suite G, Troy, MI48083, T 800-776 3942, F 313-684-9119, minimum stay 3 days, reservations cannot be made direct at the hotel), which has a minibus to collect travellers, rustic woodstoves and oil-lamps, 8-day packages available; set in high grassland near Cusárare waterfall, Jesus Manuel is a guide based here, highly rec for excellent burro hiking trips.

There are plenty of eating places in the town (but no bars).

Services Banco Serfín, on the square, very friendly, changes travellers' cheques between 1030 and 1200, but charges 5% commission, poor rates; hotels cash travellers' cheques also at poor rates. Post Office on W side of main square, Presidencia Municipal, no sign. Long-distance phone office in *Hotel Nuevo*. Laundry Santa María at López Mateos 61. General stores also on López Mateos.

Transport Buses to **Chihuahua** from 0700-1700, 9 a day (fare given above). Buses also to surrounding villages. All leave from outside *Hotel Korachi*, across railway track from square. Train schedules given above and under Los Mochis: station office is open Mon 0800-1000, 1100-1600; Tues-Fri 1000-1600, Sat 1000-1300.

NB There is a time change (1 hr back) between Creel and Los Mochis.

Excursions Creel is an excellent centre for trekking and horse riding. It is also a good centre for reaching several deep canyons, including that of the Río Urique, known as the **Barranca del Urique**, or **del Cobre** (the Urique, or Copper

Canyon—see below).

From the town footpaths lead to the Cristo Rey statue, to a viewpoint on Cerro Chapultepec and into the hills around. To the S, walk to San Ignacio mission, passing the Valle de Hongos (mushrooms), entry fee charged by local community US$3.25; continue to **Laguna Arareco** (8 km from Creel), around which one can walk (the lake is just off the Creel-Guachochi/Batopilas road), entry fee US$3.25. 20 km away, on the same road, is *Cusárare* ("place of the eagles"), with a Jesuit church (1767) painted by Indians and a 30-metre waterfall, entry fee US$1. To get to the falls: 100m after the junction to Cusárare there is a hotel sign on the right; turn right, pass the hotel and then the bridge, at the junction turn right, about 45 mins walk; it is not well-signposted. There is very good hiking around Cusárare, but as the Misión in Creel does not stock the Creel/Cusárare topographical map, a guide may be necessary (US$8.35 for guide, US$8.35 for mule to carry luggage, ask at *Margarita's*). Bus from Creel to Cusárare at 0700, US$1.75, lift in *Margarita's* transport US$4.50. Just past Laguna Arareco is an unsigned right turn onto a bumpy track which leads, in 1½ hrs in a hardy vehicle, to the top of the **Recohauta canyon**. A clear path descends in an hour or so to first a dry river, then the Río Tararécua. Follow the path along the river to where hot springs come out of the canyon's side. A pool has been made. The climb back up to the top also takes about an hour (loose scree on the path), or you can continue to other hot springs, several hours' walk, camping equipment essential (look out for the green arrows). Backpacking in the canyon is beautiful and, with a topographical map, original walks are easy to do. There are more trails than shown on maps: if the one you are on leads to a river or house if is not too difficult to find another, but many are vague and some lead to cliff edges. Do not add to the litter in the canyon.

COPPER CANYON

RESTORED HACIENDA
in the bottom of the Canyon

Hidden in the misty reaches of the Mexican Sierra Madres-at the end of an 8 hour rugged cliff-hanging dirt road, the Hacienda's shady courtyard fountains invite relaxation in another era.

You are invited.

COPPER CANYON LODGES

800-776-3942

or

810-340-7230

At Cusárare, the road bifurcates. One branch heads SE to **Norogachi**, 75 km from Cusárare, with Tarahumara school and authentic costumes worn on Sun, typical fiestas. This road continues to join the more usual route to Guachochi, which is the southern fork out of Cusárare.

Guachochi, with a wild west appearance, 156 km from Creel, buses to Creel daily at 0700, Sun at 1400, 8 hrs (check at *Korachi Hotel* for schedule from Creel); also reached from Hidalgo del Parral, bus leaves for Parral at 0800 and 1200, a dusty trip, not spectacular. Hotels of questionable quality; **E** *Chaparre*, overpriced but good restaurant; **E** *Orpimel*, in same building as bus station. There is a bank. From Guachochi one can walk 4 hrs to the impressive **Barranca de Sinforosa**. Outside the town take road to the left of a wooden hut, after 6 km take another left turn just after crossing a viaduct, carry on until you come to a gate on the left side of the road before it veers off to the right. Beyond the gate there is an orchard with a tower in the middle. It seems that you have to cross several sets of barbed wire to get to the canyon. The Canyon is not visible until you reach the edge of it. Marlen Wolf and Markus Tobler of Switzerland write: 'You will reach a point several hundred metres above the Río Verde where you can see an unforgettable extended system of immense canyons, grander than you can see from the Divisadero or on crossing the Barranca del Cobre. You can descend to the river on a path". This is not advisable for women alone.

The road S out of Cusárare leads eventually to Batopilas, passing a turn-off to El Tejabán in the Barranca del Urique/Cobre; *Basíhuare* ("Sash") village, surrounded by pink and white rock formations (40 km from Creel); Puente del Río Urique, spanning the Urique canyon, ideal camping climate. At the T junction Creel-Guachochi-Bufa is a small restaurant/hotel, **F** *La Casita*, very primitive and romantic. Just after the junction is *Samachique*, where the *rari-pame* race, consisting of kicking a wooden ball in a foot-race of 241 km without rest, often takes 2-3 days and nights in September. Stranded travellers can find a room and food at the bus stop (no more than a shack) in Samachique. *Quírare*, 65 km from Creel offers sights of Batopilas canyon, of great beauty. After Quírare there is an awesome 14 km descent at La Bufa into Batopilas Canyon.

Batopilas (on a 120-km dirt road from Creel after La Bufa mine) is a little town of 600 inhabitants, quiet, palm-fringed, subtropical and delightful, hemmed in by the swirling river and the cactus-studded canyon walls. There are good parties in the Plaza at Christmas and New Year. It is a good centre for walking—the Urique canyon can be reached. Horses, pigs, goats and chickens wander freely along the cobblestone streets. Batopilas was once a thriving silver-mining centre, with mines owned by the Shepard family. Their mansion, abandoned during Pancho Villa's campaign, is now overgrown and dilapidated. Apparently, Batopilas was the second place in Mexico, after the capital, to receive electricity (Joe Bowbeer, Rio Rancho, NM).

Hotels The owners of the *Copper Canyon Sierra Lodge* (Creel) have opened the **L** *Copper Canyon Riverside Lodge* (US reservations, T 800-776-3942), same prices for full board, renovated 19th century hacienda, with gardens, luxurious. **C** *Mari*, reservations as for *Parador de la Montaña* in Creel; **E** *Batopilas*, clean, also *Parador Batopilas*, more expensive, but not too much; **E** *Don Mario*, close to the bridge, where the bus driver stays, is popular. Basic rooms also at **F** *Restaurant Clarita* (basic accommodation) and Sra Monsé, E—ask prices first—at plaza (she sells Tarahumara violins), rooms with gas lamps. She can give information in English (which she likes to practice on tourists). *Carmen's Youth Hostel*, basic accommodation, good food, friendly. In the village there are only basic supplies in shops, no bread or alcohol. The store on the corner of the plaza, *Tienda Grande*, can change travellers' cheques at a poor rate. Pleasant unnamed restaurant in the top right-hand corner of the little plaza beyond the main Zócalo, fixed, good menu. (Bring insect repellent against locally-nicknamed 'assassin bug' or bloodsucking insect.)

Bus from Creel, Tues, Thurs, and Sat at 0700, 8-10 hrs, US$7.50, buy ticket the day before, very crowded. Tickets are sold in a blue house in the main street on the same side as *Margarita's*; the best time to try is when the bus (white with 'Batopilas' in blue on the side) stands outside from about 1225 having just arrived on its return to Creel, Mon, Wed, and Fri, leaves Batopilas at 0400.

The Porfirio Díaz mine above the bridge into town can be explored to about 3 km into the mountain (take torch); as you get into the mine there is the sickly, sweet smell of bat droppings, after about 1 km the air is thick with disturbed bats. *Satevo*, a 7-km walk from Batopilas along the river, a poor place with 15 houses, 2 of which sell drinks, has a 350-year old church whose dome has been repainted and whose interior is under repair. The family next door has the key (US$ donation appreciated). The route to Satevo can be driven on a rough jeep track. The surrounding area, but not the town, is inhabited by the Tarahumaras known as Gentiles (women don't look at, or talk to, men). If you go 'off road' here, beware of drug cultivation areas. It is possible to walk in the other direction to *Cerro Colorado* and back in a day. In this tiny village some people still mine for gold, carrying the ore down to the river by donkey where it is ground up in water-powered stone mills. You can camp in the schoolyard, or on a small beach 15 mins before the town. At **Cerro Yerbanis** there are amazing views of Batopilas Canyon. With luck you can hitch to Cerro Colorado, then walk 2 hrs to Munérache, a remote village, to meet Tarahumara Indians (best to arrange a local guide through Sra Monsé on the plaza in Batopilas as drug cultivation in this part of the canyon means some areas are unsafe). A 2-3 day hike goes from Batopilas Canyon via Urique Canyon, then get a ride to Bahuichivo for a train to Creel or Las Mochis.

The Barranca del Urique/del Cobre is a long way from Creel. Apart from the access from Batopilas (see above), or from Bahuichivo (see rail description from Los Mochis), the simplest way to see the canyon is to go to **Divisadero** or *Posada Barrancas* by road (hitch, no public transport), or by train. The *servicio estrella* leaves Creel at 1225, US$4.40, the ordinary train at 1320, US$1.10, 1½ hrs, *Posada Barrancas* is 5 mins further on, same fare (hotel reported closed since 1991). Either take the first train to Divisadero and return to Creel on the slow train (or by hitching back), nip out for ten minutes and continue to Los Mochis, or stay overnight: only *Hotel Cabañas Divisadero*, by Divisadero station, is on the canyon's edge, A, bookable at Calle 7, No 1216, Chihuahua, T 123362, full board available.
   The canyon can also be reached on foot from Divisadero or *Posada Barrancas*; from the former it is 6 km (walk or hitch) along the dirt road that runs beside the railway to the house of Florencio Manzinas (at the first group of houses you come to). He will hire out donkeys, give directions to the canyon (for a small tip), or will accompany you as guide (more expensive). He also provides food and accommodation in his house, or may let you camp free. From there it's a day's hike along narrow, slippery, often steep and sometimes overgrown trails into the canyon, descending from cool pine forest into gradually more sub-tropical vegetation as you approach the river and the canyon floor. At this point there are mango, orange and banana trees. Take plenty of water for the hike as, after descending the first section following a stream, one has to go over another hill before getting down to the river, which means several hours without access to water.

30 km NE of Creel is **San Juanito**, a little larger than Creel, with cobblestone streets which are less dusty than other towns in the region. It has an annual *fiesta* on 20-24 June (**C** *Motel Cobre*, very nice rooms). It is on the main road to Chihuahua, which continues to La Junta, a road and rail junction between Chihuahua and Madera, on one of the routes to Nuevo Casas Grandes and Ciudad Juárez. E of La Junta, some 105 km W of Chihuahua, is **Ciudad Cuauhtémoc**, a town surrounded by 20 or so Mennonite villages (*campos*), self-sufficient agricultural communities (**A** *Motel Tarahumara Inn*, corner of Allende and 5a Calle, T 22801/24865, comfortable, plenty of hot water, good restaurant, travel agency, safe parking, popular, worth booking ahead, rec; **E** *Hotel del Norte*, Calle Reforma, basic, sometimes no hot water). The Mexican Mennonites, originally from Belgium, Holland and Germany, arrived from Canada early in the 20th century. Many are blond, blue-eyed and speak old German; they can be seen in town (also in Chihuahua and Nuevo Casas Grandes) selling cheese and vegetables and buying supplies. Bus from Chihuahua US$3.80 every ½ hour after 0700 (hourly 0500-0700); also from Creel.
   A road NW from San Juanito goes 75 km to the **Basaseachi** falls, the highest single-jump waterfall in North America, 311 metres. They are at their best in July-September. The top of the falls are 3 km from town (2 km by dirt road, 1 km by signed trail); a better viewpoint is 3 km from the trailhead (can be driven to/from S of town). Free camping at trailhead, no water, and near the lookout on the other side of the canyon. Hotels: **C** *Alma Rosa*, 1 km towards Hermosillo, some

new rooms with fire places and oil lamps, TV, electricity 0800-2000, hot water; **E** *Nena*, 'downtown", bathroom in room, but no door, no electricity after dark, provides oil lamps; *Deny* also 'downtown", has own generator. From there the road goes on through beautiful mountains and forest to **Yepachic**, winding its way though Maicova, Yécora and **San Nicolás** into Sonora. From San Nicolás the road continues to the Pacific highway at Ciudad Obregón (it is paved from San Juanito to Hermosillo, but watch out for rock and mud slides in the rainy season on the older section in the mountains). The scenery is beautiful, the services in the villages limited, but you will probably not meet another tourist.

NB Unleaded fuel is only available for 320 km until 1.5 km before *Hotel Alma Rosa* (coming from Hermosillo), and the next is at La Junta, 80 km from *Alma Rosa*, on the Cd Cuanhtémoc road. There is no *magna sin* in Creel.

Hotels in Creel arrange tours to some of the places mentioned above: eg **Margarita** runs trips, minimum 8 people, to Cusárare, mission and falls, and Basíhuare; Recohuata hot springs; San Ignacio, Valle de Hongos and Laguna Arareco, all US$10; to Basaseachi US$23. These tours are pricey, but good fun and may involve more walking or climbing than advertised. Recommended for guided tours deep into the Urique Canyon is Adventure Specialists, Inc (president Gary Ziegler), Bear Basin Ranch, Westcliffe, CO 81252 (303/783-2519, 800/621-8385, ext 648), US$700-800 for 11-day tours from El Paso, vigorous, knowledgeable.

South From Chihuahua

Ciudad Camargo (Km 1,332), a small cattle town in a green valley, quiet save for its eight days of *fiesta* for Santa Rosalía beginning on 4 Sept, when there are cockfights, horse racing and dancing. Black bass fishing at the dam lake, and warm sulphur springs 5 km away.

Hotel B *Siesta Inn*, S edge of town on highway; *Santa Rosalía Courts*. **Motel D** *Victoria*, Comonfort y Jiménez, clean and cheap.

From **Ciudad Jiménez** (1,263 km from Mexico City; **B** *Motel Florido*, hot water) there are two routes to Fresnillo and Zacatecas: the Central Highway through Durango or a more direct route via Torreón (237 km from Ciudad Jiménez), passing Escalón (restaurant), **Ceballos** (**E** *Hotel San José*, basic), Yermo (restaurants) and Bermejillo (restaurant), on Route 49.

NB Roads in Durango are far worse than those in Chihuahua; between Cd Camargo and Torreón it is so badly potholed that traffic often drives along the road's shoulder.

Torreón is the principal industrial city of La Laguna cotton and wheat district. It is reported hot, polluted, without colonial atmosphere. Population, 700,000. Here is the Bolsón de Mayrán (altitude 1,137 metres) an oasis of about 28,500 square km which might be irrigated, but only about 2,000 square km have been developed and much of that is stricken with drought. On the opposite side of the mostly dry Nazas river are the two towns of **Gómez Palacio** (*feria* first half of August; **C** *Motel La Siesta*, Av Madero 320 Nte, T 140291/142840, clean, hot water, safe parking, good; **D** *Motel La Cabaña*, hot water) and Lerdo.

Hotels in Torreón A *Palacio Real*, Morelos 1280, T 60000; **A** *Paraíso del Desierto*, Independencia y Jiménez, T 61122, resort; **A** *Río Nazas*, highrise, very good, on Av Morelos y Treviño. **B/D** *Posada de Sol*, Bulevar Revolucionario, opp La Unidad de Deportes sports complex, modern motel, secure parking, small restaurant, rooms range from basic, windowless, clean *cabañas* to large, North American-style rooms with TV. **D** *Galicia*, Cepeda 273, good; **D** *Laguna*, Carrillo 333; **D** *Princesa*, Av Morelos nr Parque Central. Few decent places to eat in the centre. In **Gómez Palacio E** *Colonial*, 3 blocks S of train station, hot water, bath, only internal locks on doors, basic.

Buses Local buses on Bulevar Revolucionario go to all parts of the city. The new Torreón bus station is 5 km S of the city; if coming from the N, drivers allow you to leave the bus in the centre. There is a shuttle service between the centre and the bus station; taxis to centre operate a fixed-fare system. To **Chihuahua**, 6 hrs, US$16.50; to **Tepic**, US$30; to **Ciudad Juárez**, US$30; about 6 a day to **Durango**, 4½ hrs 2nd class. There is also an airport. Note that

Gómez Palacio has its own bus station, without a shuttle to the centre. City buses outside have frequent services to all three city centres, US$0.33. When leaving either bus terminal, make sure that your bus does not stop at the other terminal; this can cause long delays.

Between Gómez Palacio and Zacatecas are **Cuencame** (D *Motel la Posta*, hot water, N of town; hotel S of town, D, not rec, damp, dirty, but has parking); just N of Cuencame, as you turn off Ruta 49 onto Ruta 40 to Durango is *Menudo El Zancas*, 100m on left, a truckers' meal stop open 24 hrs, which is excellent, set meal US$3.45. **Río Grande** (D *Hotel Río*); **Fresnillo** (C *Motel La Fortuna*, comfortable, hot water; D *Hotel Cuauhtémoc*, basic).

From Ciudad Jiménez it is 77 km to (Km 1,138) **Hidalgo Del Parral**, an old picturesque mining town of 100,000 people with steep and narrow streets. It is rapidly becoming a modern commercial centre. See the parochial church and one dedicated to the Virgen del Rayo (Lightning Virgin). The Museum of Pancho Villa, which is also the public library, is worth seeing for the many old photos and newspaper clippings related to the 1910 revolution and Villa, who was assassinated in Parral on 20 July 1923 on the orders of Obregón and Calles.

Hotels D *Fuente*, Herrera 79, T 20016, basic but clean, can be cold, the desecrators of Pancho Villa's body stayed here; D *Savoy*, off Morelos, rec; E *Acosta*, Barbachano, T 20221, clean, hot water, friendly.
Motel *Camino Real*, Pan-American Highway, T 22050, B, good restaurant.

Restaurants *Mariscos Esquinapa*, on same block as *Hotel Fuente*, serves good seafood; *Nutrivida*, Herrera, good yoghurt and health food.

Buses There is a new bus station outside the town; 20 mins walk, taxi about US$2. To Durango, Transportes Chihuahuenses US$18, 6 hrs. To Zacatecas, Omnibuses de México, US$30, 9 hrs. To Chihuahua, frequent departures, 2½ hrs, US$7 2nd class, US$10.50 1st. Also to Guachochi (**see p 94**). Few bus lines start here so it is difficult to reserve seats.

On this road, between Rodeo and Durango, is the 'Western landscape' beloved of Hollywood film-makers. Cinema enthusiasts can visit the Western sets of Villa del Oeste (9 km from Durango) and Chupaderos (10.5 km), both decaying but smelling authentically of horse (Cía San Juan del Río buses go there).

(Victoria de) **Durango**, capital of Durango state: founded in 1563; alt: 1,924 metres; pop: 600,000, state pop 1,352,200 (Km 926—some 260 km SW of Torreón). It is a pleasant city, with parks, a Cathedral (1695) and a famous iron-water spring. Parque Guadiana at W edge of town, with huge eucalyptus trees, is a nice place to relax. Good views of the city from Cerro de Los Remedios: many flights of steps up to a chapel. Presa Victoria can be reached by bus from Durango; one can swim in the lake enclosed by the dam.

Festival *Feria* first half of July.

Hotels A *Campo México Courts*, 20 de Noviembre extremo Oriente, T 87744, F 83015, good but restaurant service poor; B *Casa Blanca*, 20 de Noviembre 811 Poniente, T 13599, F 14704, nice, big old hotel in the centre, unguarded parking lot; C *Posada Durán*, 20 de Noviembre 506 Pte, T 12412, colonial inn on Plaza de Armas, rec by AAA, good atmosphere, helpful staff; C *Reyes*, 20 de Noviembre 220, T 15050, clean; C *Villa*, P Juárez 206, T 23491, across roundabout from bus station, clean, pleasant, TV; *Roma*, 20 de Noviembre 705 Pte, T/F 20122, clean, comfortable; D *Gallo*, 5 de Febrero, with bath, good. D *Karla*, P Juárez opp bus station, T 16348, small, clean, friendly but noisy. D *Oasis*, Zarco between 20 de Noviembre y 5 de Febrero, with bath, clean, hot water, rooms on the top floor have a good view, rec *Motel Los Arcos*, nr bus station, Heroica Colegio/Militar 2204, T 72216, good restaurant. Cheap hotels: *Patoni*, Patoni entre P Suárez y 5 de Febrero, *Casa de Huéspedes Buenos Aires*, Constitución 126 Norte.

Restaurants *Buho's Bar/Restaurant*, on Zócalo, 1st floor, overlooking cathedral, reasonably-priced food, good pancakes; good breakfasts at *Café Salum*, 5 de Febrero y Progreso; *Mariscos Ramírez*, in front of the market, good sea food. *La Peña*, Hidalgo 120 N, Friday night is fiesta night with local music and singing, very popular. There is a good food store on the first block of Progreso where local foodstuffs are displayed in bulk. *El Zocabón*, off main plaza opp Cathedral, rec.

Tourist Offices Hidalgo 408 Sur and 20 de Noviembre y Independencia; both good.

Rail Daily train at 0700 to Monterrey via Torreón.

Airport 5 km from centre.

Buses Bus station out of town: minibus No 2 to centre, US$0.25. Several buses a day cross the Sierra Madre Occidental to **Mazatlán** (Transportes Chihuahuenses, 1st class, 7 hrs, US$14.80), 0400 and 1000. This is rec if you cannot do the Los Mochis-Chihuahua journey, sit on left side. Second class buses for camera buffs stop more frequently. **Guadalajara**, US$22.25; **Chihuahua**, US$32. Second class bus to **Hidalgo del Parral**, 7 hrs, US$18 with Transportes Chihuahuenses. **Zacatecas**, Omnibus de México, 4½ hrs, US$7.75. Town buses stop running early in evening, so try to arrive before dark if you wish to avoid a long walk or taxi ride to centre.

Excursions Balneario La Florida on the outskirts is pleasant (take green 'Potreros' bus on Calle Pasteur). Take a bus from Plaza Boca Ortiz to the big *hacienda* in Ferreria, a 7 km walk along mostly deserted roads leads to the Mirador la Ventana with great views. *Santiago Papasquiaro* is 3 hrs N (on the way, in Canatlán, are Mennonite colonies). **D** *Hotel División del Norte*, Madero 35, in a former convent; the owner's husband was in Pancho Villa's División del Norte. *Restaurant Mirador*, across from the market, good food. There are a number of hot springs in the area, Hervideros is the most popular, take the bus to Herreras, then ½ hr walk. *Tepehuancas*, 1 hr further on, is a small pleasant town with 2 hotels. Walk to Purísima and then to a small, spectacular canyon. A dirt road continues to **Guacevi**, a mining town in the Sierra.

Durango is on the Coast-to-Coast Highway from Mazatlán to Matamoros. The 320 km stretch of road from Durango W to Mazatlán is through splendid mountain scenery. For a one day trip, go as far as *El Salto* (96 km), 7 buses a day, but go early to get ticket.

Between Durango and Zacatecas is *Sombrerete*, a small colonial mining town with ten good churches and a superbly, partially restored Franciscan convent. (Hotels: **E** *Real de Minas*, clean, comfortable, *Avenida Real*, *Hidalgo*).

Zacatecas, founded 1548, capital of Zacatecas state; alt: 2,495 metres; pop 150,000, state pop 1,278,300 (Km 636 from capital). This picturesque up-and-down mining city is built in a ravine, pink stone houses towering above one another and scattered over the hills. The largest silver mine in the world, processing 10,000 tonnes of ore a day or 220 tonnes of silver, is at **Real de Angeles**. Places to see are the **Cathedral** (1730-52); the **San Agustín** church, with interior carvings now being restored; the Jesuit church of **Santo Domingo** and the little houses behind it (in the church, ask the sacristan to turn the lights on so you can see the frescoes in the sacristy by Francisco Antonio Vallejo); the **Museo Pedro Coronel** on Plaza Santo Domingo, admission US$4.35, which houses an excellent collection of European and modern art (inc Goya, Hogarth, Miró, Tapié) as well as folk art from Mexico and around the world (take a guide to make the most of the collections). The **Rafael Coronel Museum**, housed in the ex-Convento de San Francisco, has a vast collection of masks and puppets, primarily Mexican, nice garden, entry US$4.35, students US$1.75. **Plaza Hidalgo** and its statues; the **Casa Moneda** (better known as the Tesorería); the **Teatro Calderón**, and the chapel of **Los Remedios** (1728). The **Cerro de La Bufa** (cablecar, US$2.70 return, starts at 1200, finishes 1930 (cancelled when windy), rec for the views, nice walk, crowded Sun) which dominates the city, contains the **Museo de la Toma de Zacatecas**, commemorating Pancho Villa's victory over Huerta's forces in 1914 (entry US$1.65). There is also a statue of Villa, an observatory, and the Mausoleo de Los Hombres Ilustres, on the hill. The **Museo Francisco Goitia**, housed in what was once the governor's mansion, is by the Parque General on Enrique Estrada, Col Sierra de Alicia near the old **Acueducto del Cubo**, with modern paintings by Zacatecans, admission US$0.80. The **Mina**

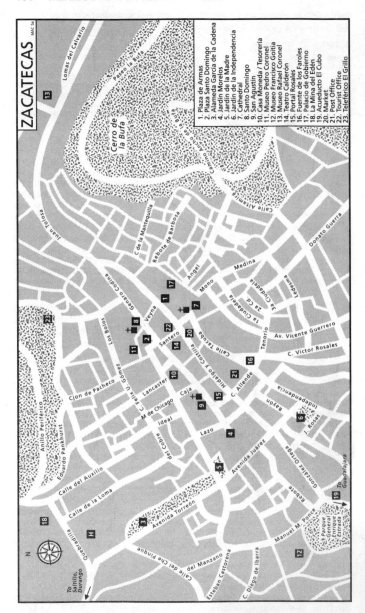

ZACATECAS

MAC 5a

1. Plaza de Armas
2. Plaza Santo Domingo
3. Alameda García de la Cadena
4. Jardín Morelos
5. Jardín de la Madre
6. Jardín de la Independencia
7. Cathedral
8. Santo Domingo
9. San Agustin
10. Casa Moneda / Tesorería
11. Museo Pedro Coronel
12. Museo Francisco Goitia
13. Museo Rafael Coronel
14. Teatro Calderón
15. Portal Rosales
16. Fuente de los Faroles
17. Palacio de Gobierno
18. Museo del Edén
19. Acueducto El Cubo
20. Market
21. Post Office
22. Tourist Office
23. Teleférico El Grillo

del Edén, Av Torreón y Quebradilla, is worth a visit, the old mine has a short section of mine railway in operation (not a proper train), tour lasts about 1 hr, commentary in fast Spanish, admission US$2.50 (accessible from the upper end of the Alameda, behind the Seguro Social hospital); there is also a disco in the mine, entry US$10, buy ticket before 2030, varied music. The market is also worth visiting.

Zacatecas is famous for its *sarapes* and has two delicacies: the local cheese, and *queso de tuna*, a candy made from the fruit of the nopal cactus (do not eat too much, it has laxative properties). Visit the small *tortilla* factories near the station, on the main road. Several good silverware shops around the Cathedral area. Zacatecas is reckoned by many travellers to be the pleasantest town in this part of Mexico.

Fiesta spreads over most of September, a rainy month here. There are bullfights on Sundays.

Hotels **A+** *Galería*, López Mateos s/n, T 23311, near old bus station, very comfortable; **A+** *Quinta Real*, Av González Ortega, T 29104, beautiful, built around old bull ring, aqueduct goes past the front door. **A** *Paraíso Radisson*, opp Cathedral, on Av Hidalgo, T 26183; **A** *Aristos*, Lomas de Soledad, T 21788; **A** *María Bonita*, Av López Velarde 319, T 24545, F 26645, hot water, heating, very good; **B** *Posada de La Moneda*, nr Cathedral, Av Hidalgo 413, T 20881, F 23693, nice and clean, but a bit noisy; **C** *Condesa*, opp *Posada de los Condes*, Av Juárez, T 21160, may negotiate to D, OK, helpful, some rooms quiet with good views of Cerro de la Bufa, cheap restaurant. **D** *Posada de los Condes*, Juárez 107, T 21093, F 21650, a bit noisy, rooms darkish. **D** *Barranca*, opp old bus terminal, Blvd López Mateos 401, T 21494, poor value, and noisy traffic; **D** *Colón*, Av López Velarde 508, T 20464, clean, showers; **D** *del Parque*, González Ortega 302, T 20479, hot shower, TV, fair, opp aqueduct; **D** *Insurgentes*, Insurgentes 114, T 23419, off Plaza del Vivar, without bath, hot showers extra; **D** *Conde de Villarreal* (was *Zamora*), Plaza de Zamora 303, T 21200, with bath, central, basic; **E** *Morelos*, Morelos 825, T 22505, economical; **E** *Río Grande*, Calzada de la Paz 217, T 25349, with bath (F without), ask for quiet room on the patio, very good value, rec; the cheap hotels (very few) are all within 5 minutes walk of the old bus station, towards Av Hidalgo. **Youth Hostel**, Parque del Encantado 103, T 21151/21891, CP 98000, on bus route to centre from bus station, F (no singles); also Av de los Deportes beside Estadio Fco Villa, CP 98064, T 29377.

Motels **C** *Del Bosque*, Fortín de la Peña, has camping facilities and hook-ups, showers and toilets, only for small cars and vans; **C** *Parador Zacatecas*, excellent, Pan-American Highway.

Trailer park at Morelos junction, about 20 mins NW of the city, where Route 54 Saltillo-Guadalajara crosses Route 49. Hook-ups, basic, US$8, behind Pemex.

Restaurants *La Cuija*, in old Centro Comercial on Av Tacuba, good food, music, atmosphere; *El Jacalito*, Juárez 18, excellent *comida corrida* and breakfast; *La Cabana*, Jardín de la Independencia, cheap, excellent set meals. *Bambi*, Juárez, good and cheap, live music in the evening; *Dragón de Oro*, Plaza Santo Domingo, cheap, good Chinese, slow service; *Burgerlandia*, beside Teatro Calderón, good; *El Carnerito*, Av Juárez 110, cheap. *Pizzería Fugazetta*, Av Guerrero 136, charming, good pizzas; *Mr Laberinto*, Av Hidalgo 342-344, luxury atmosphere, 1970s décor, quite cheap, good breakfast and dinners, rec; *El Paraíso*, Av Hidalgo y P Goytta, corner of market, bar/restaurant, nice atmosphere, closed Sun; opposite is *Nueva España*, bar with loud music, closed Sun; *La Cantera Musical*, Av Tacuba, Mexican, good atmosphere, poor a/c, good food but drinks limited after 2000. Good cafés include: *Cafetería La Terazza*, in market on a balcony, very pleasant, good *malteadas*; *Café Arús*, Centro Comercial, Av Hidalgo y Costilla, serves breakfast; *Acrópolis*, opp Cathedral, 50 year old, café and diner, good breakfast, slow service; *Café Zaz*, Av Hidalgo y Costillo 201. Several cheap restaurants along Av Independencia. *El Quixote* (at *María Bonita Hotel*), Av López Velarde, good breakfasts. Plenty of good coffee shops selling real *expresso* coffee. Many good *tamales* sold on the streets. **Health food** store at Rayón 413, fairly limited selection.

Shopping Interesting shops on Independencia selling hats, riding equipment, fruit and other produce, not touristy. Cheap postcards for sale in the toy shop and stationers on Hidalgo on the right if coming from the Cathedral.

Exchange Banamex rec. Bancomer has a Visa cash dispenser and gives cash (pesos) on Visa cards.

Post Office Calle Allende 111.

Travel Agent *Cantera Tours*, Centro Comercial El Mercado, Local A-21, T 29065, tour to Chicomostoc and Jérez at 0930, US$10.

Tourist Office Av Hidalgo y Callejón del Santero, T 28467/26683, opposite Cathedral, friendly, helpful, free maps, good hotel information, including cheaper hotels. Ask here about language classes at the University.

Trains To Mexico City 2005, arrives 0930, US$9.25 2nd class, US$15.45 1st class; from Mexico City at 2000, arrives 0930; to Querétaro, 10 hrs, US$5, 2nd class; to **Chihuahua** 1030 and 2350.

Bus New terminal 4 km N of town; red No 8 buses from Plaza Independencia, or white *camionetas* from Av González Artegú (old bus station on Blvd A López Mateos only serves local destinations). To **Durango** with Estrella Blanca, 5 hrs, US$7.75 (if continuing to Mazatlán, stay the night in Durango in order not to miss the views on the way to the coast). To **Chihuahua** via Torreón, 12 hrs, 1st class US$33; Jiménez, US$26.50; to **Hidalgo del Parral** with Chihuahuenses and Omnibus de México, US$30, 10 hrs; **San Luis Potosí** with Estrella Blanca; **Ciudad Juárez** 1st class with Omnibus de México at 1930, 11 hrs, US$43.75; to **Guadalajara**, 6½ hrs, several companies, US$14.50, but shop around for different journey times. **Aguascalientes**, every 30 mins, 2½ hrs, US$3.50. To **Leon**, 4½ hrs, US$8.80. To **Mexico City**, 8 hrs, US$23.50. Apart from buses to Mexico City, Chihuahua and a few other major towns, most buses do not have bookable seats. As the majority of buses pass through Zacatecas and don't start their journey there, long waits are probable.

Airport 25 km N of city, daily Mexicana flights to Los Angeles (CA), Mexico City and Tijuana; 4 a week to San Luis Potosí; 4 a week to Chicago, once a week to Denver. Taesa flies to Guadalajara, Mexico City, Ciudad Juárez, Morelia and Oakland (CA).

Excursions Beyond Zacatecas to the E lies the Convento de Guadalupe, a national monument, with a fine church and convent, which now houses a museum of colonial religious art; admission US$3.45 (Tues-Sun 1000-1700). Next door is Museo Regional de Historia, under development. Frequent buses, No 13, from López Mateos y Salazar, near old terminal, US$0.15, 20 mins. Visit also the *Chicomostoc* ruins 56 km S by taking the 0800 or 1100 Línea Verde bus from main terminal to Adjuntas (about 45 mins, US$0.60), on the Villanueva road. Then walk ½ hr through beautiful, silent, nopal-cactus scenery to the ruins, which offer an impressive view. There is the Palace of the Eleven Columns, a pyramid of the Sun and other remains on a rocky outcrop, in various stages of restoration. In themselves the ruins are not spectacular, but together with the setting they are worth the trip. Take water. Admission US$3.35; no information on site, so ask for explanations. Women are advised to keep at a distance from the caretaker. For the return from the junction at Adjuntas wait for a bus (possibly a long wait), or hitch back to Zacatecas. *Jerez* is an old colonial town about 65 km from Zacatecas, where the wide brimmed *sombrero charro* is still worn, worth a visit; **D** *Hotel Félix*, rec, frequent buses from new bus terminal.

(Km 508) **Aguascalientes** was founded in 1575 and is capital of its state; alt: 1,987 metres; pop: 750,000; its name comes from its hot mineral springs. An oddity is that the city is built over a network of tunnels dug out by a forgotten people. It has pretty parks, a pleasant climate, delicious fruits, and specializes in drawn linen threadwork, pottery, and leather goods. Places to see are the Palacio de Gobierno (once the castle of the Marqués of Guadalupe, with colourful murals round inner courtyards), the churches of San Marcos and San Antonio on Zaragoza and the Palacio Municipal. There is much industrial development on the outskirts.

On items of interest in Aguascalientes, Tim Connell writes:
Museo de Aguascalientes, Calle Zaragoza 505, is by the Church of San Antonio; it has a collection of contemporary art, including fine paintings by Saturnino Herrán, and works by Orozco, Angel, Montenegro and others (open from 1030 daily, except Sun and Mon). The **José Guadalupe Posada** museum is in a gallery, by the Templo del Cristo Negro, close to a pleasant garden—Díaz de León (known locally as the Jardín del Encino); it has a remarkable collection of prints by the lithographer Posada, best known for his *cadaveras*, macabre skeletal figures illustrating and satirizing the Revolution and events leading up to it. Admission

free, Tues-Sun 1000-1400, 1700-2100, shut Mon; cultural events in the courtyard on Sat and Sun. The **Casa de las Artesanías** is near the main square. The **Casa de la Cultura**, on Venustiano Carranza and Galeana Norte, is a fine colonial building. It holds a display of *artesanía* during the *feria*.

Teatro Morelos next to the Cathedral; T 5-00-97. The **University** is ½ hr from the city centre. Its administrative offices are in the ex-Convento de San Diego, by the attractive Jardín del Estudiante, and the Parían, a shopping centre. The market is not far away. There is carp fishing at El Jocoqui and Abelardo Rodríguez. The bull ring is on Avenida López Mateos.

Hacienda de San Blas, 34 km away, contains the **Museo de la Insurgencia**, with murals by Alfredo Zermeño. The area is famous for viticulture; the local wine is called after San Marcos, and the *feria* in his honour lasts for 3 weeks, starting in the middle of April, with processions, cockfights (in Mexico's largest *palenque*, seating 4,000), bullfights, agricultural shows etc. The Plaza de Armas is lavishly decorated. The *feria*, covered by national TV networks, is said to be the biggest in Mexico. Accommodation can be very difficult and prices double during the *feria*. Bullfight also on New Year's day.

Hotels A+ *Francia*, Plaza Principal, T 56080, airy, colonial style; good restaurant (*El Fausto*) for breakfast and lunch; *Fiesta Americana*, due open early 1993 - details unknown; **B** *Hotel Suites Alamo*, Alameda 129, T 5-68-85, pool; **D** *Praga*, with TV, Zaragoza 214, T 5-23-57, OK. On main square, **D** *Señorial*, Colón 104, T 52179, helpful lady speaks English. **D** *Don Jesús*, Juárez 427, T 55598, cold water, good value; **D** *Imperial*, 5 de Mayo 106, T 51984, colonial building, good, clean, hot water, **D** *Maser*, 3 blocks from Cathedral on Montaro, T 53562, *comedor* for breakfast; **D** *San José*, Hidalgo 207, T 51431, friendly. At Rep de Brasil 403, **E** *Casa de Huéspedes*, nr main square, and at No 602, **D** *Gómez*, T 70409. Cheap hotels around Juárez market (Av Guadalupe y Calle Guadalupe Victoria), eg **D** *Brasil*, Guadalupe 110, with bath, quiet, and **D** *Bahía*, No 144, with bath, **E** *México*, no bath or hot water. **Youth Hostel**, Av de la Convención y Jaime Nuno s/n, CP 20190, T 700873. **Motel A** *El Medrano*, Chávez 904, T 55500, F 68076; **B** *La Cascada*, Chávez 1501, T 61411.

Market Main one at 5 de Mayo y Unión, large and clean, with toilet on upper floor.

Bookshop Librería Universal, Madero 427.

Post Office Hospitalidad, nr El Porián shopping centre.

Tourist Office Federal tourist office in Palacio de Gobierno, T 60123.

Taxis There is a ticket system for taxis from the Central Camionera, with the city divided into different fare zones. There is no need to pay extra; a phone number for complaints is on the ticket.

Rail Twice a day to **Mexico City**, en route from Ciudad Juárez and Torreón. Train to **San Luis Potosí** daily at 0810. Train station at E end of Av Madero.

Buses Bus station about 1 km S of centre on Av Circunvalación Sur. Bus: to **Guadalajara**, 5 hrs, US$8.25 1st, US$15.50 ETN. To **Guanajuato** US$4.50 with Flecha Amarilla, 3½ hrs. To **Zacatecas**: US$3.50, every 30 mins, 2½ hrs. To **Ciudad Juárez**, US$46.25. ETN (luxury service) to **Mexico City** US$31.50. Some 170 km to the E is San Luis Potosí (**see p 76**).

Thermal Baths Balneario Ojo Caliente, E end of town beyond train station, at end of Calzada Revolución (Alameda), claims to have been founded in 1808, some private hot baths and 2 excellent public pools (US$0.75), take bus marked 'Alameda"; saunas, squash and tennis courts on the site. At end of Alameda fork right to Deportivo Ojocaliente, a large complex with several pools (not so warm water), US$0.65. 20 km N is a thermal swimming pool at Valladolid (camping is permitted in the grounds, secure, night watchman in attendance).

Encarnación de Díaz (**C** *Hotel Casa Blanca*, Anguiano 107 on the plaza, hot water, secure parking nearby, reasonable restaurant) is halfway to *Lagos De Moreno* (Km 425), a charming old town with fine baroque churches; the entry over the bridge, with domes and towers visible on the other side, is particularly impressive. See the ex-convent of the Capuchins and the Teatro Rosas Moreno. *Feria* last week of July and first of August. A road turns off right to Guadalajara,

197 km away; the same road leads, left, to Antiguo Morelos via San Luis Potosí. Lagos de Moreno has several hotels (on main plaza: **C** *La Traje*; **D** *París*; **D** *Plaza*, best rooms facing the front, small and dark at the back; just off the plaza is **C** *Colonial*; **C** *Victoria*, two blocks away, nr river) and restaurants (rec is *La Rinconada*, colonial building, old photos, on plaza 2 blocks behind Municipalidad, which is on main plaza, good *enchiladas*). 42 km SW is the colonial town of **San Juan de los Lagos**, a major pilgrimage centre, crowded during Mexican holidays, famous for glazed fruit; many hotels. There is also a fine view on entering this town: as the road descends you see the twin-towered church with its red, blue and yellow tiled dome. This road, Route 80, continues to Guadalajara; much of it is in poor condition. From Zapotlanejo to Guadalajara is a dual carriageway.

After about 1,600 km of desert or semi-arid country, we now enter, surprisingly, the basin of Guanajuato, known as the Bajío, greener, more fertile, higher (on average over 1,800 metres), and wetter, though the rainfall is still not more than 635 to 740 mm a year. The Bajío is the granary of central Mexico, growing maize, wheat, and fruit. The towns we pass through, León, Irapuato, and Celaya, have grown enormously in population and importance. Tim Connell writes that 50 km before León there are some impressive buttes (isolated, steep hills).

(Km 382) **León** (de los Aldamas), in the fertile plain of the Gómez river, is now said to be Mexico's fifth city, with a population of 1.2 million. The business centre is the Plaza de Constitución. There are a striking municipal palace, a cathedral, many shaded plazas and gardens. The Templo Expiatorio has been under construction for most of this century, catacombs open 1000-1300, well worth seeing; the Doblado theatre on Av Hermanos Aldama; the modernized zoo, reached by the Ibarilla bus. León is the main shoe centre of the country (high quality shoes in the Plaza del Zapato, Hilario Medina, and cheaper ones in places round the bus station), and is noted for its leather work (buy in the shops round the jail, and along Belisario Domínguez), fine silver-trimmed saddles, and *rebozos*. Alt: 1,885 metres. *Fiesta*: San Sebastián, 19-24 January, very crowded, good fun (if staying outside León, take an early bus out of town when leaving).

Hotels: *Real de Minas*, A López, T 43677, 5 star, rec; **A+** *Estancia*, Blvd López Mateos 1311 Pte, T 63939, restaurant rec; **B** *Condesa*, on Plaza, Portal Bravo 14, T 31120, 3 star, restaurant rec; **B** *León*, Madero 113, T 41050, 3 star; **B** *Robert*, Blvd L Mateos Oriente 1503, T 69500; **B** *Roma*, P Vallarta 203, T 61500, 3 star; **B** *Señorial*, near Plaza, Juárez 221, T 45896, **C** *Fénix*, Comonfort 338, T 32291, 2 star; *Colón*, 20 de Enero 131, T 68871, 1 star; **D** *Fundadores*, J Ortiz de Domínguez 218, T 61727, better than similarly-priced hotels in centre; **D** *Niza*, P Vallarta 102, T 31705; **D** *Tepeyac*, Av Obregón 727, T 68365, 1 star. Also several cheaper ones near market.

Restaurants Several in Colonia Jardines del Moral area in centre, including: *Ling Choy*, Chinese; *Sushito*, Japanese; *Vegas*, International; *Lupillos*, pasta and pizza; also several branches of the US fast food chains. Many restaurants in the Gran Plaza complex next to Macdonalds. Vegetarian snacks at *GFU*, on López Mateos No 17177, near IMSS building.

Buses Bus terminal has post office, long distance phones, restaurant and shops (street plan on sale, US$2.75). Plenty of buses to **Mexico City**, US$13.50 (US$27.50 ETN), **Querétaro**, US$6. Irapuato and Celaya. Frequent services to **Guanajuato**, 40 mins, US$3 ETN. To **Zacatecas**, 4½ hrs, US$8.80. To **Poza Rica**, Omnibús de México, US$21. Same company to **Monterrey**, US$25, and **Guadalajara**, every ½ hr, first at 0600, 4 hrs, US$7.75, US$15.50 ETN. Many buses run to **Ciudad Juárez**, US$50, passing through the cities mentioned above (eg Durango US$16.50, Chihuahua, US$38.50).

Airport New international airport, del Bajío, 18 km from León, 10 km from Silao: Continental to Chicago, Dallas, Denver, Midland, New York and San Antonio; AeroMéxico flies to Mexico City (with connections to external and Mexican destinations), Los Angeles (also Mexicana), Puerto Vallarta, Morelia, Tijuana; Aerolitoral to Guadalajara (also Mexicana), Monterrey, Puerto Vallarta, San Antonio (Texas); Saro to Monterrey and Acapulco.

Then highway from León to Mexico City is dual carriageway all the way. (Km 430)

Silao (hotel, bus from León US$0.70). Between León and Silao, left off Highway 45 at Km 387 (going S) are the famous swimming pools of Comanjilla fed by hot sulphurous springs (rustic, semi-tropical with hotel and restaurant at moderate rates). Eleven km beyond Silao, at Los Infantes, a short side road through the picturesque Marfil canyon leads to Guanajuato.

Guanajuato, the beautiful capital of Guanajuato state and a university city, now declared a national monument and Unesco World Heritage Zone, has been important for its silver since 1548. Its name derives from the Tarascan Quanax-Huato, place of frogs. Population, 70,000 in 1880, now 150,000, altitude, 2,010 metres (state population 1990, 3,980,200). It stands in a narrow gorge amid wild and striking scenery; the Guanajuato river cutting through it has been covered over and several underground streets opened—an unusual and effective attraction. Some, like Padre Belaunzarán, are not entirely enclosed; others, such as Hidalgo, are, so they fill with traffic fumes (as does much of the city). The Túnel Los Angeles leads from the old subterranean streets to the modern roadway which connects with the Carretera Panorámica and the monument to Pipila (see below). Taking traffic underground has not relieved the congestion of the surface streets, which are steep, twisted and narrow, following the contours of the hills. Some are steps cut into the rock: one, the **Callejón del Beso** (Street of the Kiss), is so narrow that kisses can be—and are—exchanged from opposite balconies. Over the city looms the shoulder of La Bufa mountain (you can hike to the summit up a trail which takes 2 hrs: from the Pipila monument, follow the main road for about 1 km to the hopsital then take the trail to the right; if you pass the quarry, note the quality of the stone masonry on the mason's shelter).

Guanajuato contains a series of fine museums (see below) as well as the most elegant marble-lined public lavatories in Mexico. The best of many colonial churches are **La Compañia** (Jesuit, 1765, note the brick ceiling, by the University); **San Diego** (1663) on the Jardín de la Unión; the **Parroquía del Inmaculado Corazón de María**, on Juárez, opp Mercado Hidalgo, has interesting statues on the altar; the **Basilica** (Cathedral, 1693, on Plaza de la Paz), **San Roque** (1726) on a small park between Juárez and Pocitos, and **San Francisco** (1671). The splendid church of **La Valenciana**, one of the most impressive in Mexico, is 5 km out of town on the Dolores Hidalgo road; it was built for the workers of the Valenciana silver mine, once the richest in the world. The church, dedicated to San Cayetano, has three huge, gilt altars, a wooden pulpit of sinuous design, large paintings and a cupola. The style is churrigueresque, done in grey-green and pink stone; the façade is also impressive. The mine (1548) is surrounded by a wall with triangular projections on top, said to symbolize the crown of the King of Spain. The huge stone walls on the hillside, supported by enormous buttresses, created an artificial level surface from earth excavated higher up the slope. With care you can walk freely in the whole area. A local 'Valenciana' bus starts in front of *Hotel Mineral de Rayas*, Alhóndiga 7, leaving every 30 mins during the day, US$0.10, 10 minutes ride; 10 mins walk between church and mine pit-head; don't believe anyone who tells you a taxi is necessary, but don't walk to it along the highway, it is narrow and dangerous. At the mine is a gift shop with a reasonable selection of silver. If you stay on the 'Valenciana' bus to the end of thè line, a church brightly-painted and turned into a restaurant, you will see a dirt road to the left which leads to a recreation area with reservoir and picnic area, also several walks into the hills. Local pottery can be bought in the **Mercado Hidalgo** (1910), in the centre; there is also a Casa de Artesanías behind the **Teatro Juárez** (see **Entertainment** below).

Museums A most interesting building is the massive **Alhóndiga de Granadita**, built as a granary, turned into a fortress, and now a museum (US$4.35). An unusual sight shown to visitors is of mummified bodies in the small **Museo de**

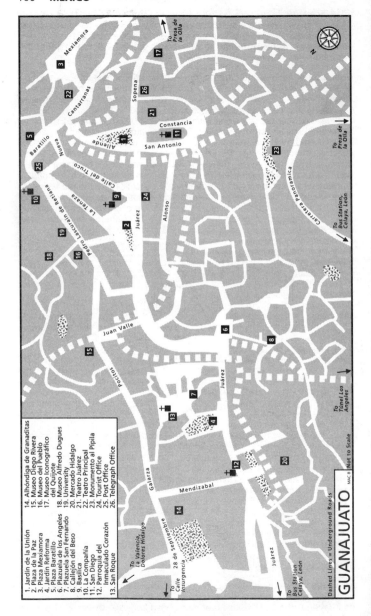

GUANAJUATO

1. Jardín de la Unión
2. Plaza de la Paz
3. Plaza Mexiamora
4. Jardín Reforma
5. Plaza Baratillo
6. Plazuela de los Angeles
7. Plazuela San Fernando
8. Callejón del Beso
9. Basílica
10. La Compañía
11. San Diego
12. Parroquia del Inmaculado Corazón
13. San Roque
14. Alhóndiga de Granaditas
15. Museo Diego Rivera
16. Museo del Pueblo
17. Museo Iconográfico del Quijote
18. Museo Alfredo Dugues
19. University
20. Mercado Hidalgo
21. Teatro Juárez
22. Teatro Principal
23. Monumento al Pípila
24. Tourist Office
25. Post Office
26. Telegraph Office

Dashed Lines = Underground Roads   MAC 8   Not to Scale

las **Momias** in the Panteón Municipal, above the city off Tepetapa; buses go there ("Momias", sign-posted Panteón Municipal, US$0.10, 10 mins, along Av Juárez), but you can walk. It's a gruesome spectacle, glass cases of naturally mummified bodies, their mouths gaping from skin contraction, some bodies with shoes and socks on, and, it is claimed, the smallest mummy in the world (entry US$2, US$0.75 to take photos, tip the Spanish-speaking guide, open 0900-1800). The **Museo Iconográfico del Quijote**, opened in 1987 at Manuel Doblado 1, is highly recommended: paintings, drawings, sculptures of the Don, entry free (see **Festivals** below for Festival Cervantino). The painter **Diego Rivera** was born in Calle de Pocitos, No 47; visit the museum there with permanent collection of his work on various floors showing his changing styles; on the ground floor are his bed and other household objects; temporary exhibitions also held (entry US$3). Also on Pocitos No 7, just across from the University is the **Museo del Pueblo** in a beautiful 17th century mansion; it has one room of work by the muralist José Chávez Morado, a room of selected items of all Mexican art forms and temporary exhibitions, Tues-Sun, 0900-1900. In the University is the **Museo Alfredo Dugues**, of natural history (Mon-Fri, 0900-1400, 1630-1900). The University was founded in 1732; its façade of coloured stone, above a broad staircase, glows richly at sunset. Also in the University is the **Sala Hermenegildo Bustos**, which holds art exhibitions. The School of Mining has a **Museo de Minería** on the Carretera Panorámica, N of the city (Mon-Fri 0900-1300, 1630-1900).

When Father Hidalgo took the city in 1810, the Alhóndiga was the last place to surrender, and there was a wanton slaughter of Spanish soldiers and royalist prisoners. When Hidalgo was himself caught and executed, along with three other leaders, at Chihuahua, their heads, in revenge, were fixed at the four corners of the Alhóndiga. There is a fine view from the **monument to Pipila**, the man who fired the door of the Alhóndiga so that the patriots could take it, which crowns the high hill of Hormiguera. Look for the 'Al Pipila' sign. Local buses go from *Hotel Central*, on the hour, to the Pipila, otherwise it's a steep climb up (about ½ hr); a number of cobbled stairways through picturesque terraces go up (or down) eg Callejón del Calvario, leading off Sopeña. Take a camera for fine panoramic views of the city. The Carretera Panorámica which encircles the city passes the Pipila monument. At its eastern end the Panorámica goes by the **Presa de la Olla**, a favourite picnic spot; good cheap meals available from roadside stalls. From the dam, Paseo de la Olla runs to the city centre, passing mansions of the wealthy silver barons and the **Palacio de Gobierno** (note the use of local stone). Also on the E side of the Panorámica is Casa de las Leyendas, with entertainment for children.

Festivals Arts festival, the Festival Cervantino de Guanajuato (in honour of Cervantes), is an important cultural event in the Spanish-speaking world, encompassing theatre, song and dance. There is a mixture of free, open-air events, and paying events. Internationally famous artists from around the world perform. The festival lasts 2 weeks, is highly rec and is very crowded; accommodation must be booked in advance (usually held the last 2 weeks in October, check dates). *Viernes de las Flores* is held on the Friday before Good Friday—starting with the Dance of the Flowers on Thurs night at about 2200 right through the night, adjourning at Jardín de la Unión to exchange flowers. Very colourful and crowded.

Hotels At the bus station you will probably be met by a tour guide who will suggest a hotel, perhaps arrange a discount, and then try to persuade you to buy a tour of the city. The guides have a hotel price list, which is higher than the official price list, which in turn differs from what hoteliers actually charge, but not by much. Most hotels charge in advance. Some also try to insist on a room with two beds, which is more expensive than with a double bed. Hotel rooms can be hard to find after 1400. There are frequent water shortages, so that hotels with no reservoirs of their own have no water on certain days; when there is water, do not drink it. **Note** Drivers should not leave their cars parked on the street since anything removable will be removed. Having said that, parking is at a premium.

On Dolores Hidalgo road exit: **A+** *Castillo de Santa Cecilia*, tourist-bus haven, T 20485; **A+** *Parador San Javier*, Plaza Aldama 92, opp side of Dolores road, T 20626, genuine hacienda style; and Motels given below. On exit to Irapuato, **A+** *Real de Minas*, Nejayote 17 at city entrance, T 21460; on the Panorámica, not far from Pipila, **A+** *Paseo de la Presa*, T 23761, quiet, good value, fantastic views, small pool, tennis courts. On Jardín de la Unión, **A+** *Posada Santa Fe*, No 12, T 20084, F 24653, good restaurant on open terrace, and **A** *San Diego*, No 1, T 21300, good bar, better run, colonial style, very pleasant; **B** *Hostería del Frayle*, Sopeña 3, next door to Teatro Juárez, T 21179, excellent in all respects, highly rec; **B** *La Abadía*, San Matías 50, T 22464; **C** *Central*, Juárez 111, T 20080, near old bus station, restaurant noisy; **C** *El Insurgente*, Juárez 226, T 22294, pleasant and quiet, good breakfasts; several others on same street: **E** *Granaditas* (No 109) clean and friendly; **D** *Posada San Francisco*, Av Juárez y Gavira, T 22084, on Zócalo, good value but noisy on outside rooms, no hot water, lovely inner patio; **D** *Reforma*, Av Juárez 113, T 20469, with bath, overpriced, little hot water. **D** *Alhóndiga*, Insurgencia 49, T 20525, good, clean, quiet, restaurant *La Estancia*. Also on Insurgencia, **C** *del Conde* (No 1, T 21465), with excellent and reasonable restaurant *Mesa de los Reyes*, and **D** *Murillo Plaza* (No 9, T 21884), hot water; **D** *El Minero*, Alhóndiga 12A, T 25251, restaurant. **D** *Mineral de Rayas*, Alhóndiga 7, T 21967, with bath, clean linen, restaurant, bar and *Danny's Bar*; **D** *Molino del Rey*, Campañero 15, T 22223, simple and quaint. **E** *Casa Kloster*, Alonso 32, T 20088, very friendly, rooms for 4 (although few with private bath, **D**, some without windows), clean, very good value, repeatedly rec, gardens, no parking (touts in town will say it is shut, but it is not). On Juárez, **D** *Granaditos*, with bath, hot showers, car park (with low clearance, just possible for a VW camper) US$1.35, **D** *Posada Juárez*, T 22559, rec, and **E** *del Comercio*, T 22065. Other hotels are mostly in our **C** range. Accommodation in private home, **F** pp *Marilu Ordaz*, Barranca 34, T 24705, friendly, 5 mins walk from market.

Motels Many on Dolores Hidalgo road exit: **A** *Villa de Plata*, T 21173. Trailer Park 1 km N of *Mineral de Rayas*, there is a sign on the Ruta Panorámica, hot showers. **B** *De Los Embajadores*, Paseo Embajadores, T 20081, Mexican décor, restaurant, famous Sun lunch; **B** *El Carruaje*, T 22140. **B** *Guanajuato*, T 20689, good pool and food, quiet, rec; **B** *Valenciana*, T 20799.

Restaurants Tourists are given the á la carte menu,; ask for the *menú de día*. Reasonable food, *comida corrida* very good value at less than US$3, at *El Retiro*, Sopeña 12, nr Jardín de la Unión; also on Sopeña, *Pizzería Mamma Fan* and *La Colmena*, Plaza Piazza, Plaza San Fernando and several other locations, cheap and good; *Cuatro Ranas*, in *Hotel San Diego*, Jardín Unión 1, good location but loud US music and overpriced; *Valadez* on Jardín de la Unión y Sopeña, excellent *menú del día*; also on Jardín de la Unión, *Bar Luna*, *El Gallo* and *El Pingüis*, popular with travellers, US$4 for *comida*, good; *La Lonja*, on the corner of the Jardín opp *Hotel San Diego*, is a pleasant and lively bar, beers (US$1.30) come with complimentary dish of tacos with salsa; meals at *Casino de Guanajuato* on Jardín de la Unión. *La Bohemia*, Calle Alonso, cheap, good sandwiches, at night it becomes a marvellous peña; *Mesón de Marco*, Juárez 25, 'rare' Mexican food, flights in balloon offered at US$100, T 27040; *La Carreta*, mostly chicken, fair, on Av Juárez about 200 metres up from Mercado Hidalgo; also on Juárez, *Tasca de los Santos*, on Plaza de la Paz, smart; *El Zaguán*, Plaza de la Paz No 48, very good and cheap food, entertainment inside courtyard; *Café Truco 7*, Callejón Truco, off Plaza de la Paz, menu of the day US$2-3, relaxed family atmosphere, rec, theatre in back room Fri and Sat pm; *La Flor Alegre* (*casa de pan pizza*), Plazuela de San Fernando 37, good, clean and cheap; *El Mexicano*, Juárez 214, good *comida corrida* with dessert and drink, US$2; *El Granero*, Juárez 25, good *comida*, until 1700. *Cafetería Neverria*, opp University, good, inexpensive. *Vegetariano*, Callejón Calixto 20, inexpensive, sells wholewheat bread; *El Unicornio Azul* on Plaza Baratillo is a good health food shop, also sells cosmetic products. You can eat well and cheaply in the market (eg *bolillos*—sandwiches, fresh fruit juices) and in the *locales* behind Mercado Hidalgo (some open till 2200; better value on 1st floor; the ladies have been forbidden by their rivals in the covered market to shout the merits of their menus, but their mime is just as engaging). Good *panaderías* also, eg *Panadería Internacional*, Contarranas y Sopena, sells wholewheat bread. Dairy products are safe, all coming from the pasteurizing plant at Silao. Also from Silao come strawberries in December. The water in Guanajuato is notorious.

Entertainment Sketches from classical authors out of doors in lovely old plazas from April to August. Teatro Juárez on Sopeña (a magnificent French-type Second Empire building, US$0.50 to view, US$0.35 to take photos), shows art films and has symphony concerts, US$1.50. A band plays in Jardín de la Unión (next to the theatre) three times a week. The Teatro Principal is on Cantarranas, by Plaza Mexiamora.

Exchange At banks, Bancomer, Banca Serfín, Banamex, 0900-1100.

Spanish Courses for foreigners at the University. Also at the University are many US exchange students so you can usually find someone who speaks English.

Laundry *Lavanderia International*, Alhóndiga 35A, self or service wash (US$3.45); *La Burbuja Express*, Plazuela Baratillo.

Post Office Corner of Subida San José, by La Compañía church. International **phone** calls from phone booths with coins, or collect. Long-distance offices in Miscelánea Unión shop, by Teatro Principal and on Pocitos, opp Alhóndiga de Granaditas.

Tourist Office 5 de Mayo y Juárez; they have all hotel rates (except the cheapest) and give away folders. Map on sale US$1.35, compared with US$2.70 for state map with town plans at bus station. Federal representative office, Juárez 250 (opp old bus station).

Bus A clean, new bus terminal has opened on the road to Silao, near toll gate, 20 mins from centre by bus, US$0.30, pick up from outside Mercado Hidalgo. At the terminal is a tourist office (reported permanently closed but with notice-board listing hotels, addresses and phone numbers, when open has free town map), post office, long-distance phone (not international; 0700-2200), restaurant, left-luggage and shops. To **Mexico City**, US$13.25, 5 hrs, about 7 companies, each with 3-4 buses daily, ETN US$24.25, 3 Estrellas de Oro at 0700 and 1500 via Dolores Hidalgo (US$2.25), **San Miguel Allende** (US$3.30—also Flecha Amarilla, 1½ hrs) and **Querétaro**, 3½ hrs (US$5.75); super express at 1700; also Omnibús de México (T 27702/20438), Estrella Blanca and Chihuahuenses (book in advance). Bus Guanajuato-Dolores Hidalgo, Flecha Amarilla, US$2, 1 hr 25 mins (of which the first 20 mins is from bus station back into Guanajuato, so catch bus outside *Hotel Mineral de Rayas*—same applies to buses for San Miguel De Allende). Similarly, alight from buses coming from Dolores Hidalgo in the town centre; don't wait for the bus station.

To **Guadalajara** 5 hrs, US$10.15, several companies, via Léon and Lagos de Moreno. To **Zacatecas**, with Omnibús de México 1st class, at 2100, US$10, 5½ hrs. Hourly service to **Morelia** Flecha Amarilla, 2nd class, 4-5 hrs, US$5.75. To **San Luis Potosí**, US$7.75 en route to Tampico (US$20 with Omnibús de México). Buses also to Monterrey, Ciudad Juárez and Nuevo Laredo, but some involve a change in León. In fact, to many destinations it is better to go to León and pick up the more frequent services that go from there (buses every 10 mins Guanajuato-León). Flecha Amarilla have more buses, to more destinations, than other companies in this area; it is not the most reliable company and buses tend to leave when full. Set fare for city buses, US$0.25.

Rail Station is off Tepetapa (continuation of Juárez), W of centre. Constitucionalista (*servicio estrella*) from Mexico City via Querétaro leaves 0700, arrives 1345; returns from Guanajuato 1420, arr Querétaro 1740 and Mexico City 2130; fare to the capital, from US$16.75 1st class only, no food or bar.

Excursions Tours of the city and outskirts by minibus cost US$6.15, rising to US$18 for tours out of town and US$40 to the S of the state; if you want a guide in English, multiply prices by 10. At the former *Hacienda de San Gabriel de Barrera* (now a 4-star hotel, A+, T 23980, F 27460), at Marfil on the Irapuato road, there are 15 patios and beautiful gardens, a chapel, museum and lovely French furniture, highly rec (take bus marked 'Marfil' from outside *Hotel Central*, 10 mins). 30 km W of Guanajuato is Cerro Cubilete, with a statue of Christ the King, spectacular view of the Bajío, local buses take 1½ hrs, US$1.15, 0700, 0900, 1100, 1400, 1600 from Guanajuato (also from Silao for US$0.75). Dormitory at the site (US$1.50) food available, but best to take your own, plus drink (and toilet paper); last bus up leaves at 1600 from Silao and Guanajuato. See also the three local silver mines of Rayas, the city's first mine, La Valenciana (se above) and La Cata. All are to the N of the city, reached from the Carretera Panorámica. It is possible to visit the separating plant at La Cata, but visitors are not admitted to mines. At the old site of La Cata mine (local bus near market), is a church with a magnificent baroque façade and the shrine of El Señor de Villa Seca (the patron of adulterers) with *retablos* and crude drawings of miraculous escapes from harm, mostly due to poor shooting by husbands.

Presa de Insurgentes, a few km up the mountain highway, has a parking area and a couple of tables for picnics; it is a nursery for plants to be planted around the countryside. 4 km up a narrow road from Presa de la Olla is Panifiel, a village with an old church. Children will take visitors into the mission whose doors are held shut against stray animals by a large, round stone just inside the doors (a child's arm is small enough to fit beneath to move the stone). Take lunch.

(Km 315) *Irapuato*, 475,000 people (*Hotel Real de Minas*, T 62380, overpriced, with equally overpriced restaurant, on Portal Carrillo Puerto, quiet rooms on church side; *Restaurant El Gaucho*, Díaz Ordaz y Lago), noted for delicious strawberries, which should on no account be eaten unwashed.

A divided-lane highway goes to (Km 265) *Celaya* (pop 420,000; altitude, 1,800 metres), famous for its confectionery, especially a caramel spread called *cajeta*, and its churches, built by Mexico's great baroque architect Tresguerras (1765-1833), a native of the town. His best church is El Carmen (1807), with a fine tower and dome; see also his fine bridge over the Laja river.

Accommodation and food C *Hotel Isabel*, Hidalgo 207, T 22095; D *Hotel Diplomático*, Carretera Panamericana, excellent restaurant, *El Gran Chaparral*, especially for steaks, good service, also *Los Guajolotes*, Insurgentes 929; there is a 24-hr pharmacy at the bus station.

From Celaya to Querétaro, to join the route from Eagle Pass (**see p 79**), there is a 56-km limited-access toll motorway (US$4.35 a car), or the old road through Apaseo el Alto.

From Guanajuato, Celaya can be reached via the historic towns of Dolores Hidalgo, Atotonilco and San Miguel Allende. 15 km from Guanajuato on the road to Dolores is *Santa Rosa*; in a story book setting in the forest is *Hotel El Crag*, D, clean; *Restaurant La Sierra* next door (the Flecha Amarilla bus stops here on the way to Dolores Hidalgo). There are two or three other places, including *Rancho de Enmiedo*, good dried meat specialities and beautiful scenery. The road corkscrews up in spectacular fashion before winding down through impressive rocky outcrops and ravines to the plain on which Dolores Hidalgo stands. The last 10 km or so are very arid.

Dolores Hidalgo (pop 135,000), the home of Father Hidalgo, is 54 km from Guanajuato, a most attractive, tranquil small town; celebrations are held on September 15 and 16. The main square, or Jardín, is lovely, dominated by a statue of Hidalgo. On one side is the church of **Nuestra Señora de los Dolores** (1712-1778) in which Hidalgo gave the Grito; the façade is impressive, and the churrigueresque side altar pieces, one of gold leaf, one of wood are more ornate than the main altar. It is not always open. In an arcade beside the church is the tourist office (limited). Also on the Jardín are many restaurants and cafés, and banks. **La Asunción**, Puebla y Sonora, has a large tower at one end, a dome at the other, with large murals and a tiled floor inside. Two blocks away, at Puebla y Jalisco, is Plaza de los Compositores Dolorenses with a bandstand. Between these 2 sites on Puebla is the post and telegraph office. Visit Hidalgo's house, **Casa Hidalgo**, Morelos y Hidalgo, open Tues-Sat 1000-1800, Sun 1000-1700, US$4.35; a beautiful building with a courtyard and wells, many memorabilia and one room almost a shrine to the Father of Independence. The **Museo de la Independencia**, on Zacatecas, entry US$0.70, was formerly a jail, now has displays of striking paintings of the path of Independence. Traditional Talavera tiles still made here and ceramics can be seen all over the town.

Hotels *Hotel María Dolores*, Av de los Héroes 13, T 20517, 2 star; C *Posada Las Campanas*, Guerrero 15, T 20427; D *Posada Cocomacan*, on the plaza, T 20018, pleasant colonial house where Juárez stayed, comfortable, good value, good food, rec. E *Posada Dolores*, on Yucatán, with bath, clean, OK, small room.

Restaurants *Caballo Blanco*, on Jardín by corner of Hidalgo and Guerrero, good value. *Fruti-Yoghurt*, Hidalgo y Guerrero, just off Jardín, delicious yoghurt, wholefood cakes and biscuits, also sells homeopathic medicines, etc. **Market** is on Tabasco, S side, between Jalisco and Hidalgo. Another market, near *Posada Dolores*, on Yucatán.

Buses Station is at Hidalgo y Chiapas, 5 mins from main square; has restaurant, toilets, left luggage, local phones. Frequent buses to Guanajuato, León (US$3.65), Mexico City (US$10.50), San Luis Potosí (US$5) and San Luis de la Paz (US$2). To Aguascalientes, US$6.50, 2nd class, via San Felipe.

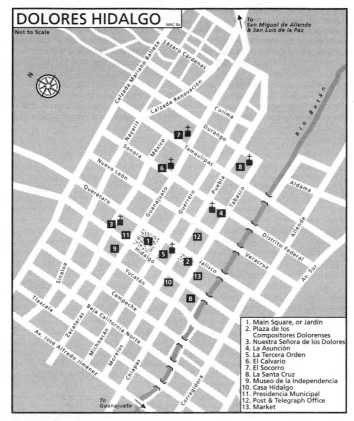

DOLORES HIDALGO MAC 8a

Not to Scale

To San Miguel de Allende & San Luis de la Paz

1. Main Square, or Jardín
2. Plaza de los Compositores Dolorenses
3. Nuestra Señora de los Dolores
4. La Asunción
5. La Tercera Orden
6. El Calvario
7. El Socorro
8. La Santa Cruz
9. Museo de la Independencia
10. Casa Hidalgo
11. Presidencia Municipal
12. Post & Telegraph Office
13. Market

Excursion About 5 km SE of town on a dirt track (walk or hitch) are the ruins of the **Hacienda de la Erre**, Padre Hidalgo's first stop on the independence route after leaving Dolores (free entrance to the untended ruins and grounds). The standing walls are only 3-4 metres high; there are about 4 rooms with ceilings; the patio, with a lot of litter is overgrown, but the chapel has been rebuilt. Outside is the huge mezquite tree under which Hidalgo is supposed to have said mass for his insurgent troops.

The walk (1½-2 hrs) starts from the plaza, then take C Guerrero to the E, take Tamaulipas to the main road. Turn left for 1 km to a gravel road on the left on a long curve. Follow this to the Hacienda in a fertile area with plenty of trees; in May there is much colour with the cacti in flower.

About 20 km further on is the small town of **Atotonilco**, where there is a church built around 1740 whose inside walls and ceiling are covered with frescoes done in black, red and grey earth: unrivalled anywhere for sheer native exuberance. It was from Atotonilco's church that Padre Hidalgo took the banner of the Virgen de Guadalupe to act as his battle standard. (Hotel: **A Parador El Cortijo**, Apdo Postal 585, San Miguel de Allende, T 91-465-21700, very good, pool open to non-residents US$3.30, below the hotel on Querétaro-Dolores Hidalgo road are Las Grutas thermal baths, which belong to the hotel. Take Dolores Hidalgo bus from San Miguel de Allende bus station, or 'Santuario' hourly bus from covered market off Plaza Allende near top of San Miguel: either passes the door.) Across the river from Atotonilco is the tiny village of San Miguelito. A short distance beyond, natural thermal waters rise from the river bed; local women construct hot tubs, called *arenas*, by piling sand around the springs in which to wash clothes and themselves. There is a spa, the Balneario Taboada (admission US$2, open Wed-Sun), between Atotonilco and San Miguel (about 20 mins bus ride direct from San Miguel market; it is a long walk from the main road, better to go by car or taxi). The Spa has a small hot pool, a fine swimming pool and good fishing in a nearby lake—very popular (café open only Sat and Sun). Near the Spa is *Hacienda Taboada* hotel (5-star, large thermal pool, swimming pool, prior booking necessary—open only to residents). Another spa is close by, Santa Verónica, with huge clean pool, open 0900-1800, US$2.50, bus stops outside, rec. From San Miguel de Allende, for either spa, catch bus from Mesones by the market.

San Miguel de Allende, a charming old town at 1,850 metres, on a steep hillside facing the broad sweep of the Río Laja and the distant blue of the Guanajuato mountains, is 50 km N of Querétaro by paved road, 90 km from Guanajuato. Population, 150,000. The city was founded as San Miguel in 1542, and Allende added in honour of the independence patriot born there. Its twisting cobbled streets rise in terraces to the mineral spring of El Chorro, from which the blue and yellow tiled cupolas of some 20 churches can be seen. It has been declared a national monument and all changes in the town are strictly controlled. In recent years there has been a large influx of American residents (now numbering over a thousand) and tourists, with a consequent rise in prices ("trendy shops run by ex-hippies"). See **Shopping**, below.

Social life centres around the market and the Jardín, or central plaza, an open-air living room for the whole town. Around it are the colonial **Palacio Municipal**, several hotels, and the **Iglesia Parroquial** (parish church), adorned by an Indian mastermason in the late 19th century, Zeferino Gutiérrez, who provided the austere Franciscan front with a beautiful façade and a Gothic tower; see also the mural in the chapel. The church of **San Felipe Neri**, with its fine baroque façade, is at the SW end of the market. Notable among the baroque façades and doors rich in churrigueresque details is the **Casa del Mayorazgo de Canal**, and **San Francisco** church, designed by Tresguerras. The convent of **La Concepción**, built in 1734, now houses an art school, the **Centro Cultural Nigromonte**, locally known as Bellas Artes (good cafeteria); the summer residence of the Condes del Canal, on San Antonio, contains an art school and a language school, the Instituto Allende, started in the 1940s by Stirling Dickinson (which has an English-language library and runs Spanish courses, usually without accommodation, but some rooms can be rented—for others, see below). Tours of old houses and gardens start from the public library, Sun 1215 4 hrs (US$8). A magnificent view of the city can be gained from the mirador on the Querétaro road (the views are also good before you get to the Mirador).

Fiestas End-July to mid-August, classical chamber music festival, information from Bellas Artes. Main ones are Independence Day (15-16 Sept); Fiesta of San Miguel (28 Sept-1 Oct, with Conchero dancers from many places); Day of the Dead (2 Nov); the Christmas Posadas, celebrated in the traditional colonial manner (16-24 Dec); the pre-Lenten carnival, Easter Week, and Corpus Christi (June).

Hotels Many weekend visitors from Mexico City: book ahead if you can. **A+** *Mansión del Bosque*, Aldama 65, T 20277, half-board; **A+** *Villa Jacaranda*, Aldama 53, T 21015, central, a couple of blocks behind cathedral, very good restaurant; **A** *Misión de los Angeles*, de luxe, 2 km out on Celaya road, T 21026, colonial style, swimming pool, convenient facilities. **A** *Posada de San Francisco*, main square, T 20072, pleasant restaurant; **A** *Posada La Aldea*, Calle Ancha de San Antonio, T 21022, colonial style, clean, quiet, swimming pool, gardens. **B** *Parador San Miguel Aristos*, at Instituto Allende, Ancha de San Antonio 30, T 20149, students given priority; **B** *Posada de las Monjas*, Canal 37, T 20171, with shower, excellent

20042   41S   465

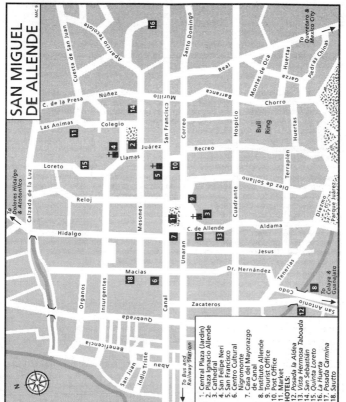

SAN MIGUEL DE ALLENDE

MAP 9

1. Central Plaza (Jardin)
2. Plaza Ignacio Allende
3. Cathedral
4. San Felipe Neri
5. San Francisco
6. Centro Cultural
7. Nigromonte
8. Casa del Mayorazgo de Canal
9. Instituto Allende
10. Tourist Office
11. Market

HOTELS:
12. Posada la Aldea
13. Vista Hermosa Taboada
14. San Sebastián
15. Quinta Loreto
16. La Huerta
17. Posada Carmina
18. Sautto

set meals in restaurant, clean and attractive, very good value, a converted convent; **B** *Rancho-Hotel El Atascadero*, T 20206, Querétaro road entrance, in an old colonial hacienda, very satisfactory; **B** *Vista Hermosa Taboada*, Allende 11, very popular, nice old colonial building, some ground floor rooms dark and noisy. Near Jardín, on Calle Vinaron, **C** *Posada La Fuente* has a few rooms, good food (by arrangement), Ancha de San Antonio 95, T 20629. **C** *Mesón San Antonio*, Mesones 80, T 20580, renovated mansion, clean, friendly, quiet; **C** *Monteverdi*, T 21814, clean, hot water; **C** *Posada Carmina*, Cuña de Allende 7, T 20485, colonial building, courtyard for meals, rec; **C** *Sautto*, Dr Macías 59, T 20072, for room with fridge, fireplace and bath, new rooms best, rustic, garden, little hot water. **C** *Quinta Loreto*, Loreto 13, T 22200, modern rooms, swimming pool, pleasant garden, splendid value, good, cheap food, restaurant closed in evening (but beware of mosquitoes); **C** *Casa de Huéspedes*, Mesones 27, T 21378, family atmosphere, popular, roof garden, nice location, good value.

D *Hidalgo*, Hidalgo 22, hot water (but not all day), rooms not always cleaned and vary in quality. **D** *La Huerta*, bath, clean, well-furnished, quiet, at the bottom of a dead-end street 4 blocks from the market in woodland, no phone; **D** *San Miguel International Hostal*, Organos 34, T 20674, 4 blocks from the central plaza, shared bath, double with breakfast, or **F** pp in 20 bed dormitory, bed linen US$2 extra, clean, kitchen and laundry facilities available, free tea and cofee, book exchange, US owners; **D** *San Sebastián*, Mesones 7, T 20707, nr market, rec, with bath, charming, large rooms with fireplace, clean, car park, noisy at front (most rooms at the back), courtyard; **D** unnamed *Casa de Huéspedes* on C Aparicio Tecolote, 150m E of Plaza Allende, clean, quiet, hot shower, toilet. **E** *Vianey*, del Fecolo; another cheap *casa de huéspedes* on Animas, just past the market building.

Motels A+ *Villa del Molino*, Mexico City road entrance; **B** *Siesta*, road to Guanajuato, with trailer park, gardens; KAO campgrounds further out on same road.

Restaurants *Mesón de San José*, Mesones 38, Mexican and international cuisine, vegetarian dishes, excellent breakfasts, nice setting, German/Mexican owners, open 0800-2200, live music Sun, gift shop, rec; *Mama Mía*, Calle Umaran W of main square, main meals not cheap but rec, free live folk music in pm, excellent cheap breakfasts, films shown in pm; *Café de la Parroquia*, Jesus 11, good, French owner speaks English; *Andale Pizza*, Hidalgo 17, good and economical pizzas, salad and *comida corrida*, rec. *Casa Mexas*, Canal 15, good American food, clean, popular with gringos, English TV. *Matador*, Hernández Macías 76, clean, excellent food, not too expensive, rec; *Italia*, hotel/restaurant, on Dr Hernández, pasta, nice; *Rincón Español*, opp Correos, good *comida corrida*, flamenco at weekends. *El Jardín*, Calle San Francisco, close to Plaza, friendly service, good food, also vegetarian, violinist plays upstairs at weekends for price of a drink; *Flamingos*, Juárez, good set lunch US$4.50; *La Princesa*, Recreo 5, set menu 1300-2000, including glass of wine, live music from 2100, cosy cellar atmosphere; *La Guarida del Zorro*, Recreo 16 entre Correo y Hospicio, excellent steaks and *parrillada*, good value, pleasant atmosphere; *Hobo*, opp Instituto Allende on San Antonio, good atmosphere, especially good for salads and vegetables, US$3-4 for main course, rec. *La Vianda*, Zacateros 56, good for cheap *comida corrida* at lunchtime; *La Vendimie*, Calle Hidalgo, English proprietor, poetry readings Monday pm (must book), occasional fish and chips; *Café Delante*, through *Remo's* on Calle Mesones, patio, fountain, homemade cakes, coffee; *El Infierno*, Mesones, just below Plaza Allende, good value. Good cheap chicken restaurant on C San Francisco between Juárez and Reloj (roast chicken in windows). *El Otro Café*, Mesones 95, quiet wholefood café, sells *The News*, English book and magazine exchange, free refills of coffee, excellent pecan pie, friendly. Try the *licuados* (fruit-shakes) in the market; ask for a *campechana*!

Shopping Handicrafts are the traditional pottery, cotton cloth and brasswork. In the Mercado de Artesanías the merchandise tends to be souvenirs rather than read handicrafts; prices are high and the selection poor. The shops on Canal have a good selection and quality is high, but so are the prices; bargaining is next to impossible. It may be better to try elsewhere for genuine handicrafts (eg the Ciudadela handicraft market in the capital). *La Casa del Vidrio*, Correo 11, offers an excellent selection of brown-glass items at fair prices (sale prices in the summer, 40% off). *Joyería Rubí*, Correo 7, good value, jewellery made to order, rec.

Bookshop *El Colibrí*, Díez de Sollano 30, French and English books. The English-language *The News* is sold on the Jardín.

Entertainment English language films at *Villa Jacarandá* hotel video bar. US$5 including alcoholic drink and popcorn.

Exchange *Casas de Cambio Deal* on Correo, opp Post Office, and on Juárez.

Laundromat on Pasaje de Allende, US$3 wash and dry, same day service; unnamed laundry at Correo 42, good.

Library English language library on Insurgentes has an excellent selection on Mexico; very extensive bilingual library, with computer centre and English-speaking staff.

Language Schools Academia Hispanoamericana, rec for language lessons and sessions on Mexican history, folklore, literature, singing and dancing; very helpful; accommodation with families. The Academia América-Española offers full time Spanish courses; Casa de la Luna teaches Spanish less formally. *Inter/Idiomas*, 20 de Enero Sur 42, Col San Antonio 37750, T 22177, F 21687, small classes, 2 hrs a day of classes. The library arranges 'amigo' sessions where Mexicans and foreigners can practice English and Spanish for free.

Consulate US Consular Agent, Plaza Colondrinas arcade, Calle Hernandes Macías, T 22357, emergencies 20068/20980, Mon and Wed 0900-1300, 1600-1900, Tues and Thur 1600-1900.

Immigration for tourist card extensions, etc, Calle Baeza, just S of Parque Juárez, has an arrangement with Guadalajara and can issue a tourist card extension, or, if qualified, a *Rentista-Visitante* permit. (Very time-consuming and many 'extra charges' until 1994 when a new official was appointed.)

Travel Agent *Viajes Vertiz*, on Hidalgo, American Express agent, mail collection and cheque cashing available.

Tourist Office on Plaza next to the church, helpful with finding hotels, English spoken.

Trains The railway station is a long way from the centre, beyond the bus terminal. Both are served by bus. The *servicio estrella* train, *El Constitucionalista*, leaves 1400 for **Mexico City** (via Querétaro); leaves the capital 0700, arrives San Miguel 1130, US$10; T 20007 for reservations. One train N to San Luis Potosí, with connections for Piedras Negras or Monterrey, at 1500 daily.   *10.30 pm*

Buses There is a new bus station on the outskirts, regular bus to the centre US$0.25, returns from the market or outside *Posada San Francisco* on the Jardín. Frequent buses to **Guanajuato** (2 hrs) with Flecha Amarilla and Estrella Blanca, via Dolores Hidalgo, US$3.30. To **Dolores Hidalgo**, US$1.50. Buses to **Mexico City** via Querétaro (US$2.20) 4 a day before 1200, US$12, 2nd class with Flecha Amarilla, crowded but interesting. Buses to **Morelia** until 2040 daily, 4 hrs, US$6.25, 2nd class. Bus to **Atotonilco** US$1, plus short walk.

   Note There are two routes between San Miguel de Allende and Guanajuato: the southerly route is faster than the northerly route through Dolores Hidalgo.

Excursions A good all-day hike can be made to the Palo Huérfano mountain on the S side of town. Take the road to just before the radio pylon then take the trails to the summit, where there are oaks and pines. Between San Miguel de Allende and Celaya is **Comonfort** (25 km); from there go 3 km N to Rancho Arias: on a hilltop to the W are precolumbian pyramids. Cross the river N of the church and climb to ruins via goat-tracks.

NOGALES—GUADALAJARA: THE PACIFIC HIGHWAY (4)

The road along the Pacific Coast gives access to several resorts (eg Guaymas, Mazatlán, Puerto Vallarta), to ferry terminals for Baja California, and to the Los Mochis end of the railway to Chihuahua. It heads inland, through Tepic, towards Guadalajara.

From Nogales (across the border from Nogales, Arizona) to Mexico City via Guadalajara is 2,235 km (1,380 miles).

In summer, W coast drivers prefer the Central Route from El Paso, Texas, unless they love heat. It is dangerous to drive on retread tyres over the hot desert. Do not drive at night and never park or sleep along the road.

   The Pacific Highway down the coast to Acapulco and Salina Cruz is completely paved but has military searches in the State of Guerrero (for narcotics and arms). There are many motels along the whole route, so that each town of any importance has one or more nearby. The American Automobile Association's annually updated *Travel Guide to Mexico* (free to AAA members, US$7.95 to non-members) lists upscale accommodation and restaurants in major Mexican tourist destinations. It is primarily oriented towards motorists.

From Nogales to Guaymas on the Gulf, the road runs along the western slopes of the Sierra Madre, whose summits rise to 3,000 metres. From Guaymas on to Mazatlán it threads along the lowland, with the Sierra Madre Occidental's bold and commanding escarpment to the E. Like the W coasts of all continents between latitudes 20° and 30°, the whole area is desert, but fruitful wherever irrigated by water flowing from the mountains. Summers are very hot, sometimes rainy, but winters are mild and very dry. Within the Sierra Madre nomadic people hunt the many wild animals; along the coasts available water determines the spots of concentrated settlement and of agriculture. Mexico gets most of its wheat from the southern part of Sonora state, and the irrigated valley bottoms (around Hermosillo) are also used for maize, cotton and beans. Farther S, in frost-free Sinaloa and Nayarit, sugar, rice, winter vegetables, tomatoes, and tobacco are grown. The three coastal states the route passes through make up 21% of Mexico's area, but include only 6% of its population.

(Km 2,403) **Nogales** lies astride a mountain pass at 1,120 metres across from

Nogales, Arizona. Population estimates range from 180,000 to 240,000, with another 20,000 on the Arizona side. Nogales is the largest town in the Pimería Alta, the area of southern Arizona and northern Sonora occupied by the Pima Indians at the arrival of the Spaniards. The Pimería Alta Historical Society, a block from the border in Nogales, Arizona, is open weekdays 0900 to 1700, Saturdays 1000 to 1600, and Sundays from 1300 to 1600; no admission charge. It has excellent exhibits on the history of the region, a valuable library and archives, and also organises tours to the Sonoran missions. The staff are a good source of information on the Mexican side. The city's commercial centre is squeezed into a few narrow blocks centred on Avenida Obregón. The town is a mining area and a busy trans-shipment point for fruit and vegetables destined for US supermarkets; walnut groves (*nogales*) and cattle ranches surround it, and the bordertown flavour is that of a miniature Tijuana: liquor stores, glass, silver and leather goods, cheap bars and colourful markets.

Festival Cinco de Mayo festival, lasting four days, celebrates the defeat of the French army at Puebla on 5 May 1862.

Hotels B *Fray Marcos de Niza*, Campillo 91, gaudy but none too good; **C** *Granada*, López Mateos y González, T 22-911; **C** *Motel Miami*, Campillo and Ingenieros, basic but friendly and good; **C** *Olivia*, Obregón 125, T 22-200, a/c, TV, reasonable; there is a wide selection of cheaper hotels on Juárez, a one-block extension of Avenida López Mateos between Campillo and the border, two blocks from the Mexican port of entry.

Restaurants *El Greco*, upstairs at Obregón and Pierson, has attractive, reasonably priced international menu. Other recommended restaurants on or near Obregón, including *El Cid* (No 124, good but dear), *Olivia*, *Casa de Maria*, *El Toro Steakhouse*. *Café Olga*, Juárez 37 next to bus station, open all hours.

Information Tourist office at the border was closed as of December 1991, but small brochures and a basic map of Nogales were available.

Crossing the border The Nogales crossing is open 24 hrs and the US downtown border post has been expanded (1994). In the event of congestion motorists may wish to explore the alternative truck crossing (open 0600 to 2000), which is reached by the Mariposa Avenue exit from Interstate 19, 2½ miles N of downtown Nogales, Arizona. Returning from Mexico to the US, follow the sign to the 'Periférico' which avoids the downtown area. Get a tourist card before crossing the border, at the International Gateway, an insurance agent, border town Mexican consulate or tourist office. Try to get your tourist card validated at the truck crossing.

Motor vehicle documents can be obtained at the Mexican Customs post 21 km S of Nogales, on the highway to Santa Ana, along with US insurance (which may also be obtained at the border proper). Two photocopies of vehicle registration, driver's licence, insurance papers, credit card and visitor's permit (approved), are required; a photocopy machine is available for use here. Drivers leaving Mexico are advised by a large sign to surrender papers here; this involves crossing the southbound traffic and joining the queues of drivers entering Mexico. It can be chaotic. The post is poorly-equipped and has few officers who speak English; high vehicles should avoid the low inspection shed.

Bus and rail passengers should seek out the immigration official at either station to obtain a tourist card.

Buses Nogales, new bus terminal is 8 km S of the city centre, along the highway to Magdalena and Hermosillo; parking US$1/hr. To Mexico City, 42 hrs with Transportes de Pacífico, daily at 2030, or twice daily with Norte de Sonora or with Tres Estrellas de Oro, US$88. To Guadalajara, 1st class, US$60, four daily with Transportes del Pacífico. Other destinations include Hermosillo (US$10), Guaymas (US$15), Los Mochis (US$24), Mazatlán (US$43), Tepic (US$53), Agua Prieta (US$8.25), Tecate (US$25), Tijuana (US$25), and Chihuahua (US$28). Recent increases in first-class train fares mean that a bus ticket to Mexico City costs no more than the train to Guadalajara, although second-class trains remain very cheap.

On the Arizona side one block from the port of entry, Citizen Auto Stage Company (T 287-5628) runs 10 buses daily between Tucson and Nogales (US$6.50); stops at Tucson airport en route. Stopovers (no additional charge) are possible to visit Tumacacori mission, N of Nogales. US Greyhound is about ¼ block from the border.

Train Pacific Railway as far as Guadalajara, and on by National Railways of Mexico. Guadalajara, 1,759 km away, is reached in 29 hrs, at a speed of 60 kmph (*servicio estrella*, dep Nogales 1500, US$93) and Mexico City (after changing in Guadalajara) in 42 hrs. From

Guadalajara, this train leaves at 0930, arriving Nogales 1150. Conditions vary in both 1st and 2nd class carriages, several unpleasant experiences reported, eg lack of air conditioning, dirt, overcrowding, etc. 2nd class train to Guadalajara 31 hrs, crowded; dep Nogales 0700, stopping at Hermosillo, Guaymas, Navojoa, Sufragio (2015), Mazatlán (0435), Tepic and many other towns. Slow train from Guadalajara leaves at 1200, arriving 1935. Fares to Guadalajara, US$81 1st class, US$23.25 2nd; to Mexico City US$115 1st class, US$32 2nd. Luggage must be checked, except hand luggage, and then must be kept an eye on. Ticket office at border immigration office open 0800-1100, 1400-1600.

A luxury train runs from Nogales into the Copper Canyon (see under Los Mochis), 5 cars, private train, one-week trip (the trip starts in Tucson and includes a tour of Alamos); details from Tauck Tours, PO Box 5027, Westport, Connecticut, CT 06881, T 06881-5027 or 800 468 2825.

Road Tolls If driving from Nogales to Mazatlán by the 4-lane, divided toll road (Route 15), there are 12 toll gates, The first is 88 km S of Nogales. If paid in full without taking deviations or roads to avoid them, the total cost is about US$74 for a car, van, large camper-van, pick-up with 2 axles, US$150 for a 4-axled vehicle (eg motor homes or a pick-up towing a trailer). No motorcycles, bicycles (**but see p 283**), pedestrians or animals are allowed on the highway, which is fenced and patrolled. The toll stations are well-lit, have good bathrooms, fuel and food. Total distance Nogales-Mazatlán is 1,118 km; the road is being extended beyond Mazatlán so that bout 70% of the entire Nogales-Guadalajara route is now 4-lane. The *autopista* sections beyond Mazatlán, eg the sections before and after Tepic, are worth taking for the time they save. It is now possible to list in this guide every toll location and every deviation to avoid it. Most deviations are dirt roads and should not be taken in the rainy season. The high toll cost on this route has led to a decline in tourism of over 50% in Sonora (1994) and similar in Sinaloa. Some drivers have been given toll discount vouchers by establishments in these states. On this, on toll routes and their avoidance, seek advice from US motoring associations and clubs (**see p 384**) as costs and conditions change rapidly.

The highway passes through the Magdalena Valley. The Cocóspera mines are near *Imuris* and there are famous gold and silver mines near **Magdalena** (*Hotel El Cuervo*, near plaza, C without TV, B with) which has a great Indian *fiesta* in the first week of October. On the Magdalena bypass is a toll, US$5, avoidable by driving through town (at N of town heading S, 95 km S of Nogales, keep left to avoid the backstreets). The free road S to Hermosillo become 'speed bump alley". **See also p 120**. Beyond, the cactus-strewn desert begins. At 120 km from Nogales is Santa Ana, where the road from Tijuana and Mexicali comes in.

From Imuris, a major highway junction with numerous inexpensive restaurants, Mexico 2 heads E to Naco and Agua Prieta through the scenic Sierra de Pintos to the historic and still important copper mining centre of **Cananea**, where a 1906 miners' strike against the American-owned Cananea Consolidated Copper Company was one of the critical events in the last years of the Porfirio Díaz dictatorship. Hundreds of Arizona Rangers crossed the border to join the Sonora militia in putting down the strike, which is commemorated at the Museo de La Lucha Obrera, the former city jail, on Avenida Juárez. There are several motels along the highway.

From Baja California Route 2 from Tijuana (**see p 353**) runs close to the border, going through Mexicali (**see p 350**), Sonoita, and Caborca to Santa Ana, where it joins the West Coast Highway (Route 15) to Mexico City. Route 15 is a divided 4-lane motorway from Nogales to Guaymas. E of Mexicali the fast 4-lane highway crosses the fertile Mexicali valley to a toll bridge over the diminished Colorado River, and continues to **San Luis Río Colorado** (pop 134,000), a cheerfully tourist-oriented border town in the 'free zone' and serving cotton country: summer bullfights, small night-life district like those of the Old West, including a so-called 'zona de tolerancia". Americans cross the border to purchase eyeglasses, prescription pharmaceuticals and have dental work done at much lower prices than in the USA. The port of entry is open 24 hrs, but there is no public transport from Yuma.

Accommodation A+ *Hotel San Angel*; *El Reuy* and others on Av Obregón, en route to Sonoita. Budget hotel: *Capra*.

Excursion N of San Luis (35 km) is Baja's last international border crossing point, the farming town of **Algodones** (pop 12,000). Border open 0600-2000, but motor vehicle documents are processed weekdays only, 0800-1500. The road N from San Luis skirts the Algodones dunes, the longest in North America. Algodones has one hotel, the rather misnamed **Motel Olímpico**, E, dozens of souvenir stands, and several decent restaurants. Mexican car insurance is readily available, and there are several *casas de cambio*.

At Andrade, on the California side, the Quechan Indians operate an RV park and campground (US$12 per site with electricity, US$8 without; includes hot showers, access to laundry room). Winter is the peak season, as the town is nearly deserted during the unbearably hot summer. From the west bank of the river, notice the abandoned Hanlon headgate for the Alamo Canal, which burst in 1905 and poured water into California's Imperial Valley for 8 months, creating the enormous 'Salton Sea".

Crossing the border There is public transportation hourly between Algodones and Mexicali but, other than taxi, there is none from Yuma, Arizona, to Andrade (although the road has recently been paved and the number of visitors is rapidly increasing). Most visitors park at the lot operated by Quechan Indians from the nearby Fort Yuma Reservation (US$1, but there is plenty of free parking with easy distance of the border, except on the busiest days).

9 km S of San Luis is **Pozos**, which 40 years ago had 60,000 inhabitants, now only 2,500. It has ruins of large buildings, churches, but no hotels. State highway 40 runs S to Riíto (gas and a few stores) then follows the railway across the edge of the barren Gran Desierto to **El Golfo de Santa Clara**, a good-sized fishing town which has a fish-processing plant, supermarket, general store, church and a couple of eating places. The tidal range at the head of the Gulf is wide but there are good sandy beaches nearby at high tide. Public camping area (no facilities) at the end of a 3 km sandy track past the town. The highway is paved, a round-trip from San Luís of 230 km.

After leaving San Luís Rio Colorado, Highway 2 crosses the sandy wastes of the **Desierto de Altar**—Mexico's own mini-Sahara. The road is very narrow in places, watch out for overloaded Mexican trucks. For 150 km there are no facilities (gas at Los Vidrios), only three houses and an enveloping landscape of sand dunes, cinder cones and a dark lava flow from the Cerro del Pinacate, so extensive that it stands out vividly on photographs from space. All the area around the central range is protected by the **Pinacate Natural Park**; a gravel road 10 km E of Los Vidrios gives access to the northern sector of the park, which contains much wildlife: eg, puma, deer, antelope, wild boar, Gila monster, wild sheep, quail, red-tailed eagle. Several volcanic craters, the treacherous lava fields and an interesting cinder mine may also be visited (the area was used to train US astronauts during the Moon missions). Visitors must register at the entrance and are restricted to the Cerro Colorado and Elegante Crater area.

After a hot and monotonous 200 km from San Luís, Route 2 reaches the sun-bleached bordertown of **Sonoita**, a short distance from Lukeville, Arizona. (Note: If coming from Lukeville to San Luís Río Colorado, make sure you turn right (W) at Sonoita and not left (S) to San Luisito; they are both on Highway 2 but 320 km apart in opposite directions!). Sonoita has little of interest itself, but there are several American-style accommodations: **C** *Motel Sol de Desierto*, air-conditioning but no heat in some rooms (request extra blankets); **C/B** *Motel San Antonio*; **B** *Motel Excelsior*. Restaurants are few and mediocre at best—the coffee shop at Lukeville is a better alternative. Transportes Norte de Sonora and Tres Estrellas de Oro both run first-class bus services. Water and snacks should be carried anywhere in this very arid region, and, if driving your own vehicle, the tank should be kept full and replenished wherever possible. Arizona's picturesque Organ Pipe Cactus National Monument is just across the border from Sonoita.

The border crossing between Lukeville and Sonoita is open from 0800 to 2400. Bus service between Phoenix and Lukeville has ceased, but call Youngstar Transportation (T 602-233-3435) to see if it will resume. Camping is possible at developed sites near visitor centre at Organ Pipe National Monument for US$8 (US$3 visitor permit is valid for 15 days).

Excursion Highway 8 goes SW from Sonoita through 100 km of sand dunes; a sign, 'Dunas—10 km", at Km 80, points to a sandy road to dramatic, desolate inland dunes through mountain-rimmed black lava fields, 4WD recommended.

Puerto Peñasco (pop 60,000) is one of the most important shrimping ports on the Gulf; the huge shrimp are too expensive for the US market and are mostly exported to Japan. It is very popular with Arizona and California RV drivers for fishing, surfing and the beach. It lies on the Mexicali railway and also has a regular air service. On the N side of the bay, 12 km, is La Choya, largely a gringo place, sandy streets, full of trailers and beach cottages, and several fine beaches. Fishing tournaments are held in the Bahía La Choya; Playa de Oro has good surf but Playa Hermosa now suffers from pollution. S of the town is the elite community of Las Conchas, security gate, US-owned beach chalets, self-contained. Navy Day is held in Puerto Peñasco, 29 May-1 June, with a colourful parade, dancing and a widely-attended sporting contest. Good souvenirs are the mirrors, necklaces and figurines locally made from coral, seashells and snail shells.

Hotels C *Viña del Mar*, Calle 1 de Junio y Blvd Malecón Kino, T 33600, modern resort, cliffside jacuzzi, video-disco, etc, attractive rooms, good value; **D** *Motel Mar y Sol*, Km 94 on Sonoita road, pleasant gardens, restaurant, a/c, friendly; **D** *Motel Señorial*, T 32065, Calle Tercera 81, 1 block from main beach, good restaurant, dearer upstairs rooms are a/c.

Camping *Playa de Oro Trailer Resort*, Matamoros 36, T 32668, 2 km E, laundry, boat ramp, 200 sites, US$12 for 2; *Playa Bonita RV Park*, on lovely Playa Bonita, T 32596, 245 spaces, restaurant, shop, laundry; *Playa Miramar*, Calle Matamoros y Final Av Campeche, T 32351, 105 spaces, laundry, boat ramp, satellite hook-ups; *Pitahaya Trailer Park*, beachfront at *Hotel Villa Granada*, E of town, 25 spaces, full hook-ups, toilets, no showers. Nominal camping fee at La Choya, showers.

Restaurants, Shopping, Services *Costa Brava Restaurant*, Kino y 1 de Junio, best in town, modest prices, exotic menu, pleasant; *Café La Cita*, 1 de Junio near the gas station, authentic Mexican, budget; *La Curva*, Kino y Calle Comonfort, T 33470, Americanized menu, popular, budget prices, little atmosphere; *La Gaviota* coffee shop at *Hotel Viña del Mar*, good breakfasts and views.

Jim-Bur Shopping Center, Beníto Juárez nr railway crossing, is the main commercial hub and has a tourist office. Try *El Vaquero* or *El Gift Shop* for souvenirs and camping supplies. Fresh fish from open-air fish market on the Malecón (old town). Laundromat Liz, Calles Altamirano y Simón Morua. 2 banks.

Recently-paved state highway 37 continues on S and E, roughly following the rail line to Caborca (180 km)—an alternative to the inland Highway 2 route.

Route 2 continues from Sonoita to Caborca (150 km), passing through a number of small towns (San Emeterio, San Luisito) and a more mountainous but still arid land. Customs and Immigration station near Quitovac (28 km S of Sonoita), where tourist cards and vehicle papers are validated as you enter the Mexican 'mainland".

Caborca (pop 38,000, alt 286m) lies on the Mexicali-Benjamín Hill railway in the midst of a gently sloping plain. *Motel Posada San Cristóbal*; **A** *Motel El Camino*; **C** *Motel San Carlos*; **D** *Hotel San Francisco*, and several hotels, service station and general facilities. A 'Grape Fair' is held 21-26 June, with wine exhibitions and industrial and agricultural show. Caborca's restored Church of Nuestra Señora de la Concepción was one of the 25 missions founded by Padre

Kino in Sonora and Arizona between 1687 and 1711. (It was also used in 1857 as a fortress during a raid by US renegades under self-styled 'General' Crabb; their defeat is still commemorated by a fair held each 6 April.) Caborca is the best base for exploring the Kino missions.

Padre Eusebio Francisco Kino was the foremost pioneer missionary of NW Mexico and Baja California. He attempted the first major settlement of the Baja peninsula (San Bruno, 1683); after its failure he was assigned to the mainland, where he blazed a *ruta de misiones* as far as present-day Tucson. Kino was a versatile and hardy Jesuit of Italian origin—astronomer, cartographer, farmer, physician, navigator, explorer and a man of unlimited faith. Most of his adobe mission buildings were later replaced by substantial Franciscan churches, such as at nearby Pitiquito, Oquitoa and at Magdalena, where his grave was discovered as recently as 1966; the remains are enclosed in glass *in situ* and the site is a colonial monument. The church of San Ignacio, between Magdalena and Imuris (**see p 117**) is in excellent repair, with a wooden spiral staircase of mesquité.

Highway 2 continues E through **Altar** (café, gas station) to join Highway 15 at **Santa Ana** (pop 12,500, alt 690m), a small town of little note. **B** *Motel San Francisco*, a/c, shower baths, restaurant; motel across the road not so nice, also B. The Fiesta of Santa Ana is held 17-26 July: horse racing, fireworks, etc 2 km W is San Francisco, with another Kino mission.

From Altar, there is a little-travelled alternative route to Sasabe, Sonora/Arizona, 68 miles SW of Tucson via Arizona Routes 86 and 286, perhaps the most isolated, forlorn and least frequented legal border crossing between the United States and Mexico. The 98-km dirt road from Altar, which passes W of the Sierra del Carrizal and Sierra de San Juan, is passable for any ordinary vehicle except after the heaviest rains (Note: the Mexican *Guía Roji* map for Sonora is very inaccurate in this area; the Pemex highway atlas is better, but not infallible). From Altar, drive 3 km NE toward Saric and bear left at the clearly signed junction; do not continue on the more inviting paved route unless you wish to visit the Kino mission sites and churches at Oquitoa and Tubutama—although maps show an equivalent dirt road beyond Saric to Sasabe, there are numerous closed gates, some of them locked, over *ejido* (community) lands. Keep an eye out for semi-wild longhorn cattle along the road to Sasabe.

The border at **Sasabe** is open from 0800 to 2000, but there is no public transportation on either side, nor is there any Mexican automobile insurance agency. For information as to road conditions, phone US Customs (T 602-823-4231); although they appear not to encourage traffic over this route, they will tell you whether vehicles have entered recently from Mexico and what drivers have said about the road.

42 km S the Pacific Highway reaches **Benjamín Hill**, where the Mexicali railway joins the main Nogales-Guadalajara track; brightening up this forgettable junction is the Children's Park, with an amusement park, lake, zoo, and a delightful scaled-down children's railway (motel, cheaper than those in Santa Ana, but only 10 mins away if not preferable). For northbound drivers there is a drug search at Benjamín Hill.

There is little of note on the straight run S to Hermosillo through semi-arid farming and rangeland, apart from the little towns of El Oasis and nearby Carbo (on the rail line)—both have gasoline supplies. 158 km from Santa Ana the land becomes greener and the irrigated fields and citrus groves begin to enclose.

Hermosillo (pop 698,300 alt 237m), capital of Sonora state (pop 1990 1,822,200), a modern city, resort town and centre of a rich orchard area. Just E, the Rodríguez Dam captures the fickle flow of the Río Sonora, producing a rich strip of cotton fields, vegetables, melons, oranges and grapes. Hermosillo's expanding industries draw many people from the hinterland, especially the new Ford assembly plant (manufacturing cars for the US market), but reminders of an illustrious colonial past can be found around the central Plaza Zaragoza (invaded by noisy blackbirds at sunset): the imposing **Cathedral of La Asunción** (1779, neoclassical, baroque dome, three naves) and the **Palacio de Gobierno**, with its intricately-carved pillars and pediment, historical murals and grandiose statues amid landscaped gardens. Highway 15 sweeps into Hermosillo from the N as a wide boulevard, vibrant in summer with orange-flowering trees, becoming Búlevar Rosales through the commercial centre before exiting S across the ring road (Periférico) for Guaymas (toll at Hermosillo US$5.35). The old traditional quarter is to the E of it, a few blocks SE of Plaza Zaragoza, where delightful houses and narrow streets wind around the base of Cerro de la Campana (fine views). On the eastern slope is the **Museo de Sonora** (Wed-Sat 1000-1730, Sun 1000-1530, free).

Not far N of downtown (Rosales y Transversal) is **University City**, with its modern buildings of Mexican architecture blended tastefully with Moorish and Mission influences. The main building contains a large library auditorium and interesting museum, open daily 0900-1300, closed holidays. There is an active fine arts and cultural life, with many events throughout the year open to visitors (check at Tourist Office for details). 2 km S of Plaza Zaragoza, near the Periférico Sur, is the wonderful **Centro Ecológico de Sonora**, a botanical garden and zoo displaying Sonoran and other desert flora and fauna in well-cared-for surroundings.

Hotels Generally poor standard of hotels, although there are **A+** *Señorial*, Blvd E Kino y Guillermo Carpena, T (621) 55155, F 55093, a/c, pool, parking, restaurant, bar; **A+** *Holiday Inn* on Blvd Eusebio Kino 368 (NE entry highway), T 51112, with restaurant, bars, entertainment, etc; 3 blocks away, No 901, is **C** *Motel El Encanto*, a/c, phone, TV, comfortable; **C** *San Alberto*, Serdán y Rosales, T 21800, with breakfast, a/c, cable TV, pool, good value; **C/D** *Kino*, Pino Suárez 151, Sur (base of Campana hill), T 24599, popular business hotel, a/c, TV, fridge; **D** *Guaymas Inn*, 5½ km N, a/c rooms with shower; **D** *Monte Carlo*, Juárez y Sonora, T 23354, a/c, old, clean, very popular, as is adjoining restaurant; **D** *Washington*, Dr Noriega Pte 68, T 31183, clean, a/c, basic rooms off narrow courts, with bath, best budget hotel, parking for motorbikes; **E** *Royal*, in centre, a/c but grubby. A/c is desirable in summer; check that it works before taking room. Cheap hotels and *casas de huéspedes* can be found around Plaza Zaragoza and along Sonora near Matamoros (red-light activity, choose carefully).
   Motel C *Bugambilia*, Padre Kino 712, T 45050. Two close to railway station.

Restaurants *Jardín Xochimilco*, Obregón 51, Villa de Seris, very good beef, not cheap; *Mariscos Los Arcos de Hermosillo*, Michel y Ocampo (4 blocks S of Plaza), fresh seafood, attractive and expensive; *Henry's Restaurant*, across the road from *Motel Encanto*, Blvd Kino Norte, nice old house, good; *La Huerta*, San Luis Potosí 109, seafood, *René's Café*, Rosales y Moreno, good value lunches, pleasant; *El Rodeo Rosticería*, Dr Noriega Pte 92, rec; *San César*, P Elias Calle 71 Pnte, excellent chop sueys, seafood and expensive 'gringo' food. Mexican specialities better value, open for breakfast.

Tourist Office Palacio de Gobierno, ground floor, T 72964.

Bus Bus station on Búlevar Transversal 400, N of University; to **Nogales** US$10, 4 hrs, hourly 0230-1830 (Tres Estrellas de Oro, 1st class); to **Agua Prieta**, 7 hrs, US$13.25, 6 a day (2nd class); to **Mexicali**; **Guaymas**, hourly round the clock, US$6, 2½ hrs; to **Los Mochis**, 1st class, US$22, 7½ hrs through scrubland and wheat fields. Bus to **Tijuana**, US$35 1st class, 11 hrs, there can be long queues, especially near Christmas. Bus to **Mazatlán** 10-12 hrs, US$30. To **Kino**, US$3.35, 4 a day, 2 hrs (2nd class).

Train Station just off Highway 15, 2½ km N of downtown; overnight to Mazatlán, worth taking a sleeper; southbound departures at 1945 1st class, 1220 2nd class, northbound for Nogales leaves in mid-morning 1st class, 1540 2nd class. Hemiosillo-Guadalajara 2nd class, US$19.60.

Air Daily to Mexico City, AeroMéxico, Taesa, Aero California; AeroMéxico and Taesa to Ciudad Obregón, Culiacán, Mazatlán; AeroMéxico and Aero California to Guadalajara, AeroMéxico also to Los Mochis, Monterrey and Tijuana. Aerolitoral to Chihuahua and Ciudad Juárez, Taesa to Durango. Arizona Airways to Phoenix and Tucson (also AeroMéxico).

Excursion A paved 118-km road runs W past the airport to *Bahía Kino*, divided into the old, somnolent and somewhat down-at-heel fishing village, and the new Kino, a 'winter gringoland' of condos, trailer parks and expensive hotels. Although the public beaches are good, most American visitors come for the sportfishing

(International Sportfishing Tournament in June). *Hotel Posada del Mar*, T 181205, F 181237, highly rec; *Hotel Sara*, 5 rooms, on beach. There is no bank in the area. The nearest is in Miguel Alemán, between Kino and Hermosillo, 48 km away (Bancomer). Camping at one of the trailer parks costs about US$12 a night (eg *Kino Bay RV Park*, Av Mar de Cortez, PO Box 857, Hermosillo, T (624) 20216/(621)53197); several others; accommodation in old Kino is not recommended, but reasonably-priced meals are available at *La Palapa* and *Marlin* Restaurants (latter next to *Islandia Marina Trailer Park*, Puerto Peñasco y Guaymas, US$10, English spoken, drinking water), extremely fresh seafood and snacks. The Seri Indians, who used to live across El Canal del Infiernillo (Little Hell Strait) from the port on the mountainous Isla del Tiburón (Shark Island), have been displaced by the navy to the mainland, down a dirt road from Bahía Kino in a settlement at Punta Chueca (no E access). They come into Kino on Sat and Sun to sell their ironwood animal sculptures (non-traditional) and traditional basketware (not cheap). They may usually be found at the *Posada del Mar Hotel*. A fine Museo Regional de Arte Seri has opened in new Kino, Calle Puerto Peñasco, 3 blocks from the main beach road. **Camping** on the beaches is possible.

At Km 1,867 (from Mexico City) the road reaches the Gulf at the port of **Guaymas** (pop 200,000), on a lovely bay backed by desert mountains; excellent deep-sea fishing, and sea-food for the gourmet. Miramar beach, on Bocachibampo bay with its blue sea sprinkled with green islets, is the resort section. Water sports on May 10. The climate is ideal in winter but unpleasant in summer. The 18th century church of San Fernando is worth a visit; so also, outside the town, is the 17th century church of San José de Guaymas. Excursions to the cactus forests. 15 km N of Guaymas is the **Bahía San Carlos**, very Americanized and touristy, where 'Catch 22' was filmed; above the bay a twin peaked hill, the Tetas de Cabra, is a significant landmark; good fishing with an international tournament each July. N of San Carlos further development is taking place on Sonora Bay. Both Miramar and San Carlos beaches are easily reached by bus. The Airport is between Guaymas and San Carlos.

Hotels in Guaymas B *Ana*, Calle 25 No 135, T 20593, near cathedral, a/c; B *Santa Rita*, Serdán and Calle 9, with bath, a/c, clean, good; D *América*, Alemán (Calle 20) y Av 18, T 21120, a/c, adequate. E pp *Casa de Huéspedes La Colimense*, basic, rooms on the inside best, with fan, near bus station; other basic *casas de huéspedes* in same area.

   Motels B *Flamingos*, Carretera Internacional, T 20960; C *Malibu*, T 22244, Carretera Internacional N.

   At Miramar Beach: A+ *Playa de Cortés*, T 11224, F 10135, also has excellent RV park (US$12.50 per day), hotel has private beach, pool, restaurant and bar, etc; A *Leo's Inn*, at opposite end of the beach, T 29490, PO Box 430, Guaymas.

   From Highway 15, it is 12 km to **San Carlos**: accommodation and services are as follows. *Condominio Pilar*, check office for rentals, good camp area; A/B *Hotel Fiesta San Carlos*, T 60229, PO Box 828, clean, good food (US$10-15), pool (opp is *Restaurant Norsa*, good, limited menu, no alcohol); *Totonaka Trailer Park*, just over 1 km up a dirt track, US$15, pool; **A+-A** *Teta Kawi Hotel Suites and RV Park* (Best Western), T 60220, F 60248, PO Box 671, Guaymas, swimming pool, bar, snack bar, disco, a/c, cable TV, trailer park rates US$14/day; *La Roca Restaurant*. 7 km from the Highway, behind the shops, are the post office and police station; the beer depository will sell by the half case. Next is *Creston Motel*, beach side, clean, good value. Then the gas station and bank opposite the phone and fax centre. *The Country Club*, with hotel and tennis, is extensive. **A+-B** *La Posada de San Carlos*, on the beach, very nice. After 10 km from the Highway a road branches right to C *Dorada Rental Units*, T 60307, PO Box 48, on beach, pleasant, and *Ferrer Apartments*. At Km 13 the road forks: left 1 km to two secluded bays with limited trailer camping, and right to the new Marina Real, the *Howard Johnson Hotel*, *Club Mediterranée*, T 60070, all on Sonora Bay, and beyond a beach with open camping.

Restaurants *Cantón*, Serdán between 20 and 21, Guaymas, good Chinese. Generally, restaurants are overpriced.

Tourist Office Av Serdán, lots of pamphlets.

Rail *Autovía* from Guaymas to Nogales leaves daily except Sat; book in advance. Trains to **Guadalajara**, and intermediate stops, and Nogales, both 1st and 2nd class, daily. All trains leave from station at Empalme, a US$4 taxi ride from Guaymas. Bus to **Empalme** will allow you to take the train at 1500 (very full at times) coming from Nogales to **Sufragio**, to catch the Los Mochis-Chihuahua train the next morning. Empalme-Guadalajara US$53.55 *primera especial*, US$17.85 2nd class.

Ferry Sematur sail from Guaymas to **Santa Rosalía**, Baja California, at 0800 every Tues and Fri, 7 hr trip, *salón* US$12, *turista* US$24, bicycles US$10, vehicles also carried; T (622) 23393.

Buses 1st class bus to **Hermosillo** (2½ hrs, US$6); **Mazatlán**, frequent, 12 hrs, US$30; **Tijuana**, 18 hrs, US$47. To **Culiacán**, 9 hrs, US$16.50.

From Guaymas to Mazatlán is 784 km. There is a toll 8 km W of Empalme, US$5; this is on the toll road which skirts Guaymas completely. An alternative route goes into Guaymas, but forks to avoid the centre from both N and S. A third route goes into the centre of Guaymas which should be avoided unless you have business there. Toll at Esperanza, US$5. First comes **Ciudad Obregón**, mainly important (180,000 people) as the centre of an agricultural region.

Hotels A *Motel Valle Grande*, M Alemán y Tetabiate, T 40940; **A** *Costa de Oro*, M Alemán 210, T 41765, well-kept and pleasant; *Dora*, California 1016 Sur, C; also 2 hotels on street of main bus station (turn right on leaving), 1 block to **La Aduana**, D, dirty, cold water, and further down, *Gema*. Youth Hostel, Laguna de Nainari s/n, CP 85000, US$2 pp, ask for bus to Seguro Social—state hospital—and walk round lake to hostel from there Villas Deportivas Juveniles campsite, T 641-41359.

From Ciudad Obregón to **Navajoa** (200,000 people) is newly-divided, 4-lane highway in splendid condition (toll at Navajoa, US$7). Navajoa has the *Motel El Rancho* (T 20004) and *Motel del Río* (T 20331) and a trailer park in the N of town on Route 15 (very good, hot showers, clean, quiet, shaded, US$10 for full hook-up, US$5 for car or small jeep, dollars preferred to pesos). W of Navajoa, on Huatabampo bay, are the survivors of the Mayo Indians; their festivals are in May.

52 km E into the hills is the delightful old colonial town of **Alamos**, now declared a national monument. House tours are given by the US community starting in the Zócalo, proceeds support the library and school children's scholarships, US$10. It is set in a mining area fascinating for rock enthusiasts. On the main road between Navajoa and Alamos is Minas Nuevas, once an important source of silver, very photogenic, bus from Alamos US$0.25.

Accommodation at Alamos A+-A *Casa Encantada*, Juárez 20, T/F 642-80482, in USA F (714) 752-2331, courtyard rooms to luxury suites, bed and breakfast, charming, small pool, will find rooms elsewhere if town is 'full"; **B** *Mansión de la Condesa Magdalena*, T 642-80221, beautifully renovated, clean, quiet, relaxing, colonial rooms, beautiful gardens, excellent food, rec; **B** *Los Portales Hotel*, T 80111, with beautiful frescoes, on plaza; **D** *Somar*, on the road into Alamos, T 80125, Madero 110. *Hotel Los Tres Tesoros*, renovated, 1993/94. *El Caracol Trailer Park*, US$8.50, rustic, good restaurant open 6 days a week; 2 other trailer parks, *Real de los Alamos*, US$10, and *Dolisa*, Calle Madero 72, T (642) 80131, US$12, also motel, with bath, TV.

Transport Bus Navajoa-Alamos every hour on the ½ hr from 0630, US$2, until 1830, 1 hr, good road—bus station for Alamos is about 8 blocks from main bus station, but you must ask directions because it is a confusing route.

NB For drivers heading N, there is a fruit and vegetable checkpoint on entering Sonora state. Toll at Sinaloa border US$5.35. Further toll and drug search 16 km N of Los Mochis, US$3.35.

Los Mochis, in a sugar-cane area, is a fishing resort 25 km from the sea with a US colony. The name is derived either from a local word meaning 'hill like a turtle", or possibly, from 'mocho", meaning one-armed, perhaps after a cowboy thus mutilated. The city was founded in 1904 around a sugar mill built by the American, Benjamin Johnson. His wife built the Sagrado Corazón church. The family lost everything in the Revolution. There are plenty of night spots and bars visited by roaming mariachis, who play excellent music. A stairway leads up the hillside behind La Pérgola, a pleasant public park near the city reservoir, for an excellent view of Los Mochis. Km 1,636.5; 200,000 people. Toll at Los Mochis US$3.65.

Hotels A+ *Santa Anita*, Leiva y Hidalgo, T 20046, comfortable, clean dining room (good), noisy a/c, has own bus service to station, safe garage to leave car whilst visiting Copper Canyon, US$4 per day; it is usually possible to change dollars. Under same ownership is *Plaza Inn*, on Leiva, the main street (also on this street, **B** *El Dorado*, 20 mins from centre, a/c, pool, friendly, very good, and *Florida*). **D** *América*, Allende Sur 655, T 21355, no hot water in early am, noisy, a/c, near bus station, has restaurant with good, cheap sandwiches; **D** *Beltrán*, Hidalgo 281 Pte, T 20688, a bit run-down but good value, rec, has all travel time-tables and will make reservations; **D** *Central*, opp 1st class bus station, with bath and a/c, front desk open 24 hrs; **D** *del Valle*, Guillermo Prieto y Independencia, T 2-01-05, a/c, bath, dirty, not rec; **D** *El Parque*, across from Parque Sinaloa; **D** *Fénix*, A Flores 365 Sur, T 22623, safe, clean, very good. **D** *Hidalgo*, opposite at No 260 Pte, T 23456, sometimes no hot water, dirty, not rec; **D** *Lorena*, Prieto y Obregón, T 20958, with bath, TV, gloomy, poor value but good cafetería; **D** *Los Arcos*, Allende (round corner from Tres Estrellas terminal), without bath, a/c, clean but dingy, fills up quickly; **D** *Montecarlo*, a/c, Independencia y Flores, T 21818. **Motel D** *Santa Rosa*, López Mateos 1051 N, modest.

Trailer Park *Río Fuerte Trailer Resort*, 16 km N of Los Mochis on Route 15, good, swimming pool, rec, US$10/car and 2 people, US$12 motor home. **Note** The Pemex Station 1.5 km S of here has a very bad reputation and bad pumps. Ask as *Río Fuerte* for which service stations are best, eg the one 16 km S on the right. There is another *Hotel Resort y Trailer Park* on Highway 15 at the turn-off to Topolobampo, sophisticated, with disco.

Restaurants *Ell Farellón*, Flores and Obregón, good seafood and service, reasonably priced; opp, on Obregón, is *España*, very good; *Café Panamá León*, Obregón 419, good meals, inc breakfast, cakes, inexpensive; *El Vaquero* in *Hotel Montecarlo*, rec; *Los Globos*, near TNS bus station, reasonable. Opposite bus terminal is *Río Rosa*, small, clean, good value, lunch US$2; next door is *El Delfín*, restaurant and bar, nice atmosphere (owner's husband is a mariachi musician). *El Taquito*, Leiva, 1 block from Santa Anita, is open 24 hrs. *Las Palmeras*, excellent, reasonably priced; good seafood at *El Bucanero*.

Exchange *Casa de Cambio Rocha*, T 25500, opp *Hotel Beltrán*; others, and banks, on Leiva. American Express at *Viajes Krystal*, Av Obregón, all services.

Hospital Fátima, Loaizo 606 Pte, T 55703/23312, private, English spoken, maybe a good place to start in an emergency.

Air To Los Angeles (California), La Paz, Baja California Sur, Guadalajara, Mexico City and Tijuana with Aero California; AeroMéxico daily to Mazatlán, Mexico City, Hermosillo and Tucson; Aerolitoral to Chihuahua and La Paz.

Bus **Mexico City**, US$60, 25 hrs. Guadalajara, frequent, Tres Estrellas de Oro, 1st class, US$31. **Ciudad Obregón**, US$16.50. **Tijuana**, US$53, several daily up to 24 hrs. **Mazatlán** US$16.50, 1st class, Tres Estrellas de Oro or Transport Norte de Sonora, hourly, also Pacífico. **Nogales**, US$27, 12 hrs. No reservations can be made for buses N or S at the terminal of Tres Estrellas de Oro and it is difficult to get on buses. Try instead Transportes de Pacífico, 3 blocks away and next to TNS terminal. First class bus to **Guaymas** 5½ hrs, US$12. To **Tepic**, Tres Estrellas de Oro, 1st class, US$25, 13 hrs. To **Topolobampo**, US$1, buses leave from lane behind Flamingo Travel.

A side road, running SW from Los Mochis crosses the salt flats to **Topolobampo** (20 km, ½ hr). The town is built on a number of hills facing the beautiful bay-and-lagoon-indented coast. In the bay, which has many outlets, there are a number of islands; sunsets here are lovely. Boats can be hired, and fishing trips are available from the jetty. It is difficult to find a beach unless one pays for a private launch. Pemex has a storage facility here and Topolobampo is being developed as a deep-water port. This is as a consequence of the full operation of the Ojinaga (**see p 92**)—Pacific railway (of which the Los Mochis-Creel-Chihuahua route forms part). Originally conceived in 1872 as an outlet for US goods from Kansas and the S to Japan, the line across the Mexican Sierra was not completed until 1961.

Hotels B *Yacht Hotel*, 3-4 km S of town, modern, a/c, clean and good food, quiet, good views, but seems to close for the winter; for other accommodation go to Los Mochis.

Ferry Topolobampo-La Paz, Baja California Sur. Ferry leaves Topolobampo daily except Sun, 0900, arriving Pichilingüe (La Paz) 1800, book ticket before 1800 on previous day (not Sun) or from 0600 on day of travel. T (686) 20141, F 20035. **See also p 372.**

Rail Connections from the Nogales-Guadalajara train are made at **Sufragio**, 37 km from Los Mochis (**see also p 351**). The *servicio estrella* passes Sufragio about 0215 going S, 0045 going N, the second class train goes through at a more civilized hour (2015 going S, 0710 going N). For **Creel and Chihuahua**, see below. **NB** If coming from Chihuahua and you don't want to stay in Los Mochis, assuming the train is not overdelayed, you can take a night bus to Mazatlán at 2200, arriving 0630. Sufragio station is open 24 hrs, including its restaurant and waiting room; warm and safe to sleep in, guards will wake you if asked; handy for those with late-night connections.

At Los Mochis station are toilets and local phones; ticket office is open Mon-Fri 0500-0830, 0900-1400, Sat, Sun and holidays 0500-0900; office in town at Hidalgo y Blvd Rosales, Ed Barriza, local 6, T 57775. The station is 8 km from town; do not walk there or back in the dark. There is a bus service from 0700, US$0.15, otherwise take the 0500 bus from *Hotel Santa Anita*, US$3.50, or taxi, of which there is only any number going into town after the arrival of the Chihuahua train. Taxis in the centre go from Hidalgo y Leiva; fare to station US$7 per car, bargaining not possible, make sure price quoted is not per person, rip-offs are common. If driving and looking for secure parking while taking the train, ask for Sr Carlos at the station ticket office, he will guard the car at his home for a modest fee. There is more expensive parking downtown.

The railway journey to Creel and Chihuahua (**see p 93**) shows the spectacular scenery of the Sierra Madre and the Barranca del Urique/Cobre (Urique, or Copper Canyon). The *servicio estrella* train leaves daily at 0600, US$19.25 to Creel (about 8 hrs), US$36 to Chihuahua (about 12 hrs, but expect delays), free snack breakfast, restaurant car selling meals, beer and coke (not cheap). Tickets must be bought in advance, not on the train, either on morning of departure or, in high season (July-August, New Year, Holy Week) a day or more before. Return tickets are valid for 30 days. Tickets can be bought at Flamingo Travel in *Hotel Santa Anita*, avoiding the queue at the station, but they will try to persuade you to book into their preferred (expensive) hotels. The ordinary train, *Tarahumara*, leaves at 0700, US$4.60 to Creel, US$8.60 to Chihuahua (can be bought on train, 25% extra—if aiming to take this train having come by ferry from La Paz, Baja California, to Topolobampo, you will have to rush). On either train, sit on the right for the best views, except when approaching Temoris, then return to the right until the first tunnel after Temoris; thereafter good views can be seen on either side. On the *servicio estrella* the windows do not open so, to take photos, stand between the carriages.

To begin with the journey is through flat country; Sufragio is reached after 40 mins, El Fuerte (see below) after $1\frac{1}{2}$ hrs, Loreto after 2 hrs. The high, long bridge over the Río Fuerte heralds the beginning of more interesting scenery (this is the first of 37 major bridges); 3 hrs from Los Mochis the first, and longest, of the 86 tunnels is passed, then, 10 mins later the Chinapas bridge (this is approximately the Sinaloa/Chihuahua border, where clocks go forward an hour). Before Temoris (4 hrs) the track loops round to the left, goes through Temoris, then enters a tunnel in which the railway turns through 180°. **Bahuichivo** (5 hrs) has a simple hotel and a few shops; if you don't want to go all the way you can return from here (Bahuichivo-Creel, 1st class, US$4). From Bahuichivo, pick-ups make the 5-hr journey to Urique, in the heart of the Barranca del Urique (not Sun). A bus from the *Misión Urique Canyon* meets the train in Bahuichivo; 2 simple hotels in Urique.

Cuiteco ($5\frac{1}{2}$ hrs) has the **B Hotel Cuiteco**, delightful, with a patio which has an unimpeded view of the mountains, quiet, oil lamps, gas stove in courtyard; San Rafael (20 mins later), where there is a 10-minute stop, is just after the La Laja bridge and tunnel; in a further 25 mins *Hotel Posada Barrancas* is reached, followed in 5 mins by Divisidero, where there is an all-too-brief, 10-minute stop to view the Barranca del Urique, buy souvenirs from the Tarahumara women, and let the down train pass. 17 km beyond Pitorreal (7 hrs) is the Lazo loop, in which the track does a 360° turn; soon afterwards the highest point, Los Ojitos, is passed. Creel is reached in 8 hrs. Creel, its surroundings, and the various accommodations in the area are described under **Creel, p 93**.

An hour NE by train from Los Mochis is **El Fuerte** (120,000). This town has recently been renovated and has interesting colonial architecture. The station is 10 km from the town; taxis US$4 pp. **D** *Hotel Oasis*, $\frac{1}{2}$ block from Calle Benito Juárez in centre, not very clean, some rooms better than others, a/c; *Hotel San Francisco*, good value. Good restaurants, nice plaza.

Some 210 km beyond Los Mochis (at Km 1,429) is the capital of Sinaloa state (pop 2,210,800), **Culiacán** (950,000 people), chief centre for winter vegetables. No longer a colonial city, but attractive and prosperous; it has a university. The safe beaches of **Altata** are 30 minutes by paved road. 18 km W of Altata on gravel, then sand (passable) is Tambor Beach, wind and waves, and fewer people than Altata.

The highway is widened and divided for 90 km S of Los Mochis to Guamúchil, where the old freeway continues to Culiacán. N of the city, the north-and southbound carriageways are on different levels with no divide (very dangerous). A new toll section of freeway heads nearer to the coast, past Navolata, bypasses Culiacán and rejoins Highway 15 a few km S of that city. Note, though that this is a very isolated stretch of road and there have been robberies on it at times. Tolls at Guasave US$1.65; first toll S of Guasave US$1.65; at turn off to Guamúchil US$3, N of Culiacán US$3; and Culiacán US$5. The area around Culiacán is also a drugs-growing region.

Hotels A *Executivo*, Madero y Obregón, T 39370. **C** *Del Valle*, Solano 180, T 39026, noisy, not rec; **D** *San Francisco*, Hidalgo 227, with bath, clean, friendly, free parking; **E** *Louisiana*. **Motels A** *Los Tres Ríos*, 1 km N of town on highway 15, trailer park, US$10, pool, resort style, good restaurant. *Pizzería Tivoli*, good, friendly. **C** *Los Caminos*, Carretera Internacional.

Airport 10 km from centre.

Transport Bus to Tepic, 8¼ hrs, US$12; to Guaymas, 9 hrs, US$16.50.

Another 208 km bring us to a roadside monument marking the Tropic of Cancer. Toll 27 km N of Mazatlán, US$11.35. Beyond the Tropic, 13 km is (Km 1,089) **Mazatlán**, spread along a peninsula at the foot of the Sierra Madre. It is the largest Mexican port on the Pacific Ocean and the main industrial and commercial centre in the W (pop 800,000). The beauty of its setting and its warm winters have made it a popular resort, but unfortunately with expansion it has lost some of its attraction. It overlooks Olas Altas (High Waves) bay, which has a very strong current. The old part of town is located around **Plaza Machado**, which is on Calle Carnival. Half a block from the plaza is the **Teatro Peralta**, the 17th century opera house, which has just been restored and reopened to the public. Tourism is now concentrated in the Zona Dorada, which includes the beaches of Gaviotas, Los Sabalos, Escondida, Delfín, Cerritos, Cangrejo and Brujas; the area is built up and accommodation is expensive. From Olas Altas the promenade, lined by hotels with a long beach at its foot, curves around the bay, first as Paseo Claussen, then Avenida del Mar which leads to Avenida Camarón Sabalo in the Zona Dorada. The sunsets are superb seen from this side of the peninsula; at this time of day high divers can be watched and the fishermen return to the N beach. There are many good beach bars from which to view the setting sun. Buses from Calle Arriba go to Zona Dorada for US$0.50. On the other side of the peninsula the Avenida del Puerto promenade overlooks a number of islands. From the ferry terminal at the southern end of Av del Puerto, a boat can be taken to Isla de los Chivos for US$1; there you can stroll along the beaches and eat at the beach bars. There are more islands in the nearby lagoons, which teem with wild life. The local Shrovetide carnival is almost as good as at Veracruz. The best beaches, 3 to 5 km

MAZATLÁN Centre MAC 10a

1. Plaza Machado
2. Plaza Revolución
3. Cathedral
4. Palacio Municipal
5. Teatro Peralta
6. Museo Arqueológico
7. Market
8. Post Office
9. Tourist Office
10. Banamex
11. High Divers
12. Monumento al Pescador
13. Cheap hotel area
14. Doney's Restaurant

from the city, are easily reached by taxi. The lighthouse, on El Faro island, is 157 metres above sea-level.

Firmly rooted and extremely popular in the State of Sinaloa is a type of orchestra known as the Banda Sinaloense or Tamborera, which can be seen and heard playing 'Chaparral' at almost any time of day or night in restaurants, dance halls, bars, at family parties or on the street. It usually has from 14 to 16 musicians: 4 saxophones, 4 trumpets, clarinets, tuba, 3-4 men on drums and other percussion instruments, including *maracas, guiro*, and loud, strong voices. It is unabashed, brutal music, loud and lively. One such Banda plays every afternoon at the *Chaparral* bar, opposite the Conasupo market near bus station.

Hotels The expensive hotels are in the area known as the Zona Dorada; budget hotels can be found around Cerro de la Nevería and on Calles Angel Flores, Aquiles Serdán and José Azueta. Ask taxi drivers for the cheaper places.

Along the northern beach, Av Camarón Sabalo or just off it, are: *Los Sábalos*, RT Loaiza 100, T 835333, Health Club facilities; *Playa Mazatlán*, same street, T 134455, good atmosphere; *El Cid*, Camarón Sabalo, with *El Caracol* nightclub and *Club 21*, T 133333; *Camino Real* (T 131111), *Oceano Palace* (T 130666), *Holiday Inn*, Camarón Sabalo 696 (T 132222, F 841287, resort facilities) all in our **A-L** ranges. **A** *Las Palmas*, Camarón Sabalo 305, Zona Dorada, PO Box 135, T 134255, good value, rec. Along Av del Mar beach are: **A+-A** *Aguamarina* (Best Western), No 110, T 817080, F 824624; **A+** *De Cima* (T 827300); **A+** *El Dorado* (T 817418); **A+** *Hacienda* (T 827000), **A** *Las Brisas*, T 830355, rec, with shower, swimming pool and on sea front, air-conditioned; **C** *Amigos Plaza*, T 830333, before *Las Brisas*, some rooms a/c, noisy at weekends, otherwise OK. **C** *The Sands*, pool, a/c, TV, garden, restaurant, rec, on beach; **C** *Tropicana*, RT Loaiza 27, T 838000, a/c, shower, large rooms, rec. Along Olas Altas beach are: **C** *Belmar*, T 820799, modernized but old. **C** *Freeman* (No 79 Sur, T 812114) old, well maintained, highrise; **C** *La Siesta*, at Olas Altas, T 812640, a/c, clean, nice patio, restaurant. On Paseo Centenario is: **C** *Olas Altas*, T 813192, with fan, efficiently run and clean, good views, restaurant. Most of the others are in the downtown area away from the beach front; **C** *Del Centro*, JM Canizales 705 Pte, T 821673, modern, behind main church; **D** *Económico*, with bath and fan, noisy, dark but very clean, next to bus station, ½ km from main beach; **E** *San Fernando*, 21 de Marzo 926, T 815980, with bath, hot water eventually, very basic, very friendly, rec, car park outside; **D** *Posada Familiar Sarita*, Mariano Escobedo, colonial, nr beach; **D** *Zaragoza*, Zaragoza 18, old and pretty, with bath, cheap cold drinks, free drinking water; **E** *Cami* (address unknown), 50m from market, very close to beach, fan, clean, good value; **E** *Casa de huéspedes El Castillo*, José Azueta 1612, 2 blocks from market, clean, family atmosphere, big rooms; **E** *Lerma*, Simón Bolívar 5, near beach, with fan and hot showers, friendly, clean, simple, but quiet and cool, highly rec; **E** *Roma*, Av Juan Carrasco 127, T 823685, very clean and friendly 2 blocks from beach, rec, with bath but some rooms noisy, clean. **E** *Vialta*, Azueta 2006, three blocks from market, without bath, friendly, helpful, comfortable.

N of the city there are undeveloped beaches with free overnight camping; some have camped alone, but it is safer in a group (take bus to Sabalos and get out where it turns round): eg *Isla de la Piedra*, friendly, huts or camping permitted if you have a meal there, good food. Beware of sandflies! At least 10 trailer parks on Playa del Norte/Zona Dorada and on towards the N, including **D** *Casa Blanca Disco*, cheapest, on beach side, dirty. Much better is **D** *La Posta*, ½ block off beach, with swimming pool and tent space, lots of shade. Big hotels rapidly expanding all along N beach seashore to Mármol.

Motels are strung all along the ocean front: **B** *Marley*, RT Loaiza 226, T 135533, rec, reservations necessary; **C** *Del Sol*, Av del Mar 200, T 814712. **C** *Papagayo*, Papagayo 712, T 816489. *La Posta Trailer Park* (turn inland at *Valentino's Disco* from northern beach road), busy, hook-ups at most sites. *Mar Rosa Trailer Park*, N of *Holiday Inn* on northern beach, T 836187, hot water, safe, own beach, rec. 4 km N of *Mar Rosa* is *Playa Escondida*, laid back, over 200 campsites, not all have water and electricity, OK. Beware of theft from trailer parks. If driving to trailer parks N of the city, pass airport on Route 15, avoid left fork 'Centro y Playas'; follow route signed 'Culiacán' but do not go onto the toll road to Culiacán which starts at the Carta Blanca agency. Keep left and 10 km further turn left at sign 'Playa Cerritos', at beach road turn left again. This leads to *Maravilla*, next to Edificio DIF, PO Box 1470, Mazatlán, T 40400, 35 spaces, US$10 daily, hot showers, clean, quiet; *Holliday*, opp beach, and *Canoa*, private club, nice, expensive. If coming to Mazatlán from the N turn right at 'Playas Mazatlán Norte' sign on Highway 15; after about 14 km you reach the junction with the Av Camarón Sabalo.

Restaurants *Doney's*, M Escobedo 610, downtown, charming old building, good home cooking; *Bruno's*, Mariano Escobedo, good food and service, highly rec; *Mamucas*, Bolívar 73, seafood expensive. *Shrimp Bucket* and *Señor Frog*, Olas Altas 11 and Av del Mar, same owners, very famous, popular, good; *Beach Boys Club*, on Malecón nr fishermans' monument, good value meals, US owned; *Balneario Playa Norte*, Av del Mar, nr Monument, friendly, reasonable prices;also on Av del Mar, Playa Norte, *Bella Mar*, good, comparatively cheap; *Lobster Trap*, Camarón Sabalo, good chicken(!). *Joncol's*, Flores 254, a/c, downtown, popular; *El Mecenas*, Belisario Domínguez 1305, excellent local dishes; *Los Comales*, Angel Flores, 2 blocks from Correo, good. Best value fish meals, US$4, above the markets near Plaza de la República (bring beer with you from supermarket opposite—not sold in cheap restaurants). Try mixed fish dish, US$15 for 2, very good. *Pastelería y Cafetería Panamá*, several branches for reasonable meals, pastries, coffee. *Casa del Naturista*, Zaragoza 809, sells good wholegrain bread. US fast food places, eg *McDonald's*, *Pizza Hut*, are more expensive than in North America.

Local transport Green and white express buses on the 'Sabalo centro' route run from Playa Cerritos to the city centre along the seafront road, US$0.35. Taxis charge an average US$3.50-5 between Zona Dorada and city centre.

Sports Fishing is the main sport (sailfish, tarpon, marlin, etc). Shrimp from the Gulf are sent, frozen, to all parts of Mexico. Its famous fishing tournament follows Acapulco's and precedes the one at Guaymas. In the mangrove swamps are egrets, flamingoes, pelicans, cranes, herons, and duck. Nearby at Camarones there is 'parachute flying', drawn by motorboats. The northern beach tourist strip offers boat trips to nearby deserted islands, snorkel hire and paragliding. For riding, see *Rancho Las Moras* in **Excursions** below. **NB** Always check with the locals whether swimming is safe, since there are strong rip currents in the Pacific which run out to sea and are extremely dangerous. There is a free Red Cross treatment station 9 blocks along the avenue opposite the Beach Man on the right. There are bull-fights at Mazatlán, good view from general seats in the shade (*sombra*), although you can pay much more to get seats in the first 7 rows—Sundays at 1600, very touristy.

Museum Museo Arqueológico de Mazatlán, Sixto Osuna 115, ½ block from *Hotel*

Freeman, small, covering state of Sinaloa.

Aquarium Av de los Deportes III, just off the beach, behind *Hotel Las Arenas*, interesting, includes sharks and blindfish, adults US$1.75, children US$0.55.

Exchange American Express, Av Camarón Sabalo 310, Zona Dorada, all services. **Banamex**, Benito Juárez and Angel Flores, also Av Camarón Sabalo 434, 0900-1330, 1530-1730. **Casas de Cambio** on same avenida, Nos 109, 1009 and at junction with Rodolfo T Loaiza; also at R T Loaiza 309.

Telephones 1 block from American Express; also 21 de Marzo y B Juárez, T 05. Computel phone and fax service, T (69) 160267/69, F 160268. Phone rental, Accetel, Calz Camarón Sabalo 310-4, T 165056. **Post Office** Benito Juárez y 21 de Marzo, opp Government Palace, T 812121. **Mail Boxes Etc**, Av Camarón Sabalo 310, T 164009, F 164011, mail boxes, courier service, fax service.

Consulate Canada, *Hotel Playa Mazatlán*, Rodolfo T Loaiza 202, T 137320/F 146655; US Consulate, T 134455 ext 285; **France**, Jacarandas 6, T 828552; **Netherlands**, Av Sabalo Cerritos, T 135155; **Germany**, Jacarandas 10, T 822809; **Italy**, Av Olas Altas 66-105, T 814855; **Norway**, F Alcalde 4, T 813237.

Emergency Call 06; Red Cross 8136901; Ambulance 851451; Police 821867.

Tourist Office Rodolfo T Loaizo 100, Local N6, T 132545; on road to northern beach, opp *Hotel Los Sabalos*. Also Av Olas Altas 1300, Edificio Bancen, Col Centro, T 851222/851847.

Travel Agent *Explora Tours*, Centro Comercial Lomas, Av Camarón Sabalo 204-L-10, T 139020, F 161322, very helpful, rec.

Bus Station Chachalaco y Ferrusquilla s/n, T 812335/815381; take 'Insurgentes' bus from terminal to Av Ejército Mexicano for the centre, via market at Calle Serdán; if you cross the boulevard and take bus in the other direction it goes to the railway station (US$0.60); taxi US$5.50. Bus fare to **Mexico City** about US$36.50, 18 hrs. (Tres Estrellas de Oro, T 813680, 1st class, express at 2100 a little more expensive; Transportes del Pacífico hourly 1st class slightly cheaper but over 20 hrs, via Irapuato and Querétaro). **Mexicali** US$50, Pullman, 21 hrs. **Guadalajara**, several companies, several times a day, US$19.25 (10 hrs). To **Chihuahua**, US$38 1st class, 19 hrs. To crossroads for **San Blas**, US$8; **Tepic** US$9.50 (5¼ hrs; Tepic is the best place to make connections to Puerto Vallarta); bus (frequent) to **Los Mochis** (7 hrs), US$16.50 with Transportes Norte de Sonora or Transportes del Pacífico, tickets available only 45 mins before departure. To **Navajoa**, US$11 1st class; 1st class Transportes del Norte bus to **Durango**, US$14.80, take an am bus to see the scenery; **Guaymas**, 12 hrs, US$30. Bus to **Rosario** US$1.65, can then with difficulty catch bus to Caimanero beach, nearly deserted. Terminal Alamos, Av Oeste Guerrero 402, 2 blocks from market, buses to **Alamos** every hour on the half hour.

Ferries La Paz (Baja California Sur), Sun to Fri (also Sat at holiday times) at 1500, arr 0900 next day, Sematur T (69) 817020, F 817023. For fares, etc, see under La Paz, Baja California section. Allow plenty of time for booking and customs procedure. Tickets from *Hotel Agua Marina*, Av del Mar 110, with 10% commission, also from travel agents. Ferry terminal is at the southern end of Av del Puerto, quite a way from centre (take bus marked 'Playa Sur", which will also go from ferry terminal to Av Ejército Méxicano near bus station). **NB** Ticket office for La Paz ferry opens 0830-1300 only, on day of departure, arrive before 0800, unclaimed reservations on sale at 1100. Don't expect to get vehicle space for same-day departure. Ferry returns from La Paz also at 1500.

Rail Take 'Insurgentes' bus out to Morelos railway station. Train to **Guadalajara**, 9 hrs, US$23.40 *primera especial*, departs 0815, but is usually late, air-conditioned (if working), scenic trip with a variety of topography and agriculture; 2nd class at 0435, 11 hrs, US$7.75. From Tepic (5½ hrs) it climbs gradually through the hills to 1,650 metres at Guadalajara, passing through some 30 or 40 tunnels. To Sufragio at 1830 1st class, 2300 2nd (US$4.35, take torch). For Creel train, spend the night at San Blas, from where there are many bus to Sufragio. Best travel 1st class; 2nd class dirty and uncomfortable. Buy tickets at agency in Pasaje Linguna in the Zona Dorada, close to Tourist Office or queue at 0730, seat numbers are not observed so sit in the first empty seat.

Tolls at Mazatlán US$14.35 (no 1) and US$14 (no 2).

Air Airport 26 km from centre. Taxi, fixed fare US$13 airport-Mazatlán; micro bus US$6 pp Daily flights to Mexican cities (inc Mexico City, Guadalajara, La Paz, Durango and Pacific coastal destinations) and US destinations (eg Los Angeles, San Francisco, Seattle—all Alaska Airlines, and Tucson—AeroMéxico). Mexicana T 827621; AeroMéxico T 141111; Delta T 823354; Alaska 144789.

MAZATLAN Orientation MAC 10

To Camarón
To Culiacán
PUEBLO NUEVO
15
200
E ZAPATA
Rafael Buelna
1 de MAYO
Ejército Mexicano
Insurgentes
Playa Las Gaviotas
Punta Camarón
Av del Mar
T
B
Pacific Ocean
Bahía del Puerto Viejo
CARRASCO
Av Gabriel Leyva
To Tepic & Durango
15
Nájera
Isla de Ocom
14
Bahía Olas Altas
Serdán
Juárez
Av del Puerto
see Centre detail
Isla de la Piedra
4
6
El Faro
5
Isla de los Chivos
0   5
km

1. Zona Dorada
2. Bull Ring
3. Aquarium
4. Ferry Port
5. Yate Fiesta
6. Star Fleet
7. Tourist Office
8. Canadian Consulate & Hotel Playa Mazatlán
9. Golf Club
10. Valentino's Disco

Hotels:
11. El Cid
12. Holiday Inn
13. Oceano Palace
14. Aguamarina
15. Sands

Cycling Beware, the road Mazatlán-Tepic-Guadalajara has been described as 'the most dangerous in the world for cyclists".

Excursions To *Islas de Piedras*, 30 km of now littered beach. Take a small boat from S side of town from Armada (naval station near brewery), regular service, US$1, walk across island (10 mins) to a clean beach where there is good surfing. Local *comedores* on beach provide primitive accommodation, or ask for permission to camp on the beach. Try smoked fish sold on a stick. Star Fleet boats may be rented at the sports fishing docks for a cruise round the Dos Hermanos rocks, where boobies and many other birds can be seen. A boat excursion on the *Yate Fiesta* cruises out at 1000 or 2000 (with dancing), from second last bus stop in the direction of Playa del Sur. Refreshments included, and you can see the wildlife in the day time. About 100 km N of Mazatlán is a turn-off to the town of *La Cruz*, with two hotels, including: **D** *Las Palmitas*, off the main street, quiet. Few tourists.

At the foot of the Sierra Madre, 30 mins from Mazatlán is **Rancho Las Moras**, a converted tequila ranch, now with 6 hotel rooms and 5 villas from US$230 to US$400/day, tennis courts, pool, laundry service, children's summer camp, restaurant and riding for all abilities (daytime activities for non-residents available), reservations T (69) 165044, F 165045, highly rec (address of office Av Camarón Sabalo 204, Suite 6, Zona Dorada 82110, Mazatlán, or 9297 Siempre Viva Rd,

Suite 15-474, San Diego, CA 92173, USA), from Route 15, take the road to La Noria for 9 km, then turn left to the Ranch.

24 km beyond Mazatlán, the Coast-to-Coast Highway to Durango (a spectacular stretch), Torreón, Monterrey and Matamoros turns off left at Villa Unión. Heading E, the road reaches **Concordia**, a delightful colonial town with a well-kept plaza and a splendid church (hotel on main road, only one, D, old-world atmosphere, swimming pool), then climbs the mountains past **Copala**, another mining ghost-town (basic hotel); **Daniel's Restaurant**, open 0900-1700. Copala can be reaching by tour bus from Mazatlán or by Auriga pick-up truck from Concordia. On this road, 40 km from Concordia, 3 km before **Santa Lucía**, there is a good German hotel, D, with poor restaurant. Santa Lucía has a small hotel, **Villa Blanca**, T 2-16-28. Before reaching La Ciudad and the plains the road goes through a spectacular section with vertical drops on both sides, called the Devil's Spine; superb views. After reaching the high plateau the road passes through pine forests to Durango.

The road to Tepic continues S from Villa Unión. At **Rosario**, 68 km S of Mazatlán, an old mining town riddled with underground workings, the church is worth a visit (**D Hotel Los Morales**, with a/c, E with fan, on main highway opp Pemex, clean, quiet, good bathrooms; there is a very good *palapa* and patio restaurant with 360° views. S of Rosario is Escuinapa (several km N of Escuinapa is **B Motel Virginia**, Carretera Internacional Km 1107-1108, T 695-32755, good clean, *palapa* restaurant next door, possible trailer parking). Here a good road turns off 30 km to the coast at **Teacapán**. The Boca de Teacapán, an inlet from the sea opening into lagoons and the mangrove swamps, is the border between Sinaloa and Nayarit. The area has palm trees, much bird and animal life, cattle ranches, and is an exporter of shrimp and mangoes. The fishing is excellent. There are fine beaches such as Las Cabras, La Tambora and Los Angeles. Buses from Escuinapa; tours from Mazatlán US$45 (eg Marlin Tours, T 135301/142690, F 164616); **B Rancho Los Angeles**, Teacapán Ecológico (Las Palmas 1-B, Col Los Pinos, Mazatlán, T/F 81-78-67), former home of a drug baron (deceased), 16 km S from Teacapán towards Escuinapa, on beach, good value, swimming pool; **D Hotel Denisse**, on square, José Morales and Carol Snobel, clean, next to phone office, good, local trips arranged; 3 trailer parks (**Oregon**, US$8, on beach in town, new Mexican hotel next door; **Las Lupitas**, US$8, rustic; another on bay, take road next to **Las Lupitas**, US$3, primitive, pretty setting). **SR Wayne's Restaurant**, on beach behind *Palmeras Hotel*, rec. Quaint little towns just off the highway between Mazatlán and Tepic: **Acaponeta** (turnoff for Novillera beach), Rosamorada, Tuxpan and Santiago Ixcuintla, all with colonial religious buildings and archaeological museums. From Highway 15, the island of **Mexcaltitán** can be reached. Turn off to Sentispac, from where a dirt road leads to La Batanga on Laguna Mexcaltitán. Boats go to the small island, which is only about 350 metres in diameter, now a fishing village, but reputed to be one of the stopping places on the Aztecs' search for a home. The name means 'place of the temple of the moon". Its *fiesta*, St Peter and St Paul, is on 28-29 June.

The resort of **San Blas** is 69 km from Tepic and is overcrowded during US and Mexican summer holidays. It has an old Spanish fortress and a smelly harbour. In August it becomes very hot and there are many mosquitoes, but not on the beach 2 km from the village (but there are other biting insects, so take repellent anyway); few tourists at this time or early in the week. The best beach is Playa de las Islas (the one in town is dirty). 7 km from San Blas (bus, taxi US$3 per car) is the beach of Matanchén, good swimming but many mosquitoes. 16 km S from San Blas is the beautiful Los Cocos beach (see over). **NB** Don't wander too far from public beach; tourists have warned against attacks and robberies.

Hotels   A+ Marino Inn, Bataillon, T 50340, a/c, friendly, pool, fair food; **A+ Las Brisas**,

Cuauhtémoc Sur 106, T 50112, very clean, highly rec, excellent restaurant; **B** *Bucanero*, Juárez Poniente 75, T 50101, with bath and fan, frequented by Americans, food good, pool, lizards abound, noisy discos 3 times a week and bar is open till 0100 with loud music; **B** *Posada del Rey*, very clean, swimming pool, excellent value, on Campeche, T 50123; *Posada de Morales* also has a swimming pool, more expensive, 1/2 block from *Posada del Rey*, T 50023; **C** *San Blas Motel*, near Zócalo, patio, fans, good value, swimming pool, safe parking; **D** *Flamingos*, Juárez Poniente 105, huge rooms, ceiling fans, colonial, clean, friendly; **D** *Posada Azul*, 4 blocks from plaza towards beach, 3-bedded room with fan and hot water, F for simple 2-bedded room without bath, cooking facilities; **D/E** *El Tesoro de San Blas*, 50m S of dock, 5 mins from centre, rooms and villas, hot water, satellite TV, US owners; **E** *María's*, fairly clean with cooking, washing and fridge facilities, without bath, D with bath and fan, friendly, rec. No camping or sleeping permitted on beaches but several pay campsites available. Sometimes free camping possible behind **E** *Playa Hermosa Hotel*, old house, only partly occupied, rooms in use clean, 2 km from town. Trailer park at town beach; all trailer parks in the centre are plagued by mosquitoes.

The best trailer park is on Los Cocos beach: *Playa Amor*, good beach, on a narrow strip of land between road to Santa Cruz and cliff, good, popular, 16 km S of town, US$7-10. Next S is **E** *Hotel Delfín*, with toilet, balcony, shared bath, good view, good value; then *Raffles Restaurant* with trailer and camping area attached (no facilities). Last on Los Cocos beach is *Hotel y Restaurante Casa Mañana*, T (324) 80610 or Tepic T/F (321) 33565, Austrian run, good food. Many apartments for rent.

Restaurants *La Familia*, try the *merequetengue dishes*, rec; *Amparo*, on main square, cheap and good; *MacDonald* just off Zócalo, good breakfast. Plenty of seafood restaurants on the beach; eg *Las Olas*, good and cheap.

Bank Banamex just off Zócalo, exchange 0830-1000 only. **Comercial de San Blas** on the main square will change money, plus commission.

Doctor Dr Alejandro Váldez, Juárez 102, T 50331, speaks some English, rec.

Bus To Tepic, frequent US$2.20, 1½ hrs. To Guadalajara, US$10, 8½ hrs.

It is possible to take a 3-hr jungle trip in a boat (bus to launching point, US$1.50) to *La Tovara*, a small resort with fresh-water swimming hole and not much else, or walking, to do. Tour buses leave from the bridge 1 km out of town and cost US$30 for canoe with six passengers. Official prices are posted but it still seems possible to shop around. There are coatis, raccoons, iguanas, turtles, boat-billed herons, egrets and parrots. Twilight tours enable naturalists to see pottos and, if very lucky, an ocelot. La Tovara is crowded at midday during the summer. A cheaper 1½-2 hr cruise is also possible. When arranging your trip make sure you are told the length of journey and route in advance. You can take a bus from San Blas towards Santa Cruz (see below under Tepic) and get off at Matanchén beach (see above). From here, a boat for ½-day hire includes the best part of the jungle cruise from San Blas.

Before reaching Tepic both road and railway begin the long climb from the lowland level over the Sierra Madre to the basin of Jalisco, 1,500 metres above sea-level. The Mirador El Aguila is on Highway 15, 11 km after the junction to San Blas; it overlooks a canyon where many birds can be seen in the morning and the late afternoon.

(Km 807) *Tepic*, capital of Nayarit state, altitude 900 metres, population 200,000 (state population 1990, 816,100), founded in 1531 at the foot of the extinct volcano of Sangagüey. It is a slightly scruffy town with much rebuilding going on and much pollution. There are many little squares, all filled with trees and flowers, but littered and dusty. The **Cathedral** (1891), with two fine Gothic towers, in Plaza Principal, has been restored; it is painted primrose yellow, adorned with gold. Worth seeing are the **Palacio Municipal**; the **Casa de Amado Nervo** (the poet and diplomat), Zacatecas 281; the **Museo Regional de Antropología e Historia**, Av México 91 Norte (open 1000-1400 and 1700-2000 hrs, closed Mon); **Plaza de los Constituyentes** (México y Juárez) with, on one side, the **Palacio de Gobierno**; and the **Convento de la Cruz**, on the summit of a hill close to the centre. The tombs in the cemetery are worth seeing.

The landscape around Tepic is wild and mountainous; access is very difficult. Here live the Huichol and Cora Indians. Their dress is very picturesque; their craftwork—bags (carried only by men), scarves woven in colourful designs and necklaces (*chaquira*) of tiny beads and wall-hangings of brightly coloured wool—is available from souvenir shops (these handicrafts are reported to be cheaper in Guadalajara, at the Casa de Artesanías). You may see some in Tepic but it is best to let Indians approach you when they come to town if you want to purchase any items.

Hotels **C** *Fray Junipero Serra*, Lerdo Poniente 23, T 22525, main square, a/c, good restaurant, friendly, good service; **C** *Ibarra*, Durango 297 A Norte, T 23870, luxurious rooms, with bath and fan (some rooms noisy), and slightly spartan, cheaper rooms without bath, very clean, DHL collection point. **C** *San Jorge*, Lerdo 124, T 21324, very comfortable, good value; **C** *Villa de las Rosas*, Insurgentes 100, T 31800, fans, friendly, noisy in front, good food, but not too clean; **D** *Altamirano*, Mina 19 Oriente, T 27131, near Palacio del Gobierno, noisy but good value; **D** *Santa Fe*, Calzada de la Cruz 85, near La Loma park, a few minutes from centre, with TV, clean, comfortable, good restaurant; **D** *Sierra de Alicia*, Av México 180 Norte, with fan, tiled stairways, friendly; **E** *Camarena*, 4 blocks from Zócalo on San Luis Norte, without bath; **E** *Juárez*, near Palacio de Gobierno, on Juárez 116, T 22112, clean room with bath, locks on room doors not very effective, limited parking in courtyard; **E** *México*, México 116 Nte, T 22354. **E** *Nayarit*, E Zapata 190 Pte, T 22183; **E** *Pensión Maty*, 3 blocks off Zócalo, hot water, clean, friendly, good value; **E** *Pensión Morales*, Insurgentes y Sánchez, 4 blocks from bus station, clean and friendly. **E** *Sarita*, Bravo 112 Poniente, T 21333, clean, good. **E** *Tepic*, Dr Martínez 438, T 31377, near bus station outside town, with bath, clean, friendly but noisy.

Motels **B** *La Loma*, Paseo la Loma 301 (swimming pool), T 32222, run down; *Bungalows and Trailer Park Koala*, La Laguna, Santa María del Oro, has bungalows at US$20, each accommodating up to 4, several trailer sites and a large campground. Fishing and waterskiing on nearby lagoon.

Restaurants *El Apacho*, opp *Hotel Ibarra*, good *sopes*, cheap; *El Tripol*, in mall, near plaza, excellent vegetarian; *Danny O* ice cream shop next door. *Tiki Room*, San Luis Norte opposite *Hotel Camarena*, restaurant, art gallery, video bar, fun. Restaurant in bus terminal, overpriced. Lots of fish stalls by market on Puebla Norte. The local *huevos rancheros* are extremely picante.

Exchange *Casas de cambio* at México 91 and 140 Norte, Mon-Sat 0900-1400, 1600-2000.

Telephones Credit card phone at Veracruz Norte y Zapata Poniente.

Tourist Office México 30 Norte, T 29546.

Travel Agencies *Viajes Regina*, tours to San Blas, 8 hrs, US$22.50; Playas de Ensueño, Fri, 8 hrs, US$15.50; Tepic city tour, Mon and Sat, 3 hrs, US$7. *Tovara*, Ignacio Allende 30.

Transport Bus station is a fairly short walk into town; bus from centre to terminal from Puebla Norte by market. At bus station there are phones, including credit card, post office, left luggage and tourist information (not always open). **Bus** to San Blas from Central Camionera: US$2.20, 0600-1600, frequent. To Guadalajara, US$7.50, frequent departures, several companies; Mazatlán, 4½ hrs, US$9.50; to Puerto Vallarta, US$6; Mexico City, US$30.25. **Train** to Guadalajara, 2nd class leaves at 1025, arrives at 1755, sit on left-hand side for best views. Train to Mexicali, 28 hrs on Tren del Pacífico, departs 1335, to Nogales, 21 hrs (same train to Benjamín Hill, where it divides); 2nd class train at 1645 to Mexicali and Nogales via B Hill. **Airport**.

Excursions One can visit Huichol villages only by air, as there are no real roads, takes at least two days. About 50 km from Tepic is an attractive lagoon, take the bus to Santa María del Oro. To various beaches along the coast, some of them off the Nogales highway, eg, **Santa Cruz**, about 37 km from Tepic (rocky beach). 2½ hrs ride by open-sided lorry, US$0.75, difficult to leave the town again, check for transport. No hotels, but accommodation at **Peter's Shop**, E, basic but pleasant and friendly. Simple food available, *Restaurant Belmar*, fish and rice, all reminiscent of the South Seas. (2 buses a day from San Blas to Santa Cruz, US$1.10.) A road runs S from Tepic through **Compostela**, a pleasant small town with an old church, El Señor de la Misericordia, built 1539 (36 km, 1½ hrs by bus from local bus station at Tepic to the coast). From Compostela one can catch an old bus to **Zacualpan**, 1½ hrs over a paved road, to visit a small enclosed park with sculptures that have been found in the area, two blocks from main square. Gate to the park must be unlocked by caretaker: inside there is a small museum. Zacualpan is a pleasant village, knock on a door to ask for the caretaker.

A road from Compostela reaches the coast at **Las Varas** (**E** *Hotel Contreras*, with fan and bath, clean, small rooms). Las Varas is connected also by good road to San Blas, N up the coast. Beaches on the coast road S to Puerto Vallarta include Chacala, lined with coconut palms and reached by an unsurfaced road through jungle; **Rincón de los Guayabitos**, which is being developed as a tourist resort with hotels, holiday village and trailer park (**C** *Coca*, among several hotels and restaurants on a rocky peninsula to the S of the beach); Los Ayala, Lo de Marcos, San Francisco (**Costa Azul Resort**, on beach, delightful, pool, apartments, restaurant), Sayulita (**Trailer Park** highly rec, US$10/day, also has bungalows, Apartado 5-585, CP 06500, Mexico DF, T Mexico City 572-1335, F 390-2750, also bungalows, turn off Route 200 at Km 123, 2½ km), **Punta de Mita**, a fishing village at the tip of a peninsula (nearby **A** *Hotel and Trailer Park Piedras Blancas*, good, also camping, US$10, hook-ups US$12-14, restaurants; excellent restaurant at Playa Desileteros not cheap but delicious food, bus from Puerto Vallarta), Cruz de Huanacaxtle, **Bucerías** (*Hotel Playa de Bucerías*, Km 154, and **B** *Marlyn*), **Peñita de Jaltemba** (**C** bungalows at N end of town, with clean rooms and kitchen; **C-D** *Hotel Mar Azul*) and others.

The road S from Tepic, through Compostela, enters Jalisco state just before **Puerto Vallarta** (population 100,000). The town is divided by the Río Cuale and on one side are the expensive hotels, many shops, the airport and the port. On the other side of the river are the bus terminal and some cheaper hotels. Latest reports indicate that every house in the old town has been turned into a tourist trap, speculation is rampant with hotels and timeshare apartments and taxi drivers are rapacious. It offers aquatic sports, particularly fishing and hunting for sharks. From the public beach you can hire parachuting equipment to be pulled by motor-boat (US$20). The Malecón is the waterfront drive. All the beaches at Puerto Vallarta are clean and there are others 8-10 km S along the coast, eg Mismaloya (crowded, reached by bus 02, US$0.50). Conchas Chinas is probably the best beach close to town, being quiet and clean (at any holiday time, though, every beach is packed); a cobblestone road leads to Conchas Chinas from Route 200 just after *Club Alexandra*. Playa de los Muertos, S of the Río Cuale, is aptly named; dangerous from underwater rocks, undertow and sewage.

Hotels   Puerto Vallarta is divided naturally into 3 sections: N of town are: **L** *Bugambilias Sheraton*, T 30404, F 20500; **L** *Fiesta Americana*, T 22010; **A-L** *Puerto Vallarta Holiday Inn*, Km 3.5 on Carretera Aeropuerto T 21700, F 25683. **A+** *Las Palmas* (Best Western), T 40650, F 40543, Blvd Medina Ascencio Km 2.5, on beach, pool, all rooms with sea view, restaurant; **A+** *Playa de Oro*, T 20348; **A+** *Plaza Vallarta*, T 24448. In town are: **A+** *Buenaventura*, México 1301, T 23742; **A** *Cuatro Vientos*, Matamoros 520, T 20161, lots of stairs; **E/F** *Central*, off main square, shared bath, basic; **D** *Paraíso*, Paseo Díaz Ordaz, on the sea but stony beach. S of Río Cuale are: **L** *Camino Real*, T 20002; *Hyatt Coral Grand*, Km 8.5 Carretera a Barra de Navidad, PO Box 448 Puerto Vallarta, T 25191, F 23496, deluxe hotel on Bahía Banderas; **A+** *Garza Blanca*, Playa Palo María, T 21023; **A+** *Molino del Agua*, Vallarta 130, T 21907, beautiful, beside the new bridge, clean, a/c, good service, pool, rec; **A+** *Oro Verde*, Gómez 111, T 215553, a/c, Swiss run, private beach, pool, rec as clean, pleasant, friendly (B out of season); **A+** *Playa los Arcos*, Olas Altas 380, T 2-3102, on beach near bus station, highly rec; **A** *Playa Conchas Chinas*, Km 2.5 on Route 200 going S towards Barra de Navidad, about 1 km before *Camino Real* on W side of road, spacious, clean rooms with kitchenettes and ocean views, connected with *El Set* restaurant which runs a *palapa* beach restaurant for breakfast and lunch; **B** *Fontana del Mar*, Diéguez 171, attractive; **B** *Posada Río Cuale*, Serdán 242, swimming pool, excellent food, a/c, highly rec; **D** *Hortensia*, Madera 336, T 22484, in old town, clean, warm water, a bit noisy, about 2 blocks from bus terminal; **D** *Posada de Roger*, Badillo 237, T 20039, fan, pool, good value, near two main city beaches, beware of thieves, popular with students; **D** *Mayo*, Badillo 300, esq Constitución, T 23403, private bath, some suites with kitchen, clean, safe parking, friendly.

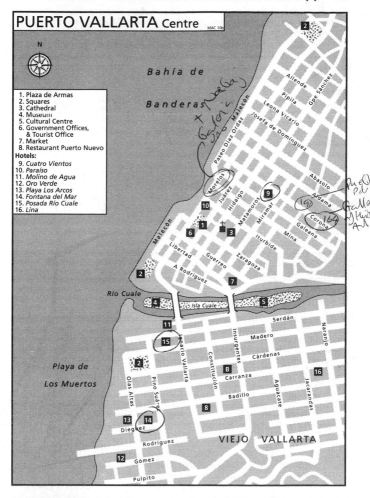

PUERTO VALLARTA Centre MAC 10b

1. Plaza de Armas
2. Squares
3. Cathedral
4. Museum
5. Cultural Centre
6. Government Offices,
   & Tourist Office
7. Market
8. Restaurant Puerto Nuevo

Hotels:
9. *Cuatro Vientos*
10. *Paraíso*
11. *Molino de Agua*
12. *Oro Verde*
13. *Playa Los Arcos*
14. *Fontana del Mar*
15. *Posada Río Cuale*
16. *Lina*

Several *casas de huéspedes* in town near bus companies' offices, eg **E** *Lina*, very nice, but rooms on street are noisy, clean. Apartments: *La Peña*, Rodríguez 174, US$30 in high season.

Camping 2 trailer parks: *Tacho*, on road to Pipala, opp Marina, 60 spaces but spacious (treat the police at the traffic lights/turn off to the trailer park with caution and respect); *Puerto Vallarta*, N of centre, just N of bypass then E 2 blocks, popular. Also at fishing village of Yelapa, best reached by boat from *Hotel Rosita* at 1130: camp under shelters (*palapas*), about US$4 each.

Restaurants *Ostión Feliz*, Libertad 177, excellent seafood. *El Dorado*, on Los Muertos beach in town, rec as best on the beach; *Santos*, 2 blocks N of *El Dorado*, between Calle Olas Altas and Los Muertos beach, rec *Gilmar*, a cheap, typical restaurant; *Tequila*, upstairs for good breakfast and a good view of what is going on; *Sr Panchos*, Cárdenas near Ignacio Vallarta, mostly seafood, good, inexpensive, free *margaritas* inc with dinner; *Los Arbolitos*,

Camino de la Rivera 184 (at end of C Lázaro Cárdenas by the river), Mexican and seafood, not too expensive, rec; *Puerto Nuevo*, S of the Río Cuale, on Badillo, expensive but good food. Good *tacos* are sold between *Hotel Playa Los Arcos* and *Oro Verde* on Olas Altas. Very good ice-cream and frozen yoghurt is sold along the Malecón and at *Bing's* near central plaza. Puerto Vallarta has an active night life, with many bars and discotheques.

Chico's Paradise, 8 km up a steep hill from Mismaloya, is a restaurant with cascades forming fresh-water pools where one can swim, jungle tours and horse riding arranged.

Shopping   Plaza Malecón, near *Hotel Río*, end of Malecón, has 28 curio shops, restaurant, music, etc.

Doctor   Dra Irma Gittelson, Juárez 479, speaks French and English, very helpful.

Consulate   Canada, Servitours, Av Hidalgo 217, T (322) 25398, F 23517. Emergency, 915-724-7900.

Immigration   Morelos 600, T 21478.

Tourist Office   Morelos 28-A; in the government building on the main square, very helpful.

Buses   By Sonora del Norte, Estrella Blanca and Autobuses del Pacífico, to **Mexico City**, 15-20 hrs, US$38.50, ETN US$66. Puerto Vallarta to **Guadalajara**, US$15.50 1st class, 6 hrs; to **Manzanillo**, US$12, midnight, Transportes Cihuatlan, Constitución y Francisco I Madero.

Air Travel   International airport 7 km from centre. Mexicana to Chicago, Denver, Los Angeles (see AeroMéxico, Air Alaska, Delta), San Francisco (also Air Alaska); American to Dallas and Nashville; Continental to Houston; Air Alaska to Seattle; AeroMéxico to San Diego. Mexican destinations served include Mexico City, Guadalajara, Acapulco, Aguascalientes, León, Los Cabos, Mazatlán, Querétaro, San Luis, Potosí and Tepic.

Warning   Those confined to wheelchairs are warned that Puerto Vallarta is a bad place, with its high kerbs and cobblestone streets.

Excursions   To *Yelapa*, Indian village with waterfall, now commercialized; by boat at least US$10, or more cheaply from the Malecón at 1130 by the local boat. Stay with Mateo and Elenita, US$25 inc breakfast, visit their waterfall.

S of Puerto Vallarta paved Route 200 continues down the coast to Melaque, Barra de Navidad and Manzanillo. Beaches and hotels on this route: at **Chamela**, Perula village at N end of Chamela beach; **C** *Hotel Punta Perula*, T (333) 70190, on beach, Mexican style; *Villa Polonesia Trailer Park*, US$12 for car and two people, rec, full hook-ups, hot showers, on lovely beach (follow signs from Route 200 on unmade road); restaurant on road to trailer park, clean, good food. Pemex at Chamela is closed, no other for miles. The excellent **A+** *Hotel Careyes* is en route, and several others, **A** *El Tecuán*, Carretera 200, Km 33.5, T (333) 70132, (lovely hotel, gorgeous beach, bar/restaurant, pool), and, 8 km further S, **A** *Hotel Tenacatita* near the village of the same name (**see p 152**), and further to Zihuatanejo and Acapulco, and finally to Salina Cruz. The road from 40 km S of Chamela to Melaque is very poor.

Route 15 leaves Tepic for Guadalajara. At Chapalilla is a turn-off to Compostela and Puerto Vallarta. At **Ahuacatlán**, 75 km from Tepic, the 17th-century ex-convent of San Juan Evangelista stands on the Plaza Principal; handicrafts on sale here. Nearby, the village of *Jala* has a festival mid-August. **E** *Hotel Cambero*, From here the **Ceboruco** volcano can be reached in a day. On the main road a lava flow from Ceboruco is visible (*El Ceboruco*, *parador turístico*, with restaurant, information, toilets and shop; buses do not stop here). 84 km (1¼ hrs by bus) from Tepic is **Ixtlán del Río** (**D** *Hotel Colonial*, Hidalgo 45 Pte, very friendly, rec; *Motel Colón*; cheaper hotels round the Zócalo are *Roma* and *Turista*). Two km out of town along this road are the ruins of *Los Toriles*, a Toltec ceremonial centre. The main structure is the Temple of Quetzalcoatl, noted for its cruciform windows and circular shape. The ruins have been largely restored, admission US$2.35, some explanatory notes posted around the site. The journey from Tepic to Guadalajara cannot easily be broken at Ixtlan for sightseeing since buses passing through in either direction tend to be full; bus on to Guadalajara

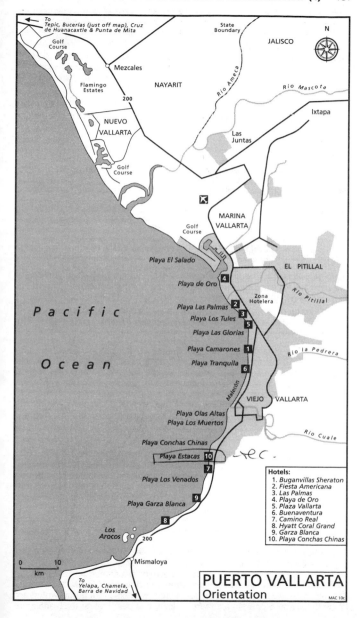

To
Tepic, Bucerías (just off map), Cruz
de Huanacaxtle & Punta de Mita

N

Golf
Course

State
Boundary

JALISCO

Mezcales

Rio Ameca

NAYARIT

Rio Mascota

Flamingo
Estates

200

NUEVO
VALLARTA

Ixtapa

Golf
Course

Las
Juntas

Golf
Course

MARINA
VALLARTA

Playa El Salado

EL PITILLAL

Playa de Oro

4

2

Playa Las Palmas

Zona
Hotelera

3

Rio Pitillal

Playa Los Tules

5

Playa Las Glorias

P a c i f i c

Playa Camarones

1

Rio la Pedrera

O c e a n

Playa Tranquila

6

Malecón

VIEJO VALLARTA

Playa Olas Altas
Playa Los Muertos

Rio Cuale

Playa Conchas Chinas

Playa Estacas

10

7

Playa Los Venados

Hotels:
1. *Buganvillas Sheraton*
2. *Fiesta Americana*
3. *Las Palmas*
4. *Playa de Oro*
5. *Plaza Vallarta*
6. *Buenaventura*
7. *Camino Real*
8. *Hyatt Coral Grand*
9. *Garza Blanca*
10. *Playa Conchas Chinas*

Playa Garza Blanca

9

8

Los
Arcos

200

0   10
km

Mismaloya

To
Yelapa, Chamela,
Barra de Navidad

PUERTO VALLARTA
Orientation

MAC 10c

3 hrs, US$4.25. There are a few souvenir shops, a Museo Arqueológico in the Palacio Municipal, a *casa de cambio* and a railway station. Harvest (maize) festival mid-September. 2 km beyond the Los Toriles site is *Motel Hacienda*, with pool. The road climbs out of the valley through uncultivated land, trees intermixed with prickly pear and chaparral cactus. Jalisco state is entered (see below) and 19 km before Tequila is Magdalena (hotel, *Restaurant Magdalena*), congested with traffic, small lake nearby. As the bus approaches Tequila there may be opportunities to buy the drink of the same name on board. The maguey cactus, from which it is distilled, can be seen growing in the pleasant, hilly countryside.

Tequila (58 km from Guadalajara road, being upgraded), is the main place where the famous Mexican drink is distilled. Tours of Cuerva (free) and Sauza (small tip) distilleries off the highway. The Sauza distillery has a famous fresco illustrating the joys of drinking tequila. Stores in town sell 4 litre wooden barrels filled with tequila, and carved with the customer's name or chosen message, for under US$15. (**D** *Motel Delicias*, on highway, good for the price; *Mario's Restaurant*, friendly.) Half-way between Tequila and Guadalajara, in the mountains, is the British-run *Rancho Río Caliente*, 8 km from the highway, a vegetarian thermal resort.

NB There is a time change between Nayarit and Jalisco; the latter is 6 hrs behind GMT, the former, as with all the Pacific coast N of Jalisco, 7 hrs behind.

GUADALAJARA TO MEXICO CITY (5)

From the second city, Guadalajara, with its fine historical centre, to the capital, an area rich in crafts and traditions, especially the music and dance of Jalisco and Michoacán. There are lakes to visit (Chapala and Pátzcuaro), volcanoes (Colima, Paricutín, Toluca), the colonial city of Morelia, and worthwhile detours to the Pacific coast and to the towns S of Toluca.

The cultural life of Jalisco state has been helped by an economy based on crafts, agriculture, and livestock, with fewer pockets of abject poverty than elsewhere in Mexico. Many villages have traditional skills such as pottery, blown glass, shoemaking, and a curious and beautiful form of filigree weaving in which miniature flower baskets, fruit and religious images are shaped from *chilte* (chicle, the raw substance from which chewing-gum is made). The state is the original home of Mexico's *mariachis*: roving musical groups dressed in the gala suits and *sombreros* of early 19th century rural gentry.

Guadalajara, Mexico's second city and capital of Jalisco state; altitude 1,650 metres, and slightly warmer than at the capital; population, 1,629,000 in 1980, but now reported as up to 4 million in the metropolitan area (state population 1990, 5,279,000), 573 km from Mexico City; founded in 1530. It used to be a fine, clean city, not unlike the towns of southern Spain, but pollution has now grown. Graceful colonial arcades, or *portales*, flank scores of old plazas and shaded parks. During the past twenty five years the city has developed to the W of Av Chapultepec, where the best shops and residential neighbourhoods are now located. The climate is mild, dry and clear all through the year, although it can be thundery at night.

The heart of the city is the Plaza de Armas. On its N side is the **Cathedral**, begun in 1561, finished in 1618, in rather a medley of styles; its two spires are covered in blue and yellow tiles. There is a reputed Murillo Virgin inside (painted 1650), and the famous La Virgen del Carmen, painted by Miguel de Cabrera, a Zapotec Indian from Oaxaca. In the dome are frescoes of the 4 gospel writers and in the Capilla del Santísimo are more frescoes and paintings of the Last Supper.

From outside you can see the sunset's rays streaming through the dome's stained glass. The Cathedral's W façade is on Plaza de los Laureles, on the N side of which is the **Palacio Municipal** (1952), which contains murals by Gabriel Flores of the founding of the city.

Also on the Plaza de Armas is the **Palacio de Gobierno** (1643) where in 1810 Hidalgo issued his first proclamation abolishing slavery (plaque). **José Clemente Orozco's** great murals can be seen on the central staircase; they depict social struggle, dominated by Hidalgo, with the church on the left, fascism on the right and the suffering peasants in the middle. More of Orozco's work can be seen in the **Congreso** (showing Reforma and Libertad) and in the main **University of Guadalajara** building, on Avs Juárez y Tolsá (re-named Enrique Díaz de León), in the dome of which is portrayed man asleep, man meditating, and man creating: lie on your back or look in a mirror. Other works by this artist can be seen at the University's main Library, at Glorieta Normal, and at the massive Cabañas Orphanage near the Mercado de la Libertad, now known as **Instituto Cultural Cabañas**. The Orphanage is a beautiful building with 22 patios, which is floodlit at night (open Tues-Sat 1015-1800, Sun 1015-1500, entry US$4.35, US$15 to take photos). The contents of the former Orozco museum in Mexico City have been transferred here, including 'Man of Fire". Also in the Instituto Cabañas, exhibitions of Mexican art are shown and other events are held, listed under **Entertainments** below.

Going E from the Cathedral is the Plaza de la Liberación, with a statue of Hidalgo, where the national flag is raised and lowered daily (with much ceremony). On the N side are the **Museo Regional** (see **Museums** below) and the **Palacio Legislativo** (neo-classical, remodelled in 1982, open to the public 0900 to 1800); it has a list of the names of all the Constituyentes, from Hidalgo to Otero (1824-57 and 1917). At the eastern end of this plaza is the enormous and fantastically decorated **Teatro Degollado** (1866, no entry except for shows, or cultural events, see **Entertainments** below).

A pedestrian mall, **Plaza Tapatía**, has been installed between the Teatro Degollado and the Instituto Cultural Cabañas, crossing the Calzada Independencia, covering 16 square blocks. It has beautiful plants, fountains, statuary, a tourist office, and is designed in colonial style. Facing Cabañas, on Morelos, is a sculpture by Rafael Zamarripa of Jalisco's symbol: 2 lions (in bronze) supporting a tree. The **Mercado Libertad** (San Juan de Dios—see **Shopping**), is S of Plaza Tapatía and between the market and Cabañas is a park, with a fine modern sculpture 'The Stampede", by Jorge de la Peña (1982).

The best churches are **Santa Mónica** (1718), Santa Mónica y Reforma, small, but very elaborate with impressive arches full of gold under a clear atrium and a richly carved façade; **La Merced**, Hidalgo y Pedro Loza, beautiful interior; **El Carmen**, Av Juárez 638, with a main altar surrounded by gilded Corinthian columns; **San José**, Alcalde y Reforma, a 19th century church with a fine gilded rococo pulpit, 8 pillars in a semicircle around the altar, painted deep red and ochre behind, give an unusual effect, the overall light blue gives an airy feel; in the plaza outside is a statue of Núñez, defender of the Reforma, who was killed in 1858; **San Miguel de Belén**, Hospital 290, enclosed in the Hospital Civil which contains three fine late 18th century *retablos*; **San Agustín**, Morelos y Degollado (16th century), quite plain, with carved stones, musical school next door; and **San Francisco** (1550) with a 3-tiered altar with columns, a feature repeated on the façade. To the N of this last church is the **Jardín San Francisco** (pleasantly shaded, starting point for horse-drawn carriages, small market), and to the W the old church of **Nuestra Señora de Aránzazu**, with three fantastic churrigueresque altarpieces; equally impressive are the coloured ceilings and the finely carved dado, the only light comes from high-up windows and from the open E door. In the shadow of San Francisco is a modern statue to teachers. **María de Gracia**,

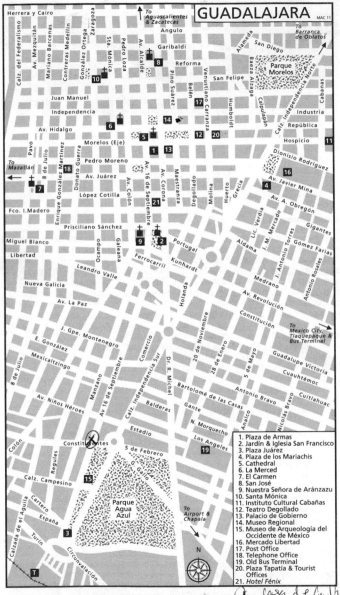

GUADALAJARA MAC 11

1. Plaza de Armas
2. Jardín & Iglesia San Francisco
3. Plaza Juárez
4. Plaza de los Mariachis
5. Cathedral
6. La Merced
7. El Carmen
8. San José
9. Nuestra Señora de Aránzazu
10. Santa Mónica
11. Instituto Cultural Cabañas
12. Teatro Degollado
13. Palacio de Gobierno
14. Museo Regional
15. Museo de Arqueología del Occidente de México
16. Mercado Libertad
17. Post Office
18. Telephone Office
19. Old Bus Terminal
20. Plaza Tapatía & Tourist Offices
21. Hotel Fénix

V Carranza y Hidalgo, is beautiful.

Other sights worth seeing are the **Parque Alcalde**, Jesús García y Av de los Maestros, to the N of the centre; the **Plaza de Los Mariachis**, Obregón and Leonardo Vicario, near Mercado Libertad; and the **Templo Expiatorio**, Av Enrique Díaz de León y Madero, with fine stained glass and intricate ceiling, gothic style, still unfinished after most of a century. On Calzada Independencia Sur, at the intersection of Constituyentes and González Gallo is **Parque Agua Azul** (open 0800-1900, US$0.20). A park with trees, flowers and fountains, it contains the **Auditorio González Cano**, an outdoor concert bowl with portraits of famous Jalisco musicians, the **Teatro Experimental** and the **Casa de las Artesanías de Jalisco** (see **Crafts** below). On the other side of Calzada Independencia Sur is **Plaza Juárez** with an impressive monument ringed by the flags of other Latin American countries (take bus 216 back to centre). There is a new, large park, zoological garden with plenty of animals in a delightful atmosphere (entry US$1) and planetarium just past the bullring going out on Calzada Independencia Norte.

There are 3 universities (visit architectural faculty near Parque Mirador, 20 mins by car from centre, or take bus 45, overlooking Barranca de Oblatos, a huge canyon).

Festivals 21 March commemorates Benito Juárez' birthday and everything is closed for the day. Ceremonies around his monument at the Agua Azul park. In June the virgin of Zapopán (see **Excursions** below), leaves her home to spend each night in a different church where fireworks are let off. The virgin has a new car each year but the engine is not started, men pull it through the streets with ropes, the streets are decorated. The climax is 12 October when the virgin leaves the Cathedral for home, there are great crowds along the route. At the end of October there is a great *fiesta* with concerts, bullfights, sports and exhibitions of handicrafts from all over Mexico. 28 October-20 December, *fiesta* in honour of the Virgin of Guadalupe; Av Alcalde has stalls, music, fair etc. In December there is one at Parque Morelos and hand-made toys are a special feature.

Hotels Many in our price ranges A and up, including: L *Camino Real*, Vallarta 5005, T 647-8000, some way from the centre; L *Fiesta Americana*, López Mateos at Minerva circle, T 625-3434, rooms not as grand as the price might suggest, but excellent views from upper floors, and impressive towering hallway; L *Quinta Real*, Av México y López Mateos, T 652-0000, small, good, large, well-furnished rooms, but slow restaurant; A+-L *Holiday Inn*, Av López Mateos 2500 Sur, opp Plaza del Sol, shopping centre, T 634-0650, F 631-9393, restaurant, night club, etc, and also opp Plaza del Sol, is L *Hyatt Regency*, Lopez Mateos Sur and Av Moctezuma, some deluxe suites with private patio, US$600 a night, high rise tower with built-in shopping centre, cavernous lobby, indoor ice-skating rink, open to the public. A+ *Calinda Roma*, Juárez 170, T 614-8650, F 614-2629; A+ *El Tapatío*, Bld Aeropuerto 3275, T 654-6050 in Tlaquepaque, nearest hotel to airport, fine view of city, extensive grounds, very attractive and comfortable rooms; A+ *Aranzazú*, Av Revolución 110 Pte, T 613-3232, F 614-5045, central, very good; A *Fénix* (Best Western), Av Corona 160, jus off López Cotilla, T 614-5714, F 613-4005, high rise block, roof garden with drinks, good restaurant; A *Francés*, Maestranza 35, T 613-1190, colonial building with central patio, oldest hotel in the city, built in 1610, have a drink there at 'happy hour' 1800-1900, to enjoy the bygone atmosphere, some rooms small but very good value penthouse suite for 4, with living room and kitchen, C pp (US$110 total), expensive parking underneath adjoining Plaza de la Liberación, US$20 for 24 hrs; A *Mendoza*, Venustiano Carranza 16, just off Plaza Tapatía, pleasant, small rooms but pretty colonial-style lobby and restaurant, rec; **B** *del Parque*, Av Juárez 845, T 625-4281, clean, friendly, courteous, problems with hot water in pm; B *Génova*, Juárez 123, T 613-7500, clean, good service, good restaurant, rec; B *Internacional*, Pedro Moreno 570, T 613-0330, clean, comfortable, safe, rec; B *Nueva Galicia*, Av Corona 610, T 614-8780, older style; B *San Francisco Plaza*, Degollado 267, T 613-8954/8971, hot water, TV, pleasant; B-C *Sevilla*, Prisciliano Sánchez 413, T 614-9037, good, clean (4 blocks S of cathedral), owner speaks English, good restaurant (not always open). B *Universo*, López Cotilla 163, T 613-2815, somewhat run down.

C *El Parador* at new bus terminal, T 659-0142 (does not take Amex), spartan rooms with TV, expensive laundry, pool, 24-hr café *El Jardín*; **D** *Estación*, Calzada Independencia Sur 1297, T 619-0051, across the main boulevard beside train station, quiet, clean, safe, luggage store, hot water, rec, station porters will carry luggage there US$0.50-1. D *Tres Estrellas*,

Calzada Independencia Sur 667, cheap, rooms on the street noisy, all rooms with bath, restaurant and garage (restaurant closed in January). There are cheap hotels along Calzada Independencia (very noisy), on 5 de Febrero and in the two blocks N of the old bus station, Calle 28 de Enero and Calle 20 de Noviembre (where there is a small market, good for breakfasts) and the side streets (although rooms can sometimes be filthy, so check); they include **E** *Canadá*, Estadio, ½ block from old bus station, in old block, C in new block, all rooms with bath, hot water, TV; **E** *Lincoln*, good, clean, helpful; **E** *Casa de Huespedes Norteña*, basic; on 5 de Febrero, **D** *San José* (No 116), *Emperador* (No 128) and *Monaco* (No 152); on 20 de Noviembre, *San Carlos* (No 728B), *Praga Central* (No 733A) and *Madrid* (No 775), all **D/E**, rec, but rooms on street are noisy.

Cheaper hotels in the centre, and near Mercado Libertad: several on Javier Mina, eg **D** *Ana Isabel*, Javier Mina 184, central, TV, clean, tiny rooms but very good value, tell them when you are checking out or room may be re-let before you have gone. **D** *Azteca*, 1½ blocks from Mercado Libertad, clean. **D** *Continental*, on Calle Corona, rec; **D** *González*, behind Mercado Corona, 4 blocks W of cathedral, González Ortega 77, good value, often full, very friendly, highly rec; **D** *Maya*, López Cotilla 39, T 614-4654, with private bath, blankets, pleasant atmosphere, rec; **D** *México 70*, Javier Mina, opp Mercado Libertad, with bath, clean, rec; **D** *Imperio*, next door, clean and popular, noisy; **D** *Morales*, on Calle Corona, rec, often fully booked; other hotels on Corona of similar quality but cheaper; **D** *Posada España*, López Cotillo 594 y 8 de Julio, with bath, nice courtyard, washing facilities, but not clean, extremely noisy, helpful manager; **D** *Posada San Pablo*, Madero 268, hot water, rec; **E** *Janeiro*, Obregón 93, by market, very clean, good value, rec; **F** *del Maestro*, Herrera y Cayro No 666, between Mariano Barcenas and Contreras Medallín, buses from Cathedral 52, 54, 231, from bus station 275), no sign, OK.

Motels A *Del Bosque*, L Mateos Sur 265, T 621-4020; **A** *Las Américas*, López Mateos Sur 2400, T 621-3857, opp Plaza del Sol shopping centre, a/c, pool, good; **A** *Posada del Sol*, López Mateos Sur 4205, T 621-0120/71. **B** *Isabel*, Montenegro 1572, sector Hidalgo, T 626-2630, pleasant, pool. There are additional ones at the end of Vallarta: Vallarta 3305, T 615-5725, A; and along López Mateos near the edge of town, before the *periférico* road.

For longer stays, a 2-bedroom, furnished apartment in a residential area costs about US$490/month; for condominium with pool, 2 bedrooms, etc, expect about US$590/month.

Youth Hostel At Prolongación Alcalde 1360, Sector Hidalgo, T 653-0044, away from centre, US$5, inc pillow and blanket, fairly clean, many mosquitoes. Bus from Cathedral 52, 54 or 231; from bus terminal No 275 (alight just after it leaves Av Alcalde to Av Camacho, then 5 mins walk). Also at Prolongación Federalismo y Lázaro Cárdenas, Unidad Deportiva, CP 44940.

Trailer Parks *La Hacienda*, 16 km out of town, off the road to Tepic, US$14, shaded, pool, clubhouse, hook-ups. Also *San José del Tajo*, 25 km from city on Route 15/80 towards Manzanillo, about 1 km from city boundary, full hook-up, hot showers, pool, laundry facilities, US$13.35 for vehicle and two people.

Restaurants *La Nueva Flor de Sahuayo*, E González Martínez 140, highly rec; *El Farol*, Pedro Moreno y Galeana, excellent dinner US$5; *Holiday Inn* does grills on Sun, 1300-1700. *Carnes Asadas Tolsa*, Enrique Díaz de León 510 and Chapultepec 189, rec. *Piaf*, Av Vallarta ⟩ nr Av Chapultepec, excellent, live music, friendly, closed Sun; *Bufalo*, Calderón de la Barca y ˙ Av Vallarta, tacos and cheap *comida corrida*, very friendly; *La Banderillas*, Av Alcalde 831, excellent food at reasonable prices.

Zanahoria, Av Las Américas 538, rec for excellent, but expensive vegetarian food; good vegetarian buffet at *La Pileca*, US$3, Colonias 279, San Javier, open 1000-1730; *Los Caias*, Tepeyac 1156, vegetarian coffee shop and cultural centre.

Madrid, Juárez y Corona, good breakfast, excellent coffee and fruit salad, very smoky (from cigarettes); *Café Makoka*, Martínez, just N of Hidalgo, excellent very early breakfasts. Many cheap restaurants in the streets near the old bus stations, esp in Calle de Los Angeles, and upstairs in the large Mercado Libertad (San Juan de Dios) in centre, but not very hygienic here. *La Trattoria*, Niños Héroes 3051, very good, reasonably priced Italian, very popular (queues form for lunch from 1400). Delicious *carne en su jugo* from *Carnes Asadas El Tapatía* in Libertad market, or *Carnes Asadas Rigo's* in Corona market, Zaragoza y Independencia, US$2-2.50 with a refresco. Goat is a speciality, roasted each day and served with radish, onion and chilli, US$3 per portion. For those so inclined, *Lido*, Colón y Miguel Blanco (Plaza San Francisco), serves *criadillas*, bull's testicles, at US$7 a plate; *Cortijo La Venta*, Federación 725, T 617-1675, open daily 1300-0100, invites customers to fight small bulls (calves) after their meal (the animals are not harmed, guests might be), restaurant serves meat, soups, salads. *El Asadero*, opp the basilica in Zapopán suburb (see **Excursions** below), is very good. *La Calle*, nr Galería de Calzado and bus terminal, expensive but good, with garden. Good *Conchería* at Morelos 99 y Gerardo Juárez, by Tourist Office. In the cloister of La Merced is a fast food place, popular with young people; *La Chata* and *Gemma*, 2 chains serving Mexican food, are usually quite good (*Gemma* does Guadalajaran 'lonches', *tortas ahogadas*). *La Pianola*, several locations, good, reasonable prices. Many bars serve snacks, *botanas*, with drinks between 1300 and 1500, free. Most of these bars are for men only, though. **NB** The bars in the centre are popular with the city's gay population, eg *Botanero el Ciervo*, 20 de Noviembre 797, corner of Calle Los Angeles, opp old bus station.

Shopping The best shops are all found in or near the Plaza Mayor (Plaza de los Tres Poderes) and the Avenida Juárez. The Plaza del Sol shopping centre, with over 100 shops, is located at Chapalita in the S of the city, while the equally modern Plaza Patria, with as many shops, is at the N end near the Zapopán suburb. There are many other shopping malls such as the Galeriá del Calzado (near the bus terminal), selling, as the name implies, only shoes.

The markets, in particular the Libertad (San Juan de Dios) which has colourful items for souvenirs with lots of Michoacán crafts including Paracho guitars and Sahuayo hats, leather jackets, and delicious food upstairs on the 1st level (particularly goat meat, *birria*, also *cocada*), but expensive soft drinks; the *tianguis* (Indian market) on Av Guadalupe, Colonia Chapalita, on Fri is of little interest to foreigners, bus 50 gets you there; the *tianguis* near the University Sports Centre on Calzada Tlaquepaque on Sundays.

Crafts Two glass factories at **Tlaquepaque** nearby where the blue, green, amber and amethyst blown-glass articles are made (bus 275 from the centre goes through Tlaquepaque en route to bus station); visit the shop of **Sergio Bustamante**, who sells his own work (good modern jewellery): expensive but well worth a look, a stream runs through this colonial house. Also, the **Casa de los Telares** (Calle de Hidalgo 1378), where Indian textiles are woven on hand looms. **Leo e Hijos**, Independencia 150, good quality leather at excellent prices, Leo himself is charming. Potters can be watched at work both in Guadalajara and at Tlaquepaque; you may find better bargains at **Tonalá** (pottery and ceramics), 15 km SW of Guadalajara on the road to Mexico City, but no glass there, market days Thur and Sun; take bus 275, bumpy 45 mins journey. Overall, Tlaquepaque is the cheapest and most varied source of the local crafts, with attractive shops set in old colonial villas; best buys: glass, papier mâché goods, leather (cheapest in Mexico), and ceramics. **Casa de Artesanías de Jalisco**, González Gallo 20, T 619-4664, open 1000-1900 (1400 Sun), free, in Parque Agua Azul: high quality display (and sale) of handicrafts, ceramics, paintings, handblown glass, dresses, etc (state-subsidized to preserve local culture, but not cheap—a percentage goes to the artisan). There is another shop-cum-exhibition at the **Instituto de Artesanía Jaliscense, Casa de Las Artesanías Normal**, Av Alcalde 1221, T 624-4624. Look out for leather belts with sewn-on tapestry. **Parián** is a covered commercial area with a whole variety of restaurants, music and handicraft shops, Calle Grecia, off Juárez. See also the **Tienda Tlaquepaque**, at Av Juárez 267-B, in Tlaquepaque, T 635-5663.   *Sandi* -Chapultepec

Bookshops English books available at a reasonable mark up, at *Sanborns*, Av Vallarta 1600 y Gen San Martín, Juárez y 16 de Septiembre, Plaza Bonita and López Mateos Sur 2718 (near Plaza de Sol). German journals at *Sanborns*, Av Vallarta branch. *Librería Británica*, Av Hidalgo 1796-B, Sector Hidalgo. Book exchange, English books, at *Happy Tiger Bookshop*, Plaza del Sol shopping complex, Chapalita, novels cost about US$1. *Sandi's*, Av Tepeyac 718, Colonia Chapalita, T 621-0863, has a good selection of English-language books and cards. *Librería México* in Plaza del Sol has US magazines and newspapers. Bookshops can be found on López Cotilla, from González Martínez towards 16 de Septiembre.

Car Rental Niños Héroes opp *Sheraton*: Quick, Budget, National, Avis, Ford and Odin. Others scattered throughout the city.

Local transport Horse-drawn carriages US$5/hr. Tourist Office in Plaza Tapatía has a full list of local buses. If in doubt ask bus driver. Some useful lines: No 275, from Zapopán-Plaza Patria-Glorieta Normal-Av Alcalde-Av 16 de Septiembre-old bus station-Tlaquepaque-new bus station-Tonalá (there are different 275s, from A to F, most follow this route); bus 60 goes along Calzada Independencia from zoo, passing Estadio Jalisco, Plaza de Toros, Mercado Libertad and Parque Agua Azul to the old bus terminal and the railway station (note, if you are going to Parque Mirador, take bus 62 north-bound, otherwise 62 has the same route as 60); bus 102 runs from the new bus terminal along Av Revolución, 16 de Septiembre and Prisciliano Sánchez to Mercado Libertad; No 258 from San Felipe (N of Cathedral) to Plaza del Sol; No 371 from Tonalá to Plaza del Sol. A shuttle bus runs between the two bus stations.

The Metro, or *Tren Ligero*, has Línea 1 running under Federalismo from Periférico Sur to Periférico Norte. Línea 2, due open in mid-1994 runs from Juárez station westbound. Fare US$0.35, one-peso coins needed to buy tokens.

Entertainment Folk dances every Sun at 1000 in the Degollado Theatre, rec, and other cultural shows, tickets US$4-16.50, US$20 for opera (book in advance); concerts and theatre in the ex-Convento del Carmen; concert every Thurs and Sun at 1900 in the Plaza de Armas, in front of the Palacio de Gobierno, free. Organ recitals in the Cathedral. Films in English are sometimes shown at the ciné-teatro in the *Instituto Cultural Cabañas* (see above), which also has a good cafetería; the Ballet Folklórico performs here every Wed at 2030, tickets US$5 . *Peña Cuicalli*, Sector Juárez, López Cotilla 1225 with Atenas, opens 2000, small cover charge, food and drink available, fills up fast—local groups perform folk and protest songs. Music also at *La Peña* on Avenida Unión. Two gay discos are: *SO'S*, Av La Paz 1413, and *Monica's* in Sector Libertad, to the E of the centre, both well known locally.

Cinema Average cost of a ticket is US$1.75.

Sport Bullfights: October to March; football throughout year; *charreadas* (cowboy shows) are held in mid-September at Unión de San Antonio; *charreada* near Agua Azul Park at Aceves Calindo Lienzo, Sun at 1200. Baseball, April-Sept; golf at: Santa Anita, 16 km out on Morelia road, championship course; Rancho Contento, 10 km out on Nogales road; San Isidro, 10 km out on Saltillo road, noted for water hazards; Areas, 8 km out on Chapala road (US$13 during the week, US$20 at weekends is the average price for a round).

Museums Museo de Arqueología del Occidente de México, Calzada Independencia Sur y Calzada del Campesino (Plaza Juárez), open Mon-Fri 1000-1430, 1600-1900, Sat-Sun 1100-1430, US$4.35: objects from Jalisco, Colima and Nayarit, pottery, ornaments, weapons, figures, illustrations of tombs, very comprehensive, small booklet in English. **Museo Regional de Guadalajara**, Liceo 60, between Hidalgo y Calle Independencia (NE of Cathedral), open Tues-Sun 0900-1545, US$4.35: in an old seminary (1710) with a good, prehistoric section (including the complete skeleton of a mammoth found in Jalisco), an interesting display of 'hidden' tombs, excellent display of Colima, Nayarit, and Jalisco terracotta figures (but less extensive than Museo Arqueológico), possibly the finest display of 17th-18th century colonial art in Mexico outside the Museo Virreinal in Mexico City, a large technology section (more complete than Museo Arqueológico), musical instruments, Indian art and one room devoted to the history of Jalisco from the Conquistadores to Iturbide (highly rec). **Albarrán hunting museum**, Paseo de los Parques 3530, Colinas de San Javier, Sat and Sun 1000-1400, with a collection of rare animals from all over the world. The **Casa de la Cultura**, Av 16 de Septiembre y Constituyentes, holds contemporary art exhibitions and lectures.

Zoo Approximately 2 km beyond bullring, worth a visit, admission (US$2 adults, US$1 children) includes entry to amusement park **Selva Mágica** which has a dolphin and seal show (3-4 times a day, US$3.75). See above for buses.

Exchange Houses There are many *casas de cambio* on López Cotilla between Independencia and 16 de Septiembre and one in Plaza del Sol. Despite what they say, *casas de cambio* close 1400 or 1500 till 1600, not continuously open 0900-1900. **American Express**, Plaza los Arcos 2440, Av Vallarta about 5 blocks E of Minerva roundabout, T 630-0200, open Sat at 0930.

Consulates Great Britain, Paulino Navarro, Av Inglaterra Moderna 1165, T 611-1678; **Austria**, Montevideo 2696, Providencia, T 641-1834; **Belgium**, Metalúrgica 2820, Parque Industrial El Alamo, T 641-1834; **Denmark**, Av Circ Agustín Yáñez 2343, T 615-8023; **Finland**, Justo Sierra 2562, 4th Floor, T 616-3623; **France**, López Cotilla 1221, T 625-1052; **Germany**, Corona 202, T 613-1414; **Netherlands**, Calz Lázaro Cárdenas 601, Zona Industrial, T 612-0740; **Italy**, Garibaldi 1849, T 616-1700; **Norway**, Pavo 135-102, T 614-4311; **Sweden**, J Gpe Montenegro 1697, T 625-1616; **Switzerland**, Calle 14 No 2412, Zona Industrial, T 611-3777; **USA**, Progreso 175, T 625-2700; **Canada**, *Hotel Fiesta Americana*, Calle Aurelio Aceves 225, local 30A, T 615-8665.

Cultural Institutes US at Enrique Díaz de León 300; **British** at Tomás V Gómez 125, Sector Hidalgo, T 616-0268, closed between 1200 and 1600. **Benjamin Franklin Library**, US Consulate, Calle Progreso 175, US papers and magazines. **Goethe Institut**, Calle Pedro Moreno y Calderón de la Barca, library, nice garden, newspapers.

Spanish Classes Centro de Estudios para Extranjeros, University of Guadalajara, Calle Guanajuato 1047, Apto Postal 1-2130 or 1-1362, 44100 Guadalajara, T (3) 653-6024/2150, lodging found with families, tuition, 5 weeks US$430 plus US$85 for registration (lodging US$495-530 extra). Centro de Estudios Intensivos, López Cotilla 66A. See also National Registration Center for Study Abroad under **Learning Spanish** Information for Visitors.

Post Office V Carranza, just behind Hall of Justice, open Mon-Fri 0800-1900, Sat, Sun and holidays 0900-1500. There are also branches at the Mercado Libertad and at the old bus station, convenient for the cheap hotels. To send parcels abroad go to Aduana Postal in same building as main post office, open Mon-Fri 0800-1300, T 614-9002. Federal Express office on Plaza Juárez. United Parcel Service at Vianova Travel Agency, Av Américas 927 and Colomos, T 641-3941/641-2042. **Telecommunications** International collect calls can be made from any coin-box phone kiosk and direct dial calls can be made from LADA pay phones, of which there are many all over the city. You can also make long-distance calls and send faxes from Computel outlets: one in front of old bus station, one on Corona y Madero, opp *Hotel Fénix*, and one on 16 de Septiembre y JP Montenegro, opp Sears. Another chain, Copyroyal, charges 3 times as much for a fax to USA. There is a credit card phone at Ramón Corona y Av Juárez, by Cathedral. 2 USA Direct phones, one within and one beyond the customs barrier at the airport.

Laundromat Aldama 125, US$3.30 per 3 kg load (walk along Independencia towards train station, turn left into Aldama).

Tourist Office Federal tourist office (Sectur) Paseo Degollado 50, Plaza Tapatía, T 614-8371 (Mon-Fri 0800-1500), has information in German and English; Jalisco state offices at Paseo Degollado 105/Morelos 102, Plaza Tapatía and a booth in capitol building. Municipal office at Los Arcos, over Juárez. The Jalisco office publishes *Guadalajara Weekly* in English, free advice and tourist news. *Siglo 21* newspaper has a good entertainments section, *Tentaciones* on Fri, every day it has good music, film and art listings. Teletur, Jalisco tourist information by phone, T 658-2222. Instituto Nacional de Estadística, Geografía e Informática, Av Alcalde 788 esq Jesús García, Sector Hidalgo, T 691-3614, for maps and information.

Rail Macull Turismo, railway ticket office in town, López Cotilla 163, 0900-1400, 1600-1900. Railway station information and tickets open 0800-1300. **Mexico City**-Guadalajara Tapatío (*servicio estrella*) leaves the capital 2030, arr 0815, returns 2100. Fares to Mexico City US$13.45 1st class, US$27 *primera especial*, US$53.75 sleeper (single) to US$208 for double cabin. The ordinary train from Mexico City to Guadalajara leaves at 1905 daily, 14-18 hrs (2nd class often sells out early; you need to be at the station 4 hrs before the train leaves, to be sure of a seat); returns from Guadalajara at 1930. Train Guadalajara-**Irapuato** leaves at 0650, which connects there with the train to Mexico City from the N. Train to **Mexicali** via Benjamín Hill, 0930 (*servicio estrella*), 31 hrs minimum, US$85.30, a/c, meals included (cold food served on trays at your seat), also to Nogales, US$68; ordinary 1200, 44-50 hrs, 2nd class US$23.20, a/c, drinks and small meals on sale. For **Tepic** and **Mazatlán** take either the *servicio estrella* or ordinary train to Benjamín Hill. There is a 2nd class train Guadalajara-**Colima-Manzanillo** at 0900 (very slow, as much as 10 hrs, US$3 to Manzanillo, 2nd class); scenery between Ciudad Guzmán and Colima is spectacular. Daily train for **Los Reyes** involves change at Yurécuaro on the line to Mexico City.

Warning Do not accept cups of coffee at the station however friendly or insistent the offer is, they may be drugged. If possible avoid arriving at night.

Airline offices Mexicana, 16 de Septiembre 495, T 613-5097, reservations T 647-2222, Mon-Fri 0900-1845, Sat-Sun 0900-1745, and other offices throughout the city, including airport, T 689-0119; AeroMéxico, Av Corona 196, T 669-0202, airport T 689-0257; Delta, López Cotilla 1701, T 630-3530 (airport 689-0048); Aero California, López Cotilla 1423 (T 626-1962); on Av Vallarta: Air France, No 1540-103 (T 630-3703), American, No 1526 (T 689-0304), Iberia, No 1540-106 (T 630-1886), KLM, No 1390-1005 (T 625-1565), Pan Am, No 1390-501 (T 625-6030), United , No 1461 (T 615-4408); British Airways, Chapultepec Sur 223-701 (T 626-6651); Continental, Plaza Astral, Locales 8-9, Hyatt Hotel (T 647-3662, airport 689-0433).

Airport Miguel Hidalgo, 20 km from town; fixed rate for 3 city zones and 3 classes of taxi: *especial*, *semi-especial* and colectivo—no tip necessary. Bus No 71 from Terminal de Autobuses, US$0.30; VW buses, Calle Federalismo Sur No 915, 'servicio terrestre', US$4 pp. Many flights daily to and from Mexico City, 50 mins. Daily to Los Mochis with Aero California. Many other Mexican and US destinations served.

Bus New bus station near the El Alamo cloverleaf, 10 km from centre; buses 102 and 275 go to the centre, US$0.15 (see **Local Transport** above), journey takes at least 30 mins; after 2230 no buses, only taxi US$5. Shuttle buses for people with luggage leave parking lot in front of the old bus terminal and go direct to the new terminal. Fixed price taxis, buy ticket at the bus terminal. Bus tickets are sold at 2 offices on Calzada Independencia underneath the big fountain on Plaza Tapatía, open 0900-1400, 1600-1900. It helps to know which company you wish to travel with as their offices are spread over a large area, in 7 modules. All modules have phones, but only Nos 1 and 2 long distance, all have left luggage, restaurants and shops; outside No 5 is a map of urban bus routes. A number of bus companies change dollars at rates marginally worse than *cambios*. At No 1: Ciénaga 1st and 2nd class (local destinations), Flecha Amarilla (T 657-7182: Colima, Manzanillo, Zamora, Morelia, Uruapan and Pátzcuaro), La Alteña (T 657-7054: Mexico City, Guanajuato, Dolores Hidalgo, León, Celaya), Servicios Coordinados (T 657-7054: Mexico City, Morelia, Guanajuato, León, Querétaro, Irapuato, Zamora, Colima). No 2: Autobuses del Occidente (T 657-6464: Mexico

City, Manzanillo, Morelia, Zamora, Uruapan, Colima, Tapalpa), La Línea (Michoacán, Jalisco), Sur (Jalisco), Mazamitla. No 3: Tres Estrellas de Oro (T 657-7225: Mexico City, Mazatlán, Puerto Vallarta, Tijuana, Tepic, Guanajuato, Morelia, Zamora, Uruapan), Unidos de la Costa (Jalisco coast), Trans del Pacífico (T 657-5184: Puerto Vallarta, Barra de Navidad, Mazatlán, Mexico City). No 4: (T 657-6330/4744: Mexico City, León, Morelia, Zamora, Pto Vallarta, Manzanillo, Mazatlán); Trans del Pacífico (T 657-4668: Mazatlán, Pto Vallarta, Mexico, Guayabitos, Las Penitas); Trans Chiuatlán (T 657-4805: Melaque, Barra de Navidad, Chamela); Elite (T 639-9830: León, Mexico, Pto Vallarta, Tijuana, Monterrey, Uruapan, Zamora). No 5: Omnibus del Oriente (Mexico City, Tampico, Querétaro, Irapuato, San Luis Potosí); services to Tepatitlán, Ajijic and León. No 6: Camiones de los Altos (T 657-6030: Acapulco, Mexico City, Mazatlán, Monterrey, Pto Vallarta, Querétaro, Tepic, Zacatecas), Estrella Blanca (T 657-6023: Mazatlán, Pto Vallarta, Zacatecas). No 7: Omnibús de México (T 657-5767: Mexico City, León, Zacatecas, Guanajuato, San Miguel Allende, Celaya, Aguascalientes, Irapuato, Monterrey, Tepic, Colima).

Sample fares: To **Uruapan**, US$9 with Flecha Amarilla about 7 hrs, and others; to **Mazatlán**, 9½ hrs, US$19.25; **Ciudad Obregón**, 15 hrs, US$41; **Hermosillo**, 19 hrs, US$54; **Mexicali**, 32 hrs, US$77 Trans del Pacífico; **Tijuana**, 36 hrs, US$82.50, same company, and **Ciudad Juárez**, US$50 (Los Altos)—US$58 (Chihuahuenses), each 5 a day. To **Monterrey**, US$33; **Mexico City**, from US$19.25 1st to 23 'plus' to 38 ETN, frequent departures, 8 hrs; **Nogales**, US$61, 26 hrs; **Guanajuato** US$10.15, several companies (if you miss a Guanajuato bus, go to León and change there, US$7). To **Durango**, US$23. To **Morelia**, frequent, US$10.35, or US$20 with ENT. **Manzanillo**, US$11, US$23 ENT, 6 hrs, **Pátzcuaro**, US$10, 4 a day with Flecha Amarilla, otherwise change at Quiroga, 6 hrs, a new road is being constructed, when open the journey will be cut by 1-1½ hrs. To **Querétaro**, US$12, 7 hrs; to **Colima**, US$14.80 1st class, US$16.25 ENT, 4 hrs. To **Puerto Vallarta** by Estrella Blanca, US$15.50, ENT US$30.25, 6 hrs. To **Acapulco**, Los Altos, US$40, 3 direct; otherwise go to **Lázaro Cárdenas**, several companies, US$21.50, and change there. To **Nuevo Laredo** with Transportes de Norte or Estrella Blanca, 9 a day, US$46.50, 18 hrs.

The old central bus station, Los Angeles y 28 Enero serves towns within 100 km. You have to pay 100 pesos to enter terminal (open 0545-2215), toilets and long-distance phones inside.

Tolls Total road toll Guadalajara – Mexico City, US$10.

Excursions 8 km to the canyon of **Barranca de Oblatos**, 600 metres deep, reached by bus 42 and others from the market to end of line (admission US$0.10), with the Río Santiago cascading at the bottom (except in dry season). Guides to the bottom. Once described as a stupendous site; now reported made hideous by littering and sewage. See especially the Cola de Caballo waterfall and the Parque Mirador Dr All. Park crowded on Sunday; Balneario Los Comachos, a large swimming pool with diving boards set on one side of the Barranca de Oblatos, has many terraces with tables and chairs and barbecue pits under mango trees; drinks and snacks on sale; now descibed as dirty. Entry US$1.50. Also to **Barranca de Huentitán**, in the canyon of the Río Lerma, access via the Mirador de Huentitán at the end of Calzada Independencia Norte, interesting flora, tremendous natural site, but also spoilt by litter. 1 hr to the bottom (no guide needed) and the Río Lerma which is straddled by the historic bridge of Huentitán. Buses to Huentitán: 42 'Jonilla Centro' from city centre; 44 'Sevilo C Médico", stops 100m short. All buses cost US$0.25.

In a NW suburb of Guadalajara are the Basílica de **Zapopán**, with a miraculous image of Nuestra Señora on the main altar, given to the Indians in 1542, and a museum of Huichol Indian art (agricultural fair in Nov). Zapopán is reached by taking the system of underground trolley buses, known as the *metro*, which also goes to Tlaquepaque, as far as the Avila Camacho station, then any bus marked Zapopán. En route for Tepic is the Bosque de Primavera, reached by town buses. Pine forests ideal for picnics, although increasingly littered; US$0.50 for a swim. Good restaurant, *Los Pioneros*, Carretera a Tesistán 2005, esq Av Hospital Angel Leaño, with bar, live music, attractions and US 'Wild West' atmosphere.

'From Guadalajara to Irapuato: via Tepatitlán (79 km, on the León road), a small unfinished market town with a *charro* centre, in an impressive setting with steep hills all around; Arandas has a curious neo-gothic church and a pleasant square with a white wrought-iron bandstand; the road then winds tightly up over a range of hills and then down into a long and heavily cultivated valley. 5-hr journey.' writes Tim Connell.

Laguna de Chapala (113 km long, 24 to 32 wide) 64 km to the SE, is near the town of Sayula from which D H Lawrence took the name when he wrote about Chapala in 'The Plumed Serpent' (return 1st class bus fare to the lake US$3.65, every ½ hr, 1 hr journey). There is an *Aldea India*, Indian settlement, on the Chapala road, with murals of the history of Jalisco.

Chapala town, on the northern shore of Laguna de Chapala, has thermal springs, several good and pricey hotels, 3 golf courses, helpful tourist office at Hidalgo 227, and is a popular resort particularly with moneyed North Americans. Watch women and children play a picture-card game called *Anachuac*. 'The house in which Lawrence wrote his novel still stands at Zaragoza 307, although a second floor and some modernization have been added. The church that figures in the last pages of 'The Plumed Serpent' still stands on the waterfront, its humble façade and interior now covered by a handsome veneer of carved stone,' writes Robert Schmitz, of Chapala. The lake is set in beautiful scenery. There are boats of all kinds for hire, water-fowl shooting in autumn and winter and sailing. Most fish in the lake have been killed by pollution, but the 5-cm 'XYZ' fish are a delicacy. Lake water must be boiled. On the Fiesta de Francisco de Asís (2-3 Oct) fireworks are displayed and excellent food served in the streets. Horses for hire on the beach, bargain. There is a handicrafts market on the SE corner of the Zocalo. Pemex sells Magna Sin.

Chagas disease was reported in the region round the Laguna de Chapala in 1989; see **Health Information** at the front of the book.

Hotels and Restaurants C *Chapala Haciendas*, Km 40, Chapala-Guadalajara highway. **D** *Nido*, T 52116, basic, clean, good restaurant, good swimming pool (not always open), parking for motorcycles beside pool; adverts for rooms and apartments for rent at pharmacy opp *Nido*; house at Calle López Cotilla 363, a few blocks away, has rooms to let, US$50 per week, US$150 per month; **E** *Casa de Huéspedes Palmitas*, Calle Juárez 531, behind market. *El Patio* is a good and cheap restaurant; also *La Viuada*, next to Chapala Realty, Hidalgo 223, pleasant garden. Chapala Realty is very helpful, T 53676, F 53528, some rentals. Good discotheque, *Pantera Rosa*.
   Trailer Park   1 km from the lake: *PAL*, Apdo Postal 1-1470, Guadalajara, T 53764 or Chapala 60040, US$13 daily, 1st class, pool, good.

Laundromat   Zaragoza y Morelos.

Postal Services   Mail Box, etc, Calle Chapala-Jocotepec 155, opp *PAL* Trailer Park, F (376) 60775.

Ajijic, 7 km to the W, a smaller, once Indian village, has an arty-crafty American colony. The Way of the Cross and a Passion Play are given at Easter in a chapel high above the town. Bus from Chapala, 1 hr, US$2.

Hotels and Restaurants B *Hotel Danza del Sol*, T (376) 60220/61080, or Guadalajara 621-8878, Av Lázaro Gárdenas 3260, Planta Baja, large complex, nice units and gardens, pool; under same management as **A+** *Real de Chapala*, Paseo del Prado 20, T 60007, F 60025, delightful, pleasant gardens; **A** *La Nueva Posada*, Donato Guerra 9, Apdo 30, T 61444, F 61344, breakfast included, horseriding, golf, tennis, theatre, gardens, swimming pool, restaurant, colonial décor, delightful; **B** *La Floresta*, E of Ajijic, lake views, motel style, kitchen, living room, bathroom, pool, good; *Posada Ajijic* bar and restaurant. **D** *Las Casitas*, motel-type with kitchen units, pool (just outside Ajijic, at Carretera Puente 20); similar is *las Calandrias* next door, furnished apartments, swimming pool, T 52819. *Mama Chuy Club*, and *Villa Chello*, on hillside, T (376) 30013 for both, good, pools, spacious, US$450/month d, good value.

Services   Clínica Ajijic, Carretera Oriente 33, T 60662/60500, with 24-hr ambulance service, Dr Alfredo Rodríguez Quintana (home T 61499).

Beyond Ajijic on the lake is the Indian town of **Jocotepec**, a sizeable agricultural centre (recently invaded by more cosmopolitan types, little budget accommodation: **Posada del Pescador**, good garden, motel-style, pool, quiet; **E** *Sajara*, clean, hot water); there is a local *fiesta* on 11-18 January. Jocotepec can be reached from Ajijic or from the Mexico-Guadalajara highway. Bus Chapala-Jocotepec US$2, every hour in each direction. The Indians make famous black-and-white *sarapes*. Tony Burton (PO Box 79, Jocotepec, T/F 376-30492), runs ecology and other tours in Western Mexico and published *Western Mexico, A Traveller's Treasury* (US$15, US$2.95 p and p), Editorial Agata, Guadalajara, ISBN 9687310448.

Between Ajijic and Jocotepec lies the small town of **San Juan Cosalá**, with thermal springs at **Balnearios y Suites Cosalá**, which has private rooms for bathing with large tiled baths. Sunbathing in private rooms also possible. Rooms to let at **Balneario Paraíso**, D. Bus service from Chapala. **NB** Route 80 from Laguna de Chapala to the Pacific Coast at Barra de Navidad is in very poor condition. Route 15 on the southern shore of Laguna de Chapala, which leads to Pátzcuaro (6 hrs) is in good condition, if slow and winding through the hills.

Due S of Lake Chapala is the colonial town of **Mazamitla**, hotel: **D** *Posada Alpina*, on square. About 4 km out of town is Zona Monteverde with pine forests, small *casitas* for rent, two good restaurants at entrance, T 161826; steep hills, access only by car or taxi.

About 130 km S of Guadalajara off the road (Jal 54) to Sayula and Ciudad Guzmán is **Tapalpa**, very pretty indeed. $3^1/_2$ hrs' drive from Guadalajara. The bus has several detours into the hills to stop at small places such as Zacoalco (Sunday market) and Amacueca. The road up to Tapalpa is winding and climbs sharply; the air becomes noticeably cooler and the place is becoming increasingly popular as a place for weekend homes. The town itself, with only 11,000 inhabitants, shows ample signs of this influx of prosperity. There are two churches (one with a curious atrium) and an imposing flight of stone steps between them, laid out with fountains and ornamental lamps. Tapalpa is in cattle country; the rodeo is a popular sport at weekends.

The main street is lined with stalls, selling *sarapes* and other tourist goods on Sundays and fresh food the other days of the week. The more expensive restaurants have tables on balconies overlooking the square—the **Restaurante Posada Hacienda** (which has a US$1 cover charge) is well placed. Others are the **Buena Vista** (which also has rooms) and **La Cabaña**, and all are visited by the mariachis. Less grand is the **D** *Hotel Tapalpa*, with huge holes in the floor, but clean and fairly cheap. Some rooms are for hire (*Bungalows Rosita*, *Posada Hacienda* has nice bungalows with fireplace and small kitchen for US$15). The only local speciality is *ponche*, an improbable blend of tamarind and mescal which is sold in gallon jars and rec only for the curious or foolhardy. If you are planning a day trip get your return ticket as soon as you arrive as the last bus back to Guadalajara (1800 on Sundays) is likely to be full.

Jalisco Route 54 continues through **Ciudad Guzmán** (formerly Zapotlán) to join Route 110, which heads SW from Zamora to Colima.

Hotels in Ciudad Guzmán: **D** *Hotel Flamingo*, nr main square, excellent value, very modern, very clean, and quiet; **E** *del Sol* (*Posada familiar*). **Buses** to Colima take 2 hrs, US$3 (Flecha Amarilla); to Uruapan involves changes in Tamazula and Zamora. **Trains** go to Guadalajara at 1658, *servicio estrella* and 1120, regular, and Manzanillo via Colima, 1205 and 1345 respectively.

Colima (pop 150,000) 96 km, capital of Colima state (pop 424,700), at an altitude of 494 metres, is a most charming and hospitable town with a 19th century, Moorish style arcade on main square and strange rebuilt gothic ruin on road beyond Cathedral (late 19th century). Also on the main square is the Palacio de Gobierno (with interesting murals of the history of Mexico) and, nearby, the church of San Felipe de Jesús (early 18th century plateresque façade) where

Miguel Hidalgo was at one time parish priest. Public swimming pool in park on Calle Degollado. Airport (daily flights from Mexico City, Aeromar).

Feria: The annual fair of the region (agriculture, cattle and industry, with much additional festivity) runs from the last Saturday of October until the first Sunday of November. Traditional local potions (all the year round) include *Jacalote* (from black maize and pumpkin seeds), *bate* (*chía* and honey), *tuba* (palm tree sap) and *tecuino* (ground, germinated maize).

Hotels A+ *Hotel América*, Morelos 162, T 20366, a/c, good restaurant, central, friendly; **C** *Posada San José*, M Chávez Madrueño 135, T 20756, phone, TV; **C-D** *Ceballos*, Torres Quintero 16, T 21354, main square, fine building beautifully remodelled in 1992, some huge rooms with a/c, clean, good food in restaurant (pricey), secure indoor parking, very good value, highly rec; **D** *Flamingos*, ex-*Gran I lotel*, pleasant rooms, Av Rey Colimán 18, T 22526, near Jardín Núñez, with bath, simple, clean, breakfast expensive, disco below goes on till 0300 on Sat and Sun; **D** *Tlayolan*, J Mina 33, T 23317, clean, quiet; **E** *Flamingo*, Gabino Barreda 12, behind the Cathedral, with bath, good value, rec; **E** *Galeana*, Medellín 142, near bus terminal, basic. **E** *Núñez*, Juárez 80 at Jardín Núñez, basic, dark, with bath; **E** *San Cristóbal*, Reforma 98, T 20515, near centre, run down. Many *casas de huéspedes* near Jardín Núñez. **D** *Rey de Colimán*, on continuation of Medellín on outskirts, large rooms; *Motel Costeño* on outskirts is rec.

Restaurants Several restaurants on the Zócalo serve inexpensive meals. *El Trébol* probably the best; *El Mesón de San Francisco*, Madero 42 Sur, luxury, mostly fish, some beef and local specialities, up to US$10 for main dish, rec; *Palomas*, behind *Hotel Ceballos*, rec; *Café Colima* more expensive, but in a park; *Giovannis*, Constitucíon 58 El Norte, good pizzas and take away. Good yoghurt and wholemeal bread at *Centro de Nutrición Lakshmi*, Av Madero 265. Try the local sweet *cocada y miel* (coconut and honey in blocks), sold in *dulcerías*.

Museums Museo de las Culturas de Occidente María Ahumada, Calzada Pedro Galván, in Casa de Cultura complex, Tues-Sun 0900-1300, 1600-1800; **Museo de la Máscara, la Danza y el Arte Popular del Occidente**, Calle 27 de Septiembre y Manuel Gallardo, folklore and handicrafts (items for sale—in the University Institute of Fine Arts); **Museo de la Historia de Colima**, on the Zócalo. Also, nearby, the Francisco Zaragoza vintage car museum (Colección de Automóviles Antiguos) the largest in Mexico, with more than 350 models from 1884-1950.

Laundry *Lavandería Shell*, 27 de Septiembre 134, open 0900-2000, inexpensive, quick.

Post Office, Av Fco I Madero y Gral Núñez.

Tourist Office on the Zócalo, opp the Cathedral, good, but no information on climbing local volcanoes.

Bus Station New, on the outskirts; buses and *kombis* run to centre, US$0.50, or taxi about US$2. If going to Uruapan it is best to go to Zamora (7-8 hrs, although officially 4) and change there. ETN bus Colima-Manzanillo US$7. ETN to Mexico City US$51.65.

Rail Colima-Manzanillo at 1613, and Colima-Guadalajara (0830) via Ciudad Guzmán, 2nd class only.

Excursions El Chanal, about 15 km to the N of Colima, is an archaeological site with a small pyramid with 36 sculptured figures, discovered in 1944.

El Hervidero, 22 km SE of Colima, is a spa in a natural lake of hot springs which reach 25°C.

Colima volcano (3,842 metres), one of the most exciting climbs in Mexico, which erupted with great loss of life in 1941, and of **El Nevado** (4,339 metres) are in the vicinity. They can be climbed by going to Ciudad Guzmán, and taking a bus to the village of Fresnito, from where it is 25 km to the hut at 3,500 metres. At weekends it may be possible to hitch. From the hut it is a strenuous 3-4 hr hike to the top. Sr Agustín Ibarra organises day trips to within a 2 hr climb of the summit, US$90 for 4, or 3 ½ hr horse ride to the refuge with a 3 hr climb, US$50. It may be possible to hitch a lift down next day with the TV maintenance crew who work at the top. Sr Ibarra provides accommodation in the village; otherwise you can camp behind the small restaurant, storing luggage there (no hotels). Hotels in Ciudad Guzmán, see above.

Comalá is a pretty colonial village near Colima, worth a few hours' visit, bus US$0.25, 20 mins every ½ hr. In the village are two popular restaurants with local

6 33 45 80
comer 4

MEXICO West Central

MAC 12

specialities, *Los Portales* and *Comalá* on Plaza Mayor; they are open until 1800. 8 km NE is the government-sponsored Escuela de Artesanía where handmade furniture, painted with fabulous bird designs, and other crafts are manufactured. Items are displayed in the school's well-laid out grounds and sold in the Sunday market at Suchitlán. About 18 km beyond Comalá (look out for signposts), is the magnificent 18th century *estancia* of *San Antonio*; set in a green valley with an impressive roman-style aqueduct leading water down from a mountain spring. Under renovation from 1993, to open as a hotel. The road continues up and over a mountain stream; about a km further on are *Las Marías*, a private mountain lake used as a picnic site, admission US$0.65.

A beautiful, 3-hr hilly route runs from Colima to **Manzanillo** (pop 150,000), which has become an important port on the Pacific, since a spectacular 257-km railway has been driven down the sharp slopes of the Sierra Madre through Colima. A new toll road has been opened between Guadalajara and Manzanillo, good, double-laned in some sections, driving time about 4 hrs, but total cost US$17 in tolls. Occupations for tourists at Manzanillo, which is not a touristy town, include deep-sea fishing (US$250 to hire a boat for a day, including beer, *refrescos* and *ceviche*), bathing, and walking in the hills. There is a bullring on the outskirts on the road to Colima. The best beach is the lovely crescent of Santiago, 8 km N, but there are three others, all of which are clean, with good swimming. Airport.

Hotels L+ *Club Las Hadas*, a Moorish fantasy ("architecture crowned by perhaps the most flamboyantly and unabashedly phallic tower ever erected, and the palpable smell of money; should on no account be missed"); **A+** *La Posada*, Calz L Cárdenas 201, near the end of Las Briasas peninsula, T 22404, US manager, beautifully designed rooms carved into the living rock of an outcrop. *Club Maeva*, T 30595, picturesque, opposite beach, clean rooms with bath and kitchen, meals included in price, several good restaurants. **A+** *Roca del Mar*, Playa Azul, T 21990, vacation centre; **B** *Las Brisas Vacation Club*, Av L Cárdenas, T 20306, some a/c, good restaurant. At Santiago beach: **A** *Playa de Santiago*, T 30344, good but food expensive; **C** *Parador Marbella*, meals extra; **C** *Anita*, built in 1940 it suffers from Mexican maintenance disease but is said to have a certain funky charm and it is clean and on the beach; *Marlyn*, third floor rooms with balcony overlooking the beach, a bargain, rec. At the port: **C** *Colonial*, good restaurant, México 100, friendly, avoid rooms above the record shop (very loud music). **D** *Casa de Huéspades Posada Jardín*, Cuauhtémoc, reasonable. **D** *Colonial*, 10 de Mayo; **D** *Emperador*, Davalos 69, good value. **D** *Flamingos*, 10 de Mayo y Madería, T 21037, with bath, quite good. Visitors can also rent apartments in private condominiums, eg *Villas del Palmar* at Las Hadas, or *Club Santiago* (contact Hector Sandoval at Hectours for information). Camping at Miramar and Santiago beaches. About 5 km N of Manzanillo is *Trailer Park El Palmar*, with a large swimming pool, run down, very friendly, coconut palms, US$13 for two in camper-van. *La Marmota* trailer park, at junction of Highways 200 and 98, cold showers, bathrooms, pool, laundry facilities, US$8 per car and 2 people.

Restaurants *Willy's Seafood Restaurant*, on the beach, French owner, primarily seafood, some meat, very good, 3-courses with wine US$15 pp; *Portofino's*, Italian, very good pizza; also Italian, *Bugatti's*; *Carlos and Charlie's*, on the beach, seafood and ribs, great atmosphere. Good but not cheap food at the two *Huerta* restaurants, the original near the centre, and *Huerta II* near the Las Hadas junction. Just N of the *Days Inn* on the main (De La Madrid) highway is *Los Hijos de Sánchez*, magnificent breakfasts, decor from Anthony Quinn film (of the book by Oscar Lewis) of the same name.

Tourist Office Juárez 244, 4th floor, helpful.

Transport Bus to **Miramar**, US$0.50, leaves from J J Alcaraz, 'El Tajo". Several to **Guadalajara**, US$11, or US$23 ENT, 6 hrs. To **Mexico City** with ETN, luxury, US$62, with Autobus de Occidente, 19 hrs, 1st class, US$25. **Barra de Navidad**, US$2.50, 1½ hrs; to **Colima**, US$4, US$7 ENT; to **Tijuana**, bus US$110, 1st class, 36 hrs. Down the coast to **Lázaro Cárdenas** and crossroads for Playa Azul (**see p 155**) by Autobus de Occidente or Galeana, US$13.50, 7 hrs. Bus terminal in Av Hidalgo outside centre, local buses go there. **Train** to **Guadalajara** 2nd class service at 0600, up to 10 hrs. For minibus to the **airport** T 32470, US$5 from the beach.

S of Manzanillo is **Tecomán** (pop 68,000) with delightful atmosphere. **B-C** *Gran Fénix*, larger rooms have a/c, smaller rooms are noisier but hotel is rec; unnamed *pensión* on the corner of the Zócalo, if you face the church it is on your left, E. Try the local deep-fried *tortillas* filled with cheese. To the W of Tecomán is the small coastal resort of **Cuyutlán**, on the fast highway between Colima and Manzanillo. It has a pleasant, black-sand beach and **D** *Hotel Bucanero*, near the N end of the front, clean rooms, good restaurant, games room and souvenir shop. Swimming here is excellent and umbrellas and wooden walkways protect feet against the hot sun and sand. The coast road continues SE to Playa Azul, Lázaro Cárdenas, Zihuatanejo and Acapulco: for 80 km beyond Manzanillo it is good, then Route 200 in some parts is in poor condition and for long stretches one cannot see the ocean. In other places there are interesting coastal spots. About 1 hr S of Tecomán is the small village of **San Juan de Lima**, on a small beach; two or three hotels, the farthest S along the beach is very basic, D. There are a couple of restaurants, one unnamed, about 200m from the hotels, serving excellent red snapper and shrimp dishes. The road to Playa Azul is very poor, lots of potholes, some sections washed out, driving time about 4 hrs. **Warning** Report received of rape and armed robbery in Río Cachán, between Tecomán and Zihuatanejo, in early 1992. Local police warn against camping in the wild in this area; similar crimes occur on a weekly basis.

Another Route to Manzanillo Route 80 goes from Guadalajara to **Melaque** bay, one of the most beautiful on the Pacific coast, but very commercialized and crowded at holiday times. The waves are not so big at San Patricio beach. The village of **Barra de Navidad** is commercial but still pleasant, where there is a monument to the Spanish ships which set out in 1648 to conquer the Philippines. Barra is 1½ hrs from Manzanillo; the beach is beautiful, very good for swimming, but at holiday times it is very crowded and a lot less pleasant. Avoid oil spillages on beach. Pemex station at Route 200/Route 80 junction, has unleaded fuel. To *new nos*

335 55018 - Sands

change money, go to Chiuatlán from Barra, buses every 30 mins; no tourist office.

Accommodation and Food In **Melaque**: *Melaque*, too big and very noisy; **B** *Bungalows Azteca*, 23 km from Manzanillo airport, for 4 at Calle Avante, San Patricio, T (333) 7-01-50, with kitchenette, pool, parking. *Club Náutico*, very pleasant, good value, small swimming pool; **D** *Flamingo*, Vallarta 19, clean with fan, balconies, water coolers on each floor; **D** *San Nicolás*, beside Estrella Blanca bus station, noisy but clean. *Trailer Park La Playa*, San Patricio, in the village, on beach, US$13 for car and two people, full hook-up, toilets, cold showers. If you follow the 'Melaque' signs, at the end of the main road is a free camping place on the beach at the bay, very good, easily accessible for RVs, popular for vehicles and tents. *Restaurant Los Pelícanos*, cheap, good, on beach.

In **Barra de Navidad**: **C** *Delfín*, Morelos 23, T 333-70068, very clean, pool, hot water, highly rec; opp is **C** *Sand's*, T 163859 (Guadalajara) or 70018 (Barra), bar, clean, some kitchen units, good value, pool; **B** *Hotel Barra de Navidad*, with balcony on beach, or bungalows where you can cook, pool, very good value; **C** *Bosantes*, on beach, with bath, clean, good value; **B** *Tropical*, on beach, seedy but pleasant; **D** *Hotel Jalisco*, hot water, safe and clean but noisy, nightclub next door with music till 0300; *San Lorenzo* is same price and much better; **E** *Posada Pacífico*, Mazatlán 136, one street behind bus terminal, clean, friendly. Ask about camping on beach. Fish restaurants eg *Antonio* on beach; many good restaurants (on the Pacific side, a couple of good restaurants; on the lagoon side, *Velero's*, delicious snapper and good views: *Amber*, Veracruz 101, half of menu vegetarian, real coffee, good breakfast and crêpes, highly rec, closed lunchtime; *Pacífico*, very good barbecued shrimp, good breakfasts).

Pretty seaside villages near Barra de Navidad include *La Manzanilla*, 14 km N of Routes 200/80 junction (*Posada del Cazador*); camping possible). 3 km N of beach is Boca de Iguanas with 2 trailer parks: *Boca de Iguanas*, US$7 pp, vehicle free, hook-ups, cold showers, toilets, laundry facilities, clean, pleasant location, and *Tenacatita* (US$9 d with hook-ups, US$7 without, cold showers, toilet, laundry facilities, restaurant. For both places take the unpaved road from Highway 200 to the abandoned *Hotel Bahía de Tenacatita*; at the T junction, turn right, pass the hotel, and the campsites are about ½ km further on the left. This place is nothing to do with the village of *Tenacatita*. This has a perfect beach complete with palm huts, tropical fish among rocks (2 sections of beach, the bay and oceanside). **D** *Hotel* (no name) in village near beach, or you can sleep on the beach under a palm shelter—but beware mosquitoes. Several km N Tenacatita is *Fiesta Americana* hotel.

The road, paved, goes S from Melaque to Manzanillo.

Continuing to Mexico City We go round the southern shores of Laguna de Chapala, and after 154 km come to **Jiquilpan** (on Route 110 to Colima). There are frescoes by Orozco in the library, which was formerly a church. At least 5 hotels; *Imperial*, on main street, E, good value.

The State of Michoacán, where the Tarascan Indians live, is a country of deep woods, fine rivers and great lakes. Fruit, game, and fish are abundant. It has some of the most attractive towns and villages in the country. Visitors are attracted by the Tarascan customs, folklore, ways of life, craft skills (pottery, lacquer), music and dance. The dance is of first importance to them; it is usually performed to the music of wooden drum, flute and occasionally, a fiddle. Masks are often worn and the dance is part of a traditional ritual. The dances which most impress outsiders are the dance of Los Viejitos (Old Men; at Janitzio, 1 January); Los Sembradores (The Sowers; 2 February); Los Moros (The Moors; Lake Pátzcuaro region, *fiestas* and carnival); Los Negritos (Black Men; *fiestas* at Tzintzuntzán); Los Apaches (4 February, at the churches); Las Canacuas (the crown dance; Uruapan, on Corpus Christi). At the weddings of fisherfolk the couple dance inside a fish net. In the local *fandango* the woman has fruits in her hand, the man has a glass of *aguardiente* balanced on his head, and a sword.

Zamora (58 km beyond Jiquilpan), with 135,000 people, is an agricultural centre founded in 1540. There is an interesting ruined gothic-style church in the centre, several other, fine churches, and a market on Calle Corregidora by the bus station.

Nearby is tiny Laguna de Camecuaro, with boats for hire, restaurants and wandering musicians; popular at holiday times.

Hotels C *Fénix*, Madero Sur 401, T 20266, near bus station, clean, swimming pool, poor ventilation, pleasant balconies; **D** *Amalia*, Hidalgo 194, T 21327, pleasant, some rooms noisy, restaurant OK; next door to *Fénix* is **D/E** *Posada Fénix*, rooms of varying quality, nice owner, good laundry service; **E** *Posada Marena*, simple, clean; other cheap *hospedajes* near market.
Motel A *Jérico*, Km 3 on La Barca road just N of town, T 25252, swimming pool, restaurant.

Buses Bus station at N edge of town, local bus to centre US$0.25, taxi US$3.50. Bus to Mexico City, 1st *plus*, US$16.50, 1st US$14.20, ETN luxury US$30 (ETN to Guadalajara US$11, and US$10 to Morelia).

On 40 km is **Carapán**, a crossroads at which a road goes N to **La Piedad**, a pleasant stopping place on the toll road between Guadalajara and Mexico City (**D** *Hotel Mansión Imperial*, parking; **E** *Gran Hotel*, on main street, OK). At Carapán a branch road runs 72 km S through pine woods to **Paracho**, a quaint, very traditional Indian village of small wooden houses; in every other one craftsmen make guitars and *mandolines* worth from US$10 to 1,000 according to the wood used. **E** Hotel on main road S of town, hot water am only. Try local pancakes. Buses to/from Uruapan.

This road continues to **Uruapan** ("Place where flowers are plentiful"), a town of 250,000 set among streams, orchards and waterfalls at 1,610 metres in the **Parque Nacional Barranca del Cupatitzio**, cool at night. Local foods are sold in the Parque and there is a government-operated trout breeding facility. The most attractive of its three plazas is the Jardín de los Mártires, with the 16th century church facing it. In the *portales* or at the market can be bought the local lacquered bowls and trays, or the delicate woodwork of the Paracho craftsmen, Patamban green pottery and Capácuaro embroideries. Restored hospital, built by Fray Juan de San Miguel in the 16th century; now a ceramics museum. Adjoining it is a 16th-century chapel now converted into a craft shop. In the same square, part of the former Collegiate church of San Francisco (17th century with later additions) houses the attractive Casa de la Cultura (small museum upstairs, free, with excellent display of the history of Uruapan). 1 km from the centre is a beautiful, tropical forest public park, named after Eduardo Ruiz, full of butterflies, streams and waterfalls at the top of Calle Venustiana with a good handicraft shop at the entrance, selling wooden boxes and bracelets (entry US$0.35). Several stalls sell food and drink. Walk there or catch a bus one block S of the Zócalo marked 'El Parque". The town suffers badly from traffic fumes. Airport.

Festivals In the first week of April the Zocalo is filled with pottery and Indians from all the surrounding villages. Around 16 September, in nearby village of San Juan, to celebrate the saving of an image of Christ from the San Juan church (see below) at the time of the Paricutín eruption. The two weeks either side of 15 September are *feria* in Uruapan, too.

Hotels **A** *Victoria*, Cupatitzio 13, T 36700, good, quiet, restaurant and garage; **B** *Concordia* on main square has nice restaurant, T 30500; **B** *Plaza Uruapan*, Ocampo 64, T 30333, good, clean, large rooms; **C** *El Tarasco*, Independencia 2, T 41500, pool, lovely, good restaurant, moderate prices; **C** *Villa de Flores*, Emilio Carranza 15, T 21650, quiet, pleasantly furnished, lovely flowers; **D** *Atzimba*, in street where the mariachis are waiting, modern, rec; **D** *Oseguera*, main square, fairly clean, hot water spasmodic; also on main square, **D** *Regis*; **D** *Moderno*, main square, with bath, water spasmodic but lovely building and friendly owners; **E** *Capri*, Portal Santos Degollado, by market, friendly. **E** *Mirador*, Av Ocampo 9 (on Zócalo), T 20473, hot water 0700-1000 and in pm, clean, rec, but rooms overlooking Zócalo are noisy; **E** *Mi Solar*, Juan Delgado 10, T 2-09-12, good value, hot water, clean, rec. **E** *Morelos*, Morelos 30, with bath, shabby; **E** *Santa Fe*, Constitución 20, without bath, adequate, beside open-air food stalls; **E** *Acosta*, opp bus station; nearby is *Sandy*, cheaper.

   Motels **A+** *Mansión del Cupatitzio*, on the road to Guadalajara, T 32100, pool, patio, restaurant, good souvenir shop, outstanding; **B** *Paricutín*, Juárez 295, T 20303, well-maintained. **B** *Pie de la Sierra*, Km 4 Carretera a Carapán, on N outskirts, T 42510, good moderately-priced restaurant; **C** *Las Cabañas*, Km 1 Carretera a México, near the bus terminal, T 34777, clean, local bus until 2200. One trailer park which takes small units only.

Restaurants *Rincón de Burrito Real* on Plaza, English-speaking owner, good local specialities, not cheap; on same side of the square in *Hotel Regis* is *Los Faroles*, *comida corrida* US$4, very good; *Oriental*, on the Plaza, near *Hotel Moderno*, clean, poor service. *Café Tradicional*, just off Plaza, on same side as *Hotel Villa de Flores*, freshly-ground coffee, home-made chocolates, light meals, rec. Locals eat at open-air food stalls under one roof at back of church, very picturesque. *La Puesta del Sol*, supermarket, Juan Ayala, has good meals. Local speciality, dried meat, *cecina*.

Laundry Emilio Carranza 51.

Tourist Office half a block from main square, at 5 de Febrero 17 (T 20633), in a small modern shopping arcade, good map, helpful.

Train Two daily to **Mexico City**: *rápido* at 0635, first class tickets from *Hotel Victoria* and Purépecha (*servicio estrella*) from Mexico City at 2100, returning 1810 (arr 0730), US$21.15 *primera especial*, US$11.20 1st, 2nd class to Mexico City US$6.75. Freight train to **Pátzcuaro**, daily, takes passengers, US$1.50, can take 5 hrs for the 62 km. Food vendors board at every stop.

Bus Bus station on the NE edge of town, necessary to get a city bus (US$0.25) into town, finishing at about 2100, or a taxi to the Plaza, US$3. To **Mexico City**, 9¼ hrs, Flecha Amarilla via Toluca leaves 0845 and then every hr, US$16.25, many stops; others less frequent but quicker, US$18.75. ETN has a deluxe service, US$28.60, several a day, hot and cold drinks, clean, good drivers. Omnibús de México has night buses and Tres Estrellas morning departures. To **Morelia**, 2nd class (Flecha Amarilla) US$4.60 (2½ hrs), nice ride. To **Colima** with Flecha Amarilla US$8.25, 5 hrs, and to **Los Reyes**, US$2.20, 1¼ hrs with same company. To **Zihuatanejo** (Galeana not rec, or Occidente) 1st or 2nd class, several a day, 6½ hrs, US$9 (2nd) along winding, intermittently wooded road via Nueva Italia and Arteaga, which turns off just before Playa Azul at La Mira and on to Lázaro Cárdenas on the Río Balsas. From there, frequent buses to Zihuatanejo (**see p 244**). Bus to **Guadalajara**, several companies, US$9, 6 hrs, ETN US$17.75. Bus to Pátzcuaro, frequent, US$2.75, 1 hr.

Excursions Through coffee groves and orchards along the Cupatitzio (meaning Singing River) to the *Tzararacua Falls* (10 km); restaurants at bus stop where you can hire a horse to the falls (US$8 pp). It is not advisable to walk to the falls alone. Good camping some 300 metres below the village under the shelter on the top of a rim, with a view down into the valley to the waterfall (1 km away) and a small lake. A bus (marked Tzararacua, or Zupomita, but ask if it goes all the way) will take you from the Zócalo at Uruapan to Tzararacua, US$0.75, erratic service. If on a tight schedule, take a taxi. Parque Cholinde, 1.5 km out of town (all uphill—take a bus), swimming pool, US$1.30; Colibrí Nurseries nearby. Balneario Caracha (frequent buses), alight at cross roads by sign, a delightful place, open daily with restaurant, hotel, several pools and beautiful gardens. *Tingambato* ruins are half way along road to Pátzcuaro, about 2 km downhill from Tingambato town (pyramid and ball court).

The volcano of *Paricutín* can be visited from Uruapan; it started erupting in the field of a startled peasant on 20 February 1943, became fiery and violent and rose to a height of 1,300 metres above the 2,200-metre-high region, and then died down after several years into a quiet grey mountain (460 metres) surrounded by a sea of cold lava. The church spires of San Juan, a buried Indian village, thrusting up through cold lava is a fantastic sight. If not taking an organized tour (with horses and guides), Paricutín is best reached by taking a 'Los Reyes' bus on a paved road to Angahuán, 34 km, US$1.75, 1 hr, 9 a day each way (hourly from 0530 to 2000) with Galeana, then hire a horse or mule or walk (1 hr). Sr José Gómez in Angahuán has mules for hire, but he is expensive; Sres Juan Rivera, Francisco Lázaro (lives in the second house on the right, coming from the *albergue*, see below), Atanacio Lázaro and his horse 'Conejo", and Lino Gómez are recommended, but there are a host of other guides (it is definitely worthwhile to have a guide—essential for the volcano—even though they are very persistent, best if you can speak Spanish, but it is expensive if you are on your own as you have to pay for the guide's mule too). A full day's excursion with mules to the area costs about US$20 per mule, with US$4-5 tip for the guide (6-7 hrs); shorter journeys cost less. To go on foot with a guide costs US$10. Distance Angahuán-San Juan ruins, 3 km, an easy walk: go from the bus stop on the main road, then take right-hand road (with your back to the church) from the plaza, which will lead you to the new hostel, from where you can see the buried church. To the peak of the volcano is 14 km, a long, tough walk (also a long day on horseback for the unaccustomed, especially if you get a wooden saddle). Walk westwards round the lava field, through an avocado plantation. Wear good walking shoes with thick soles as the lava is very rough and as sharp as glass (some cannot make the last stretch over the cricket-ball size rocks); bear in mind the altitude too, as the return is uphill. One can continue on to the volcano itself; it takes 7-9 hrs there and back. The cone itself is rather small and to reach it, there is a stiff 30 min climb from the base. A path goes around the tip of the crater, where activity has ceased. Take something to drink because it is pretty hot and dusty out on the plains. If going in one day, leave Uruapan by 0800 so that you don't have to rush. Take sweater for the evening and for the summit where it can be windy and cold after a hot climb. Last bus back to Uruapan at 1900 (but don't rely on it). Much better, though, is to stay the night in **Angahuán**, where there is an *albergue*, **E/F** pp in *cabañas* with a log fire (bunk beds), meals US$5, basic facilities, but clean and peaceful, warm and highly rec. The *albergue* is a 30 mins walk from the bus stop on the main road: walk into the village, take the 3rd turning on the left and then right at the plaza. Go straight on until the road forks at an expensive-looking wooden house with a satellite TV aerial. Take the left fork. From here, the *albergue* is about 10-15 mins walk at the end of the road. It is possible to drive to the *albergue* where they try to charge US$1.60 for the free car park. There is a panoramic view from the *albergue* of the volcano, San Juan ruins and surrounding pine forest. Camping possible near the hostel. In the village are shops selling food and drink. There is a water tap near the church; follow the signs. Just outside the village, on the dirt road to the main road, is the cemetery, which is interesting. The local Tarascan Indians still preserve their dialects.

Past Angahuán and Peribán, after the volcano, over a paved road is the little town of **Los Reyes**; good swim above the electricity generating plant in clear streams (take care not to get sucked down the feed pipe!).

Hotels C *Arias* behind Cathedral, T 20792, best, clean, friendly; **D** *Plaza*, not as good as *Arias* but nice, clean, on street facing Cathedral, T 20666; **D** *Fénix*, clean, between bus station and plaza, T 20807; **D** *Oasis*, Av Morelos 229, C for a suite, with bath, hot water, clean, pleasant; **E** *Casa de Huéspedes*, clean, basic, lovely courtyard, a little further along the same road as **E** *Villa Rica*, often no water. **Restaurant**: *La Fogata*, in main square.

Transport Buses from Uruapan to **Los Reyes** go via Angahuán (so same frequency as above), depart from Uruapan bus station, not from the plaza as the tourist office says. Bus from Los Reyes, on Av 5 de Mayo, to **Angahuán**, US$2.50, 1½-2 hrs. Bus to Los Reyes from Guadalajara with Ciénaga de Chapala 4 a day, 14 hrs, US$8.25 1st class. **Train** Guadalajara-Mexico City connects at Yurécuaro for Los Reyes, almost no wait, beautiful ride up fertile valley.

The Pacific coast of Michoacán is only just coming under development. From Uruapan Route 37 goes to **Playa Azul**, 350 km NW of Acapulco (bus US$9, 10½ hrs minimum) and 122 km from Zihuatanejo (**see p 244**), a coconut-and-hammock resort frequented much more by Mexicans than foreigners, with a few large hotels. The city of La Mira, on the main road, is larger than Playa Azul and is reported to have more hotels. 40 km of excellent deserted beaches N of Playa Azul. At night there is much beautiful phosphorescence at the water's edge. **NB** Beware of the large waves at Playa Azul and of dangerous currents; always check with locals if particular beaches are safe.

Hotels D *Costa de Oro*, clean, with fan, rec, safe parking; **D** *El Delfín*, no a/c, clean, pleasant, swimming pool; **D** *Hotel del Pacífico*, opp beach, with bath, fan, clean, hammocks on roof, friendly, a bit run-down but rec. *Hotel Playa Azul* has a trailer park with 20 spaces, full hook-up, bathrooms, cold shower, two pools, bar and restaurant, US$13 for car and two people. Many small fish restaurants along beach, but most close early; *Martita*, highly rec. Tap and shower water seems to smell of petrol.

Transport Buses ply up and down the coast road, stopping at the road junction 4 km from Plaza Azul. Colectivos take you between town and junction. If driving N it is 5 hrs to Tecomán (where the road from Colima comes down to the coast); there is nothing along this road.

Lázaro Cárdenas is the connecting point for buses from Uruapan, Manzanillo and Zihuatanejo (eg Galeana to Manzanillo 7¾ hrs, US$13.25; to Uruapan, US$10.75, 6½ hrs; to Guadalajara, US$21.50 with La Línea; to Mexico City from 1st US$36.65 to 43.35, luxury; Flecha Roja to Zihuatanejo, 2 hrs, US$3.65). If possible, book tickets in advance at the bus terminal for all journeys. Train Mexico City-Lázaro Cardenas, via Morelia, Pátzcuaro, Uruapan, dep 2100, arr 1600, returns to capital midday, arr 0730, 1st class US$17.65, *primera especial* US$33.15. Avoid *Hotel Sam Sam* (E) nr terminal; go to 5 de Mayo for *Capri* or *Costa Azul*, both E with bath, or *Verónica*, 2 blocks on left as you leave bus station, friendly, pleasant, noisy, E, restaurant in front part of hotel has nice atmosphere but indifferent food; several eating places in streets near bus terminal.

From Uruapan the Pacific coast of Michoacán, only just coming under development. There are buses from Uruapan to La Mira, then another a short distance to *Caleta de Campos*, 76 km NW up the coast from Playa Azul. In this poor village there is little food other than seafood, but there are phone services; *Hotel Yuritzi*, E pp, D in room for 4, with bath, clean, no hot water, nice; *cabañas* with hammock space at US$1 pp, NW of village, where Río Nexpa reaches the coast. *Fiesta*: 10-13 December; at 0200 on the 13th El Torito, a bull mask and sculpture loaded with fireworks appears—there are other elaborate, if dangerous fireworks. Beaches are 5 minutes away, clean, with seafood restaurants. 86 km further up the coast, to the NW, is *Maruata*, unspoilt and beautiful. This is a turtle conservation area. There are floods in the rainy season.

Back on the road **from Zamora to Morelia**, at *Zacapu* (Km 400), see Franciscan church (1548). At *Quiroga* (Km 357), a road turns off right for Pátzcuaro, heart of the Tarascan Indian country. The town is named after Bishop Vasco de Quiroga, who was responsible for most of the Spanish building in the area and for teaching the Indians the various crafts they still practise: work in wool, leather, copper, ceramics and canework; many Indians, few tourists. Fair and craft exhibitions in December. Good place to buy cheap leather jackets—most shops in town sell them. The night-time entertainment seems to be driving through town in a pick-up with blaring speakers in the back. Bus from Pátzcuaro bus station every 15 mins. Bus Quiroga-Mexico City, US$11, 1st *plus*.

Hotels C *Misión don Vasco*, Av L Cárdenas y Gpe Victoria. Three hotels on main street (Vasco de Quiroga): D *Tarasco*, colonial style, courtyard, clean, hot water, pleasant but front rooms noisy; D *Quiroga* per person and D *Tarisco* (was *San Diego*), cheapest in town, last two both modern with parking. *Cabañas Tzintzuntzan*, Km 6 Quiroga-Pátzcuaro road (Ojo de Agua), swimming pool, own pier, fully-furnished (contact *Hotel Casino*, Morelia, T 31003).

We pass through *Tzintzuntzan*, the pre-conquest Tarascan capital; the ruins are just behind the village, 5 mins walk from the monastery. The fascinating ruins of *Yácatas*, a Purépecha ceremonial centre, with 5 pyramids, are 8 km from the town. In Calle Magdalena is a monastery built in 1533 but closed over 250 years ago, which has been restored, but its frescoes have deteriorated badly. The bells of its church date from the 16th century; a guard will show you round the monastery. In the grounds are olive trees claimed to be the oldest in the world and still bearing fruit. Fortuitously they were missed in a Spanish edict to destroy all Mexican olive trees when it was thought that Mexican olive oil would compete with Spain's. A most interesting Passion play is given at Tzintzuntzan and *fiestas* are very colourful. Beautiful and extensive display of hand-painted pottery, very cheap but also brittle. (It is available in other markets in Mexico.) Other handicrafts on sale include woodcarving, leather and basketwoven Christmas tree ornaments. Good bargaining opportunities. Bus from Pátzcuaro bus station every 15 mins, US$0.50, same bus as for Quiroga, which is 8 km further on. **NB** If taking the route Uruapan-Pátzcuaro-Morelia, Tzintzuntzan and Quiroga come after Pátzcuaro.

1 2 2 Noo

Pátzcuaro is 23 km from Quiroga; altitude 2,110 metres (cold in the evenings); population 65,000, one of the most picturesque towns in Mexico, with narrow cobbled streets and deep overhanging eaves. The houses are painted white and brown. It is built on Lago de Pátzcuaro, about 50 km in circumference, with Tarascan Indian villages on its shores and many islands. The Indians used to come by huge dugout canoes (but now seem to prefer the ferry) for the market, held in the main plaza, shaded by great trees.

There are several interesting buildings: the unfinished **La Colegiata** (1603), known locally as La Basílica, with its much venerated Virgin fashioned by an Indian from a paste made with cornstalk pith and said to have been found floating in a canoe (behind the Basílica there are remains of the precolumbian town and of a pyramid in the precincts of the Museo de Artes Populares); the restored Jesuit church of **La Compañía** (and, almost opposite, the early 17th-century church of the **Sagrario**) at the top of Calle Portugal. Behind this street are two more ecclesiastical buildings: the **Colegio Teresiano** and the restored **Templo del Santuario**; on Calle Lerín is the old monastery, with a series of small patios. (Murals by Juan O'Gorman in the Library, formerly San Agustín.) On Calle Allende is the residence of the first Governor. On Calle Terán is the church of **San Francisco**; nearby is **San Juan de Dios**, on the corner of Calle Romero. Visit also the **Plaza Vasco de Quiroga**. Fifteen minutes' walk outside the town is the chapel of El Calvario, on the summit of Cerro del Calvario, a hill giving wide views; good views also from the old chapel of the Humilladero, above the cemetery on the old road to Morelia.

The very well arranged **Museo de Artes Populares** is in the Colegio de San Nicolás (1540) entrance US$7, excellent for seeing regional ceramics, weaving, woodcarving and basketware, open 0900-1900 Mon-Sat, 0900-1430 Sun, English speaking, friendly guide. Ask there for the Casa de los Once Patios, which contains boutiques selling handicrafts; you can see weavers and painters of lacquerwork in action. An 'International Hippy Crafts Market' is held every Saturday and Sunday in the courtyard in front of the Casa de Once Patios. See also the attractive Jardín de la Revolución (F Tena y Ponce de León) and, nearby, the old church of the Hospitalito. Excellent Fri and also Sat markets, often much cheaper than shops; good copperware on sale. Woodcarving is another local speciality. Some stalls open daily on the main square, selling handicrafts, and there is a friendly handicraft shop on the road down to the lake, Vicky's, with interesting toys. There is a free medical clinic, English-speaking, on the outskirts of Pátzcuaro.

Fiestas 1-2 Nov: Día de los Muertos (All Souls' Day), ceremony at midnight, 1 Nov, at almost every village around the lake; if you are in the region at this time it is well worth experiencing. The ceremony is most touristy on Janitzio island and at Tzintzuntzan, but at villages such as Ihuátzio, Jarácuaro and Uranden it is more intimate. 6-9 Dec, Virgen de la Salud, when authentic Tarascan dances are performed in front of the _basílica_. There is an interesting _fiesta_ on 12 December for the Virgin of Guadalupe; on 12 October, when Columbus reached America, there is also a procession with the Virgin and lots of fireworks. Carnival in February when the Dance of the Moors is done. On the 8th day of every month there is a religious celebration and most accommodation is full.

aff
_vt_

Hotels Rooms in some hotels are reserved 4 weeks prior to Día de los Muertos, other hotels do not take reservations, so it is pot luck at this time. **A+ _Posada de don Vasco_**, attractive, colonial-style hotel on Av de las Américas (halfway between lake and town, T 20262), breakfast good, other meals poor; presents the Dance of the Old Men on Wed and Sat at 2100, no charge, non-residents welcome but drinks very expensive to compensate; also mariachi band. **B _Las Redes_**, Av de las Américas 6, T 21275, near lake, popular restaurant; **B _Mesón del Cortijo_**, Obregón, just off Américas, T 21295, rec, but often fully booked at weekends; **C _Apo-Pau_**, between lake and town (closest to town of the non-central hotels), pleasant, friendly.

A _Mesón del Gallo_, Dr Coss 20, T 21474, F 21511, good value, flower garden, tasteful furnishings; **B _Posada La Basílica_**, Arciga 6, T 21108, nice restaurant with good views, central; **C _Los Escudos_**, Portal Hidalgo 74, T 21290, colonial style ("Baile de los Viejitos' every Sat at 2000), rec, ask for room with fireplace, good food; **B _Posada San Rafael_**, Plaza Vasco

158   **MEXICO**

1. Plaza Vasco de Quiroga
2. Plaza Bocanegra/Plaza Chica
3. Jardín de la Revolución
4. La Basílica/La Colegiata
5. La Compañía
6. El Sagrario
7. San Francisco
8. San Juan de Dios
9. El Humilladero
10. El Hospitalito
11. Museo de Artes Populares, Colegio de San Nicolás
12. Casa de los Once Patios
13. Market
14. Post Office
15. Telephone Office
16. Tourist Office

Hotels:
17. Posada San Rafael
18. Gran
19. Misión San Manuel
20. Posada de la Salud
21. El Artillero
22. Posada de la Rosa
23. Cafetería El Buho

PÁTZCUARO MAC 13

de Quiroga, T 20770, safe, poor restaurant, parking in courtyard; **A** *Mansión Iturbe*, Portal Morelos 59, restored mansion on main square, very expensive restaurant; **C** *Misión San Manuel*, Portal Aldama 12 on main square, restaurant, highly rec; **D** *Imperial*, Obregón 21, large clean rooms; these are all central. **D** *Posada de la Salud*, Benigno Serrato 9, T 20058, clean, quiet, pleasant, excellent value, some rooms with individual fireplaces, rec; **D** *El Artillero*, Ibarra 22, T 21331, hot water, with bath, gloomy, noisy, not too clean or secure, no drinking water, near Zócalo, (discounts for long stays paid in advance); **D** *Gran Hotel*, Portal Regules 6, on Plaza Bocanegra, T 20443, small rooms, clean, pleasant, good food; **D** *Casa de Huéspedes Pátzcuaro*, Ramos 9, without bath; **E** *Posada de la Rosa*, Portal Juárez 29 (Plaza Chica), with bath, F without, good value, colonial style; next door is **E** *Concordia*, with bath and hot water, cheaper without (which means use of toilet, but no bath whatsoever), clean; **E** *Valmen*, Lloreda 34, T 45412-21161, with bath, hot showers, charming colonial building but noisy, closes 2200, very popular; **E** *Posada Real*, Zaragoza 43, hot water, clean, spacious rooms. There are many *hospedajes* and hotels near the bus station. Public baths next to *Hotel Valmen*, US$0.50.

Motels B *Chalamu*, Pátzcuaro road Km 20, space for ont trailer or 3 small vans, T 20948; **B** *Hostería de San Felipe*, Cárdenas 321, T 21298, friendly, clean, fireplaces in rooms, good restaurant (closes 2030), highly rec; **B** *San Carlos*, Muelle Col Morelos, T 21359; *Pátzcuaro*, Av de las Américas 506, T 20767 (Apartado Postal 206), 1 km from centre, hot water, gardens, tennis, pleasant, also camping and caravan site. *Trailer Park El Pozo*, on lakeside, opp *Chalamu*, T 20937, hot showers am, large, delightful, well-equipped, US$10, owner speaks English, also camping (take water for drinking from the entrance rather than taps on the trailer pads).

Camping See **Motels** above.

Restaurants Local speciality is *pescado blanco* (white fish), but it is disappearing from menus as a result of over fishing and pollution. Several lakeside restaurants serve fish dishes, but it is advisable to avoid locally caught fish. Many places close before 2000. Make sure you don't get overcharged in restaurants—some display menus outside which bear no resemblance to the prices inside. *El Munjo*, main square, reasonable food but slow service. *Los Escudos* restaurant, Plaza Quiroga, open till 2200, popular, try *sopa tarasca* (a flavoursome soup made with toasted tortillas, cream and cheese), good service, value and coffee; *San Agustín*, Plaza Bocanegra, friendly, good doughnuts on sale outside in pm. *Taquería Los Equipales*, Portal Allende 57, Plaza Vasco de Quiroga (under *Hotel Mansión Iturbe*), very good *tacos*, open from mid-afternoon into the night. *Gran Hotel*, filling *comida corrida* (US$5), excellent *café con leche*; good chicken with vegetables (US$3) and *enchiladas* over the market (budget restaurants here, usually open in evening). *Cafetería Dany's*, Zaragoza between the 2 squares, *comida* for US$4, good snacks; *Cafetería El Buho*, Tejerías 8, open 0800-2200, breakfasts, meals, drinks, very good food, good value, stylish, rec. *Camino Real*, next to Pemex, 100m from *El Pozo Trailer Park*, very good *comida corrida* US$5, quick service. Excellent *paletería* and ice cream parlour at Codallos 24, also sells frozen yoghurt; fruit and yoghurt for breakfast at *El Patio*, *Plaza Chica* (not cheap, slow service). Breakfast available from small strands in the market, usually 0600-0700 (*licuadis*, *arroz con leche*, etc).

At the Plaza in Erongaricuaro, 17 km clockwise around the lake, is a Hindu vegetarian restaurant at the weekends; also a local crafts fair (take ADO bus from bus or rail station, US$0.65).

Massage Shiatsu Massage, Stephen Ritter del Castillo, Calle Mendoza 33, Mon-Fri 0900-1700, excellent, English spoken.

Tourist office Ibarra 2, Interior 3, Plaza Vasco de Quiroga, T 21214 (poorly signed); diagonally opposite NW corner of plaza, next to Veterinario. The office is 3 doors along, on the right, in the courtyard.

Transport New bus station out of town, colectivo from centre US$0.25. To **Mexico City**, Tres Estrellas de Oro, Herradura de Plata (via Morelia—rec) and Autobuses de Occidente 1st (US$15.60) and 2nd class buses (US$14.20), 6 hrs. Very enjoyable and cheaper, though slower, train ride around lake and plateau to Mexico City. Train leaves daily at 2100, from Mexico City to Pátzcuaro, arrives at 0645, beautiful views between Uruapan and Acámbaro (*fiesta*, 4 July); 1st class fare from capital US$9.50, US$18 *primera especial*. Train to Mexico City at 2115 (*servicio estrella*), 10 hrs. Take pullover. Train to **Uruapan** and **Lázaro Cárdenas**: 0645, *servicio estrella*.

Regular bus service to **Morelia**, 1 hr, US$2.20 with ADO, Herradura de Plata, Galeana and Flecha Amarilla (departs every ½ hr, US$2). Buses to **Guadalajara** go through Zamora, US$10 (Flecha Amarilla), 6 hrs; no trains to Guadalajara; to **Lázaro Cárdenas**, for connections to Zihuatenejo, Acapulco, etc, hourly from 0600, US$12.50, 8 hrs, long but spectacular ride through mountains and lakes (police checks likely); to **Uruapan**, ½ hourly, US$3.30; to **Toluca**, 1st class US$11.50, 5 hrs. Local buses from corner of market in town to lakeside (colectivo to lakeside US$0.25).

Excursions The best-known island is *Janitzio*, which despite the souvenir shops and the tourists (visit during the week if possible) has considerable charm. It is 45 mins by motorboat, leaves when full from 0800 onwards, US$12.65 return, tickets from office at dock, last boat back (return by any boat) at 1800. There is an unfortunate monument to Morelos, with mural inside, crowning a hill, US$0.30, which nevertheless affords magnificent views, and a circular path around the island. Winter is the best time for fishing in the somewhat fish-depleted lake, where Indians throw nets shaped like dragonflies. The Government is planning to improve the lake's water quality, still plenty of places sell white fish on the island, at about a quarter of the price in Pátzcuaro. On a lakeside estate is the Educational Centre for Community Development in Latin America, better known as Crefal (free films every Wed at 1930). For a truly spectacular view of the lake, the islands and the surrounding countryside, walk to Cerro del Estribo; an ideal site for a quiet picnic. It is 1½ hrs walk to the top from the centre of Pátzcuaro. Follow the cobbled road beyond El Calvario, don't take the dirt tracks off to the left. Cars go up in the afternoon, the best time for walking. No buses, 417 steps to the peak. The areas round Pátzcuaro are recommended for bird watching. If intending to drive around the lake, a high-clearance vehicle is necessary.

From Pátzcuaro one can also visit Tzintzuntzan and Quiroga by regular bus service. 30 minutes by local bus is **Ihuátzio** (US$0.25), on a peninsula 12 km N of Pátzcuaro, 8 km from Tzintzuntzan. This was the second most important Tarascan city; two pyramids are well-preserved and afford good views of the lake. Admission US$4.35. The road to the pyramids is very bad.

An excursion can be made into the hills to **Santa Clara del Cobre**, a sleepy village with red tiles and overhanging eaves, an attractive square with copper pots filled with flowers along each arcade, and a fine old church. Hand-wrought copper vessels are made here and there is a Museo del Cobre (closed Mon, free) with some excellent examples; it's ½ block from the main square. There is a Banco Serfín which changes dollars cash and cheques between 1000 and 1200. **Hotels: D** *Real del Cobre*, Portal Hidalgo 19, T 30205; **D** *Oasis*, Portal Allende 144, T 30040, both on main square; **C** *Camino Real*, Av Morelos Pte 213, T 30281. (*Fiesta*: 12-15 August.) Take a bus to Pátzcuaro bus station, then another to Ario de Rosales (every 15 mins), which passes Santa Clara, fare US$0.50 each way. Nearby is the pretty Lago Zirahuen. Past Santa Clara, on the La Huacana road, after Ario de Rosales, one descends into the tropics; fine views all along this road, which ends at Churumuco. Pátzcuaro-Ario de Rosales-Nueva Italia-Uruapan-Pátzcuaro takes about 6 hrs, beautiful tropical countryside.

(Km 314) **Morelia**, capital of Michoacán state, population 759,000 (state population 1990, 3,534,000), altitude 1,882 metres, is a rose-tinted city with attractive colonial buildings (their courtyards are their main feature), rather quiet, founded in 1541. The **Cathedral** (1640), is set between the two main plazas, with graceful towers and a fine façade, in what is called 'sober baroque"; there are paintings by Juárez in the sacristy. Other important churches are the **Virgen de Guadalupe** (also known as San Diego) with a most ornate Pueblan interior, the modernized **Iglesia de la Cruz**, and the 18th century Iglesia de las Rosas in the delightful square of the same name (its ex-Convento now houses the Conservatorio de Música). The oldest of Morelia's churches is the **San Francisco** of the Spanish Renaissance period, but lacking many of the decorative features of that style.

Even more interesting than the colonial churches are the many fine colonial secular buildings still standing. The revolutionary José María Morelos, Melchor Ocampo, and the two unfortunate Emperors of Mexico (Agustín de Iturbide and the Archduke Maximilian of Austria) are commemorated by plaques on their houses. Morelos' birthplace, at Corregidora 113, is open to visitors, admission free. The **Colegio de San Nicolás** (1540) is the oldest surviving institution of higher education in Latin America. (It has a summer school for foreign students.) Opposite is the Centro Cultural Universitario, with many free events. The fine former Jesuit college, now called the **Palacio Clavijero**, contains government offices, with a helpful tourist office on the ground floor (corner of Madero Poniente y Nigromante). Nearby on Av Madero is a library with carved wooden balconies and many historical volumes. Also notable are the **Law School**, in the former monastery of **San Diego**, next to the Guadalupe church; the **Palacio de Gobierno** (1732-70), facing the Cathedral; the **Palacio Municipal**; and the **Palacio Federal**. Visit also the churches of **La Merced**, with its lovely tower and strange, bulging *estípites* (inverted pyramidal supports), **Capuchinas** (Ortega y Montaño), which has some Churrigueresque *retablos*, and **Santa María**, on a hilltop S of the city.

Thursday and Sunday are market days: specialities are pottery, lacquer, woodcarving, jewellery, blankets, leather sandals; in this connection see the **Casa de Artesanías de Michoacán**, in the ex-Convento de San Francisco, next to the church of the same name; it is full of fine regional products for sale, not cheap. Shops close early. Free weekly concerts are held in the municipal theatre. At the E edge of the downtown area, on the road to Mexico City, are the 224 arches of a ruined **aqueduct**, built in 1788 (walk 11 blocks E from Cathedral along Av Madero). Visit the **Museo de Michoacán** (archaeological remains), Calle Allende (open 0900-1900 daily, closed Mon, 0900-1400 Sun, US$4.35), and the new **Casa de la Cultura**, Av Morelos Norte, housed in the ex-Convento del Carmen, which has a good collection of masks from various regions, crucifixes (open daily, free); also workshops (nominal fee of US$1.55 for 12 weeks). The **Museo de Estado**, in the house of Iturbide's wife (Casa de la Emperatriz), SE corner of Jardín de las Rosas, is well worth a visit (open daily). Most of the ground floor is dedicated to Tarascan history and culture, lots of information about Michoacán, and, at the front, an old pharmacy with all its bottles, cabinets, scales, etc, intact. The **Museo de Morelos**, on Morelos Sur, about three blocks S of the Cathedral, is a history museum, admission US$4.35 (described by one correspondent as 'intensely nationalistic"). Both Banamex and Bancomer have their offices in magnificent old houses; the patio of the former is especially fine. Many good language schools. Fairly good zoo in Parque Juárez, S of the centre (25 mins walk S along Galeana). Planetarium.   *91 43*

Hotels Some of the cheaper hotels may have water only in the morning; check. **A+** *Calinda Quality Inn*, Av Acueducto, T 45969, colonial-style, modern. **A** *Alameda*, Av Madero Pte 313 y Calle de Jazmines, T 22023, F 38727, 'flashy"; **A** *Virrey de Mendoza*, Portal Matamoros, T 20633, superb old-style building, service could be better, could be cleaner, poor ventilation, ask for room at front with balcony; **B** *Casino*, Portal Hidalgo 229, *180* main square, T 31003, clean, hot water, private bath. Off the Plaza de Armas and much quieter is the **B** *Posada de la Soledad*, Zaragoza 90 and Ocampo, T 21888, F 22111, fine courtyards, converted chapel as dining room, TV and fireplaces in rooms, parking opposite (free between 2000 and 0900, otherwise US$1/hr), good value, María Luisa speaks English; **B** *Catedral*, Zaragoza 37, T 30783, F 30467, close to Plaza, spacious, nice bar, restaurant closes quite early, rec; **C** *Florida*, Morelos Sur 165, T 21819, clean, good value; **D** *Carmen*, E Ruiz 63, T 21725; another **D** hotel at E Ruiz 673, good value, but small rooms, overlooks the Casa de la Cultura, hot water; **D** *Central*, Abasolo 282, T 20139, 2 blocks S of Zócalo, with hot water, F without, both payable pp, both with shared bath, simple, quiet, parking; **D** *del Matador*, E Ruiz 531, T 24649. **D** *Don Vasco*, Vasco de Quiroga 232, T 21484, with shower and hot water, clean, rec; **D** *Valladolid*, Portal Hidalgo 241, on main square, T 20027, with bath, good value for its location but a bit drab. Cheap hotels on Morelos Norte: **D** *Colonial*, corner with 20 de Noviembre 15, T 21897, pleasant; **D** *Concordia*, Gómez Farías 328, T 23052, round corner from bus station. **D** *San Jorge*, Madero Poniente 719, T 24610, with hot shower, clean, at No 670 is **E** *Vallarta*, T 24095, fair; at No 537 is **E** *Fénix*, with bath, front rooms noisy, back rooms dingy, clean, cheap. Cheap *posadas* and *casas de huéspedes* tend to be uninviting, although the half-dozen around the bus station are reported clean and cheap.

On Santa María hill, S of the city, with glorious views, are hotels *Villa Montaña*, T 40231, F 51423, each room a house on its own, run by French aristocrats, very expensive but value for money, superb restaurant, *Vista Bella* (T 20248) and **C** *Villa San José* next door and much cheaper, reached only by car.

Youth Hostel At corner of Oaxaca and Chiapas No 180, T 33177, 1 km SW of bus station (walk W to Calle Cuautla, then S along Cuautla to Oaxaca) F, pp. Camping possible in a forest about 4 km S of centre on unnumbered Pátzcuaro-signposted road.

Motels **B** *Villa Centurión*, Morelos road, T 32272, good antiques, pool, TV; **C** *El Parador*, Highway 45, with trailer park. **C** *Las Palmas*, Guadalajara road, also trailer park. Two good trailer parks on Route 126 between Morelia and the capital: *Balneario Las Ajuntas*, after Queréndaro, and *Balneario Atzimba*, hot springs at Zinapécuaro.

Restaurants *Govinda*, vegetarian, Av Morelos Sur 39, opp cathedral, delicious lunch for US$1.20, elegant setting, good breakfasts too; *Quinta Sol*, Aquiles Serdán 729, 5 blocks E of Morelos, also vegetarian, good *comida corrida*, US$4, served from 1400; both close daily at 1700 and both closed Sun. *Los Chapis*, Allende 506 esq Rayón, family-run, *comidas corridas*, US$2, good atmosphere and value, rec. *Comidas corridas* at the *Paraíso*, Madero Poniente 103 facing the cathedral; at *El Viejo Paral*, Madero Oriente and Quiroga, and in an unnamed restaurant on Gómez Farias, on right hand side heading away from bus station, US$1.50. *Pizza Tony's*, Madero Ote 698; *Pollo-Coa*, Madero Oriente 890, near aqueduct,

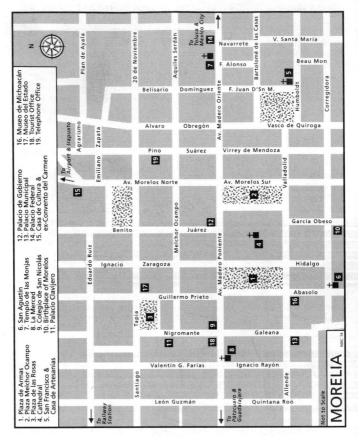

good food; *Los Pioneros*, Aquiles Serdán y Av Morelos Norte, cheap, good local food; *Café Pindaro*, Morelos Norte 150, good breakfasts. On Gómez Farías, *Boca de Río*, at No 185, good fish. Try stewed kid, best in cheaper restaurants. *Café del Olmo*, Benito Juárez 95, in a nice colonial building. There is a good cafe in *Casa de la Cultura*, with delicious home-made cakes.

The Mercado de Dulces, on Gómez Farías at W end of the Palacio Clavijero, is famous for fruit jams (*ates*), candies and *rompope* (a milk and egg nog).

Spanish Classes Centro Mexicano de Idiomas, Calz Fray Antonio de San Miguel 173, intensive weekly classes (US$280 for 1st week, other courses available inc handicrafts, accommodation with families). (See National Registration Center for Study Abroad under **Learning Spanish** in Information for Visitors). Baden-Powell Institute, Antonio Alzate 565, T 24070, from US$6.50/hr to US$8.50/hr, depending on length of course, lodging US$12/day, including 3 meals, courses for all levels, plus cultural, social science and extracurricular courses, highly rec.

Laundromat *Lavandería Chapultepec*, Calle J Ceballos 881.

Post Office in Palacio Federal is said to charge different rates from the rest of Mexico.

Tourist Office Nigromante 79, has local hotel information list and map, little English spoken, open 0900-2000 (closed Sun). Also kiosk at bus terminal.

Rail Morelia-Mexico City at 2240 (*servicio estrella*), train starts at Lázaro Cárdenas, US$8.15 1st class, US$15.35 *primera especial*. Slow train to capital at 1030.

Bus A new terminal has opened, far from the centre, local bus US$2. Many buses to **Guanajuato**, 4½ hrs, US$5.75. **Guadalajara**, US$10.35, also luxury service by ETN, US$20, T 3-74-40. To **Nuevo Laredo**, 17 hrs, US$43. **Uruapan**, US$4.60 2nd class; **Irapuato**, US$4.55 2nd class, rough ride. Several direct daily to **Querétaro**, 3½ hrs. **Mexico City**, 2nd class 6½ hrs, 4½ by 1st *plus*, US$10.50, every 90 mins from 0600 to 2000, ETN luxury service US$22 to W terminal (see also diversion, below). Bus to **Acapulco** US$36.50, 15 hrs. Bus to **Pátzcuaro** every ½ hr with ADO, Flecha Amarilla, Herradura de Plata and Parikhuni, 1 hr, US$2.20. Also about 15 a day to Zihuatanejo on the coast, US$14. For **Toluca** buses, many a day with ETN, 3 hrs, US$14.80.

Air Flights daily to and from Mexico City with Taesa and Aeromar, many daily, 50 mins. No public transport to airport, 26 km from city. Dollar and Budget car rental offices. Taxi to centre US$18.

Diversion Just after Morelia there is a good road N to two lakeside villages. At **Cuitzeo**, the first one (hotel, *Restaurant Esteban*, by post office), there is a fine Augustinian church and convent (begun in 1550), a cloister, a huge open chapel, and good choir stalls in the sacristy. The church houses a good collection of Mexican graphic art, spanning four centuries, in a gallery in the basement. Laguna de Cuitzeo, on which it stands, is the second largest lake in Mexico; the road crosses it on a causeway. Ecological damage in the past has caused the lake to dry up on occasion. From here one can go to **Valle de Santiago** (D *Hotel Posada de la Parroquia*), attractive mountain scenery. The second village, 33 km to the N, **Yuriria**, has a large-scale Indian version of the splendid church and convent at Actopán (**see p 72**). It is on Laguna de Yuriria, which looks like a grassy swamp. (Before Yuriria is Moreleón, the clothing distribution centre of Mexico—buses empty here.) The road continues to **Salamanca** (hotel, appalling traffic), where one turns left for Irapuato or right for Celaya and Querétaro. Mexico City-Morelia buses from the Central del Norte take the freeway to Celaya and then head S through Yuriria and Cuitzeo.

The road soon climbs through 50 km of splendid mountain scenery: forests, waterfalls, and gorges, to the highest point at (Km 253), Puerto Gartan, and **Mil Cumbres** (2,886 metres), with a magnificent view over mountain and valley, and then descends into a tropical valley. A new, 4-lane highway avoids the Mil Cumbres pass.

Another alternative to the Mil Cumbres pass is to take Route 126 from Morelia to **Queréndaro**, where the pavements are covered in *chiles* drying in the blazing sun, and all the shops are filled with large bags of *chiles* in the season, then at a junction 10 km short of Zinapécuaro, turn right to join Route 15 (to Toluca and Mexico City) at Huajumbaro. If, instead of turning right you carry straight on, the road climbs and descends to **Maravatío** (hotel) and then climbs steeply, towards **Tlalpujahua**, an old mining town with a museum, several churches, and cobblestoned streets, very picturesque among forests and hills (*Casa de Huéspedes*). From Maravatío Route 122 goes S to join Route 15 just E of Ciudad Hidalgo. Also from Maravatío, Route 126 to Toluca has been upgraded to a toll road, renamed 15D and is 1 hr quicker than the route over the mountains on Route 15.

NW of Maravatío, on the Río Lerma (18th century bridge), lies the town of **Acámbaro**, founded 1526. It has a Franciscan church of the same date and monastery (finished 1532), with the Capilla de Santa Gracia (mid-16th century) and its ornate fountain. It was the point from which the irrigation system for the whole area was laid out when the town was founded. Acámbaro continues to thrive as an agricultural centre and an important railway junction. It is also on the main highway from Celaya to Toluca.

Worth a glance are the façade of the 16th century church at **Ciudad Hidalgo** (Km 212, 100,000 people)—**D** *Hotel Fuente*, Morelos 37, T 40518, some rooms have no keys, clean, showers, no water in the afternoon; **E** *Florida*, damp rooms, garage US$0.50 a night; *Restaurant Manolo*, inexpensive, good; and the old colonial bridge and church at **Tuxpan** (**Michoacán**) Km 193; **D** *Mara*, on main square, clean, hot water, wood stove; *Tuxpan*, Miguel Cabrera, T 50058, noisy. At Km 183 a side road runs, right, to the spa of **San José Purúa** at 1,800 metres, in a wild setting of mountain and gorge and woods. The radioactive thermal waters are strong. First-class hotel, B, or over US$90 full board for two, beautiful spot, good restaurant but a bit run-down, reservations in Mexico City, T 510 1538/4949, helpful stall. Trailers can park outside the guarded gate (24 hrs, tip the guard for security), small charge for entry to grounds. Smaller, cheaper hotels lie on the road past the spa and in the town of Jungapeo. If driving with a trailer, do not take the downward hill to the village, your brakes may not hold.

Then comes **Zitácuaro,** with a pleasant plaza and a good covered market. Bus to Mexico City, 3½ hrs, US$5.75; to Morelia, US$4.60, 3 hrs; to Guadalajara, 11 hrs, US$14.80, 409 km.

Hotels B *Rancho San Cayetano*, 3 km out on Huetamo road, T 31926, chalets, friendly, clean, highly rec; **B** *Rosales del Valle*, Revolución Sur 56, T 31293, near bus station, fair, some rooms hired for very short stays; **B** *Salvador*, Hidalgo Pte 7, T 31107, clean and pleasant; **D** *Florida*, with bath, clean, garage US$0.50 a night; **D** *Hotel Colón*, reasonable, fan, not very quiet, friendly management, can store luggage; **D** *Posada Michoacán*, main square, TV, clean; **E** *El Turista*, Av Revolución Norte 4 (main street), with bath, restaurant with excellent meals, good value, clean, highly rec; **E** *Mary*, on main street, hot shower, clean, noisy at night from buses.

A turning off the main road at Angangueo brings one to a unique site, the wintering grounds of the Monarch butterfly in **El Campanario Ecological Reserve**, above the village of El Rosario. It can be reached by taking a half-hourly local bus (labelled Angangueo) from Zitácuaro (Av Santos Degollado Oriente) to Ocampo, 1 hr, US$0.75, and from Ocampo another local bus (3 a day from corner 2 blocks E of plaza, one at 1230, last one back at 1600, 1¼ hrs, US$0.85, 12 km on a mountainous dirt road) to El Rosario. Entry to the reserve is about US$10, including guided tour; it has a small visitors' centre and several trails to see the myriads of large orange butterflies, which migrate every year from SE Canada and NE USA. The butterflies leave in March, after which there is nothing to see until the following December/January. The reserve can no doubt be reached from other towns nearby, such as Angangueo, Ciudad Hidalgo or Tuxpan, and Aguila Tours, Amsterdam 291-C, Col Hipódromo Condesa, run tours from early December from Mexico City.

(Km 86) A branch road, right, goes to the mountain resort of **Valle de Bravo**, a charming old town on the edge of an attractive artificial lake, with another Monarch butterfly wintering area nearby. This area gets the week-end crowd from Mexico City. (1 direct bus a day Zitácuaro-Valle de Bravo, US$3.30; 1st class bus to Toluca, US$3.50.)

Hotels *Loto Azul Resort*, Av Toluca, T 20157, F 22747, 4-star; *Centro Vacacional ISSEMYM*, central, pool, restaurant, satisfactory, Independencia 404; **B** *Los Arcos*, good, is several km beyond, in pine woods, excellent restaurant. **C** *Refugio del Salto*, Fontana Brava; **D** *Mary*, main plaza, hot showers. **Trailer Park** Av del Carmen 26, T (91726) 21972 (or Toluca 91721-21580), familia Otero, English spoken, 5 hook-ups, 7 dry camping, 3 rentals, small private grounds, English spoken, rec. **NB** Drivers with trailers must approach Avándaro from the Toluca end, no other way is safe because of the hills, narrow streets and town centre.

(Km 75) A road branches off to the volcano of Toluca (**Nevado de Toluca**, or Xinantécatl; 4,558 metres, the fourth highest mountain in Mexico) and climbs to the deep blue lakes of the Sun and the Moon in its two craters, at about 4,270 metres, from which there is a wide and awe-inspiring view. It is 27 km from the turning off the main road to the heart of the craters. During winter it is possible to ski on the slopes; 2 km from the entrance is an *albergue* with food and cooking facilities. From here it is 10 km to the entrance to the crater, where there is a smaller *albergue* (cooking facilities, food sold at weekends only), and then a further 6 km to the lakes. A short cut from the small *albergue* takes 20 mins to the crater (not possible to drive). At the third refuge (21 km from the turn-off) is an attendant. Trips to the volcano are very popular at weekends. You can stay overnight at any of the refuges (F) and there is a restaurant, but the trip can be done in one day from Toluca. If walking remember the entrance to the crater is on the far left side of the volcano.

To reach the Toluca volcano take the first bus to Sultepec from Toluca at about 0700, every 2 hrs thereafter. Leave the bus where the road to the radio station branches off, just after Raices village (US$1), from there it is about 20 km to the crater, hitching fairly easy, especially at weekends. Aim to get to the crater by midday, otherwise clouds will cover everything. Visitors must leave by 1700.

(Km 64) *Toluca*, population 600,000, altitude 2,639 metres, about 4¾ hrs from Morelia by bus, is the capital of the state of México (1990 population 9,815,900). It is known mostly for its huge Friday market—reportedly less colourful than it used to be—where Indians sell colourful woven baskets, *sarapes*, *rebozos*, pottery and embroidered goods (beware of pickpockets and handbag slashers). The new market is at Paseo Tollocan e Isidro Fabela, spreading over a number of streets, open daily. As well as for textiles, the city is famous for confectionery, *chorizos* (sausages) and for an orange liqueur known as *moscos*. It is also a centre of chemical industries which causes pollution. The centre of the city is the **Plaza de los Mártires**, a very open space. On its S side is the **Cathedral**, begun in 1870, but not completed until 1978 (incorporated in its interior is the baroque façade of the 18th-century church of the Tercera Orden). Also on the S side is the **Church of Veracruz**, which houses a black Christ; its interior is very attractive. On three sides of the block which contains these two churches are **Los Portales** (Calles Bravo, Hidalgo and Constitución), arcaded shops and restaurants. NE of Plaza de los Mártires is a park, Plaza Angel María Garibay, with trees and fountains on which are the **Museo de Bellas Artes**, formerly the Convento del Carmen, with seven halls of paintings (from Colonial Baroque—18th century—to 20th century) and temporary exhibitions. A tunnel is said to run from the ex-Convento to all the central churches—in it were found the skulls of the nuns' illegitimate children. (Museum open Tues-Sun 1000-1800, students half price, booklet US$1.35.) Next door is the **Templo del Carmen**, a neoclassical church with a gold and white interior. Next to the Carmen is Plaza España. At the eastern end of Plaza Garibay is the **Cosmovitral** and **Jardín Botánico** (open Tues-Sun 0900-1700, US$1.60). From 1933-1975 the building was the 16 de Septiembre market; in 1980 it was opened in its new form, a formal garden in honour of the Japanese Eizi Matuda, who set up the herbarium of Mexico State, with fountains and exhibitions, all bathed in the blues, oranges and reds of the vast stained glass work of Leopoldo Flores Valdez, a unique sight. One block W of Plaza Garibay is the **Palacio de Gobierno**. 4 blocks W of Los Portales is the **Alameda**, a large park with a statue of Cuauhtémoc and many tall trees; on Sunday morning it is very popular with families strolling among the many stallholders. The entrance is at the junction of Hidalgo and Ocampo. At Ocampo y Morelos is the **Templo de la Merced**. The **Casa de las Artesanías** (Casart), with an excellent display of local artistic products for sale, is at Paseo Tollocan 700 (open daily 0930-1850), more expensive than Mexico City. 10 km S of the city is a good zoo, Zacango.

Hotels *Holiday Inn*, Caretera a México Km 57.5, T 164666, F 164099, restaurant, bar, parking; **C** *San Carlos*, Madero 210, T 49422; **D** *Colonial*, Hidalgo Oriente 103, T 47066, with bath, clean, TV, cheap food (good restaurant, closed Sun), rec (bus from Terminal de Autobuses to Centro passes in front); **D** *Rex*, Matamoros Sur 101, T 59300, with bath, hot water, no restaurant; on Hidalgo Poniente: **C** *La Mansión*, No 408, T 56578, with hot water, clean, garage, TV, no restaurant; **D** *Alameda*, No 508, with bath, hot water, TV, nice rooms, *El Patio* restaurant, **E** *Maya*, No 413, shared bath, hot water, clean, charming, towels extra. All the above are in the centre, not many cheap hotels. **D** *Terminal*, adjoining bus terminal, T 57960 (prices vary according to floor), restaurant next door.

Motels A+ *Del Rey Inn*, T 122122, F 122567, Km 63, Mexico City road entrance (5-star); resort facilities; on same exit road, *Paseo*, T 65730 (4-star) and *Castel Plaza Las Fuentes*, Km 57.5, T 164666, F 164798 (5-star).

Restaurants *Ostionería Escamilla*, Rayón Nte 404, good fish; *San Francisco*, Villada 108; *Café L'Ambient*, Hidalgo 231 Pte, snacks, meals, quite simple; next door is *Son Jei*, oriental; opposite, in Los Portales, is *Impala* for *comida corrida*, coffee; *Woolworth* restaurant, Hidalgo Poniente casi Matamoros, is open Sunday from 0930 for good set breakfasts; *Fonda Rosita* in Los Portales central avenue going through to Plaza de los Mártires, is also open Sun am, pleasant, Mexican; *Las Ramblas*, on Constitución side of Los Portales, Mexican food, average.

Tourist Office Lerdo de Tejada Poniente 101, Edif Plaza Toluca, 1° piso, T 50131; Federal office at Villada 123, T 48961.

Transport Bus station is some distance from the centre; inside, information is difficult to gather and all is confusion outside—look for a bus marked 'Centro'; US$0.15; from centre to terminal buses go from, among other places Ignacio Rayón Nte e Hidalgo Ote, look for 'Terminal' on window (yellow or orange bus). To Mexico City, US$2.85. Bus to **Pátzcuaro**, 6 hrs, US$11.50, several daily; to **Taxco**, 4 buses a day, book in advance, 3 hrs, US$8, a spectacular journey. To **Morelia**, several buses daily with Herrachura de Plata, 4 hrs, US$8.25, ETN US$14.80. Many buses to **Tenango de Arista** (US$0.65, ½ hr), **Tenancingo** (US$2.25); also regular buses to **Calixtlahuaca** US$2.50 (1 hr) from platform 7.

From Toluca to the coast at Ixtapa (Route 134, **see p 245**), via Tejupilco (**C** *Hotel Juárez*), Ciudad Altamirano and La Salitrera: the road is paved (deteriorating in parts), traffic is sparse and the landscape hilly and pleasant.

Excursions From Toluca take a bus to the pyramids and Aztec seminary of **Calixtlahuaca**, 2 km off the road to Ixtlahuaca; pyramids are to Quetzalcoatl (circular) and to Tlaloc; they are situated just behind the village, 10 mins walk from the final bus-stop. Entry US$4.35.

45 minutes N by car, near the town of Temoaya, is the Centro Ceremonial Otomí, a modern site for cultural events in a beautiful landscape.

See above for trips to Toluca volcano.

Along Route 55 S of Toluca, or reached from it, are a number of most interesting 'art and craft' producing villages, all with old churches. The first village is **Metepec**, the pottery-making centre of the valley, 1½ km off the road to Tenango. The clay figurines made here—painted bright fuchsia, purple, green and gold—are unique. This is the source of the 'trees of life and death", the gaudily-painted pottery sold in Mexico. Craft workshops are very spread out. Market is on Mon. Interesting convent (bus Toluca-Metepec US$0.65). A detour E off Route 55 (or S from Route 15, the Toluca-Mexico City highway) goes to the town of **Santiago Tianguistenco** (38,000). Good *cazuelas*, *metates*, baskets and *sarapes*. Between July and early November displays of wild mushrooms for sale. Try *gordas* or *tlacoyos*, blue corn stuffed with a broad bean paste. If you are brave try *atepocates*; embryo frogs with tomato and chiles, boiled in maize leaves. Try restaurant *Mesón del Cid*, good regional food, go to kitchen to see choice. Try *sopa de hongos*, mushroom soup. Market day is Wednesday. The town is crowded at weekends.

Route 55 descends gradually to **Tenango de Arista** (Toluca-Tenango bus, US$0.65), where one can walk (20 mins) to the ruins of **Teotenango** (Matlazinca culture, reminiscent of La Ciudadela at Teotihuacán, with 5 plazas, 10 structures, and 1 ball court). There is an interesting museum by the ruins of Teotenango; entry to museum and ruins US$4.35; to enter go to the end of town on the right hand side. 48 km from Toluca the road descends abruptly through gorges to

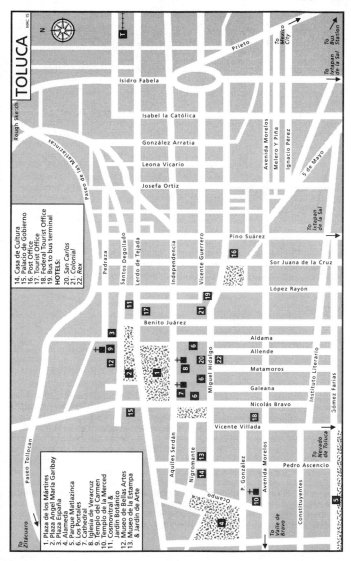

MAC 15

TOLUCA

Rough sketch

N

To
Mexico
City

To Bus
Station

To
Ixtapan
de la Sal

Prieto

Isidro Fabela

Isabel la Católica

González Arratia

Leona Vicario

Josefa Ortiz

Paseo de las Matlazincas

Avenida Morelos

Melero Y Piña

Ignacio Pérez

5 de Mayo

Pino Suárez

To Ixtapan de la Sal

Sor Juana de la Cruz

López Rayón

Pedraza

Santos Degollado

Lerdo de Tejada

Independencia

Vicente Guerrero

Benito Juárez

Aldama

Allende

Matamoros

Galeana

Nicolás Bravo

Vicente Villada

Miguel Hidalgo

Instituto Literario

Gómez Farías

Pedro Ascencio

Aquiles Serdán

Nigromante

P. González

Avenida Morelos

Constituyentes

Paseo Tollocan

To
Valle de
Bravo

To
Nevado
de Toluca

Ocampo

To
Zitácuaro

14. Casa de Cultura
15. Palacio de Gobierno
16. Post Office
17. Tourist Office
18. Federal Tourist Office
19. Bus to bus terminal
HOTELS:
20. San Carlos
21. Colonial
22. Rex

1. Plaza de los Mártires
2. Plaza Angel María Garibay
3. Plaza España
4. Alameda
5. Parque Matlazinca
6. Los Portales
7. Cathedral
8. Iglesia de Veracruz
9. Templo del Carmen
10. Templo de la Merced
11. Convento &
   Jardín Botánico
12. Museo de Bellas Artes
13. Museo de la Estampa
   & Jardín de Arte

Tenancingo, still at 1,830 metres, but with a soft, warm all-the-year-round climate. Half an hour by bus to the S (road unpaved) is the magnificent 18th century Carmelite convent of El Santo Desierto, making beautiful *rebozos*. The townspeople themselves weave fine *rebozos* and the fruit wines are delicious and cheap. Overlooking this busy commercial town is a statue of Christ on a hill. The daily market area is 2 blocks from the bus terminal (continue 1 block, turn left for 2 further blocks to the main square); market day is on Sunday. Rec hotels at Tenancingo are **C** *Lazo*, Guadalupe Victoria 100, T 20083 (1½ blocks straight on from market, away from bus terminal), with clean rooms in annex with shower, leafy courtyard, *El Arbol de la Vida* restaurant; **D** *Hotel Jardín* on main plaza, T 20108, with bath, big, airy rooms, restaurant, good value. (Frequent buses to Toluca, US$2.25 with Tres Estrellas del Centro, 1 hr; also to Ixtapan de la Sal, Taxco, Malinalco, US$1.50, and Chalma.)

On 32 km from Tenancingo, on Route 55, is **Ixtapan de la Sal**, a pleasant forest-surrounded leisure resort with medicinal hot springs. In the centre of this quiet whitewashed town is the municipal spa, adult admission US$1.60. The municipal spa's hours are 0700-1800, it is not always open. At the edge of town is Parque Los Trece Lagos. Private baths charge US$6 for admission only, everything else is extra. For the hedonist there are private 'Roman' baths, for the stiff-limbed a medicinal hot-water pool, mud baths for the vain, an Olympic pool for swimmers, rowing boats and a water slide for the adventurous. The latter is 150 metres long (prohibited to those over 40; US$1.55 entry, US$0.90 for 2 slides, US$2.20 for slides all day, free midweek 1200-1400). 'The Thirteen Lake Park' is privately run and has a train running around; there are numerous picnic spots. Market day: Sun. Fiesta: second Fri in Lent.

Ixtapan de la Sal can be reached in 2 hrs or so by car from Mexico City: turn off Route 15, the Toluca highway, at La Marquesa (see below), go through Santiago Tianguistenco and join Route 55 at Tenango. The road goes on to the Grutas de Cacahuamilpa (**see p 235**) from where you can continue either to Cuernavaca or Taxco. Bus to/from Mexico City 3 hrs, US$5.35, every 30 mins from Terminal Oriente; to Toluca every ½ hr, US$4.20, 2 hrs. Also to Taxco, Coatepec, Cuernavaca.

Hotels A+ *Ixtapan*, Nuevo Ixtapan, T 30304, food and entertainment included; **A+** *Vista Hermosa*, T 30092, next door, full board only, good, friendly; **A** *Kiss* (*Villa Vergel*), Blvd San Román y Av Juárez, T 30349, F 30842; **B** *Casablanca*, Juárez 615, T 30241, F 30842; **C** *María Isabel*, T 30122, good; **D** *Guadalajara*, with bath; **D** *Casa de Huéspedes Margarita*, Juárez, clean, rec; **E** *Casa Yuyi*, with bath, clean, good; many others. Plenty of reasonable restaurants on Av Benito Juárez, most close by 1900. Good value is *Fonda Jardín* on Zócalo.

About 11 km E of Tenancingo is **Malinalco**, from which a path winds up 1 km—20 mins—to Malinalco ruins (1188—Matlazinca culture, with Aztec additions), certainly one of the most remarkable pre-Hispanic ruins in Mexico, now partly excavated. Here is a fantastic rock-cut temple in the side of a mountain which conceals in its interior sculptures of eagle and jaguar effigies. The staircase leading to the temple has over 430 steps cut into the rock. The site is small, in a commanding position over the valley, and now overlooking the town and the wooded hills all around (open Tues-Sun 1000-1630, US$4.35, Sun free). The site is visible from the town as a ledge on the hillside; the walk up passes a tiny, blue colonial chapel. You should not fail to visit also the Augustinian Templo y Exconvento del Divino Salvador (1552), in the centre of town, the nave of which has a patterned ceiling, while the two-storey cloisters are painted with elaborate, early frescoes. Just below the main square in front of the convent is the market (market day Wednesday). There is a *fiesta* in Malinalco on 6 January.

Accommodation and Food E *Hotel Santa Mónica*, Hidalgo 109, T 29, pretty courtyard; **E** *Posada Familiar*; cabins for families at N edge of town; camping and trailer park *El Paraíso* opp the small blue chapel. Restaurant *La Playa* on road to ruins, just off square, with garden, nice place; opp is *La Salamandra*, good value; trout farm and fishery has a restaurant, superb, bring own supplies of beverages, bread, salad (trout costs US$5-6); also *El Rincón del Convento*, behind the convent on road to square.

Transport A direct road runs from Tenancingo to Malinalco, paved to the summit of a range of hills, poor at the summit, then graded to the junction with the Malinalco-San Pedro Zictepec road; pick-up truck or buses run on this direct road hourly, 40 mins, US$2.25 (in Malinalco bus leaves from corner of Av Progreso and the square). From Toluca you can go to Malinalco by leaving the Toluca-Tenancingo road after San Pedro Zictepec, some 12 km N of Tenancingo, which is paved and 28 km long. Terminal in Mexico City, Central del Poniente, opp Observatorio, at least two companies go there.

You can also get to Malinalco from Toluca, or Mexico City, by taking a 2nd class bus to **Chalma**. This is a popular pilgrimage spot, and when you get off the bus you will be offered (for sale) a corona of flowers. From the bus lot, walk up hill, past the market stalls, to the crossroads where blue colectivos leave for Malinalco until 2000 (10 km, 20 mins, US$1). Buses from Mexico City leave frequently from Central del Poniente, 2 hrs, US$3.60 direct. This is also where you make connections if coming from Cuernavaca (take a Cuernavaca-Toluca bus to Santa Marta, then wait for a Mexico City or Toluca-Chalma bus).

The basin of Toluca, the highest in the central region, is the first of a series of basins drained by the Río Lerma into the Pacific. To reach Mexico City from Toluca—64 km by dual carriageway—it is necessary to climb over the intervening mountain range. The centre of the basin is swampy. (Km 50) Lerma is on the edge of the swamp, the source of the Lerma river. The road climbs, with backward views of the snow-capped Toluca volcano, to the summit at Las Cruces (Km 32; 3,035 metres). At this point is the **Parque Nacional Miguel Hidalgo**, or **La Marquesa**, which has many facilities for weekend recreation (lakes with water sports, hiking, running, picnics etc). Here also is the turn-off for Chalma and Santiago Tianguisteco from Route 15. There are occasional great panoramic views of the City and the Valley of México during the descent (smog-permitting).

MEXICO CITY (6)

Mexico City, the capital, altitude 2,240 metres, founded by the Spaniards in 1521, was built upon the remains of Tenochtitlan, the Aztec capital, covering some 200 square km. The Valley of México, the intermont basin in which it lies, is about 110 km long by 30 km wide. Rimming this valley is a sentinel-like chain of peaks of the Sierra Nevada mountains. Towards the SE tower two tall volcanoes, named for the warrior Popocatépetl and his beloved Ixtaccíhuatl, the Aztec princess who died rather than outlive him. Popocatépetl is 5,452 metres high, and Ixtaccíhuatl (Eestaseewatl) 5,286 metres. Both are permanently snow-capped, but they are often not visible because of the smog. To the S the crest of the Cordillera is capped by the wooded volcano of Ajusco.

About 20 million people (one in four of the total population) live in this city, which has over half the country's manufacturing employment, and much of the nation's industrial smog (the worst months being December to February). Measures such as closing the huge Pemex refinery have reduced lead and sulphur dioxide emissions to acceptable levels, but the ozone level is occasionally dangerous. Common ailments are a burning sensation in the eyes (contact-lens wearers take note) and nose and a sore throat. Citizens are advised by the local authorities not to smoke and not to take outdoor exercise. The English-language daily, The News, gives analysis of the air quality, with warnings and advice.

The city suffers from a fever of demolition and rebuilding, especially since the heavy damage caused by the September 1985 earthquake. This was concentrated along the Paseo de la Reforma, Avenida Juárez, the Alameda, and various suburbs and residential districts. About 20,000 people are believed to have lost their lives, largely in multi-storey housing and government-controlled buildings, including Juárez hospital in which there were about 3,000 fatalities.

Mexico City has long burst its ancient boundaries and spread; some of the new residential suburbs are most imaginatively planned, though there are many appalling shanty-towns. Like all big centres it is faced with a fearsome traffic problem, despite the building of a new inner ring road. To relieve congestion eight underground railway lines are now operating. There is also a large traffic-free area E of the Zócalo.

Because of the altitude the climate is mild and exhilarating save for a few days in mid-winter. The normal annual rainfall is 660 mm, and most of it falls—usually in the late afternoon—between May and October. Even in summer the temperature at night is rarely above 13°C, and in winter there can be sharp frosts. Despite this, central heating is not common.

Sightseeing in and around the city can easily take up ten days. The main places of interest are listed below.

You will find, as you explore the city, that you use two thoroughfares more than any others. The most famous is Paseo de la Reforma, with a tree-shaded, wide centre section and two side lanes; it runs somewhat diagonally NE from the Bosque de Chapultepec. At the Plaza de la Reforma it bends eastwards and becomes Avenida Juárez, still fairly wide but without side lanes. Beyond the Palacio de Bellas Artes this becomes Av Madero, quite narrow, with one-way traffic. The other and longer thoroughfare is Av Insurgentes, a diagonal NS artery about 25 km long. Reforma and Insurgentes bisect at a *plazuela* with a statue of Cuauhtémoc, the last of the Aztec emperors. Much of the Centro Histórico has been refurbished; this is roughly a rectangle from Alhóndiga/Santísma, E of the Zócalo, to Guerrero, W of the Alameda; República de Honduras in the N of the Alameda; República de Honduras in the N to Arcos de Belén/Izazaga S of the Alameda and Zócala. Calle Tacuba is especially fine; street vendors have been banished from it. The *Guía Peatonal* of Sacbe (US$1.15) is rec, giving 8 suggested walking routes, all starting from metro stations. Two ways of familiarising oneself quickly with the Centro Histórico are to take a trip (US$5) on a 1910-type street car (every 30 mins from the Museo de la Ciudad de México, Pino Suárez), or to ride on a form of rickshaw (bici-taxi) from the Zocalo, US$1.65 for 30 mins.

Mexico's 'West End", the Zona Rosa (Pink Zone), used to be where most of the fashionable shops were found; it is bounded by the Paseo de la Reforma, Av Chapultepec, Calle Florencia and Av Insurgentes Sur. It has been replaced by Polanco, N of Chapultepec, a luxury residential area with many interesting art galleries and shops. It does not suffer from the tourists that crowd the Zona Rosa and other chic areas. Many old houses have carved stone façades, tiled roofs, gardens, especially on Calle Horacio, a pretty street lined with trees and parks. The Secretaría de Turismo Offices are on Av Presidente Masaryk at the corner of Hegel.

The Zócalo, the main square, or Plaza Mayor, centre of the oldest part, barred to wheeled traffic 1000-1700 Mon-Fri, is always alive with people, and often vivid with official ceremonies and celebrations. The flag in the centre of the square is taken down, with ceremony, at 1800 each day. On the N side, on the site of the Great Teocalli or temple of the Aztecs, is

The Cathedral, the largest and oldest cathedral in Latin America, designed by Herrera, the architect of the Escorial in Spain, along with that in Puebla; first built 1525; rebuilding began 1573; consecrated 1667; finished 1813. Singularly harmonious, considering the many architects employed and time taken to build it. Restoration work on the exterior has been completed; work continues inside. There is an underground crypt reached by stairs in the W wing of the main part of the building, open 1000-1300 (closed for restoration in 1993). Next to the Cathedral is the **Sagrario Metropolitano**, 1769, with fine churrigueresque façade. Behind the Cathedral are the Aztec ruins of the **Templo Mayor** or *Teocalli*, which were found in 1978 when public works were being carried out. They make a very worthwhile visit, especially since the Aztecs built a new temple every 52

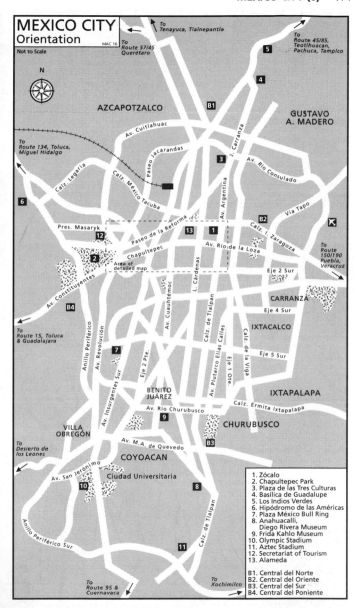

MEXICO CITY
Orientation

MAC 16

Not to Scale

N

To Tenayuca, Tlalnepantla

To Route 57/45 Querétaro

To Route 45/85, Teotihuacan, Pachuca, Tampico

AZCAPOTZALCO

GUSTAVO A. MADERO

Av. Cuitlahuac

To Route 134, Toluca, Miguel Hidalgo

Paseo Jacarandas

Calz. México Tacuba

Calz. Legaria

J. Carranza

Av. Río Consulado

Via Tapo

Pres. Masaryk

Paseo de la Reforma

Chapultepec

Area of detailed map

Av. Constituyentes

Av. Río de la Loza

Calz. I. Zaragoza

To Route 150/190 Puebla, Veracruz

CARRANZA

Eje 2 Sur

Eje 4 Sur

To Route 15, Toluca & Guadalajara

Anillo Periférico

Av. Revolución

Av. Insurgentes Sur

Eje 2 Pte.

Av. Cuauhtémoc

L. Cárdenas

Calz. de Tlalpan

Av. Plutarco Elías Calles

Eje 1 Ote.

Calz. de la Viga

IXTACALCO

Eje 5 Sur

IXTAPALAPA

BENITO JUÁREZ

Av. Río Churubusco

Calz. Ermita Ixtapalapa

CHURUBUSCO

VILLA OBREGÓN

Av. M.A. de Quevedo

To Desierto de los Leones

COYOACAN

Av. San Jerónimo

Ciudad Universitaria

Anillo Periférico Sur

Calz. de Tlalpan

To Route 95 & Cuernavaca

To Xochimilco

Av. Argentina

Av. Río de la Loza

1. Zócalo
2. Chapultepec Park
3. Plaza de las Tres Culturas
4. Basílica de Guadalupe
5. Los Indios Verdes
6. Hipódromo de las Américas
7. Plaza México Bull Ring
8. Anahuacalli,
   Diego Rivera Museum
9. Frida Kahlo Museum
10. Olympic Stadium
11. Aztec Stadium
12. Secretariat of Tourism
13. Alameda

B1. Central del Norte
B2. Central del Oriente
B3. Central del Sur
B4. Central del Poniente

years, and 7 have been identified on top of each other. A **Museum (Museo Arqueológico del Sitio)** was opened in 1987 behind the temple, to house various sculptures found in the main pyramid of Tenochtitlán and six others, including the huge, circular monolith representing the dismembered body of Coyolxauhqui, who was killed by her brother Huitzilopochtli, the Aztec tutelary god, and many other objects. The Templo Mayor and museum are at Seminario 4 y Guatemala, entrance in the corner of the Zócalo, open 0900-1730 daily except Mon, last tickets at 1700, there is a café, bookshop and left luggage office; entry to museum and temple US$4.35, free Sun, US$1.75 to take photos, US$3.45 to use video camera; guided tours in Spanish Tues-Fri 0930-1800, Sat 0930-1300, in English Tues-Sat 1000 and 1200, US$0.85 pp (sometimes cancelled at short notice). In 1993-94 Rigoberta Menchu's Nobel Peace Medal was on display at the entrance to the Templo Mayor (see Guatemala chapter **p 503**).

On Calle Maestro Justo Sierra, N of Cathedral (between Calles Guatemala and San Ildefonso—see map) is the Mexican Geographical Society (No 19), in whose courtyard is a bust of Humboldt and a statue of Benito Juárez, plus a display of documents and maps (ask at the door to be shown in); opposite are the Anfiteatro Simón Bolívar, with murals of his life in the lobby and an attractive theatre, and the Colegio San Ildefonso, open Mon-Sun 1100-1800, except Wed 1100-2100.

On the W side of the Zócalo are the Portales de los Mercaderes (Arcades of the Merchants), very busy since 1524. N of them, opposite the Cathedral, is:

The Monte de Piedad (National Pawnshop) established in the 18th century and housed in a 16th-century building. Prices are government controlled and bargains are often found. Auctions are held each Friday at 1000 (1st, 2nd and 3rd Fri for jewellery and watches, 4th for everything else), US dollars accepted.

The Palacio Nacional (National Palace) takes up the whole eastern side of the Zócalo. Built on the site of the Palace of Moctezuma and rebuilt in 1692 in colonial baroque, with its exterior faced in the red volcanic stone called *tezontle*; the top floor was added by President Calles in the 1920s. It houses various government departments and the Juárez museum (open Mon-Fri, 1000-1800), free. Over the central door hangs the Liberty Bell, rung at 2300 on 15 September by the President, who gives the multitude the *Grito*—"Viva México!' The thronged frescoes around the staircase are by Diego Rivera (including *The History of Mexico*). Open daily; guides: ask them for the US$2 booklet on the frescoes. In the Calle Moneda and adjoining the back of the Palace is the **Museo de las Culturas**, with interesting international archaeological and historical exhibits. Open 0930-1800; closed Sun. Also in Moneda are the site of the first university in the New World (building now dilapidated), the Palacio del Arzobispado, and the site of the New World's first printing press.

Museo de Artes e Industrias Populares de México Av Juárez 44, is reported to be less extensive than it was. Open Tues-Sat 1000-1400 and 1500-1800, shop 1000-1800 Mon-Sat free. Operated by Instituto Nacional Indigenista (INI). It has

---

Mexico City: Key to map

1. Zócalo; 2. Alameda Central; 3. Plaza de la República; 4. Plaza Ciudadela and market; 5. Templo Mayor; 6. Cathedral; 7. San Fernando; 8. Santo Domingo; 9. Hospital de Jesus Nazareno; 10. Colegio de las Vizcaínas; 11. Palacio Nacional; 12. Museo Nacional de Antropología; 13. Museo de Arte Moderno; 14. Castillo de Chapultepec; 15. Museo San Carlos; 16. Museo de Artes e Industrias Populares; 17. Museo de la Ciudad de México; 18. Museo Nacional de la Revolución; 19. Palacio de Iturbide; 20. Monte de Piedad; 21. Torre Latinoamericana and Casa de los Azulejos; 22. Palacio de la Minería and "El Caballito" statue; 23. Palacio de Bellas Artes; 24. Secretaría de Educación Pública; 25. Pinacoteca Virreinal; 26. San Juan market; 27. Lagunilla market; 28. Main Post Office; 29. Independence Monument; 30. Monument to Cuauhtémoc; 31. Monument to Colombus; 32. La Madre Monument; 33. Salto del Agua fountain.

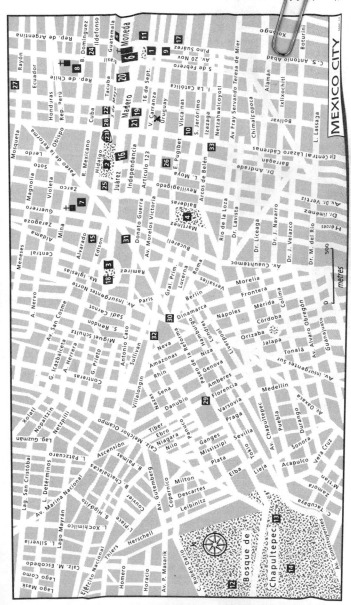

MEXICO CITY

well-arranged permanent exhibitions and the articles are for sale, although you may prefer to find cheaper goods at Ciudadela market (20% cheaper).

Suprema Corte de Justicia de la Nación, opposite Palacio Nacional, on SE corner of the Zócalo, see frescoes by Orozco.

Palacio de Bellas Artes, a large, showy building, interesting for Art Deco lovers, houses a museum and a theatre, and a *cafeteria* at mezzanine level (light, average continental food at moderate prices), and an excellent bookshop on the arts. Open Tues-Sun, 1100-1800. Its domes are lavishly decorated with coloured stone. The museum has old and contemporary paintings, prints, sculptures, and handicraft articles. The fresco by Rivera is a copy of the one rubbed out in disapproval at Radio City, New York, and there are spirited Riveras in the room of oils and water-colours. Other frescoes are by Orozco, Tamayo and Siqueiros. Daily, 1000-1730; Sun, 1000-1330, US$1.75. The most remarkable thing about the theatre is its glass curtain designed by Tiffany. It is solemnly raised and lowered before each performance of the Ballet Folclórico de México. The Palacio is listing badly, for it has sunk 4 metres since it was built. Operas are performed; there are orchestral concerts and performances by the Ballet Folclórico de México on Sun, 0930 and 2100, Wed at 2100 (check press for details)—one must book in advance. Tickets US$12 on the balcony, US$20 and US$25 (cheap balcony seats are not recommended because you see only a third of the stage set, although you can see the performers). Tickets on sale from 1100; hotels, agencies etc only sell the most expensive, cheaper tickets only at the theatre. Cheap concerts at 1200 on Sun, and also at Teatro Hidalgo, behind Bellas Artes on Hidalgo, at the same time, book in advance. Student reductions are given for some shows.

Across the road, on the 41st floor of the **Torre Latinoamericana**, is a restaurant and bar, *Muralto*, with splendid views of the city, especially at sunset and after dark (US$5 'derecho de mesa' plus US$3.30 for a drink, service criticised); on the 44th floor is a viewing platform with telescopes, US$3.30 to go up (if only going to *Muralto*, do not pay at the bottom). This great glass tower dominates the gardens of the **Alameda Central**, once the Aztec market and later the place of execution for the Spanish Inquisition. Beneath the broken shade of eucalyptus, cypress and ragged palms, wide paths link fountains and heroic statues. The park is illuminated at night. (Much rebuilding going on in this area.)

On the northern side of the Alameda, on Av Hidalgo, is the Jardín Morelos, flanked by two old churches: Santa Veracruz (1730) to the right and **San Juan de Dios** to the left. The latter has a richly carved baroque exterior; its image of San Antonio de Padua is visited by those who are broken-hearted for love. A recommended new museum, the **Franz Mayer** (opposite the Museo de la Estampa), has been opened at the Hospital de San Juan de Dios (Hidalgo 45), next to the church. The house was originally built in the second half of the 16th century and has been modified over the years. It houses fine exhibitions of Mexican colonial ceramics, Mexican and Spanish furniture, gold and silver, timepieces, European textiles, European and Mexican paintings, and has a library (open 1000-1700 except Mon, US$1.65, free on Sun, allow 3-4 hrs).

Escuela Nacional Preparatoria, N of Zócalo at Justo Sierra 27 (the street parallel to, and between, Guatemala and San Ildefonso), built 1749 as the Jesuit School of San Ildefonso in splendid baroque. There are some frescoes by Orozco and, in the Anfiteatro Bolívar, frescoes by Diego Rivera and Fernando Leal, all of which are in excellent condition. There are other Leal murals in the stairwell separating the two floors of Orozco works. The whole interior has been magnificiently restored. Occasional grand exhibitions.

Secretaría de Educación Pública, on Argentina, 3 blocks from Zócalo, built 1922, contains frescoes by a number of painters. Here are Diego Rivera's masterpieces, painted between 1923 and 1930, illustrating the lives and sufferings of the common people.

Plaza Santo Domingo, two blocks N of the Cathedral, an intimate little plaza surrounded by fine colonial buildings: (a) the Antigua Aduana (former customs house); (b) on the west side, the Portales de Santo Domingo, where public scribes and owners of small hand-operated printing presses still carry on their business; (c) on the N side, the church of Santo Domingo, in Mexican baroque, 1737—note the carving on the doors and façade; (d) the old Edificio de la Inquisición, where the tribunals of the Inquisition were held (by standing on tiptoe in the men's room one can see—if tall enough—through the window into the prison cells of the Inquisition, which are not yet open to the public). It became the Escuela Nacional de la Medicina and is now a museum of Mexican medicine. There is a remarkable staircase in the patio; it also has a theatre. The nearby streets contain some fine examples of colonial architecture.

Two blocks E of Santo Domingo are the church and convent of **San Pedro y San Pablo** (1603), both massively built and now turned over to secular use. A block N is the public market of Abelardo L Rodríguez, with striking mural decorations.

Church of Loreto, built 1816 and now tilting badly, but being restored, is on a square of the same name, surrounded by colonial buildings. Its façade is a remarkable example of 'primitive' or 'radical' neoclassicism.

La Santísima Trinidad (1677, remodelled 1755), to be seen for its fine towers and the rich carvings on its façade.

The Mercado Merced (metro Merced), said to be the largest market in all the Americas, dating back over 400 years. Its activities spread over several blocks. In the northern quarter of this market are the ruins of La Merced monastery; the fine 18th century patio is almost all that survives; the courtyard, on Avenida Uruguay, between Calle Talavera and Calle Jesús María, opposite No 171, is nearly restored.

The oldest hospital in continental America, **Jesús Nazareno,** 20 de Noviembre 82, founded 1526 by Cortés, was remodelled in 1928, save for the patio and staircase. Cortés' bones have been kept since 1794 in the adjoining church, on the corner of Pino Suárez and República de El Salvador, diagonally opposite the Museo de la Ciudad.

Avenida Madero leads from the Zócalo W to the Alameda. On it is **La Profesa** church, late 16th century, with a fine high altar and a leaning tower. The 18th century **Palacio de Iturbide,** Av Madero 17, once the home of Emperor Agustín (1821-23), has been restored and has a clear plastic roof—wander around, it is now a bank head office. To the tourist the great sight of Av Madero, however, is the **Casa de los Azulejos** (House of Tiles) at the Alameda end of the street. Now occupied by Sanborn's Restaurant, it was built in the 16th century, and is brilliantly faced with blue and white Puebla tiles. The staircase walls are covered with Orozco frescoes. (There are more Orozco frescoes at Biblioteca Iberoamericana on Cuba between 5 de Febrero and Argentina.) Over the way is the **Church of San Francisco,** founded in 1525 by the 'Apostles of Mexico", the first 12 Franciscans to reach the country. It was by far the most important church in colonial days. Cortés' body rested here for some time, as did Iturbide's; the Viceroys attended the church.

Beyond San Francisco church, Eje Lázaro Cárdenas, formerly Calle San Juan de Letrán, leads S towards **Las Vizcaínas,** at Plaza Las Vizcaínas, one block E, built in 1734 as a school for girls; some of it is still so used, but some of it has become slum tenements. In spite of neglect, it is still the best example of colonial secular baroque in the city. Not open to the public; permission to visit sometimes given.

Museo San Carlos, Puente de Alvarado 50 (metro Revolución), a 19th-century palace (open to visitors 1000 to 1700, closed Mon), has fine Mexican colonial painting and a first-class collection of European paintings. The **Escuela Nacional de Artes Plásticas** at the corner of Academía and Calle Moneda, houses about 50 modern Mexican paintings. There is another picture gallery housing a collection of colonial paintings (16th-18th century), the **Pinacoteca Virreinal**, in the former church of San Diego in Calle Dr Mora, at the W end of the Alameda, opens at 0900, interesting. (Cheap concerts on Thurs at 2000.)

Moving eastwards along Av Hidalgo, before the Palace of Fine Arts, on the right is the **Post Office**, built 1904. The postal museum (open Mon-Fri 0900-1800, Sat 1000-1400, free) on the first floor is well worth a visit: exhibits from mid-18th century.

N from the W side of the Post Office leads to the Calle Santa María la Redonda, at the end of which is **Plaza Santiago de Tlaltelolco**, next oldest Plaza to the Zócalo, heavily damaged in the 1985 earthquake. Here was the main market of the Aztecs, and on it, in 1524, the Franciscans built a huge church and convent. This is now the Plaza de las Tres Culturas (Aztec, colonial and modern): (a) the Aztec ruins have been restored, (b) the magnificent baroque church of Santiago Tlaltelolco is now the focus of (c) the massive, multi-storey Nonoalco-Tlatelolco housing scheme, a garden city within a city, with pedestrian and wheeled traffic entirely separate. In October 1968, the Plaza de las Tres Culturas was the scene of serious distubances between the authorities and students, in which a large number of students were killed (see *The Other Mexico* by Octavio Paz, or *La Noche de Tlatelolco* by Elena Poniatowska, Biblioteca Era, 1971, and the very readable, and startling, *68* by Paco Ignacio Taibo II, 1991, in Spanish).

About 4 blocks N of the Post Office off Eje Lázaro Cárdenas is **Plaza Garibaldi**, a must, especially on Friday and Saturday night, when up to 200 *mariachis* in their traditional costume of huge sombrero, tight silver-embroidered trousers, pistol and *sarape*, will play your favourite Mexican serenade for US$5 (for a bad one) to 10 (for a good one). If you arrive by taxi you will be besieged. The whole square throbs with life and the packed bars are cheerful, though there is some danger from thieves and pickpockets, particularly after dark. The Lagunilla market is held about 4 blocks NE of the plaza, a hive of activity all week. On one side of Plaza Garibaldi is a gigantic eating hall, different stalls sell different courses, very entertaining.

Palacio de Minería, Calle Tacuba 9 (1797), is a fine old building, now restored, and once more level on its foundations. From 1910 to 1954 it was the Escuela Nacional de Ingeniería; there is a permanent exhibition of meteorites found all over Mexico (up to 14 tonnes). Free. (Cheap concerts on Sun at 1700, upstairs.) Moved from the Plaza de la Reforma to Plaza Manuel Tolsá opposite the Palacio is the great equestrian statue, 'El Caballito", of King Charles IV cast in 1802; it weighs 26 tons and is the second-largest bronze casting in the world.

Museo Nacional de Arte, Tacuba 8, opp Palacio de Minería, nr main Post Office. Open Tues-Sun, 1000-1730. Built in 1904, designed by the Italian architect, Silvio Contri, as the Palacio de Comunicaciones. The building has magnificent staircases made by the Florentine firm Pignone. It houses a large collection of Mexican paintings, drawings, sculptures and ceramics dating from the 16th century to 1950. It has the largest number of paintings (more than 100) by José María Velasco in Mexico City, as well as works by Miguel Cabrera, Gerardo Murillo, Rivera, Orozco, Siqueiros, Tamayo and Anguiano. Bookshop; entry US$3.35.

Along the S side of the Alameda, running E, is Av Juárez, a fine street with a mixture of old and new buildings. Diego Rivera's huge (15m by 4.80m) and fascinating mural, the 'Sueño de una tarde dominical en la Alameda Central", was removed from the earthquake-damaged Hotel del Prado and now occupies its own purpose-built museum, the highly recommended **Museo Mural Diego Rivera**, on the N side of the new Parque de la Solidaridad (on the old Hotel Regis site) at Av Juárez 77 (open Tues-Sun 1000-1800, US$2.30, free for students with ISIC card). A stroll down Calle Dolores, a busy and fascinating street, leads to the market of San Juan. The colonial church of Corpus Christi, on Av Juárez, is now used to display and sell folk arts and crafts. The avenue ends at the small Plaza de la Reforma. At the corner of Juárez and Reforma is the Lotería Nacional building. Drawings are held three times a week, at 2000: an interesting scene, open to the public. Beyond Plaza de la Reforma is the **Monumento a la Revolución**: a great dome, soaring above supporting columns set on the largest triumphal arches in the world. Beneath the monument is the **Museo Nacional de la Revolución**, dealing with the period 1867-1917, very interesting, lots of exhibits, videos (open Tues-Sun, 1000-1700, free, but donation expected).

S of this area, on Plaza Ciudadela, is a large colonial building, **La Ciudadela**, dating from 1700. It has been used for all kinds of purposes but is now a library.

The wide and handsome but earthquake-damaged Paseo de la Reforma, 3 km long, continues to the Bosque de Chapultepec: shops, offices, hotels, restaurants all the way. Along it are monuments to Columbus; to Cuauhtémoc and a 45-metre marble column to Independence, topped by the golden-winged figure of a woman, 'El Angelito' to the Mexicans. Just before entering the park is the Salubridad (Health) Building. Rivera's frescoes in this building cannot be seen by the public, who can view only the stained-glass windows on the staircases.

Bosque de Chapultepec, at the end of Paseo de la Reforma, with its thousands of ahuehuete trees, is beautiful but is becoming spoiled by constant littering (park closes at 1700). The park is divided into three sections: the first, the easternmost, was a wood inhabited by the Toltecs and Aztecs; the second section, W of Blvd Manuel Avila Camacho, was added in 1964, and the third in 1974. The first section contains a maze of pathways, a large and a small lake, a marvellous botanical garden, shaded lawns and a zoo with giant pandas (free, closed Mon and Tues). At the top of a hill in the park is the Castillo de Chapultepec, with a view over Mexico Valley from its beautiful balconies, US$4.35 to enter the building (large bags have to be left at Museo Nacional de Historia, so go there first). It has now become the **Museo Nacional de Historia**, open 0900-1700 (long queues on Sun, closed Mon). Its rooms were used by the Emperor Maximilian and the Empress Carlota during their brief reign. There is an unfinished mural by Siqueiros (in Sala XIII, near the entrance) and a notable mural by O'Gorman on the theme of independence. Classical music concerts, free, are given on Sunday at 1200 by the Bellas Artes Chamber Orchestra; arrive early for a seat. Entrance US$4.35, free on Sun. Halfway down the hill is the new **Galería de Historia**, which has dioramas with tape-recorded explanations of Mexican history, and photographs of the 1910 Revolution. Just below the castle are the remains of the famous Arbol de Moctezuma, known locally as 'El Sargento". This immense tree, which has a circumference of 14 metres and was about 60 metres high, has been cut off at a height of about 10 metres.

The crowning wonder of the park is the **Museo Nacional de Antropología** built by architect Pedro Ramírez Vásquez to house a vast collection illustrating pre-conquest Mexican culture. It has a 350-metre façade and an immense patio shaded by a gigantic concrete mushroom, 4,200 square metres—the world's largest concrete expanse supported by a single pillar. The largest exhibit ($8\frac{1}{2}$ metres high, weighing 167 tons) is the image of Tláloc the rain god, removed—accompanied by protesting cloud bursts—from near the town of Texcoco to the museum. Open Tues-Sat, 0900-1900 and Sun, 1000-1800. Only Mexican student cards accepted. Entrance is US$7 except Sun and holidays (free). Guided tours in English or Spanish free with a minimum of 5 people. Ask for the parts you want to see as each tour only visits two of 23 halls. Excellent audio-visual introduction free (lasts 1 hr, includes 3D models). If you want to see everything, you need two days. Permission to photograph (no tripod or flash allowed) free. Upstairs is a display of folk costumes, which may be closed Sunday. Attractions include *voladores* and Maya musicians. There is an excellent collection of English, French, German and Spanish books, especially guides to Mexican ruins, including maps. Cafeteria on site is good, rec, particularly for the soup, but pricey with long queues at times. The nearest metro is Auditorio.

Also in the first section of the Bosque de Chapultepec is the **Museo de Arte Moderno** (US$2.30), which shows Mexican art only in two buildings, pleasantly set among trees with some sculptures in the grounds. The smaller building shows temporary exhibitions. The delightfully light architecture of the larger building is spoilt by a heavy, vulgar marble staircase, with a curious acoustic effect on the central landing under a translucent dome, which must have been unplanned; open 1100-1800 daily except Mon. The **Museo Rufino Tamayo**, whose interior space is unusual in that you cannot tell which floor you are on or how many there are, generally displays Mexican artists, although international modern art is in its possession, situated between the Modern Art and Anthropology Museums, US$1.70 entry, free to students with international card. In the first section there is a Plaza del Quijote and the Monumento a los Niños Héroes.

The second section has a large amusement park (there is a wonderful section for children and another for adults) with huge roller-coasters (open Wed, Fri, Sat and Sun, 1030-2000, entry US$0.10, all rides free, except roller-coaster—which has slack belts, not enough support for head and neck; on Sat and Sun only, US$0.40 – the park was closed in late 1993 following the death of a patron), bridle paths and polo grounds. Diego Rivera's famous fountain, the Fuente de Tláloc, is near the children's amusement park. Close by are the Fuentes de los Serpientes (Snake Fountains). There are two museums in this section: the **Museo de Tecnología** is free; it is operated by the Federal Electricity Commission, has touchable exhibits which demonstrate electrical and energy principles. It is located beside the roller-coasters. The **Museo de Historia Natural** is beside the Lago Menor of the second section; open 1000-1700, Tues to Sun. Both the Lago Menor and Lago Mayor are popular for boating; on the shore of each is a restaurant.

Centro Cultural de Arte Contemporáneo, Campos Eliseos y Jorge Eliot, Polanco (near *Hotel Presidente*, metro Polanco), has permanent and temporary exhibitions of painting, photography, installations (mostly Mexican), small entrance fee, highly rec.

Further places of interest to tourists are as follows:
Museo de la Ciudad, on Av Pino Suárez and República de El Salvador, shows

DIEGO RIVERA

POSTERS AND POSTCARDS

AVAILABLE FROM PRINCIPAL MUSEOS AND LIBRERIAS IN MEXICO

Published by MEXPORT UK in conjunction
with the INSTITUTO NACIONAL DE BELLAS ARTES, México.

(UK) 0272 732924   Tel-Fax   (MEX) 5 658 5376

worth visiting Condesa - Parques + cafés
San Angel.

the geology of the city and has life size figures in period costumes showing the history of different peoples before Cortés. It also has a photographic exhibition of the construction of the metro system. In the attic above the museum is the studio of Joaquín Clausell, with walls covered with impressionist miniatures. Free admittance, Tues to Thurs. Two blocks S of this museum at Mesones 139 is the **Anglican (Episcopal) Cathedral**, called the Cathedral of San José de Gracia. Built in 1642 as a Roman Catholic church, it was given by the Benito Juárez government to the Episcopal Mission in Mexico. Juárez himself often attended services in it.

Museo José-Luis Cuevas, Academia 13, new (1993) museum in a large colonial building. It houses a permanent collection of paintings, drawings and sculptures (one is two storeys high) by the controversial, contemporary Cuevas (NB the Sala Erótica), and temporary exhibitions (Tue-Fri 1000-1830, Sat-Sun 1000-1730, US$1).

Museo Nacional de las Culturas, Moneda 13, open 0930-1800, closed Sun. Exhibits of countries from all over the world and some historical information.

The **Casa del Presidente Venustiano Carranza**, Lerma y Amazonas, is a museum.

Museo de Arte Carrillo Gil, Av Revolución esq Los Leones, near San Angel; another museum of striking modern features, inside and out; paintings by Orozco, Rivera (NB some of his Cubist works), Siqueiros and others (US$3.35 entry); good bookshop and cafeteria.

Museo de Cera de la Ciudad de México (Wax Museum) in a remarkable house at Londres 6, 1100-1900 daily.

Museo de la Caricatura, Calle de Doncellas 97, free.

Instituto Nacional Indigenista, Av Revolución 1297.

Museo Universitario del Chopo, E G Martínez 10, between metro San Cosme and Insurgentes, nr Insurgentes Norte. Contemporary international exhibitions (photography, art) in a church-like building designed by Eiffel (Wed-Sun 1000-1400, 1600-1900).

Museo del Convento de Carmen, Av Revolución 4, San Angel, open 1000-1700 (has mummified nuns in upright cases in the cellar). **Museo Nacional de Culturas Populares**, Hidalgo 289 (see under Coyoacán, **Suburbs**).

Casasola Archive, Praga 16, in Zona Rosa, T 564-9214, amazing photos of the revolutionary period, reproduction for sale.

The **Siqueiros Polyforum**, on Insurgentes Sur, includes a handicraft shop and a museum of art, with huge frescoes by Siqueiros, one of the largest in the world, inside the ovoid dome. Entrance to the frescoes US$0.40; open 1000-1900, closed for lunch. Next door is the former *Hotel de México* skyscraper, which is to become Mexico's World Trade Centre.

NB For details of other museums, far from the centre, see under Suburbs, **p 195**, and Teotihuacan, **p 200**.

Modern Buildings On Avenida Insurgentes Sur (at the corner of Mercaderes) is a remarkable building by Alejandro Prieto: the Teatro de Los Insurgentes, a theatre and opera house seating 1,300 people. The main frontage on the Avenida consists of a high curved wall without windows. This wall is entirely covered with mosaic decoration, the work of Diego Rivera: appropriate figures, scenes, and portraits composed round the central motif of a gigantic pair of hands holding a mask, worth going a distance to see.

The most successful religious architecture in Mexico today is to be found in the churches put up by Enrique de la Mora and Félix Candela; a good example is the chapel they built in 1957 for the Missionaries of the Holy Spirit, in a garden behind high walls at Av Universidad 1700. (An excellent Candela church, and easy to see, is the Church of La Medalla Milagrosa, just to the E of Avenida Universidad at the junction of Avenida División Norte, metro station División del Norte.) 'All the churches and chapels built by this team have such lightness and balance that they seem scarcely to rest on their foundations.' One of the seminal works of one of Mexico's greatest modern architects, Luís Barragán, is at Los Clubes, Las Arboledas bus from Chapultepec bus station. See also the *objet trouvé* mural at the Diana cinema in the centre of the city, and Orozco's great thundercloud of composition, the 'Apocalypse", at the Church of Jesús Nazareno. Both the *Camino Real Hotel* and the IBM technical centre were designed by Ricardo Legorreto; very well worth seeing. Consult Max Cetto's book on modern Mexican architecture. In this connection, University City (**see p 197**) is also well worth a look.

The **Bull Ring** is said to be the largest in the world, and holds 60,000 spectators. Bull fights are held every Sunday at 1600 from October through March (seats from US$2 at the very top, to US$20, to US$65 in the front row—even the cheaper seats afford impressive views. Admission starts at 1600; buy ticket in morning to avoid queues. The Bull Ring is in the Ciudad de los Deportes (City of Sports), Plaza México, reached by Av de los Insurgentes; metro station San Antonio, Línea 7, is a couple of blocks away. (A little to the W of where Los Insurgentes crosses Chapultepec, and on Av Chapultepec itself between Calles Praga and Varsovia, are the remains of the old aqueduct built in 1779.) Besides the Bull Ring, the Sports City contains a football stadium holding 50,000 people, a boxing ring, a cinema, a *frontón* court for *jai-alai*, a swimming pool, restaurants, hotels, etc.

Santa María la Ribera and San Cosme (N of metro San Cosme) are two colonias which became fashionable residential areas in the late 19th century, and many elegant, if neglected façades are to be seen. In the pleasant Alameda de Santa María, between Pino and Torres Bodet, stands an extraordinary Moorish pavilion designed by Mexicans for the Paris Exhibition in 1889. On its return to Mexico, the *kiosko* was placed in the Alameda Central, before being transferred to its present site in 1910. On the W side of this square, on Torres Bodet, is the **Museo del Instituto Geológico** of UNAM; apart from its collection of fossils and minerals (and magnificent early 20th century showcases), the building itself (1904) is worth a visit: swirling wrought-iron staircases and unusual stained-glass windows of mining scenes by Zettler (Munich and Mexico); Tues-Sun 1000-1700, free.

Sullivan Park (popularly known as Colonia Park or Jardín del Arte) is reached by going up Paseo de la Reforma to the intersection with Los Insurgentes, and then W two blocks between Calles Sullivan and Villalongín. Here, each Sunday afternoon, there is a display of paintings, engravings and sculptures near the monument to La Madre, packed with sightseers and buyers; everything is for sale (beware of thieves).

Reino Aventura, S of the city near the Mall del Sur, amusement park for children along Disneyland lines, clean, orderly, popular with families.

The **Basilica of Guadalupe**, in the Gustavo A Madero district, often called La Villa de Guadalupe, in the outer suburbs to the NE, is the most venerated shrine in Mexico, for it was here, in December 1531, that the Virgin appeared three times, in the guise of an Indian princess, to the Indian Juan Diego and imprinted her portrait on his cloak. The cloak is preserved, set in gold, but was moved into the new basilica next door in 1992, as a massive crack has appeared down the side of the old building. Visitors stand on a moving platform behind the altar to view the cloak. The huge, modern basilica is impressive and holds over 20,000 people (very crowded on Sunday). The original basilica has been converted into a museum, admission US$3. It still houses the original magnificent altar, but otherwise mostly representations of the image on the cloak, plus interesting painted tin plates offering thanks for cures, etc, from about 1860s. A chapel stands over the well which gushed at the spot where the Virgin appeared. The great day here is 12 December, the great night the night before: Indian dance groups provide entertainment in front of the Basilica. There are, in fact, about seven churches in the immediate neighbourhood, including one on the hill above (Iglesia del Cerrito excellent view of the city, especially at night, free access); most of them are at crazy angles to each other and to the ground, because of subsidence; the subsoil is very soft. The Templo de los Capuchinos has been the subject of a remarkable feat of engineering in which one end has been raised 3.375 metres so that the building is now horizontal. There is a little platform from which to view this work. Buses marked La Villa go close to the site, or you can go by metro to La Villa (Line 6).

Festivals The largest is the Independence celebration on 15 September, when the President gives the *grito*: 'Viva México' from the Palacio Nacional on the Zócalo at 2300, and rings the Liberty Bell (now, sadly, electronic!). This is followed by fireworks, and on 16 September (0900-1400) there are military and traditional regional parades in the Zócalo and surrounding streets—great atmosphere.

Safety Take care in the centre at quiet times (eg Sunday pm) and in Chapultepec (where Sunday is the safest day).

Hotels Prices normally include 10% tax but not service, check in advance. The rates shown are for mid-1993 (reductions often available); check if breakfast is included in the room price. There are fair hotel reservation services at the railway station and at the airport; also services for more expensive hotels at bus stations.

The following paragraph lists, in alphabetical order, the hotels in our luxury price ranges: **L+ Camino Real**, Mariano Escobedo 700, T 203-2121; **L+ Presidente**, Campos Eliseos 218, T 327-7700, F 327-7730; **L+ Fiesta Americana Aeropuerto**, Fundidora de Monterrey 89, includes health spa, T1-800-FIESTA 1; **L+ Four Seasons Mexico**, Paseo de la Reforma 500, T 230-1818, F 230-1817, brand new (1994), beautiful, excellent restaurant; **L+ Nikko**, Campos Eliseos 204, T 203-4020. **L+-L Marquis**, Paseo de la Reforma 465, Col Cuauhtémoc, T 211-3600, F 211-5561, new, all facilities, rec as very fine; also new on Reforma, **L+ Clarion Reforma Suites**, T 207-8944, F 208-2719. **L Fiesta Americana**, Paseo de la Reforma 80, T 705-1515, with restaurants, bars, nightclubs, superior business facilities (there is also a *Fiesta Americana* at the airport, T 230-0505); **L Galería Plaza**, Hamburgo 195, T 211-0014, F 207-5867; **L Imperial**, Reforma 64, T 566-4879, very good, restaurant, café, bar, 24-hr service, business facilities, etc; **L Krystal**, Liverpool 155, T 228-9928. A rec hotel is the **L Marco Polo**, Amberes 27, T 511-1839, in the Zona Rosa; **L Royal Zona Rosa**, Amberes 78, T 525-4850, F 514-3330, good; **L+ María Isabel Sheraton**, Paseo de la Reforma 325, T 207-3933, F 207-0684, Hotel, Towers (opp Angel of Independence), 'old-fashioned", all facilities, but restaurant overpriced; **L Ramada Hotel Mexico City Airport**, Blvd Puerto Aéreo 502, T 785-8522, F 785-4605, weekend rates sometimes available; **L-A+ Century**, Liverpool 152, T 227-7272, F 525-7475 (Golden Tulip hotel).

In our categories A+ and A are: **A+ Aristos**, Paseo de la Reforma 276, T 211-0112; **A+ Genève Calinda**, Londres 130, T 211-0071, pleasant dining area; **A+ Plaza Madrid**, Madrid 2; **A+ Plaza Florencia**, Florencia 61, T 525-4800, in Zona Rosa. **A+ Bristol**, Plaza Necaxa 17 (T 533-60-60), very good; **A Cancún**, Donato Guerra 24, T 566-6083 (inc tax), restaurant, safe, clean, rec; the **A+ Cortés** (Best Western), Av Hidalgo 85, T 518-2184, F 512-1863, is the only baroque-style hotel in Mexico City, a former pilgrims' guest house, with a pleasant patio, no a/c or pool, helpful, quiet, good yet touristy floor show, but restaurant does not match the standard of the accommodation; similar reports of the **A Casa Blanca**, Lafragua 7 (1 block from Reforma and Revolución monument), T 556-3211, modern; **A Flamingos Plaza**, Av Revolución 333, T 271-7044; **A+ Howard Johnson Gran Hotel de México** 16 de Septiembre 82 (Zócalo), T 510-4040, F 512-2085, has an incredible foyer, 30's style, 4th floor restaurant and balcony good for Zócalo-watching, especially on Sun am (breakfast buffet US$10); **A+ Majestic** (Best Western), Madero 73 on Zócalo, T 521-8600, F 512-6262, interesting rooms, lots of tiles, carved wooden beams, magnificent breakfast in 7th floor restaurant with excellent views of centre; **A+-A Ritz** (also Best Western), Madero 30, T 518-1340, F 518-3466, recently renovated; **A María Cristina**, Lerma 31,

T 703-1787/566-9688, F 566-9194, attractive colonial style, comfortable, helpful, safe parking, rec (book well in advance); **A+ Regente**, París 9, T 566-8933, clean, friendly, noisy at front, restaurant; **A Capitol**, Uruguay 12, T 518-1750, F 521-1149, attractive lobby, recently remodelled; **A Ejecutivo**, Viena 8, T 566-6422, staff helpful, rec; **A Metropol**, Luis Moya 39, T 510-8661, good, clean, safe, touristy, average restaurant, good value, rec; **A Viena**, Marsella 28 (close to Juárez market and Cuauhtémoc metro), T 566-0700, quiet, Swiss decor, garage, dining room, rec.

Motels in the top price ranges include: **A Dawn Motor Hotel**, Blvd Avila Camacho 680, Naucalpan, T 373-2155; **B Park Villa**, Gómez Pedraza 68 (near Chapultepec Park), T 515-5245.

B Brasilia, excellent modern hotel, near Central del Norte bus station, on Av Cien Metros 48-25, T 587-8577, king size bed, TV, 24-hr traffic jam in front; **B Catedral**, Donceles 95, T 518-2532, behind Cathedral, clean, spacious, faded (but bed bugs); **B Jena**, Jesús Terán 12, new, central, rec (but not the travel agency on the premises). **B Lepanto**, Guerrero 90, TV, phone, modern, attractive, good restaurant; **B Mallorca**, Serapio Rendón 119, T 566-4833, clean, reasonable; **B Palace**, Ignacio Ramírez 7, T 566-2400, very friendly, good restaurant; **B Polanco**, Edgar Poe 8, T 520-6041, near Chapultepec, dark, quiet, good restaurant; **B Premier**, Atenas 72, T 566-2701, good location, clean, front rooms noisy, will store bags; **B Prim**, Versalles 46, T 592-4600, clean, good in all respects; **B San Francisco**, Luis Moya 11, T 521-8960, just off Alameda, excellent value, takes credit cards, good set meals; **B Vasco de Quiroga**, Londres and Berlín, 3 mins walk from Zona Rosa, clean, friendly, very good (ask for room away from the generator), restaurant downstairs; **B Gillow**, 5 de Mayo e Isabel la Católica 17, T 518-1440, central, large, clean, many services, attractive. **C Casa González**, Lerma y Sena (near British Embassy), full board available, shower, English spoken by Sr González, clean, quiet and friendly; **C Gilbert**, Amado Nervo 37, Col Buenavista, Mex 4DF, T 547-9260, good location but a bit spooky at night; **B Mayaland**, Maestro Antonio Caso 23, T 566-6066, with bath, good value, rec, good restaurant, remodelled 1993/94; **C Monaco**, Guerrero 12, on Jardín San Fernando, phone, TV, attractive, modern; **B Fleming**, Revillagigedo 35, T 510-4530, good value, central; **C La Villa de los Quijotes**, Moctezuma 20, near Basílica Guadalupe (metro La Villa), T 577-1088, modern, quiet, clean, expensive restaurant; **C Marlowe**, Independencia 17, T 521-9540, clean, but poor restaurant (tourist office at airport refers many travellers here—if this one is too expensive, the cheaper Concordia—see below—is round the corner); **C Pisa**, Insurgentes Norte 58, rec; **C Monte Carlo**, Uruguay 69, T 518-1418/521-2559/521-9363 (D H Lawrence's hotel), clean, friendly owner (also suites), with bath, good about storing luggage, safe car park inside the hotel premises—US$3.45, rooms in front noisy, recently renovated, very popular, can make collect calls abroad from room; **C Congreso**, with bath, hot water, good, central, clean, quiet, TV, garage, at Allende 18, T 510-9888; **C Isabel la Católica** (street of the same name, No 63, T 518-12-13) is pleasant, popular, clean, helpful, safe (taxi drivers must register at desk before taking passengers), large rooms with bath and hot water, central, quite good restaurant, luggage held, rooms on top floor with shared bathroom are cheaper; **C Galicia**, Honduras 11, T 529-7791, good; **C Ambar**, San Jerónimo 105 y Pino Suárez, shower, fan, TV, phones in rooms, safe deposit, very clean, good service, highly rec; **C Roble**, Uruguay 109 y Pino Suárez, with shower, hot water, clean, phone and TV, good; **B Sevilla**, Serapio Rendón 126 and Sullivan, T 591-0522, restaurant, garage, reasonable (not to be confused with **A+ Sevilla Palace**, Reforma 105, T 566-8877, which is smart); **C Uxmal**, Madrid 13, quite close to Zona Rosa, clean rooms, same owner as more expensive **Madrid**, next door, with access to their better facilities, rec.

The best of the cheaper hotels are in the old part of town between the Zócalo and the Alameda, and there are more N of the Plaza República. **D Carlton**, Ignacio Mariscal 32-bis, T 566-2911, clean, safe, rec; **C Oxford**, Mariscal 67, T 566-0500, very clean, radio and satellite TV, helpful rec; **C Texas**, Ignacio Mariscal 129, T 564-4626, with bath, clean, hot water, small rooms; **D Concordia**, Uruguay 13, nr Niño Perdido, excellent, lift, phone; **D Ontario**, Uruguay 87 (metro Zócalo), T 521-0952/0593, nice exterior, friendly, hot water 12 hrs a day, quiet, telephone; **D Danky**, Donato Guerra 10, with bath, central, hot water, phone, clean, easy parking (T 546-9960/61), rec; **D Habana**, República de Cuba 77, rooms dark but very clean, phone, TV, friendly and helpful staff, rec; **D Iberia**, Mina 186 y Zaragoza, with bath, rec; **D Parador Washington**, Dinamarca 42 y Londres, with bath, TV, clean, safe area, café next door; **D Encino**, Av Insurgentes, 1 block from the railway station, clean, private bath; **D Pontevedra**, Insurgentes Norte opp railway station, bath, hot water, TV, clean, helpful, will store luggage; **D Principal**, Calle Bolívar 121, with bath, central, OK, friendly owner; **D Santander**, Arista 22, not far from railway station, with bath, good value and service, clean; **D Managua**, on Plaza de la Iglesia de San Fernando, near Hidalgo metro, with bath, phone, TV, good location, car park, very friendly, run down; **D Monaco** opposite,

Guerrero 12, T 566-8333, comfortable, TV, good service; **D América**, Buena Vista 4 (nr Revolución metro), with bath, hot water, TV, good service, rec; **D Atlanta**, corner of B Domínguez and Allende, T 518-1201, good, quiet, clean and friendly, luggage store, rec; **D Florida**, Belisario Domínguez 57, TV, shower, clean, rec; **D Lafayette**, Motolinia 40 and 16 de Septiembre, with bath, and TV, good, clean, quiet (pedestrian precinct), but check rooms, there's a variety of sizes; **D Royalty**, Jesus Terán 21, opp Hotel Jena, with bath, TV, clean, very quiet, near Hidalgo metro; **D Avenidas**, Lázaro Cárdenas 38 (Bellas Artes metro), T 518-1007, with bath, central, good value, cheapest hotel that can be booked at airport; **E Cosmos**, Av Lázaro Cárdenas, next to Torre Latinoamericana, cheapest rooms on top floor; **E República**, Cuba 57 y Allende, a few blocks from Zócalo, T 512-9517, central, noisy, helpful, in-hotel parking; **E Princess**, next door at No 55, good value; **E San Pedro**, Mesones 126 and Pino Suárez, with bath, TV, tiny rooms, clean (but the occasional cockroach) and friendly, good value. Near Allende metro are **D Rioja**, Av 5 de Mayo 45, T 521-8333, shared or private baths, hot water, clean (but some cockroaches), popular, luggage store, noisy at times, well placed, rec; next door (No 47) is **C Canadá**, T 518-2106, F 521-1233, good value, friendly and helpful; opp are **C Juárez**, in small alley on 5 de Mayo, between Nos 48 and 50, 1 min walk from Zócalo, clean, with bath, phone, radio, TV, rec, and **D Zamora**, No 50, clean, cheap, hot water, some find it OK, others say it is falling apart, good Café El Popular next door; **D Washington**, 5 de Mayo 54, clean, friendly, cable TV, frequently rec; **E del Centro** on same street, No 31, T 585-0355, with bath, hot water, phone, fairly clean, try to get a quiet room on 2nd or 3rd floor away from street, even numbers, cheaper for longer stays; **E Casa Blanca**, Manuel Gutiérrez Najera 34-A, T 578-3379; **E Manolete**, Lerdo 60, nearest metro Guerrero, T 526-9697, private bath, hot water, friendly Spanish owner; **D Detriot**, Zaragoza 55, T 591-1088, hot shower, central, clean, has parking; **D Nueva Estación**, Zaragoza opp Bellavista station, with bath, clean, quiet, friendly, colour TV; **D Savoy**, Zaragoza 10, T 566-4611, near Hidalgo metro, convenient for Zócalo, with bath and hot water, clean, phone, TV, modernized, good value; **D Yale**, Mosqueta 200, 5 mins walk from Buenavista station, showers, toilet, large room with TV and phone, very good value, rec.

E Casa de los Amigos, Mariscal 132 (T 705-0521/0646), near train and bus station (metro Revolución), in dormitory, a little more expensive in double room, use of kitchen, rec, max 15-day stay, separation of sexes, run by Quakers for Quakers or peace, or development-work related travellers, other travellers taken only if space is available, good service of information on volunteer work, breakfast US$2.50 (weekdays only) and laundry facilities on roof, safe-keeping for luggage, English library, references or advance booking recommended.

For longer stays, **B Suites Quinta Palo Verde**, Cerro del Otate 20, Col Romero de Terreros (Mexico 21 DF) T 554-3575, pleasant, diplomatic residence turned guest house, near the University; run by a veterinary surgeon, Miguel Angel, very friendly, speaks English and German, but the dogs are sometimes noisy. **Suites Amberes**, Amberes 64, Zona Rosa, T 533-1306, F 207-1509, kitchenette, good value, rec; **Suites Havre**, Havre 74, near Zona Rosa, rec for longer stays, 56 suites with kitchen, phone and service. **Club Med** head office for Club Med and **Villas Arqueológicas** reservations, Calle Masaryk 183, Col Polanco, México 11570, T 203-3086/3833, Telex 1763346.

Youth Hostels Asociación Mexicana de Albergues de la Juventud, Madero 6, Of 314, México 1, D F Write for information. There is a similar organization, Comisión Nacional del Deporte (Condep), which runs the Villas Deportivas Juveniles (see below); information office at Glorieta del Metro Insurgentes, local C-11, T 525-2916/533-1291. Condep will make reservations for groups of 10 or more; to quality you must be between 8 and 65 and have a 'tarjeta plan verde' membership card, US$6, valid 2 years, obtainable within 24 hrs from office at Tlalpan 583, esq Soria, metro Xola, or a IYHF card. See also Setej, below, for information on hotels and other establishments offering lodging for students.

Camp Sites Campo Escuela Nacional de Tantoco, Km 29.5 on road Mexico-City to Toluca, T 512-2279, cabins and campsite. The Dirección de Villas Deportivas Juveniles, address above (Condep), has details of campsites throughout the country; site in the capital, T 665-5027. They have either camping, or camping and dormitory accommodation on sites with additional facilities, including luggage lockers; ask in advance what documentation is required. The nearest trailer park is Pepe's in Tepozotlán (see **Excursions** below), 43 km N of the capital; it costs about US$12 a night, 55 pads with full hook-ups, very friendly, clean, hot showers, Canadian run, rec (owner has a hotel in Mexico City it you want to leave your trailer here and stay in the capital). If you want to bring your car into the city, find a cheap hotel where you can park and leave it, while you explore the city by bus, metro or on foot. Or try camping in the parking lot of the Museum of Anthropology.

Restaurants All the best hotels have good restaurants. The number and variety of restaurants throughout the city is vast: the following is a small selection.

Mexican food: Note the *Hotel Majestic's* Mexican breakfast, Sat and Sun till 1200, excellent, US$8, go to terrace on 7th floor, otherwise food mediocre (non-residents of the hotel are not allowed in just for a drink). *San Angel Inn*, Las Palmas 50, in San Angel, is excellent and very popular, so book well in advance by bus from Chapultepec Park or by trolley bus from metro Taxqueña. *Hostelería Santo Domingo*, Belisario Domínguez, 2 blocks W of Plaza Santo Domingo, good food and service, the oldest restaurant in the city and one of the best; *La Plancha Azteca*, Río Lerma 54, good tacos and tortas, moderate prices; *La Puerta del Angel*, Varsovia y Londres, local food and specializing in American cuts, very good, US$20-25 without wine; *Fonda del Recuerdo* for excellent mole poblano, Bahía de las Palmas 39A, 17DF, with music. *Club de Periodistas de México*, F Mata 8, near Calle 5 de Mayo, open to public, OK; *Opera Bar*, 5 de Mayo near Bellas Artes, good atmosphere, expensive, see Pancho Villa's bullet-hole in ceiling (beware cocktails made with foreign spirits, 3 times as expensive as tequila). *Casa Zavala*, Bolívar y Uruguay, cheap, large selection of dishes. *Focolare*, Hamburgo 87 (swank and high priced); *Taquería Lobo Bobo*, Insurgentes Sur 2117, excellent food, quite cheap, very friendly; *Vitamar*, Ayuntamiento 8, good food, pricey, good beer from the tap, normally open till 2400; *Victor*, Ayuntamiento 169, near Buccarelli, metro Salto de Agua, very good value. A very old restaurant with interesting tile décor and not touristy is the *Café Tacuba*, Tacuba 28; it specialises in Mexican food, very good enchiladas and fruit desserts, good service, rec. *El Refugio*, Liverpool 166, tourist-oriented, good desserts, check bill carefully. *La Luna*, Oslo y Copenhague, Zona Rosa, mostly Mexican, good breakfasts. The *Vips* chain in several locations offers plentiful food at moderate prices, highly rec for set breakfasts (about US$5).

International: *Delmonico's*, Londres 87 and 16 de Septiembre 82, elegant; *Jena*, Morelos 110 (deservedly famous, à la carte, expensive); *La Cava*, Insurgentes Sur 2465 (excellent food and steaks, lavishly decorated as an old French tavern, moderate); *Andreson's*, Reforma 400, very good atmosphere, excellent local menu, not cheap; *Keops*, Hamburgo 146, near Ambere in Zona Rosa, T 525 6706, reasonable food, good live music; also in Zona Rosa are *La Calesa de Londres*, Londres 102, good meat; and *Carousel Internacional*, Hamburgo and Niza, very popular drinking-hole for smartly-dressed Mexicans, resident Mariachi, food not gourmet but fun atmosphere, about US$15 pp. *Trevi*, Dr Mora y Colón (W end of Alameda), Italian/US/Mexican, reasonable prices. *Milomita*, Mesones 87, Centro, 0800-2000, specializes in American cuts of meat (see also Polanco restaurants below).

US and other Latin American: *Shirley's*, Reforma 108 and Londres 102-B, real American food, moderate prices, esp the buffet after midday; *Sanborn's*, 36 locations (known as the foreigners' home-from-home: soda fountain, drugstore, restaurant, English language magazines, handicrafts, chocolates, etc, try their restaurant in the famous 16th century *Casa de los Azulejos*, the 'house of tiles' at Av Madero 17: many delicious local dishes in beautiful high-ceilinged room, about US$15-20 pp without wine (also has handicraft shops in basement and first floor). *New York Deli and Bagel*, Av Revolución 1321, just S of metro Barranca del Muerto, 0800-0100, good coffee and full meals available. Many US chain fast-food restaurants (eg *Burger Boy* for good value breakfasts). *Rincón Gaucho*, Insurgentes Sur 1162, Argentine food.

Spanish: *del Cid*, Humboldt 61, Castilian with medieval menu; *Mesón del Castellano*, Bolívar y Uruguay, T 518 6080, good, plentiful and not too dear, excellent steaks, highly rec; *Centro Catalán*, Bolívar 31, open 1100-1700 only, excellent paella and other Spanish cuisine (2nd floor). *Vasco*, Madero 6, 1st floor. *Moralejo*, Amberes 78 (*Hotel Royal Zona Rosa*), superb, always full; *Mesón del Perro Andaluz*, Copenhague 26, and Luis P Ogazón 89, very pleasant.

Other European: French cuisine at *Le Gourmet*, Dakota 155, said to be most expensive restaurant in Mexico, and also said to be worth it! *Ambassadeurs*, Paseo de la Reforma 12 (swank and high priced); *Les Moustaches*, Río Sena 88 (most expensive in town, probably). *Bellinghausen*, Londres y Niza, excellent food; *Chalet Suizo*, Niza 37 (very popular with tourists, specializes in Swiss and German food, moderate); *Rivoli*, Hamburgo 123 (a gourmet's delight, high priced); *Café Konditori*, Génova 61, Danish open sandwiches; *La Pérgola*, Londres 107B, in the Zona Rosa, Italian; *La Casserole*, Insurgentes Sur 1880, near Núcleo Radio Mil building, French. The *Piccadilly Pub*, Copenhague 23 and Génova, serves British food at its best, especially steak and kidney pie, expensive, smart dress preferred; very popular with Mexicans and expatriates alike. Similar (and dearer), is *Sir Winston Churchill*, Avila Camacho 67.

Seafood: *La Marinera*, Liverpool 183, best seafood restaurant in Mexico City. *El Nuevo Acapulco*, López 9, almost opposite Palacio de Bellas Artes (excellent sea food, inexpensive, closes 2100 but open 7 days a week).

Oriental At Copenhague 20, *Ginza*, good Japanese. *Mr Lee*, Independencia 19-B, Chinese, seafood, good food, value and service; *Victoria*, Bolívar 41, cheap, good Chinese.

Vegetarian: *El Vegetariano*, Filomeno Mata 13, open 0800-2000, closed Sun, 4-course meal US$7, uninspiring; *Chalet Vegetariano*, near Dr Río de la Loza; *El Bosque*, Hamburgo 15 between Berlín and Dinamarca, rec. Vegetarian restaurant at Motolinía 31, near Madero, is open Mon-Sat 1300-1800, reasonably priced. *Saks*, Insurgentes Sur 1641, close to Teatro Insurgentes, very good. *Yug*, Varsovia 3, cheap vegetarian, 4-course set lunch US$3.50 (not very special). Wholewheat bread at *Pastelería Ideal* on 16 de Septiembre 14 (near Casa de Los Azulejos). The best place to buy natural products is in the San Juan market (see **Markets** below), including tofu (*Queso de Soja*). Health food shop, *Alimentos Naturales*, close to metro Revolución, on P Arriagal; health food shops in other metro stations.

A selection of restaurants in Polanco (in the lower price ranges): *La Parrilla Suiza*, Arquímedes y Pres Masaryk, for grilled meats, *alambres*, *sopa de tortilla* and other meat-and-cheese dishes, very popular, especially 1400-1600, service fair, moderately priced, *Cambalache*, Arquímedes N of Pres Masaryk, Argentine steak house, good steaks, wide selection of wines, cosy atmosphere, not as expensive as *El Rincón Argentino*, Pres Masaryk 181, which is very expensive; *Milomita*, steak house and piano bar, Pres Masaryk 52 y Torquato Tasso. For *tacos* and other tortilla-based dishes: *Los Tacos*, Newton just S of Horacio, inexpensive; *Chilango's*, Molière between Ejército Nacional and Homero, good value and service, MTV videos, rec; *El Tizoncito*, S of Ejército Nacional just W of Pabellón Polanco mall, very popular at lunchtime. *El Jarrocho*, Homero between Emerson and Hegel, informal, eat-at-counter place, in expensive; *Embers*, Seneca y Ejército Nacional, 43 types of excellent hamburger, good French fries, rec.

Cafés etc: Many economical restaurants on 5 de Mayo, eg *Café La Blanca* at No 40, popular and busy atmosphere, rec, comparatively expensive, rec, open for Sun breakfast and early on weekdays; *París*, No 10, good breakfast and dinner; also *Popular*, between Alameda and Zócalo, on corner of alley to *Hotel Juárez*, cheap, quick, 24 hrs, meeting place; good chicken restaurant on corner of same block walking away from Zócalo; *Comida Económica Verónica*, República de Cuba, 2 doors from *Hotel Habana* (No 77), highly rec for tasty breakfasts (US$3) and set *comida corrida*, very hot *chilaquiles*, very good value and delightful staff; *El Reloj*, 5 de Febrero 50, good *comida* and à la carte; *Rex*, 5 de Febrero, nr Zócalo, good café con leche and cheap *comidas*; *Shakey's*, Monte de Piedad (at the Zócalo), self-service, large helpings of pizza and chicken; *Pastelería Madrid*, 5 de Febrero 25, one block from *Hotel Isabela La Católica*, good pastries and breakfasts. *Bamerette*, Av Juárez 52 (*Hotel Bamer*), excellent breakfast. Good small restaurants in Uruguay, near *Monte Carlo Hotel*; the *Maple*, next to *Hotel Roble* at No 109, has been rec for its *comida*, and *Pancho*, for its breakfasts and cheap meals. *Tic Tac*, Av Balderas, very good *comida corrida*, US$5 inc drink. *La Habana*, Bucareli y Morelos, not cheap but good food and excellent coffee. Another centre for small restaurants is Pasaje Jacarandas, off Génova 44: *Llave de Oro* and many others; *La Casa del Pavo*, Motolinía nr 16 de Septiembre, clean, courteous, excellent *comida corrida* for US$3.35; also Calle Motilinía between 5 de Mayo y Tacuba. Cheap cafeterias in Calle Belisario Domínguez. *Gaby's*, Liverpool y Napolés, excellent italian-style coffee, décor of old coffee machines etc. *Duca d'Este*, Av Florencia y Hamburgo, good coffee and pastries; *Il Mangiare*, opp Siqueiros Polyforum (see above), very good sandwiches (US$4-5). *El Núcleo*, Lerma y Marne, excellent fruit salads, breakfasts and lunches, closes 1800 and all day Sunday. *Dulcería de Celaya*, 5 de Mayo 39, good candy store. Highly rec unnamed place on Isabel la Católica, near metro of same name, great and cheap salads, fruit and set meals, friendly and excellent value. Good bakeries on 16 de Noviembre, near Zócalo.

Bars *Bar Jardín*, in the *Hotel Reforma*; *El Morroco*, Conjunto Marrakesh, Calle Florencia 36. *Casino*, Isabel la Católica, near *Sanborn's*, superb painted glass doors and lavish interior, also has Spanish restaurant. *Abundio*, Záragoza y Mosqueta, very friendly, free food. Many safe gay bars in the Zona Rosa in the area between Niza and Florencia, N of Londres.

Cabarets and Night Clubs Every large hotel has one. *El Patio*, Atenas 9; *Passepartout*, Calle Hamburgo; *La Madelon*, Florencia 36; *Brasileirinho*, León 160; *Guadalupana*, near Plaza Hidalgo, Coyoacán. There are many discotheques in the better hotels and scattered throughout town.

Folk Music A fine place for light refreshments and music is the *Hostería del Bohemio*, formerly the San Hipólito monastery, near Reforma on Av Hidalgo 107, metro Hidalgo: poetry and music every night from 1700 to 2200, light snacks and refreshments US$4 minimum, expensive but no cover charge.

Shopping Mexican jewellery and hand-made silver can be bought everywhere. Among the good silver shops are *Sanborn's*, *Calpini*, *Prieto*, and *Vendome*. There are also good buys in perfumes, quality leather, and suede articles. Galeria Reforma is a huge shopping complex on Reforma, not far from Plaza de las Tres Culturas, selling all sorts of gifts and goods, good cafeteria with free coffee, good toilets, a/c, very pleasant when not full of tour groups, open 0900-1900. *Woolworths* on Reforma, opp *Hotel Fiesta Americana* for cheap food, drinks, clothes, domestic goods, etc. With the extension of the ring roads around the city, hypermarkets are being set up: there are two, *Perisur* in the S of the city (with Liverpool, Sears, Sanborn's and Palacio de Hierro), open Tues-Fri 1100-2000, Sat 1100-2100; and *Plaza Satélite* in the N (with Sumesa, Sears and Liverpool), open on Sunday. There is an ISSSTE supermarket in Tres Guerras, two blocks from metro Balderas and one block from Bucaveli. Art supplies can be found on Calle San Salvador. Luggage repairs (moderate prices) at Rinconada de Jesús 15-G, opposite Museo de la Ciudad de México on Pino Suárez, but opening times can be unreliable; better try the shop in Callejón del Parque del Conde off Pino Suárez opp Hospital de Jesús church. At Pino Suárez metro station are several shops selling *charro* clothing and equipment (leggings, boots, spurs, bags, saddler, etc), eg *Casa Iturriaga*, rec.

Guatemalan Refugee shop, Yosemite 45, Col Nápoles, off Insurgentes Sur, T 523-2114.

Markets San Juan market, Calle Ayuntamiento and Arandas, nr Salto del Agua metro, good prices for handicrafts, especially leather goods (also cheap fruit and health food); open 0930-1800 (but don't go before 1000). The **Plaza Ciudadela** market (Mercado Central de Artesanías, open 1100-1800 weekdays, Sun 1100-1400), just off Balderas (metro Juárez), government-sponsored, reasonable and uncrowded, is cheaper than San Juan, but not for leather; craftsmen from all Mexico have set up workshops here (best for papier maché, lacquer, pottery and Guatemalan goods). **Mercado Lagunilla** near Glorieta Cuitláhuac (take *pesero* bus from metro Hidalgo) is a Sunday flea market where antique and collectable bargains are sometimes to be found, also a lot of rubbish. The market, which covers several blocks, now has all sorts of merchandise, including a wider range of non-silver jewellery; good atmosphere. Market (Insurgentes) in Calle Londres (Zona Rosa) good for silver, but other things expensive, stallholders pester visitors, only place where they do so. There is a market in every district selling pottery, glassware, textiles, *sarapes* and jewellery. Try also **San Angel** market, although with little choice and expensive, many items are exclusive to it; good leather belts, crafts and silver; open Sat only from about 1100. Mexican tinware and lacquer are found everywhere. Vast fruit and veg market, **Mercado Merced (see p 175)**, metro Merced. A few blocks away on Fray Servando Teresa de Mier (nearest metro Fray Servando) lies the fascinating **Mercado Sonora**: secret potions and remedies, animals and birds as well as *artesanías*. **Buena Vista craft market**, Aldama 187 y Degollado (nearest metro Guerrero), excellent quality (open 0900-1800, Sun 0900-1400). Also on Aldama, No 211, between Sol and Luna, just past international post office, the **Tianguis del Chopo** is held on Sat, 1000-1600, selling clothes, records, etc, frequented by hippies, punks, rockers, and police. You can bargain in the markets and smaller shops.

Many handicraft shops on Av Juárez: *Tienda del Arte e Industrias Populares* at Juárez 44 (reported disappointing). *Fonart*, Fondo Nacional para el Fomento de las Artesanías, a state run organisation for the promotion of *artesanías* (it holds contests in the various regions of Mexico to encourage quality; the *artesanos* receive 40% of the retail price of the goods marketed) has its main showroom at Av Patriotismo 691 (metro Mixcoac), with branches at Av Juárez 69 (metro Hidalgo), Londres 136 (Zona Rosa) and Pres Carranza 115 (Coyoacán): not cheap but quality superb. *The Mercado de Artesanías Finas Indios Verdes* is at Galería Reforma Norte SA, FG Bocanegro 44 (corner of Reforma Norte, nr Statue of Cuitlahuac, Tlatelolco); good prices and quality but no bargaining. For onyx, *Müllers*, Londres y Florencia, nr Insurgentes metro, good chess sets. There is an annual **national craft fair** in Mexico City, 1st week in Dec.

Bookshops Many good ones, eg in the Palacio de Bellas Artes, at the airport (Area D), *El Parnaso*, Jardín Centenario Coyoacán (see **Suburbs**), one of the best in the city, has a fashionable *cafetería*; *Librería Británica*, Serapio Rendón 125 (stocks this *Handbook*) has a second-hand section where you can trade in old books (as long as they're neither even slightly damaged nor 'highbrow") and buy new ones, but at poor rates; *Librería Británica*, has four other branches: Antonio Caso 127 (Instituto Anglo Mexicano), Av Universidad y Av Coyoacán (Casa del Libro, metro Coyoacán), Av Madero 30-A , and E Sada Muguerza 38; *American Book Store*, Madero 25, excellent selection of Penguins and Pelicans, low mark-up, stocks this *Handbook* (also has a large branch on Revolución, 3-5 mins by bus S of metro Barranca del Muerto); *Libros, Libros, Libros*, Monte Ararat 220, Lomas Barrilaco, T 540-47-78, hundreds of hardback and paperback English titles; the shop at the entrance to the Templo Mayor has a good selection of travel books and guides in many languages; *Librairie Française*, Reforma 250A, for French selection; *Librería Alemana*, Benjamín Hill 19-B (metro Juanacatlán), T 515-4135/1813, excellent selection of German books, also English. The *Sanborn* chain has the largest selection of English-language paperbacks, art books and magazines in the country. *Casa Libros*, Monte Athos 355 (Lomas), large stock of second-hand English book, the shop is staffed by volunteers, gifts of books welcome, all proceeds to the

American Benevolent Society. *Librería Gandhi*, Calle Miguel Angel de Quevedo (metro Quevedo), art books, discs, tapes (try coffee in restaurant upstairs). *Libros y Discos*, Madero 1. Plenty of Spanish bookshops on Calle Argentina. Second-hand book market on Independencia just past junction with Eje Lázaro Cárdenas has some English books; also Puente de Alvarado, 100m from Hidalgo metro, and Dr Bernard 42, metro Niños Héroes. Secondhand Spanish and antiquarian booksellers on Donceles between Palma and República de Brasil, about 1½ blocks from Zócalo. *La Torre de Papel*, Filomeno Mata 6-A, in Club de Periodistas, sells newspapers from all over Mexico and USA.

Photography Kodak film (Ektachrome, not Kodachrome) is produced in Mexico and is not expensive. Imported film is also available. Small shops on República de Chile N of Tacuba are cheaper than larger ones S of Av 5 de Mayo.

Traffic System The city has two ring roads, the Anillo Periférico through what were the city outskirts when first built, and the Circuito Interior running within its circumference. In the centre, there is a system of Ejes Viales. It consists of a series of freeways laid out in a grid pattern, spreading from the Eje Central; the latter serves as a focal point for numbering (Eje 2 Poniente, Eje I Oriente etc). Norte, Sur, Oriente, Poniente refer to the roads' position in relation to the Eje Central. The system is remarkably clear in its signposting with special symbols for telephones, information points, tram stops, etc. Beware of the tram lines—trams, buses, emergency services and plain simple folk in a hurry come down at high speed; and as often as not this lane goes against the normal flow of traffic! Bicycles are permitted to go the wrong way on all roads, which also 'adds to the spice of life". Driving is not too much of a problem because traffic wardens at most corners direct the flow of traffic. You must, however, have a good map (see below). **NB** Eje Lázaro Cárdenas used to be called Calle San Juan de Letrán.

City Buses Buses have been coordinated into one system: odd numbers run NS, evens EW. Fares on large buses, which display routes on the windscreen are 40 centavos (even on the '100' buses), exact fare only. There are 60 direct routes and 48 feeder (SARO) routes. We are informed that thieves and pickpockets haunt the buses plying along Reforma and Juárez. Be careful of your valuables! A most useful route for tourists (and well-known to thieves, so don't take anything you don't require immediately) is No 76 which runs from Calle Uruguay (about the level of the Juárez Monument at Parque Alameda) along Paseo de la Reforma, beside Chapultepec Park. A *Peribus* service goes round the entire Anillo Periférico (see Traffic System). The 100 bus line also insures its passengers: collection of insurance requires presentation of the ticket. Trolley buses also charge 40 centavos.

Peseros run on fixed routes, often between metro stations and other known landmarks; destination and route displayed on the windscreen. Avoid the smaller, white VW Kombis which do not have catalytic converters and which can be unpleasant. *Peseros* can be hailed almost anywhere and stop anywhere (press the button or say 'bajan"); this can make long journeys slow. If a Ruta 100 bus runs on the same route, it is preferable as it has fixed stops. Fares are 55 centavos, 80 centavos for 6-12 km, 110 centavos 13-17 km and 150 centavos over 18 km. No tip necessary; no price increase at night.

Taxis There are three types: 1) 'turismo' taxis which operate from first class hotels—the most expensive. 2) Taxis from bus terminals and the railway station (without meters), for which you pay in advance at a booth (check your change); they charge on a zone basis, US$5 for up to 4 km, rising to US$14 for up to 22 km (the same system applies at the airport—see below). 3) Taxis on unfixed routes are yellow, and green (lead-free petrol) and can be flagged down anywhere; they charge a basic fee of 2 new pesos (US$0.70), with 25 centavos for each 250 metres or 45 seconds; between 2200 and 0600 they charge 20% extra. They have meters (check they are working properly and set at zero); if you do not bargain before getting in, or if the driver does not know the route well, the meter will be switched on, which usually works out *cheaper* than negotiating a price. Note that radio-telephone taxis, and those with catalitic converters have a basic fee of 2.50 new pesos. Drivers often do not know where the street you want is; try to give the name of the intersection between two streets rather than a number, because the city's numbering can be erratic. A tip is not normally expected, except when special help has been given. At most bus terminals (but not the airport) an ordinary taxi can be found nearby, thus avoiding unscrupulous demands for extra tips. For information, or complaints, T 605-5520/6727/ 5388/ 6894; if complaining make sure you take the taxi's I.D. No.

Metro Maps of the network are usually available from ticket offices at big stations and tourist offices and are displayed at most stations. There is a metro information service at Insurgentes station on Pink Line which dispenses maps and most interchange stations have information kiosks. The *Atlas de Carreras*, US$1.65 has a map of Mexico City, its centre and the metro lines marked. *Pronto's* map of the metropolitan area displays the metro clearly. Good metro and bus maps at the Anthropology Museum, US$1.25. *Guía práctica del Metro*, US$9, explains all the station symbols; also *Guía cultural del Metro*, US$3, both for sale at Zócalo station. All the stations have a symbol, eg the grasshopper signifying Chapultepec.

There are eight lines in service, with further expansion announced in 1990. **1** from Observatorio (by Chapultepec Park) to Pantitlán in the eastern suburbs. It goes under Av Chapultepec and not far from the lower half of Paseo de la Reforma, the Mercado Merced, and 3 km from the airport. **2**, from Cuatro Caminos in the NW to the Zócalo and then S above ground to Taxqueña; **3**, from Indios Verdes S to the University City (free bus service to Insurgentes); **4**, from Santa Anita on the SE side to Martín Carrera in the NE; **5**, from Pantitlán, via Terminal Aérea (which is within walking distance of gate A of the airport, but some distance from the international gates—opens 0600), crossing Line 3 at La Raza, up to Politécnico (if using La Raza to connect with Line 5, note that there is a long walk between Lines 5 and 3, through the Tunnel of Knowledge); **6**, from El Rosario in the NW to Martín Carrera in the NE; **7**, from El Rosario in the NW to Barranca del Muerto in the SW; **9** parallels 1 to the S, running from Tacubaya (where there are interesting paintings in the station) in the W to Pantitlán in the E. Line **8** will run from Garibaldi (N of Bellas Artes, Line 2), through Chabacano (Line 9), Santa Anita (Line 4), to Constitución de 1917 in the SE. Running SE from Pantitlán, Line A, the *metro férreo* goes as far as La Paz, 9 stations in all. From Taxqueña the *tren ligero* goes as far as Xochimilco, a very convenient way to this popular destination. Music is played quietly at the stations.

Tickets 40 centavos, buy several to avoid queuing, check train direction before entering turn-stile or you may have to pay again. If you want to use the metro often, you can buy an *abono*, US$4.40 (13.50 Np, available on 1st or 16th of month from stations, Conasupo stores, special booths in the city, and some lottery sellers), which allows you to use the whole system and the 100 buses, trolleybuses, the *metro férreo* and the *tren ligero* for 15 days: remember in this case to use the blue entrances to the metro stations, or your *abono* will be lost. An efficient, modern system (virtually impossible to get lost), and the best method of getting around the city, especially when the pollution is bad. Trains are fast, frequent, clean and quiet although overcrowded at certain times (eg early morning, 1400-1500 and 1830-2000). When carriages are crowded, be alert for pickpockets (if possible don't stand near the sliding doors), but on the whole the notoriety of the metro is exaggerated, not least by those Mexicans who do not use it themselves. Between 1800 and 2100 men are separated from women and children at Pino Suárez and certain other stations. Two pieces of medium-sized luggage are permitted.

At the Zócalo metro station there is a permanent exhibit about the city, interesting. At Pino Suárez, station has been built around a small restored Aztec temple. Art in the metro: Line 1, Pino Suárez and Tacubaya; Line 2, Bellas Artes and Panteones; Line 3, La Raza, scientific display in the Tunnel of Knowledge, and S of Coyoacán; Line 4, Santa Anita; Line 5, Terminal Aérea; Line 6, all stations, Line 7, Barranca del Muerto; Line 9, Mixuca. **NB** Lines 1, 2 and 3 open 0500-2400 Mon-Fri, 0600-0100 Sat and 0700-2400 Sun and holidays; the other lines open 1 hr later. Do not take photos or make sound-recordings in the metro without obtaining a permit and a uniformed escort from metro police, or you could be arrested. For lost property enquire at Oficina de Objetos Extraviados at Fray Servando on Line 4, T 768-8175, open 0830-1600.

Car Hire Agencies Budget Rent Auto, Reforma 60; **Hertz**, Revillagigedo 2; **Avis**, Medellín 14; VW, Av Chapultepec 284-6; **National Car Rental**, Insurgentes Sur 1883; **Auto Rent**, Reforma Norte 604; quick service at Av Chapultepec 168, T 533-5335 (762-9892 airport); **Pamara**, Hamburgo 135, T 525-5572—**NB** 200 km free mileage; **Odin**, Balderas 24-A; and many local firms, which tend to be cheaper. It is generally cheaper to hire in the US or Europe.

Note When driving in the capital you must check which 'día sin auto' applies to your vehicle's number plate; if your car is on the street when its number is prohibited, you could be fined US$150. Saturday and Sunday are free.

Cycle shops *Benolto*, near Polanco metro, stocks almost all cycle spares; another good shop is between San Antonio and Mixcoac metro stations. The Escuela Médico Militar, near Pino Suárez metro station, has a very good shop, stocking all the best known international makes for spare parts.

Motocycle repairs See **Motorbikes** in Information for Visitors.

Entertainments For all cultural events, consult *Tiempo Libre*, every Thur from newsstands, US$1, or *Consejo(s) para Ver y Oir*, US$0.70 from Bellas Artes bookshop. Theatres: Palacio de Bellas Artes (for ballet, songs, dances, also concerts 2-3 times a week—**see p 174**), Fábregas, Lírico, Iris, Sullivan, Alarcón, Hidalgo, Urueta, San Rafael and Insurgentes in town and a cluster of theatres around the Auditorio Nacional in Chapultepec Park (check at Tourist Office for

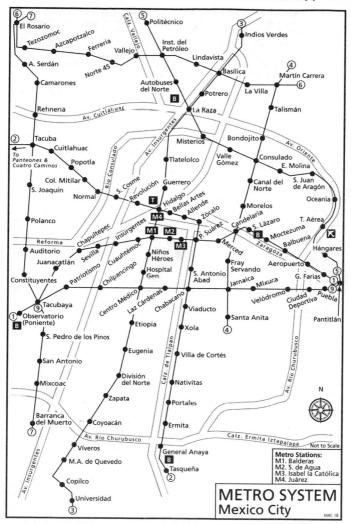

METRO SYSTEM
Mexico City

Metro Stations:
M1. Balderas
M2. S. de Agua
M3. Isabel la Católica
M4. Juárez

MAC 18

details of cheap programmes). Spectaculars (eg presidential inauguration) are often staged in the Auditorio Nacional itself. Also in Chapultepec Park is the Audiorama (behind the Castle on the Constituyentes side) where one may listen to recorded classical music in a small open ampitheatre in a charming wooded glade. A request book is provided, for the following day. There may be a free performance of a play in one of the parks by the Teatro Trashumante (Nomadic Theatre). Variety show nightly with singers, dancers, comedians, magicians and ventriloquists, very popular with locals, at Teatro la Blanquita, on Av Lazaro Cárdenas Sur near Plaza Garibaldi. The Teatro de la Ciudad, Donceles 36 (T 510-2197 and 510-2942) has the

Ballet Folklórico Nacional Aztlán, US$3-15 for tickets, very good shows Sunday am and Wednesday. On Sundays there is afternoon bull-fighting in a vast ring (**see p 180**). The balloon sellers are everywhere.

Cinemas A number show non-Hollywood films in original language (Spanish sub-titles); check *Tiempo Libre* magazine, or *Mexico City News* for details. Some recommended cinemas are: Cineteca Nacional, metro Coyoacan (excellent bookshop on the cinema and related topics, library); Cinematógrafo del Chopo, Calle Dr Atl, non-commercial films daily 1700 and 1930, US$1; good cinema in Ciudad Universitaria; Cine Latino, Av Reforma between the statue of Cuauhtémoc and El Angel; Cine Versalles, Versalles (side street off Av Reforma, near statue of Cuauhtémoc); Cine Electra, Río Guadalquivir (near El Angel); Cine Diana, Av Reforma, at the end where Parque Chapultepec starts; Cine Palacio Chino, in the Chinese *barrio* S of Av Juárez (also interesting for restaurants). The sound is often very low on sub-titled films, only option is to sit near speakers at front. All cinemas, except Cineteca Nacional, charge half-price on Wed.

Football Sun midday, Aztec and Olympic stadia (former has a great atmosphere at football matches, latter has a Rivera mural of the history of Mexican sport); also Thurs (2100) and Sat (1700). Tickets from US$3.35 at Olympic Stadium. To Aztec Stadium take metro to Taxqueña terminus, then tram en route to Xochimilco to Estadio station; about 75 mins from Zócalo. To Olympic Stadium take metro to Universidad terminus, then local bus (US$0.35) or taxi (US$1), leave Zócalo at 1045 for 1200 kick-off.

Horse Races Hipódromo de las Américas, W of Blvd Manuel Avila Camacho, off Av Conscriptos, every Tues, Thurs, Sat and Sun almost all the year. Pari-mutuel betting. Races begin at 1500 and finish at dusk; they may be watched from the exclusive restaurants (eg of the Jockey Club), or the self-service counters, from a private box or among the crowd. Beautiful track with infield lagoons and flamingoes, and plenty of atmosphere. Small entry fee with a tourist card. To get there by public transport involves 2 changes of bus, by taxi costs US$7.50.

Jai-Alai Events with the foremost players in the world every day except Friday at the Frontón México across from Monumento a la Revolución, from 2000 (1900 Sun) till 2400 (closed Mon), entry US$7, drinks expensive. It seats 4,000. Jackets and ties are needed for admission (restaurant across the sidestreet rents ties to the desperate for US$1-2). The people in the red caps are the *corredores*, who place the bets. Pari-mutuel betting. Also Frontón Metropolitano, on Bahía de Todos los Santos, near junction of Gutemberg and Calz Melchor Ocampo.

Golf at Chapultepec Golf Club and Churubusco Country Club. These are private clubs, open to visitors only if accompanied by a member. Green fees are high (US$20 upwards).

Hiking Every weekend with the Alpino and Everest clubs. Club de Exploraciones de México, Juan A Mateos 146, Col Obrero (metro Chabacano), DF 06800, T 578-5730, 1930-2400 Wed or Fri organizes several walks in and around the city on Sats and Suns, cheap equipment hire, slideshow Wed. Club Alpino Mexicano, Córdoba 234, Col Roma (metro Hospital General), T 574-9683, open Mon-Fri 1030-2030, Sat 1030-1530, small shop.

Swimming Agua Caliente, Las Termas, Elba, Centro Deportivo Chapultepec and others.

Charreadas (Cowboy displays), Rancho Grande de La Villa, at very top of Insurgentes Norte (nearest metro Indios Verdes, then walk N beyond bus station and keep asking), Sun 1100-1500, US$1.30.

Exchange Banks 0900-1330 Mon-Fri, although some branches open earlier and close later. Always see if there is a special counter where currency transactions can be effected, to avoid standing in queues which can be long, particularly on Fri. Branches of all major Mexican banks proliferate in most parts of the city. TCs in most major currencies can be cashed at any branch of Bancomer or Banco Serfín without undue delay. Banks do not charge commission for changing TCs. The exchange of foreign currency notes, apart from dollars, is difficult, although most Latin American currencies can be exchanged at a *casa de cambio* at the airport (poor rates); better to go to a main bank branch in the city centre. Before changing money, ascertain the day's exchange rate (*tipo de cambio*) from a bank or newspaper and then shop around. Bank rates are fairly uniform but those in *casas de cambio* can be unfavourable with commission charges on top. Hotels usually offer very poor rates.

Banco de Comercio (Bancomer, Visa agent), head office at Av Universidad 1200, also Venustiano Carranza y Bolívar, **Banco Nacional de México (Banamex)**, Calle Palmas, (Banamex's offices nearby, at Av Isabel la Católica 44, are in a converted baroque palace, ask the porter for a quick look into the magnificent patio; another worthwhile building is the bank's branch in the Casa Iturbide, where Agustín de Iturbide lived as emperor, at Madero 17 with Gante); **Banco Internacional** rec, they deal with Mastercard (Carnet) and Visa (usually quicker than Bancomer or Banamex for cash advances against credit card), also **Banco Serfín**, corner of 16 de Septiembre y Bolívar, or Madero 32, near Bolívar; **Citibank**, Av Insurgentes Sur, for Citicorp travellers' cheques. *American Express* office at Reforma 234 esq Havre, T 533-0380, will change cheques on Sats, 0930-1330, also open Mon-Fri until 1800 (there are 5 other AmEx offices in Mexico City, including **Campos Eliseos 204**, local 5, Polanco; **Centro Comercial Perisur**; *Hotel Crowne Plaza*, Reforma 80). For more details on Visa and Master Card, see **Information for Visitors** under **Exchange, p 391**. There are many *casas de cambio*, especially on Reforma and in the centre (eg *Euromex*, Reforma 344, outside Banamex, 0900-1300, good rates). Their hours may be more convenient, but their rates can be poor. The Perisur shopping centre, Insurgentes and Periférico Sur, has a *casa de cambio* (T 606-3698) which is usually open until 1900, with a better exchange rate in the morning. See also under **International Airport** below.

Spanish Classes The UNAM has excellent classes of Spanish tuition and Mexican culture: Centro de Enseñanza para Extranjeros, US$200 for 6 weeks, 5 different levels, free additional courses in culture, free use of medical service, swimming pool, library etc. See also National Registration Center for Study Abroad under **Learning Spanish** in Information for Visitors p 394. See also next paragraph. *$1,600 4 wks* Academo Hispano Chidua small classes

Cultural Institutions American Community School of Mexico, complete US curriculum to age of 12, Observatorio and Calle Sur 136, T 516-67-20; American Chamber of Commerce, Lucerna 78; Benjamin Franklin Library, Londres 116 (has *New York Times* 2 days after publication); Anglo-Mexican Cultural Institute (with British Council Library), Maestro Antonio Caso 127, T 566-61-44, keeps British newspapers; **Instituto Mexicano Norteamericano**, Hamburgo 115; 3-week intensive and painless courses in Spanish, 3 hrs a day; free, excellent concerts, art exhibits, conversation club, reading-room, bulletin board advertising rooms. **Instituto Italiano**, Francisco Sosa 77, Soyoacán, T 554-0044/53, has the *-4720* same courses, but less crowded. **Goethe-Institut**, Tonalá 43 (metro Insurgentes), 0900-1300, *525* 1600-1930; **Colegio Alemán**, Alexander V Humboldt, Col Huichapan, Del Xochimilco (CP 16030, México DF); **Instituto Francés de la América Latina**, Nazas 43, free films every Thurs *-3357* at 2030.

Embassies and Consulates Always check location of embassies and consulates; they tend to move frequently. Most take 24 hrs for visas; check to make sure you have a visa and not just a receipt stamp.

    Guatemalan Embassy, Explanada 1025, Lomas de Chapultepec, 11000 México DF, T 540-7520/520-9249, am only (take No 47 bus from Observatorio to Virreyes, then walk up hill, or No 76 'Km 15.5 por Reforma", or 'por Palmas", or taxi); to visit Guatemala some nationalities need a compulsory visa costing US$10 (eg Australians and New Zealanders), others need either a free visa (take a passport photo) or a tourist card (issued at the border); the current regulations are given in Guatemala—**Information for Visitors**; **Belizean Embassy**, Avenida Thiers 152-B, Anzures 2P, 11590 México DF, T 203-5960/5642, F 531-8115, open 0900-1300 Mon-Fri, visa US$10, takes a day; **Honduran Consulate**, Alfonso Reyes 220, T 515-6689/211-5425 (metro Chilpancingo), visas issued on the spot (no waiting) valid up to one year from date of issue, cost varies per nationality, up to US$20 for Australians; **Salvadorean Embassy**, Paseo de las Palmas 1930, Lomas de Chapultepec, T 596-33-90 (colectivo Las Palmas from Reforma or from Auditorio metro, 0900-1330 Mon-Fri); **Nicaraguan Consulate**, Payo de Rivera 120, Col Virreyes, Lomas de Chapultepec, T 520-4421 (bus 13 along Reforma, get out at Monte Altai and walk Son Monte Athos), visas for 30 days from date of issue, 1 photograph, US$25, plus US$5 if you want it 'on the spot"; **Costa Rican Embassy**, Río Póo 113, Col Cuauhtémoc, T 525-7764 (metro Insurgentes); **Panamanian Embassy**, Campos Eliseos 111-1, T 250-4259/4229, nr Auditorio metro, (visa US$20 for Australians); **Colombian Consulate**, Reforma 195, 3rd floor, will request visa from Bogotá by telegram (which you must pay for) and permission can take up to a month to come through.

    USA Embassy, Reforma 305, Col Cuauhtémoc, T 211-0042, F 511-9980, open Mon-Fri 0830-1730, if requiring a visa for the States, it is best to get it in your home country; **Canadian Embassy**, Schiller 529 (corner Tres Picos), nr Anthropological Museum, T 525-724-7900. **Australian Embassy**, Plaza Polanco Torre B, Jaime Balmes 11, 10th floor, Colonia Los Morales, T 395-9469; **New Zealand Embassy**, Homero 229, 8th floor (metro Polanco), T 250-59-99.

    British Embassy, Calle Río Lerma 71, T 207-2089/2449 (Apartado 96 bis, Mexico 5), open Mon and Thur 0900-1400 and 1500-1800, Tues, Wed, Fri, 0900-1500; Consular Section at Calle Usumacinta 30, immediately behind main Embassy Building; reading room in main building; poste restante for 1 month, please address to Consular section, this is not an official service, just a valuable courtesy; **British Chamber of Commerce**, Río de la Plata 30, Col Cuauhtémoc, T 211-56-54; **German Embassy**, Byron 737, Colonia Rincón del Bosque, T 545-66-55; **French Embassy**, Havre 15, near the Cuauhtémoc Monument, T 533-1361;

Netherlands Embassy, Monte Urales 635-203 (near Fuente de Petróleos), T 202-8267, F 202-6148; **Swedish Embassy**, Edificio Plaza Cornermex, Blvd M Avila Camacho 1-6, T 540-6393; **Danish Embassy**, Tres Picos 43, Colonia Polanco, Apdo Postal 105-105, 11580 México DF, T (5) 255-3405/4145/3339, open Mon-Fri 0900-1300 (nearest metro Auditorio); **Finnish Embassy**, Monte Pelvoux 111, 4th floor, 11000, Mexico, DF, T 540-6036; **Swiss Embassy**, Hamburgo 66, 5th floor, T 207-4820, open 0900-1200 Mon-Fri; **Polish Embassy**, Cracovia 40, CP 01000, T 550-4700; **Israeli Embassy**, PO Box 25389, T 540-6340, F 284-4825; Sierra Madre 215, open Mon-Fri 0900-1200. **Japanese Embassy**, Apartado Postal 5101, Paseo de la Reforma 395, Colonia Cuauhtémoc.

Delegation Building Av Central, the Ministry of Public Works is the place to report a theft; take a long book. **Customs** Dirección General de Aduanas, 20 de Noviembre 195, T 709-2900. **Immigration** Albañiles 19, esq Eduardo Molina, T 795-6685.

Setej (Mexican Students' Union), Hamburgo 301, Zona Rosa, metro Sevilla, only office to issue student card, which is required to buy a hostel card, T 211-0743 or 211-6636, deals with ISIS insurance. Open Mon-Fri 0900-1800, Sat 0900-1400.

English-Speaking Places of Worship Roman Catholic—St Patrick's, Calle Bondojito; Evangelical Union—Reforma 1870; Baptist—Capital City Baptist Church, Calle Sur 136; Lutheran—Church of the Good Shepherd, Palmas 1910; Anglican—Mexican Anglican Cathedral, Mesones 139 (**see p 179**) has services in Spanish, for services in English, Christ Church, Monte Escandinavos 405, Lomas de Chapultepec (services at 0800 and 1000, sung Eucharist, take bus Reforma Km 15 or Km 16 to Monte Alti, then down hill off opposite side of the road); First Church of Christ Scientist—21 Dante, Col Anzures. Jewish—Beth Israel, Virreyes 1140.

American British Cowdray Hospital, or the ABC, to give it its popular name, on Observatorio past Calle Sur 136. T 277-5000 (emergency: 515-8359); very helpful.

Medical Services C German, Calle Eucker No 16-601, T 545-94-34. Dr César Calva Pellicer (who speaks English, French and German), Copenhague 24, 3° piso, T 514-25-29. Dr Smythe, Campos Elíseos 81, T 545-78-61, rec by US and Canadian Embassies. For any medical services you can also go to the Clínica Prensa, US$1.20 for consultation, subsidized medicines. Hospital de Jesús Nazareno, 20 de Noviembre 82, Spanish-speaking, friendly, US$4 to consult a doctor, drugs prescribed cheaply. It is a historical monument (**see p 175**). Most embassies have a list of recommended doctors and dentists who speak languages other than Spanish.

Vaccination Centre Benjamín Hill 14, near metro Juanacatlán (Line 1). Open Mon-Fri 0830-1430, 1530-2030, avoid last half hour, also open on Sat from 0830-1430; typhoid free (this is free all over Mexico), cholera and yellow fever (Tues and Fri only) US$2; will give a prescription for gamma globulin. For hepatitis shots you have to buy gamma globulin in a pharmacy (make sure it's been refrigerated) and then an injection there (cheap but not always clean), or at a doctor's surgery or the ABC Hospital (see above). Gamma globulin is hard to find (see **pharmacies** below); try Hospital Santa Elena, Querétaro 58, Col Roma, T 574-7711, about US$50 for a vaccination. Malaria prophylaxis and advice free from San Luis Potosí 199, 6th floor, Colonia Roma Norte, 0900-1400, or from the Centro de Salud near metro Chabacano, opp Supermercado Comercial Mexicano—no typhoid vaccinations here (ask at Centro de Salud Benjamín Hill, which does not supply malaria pills). It seems that paludrine is not available in Mexico, only chloroquine.

Pharmacies Farmacía Homeopática, Calle Mesones 111-B. Farmacia Nosarco, corner of 5 de Febrero and República de El Salvador, stocks wide range of drugs for stomach bugs and tropical diseases, may give 21% discount. Sanborn's chain and El Fénix discount pharmacies are the largest chains with the most complete selection (the Sanborn's behind the Post Office stocks gamma globulin).

Laundromats Laundry on Río Danubio, between Lerma and Panuco and at Chapultepec and Toledo, nr Sevilla metro, expensive. Lavandería at Chapultepec y Toledo; Lavandería Automática at Edison 91 has automatic machines. Also at Parque España 14 and Antonio Caso 82, nr British Council.

Post Office Tacuba y Lázaro Cárdenas, opp Palacio de Bellas Artes, open for letters 0800-2400 Mon-Fri, 0800-2000 Sat, and 0900-1600 Sun (totally refurbished 1993). For parcels open 0900-1500 Mon-Fri only; parcels larger than 2 kilograms not accepted and difficult to send things other than books, records and cassettes. Philatelic sales at windows 9 to 12. Mail kept for only 10 days at poste restante window 3, rec, but closed Sat and Sun (**see p 392**). If they can't find your mail under the initial of your surname, ask under the initials of any other names you may happen to have. There is another post office at P Arriaga y Ignacio Mariscal, 2 blocks N of Monumento a la Revolución.

International Post Office (Customs) Calle Aldama 218, Colonia Buenavista, near Guerrero metro, open until 1800—airmail only (only until 1400 for parcels); take all packing materials with you, only small and expensive boxes can be bought here; or on 5 de Febrero, near the Zócalo. 1st and 2nd class airmail parcels can be sent directly from Aduana Postal, Ceylan 468 (open 0900-1300), 2nd class means that parcels are sent when there is room; they provide the box, you provide the tape and paper to cover the box. Sample price: US$37 for 2-3 kg to New Zealand. Metro to La Raza, then *pesero* to Pro-Hogar, final stop opposite post office buildings.

Telephones See **Information for Visitors** for details of the LADA phone system. Finding a phone box that works can be a problem; from many you can make local calls for nothing. Calls abroad can be made from phone booths with credit cards (via LADA system), with *fichas*, which can be bought at Parque Via 198 from 0800-2130, from a number of offices including the small office in José María Izazaga 20, near Salto de Agua metro, open until 1500, or at the International Airport. International calls can easily be made from the phone office in the Central del Oriente bus terminal. There are several places, including some shops, all officially listed, with long-distance phones. For information dial 07.

  Chief Telegraph Office for internal telegrams, Palace of Communications and Transport, Av Lazardo Gardena/Calzada Tacuba.

The **Mexican Secretariat of Tourism** (Secretaría de Turismo) is at Calle Masaryk 172, 5th floor, between Hegel and Emerson, Colonia Polanco (reached by bus No 32), T 250-8555, ext 116, F 254-2636, emergency hot line 250-0123/0151. Booking of hotels in other parts of the country possible here (reported unreliable in 1994). The tourist office produces a telephone directory in English and French. There is an office for Mexico City and the state of México at the corner of Londres and Amberes, Zona Rosa. You may refer complaints here, or to the tourist police, in blue uniforms, who are reported to be very friendly. Articles from the various craft displays can be bought. Free maps not always available, but try Cámara de Comercio de la Ciudad de México, Información Turística, open Mon-Fri 0900-1400, 1500-1800, at Reforma 42, which provides maps and brochures of the city (apparently for government employees only); may otherwise be got from Department of Public Works; or buy in bookshops. Bus and metro maps available. Information bureau outside Insurgentes metro station and on Juárez, just E of Paseo de la Reforma (closed Sun). Tourist information can be dialled between 0800 and 2000 (bilingual operator) on 525-9380. For problems, eg theft, fraud, abuse of power by officials, T 516-0490, Protectur. Incidentally, museums are closed Mon, except Chapultepec Castle, which is open daily. A weekly magazine, *The Gazer/El Mirón* gives basic information and tips for Mexico City and elsewhere in Mexico. Also *Mexico City Daily Bulletin*, free from most hotels, good listings, exchange rate information unreliable. The magazine *Donde* (US$2) gives general information, details on hotels, restaurants, crafts and entertainment.

  For information on National Parks, contact the Secretaría de Desarollo Social, Río Elba 20, piso 8, Col Cuauhtémoc, 06500 México DF, T 286-7051/553-9629; it has offices in every state. Sedue, the Dirección General de Conservación Ecológica de los Recursos Naturales, is at Río Elba, piso 10, T 286-9276/9278.

Maps Instituto Nacional de Estadística Geografía e Informática (INEGI) sells maps and has information, branches in each state capital and in the Distrito Federal in the arcade below the traffic roundabout at Insurgentes (where the metro station is), open 0800-1600, all maps available, but only one index for consultation. The Automobile Club's (AMA) street map is good, but hard to find. Good maps of the city from HFET (see **Maps** in **Information for Visitors**), *Guía Roji* (an excellent A to Z, US$9.25, but you need to know which colonia the road you are looking for is in) and *Trillas Tourist Guide* (US$6.50, rec). Street vendors on Zócalo and in kiosks sell a large city map for US$3. Good large postcard/map of Coyoacán available at many bookshops.

Travel Agencies *Thomas Cook*, Campos Eliseos 345, Col Polanco, travellers' cheques agency only; *Wagons-Lits*, Av Juárez 88, T 518-1180, also Av De Las Palmas 731, T 540-0579, very helpful and knowledgeable; *Uniclam* agent in Mexico City is Srta Rosa O'Hara, Río Pánuco 146, Apto 702, Col Cuauhtémoc, T 525-5393. *Grey Line Tours*, Londres 166, T 533-1665, reasonably priced tours, car hire, produces *This is Mexico* book (free). *American Express*, Reforma 234 y Havre, T 533-0380, open Mon-Fri 0900-1800, Sat 0900-1300, charges US$3-4 for poste restante if you do not have their travellers' cheques and US$1 if no card or cheques are held for other services, service slow but helpful. *Corresponsales de Hoteles*, Blvd Centro 224-4, T 360-3356, for hotel reservations (upmarket); *Hadad Viajes*, Torres Adalid 205, of 602, Col de Valle, T 687-0488. *Viajes Tirol*, José Ma Rico 212, Depto 503, T 534-5582/3323/1765, English and German spoken, rec; *Turisjoven*, Tuxpan 54-903 (metro Chilpancingo). For cheap tickets to Cuba, ask round agencies around Hamburgo (including Setej at No 301); *W Tours and Travel*, T 682 1718/1607, are also rec.

Finding a cheap flight to Europe is difficult. Try *Vacation Planning*, Copenhague 21-203, Zona Rosa, T 511-1604; *Cultours*, Guanajuato 72 (Col Roma), T 264-0854/574/6265, highly rec, good for flights to central and S America and for changing flight dates; *Anfitriones*, *Turismo y Convenciones*, Reforma 410, T 205-2883/3752 (ask for Marco Polo, good English), rec; *Beltravel*, Londres 51, Zona Rosa; *Viajes de Alba*, Villalongín 20-2, Col Cuauhtémoc, T 705-4180.

Railways   The central station (a remarkable, spacious building) is on Insurgentes Norte, junction Alzate with Mosqueta, nearest metro Revolución or Guerrero. Left luggage for US$1.75 per piece per day. *Cafetería* reasonable. For details of train services, see destinations in text. The *Servicio Estrella*, with reserved reclining seats in a/c cars, or single and double sleepers, meals included, has been highly rec, although the service is not immune from delays or problems with heating, etc. A monthly timetable, *Rutas Ferroviarias*, is available from the station and from ticket offices. Reservations T 597-6177, 5 lines; information T 547-1084/1097/6593. If planning a train journey, find out in advance the departure time, which floor the ticket will be sold on and when, and arrive 1 hr in advance. **NB** Lost or stolen tickets will not be replaced.

International Airport   13 km from city. There are six access points: **A** AeroMéxico arrivals; **B** Departure for internal flights (US$6.50 tax, usually included in ticket price); **C** Internal arrivals; **D** International departures (US$12 tax); **E** International arrivals; **F** Most long-haul departures. The Instituto Nacional de Bellas Artes has a permanent exhibition hall and there is an interesting mural *La Conquista del Aire por el Hombre* by Juan O'Gorman. Telephone calls abroad from booth 19 (0600-2200) and booth 8 (0700-2300); there are also LADA phones which, in theory, accept foreign credit cards. 2 USA Direct phones, outside Gates 19 and 25. Buy pesos at Bancomer or Banamex, opp B, D and F, open 24 hrs, takes cash and cheques; only US$500-worth of pesos may be changed back into dollars after you have passed through customs when leaving (there are also *cambios* at E, before you pass through immigration and customs). The exchange facilities on upper floors, for arriving and departing passengers only, are less crowded than those on the ground floor. Banco Serfín takes Mastercard. There is a post office beside A, and a small office near C, by the restaurants. Some of the shops are open 24 hrs for drinks and snacks. Left luggage on 1st floor. Mexicana bookings in annex by C and AeroMéxico bookings and timetable booklets from near A. Opp point E and F, cars are rented.

Fixed-price taxis by zone, buy tickets from booths at exits by A, E and F; cost on average N$32/US$10.65 to the centre of the city, price varies according to distance (per vehicle, not per person, beware overcharging and short-changing), drivers may not know, or may be unwilling to go to, cheaper hotels. The rates for 'authorised' taxis are extremely high; possibly their one virtue is that they are safe. A cheaper alternative (about 50%) if one doesn't have too much luggage is to cross the Blvd del Aeropuerto by the metro Terminal Aérea and flag down an ordinary taxi outside the *Ramada* hotel. Journey about 20 mins from town centre if there are no traffic jams. There are regular buses to the airport (eg No 20, along N side of Alameda) but the drawback is that you have to take one to Calzada Ignacio Zaragoza and transfer to trolley bus at the Boulevard Puerto Aéreo (ie at metro station Aeropuerto). Buses to airport may be caught every 45 mins until 0100 from outside *De Carlo Hotel*, Plaza República 35. It takes an hour from downtown and in the rush hour—most of the day—it is jam-packed. But you can take baggage if you can squeeze it in. To get to the airport cheaply, if you do not have too much luggage, take metro to Terminal Aérea and walk, or take metro to Aeropuerto and then a *pesero* marked 'Oceanía', which will leave you at the Terminal metro station.

Tourist offices at A, E and F have phones for calling hotels, no charge, helpful, but Spanish only. The Mexican Hotel Association desk at the airport will call any hotel on its list and reserve a room for you (down to US$10 a night), also has a collective taxi which will drop you at your hotel, but it does not open until 1000. For air freight contact the Agencia Aduanales, Plazuela Hermanos, Colima 114, Mon-Fri 0900-1700, US$5.75 per kilo. Smokers should note that Mexican brands in the duty free shops are charged in pesos, foreign brands in US dollars, so get the latter elsewhere.

Airline Offices   The majority are on Paseo de la Reforma: No 325, Avensa (T 208-3018/325-0990) and Aerolíneas Argentinas (T 208-1050); AeroMéxico, No 445, T 228-9910 reservations (arrivals and departures 762-4022); Air France, No 404, T 546-9140, airport 571-3206; Delta, No 381, T 202-1608; Lan Chile, No 87, T 566-5211; Copa, No 87, T 592-3535; Varig, No 80, T 591-1744; Aeronica, No 322, T 207-6447; American Airlines, No 300, T 203-9444/571-3219 (airport); Aeroperú, No 195, T 566-1174; Avianca, No 195, T 566-8550; Aerocaribe, No 157, T 592-3006; British Airways, No 10, 14th floor, T 628-0500; TAN, No 87, T 566-4549; Aviateca, No 56, T 566-5966; Iberia, No 24, T 705-0716; Aero California, No 332, T 207-1392; Canadian Airlines, No 325, T 208-1883; Taca, No 87,

T 566-1850. On Calle Hamburgo: Ladeco, No 175, T 208-0146; Swissair, No 166, T 533-6363; SAS, No 61, T 208-8533; United, No 213, T 627-0222. Mexicana, Xola 535, Col del Valle, T 325-0990; KLM, Paseo de las Palmas 135, T 202-4444; Lufthansa, Paseo de las Palmas 239, T 202-8866; Cubana, Temistocles 246, Polanco, T 250-6355; Aviacsa, Insurgentes 1228, T 559-1955; Continental, Andrés Bello 45, T 280-3434; Aeromar, Sevilla 4, T 207-1566.

Long-distance Buses For details of bus services, see destinations in text. At all bus stations there are many counters for the bus companies, not all are manned and it is essential to ask which is selling tickets for the destination you want (don't take notice boards at face value). Buses to destinations in N Mexico, including US borders, leave from **Central del Norte**, Avenida Cien Metros 4907, which has a *casa de cambio*, 24-hr cafés, left luggage, pharmacy, bakery and phone offices for long distance calls (often closed and poorly informed, very high charges). The bus station is on metro line 5 at Autobuses del Norte. City buses marked Cien Metros or Central del Norte go directly there. **Central del Sur**, at corner of Tlalpan 2205 across from metro Taxqueña (line 2), serves Cuernavaca, Acapulco, Zihuatanejo areas. Direct buses to centre (Donceles) from Central del Sur, and an express bus connects the Sur and Norte terminals. It is difficult to get tickets to the S, book as soon as possible; the terminal for the S is chaotic. The **Central del Poniente** is situated opposite the Observatorio station of line 1 of the metro, to serve the W of Mexico. You can go to the centre by bus from the 'urbano' terminal outside the Poniente terminal (US$0.10). The **Central del Oriente**, known as TAPO, Calzada Ignacio Zaragoza (metro San Lazaro, Line 1), for buses to Veracruz, Yucatán and SE, incl Oaxaca (it has a tourist information office open from 0900; luggage lockers, US$2.65 per day, key is left with guard; post office, *farmacía* changes TCs). To Guatemala, from TAPO, take a bus to Tapachula, Comitán or Ciudad Cuauhtémoc, pesos only accepted.

All bus terminals operate taxis with voucher system and there are long queues (check change carefully at the taxi office). It is much easier to pay the driver, although beware of extra charges. Easier still is to flag down a yellow VW taxi on the street outside the terminal. In the confusion at the terminals some drivers move each other's cabs to get out of the line faster and may take your voucher and disappear. Fares are given under **Taxis** above. The terminals are connected by metro, but this is not a good option at rush hours, or if carrying too much luggage.

Advance booking is rec for all trips, and very early reservation if going to *fiestas* during Holy Week, etc. At Christmas, many Central American students return home via Tapachula and buses from Mexico City are booked solid for 2 weeks before, except for those lines which do not make reservations. You must go and queue at the bus stations; this can involve some long waits, sometimes 2-2½ hrs. Even if you are travelling, you may sometimes be required to buy a *boleto de andén* (platform ticket) at many bus stations. Note that many bus companies require luggage to be checked in 30 mins in advance of departure.

Bus Companies: (tickets and bookings) **Going N**: Transportes del Norte, at Av Insurgentes Centro 137, nr Reforma (T 587-5511/5400); dep from Central Norte. Omnibús de México, Insurgentes Norte 42, at Héroes Ferrocarrileros (T 567-6756 and 567-5858). Greyhound bus, Reforma 27, T 535-2618/4200, F 535-3544, closed 1400-1500 and all day Sun; information at Central Norte from Transportes del Norte (Chihuahuenses) or Tres Estrellas bus counters, prices only, no schedules. **Going to Central States**: Autobuses Anáhuac, Bernal Díaz 6 (T 591-0533); Central Norte departures. **Going NW**: ETN, Central México Norte, T 567-3773, or Central del Poniente T 273-0251; Tres Estrellas de Oro, Calzada Vallejo 1268 Norte (Col Santa Rosa), T 391-1139/3021, Central Norte. **Going NE**: ADO, Av Cien Metros 4907 (T 567-8455/5322). **Going S** (incl Guatemala): Cristóbal Colón, Blvd Gral Ignacio Zaragoza 200, T 542-7263 to 66; from Central del Oriente; also ADO, Buenavista 9 (T 592-3600 or 542-7192 at terminal). **Going SW**: Estrella de Oro, Calzada de Tlalpan 2205 (T 549-8520 to 29).

Suburbs of Mexico City

Churubusco, 10 km SE, reached from the Zócalo by Coyoacán or Tlalpan bus, or from General Anaya metro station, to see the picturesque and partly ruined convent (1762) at Gen Anaya con 20 de Agosto, now become the **Museo Nacional de las Intervenciones** (open 0900-1800, closed Mon, US$3.35, free Sun and holidays). Seventeen rooms filled with mementoes, documents, proclamations and pictures recounting foreign invasions, incursions and occupations since independence (also has temporary exhibitions). The site of the museum was chosen because it was the scene of a battle when the US Army marched into Mexico City in 1847. Adjoining the ex-convento is the church of

San Diego (16th century, with 17th and 18th century additions). Near the church, on the other side of Calzada Gen Anaya is the delightful Parque de Churubusco. One block from Tlalpan along Héroes del 47, to the left, is the 18th century church of San Mateo. There is a golf course at the Churubusco Country Club. Churubusco has the principal Mexican film studios. The new Olympic swimming pool is here. Near enough to Coyoacán (**see p 198**) to walk there.

Tlalpan, 6½ km further out, or direct from Villa Obregón (**see p 197**) a suburb with colonial houses, gardens, and near the main square, Plaza de la Constitución, an early 16th century church (San Agustín) with a fine altar and paintings by Cabrera. Reached by bus or trolley bus from the Taxqueña metro station. Two-and-a-half km W is the suburb of Peña Pobre, near which, to the NE, is the Pyramid of ***Cuicuilco***, believed to be the oldest in Mexico (archaeological museum on site, Insurgentes Sur Km 16, intersection with Periférico, open 0800-1800, closed Mon). The pyramid dates from the 5th or 6th century BC; it is over 100 metres in diameter but only 25 high.

Another excursion can be made to ***Ajusco***, about 20 km SW of Mexico City. Catch a bus from Estadio Azteca on Calzada Tlalpan direct to Ajusco. From the summit of the extinct **Volcán Ajusco** (3,929 metres), there are excellent views on a clear day. The way up is 10 km W of the village, 400 metres W of where the road branches to Xalatlaco (there is a hut S of the road where the path goes to the mountain). Foothills are also pleasant.

Xochimilco, to the SE, in the Valley of México. Take metro to Taxqueña (terminus), go to gate J and catch a colectivo No 26 on platform L, or bus No 140, US$0.30, or, easiest of all, take the *tren ligero* to Xochimilco. Turn left out of the station to catch the bus. The bus back leaves from the street left of the main church (don't believe taxi drivers who say there is no bus back). The bus stops beside the market (cheap fruit) in Xochimilco; bad signposting, but often tours from the *embarcaderos* will meet the buses and escort you to the boats. Otherwise keep to the right of the large church on the square, on Nuevo León, carry on until Violeta then turn right for a few blocks to Hermenegildo Galeana and then turn left for 3 blocks to Embarcadero. From the *tren ligero*, bear E along Las Rosas to cross the tram line, then follow the signs to Embarcadero. Xochimilco has a maze of canals, originally part of the canal system of Tenochtitlán, which wander round fruit and flower gardens. The government has provided funds to reclaim waterways which have been lost to urbanization and an ecological park was opened in 1993 (entry US$3.25, children under 14 free, adults over 60 US$1.60). Punts adorned with flowers, poled by Indians, can be hired for US$6 pp for 45 mins (rates may change during the week, or depending on size of boat). Owners don't like trips of less than 1½ hrs. Make sure you bargain hard before boarding, don't pay a tout before checking prices thoroughly, and ensure you get all the time you paid for as many of the boats are punted by boys without watches. At the canal-side restaurants there is music and dancing. The canals are busy on Sundays, quiet midweek. There is a fine market on Saturday; Indians come from miles around. It has an important 16th century fortified monastery, San Bernardo, built on Xochimilco's main square by the Franciscans in the 16th century, which has escaped heavy-handed restoration. The main altar is a masterpiece of painting and sculpture. Only one hotel, basic, D. Many cheap souvenirs; fruit and flowers sold from boats in canals. Note that it is virtually impossible to get on to the Mexico City-Cuernavaca toll road from Xochimilco.

Ixtapalapa is at the foot of the Cerro de Estrella, whose top is reached by a paved road or a path for some ruins, a small museum and a good view of volcanoes. It has two good churches: the Santuario del Calvario (1856), and San Lucas (1664), original roof timbers restored in 19th century, main door embodies Aztec motifs, fine interior. One of the most spectacular of Mexican passion-plays begins at Ixtapalapa on Holy Thursday.

Ciudad Universitaria (University City), world-famous, is 18 km via Insurgentes Sur on the Cuernavaca highway. Perhaps the most notable building is the 10-storey library tower, by Juan O'Gorman, its outside walls iridescent with mosaics telling the story of scientific knowledge, from Aztec astronomy to molecular theory. The Rectoría has a vast, mosaic-covered and semi-sculptured mural by Siqueiros. Across the highway is the Olympic Stadium, with seats for 80,000, in shape, colour, and situation a world's wonder. Diego Rivera has a sculpture-painting telling the story of Mexican sport. A new complex has been completed beyond the Ciudad Universitaria, including the newspaper library (the Hemeroteca Nacional), Teatro Juan Ruiz de Alarcón, Sala Nezahuacoyotl (concerts etc), bookshop and post office; also the Museo Universitario Contemporáneo de Arte and the Espacio Escultórico (sculptures - a large circular area of volcanic rock within a circle of cement - monoliths; on the opposite side of the road is another large area with many huge sculptures; stick to the path as it is possible to get lost in the vegetation). In the University museum there is an exhibition of traditional masks from all over Mexico. Beyond the Olympic Stadium is also the **Jardín Botánico Exterior** which shows all the cactus species in Mexico (ask directions, it's a ½ hr walk, open 0700-1630). The University of Mexico was founded in 1551. Bus (marked CU, one passes along Eje Lázaro Cárdenas; also bus 17, marked Tlalpan, which runs the length of Insurgentes) gets you there, about 1 hr journey. Another way to the university is on metro line 3 to Copilco station (20 mins walk to University) or to Universidad station (30 mins walk). At the University City there is a free bus going round the campus. The University offers 6-week courses (US$200, plus US$35 if you enroll late, good, student card useful).

Further E is **Anahuacalli** (usually called the **Diego Rivera Museum**, open Tues-Sun 1000-1400, 1500-1800, closed Holy Week, US$1.70, free Sunday). Here is a very fine collection of precolumbian sculpture and pottery, effectively displayed in a pseudo-Mayan tomb built for it by Diego Rivera. Reached by Kombi 29 bus from the Taxqueña metro station to Estadio Azteca, or take the bus marked División del Norte from outside Salto del Agua metro. Calle Museo branches off División del Norte. There is a big display here for the Day of the Dead at the beginning of November.

Villa Obregón (popularly known as *San Angel*) 13 km SW, has narrow, cobble-stone streets, many old homes, huge trees, and the charm of an era now largely past. Most of the distinguished architecture is of the 19th century. See the triple domes of its church, covered with coloured tiles, of the former Convento del Carmen, now the **Museo Colonial del Carmen**, houses 17th and 18th century furniture and paintings (open 1000-1700). See also the beautifully furnished and preserved old house, **Casa del Risco** (photographic ID required for entry, open Tues-Sun 1000-1700, free), near the Bazar del Sábado, on Callejón de la Amargura; also the church of San Jacinto, once belonging to a Dominican convent (1566). The **Museo de Arte Carrillo Gil**, Av Revolución 1608, has excellent changing exhibits and the **Museo Estudio Diego Rivera** (Av Altavista y Calle Diego Rivera, opp Antigua Hacienda de Goicochea—now *San Angel Inn*); the museum shows many of Rivera's personal belongings, the building was built by Juan O'Gorman. The Bazar del Sábado is a splendid Saturday folk art and curiosity market. Reach San Angel by bus from Chapultepec Park or by metro line 3 to MA Quevedo. There is a YWCA (ACF) at San Angel, but it is very expensive (E) with hot water for 2 hrs in the morning only, and use of kitchen 1800-2200. Excellent restaurants: the *San Angel Inn* is first class; good *panadería* by post office (which is no good for letters abroad). Between Villa Obregón and Coyoacán is the monument to Obregón on the spot where he was assassinated in 1928 (by the junction of Av Insurgentes Sur and

Arenal); the monument is open 0900-1400. Desierto de los Leones (see below) is reached from Villa Obregón by a scenic road.

Magdalena Contreras, which has many characteristics of the old Spanish village. Up in the hills in the SW of the city, can be reached by *pesero* or bus from San Angel (or by bus direct from Taxqueña), about 30-45 mins. There is an attractive main square and an 18th century church on the site of an earlier structure. *Artesanías* and multiple *taquerías*, etc; good *comida corrida* (US$2.65) at *Restaurante del Camino* and *Local 29* in the main square. From the village take another bus (bus station behind church), or *pesero*, up to **Los Dinamos** (3½ km), site of former pumping stations, now a National Park with picnic areas, horseriding, breathtaking scenery and, above all, clean air. There are *pulquerías* invitingly placed at intervals. If walking, bear in mind that you are quite a lot higher than in the city.

(Highly recommended are knowledgeable graduate guides for small groups visiting San Angel and Coyoacán, English, French, German, Spanish spoken, T 658-5376.)

Coyoacán, the oldest part of Mexico City, is the place from which Cortés launched his attack on Tenochtitlán. It is also one of the most beautiful and best-preserved parts of the city, with hundreds of fine buildings from the 16th-19th centuries, elegant tree-lined avenues and carefully tended parks and, in the Jardín Centenario and the Plaza Hidalgo, what must be rated as two of the most attractive squares in Latin America, if not the Western world. There are no supermarkets, no high-rise buildings, no hotels, no metro stations (see below). It is an area that is best explored on foot. (An excellent postcard-cum-pedestrian map of the Centro Histórico of Coyoacán to be found in local book and gift shops.)

It is culturally one of the most lively parts of Mexico City, and it is much frequented by the inhabitants of the capital, particularly at weekends. From Villa Obregón, one can reach Coyoacán via a delightful walk through Chimalistac, across Universidad and down Av Francisco Sosa; or one can take a bus or *pesero* marked 'Tasqueña' as far as Caballocalco.

From the city centre, it is easiest to take the metro to Viveros, or General Anaya (not Coyoacán, which is a long way from the historic centre). If coming from metro Viveros (a large park in which trees are grown for other city parks), it is worth making a slight detour in order to walk the length of **Francisco Sosa**, said to be the first urban street laid down in Spanish America. At the beginning of this elegant avenue is the church of **San Antonio Panzacola** (18th century), by the side of Río Churubusco; nearby, on Universidad, is the remarkable, beautiful (and modern) chapel of **Nuestra Señora de la Soledad**, built in the grounds of the 19th century ex-hacienda El Altillo. A little way down, in Salvador Novo, is the **Museo de la Acuarela** (free admission; open Tues-Sun). The terra-cotta fronted residence at No 383 is said to have been built by Alvarado. Many fine houses follow, mostly built in the 19th century. **Santa Catarina**, in the square of the same name, is a fine 18th century church; on Sundays, at about one o'clock, people assemble under the trees to tell stories (all are welcome to attend or participate). In the same square, the **Casa de la Cultura Jesús Reyes Heroles** should not be missed, with its delightful leafy gardens. Just before arriving at the **Jardín Centenario**, with its 16th century arches, is the **Casa de Diego Ordaz**. From metro General Anaya, there is a pleasant walk along Héroes del 47 (one block along on the left, 16th century church of **San Lucas**), across División del Norte and down Hidalgo (one block along on the left, and two blocks down San Lucas is the 18th century church of **San Mateo**). The **Museo Nacional de Culturas Populares** is at Hidalgo 289, and should be seen: open Tues-Sun 1000-1600, free, permanent and temporary exhibitions, cinema-cum-auditorio; good bookshop on Mexican culture and folklore. The *pesero* from metro Anaya to the centre of Coyoacán is marked 'Santo Domingo", alight at Abasolo or at the Jardín Centenario; it also goes past the Mercado (Malintzin).

The centre of Coyoacán is dominated by the church of **San Juan Bautista** (16th century, with later additions; magnificent interior); also 16th century, Franciscan monastery. Centenario is 16th century. The building which now houses the **Delegación** (Plaza Hidalgo) was built 244 years after the Conquest, on the site of the Palacio de Cortés. The beautiful 18th century church of **La Conchita** (in square of the same name) is reached by taking Higuera from Plaza Hidalgo; on the corner of Higuera and Vallarta is what is reputed to be the house of La Laminche, Cortés' mistress. Admirers of Frida Kahlo will be pleased to know that the **Museo Frida Kahlo** (Allende and Londres) is now open again; it is preserved as lived in by Frida Kahlo and Diego Rivera, and contains drawings and paintings by both; open Tues-Sun 1000-1700, admission US$3.35. (In the Parque de la Juventud Frida Kahlo, near Plaza de La Conchita, there is a striking bronze statue of Frida.) **Trotsky's house** is at Río Churubusco 410 (between Gómez Farías and Morelos); irregular opening times; enquire locally (entry US$3.45, half-price with ISIC card). NB Also the **Museo del Retrato Hablado** (Universidad 1330-C), the **Museo Geles Cabrera** (sculpture; Xicoténcatl 181; prior appointment, T 688-3016) and the **Museo del Automóvil** (División del Norte 3752).

Coyoacán has several theatres, medium and small, and similar establishments, eg: the *Coyoacán* and *Usigli* theates (Eleuterio Méndez, 5 blocks from metro Anaya), the *Foro Cultural de Coyoacán* (Allende; most events free of charge), the Museo de Culturas Populares (Hidalgo), the *Foro Cultural Ana-María Hernández* (Pacífico 181), the *Teatro Santa Catarina* (Plaza Sta Catarina) and the new *Rafael Solana* theatre on Miguel Angel de Quevedo (nearly opposite Caballocalco). Also note *El Hábito* (Madrid) and *El hijo del cuervo* (Jardín Centenario) for avant-garde drama and cabaret, *Los talleres de Coyoacán* (Francisco Sosa) for dance and ballet, *Cadac* (Centenario) for traditional and experimental drama. Details to be found in *Tiempo Libre* and local broadsheets. At weekends there are many open-air events especially in Plaza Hidalgo. Also at weekends, the Artesanía market, in a site off Plaza Hidalgo, is well worth a visit; reasonable prices, and lots of potential for bargaining; as at most places where bargaining is possible, the best deals are to be had either early or late in the day. In Higuera, there is an excellent gift-shop (*La Casita*, reasonable prices), also a map shop (*La Rosa de Los Vientos*, No 40), with maps of all areas of the country.

Restaurants There are several pleasant *cafeterías* in the Jardín Centenario, some of which serve light snacks and *antojitos*. Two of the best-known *cantinas* in Mexico are *La Guadalupana* (Higuera) and the *Puerta del Sol* on Plaza Hidalgo. There are many places where one can have a good *comida corrida* for US$3-4.50; especially rec are the *Fonda Reli* (Higuera, opp Correos) and *El Tiburón* (Hidalgo, almost opp the Museo de Culturas Populares; excellent fish). The *Restaurante Vegetariano*, Carranza y Caballocalco, offers an excellent US$5 buffet lunch; slightly more expensive but rec are *Los Balcones*, overlooking Plaza Hidalgo, nr the Delegación, and *El Morral*, Allende. Possibly the most fashionable restaurant in the area is *Los Geranios*, Francisco Sosa, but the food is not outstanding yet is overpriced and the chairs are uncomfortable. The *Caballocalco*, on Plaza Hidalgo, is extremely expensive, although the seats are comfortable.

The **Huayamilpas Ecological Park** can be reached by *pesero* from the centre of Coyoacán. The lake and surrounding area are protected by local inhabitants. The pyramid of **Tenayuca**, 10 km to the NW, is about 15 metres high and the best-preserved in Mexico. The Aztecs rebuilt this temple every 52 years; this one was last reconstructed about 1507; well worth seeing, for it is surrounded with serpents in masonry. The easiest way to get there by car from Mexico City centre is to go to Vallejo, 11 km N of the intersection of Insurgentes Norte and Río Consulado. Admission US$4.35. By metro, take the line to the Central de Autobuses del Norte (**see p 195**), La Raza, and catch the bus there. By bus from Tlatelolco; ask driver and passengers to advise you on arrival as site is not easily visible. An excursion to Tula may go via Tenayuca. It is not far from the old town of *Tlalnepantla*: see the ancient convent (ask for the *catedral*) on the Plaza Gustavo Paz and the church (1583), which contains the first image, a Christ of Mercy, brought to the New World. 2½ km to the N is the smaller pyramid of **Santa Cecilia**, interesting for its restored sanctuary.

Los Remedios, a small town 13 km NW of Mexico City, has in its famous church an image, a foot high, adorned with jewels. See the old aqueduct, with a winding stair leading to the top of two towers. It can be reached by car or by taking the Los Remedios bus at Tacuba metro. Fiesta: 1 September to the climax 8 September.

At **Naucalpan**, NW of the city (just outside the city boundary on Blvd Toluca), pre-classic Olmec-influenced figurines can be seen in the **Museo de la Cultura de Tlatilco** (closed Mon), opposite the *Hotel Naucalpan* on Vía Gustavo Baz. This is said to be the oldest settlement in the Cuenca de México.

Excursions from Mexico City

Desierto de los Leones, a beautiful forest of pines and broad-leaved trees, made into a national park, can be reached from Mexico City (24 km) by a fine scenic road through Villa Obregón. In the woods is an old Carmelite monastery (begun 1602, finished 1611, abandoned because of cold and damp in 1780); around are numerous hermitages, inside are several subterranean passages and a secret hall with curious acoustic properties. Take a torch.

Take an hour's bus ride from Observatorio metro to La Venta and ask bus-driver where to get off for the path to the monastery (about 4 km walk). One can either get there via the paved road or via the beautiful conifer-forest path, but the latter splits frequently so stick to what looks like the main path; or take the fire-break road below the row of shops and cheap restaurants near the main road. Food stalls abound, particularly at weekends when it is crowded. We have been advised that kidnap attempts have been made at Desierto de los Leones; do not let children wander out of sight. Do not leave valuables in your car, either. Many birds may be seen in the valley reached from the picnic area 6 km S of La Venta on Route 15.

Acolman has the formidable fortress-like convent and church of San Agustín, dating from 1539-60, with much delicate detail on the façade and some interesting murals inside. Note the fine portal and the carved stone cross at the entrance to the atrium. San Agustín is closed, awaiting funds to renovate the convent and open it as a tourist centre. Reached by bus from Indios Verdes metro station, or from the Zócalo. It is 42 km NE of the city.

Teotihuacan, 45 km from Mexico City, has some of the most remarkable relics of an ancient civilization in the world. Thought to date from around 300 BC, the builders of this site remain a mystery. Where they came from and why the civilization disppeared is pure conjecture. It seems that the city may have housed 250,000 who were peace-loving but whose influence spread as far as Guatemala. So completely was it abandoned that it was left to the Aztecs to give names to its most important features. There are three main areas: the Ciudadela, the Pyramid of the Sun and the Pyramid of the Moon. The whole is connected by the almost 4 km-long Street of the Dead which runs almost due N. To the W lie the sites of Tetitla, Atetelco, Zacuala and Yayahuala (see below). To the NE lies Tepantitla, with fine frescoes on a palace. The old city is traceable over an area of 3½ by 6½ km. Reckon on about 5-8 hrs to see the site properly, arrive early before the vast numbers of the *ambulantes* (wandering sales people with obsidian, flutes, silver bangles and, in Plaza of the Sun, straw hats) and the big tourist groups at 1100. There is a perimeter road with a number of car parking places—go anticlockwise. The small pebbles embedded in mortar indicate reconstruction (most of the site apparently!).

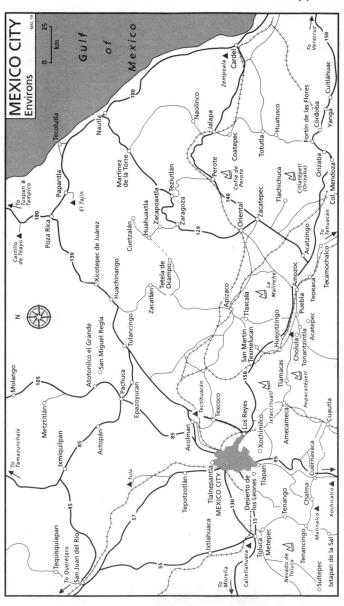

From the bus stop at the SW corner go through the museum (free). The citadel is immediately in front of you. Capable of holding 60,000 people, its main feature is the Temple of Quetzalcoatl (the Plumed Serpent, Lord of Air and Wind). Go to E side of the 1 km square. Behind the largest of the temples (take the right hand path), lies an earlier pyramid which has been partially restored. Lining the staircase are huge carved heads of the feathered serpents.

Follow the Street of the Dead to the Plaza of the Sun. You will pass small grassy mounds which are unexcavated temples. The Plaza contains many buildings, probably for the priests, but is dominated by the massive Pyramid of the Sun (64 metres high, 213 metres square at the base) and covering almost the same space as the Great Pyramid of Cheops in Egypt. The sides are terraced, and wide stairs lead to the summit. The original 4 metre covering of stone and stucco was removed by mistake in 1910. The view from the top gives a good impression of the whole site. But beware, it is a steep climb particularly between the third and fourth terrace. The car park to the N leads to Tepantitla. The murals here depict the rain god Tláloc.

The Pyramid of the Moon is about 1 km further N and on your right a tin roof covers a wall mural of a large, brightly coloured jaguar (the Jaguar Temple). The plaza contains the 'A' altars—11 in a pecular geometric pattern. The Pyramid is only half the size of the Pyramid of the Sun. A huge staircase allows access to the third terrace but you cannot go to its top. However there are excellent views looking S down the Street of the Dead.

To the W of the Plaza of the Moon lies the Palace of Quetzalpapalotl (quetzalmariposa, or quetzalbutterfly), where the priests serving the sanctuaries of the Moon lived, it has been restored together with its patio. Note the obsidian inlet into the highly decorated carved pillars. (Watch out for grey mice at the entrance!) Follow the path left under the Palace through the Jaguars' Palace with catlike murals protected from the sun by green canvas curtains to the Temple of the Feathered Shells. The base of the simple altar is decorated with shells, flowers and eagles.

You will pass several more temples on the W side of the Street of the Dead. If you want to visit Atetelco, go through the car park opposite the Pyramid of the Sun, turn right past *Restaurant Pirámides Charlies* (reputed to be the best on the site) and turn right along a small track. Alternatively to get to them from the museum, exit W and walk right up to main road, turning left after crossing the stream. They are well worth a visit; **Tetitla** a walled complex with beautiful frescoes and paintings, **Atetelco** with its three tiny temples and excellent murals and the abandoned sites of Zacuala and Yayahuala.

NB If short of time, try to get lift from a tourist bus to the Pyramid of the Moon car park. This is the most interesting area. Also take food and water—most of the shops are on the W side and you may be some distance from them. There is little by way of food apart from the expensive restaurant over the museum. There is a handicraft centre with weavings, obsidian carvings and explanations (and tastings) of the production of tequila and mescal.

Site open daily 0800-1700. (If the entrance near the bus stop is not open when it says it is, at 0800, try entrance near the Pyramid of the Moon.) Entrance, US$4.35, cars free, free on Sundays (extra charge for videos, tripods not permitted). The outside sites may be closed on Mondays. Bus from Terminal del Norte, Gate 8 (Autobuses del Norte metro), Mexico City, which takes at least 45 mins, US$2 one way (Pirámides buses are white with a yellow stripe). Bus returns from Door 1 at Teotihuacan site, supposedly every ½ hr. Some return buses to the capital terminate in the outskirts in rush hour without warning. *Son et lumière* display, costs US$4 per person (good *lumière*, not so good *son*); lasts 45 mins, 1900 in Spanish, 2015 in English (Oct-June only); take blanket or rent one. You can ride back to town with one of the tourist buses for about US$2. Note that the site is more generally known as 'Pirámides' than as 'Teotihuacan'. Train to Teotihuacan, 2 hrs, US$2.65, frequently delayed. Tours to Teotihuacan, picking you up at your hotel and usually including the Basilica de Guadalupe, normally cost US$30-35, with little time at the site. Official guidebook on sale, US$1, gives a useful route to follow. The Bloomgarden guide contains a useful map, good description and is recommended.

At the spring equinox, 21 March, the sun is perfectly aligned with the W face of the Pyramid of the Sun; many ad hoc sun worshippers hold unofficial ceremonies to mark the occasion (this is also Benito Juárez's birthday so entry is free).

Hotel A *Villas Arqueológicas*, pool (Apartado Postal 44 55800, San Juan Tesotihuacan, Edo de México, T 60909/60244, F 60928; in Mexico City, reservations at Club Med office). **Restaurants** around ruins, including that in the museum, reported high-priced and service slow.

Tepozotlán, about 43 km NW of Mexico City just off the route to Querétaro, has a splendid Jesuit church of San Francisco Javier in churrigueresque style. There are fine colonial paintings in the convent corridors. The old Jesuit monastery has been converted into a colonial art museum (Museo Nacional del Virreinato, open 1000-1700, closed Mon, entry US$4.35, US$0.20 Sun) and tourist centre with restaurants. There is a big market on Sunday. 28 km NW is the 18th century Acueducto del Sitio, 61 metres at its highest, 438 metres long.

A *Hotel Tepozotlán*, Calle Industrias, about 3 blocks from centre, TV, restaurant, swimming pool, good views, secure parking, highly rec; **Hotel San José**, Zócalo, nice rooms, poor service and value; the **Hostería del Monasterio** has very good Mexican food and a band on Sun; try their coffee with cinnamon. **Restaurant Artesanías**, opp church, rec, cheap. Also good food at **Brookwell's Posada**. Bus from near El Rosarío metro station, US$1.50, 1 hr ride. Many Querétaro or Guanajuato buses from Terminal del Norte pass the turn-off at 'Caseta Tepozotlán' from where one can take a local bus or walk (30 mins) to the town. (Do not confuse Tepozotlán with Tepoztlán, which is S of Mexico City, near Cuernavaca).

In the third week of December, *pastorelas*, or morality plays based on the temptation and salvation of Mexican pilgrims voyaging to Bethlehem, are held. Tickets are about US$10 and include a warming punch, the play, a procession and litanies, finishing with a meal, fireworks and music. Tickets from Viajes Roca, Neva 30, Col Cuauhtémoc, Mexico City.

Another half-day excursion is to *Tula*, some 65 km, thought to be the most important Toltec site in Mexico; two ball courts, pyramids, a frieze in colour, and remarkable sculptures over 6 metres high have been uncovered. There are four huge warriors in black basalt on a pyramid, the great Atlantes anthropomorphic pillars. The museum is well worth visiting and there is a massive fortress-style church, dating from 1553, near the market. Admission to site and museum, US$4.35 weekdays, free Sun and holidays. Multilingual guidebooks at entrance, fizzy drinks on sale. Site is open Tues-Sun 0930-1630 (museum open Wed-Sun till 1630). The town itself is dusty, however, with poor roads; **C** *Hotel Catedral*, clean, pleasant, TV; *Restaurant la Cabaña*, on main square, local dishes, also *Nevería*, with good soup. If driving from Mexico City, take the turn for Actopán before entering Tula, then look for the Parque Nacional sign (and the great statues) on your left.

Transport 1½ hrs by train from Buenavista station; at 0700 and 0900, returns at 1744 and 1955, US$2 (excellent breakfast for US$0.65), but can be several hours late; it follows the line of the channel cut by Alvarado to drain the lakes of Mexico Valley, visible as a deep canyon (from station walk along track ½ hr to site). One can take bus back, which leaves earlier. It can also be reached by 1st class bus, 'Valle de Mesquital", from Terminal del Norte, Avenida de los Cien Metros, goes to Tula in 1½-2 hrs; US$3 each way, 30-min service; Tula bus terminal is 3 km from the site, take a 'Pachuca' bus to the site entrance, 5 mins (badly signposted, an alternative route is: 200m to the Zócalo, to Calle Quetzalcoatl, to small bridge, sandy road to the right, and opening in the fence). Also bus or car from Actopán, on the Pan-American Highway (**see p 72**). Tula-Pachuca US$3.30; safe to leave belongings at bus station. Grey Line excursions from Mexico City have been recommended.

MEXICO CITY-VERACRUZ-MEXICO CITY (7)

A round tour by way of Tlaxcala, Cholula, Puebla, Tehuacán, Orizaba, Córdoba, Veracruz, and Xalapa. The route encompasses volcanoes, remains of the Tlaxcalan, Olmec and Totonac cultures, many fine colonial buildings in cities and villages and leads to the distinct Caribbean culture of Veracruz. A major detour goes to the Papaloapan region, in the S of Veracruz state, often neglected by visitors.

By road, the principal route is paved all the way (no Pemex service station on road between Puebla and Orizaba, a distance of about 150 km); total distance: 924 km, or 577 miles. A new toll *autopista* (motorway) now runs all the way from Mexico City to Veracruz (4 tolls which range from US$4.35 to US$9; tolls are marked on Tourist Map of Mexico). If wishing to avoid the toll route, note than the Vía Libre is very congested initially, and, at Ixtapaluca, just out of Mexico City, there is a series of *topes* (speed bumps) so high that they are a danger to ordinary saloon cars.

Our description is a trip along the old road, which goes E along the Puebla road, past the airport and swimming pools, and some spectacular shanty-towns. At (Km 19) Los Reyes, a road runs left into a valley containing the now almost completely drained Lake Texcoco, a valley early settled by the *conquistadores*. Along it we come to **Chapingo**, where there is a famous agricultural college with particularly fine frescoes by Rivera in the chapel. Next comes **Texcoco**, a good centre for visiting villages in the area. Bus from Mexico City, from Emiliano Zapata 92, near Candelaria metro station. Near Chapingo a road runs right to the village of **Huexotla** (see the Aztec wall, with ruined fortifications and pyramid, and the 16th century Franciscan convent of San Luis Obispo). Another road from Texcoco runs through the public park of Molino de las Flores. From the old *hacienda* buildings, now in ruins, a road (right) runs up the hill of Tetzcotzingo, near the top of which are the Baños de Netzahualcoyotl, the poet-prince. All the nearby villages are reported to have lost their charm; for instance (San Miguel de) **Chiconcuac** (road to San Andrés and left at its church), 4 km away, where Texcoco *sarapes* are woven. Tues is market day and there is a rousing *fiesta* in honour of their patron saint on 29 September.

At Km 29 is **Ixtapaluca** where a road on the right (S) leads to the small town of Amecameca, the starting point for Popocatépetl and Ixtaccíhuatl (see below). There is a youth hostel and Spanish countryside school at Ixtapaluca: it is open all year, caters for all abilities, small library, tourist information, economical tours. US$100/week, 5 hrs of classes daily, Mon-Fri, 3 meals a day. Youth hostel services US$3/day, meals extra. From Mexico City, take metro to Pantitlán, then a bus or *pesero* to Ixtapaluca. Behind the Mercado Municipal take another *pesero* on the 'Avila Camacho' route and get off at La Vereda (transportation from 0600-2100 daily). For information F 5-12-59-92. On the way to Amecameca, see the restored 16th century convent and church at **Chalco**, and the fine church, convent and open-air chapel of the same period at **Tlalmanalco**.

Amecameca, at 2,315m (pop 57,000), is 60 km from Mexico City, Cristóbal Colón 1st class bus every hour, 1-1½ hrs' journey, US$2, from the Central del Oriente; if hitching, take the Calzada Zaragoza, very dusty road. The zócalo is pleasant, with good taco stands; the post office is also on the Zócalo. A road reaches the sanctuary of El Sacromonte, 90m above the town (magnificent views), a small and very beautiful church built round a cave in which once lived Fray Martín de Valencia, a *conquistador* who came to Mexico in 1524. It is, next to the shrine of Guadalupe, the most sacred place in Mexico and has a much venerated full-sized image of Santo Entierro weighing 1½ kg only. From the zócalo, take the exit under the arch and head for the first white station of the cross; the stations lead to the top. Market day is Saturday. Three hotels, E, close to Amecameca's main square, and rooms at the *San Carlos* restaurant on the main square, E with bath, clean, good, modern, good food, but no hot water (sometimes no water at all). Camping is permitted at the railway station, ask the man in the office (leaving town, it's after the road to Tlamacas, on the right, 1-2 km away). Several eating-places and a good food market.

Amecameca is at the foot of the twin volcanoes ***Popocatépetl*** ('smoking mountain') and Ixtaccíhuatl ('sleeping woman'), the saddle between them, reached by car via a paved road up to the Paso de Cortés (25 km from Amecameca), gives particularly fine views. On Sats a pickup truck leaves the plaza at Amecameca, US$2 pp, for far up the mountain; also taxis for US$15 (2 people). Just before the pass, cars (but not pedestrians or taxis) pay US$0.10 entry to the national park. (Robbery and rape of car passengers at the viewpoint was reported in 1993.) The road on the other side of the pass to Cholula is rough, steep and sandy (but scenic), a sturdy vehicle is needed.

The best time to climb the volcanoes is between late October and early March when there are clear skies and no rain. From May to October the weather is good before noon; in the afternoons it is bad. Climbers are advised to spend at least a day at ***Tlamacas*** (3,950m) to acclimatize, reached from Paso de Cortés via the paved road which turns right (S), 5 km on. It is also possible to take a taxi (or hitchhike from the turn-off 2 km S of Amecameca, morning and early afternoon, best at weekends, no public transport Mon-Fri) from Amecameca to Tlamacas, US$15, up to 4 people, 32 km. There are a few houses, a small information centre for the Brigada de Rescate del Socorro Alpino de México (not always open) and, next door, a tourist hostel *Albergue de Tlamacas*, catering for day trippers from the capital, bring your own food (nearest food shop is in San Pedro, 20 km away; next restaurant in Amecameca). Sheets not provided; book in advance at weekends, US$3.50 a night in mixed dormitories (sleeping bag rec); beautiful house in wooded enclosure, poor toilet facilities, no hot water, tea and coffee available; for reservations T 553-6286/5896. 1½ km below Tlamacas is a camping and picnic area. Minibuses charge US$2.75 pp and run only Sat and Sun (from the E to Tlamacas: a bus from Cholula goes as far as San Nicolás de los Ranchos—the remaining 10 km to Paso de Cortés must be covered on foot or by hitching; colectivos from Cholula go as far as San Pedro). From Tlamacas a path goes up to Las Cruces at 4,400m (where there was once a refuge) and the snowline; from there it is 3 hrs (crampons and ice axe) to the rim of the crater (the hardest part) and thence another hour's walk round the rim to the top. Equipment hire at the hostel, check condition in advance, passport required as deposit, even for extra blankets at night, US$10 for boots, crampons and ice-axes (US$13 a set), gloves and caps for sale, or in Amecameca, but preferable to hire from Mountain Club in Mexico City. Maps available only in Mexico City. If you wish to go to the top of Popocatépetl (5,400m) leave at 0400, as the ground is more solid early on (take warm clothes and a flashlight, and sunglasses for the snow-glare).

From Paso de Cortés a road goes left (N) along another dirt road which leads past TV station for 12 km to nearest parking to summit of Ixtaccíhuatl. From there you find various routes to summit (12-15 hrs return) and 3-4 refuges to overnight (no furniture, bare floors, dirty). To climb ***Ixtaccíhuatl*** take a taxi to La Jolla, from there follow the tracks up the grassy hill on the right. There are three huts between 4,600 and 5,000m, from the last hut it is 2½ hrs to the top, over two glaciers, some rock climbing required.

Beyond Ixtapaluca the road climbs through pine forests to reach 3,196m about

63 km from Mexico City, and then descends in a series of sharp bends to the quiet town of San Martín **Texmelucan**, Km 91. The old Franciscan convent here has a beautifully decorated interior, and a former *hacienda* displays weaving and old machinery. Market day is Tuesday (**D** *Hotel San José*, D with bath, parking inside, rec, at Poniente 115).

From here a side-road leads NE for 24 km to the once quaint old Indian town of Tlaxcala; a remarkable series of precolumbian frescoes are to be seen at the ruins of **Cacaxtla** near San Miguel del Milagro, between Texmelucan and Tlaxcala. The colours are still sharp and some of the figures are larger than life size. One wall, in turquoise, depicts a battle between an army dressed as jaguars and another dressed as eagles. Also depicted are two princes, the jaguar (the native prince), and the eagle, representing the invading Huaxtecas. The jaguar also represents Venus, the night, the rainy season, north, death, while the eagle is the sun, day, the dry season, S and life (Helmut Zettl, Ebergassing, who quotes the theories of Prof Michel Graulich of the Free University of Brussels). To protect the paintings from the sun and rain, a huge roof has been constructed. (The paintings were featured in the September 1992 issue of *National Graphic*.) The site is open all day and an easily accessible visitors' centre has been opened (closed Mon). In theory there is a 'per picture' charge for photography, but this is not assiduously collected. From Puebla take a Flecha Azul bus marked 'Natividad' to just beyond that town where a sign on the right points to San Miguel del Milagro and Cacaxtla (US$1). Walk up the hill to a large sign with its back to you, turn left here for the ruins.

Back on the highway, blue buses can be flagged down for **Tlaxcala**, with its pleasant centre of simple buildings washed in ochre, pink and yellow, and its vast suburbs. It is the capital of small Tlaxcala state (pop 763,700 in 1990) whose wealthy ranchers breed fighting bulls, but whose landless peasantry is still poor. To see: the church of **San Francisco**, the oldest in Mexico (1521), from whose pulpit the first Christian sermon was preached in the New World—its severe façade conceals a most sumptuous interior (note the cedar and gold, star-spangled ceiling—and the 'No Photos' sign at the door); almost next door is the **Museo del Estado de Tlaxcala** (free), open 0900-1700, 2 floors of historical and artistic exhibits, interesting; also the extremely colourful murals (1966—still incomplete 1993) depicting the indigenous story of Tlaxcala, the history of Mexico and of mankind in the **Palacio de Gobierno**. The annual fair is held 29 Oct-15 Nov each year. Population 36,000. Altitude 2,240m. Tourist office at Juárez y Landizábal, many maps and leaflets, very helpful, no English spoken. Frequent Flecha Azul buses from Puebla, central bus station (platform 81/82) between 0600 and 2130, 45 mins, US$1.20. Tlaxcala's bus station is about a 10-minute walk to the centre.

The ruins of the pyramid of Xicohténcatl at San Esteban de **Tizatlán**, 5 km outside the town, has two sacrificial altars with original colour frescoes preserved under glass. The pictures tell the story of the wars with Aztecs and Chichimecs. Amid the archaeological digs at Tizatlán are a splendid 19th-century church and a 16th-century chapel of San Esteban. Colectivo to Tizatlán from 1 de Mayo y 20 de Noviembre, Tlaxcala, at main square, you get out when you see a yellow church dome on the left.

The **Sanctuary of Ocotlán** (1541), on a hill in the outskirts of Tlaxcala commands a view of valley and volcano. It was described by Sacheverell Sitwell as 'the most delicious building in the world', but others have been less impressed. Nevertheless, its façade of lozenge-shaped vermilion bricks framing the white stucco portal and surmounted by two white towers 'with fretted cornices and salomonic pillars' is beautiful. The golden interior was worked on for 25 years by the Indian Francisco Miguel.

(Km 106) **Huejotzingo** has the second-oldest church and monastery in Mexico, built 1529; now a museum. Market: Sat, Tues. Dramatic carnival on Shrove Tuesday, portraying the story of Agustín Lorenzo, a famous local bandit. **D** *Hotel Colonial*, secure but poor value.

(Km 122) **Cholula** is a small somnolent town (20,000 people, with the Universidad de las Américas), but one of the strangest-looking in all Mexico. When Cortés arrived, this was a holy centre with 100,000 inhabitants and 400 shrines, or *teocallis*, grouped round the great pyramid of Quetzalcoatl. In its day it was as influential as Teotihuacan. There used to be a series of pyramids built one atop another. When razing them, Cortés vowed to build a chapel for each of the *teocallis* destroyed, but in fact there are no more than about seventy. There is a very helpful tourist office opposite the main pyramid: Cholula map and guide book for US$1; the site is open 1000-1700.

Places to see are the excavated pyramid, admission US$4.35 on weekdays, free on Sun and holidays, it has 8 km of tunnels and some recently discovered frescoes inside, but only 1 km of tunnel is open to the public, which gives an idea of superimposition (the frescoes are not open to the public). Guides charge US$6.50, rec as there are no signs inside (some guides claim to speak English, but their command of the language is poor). The entrance is on the main road into Cholula. The chapel of Los Remedios on top of it gives a fine view. The Franciscan fortress church of San Gabriel (1552) is in the plaza (open 0600-1200, 1600-1900, Suns 0600-1900); and next to it, the Capilla Real, which has 48 domes (open 1000-1200, 1530-1800, Suns 0900-1800). There is a *casa de cambio* on the corner of the main plaza, and a travel agency in the Los Portales complex on the plaza.

See also the Indian statuary and stucco work of the 16th century church of Santa María de **Tonantzintla**, outside the town; the church is one of the most beautiful in Mexico (open 1000-1800 daily), and may also be reached by paved road from San Francisco **Acatepec**, which also has a beautiful, less ornate 16th century church (supposedly open 0900-1800 daily, but not always so—key is held by José Ascac, ask for his shop). They are off Highway 190 from Puebla to Izúcar de Matamoros. Both these places are easily reached from Cholula or Puebla from CAPU bus terminal, white bus, to Acatepec-Tonantzintla, 20 mins. Best light for photography after 1500. John Hemming says these two churches 'should on no account be missed; they are resplendent with Poblano tiles and their interiors are a riot of Indian stucco-work and carving.' Both churches, though exquisite, are tiny. Some visitors note that regular visiting hours are not strictly observed at Cholula, Acatepec, Tonantzintla and Huejotzingo.

One can visit Tonantzintla and Acatepec from Cholula main square with a 'peso-taxi'. Or one can take a kombi from Cholula to Acatepec or to Tonantzintla (marked Chilipo or Chipanco, ask which kombi goes to the church you want) for US$0.55 from junction of Av 5 and Av Miguel Alemán. This is 2 blocks from Zócalo, which is 3 blocks from tourist office. You can walk the 1 km to the other church, and then take a bus or kombi back to Cholula or Puebla. Acatepec from CAPU in Puebla, US$0.45, 30 mins, bus stops outside the church.

Hotels in Cholula *Villa Arqueológica*, 2 Poniente 501, T 471966; **B** *Los Sauces*, Km 122, Carretera Federal Puebla-Cholula; *Motel de la Herradura*, Carr Federal; **B** *Cali Quetzalcoatl*, on Zócalo, T 471335, clean, expensive restaurant; **C** *Hotel de las Américas*, 14 Oriente 6, T 470991, near pyramid, actually a motel, modern with rooms off galleries round paved courtyard (car park), small restaurant, clean, good value; **D** *Super Motel* on the road from Puebla as you enter town, each room with private garage, very secure; **D** *Reforma*, near main square; **E** *Trailer Park Las Américas*, 30 Oriente 602, hot showers, secure, as are the furnished apartments. *Restaurant Choloyan*, also handicrafts, Av Morelos, good, clean, friendly. Try *licuados* at market stalls, fruit and milk and 1 or 2 eggs as you wish; *mixote* is a local dish of lamb or goat barbequed in a bag. Pure drinking water sold behind the public baths, cheaper to fill own receptacle, funnel needed.

Buses Second-class Estrella Roja bus from Puebla to **Cholula** US$0.35 from 6 Poniente y 11 Norte, 9 km on a new road, 20 mins, also 1st and 2nd class Estrella Roja buses from CAPU bus terminal hourly (be ready to get out, only a quick stop in Cholula); from Cholula take a 'Pueblo Centro' bus to the city centre, or a 'Puebla-CAPU' bus for the terminal; colectivos to Cholula, US$0.40. From **Mexico City**, leave for Cholula from Terminal del Oriente with Estrella Roja, every 30 mins, US$3, 2½-3 hrs, 2nd class every 20 mins, a very scenic route through steep wooded hills. Good views of volcanoes.

Trains There is a train running to Atlixco at 0545 daily, with a stop at the pyramid. The Mexico City to Puebla train (dep 0705) also stops right by the ruins.

Just before Puebla one comes to the superb church of **_Tlaxcalantzingo_**, with an extravagantly tiled façade, domes and tower. It is worth climbing up on the roof for photographs.

(Km 134) **_Puebla_** (de los Angeles), 'The City of the Angels', one of Mexico's oldest and most famous cities and the capital of Puebla state (1990 pop 4,118,100), is at 2,060m. Unfortunately, its recent industrial growth—the population has risen to over 1 million—is rapidly destroying its colonial appearance and filling it with smog, and the centre, though still beautifully colonial, is cursed with traffic jams, except in those shopping streets reserved for pedestrians. On the central arcaded plaza is a fine **Cathedral**, notable for its marble floors, onyx and marble statuary and gold leaf decoration (closed 1230-1530). There are statues flanking the altar which are said to be of an English king and a Scottish queen. The bell tower gives a grand view of the city and snow-capped volcanoes (open 1100-1200 only, closed Mon-Tues, US$1.65). There are 60 churches in all, many of their domes shining with the glazed tiles for which the city is famous.

In the Rosario chapel of the Church of **Santo Domingo** (1596-1659), 5 de Mayo 407, the baroque displays a beauty of style and prodigality of form which served as an exemplar and inspiration for all later baroque in Mexico. There is a strong Indian flavour in Puebla's baroque; this can be seen in the churches of Tonantzintla and Acatepec (see above); it is not so evident, but it is still there, in the opulent decorative work in the Cathedral. Beyond the church, up towards the Fuerte Loreto (see below), there is a spectacular view of volcanoes.

Other places well worth visiting are the churches of **San Cristóbal** (1687), 4 Norte y 6 Oriente, with modern churrigueresque towers and Tonantzintla-like plasterwork inside; **San José** (18th century), 2 Norte y 18 Oriente, with attractive tiled façade and decorated walls around the main doors, as well as beautiful altar pieces inside; the **Congreso del Estado** in Calle 5 Poniente, formerly the Consejo de Justicia, near the post office, is a converted 19th century Moorish style town house—the tiled entrance and courtyard are very attractive—it had a theatre inside (shown to visitors on request), and is now the seat of the state government. The **Museum of Santa Rosa** (3 Norte 1203) has a priceless collection of 16th century Talavera tiles on its walls and ceilings. The **Patio de los Azulejos** should also be visited; it has fabulous tiled façades on the former almshouses for old retired priests of the order of San Felipe Neri; the colours and designs are beautiful; it is at 11 Poniente 110, with a tiny entrance which is hard to find unless one knows where to look. One of the most famous and oldest local churches is **San Francisco** (14 Oriente 1009), with a glorious tiled façade and a mummified saint in its side chapel; see also the pearl divers' chapel, given by the poor divers of Veracruz, the church thought it too great a sacrifice but the divers insisted. Since then they believe diving has not claimed a life. **Santa Catalina**, 3 Norte with 2 Poniente, has beautiful altarpieces; **Nuestra Señora de la Luz**, 14 Norte and 2 Oriente, has a good tiled façade and so has **San Marcos** at Av Reforma and 9 Norte. The Maronite church of **Belén** on 7 Norte and 4 Poniente has a lovely old tiled façade and a beautifully tiled interior. Worth visiting is also the library of Bishop Palafox, by the tourist office, 5 Oriente No 5, opposite the Cathedral; it has 46,000 antique volumes, open at 1000.

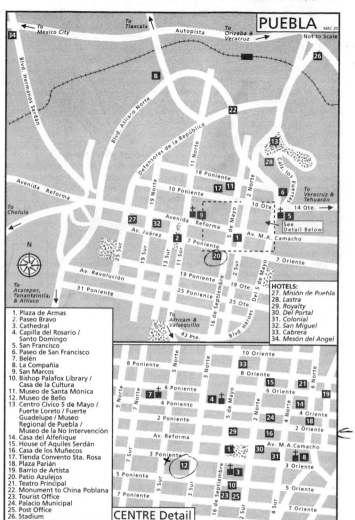

PUEBLA MAC 20
Not to Scale

To Mexico City
To Tlaxcala
Autopista
To Orizaba & Veracruz

34

Blvd. Hermanos Serdán

Blvd. Atlixco Norte

Defensores de la República

B

22

13

28

Calz. los Fuertes

26

Avenida Reforma

19 Norte

11 Norte

18 Poniente

10 Poniente

17 11

2 Norte

To Cholula

To Acatepec, Tonantzintla, & Atlixco

N

27 32

Av. Juárez

23 Sur

19 Sur

11 Sur

Avenida Reforma

2

9

7 Poniente

20

Av. Revolución

19 Poniente

31 Poniente

25 Poniente

5 de Mayo

2 Sur

Av. M.A. Camacho

5

10 Ote.

14 Ote. →

To Veracruz & Tehuacán

6

See Detail Below

1

7 Oriente

19 Ote.

Del 5 de Mayo

25 Ote.

16 de Septiembre

To Africam & Valsequillo

43 Pte.

Blvd. Heroes

HOTELS:
27. *Misión de Puebla*
28. *Lastra*
29. *Royalty*
30. *Del Portal*
31. *Colonial*
32. *San Miguel*
33. *Cabrera*
34. *Mesón del Angel*

1. Plaza de Armas
2. Paseo Bravo
3. Cathedral
4. Capilla del Rosario / Santo Domingo
5. San Francisco
6. Paseo de San Francisco
7. Belén
8. La Compañía
9. San Marcos
10. Bishop Palafox Library / Casa de la Cultura
11. Museo de Santa Mónica
12. Museo de Bello
13. Centro Cívico 5 de Mayo / Fuerte Loreto / Fuerte Guadelupe / Museo Regional de Puebla / Museo de la No Intervención
14. Casa del Alfeñique
15. House of Aquiles Serdán
16. Casa de los Muñecos
17. Tienda Convento Sta. Rosa
18. Plaza Parián
19. Barrio de Artista
20. Patio Azulejos
21. Teatro Principal
22. Monument to China Poblana
23. Tourist Office
24. Palacio Municipal
25. Post Office
26. Stadium

CENTRE Detail

10 Oriente

33

8 Poniente

5 Norte

3 Norte

8 Oriente

15 21

6 Norte

9 Norte

7 Norte

6 Poniente

7

4 Poniente

4

5 de Mayo

6 Oriente

14

19

2 Poniente

2 Norte

4 Norte

24

4 Oriente

18

2 Oriente

Av. Reforma

29

16

1

30

Av. M.A. Camacho

3 Poniente

5 Sur

3 Sur

31

8

12

3 Oriente

5 Poniente

3

5 Oriente

7 Poniente

10

23 25

16 de Septiembre

2 Sur

4 Sur

7 Oriente

Besides the churches, the fragile-looking and extravagantly ornamented **Casa del Alfeñique** (Sugar Candy House), Av 4 Oriente 418, a few blocks from the Cathedral is worth seeing, now the **Museo Regional del Estado** (entry US$0.40). Nearby is Plaza y Mercado Parián, with onyx souvenir shops (6 Norte and 4 Oriente). Onyx figures and chess sets are attractive and cheaper than elsewhere, but the *poblanos* are hard bargainers; another attractive buy is the very tiny glass animal figures. In the adjoining Barrio del Artista the artists' studios are near to

Hotel Latino. Live music and refreshments at small *Café del Artista*. The University Arts Centre offers folk dances at various times, look for posters or enquire direct—free admission.

The Cinco de Mayo civic centre, with a stark statue of Benito Juárez, is, among other things, a regional centre of arts, crafts and folklore and has a very worthwhile **Museo Regional de Puebla**, open 1000-1700, **Museo de Historia Natural**, auditorium, planetarium, fairgrounds and an open air theatre all nearby. In the same area, the forts of Guadalupe and Loreto have been restored; they were the scene of the Battle of Puebla, in which 2,000 Mexican troops defeated Maximilian's 6,000 European troops on 5 May 1862 (although the French returned victorious ten days later). Inside the **Fuerte Loreto** (excellent view of the city—and of its pollution) is a small museum (Museo de la No Intervención) depicting the battle of 1862 (open 1000-1700, closed Mon, entry US$2). 5 May is a holiday in Mexico. ⁀ *middle one name*

Three other Museums: **Museo de Bello**—the house of the collector and connoisseur Bello—has good displays of Chinese porcelain and Talavera pottery, Av 3 Poniente 302; the building is beautifully furnished (entry US$1, guided tours, closed Mon). **Museo de Santa Mónica** (convent) at 18 Poniente 103, open 1000-1800, closed Mon; generations of nuns hid there after the reform laws of 1857 made the convent illegal. **Museo Amparo**, 2 Sur 708, has a good anthropological exhibition, modern, audiovisual explanations in Spanish, English, French and Japanese, open am and 1600-1800, closed Thur, Mon free, US$1.65 other days, students half-price, rec.

Also worth seeing are the church and monastery of **El Carmen**, with its strange façade and beautiful tile work; the **Teatro Principal** (1550), Av 8 Oriente y Calle 6 Norte, possibly the oldest in the Americas; the grand staircase of the 17th century **Academia de las Bellas Artes** and its exhibition of Mexican colonial painting; and the Jesuit church of **La Compañía** (Av Maximino Avila Camacho y 4 Sur) , where a plaque in the sacristy shows where China Poblana lies buried. This mythical figure, a Chinese princess captured by pirates and abducted to Mexico, is said to have taken to Christianity and good works and evolved a penitential dress for herself which has now become the regional costume; positively dazzling with flowered reds and greens and worn with a strong sparkle of bright beads. Also worth visiting is the house of Aquiles Serdán (6 Oriente 206), a leader of the Revolution, preserved as it was during his lifetime. The tiled façade of the **Casa de los Muñecos**, 2 Norte No 1 (corner of the main square) is famous for its caricatures in tiles of the enemies of the 17th century builder. Avenida Reforma has many fine buildings, eg No 141 (*Hostal del Halconeros*), which is tiled inside and out.

Festivals *Feria* in mid-April for two weeks.

Hotels A+ *Del Portal*, Portal Morelos 205, T 460211, very good, but ask for room away from Zócalo side (noisy), restored colonial, does not accept Amex; **A+ *Misión de Puebla***, 5 Poniente 2522, helpful staff, restaurant not open in evening; **A** *Lastra*, Calz de Los Fuertes, T 351501; **A-B** *Royalty*, Portal Hidalgo 8, T 424740, F 424740 ext 113, pleasant, central, quiet, restaurant good but expensive and service slow; **A** *Colonial*, 4 Sur 105, old-fashioned and charming, has excellent restaurant and accepts American Express cards, ask for back room, with bath; **A** *San Leonardo*, 2 Oriente No 211, T 460555, F 421176, modern but wonderful colonial entrance hall, remodelled 1993; **B** *Gilfer*, 2 Oriente No 11, T 460882, F 428990, large rooms, reasonable restaurant, excellent service; **C** *Hostal de Halconeros*, Av de la Reforma 141, with bath, tiled throughout, good; **C** *Imperial*, 4 Oriente 203, T 463825, basic, shower, noisy, parking; **D** *Cabrera*, 10 Oriente 6, with shower and phone, clean, quiet in interior rooms, don't be put off by outward appearance of hardware store, no restaurant; **D** *del Paseo*, 10 Sur No 404, across Héroes, no entry from 2300-0600, but central, parking, hot water, quiet; **D** *Mendoza*, 3 Poniente 912, pleasant, clean, friendly, owner; **D** *Ritz*, 2 Norte 207 y 4 Oriente, T 414457, 2 blocks from Zócalo, reasonable, front rooms with balcony quieter, no hot water; **D** *Victoria*, near Zócalo, 3 Poniente 309, T 418992, clean; **E** *Teresita* opposite, for rooms on 4th floor, shared bath, hot water, friendly, rec; **E** *Casa de Huéspedes*,

5 Poniente 111, hot showers, clean, simple, big bright rooms towards street, rec; **E** *Embajadores*, 5 de Mayo 603, T 412637, 2 blocks from Zócalo, without bath but limited water and insalubrious; other cheap places on pedestrian mall on this street; several basic *casas de huéspedes*, near market. Very cheap hotel (F), 2 blocks S of train station, *20 de Noviembre*, big rooms, no water 2000 to 0700, clean, bus to town.

Motels A+ *Mesón del Angel*, good, pool, gardens, Hermanos Serdán 807, T 482100, F 487935, near first Puebla interchange on Mexico-Puebla motorway, possibly best in town, but far from the centre: **B** *Panamerican*, Reforma 2114, T 485466, restaurant, bar, rec.

Camping Possible on the extensive university grounds about 8 km S of centre.

Food Specialities *Mole poblano* (meat or chicken with sauce of chiles, chocolate and coconut); best at *La Poblanita* D, 10 Norte 1404-B, and *Fonda Santa Clara*, 3 Poniente 307, good for local specialities. *Camotes* (candied sweet potatoes) and *dulces* (sweets). Also *nieves*—drinks of alcohol, fruit and milk—worth trying, and excellent *empanadas*. Also noted are *quesadillas*—fried tortillas with cheese and herbs inside.

Other Restaurants *El Vasco*, on Zócalo, very good, most dishes US$3, US$6 for *plato mexicano*; several others to choose from on Zócalo, eg *Mac's*, US-style diner, slow service but good variety. Cheap *comidas* at *Hermilo Nevados*, 2 Oriente 408, good value, rec; also *Munich*, 3 Poniente y 5 Sur. Many cheap places near main square with menus prominently displayed. *Woolworth's*, 1½ blocks from NW corner of Plaza Mayor, 0800-2100, good range of cheap, reasonable meals and some dearer dishes. *Café bar El Molino Rojo*, 3 Poniente 512, between 7 and 5 Sur, open 1100-2200 Mon-Sat, live local music nightly, nice atmosphere. *El Vegetariano*, 3 Poniente 525, good (near *Hotel San Agustín*); *Centro Botánico Azteca*, Av 7 Poniente entre 16 de Septiembre y Calle 3 Sur, excellent vegetarian. *Pizza Hadis*, 3 Norte between 3 Poniente y Reforma, cheap, good, friendly; *Librería Cafetería*, Reforma y 7 Norte, good coffee; *Super-Soya*, 5 de Mayo, good for fruit salads and juices; several other good places for *comidas corridas* on 5 de Mayo; *Teorema* Reforma 540, near 7 Norte café, books and art, live music, good coffee and snacks, rec *Cafetería Tres Gallos*, 4 Poniente 110, good coffee and pastries. *Jugos y Licuados*, 3 Norte No 412, rec; *Tony's Tacos*, 3 Norte, and Reforma, quick and very cheap.

Shopping Craft shop sponsored by the authorities. *Tienda Convento Santa Rosa*, Calle 3 Norte 1203, T 2-89-04. The famous Puebla tiles may be purchased from factories outside Puebla, or from *Fábrica de Azulejos la Guadalupana*, Av 4 Poniente 911; *D Aguilar*, 40 Poniente 106, opposite Convent of Santa Mónica, and *Casa Rugerio*, 18 Poniente 111; *Margarita Guevara*, 20 Poniente 30. **Bookshop**: *Librería Británica*, Av 25 Pte 1705.

Exchange Bancomer, 3 Poniente 110, changes travellers' cheques 1000-1230, good rates.

Laundry In large commercial centre on Av 19 Poniente y Calle 7 Sur, US$4 wash and dry, 3 hrs.

Post Office 5 Oriente between 16 de Septiembre and 2 Sur.

Tourist Office 5 Oriente 3, Av Juárez behind the Cathedral, T 46-09-28, closed Sat and Sun. Also 3 Sur 1501, 8th floor and at the bus station.

Tour guide Emilio Hernández guides visitors through the city, especially the historic part, very interesting, speaks English, T 466537, his grandparents, or Roberto Méndez, 12 Poniente 119, T 468093.

Roads and Buses A 4-lane highway, 70 mins, to **Mexico City**, toll US$2.35; ADO express buses every 7 mins, 2 hrs, US$5; Mexico City-Puebla buses also with AU (cheapest) and Estrella Roja from Central del Oriente. 2-lane highway to Orizaba, toll US$3.45. For the road from Puebla S through Oaxaca to Guatemala, see p 251. Bus to **Oaxaca** costs US$16.50 (6-8 hrs, 1st class, ADO, Flecha Roja and Autobuses Unidos). Bus to **Veracruz** 1st class, US$9. Bus to **Xalapa** (see p 226) ADO, 4 hrs. To **Tuxtla Gutiérrez** (via Orizaba, Tuxtepec and Paso Real), 15 hrs, US$35 with ADO at 2025 or Cristóbal Colón at 1950; to **Villahermosa**, US$25. To **Mérida**, 1 day, 2130, arrives 1730, US$43. To **Pachuca**, 0800, 1430, 1800, 4 hrs, 2nd class, US$4.40. New, huge CAPU bus terminal for all 1st and 2nd class buses N of city, has left luggage, Banco Serfín (Mon-Fri), shops, restaurants: to the centre take Kombi No 14, US$0.30, which stops at 11 Norte and Reforma at Paseo de Bravo (make sure it's a No 14 'directo', there is a No 14 which goes to the suburbs). From the centre to the terminal, take any form of transport marked 'CAPU', many colectivos on Av 9 Norte. Taxi touts abound in the terminal, but there are several booths selling fixed price taxi tickets, US$3 to centre.

Rail Station is a long way from centre. Trains from **Mexico City**, 2nd class to Puebla via Cuautla at 0705, very slow (10-11 hrs, stops at the ruins of Cholula, see p 207); train to **Oaxaca** (2nd class), leaves Puebla 0720, 12 hrs, no advance booking, US$3.50, superb scenery. The line weaves through cactus laden gorges recalling the Wild West. On clear days one gets a good view of Popocatépetl. The Oaxaqueño train from Mexico City leaves at 1900 and stops at 2350 at Puebla on its way to Oaxaca (tickets sold 1200-1400 for reserved seats, breakfast included, supposed to arrive in Oaxaca 0925, often delayed). Fares from Mexico City: US$2.80 2nd class, US$4.75 1st, US$9.50 *primera especial*.

Excursions On the Prolongación Av 11 Sur is Agua Azul, in the suburbs, a complex with sulphur springs, playing fields, amusement park etc, popular with families (entry US$6, bus from centre). 15 km S of Puebla lies Lago Valsequillo, with **Africam**, a zoo of free-roaming African animals. Entry US$2.40, open Mon-Fri 1000-1730, Sat, Sun and holidays 0900-1800. Information from 11 Oriente, T 460888. A good, one-day excursion is a round trip Puebla- Cacaxtla- Tlaxcala- Tizatlán- Puebla: details are given on **p 206**.

Interesting day-trip to **Cuetzalán** market (via Tetela-Huahuaztla) which is held on Sun in the Zócalo (3 hr walk up). In first week of October each year dancers from local villages gather and *voladores* 'fly' from the top of their pole. Nahua Indians sell cradles (*huacal*) for children; machetes and embroidered garments. The Día de los Muertos (2 Nov) is interesting here. Big clay dogs are made locally, unique stoves which hold big flat clay plates on which *tortillas* are baked and stews are cooked in big pots. Also available in nearby Huitzitlán. Women decorate their hair with skeins of wool. You can also go via Zaragoza, Zacapoaxtla and Apulco, where one can walk along a path, left of the road, to the fine 35-metre waterfall of La Gloria. It can be very foggy at Cuetzalán, even when it is fine in Puebla. Tourist information, Calle Hidalgo y Bravo, helpful, good map.

From Cuetzalán it is a 1½ hr walk to the well-preserved, niched pyramids of **Yohualichan** (Totonac culture); there are five excavated pyramids, two of them equivalent to that at El Tajín, and three still uncovered. There has been earthquake damage, though. Take a bus from Calle Miguel Alvarado Avila y Calle Abosolo, more frequent in morning and market days to San Antonio and get off at the sign Pirámides Yohualichan (30 mins, bad road), then walk 2 km to the site, closed Monday and Tuesday, entry US$2. In the Cuetzalán area are 32 km of caverns with lakes, rivers and wonderful waterfalls. These include Tzicuilan (follow Calle Emiliano Zapata, E of town) and Atepolihuit (follow Carretera Antigua up to the Campo Deportivo, W of town). Children offer to guide visitors to the ruins and the caves. (Claudio Rivero, Buenos Aires.)

Accommodation and Food Several cheap, quite clean hotels, eg **E** *Hotel Rivello*, G Victoria 3, T (91) 2331-01-39, 1 block from Zócalo, with bath, F without, basic, friendly, clean; **E** *Posada Jackelin*, upper end of plaza, near market, behind church, pleasant; **E** *Posada Vicky*, on G Victoria; *Posada Quetzal*, Calle Zaragoza. Good, cheap restaurant: *Yokoxochitl*, 2 de Abril, good for breakfasts, huge juices; *Casa Elvira Mora*, Hidalgo 54, rec; *Villacaiba* for seafood, Francisco Madero 6; *Ritz*; *Café-Bazar Galería* in centre, good sandwiches and tea, nice garden, English magazines, rec.

Buses Direct buses from Puebla (Tezuitecos line only) 5 a day from 0500 to 1530, US$6.50; quite a few return buses, but if none direct go to Zaragoza and change buses there. There are many buses to Zacapoaxtla with frequent connections for Cuetzalán.

(Km 151) **Amozoc**, where tooled leather goods and silver decorations on steel are made, both mostly as outfits for the *charros*, or Mexican cattlemen. Beyond Amozoc lies **Tepeaca** with its late 16th century monastery, well worth a visit; its weekly market is very extensive. An old Spanish tower or *rollo* (1580) stands between Tepeaca's main square and the Parroquia. Beyond Tepeaca, 57½ km from Puebla, lies **Tecamachalco**: vast 16th century Franciscan monastery church with beautiful murals on the choir vault, in late medieval Flemish style, by a local Indian. **Language school**: Patricio O Martínez, Calle 29 Sur 303, Barrio de San Sebastián, Tecamachalco, CP 75480, Apartado Postal 13, T 91-242-21121, very good; US$70 for one week, 4 hrs a day, possible to live with families. There is a good seafood restaurant; enquire at José Colorado's *tienda* near the school.

Beyond, the road leads to **Tehuacán** (population 113,000, altitude 1,676m),

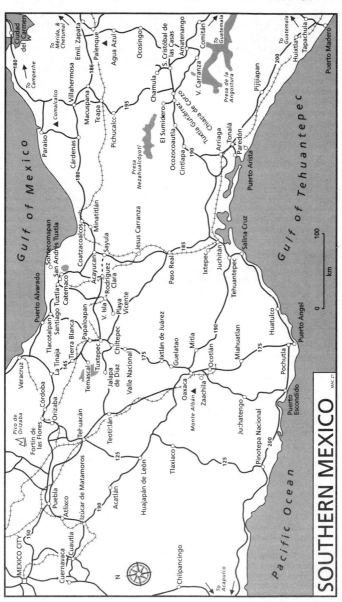

SOUTHERN MEXICO

MAC 21

a charming town with a pleasant, sometimes cool, climate. It has some old churches. Water from the mineral springs is bottled and sent all over the country by Garci Crespo, San Lorenzo and Peñafiel. From the small dam at Malpaso on the Río Grande an annual race is held for craft without motors as far as the village of Quiotepec. The central plaza is pleasant and shaded; the nights are cool. The Ayuntamiento on the Zócalo is decorated inside and out with murals and tiles. From Tehuacán there are two paved roads to Oaxaca: one, very scenic, through Teotitlán del Camino (US$1.65 by 2nd class bus), and the other, longer but easier to drive, through Huajuapan (**see p 262**). Railway junction for Oaxaca and Veracruz; no passenger trains on line to Esperanza. Wild maize was first identified by an archaeologist at Coxcatlán Cave nearby. There is an airport.

Spas A short bus ride beyond Peñafiel Spa (refurbished in 1993) is the spa of **San Lorenzo** with spring-fed pools surrounded by trees, US$2 entry.

Hotels and Restaurants *México*, Reforma Norte and Independencia Poniente, one block from Zócalo, T 20019, garage, TV, restaurant, renovated colonial building, pool, quiet; **C** *Iberia*, Independencia 217, T 21122, with bath, clean, airy, rec, pleasant restaurant, public parking nearby at reduced fee with voucher from hotel; **D** *Inter* above restaurant of same name, close to bus station (ask there), hot shower, clean, modern; **D** *Madrid*, 3 Sur 105, T 20272, opp Municipal Library, comfortable, cheaper without bath, rec. Several *casas de huéspedes* along Calle 3 (Norte and Sur) but low standards. Many eating places on Zócalo with reasonable prices (eg on same corner as Cathedral, good breakfast). The main meal is served at midday in Tehuacán. Try *Restaurant Santander*, good but pricey. *Cafetería California*, Independencia Oriente 108, excellent juices and *licuados*; *Pizzería Richards*, Reforma Norte 250, quite good pizzas, good fresh salads; excellent taco stands.

Museum Museo de Mineralogía Romero, 7 Norte 356, open 0900-1200, 1600-1800, am only on Sat, free, one room with good collection of minerals from all over the world.

Buses ADO bus station on Av Independencia (Poniente). Bus direct to **Mexico City**, 5 hrs, US$10; to **Puebla**, 2½ hrs, US$4.50; to **Oaxaca** (US$10.75, 5½ hrs, AU at 1430, coming from Mexico City, may be full), **Veracruz**, US$7.75, and the Gulf: Autobuses Unidos, 2nd class on Calle 2 Oriente with several buses daily to Mexico City and Oaxaca. Local bus to **Huajuapan** 3 hrs, US$5; from there, frequent buses to Oaxaca.

Teotitlán del Camino, en route to Oaxaca, is a glaringly bright town with a military base. Vehicles are stopped occasionally; make sure, if driving, that your papers are in order. From Teotitlán it is possible to drive into the hills, to the Indian town of *Huautla de Jiménez*, where the local Mazatec Indians consume the hallucinogenic 'magic' mushrooms made famous by Dr Timothy Leary. Huautla has 'all four seasons of the year in each day; springlike mornings; wet, foggy afternoons; fresh, autumn evenings; and freezing nights.' There are many police and military. Drivers may be waved down by people in the road up to Huautla; do not stop for them, they may be robbers.

The road from Tehuacán to the coast soon begins to climb into the mountains. At Cumbres we reach 2,300m and a wide view: the silvered peak of Citlaltépetl (or Orizaba—**see p 230**) volcano to the E, the green valley of Orizaba below. In 10 km we drop down, through steep curves, sometimes rather misty, to Acultzingo 830m below. The road joins the main toll road from Puebla to Orizaba at Ciudad Mendoza, where it has emerged from the descent through the Cumbres de Maltrata, which are usually misty and need to be driven with care and patience. (The expensive toll road Puebla-Orizaba is a much safer drive than the route we have described; it, too, is scenic.)

(Km 317) *Orizaba*, the favourite resort of the Emperor Maximilian (population 115,000, altitude 1,283m), lost much of its charm in the 1973 earthquake, when the bullring, many houses and other buildings were lost, and is now heavily industrialized. In the distance is the majestic volcanic cone of Orizaba. The town developed because of the natural springs in the valley, some of which are used by the textile and paper industries and others are dammed to form small pools for bathing beside picnic areas; Nogales (restaurant) is the most popular, Ojo de Agua is another. The Cerro del Borrego, the hill above the Alameda park, is a favourite early-morning climb. The Zócalo at one time lost much of its area to permanent snack bars, but these have been removed. On the N side is the market, with a wide variety of local produce and local women in traditional dress, and the many-domed San Miguel church (1690-1729). There are several other quite good churches, and there is an Orozco mural in the Centro Educativo Obrero on Av Colón. The Palacio Municipal is the actual cast-iron Belgian pavilion brought piece by piece from France after the famous 19th century Paris Exhibition—an odd sight.

Hotels **B** *Aries*, Oriente 6 No 265, T 51116 (nightclub on top floor); **B** *Trueba*, Oriente 6 and Sur 11, T 42744, resort facilities; **C** *De France*, Oriente 6 No 186, T 52311, and US$0.25 for parking in courtyard, charming building, clean, comfortable, shower, reasonable if uninspiring restaurant; **E** *Mirabel*, 7 Norte 235, with bath, clean, friendly, a bit noisy; **E** *Vallejo*, Madero Norte 242, rec.

Restaurants *Romanchu* and *Paso Real*, on the main street, have excellent cuisine. Hare Krishna vegetarian restaurant, *Radha's*, on Sur 4 between Oriente 1 and 3, excellent. In the market, try the local morning snack, *memelita picadita*.

A road leaves Orizaba southwards, up into the mountains of **Zongolica**, a dry, poor and isolated region, cold and inhospitable, inhabited by various groups of Indians who speak Nahuatl, the language of the Aztecs. Zongolica village is a good place to buy *sarapes*; take early bus from Orizaba (ask for direct one) to get clear views of the mountains.

Beyond Orizaba the scenery is magnificent. The road descends to coffee and sugar-cane country and a tropical riot of flowers. It is very pleasant except when a northerly blows, or in the intolerable heat and mugginess of the wet season.

(Km 331) **Fortín De Las Flores**, a small town devoted to growing flowers and exporting them. Sometimes Indian women sell choice blossoms in small baskets made of banana-tree bark. Near Fortín there is a viewpoint looking out over a dramatic gorge (entry free). The *autopista* from Orizaba to Córdoba passes over this deep valley on a concrete bridge.

Hotels **B** *Posada la Loma*, Km 333 Carretera Norte 150, T 30658, very attractive, tropical garden with butterflies, distant view of snow-capped volcano in early morning, moderately expensive. There are others, slightly cheaper, which also offer tropical gardens for relaxation. Note that Veracruz-Mexico City night trains sound their horns when passing Fortín which can be disturbing.

Córdoba (population 126,000, altitude 923m), 8 km on in the rich valley of the Río Seco, an old colonial city, is also crazy with flowers. Its Zócalo is spacious, leafy and elegant; three sides are arcaded; two of them are lined with tables. On the fourth is an imposing church with a chiming clock. There are several hotels in the Zócalo, which is alive and relaxed at night. In one of them, the *Hotel Zevallos*, Gen Iturbide signed the Treaty of Córdoba in 1821, which was instrumental in freeing Mexico from Spanish colonial rule. There is a local museum at Calle 3, No 303, open 1000-1300 and 1600-2000. Córdoba has the highest rainfall in Mexico, but at predictable times. The area grows coffee.

Hotels **B** *Mansur*, Av 1 y Calle 3, T 26600, on square, smart; **C** *Hostal de Borreña*, Calle 11 308, T 20777, modern, clean, really hot water, some traffic noise but good value. Near the ADO terminal are **C** *Palacio*, Av 3 y Calle 2, T 22186; **C** *Marina* (T 22600), **D** *Iberia* (T 21301), **D** *Trescado* (T 22366) and *Casa de Huéspedes Regis* are all on Avenida 2; **E** *Las Carretas*, Av 4 No 512, with bath, clean, friendly, can wash clothes; *Casa de Huéspedes La Sin Rival* and **E** *La Nueva Querétana* are at 511 and 508 of Avenida 4, respectively (latter is basic but cheap); **E** *Los Reyes*, rec, shower, hot water, street rooms double-glazed, street parking OK.

Restaurant *Brujes*, Av 2 No 306, good *comida corriente*.

Car Service Nissan, Chevrolet and Dodge dealers, mechanics all on Calle 11.

Exchange *Casa de Cambio* on Av 3 opp Bancomer, rec.

Buses Direct services to **Veracruz**, 2 hrs, US$4; **Puebla**, 3 hrs, US$7.70; **Mexico City**, hourly, 5 hrs, US$14; **Oaxaca** and many others.

The direct road from Córdoba to Veracruz is lined, in season, by stalls selling fruit and local honey between *Yanga* and Cuitláhuac. Yanga is a small village named after the leader of a group of escaped black slaves in colonial times. A slightly longer but far more attractive road goes from Fortín de las Flores northwards through Huatusco and Totutla, then swings E to Veracruz.

(Km 476) ***Veracruz***, the principal port of entry for Mexico (population approaching 1 million, according to latest local estimates) lies on a low alluvial plain bordering the Gulf coast. Cortés landed near here at Isla de Sacrificios, on 17 April 1519. The first settlement was called Villa Rica de la Vera Cruz; its location was changed various times, including to La Antigua, now a pleasant little colonial town with the ruins of Cortés' house (it is 1.5 km off the road to Cardel, some 30 km N of Veracruz). The present site was established in 1599.

NB If planning to visit Veracruz or the hills inland (eg Xalapa) between July and September, check the weather forecast because many tropical storms blow themselves out in this region, bringing heavy rain. From October to January the weather tends to be changeable, with cold, damp winds from the N. At this time the beaches and Malecón are empty and many resorts close, except over Christmas and New Year when the tourists flood in and all road transport is booked up 5 days in advance. Otherwise it is generally hot.

Veracruz is a mixture of the very old and the new; there are still many picturesque white-walled buildings and winding side-streets. It has become a great holiday resort, and is reported touristy and noisy. The heart of the city is **Plaza Constitución** (Zócalo); make at once for the traditional *La Parroquia* café, cool and tiled. (The newer café of the same name on the Malecón does not have the same atmosphere.) The square is white-paved, with attractive cast iron lampstands and benches, and surrounded by the cathedral, with an unusual cross, depicted with hands, the governor's palace and colonial-style hotels. The plaza comes alive in the evening at weekends: an impressive combination of the crush of people, colour and marimba music in the flood-lit setting. From 15 July to the end of August there is jazz in the Zócalo from 1900.

Culturally, Veracruz is a Caribbean city, home not only to the *jarocho* costume (predominantly white), but also to *jarocho* dance and music which features harps and guitars. The most famous dances, accompanied by the Conjunto Jarocho, are the *bamba* and *zapateado*, with much stamping and lashing of feet related to flamenco of Andalucía. Mexico's version of the Cuban *danzón* music and the indigenous *música tropical* add to the cultural richness. Many cultural events can be seen at the Instituto Veracruzano de Cultura, a few blocks from the Zócalo with a good, new café and library; a nice place to relax and mingle with students. At night the Malecón is very lively, and sometimes fire-eaters and other performers entertain the public. The Shrovetide carnival 7 weeks before Easter is said to be Mexico's finest, rivalling those of New Orleans, Brazil and Trinidad. The carnival starts a week before Shrove Tuesday and ends on Ash Wednesday; Saturday-Tuesday are the main days with parades. At this time it is very difficult to find higher-priced accommodation (especially on the Saturday), or tickets for transportation.

The food is good, the fishing not bad, and the people lively and welcoming. The local craft is tortoiseshell jewellery adorned with silver, but remember that the import of tortoiseshell into the USA and many other countries is prohibited.

There are two buildings of great interest: the very fine 17th-century **Palacio Municipal**, on Plaza Constitución, with a splendid façade and courtyard, and the castle of **San Juan de Ulúa** (1565), on Gallega Island, now joined by road to the mainland; take bus marked Ulúa from Malecón Av República (it is not advisable

1. Plaza Constitución / Zócalo
2. Parque Zamora
3. Parque La Madre
4. Cathedral
5. Palacio Municipal
   & Tourist Office
6. Castillo de San Juan de Ulúa
7. Museo de la Ciudad
8. Baluarte de Santiago
9. Museo y Faro Carranza
10. Instituto Veracruzano
    de Cultura
11. Mercado de Artesanías
12. Mercado Hidalgo
13. Boat Trips
14. ADO Terminal
15. Post Office x2
16. La Parroquia (original)
17. La Parroquia (new)
18. Restaurante El Pescador
19. Restaurante Submarino
    Amarillo

To
Ruta 180 (N), Cardel,
Xalapa, & Mexico City

de Quevedo

Montesinos

Benito Juárez

M. Arista

Av. Cuauhtémoc

J. Soto

Campero

Zaragoza

Independencia

Av. I. Allende

See Detail

Salvador Díaz Mirón

20 de Noviembre

Av. I. Allende

Fco. del Paso y Troncoso

Juan Enrique

Juan de Dios Peza

To
Ruta 150,
Airport,
Xalapa

1 de Mayo

Playa de Hornos

Playa Villa del Mar

Golfo de

México

0   350
metres

N

Port

Morelos

Insurgentes

Blvd. M. Avila Camacho

José Martí

Simón Bolívar

Esteban Morales

F. Canal

Rayón

Mariano Arista

Av. Independencia

Zaragoza

Av. 16 de Septiembre

Xicoténcatl

M. Lerdo

Aquiles Serdán

Av. S de Mayo

M. Hidalgo

Costa Verde

Framboyanes

Cárdenas Jardines

Las Palmeras

Blvd. del Mar

Av. Adolfo Ruiz Cortines

Costa Verde

Costa
de
Oro

To
Ruta 150,
Airport,
Xalapa

Carretera Boticaria Mocambo

To
Boca del Río, Ruta 180 (S),
Ruta 150, Córdoba,
Orizaba, & Mexico City

Mocambo

Hotels:
20. Emporio
21. Baluarte
22. Colonial
23. Hostal de Cortés
24. Amparo
25. Mar y Tierra
26. Oriente
27. Mocambo

VERACRUZ
& Centre Detail   MAC 22

to walk there—entry to the castle US$4.35). It failed to deter the buccaneers and later became a political prison. Mexico's 'Robin Hood', Chucho el Roto, was imprisoned there, and escaped three times. There is a **city historical museum** with a good collection of photographs, well displayed; it traces history from the Conquest to 1910; it is at Zaragoza 397 (entry US$1, open on Sun 0900-1300 and other days, English booklet available). The **Baluarte de Santiago**, a small fort which once formed part of the city walls, is at Francisco Canal y Gómez Farias, open 0900-1900, Sun and holidays, 1600-1900, closed Tues (entry US$4.35). The **Carranza museum** on the Malecón, Tues-Sun 0930-1400, 1600-1800, has photos of the revolution, the life of Carranza and his battles against the Huerta Regime (the last room shows a picture of Carranza's skeleton and the trajectory of the bullet that killed him), entry free. The **aquarium** has moved from the harbour breakwater to a new building at Villa del Mar; large underwater viewing tank, watch sharks and other exotic species, admission US$3.45. **Plazuela de la Campana**, by Serdán and Zaragoza, is an attractive small square.

The beach along the waterfront, and the sea, are filthy. There is much pollution from the heavy shipping. Amber from Simojordis is sold on the town beach. A short bus ride from the fish market takes you to **Mocambo** beach, which has a superb, 50-metre swimming bath (with restaurant and bar, admission US$3.30), beach restaurants, Caribbean-style beach huts and the water is quite a bit cleaner though still rather uninviting in colour. There are crabs and mosquitoes and much pestering by sellers. The Gulf is even warmer than the Caribbean. The beach is crowded. At holiday time cars race up and down, there are loud radios, etc. There is little shade near the beach. There is a fine beach at Chachalacas, 50 km N, not crowded (see p 227).

NB Travellers are warned to be particularly wary of overcharging.

Hotels Note, because of the liveliness of the Zócalo at night, hotels on the square can be noisy. **A+** *Veracruz*, Av Independencia esq Lerdo, nr Zócalo, probably the best in the centre; **A** *Mocambo*, Boca del Río, T 371661, 8 km out on Mocambo beach, 1930s palace, good service and food, highly rec; **A** *Emporio*, very good, with bath, swimming pool, inexpensive *comida corrida*, rather old-fashioned, on Paseo del Malecón (Insurgentes Veracruzanos y Xicoténcatl, T 320020, F 312261); a block before the *Emporio* when approaching from the Zócalo is **A** *Puerto Bello* (aka *Howard Johnson's*), Avila Camacho 1263, T 310011, F 310867, good, clean, friendly, most rooms have sea-view, rec; **B** *Baluarte*, opp the small fort of Baluarte, Canal 265, T 360844, good, clean, rec; **B** *Colonial*, on Zócalo, T 320193, swimming pool, indoor parking, rec; **B** *Hostal de Cortés*, 3 star, convenient for clean beaches, Avila Camacho y de las Casas, T 320065, F 315744; **C** *Cristóbal Colón*, Avila Camacho 681, T 823844, small, quiet, some rooms with sea-view balconies; clean; **C** *Oriente*, M Lerdo 105, T 312440, secure parking, clean, friendly, balconies (noisy from street), good fans, some a/c, rec; **C** *Central*, Mirón 1612, T 372222, next to ADO bus terminal, clean, fair, noisy, erratic hot water, unhelpful, get room at back, esp on 5th floor, laundry facilities; **D** *Impala*, Orizaba 650, T 370169, with bath, cold water, mosquitoes but clean, near bus station; **D** *Mar y Tierra*, Figueroa y Malecón, T 313866, good value, some rooms with balconies overlooking the harbour; **D** *Príncipe*, Collado 195, some distance from centre, very clean with hot shower and toilet; **D** *Royalty*, Abasolo 34, T 361041, average, near beach, 20 min walk from Zócalo, rec, but noisy as it caters mainly to student groups; **C** *Ruiz Milán*, Malecón y Gómez Farias, T 361877, F 361339, good; **D** *Amparo*, Serdán 482, T 322738, with fan, insect screens, good value, rec; opp is **D** *Santo Domingo*, with bath, fan, OK, bakery attached; nearby on Serdán is **D** *Mallorca*, with bath and fan, radio, newly furnished, very clean, highly rec; **D** *La Paz*, Av Díaz Mirón 1242, T 325399, right from ADO bus station 4 blocks, with bath, highly rec, clean and helpful; **D** *Casa de Huéspedes*, on Morelia, nr Zócalo, new, exact location not known, with bath, hot water, quiet, clean, use of mosquito net needed, economical restaurant next door; **E** *Hatzin*, Reforma 6 and Avista, rec; **E** *Ortiz*, M Lerdo 95, on Zócalo, no hot water, a bit dirty but pleasant; around the corner, on the large plaza on which is the railway station, is **E** *Rex*, colonial-style, large courtyard, basic seedy rooms; many others in port area, reached by bus from the bus terminal. Two more on Miguel Lerdo, near the Portales: *Rías* and *Concha Dorada*.

Youth Hostel, Paso Doña Juana, Municipio de Ursulo Galván, T 320878, 2 hrs by bus from town, US$2.30 a night; for information on Villas Deportivas Juveniles—see under Mexico City

Camp Sites.
The only **trailer park** is behind *Hotel Mocambo* (see above), dry camping, showers and bathrooms dirty, swimming pools empty, US$6.50 for vehicle and two people.

Restaurants Torros are the local drinks made of eggs, milk, fruit and alcohol—delicious and potent. *La Parroquia* (original) has fans, white tiled walls, cement floors and waiters in white jackets, facing the Cathedral; wonderful coffee, food not marvellous but place is crowded. In the main market, H Cortés y Madero, there are inexpensive restaurants in the mezzanine, overlooking the interior (watch out for extras that you did not order). In the fish market for excellent fish and shrimp cocktails, and opp are *La Garlopa* and *Doña Paz/Normita*, good seafood. There is a good local fish restaurant, *Olympica*, Zaragoza 250, near the fish market, 2 blocks from the Zócalo. Recommended: *El Pescador*, for fish, Zaragoza 335 y Morales (not evenings); and the steakhouse *Submarino Amarillo*, Malecón 472. *Karen*, Arista 574 between Landero y Coss and Zaragoza, good fish restaurant. *El Azteca de Cayetano*, Mario Molina 94, where *mondongos de fruta* (a selection of all the fruits in season, plus fruit-flavoured ice) are prepared on one plate; also *Mondongo de Fruta*, M Molina 88, not cheap but delicious for fruits, juices and ices. Also on Molina, *Amparo* and *Santo Domingo*. An interesting place is *Tiburón*, Av Landero y Coss 167, esquina A Serdán, 2 blocks from Zócalo, run by 'Tiburón' González, the 'Rey de la Alegría', or 'Rey Feo' of carnival; the walls are covered in pictures of him and his *comparsas*, dating back to at least 1945, has inexpensive, good food too. *La Paella*, Plaza Constitución, No 138, has its name written into the concrete of the entrance floor as well as a sign, good *comida corrida*. *Pizza Palace*, Zamora, buffet 1200-1700, US$5; *Emir Cafeteria*, Independencia 1520, nr F Canal, good breakfast. *La Quinta del Son*, on paved side street off Serdán, bar and restaurant, food nothing special but excellent Cuban-style *trova* band in pm. Good shellfish at Boca del Río. *Nevería y Refresquería Aparito*, A Serdán y Landero y Coss, nr fish market, good for fruit and juices.

Exchange Bancomer, Independencia y Juárez (changes TCs 1000-1215), **Banco Serfín**, Díaz Mirón, 2 blocks from bus station, changes US$ cash and TCs; and Banamex (not Amex) changes money. American Express agency is *Viajes Olymar*, Blvd M Avila Camacho 2221, T 31-34-06. 2 *casas de cambio*: *La Amistad*, Juárez 112 (behind the hotels on the Zócalo), rates not as good as the banks but much quicker; *Hotel Veracruz* changes money at similar rates.

US Consular Agency, Calle Víctimas del 25 de Junio 388, in centre.

Post Offices Main post office by bridge to San Juan de Ulúa fortress, also at Palacio Federal, 5 de Mayo y Rayón, 0800-1900.

Tourist Offices Palacio Municipal on the Zócalo, T 32-99-42, helpful but no hotel price list; Federal office, T 32-16-13.

Airport at Las Bajadas, to the capital several flights daily with Mexicana (Av 5 de Mayo y A Serdán, T 32-22-42, airport 34-69-16), and AeroMéxico (García Auly 231, T 35-52-87, airport 34-66-20). Litoral, T 315232, for flights up and down the coast: Monterrey, Tampico, Minatitlán, Villahermosa, and to McAllen (Texas). Aero Caribe to Ciudad del Carmen and Mérida daily. Continental Houston and Dallas 4 times a week.

Rail Rail to Mexico City: El Jarocho (*servicio estrella*) leaves Mexico City at 2115, arr Veracruz 0710; leaves Veracruz 2130, arr 0740, fares US$17.85 *primera especial*, US$38.35 sleeper for one, US$63.25 for 2, snacks and drinks for sale; ordinary trains to Mexico City at 0725 via Xalapa, at 0800 and 2200 via Córdoba, 2nd class, 10 hrs minimum, US$5.75, comfortable, empty (even at holiday times).

Buses The majority of buses are booked solid for three days in advance throughout summer; at all times queues of up to 2 hrs possible at Mexico City booking offices of bus companies (best company: ADO). Book outward journeys on arrival in Veracruz, as the bus station is some way out of town and there are often long queues. ADO terminal, Díaz Mirón y Jalapa, T 376790; Autobuses Unidos, Lafragua y Jalapa, T 372376. For local buses, get accurate information from the tourist office. Buses to the main bus station along Av 5 de Mayo; marked ADO; and from the station to the centre, blue and white or red and white buses marked Díaz Mirón; pass one block from the Zócalo, US$0.35, or colectivos, also US$0.35. Taxi to ADO terminal from centre US$2.50. Bus to **Mexico City**, ADO, US$16.50, US$20.35 *primera plus* (7 hrs), via Xalapa, stops only at Perote, misses out Orizaba, Fortín and Córdoba; to **Villahermosa** US$14.30 (7½ hrs), or with UNO, deluxe sleeper service, 3 seats to a row, US$41, 6½ hrs; to **Puebla**, US$9; to **Oaxaca**, ADO, 11 hrs, US$13.25; to **Mérida** US$38.50 (16 hrs).

Connections with Guatemala There are no through buses to Guatemala, but there are connecting services. The 'directo' train leaves Veracruz 2100 daily for Ixtepec and Tapachula

(US$11.75); scheduled to take almost 24 hrs, more like 38; not recommended, foul toilets, no lighting so high likelihood of robbery. Take your own toiletries and food, although there is a restaurant car—food is available at every stop. No sleeping accommodation. Local bus services run Tapachula-border and border-Guatemala City; quicker than the much more mountainous route further N. Bus Veracruz-Tapachula 14 hrs, one half-hour meal stop (at 0230), 4 ten-minute station stops, US$30.75, 'plus' service US$50, 1900 every night, 13 hrs, video, reclining seats. Alternatively, take ADO bus to Oaxaca, then carry on to Tapachula (12 hrs) by bus. This allows you to stop at intermediate points of your choice, has few 'comfort' stops. Buy bus tickets out of Veracruz in advance.

The road is very winding from Orizaba so take travel sickness tablets if necessary. Philippe Martin, of the Touring Club Suisse, writes: 'The road from Veracruz to Oaxaca is spectacular but tiresome to drive and will take about a day. The road from Veracruz to La Tinaja and Tierra Blanca is good and fast although there are many lorries. From there to Miguel Alemán the road is bad, speed reasonable, still many lorries. The Tuxtepec area has lovely lowland, jungle areas, charming villages, and the traffic is sparser between Tuxtepec and Oaxaca, while there are no more gasoline stations. The road is very bad and winding and the fog only lifts after you leave the pines at 2,650m above sea level. After a descent and another pass at 2,600m you enter the bare mountainous zone of Oaxaca. Very few eating places between Tuxtepec and Oaxaca.'

Excursions Harbour trips from the Malecón US$3.30 pp for 35 mins if 15 people turn up. Isla de Sacrificios (see above) is no longer included as damage from tourism has caused it to be closed to visitors. **Excursion to Zempoala (see p 227)**, buses from ADO terminal $\frac{1}{2}$ hr each way, via Cardel, or less frequent direct 2nd class buses; a local bus from Cardel goes to La Antigua, US$0.50. On Sunday, to Mandinga for cheap fresh sea food (big prawns), and local entertainment.

The Papaloapan Region At *Puerto Alvarado* ($1\frac{1}{2}$ hrs S from Veracruz by bus), a modern, fishing port, none too pleasant for women on their own, many bars and drunks; **D** *Hotel Lety*, reasonable but for grim plumbing system; **D** *Hotel del Pastor*, avoid next-door restaurant; **D** *María Isela*, quiet, clean with fan, rec; beware of small boys with pea-shooters in the plaza; exchange services 1000-1200; fair/carnival 31 March-5 April), cross the Río Papaloapan (Butterfly River) by a toll bridge (US$1.70), go along Route 180 into the sugar-cane area around Lerdo de Tejada and Angel R Cavada. At El Trópico shop a dirt road turns left to some quiet beaches such as Salinas and Roca Partida. Only at Easter are the beaches crowded: they are normally the preserve of fishermen using hand nets from small boats. In the dry season (Dec-May) the road is passable around the coast to Huatusco.

At Tula, a little further along the main road, is a spectacular waterfall, El Salto de Tula; a restaurant is set beside the falls. The road then climbs up into the mountainous volcanic area of Los Tuxtlas, known as the Switzerland of Mexico for its mountains and perennial greenness.

Santiago Tuxtla, set on a river, is a pleasant town of colonial origin. In the main square is the largest known Olmec head, carved in solid stone, and also a museum (open 0900-1500, Sat-Sun 0900-1200 and 1500-1800), containing examples of local tools, photos, items used in witchcraft (*brujería*), and the first sugar-cane press used in Mexico and another Olmec head. There is dancing to *jarana* bands in the Christmas fortnight. (**C** *Hotel Castellanos*, on Plaza, hot shower, clean, swimming pool (US$1 for non-residents), rec; **D** *Morelos*, family run, quiet, nicely furnished.) Exchange at Banco Comermex on Plaza, travellers' cheques 0900-1330. AU bus from Veracruz, 2nd class, 3 hrs, US$2.

The archaeological site of *Tres Zapotes* lies to the W; it is reached by leaving the paved road S towards Villa Isla and taking either the dirt road at Tres Caminos (signposted) in the dry season (a quagmire from May-Dec), or in the wet season access can be slowly achieved by turning right at about Km 40, called Tibenal, and following the dirt road N to the site of the Museum which is open 0900-1700, entrance US$1.65. (If it is closed, the lady in the nearby shop has a key.) A bus from Santiago Tuxtla goes at 1200 to the village of Tres Zapotes, the site is 1 km walk (the bus cannot reach Tres Zapotes if rain has swollen the river that the road has to cross). Travellers with little time to spare may find the trip to Tres Zapotes not worth the effort. There is an Olmec head, also the largest carved stela ever found and stela fragments bearing the New World's oldest Long Count Date, equal to 31 BC. Not far from Tres Zapotes are three other Olmec sites: Cerro de las Mesas, Laguna de los Cerros, and San Lorenzo Tenochtitlán.

Overlooking Santiago Tuxtla is the hillside restaurant *El Balcón*, which serves excellent fish and seafood for about US$4 per dish and *horchata de coco*, a drink made from the flesh and milk of coconut.

15 km beyond lies **San Andrés Tuxtla** (112,000), the largest town of the area, with narrow winding streets, by-passed by a ring road. This town is also colonial in style and has a well-stocked market with Oaxacan foods such as *totopos*, *carne enchilada*, and *tamales de elote* (hard tortillas, spicy meat, and cakes of maize-flour steamed on leaves). It is the centre of the cigar trade. One factory beside the main road permits visitors to watch the process and will produce special orders of cigars (*puros*) marked with an individual's name in $1/2$ hr. (Bus San Andrés Tuxtla-Villahermosa US$11, 6 hrs; to Mexico City, 1st class, 9 hrs, US$22.)

Hotels D *Catedral*, nr Cathedral, very nice; D *Figueroa*, Pino Suárez 10; D *del Parque*, Madero 5, a/c, very clean, good restaurant; D *Zamfer*, $1/2$ block from Zócalo; E *Casa de Huéspedes la Orizabana*, in the centre of town, without bath, clean, hot water, friendly; E *Juárez*, across from 2nd class bus station, clean, friendly; E *Ponce de León*, primitive, pleasant patio.

Restaurants Near the the town centre is the restaurant *La Flor de Guadalajara*; it appears small from the outside but is large and pleasant inside, well rec; sells *tepachue*, a drink made from pineapple, similar in flavour to cider, and *agua de Jamaica*.

Catemaco is a pleasant town (31,000 people) with large colonial church and picturesque situation on lake, 13 km from San Andrés Tuxtla. There are stalls selling handicrafts from Oaxaca, and boat trips out on the lakes to see the shrine where the Virgin appeared, the spa at Coyame and the Isla de Changos, and to make a necklace of lilies, are always available (boat owners charge US$30-35 per boat). The town is noted for its *brujos* (sorcerers), although this is becoming more of a tourist attraction than a reality, and the Monte del Cerro Blanco to the N is the site of their annual reunion. Catemaco can be reached by direct AU 2nd class bus from Veracruz, every 10 mins, many stops, 4 hrs, US$5, also ADO 1st class; buses also from Santiago Tuxtla, 2nd class. It is about 120 km NW of Minatitlán (**see p 285**); buses also from/to Villahermoso, 7 hrs, US$10 (ADO). To Tuxtepec, change in San Andrés Tuxtla.

Hotels A number of hotels are situated at the lakeside; A *La Finca*, just outside town, T 30430, pool, attractive grounds, beautiful setting beside lake, full at weekends, a/c, comfortable rooms, but poor food and service; B *Motel Playa Azul*, 2 km on road to Sontecomapan, T 30042, modern, a/c; in a nice setting, comfortable and shady, with water-skiing on lake, will allow trailers and use of showers; C *Posada Komiapan* (swimming-pool and restaurant), very comfortable, T 30063; C *Catemaco*, T 30203, excellent food and swimming pool, and *Berthangel*, T 30411, a/c, satellite TV, similar prices; both on main square; D *Del Cid*, 1 block from ADO bus terminal, with fan and bath, OK; D *Los Arcos*, T 30003, clean, fan, good value; D *del Brujo*, Ocampo y Malecón, fan, a/c, shower, nice clean rooms, balcony overlooking the lake, rec; E *Posada Viki*, on Zaragoza, next to *Gallardo*; E *San Francisco*, Matamoros 26, with bath, basic, but good and clean.

Camping Trailer park at Solotepec, on the lakeside on the road to Playa Azul, US$6.50 per vehicle, very clean, hook-ups, bathrooms, rec; also *La Ceiba*, restaurant and trailer park, Av Malecón, 6 blocks W of Zócalo, by lakeshore, camping and hook-ups, bathrooms with hot water, restaurant and lakeside patio.

Restaurants On the promenade are a number of good restaurants—*María José*, best; *7 Brujas*, wooden restaurant open till 2400, good, try *mojarra* (local fish); *La Julita*, also lets rooms, E, with bath, pleasant, rec; *La Ola*, built almost entirely by the owner in the local natural materials, and *La Luna*, among others. At the rear of the market, diagonally from the back of *La Luna*, are some inexpensive, good restaurants serving *comida corrida* for

US$2-2.50, *La Campesina* is rec. Restaurant on 1st floor opp Cathedral, nice atmosphere. Best value are those not directly on the lake, eg *Los Sauces*, which serves *mojarra*. *Bar El Moreno*, 2 de Abril, at the beach, 'not too fancy' but good cuba libres and live synthesizer music.

Excursion At Sihuapan, 5 km from Catemaco, is a turning to the right on to a paved road which leads to the impressive waterfall of Salto de *Eyipantla* (well worth a visit); there are lots of butterflies. There is a stairway down to the base and a path winding through a small village to the top. Small boys at the restaurant near the falls offer their services as guides. Take 2nd class AU bus Catemaco-Sihuapan; from 1030 buses leave every 30 mins from Sihuapan to Eyipantla, otherwise it's a 20-min walk to Comoapan, then take a taxi for US$2.

The Gulf Coast may be reached from Catemaco along a dirt road (which can be washed out in winter). It is about 18 km to Sontecomapan, crossing over the pass at Buena Vista and looking down to the Laguna where, it is said, Francis Drake sought refuge. The village of **Sontecomapan** (1,465 pop, *Hotel Sontecomapan*) lies on an entry to the Laguna and boats may be hired for the 20-min ride out to the bar where the Laguna meets the sea (US$10 return). A large part of the Laguna is surrounded by mangrove swamp, and the sandy beaches, edged by cliffs, are almost deserted except for local fishermen and groups of pelicans. Two good restaurants in Sontecomapan. Beaches are accessible to those who enjoy isolation—such as Jicacal and Playa Hermosa. Jicacal can be reached by going straight on from the Catemaco-Sontecomapan road for 9 km on a good dirt road to La Palma where there is a small bridge which is avoided by heavy vehicles; immediately after this take left fork (poor dirt road, there is a bus) for Monte Pío, a pretty location at the mouth of the river (basic rooms to let, E, and a restaurant), and watch out for a very small sign marked Playa Escondida; road impassable when wet, about 2 km, and then continuing for about 4 km from there. Playa Jicacal is long and open, the first you see as you near the water. The track reaches a T-junction, on the right Jicacal, to the left to Playa Escondida, *Hotel*, E and restaurant. It is not recommended to sleep on the beaches (assaults and robberies) although at Easter time many people from the nearby towns camp on the beaches. The place is busy at weekends.

At **Acayucán**, a pleasant town with several cinemas (**D** *Hotel Joalicia*, Zaragoza 4; **D** *Los Angeles*, cheaper without TV, clean, fans, friendly, pool, owners speak some English, space for car inside; **E** *San Miguel*, with bath, hot water and fan, not very affordable, but OK; **E** *Hotel Ritz*, adequate; **E** *Iglesias*), 267 km from Veracruz (1st class buses 'de paso', very hard to get on, 4 hrs to Veracruz, 2nd class 5½ hrs), turn right for Route 185 if you want to go across the Isthmus to Tehuantepec, Tuxtla Gutiérrez and Central America, but continue on Route 180 for Minatitlán, Coatzacoalcos and Villahermosa (Tabasco). The road across the Isthmus is straight but is not always fast to drive because of high winds (changing air systems from Pacific to Atlantic). Gasoline and food on sale at the half-way point, **Palomares**, where there is a paved road to Tuxtepec (**see p 224**), 2½ hrs' drive. A few kilometres S of Palomares a gravelled road enters on the eastern side; this passes under an imposing gateway 'La Puerta de Uxpanapa' where some 24,500 families are being settled on land reclaimed from the jungle. An hour's drive further S the road crosses the watershed and passes across the flat coastal plain to Juchitán (**see p 265**).

About 15 km from Alvarado a new bridge replaces the old ferry-crossing at Buenavista over the Papaloapan River and the road heads southwards to the fishing village of **Tlacotalpan** where the Papaloapan and San Juan rivers meet. This town, regarded as the centre of Jarocho culture (an amalgam of Spanish, mainly from Seville, African and Indian cultures), has many picturesque streets with one-storey houses all fronted by stuccoed columns and arches painted in various bright pastel colours. Two churches in the Zócalo, and a Casa de las Artesanías on Chazaro, 1½ blocks from the Zócalo. The Museo Funster contains interesting local paintings and artefacts. There is a famous *fiesta* there on 31

January which is very much for locals rather than tourists (accommodation is impossible to find during *fiesta*).

Hotels and Restaurants The **D** *Viajero* and *Reforma*, hotels are good; so is the **C** *Posada Doña Lala*, Carranza II, T 42580, F 42111, with a/c and TV, restaurant expensive; **E** *Jarocho*, seedy. Excellent *sopa de mariscos* and *jaiba a la tlacotalpina* (crab) at the *Restaurant La Flecha*.

Transport Buses go to Veracruz via Alvarado (US$2, 45 mins), to San Andrés, Tuxtla Gutiérrez, Santiago Tuxtla (US$2.50, 1½ hrs) and Villahermosa.

Cosamaloapan, some 40 km beyond Tlacotalpan (103,000 people), is the local market centre with a number of hotels, and the staging point for most bus lines from Veracruz, Orizaba and Oaxaca. One of the largest sugar mills in Mexico is situated just outside the town—Ingenio San Cristóbal—and there is a local airstrip. From Cosamaloapan to Papaloapan the banks on either side of the river are lined with fruit trees. Chacaltianguis, on the E bank of the river, reached by car ferry, has houses fronted by columns.

40 km beyond Cosamaloapan is a ferry to ***Otatitlán***, also on the E bank of the river (it leaves whenever there are sufficient passengers, US$0.25 the ride). The town, also known as El Sanctuario, dates back to early colonial times, its houses with tiled roofs supported by columns, but most interesting is the church. The padre maintains that the gold-patterned dome is the largest unsupported structure of its kind in Mexico, measuring 20m wide and 40 high. El Sanctuario has one of the three black wooden statues of Christ brought over from Spain for the son of Hernán Cortés. During the anti-clerical violence of the 1930s attempts to burn it failed, although the original head was cut off and now stands in a glass case. The first weekend in May is the saint's day and fair, for which pilgrims flock in from the *sierra* and from the Tuxtlas, many in local dress. (*Restaurant-Bar Pepe* serves delicious local, but unusual food; *Restaurant-Bar Ipiranga III* also offers excellent cooking; both by embarkation point.)

At ***Papaloapan*** on the eastern bank of the river, the main road from Orizaba to Rodríguez Clara crosses the main road from Alvarado to Oaxaca; the railway station has services to Yucatán and Chiapas, and to Orizaba or Veracruz. On the W bank is the bus terminal of Santa Cruz (almost under the railway bridge) where all second class buses stop. A passenger ferry may be taken from here to Papaloapan (US$0.50). Although Papaloapan is the route centre for the area the most convenient centre is Tuxtepec, 9 km further S (see below).

The river basin drained by the Papaloapan and its tributaries covers some 47,000 sq km—about twice the size of the Netherlands—and is subject to a programme of regional development by the Comisión del Papaloapan, which includes the construction of two large dams to control the sometimes severe flooding of the lower basin. The lake formed behind Presidente Alemán dam at Temascal is scenically very attractive and boats may be hired to go to Mazatec Indian settlements on the islands or on the other side. There is also a daily ferry passing round the lake. ***Soyaltepec*** is the closest settlement, situated high above the water on an island, the peak crowned by a church. ***Ixcatlan*** lies on a peninsula jutting into the lake on the SE side; it has one hotel and one restaurant, as well as a large beer repository. Ixcatlan may also be reached by dirt road from Tuxtepec, but it is less nerve-racking to take a ferry.

Temascal (Sun is the most active day) may be reached by taking Route 145 from Papaloapan through Gabino Barreda, Ciudad Alemán (no facilities, centre of the Papaloapan Commission), Novara (petrol and 3 restaurants of varying prices, 1 air-conditioned), as far as La Granja where the turn to Temascal is clearly marked. (In Temascal there is a woman who offers very basic accommodation.) Route 145 continues paved and straight past Tres Valles (cheap, good regional food; annual fair mid-Nov), and on to ***Tierra Blanca***, a railway junction on the

Tapachula-Veracruz and Mérida-Córdoba-Mexico City lines (Hotels **E** *Balun Canán*, cheap, hot; **D** *Principal*, own shower and fan, clean, just above bus station, noisy; *Bimbis* restaurant by ADO bus station, good; shopping centre, market, car repairs, eg Volkswagen agent). Route 145 passes under a sign saying 'La Puerta del Papaloapan', to join the main Orizaba-Veracruz road (Route 150) at *La Tinaja*, a second-class bus junction, also gasoline, and restaurants (1 air-conditioned at service station). Papaloapan to La Tinaja takes about 1 hr, the road often has a lot of lorries and in the cane-cutting season great care should be taken at night for carts travelling on the road without lights. There are three railway crossings on the road, also poorly marked, two near La Granja and one near Tierra Blanca. The tarmac is often damaged in the wet season (June-Dec).

From Papaloapan a paved road runs eastwards to Rodríguez Clara and on to Sayula on the Trans-Isthmian road. This road passes through the main pineapple-producing region of Mexico, which has encouraged the development of towns such as *Loma Bonita* (local airstrip, hotels, restaurants and gasoline) and *Villa Isla* (Hotels: *La Choca* restaurant good, railway station, ADO bus terminal, and centre for the rich cattle-producing area that surrounds it).

From Villa Isla a good dirt road runs S to *Playa Vicente* (6,974 pop), another ranching town, located beside a wide river; excellent crayfish may be eaten at the *Restaurant La Candileja*, while the café on the central plaza serves tender steaks. Another dirt road leaves the Villa Isla-Playa Vicente road for *Abasolo del Valle* (2,000 pop), but only reaches to within 7 km. The last few kms can be impassable by vehicle in the wet season. The town is set beside a lagoon and the houses are surrounded by fruit trees (no hotels or restaurants). Gasoline can be bought—ask at a shop who has some to sell.

At the cross-roads of the Papaloapan-Sayula road about 80 km from Papaloapan, where the S turn is to Villa Isla, the N turn is a paved road which in about ½ hr will take you past two turnings to Tres Zapotes and up to Santiago Tuxtla.

The road from Papaloapan continues E to a point just N of *Rodríguez Clara*, which is reached by branching off S down a dirt road. This is a compact, thriving town. There are 2 hotels, the better is in the centre of the town, **D** *Hotel Roa*; *Restaurant Mexicana* rec.

Tuxtepec is the natural centre for a stay in the Papaloapan area. It is a large city in the state of Oaxaca, some 9 km S of Papaloapan (toll for Caracol bridge, US$0.40). There is a fascinating mixture of the music and exuberance of Veracruz with the food and handicrafts of Oaxaca. The town is built on a meander of the Río Santo Domingo and a good view can be had from the rear balcony of the market on Av Independencia; there are other viewpoints beyond the main shops. A hand-pulled ferry crosses the river from below the viewpoint next to *Hotel Mirador*.

NB Near the river watch out for gnats (*rodadores*), which bite sensitive skins leaving itchy welts.

NB Also many street names and numbers are not marked.

Hotels *El Rancho*, Avila Camacho 850, T 50641, restaurant, bar, evening entertainment, most expensive, accepts travellers' cheques as payment, rec; **C** *María de Lourdes*, Av 5 de Mayo 1380, T (91-287)5-0410, hot water, clean, excellent car park, rec; *Tuxtepec*, Matamoros 2, T 50944, good value; **D** *Catedral*, Calle Guerrero, nr Zócalo, very friendly, fan and shower; **D** *Mirador*, Av Independencia, hot showers, fairly safe car park, with view of filthy river, good; nearby on same Avenida, **E** *Posada Guadelupana*, and **E** *Posada Real*; **E** *Sacre*, Calle Libertad, good, quiet; nearby is **E** *Casa de Huéspedes Ocampo*, with bath, clean, friendly, room 10 is the best. Very good value is the **E** *Avenida* in Independencia round the corner from ADO bus station, with bath and fan, basic, clean but restaurant below not very good value; **E** *Posada del Sol*, basic and noisy, opp Fletes y Pasajes bus station.

Restaurants *El Estero*, in a side street opp market on Av Independencia (fish dishes and local cuisine excellent), *El Mino* (near Fletes y Pasajes bus terminal), *Mandinga*, Av 20 de Noviembre, for fish dishes, *Avenida*, next to hotel of same name; *Pata Pata*, around corner, on side street, half way down the block. *Ronda*, Calle Independencia, cheap and good; *La Mascota de Oro*, 20 de Noviembre 891, very friendly, cheap. *Las Palmas*, Riva Palacios, palm-thatched, excellent local food, friendly, heartily rec. Beer from the barrel can be bought from the bar next to the Palacio Municipal, and the best ices are found in *La Morida*.

Transport There are four bus terminals in town, clear street signs for each one. ADO bus services to **Mexico City** (Thurs, US$16.50), **Veracruz** and regular daily minibus (taking 5-6 hrs) to **Oaxaca** leaving at 2230. AU (Autobuses Unidos, on Matamoros, ½ block from Libertad) daily to wide variety of destinations. AU to Oaxaca, US$10 2nd class, 8 hrs, slow, Buses Cuenca del Papaloapan, direct route, every 2 hrs in am and pm, US$8.25, ADO at 2230, 10 hrs, US$16.50. Also Transportes Chinantecos. The Tuxtepec-Palomares road provides a short cut to the Transístmica; it passes through many newly cleared jungle areas. Armed robberies are said to be a danger on this road, the route via Sayula is 20 km longer, but safer as well as quicker. Bus to **Acayucán**, ADO, 4 hrs, US$3.30.

There are scattered villages, the main halt being at María Lombardo (some 2 hrs from Tuxtepec where food is sold); Zócalo is attractive. Gas station 4 km further on at Cihualtepec junction, a village of Indians moved from the area flooded by the Temascal dam.

Excursions To Temascal to see the dam (see above); also a visit to the Indian villages of *Ojitlán* and *Jalapa de Díaz* (bus leaves from the end of Calle 20 de Noviembre, US$5, 2½ hrs; hotel, E and food stores, good and cheaper *huipiles* from private houses) is well worth the ride; easily reached by car along semi-paved road and also by AU bus service (from Mercado Flores Magón, 20 de Noviembre y Blvd Juárez, every hour on the half hour). The Chinantec Indians' handicrafts may be bought on enquiry; hotels non-existent and eating facilities limited but some superb scenery, luxuriant vegetation and little-visited area. Ojitlán is best visited on Sunday, market day, when the Chinanteca *huipiles* worn by the women are most likely to be seen. Part of the area will be flooded when the Cerro de Oro dam is finished and the lake will join that of Temascal. Heavily armed checkpoint on the road from Tuxtepec to Tierra Blanca (bus 1½ hrs, US$1.50), non-uniformed men, very officious, do not get caught with any suspicious goods.

The road to Tuxtepec N from Oaxaca (Route 175) is in bad repair but is a spectacular, steep and winding route, cars need good brakes and it is reported to be difficult for caravans. A correspondent drove it in 1992: 'the road is good from Oaxaca as far as the national shrine at Juárez's birthplace in Ixtlán. N from there to the crestline of the mountain range is pretty dreadful - potholed and rutted with a scrubby pine forest cutting off any views for almost the whole route. It gets much better coming down the other side, however. The surface is smooth, the curves are well-engineered and the descent from alpine evergreen down into tropical rainforest is fascinating and exhilarating. Valle Nacional, at the bottom of the descent, is notable for what are surely the highest and most diabolically-shaped *topes* in the Mexican republic: at any speed, at any angle of approach, it was almost impossible to keep a VW from bottoming out on them'. (Eric Mankin, California, USA).

It takes about 5 hrs to drive this journey in reverse, up *Valle Nacional*. This valley, despite its horrific reputation as the 'Valle de los Miserables' in the era of Porfirio Díaz, for political imprisonment and virtual slavery from which there was no escape, is astoundingly beautiful. The road follows the valley floor, on which are cattle pastures, fruit trees and a chain of small villages such as Chiltepec (very good bathing in the river), Jacatepec (reached by ferry over the river, produces rich honey and abounds in all varieties of fruit), Monte Flor (where swimming and picnicking are possible beside natural springs, but *very* cold water, and an archaeological site) and finally Valle Nacional. (Bus to Valle Nacional from Tuxtepec, 1½ hrs, basic hotel, restaurants, stores, and gasoline available; river swimming.) The road climbs up into the Sierra, getting cooler, and slopes more heavily covered with tropical forest, and there are panoramic views.

San Pedro Yolox lies some 20 minutes' drive W of this route down a dirt road; it is a peaceful Chinantec village clustered on the side of the mountain, while Llano de Flores is a huge grassy clearing in the pine forest with grazing animals and cool, scented air. Wood from these forests is cut for the paper factory in Tuxtepec. Ixtlán de Juárez has gasoline. While houses in the lowlands are made of wood with palm roofs, here the houses are of adobe or brick. From Guelatao (**see p 263**) it is about 1½ hrs' drive, mainly downhill, to Oaxaca (**see p 253**), with the land becoming drier and the air warmer. About 30 km before Oaxaca is **Restaurant del Monte**, by the roadside, ranch-style, good views, tasty soup, meat indifferent.

Veracruz to Mexico City

By the road followed to Veracruz, the driving time from Mexico City is about 9 hrs. One can return to the capital by a shorter route through Xalapa which takes 6 hrs; this was the old colonial route to the port, and is the route followed by the railway.

Xalapa (also spelt Jalapa), capital of Veracruz state (pop 1990 6,215,100), 132 km from the port, is in the *tierra templada*, at 1,425m. The weather is variable, hot with thunder storms, the clouds roll down off the mountains in the evening. There was a passion for renovation in the flamboyant gothic style during the first part of the 19th century. It is yet another 'City of Flowers', with walled gardens, stone-built houses, wide avenues in the newer town and steep cobbled crooked streets in the old. The 18th century cathedral, with its sloping floor, has been recently restored. Population 213,000. Just outside, on the road to Mexico City, is an excellent, modern museum (opened Oct 1986) showing archaeological treasures of the Olmec, Totonac and Huastec coastal cultures. The three colossal heads displayed in the grounds of the museum, are Olmec; the museum has the best collection of Olmec monumental stone sculptures in Mexico (open 1000-1700, take the Foviste de Tejada bus). Xalapa has a University; you can take a pleasant stroll round the grounds, known as El Dique. Pico de Orizaba is visible from hotel roofs or Parque Juárez very early in the morning, before the haze develops. 2.5 km along the Coatepec road are lush botanical gardens with a small museum.

Festival Feria de Primavera, mid-April.

Hotels Cheaper hotels are up the hill from the market, which itself is uphill from Parque Juárez (there is no Zócalo). **L** *Xalapa*, Victoria y Bustamante, T 82222, good restaurant, excellent bookshop, changes travellers' cheques; **A** *María Victoria*, Zaragoza 6, T 80268, good; *Hostal del Tejar*, 20 de Noviembre Ote 552 esq Av del Tejar, T 72459, F 83691, 3-star, a/c, pool, parking; **C** *Hotel Suites Araucarias*, Avila Camacho 160, T 73433, with large window, balcony and view (D without), TV, fridge, good cheap restaurant; **C** *México*, Lucio 4, T 75030, clean, with shower, will change dollars; **C** *Salmones*, Zaragoza 24, T 75435, restaurant, excellent view of Orizaba from the roof, good restaurant, rec; **E** *Amoro*, nr market, no shower but public baths opp, very clean; **C** *Limón*, Revolución 8, ½ block up from Cathedral, tiled patio, laundry, poor value, uncomfortable; **E** *Continental*, on Enríquez, owner speaks some English, good lunches, friendly; **E** *Plaza*, Enríquez, clean, safe, friendly, will store luggage, good view of Orizaba from the roof.

Restaurants *La Casona del Beaterío*, Zaragoza 20, good atmosphere; *Quinto Reyno*, Juárez 67 close to Zócalo, lunches only, excellent vegetarian with health-food shop, very good service. *Terraza*, opp Parque Juárez, the cheapest breakfast in the centre; *Estancia*, opp Barranquilla, good food; *Aladino*, Juárez, up from ADO, excellent Mexican food; *Pizzaría*, Ursulo Galván; *La Tasca*, a club, good music, rec; another club is *La Cumbre* (rock). Health food shops, Ursulo Galván, nr Juárez, good bread and yoghurt, another opp the post office on Zamora. The famous Xalapeño chilli comes from this region.

Shopping *Artesanía* shop on Alfaro, more on Barcenas, turn off Enríquez into Madero, right again at the top, the owner of *El Tazín* on the corner speaks English.

Books *Instituto de Antropología*, Benito Juárez, has books in English and Spanish, student ID helps.

Moped Hire in Camacho US$4-6/hr, Visa accepted.

Theatre Teatro del Estado, Av Avila Camacho; good Ballet Folklórico Veracruzano and fair symphony orchestra.

Entertainments Centro de Recreación Xalapeño has exhibitions; live music and exhibitions in Ayora, underneath Parque Juárez; 10 pin bowling, Plaza Cristal, next to cinema. There are 2 cinemas next to *Hotel Xalapa*, off Camacho; 3-screen cinema in Plaza Cristal; cinemas in the centre tend to show soft porn and gore.

Exchange Houses Banco Serfín will change TCs, Bancomer will not. *Casa de Cambio*, on right side of Zamora going down hill, English spoken. Banks are slow, money transferred from abroad comes via Mexico City, banks prefer to issue pesos, with persistence and tact it may be possible to obtain dollars. **American Express** at Viajes Xalapa, Carrillo Puerto 24, T 76535, in centre, sells cheques against Amex card. The liquor shop in Plaza Cristal will change dollars.

Laundromat 2 on Ursulo Galván, same day service.

Health Hospital, Nicolás Bravo, entrance in street on right. Dr Blásquez, Hidalgo, speaks English. There are 2 dentists on Ursulo Galván.

Communications Radio-telephone available opposite *Hotel María Victoria*; long distance phone in shop on Zaragoza, with a sign outside, others behind the government palace also in Zaragoza. Letters can be sent to the Lista de Correos in Calle Diego Leño, friendly post office, and another at the bottom of Zamora. There is a telegraph office next door where telegrams marked Lista de Correos are kept.

Travel Agents There are 4 on Camacho, the one nearest Parque Juárez is very helpful.

Tourist Office Av Camacho, a long walk or short taxi ride. Look out for *Toma Nota*, free sheet advertising what is on, available from shop in front of *Hotel Salmones*.

Airport 15 km SE, on Veracruz road.

Transport A new 1st and 2nd class bus station has been built; taxi from centre US$1.75. 5 hrs from Mexico City by AU or ADO, from the Central de Oriente (TAPO). Frequent ADO service Xalapa-Veracruz, US$3.30. To **Puebla**, ADO, 4 hrs. To **Villahermosa**, ADO, 3 a day, 10 hrs. To **Poza Rica**, the coast road is faster, while the impressive route via Teziutlán requires a strong stomach for mountain curves. Railway station on outskirts, buses from near market to get there. Train to **Mexico City** at 1140 (unreliable, dirty, crowded), to **Veracruz** at 1530 (4 hrs).

Excursions Hacienda Casa de Santa Ana, 20 minutes' drive, was taken over in the revolution and is now a museum with the original furniture, entrance free, no bags allowed in. To ruins of **Zempoala**, 65 km N of Veracruz (hotel, **Chachalaca**, near sea, spotless, rec), the coastal city which was conquered by Cortés and whose inhabitants became his allies. The ruins are interesting because of the round stones uniquely used in construction. (Entry US$3.45, small museum on site.) Take 2nd class bus to Zempoala via Cardel, which will let you off at the ruins, or take a taxi from the Plaza of Zempoala, US$3 return. You can also get there from Veracruz. To **Texolo** waterfalls, some 15 km away near the village of Jico, just beyond the neighbouring town of Coatepec (famous for its ice-cream); there is a deep ravine and an old bridge, as well as a good, cheap restaurant at the falls. It's a 5 km walk through Jico to the falls. The village itself is pretty, US$0.60 by bus from Xalapa every ½ hr. (The film *Romancing the Stone* used Texolo as one of its locations.)

Tim Connell writes: '**Naolinco** is ½ hr ride, 40 km NE of Xalapa up a winding hilly road, *Restaurant La Fuente* serves local food; has nice garden. Las Cascadas, with a *mirador* to admire them from, are on the way into the town: two waterfalls, with various pools, tumble several thousand feet over steep wooded slopes. Flocks of *zopilotes* (buzzards) collect late in the afternoon, soaring high up into the thermals. Baños Carrizal: 8 km off main road, 40 km from Veracruz. **Chachalacas** is a beach with swimming pool and changing facilities in expensive hotel of same name, US$1 adults. Thatched huts; local delicacies sold on beach, including *robalito* fish.'

The coast road from Veracruz heads to **Nautla** (one hotel, E, rec, on main street; pleasant town, but nothing to see or do) 3 km after which Route 131 branches inland to Teziutlán (see below). 42 km up the coast from Nautla is **Tecolutla**, a very popular resort on the river of that name, toll bridge US$2.50.

Accommodation B Hotels Villas de Palmar; **D** Playa, good; **D** Tecolutla, best, and Marsol (run down) are on the beach; **E** Posada Guadalupe and **E** Casa de Huéspedes Malena (pleasant rooms, clean) are on Avenida Carlos Prieto, near river landing stage. Newer hotels, D, on road to Nautla. Torre Molina trailer park, 16 km before Nautla on coastal route 180 (coming from Veracruz), electricity, water and sewage disposal, hot showers, bathrooms, swimming pool, on beach, US$10 per vehicle with 2 people, rec. **Restaurant** Paquita, next to Hotel Playa, rec.

El Pital (15 km in from the Gulf along the Nautla river, 80 km SE of Papantla and named after a nearby village), was identified early in 1994 as the site of an important, sprawling precolumbian seaport (approx AD 100-600), which lay hidden for centuries under thick rainforest. Now planted over with bananas and oranges, the hundred or more pyramid mounds (some reaching 40m in height) were assumed by plantation workers to be natural hills. Little excavation or clearing has yet been done, but both Teotihuacan-style and local-style ceramics and figurines have been found, and archaeologists believe El Pital may mark the principal end point of an ancient cultural corridor that linked the north-central Gulf Coast with the powerful urban centres of Central Mexico. As at nearby El Tajín, ball courts have been discovered, along with stone fragments depicting what may be sacrificed ball players.

Some 40 km inland from Tecolutla is **Papantla** (280,000 people), built on the top of a hill overlooking the lush plains of northern Veracruz. It was the stronghold of a Totonac rebellion in 1836. Traditional Totonac dress is common: the men in baggy white trousers and sailor shirts and the women in lacy white skirts and shawls over embroidered blouses. The **Zócalo**, formally known as Plaza Téllez, is bordered by Enríquez on its downhill N edge; on the S uphill side is the Cathedral of **Señora de la Asunción** with a remarkable 50m-long mural in its northern wall called Homenaje a la Cultura Totonaca, with the plumed serpent Quetzalcoatl along its entire length. Voladores perform each Sun at 1100 in the church courtyard and as many as three times daily during the colourful 10 days of Corpus Christi (late May or early June), along with games, fireworks, artistic exhibitions, dances and cockfights. For a sweeping view of the area walk up Reforma to the top of the hill where the giant **Monumento al Volador** was erected in 1988. Murals and mosaic benches in the Zócalo also commemorate Totonac history and their conception of creation. Beside the main plaza is the Mercado Juárez (poultry and vegetables); more interesting is **Mercado Hidalgo**, 20 de Noviembre off the NW corner of the Zócalo (open daily 0600-2000), where traditional handmade clothing is sold amid fresh produce and livestock. Papantla is also the centre of one of the world's largest vanilla-producing zones, and the distinctive odour often lingers over the town. Small animal figures, baskets and other fragrant items woven from vanilla bean pods are sold at booths along Highway 180, as well as the essence; packaged in tin boxes, these sachets are widely used to freshen cupboards and drawers. The vanilla is processed in Gutiérrez Zamora, a small town about 30 km E (closed to Tecolutla), and a 'cream of vanilla' liqueur is also produced. The Fiesta de la Vainilla is held throughout the area in early June.

Hotels C Pulido, Enríquez 205, modern, T 20036, but noisy, with bath, reported dirty, parking; **C** Tajín, Calle Dr Núñez 104, T 21064, restaurant with good value breakfast and bar, reasonable; Papantla, on Zócalo; **E** Trujillo, Calle 5 de Mayo 401, rooms with basin, friendly. (It is better to stay in Papantla than in Poza Rica if you want to visit El Tajín.)

Restaurants (most open 0700-2400) Las Brisas del Golfo, Calle Dr Núñez, reasonable and very good. Enríquez, Enríquez 103, attached to Hotel Premier, modern, expensive seafood, popular, pleasant; Terraza, 20 de Noviembre, overlooking Zócalo, simple, pleasant; Sorrente,

Zócalo, covered in decorative tiles, good, cheap, rec; *Cathedral*, Núñez y Curado, behind Cathedral, plain, clean, cheap breakfasts and good 'fast' meals, 0630-2100.

Services Post Office: Azueta 198, 2nd floor, Mon-Fri 0900-1300, 1500-1800, Sat 0900-1200. **Exchange**: Bancomer and Banamex, on Zócalo, 0900-1300, change cash and TCs till 1200; **Serfín**, between the two, does not change TCs. *Farmacia Aparicio*, Enríquez 103, daily 0700-2200.

Tourist Office On 1st floor of Palacio Municipal, on the Zócalo, T 20177, no maps, no English, leaflet sold (US$0.75), Mon-Fri 0900-1500, Sat 0900-1300, often closed pm.

Buses ADO terminal, Juárez 207, 5 blocks uphill from centre. To Mexico City, 4 a day, 5 hrs via Poza Rica, US$7; **Poza Rica**, 8 daily, 1/2 hr, US$0.50; to **Xalapa**, 8 daily, 6 hrs, US$6.25; 4 hrs to **Veracruz**, US$11. 2nd class terminal (Transported Papantla), 20 de Noviembre 200, many services to local destinations, inc El Tajín, buses leave when full. Occasional minibus to El Tajín from SW corner of Zócalo, US$2, unreliable schedule about every 1-11/2 hrs.

About 12 km away, in the forest, is *El Tajín*, the ruins of the capital of the Totonac culture (6th to 10th century AD—the name means 'hurricane') entry, US$4.35, free on Sun. Guidebook US$1.25, available in Museo de Antropología, Mexico City. At the centre of this vast complex is the Pyramid of El Tajín, whose 365 squared openings make it look like a vast beehive. There is a small museum, described as 'just a dark shed but with some interesting carvings', and the remains of some columns, propped up next to another building on the site. Traditionally, on Corpus Christi, Totonac rain dancers erect a 30-metre mast with a rotating structure at the top. Four *voladores* (flyers) and a musician climb to the surmounting platform. There the musician dances to his own pipe and drum music, whilst the roped *voladores* throw themselves into space to make a dizzy spiral descent, sometimes head up, sometimes head down, to the ground. *Voladores* are now in attendance every day, most of the day, and fly if they think there are enough tourists, they charge US$5-7. The tourist office near the Zócalo will show you bus schedules.

21 km NW of Papantla is *Poza Rica*, an oil city (pop 210,000), with an old cramped wooden market, but little else to recommend it. The streets are busy, there are several comfortable hotels and bus connections are very good. Flaring gas burn offs light up the night sky.

Hotels B *Poza Rica Inn*, carretera a Papantla, Km 4, 'Holiday Inn look-a-like', poor restaurant; **B** *Robert Prince*, Av 6 Norte, 10 Oriente, T 25455, Col Obrera; **C** *Nuevo León*, Av Colegio Militar, T 20528, opp market, rooms quite spacious, fairly clean and quiet, rec; **C** *Poza Rica*, 2 Norte, T 20134, fairly comfortable, good *comida corrida* in restaurant; **C** *Salinas*, Blvd Ruiz Cortines, 1000, T 20706, good central hotel, a/c, TV, restaurant, pool, secure parking; **E** *Aurora*, Bolívar 4, basic but quiet and fairly clean; **E** *Fénix*, basic, opposite ADO bus station; **E** *Juárez*, Cortines y Bermúdez, average; **E** *San Román*, 8 Norte 5; **F** *Cárdenas*, Bermúdez y Zaragoza, T 26610, basic, not central; *Madrid*, basic.

Bus All buses leave from new terminal about 11/2 km from centre, take white bus from centre. Terminal is divided into ADO and all others, good facilities, tourist office. ADO 1st class to **Mexico City** and **Tampico**, 21 daily each, 5 hrs, US$11. Estrella Blanca 2nd class to Mexico City, 23 daily, US$7.25. To **Monterrey**, 4 a day, US$11. To **Veracruz**, 4 hrs, US$13.75. To **Pachuca**, Estrella Blanca, 41/2 hrs, US$6, change in Tulancingo. To **Tecolutla** (see below), US$2.20, 11/4 hrs. 2nd class with Transportes Papantla to **El Tajín**, 10 per day (with different destinations), US$0.40.

Air Airport 8 km S; 3 flights a week to both Ciudad Victoria and Mexico City, AeroMéxico (Edificio Geminis, Parque Juárez, T 26142/28877).

From Poza Rica you can visit the *Castillo de Teayo*, a pyramid with the original sanctuary and interesting carvings on top, buses every 1/2 hr, change halfway. 25 km along Route 8 is Barra de Cazones with a little developed, good beach.

On the coast, 55 km from Poza Rica, 189 km S of Tampico is *Tuxpan* (*Veracruz*), tropical and humid, 12 km from the sea on the Río Tuxpan. Essentially a fishing town (shrimps a speciality), it is now decaying from what must have been a beautiful heyday. Interesting covered market, but beware of the bitter, over-ripe avocados; fruit sold on the quay. Beach about 2 km E of town, reached by taxi or bus (marked 'Playa'), at least 10 km long. White sands, few people, no hasslers, some sandflies; hire deckchairs under banana-leaf shelters for the day (US$2). Many restaurants line the beach, with showers for the use of bathers (US$0.35); *El Arca* restaurant serves good fish and shrimp and the owners are very friendly and helpful; also *Bremen*, a/c, food good and cheap. Bus to Mexico City (Terminal del Norte), US$14.80, 6½ hrs via Poza Rica. (**B** *Hotel Florida*, Av Juárez 23, clean, hot water; **D** *California*, clean, hot water, good breakfast; **E** *Tuxpan*, OK; and others. Entertainment: *Hotel Teján*, over the river, S side, then about 1 km towards the sea, very plush, good singers but US$6.50 cover charge; *Aeropolis* disco, dull, no beer.)

The road towards the capital continues to climb to *Perote*, 53 km from Xalapa. The San Carlos fort here, now a military prison, was built in 1770-77; there is a good view of Cofre de Perote volcano. A road branches N to *Teziutlán* (**D** *Hotel Valdez*, hot water, car park), with a Friday market, where good *sarapes* are sold, a local fair, *La Entrega de Inanacatl*, is held in the 3rd week in June. The old convent at *Acatzingo*, 93 km beyond Perote, is worth seeing. Another 10 km and we join the road to Puebla and Mexico City.

Pico De Orizaba (Citlaltépetl) is the highest mountain in Mexico (5,760m). It is not too difficult to climb although acclimatization to altitude is advised and there are some crevasses to be negotiated. From Acatzingo one can go via a paved road to Tlachichuca (35 km, or you can take a bus from Puebla to Tlachichuca). Either contact Sr Reyes who arranges trips in a four-wheel drive car up an appalling road to 2 huts on the mountain. He charges about US$80-100, including one night at his house (**D** full board). Alternatively, stay at **E** *Hotel Margarita*, no sign, then, early in the morning hitch hike to the last village, Villa Hidalgo (about 15 km). From there it's about 10 km to the huts. Take the trail which goes straight through the forest, eventually to meet the dusty road. The huts, one small, one larger and colder, are at 4,200m (small charge at each). There is no hut custodian; it's usually fairly empty, except on Sat night. No food or light, or wood; provide your own. Water close at hand, but no cooking facilities. Start from the hut at about 0500, first to reach the glacier at 4,700m, and then a little left to the rim. It's about 7-8 hrs to the top; the ice is not too steep (about 35-40°), take crampons, if not for the ascent then for the descent which takes only 2½ hrs. At the weekend you're more likely to get a lift back to Tlachichuca.

Volker Huss of Karlsruhe (Germany) informs us of an alternative route up the volcano; this is easier, because there is no glacier and therefore no crevasses, but can only be done in the rainy season (April to October), when there is enough snow to cover the loose stone on the final stage. Crampons and ice-axe are necessary. The route is on the S face of the volcano. Stay in Orizaba and take a very early bus to Ciudad Serdán (departs 0530), or stay in Ciudad Serdán. At Serdán bus station take a colectivo to the trail's starting point (US$15): the route is Esperanza, San Antonio, Asisintla, Texmalaquila; the driver will know the way. 8 hrs from the start is the Fausto González hut at 4,800m (take own food and water). Spend the night there and climb the final 1,000m early in the morning, about 5 hrs. From the top are fine views, with luck even to Veracruz and Mexico City. In the rainy season the summit is usually free of cloud until midday. The entire descent take 6 hrs and can be done the same day.

MEXICO CITY-CUERNAVACA-TAXCO-ACAPULCO (8)

From the capital to the Pacific, with long-established resorts such as Acapulco, newer developments (Puerto Escondido, Huatulco) and the only-recently discovered (Zipolite). The route passes through Cuernavaca, the country seat of Aztecs and Spaniards, now a major tourist town, and the silver city of Taxco.

A 406-km 4-lane toll motorway connects Mexico City with Acapulco. (Total toll for the route at 8 booths is US$89) Driving time is about 3 hrs. The highest point, La Cima, 3,016m, is reached at Km 42. The road then spirals down through precipitous forests to (Km 75):

Cuernavaca, capital of Morelos state (originally Tlahuica Indian territory); at 1,542m; 724m lower than Mexico City Population approaching 1 million because of a new industrial area to the S. The temperature never exceeds 27°C nor falls below 10°C, and there is almost daily sunshine even during the rainy season. The city has always attracted visitors from the more rigorous highlands and can be overcrowded. The Spaniards captured it in 1521 and Cortés himself, following the custom of the Aztec nobility, lived there. The outskirts are dotted with ultra-modern walled homes and it has lost most of its charm as a result of rapid growth.

The **Cathedral**, finished in 1552, known as Iglesia de la Asunción, stands at one end of an enclosed garden. 17th-century murals were discovered during restoration; also, on the great doors, paintings said to have been done by an Oriental convert who arrived by a ship from the Philippines, relating the story of the persecution and crucifixion of 24 Japanese martyrs. The Sunday morning masses at 1100 are accompanied by a special *mariachi* band. *Mariachis* also perform on Sunday and Wednesday evenings in the Cathedral. By the entrance to it stands the charming small church of the **Tercera Orden** (1529), whose quaint façade carved by Indian craftsmen contains a small figure suspected to be one of the only two known statues of Cortés in Mexico. (The other is a mounted statue near the entrance of the *Casino de la Selva* hotel.)

The palace Cortés built in 1531 for his second wife stands by the city's central tree-shaded plaza; on the rear balcony is a Diego Rivera mural depicting the conquest of Mexico. It was the seat of the State Legislature until 1967, when the new legislative building opposite was completed; it has now become the **Museo Regional de Historia Cuauhnáhuac**, showing everything from dinosaur remains to contemporary Indian culture (closed Thurs, as are other museums in Cuernavaca). The 18th century **Jardín Borda**, on Calle Morelos, was a favourite resort of Maximilian and Carlota; it has been restored and is in fine condition (open-air concerts). The weekend retreat of the ill-fated imperial couple, in the Acapantzingo district, is being restored. Another museum is the **Herbolario y Jardín Botánico**, Matamoros 200, Col Acapatzingo (no one seems to know exactly where it is), peaceful, interesting, free. Other places worth seeing are the three plazas, Calle Guerrero, and, some distance from the main plaza, the new market buildings on different levels. The house of David Alfaro Siqueiros, the painter, is now a museum (**Taller Siqueiros**) at Calle Venus 7 and contains lithographs and personal photographs. The very unusual **Teopanzolco** pyramid is to be found near the railway station (entry US$2.65). Remarkable frescoes have recently been found in the old Franciscan church of **La Parroquia**. There are occasional concerts at the San José open chapel. Many spas in surrounding area, at Cuautla, Xocitepec, Atrotomilco, Oaxtepec and others.

Hotels Good value, cheap hotels are hard to find. **L** *Las Mañanitas*, Linares 107, T 12-4646 (one of the best in Mexico), Mexican colonial style, many birds in lovely gardens, excellent food; **A+** *Hacienda de Cortés*, Atlacomulco suburb, T 160867/158844, 16th century sugar *hacienda*, magnificent genuine colonial architecture, garden, suites, pool, excellent restaurant, access by car; **A+** *Hostería Las Quintas*, Av las Quintas (Pte Díaz Ordaz) 107, T 183949, F 183895, built in traditional Mexican style, owner has splendid collection of bonsai trees, restaurant, pool, magnificent setting, fine reputation; **A+** *Posada Jacarandas*, Cuauhtémoc 805, T 15-7777, garden, restaurant, parking; **A+** *Posada San Angelo*, Privada la Selva 100, T 14-1499, restaurant, gardens, pool; **A+** *Posada Xochiquetzal*, Francisco Leyva 200, T 12-0220, near Zócalo, restaurant, pool, garden; **A** *Casino de la Selva*, Leandro Valle 26, T 12-4700, with huge mural by Siqueiros on the future of humanity from now till AD 3000, shops, restaurant, bars, gardens; **A** *Suites Paraíso*, Av Domingo Díaz 1100, T 13-3365, family accommodation; on same avenue, *Villa Bejar*, No 2350, T 175000, F 174953, Gran Turismo class, all facilities; **B** *Papagayo*, Motolinia 13, T 14-1711, 5 blocks from Zócalo, 1 block from Estrella Roja bus station, on Fri-Sat rooms are available only if one takes 3 meals a day, on other days price is room only, pool, gardens, convenient, noisy, unhelpful reception, insist on a good room, suitable for families, parking; **B** *Posada Quinta Las Flores*, Tlaquepaque 210, Colonia Las Palmas, T 141244/125769, including breakfast, no TV, pool, gardens, restaurant, small parking space, very pleasant, highly rec; **C** *Hostería Peñalba*, Matamoros 204, T 12-4166, beautiful courtyard with exotic birds and a monkey, restaurant with famous Spanish food (long-term guests only), was once Zapata's HQ during the Revolution, very atmospheric and friendly but disappointing facilities, much insect life, rooms on street are very noisy; **D** *Roma*, Matamoros 405, T 12-0787, good value, with hot water 0700-0800 and shower. Several cheaper hotels in Calle Aragón y León between Morelos and Maramoros: eg **E** *América*, No 111, safe, good value but noisy (couples only), clean, basic; some rent rooms by the hour.

Motels A *Posada Cuernavaca*, Paseo del Conquistador, T 13-0800, view, restaurant, grounds; **B** *El Verano*, Zapata 602, T 17-0652; **D** *Royal*, Matamoros 19, hot water 0700-2300, rec; *Suites OK Motel* with *Restaurant Las Margaritas*, Zapata 71, T 13-1270, special student and long-term rates, apartments, trailer park, swimming pool and squash courts.

Camping D *San Pablo* (aka *El Paraíso*), Highway 95, 9 km out of town, near the road, showers, friendly, US$8.50 for two in camper van; *Monasterio Benedito* on road to Tepoztlán, ½ hr by bus to the centre, very quiet, hot showers, rec, trailers/vehicles about US$15, coleman fuel, white gas available in Ocotepec, the village nearby.

Restaurants *Hacienda de Cortés*, (see above); *Las Mañanitas*, Ricardo Linares 107, beautiful but expensive, no credit cards accepted; with similar prices and also beautiful is *Casa de Campo*, Abasolo 101, Centro, T 182635/89, reservations required at weekends; *Harry's Grill*, on Hidalgo, excellent Mexican food, good food but high prices; *Andiamo*, on Zócalo,

Study Spanish where it's spoken!!!

CEMANAHUAC
EDUCATIONAL COMMUNITY

•**Intensive study of Spanish language at all ability levels**
•**Special summer programs for language and bilingual teachers**
•**Small groups (never more than 5 students) allow individualization**
•**Latin American Studies program, "Thought and Culture of Mexico"**
•**Field study, led by anthropologists, to historic/archeological sites**
•**Rural studies program in Mexican village available**
•**Housing program with Mexican families**
•**Begin any Monday, year-round program**

For information, call, write or fax:

Vivian B. Harvey, Educational Programs Coordinator
Cemanahuac Educational Community
Apartado 5-21
Cuernavaca, Morelos   MEXICO
Telephone (52-73) 18-6407 or 14-2988   Fax (52-73) 12-5418

good, foreigners meeting place, live Mexican music Wed 2000. There are other popular places on the Zócalo. *Marco Polo*, opp Cathedral, good, Italian, good pizzas, popular meeting place; rec for pizzas is *La Pizzería* on MA Camacho; *La Strada*, N side of Palacio de Cortés on stairway, good pizzas, moderate prices, closed Mon, nice atmosphere; *Casa de Gardenias*, opp Cortés' palace, open air, food at US$2 a dish; *Baalbek*, Netzahualcoyotl 300, gorgeous garden, best Lebanese food in town, expensive but worth it; *Vienés*, Lerdo de Tejada 4, German-Swiss food, very good; *Pollo y Más*, Juárez, decent, cheap, US$2 for *comida corrida*. *MacDonalds* on the Zócalo.

Bookshop Secondhand English books at Guild House, Calle Tuxtla Gutiérrez, Col Chipitlán, T 12-51-97.

Handicrafts Market Behind Cortés' palace on the main plaza, moderately priced and interesting silver, textiles and souvenirs.

Local Transport City buses cost US$0.30.

Language Schools There are about 12 Spanish courses on offer. These start from US$100 per week, plus US$60 registration at the *Centro de Lengua, Arte e Historia para Extranjeros* at the Universidad Autónoma del Estado de Morelos, Río Panuco 20, Col Lomas del Mirador, T 16-16-26 (accommodation with families can be arranged). Private schools charge US$100-150 a week, 5-6 hrs a day and some schools also have a US$50-75 registration fee. The peak time for tuition is summer: at other times it may be possible to arrive and negotiate a reduction of up to 25%. There is a co-operative language centre, *Cuauhnahuac*, with Spanish courses, at 1414 Av Morelos Sur, efficient, helpful, no credit cards, registration US$70, 6 hrs a day US$124/week, accommodation with families US$14/day (low season). *Center for Bilingual Multicultural Studies*, Apdo Postal 1520, T 17-10-87/17-24-88, F 17-05-33 or Los Angeles, LA, 213-851-3403; *Instituto Fénix*, Salto Chico 3, Col Tlaltenango, T 13-17-43, which also has excursions and minor courses in politics, art and music; *Cetlalic*, Apdo Postal 1-201, 62001 Cuernavaca, T 13-35-79, F 18-77-99, a non-profit organization teaching the Spanish language, plus Mexican and Central American history and culture; *Cemanahuac*, Calle San Juan 4, Las Palmas, claims high academic standards, field study, also weaving and pottery classes; *Experiencia*, which encompasses all these features, free 'intercambios' (Spanish-English practice sessions) Tues and Wed pm, Calle Leyva, Colonia Las Palmas; *Cidoc*, Av Río Balsas 14, Colonia Vista Hermosa; *Universal*, JH Preciado 332, Col San Anton, T 12-49-02 (Apdo Postal 1-1826), 3 levels of language course, tutorials and mini courses on culture; and *Idel*, Apdo 1271-1, Dr Manuel Mazari 100, Col Miraval, T and F 13-25-62, US$100 registration, 5 levels of course. Staying with a local family will be arranged by a school and costs US$12-20 a day incl meals; check with individual schools, as this difference in price may apply even if you stay with the same family. See also *National Registration Center for Study Abroad*, which represents three schools in Cuernavaca, under **Learning Spanish** in Information for Visitors.

Telephones Long-distance calls from booth at Av Salazar 1, on W side of the Zócalo; credit cards accepted, collect calls possible from public phones.

Tourist Office Av Morelos Sur 802, many maps. For cultural activities, go for information to the university building behind the Cathedral on Morelos Sur.

Railway Station at Calle Amacuzac; only passenger service is daily train to Iguala and Apipilulco.

SPANISH LANGUAGE SCHOOL SINCE 1972

Cuauhnahuac

Esc. C.I.C.L.C.

OFFERS: • Intensive Spanish classes • Maximum of 4 student per teacher • 6 hours per day, 5 days per week • Lodging with Mexican Families

• Excursions & other Cultural Activities • Classes begin every Monday

For more information contact: CUAUHNAHUAC, APDO 5-26, CUERNAVACA, MORELOS, 62051, MEXICO. Tel: (52-73) 12-36-73, 18-92-75, Fax: (52-73) 18-26-93

Or visit us at Morelos Sur 1414

Buses Each bus company has its own terminal; Estrella de Oro, Las Palmas y Morelos Sur; Pullman de Morelos on Plan de Ayala across from railway; Flecha Roja on Morelos y Arista (left luggage open 0700 to 2100 daily, US$0.25/hr per item); Estrella Roja, S of the centre, 1 block S of *Baalbek* restaurant; many minibuses and 2nd class buses leave from a terminal by the market. To **Mexico City** 0600-2200, every 10 mins, fares US$3.65 ordinary—to US$6 luxury (*ejecutiva*): Pullman de Morelos is said to be the most comfortable and fastest, from Southern Bus Terminus, Mexico City. Pullman de Morelos sometimes has a bus service to Mexico City Airport from Selva bus station. A taxi service, Aerotransporte Terrestre, runs from Mexico City Airport to Cuernavaca, service until 2130, takes 7 passengers, 1 hr, fare for 2 US$40.

To **Acapulco**, 6 hrs, Estrella de Oro, US$10. For advance tickets for Acapulco or other points on the Pacific Coast, be at Estrella de Oro office between 1645 and 1700, 2-3 days before you want to travel, this is when seats are released in Mexico City and full fare from Mexico City to the coast must be paid. To **Taxco**, Flecha Roja, 2nd-class buses, hourly on the half-hour, or Estrella de Oro, 1st class, US$3; to **Puebla**, Estrella Roja, US$5.75, 3½ hrs, fairly comfortable; **Cuautla** (p 252) either Estrella Roja every 20 mins, or 2nd class or minibus from market terminal, US$1.65, via Yautepec every hour, 1 hr, interesting trip; go there for long-distance buses going S (Puebla buses do not stop at Cuautla).

Warning Theft of luggage from waiting buses in Cuernavaca is rife; don't ever leave belongings unattended. It has also reported that ticket sellers are in league with thieves, who are told which buses will be a good target: travel in small groups, don't buy tickets in advance and if possible, get a Mexican to buy tickets for you. Robberies have been reported on the non-toll mountain road to Taxco.

Note to Drivers Cuernavaca to points W of Mexico City: on the toll road, 95D from Cuernavaca is a sign at Las Tres Marías to Toluca. Do not be tempted to take this route; it is well-surfaced but narrow over the pass before leading to the lakes at Zempoala, but thereafter it is almost impossible to navigate the backroads and villages to Toluca. Among the problems are livestock on the road, unsigned intersections, signposts to villages not marked on the Pemex atlas, heavy truck traffic, potholes, *topes* and congested village plazas. (Eric Mankin, Venice, CA.)

Excursions To the Chapultepec Park, W end of town, with boating facilities, small zoo, water gardens, small admission charge. To the suburb of Sumiya with a 200-year old Japanese villa, exquisite decor, must be seen (restaurant). To the potters' village of **San Antón**, perched above a waterfall, a little W of the town, where divers perform Sun for small donations. To the charming suburb of **Acapantzingo**, S of the town, another retreat of Maximilian. To **Tepoztlán**—24 km—at the foot of the spectacular **El Tepozteco national park**, wild view, with Tepozteco pyramid high up in the mountains (US$3, open anytime between 0900 and 1030 (officially 1000)-1630, the climb is an hour long, and strenuous, climb up before the sun is too high—the altitude at the top of the pyramid is 2,100m—but the view is magnificent). The town (pop 4,000) has picturesque steep cobbled streets, an outdoor market and a remarkable 16th century church and convent (entry US$0.45, site closes at 1630): the Virgin and Child stand upon a crescent moon above the elaborate plateresque portal, no tripod or flash allowed. Tepoztlán, formerly a 'hippy' hang-out, has become a centre for artists, 'eccentrics', fortune-tellers and witch doctors. There is a Sat/Sun arts and crafts market on the plaza with a good selection of handicrafts from Mexico, Guatemala and East Asia, expensive. There is a small archaeological museum behind the church. Every November, first week, there is an arts festival with films and concerts (open air and in the main church's cloister). This was the village studied by Robert Redfield and later by Oscar Lewis. Local bus from Cuernavaca market terminal, takes 1 hr, US$1; bus to Mexico City, US$3.35 1st class, US$3.65 *primera plus*, hourly.

Tepoztlán Hotels and Restaurants A *Posada del Tepozteco*, a very good inn, quiet, old fashioned, with swimming pool, excellent atmosphere and view; **B** *Hotel Tepoztlán*, largest hotel, towering over the village, grand pool, popular, crowded at weekends—as they all are; **D** *Mesón del Indio*, Av Revolución 44, no sign, Sr Lara, basic; **D** *Mexique*—*Casa Iccemanyan*, Familia Berlanga, Calle del Olvido 26, Casa Postal 65520, Tepoztlán, T (91-739) 50096 (C full board), 4 cabañas, swimming pool, clothes washing facilities, laundry,

restaurant, English, French and German spoken. Budget travellers would d
Cuernavaca. The restaurants are all overpriced but, near the plaza, are
vegetarian, and *Tapatía*, good food and pleasant view from 1st floor.

(Km 100) **Alpuyeca**, whose church has good Indian murals. A roa
runs to *Lago Tequesquitengo* (*Paraíso Ski Club*) and the lagoon a
baths of Tehuixtla. Near the lake a popular resort—swimming, boati   water
skiing and fishing—is *Hacienda Vista Hermosa* (A), Hernán Cortés' original
ingenio (sugar mill), and several lakeside hotels. E of the lake is **Jojutla**
(**D** *Hotel del Sur*, central, clean, simple; and others). Near Jojutla is the old Franciscan
convent of *Tlaquiltenango* (1540), frequent bus service from Cuernavaca. The
route through Jojutla can be used if coming from the coast heading for Cuautla
and wishing to avoid Cuernavaca. Enquire locally of road conditions off the major
highways.

From Alpuyeca also a road runs W for 50 km to the **Cacahuamilpa** caverns
(known locally as 'Las Grutas'); some of the largest caves in North America, open
1000 to 1700 (well lit, but take a torch nonetheless); strange stalactite and
stalagmite formations; steps lead down from near the entrance to the caverns to
the double opening in the mountainside far below, from which an underground
river emerges (entry, US$1, US$5 inc 1¼ hr guided tour, up to 1600—crowded
after 1100 and at weekends). Guided tours, take you 2 km inside; some excursions
have gone 6 km; the estimated maximum depth is 16 km. Don't miss the descent
to the river exits at the base of the cliff, called Dos Bocas, tranquil and
less-frequently visited.

Warning The disease *histoblastose* is present in the bat droppings in the cave (if you breathe
in the tiny fungus it can cause a tumour on the lungs); to avoid it you can buy a dentist's face
mask (*protección de dentista*) at a pharmacy.

Pullman de Morelos buses going to Cacahuamilpa from Cuernavaca leave every 20 mins
between 1000 and 1700 (1-2 hrs, US$2); they are usually overcrowded at weekends; enquire
about schedules for local buses or buses from Taxco to Toluca, which stop there (from Taxco,
30 km, 40 min).

At 15 km on the westerly road from Alpuyeca is the right-hand turn to the
Xochicalco ruins (36 km SW of Cuernavaca), topped by a pyramid on the peak
of a rocky hill, dedicated to the Plumed Serpent whose coils enfold the whole
building and enclose fine carvings which represent priests. The site is large: needs
2-3 hrs to see it properly (it closes at 1700).

Xochicalco was at its height between 650 and 900 AD. It is one of the oldest
known fortresses in Middle America and a religious centre as well as an important
trading point. The name means 'place of flowers' although now the hilltops are
barren. It was also the meeting place of northern and southern cultures and both
calendar systems were correlated here. The sides of the pyramid are faced with
andesite slabs, fitted invisibly without mortar. After the building was finished,
reliefs 3-4 inches deep were carried into the stone as a frieze. There are interesting
underground tunnels (open 1100-1400); one has a shaft to the sky and the centre
of the cave. There are also ball courts, an avenue 18.5m wide and 46m long,
remains of 20 large circles and of a palace and dwellings. Xochicalco is well worth
the 4 km walk from the bus stop (try hitching up the hill, there are occasional
colectivos, US$0.20, or taxis); take a torch for the underground part—if you do
not want a guide, entry US$4.35. To get to Xochicalco, take a bus from
Cuernavaca en route to El Rodeo, 2 km from the ruins (last bus back to Cuernavaca
at 1900); buses to Las Grutas/Cacahuamilpa (see above) or Ixtapan de la Sal pass
the turn-off; bus Cuernavaca-Alpuyeca (2 hrs, US$2), then Kombi to turn-off
US$0.60, then hitch or taxi (taxi from Alpuyeca US$4.50). Alpuyeca is also easily
reached from Taxco by bus.

From the toll road at Amacuzac (Km 121) an old road (39 km) runs to **Taxco** (pop
120,000), a colonial gem, with steep, twisting, cobbled streets and many

...uresque buildings. The first silver shipped to Spain came from the mines of Taxco. José de la Borda made and spent three fortunes here in the 18th century; he founded the present town and built the magnificent twin-towered, rose-coloured parish church of **Santa Prisca** which soars above everything but the mountains. Well worth a visit are the **Museum of the Viceroyalty** (formerly Casa Humboldt), where Baron von Humboldt once stayed, recently renovated with beautiful religious art exhibits, many from Santa Prisca, admission US$4.35, students US$1.75, open only Fri-Sun, and the **Casa Figueroa**, the 'House of Tears' (closed for restoration since June 1992), so called because the colonial judge who owned it forced Indian labourers to work on it to pay their fines. **Museo Guillermo Spratling**, behind Santa Prisca, is a museum of Mexican artifacts and Spratling's life, entry US$3.30. Large paintings about Mexican history at the Post Office. The roof of every building is of red tile, every nook or corner in the place is a picture, and even the cobblestone road surfaces have patterns woven in them. It is now a national monument and all modern building is forbidden. Gas stations are outside the city limits. The plaza is 1,700m above sea-level. A good view is had from the Iglesia de Guadalupe. There are superb views also from the *Teleférico* to Monte Taxco, US$3 one way (take photos on the way down), reached by microbus along the main street from Santa Prisca. The climate is ideal, never any high winds (for it is protected by huge mountains immediately to the N); never cold and never hot, but sometimes foggy. The processions during Holy Week are spectacular. The main central area is full of shops and shopping tourists; the district between the four-storey Mercado and the Carretera Nacional is quieter and free of tourists. Also quieter are those parts up from the main street where the taxis can't go. Wear flat rubber-soled shoes to avoid slithering over the cobbles. Silverwork is a speciality and there are important lead and zinc mines.

Vendors will bargain and cheap silver items can often be found. Beware of mistaking the cheapish pretty jewellery, *alpaca*, an alloy of copper, zinc and nickel, for the real stuff. By law, real silver, defined as 0.925 pure, must be stamped somewhere on the item with the number 925. The downtown shops in general give better value than those on the highway, but the best value is among the booth-holders in the Pasaje de Santa Prisca (from the Zócalo). On the 2nd Sunday in December there is a national silversmiths' competition. The colourful labyrinthine produce and general market beneath the Zócalo, is spectacular among Mexican markets; reasonable meals in the many *fondas*.

NB All silver jewellers must be government-registered. Remember to look for the 925 stamp and, if the piece is large enough, it will also be stamped with the crest of an eagle, and initials of the jeweller. Where the small size of the item does not permit this, a certificate will be provided instead.

One of the most interesting of Mexican stone-age cultures, the Mezcala or Chontal, is based on the State of Guerrero in which Taxco lies. Its remarkable artefacts, of which there are many imitations, are almost surrealist. The culture remained virtually intact into historic times.

There is much festivity in Semana Santa (Holy Week); at this time the price of accommodation rises steeply. At any time it is best to book a room in advance because hoteliers tend to quote inflated prices to those without reservations.

Hotels A+ *De la Borda*, on left as you enter Taxco, largest, all facilities, great views, T 20225, dearest and best; **A+** *La Cumbre Soñada*, 1.5 km or so towards Acapulco on a mountain top, colonial, exquisite; **A+** *La Hacienda del Solar*, Acapulco exit of town, T 20323, best restaurant in Taxco (*La Ventana*); **A+** *Rancho Taxco-Victoria*, Soto la Marina 15, walk to centre, fantastic view, good restaurant, rec; **A** *Posada de la Misión* Cerro de la Misión 32 (Mexico City—Cuernavaca buses stop outside), T 20063, F 22198, Juan O'Gorman mural, restaurant, good, pool, no a/c, quiet, rec; **B-C** *Los Arcos*, Juan Ruiz de Alarcón 2, T 21836, magnificently reconstructed 17th century ex-convent, charming, friendly, breakfast available, rooms overlooking street are noisy, otherwise rec; **B** *Posada Don Carlos*, Cerro de Bermeja

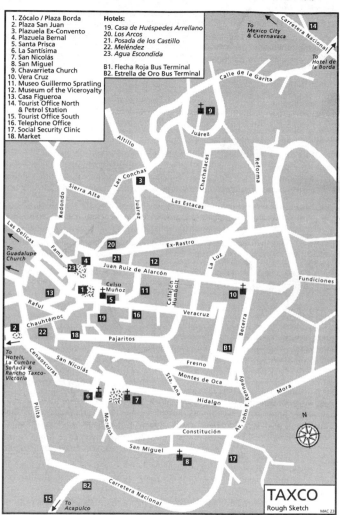

1. Zócalo / Plaza Borda
2. Plaza San Juan
3. Plazuela Ex-Convento
4. Plazuela Bernal
5. Santa Prisca
6. La Santísima
7. San Nicolás
8. San Miguel
9. Chavarrieta Church
10. Vera Cruz
11. Museo Guillermo Spratling
12. Museum of the Viceroyalty
13. Casa Figueroa
14. Tourist Office North
   & Petrol Station
15. Tourist Office South
16. Telephone Office
17. Social Security Clinic
18. Market

Hotels:
19. *Casa de Huéspedes Arrellano*
20. *Los Arcos*
21. *Posada de los Castillo*
22. *Meléndez*
23. *Agua Escondida*

B1. Flecha Roja Bus Terminal
B2. Estrella de Oro Bus Terminal

TAXCO
Rough Sketch

6, converted old mansion, restaurant, good view; **B** *Agua Escondida*, near Zócalo at Calle Guillermo Spratling 4, T 20726, with bath, nice view; **B** *Posada San Javier*, down a small street opp Municipalidad, clean, lovely garden, pool, excellent value; **C** *Meléndez*, T 20006, clean, somewhat noisy as it is near market, good breakfast, excellent good value lunch; **C** *Posada de los Castillos*, Alarcón 7, off main square, Mexican style, friendly, excellent value; **D** *Casa Grande*, Plazuela San Juan 7, T 20123, check bathrooms; **D** *Casa de Huéspedes Arellano*, Pajaritas 23, by Santa Prisca and Plaza Borda, with bath (E without), clean but basic, no single rooms, old beds, hot water; **D** *Posada Santa Anita*, John F Kennedy 106, T 20752, close to Flecha Roja buses, (certainly D in Holy Week), with hot shower and toilet, cheaper without, smelly, basic, overpriced, noisy at night, friendly; the cheapest hotels are in this area. **E** *El Jumil*, just-off Calle de la Garita, nr Tourist Office North, without bath, hot water, OK but noisy.

Restaurants Restaurants tend to be pricey. There are many places on the Zócalo: *Alarcón*, overlooking Zócalo, very good; *Sr Costilla*, next to church on main square, good drinks and grilled ribs; *Cielito Lindo*, on Zócalo, good food, service and atmosphere; next door is *Papa's Bar*, a discotheque and a small pizza place in an arcade; *Bora-Bora*, overlooks Zócalo, Guadalupe y Plaza Borda, good pizzas; *Pizzería Mario*, Plaza Borda, beautiful view over city, excellent pizzas, the first pizzeria in town, opened 30 years ago, highly rec; *La Hacienda*, Plaza Borda 4 (entrance is off the square), excellent, fair prices; *Mi Taverna* next to the Post Office, excellent Italian food, friendly; *Concha Nuestra*, Plazuela San Juan, food and music excellent; *Pozolería Betty*, Mora 20 (below bus station), good food including the local beetle (jumil) sauce. Many small restaurants just near *Hotel Meléndez*. Excellent *comida corrida* (US$6) at *Santa Fe*, opp *Hotel Santa Prisca* but disappointing *enchiladas*. Cheap *comida corrida* in market.

Post Office On Carretera Nacional about 100m E of Estrella de Oro bus terminal.

Buses Book onward tickets to Mexico City on arrival. (Taxis meet all buses and take you to any hotel, approx US$2.) Taxco is reached from **Mexico City** from the Central del Sur, Estrella de Oro, luxury US$10.65, *plus* US$8.65, non-stop, with video, 3 a day, 1st class US$7.65, only one stop in Cuernavaca, quick, no overcrowding, 3 a day (3 hrs); last bus back to Mexico City at 1800, but computerised booking allows seat selection in the capital, also five Flecha Roja, a day for US$7.50, up to 5 hrs. Buses to **Cuernavaca**; 1st class buses at 0900, 1600, 1800 and 2000 (Estrella de Oro), 2nd class about 5 a day, 2½ hrs (Flecha Roja), US$3 but can be erratic and crowded (watch out for pickpockets); buses en route to Mexico City drop passengers on the main highway, away from centre of Cuernavaca. Little 24-seaters, 'Los Burritos' (now called 'Combis'), take you up the hill from the bus terminal on main road, US$0.35, same fare anywhere in town. Spectacular journey from **Toluca**, missing out Mexico City, 2nd class buses only, from Flecha Roja Terminal, change at Toluca for Morelia. To **Acapulco**, Estrella de Oro, or Flecha Roja, US$11, 5 hrs.

If driving from Taxco to Oaxaca or beyond, go through Cuautla, not Cuernavaca which is a difficult city to negotiate.

Excursions Visit *Posada Don Carlos*, Bermeja 6, also Ventana de Taxco in *Hacienda del Solar* for view. 'Combi' to Panorámica every 30 mins from Plaza San Juan, US$0.20, or you can walk up the steep hill from Plaza San Juan for views of the hills and volcanoes. About 20 km out of Taxco a rodeo is held on Sat, guides available, admittance US$1.50. 12 km from Taxco to Acuitlapán waterfalls, with colectivo or Flecha Roja bus; hire a horse to travel down 4 km path to large clear pools for swimming. Taxis about US$7.50/hr. To **Cacahuamilpa** for caverns, 40 minutes, **see p 235.** Buses from 0820 but service erratic, US$1.65, or take a long white taxi marked 'Grutas' from opposite the bus station, US$3.50. Take an Ixtapan bus from Flecha Roja bus terminal, US$1.50, 1 hr, which passes the turn off to the site, 1 km downhill; Ixtapan-Taxco buses go to the site car park. Alternatively, to return, take bus coming from Toluca at junction, ½ km from the caves. Visit the villages where *amate* pictures are painted (on display at Museum of the Viceroyalty/Casa Humboldt and in the market). Xalitla is the most convenient as it is on the road to Acapulco, take 2nd class bus there. Other villages: Maxela, Ahuelicán, Ahuehuepán and San Juan, past Iguala and before the Río Balsa.

To reach the **Grutas de Juxtlahuaca** caves, drive to Petaquillas on the non-toll road then take a side road (paved, but poor in parts) through several villages to Colotlipa. Ask at the restaurant on the corner of the Zócalo for a guide to the caves. They can only be visited with a guide (3-hr tour US$60-80, popular at weekends for groups; if on your own, try for a discount). The limestone cavern has an intricate network of large halls and tunnels, stalagmites and stalactites, a few paintings and artefacts. Take a torch, food and drink and a sweater if going a long way in.

The road descends. The heat grows. We join the main road again at **Iguala**, 36 km beyond Taxco (**E** *Hotel Central*, basic; **E** *Pasajero*; bus to Taxco US$1, to

Mexico City from US$9.35 to US$15.35). Beyond the Mexcala river, the road passes for some 30 km through the dramatic canyon of Zopilote to reach **Chilpancingo** (pop 120,000, altitude 1,250m), capital of Guerrero state (population 1990 2,622,100), at Km 302. The colourful reed bags from the village of Chilapa are sold in the market (see below). The Casa de las Artesanías for Guerrero is on the right-hand side of the old main highway Mexico City—Acapulco. It has a particularly wide selection of lacquerware from Olinalá. Its *fiesta* starts on December 16 and lasts a fortnight. It has a University. Hotel: *La Posada Meléndez*, large rooms, helpful, swimming pool, cheap *comida corrida* in restaurant, rec; a cheap place is on Calle 5 de Mayo, about 5 blocks from Zócalo on left-hand side. Not far from Chilpancingo are Oxtotitlán and Juxtlahuaca, where Olmec cave paintings can be seen (see above for the latter). Buses Mexico City-Chilpancingo from US$11 to US$23.35 super luxury. **Chilapa** is accessible by several local buses and is worth a visit (about 1 hr journey). On Sunday there is an excellent craft market selling especially good quality and well-priced Olinala lacquer boxes as well as wood carvings, textiles, leather goods, etc.

The new section of 4-lane toll freeway runs from Iguala W of the old highway as far as Tierra Colorada, where it joins the existing 4-lane section to Acapulco. Chilpancingo is bypassed, but there is an exit. This is the third improvement: the first motor road was pushed over the ancient mule trail in 1927, giving Acapulco its first new lease of life in 100 years; when the road was paved and widened in 1954, Acapulco began to boom.

About 20 km from the coast, a branch road goes to the NW of Acapulco; this is a preferable route for car drivers because it avoids the city chaos. It goes to a point between Pie de la Cuesta and Coyuca, is signed, and has a drugs control point at the junction.

Warning Do not travel by car at night in Guerrero, even on the Mexico City-Acapulco highway and coastal highway. Always set out early to ensure that you reach your destination in daylight. Many military checkpoints on highway. *Guerrilleros* have been active in recent years, and there are also problems with highway robbers and stray animals.

Acapulco (population now thought to be over a million) is the most popular resort in Mexico, particularly in winter and spring. During Holy Week there is a flight from the capital every 3 mins. It does not fit everyone's idea of a tropical beach resort. The town stretches for 16 km in a series of bays and cliff coves and is invading the hills. The hotels, of which there are 250, are mostly perched high to catch the breeze, for between 1130 and 1630 the heat is sizzling; they are filled to overflowing in January and February. It has all the paraphernalia of a booming resort: smart shops, night clubs, red light district, golf club, touts and street vendors and now also air pollution. The famous beaches and expensive hotels are a different world from the littered streets, dirty hotels and crowded shops and buses which are only two minutes walk away. The Zócalo is lively in the evenings, but the surrounding streets are grimy. There are some twenty beaches, all with fine, golden sand; deckchairs on all beaches, US$0.50; parachute skiing in front of the larger hotels at US$12 for 5 mins. Every evening, except Monday, there is a water skiing display opposite Fuerte de San Diego. The two most popular are the sickle-curved and shielded Caleta, with its smooth water and now dirty sands, and the surf-pounded straight beach of Los Hornos. Swimmers should look out for motor boats close in shore. Take local bus to Pie de la Cuesta, 12 km, now preferred by many budget travellers to Acapulco itself, but also commercialized. There are several bungalow-hotels and trailer parks (see below), lagoon (6-hr boat trip US$10), now used for laundry, and big beaches (warning: the surf is dangerous on the beach W of the road and the beaches are unsafe at night). At Pie de la Cuesta you drink *coco loco*—fortified coconut milk—and watch the sunset from a hammock. One can swim, and fish, the year round. Best free map of Acapulco can be obtained from the desk clerk at *Tortuga Hotel*.

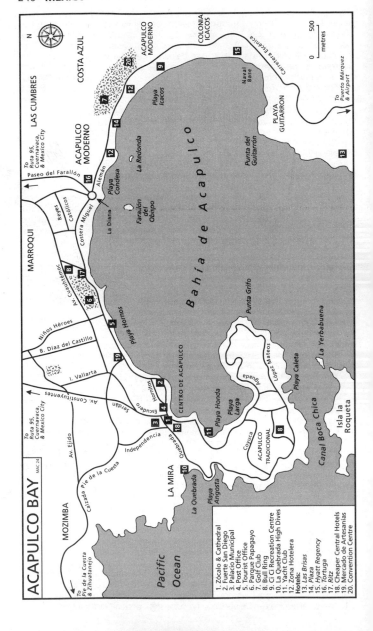

ACAPULCO BAY

MAC 24

Pacific Ocean

MOZIMBA

LA MIRA

La Quebrada

Playa Angosta

Calzada Pie de la Cuesta

To Pie de la Cuesta & Zihuatanejo

Av. Ejido

To Ruta 95, Cuernavaca, & Mexico City

Av. Constituyentes

I. Vallarta

B. Díaz del Castillo

Niños Héroes

Av. Cuauhtémoc

MARROQUI

Reyes Católicos

Paseo del Farallón

To Ruta 95, Cuernavaca, & Mexico City

LAS CUMBRES

COSTA AZUL

ACAPULCO MODERNO

ACAPULCO MODERNO

COLONIA ICACOS

Costera Miguel Alemán

Independencia

Quebrada

Serdán

Escudero

Hornitos

Playa Hormos

CENTRO DE ACAPULCO

ACAPULCO TRADICIONAL

Coyuca

Playa Honda

Playa Larga

Ipeneby

López Mateos

Covuca

ACAPULCO TRADICIONAL

Playa Caleta

La Yerbabuena

Isla la Roqueta

Canal Boca Chica

Punta Grifo

Bahía de Acapulco

Playa Condesa

La Redonda

La Diana

Farallón del Obispo

Punta del Guitarrón

Playa Guitarrón

PLAYA GUITARRON

Naval Base

Playa Icacos

Carretera Escénica

To Puerto Márquez & Airport

N

0   500
metres

Hotels:
1. Zócalo & Cathedral
2. Fuerte San Diego
3. Palacio Municipal
4. Post Office
5. Tourist Office
6. Parque Papagayo
7. Golf Club
8. Bull Ring
9. Ci Ci Recreation Centre
10. La Quebrada High Dives
11. Yacht Club
12. Zona Hotelera

Hotels:
13. Las Brisas
14. Plaza
15. Hyatt Regency
16. Ritz
17. Tortuga
18. Cheaper Central Hotels
19. Mercado de Artesanías
20. Convention Centre

Acapulco in colonial times was the terminal for the Manila convoy. Its main defence, Fuerte de San Diego, where the last battle for Mexican independence was fought, in the middle of the city and is worth a visit. (Open 1000-1800, Tues and Sun only, free admission.)

Hotels can cost up to US$200 a night double; cheaper for longer stays, but this also means less expensive hotels insist on a double rate even for 1 person and for a minimum period. In the off-season (May-November) you can negotiate lower prices even for a single for one night, but you are unlikely to find anything under US$12 for a double. For cheap hotels in Acapulco you can make reservations at the bus terminal in Mexico City; similarly, at the 1st class bus station in Acapulco you can arrange hotel packages, eg 3 nights in 4 star accommodation for US$60. Hotel recommendations, and reservations, made at the bus terminal, often turn out to be dingy downtown hotels. If seeking a hotel in the D or C range, go to the *Ritz*, at Costera Miguel Alemán y Magallanes, or the *Playa Doral*, on Hornos beach, and use either as a base for exploring the hotels in surrounding streets.

The fabulous **L+** *Club Residencial de las Brisas*, a hotel where the services match the astronomical price. (It begins at sea-level and reaches up the mountain slope in a series of detached villas and public rooms to a point 300m above sea-level. Each room has own or shared swimming pool. Guests use pink jeeps to travel to the dining-room and recreation areas.) **L** *Villa Vera Raquet Club*, luxurious celebrity spot, T 40333; **A+-L+** *Acapulco Plaza*, Costera 123, T 59050, 3 towers, 2 pools, 5 bars, 4 restaurants, a city in itself; *Hyatt Regency*, next to naval base, Av Costera M Alemán 1, T 42888, F 43087; **A+** *Acapulco Tortuga* (T 48889), and **A+** *Romano's Le Club* (T 45332), both on Costera, many groups; **A+** *Caleta*, Playa Caleta, T 39940, remodelled; **A+** *Condesa del Mar*, Costera at Condesa beach, T 42828, all facilities; **A+** *Elcano*, Costera near golf club, T 41950; **A+** *Maralisa*, Enrique El Esclavo, T 40976, smallish and elegant, Arab style, rec; **A+** *Maris*, Alemán y Magallanes, T 42800, very good; **B** *Casa Blanca Tropical*, Cerro de la Pinzona, T 21217, with swimming pool, is rec; **A** *Acapulco Imperial*, Costera 251, T 41865; **A** *Diana*, street beside Costera M Alemán, a/c, clean, quiet, pool. The *Acapulco Princess Country Club*, part of the *Acapulco Princess*, 20 km away on Revolcadero beach, is highly fashionable, delightful resort, all facilities, taxi to town US$10; **B** *Costa Linda*, Costera Miguel Alemán 12, T 22549, near Yacht Club, a/c; **B** *do Brasil*, Costera Miguel Alemán on Hornos beach, shower, TV, all rooms with sea view balcony, pool, restaurant, bar, travel agency, friendly, rec; **B** *Playa Doral*, Hornos beach, a/c, pool, ask for front upper floors with balcony, good value; **B** *Posada del Sol*, clean, friendly, on the beach, pool, good food, Playa del Coco opp new convention centre, T 41010; *Playa Hornos*, Calz Pie de la Cuesta, T 33940, clean, friendly; **B** *Villa Lucía*, built around pretty swimming pool, with kitchens in rooms, mostly frequented by Mexicans, a/c, one block from sea and one block from *Ritz* (see above), acceptable; *Boca Chica*, Playa Caletillo, T 32835, on promontory opp island, pool, clean, direct access to bathing, free drinking water on each floor; **B** *Club Majestic*, nr Yacht Club and above city (a little hard to find), quiet, reasonable, good views; **C** *Vacaciones*, Costera Alemán 63, T 21637, Caleta, good value. **C** *El Cid*, Hornos beach, T 51024, clean, pool, rec; **C** *Jungla*, Miguel Alemán 86, T 20255; opposite *Costa Linda* is **D** *Casa de Huéspedes Johnny*, hammocks on porch, etc, OK; **D** *San Francisco*, Costera 219, T 20045, old part of town, friendly, good value, noisy in front.

Most cheaper hotels are grouped around the Zócalo, especially Calles La Paz and Juárez; about 15 mins from the 2nd class bus station (Flecha Roja) on Av Cuauhtémoc. **C** *Acuario*, Azueta 11, T 21784, popular; **C** *Añorve*, Juárez 17, T 22093, 2 blocks off Zócalo, clean, with bath, front rooms better than back; opp *Añorve* is *Mama Helène*, who owns two hotels in same price range, and offers laundry service, US$5; **C** *Fiesta*, clean and nice, with bath, fan, 2 blocks NW from Zócalo, Azueta 16, T 20019; **C** *Misión*, Felipe Valle 12, T 23643, very clean, colonial, close to Zócalo; **D** *California*, La Paz 12, T 22893, 1½ blocks W of Zócalo, good value, fan, hot water, pleasant rooms and patio; **D** *Casa García*, clean, cold shower, clean but very basic, 3 blocks SW of Zócalo; **D** *Colimense*, JM Iglesias II, off Zócalo, T 22890, pleasant, limited parking; **D** *Isabel*, La Paz y Valle, T 22191, with fan, rec, near Zócalo; **D** *Lucía*, López Mateos 33, T 20441, family-owned, will negotiate if not full, good value; **D** *Sacramento*, E Carranza y Valle, with bath and fan, no towel, soap or loo paper, friendly, noisy, OK, purified water, T 20821; **D** *Santa Cecilia*, Francisco Madero 7, off Zócalo, with bath and fan, noisy, but otherwise fine; **E** *La Posada*, Tte Azueta 8, nr Zócalo, with bath, more expensive in high season; **F** *Chamizal*, López Mateos 32, close to Zócalo, shower, good.

Many cheap hotels on La Quebrada, basic but clean with fan and bathroom, including **D** *El Faro* (No 63, T 21365, clean); **D** *Casa de Huéspedes Aries* (with bath, nice); **E** *Corral* (No 56, T 20756, good value); **E** *Sagamar* (No 51), with bath, basic, friendly, some English spoken, use mosquito coil; **E** *Biarritz*, 3 blocks from Flecha Roja terminal, 2 from beach, for more than one night, central, fan, shower, pool; **D** *Betty*, Belisario Domínguez 4, T 35092, 5 mins from bus station, with bath, fan, short stay, dirty, not rec; just around corner on same street is **E** *Alberto*, much better. Turn left at *Betty* for several cheap *casas de huéspedes*.

Several nice places at Pie de la Cuesta, D, in clean rooms with shower: **C** *Villa Nirvana*, Pie de la Cuesta, Canadian/Mexican owners, (depending on season) with kitchen, pool, good value, rec; *Puesta del Sol*, expensive places for hammocks; **D** *Quinta Dora Trailer Park*, for hammock, managed by American, helpful.

The student organization Setej offers dormitory accommodation, D, if one has a valid international student card, at Centro Vacacional, Pie de la Cuesta, 0700-2400. For longer (1 month plus) stays, try *Amueblados Etel*, Av la Pinzona 92 (near Quebrada) for self-catering apartments, cheap off-season (before November); **C** *Apartamentos Maraback*, Costera M Alemán. The Tourist Bureau is helpful in finding a hotel in any price range.

Motels B *Impala*, *Bali-Hai*, *Mónaco*, *Playa Suave*, all along the Costera; **B** *Ofelia*, *Victoria*, Cristóbal Colón, 1 block behind Costera.

Camping *Trailer Park El Coloso*, in La Sabana, small swimming pool, and *Trailer Park La Roca* on road from Puerto Márquez to La Sabana, both secure. *Estacionamiento Juanita* and *Quinta Dora* at Pie de la Cuesta (latter is 13 km up the coast on Highway 200, palapas, bathrooms, cold showers, hook-ups, US$12 for 2 plus car, US$4 just to sling hammock), *Quinta Carla*, *Casa Blanca*, *U Kae Kim*, all US$50 a week upwards, but negotiable.

Restaurants There are a number of variously-priced restaurants along and opposite Condesa beach, including *Embarcadero* on the Costera, Thai/Mexican/US food, extraordinary decor with waterfalls, bridges, bamboo huts and 'a hall of mirrors on the way to the loo', expensive but worth it for the atmosphere; many cheap restaurants cluster in the blocks surrounding the Zócalo, especially along Juárez; for example, *Nacho's*, very popular, excellent prawns; *El Amigo Miguel*, *San Carlos*, Juárez (near Zócalo), fixed menu lunch, good; opp is *100% Natural*, mostly vegetarian, other branches on Costera Miguel Alemán, and up the hill from the yacht club. By La Diana roundabout is *Pizza Hut*, reliable, with 'blissful air conditioning'; *Italianissimo*, nearby, decent pizza and garlic bread, average price for area; *El Zorrito*, opp *Ritz Hotel*, excellent local food with live music, average prices, reputedly popular with Julio Iglesias when he is in town. The *cafetería* at the SE corner of the Zócalo serves good coffee. Another group along the Caleta beach walkway; yet another group of mixed prices on the Costera opp the *Acapulco Plaza Hotel*. 250 or so to select from.

Night Clubs There are dozens of discos including *Discotheca Safari*, Av Costera, free entry, 1 drink obligatory, good ambience; every major hotel has at least one disco plus bars. Superb varied night-life always.

City Transport Taxis US$9 an hour; sample fare: Zócalo to Condesa Beach US$3.65. Several bus routes, with one running the full length of Costera Miguel Alemán linking the older part of town to the latest hotels, marked 'Caleta-Zócalo-Base', US$0.50, another operating to Caleta beach. Buses to Pie de la Cuesta, 12 km, US$0.50. Bus stops on the main thoroughfare are numbered, so find out which one you need. Many buses along the beach front may turn off at right angles; read the destination boards carefully.

British Consul (Honorary) Mr DB Gore, MBE, *Hotel Las Brisas*, T (91-748) 46605. **Canadian Consul**, *Hotel Club del Sol*, Costera Miguel Alemán, T 56621.

Laundromat *Tintorería Bik*, 5 de Mayo.

Telephones Public offices will not take collect calls; try from a big hotel (ask around—there will be a surcharge).

Post Office Costera, 2 blocks S of Zócalo.

Tourist Information Costera Miguel Alemán at Hornos beach, helpful, but double-check details; useful free magazines, *Aca-Sun* and *Acapulco guide*. Also at 'Flechas' bus station, very helpful, will make hotel bookings, but not in cheapest range.

Buses Mexico City, 406 km, 8 hrs; de luxe air-conditioned express buses (*futura*), US$28.35 and super luxury US$36.65; ordinary bus, US$21.65 1st and US$25.65 *plus*, all-day services from Estación Central de Autobuses del Sur by the Taxqueña metro station, Mexico City, with Estrella de Oro (10 a day, one stop) or Flecha Roja (part of Líneas Unidas del Sur, hourly). 1st class bus depot at Av Cuauhtémoc 1490, T 26450. Taxi to Zócalo, US$5.50; bus, US$0.50. To **Cuernavaca**, with Estrella de Oro, 6 hrs, US$10. To **Oaxaca**, 402 km: 6 hrs on main road, 264 km, 6 hrs on good road through mountains by bus, change at Pinotepa Nacional after 3 hrs. Several 1st class buses, Estrella de Oro, 5 hrs, and Flecha Rosa buses a day to **Taxco** US$11. Bus to **Puerto Escondido** every hour on the half-hour from 0430-1630, plus 2300, 2400, 0200 and *directo* at 1330 and 2300, US$20, 8½ hrs, seats bookable, advisable to do so the day before, 7½ hrs, many check points; Flecha Roja, Transportes Gacela (US$15.65). To

Tapachula: take Impala 1st class bus to Huatulco, arriving 1930; from there Cristóbal Colón at 2030 to Salina Cruz, arriving about midnight, then take 1st or 2nd class bus.

Air Services Airport 26 km from Acapulco. Direct connections with New York, Chicago, Dallas, Houston, Los Angeles and other US cities, by Mexican and US carriers. Cancún, 4 hrs 20 mins, via Mexico City; Mérida, via Mexico City, at least 3 1/2 hrs. Mexico City, 50 mins. AeroMéxico and Mexicana offices in Torre Acapulco, Miguel Alemán 1252, Mexicana T 846890, AeroMéxico T 847009. Flights to Mexico City are worth booking at least a week in advance, especially in high season. Transportaciónes de Pasajeros Aeropuerto taxi service charge return trip (*viaje redondo*) when you buy a ticket, so keep it and call 24 hrs in advance for a taxi, US$11. Airport bus takes 1 hr, US$3.35 and *does* exist (ticket office outside terminal)!

Excursions Daily, amazing 40-metre dives into shallow (polluted) water by boys can be watched from the Quebrada (US$1.70, 4 times a day, the first at 1230, the last, with torches, at 2130). The lagoons can be explored by motor boats; one, **Coyuca Lagoon**, is over 110 km long (38 km N of Acapulco); strange birds, water hyacinths, tropical flowers. 2 hotels at Coyuca: **E** *Imperial*, off the main square, *El Provincial*. There is a *jai-alai* palace. At Playa Icacos there is a marineland amusement park *Ci-Ci*, with a waterslide, pool with wave-machine and arena with performing dolphins and sea-lions, US$5.70 for whole day (nothing special). Pleasant boat trip across beach to Puerto Marqués, US$2 return (or 1/2 hr by bus); one can hire small sailing boats there, US$12 an hr. Bay cruises, 2 1/2 hrs, from Muelle Yates, US$5, at 1100, 1630 and 2230. Visit island of La Roqueta, glass-bottomed boat, US$3 return, 2 hrs; once on the island follow the path which goes over the hill towards the other side of the island (towards the right) where there is a small, secluded and usually empty bay (about 15 mins walk). Parachute sailing (towed by motor boats), US$12 for a few minutes, several operators. There is an Aqua Marine museum on a little island (Yerbabuena) off Caleta beach, with sharks, piranhas, eels, stingrays in an aquarium, swimming pool with water-chute, and breezy bar above, entry US$7.

Coast NW of Acapulco

Between Acapulco and Zihuatanejo are Coyuca de Benítez, a lagoon with little islands 38 km from Acapulco, also a market town selling exotic fruit, cheap hats and shoes. Pelicans fly by the lagoons, there are passing dolphins and plentiful sardines, and young boys seek turtle eggs. 1 1/2 km beyond Coyuca is a turn-off to *El Carrizal* (7 1/2 km), a village of some 2,000 people, a little paradise with a beautiful beach (many pelicans) with a steep drop-off (unsafe for children), dangerous waves and sharks behind them; good restaurant (opposite *Hotel-Bungalows El Carrizal*) which has 6 rooms with bath and toilet, E, closes early (1800 for food), poor food, not very clean; more basic; **E** *Aida*, friendly, rec, but little privacy, Mexican food (good fish). Shops will change dollars (eg Doña Joaquina's shoe shop, the video shop), and long-distance phone calls can be made from the *farmacia*. Frequent VW minibuses from Acapulco or Pie de la Cuesta, US$0.55. If driving, take Route 200, direction Zihuatanejo. If heading towards Mexico City, it is better to go via Acapulco, from where there is a new, fast toll-road to Chilpancingo, than via Ciudad Altamirano, **see p 246**. Highway 200, between Tecomán and Acapulco, has many badly potholed stretches.

A couple of km SE of El Carrizal is *El Morro* on an unpaved road between the ocean and the lagoon: the waves on the ocean side are very strong, while swimming in the lagoon is excellent. El Morro is a small fishing village (carp) reminiscent of African townships as it is constructed entirely of *palapa* (palm-leaf and wood). Every other house is a 'fish-restaurant'; ask for bungalow rental (F), no running water but there is a toilet, mosquito nets on requests. One shop sells basic provisions; fruit and vegetables from Coyuca may be available. At El Morro you can rent a canoe for US$2/hr and sail down river, past El Carrizal; you can also go up river to the lagoon, an all day trip, very beautiful with plenty of birdlife.

Minibuses run Coyuca-El Carrizal-El Morro. *San Jerónimo*, 83 km from Acapulco, has an 18th century parish church, you can make canoe trips up river to restaurants; *Tecpan de Galeana*, 108 km from Acapulco, is a fishing village. 10 km N of Tecpan is a turn-off to another El Carrizal, which is 7 km from the Pacific Highway. There is some public transport from Tecpan, but plenty of cars go there (the road is rough). Very little accommodation, but plenty of hammock space; there is a beautiful beach and lagoon and the place is very friendly. There is a beach further on at *Cayaquitos* where a series of small rivers join the ocean and there is a large variety of birds and dense vegetation; three restaurants offer fish dishes, there is a reasonable modern hotel, *Club Papánoa*, with lovely views, and a camping site; and one can also visit the lovely bay of Papanóa.

Zihuatanejo (pop 22,000), is a beautiful fishing port and expensive, commercialized tourist resort 237 km NW of Acapulco by the paved Route 200, which continues via Barra de Navidad along the Pacific coast to Puerto Vallarta (**see p 134**); 1st class bus from Acapulco, 4 hrs. (This road goes through coconut plantations where you can buy *tuba*, a drink made from coconut milk fermented on the tree, only slightly alcoholic.) Despite being spruced up, 'Zihua', as it is called locally, still retains much of its Mexican village charm. There are about ten square blocks of cobbled alleys, an Indian handicraft market by the church, some beachside cafés and a small Museo Arqueológico, in the old Customs and Immigration building on Av 5 de Mayo. At sunset thousands of swallows meet in the air above the local cinema in the centre of town and settle for the night within one minute on the telephone poles. The *plaza de toros* at the town entrance with seasonal *corridas*. The yacht, *Fandango Zihua*, takes bay cruises from the municipal pier. There are 5 beaches in the bay, including Playa de la Madera, near town and a bit dirty; better is Playa de la Ropa, 20 min walk from centre, with the *Sotavento* and other hotels, and some beach restaurants. Also good is Las Gatas beach, secluded, a haven for aquatic sports and can be reached by boat from the centre (US$2 return) or a 20-min walk from La Ropa beach over fishermen-frequented rocks (the boat is much safer, muggings on the path have occurred). Watch out for coconuts falling off the trees! Off the coast there are rock formations, to which divers go, and Isla Ixtapa, a nature reserve with numerous restaurants. Difficult to find accommodation in March, and around Christmas/New Year.

Hotels L+ *Villa del Sol*, Playa La Ropa, T 42239, F 4758, Apartado 84, no children under 12 in high season, very expensive but highly regarded; *Fiesta Mexicana*, Playa La Ropa, T 43776, F 43738, a/c, satellite TV, fine views, pool, restaurant, bar; A+ *Catalina* and *Sotavento*, Playa la Ropa, T 42032, F 42975, 105 steps to hotel, same facilities; B *Las Uraccas*, Playa La Ropa, T 42049, cooking facilities, good value; A+ *Irma* (Playa la Madera), T 42025, F 43738, good hotel but not best location; B *Bungalows Pacíficos*, T 42112, highly rec, advance reservation necessary; B *Palacios* (T 42055, good), on Playa de la Madera. Several other hotels along Playa Madera, try A *Villas Miramar*, T 42106, F 42149, suites, pool, lovely gardens, rec. Central hotels: B *Avila*, Juan N Alvarez 8, T 42010, a/c, phone; C *Posada Citlali*, Vicente Guerrero 3, T 42043; C *Zihuatanejo Centro*, Agustín Ramírez 2, T 42669, bright rooms, a/c, rec; D *Las Tres Marías*, Calle La Noria 4, T 42191 (take a boat across canal, US$0.20, or cross the wooden footbridge) very pleasant with large communal balconies overlooking town and harbour, clean but sparely decorated, tiny baths, nice plants, hotel has an annex on Calle Juan Alvarez 52, part of restaurant, similar rooms and tariffs, best on 2nd floor, both rec for budget travellers (note that price doubles during Christmas holidays); D-E *Casa Elvira* hotel-restaurant, Paseo del Pescador 16, T 42061, in older part of town on waterfront, very basic but clean, noisy from 0730, fan, share bath, the restaurant is on the beach front (*the* place to watch the world go by), good and reasonable; D-E *Casa La Playa*, similar to *Elvira*, but not as good; D-E *Casa Aurora* (N Bravo 27, clean with bath and fan, not all rooms have hot water), and D-E *Casa Bravo*, T 42528; C *Imelda*, Catalina González 11, T 43199, clean, rec, no restaurant.

Youth Hostel, Av Paseo de las Salinas s/n, CP 40880, T 44662.

Restaurants On Playa la Ropa: *La Perla* (very popular, good food, slow service), *Elvira* (by

Hotel Sotavento, small, good value) and *Rossy* (good, live music at weekends). In Zihuatanejo: many including *El Patío*, excellent food and atmosphere, beautiful patio/garden, live music occasionally; *Il Piccolo*, restaurant and video bar, excellent value, good pizzas; *Gitano's*, *Coconuts* (good atmosphere, pricey, dinner only, rec), *La Marina* (popular, rec). *Puntarenas*, close to *Hotel Las Tres Marías*, excellent cooking, friendly, not expensive, popular, slow service. *Stall 27* at marketplace is very popular, cheap and good. Try local lobster for about US$10; most meals cost US$6 or over.

Car Hire Hertz, N Bravo and airport, T 43050 or F 42255; also with offices at the airport and in Ixtapa hotels: **Avis, Budget, Dollar, Economy.**

Scuba Diving Hire of all equipment and guide from Zihuatanejo Scuba Center, T 42147, English spoken. Off Playa de las Gatas is an underwater wall built, according to legend, by the Tarascan king Calzonzin, to keep the sharks away while he bathed; the wall is fairly massive and can be seen clearly while scuba diving. Many fish too. US$3 a day for mask, snorkel and flippers.

Exchange Banca Serfín will change travellers' cheques at lower commission than in banks in hotel district; **Banamex; Bancomer.** Good rates at **Mario's** leather shop; several *casas de cambio.*

Addresses Immigration, T 42795; Customs at airport, T 43262; Red Cross (ambulances), T 42009; Police, T 42040; Ministerio Público (to report a crime), T 42900; Tourist Office and Complaints, see under Ixtapa, below.

Buses and Roads Estrella de Oro operates its own terminal on Paseo Palmar, serving Zihuatanejo, Acapulco and **Mexico City**; to the capital 0830, 1130, 1930 (with stops), US$24.20, direct (no stops) at 2000; 'Diamante' (wider seats, movie, stewardesses serving free drinks) non-stop 2100, arriving 0600, US$50; *plus* (wider seats, non-stop) 2200 arriving 0700, US$33. To **Lázaro Cárdenas** at 0600, 1500 and 1900, US$3.65. Direct to **Acapulco** 0600, US$8, *plus* at 1630.

The Central de Autobuses is on the Zihuatanejo-Acapulco highway opp Pemex station; 3 lines operate from here, all using good, 32-seater buses. The terminal is clean, with several snackbars. Estrella Blanca: to Mexico City almost hourly from 0600-2130, US$24.20; to Lázaro Cárdenas daily, for connections further N and to the interior, US$4; to Acapulco US$9; to **Laredo** at 1730, 30 hrs, US$65. Blancas Fronterea to Mexico City 2100 or 2200, US$33 (direct); to Acapulco 0100, 0900 and 1700, US$10.65; to Lázaro Cárdenas 4 a day, US$4.75; to **Puerto Escondido** and **Huatulco**, 2130, US$34. Cuauhtémoc serves all towns between Zihuatanejo and Acapulco almost half-hourly from 0400 to 2000. The old Central de Autobuses is half a block from the new; old buses use it, with erratic service to Mexico City via the less-used dangerous road through Altamirano (to be avoided if possible, robberies).

By road from Mexico City via the Toluca-Zihuatanejo highway (430 km) or via the Acapulco-Zihuatanejo highway (405 km). To Acapulco can be done in 4 hrs, but usually takes 6 hrs. To Lázaro Cárdenas, 103 km, takes 3$^{1}/_{2}$ hrs, the road is very bad.

Airport Ixtapa/Zihuatanejo international airport, 19 km from town, T 42070/42100. Many flights from Mexico City and others from Guadalajara and, in the USA, Los Angeles and Minneapolis. Other destinations via Mexico City. AeroMéxico, T 42018/32208/09; Delta (airport), T 43386/686; Mexicana, *Hotel Dorado Pacífico*, Ixtapa, T 32208-10.

From Zihuatanejo one can drive 7 km or take a bus (US$0.50) or taxi (US$5, colectivo, US$1) to *Ixtapa*, 'where there are salt lakes' (pop 32,000). The resort, developed on a large scale, boasts 14 beaches: La Hermosa, Del Palmar, Don Juan de Dios, Don Juan, Don Rodrigo, Cuata, Quieta, Oliveiro, Linda, Larga, Carey, Pequeña, Cuachalate and Varadero. There are turtles, many species of shellfish and fish, and pelicans at El Morro de los Pericos, which can be seen by launch. There is an island a few metres off Quietas beach; boats go over at a cost of US$5. Ixtapa has ten large luxury hotels and a Club Méditerranée (all obtain food-supplies from Mexico City making food more expensive, as local supplies aren't guaranteed); a shopping complex, golf course, water-ski/parachute skiing and tennis courts. There are a yacht marina and an 18-hole golf club, Palma Real. Isla Grande has been developed as a nature park and leisure resort. **NB** The beach can be dangerous (strong undertow—small children should not be allowed in the sea unaccompanied). Also, there are crocodiles in the beautiful lagoons at the end of the beach.

Hotels All in **L-A** range: *Westin Resort Ixtapa*, T 32121, F 31091, spectacular, in a small jungle; **Krystal** (highly rec, book in advance, T 30333, F 30216), **Dorado Pacífico** (T 32025, F 30126), **Sheraton** (Blvd Ixtapa, T 31858, F 32438), with panoramic lift, A+, reductions for AAA members, rec, **Stouffer Presidente**, T (753) 30018, F 32312; **Aristos** (T 31505, the first to open in Ixtapa); **A+ Best Western Posada Real**, next to *Carlos and Charlie's Restaurant*, T 31745, F 31805; **Fontan Ixtapa** (T 30003); **Holiday Inn SunSpree Resort**, Blvd Ixtapa, T 800-09346, F 31991. Taxi between centre and main hotels, US$3.

Camping *Playa Linda Trailer Park*, on Carretera Playa Linda at *Playa Linda Hotel*, just N of Ixtapa, 50 spaces, full hook-ups, restaurant, recreation hall, baby sitters, on beach, US$14 for 2, comfortable.

Restaurants Besides those in every hotel, there are many others, including **Villa de la Selva** (rec for food and views, book in advance, T 30362), **El Sombrero** (Mexican, very good), **Montmartre** (French), **Onyx**, **Bogart's** (opp *Hotel Krystal*), **Gran Tapa**, all more costly than in Zihuatanejo.

Nightclubs Every hotel without exception has at least one night club/disco and two bars.

Tourist Office In Ixtapa Shopping Plaza, T 31967/68.

Note for motorists Although paved Highway 134 leads directly from Mexico City and Toluca to Ixtapa, there is no fuel or other supplies after **Ciudad Altamirano** (188 km, pleasant motel on SW edge of city, C with a/c). This road also runs through remote country, prone to landslides, and there is occasional bandit activity, with unpredictable army check-points (looking for guns and drugs). It is not recommended for non-Spanish speaking, or lone motorists.

The coastal route continues NW to Lázaro Cárdenas and Playa Azul in Michoacán (**see p 155**).

Coast E of Acapulco

Highway 200, E from Acapulco along the coast, is paved all the way to Puerto Escondido; the stretch is known as the Costa Chica (there is a bridge missing about 55 km from Acapulco, near Playa Barra Vieja on the road along the coast, take the inland road to San Marcos and Sabana Grande). This road, which is windy, hilly and with few services and little traffic, has been reported dangerous due to bandit hold ups of lone cars, check locally before driving this route.

Some 100 km from Acapulco is **Morcelia**, with excellent beaches about 3 km from town (transport well nigh impossible); there are no hotels, but you can spend the night in a hammock in one of the little restaurants on the beach. The restaurant owners will look after luggage, but keep an eye on it anyway. There is no charge, but you should eat at the restaurant that provides the hammock space; very good seafood, about US$3 per meal. Bus to Puerto Escondido US$7.35, 5-6 hrs, very full coming from Acapulco.

'From **Pinotepa Nacional** (**D** *Hotel Carmona*, restaurant, good value but poor laundry service, parking; **D** *Massiel*; **E** *Tropical*, fan, clean, large rooms, quiet, parking), you can visit the Mixtec Indian village of **Pinotepa de Don Luis** by *camioneta*. These leave from the side street next to the church in Pinotepa Nacional, taking a dirt road to Don Luis (last one back to Pinotepa Nacional at 1300, or wait till next morning, nowhere to stay). The women there weave beautiful and increasingly rare sarong-like skirts (*chay-ay*), some of which are dyed from the purple of sea snails. Also, half-gourds incised with various designs and used both as caps and cups can be found. The *ferias* of Don Luis (20 January) and nearby San Juan Colorado (29-30 November) are worth attending for the dancing and availability of handicrafts.' (Dale Bricker, Seattle)

Puerto Escondido, 144 km E of Pinotepa Nacional, is on a beautiful bay almost due S of Oaxaca (population 25,000) very touristy, good surfing. Palm trees line the beach, which is not too clean. The expansion of the SE end of town, 'to make it the next Acapulco' (in the words of one developer) is well-advanced. Many visitors are disappointed by the high costs and the commercialization in the main part of the town. There are, however, a number of beaches to visit and villages close by. Next to the Bahía Principal is Playa Marinero, with small bars, restaurants and handicrafts market. Further SE is Zicatela, good for surfing. 2 km W of the centre is Puerto Angelito, recommended by locals as a safe and clean beach. Launches take passengers from the bay in Puerto Escondido, US$3.50 pp for max 10, or taxi US$2. At Manzanillo, with a small creek, is a coral reef and tropical fish; access to the beach on foot only. 15 mins by taxi or bus to the W is Manialtepec, with a lagoon, wild birds and watersports such as water skiing; the village has rivers and hot springs. Villages inland include San Pedro and San Gabriel Mixtepec on the direct road to Oaxaca and, just off this road, Santa Catarina Juquila, with a sanctuary.

NB   There can be dangerous waves, and the cross-currents are always dangerous; non-swimmers should not bathe except in the bay on which the town stands. Also, a breeze off the sea makes the sun seem less strong than it is—be careful. Do not stray too far along the beach; armed robbery by groups of 3-5 is becoming more and more frequent, even in daylight, take as little cash and valuables as possible, US$ sought after. Also at La Barra beach 10 km away. Be alert for dogs.

Hotels   Very crowded during Holy Week; prices rise on 1 November because of the local Fiesta de Noviembre. Most hotels are on the beach, little air-conditioning. Many cheaper hotels have no hot water and cheap *cabañas* are often full of mosquitoes.

   A+ *Best Western Posada Real* (ex-*Bugambilias*), T 20133, F 20192, about 2½ km from town, off road to Acapulco, very pleasant, lovely gardens, pool, path to beach, attentive, a/c, good service, food included (à la carte, also lobster); **A** *Paraíso Escondido*, Unión 1, T 20444, noisy a/c, not on beach (up the hill almost all the way to the Grucero) but with own swimming pool, management cool, but rec, clean, colonial style, in summer when not full bar and restaurant open according to demand; **B** *Bungalows Barlovento*, very comfortable, highly rec, but a little way out of town and not advisable to walk there at night; **B** *El Rincón del Pacífico*, Pérez Gasca 900, T 20056, very popular, always full, on beach, with restaurant, hot water; **B** *Loren*, Pérez Gasca 507, T 20448, clean, friendly, safe, rec; **B** *Nayar*, Pérez Gasca 407, T 20113, big rooms, views, some with bath and fan, more expensive with a/c, no hot water, restaurant, not rec; **B** *Hotel Santa Fe*, Carretera Costera, on beach at N end of bay, restaurant expensive but very good food; **B** *Cabañas Zikatela*, on Zicatela beach, a bit further down from the *Arco Iris*, large clean rooms with fan and mini-fridge, swimming pool, bar service, small restaurant serving breakfast and cheese burgers; **C** *Casa Blanca*, Pérez Gasca, middle of beach, with fan and hot water, clean and well-furnished, balconies, pool; **C** *Margot's*, 30m S of the pedestrian zone in the centre, nice big rooms, good, cheap food, not very friendly; **C** *Rocamar*, Pérez Gasca 601, T 20339, by beach, upper rooms a/c and balconies, fans, hot water, restaurant, rec. **D** *Alderete*, opp bus station, with private bath; **D** *Art and Harry's*, on oceanfront, free board use, great barbecues, good food; **D** *Bungalows Villa Marinero*, on beach, a bit run down, own cooking possible, friendly, restaurant a little dear but good; **D** *Cabañas San Diego*, down a sand road just before bridge on road to Puerto Angel, safe, nice grounds but few facilities; **D** *Central*, 2 minutes uphill from bus terminal, clean, friendly; **D** *La Posada Económica*, one big dormitory, attached to restaurant, but also runs hotel across the road, ask for a room opp the flat, good *huachinango*; **D** *Real del Mar*, nr bus station (cheaper for longer stays), bath, clean, nice view; **D** *Ribera del Mar*, behind Iglesia de la Soledad, uphill, fan, quiet, no hot water, laundry facilities, rec; **D** *San Juan*, downhill from bus station, some rooms with seaview, no English spoken, fair. **E** *Alojamiento Las Cabañas* has dormitories with bunks, on main road (S side), friendly, very nice, food is good, you will be charged for all beds regardless of whether they are occupied, unless you share the cabin; *Cabañas Cocoa Beach*, in the town near the church, US$4.50 per cabin (6 or 7 available), mosquito nets, cold shower, family-run; **E** *Cabañas Cortés*, for small, basic huts or large, basic huts—in all cases, take mosquito nets; **E** *Casa de Huéspedes Las Dos Costas*, fairly clean, acceptable for budget travellers. Lots of bungalows and *cabañas* at S end of the beach.

Apartments   *La Maison*, Andador Puerto Juárez C, Lomas de Puerto, Box 243, Puerto Escondido, Oax 71980, F (010-52) 958-20612 'para entregar a Pierre', 1 room (shared kitchen and patio), 3 apartments for 2, 3 and 5 people, with kitchen, all with bath, hot water, rates from US$180 for 2 to US$480 for 5 per week, high season (Christmas/New Year, Easter and 15 July to 31 August), low season US$130-370, reductions for long stays.

Camping   If camping, beware of clothes being stolen. *Carrizalillo Trailer Park*, near old airport on W side of town (follow signs from Tourist Office), on cliff top with path leading down to secluded beach, bathroom, cold showers, laundry facilities, swimming pool and bar, very pleasant, prices from US$8 to US$20 for 2 plus car depending on location and whether you have hook-up. *Neptuno* campsite for vehicles, tents and hammocks on water front in centre of town, vehicles and tents accepted, swimming pool, electricity, cold showers, US$10 per car with 2 people, rather rundown and noisy; next door is *Las Palmas* (better), about US$10 for 2 plus car. *Hotel Playa Azul* has a constricted trailer park (not very convenient for large vehicles), access from a side road, has a good swimming pool.

Restaurants Many restaurants on main street, Pérez Gasca, eg: *Lolys*, cheap and good, try *pescado a la parrilla*, with sweet onion sauce, and lemon pie after; *San Angel* for fish; *La Estancia*, good but expensive; *La Sardino de Plata*, popular; *Lisa's Restaurant*, nice location on beach (just off Carretera Costera) good food, also has rooms to let, D off season, with fan, very clean, safe deposit, highly rec; *Los Crotos*, also on the beach, good and varied food at reasonable prices, good service, rec. The vegetarian restaurant in front of *Farmacia La Moderna* (see below) is not good. *Cappuccino*, Pérez Gasca, good coffee, fruit salads, some dishes pricey. Good *licuados* at *Bambú Loco*, also fish. *Las Palapas*, good, it is just over the stream (sewer) on the right. *Pepe's*, great sandwiches. *Alicia*, in town, best value but be careful with seafood. Food is good quality, but very expensive near the beach.

Shopping Small selection of foreign language books at *Papi's*, souvenir shop 3 doors from Mercado de Artesanías, buy or swap. Local crafts best not bought from vendors on the beach, but in the non-gringo part of town up the hill near where the buses stop.

Discos *Tequila Bum-Bum* (pronounced Boom-Boom), downtown, international crowd, varied music, open air; *Bacocho*, popular with locals, Mexican pop, indoors.

Banks Bancomer, Pérez Gasca, open 0900-1200, slow service, US$2 commission on each cheque; *Banpeco*, open 0900-1330. *Casa de cambio*, on Pérez Gasca, open till 2000, poor rates.

Health Dr Francisco Serrano Severiano, opp Banpeco, speaks English, 0900-1300, 1700-2000. *Farmacia La Moderna*, Av Pérez Gasca 203, T 20214, open 24 hrs.

Transport It is best to go from Oaxaca to Puerto Escondido by the road to Puerto Angel, turning off at Pochutla (see below). Bus drivers on the paved route have a radio for checking road conditions. The direct highway to Oaxaca is being upgraded. Don't take a stopping bus to Oaxaca on the direct road as robberies have been reported. Bus to **Oaxaca**, 3 a day (including overnight), US$11.50 1st class, US$18.75 *plus* with Trans Oaxaca-Pacífico (direct), advertised as 7 hr trip, but can take up to 17 hrs; also Estrella del Valle (1st class, from 2nd class terminal); Auto Transportes Oaxaca-Pacífico, via Pochutla, 10-18 hrs (depending on roadworks)—leaves at 0700, 2nd class, 2300 1st class; all have bookable seats. Puerto Escondido-**Pochutla**, for Puerto Angel, several hourly from 0500 to 2000, about 1 hr, US$2.50, and on to **Salina Cruz**, Oaxaca-Pacífico company rec. The road to Salina Cruz is now paved (bus US$9.75, about 7 a day, 10 hrs). Bus to **Acapulco**, US$15.65, Flecha Roja (near La Solteca terminal), at least 7½ hrs, not exciting. The 1030 bus stops for 2 hrs' lunch at Pinotepa, book tickets at least one day in advance. First bus to Acapulco at 0400, hourly up to 2100 thereafter. Transportes Gacela run 3 direct buses a day to Acapulco at 1030, 1330 and 2300, only 2 short stops. The road is in bad condition. To/from **Mexico City** US$38.35 1st class, US$40.35 *plus*. To **Tehuantepec**, go to Salina Cruz and change there; two direct buses a day to San **Cristóbal de las Casas**, US$21.

Flights Airport 10 minutes drive from town, orange juice and coffee sold. Puerto Escondido-Mexico City, with Mexicana 5 days a week, non-stop. Puerto Escondido-Oaxaca, see under Oaxaca **Air Services**. Taxis to centre in VW combis, US$2.25 pp, Colectivos Combi, T 20030.

Also S of Oaxaca (240 km, paved road, but many curves) is **Puerto Angel**, a coffee port on the Pacific with a good, safe and popular beach , 69 km from Puerto Escondido, with road connection but no direct buses; all services involve change at Pochutla; transport details given below. It is 8 hrs by bus from Oaxaca, see under Oaxaca **Buses**. Just before Puerto Angel, a dirt road leads left to some small bays which have no people, are good for snorkelling, but can have dangerous waves.

In Puerto Angel take care of your belongings, but, more important, take extra care in the sea, the currents are very dangerous. The sea water is said to be polluted from animals on the beach, 'immediate stomach problems' reported.

Fiesta 1 October.

Hotels Luxury hotel on a hill away from the beach, **D** *Angel del Mar*, fan, clean, friendly, helpful, good view, rec; **D** *Buena Vista*, nice rooms up hill, clean, relaxing; **D** *Cabaña*, near the *Cañón de Vata*, fan, free coffee in morning, friendly owner, no restaurant, rec; **D** *El Rincón*

Sabroso, beautiful views, clean, quiet, friendly, no hot water; **D** *Hotel Soraya*, fan, bath, very clean (changes dollars and TCs); **E** *Anahi*, on road to *Angel del Mar*, with fan, Indonesian-style wash basins; **E** *Casa de Huéspedes Gladys*, just above *Soraya*, balcony, fine views, clean, rec, owner can prepare food, no hot water; **D** *Casa de Huéspedes Gundi* (Gundi and Tomás López), without bath, clean, or hammocks (G), popular with travellers, will store luggage, good value, snacks and breakfast (US1.50-3), sells food and beverages, rec; Gundi also runs **Pensión El Almendro**, with café (good ice cream) and library. Similar is the **E** *Pensión Puesta del Sol*, run by Harald and Maria Faerber (suite D), very friendly, English and German spoken, restaurant, on road to Playa Panteón, clean, rec; **E** *San Juan*, with bath, good view, pleasant; for *cabañas* and hammock places ask at *Susanna's Restaurant* (Susana y Mateo, Apartado Postal 74, Pochutla) near the football pitch, Playa Panteón; *Noah's Arc*, at the end of the beach, for the 'flower-powered'; hammocks at **F** *Gustavos*; **D** *Posada Cañón de Vata*, on Playa Panteón, Apartado Postal 74, Pochutla 70900, nice, very clean, lovely setting, booked continuously, quite good restaurant, mainly vegetarian. Possible to sleep on beach away from the naval base and soldiers who will move you on. Good restaurant *Capis* (has 10 rooms above). *Beto's* restaurant, just up hill on road to Zipolite, 5 mins walk from centre, good fish (tuna) and cheap beer; *Ma Bell* restaurant, good and cheap; *Cabaña de Ferdinand* on the main street, good food and very friendly owner; *Two in One* restaurant on Cementerio beach is a great place to eat and drink, Many fish restaurants along the main street. *Estacahuite*, a beautiful, clean beach, 1 km from town, 20 mins walk, has cabins (beware of jelly fish on the beach). There is a hut at the beach selling beer and fries, and it lends snorkelling gear.

Camping There is a new campsite half way between Puerto Angel and Pochutla, very friendly, driveway is too steep for large vehicles, US$8.50 for two in camper van, rec.

Services Long distance phone next to *Soraya*; for post office, go to Customs office; for other services go to Pochutla (eg exchange).

Four km W (30 mins walk) is **Zipolite** beach (name means 'the killing beach', according to legend, one drowning a month). It is dangerous for bathing if you swim behind the waves or when the tide changes. It may be the last nude beach in Mexico (only at the far end), but do not walk to the beach at night, packs of dogs have attacked people. It has much less of a Mexican atmosphere than Puerto Angel, but is very popular with travellers. Bus service from Pochutla to Zipolite every 20 mins from 0600 to 1830, last bus back from Zipolite to Pochutla at 1900, US$0.70; fare to Puerto Angel US$0.35. Buses stop on the paved road behind the beach just after the 'Zipolite/Playa de los Muertos' sign. Taxi Puerto Angel-Zipolite, US$3.50 pp for any amount of passengers; to Pochutla US$5 (add US$3.50 to be taken to your *cabaña* door).

Accommodation and food Places to stay are usually either basic or overpriced. Hammock spot and vegetarian restaurant *Shambhala* run by Gloria, an American woman, very friendly, best on the beach ($\frac{1}{2}$ hr walk to far end coming from Puerto Angel), very fresh food, F pp with hammock or US$10; *Lo Cósmico*, just before *Shambhala*, *cabañas* and very good crêpes, open all year; hammocks for rent from Philippe at 'Gloria end' of the beach, US$1; also at 'Gloria end', *Cristóbal Cabañas*, family run, clean, good meals, E for room, F basic *cabaña*, US$1.65 for hammock, shared bathrooms; **E** *Cabañas El Tao*, 'rooms with a view', clean, friendly, shared bath, expensive breakfast; *Cabañas Montebello*, next to *La Puesta* bar, with hammocks, quiet and very clean, run by Luis and María; *Hamacas La Choza*, on way to *Shambhala*, with restaurant, family atmosphere, hammocks to rent for under US$2 per night, luggage store. *Restaurant Genesis*, 3rd on beach, ask for rooms, E, clean, charming, helpful, good meals (ask for house on the hill). There is a campsite suitable for tents only, water and bathroom: follow paved road, then unpaved road for 1 km, then small road to the left. RVs can stay overnight in the parking lot, but no facilities. Every hut on the beach is a fish restaurant with cold drinks and hammock space, US$2 pp but lots of mosquitoes. There are a couple of informal discos. At the E end of the beach is *Lola's*, excellent food; good pizzas at *Gemini Pizzas*; there is a good *Panadería* on the road behind the beach, through the green gate.

Several km further up the coast is San Agustín beach, accessible by a path behind Shambhala (ask directions), beautiful, safe for swimming, with an extraordinary cave in the cliffs. Accommodation is now available. About 15 km from Zipolite on a dirt road is a sign to Ventanilla beach; follow the rough track until you find a thatched ranch and ask for Hilario Reyes. The beach is long and empty and there are 2 lagoons with fresh water. There are no cabins: you need your own tent (or hammock/ mosquito net). Ventanilla beach is also dangerous for bathing.

You can go to Salina Cruz from Puerto Angel via Pochutla: take bus or taxi to **Pochutla** and catch hourly bus to Salina Cruz (US$5, 4 hrs), to which a new road is finished (occasionally closed by landslides). Pochutla-Puerto Angel, same regular service as for Zipolite, above; alternatively take a colectivo, about US$4 for up to 6, bargain hard and beware of taxi rip-offs. Pochutla-Oaxaca, either direct, on a paved, winding road (a safer route than Puerto Escondido-Oaxaca) from 0500-2300, 6½-9 hrs, US$18 (Estrella del Valle, 1st class), 1st class not always available, 2nd class US$8.25, 7 hrs (Oaxaca-Pacífico); San José del Pacífico is a pleasant stop on the way, with good restaurant; or via Salina Cruz, US$13.25, 8 hrs (2nd class cheaper). The bus service between Pochutla and Puerto Escondido (US$2.50, several every hour from 0500 to 2000) links with the bus to Puerto Angel. Bus Pochutla-San Cristóbal de las Casas at 1000 and 2200, 12-15 hrs, 1st class (Cristóbal Colón, US$19, bus starts at Puerto Escondido so very few seats available in Pochutla, book in advance if possible), goes via Huatulco, Salina Cruz, Tehuantepec and Tuxtla Gutiérrez; to Acapulco at 2200 direct, 1st class, 12 hrs, US$20. At Pochutla there is a prison; you can buy black coral necklaces made by prisoners very cheaply (but remember that black coral is an endangered species); they make and sell other handicrafts. Take vitamins or other useful small items to trade or give away. Leave documents and valuables outside (an 'interesting, eye-opening, if noisy, shopping trip'). A **Costa del Sol**, on main street near the market, with a/c, C with ceiling fan, credit cards, bar, restaurant; **D** *Hotel Ipsala*, on main street behind plaza, shower, fan, clean comfortable. Excellent ice cream factory.

Services in Pochutla Exchange: Bancomer, only 0930-1100, exchanges AmEx and Visa travellers' cheques; **Banamex** handles AmEx and Mastercard. Also a **post office**. Snorkel equipment can be bought in Pochutla.

Health There is a hospital outside Pochutla, US$2 for a consultation, medicines free. There is also a private doctor in Puerto Angel, but he charges US$17 minimum for a consultation, and it is hard to find him home.

E of Puerto Angel (50 km, 1 hr) and 112 km W of Salina Cruz, on the coast road, is the new resort of **Huatulco** being built on about 34,000 hectares around nine bays. Some estimate that it will surpass Cancún by the year 2000. Population in 1992 was 15,000, and growing as more hotels and businesses spring up. Santa María Huatulco, near the airport, is now the town for the construction workers, while Santa Cruz Huatulco, the original village, is destined to become an 'authentic Mexican village' for the tourists. There are 3 separate areas of development: Zona Hotelera on Tangolunda Bay, with 4 luxury hotels, **Sheraton**, L (T 958-10055, F 10335), **Royal Maeva**, **Holiday Inn Crowne Plaza**, Blvd Benito Juárez 8, T 928-10044, F 958-10221, and the **Club Méditerranée** (5-star, reservations are cheaper when made at head office in Calle Masaryk, Mexico City). Near Santa Cruz Bay are a hotel, 3 banks, a tourist market and boats for hire. The third area is Crucecita, downtown, with 5 hotels, all C, all within one block W of Plaza Principal (**Suites Bugambilias**, T 70018, rec, clean). There are 18 restaurants, some overpriced, and many *comedores*. **Palma Real**, opp Cristóbal Colón bus terminal, rec. There are also a number of shopping centres around Plaza La Crucecita, with *artesanías* and boutiques. *Colectivos*, US$0.20, and taxis connect the three areas. The nearest beach to Crucecita is Chahue Bay, about 3 km, dangerous undertow, better to go to the Zona Hotelera, about 6 km, which has a good beach. Other beaches are accessible by car or boat. There is a trailer park at Chahue (bathrooms, snackbar, but sites are quite stark). *Lanchas* can be hired from Cooperativa Tangolunda for exploring the coves, US$10/day. Guided tours of the Bahías de Huatulco from the major hotels or from Agencia de Viajes García Rendón, Av Alfonso Pérez Gasca, Puerto Escondido, T 20114. Tourist office is on Av Guamuchl. Three bus companies: Gacela has direct buses to Acapulco at 0815 and 1315, and to Puerto Escondido at 1015. Several buses to Salina Cruz. The airport (Bahías de Huatulco) is open with daily, non-stop flights from Mexico City and Oaxaca with Mexicana (T 32208, airport 42805), and daily from Mexico City with AeroMéxico (T 10336).

Great care is to be taken to blend the resort into the landscape: about 80% of the total area is to be set aside as a nature reserve. The name means 'place of the wood', which refers to a cross planted on the beach, legend tells, by Quetzalcóatl. After resisting efforts to pull it down, it was found to be only a few feet deep when dug up; small crosses were made from it. A more likely history of the cross is told by Michael Turner in his research into Francis Drake's voyages. Until the establishment of Acapulco as the departure point for the Spanish Pacific fleet, Huatulco (Guatulco) was the main port on the Pacific, its heyday being from about 1537 to 1574. Drake sacked the port on his voyage around the world (1577-80) and Thomas Cavendish raided it in 1587. Cavendish burnt the church to the ground, but the crucifix (La Santa Cruz) survived, thereafter being incorporated into the village's name. The Spanish viceroy ordered Huatulco's abandonment in 1616.

MEXICO CITY TO GUATEMALA (9)

Out of a number of routes, we describe that through Oaxaca, a popular tourist town with many fine colonial buildings, markets, Indian traditions and, close by, several magnificent archaeological sites (Monte Albán, Mitla, and others). From Oaxaca, there is a coastal route to Guatemala and the more interesting Chiapas highland route. The main town of interest on the latter is San Cristóbal de Las Casas, which gives access to Maya villages, archaeological sites and lakes.

The National Railway runs daily from Mexico City to Tapachula. Taxi to Talismán, on the Guatemalan border, for bus to Guatemala City (also accessible from Puebla). There is a new bridge which links Ciudad Hidalgo with Tecún-Umán (formerly Ayutla) in Guatemala. Cristóbal Colón bus Mexico City-Guatemala City takes 23 hrs, with a change at the border to Rutas Lima. Mexico City-Tapachula, 20 hrs.

Note Motorists who know the area well advise that anyone driving from Mexico City to Tehuantepec should go via Orizaba-La Tinaja-Papaloapan-Tuxtepec-Palomares. This route is better than Veracruz-Acayucán and, if drivers are in a hurry, far preferable to the route which follows, via Izúcar de Matamoros and Oaxaca. Between Oaxaca and Tehuantepec the road, although paved throughout and in good condition, serpentines unendingly over the Sierras and is quite beautiful. But as the Oaxaca route is far more interesting and spectacular we describe it below. For the alternative journey through the Papaloapan region, see p 220.

Tolls Total road toll Mexico City—Oaxaca, US$8.35.

This road through southern Mexico is 1,355 km long. It can be done in 3 or 4 days' driving time. There are bus services from Mexico City along the route through Oaxaca to Tehuantepec and on to the Guatemalan frontier through San Cristóbal de Las Casas to Ciudad Cuauhtémoc or through Arriaga to Tapachula. A road now runs (still rough in places) from Paso Hondo near Ciudad Cuauhtémoc via Comalapa and Porvenir to Huixtla on the S road, and from Porvenir to Revolución Mexicana.

From Cuernavaca to Oaxaca: take Route 160 via Yantepec to the semi-tropical town of *Cuautla* (94,000 people), with a popular sulphur spring (known as *aguas hediondas* or stinking waters) and bath, a crowded week-end resort for the capital. Tourist Cuautla is divided from locals' Cuautla by a wide river, and the locals have the best bargain: it is worth crossing the stream. The plaza is pleasant, traffic-free and well maintained. There is a market in the narrow streets and alleyways around 5 de Mayo. The tourist office is opp *Hotel Cuautla*, on Av Obregón, satisfactory.

Hotels and Restaurants **C** *Jardín de Cuautla*, Dos de Mayo 94, opp Colón bus station, modern, clean, but bad traffic noise, pool; one block from *Jardín de Cuautla* is **C** *Colonial*, modern, pool; **D** *Hotel Colón* in Cuautla is on the main square, good, clean; *Hotel-restaurante Valencia*, 4 blocks N of Cristóbal Colón terminal; **E** *Hotel España*, Dos de Mayo 22, very good, clean, rec; **D** *Hotel Madrid*, Los Bravos 27. **Youth Hostel**, Unidad Deportiva, T 20218, CP 60040. Try the delicious *lacroyas* and *gorditas*, tortillas filled with beans and cheese. 4 good restaurants in main square, all serving cheap *comidas*; good restaurant at *Hotel Granada*, Defensa de Aguas 34. 11 km from Cuautla, on road to Cuernavaca is the **A+** *Hacienda de Cocoyoc*, an old converted *hacienda* with a swimming pool backed by the mill aqueduct. Glorious gardens, 18-hole golf-course, tennis and riding, but isolated, Amex not accepted, reservations at Centro Comercial El Relox, Local 44, Insurgentes Sur 2374, México 01000 DF, T 550-7331.

Buses from Mexico City to **Cuautla** from Central del Oriente. Buses from Cuautla at Cristóbal Colón terminal, 5 de Mayo and Zavala, to **Mexico City** hourly US$3.65 1st class, US$4.65 *plus*; Estrella Roja 1st class, 2nd class buses or minibuses to **Cuernavaca** at least hourly, 1 hr, US$1.65; to **Oaxaca**, US$14.80, five Cristóbal Colón buses per day (1st class 0800 and 1300), 7-8 hrs, also ADO, most overnight and en route from Mexico City so book ahead, also try Fletes y Pasajes 2nd class buses, or change twice, at Izúcar de Matamoros and Huajuapan. A road leads to Amecameca (p 204).

From Cuautla, the interesting Olmec sanctuary of *Chalcatzingo* can be reached. It has an altar, a pyramid and rock carvings, one of which depicts a procession of warriors led by a prisoner with a beard and horned helmet (a Viking, some say), others depict battles between jaguars and men. To get there take Route 140 SE, direction Izúcar de Matamoros; at Amayuca turn right towards Tepalcingo. 2 km down this road turn left towards Jonacatepec and it's 5 km to the village of Chalcatzingo (take a guide). There are buses from Puebla to Amayuca. A taxi from Amayuca costs US$5. Near Jonacatepec are the ruins of Las Pilas. Some 7 km further down the road to Tepalcingo is Atotonilco where there is a *balneario* for swimming (bus from Cuautla). (We are grateful to Helmut Zettl of Ebergassing for much of this information.)

After Cuautla take Route 160 with long descent and then ascent to *Izúcar de Matamoros*, 58,000 people (**C** *Premier*, on Zócalo, new in 1993; **D** *Hotel Ocampo*, next to bus station; **E** *Las Fuentes*, bath and hot water, clean, quiet, TV, courtyard, rec), famous for its clay handicrafts, 16th-century convent of Santo Domingo, and two nearby spas, Los Amatitlanes (about 6 km away) and Ojo de Carbón. A side road leads from Izúcar to *Axochiapan* (Morelos state; **E** *Hotel Primavera*, bath, hot water, clean, tiny room), leading to a paved road to the village of *Jolalpan* with the baroque church of Santa María (1553). Very few restaurants in Jolalpan; ask where meals ae to be had. Bus from Axochiapan stops in front of the church in Jolalpan. The road (and bus) continues to Atenango del Río in Guerrero state, the last 20-30 km unpaved.

Route 190 heads N from Izúcar to Puebla via Huaquechula (16th-century renaissance-cum-plateresque chapel) and *Atlixco* ('the place lying on the water'), with interesting baroque examples in the Capilla de la Tercera Orden de San Agustín and San Juan de Dios. There is an annual festival, the Atlixcayotl, on San Miguel hill (**E** *Hotel Colonial* behind parish church, shared bath; nearby—20 mins—are the curative springs of Axocopán). Thence to Acatepec (p 207) and, 30 km, Puebla.

OAXACA MAC 25

Not to Scale

1. Zócalo
2. Paseo Juárez
3. Jardín Conzatti
4. Cathedral
5. Santo Domingo
6. La Soledad
7. San Felipe Neri
8. San Juan de Dios
9. San Agustín
10. Regional Museum
11. Rufino Tamayo Museum
12. Teatro Macedonio Alcalá
13. Tourist Office
14. Federal Tourist Office
15. Post Office
16. Mercado de Abastos
17. Mercado Artesanal
18. Benito Juárez Market
19. Mercado 20 de Noviembre
20. Arcos de Xochimilco
21. Alameda de León
22. Monument to Juárez
23. Guelaguetza Stadium

Hotels:
24. Señorial
25. Mesón del Rey
26. Francia
27. Monte Albán
28. Central
29. Santo Tomás
30. Vallarta
31. Virreyes
32. Principal
33. Nacional
34. Mesón del Angel

B1. 1st Class Bus Station
B2. 2nd Class Bus Station

excellent collection with a good library (free, but donation appreciated). At Alcalá 202 is **Museo de Arte Contemporáneo**, good exhibition with library, also free but donation appreciated. **Museo Rufino Tamayo**, Av Morelos 503, has a very good display of precolumbian artefacts dating from 1250 BC to AD 1100 (1000-1400, 1600-1900, Sun 1000-1500, closed Tues); entry for US$4.35. **Teatro Macedonio Alcalá**, 5 de Mayo with Independencia, beautifully restored theatre from Porfirio Díaz' time (closed or restoration in February 1994). Visit also the Street of the Little Arches (Arcos Xochimilco—on García Vigil, some 10 block N of the Zócalo), a picturesque, narrow, cobbled street with archways along the sides. There is a grand view from the amphitheatre on the Cerro de Fortín. The monument to Juárez is in the valley below. The house of the Maza family, for whom Bénito Juárez worked and whose daughter he married, still stands at Independencia 1306 (a plaque marks it). Similarly, a plaque marks the birthplace of Porfirio Díaz at the other end of Independencia, in a building which is now a kindergarten, near La Soledad. DH Lawrence wrote parts of 'Mornings in Mexico' here, and revised 'The Plumed Serpent'; the house he rented is in Pino Suárez, a block S of the Llano (the main park), NE corner. There is an observatory and planetarium on the hill NW of the town, two shows each evening, entrance US$0.20.

Specialities: black earthenware, tooled leather, blankets, ponchos, shawls, embroidered blouses, the drink *mescal*. The best *mescal* in the region is El Minero. *Mescal* sours are good at the bar of *Misión Los Angeles*. The poor man's drink is *pulque*. Local *sarapes* are more varied and cheaper than in Mexico City.

The Zapotec language is used by over 300,000 people in the State as a first or second language (about 20% of Oaxaca State population speaks only an Indian language). The Zapotec Indians, who weave fantastic toys of grass, have a dance, the *Jarabe Tlacolula Zandunga* danced by barefooted girls splendid in most becoming coifs, short, brightly coloured skirts and ribbons and long lace petticoats, while the men, all in white with gay handkerchiefs, dance opposite them with their hands behind their backs. Only women—from Tehuantepec or Juchitán—dance the slow and stately *Zandunga*, costumes gorgeously embroidered on velvet blouse, full skirts with white pleated and starched lace ruffles and *huipil*.

Festivals Los Lunes del Cerro, on the first two Mondays after 16 July (the first is the more spontaneous, when Indian groups come to a hill outside the city to present the seven regional dances of the State in a great festival, also known as La Guelaguetza). Upper seats (rings C and D) free, ring B US$23, ring A US$35, be there 1½ hrs in advance to get a good seat, tickets from Tourist Office. After each dance the dancers exchange presents and throw gifts to the audience in ring A. Hotels get booked early for the Guelaguetza and for the Day of the Dead, as does transport to Oaxaca on the days beforehand. El Señor del Rayo, a nine-day event in the third week of October, including excellent fireworks. 2 Nov, the Day of the Dead, is a mixture of festivity and solemn commemoration, best appreciated at the Panteón General; the decoration of family altars is carried to competitive extremes (competition in Calle 5 de Mayo between Santo Domingo and the Zócalo on 1 Nov); traditional wares and foods, representing skulls, skeletons, coffins etc are sold in the market. Also celebrated more traditionally, in the outlying villages, especially in the cemetery of Acotlán. Ask before photographing. 8 to 18 Dec with fine processions centred around the Church of Soledad and throughout the city, and 23 (Rábanos) with huge radishes carved in grotesque shapes sold for fake money; *buñuelos* are sold and eaten in the streets on this night, and the dishes ceremonially smashed after serving. Night of 24 Dec, a parade of floats (best seen from balcony of *Merendero El Tule* on the Zócalo; go for supper and get a window table). Posadas in San Felipe (5 km N) and at Xoxo, to the S, the week before Christmas. Bands play in the Zócalo every evening except Sat, and there are regional folk dances twice a week.

Hotels A+ *Victoria*, colonial house turned into hotel, bedrooms with showers built round the garden, good value, swimming pool, TV (with 2 US satellite channels), discount for elderly couples who book directly, up to 30%, many tour groups, but out of town (around 15-min walk) at Km 545 on Pan-American Highway, T 52633, F 52411; **A+-A** *Hacienda La Noria* (Best Western), Periférico con La Costa, T 67555, F 65347, motel-type, pool, good and convenient; Best Western also has **A+** *Hostal de la Noria*, Hidalgo 918, T 147844, F 163992, 2 blocks from Zócalo, new colonial style; **A** *Calesa Real*, García Vigil 306, T 65544, modern colonial but many small dark rooms, good but expensive, *Los Arcos* restaurant, parking, central, slow service; **A** *Misión de Los Angeles*, Porfirio Díaz 102, T 51500, F 51680, motel-style, 2 km from centre, quiet and most attractive, with swimming pool, good food; **A** *Misión Oaxaca*, San Felipe del Agua, some way out, attractive; **B** *Gala*, Guerrero y Bustamante 103, SE corner of Zócalo, with a/c, very nice (no elevator); **B** *Mesón del Angel*, Mina, nr Díaz Ordaz, clean, large rooms, good services, with pool, tours to ruins (see below), bus to Pochutla passes hotel at 0800 and 2200, rec; **B** *Posada San Pablo*, M Fiallo 102,

T 64914, with bath, hot water, kitchen, large rooms in old convent, quiet, safe, clean, must stay more than 2 nights, highly rec; **C** *California*, Chapultepec 822, T 53628, near 1st class bus station, with bath, friendly, pleasant, restaurant; **C** *Del Arbol*, Calzada Madero 131, T 64887, modern, comfortable, bath; **C** *Del Bosque*, exit road to Mitla, T 52122, modern, restaurant; **C** *Las Rosas*, Trujano 112, nice patio, clean; **C** *Margarita*, Madero 1254, at N entrance to city, T 64865, good and reasonable, safe parking, rec; **C** *Mesón del Rey*, Trujano 212, T 60033, 1 block from Zócalo, clean, modern, parking, value, restaurant and travel agency; **C** *Monte Albán*, Alameda de León 1, T 62777 friendly, colonial style, opp Cathedral; regular folk dance performances are given here at 2030, US$2.50, photography permitted; **C** *Plazuela*, La Bastida 115, pleasant, friendly; **C** *Primavera*, Madero 438, T 64508, opp railway station, with bath, warm water, front rooms noisy; 2 blocks from the Zócalo at 5 de Mayo 208 is **C** *Principal*, T 62535, colonial house, very clean, private shower with hot and cold water, English spoken, heavily booked; **C** *Santo Tomás*, Abasolo 305, T 63800, clean, private shower, helpful, kitchen for use of guests, some comfort, washing facilities, quiet, parking, rec; **C** *Señorial*, Portal de Flores 6, T 63933, will store luggage, suites or rooms, with bath, swimming pool, on main square, good restaurant, will change TCs for guests, very good value, rec; **C** *Veracruz*, Chapultepec 1020, T 50511, next to ADO bus station, spotless; **C** *Vallarta*, Díaz Ordaz 309, T 64967, clean, good value, enclosed parking.

D *Antonio's*, Independencia y 20 de Noviembre, with bath, hot water, spotless; **D** *Central*, 20 de Noviembre 104, T 65971, private bathroom, hot water, good value but very noisy, fills up early; **D** *Chayo*, 20 de Noviembre 508, bath but no fan, water not always hot, clean, large courtyard used as carpark; **D** *Francia*, 20 de Noviembre 212, T 64811, around enclosed courtyard, popular, some rooms scruffy without windows, friendly and helpful, rec. **D** *Posada Margarita*, La Bastida 115, with shower, clean, quiet, near Santo Domingo; **D** *Reforma*, Av Reforma between Independencia and Morelos, back rooms quieter, upper floors have good views, terrace on roof, friendly, rec; **D** *Asunción*, Aldama 410 and García (bargaining possible), popular but few good reports (eg cockroaches in shower, few locks, basic, noisy); **D/E** *Casa Arnel*, Aldama 404, clean and comfortable, rec; **D** *Aurora*, Bustamante 212, T 64145, no private bath, 2 blocks from Zócalo, being remodelled (1993); **D** *Villa Alta*, Cabrera 303, T 62444, 4 blocks from Zócalo, friendly service, clean. Many cheap hotels in the block Mina, Zaragoza, Díaz Ordaz y García; **D** *Fortín*, Díaz Ordaz 312, nr S side of main market, clean, some rooms good, others basic, noisy at ground floor level, with bath, hot water am only; **D** *del Valle*, Díaz Ordaz 105, with bath, run down, friendly, a bit noisy, poor breakfast, next door to tourist bus to Monte Albán; **D** *Pasaje*, Mina 302, near market, in doubtful neighbourhood, with bathrooms, parakeets in patio (Lorenzo is most entertaining—'mercifully covered at night'), noisy, water supply unreliable, clean. Next door to *Fortín* at 316 is **E** *Díaz Ordaz*, clean and friendly, similar water problem; and on the other side of *Fortín* is **E** *Lupita*, large, pleasant rooms, rec; **E** *Yagul*, Mina 103 near market and Zócalo, family atmosphere, use of kitchen on request, very clean; **E** *La Cabaña*, Mina 203, near M Cabrera, cheap, safe, clean, hot water 0700-1000, 1800-2100; next door to *Pasaje*, but not so nice, is **E** *Mina*, cheap, without bath, more with, noisy. **E** *Pombo*, Morelos 601 y 20 de Noviembre, near Zócalo, gringo hotel, hot shower, clothes washing not allowed, mixed reports; **E** *Virreyes*, Morelos y Reforma, hot water, quiet, a bit tatty, rooms on street a bit noisy, otherwise rec; **E/F** *Posada El Palmar*, Calle JP García 504 and Aldama (2 blocks from the market), reasonable, friendly and cheap; **E** *San José*, Trujano 412, basic, dirty, cheap, lively, friendly. Many other cheap hotels in 400 block of Trujano. There is also accommodation in private houses which rent rooms (*casas de huéspedes*); **E** *Casa de Huéspedes Farolito*, Calle de Las Casas 508, more expensive with bath, basic, quiet, clean; **E** *Posada Las Palmas*, Av Juárez 516, without bath, restaurant, rec.

Villa María, Arteaga 410, 5 blocks from the Zócalo, pleasant modern well furnished apts, maid service if required, rec. On the road to Tehuantepec (Km 9.8); **C** *Hotel Posada Los Arcos*, Spanish-style motel at San Sebastián Totla.

Youth hostel *El Pasador*, Fiallo 305, T 61287, F pp in dormitories, kitchen and laundry facilities, stores luggage, purified water. Villa Deportiva Juvenil, office at Belisario Domínguez 920, Col Reforma, bus from Las Casas y JP García in centre, 5 mins, US$0.15, cold water, dormitories, clean, friendly, G with YHA card, F without, sheets and blankets provided.

Camping Oaxaca Trailer Park S of town off the road to Mitla at a sign marked 'Infonavit' (corner of Calles Pinos and Violetas), US$8.65 for a tent, US$10.35 for a camper van, secure, clothes washing facilities not always available; bus 'Carmen-Infonavit' from downtown.

Restaurants Most restaurants on the main square cater for tourists, for instance, *El Jardín*, rec for people-watching; several are deemed to be overpriced, also very slow service, up to 1½ hrs to get complete order. It is, however, a nice place to sit and watch all the activity (music, parades, aerobics, etc) in the Zócalo. *Guelatao*, on main square, good for breakfast and snacks, cheap beer; *Portal*, next door, similar to *Guelatao* but better, good soup and sandwiches, quick service; *El Asador Vasco*, 2nd floor overlooking Zócalo, live (and loud) Mexican music, good food; *Flor de Oaxaca*, Armenta y López 311, pricey but excellent meals and delicious hot chocolate; *Los Arcos*, García Vigil 306 under *Calesa Real* hotel, good food in pretty setting and friendly service. *La Fuente de la Catedral*, corner of Gral García Vigil and Morelos, 1 block from Cathedral, good for international and local specialities—steaks, good *tamales*, classical music. *Alameda*, JP García between Trujano and Hidalgo, excellent regional food, crowded Sun. *Flami*, on Trujano near Zócalo, good food. *Hostería Alcalá*, Calle Macedonio Alcalá, 5 mins from Zócalo, not cheap but excellent food and quiet atmosphere, good service. *La Quebrada*, Armenta y López, excellent fish, open only to 1800. *Guitarra, Pan Y Vino*, Morelos 511, regional food, music *soirées*. *Quince Letras*, Abasolo opp *Hotel Santo Tomás*, excellent food, friendly service.

Vegetarian: *Flor de Loto*, Av Morelos 512, next to Rufino Tamayo museum, noisy (US$3.30 a meal, beautifully clean, cheap, very friendly, owner is into yoga); next door, *Plaza Gourmet* has vegetarian meals, rec; *Café Fuente y Señor de Salud*, Juárez just N of Morelos, pleasant, reasonable food; *Arco*, dearer, opp ADO bus station, Niños Héroes de Chapultepec, loud music; *Comedor Piscis*, Hidalgo y Díaz Ordaz, rec, open 1300 to 1900.

Gino's Pizza, pleasant café, inexpensive in Independencia 503, mixed reports on the food; *Pizza, pasta y más*, Av Hidalgo on Zócalo, good if a bit pricey; *Alfredo's Pizzería*, Alcalá, about 4 blocks N of the Zócalo, excellent food, expensive wine by the glass; *El Sol y la Luna*, on Murguia, good although not cheap, live music some nights, open evenings only. At M Cabrera 413 is an unsigned restaurant with nice patio and garden, US$7 for 5-course lunch, no dinner, good atmosphere. *Las Chalotes*, Fiallo 116, French food, friendly service, moderate prices. The best Oaxacan food is found in the *comedores familiares* such as *Clemente, Los Almendros, La Juchita*, but they are way out of town and could be difficult to get to, or in *comedores populares* in the market; also try *El Bicho Pobre*, Tacubaya y Abasolo, local food, open 1330-1800, excellent value; also *El Bicho Pobre II*, Calzada de la República, highly rec, lunch only, very popular; *La Verde Antequera*, Matamoros 3 blocks N of Zócalo, good daily lunch specials; *El Mesón*, good tacos, clean, quick service, on Hidalgo at NE corner of Zócalo; good Sunday buffet also at *El Laurel*, M Bravo 210, tasty home-style cooking, open to 1800 Tues-Thurs and Sun, and to 2200 on Fri and Sat; *Café Tito*, near Zócalo on García Vigil, good value for breakfast; on same street, also close to Zócalo, *Bamby*, good breakfast; *El Paisaje*, 20 de Noviembre, good, cheap chicken dishes; *Los Canarios*, 20 de Noviembre, near *Hotel Chayo*, good *comida corrida* and drink for US$2; *María Cristina's* in Mercado 20 de Noviembre, excellent *caldos* and *comidas*; *El Hipocampo*, Hidalgo 505, cheap, good; *La Pinata*, Hidalgo (just E of Zócalo), good chicken in mole lunches; *Café Pitapé*, García Vigil 403 y M Bravo, friendly, good value; *Fiesta*, Las Casas 303, good for breakfast or *comida corrida*; *Gala*, Bustamante, just off Zócalo, opens 0730 for good coffee and breakfast; *Trece Cielos*, Matamoros 101, good, cheap daily *menú*; *Cafetería Chips*, Trujano (in 1st block W of Zócalo), good coffee and milkshakes; next door is *French Pastry Shop*, 1 block W of Zócalo, good coffee, pastries, desserts; *Cafetería Alex*, Díaz Ordaz y Trujano, good *comida corrida*, coffee and breakfasts, delicious pancakes with fruit, good value; *Tartamiel*, Valerio Trujano, ½ block E of Zócalo, good bakery and cake shop; as is *La Luna*, Independencia 1105, 5 blocks E of cathedral. Good restaurant opposite 1st class bus station, good value, one of the only sit-down places among taco stands. Good *dulcería* (sweet shop) in the 2nd class bus station; *Pastelería Quemen*, Morelos y Reforma, excellent cakes. Good ice cream and cheese in the market. In Calle Mina and near the market are several mills (La Soledad, rec), where they grind cacao beans, almond, sugar and cinnamon into a paste for making delicious hot chocolate. Good chocolate shop on 20 de Noviembre between Mina and Zaragoza. A local bread called *pan de yema*, is made, with egg-yolk, at the Mercado de Abastos (the Hermanas Jiménez bakery is most rec).

Shopping There are endless temptations such as green and black pottery, baskets and bags made from cane and rushes, embroidered shirts, skirts, and blankets; Saturdays are the best for buying woollen *sarapes* cheaply. Unfortunately some of the woven products are of a different quality from the traditional product—more garish dyes and synthetic yarns are replacing some of the originals; but you can still find these if you shop around. *Aripo*, on García Vigil, cheaper and better than most, service good, with very good small market nearby on junction of García Vigil and Jesus Carranza, for beautiful coloured belts and clothes. *Casa Breno*, near Santo Domingo church, has unusual textiles and spindles for sale, happy to show visitors around the looms. *Lo Mexicano*, García Vigil, at end furthest from centre, excellent selection of high quality crafts at reasonable prices, run by young Frenchman. *Pepe*, Avenida Hidalgo, for jewellery; cheap local crafts. Good for silver, *Plata Mexicana*, 20 de Noviembre 209-C. *Yalalag*, Alcalá 104, has good selection of jewellery, rugs and pottery, somewhat overpriced; *El Palacio de Gemas*, next door, is rec for gemstones, good selection at reasonable prices; cheapest and largest selection of pottery plus a variety of fabrics and sandals at *Productos Típicos de Oaxaca*, Av Dr B Domínguez 602; city bus near ADO depot goes there. *Casa Aragón*, JP García 503, famous for knives and *machetes*; a large **Mercado Artesanal** also at JP García y Zaragoza. Fine cream and purple-black pottery (Zapotec and Mixtec designs) available at *Alfarería Jiménez*, Zaragoza 402. Other **potteries** at Las Casas 614, makers of the Oaxacan daisy design, and Trujano 508, bold flower designs. The nearby village of Atzompa (NW of the city, buses from 2nd class terminal) is worth a visit for its interesting ceramics; local potters are very friendly.

Markets The **Mercado Juárez**, just SW of the Zócalo on 20 de Noviembre below Las Casas, sells fruit, vegetables, meat, cheeses and some handicrafts (good leather bags are sold in and around this market). Immediately S of Mercado Juárez is **Mercado 20 de Noviembre**, for baked goods, with lots of *comedores*. The **Mercado de Abastos**, open daily, which sells just about everything including baskets and pottery, is close to the 2nd class bus station. There is a large and interesting straw section here. Gilberto Segura T, 2 Galería de Artesanías, puesto 140, Mercado de Abastos, makes hammocks to your own design and specification, price depends on size, about US$20 for a single. Sr Leonardo Ruiz of Teotitlán del Valle, has an excellent carpet stall here. Market stallholders drive very hard bargains and often claim 'no change'; it may be possible to barter rather than bargain. Those disappointed with it should go to the Sunday market at **Tlacolula**.

Local Buses Local town minibuses, mostly US$0.30. To the bus station, buses marked 'VW' go from Av Juárez.

Entertainment *Guajiros*, Macedonia Alcalá, live salsa music; folk dancing at the *Hotel Señorial* most nights of the week, advance booking rec. **Cinemas** *Ariel 2000*, Juárez y Berriozabal (3 blocks E, 7 N of Zócalo); *Cine Versalles*, Av Melchor Ocampo, N of Hidalgo (3 blocks E, ½ block N of Zócalo); *Cine Oaxaca*, Morelos nr Alcalá; another cinema on Trujano, 1 block W of Zócalo.

Exchange Get to banks before they open, long queues form. **Bancomer**, 1 block from Zócalo, exchanges TCs, 0900-1330, on García Vigil, and has cash dispenser for Visa card. **Banpais** at corner of Zócalo has a better service. For Thomas Cook cheques, **Banco Internacional**. **Amex** office Viajes México Istmo y Caribe, at Valdivieso 2, T 62700, on Zócalo, very helpful, but lots of paperwork: will change cheques into dollars cash as long as you

Your Best Choice!

becari

L A N G U A G E　S C H O O L

Private and group Spanish lessons adapted to individual needs. Discover the indigenous culture in the beautiful region of Oaxaca.

**M. Bravo 210, Plaza San Cristóbal
Oaxaca, Oax., 68000, México
Tel. (951) 6 88 32 / Fax 4 70 52**

change some into pesos (no travel reservations). *Interdisa*, Valdivieso near Zócalo, Mon-Sat 0800-2000, Sun 0900-1700, cash, TCs, sells quetzales and exchanges many Western currencies. *Casa de Cambio*, Abasolo 105, 0800-2000 changes travellers' cheques. *Casa de Cambio* at Armenta y López, nr corner with Hidalgo, 0800-2000 Mon-Sat, shorter hours on Sun. No problem to change TCs at weekends, many *casas de cambio* around the Zócalo.

Consulates US Consular Agency, Alcalá 201, suite 204, T 43054; **Canadian Honorary Consul**, Dr Liceaga 119-8, T 33777; combined **Honorary British** and **German** consul.

Library/Cultural attractions English lending library with very good English books, a few French and Spanish, also English newspapers (*The News* from Mexico City), used books and magazines for sale, at Macedonio Alcalá 305—looks like an apartment block on a pedestrian street, a few blocks N of Zócalo (open Mon-Fri, 1000-1300, 1600-1800). *The News* is also sold round the Zócalo by newsboys, from mid-morning, or from street vendor at Las Casas y 20 de Noviembre. The local library at Alcalá 200 (no sign) has a lovely courtyard and a reading room with Mexican newspapers and magazines. Next door is the library of the Museo de Arte Contemporáneo.

Language courses Instituto de Comunicación y Cultura, M Alcalá 307-12, 2nd floor, T 63443, US$75/week; accommodation can be arranged (part of the National Registration Center for Study Abroad consortium; see **Learning Spanish** in Information for Visitors). Centro de Idiomas, Universidad Autónoma Benito Juárez, Calle de Burgoa, 4 blocks S of Zócalo, weekly or monthly classes (US$200 per month), or private tuition, very professional and good value for money, rec. Other schools include Becari, M Bravo 210, Plaza San Cristóbal, T 68832, F 47052.

In addition to Spanish classes, local crafts (including cooking, weaving and pottery) are also taught at the Instituto Cultural Oaxaca, Av Juárez 909, T 53404/51323, not cheap but rec.

Health Doctor Dr Victor Tenorio, Clínica de Carmen, Abasolo 215, T 62612, close to centre (very good English); Dr Marco Antonio Callejo (English-speaking), Belisario Domínguez 115, T 53492, surgery 0900-1300, 1700-2000. **Dentist** Dra Marta Fernández del Campo, Armenta y López 215, English-speaking, very friendly, rec. **Chemist/pharmacy** 20 de Noviembre y Ignacio Aldama, open till 2300.

Washing Self: Baños Reforma, Calle Reforma 407, open 0700-1800, US$4 for steam-bath for two, sauna for one, US$3. Clothes: ELA, Super Lavandería Automática, Antonio Roldán 114, Col Olímpica, washes and irons. About US$3.30 for 3.5 kg.

Luggage Storage Servicio Turístico de Guarda Equipaje y Paquetería, Av Tinoco y Palacios 312, Centro, T 60-432, open 24 hrs.

Telephone Self-service, long-distance phone at pharmacies at 20 de Noviembre y Hidalgo, Porfirio Díaz y Av Morelos, and at Calle Rayón 504. Computel, for long distance calls and fax, Trujano, 2 blocks W of Zócalo.

Tourist Office 5 de Mayo y Av Morelos, excellent free map of city and surroundings. Federal tourist office Matamoros 105 y García Vigil. Tourist Police on Zócalo near Cathedral, friendly and helpful. Instituto Nacional de Estadística, Geografía e Informática, Calz Porfirio Díaz 241A, for maps.

Railway Station on Calzada Madero at junction with Periférico, 15 min walk from Zócalo. From Mexico City, 563 km, 14½ hrs, magnificent scenery after dawn in either direction, El Oaxaqueño, with *primera especial*, 1st and 2nd class, no sleepers; take food for 2nd and 1st class (although there are colourful foodsellers on the train), at 1900 daily. To **Mexico City** daily also at 1900. Tickets must be bought the same day; the office is open 1400-1530, long queues. Numbered seats in 2nd class, US$7.70; 1st class US$12.70; *primera especial* US$25.85. Route is via Tehuacán and Puebla to the capital.

Buses 1st class terminal is NE of Zócalo on Calzada de Niños Héroes (no luggage office, taxi from centre US$3.35); 2nd class, Autobuses Unidos (AU), is W of Zócalo on Calz Trujano (referred to as 'Central'), has left-luggage office. Beware of double-booking and short-changing, especially when obtaining tickets from drivers if you have not booked in advance; beware also of thieves at both bus terminals, but especially on arrival of *plus* services. Cristóbal Colón to **Mexico City**, 10 hrs, about 8 a day, mostly evenings; 2nd class by Fletes y Pasajes, 12 hrs, comfortable; about 10 a day with ADO, 8 hrs, robberies have been reported on these buses. Fares to the capital: 1st class US$21.65 *plus*, US$24.20 and luxury *futura* service US$34.65. If buses to the capital are fully booked travel via Puebla. It is difficult to get tickets for buses from the capital to Oaxaca on Fri pm without booking in advance (you can book in advance and pay on day of travel); bus companies require 2 hr checking-in time in

Mexico City on this route. 1st class to **Cuautla**, US$14.80 with ADO, 7 hrs (change there for Cuernavaca and Taxco); **Puebla** (1st class, 6-8 hrs, US$16.50, several companies); to **Tuxtepec**, 1st class, 6 hrs, US$16.50 with ADO, from same terminal, Cuenca goes by a more direct, but still beautiful route 1st class US$8.25 (police have reported robberies on this route). To **Veracruz**, ADO, 2 a day from 1st class bus station, via Huajuapan, Tehuacán and Orizaba, 11 hrs, US$13.25, book early, or change as above, allow 16 hrs. Cristóbal Colón to **Villahermosa**, US$24, book well ahead, 12 hrs, daily at 1700 and 2100. 1st class; **San Cristóbal de Las Casas** (US$21.50, at 0900, 12 hrs) book 1-2 days in advance with C Colón; and Tapachula, 10 hrs, US$22.50 (2200, Cristóbal Cólon, also Fipsa, same price, 3 in pm from 2nd class terminal). Book well in advance as buses often come almost full from Mexico City. To **Tuxtla Gutiérrez**, C Colón, 3 a day, 12 hrs, *especial* at 2230, US$22.50; by 1st class (ADO), 10 hrs, US$18, 5 a day. To **Tehuantepec**, scenic, 5 a day, 2nd class US$6.50, Cristóbal Colón US$8, 7½ hrs. To **Ciudad Cuauhtémoc**, US$33, 12 hrs. To **Arriaga** US$20, 5 a day. To **Puerto Escondido**, US$11.50 1st class, US$18.75 *plus*, gruelling 13 hrs journey (can be longer) 3 a day, partly along dirt roads, interesting scenery. Night bus 5 hrs faster. Probably better to go Oaxaca-**Pochutla** on new road with spectacular scenery, especially the cloud forest and 2-hr descent into Pochutla, 6½-10 hrs, US$18, 1st-class Estrella del Valle buses at 0800 and 2200, then change for Puerto Angel/Puerto Escondido. Oaxaca-Pacífico has good 2nd class buses (five a day to Pochutla, US$8.25, one a day to Puerto Angel at 1730 arrives in middle of the night). 1st class buses from 2nd class terminal to Pochutla via Salina Cruz and Huatulco, 7 hrs, several daily. Buses to most local villages go from this terminal, too.

Air Services The airport is about 8 km S, direction Ocotepec. The airport taxis (*colectivos*) cost US$5 pp. Book at Transportaciones Aeropuerto Oaxaca on Alameda de León No 1-6, opp the Cathedral in the Zócalo (T 64350) for collection at your hotel to be taken to airport, office open Mon-Sat 0900-1400, 1700-2000.

From Mexico City at least twice daily by AeroMéxico in less than an hr, or Mexicana at least four daily (US$63 one way). Aero Caribe and Aviacsa fly daily to Tuxtla Gutiérrez, and Aero Caribe to Villahermosa, 90 mins, continuing to Mérida and Cancún. Aviacsa's Tuxtla flight continues to Mérida. Aviacsa also has a daily flight to Mexico City, book at its agency on the Zócalo, take ticket to airport shuttle bus beside *Hotel Monte Albán* (US$2). Flights to other Mexican, and to any US destination, except Los Angeles with Mexicana daily, involve a connection in Mexico City. Daily flights to Puerto Escondido, 40 mins, eg Aero Caribe; Aerovías Oaxaqueñas at 1100, returns at 0730 or 1200; Líneas Aéreas Oaxaqueñas fly at 1030 Mon-Sat and 0830 Sun; Aeromorelos at 0730, returns at 0830, US$64 one way (new 40-seater Fokker). Most flights are in small, modern planes, 35-mins journey, spectacular, eg Aero Veca. Be very careful when booking flights to Puerto Escondido on a small airline, they tend to be very erratic. Once weekly flights also to Pochutla. Líneas Aéreas Oaxaqueñas office at Av Hidalgo 503, T 65362, airport 61280. There is a Mexicana office at Fiallo 102 y Av Independencia, T 68414 (airport T 62337); AeroMéxico, Av Hidalgo 513 Centro, T 67101 (airport T 64055); Aviacsa T 31809/51500 (airport T 62332); Aero Caribe, at *Hotel Misión de los Angeles*, T 56373 (airport T 62247).

Excursions For good hikes, take local bus to San Felipe (N of the city); at the end of the line follow the dirt road to the left along the valley, cross the bridge and turn right (uphill) after the bridge, trails go into the mountains and to a waterfall (ask for La Cascada).

To **Monte Albán** (open 0830-1700) about 10 km (20 mins) uphill from Oaxaca, to see the pyramids, walls, terraces, tombs, staircases and sculptures of the ancient capital of the Zapotec culture. The place is radiantly colourful during some sunsets, but permission is needed to stay that late (take a torch/flashlight). Beware of fake 'antique' sellers. Autobuses Turísticos depart from behind *Hotel Mesón del Angel*, Mina nr Díaz Ordaz (bus tickets available from hotel lobby) hourly on the half-hour from 0830 to 1530 fare US$4 return, last bus back at 1730; 2 hrs at the site, allowing not enough time to visit ruins before returning (you are permitted to come back on another tour on one ticket for an extra US$0.55 but you will not, of course, have a reserved seat for your return). There is a shuttle bus from *Hotel Trébol*, 1 block S of Zócalo, US$2.50, leaves in am, allowing 3 hrs at the site. Local buses also run from outside *Hotel Mesón del Angel*, which leaves you to walk up the pleasant trail from the end of the line; alternatively hitch the last bit. Taxi US$10. To give yourself enough time (3 hrs is adequate at the site), you can walk 4 km downhill from the ruins to Colonia Monte Albán and get a city bus back

To Tehuacán
131
To Tuxtepec
Guelatao○ ○Ixtlán de Juárez
San Francisco
○Telixtlahuaca
190
175
To
Yanhuitlán,
Huajapan de Léon,
Cuernavaca, &
Mexico City
190
○Etla
San Antonio
Nevería○ ○Cuajimoloyas
Atzompa○
OAXACA
○El Tule
Monte Albán▲ ○Teotitlán del Valle
Cuilapan○ Tlacochuaya▲
Tlacolula
Zaachila○ Dainzú▲ Lambityeco
○ San Bartolo Yagul
Coyotepec
Mitla
Zimatlán de Alvarez
○Santo Tomás
San Pablo Huixtepec Jalieza 190
○Ocotlán
Santiago
Matatlán○
N
0 10 20
Km approx
131
○San Jerónimo San Pedro
San Sebastián Taviche Totolapan
de las Grutas
OAXACA ○ To To To
Environs Puerto Puerto Angel Tehuantepec
MAC 26 Escondido

from there, or 1½ hrs all the way to the Zócalo. Some prefer to walk up and take the bus back. Entrance to ruins US$4.35, closed Monday, free on Sun and public holidays (and for students with international card on request). Most people go in the morning, so it may be easier to catch the afternoon bus. Next to the gift shop is a museum with pottery, a grave with skeleton, and engraved stones, free.

To the right, before getting to the ruins, is Tomb 7, where a fabulous treasure trove was found in 1932 (take a torch); most items are in the Museo Regional in the convent of Santo Domingo and the entrance is closed off by a locked gate. Tomb 172 has been left exactly as it was found, with skeleton and urns still in place. Tomb 104 contains an interesting statue of the rain god, Tlaloc. The remarkable rectangular plaza, 300 by 200m, is rimmed by big ceremonial platforms: the Ball Court, and possibly a palace to the E, stairs rising to an unexcavated platform to the S, several platforms and temples to the W and one—known as Templo de los Danzantes but in reality, probably a hospital—with bas-reliefs, glyphs and calendar signs (probably 5th century BC). A wide stairway leads to a platform on the N side. Most of the ruins visible are early 10th century, when the city was abandoned and became a burial place. Informative literature is available at the site. (Recommended literature is the Bloomgarden *Easy Guide* to Monte Albán or *Easy Guide* to Oaxaca covering the city and all the ruins in the valley, with maps. In major hotels or the bookshop at Guerrero 108, and all the ruins.) Restaurant *Jade* at the visitors' centre is good value.

Only 72 km NW of Oaxaca on Route 190 is **Yanhuitlán**, with a beautiful 400-year-old church, part of a monastery (Santo Domingo). Yanhuitlán is in the Sierra Mixteca, where Dominican friars began evangelizing in 1526. Two other important centres were San Juan Bautista at Coixtlahuaca and the open chapel at Teposcolula. The scenery and the altars, the huge convents in such a remote area, are a worthwhile day trip from Oaxaca by car, or by bus from the 2nd class bus terminal (with thanks to Claudio Rivero). NW of Yanhuitlán is **Huajuapan De León**, with *Hotel García Peral*, on the Zócalo, good restaurant; *Hotel Casablanca*, Amatista 1, Col Vista Hermosa, also good restaurant (just outside Huajuapan on the road to Oaxaca); **C-D** *Plaza de Angel*, Central, nice, clean; **D** *Playa*, El Centro, hot water, clean, big windows, good value; and **D** *Hotel Bella Vista*; and **D** *Colón*, very good. 2nd class bus from Oaxaca to Huajuapan, four a day, US$3.50.

To Mitla, paved road (Route 190), 42 km from Oaxaca past (1) **El Tule** (12 km from Oaxaca) which has what is reputed the world's largest tree, a savino (*Taxodium mucronatum*), estimated at 2,000 years old, 40m high, 42m round at base, weighing an estimated 550 tons, fed water by an elaborate pipe system, in churchyard—US$0.35 entry (bus from Oaxaca, 2nd class bus station, every ½ hr, US$0.75, buy ticket on bus, sit on the left to see the Tule tree; bus El Tule-Mitla US$0.40); El Tule has a good market with good food on sale and *La Sonora* restaurant on eastern edge of town has quite tasty food. (2) **Tlacochahuaya**, 16th century church, vivid Indian murals, carpets and blouses sold in market nearby, admission US$0.45 to church. (3) An unpaved road leads off Route 190 to **Teotitlán Del Valle**, where Oaxaca *sarapes* and *tapetes* (rugs) are woven, which is now becoming rather touristy. If you knock at any door down the street, you will get them only a little cheaper than at the market, but there is greater variety. The best prices are to be had at the stores along the road as you come into town, but may be even cheaper in Oaxaca where competition is stronger. (Make sure whether you are getting all-wool or mixture.) Buses leave every 1-1½ hrs from 0800 from 2nd class bus terminal (US$0.75); the 3rd class bus may provide all the contacts you need to buy all the weavings you want! *Juvenal Mendoza*, Buenavista 9, will make any design any size into a rug to order (daily at 1100). Recommended for rugs is Pedro Guitiérrez, Cuauhtémoc 29. Just before the turning for Teotitlán, turn right for **Dainzu**, 1 km off the road, another important ruin recently excavated (US$4.35). Its pyramid contains figures, probably ball players, similar to the Monte Albán dancers. The nearby site of **Lambytieco** is also well worth visiting, to see several fine and well-preserved stucco heads.

(4) **Tlacolula** (**E** *Hotel Glish Bal*, Zaragoza 3, reported clean), with a most interesting Sunday market and the renowned Capilla del Santo Cristo in the church, elaborate decorations and gruesome figures of saints (fiesta 9 October). A band plays every evening in the plaza, take a sweater, cold wind most eves, starts at 1930. Tlacolula can be reached by bus from Oaxaca, from the 2nd class bus station every 30 mins, but every 15 mins on Sun, US$0.75.

(5) Fletes y Pasajes buses and taxis from Oaxaca go to the ruins of **Yagul** (on the way to Mitla, ask to be put down at the turn-off to Yagul, 2 km from road), guided tours in English leave on Tues from *Mesón del Angel*, Mina, in Oaxaca, US$10, an outstandingly picturesque site where the ball courts and quarters of the priests are set in a landscape punctuated by candelabra cactus and agave (admission US$4.35). Yagul was a large Zapotec and Mixtec religious centre; the ball courts are perhaps the most perfect discovered to date; also fine tombs (take steep path from behind the ruins) and temples. You will have to walk from the bus stop to the site, and you can return the same way or walk 3 km to Tlacolula to catch a bus (signposted). The 2 km-long side road off the main road is paved.

From the main road a turn left leads 4 km to **Mitla** (whose name means 'place of the dead') where there are ruins of four great palaces among minor ones. Some of the archaeology, outside the fenced-in site, can be seen within the present-day town. Entry US$4 (Sun free), open 0830-1800, literature available on site. See in particular the magnificent bas-reliefs, the sculptured designs in the Hall of Mosaics, the Hall of the Columns, and in the depths of a palace La Columna de la Muerte (Column of Death), which people embrace and measure what they can't reach with their fingers to know how many years they have left to live (rather hard on long-armed people). The museum just W of the Zócalo in the village is interesting (free). There is a soberly decorated colonial church with three cupolas, and a rash of guides and pedlars. Beautiful traditional Indian clothes and other goods may be bought at the new permanent market, bargaining possible. Also good *mescal*.

Accommodation B *Casa Liooba*, hotel/trailer park, near ruins, scenic location, clean, friendly, German owner speaks English, homely rooms, good restaurant, trailer and tent sites with all facilities, self-catering possible, rec; to get there follow traffic route to Mitla ruins, turn left after handicrafts market and it's about 800m to end of street; **C** *Hotel Mitla*, clean, local food; **C** *Hotel La Zapuleca*, on road to ruins, newer and better than *Mitla*, cheaper food, good. The University of the Americas has a small guest-house, and runs the small Frissell museum in the Zócalo at Mitla, with very good and clean restaurant, *La Sorpresa*, in a patio; restaurant opp site, *Santa María*; *María Elena* restaurant 100m from site towards village, good *comida corrida*. The local technical college provides accommodation, showers and a bathroom; good shopping too.

Transport Taxi costs US$10 each to Mitla for 4 sharing, with time to take photographs at Tule and Mitla and to buy souvenirs at ruins. Tours (1000 till 1300, rather rushed) to Tule, Mitla and Tlacolula from *Hotel Mesón del Angel*, cost US$7.50, not including entry fees. Fletes y Pasajes bus from Oaxaca, 2nd class bus station, every 20 mins to Mitla, 1 hr, US$1; the ruins are 10-min walk across the village (from the bus stop). Minibuses from Oaxaca leave a shorter walk to the ruins than regular buses.

From Mitla take a bus towards Ayutla and get off at the turning to 'Hierve El Agua': this is a cliff over which water from pools flows, but is has also created a stalactite, which looks like a petrified waterfall. From the turn-off it is 1½ hrs walk, or by hitching to San Lorenzo, from where it is 10 mins. On Sundays there are sometimes bus excursions to Oaxaca.

Friday trips from Oaxaca to market at **San Antonio Ocotlán** on the road to Puerto Angel, good prices for locally woven rugs and baskets, also excellent fruit and veg; buses leave every 30 mins for Ocotlán from the co-operative bus station opposite Oaxaca Mercado de Abastos (½ hr journey, US$1). Stop in **San Bártolo Coyotepec** to see black pottery (Doña Rosa's—she's been dead for years but her name survives—is a target for tours, but other families are just as good) and don't try to bargain (also red and green ceramics in the village), and in **Santo Tomás Jalieza**, where cotton textiles are made.

17 km SW of Oaxaca is **Cuilapan**, where there is a vast unfinished 16th-century convent, now in ruins, with a famous nave and columns, and an 'open chapel', whose roof collapsed in an earthquake. 'At the back of the unfinished chapel is a board on which the Zapotec and Mixtec calendars had been correlated. On the left side is the date 1555 in Arabic numerals; the two calendars differed by 13 years, Zapotec 1555, Mixtec 1568. The last Zapotec princess, Donaji, daughter of the last ruler Cosijoeza, married a Mixtec prince at Tilantengo and was buried at Cuilapan. On the grave is an inscription with their Christian names, Mariana Cortez and Diego Aguilar'. (Helmut Zettl, Ebergassing). Reached by bus from Oaxaca from 2nd class bus station, on Calle Bustamante, near de Arista (US$0.50), take bus to Zaachila (US$0.60) which leaves every 30 mins, then walk to unexcavated ruins in valley. **Zaachila** is a poor town, but there are ruins, with two Mixtec tombs, with owls in stucco work in the outer chamber and carved human figures with skulls for heads inside, admission US$4.35. No restrictions on flash photography. There is an Indian market on Thursday. 80 km S on Route 131 is San Sebastián (about 10 km off the road) where there are caves. Ask for a guide at the Agencia Municipal next to the church; guide obligatory, US$1.50. Take bus 175 from Oaxaca.

To San Pablo de **Guelatao** (65 km from Oaxaca), the birthplace of Benito Juárez. The town is located in the mountains NE of Oaxaca and can be reached by bus (3 hrs) along a paved but tortuously winding road. There are a memorial and a museum to Juárez on the hillside within the village (entry, US$0.20), and a pleasant lake with a symbolic statue of a shepherd and his lambs.

We are approaching a more traditional part of Mexico; Tehuantepec isthmus and the mountains of Chiapas beyond, a land inhabited by Indians less influenced than elsewhere by the Spanish conquest. Only about 210 km separate the Atlantic and the Pacific at the hot, heavily-jungled Isthmus of Tehuantepec, where the land does not rise more than 250m. There are a railway (to be renewed) and a Trans-Isthmian Highway between Coatzacoalcos and Salina Cruz, the terminal cities on the two oceans. Winds are very strong on and near the isthmus, because of the intermingling of Pacific and Caribbean weather systems. Drivers of high-sided vehicles must take great care.

NB In southern Mexico the word 'Zócalo' is not often used for the main square of a town: 'Plaza (Mayor)' is much more common.

Route 190 heads SE from Oaxaca towards the Golfo de Tehuantepec and the Pacific. At Km 116, in San José de Gracia, is a huge *casa de huéspedes* overlooking a beautiful valley, parking in front.

(Km 804) **Tehuantepec** (population 45,000, altitude 150m) is 257 km from Oaxaca. A colourful place, it is on the bend of a river around which most of its activities are centred and which makes it very humid. Tehuantepec is probably a better place to break the journey to Tapachula than Salina Cruz, but some find it a smelly, rundown city, others find it friendly nonetheless. The plaza has arcades down one side, a market on the other, and many stands selling *agua fresca*, an iced fruit drink. At dusk the trees of the square are filled with black birds roosting and making an incredible noise. There is more noise from the music played through loud speakers at high volume. Houses are low, in white or pastel shades. The Indians are mostly Zapotecs whose social organization was once matriarchal: the women are high-pressure saleswomen, with some Spanish blood; their hair is sometimes still braided and brightly ribboned and at times they wear embroidered costumes. The men for the most part work in the fields, as potters or weavers, or at the nearby oil refinery. Hammocks made in this area are of the best quality. The town is divided into 15 wards, and each holds a *fiesta*, the main one at the end of Holy Week, when the women wear their finest costumes and jewellery. There is another splendid *fiesta* in honour of St John the Baptist on 22-25 June. January and February are good months for the ward *fiestas*.

Hotels Mostly overpriced and basic. **D** *Donaji*, Juárez 10, fan, nr market, clean, friendly, rec; **D** *Oasis* (central and good atmosphere), with bath and fan, simple, near Plaza, safe parking; **D** *Posada Tehuanita*, central, rec; **D** *Posada Villa Real*, nice courtyard; **D** *Posada del Istmo*, just off the main plaza, quiet, basic, with lovely patio, but unfriendly, quite dirty, poor value; *Calli* has simple rooms, but good food in *Restaurant Tequendama*; cheapest is **E** *Posada San Sebastián*, 'a filthy hole', there is also a *casa de huéspedes* whose prices, at **F** pp, have been called 'crazy'.

Santa Teresa Trailer Park, E side of town, 8 km off Route 190 (take side road at *Hotel Calli* and follow signs), US$6.50 for car and 2 people, cold showers, restrooms, drinking water, restaurant.

Restaurants Cheap food on top floor of market. *Colonial*, good *comida corrida*, US$4. The local *quesadillas* made of maize and cheese are delicious; sold at bus stops. Tehuantepec is noted for its mangoes.

Bus There is a bus station at N end of town, taxi to Zócalo US$1.35, or 15 mins walk. One bus a day to **San Cristóbal** at 1230, it may be full, standing is not allowed but the driver may accept a present and let you on (7½ hrs, US$14.80). To **Coatzacoalcos** at 0730, 9-10 hrs, US$8 2nd class. Bus to **Arriaga** at 0600, 0800, 1800 to connect to Tonalá. To **Tuxtla Gutiérrez**, 2130, 2200, 0030, 0400, 4½ hrs, 2nd class at 0130, and Tapachula, US$14.80 (Cristóbal Colón). Bus to **Tonalá** (Cristóbal Colón) at 0030 and 0130. To **Oaxaca**, US$6.50, 5 hrs, with Istmo, US$8 Cristóbal Colón US$7 2nd class; to **Salina Cruz**, US$0.75; to **Villahermosa**, Cristóbal Colón 1st class, US$14, 8 hrs, 2nd class US$10.50. (**NB** Some buses from Salina Cruz do not stop at Tehuantepec.)

Roads The highway between Tehuantepec and Tapachula is being made into a dual carriageway; the construction work may cause delays to road transport.

Excursions To neighbouring villages for *fiestas*. Near the town are the ruins of *Guingola*, 'the Mexican Machu Picchu', so called because of its lonely location on a mountain. It has walls up to 3m high, running, it is said, for 40 km; there are the remains of two pyramids and a ball court. This last fortress of the Zapotecs was never conquered; Alvarado and his forces marched past it in 1522. Take the 0500 bus Tehuantepec towards Oaxaca and alight at Km 141, at the bridge (8 km from Tehuantepec). Take the turn at the signpost 'Ruinas Guingola 7 km'. Walk 5 km then turn left, uphill, to the car park. From here it is 1½ hrs to the ruins. Try to return before 0900 because it gets very hot; take plenty of water. Alternatively, take a taxi to the car park and ask the driver to return for you 3 hrs later, or drive there. (With thanks to Helmut Zettl of Ebergassing for these details.)

Salina Cruz (43,000), 21 km from Tehuantepec, is a booming and evil-smelling port with a naval base, extensive oil-storage installations and an oil refinery. Bathing is dangerous because of the heavy swell from Pacific breakers and also sharks. Beware of overcharging in the marketplace. Car drivers should not park close to the beach in windy weather unless they want their vehicle sandblasted.

Hotels *Fuente*, bath, basic. *Río*, reasonable, nr Cristóbal Colón bus station. Avoid the *Magda*, overpriced, unfriendly. *Posada del Jardín*. All **D** or above.

Restaurant *Costa del Pacífico*, hires shower cabin, stores luggage.

Buses 2 daily buses from Salina Cruz to **San Cristóbal** come from Oaxaca and are very often full (2nd class, US$14); take instead a 2nd class bus to **Juchitán**, then to Arriaga and from there to Tuxtla and San Cristóbal; a long route. To **Coatzacoalcos**, US$12.15, 6 hrs. Salina Cruz-**Pochutla**, US$5, 4 hrs; 2nd class to **Puerto Escondido**, 6 hrs, slow, US$9.75. Frequent buses to **Tehuantepec**, 30 mins, US$0.75. To **Tapachula** by Cristóbal Colón 2nd class, along the coast, 9-10 hrs, 0740 and 2030, US$14.50, 1st class bus at 2000. No luggage storage at bus station. **NB** The Cristóbal Colón terminal is not in a safe area.

Ten km to the S is a picturesque fishing village with La Ventosa beach which, as the name says, is windy. Buses go to the beach every 30 mins from a corner of the main square. Accommodation: **D** *La Posada de Rustrian*, overlooking the sea, with bath in new block, half in old block, poor value; unnamed *pensión*, E, on right of road before asphalt ends. Friendly family at the top of the dirt road coming from Salina Cruz (on the right) and 200m after the first path that leads down to the beach, rents hammocks, US$1 a night, fried fish US$1. *Champas*, or hammocks under thatch shelters by the beach, US$1 a night. The owners serve drinks and food (fish, shrimps, crabs just caught) from early morning on. Prices often high.

Warning Do not wander too far off along the beach as many people have been attacked and robbed. Do not sleep on the beach or in your car.

27 km beyond Tehuantepec on the road to Tuxtla Gutiérrez is **Juchitán** (E *Hotel Don Alex*, clean, cheapest; *El Palacio de Gemas*, next door, is recommended for gemstones, good selection at reasonable prices; **D** *Hotel Casa Río*, has an Indian name, *Coty*, not posted, next to Casa Río shop, nr market, clean; be prepared to bargain in cheap hotels), very old, Indian, with an extensive market, many *fiestas* and a special one on 19 June (2nd class bus Oaxaca-Juchitán, at least twice a day, US$8.25, 6 hrs, frequent Juchitán-Tuxtla, 1st class, 4 hrs, US$7.15). Connect here with train from Veracruz to Tapachula, but Juchitán station is very dangerous (at night you are strongly advised to wait for the train in Ixtepec). A road runs 6 km N to **Ixtepec** (airport), railway junction on the lines Veracruz-Tapachula and Salina Cruz-Medias Aguas (Hotels: **E** *Casa de Huéspedes San Gerónimo*, close to train station and market, clean, good; **E** *Panamericano*, noisy from railway station; **E** *San Juan*, bath, acceptable; *Colón*). Buses from Ixtepec to, eg Tehuantepec. Natural and man-made pools are fed by springs rising in Santiago Laollaga, free bathing, popular with Mexicans.

The Trans-Isthmian highway goes N from Juchitán, with a good hotel at **Matías**

Romero, Real del Istmo, a/c, by the road, safe parking; good restaurant in the same building. At Las Cruces (restaurant), a road runs right through **Zanatepec** (Motel: **C** *Posada San Rafael*, very comfortable); **Tapanatepec** (**D** *Motel La Misión* on Highway 190 on northern outskirts, T (91971) 70140, fan, hot water, clean, TV, hammock outside each room, affiliated restaurant, very good), at another junction where Highway 190 heads NE to Tuxtla Gutiérrez and Highway 200 continues SE to **Arriaga** (12,000 people); a good stopping place; many banks around Zócalo for exchange. Hotels: **C** *Ik-Lumaal*, near Zócalo, a/c, clean, quiet, good restaurant; *El Parador*, Km 47 on road to Tonalá, T 20199, clean with swimming pool; **D** *Colonial*, Callejón Ferrocarril, next to bus station, clean, friendly, quiet, limited free parking; **E** *Arbolitos*, fan, basic, clean, off main road; *Restaurant Xochimilco* near bus stations; buses to many destinations, mostly 1st class, to Mexico City, US$26.50, 12-13 hrs, at 1645. The road then goes to **Tonalá**, formerly a very quiet town but now noisy and dirty, with a small museum; good market (bus Tonalá-Tapachula, 3 hrs, US$6.75; also buses to Tuxtla). Beyond Tonalá the road is mostly straight and is being improved (1994). This is by far the most direct road for travellers seeking the quickest way from Mexico City to Guatemala.

Hotels B *Galilea*, Av Hidalgo y Callejón Oriente, T 30239, with bath, air-conditioned, good, basic cheap rooms on 1st floor, balconies, on main square, with good restaurants; **D** *Tonalá*, Hidalgo 172, T 30480, opposite museum; **E** *Casa de Huéspedes El Viajero*, Avenida Matamoros, near market, with bath, rough but OK; **E** *Faro*, 16 de Septiembre 24, near Plaza; *Santa Elena Restaurant*, at the S end of town, near Cristóbal Colón bus station on outskirts, good. On the Plaza, *Restaurant Nora*. Numerous Chinese-named restaurants; good breakfast at restaurants on Zócalo.

Route 200 runs more-or-less parallel to the coast from Tonalá to Tapachula, passing several fine-looking and undeveloped beaches (although waves and/or currents are dangerous). **Puerto Arista** is now being built up and spoiled; bus from Tonalá every hour, 45 mins, US$0.50, taxi US$2; plenty of buses to Arriaga, US$0.75. Many hotels, motels and restaurants on the beach; hot, muggy, lots of mosquitoes and, in the wet season, sandflies. Take your own water. **E** *Casa Diana*, N end of beach road, run by 2 Canadians, with breakfast, nice, friendly. Some restaurants (closed by 2000) have rooms to rent, eg *Restaurant Turquesa*; small hotel/restaurant 3 blocks down on the right from where the road reaches the beach coming from Tonalá and turns right, next to bakery, no fan, basic, F. Buses also from Tonalá to Boca del Cielo further down the coast, which is good for bathing but has no accommodation, and similarly Cabeza del Toro. **Paredón**, on the huge lagoon Mar Muerto near Tonalá, has excellent seafood and one very basic guest house. One can take a local fishing boat out into the lagoon to swim; the shore stinks because fishermen clean fish on the beach among dogs and pigs. Served by frequent buses. En route for Tapachula one passes through **Pijijiapan** where there is the *Hotel Pijijilton*(!) next to the Cristóbal Colón bus station; also **C** *Hotel El Estraneo*, very nice, parking in courtyard and **E** *Sabrina*, nice, clean and quiet, safe parking; many on Ruta México 200 (the main road from Tehuantepec to Tapachula), eg *El Navegante Los Reyes*, E per bed, doubles only. Also **Huixtla**, which has a good market, no tourists (**E** *Casa de Huéspedes Regis*, Independencia Norte 23).

Tapachula (pop 144,000) is a pleasant, neat, but expensive, hot commercial town (airport; cinemas in centre). Avenidas runs N-S, Calles E-W (Oriente-Poniente). Odd-numbered Calles are N of Calle Central, odd Avenidas are E of Av Central. It is the road and rail junction for Guatemala (road crossings at the Talismán bridge, or at Ciudad Hidalgo). It is also home to many refugees and has a rough atmosphere.

Hotels A *Motel Loma Real*, Carretera Costera No 200, Km 244, T 61440, 1 km N of city, operates as a 1st class hotel, use of swimming pool, cold showers; **C** *Fénix*, 4 Av Norte 19,

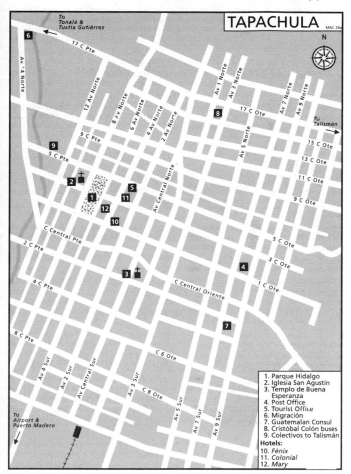

TAPACHULA MAC 26a

To Tonalá & Tuxtla Gutiérrez

To Talismán

To Airport & Puerto Madero

17 C Pte

Av 14 Norte

12 Av Norte

8 Av Norte

6 Av Norte

4 Av Norte

2 Av Norte

9 C Pte

5 C Pte

Av 1 Norte

Av 3 Norte

Av 5 Norte

Av 7 Norte

Av 9 Norte

17 C Ote

15 C Ote

13 C Ote

11 C Ote

9 C Ote

5 C Ote

3 C Ote

1 C Ote

Av Central Norte

C Central Pte

2 C Pte

4 C Pte

C Central Oriente

C 6 Ote

C 8 Ote

8 C Pte

Av 4 Sur

Av 2 Sur

Av Central Sur

Av 3 Sur

Av 5 Sur

Av 7 Sur

Av 9 Sur

1. Parque Hidalgo
2. Iglesia San Agustín
3. Templo de Buena Esperanza
4. Post Office
5. Tourist Office
6. Migración
7. Guatemalan Consul
8. Cristóbal Colón buses
9. Colectivos to Talismán
Hotels:
10. Fénix
11. Colonial
12. Mary

T 50755; **C** *San Francisco*, Av Central Sur 94, T 61454, 15 mins from centre, good, a/c; **C** *Santa Julia*, next to Cristóbal Colón terminal, bath, phone, TV, a/c, clean, good. In centre within 1 block of Plaza Central; **C** *Don Miguel* (1a Calle Pte No 18, T 61143) and **D** *Posada Michel* (5a Calle Pte No 23, T 52640); **E** *Cinco de Mayo*, 5 Calle Poniente y 12 Av Norte, with bath (cheaper without), not very clean, convenient for Talismán colectivos which leave ½ block away; **E** *El Retorno*, opp, on 5a Calle Poniente, is unhelpful and noisy; **E** *Colonial*, 4a Av Norte 31, attractive courtyard, about 1 block from central square, good value, but door locked at all times; **E** *Rex*, 8a Av Norte 43, T 50376, similar *Hospedaje Carballo*, 6a Av Norte 18, T 64370; **D** *Tabasco*, with shower, close to first-class bus station, poor value but friendly. On 11a Call Pte: **D** *Alfa*, No 53, T 65442, clean, fan, cold shower, similar *Posada de Calu*, No 34, T 65659; **E** *Hospedaje Santa Cruz*, No 36, clean, fan, bath, no windows in some rooms; all a long way from Cristóbal Colón 2nd class terminal (15-20 blocks). Many hotels along Avenidas 4, 6, 8 (near Plaza); **E** *Pensión Mary* (Av 4 Norte No 28, T 63400) has cheap *comidas*; **E** *Atlántida*, 6 Av N, Calle 11/13 Pte, T 62136, not very clean, cheaper without window, fans, noisy, unhelpful, safe parking for 2; **E** *Hospedaje Madrid*, 8 Av Norte, No 43, T 63018, shared bath. Good **restaurant** next to Cristóbal Colón terminal and on main square.

Viva Pizza, Av Central, good pizza, reasonable price. Good, cheap chicken on Central Norte; good but expensive restaurant on main square.

Shopping *Rialfer*, supermarket, Blvd Díaz, 2 doors from Banamex.

Laundromat There is a laundry, at Av Central Norte 99 between Calles 13 and 15 Oriente, US$3 wash and dry, 1 hr service, about 2 blocks from Cristóbal Colón bus station, open Sun. Also on Central Norte between Central Oriente y 1a Calle, opens 0800, closed Sun.

Exchange Avoid the crowds of streetwise little boys at the border; exchange is rather better in the town, bus station gives a good rate (cash only). **Banamex**, Blvd Díaz Ordaz, open 0830-1230, 1400-1600, disagreement over whether TCs are charged. *Casa de cambio*, Av 4 Norte y Calle 3 Poniente, changes dollars, TCs, pesos, quetzales, lempiras and colones (open late Mon-Sat and on Sun am), but not rec.

Guatemalan Consulate, 2 Calle Oriente 33 and 7 Av S, T 6-12-52, taxi from Colón terminal, US$1. (Open Mon-Fri 0800-1600; visa US$10, friendly and quick, take photocopy of passport, photocopier 2 blocks away—the consul may give a visa on Sat if you are willing to pay extra.)

Telephones Several long-distance phone offices, eg *Esther*, 5 Av Nte No 46; *La Central*, Av Central Sur No 95; *Monaco*, Calle 1 Pte No 18.

Migración/Gobernación 14 Av Norte No 57, T 61263.

Travel Agent *Viajes Tacaná*, operated by Sr Adolfo Guerrero Chávez, 4a Av Norte, No 6, T 63502/63501/63245; trips to Izapa ruins, to mountains, beaches and can gain entry to museum when closed.

Tourist Office 4 Norte No 35, Edificio del Gobierno del Estado, 3rd floor, between 3 and 5 Poniente, T 65470, F 65522, Mon-Fri, 0900-1500, 1800-2000, helpful.

Air Services Aviacsa (Calle Central Nte No 52-B, T 63147, F 63159) flies daily Tapachula-Tuxtla Gutiérrez-Mexico City, T 63159; Aviacsa also flies 4 days a week to Guatemala City. AeroMéxico (2a Av Norte No 6, T 63282) flies daily to Mexico City. Kombis to airport from 2 Calle Sur No 40, T 51287. From airport to border, minibuses charge US$26 for whole vehicle, so share with others, otherwise take colectivo to 2nd class bus terminal and then a bus to Ciudad Hidalgo.

Into Guatemala It is 8 km from Tapachula to the frontier at the Talismán bridge (open 24 hrs a day); kombi vans run from near the Unión y Progreso bus station, about US$1; *colectivo* from outside *Posada de Calu* to Talismán, US$0.60, also from Calle 5 Poniente between Avs 12 y 14 Norte. Taxi Tapachula-Talismán, negotiate fare to about US$2, exit tax US$0.45. There is a *hospedaje* at the border. The Guatemalan customs post is 200m from the Mexican one. Exchange in town rather than with men standing around customs on the Guatemalan side (check rates before dealing with them, and haggle; there is no bank on the Guatemalan side). Crossing into Guatemala by car can take several hours. If you don't want your car sprayed inside it may cost you a couple of dollars. Guatemalan buses (Galgos) leave Talismán bridge 7 times a day for Guatemala City (6½ hrs), entry tax US$1/5 quetzales; insist that you are given 90 days' stamp, this may not be possible in all cases, and watch out for bribes. The toilet at immigration at the crossing is dangerous, hold-ups have been reported day or night.

There is another crossing S of Tapachula, at *Ciudad Hidalgo*, with road connection to Mazatenango. From Calle 7 Poniente between Av 2 Norte and Av Central Norte, Tapachula, buses go to 'Hidalgo', US$1.25. A few blocks from town square is Mexican immigration, at the foot of the kilometre-long bridge across the Río Suchiate; cycle taxis cross the bridge for about US$1, pedestrians pay US$0.15.

There are few buses between the Talismán bridge and Oaxaca or Mexico City (though they do exist); advisable therefore to travel to Tapachula for connection, delays can occur there at peak times. Buses (Cristóbal Colón 1st class, Av 3 Norte y 17 Oriente, T 62880; 2nd class Prolongación 9 Pte s/n, T 61161) to/from Tapachula to **Mexico City**, US$46, five a day, all pm, 18 hrs in theory (frequent stops for toilets and food, also frequent police checks, no toilet or a/c on bus), much better to take 'plus' service, 1915, US$58. Bus to **Oaxaca**, Cristóbal Colón and Fipsa (9a C Oriente, T 67603) has luggage store, US$22.50, 14 hrs, many passport checks (Fipsa has 4 a day, continuing to Puebla and Córdoba, take 1830 to see sunrise over the Sierra Madre; also has 2 a day to Mexico City). Cristóbal Colón, 1st class to Puebla, US$50. Buses from Mexico City will all leave pm also; the 1545 and 1945 go on to Talismán. Cristóbal Colón and Salina Cruz 0915, 8 hrs, US$14.80; to San Cristóbal de las Casas and Tuxtla Gutiérrez at 1100. A taxi from Guatemala to Mexican Immigration will cost US$2, but it may be worth it

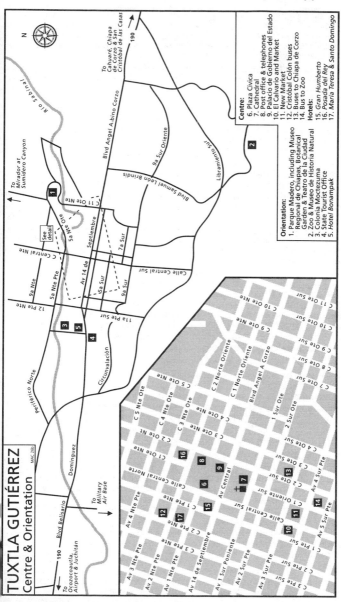

TUXTLA GUTIÉRREZ
Centre & Orientation

MAC-286

Orientation:
1. Parque Madero, including Museo Regional de Chiapas, Botanical Garden & Teatro de la Ciudad
2. Zoo & Museo de Historia Natural
3. Colonia Moctezuma
4. State Tourist Office
5. *Hotel Bonampak*

Centre:
6. Plaza Cívica
7. Cathedral
8. Post office & telephones
9. Palacio de Gobierno del Estado
10. El Calvario and Market
11. New Market
12. Cristóbal Colón buses
13. Buses to Chiapa de Corzo
14. Bus to Zoo

Hotels:
15. *Gran Humberto*
16. *Posada del Rey*
17. *María Teresa & Santo Domingo*

if you are in a hurry to catch an onward bus. Hitchhikers should note that there is little through international traffic at Talismán bridge.

The train journey from Mexico City to Tapachula involves a change at Veracruz (see under Veracruz). If travelling in the reverse direction, board train at Tapachula hours in advance of departure to get seats, and guard them. Train departs daily at 0730 for Veracruz (2nd class fare Tapachula-Veracruz US$11.75) from where 2 trains run to Mexico City.

Motoring into Mexico See **Information for Visitors, Automobiles**, on the temporary importation of vehicles, **p 382**. Car papers are issued at the Garita de Aduana on Ruta 200 out of Tapachula. There is no other road, you can't miss it. Photocopies of documents must be made in town; no facilities at the Garita.

The coastal town of **Puerto Madero**, 20 km from Tapachula (bus US$1.80), is worse than Puerto Arista, because it is more built up and the beaches stink from rubbish being burned. Intense heat in summer. (**E** *Hotel Pegado*, run down, not rec, better is unnamed *hospedaje*, also E; **F** *Hotel Puerto Madero*, accommodation in what are really remains of cement block room.) Water defences are being built, but the graveyard is under threat of being washed into the sea (watch out for skulls, etc). Many fish restaurants on beach.

Visit the ruins of **Izapa** (proto-classic stelae, small museum) just off the road to Talismán; the part of the site on the N is easily visible but a larger portion is on the S side of the highway, about 1 km away, ask caretaker for guidance. These buildings influenced Kaminal Juyú near Guatemala City and are considered archaeologically important as a Proto-Mayan site. 45 km beyond Tapachula, beyond the turning to Talismán is **Unión Juárez** (**E** *Hotel Alijoat*, hot shower, reasonable restaurant; **E** *Hotel Colonial*; *Restaurant Carmelita* on the square is modest with fair prices). In Unión Juárez one can have one's papers stamped and proceed on foot via Talquián to the Guatemalan border at Sibinal. Take a guide.

A worthwhile hike can be made up the **Tacaná volcano** (4,150m), which takes 2-3 days from Unión Juárez. Ask for the road to Chiquihuete, no cars. The Tapachula tourist office can help; in Unión Juárez ask for Sr Umberto Ríos at *Restaurante Montaña*, he will put you in touch with guide Moises Hernández, who charges US$15 a day. It is possible to stay overnight in Don Emilio Velásquez' barn half way up, US$2; he offers coffee and tortillas. At the top are some *cabañas* in which you sleep for free, sleeping bag essential.

Beyond Las Cruces (near the Oaxaca-Chiapas border) we enter the mountainous Chiapas state, mostly peopled by Maya Indians whose extreme isolation has now been ended by air services and the two main highways. Chiapas ranks first in cacao production, second in coffee, bananas and mangoes, and cattle-grazing is important. Hardwoods are floated out down the rivers which flow into the Gulf.

Note Following the EZLN uprising in early 1994, check on political conditions in Chiapas state before travelling in the area. At the time of going to press, there was no fighting between the EZLN and the Mexican army.

Mike Shawcross writes: Anyone with a vehicle who has time to visit or is looking for a place to spend the night would find it well worth while to make a 4-km detour. 50 km beyond Las Cruces a gravel road leads N (left—last km very rough) to the beautiful waterfall in **El Aguacero** national park (small sign), which falls several hundred feet down the side of the Río La Venta canyon. There is a small car-park at the lip of the canyon. 798 steps lead down to the river and the base of the waterfall. Good camping.

From Las Cruces to Tuxtla Gutiérrez, Route 190 carries on to **Cintalapa** (restaurant) whence there is a steep climb up an escarpment. Carry on to **Ocozocoautla** (airport for Tuxtla, hotel, E), make a long ascent followed by descent to

(Km 1,085) **Tuxtla Gutiérrez**, capital of Chiapas; pop: 240,000 (state pop 1990, 3,203,900); alt: 522m, 301 km (183 miles) from Tehuantepec. It is a hot, modern, some say ugly, city with greatest interest to the tourist during the fair of

Guadalupe, on 12 December. The market is worth a look. In the Parque Madero at the E end of town (Calzada de los Hombres Ilustres) is the **Museo Regional de Chiapas** with a fine collection of Mayan artefacts, open daily (US$3.45); nearby is the botanical garden. Also in this park is the Teatro de la Ciudad. There is a superb **zoo** some 3 km S of town up a long hill (too far to walk), which contains only animals and birds from Chiapas, wild and in captivity. It is said to be the best zoo in Mexico, if not Latin America—good for birdwatchers too (open Tues-Sun, 0830-1700, aviary closes 1400, free, but voluntary donation to ecological work recommended, shirts and posters for sale); the colectivos 'Zoológico' and 'Cerro Hueco' from Mercado, Calle 1a Oriente Sur y Av 5a Sur Oriente, pass the entrance every 20 mins; taxi US$2.50 from centre. Town buses charge US$0.15.

The street system here is as follows: Avenidas run from E to W, Calles from N to S. The Avenidas are named according to whether they are N (Norte) or S (Sur) of the Avenida Central and change their names if they are E (Oriente) or W (Poniente) of the Calle Central. The number before Avenida or Calle means the distance from the 'Central' measured in blocks. Drivers should note that there are very few road signs.

Hotels A *Bonampak* (Best Western), Blvd Belisario Domínguez 180, T 32050, F 22737, W end of town, the social centre, clean, noisy at night, expensive and poor restaurant; *Flamboyant*, Blvd Belisario Domínguez 1081, T 29730, F 11236, comfortable, good swimming pool; **B** *Palace Inn*, Blvd Belisario Domínguez Km 1081, 4 km from centre, T 24343, generally rec, lovely garden, pool, noisy videobar, some a/c doesn't work; **B** *Gran Hotel Humberto*, Av Central Pte 180, T 22080, central, a/c (doesn't always work), noisy disco, not rec; **C** *Posada del Rey*, 2 Av Norte Oriente 310, T 22911, a/c, but damp; **C** *La Mansión*, 1 Poniente Norte 221, T 22151, a/c, bath, safe, clean, but street-facing rooms are noisy and affected by traffic fumes; all centrally located; **C** *Mar-Inn*, pleasant, clean, 2a Av Norte Oriente 347, T 22715; **C** *Regional San Marcos*, 1 Sur y 2 Oriente No 176, T 31940, cheaper without TV, close to Zócalo, bath, fan or a/c, clean; **D** *Plaza Chiapas*, 2 Av Norte Oriente y 2 C Norte Oriente, new, clean, with fan and hot shower, rec. Opp Cristóbal Colón bus station are **D** *María Teresa* (2a Norte Pte 259-B, T 30102), not rec, and **E** *Santo Domingo*, with shower, good if you arrive late, but noisy and very basic; **E** *Estrella*, 2a Oriente Norte 322, T 23827, good; **E** *Posada del Sol*, 3a Norte Poniente, 1 block from Cristóbal Colón buses, with warm shower; **E** *Posada Maya*, 4 Poniente Sur 322, clean; *Posada Muñiz*, 2a Sur Ote 245, near 2nd class bus station, not rec, but useful for early departures; **F** *Santa Elena*, Oriente Sur 346, basic. **Youth Hostel**, Calz Angel Albino Corzo 1800, T 33405, CP 29070, meals available.

Motels C *Costa Azul*, Libramiento Sur Oriente No 3722, T 13364/13452, new, comfy, clean, but everything designed for short-stay couples; **C** *El Sumidero*, Panamericana Km 1093, on left as you enter town from E, a/c, comfortable, but much passing trade; **C** *La Hacienda*, trailer-park-hotel, Belisario Domínguez 1197 (W end of town on Route 190), T 27832, camping US$7-8 per tent, 4 spaces with hook-up, hot showers, restaurant, minipool, US$13.50 for car and 2 people, a bit noisy and not easily accessible for RVs over 6m, owner speaks English.

Restaurants *Parrilla La Cabaña*, 2a Oriente Nte 250, excellent *tacos*, very clean; *Los Arcos*, Central Poniente 806, good international food; *Las Pichanchas*, pretty courtyard, *marimba* music between 1400-1700 and 2000-2300, on Av Central Oriente 857, worth trying; good pizza restaurant by cinema on Plaza, reasonable; *Mina*, Av Central Oriente 525, nr bus station, good cheap *comida*, unfriendly service; *Café Mesón Manolo*, Av Central Poniente 238, good value, reasonably priced; *La Parcela*, 2C Oriente, nr *Hotel Plaza Chiapas*, good, cheap, good breakfasts, rec; *Los Gallos*, 2a Av Norte Poniente, 20m from Cristóbal Colón terminal, open 0700-2400, good and cheap; *Las Delicias*, 2 Poniente between Central and 1 Norte, close to Cristóbal Colón terminal, good breakfasts and snacks; *Pizzería San Marco*, behind Cathedral, good; *Bing*, 1a Sur Poniente 1480, excellent ice cream; many others. Coffee shop below *Hotel Serrano*, Av Central Pte 224, serves excellent coffee.

Exchange Bancomer, la Sur Pte 1600, near *Hotel Bonampak* for Visa, open 0900-1330. For cheques and cash at 1a Sur Pte 350, near Zócalo.

Post Office on main square. International **phone** calls can be made from 1 Norte, 2 Oriente, directly behind post office, 0800-1500, 1700-2100 (1700-200 Sun).

Travel Agency *Carolina Tours*, Sr José Narváez Valencia (manager), Av Central Poniente 1138, T 2-42-81; reliable, recommended; also coffee shop at Av Central Poniente 230.

Tourist Office For Chiapas Av Central Poniente 1500 block (on left-hand side going up), next to Bancomer building, in a complex with *artesanía* shop and cheap, a/c café, Col Moctezuma, has information on all Chiapas, including very useful state map, free; also in Zoo, am only.

Roads and Buses 35 km E of Tuxtla, just past Chiapa de Corzo (see below), a road runs N, 294 km, to Villahermosa via Pichucalco (**see p 289**), paved all the way. If driving to Villahermosa, allow at least 5 hours for the endless curves and hairpins down from the mountains—a very scenic route, nevertheless.

Cristóbal Colón 1st class bus terminal is at 2 Av Norte Poniente 268; has buses daily to **Villahermosa** at 0620, 1300 and 1730, 8½ hrs, US$14.80; to **Oaxaca** 4 a day, 12 hrs, US$17 1st class, US$22.50 deluxe 'servicio plus'; ADO to **Puebla**, US$35, departs 1845; ADO to **Veracruz**, US$25, at 2100; 8 a day to **Mexico City**, US$39, plus frequent buses 0430 to 2115 to **San Cristóbal de Las Casas**, 2 hrs, US$3, superb mountain journey. To **Comitán** 0530 then each hour to 1800, Cristóbal Colón, US$5.80; to Ciudad Cuauhtémoc, same company, US$8, 0730 and 1245. Tuxtla-**Tapachula**, US$11, 4 a day; there are more 1st class than 2nd class to the Talismán bridge (1st class is less crowded). Oaxaca Pacífico buses to Salina Cruz, from 1st class bus terminal. Take travel sickness tablets for Tuxtla-Oaxaca road if you suffer from queasiness. To **Palenque**, 2nd class, US$11. To **Mérida** change at Villahermosa if no direct service at 1330, US$35. The scenery between Tuxtla and Mérida is very fine, and the road provides the best route between Chiapas and Yucatán.

By Air The new airport (San Juan) for Tuxtla is way out at the next town of Ocozocoautla, a long drive to a mountain top. It is often shrouded in cloud and has crosswinds: there are times when aircraft do not leave for days! There are VW taxis at the bus station and opp *Hotel Humberto*, but they will not drive to the airport unless they have a full passenger load and may tout hotels before going there. Journey takes 45-50 mins, US$3.50 by colectivo from AeroMéxico and Mexicana agency, Av Central Poniente 206, T 20020/25402. Good facilities, including restaurant. This airport is used by AeroMéxico and Mexicana. Aviacsa and Aerocaribe fly from Terán airport, 10 mins by taxi from the centre, US$2.

Tuxtla Gutiérrez to Tapachula, daily with Aviacsa (Av Central Pte 1144, T 26880/28081, F 27086), new jets, 40 mins; to Villahermosa daily, 30 mins, Aerocaribe daily, Aviacsa 4 times a week. Frequent to Mexico City, direct 1 hr 20 mins, Mexicana and Aviacsa daily (the latter's 1610 flight stops at Oaxaca). Aerocaribe also flies to Oaxaca and to Mérida and Cancún. There is a 40 min flight by Britten-Norman Islander to Palenque, very exciting, no reservations or tickets available. You must be at the airport before dawn, flights leave at about 0700, Sumidero canyon can be seen during flight.

Excursions Two vast artificial lakes made by dams are worth visiting: the Presa Netzahualcoyotl, or Mal Paso, 77 km NW of Tuxtla, and La Angostura, SE of the city. Information from the tourist office. Mal Paso can also be visited from Cárdenas (**see p 286**). By paved road in excellent condition, to the rim of the tremendous ***Sumidero Canyon***, over 1,000m deep (tour US$35; taxi fare US$25 return; try to get a group together and negotiate with a *kombi* driver to visit the viewpoints on the road into the canyon, US$15 per vehicle). To get to the first viewpoint only, take colectivo marked 'Km 4', get out at the end and walk about 3 km up the road. With your own car, you can drive up to the last mirador (restaurant), especially recommended at sunset (2-3 hrs trip, 20 km W of the city). Indian warriors unable to endure the Spanish conquest hurled themselves into the canyon rather than submit. The canyon is in a national park, open 0600-1800, camping permitted outside the gate. At Cahuaré, 10 km in the direction of Chiapa de Corzo, it is possible to park by the river. If going by bus, get out just past the large bridge on the Chiapa de Corzo road. Boat trip into the Sumidero Canyon costs US$50 for the boat for 1½ hrs; boats often set out with 6 passengers but can take 10, when cost is US$6 pp (take a sweater, the boats go very fast). It is easier to find people to make up numbers in Chiapa de Corzo than in Cahuaré, as the former is a livelier place with more restaurants, launches and other facilities.

Excursions by air to Bonampak and Yaxchilán cheaper from San Cristóbal (see below).

Chiapa de Corzo (pop 35,000), 15 km on, a colonial town on a bluff overlooking the Grijalva river, is more interesting than Tuxtla: see a fine 16th century crown-shaped fountain, a church whose engraved altar is of solid silver, and famous craftsmen in gold and jewellery and lacquer work who travel the fairs. Painted and lacquered vessels made of pumpkins are a local speciality. There is a small lacquer museum. The *fiestas* here are outstanding: they reach their climax on 20-23 January with a pageant on the river, but there are daylight *fiestas*, Los Parachicos, on 15, 17 and 20 January, and the Chunta *fiestas*, at night, from 9-23 January. The musical parade is on 19 January. There is another *fiesta* in early February. **D** *Hotel Los Angeles*, on Plaza, often full, warm shower, fan, only one; *Jardín Turístico* on main plaza, good restaurant (*plato jardín* is a selection of different regional dishes); good seafood restaurants by the riverside. Plaza filled with bars playing jukeboxes. Chiapa de Corzo was a preclassic and proto-classic Maya site and shares features with early Maya sites in Guatemala; the ruins are behind the Nestlé plant, and some restored mounds are in a field near modern houses. Ask the householders' permission to climb over the fence as the ruins are on private property. Bus from Tuxtla Gutiérrez, 380 Calle 3C Oriente Sur, US$0.50, frequent; several buses a day (1 hr) to San Cristóbal de Las Casas, 2nd class, US$3.50. Cristóbal Colón from Mexico City, 1815, US$36.50.

Mike Shawcross tells us: The waterfall at the **Cueva de El Chorreadero** is well worth a detour of 1 km (one restaurant here, rec). The road to the cave is 10 km past Chiapa de Corzo, a few km after you start the climb up into the mountains to get to San Cristóbal.

(Km 1,170) **San Cristóbal de Las Casas** (population 90,000), 85 km beyond Tuxtla Gutiérrez, was founded in 1528 by Diego de Mazariegos and was the colonial capital of the region. It stands in a high mountain valley at 2,110m. It was named after Las Casas, protector of the Indians, its second bishop. There are many old churches; two of them cap the two hills which overlook the town. **Santo Domingo**, built in 1547, has a baroque façade, a gilt rococo interior and a famous carved wooden pulpit (see below). Museum in the **Convent of Santo Domingo** gives a very good history of San Cristóbal, and has a display of local costumes upstairs (closed for renovation since 1992). Other churches include **San Nicolás**, with an interesting façade, **El Carmen**, **La Merced**, and **La Caridad** (1715). From the **Temple of Guadalupe** there is a good view of the city and surrounding wooded hills (from the N side of the Zócalo, go E along Calle Real de Guadalupe). At the opposite side of the city, behind the **Iglesia de San Cristóbal** at the top of Cerrito San Cristóbal is a crucifix made of licence plates (reached via Hermanos Domínguez at Ignacio Allende); parking area with stone benches, popular with picnickers, also good view over city. Churches are closed Sunday pm. 25 July is *fiesta* day, when vehicles are taken uphill to be blessed by the Bishop. There is also a popular spring festival on Easter Sunday and the week after. Various kinds of craftwork are sold in the new market, open daily, and in the Sunday markets of the local Indian villages. There is a small American colony. There is a remarkable **cemetery** on the road to Tuxtla Gutiérrez, 2-3 km from the centre of town.

Most Indian tribes here are members of the Tzotzil and Tzeltal groups. The Tenejapans wear black knee-length tunics; the Chamulans white wool tunics; and the Zinacantecos multicoloured outfits, with the ribbons on their hats signifying how many children they have. The Chamula and Tenejapa women's costumes are more colourful, and more often seen in town, than the men's.

NB Check on the situation before you visit the surrounding villages. Travellers are strongly warned not to wander around on their own, especially in the hills surrounding the town where churches are situated, as they could risk assault. Warnings can be seen in some places frequented by tourists. Heed the warning on photographing, casual clothing and courtesy (**see p 280**). It is cold at night, in winter extremely so, bring warm clothing and night clothes.

Hotels A *Bonampak*, Calzada México 5, T 81622, F 81621; **A** *Arrecife de Coral*, Crescencio Rosas 29, T 82125/82098, modern, clean, TV, hot water, garden, off-street parking, friendly owners; **B** *Casa Mexicana*, 28 de Agosto 1, T 80698, F 82627, cable TV, telephone, indoor patio with fountain, very plush and comfy, same owner as *La Galería*

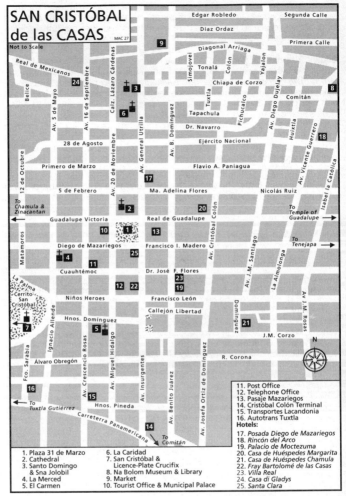

SAN CRISTÓBAL de las CASAS MAC 27
Not to Scale

Map labels:
Edgar Robledo — Segunda Calle
Díaz Ordaz — Primera Calle
Real de Mexicanos — Diagonal Arriaga
Simojovel — Tonalá — Colón — Yajalón
Chiapa de Corzo
Belice — Av. 5 de Mayo — Av. 16 de Septiembre — Calz. Lázaro Cárdenas — Tuxtla — Pichucalco — Av. Diego Dujelay — Comitán
Tapachula
Dr. Navarro
28 de Agosto — Av. 20 de Noviembre — Av. General Utrilla — Av. B. Domínguez — Ejército Nacional — Av. Vicente Guerrero — Huixtla
Primero de Marzo — Flavio A. Paniagua
12 de Octubre — 5 de Febrero — Ma. Adelina Flores — Nicolás Ruiz — Isabel la Católica
To Chamula & Zinacantan
Guadalupe Victoria — Real de Guadalupe — To Temple of Guadalupe
Matamoros — Diego de Mazariegos — Av. Cristóbal Colón — Av. J.M. Santiago — La Almolonga — To Tenejapa
Francisco I. Madero
Cuauhtémoc — Dr. José F. Flores
La Palma — Cerrito San Cristóbal — Niños Héroes — Francisco León — Av. J.M. Rosas
Ignacio Allende — Hnos. Domínguez — Callejón Libertad — Domínguez
Sarabia — Fco. Sarabia — Álvaro Obregón — Av. Crescencio Rosas — Av. Miguel Hidalgo — J.M. Corzo
R. Corona
To Tuxtla Gutiérrez — Hnos. Pineda — Av. Insurgentes — Av. Benito Juárez — Av. Josefa Ortiz de Domínguez
Carretera Panamericana — To Comitán

1. Plaza 31 de Marzo
2. Cathedral
3. Santo Domingo & Sna Jolobil
4. La Merced
5. El Carmen
6. La Caridad
7. San Cristóbal & Licence-Plate Crucifix
8. Na Bolom Museum & Library
9. Market
10. Tourist Office & Municipal Palace
11. Post Office
12. Telephone Office
13. Pasaje Mazariegos
14. Cristóbal Colón Terminal
15. Transportes Lacandonia
16. Autotrans Tuxtla

Hotels:
17. Posada Diego de Mazariegos
18. Rincón del Arco
19. Palacio de Moctezuma
20. Casa de Huéspedes Margarita
21. Casa de Huéspedes Chamula
22. Fray Bartolomé de las Casas
23. Villa Real
24. Casa di Gladys
25. Santa Clara

restaurant, highly rec; **B** *Español*, 1 de Marzo 16, T 80045, hot water morning and evening, clean, beautiful courtyard, restaurant, some rooms noisy; **B** *Molino de La Alborada*, Periférico Sur Km 4, S of airstrip, T 80935, modern ranch-house and bungalows; **A** *Posada Diego de Mazariegos*, María A Flores 2, T 81825, F 80827, 1 block N of Plaza, rec, comfortable, quiet, reception at 5 de Febrero, restaurant, live music regularly in the evening in bar *El Jaguar*; *Parador Ciudad Real*, Diagonal Centenario 32, T 81886, F 82853, W edge of city; **B** *Rincón del Arco*, 8 blocks from centre, friendly, Ejército Nacional 66, T 81313, F 81568, warmly rec, bar, restaurant, discotheque; **B** *Santa Clara*, Insurgentes 1, on Plaza, T 81140, F 81041, colonial style, clean, good restaurant, pool, highly rec; **B/C** 2 *Hoteles Mónica*, larger at Insurgentes 33, T 80732, F 82940, nice patio, restaurant, bar, rec, and smaller at 5 de Febrero 18, T 81367 (also have furnished bungalows to rent on road to San

Juan Chamula); **C** *Palacio de Moctezuma*, Juárez 16, T 80352, F 81533, colonial style, good Mexican food; **C** *Maya Quetzal*, on Pan-American Highway, Km 1171, T 81181, F 80984, adjoining restaurant; **C** *Mansión del Valle*, C Diego de Mazariegos 39, T 82582/3, F 82581, chic; **C** *Parador Mexicano*, Av 5 de Mayo 38, T 81515, tennis court, quiet and pleasant; **C** *Capri*, Insurgentes 54, near Cristóbal Colón bus terminal, T 80015, clean, helpful, rec; **C** *Ciudad Real*, Plaza 31 de Marzo 10, T 80187, F 80469, clean, good value, good restaurant, attractive rooms, but noisy parrot talks a lot; **C** *Posada de los Angeles*, Madero 17, T 81173, F 82581, very good value, hot water, with bath and TV; **C** *Real del Valle*, Av Real de Guadalupe 14, T 80680, F 83015, next to Plaza, very clean, friendly, rec, washing facilities on roof, new wing added, very nice, hot water, but no heating, good café, English spoken, laundry, credit cards accepted, parking; **C** *Fray Bartolomé de Las Casas*, Insurgentes and Niños Héroes, T 80932, with bath, nice rooms (some dark) and patio with *Café Kate*, can be noisy, extra blankets available, safe parking; **D** *Pensión Ramos*, Cuauhtémoc 12, with bath and hot water, small, rec; **D** *San Cristóbal*, Insurgentes 2 near Plaza, with bath, colonial style, renovated, pleasant; **D** *San Martín*, Real de Guadalupe 16, T 80533, near Plaza, clean, highly rec, hot water, left-luggage; **D** *Casa de Huéspedes Margarita*, Real de Guadalupe 34, T 80957, in private room without bath, spotless communal sleeping E-F, washing and toilets, clean, friendly, hot water, laundry possible, rec, popular with backpackers, attractive restaurant serves good breakfast and dinner, not cheap, wholefood, horses and guides arranged for visits to nearby villages or caves in the mountains, US$16 incl guides for 4 hrs. Next door is **D** *Posada Santiago* (No 32, T 80024), with private bath, clean, hot water, good cafeteria, rec; **D** *Posada Tepeyac*, Real de Guadalupe 40, one block from *Margarita*, with bath, friendly, clean, hot shower, avoid ground floor rooms, dark and gloomy, rec; **D** *Posada Los Morales*, Ignacio Allende 17, cottages with open fires (wood US$0.80), kitchen and hot showers, beautiful gardens overlook city, but dirty (some cottages are very basic, with no water); **D** *Posada Virginia*, Calle Cristóbal Colón and Guadalupe, for 4 in room with bath, hot water, clean, rec; **D** *Villa Real*, Av Benito Juárez 8, T 82930, clean, hot water, luggage deposit, safe, rec.

E pp *Villa Betania*, Madero 87, T 84467, airy rooms with bath and fireplace, hot water, clean, meets 1st class buses with jeep transport to hotel; **E** *Casa di Gladys* (Privates Gästelhäus Casa Degli Ospiti), Real de Mexicanos 16, Caja Postal 29240, 2 blocks from Santo Domingo, or F pp in dormitory, patio, hot showers, clean bathrooms, comfortable, breakfast available, Gladys meets Cristóbal Colón buses, highly rec, laundry facilities, horseriding arranged, luggage store; **E** *Casa de Huéspedes Chamula*, Calle Julio M Corzo, clean, hot showers, washing facilities, friendly, parking, noisy, with shared bath, some rooms without windows, rec. **E** *Casa de Huéspedes Santa Lucía*, Clemente Robles 21, T 80315, shared bath, ask for hot water, refurbished, clean, rec, one of the cheapest. **E** *Posada Casa Blanca*, Insurgentes 6-B, 50m S of Zócalo, with shower, clean, hot water, friendly owner; **E** *Posada Insurgente*, Av Insurgentes 73, clean, refurbished, good bathrooms with hot water, one block from Cristóbal Colón station; **E** *Posada Lupita I*, Benito Juárez 12, T 81421, beds like hammocks, strict controls of hot water and *No II* at Insurgentes 46, T 81019; **E** *Posada Poganda*, Insurgentes, nr Cristóbal Colón terminal, good laundry, hot showers, comfortable; **E** *Posada Lucella*, Av Insurgentes 55, T 80956, opp Iglesia Santa Lucía, some rooms with bath, hot water, others shared, good value, clean, safe, quiet rooms around patio, well-furnished, rec. **E** *Jovel*, Calle Flavio Paniagua 28, T 81734, shared bath, clean, quiet, good, hot water, extra blankets available, friendly, will store luggage, restaurant, horses (OK) for hire, highly rec; **E** *Posadita*, Flavio Paniagua 30, with bath, clean, friendly, laundry facilities, rec; **E** *Posada del Candil*, Mexicanos, hot shower, but hot water (even water) not always available, clean, laundry facilities, good value; **E** *Posada El Cerillo*, Av B Domínguez 27, hot showers, washing facilities, no electricity 1300-1700, reports vary; **E** *Posada Isabel*, Francisco León 54, near Av JM Santiago, with shower, clean, quiet, good value, parking; **E** *Santo Domingo*, 28 de Agosto 4, 3 blocks from Zócalo, with bath, F without, clean, hot showers, very friendly. **F** *Baños Mercederos*, Calle 1° de Marzo 55, shared quarters, good cheap meals, steam baths (highly rec, $2 extra). Look on the bulletin board outside the tourist office for guesthouses advertising rooms at US$3.50 pp, bed and breakfast (ie *Madero 83*, clean, safe, good breakfast, popular with backpackers, frequently rec), US$5 with lunch or dinner.

Camping *Rancho San Nicolás*, at end of Calle Francisco León, 1½ km E of centre, beautiful, quiet location, is a trailer park, but do take warm blankets or clothing as the temperature drops greatly at night, hot showers, US$5 for room in cabaña, US$3.30 to camp, US$10 for camper van with 2 people (electricity hook-up), children free, laundry facilities, rec. Trailer Park *Bonampak* on Route 190 at W end of town, 22 spaces with full hook-up, hot shower, heated pool, restaurant, US$10 per vehicle and 2 people. 'White gas' available at small store on corner across from NE corner of main market (Chiwit).

Restaurants *La Parrilla*, Av Belisario Domínguez 32, closed Sat, not cheap but excellent grilled meats and cheese, open fire, cowboy decor with saddles as bar stools, rec; *La Pergola*,

Plaza de la Calle Real, Real de Guadalupe 5, very good pasta and coffee; *La Taverna*, Real de Guadalupe, good pizza, concerts almost nightly, rec; *El Mural*, 20 de Noviembre 8, good, excellent coffee and cakes; *El Bazar*, Paniagua 2, hippy, good local dishes, good value, live music; *La Galeria*, Hidalgo 3, a few doors from Zócalo, popular with tourists, best coffee, good breakfast, international (many German) newspapers, art gallery, videos at night; *La Plaza*, upstairs, SW corner of Plaza, clean; *El Unicornio*, Av Insurgentes 33a (US$20 for 2), good; *Capri*, Insurgentes 16, good food, set meals at reasonable prices; *Tikal*, Insurgentes 77A, near bus station, excellent and not expensive, good breakfasts, bright and pleasant, sells toys made by SODAM (see below); *Cafetería Palenque*, on Insurgentes nr C Colón terminal, cheap, good and friendly, open 0800-1900, closed Sun; *Tuluc*, Insurgentes 5, open 0615-2200, good value, near Plaza, popular, classical music, art for sale and toys on display (sold at SODAM, see below), rec; *Merendero*, JM Corzo y Insurgentes, OK, cheap; *Casa de las Imágenes*, Av Belisario Domínguez 11, near *Margarita* restaurant, gallery, cinema, bookstore, live concerts with local musicians, good café, rec; *El Teatro*, 1 de Marzo 8, café, bar, restaurant; *La Chimenea*, 1 de Marzo, very good and cheap set meal, friendly, highly rec; *Oasis*, also 1 de Marzo, excellent milk shakes; *París-México*, Madero 20, smart, French cuisine, reasonably-priced *comida corrida*, US$4, classical music; *Los Arcos*, Madero 6, varied menu, family run, inexpensive, good, closes 2130; several other cheap, local placed on F Madero E of Plaza 31 de Marzo; *Fulano*, on Madero 12, near Plaza, excellent set meal at reasonable price; *La Langosta* opposite, Madero 9, good *comida corrida*; *Flamingo*, Madero 14, nice décor, reasonable food (good paella); next door is *El Mirador II*, good local and international food. *Jardín de Cantón*, Calle 28 de Agosto 19, open Tues-Sun 1300-1900, excellent and not expensive Chinese cuisine, open garden in back, attentive service, peaceful atmosphere, highly rec; *Cactus Crazy*, Guadalupe Victoria 59, bar and restaurant, good atmosphere, friendly owner.

The town is a 'health food and vegetarian paradise'; shop around. *Madre Tierra*, Insurgentes 19 (opp Franciscan church), Anglo-Mexican owned, European dishes, vegetarian specialities, good breakfasts, wholemeal breads from bakery (also take-away), pies, brownies, chocolate cheese cake, classical music, popular with travellers, not cheap, good night life; *Las Estrellas*, Escuadrón 201 No 2B, good cheap food, inc vegetarian, good brown bread, live music from 2030, nice atmosphere, Mexican/Dutch owned, rec; *El Trigal*, Flavio Paniagnua, between Utrilla and B Domínguez, restaurant, vegetarian, good and cheap; *Tienda Vegetariana* at 28 de Agosto 2, sells a variety of health foods; *Café San Cristóbal* on Cuauhtémoc, good coffee sold in bulk too. Many others. San Cristóbal is not lively in the evenings: main meeting place is around *ponche* stall on Plaza.

Shopping Part of the ex-convent of Santo Domingo has been converted into a cooperative, *Sna Jolobil*, selling handicrafts from many Indian villages (best quality, so expensive; also concerts by local groups). *SODAM* (Mutual Aid Society) with their shop at Casa Utrilla, Av Gral Utrilla 33, is a cooperative of Indian craftsmen selling beautiful wooden dolls and toys. Sales go towards a training fund for Chamula Indians, with a workshop based at Yaalboc, a community near San Cristóbal. For local goods try *Miscelánea Betty*, Gen Utrilla 45, good value. Souvenir markets on Gral Utrilla between Real de Guadalupe and Dr A Navarro. Amber museum in Plaza Sivan shop, Gen Utrilla 10, T 83507. Many shops on Av Real de Guadalupe. For good leather cowboy boots: *Santiag*, Calle Real de Guadalupe 5; very good prices. *Postelería*, Real de Guadalupe 24, open late for maps, postcards, water and cakes. Main market is worth seeing as well. Pasaje Mazariegos (in the block bounded by Real de Guadalupe, Av B Dominguez, Madero and Plaza 31 de Marzo) has luxury clothes and bookshops, restaurants and travel agents. Bookshop *Soluna*, has a few English guidebooks, a wide range of Spanish titles and postcards. *Librería Chilam Balam*, Casa Utrilla, Av Gral Utrilla 33, good range of books, mostly in Spanish, also cassettes of regional music. *Librería El Rincón*, Diego de Mazariegos, some 2nd hand books, exchange only, 2 for 1.

Culture and Entertainment Na Bolom, Vicente Guerrero 33, the house of the archaeologists Frans (died 1963) and Trudi Blom, and a beautiful 15-room guest house (previous reservation necessary, double room US$44 with bath and fireplace, breakfast US$3.50, lunch US$5, dinner US$6.65—lunch and dinner require 3 hrs' notice), with good library (closed to visitors in 1993), run by Mrs Trudi Blom. At 1630 sharp guides take you round display, rooms of beautiful old house, and garden (1½ hrs, US$2.35 plus video—a US PBS TV programme—at 1800, US$1, rec). Entrance US$3.50. It is well worth visiting: beautifully displayed artefacts, pictures of Lacandón Indians, with information about their history and present way of life (in English). Also only easily-obtainable map of Lacandón jungle.

The *Casa de Cultura*, opp El Carmen church on junction of Hnos Domínguez and Hidalgo, has a busy range of activities on offer: concerts, films, lectures, art exhibitions and conferences. The *Casa de Las Imagenes* (see Restaurants, above) is also recommended for its cultural events.

Car hire Budget, Mazariegos 36.

Laundromat *Super Clean*, Calle Crescencio Rosas 48, US$3 for washing and drying for up to 3 kg, for collection after 5 hrs. Lavorama at Guadalupe Victoria 20A; another opp *Posada del Candil*, 6 hrs, US$1 per kg.

Exchange *Casa Margarita* will change dollars and TCs. Banks are usually open for exchange between 0900 and 1100 only, check times; this leads to queues. **Bancomer** charges commission, doesn't take Visa, only American Express or Citicorp TCs, good rates and service; **Banamex** does not change cheques; **Banco Serfin** on the Zócalo, changes Euro and Mastercard TCs. **Casa de Cambio Lacantún**, Real Guadalupe 12, open daily 0900-1400, 1600-1900, Sun 0900-1300 (supposedly, may close early), no commission, fair rates, at least US$50 must be changed. Quetzales can be obtained for pesos or dollars in the *cambio* but better rates are paid at the border.

Language Schools Roberto Rivas Bastidas, Centro Bilingüe, Insurgentes 57-D, Santa Lucía, Caja Postal 29250, T 84157, F 83723 (English programme) and Centro Cultural *El Puente*, Real De Guadalupe 55, Caja Postal 29230, T/F 83723 (Spanish programme), rates range from US$4.50/hr to US$7.50/hr depending on number in class and length of course, home stay programmes available, registration fee US$100; *El Puente* has café, bookshop, information centre, travel agency, phones and gallery, rec (also contact William English, T/F 82250). Universidad Autónoma de Chiapas, Av Hidalgo 1, Departamento de Lenguas, offers classes in English, French and Tzotzil. Instituto Jovel, María Adelina Flores 21, Apartado Postal 62, T/F 84069, runs language classes and handicraft workshops, tours offered, accommodation with families, US$285 for 2 weeks, US$130 each subsequent week, homestay US$80-95/week, deposit US$80. Ask Mercedes (see below) about her sister's language lessons.

Post Office Cuauhtémoc 13, between Rosas and Hidalgo, Mon-Fri 0800-1900, Sat 0900-1300.

Telephones Long distance phone calls can be made from the *Boutique Santo Domingo* on Utrilla, esquina Paniagua, takes credit cards, collect possible; and at shops at Av 16 de Septiembre 22 and Av Insurgentes 60. Cheap international calls from 2nd class bus station, no waiting. No operator-assisted phone calls are possible on Sundays after 2000 in Chiapas.

Tourist Office Helpful, at the Palacio Municipal, W side of main Plaza, some English spoken. Ask here for accommodation in private house. Good free map of town and surroundings. Maps of San Cristóbal US$0.35, also on sale at Kramsky, Diego de Mazariegos y 16 de Septiembre, behind Palacio Municipal (one way traffic shown for Av 16 de Septiembre and Av Ignacio Allende actually goes in the opposite direction).

Tour Guides Mercedes Hernández Gómez, leads 5-6 hr tours of local villages, including the 1-hr walk from Chamula to Zinacantán, starting at 0900 from Kiosk on the Plaza 31 de Mayo, returns about 1500, about US$13.50 pp, repeatedly recommended (take along unwanted medicines and small change). Many others take tours for same price, eg Raul and Alejandro who leave from in front of the cathedral at 0930 in VW minibus.

Horse hire Carlos, T 81873/81339; Olivier at *Bar-Restaurante La Galería*, Hidalgo 3, T 81547, reserve 1600-2230, US$20 pp, groups of 4-6, not for the inexperienced. Horses can be hired from *Casa de Huéspedes Margarita*, prices US$16-20 for horse and guide, reserve the day before; or from Sr José Hernández, Calle Elias Calles 10 (one block from Av Huixtla and Calle Chiapa de Corzo, not far from Na Bolom), T 81065, US$10 for half a day, plus guide US$11.50; the tourist office also has a list of other stables which hire out horses.

Buses Beware of highly proficient pickpockets at bus stations. From Mexico City direct, Cristóbal Colón at 1415, 1815, 2300. Cristóbal Colón 1st class bus to **Oaxaca**, about 12 hrs, at 1815 daily, book well in advance, monotonous trip, US$21.50, 622 km, robberies have been reported on these buses. To do the trip in daytime, you need to change at Tuxtla Gutiérrez (0745 Cristóbal Colón to Tuxtla, then 1100 on to Oaxaca), C Colón has hourly buses to Tuxtla between 0630 and 2030, US$3; to **Mexico City**, via Tuxtepec, about 18 hrs, 1,169 km at 2200, US$40; to **Tapachula**, 9 hrs, at 1200, US$14.80, 483 km; to **Puebla** at 1400, US$26.50, 1,034 km. Bus to **Huatulco**, 0730. Book tickets as far in advance as possible—during Christmas and Holy Week buses are sometimes fully booked for 10 days or more.

Cristóbal Colón has its own bus station on Insurgentes, 1st class; to **Villahermosa**, 6 hrs, US$11 (direct at 0700); to **Arriaga**, at 1200 via Tuxtla Gutiérrez, 235 km, US$6; to **Coatzacoalcos** at 0630, 576 km, US$14.80; to **Orizaba** 845 km; to **Chiapa de Corzo**, 64 km, several daily at 0800, 0830, 1100, 1400, 2 hrs, US$3.35; *servicio plus* to Campeche 2100; direct to **Mérida** at 2000, to **Chetumal** at 1900. To **Puerto Escondido** with Cristóbal Colón, 1st class overnight daily, US$21. There is a new 210 km paved road with fine views to

Palenque; Lacandonia 2nd class bus to Palenque from 2nd class bus station on Calle Allende (where the 1st class bus station is also) 7 a day between 0100 and 2015, US$6 (via Agua Azul, US$4); Cristóbal Colón, 1st class service, up to 4 times daily (including at least one *servicio plus*) US$8.25, bookings 5 days in advance; new company with a/c buses, Rodolfo Figueroa, 3-4 times a day, US$8.25. Other buses leave one at Ocosingo; Lacandonia 2nd class to Ocosingo, 3 hrs, US$2.75. Refunds of fares to Palenque when reaching Ocosingo are not rare, and you then have to make your own way. Autotransportes Na-Bolom to Tuxtla Gutiérrez, Comitán and Palenque from just E of 1st class bus terminal (across the bridge): to Tuxtla 13 departures (1600 *servicio plus*), US$3, 2 hrs, to Palenque 0700 and 1300, US$6.50, to Comitán 1100 and 1500, US$2.75, 2 hrs. Autotrans Tuxtla, F Sarabia entre Carretera Panamericana y Alvaro Obregón 2nd class to Palenque, reserved seats, US$5.

Into Guatemala Cristóbal Colón, S end of Av Insurgentes (left luggage facilities open 0600-2000 exc Sun and holidays), clean station, direct 1st class buses to the Guatemalan border at Ciudad Cuauhtémoc, 170 km, several daily from 0600 or 0630, 3 hrs, US$5.50 (leave bus at border, not its final destination). Cristóbal Colón to Comitán (if you can't get a bus to the border, take one to Comitán and get a colectivo there), 8 a day from 0700, US$2.75, 87 km (a beautiful, steep route). 2nd class to border with Autotrans Tuxtla, US$3.75 (do not take 1430 ACL 2nd class, next to Trans Lacandonia, on Carretera Panamericana, it arrives too late for onward transport). For details on crossing the border at La Mesilla **see p 282**.

Air Services San Cristóbal no longer has an airport; it has been consumed by urban growth. The nearest airport is at Ocosingo (**see p 280**) about 50 km along the Palenque road. To Tuxtla Gutiérrez Tues, Thurs, Sat at 1345, 84 km (Tuxtla is the major local airport but **see p 272**). Regular daily flights, except Sundays, to Palenque, 0715 (some crashes); booking only at airport. Charter flights to see Lacanjá, Bonampak and Yaxchilán on the Usumacinta River, 7 hrs in all (US$100 pp if plane is full, more if not). All with Aerochiapas at airport. Aviacsa, Pasaje Mazariegos, local 16, T 84441, F 84384, for flights from Tuxtla Gutiérrez to Mexico City and Yucatán.

Excursions Caves (Las Grutas de San Cristóbal) 10 km SE of the town (entrance US$5.25) contain huge stalagmites and are lit for 800m. Horses can be hired at Las Grutas for US$13 for a 5-hr ride, guide extra, for rides on beautiful trails in the surrounding forest. Some of these are best followed on foot. Yellow diamonds on trees and stones mark the way to beautiful meadows. Las Grutas are reached by Autotransportes de Pasaje/31 de Marzo colectivos every 15 mins (0600-1900) from Av Benito Juárez 37B, across the Pan-American Highway just S of Cristóbal Colón bus terminal. Colectivos are marked 'San Cristóbal, Teopisca, Ciudad Militar, Villa Las Rosas', or ask for minibus to 'Rancho Nuevo'. To the bus stop take 'San Diego' colectivo 1 block E of Zócalo to end of Benito Juárez. When you get to Las Grutas, ask the driver to let you out at Km 94, caves are poorly signed.

You are recommended to call at Na Bolom before visiting the villages, to get information on their cultures and seek advice on the reception you are likely to get. Photography is resisted by some Indians (see below) because they believe the camera steals their souls, and photographing their church is stealing the soul of God. Many Indians do not speak Spanish. On Sun you can visit the villages of San Juan Chamula Zinacantán and Tenejapa. While this is a popular excursion, especially when led by a guide (see above), several visitors have felt ashamed at going to look at the villagers as if they were in a zoo; there were many children begging and offering to look after private vehicles in return for not damaging them.

Zinacantán is reached by VW bus from market, US$0.75, $\frac{1}{2}$ hr journey, sometimes frequent stops while conductor lights rockets at roadside shrines. The men wear pink/red jackets with embroidery and tassels, the women a vivid pale blue shawl and navy skirts. At midday the women prepare a communal meal which the men eat in shifts. Main gathering place around church; the roof was recently destroyed by fire (US$1 charged for entering church; photography inside is strictly prohibited).

You can catch a VW bus ride from the market to **Chamula** every 20 mins, last at 1700, last one back at 1900, US$0.65 pp (or taxi, US$10) and visit the local church; another popular excursion. A permit (US$1) is needed from the village tourist office and photographing inside the church is absolutely forbidden. There are no pews but family groups sit or kneel on the floor, chanting, with rows of candles lit in front of them, each representing a member of the family and certain significance attached to the colours of the candles. The religion is centred around the 'talking stones', and three idols and certain Christian saints. Pagan rituals held in small huts at the end of August. Pre-Lent festival ends with celebrants running through blazing harvest chaff. Just after Easter prayers are held, before the sowing season starts. Festivals in Chamula should *not* be photographed, if you wish to take other shots ask permission, people are not unpleasant, even if they refuse (although children may pester you to take their picture for US$0.15). The men wear grey, black or light pink tunics, the women bright blue blouses with colourful braid and navy or bright blue shawls. There are many handicraft stalls on the way up the small hill SW of the village. This has a good viewpoint of the village and valley: take the road from SW corner of square, turn left towards ruined church then up flight of steps on left.

Interesting walk from San Cristóbal to Chamula along the main road to a point one km past the crossroads with the Periférico ring road (about 2½ km from town centre); turn on to an old dirt road to the right—but first fork you come to between some farmhouses. Then back via the road through the village of Milpoleta, some 8 km downhill, 5 hrs for the journey round trip (allow 1 hr for Chamula). Best not done in hot weather. Also, you can hike from Chamula to Zinacantán in 1½ hrs: when leaving Chamula, take track straight ahead instead of turning left onto San Cristóbal road; turn left on small hill where school is (after 30 mins) and follow a smaller trail through light forest. After an hour you reach the main road 200m before Zinacantán.

Note Signs in Chamula warn that it is dangerous to walk in the area, robberies have occurred between Chamula and both San Cristóbal and Zinacantán (these warnings have persisted in 1992, 1993 and 1994; the police in San Cristóbal are reported to charge for statements of robberies). Also seek full advice on any travel outside San Cristóbal de las Casa in the wake of events in early 1994 (see above).

3½ km from San Cristóbal, on the road to Chamula, is the **Huitepec** nature reserve; entrance US$1, 2½ km trail with Spanish and English information, administered by Pronatura-Chiapas. The 135-ha reserve contains grassland, oakwood forest, rising to cloud forest at 2,400m. As well as a wide diversity of plants, there are many birds, including some 50 migratory species. Colectivos go there. On Thursdays there is an early birdwatching tour; meet in Zócalo at 0600, but check at tourist office beforehand.

The Sun market at **Tenejapa** (F *Hotel Molina*, simple but clean; several *comedores* around the market) is traditionally fruit and vegetables, but there are a growing number of music cassette and shooting gallery stalls. Excellent woven items can be purchased from the weavers' cooperative near the church. They also have a fine collection of old textiles in their regional ethnographic museum adjoining the handicraft shop. The cooperative can also arrange weaving classes. The village is very friendly and many men wear local costume. Buses leave from San Cristóbal market at 0700 and 1100 (1½ hr journey), and colectivos every hour. The dirt road is very bumpy, not recommended for an ordinary car in the wet. Ask permission to take pictures and expect to pay. Market thins out by noon.

Two other excursions can be made, by car or local bus, from San Cristóbal S on the Pan-American Highway (½ hr by car) to **Amatenango Del Valle**, a Tzeltal village where the women make and fire pottery in their yards, and then SE (15 min by car) to **Aguacatenango**, picturesque village at the foot of a mountain. Continue 1 hr along road past Villa las Rosas (hotel) to **Venustiano Carranza**, women with fine costumes, extremely good view of the entire valley.

Get to outlying villages by bus or communal VW bus (both very packed); buses leave very early, and often don't return until next day, so you have to stay overnight; lorries are more frequent. To Zinacantán catch also VW bus from market. Buses from the market area to San Andrés Larrainzar (bus at 1000, 1100, 1400, with return same day, US$0.80 one way) and Tenejapa. Transportes Fray Bartolomé de Las Casas has buses to Chanal, Chenalhó (US$15 with taxi, return, one hr stay), Pantelhó, Yajalón and villages en route to Ocosingo. Transportes Lacandonia on Av Crescencio Rosas also go to the villages of Huistán, Oxchuc, Yajalón, on the way to Palenque, Pujiltic, La Mesilla and Venustiano Carranza. If you are in San Cristóbal for a limited period of time it is best to rent a car to see the villages.

NB Remember that locals are particularly sensitive to proper dress (ie neither men nor women should wear shorts, or revealing clothes) and manners; persistent begging should be countered with courteous, firm replies. It is best not to take cameras to villages: there are good postcards and photographs on sale. Drunkenness is quite open and at times forms part of the rituals—best not to take umbrage if accosted.

Palenque (**see p 289**) can be reached by paved road from San Cristóbal de Las Casas, a beautiful ride via *Ocosingo*, a not particularly attractive place (70,000 people) which has a local airport and several hotels (**D** *Central* on Plaza, shower, clean, verandah; **E** *Bodas de Plata*, 1 Av Sur, clean, hot water; *San José*; **E** *San Jacinto*, just off lower side of plaza, with bath, hot water, clean, friendly; *Posada Morales*) and clean restaurants. It was one of the centres of fighting in the Ejército Zapatista de Liberación Nacional uprising in January 1994. Bus to Palenque, 2½ hrs, US$3.30.

Road to ruins of *Toniná*, 12 km away, is unpaved but marked with signs once you leave Ocosingo (possible in ordinary car, taxi US$25); a tour from San Cristóbal costs US$15. To walk from Ocosingo, start in front of the church on the plaza and follow the signs, or take the 0900 bus from the market to the jungle and get off where the road forks (ask). There is a short cut through the fields: after walking for 2 hrs you come to an official sign with a pyramid on it: don't follow the arrow but take the left fork for about 15 mins and go through a wooden gate on your right; follow the path for 2-3 km (across a little stream and two more gates, ask farmers when in doubt). You end up in the middle of the site, with the palace high on a hill to your left. It is well worth visiting the ruins excavated by a French government team (open 0900-1600). Temples are in the Palenque style with internal sanctuaries in the back room. The huge pyramid complex is 10m higher than the Temple of the Sun at Teotihuacan. Stelae are in very diverse forms, as are wall panels, and some are in styles and in subject unknown at any other Maya site. A beautiful stucco mural was discovered in December 1990. Ask guardian to show you second unrestored ballcourt and the sculpture kept at his house. He will show you round the whole-site; there is also a small museum. Entry US$4.35. (Drinks available at the site.) Beside the Ocosingo-Toniná road is a marsh, frequented by thousands of swallows in January.

Some 15 km from Ocosingo on the road to San Cristóbal de las Casas is a beautiful cave with stalagmites and stalactites and bats. It is visible from the road on the left (coming from Ocosingo), close to the road, but look carefully for it. Take a torch/flashlight and walk 15m to a 10m diameter chamber at the end of the cave (don't touch the geological formations as many stalactites have already been damaged).

For Guatemala, follow the 170-km paved road via *Teopisca* (*pensión*, **E**, comfortable; *La Amistad* trailer park, run down, one dirty shower and bathroom, no electricity, not rec), past *Comitán* (85 km), a lively, attractive town of 87,000 people at 1,580m above sea level with a large, shady Plaza. Buses from San Cristóbal de la Casas with Cristóbal Colon, frequent between 0730 and 2030, US$2.75, 2 hrs, last bus back at 1930. Buses, kombis and pick-up trucks from Comitán run to the border at Ciudad Cuauhtémoc: not a town, despite its name; just a few buildings; the Cristóbal Colón bus station is off the main highway, with an overpriced restaurant and an excellent **E/F** *Hospedaje*, extremely clean and quiet, highly rec, with OK *comedor* across the street. Unleaded petrol is available in Comitán, but the location of the filling station is not known to us.

Hotels in Comitán Accommodation inferior in quality and almost twice the price of San Cristóbal. **B** *Internacional*, Av Domínguez 22, T 20112, near Plaza, good, decent restaurant. **B** *Los Lagos de Montebello*, T 20657, on Pan-American Highway, noisy but good; **B** *Real Balún Canán*, 1 Av Poniente Sur, T 20031, restaurant. **D** *Delfín*, on Plaza, fairly clean, as is **E** *Hospedaje Santo Domingo*, Calle Central B Juárez 45; **E** *Ideal*, 2a Sur Oriente, clean, friendly, centrally located. **F** *Casa de Huéspedes Río Escondido*, next to *Real Balún Canán* (No 7), shared bath, friendly, reasonable. **F** *Hospedaje Primavera*, Calle Central Poniente, 1/2 block off Plaza, looks OK; **F** *Posada Panamericana*, basic, and **F** *Posada Maya*, both on 1 Av Poniente Norte.

Restaurants *Nevelandia*, Central Nte 1, clean, rec, and **Café** *Casa de La Cultura*, on the Plaza. *L'Uccello*, Italian, 1 Av Poniente Norte, rec. **Puerto Arturo** on Blvd Dr Belisario Domínguez is good. Several small *comedores* on the Plaza.

Exchange Bancomer, on plaza will exchange Amex travellers' cheques; 2 others on plaza, none changes dollars after 1200; also a *casa de cambio*. Poor rates for both pesos and quetzales.

Guatemalan Consulate Open Mon-Fri 0800-1200, 1400-1700, Sat 0800-1400 at 2a Av Poniente Norte 28, T 2-26-69; visa (if required) US$10 (even for those for whom it should be free), valid 1 year, multiple entry: tourist cards available at border.

Tourist Office On main square, in Palacio Municipal, ground floor, open till 2000.

A road branches off the Pan-American Highway 16 km after Comitán to a very beautiful region of vari-coloured lakes, the **Lagunas de Montebello** (a national park). Off the road to Montebello, 30 km from the Pan-American Highway, lie the ruins of **Chinkultic**, with temples, ballcourt, carved stone stelae and *cenote* (deep round lake—good swimming) in beautiful surroundings; from the signpost they are about 3 km along a dirt road and they close at 1600 (entry US$3). Watch and ask for the very small sign and gate where road to ruins starts (about 1 km back along the main road—towards Comitán—from Doña María's, see below—don't attempt any short cuts), worth visiting when passing. Colectivo from Comitán US$1.

Kombi vans marked Tziscao to the Lagunas de Montebello (60 km from Comitán, US$1.80 about 1 hr), via the Lagunas de Siete Colores (so-called because the oxides in the water give varieties of colours) leave frequently from 2 Av Poniente Sur y 3 Calle Sur Poniente, 4 blocks from Plaza in Comitán; buses go as far as Laguna Bosque Azul, US$1.50, 1 hr journey; *Tziscao* is 9 km along the road leading right from the park entrance, which is 3 km before Bosque Azul; five buses a day Comitán-Tziscao, bumpy ride; the last bus and colectivo back is at 1600 and connects with the 1900 bus to San Cristóbal. A trip to the Lagunas de Siete Colores from Comitán can be done in a day (note that the less accessible lakes are hard to get to even if staying in the vicinity). It is also possible to hire a Kombi, which takes 12 people, to go to the Lakes and Chinkultic for US$15/hr. A day trip to Chinkultic and the lakes from San Cristóbal de Las Casas is also possible. The Bosque Azul area is now a reserve: there are, as well as picnic areas, an *Albergue Turístico* on the shores of Lake Tziscao (10 km, F pp, rooms for 4-6, toilet, blankets available, no hot water, reasonable kitchen facilities and bathrooms, reasonably-priced meals, dinner US$3.50, camping US$1.60 per site incl use of hotel facilities; boats for hire); a small, family-run restaurant at Laguna Bosque Azul with a wooden hut for sleeping, G, bring sleeping bag, two very basic food shops in the village (best to bring your own food from Comitán market), and there are small caves. The area is noted for its orchids and birdlife, including the famous *quetzal*; very crowded at weekends and holidays. Horse hire US$5/hr. *Posada Las Orquídeas* (better known as 'Doña María'), Km 31, on the road to Montebello near Hidalgo and the ruins of Chinkultic, dormitory or cabin, G pp, family-run, very basic (no washing facilities, rudimentary hot shower, 2 toilets—urn in a shack) but friendly, small restaurant serving plentiful Mexican food. **Youth Hostel**, Las Margaritas. *Hotel Bosque Bello*, 34 km, reservations in Tuxtla, T 10966, or Comitán T 21702. **NB** Mexican maps show a road running along the Guatemalan border from Montebello to Bonampak and on to Palenque; this road is not complete and no public transport or other traffic makes the trip.

From Hidalgo you can get to Comitán by pick-up or paying hitchhike for US$1; to the Guatemalan border go from Hidalgo to La Trinitaria and catch a bus or pick-up there.

From Comitán the road winds down to the Guatemalan border at Ciudad Cuauhtémoc via La Trinitaria (near the turn-off to Lagunas de

Montebello—restaurant but no hotel). In Ciudad Cuauhtémoc, cross the road from the bus terminal to Mexican immigration, show passport, etc, then take a pick-up to the Guatemalan border, US$1.65. Walk 100m to immigration and customs. Beyond the Guatemalan post at La Mesilla, El Tapón section, a beautiful stretch, leads to Huehuetenango, 85 km. Allow 10 hrs to reach Guatemala City by bus, not 6 as advised. It is cheaper to pay initially only to Huehuetenango and buy a ticket onwards from there (no change of bus necessary). Sometimes there is a minibus going straight to Panajachel for US$8. Do not buy a ticket at the border until a bus leaves as some wait while others come and go. If you miss the last bus to Huehuetenango, you may be able to negotiate a ride out of La Mesilla, If not, the border officials are helpful with accommodation. This route is far more interesting than the one through Tapachula; the border crossing at Ciudad Cuauhtémoc is also reported as easier than that at Talismán.

A tourist card for Guatemala can be obtained at the border, normally available for 30 days, renewable in Guatemala City. See under **Guatemala—Information for Visitors** for those who need visas. Visas are not available at the border for all nationalities who need them (eg Australians) and buses do not wait for those who alight to obtain them. It is advisable to obtain a visa in advance, ie from Comitán. You pay US$1/5 quetzales to enter Guatemala, and the border is open until 1900 (beware of 'overtime charges', etc).

Have your Mexican tourist card handy as it will be inspected at the Río San Gregorio, about 20 km before the border. Be sure to surrender your tourist card and get your exit stamp at Mexican immigration before boarding a pick-up for Guatemalan immigration; you will only have to go back if you don't.

Don't change money with the Guatemalan customs officials: the rates they offer are worse than those given by bus drivers or in banks (and these are below the rates inside the country). There is nowhere to change travellers' cheques at the border and bus companies will not accept cheques in payment for fares. The briefcase and dark glasses brigade changes cash on the Guatemalan side only, but you must know in advance what quetzal rates are.

Buses are 'de paso' from San Cristóbal so no advance booking is possible. The Cristóbal Colón bus leaves Comitán 0800, 1100 (coming from San Cristóbal) and in pm for the border at Ciudad Cuauhtémoc, fare US$2.75. Pick-ups charge US$2 Comitán-border; beware short-changing. From here take a taxi or colectivo to the Guatemalan side (3.7 km uphill, US$1 pp, minimum 3 people) and get your passport stamped to allow entry for a month. Cristóbal Colón (terminal near the Pan-American Highway, Comitán) has 1st class buses to **Mexico City** at 0900, 1100 and 1600 (which leave the border 2½ hrs earlier), fare US$40.75 (from Mexico City to Comitán at 1415 and 2040, fully booked 2 hrs in advance); to **Oaxaca** at 0700 and 1900, US$33; to **Tuxtla Gutiérrez** at 0600 and 1600, US$8, and to **Tapachula** (via Arriaga) at 1200 and 2000, US$20. Entering Mexico from Guatemala, if no bus is available to San Cristóbal, take a truck or colectivo to Comitán and travel on from there.

Airport Flights available from Comitán to Lacanjá, Bonampak, Yaxchilán, contact Capitán Pérez Esquinca, T Comitán 4-91.

NB Entering Mexico from Guatemala, 1) tourist cards are available at the border; 2) it is forbidden to bring in fruit and vegetables; rigorous checking at two checkpoints to avoid the spread of Mediterranean mosquito. Drivers entering Mexico are not given a tourist sticker for the car (as you are when entering from the USA); car entry is stamped on the back of your tourist card. There is no fee for *migración* or customs, but US$1.35 for fumigation.

YUCATAN PENINSULA (10)

The states of Yucatán and Quintana Roo, sold to tourists as the land of Maya archaeology and beach and island resorts (Cancún, Cozumel, etc). It pays to explore beyond the main itineraries, for lesser-known Maya sites, caves, lagoons, flamingo feeding grounds and villages with old churches. There are two road and river routes into Guatemala, and the main road access to Belize.

The peninsula of Yucatán is a flat land of tangled scrub in the drier NW, merging into exuberant jungle and tall trees in the wetter SE. There are no surface streams. The underlying geological foundation is a horizontal bed of limestone in which rainwater has dissolved enormous caverns. Here and there their roofs have collapsed, disclosing deep holes or *cenotes* in the ground, filled with water. Today this water is raised to surface-level by wind-pumps: a typical feature of the landscape. It is hot during the day but cool after sunset. Humidity is often high. All round the peninsula are splendid beaches fringed with palm groves and forests of coconut palms. The best time for a visit is from October to March.

The people are divided into two groups: the Maya Indians, the minority, and the *mestizos*. The Maya women wear *huipiles*, or white cotton tunics (silk for *fiestas*) which may reach the ankles and are embroidered round the square neck and bottom hem. Ornaments are mostly gold. A few of the men still wear straight white cotton (occasionally silk) jackets and pants, often with gold or silver buttons, and when working protect this dress with aprons. Carnival is the year's most joyous occasion, with concerts, dances, processions. Yucatán's folk dance is the Jarana, the man dancing with his hands behind his back, the woman raising her skirts a little, and with interludes when they pretend to be bullfighting. During pauses in the music the man, in a high falsetto voice, sings *bambas* (compliments) to the woman.

The Maya are a courteous, gentle, strictly honest and scrupulously clean people. They drink little, except on feast days, speak Mayan, and profess Christianity laced with a more ancient nature worship. In Yucatán and Quintana Roo, the economy has long been dependent on the export of *henequén* (sisal), and chicle, but both are facing heavy competition from substitutes and tourism is becoming ever more important.

The early history and accomplishments of the Maya when they lived in Guatemala and Honduras before their mysterious trek northwards is given in the introduction to the book. They arrived in Yucatán about AD 600 and later rebuilt their cities, but along different lines, probably because of the arrival of Toltecs in the ninth and tenth centuries. Each city was autonomous, and in rivalry with other cities. Before the Spaniards arrived the Maya had developed a writing in which the hieroglyphic was somewhere between the pictograph and the letter. Fray Diego de Landa collected their books, wrote a very poor summary, the *Relación de las Cosas de Yucatán*, and with Christian but unscholarlike zeal burnt all his priceless sources.

In 1511 some Spanish adventurers were shipwrecked on the coast. Two survived. One of them, Juan de Aguilar, taught a Maya girl Spanish. She became interpreter for Cortés after he had landed in 1519. The Spaniards found little to please them: no gold, no concentration of natives, but Mérida was founded in 1542 and the few natives handed over to the conquerors in *encomiendas*. The Spaniards found them difficult to exploit: even as late as 1847 there was a major revolt, arising from the inhuman conditions in the *henequén* plantations and from the discrimination against the Maya in the towns. In July 1847 a conspiracy against the Blancos, or ruling classes from Mexico, was uncovered in Valladolid and one

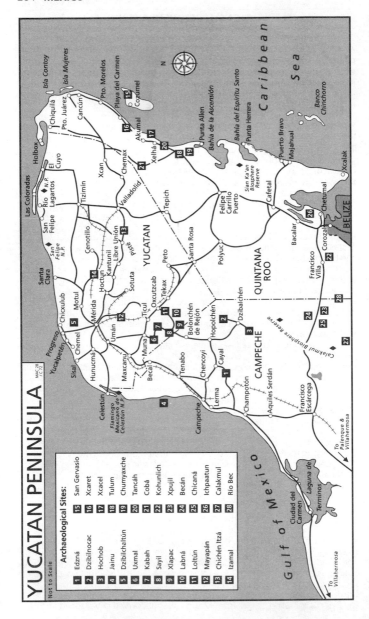

YUCATAN PENINSULA

MAC.28 /C.72

Not to Scale

Archaeological Sites:

1 Edzná	**8** Sayil	**15** San Gervasio	**22** Xpujil
2 Dzibilnocac	**9** Xlapac	**16** Xcaret	**23** Becán
3 Hochob	**10** Labná	**17** Xcacel	**24** Chicaná
4 Jainu	**11** Loltún	**18** Tulum	**25** Ichpaatun
5 Dzibilchaltún	**12** Mayapán	**19** Chumyaxche	**26** Calakmul
6 Uxmal	**13** Chichén Itzá	**20** Tancáh	**27** Rio Bec
7 Kabah	**14** Izamal	**21** Cobá	**28**

of its leaders, Manuel Antonio Ay, was shot. This precipitated a bloody war, the Guerra de Castas (Caste War) between the Maya and the Blancos. The first act was the massacre of all the non-Maya inhabitants of Tepich, S of Valladolid. The Maya took control of much of the Yucatán, laying siege to Mérida, only to abandon it to sow their crops in 1849. This allowed the governor of Yucatán to counter-attack, driving the Maya by ruthless means into southern Quintana Roo. In Bacalar, now called Felipe Carrillo Puerto, one of the Maya leaders, José María Barrera, accompanied by Manuel Nahuat, a ventriloquist, invented the 'talking cross", a cult that attracted thousands of followers. The sect, called Cruzob, established itself and renewed the resistance against the government from Mexico City. It was not until 1901 that the Mexian army retook the Cruzob's domain.

Many tourists come to Yucatán, mostly to see the ancient Maya sites and to stay at the new coastal resorts. A good paved road runs from Coatzacoalcos through Villahermosa, Campeche and Mérida (Route 180—one ferry crossing). All the great archaeological sites except Palenque are on or just off this road and its continuation beyond Mérida. An inland road from Villahermosa to Campeche gives easy access to Palenque. If time is limited, take a bus from Villahermosa to Chetumal via Escárcega, which can be done overnight as the journey is not very interesting (unless you want to see the Mayan ruins off this road—see p 347). From Chetumal travel up the coast to Cancún, then across to Mérida. A train from Mexico City to Mérida goes through Palenque; Pullman passengers can make the whole trip without leaving the car in 2 nights. Route 307 from Puerto Juárez and Cancún to Chetumal is all paved and in very good condition. Air services from the USA and Mexico City are given under Villahermosa, Mérida, Cancún and Cozumel. Details of the road route between Guatemala and Yucatán are given on **pages 293 and 311**. The state of Quintana Roo is on the eastern side of the Yucatán Peninsula and has recently become the largest tourist area in Mexico with the development of the resort of Cancún, and the parallel growth of Isla Mujeres, Cozumel and the 100-km corridor S of Cancún to Tulum. Growth has been such, in both Yucatán and Quintana Roo, that there are insufficient buses at peak times, old 2nd class buses may be provided for 1st class tickets and 2nd class buses take far too many standing passengers. There is a lack of information services. Where beaches are unspoilt they often lack all amenities. Many cheaper hotels are spartan. **Warning** So many of the tourists coming to the coastal resorts know no Spanish that price hikes and short-changing have become very common there, making those places very expensive if one is not careful. In the peak, winter season, prices are increased anyway, by about 50%.

NB The use of tripods for photography at sites is subject to an extra fee of US$3.50, but for using video cameras the fee is US$8.50. Since the major archaeological sites get very crowded, it is best to visit them just before closing time. Note also that in spring and summer temperatures can be very high; taking plenty of drinking water and adequate protection against the sun if walking for any length of time (eg around a large Maya site).
See p 394 for recommended reading.

Coatzacoalcos, 186,000 people, the Gulf Coast gateway for Yucatán, was 1½ km from the mouth of its wide river, but now has expanded down to it. It is hot, frantic and lacking in culture, and there is not much to do save watch the river traffic (river too polluted for fishing and swimming—less than salubrious discos on the beach by the pier at the river-mouth; beach is dangerous at nights, do not sleep there or loiter). Ocean-going vessels go upriver for 39 km to *Minatitlán*, the oil and petrochemical centre (145,000 people; airport), whose huge oil refinery sends its products by pipeline to Salina Cruz on the Pacific. Pollution can be bad at times. The road between the two towns carries very heavy industrial traffic. The offshore oil rigs are serviced from Coatzacoalcos. Sulphur is exported from the mines, 69 km away.

Coatzacoalcos Hotels Very difficult as all hotels are used by oil workers. Don't spend the night on the street if you can't find lodging. Prices double those of hotels elsewhere. A *Enríquez*, Ignacio de La Llave, good; **D** *Oliden*, Hidalgo 100, with fan, clean, noisy (other similar hotels in this area); **D** *San Antonio*, Malpica 205, near market. *Motel Colima* at Km 5, Carretera Ayucan-Coatzacoalcos, may have rooms if none in Coatzacoalcos; it is clean, in a quiet position, but does have a lot of red-light activity.

Minatitlán Hotels **B** *Cesar*; **B** *Palacio* on main street; **B** *Plaza*; **C** *Tropical*, with bath, no hot water. **D** *Hotel Nacional*, opposite *Palacio*, with bath, fan, hot water, clean, rec.

Coatzacoalcos Restaurants *Los Lopitos*, Hidalgo 615, good *tamales* and *tostadas*. Cheap restaurants on the top floor of the indoor market near the bus terminal. *Cafetería Sanborn*, Carranza 406 on Plaza Independencia, good breakfast. There is a 24-hr restaurant in one of the streets just off the main Plaza, good empanadas with cream.

Post Office Carranza y Lerdo, Coatzacoalcos.

Bus To Mexico City, US$26.50; to **Mérida** US$29. To Veracruz (312 km), US$9, 7¼ hrs, **Ciudad del Carmen**, US$16.50, **Salina Cruz**, US$12.15; to **Minatitlán**, to which taxis also ply. To **Villahermosa**, US$7.

Buses from Minatitlán, ADO to many destinations: Mexico City, Puebla, Villahermosa, Veracruz, Mérida Palenque, Chetumal, but not Cancún.

Rail Railway station is 5 km from town at Cuatro (for Mexico City and Mérida) at end of Puerto Libre bus route and on Playa Palma Sola route, smelly and dingy, the through train is swept out here; irregular bus services. Better walk about ½ km to the main road and get a bus there, US$0.25. Train to **Mérida**, via Palenque and Campeche at 1540. Another station, in the city centre, serves Tehuantepec and Salina Cruz, via Medias Aguas. The train to **Salina Cruz** leaves daily at 0605, 9½ hr journey 2nd class.

Air Services Minatitlán airport, 30 mins.

39 km E of Coatzacoalcos, on a side road off Route 180 is **Agua Dulce**, where there is a campground, *Rancho Hermanos Graham*, nice location, full hook-up, cold showers, only one bathroom for whole site, US$6.50 for car and 2 people.

On the Gulf Coast, further E (turn off Route 180 at Las Piedras, 70 km from Coatzacoalcos, signposted), is **Sánchez Magallanes**, a pleasant, friendly town. You can camp safely on the beach.

Cárdenas 116 km from Coatzacoalcos and 48 km from Villahermosa, is headquarters of the Comisión del Grijalva, which is encouraging regional development. Between Cárdenas and Villahermosa are many stalls selling all varieties of bananas, a speciality of the area, and the road passes through the Samaria oilfield. (From Chontalpa there is irregular transport to Raudales on the lake formed by the Netzahualcoyotl dam.) It is very hard to find accommodation in Cárdenas, **D** *Hotel Yak-Xol*, cheapest, with bath, a/c, parking, clean, on main plaza.

Villahermosa (pop 275,000) capital of Tabasco state (pop 1990 1,501,200), is on the Río Grijalva, navigable to the sea. It used to be a dirty town, but is now improving, though it is very hot and rainy. The **cathedral**, ruined in 1973, has been rebuilt, its twin steeples beautifully lit at night; it is not in the centre. There is a warren of modern colonial-style pedestrian malls throughout the central area. The **Centro de Investigaciones de las Culturas Olmecas** (CICOM) is set in a new modern complex with a large public library, expensive restaurant, airline offices and souvenir shops, a few minutes' walk S out of town along the river bank. The **Museo Regional de Antropología Carlos Pellicer Cámara** on three floors, has well laid out displays of Maya and Olmec artefacts, with an excellent bookshop. Entry US$1, open 0900-2000.

At the NW side of town (W of the downtown area) is Tabasco 2000, a futuristic mall/hotel/office area with an original statue of fishermen.

In 1925 an expedition discovered huge sculptured human and animal figures, urns and altars in almost impenetrable forest at La Venta, 96 km from Villahermosa. Nothing to see there now: about 1950 the monuments were threatened with destruction by the discovery of oil nearby. The poet Carlos Pellicer got them hauled all the way to a woodland area near Villahermosa, now the **Parque Nacional de La Venta**, Blvd Adolfo Ruíz Cortines, with scattered lakes, next to a children's playground and almost opposite the old airport entrance (W of downtown). There they are dispersed in various small clearings. The huge heads—one of them weighs 20 tons—are Olmec, a culture which flourished about 1150-150 BC; this is an experience which should not be missed. Be sure to take insect-repellent for the visit. It takes 1 hr to walk around, excellent guides, speak Spanish and English (US$6.65 for 1 hr 10 mins). There is also a zoo of lonely, dispirited and wretched creatures from the Tabasco jungle: monkeys, alligators, deer, wild pigs and birds. Open 0900-2000, entrance US$4.35, bus, marked 'Gracitol' from bus terminal US$0.30 (don't take a bus going to 'La Venta"—if in doubt, ask). Bus Circuito No 1 from outside 2nd class bus terminal goes past Parque La Venta (taxi to La Venta park US$2).

Villahermosa is heaving under pressure from the oil boom, which is why it is now such an expensive place. Buses to Mexico City are often booked up well in advance, as are hotel rooms, especially during the holiday season (May onwards). Overnight free parking (no facilities) in the Campo de Deportes. It is hard to find swimming facilities in Villahermosa: Ciudad Deportiva pool for cardholders only. There is a bull ring. Ash Wednesday is celebrated from 1500 to dusk by the throwing of water in balloon bombs and buckets at anyone who happens to be on the street.

Hotels The price difference between a reasonable and a basic hotel can be negligible, so one might as well go for the former. Best is **L** *Exalaris Hyatt*, Juárez 106, T 34444, F 55808, all services, remodelled 1992; **A+** *Holiday Inn Villahermosa Plaza*, Paseo Tabasco 1407, T 64400, F 64569, 4 km from centre, restaurant, bar, entertainment; **A** *Maya-Tabasco* (Best Western), Blvd Ruiz Cortines 907, T 21111, F 21133, all services; **B** *Don Carlos*, Madero 418, T 22493, F 24622, central, clean, helpful, good restaurant (accepts American Express card—one of the few that does) nearby parking; **B** *Plaza Independencia*, Independencia 123, T 21299, F 44724; **C** *Chocos*, Merino 100, T 129444, F 129649, friendly, clean, a/c, near ADO terminal; **C** *María Dolores*, Aldama 104, a/c, hot showers, excellent restaurant (closed Sundays); **C** *Palma de Mallorca*, Madero 516, T 20144; many other hotels along Madero (eg **D** *La Paz*, central). **D** *Madero*, Madero 301, T 20516, hot water, good value, some rooms for 4 are cheaper; **D** *Oviedo*, Lerdo 303, good; **D** *San Miguel*, Lerdo 315, T 21500, good value, but some rooms damp, no hot water pm; **D** *Sofia*, Zaragoza 408, T 26055, central, tolerable but overpriced, a/c. **E** *Los Carlos*, Hnos Basta-Zozoya 624, T 26409, a/c, basic, dirty, noisy, from ADO terminal, cross main street, go 2 blocks then left 2 blocks; **E** *Oriente*, Madero 441, clean, hot shower, fan, rec, good restaurant; **E** *Tabasco*, Lerdo 317, T 20077, not too clean, cold water, mosquitoes; several others on Lerdo. Cheap hotels, from **E** pp, on Calle Constitución (come out of main entrance of bus terminal, turn right then 1st left and continue for 5 blocks, but it's the red-light district). There is a **youth hostel** at the Ciudad Deportiva, but it doesn't accept travellers arriving in the evening (4 km SW of the bus station), CP 80180, T 56241.

NB Tourists are often wiser to go directly to Palenque for accommodation; cheaper and no competition from business travellers. Villahermosa can be difficult for lone women: local men's aggressive behaviour said to be due to the effect of eating iguanas.

Restaurants A good restaurant at *Hotel Madan*, Madero 408, good breakfast, pricey, unfriendly service; *Cafetería La Terraza*, Reforma 304, in *Hotel Miraflores*, good breakfast; *Café Casino*, Suárez 530, good coffee; *Bruno's*, Lerdo y 5 de Mayo, cheap, good, noisy, good atmosphere; *Café La Barra*, Lerdo, near *Bruno's*, good coffee, quiet, pleasant; *El Torito Valenzuela*, next to *Hotel Madero*, Mexican specialities; *El Fogón*, Av Carlos Pellicer 304-A, good value; *Blanca Mariposa*, near entrance to Parque La Venta, rec. Avoid the bad and expensive tourist eating places on and near the river front.

Local Transport Taxis now mainly on a fixed-route collective system (US$1 per stop), which can be a problem if you want to go somewhere else. You may have to wait a long time before a driver without fares agrees to take you.

Museums See above for CICOM and La Venta. **Museo de Cultura Popular**, Zaragoza 810, open daily 0900-2000; **Museo de Historia de Tabasco**, Av 27 de Febrero esq Juárez, same hours.

Exchange Banco Internacional, Suárez y Lerdo, changes travellers' cheques; **Banamex**, Madero y Reforma; **American Express**, Turismo Nieves, Sarlat 202, T 41818.

Postal Services DHL, parcel courier service, Paseo Tabasco.

Tourist Office in the 1st class bus station (English spoken) and another not far from La Venta park, in Edificio Administrativo Tabasco 2000, at Paseo Grijalva and Paseo Tabasco (T 163633, F 163632), both good, closed 1300-1600.

Travel Agencies Viajes Villahermosa, 27 de Febrero 207.

Airport Daily services to Mexico City, Mérida, 1 hr, Oaxaca, Chetumal, Minatitlán, Veracruz and Cancún, from airport 15 km SE, out along the Palenque road, VW bus to town US$3 pp, taxi US$9.50 for 2. To Mexico City with AeroMéxico, Mexicana and Aviacsa, all daily. To Oaxaca with Aerocaribe, Fco Javier Mina 301-A, T 43202 (Airport 44695), dep 1100 (via Tuxtla Gutiérrez 1 hr 45 mins); Aerocaribe also flies to Mérida and Cancún, Minatitlán, Tampico and Veracruz. Aviacsa (T 45780) to Tuxtla Gutiérrez, 4 days a week, Mérida, at 0715 4 days a week (continuing to Cancún) and 2050 daily. Aerolitoral has a daily flight McAllen (Texas), Monterrey, Tampico, Veracruz, Villahermosa. AeroMéxico office, Periférico Carlos Pellicer 511, T 26991 (airport 41675); Mexicana, Av Madero 109, or Desarollo Urbano Tabasco 2000, T 21169 (airport 21164).

Buses 1st class, ADO bus terminal is on Javier Mina between Méndez and Lino Merino, 12 blocks N of centre, computerized booking system, staff unhelpful. Left luggage at ADO terminal, 0700-2300, US$0.20 per piece per hour, alternatively, go to Sra Ana in minute restaurant/shop at Pedro Fuentes 817, 100m from ADO, reliable, open till 2000, small charge made. Other private luggage depositories by the bus station also make a small charge. The Central Camionera 2nd class bus station is on Av Ruiz Cortines, near roundabout with fisherman statue, 1 block E of Javier Mina, opp Castillo, 4 blocks N of ADO (ie 16 from centre); usually in disarray and it is difficult to get a ticket. Mind your belongings.

Several buses (1st class) to **Mexico City**, US$30, 12 hrs, direct bus leaves 1815 (Cristóbal Colón) or 1650 (ADO) then frequent through the night, expect to wait a few hours for Mexico City buses and at least ½ hr in the ticket queue. To **Jalapa** with ADO, 3 a day, 10 hrs; to **Campeche**, US$16.50 (6 hrs), reservation required; to **Coatzacoalcos**, US$7; to **Tapachula**, US$20, 14 hrs. Many buses a day to **Mérida** 8-10 hrs, with ADO, US$19.50, 11 a day, or Cristóbal Colón at 1030 and 2230, US$22; or go 2nd class from Palenque; if coming from Oaxaca to make a connection for Mérida, be prepared for long queues as most buses pass through en route from México City. To **San Andrés Tuxtla**, 6 hrs, US$12.50. To **San Cristóbal**, US$11, 6 hrs; also 2nd class bus with one change at Tuxtla, leaves 0800, arrives 2100, fine scenery but treacherous road. Cristóbal Colón from ADO terminal to **Oaxaca** via Coatzacoalcos and Tehuantepec at 1930 and 2130, 1st class, stops at about 7 places, US$24. Bus to **Veracruz**, many a day with ADO, 7 hrs, US$14.30; to **Chetumal**, US$18, 10 hrs, but the road is now in a very bad state and it can take much longer, four buses, erratic service. To **Catazajá**, US$4, 1½ hrs. To **Palenque**, US$5.50, 1st class, US$4.50, 2nd class, 2½ hrs, 8 a day in all from 0430 (difficult to get on a bus on Sunday). Circuito Maya, US$5.60, ADO; 1st class 1000 (buy ticket day before) and 1700. To Emiliano Zapata and Tenosique (for Río San Pedro crossing into Guatemala—**see p 293**), buses 0700, 0800, 1330, 3-4 hrs.

Excursion NW of Villahermosa are the Maya ruins of **Comalcalco**, reached by bus (2 a day by ADO, 1230 and 1800, US$2.50, or local Somollera bus, US$2, 1½ hrs over dirt roads—Somollera bus leaves from near the bridge where Av Universidad crosses Ruiz Cortines, 4-5 blocks N of Central Camionera in Villahermosa), then taxi to the ruins US$4.50 or to the entrance, US$0.35, and walk 1 km, or walk the full 3 km. The ruins are unique in Mexico because the palaces and pyramids are built of bricks, long and narrow like ancient Roman bricks, and not of stone (entry US$4.35). From Comalcalco go to **Paraíso** near the coast, frequent buses from town to the beach 8 km away. Interesting covered market, good cocoa. **D** *Centro Turístico* beach hotel, clean, no hot water, food and drink expensive. Also **E** *Hotel Hidalgo*, in centre, clean.

Further Travel If the Villahermosa-Mexico City bus is booked up, try taking the train from *Teapa* (buses run hourly between Teapa and Villahermosa on a paved road, 50 km 1 hr, US$1.65). The dining car is good but very expensive. Check in rainy season whether bridges are OK. (It took one passenger 56 hrs to travel some 950 km after being diverted.) Vendors ply the train with local foods and drinks. Journey 14 hrs. Teapa is a nice, clean little town with several hotels (**C** *Quintero*,

Eduardo R Bastar 108, T 20045, behind Zócalo, a/c, fan, clean, friendly, enthusiastic restaurant; **E** *Casa de Huéspedes Miye*, in the main street; good restaurant on main square, *El Mirador*) and beautiful surroundings. The square is pleasant, and you can swim in the river or in the sulphur pool, El Azufre and cavern of Cocona (dear). From Teapa, Tapijulapa on the Chiapas border can be visited, beautiful views. Bus to Chiapa de Corzo at 0730, 7 hrs, US$10, lovely, mountainous landscape (**see p 272**).

80 km SW of Villahermosa on Route 195 is **Pichucalco**, an affluent town with no beggars and a lively and safe atmosphere. The Zócalo is thronged in the evening with people on after-dinner *paseo*. There are many good restaurants and bars. **D** *Hotel La Loma*, Francisco Contreras 51, T 30052, bath, a/c, or fan, ample parking, clean (opposite is a cheaper *posada* with resident monkey); **E** *Hotel México*, on left turn from bus station, with bath, fan, clean but musty, *Vila*, on Plaza, **D** *Jardín*, noisy, **D** *La Selva*. Buses almost every hour to Villahermosa, US$4.

Villahermosa to Guatemala by car: 1) via Palenque to San Cristóbal de Las Casas (see below); 2) by route 195 and 190 to Ciudad Cuauhtémoc via San Cristóbal de Las Casas (Highway 195 is fully paved, but narrow and winding with landslides and washouts in the rainy season, high altitudes, beautiful scenery). If this route is impassable, travel back by route 180 to Acayucan, to 190, via 185 and go to Ciudad Cuauhtémoc or by route 200 to Tapachula.

From Villahermosa to Campeche there are two roads, both described in more detail after Palenque, which is reached by turning off the inland Highway, 186, at **Playas de Catazajá**, 117 km from Villahermosa (no petrol stations until Catazajá; unleaded Magna-sin is available in Catazajá; if you look like running out, turn left half-way for **Macuspana**, where there is one; hotel in Macuspana; **D** *America*, basic, clean, comfortable, safe parking). (Macuspana municipal *fiesta* 15-16 August.) Palenque is 26 km away on a good paved but winding road. (If short of time you can fly Aviacsa Mérida-Villahermosa at 0645, hire car at Villahermosa airport, drive to Palenque and back with 3½ hrs at ruins, and catch 2100 AeroMéxico or 2145 Mexicana flight from Villahermosa to Mexico City.) Coming from Campeche it is 5 hrs' drive on a good road, apart from one rough stretch about 1 hr from Palenque; toll bridge US$0.60.

Palenque (143 km from Villahermosa), is a splendid experience, with its series of Maya hilltop temples in remarkably good condition. It is best to visit the ruins just before they close to avoid the crowds, but to avoid the heat arrive early. The site is in a hot jungle clearing on a steep green hill overlooking the plain and crossed by a clear cascading brook. Interesting wildlife, mainly birds, also includes howler monkeys and mosquitoes. The ruins are impressive indeed, particularly the Templo de las Inscripciones, easy to climb from the back, in the heart of which was discovered an intact funerary crypt with the Sarcophagus of Lord Pacal, Palenque's greatest ruler, buried in AD 683 (you walk from the top of the pyramids into a staircase, descending to ground level, very humid; usually illuminated when the site is open, but check). The temples around, with fantastic comb-like decorations on their intact roofs, and the sculptured wall panels, are undoubtedly the most exquisite achievement of the Maya. Explanations in 4 languages on each temple are now illegible (pamphlet with brief explanations in English available at the ticket office, US$1.30). A path (closed in 1994) behind the Templo de las Inscripciones leads through jungle to a small ruined temple—if you continue for 8 km the path leads to a friendly village. You can also wander around in the jungle, many unexcavated ruins, take a torch and look out for spiders and snakes. An excellent museum about 1 km outside the ruins has some fine Maya carvings—stuccos, jade pieces, funerary urns, pottery and other artefacts excavated at the site (open 1000—more like 1100—to 1700). Entry to ruins, US$4.35 (Sun free), charge for car parking. The site opens at 0800 and closes at 1700 (guide, up to 10 people).

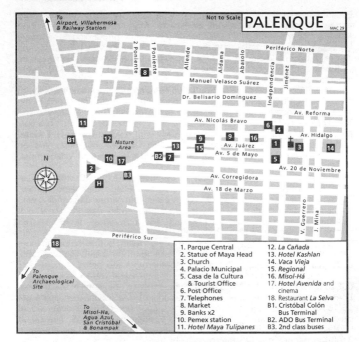

PALENQUE MAC 29

To Airport, Villahermosa & Railway Station

Periférico Norte

Manuel Velasco Suárez

Dr. Belisario Dominguez

Av. Nicolás Bravo

Av. Reforma

Av. Hidalgo

Av. Juárez

Av. 5 de Mayo

Av. 20 de Noviembre

Av. Corregidora

Av. 18 de Marzo

Periférico Sur

To Palenque Archaeological Site

To Misol-Ha, Agua Azul, San Cristóbal & Bonampak

1. Parque Central	12. La Cañada
2. Statue of Maya Head	13. Hotel Kashlan
3. Church	14. Vaca Vieja
4. Palacio Municipal	15. Regional
5. Casa de la Cultura	16. Misol-Há
& Tourist Office	17. Hotel Avenida and
6. Post Office	cinema
7. Telephones	18. Restaurant La Selva
8. Market	B1. Cristóbal Colón
9. Banks x2	Bus Terminal
10. Pemex station	B2. ADO Bus Terminal
11. Hotel Maya Tulipanes	B3. 2nd class buses

Beware of thieves at all times. A restaurant by the cascades serves a limited range of food, basic but friendly (stores luggage for US$0.25); shops quick to overcharge and souvenirs are dearer than elsewhere. The ruins are 8 km from the town. A path runs from the museum to the main road via waterfalls with good swimming. Hail a colectivo on the road, US$0.35 to town. The climate is hot and dry March-April, the coolest months are October to February. **Warning** The area can have many mosquitoes; make sure you're up-to-date with your tablets (Dec-April usually few mosquitoes).

Fiesta Santo Domingo, first week in August.

Micro buses run back and forth along the main street, passing the bus station area, to and from the ruins, every 10 mins, US$0.85. Taxi US$5. It is convenient to stay at hotels near the Pemex service station, as they are also nearer the ruins and the bus stations.

Hotels (Prices treble around *fiesta* time.) **A+ *Misión Palenque***, far end of town in countryside, T 50241, F 50499, complete resort, noisy a/c, although poor service in restaurant reported, has a minibus service from Villahermosa airport for about US$20 return (2 hr journey—avoids backtracking from airport into Villahermosa for transport to Palenque), has courtesy bus to ruins and to airfield for trips to Bonampak and Yaxchilán. **A+ *Motel Chan-Kah Inn***, at Km 03 Carretera Ruinas, T 51100, F 50820, closest to ruins, swimming pool fed from river, beautiful gardens, perfectly clean, restaurant, with marimba music Fri-Sun, and affiliated to **B** *Chan Kah Centro*, corner of Juárez and Independencia, T 50318, F 50489, a/c, restaurant, terrace bar with happy hour; **A+** *Best Western Plaza Palenque*, Km 27, Carretera Catazajá-Palenque, T 450555, F 450395, free transport Mon-Sat 0800-1700, a/c, disco, 1.5 km from centre, 8 km from ruins; **A** *Maya Toucan*, on road into town, pool, a/c, bar, restaurant, lovely views from rooms; **A** *Hotel Maya Tulipanes*, Calle Cañada 6, T 50201, F 50230, a/c, cable TV, garage, pool, bar/restaurant next door; **B** *Motel Los Leones*, Km 2.5, about 5 km before ruins on main road, T 50209, F 50033, hot water, a/c, TV, quiet, large restaurant; **B** *Hotel La Cañada*, T and F 50446, C out of season, very rustic but very clean, with fan, good value, lovely garden, expensive but good restaurant, the owner, Sr Morales, is an expert on the ruins (nearby is **C** *Zchibalal*, reductions for stays over 2 nights, spacious rooms, clean, hot water, a/c, fan, rec); **D** *Lacroix*, Hidalgo, next to church, with bath, fan, no hot water, some cheaper rooms, pleasant place; **C** *Palenque*, 5 de Mayo 15, off Plaza, T 50103, F 50030, with bath, a/c restaurant, vast, rambling menage, 'going downhill fast", pool; **D** *La Posada*, at La Cañada, 200m from Cristóbal Colón buses, T 50437, hot water, fans, modern, simple, 'designed for young travellers, international ambience", peaceful, excellent value, rec; **D** *Avenida*, Juárez 173, T 50116, opp 2nd-class bus station (can be very noisy), with restaurant, clean, large rooms with fan, parking, but does not display price in rooms so ask for government list to check, no hot showers, some rooms with balcony; **C** *Casa de Pakal*, Juárez 10, T 50042, 1 block from Plaza, a/c, good but not very friendly; next door is **D** *Misol-Há*, at Juárez 14, T 60082, fan, with bath, hot water, clean, owner Susana Cuevas speaks English; **C** *Kashlan*, 5 de Mayo 105, T 50297, F 50309, with bath, fan, hot water, quiet, clean, will store luggage, video each pm, mosquito nets, helpful owner Ada Luz Navarro, laundry opp, good restaurant with vegetarian food in same building, tours offered; **D** *Vaca Vieja*, 5 de Mayo 42, T 50388, 3 blocks from Plaza, popular with gringos, good restaurant; **D** *Posada Mallorca*, on highway, new, small rooms, comfortable; **D** *Regional*, Av Juárez 79, 3 blocks from Plaza, 100m from bus station, hot showers (US$1.50 extra), noisy; **E** *Santa Elena*, 100m down dirt track by *Restaurant Oaxaqueña*, with bath, good value, 2 blocks from ADO terminal, clean, simple and quiet, safe parking; **D** *Posada San Juan*, T 50616 (from ADO go up the hill and first right, it's on the 4th block on the left), with bath, cheaper without, cold water, and fan, clean, quiet, 1st floor rooms more airy, very good for budget accommodation, safe parking available (also near ADO, *Santo Domingo*, 20 de Noviembre 1191, T 50146, stores luggage); **E** *Posada Alicia*, Av Manuel Velásquez Suárez, between new market and Calle Novelos, with fan (ask for one), cold water, no towels, cheap, grubby, rooms on left as you enter are cooler, ask for rooms with communal bathroom; **E** *Casa de Huéspedes León*, Hidalgo (s/n) near junction with Abasolo, T 50038, with bath, only cold water, some mosquitoes; **E** *Casa de Huéspedes San Francisco*, Hidalgo 134 and Allende, with bath, good. **E** *Posada Charito*, Av 20 de Noviembre 10, clean, friendly, family run, very good value, mixed reports on security, some rooms very airless; **E** *TRF*, above 2nd class bus terminal, with bath, not noisy, rec; **E** *Yax-Ha*, opp *La Posada* on La Cañada, big rooms, very friendly family, also information centre and books, videos for sale, tours organized, rec. **E-F** *Posada Canek*, 20 de Noviembre, dearer rooms have bath, all with fan and toilet, very clean, ground floor rooms near reception noisy, prices are pp and sharing is often required (regardless of sex), fills up early, arrive before 1000 check-out time.

Camping *Trailer Park Mayabel*, on road to ruins 2 km before entrance (bus from town US$0.30) for caravans and tents, US$8 per vehicle with 2 people. US$2.35 for tent or to sling hammock (an *ambulante* sells hammocks once a day), palmleaf huts, bathrooms, cold showers, good value, restaurant, with good food and reasonable prices, nice setting, popular so can be noisy, the place is not to everyone's taste; many mosquitoes and many ticks in long grass (we're told they avoid people who eat lots of garlic!) Watch your belongings; management sometimes stores luggage during the day (reluctant to store valuables. At night, around 0100, one can often hear the howler monkeys screaming in the jungle; quite eerie. The path between the campground and the ruins is not open; do not attempt to use this path. *Trailer Park María del Mar*, 5 kms from Palenque, along road to ruins, US$12 for 2 in camper van with hook-up, camping US$5, restaurant and swimming pool, cold showers, clean, pretty setting (check that water is turned on). Good swimming at *Balneario and Hotel Nututún* (entry US$1), 3 km along Palenque-Ocosingo road, US$3.30 pp, vehicle free, US$2 per camping site per night, rather run down, no tent rentals, toilets and bath, disco bar, at restaurant with laughable service and high prices; and beautiful lake and waterfall open to the public for a small fee. Misol-Ha, 2 km off same road at Km 19, see below.

Restaurants Water is often hard to get. Some restaurants accept dollars, but at less than the current rate. *Montes Azules*, Juárez 120, very tasty food in generous portions and at low prices, friendly and helpful owner, live marimba music Fri, Sat, Sun nights; *Lakan-Ha*, Juárez 20, fast, cheap, efficient; also on Av Juárez, *La Jícara Pícara*, Allende junction, very good value and very friendly, specialises in *pozole*, a maize stew; *El Rodeo*, Juárez 7, near Plaza, does breakfasts and meat dishes, not too good but popular with travellers, good source of information; *La Ceiba* (Hnos Cabrera) on Juárez, good café for breakfast; *Girasoles*, Juárez 189, very good food and value, popular with backpackers, good breakfasts; *Francesca*, Juárez, two doors down from ADO bus office, nothing French but reasonable steak and chips; *Mariscos and Pescados*, off Juárez, opp large *artesanía* market; *Las Tinajas*, 20 de Noviembre y Abasolo, good, family run, excellent food, huge portions foodbut not cheap; *Los Portales*,

Av 20 de Noviembre e Independencia, cheap, good, rec; *Artemio*, Av Hidalgo, nr Plaza, reasonably-priced food, rec; *Chan Kah*, on Plaza, steak, rec, good value, accepts credit cards; *La Oaxaqueña*, right after entering town from ruins, very good, typical, quite expensive, rec. At Km 0.5 on Hidalgo (road to ruins) is *La Selva*, expensive, but excellent, smart dress preferred, live music at weekends; *Yunuen*, at *Hotel Vaca Vieja*, generous portions at reasonable prices, good steaks, popular with local ranchers. *La Palapa de Apo-Hel*, Av 5 de Mayo, s/n, between Independencia and Abasolo, a delightful little bamboo shack specialising in sea food, rec; *California*, Av 5 de Mayo, opp *Avenida*, nr 2nd class buses, good value, Mexican specialities; opp *Hotel Kashlan*, *Café de los Altos*, good coffee; *El Rinconcito*, Allende, across from *Kashlan*, good, economical; *El Fogón de Pakal*, Calle Merle Green, La Cañada, delightful, good and varied menu. *Los Caminantes*, opp bus station and a few metres further into town, good value, cheap coffee, friendly. Good *pollo rostizado* in restaurant inside ADO office. Try the ice cream at *Holanda* on Av Juárez, s/n, 4 doors W of Banamex, in the centre.

NB Visitors should respect the local customs and dress so as not to offend—footwear and shirts should always be worn.

Horse riding Tours can be booked at the Clínica Dental Zepeda, Av Juárez s/n. The dentist is the owner of the horses.

Exchange Exchange rate only comes through at 1000, then banks open until 1200. **Bancomer** does not charge commission; Banamex, both very slow for cashing TCs. **Yax-Ha Cambio** on Juárez, next to Banamex, open 0700-2000 daily, changes US$ cash and TCs. *Restaurante El Rodeo* also changes TCs at bank rate. At weekends TCs can be changed at many travel agencies and other shops on Av Juárez; also, the owner at Farmacia Central will change US$ at a reasonable rate.

Post Office Independencia, next to Palacio Municipal, helpful. **Long-distance telephones** at ADO bus terminal, cheaper than many other telephone offices; at *Mercería* bookshop in Aldama near Juárez, and a shop by *Hotel Palenque* in Zócalo.

Laundromat Opposite *Hotel Kashlan*.

Travel Agencies *ATC Tours*, Calle Allende y Juárez, local 6, T 50210, run private tours to other Mayan sites (Bonampak, Yaxchilán, also flights, see below, Tikal, all min 5 people), local attractions (Agua Azul, Mi Sol Ha waterfall at 0930, US$5), horseriding in the jungle (US$25, more defforestation than jungle on some rides, but pleasant), etc; helpful, English spoken. *Shivalva* (Marco A Morales), Merle Green 1, La Cañada, T 50411, F 50392, tours of Palenque, Yaxchilán, Bonampak, Tikal, Guatemala City, Belize, Copán (also offers hotel booking for San Cristóbal de las Casas, but it's best to make your own choice).

Tourist Office in the Casa de la Cultura on plaza entrance at side of building, corner of Jiménez and 5 de Mayo, open 0900-1300 and 1700-2000, useful map with hotel and restaurant listings, helpful and informative staff.

Trains Railway station for Palenque is 10 km outside town (bus goes from in front of *Posada Alicia* at 2000; from station to town, irregular service, be patient). Much better is a taxi colectivo to/from railway station and Pemex service station US$1.50 for 2. Latest timetables show trains to Palenque and Mérida starting at Córdoba at 0630, which would mean taking El Jarocho from Mexico City at 2115 to get to Córdoba at 0445 (or the 0745 to arrive 1610 the day before). 16$\frac{1}{2}$ hrs Córdoba-Palenque US$9.25 2nd class. The train to **Campeche** and **Mérida** leaves Palenque in theory at 2249, 7$\frac{1}{2}$ hrs to Campeche, 10$\frac{1}{2}$ to Mérida, US$6.65 1st class): keep your luggage with you, 1st (only one car, no sleeper) is very comfortable, 2nd, dirty and smelly and no light, take a torch and insect repellent. Also *Mixto* to Campeche at 1600, US$4. Tickets on sale one hour before train arrives. The train may be crowded so it may be necessary to stand all the way. It is reported that the trains are 'a disaster", unreliable with delays of up to 11 hrs. The station is not a pleasant place to wait in the dark. Do not rely on timetables, check all times in person before travel. **NB** If returning from Palenque to Mérida by train, bear in mind that in Dec and Jan it is nearly impossible to make reservations.

Air Travel Light aircraft Palenque-Mérida US$90. For flights to Bonampak and Yaxchilán, see below.

Buses All bus companies have terminals at W end of Av Juárez. The Cristóbal Colón terminal is 200m N of junction with road to ruins. Buy ticket to leave on arrival, ADO 1st class on sale the day before, buses are often full, very heavy ticket sales on 1 and 15 of each month when salaries are paid. 1st class bus to/from **Mexico City**, ADO, at 1600 and 1800, 16 hrs, 1,006 km, US$38.50. First-class bus to **Villahermosa** with ADO, 6 a day between 0700 and 1900, 2$\frac{1}{2}$ hrs, US$5.50. 2nd class bus to Villahermosa at 0800 and 1200, US$4.50. To Veracruz, only via Villahermosa, from there 6 hrs with ADO, many a day, US$14.80. ADO buses, seven a day, to **Ciudad del Carmen**, US$13.25.

Direct bus to **Campeche** from Palenque at 1700, 2nd class (Transportes del Sur), 5 hrs, US$10.65, or 2 with ADO, 0800 and 2100, US$15, 8½ hrs, change here for Mérida (a further 2½ hrs). Daily ADO 1st class bus direct to **Mérida** at 0800, 2100 and 2200 (arr 0530), US$20, 8 hrs, luxury service at 0100 daily, Cristóbal Cólon. 2nd class to Mérida US$14.50. Another possibility is to go for connections to Campeche or Mérida at Emiliano Zapata, bus from Palenque at 0900 and 1400, bus to Palenque at 0600 and 1230 (taxi Emiliano Zapata-Palenque US$28). See p 295. Another possiblity is to take a bus to Catazajá (see p 288), where the 1500 Cristóbal Colón bus Villahermosa-Campeche bus stops.

To **Chetumal** with ADO, daily at 2030, with a/c, toilets, stops at Escárcega for a meal, 8-10 hrs, US$15.50; also 2nd class with Lacandonia at 0100 from their office next to *Restaurante Oaxaqueña*, US$14.80.

To **San Cristóbal de Las Casas**, good road throughout, 5 hrs journey, Rodolfo Figueroa, new company, a/c, TV, toilet, 3-4 a day, US$8.25 (beware car sickness); new luxury service with Cristóbal Colón, a/c, video, 0230 and 2300 daily, also goes on to Tuxtla Gutiérrez. **Tuxtla Gutiérrez**, 5 a day, 377 km, US$11, 3½ hrs, 2nd class, via San Cristóbal de Las Casas.

Bus and River Travel to Guatemala: 1) The Río San Pedro route starts at *Tenosique*, a friendly place (money exchange at clothing shop Ortiz y Alvarez at Calle 28, No 404, good rates for dollars to quetzales, poor for dollars to pesos). **Hotels**: **E Garage**, a/c, on main square with restaurant, very clean; **E Rome**, Calle 28, No 400, T 20151, clean, will change dollars for residents, bath, not bad; **E Azulejos**, Calle 26 No 416, with bath, fan, clean, hot water, friendly, helpful owner speaks some English, opp church; *Casa de Huéspedes La Valle*, Calle 19, E with bath, clean, good, and others. For planes to Bonampak contact Sr Quintero, T 20099. For overland trips ask at restaurant opp new market, owner goes in his camioneta to Bonampak and Yaxchilán: negotiate price.

You can get to Tenosique from Villahermosa by ADO bus (0700, 0800, 1330), 4 hrs, from Emiliano Zapata by frequent 1st or 2nd class bus, US$2, or on the México-Mérida railway line, 1 hr E by train from Palenque. From Palenque by road minibuses Libertad leave from 20 de Noviembre y Allende from 0500 to Emiliano Zapata, 1 hr, US$2.50 (take 0630 to be sure of making the boat at La Palma); and from there to Tenosique at 0830 or 0900, 90 mins, US$2. Many travel agents in Palenque organize colectivos direct to La Palma at 1000, US$14 pp to connect with the boat to El Naranjo. Alternatively, take a colectivo before 0645 to Playas de Catazajá from the stop just up from ADO (US$1, ½ hr); alight at the El Crucero de la Playa crossroads on the Villahermosa—Tenosique road and wait for the bus to pass at 0730 (2 hrs to Tenosique, US$2). Similarly, from Tenosique to Palenque, take the Villahermosa bus (every hour or so during the day) as far as El Crucero de La Playa, and then take one of the regular minibuses running to Palenque. Bus also from Mexico City, ADO, 16½ hrs, arrives 0700.

From Tenosique to *La Palma* on the Río San Pedro, orange *colectivos*, 1 hr, US$1.70, and buses at 1130 and 1200 (also earlier) leave from Calles 28 y 31, beside church, 2 hrs (from Tenosique bus station, which is outside town, take taxi, US$1.70 or colectivo to 'Centro', or walk 20 mins). From La Palma boats leave to El Naranjo (Guatemala) at 1400, at least 4½ hrs, US$20 (to check boat times, T 30811 Rural at the Río San Pedro, or seek out Sr Valenzuela, Calle 28 No 142, Tenosique, who nowadays is reported to be more interested in selling drinks and food, persistence is required). Be at boat 1 hr early, it sometimes leaves ahead of schedule; if this happens ask around for someone to chase it, US$3-4 pp for 3 people. It is a beautiful boat trip, through mangroves with flocks of white herons and the occasional alligator, dropping people off at homesteads. There is a stop at the border post 2 hrs into the journey to sign out of Mexico, a lovely spot with a lake and lilies. In the rain, luggage will get wet; take a raincoat and good shoes for the muddy landing at El Naranjo. Take a torch, too. In La Palma, restaurant and exchange are poor value; Nicolás Valenzuela offers both services, and lodging (US$2 to sling hammock), very helpful. There are no officials on arrival at the jetty in El Naranjo; immigration is a short way uphill on the right (entry will cost US$5 in quetzales or dollars, beware extra unofficial charges at customs); bus tickets to Flores sold here.

At El Naranjo there are hotels (basic), a video cinema (US$0.50) and restaurants (you can wait in a restaurant till the 0100 bus departs, but electricity is turned off at 2300). The grocery store opposite immigration will change dollars into quetzales at a better rate than in La Palma, but still at a poor rate. From **El Naranjo** there is a dirt road through the jungle to Flores; buses leave at 0100, 0400 and 1200 for Flores (minimum 4½-5 rough, crowded hours) or hitchhiking apparently possible.

Travel agencies in Palenque do the trip to Flores via La Palma and El Naranjo, US$55 pp, 4 passengers minimum (agencies will make up the numbers), dep 0500, arrive Flores 1900; via Yaxchilán and Bonampak, with overnight camping, US$88 pp, minimum 5 people.

2) The Río Usumacinta route: 4 buses run daily from Palenque to Benemérito, on the

Mexican side of the Usumacinta, at least 7 hrs. Alternatively, one bus a day runs Palenque-Frontera Echeverría, 0930 (Autotransportes Comitán Lagos de Montebello company, Av Manuel Velasco Suárez, 3 blocks from food market), 6-8 hrs, US$5. Echeverría is also called Corozal. From Echeverría/Corozal there is a 40-minute launchride to Bethel in Guatemala, from where a regular bus service goes to Flores (see Guatemala chapter—**El Petén**). At Echeverría/Corozal there is an immigration office which has a basic room where people can stay for US$3.50 (the only place to stay if stuck here).

The Río Usumacinta, on the Chiapas border with Guatemala, is to be dammed. Three dams are projected just downstream from Piedras Negras ruins, but in 1992 Mexico shelved these plans at least until 1994. The ruins are accessible only by white water rafts, no road, no airstrip, unspoiled jungle (NW of Yaxchilán).

Other Sites Flights from Palenque to *Bonampak* and *Yaxchilán* , in light plane for 5, about US$600 per plane, to both places, whole trip 6 hrs. Prices set, list available; Viajes Misol-Ha run charter flights to Bonampak and Yaxchilán for US$150 pp return, minimum 4 passengers. ATG Travel Agency, agents for Aviacsa, at Av Benito Juárez and Allende, open 0800-1800 daily except Sunday, to Bonampak; book at airport, may be cheaper from Tenosique, best to visit in May—the driest month; Yaxchilán, which is being excavated (season March-June) and where there are more howler monkeys than people, is judged to be more interesting. Do not visit ruins at night, it is forbidden.

From Palenque, a 2-day road and river trip to Bonampak and Yaxchilán is sold by travel agencies, US$100 pp, all transport and food included; or one day trip to Yaxchilán, US$60; entrance to sites not included in cost. Strenuous, but good value: the usual schedule is 4-hr bus ride to Echeverría/Corozal, 1 hr boat to Yaxchilán, next day boat to Echeverría, 1 hr bus to Bonampak turn-off, walk to Bonampak and back (see over), 6 hr bus to Palenque (arriving 2200). Colectivos Chambala at Hidalgo y Allende, Palenque, also run 2-day trips, slightly cheaper, again all inclusive, minimum 6 passengers. However you go, take suitable footwear and rain protection for jungle walking, drinking water, insect repellent and passport. Bonampak is over 30 km from Frontera Echeverría/Corozal (see above for how to get there—food, petrol and accommodation; you must register the Migración office) and can be reached only on foot from the crossroads to Lacanjá on the road to Echeverría. Autotransportes Comitán Lagos de Montebello buses at 0300, 0430, 0630, 0900 and 2000 all pass the turn off to Bonampak, US$5.50, check details in advance. It is a 12 km walk from the crossroads to the ruins, 2-4 hrs depending on mud and fitness (all maps are inaccurate, directions must be asked frequently). Beware of sandflies, black flies which cause river blindness, and mosquitoes; there is basic accommodation at the site, take hammock and mosquito net. The workers are not to be trusted. There are many new tracks criss-crossing the Selva Lacandona (jungle), most going to Echeverría.

Yaxchilán is reached by 1-hr boat journey from Echeverría (US$40 to hire a motorboat for the round trip); a beautiful ride, and beautiful ruins. The custodian of the ruins is very helpful; outside the excavation season you can sling a hammock anywhere.

Agua Azul, a series of beautiful waterfalls aptly named for the blue water swirling over natural tufa dams on 7 km of fast-flowing river, is a popular camping spot reached by a 4-km paved road (in fair condition) from the junction with the paved road to San Cristóbal, 65 km from Palenque. Best visited in dry season as in the rainy season the water is less blue and it is hard to swim because of the current (don't visit if it was raining the day before). **Warning** One of the falls is called 'The Liquidiser" , an area of white water in which bathing is extremely dangerous. On no account should you enter this stretch of water; many drownings have occurred. Obey the notice posted in an adjacent tree. If you walk some way up the lefthand side of the river you come to uncrowded areas where the river is wider and safer for swimming. 3 km upstream is the Balcón Ahuau waterfall, good beach for sunbathing. It is extremely popular at holiday time (visit in the morning, less crowded). Entrance fee to this *ejidal* park US$0.65 on foot, US$1.65 for cars. There are a few restaurants and many food stalls (if on a tight budget, bring your own). There are 2 places with *cabañas* for hammocks (hammock rental US$1.50 and up, US$3.45 pp in beds in dormitory); if staying, be very careful of your belongings; thefts have been reported. *Camping Agua Azul* is popular and reliable, opposite the parking lot; camping costs US$1.75, US$3.30 for 2 in camper van, and US$0.15 for use of toilets (100m further on are free public toilets), no other facilities. RVs can stay overnight at Agua Azul, using the facilities, without paying extra (as long as you do not leave the park). Plenty of food stalls, two restaurants. Follow the path up the falls to a second site, cheaper, less crowded. There are also more *cabañas* and nice places to sling a hammock further upstream, all cheaper and less touristy than lower down. *Hamacas Casa Blanca* next to *Comedor El Bosque*, 2 km upstream, big room with mosquito-netted windows, accommodates 10, shared toilet, US$2 pp (US$1.70 with own hammock), free locked luggage store. Horses can be rented for riding downstream. It is possible to walk upriver to the rainforest; follow the river till you come to a rickety bridge across a stream, cross this and continue through a meadow until you rejoin the river; carry on to a lovely beach with trees and the river thundering through a gorge. Further progress is difficult. Beware of ticks when camping in long grass, use kerosene to remove them (or eat raw garlic to repel them!). Flies abound during the rainy season (June-November). The river near the campsite is often badly polluted with soap and detergents.

Between Palenque and Agua Azul are the *Misol-Ha* waterfalls (entry US$0.65, US$1.65 for a car). Coop Chambalum, Calle Allende, and Viajes Aventura Maya, Av Juárez 123, Palenque run tours to Agua Azul and Misol-Ha for US$8.35, leaving 1000 returning 1630, and 1200 returning 1900 (30 mins at Misol-Ha, 4 hrs at Agua Azul, take swimsuit). Other minibuses from minibus terminal (nr 4 Esquinas): they leave 0930-1000 from Palenque, 2 hrs at Agua Azul, arriving back in Palenque at 1500, stopping for 15 minutes at Misol-Ha, US$6.65-8 ($\frac{1}{2}$ price one way). Colectivos from Hidalgo y Allende, Palenque, for Agua Azul and Misol-Ha, 1000-1500, US$5; colectivos can also be organized between Misol-Ha and Agua Azul, in either direction. Several buses from Palenque daily (direction San Cristóbal de las Casas or Ocosingo), to crossroads leading to the waterfall, US$3.35, 2nd class, $1\frac{1}{2}$ hrs. From the crossroads walk the 4 km downhill to the falls (or hitch a ride on a minibus for US$0.20). There is an interesting cave to the right of the big falls, about 25m deep, with a pool inside and another waterfall; take a torch and beware of bats! Back from the junction 1400-1600 with Transportes Maya buses. There are buses between San Cristóbal de Las Casas and Palenque (to 2nd class bus station, Transportes Maya) which will stop there, but on a number of others you must change at Temo, over 20 km away, N of Ocosingo, which may require a fair wait.

Two highways lead **from Villahermosa to Campeche**: inland Highway 186, via Escárcega, with two toll bridges (cost US$4.25), and the slightly longer coastal route through Ciudad del Carmen, Highway 180, on which all but one of the former ferries have been replaced by bridges; both converge at Champotón, 66 km S of Campeche. Highway 186 passes Villahermosa's modern international airport and runs fast and smooth in a sweeping curve 115 km E to the Palenque turnoff at Playas del Catazajá; beyond, off the highway, is *Emiliano Zapata* (pop 13,000, *fiesta* 26 October), a busy cattle centre, with Pemex station (Hotels: **C** *Maya Uscumacinta*, **D** *Ramos*, opp bus station, with a/c, **E** with fan, reasonable restaurant, friendly; *Bernat Colonial*, all basic); the river town of *Balancán* is a further 60 km NE and has a small archæological museum in its Casa de Cultura (**E** *Hotel Delicias*); *fiesta* 14 December. In ten kilometres the main highway has crossed the narrow waist of Tabasco state and entered Campeche amid thick tropical vegetation filled with wildlife (jaguar, ocelot, tapir, wild turkey, boa and iguana), a popular destination for hunters and fishermen.

Transport from Emiliano Zapata, all ADO: to **Tenosique**, frequent, first at 0700, 0830, 0900, last at 2000, 2100, US$2, 90 mins (plus 2 2nd class companies); to **Villahermosa**, 17 departures between 0600 and 1700, US$3; to **Mérida**, 5 a day between 0900 and 2200, US$16.50; to **Escárcega**, 5 between 0630 and 2100, US$5.50; to **Chetumal**, 2130, US$14.

Route 186 is paved for the 140 km run to **Escárcega** (officially Francisco Escárcega). The condition of this route varies, poor up to Escárcega, but good around the town itself, good around Champotón (see below), but worsening as it approaches Campeche. Escárcega is a hot, straggling town of 16,700 which relies heavily on the many buses passing through. Service stations, a few overpriced hotels and cafés and the ADO 1st class bus station cluster near the junction of Highways 186 and 261. The rest of town spreads 2 km E along the Chetumal highway (186) and Calle Justo Sierra (which parallels it a block S) to the 2nd class Autobuses del Sur terminal just E of the railway crossing. The oil boom has expanded the town's services considerably in recent years.

Hotels and Services D *Casa de Huéspedes Lolita* on Chetumal highway at E end of town, pleasant; **D** *Berta Leticia*, Calle 29 No 28, with bath, fairly clean; **C** *Motel Akim Pech*, on Villahermosa highway, a/c or fans and bath, reasonable rooms, restaurant in motel, another across the street, also Pemex station opposite (sells unleaded *magna sin*); **D** *María Isabel*, Justo Sierra 127, a/c, restaurant, comfortable, back rooms noisy from highway; **D** *Escárcega*, Justo Sierra 86, T 40-186, C with a/c, best value, good restaurant, small garden, about ½ km E of ADO; **E** *San Luis*, Calle 28 facing the Zócalo, simple and lazily-maintained; **E** *El Yucateco*, Calle 50 No 42-A, T 40-065, D with a/c, central, tidy, fair value. **E** *Las Gemelas*, behind Pemex on Highway 186 W of intersection and ADO, noisy, decrepit, overpriced. **Restaurants** *La Choza*, on Chetumal highway by railway line, local atmosphere, good, inexpensive; budget prices and *típico* fare also at *Juanita*, same building as *Akim-Pech*; nearby is *Mi Ranchito*, grilled meal or chicken, popular; plenty of food in the town market (begins at Calle 31 on the corner of the plaza) **Post Office** on Calle 28a, and **Bancomer**, Calle 31 No 26 with limited currency exchange facilities.

Transport Escárcega is an important transport hub and buses run regularly from the 2nd class bus station to Palenque beginning at 0430 (US$6.60, 3 hrs); for other connections to Palenque, go to Emiliano Zapata, not all Villahermosa buses stop there, though. 1st class services on to Campeche, Mérida and Villahermosa depart from the ADO terminal; buses plying beautifully-surfaced Highway 186 E to Chetumal are ADO, 4 a day, and Autobuses del Sur, 3 at night, US$5 and US$4.60 respectively, 4 hrs. Off this road are many interesting ruins (see p 347), such as Balamku (105 km, discovered only in 1990), **Chicanná** (145 km), **Becán** (watch for very small sign) and **Xpujil** (153 km); little excavation has yet been undertaken in this region, but these ruins do give a good idea of how such sites look when stumbled upon by archæologists.

Highway 261 runs 86 km due N from Escárcega through dense forest to the Gulf of Mexico, where it joins the coastal route at **Champotón** (pop 70,000), a relaxed fishing and shrimping port spread along the banks of the Río Champotón. In prehispanic times it was an important trading link between Guatemala and Central Mexico; Toltec and Maya mingled here, followed by the Spaniards (where their first blood was shed on Mexican soil when Francisco Hernández de Córboba was fatally wounded in a skirmish with the inhabitants in 1517). On the S side of town can be seen the remnants of a 1719 fort built as a defence against the pirates who frequently raided this coast. The Feast of the Immaculate Conception (8 Dec) is celebrated with a joyous festival lasting several days.

Hotels and Services C *Snook Inn*, Calle 30 No 1, T 80088, a/c, fan, pool, owner speaks English, favourite with fishing enthusiasts and bird hunters; for larger game (plentiful in the surrounding jungle) there are three primitive but comfortable jungle camps to the S; rec guide is José Sansores (*Hotel Castelmar*, Campeche); *Gemenis*, Calle 30 No 10; *D'Venicia*, Calle 38; *Imperial*, Calle 28 No 38, all **E**, simple, with fans, river views, regular food. A few unpretentious restaurants, usually seafood menus but venison (*venedo*) and *pato* plentiful in season. Gasoline available, several banks: try the **Banco del Atlántico** for currency transactions, open Mon-Fri 0900-1230.

Villahermosa to Campeche via the coast Although Highway 180 is narrow, crumbling into the sea in places and usually ignored by tourists intent on visiting Palenque, this journey is a beautiful one. The road threads its way from Villahermosa 78 km N through marshland and rich cacao, banana and coconut plantations, passing turnoffs to several tiny coastal villages with palm-lined but otherwise mediocre beaches, to the river port of **Frontera** (pop 28,650), from where Graham Greene began the research journey in 1938 for his novel *The Power and the Glory*. (**Hotels:** *Zócalo*, showers, clean and pleasant, *Maya del Grijalva, San Agustín*, all **E**); toll bridge across the Río Grijalva (US$2.50). The Fería Guadalupana is held from 3-13 December, agricultural show, bullfights, *charreadas*, regional dances.

The road briefly touches the coast at the Tabasco/Campeche state border before running E beside a series of lakes (superb bird watching) to the fishing village of **Zacatal** (93 km), at the entrance to the tarpon-filled **Laguna de Términos** (named for the first Spanish expedition which turned back here). The only remaining car ferry on this route takes the traveller across the lake's mouth to Ciudad del Carmen (US$0.70 passengers, US$8 cars, 40 mins, first at 0330, last at 1730, returns an hour later, met by the bus for Frontera and Villahermosa, no after-dark services on Sun; plenty of room for foot passengers, usually has to turn away last cars, motorbikes easily accommodated). Just before Zacatal is the lighthouse of **Xicalango**, an important precolumbian trading centre where Cortés landed in 1519 on his way to Veracruz and acquired 'La Malinche', the Indian princess baptized as Doña Marina who, as the Spaniards' interpreter, was to play an important rôle in the Conquest.

Ciudad del Carmen (pop 151,400) is the hot, bursting-at-the-seams principal oil port of the region and is being developed into one of the biggest and most modern on the Gulf. Its important shrimping and prawning fleets are also expanding (good photo possibilities along the trawler-filled docks E of the ferry landing) and much ship building is undertaken. The site was originally established in 1588 by a pirate named McGregor as a lair from which to raid Spanish shipping; it was infamous until the pirates were wiped out by Alfonso Felipe de Andrade in 1717, who then named the town after its patroness, the Virgen del Carmen. Her attractive, cream-coloured **Cathedral** (notable for its stained glass), along with the Palacio Municipal and Library, stands on the **Plaza Principal**, or Plaza Zaragoza, a lush square conveniently sited on the waterfront at the ferry terminal, with wooden gazebo (free band concerts Thur and Sun evenings), Spanish lanterns, brick walkways and elegant wrought iron fencing. There is a modest **Archæological Museum** in the Liceo Carmelita showing locally-excavated items (US$0.25 admission). The town's patroness is honoured with a cheerful fiesta each 15-30 June, bullfights, cultural events, fireworks, etc. Carmen is inescapably associated with the ugliness accompanying an oil boom and is little-frequented by tourists; nevertheless, it is a good place for those curious to see the development of the Mexican oil and fishing industries: there is a wide range of facilities available and it is a convenient place to break the journey to Campeche. Delays and long queues at the ferry (which in extreme weather can be seriously disrupted) may sometimes force a stopover. Calle 20 is the seaside *malecón*, even-numbered streets run parallel to the E, with 20a, b, c, etc, being separate streets.

Hotels A *EuroHotel*, Calle 22a No 208, T 31030, large and modern, two restaurants, pool, a/c, disco, built to accommodate the flow of Pemex traffic; **B** *Isla del Carmen*, Calle 20 No 9, T 22350, a/c, restaurant, bar, parking; **B** *Lli-Re*, Calles 32a & 29a, T 20588, commercial hotel with large sparsely-furnished a/c rooms, TV, servibars, oddly old-fashioned but comfortable, restaurant with good but not cheap fish dishes; **C** *Aquario*, Calle 51 No 60, T 22547, a/c, comfortable; **C** *Lino's*, Calle 31 No 132, T 20738, a/c, pool, restaurant, also has 10 RV spaces with electricity hook-ups; **D** *Zacarías*, Calle 24a No 58, T 20121, modern, some cheaper rooms with fans, brighter a/c rooms are better value, rec; **E** *Internacional*, Calle 20a

No 21, T 21344, uninspiring outside but clean and friendly, one block from Plaza, some a/c; **E** *Roma*, on Calle 22, fan, cold showers, good value; other budget class places nearby are *Casa de Huéspedes Carmen*, Calle 20 No 142, *Villa del Mar*, Calles 20 y 33; and *Hotel del Parque*, Calle 33 No 1.

Restaurants The better hotels have good restaurants (the shrimp and prawns are especially tasty); others rec are *Pepe's*, Calle 27a No 15, a/c, attractive seafood dishes; *Vía Veneto*, in the *EuroHotel*, reasonable prices, good breakfasts; *El Kiosco*, in *Hotel del Parque* with view of Zócalo, modest prices, eggs, chicken, seafood and Mexican dishes; *La Mesita*, outdoor stand across from ferry landing, well-prepared shrimp, seafood cocktails, extremely popular all day; *La Fuente*, Calle 20a, 24-hr snack bar with view of the Laguna; for 'best coffee in town' try *Café Vadillo* or other tiny cafés along pedestrian walkway (Calle 33a) near the Zócalo; inexpensive snacks also in the thriving Central Market (Calles 20a & 37a, not far NW of Zócalo), many bakeries and supermarkets throughout the city, eg *Conasuper*, Calles 20a y 37a.

Car rentals (not cheap) **Auto-Rentas del Carmen**, Calle 33 No 121 (T 22376); **Fast** (T 22306), and **Auto Panamericana**, Calle 22 (T 22326).

Exchange Banco del Atlántico or Banamex, both at Calles 24a y 31a.

Post Office at Calles 29 y 20b, one block from the Plaza.

Tourist Office on Calle 20c near Calle 23 has little to promote in this non-tourist town, emphasis is on fishing excursions, basic street map available. **Fishing excursions** can be arranged through the *Club de Pesca Nelo Manjárrez* (T 20073) at Calles 40a and 61a, coastal lagoons are rich in tarpon *(sábalo)* and bonefish.

Buses Bus station conveniently located near city centre. At least 8 ADO services daily to **Campeche** (3 hrs) and **Mérida** (9 hrs, US$14.80), including three departures between 2100 and 2200 (worth considering if stuck for accommodation); several to **Villahermosa** via the coast, normally 8 hrs, but may depend on waiting time at the Zacatal ferry. A connection can be made to **Palenque** at 2330 or 0400, a slow but worthwhile trip. Buses also travel via **Escárcega**, where connections can be made for Chetumal and Belize.

Air Carmen's efficient airport (Av Aviación, only 3 km E of the Plaza) has also benefited from the oil traffic, with Mexicana (Calles 22 & 37, T 21171) flights daily to Mexico City and Aero Caribe daily to Villahermosa, Minatitlán, Veracruz and Mérida (more frequent at certain times of year); Aero-Campeche and Aviatur service many regional towns and oilfields.

11 km beyond Carmen is the *Rancho El Fénix*, with an interesting iguana (*lagarto*) hatchery. Highway 180 runs NE along the 38-km length of the Isla del Carmen and is now linked to the 'mainland' at Puerto Real by the 3.25 km long Puente de la Unidad (US$1.85 toll), built in 1982 and claimed to be the longest bridge in Mexico. Isla del Carmen is little more than a narrow sandspit, heavily forested (coconuts) and with Playa Norte occupying most of the Gulf side; Playa Bahamita extends it to the bridge at Puerto Real. Both have gritty sand mixed with shells and generally good swimming (although oil processing in the region can periodically affect the water), few facilities but a great place for beachcombing; camping is poor because of the shells and biting chiggers. The bridge crosses to the **Isla Aguada** (**C** *Hotel Tarpon Tropical*, **D** *Motel La Cabaña* and Trailer Park at former boatlanding just after the toll bridge, full hook-up, hot showers, laundry facilities, quiet, US$12 for vehicle and 2 people), actually a narrow peninsula with more deserted shell-littered beaches on the Gulf shore, and undulates its way NE through tiny fishing villages towards Campeche; there are many offshore oil rigs to be seen. At Sabancuy (85 km from Carmen) a paved short cut (57 km) crosses to the Villahermosa-Escárcega highway, a way of avoiding the Zacatal ferry if heading S. 63 bumpy km later, Highway 180 reaches Champotón (see above).

Continuing N, Highways 180 and 261 are combined for 17 km until the latter darts off E on its way to Edzná and Hopelchen (bypassing Campeche, should this be desired). A 66-km toll *autopista*, paralleling Highway 180, just inland from the southern outskirts of Champotón to Campeche, is much quicker than the old highway. Champotón and Seybaplaya are bypassed. We describe the places reached from Highway 180, narrow and slow (beware many speed bumps), which runs on a little further to the resort of **Sihoplaya**. Here is the widely-known **C** *Hotel Siho Playa* (T 62989), a former sugar hacienda with a beautiful setting and beach facilities, pool, disco/bar, breezy rooms, etc, but, despite remodelling in the past, it has seen better days; camping possible, US$5; restaurant is overpriced and poor but nowhere else to eat nearby; very popular, nonetheless, with *campechano* families and good views from the iguana-covered jetty of pelicans diving for their supper. Regular buses from Campeche US$1. A short distance further N is the larger resort of **Seybaplaya**, an attractive place where fishermen mend nets and pelicans dry their wings on posts along the beach. On the Highway is the open-air *Restaurant Veracruz*, serving delicious red snapper (fresh fish at the seafront Public Market is also good value), but in general there is little to explore; only the **Balneario Payucán** at the N end of the bay makes a special trip worthwhile; this is probably the closest decent beach to Campeche (33 km) although a little isolated, since the water and sand get filthier as one nears the state capital.

Our road now approaches **Lerma**, virtually a small industrial suburb of Campeche, with large shipyards and fish processing plants; the afternoon return of the shrimping fleet is a colourful sight; *Fiesta de Polk Kekén* held on 6 Jan, traditional dances. Close by is **Playa Bonita**, touted as a wonderful place to go (and hordes of Yucatecanos do during the *temporada* season); the beach has lockers, showers, *palapas* and dressing sheds but the water is now polluted and the sand hopelessly littered. Oil storage tanks nearby do little to improve the view, but the *malecón* is useful for car parking. Rickety buses marked 'Lerma' or 'Playa Bonita' run from Campeche, crowded, US$1, 8 km. A short distance to the S is the slightly better but less accessible San Lorenzo beach, rocky and peaceful but littered with cans and bottletops nonetheless.

Highway 180 enters the city of **Campeche** as the divided Avenida Resurgimiento, which passes either side of the huge **Monumento al Resurgimiento**, a stone torso holding aloft the torch of Democracy. The city, capital of Campeche state (pop 230,000, state pop 1990 528,800) is beautifully set on a small bay on the western coast of Yucatán, 252 km from Mérida and 444 km from Villahermosa. Originally the trading village of Ah Kim Pech, it was here that the Spaniards, under Francisco Hernández de Córdoba , first landed on Mexican soil (20 March 1517) and thus made the first contact between Maya and European. The city was founded by Francisco de Montejo in 1540; export of local dyewoods, chiclé, timber and other valuable cargoes soon attracted the attention of most of the famous buccaneers, who constantly raided the port from their bases on Isla del Carmen, then known as the Isla de Tris. Combining their fleets for one momentous swoop, they fell upon Campeche on 9 February 1663, wiped out the city and slaughtered its inhabitants. Five years later the Crown began fortifying the site, the first Spanish colonial settlement to be completely walled. Formidable bulwarks, 3m thick and 'a ship's height", and eight fortress/bastions (*baluartes*) were built in the next 36 years; the walls extended into the sea allowing ships to sail directly into the port through huge gates! All these precautions soon defeated pirate attacks and Campeche prospered until Mexican independence (only Campeche and Veracruz had the privilege of conducting international trade), after which it declined into an obscure fishing and logging town. Only with the arrival of a road from the 'mainland' in the 1950s and the oil boom of the 1970s has Campeche begun to see visitors in any numbers, attracted by its impressive historical monuments, modest prices and relaxed atmosphere (*campechano* has come to mean an easy-going, pleasant person).

Seven of the *baluartes* and an ancient fort (now rather dwarfed by two big white hotels on the seafront) near the cathedral remain, and are a photographer's delight. Some house museums: **Baluarte La Soledad** (just W of the Central Plaza), the largest of the seaward defences, with a small room of poorly maintained Maya stelae and a collection of colonial arms and seafaring equipment, friendly and informative caretaker (open Tues-Sat, 0900-1400, 1600-2000; Sun 0900-1300, free); **Baluarte San Carlos** (near the Palacio de Gobierno) with interesting scale models of the 18th century defences, small library, a fine view from the cannon-studded roof, dungeons and a government-sponsored handicrafts market; for a few pesos, guides will conduct you through underground passageways which once provided escape routes from many of the town's houses (most have now been bricked up), open 0800-2000 Tues-Sat, 0800-1300 Sun, US$0.15; **Baluarte San Pedro** (Calles 18 y 51, 5 blocks S of the Plaza) has a permanent *artesanía* exposition open Mon-Fri, 0900-1300, 1700-2000, free; **Baluarte Santiago**, 1 block N of the Plaza, with the Xmuch Haltun Botanical Gardens: 250 species of Yucatecan plants exhibited in a courtyard of fountains, a delightful spot to relax (small fee, open Tues-Sat, 0900-2000; Sun 0900-1300). The **Fuerte de San Miguel**, on the Malecón 4 km SW, is the most atmospheric of the forts (complete with drawbridge and a moat said to have once contained either crocodiles or skin-burning lime ... take your pick!); it houses the **Museo Arqueológico**, with fine Olmec and Maya figurines from Edzná and Jaina (many are cross-eyed, a mark of beauty to the Maya) and such intriguing artefacts as a wooden device for deforming the heads of new-born infants (another desirable feature to the ancient Maya); closed for renovation January 1994. Like many of the Yucatán's towns, Campeche's streets in the Old Town are numbered rather than named. Even-numbers run N/S beginning at Calle 8 (no-one knows why) near the Malecón, E to Calle 18 inside the walls; odd-numbers run E (inland) from Calle 51 in the N to Calle 65 in the S. Most of the points of interest are within this compact area. The full circuit of the walls is a long walk; buses marked 'Circuito Baluartes' provide a regular service around the perimeter. Running in from the NE is Avenida Gobernadores, on which are situated the bus and railway stations.

The heart of Campeche is its **Plaza Principal** or Zócalo, bounded by Calles 8, 10, 55 and 57 and filled with a strange mixture of colonial past and ultramodern; an atmosphere of small-town Spain gives it a delightful ambience during the evening *paseo*. The somewhat dull and crumbling Franciscan **Cathedral** (1540-1705), facing the Plaza, the oldest church in the Yucatán, has an elaborately carved façade and the Santo Entierro (Holy Burial), a sculpture of Christ in a mahogany sarcophagus with silver trim. There are, however, several better 16th and 17th century churches. The most interesting are **San Francisquito** (16th century with wooden altars painted in vermilion and white), Jesús, San Juan de Dios, Guadalupe and Cristo Negro de San Román. Also on the Zócalo is the **Regional Museum**, housed in the 18th century Casa del Teniente del Rey, with a well-documented display of precolumbian exhibits on the ground floor and an historical overview of colonial Campeche on the upper level (open Tues-Sat, 0900-2000, Sun 0900-1300, admission US$2.20, recommended). The old houses within the walls are warmly coloured but often in a bad state of repair; efforts are now being made to spruce the place up. The best way to see the Old City is to walk its narrow streets; the shady **Alameda** (bottom of Calle 57 opposite the Baluarte San Francisco) offers respite from the sun and contains the unusual **Puente de los Perros** (Bridge of the Dogs), a colonial bridge guarded by carved stone dogs honouring the Dominican missionaries called the 'Hounds of God' for their zealous pursuit of converts.

Representative of the city's increasing modernity are big white luxury hotels on the sea-front, and the square glass Palacio de Gobierno (colourful murals) and adjoining concrete Congreso; although both were designed to blend in with the native architecture, conservative Campechanos dismiss them as 'The Jukebox' and 'The Flying Saucer' respectively. The futuristic Ciudad Universitaria (near Youth Hostel) almost rivals that of Mexico City. Other interesting sights include: the **Fuerte José El Alto**, some distance NE on Calle 7 beyond the railway ("San José El Alto' bus from the market), with excellent views, and adjacent refurbished church and Jesuit college (1756), now a museum and cultural centre with frequently changing exhibits, gift shop; incorporated into the church is Yucatán's first lighthouse (1864). Remnants of the **Convento de San Francisco** (1546) lie 20 min walk NE along the seafront, where the first Mexican Mass was celebrated and Cortés' grandson, Jerónimo, was baptized (1563) in the font, which is still in use; close by is **Pozo de la Conquista**, the spring from which Hernández de Córdoba's men filled their casks in 1517.

Festivals *Fería de San Román*, second two weeks of September; *Fiesta de San Francisco*, 4-13 Oct; good Carnival in February/March; 7 August is a state holiday.

Hotels In general, beware of overcharging and, if driving, find a secure car park. **A** *Alhambra*, Av Resurgimiento 85, T 66822, F 66132, 4-star, S end of town, a/c, disco, pool, satellite TV, quiet but popular with Mexican families in summer; **A** *Ramada Inn*, Av Ruiz Cortines 51, T 62233, F 11618 (5 stars), on the waterfront; **B** *Baluartes*, Av Ruiz Cortines, T 63911, nice, parking for campers, who can use the hotel washrooms, very good restaurant, pool; **D** *López*, Calle 12, No 189, T 63344, clean if a bit musty, with bath, a/c, friendly, better food; **D** *Castelmar*, Calles 8 y 61, T 65186, good location in colonial building at S end of Plaza Central, large rooms with bath, clean, friendly, ceiling fans, some balconies, patio, poor value. Several on Calle 10: **B** *América*, No 252, T 64588, hot water, clean, fans but hot, OK; **D** *Posada Del Angel*, No 307, T 67718 (opp cathedral), a/c, attractive, clean, rec, and **E** *Roma*, No 254, T 63897, running down, not safe (often full); **D** *Reforma*, Calle 8 No 257, T 64464, upper floor rooms best, clean bathrooms, reasonable value; **D** *Autel El Viajero*, López Mateos 177, overcharges, but often only one left with space in the afternoon, T 65133; **D** *Central*, on Gobernadores opp ADO bus station, misleadingly named, overpriced but may negotiate, a/c, hot water, clean, friendly, noisy; **C** *Colonial*, clean, good, Calle 14 No 122, T 62222, several blocks from Zócalo, not very friendly; **D** *Campeche*, Calle 57 No 1, across from the park at the end of Calle 57, T 65183, fan, cold water, washing facilities, dirty, noisy, not rec; **E** *Hospedaje Teresita*, Calle 53 No 31, 3 blocks NE of Plaza, quiet, welcoming, spartan rooms with fans, no hot water.

Youth Hostel Av Agustín Melgar s/n, Col Buenavista, CP 24020, T 61802/67718, in the S suburbs, nr University, Fuerte San Miguel and Trailer Park, take Samulá or ISSSTE bus from market US$0.15 (ISSSTE bus also from bus station), segregated dormitories with bunk beds (US$3 pp), lovely grounds, pool, cafeteria (breakfast 0730-0930, lunch 1400-1600, dinner 1930-2130, about US$1.50), clean and friendly, towels provided.

Camping *Trailer Park Campeche*, on Agustín Melgar & Calle 19a, 5 km S of centre, close to the Bay in uninviting suburb of Samulá (signposted), 25 spaces and tent area, full hook-ups, good amenities, cold showers, pleasant site, owners speak some English, US$3.25 pp, US$6.50 for car with 2 people, 'Samulá' bus from market (US$0.15) or a 'Lerma' bus down coast road, alight at Melgar and walk. Tourist Office often gives permission to pitch tents in their grounds, as will the Youth Hostel. There is a trailer park near the tourist office, open evenings only, until 2000, no tent or hammock facilities.

Restaurants *La Perla*, Calle 10 No 345, good fish, busy and popular, venison, squid; locals' haunt, sometimes erratic service, off Plaza; *Lonchería Puga*, Calle 8 No 53, open 0700, rec; *Pizzería Gato Pardo*, corner of Calle 10 and 49, on Jardín San Martín, outside the wall, excellent pizzas, loud music. *Café Artista*, on Zócalo, good fish from 1200-1400, also popular in evening; *Los Portales*, on main square, good value, especially seafood. *Marganza*, Calle 8, good breakfast and meals, excellent service; *Heladería Bing*, Calle 12 No 59, good ice cream. *Ave Fénix*, on Juárez where the street bends towards the terminal, generous breakfasts. Good food in the market, but don't drink the tap water. It is hard to find reasonably-priced food before 1800; try the restaurant at the ADO terminal, or *La Parroquia*, Calle 55 No 9, open 24 hrs, good local atmosphere, friendly and clean, rec. *Disco Bar Bali Hai*, on Malecón S of town, good drinks and *tapas*, moderately priced.

Campeche is widely-known for its seafood, especially large shrimps (*camarones*), black snapper (*esmedregal*) and *pan de cazón* – baby hammerhead shark sandwiched between corn tortillas with black beans. Food stands in the Market serve *típico tortas, tortillas, panuchos* and *tamales* but hygiene standards vary widely; barbequed venison is also a marketplace speciality. Fruit is cheap and in great variety; perhaps best to resist the bags of sliced mangoes and peel all fruit yourself. (The word 'cocktail' is said to have originated in Campeche, where 17th century English pirates enjoyed drinks adorned with palm fronds resembling cock's tails.)

Shopping Excellent cheap Panama hats *(jipis)*, finely and tightly woven so that they retain their shape even when crushed into your hand luggage; cheaper at the source in Becal (see under **From Campeche to Mérida**). Handicrafts are generally cheaper than in Mérida. The attractive new market, from which most local buses depart, is beside Alameda Park at the S end of Calle 57 and is worth a visit. Plenty of bargains here, especially Mexican and Maya clothes, hats and shoes, fruit and vegetables; try ice cream, though preferably from a shop rather than a barrow. *Super 10* supermarket behind the post office has some English magazines. There are souvenir shops along Calle 8a, such as *Artesanía Típica Naval* (No 259) with exotic bottled fruit like *nance* and *marañón*, or *El Coral* (No 255) with a large variety of Maya figurines; many high-quality craft items are available from the *Exposición* in the Baluarte San Pedro. Camping and general supplies, and laundrette, at *Superdíaz* supermarket in reclaimed Akim-Pech shopping area at Av Miguel Alemán y Av Madero, some distance N of the Zócalo (open 0800-2100).

Car Hire next to *Hotel Ramada Inn*, Av Ruiz Cortines 51, T 62233.

Exchange Banamex, Calle 10 No 15; **Bancomer**, opp the Baluarte de la Soledad; **Banco del Atlántico**, Calle 50 No 406; open 0900-1300 Mon-Fri; all change TCs and give good service. **American Express** (T 11010), Calle 59 in Edificio Belmar, oficina 5, helpful for lost cheques, etc.

Post Office Av 16 de Septiembre (Malecón) & Calle 59 in the Edificio Federal (go to the right upon entry for telegraph service); open Mon-Fri 0800-2000, Sat 0900-1300 for *Lista de Correos*, registered mail, money orders and stamps.

Transport ADO bus terminal at Gobernadores 289, esq Chile, on way to train station ("Gobernadores' or 'Centro' buses to the Plaza Principal, taxis about US$2.50, or 30 mins walk). First class buses almost hourly to Mérida, 3 hrs, US$6.25. First class buses go by the Vía Corta, which does *not* pass through Uxmal, Kabah, etc. Take a really quite comfortable 2nd class bus from the same terminal, Vía Larga, have 3 hrs at Uxmal (if you take the 0600 or 0900 bus, not the 1200, 1430 or 1500), and catch the next bus to Mérida, but don't buy a through ticket to Mérida; you'll have to pay again when you board the bus (2nd class to Mérida is US$5). Check bus times, as there are fewer in the afternoon. Bus Campeche-Uxmal, US$4.50, 2nd class, 3 hrs, 5 a day (but none between 0900 and 1200 - only the 0600 or 0900 give enough time at Uxmal ruins, unless you stay the night there). Buses along inland road to **Villahermosa**; take posted times with a pinch of salt, 2nd class, 5 a day, US$14.25, 1st class US$16.50, 6½ hrs, 2300 bus comes from Mérida but empties during the night. Bus via Emiliano Zapata (US$7.75, 2 hrs before Villahermosa) to **Palenque**, change at Emiliano Zapata, or direct, 1 daily, 2nd class (Transportes del Sur), US$10.65, 2 with ADO, US$15, **see p 293**. ADO bus to **Mexico City**, US$56.

Trains Railway station is at Gobernadores y Av Héroes de Nacozari (3 km), plenty of 'Centro' buses; some banditry in this region, trains from Campeche not really rec. Train to Mexico City, 34 hrs, comfortable. Mexico City-Campeche train leaves at 2115 daily, very crowded in holiday times. Train Campeche-**Palenque**, 1st and 2nd class train at 2140, 7 hrs (coming from Mérida, and continuing for Córdoba for Mexico City). To Mérida at 0545 (1st and 2nd class, 3½ hrs).

Air Modern and efficient airport on Porfilio, 10 km NE. AeroMéxico direct daily to Mexico City (T 65678), Hertz and Autorent car rentals at airport (good for neighbourhood excursions); if on a budget, walk 100m down service road (Av Aviación) to Av Nacozari, turn right (W) and wait for 'China-Campeche' bus to Zócalo.

Maya Sites in Campeche State A number of city remains (mostly in the unfussy Chenes architectural style) are scattered throughout the rainforest and scrub to the E of Campeche; little excavation work has been done and most receive few visitors. Getting to them by the occasional bus service is possible in many cases, but return trips can be tricky. The alternatives are one of the tours run by some luxury hotels and travel agencies in Campeche (see below) or renting a vehicle (preferably with high clearance) in Campeche or Mérida. Whichever way one travels, carrying a canteen of drinking water is strongly advised.

The closest site to the state capital is *Edzná* ("House of Grimaces"), reached by the highway E to Cayal, then right turn onto Highway 261 (the road to Uxmal, **see p 304**), a total distance of 61 km. A paved short cut SE through China and Poxyaxum (good road) cuts off 11 km; follow Av Nacozari out along the railway track. Gracefully situated in a lovely valley with thick vegetation on either side, Edzná was a huge ceremonial centre, occupied from about 600 BC to AD 200, built in the simple Chenes style mixed with Puuc, Classical and other influences. Centrepiece is the magnificent, 30 metre-tall, 60 square metre **Temple of the Five Stories**, a stepped pyramid consisting of four levels of living quarters for the priests and a shrine and altar at the top; 65 steep stairs ascend it from the Central Plaza. Opposite is the recently-restored **Paal U'na**, Temple of the Moon.

Excavations are being carried out on the scores of lesser temples by Guatemalan refugees under the direction of Mexican archaeologists, but most of Edzná's original sprawl remains hidden away under thick vegetation; imagination is still needed to picture the extensive network of irrigation canals and holding basins built by the Maya along the below-sea-level valley. Some of the site's stelae remain in position (two large stone faces with grotesquely squinting eyes are covered by a thatched shelter); others can be seen in various Campeche museums. There is also a good example of a *sacbe* (white road). Edzná is especially worth considering in July (date varies) when a Maya ceremony to Chac is held, either to encourage or to celebrate the arrival of the rains.

Edzná is open Tues-Sun 0800-1700, US$4.35 admission; *comedor* at the entrance. At weekends take a bus towards Pich from Campeche market place at 0800 (1 hr trip) but may leave hours late, return buses passing the site (500m walk from the Highway) have been reported at 1130, 1245 and 1345, none allowing an extended visit. In the week, the Pich bus leaves Campeche at 1400, which is only of any use if you are prepared to sleep rough as there is nowhere to stay in the vicinity; hitching back is difficult, but you may get a ride to El Cayal on the road to Uxmal. *Viajes Programados*, Calle 59, Edificio Belmar, in Campeche offers daily 2-hr tours at 1000 ($15 pp); the Tourist Office can also recommend reliable guides for regional tours, eg Sr Antonio Romero.

Of the remoter and even less-visited sites beyond Edzná, Hochob and Dzibilnocac are the best choices for the non-specialist. **Hochob** is reached by turning right at **Hopelchén** on Highway 261, 85 km E of Campeche. This quiet town has an impressive fortified 16th century church but only one hotel, **D Los Arcos**; a traditional honey and corn festival is held on 13-17 April, another *fiesta* takes place each 3 May on the Día de la Santa Cruz. From here a narrow paved road leads 41 km S to the village of **Dzibalchén**; no hotels but hammock hooks and toilet facilities upon request at the Palacio Municipal, there are some small eating places around the Zócalo; directions can be obtained from the church here (run by Americans); essentially you need to travel 11 km SW on a dirt road (no public transport, hopeless quagmire in the rainy season) to the village of Chenko, where locals will show the way (a complicated 4 km into the jungle). Remember to bear left when the road forks; it ends at a small *palapa*, from which the ruins are a kilometre's walk up a hill with magnificent view over the surrounding forest. Hochob covered a large area but, as at Edzná, only the hilltop ceremonial centre (the usual Plaza surrounded by elaborately decorated temple buildings) has been properly excavated; even so, most of these are little more than rubble mounds, but the site is perfect for contemplating deserted yet accessible Maya ruins in solitude and silence. The one-room temple to the right (N) of the plaza is the most famous structure: deep-relief patterns of stylized snakes moulded in stucco across its façade were designed to resemble a mask of the ferocious rain god Chac, a door serving as the mouth (some concentration is need to see this due to erosion of the carvings; a fine reconstruction of the building is on display at the Museo de Antropología in Mexico City). Open daily 0800-1700, US$4.35. Early-morning 2nd class buses serve Dzibalchén but, as always, returning to Campeche later in the day is often a matter of luck.

Dzibilnocac, 20 km NE of Dzibalchén at Iturbide, can be reached by a bus which leaves Campeche at 0800, 3 hrs, return 1245, 1345 and 1600, US$3.35 to Campeche. If driving your own vehicle, well-marked 'km' signs parallel the rocky road to Iturbide (no accommodation); bear right around the tiny Zócalo and its attendant yellow church and continue on (better to walk in the wet season) for 50m, where the right branch of a fork leads to the ruins, one of the largest in Chenes territory; open daily 0800-1700, US$4.35. Only three temples have been excavated here (many pyramidal mounds in the forest and roadside *milpas*); the first two are in a bad state of preservation, but the third is worth the visit: a unique narrow edifice with rounded corners and remains of a stucco façade, primitive reliefs and another grim mask of Chac on the top level. Much of the stonework from the extensive site is used by local farmers for huts and fences, keep an eye out in the vegetation for thorns and snakes. Other sites in the region would require four-wheel drive transport and be likely to appeal only to professional archaeologists.

The small limestone islands of **Jaina** and **Piedra** lie just off the coast 40 km and 55 km N of Campeche. Discovered by Morley in 1943, excavations here have revealed the most extensive Maya burial grounds ever found, over 1000 interments dating back to AD 652. The bodies of religious and political leaders were carried long distances from all over the Yucatán and Guatemala to be buried beneath the extremely steep **Pyramids of Zacpol** and **Sayasol** on Jaina. The corpses were interred in jars in crouching positions, clutching statues in their folded arms, some with jade stones in their mouths; food, weapons, tools and jewellery accompanied the owner into the afterlife. Terracotta burial offerings (including figurines with movable arms and legs) have provided a revealing picture of Maya customs, dress and living habits; many of these are now on display in Campeche or in the museum at Hecelchakán (see below). Although a vehicular track from Hecelchakán on Highway 180 leads W to the beach opposite Jaina, the islands are Federal property and are guarded; consequently, written official permission is needed to visit. Some tour operators in Campeche are allowed to run boat tours if there are enough people (about US$10 pp, but bargain), 3 hrs each way. This is practically the only way for a non-professional foreigner to make the excursion. The Tourist Office can provide details.

There are two **routes between Campeche and Mérida**: the so-called 'Camino Real", Vía Corta or Short Route (173 km via the shortcut along the railway line to Tenabó), using Highway 180 through Calkiní, Becal and Umán (taken by all first class and *directo* buses), and the 'Ruta Maya' or Long Route (254 km), Highway 261 through Hopelchén and Muná, which gives access to many of the Peninsula's best-known archaeological sites, especially Uxmal.

On the direct route, State Highway 24 provides a convenient link from Campeche to Highway 180 at **Tenabó** (36 km against 58 km), from where the well-paved road runs on through rising ground and sleepy villages, each with its traditional *zócalo*, solid church and stone houses often made from the materials of nearby Maya ruins, to **Hecelchakán** (18 km, large service station on the bypass), with a 1620 Franciscan church and the rustic Museo Arqueológico del Camino Real on the Zócalo. Although dusty, the museum's five rooms give an informative overview of Mayan cultural development with the help of maps, stelae, a diorama and many Jaina burial artefacts (open Tues-Sat 0900-1400, US$1.85).

The highway bypasses **Calkiní** (F *Posada del Viajero*, good, also restaurant; service station) and after 33 km arrives at **Becal** (pop 4000), the centre for weaving Panama hats, here called *jipis* (pronounced 'hippies") and ubiquitous throughout the Yucatán. Many of the town's families have workshops in cool, moist backyard underground caves, necessary for keeping moist and pliable the shredded leaves of the *jipijapa* palm of which the hats are made; most vendors are happy to give the visitor a tour of their workshop, but are quite zealous in their sales pitches. Prices are only marginally higher for *jipis* and other locally-woven items (cigarette cases, shoes, belts, etc) in the *Centro Artesanal, Artesanías de Becaleña* (Calle 30a No 210a), or the shops near the Plaza, where the hat is honoured by a hefty sculpture of three concrete sombreros! More celebrations of homage take place each 20 May during the *Feria del Jipi*.

Just beyond Becal, the Highway passes under a 19th century stone arch which is supposed to mark the Campeche/Yucatán border (although nobody seems totally sure of where the line is) and runs 26 km to **Maxcanu**. Here the road to Muná and Ticul branches right (**see p 314**); a short way down it (right) is the recently-restored Maya site of *Oxkintoc*. The Pyramid of the Labyrinth can be entered (take a torch) and there are other ruins, some with figures; entrance US$3, ask for a guide at Calcehtoc which is 4 km from the ruins and from the Grutas de Oxkintoc (no bus service). These, however, cannot compare with the caves at Loltún or Balancanché. Highway 180 continues N towards Mérida through a region of numerous *cenotes*, soon passing a turnoff to the turn-of-the-century Moorish-style *henequén* (sisal) hacienda at **San Bernardo**, one of a number in the state which can be visited (another to the E at Yaxcopoil on Highway 261); an interesting colonial museum chronicling the old Yucatán Peninsula tramway system is located in its lush and spacious grounds. Running beside the railway, the highway continues 47 km to its junction with the inland route at **Umán**, an *henequén* processing town of 7000 with another large 17th century church and convent dedicated to St Francis of Assisi; there are many *cenotes* in the flat surrounding limestone plain. Highway 180/261 is a divided four-lane motorway for the final 18 km stretch into Mérida.

Mérida, capital of Yucatán state (pop 700,000, state pop 1990 1,363,000), was founded in 1542 on the site of the Mayan city of Tihoo. Its centre is the Plaza Mayor, green and shady; its arcades have more than a touch of the Moorish style. It is surrounded by the severe twin-towered 16th century **Cathedral**, the Palacio Municipal, the Palacio de Gobierno, and the **Casa Montejo**, originally built in 1549 by the *conquistador* of the region, Francisco de Montejo, rebuilt around 1850 and now a branch of the Banco Nacional de México (Banamex). The **Casa de los Gobernadores**, or Palacio Cantón, on Paseo de Montejo at Calle 41, is an impressive building in the turn-of-the-century French style of the Porfirio Díaz era. It now houses the **Museo de Antropología e Historia**, closed on Mon (open 0800-1400 Sun, 0800-2000 all other days, US$4.35). The **Museo de Arte Popular** (Museum of Peninsular Culture—Calle 59, between 50 and 48), run by the Instituto Nacional Indigenista (INI), a contemporary crafts museum, is well worth visiting (inexpensive gift shop, small stock). There are several 16th and 17th century churches dotted about the city: La Mejorada, behind the Museum of Peninsular Culture (Calle 59 between 48 and 50), Tercera Orden, San Francisco and San Cristóbal (beautiful, in the centre). Along the narrow streets ply horse-drawn cabs of a curious local design. In all the city's parks you will find *confidenciales*, S-shaped stone seats in which people can sit side by side facing each other. The **Ermita**, an 18th century chapel with beautiful grounds, is a lonely, deserted place 10-15 mins from the centre.

In the **Palacio de Gobierno**, on the Plaza Mayor, there is a series of superb symbolic and historical paintings, finished 1978, by a local artist, Fernando Castro Pacheco. The Palacio is open evenings and very well lit to display the paintings.

All the markets, and there are several, are interesting in the early morning. One can buy traditional crafts: a basket or *sombrero* of sisal, a filigree necklace, also a good selection of Maya replicas. Tortoiseshell articles are also sold, but cannot be imported into most countries, as sea turtles are protected by international convention. The Mérida market is also particularly good for made-to-measure sandals of deerskin and tyre-soles, panama hats, and hammocks of all sizes and qualities. Some of the most typical products are the *guayabera*, a pleated and/or embroidered shirt worn universally, its equivalent for women, the *guayablusa*, and beautiful Mayan blouses and *huipiles*. In **Parque El Centenario** is a zoo; a popular place for family outings on Sunday. In the Parque de las Américas is an open-air theatre giving plays and concerts, and bands play in various plazas in the evenings. Enquire at hotels about the house and garden tours run by the local society women for tourists to raise money for charity. Every Thursday evening there is free local music, dancing and poetry at 2100 in the Plaza Santa Lucía, two blocks from the Plaza Mayor (Calles 55 and 60), chairs provided. Every Sunday

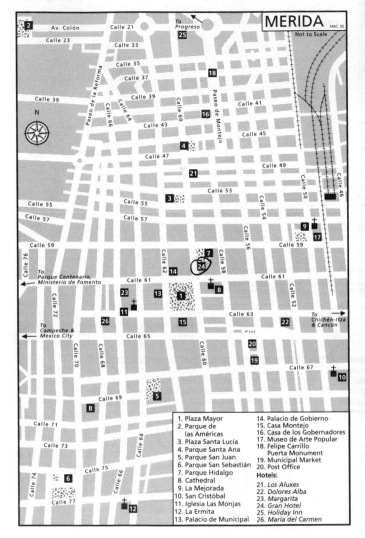

MERIDA MAC 30
Not to Scale

To Progreso

To Parque Centenario,
Ministerio de Fomento

To Campeche &
Mexico City

To Chichén-Itzá
& Cancún

1. Plaza Mayor
2. Parque de
   las Américas
3. Plaza Santa Lucía
4. Parque Santa Ana
5. Parque San Juan
6. Parque San Sebastián
7. Parque Hidalgo
8. Cathedral
9. La Mejorada
10. San Cristóbal
11. Iglesia Las Monjas
12. La Ermita
13. Palacio de Municipal

14. Palacio de Gobierno
15. Casa Montejo
16. Casa de los Gobernadores
17. Museo de Arte Popular
18. Felipe Carrillo
    Puerta Monument
19. Municipal Market
20. Post Office

Hotels:
21. Los Aluxes
22. Dolores Alba
23. Margarita
24. Gran Hotel
25. Holiday Inn
26. María del Carmen

(from 0900 to 2100) all the roads in the centre are closed to motor traffic: everyone takes to the streets to stroll, chat, cycle around or ride in a horse-drawn open carriage ("the best time to be in the city"). There is a weekly programme of events organized by the Municipality (every night except Saturday), including regional dancing and folk guitar concerts. The Tourist Office has details. The Casa de Cultura (Calle 63 and 64) has several rooms; an open-air theatre, concert hall, art gallery and display of regional handicrafts. There are monuments to Felipe Carrillo Puerto, an agrarian labour leader prominent in the 1910 revolution.

In Paseo de Montejo, together with many shops and restaurants, there are a few grand late 19th century houses. Calle 65 is the main shopping street and the Plaza Mayor is between Calles 61/63 and 60/62. Odd-number streets run E and W, even numbers N and S. In colonial times, painted or sculpted men or animals placed at intersections were used as symbols for the street: some still exist in the small towns of Yucatán. All streets are one-way. The houses are mostly of Spanish-Moorish type, painted in soft pastel tones, thick walls, flat roofs, massive doors, grilled windows, flowery patios. The water supply, once notorious, is improved. Redevelopment is rapid; many of the old houses are being pulled down. The city suffers from pollution caused by heavy traffic, narrow streets and climatic conditions favouring smog-formation. Mérida is a safe city in general (though be careful on Calle 58 and near the market), but the large influx of visitors in recent years is creating 'mostly quiet hostility' towards them. Begging and much molestation from car-washers, shoe-shiners, souvenir-peddlers and others wishing to 'help you find the right hammock, just to practise English".

Fiesta Carnival during the week before Ash Wednesday (best on Sat). Floats, dancers in regional costume, music and dancing around the Plaza and children dressed in animal suits. **NB** Banks closed Monday following carnival.

Addresses Check that the address you need is in the centre; there are many *fraccionamientos* (estates) around the town.

Hotels Cheaper hotels tend to be S of the main Plaza (odd streets numbered 63 and higher), near the market and especially the bus station (Calles 69 and 68). More expensive hotels are on the N side of the city and near the Paseo Montejo. The narrow streets in the city centre tend to amplify noise making it difficult to sleep in hotels in this part of town.
  L *Hyatt Regency*, Calle 60 No 344 x Colón, T 256722, F 257002, new luxury hotel with boutiques, car hire, money exchange, tennis, gym, *Peregrina* restaurant; opp and due open Oct 1994 is a *Fiesta Americana*; **A+** *Best Western María del Carmen*, Calle 63, No 550 x 68, T 239133, F 239290, pool, a/c, good value; **A+** *Calinda Panamericana*, Calle 59, No 455 x 52, T 239111, F 248090, good, expensive, with elaborate courtyard in the Porfirian style, very spacious and airy, ordinary rooms in new building behind, good buffet breakfast, with swimming pool, 5 blocks from centre; **A+** *Casa del Balam*, Calle 60, No 488 x 57, T 248844 (Mayaland Resort, T in USA 305-344-6547/800-451-8891), a/c, close to centre, noisy at front, restaurant, bar, pool, neocolonial style, facilities rather below 5-star; **A+** *Castellano*, Calle 57, No 513 x 62, T 230100, modern, clean but a bit run-down, friendly, pool; **A+** *El Conquistador*, Paseo del Montejo 458 x 35, T 262155, modern, specializing in package tours, unhelpful, poor value for independent travellers, good buffet breakfast; **A+** *Holiday Inn*, Av Colón No 489 x Montejo, T 256877, F 247755 (connected with LADA international direct dialling), all facilities, elegant but a long way from the centre; **A+** *Los Aluxes*, Calle 60 No 444, T 242199 x 49, delightful, pool, restaurants, very convenient, first class, two large new wings away from traffic noise due open 1994; **A** *Del Gobernador*, Calle 59, No 533 x 66, T 237133, a/c, big rooms, quite good; and others in our A range and above.
  B *Caribe*, Parque Hidalgo, Calle 59 No 500, T 249022, F 248733, tiny pool, a/c, cheaper with fan, modern, tasteful patio, renovated 1993; **B** *Gran Hotel*, Parque Hidalgo, Calle 60 No 496, T 247730, F 247622, does not accept Amex card, with a/c, TV, hot water, phone, clean, helpful, owner speaks English, turn-of-the-century atmosphere (inaugurated 1901, renovated 1993 not to everyone's taste), Fidel Castro has stayed here frequently, as have other politicians, film and stage stars, good restaurant attached, free parking nearby on Calle 61 between 56 and 54 (opp Banco BCH, ask front desk to stamp the parking receipt); **B** *Maya Yucatán*, Calle 58 No 483 x 57, between Calles 55 y 57, T 235395, F 234642, with bath, a/c, clean, swimming pool, TV, good restaurant; **B** *Posada Toledo*, Calle 58, No 487 x 57, T 231690, good, central, in charming old house, lots of plants, has paperback exchange; **B** *Reforma*, Calle 59, No 508 x 62, T 247922, swimming pool, refurbished, nice; **C** *Colón*, Calle 62, No 483, T 234355, good value, pool; **C** *Del Parque*, Calle 60 No 495 x 59, T 17840, with bath and fan, clean, friendly, rec; **C** *Dolores Alba*, Calle 63 No 464 x 54, T (99) 285650, F (99) 283163, does not take credit cards, with bath and fan, some with a/c, good, pool, clean, cool on 1st floor, have to pay for children under 10, breakfast 0700-1000, US$3.35, will make reservations for sister establishment at Chichén Itzá; **C** *Flamingo*, Calle 58 y 59, T 17740, near Plaza, with private shower, swimming pool, noisy, so get room at the back, in poor

condition; **C** *México*, Calle 60, No 525 x 67, T 19255, good restaurant, attractive; **C** *Montejo*, Calle 57 No 507 entre 62 y 64, T 280277, clean, comfortable, convenient, safe, rec; **C** *Peninsular*, Calle 58, No 519 x 65 y 67, T 236996, 1 block from post office and market, small pool, a/c, clean, comfortable, convenient, friendly; **C** *Posada del Angel*, Calle 67, No 535, x 66 y 68, T 232754, clean, excellent value (don't bother with the restaurant next door); **C** *Príncipe Maya Airport Inn*, T 14050, noisy from night club, convenient for airport. **C** *Santa Lucía*, Calle 55 No 508, almost opp Plaza Santa Lucía, TV, a/c, very clean, very good value, rec; **C** *Sevilla*, Calle 62, No 511 x 65, T 15258, near Zócalo, private bath, clean, quiet, fan, but rooms without proper windows; **C** *Trinidad*, Calle 62, No 464 x 55, T 213029, old house, cheaper rooms with shared bath, clean bathrooms, tranquil, courtyard, sun roof, lovely garden, can use pool at the other hotel; **C** *Trinidad Galería*, Calle 60, esq 51, T 232463, F 242319, excellent value, pool, hot water, fan, nice atmosphere and arty décor, laundry service, mixed reports; same ownership.

D *América*, simple, private shower and toilet, noisy, will look after luggage, Calle 67, No 500, x 58 y 60, T 15133, about 10 mins from bus station and near centre, rec; **D** *Casa Becil*, Calle 67 No 550-C, x 66 y 68, convenient for bus station, bath, hot water, clean, safe, popular, owner speaks English; **D** *Casa Bowen*, restored colonial house (inside better than out), corner of Calle 66, No 521-B, x 65, rooms on the main street noisy, bath (E without), hot water, exchanges dollars, cheap laundry service, stores luggage, clean, pleasant, some rooms with kitchen (but no utensils), near ADO bus station; **D** *Latino*, Calle 66 y 63, T 213841, with fan and shower (water supply problems), friendly and clean; **D** *Mucuy*, Calle 57, No 481 x 56 y 58, T 211037, good, but 1st floor rooms very hot, with shower, use of fridge, washing facilities, efficient, nice gardens, highly rec (although owner can be irritable, his wife is nice), but long way from bus station; **D** *Oviedo*, Calle 62, next to *Sevilla*, near main Plaza, clean, luggage deposit, quieter rooms at the back; **D** *San Jorge*, across from ADO bus terminal, T 19054, clean, but take interior room as the street is noisy; **D** *Hospedaje San Juan*, 1 block N of arch by Iglesia San Juan, 3 blocks S of main bus station, clean rooms with fan and bath; **D** *San Luis*, Calle 61, No 534 x 68, T 17580, with fan and shower (and US$2.25 for noisy a/c), basic, friendly, patio pool, restaurant; **D** *María Teresa*, Calle 64 No 529 x 65 y 67, T 11039, friendly, safe, central, with bath and fan, a bit noisy, some rooms E, rec; **D** *Del Mayab*, Calle 50, No 536A entre 65 y 67, T 285174, with bath, reasonable, swimming pool and car park. **E** *Alamo*, T 18058, double rooms much better than singles, with bath, clean, next to bus station (noisy), on Calle 68, rec, storage; **E** *Casa de Huéspedes*, Calle 62, No 507 entre 63 y 65, shared Victorian showers and toilets, very poor water supply but drinking water available, run down, will keep luggage for small fee, mosquitoes, so take coils or net, pleasant and quiet except at front, laundry expensive; **E** *Centenario*, with bath, friendly, clean, safe on Calle 84, entre 59 y 59A, T 32532; **E** *Margarita*, Calle 66, No 506 x 63, T 13213, with shower, some rooms windowless and dirty, friendly; **E** *Rodríguez*, Calle 69, Calles 54 y 56, central, clean, safe; **E** *San José*, W of Plaza on Calle 63, bath, hot water, basic, not too clean but friendly, one of the cheapest, will store luggage. *Pantera Negra*, Calle 67 No 547B entre 68 y 70, T 240251, inc breakfast, beautiful old Mexican house, clean, very friendly English owner, rec (price not known, 1994).

Camping *Trailer Park Rainbow*, Km 8, on the road to Progreso, is preferable, US$5 for one or two, hot showers. *Oasis Campground*, 3 km from Mérida on Highway 180 to Cancún, F (011-52-99) 432160, with hook-ups, hot showers, laundry, US manager, US$11 for car and 2 people.

Restaurants *Soberanis*, Calle 60 No 503, entre 63 y 65, serving delicious fish dishes, seafood cocktails highly rec, but expensive, closed Mon. On main plaza: *Nicte Há*, good regional specialities; *Louvre* (NW corner), good, cheap, quick friendly service; *Lido* (Calles 62 y 61), good value meals and breakfast; *Pizza Bella*, good meeting spot, pizzas US$4-7. *La Choza*, Av Reforma y Calle 23 (near Plaza de Toros), bands play there daily except Mon, from 1300-2100. *Los Almendros*, Calle 50A, No 493 x 59, in high-vaulted, whitewashed thatched barn, for Yucatán specialities, expensive, mind the peppers, esp the green sauce, sometimes live music played, very good, and very popular! *Pórtico del Peregrino*, Calle 57, entre 60 y 62, dining indoors or in a leafy courtyard, good, moderate prices; next door is *Pop*, excellent snacks, popular with foreigners, very charming; *Patio de las Fajitas*, Calle 60 No 482 x 53, about 3 blocks from Zócalo, not cheap but pleasant open air setting; meat served on a hot griddle at the table; also in the same building is *La Casona*, Italian dishes, quite smart. The *Patio Español*, inside the *Gran Hotel*, well cooked and abundant food, local and Spanish specialities, moderate prices; *La Bella Epoca* in *Hotel Parque*, pricey but good with vegetarian selections and nice atmosphere on 1st floor; another excellent hotel restaurant for value and cooking is *El Rincón* in *Hotel Caribe*. *Fau-San*, Calle 64 next to *Hotel María Teresa*, good cheap meals and drinks, also free *botanos* (tapas), rec. *La Prosperidad*, Calle 53 and 56, good Yucateca food, live entertainment at lunchtime; *El Escorpión*, just off plaza on Calle

61, good cheap local food. *Tianos*, Calle 59 No 498, corner of Calle 60 (outdoor seating), friendly, with music, but beware overcharging; next door, on Parque Hidalgo, is *El Mesón*, pleasant with tables on the square. *El Faisán y El Venado*, Calle 59 No 617 entre 80 y 82, expensive, regional food, Mayan dance show, near zoo. *Pizzería Vita Corleone*, Calle 59 No 508, near Plaza, good; *Restaurant Vegetariano y Pizza Ananda Maya Gynza*, Calle 59 No 507, entre 60 y 62 with open courtyard and covered patio, good food, poor service, try *chaya* drink from the leaf of the *chaya* tree, their curry, and home-made bread, are also very good, open 1200-2200, closed on Sundays; *Mily's*, Calle 59 entre 64 y 66, good quality and quantity *comida corrida* for US$3.45; *La Pérgola*, warmly rec (both drive-in and tables), at corner Calles 56A and 43, good veal dishes; also in Colonia Alemán at Calle 24 No 289A. *Los Cardenales*, Calle 69 No 550-A x 68, close to bus station, good food at reasonable prices, but service a bit wanting, good value, open for breakfast, lunch and dinner. Cold sliced cooked venison (venado) is to be had in the Municipal Market.

For excellent coffee and breakfast, *Hotel Colonial*, Calle 62 No 476. *Café Restaurante Express*, on Calle 60, at Parque Hidalgo, good food (especially fruit salad), breakfast, traditional coffeehouse where locals meet; *Mil Tortas*, good cheap sandwiches, Calle 62 with 65 and 67; *Tortacos*, Calles 62 y 65, good, cheap Mexican food; many other *torta* places on Calle 62, but check them carefully for best value and quality. *El Jardín*, Calle 55 No 496, entre 60 y 58, open until 1600, a good range of vegetarian dishes, fruit juices, at reasonable prices, pleasant atmosphere, also makes wholemeal bread and pastries to take away; *Naturalmente*, Calle 20 No 104, corner of Calle 23, Colonia Chuburrá, not in centre, vegetarian, rec; banana bread and wholemeal rolls at *Pronat* health shop on Calle 59, No 506, corner of Calle 62. *Jugos California*, good, expensive fruit juices, Calle 60, in Calle 65, at the main bus station and many other branches all over city. *Bing*, Paseo Montejo (56A) y Calle 37, 13 blocks from centre, about 30 different flavours of good ice cream. Good *panadería* at Calles 65 y 60, banana bread, orange cake, US$0.15. Another good bakery at Calles 62 y 61.

Shopping The Mercado de Artesanías has many nice things, but prices are high and the salespeople pushy. Good postcards for sale, though.

The best hammocks are the so-called 3-ply, but they are difficult to find, up to about US$55 (cheaper than in Campeche for cotton). Never buy your first hammock from a street vendor and never bargain then accept a packaged hammock without checking the size and quality. The surest way to judge a good hammock is by weight: 1,500 grams (3.3 lbs) is a fine item, under 1 kg (2.2 lbs) is junk (advises Alan Handleman, a US expert). Also, the finer and thinner the strands of material, the more strands there will be, and the more comfortable the hammock. There are three sizes: single, matrimonial and family (buy a matrimonial at least for comfort). If judging by end-strings, 50 would be sufficient for a child, 150 would suit a medium-sized adult, 250 a couple. There are four frequently recommended shops (there is little agreement about their respective merits, best to compare them all and let them know you are comparing): *El Hamaquero*, Calle 58 No 572 entre 69 y 71, popular, but beware the very hard sell; *El Campesino*, moved to the market (from Calle 58 No 543), Eustaquio Canul Cahum and family, will let you watch the weaving; *El Mayab*, friendly, limited choice but good deals available; and *El Poblano*, Calle 65, will bargain, especially for sales of more than one, huge stock; also *Jorge Razu*, Calle 56 No 516B, entre 63A y 63, rec, very convincing salesman, changes TCs at good rates; *Aguacate*, Calle 58 No 604, corner of Calle 73, good hammocks, not cheap; *Rada*, Calle 60 No 527, entre 65 y 67, T 241218, F 234718, good. All shops will mail abroad, but this is very expensive. In the market prices are cheaper but quality is lower and sizes smaller. There are licensed vendors on the streets and in the main plaza; they will bargain and may show you how hammocks are made; some are very persistent.

Good silver shops and several antique shops on Calle 60 between Calle 51 and 53; *Bacho Arte Mexicano*, Calle 60 No 466, between Calle 53 and 55, also sells other jewelry and ornaments. Good panama hats at *El Becaliño*, Calle 65 No 483, esq 56A, diagonally opp Post Office. **Guayaberas**: *Paty*, Calle 64 No 549, between Calle 67 and 69, stocks reputable 'Kary' brand, also sells hammocks. Calle 62, between Calle 57 and 61, is lined with *guayabera* shops, all of a similar price and quality. Embroidered *huipil* blouses cost about US$25. Clothes shopping is good along Calle 65 and in the García Rejón Bazaar, Calle 65 y Calle 60. Good leather sandals with soles made from old car tyres, robust and comfortable, from the market, US$10. Excellent cowboy boots for men and women, maximum size 10, can be bought around the market for US$46. *Casa de las Artesanías*, Calle 63 between 64 and 66, good. There is a big supermarket, *Blanco*, on Calle 67 and 52, well stocked. **Bookshop** *Librerías Dante*, Calle 59, No 498 entre 58 y 60.

Try Xtabentun, the liqueur made from sweet anise and honey since ancient Mayan times.

Cameras and Film Repairs on Calle 53/62. Mericolor, Calle 67 y 58, rec for service and printing. Many processors around crossing of Calles 59 and 60. Prices are high by international standards.

Taxis We are warned that taxi drivers are particularly prone to overcharge by taking a long route, so always establish the journey and fare in advance. There are a dozen taxi stands in the city, eg beside the Cathedral (T 212136), at Calle 57A y 60 (T 212133), at Calle 59 y 60 (T 212500), and at the airport (T 230391). Stands display fixed charges. Taxi from centre to bus terminal, US$3.80. Taxis are hard to find on Sun pm.

Car Hire Car reservations should be booked well in advance wherever possible; there is a tendency to hand out cars which are in poor condition once the main stock has gone, so check locks, etc, on cheaper models before you leave town. **Avis**, Calle 57 No 507A x 62, T 236191; **Hertz**, Calle 55, No 479, x 54, T 242834; **Budget**, Prol Paseo Montejo 49, T 272708; **Panam**, *Hotel Montejo Palace*, T 234097, or Calle 56A No 483 x 43, T 231392; **Ximbal**, C 44, No 500, Col Jesús Carranza (owner Roger de Jesús García Pech), English spoken, VW Beetles in good condition, accepts Amex; **Easy Way** (Turismo Planeta), Calle 59, No 501 x 60, T 281560, collect rates from other agencies, they will offer a lower price, new cars. Most car hire agencies have an office at the airport and, as all share the same counter, negotiating usually takes place. Many agencies also on Calle 60 (eg **Executive**, down from *Gran Hotel*, good value). Some agencies allow vehicles to be returned to Cancún at an extra charge (US$53).

Motorcycles *Merimotos*: Honda, on Calle 47 y 90, and Kawasaki on Calle 74 y 59.

Car Service Servicillos de Mérida Goodyear, very helpful and competent, owner speaks English, serves good coffee while you wait for your vehicle.

Nightlife Most bars close at 2300 (they open at 1000), but a few expensive discos remain open until 0300. 7 good cinemas regularly show films in English, US$2. 2 recommended spots: *El Tuche*, Calle 60 No 482 x 55 y 57, just N of Plaza, cabaret with live music and dance, salsa, local bands, good food at reasonable prices, very popular with locals; *Trovador Bohemia*, Parque Santa Lucía, guitar trios (*trova*) nightly at 2100, entrance US$3.

Exchange Banamex (passport necessary) on Plaza (Mon-Fri 0900-1300, 1600-1700, very crowded and slow service), and at Calles 56 y 59. **Banco Atlántico**, Calle 61 y 62, quick, good rates. Many banks on Calle 65, off the Plaza. Most banks on Calle 64 have ATM cash machines, open 24 hrs, giving cash on Visa or Mastercard with PIN-code. Cash advance on credit cards possible only between 1000 and 1300. **Centro Cambiario**, Calle 61 entre Calles 54 y 52; *casa de cambio* in Casa Montejo has slightly better rates than banks, busy in am, quiet in pm. *Casa de Cambio*, Calle 56 No 491 entre 57 y 59, open 0900-1700 Mon-Sun, but bank's rates better.

Cultural Institute Alliance Française, Calle 56 No 476, between Calle 55 and 57, has a busy programme of events, films (Thur 1900), a library and a cafeteria open all day.

Consulates British Vice Consul, also **Belize**, Major A Dutton (retd), MBE, Calle 58-53 No 450, T (010-5299) 286152, 0900-1600. Postal address Apdo 89. **US**, Paseo Montejo 453 y Av Colón (T 255011). **Canada**, Av Colón, No 309-D-19 x 62, T 256419. **Cuba**, Calle 60, No 285, at 23 y 25, T 256419.

Immigration Office Calle 60, No 448, Dpto 234, 1st floor, T 214824/211714, Pasaje Camino Real, extension of stay easy and quick, open 0830-1430. Also helpful in the case of lost tourist cards.

Hospital IDEM, Calle 66 entre 67 y 65, open 24 hrs, specialises in dermatology. **English-Speaking Doctor** Dr A H Puga Navarrete (also speaks French), Calle 13 No 210, between Calles 26 and 28, Colonia García Gineres, T 250709, open 1600-2000.

Laundry Calle 59 between Calles 72 and 74, at least 24 hrs. *Lavandería* Calle 69, No 541, 2 blocks from bus station, about US$3 a load. *La Fe*, Calle 61 No 518, near Calle 64, US$3.30 for 3 kg, highly rec. Self-service hard to find.

Post Office Calle 65 y 56, will accept parcels for surface mail to USA only, but don't seal parcels destined overseas: they have to be inspected. For surface mail to Europe try Belize, or mail package to USA, *poste restante*, for collection later if you are heading that way. Also branches at airport (for quick delivery) or on Calle 58, instead. Telegrams and faxes from Calle 56, between 65 and 65A (same building as Post Office, entrance at the back), open 0700-1900, Sat 0900-1300. DHL on Av Colón offers good service, prices comparable to Post Office prices for air mail packages over 1 kg (eg US$16.50/1 kg to US$50/5 kg).

International Calls Possible from central bus station, airport, the shop on the corner of Calles 59 and 64, or public telephones, but not from the main telephone exchange. Many phone card and credit card phone booths on squares along Calle 60, but many are out of order. Collect calls can be made on Sat or Sun from the *caseta* opp central bus station, but beware overcharging (max US$2).

Tourist Office Corner of Calles 57 and 60. Also tourist office at the airport, which has maps, and at the bus station. Instituto Nacional de Estadística, Geografía e Informática, Paseo Montejo 442, Ed Oasis, for maps and information.

Travel Agents *Wagon-Lits (Cooks)*, helpful, Av Colón 501 (Plaza Colón), T 55411; *Yucatán Trails*, Calle 62, No 482, is very helpful, run by Canadian, Denis Lafoy; *Yucamex Travel Service*, Calle 65 No 498 x 58 y 60, T 244252, rec; *Viajes T'Ho*, lobby of *Hotel Reforma*, Calle 59, No 508 y 62, T 236612/247922, for tours in private cars, also for flights to Havana and to Palenque; *Ecoturismo Yucatán*, Calle 3 No 235, entre 32-A y 34, Col Pensiones, T 252187, F 259047, Alfonso Escobedo.

Trains Fees for red-capped porters posted at the station (Calles 48 and 55). From Mexico City at 2115, via Córdoba. Tickets have been refused to lone travellers on the ground that it is not safe. To **Mexico City**, leaves Mérida at 1815 (37 hrs but often more like 45 to 72); book ticket on day of departure at station, but queue long before departure. 2nd class (US$17 to Córdoba) not rec, dirty, live animals. No clean running water, lavatory dirty. Beggars get on at every stop; thieving. No food except for vendors at stations, stock up. Many stops up to Coatzacoalcos. Possible to break journey at Palenque but not on one ticket. Mérida-**Palenque**, US$6.65 (on same train as to Mexico City), takes 12 hrs, 1st class also dirty and crowded, travelling time unpredictable, no *dormitorio* now available. Track recently improved, train rocks rather than jerks as it did, speed about 50 km an hour. Air conditioning improves as you leave the station, but not spectacularly. Fruit near station, bread and cheese a couple of streets away from station, better bought before leaving centre.

To **Progreso** (service reintroduced in March 1992), Mon-Fri 0605 (via Xcanatún) and 1500 (non-stop), returning 0730 (non-stop) and 1620 (via Xcanatún); Sat 0605 (via Xcanatún) 1015 and 1330 (non-stop), returning 0730 (non-stop), 1140 (via Xcanatún), and 1630 (non-stop), approx 1-1½ hrs; Sun 0700 and 1000 returning at 0815 and 1630 (Sunday service more unreliable, check in advance). To **Tizimín** at 0600, about 6 hrs, arrives back in Mérida at 1750, US$1.60 one way. There are two picturesque railway lines SE of Mérida—one to **Sotuta** and the other to **Peto** (dep 1425) via Ticul and Oxcutzcab.

Buses Almost all buses except those to Progreso, or Tizimín etc (see below) leave from terminal on Calle 69 between Calles 68 and 70. The station has lockers; it is open 21 hrs a day. About 20 mins walk to centre, taxis are expensive (US$4). Most companies have computer booking. To **Mexico City**, US$55, 24-28 hrs, about 6 rest stops (eg ADO, 6 a day); direct Pullman bus Mexico City 2200. 14 hrs to **Coatzacoalcos**, US$29. Bus to **Veracruz**, 1730, 2130, US$38.50, 16 hrs; to **Chetumal**, see **Road to Belize** below. To **Ciudad del Carmen** 8 a day, 1st class, ADO, US$14.80, 9 hrs. Seven buses to **Tulum**, mostly via Chichén Itzá, Valladolid, Cancún and Playa del Carmen, some via Cobá junction, first at 0630, last at 2300, 8 hrs, US$12, drops you off about 1 km from the ruins. For buses to Uxmal and Chichén Itzá see under those places. Regular 2nd class buses to **Campeche** (US$5, 4½ hrs) also pass Uxmal, 6 a day between 0630 and 1900; 1st class fare (not via Uxmal) US$6.25. Buses to **Puerto Juárez** and **Cancún** (Autobuses de Oriente), every hr 0600 to 2200, US$14 1st class, US$20 *plus*, 4½ hrs. Buses to and from Cancún stop at Calle 50, between Calles 65 and 67. If going to Isla Mujeres, make sure the driver knows you want Puerto Juárez, the bus does not always go there, especially at night. Buses to **Progreso** (US$1.65) with Auto Progreso, leave from the bus station on Calle 62, between Calle 65 and 67 every 15 mins from 0500-2100. To **Valladolid**, US$5.30 2nd class, US$6, 1st express (5 a day). Many buses daily to **Villahermosa**, US$22, 1st class in pm only, but better than 2nd class, 11 hrs, US$19.50; one direct bus daily at 1330 via Villahermosa and Campeche to **Tuxtla Gutiérrez**, arrives 0630 next day, US$35 with Autotransportes del Surente de Yucatán.

Buses to **Palenque** (US$20) and 2330 (US$15.50) from ADO terminal, 8-9 hrs, alternatively take Villahermosa bus to Playas de Catazajá, US$16.50, 8½ hrs, then minibus to Palenque US$1.15, ½ hr, or go to Emiliano Zapata, 3 buses a day US$16, and local bus (**see p 293**). To **San Cristóbal de las Casas**, at 1800, US$27.50 (arr 0800-0900), and one other at 0700 (Autotransportes del Sureste de Yucatán).

Buses to Celestún and Sisal from corner of Calle 50 entre 65 y 67. To **Tizimín**, **Cenotillo** and **Izamal** buses leave from Calle 50 entre Calles 65 y 67.

Route 261, Mérida-Escárcega, paved and in very good condition.

There is a toll road from Kantunil, 68 km E of Mérida, to Xcan, whereafter it is a divided free way to Cancún; the toll is US$20, which has to be paid in full however little of the road you use. The only exits from the toll road are at Chichén-Itzá and Valladolid.

To Guatemala by public transport from Yucatán, take a bus from Mérida to San Cristóbal and change there for Comitán. A more expensive alternative would be to take the bus from Mérida direct to Tuxtla Gutiérrez (times given above), then direct either Tuxtla-Ciudad Cuauhtémoc or to Tapachula.

Road to Belize: paved all the way to Chetumal. Bus Mérida-Chetumal US$16.50, 1st class, 16 a day, takes 7 hrs (Autotransportes del Caribe, Autotransporte Peninsular), US$13 2nd class. Bus station on corner of Calle 68 and 69.

By Air Mexicana office at Calle 58 No 500 x 61 T 246633, and Paseo Montejo 493, T 247421 (airport T 461332). AeroMéxico, Paseo Montejo 460, T 279000, airport T 461400. From Calle 67 and 60 bus 79 goes to the airport, marked Aviación, US$0.20. Taxi US$8, voucher available from airport, you don't pay driver direct; colectivo US$2.50. The airport has no announcements or departures board; one departure lounge for all and flights are called 'discreetly in Spanish". There is a tourist office with a hotel list.

Mexicana and AeroMéxico both have about 12 flights between them to Mexico City daily, 1¾ hrs, both also fly Miami-Mérida daily (about 2 hrs). Aviacsa daily to Mexico City, Ciudad Juárez, Monterrey, Cancún, Villahermosa, Tuxtla Gutiérrez and Oaxaca, T 269173/263253. Aero Caribe (Paseo Montejo 500-B, T 286790, airport 461361) flies daily to Oaxaca (4 hrs 20 mins) daily to Cancún, 45 mins; Cozumel, 1 hr; Tuxtla Gutiérrez, 2 hrs; Villahermosa, 80 mins; Minatitlán and Veracruz. Aviateca flies 4 days a week to Guatemala City. Mexicana to Cuba, Wed and Sun; package tours Mérida-Havana-Mérida are available (but book through an agency or Mexicana in Mexico City, not Mexicana in Mérida). See **To Cuba** in **Information for Visitors** (page 380) for details. A description of Cuba will be found elsewhere in this volume. For return to Mexico ask for details at Secretaría de Migración, Calle 60, No 285. The smaller airlines tend to offer cheaper flights, on older aircraft. Food and drinks at the airport are very expensive.

Excursions: **West of Mérida** (29 km) is *Hunucmá* , an oasis in the dry Yucatán, about ½ hr from the Central Camionera bus station, US$0.50. The road divides here, one branch continuing 63 km W to Celestún, the other running 24 km NW to the coast at *Sisal*, a languid, faded resort which served as Mérida's port from its earliest days until replaced by Progreso last century; the old Customs House still retains some colonial flavour, snapper and bass fishing from the small wharf is rewarding; the windy beach is acceptable but not in the same league as Celestún's. Sisal's impressive lighthouse, painted in traditional red-and-white, is a private residence and permission must be sought to visit the tower, the expansive view is worth the corkscrew climb. Frequent buses (0500-1700) from Mérida, Calle 50 between Calles 65 and 67, 2 hrs, US$1.50. **Hotels**: *Sisal del Mar Hotel Resort*, luxury accommodation, T in USA 800-451-0891 or 305-341-9173. More modest are **E** *Club Felicidades*, a 5-min walk E of the pier, bathrooms not too clean; **E** *Club de Patos*, similar but a slight improvement.

Celestún, a small, dusty fishing resort much frequented in summer by Mexicans, stands on the spit of land separating the Río Esperanza estuary from the ocean. The long palm-lined beach is relatively clean except near the town proper (litter, the morning's fishing rejects, insects, weeds that stick to feet, etc), with clear water ideal for swimming, although rising afternoon winds usually churn up silt; along the beach are many fishing boats bristling with *jimbas* (cane poles), used for catching local octopus. A plain zócalo watched over by a simple stucco church is the centre for what little happens in town. Cafés (some with hammock space for rent) spill onto the sand, from which parents watch offspring splash in the surf. Even the unmarked post office operating Mon-Fri, 0900-1300, is a private residence the rest of the week. There is a *Banco del Atlántico* branch for exchange (Mon-Fri 0800-1200) but easier in Mérida.

The immediate region is a National Park, created to protect the thousands of migratory waterfowl (especially flamingoes and pelicans) who inhabit the lagoons; fish, crabs and shrimp also spawn here, and manatees, toucans and crocodiles may sometimes be glimpsed in the quieter waterways. Boat trips to view the wildlife can be arranged with owners at the river bridge 1 km back along the Mérida road (US$30 for one large enough for 6-8, 1½ hrs, bargaining possible), ensure that the boatman will cut his motor frequently so as not to scare the birds; morning is the best viewing time, important to wear a hat and use sun-screen. Hourly buses to Mérida 0530-2030, 1 hr, US$3.

Hotels D *Gutiérrez*, Calle 12 (the *malecón*) No 22, large beds, fans, views, clean; **D** *María* *del Carmen*, new, spacious and clean, rec; **E** *San Julio*, Calle 12 No 92, also large bright rooms and clean bathrooms. **Eating:** Many beachside restaurants along Calle 12, but be careful of food in the cheaper ones; rec is *La Playita*, for fried fish, seafood cocktails; bigger menu and more expensive is *Restaurant Chemas*, for shrimp, oysters and octopus; *Restaurant Avila* also safe for fried fish; food stalls along Calle 11 beside the bus station should be approached with caution.

Halfway to Progreso turn right for the Maya ruins of *Dzibilchaltún*, open 0800-1700 (entry US$3). This unique city, according to carbon dating, was founded as early as 1000 BC. The most important building is the Templo de las Siete Muñecas (Seven Dolls—partly restored and on display in the museum); museum at entrance, where you can buy drinks and 1 km beyond is the ticket office. The Cenote Xlaca contains very clear water and is 44m deep (you can swim in it); ruined church nearby; very interesting nature trail starting half way between temple and cenote; rejoins the sacbé ("white road") half way along. VW combis leave from Parque San Juan, corner of Calle 62 and 67A, every one or two hours between 0500 and 1900, stopping at the ruins en route to Chablekal, a small village further along the same road. There are also 5 direct buses a day, from Parque San Juan, marked 'Tour/Ruta Polígono"; bus returns from site entrance on the hour, passing the junction 15 mins later, taking 45 mins from junction to Mérida (US$0.60).

Progreso, the port 39 km away, is reached by road (45 mins) or railway (1-1½ hrs). Population 14,000; temperatures range from 27° to 35°C. Main export: *henequén*. It claims to have the longest stone-bridge pier in the world (it is being extended to 6 km). The beach is usually dirty and plenty of new hotels and houses have been built. Most of the palm trees along the front are dying from a virus (*amarrillamiento letal*). It is very popular with Mexican tourists at weekends and holiday times (July-August), but is quiet otherwise.

Hotels On beach: **C** *Progreso*, clean, friendly, traffic noise; **C** *Tropical Suites* (more with kitchen), clean, rec; **D** *San Miguel*, Calle 78 No 148, hot shower, fan, clean, traffic noise; *Playa Linda* and *Real del Mar*, both by beach, similar prices, quiet; **E** *Hostal*, clean, big rooms. Good **restaurants** are *Capitán Marisco*, and *Charlie's* expensive but good; *Soberanis*, for seafood tacos; *El Cordobés*, rec, good service; *La Terraza*, variable results, expensive; *Pelícanos*, corner of Calle 21 and 20 on sea front, good and friendly, rec. Many good restaurants along the beach. Police permit free beach camping; huts for hammocks. Many homes, owned by Mexico City residents, available for rent, services included. Good local market with lowest food prices in Yucatán, esp seafood. You can buy fresh shrimps cheaply in the mornings on the beach. Bus, Progreso-Mérida US$1.15 every 15 mins. The bus and train stations are close together, 3 blocks inland, 5 mins walk E of the pier. The beach front by the pier is devoted to cafés with seafood cocktails as their speciality. They also have little groups performing every weekend afternoon in summer; and the noise can be both spirited and deafening. 2 cinemas.

Boats can be hired to visit the reef of Los Alacranes where many ancient wrecks are visible in clear water.

A short bus journey (4 km) W from Progreso are **Puerto Yucalpetén** and **Chelem**, a dusty resort. Balneario Yucalpetén has a beach with lovely shells, but also a large naval base. A *Fiesta Inn* on the beach and *Mayaland Club* (Mayaland Resorts, T in USA 800-4510-8891/305-341-9173), villa complex. Yacht marina, changing cabins, beach with gardens and swimming pool. Between the Balneario and Chelem there is a nice hotel with some small bungalows, *Hotel Villanueva* (2 km from village, hot rooms), and also *Costa Maya*, on Calle 29 y Carretera Costera, with restaurant. In Chelem itself is a new hotel, **B** *Las Garzas*, Calle 17 No 742, T 244735, a/c, cable TV, bar, good restaurant, private beach club, pool, pleasant. Fish restaurants in Chelem, *Las Palmas* and *El Cocalito*, reasonable, also other small restaurants. 5 km E of Progreso is another resort, *Chicxulub*; it has a narrow beach, on which are many boats and much seaweed. The beaches on this coast are often deserted and, between December and February, 'El Norte' wind blows in every 10 days or so, making the water turbid and bringing in cold, rainy weather.

Uxmal (pronounced Ooshmál) is 74 km from Mérida, 177 km from Campeche, by a good paved road. If going by car, there is a new circular road round Mérida: follow the signs to Campeche, then Campeche via *ruinas*, then to Muná via Yaxcopoil (long stretch of road with no signposting). Muná-Yaxcopoil about 34 km. The Uxmal ruins are quite unlike those of Chichén Itzá (see below), and cover comparatively little ground. Uxmal, the home of the Xiu tribe, was built during the Classic Period (AD600-900). Its finest buildings seem to have been built much later. See El Adivino (the Sorcerer, a 3m high pyramid, topped by two temples with a splendid view); the Casa de las Monjas (House of Nuns), a quadrangle with 88 rooms much adorned on their façades; the Casa del Gobernador (House of the Governor), on three terraces, with well preserved fine sculptures; the Casa de las Tortugas (Turtle House) with seven rooms; the Casa de las Palomas (House of Doves), probably the oldest; and the so called 'Cemetery Group".

Ruins open at 0800, close at 1700, entrance US$6.50 weekdays, free on Sundays. A new visitors' centre at the entrance to the ruins houses a museum, souvenir shops and an expensive restaurant (no refreshments sold in the ruins); also a good selection of guide books here. A free film is shown in English at 1000 and 1200. Guided tours cost US$20. Luggage can be left at the visitors' centre. There is a car park, US$1.50. There are caves which go in for about 100m near the main entrance (rather dull). Many iguanas (harmless) wandering about, watch out for occasional scorpions and snakes, and beware of biting insects in the long grass. There is a *son et lumière* display at the ruins nightly—English version (US$2.50) at 2100, Spanish version (US$2) 1900 (check for times), highly rec (special bus for Spanish version only leaves at 1730 from terminal at Calle 69, between 68 and 70, returning 2100, US$4.10 return). 2nd class bus from Mérida to Campeche ("Via Ruinas") passes Uxmal, can buy tickets on bus, 2 hr journey, 4 hrs just enough to see ruins. From Mérida at least six 2nd-class buses a day from 0600, US$2.50, 1st class bus (Autotransportes del Sur) at 0800, returns 1430 (can be overcrowded). Advance seat booking is strongly recommended. ATS buses stop outside main entrance to site to drop off and pick up passengers, including those going on to Campeche. After the Spanish show it may be possible for those without tour bus tickets to get a ride to Muná from where the last bus to Mérida leaves at 2200. (There may be spare seats in VW colectivos for those without return tickets, US$4) There is, however, a bus to Campeche at 2315 (can be crowded). Good service with Yucatán Trails (**see p 311**). For best photographs early morning or late afternoon arrival is essential.

Hotels A-B *Hacienda Uxmal*, T 247142, 300-400m from ruins, is good, efficient and relaxing, (3 restaurants open 0800-2200), a/c, gardens, swimming pool (the pottery that decorates the rooms is made by Miguel Zum, Calle 32, Ticul). **A+** *Misión Park Uxmal*, T and F 247308, Km 78, 1-2 km from ruins on Mérida road, rooms a bit dark. Club Méditerranée **A+** *Villa Arqueológica*, T 47030, beautiful, close to ruins, good, swimming pool. For cheap accommodation, go to Ticul, 28 km away (see below). New restaurant at ruins, good but expensive; restaurant of **D** *Hacienda Uxmal*, about 4 km N of ruins, reasonable food but not cheap. **NB** There is no village at Uxmal, just the hotels.

No camping allowed, but there is a campsite, *Sacbe*, at Santa Elena, about 15 km S, between Uxmal and Kabah, on Route 261, Km 127 at S exit of village (2nd class buses Mérida-Campeche pass by, ask to be let out at the Campo de Baseball), 9 electric hook-ups (US$7-10 for motor home according to size), big area for tents (US$2.65 pp with tent), palapas for hammocks (US$2.65 pp), cars pay US$1, showers, toilets, clothes washing facilities also 3 bungalows with ceiling fan (D), breakfast and dinner available (US$2.65 each), French and Mexican owners, a beautifully landscaped park, fastidiously clean, and impeccably managed, highly rec. *Restaurante Rancho Uxmal*, 3 km N of Uxmal, T 20277, has rooms with hot and cold water, fan, also camping for US$5 and a pool, also good local food.

On the road from Uxmal to Mérida is **Muná** (15 km from Uxmal, 62 from Mérida);

delightful square and old church, no hotel, but ask in *Restaurant Katty*, just on plaza, whose owner has 2 rooms with 2 double beds at his home, E, clean, friendly, hot showers, rec (restaurant has good, cheap *enchiladas en mole*). Also ask in shops by bus stop in town centre for accommodation in private homes. There is a new direct road (Highway 293) from Muná to Bacalar, Quintana Róo, just N of Chetumal.

On either side of the main road, 37 km S of Uxmal and often included in tours of the latter, are the ruins of **Kabah**; on one side there is a fascinating Palace of Masks (or Codz-Poop), whose façade bears the image of Chac, mesmerically repeated over and over again about two hundred and fifty times, each mask made up of thirty units of mosaic stone: even the central chamber is entered via a huge Chac mask whose curling snout forms the doorstep. On the other side of this wall, beneath the figure of the ruler, Kabal, are impressive carvings on the door arches which depict a man about to be killed, pleading for mercy, and of two men duelling. This side of the road is mostly reconstructed; across the road the outstanding feature is a reconstructed arch marking the start of the sacbe (sacred road), which leads all the way to Uxmal, and several stabilized, but unclimbable mounds of collapsed buildings. The style is classic Puuc. Watch out for snakes and spiders. Admission, US$4.35, free on Sunday.

Further S of Uxmal, about half-way between Mérida and Campeche, a paved road branches off to the left to the *Sayil* ruins (5 km), *Xlapak* (about 11 km) and *Labná* (about 14 km). Both Sayil and Labná are in low, shrubby bush country. Sayil has several fine structures scattered over a wide area, including the massive Gran Palacio with a colonnaded façade; walks of several hundred metres are involved, but do not stray from the marked paths as many mapping trails merely lead off into the forest (admission, US$4.35). Xlapak has one, well-reconstructed palace and two partially reconstructed buildings (entry US$1.65). Labná has an astonishing arch, two palace structures and a pyramid all within a 200-metre radius, quiet, lovely setting among trees (admission US$4.35). These sites can each be explored in 1-2 hrs (all are free on Sunday). Refreshments and water are available, at the sites. From Labná, continue to immense galleries and caves of **Bolonchen** which are now illuminated (bus from Mérida).

Autotransportes del Sur run a 'Tour Puuc' bus at 0800 from the main bus terminal in Mérida, which passes Uxmal at 0930 before leaving passengers for ½ hr each at Labná, Sayil and Kabah, returning to Uxmal at 1330 for 1½ hrs; back to Mérida at 1400; cost is US$10. The only disadvantage is that you get to Uxmal in the midday heat when the crowds are there. If visiting Sayil, Xlapak and Labná only, you can take a taxi from the village of Santa Elena at the turn-off (see camping *Sacbe*, above), costing US$22 for 1-3 persons. By hire-car one can continue to Oxcutzcab (see below).

The road from Mérida (and also from Uxmal) to Chetumal is through Muná, *Ticul* (where pottery, hats and shoes are made; quite a good base for visiting Uxmal and Loltún; **Hotels: C** *Motel Bougambileas*, Calle 23, clean but overpriced; **D-E** *Sierra Sosa*, shower, fan, cheapest rooms dungeon-like but clean, helpful, friendly; **E** *San Miguel*, Calle 28 nr Plaza, fan, quiet, good value, parking, rec; next door is a good little *pizzería*; next door again is *Los Almendros* restaurant, opp Cinema Ideal; post office chaotic), **Peto** (best avoided, via Tzucacab-Santa Rosa bypass, no restaurant) and Felipe Carrillo Puerto. Between Ticul and Peto is **Oxcutzcab**, a good centre for catching buses to Chetumal, Muná, Mayapán and Mérida (US$2.20). It is a friendly place with a large market on the side of the Plaza and a church with a 'two-dimensional' façade on the other side of the square. Accommodation: **D** *Tucanes*, with a/c, E with fan, by Pemex station; **E** *Casa de Huéspedes*, near bus terminal, large rooms with bath, TV, fan, friendly, rec; *Bermejo*, Calle 51, No 143; **E** *Trujeque*, just S of main plaza, a/c, TV, clean, good value, discount for stays over a week. Hammocks provided in some private houses, usually full, fluent Spanish needed to find them. (No money exchange facilities;

go to Banco Atlántico in Tekax, 25 minutes away by bus). Nearby, to the S, are the caverns and precolumbian vestiges at **Loltún** (supposedly extending for 8 km). Caves are open Tues-Sun, admission at 0930, 1100, 1230 and 1400 (US$5.50 with obligatory guide, 1 hr 20 mins). Caretaker may admit tours on Mon, but no lighting. Take pickup (US$0.30) or truck from the market going to Cooperativa (an agricultural town). For return, flag down a passing truck. Alternatively, take a taxi, US$10 (can be visited from Labná on a tour from Mérida). The area around Ticul and Oxcutzcab is intensively farmed with citrus fruits, papayas and mangos. Between Oxcutzcab and Peto is **Tekax** with restaurant *La Ermita* serving excellent Yucateca dishes at reasonable prices. From Tekax a paved road leads to the ruins of **Chacmultun**. From the top one enjoys a beautiful view; there is a caretaker. All the towns between Muná and Peto have large old churches. Beyond Peto the scenery is scrub and swamp as far as the Belizean frontier.

Mayapán is a large, peaceful late Maya site easily visited by bus from Mérida (every 30 mins from terminal at Calles 50 y 67 behind the municipal market, 1 hr, US$1 to Telchquillo). It can be reached from Oxcutzcab. Beware of snakes at site (entrance US$4.35); also two large pyramids in village of **Acanceh** en route. Before Acanceh, on the road to Mayapán, is a restaurant at **Kanasin**, *La Susana*, to which there are frequent buses. It is known especially for local delicacies like *sopa de lima*, *salbutes* and *panuchos*. Clean, excellent service and abundant helpings at reasonable prices. Between Acanceh and Mayapán is Tecóh, with the caverns of **Dzab-Náh**; you must take a guide as there are treacherous drops into *cenotes*.

Chichén Itzá is 120 km by a paved road running SE from Mérida. The scrub forest has been cleared from over 5 square km of ruins. The city was built by the Maya in late Classic times (AD 600-900). By the end of the 10th century, the city was more-or-less abandoned. It was reestablished in the 11th-12th centuries, but much debate surrounds by whom. Whoever the people were, they were heavily influenced by the Toltecs of Central Mexico. The major buildings in the N half display this Toltec influence. Dominating them is El Castillo, its top decorated by the symbol of Quetzalcoatl, and the balustrade of the 91 stairs up each of the four sides is decorated at its base by the head of a plumed, open-mouthed serpent. There is also an interior ascent of 61 steep and narrow steps to a chamber lit by electricity where the red-painted jaguar which probably served as the throne of the high priest burns bright, its eyes of jade, its fangs of flint (see below for entry times). There is a ball court with grandstand and towering walls each set with a projecting ring of stone high up; at eye-level is a relief showing the decapitation of the winning captain (sacrifice was an honour—some theories, however, maintain that the losing captain was killed). El Castillo stands at the centre of the northern half of the site, and almost at right-angles to its northern face runs the sacred way to the Cenote Sagrado, the Well of Sacrifice. Into the Cenote Sagrado were thrown valuable propitiatory objects of all kinds, animals and human sacrifices. The well was first dredged by Edward H Thompson, the US Consul in Mérida, between 1904 and 1907; he accumulated a vast quantity of objects in pottery, jade, copper and gold. In 1962 the well was explored again by an expedition sponsored by the National Geographic Society and some 4,000 further artefacts were recovered, including beads, polished jade, lumps of copal resin, small bells, a statuette of rubber latex, another of wood, and a quantity of animal and human bones. Another *cenote*, the Xtoloc Well, was probably used as a water supply.

Old Chichén, where the Maya buildings of the earlier city are found, lies about ½ km by path from the main clearing. The famous El Caracol, or observatory is included in this group as is the Casa de las Monjas, or Nunnery. A footpath to the right of Las Monjas takes one to the Templo de los Tres Dinteles (the Three Lintels) after ½ hr walking. It requires at least one day to see the many pyramids, temples, ballcourts and palaces, all of them adorned with astonishing sculptures, and excavation and renovation is still going on. Interesting birdlife can be seen around the ruins.

Entry to Chichén Itzá, 0800-1700, US$6.50 (free Sun and holidays, when it is incredibly crowded); check at entrance for opening times of the various buildings. Best to arrive before 1030 when the mass of tourists arrives. Son et lumière (US$1.85 in English, US$1.35 in Spanish) at Chichén every evening, in Spanish at 1900, and then in English at 2100; nothing like as good as at Uxmal. A tourist centre has been built at the entrance to the ruins with a restaurant, free cinema (short film in English at 1200 and 1600), a small museum, books (good selection) and souvenirs shops (if buying slides, check the quality), with exchange facilities at the latter; luggage deposit free, open 0800-1700. Car park US$1.50. Entry to see the jaguar in the substructure of El Castillo along an inside staircase at 1100-1300, 1600-1700. Try to be among the first in as it is stuffy inside and queues form at busy times. Drinks and snacks available at entrance, also guidebooks, clean toilets. Also toilets on the way to old Chichén, and a drinks terrace with film supplies. The site is hot, take a hat, sun cream, sun glasses, shoes with good grip and drinking water. The Easy Guide by Richard Bloomgarden is interesting though brief, available in several languages; Panorama is the best. José Díaz Bolio's book, although in black and white (and therefore cheaper) is good. Guides charge US$4-6 pp for a 1½-hr tour (they are persistent and go too fast).

There are tours daily to the **Balankanché** caves, 3 km E, just off the highway (caretaker turns lights on and off, answers questions in Spanish—every hour on the hour, 0900-1600, US$5.30, US$2 on Sun); minimum 6, maximum 20 persons. Worth the trip: there are archaeological objects, including offerings of pots and metates in a unique setting, except for the unavoidable, 'awful' son et lumière show (5 a day in Spanish; 1100, 1300 and 1500 in English; 1000 in French; it is very damp and hot, so dress accordingly). Open 0900-1700, US$3.45, free Sun (allow about ¾ hr for the 300-metre descent), closed Sat and Sun afternoons. Bus Chichén Itzá or Pisté— Balankanché hourly at a quarter past, US$0.50, taxi US$15.

Hotels All are expensive for what they offer. The three hotels closest to the ruins are **A+** Hacienda Chichén, once owned by Edward Thompson with charming bungalows; **A+** Villas Arqueológicas, T (985) 6-28-30, Apdo Postal 495, Mérida, 1st class, pool, tennis and good restaurant. Both are on the other side of the fenced-off ruins from the bus stop; rather than walk through ruins take taxi (US$1-1.50); **A+** Mayaland Hotel, incl breakfast and dinner, pool, but sometimes no water in it, no a/c, just noisy ceiling fans, but good service and friendly (T in USA 800-451-8891/305-341-9173). Others are further away: **B** Sunset Club, 10 mins walk from Pisté village, 30 mins from Chichén Itzá, takes credit cards, room with bath, hot water, fan, TV, swimming pool, rec; nearby is **B** Pirámide Inn, 1½ km from ruins, at the Chichén end of Pisté, with food (slow service), swimming pool, Trailer Park and camping US$6.50 for 2 plus car in front of hotel, US$10 in campground (different ownership from hotel, but still check in at hotel reception, dirty bathrooms, cold showers, rundown). **A** Lapalapa Chichén, with breakfast and dinner, a few km from the ruins, excellent restaurant, modern, park with animals; **C** Dolores Alba, small hotel (same family as in Mérida, where you can make advance reservations, advisable in view of long walk from ruins), 2½ km on the road to Puerto Juárez (bus passes it), in need of renovation, with shower; has swimming pool and serves good, expensive meals, English spoken, RVs can park in front for US$5, with use of restroom, shower and pool, free transport to the ruins (be careful if walking along the road from the ruins after dark, there are many trucks speeding by—carry a flashlight/torch).

Other hotels at **Pisté** about 2 km before the ruins if coming from Mérida (taxi to ruins US$2.65): no accommodation under US$10. **B-C** Stardust Posada Annex, good value, especially if you don't want TV or a/c (fans available), swimming pool, popular with German tour groups, average restaurant; **D** Posada Chac Mool, fan, shower, clean, laundry service, rec; nearby is **D** *Posada Maya*, with bath, clean, hot water, but restaurant not rec; **D** *Posada Olalde*, quiet, 100m from main road at end of Calle 6; **E** *Posada Novelo*, near *Pirámide Inn*, run by José Novelo who speaks English, restaurants nearby, not very good value, sanitation in poor condition. *Hotel Cunanchén*, on Plaza, prices negotiable with owner, not rec; ask to see private *cenote*. **D** *Posada el Paso*, on main road into village from Chichén, with shower, good value, very friendly, safe parking. A lot of traffic passes through at night, try to get a room at the back.

There is a small pyramid in the village opp the **A+** *Hotel Misión Chichén Itzá*, a/c, pool (disappointing), not easily seen from the road; it has staircases with plumed serpents and a big statue facing N on top; close by is a huge plumed serpent, part coloured, almost forming a circle at least 20m long. Unfortunately the serpent has been largely destroyed to make way for the *Posada Chac Mool*. There is no sign or public path, climb over gate into scrubland, the serpent will be to right, pyramid to left. The whole construction is an unabashedly modern folly made 25 yrs ago by a local stone-mason who used to work on the archaeological expeditions. Bank in Pisté, Banamex, open 0900-1300.

Restaurants Mostly poor and overpriced in Chichén itself (cafés inside the ruins are cheaper than the restaurant at the entrance to the ruins, but they are still expensive). *Hotel Restaurant Carrousel* (rooms D); *Las Redes*; *Nicte-Ha* opposite is cheaper and has chocolate milk shakes; *Fiesta* in Pisté, Calle Principal, Yucatec specialities, touristy but good. Next door is a place serving good *comida corrida* for US$5.35; *Poxil*, Mérida end of town, for breakfast; *El Paso* in Pisté, good meals but doesn't open for breakfast as early as it claims. Restaurants in Pisté close 2100-2200.

Shopping Hammocks are sold by *Mario Díaz* (a most interesting character), excellent quality, huge, at his house 1/2 km up the road forking to the left at the centre of the village. A few km from Chichén is Ebtún, on the road to Valladolid. A sign says 'Hammock sales and repairs": it is actually a small prison which turns out 1st class cotton or nylon hammocks—haggle with wardens and prisoners; there are no real bargains, but good quality.

Telephone International calls may be placed from Teléfonos de México, opposite *Hotel Xaybe*.

Transport If driving from Mérida, follow Calle 63 (off the Plaza) out as far as the dirt section, where you turn left, then right and right again at the main road, follow until hypermarket on left and make a left turn at the sign for Chichén Itzá. Hitch hiking to Mérida is usually no problem.

Chichén Itzá is easily reached (but less easily during holiday periods) from Mérida by 1st at 0845, US$9.20 (return), bus station at Calle 69 between 68 and 70 (return 1445-1500), and hourly 2nd class (ADO) buses from 0500 (US$5.75 return), bus station on Calle 50 between 65 and 67, about 11/2 or 3 hours' journey. Buses drop off and pick up passengers at the junction, 500m from the ruins until 1700 (thereafter take a taxi to Pisté or colectivo to Valladolid for buses). Mon am 2nd class buses may be full with workers from Mérida returning to Cancún. 1st class buses on the Mérida-Cancún route pass every 30 mins (between 0430 and 2300), 2nd class every 60 mins. Many buses a day go to **Cancún** and **Puerto Juárez**, US$6.20. The first bus from Pisté to Puerto Juárez is at 0730, 3 hrs. ADO bus office in Pisté is between *Stardust* and *Pirámide Inn*. Budget travellers going on from Mérida to Isla Mujeres or Cozumel should visit Chichén from Valladolid (see below). Buses from **Valladolid** go every hour to the site, the 0715 bus reaches the ruins at 0800 when they open, and you can return by standing on the main road 1 km from the entrance to the ruins and flagging down any bus going straight through. Colectivo entrance-Valladolid, US$1.65. Bus Pisté-Valladolid US$1.50; Pisté-**Tulum**, US$5.75.

An interesting detour off the Chichén—Mérida highway is to turn in the direction of Yaxcaba at Libre Unión, after 3 km turn on to a dirt road, singposted to cenote *Xtojil*, a beautiful cenote with a Maya platform, which has well-preserved carvings and paintings.

On the way back, turn to the right at Kantunil (68 km from Mérida) for a short excursion to the charming, friendly little city of *Izamal* (pop 15,385). (It can be reached by direct bus either from Mérida or Valladolid—a good day excursion.) Once a major Classic Maya religious site (founded by the priest Itzamná), Izamal became one of the centres of the Spanish attempt to christianize the Maya. Fray Diego de Landa, the historian of the Spanish conquest of Mérida (to whom there is a statue in the town), founded the huge convent and church which now face the main Plaza de la Constitución. This building, constructed on top of a Maya pyramid, was begun in 1549 and has the second largest atrium in the world. The image of the Inmaculada Virgen de la Concepción in the magnificent church was made the Reina de Yucatán in 1949 and the patron saint of the state in 1970. Just two and a half blocks away, visible from the convent across a second square, are the ruins of a great mausoleum known as Kinich-Kakmo pyramid. The entrance is on Calle 27, next to the tortilla factory (open 0800-1700, free). You climb the first set of stairs to a broad, tree-covered platform, at the end of which is a further pyramid (still under reconstruction). From the top there is an excellent view of the town and surrounding *henequén* and citrus plantations. Kinich-Kakmo is 195m long, 173 wide and 36 high, the fifth highest in Mexico. In all, 20 Maya structures have been identified in Izamal. Another startling feature about the town is that the entire colonial centre, including the convent, the arcaded government offices on Plaza de la Constitución and the arcaded second square, is painted a rich yellow ochre, giving it the nickname of the 'golden city".

Four blocks up Calle 27, at the junction with Calle 34 is a small church on a square. The front door may be locked, but a little door outside leads to a spiral staircase to the interior gallery (note the wooden poles in the ceilings) and to the roof. The treads on the stair are very narrow.

Lodging, Food, Services Hotels: On Plaza de la Constitución, **D** *Kabul*, poor value, cell-like rooms; **D** *Canto*, minimum services. Several **restaurants** on Plaza de la Constitución; *Gaby* just off the square on Calle 31; *El Norteño* at bus station, good, cheap. Activity in town in the evening gets going after 2030. **Market**, Calle 31, on Plaza de la Constitución, opposite convent, closes soon after lunch. **Bank** on square with statue to Fray Diego de Landa, S side of convent. **Post Office** on opposite side of square to convent.

Transport Buses bus station is on Calle 32 behind government offices, can leave bags; 2nd class to **Mérida**, every 45 mins, 2 hrs, US$2, lovely countryside; bus station in Mérida, Calle 50 entre Calles 65 y 67. 6 a day to/from **Valladolid** (96 km), about 2 hrs, US$2.30-3. **Train** Mérida-Izamal leaves at 0600, returns 1520.

From Izamal one can go by bus to **Cenotillo**, where there are several fine *cenotes* within easy walking distance from the town (avoid the one *in* town), especially Ucil, excellent for swimming, and La Unión. From Mérida, take 0600 train to Tunkas, and then bus to Cenotillo (direct bus from Mérida, same service as to Izamal), the train continues from Tunkas to Tizimín, arr 1140. Lovely train ride, $2\frac{1}{2}$ hrs, US$1.50. Past Cenotillo is Espita and then a road forks left to Tizimín (see below).

The cemetery of **Hoctun**, on the Mérida-Chichén road, is also worth visiting, impossible to miss, there is an 'Empire State Building' on the site. Take a bus from Mérida (last bus back 1700) to see extensive ruins at **Aké**, unique structure. Public transport in Mérida is difficult: from an unsigned stop on the corner of Calles 53 and 50, some buses to Tixcocob and Ekmul continue to Aké; ask the driver.

Beyond Chichén Itzá, and easily reached from Mérida is **Valladolid** (pop 70,000), a pleasant Yucatecan town bypassed by the paved road between Mérida and Puerto Juárez/Cancún. Here also is a large Franciscan church, situated on the pleasant plaza, in the middle of which is a fountain with a statue of a woman wearing a *huipil*, pouring water from a jar. At dusk in the plaza there is a cacophony of birdsong. In the western outskirts, in the Barrio del Convento de Sisal, is the former convent of San Bernardino de Siena; built in 1552, it is the oldest church in the Yucatán.

Hotels B *Mesón del Marqués*, N side of Plaza Principal, T 62073, F 622680, takes Visa and Master Card, a/c, with bath, on square, with good restaurant and shop (helpful for information), cable TV, swimming pool, excellent value, rec. **C** *María de la Luz*, Calle 42 No 193-C, Plaza Principal, T 6-20-71, good, swimming pool (non-residents, US$0.50) and small night-club, excellent restaurant, buffet breakfast US$3.50, closes at 2230; **C** *San Clemente*, Calle 41 and 42 No 206, 62208, with a/c, spacious, clean, has car park, small swimming pool, restaurant, opposite Cathedral, in centre of town, good. **C-D** *Zací*, Calle 44 No 191, a/c,

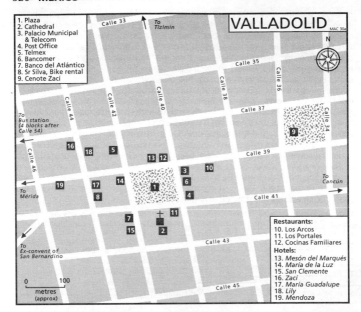

Map key:
1. Plaza
2. Cathedral
3. Palacio Municipal & Telecom
4. Post Office
5. Telmex
6. Bancomer
7. Banco del Atlántico
8. Sr Silva, Bike rental
9. Cenote Zací

VALLADOLID MAC 30a

Restaurants:
10. Los Arcos
11. Los Portales
12. Cocinas Familiares
Hotels:
13. Mesón del Marqués
14. María de la Luz
15. San Clemente
16. Zací
17. María Guadalupe
18. Lily
19. Mendoza

cheaper with fan, TV, pool, clean, quiet, good value; **D** *María Guadalupe*, Calle 44 No 188, T 62068, quiet, clean and good value, hot water, but uncertain water supply. **D** *Lily*, Calle 44 No 190, with hot shower, cheaper with shared bath, fan, basic, laundry facilities, safe motorcycle parking, friendly; **D** *Maya*, Calle 41 No 231, between 48 and 50, T 62069, fan or a/c, clean, good value, also runs good restaurant two doors away; **D** *Mendoza*, Calle 39 No 204C (between Calles 44 and 46), T 62002, good, clean, hot water, noisy, cheaper with shared bath (but communal toilets dirty).

Restaurants *Los Arcos*, Calle 39 just E of plaza, smart, mid-price range, good service and food, inc vegetarian soup, good value set lunch US$5; *Los Portales* on SE corner of main square, very good; *La Sirenita*, Calle 41 No 168-A, a few blocks E of main square, highly rec for seafood, popular; *Spago*, Calle 43, behind church, pizzas and good pastas, cheap. Next to *Hotel Lily* are *Panadería La Central* and *Taquería La Principal*. Good, cheap food at the *cocinas familiares*, Yucatecan food, pizzas, burgers, etc, NE corner of Plaza Principal, next to *Mesón del Marqués*.

Bike rental Sr Silva, Calle 44, between Calles 39 and 41, US$1/hr.

Post Office On E side of Plaza, 0800-1900 (does not accept parcels for abroad); Telecom telegraph office on same side of Plaza, next to Palacio Municipal. **Telephones** Telmex phone office on Calle 42, just N of square; expensive Computel offices at bus station and next to *Hotel San Clemente*; Ladatel phonecards can be bought from *farmacias* for use in phone booths.

Bank Bancomer on E side of square, changes TCs from 0900; Banco del Atlántico, corner of Calle 41 and 42, quick service for TCs, from 1000.

Buses New bus station is at Calles 54 y 37, 6 blocks W of plaza, taxi US$1.35 (old terminal is at Calles 46 y 39). To **Chichén Itzá**, take Mérida bus, 2nd class, US$1.50, frequent, from 0600-2400, 1 hr ride, also to Balankanché caves; many buses go to **Mérida**, first at 0300, US$6, 2nd class US$5.30 (3 hrs); and to **Cancún** from 0130 to 1400, US$5.20, 2 hrs, US$5 2nd class (can take 3½ hrs), from 0700. To **Playa del Carmen** at 0430 (reservations available) and 1315 via Cobá and the crossroads 1 km from Tulum, US$8 (3½ hrs), more frequently via Cancún from 0130 to 1400, US$8.25 1st class, US$8 2nd class (4 hrs); to **Tizimín**, hourly 2nd class, 1 hr, US$1.75; **Felipe Carrillo Puerto**, at 0600 and 0930 and others for **Chetumal** (most 'de paso", buy tickets on the bus, only two direct, at 0630 and 1330), 2nd class, US$8, 5 hrs.

A lovely *cenote*, Zací, with a thatched-roof restaurant and lighted promenades, is on Calle 36 between Calle 37 and 39, but you cannot swim in it because of the algae, admission US$0.80 (children half-price). Road turns left from Cancún road a couple of blocks from main plaza.

One can swim in the very clean electrically-lit *cenote* of Xkeken at **Dzit-Nup**, a huge cave with blue water —"wonderful' but take a torch for exploring (entry US$1.30, open until 1700, taxi US$6 one way from Valladolid 7 km away). Colectivos leave several times a day from in front of *Hotel María Guadalupe*, or take Valladolid-Mérida bus and alight at Dzit-Nup junction, US$0.50, then hitch or walk the last couple of km, or it's ½ hr by bicycle (take Calle 39 towards Mérida; leaving town you reach a fork in the road, go left, unsigned for Mérida and after 10 mins or so—in a car—you'll see the sign for Dzit-Nup; turn left and cenote is on the left).

A paved road heads N (buses) from Valladolid to **Tizimín** (pop 30,000), a pleasant, busy town with an austere 16th-century church and a convent (both may be closed), open squares and streets with low houses. It has a famous New Year *fiesta*. There are several hotels, eg **D** *San Jorge*, on main plaza, a/c, good value; **D** *posada* next to church. There is a good but expensive restaurant, *Tres Reyes*, and others, including many serving cheap *menú del día* around the plaza. Long-distance phone at Calle 50 No 410, just off plaza. On the edge of town is a vast pink disco, popular with Meridanos. There is also a local *cenote*, Kikib, and the Maya ruins of **Kulubá** are 1 hr, 50 km away (taxi US$18.50).

Bus from Mérida from Calle 50 entre Calles 65 y 67, 1st class, 3 hrs, US$6. In Tizimín there are two bus terminals side-by-side: Expreso del Oriente for Valladolid, Mérida, Cancún, and Playa del Carmen, and Pullman Ejecutivo Noreste for Mérida (3 *ejecutivo* and at least 7 1st class), Río Lagartos (3 1st class and 11 2nd class between 0515 and 1900, US$2.20), San Felipe (2 1st, 5 2nd class), Chiquilá, Valladolid (5 a day, US$1.75), and Felipe Carrillo Puerto, Bacalar and Chetumal (0530 and 1430).

The road continues N over the flat landscape to **Río Lagartos**, itself on a lagoon, where the Maya extracted salt. Río Lagartos has been declared a nature reserve to protect waterfowl habitat (local and migratory) and turtle nesting beaches. (**C** *Hotel Nefertiti*, but bargaining possible, uncertain water supply, run down, fish restaurant; *Cueva Macumba* restaurant near harbour, good Mexican food, friendly, will arrange breakfast if requested in advance; restaurant at seashore, good, well decorated, evening only; *lonchería*, opp hotel open for lunch. There are a number of small eating-places. *Fiesta*, 12 December, La Virgen de Guadalupe.) There are frequent buses from Tizimín (see above), and it is possible to get to Río Lagartos and back in a day from Valladolid, if you leave on the 0630 or 0730 bus (taxi Tizimín-Río Lagartos US$25, may be bargained down to US$17) and last bus back from Río Lagartos at 1730. Swimming from island opposite Río Lagartos, where boats are moored; access to beach by boat only. Bus from Río Lagartos to **San Felipe** (13 km), can bathe in the sea, access to beach here, too, only by boat; good cheap seafood at *El Payaso* restaurant; on a small island with ruins of a Maya pyramid, beware of rattlesnakes. One can also go from Río Lagartos to **Los Colorados** (15 km) to swim and see the salt deposits with red, lilac and pink water (no shade, beware of sunburn). Early morning boat trips can be arranged in Río Lagartos to see the flamingoes (US$40, in 8-9 seater, 2½-3 hrs, cheaper in 5-seater, but no shade, fix the price before embarking; in mid-week few people go so there is no chance of negotiating, but boat owners are more flexible on where they go; at weekends it is very busy, so it may be easier to get a party together and reduce costs). There are often only a few pairs of birds (but thousands in July-August) feeding in the lagoons E of Los Colorados; ask for

Adriano who is a good guide and bird expert, or for Manuel at the Río Lagartos bus stop. Make sure you are taken to the furthest breeding grounds, to see most flamingoes, and pelicans. There is also a road around the main congregating area. (Check before going whether the flamingoes are there. Salt mining is disturbing their habitat.) Not a lot else here, certainly no accommodation, but if you are stuck for food, eat inexpensively at the *Casino* (ask locals).

The road goes on to **El Cuyo**, rough and sandy, but passable. El Cuyo has a shark-fishing harbour. Fishermen cannot sell (co-op) but can barter fish—fry your shark steak with garlic, onions and lime juice. El Cuyo is a very quiet, friendly place with a beach where swimming is safe (there is less seaweed in the water the further from town you go towards the Caribbean). *La Conchita* restaurant (good value meals) has *cabañas* with bath, double bed and hammock (D). Opposite *La Conchita* bread is sold after 1700. From Tizimín there are kombis (US$2.70, 1½ hrs) and buses (slower) to El Cuyo, or take a kombi to Colonia and hitch from there (Sheila Wilson, Stoke Poges, UK).

Also N of Valladolid, turning off the road to Puerto Juárez after Nuevo Xcan, is **Holbox Island**. Buses to **Chiquilá** for boats, 3 times a day, also direct from Tizimín at 1130, connecting with the ferry, US$2.20. The ferry leaves for Holbox 0600 and 1430, 1 hr, US$1, returning to Chiquilá at 0500 and 1300. A bus to Mérida connects with the 0500 ferry. If you miss the ferry a fisherman will probably take you quite cheaply (say US$2). You can leave your car in care of the harbour master for a small charge; his house is E of the dock. Take water with you if possible. The beach is at the opposite end of the island to the ferry, 10 mins walk; Hurricane Hugo uprooted or broke all the palm trees. During 'El Norte' season, the water is turbid and beach is littered with seaweed.

Lodging and food E *Hotel Holbox* at dock, clean, quiet, cold water, friendly; house with 3 doors, ½ block from plaza, rooms, some beds, mostly for hammocks, very basic, very cheap, outdoor toilet, no shower, noisy, meals available which are rec; rooms at pink house off plaza, D, clean, with bath; *cabañas*, D, usually occupied; take blankets and hammock (ask at fishermen's houses where you can put up), and lots of mosquito repellent. Best camping on beach E of village (N side of island). *Lonchería* on plaza; restaurant on main road open for dinner; all bars close 1900; bakery with fresh bread daily, good; fish is generally expensive. Disco opens 2230, admission US$2.75.

There are five more uninhabited islands beyond Holbox. Beware of sharks and barracuda, though few nasty occurrences have been reported. Off the rough and mostly unpopulated bulge of the Yucatán coastline are several islands, once notorious for contraband. Beware of mosquitoes in the area.

At the border between Yucatán and Quintana Roo states, Nuevo Xcan (**see p 342**), police searches are made for those leaving Quintana Roo for items which may transmit plant and other diseases.

The Caribbean Coast

Further to the information given in the introduction of this section (**see pages 283**), Quintana Roo (and especially Cozumel) is the main area for Diving and Watersports in the Yucatán Peninsula. More dive sites are found off the Belize Cayes. The text below gives information on some of the options available, with addresses of dive shops, etc. It should be noted that watersports in Quintana Roo are expensive and touristy, but operators are generally helpful; snorkelling is often organized for large groups. On the more accessible reefs the coral is dying and there are no small coral fishes as a necessary part of the coral life cycle. Further from the shore, though, there is still much reef life to enjoy.

The famous resort of **Cancún**, near the north-eastern tip of the Yucatán peninsula, is a thriving holiday resort and town. The town is on the mainland; the resort, usually known simply as the Zona Hotelera (Hotel Zone), is on an island shaped like the number 7, encompassing the Laguna Nichupté. The population

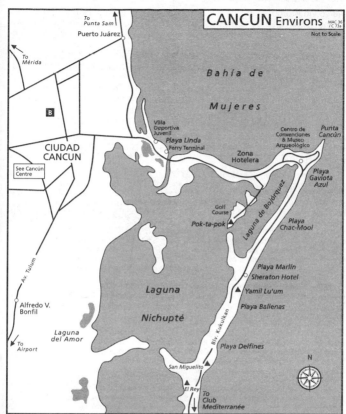

CANCUN Environs MAC 36 / C 73a
Not to Scale

is about 30,000, almost all dedicated to servicing the tourist industry. A bridge at each end of the island links the hotel zone with the mainland in a seamless ribbon, not yet developed along its entire length, but not far off. Beaches stretch all along the seaward side of the Zona Hotelera; both sand and sea are clean and beautiful. Watersports take place on the Caribbean and on the Laguna, but when bathing, watch out for the warning flags at intervals along the shore.

The scale of the Zona Hotelera is huge, with skyscraper hotels and sprawling resorts between the beach and Bulevar Kukulkán, which runs the length of the island. At the northern end are shopping malls and an archaeological museum with local finds, next to the old Convention Centre (a new Convention Centre has been constructed opposite the *Fiesta Americana Coral Beach*.) There are vestiges of Maya occupation here, San Miguelito and El Rey towards the S of the island, a small temple in the grounds of the *Sheraton* and Pok-ta-Pok on a peninsula at the N of the Laguna, but they are virtually lost in the midst of the modern concrete and the architectural fantasies. Near El Rey (open 0800-1630), land is being reclaimed for the construction of a golf course, marina, hotel and commercial centre. Prices are higher on Cancún than elsewhere in Mexico because everything is brought in from miles outside. Buses, marked 'Hoteles", run every 5 minutes for US$0.80 from the southern end of the Zona Hotelera to the town and back. At busy times they are packed with holidaymakers trying to locate where they should get off.

It is about 4 km from the Zona Hotelera to the town, which is full of tourist shops, restaurants and a variety of hotels which are cheaper than on the island. The town is divided into 'supermanzanas", indicated by SM in addresses, each block being divided further by streets and avenues. The two main avenues are Tulum and Yaxchilán, the former having most of the shops, exchange facilities, many restaurants and hotels. Its busiest sector runs from the roundabout at the junction with Bulevar Kukulkán to the roundabout by the bus station.

Hotels   Hotels fall roughly into two categories: those in the Zona Hotelera, which are expensive and tend to cater for package tours, but which have all the facilities associated with a beach holiday; those in the town are less pricey and more functional. The list below gives more detail on the latter.

In the Zona Hotelera: *Camino Real*, T 83-01-00, F 83-17-30; *Sheraton Cancún Resort and Towers*, in the **L+** range (PO Box 834, Cancún, T 83-19-88, F 85-02-02); *Hyatt Cancún Caribe*, T 83-00-44, F 83-15-14, and *Hyatt Regency*, T 83-09-66, F 83-13-49; **L** *Stouffer Presidente*, T 83-02-00, F 83-25-15, *Miramar Misión Park Plaza*, T 83-17-55, F 83-11-36. **A+** *Playa Blanca*, T 83-00-71, F 83-09-04, resort facilities; and *Krystal*, T 83-11-33, F 83-17-90. Slightly less expensive: *Aristos*, T 83-00-11, F 83-00-78, **A+** *Calinda Quality Cancún Beach*, T 83-08-00, F 83-18-57, and *Calinda Viva*, same phone, F 83-20-87; *Club Lagoon Marina*, T 83-11-01, F 83-13-26. Also represented are hotels in the *Fiesta Americana* chain (three in all), *Days Inn*, *Holiday Inn* (two, one in the *Zona Hotelera*, one in the centre), *Marriott*, *Meliá* (two), *Radisson* (also two), and many more hotels, suites and villas. At the southern end of the island is the *Club Méditerranée* with its customary facilities (T 85-29-00, F 85-22-90).

Youth hostel   **E** *Villa Deportiva Juvenil*, is at Km 3.2 Av Kukulkán, T 83-13-37, on the beach, 5 mins walk from the bridge towards Cancún town, next to *Club Verano Beat*, dormitory style, price per person, US$10 deposit, 25% discount with membership card, 12 people per room, basic, dirty, plumbing unreliable, sketchy locker facilities, meals at set times, small shop, camping US$5.

Hotels in Cancún town: most are to be found on Av Tulum and Av Yaxchilán and the streets off them. In Cancún town you will be lucky to find a double under US$20; many do not serve meals. **A+÷-A** *Best Western Plaza Caribe*, Av Tulum y Uxmal, T 84-13-77, F 84-63-52, opposite bus terminal; **A+** *Plaza del Sol*, Yaxchilán y Gladiolas, T 84-38-88, F 84-43-93, modern, comfortable; **A** *Caribe Internacional*, at the junction of Yaxchilán and Sunyaxchén, T 84-34-99, F 84-19-93. In our **B** range: *Antillano*, Av Tulum y Claveles, T 84-15-32, F 84-11-32, a/c, TV, phone, pool; *Cancún Rosa*, Margaritas 2, local 10, T 84-28-73, F 84-06-23, close to bus terminal, a/c, TV, phone, comfortable rooms; *El Alux*, Av Uxmal 21, T 84-06-62, 2 blocks from bus terminal; *El Rey del Caribe*, Av Uxmal y Náder, T 84-20-28, F 84-98-57, a/c, kitchenettes, pool, garden with hammocks, parking, older style, rec; *Hacienda*, Sunyaxchén 38-40, a/c, TV; *Margarita*, Yaxchilán y Jazmines, T 84-93-33, F 84-92-09; *María de Lourdes*, Av Yaxchilán SM 22, T 84-47-44, F 84-12-42; *Parador*, Av Tulum 26, T 84-13-10, F 84-97-12, close to bus terminal, inefficient, a/c, TV, phone, pool, restaurant attached, clean. In our **C** range: *Colonial*, Tulipanes 22 y Av Tulum, T 84-15-35, a/c, cheaper with fan, quiet, TV, phone; *Coral*, Sunyaxchén 30 (towards post office), T 84-29-01; *Cotty*, Av Uxmal 44, T 84-05-50, near bus station, a/c, TV, reports vary on cleanliness; *Lucy*, Gladiolas 25, between Tulum and Yaxchilán, T 84-41-65, a/c, kitchenettes, takes credit cards; *María Isabel*, Palmera 595, T 84-90-15, near bus station and Av Tulum, fan and a/c, hot water, TV, small and clean, friendly, helpful; *Novotel*, Av Tulum y Azucenas, T 84-29-99, F 84-31-62, close to bus station, rooms start at under US$30 with fan, but rise to **B** range with a/c, popular, noisy on Av Tulum side; *Rivemar*, Av Tulum 49-51 y Crisantemas, T 84-17-08, a/c, phone, TV; *Villa Maya Cancún*, Uxmal 20 y Rubia, T 84-28-29, F 84-17-62, a/c, pool, *La Francesa* bakery next door; *Villa Rossana*, Yaxchilán, opposite *Plaza del Sol*. **D** *Piña*, hot showers, fan, clean, rec; **D** *Tropical Caribe*, Cedro 10 SM 23, T 41-14-42, bath and fan, quiet, secure, not too clean (walk N up Av Tulum from junction with Uxmal for about 5 blocks, from left at Disco Salsa and hotel is on the right).

Camping is not permitted in Cancún town except at the Villa Deportiva youth hostel. There is a trailer park, *Rainbow*, just S of the airport.

Restaurants   There is a huge variety of restaurants, ranging from hamburger stands to 5-star,

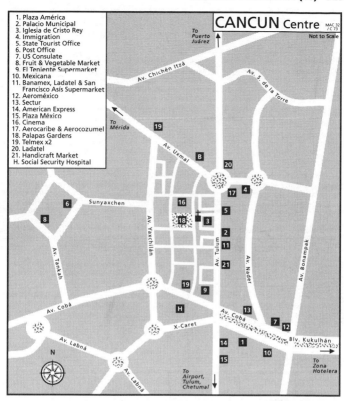

CANCUN Centre MAC 32 / C 73
Not to Scale

1. Plaza América
2. Palacio Municipal
3. Iglesia de Cristo Rey
4. Immigration
5. State Tourist Office
6. Post Office
7. US Consulate
8. Fruit & Vegetable Market
9. El Teniente Supermarket
10. Mexicana
11. Banamex, Ladatel & San Francisco Asís Supermarket
12. Aeroméxico
13. Sectur
14. American Express
15. Plaza México
16. Cinema
17. Aerocaribe & Aerocozumel
18. Palapas Gardens
19. Telmex x2
20. Ladatel
21. Handicraft Market
H. Social Security Hospital

gourmet places. Just about every type of cuisine can be found. The best buys are on the side streets of Cancún town, while the largest selection can be found on Avs Tulum and Yaxchilán. The ones on the island are of slightly higher price and quality and are scattered along Av Kukulkán, with a high concentration in the shopping centres (of which there are about ten). If you are in no hurry to eat, look at what the restaurants are offering in the way of dishes, prices and drinks specials, then decide, if you can resist the pressurized selling.

The best is said to be *100% Natural*, opposite *Hotel Caribe Internacional* on Yaxchilán y Sunyaxchén freshly-prepared food, friendly staff, 'invigorating eating"; *Los Braceritos*, Yaxchilán 35, open 24 hrs; *La Estancia*, Gladiolas 25 next to *Hotel Lucy*, good; *Los Huaraches*, on Uxmal opposite Yaxchilán, fast food, cheap *empanada* specials after 1300; many others on Av Uxmal, not too expensive. *Los Almendros*, Av Bonapak y Sayil, Lote 60, 61 and 62, good local food. *La Bodeguita del Medio*, Tulipanes SM 22 y Av Tulum, good food and service, 'Cuban"; *El Pescador*, Tulipanes 28, good seafood but expensive; *Pop*, next to *Hotel Parador*, for quicker-type food; *Bing*, Av Tulum y Uxmal, close to Banpais bank, best ice cream. *Jaguari*, Zona Hotelera, Brazilian, opens 1700, US$15.95 + tax, set price, has been rec. *Piemonte Pizzería*, Av Yaxchilán 52, good food and value, appetizing aperitifs on the house, rec; *Las Tejas*, Av Tulum, central end, good food at reasonable prices; also on Av Tulum, *Olé Olé*, good meat, friendly. *Tacolote*, Av Cobá 19, good food and excellent value, cheerful, popular; taco stands can be found each evening on and around the squares between Avs Tulum and Yaxchilán, good family atmosphere. *Comida Casera*, Av Uxmal opp bus terminal, good coffee. The native Mexican restaurants in the workers' colonies are cheapest. Best bet is to buy food and beer in a store and take it to the beach, spending the day on a lounger.

Shopping The market, at Av Tulum 23, is basically a handicrafts market, with jewellery, clothing, hats, etc. Downtown there are several supermarkets, big and small, for food and drink, eg *Comercial Mexicana*, nr Ladatel; *San Francisco de Asís*. Next to *Hotel Caribe Internacional*, on Yaxchilán, are two 24-hr *farmacias*. **Bookshop** *Fama*, Av Tulum 105, international books and magazines, English, French, German.

Entertainment Ballet Folclórico de México, nightly dinner shows at 1900 at *Continental Villas Plaza Hotel*, Zona Hotelera, T 85-14-44, ext 5706. *La Boom* disco, almost opposite Playa Linda dock, near the youth hostel, US$7 for all you can drink. Salsa club *Batachá* in *Miramar Misión* hotel, US$5 entry charge, popular with locals, good music. Crococun crocodile ranch, 30 km on road to Playa del Carmen.

Sports Parasailing from beaches on Zona Hotelera; **sailing**; many other water sports; **bungee jumping** also available, from a crane hoist.

Exchange Many Mexican banks. Many small *casas de cambio*, which change cash and TCs (latter at poorer rates) until 2100; rec is *Cunex*, Av Tulum 13, close to Av Cobá. Rates are better in town than at the airport. It is possible to change dollar TCs into dollars cash, but not one-for-one.

Car Hire Budget Rent-a-Car in Cancún has been rec for good service. **Avis**, Plaza Caracol, cheapest but still expensive. There are many car hire agencies, with offices on Av Tulum, in the Zona Hotelera and at the airport; look out for special deals, but check vehicles carefully. Rates vary enormously, from US$40 to US$80 a day for a VW Golf (VW Beetles are cheaper), larger cars and jeeps available.

Consulates Downtown, unless stated otherwise, most open am only: **Costa Rica**, Calle Mandinga, manzana 11, SM 30, T 84-48-69; **USA**, Av Náder 40, T 84-24-11, 0900-1400, 1500-1800; **Canada**, Plaza México 312, 2nd floor, T 84-37-16, 1100-1300; **Germany**, Punta Conoco 36, SM 24, T 84-18-98; **Sweden**, Av Náder 34, SM 2-A, T 84-72-71, 0800-1300, 1700-2000; **Spain**, Cielo 17, Depto 14, SM 4, T 84-18-95; **Italy**, La Mansión Costa Blanca Shopping Center, Zona Hotelera, T 83-21-84; **France**, Instituto Internacional de Idiomas, Av Xel-Há 113, SM 25, T 84-60-78, 0800-1100, 1700-1900.

Post Office At end of Av Sunyaxchen, a short distance from Av Yaxchilán. **Telephones** Telmex *caseta* just off Av Cobá on Alcatreces; another *caseta* on Av Uxmal next to *Los Huaraches* restaurant. Ladatel phones in Plaza América, at San Francisco de Asís shopping centre and opposite the bus station on the end wall of a supermarket at Tulum y Uxmal. Computel phone and fax, more expensive, at Yaxchilán 49 and other locations.

Tourist Information State Tourist Office, Av Tulum, between Comermex and city hall; Sectur Federal Tourist Office, corner of Av Cobá and Av Náder, closed weekends, but kiosk on Av Tulum at Tulipanes is open sometimes at weekends. There are kiosks in the Zona Hotelera, too, eg at Mayfair Plaza. Downtown and in the Zona Hotelera closest to downtown most street corners have a map. See free publication, *Cancún Tips*, issued twice a year, and *Cancún Tips Magazine*, quarterly, from Av Tulum 29, Cancún, QR 77500, Mexico.

Buses Local bus ("Hoteles' Route), US$0.80 (taxis are exorbitant); to Puerto Juárez from Av Tulum, marked 'Puerto Juárez or 'Colonia Lombardo", US$0.55.

   Cancún bus terminal, at the junction of Avs Tulum and Uxmal, is the hub for routes W to Mérida and S to Tulum and Chetumal. The station is neither large nor very well organized. It is open 24 hrs. Many services to **Mérida**, 4 hrs, ranging from *plus* with TV, a/c, etc, US$20, to 1st class US$14; all services call at **Valladolid**, US$5.50 1st class, US$5 2nd class; to **Chichén Itzá**, Expreso de Oriente 1st class en route to Mérida, US$6.20. Expreso de Oriente also has services to Tizimín, Izamal, Cenotillo and Chiquilá. Caribe Express has a 1330 service to **Campeche** via Mérida, US$38. Caribe Inter 3 times a day to Mérida via Francisco Carrillo Puerto, US$17.50, calling at Polyuc, Peto, Tekax, Oxkutzcab, Tikul, Muná and Uman. To **Villahermosa**, US$60.

   Inter Playa Express every 30 mins to **Puerto Morelos**, US$1, **Playa del Carmen**, US$2.25 and **Xcaret**, US$2.25; 3 times daily to **Puerto Aventuras**, US$2.50, **Akumal**, US$3, **Xel-Há**, US$3.30 and **Tulum**, US$4. Other services to Playa del Carmen and Tulum are more expensive, eg 1st class Caribe Inter to Playa del Carmen US$3, 2nd class US$2.35 to Playa del Carmen and US$4.75 to Tulum. Last bus to Playa del Carmen 2000. These services are en route to **Chetumal** (US$33 1st class, US$15-17.75 2nd). Several other services to Chetumal, including Caribe Express, deluxe service with a/c.

Boat Services The Playa Linda boat dock is at the mainland side of the bridge across Canal Nichupté, about 4 km from centre, opposite the *Calinda Quality Cancún Beach*. It has shops, agencies for boat trips, a snack bar and Computel. Trips to Isla Mujeres, with snorkelling, bar, shopping, start at US$27.50, or US$35 with meal; ferry to Isla Mujeres 0900, 1100, 1330, returning 1600 and 2000, US$6.65 one way. Cheaper ferries go from Puerto Juárez, see below.

Trips to Isla Contoy (see under Isla Mujeres), were suspended in mid-1993 owing to excessive disturbance of bird habitats. *Nautibus*, a vessel with seats below the waterline, makes trips to the reefs, 1½ hrs, a good way to see fish, Playa Linda dock, T 83-35-52. There are a number of other cruises on offer.

Air Services Cancún airport is 16 km S of the town (very expensive shops and restaurant, exchange facilities—double check your money, especially at busy times, 2 hotel reservation agencies, no rooms under US$45). AeroMéxico, Av Cobá 80, T 84-11-86; Mexicana, Av Cobá 13, T 87-14-44; Aerocaribe and Aerocozumel, Av Tulum 29, T 84-20-00; Aviacsa, T 42311, F 76795. American Airlines, Aeropuerto, T 86-00-55; Continental, Aeropuerto, T 86-00-40: NW, Aeropuerto, T 86-00-46. From Cancún by AeroMéxico to Miami, Mérida, Mexico City, and other Mexican destinations. Aviacsa (Av Cobá 55, T 87-42-14) daily to Mérida, Villahermosa, Tuxtla Gutiérrez, Monterrey and Ciudad Juárez. Continental flies to Houston, New York and Chicago. To Los Angeles daily with Mexicana (less frequent out of high season). Cheap flights to USA and Canada can be found. Flights to Mexico City are heavily booked; try stand-by at the airport, or go instead to Mérida. Aviateca (Av Tulum 200, T 84-39-38) to Guatemala City Wed, Thur, Sat, Sun, schedules change. Aerocaribe to Flores (Tikal ruins) on Mon, Wed, Fri 0715, returning at 1730, also Aviateca 4 times a week (as for Guatemala City). Lacsa (Av Bonampak y Av Cobá, T 87-31-01) flies Cancún-San Pedro Sula and San José, and on to Panama. From Amsterdam direct, once a week with Martin Air. Nouvelles Frontières fly charter Zürich-Cancún, 66 Blvd St Michel, 75006 Paris, France. Many charters from North America. Reconfirm flights at a travel agent, they charge, but it is easier than phoning.

On arrival at Cancún, make sure you fill in documents correctly, or else you will be sent back to the end of the long, slow queue. At customs, press a button for random bag search. Colectivo taxi buses run from the airport to Cancún town via the Zona Hotelera, US$7; taxis on the same route charge US$25.35. Only taxis go to the airport, US$8 minimum, usually US$11.50 (beware of overcharging; even if you take a 'Hotelera' bus to the last hotel, the taxi fare remains the same). Irregular bus from Cancún to the airport four times a day, US$3, allow 1 hr. At Cancún airport, official ticket for taxi to Playa del Carmen costs US$50, paid in advance. If you leave the airport area on foot, walk along main road to Cancún, about ½ km outside the area is a control booth; behind it taxis are allowed to pick you up for Playa del Carmen for about US$25 after bargaining. From the airport to the main road is 4 km; you can hitch on the main road.

Puerto Juárez is about 3 km N of Cancún. It is the dock for the cheaper ferry services to Isla Mujeres; there is also a bus terminal, but services are more frequent from Cancún. There are many buses between Cancún and Puerto Juárez, eg No 8 opposite bus terminal (US$0.65), but when the ferries arrive from Isla Mujeres there are many more taxis than buses (taxi fare should be US$3, beware overcharging).

Hotels and Restaurants A *Hotel Caribel*, resort complex, with bath and fan; in the same price range is *San Marcos*; other hotels include **C** *Kah Che*, first hotel on right coming from Cancún, in room for 3, fan, clean, swimming pool on beach, good value; *Posada Hermanos Sánchez*, 100m from bus terminal, on road to Cancún; **D** *Fuente Azul* opposite the dock. Restaurants *Natz Ti Ha* and *Mandinga* by the ferry dock, serve breakfast. *Cabañas Punta Sam*, clean, comfortable, on the beach, **D** with bath (**C** in high season). Possible to camp, with permission, on the beach near the restaurant next door. A big trailer park is being built opposite *Punta Sam*. Irregular bus service there, or hitchhike from Puerto Juárez. Check to see if restaurant is open evenings. No shops nearby. Take mosquito repellent.

Ferries Passenger ferry to Isla Mujeres leaves from the jetty opposite the bus terminal at Puerto Juárez 16 times a day between 0600 and 2100, returning 0500-1930; sometimes leaves early, last boats back may not sail at all (US$1.50, 1 hr, 5 vessels; *Caribbean Queen* is faster, US$3.35; *Caribbean Express* is faster still). There are also small water taxis, but these are much more expensive (US$6 at least to the town or El Garrafón). At the jetty is a luggage store (0800-1800) and a tourist information desk. Car ferry from Punta Sam to Isla Mujeres (about 75 cars carried), 5 km by bus from Cancún via Puerto Juárez (facilities to store luggage), US$1.50 pp and US$6-7 per car; six times a day between 0830 and 2200, returning between 0715 and 2200 (45-min journey).

Buses On the whole it is better to catch outgoing buses in Cancún rather than in Puerto Juárez: there are more of them.

Isla Mujeres (which got its name from the large number of female idols first found by the Spaniards) once epitomized the Caribbean island: long silver beaches (beware sandflies), palm trees and clean blue water at the N end (although the large *Del Prado* hotel dominates the view there) away from the beach pollution of the town, and the naval airstrip to the SW of the town. There are limestone (coral) cliffs and a rocky coast at the S end. A lagoon on the W side is now fouled up. The island has suffered from competition from Cancún and although it is touristy, it is worth a visit. A disease destroyed practically all the palms which used to shade the houses and beach, but new, disease-resistant varieties have been planted and are growing to maturity. There was considerable damage from hurricane Gilbert. The main activity in the evening takes place in the square near the church, where there are also a supermarket and a cinema. Between 1-8 December there is a fiesta for the Virgin of the island, fireworks, dances until 0400 in the Plaza. In October there is a festival of music, with groups from Mexico and the USA performing in the main square. The Civil Guard patrol the beaches at night.

At *El Garrafón*, 7 km (entry US$2, and the same for a locker with an extra US$3.35 key deposit), there is a tropical fish reserve (fishing forbidden) on a small coral reef. Take snorkel (rental US$2.65 a day for mask and snorkel, same again for fins, US5 for underwater camera, plus deposit of US$30, passport, driver's licence, credit card or hotel key, from shops in the park) and swim among a variety of multicoloured tropical fish—they aren't at all shy, but the coral is dead and not colourful. Reef trips by boat cost US$11.65 without equipment hire, US$15 with hire. El Garrafón is a very popular excursion on the island and from Cancún; the water is usually full of snorkellers between 1100 and 1400. It is open 0800-1630; there are showers, toilets, expensive restaurants and bars, reasonable snack bar, shops and a small museum-cum-aquarium.

Taxi from the town to El Garrafón costs about US$6, maybe more for the return. It is cheaper to take a taxi from El Garrafón to the Casa Mundaca (see below), US$2.65, the another back to town, US$1.65. There is a bus which goes half-way to El Garrafón, the end of the line being at the bend in the road by the entarnces to Casa Mundaca and Playa Paraíso (bus fare US$0.35). This beach, and its neighbour, Lancheros, is quite clean, with palms, restaurants and toilets. The area of sand is quite small. Sadly, there are pens at the shore containing nurse sharks, which swim up and down their cages like big cats in a zoo. If so moved, you can join them in the water. Playa Indios, S of Lancheros, towards El Garrafón, has similar facilities and 'entertainment".

The curious remains of a pirate's domain, called Casa de Mundaca, is in the centre of the island; a big, new arch gate marks its entrance. Paths have been laid out among the large trees, but all that remains of the estate (called Vista Alegre) are one small building and a circular garden with raised beds, a well and a gateway. Fermín Mundaca, more of a slave-trader than a buccaneer, built Vista Alegre for the teenage girl he loved. She rejected him and he died, broken-hearted, in Mérida. His epitaph there reads 'Como eres, yo fui; como soy, tu serás' (what you are I was; what I am you shall be). See the poignant little carving on the garden side of the gate, 'La entrada de La Trigueña' (the girl's nickname).

At the southern tip is a small, ruined Mayan lighthouse or shrine of Ixtel, just beyond a modern lighthouse. The lighthouse keeper sells coca-cola for US$1, hammocks and conch shells. The view from the Maya shrine is beautiful, with a pale turquoise channel running away from the island to the mainland, deep blue water surrounding it, and the high-rise hotels of Cancún in the distance. Looking N from the temple you see both coasts of the island stretching away from you.

The town is at the NW end of the island; at the end of the N-S streets is the northern beach (Playa Coco), the widest area of dazzling white sand on the island (watersports equipment is rented at very high prices). The island is best visited

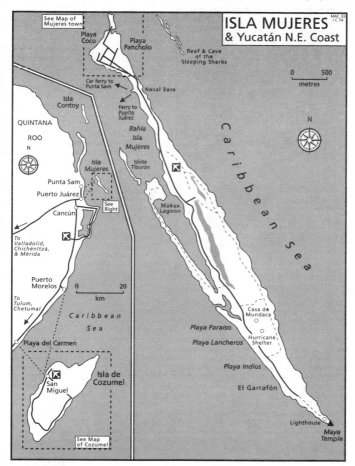

April to November, off-season (although one can holiday here the year round).
NB Bathing on the Caribbean side of the island can be unsafe because of strong
undertows and cross-currents.

Trip to **Isla Contoy** (bird and wildlife sanctuary), while suspended from
Cancún, are still possible form Isla Mujeres, US$40, 9 hrs, with excellent lunch,
two hours of fishing, snorkelling (equipment hire extra, US$2.50) and relaxing.
Boats from the cooperative at the town pier may not leave until full. From the
same point boat trips go to the lighthouse at the entrance to the harbour, Isla
Tiburón, El Garrafón and Playa Lancheros for lunch, 3-4 hrs, US$16.65 pp. You
will be approached by boatmen on the boat from Puerto Juárez, and on arrival.

There is public transport on Isla Mujeres, ie taxis at fixed prices, and the bus service mentioned
above. You can walk from one end of the island to the other in 2½ hrs. At the top of the rise

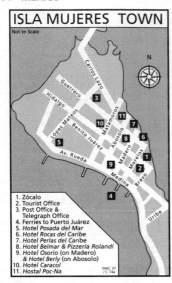

ISLA MUJERES TOWN

Not to Scale

1. Zócalo
2. Tourist Office
3. Post Office &
   Telegraph Office
4. Ferries to Puerto Juárez
5. Hotel Posada del Mar
6. Hotel Rocas del Caribe
7. Hotel Perlas del Caribe
8. Hotel Belmar & Pizzería Rolandi
9. Hotel Osorio (on Madero)
   & Hotel Berly (on Abosolo)
10. Hotel Caracol
11. Hostal Poc-Na

MAC 37
/ C 74a

before El Garrafón, by the speed humps and the houses for rent, is a point where you can see both sides of the island. A track leads from the road to the Caribbean coast, a couple of minutes stroll. You can then walk down the east coast to the southern tip. Worth hiring a bicycle, US$5 a day (about US$7 deposit eg *Sport Bike*, Av Juárez y Morelos), or a moped (US$5/hr, US$20-25 all day, US$35-40/24 hrs, credit card, passport or money deposit, helmet not required), to explore the island in about 2 hrs. Do check if there is any damage to the bicycle *before* you hire. Bicycles for hire from several hotels. Try Ciro's Motorrentor by *Hotel Caribe* for good motorbikes. You can rent skin and scuba diving equipment, together with guide, on the waterfront N of the public pier, a boat and equipment costs about US$50 pp for ½ day, check how many tanks of air are included and shop around. They can set up group excursions to the Cave of the Sleeping Sharks; English spoken. It is no cheaper to hire snorkel gear in town than on the beach. Deep sea fishing for 10 in a boat from *Aguamundo*. Diving is not in the class of Cozumel.

Hotels At Christmas hotel prices are increased steeply and the island can heave with tourists, esp in January. The island has several costly hotels and others, mainly in the D category, and food, especially fresh fruit, is generally expensive.

Reasonable hotels to stay at on Isla Mujeres are **A** *Posada del Mar*, Alte Rueda 15, T 20212, (including meals) has pleasant drinks terrace but expensive drinks, restaurant for residents only; **A** *Las Perlas del Caribe*, Caribbean side of town, clean, pool, rec; **A-B** *Belmar*, Av Hidalgo 110 entre Madero y Abasolo, T 70430, F 70429, a/c, TV, restaurant Pizza Rolandi downstairs; **A-B** *El Mesón del Bucanero*, Hidalgo 11, T 20210, F 20126, all rooms with fan; **C** *Berny*, Juárez y Abasolo, T 20025, with bath and fan, basic, swimming pool, long-distance calls possible, residents only, but does not even honour confirmed reservations if a deposit for one night's stay has not been made. **C** *El Paso*, Morelos 13, with bath, clean, facing the pier, 2nd floor; **C** *Isla Mujeres*, next to church, with bath, renovated, run by pleasant Englishman; **D** *María José*, Madero 25, T 20130, clean, fans, friendly, scooter hire; **C** *Rocas del Caribe*, Madero 2, 100m from ocean, cool rooms, big balcony, clean, good service; **C** *Vistalmar*, on promenade about 300m left from ferry dock (D for longer stays—negotiate), ask for rooms on top floor, bath, balcony, fan, insect screens, good value; **C** *Caracol*, Matamaros 5, T 70150, F 70547, cheaper with fan, hot water, terrace balcony, stoves for guests' use, bar, coffee shop, laundry, central, clean, good value; **D** *Caribe Maya*, Madero 9, central, modern, a/c, cheaper with fan, very clean and comfy; **C** *Carmelina*, Guerrero 4, T 70006, central with bath and a/c, clean, comfortable, safe, rec, rents bikes and snorkelling gear, advance payment for room required daily; **D** *Las Palmas*, central, Guerrero 20, 2 blocks from N beach, good, clean; **D** *Osorio*, Madero, 1 block from waterfront, clean, fan, with bath and hot water, rec, *La Reina* bakery nearby; **D** *Xul-Ha*, on Hidalgo towards N beach, with fan. **E** *Isleñas*, without bath, D with, very clean, helpful; **F** *Poc-Na Hostal*, price pp, is cheapest, dormitories, try for central section where there are fans, clean, everything works, no bedding, but linen is included in price, gringo hang-out, good and cheap café, video, take insect repellent (San Jorge laundry is just 1 block away, US$2 per kg). There is a trailer park on the island, with a restaurant. At Playa Indios is *Camping Los Indios* where you can put up your hammock. **NB** If you arrive late, book into any hotel the first night and set out to find what you want by 0700-0800, when the first ferries leave the next morning.

Restaurants Many beach restaurants close just before sunset. *El Limbo* at *Roca Mar Hotel* (Nicolás Bravo y Guerrero), excellent seafood, good view, reasonable prices; *Miriti*, opp ferry, quite good value; *Pizza Rolandi*, see above, good breakfast, popular. *Gomar*, Madero y

Hidalgo, expensive, possible to eat outside on verandah or in the colonial-style interior, popular; *Chen Huayo*, Hidalgo, excellent Mexican food, cheap; *Las Gemelas*, also on Hidalgo, US-owned, vegetarian options, good value; *Mano de Dios*, near the beach, probably cheapest on island, quite good. *Eric's*, very good inexpensive Mexican snacks; *Tropicana*, 1 block from pier, simple, popular, cheap; *Cielito Lindo*, waterfront, open air, good service; good fish restaurant 50 metres to left of jetty, US$3-4; *Peña*, overlooks beach, good pizzas, nice atmosphere; *La Langosta*, good Mexican dishes, lovely view; *Bucanero*, downtown, steak, seafood, prime rib, classy for Islas Mujeres. *Sergio's* on main square, expensive, very good, also *Robert's* on square, cheap and good; *Giltri*, in town, good value; *Café Cito* on B Juárez, 1 Block W of *Tequila*, best breakfast, good health food, rec. *Ciro's* lobster house, not too good but *Napolito's*, opp, is excellent. Small restaurants round market are good value. Daily fish barbecue at El Paraíso beach. At Garrafón Beach; *El Garrafón*, *El Garrafón de Castilla*, catering for tour boats from Cancún; between Playa Indios and El Garrafón, *María's Kankin Hotel and Restaurant*, French cuisine.

Shopping Opposite the restaurant *Gomar* are several souvenir shops, selling good stone Maya carvings (copies), macramé hangings and colourful wax crayon 'Maya' prints. *El Paso Boutique*, opp ferry, trades a small selection of English novels.

Disco-bars *Tequila*, on Hidalgo, video bar and restaurant. *Bad Bones* has live rock-and-roll.

Services Exchange Banco del Atlántico, Av Juárez 5, 1% commission. **Telephones** Ladatel cards are sold at *Artesanía Yamily*, Hidalgo, just N of the square. **Tourist Information** Tourist office on square, opposite the basketball pitch.

Puerto Morelos, not far S of Cancún (bus US$1), has 3 hotels, two expensive, one basic, *Amor*, E, near bus stop; also free camping. Popular with scuba divers and snorkellers, but beware of sharks.

Playa del Carmen is a fast growing beach centre, with many new hotels and restaurants. In Maya times it was a departure point for boats to Cozumel; modern services have resumed with the development of Playa del Carmen as a resort. This has only happened more-or-less concurrently with the expansion of Cancún. 'Playa", as it is usually known, has several kilometres of white sand beaches, which are relatively clean; those to the N of town are the most pleasant (there are sandflies, though). Avenida Juárez runs from Highway 307 to the park which fronts the sea. One block S of the park is the ferry terminal. All along Avenida 5, the street which parallels the beach, are restaurants and shops, with hotels on the streets running back from the beach. Playa is conveniently placed between Cancún and Tulum, giving easy access to these and other tourist sites on the coast and inland.

Hotels Hotels fill up early; cheaper rooms are hard to find in January. Outside town are: at Km 297/8, N of Playa del Carmen, **A+** *Cabañas Capitán Lafitte*, very good, pool, excellent cheap restaurant on barren beach; under same ownership is **A+** *Shangri-Lá Caribe*, T 22888, 7 km S, closer to town (at N end of the bay N of Playa), cabins, equally good, excellent beach with diving (Cyan-Ha, PADI) and snorkelling, sailing, easy birdwatching beside hotel; beside *Shangri-Lá* is **L** *Las Palapas*, breakfast and dinner included, cabins with hammocks outside, good, T 22977, F 41668 (F Mexico City 379-8641); at Km 296, **A+** *El Marlín Azul*, swimming pool, good food.

Most luxurious is *Continental Plaza Playacar*, T 30100, F 30105, a huge new development just S of the ferry terminal; in the same development as this 5-star hotel is the 5-star *Diamond Resort*, Apdo Postal 149, T 30340, F 30348 and the 4-star *Caribbean Villages*, T 30434, F 30437, both all-inclusive club operations, the latter in the middle of the golf course; there are also villas for rent from US$65 to US$280, PO Box 139, Playa del Carmen, T/F 30148. At the N end of town, on a popular stretch of beach between Calles 12 and 14, is **A+-B** *Blue Parrot*, T 30083, F 44564 (reservations in USA 904- 775 6660, toll free 800-634 3547), price depends on type of room and facilities, has bungalows, with excellent bar (Happy Hour 2200) and café, volley ball court, deep sea fishing expeditions, highly rec; **A+** *Molcas*, T 30070, nr ferry pier, pool, luxurious, although restaurant is poor; **A** *Hotel Maranatha*, Av Juárez between Avs 30 and 35, T 30143, F 30038 (Us Res T 1-800-3298388), luxury with all facilities; **B** *Rosa Mirador*, behind the *Blue Parrot*, **A** in high season, hot showers, fan, best views from 3rd floor, owner Alberto speaks English, rec; **B** *Azul Profundo*, next to *Blue Parrot*, with bath and balcony; **B** *Costa del Mar*, T 30058, on little road between Calles 10 and 12, restaurant and bar, pool; **B-F** *Cabañas Alejari*, Calle 6 going down to beach, T 30374, very nice, shop has long distance phones; next to *Alejari* on the beach is **C** *Albatros* and,

PLAYA DEL CARMEN

MAC 33a

To
Cancún

To
Tulum

Highway 307

Avenida 40
Avenida 35
Avenida 30
Avenida 25
Avenida 20
Avenida 15
Avenida 10
Avenida 5

Calle 14
Calle 12
Calle 10
Calle 8
Calle 6
Calle 4
Calle 2

Avenida Juárez

Calle 1

Parke

To
Las Palapas
& Shangri-Lé
(along beach)

N

Restaurants:
25. *Máscaras*
26. *Da Gabi*
27. *El Pescador*
28. *Pez Vela*
29. *Karen's*
30. *Chicago*
31. *Bip Bip & La Opción*
32. *El Capitán*

B1. Playa Express buses
B2. Caribe buses
B3. Expreso Oriente buses

1. Tourist Kiosk
2. Bank
3. Post Office
4. Telephone Office
5. Ferry terminal
   for Cozumel
6. Taxis
HOTELS:
7. *Continental Plaza
   Playacar*
8. *Blue Parrot*
9. *Las Molcas*
10. *Costa del Mar*
11. *Cabiñas Alejari
    & Phones*
12. *Yax-Ha*
13. *Cabañas Banana*
14. *Cabañas Tuxatah*
15. *Nuevo Amanecer*
16. *Maya Bric &
    Tank-Ha diving*
17. *Sian Ka'an*
18. *Playa del Carmen*
19. *Posada Lily*
20. *Cabañas Tucán*
21. *Mi Casa*
22. *Villa Deportiva Juvenil*
23. *Las Brisas*
24. *La Ruina*
25. *Plaza Marina Playacar*
26. *Mom's Hotel &
    Restaurant*

more expensive, **A** *Albatros Royale*, T 30001, clean, very good, no pool. **B** *Mom's*, Av 30 y Calle 4, T 30315, about 5 blocks from bus station or beach, clean, comfortable, small pool, good restaurant with US home cooking and plenty of vegetables, good value. **A-C** *Yax-Ha* cabins, on the beach, via Av 5 by Calle 10, (price depending on size and season), excellent. **B-C** *Cabañas Banana*, Av 5 entre Calles 6 y 8, T 30036, cabins and rooms, kitchenettes; **B-C** *Casa de Gopala*, Calle 2 Norte and Av 10 Norte (PO Box 154), T/F 30054, with bath and fan, quiet and central, pool, American/Mexican owned, large rooms, quiet and comfortable, rec; **C** *Cabañas Tuxatah*, 2 minutes from sea, 2 blocks S from Av Juárez (Apdo 45, T 30025), German owner, Maria Weltin speaks English and French, with bath, clean, comfortable, hot water, laundry service, beautiful gardens, rec, breakfast US$4. **C** *Delfín*, Av 5 y Calle 6, T 30176, with bath; **C** *Nuevo Amanecer*, Calle 4 W of Av 5, very attractive, fans, hot water, hammocks, mosquito nets, clean, laundry area, pool room, helpful, rec; **C** *Maya Bric*, Av 5, between Calles 8 and 10, T 30011, hot water, clean, friendly, pool, Tank-Ha dive shop (see below). **C** *Sian Ka'an*, Av 5 y Calle 2, T 30203, 100m from bus station, modern rooms with balcony, clean, rec. Others in the **C** range include *El Elefante*, Av 10 y Calle 10, T 30037, with bath, modern but basic, unwelcoming, and *Playa del Carmen*, Av Juárez, between Avs 10 y 15, T 30293, opp bank, not rec. **D** *Posada Fernández*, Av 5 opp Calle 1, with bath hot water and fan, friendly, rec; **D** *Posada Lily*, with shower, fan, safe, clean, rec, but noisy in am and cell-like rooms, Av Juárez at Caribe bus stop; under same ownership *Dos Hermanos*, three blocks W and two blocks N of *Posada Lily*, clean, hot showers, fan, quiet. **D** *Cabañas Tucan*, Av 5 beyond Calle 14, new, clean, good, mosquito net, highly rec (there is also *Casa Tucan* on Calle 4); **E-F** *Cabañas La Ruina*, at the beach end of Calle 2, popular, noisy, clean, well-organized, rec, lots of options and prices, from 2- to 3-bedded cabins, hammock space under *palapa*, with or without security locker, hammock in open air, camping, space for vehicles and camper vans, linen rental, bath extra, cooking facilities; **F** *Mi Casa* (unmarked), Av 5 opp *Maya Bric*, price per person, with bath and fan, cold water, clean, friendly manager speaks English, mosquito coils necessary. Lots of new places going up, none under US$10 a night. Youth Hostel *Villa Deportiva Juvenil*, from US$5 in dormitory to US$20 for up to 4 in cabin with fan and private shower, comfortable, with basketball court and good café, rec, but difficult to find, especially after dark, but it is signposted—it's 5 blocks up from Av 5, on Calle 8 (T 525-2548).

Camping See above under *La Ruina*; also *Camping Las Brisas* at the beach end of Calle 4.

Restaurants *Belvedere*, on square between ferry and bus station, good pasta. *Máscaras*, on square, highly rec; also on the square, *El Tacolote*, tacos, etc, and *Las Piñatas*. *Da Gabi*, just up Calle 12 from *Blue Parrot*, good pastas, Mexican dishes, breakfast buffet, also has rooms in C range. Next to *Cabañas Yax-Ha* is *El Pescador*, fish, has a variety of beers. On or near Av 5: *Pez Vela*, Av 5 y Calle 2, good atmosphere, food, drinks and music (closed 1500-1700); *Nuestra Señora del Carmen*, Av 5 y Calle 2, family-run, cheap, generous portions, rec; *Playa Caribe*, 1 block up Av 5 from plaza, fish and seafood specialities, good breafast, nice atmosphere, cheap, and popular with budget minded travellers; *Karen's Pizza*, Av 5 entre Calles 2 y 4, pizzas, Mexican dishes, cable TV, popular; *El Capitán*, Calle 4 just off Av 5, good meals and music, popular; next door is *Sabor* for sandwiches, juices, breakfast. In Plaza Plaza on Av 5 entre Calles 4 y 6, *Restaurante y Tropical Bar*, good service. *Limones*, Av 5 y Calle 6, good food, popular, reasonable prices; opposite is *Chicago*, steakhouse, American-owned, also serves seafood and breakfast (US$2.50 on terrace with seaview), good, CNN TV; across Calle 6, still on Av 5 is *Flippers*, good atmosphere, good food especially fish, moderately priced. *Bip Bip*, Av 5 between Calles 4 and 6, best pizza in town; *La Hueva del Coronado*, same block, seafood and local dishes, reasonable; *La Deseada House of Deserts* (sic) and *Calypso House* also in same block. *La Lunada*, Av 5 entre Calles 6 y 8. *El Correo*, just beyond *Posada Fernández*, Mexican, cheap, rec. *Panadería del Caribe*, Av 5 entre Calles 4 y 2, for breads and cakes; *Zermat Bakery* at extreme end of pedestrian Calle Norte, 5 blocks from bus station, rec for pastries. Various places serve breakfast close to Post Office. Many places have 'happy hour", times vary, shop around.

Entertainment *La Opción*, Av 5 beside *Bip Bip*, upstairs, shows video films, usually 2 a night. *Ziggy's Bar and Disco* on the square, very busy Fri/Sat night, expensive drinks; live music in a number of places at night, look for notices. *Pez Vela* has live music at about 2000 followed by Happy Hour.

Diving Tank-Ha Dive Center, at *Maya Bric Hotel*, resort course US$60 (diving lesson in the hotel pool before first dive), 1-tank dive US$35, 2-tank US$50, packages from US$90-395, PDIC certification course US$350. Dive shop at *Yax-Ha Cabañas*. Also El Oasis Dive Shop, Calle 4 between Avs 5 and 10; Albatros Water Sports; Costa del Mar Dive Shop, beside *Blue Parrot*; and others.

Car Hire Continental Car Rental, Av Juárez; car and motorcycle hire on Av Juárez, opposite bus office, beside Caribe Express. **Playa**, at Plaza Marina Playacar; **National** at *Hotel Molcas*.

Bank Banco del Atlántico on Av Juárez y Av 10, two blocks up from plaza; **Bancomer**, Av Juárez, 5 blocks W of Av 5, *casa de cambio* on Av 5 opp tourist information booth, reasonable rates for US$ cash, no commission.

Post Office Av Juárez y Av 15, open 0800-1700 Mon-Fri, 0900-1300 Sun and holidays. **Telephones** Computel next to bus station on Av Juárez. Long distance phones at shop at *Cabañas Alejari*. International fax service at Turquoise Reef Realty, in same block as *Hotel Playa del Carmen*, cost of phone call plus US$3.65 for first sheet, US$1.65 for second.

Launderette Av Juárez, 2 blocks from bus station; another on Av 5.

Tourist Information Tourist kiosk on square, with information and leaflets, books guided tours to Tulum and Cobá, US$30 including transport, entry to site, and English-speaking guide,

Mon and Fri, 0930. *Destination Playa del Carmen* bulletin gives details of many of the services in town, plus map.

Transport Ferry for **Cozumel**, two companies, *Mexico I* and *Mexico II* waterjets, US$8.35 one way, minimum 30 mins journey, and Caribe Tours, which has 2 classes of boat, US$8.35 5 times a day, and US$5 3 times (40 mins). Each company has 8-9 a day from 0530-2045, returning 0400-2000 (schedules change frequently).

Buses: to/from **Cancún**, 1 hr 15 mins, Playa Express (Av Juárez, between Avs 5 y 10) goes every 30 mins, US$2.25; also Caribe (Av Juárez, by *Posada Lily*) to Cancún luxury bus at 1215, 1st class 3 times a day. To Cancún international airport, take a 2nd class bus to the crossroads (US$2.50) and walk, or take a taxi (US$1.65) the 4 km to the terminal. Caribe luxury buses to **Mérida**, US$25.30, **Campeche** US$42, and **Chetumal** US$16.50, also 1st and 2nd class (US$10) to Chetumal, Felipe Carrillo Puerto; 2nd class calls at **Tulum**, US$2.20. Expreso Oriente (Av Juárez y Av 5) has luxury, 1st and 2nd class buses to Mérida via Cancún, many a day, US$17.50, US$14.30 and US$12 respectively; also to **Valladolid** 1st class US$8.50, US$6 2nd; Tizimín, US$9, and 2nd class Tulum (US$1.80), **Cobá** (US$3.30), Valladolid (US$8.50) at 0500, 1000 and 1700. In all, several buses a day to Tulum between 0530 and 1845, 1 hr.

Tours to Tulum and Xel-Há from kiosk by boat dock US$30; taxi tours to Tulum, Xel-Há and Xcaret, 5-6 hrs, US$60; taxi to Xcaret US$6.65. Taxis congregate on the Av Juárez side of the square (Sindicato Lázaro Cárdenas del Río, T 30032/30414).

Cozumel island is not only a marvellous place for snorkelling and scuba diving, but is described as a 'jewel of nature, possessing much endemic wildlife including pygmy species of coati and raccoon; the bird life has a distinctly Caribbean aspect and many endemic forms also"—Jeffrey L White, Tucson, Arizona. A brief visit does afford much opportunity to see the flora and fauna on land; the forested centre of the island is not easy to visit, except at the Maya ruins of San Gervasio (see below), and there are few vantage points. On the other hand, the island has a great deal to offer the tourist. The name derives from the Maya 'Cuzamil", land of swallows.

Maya pilgrims hoped to visit once in their lifetime the shrine to Ix-Chel (goddess of the moon, pregnancy, childbirth, all things feminine, but also floods, tides and destructive waters), which was located on the island. By the 14th century AD, Cozumel had also become an important trading centre. The Spaniards first set foot on the island on 1 May 1518 when Juan de Grijalva arrived with a fleet from Cuba. Spanish dominance came in 1520. By the 18th century, the island was deserted. In all, there are some 32 archaeological sites on Cozumel, those on the east coast mostly single buildings (lookouts, navigational aids?). The easiest to see are the restored ruins of the Maya-Toltec period at **San Gervasio** in the N (7 km from Cozumel town, then 6 km to the left up a paved road, toll US$1). Entry to the site is US$4.35; guides are on hand, or you can buy a self-guiding booklet at the *librería* on the square in San Miguel, or at the *Flea Market*, for US$1. It is an interesting site, quite spread out, with *sacbes* (Maya roads) between the groups of buildings. There are no large structures, but a nice plaza, an arch, and pigment can be seen in places. It is also a pleasant place to listen to birdsong, see butterflies, animals (if lucky), lizards and landcrabs (and insects). Castillo Real is one of many sites on the northeastern coast, but the road to this part of the island is in very bad condition. *El Cedral* in the SW (3 km from the main island road) is a two-room temple, overgrown with trees, in the centre of the village of the same name. Behind it is a ruin, and next to it a modern church with a green and white façade (an incongruous pairing). In the village are large, permanent shelters for agricultural shows, rug sellers, and locals who pose with *iguanas doradas*. El Caracol, where the sun, in the form of a shell, was worshipped is 1 km from the southernmost Punta Celarain. At Punta Celarain is an old lighthouse.

The main town is *San Miguel de Cozumel*, on the sheltered west coast. Here the ferries from the mainland and the cruise ships dock. The waterfront, Av Rafael Melgar, and a couple of streets behind it are dedicated to the shoppers and restaurant-goers, but away from this area the atmosphere is quite Mexican. Fishermen sell their catch by the passenger ferry pier, which is in the centre of

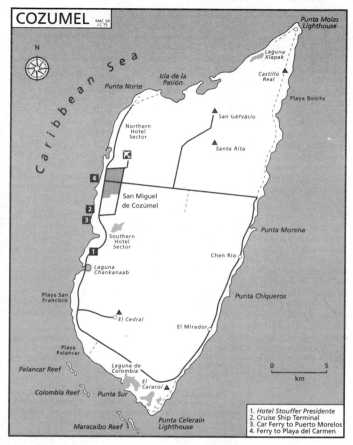

COZUMEL MAC 34 /C 75

Punta Molas Lighthouse

Caribbean Sea

N

Laguna Xlapak

Isla de la Pasión

Castillo Real

Punta Norte

Playa Bonita

▲ *San Gervasio*

Northern Hotel Sector

▲ *Santa Rita*

✈

4

2

3

San Miguel de Cozumel

Punta Morena

1

Chen Río

Southern Hotel Sector

Laguna Chankanaab

Playa San Francisco

Punta Chiqueros

▲ *El Cedral*

El Mirador

Playa Palancar

Palancar Reef

Laguna de Colombia

0   5
km

Colombia Reef

El Caracol ▲

Punta Sur

Maracaibo Reef

Punta Celerain Lighthouse

1. *Hotel Stouffer Presidente*
2. *Cruise Ship Terminal*
3. *Car Ferry to Puerto Morelos*
4. *Ferry to Playa del Carmen*

town. It is a friendly town, with a good range of hotels (both in town and in zones to the N and S) and eating places. The best public beaches are some way from San Miguel town: in the N of the island they are sandy and wide, although those at the Zona Hotel Norte were damaged in 1989 and are smaller than they used to be. (At the end of the paved road, walk up the unmade road until it becomes 'dual carriageway"; turn left for the narrow beach, which is a bit dirty. Cleaner beaches are accessible only through the hotels.) S of San Miguel, San Francisco is good if narrow (clean, very popular, lockers at *Pancho's*, expensive restaurants), but others are generally narrower still and rockier. All the main hotels are on the sheltered west coast. The E, Caribbean coast is rockier, but very picturesque; swimming and diving on the unprotected side is very dangerous owing to ocean underflows. The only safe place is at a sheltered bay at Chen Río.

A circuit of the island on paved roads can easily be done in a day (see **Local Transport** below). Head due E out of San Miguel (take the continuation of Av Benito Juárez). Make the detour to San Gervasio before continuing to the

Caribbean coast at *Mescalito's* restaurant. Here, turn left for the northern tip (road unsuitable for ordinary vehicles), or right for the S, passing Punta Moreno, Chen Río, Punta Chiqueros (restaurant, bathing), El Mirador (a low viewpoint with sea-worn rocks, look out for holes) and Paradise Cove. At this point, the paved road heads W while an unpaved road continues S to Punta Celarain. On the road W, opposite the turnoff to El Cedral, is a sign to *Restaurante Mac y Cía*, an excellent fish restaurant on a lovely beach, popular with dive groups for lunch. Next is Playa San Francisco (see above). A few more km lead to the former *Holiday Inn*, the last big hotel S of San Miguel. Just after this is Parque Chankanab, which used to be an idyllic lagoon behind the beach (9 km from San Miguel). After it became totally spoilt, it was restored as a National Park, with the lagoon, crystal clear again, a botanical garden with local and imported plants, a 'Maya Area' (rather artificial), swimming (ideal for families with young children), snorkelling, dive shops, souvenirs, expensive but good restaurants and lockers (US$2). Entry costs US$4, snorkelling mask and fins US$5, use of underwater camera US$25, open 0800-1600. Soon the road enters the southern hotel zone at the *Stouffer Presidente*, coming to the cruise ship dock and car ferry port on the outskirts of town.

Diving The island is famous for the beauty of its underwater environment. The best reef for scuba-diving is Palancar, reached only by boat. Also highly recommended are Santa Rosa and Colombia. There are at least 20 major dive sites. There are also over 20 dive operators. PADI, NAUI or SSI certification are all available; most trips are two-tank dives, but one-tank and nighttime dives are easily arranged. The better establishments have more dive masters accompanying reef trips. There are two hyperbaric chambers on the island. A resort course costs on average US$60, a 3-4 certification course US$350, including equipment. Lots of packages are available. The following operators have been recommended: *Chino's Scuba Shop*, T/F 24487, ask for Ruben Maldonado; *Caribbean Diver's*, T 21080, F 21426; there are many others, shop around.

Hotels (Prices rise 50% around Christmas.) **L+-L** *Meliá Mayan Cozumel*, in northern hotel zone, 5 km from airport, T 20072, F 21599; *El Cozumeleño*, also in N zone, T 20149, F 20381, good, but like all hotels in this area, a bit inconvenient. S of San Miguel are *Stouffer Presidente*, T 20322, F 21360, first class, but some distance from town; *Fiesta Americana*, T 22900, F 21301, linked to beach by tunnel; *La Ceiba*, T 20844, F 20065, and others (all in the **L-A+** range).

Hotels in San Miguel town: **A** *Bahía*, Av Rafael Melgar y Calle 3 Sur (above *Kentucky Fried Chicken*), a/c, phone, cable TV, fridge, even-numbered rooms have balcony, T 20209, F 21387, rec; **A** *Barracuda*, Av Rafael Melgar 628, T 20002, F 20884, popular with divers; **A** *Mesón San Miguel*, on the plaza, T 20233, F 21820; **A** *Plaza Cozumel*, Calle 2 Norte 3, T 22711, F 20066, a/c, TV, phone, pool, restaurant, car hire, laundry; **B** range hotels include *Maya Cozumel*, Calle 5 Sur 4, T 20011, F 20781, a/c, pool; *Safari*, T 20101, F 20661, a/c; *Soberanis*, Av Rafael Melgar 471, T 20246, a/c, restaurant terrace bar; and *Vista del Mar*, Av R Melgar 45, T 20545, pool, a/c, restaurant, parking. **C** *Al Marestal*, Calle 10 y 25 Av Norte, T 20822, spacious, clean rooms, fan or a/c, cool showers, swimming pool, very good; **C** *Elizabeth*, Adolfo Rosado Salas 44, T 20330, a/c, suites with fridge and stove, also has villas at Calle 3 Sur con Av 25 Sur; 2 doors away is **C** *Flores*, a/c, D with fan; **C** *Flamingo*, Calle 6 Norte 81, T 21264, showers, fan, clean, good value; **C** *López*, on plaza, Calle Sur 7-A, T 20108, hot showers, clean, main square, no meals; **C** *Marqués*, 5 Av Sur between 1 Sur and A R Salas, T 20677, a/c, cheaper with fan, rec; close by are *Mary Carmen* and *El Pirata*, both C but cheaper with fan; **C** *Pepita's*, 15 Av Sur 120, T 20098, a/c, fan, fridge, owner, Eduardo Ruiz, speaks English, Spanish, French, Italian, German and Mayan, highly rec as best value on island; *Posada Cozumel*, Calle 4 Norte 3, T 20314, pool, showers, a/c, cheaper with fan, clean; **D** *Blanquita*, 10 Norte, T 21190, comfortable, clean, friendly, owner speaks English, rents snorkelling gear and motor-scooters, showers; *José de León*, Av Pedro J Coldwell y 17 Calle Sur, fairly clean, showers; *Posada del Charro*, one block E of *José de León*, same owner, same facilities; *Kary*, 25 Av Sur y A R Salas, T 22011, a/c, showers, pool, clean; *Paraíso Caribe*, 15 Av Norte y 10 Calle, fan, showers, clean; **D** *Saolima*, A R Salas 260, T 20886, clean, fan, showers, cold water, rec; **D** *Posada Letty*, Calle 1 Sur y Av 15 Sur, clean, hot water, good value.

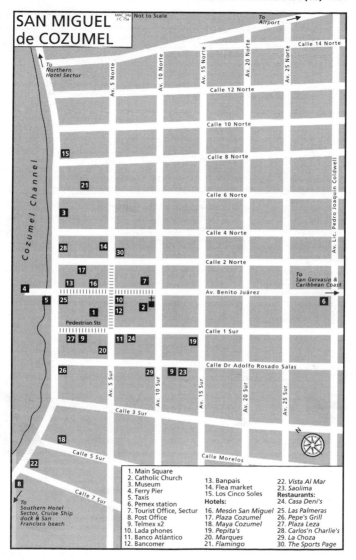

SAN MIGUEL de COZUMEL

MAC 34a / C 75a Not to Scale

To Airport

Calle 14 Norte

Calle 12 Norte

Calle 10 Norte

Calle 8 Norte

Calle 6 Norte

Calle 4 Norte

Calle 2 Norte

Av. Benito Juárez

Calle 1 Sur

Calle Dr Adolfo Rosado Salas

Calle 3 Sur

Calle Morelos

Calle 5 Sur

Calle 7 Sur

To Northern Hotel Sector

Cozumel Channel

Av. 5 Norte

Av. 10 Norte

Av. 15 Norte

Av. 20 Norte

Av. 25 Norte

Av. Lic. Pedro Joaquín Coldwell

To San Gervasio & Caribbean Coast

Pedestrian Sts

Av. 5 Sur

Av. 10 Sur

Av. 15 Sur

Av. 20 Sur

Av. 25 Sur

N

To Southern Hotel Sector, Cruise Ship dock & San Francisco beach

1. Main Square
2. Catholic Church
3. Museum
4. Ferry Pier
5. Taxis
6. Pemex station
7. Tourist Office, Sectur
8. Post Office
9. Telmex x2
10. Lada phones
11. Banco Atlántico
12. Bancomer

13. Banpais
14. Flea market
15. Los Cinco Soles
Hotels:
16. *Mesón San Miguel*
17. *Plaza Cozumel*
18. *Maya Cozumel*
19. *Pepita's*
20. *Marques*
21. *Flamingo*

22. *Vista Al Mar*
23. *Saolima*
Restaurants:
24. *Casa Deni's*
25. *Las Palmeras*
26. *Pepe's Grill*
27. *Plaza Leza*
28. *Carlos'n Charlie's*
29. *La Choza*
30. *The Sports Page*

Camping is not permitted although there are two suitable sites on the S shore. Try asking for permission at the army base.

Restaurants In general, it is much cheaper to eat in town than at the resort hotels to the N or S. Very few hotels in town have restaurants since there are so many other places to eat.

Las Palmeras, at the pier (people-watching spot), rec, very popular for breakfast, opens 0700, always busy; *Morgans*, main square, elegant, expensive, good; *Plaza Leza*, main square, excellent and reasonable; *La Choza*, A R Salas 198, reasonable, Mexico City food, rec; *Karen's Pizza and Grill*, Av 5 Norte between Av B Juárez and Calle 2 Norte, pizza cheap, good; *Gatto Pardo*, 10 Av Sur 121, good pizzas and try their 'tequila slammers"; *Café del Puerto*, 2nd floor by market, South Seas style; *El Moro*, 75 Bis Norte 124, between 4 y 2, good, closed Thur; *Santiago's Grill*, 15 Av Sur y A R Salas, excellent, medium price-range, popular with divers; also popular with divers is *Las Tortugas*, 10 Av Norte, just N of square, good in the evening; *El Capi Navegante*, 2 locations: by market for lunch, and C 3 y 10 Av Sur, more up market, seafood at each; *La Yucatequita*, 9 C Sur y 10 Av Sur, genuine Mayan food, closes at 2130, best to go day before and discuss menu; *La Misión*, Av Benito Juárez y 10 Av Norte, good food, friendly atmosphere; *Pepe's Grill*, waterfront, 2 blocks S of pier, expensive and excellent, service not always courteous; *Acuario*, on beach 6 blocks S of pier, famous for seafood, aquarium in restaurant (ask to see the tanks at the back). *Carlos and Charlie's* restaurant/bar, popular, 2nd floor on waterfront 2 blocks N of pier. *Pancho's Backyard*, Rafael Melgar 27, in *Los Cinco Soles* shopping complex, Mexican food and wine elegantly served, good food. *Mi Chabalita*, 10 Av Sur between Calle 1 Sur and Calle Salas, friendly, good Mexican food. *Casa Deni's*, Calle 1 Sur 164, close to Plaza, open air restaurant, vey good, moderate prices. *The Sports Page*, Calle 2 Norte y Av 5, US-style, breakfasts, burgers, steaks, lobster, satellite TV, money exchange, phones for USA; US-style breakfasts also at *Los Cocos*, next to ProDive on A R Salas.

Naked Turtle, on E side (has basic rooms to let); *Mescalito's*, see above, another place, like *The Sports Page*, to write a message on your T-shirt and leave it on the ceiling; several other bar restaurants on the E side.

Nightclubs *Joman's* (very seedy), *Scaramouche* (the best, Av R Melgar y Calle A R Salas), *Neptuno* (Av R Melgar y Calle 11, S of centre, these two are state-of-the-art discos), as well as hotel nightclubs.

Exchange 4 banks on the main square, all exchange money in am only, but not at same hours; **Bancomer** has ATM machines. *Casas de cambio* on Av 5 Norte (eg next to Banco Atlántida) and around square, 3.5% commission, open longer hours.

Local Transport The main road around Cozumel is paved, but public buses serve only the expensive hotels N of town. It is best to hire a bicycle (quiet) when touring around the island so one can see wildlife—iguanas, turtles, birds. Rental charges are US$5 for 12 hrs, US$8 for 24 hrs, eg from *Splash*, on Calle 6 Norte, T 20502, 0800-2000. **Vehicle rental** Many agencies for cars, jeeps and mopeds. Eg Avis, Budget, Hertz, National, and local companies. Car hire ranges from about US$55 a day for a VW Beetle to US$70 minimum for a jeep. Scooter rental is US$27 a day high season, US$22 low. One Pemex filling station, at Av Juárez y Av 30; beware overcharging. If taking a moped be aware of traffic laws, helmets must be worn, illegal parking is subject to fines, etc (single women should not ride alone on the eastern side of the island).

Taxis All carry an official price list. Downtown fare US$1.15; to N or S hotel zones US$2.35; San Francisco beach US$10; Maya ruins US$30; island tour including San Gervasio US$50.

Museum On waterfront between Calles 4 and 6, history of the island, well laid-out (entry US$3). Bookshop, art gallery, rooftop restaurant has excellent food and views of sunset, good for breakfast, too from 0700 ("The Quick' is excellent value). Recommended.

Film Two shops develop film, both quite expensive (about US$20 for 36 prints). Best to wait till you get home.

Laundry On A R Salas between Avs 5 and 10, coin op or service wash.

Post Office Av Rafael Melgar y Calle 7 Sur. **Telephones** Credit card LADA phones on main square at corner of Av Juárez y Av 5, or on A R Salas, just up from Av 5 Sur, opp *Roberto's Black Coral Studio* (if working). For calls to the USA go to *The Sports Page*. Telmex phone offices on the main square next to *Restaurant Plaza Leza*, open 0800-2300, and on A R Salas between Avs 10 and 15. There are also expensive Computel offices in town, eg at the cruise ship dock.

Tourist Information Sectur tourist office in Plaza Cozumel on Av Juárez, between 5 Av and 10 Av, 1st floor, English-speaking service in am, opens 1800 in pm. On arrival, cross the road from the pier to the square where lots of information kiosks give maps, tour information, etc. A good map (*The Brown Map*), including reef locations, is available from stores and shops. *The Blue Guide*, free, has maps and practical details, available everywhere. Booklets on archaeological sites and the region, and Mexico City newspapers are available at the *papelería* on the E side of the square.

Ferries See under Playa del Carmen for passenger ferries. Car ferry goes from Puerto Morelos twice a day: US$27 for a car, US$4 per passenger; the entrance to the car ferry on Cozumel is just past the cruise ship dock.

Air Services Cozumel-Mexico City direct with Mexicana; Mexicana also flies to Miami; Continental to Houston; Aero Caribe to Cancún, Mérida (as does Mexicana) and Playa del Carmen (several daily).

There are some Maya ruins on the mainland at *Xcaret*, a turnoff left on Route 307 to Tulum, after Playa del Carmen. This was once an undeveloped spot, with the unrestored ruins near three linked *cenotes* and sea water lagoons. The Maya site, called Pole, was the departure point for voyages to Cozumel. It has now been redesigned as a daytrip from Cancún. The ruins and lagoons form part of a clean, well-tended park, catering exclusively for day-trippers, which costs US$17 to enter. This entitles you to visit the small ruins, the beach, lagoon and inlet, to take an underground river trip (life vest included) and to use all chairs, hammocks and *palapas*. Everything else is extra: food and drink (none may be brought in), snorkel rental (US$7), snorkel lessons, reef trips (US$10), diving, horse riding (US$30) and lockers (for which you have to pay US$1 each time you lock the door). There are also dolphins in pens with which you may swim for US$50. No sun tan lotion may be worn in the sea, but there is a film of oils in the sea nonetheless. Buses from Playa del Carmen leave you at the turnoff (US$0.65), by a roadside restaurant which is very clean (accepts Visa). This is a 1 km walk from the entrance to Xcaret. The alternative is to take a taxi, or a tour from Playa del Carmen or Cancún (in a multicoloured bus). You can also walk along the beach from Playa del Carmen, 3 hrs.

Paamul, about 92 km S of Cancún, is a fine beach on a bay, planned for development, with chalets (C with bath, fan, terrace for hammocks, comfortable, pretty, clean, rec) and campsites (recommended). Snorkelling and diving. 2nd-class buses from Cancún and Playa del Carmen pass. *Playa Aventuras* is a huge beach resort 96 km from Cancún. Two ferries run daily to Cozumel.

Akumal, a luxury resort, is 20 km N of Tulum, and reached easily by bus from there or from Playa del Carmen (30 mins). Cove owned by Mexican Skin-Divers Society, 102 km S Cancún. **L Hotel Club Akumal Caribe**, restaurant (there is a small supermarket nearby at Villas Mayas), poor service, overpriced, no entertainment, excellent beach, linked to two buildings separated by *Villas Mayas*, with coral reef only 100m offshore. Eat at restaurant marked *Comidas Económicas* outside the gate. In addition at *Villas Mayas*, bungalows A+, with bath, comfortable, some with kitchens, on beach, snorkelling equipment for hire, US$6 per day, restaurant with poor service. Recommended as base for excursions to Xelhá, Tulum and Cobá. There is a small lagoon 3 km N of Akumal, good snorkelling. Not far from Akumal are **Chemuyil** (*palapas*—thatched shelters for hammocks—US$4, plus US$1 for shower, expensive restaurant, laundry facilities) and **Xcacel** beaches and campsites down new roads, with restaurants (very expensive at Xcacel, where the beach is oily). Campground has water, bathrooms, cold showers and restaurant, very clean, US$3.50 pp, vehicles free, beautiful swimming in the bay. Xcacel has a cenote, with excellent clear water and underwater rock formations (dive shop with gear for hire). Ask guards if you can go on turtle protection patrol at night (May-July).

N of Tulum, 122 km from Cancún (bus from Playa del Carmen, 45 mins) is a beautiful clear lagoon, **Laguna Xelhá**, full of fish, but no fishing allowed as it is a national park (open 0800-1630), entry US$5, get a receipt if you want to leave and come back next day. Snorkelling gear can be rented at US$7 for a day, but it is often in poor repair; better to rent from your hotel. Arrive as early as possible to see fish as later buses full of tourists arrive from Cancún, watch for sting-rays (you need to dive down about a metre because above that level the water is cold and fresh with few fish; below it is the warm, fish-filled salt water). Bungalows being built. Very expensive food. There is a marvellous jungle path to one of the lagoon bays. Xelhá ruins (known also as Los Basadres) are located across the road from the beach of the same name. Entry US$3.35, few tourists but not much to see. You may have to jump the fence to visit; there is a beautiful cenote at the end of the ruins where you can have a lovely swim. Small ruins of **Ak** are near Xelhá. Closer to Tulum, at **Tancáh**, are newly-discovered bright post-classical Maya murals but they are sometimes closed to the public.

Tulum The Tulum ruins, Maya-Toltec, are 131 km S of Cancún, 1 km off the main road. They are 12th century, with city walls of white stone atop coastal cliffs. The temples were dedicated to the worship of the Falling God, or the Setting Sun, represented as a falling character over nearly all the west-facing doors (Cozumel was the home of the Rising Sun). The same idea is reflected in the buildings, which are wider at the top than at the bottom. The main structure is the Castillo, which commands a view of both the sea and the forested Quintana Roo lowlands stretching westwards. All the Castillo's openings face W, as do most, but not all, of the doorways at Tulum. Look for the alignment of the Falling God on the temple of that name (to the left of the Castillo) with the pillar and the back door in the House of the Chultún (the nearest building in the centre group to the entrance). The majority of the main structures are roped off so that you cannot climb the Castillo, nor get close to the surviving frescoes, especially on the Temple of the Frescoes. In 1993 the government began a major improvement and conservation programme to improve facilities at the site. The site is open 0700-1700, about 2 hrs needed to view at leisure (entry US$4.35, half-price for Mexican students if more than one in group, Sun free).

Tulum is these days crowded with tourists (even at 0800 on some days). The best time to visit is at sunset; fewer people and a good light for photographs. Take towel and swimsuit if you wish to scramble down from the ruins to one of the two beaches for a swim (the larger of the two is less easy to get to). The reef is from 600 to 1,000m from the shore, so if you wish to snorkel you must either be a strong swimmer, or take a boat trip.

Public buses drop passengers at El Crucero, a crossroads 1 km from Tulum Ruinas (an easy walk); at the crossroads are 2 hotels, a shop, on the opposite side of the road a naval base and airstrip, and a little way down Highway 307 a Pemex station. The village of Tulum is 4 km S of El Crucero. It is not very large and has a post office but no bank; travellers' cheques can be changed at the offices of the GOPI Construction Company, though not at a very good rate; there are shops and a hotel, **C** *Hotel Maya* (clean, noisy, friendly).

There is a large car-park at the entrance to the ruins (here you can leave luggage), which is ringed by small shops (selling dresses, souvenirs, etc), and two restaurants, the *México* (not rec) and the *Garibaldi* (with a store). There are three tourist information kiosks. Guide books can be bought in the shops; Panorama guide book is interesting, others available. The paved road continues through the parking lot, along the coast, to Bocapaila and the northern access to the Sian Ka'an Biosphere Reserve.

Accommodation When arriving by bus, alight at El Crucero for the ruins and accommodation, not at the town. At El Crucero: **B** *El Faisán y El Venado*, TV, a/c, restaurant serving pizzas, Mexican dishes and very expensive drinks; across the road is **E** *Hotel El Crucero de Tulum*, much more basic, but a/c, hot water, staff unhelpful, good restaurant with shop attached. Almost opp bus stop is *Ambrosio's* restaurant (24 hrs), good food and service; and *Chilam-Balam*, across the road, also serves good food.

It is possible to sleep outside the entrance, beneath the vendor's stalls, the guards will allow it until 0500, but beware rats and mosquitoes. A new hotel is under construction at the site.

On the road between the parking lot and Bocapaila (none served by public transport): *Cabañas El Mirador*, small, quiet, cabins from US$3.35 pp to US$10 (won't rent to singles), hammocks available (F), camping US$1.65 pp, sanitation very limited (one toilet for whole camp, manager has key, well for washing in), 5 mins walk from ruins; next is *Santa Fe*, about

1½ km from the ruins (a path leads along the beach and then through forest to the ruins, 20 mins), where basic *cabañas* are rented for US$7.50, hammocks or tents US$1.60 pp (free camping possible further up the beach), has a restaurant, good fish dinners, reggae music, English, French and Italian spoken, basic toilets, frequently rec; next, with good management, are **Cabañas Don Armando**, T 43856/44539/44437, *cabañas* from E s or d to C for up to 4, prices variable, the best, most (but not all) staff are friendly and helpful, mixed reports on atmosphere, good restaurant, bar with disco till 0200. **C-E *Los Gatos***, cabins on beach, clean, nice atmosphere, price depends on whether in room or hammock, torch/flashlight necessary; **E *Cabañas Mar Caraibe***, 15 mins from ruins, new. **C *Bungalows Paraíso***, 3 km from ruins, nice cabins with fan, hot shower, clean, electricity 1800-2200. **B *Sian Ka'an/Osho Oasis*** (owned by Samyasins), 5 km S from ruins, wooden huts, well-equipped, electricity, mosquito net, good showers, washing facilities, clean, expensive restaurant, but full board option for US$18, excellent food, nice, relaxed. *La Perla*, 5 km S of Tulum, *cabañas*, camping and restaurant, comfortable, good food, family atmosphere, near beach, rec (Monica Koestinger, Lista de Correos, Tulum, Quintana Roo); **C *Hotel Posada Tulum***, 8 km S of the ruins on the beach, has an expensive restaurant. *Anna y José* restaurant, rec, which also has *cabañas*, very hospitable. For places to stay in Sian Ka'an Biosphere Reserve, see below.

Diving Buzos Maya, near *Don Armando*, run by American, John, good value, rec for scuba, snorkelling and fishing. Many untrained snorkelling and diving outfits, take care.

Telephones Long-distance phones in ADO terminal in town.

Buses 2nd class buses on the Cancún-Playa del Carmen-Felipe Carrillo Puerto-Chetumal route stop at Tulum; also 3 Inter Playa buses a day from Cancún, US$4. To Felipe Carrillo Puerto, several between 0600-1200 and 1600-2200, 1 hr, US$2, continuing to **Chetumal**, 2nd class, US$7, 4 hrs. To **Cobá**: the Playa del Carmen-Tulum-Cobá-Valladolid bus passes El Crucero at 0545, 1045 and 1745 (in the other direction buses pass Tulum at 0715 and 1545, all times approximate, may leave 15 mins early). Fare Tulum-Cobá US$1.35, 45 mins. To **Mérida**, several daily, US$12. To Tizimín daily at 1400, via Cancún and Valladolid. Autobuses del Caribe offices are next door to *Hotel Maya*. Buy tickets here rather than wait for buses at the crossroads, but this still does not ensure getting a seat. It may be better to go to Playa del Carmen for more connections to nearby destinations. If travelling far, take a bus to Felipe Carrillo Puerto and transfer to ADO there.

Taxi Tulum town to ruins US$2; to the hotels beyond US$2.65.

The ***Sian Ka'an Biosphere Reserve***, covers 1.3 million acres of the Quintana Roo coast. About one third is covered in tropical forest, one third is savannas and mangrove and one third coastal and marine habitats, including 110 km of barrier reef. Mammals include jaguar, puma, ocelot and other cats, monkeys, tapir, peccaries, manatee and deer; turtles nest on the beaches; there are crocodiles and a wide variety of land and aquatic birds. For all information, go to the office of Los Amigos de Sian Ka'an, Plaza América, Av Cobá 5, 3rd floor, suites 48-50, Cancún (Apartado Postal 770, 77500 Cancún, T 84-95-83), open 0900-1500, 1800-2000, very helpful. Few locals have information or know how to get there. Do not try to get there independently without a car. Los Amigos run tours to the Reserve, US$115 for a full day, starting at 0700, everything included: in winter the tour goes through a canal, in summer it goes birdwatching, in both cases a visit to a Maya ruin, a cenote, snorkelling, all equipment, breakfast and evening meal are included. Two-day camping trips can be arranged. It is possible to drive into the Reserve from Tulum as far as Punta Allen (beyond that you need a launch). At Punta Allen is a small fishing village with houses for rent (cooking facilities), and a good, non-touristy restaurant, *La Cantina* (US$3-4 for fish, highly rec). From the S it is possible to drive to Punta Herrero (unmade road). No explanations are available for those going independently. Punta Herrero is 6 hrs from Chetumal, 10 from Cancún; *rancheros* are very hospitable, camping is possible but take all food and plenty of insect repellent. In the Reserve, 8 km S of Tulum, are the quiet, pleasant **A *Cabañas Los Arrecifes***, with smart chalets on the beach and others behind, cheaper, with good fish restaurant shaped like a ship (no electricity), limited menu. 100m away are **D *Cabañas de Tulum***, also with good restaurant, clean cabins with shower, electricity 1730-2100; interesting fish in the cenote opposite, take taxi there (US$5-6 from ruins car park), empty white beaches; *Pez*

Maya and *Boca Paila* are expensive fishing lodges; *Casa Blanca* is an exclusive hotel reached only by small plane; *Rancho Retiro*, camping US$2, food and beer served, very relaxed atmosphere.

The ruins of **Chumyaxche**, three pyramids (partly overgrown), are on the left-hand side of the road to Felipe Carrillo Puerto, 18 km S of Tulum (they are mosquito-infested). Entry US$4. Beyond the last pyramid is Laguna Azul, which is good for swimming and snorkelling in blue, clean water (you do not have to pay to visit the pool if you do not visit the pyramids).

The road linking Tulum with the large but little-excavated city of Cobá (see below) turns off the main Highway 307 just before Tulum Pueblo. This road joins the Valladolid-Cancún road at **Nuevo Xcan**, thus greatly shortening the distance between Chichén Itzá and Tulum. The Cobá-Valladolid bus passes Nuevo Xcan (no hotel but the owner of the shop where the road branches off to Cobá may offer you a room). There is an *aduana* post in Nuevo Xcan. If going from Valladolid or Cancún to Cobá, look for the *Villas Arqueológicas* sign at Nuevo Xcan. Note, many maps show a road from Cobá to Chemax, W of Xcan. This road does not exist; the only road from the N to Cobá is from Nuevo Xcan.

Between Nuevo Xcan and Cobá is the tiny village of **Punta Laguna**, which has a lake and forest, preserved through the efforts of ecotourists. Ask for Serapio to show you round; he does not speak English, and depends mainly on tourist for his income.

Cobá, an important Maya city in the 8th and 9th centuries AD, whose population is estimated to have been between 40,000 and 50,000, but which was abandoned for unknown reasons, is 47 km inland from Tulum. The present day village of Cobá lies on either side of Lago Cobá, surrounded by dense jungle. The entrance to the ruins is at the end of the lake between the two parts of the village. A second lake, Lago Macanxoc, is within the site. Both lakes and their surrounding forest can be seen from the summit of the Iglesia, the tallest structure in the Cobá group. There are three other groups of buildings to visit: the Macanxoc group, mainly stelae, about 1.5 km from the Cobá group; Las Pinturas, 1 km Neast of Macanxoc, a temple and the remains of other buildings which had columns in their construction; the Nohoch Mul group, at least another km from Las Pinturas. Nohoch Mul has the tallest pyramid in the northern Yucatán, a magnificent structure, from which the views of the jungle on all sides are superb. You will not find at Cobá the great array of buildings which can be seen at Chichén Itzá or Uxmal, nor the compactness of Tulum. Instead, the delight of the place is the architecture in the jungle, with birds, butterflies, spiders and lizards, and the many uncovered structures which hint at the vastness of the city in its heyday (the urban extension of Cobá is put at some 70 square km). An unusual feature is the network of ancient roads, known as *sacbes* (white roads), which connect the groups in the site and are known to have extended across the entire Maya Yucatán. Over 40 *sacbes* pass through Cobá, some local, some of great length, such as the 100 km road to Yaxuná in Yucatán state.

Cobá is becoming more popular as a destination for tourist buses, which come in at 1030; arrive before that to avoid the crowds and the heat (ie on the 0430 bus from Valladolid, if not staying in Cobá). Take insect repellent. The site is open 0800-1700, entry US$5, free on Sun. Guide books: Bloomgarten's *Tulum and Cobá*, and *Descriptive Guide book to Cobá* by Prof Gualberto Zapata Alonzo, which is a little unclear about dates and details, but is still useful and has maps. Free map from *Hotel Restaurant Bocadito*.

At the lake tucans may be seen very early; also look out for greenish-blue and brown mot-mots in the early morning. The guards at the site are very strict about opening and closing time so it is difficult to gain entry to see the dawn or sunset from a temple. Swim in the lake in the village.

Lodging and Transport: A+ *Villas Arqueológicas* (Club Méditerranée), about 2 km from site on lake shore, open to non members, excellent, clean and quiet, a/c, swimming pool, expensive food. Do not arrive without a reservation, especially at weekends; on the other hand, making a reservation by phone seems to be practically impossible. In the village, on the street leading to the main road, are **E** *Hotel Restaurant Bocadito*, clean, spartan rooms with fan and cold water in shower, poor security, good restaurant (which is popular with tour groups), helpful, books and handicrafts for sale, rec; next door is **E** *Isabel*, cabañas, basic, but very good value, restaurant quite good. There are plenty of restaurants in the village, on the road to *Villas Arqueológicas* and on the road to the ruins, also a grocery store by *El Bocadito* and souvenir shops.

The paved road into Cobá ends at Lago Cobá; to the left are the ruins, to the right *Villas Arqueológicas*. Buses into the village turn round at the road end. There are three a day to Valladolid, coming from Playa del Carmen and Tulum, passing through at 0630, 1130 and 1830, 2 hrs to Valladolid, US$2; two buses a day to Tulum and Playa at 0630 and 1500, US$1.35 to Tulum. If you miss the bus there is a taxi to be found at *El Bocadito*.

At **Felipe Carrillo Puerto**, the cult of the 'talking cross' was founded (**see p 285**). The Santuario de la Cruz Parlante is 5 blocks W of the Pemex station on Highway 307. The beautiful main square is dominated by the Catholic church, which is built on a Maya temple. The church is not fully enclosed, so mass can be heard from the plaza. Legend has it that the unfinished bell tower will only be completed when the descendants of those who heard the talking cross reassert control of the region. In the plaza is lots of playground equipment for children. (With thanks to Suzanne Elise Tourville, St Louis, Missouri.)

Hotels and restaurants *Hotel Carrillo Puerto* has been rec; **C** *El Faisán y El Venado*, 2 blocks NE of main square, mixed reports on cleanliness, but hot water and good value restaurant; **D** *Tulum*, with better restaurant; **E** *Chan Santa Cruz*, just off the plaza, good, very clean and friendly; **E** *Hotel Esquivel*, just off Plaza, fair, noisy; **E** *San Ignacio*, nr Pemex, good value, bath, towels, TV, secure car park; next door is restaurant *Danburger Maya*, good food, reasonable prices, helpful; *Restaurant Addy*, on main road, S of town, good, simple.

Transport Bus station is on Calle 69, opposite Pemex. Autotransportes del Caribe (Playa Express) to Cancún daily from 0600, 1st and 2nd class to Tulum, US$2, and Playa del Carmen en route. Bus Felipe Carrillo Puerto-Mérida, via Muná, US$10, 4½ hrs; to Valladolid, 2nd class, 2 hrs, US$3.75; to Chetumal, 1st class, 2 hrs, US$3.35.

Chetumal (pop 120,000), the capital of the state of Quintana Roo (state pop 1990 493,600), now being developed for tourism (albeit slowly), is a free port with clean wide streets, and a pleasant waterfront with walks, parks and trees. It is 240 km S of Tulum. The 'paseo' near the waterfront on Sunday night is worth seeing. The State Congress building has a mural showing the history of Quintana Roo. Good for foreign foodstuffs—cheaper at covered market in outskirts than in centre. A new commercial centre is being built at the site of the old bus station; a new cultural and historical museum opened on Av Héroes de Chapultepec in December 1993.

Hotels (Accommodation may be a problem during the holiday season.) A+ *Los Cocos*, Héroes de Chapultepec 138, T 20544, reductions for AAA members, a/c, pool, restaurant not too good; A+ *Continental Caribe* (Best Western), Av Héroes 171, T 21100, F 21676; A *El Marqués*, Av Lázaro Cárdenas 121, T 22998, 5 blocks from centre, fan, a/c, hot water, restaurant, rec; *Marlon*, Av Benito Juárez, new, no details as yet; C *Caribe Princess*, Av A Obregón 168, T 20520, a/c, TV, good, no restaurant, rec; C *Real Azteca*, Belice 186, T 20720, cheerful, friendly, but no hot shower (2nd floor rooms best, but still not good); D *Brasilia*, Aguilar 186, T 20964, clean, quiet, good value, rec; D *El Dorado*, Av 5 de Mayo 21, T 20316, hot water, a/c, overpriced (no restaurant); D *Jacaranda*, Av Obregon 201, T 21455, clean; D *Ucum*, Gandhi 4, T 20711 (no singles) with fan and bath, clean, pleasant, quiet, good value; D *Big Ben*, Héroes 48-A, T 20965, clean, pleasant and safe, cheaper rooms for 4, with bath; D *Luz María*, Carmen de Merino 204, T 20202, friendly but not very clean, owner speaks English; D *María Dolores*, Alvaro Obregón 206, T 20508, bath, hot water, fan, clean, rec, restaurant downstairs not too good; E *Motel Casablanca*, Alvaro Obregón 312, clean, quiet and friendly; D *Tulum*, Héroes 2, T 20518, above market, noise starts 0530, but clean, fan, friendly, large rooms. E-F *Boston*, Belice 290, between bus station and centre, a/c, not very good; F *Ejidal*, Av Independencia entre Obregón y P Blanco, bath, clean. Plenty more. **Youth Hostel**, F pp, No 66 Alvaro Obregón y General Anaya (one street), T 23465, CP 77050, hot

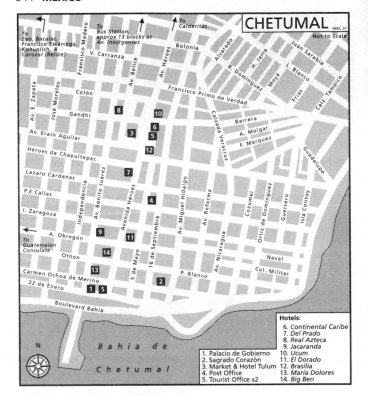

CHETUMAL MAC 31
Not to Scale

N

Bahia de Chetumal

Hotels:
6. *Continental Caribe*
7. *Del Prado*
8. *Real Azteca*
9. *Jacaranda*
10. *Ucum*
11. *El Dorado*
12. *Brasilia*
13. *María Dolores*
14. *Big Ben*

1. Palacio de Gobierno
2. Sagrado Corazón
3. Market & Hotel Tulum
4. Post Office
5. Tourist Office x2

water, clean, rec, camping US$2.

Camping *Sunrise of the Caribbean*, Trailer Park on the road to Calderitas, US$12 for car and 2 people, cold showers, electricity, laundry facilities, *palapas*, boat ramp.

Restaurants Next door to *Hotel Ucum*, reasonable, good value, rec. Cheap snacks at *Lonchería Ivette* on Mahatma Gandhi 154. *La Charca de las Ranas Verdes*, Boulevard Bahía, opp bandstand, cheap and good; *Pérez Quintas*, next door, good; *Sergio Pizza*, Obregón 182, good pizzas, good but expensive steak meals, a/c, good drinks too; *María's*, 5 de Mayo and Obregón, smart, large menu, not cheap; *La Cabaña Azul*, 5 de Mayo near waterfront, good and cheap; *Mar Caribe*, 22 de Enero entre F Madero y Independencia, snacks only. Several W of intersection of Héroes y Obregón, eg *Bienvenidos*, good. *Arcada*, Héroes y Zaragoza, open 24 hrs, with supermarket at the back. Another area with many restaurants is about 4 blocks N of market, then 3 blocks W, eg *Barracuda*, good seafood. *Pacho Tec*, small lunch room next to electricity plant, try the chicken broth. Delicious yoghurt ice in shop opp market; *Cafetería Don Artur*, Av Héroes 2, ground floor of *Hotel Tulum*, good value breakfasts. Try *Safari* roadhouse in Calderitas suburb for enterprising nightlife.

Shopping Shops are open from 0800-1300 and 1800-2000. *Super San Francisco* supermarket, nr bus station, is better than the one behind *Arcada* restaurant.

Local transport No city buses; taxis operate on fixed price routes, US$0.50 on average. Cars with light-green licence plates are a form of taxi.

Fuel *Magna Sin* (unleaded fuel) is sold at the petrol station just outside Chetumal on the road north at the beginning of the road to Escárcega. Fill up here as there is none until

Escárcega if heading W.

Garage Talleres Barrera, helpful, on Primo de Verdad; turn right off main street that passes market, then past the electrical plant.

Exchange For exchange, **Banamex**, Héroes y Carmen Ochoa de Merino, changes TCs; **Banco Mexicano**, Juárez and Cárdenas, TCs or US$ cash, quick and courteous service. Banks do not change quetzales into pesos. Good rates at *Bodegas Blanco* supermarket beside bus terminal; will change US dollars and Belize dollars (only if you spend at least 15% of the total on their groceries!). Batty Bus ticket counter will change pesos into Belizean dollars.

Consulates **Guatemala** Av Héroes de Chapultepec 354, T 26565, open for visas, Mon-Fri 0900-1700. Although there is a Guatemalan consul in Belize, **visas to Guatemala** may be more easily obtained in Chetumal, see Guatemala **Information for Visitors** for requirements and fees, usually takes 15 minutes, 30 days only available, passport photo and photocopy of passport required. **Belize** Hon Consul, Lic Francisco Lechón Rosas, Av Alvaro Obregón 232-1, T 24908; visas usually given in 10 mins (US$25). **NB** A list of nationalities who do *NOT* need a visa for Belize is given in the Belize **Information for Visitors** section. All others **must** have a visa in advance. The surest place to get one is in Mexico City at the Belize Embassy, or in Mérida.

Health Malaria prophylaxis available from Centro de Salud, opposite hospital (request tablets for 'paludismo').

Laundry *Lavandería Automática* 'Lava facil', corner of Héroes and Confederación Nacional Campesina.

Tourist Information Office on Boulevard Bahía and 5 de Mayo, useful city booklet and map of Quintana Roo; also a kiosk in the small plaza on Héroes and Aguilar. Turismo Maya at *Hotel Continental Caribe* will arrange flights in Belize, T 2-05-55.

Airport with flights to Cancún (Taesa), Mexico City (Aviacsa, T 27765) and Belize City (Bonanza).

Buses The main bus station is 2-3 km out of town at the intersection of Insurgentes y Belice, clean facilities, reasonable café; all passengers have to go through the customs *semáforo* (red/green light) on entry. Colectivo taxi from town US$1.60, bus to town from Av Belice. Left luggage US$0.30/hr. Many buses going to the border, US$0.30; taxi from Chetumal to border, 20 mins, US$6 for two. Buses are often all booked a day ahead so avoid unbooked connections. Expect passport checks on buses leaving for Mexican destinations. Autobuses del Caribe to **Mexico City**, 22 hrs, US$66, four daily via **Villahermosa** (US$18, 10 hrs, the road is bad and it can take longer); bus to **Escárcega**, four between 1300 and 2100, 3½ hrs, US$7.25, 2nd class; from Chetumal to **Palenque**, ADO/Caribe 1st class at 2215, US$15.50, 9 hrs (2 stops), 2nd class at 2130, US$14.80, otherwise a change is necessary at Emiliano Zapata (bus to there at 0900, 1300, US$11.50), then change again at Catazajá, or Catazajá itself (then take a colectivo), or Escárcega. Lacandonia has 2nd class bus to **San Cristóbal** and Palenque at 2130, US$20. Bus to **Mérida**, 16 a day, US$16.50 1st class, about 7 hrs, 2nd class US$13. To **Felipe Carrillo Puerto**, US$3.35, 1½ hrs, many, on excellent road. To **Cancún**, 6 hrs, boring road, about 8 daily, between 0630 and 2400 (US$33 at 1500, hourly service US$15-17.75). To **Tulum**, several 2nd class from 0630, 1st class from 0700, 4 hrs, US$57, 2nd class. To **Minatitlán**, 12 hrs, US$22.50. There are also buses to Veracruz, Campeche, Villahermosa, Córdoba, X-Pujil and Puerto Juárez. Green *colectivos* at Francisco Primo de Verdad y Av Hidalgo go along the coast to Cancún.

To Belize Batty Bus from bus terminal to **Belize City**, several a day, schedules change frequently, taking 4-5 hrs on paved road, US$6 in pesos, US dollars or Belize dollars. Venus Bus to Belize City leaves from the square by Mercado Nuevo on Calzada Veracruz, 3 blocks from main terminal (US$1 taxi ride), again frequent schedule changes. Be there in good time; they sometimes leave early if full. If intending to stay in Belize City, do not take a bus which arrives at night as it is not recommended to look for a hotel in the dark. Bus Chetumal-**Orange Walk**, 2½ hrs, US$4.50. Caribe Express has a direct service to Flores (US$30) and Tikal (US$40) in **Guatemala**, at 1330, 8 hrs.

Money checked on entering Belize. Excess Mexican pesos are easily changed into Belizean dollars with men waiting just beyond customs on the Belize side, but they are not there to meet the early bus. Mexican customs procedure can be slow; bus passengers en route to Belize walk across the bridge, with personal luggage, for Belizean passport control, where the buses wait. Visitors who have been to Ecuador, or any of its neighbouring countries recently, require a health certificate, available from the Centro de Salud at the border.

It is difficult to hitch to the Belizean border. To hitch once inside Belize, it is best to take the *colectivo* from in front of the hospital (1 block from the bus station, ask) marked

'Chetumal-Santa Elena", US$1. You can change US for Belizean dollar bills in the shops at the border, this is not necessary as US$ are accepted in Belize. On entering Belize you must purchase car insurance. Entering Mexico, tourist cards are available at the border.

Excursions 6 km N of Chetumal are the stony beaches of **Calderitas**, bus US$0.25 or taxi, US$5, many fish restaurants. 16 km N **Laguna de los Milagros**, a beautiful lagoon for swimming, and 34 km N of Chetumal, on the road to Tulum (**page 340**), is **Cenote Azul**, over 70m deep, with an expensive waterside restaurant serving good regional food (but awful coffee) until 1800 and a trailer park (Apartado 88, Chetumal, relaxing place to camp; other *cenotes* in area). About 3 km N of Cenote Azul is the village of **Bacalar** (nice, but not special) on the Laguna de Siete Colores; swimming and skin-diving; colectivos from Chetumal, corner of Miguel Hidalgo y Primo de Verdad, from 0700-1900, US$1.60, also buses from Chetumal bus station every 2 hrs or so, US$1.60. There is a Spanish fort there overlooking a beautiful shallow, clear, fresh water lagoon; abundant birdlife on the lakeshore. This is the fort of San Felipe, said to have been built around 1725 by the Spanish to defend the area from the British (there is a plaque praying for protection from the British). Spanish galleons were repaired in the lagoon, where they kept their bullion hidden from the pirates. The British ships roamed the islands and reefs, looting Spanish galleons laden with gold, on their way from Peru to Cuba. There are many old shipwrecks on the reef and around the Chinchorro Banks, 50 km out in the Caribbean (information kindly provided by Coral Pitkin of the Rancho Encantado, see below). Hotel and good restaurants on the Laguna. At Bacalar is **D** *Hotel Refugio*, with bath, 10 mins walk from main plaza, N, lovely gardens and thatched bar overlooking lagoon, but facilities in poor condition (dirty, no hot water) quiet, friendly; *Restaurant La Esperanza*, 1 block from plaza on same road, thatched barn, good seafood, not expensive and two cheap places on the plaza, **Punta y Coma** and **Orizaba**. Several lakeside bars also serve meals, mostly fish: **Ojitos**, **Los 6 Hermanos**, **Sian Kaan**, **El Pez de Oro**, **El Fuerte**, but no details on any of these. Camping possible at the end of the road 100m from the lagoon, toilets and shower, US$0.10, but lagoon perfect for washing and swimming; Balneario Ejidal, with changing facilities and restaurant (good fried fish), rec; gasoline is sold in a side-street. About 2 km S of Bacalar (on left-hand side of the road going towards the village) is **C** *Hotel Las Lagunas*, very good, clean, comfortable, hot water, swimming pool and opp a sweet-water lake; restaurant is, however, overpriced. 3 km N of Bacalar is the resort hotel **A+** *Rancho Encantado*, on the W shore of the lagoon, half-board also available, Aptdo 233, Chetumal, T/F 983-80427 (USA res: 800 748 1756 or F 505-751-0972. PO Box 1644, Taos, New Mexico), with private dock, tour boat, canoes and windsurf boards for rent, private cabins with fridge and hammock, vey good. N of Bacalar a direct road (Route 293) runs to Muná, on the road between Mérida and Uxmal.

Just after the turn off to Muná, at Cafetal, is a paved road E to Majahual on the coast (56 km from Cafetal). About 2 km before Majahual a paved road to the left goes to Puerto Bravo and on to Placer and Punta Herrera (in the Sian Ka'an Biosphere Reserve). 3.5 km along this road a right turn goes to the **Sol y Mar** restaurant, with rooms to rent, bathrooms and spaces for RVs, also coconut palms and beach. 10.5 km along the Punta Herrero road, again on the right, is **Camidas** Trailer Park, with palm trees, *palapas*, restaurant and restrooms, space for 4 RVs, US$5 pp, car free.

Across the bay from Chetumal, at the very tip of Quintana Roo is **Xcalak**, which may be reached from Chetumal by private launch (2 hrs), or by same unpaved road from Cafetal to Majahual, then turning S for 55 km (186 km from Chetumal, suitable for passenger cars but needs skilled driver). Daily colectivos from 0700-1900, from 16 de Septiembre y Mahatma Ghandi, but the only one back is at 1300. Bus runs Fri 1600 and Sun 0600, returning Sat am and Sun pm (details from Chetumal tourist office). Xcalak is a fishing village (250 pop) with a few shops with beer and basic supplies and one small restaurant serving Mexican food. A few km N of Xcalak are two hotels, *Costa de Cocos* and *Villa Caracol*, both American run, latter is good, comfortable *cabañas*, expensive. From, here trips can be arranged to the Banco Chinchorro or to San Pedro, Belize. *Villa Caracol* has sport fishing and diving facilities. In the village you may be able to rent a boat to explore Chetumal Bay and the unspoiled islands of Banco Chinchorro. N of Chetumal are also the unexcavated archaeological sites of *Ichpaatun* (13 km), Oxtancah (14) and Nohochmul (20). Do *not* try to walk from Xcalak along the coast to San Pedro, Belize; the route is virtually impassable.

30 km S of Chetumal is *Palmara*, located along the Río Hondo, which borders Belize, swimming holes and restaurant.

From Chetumal one can visit the fascinating Mayan ruins that lie on the way to Escárcega (see above re **Fuel**; the road is bad in places, although under repair. Leaded fuel is available half-way between Chetumal and Escárcega). Just before Francisco Villa (61 km from Chetumal) lie the ruins of *Kohunlich* 8.4 km S of the main road, 1½ hrs walk, take plenty of water (hitching difficult), where there are fabulous masks (early classic, AD 250-500) set on the side of the main pyramid, still bearing red colouring; they are unique of their kind (allow an hour for the site). 200m W of the turning is a *migración* office and a stall selling beer; wait here for buses, which have to stop, but 1st class will not pick up passengers. Colectivos 'Nicolás Bravo' from Chetumal, or bus marked Zoh Laguna from bus station pass the turning. Seven km beyond *Xpujil* (119 km from Chetumal, all that remains of one large pyramid, 8th century AD, recently restored, about 1 km W of bus terminal/junction), lies the large Maya site of *Becán*, shielded by the forest with wild animals still wandering among the ruins, surrounded by a water-less moat and a low wall, now collapsed, with vast temples and plazas and a decayed ball court (site is visible from road, entry US$4.35, lots of mosquitoes, RVs may be parked at the ruins, no facilities).

Two km further on and 10 mins down a paved road lies *Chicanná*, with a superb late classic Maya temple with an ornate central door which has been formed in the shape of the open-fanged jaws of the plumed serpent. A 10-minute path leads from the first site to a second, which has a pyramid with lovely Chac masks (about 1 hr is enough to see both sites). Nearest accommodation is a few rooms to let in Xpujil; no camping permitted at either site.

Two sites, a bit further away, accessible from Xpujil village are *Hormiguero* (Hill of the Ants), and *Río Bec*. Helmut Zettl (Ebergassing) writes: 'The latter was discovered in 1912 by an American, but was later lost for almost 60 years. It was rediscovered in 1973 by an American couple who were researching a documentary on the Maya and were shown the overgrown temple by a *chiclero*. Try to find a driver and guide in Xpujil to make the 6-7 hr expedition, well worth it, but only possible in the dry season (December-March)". On either side of the Chetumal-Francisco Escárcega road at this point stretches the **Calakmul Biosphere Reserve** (S it reaches to the Guatemala border). 180 species of birds have been registered here, including the endangered king vulture, 2 species of eagle, and others.

Buses leave from Chetumal bus terminal along the road to Francisco Villa and Xpujil, passing the entrance to Becán. Many taxis and colectivos in Xpujil for the ruins (US$8 for taxi including waiting time). If stuck overnight there is a basic lodge in Xpujil, with *cabañas*. 2nd class buses from Chetumal to Xpujil at 0630, 1200, 1930 and others later, stopping service; 1st class (direct), US$3.30, 0900,1130, 1230, 1300 and others; 2nd class fare Chetumal-Francisco Villa US$1.65, 1 hr 10 mins, Francisco Villa-Xpujil US$2.20, 2 hrs 20 mins. Last bus from Xpujil to Chetumal at 1700 (1st class ADO); similarly, last bus back from Becán is just before 1700. Colectivos, a bit more expensive, leave from E of the electricity plant in Chetumal. Xpujil, Becán and Chicanná are in Campeche state and, at the state border, passports and tourist cards must be shown.

Maps of roads in Quintana Roo are obtainable in Chetumal at Junta Local de Caminos, Secretaría de Obras Públicas.

BAJA CALIFORNIA (11)

A land of hot, parched deserts, but deserts of infinite variety and everchanging landscapes, clothed in a fascinating array of hardy vegetation. Most visitors find Baja a magical place of blue skies, fresh air, solitude and refuge from the rat race N of the border.

Baja California (Lower California) is that long narrow arm which dangles southwards from the US border between the Pacific and the Gulf of California for 1,300 km. It is divided administratively into the states of Baja California and Baja California Sur, with a one-hour time change at the state line. The average width is only 80 km. Rugged and almost uninhabited mountains split its tapering length. Only the southern tip gets enough rain: the northern half gets its small quota during the winter, the southern half during the summer. Not only the northern regions near the US, but also the southern Cape zone is attracting increasing numbers of tourists. The US dollar is preferred in most places N of La Paz.

Stretching 1,704 km from Tijuana to Cabo San Lucas, Highway 1 is in good repair, although slightly narrow and lacking hard shoulders. Service stations are placed at adequate intervals along it, but motorists should fill their tanks at every opportunity and carry spare fuel, particularly if venturing off the main roads. Stations in small towns may not have fuel, or may sell from barrels at inflated prices. The same conditions apply for Highways 5 (Mexicali-San Felipe), 3 (Tecate-Ensenada-San Felipe road) and 2 (Tijuana 196 Mexicali-San Luís-Sonoita). Hitchhiking is difficult, and there is very little public transport off the main highway.

There is no immigration check on the Mexican side of the border—the buffer zone for about 120 km S of the frontier allows US citizens to travel without a tourist card. Some have reported travelling in Baja California Sur without a tourist card. If you are bringing in a vehicle you should try to get a tourist card/vehicle permit in Tijuana (**see page 355**); if you are travelling beyond Baja California, with or without a vehicle, getting a tourist card in Tijuana will save a lot of trouble later. Immigration authorities are also encountered at Mexicali, at Ensenada, at Quitovac, 28 km S of Sonoita (Sonora) on Highway 2, and when boarding the ferries to cross the Gulf. Ferries ply from Pichilingüe (N of La Paz) and Santa Rosalía to various places on the mainland (see text). As a car needs an import permit, make sure you get to the ferry with lots of time and preferably with a reservation if going on the Pichilingüe-Mazatlán ferry. (See under La Paz below.)

Recommended guides and clubs The Automobile Club of Southern California's *Baja California*, which contains plenty of information and detailed driving logs for all of Baja's roads; *Baja California: A Travel Survival Kit*, Lonely Planet (1988); and *The Magnificent Peninsula*, by Jack Williams, which includes a km by km log to the highways as well as an enormous amount of background detail. *Baja Adventure Book*, by Walt Peterson, Wilderness Press, 2440 Bancroft Way, Berkeley, CA 94704.

Insurance and Medical Services Insurance covering bodily injury is not available locally. Motorcycle insurance costs about US$3 a day. If you require x-ray facilities after an accident it appears that the only place between Tijuana and Los Cabos with X-ray equipment and an on-call technician is Ciudad Constitución.

Maps There are only two really comprehensive maps—the road map published by the ACSC, which gives highly detailed road distances (but in miles) and conditions, and which is available only to AAA members (the AAA also publishes a *Guide to Baja California* for members only); and International Travel Map (ITM) Production's *Baja California 1:1,000,000* (2nd edition 1992-93), which includes extra geographical and recreational detail on a topographic base. Many specialist maps and guides are available in book stores in Southern California. Both guidebooks and maps are sadly rare in Baja itself.

The Value Added Tax (IVA) is only 6% in Baja California compared with 10% on the mainland (although costs of food and accommodation are more expensive than the rest of Mexico, but

NORTHERN BAJA CALIFORNIA MAC 31a

U.S.A.

Tijuana
Rosarito — Tecate — Calexico
La Rumorosa — Mexicali
Laguna Salada
Ensenada — PN Constitucion de 1857 — San Luis Río Colorado
Maneadero
Santo Tomás — To Sonoita
San Vicente — Golfo de Santa Clara
Crucero la Trinidad
Colonet — Sierra San Pedro-Martir
Pacific Ocean — Picacho del Diablo — San Felipe
San Quintín
El Rosario
Punta Baja — Puertecitos
Cataviña — Bahía San Luis Gonzaga

0 — 50 km

less than in the USA). Tijuana, Ensenada and La Paz all have a good range of duty-free shopping. Stove fuel is impossible to find in Baja California Sur. Beware of overcharging on buses and make a note of departure times of buses in Tijuana or Ensenada when travelling S: between Ensenada and Santa Rosalía it is very difficult to obtain bus timetable information, even at bus stations. Don't ask for English menus if you can help it—prices often differ from the Spanish version. Always check change, overcharging is rife. Note also that hotels have widely divergent winter and summer rates; between June and November tariffs are normally lower than those given in the text below (especially in expensive places).

Cortés attempted to settle at La Paz in 1534 after one of his expeditions had become the first Europeans to set foot in Baja, but the land's sterile beauty disguised a chronic lack of food and water; this and sporadic Indian hostility forced the abandonment of most early attempts at settlement. Jesuit missionary fathers arrived at Loreto in 1697 and founded the first of their 20 missions. The Franciscans and then Dominicans took over when the Jesuits were expelled in 1767. The fathers were devoted and untiring in their efforts to convert the peninsula's three ethnic groups, but diseases introduced unknowingly by them and by ships calling along the coasts soon tragically decimated Indian numbers; some Indians remain today, but without tribal organization. Scattered about the Sierras are the remains of 30 of these well-meaning but lethal missions—some beautifully restored, others only eroded adobe foundations. Most are within easy reach from Highway 1, although 4-wheel drive is necessary for remoter sites such as San Pedro Mártir and Dolores del Sur.

Baja became part of Mexico after the signing of the peace treaty with the United States in 1848, ceded in exchange for Alta California. Battles were fought on the peninsula during the Mexican Revolution. Today's population of about 2.8 million has increased by two-thirds in the past decade through migration from Mexico's interior and Central Pacific coast. The development of agriculture, tourism, industry, migrant labour from California, and the opening of the Transpeninsular Highway has caused an upsurge of economic growth and consequently of prices, especially in areas favoured by tourists.

The Morelos dam on the upper reaches of the Colorado River has turned the Mexicali valley into a major agricultural area: 400,000 acres under irrigation to grow cotton and olives. The San Quintín Valley and the Magdalena Plain are other successful areas where crops have been wrenched from the desert. Industries are encouraged in all border regions by investment incentives; called *maquiladoras*, they are foreign-owned enterprises which import raw materials without duty, manufacture in Mexico and ship the products back to the United States.

Mexicali (pop 850,000), capital of Baja California state (1990 pop 1,657,900), is not as geared to tourism as Tijuana and thus retains its busy, business-like border town flavour. It is a good place to stock up on supplies, cheap clothing and footware, and souvenirs.

The new **Centro Cívico-Comercial**, Calzada López Mateos, is an ambitious urban development comprising government offices, medical school, hospitals, bullring, bus station, cinemas, etc. The **City Park**, in the SW sector, contains a zoo, picnic area and **natural history museum** (open Tues-Fri 0900-1700; weekend 0900-1800). University of Baja California's **Regional Museum**, Av Reforma y Calle L; interesting exhibits illustrating Baja's archaeology, ethnography and missions (Tues-Fri 0900-1800; weekend 1000-1500, admission free). **Galería de la Ciudad**, Av Obregón 1209, between Calles D y E, former state governor's residence, features work of Mexican painters, sculptors and photographers (Mon-Fri 0900-2000). There are *charreadas* (rodeos), held on Sundays during the April-October season, at two separate *charro* grounds on eastern and western outskirts of Mexicali. Mexicali has numerous Chinese restaurants, the legacy of immigration which began in Sonora in the late 19th century.

Calexico, the much smaller city on the California side of the border, is so thoroughly Mexicanized that it can be difficult to find a newspaper from San Diego or Los Angeles. Mexican shoppers flock here for clothing bargains.

Hotels A+ *Holiday Inn*, Blvd Benito Juárez 2220, T (656) 61300, F 664901, a/c, best in town; also **A+** *Crowne Plaza*, Blvd López Mateos y Av de los Héroes 201, T 573600, F 570555; **A** *Castel Calafia*, Calzada Justo Sierra 1495, T 682841, a/c, plain but comfortable, dining room; **A** *Lucerna*, Blvd Juárez 2151, T 541000, a/c, meeting rooms, bar, nightclub; **B** *Del Norte*, Calle Melgar y Av Francisco Madero, T 540575, some a/c and TV, across from border crossing, pleasant but a little noisy, has free parking for guests and offers discount coupons for breakfast and dinner in its own restaurant. **C** *La Siesta*, Justo Sierra 899, T 541100, reasonable, coffee shop. **D** *Rivera*, near the railway station, a/c, best of the cheaper hotels; *Fortín de las Flores*, Av Cristóbal Colón 612, T 524522; and **D** *Las Fuentes*, Blvd López Mateos 1655, T 571525, both with a/c and TV but noisy, tolerable if on a tight budget. **Youth hostel** Av Salina Cruz y Coahuila 2050, CP 21050, T 551230.

Motels B-C *Azteca de Oro*, Calle Industria 600, T 571433, opposite the train station and only a few blocks from the bus terminal, a/c, TV, a bit scruffy but convenient. Others around town and in Calexico just across the border around E 4th St. **B-C** *Hotel De Anza*, on the Calexico side, excellent value for money.

Many good night clubs on Av Justo Sierra, and on your left as you cross border, several blocks away.

Exchange All major banks: currency exchange is only from 0900-1330. *Casas de cambio* in Calexico give a slightly better rate. Several *cambios* on López Mateos.

Crossing the border The border is open 24 hrs a day for all formalities. Day visitors may prefer to park on the California side, since the extremely congested Avenida Cristóbal Colón, which parallels the frontier fence, is the only access to the US port of entry; entering Mexico, follow the diagonal Calzada López Mateos, which leads to the tourist office and train and bus stations. Mexican automobile insurance is readily available on both sides of the border.

Pedestrians travelling from Mexicali to Calexico should take the underpass beneath Calzada López Mateos, which passes through the utterly indifferent Mexican immigration office before continuing to the US side.

Tourist Office State Tourism Office, Calle Comercio, between Reforma and Obregón ("Centro Cívico" bus); better is **Tourist and Convention Bureau**, Calzada López Mateos y Calle Camelias, helpful, English spoken, open Mon-Fri 0800-1900, Sat 0900-1300. The Procuraduría de Protección al Turista, which provides legal assistance for visitors, is in the same building as the State Tourism office.

Airport 18 km E, Blvd Aviación; daily flights to Mexico City, Guadalajara and Hermosillo. Air LA flies 5 times a week between Los Angeles and Mexicali. Charter services.

Train The railway station to the S is about 3½ km from the tourist area on the border and Calle 3 bus connects it with the nearby bus terminal. There is a passport desk at the station. The ticket information office closes at 1230 but there are timetables on the wall. Phone 57-23-86 (1000-1200) or 57-21-01 to verify departure times and make reservations. The ticket office is open 0900-1100 for 1st class tickets for following day. For the slow train the office is open from 1630 to 2040. A special 1st class train, *servicio estrella* El Tren del Pacífico, leaves at 0900 daily for the **capital**, via Guadalajara, fare includes meals, a/c, book in advance. On this train the sleeping car and dining room are connected to the Nogales-Guadalajara train at Benjamín Hill; all other passengers have to change carriages to the Nogales train which is often very full on arrival. Slow train (leaves 2050, 2nd class cars) to **Guadalajara** and **Mexico City** takes 57 hrs. On this train the special first class and dining cars are detached, the others go all the way to Guadalajara. Be sure to take your own food. Dining cars can run out of food when there are delays. Food and drink sold on station platforms. Make sure you are on the right car, not one that will be disconnected—guards not always reliable, thieves especially active if lights are turned off. Thorough police luggage searches for drugs and guns possible. Toilets in each class are inefficient and therefore unpleasant. There is no air conditioning except in *dormitorio* cabins for 1-2 persons. Price difference between cabins and roomettes minimal, but cabin vastly preferable. 1st class seats are comfortable. Very hot and dusty in desert part of trip, though train is cleaned twice, cold at night between Los Mochis and Mexico City, take a blanket. Some fares and times: **Puerto Peñasco**, US$8.70; **Caborca**, US$16.25; **Hermosillo**, US$24, 9½ hrs; **Empalme**, US$31.25; **Ciudad Obregón**, US$36.50; **Navajoa**, US$37.50; **Culiacán**, US$49; **Mazatlán**, US$57, 22 hrs; **Tepic**, US$68.50; **Guadalajara**, US$82.30 *servicio estrella*, US$50 ordinary 1st class. 2nd class fares on the slow train are less than one third of 1st class fares (to Mexico City 2nd class US$36.50).

If you come from the N on the slow train and want to go to Chihuahua you'll arrive at 2015 at the junction, **Sufragio** (the Tren del Pacífico arrives at 0215, easy to miss in the drak, but can be too late for the Chihuahua connection). For a hotel, go to San Blas, where the train also stops (US$9.70 from Mexicali), 5 mins away by local bus (every 15 mins from 0500 in either direction), where there are 3 hotels: *Santa Lucía*, *San Marco*, both often full; *Pérez* dirty, cold water, but adequate, E. If the next morning you are refused a ticket because the train is full, try getting in and getting a ticket on the train.

Bus Tijuana, 3 hrs, US$16.50 luxury liner, US$8 1st class, US$5 2nd class, sit on right for views at the Cantú Grade; **San Felipe**, 3 hrs, 4 a day, US$8, **Guadalajara**, US$77. **Mazatlán**, US$50. **Hermosillo**, 10 hrs, US$22. **Mexico City**, US$96. **Ensenada**, US$9. **Santa Rosalía**, US$33. **La Paz**, daily 1630, 24 hrs, US$60.50. All trips leave from the new central bus station (Camionera Central) on Av Independencia; four major bus companies have their offices here under one roof. Autotransportes Tres Estrellas de Oro serves both Baja and the mainland. Golden State buses from Mexicali to Los Angeles (US$40) tickets available at trailer/kiosk across from *Hotel del Norte*. Greyhound from Los Angeles to Calexico (901 Imperial Av), US$33, 6 hrs. San Diego to Calexico via El Centro, US$20, 3 to 4 hrs. The 1200 bus from San Diego connects with the Pullman bus to Mazatlán, US$40, 21 hrs. Local buses are cheap, about US$0.55. 'Central Camionera' bus to Civic Centre and bus station.

Paved Highway 5 heads S from Mexicali 196 km to San Felipe, passing at about Km 34 the Cerro Prieto geothermal field. After passing the Río Hardy (one of the peninsula's few permanent rivers) and the **Laguna Salada** (Km 72), a vast dry alkali flat unless turned into a muddy morass by rare falls of rain, the road continues straight across sandy desert until entering San Felipe around a tall, white, double-arched monument. Floods in January 1993 cut the road across the Laguna Salada; until it is reopened motorists have to use Highway 3 from Ensenada to get to San Felipe.

San Felipe is a pleasant, tranquil fishing and shrimping port on the Gulf of California with a population of about 13,000, with about 3,000 North American RV temporary residents and a further 3,000 on winter weekends. Long a destination for devoted sportfishermen and a weekend retreat for North Americans, San Felipe is now experiencing a second discovery, with new trailer parks and the paving of many of the town's sandy streets. A public library is planned, recycling plant, artificial breakwater reef and two golf courses are under construction. Even the *Las Macetas* hotel (the 'grey ghost") may see completion in the near future. A new airport 8 km S now takes international flights. San Felipe is protected from desert winds by the coastal mountains and is unbearably hot during the summer; in winter the climate is unsurpassed, and on weekends it can become overcrowded and noisy. A good view of the wide sandy beach can be had from the Virgin of Guadalupe shrine near the lighthouse.

Navy Day is celebrated on 1 June with a carnival, street dancing and boat races.

Hotels A *Aquamarina Condohotel and Villas*, 4 km S on Punta Estrella road, B Sun-Thur, on beach, pool, attractive rooms, a/c; **A** *Castel*, Av Misión de Loreto 148, T 71282, a/c, 2 pools, tennis etc, best in town; **B** *La Trucha Vagabunda*, Mar Báltico, near *El Cortés Motel*, T 71333, also a few RV spaces and *Restaurant Alfredo* (Italian), seafood, international cuisine; **B** *Vagabond Inn*, on same street, 3 km S of town, a/c, pool and beach; **B** *Villa del Mar*, pool, volley ball court, restaurant; **C** *Fiesta San Felipe*, 9 km S on the airport road, isolated, every room has Gulf view, tennis, pool, restaurant, renovated in 1991, VAT (IVA) not included in bill. **C** *Riviera*, 1 km S on coastal bluff, T 71185, a/c, pool, spa, restaurant.

Motels B *Chapala*, some a/c, free coffee, clean but pricey, on beachfront, T 71240. **B** *El Capitán*, Mar de Cortés 298, T 71303, a/c, some balconies, pool, lovely rancho-style building, hard beds but otherwise OK; **B** *El Cortés*, on Av Mar de Cortés, T 71055, beachside esplanade, a/c, pool, palapas on beach, launching ramp, disco, restaurant; **C** *El Pescador*, T 71044, Mar de Cortés and Calzada Chetumal, a/c, modest but comfortable.

Camping Many trailer parks and campgrounds in town and on coast to N and S, inc *El Faro Beach and Trailer Park*, D, on the bay 18 km S; *Ruben's*, *Playa Bonita*, *La Jolla*, *Playa de Laura*, *Mar del Sol*, and the more primitive *Campo Peewee* and *Pete's Camp*, both about 10 km N. All from US$8 per night for two.

Restaurants *Green House*, Av Mar de Cortés 132 y Calzada Chetumal, good food (beef or chicken *fajitas* a speciality) and friendly service, cheap breakfasts, 'fish filet for a fiver"! 0730-0300 daily. *Clam Man's Restaurant*, Calzada Chetumal, 2 blocks W of Pemex station, used to belong to the late, famous Pasqual 'The Clam Man", oddly decorated, but excellent clams, steamed, fried, barbecued, at budget prices. *Los Misiones* in *Mar del Sol* RV park, small menu, moderately-priced, seafood crêpes a speciality, popular with families, good service. *Las Redes*, Mar de Cortés Sur; *Ruben's Place*, Junípero Serra, both favourites for seafood; *El Toro II*, Chetumal, Mexican and American food, popular for breakfasts; other pleasant places on Avenida Mar de Cortés: No 300 *Corona*, No 348; *El Nido*, grilled fish and steaks (closed Wed), No 358; *Puerto Padre* (Cuban); *George's*, No 336, steaks, seafood, live music, pleasant, friendly, popular with US residents, rec.

Tourist Office Mar de Cortés y Manzanillo, opp *El Capitán Motel*, helpful, little handout material, open Tues-Sun 0900-1400 and 1600-1800.

Bus Transportes ABC and TNS buses to **Ensenada**, direct, over the mountains, at 0800 and 1800, 3½ hrs, US$9. Bus to **Mexicali** US$8, 4 a day from 0730, 2 hrs. Hitching to Mexicali is not difficult (much traffic), but beware the desert sun. Bus station is on Mar Báltico near corner of Calzada Chetumal, in town centre.

Airport Air LA flies 3 times a week from Los Angeles, CA.

The coastal road S of San Felipe has been paved as far as Puertecitos, a straggling settlement mainly of North American holiday homes. There is an airstrip, a simple grocery store, a Pemex station and the 8-room *Puertecitos Motel*. Fishing is good outside the shallow bay and there are several tidal hot springs at the SE point. The road continues S along the coast (well graded with improvements continuing, acceptable for standard vehicles), leading to the tranquil **Bahía San Luís Gonzaga**, on which are the basic resorts of Papa Fernández and Alfonsinas; the beach here is pure sand, empty and silent. From here, the 'new' road heads W over hills to meet Highway 1 near Laguna Chapala, 53 km S of Cataviña, opening up a circular route through northern Baja California.

Highway 2 runs E from Mexicali through San Luis Río Colorado, Sonoita and Caborca to join the Pacific Highway at Santa Ana; see page 120.

The road from Mexicali W to Tijuana is fast and well surfaced, it runs across barren desert flats, below sea level and with organ-pipe cacti in abundance, until reaching the eastern escarpment of the peninsula's spine; it winds its way up the Cantú Grade to **La Rumorosa**, giving expansive, dramatic vistas of desert and mountain. The numerous wrecked trucks and cars which litter the canyons along the Cantú Grade, together with countless crosses, emphasise the need for careful driving and better than adequate brakes. If pulling off the highway for the view, do so only on wide shoulders with good visibility in both directions. La Rumorosa, sited high enough on a boulder- strewn plateau to receive a sprinkling of snow in winter, has a service station. There are three more Pemex stations along the highway before it reaches Tecate after 144 km.

Visitors will find that placid *Tecate* (population 40,000) more resembles a Mexican city of the interior rather than a gaudy border town, perhaps because there is no population centre on the US side. It is a pleasant place to break the journey, especially around the shady Parque Hidalgo, where families promenade on weekends. The Baja California Secretary of Tourism, opposite the park at Libertad 1305, provides a useful map of the town and other information. English spoken.

The border crossing is open from 0700-2400. To get to border immigration facilities, go N 3 blocks, uphill, from the W side of the Parque. You will pass the theatre. Mexican offices are on the left, US on the right. The orderly and friendly Mexican immigration and customs officers will only process vehicle papers between 0800 and 1600; at other hours, continue to Mexicali or Sonoita. Tourist cards may also be obtained at the bus terminal; services to the interior resemble those from Tijuana (Tres Estrellas de Oro to Mexico City, US$93.50).

Brewing is the most important local industry; the landmark Tecate Brewery, which produces Tecate and Carta Blanca beers, offers tours on the first three Saturdays of the month between 0800 and 1200. There are many *maquiladora* industries.

Accommodation **A** *Motel El Dorado*, Juárez 1100, T 41102, a/c, central, comfortable; **C** *Hotel Hacienda*, Juárez 861, T 41250, a/c, clean; **C** *Hotel Paraíso*, Aldrete 83, T 41716. Ten km S of Tecate, on the road to Ensenada, is **A** *Rancho Tecate*, T 40011.

Budget-minded travellers may try **E** *Hotel México*, Juárez 230, gloomy rooms with or without bath, rumoured to be a staging post for unauthorised border crossings; **D** *Hotel Frontera*, Callejón Madero 131, T 41342, basic but clean and friendly, is probably a step up in quality (Antonio Moller Ponce, who resides here, is knowledgeable on the area's history and ethnohistory).

Restaurants Excellent Mexican and Italian specialities at *El Passetto*, Libertad 200 near Parque Hidalgo. Many other good ones.

The highway continues W past the Rancho La Puerta, a spa and physical fitness resort, strictly for the rich, vegetarian meals, petrol station. Leaving the Rodríguez Reservoir behind, Highway 2 enters the industrial suburb of La Mesa and continues into Tijuana as a 4-lane boulevard, eventually to become Av Revolución, one of the city's main shopping streets.

A new alternative to Route 2 is the only completed segment of the four-lane Tijuana-Mexicali motorway, between Tecate and Otay Mesa, Tijuana. It is very fast, but carries almost no traffic because of the US$4 toll.

Tijuana (pop 1,500,000), on the Pacific, is where 35 million people annually cross the border, fuelling the city's claim to be 'the world's most visited city". It came to prominence with Prohibition in the United States in the 1920s when Hollywood stars and thirsty Americans flocked to the sleazy bars and enterprising nightlife of Tijuana and Mexicali. Today, tourism is the major industry; although countless bars and nightclubs still vie for the visitor's dollar, it is duty-free bargains, horse racing and inexpensive English-speaking dentists which attract many visitors. This area is much more expensive than further S, especially at weekends. Modern Tijuana is Mexico's fourth-largest city and one of the most prosperous.

Points of interest: **Centro Cultural**, Paseo de los Héroes y Av Independencia (museum, handcraft shops, restaurant, concert hall, and the ultra-modern spherical Omnimax cinema, where three films are shown on a 180° screen, best to sit at the back/top so you don't have to lean too far back: English performance at 1400 daily, US$4.50—Spanish version at 1900 costs US$3.75); **Casa de la Cultura**, a multi-arts cultural centre with a 600-seat theatre; the Cathedral of **Nuestra Señora de Guadalupe**, Calle 2. The **Jai-Alai Palace** (Palacio Frontón) is at Av Revolución y Calle 7 (games begin at 2000 nightly except Weds; spectators may bet on each game). Tijuana has two bullrings, the **Plaza de Toros Monumental** at Playas de Tijuana (the only one in the world built on the sea

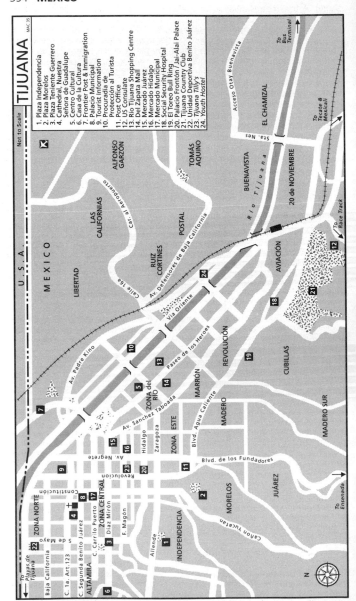

MAC 35

Not to Scale **TIJUANA**

1. Plaza Independencia
2. Plaza Morelos
3. Plaza Teniente Guerrero
4. Cathedral, Nuestra
   Senora de Guadalupe
5. Centro Cultural
6. Casa de la Cultura
7. Frontier Post & Immigration
8. Palacio Municipal
9. Tourist Information
10. Procuradía de
    Protección al Turista
11. Post Office
12. US Consulate
13. Río Tijuana Shopping Centre
14. Del Zapata Mall
15. Mercado Juárez
16. Mercado Hidalgo
17. Mercado Municipal
18. Social Security Hospital
19. El Toreo Bull Ring
20. Palacio Frontón / Jai-Alai Palace
21. Tijuana Country Club
22. Unidad Deportiva Benito Juárez
23. Tijuana Tilly's
24. Youth Hostel

shore). A few metres away is an obelisk built into the border chain-link fence commemorating the Treaty of Guadalupe Hidalgo, 1848, which fixed the frontier between Mexico and the USA. **El Toreo** bullring is 3 km E of downtown on Búlevar **Agua Caliente**; *corridas* alternate between the two venues between May and September; Sun at 1600 sharp. Tickets from US$4.50 (*sol*) to US$16 (*sombra*). Horse and dog racing is held at the Agua Caliente track, near the Tijuana Country Club; horse racing Sat and Sun from 1200; greyhound meetings Wed-Mon at 1945, Mon, Weds, Fri at 1430. Admission US$0.50, reserved seats US$1. *Charreadas* take place each Sunday from May to Sept at one of four grounds, free. Tourism office will give up-to-date information. A walk along the barrio beside the border (don't go alone) to see the breached fence will demonstrate the difference between the first and third worlds.

Immigration There is no passport check at the border, although US freeways funnelling 12 lanes of traffic into three on the Mexican side means great congestion, particularly at weekends. A quieter recommended alternative is the **Otay Mesa** crossing (open 0600-2200) 8 km E of Tijuana, reached from the US side by SR-117. Car insurance, as well as immigration and vehicle documents, are available at Otay, where traffic is less frantic and parking much easier. From the Mexican side it is harder to find: continue on the bypass from Highway 1-D to near the airport to 'Garita de Otay' sign.

If travelling on into Mexico, don't follow the crowds who cross without visiting immigration: try to deal with US exit formalities and get an entry stamp at the border as it will avoid serious problems later on. Note that Los Angeles—Tijuana Greyhound buses do not stop at Mexican Immigration. The Migración office is difficult to find: try the right hand lane marked 'Customs". When entering with a vehicle or motorcycle you should be able to obtain your tourist card/vehicle permit at this office, then you are supposed to get a stamp from a vehicle registry office about 100m S. The officials will ask for copies of your documents, including the vehicle permit. As they have no photocopier you can look for the copy shop opposite, above a liquor store, or return to the USA, go 2 blocks N and look for the mail box rental company opposite the *Jack-in-the-Box*. There is an immigration office for tourist cards and vehicle documents on the righthand side of Highway 1 as it enters Ensenda. Alternatively, you can forget the stamp and hope you won't be asked for it later (do not do this if going beyond Baja California). Going into the USA, be prepared for tough immigration procedures.

If entering without a vehicle, get a tourist card in advance; there is no passport check at the border but there is a small immigration office for entry stamps. Money changers operate in the shopping centre 200m from the border and opposite this is the bus stop for the bus terminal. A tourist office at the border gives out maps of the border area explaining money changing, buses, etc. When leaving the USA without a vehicle, there is nowhere to surrender your US entry card because there is no passport check on the US side. You can send your card to a US Consulate.

Those visiting Tijuana for the day often find it easier to park on the San Ysidro side and walk across the footbridge to the city centre. (Parking fees near the border range from US$5 to US$7 per day—24 hrs.) Alternatively, the 'San Diego Trolley' is an entertaining way to reach the border, taking visitors from downtown San Diego to 'la línea' from US$1-3; departures every 15 mins between 0500 and 0100 (tickets sold from machines at stops). There is a visitor information kiosk at the Trolley's southern terminus.

Hotels L *Fiesta Americana Tijuana*, Blvd Agua Caliente 4500, T 817000, heated pool, suites, etc, first rate; **A**: *Country Club*, Blvd Agua Caliente y Tapachula 1, T 817733, F 817066, *Hacienda de Río*, Blvd Sánchez Taboada 10606, T 848644, F 848620, and *La Mesa Inn*, Blvd Díaz Ordaz 50 y Gardenia, T 816522, F 812871; **A** *Centenario Plaza*, Blvd Agua Caliente 22400, T 818183; **A** *Lucerna*, Héroes y Av Rodríguez in new Río Tijuana development, T 841000, a/c, pool, piano bar, popular with business travellers; **A** *Paraíso-Radisson*, Blvd Agua Caliente 1 at the Country Club, T 817200, pool, sauna, bar, a/c, etc; **A/B** *El Conquistador*, Blvd Agua Caliente 700, T 817955, colonial style, a/c, pool, sauna, disco; **B** *Calinda Tijuana*, near the Paraíso-Radisson, a/c, pool, disco, convention centre; **B** *Palacio Azteca*, Highway 1 S, T 865301, a/c, modern, cocktail bar, extensively remodelled, in older, congested part of city; **B/C** *Hotel Caesar*, Calle 5a y Av Revolución, T 851606, a/c, restaurant, decorated with bullfight posters, unique character, good; **C** *La Villa de Zaragoza*, behind the Jai-Alai *frontón*, a/c, comfortable; **C** *Nelson*, Av Revolución 502, T 854302, central, simple clean rooms, coffee shop; **D** *Hotel del Pardo*, Calle 5a y Niños Héroes, acceptable, noisy in parts; **D** *Rey*, Calle 4a 2021, central, old but comfortable; **D** *St Francis*, Benito Juárez 2A, more with bath, recommended, central. **D** *París*, Calle 5a 1939, adequate, value-for-money budget hotel; **E** *Adelita*, hot showers, clean, basic, Calle 4a 2770; **E** *Hotel del Mar*, Calle

1a 1448, opposite *Nelson*, central but in a poor section, communal bathroom, good budget hotel. Recommended along Calle Baja California are **E** *Hotel Virrey* and **F** *Pensión Noche Buena*; nearby and as good are **D** *Rivas*, on Constitución, friendly, clean, a little noisy; **E** *Chula Vista*, Niños Héroes 380 and **E** *Fénix*, Miguel Martínez 355; **E** *Machado*, restaurant, basic, reasonable, Calle 1 No 1724; **E** *San Jorge*, Av Constitución 506, old but clean, basic. **Youth hostel** T 832680/822760, far from centre, Vía Oriente y Puente Cuauhtémoc, Zona del Río, dirty, not rec, inexpensive cafeteria on premises, open 0700-2300.

Motels B/C *León*, Calle 7a 1939, T 856320; **C/D** *La Misión*, in Playas de Tijuana near the bullring, T 806612, modern, a/c, restaurant, pool, popular with businessmen; **D** *Golf*, (T 862021), opposite each other on Blvd Agua Caliente, next to Tijuana Country Club, both OK, and **D** *Padre Kino*, (T 864208), *Golf*, an older-type motel.

If entering from the USA: it is easier to sightsee in Tijuana without luggage, so stay in San Diego and make a day excursion before travelling on. 2 rec places: **C** *Park Regency Hotel*, nr Balboa Park, 3 room apartment, good value; **E** *Imperial Beach Youth Hostel*, the grade for members, take bus 933 from trolley station Palm City to 3rd Street.

Restaurants *Capri*, cheap; *Tijuana Tilly's*, excellent meal, reasonably priced. *La Leña*, downtown on Av Revolución between Calles 4a y 5a, excellent food and service, beef and Mexican specialities; countless others, including new complex near border crossing. *Casa del Taco*, Revolución y Hidalgo, has taco buffet for US$2.30.

Night Clubs recommended: *Flamingos*, S on old Ensenada road; *Chantecler*.

Shopping The Plaza Río Tijuana Shopping Centre, Paseo de Los Héroes, is a new retail development; opposite is the Plaza Fiesta and Plaza del Zapato malls, the latter specializing in footwear! Nearby is the colourful public market. Downtown shopping area is Avs Revolución and Constitución. Bargaining is expected at smaller shops, and everyone except bus drivers is happy to accept US currency.

Exchange Many banks, all dealing in foreign exchange. For Visa TCs, go to **Bancomer**. Better rate than *cambios* but less convenient. Countless *casas de cambio* throughout Tijuana open day and night. Some *cambios* collect a commission (up to 5%), even for cash dollars; ask before changing.

US Consulate Calle Tapachula 96, between Agua Caliente racetrack and the Country Club, Mon-Fri 0800-1630, T 681-7400. **Canadian Consul** Calle Germán Gedovius 5-201, T 84-0461.

Mexican Consulate-General in San Diego, CA, 610 'A' Street, T (619) 231-8414/8427, Mon-Fri 0900-1400, for visas and tourist information.

Telephones Computel, Calle 7 y Av Negrete, metered phones, fax, computer facilities.

Emergency Phone Numbers Police 134; Fire 135; Red Cross 132; valid for Tijuana, Rosarito, Ensenada, Tecate, Mexicali and San Luis Río Colorado.

Tourist Information State Tourism Secretariat, main office on Plaza Patria, Blvd Agua Caliente, Mon-Fri 1000-1900. Branch offices at airport, first tollgate on Highway 1-D to Ensenada, and at the Chamber of Commerce, Calle 1 and Av Revolución, English-speaking staff, helpful, Mon-Fri 0900-1400, 1600-1900; Sat 0900-1300. Brochures and schematic maps available; no hotel lists. Chamber of Commerce also offers rest rooms and first aid facilities to visitors. Procuraduría de Protección al Turista is in the Government Centre in the Río Tijuana development; 0800-1900.

Buses Local buses about US$0.30, taxis ask US$10 (but shouldn't be that much), 'Central Camionera' or 'Buena Vista' buses to bus station, downtown buses to border depart from Calle 2a near Av Revolución. Local buses also go to the border from the bus station, every half hour up to 2300, marked 'La Línea/Centro". New bus station is 5 km SE of centre on the airport road at the end of Vía Oriente (at La Mesa). It is very crowded and inefficient; take advantage of toilet facilities as long distance buses are usually so full of luggage and goods that getting to the toilet at the back is impossible. There is a bank which changes travellers' cheques. Parking at bus terminal US$1/hr.

To **Mexico City** (every couple of hours) 1st class (Tres Estrellas de Oro, T 869515/869060), normal about 46 hrs, US$93.50, express US$105 (still a 2nd class bus), 40 hrs, *plus* service US$110, or special (with video and more comfort), US$126, 38 hrs. (Transportes del Pacífico, similar fares, express only). 2nd class (Transportes del Norte de Sonora), US$86. Other 1st class routes: **Guadalajara**, 36 hrs, US$82.50; **Hermosillo**, 12 hrs, US$35; **Los Mochis**, 22 hrs, US$53, Tres Estrellas de Oro; **Mazatlán**, 29 hrs, US$62.75; Sonoita US$16.50, Culiacán US$54; Querétaro US$99. By ABC line: **Ensenada**, about hourly 0500-2400, 1½ hrs, US$3.70; **Mexicali**, hourly from 0500-2200, US$8; **San Quintín**, 7 a day, US$7.15; **Santa Rosalía**, 1600, direct, US$27; La Paz, 0800, US$60.50, packed full; Tres Estrellas to La Paz, cheaper, 4 a day, 24 hrs. There are also many services E and S from the old bus station at Av Madero and Calle 1a (Comercio). From Tijuana bus terminal Greyhound has buses every 2 hrs to San Diego via the Otay Mesa crossing, except after 2200, when it uses the Tijuana crossing. Walk across 'La Línea' border and catch a Golden State bus to downtown Los Angeles, US$13 (buy ticket inside *McDonalds* restaurant), 12 a day, or take trolley to downtown San Diego and there get Greyhound, US$20, or Amtrak train, US$25, to Los Angeles. Golden State is the cheapest and fastest; it stops 1 block from Greyhound terminal in downtown LA, but stops first at Santa Ana and elsewhere if requested. If travelling beyond Los Angeles, ask about layovers in LA before buying a through ticket. Tijuana is a major transportation centre and schedules are complex and extensive.

International Airport 5 km E, 20 mins from San Diego, CA; cheaper flights than from the US. Aero California, daily flights to Los Mochis, and to La Paz, Aguascalientes, Colima, Guadalajara, Durango, Culiacán, Mazatlán, Puebla, Tepic and Torreón. Mexicana: To Mexico City, Guadalajara, León and Zacatecas; direct AeroMéxico jet services to La Paz, 1 hr 45 mins; AeroMéxico to the capital, many cities N of Mexico City and on the Pacific coast. Aeromar and Air LA to Los Angeles; Taesa to Aguascalientes, Ciudad Juárez, Guadalajara, León, Mexico City, Morelia and other cities. Saro to Puebla, Tepic, Torreón, Mexico City and Culiacán. Taxi between airport and centre is quoted at US$15 (bargaining may be possible from centre to airport); colectivo from airport to border, 'La Línea", US$3.20. Mexicoach run from San Diego to Tijuana airport for US$15, combination bus to Plaza La Jolla and taxi to airport.

A dramatic 106-km toll road (Highway 1-D) leads along cliffs overhanging the Pacific to Ensenada; the toll is in three sections of US$2 each. There are emergency phones approximately every 2 km on the toll road. This is the safest route between the two cities and 16 exit points allow access to a number of seaside developments and villages along the coast.

Largest is **Rosarito** (pop 50,000), variously described as a drab resort strung out along the old highway, or 'a breath of fresh air after Tijuana", with numerous seafood restaurants, curio shops, etc. There is a fine swimming beach; horseriding on N and S Rosarito beaches US$4/hr. In March and April accommodation is hard to find as college students in great numbers take their holiday here. Many hotels and motels, including: **A/B** *Festival Plaza*, Blvd Benito Juárez, T 20842, F 20224, deluxe, pool, shopping, 1 block from beach; **A/B** *Quinta del Mar Resort Hotel*, pool, sauna, tennis, also condos and townhouses with kitchens (L, T 21145), *Beachcomber Bar*, good food, relatively cheap, good for watching the sunset; *Motel Quinta Chico*; **B/C** *Motel Colonial*, (T 21575); **D** *Rene's Motel* (T 21020), plain but comfortable; **D** *Motel La Prieta*. Best is the **A/B** *Rosarito Beach Hotel*, T 21106 (US toll free 1-800-343-8582), Benito Juárez 31, which was one of the casinos which opened during Prohibition; its architecture and decoration are worth a look. Tourist office, Quinta Plaza Mall, Benito Juárez 96, 0900-1600 daily.

The coast as far as Puerto Nuevo and nearby **Cantamar** (Km 26 and 28) is lightly built-up (toll between Cantamar and Highway 1 US$1.35, none heading towards Cantamar); there are several trailer parks and an amazing number of restaurants specializing in lobster and seafood (impressive is *Jatay*, built on 4 levels—Puerto Nuevo). There is fine surfing to the N and 'hassle-free' hang-gliding areas S of Cantamar. 11 km S is an archaeological garden (Plaza del Mar) with an exhibition of precolumbian stone art, open to visitors. At **Punta Salsipuedes**, 51 km S of Tijuana by the tollway, a *mirador* affords sweeping views of the rugged Pacific coast and the offshore Todos Santos Islands. The section of Highway 1-D for several km beyond this point is subject to landslides.

Ensenada (pop 255,700) is Baja's third city and leading seaport. It is a delightful city on the northern shore of the Bahía de Todos Santos, whose blue waters sport many dolphins and underline the austere character of a landscape reduced to water, sky and scorched brown earth. Sport and commercial fishing, canning, wineries, olive groves and agriculture are the chief activities. Tourist activity concentrates along Av López Mateos, where most of the hotels, restaurants and shops are located. The twin white towers of **Nuestra Señora de Guadalupe**, Calle 6a, are a prominent landmark; on the seafront boulevard is the new **Plaza Cívica**, a landscaped court containing large busts of Juárez, Hidalgo and Carranza. A splendid view over city and bay can be had from the road circling the Chapultepec Hills on the western edge of the business district. Steep but paved access is via the W extension of Calle 2a, two blocks from the bus station. The **Bodegas de Santo Tomás** is Mexico's premier winery, Av Miramar 666, between Calles 6 and 7, T 82509; daily tours at 1100, 1300, 1500, US$2. *Charreadas* are held on summer weekends at the *charro* ground at Blancarte y Calle 2a. A weekend street market is held from 0700-1700 at Av Riversoll y Calle 7a; the fish market at the bottom of Av Macheros specializes in 'fish tacos' (a fish finger wrapped in a taco!). *Ensenada Clipper Fleet* runs daily fishing trips (0700-1500) from the sportfishing terminal, US$30 inc rod, reel, line, bait and licence. Also seasonal whale-watching trips and bay and coastal excursions.

Hotels L *Las Rosas Hotel and Spa*, on Highway 1, 7 km W of town, suites, spectacular ocean views, pool, sauna, restaurant; **L** *Punta Morro Hotel Suites*, on coast 3 km W of town, rooms have kitchens and fridges, 2 and 3-bedroom apartments available, pool; **L** *San Nicolás Resort Hotel*, López Mateos y Av Guadalupe, T 61901, a/c, suites, dining room, disco; **A+-A** *Villa Marina*, Av López Mateos y Blancarte, T 83321, heated pool, coffee shop; **A** *La Pinta*, Av Floresta y Blvd Bucaneros (on Fri-Sat, B Sun-Thurs), TV, pool, restaurant; **A** *Punta Morro*, 3 km N on Highway 1, rooms and suites, a/c, pool, kitchens, etc; **A** *Quintas Papagayo*, 1½ km N on Highway 1, T 44575, landscaped beach resort complex with all facilities, Hussong's *Pelicano* restaurant attached, seafood and local specialities, 0800-2300, best value for an Ensenada 'splurge'; **B** *Bahía*, López Mateos, T 82101, balconies, suites, fridges, quiet, clean, parking, a/c, good value, popular; **B** *Misión Santa Isabel*, López Mateos and Castillo, T 83616, pool, suites, Spanish Mission-style, attractive; **C** *México*, Av Ruiz y Calle 4, No 381, T 40573, central, a/c, TV, phone, coffee shop, parking; **D** *América*, López Mateos opp State Tourist Office, T 61333, basic, hard beds, budget. **D** *Plaza*, López Mateos 540, central, plain but clean, rooms facing street noisy. Several cheaper hotels around Miramar and Calle 3, eg **C-D** *Perla del Pacífico*, Av Miramar 229, quite clean, hot water; **E** *Río*, Av Miramar, basic. **E** *Pacífico*, Calle 2, clean, hot water, helpful. Note that some of the larger hotels have different rates for summer and winter; cheaper tariffs are given above— check first! All hotels are filled in Ensenada on weekends, get in early.

Motels *Ensenada Travelodge*, Av Blancarte 130, T 81601, a/c, heated pool, whirlpool, family rooms available, restaurant; **A+-A** *Cortés*, López Mateos 1089 y Castillo, T 82307, F 83904; **A+-A** *Casa del Sol*, López Mateos 101, T 81570, F 82025; both part of Best Western chain, a/c, TV, pool, comfortable; **A** *El Cid*, on Fri-Sat, B on Sun-Thurs, Av López Mateos 993, T 82421, Spanish-style building, a/c, fridges, suites available, dining room, lounge, disco; **C** *Balboa*, Guerero 172 y Cortés, T 61077, modern, comfortable, some way E of downtown; **C** *Villa Fontana*, López Mateos y Calle Blancarte, T 83434, good location, old but large clean rooms, cheerful, English spoken; **D** *Costa Mar*, Av Veracruz 319 at Playa Hermosa (1 km S), ½ block from beach, T 66425, TV, phones, etc, agreeable; **E** *Pancho*, Av Alvarado 211, shabby but clean rooms, opposite the *charro* ground, cheapest habitable motel in town. A great many good trailer parks.

Restaurants *El Rey Sol*, López Mateos 1000 y Blancarte, French/Mexican, elegant, reasonable prices; *La Góndola*, López Mateos between Miramar and Macheros, clean, Mexican dishes and pizzas—including lobster pizza!; *Mesón de Don Fernando*, López Mateos, good breakfasts, tacos and seafood, good value; *Taco Factory*, López Mateos y Av Gastelum, good tacos, many varieties. *Cantina Hussong's*, Avenida Ruíz 113, an institution in both the Californias, 1000-1400. *Cha-Cha Burgers*, Blvd Costero 609, 'American style burgers', fish, chicken, fast food 1000-2200; *Pancho's Place* (don't confuse with *Motel Pancho*), Ejército Nacional (Highway 1) y San Marcos, well-run, wide menu, pleasant; *Restaurant Muylam*, Ejército Nacional y Diamante, seafood and Chinese cuisine, 1200-2400; *China Land*, Riveroll 1149 between Calles 11 y 12, Sichuan, Mandarin and Cantonese cuisine, authentic, not cheap, 1200-2300; *El Pollo*, Macheros y Calle 2, grilled chicken 'Sinaloa style', fast food 1000-2200 every day of year; *Las Brasas*, López Mateos 486, between Ruíz and Gastelum barbeque chicken and fish, Mexican specialities, attractive patio dining, 1100-2200, closed Tues; *Mandarin*, López Mateos 2127, between Soto and Balboa (Chinese), elegant surroundings, good food, expensive, considered to be the best *chifa* in Ensenada. *Domico's*, Av Ruíz 283, also Chinese restaurants in same avenue; *Lonchería la Terminal*, opp bus station, cheap and filling *comida*, good but basic.

Tourist Office Av López Mateos y Espinoza, part of the Fonart artesan centre, Mon-Sat 0900-1900, accommodation literature; the Procuraduría is next door, same hours plus Sun 0900-1600. Tourist and Convention Bureau, Lázaro Cárdenas y Miramar, Mon-Sat 0900-1900, Sun 0900-1400, helpful; free copies of *Ensenada News and Views*, monthly English-language paper with information and adverts on northern Baja, Tijuana and Ensenada.

Airport 8 km S; scheduled flights to Tijuana, Guerrero Negro, Cedros Island, La Paz, etc.

Highway 3 E to San Felipe leaves Ensenada at the Benito Juárez *glorieta* monument as the Calzada Cortés. 26 km out of Ensenada, an 8-km dirt road branches S for a steep descent to the basic resort of **Agua Caliente** (C *Hotel Agua Caliente*, restaurant, bar, closed in winter; adjoining is a campground and large concrete pool heated to 38° by nearby hot springs; access road should not be attempted in wet weather).

At Km 39, a paved road leads off 3 km to Ojos Negros, continuing E (graded, dry weather) into scrub-covered foothills. It soon climbs into the ponderosa pine forests of the Sierra de Juárez. 37 km from Ojos Negros, the road enters the **Parque Nacional Constitución de 1857**. The jewel of the park is the small Laguna Hanson, a sparkling shallow lake surrounded by Jeffery pines; camping here is delightful, but note that the lake is reduced to a boggy marsh in dry seasons and that the area receives snow in mid-winter. A high-clearance vehicle is necessary for the continuation N out of the park to Highway 2 at El Cóndor 15 km E of La Rumorosa.

At Km 92½, Ejido Héroes de la Independencia, a graded dirt road runs 8 km E to the ruins of Mission Santa Catarina, founded in 1797 and abandoned after a raid by the Yuman Indians in 1840; the Paipái women in the village often have attractive pottery for sale.

Highway 3 descends along the edge of a green valley to the rapidly developing town of Valle de Trinidad. A reasonable dirt road runs S into the **Parque Nacional Sierra San Pedro Mártir** and Mike's Sky Rancho (35 km), a working ranch which offers motel-style accommodation, a pool, camping and guided trips into the surrounding mountains; rooms about US$8-10 per night, good meals.

After leaving the valley, the highway follows a canyon covered in dense stands of barrel cacti to the San Matías Pass between the Sierras Juárez and San Pedro Mártir which leads onto the desolate Valle de San Felipe. The highway turns E and emerges onto open desert hemmed in by arid mountains. 198½ km from Ensenada it joins Highway 5 at the La Trinidad T-junction, 148 km from Mexicali and 50 km from San Felipe.

Highway 1 S from Ensenada passes turn-offs to several beach resorts. Just before the agricultural town of **Maneadero**, a paved highway runs 23 km W onto the Punta Banda pensinula, where you can see **La Bufadora** blowhole, one of the most powerful on the Pacific. Air sucked from a sea-level cave is expelled as high as 16m through a cleft in the cliffs. Concrete steps and viewing platform give easy access. Tourist stalls line the approach road and boys try to charge US$1 for parking (restaurants **Los Panchos** and **La Bufadora**, Mesquite-grilled seafood, *palapa* dining, both 0900 to around sunset). This is one of the easiest side trips off the length of Highway 1.

NB Tourist cards and vehicle documents of those travelling S of Maneadero are supposed to be validated at the immigration checkpoint on the southern outskirts of the town; the roadside office, however, is not always in operation. If you are not stopped, just keep going.

Chaparal-clad slopes begin to close in on the highway as it winds it way S, passing through the small towns of **Santo Tomás** (D *El Palomar Motel*, restaurant, bar, general store and gas station, RV park with full hook-ups, campsite with swimming pool, clean, refurbished, US$7, nearby ruins of the Dominican Mission of 1791, local Santo Tomás wine— cheaper out of town) and **San Vicente** (2 Pemex stations, cafés, tyre repairs, several stores), before reaching Colonet. This is a supply centre for surrounding ranches; several services. A dry weather dirt road runs 12 km W to **San Antonio del Mar**: many camping spots amid high dunes fronting a beautiful beach renowned for surf fishing and clam-digging.

14 km S of Colonet a reasonable graded road branches to San Telmo and climbs into the mountains. At 50 km it reaches the **Meling Ranch** (also called San José), which offers resort accommodation for about 12 guests. 15 km beyond San José the road enters the **Parque Nacional Sierra San Pedro Mártir** and climbs through forests to three astronomical observatories perched on the dramatic eastern escarpment of the central range. The view from here is one of the most extensive in North America: E to the Gulf, W to the Pacific, and SE to the overwhelming granite mass of the **Picacho del Diablo** (3,096m), Baja's highest peak. The higher reaches of the park receive snow in winter. The observatories are not open to visitors.

179 km from Ensenada **San Quintín**, a thriving market city (pop 15,000) almost joined to Lázaro Cárdenas 5 km S. There are service stations in both centres and San Quintín provides all services. Rising out of the peninsula W of San Quintín bay is a line of volcanic cinder cones, visible for many kilometres along the highway; the beaches to the S near Santa María are hugely popular with fishermen, campers and beachcombers.

Festival 20 November, Day of the Revolution, street parades with school children, bands and the military.

Hotels A *La Pinta*, isolated beachfront location 18 km S of San Quintín then 5 km W on paved road, a/c, TV, balconies, tennis, nearby airstrip, reasonably priced breakfasts, even for non-residents; **E** *Hada's Rooms*, just N of Benito Juárez army camp in Láraro Cárdenas, cheapest in town, shabby, basic, sometimes closed when water and electricity are cut off.

   Motels C *Cielito Lindo*, 2 km beyond the *La Pinta Hotel* on S shore of bay, restaurant, cafeteria, lounge (dancing Sat nights), electricity Mon-Sat 0700-1100, 1500-2400, Sun 0700-2400, modest but pleasant, last km of access road unpaved, messy after rain; **A-C** *Molino Viejo/The Old Mill*, on site of old English mill—part of an early agricultural scheme, upgraded by new American owners, new wing, new bar and dining room with good food and drink, on bay 6 km of W of highway and S of Lázaro Cárdenas, rough access road, some kitchenettes, also one 6-bed dormitory, 15 RV spaces with full hook-up (US$15), camping (US$10), electricity 0800-0900, 1800-2200, various sizes of boat for rent, rec as 'delightfully well-run and cosy' (in USA, representative is The Baja Outfitter, 223 Via de San Ysidro, Ste 76, San Ysidro, CA 92173, T 619-428-2779, F 619-428-6269, or T 800-479-7962); **D** *Ernesto's*, next door, rustic, overpriced, popular with fishermen, electricity 0700-2100; **D** *Muelle Viejo*, between *Ernesto's* and the old English cemetery, restaurant, bad access road, hot showers, bay views; **D** *Chávez*, on highway N of Lázaro Cárdenas, family-style, clean rooms, plain but good value; **E** *Romo*, about 200m from post office, clean, OK, convenient if arriving late; **E** *Uruapan*, very clean and friendly.

Camping *Honey's RV Campground*, 15 km S and 2 km W on coast, 200 spaces, no electricity, disposal station, toilets, showers, beach access, US$5 per vehicle, great area for clam-digging. *Posada Don Diego*, off Highway in Colonia Guerrero (S of town, Km 174), wide range of facilities, laundry, restaurant, etc, 100 spaces, US$7; nearby is *Mesón de Don Pepe RV Park*, smaller and more modest, full hook-ups, restaurant, US$5. *Campo Lorenzo* is just N of Molino Viejo, 20 spaces, full hook-up but mostly permanent residents. Trailer park attached to Cielito Lindo Motel, comfortable.

Restaurants *El Alteño*, on highway next to the cinema, bare but clean roadhouse, fresh seafood and Mexican dishes, Mariachi music, moderate prices, closed July-September; *Tres Estrellas de Oro*, where the bus company stops for lunch, reasonably priced and sized meals. *Muelle Viejo*, next to motel, overlooks old pier, reasonably-priced seafood, modest decor. *Mi Lien* on Highway 1, N end of town, very good Chinese food.

Services Post office on highway opposite the *El Alteño*. **Banco Internacional**, off highway behind the Pemex station and small plaza.

After leaving the San Quintín valley, bypassing Santa María (fuel), the Transpeninsular Highway (officially the Carretera Transpeninsular Benito Juárez) runs near the Pacific before darting inland at El Consuelo Ranch. It climbs over a barren spur from which there are fine views, then drops in a succession of tight curves into **El Rosario**, 58 km from San Quintín: **D** *Motel Rosario*, small, very clean; new motel at S end of town; **D-E** *Sinai*, comfortable, very clean, small RV park. This small, agricultural community has a Pemex station, small supermarket, a basic museum, and meals, including Espinosa's famous lobster *burritos* and omelettes, also a good *taco* stand outside the grocery store at night. 3 km S is a ruined Dominican Mission, founded 1774 upstream, then moved to its present site in 1882; take the graded dirt road to Punta Baja, a bold headland on the coast, where there is a solar-powered lighthouse and fishing village.

Highway 1 makes a sharp 90° turn at El Rosario and begins to climb into the central plateau; gusty winds increase and astonishingly beautiful desertscapes gradually become populated with many varieties of cacti. Prominent are the stately *cardones*: most intriguing are the strange, twisted *cirios* growing to heights of 6 to 10 m—they are unique to this portion of Baja California as far S as the Vizcaino Desert, and to a small area of Sonora state on the mainland. At Km 62 a 5 km track branches S to the adobe remains of Misión San Fernando Velicatá, the only Franciscan mission in Baja, founded by Padre Serra in 1769. 5 km further on, Rancho El Progreso offers expensive meals and refreshments (possible to camp behind Rancho—fill up with water if possible). The highway is now in the **Desierto Central de Baja California Natural Park** (as yet not officially recognised). About 26 km N of Cataviña a strange region of huge boulders begins, some as big as houses; interspersed by cacti and crouching elephant trees, this area is one of the most picturesque on the peninsula.

Cataviña is only a dozen buildings, with a small grocery store/*Café La Enramada*, the only Pemex station on the 227-km stretch from El Rosario to the Bahía de Los Angeles junction (there are in fact 2 fuel stations, but do not rely on either having supplies), and the attractive **A** *La Pinta Hotel*, a/c, pool, bar, electricity 1800-2400, good restaurant, tennis, 28 rooms. Attached to the *La Pinta* is the *Parque Natural Desierto Central de Baja California Trailer Park*, flush toilets, showers, restaurant, bar, US$3 per site. 2 km S of Cataviña is Rancho Santa Inés, which has dormitory-style accommodation (E), meals and a paved airstrip.

Highway 1 continues SE through an arid world of boulder-strewn mountains and dry salt lakes. At 53 km the new graded road to the Bahía San Luís Gonzaga (see under San Felipe) branches off to the E. After skirting the dry bed of Laguna Chapala (natural landing strip at southern end when lake is totally dry), the Transpeninsular Highway arrives at the junction with the paved road E to Bahía de Los Angeles; **C** *Parador Punta Prieta*, fair, 20 RV spaces with full hook-ups, few facilities; café and gas station at junction, fuel supply sometimes unreliable.

Excursion The side road runs 68 km through *cirios* and *datilillo* cactus-scapes and crosses the Sierra de la Asamblea to **Bahía de Los Angeles** (no public transport), a popular fishing town which, despite a lack of vegetation, is one of Baja's best-known beauty spots. The bay, sheltered by the forbidding slopes of Isla Angel de la Guarda (Baja's largest island), is a haven for boating (winds can be tricky for kayaks and small craft). The series of tiny beaches at the foot of the Díaz *cabañas* are good for swimming, but watch out for stingrays when wading. There is good clamming and oysters. Facilities in town include: gas station, bakery, stores, two trailer parks and four restaurants, paved airstrip; water supply is inadequate, a water truck visits weekly, electricity is cut off about 2200 nightly. There is also a modest but interesting museum in town, good for information on the many mines and mining techniques used in the region around the turn of the century, such as the San Juan Mine high in the mountains 24 km SSW which had its own 2-ft guage railway and wire rope tramway down to a smelter at Las Flores as early as 1895; the relic steam locomotive and mine car on display beside the airstrip are from this remarkable mine (which returned US$2 million in gold and silver before closing down in 1910). **B** *Villa Vita Motel*, modern, a/c, pool,

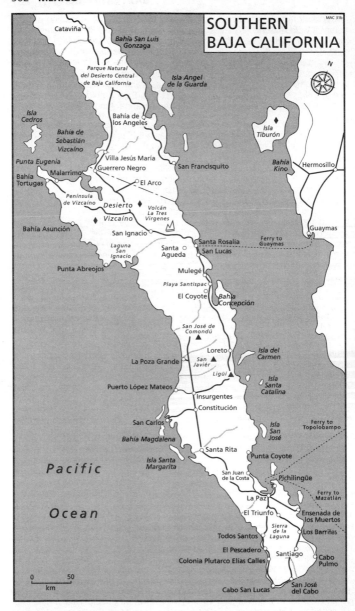

MAC 31b

SOUTHERN
BAJA CALIFORNIA

N

Cataviña

Bahía San Luis Gonzaga

Parque Natural del Desierto Central de Baja California

Isla Angel de la Guarda

Isla Cedros

Bahía de Sebastián Vizcaíno

Bahía de los Angeles

Isla Tiburón

Punta Eugenia

Villa Jesús María

Guerrero Negro

San Francisquito

Bahía Kino

Hermosillo

Malarrimo

Bahía Tortugas

El Arco

Península de Vizcaíno

Desierto

Vizcaíno

Volcán La Tres Vírgenes

Bahía Asunción

San Ignacio

Laguna San Ignacio

Santa Rosalia

San Lucas

Ferry to Guaymas

Guaymas

Santa Agueda

Punta Abreojos

Mulegé

Playa Santispac

El Coyote

Bahía Concepción

San José de Comondú

Loreto

Isla del Carmen

La Poza Grande

San Javier

Ligüí

Isla Santa Catalina

Puerto López Mateos

Insurgentes

Constitución

San Carlos

Bahía Magdalena

Isla San José

Ferry to Topolobampo

Isla Santa Margarita

Santa Rita

Punta Coyote

San Juan de la Costa

Pichilingüe

Pacific

Ocean

La Paz

Ferry to Mazatlán

El Triunfo

Ensenada de los Muertos

Sierra de la Laguna

Los Barriles

Todos Santos

El Pescadero

Colonia Plutarco Elías Calles

Santiago

Cabo Pulmo

0   50
km

Cabo San Lucas

San José del Cabo

jacuzzi, boat launch, trailer park, electricity 0700-1400, 1700-2000, bar, dining room; **C** *Casa de Díaz*, 15 rooms, restaurant, grocery store, campground, boat rentals, clean, well-run, popular; *Guillermo's Trailer Park*, flush toilets, showers, restaurant, gift shop, boat ramp and rentals; *Guillermo's* also has a new restaurant in a white building on main street, above the gift shop, well-prepared Mexican food, attractive, reservations advised at weekends; *La Playa RV Park*, on beach, similar facilities and tariff (US$4 per site). *Restaurant Las Hamacas*, on N edge of town, budget café with bay view, slow service, popular for breakfast. La Gringa is a beautiful beach 13 km N of town, many camping sites, pit toilets, rubbish bins, small fee.

Lynn and Walt Sutherland from Vancouver write: 'Bahía de los Angeles (pop 1,245) is worth a visit for its sea life. There are thousands of dolphins in the bay June-December. Some stay all year. In July and August you can hear the whales breathe as you stand on shore. There are large colonies of seals and many exotic seabirds. Fishing is excellent. A boat and guide can be rented for US$40 a day; try Raúl, a local fisherman, who speaks English.' Camping free and safe on beach.

The highway now runs due S through *Villa Jesús María* (gas station, store, cafés) to the 28th parallel, the state border between Baja California and Baja California Sur (soaring stylized eagle monument and **A** *Hotel La Pinta*, a/c, pool, dining room, bar, trailer park attached, 60 spaces, full hook-ups, US$5, laundry and gasoline at hotel). Before you enter Baja California Sur you pass Punta Prieta (3 stores) and Rosarito (1 store and 1 restaurant).

NB Advance clocks one hour to Mountain time when entering Baja California Sur, but note that Northern Baja observes Pacific Daylight Saving Time from first Sunday in April to last Sunday in October; time in both states and California is thus identical during the summer.

Guerrero Negro (9,000 people) is 3 km beyond the state line and 4 km W of the highway; 714 km S of Tijuana, 414 from San Quintín, it is halfway point between the US border and La Paz. There are 2 gas stations, bank, hospital, cafés, stores, an airport with scheduled services (just N of the Eagle monument), and the headquarters of Exportadora de Sal, the world's largest salt-producing firm. Seawater is evaporated by the sun from thousands of salt ponds S of town; the salt is loaded at the works 11 km SW of town and barged to a deepwater port on Cedros Island. From there ore carriers take it to the USA, Canada and Japan. Flights to Cedros Island and Bahía Tortugas cost US$20 one way; information from airfield downtown.

Hotel E *Cuartos de Sánchez-Smith*, Calle Barrera, W end of town, basic rooms, some with showers, cheapest in town. **Motels D** *El Morro*, on road into town from highway, modest, clean; **E** *Las Dunas*, few doors from *El Morro*, modest, clean; **E** *Gámez*, very basic, near city hall. **Camping** *Malarrimo Trailer Park*, on highway at junction to town, next to *Malarrimo Restaurant*, flush toilets, showers, bar US$5 per vehicle. Good restaurant at bus station.

Restaurants *Malarrimo Restaurant-Bar*, fishing decor, good fish and steak menu, moderate prices, music, open for breakfast; *Mario's Restaurant-Bar*, next to *El Morro*, modest surroundings and fare, disco. Good bakery on main street.

Whale watching is the main attraction on nearby *Laguna Ojo de Liebre*, usually known as *Scammon's Lagoon* after the whaling captain who first entered in 1857. California Grey Whales mate and give birth between end-December and February, in several warm-water lagoons on central Baja's Pacific coast, most leave by the beginning of April, but some not departing until as late as May or June. They can be seen cavorting and sounding from the old salt wharf 10 km NW of Guerrero Negro on the Estero San José, or from a designated 'whale watching area' with observation tower on the shore of Scammon's Lagoon 37 km S of town, access road branches off Highway 1, 8 km E of junction (if going by public transport, leave bus at the turn off and hitch). US$3 is charged to enter the park. Local personnel may collect a small fee for camping at the watching area—this pays to keep it clean. The shores of Scammon's are part of the **Parque Natural**

de Ballena Gris. Watch between 0700 and 0900 and again at 1700. The authorities in Guerrero Negro say that boats are not allowed on to the lagoon to watch whales, but reports indicate that *pangas* are still available for hire (US$10 pp).

The road to the park was repaired in 1991 and now has little whale signs at regular intervals. It is still sandy in places, so drive with care.

After Guerrero Negro the highway enters the grim Vizcaíno Desert. A paved but badly potholed road leads due E (42 km) to El Arco, other abandoned mining areas and crossing to **San Francisquito** on its beautiful bay on the Gulf (77 km), and to Santa Gertrudis Mission (1752), some of whose stone ruins have been restored; the chapel is still in use. It should be stressed that these minor Bajan roads require high-clearance, preferably 4x4, vehicles carrying adequate equipment and supplies, water and fuel. A new gravel road from Bahía de Los Angeles (135 km) gives easier road access than from El Arco and opens up untouched stretches of the Gulf coast.

Vizcaíno Peninsula which thrusts into the Pacific S of Guerrero Negro is one of the remotest parts of Baja. Although part of the Vizcaíno Desert, the scenery of the peninsula is varied and interesting; isolated fishcamps dot the silent coast of beautiful coves and untrodden beaches. Until recently only the most hardy ventured into the region; now an improved dry-weather road cuts W through the peninsula to Bahía Tortugas and the rugged headland of Punta Eugenia. It leaves Highway 1 at Vizcaíno Junction (also called Fundolegal, Pemex station, café, market, pharmacy and auto parts store; *Motel Oliva* at Vizcaíno is overpriced, with cold water), 70 km beyond Guerrero Negro and is paved for 8 km to Ejido Díaz Ordaz. The new road passes Rancho San José (116 km) and the easily-missed turnoff to Malarrimo Beach (where beachcombing is unparalled). After another bumpy 50 km is **Bahía Tortugas**, a surprisingly large place (pop 3,200) considering its remoteness. Many facilities including eating places, health clinic, gas station, airport with services to Cedros Island and Ensenada, and the small **D/E** *Vera Cruz Motel*, restaurant, bar, very modest but the only accommodation on the peninsula apart from a trailer park at Campo René, 15 km from Punta Abreojos. Two roads leave the Vizcaíno-Bahía Tortuga road for Bahía Asunción (pop 1,600), which has the peninsula's only other gas station, then following the coast to Punta Prieta, La Bocana and Punta Abreojas (93 km). A lonely road runs for 85 km back to Highway 1, skirting the Sierra Santa Clara before crossing the salt marshes N of Laguna San Ignacio and reaching the main road 26 km before San Ignacio.

The Highway continues SE on a new alignment still not shown on most maps and, 20 km from Vizcaíno Junction, reaches the first of 23 microwave relay towers which follow Highway 1 almost to the Cape. They are closed to the public but make excellent landmarks and, in some cases, offer excellent views. 143 km from Guerrero Negro is the turnoff for **San Ignacio** (pop 2,200). Here the Jesuits built a mission in 1728 and planted the ancestors of the town's date palm groves. On the square is the beautifully-preserved mission church, completed by the Dominicans in 1786. The town is very attractive, with thatched-roof dwellings and pastel-coloured commercial buildings; there is limited shopping but several restaurants, service station, mechanical assistance and bank.

Hotel A *La Pinta*, on road leading into town, a/c, pool, all facilities, built in mission style, attractive but overpriced; **E** *Cuartos Glenda*, with shower, basic but cheapest in town, on highway E. **Motel D** *La Posada*, on rise 2 blocks from zócalo (difficult to find), well-maintained, fans, shower, best value in town, worth bargaining (owner can arrange trips to the cave paintings for US$25 pp).

Camping *San Ignacio Transpeninsula Trailer Park*, Government-run, on Highway 1 behind Pemex station at the junction, full hook-ups, toilets, showers US$4 per site; basic campground on left of road into San Ignacio, grass, rec, helpful owner, Martín, cheap dates in season; one other basic site on this road, insects, not recommended.

Loncheria Chalita, on Zócalo, excellent value; *Restaurant Tota* has received poor reports.

A 70-km road from San Ignacio leads to **Laguna San Ignacio**, one of the best whale viewing sites; mothers and calves often swim up to nuzzle boats and allow their noses to be stroked. The Cooperativa Laguna de San Ignacio, Calle Juárez 23, off the Zócalo in San Ignacio, takes fishermen to the lagoon every day and can sometimes accommodate visitors. The road is rough and requires a high clearance vehicle.

There are many cave painting sites around San Ignacio; colourful human and animal designs left by Baja's original inhabitants still defy reliable dating, or full understanding. To reach most requires a trek by mule over tortuous trails; Oscar Fischer, owner of the *La Posada Motel*, arranges excursions into the sierras (about US$10 per person to Santa Teresa cave). The cave at the **Cuesta del Palmarito**, 5 km E of Rancho Santa Marta (50 NW of San Ignacio), is filled with designs of humans with uplifted arms, in brown and black; a jeep and guide (if one can be found) are required. A better road leads E from the first microwave station past Vizcaíno Junction up to **San Francisco de la Sierra**, where there are other paintings and petroglyphs in the vicinity (US$120 pp for trip with own car).

Highway 1 leaves the green *arroyo* of San Ignacio and re-emerges into the arid central desert. To the N, the triple volcanic cones of **Las Tres Vírgenes** come into view, one of the most dramatic mountain scenes along this route. Dark brown lava flows on the flanks are evidence of relatively recent activity (eruption in 1746, smoke emission in 1857). The highest peak is 2,149m above the Gulf of California; the sole vegetation on the lunar-like landscape is the thick-skinned elephant trees.

2½ million hectares of the Vizcaíno Desert are now protected by the **Reserva de la Biósfera El Vizcaíno**, supposedly the largest in Latin America. It was decreed in November 1988 and has absorbed the Parque Nacional Ballena Gris. It runs S from the state border to the road from San Ignacio to Laguna San Ignacio and Highway 1 near Santa Rosalía; it stretches from the Pacific to the Gulf. Encompassed by the reserve are the desert, the Vizcaína Peninsula, Scammon's Lagoon, Las Tres Vírgenes volcano, the Laguna San Ignacio and several offshore islands.

72 km from San Ignacio is *Santa Rosalía*, a bustling city of 14,500. It was built by the French El Boleo Copper Company in the 1880s, laid out in neat rows of wood frame houses, many with broad verandahs, which today give Santa Rosalía its distinctly un-Mexican appearance. Most of the mining ceased in 1953; the smelter, several smokestacks above the town and much of the original mining operation can be seen on the N of town. There is a small museum off Calle Francisco next to the Impecsa warehouse, historic exhibits of mining and smelting. The port was one of the last used in the age of sail. The church of Santa Bárbara (Av Revolución y Calle C, a block N of the main plaza), built of prefabricated galvanized iron for the 1889 Paris Worlds' Fair from a design by Eiffel, was shipped around the Horn to Baja. A car ferry leaves for Guaymas at 0800 on Sun and Wed, from the small harbour, 7 hrs (T 20014, fares are the same as for the La Paz-Topolobampo ferry, see below).

Drivers should note that Santa Rosalía's streets are narrow and congested; larger vehicles should park along the highway or in the ferry dock parking lot. The Pemex station is conveniently located on the highway, unlike at Mulegé (see below), so larger RVs and rigs should fill up here.

Hotels and Restaurants D *El Morro*, on Highway 2 km S of town, T 20414, on bluff with Gulf views, modern, Spanish-style, a/c, bar, restaurant (good food, generous portions, reasonable prices); **D** *Francés*, Av 11 de Julio on the N Mesa, T 20829, a/c, restaurant, bar, pool not always filled, historic 2-storey wooden French colonial building overlooking smelter and Gulf, photos of sailing vessels on walls. **D** *Olvera*, on main plaza, 2nd floor, a/c, showers, clean, good value; **D** *Playa*, Av La Playa between Calles B y Plaza, central, fans, bathrooms, good budget hotel; **D** *Real*, Av Manuel Montoya near Calle A, similar to *Olvera*, rec; **E** *Blanca y Negra*, basic but clean, Av Libertad at end of Calle 3. Camping possible on the beach under *palapas*, access via an unmarked road ½ km S of *El Morro*, free, no facilities, a beautiful spot.

Balneario Selene, T 20685, on Highway opposite Pemex; *Palapa Mauna Loa*, T 21187, on Highway below copper smelter, good spaghetti and pizzas, popular; *Panadería El Boleo*, widely noted for its delicious French breads.

Post Only from here and La Paz can parcels be sent abroad; customs check necessary first, at boat dock.

Bus Tres Estrellas de Oro bus station (T 220150) near tourist office and Pemex station 2 km S of ferry terminal; stop for most Tijuana-La Paz buses, several per day. To **La Paz**, 1100, US$17.50. Autobus Aguila, Calle 3a y Calle Constitución, T 20374.

Painted cave sites can be visited from the farming town of **Santa Agueda**, turnoff 8 km S of Santa Rosalía then rough dirt road for 12 km. (4WD necessary, guide can be arranged at the Delegado Municipal, Calle Madero, Mulegé.) The caves are in the San Borjita and La Trinidad deserts; the drawings depict animals, children and, some claim, female sexual organs. The fishing village of **San Lucas**, on a palm-fringed cove, is 14 km S of Santa Rosalía; camping is good and popular on the beaches to N and S. *San Lucas RV Park*, on beach, no hook-ups, flush toilets, boat ramp, ice, restaurant, US$5 per vehicle, 35 spaces, rec. Offshore lies Isla San Marcos, with a gypsum mine at the S end.

Just beyond **San Bruno** is a reasonable dirt road to **San José de Magdalena** (15 km), a picturesque farming village dating back to colonial days; ruined Dominican chapel, attractive thatched palm houses, flower gardens. An awful road leads on for 17 km to Rancho San Isidro, from where the ruined Guadalupe Mission can be reached on horseback. At San Bruno, *Costa Serena* beach camping, no hook-ups, one shower, clean beach with good fishing and shrimping. Similar is *Camp Punta Chivato*, just before Mulegé, no hook-ups but clean toilets and shower, beautiful location.

Mulegé, 61 km S of Santa Rosalía, is another oasis community (pop 5,000) whose river enters the gulf as a lushly-vegetated tidal lake. There are lovely beaches, good diving, snorkelling and boating in the Bahía Concepción. The old Federal territorial prison (La Cananea) is being converted into a museum. There is a good cheap fish restaurant 40 mins walk along the river; the lighthouse, 10 mins further on provides tremendous views and the sunsets are unforgettable. S of the bridge which carries the highway over the river is the restored Mission of Santa Rosalía de Mulegé, founded by the Jesuits in 1705; good lookout point above the mission over the town and its sea of palm trees. Locals swim at an excellent spot about ½ km inland from the bridge and to the right of the track to the Mission. The bank will only change a minimum of US$100. **NB** one Pemex station is in the centre; not convenient for large vehicles, and a one-way system to contend with, but there is another Pemex station 4½ km S of the bridge, on the road out of town towards Loreto, with restaurant and mini-market.

Hotels B *Baja Hacienda*, Calle Madero 3, lovely courtyard, pool, rooms refurbished, bar, trips to cave paintings and kayaking offered (US$25 pp), rec; **B** *Serenidad*, 4 km S of town near the river mouth on beachside road, delightful, a/c, pool, sophisticated dining room, bar, banquet/mariachi band Wed and Sat nights, cottages, trailer park, T 20111, rec; **B** *Vista Hermosa*, opp the *Serenidad*, a/c, pool, excellent restaurant, bar with satellite US TV; **C** *Las Casitas*, Callejón de los Estudiantes y Av Madero, central, a/c, showers, restaurant next door, shady garden patio, fishing trips arranged, pleasant older hotel, well-run; **D** *Suites Rosita*, Av Madero near main plaza, a/c, kitchenettes, clean and pleasant; **D** *Terraza Motel*, Calles Zaragoza y Moctezuma, in business district, 35 rooms, rooftop bar, basic, clean; **E** *Casa de Huéspedes Manuelita*, sloppily run but reasonably clean; **F** *Casa Nachita*, next door, with fan, basic and pleasant, fairly clean, hot water in am. **E** *Huesped Canett*, Madero, next to church by riverside, shared bath, basic, clean and friendly, fan supplied, ground floor rooms with bath.

Camping *The Orchard (Huerta Saucedo) RV Park*, on river S of town, partly shaded, off

Highway 1, pool, boat ramp, fishing, up to US$10.50 for two; *Villa María Isabel RV Park*, on river and Highway E of *Orchid*, pool, recreation area, disposal station, American-style bakery; *Jorge's del Río Trailer Park*, grassy, on river at E end of Highway bridge by unpaved road, hot water, clean, plenty of shade but watch belongings at night; *Pancho's RV Park*, next to *María Isabel*, off Highway 1, little shade; *Oasis Río Baja RV Park*, on same stretch as those above, reasonable. All the foregoing have full hook-ups, flush toilets, showers, etc. From here on down the Bahía Concepción coast and beyond are many *playas públicas* (*PP*); some have basic facilities, most are simple, natural camping spots on beautiful beaches where someone may or may not collect a fee. At Mulegé is the Playa Sombrerito at the hat-shaped hill (site of Mexican victory over US forces in 1847), restaurant and store nearby. White gas is sold at the *ferretería* 'on the far side of town from the main entrance' in large cans only.

Restaurants *Patio El Candil*, Calle Zaragoza, simple outdoor dining; *Azteca* and *Vista Hermosa* at *Hotel Terraza*, good food, budget prices; *Paco y Rosy's*, signed turnoff from Highway 2 km S, rustic, friendly, Chinese, open from 1800. *Tandil* and *Las Casitas*. *Equipales*, Calle Zaragoza, 2nd floor, rec for good local cooking and for breakfasts; *Baja Burger*, between *Las Casitas* and *Hotel Baja Hacienda*, traditional burgers and *quesadillas*, ice cream. *Doney's Tacos*, Fco Madero, end farthest from centre, good food and clean. Good pizza place under the bridge, on the river between *Jorge's Trailer Park* and town, reasonable prices, English book exchange. In the plaza next to the *Hacienda* is a good *taco* stand in am and vendors selling chips and *churros* in pm. Next to *Doney's* on Madero is a Corona beer store, selling ice-cold beer with plastic bags of ice supplied.

Dive Shop Calle Madero 45, rents equipment and runs trips around Bahía Concepción.

Launderette *Lavimática*, Calle Doblado, opp Tres Estrellas bus station.

Beyond Mulegé the Highway climbs over a saddle and then runs along the shores of the bay for 50 km. This stretch is the most heavily-used camping and boating area on the Peninsula; the water is beautiful, swimming safe (although one disturbing warning received of 'stinging seaweed"), camping excellent, varied marine life. Bahía Concepción and Playa Santispac, 23 km S of Mulegé, are recommended, many small restaurants (eg *Ana's*, which sells water, none other available, food good value) and *palapas* (shelters) for hire (day or overnight, US$2.50). Beyond Santispac is Playa Burro and, beyond that, an unnamed beach. Further S from El Coyote is Playa Buenaventura, which has *palapas* and 3 *cabañas* for rent (US$20), and a restaurant serving wine, burgers and spaghetti. From the entrance to the beach at Requesón, veer to the left for Playa La Perla, which is small and secluded. In summer this area is extremely hot and humid, the sea is too salty to be refreshing and there are many midges.

A new graded dirt road branches off Highway 1 to climb over the towering **Sierra Giganta**, whose desert vistas of flat-topped mesas and *cardón* cacti are straight out of the Wild West; it begins to deteriorate after the junction (20 km) to San José de Comondú and limps another 37 km into San Isidro after a spectacular drop into the La Purísima Valley. San Isidro has a population of 1,000 but little for the visitor; 5 km down the valley is the more attractive oasis village of La Purísima (pop 800). The road leads on southwards to Pozo Grande (52 km) and Ciudad Insurgentes (85 km), it is now beautifully paved and is probably the fastest stretch of road in Baja. Two side roads off the San Isidro road lead down to the twin towns of San Miguel de Comondú and San José de Comondú (high-clearance vehicles are necessary); both oasis villages of 500 people each. One stone building remains of the mission moved to San José in 1737; the original bells are still at the church. A new graded road leads on to Pozo Grande and Ciudad Insurgentes.

Loreto (pop 7,300), 1,125 km from Tijuana, is one of the most historic places in Baja. Here settlement of the Peninsula began with Father Juan María Salvatierra's founding of the Mission of Nuestra Señora de Loreto on 25 October 1697. The Mission is on the Zócalo, the largest structure in town and perhaps the best-restored of all the Baja California mission buildings. It has a gilded altar. The museum beside the church is worth a visit: there are educational displays about the missions, Bajan history and historic horse and ranching equipment, book shop, open Tues-Sat 0900-1700. Inscription over the main door of the mission announces: 'Mother of all the Missions of Lower and Upper California". Nestled between the slopes of the Sierra Giganta and the offshore Isla del Carmen, Loreto has experienced a tourist revival; fishing in the Gulf here is some of the best in Baja California.

Hotels **A** *Oasis*, Calles de la Playa y Baja California, T 30112, on bay at S end of Loreto in palm grove, large rooms, pool, tennis, restaurant, bar, skiffs (pangas) for hire, fishing cruises arranged, pleasant and quiet, a/c; **A-B** *La Pinta*, on Sea of Cortés 2 km N of Zócalo, a/c, showers, pool, tennis, restaurant, bar, considered by many the best of the original 'Presidente' paradores, 30 rooms, fishing boat hire, recommended; **C** *La Siesta Bungalows*, small, manager owns the dive shop and can offer combined accommodation and diving trips; **C** *Misión de Loreto*, Calle de la Playa y Juárez, T 30048, colonial-style with patio garden, a/c, pool, dining rooms, bar, fishing trips arranged, very comfortable, but poor service, check for discounts; **D** *Villa del Mar*, Colina Zaragoza, near sports centre, OK, restaurant, bar, pool, bargain rates, on beach. **Motel** **D** *Salvatierra*, Calle Salvatierra, on S approach to town, a/c, hot showers, clean, good value; **E** *Davis*, Calle Davis, (bargaining possible), basic, fair, ask for directions, it's down a sidestreet. **E** *Casa de huéspedes San Martín*, with shower, address not known.

Camping *Ejido Loreto RV Park*, on beach 1 km S of town, full hook-ups, toilets, showers, laundry, fishing and boat trips arranged, US$7.50 per site. *Flying Sportsman*, just S of town, 31 spaces with full hook-ups, laundry. *PPs* in the area average US$2-3 pp. Butter clams are plentiful in the sand.

Restaurants on Calle de la Playa, *Embarcadero*, owner offers fishing trips, average prices for food; *El Nido* and *El Buey*, both good (latter barbecues); several *taco* stands on Calle Salvatierra. *Playa Blanca*, Hidalgo y Madero, rustic, American meals, reasonable prices; *César's*, Emiliano Zapata y Benito Juárez, good food and service, candelit, moderate prices; *Café Olé*, Madero 14, Mexican and fast food, palapa-style, open-air breakfasts, budget rates.

Diving Scuba and snorkelling information and equipment booth on municipal beach near the fishing pier; the beach itself stretches for 8 km, but is dusty and rocky.

Airport International, 4 km S; Aero California to La Paz and Los Angeles.

Bus Bus station at Calle Salvatierra opposite intersection of Zapata; to **La Paz** 6 a day, from 0700, US$10.75; to **Tijuana** 1500, 1800, 2100, 2300, US$30, 17 hrs.

Just S of Loreto a rough road runs 37 km through impressive canyon scenery to the village of ***San Javier***, tucked in the bottom of a steep-walled valley; the settlement has only one store but the Mission of San Javier is one of the best-preserved in North America; it was founded by the Jesuits in 1699 and took 59 years to complete. The thick volcanic walls, Moorish ornamentation and bell tower are most impressive in so rugged and remote a location. Near San Javier is Piedras Pintas, close to Rancho Las Parras; there are eight prehistoric figures painted here in red, yellow and black. The road to San Javier Mission, having been washed out in 1991, has been patched up enough for sturdy vehicles, but it is in poor shape nonetheless.

The highway S of Loreto passes a picturesque stretch of coast. Fonatur, the government tourist development agency, is building a resort complex at ***Nopoló*** (8 km), which it hoped would one day rival its other resort developments at Cancún, Ixtapa and Huatulco. An international airport, streets and electricity were laid out, then things slowed down; today there is the 15-storey **L** *El Presidente Hotel*, T 30700; international class, self-contained, on its own imported-sand beach; nearby lighted Loreto Tennis Center, half-finished foundations, weeds and an absence of people. 16 km further on is Puerto Escondido, with a new yacht harbour and marina; although the boat landing and anchoring facilities are operating, the complex is still far from complete, slowed by the same diversion of funds to other projects as Nopaló. There is, however, the *Tripui Trailer Park*, claimed to be the best in Mexico (PO Box 100, Loreto), landscaped grounds, paved roads, coin laundry, groceries, restaurant and pool, lighted tennis court, playground; 116 spaces (most rented by the year), US$17 for 2, extra person US$5

(T 706-833-0413). There are three lovely *PP*s between Loreto and Puerto Escondido (none has drinking water); Notrí, Juncalito and Ligüí—palm-lined coves, which are a far cry from the bustle of the new resort developments nearby. Beyond Ligüí (36 km S of Loreto) Highway 1 ascends the eastern escarpment of the Sierra Giganta (one of the most fascinating legs of Highway 1) before leaving the Gulf to strike out SW across the Peninsula again to Ciudad Constitución. It passes by **Ciudad Insurgentes**, a busy agricultural town of 13,000 with two service stations, banks, auto repairs, shops and cafés (no hotels/motels), then runs dead straight for 26 km to **Ciudad Constitución**, which is the marketing centre for the Magdalena Plain agricultural development and has the largest population between Ensenada and La Paz (50,000). Although not a tourist town, it has extensive services of use to the visitor: department stores, restaurants, banks, public market, service stations, laundries, car repairs, hospital (see introduction to this section, **Insurance and Medical Services**) and airport (near Ciudad Insurgentes). Many businesses line Highway 1, which is divided and doubles as the palm-lined main street, with the first traffic lights since Ensenada, 1,158 km away.

Hotels D *Maribel*, Guadalupe Victoria y Highway 1, T 20155, 2 blocks S of San Carlos road junction, a/c, TV, restaurant, bar, suites available, clean, fine for overnight stop; **D** *Casino*, a block E of the *Maribel* on same street, T 20754, quieter, 37 clean rooms, restaurant, bar; **E** *El Arbolito*, basic, clean, central.

Camping *Campestre La Pila*, 2½ km S on unpaved road off Highway 1, farmland setting, full hook-ups, toilets, showers, pool, laundry, groceries, tennis courts, ice, restaurant, bar, no hot water, US$10-13 for 4.

Food *Panadería Superpan*, N of market hall, excellent pastries.

Excursion Deep artesian wells have made the desert of the Llano de Magdalena bloom with citrus groves and a chequerboard of neat farms growing cotton, wheat and vegetables; this produce is shipped out through the port of San Carlos, 58 km to the W on **Bahía Magdalena**. Known to boaters as 'Mag Bay", it is considered the finest natural harbour between San Francisco and Acapulco. Protected by mountains and sand spits, it provides the best boating on Baja's Pacific coast. Small craft can explore kilometres of mangrove-fringed inlets and view the grey whales who come here in the winter season. On the narrow S end of Magdalena Island is Puerto Magdalena, a lobstering village of 400. 7 km away is a deepwater port at Punta Belcher. Whales can be seen at Puerto López Mateos; no hotel, but take a tent and camp at the small harbour near the fish plant, or stay in Ciudad Constitución, several daily buses. On Santa Margarita Island are Puertos Alcatraz (a fish-canning community of 300) and Cortés (important naval base); neither is shown on the ACSC map.

Highway 1 continues its arrow-straight course S of Ciudad Constitución across the flat plain to the village of Santa Rita, where it makes a 45° turn E 28 km beyond Santa Rita, a road of dubious quality runs to the remote missions of San Luis Gonzaga (64 km) and La Pasión (49 km); it is planned to extend it to the ruins of Dolores del Sur (85 km) on the Gulf of California, one of Baja's most inaccessible mission sites. There is a service station at the village of El Cien; meals and refreshments are available at the Rancho San Agustín, 24 km beyond.

La Paz, capital of Baja California Sur (state pop 1990 317,300), is a fast-changing, but relaxed modern city (population 168,000, 1991), nestled at the southern end of La Paz Bay (where Europeans first set foot in Baja in 1533). Sunsets can be spectacular. Prices have risen as more tourists arrive to enjoy its winter climate, but free port status ensures that there are plenty of bargains (although some goods, like certain makes of camera, are cheaper to buy in the USA). Oyster beds attracted many settlers in the 17th century, but few survived long. The Jesuit mission, founded here in 1720, was abandoned 29 years later. La Paz became

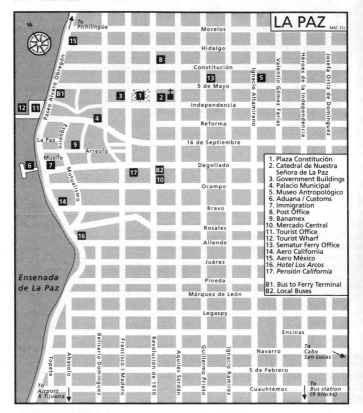

LA PAZ MAC 31c

1. Plaza Constitución
2. Catedral de Nuestra Señora de La Paz
3. Government Buildings
4. Palacio Municipal
5. Museo Antropológico
6. Aduana / Customs
7. Immigration
8. Post Office
9. Banamex
10. Mercado Central
11. Tourist Office
12. Tourist Wharf
13. Sematur Ferry Office
14. Aero California
15. Aero México
16. Hotel Los Arcos
17. Pensión California
B1. Bus to Ferry Terminal
B2. Local Buses

the territorial capital in 1830 after Loreto was wiped out by a hurricane. Although bursting with new construction, there are still many touches of colonial grace, arched doorways and flower-filled patios. The early afternoon *siesta* is still observed by many businesses, especially during summer.

Heart of La Paz is the **Plaza Constitución**, facing which are the Government Buildings and the graceful **Cathedral of Nuestra Señora de la Paz**, built in 1861-65 on or near the site of the original mission. The Post Office is a block NE at Revolución de 1910 y Constitución. The street grid is rectangular; westerly streets run into the Paseo Alvaro Obregón—the waterfront **Malecón**—where the commercial and tourist wharves back onto a tangle of streets just W of the main plaza; here are the banks, City Hall, Chinatown and many of the cheaper *pensiones*. The more expensive hotels are further SW. A must is the **Museo Antropológico de Baja California Sur**, Ignacio Altamirano y 5 de Mayo (4 blocks E of the Plaza), with an admirable display of peninsula anthropology, history and pre-history, folklore and geology. (The bookshop has a wide selection on Mexico and Baja. Open Tues-Sat 0900-1800; entry free.) A carved mural depicting the history of Mexico can be seen at the **Palacio de Gobierno** on Isabel La Católica, corner of Bravo. There are boat tours from the Tourist Wharf on the

Malecón around the bay and to nearby islands like Espíritu Santo.

Festival Pre-Lenten Mardi Gras (carnival) in February or March, inaugurated in 1989, is becoming one of Mexico's finest. The Malecón is converted into a swirling mass of dancing, games, restaurants and stalls, and the street parade is happy and colourful. Well worth a visit, but book accommodation far in advance.

Hotels **A+** *Los Arcos*, Paseo Alvaro Obregón 498 at Allende, T 22744, a/c, pool, restaurant, coffee shop, across the Malecón from the beach, walking distance of centre, fishing trips arranged, excellent value; **A+** *Cabañas de los Arcos*, opposite with shared facilities, a/c, pool, slightly cheaper, T 22297; **A+** *Gran Hotel Baja*, 'the only high-rise structure S of Ensenada", so easy to find, T 23844, restaurant, bar, pool, disco, etc, on beach, trailer park adjacent; **A+** *La Posada*, on bay 3½ km SW of centre, 5 blocks off Highway 1 on Colima, T 20653, a/c, pool, tennis, bar, restaurant, quiet and relaxing, recommended but away from the centre. **A** *El Morro*, 3½ km NE on Palmira Beach, Moorish-style, a/c, TV, fridges, apartments with kitchenettes, pool, restaurant, bar; **A** *El Presidente Sur*, 6½ km NE at Caimancito Beach, T 26544, good location but furthest from town, a/c, pool, restaurant, bar, next door to Governor's mansion; **A** *Misiones de La Paz*, on El Mogote sandspit, isolated, accessible by launch from *Hotel La Posada*, T 24021, a/c, showers, pool, restaurant, cocktail bar, quiet; **A** *Palmira*, T 24000, 3½ km NE of Pichilingüe road, a/c, pool, tennis, restaurant, disco, convention facilities, fishing trips arranged, popular with families; **C** *La Perla*, on the water front, T 20777, clean, a/c, friendly, restaurant expensive, locked garage; **C** *María Dolores Gardenias*, Aquíles Serdán y Vicente Guerrero, a/c, pool, restaurant (good), excellent, value. **D** *Hospedaje Marelí*, Aquíles Serdán 283 y Bravo, a/c, clean, 10 min walk to Plaza Constitución, pleasant, recommended; **D** *Hostería del Convento*, Calle Madero 85, fans, clean, shower, tepid water between 0700 and 0900, beautiful patio; **D** *Lorimar* on Bravo, hot showers, clean, very helpful, run by a Mexican/American couple, good value restaurant, free ferry booking service; **D** *Veneka*, Madero 1520, T 54688, nice, clean and friendly, safe parking, chained monkey in courtyard, not rec for animal lovers. **E** *Cuartos Jalisco*, Belisario Domínguez 251, very basic; **E** *Palencia*, Calle 16 de Septiembre nr Francisco Madero, central, basic, fans, seedy, not recommended; **E** *Pensión California*, Calle Degollado 209 near Madero, fan, shower, garden patio, noisy, friendly, basic and not too clean, but popular; **E** *Posada San Miguel*, Calle Belisario Domínguez Norte 45, near plaza, colonial-style, bathroom, clean, hot water morning and evening, OK. **F** *Miriam*, Av 16 de Septiembre, price per person, cheapest. **Youth Hostel** on Carretera al Sur (Highway 1), Blvd Forjadores de Sudcalifornia Km 3, CP 23040, T 24615, dormitory bunk US$1.60 per night, open 0600-2300, good value, '8 de Octubre' bus from market.

Camping *El Cardón Trailer Park*, 4 km SW on Highway 1, partly-shaded area away from beach, full facilities, US$11 for 2; *Aquamarina RV Park*, 3½ km SW, 400m off Highway 1 at Calle Nayarit, on bay, nicely landscaped, all facilities, marina, boat ramp, fishing, scuba trips arranged, US$17 for 2; *La Paz Trailer Park*, 1½ km S of town off Highway 1, access via Calle Colima, deluxe, nearest RV Park to La Paz, very comfortable, US$12 for 2. The ferretería across from the main city bus terminal sells white gas stove fuel (*gasolina blanca*). *La Perla de la Paz* department store, Calles Arreola y 21 de Agosto, sells general camping supplies. CCC Supermarket, opp Palacio de Gobierno, is good for supplies.

Restaurants *Palapa Adriana*, on beachfront, open air, excellent service but beware overcharging; *Antojitos*, next to *Pirámide* on 16 de Septiembre de 1810, friendly, good value. *Rossy*, Av 16 de Septiembre, good for breakfast, fish, cheap; *Café Chanate*, behind tourist office, open evening only, good atmosphere, jazz music, sometimes live. *La Caleta* on the waterfront near La Paz Lapa, rec; *Mar Vino y Queso*, Paseo Obregón, near tourist office, small, a/c, good fish, good service. *La Tavola Pizza*, good value. Restaurant of *Aquarius Hotel*, rec, fish burgers, free coffee. *Imperial Palace*, Degollado 213, next to *Pensión California*, Chinese, excellent, cheap. Vegetarian restaurant *El Quinto*, Independencia y B Domínguez, expensive (whole wheat bread is half the price at the *panadería* in the market place). Excellent and cheap tacos at a restaurant with no name on Av 16 de Septiembre, near the bus station. Good *lonchería* and juice bars in the market.

Shopping A duty-free port (but see above). *Casa de las Artesanías de BCS*, Paseo Alvaro Obregón at Mijares, just N of *Hotel Los Arcos*, for souvenirs from all over Mexico; *Centro de Arte Regional*, Chiapas y Encinas (5 blocks E of Isabel La Católica), pottery workshop, reasonable prices; *Fortunato Silva*, Highway 1 (Abasolo) y Jalisco at S end of town, good quality woollen and hand-woven cotton garments and articles. *Bazar del Sol*, Obregón 1665, for quality ceramics and good Aztec art reproductions; *Solco's*, Obregón y 16 de Septiembre, large selection of Taxco silver, leather, onyx chess sets. The Mercado Central, Revolución y Degollado, and another at Bravo y Prieto, have a wide range of goods (clothes, sandals, guitars, etc), plus fruit and vegetables. Tourist shops are concentrated along the Malecón between the Tourist and Commercial Wharves.

Rentals *Viajes Palmira* rents cycles and mopeds, Av Obregón, opp *Hotel los Arcos*, T 24030. Budget, Avis, Hertz, **Auto Renta Sol** and **Auto Servitur** booths at airport. *Baja Diving and Service*, Obregón 1680, hires equipment and takes diving trips (US$320 for 4-day PADI course); snorkelling day trip about US$35, very good.

Exchange Banks will not exchange TCs after 1100. **Banamex**, Calles Arreola y Esquerro.

Laundry *Laundromat Yoli*, Calles 5 de Mayo y Rubio.

Immigration Second floor of large building on Paseo Alvaro Obregón, opp the pier.

Tourist Office On Tourist Wharf at bottom of 16 de Septiembre, helpful, English spoken, open Mon-Fri 0800-1500, Sat 0900-1300, 1400-1500, open till 1900 high season, will make hotel reservations, some literature and town maps.

Buses Local buses about US$0.50, depot at Revolución de 1910 y Degollado by the Public Market. Central Bus Station (Central Camionera): Jalisco y Héroes de la Independencia, about 16 blocks from centre, terminal for Tres Estrellas de Oro and Autotransportes Aguila; Autotransportes de La Paz leave from Public Market. **Ciudad Constitución** 13 departures a day, US$7.70; **Loreto** 3 per day, US$11.50; **Guerrero Negro** 6 per day, US$24; **Ensenada** US$43; **Tijuana** US$60.50, **Mexicali** US$55. To the Cape: **San Antonio** US$1.75, **Miraflores** US$5, **San José del Cabo** US$6.60, **Cabo San Lucas** US$8 (all 10 departures per day). **Todos Santos**, 6 per day, US$4.40; Cabo San Lucas via W loop US$7.70.

Air General Manuel Márquez de León International Airport, 11 km SW on paved road off Highway 1. Taxi fare US$6, supposedly fixed, but bargain. AeroMéxico and Aero California: to Tijuana non-stop, Mexico City, Culiacán, Guadalajara, also to Los Angeles, California. AeroMéxico to Guaymas and Tucson, Arizona. Aero California: to Los Mochis, daily 0725. Loreto and Mazatlán; city office at Malecón y Calle Bravo. Aero Litoral to Chihuahua, Ciudad Obregón, El Paso (Texas), and Los Mochis.

Ferry Services Modern ferry terminal at Pichilingüe, 21 km N on paved highway. Tickets may be bought at Sematur, 5 de Mayo y Guillermo Prieto, between Reforma and Independencia, T 53833/54666, F 56588, open 0700-1200, but tickets are *not* sold at the terminal itself. (In Mexico City, Sematur, Paseo de la Reforma 509, 4th floor, T 553-7957, F 553-7935.) Travel agents sell ferry tickers, eg *Turismo Express*, Esplanada Alvaro Obregón y 16 de Septiembre, 23000 La Paz, T 56310-3, F 20706. Tourist cards must be valid, allow 2 hrs as there are long queues—trucks have loading priority. It should be noted that many motorists have had difficulty getting reservations or having them honoured. **NB** Vehicles must have car permits, as of July 1992, not obtainable at ferry ports, best to get at Registro Federal de Vehículos in Tijuana; automobile clubs will provide information. Four classes of service: *salón* (reserved non-reclining seat, not particularly comfortable when crowded), *turista* (roomette with with two bunks and a sink), *cabina* (bedroom with shower), *especial* (first class suite). The ferry journeys have not received favourable response; 'expensive, dirty, smelly and a cockroach haven."

To Topolobampo Daily except Mon, dep 2000, arr mainland 0600. Tickets sold on day of departure only (0800-1400, or passenger list taken at terminal at 1500, but many people turned away); apparently no women or children are carried on Friday (dangerous cargo). Fares *salón*, US$13.35.

To Mazatlán Sun-Fri (daily at holiday times), dep 1500, arr mainland 0900 next day; tickets sold one day in advance; stand firm. Fares *salón*, US$20; *turista*, US$40; *cabina*, US$55; *especial*, US$88; motorcycle US$20 (bicycles free). Cars (US$110) and motorhomes also carried. Children of 2-11 go half price. The deck gets wet during the night, but the top deck is very refreshing in summer; toilets quickly get blocked and are then locked up, so make an early call. To get a tourist cabin, insist that you will share with strangers—a friendly chat may help. The queue for seats starts at 0630. Book cars 4 weeks in advance. On arrival, buses to Mazatlán may be full, ask about rides on the ferry.

Bus to ferry terminal from Medrita Travel Agency, Paseo Alvaro Obregón y Calle 5 de Mayo, frequent departures; from terminal, Calle Ejido (first on the left after leaving the ferry). Reasonable facilities at terminal but crowded; large parking lots—officials may permit RVs to stay overnight while awaiting ferry departures.

NB On all ferry crossings, delays can occur from September if there is bad weather, which could hold you up for 3 days; fog at the entrance to Topolobampo harbour is often a problem; mechanical breakdowns are not unknown! Keep a flexible schedule if travelling to the mainland.

Beaches Many, most popular on the Pichilingüe Peninsula, most have restaurants. Going N from La Paz to ferry terminal on Highway 11; Palmira, Coromuel (popular with paceños), El Caimancito, Tesoro. Wind surfing and catamaran trips can be arranged on the main beach, if the English speaking owner likes you. Pichilingüe (bus at 0800 then hourly from 1000-1700, US$1 from station at Paseo Alvaro Obregón y Independencia), 100m N of ferry terminal is a *playa pública*. Balandra (rubbish bins, *palapas*, US$2), Tecolote (same) and El Coyote (no water or facilities), reached by the road beyond the ferry terminal (paved for some distance beyond this point), ends at a gravel pit at Playa Cachimba (good surf fishing), 13 km NE of Pichilingüe; beaches facing N are attractive but can be windy, some sandflies. El Comitán and El Mogote, are to SW of La Paz on bay, tranquil, no surf. In October (at least) and after rain, beware stinging jelly fish in the water.

Excursions All travel agencies offer a daily boat tour to **Los Lobos Islands** for US$10; the tour should include lunch and snorkelling, 6 hrs, you can see pelicans, sealions and dolphins, with luck whales, too. 17 km W of La Paz a paved road branches NW off Highway 1 leading to the mining village of **San Juan de la Costa**, allowing a closer look at the rugged coastal section of the Sierra de la Giganta. Pavement ends after 25 km, road becomes wide, rolling, regularly graded; OK for large RVs to San Juan, which is a company town of neat-rowed houses; phosphorus is mined and loaded by conveyor and deep-water dock, to be shipped to processing plants for fertilizer production. After San Juan (45 km), the road is passable for medium-size vehicles to Punta Coyote (90 km), closely following the narrow space between mountains and coast; wonderful untouched camping spots. From Coyote to **San Evaristo** (27 km) the track is poor—rugged vehicle recommended, travel time from Highway 1 about 4½ hrs; San Evaristo is a sleepy fishing village on a delightful cove sheltered on the E by the Isla San José. Ideal boating area but as yet undiscovered. Visit the salt-drying operations near San Evaristo or on San José. This is a rewarding excursion for those with smaller, high-clearance vehicles (vans and pick-ups with shells) for the steep final 20 mile stretch.

State Highway 286 leads SE out of La Paz 45 km to **San Juan de Los Planes** (pop 1,350), a friendly town in a rich farming region. A fair road continues another 15 km to the beautiful **Ensenada del los Muertos**, good fishing, swimming and 'wild' camping. A further 11 km is the headland of **Punta Arena de la Ventana**, with a magnificent view of the sterile slopes of Isla Cerralvo. (**L** *Hotel Las Arenas*, resort overlooking Ventana Bay). 6 km before Los Planes, a graded road leads to the Bahía de la Ventana and the small fishing villages of La Ventana and El Sargento; lovely beaches facing Cerralvo Island.

S of La Paz and its plain, the central mountain spine rises again into the wooded heights of the Sierra de la Laguna and bulges out into the 'Cape Region", Baja's most touristically-developed area. The highway winds up to **El Triunfo**, a picturesque village (almost a ghost town); silver was discovered at nearby **San Antonio** in 1748 and at El Triunfo in 1862. The latter exploded with a population of 10,000 and was for a while the largest town in Baja. The mines closed in 1926 but small-scale mining has resumed in places. *Warning*: present-day miners are using arsenic in the old mine tailings; these areas are fenced and signed. There is a craft shop at the village entrance where young people make palm-leaf objects. 8 km further on is the lovely mountain town and farming centre of San Antonio (gasoline, groceries, meals), which was founded in 1756 and served briefly as Baja's capital (1828-30) when Loreto was destroyed. 8 km S of San Antonio was the site of Santa Ana, where silver was first discovered in 1748. It was from this vanished village that the Viceroy and Padre Junípero Serra planned the expedition to establish the chain of Franciscan missions in Alta California.

Highway 1 climbs sharply from the canyon and winds past a number of ancient mines, through the peaceful orchard-farming town of San Bartolo (groceries and meals) and down to the coastal flats around **Los Barriles**, a small town with fuel, meals and limited supplies. A number of resort hotels are situated near here along the beautiful Bahía de Palmas and at nearby Buena Vista; none is in the 'budget' class but all are popular (**A+ Hotel Palmas de Cortez**, nice beach location, but a bit run down and poor service).

The Highway turns inland after Los Barriles (106 km from La Paz). An 'East Cape Loop' turns E off the Highway through La Rivera (well paved), where a new spur leads towards **Cabo Pulmo**; it is being paved at a rapid rate and will eventually take a slightly inland route paralleling the coast to San José del Cabo (the present coastal track was badly damaged by a severe storm in 1991). Off Cabo Pulmo, a beautiful headland, is the Northern Pacific's only living coral reef; fishing, diving and snorkelling are excellent (56 km from Los Barriles). There are many camping spots along the beautiful beaches of this coast.

Santiago is a pleasant, historic little town (pop 2,000) 3 km off Highway 1. On the tree-lined main street are a Pemex station, café and stores grouped around the town plaza. A kilometre further W is the Parque Zoológico, the Cape's only zoo—modest but informative, free admission. The Jesuits built their 10th mission in Santiago in 1723 after transferring it from Los Barriles. The town was one of the sites of the Pericué Indian uprising of 1734. (**Hotel D Palomar**, a/c, hot showers, restaurant, bar, on main street, modest, good meals).

3½ km S of the Santiago turnoff Highway 1 crosses the Tropic of Cancer, marked by a large concrete sphere, and runs S down the fertile valley between the lofty Sierra de la Laguna (W) and the Sierra Santa Clara (E) to the Cabos International Airport (direct jet services to Los Angeles, San Francisco, San Diego in California, Phoenix, Arizona and Seattle, USA, and Mexican destinations; modern terminal, expensive store, parking and good transportation to San José del Cabo, 10 km S and Cabo San Lucas, bus 1 hr, US$9).

San José del Cabo, the largest town S of La Paz, has a population of 10,000. Although founded in 1730, it is now essentially a modern town divided into two districts: the resort sectors and new Fonatur development on the beach, and the downtown zone to the N, with the government offices and many businesses grouped near the tranquil Parque Mijares, and numerous shops and restaurants along Calles Zaragoza and Doblado. The N end of Blvd Antonio Mijares has been turned into a 'mini-gringoland ... which could have been transplanted from the Main St of Disneyland' (Scott Wayne). San José also has two service stations, hospital, auto parts and mechanical repairs. The attractive church on the Plaza Mijares was built in 1940 on the final site of the mission of 1730; a tile mosaic over the entrance depicts the murder of Padre Tamaral by rebellious Indians in 1734. Most of the top hotels are located W of San José along the beaches or nearby estero; the Fonatur development blocks access to much of the beach near town; best are Playas Nuevo Sol and California, about 3 km from downtown. Unofficial camping is possible on those few not fronted by resort hotels.

Note A severe storm in November 1993 caused extensive damage in San José del Cabo, Cabo San Lucas and the road between the two. Several bridges were washed away. Check on road conditions before driving in this area.

Hotels L Palmilla, one of the top resorts in Baja, 8 km W at Punta Palmilla (outstanding surfing nearby), some a/c, showers, pool, beach, tennis, narrow access road, restaurant, bar, skin diving, fishing cruisers and skiffs for hire (daily happy hour allows mere mortals to partake of margarita and appetizers for US$3 and see how royalty and film stars live!). **L Stouffer Presidente Los Cabos**, Blvd Mijares s/n, T 20038, F 20232, on lagoon S of town, a/c, all facilities, boat rentals, centrepiece of the Fonatur development at San José del Cabo; **A Castel Cabo**, on beach off Paseo San José S of town, T 20155, a/c, another Fonatur hotel; **A+ Posada Real Cabo**, next door, T 20155, F 20460, a/c, colour TV, showers, pool, tennis, restaurant, bar, gift shop, fishing charters; **A Calinda Aquamarina-Comfort Inn**, next to Posada Real Cabo, T 20077, US Comfort Inn chain, a/c, beach, pool, restaurant, bar, fishing, clean and comfortable; **Aston Cabo Regis Resort and Beach Club**, in hotel zone on Blvd Finisterra, a/c, colour TV, showers, kitchenettes, private balconies, pool, tennis, golf course, restaurant; **C Nuevo Sol**, on beach S of intersection of Paseo San José and Highway 1, pool, restaurant, sports facilities, nicely-landscaped, acceptable and good beachside value; **C San José Inn**, on last paved street N of beach, clean, quiet, cool, comfortable, ceiling fans, good value; **D Collí**, in town on Hidalgo above Budget Rent-a-Car, T 20052, fans, hot showers, 12 clean and adequate rooms; **D** *Pagamar*, Obregón between Degollado y Guerrero 3½ blocks from plaza, fans, café, hot showers, clean, good value; **E** *Ceci*, Zaragoza 22, 1 block W of plaza, T 20051, fans, hot showers (usually), basic but clean, excellent value, central. **Youth hostel**, Domicilio Conocido Anikan s/n.

Motel D *Brisa del Mar*, on Highway 1, 3 km SW of town near Hotel Nuevo Sol, 10 rooms, restaurant, bar, pool, modest but comfortable, at rear of trailer park on outstanding beach.

Camping *Brisa Del Mar Trailer Park*, 100 RV sites in fenced area by great beach, full hook-ups, flush toilets, showers, pool, laundry, restaurant, bar, fishing trips arranged, popular, rec, good location ("unofficial' camping possible under *palapas* on beach).

Laundry Self-service at Playa de California.

Bus Bus station on Calle Manuel Doblado opp hospital, about 7 blocks W of plaza. To **Cabo San Lucas** (Tres Estrellas) daily from 0700, US$1.25, ½ hr; to **La Paz** daily from 0630, US$6.60, 2 hrs.

All the beaches and coastal areas between San José del Cabo and Cabo San Lucas have become public after protests by local inhabitants against private developments. These include: **L** *Hotel Cabo San Lucas*, **L+** *Twin Dolphin* (T 30140), and **L** *Calinda Cabo Baja-Quality Inn* (T 30045), part of Cabo Bello residential development. At Km 25, just after the *Twin Dolphin*, a dirt road leads off to Shipwreck Beach, where a large ship rots on the shore. 5 km before Cabo a small concrete marker beside the highway heralds an excellent view of the famous Cape. The Highway enters Cabo San Lucas past a Pemex station and continues as Blvd Lázaro Cárdenas to the Zócalo (Guerrero y Madero) and the Kilómetro 0 marker.

Cabo San Lucas has grown rapidly in recent years from a sleepy fishing village (pop 1,500 in 1970) to a bustling, expensive international resort with a permanent population of 8,500. There are trailer parks, many cafés and restaurants, condominiums, gift shops, discos and a marina to cater for the increasing flood of North Americans who come for the world-famous sportfishing or to find a retirement paradise. The town fronts a small harbour facing the rocky peninsula that forms the 'Land's End' of Baja California. Francisco de Ulloa first rounded and named the Cape in 1539. The sheltered bay became a watering point for the treasure ships from the Orient; pirates sheltered here too. Now it is on the cruise ship itinerary. A popular attraction is the government-sponsored regional arts centre, where distinctive black-coral jewellery is made and sold, located at the cruise liner dock. Post Office is at Morelos y Niños Héroes.

Hotels L *Finisterra*, perched on promontory near Land's End, T 30000, a/c, TV, shower, pool, steps to beach, poolside bar with unsurpassed view, restaurant, entertainment, sportfishing cruisers; **L** *Giggling Marlin Inn*, central on Blvd Marina y Matamoros, a/c, TV, showers, kitchenettes, jacuzzi, restaurant, bar, fishing trips arranged, lively drinking and poor food in attached cocktail bar; **L** *Hacienda Beach Resort*, at N entrance to harbour, some a/c, showers, pool, tennis, yacht anchorage, various water sports, hunting, horseriding, restaurant, etc, claims the only area beach safe from strong Pacific swells; **L** *Marina Sol Condominiums*, L:16 Oct-30 June, A: rest of year, on 16 de Septiembre, between Highway 1 and Bay, full hotel service in 3- and 7-storey buildings; **L** *Solmar*, T 30022, the southernmost development in Baja California, a/c, showers, ocean view, pool, tennis, diving, restaurant, poolside bar, fishing cruisers, beach with heavy ocean surf; **B** *Mar de Cortez*, on Highway 1 at Guerrero in town centre, T 30032, a/c, showers, helpful, pool, outdoor bar/restaurant, good value; **C** *Casablanca*, Calle Revolución between Morelos y Leona Vicario, central, ceiling fan (D in rooms with floor fan), hot shower, clean, but basic in cheaper rooms, quiet and friendly; **C** *Marina*, Blvd Marina y Guerrero, T 30030, central, a/c, restaurant, bar, can be noisy, pricey. **D** *Dos Mares*, Hidalgo, a/c, TV, clean, small pool, parking space, rec. Nothing cheaper than US$12d. **D** *Youth Hostal* Av de la Juventud s/n, T 30148, private bath, F pp in dormitory, not very central, but quite smart and clean.

Motel C *Los Cabos Inn*, Abasolo y 16 de Septiembre, central, 1 block from bus station, fans, showers, central, modest, good value.

Camping *El Arco Trailer Park*, 4 km E on Highway 1, restaurant; *El Faro Viejo Trailer Park*, 1½ km NW at Matamoros y Morales, shade, laundry, ice, restaurant, bar, clean, out-of-town but good; *Vagabundos del Mar*, 3½ km E on Highway 1, pool, snack bar, laundry, good, US$15 for 2; *Cabo Cielo RV Park*, 3 km E on Highway 1; *San Vicente Trailer Park*, 3 km E on Highway 1, same as Cabo Cielo plus pool, both reasonably basic, rates unknown. All have full hook-ups, toilets and showers. Several *playas públicas* on coast E of town, inc Cabo Real, 5 km, showers and restrooms, modest fee; 'Barco Barrado' (Shipwreck Beach), 10 km, lovely beach.

Restaurants As alternatives to expensive restaurants, try the two pizza places just beyond *Mar de Cortez*, one next to the telphone office, the other in the block where the street ends; also *Flor Guadalajara*, Calle Lázaro Cárdenas, on the way out of town a few blocks beyond 'Skid Row", good local dishes. Half a block uphill from *Hotel Dos Manes*, is *San Lucas*, Hidalgo s/n, good food at very reasonable prices, highly rec. There is a good bakery in front of the large modern supermarket in the centre of town. The supermarket is stocked with a full range of US foodstuffs.

Tourist Office Next to ferry landing, town maps, Fonatur office. Note that there are no ferries from Cabo San Lucas to Puerto Vallarta.

Bus Bus station at 16 de Septiembre y Zaragoza, central, few facilities. To **San José del Cabo**, 8 departures a day, US$1.25. To **La Paz** 6 a day from 0630, US$8; **Tijuana** US$44, 1600 and 1800 daily via La Paz.

To Los Cabos International Airport take a local bus, US$3, which drops you at the entrance road to the airport, leaving a 2-km walk, otherwise take a taxi.

Ringed by pounding surf, columns of fluted rock enclose Lover's Beach (be careful if walking along the beach—huge waves sweep away several visitors each year), a romantic sandy cove with views out to the seal colonies on offshore islets. At the very tip of the Cabo is the distinctive natural arch ("el arco"); boats can be hired to see it close-up, but care is required because of the strong rips. At the harbour entrance is a pinnacle of rock—Pelican Rock—which is home to vast shoals of tropical fish; it is an ideal place for snorkelling and scuba diving or glass-bottomed boats may be rented at the harbourside. (45 min harbour cruise in glass-bottomed boat to 'el arco", Lover's Beach, etc US$5 pp.)

Many firms rent aquatic equipment and arrange boating excursions, etc; the beaches E of Cabo San Lucas offer endless opportunities for swimming, scuba diving and snorkelling. Boat trips to Lover's Beach about US$20 for 4; most hotels can arrange hire of skiffs to enable visits to the Arch and Land's End, about US$5-10/hr.

Highway 19, the western loop of the Cape Region, was not paved until 1985 and the superb beaches of the west coast have yet to suffer the development and crowding of the E. The highway branches off Highway 1 just after San Pedro, 32 km S of La Paz, and runs due S through a cactus-covered plain to **Todos Santos**, a quiet farming town of 4,000 only a few hundred metres N of the Tropic of Cancer. There is a Pemex station, cinema, stores, cafés, a bank, clinic and market, a museum—the Casa de la Cultura (Calles Topete y Pilar)—and **B** *Hotel California*, formerly the *Misión de Todos Santos Inn*, historic brick building near town centre, Calle Juárez next to Pemex station a block N of Highway 19, fans, showers, pool, a/c, dining room; opp is **D** *Motel Guluarte*, fan, fridge, good value. *El Molino Trailer Park*, off Highway at S end of town, 30 mins from beach, full hook-ups, flush toilets, showers, laundry, American owner, very helpful, US$8 for 4, better value than the hotels! Even cheaper is *Trailer Park San Pedrito*, on the beach, G, very good.

Todos Santos was founded as a Jesuit mission in 1734; a church replacing the abandoned structure, built in 1840, stands opposite the Civic Plaza on Calle Juárez. The ruins of several old sugar mills can be seen around the town in the fertile valley. Fishing is also important.

2 km away is the Pacific coast with some of the most beautiful beaches of the entire Peninsula. Nearest is **Playa Punta Lobos**, a popular picnic spot, but too much rubbish and unfriendly dogs for wild camping; better is the sandy cove at **Playa Pedrito** (4km SE). Backed by groves of Washingtonia fan palms and coconut palms, this is one of the loveliest camping spots anywhere. Opposite the access road junction is the Campo Experimental Forestal, a Botanical Garden with a well-labelled array of desert plants from all regions of Baja. Here too is the *San Pedrito RV Park*, an open area on the beach, full hook-ups, flush toilets, showers, pool, laundry, restaurant, bar, US$3 for tent, US$8 for RVs, one of the most beautifully-sited RV parks in Baja, very good value. 11 km S of Todos Santos is *El*

Pescadero, a fast-growing farming town with few facilities for visitors.

Excursion In the rugged interior E of Todos Santos is the **Parque Nacional Sierra de la Laguna** (under threat and not officially recognized). Crowning peak is the Picacho La Laguna (2,163m), beginning to attract a trickle of hikers to its 'lost world' of pine and oak trees, doves and woodpeckers, grassy meadows and luxuriant flowers; there is nothing else like it in Baja. Trail is steep but straight forward; the panoramic view takes in La Paz and both the Gulf and Pacific. Cold at night. Best reached from Todos Santos by making local enquiries; 3-day guided pack trips are also offered by the Todos Santos Inn, US$325 per person.

7 km S of El Pescadero is *Los Cerritos RV Park* on a wide sandy beach, 50 RV or tent sites but no hook-ups, flush toilets, US$3 per vehicle. Playa Los Cerritos is a *playa pública*; there are several camping areas but no facilities, US$2 per vehicle. The succession of rocky coves and empty beaches continues to Colonia Plutarco Elías Calles, a tiny farming village in the midst of a patchwork of orchards. The highway parallels the coast to Rancho El Migriño, then continues S along the coastal plain; there are no more camping spots as far as Cabo San Lucas. Many now prefer the W Loop to the main highway; it is 140 km from the junction at San Pedro, thus cutting off about 50 km and up to an hour's driving time from the Transpeninsular Highway route.

INFORMATION FOR VISITORS

Documents A passport is necessary, but US and Canadian citizens need only show birth certificate (or for US, a naturalization certificate). Tourists need the free tourist card, which can be obtained from any Mexican Consulate or Tourist Commission office, at the Mexican airport on entry, from the offices or on the aircraft of airlines operating into Mexico, ask for at least 30 days (maximum 180 days); if you say you are in transit you may be charged US$8, with resulting paper work. **NB** Not all Mexican consuls in USA are aware of exact entry requirements; it is best to confirm details with airlines which fly to Mexico. Some nationalities appear no longer to need a tourist card. Best to say you are going to an inland destination. (Airlines may issue cards only to citizens of W European countries, most Latin American countries—not Cuba, Chile or Haiti—the USA, Canada, Australia, Japan and the Philippines.) Also at border offices of the American Automobile Association (AAA), which offers this service to members and non-members. There is a multiple entry card valid for all visits within 6 months for US nationals. The normal validity for other nationals is 90 days, but sometimes only 30 days are granted at border crossings; insist you want more if wishing to stay longer.

Renewal of entry cards or visas must be done at Secretaría de Gobernación, Dirección General de Servicios Migratorios, Albañiles 19, esq Eduardo Molina, Col 20 de Noviembre, Mexico City, 1st floor, 1st door on right, takes 15 mins, only 60 days given, open 0830-1500, T 795-6685 (Metro San Lázaro, or Morelos), or in Guadalajara, or at international airports (there is a helpful office at Room 78 in the International Airport). To renew a tourist card by leaving the country, you must stay outside Mexico for at least 72 hrs. Take travellers' cheques as proof of finance. Best to collect visa, not have it forwarded by post. Travellers not carrying tourist cards need visas (Israelis and French need a visa), multiple entry not allowed, visa must be renewed before re-entry. Tourist cards are not required for cities close to the US border, such as Tijuana, Mexicali, etc. Businessmen who want to study the Mexican market or to appoint an agent should apply for the requisite visa and permit. (Since 1 April 1994, business visas for US and Canadian citizens are free.) For a *Visitante Rentista* visa (non-immigrant pensioner) for stays over 6 months the following are required: passport, letter from your bank showing minimum income of US$1,000/month, good conduct letter from police department, 3 passport photos, cost US$71.

At border crossings make sure the immigration people don't con you to pay a dollar for the card or visa. It is free and the man typing it out is only doing his job. We would warn travellers that there have been several cases of tourist cards not being honoured, or a charge being imposed, or the validity being changed arbitrarily to 60 days or less. In this case, complaint should be made to the authorities in Mexico City. Some border stations do not issue tourist cards; you are therefore strongly advised, if travelling by land, to obtain a card before arriving at the border. If, on leaving Mexico, your tourist card is not taken from you, post it to the Mexico City address above. Above all, do not lose your tourist card—you cannot leave the country without it and it can take up to a week to replace. If you want to return to Mexico after leaving there to visit Belize or Guatemala, remember that you will need a new visa/tourist card if yours is not marked for multiple entry.

At the land frontiers with Belize and Guatemala, you may be refused entry into Mexico if you have less than US$200 (or US$350 for each month of intended stay, up to a maximum of 180 days). This restriction does not officially apply to North American and European travellers. In most cases entering Mexico from Belize and Guatemala only 30 days entry is given, possibly renewable for up to 60 days.

British business travellers are strongly advised to read *Hints to Exporters: Mexico*, obtainable from the DTI Export Publications, PO Box 55, Stratford-upon-Avon, Warwickshire, CV37 9GE. The US State Department publishes *Tips for Travelers to Mexico*, available from the Superintendent of Documents, US Government Printing Office, Washington, DC 20401, US$1.

Student cards: only national, Mexican student cards permit free entry to archaeological sites, museums, etc. The surest way to get in free is to go on Sunday, when all such places have no entry charge, but are crowded in consequence.

Airport Departure Tax   US$12 on international flights (dollars or pesos accepted); US$6.50 on internal flights, may be included in ticket price.

NB VAT is payable on domestic plane tickets bought in Mexico. Domestic tax on Mexican flights is 10%, on international flights 3.75%.

How to Get There by Air   Several airlines have regular flights from Europe to Mexico City. Air France from Paris twice direct, or 4 a week via Houston, daily except Wednesday, also AeroMéxico, twice a week direct, twice via Cancún; Iberia, Delta (via Atlanta) and AeroMéxico from Madrid; KLM from Amsterdam, direct; British Airways direct from London (Heathrow) 3 times a week; Lufthansa from Frankfurt non stop, 5 times a week (LTU and Condor charter flights from Germany to Mexico City or Cancún). AeroMéxico also fly from Frankfurt twice a week. Aeroflot fly to Mexico City from Moscow via Shannon on Wed.

Mexico City from New York, under 4 hrs (Delta, AeroMéxico, Continental, Mexicana, Taesa); from Chicago, 3 hrs (Mexicana, Taesa, Continental, United and American Airlines); from Los Angeles, $4\frac{1}{2}$ hrs with Mexicana, AeroMéxico, Lacsa, Continental, Delta, United, Aero California; from Houston, 1 hr (AeroMéxico, Continental, Air France); from Washington, with United Airlines, or Continental (via Houston). Other flights from the USA include: San Antonio (Mexicana, Aeromar, Continental), Denver (Mexicana and Continental), Dallas (many lines), Miami (United, Continental, American, AeroMéxico), San Francisco (Mexicana, United, Continental, Delta), Tucson (AeroMéxico and America West), Seattle (United and Delta). Other flights from the USA to Mexican cities are given in the text. Japan Airlines twice weekly flight from Tokyo stops at Vancouver.

Flights from South and Central America: Aerolíneas Argentinas from Buenos Aires (three a week via Lima or Bogotá), also Ladeco (via Santiago and Guayaquil or San José), Aero-Perú also from Lima; Avensa from Caracas; Avianca from Bogotá, also Mexicana and Varig en route from Rio and São Paulo; Aviateca, Lacsa, United, KLM and Mexicana from Guatemala City; Taca and Copa from Managua; Copa and Aeroperú from Panama; Lacsa, United and Mexicana from San José, Costa Rica; Taca from Tegucigalpa, who fly from San Salvador (as do United).

To Cuba Return flight to Cuba, Sun and Wed, with stop at Mérida if plane is not fully booked (Mexicana); Mexicana direct on Mon, Thur and Fri, Cubana Wed and Sat (liable to breakdowns and delays, US$165 return). Cuba package tours with Mexicana start at US$411 (Wed-Sun, or Sun-Sun), depending on hotel category and season, visa (US$18) included, but not tax, staying in Havana; 'Sun, sea and sand' packages cost from US$510. There are other packages available. In all cases, tours starting from Mérida cost US$189 less. High season is mid-Dec to early Jan, mid- to end-March and mid-July to mid-August. *Cuba-Mex SA* (reliable), Calle 63, No 500, Depto D, Edificio La Literaria, Mérida, Yucatán (Apdo Postal 508, CP 97000, Telex 753806 Cumeme, T 23-91-99/97-25, F 28-33-68), with branch at Manzanillo 123, D 104, esq Baja California, Colonia Roma Sur, T 574-0813/584-2465, F 584-6814, México, DF. Also *Cubana Tours*, Reforma 400 C, local 'B', Av Colón, Mérida, T 25-79-91, Telex 75-36-22, or Baja California 255, Edif, 'B' Despacho 103, Col Hipódromo Condesa, México DF, Casilla Postal 06100, T 564-7839/5208, F 264-2865, Telex 176-1240. Ask around Hamburgo in Mexico City for cheap tickets: might pick them up for as little as US$120 or so. If you pay in dollars make sure the fact is noted on the ticket; if you pay in new pesos and use the ticket later you may be surcharged if the peso price has risen meanwhile. Visas for Cuba available through *Viñales Tours*, Oaxaca 80, Colonia Roma, T 208-99-00/564 4417 (metro Insurgentes, very helpful), or other travel agencies; you have to show your return ticket for Cuba. Tourist visas only are issued in Mexico, valid for the length of your tour. To extend a tourist visa in Cuba will cost US$120. The Cuban consulate in Mexico City does not give visas to individual travellers. Once in Cuba, check with the Mexican Embassy (Calle 12, No 518, between 5 y 7, Miramar, T 33-2142/2489, Mon-Fri 0900-1200) on procedures for reentering Mexico.

Overland Toronto to Mexico City, via Chicago-St Louis-Dallas-San Antonio-Laredo-Monterrey, with Greyhound bus (74 hrs) on a 15-day pass. Montreal-Laredo via New York, Washington, Atlanta, New Orleans, Houston and San Antonio, 60 hrs. Both Greyhound and Trailways provide services from Miami to the Mexican border and on to Mexico City. It's cheaper to make booking outside the US, but the information is hard to come by in Mexico City. Trailways in London, c/o Holiday Inn, Heathrow Airport, Stockley Rd, West Drayton, Middlesex, UB7 9NA. Los Angeles-Mexico City, 44 hrs; New York-Mexico City, 70 hrs; San Antonio-Mexico City, 20 hrs. If coming from the US it is usually cheaper to travel to the border and buy your ticket in the Mexican border town from the Mexican company. If going to the US it is worth checking Greyhound bus passes, cheap offers have been reported, check with Transportes del Norte or Wagon Lits offices in Mexico.

Customs Regulations The luggage of tourist-card holders is often passed unexamined. If flying into Mexico from South America, expect to be thoroughly searched (body and luggage) at the airport. US citizens can take in their own clothing and equipment without paying duty, but all valuable and non-US-made objects (diamonds, cameras, binoculars, typewriters, etc), should be registered at the US Customs office or the port of exit so that duty will not be charged on returning. Radios and television sets must be registered and taken out when leaving. Anyone entering Mexico is allowed to bring in: clothing, footwear and personal cleaning items suitable for the length of stay; camera, or video recorder, and 12 rolls of film, or videocassettes; books and magazines; one used article of sporting equipment; 20 packs of cigarettes, or 50 cigars, or 250 grams of tobacco; medicines for personal use. Foreigners who reside legally outside Mexico are also allowed: a portable TV, stereo, 20 records or audio cassettes, a musical instrument, 5 used toys, fishing tackle, tennis racket, a pair of skis, a boat up to 5m without an engine, camping equipment, a tent. Those entering by trailer, private plane or yacht may also bring a videocassette recorder, bicycle, motorbike and kitchen utensils. Anything additional to this list with a value of over US$300, if entering by land, air or sea, is taxable and must be declared as such (for Mexicans returning by land the value is US$50). There are no restrictions on the import or export of money apart from gold but foreign gold coins are allowed into the US only if they are clearly made into jewellery (perforated or otherwise worked on). On return to the US a person may take from Mexico, free of duty, up to US$100 worth of merchandise for personal use or for personal gifts, every 31 days, if acquired merely as an incident of the trip. 1 litre of alcoholic drinks may be taken across the border from Mexico (beer is counted as an alcoholic drink); Texas will allow you to pay the small state tax, Arizona will not. All foreign citizens are subject to this law. Archaeological relics may not be taken out of Mexico. US tourists should remember that the US Endangered Species Act, 1973, prohibits importation into the States of products from endangered species, eg tortoise shell. The Department of the Interior issues a leaflet about this. Llama, alpaca, etc, items may be confiscated at the airport for fumigation and it will be necessary to return to the customs area on the Mexico City airport perimeter 2-3 days later to collect and pay for fumigation. Production of passport will be required and proof that goods are to be re-exported otherwise they may also be subject to import duties. Duty-free goods from Aeroboutiques at Mexico City, Mazatlán, Puerto Vallarta, Guadalajara, Monterrey, Mérida and Acapulco airports.

Travel in Mexico By Air Note that the majority of internal routes involve a change in Mexico City, eg there is no direct flight Acapulco-Cancún. Promotional packages for local tourism exist, with 30-40% discount, operated by hoteliers, restauranteurs, hauliers and AeroMéxico and Mexicana. These may be the best value if going from and returning to the same city. Their tickets are not interchangeable. Mexicana offer MexiPass tickets, which are 2-, or 4-coupon tickets for 5 zones of the country (Colonial, Maya, Pleasure, Golden and Central, which includes Guatemala); the pass is eligible only to those arriving on international flights, valid 2-45 days. Fares range from US$124 to US$683; extra coupons may be brought. Mexicana also has 50% discounts on domestic flights between 2300 and 0600. There are several other airlines flying internal routes (a few with international flights as well), eg Aero California, Aeromar, Aerolitoral, Taesa, Saro, Aviacsa and Aero Caribe (details are given in the text above).

Local Road Services Bus services have been upgraded in recent years, but the ordinary traveller should not be beguiled into thinking that it is necessary to purchase an expensive ticket in order to travel comfortably. On many routes, the 2nd, or 'normal", class has disappeared. 1st class is perfectly satisfactory, but there now exist three superior classes, usually called 'Primera Plus", 'Futura' and 'Ejecutiva", which offer various degrees of comfort and extra services. Companies offering these services include UNO (rec) and ETN, as well as the major bus companies. The extras are reclining seats, toilets, drinks, videos, etc, and prices about 35-40% (in some cases double) above regular 1st class. The superior classes are probably best for journeys over 6 hrs, but take a warm garment at night because a/c can be very cold. On day time journeys consider whether you want to see the scenery or a video. First-class buses and above assign you a seat and you may have to queue for 1-2 hrs to get a ticket. It is not easy to choose which seat or to change it later. If going on an overnight bus, book seats at the front as toilets get very smelly by morning. No standing (in theory), and you may have to wait for the next one (next day, perhaps) if all seats are taken. You *must* book in advance for buses travelling in the Yucatán Peninsula, especially around Christmas, but it is also advisable to book if going elsewhere. Some companies, eg ADO, are computerised in main cities, so advance reservations can be made. Bus seats are particulary hard to get during school holidays, August and the 15 days up to New Year when many public servants take holidays in all resorts; transport from Mexico City is booked up a long time in advance and hotels are filled, too. In the N especially, try to travel from the starting-point of a route; buses are often full at the mid-point of their routes. Beware of 'scalpers' who try to sell you a seat at a higher price, which you can usually get on a stand-by basis, when somebody doesn't turn up, at the regular price. Sometimes it helps to talk to the driver, who has two places to use at his discretion behind his seat (don't sit in these until invited). Lock your luggage to the rack with a cycle lock and chain. If protecting luggage with chicken wire it will set off metal detectors used by Cristóbal Colón bus line in southern Mexico. Stowing your luggage on the roof is not advisable on night buses since theft can occur. Luggage racks on both classes of long-distance bus are spacious and will take a rucksack with a little persuasion (either of the rucksack itself, or the bus driver). However well-organized a company (eg ADO), always check that your luggage is on your bus if your are putting it in the hold.

Second-class buses usually operate from a different terminal from 1st class buses and are often antiques (interesting, but frustrating when they break down) or may be brand new. The passengers are invariably more entertaining and courteous than in first-class buses. They call at towns and villages and go up side roads the first-class buses never touch. They stop quite as often for meals and toilets as their superiors do and—unlike the first-class buses—people get on and off so often that you may be able to obtain a seat after all. Autobuses Unidos (AU) are usually a little cheaper than other services, but they stop more often, including at the roadside when flagged down. They will not stop on curves—walk until you find a straight stretch. It is not unusual to have to stand on these buses. Some second class seats are bookable (eg in Baja California), others are not, it depends on the company. In general, it is a good idea to take food and drink with you on a long bus ride, as stops may depend on the driver. When a bus stops for refreshment, remember who your driver is and follow him; also memorize your bus' number so you do not miss it when it leaves. First class fares are usually 10% dearer than 2nd class ones (see **Cost of Living**, below, on fares). Some companies give holders of an international student card a 50% discount on bus tickets; persistence may be required. If making a day trip by bus, do not lose your ticket; you will have to show the driver and operator proof that you have paid for the return. There seem always to be many buses leaving in the early morning. All classes of bus invariably leave on time. Buses are sometimes called *camiones*, hence *central camionero* for bus station. A monthly bus guide is available for US$1 (year's subscription) from Guía de Autotransportes de México, Apartado 8929, México 1, DF.

Rail Much of the passenger equipment in use dates from the forties or fifties, including a number of *autovías*. There are modern trains between Mexicali and Guadalajara in 36 hrs, and overnight good Pullman trains between Mexico City and Monterrey, Guadalajara, Veracruz and Mérida. The *servicio estrella* services (see text for routes) provide good accommodation and all meals (usually cold, served on a tray at your seat), and have been much recommended. They have 1st class and 1st class special seats, the latter being much more comfortable. The railways claim that you can see more from a train than from any other form of transport; this may well be true, but trains are slower than the buses (they can, however, be very crowded); they sometimes have comfortable sleeper cars with *alcobas* (better berths) and *camarines* (small sleepers). The special first class has air-conditioning and reclining seats and costs about 10% more than the regular 1st class, which costs about twice the 2nd class fare. Tickets are best booked at the stations: agencies tend to add a large commission and the tickets they issue sometimes turn out not to be valid. A condensed railway timetable is published monthly, see under Mexico City, **Railways**.

If you should get caught during the holiday season try to book a 2nd class train, but this may involve queuing 12 hrs or more if you want a seat. More first-class tickets are sold than the total number of first-class seats; first-class passengers are allowed on first, so you may still find a 2nd class seat. Some travellers have remarked that the last carriage of a 2nd class train is often half full of soldiers, who might deter would-be thieves from taking one's personal belongings if one shares their carriage. We have received a report of conductors turning out lights on night trains, enabling thieves to operate with impunity; take great care under these circumstances.

Automobiles These may be brought into Mexico on a Tourist Permit for 180 days each year (insist on the maximum on arrival—ie you have to wait until a year has passed before returning to Mexico with a vehicle). The necessary documents are: passport, birth certificate or naturalization papers; tourist card; vehicle registration (if you do not own the car, a notarized letter from the vehicle's owner, be it the bank, company, whoever, is necessary); a valid driver's licence. National or international driving licences are accepted. The original and 2 photocopies are required for each. Entry and exit will be recorded in your passport. It takes 10 days to extend a permit, so ask for more time than you expect to need. Don't overstay—driving without an extension gets a US$50 fine for the first five days and then rises abruptly to *half the value of the car!* US$12 is charged for the permit, payable only by credit card (Visa, Mastercard, American Express or Diners Club), not a debit card, in the name of the car owner, as recorded on the vehicle registration. The American Automobile Association (AAA) is permitted to issue Tourist Permits for 'credit card' entry, free to members, US$20 to non-members, but this service in California is available only to members. If you do not have a credit card, you have to buy a refundable bond in cash to the value of the vehicle according to its age (a set scale exists), which is repaid on leaving Mexico. In theory, 100% of the bond is repaid, in practice this is open to question. The bond is issued by Afianziadora Mexicana at US/Mexican border crossings, or by Sanborn's (see below).

English versions of leaflets giving the rules on temporary importation of vehicles state that you must leave at the same crossing by which you entered. The Spanish versions do not say this and in practice it is not so. The temporary importation permit is multiple entry for 180 days; within that period you can enter and leave by whatever crossing, and as often as you like. When you finally leave Mexico, you are advised to use the crossing you entered by, but can use another if you notify the original border and the head office Afianziadora Mexicana (Monte de Piedad 11, Edif Amsa, CP 06000 México DF, T 726-9007, F 518-3915) in writing in advance. Experiences differ on this point.

On entry, go to Migración for your tourist card, then to 'Copias' for photocopies of all papers (it is wise to bring your own photocopies of documents from home). At the next desk sign a 'Promesa de retornar el vehíanlo", which bears all vehicle and credit card details so that, if you sell your car illegally, your credit card account can be debited for the import duty. Next you purchase the 'Solicitud de importación temporal", which costs the US$12; it bears a hologram which matches the dated sticker which must be displayed on the windscreen. This sticker and other entry documents must be surrendered on departure. They can only be surrendered at a Mexican border crossing, with date stickers cancelled by Banjército at Immigration. If you neglect to do this, and re-enter Mexico with an expired uncancelled sticker on you car, you will be fined heavily for each 15-day period that has elapsed since the date of expiry. If entry papers are lost there can be much delay and expense (including enforcement of the bond) in order to leave the country. Banjércitco (Banco del Ejército) offices at borders are open daily, for 24 hrs, except at Naco (daily 0800-2400), Tecate (daily 0800-1600), Tijuana (Mon-Fri 0800-2200, Sat 0800-1800, Sun 1200-1600), Columbia, Texas (Mon-Fri 1000-1800), Ojinaga (Mon-Fri 0730-2100, Sat 0730-1600, Sun 0800-1600). Each vehicle must have a different licensed driver (ie, you cannot tow another vehicle into Mexico unless it has a separate driver).

On arrival, you have to find the place where car permits are issued; this may not be at the border. If driving into Mexico from California, Nogales is probably the easiest crossing, which means going first into Arizona. The main car documentation point here is Km 21, S of Nogales. Entering at Tijuana, it seems that car entry permits are given at Mexicali (which means taking the very busy Route 2 through Tecate), or, if you drive through Baja California, at the ferry offices in Santa Rosalía or La Paz. This does not apply if you are not going beyond Baja. In Nuevo Laredo permits are issued at a new complex in town, opposite the train station.

According to latest official documents, insurance for foreign cars entering Mexico is not mandatory, but it is highly recommended to be insured. Arranging insurance when crossing from the USA is very easy as there are many offices at US border crossings. Policy prices vary enormously between companies, according to age and type of vehicle, etc.

Sanborn's Mexican Insurance Service, for example, with offices in every US border town, and many more, will provide insurance services (many comprehensive plans available, including full-year cover) within Mexico and other parts of Latin America, and provides free 'Travelogs' for Mexico and Central America with useful tips. A selection of offices: Brownsville, Johnny Ginn Travel Center, 1845 Expway US, 77-83 exit, T 512-542-5457; El Paso, Associated Insurance Agency, 440 Raynolds off IH-10, T 915-779-3588; Nogales, PO Box 1584, 3420 Tucson Hwy (US-89), T 602-281-1873; San Antonio, Broadway Insurance Agency, 8107 Broadway, S off loop 410-E, T 512-828-3587. Also, Tepeyac, with offices at most Mexican cities, towns and border crosings (including Tapachula), and in USA (eg in San Diego, Mexican American Insurance Agency, corner of 6th and A streets, downtown, T 233-7767); Aseguradora Mexicana SA (Asemex), with offices in Tijuana, T 85-03-01/04, 24 hrs, Ensenada, Mexicali, La Paz, and adjusters throughout Baja California and that border zone; International Gateway Insurance Brokers (also offers insurance for Mexican residents visiting USA), PO Box 609, Bonita, CA 92002-0609, T (619) 422-3022, F (619) 422-2671; also 2981 N Grande Ave, Nogales, T 281-9141, F 281-0430; 1155 Larry Mahan, Suite H, El Paso, T 595-6544, F 592-1293; Hidalgo 79F, Riberas del Pilar, Centro Comercial Máscaras, Chapala, T 52559, F 543-16; Escuela Militar de Aviación 60, Chapultepec, Guadalajara, T 152992, F 341448; Misión de San Diego, No 1517 Despacho 1C, Tijuana, T 341446, F 341448; Revolución Morelos s/n, Cabo San Lucas, T 31174, F 30793; Blvd Costera Miguel de la Madrid, Km 10, Plaza Galerías local 3, Manzanillo. Mex-Insur in San Diego CA, T 425-2390, will issue a policy and refund each full 24 hrs not used as long as you return over the Mexican/US border.

Entering Mexico from Guatemala presents few local insurance problems now that Tepeyac (see above), has an office in Tapachula, and Seguros La Provincial, of Av General Utrillo 10A, upstairs, San Cristóbal de las Casas, have an office in Cuauhtémoc, Av Cuauhtémoc 1217 PB, Sr García Figueroa, T (5) 6-04-0500. Otherwise, try in Tuxtla Gutiérrez (Segumex). In Mexico City, try Grupo Nacional Provincial, Río de la Plata 48, T 286-7732, who have offices in many towns. Minimum cover costs US$3/day plus US$5 tax and handling (they prefer to be paid in dollars).

British AA and Dutch ANWB members are reminded that there are ties with the AAA, which extends cover to the US and entitles AA members to free travel information including a very useful book and map on Mexico (note that some AAA offices are not open at weekends or on US holidays). Luggage is no longer inspected at the checkpoints along the road where tourist cards and/or car permits are examined.

Spare parts: the only Japanese makes for which spare parts are sold in Mexico are Datsun and Nissan. Most other cars are US makes.

Gasoline is either unleaded, 85 octane and 90 octane, called *magna sin*, which costs about US$0.43/litre and US$0.45 respectively (take additive if you have to use 85 octane), and *nova*, leaded, 80 octane, US$0.39/litre. *Magna sin* is sold from green pumps from green and white Pemex stations; *nova* from blue pumps and diesel (US$0.29) from purple pumps are sold in both green and white and blue and orange Pemex stations. Unleaded petrol is supposed to be available every 80 km or so. It is signed on major roads, but filling stations sometimes run out of it, which is not much good when rental cars often require it. Always fill up when you can. If your own vehicle is fitted with a catalytic converter you can remove it to use either leaded or unleaded fuel. (Mexican petrol is not very clean, so check spark plugs frequently; most mechanics will let you use their wire brushes free of charge.) There are dozens of minor swindles, including overcharging, practised at filling stations. Make sure you are given full value when you tank up, that the pump is set to zero before your tank is filled, that both they and you know what money you've proffered, that your change is correct, that the pump is correctly calibrated, and that your filler cap is put back on. There is no legal surcharge for service at night, nor additional taxes: two more games frequently tried.

The Free Assistance Service of the Mexican Tourist Department's green jeeps ("*ángeles verdes*") patrol most of Mexico's main roads. Every state has an Angeles Verdes Hotline and it is advisable to find out the relevant number when entering each state. The drivers speak English, are trained to give first aid and to make minor auto repairs and deal with flat tyres. They carry gasoline and have radio connection. All help is completely free. Gasoline at cost price. Parking: Multi-storey car parks are becoming more common but parking is often to be found right in city centres under the main square.

A useful source of information and advice (whose help we acknowledge here) is the Recreation Vehicle Association of British Columbia, Box 2977, Vancouver, BC, V6B 3X4 (members receive *RV Times* publication; Mexican insurance arranged for members). Another recommended source of information in Canada is *Mexi-Can Holidays Ltd*, 150-332 Water St, Vancouver, BC V6B 1B6, T (604) 685-3375, F (604) 685-3321. Motorists are referred to: *Clubmex*, PO Box 1646, Bonita, California 91908, USA, T (619) 585 3033, F (619) 420 8133, publishes a regular newsletter for its members (annual subscription US$35). The newsletter gives useful information and advice for drivers, specialist trips for sport fishing enthusiasts, and some interesting travel articles. *Clubmex* also arranges insurance for members. *Mexico Travel Monthly Report*, Carolyn Files, Box 1498, Imperial Beach, CA 91933-1498, T/F 619-429-6566, has also been recommended. *Points South Caravan Tours*, 11313 Edmonson Ave, Moreno Valley, CA 92560-5232, T (909) 247-1222 or toll free USA and Canada 1-800-421-1394, offers Mexican insurance. *Winter in Mexico Caravans Inc*, with newsletter of *The Escapees Club* (see 'Mexico Connexion' chapter), 101 Rainbow Drive, Livingston, Texas 77351, T (303) 761-9829, offers advice on caravan trips to Mexico, runs tours for caravanners, including a birdwatching tour. Also *Aim*, on retirement and travel in Mexico, Apdo postal 31-70, Guadalajara 45050, Jalisco.

Car Rental is very expensive in Mexico and 10% VAT is added to rental costs. Cheapest rates are about US$34 a day for VW beetle, rising to US$75 a day for a jeep (mileage extra US$0.25-0.66/km) collision protection US$11.65. Rates will vary from city to city. Apart from some local companies, Budget was reported to be the best value in 1993-94. It is cheaper to arrange hire in the US or Europe, but rentals booked abroad cannot be guaranteed (though usually they are). Proceed with caution. Renting a vehicle is nearly impossible without a credit card. It is twice as expensive to leave a car at a different point from the starting point than a round trip. Check the spare tyre, that the fuel gauge works and that you have been given a full tank, that the insurance is valid on unmade roads and that you know how the alarm (if fitted) turns off—the car will not go if the alarm is set off. A short length of strong chain and a padlock for securing the trunk are worthwhile, for VW beetles (Mexican models are the cheapest cars available for hire but do not come with any frills - a/c, radio, etc). Note that caution is also required when driving in Chiapas: a rented VW Beetle can cope with the roads, but potholes, subsidence and collapses at the edge of sheer drops are common.

Airport Taxis To avoid overcharging, the Government has taken control of taxi services from airports to cities and only those with government licences are allowed to carry passengers from the airport. Sometimes one does not pay the driver but purchases a ticket from a booth on leaving the airport. No further tipping is then required, except when the driver handles heavy luggage for you. The same system has been applied at bus stations but it is possible to pay the driver direct.

Motorbikes Grant and Susan Johnson, of Horizons Unlimited, Vancouver, tell us that motor-cycling is good in Mexico as most main roads are in fairly good condition and hotels are usually willing to allow the bike to be parked in a courtyard or patio.

In the major tourist centres, such as Acapulco, Puerto Vallarta or Cancún, motorbike parts can be found as there are Honda dealers for bike and jet ski rentals. All Japanese parts are sold only by one shop in Mexico City at extortionate prices (but parts and accessories are easily available in Guatemala at reasonable prices for those travelling there). Robert S Kahn recommends Señor Romano's shop, Av Revolución 1310, Mexico City, for bike repairs. Sr Romano, a Belgian-Mexican, speaks French and English. For BMW repairs and some parts, Ashley Rawlings recommends BMW Mexico City, Grupo Baviera SA de CV, Calzada de Tlalpan 4585, Apdo postal 22-217-CP 14330, T 573-4900. Some motorbike travellers have warned that particularly in Mexico City groups of plain clothes police in unmarked cars try to impound motorbikes by force of arms. Uniformed police are no help here.

In Case of Accident Do not abandon your vehicle. Call your insurance company immediately to inform it of the accident. Do not leave Mexico without first filing a claim in Mexico. Do not sign any contract or agreement without a representative of the insurance company being present. Always carry with you, in the insured vehicle, your policy identification card and the names of the company's adjusters (these are the recommendations of Asemex). If, in an accident, bodily injury has occurred or the drivers involved cannot agree who is at fault, the vehicles may be impounded.

Warnings On all roads, when two vehicles converge from opposite directions, or when a vehicle is behind a slow cart, bicycle, etc, the driver who first flashes his lights has the right of way. This also applies when a bus or truck wishes to turn left across the opposing traffic: if the driver flashes his lights he is claiming right of way and the oncoming traffic must give way. Don't drive fast at night; farm and wild animals roam freely. In fact, it is advisable to drive as little as possible at night as robberies are on the increase especially in Guerrero and Oaxaca States. Some motorists report that it is better not to stop if you hit another car, as although Mexican insurance is proof of your ability to pay, both parties may sometimes be incarcerated until all claims are settled. 'Sleeping policemen' or road bumps can be hazardous in towns and villages as often there are no warning signs; they are sometimes marked *'zona de topes'*, or incorrectly marked as *vibradores*. In most instances, their distinguishing paint has worn away.

Searches of foreigners for drugs on the west coast were reinstated in 1993. The following precautions should help towards an incident-free passage of a drug search. Carry copies of all prescriptions for medicines (typed). Keep medicines in the original container. Carry a notice of all medical conditions that need a hypodermic syringe or emergency treatment. Never take packages for another person. Never take hitchers across a border. Always cross a border in your own vehicle. Check your vehicle carefully for suspicious packages secreted by someone other than yourself. If you have bodywork done in Mexico, supervise it yourself and keep records, even photos, of the workshop that did it. If you did have work done on your vehicle, call for a sniffer dog to cover yourself. Prior to inspections, open all doors, hatches, etc. Put away all money and valuables. Offer no drinks, cigarettes or gifts to the inspectors; accept none. When searched, cooperate with narcotics officers (who wear black); do not intrude, but watch the proceedings closely.

If you are stopped by police in town for an offence you have not committed and you know you are in the right, do not pay the 'fine' on the spot. Take the number of the policeman from his cap, show him that you have his number and tell him that you will see his chief (*jefe*) at the tourist police headquarters instead. It is also advisable to go to the precinct station anyway whenever a fine is involved, to make sure it is genuine. If stopped in a remote area, though, it is not advisable to get into a dispute with a policeman; drugs may be planted in your vehicle or other problems may occur.

When entering Mexico from Belize by car point out to the authorities that you have a car with you, otherwise they may not note it and you could be arrested for illegally importing a car.

In the US-Mexico border areas do not give lifts to strangers; if at all possible do not cross at night. It was reported in January 1992 that the Mexican authorities were working to eradicate corruption in the border zone.

Tourists' cars cannot, *by law*, be sold in Mexico. This is very strictly applied. You may not leave the country without the car you entered in, except with written government permission with the car (and trailer if you have one) in bond.

Road Tolls (See also p 117.) A toll is called a 'cuota", as opposed to a non-toll road, which is a 'vía libre" . There are many toll charges, mostly of US$1 to 2, on roads and bridges. Some new freeways bypassing city centres charge US$7 or more for 50 km, expensive but much quicker for those in a hurry. With the privatization of many freeways, hefty tolls are charged to roadusers (double the car fee for trailers and trucks). Some can be avoided if you seek local, or motoring club (see above) advice on detours around toll gates (follow trucks). This may involve unpaved roads which should not be attempted in the wet.

Cycling Peter Cossins (of Bath) writes: 'Considering that it is a large country with many sparsely populated areas, Mexico offers plenty of enjoyable places for riding. The main problems facing cyclists are the heavy traffic which will be encountered on many main roads, the poor condition of the same main roads and the lack of specialized spare parts particularly for mountain bikes. It is possible to find most bike spares in the big cities, but outside these places it is only possible to find the basics—spokes, tyres, tubes etc. Traffic is particularly bad around Mexico City and on the road between Mazatlán and Guadalajara. The easiest region for cycling is the Gulf of Mexico coast, however the roads are dead flat, straight and generally boring. The mountains may appear intimidating, but gradients are not difficult as clapped-out buses and trucks have to be able to climb them. Consequently, much of the best riding is in the sierra. If cycling in Baja, avoid riding in mid-Summer—even during October temperatures can reach 45°C+ and water is very scarce all the time. Also beware of Mexican bike mechanics who will attempt to repair your bike rather than admit that they don't know what they are doing, particularly when it comes to mountain bikes.' Wolfgang Schroppel from Urbach and Friedemann Bar from Plüderhausen in Germany also advise that: 'for cyclists the toll roads are generally preferable to the ordinary highways. There is less traffic, more lanes and a wide paved shoulder. Some toll roads have 'no cyclists' signs but even the police pay no attention. If you walk your bicycle on the sidewalk through the toll station you don't have to pay. Overland buses, especially on the Pacific Coast highway from Tijuana to Guadalajara, forced us off the road several times as there is no shoulder. They believe more in God than in their brakes. This is very dangerous for cyclists. It is useful to fit a rear mirror, so you can jump off the road before you get hit" .

Hitchhiking is usually possible for single hikers, but apparently less easy for couples. It is generally quick, but not universally safe (seek local advice). Do not, for example, try to hitch in those parts of Guerrero and Oaxaca States where even driving alone is not recommended. In more out of the way parts, short rides from village to village are usually the rule, so progress can be slow. Getting out of big cities is best done by taking a local bus out of town in the direction of the road you intend to take. Ask for the bus to the 'Salida' (exit) to the next city on that road. From Mexico City to the US border, the route via Tula, Ciudad Valles and Ciudad Victoria, the Sierra Madre Oriental, is scenic but slow through the mountains. The quicker route is via Querétaro, San Luis Potosí and Matehuala. Elsewhere, the most difficult stretches are reported to be Acapulco-Puerto Escondido, Santa Cruz-Salina Cruz and Tulum-Chetumal. It is very easy to hitch short distances, such as the last few km to an archaeological site off the main road; offer to pay something, like US$0.50.

Walking Walkers are advised to get *No Frills Guide to Hiking in Mexico*, edited by Jim Conrad (Bradt Publications, 41 Nortoft Road, Chalfont St Peter, Bucks, SL9 0LA, UK, updated every 6 months or so, readers' suggestions welcome). Do not walk at night on dark, deserted roads or streets.

Camping Most sites are called Trailer Parks, but tents are usually allowed. For camping and youth-hostel accommodation, see under **Camp Sites**, Mexico City (**page 183**) for *Villas Deportivas Juveniles*. Beware of people stealing clothes, especially when you hang them up after washing. *Playas Públicas*, with a blue and white sign of a palm tree, are beaches where camping is allowed. They are usually cheap, sometimes free and some have shelters and basic amenities. Paraffin oil (kerosene) for stoves is called *petróleo para lámparas* in Mexico; it is not a very good quality (dirty) and costs about US$0.05 per litre. It is available from an *expendio*, or *despacho de petróleo*, or from a *tlalalpería*, but not from gas stations. Calor gas is widely available, as it is throughout Central America. Gasolina Blanca may be bought in *ferreterías*, ironmongers, prices vary widely, also ask for Coleman fuel. Alcohol for heating the burner can be obtained from supermarkets. Repairs to stoves at Servis-Coleman at Plaza de San Juan 5, Mexico City. Katadyn water-purifying filters can be bought in Mexico City at Katadyn/Dispel, Distribuidores de Purificadores y Electrodomésticos, Fco Javier Olivárez Muñoz, Sinaloa 19 PB, Colonia Roma, CP 06700, Mexico DF, T 533-0600, F 207-7174, spare parts also available.

Youth Hostels 21 *albergues* exist in Mexico, mostly in small towns, and generally of poor quality. The hostels take YHA members and non-members, who have to pay more. You have to pay a deposit for sheets, pillow and towel; make sure that this is written in the ledger or else you may not get your deposit back. Hostels have lockers for valuables; take good care of your other possessions.

Hotels Hotel rates were freed from government control in early 1993; some establishments may raise prices above the rate of inflation, so some bargaining, or shopping around, may be required to find the best value. Complaints about standards, etc, may be reported to the Department of Tourism, Presidente Masaryk 172, Colonia Polanco, Mexico City, T 250-1964 and 250-8555. English is spoken at the best hotels.

Casas de huéspedes are usually the cheapest places to stay, although they are often dirty with poor plumbing. Usually a flat rate for a room is charged, so sharing works out cheaper, say US$3-5 pp. There are very few places with double beds (*matrimonial*) under US$9 double. Sleeping out is possible anywhere, but is not advisable in urban areas. Choose a secluded, relatively invisible spot. Mosquito netting (*pabellón*) is available by the metre in textile shops and, sewn into a sheet sleeping bag, is ample protection against insects.

Beware of 'helpfuls' who try to find you a hotel, as prices quoted at the hotel desk rise to give them a commission. If backpacking, best for one of you to watch over luggage while the other goes to book a room and pay for it; some hotels are put off by backpacks. During peak season (November-April), it may be hard to find a room and clerks do not always check to see whether a room is vacant. Insist, or if desperate, provide a suitable tip. The week after Semana Santa is normally a holiday, so prices remain high, but resorts are not as crowded as the previous week. When using a lift, remember PB (*Planta Baja*) stands for ground floor. Discounts on hotel prices can often be arranged in the low season (May-October), but more difficult in Yucatán and Baja California. There is not a great price difference between single and double rooms. Rooms with double beds are usually cheaper than those with 2 singles. Check out time from hotels is commonly 1400. When checking into a hotel, always ask if the doors are locked at night, preventing guests from entering if no nightguard is posted. Always check the room before paying in advance. Also ask if there is 24-hr running water.

Motels and Auto-hotels, especially in central and South Mexico, are not usually places where guests stay the whole night (you can recognise them by curtains over the garage and red and green lights above the door to show if the room is free). If driving, and wishing to avoid a night on the road, they can be quite acceptable (clean, some have hot water, in the Yucatán they have a/c), and they tend to be cheaper than respectable establishments.

Note In the highlands, where it can be cold at night, especially in winter, many hotels do not have heating; be prepared. This applies in popular tourist centres such as San Cristóbal de las Casas, Oaxaca, Pátzcuaro.

Experiment in International Living Ltd, 'Ostesaga", West Malvern Road, Malvern, Worcestershire, WR14 4EN, T 0684-562577, F 562212, or Ubierstrasse 30, 5300 Bonn 2, T 0228-95-7220, F 0228-35-8282, with offices in 38 countries, can arrange stays with families in Mexico from 1 to 4 weeks. This has been recommended as an excellent way to meet people and learn the language.

Food Usual meals are a light breakfast (although this can consist of several courses), and a heavy lunch between 1400 and 1500. Dinner, between 1800 and 2000, is light. Many restaurants give foreigners the menu without the *comida corrida* (set meals), and so forcing them to order *à la carte* at double the price; watch this! Try to avoid eating in restaurants which don't post a menu. Meals in modest establishments cost about US$2.25-3.25 for breakfast, US$2.65-4 for lunch (*comida corrida*, US$5.25-8 for a special *comida corrida*) and US$8.35-12 for dinner (generally no set menu). A la Carte meals at modest establishments cost about US$10; a very good meal can be had for US$16.50 at a middle level establishment. Much higher prices are charged by the classiest restaurants (eg, in Mexico City, US$25-30 medium class, US$40 1st class, US$50 plus luxury). The best value is undoubtedly in small, family-run places. For those who are self-catering the cost of food in markets and supermarkets is not high. In resort areas the posh hotels include breakfast and dinner in many cases. Check bills and change, even if service is included waiters may deduct a further tip from the change, they will hand it back if challenged. In some restaurants, beer will not be served unless a meal is ordered.

Among the least appetizing places to eat in Mexico are fast food chain restaurants named after their American counterparts.

What to Eat *Tamales*, or meat wrapped in maize and then banana leaves and boiled. Turkey, chicken and pork with exotic sauces—*mole de guajolote* and *mole poblano* (*chile* and chocolate sauce with grated coconut) are famous. *Tacos* (without *chiles*) and *enchiladas* (with all too many of them) are meat or chicken and beans rolled in *tortillas* (maize pancakes) and fried in oil; they are delicious. Try also spring onions with salt and lime juice in *taquerías*. Indian food is found everywhere: for instance, *tostadas* (toasted fried tortillas with chicken, beans and lettuce), or *gorditas*, fried, extra-thick tortillas with sauce and cheese. Black kidney beans (*frijoles*) appear in various dishes. Try *crepas de cuitlacoche*, best during rainy season—this consists of a pancake stuffed with maize fungus, which has a delicate mushroomy taste— very moreish. In the Pátzcuaro area ask for *budín de cuitlacoche*, with tomato, cream and *chiles*. Red snapper (*huachinango*), Veracruz style, is a famous fish dish, sautéd with *pimientos* and spices. Another excellent fish is the sea bass (*robalo*). Fruits include a vast assortment of tropical types—avocados, bananas, pineapples, *zapotes*, pomegranates, guavas, limes and *mangos de Manila*, which are delicious. Don't eat fruit unless you peel it yourself, and avoid raw vegetables. Try *higos rebanados* (delicious fresh sliced figs), *guacamole* (a mashed avocado seasoned with tomatoes, onions, coriander and *chiles*) and of course, *papaya*, or pawpaw. Mexico has various elaborate regional cuisines. Some Maya dishes are *sopa de lima* (chicken, rice, *tostada* and lime), *pok chuk* (pork in achiote sauce), *pibil* (a mild sauce on meat or chicken, cooked in banana leaves), *longanizo* sausage from Valladolid. Chinese restaurants, present in most towns, generally give clean and efficient service.

European continental breakfast is very hard to find. For those who like a light, sweet breakfast, try *avena*, a fairly liquid porridge prepared with milk or water, with liberal amounts of cinnamon. Mexican chocolate made with milk is quite filling. In markets, *arroz con leche* is rice boiled in milk until it starts to dissolve, flavoured with cinnamon and sugar. Milk is only safe when in sealed containers marked *pasteurizado*. Fried eggs are known as *huevos estrellados*. On 6 January,

Epiphany, the traditional *rosca*, a ring-shaped sweet bread with dried fruit and little plastic baby Jesuses inside, is eaten. The person who finds a baby Jesus in his piece must make a crib and clothes for Him, and invite everyone present to a *fiesta* on 2 February, Candelaria.

Drink The beer is good: brands include Dos Equis-XX, Montejo, Bohemia, Sol and Superior (last two not as good). Negra Modelo is a dark beer, it has the same alcohol content as the other beers. Local wine is cheap; try Domecq, Casa Madero, Santo Tomás, etc; the white sold in oyster restaurants *ostionerías* is usually good. The native drinks are *pulque*, the fermented juice of the agave plant (those unaccustomed to it should not over indulge), *tequila*, made mostly in Jalisco, and *mescal* from Oaxaca; the last two distilled from agave plants. Mescal usually has a 'gusano de maguey' (worm) in the bottle, considered by Mexicans to be a particular speciality. Tequila and mescal rarely have an alcoholic content above 40-43%; tequila Sauza and Cuervo have been recommended. Also available is the Spanish aniseed spirit, *anís*, which is made locally. Imported whiskies and brandies are expensive. Rum is cheap and good. *Puro de caña* (called *chingre* in Chinanteca and *posh* in Chamula) is distilled from sugar cane, stronger than mescal but with less taste; it is found in Oaxaca and Chiapas. There are always plenty of non-alcoholic soft drinks (*refrescos*)—try the *paletas*, safe and refreshing (those of Michoacán are everywhere)—and mineral water. Fresh juices (as long as not mixed with water) and milk shakes (*licuados*) are good and usually safe. If you don't like to drink out of a glass ask for a straw, *popote*. Herbal teas, eg camomile, are available. There are few outdoor drinking places in Mexico except in tourist spots.

Tipping is more or less on a level of 10-15%; the equivalent of US$0.25 per bag for porters, the equivalent of US$0.20 for bell boys, theatre usherettes, and nothing for a taxi driver unless he gives some extra service. It is not necessary to tip the drivers of hired cars.

Security   Mexico is generally a safe country to visit, although the usual precautions should be taken as the number of assaults is rising, especially in Mexico City. Never carry valuables visibly or in easily picked pockets. Leave passports, tickets and important documents in an hotel safety deposit, not in your room. Underground pedestrian crossings are hiding places for thieves, take extra care at night. Cars are a prime target for theft. As with driving at night in the States of Guerrero and Oaxaca, avoid travelling by bus at night in these districts; if at all possible make journeys in day light. Also (and it is very sad having to write this), beware of getting too friendly with young gringos who seem to be living in Mexico permanently—unless, of course, they have jobs. Many of them stay in Mexico for the cheap drugs, and are not above robbery and assault to finance their habit. Couples, and even more, women on their own, should avoid lonely beaches. Those on the west coast are gaining a reputation as drug landing points. Some women experience problems, whether accompanied or not; others encounter no difficulties at all. (In discos women are supposed to wait until asked to dance by a man.) The police service has an equivalent to the Green Angels (see above), the Silver Angels, who help victims of crime to file a report. US citizens should present this report to the nearest embassy or consulate.

Speaking Spanish is a great asset in avoiding rip-offs for gringos, especially short changing and overcharging (both rife), and to make the most of cheap *comedores* and market shopping.

Gay travellers should be aware of 'public decency' laws which allow the police much latitude: for as little as holding hands on the beach you can be arrested, even in Acapulco which has many attractions for gay visitors.

Drugs Note that anyone found in possession of narcotics, in however small a quantity, is liable to a minimum prison sentence of 10 years, with a possible 1-year wait for a verdict. Narcotics include 'magic mushrooms".

Health The Social Security hospitals are restricted to members, but will take visitors in emergencies; they are more up to date than the Centros de Salud and Hospitales Civiles found in most centres, which are very cheap and open to everyone. There are many homeopathic physicians in all parts of Mexico. You are recommended to use bottled or mineral water for drinking, except in hotels which normally provide purified drinking water free. Ice is usually made from *agua purificada*. Coffee water is not necessarily boiled. Bottled water is available everywhere. Tehuacán mineral water is sold all over Mexico; both plain and flavoured are first class. Water-sterilizing tablets and water purification solution, Microdyn, can be bought at pharmacies. Raw salads and vegetables, and food sold on the streets and in cheap cafés, especially in Mexico City, may be dangerous. Women who are breast-feeding should avoid eating chile. Advisable to vaccinate against typhoid, paratyphoid and poliomyelitis if visiting the low-lying tropical zones, where there is also some risk of malaria; advice and malaria pills from 6th floor, San Luis Potosí 199, Colonia Roma Norte, Mexico City, 0900-1400 (chloroquine is available in most large chemists/pharmacies under the brand name Aralen; mefloquire-Larium, is not available). Gamma globulin is available at better pharamacies/chemists. Heavy eating and drinking of alcohol is unwise in the capital because of its altitude; so is overdoing it physically in the first few days. Some people experience nose-bleeds in Guadalajara and Mexico City because of pollution; they cease with fresh air. Locals recommend Imecol for 'Montezuma's Revenge' (the very common diarrhoea).

Clothing People are usually smartly dressed in Mexico City. There is little central heating, so warm clothing is needed in winter. Four musts are good walking shoes, sun hats, dark glasses, and flip-flops for the hot sandy beaches. Topless bathing is now accepted in parts of Baja California, but ask first, or do as others do. Men may need a jacket and tie in some restaurants. It is difficult to obtain shoes over US size 9 1/2, but it is possible to have them made.

Hours of Business in Mexico City are extremely variable. All banks are open from 0900 to 1330 from Mon to Fri, some stay open later, and (head offices only) 0900 to 1230 on Sat. Business offices usually open at 0900 or 1000 and close at 1300 or 1400. They reopen at 1400 or 1500, but senior executives may not return until much later, although they may then stay until after 1900. Other businesses, especially those on the outskirts of the city, and many Government offices, work from 0800 to 1400 or 1500 and then close for the rest of the day. Business hours in other parts of the country vary considerably according to the climate and local custom. In Monterrey they are roughly as in Britain.

National Holidays Sunday is a statutory holiday. Saturday is also observed as a holiday, except by the shops. There is no early-closing day. National holidays are as follows:
New Year (1 January), Constitution Day (5 February), Birthday of Benito Juárez (21 March), Maundy Thursday, Good Friday and Easter Saturday, Labour Day (1 May), Battle of Puebla (5 May), President's Annual Message (1 September), Independence Day (16 September), Discovery of America (12 October), Day of the Revolution (20 November), Christmas Day (25 December).

All Souls' Day 2 Nov and Our Lady of Guadalupe 12 Dec, are not national holidays, but are widely celebrated.

Standard Time The same as US Central Standard Time, 6 hrs behind GMT. In Sonora, Sinaloa, Nayarit and Baja California Sur, 7 hrs behind GMT; and in Baja California Norte 8 hrs behind GMT (but 7 hrs behind GMT between 1 April and end October). The states N of the Tropic of Cancer have adopted a summer time (Zacatecas, León, Tamaulipas, Durango, Coahuila, Nuevo León, Chihuahua).

The **best season** for a business visit is from late January to May, but for pleasure between October and early April, when it hardly ever rains in most of the country. August is not a good time because it is a holiday month throughout Central America and most internal flights and other transport are heavily booked (also see above under **Travel in Mexico**).

Currency Until 1 January 1993, the monetary unit was the Mexican peso (represented by an 'S' crossed with one vertical line—unlike two vertical lines on the US dollar sign), divided into 100 centavos. On that date three zeros were eliminated from the peso, so that 1,000 peso now equals 1 new peso. The new symbol is N$. The smallest note is for 2 new pesos, 2,000 pesos, then 5/5,000,

10/10,000, 20/20,000, 50/50,000 and 100/100,000 pesos (2 and 5 peso notes are disappearing fast). Colours of notes to remain the same. New coins: 5C, 10C, 20C (dodecagonal), 50C (notched dodecagonal), N$1, 2, 5 and 10, all circular except those indicated. It is wise to check the number on coins. Local cheques are easier to cash in the issuing branch. There is a charge for cashing a cheque in a different city; if you can take someone along as a guarantor who has an account in the branch it helps.

Exchange In the border states such as Baja California Norte, the most-used currency is the US dollar, and the Mexican peso is often accepted by stores on the US side of the border. Travellers' cheques from any well-known bank can be cashed in most towns if drawn in US dollars; travellers' cheques in terms of sterling are harder to cash, and certainly not worth trying to change outside the largest of cities. The free rate of exchange changes daily and varies from bank to bank (Banamex usually has the best rates). Until the new day's rate is posted, at any time between 1000 and 1100, yesterday's rate prevails. Many banks, including in Mexico City, only change foreign currency during a limited period (often between 1000 and 1200, but sometimes also 1600-1800 in Banamex), which should be remembered, especially on Fridays. *Casas de cambio* are generally quicker than banks for exchange transactions, but their rates are not as good. Telegraphic transfer of funds *within* Mexico is not reliable. Beware of short-changing at all times. American Express, Mastercard and Visa are generally accepted in Mexico and cash is obtainable with these credit cards at certain banks. Automatic Teller Machines (ATM, *cajero automático*) of Banamex accept Visa, Mastercard and ATM cards of the US Cirrus ATM network for withdrawals up to 300 new pesos. ATM withdrawals on Visa can also be made at branches of Bancomer and Cajeros RED throughout the country. Many banks are affiliated to Mastercard but locations of ATMs should be checked with Mastercard in advance. There have been repeated instances of Banamex ATMs stating that cash cannot be given, 'try again later", only for the card holder to find that his/her accounts has been debited anyway. If you get a receipt saying no cash dispensed, keep it. **NB** An American Express card issued in Mexico states 'valid only in Mexico", and is used only for peso transactions. All other American Express cards are transacted in US dollars even for employees living in Mexico. Amex travellers' cheques are readily accepted and can easily be purchased with an Amex credit card. There is a 6% tax on the use of credit cards.

Cost of Living Budget travellers should note that there is a definite tourist economy, with high prices and, on occasion, unhelpful service. This can be avoided by seeking out those places used by locals; an understanding of Spanish is useful. The prices of accommodation and transport in this chapter can only be taken as representative. You are advised to check all local prices before booking. VAT (IVA) is charged on all but some basic goods; it ranges from 6% on food to 15% on almost all consumer goods, including hotel and restaurant bills, to 25% on luxury items. VAT is already included in the final price of the good or service. Hotels can be expensive for what is offered, especially cheaper hotels in smaller towns: cheap double room from US$13 (Mexico City) to US$22 (eg Taxco). The bus fares given in this chapter were current in March 1994; further rises in public transport fares, especially in cities, can be expected. As a very rough guide, allow US$22-27 a day if planning to stay in E-D range hotels, travel by bus and take taxis from bus stations to a hotel. Laundry in a laundromat costs on average US$5 for 5 kg load, wash and dry. This cost of living for travellers is about 2-3 times more expensive than Guatemala or Honduras (1993). For travellers, Mexico is in some respects cheaper than the USA in that 1st class bus travel is less, there are local bus services which many US cities lack, and cheap hotel accommodation exists in city centres where, in the USA, there is little more than YMCAs and youth hostels. In other respects, though, Mexico can be more expensive than the USA. In comparison with most Western European countries, Mexico is considerably cheaper. The only areas in which travellers will find Mexico more expensive than the UK are luxury hotels, coffee, beer, long-distance and international phone calls, international postage, theatres and especially car hire. Doctors and dentists provide good quality care at high prices (taking appropriate insurance is highly rec). Film is reasonably cheap, but developing is expensive and of poor quality.

Weights and Measures The metric system is compulsory.

Postal Services Rates are raised periodically in line with the peso's devaluation against the dollar but are reported to vary between towns. They are posted next to the windows where stamps are sold. Rates in March 1994 were: to North and Central America and the Caribbean: letters N$2 (20g), N$3.70 (50g), N$5.50 (100g), postcards N$1.50; South America and Europe N$2.50, 4.40, 7.70, postcards N$1.80; Asia and Africa N$2.80, 5.20, 8.60, postcards N$2.10 (an increase was due later in 1994). International service has improved and bright red mail-boxes, found in many parts of the city, are reliable. Weight limit from the UK to Mexico:

22 lb, and 5 kg in the reverse direction. About 3 months to Europe. Small parcel rate cheaper. Parcel counters often close earlier than other sections of the post office in Mexico. As for most of Latin America, send printed matter such as magazines registered. International parcels must be examined by the Customs at Aldama 218, Colonia Buenavista, near Guerrero metro, open 0900-1400; or Correo Central at Calle Tacuba, open 0800-1300, window No 48 from which only books or records can be sent; parcels with books in them must be less than 5 kg before posting. No more than 3 parcels may be sent at a time; maximum parcel size: 40 cm X 60 cm; registered letters received here. Cheaper, 2nd class airmail parcels from Aduana Postal, Ceylán 468 (see under Mexico City, **International Post Office**). We have heard that the Customs Department at the airport holds up registered parcels coming in from abroad. Many travellers have also recommended that one should not use the post to send film or cherished objects as losses are frequent. A permit is needed from the Bellas Artes office to send paintings or drawings out of Mexico. Not all these services are obtainable outside Mexico; delivery times in/from the interior may well be longer than those given above. Poste restante ("general delivery' in the US, *lista de correos* in Mexico) functions quite reliably, but you may have to ask under each of your names; mail is sent back after ten days (for an extension write to the Jefe de la Administración of the post office holding your mail, any other post office will help with this). Address '*favor de retener hasta llegada*' on envelope. Within Mexico many businesses use 1st and 2nd class passenger buses to deliver letters and parcels. Each piece is signed for and must be collected at the destination. The service is considered quick and reliable. Should it be necessary to send anything swiftly and safely (in Mexico and other countries), there are many courier firms; the best known is DHL (Mexico City T 227-0299), but it is about twice the cost of Estrella Blanca (T 368-6577) or Federal Express (T 228-9904).

Telephones Pay telephones (black) for local calls take coins, or *fichas*, also for collect long-distance calls. In the capital *fichas* are available at Parque Vía 198, although often no money is needed to make a call within the Mexico City. Public telephones are still being adjusted to take the new coins. Phones that take cards are more common at airports and other terminals. Follow local procedures, then dial 02 for calls inside Mexico and 09 for international calls, and be patient. AT&T's USA Direct service is available, for information in Mexico dial 412-553-7458, ext 359. From LADA phones (see below), dial **01, similar for AT&T credit cards. To use calling cards to Canada T 95-800-010-1990. March 1994 rates for phone and fax: Europe N$9.30, cheap rate 6.20; USA/New York N$5.60, cheap rate 3.73; Australia N$11.85, cheap rate 7.90; plus 10% VAT. Commercially-run *casetas*, or booths (eg Computel), where you pay after phoning, are 2-3 times more expensive, and charges vary from place to place. It is better to call collect from private phones, but better still to use the LADA system. Collect calls on LADA can be made from any blue public phone, silver phones for local and direct long distance calls, some take coins. Others take foreign credit cards (Visa, Mastercard, not Amex—"a slot machine scenario", not all phones that say they take cards accept them, others that say they don't do), still others take plastic cards worth from 5 to 50 new pesos, purchasable from phone company offices, supermarkets, etc. LADA numbers are: 91 long distance within Mexico, add city code and number (half-price Sunday); 92 long distance in Mexico, person to person; 95 long distance to USA and Canada, add area code and number; 96 to USA and Canada person to person for collect calls; 98 to rest of the world, add country code, city code and number; 99 to rest of the world, person to person; it is not possible to call collect to Germany, but it is possible to Israel. Cheap rates vary according to the country called. For information dial 07 or 611-1100. Foreign calls (through the operator, at least) cannot be made from 1230 on 24 December until the end of Christmas Day. The *Directorio Telefónico Nacional Turístico* is full of useful information, including LADA details, federal tourist offices, time zones, yellow pages for each state, places of interest and maps.

Telecommunications Telégrafos Nacionales maintains the national and international

To use AT&T USADirect® Service for Calling Card or collect calls from Mexico just dial **95-800-462-4240**. If you require assistance, please call the AT&T offices in Mexico City **(91-5) 327-2883**, Guadalajara **(91-3) 616-1212**, or Monterrey **(91-8) 340-82-82**.

AT&T USADirect® Service.

telegraph systems, separate from the Post Office. There is a special office at Balderas 14-18, just near corner of Colón, in Mexico City to deal with international traffic (open 0800-2300, Metro Hidalgo, exit Calle Basilio Badillo). There are three types of telegraph service: *extra urgente*, *urgente* and *ordinario*; they can only be prepaid, not sent collect. There is a telegraph and telex service available at Mexico City airport. Fax is common in main post offices.

Press The more important journals are in Mexico City. The most influential dailies are: *Excelsior, Novedades, El Día* (throughout Mexico), *Uno más Uno; The News* (in English, now available in all main cities); *El Universal* (*El Universal Gráfico*); *La Jornada* (more to the left), *La Prensa*, a popular tabloid, has the largest circulation. *El Nacional* is the mouthpiece of the Government; *El Heraldo*; *Uno más Uno* publishes a supplement, *Tiempo Libre*, on Thursdays, listing the week's cultural activities. In Guadalajara, *El Occidental, El Informador* and *Siglo 21*. There are influential weekly magazines *Proceso*, and *Siempre*; *Epoca*, weekly also. The political satirical weekly is *Los Agachados*.

Local Information All Mexican Government tourist agencies are now grouped in the Department of Tourism building at Avenida Masaryk 172, near corner of Reforma. See under Mexico City for full details. A few cities run municipal tourist offices to help travellers. The Mexican Automobile Association (AMA) is at Orizaba 7, 06700 México DF, T 208-8329, F 511-6285; they sell an indispensable road guide, with good maps and very useful lists of hotels, with current prices. The ANA (Asociación Nacional Automobilística) sells similar but not such good material; offices in Insurgentes (Metro Glorieta) and Av Jalisco 27, México 18 DF. For road conditions consult the AMA, which is quite reliable. A calendar of *fiestas* is published by *Mexico This Month*.

There are a series of telephone number that tourists can call to clarify problems. In USA, phone Mexican Turismo, Miami, 1-800-446-8277. In Houston T 1-800-44-639-420, for English information for US and Canadian citizens. There is another Houston number which anyone can call, 1-713-880-8772 for information on surface tourism. In Mexico, tourists can call 91-800-00148 and in Mexico City 604-1240. The Secretaría de Turismo has an emergency hot line, open 24 hrs a day: (05) 250-0123/0151.

In a similar vein to the Ruta Maya (see the Introduction to this book), but purely Mexican, is the Colonial Cities Schedule, which links 51 cities in 8 circuits. Full details are available from the Secretaría de Turismo, T/F 250-7414.

Tourist Information **Canada**, 2 Bloor Street West, Suite 1801, Toronto, Ontario, M4W 3EZ, T 416 925-0704; **France**, 4 Rue Notre Dame des Victories, 75002 Paris, T 331 4020-0734; **Germany**, Welsenhuttenplatz 26, D600 Frankfurt am Main 1, T 4969 25-3413; **Italy**, Via Barberini 3, 00187 Rome, T 396 474-2986; **Mexico**, Subsecretaria de Turismo, Martano Escobedo No 726, CP 11590, Mexico DF, T 525 211-0099; **UK**, 60-61 Trafalgar Square, 3rd Floor, London, WC2N 3DS, T 0171 839-3177; **USA**, 405 Park Avenue, Suite 1401, New York, NY 10022, T 212 755-7261.

If you have any complaints about faulty goods or services, go to the Procuraduría Federal de Protección del Consumidor of which there is a branch in every city (head office in Mexico City, José Vasconcelos 208, CP 06720, México DF, T 761-3801/11). Major cities, like Acapulco, also have a Procurador del Turista. The Tourist Office may also help with these, or criminal matters, while the Agente del Ministro Público (Federal or State District Attorney) will also deal with criminal complaints.

Maps The Mexican Government Tourist Highway map is available free of charge at tourist offices (when in stock). If driving from the USA you get a free map if you buy your insurance at Sanborn's in the border cities. The official map printers, Detenal, produce the only good large-scale maps of the country.

The Dirección General de Oceanografía in Calle Medellín 10, near Insurgentes underground station, sells excellent maps of the entire coastline of Mexico. Good detailed maps of states of Mexico and the country itself from Dirección General de Geografía y Meteorología, Av Observatorio 192, México 18, DF, T 515-15-27 (go to Observatorio underground station and up Calle Sur 114, then turn right a short distance down Av Observatorio). Best road maps of Mexican states, free, on polite written request, from Ing Daniel Díaz Díaz, Director General de Programación, Xola 1755, 8° Piso, México 12 DF Building is on the corner of Xola with Av Universidad. Mapas Turísticos de México has Mexican (stocks Detenal maps) and world-maps, permanent exhibition at Río Rhin 29, Col Cuauhtémoc, Mexico 5, T 566-2177. Maps also available from Instituto Nacional de Estadística, Geografía e Informática (INEGI), which has branches in Mexico City **(see page 193)** and in state capitals. Pemex road atlas, *Atlas de Carreteras y Ciudades Turísticas*, US$5 in bookshops (eg Sanborns), has 20 pages of city maps, almost every road one may need, contour lines, points of interest, service stations, etc (it is rarely on sale in Pemex stations), rec. As well as its maps of *Mexico*

City and Baja California, ITM of Vancouver (PO Box 2290, Vancouver, BC, V6B 3W5, Canada) publish a map of Mexico (1:3,300,000, 1993-94), Mexico: South (1:1,000,000, 1992-93) and Yucatán (1:1,000,000, 3rd edition, 1993-95). The AAA road map is fine for major roads, less good off the beaten track. Also rec, maps published by HFET SA, Fresas 27, Col de Valles, Mexico DF, T 559-2310/559-2320, Mexico City, Estado de México and Mapectual Road Atlas of whole country, US$6 (from Sanborns).

Guidebooks Travellers wanting more information than we have space to provide, on archaeological sites for instance, would do well to use the widely available Panorama guides and the Easy Guides written by Richard Bloomgarden, with plans and good illustrations. You will appreciate archaeological sites much more if you do some research before visiting them. A Field Guide to Mexican Birds, Peterson and Chalif, Houghton Mifflin, 1973, has been recommended. For ornithologists: Finding Birds in Mexico, by Ernest P Edwards, Box AQ, Sweet Briar, Virginia 24595, USA, recommended as detailed and thorough. 2 books by Rudi Robins: One-day Car Trips from Mexico City, and Weekend trips to Cities near Mexico City. Highly recommended, practical and entertaining is The People's Guide to Mexico by Carl Franz (John Muir Publications, Santa Fe, NM), now in its 8th edition, 1990; there is also a People's Guide Travel Letter. Back Country Mexico, A Traveller's Guide and Phrase Book, by Bob Burlison and David H Riskind (University of Texas Press, Box 7819, Austin, Texas, 78713-7819) has been recommended. Mexico From The Driver's Seat, by Mike Nelson, is published by Sanborn's (see **Automobiles**, above). Also Hidden Mexico by Rebecca Brüns. More Maya Missions. Exploring Colonial Chiapas, written and illustrated by Richard D Perry (Espadaña Press, PO Box 31067, Santa Barbara, CA 93130, USA) is the latest in a series; also published, Maya Missions (in Yucatán) and Mexico's Fortress Monasteries (Central Mexico and Oaxaca). Fielding's Mexico by Lynn V Foster and Lawrence Foster has been recommended for its non-specialist archaeological and historical text (Fielding Travel Books, Wm Morrow and Co, New York).

Recommended reading for the Maya archaeological area: The Maya, by M D Coe (Pelican Books, or large format edition, Thames and Hudson); C Bruce Hunter, A Guide to Ancient Mayan Ruins (University of Oklahoma Press, 1986); Joyce Kelly, An Archaeological Guide to Mexico's Yucatán Peninsula (the states of Yucatán, Quintana Roo and Campeche) (University of Oklahoma Press, Norman and London, 1993, with maps, photos, 364 pp, accessible, informative and very good). For the Puuc region, Guide to Puuc Region, Prof Gualberto Zapata Alonzo (US$7.30), has been recommended. The Panorama series of guide books to the Maya sites is always good, but not always available. Bloomgarden guides also cover the major sites. For a contemporary account of travel in the Maya region, see Time among the Maya, by Ronald Wright. Perhaps the most descriptive of travel in the region is John L Stephens, Incidents of Travel in Central America, Chiapas and Yucatán, with illustrations by Frederick Catherwood (several editions exist).

Photography The Instituto Nacional de Antropología e Historia (INAH), Córdoba 44, Colonia Roma, Mexico City, will grant teachers, archaeologists, etc, written permission to take any type of photograph at sites and museums, including photos which general public may not take. It also issues admission discounts. The use of video cameras at historical sites costs US$8.50.

Books If looking for something to read in English, German or French, ask at the front desk of a first class hotel. Previous visitors may have left books behind which the receptionist may give you, often without charge.

Learning Spanish in Mexico: the National Registration Center for Study Abroad, 823 N 2nd St, PO Box 1393, Milwaukee, WI 53201, USA, T (414) 278-0631, F (414) 271-8884, Telex 8100071205, will advise on tuition within a worldwide consortium of language schools. It will also make all arrangements for study in Mexico. The catalogue costs US$3; phone for information and newsletter. Affiliated schools in Mexico are in San Miguel de Allende, Cuernavaca, Mazatlán, Mérida, Morelia, Guadalajara, Puebla, Acapulco, Mexico City, Aguascalientes, Toluca, Saltillo, Oaxaca.

Friends To meet interesting people, it is probably a good idea to visit the Casa de Cultura in any sizeable town.

For their invaluable assistance we are most grateful to Lynne Anderson (Cornhill-on-Tweed, Northumberland) Janet Arnold (Melbourne, Australia) Dr P Aylett (London SW15) Susanne Baader (Bremen, Germany), Jack Bailey & Diana Musacchio (Santa Barbara, CA, USA), Sheldon A Bass (Las Vegas, Nevada, USA), David Beasley & Liz Brooks (Horsham, West Sussex) Alexander Beck (Altessing, Germany), Adrian Stöckli (Birsfelden, Switzerland) Diego Bittel (Visp, Switzerland) Sybille Böhme (Kahl/Main, Germany), Sarah & Philippe Bonay (Auterine, France), Debra Brender (Davis, CA, USA) Ajues Burger (Germany), Christof Popp (Germany) & Christoph Durr (France) Jon Chambers (Moreton-in-Marsh, Gloucestershire) & Marianne Mller (Denmark) Jay Connerley (Fremont NE, USA) Christof Dillenberger & Claudia Kurz

(Holzgerlingen, Germany), Joe Docherty (Bath, UK) R Drost (Berlin, Germany) Frank Dux (Passau, Germany), Axel Ebert (Essen, Germany), Urs Eggli (Zurich, Switzerland) Frank Engler (Birsfelden/Basel, Switzerland) Gerard Klein Essink & Truus W de Graaf (Groningen, The Netherlands) Ariane Fässler (Wettswil, Switzerland) Matthias Fehrenbach (Immenstaad, Germany) Joy Hale & Derek Fess (Columbus, Ohio) Karin Fischli & Veli Hermann (Reichenburg, Switzerland), Ann Frechette & Jean Luc Massicotte for Charles Huot (Montréal), Darrel Freeman (Lancaster, PA, USA), P D Gadd & R del Tufo (London N1) Fränzi Gäggel (Glahfelden, Switzerland) Alessandra Gavirati (Arese, Italy), Karl Gebert (San Antonio, Texas), Julio Gonzalez (Saint-Bonnet près Riom, France) J Roy Goodall (Belize City) Thomas Gredig (Zurich, Switzerland) Heidi Gürtler (Friedrichshafen, Germany), Stefan Hansson (Lund, Sweden), Pasi Hannonen (Jy vä Skylä, Finland) Sally & Mike Hayden (Cheltenham, Glos), Mary Hayward (Edinburgh) Roger Hillen (Germany) Markus Hohl (London W11) Lorraine Hunter (Irish Town, Jamaica) Bente Iren Jakobsen (Oslo, Norway) Noel, Nenagh & Zoë Kemp (Lindisfarne, Australia), Dr Jürgen Koch (Leonburg, Germany) Ariane Kolckmann (Afdorf, Germany) Thomas Kuner (Rüti, Switzerland) Christopher Kwasizur (La Cañaada, CA, USA), Russel Lane (Salt Lake City, Utah), Luz (Pátzcuaro, Michoacán, Mexico) Eric Mankin (Venice, CA) Michelle Mason (Brightwalton Green, Berkshire), Richard W Middaugh (Glendale, CA, USA) Rob Minnee (Lisse, The Netherlands) Andrea Neumann, F Stehlik & A Mikula (Vienna, Austria) Rodney North & Donna Desrochers (Halifax, Nova Scotia), Bill & Michelle Osment (London), Francesca Pagnacco (Exeter, Devon) for a very helpful contribution, Antoine Pecard (Paris) Roma & Leo Pedenser (Oliver, BC, Canada) Thea Fischer & Michael Perch (Kbh K) Michael Pohl (Bad Honnef, Germany) Lisa Pollitt (Newcastle, UK) Warren Post (Santa Rosa de Copán, Honduras), Nigel & Maggie Potter (San José, Honduras), Helmut Quitt (Rosenheim, Germany), (Sandy) Alexandra Reid (Leichhardt, NSW, Australia) Michael Reiterer (Vienna, Austria) Sarah Ringles (Santa Cruz, CA, USA), Claudio Rivero (Buenos Aires) Richard Robinson (Tring, Herts), Jean Pierre Roose (Beersel, Belgium),

Dr Robert Rosen Jacobson (Amsterdam), Frank & Christine Ruiz (Brossard, Quebec), Dr Nick Saunders (Kingston, Jamaica) Johannes Schmeer (Munich, Germany), Jan & Truus van Ingen Schenau (Amsterdam) Adrian van Schie (New Zealand) Nina Schramm (Sheringham, Norfolk) Mary Nicoll & Charlie Schreiber (London NW5) Mark Schuringa (Amsterdam, Holland) Harald Schwender & Birgitte Hächer (Sandhausen, Germany) Peter Selley (London SW11) Michael Snowden (Ongar, Essex), Bjorn Sorlie (Berg I Ostfold, Norway), David Spencer (Santa Monica, CA) Stefan Cotting (Nevenegg, Switzerland), Glen Stephens (Castlecrag, NSW, Australia), Jan Svoboda (Vancouver, BC, Canada), George Tanber (Anniston, Alabama) Karin Taraschewski (Plüderhausen, Germany) Dan Toporoski (San Diego, CA) Suzanne Elise Tourville (St Louis, MO, USA), Eric H Tucker (Coulsden, Surrey) Christopher J S Tuppen (Southampton), Bill Vallis (Surbiton, Surrey), Edwin van der Werf & Harold Bierens (Holland) Anke & Herman Van Weeghel (Wychen, The Netherlands) Nina Vester (Mexico City) Benderoth Vitus (Hadamar), Volker Huss (Karlsruhe, Germany) Andy Walter (Swindon, Wiltshire), Tonya Ward (Middletown, CT, USA) Simon Watson Taylor (Goa) Dirk & Laura Weisheit (Mexico City) Sheila Wilson (Stoke Poges, Slough) Roberta Yamada (Milwaukee, WI, USA), Giulio Zanetti (Ivrea, Italy) Dirk Zeiler (Giessen, Germany), Christoph Zimmermann (Jona, Switzerland).

WILL YOU HELP US?

We do all we can to get our facts right in the MEXICO & CENTRAL AMERICAN HANDBOOK. Each section is thoroughly revised each year, but the territory is vast and our eyes cannot be everywhere. We are always pleased to hear about your travels; do write to us in as much detail as possible. In return we will send you information about our special guidebook offer.

TRADE & TRAVEL *Handbooks*

Write to The Editor, Mexico & Central American Handbook, Trade & Travel, 6 Riverside Court, Lower Bristol Road, Bath BA2 3DZ. England

CUBA

INTRODUCTION

THE ISLAND OF CUBA, 1,250 km long, 191 km at its widest point, is the largest of the Caribbean islands and only 145 km S of Florida. The name is believed to derive from the Arawak word 'cubanacan', meaning centre, or central. Gifted with a moderate climate, afflicted only occasionally by hurricanes, not cursed by frosts, blessed by an ample and well distributed rainfall and excellent soils for tropical crops, it has traditionally been one of the largest exporters of cane sugar in the world.

About a quarter of Cuba is fairly mountainous. To the W of Havana is the narrow Sierra de los Organos, rising to 750m and containing, in the extreme W, the strange scenery of the Guaniguánicos hill country. S of these Sierras, in a strip 145 km long and 16 km wide along the piedmont, is the Vuelta Abajo area which grows the finest of all Cuban tobaccos. Towards the centre of the island are the Escambray mountains, rising to 1,100m, and in the E, encircling the port of Santiago, are the most rugged mountains of all, the Sierra Maestra, in which Pico Turquino reaches 1,980m. In the rough and stony headland E of Guantánamo Bay are copper, manganese, chromium and iron mines. About a quarter of the land surface is covered with mountain forests of pine and mahogany. The coastline, with a remarkable number of fine ports and anchorages, is about 3,540 km long.

Some 66% of Cubans register themselves as whites: they are mostly the descendants of Spanish colonial settlers and immigrants; 12% are black, now living mostly along the coasts and in certain provinces, Oriente in particular; 21% are mulatto and about 1% are Chinese; the indigenous Indians disappeared long ago. Some 70% live in the towns, of which there are 9 with over 50,000 inhabitants each. The population is estimated at 10.9 million, of which 19% live in Havana (the city and that part of the province within the city's limits).

History Cuba was visited by Columbus during his first voyage on 27 October 1492, and he made another brief stop 2 years later on his way to Jamaica. Columbus did not realize it was an island; it was first circumnavigated by Sebastián de Ocampo in 1508. Diego de Velázquez conquered it in 1511 and founded several towns, including Havana. The first African slaves were imported in 1526. Sugar was introduced soon after but was not important until the last decade of

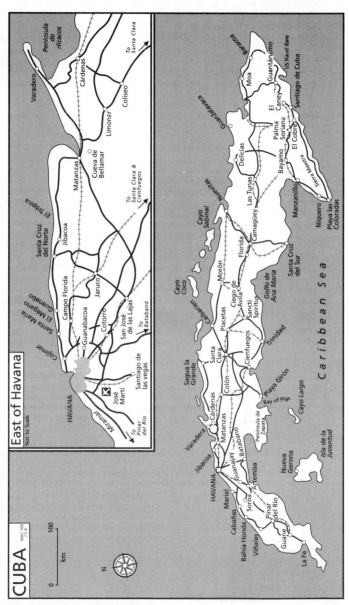

the 16th century. When the British took Jamaica in 1655 a number of Spanish settlers fled to Cuba, already famous for its cigars. Tobacco was made a strict monopoly of Spain in 1717. The coffee plant was introduced in 1748. The British, under Lord Albemarle and Admiral Pocock, captured Havana and held the island in 1762-63, but it was returned to Spain in exchange for Florida.

The tobacco monopoly was abolished in 1816 and Cuba was given the right to trade with the world in 1818. Independence elsewhere, however, bred ambitions, and a strong movement for independence was quelled by Spain in 1823. By this time the blacks outnumbered the whites in the island; there were several slave rebellions and little by little the Créoles (or Spaniards born in Cuba) made common cause with them. A slave rising in 1837 was savagely repressed and the poet Gabriel de la Concepción Valdés was shot. There was a 10-year rebellion against Spain between 1868 and 1878, but it gained little save the effective abolition of slavery, which had been officially forbidden since 1847. From 1895 to 1898 rebellion flared up again under José Martí and Máximo Gómez. The United States was now in sympathy with the rebels, and when the US battleship *Maine* exploded in Havana harbour on 15 February 1898, this was made a pretext for declaring war on Spain. American forces (which included Colonel Theodore Roosevelt) were landed, a squadron blockaded Havana and defeated the Spanish fleet at Santiago de Cuba. In December peace was signed and US forces occupied the island. The Government of Cuba was handed over to its first president, Tomás Estrada Palma, on 20 May 1902. The USA retained naval bases at Río Hondo and Guantánamo Bay and reserved the right of intervention in Cuban domestic affairs, but granted the island a handsome import preference for its sugar. The USA chose to intervene several times, but relinquished this right in 1934.

From 1925 to 1933 the 'strong man' Gerardo Machado ruled Cuba as a dictator. His downfall was brought about by Fulgencio Batista, then a sergeant. Corrupt, ineffectual governments held office in the 1940s, until Batista, by then a self-promoted general, staged a military coup in 1952. His harshly repressive dictatorship was brought to an end by Fidel Castro in January 1959, after an extraordinary and heroic 3 years' campaign, mostly in the Sierra Maestra, with a guerrilla force reduced at one point to twelve men.

From 1960 onwards, in the face of increasing hostility from the USA, Castro led Cuba into communism. All farms of over 67 hectares have been taken over by the state. Rationing is still fierce, and there are still shortages of consumer goods. However, education, housing and health services have been greatly improved. Considerable emphasis is placed on combining productive agricultural work with study: there are over 400 schools and colleges in rural areas where the students divide their time between the fields and the classroom. Education is compulsory up to the age of 17 and free.

Before the Revolution of 1959 the United States had investments in Cuba worth about US$1,000mn, covering nearly every activity from agriculture and mining to oil installations; it took 66% of Cuba's exports and supplied 70% of the imports in 1958. Today all American businesses, including banks, have been nationalized; the USA has cut off all imports from Cuba, placed an embargo on exports to Cuba, and broken off diplomatic relations. Promising moves to improve relations with the USA were given impetus in 1988 by the termination of Cuban military activities in Angola under agreement with the USA and South Africa. However, developments in Eastern Europe and the former USSR in 1989-90 provoked Castro to defend the Cuban system of government; the lack of political change delayed any further rapprochement with the USA. Prior to the 1992 US presidential elections, President Bush approved the Cuban Democracy Act (Torricelli Bill) which strengthened the trade embargo by forbidding US subsidiaries from trading with Cuba. Many countries, including EC members and Canada, said they would not allow the US bill to affect their trade with Cuba and the UN General Assembly voted in November in favour of a resolution calling for an end to the embargo. The defeat of George Bush by Bill Clinton did not, however, signal a change in US attitudes, in large part because of the support given to the Democrat's campaign by Cuban exiles in Miami. Members of some Cuban exile groups were invited to Havana in April 1994 to discuss issues such as travel and family unification. Not included were those groups which support the US blockade. Even though a number of exiles began to press for a more flexible US line, President Clinton made no move to relax US policy and Cuban officials stated that, should any change occur, normalization of relations would be very difficult. Meanwhile, the number of Cubans fleeing to Florida by boat increased by over 40% in 1993. The defection of President Castro's daughter, Alina Fernández Revuelta, received much publicity.

In 1989 the country was shaken by the trials and executions of high-ranking officials for narcotics trafficking, abuse of power and corruption. President Castro pledged to fight against corruption and privilege and deepen the process of rectification begun in 1986. In an effort to broaden the people's power system of government introduced in 1976, the central committee of the Cuban Communist Party adopted resolutions in 1990 designed to strengthen the municipal and provincial assemblies and transform the National Assembly into a genuine parliament. In February 1993, the first direct, secret elections for the National Assembly and for provincial assemblies were held. Despite calls from opponents abroad for voters to register a protest by spoiling their ballot or not voting, the official results showed that 99.6% of the electorate voted, with 92.6% of votes cast valid. All 589 official candidates were elected.

Economic difficulties in the 1990s brought on by the changes in the former Soviet economy and Eastern Europe, together with higher oil prices because of the Gulf crisis, forced the Government to impose emergency measures and declare a special period in peace time. Rationing was increased, petrol became scarce, the bureaucracy was slashed and several hundred arrests were made in a drive against corruption. As economic hardship continued into 1993, Cuba was hit on 13 March by a winter storm which caused an estimated US$1bn in damage. Agricultural production, for both export and domestic consumption, was severely affected, which additional disruption to food supplies increased concern over the nation's health as an outbreak of a disease attacking the nervous system, thought to have been caused in part by vitamin deficiency, affected about 50,000 people. The Cuban health services contained the illness by September, but its exact cause remained a mystery.

As the economic crisis persisted into 1994, the government adopted measures (some of which are outlined below) which opened up many sectors to private enterprise and recognized the dependence of much of the economy on dollars. The partial reforms did not eradicate the imbalances between the peso and the dollar economies, and shortages remained for those without access to hard currency. Further reforms were proposed in May 1994 aimed at giving the state greater access to the quantity of dollars in circulation and reducing the huge fiscal deficit. Great emphasis was given to the confiscation of black marketeers' illicit profits. At the time of going to press, the exact measures involved had not been published.

Government In 1976 a new constitution was approved by 97.7% of the voters, setting up municipal and provincial assemblies and a National Assembly of the People's Power. The membership of the Assembly was increased to 589 in 1993, candidates being nominated by the 169 municipal councils, and elected by direct secret ballot. Similarly elected are numbers of the 14 provincial assemblies. The number of Cuba's provinces was increased from 6 to 14 as a result of the decisions of the First Congress of the Communist Party of Cuba in December 1975. Dr Fidel Castro was elected President of the Council of State by the National Assembly and his brother, Major Raúl Castro, was elected First Vice-President.

The Economy Following the 1959 revolution, Cuba adopted a Marxist-Leninist system. Almost all sectors of the economy are state controlled and centrally planned, the only significant exception being agriculture where some 12% of arable land is still privately owned by 192,000 small farmers. Economic pressures in 1993 forced a number of reforms which, as well as permitting Cubans to hold dollars and other currencies, turned state-owned farms into semi-autonomous cooperatives, and legalized 117 categories of self-employment.

The Government has made diversification of the economy away from sugar the prime aim of economic policy. Some progress towards this has been made, but the overwhelming reliance on sugar remains and there is little expectation of achieving balanced and sustained growth in the foreseeable future. Aid from the USSR was traditionally estimated at about 25% of gnp. Apart from military aid, economic assistance took 2 forms: balance of payments support (about 84%), under which sugar and nickel exports were priced in excess of world levels and oil imports were indexed against world prices for the previous 5 years; and assistance for development projects. About 13 million tonnes of oil were supplied a year, allowing 3 million to be re-exported, providing a valuable source of foreign exchange earnings. There is, however, a trend towards more trade credits, which are repayable, rather than trade subsidies, and all trade agreements are being renegotiated over the next few years. From 1991, trade between Cuba and the former Soviet Union has been denominated in convertible currencies. Trade agreements with the ex-USSR, involving oil and sugar, survived US pressure on Russia to end oil shipments in order to receive US aid. Other oil producers have been supplying fuel, for example Iran and Colombia, and Cuba stepped up its own production to an estimated 1.1 million tonnes in 1993, providing 30-40% of electricity generation. Foreign companies have been encouraged to explore for oil on and off-shore and a consortium led by Total of France was to start exploratory drilling off the N coast in 1994. Cooperation is also being sought in upgrading Cuba's refining capacity. 1993 oil imports were put at 6 million tonnes, compared with 13 million in 1989. The shortage of fuel, combined with a lack of spare parts for ex-Soviet and Czechoslovakian generating plants, caused power cuts of up to 10 hrs a day in Havana in 1994. Furthermore, Cuba's domestically-produced oil has corrosive effects on some machinery. A major increase in spending on installed capacity was planned for 1994.

The sugar industry (70% of export earnings) has consistently failed to reach the targets set. Cuba's dream of a 10m tonne raw sugar harvest has never been reached and the 1991-92 crop reached only 6.2 million tonnes because of poor weather and shortages of oil and spare parts. The same factors further restricted the 1992-93 harvest, exacerbated by the March 1993 storm and by further torrential rain at the end of the season. Under normal circumstances, Cuba would expect to be the world's second-largest producer after Brazil and the world's leading exporter, but 1993's disastrous results (little over 4 million tonnes) undermined all exports, including the sugar-for-oil trade with Russia. The sugar harvest for 1993-94 showed improvement at an estimated 5 million tonnes. Earnings from sugar exports are now devoted to purchasing oil. While sugar mills now use bagasse as fuel, the canefields use large quantities of oil for machinery to cut and transport the cane. Much of the machinery was idle in 1993 owing to lack of fuel. Cuba became a member of the International Coffee Agreement in February 1985, and was allocated an export quota of 160,000 bags of 60 kg compared with production of 375,000 bags. Citrus has become the second-most important agricultural export. Production of food for domestic consumption has been encouraged as foreign exchange for imports has dwindled.

Construction and industry have been the main growth motors in recent years. A major construction project, initiated before the economic crisis, was the building

CUBA : FACT FILE

Geographic

Land area	110,861 sq km
forested	25.1%
pastures	27.1%
cultivated	30.3%

Demographic

Population (1992)	10,848,000
annual growth rate	1.0%
urban	72.8%
rural	27.2%
density	97.9 per sq km
Religious affiliation	
Roman Catholic	39.6%
Non religious	48.7%
Birth rate per 1,000 (1991)	18.0
	(world av 26.4)
Death rate per 1,000 (1991)	7.0
	(world av 9.2)

Education and Health

Life expectancy at birth,	
male	73 years
female	78 years
Infant mortality rate	
per 1,000 live births (1989)	11.1
Physicians (1989)	1 per 303 persons
Hospital beds	1 per 141 persons
Calorie intake as %	
of FAO requirement	135%
Population age 25 and over	
with no formal schooling	39.6%
Literacy (over 15)	96.0%

Economic

GNP (1990 market prices)	
	US$20,900mn
GNP per capita	US$2,000
Public external debt (1989)	
	US$6,800mn
Tourism receipts (1990)	US$246mn
Inflation	na
Radio	1 per 3.1 persons
Television	1 per 4.3 persons
Telephone	1 per 18 persons

Employment

Population economically active (1988)	
	4,570,236
Unemployment rate	6.0%
% of labour force in	
agriculture	20.4
mining and manufacturing	21.8
construction	9.8
Military forces	175,500

Source *Encyclopaedia Britannica*

of facilities for the 1991 Panamerican Games, 5 miles E of Havana, including a stadium seating 35,000 spectators, a swimming complex, a cycle racetrack and housing for 8,000 visitors. Tourism is set to expand considerably with the construction of 5,000 new hotel rooms. In 1993, about 700,000 tourists visited Cuba, mostly from Western countries, generating earnings of US$220mn, compared with 460,000 visitors in 1992. Daily spending by tourists rose from US$67 per person in 1990 to US$89 in 1992, with US$100 predicted for 1995.

Commercial relations with market economies deteriorated in the late 1980s because of lack of progress in debt rescheduling negotiations. By the 1990s, however, a change in emphasis was noted following the demise of the Eastern European trading bloc, upon which Cuba was so dependent. Exports fell from US$8.1bn (1989) to US$1.7bn (1993), according to government sources, and since Cuba could no longer rely on trade agreements with the USSR and Eastern Europe, it began to concentrate on improving commercial relations with Western Europe, Latin America and the Caribbean. Progress was constrained by a serious lack of hard currency reserves and the US$7.5bn foreign currency debt, including substantial arrears to banks and suppliers. Trade agreements were also signed with China, Iran and North Korea. The debt with the former USSR is a secret: estimates range from US$8.5bn (eq) to US$34bn (eq).

Culture The Cuban Revolution has had a profound effect on culture both on the island itself and in a wider context. Domestically, its chief achievement has been to integrate popular expression into daily life, compared with the pre-revolutionary climate in which art was either the preserve of an elite or, in its popular forms, had to fight for acceptance. The encouragement of painting in people's studios and through a national art school, and the support given by the state to musicians and film-makers has done much to foster a national cultural identity. This is not to say that the system has neither refrained from controlling what the people should be exposed to (eg much Western pop music was banned in the 1960s), nor that it has been without its domestic critics (either those who lived through the Revolution and took issue with it, or younger artists who now feel stifled by a cultural bureaucracy). Furthermore, while great steps have been made towards the goal of a fully-integrated society, there remain areas in which the unrestricted participation of blacks and women has yet to be achieved. Blacks predominate in sport and music (as in Brazil), but find it harder to gain recognition in the public media; women artists, novelists and composers have had to struggle for acceptance. Nevertheless, measures are being taken in the cultural, social and political spheres to rectify this.

The major characteristic of Cuban culture is its combination of the African and European. Because slavery was not abolished until 1886 in Cuba, black African traditions were kept intact much later than elsewhere in the Caribbean. They persist now, inevitably mingled with Hispanic influence, in religion: for instance *santería*, a cult which blends popular Catholicism with the Yoruba belief in the spirits which inhabit all plant life. This now has a greater hold than orthodox Catholicism, which lost much support in its initial opposition to the Revolution. Catholicism in Cuba today is in sympathy with the liberation theology professed elsewhere in Latin America.

Music is incredibly vibrant on the island. It is, again, a marriage of African rhythms, expressed in percussion instruments (batá drums, congas, claves, maracas, etc), and the Spanish guitar. Accompanying the music is an equally strong tradition of dance. A history of Cuban music is beyond the scope of this book, however there are certain styles which deserve mention. There are 4 basic elements out which all others grow. The *rumba* (drumming, singing about social preoccupations and dancing) is one of the original black dance forms. By the turn of the century, it had been transferred from the plantations to the slums; now it is a collective expression, with Saturday evening competitions in which anyone can partake. Originating in eastern Cuba, *son* is the music out of which *salsa* was born. *Son* itself takes many different forms and it gained worldwide popularity after the 1920s when the National Septet of Ignacio Piñeiro made it fashionable. The more sophisticated *danzón*, ballroom dance music which was not accepted by the upper classes until the end of the last century, has also been very influential. It was the root for the *cha-cha-cha* (invented in 1948 by Enrique Jorrin). The fourth tradition is *trova*, the itinerant troubadour singing ballads, which has been transformed, post-Revolution, into the *nueva trova*, made famous by singers such as Pablo Milanés and Silvio Rodríguez. The new tradition adds politics and everyday concerns to the romantic themes.

There are many other styles, such as the *guajira*, the most famous example of which is the song 'Guantanamera'; *tumba francesa* drumming and dancing; and Afro-Cuban jazz, performed by internationally renowned artists like Irakere and Arturo Sandoval. Apart from sampling the recordings of groups, put out by the state company Egrem, the National Folklore Company (Conjunto Folklórico Nacional) gives performances of the traditional music which it was set up to study and keep alive.

In Havana, a weekly guide (*Urbe*, US$1 from major hotels) appears every Thursday, with listing of concerts, theatre programmes, art exhibitions, etc. It also carries the names, addresses and programmes of the Casas de Cultura and Casas de la Trova, houses where traditional Cuban music can be heard for free, thoroughly recommended.

In Vedado, the National Folklore Company, Calle 2 entre Calzada y 5ta, sometimes stage 'Rumba Saturday' at 1500, 1 peso.

Festivals of dance (including ballet), theatre, jazz, cinema and other art forms are held frequently—tickets (in dollars) from lobbies of the major hotels. Outside

Havana, ask in hotels for detailed information.

   NB Last-minute changes and cancellations are common.

The Cuban Revolution had perhaps its widest cultural influence in the field of literature. Many now famous Latin American novelists (like Gabriel García Márquez, Mario Vargas Llosa and Julio Cortázar) visited Havana and worked with the Prensa Latina news agency or on the *Casa de las Américas* review. As Gordon Brotherston has said, 'an undeniable factor in the rise of the novel in Latin America has been a reciprocal self-awareness among novelists in different countries and in which Cuba has been instrumental.' (*The Emergence of the Latin American Novel*, Cambridge University Press, 1977, page 3.) Not all have maintained their allegiance, just as some Cuban writers have deserted the Revolution. One such Cuban is Guillermo Cabrera Infante, whose most celebrated novel is *Tres tristes tigres* (1967). Other established writers remained in Cuba after the Revolution: Alejo Carpentier, who invented the phrase 'marvellous reality' to describe the different order of reality which he perceived in Latin America and the Caribbean and which now, often wrongly, is attributed to many other writers from the region (his novels include *El reino de este mundo, El siglo de las luces, Los pasos perdidos*, and many more); Jorge Lezama Lima (*Paradiso*, 1966); and Edmundo Desnoes (*Memorias del subdesarrollo*). Of post-revolutionary writers, the poet and novelist Miguel Barnet is worth reading, especially for the use of black oral history and traditions in his work. After 1959, Nicolás Guillén, a black, was adopted as the national poet; his poems of the 1930s (*Motivos de son, Sóngoro cosongo, West Indies Ltd*) are steeped in popular speech and musical rhythms. In tone they are close to the work of the *négritude* writers of Africa and the Caribbean, but they look more towards Latin America than Africa. The other poet-hero of the Revolution is the 19th-century writer and fighter for freedom from Spain, José Martí. Even though a US radio and TV station beaming propaganda, pop music and North American culture has usurped his name, Martí's importance to Cuba remains undimmed.

National Parks The National Committee for the Protection and Conservation of National Treasures and the Environment was set up in 1978. There are 6 national parks, including 3 in Pinar del Río alone (in the Sierra de los Organos and on the Península de Guanahacabibes), the swamps of the Zapata Peninsula and the Gran Piedra near Santiago. The Soledad Botanical Gardens near Cienfuegos house many of Cuba's plants. The Royal Palm is the national tree. Over 200 species of palms abound, as well as flowering trees, pines, oaks, cedars, etc. Original forest, however, is confined to some of the highest points in the southeastern mountains and the mangroves of the Zapata Peninsula. The manatee (sea cow), which has been hunted almost to extinction, is now protected; it lives in the marshes of the Zapata Peninsula. Also living in the mangrove forests is the large Cuban land crab.

   Reptiles range from crocodiles to iguanas to tiny salamanders. Cuba claims the smallest of a number of animals, for instance the Cuban pygmy frog (one of some 30 small frogs), the almiqui (a shrew-like insectivore, the world's smallest mammal), the butterfly or moth bat and the bee hummingbird (called locally the *zunzuncito*). The latter is an endangered species, like the *carpintero real* woodpecker, the cariara (a hawk-like bird of the savannah), the pygmy owl, the Cuban green parrot and the *ferminia*. The best place for birdwatching on the island is the Zapata Peninsula, where 170 species of Cuban birds have been recorded, including the majority of endemic species. In winter the number increases as migratory waterbirds, swallows and others visit the marshes. The national bird is the forest-dwelling Cuban trogon (the *tocororo*).

   There are, of course, a multitude of flowers and in the country even the smallest of houses has a flower garden in front. To complement the wide variety of butterflies that can be found in Cuba, the buddleia, or butterfly bush, has been named the national flower.

Carnival During July, carnivals are held in Havana and Santiago, reaching fever pitch with the 26 July festivities. Similar events are held in all Cuban cities and large towns at different times during the summer months. They generally last 1-2 weeks.

HAVANA

Havana, the capital, is situated at the mouth of a deep bay; in the colonial period this natural harbour was the assembly point for ships of the annual silver convoy to Spain. Its stategic and commercial importance is reflected in the extensive fortifications, particularly on the E side of the entrance to the bay (see below). Before the Revolution, Havana was the largest, the most beautiful and the most sumptuous city in the Caribbean. Today it is rather run-down, but thanks to the Government's policy of developing the countryside, it is not ringed with shantytowns like so many other Latin American capitals.

With its suburbs Havana has 2.1 million people, half of whom live in housing officially regarded as sub-standard. Many buildings are shored up by wooden planks. Some of it is very old—the city was founded in 1515—but the ancient palaces, plazas, colonnades, churches and monasteries merge agreeably with the new. The old city is being substantially refurbished with Unesco's help, as part of the drive to attract tourists and has been declared a World Heritage Site by the United Nations. There are good views over the city from the top floor restaurant and bar of *Hotel Habana Libre* and of the *Hotel Sevilla*.

The centre is divided into 5 sections, 3 of which are of most interest to visitors, Habana Vieja (Old Havana), Central Havana and Vedado. The oldest part of the city, around the Plaza de Armas, is quite near the docks where you can see cargo ships from all over the world being unloaded. Here are the former palace of the Captains-General, the temple of El Templete, and La Fuerza, the oldest of all the forts. From Plaza de Armas run 2 narrow and picturesque streets, Calles Obispo and O'Reilly. There are several old-fashioned pharmacies on Obispo – traditional glass and ceramic medicine jars and decorative perfume bottles in shops gleaming with polished wood and mirrors. Obispo and O'Reilly go W to the heart of the city: Parque Central, with its laurels, poincianas, almonds, palms, shrubs and gorgeous flowers. To the SW rises the golden dome of the Capitol. From the NW corner of Parque Central a wide, tree-shaded avenue, the Paseo del Prado, runs to the fortress of La Punta; at its northern sea-side end is the Malecón, a splendid highway along the coast to the western residential district of Vedado. The sea crashing against the seawall here is a spectacular sight when the wind blows from the N. On calmer days, fishermen lean over the parapet, lovers sit in the shade of the small pillars, and joggers sweat along the pavement. On the other side of the 6-lane road, buildings which look stout and grand, with arcaded pavements, balconies, mouldings and large entrances, are salt-eroded, faded and sadly decrepit inside.

Further W, Calle San Lázaro leads directly from the monument to General Antonio Maceo on the Malecón to the magnificent central stairway of Havana University. A monument to Julio Antonio Mella, founder of the Cuban Communist Party, stands across from the stairway. Further out, past El Príncipe castle, is Plaza de la Revolución, with the impressive monument to José Martí at its centre. The large buildings surrounding the square were mostly built in the 1950s and house the principal government ministries. The long grey building behind the monument is the former Justice Ministry (1958), now the HQ of the Central Committee of the Communist Party, where Fidel Castro has his office. The Plaza is the scene of massive parades and speeches marking important events.

From near the fortress of La Punta a tunnel runs eastwards under the mouth of the harbour; it emerges in the rocky ground between the Castillo del Morro

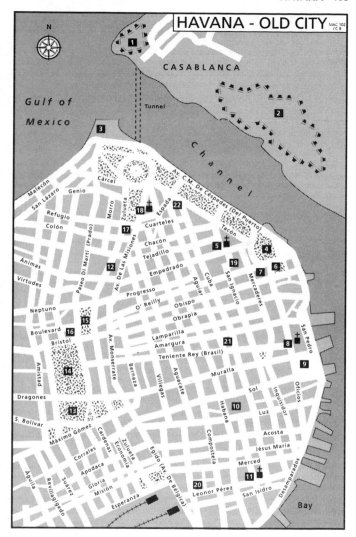

and the fort of La Cabaña, some 550m away, and a 5-km highway connects with the Havana-Matanzas road.

The street map of Old Havana is marked with numerals showing the places of most interest to visitors.

1 Castillo del Morro was built between 1589 and 1630, with a 20-m moat, but has been much altered. It stands on a bold headland; it was one of the major fortifications built to

protect the natural harbour and the assembly of Spain's silver fleets from pirate attack. The flash of its lighthouse, built in 1844, is visible 30 km out to sea. The castle is open to the public, Wednesday-Sunday, 1000-1800, as a museum with a good exhibition of Cuban history since Columbus. On the harbour side, down by the water, is the Battery of the 12 Apostles, each gun named after an Apostle. It can be reached by bus through the tunnel to the former toll gates.

2 Fortaleza de la Cabaña, built 1763-1774. Fronting the harbour is a high wall; the ditch on the landward side, 12m deep, has a drawbridge to the main entrance. Inside are Los Fosos de los Laureles where political prisoners were shot during the Cuban fight for independence. Open to visitors at the same hours as El Morro.

The National Observatory and the railway station for trains to Matanzas are on the same side of the Channel as these 2 forts.

3 Castillo de la Punta, built at the end of the 16th century, a squat building with 2½-m thick walls, is open to the public, daily 1400-2200. Opposite the fortress, across the Malecón, is the monument to Máximo Gómez, the independence leader.

4 Castillo de la Fuerza, Cuba's oldest building and the second oldest fort in the New World, was built 1538-1544 after the city had been sacked by buccaneers. It is a low, long building with a picturesque tower from which there is a grand view. Inside the castle is the Museo de Armas. The downstairs part is used for art exhibitions. The Castillo has reopened (1994) after renovation. *Note*: There are 2 other old forts in Havana: Atarés, finished in 1763, on a hill overlooking the SW end of the harbour; and El Príncipe, on a hill at the far end of Av Independencia (Av Rancho Boyeros), built 1774-1794, now the city gaol. Finest view in Havana from this hill.

5 The Cathedral, built in 1704 by the Jesuits, who were expelled in 1767. On either side of the Spanish colonial baroque façade are belltowers, the left one (W) being half as wide as the right (E). There is a grand view from the latter. The church is officially dedicated to the Virgin of the Immaculate Conception, but is better known as the church of Havana's patron saint, San Cristóbal, and as the Columbus cathedral. The bones of Christopher Columbus were sent to this cathedral when Santo Domingo was ceded by Spain to France in 1795; they now lie in Santo Domingo. The bones were in fact those of another Columbus. The Cathedral is open Monday-Friday 0900-1130 and Saturday 1530-1730. On Saturdays there is a handicraft market on the square in front of the Cathedral, and in adjacent streets.

6 Plaza de Armas, has been restored to very much what it once was. The statue in the centre is of Céspedes. In the NE corner of the square is the church of El Templete; a column in front of it marks the spot where the first mass was said in 1519 under a ceiba tree. A sapling of the same tree, blown down by hurricane in 1753, was planted on the same spot, and under its branches the supposed bones of Columbus reposed in state before being taken to the cathedral. This tree was cut down in 1828, the present tree planted, and the Doric temple opened. There are paintings by Vermay, a pupil of David, inside. On the N side of the Plaza is the Palacio del Segundo Cabo, the former private residence of the Captains General, now housing the Feria Cubana del Libro. Its patio is worth a look.

7 On the W side of Plaza de Armas is the former palace of the Captains General, built in 1780, a charming example of colonial architecture. The Spanish Governors and the Presidents lived here until 1917, when it became the City Hall. It is now the Museo de la Ciudad, the Historical Museum of the city of Havana (open Tuesday-Sunday 0930-1700, T 61-0722, entry US$2). It is best to go at 1130 when the upper floor is open. The building was the site of the signing of the 1899 treaty between Spain and the USA. The arcaded and balconied patio is well worth a visit. The museum houses a large collection of 19th-century furnishings which illustrate the wealth of the Spanish colonial community. There are no explanations, even in Spanish. Outside is a statue of Ferdinand VII of Spain, with a singularly uncomplimentary plaque. Also in front of the museum is a collection of church bells. The former Supreme Court on the N side of the Plaza is another colonial building, with a large patio.

8 The church and convent of San Francisco, built 1608, reconstructed 1737; a massive, sombre edifice suggesting defence rather than worship. The 3-storeyed tower was both a landmark for returning voyagers and a look-out for pirates. Having been restored to the Franciscan order, it is now open to the public on Sunday mornings or at other times immediately after services. Most of the treasures were removed by the government and some are in museums.

9 The Corinthian white marble building on Calle Oficinas S of the Post Office was once the legislative building, where the House of Representatives met before the Capitol was built.

10 The Santa Clara convent was built in 1635 for the Clarisan nuns. The quaint old patio has been carefully preserved; in it are the city's first slaughter house, first public fountain and

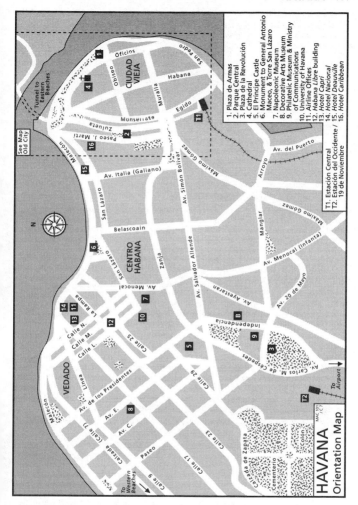

HAVANA
Orientation Map

1. Plaza de Armas
2. Parque Central
3. Plaza de la Revolución
4. Cathedral
5. El Príncipe Castle
6. Monument to General Antonio Maceo, & Torre San Lázaro
7. Napoleonic Museum
8. Decorative Arts Museum
9. Philatelic Museum & Ministry of Communications
10. University of Havana
11. Airline Offices
12. Habana Libre building
13. Hotel Capri
14. Hotel Nacional
15. Hotel Deauville
16. Hotel Caribbean

T1. Estación Central
T2. Estación del Occidente / 19 de Noviembre

public baths, and a house built by a sailor for his love-lorn daughter. You can still see the nuns' cemetery and their cells.

11 La Merced church, built in 1746, rebuilt 1792. It has a beautiful exterior and a redecorated lavish interior.

12 The Museo Nacional Palacio de Bellas Artes (T 61-2332). It also has a large collection of relics of the struggle for independence, and a fine array of modern paintings by Cuban and other artists. Its huge collection of European paintings, from the 16th century to the present, contains works supposedly by Gainsborough, Van Dyck, Velázquez, Tintoretto, Degas, et al. There are also large chambers of Greek, Roman, Egyptian sculpture and artefacts, many very impressive. Descriptions are in Spanish only and labels, on small cards, may be hard to read.

The museum also has temporary exhibitions. Open Wednesday-Sunday 1030-1830—US$3.

13 Parque Fraternidad, landscaped to show off the Capitol, N of it, to the best effect. At its centre is a ceiba tree growing in soil provided by each of the American republics. In the park also is a famous statue of the Indian woman who first welcomed the Spaniards: La Noble Habana, sculpted in 1837. From the SW corner the handsome Avenida Allende runs due W to the high hill on which stands Príncipe Castle (now the city gaol). The Quinta de los Molinos, on this avenue, at the foot of the hill, once housed the School of Agronomy of Havana University. The main house now contains the Máximo Gómez museum (Dominican-born fighter for Cuban Independence). Also here is the headquarters of the young writers and artists (Asociación Hermanos Saiz). The gardens are a lovely place to stroll. N, along Calle Universidad, on a hill which gives a good view, is the University.

14 The Capitol, opened May 1929, has a large dome over a rotunda; it is a copy, on a smaller scale, of the US Capitol in Washington. At the centre of its floor is set a 24-carat diamond, zero for all distance measurements in Cuba. The interior has large halls and stately staircases, all most sumptuously decorated. Entrance for visitors is to the left of the stairway. The Capitol now houses the Museo Nacional de Historia Natural, which is open Tuesday to Saturday 1015-1745, and Sunday 0915-1245.

15 Parque Central.

16 Gran Teatro de la Habana, a beautiful building.

17 Presidential Palace (1922), a huge, ornate building topped by a dome, facing Av de las Misiones Park; now contains the Museo de la Revolución (T 62-4091). Open Tuesday-Friday 1000-1700, Saturday-Sunday 1000-1800, 1400-2000, entry US$3, no cameras allowed either inside or in the adjoining park, although photographs are permitted in the park in front of the building. (Allow several hours to see it all, explanations are all in Spanish.) The history of Cuban political development is charted, from the slave uprisings to joint space missions with the ex-Soviet Union. The liveliest section displays the final battles against Batista's troops, with excellent photographs and some bizarre personal momentos, such as a revolutionary's knife, fork and spoon set and a plastic shower curtain worn in the Sierra Maestra campaign. The yacht *Granma*, from which Dr Castro disembarked with his companions in 1956 to launch the Revolution, has been installed in the park facing the S entrance, surrounded by planes, tanks and other vehicles involved, as well as a Soviet-built tank used against the Bay of Pigs invasion and a fragment from a US spy plane shot down in the 1970s.

18 The Church of El Santo Angel Custodio was built by the Jesuits in 1672 on the slight elevation of Peña Pobre hill. It has white, laced Gothic towers and 10 chapels, the best of which is behind the high altar.

19 Museo de Arte Colonial, Plaza de la Catedral (in the former Palacio de los Condes de Casa Bayona), open 1000-1730 (closed Tuesday), US$2, contains colonial furniture and other items, plus a section on stained glass (T 61-1367).

20 Birthplace of José Martí, Leonor Pérez 314, opposite central railway station (Tuesday-Saturday 1315-2030, Sunday 0900-1230, T 6-8852).

21 Museu Histórico de Ciencias Carlos J Finlay, Calle Cuba 460 (Monday-Friday 0800-1200, 1300-1700, T 6-8006).

22 Palacio Pedroso, now the Palacio de la Artesanía; see **Shopping** below.

Other Museums Museo de Alfabetización, Plaza de la Catedral, Monday-Friday 0800-1200, 1300-1600, T 20-8054; **Napoleonic Museum**, Calle Ronda (Tuesday-Saturday 1100-1830; Sunday 0900-1300), houses paintings and other works of art, a specialized library and a collection of weaponry (T 79-1412); **Museo de Artes Decorativas**, Calles 17 y Este Vedado (Wednesday-Sunday 0900-1700 T 32-0924); **Postal Museum**, Ministry of Communications, Plaza de la Revolución (Monday-Friday 1000-1900, working Saturdays 0900-1800, T 70-5193); also **Numismatic Museum**, (Calle Oficios 8 between Obispo and Obrapía, T 63-2521, Tuesday-Saturday 1300-2100, Sunday 0900-1300). **Museo de Finanzas**, Obispo y Cuba, in the old Ministry of Finance building, has a beautiful stained-class ceiling in the foyer, Monday-Friday 0830-1700, Saturday till 1230 only. **Vintage Car Museum**, Oficios y Jústiz (just off Plaza de Armas; there are a great many museum pieces—pre-revolutionary US models—still on the road especially outside Havana, in among the Ladas, VWs and Nissans), **Casa de los Arabes** (with restaurant) opposite, on Oficios between Obispo and Obrapía, open Tuesday-Saturday 1330-2030; **Casa de Africa**, on Obrapía between San Ignacio and Mercaderes (Tuesday-Sunday 1300-2000), small gallery of carved wooden artefacts and handmade costumes. **Museo de la Música**, Capdevilla 1, Habana Vieja; small and beautifully furnished old house; interesting collection of African drums and other instruments from all around the world, showing development of Cuban *son* and *danzón* music. The *Hotel Ambos Mundos*, Calle Obispo 153, between San Ignacio and Mercaderes, has kept room 511 where Ernest Hemingway lived, as a showpiece for visitors. Hemingway lived here for 10 years before moving to La Vigía in 1939. His room has some of the finest views over the old part of the city. Always check opening times in advance.

Suburbs The western sections of the old city merge imperceptibly into Vedado. W of it, and reached by a tunnel under the Almendares river, lies Miramar, some 16 km W of the capital, and easily reached by bus. Miramar was where the wealthy lived before the Revolution; today there are several embassies and government buildings, and also many old, abandoned villas.

The Cuban pavilion, a large building on Calle 23, Vedado, is a combination of a tropical glade and a museum of social history. It tells the nation's story by a brilliant combination of objects, photography and the architectural manipulation of space.

The National Arts College, located in the grounds of the former Havana Country Club in Cubanacan, SW of Miramar, houses schools for different arts and was designed by Ricardo Porro. Architects will be interested in this 'new spatial sensation'.

The Cementerio Colón should be visited to see the wealth of funerary sculpture, including Carrara Marbles; entry US$1.

Pabexpo, completed in January 1989, a sprawling new facility SW of Havana, past Lenin Park, near the botanical gardens, features a score of pavilions showing Cuba's achievements in industry, science, agriculture and the arts and entertainment. Open weekdays Wednesday-Friday 1400-1600 and Saturday-Sunday 1000-1800 (times subject to change). Special trains leave from main terminal in Old Havana. Information on times (and special buses) from hotels.

Beaches The beaches in Havana, at Miramar and Playa de Marianao are rocky and generally very crowded in summer (transport may also be difficult and time consuming). The beach clubs belong to trade unions and may not let non-members in. Those to the E, El Mégano, Santa María del Mar and Bacuranao, for example, are much better (see also **East from Havana**). To the W of Havana are Arena Blanca and Bahía Honda, which are good for diving and fishing but difficult to get to unless you have a car.

Hotels (Payment for hotels used by tourists is in US$). Foreign tourists can obtain a reservation through an accredited Cubatur agent (see **Travel Agencies** at the end of this chapter), through a travel agent in Cuba, or simply by booking at reception. Always tell the hotel each morning if you intend to stay on another day. Do not lose your 'guest card' which shows your name, room number and meal arrangement. Tourist hotels are a/c, with 'tourist' TV (US films, tourism promotion), restaurants with reasonable food, but standards are not comparable with Europe and plumbing is often faulty, or affected by water shortages. The Vedado hotels (the best) are away from the old centre; the others reasonably close to it.

L *Nacional de Cuba*, 21 y O, Vedado, T 7-8980/89, F 33-5054, grand building by the Malecón, all services; **A+** *Capri*, 21 y N, Vedado, T32-0511, F 32-0525; **A+** *Habana Libre*, L y 23, Vedado, T30-5011, F 32-8722, prices depend on the floor number, the hotel has an ugly exterior but most facilities are here, eg hotel reservations, excursions, Post Office, airlines nearby; the buffet breakfast has been recommended, as have the pizzas. **A** *Hostal Valencia*, Oficios 53, esq Obrapia, T 62-38-01, old Havana, a joint Spanish/Cuban venture modelled on the Spanish paradores, 11 rooms, each named after a Valencian town, tastefully restored building, nicely furnished, good buffet breakfast; **A+** *Presidente*, Calzada y G, Vedado, T 32-7521, F 32-3577, good buffet breakfast; **A+** *Habana Riviera*, Paseo y Malecón, Vedado, T 30-5051, F 31-1345, comfortable, good breakfast and pizzas; **A+** *Sevilla*, Trocadero 55 entre Zulueta y Prado, T 33-8560, F 33-8582, bars, restaurant, swimming pool, Havanautos office, breakfast buffet US$3.50, rec. **A+** *Plaza*, Zulueta y Neptuno, T 62-2006, F 63-9620, comfortable, good buffet breakfast and dinner, street front rooms very noisy, ask for one on the inner courtyard. **A+** *Victoria*, 19 y M, Vedado, T 32-6531, F 33-3109, small, quiet, pleasant, tasteful if conservative, rec; **A** *Deauville*, Galiano y Malecón, T 62-8051, refurbished in 1993; **A+** *Inglaterra*, Paseo del Prado 416 entre San Rafael y Neptuno, T 62-8351, F 33-8452, Parque Central, next to Teatro Nacional, old style, beautifully restored, highly recommended (**A** without balcony overlooking Parque Central), helpful staff, several of whom speak English, lovely old tiled dining room, open to non-guests, also Italian *Ristorante La Stella*, snacks available in pleasant inner courtyard, piano music at meal times in *Restaurante Colonial*, the bar often has music or shows at 2200. **A** *Tritón*, 3 Av y Calle 74, Miramar, T 22-6081; **A** *Vedado*, Calle O, No 244, T32-6501. **B** *Colina*, L y 27, Vedado, T 32-3535, popular with airport Cubatur desk, small rooms, poor breakfast; **B** *St John's*, O, entre 23 y 25, Vedado, T32-9531. **B** *Lincoln*, Galiano y Virtudes, T 62-8061.

The cheaper hotels are usually hard to get into; often full. **C** *Caribbean*, Paseo Martí 154 (bus 82 from Vedado), T 62-2071, popular with travellers, hot water, fan and TV, clean, old city, but avoid noisy rooms at front and lower floors at back over deafening water pump, and beware of petty theft from rooms, small, cafe serves mostly sandwiches and eggs at a low price, recommended. **C** *Ambos Mundos*, Obispo 153 between San Ignacio and Mercaderes, T 61-4887, F 62-2547, a/c, cheaper with fan, friendly, clean, retrains some of its early 20th century charm, wonderful location with great view of old city from roof terrace restaurant, Hemingway's room is open to visitors (see under *Museums* above), rec. **C** *Lido*, on Consulado near corner of Animas, T 62-5231, good, choose a room away from the alley alongside, excellent breakfast 0800-1000 and some food available in coffee shop, running water all day, say staff, bar on roof terrace, sometimes live music, recommended. **D** *Bruzón*, on Calle Bruzón near the Plaza de la Revolución and the bus station, fan, bath, TV in some rooms, no hot water, drinking water on each floor, back rooms noisy from bus station, staff from sleepy to helpful, aggressive lady in charge of breakfasts, poor restaurant. It is quite impossible for tourists to stay in 'peso hotels' in Havana.

If you have a car, the eastern beaches are good places to stay for visiting Havana. The hotels are usually booked up by package tours but you can rent an apartment on the beach away from the main tourist area for US$30. The office is at the end of the main road running along the beach nearest to Havana and furthest from the main hotel area.

Restaurants Restaurants are not cheap. The choice of food is limited except in 'dollar' restaurants, recognizable by the credit card stickers on the door, where meals are about US$10-15, paid only in US dollars. Check the bill carefully as overcharging is common in some Havana 'dollar' restaurants, also the bill may not record what you actually ate. As a rule, in Havana, outside the hotels, the 'dollar' places are the only option since by mid-1993 there was no food on sale in pesos for foreigners (or Cubans, for that matter). In 1993-94, many private houses began operating as restaurants, charging for meals in dollars. A government clamp-down on these activities did not stop the business, but many places became caterers rather than restaurants.

The *Bodeguita del Medio*, Empedrado 207, near the Cathedral, made famous by Hemingway and should be visited if only for a drink (*mojito*—rum, crushed ice, mint, lemon juice and carbonated water—is a must). Excellent food and wide range for vegetarians, about US$25 for 2, drinks extra, colourful atmosphere and nice roof terrace. Book in advance or go early for a meal, very popular. *Floridita*, on the corner of Obispo and Monserrate, next to the Parque Central, was another favourite haunt of Hemingway. It has had a recent face-lift and is now a very elegant bar and restaurant reflected in the prices (US$5 for a daiquiri), but well worth a visit if only to see the sumptuous decor and 'Bogart atmosphere'. Another pre-Revolution haunt, *Sloppy Joe's*, was due for refurbishment and reopening in 1994. *El Patio*, Plaza Catedral, nearby, is recommended for national dishes and sandwiches and *La Mina*, on Plaza de Armas, traditional Cuban food but both have uneven service, waits can be long and cooking gas shortages are common; nearby, *El Oasis*, Paseo Martí 256-58, in Arab Cultural Institute, cold a/c, very good hummus and lamb dishes; and *D'Giovanni*, Italian, Tacón between Empedrado and O'Reilly, lovely old building with patio and terrace, interesting tree growing through the wall, but food very bland. Handicrafts shop in doorway specializes in miniature ornaments. *Hostal Valencia* restaurant features paella, good food, charming; *El Tocororo* (national bird of Cuba), excellent food at US$30-35 a head, old colonial mansion with nice terrace, recommended as probably the best restaurant in town; *La Cecilia*, Calle 5a, Miramar, good international food, mostly in open air setting, rec. *La Divina Pastora*, fish restaurant, not far from Castillo del Morro, dollars only, expensive, food praised; *Doce Apostolos*, nearby, fish and good criollo food (but not as good as the *Bodeguita del Medio*), good views of the Malecón. *El Pacífico*, Chinese restaurant, popular with Cubans. *Las Ruinas* in Parque Lenín, Cuba's most exclusive restaurant—and aptly named for its prices—is most easily reached by taxi; try to persuade the driver to come back and fetch you, as otherwise it is difficult to get back. Visit *Dulcería Doña Teresa* (end of Obispo) for the caramel pudding. Reasonable cafeteria-style meals are available at *Wakamba*, opposite *St John's* hotel; nearby is the *Pizzería Milán*; *Budapest*, near Parque Central, expensive but not rec. In Vedado, *El Cochinito*, Calle 23 (national criollo dishes); *El Conejito*, Calle North, and *La Torre* (17 y M, at top of Edificio Fosca, poor food but good view), are quite expensive. In the *Habana Libre Hotel*, try *El Barracón*, traditional Cuban with good fish and seafood at lobby level, open 1200-midnight, and *Sierra Maestra* restaurant and *Bar Turquino* on the 25th floor (spectacular views of Havana which makes the food acceptable). Also expensive, *'1830'* on Malecón. Along and near La Rampa there are some cheaper pizzerías and self-service restaurants. On Paseo Avenue and Calle 1, near the *Riviera*, there is a cafetería in the

'Diploferretería' (dollar hardware store), open 1000-2200 every day for sandwiches (usual limited selection), beer and soft drinks, quicker and cheaper than hotel cafés. The cafetería at the Museo Nacional is OK, usually no queues, juice and sandwiches, open about 1000-1200 for sandwiches. At Marianao beach there are also some cheaper bars and restaurants. Inside the hard currency shopping centre, Av 5 and Calle 42 in Miramar, is an outdoor fast-foodery and an indoor restaurant, the latter with moderate dollar prices.

A visit to the **Coppelia** ice-cream parlour, 23 y L Vedado, is recommended. It tends to be very crowded in the evenings as it and La Rampa are very popular with young people. To get an ice-cream, pay first, collect a dish and then the ice. Alternatively, sample the Coppelia ice-cream in the tourist hotels and restaurants. Coppelia ices were reported subject to rationing in mid-1994.

Bars Visitors often find that ordinary bars *not* on the tourist circuit will charge them in dollars. Unfortunately even if it is a local bar and the Cubans are all paying in pesos, you will have to pay in US dollars. Even so, the prices in most places are not high by Caribbean standards.

The best bar in Old Havana is *La Bodeguita* (see above), also for *Floridita*. *La Casa del Agua La Tinaja*, on SW corner of the Plaza de Armas is a nice place selling drinking water for 5 cents. Try a *mojito* in any bar.

Shopping Local cigars and rum are excellent. Original lithographs and other works of art can be purchased directly from the artists at the Galería del Grabado, Plaza de la Catedral (Monday-Friday 1400-2100, Saturday 1400-1900). On Saturday afternoons there are handicraft stalls in the Plaza. Reproductions of works of art are sold at La Exposición, San Rafael 12, Manzana de Gómez, in front of Parque Central. There is a special boutique, the *Palacio de la Artesanía*, in the Palacio Pedroso (built 1780) at Calle Cuba 64 (opposite Parque Anfiteatro) where the largest selection of Cuban handicrafts is available; the artisans have their workshops in the back of the same building (open, Monday-Saturday 1230-1930); it has things not available elsewhere: jewellery, Cuban coffee, local and imported liqueurs, soft drinks, T-shirts, postcards and best retail selection of cigars (2 cigar-makers in attendance, lower prices than at factory); Visa and Mastercard accepted, passport required. Similar, and good, is *El Palacio del Turismo*, Obispo 252, T 63-6095, open 24 hrs, with shops, bar/café, information bureau, phones (open 0900-2100 daily) and other services (see **Travel Agents** below). The *Caracol*, formerly 'Intur-shops' in tourist hotels (eg *Habana Libre*) and elsewhere, which sell tourists' requisites and other luxury items, require payment in US$ (or credit cards: Mastercard, Visa) and will generally cash travellers' cheques and give change in US$ cash. *La Maison* is a luxurious mansion on Calles 7 and 16 in Miramar, with dollar shops selling cigars, alcohol, handicrafts, jewellery and perfume. There is sometimes live music in the evening in a lovely open-air patio, and fashion shows displaying imported clothes sold in their own boutique, free entry. The large department stores are along Galiano (Av Italia) near San Rafael and Neptuno. Large diplomatic store, Diplomercado, at Miramar (Av 5 y C 42) accepts all foreign currencies (no pesos) and has a variety of goods (including foodstuffs) at prices way below the government *Caracol* dollar shops. Rationed goods are distinguished by a small card bearing the code number and price but a great deal is now sold freely and these articles bear only the price. Most stores are open only in the afternoon.

If buying food, go to the Diplomercado; if there is no bread, there is a good *panadería* next door. There are tourist food shops in the hotels *Habana Libre* and *Riviera*, but they do not sell fresh food.

Bookshops International bookstore at end of El Prado, near Parque Fraternidad and Capitol, English, French, German books but selection poor and payment has to be in dollars. Other good bookshops near Parque Central and La Moderna Poesía on Calle Obispo (books are very good value). Librería La Bella Habana, in the Palacio del Segundo Cabo, O'Reilly 4 y Tacón, open Monday-Friday 0900-1630, has both Cuban and international publications. Good art books (weighty) at the Maxim Gorky Soviet bookshop. Universal (San Rafael) and El Siglo de las Luces (Neptuno), both near Capitolio, are good places to buy *son*, *trova* and jazz (rock) records.

Cigar Factory Partagas on Calle Inglaterra behind the Capitolio, gives tours twice daily, in theory, at 1000 and 1300, US$10 including drink and pack of small cigars. The tour lasts for about an hour and is very interesting. You are taken through the factory and shown the whole production process from storage and sorting of leaves, to packaging and labelling (explanation in Spanish only). Four different brand names are made here; Partagas, Cubana, Ramón Allones and Bolívar (special commission of 170,000 cigars made for the Seville Expo, Spain 1992). These and other famous cigars can be bought at their shop here, as well as rum, at good prices (credit cards accepted). Cigars are also made at many tourist locations (eg Palacio de las Artesanías, the airport, some hotels).

Photography Films developed at *Publifoto*, Edificio Focsa, Calle M entre 17 y 19, and

Photoservice, Galiano 572 entre Reina y Salud (another branch in Varadero, Villa Cuatro Palmas, casa 526).

Night Clubs The *Tropicana* (closed Monday) is a must; book with Cubatur or through a tourist hotel, US$40-55, depending on seat, entry only, transport US$5 and drinks extra (2030-0200). Despite being toned down to cater for more sober post-revolutionary tastes, it is still a lively place with plenty of atmosphere, open-air (entry refunded if it rains). Drinks are expensive: a bottle of rum is US$60; payment in dollars. Bringing your own bottle seems acceptable. Foreigners showing their exchange paper at the door may be admitted without booking if there is room. Next door is *Arcos de Cristal*, with live music till 0200. All the main hotels have their own cabarets, enquire at Cubatur and make a reservation. *Capri* is recommended, at US$15 and longer show than *Tropicana* but the drinks are expensive at US$40 for a bottle of best rum. Best to reserve through Cubatur. Also *Pico Blanco* (*Rincón del Feeling*) at *Hotel St John's*; the *Commodore* disco (US$10), crowded, Western-style, free to *Hotel Neptune* guests; *La Finca* at Playas del Este. *El Galeón* is a disco on a ship which sails at night from El Morro, 2 dance floors (1 salsa, 1 Cuban music), US$10. The *Cabaret Nacional*, San Rafael y Prado, costs US$10 for 2 shows (first with dancing, second a band, with everyone dancing between the 2); you must enter with a Cuban and leave passport details at the door.

Theatres *Teatro Mella*, Línea entre A y B, Vedado, specializes in modern dance; more traditional programmes at *Gran Teatro de la Habana* on the Parque Central next to *Hotel Inglaterra*. The Conjunto Folklórico Nacional dance company sometimes performs here, highly recommended, 2 pesos (local currency accepted). Havana has some very lively theatre companies.

Casa De La Trova San Lázaro, entre Belascoán y Gervasio.

Jazz *Maxim Club*, Calle 10, T 33981, free entry, music starts at 2100, worth arriving early, recommended but beware of 'friends' drinks appearing on your bill; *Coparrun*, *Hotel Riviera* (big names play there), jazz in the bar recommended.

Cinemas Best are *Yara* (opposite *Habana Libre* hotel); *Payret*, Prado 503. Many others.

Jardín Botánico Nacional de Cuba, Km 3½, Carretera del Rocía, S of the city, beyond Parque Lenín (take Bus 4 from the end of the Prado to Vivara, then take Bus 31 and ask; taxi to Varadero US$80). Open daily 0900-1700 (1000-1800 in summer), US$0.30. The garden is well-maintained with excellent collections; it has a Japanese garden with tropical adaptations. Rosa Alvarez, one of the guides, is knowledgeable and speaks some English.

Zoos *Parque Zoológico Nacional*, Calzada de Bejucal y Avenida 200-Lenin, o Boyeros y Fontanar, Wed-Sun, 0900-1515, T 44-7614. *Parque Zoológico de la Habana*, Av 26, Vedado (open Tues-Sun 0900-1800).

El Bosque de La Habana Worth visiting. From the entrance to the City Zoo, cross Calle 26 and walk a few blocks until you reach a bridge across the Almendares. Cross this, turn right at the end and keep going N, directly to the Bosque which is a jungle-like wood.

Aquaria National Aquarium, Calle 60 and Av 1, Miramar, specializes in salt-water fish and dolphins (open Tuesday-Friday 1300-1730, Saturday and Sunday 1000-1730) while the Parque Lenín aquarium has fresh-water fish on show.

Banks Banco Nacional and its branches. (See also under **Currency** below.)

Post Office There is a post and telegraph office in the *Hotel Habana Libre* building. Also on Calle Ejido next to central railway station and under the Gran Teatro de la Habana. For stamp collectors the Círculo Filatélico is on Calle San José 1172 between Infanta and Basarrata, open Monday-Friday, 1700-2000, and there is a shop at Obispo 518 with an excellent selection (Cuban stamps are very colourful and high quality).

Telephones and cable offices Calle Obispo 351, T 6-9901/5; Telegraph in *Habana Libre* building. Ministerio de Comunicaciones, Plaza de la Revolución, T 70-5581. The international telephone, telex and fax centre in the *Habana Libre* is open round the clock (also see **Travel Agents** below).

Travel Agents See **Excursions** in **Information for Visitors** on tours offered by *Cubatur*. *Gaviota Travel*, Avenida 47 No 2821, T 294694/294528, claim to be the only private travel company in Cuba, recommended. *The Palacio del Turismo*, Obispo 252, on the corner of Cuba, is also recommended for arranging tours around the country (bearing in mind the warnings in **Information for Visitors**, **Excursions**); see also **Shopping** above. **Travel Assistance** Asistur, Av del Prado 254, between Trocadero y Animas, La Habana Vieja, T 62-5519/63-8284, F 33-8087, open 0830-1700, in case of emergency 24 hrs, some English spoken, maps sold, hotel and train ticket reservations, has links to many worldwide insurance companies, very helpful (cost of insurance US$1.50/day). Asistur also has a shop selling souvenirs.

Transport The economic crisis and shortage of fuel has led to severe transport problems. There is now very little local traffic, there are long queues at petrol stations and public transport has dwindled. Tourists are officially encouraged to use dollar transport, such as taxis or hired cars (when available), or not travel at all. Organized tours out of town are rarely more than day trips. Always check when booking that departure is definite, agencies will cancel through lack of passengers or fuel. A fleet of white **'Turistaxis'** with meters has been introduced for tourists' use; payment in US$: sample fare, Ciudad Vieja to Vedado US$3.50. *Panataxi* (T 81-0153/1175/7931), 24 hrs, cheaper than most as they use Ladas instead of Nissans, and are not air-conditioned, US$1 call-out charge. If you ask your hotel to book a taxi for you they are more likely to call for the luxury variety (US$2 call-out charge). Some ordinary taxis are only allowed to operate in a restricted area (indicated by a sign in the window). If you want to go further afield look for one without a sign. The newer taxis have meters which should be set at No 1 during the daytime and at No 2 at night (2300-0700); they carry a maximum of 4 passengers (drivers may take a fifth if he/she is prepared to hide when passing the police). In the older taxis there are no meters and there is normally a fixed charge between points in or near the city. The fare should be fixed before setting out on a journey. **Ordinary taxis** are not allowed to accept US dollars (latest reports indicate that peso taxis have stopped running completely). Beware of unofficial taxis at the airport arrival gate who will overcharge. Private cars also wait at bus and train stations and will negotiate a price (their preference is for dollars).

Town buses used to be frequent and cheap but the crisis since 1993 means that they have stopped running too.

The **out-of-town bus services** leave from the Terminal de Omnibus Interprovinciales, Av Rancho Boyeros (Independencia), but practically none has run since mid-1993. See **Information for Visitors** for advance booking addresses.

Trains leave from the Estación Central in Av Egido (de Bélgica), Havana, to the larger cities. The Estación Central has what is claimed to be the oldest engine in Latin America, *La Junta*, built in Baltimore in 1842. Trains for Pinar del Río leave from the W (Occidente or 19 de Noviembre) station. A third station, Cristina, near Plaza de Cuatro Caminos and the old central market (a run-down area, walk down Gómez from the Prado, or take taxi) serves Guanabo beach, see below. It is sometimes easier to get a seat on a train than on a bus (though there are waiting lists for buses), but all public transport out of Havana is heavily booked in advance and difficult to get on. Staff at the train station have been said to be unhelpful in providing information on departures, with little interest in helping you travel. *Ferrotur*, Calles Arsenal y Egido, use side entrance for dollar tickets, is very helpful. For details of services, **see below**.

The **peso taxi** base is beside the Interprovincial bus terminal (see also **Information for Visitors**).

Bicycle Hire from **Panataxi**, car-park in corner of O'Reilly and Cuba, T 81-0153, US$1 per hour, US$12 per day. *Hotel Neptune* charges US$3 for the first hour then US$1 for each subsequent hour. Also *Hotel Riviera* and *Palacio del Turismo*, Obispo 252. Check the bicycle carefully (take your own lock, pump, even a bicycle spanner and puncture repair kit; petrol stations have often been converted into bicycle stations, providing air and tyre repairs). Cycling is a good way to see Havana, especially the suburbs; some roads in the Embassy area are closed to cyclists. The tunnel underneath the harbour mouth has a bus designed specifically to carry bicycles and their riders. Take care at night as there are few street lights and bikes are not fitted with lamps.

Airport José Martí, 18 km from Havana. Turistaxi to airport, US$16-18 depending on time of day or night and destination. The Cubatur desk in arrivals will book a taxi for you from the airport. The duty free shop at the airport is good value.

EAST FROM HAVANA

Short ferry rides across Havana Bay to Casablanca and Regla (50 centavos) are fun and a good way of looking at these 'across the bay' villages and Havana itself from a different perspective. The best view of Havana is from Morro Castle.

An easy excursion is to Cojímar, the seaside village featured in Hemingway's *The Old Man and the Sea*. The coastline is dirty because of effluent from tankers, but it is a quiet, pretty place to relax. *La Terraza* is a restaurant ('dollars') with a pleasant view, reasonably priced seafood meals. Further E is Santa María del Mar, to which Cubatur runs day excursions for US$10 (min 6 people). Another easy excursion is by train to Guanabo (4 departures daily), a pleasant, non-touristy beach; no dollar facilities, few peso ones. The quietest spot is Brisas del Mar, at the eastern end. Taxi from Havana US$20. Hotels: **A** *Itabo*, Laguna Itabo entre Santa María del Mar y Boca Ciega, T 2581, good accommodation, poor food, dirty pool; **B Hotel Atlántico**, Av Las Terrazas, Santa María del Mar, T 3308, also has an *Aparthotel* (opp the hotel is the self-catering complex's shop selling fresh food, including eggs, bread, cheese and meat). It may be possible to find 'black market' appartments in Guanabo for US$15 a night with kitchen; ask around. **C** *Villa Playa Hermosa*, 5 Av entre 472 y 474, T 2774, Guanabo, rents bikes (in poor condition).

Guanabacoa is 5 km to the E of Havana and is reached by a road turning off the Central Highway, or by launch from Muelle Luz (not far from No 9 on the map) to the suburb of Regla, then by bus direct to Guanabacoa. It is a well preserved small colonial town; sights include the old parish church which has a splendid altar: the monastery of San Francisco; the Carral theatre; and some attractive mansions. The Historical Museum of Guanabacoa, a former estate mansion, has an unusual voodoo collection in the former slave quarters at the back of the building, Calle Martí 108, between San Antonio and Versales, T 90-09117. Open: Monday and Wednesday to Saturday 1030-1800, Sunday 0900-1300.

A delightful colonial town, **Santa María del Rosario**, founded in 1732, is 16 km E of Havana. It is reached from Cotorro, on the Central Highway, and was carefully restored and preserved before the Revolution. The village church is particularly good. See the paintings, one by Veronese. There are curative springs nearby.

Hemingway fans may wish to visit the house in **San Francisco de Paula**, 11 km from the centre, where he lived from 1939 to 1960 (called the **Museo Hemingway**, T 082-2515). 11 km from the centre of Havana. The signpost is opposite Post Office, leading up short driveway. Open Monday, Wednesday-Saturday, 0900-1600, Sunday 0900-1200 (closed Tuesday and on rainy days). Entry US$2. Visitors are not allowed inside the plain whitewashed house which has been lovingly preserved with all Hemingway's furniture and books, just as he left it. But you can walk all around the outside and look in through the windows and open doors, although vigilant staff prohibit any photographs. There is a small annex building with 1 room used for temporary exhibitions, and from the upper floors there are fine views over Havana. The garden is beautiful and tropical, with many shady palms. Next to the swimming pool (empty) are the gravestones of Hemingway's pet dogs, shaded by a flowering shrub. There is a bust of the author in the village of Cojímar.

Some 60 km E of Havana is **Jibacoa** beach, which is excellent for snorkelling as the reefs are close to the beach. (*Camping de Jibacoa*, cabins for 4 or 2, US$12 pp, US$16 d. Food is rather expensive: 1.40 pesos for breakfast, 5 for lunch, 5 for dinner.)

The old provincial town of **Matanzas** lies 104 km E of Havana along the Vía Blanca, which links the capital with Varadero beach, 34 km further E (many small oil wells producing low-grade crude are passed en route). There are frequent buses but the journey via the Hershey Railway is more memorable (4 trains daily—3 hrs, 1.03 pesos—from the Casablanca station, which is reached by public launch from near La Fuerza Castle, 0.50 peso). Those who wish to make it a day trip from Havana can do so, long queues for return tickets, best to get one as soon as you arrive. There are 3 peso hotels, always full, and nowhere for tourists to eat.

The old town is on the W bank of the estuary, the new town on the E; both the rivers Yumurí and San Juan flow through the city. In Matanzas one should visit the Pharmaceutical Museum (Monday-Saturday 1400-1800, 1900-2100), the Matanzas Museum (Tuesday-Sunday 1500-1800, 1900-2200), and the cathedral, all near Parque La Libertad. There is a wonderful view of the surrounding countryside from the church of Montserrat. Bellamar Cave is only 5 km from Matanzas. (Hotel: **B** *Canimao*, Km 4 Carretera Matanzas a Varadero, T 6-1014, good restaurant.)

From Matanzas one can continue on a good dual carriageway to **Varadero**, 144 km from Havana, Cuba's chief beach resort with all facilities. It is built on a 20-km sandspit, the length of which run 2 roads lined with about a dozen large hotels, some smaller ones, and many chalets and villas. Many of the villas date from before 1959. It is undergoing large scale development of new hotels and cabins and joint ventures with foreign investors are being encouraged. 5,000 rooms had been built by 1991, with the aim of expanding to 30,000 rooms by the turn of the century. A Cuban-Spanish joint venture has opened 2 resort hotels managed by Sol/Meliá Hotels of Spain: **L** *Sol Palmeras* (T 566110) and the **L** *Meliá Gran Varadero* (T 66220). Jamaican investors have built the 160-room *Cactus* to be followed by a 250-room hotel later. In Varadero all hotels, restaurants and excursions must be paid in US dollars; pesos only for local bus rides and the cinema. Book excursions at any hotel with a Playazul Travel Agency office, or at 1 Av entre 13 y 14, T 6-2384. Cubatur office: Calle 39 entre 1 Av y Playa, T 6-4143. Despite the building in progress it is not over exploited and is a good place for a family beach holiday. The beaches are quite deserted, if a bit exposed, but there is not a lot to do. Distances are large. Avenida 1, which runs NE-SW the length of the spit, has a bus service; calle numbers begin with lowest numbers at the SW end and work upwards to the NE peninsula. There is a Municipal Museum at Calle 57 y Av de la Playa. The Centro Recreativo Josone, Av 1 y Calle 59, is a large park with pool, bowling, other activities and a café. Each November a festival is held in Varadero, lasting a week, which attracts some of the best artists in South America. Entrance US$2-10 per day.

From Varadero it is possible to explore the interesting town of **Cárdenas**, where the present Cuban flag was raised for the first time in 1850. The sea here is polluted with oil and the air smells of phosphorous. Another excursion is to Neptune's Cave (thought a more appealing name than the old one, Cepero), which is S of the town of Carboneras, half-way between Matanzas and Varadero. It has an underground lagoon, stalagmites and stalactites, evidence of Indian occupation and was used as a clandestine hospital during the war of independence. Boats moored at the jetty opposite the *Hotel Paradiso* offer 1 hr cruises up and down the coastline, US$10 pp.

Hotels in Varadero (All prices high season, double. Hotels can be booked in the tourist office.) At the S end: **L** *Paradiso*, US$140, attached to **L** *Puntarena*, T 6-3917 (Paradiso), 6-3919 (Puntarena), F 33-7074, with all resort facilities, 3 pools, watersports, all shared by both hotels, good restaurants, fresh seafood, recommended; **L** *Varadero Internacional*, Carretera a Las Américas, T 6-3011, 2 grades of rooms, all facilities (including 5 restaurants), connected with **A** *Villas Cabañas del Sol*. In our **A+** range: *Cuatro Palmas Resort (Four Palms)*, Av 1 y Calle 60, T 6-2893 (**A** in bungalows and villas), very pleasant; *Los Cactus*. In our **A** range: *Acuazul*, Av 1 entre Calles 13 y 14, T 6-3918, with pool; *Hotel y Villa Kawama*, Carretera de Kawama y Calle 0, T 6-3015. **B** *Varazul*, Av 1 entre Calles 14 y 15, T 6-2512, quiet; **B** *Villa Sotavento*, Calle 13 entre 1 y Camino del Mar, T 6-2953, dependency of *Acuazul*, next to beach, clean, with bath, breakfast, US$5, buffet, very good. **A** *Villa Punta Blanca*, T 6-3916, made up of a number of former private residences with some new complexes; **A** *Villas Solymar* (adjacent to *Hotel Internacional*, whose facilities can be shared), rec, pool, bar and shop but no restaurant; **B** *Villa Caribe*, Av 1 y Calle 30, T 6-3310; **B** *Pullman*, Av 1 entre Calle 49 y 50, T 6-2575, best value for the independent traveller, only 12 rooms, very popular; **A** *Ledo*, Av Playa y C44 T 6-3206, not rec; **A** *Villa La Herradura*, Av Playa entre 35 y 36, T 6-3703, well-equipped suites, balcony, restaurant, bar, *Caracol* shop, etc; **B** *Los Delfines*, Av Playa y Calle 39, T 6-3815. If you need to change a little money, go to *Hotel Bellamar*.

Restaurants Recommended restaurants, all between US$9-15, are *Mi Casita* (book in advance), *La Cabañita*, *Halong*, *La Esquinita*, *El Mesón del Quijote* (Spanish) and buffets at the restaurant of hotel *Kawama*. *Albacora*, disappointing, all dishes except *pescado*, US$12-18, but if you want fish you may be told '*no hay*'; *Terrace* cafeteria at the *International* for the best lunches; *Bodegón Criollo*, pleasant atmosphere, popular, no vegetarian food. *Coppelia*, C 46 y 1 Av, in town centre, ice cream US$0.90. It is now easier to buy food in Varadero because the Aparthotels (*Varazul*, *La Herradura*) have a small food store.

Car hire Havanantos, T 6-3433, or through many hotels. **Moped rental** US$5 per hour, US$15 3 hrs, US$24 for 24 hrs, a good way to see the city. **Bicycle hire** from *Villa Calleta*, Av 1 y Calle 33, US$1/hour.

Services Bank: Banco Financiero Internacional, Av Playa y C 32, T 6-3144. **Phones, telex and telegrams**: C 64 y 1 Av, T 6-2103. **Clinic**: 1 Av y C 61, T 6-2122. **Police**: C 39 y 1 Av, T 116.

A cheap, recommended method of getting to Varadero is to take the train to Matanzas (see above), then a taxi to Matanzas bus terminal (3 pesos) from where you catch a bus, 0.40 pesos, about 1 hr (state destination, take ticket, wait for bus and then your number to be called, and run for the bus). About 5½ hrs in all, if buses are running. Bus station in Varadero is at Calle 36, but there is a wait of several days for a bus to Havana. There is an airport; bus to hotels US$10 pp.

Santa Clara, 300 km from Havana and 196 km from Varadero, is a pleasant university city in the centre of the island. It was the site of the last battle of the Cuban revolution before Castro entered Havana, and the Batista troop train captured by Che Guevara can be seen near the cathedral. There are 2 'dollar hotels', **B** *Motel Los Caneyes*, Av de los Eucaliptos y Circunvalación, T 4512 (outside the city), chalet-style cabins, hot showers, good buffet, supper US$12, breakfast US$4, excellent value, and **C** *Santa Clara Libre* (central, on Parque Vidal, T 7540), reasonable lunch. At Corralillo is **C** *Hotel Elguea*, at the spa of that name, a/c rooms, bath, sports facilities, T 9-6240.

Cienfuegos, on the S coast, is an attractive seaport and industrial city 80 km from Trinidad and 70 km from Santa Clara. Interesting colonial buildings around the central Parque Martí. There are one 'dollar hotel', 45 mins walk from station, **B** *Jagua*, Punta Gorda, T 6302, comfortable, palatial restaurant next door, gorgeous decor, live piano music, simple but good food in snack bar (expensive restaurant next door). **B** *Hotel Pasacaballo*, Carretera a Rancho Luna, T 96-212, and **B** *Rancho Luna*, T 432-5929, are seaside complexes with cafeteria etc.

From Cienfuegos take a taxi to **Playa Girón** and the **Bay of Pigs** (26 pesos, 1½ hrs). Ask the driver to wait while you visit the beach and tourist complex, and the site of national pilgrimage where, in 1961, the disastrous US-backed invasion of Cuba was attempted. (Hotel: **C** *Playa Girón*, T 59-7810, a/c with bath, good self-service meals.) Further W from Girón is the **Zapata Peninsula**, an area of swamps, mangroves, beaches and much bird and animal life. Access from Playa Larga or Guamá, inland. You can rent a cabin at Playa Larga (**C**, T 7219), or there is the **B** *Centro Turístico Guamá*, Laguna del Tesoro, Zapata, T 2979, a/c rooms with bath, restaurant and other services. There is a crocodile farm at the Zapata Tourist Institute in Guamá, which can be visited. Varadero hotels organize day excursions for US$35 pp which includes lunch, English-speaking guide and a boat ride on the lagoon.

Trinidad, 133 km S of Santa Clara is a perfect relic of the early days of the Spanish colony: beautifully preserved streets and buildings with hardly a trace of the 20th century anywhere. It was founded in 1514 as a base for expeditions into the 'New World'; Cortés set out from here for Mexico in 1518. The 5 main squares and 4 churches date from the 18th and 19th centuries; the whole city, with its fine palaces, cobbled streets and tiled roofs, is a national monument. The **Museo Romántico**, next to the church of Santíssima Trinidad on the main square, is excellent. It has a collection of romantic-style porcelain, glass, paintings and ornate furniture displayed in a colonial mansion, with beautiful views from the upper floor balconies. Admission US$3, no cameras allowed. **Museo de Historia Nacional** is on Calle Simón Bolívar, an attractive building but rather dull displays, admission US$3. The **Museo de Arte**, on the corner of Simón Bolívar and the main square, has a small collection of works by local artists, plus a few prints of old masterpieces, such as the Mona Lisa, admission US$3. 1 block from the church is the *Casa de la Trova*, open weekend lunchtimes and evenings, entry free. Excellent live Cuban music with a warm, lively atmosphere. There are mostly Cubans here, of all age groups, and it's a great place to watch, and join in with, the locals having a good time. All drinks paid for in dollars. Another venue for live music is *La Canchanchara*, Calle Real 44, T 4345. Open 0900-1700, cocktails, no food. More touristy than *Casa de La Trova* (cigar and souvenir shop), but good traditional music at lunchtimes. **Restaurant El Jigue**, lunch only, live music, good food and atmosphere. Nearby are the excellent beaches of La Boca (8 km), a small fishing village, restaurant on beach, some buses or taxi. Inland from Trinidad are the beautiful, wooded Escambray mountains. There is no public transport but day trips are organized to Topes de Collantes by the *Hotel Ancón*, for US$43 pp. Their tour includes lunch, cocktail (at 1000) and visits coffee plantations, a crystal clear swimming pond and a pretty waterfall. Half-way up the mountainside, the paved road gives way to dirt track. Passengers transfer from air-conditioned mini-bus to Russian 4-wheel drive lorry, an exhilarating experience! You can see hummingbirds and the tocororo, the national bird of Cuba. A great day out. There is also a huge hospital in the mountains, which offers special therapeutic treatments for patients from all over the world, and a hotel **Los Helechos**, US$26d — details about both places at the *Hotel Ancón*.

Hotels In Trinidad Hard to find, particularly in summer. **B** *Motel Las Cuevas*, Finca Santa Ana, T 2324/2368, on a hill 10 mins walk from town (good road), chalets with balconies, very comfortable rooms with air-conditioning, TV, fridge, hot water, and very clean, 2 swimming pools, bar, discotheque (most rooms are far enough away not to be disturbed by noise), dollar shop, restaurant (good self-service meals), very good value, recommended. **B** *Costa Sur*, good value, 11 km SE of town at Playa Ancón, T 2524, good food, pool and a/c, poor beach, taxi fare approximately US$9. Pesos hotels are now closed down. Campsites at Ancón beach and La Boca (5-bed apartments). Camping at Base Manacal in the mountains: tent or small hut for US$5 per day; take No 10 bus from Cienfuegos. The only restaurant seems to be the **Mesón del Regidor** on Calle Simón Bolívar, small menu but elegant setting. There are also a couple of dollar tiendas in the centre selling souvenirs, postcards and imported snacks. On the road to Cienfuegos, *Hacienda María Dolores*, serving creole food, 0900-1600, has a collection of tropical birds, cockfighting and a fiesta on Thursday, 1800-2300.

Transport from Havana: a/c buses at 0335 (arrive 0905) and 1220 (arrive 1750), if running. Train from Estación 19 de Noviembre (on Tulipán) to Cienfuegos, number 1301 departs 2146 arrives 0440, number 1303 departs 0725 arrives 1420, 7 hrs to travel 250 km, US$8. If you can get on a tour bus returning to Havana, the fare, including lunch, will be US$25 pp. Taxi Cienfuegos-Trinidad US$75; tour US$30 pp including lunch. From Santa Clara to Cienfuegos there are about 10 buses daily; from Santa Clara to Trinidad only 2. Transport to the E of Cuba is difficult from Trinidad as it is not on the Carretera Central. Best to go to Sancti Spiritus (see below) and bus from there, about 1½ hrs through beautiful hilly scenery, 50 cents. As elsewhere, severe shortages and huge queues, trucks and tractors with trailers may be laid on as a back-up.

13 km from Trinidad is Playa Ancón (not a town as such — just 2 resort hotels: *Costa Sur*—see above—and *Ancón*). The **B** *Ancón*, T 4011/3155, is (US$45d) with air-conditioning though they encourage you to take the daily package rate of US$100 including 3 meals, drinks and such extras as snorkels, bicycles and horse riding. Good restaurant, snack bar and many facilities, popular for families. The beach is lovely, pure white sand and clean turquoise water, highly recommended.

Sancti Spiritus, about 80 km E of Trinidad and 90 km SE of Santa Clara, can be reached by road from Cienfuegos, Santa Clara or Trinidad (2 hrs over a mountain road through the Escambray). In the San Luis valley, between Trinidad and Sancti Spiritus are many 19th century sugarmills. Among them is the 45-m Manacas-Iznagas tower (entry US$1), with a café nearby. Daily train from Havana, 0645, 6 hrs (but may take 9 or more). The train seats are very comfortable, though the journey is hot and stuffy through flat countryside, endless fields of sugar cane and a few villages. Buffet car on board (serving tinned grapefruit juice, bread with oil, rice and beans), intriguing queueing system with cards, giving priority to pregnant mothers, the elderly, the disabled and children. It is one of Cuba's 7 original Spanish towns and has a wealth of buildings from the colonial period. The former is a crumbling 19th century stuccoed building in splendid baroque decay, the latter is seedy and lacks the grandeur of the *Perla*. Refreshments in town available at the *Casa de las Infusiones*. The nearest tourist hotel is the **B** *Zaza*, T 2-6012/5334, 10 km outside the town on the Zaza artificial lake, rather run down but service and food praised by Cubans.

The next province E is **Ciego de Avila**, largely flat, with mangrove swamps on the coasts and cayes to the N. 2 km outside the province's capital is **B** *Hotel Ciego de Avila*, T 2-8013, with good food. At Morón, N of Ciego de Avila, is a hotel called **B** *Morón*, very smart, being renovated early 1994, good a/c and food. There is also a hotel on Cayo Guillermo (**A**, T 2-2352/5343), a/c, bath, restaurant, watersports, etc.

The Museo Ignacio Agramonte in the large city of **Camagüey**, half-way between Santa Clara and Santiago, is one of the biggest and most impressive museums in the country. **B** *Hotel Camagüey*, Av Ignacio Agramonte, T 8-2490, good condition, good buffet restaurant; **B** *Puerto Príncipe*, Av de los Mártires y Andrés Sánchez, La Vigía (in town), T 7575/78; **B** *Gran Hotel*, Maceo 67, T 2093/4, and **B** *Plaza*, are the 'dollar' hotels.

Two tourist enclave developments have been built at Santa Lucía near Nuevitas, on the coast N of Camagüey, and at Marca del Portillo, on the coast S of Camagüey. Nuevitas was the original site of Camagüey, founded in 1514 by Diego de Velázquez as Santa María del Puerto del Príncipe. Constant pirate attacks forced the town to be moved inland.

In the province of Las Tunas there is a hotel called **B** *Villa El Saltón*, in a wooded valley beside a river S of Contramaestra, run by Cubanacan, hard to find, rustic style, good restaurant.

Holguín, a provincial capital in the E, near Santiago, has the **B** *Hotel Pernik*, Av Jorge Dimitrov y Av XX Aniversario, T 48-1663, plentiful food; **C** *Motel El Bosque*, and **C** *Motel Mirador de Mayabe*, T 4-2660. From Holguín the beautiful Atlantic resort of **Guardalavaca** (**B** *Hotel Guardalavaca*, pool, recommended, 'dollar hotel'), with good beach, can be reached by bus.

Santiago de Cuba, near the E end of the island, 970 km from Havana and 670 km from Santa Clara, is Cuba's second city and 'capital moral de la Revolución Cubana'. It is a pleasant colonial Caribbean city, with many balconies and *rejas* (grills), for instance on Calles Aguilera and Félix Pena. Of the several museums, the best is the **Colonial Museum** located in Diego de Velázquez' house (the oldest in Cuba, started by Cortés in 1516, completed 1530), at the NW corner of Parque Céspedes. It has been restored after its use as offices after the Revolution and is in 2 parts, one 16th century, one 18th century (each room shows a particular period; there is also a 19th-century extension; open Tues-Sat 0800-2200, Sun 0900-1300, Mon 0800-1200, 1400-1800, free). On the S side of Parque Céspedes is the Cathedral (1522). 2 blocks E of the Parque, opposite the Palacio Provincial is the **Museo Bacardí** (exhibits from prehistory to the Revolution downstairs, paintings upstairs), closed indefinitely in 1992. Visit the **Moncada** barracks museum and the house of Frank País (General Bandera 226), leader of the armed uprising in Santiago on 30 November 1956, who was shot in July 1957. The national hero, José Martí, is buried in Santa Efigenia cemetery, just W of the city. The **Museo de la Clandestinidad** has an exhibition of the citizens' underground struggle against the dictatorship. It was orginally the residence of the Intendente, then was a police HQ. It is at the top of picturesque Calle Padre Pico (steps), corner of Santa Rita, and affords good views of the city. Another historical site is the huge ceiba tree in the grounds of the *Leningrado* hotel, beneath which Spain and the USA signed the surrender of Santiago on 16 July 1898; at the Loma de San Juan nearby are more monuments of the Hispano-Cuban-American war (only

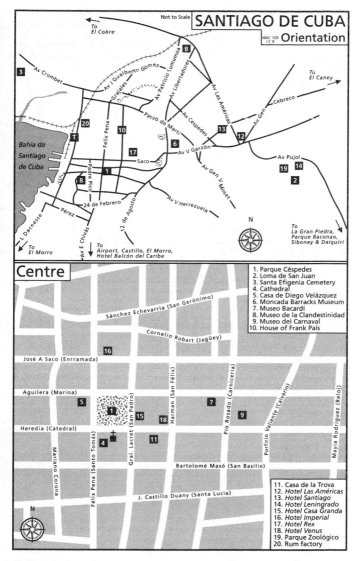

Not to Scale **SANTIAGO DE CUBA**

MAC 103 /C 9 **Orientation**

To El Cobre

Av Crombet

Av J Gualberto Gómez

Av Patricio Lumumba

Av Libertadores

Av Las Américas

Av Gen Cebreco

To El Caney

Grajales

Paseo de Marti

Av Céspedes

Félix Pena

Bahía de Santiago de Cuba

Saco

Av V Garzón

Av Gen V Minet

Av Pujol

Padre Pico

24 de Febrero

Pérez

L Darnesse

12 de Agosto

Av V Herrezuela

To El Morro

Av E Chivás

To Airport, Castillo, El Morro, Hotel Balcón del Caribe

To La Gran Piedra, Parque Baconao, Siboney & Daiquirí

N

Centre

1. Parque Céspedes
2. Loma de San Juan
3. Santa Efigenia Cemetery
4. Cathedral
5. Casa de Diego Velázquez
6. Moncada Barracks Museum
7. Museo Bacardí
8. Museo de la Clandestinidad
9. Museo del Carnaval
10. House of Frank País

Sánchez Echevarria (San Gerónimo)

Cornelio Robart (Jagüey)

José A Saco (Enrramada)

Aguilera (Marina)

Heredia (Catedral)

Mariano Corona

Félix Pena (Santo Tomás)

Gral. Lacret (San Pedro)

Harman (San Félix)

Pío Rosado (Carnicería)

Porfirio Valiente (Calvario)

Mayia Rodríguez (Reloj)

Bartolomé Masó (San Basilio)

J. Castillo Duany (Santa Lucía)

N

11. Casa de la Trova
12. *Hotel Las Américas*
13. *Hotel Santiago*
14. *Hotel Leningrado*
15. *Hotel Casa Granda*
16. *Hotel Imperial*
17. *Hotel Rex*
18. *Hotel Venus*
19. Parque Zoológico
20. Rum factory

worth visiting if staying at the *Leningrado*, or going to the zoo and amusement park behind the hotel).

The Festival de Caribe runs from 16 to 19 April, with traditional African dancing and beautiful costumes. There is daily live music, free, and singing every weekend at the Casa de la Trova at Calle Heredia 206-8 (but hope that there is no modern music at the Casa de Estudiantes Josué País García next door to drown out the more traditional thing).

For stamp and coin collectors, the *círculo filatélico* and *numismático* is held every Sunday morning on the Plaza de la Catedral near the hotel reservations office.

Hotels In Santiago A+ *Hotel Santiago*, Av las Américas (10) y M, 5-star, clean, good service, pool, *A La Cubana* restaurant, highly rec, swimming pool, tennis, sauna; **B** *Balcón del Caribe*, next to Castillo del Morro, T 9-1011, overlooking the sea, quiet, pool, basic food, cold water in bungalows, pleasant but inconvenient for the town; **B** *Las Américas*, Av de las Américas y Gen Cebreco, T 4-2011, not too far out of town, lively, recommended (turistaxi US$2.35), expensive restaurant (although cheap sandwiches and spaghetti are available), non-residents may use swimming pool, bicycle hire; **B** *Leningrado*, Km 1 Carretera a Siboney, T 4-2434 (too far out of town, turistaxi US$3.95), a complex with cabins, pool, bar and several restaurants for which there are always queues, water shortages, **D** pp *MES*, Calle L y 7 Terraza (about 5 blocks N of *Las Américas*), T 4-2398, cheapest dollar hotel, with TV and fan, 2 rooms share bath and fridge; **C** *Hotel Tropical*, flats built for Russian technicians, 2 double beds, kitchen, TV, fridge, good value, reasonable restaurant. *Casa Granda* on Parque Céspedes is closed as a hotel (since 1992), but its café is open and is good. You can reserve beach accommodation in Santiago, eg a Siboney apartment, 2 rooms, 4 people, Mar Verde, crowded at weekends, a *cabaña*, basic, 3 people.

Shopping *Diplomercado* outside airport; take passport.

Telephones For calls outside Santiago, Centro de Comunicaciones Nacional e Internacional, Heredia y Félix Pena, underneath the cathedral.

Train Havana-Santiago every other day at 1659; Santiago-Havana, every other day at 1859: US$35 single for foreigners, 16 hrs; train Santiago-Camagüey 1810, arrives 2300, also Tues, Thur, Sat 1000, arrive 1500, US$13 one way. No tourist taxis at the station, only local drivers, who charge, for example, US$4 to *Hotel Las Américas*.

Bus Terminal near Plaza de la Revolución for reservations.

Excursions Excellent excursions can be made to the **Gran Piedra** (32 km E) a viewpoint from which it is said you can see Haiti and Jamaica on a clear day, more likely their lights on a clear night. It is a giant rock weighing 75,000 tons, 1,234m high, reached by climbing 454 steps from the road ('only for the fit'). Santiago-La Gran Piedra buses are no use because daily buses leave La Gran Piedra early morning and return in the evening (the *Turismo Buró* in any hotel will arrange a tour, good value). 2 km before La Gran Piedra are the Jardines de la Siberia, on the site of a former coffee plantation, an extensive botanical garden; turn right and follow the track for about 1 km to reach the gardens. The Museo La Isabelica is 2 km past La Gran Piedra, a ruined coffee plantation, the buildings of which are now turned into a museum housing the former kitchen and other facilities on the ground floor. Upstairs is the owners' house in authentic 19th-century style. On view in the ground floor are instruments of slave torture. After the slave revolt in Haiti, large numbers of former slave owners were encouraged to settle in the Sierra de la Gran Piedra. Here they built 51 *cafetales*, using slave labour. During the Ten Years War (1868-78) the revolutionaries called for the destruction of all the *cafetales*. This influx led to the impact of Haitian/French culture on Santiago, especially in music.

The Ruta Turística runs along the shore of the Bahía Santiago to the Castillo del Morro, a clifftop fort with a museum of the sea, piracy and local history (open all week, but only morning on Monday). Recommended, even if only for the view. Turistaxi to El Morro, US$5.50-6 round trip with wait. Transport along the road passes the ferry at Ciudadmar to the resorts of Cayo Granma and La Socapa in the estuary (5 cents each way). *Cayo Granma* was originally Cayo Smith, named after its wealthy owner; it became a resort for the rich. Now most of its 600 inhabitants travel to Santiago to work. There are no vehicles; fish restaurant and bar (try the house speciality in the restaurant) in an idyllic setting looking across the bay towards Santiago.

Another excursion can be made to **Siboney**, the nearest beach to Santiago, pleasant and unpretentious (peso hotel, no dollar facilities). Take bus 214 from near bus terminal. Very crowded at weekends. Even nicer is Junagua beach, bus 207, along the same road; further development is projected in this area. 12 km E of Santiago is La Granja Siboney, the farmhouse used as the headquarters for the revolutionaries' attack on the Moncada barracks. It now has a museum of uniforms, weapons and artefacts as well as extensive newspaper accounts of the attack (entry US$1). Further E is Parque Bacanao, a wonderful amusement park in which you can visit El Valle Prehistórico (with lifesize replicas of dinosaurs), an old car and trailer museum (free, rec) and the Daiquirí Beach and Hotel, basic facilities, quiet. There are buses Nos 14, 35 & 62 (if running) to the public beaches in the park.

10 mins from the centre of Santiago there is a rum factory, open to visitors, US$6 for a guided tour with English-speaking guide, including free sample. From Santiago, it is possible to visit El Cobre (bus No 3) where the shrine of Cuba's patron saint, the Virgen de la Caridad del Cobre, is located (there is a hotel and reasonable restaurant). Interesting collection of personal offerings at foot of the statue, including a gold model of Fidel Castro.

Baracoa, 150 km E of Santiago, close to the most easterly point of the island, is an attractive place surrounded by a fruitful countryside. It was the first settlement founded by Diego de Velázquez on the island, in 1512 (Nuestra Señora de la Asunción de Baracoa). It is well worth the trip from Santiago (4 hrs drive) for the scenery of the last section of road, called La Farola, which winds through lush tropical mountains and then descends steeply to the coast. 'Dollar hotels' **B** Castillo, Calixto García, Loma del Paraíso, T 4-2103/2147, rec, friendly staff, food OK, nice views, good swimming pool; on the road to the airport is the **A+-A** Porto Santo, T 4-3581, rooms and cabins, pool, car hire, etc. The Cubana office is on Plaza Martí. The taxi base is in front of the hospital. Bus to Guantánamo takes 4 hrs.

Guantánamo 80 km from Santiago on the Baracoa road, is close to the US base of the same name (which cannot be easily visited from Cuba). 'Dollar hotel' **C** Guantánamo, Plaza Mariana Grajales, T 3-6015.

Guardalavaca see p 418 on the N coast is a lovely drive through the mountains from Santiago. Take a day driving to Frente II (eat at Rancho México), down to Sagua and across to Guardalavaca. You can stay at Don Lino beach, which is small but pleasant, where there are comfortable huts (US$14) with refrigerator for cooling beer. Restaurant food is basic.

W from Santiago runs a wonderful coastal road along the Sierra Maestra with beautiful bays and beaches, completely deserted, some with black sand. It is only possible to visit by car. At **La Plata**, about 150 km from Santiago, is a little museum about the Cuban guerrillas' first successful battle. There is no curator so ask the local people to open it. En route you pass **Las Coloradas**, the beach where Granma landed. You can make a circular route back to Santiago via Manzanillo, **Bayamo** (both in Granma province; in Bayamo **B** Hotel Sierra Maestra, on Santiago road, T 4-5013, a/c, bath, restaurant, pool and other usual facilities) and Palma Soriano.

WEST FROM HAVANA

W from Havana a dual carriage highway has been completed almost to **Pinar del Río**, the major city W of Havana. The province of Pinar del Río produces Cuba's best cigars. The city itself has many neoclassical villas with columns. At the eastern entrance to the city is the modern **B** Hotel Pinar del Río, Calle Martí final, T 5071/78, swimming pool, night club etc. For travel to Pinar del Río, train from

Havana's Estación 19 de Noviembre/del Occidente, rather than bus, is recommended (leaves Havana 0500, book 1300 day before, leaves Pinar del Río 1702, 8 hrs); slow but comfortable.

If travelling by car on this route, you can make a detour to **Soroa** in the Sierra de Rosario, 81 km SW of the capital. It is a spa and resort in luxuriant hills. As you drive into the area, a sign on the right indicates the Mirador de Venus and Baños Romanos. Past the baths is the **Bar Edén** (open till 1800), where you can park before walking up to the Mirador (25 mins). From the top you get fine views of the southern plains, the palm-covered Sierra and the tourist complex itself; lots of birds, butterflies, dragonflies and lizards around the path; many flowers in season.

The road continues into the complex where there is an orchidarium with over 700 species (check if they are in bloom before visiting, guided tours between 0830-1140, 1340-1555 daily, US$2) and the **Castillo de las Nubes** restaurant (1130-2200, entrees US$5-6), a mock castle. Across the road from the orchidarium is a waterfall (250m, paved path, entry US$1), worth a visit if you are in the area. At the resort are cabins (B high season, T 2122), restaurant **El Centro** (quite good), disco, bar, olympic swimming pool, bike rental, riding nearby and handicrafts and dollar shops. Despite the ugly, gloomy cabins, it's a peaceful place and would be more so without the loud juke box.

Nearer Pinar del Río another detour N off the main road is to the spa of **San Diego de los Baños**, also in fine scenery in the Sierra de los Organos.

N of Pinar del Río, on a road which leads to the N coast and eventually back to Havana is **Viñales**, a delightful small town in a dramatic valley. Stands of palm and tobacco fields with their drying barns (*vegas*, steep, thatch-roofed buildings which you can enter and photograph with ease) lie amid sheer and rounded mountains (*mogotes*) reminiscent of a Chinese landscape, especially at dawn and dusk. These massifs were part of a cave system which collapsed millions of years ago and, on some, remnants of stalactites can still be seen.

2 km N (27 km N of Pinar del Río) is the Mural de la Prehistoria, painted by Lovigildo González, a disciple of Diego Rivera, between 1959 and 1976; tourist restaurant nearby. 6 km beyond Viñales is the **Cueva del Indio** which can be approached from 2 ends, neither far apart. Inside, though, you can travel the cave's length on foot and by boat (US$2 for foreigners), very beautiful. There is a restaurant at the cave (also at a smaller cave nearer Viñales).

Viñales itself is a pleasant town, with trees and wooden colonnades along the main street, red tiled roofs and a main square with a little-used cathedral and a Casa de Cultura with art gallery.

Hotels In Viñales B *Motel Los Jazmines*, 3 km before the town, T 9-3265, in a superb location overlooking the valley, good restaurant, bar with snacks available, shops, swimming pool, riding, easy transport, recommended; **B** *La Ermita*, 3 km from town with good view, T 9-3204, pool (not always usable), good food, recommended as beautiful; **B** *Rancho San Vicente*, near Cueva del Indio, T 9-3200, nice pool, pleasant. Book your hotel before you arrive as everywhere is often full.

Turistaxi from Havana to *Motel Los Jazmines* takes 2½ hrs, bus back to the capital, 3½ hrs, 2.70 pesos.

From Viñales to Havana along the coast road takes about 4 hrs by car. It is an attractive drive through sugar and tobacco plantations, pines, the mountains inland, the coast occasionally visible. You pass through La Palma, Las Pozas (which has a ruined church with a boring new one beside it), Bahía Honda and Cabañas; many agricultural collectives along the way. After Cabañas the road deteriorates; either rejoin the motorway back to the capital, or take the old coast road through the port of Mariel to enter Havana on Av 5. Near Mariel is **El Salado** beach, small, secluded, with calm, clear water, although some parts are rocky. Taxi from Havana US$25. There is a reasonably-priced restaurant, part of a small hotel used by

German holidaymakers; the hotel has good value tours. Taxis back to Havana can be ordered at the hotel, but you may have to wait. Off Avenida 5 is the Marina Hemingway tourist complex, with *El Viejo y El Mar*; live music in *La Tasca Española* nightclub, entrance US$5, popular with Cubans and foreigners. There are 4 restaurants (*La Cova*, *Fiesta*, *Papa's* and *Los Caneyes*), bungalows for rent, shopping, car hire, watersports, facilities for yachts, sports, yacht trips (US$45, 0900-1630) and a tourist bureau. T 22-5590/93; VHF radio channels 16, 68 and 72, or 55B 2790. Also in this area is *Hotel Tritón* (see Havana **Hotels**), operated by Cubanacán.

The Islands

In the Gulf of Batabanó is the *Isla de la Juventud* (Isle of Youth), 97 km from the main island, reached by daily Cubana flights. At about 3,050 sq km, it is not much smaller than Trinidad, but its population is only 60,000. It gets its present name from the educational courses run there, particularly for overseas students. Columbus, who landed there in 1494 called the island Evangelista and, until recently, it was called the Isla de Pinos. From the 19th century until the Revolution its main function was as a prison and both José Martí and Fidel Castro served time there. Today the main activities are citrus-growing, fishing and tourism. There are several beaches and ample opportunities for water sports. The capital is Nueva Gerona, with a museum in the old Model Prison (El Presidio) and 4 others. Main tourist hotel is **A** *El Colony* (high season, T 9-8296).

Cayo Largo, E of Isla de la Juventud, is a westernized island resort reached by air from Havana (US$75 return), or by light plane or boat from Juventud, or by charter plane from Grand Cayman. There are 5 hotels here at present, with all facilities shared and included in their package costs (all A+ in high season, US$120-140 per person and include 3 meals and free use of all water sports and other activities). *Villa Capricho*, *Isla del Sur*, *Pueblito* (Villa Coral), *Hotel y Villa Pelícano* and *Club* (Villa Iguana). The hotels and the thatched *cabañas* are low-lying and pleasantly spread out in gardens by the beach. Snorkelling and scuba-diving can be done at Playa Sirena, 10 mins boat ride away. Very tame iguanas can be spotted at another nearby cay, Cayo Rico (day-trips available for US$37). Cayo Largo can also be visited for the day, from Havana or Varadero, price includes return flight and lunch etc (organized in Cuba by *Turcimex*, 5ta Avenida No 8203, Miramar, Havana, T 22-8230). There are several restaurants attached to the hotels, including a highly recommended Italian place and a good pizzería. As with many Cuban resort hotels restaurants are run on a self-service buffet basis and food is reported to be plentiful and fresh. Cayos Rosario and Avalos, between Juventud and Largo, have not yet been developed.

INFORMATION FOR VISITORS

Documents Visitors from the majority of countries need only a tourist card to enter Cuba, as long as they are going solely for tourist purposes. A tourist card may be obtained from Cuban embassies, consulates, or approved Cubatur agents (price in the UK £10 from the consulate, £12-13 from travel agents, some other countries US$15). From some countries (eg Canada) tourist cards are handed out on the plane and checked by visa control at the airport; the first one is free but replacements cost US$10. Nationals of other countries without visa-free agreement with Cuba, journalists and those visiting on other business must check what visa requirements pertain (in the UK a business visa costs £25, plus US$13 for any telex that has to be sent in connection with the application). The US government does not normally permit its citizens to visit Cuba. They should contact Marazul Tours, 250 W 57th Street, Suite 1311, New York City, 10107

New York, T 212-582 9570, or Miami T 305-232 8157 (information also from Havanatur, Calle 2 No 17, Miramar, Havana, T 33-2121/2318). A possibility is to go via Mexico, asking Cuban officials not to stamp any record of the visit in the passport. In the USA, the Swiss Embassy in Washington, DC now represents the Cuban interests section and will process applications for visas. Visas can take several weeks to be granted, and are apparently difficult to obtain for people other than businessmen, guests of the Cuban Government or Embassy officials. When the applicant is too far from a Cuban consulate to be able to apply conveniently for a visa, he may apply direct to the Cuban Foreign Ministry for a visa waiver. The Cuban Consulate in Mexico refuses to issue visas unless you have pre-arranged accommodation and book through a travel agent; even then, only tourist visas are available. Weekend packages can be extended in Mexico. Visitors may stay in Cuba for 72 hrs in transit without tourist card or visa.

Visitors travelling on a visa must go in person to Cubatur or the Immigration Office for registration the day after arrival. The office is on the corner of Calle 22 and Av 3, Miramar. (If buses are running, take No 132 from the old city centre, get off at second stop after the tunnel; also bus 32 from La Rampa or *Coppelia* ice-cream parlour in Vedado, alight at same stop.) When you register you will be given an exit permit.

Travellers coming from or going through infected areas must have certificates of vaccination against cholera and yellow fever.

The Cuban authorities will not insist on stamping your passport in and out if you ask them not to. They will stamp your tourist card instead.

British business travellers should get 'Hints to Exporters: Cuba', from DTI Export Publications, PO Box 55, Stratford-upon-Avon, Warwickshire, CV37 9GE. US citizens on business with Cuba should contact Foreign Assets Control, Federal Reserve Bank of New York, 33 Liberty St, NY 10045. Another useful leaflet 'Tips For Travelers to Cuba' is available from the Passport Office, US Department of State, Washington DC 20524.

Airport Tax US$11 on departure.

Air Services From Europe, Cubana flies Stansted-Gander-Havana once a fortnight on Sunday, returning on a Saturday. Cubana flies from Berlin, Brussels and Paris (also AOM French Airlines), Iberia and Cubana from Madrid. LTU from Dusseldorf. Cubana and Aeroflot from Moscow. Aeroflot has one route via Luxembourg and one via Shannon (Eire). Some Aeroflot flights continue on to Lima. It is essential to check Aeroflot's flights to make sure there really is a plane going. Since Havana no longer enjoys the close relationship with Moscow that it used to have, these flights are now reported to be increasingly unreliable.

From the American mainland, Cubana from Montréal, Cubana and Mexicana de Aviación from Mexico City with some Mexicana flights via Mérida, Ladeco from Cancún, Viasa and Aeropostal from Caracas, Lacsa from San José, Costa Rica, Aeroflot from Managua, Cubana from Buenos Aires, Cubana from São Paulo, Cubana and Aeroflot from Panama and Cubana and Ladeco from Santiago de Chile (Ladeco via Iquique and Bogotá). Within the Caribbean Cubana flies to Kingston, Jamaica and ALM from Curaçao.

The frequency of these flights depends on the season, with twice weekly flights in the winter being reduced to once a week in the summer. Some of the longer haul flights, such as to Buenos Aires, are cut from once every 2 weeks in winter to once a month in summer. There are daily charters to Miami (US$157, but lots of restrictions on who can use this route) and twice a week to Cancún, Mexico, with ABC/Celimar, enquire at Havanatur. Weekly charter flights between Santiago de Cuba and Montego Bay, Jamaica. Regular charters between Cayo Largo and Grand Cayman. Martinair has charters from Amsterdam to Varadero and Holguín. At certain times of year there are special offers available from Europe; enquire at specialist agents (see **Travel Agents** below). There are also many combinations of flights involving Cuba and Mexico, Venezuela, Colombia and the Dominican Republic; again ask a specialist agent.

Mexicana de Aviación organizes package tours (for full information see Mexico chapter, **Information for Visitors**). Unitours (Canada) run package tours to Cuba for all nationalities. Package tours also available from Venezuela. In Cuba, enquire at Havanatur.

It is advisable to book your flight out of Cuba before actually going there as arranging it there can be time-consuming. Furthermore, it is essential to reconfirm onward flights as soon as you arrive in Cuba, otherwise you will lose your reservation. Independent travellers should have tickets stamped in person, not by an agent and, for Mexico, should make sure they have a Mexican tourist card and that Cuban departure tax is collected.

No passenger ships call regularly. In late 1993, Havanatur and European investors started cruises out of Havana on the *Santiago de Cuba*, doing day trips out of territorial waters with gambling on board.

Internal Air Services Cubana de Aviación services between most of the main towns. From Havana to Camagüey (US$38), Holguín ((US$44), Baracoa (US$58), Guantánamo (US$54), Manzanillo (US$44), Moa (US$54), Nueva Gerona/Isla de Juventud (US$12), Bayamo (US$44), Ciego de Avila (US$32), Las Tunas (US$42), and Santiago (US$68); all have airports. Tourists must pay airfares in US$; it is advisable to prebook flights at home as demand is very heavy. It is difficult to book flights from one city to another when you are not at the point of departure, except from Havana, the computer is not able to cope. Airports are usually a long way from the towns, so extra transport costs will be necessary. Delays are common.

Airline Offices All are situated in Havana, at the seaward end of Calle 23 (La Rampa), Vedado: eg Cubana, Calle 23 esq, Infanta, T 7-4911; Aeroflot, Calle 23, No 64, T 79-6138. Iberia, T 33-5041; Mexicana, T 79-2041, Viasa, T 30-5011. If staying at Old Havana, allow sufficient time if you need to visit an airline office before going to the airport.

Customs Personal baggage and articles for personal use are allowed in free of duty; so are 200 cigarettes, or 25 cigars, or 1 lb of tobacco, and 2 bottles of alcoholic drinks. Many things are scarce or unobtainable in Cuba: take in everything you are likely to need other than food (say razor blades, soap, medicines and pills, insecticides against mosquitoes, cockroaches, etc, tampons, reading and writing materials and photographic supplies).

Buses The local word for bus is *guagua*. In 1993-94 it was very difficult to get on a bus, not many were running because of the fuel shortages, some would take you a maximum of 60 km and others made it almost impossible for a foreigner to get on. A minimum of 3 days' wait in the station for a ticket is possible. Because it is so difficult for visitors to use public buses and until the economic problems facing Cuba improve, we do not give bus fares or schedules. Some are given in the text above, but do not bank on them running. The urban bus fare throughout Cuba is 10 centavos and you have to have the exact fare. In the rush hours they are filled to more than capacity, making it hard to get off if you have managed to get on. Cubans are very helpful if you are lost or have got on the wrong bus.

Bus Reservations Tickets between towns must be purchased in advance from: Oficina Reservaciones Pasajes, Calle 21, esq 4, Vedado; Plazoleta de la Virgen del Camino, San Miguel del Padrón; Calzada 10 de Octubre y Carmen, Centro; Terminal de Omnibus Nacional, Boyeros y 19 de Mayo (all in Havana). However, the booking offices are often shut, increasing the difficulties of travelling around Cuba. Cubatur directs travellers to the office on the corner of Calles 21 and 4. This is the main booking office for buses and trains from Havana to anywhere in the country, one-way only. It is open Monday to Friday, 1200-1745, organized chaos. Bus tickets are sold up to 1 day in advance, train tickets up to 3 days, payable in pesos. Look for notices in the window for latest availabilities, find out who is last in the queues (separate queues for buses and trains, sometimes waiting numbers issued), and ask around for what is the best bet. Maximum 3 tickets sold per person, buses usually harder to get on than trains (see **Travel Assistance**, Havana).

Trains Recommended whenever possible, although delays and breakdowns must be expected. Be at station at least 30 mins before scheduled departure time, you have to queue to reconfirm your seat and have your ticket stamped. See above for latest booking procedures. Fares are reasonable, eg US$8 for the 6 hr journey to Sancti Spiritus (nearest station for Trinidad). Alternatively *Ferrotur*, Calles Arsenal y Egido, near Estación Central, T 62-1770, Havana, very helpful, sells train tickets to foreigners, in dollars, as do *Hoteles Habana Libre*, *Inglaterra* and *Plaza*; eg to Santiago de Cuba US$70 return, US$35 one way. Tourists will find it much easier to pay for rail tickets out of Havana in dollars, but may be able to pay for the return in pesos. Food on trains can be paid for in pesos. See the text above for details. Bicycles can be carried as an express item only.

NB In major bus and train terminals, ask if there are special arrangements for tourists to buy tickets without queuing; payment would then be in dollars. You can waste hours queuing and waiting for public transport. Travel between provinces is usually booked solid several days or weeks in advance. If you are on a short trip you may do better to go on a package tour with excursions. Trains and some buses are air-conditioned—you may need a warm jersey.

Taxis In 1993-94 foreigners were unable to pay for any taxi ride in pesos. The best you can do is avoid the most expensive tourist taxis. See **Transport** under Havana.

Dollar tourist taxis can be hired for driving around; you pay for the distance, not for waiting time. On short routes, fares start at US$1. Airport to Havana (depending on destination), US$16-18, to Playas del Este US$25, to Varadero US$71; Havana to Varadero US$65; Varadero airport to Varadero hotels US$13; Santiago de Cuba airport to *Hotel Las Américas* US$8, to *Balcón del Caribe* US$5.

Car Hire Through Havanautos at a caravan in the car park of the International Airport, *Hotels Capri* and *Victoria* in Havana, at *Tropicoco Beach Club*, Santa María del Mar (T 2531), at Varadero beach (eg *Paradiso* and *Puntarena Resort, Barlovento, Villa Tortuga, Club Herradura* and others), *Hoteles Ancón* and *Costasur, Motel Las Cuevas, Hotel Zaza*, in Trinidad province; and *Hotel Porto Santo*, Baracoa. Maximum 4 passengers allowed; vehicles can be returned to any depot but you will be charged extra. Minimum US$55 a day (or US$60 for a/c) plus US$0.30 each km after the first 100 km, and US$5 a day optional insurance. The overall cost may work out at around US$65-70 a day. Buggies are available, mostly for use on the beach, at US$30 a day plus US$0.15 each km after the first 100 km. Visa and Mastercard accepted for the rental, or US$100-150 deposit; you must also present your passport and home driving licence. Petrol coupons must be purchased, in 20 litre amounts, when you rent the car, so work out how much you'll need; unused coupons are returnable or you can use them for onward transport like peso taxis. Petrol, if you can find it, costs US$0.30 per litre. If possible, get Havanautos to fill the car with fuel, otherwise your first day will be spent looking for petrol. Get clear directions on which filling stations will serve foreigners: some accept only pesos, some do not have 'Especial' fuel, and some refuse coupons, asking for dollars instead. In the last case, ask the attendant his name, write it down, and then he'll probably accept your coupons. Hiring a car is recommended, in view of difficulties of getting seats on buses and trains and you can save a considerable amount of time but it is the most expensive form of travel. Breakdowns are not unknown, in which case you may be stuck with your rented car many kilometres from the nearest place that will accept dollars to help you. Be careful about picking up hitchhikers, although it can be an interesting and pleasant way of meeting Cubans.

Excursions Cubatur, the national tourist office, offers day trips to many parts of the island as well as tours of colonial and modern Havana. Examples (one day, except where indicated): Viñales, including tobacco and rum factories, US$39; Soroa, US$23; Varadero, US$29; Cayo Largo (by air), US$89; Trinidad (by air), US$79; Trinidad and Cienfuegos (2 days), US$109; Santiago de Cuba (by air), US$99. Tours can also be taken from Varadero, eg to Pinar del Río, 2 days, US$105. Guides speak English, French or German; the tours are generally recommended as well-organized and good value. It is also possible to go on a 'Vuelta a Cuba', 7-day round-trip of the island, travelling by bus to Santiago and returning by air. Details from the Cubatur office. A common complaint from individual tourists is that, when they sign up for day trips and other excursions (eg Cayo Largo), they are not told that actual departure depends on a minimum number of passengers. The situation is made worse by the fact that most tourists are on pre-arranged package tours. They are often subject to long waits on buses and at points of departure and are not informed of delays in departure times. Always ask the organizers when they will know if the trip is on or what the real departure time will be.

In mid-1993 it was possible to hire a car with driver and English-speaking guide for 3 hrs, costing US$30 for 2 passengers; good value.

Hotel Reservations It is advisable to book hotel rooms before visiting any of the provinces otherwise you may have to return to Havana. This can be done abroad through travel agencies, accredited Cubatur agencies, or through the

Cubatur office, Calle 23, No 156, Vedado, La Habana 4; telex 511243; T 32-4521, or through Turismo Buró desks in main hotels. It is slightly cheaper to book through Cubatur than direct at a hotel. It used to be a requirement to book the first night's hotel at the airport on arrival, if you have not done so beforehand, but this system has been abandoned since mid-1993. Cubana give a 1-night hotel voucher to their passengers. Cubatur will inform you only about the hotels which it operates. It is a good idea to book hotel rooms generally before noon. In the peak season, July and August (carnival time) and December to February, it is essential to book in advance. At other times reservations can be made at hotel reception. Prices given in the text are high season (December-April, July-August); low season prices (May-June, September-November) are about 20% lower. After 31 August many hotels go into hibernation and offer limited facilities, eg no restaurant, no swimming pool.

Camping Official campsites are opening up all over the island, charging 5-8 pesos a night (in pesos); they are usually in nice surroundings and are good value. One such is El Abra International Campsite halfway between Havana and Varadero, which has extensive facilities (car hire, bicycles, mopeds, horses, watersports, tennis etc) and organizes excursions.

Note Cuba is geared more to package tourism than to independent visitors and this has become more evident with the local petrol shortage. Camping out on the beach or in a field is forbidden. Lodging with a family is reportedly possible (at US$12 per day); make enquiries locally. Because of rationing it is difficult to buy food in the shops. Do not take photographs near military zones. Also be prepared for long waits for everything: buses, cinemas, restaurants, shops etc. Service has improved somewhat in Havana tourist facilities with the passage of new legislation allowing employees to be sacked if they are not up to the job, but inefficiency is rife. Take care with unofficial guides or 'friends' you make; if they take you to a bar or nightclub or restaurant you will be expected to pay for them and pay in dollars.

This chapter catalogues a great many difficulties for the independent traveller, but if on a package, with a couple of days in Havana and a few days on the beach, the visitor should have no problems at all. Similarly, if travelling independently in a rented vehicle, there should be no problems.

Eating Out Visitors should remember that eating is often a problem and plan ahead. It is generally impossible to have an evening meal and go on to a concert or the theatre (performances start at 2030 or 2100 in Havana).

Breakfast can be particularly slow although this is overcome in the larger hotels who generally have buffets (breakfast US$3, lunch and dinner US$10-18). If not eating at a buffet, service, no matter what standard of restaurant or hotel, can be very slow (even if you are the only customers). Look out for the *oferta especial* in small hotels which gives guests a 25% discount on buffet meals in larger hotels. Also, the 'all-you-can-eat' vouchers for buffets in tourist hotels do not have to be used in the hotel where bought. Breakfast and one other meal may be sufficient if you fill in with street or 'dollar shop' snacks.

In Havana the peso food situation is poor. Outside Havana, including Havana province, it is much worse according to a cyclist who found little or no food to buy. Self-catering is extremely difficult as supermarkets (as opposed to *Diplomercados*) are not accessible without ration cards and only occasionally do you find street vendors of fruit. For vegetarians the choice is very limited, normally only cheese, sandwiches, spaghetti and omelettes. Generally, although restaurants have improved in the last few years, the food in Cuba is not very exciting or enjoyable. There is little variety in the menu and menu items are frequently unavailable. Always check restaurant prices in advance and then your bill. The national dish is *arroz moro* (rice mixed with black beans), roast pork and yucca (manioc). Salads in restaurants are mixed vegetables which are slightly pickled and not to everyone's taste.

Tipping Tipping customs have changed after a period when visitors were not allowed to tip in hotels and restaurants. It is now definitely recommended. Tip a small amount (not a percentage) in the same currency as you pay for the bill (typically US$1-2 on a US$25 meal, 1 peso on amount over 6-7 pesos). At times taxi drivers will expect (or demand) a tip. Turistaxis are not tipped, but the drivers still appreciate a tip. If you want to express gratitude, offer a packet of American cigarettes. Hotel staff are always happy to accept your left over pesos when you depart. Leaving basic items in your room, like toothpaste, deodorant, paper, pens, is also recommended.

Shopping Essentials—rent and most food—are cheap; non-essentials are very expensive. Everything is very scarce, although imported toiletries and camera film (Kodak print only, from Mexico), is reasonably priced. Compared with much of Latin America, Cuba is expensive for the tourist, but compared with many Caribbean islands it is not dear.

Language Spanish, with local variants in pronounciation and vocabulary. Little English is spoken.

Currency The monetary unit is the peso, US$1=1.10 peso. There are heavy penalties for Cubans caught exchanging money on the black market, though a tourist will be approached, especially on the E side of La Rampa, in front of the *Hotel Caribbean*, in the Parque Central and along the Malecón in Havana (beware muggers). These 'hasslers' can be extremely persistent and even charming — at first. However their conversation soon turns to money and, once you have shown them any sign of attention, they are very hard to shake off. Do not change money where there are groups of black marketeers or where you are outnumbered, you may be tricked. Do not give them the name of your hotel. The best policy is to ignore them completely — rude but effective! Taxi drivers can be a good source of information. The extent of hustling for dollars depends on whether there is a government crackdown in operation. There has also been a reduction in activity in Havana and Varadero since it has become almost impossible for tourists to spend pesos; this is less true outside Havana and the beach resorts. The going rate was 100 pesos = US$1 in May 1994, when it was still possible to change on the black market with caution, only worth changing the absolute minimum (if at all) as there is so little available to buy with pesos. (Food on trains, and books—but not in every shop—can be bought in pesos.) Visitors on pre-paid package tours are best advised not to change any pesos at all. Bring US$ in small denominations for spending money, dollars are now universally preferred. Watch out for pre-1962 peso notes, no longer valid. There are notes for 3, 5, 10, and 20 pesos, and coins for 5, 20, and 40 centavos and 1 peso. You must have a supply of 5 centavo coins if you want to use the local town buses (10 centavos) or pay phones (very few work). The 20 centavo coin is called a *peseta*. US dollars are accepted by hotels and in all tourist establishments. Credit cards acceptable in most places are Visa, Master, Access, Diners, Banamex (Mexican) and Carnet. No US credit cards accepted so a Visa card issued in the USA will not be accepted. American Express, no matter where issued, is unacceptable.

Currency Control The visitor should be careful to retain the receipt every time money is changed officially; this will enable Cuban pesos remaining at the end of the stay to be changed back into foreign currency (to a maximum of US$10 equivalent).

Travellers' cheques expressed in US or Canadian dollars or sterling are valid in Cuba. Travellers' cheques issued on US bank paper are generally not accepted so it is best to take Thomas Cook. Don't enter the place or date when signing cheques, or they may be refused. You can occasionally get US dollars change when paying a hotel bill with travellers' cheques, but you can not cash travellers' cheques for US dollars, nor even for Cuban pesos. Instead you receive Dinero Intur (also known as Monopoly money or funny money) which can be used at any dollar store, including the Cubatur *tiendas*. Do not get left with Dinero Intur as it cannot be changed into dollars late at night or when the airport bank is closed.

There is a branch of the Banco Nacional at the 42nd Street 'diplomatic' shopping centre in Havana for changing money legally. It is useful for changing non-dollar currencies into dollars and also for changing travellers' cheques. Visitors have difficulties using torn or tatty US dollar notes.

Sale Of Possessions, Gifts etc Tourists willing to take risks can earn extra spending money by taking along consumer goods to sell to Cubans. It has been reported that you need to guard your clothes more closely than your camera and a T-shirt is greatly appreciated as a gift (you may be asked to sign it, to show that it *is* a gift). Cubans are now rationed to one pair of new trousers a year. Any foreigner sitting in the Parque Central with a flight bag at his side is soon approached by buyers. One can usually get about 3 times what was paid for the articles. Also appreciated as gifts are household medicines, cosmetics and, for children, pens, chewing gum and sweets. It's inadvisable to bring in too many of a single item or you may have trouble at Customs. Since Cubans may only enter 'dollar' establishments with a foreigners, tourists may find themselves in a very 'priviliged' position.

Security In general the Cuban people are very hospitable. The island is generally safer than many of its Caribbean and Latin neighbours, but certain precautions should be taken. Visitors should never lose sight of their luggage or leave valuables in hotel rooms (most hotels have safes). Do not leave your things on the beach when going swimming. Pickpocketing and pursesnatching on buses is quite common in Havana (especially the old city) and Santiago. Also beware of bagsnatching by passing cyclists. In the capital, street lighting is poor so care is needed when walking or cycling the city at night. Visitors should remember that the government permitting Cubans to hold dollars legally has not altered the fact that the local population will often do anything to get hard currency, from simply asking for money or dollar-bought goods, to mugging. Latest reports suggest that foreigners will be offered almost anything on the street 'from cigars to cocaine to chicas.' Cubans who offer their services in return for dollars are known as *jineteros/-as* (because they 'ride on the back' of the tourists). Offers to drive you around Havana in a Cadillac should be treated with suspicion. The police are very helpful and thorough, but you may have to insist on a written police report for insurance purposes. In the event of a crime, make a note of where it happened. Take extra passport photos and keep them separate from your passport. You will waste a lot of time getting new photos if your passport is stolen.

Health Sanitary reforms have transformed Cuba into a healthy country, though tap water is generally not safe to drink except in Havana; bottled and mineral water are recommended.

Medical service is no longer free for foreign visitors in Havana and Varadero, where there are clinics that charge in dollars. Visitors requiring medical attention will be sent to them. Emergencies are handled on an ad hoc basis. Check with your national health service or health insurance on coverage in Cuba. Charges are high, but reasonable and generally lower than those charged in western countries. According to latest reports, visitors are still treated free of charge in other parts of the country, with the exception of tourist enclaves with on-site medical services.

The Cira García Clinic in Havana (payment in dollars) sells prescription and patent drugs and medical supplies that are often unavailable in chemists.

Between May and October, the risk of sunburn is high—sun blocks are recommended when walking around the city as well as on the beach. In the cooler months, limit beach sessions to 2 hrs.

Climate Northeast trade winds temper the heat. Average summer shade temperatures rise to 30°C (86°F) in Havana, and higher elsewhere. In winter, day temperatures drop to 19°C (66°F). Average rainfall is from 860 mm in Oriente to 1,730 mm in Havana; it falls mostly in the summer and autumn, but there can be torrential rains at any time. Hurricanes come in June-October. The best time for a visit is during the cooler dry season (November to April). In Havana, there are a few cold days, 8°-10°C (45°-50°F), with a N wind. Walking is uncomfortable in summer but most offices, hotels, leading restaurants and cinemas are air-conditioned. Humidity varies between 75 and 95%.

NB The summers are unbearably hot and travel between Havana and Santiago is extremely difficult during Carnival (July) and also during the Christmas-New Year period.

Dress Generally informal. Summer calls for the very lightest clothing. A jersey and light raincoat or umbrella are needed in the cooler months.

Hours Of Business Government offices: 0830-1230 and 1330-1730 Monday to Friday. Some offices open on Saturday morning. Banks: 0830-1200, 1330-1500 Monday to Friday,

0830-1030 Saturday. The Banco Nacional de Cuba is the only bank in the country. Shops: 1230-1930 Monday to Saturday, although some open in the morning 1 day a week. Hotel tourist (hard currency) shops generally open 1000-2100.

Time Zone Eastern Standard Time, 5 hrs behind GMT; Daylight Saving Time, 4 hrs behind GMT.

Holidays Liberation Day (1 January), Victory of Armed Forces (2 January), Labour Day (1 May), Revolution Day (26 July and the day either side), Beginning of War of Independence (10 October).

Weights And Measures The metric system is compulsory, but exists side by side with American and old Spanish systems.

Electric Current 110-230 Volts. 3 phase 60 cycles, AC. Plugs are of the American type, an adaptor for European appliances can be bought at the Intur shop at the *Habana Libre*.

Post, Telecommunications When possible correspondence should be addressed to post office boxes (Apartados), where delivery is more certain. Telegraphic services are adequate. You can send telegrams from all post offices in Havana. Telegrams to Britain cost 49 centavos a word. The night letter rate is 3.85 pesos for 22 words. Local telephone calls can be made from public telephones for 5 centavos. A telephone call to Britain costs US$18 for the first 3 mins, US$6 a minute thereafter. The cost of phoning the USA is US$4.50 a minute from Havana, US$3 from Varadero. 'Collect' calls are not permitted. Air mail rates to Britain are 31 centavos for half an ounce and 13 centavos to Canada. Postcards to North, Central America and Caribbean 20 centavos, to South America 25 centavos, Europe 30 centavos, USA, Asia, Africa 50 centavos. Stamps can only be bought in dollars at Post Offices, or at the *Habana Libre*. All postal services, national and international, have been described as appalling. Letters to Europe, for instance, take at least 4-5 weeks, up to 3 months.

Newspapers A shortage of newsprint has led to cuts in newspaper and magazine production. *Granma*, mornings except Sunday and Monday; *Trabajadores*, Trade Union weekly; and *Juventud Rebelde*, now also only weekly. *Granma* has a weekly English edition (also French and Portuguese editions available, International annual subscriptions US$40, main offices: Avenida General Suárez y Territorial, Plaza de la Revolución, La Habana 6, T 70-8218, Telex: 0511 355; in UK 928 Bourges Boulevard, Peterborough PE1 2AN). The Financial Times, Time, Newsweek and The International Herald Tribune are on sale at the telex centre in *Habana Libre* and in the *Riviera* (also telex centre, open 0800-2000). The previous day's paper is available during the week. Weekend editions on sale Tuesday. FT costs US$2, IHT US$1.50.

Embassies and Consulates All in Miramar, unless stated otherwise: **Argentina**, Calle 36 No 511 between 5 and 7, T 33-2972/2549; **Austria**, Calle 4 No 101, on the corner with 1st, T 33-2825; **Belgium**, Av 5 No 7408 on the corner with 76, T 33-2410; **Brazil**, Calle 16 No 503 between 5 and 7, T 33-2139/2786; **Canada**, Calle 30 No 518, on the corner with 7, T 33-2516/2527; **UK**, Calle 34, No 708, T 33-1771, telex 511656 UKEMB CU; **Germany**, Calle 28 No 313, between 3 and 5, T 22-2560, 22-2569; **France**, Calle 14 No 312 between 3 and 5, T 33-2539/2460; **Mexico**, Calle 12 No 518 between 5 and 7, T 33-2142/2489, open 0900-1200, Monday-Friday; **Netherlands**, Calle 8 No 307 between 3 and 5, T 33-211/2; **Peru**, Calle 36 No 109 between 1 and 3, T 22-2777; **Venezuela**, Calle 36A No 704 corner of 42, T 33-2662. In Vedado, **The US Interests Section**, at the Swiss Embassy, Calzada between L and M, T 33-3550/9; **Italy**, Paseo No 606 between 25 and 27, T 33-3378; **Japan**, Calle N No 62, on the corner with 15, T 33-3454/8598. In the old city, **Spain**, Cárcel No 51 on the corner of Zulueta, T 33-8025-6.

Working in Cuba Those interested in joining International Work Brigades should contact Cuba Solidarity Campaign, c/o The Red Rose, 129 Seven Sisters Road, London N7 7QG, T 071-263 6452. The CSC publishes a quarterly magazine called *Cuba Sí* (£1). Also contact 119 Burton Road, London SW9 6TG.

Language Study Any Cuban embassy will give details, or, in Santiago, contact Cecilia Suárez, c/o Departamento de Idiomas, Universidad de Oriente, Av Patricio Lumumba, Código Postal 90500, Santiago de Cuba.

Travel Agents In the UK, agents who sell holidays in Cuba include Regent Holidays, 15 John Street, Bristol BS1 2HR, T 0272-211711, F 0272-254866, ABTA members, holding ATOL and IATA Licences; South American Experience Ltd, 47 Causton Street, Pimlico, London SW1P 4AT, T 071-976 5511, F 071-976 6908, ATOL, LATA; Progressive Tours, 12 Porchester Place, Marble Arch, London W2 2BS, T 071-262 1676, F 071-724 6941, ABTA, ATOL, IATA. Check with these agents for special deals combined with jazz or film festivals. The Cuban Consulate in

London has a full list of all authorized Cubatur agents in the UK. A recommended agents in Eire for assistance with Aeroflot flights is Concorde Travel, T Dublin 763232; Cubatur agent is Cubatravel, T Dublin 713385. See above under **Documents** for Marazul Tours in the USA. If travelling from Mexico, many agencies in the Yucatán peninsula offer packages, very good value and popular with travellers wanting to avoid Mexico City. Full details are given in the **To Cuba** paragraph in the Mexico chapter, **Information for Visitors**. From Venezuela, Ideal Tours, Centro Capriles, Plaza Venezuela, have 4-day package tours for US$406-497 low season, US$449-517 high season, 8-day tours US$500-640 low season, US$575-706 high season.

Tourist Information The main Cubatur office is at Calle 23, No 156 between N and O, La Rampa, Vedado, T 32-4521/3157 (open Monday-Friday 0800-1700, Saturday 0800-1200), and reservations for all Cuban hotels, restaurants, and night clubs can be made here. Cubatur is both a tourist information bureau and an agency offering tours. In practice, staff concentrate on the latter, assuming that visitors wish to take tours (see **Excursions** above). Consequently they do not provide a great deal of information. The Oficina de Turismo Individual is in the main Cubatur office on Calle 23; all problems with pre-booked accommodation, transport, etc should be dealt with here. Sr Justo Pérez handles British and Irish clients and is very helpful. Most tourist hotels have a Turismo Buró, which will arrange bookings, etc, but many have better information than Cubatur's main office. The magazine, *Urbe*, in Havana, twice monthly, US$1, lists shows, events, trips, useful addresses and has articles.

Cubatur also has offices in: **Canada**, 440 Blvd René Levesque, Suite 1402, Montréal, Quebec H2Z 1V7, T (514) 875-8004/5, F 875-8006; 55 Queen St E, Suite 705, Toronto, M5C 1R5, T (416) 362-0700/2, F 362-6799; **Spain**, Paseo de la Habana No 27, 2° izquierda, T 411-3097, F 564-5804; **France**, 24 rue du 4 Septembre, Paris 75002, T 47-42- 54-15, F 40-07-02-13; **Germany**, Steinweg 2, D-6000 Frankfurt am Main 1, T (069) 288322, F 296664; **UK** (Cuban Consulate), 15 Grape Street, London WC2H 8DR, T 071-379-1706, F 071-836-2602; **Mexico**, Insurgentes Sur 421 y Aguascalientes, Complejo Aristos, Edificio B, Local 310, México DF 06100, T 574-9651, F 574-9454; **Russia**, Hotel Belgrado, Moscow, T 2-48-2454/3262; **Argentina**, Paraguay 631, 2° piso A, Buenos Aires, F 311-4198, T 311-5820; **Italy**, Via General Fara 30, Terzo Piano, 20124 Milan, T 66981463, F 6690042.

Maps Mapa Turístico de la Habana, Mapa de la Habana Vieja, and similar maps of Santiago de Cuba, Trinidad, Camagüey and Varadero are helpful, but not always available. There is a series of good provincial road maps, 1:300,000, but not all sheets are available.

We are most grateful to Christina Gibbons of Regent Holidays (Bristol), Richard Laker, South American Experience, London, Jorge Valle-Aguiluz (Tegucigalpa) for help in updating this chapter. We thank also the following travellers: David Beasley & Liz Brooks (Horsham, West Sussex) Luis Hernández (Winter Park, FL, USA), Glen Stephens (Castlecrag, NSW, Australia), Ken Welsh (Málaga, Spain) and those travellers who wrote to the *Caribbean Islands Handbook*.

WILL YOU HELP US?

We do all we can to get our facts right in the MEXICO & CENTRAL AMERICAN HANDBOOK. Each section is thoroughly revised each year, but the territory is vast and our eyes cannot be everywhere. We are always pleased to hear about your travels; do write to us in as much detail as possible. In return we will send you information about our special guidebook offer.

 **TRADE & TRAVEL** *Handbooks*

Write to The Editor, Mexico & Central American Handbook, Trade & Travel, 6 Riverside Court, Lower Bristol Road, Bath BA2 3DZ. England

CENTRAL AMERICA

CENTRAL AMERICA comprises the seven small countries of Guatemala, Belize (formerly British Honduras), El Salvador, Honduras, Nicaragua, Costa Rica and Panama. Together they occupy 544,700 square km, which is less than the size of Texas. The total population of Central America in 1992 was about 30.5 million and it is increasing by 2.7% each year.

The degree of development in these countries differs sharply. Costa Rica and Panama have the highest standard of living, with two of the highest rates of literacy in all Latin America. At the other end of the scale, Honduras and Nicaragua have the lowest standards of living.

Geographically, these countries have much in common, but there are sharp differences in the racial composition and traditions of their peoples. Costa Ricans are mostly white, Guatemalans are largely Amerindian or *mestizo*; Hondurans, Nicaraguans and Salvadoreans are almost entirely *mestizo*. Panama has perhaps the most racially varied population, with a large white group. Most of these countries also have a black element, the largest being found in Panama, Nicaragua and Belize.

Early, Post-Conquest History　At the time of the coming of the Spaniards there were several isolated groups of Indians dotted over the Central American area: they were mostly shifting cultivators or nomadic hunters and fishermen. A few places only were occupied by sedentary agriculturists: what remained of the Maya (see **Precolumbian Civilizations**) in the highlands of Guatemala; a group on the south-western shores of Lakes Managua and Nicaragua; and another in the highlands of Costa Rica. The Spanish conquerors were attracted by precious metals, or native sedentary farmers who could be christianized and exploited. There were few of either, and comparatively few Spaniards settled in Central America.

It was only during his fourth voyage, in 1502, that Columbus reached the mainland of Central America; he landed in Panama, which he called Veragua, and founded the town of Santa María de Belén. In 1508 Alonso de Ojeda received a grant of land on the Pearl Coast E of Panama, and in 1509 he founded the town of San Sebastián, later moved to a new site called Santa María la Antigua del Darién. In 1513 the governor of the colony at Darién was Vasco Núñez de Balboa. Taking 190 men he crossed the isthmus in 18 days and caught the first glimpse of the Pacific; he claimed it and all neighbouring lands in the name of the King of Spain. But from the following year, when Pedrarias de Avila replaced him as Governor, Balboa fell on evil days, and he was executed by Pedrarias in 1519. That same year Pedrarias crossed the isthmus and founded the town of Panamá on the Pacific side. It was in April 1519, too, that Cortés began his conquest of Mexico.

Central America was explored from these two nodal points of Panama and Mexico. Cortés' lieutenant, Pedro de Alvarado, had conquered as far S as San Salvador by 1523. Meanwhile Pedrarias was sending forces into Panama and Costa Rica: the latter was abandoned, for the natives were hostile, but was finally colonized from Mexico City when the rest of Central America had been taken. In 1522-24 Andrés Niño and Gil Gonzales Dávila invaded Nicaragua and Honduras.

Many towns were founded by these forces from Panama: León, Granada, Trujillo and others. Spanish forces from the N and S sometimes met and fought bitterly. The gentle Bartolomé de Las Casas, the 'apostle of the Indies', was active as a Dominican missionary in Central America in the 1530s.

Settlement The groups of Spanish settlers were few and widely scattered, and this is the fundamental reason for the political fragmentation of Central America today. Panama was ruled from Bogotá, but the rest of Central America was subordinate to the Viceroyalty at Mexico City, with Antigua Guatemala as an Audiencia for the area until 1773, thereafter Guatemala City. Panama was of paramount importance for colonial Spanish America for its strategic position, and for the trade passing across the isthmus to and from the southern colonies. The other provinces were of comparatively little value.

The small number of Spaniards intermarried freely with the local Indians, accounting for the predominance of *mestizos* in present-day Central America. In Guatemala, where there were the most Indians, intermarriage affected fewer of the natives, and over half the population today is pure Indian. On the Meseta Central of Costa Rica, the Indians were all but wiped out by disease; as a consequence of this great disaster, there is a buoyant community of over 2 million whites, with little Indian admixture, in the highlands. Blacks predominate all along the Caribbean coasts of Central America; they were not brought in by the colonists as slaves, but by the railway builders and banana planters of the nineteenth century and the canal cutters of the twentieth, as cheap labour.

Independence and Federation On 5 November 1811, José Matías Delgado, a priest and jurist born in San Salvador, organized a revolt in conjunction with another priest, Manuel José Arce. They proclaimed the independence of El Salvador, but the Audiencia at Guatemala City quickly suppressed the revolt and took Delgado prisoner.

It was the revolution of 1820 in Spain itself that precipitated the independence of Central America. When on 24 February 1821, the Mexican general Agustín de Iturbide announced his Plan of Iguala for an independent Mexico, the Central American *criollos* decided to follow his example, and a declaration of independence, drafted by José Cecilio del Valle, was announced in Guatemala City on 15 September 1821. Iturbide invited the provinces of Central America to join with him, and on 5 January 1822, Central America was declared annexed to Mexico. Delgado refused to accept this decree, and Iturbide, who had now assumed the title of Emperor Agustín the First, sent an army S under Vicente Filísola to enforce it in the regions under Delgado's influence. Filísola had completed his task when he heard of Iturbide's abdication, and at once convened a general congress of the Central American provinces. It met on 24 June 1823, and established the Provincias Unidas del Centro de América. The Mexican republic acknowledged their independence on 1 August 1824, and Filísola's soldiers were withdrawn.

The congress, presided over by Delgado, appointed a provisional governing *junta* which promulgated a constitution modelled on that of the United States on 22 November 1824. The Province of Chiapas was not included in the Federation, for it had already adhered to Mexico in 1821. No federal capital was chosen, but Guatemala City, by force of tradition, soon became the seat of government.

Breakdown of Federation The first President under the new constitution was Manuel José Arce, a liberal. One of his first acts was to abolish slavery. El Salvador, protesting that he had exceeded his powers, rose in December, 1826. Honduras, Nicaragua, and Costa Rica joined the revolt, and in 1828 General Francisco Morazán, in charge of the army of Honduras, defeated the federal forces, entered San Salvador and marched against Guatemala City. He captured the city on 13

April 1829, and established that contradiction in terms: a liberal dictatorship. Many conservative leaders were expelled and church and monastic properties confiscated. Morazán himself became president of the Federation in 1830. He was a man of considerable ability; he ruled with a strong hand, encouraged education, fostered trade and industry, opened the country to immigrants, and reorganized the administration. In 1835 the capital was moved to San Salvador.

These reforms antagonized the conservatives and there were several risings. The most serious revolt was among the Indians of Guatemala, led by Rafael Carrera, an illiterate *mestizo* conservative and a born leader. Years of continuous warfare followed, during the course of which the Federation withered away. As a result, the federal congress passed an act which allowed each province to assume what government it chose, but the idea of a federation was not quite dead. As a result, Morazán became President of El Salvador. Carrera, who was by then in control of Guatemala, defeated Morazán in battle and forced him to leave the country. But in 1842, Morazán overthrew Braulio Carrillo, then dictator of Costa Rica, and became president himself. At once he set about rebuilding the Federation, but was defeated by the united forces of the other states, and shot on 15 September 1842. With him perished any practical hope of Central American political union.

The Separate States Costa Rica, with its mainly white population, is a country apart, and Panama was Colombian territory until 1903. The history of the four remaining republics since the breakdown of federation has been tempestuous in the extreme. In each the ruling class was divided into pro-clerical conservatives and anti-clerical liberals, with constant changes of power. Each was weak, and tried repeatedly to buttress its weakness by alliances with others, which invariably broke up because one of the allies sought a position of mastery. The wars were rarely over boundaries; they were mainly ideological wars between conservatives and liberals, or wars motivated by inflamed nationalism. Nicaragua, for instance, was riven internally for most of the period by the mutual hatreds of the Conservatives of Granada and the Liberals of León, and there were repeated conflicts between the Caribbean and interior parts of Honduras.

Of the four republics, Guatemala was certainly the strongest and in some ways the most stable. While the other states were skittling their presidents like so many ninepins, Guatemala was ruled by a succession of strong dictators: Rafael Carrera (1844-1865), Justo Rufino Barrios (1873-1885), Manuel Cabrera (1898-1920), and Jorge Ubico (1931-44). These were separated by intervals of constitutional government, anarchy, or attempts at dictatorship which failed. Few presidents handed over power voluntarily to their successors; most of them were forcibly removed or assassinated.

Despite the permutations and combinations of external and civil war there has been a recurrent desire to reestablish some form of *la gran patria centroamericana*. Throughout the 19th century, and far into the 20th, there have been ambitious projects for political federation, usually involving El Salvador, Honduras and Nicaragua; none of them lasted more than a few years. There have also been unsuccessful attempts to reestablish union by force, such as those of Barrios of Guatemala in 1885 and Zelaya of Nicaragua in 1907.

During colonial times the area suffered from great poverty; trade with the mother country was confined to small amounts of silver and gold, cacao and sugar, cochineal and indigo. During the present century the great banana plantations of the Caribbean, the coffee and cotton trade and industrialization have brought some prosperity, but its benefits have, except in Costa Rica and Panama, been garnered mostly by a relatively small landowning class and the middle classes of the cities. Nicaragua is now a case apart; extensive and radical reforms were carried out by a left-leaning revolutionary government, but protracted warfare and mistakes in economic management have left the country still extremely poor. Poverty, the fate of the great majority, has brought about closer economic cooperation between the five republics, and in 1960 they established the Central American Common Market (CACM). Surprisingly, the Common Market appeared to be a great success until 1968, when integration fostered national antagonisms, and there was a growing conviction in Honduras and Nicaragua, which were doing least well out of integration, that they were being exploited by the others. In 1969 the 'Football War' broke out between El Salvador and Honduras, basically because of a dispute about illicit emigration by Salvadoreans into Honduras, and relations between the two were not normalized until 1980. Despite the handicaps to economic and political integration imposed by nationalist feeling and ideological differences, hopes for improvement were revived in 1987 when the Central American Peace Plan, drawn up by President Oscar Arias Sánchez of Costa Rica, was signed by the Presidents of Guatemala, El Salvador, Honduras, Nicaragua and Costa Rica. The plan proposed formulae to end the civil strife in individual countries, achieving this aim first in Nicaragua (1989), then in El Salvador (1991). In October 1993, the presidents of Guatemala, El Salvador, Honduras, Nicaragua and Costa Rica signed a new Central American Integration Treaty Protocol, to replace that of 1960 and set up new mechanisms for regional integration. The Treaty was the culmination of a series of annual presidential summits since 1986 which, besides aiming for peace and economic integration, has established a Central American Parliament and a Central American Court of Justice.

WILL YOU HELP US?

We do all we can to get our facts right in the MEXICO & CENTRAL AMERICAN HANDBOOK. Each section is thoroughly revised each year, but the territory is vast and our eyes cannot be everywhere. We are always pleased to hear about your travels; do write to us in as much detail as possible. In return we will send you information about our special guidebook offer.

TRADE & TRAVEL *Handbooks*

Write to The Editor, Mexico & Central American Handbook, Trade & Travel, 6 Riverside Court, Lower Bristol Road, Bath BA2 3DZ. England

GUATEMALA

INTRODUCTION

GUATEMALA is the most populous of the Central American republics and the only one which is largely Indian in language and culture. It still has large areas of unoccupied land, especially in the N; only about two-thirds is populated. Two-thirds of it is mountainous and about the same proportion forested. It has coastlines on the Pacific (240 km), and on the Caribbean (110 km).

A lowland ribbon, nowhere more than 50 km wide, runs the whole length of the Pacific shore. Cotton, sugar, bananas and maize are the chief crops of this lowland, particularly in the Department of Escuintla. There is some stock raising as well. Summer rain is heavy and the lowland carries scrub forest.

From this plain the highlands rise sharply to heights of between 2,500 and 3,000m and stretch some 240 km to the N before sinking into the northern lowlands. A string of volcanoes juts boldly above the southern highlands along the Pacific. There are intermont basins at from 1,500 to 2,500m in this volcanic area. Most of the people of Guatemala live in these basins, drained by short rivers into the Pacific and by longer ones into the Atlantic. One basin W of the capital has no apparent outlet and here, ringed by volcanoes, is the splendid Lake Atitlán. The southern highlands are covered with lush vegetation over a volcanic subsoil. This clears away in the central highlands, exposing the crystalline rock of the E-W running ranges. This area is lower but more rugged, with sharp-faced ridges and deep ravines modifying into gentle slopes and occasional valley lowlands as it loses height and approaches the Caribbean coastal levels and the flatlands of El Petén.

The lower slopes of these highlands, from about 600 to 1,500m, are planted with coffee. Coffee plantations make almost a complete belt around them. Above 1,500m is given over to wheat and the main subsistence crops of maize and

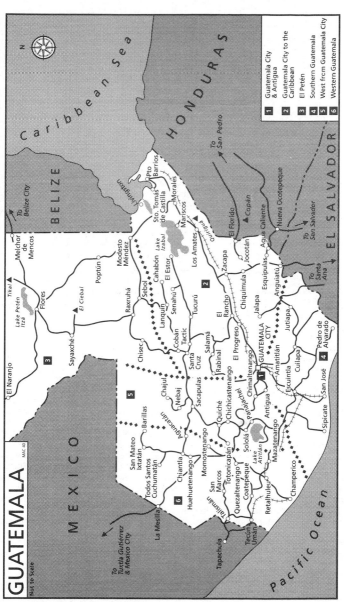

GUATEMALA MAC 40

Not to Scale

1 Guatemala City & Antigua
2 Guatemala City to the Caribbean
3 El Petén
4 Southern Guatemala
5 West from Guatemala City
6 Western Guatemala

beans. Deforestation is becoming a serious problem. Where rainfall is low there are savannas, where water for irrigation is now drawn from wells and these areas are being reclaimed for pasture and fruit growing.

Two large rivers flow down to the Caribbean Gulf of Honduras from the highlands: one is the Río Motagua, 400 km long, rising among the southern volcanoes; the other, further N, is the Río Polochic, 298 km long, which drains into Lake Izabal and the Bay of Amatique. There are large areas of lowland in the lower reaches of both rivers, which are navigable for considerable distances; this was the great banana zone.

To the NW, bordering on Belize and Mexico, in the peninsula of Yucatán, lies the low, undulating tableland of El Petén (36,300 square km). In some parts there is natural grassland, with woods and streams, suitable for cattle, but large areas are covered with dense hardwood forest. Since the 1970s large-scale tree-felling has reduced this tropical rain forest by some 40%, especially in the S and E. However, in the N, which now forms Guatemala's share of the Maya Biosphere Reserve (with Mexico and Belize), illegal logging still takes place. Deep in the tangled rain forest lie the ruins of Maya cities such as Tikal and Uaxactún. In the Department of Petén, almost one-third of the national territory, there are only 250,000 people.

Climate, which depends upon altitude, varies greatly. Most of the population lives at between 900 and 2,500m, where the climate is healthy and of an even springlike warmth—warm days and cool nights. The pronounced rainy season in the highlands is from May to October; the dry from November to April.

History For early history see the introductory chapter to Central America. Cochineal and indigo were the great exports until 1857, when both were wiped out by competition from synthetic dyes. The vacuum was filled by cacao, followed by coffee and bananas, and essential oils. The upland soil and climate are particularly favourable to coffee.

Only coffee of the Bourbon variety is planted below 600m, and until 1906, when bananas were first planted there, the low-lying *tierra caliente* had been used mostly for cane and cattle raising. The first plantations of the United Fruit Company were at the mouth of the Motagua, near Puerto Barrios, then little more than a village. Blacks from Jamaica were brought in to work them. The plantations expanded until they covered most of the *tierra caliente* in the NE—along the lower Motagua and around Lake Izabal.

In the 1930s, however, the plantations were struck by disease and the Company began planting bananas in the Pacific lowlands; they are railed across country to the Caribbean ports. There are still substantial plantations at Bananera, 58 km inland from Puerto Barrios, though some of the old banana land is used for cotton and *abacá* (manila hemp).

Jorge Ubico, an efficient but brutal dictator who came to power in 1931, was deposed in 1944. After some confusion, Juan José Arévalo was elected President and set out to accomplish a social revolution, paying particular attention to education and labour problems. He survived several conspiracies and finished his term of six years. Jacobo Arbenz became President in 1950, and the pace of reform was quickened. His Agrarian Reform Law, dividing large estates expropriated without adequate compensation among the numerous landless peasantry, aroused opposition from landowners. In June 1954, Colonel Carlos Castillo Armas, backed by interested parties and with the encouragement of the United States, led a successful insurrection and became President. For the following 29 years the army and its right-wing supporters suppressed left-wing efforts, both constitutional and violent, to restore the gains made under Arévalo and Arbenz; many thousands of people, mostly leftists but also many Indians, were killed during this period. In August 1983 General Oscar Mejía Víctores took power. He permitted a Constituent Assembly to be elected in 1984, which drew up a new constitution and worked out a timetable for a return to democracy. Presidential elections, held in December 1985, were won by Vinicio Cerezo Arévalo of the Christian Democrat party (DC), who took office in January 1986. In the 1990 elections the Christian Democrats fared badly, their candidate failing to qualify for run-off elections between Jorge Serrano Elías, the eventual winner, of the Solidarity Action Movement (MAS) and Jorge Carpio of the National Centrist Union (UCN). One of the earliest moves made by President Serrano was to speed up a process of talks between the government and the Guatemalan National Revolutionary Unity (URNG), which began in Oslo in March 1990. The sides, including the military, met in Mexico City in April 1991 to discuss such topics as democratization and human rights, a reduced role for the military, the rights of indigenous people, the resettlement of refugees and agrarian reform. Progress was slow and several rounds of talks were held with little achieved. The URNG remained active, but in late 1993 negotiations recommenced, leading to a Global Human Rights accord signed between the government and rebels on 29 March 1994. Further talks and the setting up of a Civil Society Assembly (to deliberate on the displaced and victims of war, a truth commission and other issues) raised hopes for a solution to the civil war by the end of 1994.

By 1993 when President Serrano's government reached mid-term, the country was in disarray. Political, social and economic policies pursued by the government had alienated nearly everybody and violence erupted on the streets led by a wave of student riots. The Christian Democrats and the UCN centrists withdrew their support in Congress, leaving the government without a majority. Amid growing civil unrest, President Serrano suspended the constitution, dissolved Congress and the Supreme Court and imposed press censorship, with what appeared to be military support for his auto-coup. International and domestic condemnation for his action was immediate and most foreign aid was frozen. After only a few days, Serrano was ousted by a combination of military, business and opposition leaders and a return to constitutional rule was promised. Congress approved a successor to Serrano immediately, electing Ramiro de León Carpio as present. Sr de León had previously been the human rights ombudsman and had been one of the officials arrested by former President Serrano. This spectacular choice led to much optimism, which proved short-lived. Although progress was made in talks between the government and URNG, assassinations and kidnapping continued. Some communities, displaying no faith in the security and justice systems, took the law into their hands to deal with criminals. Land invasions also continued and a 10-week public sector strike in early-1994 disrupted most government services. In addition, attacks by mobs on two US women who were suspected of kidnapping children (there was no evidence of this), heightened the sense of crisis. In this climate, the public's distaste at corrupt congressional deputies and ineffectual government was not diminished. By mid-1994, the president seemed powerless to restore any confidence because Congress deliberately failed to approve bills on constitutional, police, or tax reform, and other laws. The reform of election procedures and political parties had been called for by a referendum on 30 January (albeit with a very small voter turnout). This obliged Congressional elections to be called for 14 August. Even these were in doubt as the constitutionality of the elections was challenged in the courts.

The People About half the total population are classed as Amerindian. (Estimates of the Amerindian population vary, from 40% to 65%.) Over 40% are ladino, while 5% are white, 2% black and 3.9% other mixed race or Chinese. UN statistics show that 87% of the population live in poverty and 72% can not afford a minimum diet. Some 65% of the people live at elevations above 1,000m in 30% of the total territory; only 35% live at lower elevations in 70% of the total territory.

The indigenous people of Guatemala are mainly of Maya descent. There are

22 recognized language groups of the Guatemalan Maya, with 100 or more dialects. Among the groups are the Mam, Cakchiquel, Kekchi, Quiché, Chuj, Maya-Mopan and Ixil. A brief description of their culture follows.

Culture When the Spaniards arrived from Mexico City in 1523 they found little precious metal: only some silver at Huehuetenango. Those who stayed settled in the intermont basins of the southern highlands around Antigua and Guatemala City and intermarried with the groups of native subsistence farmers living there. This was the basis of the present *mestizo* population living in the cities and towns as well as in all parts of the southern highlands and in the flatlands along the Pacific coast; the indigenous population is still at its most dense in the western highlands and Alta Verapaz. They form two distinct cultures: the almost self-supporting indigenous system in the highlands, and the *ladino* commercial economy in the lowlands. At first sight the two seem to have much in common, for the Indian regional economy is also monetary, but a gulf opens between the two systems when it is realized that to an Indian trade is seen as a social act, not done out of need, and certainly not from any impulse to grow rich.

The scenery of the Indian regions W of the capital is superb and full of colour. In the towns and villages are colonial churches, some half ruined by earthquakes but often with splendid interiors. The coming of the Spaniards transformed outer lives: they sing old Spanish songs, and their religion is a compound of image-worshipping paganism and the outward forms of Catholicism, but their inner natures remain largely untouched.

Their markets and *fiestas* are of outstanding interest. The often crowded markets are quiet and restrained: no voice raised, no gesture made, no anxiety to buy or sell; but the *fiestas* are a riot of noise, a confusion of processions, usually carrying saints, and the whole punctuated by grand firework displays and masked dancers. The chief *fiesta* is always for a town's particular patron saint, but all the main Catholic festivals and Christmas are celebrated to some extent everywhere.

Indian dress is unique and attractive, little changed from the time the Spaniards arrived: the colourful head-dresses, *huipiles* (tunics) and skirts of the women, the often richly patterned sashes and kerchiefs, the hatbands and tassels of the men. It varies greatly, often from village to village. Unfortunately a new outfit is costly, the Indians are poor, and denims are cheap. While men are adopting western dress in many villages, women are slower to change. As a result of the increase in employment opportunities and the problems of land distribution (see below), many Indians are now moving from the highlands to the *ladino* lowland areas; other Indians come to the southern plains as seasonal labourers whilst retaining their costumes, languages and customs and returning to the highlands each year to tend their own crops.

NB The word *ladino*, used all over Central America but most commonly in Guatemala, applies to any person with a 'Latin' culture, speaking Spanish and wearing normal Western clothes, though he may be pure Amerindian by descent. The opposite of *ladino* is *indígena*; the definition is cultural, not racial.

The Economy The equitable distribution of occupied land is a pressing problem. The Agrarian Census of 1950 disclosed that 70% of the cultivable land was in the hands of 2% of the landowners, 20% in the hands of 22%, and 10% in the hands of 76%—these figures corresponding to the large, medium and small landowners. A quarter of the land held by the small owners was sub-let to peasants who owned none at all. There were 531,636 farms according to the 1979 census, of which 288,083 (54%) were of less than 1.4 hectares, 180,385 (34%) were of under 7 hectares, while 482 (less than 1%) were of more than 900 hectares. Between 1955 and 1982, 665,000 hectares were redistributed (compared with 884,000 between 1952 and 1954), but it was estimated that in 1982 there were 420,000 landless agricultural workers. A peaceful movement of *campesinos* (farm labourers) was formed in 1986 to speed land distribution.

GUATEMALA : FACT FILE

Geographic
Land area	108,889 sq km
forested	34.6%
pastures	12.9%
cultivated	17.4%

Demographic
Population (1992)	9,442,000
annual growth rate (1987 92)	2.8%
urban	38.3%
rural	61.7%
density	86.7 per sq km
Religious affiliation	
Roman Catholic	75%
Protestant	25%
Birth rate per 1,000 (1989)	39.4
	(world av 26.4)
Death rate per 1,000 (1989)	7.3
	(world av 9.2)

Education and Health
Life expectancy at birth,	
male	59.7 years
female	64.4 years
Infant mortality rate	
per 1,000 live births (1989)	43.6
Physicians (1987)	1 per 2,356 persons
Hospital beds	1 per 602 persons
Calorie intake as %	
of FAO requirement	103%
Population age 25 and over	
with no formal schooling	50.0%
Literate males (over 15)	69.7%
Literate females (over 15)	51.7%

Economic
GNP (1990 market prices)	US$8,309mn
GNP per capita	US$900
Public external debt (1990)	US$2,100mn
Tourism receipts (1990)	US$185mn
Inflation	
(annual av 1986-91)	21.1%
Radio	1 per 23 persons
Television	1 per 19 persons
Telephone	1 per 36 persons

Employment
Population economically active (1989)	
	2,898,316
Unemployment rate	2.9%
Underemployment rate	63%
% of labour force in	
agriculture	48.9
mining	0.2
manufacturing	13.4
construction	3.9
Military forces	44,600

Source *Encyclopaedia Britannica*

In international trade the accent is still heavily on agriculture, which accounts for over two thirds of total exports. Coffee is the largest export item, followed by sugar, but bananas, vegetables, sesame and cardamom are also important crops. There has been an attempt to diversify agricultural exports with tobacco, fruit and ornamental plants, and beef exports are increasing.

The industrial sector has been growing steadily; the main activities, apart from food and drink production, include rubber, textiles, paper and pharmaceuticals. Chemicals, furniture, petroleum products, electrical components and building materials are also produced. The encouragement of *maquila* industries in the mid-1980s has attracted foreign investment, much of it from the Far East, and has created low-paid jobs for about 80,000 Guatemalans, mostly in garment manufacturing. *Maquila* exports rose from US$20mn in 1986 to nearly US$207mn in 1990.

Petroleum has been discovered at Las Tortugas and Rubelsanto in the Department of Alta Verapaz and in the northern Petén in a basin known as Paso Caballos. The Rubelsanto find is estimated to have proven and probable reserves of 27.3mn barrels, with production from this field and from W Chinajá running at 4,000 bpd. A pipeline transports oil from Rubelsanto to the port of Santo Tomás de Castilla. Several new wells are under development in El Petén and oil companies are optimistic that by the mid-1990s Guatemala will be nearly self-sufficient. 1993 production was estimated at an average 7,000 bpd. Offshore exploration has so far been unsuccessful. There are three oil refineries. In order to lessen imports of petroleum, five hydroelectricity projects have been developed including Aguacapa (90 Mw) and Chixoy (300 Mw).

Guatemala's poor growth record in first half of the 1980s was attributable to the world recession bringing low agricultural commodity prices, particularly for coffee, and political instability both at home and in neighbouring Central American countries. The return to democracy and economic restructuring brought confidence and higher rates of growth as inflows of foreign funds were renewed. Other factors improving the balance of payments included moderate imports, rising exports, a rebound in tourism and selective debt rescheduling arrangements. An attempt at economic liberalization in 1989, involving the floating of the exchange rate, was reined in in 1990. The Government reintroduced control over the rate after it fell sharply, causing a surge in inflation. Measures were announced to reduce liquidity and curb the fiscal deficit by raising tax income, although two previous efforts to increase taxes were followed by military coup attempts and had to be diluted. The Government which took office in January 1991 sought an agreement with the IMF to reduce the fiscal deficit and inflation and stablilize the exchange rate. Efforts were also made to refinance the external debt owed to official international financial institutions. Inflation was cut from 41.1% in 1990 to 33.2% in 1991 and 10.1% in 1992. In 1993, the rate of inflation rose to 13%, mainly as a result of increased food prices following poor harvests and an excess of liquidity as a result political unrest. A target of 8% inflation was set for 1994. Gdp rose by 3.2% in 1991 and 4.8% in 1992. Growth slowed to 4% in 1993 as investment was restricted after the insecurity of the Serrano *autogolpe*; agriculture and manufacturing did not perform well and reduced exports also contributed to the lower growth. High interest rates attracted capital inflows and international reserves increased from US$19mn in 1990 to US$900mn by March 1994. A 15-month standby arrangement was signed with the IMF in December 1992 but had to be renegotiated by the de León Carpio government. A new agreement was signed in late 1993 and much of the administration's economic planning was tied to IMF structural adjustment. The IADB funded a US$130mn Financial Modernization Programme to assist with the deregulation of the economy. All these accords were in abeyance in May 1994 as Congress failed to approve any of the relevant bills.

Government Guatemala is a Republic with a single legislative house with 116 seats. The Head of State and of government is the President. The country is administratively divided into 22 Departments. The Governor of each is appointed by the President, whose term is for 5 years. The latest constitution was dated May 1985.

Religion There is no official religion but about 75% consider themselves Roman Catholic. The other 25% are Protestant, mostly affiliated to evangelical churches.

Education 50% of the population aged 25 and over have had no formal schooling and a further 22% failed to complete primary education.

Communications There are 18,000 km of roads, 16% of which are paved. A railway links the Caribbean seaboard with the Pacific, running from Puerto Barrios up the Motagua valley to Guatemala City and on to the port of San José. From Santa María a branch line runs W through Mazatenango to the port of Champerico and the Mexican frontier. From Zacapa, half-way from Puerto Barrios to the capital, a branch line runs S to San Salvador. Apart from Guatemala City – Puerto Barrios, there are only freight services on Guatemala's railways. There are 867 km of public service railways and 290 km of plantation lines.

Conservation The quetzal, a rare bird of the Trogon family, is the national emblem. A stuffed specimen is perched on the national coat of arms in the Presidential Palace's ceremonial hall and others are at the Natural History Museums in Guatemala City, Quezaltenango, the Camino Real Hotel in Guatemala City and in the Historical Exhibit below the National Library. (Live ones may be seen, if you are very lucky, in the Biotopo on the Guatemala City-Cobán road, or in heavily forested highlands.)

Cecon (Centro de Estudios Conservacionistas) and Inguat (addresses under **Tourist Information**, Guatemala City) are setting up Conservation Areas (Biotopos) for the protection of Guatemalan wildlife (the quetzal, the manatee, the jaguar, etc). Several other national parks (some including Maya archaeological sites) and forest reserves have been set up or are planned. The main ones are given in the text. Those interested should see Thor Janson's books *Animales de Centroamérica en Peligro*, *Maya Nature* and *The Quetzal* (in English) available at Editorial Piedra Santa bookstores in Guatemala City.

GUATEMALA CITY AND ANTIGUA (1)

The present capital, commercial and administrative centre of the country, smog-bound and crowded, and the former capital, now one of Latin America's most popular places for learning Spanish. Antigua has many major ruins, evidence of the earthquakes that have bedevilled its history. Both cities are overlooked by volcanoes active and dormant.

Guatemala City, at 1,500m, was founded by decree of Charles III of Spain in 1776 to serve as capital after earthquake damage to the earlier capital, Antigua, in 1773. The city lies on a plateau in the Sierra Madre. The lofty ranges of these green mountains almost overhang the capital. To the S looms a group of volcanoes. Population, 1,100,000.

The climate is temperate, with little variation around the year. The average annual temperature is about 18°C, with a monthly average high of 20° in May and a low of 16° in December-January. Daily temperatures range from a low of 7°C at night to a high of about 29° at midday. The rainy seasons are from late April to June (light), September to October, with an Indian summer (*canicula*) in July and August; the rain is heaviest in early September. It averages about 1,270 mm a year, and sunshine is plentiful. The city has a serious smog problem.

The city was almost completely destroyed by earthquakes in 1917-18 and rebuilt in modern fashion or in copied colonial; it was further damaged by earthquake in 1976, but most of the affected buildings have been restored. A plaza called Parque Central lies at its heart: it is intersected by the N-S running 6 Avenida, the main shopping street. The eastern half has a floodlit fountain; on the W side is Parque Centenario, with an acoustic shell in cement used for open-air concerts and public meetings. To the E of the plaza is the Cathedral; to the W are the Biblioteca Nacional and the Banco del Ejército; to the N the large Palacio Nacional. Behind the Palacio Nacional, built of light green stone, is the Presidential Mansion.

Guatemala City is large. Any address not in Zona 1—and it is absolutely essential to quote Zone numbers in addresses—is probably some way from the centre. Addresses themselves, being purely numerical, are easy to find. 19 C, 4-83 is on 19 Calle between 4 and 5 Avenidas.

Many of the hotels and boarding houses are in the main shopping quarter between 2 and 11 Avenidas and between 6 and 18 Calles, Zona 1. The railway station is in the southern part of Zona 1, at 10 Av, 18C, facing the Plaza named for Justo Rufino Barrios, to whom there is a fine bronze statue on Av las Américas, Zona 13, in the southern part of the city. To see the finest residential district go S down 7 Avenida to Ruta 6, which runs diagonally in front of Edificio El Triángulo, past the Yurrita chapel (Zona 4), into the wide tree-lined Avenida La Reforma. Just S are the Botanical Gardens (1C in Zona 10, open Mon-Fri, 0800-1200, 1400-1800, Sat 0830-1230) and the Natural History Museum of the University of San Carlos at Calle Mariscal Cruz 1-56, Zona 10 (same hours as the Botanical Gardens). The Botanical Gardens were opened in 1922 and there are over 700

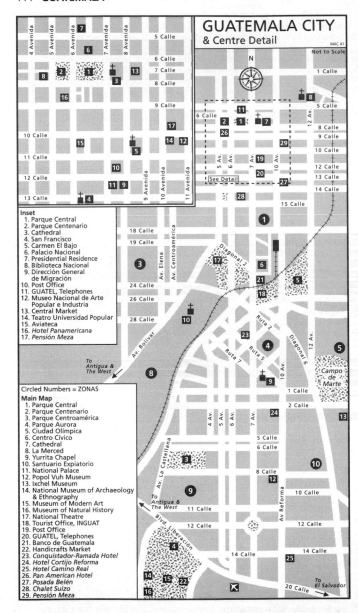

GUATEMALA CITY
& Centre Detail

MAC 41

Not to Scale

Inset
1. Parque Central
2. Parque Centenario
3. Cathedral
4. San Francisco
5. Carmen El Bajo
6. Palacio Nacional
7. Presidential Residence
8. Biblioteca Nacional
9. Dirección General
   de Migración
10. Post Office
11. GUATEL, Telephones
12. Museo Nacional de Arte
    Popular e Industria
13. Central Market
14. Teatro Universidad Popular
15. Aviateca
16. *Hotel Panamericana*
17. *Pensión Meza*

Circled Numbers = ZONAS

Main Map
1. Parque Central
2. Parque Centenario
3. Parque Centroamérica
4. Parque Aurora
5. Ciudad Olímpica
6. Centro Cívico
7. Cathedral
8. La Merced
9. Yurrita Chapel
10. Santuario Expiatorio
11. National Palace
12. Popol Vuh Museum
13. Ixchel Museum
14. National Museum of Archaeology
    & Ethnography
15. Museum of Modern Art
16. Museum of Natural History
17. National Theatre
18. Tourist Office, INGUAT
19. Post Office
20. GUATEL, Telephones
21. Banco de Guatemala
22. Handicrafts Market
23. *Conquistador-Ramada Hotel*
24. *Hotel Cortijo Reforma*
25. *Hotel Camino Real*
26. *Pan American Hotel*
27. *Posada Belén*
28. *Chalet Suizo*
29. *Pensión Meza*

species of plants; most of them labelled. Admission free. Parque El Obelisco (also known as Próceres or Independencia), with the obelisk to Guatemalan independence, is at the S end of the Avenida. La Aurora international airport, the Zoo (entry US$1, newer areas show greater concern for the animals' well-being), the Observatory, the Archaeological and the Modern Art Museums and racetrack are in Parque Aurora, Zona 13, in the southern part of the city.

There is a magnificent view all the way to Lake Amatitlán from Parque de Berlín at the S end of Av las Américas, the continuation of Av La Reforma, though some recent poor quality building has spoilt the foreground.

In the northern part (Zona 2) is the fine **Parque Minerva**, where there is a huge relief map of the country made in 1905 to a horizontal scale of 1 in 10,000 and a vertical scale of 1 in 2,000 (open 0800-1700). Buses 1 (from Av 5, Zona 1) and 18 run to the park, where there are basketball and baseball courts, swimming pool, bar and restaurant and a children's playground (it is unsafe at night).

The most notable public buildings built 1920-44 after the 1917 earthquake are the Palacio Nacional (the guards have keys and may show you round the rooms of state), the Police Headquarters, the Chamber of Deputies and the Post Office. The modern civic centre includes the City Hall, the Supreme Court, the Ministry of Finance, the Banco de Guatemala, the mortgage bank, the social-security commission and the tourist board.

The Teatro Nacional dominates the hilltop of the W side of the Civic Centre. There is an excellent view of the city and surrounding mountains from the roof. An old Spanish fortress provides a backdrop to the Open Air Theatre adjoining the blue and white mosaic-covered Teatro Nacional; open Mon-Fri (unaccompanied tours not permitted in the grounds).

On the W outskirts in Zona 7 are the Mayan ruins of *Kaminal Juyú* (Valley of Death). About 200 mounds have been examined by the Archaeological Museum and the Carnegie Institute. The area is mainly unexcavated, but there are three excavated areas open to the public, and a sculpture shed.

Churches

Cathedral Begun 1782, finished 1815. Paintings and statues from ruined Antigua. Solid silver and sacramental reliquary in the E side chapel of Sagrario. Next to the Cathedral is the colonial mansion of the Archbishop.
Cerro del Carmen A copy of a hermitage destroyed in 1917-18, containing a famous image of the Virgen del Carmen, situated on a hill with views of the city, was severely damaged in 1976 and remains in poor shape (1994).
La Merced (11 Av and 5 C, Zona 1), dedicated in 1813, which has beautiful altars, organ and pulpit from Antigua as well as jewellery, art treasures and fine statues.
Santo Domingo church (12 Av and 10 C, Zona 1), 1782-1807, is a striking yellow colour, reconstructed after 1917, image of Nuestra Señora del Rosario and sculptures.
Santuario Expiatorio (26 C and 2 Av, Zona 1) holds 3,000 people; colourful, exciting modern architecture by a young Salvadorean architect who had not qualified when he built it. Part of the complex (church, school and auditorium) is in the shape of a fish.
Las Capuchinas (10 Av and 10 C, Zona 1) has a very fine St Anthony altarpiece, and other pieces from Antigua.
Santa Rosa (10 Av and 8 C, Zona 1) was used for 26 years as the cathedral until the present building was ready. Altarpieces again from Antigua (except above the main altar).
San Francisco (6 Av and 13 C, Zona 1) has a sculpture of the Sacred Head, originally from Extremadura. Interesting museum with paintings at the back, though in poor condition.
Capilla de Yurrita (Ruta 6 and Vía 8, Zona 4), built in 1928 on the lines of a Russian Orthodox church as a private chapel. It has been described as an example of 'opulent 19th century bizarreness and over-ripe extravagance.' There are many wood carvings.
Carmen El Bajo (8 Av and 10 C, Zona 1) built in the late 18th century; the façade was severely damaged in 1976.

Festival 7 December, Devil's Day, hundreds of street fires are lit, any old rubbish burnt so the smell is awful, but it's spectacular.

Warning Thieves and handbag snatchers operate openly throughout the centre of Zona 1, especially between 4 Av and 8 Av from the Cathedral to 18 Calle. Some operate in pairs on motorbikes. Take extra care walking at night. Do not park on the street, either day or night, or your car may well be broken into. There are plenty of lock-up garages and parking lots (*estacionamientos*).

Hotels (Av=Avenida; C=Calle). **Note** Hotel prices are subject to 7% VAT and 10% service. Thefts from hotel rooms and baggage stores have been reported; do not leave valuables unsecured. Better prices in the more expensive hotels may be obtained by booking corporate rates through a reputable travel agent. More expensive, Zona 1: **A+** *Ritz Continental*, 6 Av 'A', 10-13, T 81671, clean, TV, a/c, pool, restaurant, rec; **A** *Pan American*, 9 C, 5-63, T 535991, central and rec as quiet and comfortable, TV and baths with plugs, try to avoid rooms on the main road side, restaurant with good and reasonably-priced food (lunch rec, served by staff in typical costumes), parking.

Zona 4: **A+** *Ramada Conquistador*, Vía 5, 4-68, T 364691, luxurious; **A** *Plaza*, Vía 7, 6-16, T 316173, outdoor pool, squash court, satisfactory.

Zona 9: **L** *El Dorado Americana*, 7 Av, 15-45, rowdy, loud music, lifts break down, too noisy for business visitors; **A+** *Princess*, 13 Calle 7-65, T 344545, F 344546, small, beautiful, a/c, cable TV, phone, Hertz, travel agency; **A** *Apartotel Alamo*, 10C, 5-60, T 324942, large rooms, bare walls and under airport flight path; **L** *Cortijo Reforma*, Av La Reforma 2-18, T 322713, attractive rooms, suites, good restaurant, rec; **C** *Carillon*, 5 Av, 11-23, T 324036, noisy, uncomfortable beds, only breakfast in restaurant; **A** *Villa Española*, 2 C, 7-51, T 365515, reasonably clean and modern, restaurant, bar, reasonable prices, parking, colonial atmosphere, good security, rec.

Zona 10: **L+-L** *Camino Real*, Av La Reforma and 14 C, T 334633, no airport transfers, good restaurant but hotel reported overpriced; **L** *Radisson Suites Villa Magna*, 1 Av, 12-46, T 329797, F 329772, large, luxurious suites with kitchenette, no restaurant but many nearby, good for long rental; **A+** *Guatemala Fiesta*, 1 Av, 13-22, T 322555; **A** *Residencial Reforma* (*Casa Grande*), Av La Reforma 7-67, T 310907, near US Embassy, rec.

Zona 13: **L** *Las Américas*, Av Las Américas, 9-08, T 390676, F 326686, new, suites available; **Apartotel Casa Blanca**, Av Américas 5-30, US$920 a month, new, pleasant, a bit noisy from highway and airport; **Aeropuerto Guest House**, 15 C 'A', 7-32, see under **Airport** below.

Medium price, all in Zona 1 unless otherwise stated: **B** *Hotel del Centro*, 13C, 4-55, T 81519, 80639, F 300208, large comfortable rooms, cable TV, good restaurant, live entertainment in bar, excellent service, rec; **C** *Centenario*, 6 C, 5-33, T 80381, clean, clothes washing facilities on top floor; **C** *Chalet Suizo*, 14 C, 6-82, T 513786, with or without shower (triples available) popular, often crowded, locked luggage store US$0.50/day but theft reported from locked store, noisy rooms on street (avoid rooms 9 to 12, noisy pump will disturb sleep), nice new extension, big rooms, constant hot water, *Café Suizo*, next door, breakfast (with muesli) and snacks, reasonable prices; **B-C** *Posada Belén*, 13 C, 'A' 10-30, with bath in a colonial-style house, quiet, good laundry service, friendly, Francesca and René Sanchinelli speak English, highly rec, often full, will store luggage safely, good dining room, avoid rooms next to front door, rather noisy (T 29226, 534530, F 513478); **C** *Colonial*, 7 Av, 14-19, T 26722, reasonable restaurant for breakfast, quiet and rec, although ground floor rooms are small and poorly ventilated, ask for 2nd floor; **D** *Alameda Guest House*, 4 Av, 14-10, Zona 10, rather run down; **D** *Spring*, 8 Av 12-65, with shower and hot water, cheaper without, quaint, good breakfasts, cable TV, guarded parking lot nearby, highly rec; **D** *Maya Excelsior*, 7 Av, 12-46, T 82761, crowded, noisy and commercial but comfortable rooms, good service and rec restaurant.

In our **E** range: *Lessing House*, 12 C, 4-35, T 513891, small, clean, friendly; *Hernani*, 15 C, 6-56, no restaurant, clean, friendly, safe to leave luggage while travelling, the Spanish owner is severe in manner but noble in spirit! *Costa del Sol*, 17C, 8-35, bath, hot water, noisy, adjoining *cafetería* poor value; *La Fuente*, 16 C, 3-46, T 539924, quiet, will store luggage; *Maya Quiché*, 10 Av y 12 C, very friendly, many families use it, good restaurant attached; *Ritz*, 6 Av, 9-28, 2nd floor, central, hot water, all the breakfast you can eat for US$2, German owner speaks English, very helpful but not too clean; *San Diego*, 15 C, 7-37, unfriendly, run down, uncomfortable beds, no bag storage facilities, theft reported 1993, annex opp, F, good value, full by 1000; *CentroAmérica*, 9 Av 16-38, with 3 meals, US$1 extra with bath, clean, bright, hot water, iced drinking water, peaceful, highly rec; next door is *Albergue*, courtyard, friendly, very basic but pleasant; *Capri*, 9 Av 15-63, T 513737, with shower, F without, some rooms noisy, clean, helpful, good restaurant, hot water, cable TV; *Venecia*, 4 Av 'A', 6-90, Zona 4, very comfortable, with bath, meals poor but cheap; *Aguilar*, 4 Av, 1-51 Zona 9, T 347164, next to bus station, modern, good cheap food, a bit noisy, handy if you are going on to El Salvador by bus.

Inexpensive, all in Zona 1 and in our **F** range unless otherwise stated: *Bilbao*, 8 Av y 15 C, some English spoken, shared showers, good toilets; also **E** *Bilbao II*, fairly clean, functional, safe; *Bristol*, 15 C, 7-36, shared bath, pleasant, back rooms are brighter; *Diligencia*, 14 C, 7-36, reasonable but unfriendly; *Fénix*, 7 Av, 16-81, some rooms with bath, clean, safe, very helpful, corner rooms noisy, good meals US$1.25 and 1.50, breakfast available; *San Martín*, 16 C, 7-59, round the corner from the *Fénix*, same management, with or without bath, modern, clean, a bit noisy; *San Angel*, 14 C between 10 and 11 Av, with or without bath, large rooms, good beds, intermittent hot water, clean, bad electric wiring in some rooms and rats, kitchen; **E** *Ajau*, 8 Av, 15-62, T 20488, convenient for El Petén and El Salvador buses. *Pensión Meza*, 10 C, 10-17, beds in dormitories **G**, other rooms **F**, popular, helpful staff, English spoken, hot electric showers, noisy, dirty, damp, inhabited mainly by young travellers, good place to arrange travel with others, basic, beware of petty theft; *El Virrey*, 5 Av, 13-52, OK.

NB The water supply in hotels tends to be spasmodic, and water for showering is often unobtainable between 1000-1800. Hotels are often full at holiday times, eg Easter, Christmas, when visitors from other countries and the interior come to shop. At the cheaper hotels it is not always possible to get single rooms. There are many other cheap *pensiones* near bus and railway stations and market; those between Calles 14 and 18 are not very salubrious.

Camping For campsites within easy access of Guatemala City **see p 487** under Amatitlán. Parking is available free at the Airport from 1900-0700. Camping-gas cartridges not hard to find (they are stocked at Almacén Orval, 11 C, y 8 Av, Zona 1 and *Supermercado Norte*, 6 Av, 2-47, Zona 1). For equipment, try *El Globo*, 7 Av, 9-61 Zona 1.

Restaurants (Restaurants at hotels. Food prices vary less than quality.) In the capital, the tourist can easily find everything from the simple national cuisine (black beans, rice, meat, chicken, soup, avocado, cooked bananas—*plátanos*—and tortillas with everything) to French, Chinese, Italian and German food (and pastries). A meal in a smart restaurant will cost between US$15 and 20 (1993). A simple, but nourishing, three-course meal can be had for US$1 at any *comedor*. For local food served in 14 different 'menus', try *Los Antojitos*, 15 C, 6-28, Zona 1, with music, though a bit pricey. Fashionable places, such as *Hola* (French and Italian), Av Las Américas, Zona 14, *Romanello* (Italian), 1 Av, 13-38, Zona 10, *El Parador*, 4 Av y 10 C, Zona 10, good Japanese; *El Quixote*, 11 C between 5 and 6 Av, Zona 9, and *Altuna*, 5 Av, 12-31 Zona 1, about US$6 main course, excellent service, both good Spanish; *Arrin Cuan*, 5 Av, 3-27 Zona 1, serving food from Cobán, with music; *Palo Alto*, 14C, 4 Av, Zona 10, superb but dear; *Mediterráneo*, 7 Av, 3-31, Zona 9, Italian/Spanish with nice garden, good food; *El Rodeo*, 7 Av, 14-84, Zona 9, excellent steaks, about US$15 pp without wine. Fast food is available in all parts of the city, and is relatively safe, eg *Picadilly*, 6 Av y C11, good, modern, bright, busy, Italian food; *Las Cebollines*, several locations in Zona 1, and in Zona 10: 6 Av, 9-77, Mexican, inexpensive, good (accepts Visa cards). *El Gran Pavo*, 13 C, 4-41, Zona 1, regional Mexican, well patronised. *Lido*, on 11 C between 7 Av y 8 Av, Zona 1, good, inexpensive set lunch; *Ritz*, near *Pensión Meza*, good buffet breakfast about US$2.50; connected to *Pensión Meza* is *Chez André*, French owned, happy hour is good value. A rec pizza chain is *A Guy from Italy* (in Zona 1, 12 C, 6-33 and 5 Av, 5-70), good daily lunch menu; another is *La Spaghettería*, eg Av Reforma y 11 Calle, Zona 10; *Las Vegas*, 12 C, 6-37, good atmosphere, reasonable prices. Rec vegetarian restaurants: *Productos Integrales*, 8 C, 5-36, Zona 1; *Señor Sol*, 5 C, 11-32, Zona 1; *Vegitariano*, 14 C, 6-72, Zona 1; and *Comida de Vegetales* chain, several branches (eg corner of 8 Av and 11 C, Zona 1), also take-away.

The best cafeterias for pies, pastries and chocolates (German, Austrian and Swiss styles) are *Zurich*, 6 Av, 12-52; *Los Alpes*, 10 C, 1-09, Zona 10; *Jensen*, 14 C, 0-53, Zona 1. *Dixie Deli* (formerly *Café Austria*), 12 C between Avs 6 y 7, less than one block up from the main post office in Zona 1, excellent coffee, good cakes (authentic *Stollen*) and set lunch. The *Pastelería Lins* chain (4 or 5 in Zona 1) has been rec. *American Doughnuts*, 5 Av, 11-47, Zona 1, and several other branches in the capital. *El Jardín*, 9 Av, 15-80, *comida corriente*, open 24 hours. For German food eg sausages and other European specialities, try *Gourmet Center*, 18C between 8-9 Av, Zona 10.

Clubs The American Club (introductions can be arranged for temporary membership). Lions Club. Rotary Club. Von Humboldt (German). Italian Club.

Shopping The **Central Market** was destroyed in the 1976 earthquake but a new one operates behind the Cathedral, from 7 to 9 Av, 8 C, Zona 1; one floor is dedicated to native textiles and crafts, and there is a large, cheap basketware section on the lower floor. Apart from the **Mercado Terminal** in Zona 4 (large, watch your belongings), there is the **Mercado del Sur**, 6 Av, 19-21, Zona 1, primarily a food market though it has a section for popular handicrafts. There is also a new *artesanía* market in Parque Aurora, near the airport, where marimba music is played, and which is strictly for tourists. *La Placita* by the Church of Guadalupe at 18 C and 5 Av is good for conventional clothes, leather suitcases, etc. Silverware is cheaper at the market than anywhere else in Guatemala City, but we are told that a better place for silverware is Cobán. The market is, however, rec for all local products. Bargaining is necessary at all markets in Guatemala. Also, *4 Ahau*, 11 C, 4-53, Zona 1, very good for *huipiles*, other textiles, and crafts and antiques; hand-woven textiles from *Miranda* factory, 8 Av, 30-90, Zona 8; *El Patio*, 12 C, 3-57, Zona 1; *Rodas Antiques*, 5 Av, 8-42, Zona 1 and *Barrientos Antigüedades*, 10 C, 4-64, Zona 1, have high priced silver and antiques. *Mayatex*, 12 C, 4-46, good choice, wholesale prices. *Maya Exports*, 7 Av, 10-55, credit cards accepted. Opp is *Sombol*, Av Reforma 14-14 and Calle 7-80, good for handicrafts, dresses and blouses. *La Momosteca* has a stall in Plaza Barrios and a shop at 7 Av, 14-48, Zona 1, and sells both textiles and silver. *Pasaje Rubio*, 9 C near 6 Av, Zona 1, is good for antique silver charms and coins. Shop hours 0900-1300, 1500-1900 weekdays; may open all day on Sats.

Bookshops *Geminiz*, 6 Av, 7-24, Zona 9, T 310064 (good selection), has English books; *La Plazuela*, 12C, 6-14, Zona 9, US magazines, English and Spanish books, large selection of 2nd hand books (very poor resale value, better to buy); *Vista Hermosa* 2 C, 18-50, Zona 15, T/F 691003 (English, German, Spanish); *Don Quijote*, Av Reforma y 14 C, Zona 10 (in Galería), good selection in Spanish. Museo Popol Vuh bookshop, Av La Reforma 8-60, Zona 9, has a good selection of books on precolumbian art, crafts and natural history; also bookshop of *Camino Real* hotel which has US newspapers. Bookshops also at *Conquistador-Ramada*, Museo Ixchel, and the airport. *Librería Arnel*, 7 Av y 9 C, Zona 1, German, French and English books. Instituto Guatemalteco Americano (IGA), Ruta 1 and Vía 4, Zona 4 (also library). *Eximia*, 12C, 0-85, Zona 9, Local 5, Plaza Lorenzo, a good place to browse, stocks English and Spanish books on ecology, mysticism, psychology, also posters, cards, crystal, quartz and gemstones. *Piedra Santa*, 11 C, 6-50, Zona 1 and 7 Av, 4-45, Zona 1.

Car Rental Hertz, 7 Av, 14-76, Zona 9, T 510202; *Avis*, 12 C, 2-73, Zona 9, T 316990; **Budget**, Av Reforma y 15 C, Zona 9, T 316546; **National**, 14 C, 1-42, Zona 10, T 680175; **Dollar**, 6 Av 'A', 10-13, Zona 1, T 23446 (at *Hotel Ritz*); **Tikal**, 2 C, 6-56, Zona 10, T 316490; **Quetzal**, 5 Av, 12-53, Zona 9, T 364192; **Ambassador**, Av 9-31, Zona 1, T 85987; **Tabarini**, 2 C, 'A', 7-30, Zona 10, T 316108, airport T 314755 (have Toyota Land Cruisers); **Rental**, 11 C, 2-18, Zona 9, T 341416, good rates, also motorbikes. **Tally**, 7 Av, 14-74, Zona 1, T 514113 (have Nissan and Mitsubishi pick-ups). **Ahorrent**, at airport, good service, hotel delivery. Check carefully the state of the car when you hire. You may be charged for damage already there. Average rates are US$50-60 all included (US$60-80 Hertz, or Avis) per day. Local cars are usually cheaper than those at international companies; if you book ahead from abroad with the latter, take care that they do not offer you a vehicle which is not available. If you wish to drive to Copán, you must check that this is permissible; Tabarini and Hertz do allow their cars to cross the border. Insurance rate (extra) varies from US$4-6 a day, check carefully what excess will be charged.

Motor Bike Rental Moto-Rent, 11 C, between 2 and 3 Av, Zona 9. Good Hondas for rent at reasonable prices, about US$15 per day for a Honda XL 185. Bikes can also be rented at the airport, a Jawa 180 cc for US$15, primitive but it works. Rec to take jacket and gloves, particularly when touring the countryside. Avoid riding a bike in Guatemala City, it is very polluted.

Local Buses in town, US$0.20 per journey. Not many before 0600 or after 2000.

Taxis are from US$1 for a short run to US$5-9 for longer runs inside the city (eg US$6 Zona 9 to centre). Hourly rates are from US$5. Prices double at night. Taxis of the Azules, Concordia and Palace companies rec, otherwise service is generally bad. Agree fares in advance; no meters. Taxis always available in Parque Central and Parque Concordia (6 Av and 15 C, Zona 1) and at the Trébol (the main crossroads outside city if coming from Pacific or Highlands by bus, convenient for airport).

Traffic Some traffic lights operate at rush hours; at dangerous junctions they operate 24 hrs. Avenidas have priority over Calles (except in Zona 10, where this rule varies).

Night Clubs *La Quebrada*, 6 Av, 4-60, Zona 4; *Plaza Inn, Motel Plaza*, Vía 7, 6-16, Zona 4; *Brasilia* in *Hotel Ritz Continental*. Discothèques: *After Eight*, Ed Galerías España, Zona 9;

The widest range of destinations to Mexico and Central America.

It shouldn't surprise you that Iberia knows more about flying to Latin America than anyone else. After all, Spain's trade and cultural links there stretch back some five centuries.

Five decades ago, Iberia was the first airline to link Europe with Latin America.

Serving 21 cities in 19 countries, no other airline can offer more frequent flights or a wider choice of destinations between the two continents.

Should you decide to take advantage of Iberia's FREE stopover in Madrid, there's lunch or dinner plus hotel accommodation with transfers to and from the airport. If time allows there's also a free sightseeing tour of the city.

When you arrive at your chosen destination you'll be ready for all that Latin America has to offer.

Be it adventure, seeking lost cultures or just winding-down on tropical beaches, Iberia can show you how best to discover a world we've known for centuries.

For more details telephone Iberia on 071 830 0011.

Mexico

Belize

Guatemala

Costa Rica

Belize
Costa Rica,
Guatemala & Mexico

These four exciting
countries offer you
pleasures as diverse as
coral reefs and rain
forests, orchids and exotic
birds, the remains of the
great Mayan civilisation
and the dynamic
colourful culture of today.

For all enquiries and a copy of our
colour brochure contact

Twickers World

20/22 Church Street, Twickenham TW1 3NW
Telephone 081 892 8164, Fax 081 892 8061
24 hour brochure service 081 892 7851
ABTA 60340   IATA   PATA   ATOL 1996

Kahlúa, 1 Av, 13-21, Zona 10; *Manhattan*, 7 Av opp *Hotel El Dorado*, Zona 9; *El Optimista*, Av La Reforma 12-01, Zona 10; *La Petite Discothèque*, La Manzana, Ruta 4, 4-76, Zona 4. *La Bodeguita*, 12C, 3 Av, Zona 1, rec dance club; *El Establo*, Av La Reforma 11-83, Zona 10, is a bar with excellent music. *Pandora's Box*, Ruta 3-38, Zona 4, popular. Another popular bar with live music is *Concierto de los 60*, 7 Av y 8C, Zona 1, no entrance charge and normal prices for drinks. Also in Zona 1 are *Madrid*, 8 Av y 12 C, opposite Guatel, good, and *Cavi*, 17 C between 7 and 8 Av, both Spanish style bars.

Guatemala (with southern Mexico) is the home of marimba music (see **Music** in the Introduction). The marimba is a type of xylophone played with drum sticks by from one to nine players. Up country the sounding boxes are differently sized gourds, the *marimbas de tecomates*. The city ones are marvels of fine cabinet work.

Theatres Teatro Nacional. Teatro Gadem, 8 Av, 12-15, Zona 1; Antiguo Paraninfo de la Universidad, 2 Av, 12-30, Zona 1; Teatro Universidad Popular, 10 C, 10-32, Zona 1; Teatro Artistas Unidos, 3 Av, 18-57, Zona 1. Occasional plays in English, and many other cultural events, at Instituto Guatemalteco Americano (IGA), Ruta 1 and Vía 4, Zona 4. List of current offerings outside Teatro del Puente, 7 Av, 0-40, Zona 4, and in local English-language publications and city newspapers.

Cinemas are numerous and often show films in English with Spanish subtitles. Prices are US$1.

Concerts Concerts of the Philharmonic Orchestra take place in the Teatro Nacional, Civic Centre, 24 Calle, Zona 1. During the rainy season at the Conservatorio Nacional, 5 C, y 3 Av, Zona 1, and occasionally in the Banco de Guatemala.

Sports There is an 18 hole golf course at the Guatemala Country Club, 8 km from the city, and a 9 hole course at the Mayan Club. The Guatemala Lawn Tennis Club and the Mayan Club are the chief centres for tennis.

Swimming Pools Apart from those at the Parque Minerva (**p 445**) there are pools at Ciudad Olímpica, 7 C y 12 Av, Zona 5 (monthly membership only, US$2.50 a month— photograph required; you may be allowed in for a single swim); Piscina Ciudad Vieja, Zona 15; Baños del Sur, 13 C 'A' 7-34, Zona 1, has hot baths for US$0.50, saunas for US$1.50. Try also the hotels and the campsites near Amatitlán. The *Camino Real* sells tickets for its pool to non-guests.

Other Sports Bowling Ten-pin variety and billiards at Bolerama, Ruta 3, 0-61, Zona 4, 2 blocks from *Ramada-Conquistador* hotel. **Hang Gliding**: Asociación de Vuelo Libre, 12 C, 1-25, Zona 10 Oficina 1601, Edif Geminis 10, T 353215, flying over Lakes Atitlán and Amatitlán, best time November to May.

Museums The National Museum of Archaeology and Ethnology, Salón 5, Parque Aurora, Zona 13, T 720489, contains stelae from Piedras Negras and typical Guatemalan costumes, and good models of Tikal, Quiriguá and Zaculeu, and other Maya items. (Open 0900-1600, Tues-Fri, 0900-1200, 1400-1600 Sat-Sun) Admission US$0.40, Sun free for Guatemalans only. Contains sculpture (including stelae, murals, etc), ceramics, textiles, and a collection of masks. Its excellent jade collection is closed at weekends.

The **Museum of Modern Arts**, Salón 6, Parque Aurora, Zona 13, 'modest, enjoyable collection'. Open Tues-Fri, 0900-1600, US$0.12.

National Museum of Natural History, collection of national fauna: stuffed birds, animals, butterflies, geological specimens etc, in Parque Aurora, 7 Av, 6-81, Zona 13, T 720468; open Tues-Fri, 0900-1600, Sat-Sun, 0900-1200, 1400-1600 free.

Museum of Natural History, Calle Mariscal Cruz 1-56, Zona 10, T 346065, free, open Mon-Fri, 0800-1200, 1400-1800, closed 1 December—15 January, Holy Week and holidays, botanical garden and stuffed animals.

National Museum of Arts and Industry, 10 Av, 10-72, Zona 1, T 80334, small exhibition of popular ceramics, textiles, silversmiths' work etc. Hours Tues-Fri 0900-1600, Sat and Sun 0900-1200, 1400-1600 (US$0.12).

Museo Ixchel del Traje Indígena, Complejo Cultural del Campus de la Universidad Francisco Marroquín, 6A Calle Final, Zona 10, has a collection of Indian costumes. Open Mon-Fri 0830-1730, Sat 0900-1300, entrance US$2. Costumes are not yet on display in the new premises, but photos from early 20th Century, paintings and video. Has an excellent shop selling textiles not usually available on the tourist market, prices are fixed and reasonable, giving an idea of what to bargain for in markets.

Popol Vuh Museum of Archaeology, Edificio Galerías Reforma, Av La Reforma 8-60, Zona 9 (6th floor, T 347121). Extensive collection of precolumbian and colonial artefacts. Has a replica of the Dresden Codex, one of only 3 Maya parchment manuscripts in existence. Open Mon-Fri, 0900-1700, Sat, 0900-1600. Admission US$1.20 (students US$0.60, children US$0.10-20). US$5 charge to take photographs.

National Museum of History, 9 C, 9-70, Zona 1, T 536149 (Mon-Fri 0830-1600), historical documents, and objects from independence onward; and colonial furniture and arms.

Fray Francisco Vásquez Museum, 13 C, 6-34, Zona 1, 18th century paintings, Mon-Fri 0900-1200.

NB Each museum has a sign in 4 languages to the effect that 'The Constitution and Laws of Guatemala prohibit the exportation from the country of any antique object, either precolumbian or colonial'. The USA in fact prohibits the import of such items and penalties are severe.

Exchange Banks change US dollars into quetzales at the free rate. **Banco de Guatemala** (in Edificio Correos, main post office, or 7 Av and 22 C, Zona 1) open Mon-Thurs 0830-1400, Fri 0830-1430. There is a **Banco de Quetzal** office open 7 days a week at the airport, weekdays 0800-2100, Sat, Sun and holidays 0800-1100, 1500-1800 (only place to change foreign banknotes). When shut, try airport police or porters who may be able/willing to change US$ cash for quetzales. There are several banks on 7 Av, open from 0830. Try the **Banco Industrial** (which sometimes advances quetzales on Visa cards, no commission, on Av 7, nr Central Post Office, will only change TCs with proof of purchase), **Banco Internacional**, or **Bandesa**, 9 C between 9 and 10 Avs, Zona 1. **Lloyds** Bank plc (6 Av, 9-51, Edifico Gran Vía, Zona 9); agencies at El Reformador, Av Roosevelt, Zona 1, Zona 10, La Parroquía and Petapa. Open weekdays, 0900-1550. **American Express** at Banco del Café, Av La Reforma, 9-00 planta baja, Zona 9, T 311311 ext 1113, F 311418 (bus 101 from Av 10), open Mon-Fri 0900-1630, for all services (agencies throughout the country). Quetzales may be bought with Visa or Mastercard at Crediomatic, minimum withdrawal US$100, in the basement of 7 Av, 6-22, Zona 9 (open until 2000, Mon-Fri). You can also draw quetzales on Diners Club card, not less than US$125 or more than US$1000 equivalent, once every 2 weeks maximum, 12 C, 4-74, Zona 9, Edif Quinta Montufar, 4th floor.

The **legal street exchange** for cash and cheques may be found on 7 Av, 12-14 C, near the Post Office (Zona 1). Be careful when changing money on the street; never go alone.

Cultural Institutes Goethe Institut, 11 C between 3 and 4 Av, German newspapers. Alianza Francesa, 4 Av, 12-39, Zona 1, free film shows on Mon, Wed and Sat evenings; other activities on other evenings, rec. Sociedad Dante Alighieri (Italian cultural centre), 4 Av, 12-47. Instituto Guatemalteco Americano (IGA) offers 6-week Spanish courses, 2 hrs a day, for US$60. Several other schools in the city.

Embassies and Consulates Addresses change frequently.
USA, Av La Reforma 7-01, Zona 10 (T 311541-55, 366205/9), Mon-Fri 0800-1200, 1300-1500. **Canada,** Galería España, 7 Av, 1-59, Nivel 6, Zona 9, T 321411/353604, Mon-Fri 0900-1300. **Mexico**, Consulate, 13 C, 7-30, Zona 9, T 325249/319573, open 0900-1100 for tourist card applications and issues cards at 1500 that afternoon, those with straightforward applications, eg US, can get them at the border and avoid queues. **El Salvador**, 12 C, 5-43, Zona 9, T 629385, 0800-1400, for visa take a passport photo, a photocopy of your passport, letter of recommendation from police authorities in country of origin or residence, visa normally costs US$30 and takes 24 hrs. **Honduras**, 15C, 3-20, Nivel 8, Zona 10, T 370663 (visas take 24 hrs, quicker in Esquipalas). **Nicaragua**, 10 Av, 14-72, Zona 10 (open Mon-Fri 0900-1300, visas on the spot, US$25 in cash, English spoken). **Costa Rica**, Edificio Galerías Reforma Oficina 320, Av Reforma, 8-60, Zona 9, T 325768. **Panama**, 5 Av, 15-45, Centro Empresarial 1, Zona 10, 0830-1300 Mon-Fri, visa given on the spot, US$10, valid for 3 months for a 30-day stay, English spoken.

Argentina, 2 Av, 11-04, Zona 10. **Bolivia**, 12 Av, 15-37, Zona 10. **Brazil**, 18 C, 2-22, Zona 14, T 370949. **Colombia**, Edificio Gemini 10, 12 C, 1 Av, Zona 10, T 320603/4. **Chile**, 13 C, 7-85, Zona 10. **Ecuador**, Diagonal 6, 13-08, Zona 10 (T 316119). **Paraguay**, 7 Av, 7-78 (8th floor), Zona 4. **Peru**, 2 Av, 9-48, Zona 9 (T 318409). **Uruguay**, 20 C, 8-00, Zona 10. **Venezuela**, 8 C, 0-56, Zona 9.

Israel, 13 Av 14-07, Zona 10 (T 371303). **Japan**, Ruta 6, 8-19, Zona 4. **South Africa**, 10 Av, 30-57, Zona 5 (T 62890).

Austria, Trade Council, 6 Av, 20-25, Zona 10; Consulate, 5 Av, 10-52, Zona 9, T 362019 Mon to Fri 1100 to 1300. **Belgium**, Av La Reforma 13-70 (2nd floor), Zona 9. **Denmark**, 7 Av 20-36 (Apartment 1, 2nd floor), Zona 1. **Finland**, 10 C, 6-47, Zona 1. **France**, 16 C, 4-53, Zona 10, T 370480. **Germany**, 6 Av, 20-25, Edificio Plaza Marítima 2nd floor, Zona 10, T 370028, 370031, open 0900-1200 (bus 14 goes there). **Netherlands**, Consulate General, 12 C, 11-91, Edif La Curaçao, Zona 9, 4th floor, T 313505 (open 0900-1200). **Italy**, 5 Av, 8-59, Zona 10, T 374888/578, Mon, Wed, Fri 0800-1430, Tues, Thur 0800-1330, 1500-1800; **Portugal**, 5 Av, 12-60, Zona 9; **Spain**, 10 C, 6-20, Zona 9. **Sweden**, 8 Av, 15-07, Zona 10, T 680621 (Norwegian interests dealt with here). **Switzerland**, Edif Seguros Universales, 4 C,

7-73, Zona 9, T 347647, 349734, Mon-Fri 0900-1130; **British Embassy**, Ed Centro Financiero, Torre 2, 7th floor, 7 Av 5-10, Zona 4 (T 321601/02/04/06), Mon-Thur 0900-1200, 1400-1600, Fri 1330-1700.

Immigration Office 41 C, 17-36, Zona 8, T 714670, F 714678 (for extensions of visas, take photo to 'Inspectoria'). Take bus 71 'Terminal' from 10 Av. See **Documents** under **Information for Visitors**.

Central Post Office 7 Av, 12 C, Zona 1. Ground floor for overseas parcel service (airmail only, very expensive), at the back (allow plenty of time). Watch your belongings when standing in queues here. This is the only post office in the country from which parcels over 2 kg (other than books) can be sent abroad. You have to show your goods, which will be weighed, make a customs list before packing (cardboard box or flour sack, staff will lend a needle and give instructions), all in an office at the back of the building. 1-3 kg US$34 airmail, 3-5 kg US$50, 5-10 kg US$85, 10-15 days, receipt given, refunds available if the item is lost, but receipt has to be shown in Guatemala for this. Poste restante keeps mail for 2 months (US$0.03 per letter). Open Mon-Fri 0800-1630. If you are awaiting an incoming parcel, the Post Office will inform you at a private address that the item has arrived. You must then clear customs, Aduana de Fardos Postales, 10 C, 13-92, Zona 1, and pay the charges, which may be high. At customs, there are lists of parcels received, which you can ask to see. There may also be information in rooms 110 and 233 in the main post office.

Telecommunications Empresa Guatemalteca de Telecomunicaciones (Guatel), 7 Av, 12-39, Zona 1 for international calls; 24-hr national and international telephone service. Local telegrams from central post office.

Non-Catholic Churches Episcopalian Church of St James, Av Castellana 40-08, Zona 8, and the Union Church of Guatemala (Plazuela España, Zona 9). Sun morning service in English at the first: 0930; at the second: 1100.

Synagogue 7 Av, 13-51, Zona 9. Service at 0930 Sat.

Voluntary Work Casa Guatemala, 14 C, 10-63, Zona 1, T 25517, can arrange voluntary work in an orphanage in Río Dulce (Fronteras) near the road bridge.

Health Centro Médico Hospital, 6 Av, 3-47, Zona 10, private, but reasonably priced, all senior doctors speak English; very helpful. Dr Mariano A Guerrero, 5 Av, 3-09, Zona 1, German-speaking, understands English (US$10 for treatment). Dr Manuel Cáceres, 6 Av, 8-92, Zona 9, 1600-1800, speaks English and German. Dr Castillo, 6 Av, 7-55, Zona 10, office 17, T 366 7715, rec. Also Dr Román Ferrate Felice at 5 Av, 2-63, Zona 1, rec for consultation (US$6) by tourist who had amoebic dysentery. Dentists: Dr Freddy Lewin, Centro Médico, 6 Av 3-69, Zona 10, T 325153 (German, English); Dr Bernal Herrera, 6 C, 1-50, Zona 1, T 518249 (English, Japanese). Amicelco, 5 Av, 4-12, Zona 1, sells drugs to pharmacies but will also supply gamma globulin etc to the public at reasonable prices.

Laundromats Lava-Centro Servimatic, Ruta 6, 7-53, Zona 4 (opposite Edificio El Triángulo) sometimes has hot water; **Express** (dry cleaners), 7 Av, 3-49, Zona 4; El Siglo (dry cleaners), 7 Av, 3-50, Zona 4, 11 Av, 16-35, Zona 1, and 12 C, 1-55, Zona 9, 4 Av, just up from 13 C, Zona 1. Dry cleaner also at Vía 2, 4-04, Zona 4, open Mon-Fri, 0730-1830.

Car Insurance Granai y Townson, 7 Av, 1-82, Zona 4.

Car Repairs Christian Kindel, 47 C, 16-02, Zona 12. Honda **motorcycle** parts from FA Honda, Av Bolívar 31-00, Zona 3; general manager and chief mechanic are German, former speaks English. Car and motorcycle parts from FPK, 7 Av, 8-08, Zona 4, T 319777. **Motorcycle Repairs** Mike and Andy Young, 13C, 73, Zona 5, T 319263, open 0700-1530, excellent mechanics for all vehicles.

Camera Repairs Fototécnica, Av Centro América 15-62, efficient, good stock. Batteries for cameras hard to come by but try Celcomer in Centro Comercial Montufar on 12 C in Zona 9. Kodak's main local distributor is near the zoo for a wide supply of camera products. Film is easy to find; slide film, Ektachrome 36 exp 100 ASA costs around US$10, shops at 9C, 6-88, 6A, 11C and others.

Tourist Information Inguat, 7 Av, 1-17, Zona 4 (Centro Cívico), T 311333/47, F 318893/314416. Very friendly, English and some German spoken. Provides hotel list from the inexpensive to the most expensive, has general information on buses, market days, museums, etc. Open Mon-Fri 0815-1600, accurate map of city, other maps, information, major tourist attractions. The Citur office on the 2nd floor of the Inguat building can arrange air fare discounts for International Student Identity card holders. A letter from a Guatemalan language school may work. Information on nature from Inafor, 7 Av y 13 C, Zona 9, T 325064. For information on the Biotopos (Nature reserves) contact CECON, Av Reforma 0-63 Zona 10,

T 310904, who can also advise on voluntary work opportunities.

Maps Maps can also be bought from the Instituto Geográfico Nacional, Av Las Américas 5-76, Zona 13, open 0800-1600 Mon to Fri, closed Sat and Sun; some of the more detailed maps can only be obtained by post, and permission must be obtained from the Ministry of Defence before buying maps of 'sensitive areas'. A 'papel sellado' may be required before purchase is allowed. Those that cannot be bought may be copied by hand from the book containing all the 1:50,000 and 1:250,000 maps of the country. Also good map of city on back of map of country, from Hertz at airport when in stock.

Travel Agents *Clark Tours*, 7 Av y Vía 6, no exchange, in Edif El Triángulo, Zona 4, T 310213, long established, very helpful, tours to Copán, Quiriguá, etc. For address of **American Express**, see under **Exchange** above; *Setsa Travel*, 8 Av, 14-11, very helpful, tours arranged to Tikal, Copán, car hire; *Aire, Mar y Tierra*, Plaza Marítima, 20 C, y 6 Av, Zona 10, and Ed Herrera, 5 Av y 12 C, Zona 1; *Tourama*, Av La Reforma 15-25, Zona 10, both rec, German and English spoken. *Izabal Tours*, Alfredo Toriello, 7a Av 14-44, Zona 9, Local 10, T 234-0323, F 234-0324, highly rec for special interest and educational tours, very knowledgeable. *Servicios Turísticos del Petén*, 2 Av, 7-78, Zona 10, trips to Flores and Tikal (owns *Hotel Maya Internacional*, Flores). *Maya Expeditions*, 3 Av, 16-52, Zona 10, T 683010/562551, varied selection of short and longer river/hiking tours. *Interconti Travel*, 14 C, Zona 10, opposite *Camino Real*, English and German, T 373102. *Nancy's*, 11 Calle, 5-16, Zona 1, T 2516996, very helpful. *Aventuras Vacacionales*, 4 C, 6-63, Zona 13, T/F 736253, for sailing trips from Río Dulce to local destinations and the Belize Cayes (see **p 474**). For the cheapest flights out of Guatemala, speak to Josefina at 6 Av, 9-28, Zone 1, T 536346, in English, German or French. *Viajes de Guatemala*, 15 C, 7-75, Zona 10, T/F 682252, arranges helicopter flights from Flores to Uaxactún, Río Azul and Mirador, and helicopter rental.

Archaeological Tours Turismo Kim'Arrin, Edificio Maya, Office No 103, Vía 5, 4-50, Zona 4, and Panamundo Guatemala Travel Service also arrange tours to Maya sites.

Airline Agents Local airlines: Aviateca, 10 C, 6-30, Zona 1, poor service, and at airport; Aeroquetzal, at airport, fly to Flores and Cancún, Aerovías (T 81463/316935), for Flores and Belize City, Tapsa for Flores: these 3 have offices at Av Hincapié and 18 C, Zona 13 at the national part of the airport. Copa, in Edif El Triángulo, 7 Av and Ruta 6, Zona 4, T 318256; Avianca and SAM, Edif Reforma Montufar, Av Reforma 12-01, Zona 10; Lacsa, 7 Av, 14-44, Zona 9, Ed Galeria, T 310906. Agencia de Viajes Mundial, 5 Av, 12-44, Zona 1, is very good. Iberia (Ed Galerías Reforma, Av La Reforma, 8 C, Zona 9), Aero México, 13 C, 8-44, Zona 10, T 336001, Mexicana, KLM (20 C and Av 6, Zona 10—bus 2, black or 14 from Av 10, Zona 1, open 0900-1700), Aerolíneas Argentinas, T 311276, United, T 326084, and the Central American airlines all have offices, so has Lufthansa, Plaza Marítima, 6 Av, 20-25, Zona 10.

Airport At La Aurora, 8 km S; restaurant with cheap 'meal of the day'; all prices marked up in the shops. Tourist information desk close to immigration office, open 0600-2100, T 314256, has maps and general information. No left luggage facilities. Banco de Quetzal for exchange, see above. Taxi to town, US$7-8, bargaining difficult (airport tourist office supplies official taxi-fare chits). Buses nos 5 (in black not red), 6, 20 and 83 from 8 Av, Zona 1, and the Zona 4, 4 Av, 1 C, bus terminal, run the ½ hour's journey between airport and centre (US$0.20). (Bus 20 runs from Centro Cívico to Aeropuerto Local.) There is also a bus to 7 Av, 18 C (price increases at night). From airport, buses leave just outside the upper level. Some domestic flights (check!) to Flores (see **p 476**) leave from a separate terminal at La Aurora. It is 150m to Avenida Américas and buses to town. All other domestic flights must be chartered. NB The airport is closed from 2100-0400, so you cannot stay the night there, but there is **C** *Aeropuerto Guest House*, 5 mins walk from the airport at 15 Calle A, 7-32, Zona 13, T 323086, with free transport to and from the airport, shared baths, clean, safe, rec.

Rail Guatemalan Railways to **Puerto Barrios**, 0700, Sat, US$2 each way (a slow way of getting a first impression of the country, takes 23 hrs, trains are usually delayed, all windows broken, thefts occur, so don't fall asleep). Return Sun 0600. The train usually calls at Quiriguá. No cooked meals are served in trains, although sandwiches and light refreshments, iced beer and soft drinks can be bought at inflated prices. Station at 18 C, 9 and 10 Av, Zona 1, on E side of Plaza Barrios (T 83031/39). No passenger connections to El Salvador, nor from Escuintla to the Pacific port of San José.

Buses Note Information on interior bus services is available at Inguat, see Tourist Information above.

The Zona 4 bus terminal between 1-4 Av and 7-9 C serves the Occidente (West), the Costa Sur (Pacific coastal plain) and El Salvador. The area of 19 C, 8-9 Av Zona 1, next to the Plaza Barrios market, contains many bus offices and is the departure point for the Oriente (East), the Caribbean zone, Pacific coast area toward the Mexican border and the N, to Flores and

Tikal. First class buses often depart from company offices in the south-central section of Zona 1. The following companies operate from Guatemala City: **Transportes Unidos**, 15 C, 3-4 Av, Zona 1, T 24949, 536929 (Antigua); **Delta y Tropical**, 1C y 2 Av, Zona 4; **Escobar y Monja Blanca**, 8 Av, 15-16, Zona 1, T 511878, 81409 (Biotopo del Quetzal and Cobán); **Veloz Quichelense** (Chichicastenango), **Chatia Gomerana** (La Democracia), **Transportes Cubanita** (Reserva Natural de Monterrico) all at Zona 4 terminal; **Galgos**, 7 Av, 19-44, Zona 1, T 23661, 534868 (Quezaltenango), Mexican border—rec); **Rutas Orientales**, 19C, 8-18, Zona 1, T 536714, 512160 (Honduran border); **Buses Vilma**, Parque de Chiquimula (Florido); **Los Halcones**, 7 Av, 15-27, Zona 1, T 81929 (Huehuetenango); **Transportes Velásquez**, 20C, 2 Av, Zona 1 (Mexican border); **Transportes Rebuli**, 21C, 1-34, Zona 1, T 513521 (Panajachel); **Transportes Litegua**, 15C, 10-42, Zona 1, T 538169 (Puerto Barrios); **Transportes Esmeralda**, 32C, 0-49, Zona 3, T 710327 (Pacific coast); **Fuentes del Norte**, 17C, 8-46, Zona 1, T 513817 (Río Dulce); **Maya Express**, 17C, 9-36, Zona 1, T 21914 (Petén); **Melva Internacional**, 3 Av, 1-38, Zona 9, T 310874 (El Salvador border); **Transportes Poaquileña**, 20C, Av Bolívar, Zona 1 (Tecpán); **Transportes Fortaleza**, 19C, 8-70, Zona 1, T 23643, 517994 (Tecún Umán—not rec). See under destinations for schedules and fares.

International buses To **San Salvador**: Mermex, 20 C, 6-39, Zona 1, T 539952, twice daily, US$6; Transportes Centroamérica, 7 Av, 15-59, Zona 1, T 23432 (minibus service to hotel on request), daily, 0730 after all passengers have been collected. Melva, 3 Av, 1-38, Zona 9, departures from 0530-1630, US$6, Pezzarossi 6 departures daily, 6 hrs; both rec, own terminal in Zona 4 (office at 4 Av, 1 C, Zona 9), at edge of bus station at 4 Av y 7 C; Tica Bus (7 Av, 19-44 Zona 1, same as Galgos, T 534868) at 1230 daily, to San Salvador (US$8.25) with connections to Tegucigalpa, US$24, Managua, US$45, San José, US$61, and Panama, US$87. Reserve the day before if you can (all except Pezzarossi go also to Santa Ana). Quality, Círculo Maya, 6 Av, 9-85, Zona 9, T 347954, leaves from *Hotel Villa Española* (0615 and 1515) and *Hotel Guatemala Fiesta* (0630 and 1530) daily for San Salvador, about 5 hrs, bus takes care of border formalities, a/c,video, snacks, US$22 one way, US$40 return (valid 90 days).

To **Honduras** avoiding El Salvador, take bus to Esquipulas (see below), then minibus to border.

To **Mexico**: Fortaleza has buses to Tecún Umán, US$4; Galgos have several buses daily to Talismán, US$5, connections with Cristóbal Colón bus line— rebookings at the border may be necessary. Velásquez have 0830 bus daily to La Mesilla, connections with Cristóbal Colón. No Guatemalan bus goes into Mexico.

The shortest route to **Antigua** is 45 km via San Lucas Sacatepéquez (**see p 462**) by paved double-lane highway passing (25 km out) El Mirador (1,830m), with fine view of the capital. Road then rises to 2,130m and gradually drops to 1,520m at Antigua. The main road between Guatemala City and Antigua suffers from heavy traffic at weekends.

Antigua was the capital city until it was heavily damaged by earthquake in 1773. Population today: 30,000. Founded in 1543, after destruction of a still earlier capital, Ciudad Vieja, it grew to be the finest city in Central America, with a population of 60,000, numerous great churches, a University (1680), a printing press (founded 1660), and famous sculptors, painters, writers and craftsmen. Centre of the city is the Parque Central, the old Plaza Real, where bullfights and markets were held. The Cathedral (1534) is to the E (entry US$0.15), the Palace of the Captains-General to the S (1769), the Municipal Palace (Cabildo) to the N (all have been repaired since the 1976 earthquake) and an arcade of shops to the W. Alvarado was buried in the Cathedral, but whereabouts is not known. All the ruined buildings, though built over a period of three centuries, are difficult to date by eye, partly because of the massive, almost romanesque architecture against earthquakes: cloisters of the convent of Capuchinas (1736), for example, look 12th century, with immensely thick round pillars (entrance, US$1). The most interesting ruins (apart from those mentioned) are of the monastery of San Francisco, the convent of Santa Clara (1723-34, entrance US$1), El Carmen, San Agustín (the last two may only be viewed from outside), La Compañía de Jesús (being restored with a Unesco grant), Santa Cruz, Escuela de Cristo church, La Recolección (1703-17) off the road, set among coffee groves (particularly worth a visit), Colegio y Hermita de San Jerónimo (Real Aduana), open every day except Mon, 0800-1700, La Merced (being restored, said to have largest fountain in the New World), the Hospital (badly damaged by 1976 earthquake, and no longer

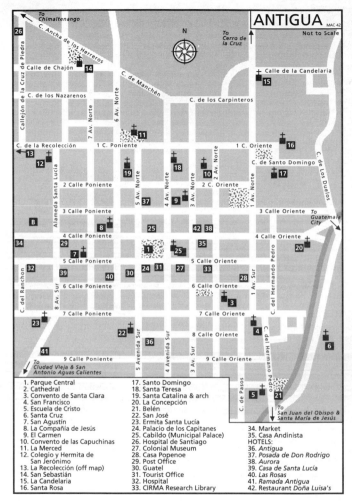

ANTIGUA MAP 42
Not to Scale

1. Parque Central
2. Cathedral
3. Convento de Santa Clara
4. San Francisco
5. Escuela de Cristo
6. Santa Cruz
7. San Agustín
8. La Compañía de Jesús
9. El Carmen
10. Convento de las Capuchinas
11. La Merced
12. Colegio y Hermita de San Jerónimo
13. La Recolección (off map)
14. San Sebastián
15. La Candelaria
16. Santa Rosa

17. Santo Domingo
18. Santa Teresa
19. Santa Catalina & arch
20. La Concepción
21. Belén
22. San José
23. Ermita Santa Lucía
24. Palacio de los Capitanes
25. Cabildo (Municipal Palace)
26. Hospital de Santiago
27. Colonial Museum
28. Casa Popenoe
29. Post Office
30. Guatel
31. Tourist Office
32. Hospital
33. CIRMA Research Library

34. Market
35. Casa Andinista
HOTELS:
36. *Antigua*
37. *Posada de Don Rodrigo*
38. *Aurora*
39. *Casa de Santa Lucía*
40. *Las Rosas*
41. *Ramada Antigua*
42. *Restaurant Doña Luisa's*

functioning), and the Museum. Other ruins, such as Santa Isabel, San Cristóbal, El Calvario and San Gaspar Vivar, all S of the town, are well worth visiting. Many sculptures, paintings and altars have been removed to Guatemala City. The Casa Popenoe, 1 Av Sur, between 5 and 6 C Oriente, is a restored colonial house with a few original 16th-century parts (the kitchen, herb garden), and contains many old objects from Spain and Guatemala; 1400-1600, Mon to Sat (it's still a private house), entry US$0.25.

Antigua is so restored that only convents and churches are in ruins, and San Francisco church has been rebuilt. Indian women sit in their colourful costumes amid the ruins and in the Parque Central. Most picturesque. In the late afternoon light, buildings such as Las Capuchinas are very attractive. Good views from the Cerro de la Cruz, 15 mins' walk from the northern end of town.

This is certainly the cultural centre of Guatemala as shown by the sections on museums and shopping below. Indigenous music can be heard everywhere, and the Marimba Antigua plays Bach and Mozart.

Warning This is an important historic centre with an air of tranquility. Unfortunately it has attracted a good number of undesirables. Petty theft, street robberies and violent crimes have been reported. Take care and take advice on where not to go (eg from Casa Andinista or the Tourist Office). Cerro de la Cruz is a notorious area for muggings, check whether the tourist police are on duty there before going up. Report incidents to police, tourist office and Casa Andinista.

Orientation Agua volcano is due S of the city and the market is to the W. Avenidas are numbered upwards running from E (Oriente) to W (Poniente), and Calles upwards from Norte to Sur. Avenidas are Norte or Sur and Calles Oriente or Poniente in relation to the central Plaza; however, unlike Guatemala City, house numbers do not give one any clue towards how far from the central Plaza a place is. There are authorized guides whose tours of Antigua and surroundings are good value.

Fiestas Holy Week. The most important and colourful processions are those leaving La Merced on Palm Sunday and Good Friday, and Escuela de Cristo and the Church of San Felipe de Jesús (in the suburbs) on Good Friday. Bright carpets, made of dyed sawdust and flowers, are laid on the route. The litter bearers wear purple until 1500 on Good Friday afternoon, and black afterwards. Only the litter bearing Christ and His Cross passes over the carpets, which are thereby destroyed. Also 21-26 July and 31 Oct-2 Nov. (All Saints and All Souls, in and around Antigua). On 7 December, the citizens celebrate the Burning of the Devils by lighting fires in front of their houses thereby starting the Christmas festivities.

Hotels In the better hotels, advance reservations are advised for weekends and Dec-April. During Holy Week hotel prices are generally double. **A+** *Antigua* (best), 5 Av Sur and 8 Calle (4 blocks S of Parque), T 320288, beautiful gardens, pool (see **Bathing** below); **A+** *Casa de Santo Domingo*, 3 Calle Oriente No 28, T 320140, F 320102, inc breakfast, beautifully designed in ruins of 17th century convent, good service, beautiful gardens, good restaurant; **L-A+** *Ramada Antigua*, 9 C Poniente and Carretera Ciudad Vieja, T 320011-5, F 320237, two pools (see below), horse hire and riding, tennis courts, discotheque, gymnasium, sauna; **A** *Posada de Don Rodrigo*, 5 Av Norte 17, T 320291, very agreeable if a little worn, good food, buffet breakfast rec, in colonial house (Casa de los Leones), marimba music pm; **B** *Posada del Farol*, Calle Los Nazarenos No 17, T 323316, F 320642, 7 rooms with bathroom, hot water, fridge, cable TV, laundry, lots of original artwork as owner also runs *Galería de Arte Estípite*, English, French, German, Italian and Spanish spoken, convenient, friendly, clean, rec; **B** *Aurora*, 4 C Oriente 16, T 320217, breakfast available, the oldest hotel in the city, old plumbing but it works, clean, quieter rooms face the patio, beautiful gardens, garage for parking, good value; **C** *Posada San Sebastián*, 7 Av Norte No 67, T 320465, near Parque San Sebastián, breakfast and laundry available, and *Posada San Sebastián 2*, 3 Av Norte No 4, T 322621, same facilities and price, English-speaking owner, both good; **B** *Convento Santa Catalina*, 5 Av Norte 28, T 323080, F 322925, under the arch, some rooms dark and small; **C-D** *Santa Clara*, 2 Av Sur 20, T 320312, 8 rooms, 4 with private bath, hot water, very clean, Doña María Panedes, the owner very helpful; **D** *El Descanso*, 5 Av Norte 9, T 320442, 2nd floor, with private bath, clean, pleasant, family atmosphere; **C** *El Rosario Lodge*, 5 Av Sur 36, T 320 336, very quiet with garden, some bungalow rooms with fireplace.

D *Las Rosas*, 6 Av Sur 8, T 320644, clean, comfortable, quiet, hot water; **E** *Los Capitanes*, 5 Av Sur, between 5 and 6 C, all rooms with bath, restaurant downstairs, commercial; **E** *Casa de Santa Lucía*, Alameda de Santa Lucía 5, near bus terminal, very popular, highly rec, luggage stored, with bath, hot water 1000-1800 (better in the upstairs rooms), good value; near to *Casa de Santa Lucía*, **E** *Posada Asjemenou*, Calle del Arco No 31 near La Merced, T 322865, nice gardens, friendly, popular with tour groups; **F** *Posada El Refugio*, 4 C Poniente 28, with or without showers, hot water, popular, cooking facilities, laundry facilities, secure parking Q2; **E** *Posada de Doña Angelina*, 4 C Poniente 33, with hot shower, F without (rooms in new part more expensive, but good), noisy, near market and bus station. **E** *Posada Landivar*, 5 C Poniente 23, close to bus station, safe, hot water all the time, clothes washing facilities, rec, but little privacy and noisy pm and early am. Opposite is **D** *Don Valentino*, 5 C Poniente 28, T 320384, clean, with bath; **E** *Posada La Merced*, 7 Av Norte, 43A, no sign, hot shower, clean, rec; **E-F** *Primavera*, 3 C Poniente near Alameda de Santa Lucia and bus station, clean and friendly, good value; **E** *Posada Pedro de Alvarado*, 4 C Poniente 27, above gas station, nr bus station, with bath, cheaper without, clean, laundry and cooking facilities, see also **Language Schools** below; **F** *Posada Ruiz*, Alameda de Santa Lucía 17, clean, basic, friendly, good café opposite, near bus station; **F** *Posada Ruiz No 2*, 2 Calle Poniente between 6 and 7 Av Norte, hot water, safe, busy.

F *Hospedaje El Pasaje*, Alameda de Santa Lucía 3, clean, friendly, washing facilities, will store luggage for US$0.50, doors shut at 0100, good view of volcanoes from roof, rec; **F** *Pensión El Arco*, 5 Av N between 1 and 2 C Poniente, clean, shared bath, hot shower, quiet, good value, single rooms available; **E** *Placido*, Calle del Desengaño, 3 blocks from Parque Central, cheaper rates for 3 nights or more, clean, friendly, good, not all rooms have hot water, beautiful courtyard complete with parrot which will bite your toes, cooking facilities, rec; **E** *Plaza Real*, 5 Av, S of main square, basic, friendly, hot water, cheap restaurant downstairs; **F** *Colonial*, 2 C Poniente 2, picturesque, with or without bath, cheaper rates for longer stays, ask for upstairs rooms, clean (beware of dog); **F** *Posada La Antigüeñita*, 2 C Poniente, very basic; *Angélica Jiménez*, 1 C Poniente 14A, offers accommodation and meals, cheap, clean; **E-F** *Villa San Francisco*, 1 Av Sur 15, T/F 323383, clean, quiet, helpful staff, video bar upstairs, bicycle rental, rec. **G** *San Francisco*, 3 C Oriente 19, clean. Rooms, from about US$50 per month, and houses, from about US$150 per month, can be found on the noticeboard at Casa Andinista (see **Bookshops**) and sometimes advertised in the Tourist Office and in Doña Luisa's café. You do not have to be on a language course to stay with local families, it is cheap and convenient, about US$30-35 a week inc meals, and a good way of meeting local people. Look on noticeboards for rec families or ask in shops outside central area of town. Gladys Rivera, 7 C Oriente 33, very nice house with patio and roof terrace, US$30 per week with board; Martha, 2 Av Sur 53, US$48 for two, inc meals, for a week. Estela López, 1 Calle Poniente No 41A, US$35/week for room and 3 meals per day, clean, friendly. Good accommodation in Jocotenango, 15 mins' walk, 5 mins in kombi (on road to Chimaltenango), Doña Marina's, 13 C 1-69, Colonia los Llanos; Carmen Urrutia, 12 C 1-69, Colonia Los Llanos, Jocotenango, T 322216, excellent house and food.

Camping Ask at the Tourist Office or at *Doña Luisa's* for possibilities.

Restaurants In several of the more expensive hotels. *El Sereno*, 6 C Poniente 30 (T 320073), well-prepared meals in beautifully-reconstructed colonial-style house, open 1200-1500, 1830-2200 Wed to Sun, expensive but highly rec, reservations advised, especially Sun lunch (children under 8 not served), chamber music recitals often on Mon and Tues, art exhibitions, handicrafts and old books on display and for sale. *Welten*, 4 C Oriente 21, not cheap but very good, interesting food in a delightful garden setting, reservations T 320630, closed Tues, also shows films most evenings. *Panadería y Pastelería Doña Luisa Xicotencatl* ('*Doña Luisa's*'), 4 C Oriente 12, 1½ blocks E of the Plaza, cable TV, a popular meeting place with an excellent bulletin board, serves pies and bread, breakfasts, ice cream, good coffee, but meals and service criticized in 1993; *Café Mistral* (opposite *Doña Luisa's*), for good food, soup and pasta rec, good cocktails, *licuados*, juices and snacks, satellite TV shows CNN. *Café de las Américas*, 5 C y 6 Av, best cakes and chocolates in town, though others now claim *La Cenicienta* on Av 5 Norte, takes that honour, eg cinnamon roll, New York cheesecake, etc. Near Plaza are *La Estrella*, 5 C Poniente No 6, Chinese and other food; *Café Flor*, 4 Av Sur, good, helpful owners, Mexican food, and *El Churrasco*, steakhouse, 4 C Poniente. *Katok*, 4 Av Norte 7, small patio, good food; *Martedino*, 4 C, between Av 5 and 6, consistently good cheap Italian food; *El Mesón Panza Verde*, 5 Av Sur 19, expensive but excellent (has 4 excellent rooms to let, D range). *El Oasis*, 7 Av Norte, European dishes, good brunch on Sundays, challenge the owner to a game of darts and he will offer you a beer. *Su Chow*, 5 Av Norte near La Merced, good and inexpensive; *Fonda de la Calle Real*, 5 Av Norte No5, speciality is *queso fundido*, guitar trio on Sun evenings, good; *Quesos y Vino*, 5 Av Norte 31A, good Italian food, open late; *El Capuchino*, 6 Av, between C 4 and 5, good Italian food and salads, try the garlic spaghetti, friendly English-speaking owner from Philadelphia, has US cable TV; *Café Opera*, 6 Av Norte y 2 C Poniente, Italian owned, good food and atmosphere; *Angeletti*, 5 C Poniente 18 also good Italian; *Emilio*, on 4 C Poniente (great noodles), and *Gran Muralla* opposite, both sell reasonable Chinese food; *El Peregrino*, 4 Av Norte, rec; as is *Luna Llena*, 6 Av Norte 32. *San Carlos*, on main square, sells good set meals; *Café Jardín*, on W side of main square, good value, nice atmosphere; *Hamburguesa Gigante* on main square, cheap; *Panchoy's*, 6 Av near 4 C, good beef and fondue; *Comedor Veracruz* in the market, good; *Asjemenou*, 5 C Poniente No 4, serves Italian dishes, good food, very small, therefore always full, slow service, but rec; *Lina*, near market on Alameda de Santa Lucía, serves good, cheap meals; *Santa Bárbara*, 4 C Oriente 53, 'super asados', seafood, grilled meats, etc, music, good for breakfast too, rec. *Sueños del Quetzal*, 5 Av Norte 3, upstairs, vegetarian, Cable TV, vegetarian tamales, good breakfast, message board; *Café/Restaurant Wiener Terraza*, Austrian and Guatemalan food, Alameda Santa Lucía and

C 3-4, near bus station, good value, jazz, good vegetarian selection; also on Alameda Santa Lucía *Peroleto*, for fruits and yoghurt; *Tostaduría Antigua*, 6 Av Sur No 12A, coffee shop, pies, cheap, friendly American owner; *Rainbow Room*, 7 Av, 6 C, bookshop with vegetarian food, popular with travellers, see under **Bookshops**; *La Condesa*, W side of main plaza, through *Casa del Conde* bookshop, favourite gringo hangout, capuccino, breakfast, desserts, friendly, not cheap; *Don Diego's*, 1C Poniente with Alameda Santa Lucía, cheap, good Tex Mex food; *Pastelería Okrassa*, 6 Av, C, 1-2, for meat and fruit pies. *Panificadora Colombia*, 4 C Poniente 34, close to bus terminal, poor breakfasts. Good coffee roasted and brewed at 6 Av Sur No 12A, *Tostaduría*, Antigua, *tinca* tour available proceeds to workers.

Note Some establishments have introduced microwave ovens; make sure your food is piping hot.

Bars *Bar Picasso*, Av 7 Norte, popular; *Latinos*, nearby, (live music occasionally, good dance floor), also *Abstracto*, (diagonally opp *Picasso*) loud music, crowded after 2200, party atmosphere. *Moscas y Miel*, 2 blocks from Parque Central, open late. *Jazz Gruta*, near Post Office, 2 blocks N of bus station, live jazz. *Bar Chimenea*, 4 C Poniente, nr main square, large dance floor, cheap drinks (opp is *Los Pollos*, 24-hr takeaway, 'lousy food'). *Macondo*, C del Arco, 'English-style pub', good Western and local music, rec.

Market There is an extensive daily market, particularly on Mon, Thurs and Sat (best) next to the bus terminal at end of 4 Calle Poniente, W of Alameda Santa Lucía. Good handmade textiles, pottery and silver, but you will probably pay less in Guatemala City or elsewhere.

Shopping Mercado de Artesanías is at 7 Av between 4 and 3 Calles (in La Compañía ruins, touristy). Main market is by the bus terminal. *Casa de Artes* for traditional textiles and handicrafts, antiques, jewellery, etc, 4 Av Sur. *Casa de los Gigantes* for textiles and handicrafts and *Concha's Footloom*, both opposite San Francisco Church. *Fábrica de Tejidos Maya*, 1 Av Norte, C, 1-2, makes and sells good cheap textiles, wall hangings, etc. The *Utatlán* cooperative on 5 Av Norte specializes in good handicrafts and antiques (expensive). Doña María Gordillo's sweet (candy) shop on 4 C Oriente is famous throughout the country. There are many other stores selling textiles, handicrafts, antiques, silver and jade on 5 Av Norte and 4 C Oriente (*Ixchel* on 4 C Oriente sells blankets from Momostenango; *Kashlan P'ot*, in Galería La Fuente, 4 C Oriente 14, T 322676). *Galería Klaske*, 3 C Poniente, good quality. *Galería de Arte Estípite*, 3 Av Norte 9-A, Central American artists, will ship works of art abroad. A number of jade-carving factories may be visited, eg *Jades, SA*, 4 C Oriente 34 (branches on same street Nos 1 and 12), open daily 0900-2100 (also coffee shop), *La Casa del Jade*, 4 C Oriente 3 (open daily 0900-1800) or *JC Hernández*, 2 Av Sur 77, *San José*, Calzada Santa Lucía N, No 23 A. Jade is sold on the Parque Central on Sats more cheaply. Painted ceramics can be obtained from private houses in 1 Av del Chajón (Calle San Sebastián) near Calle Ancha, and glazed pottery from the *Fábrica Montiel*, N of Calle Ancha on the old road to San Felipe. Near San Felipe is the silver factory where many of the silver ornaments sold in Antigua and Guatemala City are made. Various local handicrafts at *Hecht House* in the same area. Ceramic birds at handicrafts shop in the *Posada de Don Rodrigo* (see under Hotels above). *Calzado Fase*, 6 Av Norte 61, makes made-to-measure leather boots.

Bookshops *Casa Andinista*, 4 C Oriente 5A, sells books in Spanish and English (including the *Mexico and Central American* and the *South American Handbooks*), photographs, posters, rubbings, maps (easier than the Instituto Geográfico in Guatemala City), large selection of postcards, cards, weavings from Ixil Triangle, camping gear for rent (opp *Doña Luisa's*, which sells *Time* and *Newsweek*), has photocopying machine, repeatedly recommended. *Un Poco de Todo*, on W side of Plaza, sells English language books, postcards, maps. *Librería Pensativo*, 5 Av Norte 29, good for books in Spanish about Central America. *Librería Marquense*, 6 C Poniente between 5 and 6 Av. *Rainbow Reading Room*, 7 Av Sur, No 8, 6 C, campfire in evenings with musicians, nice atmosphere, videos, secondhand books, popular with travellers. *Casa del Conde*, W side of plaza, good for books on Central America.

Car Rental Avis, 5 Av Norte between the square and the arch. Also 6 Av Norte 594.

Motorcycle hire Jopa, 6 Av Norte 3, Yamaha 225 or 175, Honda 185, ask for Juan Pablo, who is very knowledgeable about what excursions to make; US$130/week, also daily, hourly and monthly rates. Good bikes, locks, tools and helmets (in poor shape, but better than nothing) available.

Bike Hire Bicycles (US$1/hour, US$5/day) and motorcycles (US$50 for 3 days) for hire at *Jopa*, 6 Av Norte No 3. Mayan Mountain Cycle Tours offer tours around Antigua, Lake Atitlán and other areas, 6 Av Sur No 12B, T/F 323316, Spanish, English, German, French, Italian spoken, US$15 for half day with guide, US$30 full day, rec.

Bathing Non-residents may use the pool at the *Hotel Antigua* for a charge of US$4, US$7 on Sunday, (US$45/month) you may be obliged to have a buffet meal (eg breakfast) as well, also, at *Ramada Antigua* for US$3 a day, US$35 a month. Both hotels have special Sunday prices for buffet lunch, swimming and marimba band (the *Ramada* also has children's shows). At the latter, weekly and monthly rates for use of sports facilities can be negotiated. Massage and sauna at *Natura*, corner of 7 C and 5 Av, sauna US$3, massage US$5, also good restaurant. *Antigua Spa Resort*, T 311456, swimming pool, steam baths, sauna, gymnasium, jacuzzi, beauty salon. Warm mineral springs (public pool and private cubicles, less than US$1) at San Lorenzo El Tejar: Chimaltenango bus to San Luis Las Carretas (about 8 km) then 2 km walk to 'Balneario', or direct bus to San Lorenzo and a 5 minute walk, popular with local families on Sunday, good day trip by motorbike. At Jocotenango, *Fraternidad Naturista Antigua*, Calle Real 30, T 322443, with public saunas US$2, massage US$5.20, health foods, medicinal herbs, dietary advice, open Sun-Thur 0700-1800, Fri 0700-1300, closed Sat, 2 km NW of Antigua. Pool El Pilar 30 min walk on road to San Juan del Obispo, US$0.60 entrance.

Sports Karate school: Bie Sensei (Danish), 3rd degree black belt gives hour long lessons. Also Mexican black belt instructor, Alameda Santa Lucía and 2 C Poniente.

Museums Colonial Art museum, C 5 Oriente, 1/2 block from Parque Central, mostly 17-18th century religious art, well-laid out in large airy rooms round a colonial patio, US$0.05 (open Tues-Fri 0900-1600, Sat-Sun 0900-1200, 1400-1600). **Museo de Santiago** in municipal offices to N of Plaza, contains replica of 1660 printing press (original is in Guatemala City), old documents, collection of 16th-18th-century books (1500 volumes in library, open afternoons, US$0.05), and the **Museo de Armas** weapons collection. Open Mon-Fri 0900-1600, Sat and Sun 0900-1200, 1400-1600. Admission US$0.05 (free Sundays). Also small museum in **Convento de Capuchinas**. **Museum of Indian Music**, K'ojam, Calle de Recoletos 55, next to churchyard behind market, good collection of traditional musical instruments, slide shows on music and culture with free coffee, open 0930-1230, 1400-1700 Mon-Sat, US$1.

Cinemas Los Capitanes on 5 Av Sur. Showings several days a week. English films with Spanish subtitles often shown, US$0.80. Cinemala, 3 Av Norte 9, round the corner from *Doña Luisa*, good films. Also *Restaurant Welten*, above. Lots of places show videos, adverts in *Doña Luisa's* and elsewhere.

Concerts Music festival in November, excellent. The Alianza Francesa, 3 C Oriente 19, has French music on Fridays between 1600 and 2000, regular talks and slide shows, films (information from Casa Andinista or *Doña Luisa's*), also French newspapers. Concerts also at Capuchinas convent and *El Sereno* restaurant (see above).

Dance lessons Escuela de Danza Antigua, Av El Desengaño 20A, US$4/hr, private lessons also, highly rec, 1800-2000.

Exchange Lloyds Bank plc, 4 C Oriente 2 on NE corner of Plaza, Mon-Fri 0900-1500; **Banco del Agro**, N side of Plaza, same times but is also open Sat; **Banco Industrial**, 5 Av Sur 4, near Plaza, gives cash on Visa credit card at normal rates, no commission. Branch of **Banco del Agro**, Alameda Santa Lucía y 5 C, near Post Office, open 0900-1800, Mon-Sat. US dollars not obtainable. May exchange personal cheques for quetzales. Cash advances on a MasterCard were not available in 1993, only in Guatemala City.

Spanish Language Schools There are dozens, consequently Antigua is full of foreigners learning Spanish. Not all schools are officially authorized by the Ministry of Education and Inguat. Rates depend on how many hours tuition you have a week and vary from school to school; as a rough guide the fee for 4 hrs a day, 5 days a week starts at US$2.50 per hour. You will benefit more from the classes if you have done some study before you arrive. There are guides who take students around the schools and charge a commission (make sure this is not added to your account). They may tackle tourists on the bus from the capital. Before making any commitment, find somewhere to stay and shop around at your leisure. Some points to bear in mind: accommodation with families is often linked to a particular school so be sure about one before you pay a week in advance for the other. Average accommodation rates with a family with three meals a day are US$30-40 per week (1993). In some cases lodging is group accommodation; if you prefer single accommodation, ask for it. All schools offer one-to-one tuition; if you can meet the teachers in advance, so much the better, but don't let the director's waffle distract you from asking pertinent questions. Paying more does not mean you get better teaching and the standard of teachers varies within schools as well as between schools. Some schools are cheaper in the afternoons than in the mornings. Beware of 'hidden extras' and be clear on arrangements for study books. Some schools have an inscription fee. Several schools use a portion of their income to fund social projects. Latest indications are that learning Spanish in Quezaltenango or Huehuetenango is preferable to Antigua if you want to avoid Antigua's international atmosphere.

We list only those schools of which we have received favourable reports from students: **Proyecto Lingüístico Francisco Marroquín**, 4 Av Sur 4, T/F 320406, Apartado Postal 237, 03901 Antigua; **Sevilla Academia de Español**, Apartado Postal 380, 6 C Oriente No 3, Parque La Unión, T/F 323609; **CSA (Academia Cristiana de Español)**, 6 Av Norte No 15, Apartado Postal 320, T/F 320367; **Maya**, 5 C Poniente 20, T/F 320656; **Nahual**, 6 Av Norte 9, T 322548; **Tecún Umán**, 6 C Poniente 34, T/F 322792; **Quiché**, 3 Av Sur No 15A, T 320575, F 322893; **Español Dinámico**, 6 Av Norte 63, T 322440; **Jiménez**, near La Merced, 1 C Poniente 41; **Don Pedro de Alvarado**, 4 C Poniente No 27, T 322266 (also a hotel, see above); **Instituto Antigüeño de Español**, 1 C Poniente No 33, T 322682; **El Quetzal**, 7 C Poniente 7, Apartado Postal 426, T 323331; **Arcoíris**, 7 C Oriente No 19, T 322933; **Academia de Español Cervantes**, 5 C Poniente No 42, T/F 320635, Apartado Postal 427; **Centro Lingüístico Atabal**, 1 Av Norte 6, T 320791. **Popal Vuh Professional Language School**, 7 Av Norte No 82, PO Box 230, Roberto King and Lesvia Arana Gallardo (directors); **La Enseñanza**, Calle El Portal 1, T 7320692, run by Aura and Paty Miranda; **Hombres de Maíz**, Callejón Camposeco 5, 2 blocks from La Merced run by Rosa and Nery Méndez; **Don Quijote**, 9 C Poniente 7, T 320651; **Academia de Español Colonial** (ACADEC), Calzada Santa Lucía Sur, Pasaje Matheu No 7, Director Alvaro Coronado Estrada; **Alianza Lingüística 'Cano'**, 2 Av del Chajón No 8A, PO Box 366. Highly rec private teacher, Julia Solís, 5 C Poniente 36, another is María Elena Estrada, *La Ceniciento*, 5 Av Norte 7, a third, Sandra Rosales, 7 C Oriente 21; also Amalia Jarquín, Av El Desengaño No 11, T 322377. Also check advertisements in Doña Luisa's and the Tourist Office (Director helpful) for private lessons (about US$2 per hour).

Laundromat 5 Av Sur 24. Also 5 Calle Poniente, between 5 and 6 Av. **Summer**, 7 Av Norte No 78 and other locations, About US$3 for 4.5 kg of laundry, ready in 3 hrs.

Post Office, Telephone, Cables Post Office at Alameda Santa Lucía and 4 C, near market (local cables from here); *lista de correos* keeps letters for a month. Boxes of books up to 2 kg can be sent from the post office, but other packages weighing more than 2 kg must be posted from Guatemala City (do not seal parcels before going to the capital). There are strict rules on how to wrap parcels, see instructions at counter 3. International cables in Guatel building, SW corner of main square. You can make collect calls from a public phone to some countries (see **Post and Telecommunications** in **Information for Visitors**). Some hotels and restaurants will also let you use their fax machines to send and receive messages eg *Villa San Francisco*, 1 Av Sur; (*Maya Communications* – linked to similar offices in Panajachel and Quezaltenango); *Sueños del Quetzal* restaurant. For a small charge you can phone abroad, leave the number and be called back. *Conexión* is an electronic mail service, fax, telex, EMail, telegrams, send and receive, message service, translations, word processing, computers available for customers' use, 4 C Oriente No 14, T 323768, F 320602.

Research Library The Centro de Investigaciones Regionales de Mesoamérica (Cirma), 5 C Oriente 5, offers good facilities for graduate students and professional scholars of Middle American history, anthropology and archaeology.

Public Library On E side of Plaza, due to reopen late 1992. The Granai y Townson library, on W side of Plaza, is open to the public, Mon-Fri 1000-1200, 1400-1900.

Doctor Dr Julio R Aceituno, 2 C Poniente, No 7, T 320512, speaks English; Dr José del Valle Monge, 8 C Oriente 5, good English and German, US$4 for consultation; Dr Joel Alvarado, 4 C Poniente 21, keeps regular hours and a quick cure for dysentery. Dr Sergio Castañeda, 6

Sevilla
ACADEMIA DE ESPAÑOL

Intensive one-to-one Spanish instruction
- ■ ONE teacher – one student
- ■ FREE activities programme
- ■ LEARN at your own pace
- ■ LIVE with a Guatemalan family
- ■ 4 - 8 hours' intensive study daily for any number of weeks

100% TRUE LANGUAGE IMMERSION
SEVILLA Spanish Academy, 6a Calle Oriente #3, Apartado Postal 380, Antigua Guatemala

Av Norte 52, rec by Alianza Francesa. Centro Diagnóstico, 4 Av near the police station will test for amoebae, US$6. **Dentist** Dr Asturias, a few doors up from *Doña Luisa's*.

Tourist Offices E corner of Palace of the Captains-General, S side of Plaza (street plan available, US$0.10); English and a little German spoken. Open: 0800-1800 (7 days a week), T 320763. The tourist office can arrange guides for visits to monuments for between US$3 and US$6 per day. Ask here for campsite details (there are no caravan parks). *Turansa*, 9 Calle y Salida a Vieja Antigua, T 320011/15, good for flights, eg to Tikal.

Travel Agents *Connection Travel*, at *Ramada Antigua*, rec. *Tivoli Travel*, above *Un Poco de Todo* bookshop, highly rec, helpful with any travel problem, speak English, French, Spanish, reconfirm tickets, good value tours. *Ceprotur*, 4 C, W of main square, friendly, helpful, speak English. *Centro de Viajes*, 5 Av Norte, 15A 2nd block away from plaza, rec (Roberto and Claudia). *Adventure Travel Center-Viareal*, 4 C Oriente No 7, T/F 323228, weekend trips to Guatemalan destinations (especially Río Dulce sailing, river and volcano trips), El Salvador, Honduras; *Total Petén*, 6 C Poniente No 6, T 320478, good service to El Petén. Elizabeth Bell, *Antigua Tours*, 4 Av Norte No 25, T 320228, F 320602, author of *Antigua Guatemala: An Illustrated History of the City and its Monuments* (9th ed, 1993), offers walking tours of the city and 45 min slide lecture (in USA contact Section 710/Guatemala, 2898 NW 79th Avenue, Miami, FL33122). Shop around for tours.

A bi-weekly magazine, *The Classifieds Revue* (4 C Oriente No 14, T/F 320082), has information, articles and advertisements in English, there.

Buses Half-hourly from **Guatemala City**, from 0700 to 1900, US$0.50, 45 mins, from several locations: Av Bolívar, 32 Calle, Zona 3, 2 Av 19-62, Zona 1, C, 15 between Avs 3 y 4, Zona 1 and C 21, Av 2-3 (at least 10 bus lines, ask your hotel in the capital which is nearest). Buses to Guatemala City leave from Alameda Santa Lucía near the market, with the same time and schedules as buses to Antigua. To **Chimaltenango**, on the Pan-American Highway, hourly, US$0.25, for connections to Los Encuentros (for Lake Atitlán and Chichicastenango), Cuatro Caminos (for Quezaltenango) and Huehuetenango (for the Mexican border). It is possible to get to Chichicastenango and back by bus in a day. Direct buses to **Panajachel** Wed, Fri and Sun, US$2, 2½ hrs; tourist minibus costs US$12. To **Escuintla**, Grenadiña and Ruta América, at 0600, 0630 and 1300, 2 hrs, US$0.60. Buses and minibuses also to nearby villages.

Buses Inter-Hotel y Turismo run a transfer service (1 hr) from Antigua to **La Aurora airport**, at 0440, 1100 and 1500, starting at *Ramada*, calling at *Antigua Hotel*, *Posada Don Rodrigo*, *Doña Luisa's* and *Hotel Aurora*; for tickets T 320011/15, US$7. Tickets available at *Doña Luisa's* and Casa Andinista. Other services will collect, see noticeboards, US$5. Direct buses to Panajachel from Inter-Hotel y Turismo on Tues, Thur and Sun. Turismo Yax Be runs a similar service. Taxi to Guatemala City US$20, same rate to airport.

Excursions To *Ciudad Vieja*, 5½ km SW at the foot of Agua volcano. In 1541, after days of torrential rain, an immense mud-slide came down the mountain and overwhelmed the city. Alvarado's widow, newly elected Governor after his death, was among the drowned; you can see the ruins of the first town hall. Today it is a mere village (*Hospedaje Shigualita*, cheap, at S end of village), but with a handsome church, founded 1534, one of the oldest in Central America. *Fiesta*: December 5-9. Bus US$0.10. At *San Juan del Obispo*, not far, is the restored palace of Francisco Marroquín, first bishop of Guatemala, now a convent. The parish church has some fine 16th century images. Ask behind the church if you wish to hire horses.

Behind San Juan del Obispo, on side of Agua volcano, is the charming village of *Santa María de Jesús*, with a beautiful view of Antigua. In the early morning, there are good views of all 3 volcanoes 2 km back down the road towards Antigua. Beautiful *huipiles* are worn, made and sold from a couple of stalls, or ask at the shops on the plaza. Frequent buses from Antigua on main market days US$0.10 (Mon, Thurs, Sat) otherwise 0700 only; last bus returns at 1700. *Fiesta* on 10 Jan, accommodation at *municipalidad* **G**; **E** *Hospedaje y Comedor El Oasis* on road to Antigua has clean, pleasant rooms; **F** *San José*, basic and noisy. The road, very steep in places, high clearance vehicle necessary, continues on to the main road to Escuintla at Palín. Excellent views of Pacaya Volcano.

About 3 km NW of Ciudad Vieja is *San Antonio Aguas Calientes*, a village with many small shops selling locally made textiles; *Carolina's Textiles* is recommended for a fine selection, while just down the road *Alida* has a shop almost as large. Carmelo and Zoila Guarán give weaving lessons for US$1 per hr, as do Rafaela Godínez, very experienced, and Felipa López Zamora, on the way to the church, 30m from bus station (bring your own food and she will cook it with you), US$2 daily. Sra María Natividad Hernández is also recommended. You will need some time (say several afternoons) to make some progress. *Fiestas*: 16-21 January; 13 June; 1 November. Frequent buses from Antigua.

Volcanoes The three nearby volcanoes provide incomparable views of the surrounding countryside and are best climbed on a clear night with a full moon or with a very early morning start. Altitude takes its toll and plenty of time should be allowed for the ascents. Plenty of water must be carried and the summits are cold. Ankle boots, preferably full climbing boots recommended, especially on Fuego to cope with the cinders. Descents take from a third to a half of the ascent time. Tourist Office in Antigua helpful. Enquire there about conditions (both human and natural) before setting out. There is a volcano-climbing club: Club de Andinismo, Chigag, Volcano Tours, Daniel Ramírez Ríos (helpful), 6 Av Norte, No 34, Antigua, T/F 323343, the only (1993) guide certified by the Guatemalan Tourist Commission (he has a guest house, *Albergue Andinista*, with use of kitchen). Recommended for volcano tours are Quetzal Expeditions on Alameda Santa Lucía 6, T 320892, Volcanoes Tour, 6 Av Norte No 9, T 322548, ICO's Expeditions, Calle del Desengaño 2, and Carlos Chiroy, of Popeye Tours, 4 C Poniente No 38, T 320748. Prices from US$6/8 pp. **Warning** Robberies and rapes have occurred even where large parties are climbing these volcanoes. See also under Pacaya at the end of this section. Check with the tourist office before climbing.

Agua Volcano 3,760m, the easiest of the three (or the least difficult as one traveller described it!), is climbed from Santa María de Jesús (directions to start of ascent in village). Crater (with football field) with small shelter (dirty), which is/was a shrine, and 5 antennae at top. Fine views (though not guaranteed) of Volcán de Fuego; 3 to 5 hrs' climb if you are fit, 2 hrs down. Make sure you get good directions; there is an old avalanche you have to cross and regain the trail, if you do not you may get lost. To get the best views before the clouds cover the summit, it is best to stay at the radio station at the top. Climbing at night is recommended by torchlight/moon with help from fireflies. Bus from Antigua to Santa María de Jesús at 0500, later on Sundays (irregular) allows you to climb the volcano and return to Antigua in one day. Guided tours US$10; information from *El Oasis* restaurant.

Agua can also be climbed from *Alotenango*, a village between Agua and Fuego volcanoes (*fiesta* 18-20 January), S of Ciudad Vieja, 9 km from Antigua. Looking at the market building, take the left route up; turn left at the T junction, then first right and up. Only two decision points: take the right fork, then the left. It is not advisable to descend Agua towards Palín (SE—**see p 487**) as there is precipitous forest, steep bluffs, dry watercourses which tend to drop away vertically and a route is hard to plot.

Acatenango Volcano 3,976m. The best trail (W of the one shown on the 1:50,000 topographic map) heads S at La Soledad (15 km W of Ciudad Vieja on Route 10) 300m before the road (Route 5) turns right to Acatenango (good *pensión*, G, with good cheap meals). A small plateau, La Meseta on maps, known locally as El Conejón, provides a good camping site two-thirds of the way up (3-4 hrs). From here it is a further 3-4 hrs harder going to the top. There is a shelter, holding up to 15 people, on the lower of the 2 summits. Excellent views of the nearby (lower) active crater of Fuego and you can watch the activity of Pacaya at night. To reach Acatenango, take a bus heading for Yepocapa or Acatenango (village) and get off at Soledad, or from Antigua to San Miguel Dueñas, and then hitch to Soledad. Alternatively, take an early bus to Ciudad Vieja from where you can hitch to Finca Concepción Calderas (bus Ciudad Vieja-Calderas 0645 Sat only), then 1 hr walk to La Soledad. Be sure to take the correct track going down (no water on the way). Guided tours US$14.

Fuego Volcano 3,763m, for experienced hikers only. Can be climbed either via Volcán de Acatenango (sleeping on the col between the two volcanoes where there is a primitive shelter), up to 12 hrs hiking, or from Alotenango. For the first hour or so, until the trees, take a guide, or follow these instructions (given by Will Paine, Maidstone): down from Alotenango market place, over river, and at the concrete gateway turn right, up the main track. Ignoring the initial left fork, plantation/orchard entrances and all 90° turnoffs, take the next three left forks and then the next two right forks. Do not underestimate water needed for the climb. It is 7 hrs ascent with an elevation gain of 2,400m. A very hard walk, both up and down, and easy to lose the trail. Steep, loose cinder slopes, very tedious in many places. It is possible to camp about three quarters of the way up in a clearing. Fuego has had frequent dangerous eruptions in recent years though generally not without warning. Check in Antigua before attempting to climb.

At the village of **San Felipe** (US$0.05 by bus, or 15 min walk from Antigua) is a figure of Christ which people from all over Latin America come to see. *Restaurant El Prado* is rec. There is a small silver workshop which is worth visiting. Robbery in the village reported.

Three Indian villages N of Guatemala City are easily reached by bus. At **Chinautla** (9½ km), the village women turn out hand-made pottery. Eight km beyond is another small village, **San Antonio las Flores**: good walking to a small lake (70 mins) for bathing. **Santo Domingo Xenacoj** can be reached by bus from the Zona 4 terminal, Guatemala City. It has a fine old church and produces good *huipiles*.

At **San Lucas Sacatepéquez**, the Fábrica de Alfombras Típicas Kakchikel at Km 29½, Carretera Roosevelt (usually known as the Pan-American Highway), will make rugs for you. Restaurants: *La Parrilla, La Cabaña, Nim-Guaa, La Diligencia*, and *El Ganadero*, all good for steaks; *Delicias del Mar* for seafood. 5 km beyond San Lucas is **Santiago Sacatepéquez**, whose *fiesta* on Nov 1 is characterized by colourful kite-flying. Market Wed and Fri.

A most interesting short trip by car or bus from the capital is to **San Pedro Sacatepéquez**, 22½ km NW. Good view over Guatemala valley and mountains to the N. Its inhabitants, having rebuilt their village after the 1976 earthquake, are returning to the weaving for which the village was renowned before the disaster. Bus from Guatemala City, Zona 4 bus terminal, US$0.20, 1 hr. *Fiestas*: Carnival before Lent; 29 June (rather rough, much drinking) and great ceremony on 15 March when passing the Image of Christ from one officeholder to the next, and in honour of the same image in May.

6½ km beyond, through flower-growing area, is **San Juan Sacatepéquez**, where textiles are also made.

28 km N of San Juan Sacatepéquez is **Mixco Viejo**, the excavated site of a post-classic Mayan fortress, which spans 14 hilltops, including 12 groups of pyramids. Despite earthquake damage it is worth a visit, recommended. It was the 16th century capital of the Pokomam Maya; there are a few buses a day from the Zona 4 bus terminal in Guatemala City, departures at 1000 and 1700. The bus goes to Pachalum; ask to be dropped at the entrance. A new bridge now enables you to reach the site.

The village of **Rabinal** was founded in 1537 by Las Casas as the first of his 'peaceful conquest' demonstrations to Emperor Charles V. It has a handsome 16th century church (under reconstruction), Sun market interesting; brightly lacquered gourds, beautiful *huipiles* and embroidered napkins, all very cheap. The local pottery is exceptional. Local festival on 16 Feb with mask dancers. *Pensión Motagua*, F, friendly, has bar attached, not rec for women travelling alone. *Hospedaje Caballero*, 1 C, 4-02, F without bath, nearby. *Restaurant El Cevichazo* has good food. Bus from Guatemala City 5½ hrs, a beautiful, occasionally heart-stopping ride. Buses go N through Rabinal to Cobán (see p 465).

The town of **Salamá**, capital of Baja Verapaz, is normally reached from the capital through El Rancho on the Atlantic Highway, paved all the way. Alternatively, it can be reached from San Juan Sacatepéquez and Rabinal through San Miguel Chicaj along another road which offers stunning views (bus Rabinal-Salamá US$0.50, takes 1-1½ hrs; Salamá-Guatemala, US$1.60). Its church contains carved gilt altarpieces. Market day is Monday; worth a visit. **E** *Hotel Tezulutlán*, best, with bath, cheaper without, good restaurant but service a bit slow, Ruta 4, 4-99, Zona 1, just off plaza; **F** pp *Pensión Verapaz*, 3 C, 8-26 and **F** pp *Hospedaje Juárez*, 10 Av, 5-55, both with bath, cheaper without. Exchange at Banco de Guatemala, 5 Av, 6-21; *Restaurante Las Tejas*, opp Shell station as you enter town from the E, good, specialty is *caldo de chunto* (turkey soup).

Another popular excursion is to the still active **Pacaya** volcano (last major eruption January 1987, but some continuing dangerous activity in 1994). Tours are available for US$8-14, depending on the number in the party, with Ceprotur, Tivoli and other Antiguan tour agencies, 1400-2230 (Popeye Tours 4 C Poniente No 38, Antigua, has been rec, 2 guides and security guard in small vans, proper torches for everybody. Tours on large buses do not always provide enough guides/torches and people get lost on the descent). It can be reached by private vehicle, the road from Antigua is unpaved. Alternatively take a bus from the central bus station in Zona 4 to **San Vicente de Pacaya**, 0700 and 1530 (US$0.35); then one must walk to **San Francisco** (1½ hrs); or Guatemala City-Palín bus to turn-off to San Vicente, wait for bus to San Vicente and San Francisco, last at 1800 (buses from San Francisco to junction on Guatemala City-Escuintla road 0500, 0900, 1200 and 1500). The road to San Francisco is not easy to drive, even in 4WD. From San Francisco, walk up 1 hr to the TV station at the first ridge. At a push, a 4WD will take you almost to the antennae, 20 min from the *meseta*, the best viewing spot. It is sometimes not possible to go to the old cone (2 hrs) above the active cone because of the continuing eruptions; in this case, the eruptions can be seen clearly from the first ridge, slightly below the active one. Check the situation in advance in San Francisco for both climbing and camping (if safe, take torch, warm clothing and a handkerchief to filter dust and fumes). Robert Francis (1991) strongly recommends going up overnight with a good camera, tent and sleeping bag needed, camp at a respectful distance from the cone or at a local home, all arranged by a guide from ICO's Expeditions (see above). To get good photographs, a tripod or similar requires for exposure 8 seconds at f2.8 on 100 ASA film. Beware cold and cloud; however, you can warm your hands on the lava blocks! Sunrise comes with awesome views over the desolate black lava field to the distant Pacific (airborne dust permitting) and the peaks of Fuego, Acatenango and Agua. An Austrian traveller (1989) recommended leaving San Francisco at 0500 for the sunrise near the cone. 'An unforgettable experience in a magical world.' He was offered coffee, tortillas and beans on his return by his hosts of the previous night. People do scramble up from the 40-metre view-point to watch the venting in the crater below ('scary but unmissable'). Be warned, though, that this can be dangerous.

If you miss the last bus back to Palín or San Vicente, you can stay overnight with Luis the Mexican in San Francisco (a good guide), or you can sleep in the porch at the school in El Cedro, the village below San Francisco, or in a house at the entrance to San Vicente (US$1), or with other locals. Another recommended guide is Salvador, whose house is near the bus stop for Guatemala. **Warning**: In February 1991 a group of over 20 foreigners was robbed at gunpoint, and 3 women were raped, by a gang. The incident created outrage and, although strong representations were made to the authorities, at the time little action was taken to improve safety on Pacaya. Tourists should seek advice before visiting this volcano. Climbers since then have not reported any molestation or threats to safety. Any attack should be reported to your embassy.

GUATEMALA CITY TO THE CARIBBEAN (2)

The Atlantic Highway is the main road to Guatemala's Caribbean coast with its two main ports. From Puerto Barrios there is access by the Jungle Trail to Honduras; also to Lake Izabal in which is the Biotopo del Manatí. Another Biotopo, of the national quetzal bird, is found just off an alternative route to Lake Izabal, through Alta Verapaz (via Cobán: nearby are natural rock formations at Lanquín and Semuc Champey). Easier routes to Honduras go through Chiquimula, either to Esquipulas, or to the Maya site at Copán across the border.

From the SE corner of Guatemala City (Zona 10) the Pan-American Highway leads out toward the Salvadorean border. After a few kilometres a turning to **San José Pinula** (G *Hotel San Francisco*, large rooms, no running water, but they will fill a tub for you; most people don't stay the whole night; one other hotel, poorer) leads to an unpaved winding branch road, 203 km long through fine scenery to **Mataquescuintla** (G *Pensión Olimpia*, small rooms, clean, cold showers, good value), Jalapa, San Pedro Pinula, San Luis Jilotepeque, and Ipala to Chiquimula (see p 468). This road is impassable in the wet; buses San José Pinula to

Mataquescuintla at 1130, and Mataquescuintla-Jalapa, several. It was the route to the great shrine at Esquipulas, but visitors now use the Atlantic Highway to Río Hondo and the new road to Honduras past Zacapa (**see p 467**) and Chiquimula.

Jalapa, capital of Jalapa Department, 114 km from Guatemala City, is set in an attractive valley at 1,380m. Bus to Esquipulas 0900, 7½ hrs, US$1.60; to Chiquimula, 8 hrs. Population 42,000.

Hotel F *Méndez*, 1 C 'A', 1-27, Zona 2, T 424835, 1 block from market, hot water, towels, rec; *Pensión Casa del Viajero*, 1 Av 0-70, T 424086, clean, bath, warm water. At least two other *hospedajes*. **Restaurant** *Casa Real*, one block from market, reasonable prices, pleasant.

The Atlantic Highway from Guatemala City to the Caribbean port of Puerto Barrios (Route CA9) is fully paved and gives access to the Honduran border, Cobán and the Petén. Note that the distances between filling stations are greater than in other parts of the country. At Km 19 the San Juan bridge was destroyed by URGN guerrillas in March 1994. The army has put in a one-way pontoon bridge and is urgently rebuilding the main bridge. There were long delays to traffic in mid-1994 as there is no reliable alternative route. Along the way is **Sanarate** (**F** *Hotel Las Vegas*, 1 Av 1-21), **El Progreso** (also known as Guastatoya—**E** *Hotel Guastatoya*, T 341589, bath, swimming pool, good restaurant, relaxed, friendly), **Teculután** (one hotel), and Santa Cruz (for some reason a whole clutch of hotels). Shortly after Santa Cruz is Río Hondo (**see p 467**) and the turn off for the new road to Esquipulas and the Honduran border.

The branch road to Cobán is at **El Rancho**, Km 85, between El Progreso and Teculután; this is a better alternative to the route through Rabinal and Salamá (**see p 462**). N of El Rancho is San Agustín, the entrance for the **Sierra de las Minas** National Park. Get a *permiso* in Salamá at the Oficina Defensores Naturales.

Between Cobán and Guatemala City at Km 163, 4 km S of Purulhá and 53 km from Cobán, is the **Biotopo del Quetzal**, a reserve established by Mario Dary Rivera, a biologist of San Carlos university, for the preservation of the quetzal bird and its cloud-forest habitat; trails in the jungle.

Mike Shawcross writes: 'I saw my first quetzal late in 1980, and consider the sighting a highlight of all my time here; it really is an incredibly beautiful bird. A series of trails, taking up to 3 hrs to cover on foot, lead more than 300m up the mountainside'. The reserve is in two parts. The lower part has two trails, the other is inaccessible except with permission. Most animals have naturally retreated from tourists and buses in the former to the latter. Nevertheless, there are now reported to be increasing numbers of quetzales in the Biotopo, but still very elusive. They feed on the fruit of the aguacatillo and guaramo trees early in the morning or early eveningl. Ask for advice from the rangers. Open 0600 to 1600, nominally free but you are asked for a donation of US$1 pp. (Bus Cobán-Purulhá, US$0.50; from Guatemala City, take a Cobán bus and ask to be let out at the Biotopo; more difficult to get a bus back to the capital, last one at 1600; bus El Rancho-Biotopo, US$0.80, 1 hr).

At Km 156 is the new hotel and restaurant **B** *Posada Montaña del Quetzal*, highly rec, café, bar, swimming pool, gardens (T 351805 in Guatemala City for reservations although they may get lost by inefficient front desk staff, book in advance, especially at weekends). 100m N of the entrance to the Biotopo is the **E** *Hospedaje Los Ranchitos*, in 3-room, 10-bed cabins, fairly basic, also 2 stone houses each with 4 double rooms with bathrooms, spacious, clean, hot water, limited restaurant; they allow you to cook your own food in the kitchen. The *Hospedaje* is a good place to see the bird (not frequent, but most likely in the early morning August to Nov). The *farmacía* at **Purulhá** has rooms to let, F. *Comedor San Antonio* in Purulhá, simple meals. Electricity is a problem, a torch is handy in this area.

Tactic, on the main Guatemala City-Cobán road, is famous for beautiful *huipiles* and for its 'living well', in which the water becomes agitated as one approaches. (Ask for the Pozo Vivo; it is along a path which starts opp the gas station on the main road—now reported dirty and disappointing.) Colonial church with Byzantine-influenced paintings, well worth a visit. Market Sun and Thur. *Fiesta* 3rd week in August. (**G** *Hotel Sulmy*, nice, clean, meals, US$0.75; **G** *Pensión Central*, clean, hot showers, cheap meals; and **G** *Hospedaje Pocompchi*, less good) Doña Rogelia sells *huipiles* made in the surrounding area, and the silversmith near her shop will make silver buttons etc to order. The Cooperativa Origen Maya Pocom 'Ixoq Aj Kemool', is an association of 60 weavers just W of El Calvario church on road to Cobán, open Tues, Thur, Sun, 0900-1700 for sales, orders and to watch the women weaving.

15 km NW of Tactic is **San Cruz Verapaz**, at the junction with the road to Uspantán (**see p 503**) which has a fine 16th century church and a festival 1-4 May. **C** *Hotel Park*, on main road, T 514539, opened 1993, 48 rooms, some bungalows, restaurant, bar, excellent gardens small zoo, Italian owner, rec. 6 km W towards Uspartán is **San Cristóbal Verapaz** , which has a large colonial church with interesting altar silver and statue of San Joaquín (*Hospedaje Viajeros* and *Hospedaje Oly*, both G). The lake is popular for fishing and swimming. Market: Sun; festival 21-26 July.

Cobán, capital of Alta Verapaz Department, is the centre of a rich district producing coffee and cardamom, of which Guatemala is the world's largest exporter. The plant is tall, reed-like, with coarse leaves and white spiky flowers. Population 59,307, altitude 1,320m, climate semi-tropical. It is 135 km by road S to El Rancho on the Guatemalan Railway and the highway to Guatemala City. Founded by Apostle of the Indies, Las Casas, in 1544. See the church of El Calvario (1559), now completely renovated, original façade still intact. Daily market. *Fiestas*: Holy Week (which is said to be fascinating), Rabín Ahau, in July, meeting of cultural groups from the whole country and election of a 'reina indigenista', and 3 August (procession of saints with brass bands, pagan dancer dancers and people enjoying themselves), followed by a folklore festival, 22-28 August. Cobán is a good place for finding textiles. There are several cinemas near the main square.

Hotels B *La Posada*, 1 C, 4-12, T 511495, attractive hotel with well-kept gardens, full board available, reasonable, no credit cards; **E** *Oxib Pec*, 1 C, 12-11, T 511039, with bath; **E** *Central*, 1 C, 1-79, T 511442, no sign, check you are not overcharged, very clean, with hot shower, good restaurant entered through *Café San Jorge*; **E** *El Recreo*, 10 Av 5-01, Zona 3, T 512160, F 512333, clean, good breakfast; *La Colonial*, 2a C Zona 4, clean, hot water sometimes, restaurant, family-owned, friendly, car parking. **F** *Hospedaje Maya*, opp Ciné Norte, hot showers, friendly, rec; **F** *La Paz*, 6 Av, 2-19, T 511358, with extension which is rec, pleasant, comfortable beds, garden; **F** *Monterrey*, 6 Av, 1-12, T 511131, rec; **E** *La Fe*, on corner near the Monja Blanca bus terminal on 8 Av, Zona 1, good facilities; **F** pp *Hospedaje Ascuña*, owner's wife is from USA, clean, sons make trips to Lanquín; **F** hotel opp bus station on 4 Calle, Zona 3, hot shower; **G** *El Carmen*, on main square, clean; **G** *Chipi-Chipi*, clean, dark and noisy, hot water in morning, but very friendly and how can you pass up the name (the name, in fact, means 'light rain', of a type frequent in Cobán); **G** *Pensión Familiar*, Diagonal 4, 3-36, Zona 2, 1 block N of Parque Central, cold water, basic, cockroaches, airless rooms in cellar; **G** *Valenciana*, (you can sleep on the balcony for US$0.50), basic; nameless *pensión* at 1-12 Av Estado (near *Hotel La Paz*), clean. Accommodation is hard to find in August and even at other times of the year in the town centre. At no time be tempted to spend the night in the covered market, very dangerous.

Restaurants *La Posada* (address above), rec, good lunch menu, US$6; *Comedor Chinita*, Parque Central, good *comidas corridas*, *Café Norte* (good fast food), *El Refugio* (near the bus terminal, good) and *Las Delicias* serve meals for less than US$1; *Cafe El Tirol*, on main square, 33 different coffees, also homemade wholemeal bread, good cakes, nice garden, slow service; *El Chino*, small, good typical dishes (good new hotel of same name nearby, exact address not known).

Electric Current 110 volts. It has been recommended not to use standard electrical appliances in Cobán as the voltage is variable.

Exchange Banco de Guatemala, 1 C, 5-24, Zona 2.

Doctor Dr Juan José Guerrero P, 3 Av, 1-47, Zona 3, T 512041/513175, rec.

Telephones You cannot make international calls from Guatel. Try the phone directly opposite, outside the abandoned building.

Tourist Office on main square, run by knowledgeable Acuña family, who also run day trips to the caves of Lanquín and Semuc Champey, from US$21, highly rec, stop several times on the way to look at plants and taste fruits, T 511268, English spoken. For local trips also ask for Alejandro Díaz, T/F 512149.

Buses from Guatemala City: US$3. Transportes Escobar-Monja Blanca (hourly from 0400 till 1700, 4 hrs, arrive early in the morning and book a seat on the first available bus, or book in advance). The bus from **El Estor** takes 9 hrs, 3 services a day (0500, 0800, 1000). Return buses leave in the morning from the terminal, top of the bus rec. The trip from the capital via Rabinal, along an old dirt road, takes about 12 hrs (change buses in Salamá). To **Huehuetenango** 0600, every other day (to be increased to daily), owner is Sr Castro of Uspantán. Cobán can also be reached from **Sacapulas** and **Quiché** (p 502) and from **Huehuetenango** (p 511). There are also buses from **Flores** via Sayaxché and Sebol.

Excursions Near Cobán is the old colonial church of **San Juan Chamelco**, well worth a visit. **San Pedro Carchá** (5 km E of Cobán, bus US$0.10, 15 mins, frequent; buses from the capital as for Cobán; Hotel La Reforma, 4 C, 8-45 'A', T 511448, G) used to be famous for its pottery, textiles and wooden masks, and silver, but only the pottery seems to be available at the Tues market. Small local museum displays examples of local crafts. Truck to Sebol (**see p 484**), 7 hrs, US$1.20. Also visit the orchid farm of Otto Mittelstaedt, more than 23,000 specimens.

From Cobán a road runs 70 km to **Lanquín** cave, in which the Lanquín river rises. The road is rough, and particularly bad for the last 12 km. You can camp at the cave. If you want to visit the cave ask in the morning if possible, at the police station in the village (2 km) to turn the lights on (US$2 entry, lights left on for 45 mins only). The bats flying out at dusk is impressive. The cave is very slippery and the ladders and handrails are poor, so wear appropriate shoes and take a torch for additional lighting. It may take you up to 1$\frac{1}{2}$ hrs to go to the end of the caves and back. Outside the cave you can swim in the deep, wide river, and camp (free) or sling a hammock under a large shelter. From Lanquín one can visit the natural bridge of **Semuc Champey** stretching 60m across the Cahabón gorge, 10 very hard km walk, or up to 4 hrs along a new road which runs to the footbridge over the river, 20 mins from Semuc Champey. At the end of the road, which is very steep in places, is a car park (quite a few cars, lifts possible). A steep track heads down to the new bridge half-way along the road (the route is not signposted so ask frequently for the shortest route). People may try to charge you to cross the new bridge but you can argue and not pay. The natural bridge has water on top of it as well as below, and the point where the river Cahabón goes underground is spectacular. One can swim in the pools on top of the bridge. The further upstream you go the less safe it is, stone throwing has been reported. At Semuc Champey are places where you can camp. Insect repellent is essential. If planning to return to Lanquín the same day, start early to avoid the midday heat. There are a couple of places en route where you can get a drink.

At Lanquín there is **G** *Hospedaje Mary*, pleasant, cheap, basic, and small restaurants and **G** *Hospedaje La Divina Providencia*, no hot water and a good (for Lanquín), cheap restaurant, friendly; neither very clean. There is a cleaner *comedor* in town, which is good. **E** *Hotel El Recreo*, T 512160, (through hotel of same name in Cobán) new, at entrance to the village, clean, good meals, friendly, rec. The church has fine images and some lovely silver. Several buses from Cobán, first at 0530, 4 hrs, US$0.75 including breakfast stop en route, also 1300, 1500; returns at 0500, 0700 and 1400; also to and from San Pedro Carchá, 0530 (you can try hitching from San Pedro Carchá, from the fumigation post, where all trucks stop, to the turn-off to Lanquín, then 12 km walk—very little traffic). There are buses at 0500 and 0730 from **Lanquín to Pajal** (12 km, 1 hr, US$0.30) from where one can go to **Sebol** US$4, 0830, 5½ hrs (**p 483**); Pajal is just a shop. Pick-up Lanquín-Sebol, US$1. You can also hike from Cobán or San Pedro Carchá to Lanquín via Semuc Champey in five or six days camping beside rivers, visiting caves and canyons in this limestone region. There are coffee, cardamom and banana plantations on the way. Unless you speak Kekchí, conversation is difficult with the people in the countryside, few of whom speak Spanish.

From Tactic, a reasonable and very beautiful unpaved road runs down the Polochic valley to El Estor, quite easy to hitch (**see p 475**). *Tamahú* (12 km) and *Tucurú* (28 km) produce pretty *huipiles*; main market day is Sun and there are interesting images in the Tucurú church. 47 km beyond Tucurú is a turnoff to **Senahú** (the journey from Cobán takes 8 hrs, Autotransportes Valenciano and Brenda, departures from Cobán at 0500 and 1000 (but check), US$1.25, particularly crowded on Sun, difficult to hitch to Senahú). Climb to the cemetery for good views. (*Pensiones* at Senahú: *Senahú*, same group as *El Recreo* in Cobán; **G** *González*, good meals for US$0.60, at entrance to village, no sign, old finca, romantic exterior, rundown interior; **G** *Edilson*, good for information on hikes: *Pensión Oly* in centre, not rec; **G** *Gladys*, near main square, meals for US$0.55.) Walking in the Senahú district is magnificent. It is possible to cross the mountains to the village of **Cahabón** (24 km E of Lanquín), which will take a full day, or, if you can get a lift to Finca Volcán, only 6 hrs (either way is quicker than by road). There is accommodation, G, in Cahabón. Beyond the turn-off to Senahú, the road continues to *Telemán* (bus from Senahú at 0300 and 1030), *Panzós* (pick-up from Telemán; guest house; bus to El Estor pm) and Cahaboncito (6 km from Panzós). Here you can either carry on to El Estor, or take an appalling road (av speed 10 kmph) to Cahabón and Lanquín. Coming from El Estor, alight at the Senahú turn off, hitch or wait for bus from Cobán which should pass on its way to Senahú around 1200 and 1600. Trucks take this road, passing the turning at about 0800, on Fri and Sun, and possibly Thur, otherwise no traffic (the alternative is to go back to Cobán and go from there to Lanquín).

To the W of Cobán is Nebaj which can be reached by taking the Huehuetenango bus to Sacapulas (preferable to ride on the roof) and either hitching from there or waiting for the bus from Quiché. **See p 503** and **513** for places en route to Sacapulas, Nebaj and Huehuetenango.

At Km 126 on the Atlantic Highway is the **B** *Motel Longarone*, T 410314, with bungalows and a/c, good service, good food, pool, in a delightful setting, good place for trips to Quiriguá and Copán. Nearby is **B** *Hotel Atlántico*, T 417160, also good, with good value restaurant. **F** *Hotel Santa Cruz*, bath, fan, no a/c, clean, good value. The Pasabien waterfall and swimming hole is a few km N at the bottom of the Sierra de las Minas at the end of a dirt road, pleasant. Geologists will be interested in the Motagua fault near Santa Cruz. At **Río Hondo**, 138 km from Guatemala City there is **F** *Hotel Hawaii*, helpful, rather individual idea of door locks, clean except for resident cockroaches. Also *Posada del Río*, Km 137. From here a paved road runs S to **Zacapa**. Population 15,000, altitude 187m. Sulphur springs for rheumatic sufferers at Baños de Agua Caliente, well worth a visit (closed on Mon: two baths, one private, US$3, good value, the other state-owned, usually closed. No bus but the train passes the *baños*—ask the driver to stop for you). It is an attractive town with a colourful market, 148 km from Guatemala City. Climate hot and dry. *Fiestas*: 29 June, 1-9 Dec, 30 April-1 May, small local ceremony. Just outside the town is Estanzuela (minibus, US$0.30), a village whose museum houses a complete skeleton of a prehistoric monster.

Hotels F *De León*, G without bath, clean, good value but make sure your room is securely locked; **E** *Wong*, 6 C, 12-53, with bath; next to station is **D** *Ferrocarril*; other *pensiones* (basic) opp; **G** *Central*, opp market, clean, friendly, noisy parrots, very good, delightful setting, rec. **F** *Posada Doña María*, E of Zacapa at Km 181 on road to Puerto Barrios, with bath, rec.

Restaurant *Comedor Lee*, 50m from *Pensión Central*, good rice, friendly Chinese owners. *Chow Mein*, Chinese food and satelite TV, varying reports.

Exchange Banco de Guatemala, 4 C, 14-21, near central market, changes TCs.

Transport Bus from Guatemala City to **Zacapa**, US$1.25 with Rutas Orientales, every ½ hr, 3½ hrs. Bus to **Esquipulas** 0700 daily, Rutas Orientales, US$0.80, 1½ hrs. Train to **Quiriguá** and on to **Puerto Barrios** 1330, Tues, Thur, Sat, usually late.

From Zacapa the paved road runs S to Chiquimula and Esquipulas. *Chiquimula* (21 km), capital of its Department, population 42,000, has a number of interesting churches including the 'Templo Santuario' facing the plaza, with a colonnaded vault, dome and fine stained glass windows. On the outskirts is the 'Iglesia Vieja', a church ruined by 1765 earthquake. Daily market. The town has an attractive central plaza surrounded by a circle of ceiba trees. A road, 203 km, runs W through splendid scenery to the capital (**see p 464**). *Fiestas*: 12-18 August, Virgen del Tránsito, 12 December.

Hotels E *Victoria*, 2 C, 9-99, T 422238, next to bus station, all rooms with bath, TV, towels, soap, shampoo, drinking water all provided, good café next door; **E** *Posada Perla del Oriente*, 2 C y 11 Av, T 420152, restaurant, quiet, rec; **F** *Cabrera*, green building to right of bus stop, market outside, shower, fan, clean, friendly; **F** *Hospedaje Río Jordan*, 3 C, 8-81, between main plaza and bus station, without or with bath, basic, pleasant owners; **E** *Chiquimulja*, 3 C, 6-51, T 420387, with bath, good quality, clean, but poor staff; **F** *Darío*, 8 Av, 4-40, 1/2 block from main square, with or without bath, rec. **F** *Hotel Hernández*, good, cheap, swimming pool, friendly; **G** *Los Eros*, close to market and bus station, shared bath, cold shower, clean, 3 C, 7-41, good value, plant-filled courtyard, good cheap food next door; **G** *España*, a few doors along from *Hotel Hernández*. The town's water supply is often cut off.

Restaurants *Las Vegas*, 7 Av, S side of Plaza, extensive menu, good typical dishes, also pizza, good selection of wines and beers, good mains US$4-7, rec; *El Tesoro*, also on Plaza, good Chinese; *El Chino*, just off the Plaza, also Chinese, very large helpings, opp is El Lugar, very good, and around corner from *El Chino* is *Topsy* ice cream parlour. *Panadería Las Violetas* is a good bakery near the church.

Exchange Banco de Guatemala, 3 C, 5-91, Zona 1, corner of main square, Mon-Fri 0830-1400; Banco del Agro (will change Amex cheques, helpful, good rates, fast service); Bancafé and Banco Granai y Townson have extended opening hours. Also Almacén Nuevo Cantón, on the Plaza, will change quetzales into dollars.

Bus from Guatemala City, Transportes Guerra, 3 1/2 hrs, 0700, US$2.50, Rutas Orientales, frequent, US$2.50 pullman, 3 hrs; from Zacapa US$0.12, from Quiriguá, US$1, from Puerto Barrios US$3, 4 hrs, several companies, and from Cobán via El Rancho (where a change must be made) US$1.65. Buses to El Florido (Honduras border), 3 hrs, US$1.50, most leave 0630-0700.

At *Vado Hondo* (10 km from Chiquimula) on the road to Esquipulas, a smooth dirt road branches E to the Honduran border (48 km) and on (11 km) to the great Mayan ruins of Copán (see Honduras section, **Copán and Western Honduras**). It goes through the small town of *Jocotán* (**G** *Pensión Ramírez*, showers, pleasant, very friendly, good local food from *comedor*; **G** *Pensión Sagastume*, very friendly, garden, safe parking for motorcycles, bus will stop outside, good meals on request. Meals also at the bakery; exchange at *farmacia*, with 10% commission). Good place to buy cheap hammocks in the market. *Fiesta* 25 July. Hot springs 4 km from town. The road goes on to the border at *El Florido* and to Copán (paved on the steep parts, dirt on the flat road). The drive to Copán (by car) takes 4-5 hrs from Guatemala City, or 2 from Vado Hondo, including the frontier crossing.

To Copán There are through buses from Chiquimula to El Florido at 0600, 0900, 1130 and 1300 (Transportes Vilma, US$2.50, 3 1/2 hrs). At 0900, 1430, 1730 a bus goes as far as Jocotán (no connection to border on last bus). Bus Jocotán to the border, US$0.50, taxi, US$5. Transportes Rutas Orientales buses from Guatemala City run to Chiquimula from 0500, half-hourly (3 1/2 hrs, US$2, US$2.50 Pullman), any before 0730 should make this connection, but if you take the 1300 bus to the border, you won't get to Copán in time to visit the ruins, which close at 1600. There is a Vilma bus from Zacapa to the border at 0530, US$1, which will enable you to spend 2-3 hrs at Copán and return the same day. From the border to Copán there are minibuses, US$1 (leave when full; don't believe pick-up drivers who say there are no minibuses. If short of time and no minibus appears, it is possible to hire a pick-up for US$15 to take you to the ruins and collect you later to go back to the border if only staying one day). Those travelling by bus will find that it is impossible to visit Copán from Guatemala City and return in one day. It is best to spend the night in Copán village. Bus to border at 0715 connects with the first bus from the border to Chiquimula, which departs at 0830; others at 0900 and 1400. Last bus Copán-El Florido 1300 for connecting bus from Jocotán to Chiquimula at

1700; last bus Chiquimula-Guatemala City at 1800. Taxi Chiquimula to the border, US$10 (there may be colectivos for US$2); Chiquimula to Copán and back in same day, US$20. Travel agents do a one-day tour from Guatemala City to Copán and back, for about US$35 pp. You can sometimes get a lift to Guatemala City with tourist agency guides whose minibuses are not full—cost about US$2. You may also be able to hitch a ride from the border to Copán for US$1.

If you are coming in to Guatemala at this point and need a visa it is advisable to get one in advance. Tourist cards, however, are available at the border. There is no transport from the border after 1700. If returning to Guatemala remember that you must have a new visa or tourist card (see p 518, Documents). However the Guatemalan border official will give a 72-hr exit pass to visit Copán, stapled into passport (this avoids having to get a new visa or tourist card to reenter), but if you try to reenter at a different border post, the pass may not be recognized. If you do have undue difficulties at this crossing, ask to speak to the delegado. Make sure that the customs official stamps your papers. You have to pay all exit and entry taxes. Offically there is no entry/exit charge for Honduras. Any fees requested should have a receipt. Crossing the border by car takes $\frac{1}{2}$-1 hr; altogether you need 11 stamps, 5 in Guatemala, 6 in Honduras, and you have to pay for practically every one. Leaving Guatemala costs US$4, returning to Guatemala costs US$7.50 (ask for a receipt, or bargain); it is all very civil, but the vehicle will be sprayed (make sure none of the disinfectant gets inside). Unfortunately the border officials of the two countries do not keep the same hours: Guatemalan hours are 0700-1200, 1400-1800; Honduran hours 0700-1800. If you leave Guatemala outside business hours there is an extra charge of US$0.50. Note: this is the best information we have but travellers frequently find that their experience differs. This particular border point seems to depend on the individual officials rather than standard tariffs.

To visit the Mayan ruins of El Petén, take a bus from Chiquimula to Río Hondo (US$0.35, 1 hr) to connect with the 0730 bus from Guatemala City to Flores which leaves Río Hondo at 1030, cost US$3, or a bus to Bananera (Morales) and change there.

The main road continues S from Vado Hondo to San Jacinto and **Quezaltepeque** (no hotel, but a *comedor* 1 km towards Esquipulas has rooms). Thence to Padre Miguel where you turn E to **Esquipulas** (population: 7,500, 940m), a typical market town in semi-highland and pleasantly cool. At the end of its 1½-km main avenue is a magnificent white basilica, one of the finest colonial churches in the Americas. In it is a black Christ carved by Quirio Catano in 1594 which draws pilgrims from all Central America, especially on 27-30 January and during Lent and Holy Week. The image was first placed in a local church in 1595, but was moved to the basilica, built to house it, in 1758. The old quarter near the Municipal Building is worth a visit.

The Benedictine monks who look after the shrine are from Louisiana and therefore speak English. They show visitors over their lovely garden and their extensive library. If you wish to see this, go midweek; on Sundays in particular the town is very busy with pilgrims.

Hotels Plenty of hotels, *pensiones* and *comedores* all over town. **A+** *Gran Chorti*, at Km 222 on the highway to Chiquimula, T 431134, all you would expect from a luxury hotel; 2 km S on road to Honduras at Km 224 is **D** *Posada del Cristo Negro*, T 431182, motel style, swimming pool, restaurant, good. Near the basilica are **B** *Payaquí*, D in annex, T 431371, hot water and drinking water, swimming pool, protected car parking; **C** *Los Angeles*, with bath, D without, rec, T 431254; **E** *El Angel*, with bath, cold water; **F** *Pensión Casa Norman*, nice rooms with bath; **F** *Pensión Santa Elena*, behind market; near the Rutas Orientales bus stop, **E** *Santa Rosa* (1 block opp), hot water; **G** *París*, 2 Av, 10-48. Several good restaurants on main road.

Exchange Bancafé and Banco Granai y Townson, latter changes TCs. No bank will exchange anything for lempiras. Plenty of moneychangers in the centre. Better rates than at the borders.

Honduran Consulate in the lobby of the *Hotel Payaquí*, very helpful. Quicker to get your Honduran visa here than in the capital.

Transport Buses from the capital every 30 mins 0400-1800, US$3.25 (4-5 hrs), Rutas Orientales and Rutas Guatesqui (unreliable). The road goes on to **Atulapa**, on the Honduran border (minibuses when full, US$0.60, plus US$0.25 across border), and continues to the Honduran town of **Nueva Ocotopeque** and S to **San Salvador**. Minibuses to border will overcharge to 'help you use up left over quetzales'. On the Honduran side buses run directly to San Pedro Sula.

El Salvador may be reached from Guatemala City by leaving the Esquipulas bus at the

Padre Miguel junction, from where colectivos run to **Anguiatú** on the border, or from Esquipulas by taking the road to Concepción Las Minas and then on to Anguiatú. From there a good road goes to Metapán.

Part of the Department of Chiquimula falls within the International Biosphere **La Fraternidad**, a reserve of cloud forest and its surroundings in the Montecristo range. The reserve will be administered jointly by Guatemala, Honduras and El Salvador.

Quiriguá is about half way between Zacapa and Puerto Barrios on the Atlantic Highway and about 4 km from some remarkable Maya late classic period remains: temple, carved stelae, etc. In 1975 a stone sun-god statue was unearthed here. The tallest stone is over 8m high with another 3m or so buried. Some stelae have been carved in the shapes of animals, some mythical, all of symbolic importance to the Maya. Many of the stelae are now in a beautiful park (but all have shelters which makes photography difficult), where refreshments are served. Open 0800-1800, entry US$0.25. In August 1989 a tornado did considerable damage to the area and the site was closed for some months, but it is now better maintained than Copán.

From the main highway to the ruins, there is an occasional bus; alternatively ride on the back of a motorbike, US$0.50, walk or take a taxi. **F** *Hotel Royal*, with bath, clean, mosquito netting on all windows, poor meals US$1.60, unfriendly; camping in car park of the ruins, US$0.50. From *Hotel Royal* walk past church towards train station, follow tracks branching off to right through banana plantation for about 45 mins to the ruins. Reached by road from Guatemala City to Los Amates, then a 3½-km dirt road (ask to be put down at the 'ruinas de Quiriguá', 4 km after Los Amates), Velázquez bus at 0700, US$1.25, 3½ hrs. If driving the road branches off the Atlantic Highway at Km 205 which is where the bus stops. Train Guatemala City to Quiriguá Sat 0700, 12 hrs. Take insect-repellent. The best reference book is S G Morley's *Guide Book to Ruins of Quiriguá*, which should be obtained before going to the ruins.

Puerto Barrios, on the Caribbean (population 37,800), 297 km from the capital by the Atlantic Highway (toll, free for motorcycles) and with rail connections also, has now been largely superseded as a port by Santo Tomás. It is the capital of the Department of Izabal. The beach of Escobar on the northern peninsula is recommended. Toll, US$0.25. The launch to Livingston leaves from here, and one can take a boat to Puerto Modesto Méndez, on the Sarstún river.

Hotels D *Del Norte*, 7 C, and 2 Av, T 480087, 'rickety old wooden structure' on sea front (rooms 5 and 7 have bath), a timeless classic, but with a concrete newer part, will change US$ cash at good rate, expensive restaurant; **C** *El Reformador*, 16 C y 7 Av, T 481533, rooms on two levels around a green courtyard, restaurant, clean, quiet, rec; **D** *Calypso*, 7 C 6 y 7 Av, T 480494, a/c, TV, parking, cold shower, clean, boat trips; **E** *Español*, 13 C between 5 and 6 Av, T 480738, with bath, clean, friendly; **F** *Caribeña*, 4 Av, between 10 and 11 C, T 480860, rec, close to boat and bus terminals, has popular restaurant; **F** *El Dorado*, 13 C between 6 and 7 Av, with bath, noisy, friendly; **F** *Europa*, 8 Av, 8 and 9 C, new, clean, with bath, good restaurant, car parking outside hotel; **F** *San Marcos*, 7 C, 7 Av 63, with bath, 3 good meals, US$4.25; **G** *Hotel Xelajú*, 9 C between 6 and 7 Av, clean, friendly, by market and bus station, noisy; **G** *Pensión Xelajú*, 8 Av, between 9 and 10 C, quiet, clean. There are other cheap hotels on 7 and 8 Calles between 6 and 8 Avenidas (eg **F** *Canadá*, 6 C, between 6 and 7 Av), and on and near 9 Calle towards the sea.

Restaurants Most hotels. *Cafesama*, 7 C, and 6 Av, open 24 hrs, reasonable. *Ranchón La Bahía*, 7 C and 6 Av, good seafood, snacks and sandwiches, reasonable prices but watch the bill; *Al Mar Caribe*, on the waterfront, has open air section where you can sit and watch the cargo boats loading; *Pizzería Pastelería Salinas*, 7 C and 7 Av, clean, pleasant, cheap; *Copos* and *Frosty* ice-cream parlours, 8 C between 6 and 7 Av, both good and clean; *Frutiland*, good juices, sandwiches. Numerous others, undistinguished, in centre and on 9 Calle. Avoid *Quick Burger*. Nightlife is aimed at visiting seamen, with lots of night clubs and prostitutes.

Market In block bounded by 8 and 9 C and 6 and 7 Av. Footwear is cheap.

Cinemas *Palacio Del Cine*, 7 Av y 7 C, historic building. Also cinema next to the Banco Granai y Townson. Both show US movies.

Exchange Lloyds Bank, 7 C and 2/3 Av, open 0900-1500, Mon-Fri; **Banco de Guatemala** on seafront (9 C Final), opens and closes ½ hr earlier; **Bancafé**, 13 C and 7 Av, open Mon to Fri until 2000 and on Sat 1000-1400; **Banco Granai y Townson**, 7 C and 6 Av, also opens late. *Quinto* store in the market place changes money.

Post Office 3 Av and 7 C, behind Bandegua building.

Cables/Telephones Guatel, 10 C and 8 Av.

Buses to **capital** (Zona 4 terminal), Litegua, regular bus 8 a day from 0700, US$5, pullman US$6.20, 7 daily, first at 0630 and 0730, good sandwiches sold on bus, 6 hrs, address in Puerto Barrios 6 Av entre 9 y 10 C. Fuentes del Norte runs a regular service; Unión Pacífica y Las Patojas (9 Av, 18-38, Zona 1, Guatemala City), has 4 2nd-class buses and one semi-pullman to capital a day, with luggage on top, (US$5). Bus to **El Rancho** (turn-off) for Biotopo del Quetzal and Cobán, US$2.40, 4 hrs. To **Chiquimula**, first at 0500 operated by Carmencita, 4 hrs, US$3.

Train to **Guatemala City** (schedule under Guatemala City **Rail**).

Air Daily flight to Guatemala City.

Ferry to Belize Passenger boat to **Punta Gorda**, Belize, Tues and Fri 0800, from Puerto Barrios, 2½ hrs, US$5; return same days at about 1400. Get your tickets in good time from Agencia Líneas Marítimas (ALM) offices at 1 Av, between 11 C and 12 C; trips are often sell-outs. You must have your exit stamp before you can buy a ticket. **NB** There are immigration offices in both Livingston (Calle 9, near landing) and Puerto Barrios (Calle 7, 100m from sea front); to avoid confusion, get your exit (Q6) and entry stamp in Puerto Barrios. We understand the only justified charge by immigration is if you do not have a tourist card (US$5) or, if your passport requires it, a visa (see **Information for Visitors**). There is an immigration service on Sat and Sun. You can obtain entry visas for Belize at the police station in Punta Gorda (US$8). Be warned also that your luggage will get wet and the boats do not handle well in rough weather (see also the corresponding comments under Belize). While waiting for the ferry in Puerto Barrios, you can buy a good quality hammock from the prison (penitenciaria).

Jungle Trail to Honduras On the possibility of crossing from Guatemala to Honduras in this region, Piero Scaruffi of Redwood City, CA, writes: If you want to go from Puerto Barrios (Guatemala) to nearby Puerto Cortés (Honduras) there is no road, but there is a way. It's a one-day trip (guaranteed), even if you have luggage and need frequent stops. You leave around 0600 from the market of Puerto Barrios on the bus to Entre Ríos. At the terminal in Entre Ríos you can take the small 4-wheel railway maintenance vehicles (it costs less than US$1). The railway ends at Finca Chinoq, where you have to walk to the river and hire a boat to take you to El Cinchado (US$3 or so). Mind: the locals go to El Cacao, but there is no immigration there; the only legal way to cross the border is through El Cinchado. The boat leaves you at the immigration. Get an exit stamp (wait a few minutes if the office is closed) and ask for directions to walk to Corinto. It's a three hour walk in the middle of nowhere and under hot sunshine. You will get lost because the trail disappears pretty soon. Look for the tree trunks they use as bridges between the canals; they follow the trail. Alternatively, wait for a local to show up. One hour of walk leads you to a village called Jimeritos, where you can rest and buy drinks and fruit. From there the trail is much better but there are many forks; you should meet considerably more people as all around are farms and plantations, and thus all you have to do is ask for directions. Two more hours of good walking get you to Corinto, which is in Honduras. You can sleep at *Victorio's* for about US$3 or get on a camioneta going to Cuyamel (offer US$1 for the ride). Gorgeous scenery on the way (hills, jungle, pueblos, streams). From Cuyamel or Corinto you may catch a bus to Puerto Cortés. There are immigration offices in Puerto Cortés (closed Sun) where you can get your entry stamp. The trip is not recommended if the sky is overcast: storms are sudden and wild. Going the other way is slightly more complicated, but you can still do it in one day. (See reports under Honduras, **North Coast** section.)

Some correspondents have stressed that this 'Jungle Trail' is only possible in the driest of weather, others have crossed in the wet season but had to wade 'through mud a foot deep hoping not to tread on any snakes'. Take your pick. There also seems to be disagreement on the trail's safety (both from the terrain and robbers), so seek local advice. The nearest car crossings are at Copán or Esquipulas.

Mark Simmerman of Mayetta, Kansas, writes of an alternative route: from the bus station in Puerto Barrios take a bus to Entre Ríos (US$1). They leave many times each day and the trip takes about 45 mins. From there take the Banana Finca bus (US$0.20, every 30 mins) all the way to the end of the route (45 mins) through miles of Chiquita banana fields. Ask to be dropped where the *lanchas* leave on the Río Pinto Negro for Honduras. This motor canoe will cost US$2 and take about 30 mins. You will have to change canoes at the border station which is almost always devoid of personnel. A few families live here and can change your quetzales, offer warm sodas and very local food from their hunting and fishing. The next canoe ride lasts about 1½ hrs and costs US$2.20. It is a beautiful experience winding through the jungle on cool, narrow streams nearly choked with vegetation. The view of the Honduran mountains is priceless but the biting flies and relentless sun can take their toll. Make certain that the canoe takes you all the way to the bridge at Tegucigalpita, the driver may be tempted to leave you where a fence crosses the river some 2 km short of town. At Tegucigalpita, wait for the bus which comes about every 1½ hrs and can take you to many different towns, including the beach town of Omoa (two *pensiones*). To get your passport stamped you must go to Puerto Cortés by the next day or you will get more than the usual amount of disgruntled looks from the immigration officials for entering Honduras in this beautiful and somewhat unapproved manner.

Boats can be hired in either Livingston or Puerto Barrios to take you directly to Puerto Cortés, which may be worth it if there is a group of you. Pay no more than US$200 after bargaining.

Santo Tomás de Castilla, a few km S of Puerto Barrios on Santo Tomás bay, is now the country's largest and most efficient port on the Caribbean. It handles 77% of the exports and half the imports as well as 20% of El Salvador's imports and 10% of its exports. Cruise ships put into Santo Tomás. Apart from *Hotel Puerto Libre* (see below), no good hotel or eating place as yet, and no shops, and nothing to do save sea bathing; the sea and beach are none too clean. There is fresh water bathing past the port and the garrison.

Hotel D *Puerto Libre*, 25 rooms, at highway fork for Santo Tomás and Puerto Barrios, a/c and bath, TV, phone for international calls, restaurant and bar, swimming pool (hotel reported damaged by fire in 1992).

Shipping It is possible to ship a car to New Orleans: the cost depends on size of car.

Transport To Guatemala City one has either to take a local bus to Puerto Barrios to connect with the train, or to Puerto Barrios or the highway fork by the *Hotel Puerto Libre* to catch the Pullman bus.

A ferry from Puerto Barrios to **Livingston** (22½ km), at the mouth of the Río Dulce, leaves daily, 1000 and 1700, taking 1½ hrs; arrive at least 1 hr in advance to ensure a seat, cost US$0.70. Tickets on the boat, or from the ALM shipping office, 1 Av, between 11 C and 12 C, who will advise if there are other sailings and details of excursions. Launch returns to Puerto Barrios 0500 and 1400 daily, buy ticket previous afternoon, office in front of *Tucán Dugú*. The ferry has been referred to as the 'barfy barque', there is much pitching and heaving. Private launches taking 10-12 people also ply this route, 30-40 mins, US$2.75, much better, leave when full, about once an hour. Livingston is very quiet, now there is little trade save some export of famous Verapaz coffee from Cobán, and bananas. It is the centre of fishing and shrimping in the Bay of Amatique. Population: 5,000, mostly Garifuna blacks, a few English-speaking. Many young travellers congregate here for the Caribbean atmosphere. Beach discotheques at the weekend are popular. Some hotels will change TCs, as will the Chinese shop. No phone service between 1900 and 0700. Outside Livingston along the beach is a terrarium (snakes and spiders) run by Frenchman William Martin, who is very knowledgeable and also runs jungle tours and jungle survival training courses.

Warning Don't stroll on the beach after dark, or in daylight at the Siete Altares end as there is a serious risk of robbery. Never drink from unsealed liquor bottles; they may be drugged as a prelude to robbery.

Hotels at Livingston: **A+** *Tucán Dugú* (Fri-Sun, less in week—all rooms with bath), sea view, swimming pool, very good, restaurant (but overpriced breakfasts), bars, laundry service, mini zoo, to book T 481572/588, or Guatemala City 321259, Telex 5139; **B-D** *Hospedaje Doña Alida*, 200m beyond Tucán Dugú, on right, T 481567, clean, tepid water, in bungalows or rooms, with or without bath, variety of prices and standards, pleasant, quiet charming owner; **D** *Henry Berisford*, T 481568, near *Casa Rosada*, 28 rooms, opened 1991, restaurant; **E** *Garifuna*, first paved road to the right on the way to the *African Place*, halfway to the beach, 10 rooms some with private bath, comfortable, laundry, rec; **E** *Casa Rosada*, 800m first left from dock, 5 thatched cabins for 2-3 persons each, swimming and trips can be arranged, peaceful, rec, call Guatel in Livingston for reservations, hotel will call back, American owner, Jean Swanson; **E** *Flamingo*, turn right near *African Place* then left along the beach, with garden, clean, comfortable cottages, own water supply and generator, German owner; **E** *African Place*, looks like a cross between a mosque and a castle, main street 800m from dock, with bath, F without, clean, huge rooms, pleasant, restaurant, good breakfasts, left on paved road at top of hill, rec; **F** *Caribe*, T 481073, 100m first left from dock, same road as *Casa Rosada* and *Henry Berisford*, with bath, cheaper rooms without, noisy but good. **F** *El Viajero*, from port turn left, clean, friendly, rec; **F** *Minerva*, left off road to *African Place*, near *Restaurant Margoth*, basic but clean; **G** *Río Dulce*, 300m from dock on the main street, basic, clean, but beware of the odd rat. Beach bungalows can be rented just outside Livingston on the way to Siete Altares, **E**, *Livingston Seagull Bungalows*, owned by Manuel García de la Peña, T 313908, 318449, F 310784. Camping is said to be good around Livingston, but check on security. Beware of theft from hotel rooms.

Restaurants *El Tiburón*, restaurant of the *Tucán Dugú*, very good but expensive; *El Malecón*, 50m from dock, on left, reasonable; *African Place*, reasonable and friendly, Spanish owner; *Margoth*, don't be put off by the building, the food is good and reasonably priced; *La Cabaña*, good but a little pricey, rec; *El Jaguar*, main street, Caribbean style, Garifuna background music, fish and seafood, good; *La Cueva*, opposite Catholic church, nice decoration, music, extensive menu; *Cafetería Coni*, clean, good, cheap; *Café McTropic*, opp *Hotel Río Dulce*, great breakfasts, 2 menus lunch and dinner; good breakfast at *Doña Luisa* on main street; *Café Lily*, cheap, friendly, food OK. Fresh fish is available everywhere. Women sell *pan de coco* on the streets. You can buy cold, whole coconuts, US$0.20, from the orange crush stand on the main street, which they split for you with a machete.

NW along the coast towards the Río Sarstún, which is the border with Belize, is Río Blanco beach followed by **Playa Quehueche** (also spelt Keueche), where there is *Hotel El Chiringuito*, thatched roof, good music, relaxing atmosphere and good food, with 6 bungalows available—a good place to stop for a few days. Guided jungle trips arranged. 5 mins before *El Chiringuito* is **E** *Hotel Seaguilan*, bungalows with bath, comfortable, clean, shop nearby, good and cheap breakfast and dinner, rec. 10 mins walk further on, about 6 km from Livingston, is **Los Siete Altares**, beautiful waterfalls and pools, at their best during the rainy season (well recommended). Early Tarzan movies were filmed here. Beware of theft when leaving belongings to climb the falls. **Warning** people are frequently robbed on their way to the Falls, single women should not go. Also paddle up the Río Dulce gorge. *Cayucos* can be hired near Texaco station, US$5 per day. You need a boat to visit these beaches from Livingston, the river is too deep to wade.

Boats From Puerto Barrios-Livingston to Río Dulce, with stops at Agua Caliente and Biotopo, cost about US$7-8 one way, easy to arrange, enquire at the ALM office in Puerto Barrios. One can get the mail boat from Livingston up to the new bridge at Río Dulce (from where you can catch the bus to Tikal) at 0930, Tues and Fri (0600 in the other direction) but schedules subject to change, US$6. Take food and drink along with you, though there are some places for refreshments on the way. *Cayucos* are cheaper than *lanchas*, and if you want to share, get a group together; fare about US$10 pp. Taking a boat is the best way to reach Livingston, travelling through beautiful scenery. Try asking for Carlos at the *Cafetería Coni* who can arrange trips and act as guide (Spanish). Rec boats: Nery's boat *Yertzy*; Mariel or Cambell with *Lidia II* (speaks good English).

Boats can also be hired in Livingston to cross Amatique Bay to the N to the tip of the long finger of land beyond Puerto Barrios. At *Estero Lagarto*, near Punta Manabique, there is a laid-back resort called *Pirate's Point*, thatched *cabañas*, **E**, restaurant, campsite, **G**, American owned (Jimmy and Ingrid Overman), miles of white sand, good snorkelling, fishing and birdwatching. A boat for the day costs about US$25-30 shared between several passengers, 45-60-minute crossing. Transport may also be arranged through the Empresa Portuaria in Puerto Barrios or with one of the fishermen whose boats leave from the house of Doña Licha, near *African Place*. At the 'neck' of the peninsula there is a channel (Canal Ingleses) which connects the bay with the Caribbean. You can take a boat through the channel.

To Punta Gorda in Belize, wait at the jetty or the Immigration Office, depart about 0700, 2 hrs journey, US$15, expect to have to pay an unofficial exit tax of about US$2. Anyone who says they will take you must have a manifest with passengers names stamped and signed at Immigration Office. Boats can be hired to go to southern Belize cayes, US$14 per day, max 6 passengers, rec.

Near **Fronteras**, commonly known as **Río Dulce**, 23 km upstream at entrance to **Lago de Izabal** (site of new bridge, toll US$1), is **A** *Turicentro Marimonte*, 500m to right at Shell station, bungalows (T 478585 for reservations), restaurant, pool, mixed reports, no real camp site but you can park a camper van overnight,

US$2 per car, US$6 pp, use of showers and pool; C *Izabal Tropical*, bungalows, T 478115, over the bridge look for sign in the village, 4 km to hotel on lake shore (it is 1 km from Castillo San Felipe), charming setting, rec, you may also park your car and sleep in it for a tip of US$1; F *Marilú*, El Relleno on N side, with bath, but rooms are sheds full of holes, uncertain water supply, no electricity late pm, beware of overcharging; F *Hospedaje Riverside*, cold water, shared bath, fan, friendly, good (no water in late pm), about 200m on left from bridge (the first hotel on the right after the bridge going NE is not rec, overcharges, unfriendly); G *Hotel Río Dulce*, by railway, brothel but cheapest and friendly; F *Hospedaje* at Río Dulce bus stop, clean, shower, reports vary. The US-owned B *Catamaran* (taxes extra), T 478361, bungalows, pool, friendly and helpful, expensive restaurant but good food, is reached by outboard canoe (US$1.50 from Río Dulce, 2 km or 10 mins downstream, T 364450, Guatemala City, for reservations). A *Hotel Del Río*, a few km downstream, inc 3 meals, F without meals, has seen better days (Guatemala City 310016 for reservations). *Comedor El Quetzal*, near the bridge at Río Dulce, has excellent sea food; *Restaurant Olimar*, Swiss-run, on waterfront nr Hacienda Tijax, good. *Hacienda Tijax* near the bridge at Río Dulce, has 4 jungle lodges, A-E, depending on season. Good breakfasts at the *Bar Hotel California*, overlooking the river by the bridge, known as *Tom's Place*. Enquire here about Punta Bacadilla, 30 mins downstream, where there is a bar, restaurant and a place to sling your hammock for US$1 per night, tent sites and hammock rentals available. Mosquitoes abound however, and not all reports are favourable. There are yachting facilities at Río Dulce. *Once Around Suzanna Laguna Marina* is reached by 2-min shuttle boat from NE corner of the bridge across the Río Dulce; good, inexpensive food and drinks at the Marina. In the Río Dulce there are hot springs at Aguas Calientes; there is no beach so you have to swim to them from a boat.

Captain John Clark offers sailing trips on his 46-foot Polynesian catamaran, highly rec. One 2-3 day sail is to Río Dulce canyon, Livingston, Lago Izabal, hot waterfalls, Castillo de San Felipe, US$80-121 pp double occupancy. The other 7-day sail is to Río Dulce, Livingston and the Belize Cayes, US$279 pp double occupancy, inc food, taxes, snorkelling and fishing gear, windsurf boards. Trips leave on Fridays, credit cards accepted. Contact Aventuras Vacacionales, 4 C, 6-63, Zona 13, 01013 Guatemala City, T/F 736253, or in Panajachel T/F 622029, or Antigua T 323041, F 320892, or the USA, 7570 La Madre Way, Las Vegas, Nevada 89129, F (702) 2553641.

At the entrance to Lake Izabal, 2 km upstream, is the old Spanish fort of **Castillo de San Felipe** (entrance US$2) with a pleasant park, restaurant and swimming pool, US$0.40 (boat from El Relleno, Río Dulce—below the new bridge—US$2.50 return for one, US$0.50 pp in groups; it is a 5 km walk, practically impossible after rain). The fortification was first built about 1600, was rebuilt and expanded in 1688 and restored as a national monument in 1955-56. E *Hotel Don Humberto*, at San Felipe; also basic *pensión*, G, which is not recommended. The Lake Izabal area is a habitat for the manatee (sea cow). A reserve, the **Biotopo Chacón-Machaca del Manatí**, has been set up halfway between San Felipe and Livingston on the northern shore of El Golfete, where the Río Dulce broadens into a lake 5 km across. The reserve has been set up to protect the mangrove swamps and the local wildlife including jaguars and tapirs as well as the endangered manatee. It covers 135 sq km, with both a land and an aquatic trail. (The Park, like the Biotopo del Quetzal, is run by Centro de Estudios Conservacionistas - Cecon - and Inguat; entry US$2). A boat from the bridge to Livingston costs US$60 for 2 people, a day trip with a stopover at the Biotopo, Aguas Calientes and some lagoons, highly rec. It is probably cheaper to hire a boat here than in Livingston for this trip. All prices, tours and numbers of passengers negotiable. The likeliest way to see manatees is to hire a rowing boat and allow plenty of time; the animals are allergic to the noise of motor boats.

On the NW shore of Lago de Izabal is *El Estor*—its name dates back to the days when the British living in the Atlantic area got their provisions from a store situated at this spot—where nickel-mining began in 1978 but was suspended after the oil crisis of 1982 because the process depended on cheap sources of energy. The mine is still closed, but oil prospecting has started. It is a good place to relax, quiet, cheap and in a beautiful setting. One can hire a boat from Río Dulce to El Estor for about US$60, which alternatively can be reached by going to Mariscos on the S side of Lago de Izabal, then crossing on the boat (US$1.50, 0800 and 1300) to El Estor, to which there is no direct road. Coming by road from Guatemala City or Puerto Barrios, get off at La Trinchera and continue by pick-up to Mariscos. For the routes from El Estor to Cobán via either Panzós and Tactic, or Cahabón and Lanquín, **see p 467**. (Note that if taking the 1300 boat from Mariscos to El Estor, there is no bus connection on to Lanquín or Cobán. All buses leave El Estor in the morning.)

Lodging and Food F *Hotel Los Almendros*, rec; **D** *Hotel Vista al Lago*, 6 Av, 1-13, owned by Oscar Paz who will take you fishing; **F** *Villela*, big rooms with bath, nice, clean, friendly, patio, rec; **F** *Santa Clara*, friendly, basic, clean, others at similar prices. Also restaurants: *Hugo's*, good; *Rancho Mery*, fish and beer only, big helpings, delicious; a very good one at ferry point for Mariscos; a *comedor* 1 block from *Hotel Vista al Lago* on waterfront is good and cheap, eggs, beans and coffee for US$0.50.

On the shore of Lago de Izabel is *Casa Guatemala*, a children's orphanage, run by a lady called Angie, where you can work in exchange for basic accommodation and food. There are about 200 children. Ask for information in Fronteras.

A ferry leaves El Estor at 0600 for Mariscos (US$1, 1 hr 50 mins, returns 1300) from where there are buses to the twin town of ***Bananera/Morales***, US$0.60 and Puerto Barrios, US$1; from Bananera there are buses to the Río Dulce crossing (road paved, 30 km, US$0.80 in minibus), Puerto Barrios and the Petén (US$4, 10 hrs to Flores); return buses from Río Dulce to Bananera start at 0600. Morales is a short distance off the main road, check carefully where the bus you want will stop. Train to Guatemala City is supposed to leave at 0915. At Bananera, **G** *Hospedaje Liberia*, basic, but OK; *Simon's*, basic, dirty, not rec; **G** *Pensión Montalvo*, next to station, basic but clean, friendly, quiet. Best place to eat cheaply, *Carnita Kelly*, good meat, homemade tortillas. One decent restaurant in Morales, *Nineth*.

At ***Mariscos***, **F** *Hospedaje Karilinda*, good food, right on the lake, rec; **G** *Cafetería/Hospedaje Los Almendros*, good. Many Guatemalans have holiday homes on Lago de Izabal, particularly around Mariscos. *Cauca* (dory) trips can be arranged to Livingston, via San Felipe, from Mariscos, 5 hrs, US$18 for 3 people.

EL PETEN: THE MAYA CENTRES AND THE JUNGLE (3)

Mostly deep in the jungle and reached only in the dry season, or, as with the majestic Tikal, full-blown tourist sites, ancient Maya cities are the main attraction of El Petén. Flores on Lake Petén Itzá is the chief starting point; another, but less developed and less-easily accessible is Sayaxché. From both there are tough road and river routes into Mexico; from Flores is the principal road route to Belize.

El Petén Department in the far N, which was so impenetrable that its inhabitants, the Itzáes, were not conquered by the Spaniards until 1697, is now reached by road either from Km 245, opposite Morales, on the Atlantic Highway, or from Cobán, through Sebol and Sayaxché, or by air. The local products are chicle and timber (the tropical forest S of Flores is being rapidly destroyed)—and mosquitoes in the rainy season; take plenty of repellent, and re-apply frequently.

From either Guatemala City or Puerto Barrios, the road from the Atlantic

Highway is paved to **Modesto Méndez** (no accommodation, but you can borrow a hammock). A new bridge has been built over the Río Sarstún, then 215 km on a road which is narrow and winding in stretches, otherwise broad, dusty and potholed. Despite the first, paved 40 km it takes 7 hrs to drive in a private car.

Never drive at night. Some drivers suggest driving in front of a truck and, if you break down, do so across the road, then you will be assured of assistance. Alternatively after rain, it is advisable to follow a truck, and do not hurry.

NB Since Tikal is a 'must' on the visitor's itinerary, there are many tourists at Flores and the ruins. Demand has outstripped supply, prices are therefore high and quality of service often poor. If you have several days available, consider staying in Flores/Santa Elena and making the easy trip to the ruins each day. This will involve paying daily to enter the Park. Sadly theft is common, and watch out for rip-offs. Tikal, however, will not disappoint you.

Flores, the Department's capital, lies in the heart of the Petén, and is built on an island in the middle of Lake Petén Itzá. It is linked by a causeway with Santa Elena (airport). Its population is 5,000. There have been heavier than average rains in the past few years and the level of the lake, which has no surface outlet, has been rising, giving problems to some lakeside properties and making the causeway difficult. There is a ferry. From Flores the ruins of Tikal and other Maya cities can be reached. (For description of Maya culture **see the Introduction to this book**). There is a collection of stelae, altars, etc, from Naranjo and other remote Maya sites, in a park W of the airport; no labels or guide book. *Fiesta*: 1-14 January.

Hotels In Flores: **C** *La Casona de las Islas*, T 501318, F 501258, on the lake (water encroaching), elegant rooms, fans, clean, friendly, good restaurant, bar, garden, takes major credit cards; **C** *Sabana*, inc breakfast and evening meal, huge rather spartan rooms, good service, clean, pleasant, good view, manager from Belize, caters for European package tours; **D** *Yum Kax*, with bath and a/c; **D** *La Mesa de los Mayas*, T 501240, clean, friendly, good bathrooms, rec; **D** *Santa Rita*, with bath, clean, excellent service, rec; **D** *Petén*, T 500692, F 500662, with hot water, C with lake view, clean, rec, breakfast a little extra, helpful travel agency (will change TCs) rec minibus service to Tikal, may give free ride to airport, very obliging, will store luggage, ask for the new rooms at the front; **E** *Casa Blanca*, rooms with 2 double beds, can sleep 4, clean sheets, hot showers downstairs, drinking water available, very accommodating, can arrange Tikal trip; **E** *El Itzá*, basic, no hot water, dangerous fixtures, unfriendly, avoid; **E** *El Itzá II*, new, nice rooms, shower, but watch your belongings; **F** *Tucán*, on the lakeside and becoming flooded, four rooms only, run by Dutch woman and her Guatemalan husband, comfortable, restaurant in garden with collection of birds, friendly, excellent food, highly rec; **E** *Villa del Lago* next door, T 501446, new, smart, very clean, small balcony over lake, no food, cold drinks, friendly, rec.

At Santa Elena: **A** *Del Patio Tikal*, T 501229, clean, hot water, a/c, modern, colour TV, expensive restaurant, best booked as part of package; **B** *Maya Internacional*, T 501276, tax extra, beautifully situated on the lake front, but firmly under water in 1993; **A** *Tziqui Na Ha*, near airport, T 501359, a/c pool, overpriced; **C** *Costa del Sol*, T 501336, 1 block from bus station, pool, friendly; **D** *San Juan I* close to the Catholic Church, bus stop outside, travel agency inside acts as Aviateca office, tours arranged, pleasant, full of budget travellers, luxurious remodelled rooms and older rooms, credit cards accepted, also cash advances on credit cards and TC exchange, clean, safe, not to be confused with *San Juan II*. **D** *Sac Nicte*, by lake below road to Flores, small rooms, electric shower, fan, some trouble with water and electricity, not very clean, friendly, minibus to Tikal; **E** *Alonzo*, 6 Av, 4-99, T 500105, with bath, F without, clean, fan, quiet, minibus to Tikal; **G** *Jade*, very simple, intermittent electricity, clean, helpful, just by the causeway to Flores, will store luggage; **F** *Leo Fu Lo*, on lake, quiet, hot water, restaurant (Chinese, good); **F** *Don Quijote*, next door, on lake, friendly and good restaurant (eg paella), will store luggage, but reported to be deteriorating. **F** *San Juan II*, close to the lake, cheaper without bath, front rooms noisy, staff helpful and friendly, luggage store, money exchange; **G** *Ahauna-Ula*, good restaurant.

Between Santa Elena and Tikal: **L** *Camino Real*, T 500204, 30 km from Santa Elena, at El Remate **see p 479**, on shore of lake, all rooms have views, free minibus from airport, good restaurant, a/c, free use of boats on the lake, cable TV etc; **B** *Villa Maya*, 5 km from Santa Elena airport on road to Tikal, bungalows, nice setting beside lake, helpful, pool, rec, only drawback is set menu, if you do not like it you are a long way from an alternative restaurant.

Restaurants At Flores: *El Jacal*, on road to left of causeway, good regional dishes, animal skins on walls; *Gran Jaguar*, pleasant, very good, rec, relocated to other side of lake because of flooding; *La Jungla*, reasonably priced, rec; *El Faisán*, reasonable prices, good food; *El Tucán*—see **Hotels**, the best place at sunset; *La Mesa de los Mayas*, good food, clean, toucan in cage; *Chez Michel*, enterprising menu, eg wild game fondue and figs in port with vanilla ice cream.

At Santa Elena: *El Rodeo*, 2 C y 5 Av, excellent, reasonable prices, classical music; *El Lago Azul*, good value; *La Parranda* on the lake. Santa Elena market, well-stocked, 2 blocks from *Hotel San Juan*, just off Guatel road.

NB In restaurants, do not order *tepezcuintle*, a rabbit-sized jungle rodent that is endangered.

Laundry *Lavandería Fénix* with dryer, US$2 wash and dry.

Dugouts or fibreglass one or two-seaters can be hired to paddle yourself around the lake (US$2 per hour). Check dugouts for lake-worthiness. You can swim from 'Radio Petén' island, the small island which used to have a radio mast on it, US$0.12 by boat, though there are signs of increasing water contamination. Petenito (La Guitarra) island in the lake is being developed for tourism (known as 'Paraíso Escondido'); there is a small zoo of local animals, birds and reptiles (the conditions are not good), 2 water toboggan slides, and plant-lined walks, rec, but popular at weekends. Dugout to island, US$3 pp. Boat tours of the whole lake cost about US$10 per boat, calling at these islands, a lookout on a Maya ruin and *Gringo Perdido* (see p 479); whatever you may request, the zoo will almost certainly be included in the itinerary.

San Benito, a US$0.05 (US$0.10 after 1800) ride across the lake (or walk from Santa Elena), has some small restaurants (eg *Santa Teresita*), which are cheaper but less inviting than those in Flores. **G** *San Juan*, clean; **G** *Hotel Rey*, friendly, untidy, noisy; **F** *Hotel Miraflores*, good, private showers. A dirty village, but good football matches at weekends. Regular launch service from San Benito across the lake to San Andrés (US$0.12) and San José (US$0.15) on NW shore. **G** *Hospedaje El Reposo Maya*, at San Andrés.

10 mins by road from Santa Elena are the Aktun Kan caves, a fascinating labyrinth of tunnels.

Car Hire at airport, mostly Suzuki jeeps; Jade agency is rec.

Exchange Flores: **Banco de Guatemala**, C Rosario y Av Santa María, open Mon-Thur, 0830-1400, Fri 0830-1430, changes Amex TCs; **Banco Hipotecario**. Santa Elena: **Banco Granai y Townson**. The major hotels and travel agents change cash and TCs.

Telephones Guatel in Santa Elena.

Travel Agents Flores: *Petén Travel Agency*, can arrange trips in Tikal, Sayaxché and region and to other Maya sites. *Total Petén*, T 500662/501318, F 500662, F 501258. Santa Elena: *San Juan Travel Agency*, T/F 500041/2, reliable transport to Tikal 0400 (in time to see sun rise), 0600, 0800, 1000, returns, 1200, 1400, 1600, 1700, US$6 return, US$30 inc tour, also excursions to Ceibal US$30, and Uaxactun US$20, with non-bilingual guide. Excellent service to Belize, US$20 (except driver sometimes stops for breakfast after only 30 mins) 0500, arrives 1100, wake up call if you stay at *San Juan* hotel, otherwise collect from your hotel, bus links with Chocolate's boat to Caye Caulker, ticket US$8 from *San Juan* hotel US$6 in Belize. *Transportes Inter-Petén*, 10 C, 10-32, Zona 1, San Benito, T 500574, for transport to archaeological sites, Belize, etc.

Airport 4 companies fly from Guatemala City to Flores: Aviateca, Aerovías, Tikal Jet and Aviones Comercial (small plane, irregular). Aviateca charges US$160 return, the others less, but enquire about special offers: eg Aviateca may offer reduction if you buy an international ticket from them. Aviateca and Aero Caribe fly to and from Cancún (Mexico) three days a week. Prices reported to us (1993) range from US$60-90 one way, but one reader found a special deal of US$50 return. Be early for flights, overbooking is common and reconfirming is no help. The schedules appear to change frequently, but all fly daily at 0700 or 0800; flights back leave between 1600 and 1700, but check. See **Information for Visitors** for flights to other countries. You must have passport (or identity documents) to pass through Santa Elena airport. *Inguat Tourist Office* at Santa Elena airport, T 500533.

Buses The Flores bus terminal is in Santa Elena, a 10-min walk from Flores (urban bus US$0.10, taxi whatever you can bargain). Services from the capital are run by Maya Express, T 501232, US$10, no stops, at 1600, 1800 and 2000 daily, from Santa Elena, 1700, 1800, 2000 to *Guatemala City*, 12 hrs. Also by La Petenera, T 500070 (early morning and late afternoon each way) US$10, 15 hrs; Tikal Express, T 500574 and Fuente del Norte, throughout the day including express buses, US$10, and ordinary buses, US$7, 12-15 hrs with refreshment stops, take food anyway and your passport in case of army checks, very crowded (try riding on roof for breathing space). If you are going only to Poptún or Fronteras/Río Dulce make sure you do not pay the full fare to Guatemala City. Route is via Morales and Modesto Méndez;

GUATEMALA

BELIZE

Tenosique
La Palma

Reserva
Biósfera
Maya

Dos Lagunas

To
Belize
City

Carmelita

El Pedregal

Río San Pedro

Ontario

BELMOPAN

El Naranjo

P.N. Sierra
de Lacandón

Lago
Petén
Itza

El Remate

San Ignacio

To
Palenque

Frontera Echeverría

Melchor
de
Mencos

Benque
Viejo
del Carmen

Reserva
Biósfera
Montes Azules

Benemérito

Flores

El Cruce

R. Pasión

Sayaxché

To
Dangriga

Dolores

San Pedro

MEXICO

Río Machaquila

Poptún

San Antonio

Río Lacantún

San Luis

Pt.
Gorda

Playa
Grande

Xuctzul

Raxrujá

F. Bartolomé
de las Casas

Modesto
Méndez

R. Sarstún

Barillas

N

Chisec

Sebol

Cahabón

Castillo de
San Felipe

El Estor

To Pto.
Barrios

Livingston

Lago de
Izabal

Pajal

Lanquín

San Pedro Carchá

Semuc
Champey

Senahú

Cahaboncito

Morales

Mariscos

To
Sacapulas &
Huehuetenango

Cobán

Tamahú

Tucurú

Telemán

MAC 43

Uspantán

San
Cristóbal
Verapaz

Tactic

To
Guatemala City &
Biotopo del Quetzal

To
Guatemala City

Not to Scale

Archaeological Sites

1. El Mirador
2. Río Azul
3. Uaxactún
4. El Zotz
5. Tikal
6. Nakum
7. Yaxhá

8. Xunantunich
9. Piedras Negras
10. Yaxchilán
11. Bonampak
12. Caracol
13. Nimli Punit

14. Lubaantun
15. Naj Tunich Cave
16. Ixcún
17. El Ceibal
18. Aguateca

19. Dos Pilas
20. Altar de los
Sacrificios
21. Itzán
22. Quiriguá

EL PETEN
& ALTA
VERAPAZ

from Flores 'the first 6 hrs are terrifying, a virtual rollercoaster: book early if you want a front seat!'. Also minibus, more expensive, faster but beware owner saying nothing else is available. Bus Flores to **Río Dulce**, US$4, Fuente del Norte, 8 hrs. Bus between Flores and *Quiriguá* (**see p 470**), US$5, 11 hrs. In the rainy season the trip can take as much as 28 hrs, and in all weathers it is very uncomfortable and crowded (flights warmly rec). There is a minibus to *Belize City* at 0500, US$20, 5 hrs, 3 hrs to border, see below.

Maya ruins fans wishing to economize can travel to **Copán** by bus from Flores to Morales, then from Morales to Chiquimula, then from Chiquimula to El Florido (**see p 468**) and finally from there to Copán.

Those who wish to break the journey could get off the bus and spend a night in Morales, Río Dulce, **San Luis** (**G** *Pensión San Antonio*, nice; *Comedor Oriente*, cheap, good) or Poptún. **Poptún** is 100 km from Flores; 5 minibuses a day from Flores, US$3 or take Fuente del Norte bus, US$1.15, 4 hrs; bus Poptún-Guatemala City at 0900 and 2400 (en route from Flores), 11 hrs, US$6, long and bumpy; take this bus also for Cobán, alight at the turn-off to Sebol, 5 km before Modesto Méndez, hitch to Fray Bartolomé de las Casas (**see p 484**), then take 0500 bus to Cobán. Alternatively, take bus (4 daily, 2½ hrs, US$1) to Sayaxché and to Cobán via Chisec with pick up truck or hitch, a long ride, need a day to recover from bruises (**see p 485**). La Pinita has a service from Flores to Poptún and Sayaxché, see below. Bus Poptún-Río Dulce US$5. *Pensión Isabelita*, F, clean, rec, but no electricity at night; *Pensión Gabriel*, G. At certain times of the year delicious mangoes are on sale in this area. Good view of the town from Cerro de la Cruz, a 15-minute walk from the market.

3 km S of Poptún is *Finca Ixobel*, a working farm owned by Carole DeVine (only rarely

there). At this highly acclaimed 'paradise', one may camp for US$1 pp. There are shelters, tree houses, showers, free firewood, one unforgettable parrot, swimming, riding, rafting, many short and longer treks in the jungle, farm produce for sale; excellent family-style meals available, and there is a small guest house, F, travellers' cheques exchanged. This is a popular stop for backpackers. They have a restaurant-bar (also called *Ixobel*, excellent too, and *hospedaje* next door) in the centre of Poptún where the buses stop. Ask there for transport to the *Finca*. Two cave expeditions are organized; the one day River Cave Trip is rec. Unfortunately, the 3-day mule hike to the Cueva de las Inscripciones (Naj Tunich), once used by Maya, has been suspended after vandals in 1989 rubbed off some of the marvellous glyphs. The cave is now closed but 3-day jungle expeditions are organized instead. Hector Gómez, Barrio Santa María Poptún, T 507327, also offers jungle treks of 4 days visiting caves and forest on his own property with groups of 4-12 people, rec. A novel way of returning to Guatemala City from *Finca Ixobel* is to leave at midnight and take the bus to Morales to catch the train for Guatemala. It will cost you US$8 on the bus and you must walk from the main road to Morales (4 km) at 0430 to await the train at 0930. You arrive at 0200, in theory, the next day.

24 km N of Poptún, 8 km NE of Dolores, is the small Maya site of *Ixcún*, unexcavated, with a number of monuments (some carved), and a natural hill topped by the remains of ancient structures. The access road is impassable in the rainy season.

In 1982, the **Cerro Cahui Conservation Park** was opened on the northern shore of Lake Petén Itzá; this is a lowland jungle area where one can see 3 species of monkeys, deer, jaguar, peccary, some 450 species of birds; run by Cecon and Inguat. There are several trails through hilly country with good views of the lake. Almost at the entrance to the Cerro Cahui Conservation Park is **C** *El Gringo Perdido Parador Ecológico* (T Guatemala City 25811, F 538761, Viajes Mundial, 5 Av, 12-44, Zona 1), with a restaurant, cabins, camping (US$3 a night) and good swimming in the lake, good meals available at US$1.25 or C pp for dinner, bed and breakfast and sandwich lunch, owner keen on triathlon. Canoes (US$4 per day); mountain bikes, horses and guides are available. Good walking. It is about 4 km from El Cruce on the Tikal road, turning off to the left along the N shore of the lake. To get there walk 3 km from El Remate, or ask for a boat in *El Gringo Perdido* store, El Remate. The road from El Remate to *El Gringo Perdido* is often flooded. There is also accommodation up the hill overlooking **El Remate**: *Eco-Camping*, El Mirador del Duende, El Remate, Km 30 on road to Tikal, T/F 500269, run by Manuel Soto Villafuente and his family, overlooks lake Petén Itzá, G pp for bed or hammock, jungle trips highly rec, US$25/day. No electricity, take flashlight. In El Remate is a handicraft shop selling carvings in tropical hardwood made by a group of local farmers; items cost from US$6 to US$60, rec. Tourist and minibuses stop here.

Tikal The great Maya ruins of vast temples and public buildings are reached by bus from Santa Elena (see below). Tikal lasted from the third century AD until the tenth. An overall impression of the ruins (a national park) may be gained in 4-5 hrs, but you need at least 2 days to see everything. Ruins (open 0600-1730 daily) charge US$6 per day. The **Museum** is worth a visit; a good collection of Maya ceramics and a reproduction of the tomb of the ruler Chac, entrance US$2 (open Mon-Fri 0900-1700, Sat and Sun 0900-1600). Extended passes to see the ruins at sunrise/sunset (until 2100) are easy to obtain from the Inspectoría office on the slope by the path to the ruins (especially good for seeing animals). It is best to visit the ruins after 1400, or before 0900 (fewer tourists). All the pyramids can be climbed except Temple I; Temple IV, the highest, especially recommended. A network of tunnels linking some of the temples has recently been discovered near El Mundo Perdido. Ask a guard to show you. Also recommended to see the wildlife around Temple III between sunrise and 0800. There is officially nowhere to store luggage at Tikal while you are visiting the ruins but you may be able to persuade the Inspectoría to help. The guide book (Spanish or English), *Tikal*, by W R Coe, has an essential map (updated 1988) price US$11 in the capital, US$10 at Casa Andinista, Antigua, or slightly more at the Tikal Museum and the entrance to the park; some visitors find the text difficult to connect with what is seen. Without a guide book, a guide, US$10-20, is essential (Maximiliano has been rec, he will meet you at 0500, US$20, speaks Spanish), as outlying structures can otherwise easily be missed—and there are many km of trails. Guides are available by the hotels, at the Rangers' Office (Inspectoría), or where the buses park. A Land Rover trip through the ruins costs US$2.50.

Marvellous place for seeing animal and bird life of the jungle. Take binoculars. There is a secluded part, called 'El Mundo Perdido', in which wildlife can be seen. *Birds of Tikal*, by Frank B Smithe, available at the museum, but for the serious bird watcher, Peterson's *Field Guide to Mexican Birds* is recommended (covers most Central American birds also) and a quality guide to North American birds is helpful if visiting Tikal in the early months of the year. Ask for Normandy Bonilla González if you would like a local expert. Wildlife includes spider monkeys, howler monkeys (re-established after being hit by disease), three species of toucan (most prominent being the 'Banana Bill'), deer, foxes and many other birds and insects. Mosquitoes can be a real problem even during the day if straying away from open spaces. It rains here most days for a while between April and December. It is busiest November to January and during the Easter and Northern Hemisphere summer holidays.

To visit Tikal you can take package tours from Guatemala City, but due to tourist demand these are now expensive, at least US$250 for 3 days/2 nights with not necessarily much time to see the ruins. A one day inclusive air trip can cost US$250, which includes the bus to Tikal, lunch while there and a guide. If you are in a party of say 6 to 10 it may be worth investigating a private plane, cost similar to the US$250 pp quoted, and more time flexibility at Tikal. Servicios Turísticos del Petén, 2 Av 7-78, Zona 10, Guatemala, T 363909/346235, highly rec. Buses from Guatemala City are all on 17 C between 8-10 Avs, and cost under US$10: La Petenera, dep 1600, 1800, 2000; Fuentes del Norte, 0100, 0200, 0300, 0700, 2100; Maya Express, 1600, 2000. If you wish to drive, you will need a sturdy vehicle though not 4-wheel drive.

From Santa Elena, it is possible to visit Tikal in a day. San Juan Travel Agency minibuses leave 0400, 0600, 0800, 1000, return 1200, 1400, 1600, 1700, 1 hr, US$6 return. Several other companies and hotels also run minibuses at the same price although out of season you can bargain. If you have not bought a return ticket you can often get a discounted seat on a returning bus if it is not full. The 0400 bus should get you to Tikal in time to see the sunrise, but do not rely on it. Minibuses meet Guatemala City-Flores flights to take visitors to Tikal, but check arrangements with your airline or hotel. Taxi to Tikal costs US$16 per vehicle, or US$24 waiting for return. Mario Grijalba, T 500624, has been rec.

Hotels Note: It is advisable to book a hotel room or camping space as soon as you arrive—in high seasons, book in advance. **B** *Jaguar Inn*, full board, triple room C (without board: D), will provide picnic lunch at US$1.30. Its electricity supply is the most reliable (1800-2200); will store luggage, you may share your room with bugs and lizards. Tents can be hired at about US$10, to use in their campground, inc mattress, sleep 2-3. Wife of proprietor, Patricia (English) is very knowledgeable on local wildlife. **B** *Tikal Inn*, in rooms (1 to 4 people) and B for up to four in a lodge, cheap accommodation without electricity also available, guests only restaurant, breakfast and dinner included in room price, mediocre food, pool (dirty), they have a pet ocelot who is very cute but its teeth are sharp; **A** *Jungle Lodge*, reservations direct T 501519, or may be made at 29 C, 18-01, Zona 12, Guatemala City, T 768775, although this is not recommended as you have to pay for one night in advance and we have been repeatedly told that reservations get lost somewhere down the line, with bath and fan (electricity 1800-2230 max), C without bath. It is cheaper to pay in quetzales than dollars at the lodge, they will cash TCs, new bungalows have been built but rooms reported dirty with used bed linen, full board available (food fair, but service slow and portions small); has its own campsite with toilets and cold shower facilities where you can sling your hammock for US$6 and rent tent for about US$7.60. Some mosquito nets for rent but better take your own, without one you will not sleep. Jungle Lodge's Tikal tours (US$5) have been rec; runs bus to meet incoming flights, US$2.50 one way.

Comedores: *Comedor Tikal*, good food, rec; you can put up your hammock at the back; *Imperio Maya* (opens 0530), good food and lots of it at reasonable prices, friendly, very slow; *Restaurant del Parque*, annex to the stelae museum, hygiene neglected, staff rude. Sometimes the restaurants only have chicken on the menu. Economical travellers are best advised to bring their own food (you can pay US$2 for a candy bar), and especially drink. Everyone should take drinking water.

Camping There is one campsite (US$6), by the old airstrip (which is closed except for emergencies for ecological reasons), rents a few small hammocks with mosquito netting for US$3 best to bring your own, very popular. Take your own water as the supply is very variable, sometimes rationed, sometimes unlimited, depending on season. Bathing is possible in a pond at the far end of the airstrip (check first). Beware of chiggers in the grass.

Wear light cotton clothes, a broad-brimmed hat and take plenty of insect repellent. The nights can be cold, however; at least one warm garment is advisable. Soft drinks are available near every major temple or pyramid (US$0.75). No banking services available, and exchange rates locally in hotels, etc are poor. Bring enough quetzales with you. Take a torch, electricity at Tikal is only available 1800-2200 and then is intermittent.

Warning There are increasing numbers of bats in Tikal, and anyone bitten must seek medical aid right away. This means an immediate return to Guatemala City and a visit to the Centro de Salud, 9 C between Av 2 and 3 for treatment, including tetanus shots if necessary. The treatment is free.

Note Heavy rains and flooding can close the road between Tikal and Flores, but the 65 km is paved all the way. 30 km from Santa Elena is Puente Ixlu, known as El Cruce where the main road turns E to the Belize border. Most of this 81 km is unpaved, 4 WD needed in the wet season and hard to average more than 30 kmph when it is dry.

25 km N of Tikal is **Uaxactún**, which has a stuccoed temple with serpent head decoration. Uaxactún is one of the longest-occupied Maya sites and contains the oldest complete Mayan astronomical complex. The road from Tikal is in good condition and takes less than 1 hr in any vehicle. There are 2 buses a day from Santa Elena, 0600, 1300 via Tikal 0830, 1530, arrive 0930, 1630, returning 0500, 1100. A campsite 150m from the ruins has toilets, showers and guard service, G pp. The village has laundry service, *comedores* and a tourist office. *Hotel Campamento El Chiclero* has hammocks or rooms, a zoo and museum of the life and work of the *chicleros*. Contact the Association of Eco-Cultural Guides of Uaxactún for tours and expeditions to Xultún, Río Azul, El Zotz, Nakbe and El Mirador. A guided tour of the ruins is US$15 for 2 people, US$20 for 3 or more; jungle treks inc food, mules, guides etc are US$30 pp/day for 8-10 days. Nearby is *El Zotz*, another large site, reachable by a reasonable dirt road. In the far N of El Petén is *Río Azul*, which has impressive early tomb murals and early classic standing architecture (under investigation each dry season). The road to Río Azul goes via Dos Lagunas, beyond which it is very bad, 2-3 days from Tikal by 4-wheel drive (the army sometimes restricts travel N of Dos Lagunas). All the sites are accessible by jeeps in the dry season.

The largest Maya site in the country is at *El Mirador*, just short of the northern border with Mexico, 36 km direct from **Carmelita**, very many more by jungle trail from Flores (a 3-5 day trek—a guide is essential, take plenty of food; only possible by 4-wheel drive in dry season). No permission is needed to visit the site because there are permanent guards there. If you are uncertain, check with the Archaeology Dept behind the Gobernación in Flores. The larger of the two huge pyramids, called La Danta, is 70m high. Don't expect too much, the view from the top is simply of endless jungle, and there has so far been only minimal clearing and excavation. There are paintings and other treasures; guards at the site will show you around if no one else is on hand. Camping is possible. Free water purification tablets for the trip can be obtained at the pharmacy of the army barracks by the airport. Drive or hitch-hike to Carmelita (no bus service beyond San Andrés on Lake Petén Itzá); a hard 65 km that can take 5 hrs—after rain four-wheel drive, a winch and shovel are necessary. Take sufficient food and water, or at least water purification tablets, from Flores as the local *tiendas* in Carmelita are notoriously understocked. Normally one truck a day leaves San Andrés for Carmelita. At Carmelita, ask around for space to sling your hammock or camp. Also ask for guides who go with mules to El Mirador (Sebastián Hernández and Rudy are rec; Chepe who lives next to the doctor is not, he doesn't have mules and may not be able to obtain them): US$12 per day for mule and guide. Allow 2 days each way unless you want a forced march. Take water, food, hammocks, mosquito nets, tents and torches; cooking gear is not essential because guides will make a fire and the guards may let you use their kitchen if you're polite (they also appreciate gifts, eg a giant can of peaches). You will pass 'chicleros' camps on the way, who are very hospitable, but very poor also. Gifts in return for staying with them are much appreciated, food, batteries for torches (used to guard against nocturnal snakes) for example. For staying overnight there are fewer mosquitoes at El Arroyo than at Tintal camp. Ticks can be a menace in the jungle and scorpions at El Mirador camp. You need reasonable Spanish to get the most from this sort of excursion.

About 30 km from Flores, on the road towards the Belize border, is Lake Yaxhá. On the northern shore is the site of *Yaxhá*, the third-largest known classic Maya site in the country, accessible by causeway (little excavation has yet been done). In the lake is the site of Topoxte. (The island is accessible by boat.) The site is unique since it flourished between the 12th and 14th centuries, long after the abandonment of all other classic centres. 20 km further N lies **Nakum**, with standing Maya buildings. It is possible to drive part of the way (dry season, April-May) only, or else to walk, but since there are numerous forks in the track, it is essential to hire a guide (no overland transport or flights in the off-season).

To Belize Since the establishment of formal diplomatic relations between Guatemala and Belize in September 1991, travel between the two countries has improved and been simplified. There are several buses from Santa Elena to **Melchor de Mencos**, starting at 0500, about 3$\frac{1}{2}$ hrs inc breakfast stop, US$2. Bus from Melchor de Mencos to Flores include Autobuses de Rosita, on main street near *Hotel Mayab*. These buses call at El Cruce (the turn off for Tikal). Connecting buses for San Ignacio, Belmopan and Belize City wait at Melchor de Mencos (if you catch the 0500 bus from Santa Elena you can be in Belize City by noon). In addition, there is a non-stop minibus service at 0500 to Belize City, reserve previous day with travel agents, cost US$20. This service terminates at the Shell Station in Belize from where boats to the Cayes leave. If driving from Flores/Tikal to Belize, take spare fuel. Transport from the border direct to Tikal costs US$10 pp, minimum 4 passengers. **NB** If you need a visa to enter either Belize (other than transit) or Mexico, it is safer to get it before crossing from Guatemala at this point though you may be able to get one at the border for US$5. You may also get asked for another US$1 on your departure if you bought your visa at the border. You can also fly from Flores to Belize City (see above).

Accommodation and Services at Melchor de Mencos: **E** *Mayab*, clean, comfortable, fan, F with shared showers and toilets, hot water, rec, safe parking; **G** *Zacaleu*, clean, good value, shared toilets/showers; *La Chinita*, 1 block from *Mayab*, good dinner under US$2; *El Hilton*, good meals, reasonable prices; *Ribera*, at the border, good, pleasant view. Also at the border the new *Hotel Frontera*, with restaurant, car rental services, on the banks of the Río Mopan, T 505196. Tienda Unica will change TCs, but at a poor rate. Banco de Guatemala at the border, open 0800-1400 Mon-Thur, to 1430 on Fri, gives better rates than money changers, but does not take Belize dollars. There is a street market in Belizean dollars (street changers accept TCs when bank is closed).

To Mexico From Flores or Tikal to Chetumal in a day is possible if the 0500 bus from Flores to Melchor de Mencos, or 0630 from Tikal (change at El Cruce) connects with a bus at 0920 from the border to Belize City, from where you can take an afternoon bus to Chetumal. Total cost about US$30. 72-hour transit visas for Belize can be obtained at the border, but make sure you have all necessary documentation for Mexico before leaving Belize City. There are also daily minibuses Santa Elena to Chetumal, US$30, 0500, with San Juan Travel Agency, although reports vary; some say the bus will not cross the border, so you have to walk across with your luggage, others differ on whether the bus goes to Belize City or bypasses it.

A rough, unpaved road runs 160 km to **El Naranjo** on the Río San Pedro—a centre for oil exploration, unfriendly—near the Mexican border. There is a big army base there. There are daily buses from Santa Elena at 0500 and 1230 from *Hotel San Juan* (US$4, 5$\frac{1}{2}$ hrs at least; bus from El Naranjo to Flores at 0100, 0400 and 1200). Get there early for the bus or you may have to stand all the way (or sit on the top). When coming from El Naranjo to Flores, ask customs officers what the bus fare is to avoid overcharging. You can change money at the grocery store opposite immigration, which will give you a better US$/Q rate than the Mexican side of the border, but it is still poor. At **G** *Posada San Pedro*, basic (under same ownership as *Maya Internacional* in Santa Elena) there is information, group travel, guides, and arrangements for travel as far as Palenque; reservations can be made through travel agencies in Guatemala City; there is one other basic hotel and accommodation by the landing stage. The restaurant by the dugouts is expensive, others in town better value. Also bungalows in El Naranjo, which has an immigration office. Electricity is turned off at 2200. An orphanage, run by an American and his Guatemalan wife, advertises for volunteers in *Doña Luisa's*, Antigua (they have a clinic, school, garden, etc).

If you take the midday bus from Flores, go to immigration next morning and have your passport stamped (if not travelling alone, make sure everyone gets a stamp). From El Naranjo, daily boats leave at 0600 and sometime after 1100 (on arrival of the 0500 Flores bus), for La Palma in Mexico (US$20—cheaper to pay in quetzales, 4-5 hrs inc Mexican border crossing), from where buses go to Tenosique and on to Palenque. Return from La Palma to El Naranjo at 1400. Bus La Palma-Tenosique at 1700, and one other; it is not possible to go Palenque the same day unless you hire a taxi in La Palma. Mexican tourist cards can be obtained at the border. Beautiful trip, but take waterproofs, a torch and some food with you. Beware mosquitoes. Expect thorough searches on both sides of the border.

A third route to Mexico is to take a bus from Santa Elena to Bethel (regular service), then a 40-minute launch ride to **Frontera Echeverría**/Corozal on the Río Usumacinta. From Frontera Echeverría it is 6-8 hrs by bus to Palenque, US$4.75. Alternatively, go from Santa Elena to Sayaxché (see below), then take a boat down the Río de la Pasión to the military post at **Pipiles** (exit stamps must be given here) or to the town of **Benemérito** on the Río Usumacinta (trading boat twice a week US$4-5, 2 days; private launch US$100, 4 hrs). The trading boats (maize) give a good insight into riverside life, stopping frequently at hamlets to drop and pick up passengers. Grapefruit are in such plentiful supply that no one bothers to sell them (still, it is polite to ask before picking them up off the ground). If stuck at Pipiles, a farmer who lives 800m upstream may take you to Benemérito in his launch. If there is more than one maize boat at Pipiles move up to the first one because they often wait up to 3 days to get a better price. At Benemérito, a shop near the river lets out rooms at the back, no electricity, water from well. From Benemérito, buses go at 0600, 0700, 0800 and 1300 to immigration just past the Río Lacantún (or hitch in a truck); unpaved road, 7 hrs by bus Benemérito-Palenque (more in the wet). There are also boats from Sayaxché to Frontera Echeverría/Corozal, but they charge from US$275 for a 20-seater. Get Mexican tourist card in advance to avoid offering bribes at border, and get your exit visa in Flores. Take also hammock, mosquito net, food and insect repellent; there are no hotels between Sayaxché and Palenque and dollars cannot be exchanged. Yaxchilán and Bonampak in Mexico can be visited from the road Benemérito-Palenque.

Sayaxché is a good centre for visiting the Petén, whether your interest is in the wildlife or the Maya ruins. To cross the ferry near the village costs US$2 for a car.

Accommodation and Food **D-E** *Hotel Guayacán*, known locally as *Hotel de Godoy* after the owner Julio Godoy, is a good source of information on the area, on S bank of river, close to ferry, 2 rooms with bathrooms, rest are dark, dirty and damp, unfriendly, building work in 1993 so may improve; **G** *Casa de Huéspedes Carmen Kilkan*, with breakfast, very friendly, rec, ask there for Juanita (American), knowledgeable, will arrange trips and accompany you; **F** *Hotel Mayacán*, S bank near ferry, no water or electricity after 2200, new rooms built; or **G** *Hotel Sayaxché*, basic, dirty, food not bad. *Yaxquín*, good food, friendly, cheap, owner speaks English, very informative; *Restaurant Montaña*, Julian Mariona Morán, T/F 506114, will give you information, he also owns **B** *Posada Caribe* at Laguna Petexbatún (see below), and at *Los Charros*, Maguin is helpful, good food, nice. If travelling S, stock up with fruit in the market and, if driving, fuel at the service station.

You can change US$ bills at various places in town but not TCs. Pesos can be bought in the store *La Moderna* or *Hotel Guayacán*. Viajes Don Pedro runs launches to El Ceibal, Petexbatún and Aguateca, 4 hrs, and 2-day trips to Yaxchilán (see Mexico chapter, **Other Sites**, under Palenque). Although Don Pedro organizes interesting jungle tours, his son, the guide, tends to change the plans and alter the length of the trip once you have started. *Viajes Twísticos La Montaña*, (Julián Mariona Morán, see above); good guide Antonio Chiquín Cocul, at *Hotel Mayacán*, good tours to Maya sites, US$7 pp. Ask around for alternative tours, eg at *Hotel Guayacán*.

There are buses to and from Guatemala City via Sebol from 0700 but you can also catch pickup trucks to Sebol from 0630, 7½ hrs, terrible road, police checks, reported great fun! Also buses to and from Santa Elena, Flores, 0600, 1300 (US$0.80, 3 hrs); La Pinita has a bus to Flores, US$2 (no transport S in the rainy season). If hitching to Flores, try for a ride on an oil truck at the river crossing in Sayaxché to La Libertad (oil refinery under construction here), then truck or bus to Flores.

100 km NE of Cobán, 40 km N of Lanquín is **Sebol** from where roads go N into the Petén and E to Izabal. The Río Sebol (part of the Río de la Pasión system) offers good bathing a short distance to the N (follow the signs to La Playa). 2 hrs N at Balneario Las Islas there is also good swimming and walks, well signposted, crowded at weekends, good camping, good *comedor* (US$3 by boat, 1½-2 hrs). On 24 August, all-night mass is celebrated in Sebol (free food at 0100) with games played on the church lawn in the daylight hours. 10 km from Sebol is **Fray Bartolomé de Las Casas** (F *Hospedaje Ralíos*, shared bath, OK; F *Damelito*, on main sqare, own generator, clean friendly, good breakfast; F *Evelyne*, main street, no meals; restaurants), a pleasant village which has a *fiesta* (parade and rodeo) on 1 May. No bus service to Fray Bartolomé from 16 Jan to end of wet season, bargain with pick-up drivers to/from Sebol. There is an airstrip nearby, charters possible. A rough dirt road links Sebol with Sayaxché via **Raxrujá**, ' a hole', with strong military presence. Most of this 120-km road is in poor condition, particularly the section from Raxrujá to (Cruce) El Pato. Thereafter going N, the road improves though it can be very difficult in the wet season (coming S it is often not possible to travel Sayaxché-Sebol in one day and you get stuck overnight in Raxrujá, from where transport only leaves in the morning). Hitching with oil tankers is possible. Near to Raxrujá is an extensive river cave. Accommodation in Raxrujá: G *Pensión Aguas Verdes*, basic, pleasant; G *Pensión La Reina*, rough, no water, dirty, bad; good *pensión* nr bridge, G pp, no bath (except the river!) *comedor* opposite; many *comedores*, eg *El Piloto*, good, meal US$1; *El Ganadero*, quite good and in **El Pato**: 2 *hospedajes*, first at the port, dirty, monkey in garden; second at G *Farmacía Margarita/Hospedaje El Amigo*, better, basic, mosquito net necessary, owner's son has pick-up transport; good *comedor*, *Tonito*, behind soccer field. In the wet season there is occasional boat transport Sebol-El Pato-Sayaxché.

Local transport connects most of these towns, but do not travel at night (guerrilla activity): from Sayaxché there are buses at 0730 and 1430 to within 20 km of Raxrujá, at which point you have to change to a pick-up because buses cannot cope with the road; there are also pick-ups all the way, check times, several a day, 6 hrs, US$2.60; after about 2½ hrs is a road junction with a *comedor*, at least 2 buses a day from here to Sayaxché (one at midday), 3½ hrs. There are many more roads in this area than maps show, there are also plenty of military camps, so expect checks by the army and other types of (non-military) hold-up. El Pato-Raxrujá (minibus 0500 daily); Raxrujá-Sebol, occasional bus, US$0.40, pick-up from 0700 more common, US$0.75 (very bad road, 2 hrs for 25 km) or El Pato-Sebol; Fray B de Las Casas-Cobán, 0500, 9 hrs, US$1.50 (Cobán-Sebol at 0530). You can also go from Lanquín to Sayaxché via Pajal, Las Casas, Sebol and Raxrujá (**see p 466**) (not rec as a 1-day journey, better to rest in Raxrujá).

The road from Raxrujá via Chisec to Cobán is very steep and rocky (part, over the Sierra de Chamá, is known as the staircase!), but passable in the dry season with high clearance vehicle. Recommended for spectacular scenery but you need lots of time. Even well after the wet season, ie mid-January, a bus may not be able to get all the way from Sayaxché to Cobán, even though tickets may be sold. Pick-ups will do the trip via Chisec, 11-12 hrs, US$4, a terrible squash, but ask as many people as possible before embarking if a bus is running via Sebol. **Chisec** to Cobán takes 5 hrs driving in normal conditions; if driving 'just keep cool, it's a wonderful trip'. There is a petrol station in Chisec (on the right heading for Cobán). The owner of *Pinchazo* workshop also owns *Costa Sur* hotel and restaurant, on right entering from Sayaxché; meals US$1, car park outside, friendly, good advice on road conditions.

From Sebol, there is an 0300 bus to Poptún (see p 478), via Fray Bartolomé de Las Casas and San Luis (on the Morales-Río Dulce-Poptún-Flores road). This route is impassable in the rainy season. From San Luis there is an 0630 bus to Flores, stopping at Poptún (4½ hrs). It is easy to get a ride on one of the many trucks which run on all these routes. You can also go from Sebol to Modesto Méndez on the Morales-Flores road but a correspondent (1990) told us that it took 2 days on motorbikes in the wet season. Another in 1991 reported that he got as far as Chahal by bus, but hitching thereafter was difficult and it took 3 days in all. In 1993 it took 2 days driving 0-15 kmph in a 4WD jeep from Modesto Méndez to Cobán via Sebol because of potholes, winding narrow roads, big rocks.

Up the Río de la Pasión from Sayaxché is *El Ceibal*, where the ruins were excavated by Peabody Museum and Harvard. Some of the best preserved *stelae* in Guatemala are found in a jungle park setting. There is now a difficult road linking Sayaxché with El Ceibal—impassable in the wet (leave bus at El Paraíso on the main road—local pick-up from Sayaxché US$0.20—then walk to the ruins, a further 7 km, 1½ hrs) so the trip can be made either by road or by river (launch hire US$25, 2 hrs—*pensión* G). You can sling a hammock at El Ceibal and use the guard's fire for making coffee if you ask politely—a mosquito net is advisable, and take repellent for walking in the jungle surroundings. If you leave belongings at El Ceibal, make sure they are in reliable care, theft is not uncommon. From Sayaxché the ruins of the *Altar de Sacrificios* at the confluence of the Ríos de la Pasión and Usumacinta can also be reached. Further down the Usumacinta river is Yaxchilán, just over the border in Mexico (temples still standing, with sculptures and carved lintels—**See Mexico, Section 9, Yucatán Peninsula**). Still further down the Usumacinta in the W of Petén department is *Piedras Negras*, with little standing architecture, and most sculpture removed to the National Museum in Guatemala City (imagination needed), which can be reached by special rafts suitable for light rapids, at some considerable expense. The Usumacinta river has been dammed by Mexico below Piedras Negras; so river trips are no longer possible.

The Río de la Pasión is a good route to visit other, more recently discovered Maya ruins. From *Laguna Petexbatún* (16 km), a fisherman's paradise, which can be reached by outboard canoe from Sayaxché (US$10 or more for 6 people and luggage) excursions can be made to unexcavated ruins: these include *Arroyo de la Piedra* (a small site with a number of mounds and stelae, between Sayaxché and Dos Pilas), *Dos Pilas* itself (many well-preserved stelae, important tomb find of a King here in 1991), *Aguateca*, where the ruins are so far little excavated, giving a feeling of authenticity, and where an excursion can be made over the only known Maya bridge and down into a huge chasm, and *Itzán*—discovered in 1968. Lagoon fishing includes 150-lb tarpon, snoek and local varieties. Many interesting birds, including toucan and *guacamayo*. Highly rec for accommodation is **B** pp *Posada Caribe*, run by Julian Mariona Morán, T/F 506114, inc 3 meals, comfortable *cabañas* with bathroom and shower, excursion to Aguateca or El Ceibol by launch and a guide for jungle excursions where you can see lots of animals and birds. The only other hotel, **A+** *Posada Mateos*, with bath, hot water, electricity, in bungalows, T 500505, or can be booked in advance by tour agencies. Jungle guides can be hired for US$1.50-2.50 per day.

SOUTHERN GUATEMALA (4)

From Guatemala City to San Salvador, and to the Pacific ports of San José and Puerto Quetzal: some of the busiest roads in the country passing through major agricultural areas. Several beach resorts, and bird and turtle reserves near Monterrico.

Routes to El Salvador

There are 3 routes through Southern Guatemala to El Salvador. The first is the paved Pan-American Highway through Barberena and Cuilapa which keeps to the crest of the ridges most of the way to the border, 166 km. At **Cuilapa**, capital of Santa Rosa Department, **F Hospedaje Posada K-Luy**, 4 C, 1-166, T 475372, clean, comfortable, cable TV. Beyond Cuilapa the Highway crosses the Río de los Esclavos by a bridge first built in the 16th century. At **Los Esclavos** is **D Turicentro Los Esclavos**, T 875571, F 875158, pool, hot water, restaurant, a/c. 50 km on is **Jutiapa** (population 9,200, a pleasant, lively town with a big food market in Zona 3; at least 6 hotels/hospedajes nearby, eg **B Linda Vista**, 4 Av, 3-55, Zona 3, a/c, parking; **E Ordóñez**, 4C, 8-33, Zona 3, T 441273, a/c, restaurant, parking; **E Posada del Peregrino**, C 15 de Sep 0-30, Zona 3, T 441770; **F Posada Belén**, T 441767). Beyond, it goes through the villages of El Progreso and Asunción Mita, where another road runs left to Lago de Güija. Between Jutiapa and El Progreso is the Centro Turístico Guantepec, swimming pool and restaurant, camping permitted (free). Before reaching the border at San Cristóbal it dips and skirts the shores (right) of **Lago Atescatempa**, an irregular sheet of water with several islands and set in heavy forest. From the border to San Salvador is 100 km.

A right turn after Cuilapa (just before Los Esclavos) towards Chiquimulilla (road No 16, with old trees on either side, some with orchids in them) leads after 20 km to a sign to Ixpaco. A 2-3 km steep, narrow, dirt road goes to the **Laguna de Ixpaco**, an impressive, greenish-yellow lake, boiling in some places, emitting sulphurous fumes, set in dense forest. There is a bus service.

The second, quicker way of getting to San Salvador is to take a paved highway which cuts off right from the first route at Molino, about 7 km beyond the Esclavos bridge. This cut-off goes through El Oratorio and **Jalpatagua** (F **Hotel El Centenario**, clean, a/c, pool) to the border, continuing then to Ahuachapán and San Salvador. (Try **F Motel Martha**, 15 km from frontier on Guatemalan side, excellent breakfast, swimming pool.)

The third route goes SW from Guatemala City past Amatitlán to Escuintla where it joins the Pacific Highway. E from Escuintla the road is paved through Guazacapán to the border bridge over the Río Paz at La Hachadura (El Salvador), then through the coastal plain to Sonsonate and on to San Salvador, 290 km in all; this road gives excellent views of the volcanoes. It takes 2 hrs from Escuintla to the border, 10 mins to go through border formalities, then 3 hrs on a bad road to Sonsonate. At **Pedro de Alvarado** (formerly Pijije) on the border there are several hospedajes (all G, basic). If stuck at La Hachadura (the last bus for Sonsonate leaves at 1800), you can get food at the service station restaurant and there is a very basic hospedaje, G, nearby—not recommended for lone women.

Guatemala City to the Pacific Coast

The first part of this route to Escuintla is one of the busiest roads in the country, paved throughout, much of it a divided highway. It connects the capital with all the Pacific ports and with the most important agricultural area of the country. In 1994 this highway was particularly dangerous because most of it is in a poor state of repair.

Amatitlán is 37 km by rail and 27 by road SW of the capital, on Lake Amatitlán, 12 by 4 km (but diminishing in size as a result of sedimentation in the Río Villalobos which drains into it—caused by deforestation). Fishing and boating; bathing is not advisable, as the water has become seriously contaminated. Sunday boat trips cost US$1, or less, for 30 mins; beware of people offering boat trips which last no more than 10 mins. Very popular and colourful at weekends. The thermal springs on the lake side, with groves of trees and coffee plantations, feed pools which *are* safe to bathe in. The lake is surrounded by picturesque chalets with lawns to the water's edge. Altitude 1,240m, pop 12,225. Grand view from the United Nations Park, 2½ km N, above Amatitlán. A road goes round the lake; a branch runs to the slopes of Pacaya volcano, US$0.15 by bus **(see p 463)**. The town has two famous ceiba trees; one is in Parque Morazán. Bank changes dollars cash but not TCs. Buses from Guatemala City (every ½-hr, US$0.20) go right to the lakeside.

Fiesta Santa Cruz, 2-3 May.

Hotels D *Blanquita*, on the road to Guatemala City, room with bath; **E** *Los Arcos y Anexo Rocareña*, on lakeside, T 330337, with bath, pool, a/c, parking, restaurant; **F** *Hospedaje y Comedor Kati*, clean, pleasant dining room; **F** *Pensión Karla*, clean, friendly, family-run; **E** *Amatitlán*, three blocks from *Karla*, parking inside, dirty bathrooms, overpriced, friendly but noisy.

Many **restaurants** are near the lake—beware of local fish because of water pollution.

Camping The by-road to the UN Park (turning at 19½ km from Guatemala City) ends at camping sites and shelters; it is rather steep and narrow for caravan trailers. View of Lake Amatitlán and Pacaya Volcano, US$0.12 entrance fee. On the main highway S of Amatitlán, accessible by any bus going to Palín, Escuintla or beyond, is *Automariscos* (Km 33.5, T (330479), English-speaking owner, electric and water hook-ups, large warm swimming pool (thermal), hot jacuzzi, baby pool, good toilets, restaurant, noisy at weekends. A third, next door in the direction of Escuintla, is *La Red*, which has swimming pools fed by volcanic springs (US$0.60 each); quieter, restaurant/bar and good toilet facilities (camping G). Bus, Guatemala City to any of these 3, US$0.25.

Palín, 14½ km from Amatitlán, has a Sunday Indian market in a square under an enormous ceiba tree. Grand views to E, of Pacaya, to NW, of Agua volcano, to W, of Pacific lowland. Power plant at Michatoya falls below town. An unpaved road runs NW to Antigua through Santa María de Jesús **(see p 460)**. See old Franciscan church (1560). *Fiestas*: 8 December, first Sunday January, 3 June, and movable feasts of Holy Trinity and Sacred Heart. Textiles here are exceptional, but are becoming hard to find. **G** *Pensión Señorial*, basic; **G** *Napolitana*, also basic.

Escuintla, 18 km from Palín on the road to San José, is a market town in a rich tropical valley at 335m. Population 62,500. Famous for its medicinal baths and fruits. There is a large market on Sunday, and a daily market over 2 blocks exceptional, interesting building). ear the market is police HQ, fortress-like, painted sky blue. Marimbas frequently play in the central plaza, the local banana bread is worth trying and *basitas*, real fruit ice-lollies. The town is crowded with lots of streetlife, eating places, bars (many with prostitutes from San Salvador) and, at weekends, much drunkenness. Agua volcano looms to the N. Road N to Antigua. Beyond Escuintla the railway branches W at the station of Santa María to Mexico.

There is a meat packing plant. *Fiesta*: 8 (holiday) to 12 December. Many buses to the capital (US$0.50) also direct to Antigua at 0730 and 1500, US$0.60 (poor road).

Hotels (each with acceptable restaurant) **A** *Hotel Sarita*, Av Centroamérica 15-32, Zona 3, T 880482, pool; **F** *Campo Real*, 10 C behind market, with fan, very clean, pleasant owners; **E** *Carlos Paz*, very clean, a/c, cold water, parking, rec; **E** *Costa Sur*, 12 C, 4-13, Zona 1, T 881109, a/c, TV, clean, friendly owner, speaks English, good value; **F** *Las Rosas*, about 400m from bus terminal heading into town, for a clean, basic room, better rooms also; **G** *La Castilia*, near market, basic, clean.

Several Chinese restaurants, bakeries, hamburger and sandwich places with good milk shakes.

Exchange Lloyds Bank (agency) 7 Calle 3-09, Zona 1. Open 0830-1200, 1400-1600. **Banco de Guatemala**, 4 C, 6-98, Zona 1.

Consulate El Salvador, 16 Calle, 3-20, near the Esso Station, will issue visas.

The Department of Escuintla, between the Pacific and the chain of volcanoes, is the richest in the country, producing 80% of the sugar, 20% of the coffee, 85% of the cotton, and 70% of the cattle of the whole country.

The Pacific Highway goes W to the Mexican border at Tecún Umán (200 km). As a route to Mexico, it is shorter, faster and easier to drive, but hotter and much less picturesque, than the El Tapón route to the N. The road is paved all the way but has a lot of heavy traffic; be wary of the large, decrepit tractor-trailers carrying sugar cane to the several large mills in the season.

Between Escuintla and **Santa Lucia Cotzumalguapa** at Siquinalá is a turn off S to **La Democracia** (7 km), where sculptures found on the Monte Alto and Costa Brava estates (*fincas*) are displayed. These are believed to date from 400 BC or earlier and have magnetic navels or temples. Visit the Museo del Pueblo on the main square (closed Mondays). This road continues 40 km to **Sipacate** on the coast with a half hourly bus service to Guatemala City. Bus every 30 mins La Democracia-Sipacate, from where pick-ups in the market go to *Rancho El Coco*, with an unspoilt beach and pool, rooms (F), delicious food, excellent value, basic but quiet and mosquito-free. At Santa Lucía, a friendly town, is the 9th century site of **Bilbao** (or **Cotzumalguapa**), which shows Teotihuacán and Veracruz influences. **El Baúl**, a pre-classic monument (stelae) which dates back to the Izapan civilization (see the Introduction to this book), is 6 km from Santa Lucía: cross bridge, keep left and follow the road to the timberyard where numerous interesting stelae are displayed. From this early art, the classic Maya art developed. El Castillo, between Bilbao and El Baúl, has some small sculptures dating back to Maya times. On the Las Ilusiones and Finca Pantaleón estates are ruined temples, pyramids and sculptures, and there are other stelae to be found in the area, though most items have now been transferred to museums in Guatemala City.

Hotels at Santa Lucía: **C** *Santiaguito*, swimming pool, good restaurant, T 845435, rec; **D** *El Camino*, T 845316, both at Km 90.5. At La Democracia: **F** *El Reposo*; **G** *Galeano*; **G** *El Carmen*. Buses from the Zona 4 terminal in the capital run to both places.

23 km beyond Santa Lucía is **Cocales**. A few km before Cocales a bridge was destroyed by guerrillas as a 'Christmas present' in 1989. Since that time, there has been very little activity though the military are in evidence, and set up road blocks from time to time. Two other bridges between here and Mazatenango suffered the same fate. The bridge near Cocales was reopened in 1994 and there are serviceable pontoons meanwhile at the other locations.

At Cocales a road N leads to Patulul and in 30 km to Lake Atitlán at San Lucas Tolimán. This is a good surfaced road which climbs up from the Pacific plains to the coffee region dominated by volcanoes, Agua and Fuego to the right and Atitlán in front. Excellent cheese, ice cream and other dairy products at Lacteos Parma, 16 km short of San Lucas. This area suffered an earthquake in 1991 with the epicentre near Pochuta, 20 km N of Cocales. There were many landslides including one affecting a steep half km just short of San Lucas which still needs high clearance to drive (1994).

60 km S of Cocales on a good paved road is the coastal resort of **Tecojate**, popular with Guatemalans specially at holiday times. The road stops at the *estero* (tidal lagoon) and motor launches cross to the excellent black sand beach, 5 min, US$0.25 pp, or you can paddle across at low tide. Private, rustic beach houses, but no formal public accommodation. Beachside places to eat. Buses from Guatemala City and other closer centres mostly passing though Cocales. Parking for the day US$1, more at holiday times. Do not bathe in the *estero*.

The Pacific Highway continues through San Antonio Suchitepéquez to Mazatenango, see Section 6, below.

S of Esquintla, the railway follows the road for 11 km to **Santa María**, near Masagua where the line to Mexico branches W. The railway (now freight only), the road and a new motorway completed 1991 continue S to **San José**, 52 km beyond Escuintla, 109 km by road from the capital. San José used to be the country's second largest port. Population 8,000. The climate is hot, the streets and beaches filthy and at weekends the town fills up with people from the capital. Fishing, swimming, though beware the strong undercurrent. *Fiesta*: 19 March, when town is crowded and hotel accommodation difficult to get. San José has the big disadvantage of requiring most ships to anchor offshore and discharge by lighter. A new harbour, **Puerto Quetzal**, to take all shipping alongside, has been completed, 3 km to the E, although the oil terminal remains at San José.

Hotels at San José A *Turicentro Agua Azul*, Km 106, T 841667, 4 different swimming pools, food reasonable, 24 rooms; **D** *Turicentro El Coquito*, on the road to Escuintla; **B** *Posada Quetzal*, Av 30 de Junio, T 841601 and **A** *Posada Quetzal II*, Barrio Miramar No 26, T 841892, 500m from the mole, rec; **E** *Viñas del Mar*, on the beach, with bath, run down, friendly; **G** *Veracruz*, on the main street, very basic, dark but friendly. No accommodation at present in Puerto Quetzal. **Restaurant** *Papillon*, on the beach, serves *cacerolas* (fish and shrimp soup), also has rooms, E.

Bus San José-Guatemala City (Transportes Unidas), half hourly from 0530, US$1.50, 2 hrs 30 mins; from **Iztapa** to San José US$0.12. To **Escuintla**, US$0.50.

5 km to the W of San José is **Chulamar**, a popular beach at weekends, good bathing; **B** *Santa María del Mar*, T 841283. Some chalets can be hired. Many new houses are being built. It is lifeless during the week with nowhere but expensive resorts to stay. To the E of San José is the smart resort of **Likin**, which fronts on both the Chiquimulilla canal and the Pacific. The construction of Puerto Quetzal has altered the configuration of the coast and the outer beach, with bungalows and restaurant, has been temporarily affected by tides and sand. Interesting trip can be taken through Chiquimulilla canal by launch from the old Spanish port of **Iztapa**, now a bathing resort a short distance to the E. At Iztapa you can camp on the beach (dirty and not particularly pretty) and rent launches. By road you need to cross the canal by ferry which takes cars. At Iztapa **E** *Playa del Sol*, with swimming pool, non-residents US$2, friendly staff, rooms OK, good food; **F** *Pollo Andra*, nice beds, overhead fans, attached restaurant good value; **F** *Brasilia*, 1C, 4-27, Zona 1, basic; some local people may put you up. Cabins along the beach for hire but few have water and they are very rustic; those run by 'Tex Mex' (from Tennessee) have running water, E, over friendly.

Further E is the less expensive resort of **Monterrico**, best approached from Taxisco on the main lowland route to El Salvador. It is a small black sand resort (beach shoes advisable), a few shops and *comedores*. Its popularity is growing fast. Bird and turtle reserves in the mangrove swamps nearby, operated by the Conservation Department of the Public University (USAC) and Inguat, combine estuarine and coastal ecosystems with a great variety of waterbirds and aquatic plants. Turtles normally visit Oct-Dec. Free, but donations welcome. Take insect repellent, guides available. Well worth taking a boat trip at sunrise or sunset, negotiate the price. This reserve is also on the migratory routes of North and South American birds. Stay at **D** *Johnny's Place*, cabins for 4, well-furnished, refrigerator, stove for rent, fan, nets on windows, or **E** *Baule Beach Hotel*, with bath, mosquito nets, run by ex Peace Corps volunteer, Nancy, seafood restaurant, mixed reports, good surfing but busy at weekends. Look for a good plate of shrimps at *comedores* on the main street. *Comedor Susy* is good. Rigoberta Menchu Language School in Antigua (5 Av Sur) has a school in Monterrico (rec). Bus to San José nominally at 0500 and 1100, but check. Best to take a boat from Monterrico 'inland' through the canals to **La Avellana** (US$0.50) and then by bus to Taxisco. Buses run by Cubanita from Guatemala City, Terminal Zone 4, to La Avellana via Taxisco at 1030, 1230 and 1430, 5 hrs.

WEST FROM GUATEMALA CITY (5)

There is some beautiful scenery W of the capital, with interesting markets and colourful Indian costumes in the towns and villages. Lake Atitlán, in the shadow of three volcanoes, is a jewel of the region, the villages around it having acquired varying degrees of tourist consciousness. In the highlands is the famous market of Chichicastenango; N of here are the Quiché and Ixil regions, very traditional and yet suffering heavily in Guatemala's bloody recent past.

The Pacific Highway goes W from Guatemala City to Tapachula in Mexico. The Pan-American Highway (fully paved) cuts off NW at San Cristóbal Totonicapán and goes into Chiapas by El Tapón, or Selegua, canyon. This is a far more interesting route, with fine scenery. A railway also runs through southwestern Guatemala from Guatemala City to the Mexican frontier.

Some 6½ km W of the capital a road (right) leads to San Pedro Sacatepéquez (see p 462) and Cobán (see p 465). Our road twists upwards steeply, giving grand views, with a branch to Mixco (16½ km from Guatemala City). At Km 18.5, *Restaurante Los Tilos*, open 1000-1900, good lunches, pies a specialty, rec. About 14 km beyond, at San Lucas Sacatepéquez, the road to Antigua turns sharp left. **Sumpango**, which is a little over 19 km beyond this turn-off, has a Sun market, and *huipiles* can be bought from private houses; they are of all colours but preponderantly red, as it is believed to ward off the evil eye. Good font in church. At **Chimaltenango**, another road runs left, 20 km, to Antigua; this road is served by a shuttle-bus (US$0.25 or US$0.40 in minibus), so Antigua can be included in the Guatemala-Chichicastenango circuit. Chimaltenango is the capital of its Department. **G** *Pensión La Predilecta*, pleasant rooms, shared toilets/showers, cold water, clean, helpful, rebuilt since the earthquake; **G** *Pensión Río*, OK. Good restaurant nearby: *La Marylena*. 4-5 km W of Chimaltenango is **D** *Hotel y Restaurant La Villa*, T 391130. Widows' cooperative selling weavings to support widows and orphans of the disappeared: contact Margarita de Similax, Segunda Calle 8-72, Chimaltenango. Exchange at Banco de Guatemala, 2 Av, 2-20, Zona 3. Excellent views at 1,790m, from which water flows one side to the Atlantic, the other side to the Pacific. Thermal swimming pool at San Lorenzo El Tejar, which can be reached by bus from Chimaltenango. Market: Wed. *Fiesta*: 18-20 January. Buses to Antigua pass the famous park of **Los Aposentos**, 3 km (lake and swimming pool). Also between Chimaltenango and Antigua is the *Sanatario Naturista*, a health clinic, T 717227, which is rec as friendly, good food, fluent English. Bus to Panajachel, US$1.70. At **San Andrés Itzapa** (2 km off Antigua road, 4 km from Chimaltenango) there is a very interesting chapel to Maximon (San Simón) which is well worth a visit. Shops by the chapel sell prayer pamphlets and pre-packaged offerings.

A side-road runs 21 km N to San Martín **Jilotepeque** over deep *barrancas*; markets on Sun, Thur. Bus from Chimaltenango, US$0.50. *Fiesta*: November 11. Fine weaving. Striking *huipiles* worn by the women. 10 km beyond Chimaltenango is Zaragoza, former Spanish penal settlement, and beyond that (right) a road (13 km) leads N to the interesting village of **Comalapa**: markets 1000-1430, Mon-Tues, bright with Indian costumes. Fine old church of San Juan Bautista (1564). *Fiestas*: 24 June, 8, 12 Dec.

There are several local artists working in Comalapa; no studios, so best to ask where you can see their work (Artexco cooperative, *Figura Antigua*). There is a *pensión* here, G.

6 km beyond Zaragoza the road divides. The southern branch, the old Pan-American Highway, goes through Patzicía and Patzún to Lake Atitlán (see below), then N to Los Encuentros. The northern branch, the new Pan-American Highway, much faster, goes past Tecpán and over the Chichoy pass, also to Los Encuentros. From Los Encuentros there is only the one road W to San Cristóbal Totonicapán, where the new road swings NW through El Tapón and La Mesilla to Ciudad Cuauhtémoc, the Mexican border settlement; and the old route goes W through Quezaltenango and San Marcos to Tapachula, in Mexico.

The northern road to Los Encuentros: from the fork the Pan-American Highway runs 19 km to near *Tecpán*, which is slightly off the road at 2,287m. It has a particularly fine church: silver altars, carved wooden pillars, odd images, a wonderful ceiling which was severely damaged by the 1976 earthquake. The church is being slowly restored: the ceiling is missing and much of its adornment is either not in evidence, or moved to a church next door. The women wear most striking costumes. Market: Thur and Sun (glorious photo opportunities). *Fiestas*: 3 May (Santa Cruz), 1-8 October, and 8 December. *Hotel Iximché*, **G** *Posada de Doña Ester*, clean, hot water; *Restaurant de la Montaña*, 1 km after the road to Tecpán; the owner of *Zapatería La Mejor* has a guest house, G. Also *Restaurante Katok*, on the highway, good *parrillados*, but expensive, and opposite *El Encinal del Río*, opened late 1993, wider menu, expensive. Better value at *El Pedregal*, just off the main road toward Xetzac, run by a German family. Buses from Guatemala City (Zona 4 terminal), 2¼ hrs, every hour; easy day trip from Panajachel.

Near Tecpán are the very important Mayan ruins of *Iximché*, once capital and court of the Cakchiqueles, 5 km of unpaved road from Tecpán (nice walk), open 0800-1700 (admission US$0.10). Iximché was the first capital of Guatemala after its conquest by the Spaniards; followed in turn by Ciudad Vieja, Antigua and Guatemala City. The ruins are well-presented with 3 plazas, a palace, and 2 ballcourts on a promontory surrounded on 3 sides by steep slopes. There is a museum at the site.

Beyond Tecpán the road swings up a spectacular 400m to the summit of the Chichoy pass. The pass is often covered in fog or rain but on clear days there are striking views. 58 km from the fork is Los Encuentros (and the road to Chichicastenango) and 3 km further on the new northern road joins the old southern one from Sololá. 12 km before Los Encuentros is a new road to Godínez (see below); buses may now run along it, but it's worth taking if in a car; the paved road down to the lake has many small potholes.

Sololá, at 2,113m, 11 km from the junction, has superb views across Lake Atitlán. Population 40,785. Fine Tues and Fri markets, to which many of the Indians go (mornings only, go early, Fri market gets underway on Thur). Good selection of used *huipiles*. Note costumes of men. Great *fiesta* around 15 August. Hot shower 500m from market on Panajachel road, behind Texaco station, US$0.18.

Tightly woven woollen bags are sold here: far superior to the usual type of tourist bags. Prices are high because of nearness of tourist centres of Panajachel and Chichicastenango.

Hotels **E** *Del Viajero*, 7 Av, 10-45, on main square, no windows or bath but spacious, clean and friendly, good food; **F** *Tzoloj-yá*, 11 C, 7-70, T 621266, near main square, tepid shower, mixed reports; **F** *El Paisaje*, 9 Calle, 5-6 Av 2 blocks from central square, pleasant colonial courtyard, shared baths and toilets, clean, cold water, family run, laundry facilities; **F** *Santa Ana*, 6 Av, 8 C, basic, clean, friendly, rooms around a lawn, shared facilities, good value.

Restaurants *El Cafetín*, Parque Central, delicious lake fish, *mojarra*; *Cafetería Karol* and *Café Favy*, open all day for cheap meals and snacks; *Helados Topsy* for ice cream, all within a block of Parque Central.

Exchange Banco G y T, 7 Av y 9C, Zona 2.

Bus to Chichicastenango US$0.35, 2 hrs. Bus to Panajachel, US$0.25, or 1½-2 hour walk; to **Chimaltenango**, US$1; to **Quezaltenango** at 1200, US$1.50. Colectivo to **Los Encuentros**, US$0.15; to **Guatemala City** (Rebuli 1) direct US$1.50, 3 hrs.

From Sololá the old Pan-American Highway drops 550m in 8 km to Panajachel: grand views on the way. Take the bus up (US$0.25, they stop early in the evening). It is quite easy to walk down (the views are superb, particularly early in the morning), direct by the road, recommended (you also miss the unnerving bus ride down!). You can return to Panajachel either by taking the southern road from the plaza, which rejoins the main road, off which another road S strikes through a very steep, wooded hill down to the tower block flats. Alternatively, take the western road out of Sololá's plaza direct to the lake shore. Once you get to the tower blocks, it is impossible to carry on along the shore because of fenced-off private land; you must return to the main road. It is a 2-hour walk. A longer, but rewarding walk is along the road W from Sololá to San José Chacayá, then down to the lake through the Finca María Linda. About 4-5 hrs to Santa Cruz La Laguna on the lake and another 3 hrs along, below San Jorge to Panajachel.

The southern road from Zaragoza to Los Encuentros (much more difficult than the northern, with some steep hills and hairpin bends, bus, US$0.35) goes through **Patzicía**, a small Indian village founded 1545 (no accommodation). Market on Wed and Sat. *Fiesta* for the patron, Santiago, on 23-26 July. The famous church, which had a fine altar and beautiful silver, was destroyed by the 1976 earthquake; some of the silver is now in the temporary church. 14 km beyond (road in good condition, with one steep climb) is the small town of **Patzún**; its famous church, dating from 1570, was severely damaged; it is still standing, but is not open to the public. Sun market, which is famous for the silk (and wool) embroidered napkins worn by the women to church, and for woven *fajas* and striped red cotton cloth; other markets Tues and Fri. *Fiesta*: 17-21 May (San Bernardino). Lodgings at the tobacco shop, G, or near market in unnamed *pensión*.

The road descends in two stages, then climbs steeply to **Godínez**, 19 km W of Patzún, where there is a good place for meals (no bus Patzún-Godínez, very little motor traffic of any sort). A good paved road turns off S to the village of San Lucas Tolimán and continues unpaved to Santiago Atitlán; the latter can be reached by a lake boat from Panajachel. The main road continues straight on for Panajachel; it is good between Godínez and San Andrés Semetebaj, dirt and poor thereafter. The high plateau, with vast wheat and maize fields, now breaks off suddenly as though pared by a knife. From a viewpoint here, there is an incomparable view of Lake Atitlán, 600m below; beyond it rise three 3,000m-high volcano cones, Tolimán, Atitlán and San Pedro, to the W. The very picturesque village of San Antonio Palopó is right underneath you, on slopes leading to the water. It is about 12 km from the viewpoint to Panajachel. For the first 6 km you are close to the rim of the old crater and at the point where the road plunges down to the lakeside is **San Andrés Semetebaj** with a beautiful ruined early 17th century church. Market on Tues.

Shirley Hudson (Mosier, Oregon) writes: The road from Patzicía to Godínez is about as wide as a good bike path, is about half dirt and is often partly covered in pineneedles or vegetation. The hills are extremely steep and there are many people walking. On a bike it is 'adventurous, but fascinating', but also extremely difficult. Guatemala has a lot of steep hills, but these were the most extreme. If cycling in this area go from Patzún to Panajachel; the road down to Panajachel from above Sololá is too steep and rough to be much fun on a bicycle.

Note Do not drive to Panajachel via Patzicía and Patzún; there is a bridge missing and ordinary cars cannot ford the river in the rainy season (1994). The road is reported unsafe at night. The best route by car is via the new road from the Pan-American Highway to Godínez (see above).

Lake Atitlán is 147 km from the capital via the northern road and Los Encuentros, 116 km via the southern road and Patzún, and 148 km via Escuintla and Cocales to San Lucas Tolimán (see Section 4). It is a further 31 km from San Lucas to Panajachel. The lake, 1,562m above sea-level, about 7-10 km across and 18 km long, is one of the most beautiful and colourful lakes in the world. It changes

PANAJACHEL MAC 44

Not to Scale

To Los Encuentros & Guatemala City

C. los Árboles

Calle Tucán Ya

Calle Principal

C. el Embarcadero

Av. Santander

15 de Febrero

1 Calle

14 de Febrero

Av. Rancho Grande

Av. el Frutal

Calle del Rio

Rio Panajachel

Av. Salpores

To Godínez & San Lucas Tolimán

To Santa Catarina Palopó

Lago de Atitlán

N

1. Church
2. Market
3. Post Office
4. Guatel
5. Tourist Office
6. Bank
7. Texaco Station
8. Public beach, boats.
9. Boats for
   Santiago Atitlán

10. *Hotel del Lago*
11. *Hotel Playa Linda*
12. *Hotel Monterrey*
13. *Cacique Inn*
14. *Hotel Rancho Grande*
15. *Hotel Regis*

16. *Hospedaje Santander*
17. *Fonda del Sol*
18. *Hospedaje Santa Elena*
19. *Hotel Tzanjuyu*
20. *El Aguacatal*
21. *Mayan Palace*

22. *Maya Kanek*
23. *Mario's*
24. *The Last Resort*
25. *Blue Bird*
26. *Circus Bar*
27. *Zanahoria*

colour constantly—lapis lazuli, emerald, azure—and is shut in by purple mountains and olive green hills. Over a dozen villages on its shores, some named after the Apostles, house three tribes with distinct languages, costumes and cultures. The lake was the only place in the world where the *poc*, a large flightless water grebe, could be seen (**see p 498**). There is no surface outlet now, though at some time in the past it presumably drained through the gap S of San Lucas, at present 30m above the water surface. The water level varies, but has been falling slowly for several years.

Visitors to Lake Atitlán tend to stay at or near **Panajachel**, 1 km from the lake. Six hotels are actually on the lakeshore: *Atitlán, Visión Azul, Monterrey, Del Lago, Playa Linda* and *Tzanjuyu*. The main attraction is the scenery. (Visitors planning to travel round the lake should note that the only bank is here.) The town is a popular tourist resort and inhabited by many *gringos* ('Gringotenango'). The main tourist season is the second half of November to February. There is water-skiing (at weekends), private boating (kayaks for hire) and swimming in fresh clear water. The town has a newly laid out promenade. Good market in the upper part of town on Sun mornings, especially for embroidery; you are expected to bargain (despite the amount of tourism and some hassling, prices are reasonable). Visit La Galería (near *Rancho Grande Hotel*), where Nan Cuz, an Indian painter, sells her pictures which evoke the spirit of village life. The village church, originally built in 1567, was restored, only to be badly damaged by the 1976 earthquake. *Fiesta*: 2-6 Oct.

Hotels A+ *Atitlán* (check price beforehand), T 621416, 3 meals US$10 (breakfast is very good, less choice at other 2 meals—restaurant caters for travel groups), 1 km W of centre on lake, excellent rooms and service; **A+** *Del Lago*, T 621555, on lakeshore, pool (non-residents US$2), rec, although the restaurant is not as good for other meals as it is for breakfast; **A+** *Tzanjuyu*, T 621317, 3 meals US$10, on the lake, balconies and private beach; **A** *Cacique Inn* (full board available), T 621205, large comfortable rooms, no credit cards, swimming pool, magnificent house and garden, English spoken, good food, rec; **A** *Turicentro Los Geranios*, T 621433, near *Hotel del Lago*, has fully-equipped new bungalows which sleep 6, this price on Sat and Sun, C, on other days, outdoor pool; **A** *Monterrey*, T 621126, without breakfast, discounts for longer stays, clean, friendly, good food, restaurant open 1100-1400, 1900-2100; **B** *El Aguacatal*, T 621482, also near *Hotel del Lago*, has bungalows, for 4, US$67 pp; **C** *Bungalows Guayacán*, T 621479, beautifully located among coffee bushes 700m from centre on road to Santa Catarina Palopó; **D** *Fonda del Sol*, Calle Principal, T 621162, with bath, occasional hot water, or E without, noisy but comfortable; **E** *Galindo*, Calle Principal, with bath, dirty, thin walls, check for bedbugs, nice garden and good set meal, US$3.50; **D** *Mayan Palace*, Calle Principal, with shower, hot water, nice furnishings, clean, friendly, but a bit small and noisy; **A** *Playa Linda*, T 621159, above public beach, rooms sleep up to 6, fireplace, beautiful view, slow service in restaurant; **A** *Rancho Grande*, T 621554, cottages in charming setting, 4 blocks from beach, popular for long stay, good, simple food, inc breakfast, rec; **B** *Regis*, T 621149, Swiss-owned, well-kept house, rooms or apartments, garden, friendly, if you pay by credit card you may be charged an extra 17%, do not pay it; **A** *Visión Azul*, T 621426, near *Hotel Atitlán*, friendly staff, good meals but grubby pool, hot water in evenings; **E** *Del Camino*, next to Texaco, with bath (private bathrooms separate from bedrooms), clean, comfortable; **D** *Hospedaje Santa Isabel*, T 621462, near the jetty, new rooms built in an orchard, private bath, safe; **E** *Maya Kanek*, T 621104, good, clean, friendly, good value; **C** *Mini Motel Riva Bella*, T 621353, bungalows, with bath, good, clean, rec; **D** *Primavera*, Calle Santander, T 621427, clean, expensive restaurant serves German food, rec; **E** *Casa Linda*, 1 Calle, clean, hot-shower, nice garden, friendly, central, quiet; **E** *Posada La Casita*, with bath, hot shower, next to police station and market, buses stop outside but quiet at night; **F** *Del Viajero*, on main street, basic; **F** *Viajero Annex*, camping US$0.75 pp; **F** *Posada de Doña Carmen*, Av Rancho Grande, new, hot water, garden, quiet, motor cycle parking; **F** *Cabaña Country Club*, Av Rancho Grande, cheaper rooms, hot showers extra, clean, sheets 100% nylon, parking for 2 cars; **F** *Vista Hermosa*, Calle 15 de Febrero, basic, hot showers, pleasant family; **F** *Hospedaje Santa Ana*, off Calle Los Arboles, without bath, simple, adequate; **F** *Hospedaje Santa Elena* Calle Principal/Av Santander, with bedding, cheaper without, all facilities charged extra, friendly, safe parking for motorcycles; has annex (off Guatel road), also F, hot showers US$0.40, clean, family atmosphere; **F** pp *Hospedaje García*, Calle 14 de Febrero, shared shower, hot water extra, mixed reports.

There are a number of cheap *pensiones* on Av Santander, same road to the beach as Guatel building, including **E** *Bungalows El Rosario*, T 621491, about 1/2 block S of *Hotel del Lago*, safe, clean, run by Indian family, hot water 0800-1800; **E** *Hospedaje Mi Chosita*, just beyond *Last Resort*, clean, friendly, family atmosphere, but very small cabins; **F** *Hospedaje Pana*, on side street opposite *Restaurant Zanahoria*, clean, friendly, hot water, gymnasium; **E** *Hospedaje Ramos*, close to lake shore, run by an Indian family, friendly, safe, loud music from nearby cafés; **F** *Hospedaje Zulema*, Calle Rancho Grande y 5 C, near *Hotel del Lago*, clean, hot showers, rec; **F** *Mario's Rooms*, T 621313, with garden, clean, hard beds (try to pick your room), laundry, hot showers US$0.20 (sheets US$0.35), good breakfast US$0.55), **F** *Salvavidas*, without bath, hot shower US$0.50, cold free, nice family, lovely gardens, very popular, arrive before 1000; **F** *Santander*, friendly, nice rooms, lovely garden, rec; **F** *Santo Domingo*, 30m from *Vista Hermosa*, shared bath, new, clean, quiet, relaxing, nice garden, good for people travelling alone, rec; **F** *Villa Martita*, friendly, rec. **G** *Hospedaje Buena Vista*, without bath, F with, hot showers extra, basic but clean and secure.

For long stay, ask around for houses to rent; available at all prices from US$125 a month for a basic place, to US$200, but almost impossible to find in November and December. Domingo Can, whose office is in the same building as Gallery Bookstore, rents pretty houses with fireplaces, electric showers, private yards. Break-ins and robberies of tourist houses are not uncommon. The water supply is variable, with water sometimes only available 0630-1100.

Camping No problem, but campsites (US$0.50 pp) are dirty. Camping on the lakeshore is currently allowed in a designated area.

Restaurants Many of the higher priced hotels have restaurants open to the public, as does *Fonda del Sol* (large varied menu, reasonable prices, rec). *Casa Blanca*, Calle Principal, a bit expensive, but good, German owned; next door is *La Fontana*, good, Italian, but expensive. Opposite is *La Laguna*, excellent cooking, nice garden, log fire indoors. Also on Calle Principal, **Rancho Mercado Deli/Restaurant**, good delicatessen and fine restaurant, good soups, sandwiches, moussaka, homemade bread, honestly priced wine, lending library, rec. *The Last Resort*, C 14 de Febrero, 'gringo bar', breakfast, reasonable prices, bar (open 1800), table tennis, good information. *El Patio*, Av Santander, good food, very good breakfast, often crowded. *El Cisne*, opposite *Hotel del Lago*, attractive, clean, good cheap set meals; also nearby *Tres Hermanas*, good pies, slow service. *Brisas del Lago*, good meals at reasonable prices, on lake shore; a number of others on beach front, eg *El Pescador* for fish (good bass), about US$4. Next door *Los Pumpos*, good fish dishes, and nearby *El Xocomil*, good steaks, friendly, good service. There are a number of vegetarian restaurants: *Comedor Hsieh*, Calle Los Arboles, great variety of dishes inc vegetarian, rec, *Casa de Pays*, Calle Los Arboles (pie shop, also known as *La Zanahoria*, or *The Carrot*), good food, good value, clean and friendly, also has rooms (shows English language videos in evening US$1); *El Dragón*, Av Santander, vegetarian, Eastern and international dishes, only use purified water, good; *Elisabeth*, Av Santander, cheap, good crêpes. *El Unico Deli*, coffee shop, dear, but nice food including bagels and cream cheese, imaginative vegetarian food, good coffee, rec; also *Deli 2* at end of Av Santander both rec for all meals; *Tocoyal*, on beach near *Hotel del Lago*, good value; *Bar y Restaurant Las Gaviotas*, 2nda Av Rancho Grande, very good, national and international food; *Paradise Gardens*, opposite the *Casa Blanca*, good food. Go to *Panadería San Martín* at 1500 for fresh brown and banana bread; *Pana Pan* also has excellent wholemeal breads and pastries, banana bread comes out of the oven at 0930, wonderful, cinnamon rolls also rec; *Pizza Hot* at Centro Comercial, US run, excellent pizzas and banana pie, newspapers to read; pizzas also at *Yax Che*, which caters for vegetarians. *Circus Bar*, has pizzas, German/French owners, popular. *Ranchón Típico*, Av Santander. *El Bistro*, Swiss-owned, 'overpriced, bland food', near beach on same road as Guatel; *Chisme*, Calle Los Arboles, good food, try eggs McChisme for breakfast, excellent banana cake, good atmosphere, popular, English and German magazines; next to *Rooms Santander* is *Amigos*, US-run, local and European dishes, very crowded, good. The yoghurt dishes at *Mario's* restaurant are good, his crêpes filled with yoghurt and fruit are rec. *Jebel Rancho*, Av Santander, steak specialities, ceviches, crêpes, good yoghurt, slow service, otherwise rec; *Connections*, Av Santander, good value.

Entertainment *Chapiteau*, discotheque, open 2000 to early morning Tue to Sat. Opp *Hotel del Lago*, *Circus Bar*, good live music at weekends. *Grapevine Video Bar*, Av Santander, 2 screens, about 10 films a day, US$1.15, good coffee and brownies and excellent set dinner US$3. *Nuan's Bar*, in small shopping arcade just down road from *Circus Bar*, happy hour 2200-2300, small dance floor. A number of other video bars.

Shops Many small stores selling local handicrafts. *The Chocolate Factory* (*Casa de Pájaros*) sells books as well as chocolate. Another chocolate shop is on the other side of the main street, near the bank, good, but expensive. Also on road to San Andrés Semetebaj is the *Idol's House*, an antique shop where you must bargain. Indians sell their wares cheaply on the lakeside; varied selection, bargaining easy/expected. You can buy daily Guatemalan and international newspapers at *Almacén Rosales*, Calle Principal 0-32.

Car rental two doors down from post office, cheapest US$40 a day with unlimited mileage. **Motorcycle rental** about US$6/hr, plus fuel and US$20 deposit. Shop near the Church, another at the junction of Calles Principal and Santander, and two places near *Circus Bar*. Bikes generally poor, no locks or helmets provided. **Bicycle Hire** US$1/hr or US$5 for 8 hrs. Mayan Mountain Cycle Tours offers mountain bike tours around Antigua, Lake Atitlán and other places (see under Antigua). **Horse hire** at riding club close to *Hotel Atitlán*, US$8/hr. **Kayak hire** US$1.70 per hour, good Kayaks. **Ultralight flights** US$20 for 15 mins, thrilling and nerve-racking first time up, but a good way to see the lake.

Health Centro de Salud on Calle Principal, just downhill from the road to San Antonio Palopó. Dr Hernández Soto, office near Texaco station, US$5 for a short consultation. There are good clinics at Santiago Atitlán and San Lucas Tolimán, which specialize in treating dysentery. Outbreaks of cholera have been reported in the lake area since 1991; enquire locally about the safety of water, lake fish, etc. Amoebic dysentery and hepatitis are less common than in the past. Treatment free, so a donation is appropriate. Fleas endemic. Take care to treat bites in case of infection. 1 litre plastic bags of water are sold in Panajachel, bring your own container.

Exchange Banco Inmobilario on Calle Los Arboles, open Mon-Thur 0900-1500, Fri to 1530, Sat 0900-1300 will change TCs. Also Banco Industrial, Calle Santander, and Banco Agrícola Mercantil, Call Principal, also changes TCs. There is a *cambio* on the street near *Mayan Palace* for US dollars cash and TCs, good rate. The barber's shop near the bank will change TCs. The

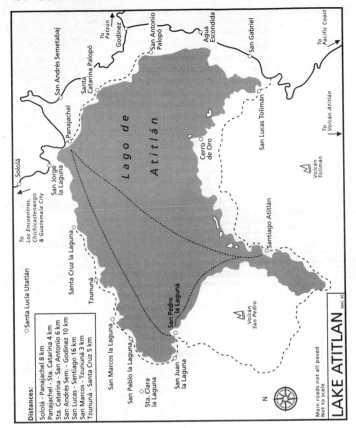

Distances:
Sololá - Panajachel 8 km
Panajachel - Sta. Catarina 4 km
Sta. Catarina - San Antonio 6 km
San Andrés Sem. - Godínez 10 km
San Lucas - Santiago 16 km
San Marcos - Tzununá 3 km
Tzununá - Santa Cruz 5 km

Main roads not all paved
Not to scale

LAKE ATITLAN

Kodak Camera Club near the Tourist Office, slightly better rates.

Language Classes Mayalingua, Santander y Callejón Londres, T 612707, 4, 5 or 6 hrs a day. Pana Atitlán Language School, Calle de la Navidad 0-40, rec.

Post Office Near the church. Will not arrange for parcels to be sent, or received from, abroad. Next to *Restaurant Chisme*, a parcel service in the handicrafts shop claims economy rates to USA cheaper than post office (more expensive to Europe); can send over 2 kg. Central America Link sends parcels to USA, US$18.50 plus US$4.10 per kg, and to Europe US$24.50 plus about US$10 per kg, 6 days to Miami. If you can collect your parcel in Miami and mail it from there to Europe it is cheaper (7790 NW 64th Street, Miami, FL 33166, T (305) 592 5219). **Telephones** Good service from Panajachel, internal and external. The *Grapevine* bar allows you to phone abroad, leave a message and be called back, cheaper than Guatel and useful if there is no collect call facility (this is a *Maya Communications* office, T/F 502-9-622194, interlinked with Antigua and Quezaltenango).

Tourist Office Inguat is on Av Santander, T 621392. Open Wed-Sun, 0800-1200 and 1400-1800, Mon 0800-1200, Tues closed; has maps. Bus and boat timetables posted on door when closed. Hector is very helpful and speaks excellent English. They can also help booking internal flights, sometimes with discounts. Check with Inguat whether it is safe to climb the volcanoes.

Bus Rebuli to **Guatemala City**, 3 hrs, US$1.75, crowded; hourly service 0700-1500. Direct bus to **Quezaltenango** 0545, 0645, 0745, 1100, US$2 (from there to Mexico, bus to Tecún Umán via Coatepeque). There are direct buses to **Los Encuentros** on the Pan-American Highway (US$0.50, the junction for routes to the capital, Quezaltenango and Chichicastenango and the cheapest way to travel). To **Chichicastenango** direct, 0645 and hourly thereafter, US$3, although a minibus tour can cost US$6.50 (no buses from Los Encuentros to Panajachel after 1830). There are direct buses to **Cuatro Caminos**, US$0.50 (**see p 505**) from 0530, for connections to Totonicapán, Quezaltenango, Huehuetenango, etc. Bus to **Chimaltenango** (for Antigua), US$1.70, change there for **Antigua**. There is also a direct bus 1100 and 1400, US$2, which leaves from opp the bank and a tourist minibus, US$12, Antigua-Panajachel. Bus to **Sololá**, US$0.25. Best to wait for buses by the market, not by the Guatel road to the lake.

Excursions There are regular boat trips across the lake, mainly to Santiago Atitlán and San Pedro La Laguna—but there are a number of stopping services to places along the W shore, so you can take a boat to eg Santa Cruz, walk on to San Marcos and catch a boat back from there. (Note that for return to Panajachel boats may not stop at Santa Cruz and San Pablo unless someone is going to get off.) It is best to buy single tickets as some boat owners will not recognize a return and make you pay again. You can also hire boats for trips (a 6-hr tour costs about US$6.50). The Tourist Office has the latest information on boats pinned on its door, schedules change too frequently for us to publish.

The lake is some 50 km in circumference and you can walk on or near the shore for most of it. Here and there the cliffs are too steep to allow for easy walking and private properties elsewhere force you to move up 'inland'.

Santa Catarina Palopó is within walking distance of Panajachel (about 4 km, path goes through many tiny farms, very friendly and pleasant; truck US$0.12). The town has an attractive adobe church. Reed mats are made here, and you can buy *huipiles* (beautiful, green, blue and yellow) and men's shirts. Must bargain for articles. Hotel, **A** *Villa Catarina*, T 621291, nice setting; also **A** *Bella Vista*, T local 621566/26807-9 (Guatemala City), on road to San Antonio Palopó, overlooking lake, quiet, highly rec. Houses can be rented here. From Santa Catarina you can walk to the Mirador of Godínez for views, but the path is very steeply uphill for quite a while.

San Antonio Palopó (6 km beyond Santa Catarina), has another splendid church; it lies in an amphitheatre formed by the mountains behind. The village is noted for the costumes and headdresses of the men, and *huipiles* and shirts are cheaper than in Santa Catarina. *Fiesta*: June 14. The Artexco cooperative is called by the name of the village. **D** *Hotel Terrazas del Lago*, T 28741 (Guatemala City), on the lake with the view, bath, clean, restaurant, nice atmosphere, Polish born owner speaks German and English; **E** *Hotel Casa de don Félix* (or *Casa del Lago*), superb views and good bathing, only a few rooms but gradually being expanded, good restaurant; you can stay in private houses (eg Don Tiedera nr the Post Office) or rent rooms (take sleeping bag). A good hike is to take the bus from Panajachel to Godínez, walk down from there to San Antonio Palopó (1 hr) and then along the new road back to Panajachel via Santa Catarina Palopó (3 hrs). The only bus from Panajachel to San Antonio is at 1600, but there are pick-ups.

You can walk on round the lake from San Antonio, but you must eventually climb steeply up to the road at Agua Escondida. 1½ km S along the road is *Panaranjo* from where a track leads towards the lake and down to Finca Tzanpetey, 30-40 mins. From there it is possible to walk to San Lucas Tolimán but the path is narrow and delicate in places where it climbs up 50-100m to negotiate the steepest drops to the lake. After 1 km you reach the N end of the San Lucas lake shore and it is an easy walk. Less strenuous is to walk on from Panaranjo to San Gabriel, ask for the 'extravio para San Lucas' for a delightful route through fields of corn, tomato, potatoes, chillies, beans and coffee, then following a deep dry water course to a spectacular view of the lake and volcanoes. A traverse follows to a band of cypress where the path descends using the roots of trees to help you, alpine-style, down to San Lucas. Good footwear essential.

At **San Lucas Tolimán**, on the southern tip of the lake, there is accommodation at **E** *Villa del Lago*, with bath, hot water, restaurant, parking; **E** *Brisas del Lago*, prominent position overlooking the lake, 10 rooms at present, restaurant, bar; **E** *Pensión Central*, with private bath, F without, hot water, meals US$1. *Cafetería Santa Ana*, shop and café, will put you up for US$2, clean. Restaurants: *Comedor Victoria*, Guatemalan food; *Café Tolimán*, on the lakeside, home made yoghurt and local dishes, rec; *La Fonda*, ½ block N of plaza, clean, food local food. Camping possible near the lake but ask, and check for safety. *Fiestas* include Holy Week with processions, arches and carpets on the Thurs and Fri. Many Indians in their finest clothes take part. There is a market on Tues, Fri and Sun. There are boats to and from Panajachel and San Antonio on market days, enquire. Though there are plans for a scheduled service, this has not yet materialized. Bus to San Lucas from Panajachel at 0630 and 1600 daily, 1 hr, US$0.50. A bus leaves San Lucas to Panajachel, 0700 and 1800; to Santiago, hourly between 0900 and 1800, 1 hr, returning hourly between 0300 and 1300. Bus San Lucas to Quezaltenango, US$1.50, 0430 and 0600.

From San Lucas the cones of *Atitlán*, 3,535m, and *Tolimán*, 3,158m, can be climbed. The route leaves from the S end of the town and makes for the saddle (known as Los Planes, or Chanán) between the two volcanoes. From there it is S to Atitlán and N to the double cone and crater of Tolimán. Though straightforward, the climb of both is complicated by many working paths and thick cover above 2600m. Cloud on the tops is common, least likely Nov-March. If you are fit, either can be climbed in 8 hrs, 5 hrs down. Ask at the Municipalidad for information on guerrilla/bandit activity, which has noticeably declined since 1991, and for available guides. Though formal permission is not required, they will give you a note to indicate your excursion is registered, which could be useful. Maps are not available locally.

This area was affected by the earthquake of November 1991, which caused landslides, damage to roads and buildings. The church in San Lucas was damaged and the façade is being rebuilt.

From San Lucas, a poor dirt road, passable only with high clearance, preferably 4WD, goes 16 km to *Santiago Atitlán*. On the right is the hill, *Cerro de Oro*, with a small village of that name on the lake. You can also reach Santiago from Panajachel by boat, lots available, check schedule at Tourist Office. The women wear fine costumes and the men wear striped, half-length embroidered trousers. There is an Artexco cooperative: *Flor del Lago*. There is a daily market, best on Friday. *Fiesta*: 5 June and 25 July. The celebrations of Holy Week are worth seeing, but it may be hard to find a room. The celebrations include the display of Maximon, whose idol is housed in the town. The Franciscan church dates back to 1568. Nearby were the ruins of the fortified Tzutuhil capital on the Cerro de Chuitinamit (nothing new to see). **B** *Posada de Santiago*, to leave message, T 9627158/7168, cabins, including breakfast, American owners, 2 km on the road to San Pedro, good restaurant, boat trips on lake for US$5 per hour. **F** *Pensión Rosita*, near the church, dirty; **E** *Hospedaje Chi-Nim-Ya*, good (good café opposite, also 50m away, huge Pepsi advert on wall, cheap, large helpings). Houses can be rented, but be extremely careful to check for, and protect against, scorpions and poisonous spiders in the wooden frames. *Santa Rita* restaurant good and cheap. The *Galería Nim Pot* is worth a visit, near the school, the family Chávez exhibit their own paintings and carvings and sell hand woven cloth, etc. Bus to Guatemala City, US$1.50 (5 a day, first at 0300). Buses to Panajachel at 0600, 2 hrs, or take any bus and change on the main road just S of San Lucas.

5 km N of Santiago Atitlán is the **Parque Nacional Atitlán** which had a small reserve for the *poc*, the Atitlán grebe. The *poc* is now extinct because of loss of habitat, increased human population, pollution and the introduction of non-native fish. The British Royal Society for the Protection of Birds also cites replacement by, or hybridization with, the pied-billed grebe, which it closely resembled. Safe camping, take food and water; the guards may put you up in one of their cabins. Also in the reserve is a tame *pavo del cacho* (a big black bird with a red horn on its head), though there is some doubt if any are now left there. To get there, go by canoe from Santiago (US$0.65), with the reserve workers, or on foot, about ½ hr on the San Lucas Tolimán road, but ask directions.

7 km S of Santiago Atitlán is a mirador and *refugio* called **Quetzal Reserve** where a path winds up and down through rain forest. Follow the path past the *Posada de Santiago*, then go left at the fork and stay on the road until you come to the reserve and viewpoint, both on the left.

6-7 *lanchas* a day leave from Panajachel for *San Pedro La Laguna*, 20 km by dreadful road beyond Santiago (not rec for motorcycles unless you are an expert off-roader. The boat fare is about US$1.10 (US$5 to take motorcycle in boat). There is a launch from Santiago to San Pedro which leaves when full (45 mins, US$1). **NB** There are two landing stages in San Pedro, the 'pier' and the 'beach'. There is an unreliable, uncomfortable bus to San Pedro, not rec, better take the boat. There is also one daily bus San Pedro-Quezaltenango, 0430, 3½ hrs, cold, US$2. San Pedro is at the foot of the **San Pedro volcano**, which can be climbed in 4-5 hrs, 3 hrs down, not difficult except for route finding through the coffee plantations and heavy cover. A guide is therefore advisable unless you walk part of the way the day before to make sure you know where you are going; after 1 hr there is only one path and you cannot get lost. A rec guide is Ventura Matzar González, Calle Principal, Cantón Chuacante, San Pedro, T 621140, US$2.4 pp. Go early (0530) for the view, because after 1000 the top is usually smothered in cloud; also you will be in the shade all the way up and part of the way down. The route around the volcano to Santiago Atitlán can be cycled (boats charge half fare for a bike from Panajachel—beware overcharging); it is a tough 3-4 hr ride requiring some experience and good brakes. If hiring a bike in Panajachel, check the machine carefully. Set out early and allow enough time to catch the last boat back.

Canoes are made here (hire, US$0.50 a day) and a visit to the rug-making cooperative on the beach is of interest. Backstrap weaving is taught at some places, about US$0.50 per day. Try Rosa Cruz, past the 'Colonel's Place', turn right up the hill. Local people in San Pedro speak Tzutuhil. Market days Thur and Sun (better). Fiesta 26-29 June with traditional dances. Dugouts can be hired for US$0.50 per day. Horse hire in San Pedro from two houses next to each other on path closest to beach, US$5 for 3 hrs with guide to neighbouring villages (rather primitive saddles leave you bow-legged). You can also walk from San Pedro to San Juan along the lake and up to *Santa María Visitación*, an attractive village with spectacular views.

San Pedro de la Laguna has become rather a hippie commune of immigrants escaping from the industrialized countries; they sell home-made jewellery and other substances. Samuel Cumes Pop has been rec as a qualified Spanish teacher, US$1.50/hr, he was building a school in 1993.

There are many *pensiones*, including two on the public beach, at about US$0.50. All beach *pensiones* have a water supply problem so bathrooms are often smelly. (**G** *Pensión Balneario*, not rec, 100m to the right is **G** *Villa Sol*, better, nothing fancy, no bath, excellent banana pancakes, helpful owner; **F** *Pensión Chuazanahi* (known as the Colonel's Place), bedding US$0.50 pp, boating and swimming, you can sling your hammock for US$1, reasonable meals, friendly staff; next door is **G** *Tikaaj*, good, wooden cabins a few yards from second dock, popular with backpackers; rooms also at **G** *Blue House* down road beside *Chuazanahi*; **G** *Johanna*, near landing stage for Panajachel mail boat, nice rooms without bath, cold water only, also *cafetería*, good wholemeal pancakes, but reported dirty with fleas; **G** *Domingo's*, chalets, communal toilets and cold showers; all are basic; houses can be rented from US$5 a week to US$50 a month). Good food is available at *Restaurant Chez Michel*, friendly (some French spoken), cheap but slow, turn right from landing stage along beach road, past *Pensión Chuazanahi*; *Sascha*, run by Dutch woman, on right side of first pier you come to by boat, good lasagne, cakes, popular; *Restaurant Francés*, good for pancakes (chocolate and banana), cheap, steaks US$1.50, go through coffee plantation from first pier to the next one; good food but slow service at *Comedor Ranchón*, opp *Chuazanahi*; *Pachanay*, 150m from *Villa Sol*, lunch and dinner, good, cheap, 'hippy'-type atmosphere; *Otty's* also has good, cheap food. Buy banana bread from the *Panadería El Buen Gusto*, near centre of town; *Comedor la Ultima Cena*, opposite the Municipalidad, good pizzas, pancakes, very popular, service for food can be very slow but beer comes quickly; *Restaurant Rosalinda* reported very good especially for local fish and for the banana and chocolate cakes; *Tulipán* has wide variety and vegetarian dishes. Village café, meals US$0.30. Be careful of drinking water in San Pedro, both cholera and dysentry exist here. Centro Médico opp Educación Básica school, good doctor who does not speak English.

From San Pedro, you can walk to Panajachel through San Juan (look for *Artesanía Juanera*, T 621156, cheap, mostly for export), San Pablo, San Marcos and finally Santa Cruz (a difficult track). You can get beautiful views of the lake and volcanoes in the early morning light. Sisal bags and hammocks are made at *San Pablo La Laguna* (**G** *Hospedaje Bisente*, nice patio, the family makes meals). If hiking around the lake, the only hotel between San Pedro and Panajachel is **E** *Arco de Noa*, the bungalow accommodation of Americans Rarin and Guido Bondioli in *Santa Cruz* (Aptdo Postal 39, Panajachel), with small restaurant, excellent food, 5-course dinner with fresh home-made food US$4, very friendly, highly rec; there is also **G** *Hospedaje Hernández*, in the village, clean, friendly, cold water only, and an interesting 16th century church with many curious wooden statues. *Flor del Lago* restaurant serves good chicken, the owner speaks only Calchiquel, but her daughter speaks Spanish. Boat to Panajachel about 1300.

Warning Not a safe area for women to go walking alone. Beware of theft, including of clothes hanging out to dry, in the Lake Atitlán area. Equally, there are stories of money stolen from tourists being recovered and returned to owners by local people. Also beware of overcharging on private boats crossing the lake: practices include doubling the price half-way across and if you don't agree, out you get.

Los Encuentros The old and new Pan-American Highways rejoin 11 km from Sololá. 3 km E is Los Encuentros, the junction of the Pan-American Highway and the road 18 km NE to Chichicastenango. Altitude 2,579m. (Very poor accommodation available, G, if you miss a bus connection, easy to do as they are all full.) Buses for Panajachel stop outside the green police office, about 250m from where the bus stops en route between the border and capital.

Chichicastenango (also known as Santo Tomás) is the hub of the Maya-Quiché highlands, and is very popular with tourists. Altitude 2,071m, and nights cold. About 1,000 *ladinos* in the town, but 20,000 Indians live in the hills nearby and flood the town, almost empty on other days, for the Thur and Sun markets. The town is built around a large square plaza, with two churches facing one another: Santo Tomás parish church and Calvario. Santo Tomás is now open again to visitors, although restoration work is still going on; photography is not allowed, and visitors are asked to be discreet and enter by a side door. Groups burn incense and light candles on steps and platform before entering. Inside, from door to high altar, stretch rows of glimmering candles, Indians kneeling beside them. Later they offer copal candles and flower-petals to the 'Idolo', a black image of Pascual Abaj, a Maya god, on a hilltop 1½ km SW of the plaza (beware of armed robbery on the way), boys act as guides for US$1; be very respectful at the ceremony and do not take photographs. Next to Santo Tomás are the cloisters of the Dominican monastery (1542) where the famous Popol Vuh manuscript of Maya mythology was found and translated into Spanish in 1690; Father Rossbach's jade collection can be seen in the municipal museum on the main square (open 0800-1200, closed Tues), and so is the house of a mask-maker on the way up to the 'Idolo', who rents masks and costumes to the dancers and will show visitors the path to the idol (boys often don masks and do a dance for the tourists, for a small fee). This is a little difficult to find even then, and clear instructions should be obtained before setting out.

Derivation of town's name: *chichicaste*—a prickly purple plant like a nettle, which grows profusely—and *tenango*, place of. The town itself is charming: winding streets of white houses roofed with bright red tiles wandering over a little knoll in the centre of a cup-shaped valley surrounded by high mountains. Fine views from every street corner. The costumes are particularly splendid: the men's is a short-waisted embroidered jacket and knee breeches of black cloth, a gay woven sash and an embroidered kerchief round the head. The cost of this outfit, over US$200, means that fewer and fewer men are in fact wearing it. Women wear *huipiles* with red embroidery against black or brown and skirts with dark blue stripes. The Sun market is more colourful than the one on Thur: more Indians, brighter costumes and dancing to marimba bands, but it certainly becomes very touristy after the buses arrive from Guatemala City (bargains may be had after 1530 when the tourist buses depart). Articles from all over the Guatemalan highlands may be bought including rugs, carpets and bedspreads. In fact the markets begin on the previous pm. You must bargain hard, although reductions may be limited owing to the non-bargaining of package tourists. Good value handicrafts at the shop next door to Cooperativo Santo Tomás, opp. *Mayan Inn* on market place; also from *Popol Vuh*, opposte *Pensión Girón*, which has a good range of clothing in modern designs, good value.

Fiestas Santo Tomás, 17-21 December: processions, dances, marimba music (well worth a visit—very crowded); New Year's Eve; Holy Week; 1 November; 20 January; 19 March; 24 June (shepherds). There is also a *fiesta* at the end of May.

Hotels You won't find accommodation easily on Sat evening and the prices rise to E and over. **A+** *Santo Tomás*, 7 Av, 6-32, T 561061, very attractive building with beautiful colonial furnishings (a museum in itself), often full at weekends, very good, friendly service, helpful owner (Sr Magermans), pool, good restaurant (set meals US$6) and bar, marimba music pm, same day laundry, nice patio; **A+** *Mayan Inn*, T 561176, colonial style courtyard hotel, huge rooms, simple, antique furniture, fireplaces, friendly staff, bar, marimba music, laundry service, restaurant overpriced; **C** *Maya Lodge*, 6 C, 4-08, T 561177, with bath, with breakfast, mixed reports; **C** *Pensión Chigüilá*, 5 Av, 5-24, T 561134, clean, good, D without bath, meals another US$3.85 (some rooms have fireplaces, wood costs US$0.90 a day extra), front rooms noisy otherwise rec; **F** *Posada Belén*, 12 C, 5-55, T 561244, more expensive with bath, hot water, balcony, clean, friendly, will do laundry, fine views; **E** *El Salvador*, 10 C, 4-47, 2 blocks from main square, in large rooms with bath and fireplace (wood available in market), good views, F in small rooms without bath, mixed reports (1993), several complaints about overcharging, theft, dirt, fleas and rudeness; **F** *El Torito*, near where the buses stop, clean, comfortable; **D-E** *Pensión Girón* (cheaper without bath), on 6 Calle, 4-60, Edif Girón, T 561156, good, hot water, helpful, clean, ample parking; **E** *Pasqual Abaj*, 5 Av, on the road to Quiché, T 561055, rooms around a central courtyard, hot showers, good value; **F** *Posada Santa Marta*, 5 Av, 3-27, with cold water, bath and sheets (G without either); **F** *Posada El Arco*, 4 C, 4-36, helpful, clean, large rooms, English spoken, cold water, garage. Local boys will show you other cheap lodgings, G. Try the fire station (Los Bomberos) at weekends.

Restaurants At hotels; *Tapena*, 5 Av, 5-21, clean, very good; *El Torito*, on the second floor of Edif Girón, steaks, fish, good breakfasts, 3-course meal and drink US$5-6, rec; *Eben Ezer*, good breakfasts; *Tziguan Tinamit*, 5 Av y 6 C, some local dishes, steaks, breakfasts, good; *Tita*, average quality, expensive; *La Fonda de Tzijolaj*, 2nd floor of Centro Comercial Municipal Santo Tomás, N side of main square, good meals, good service, reasonable prices (ask the waitress for the booklet written by the owner, a useful English-Spanish-Quiché phrase book). Also above the market at local 17 is *Buenaventura*, reasonable, friendly owner, Manuel Ventura. *Antojitos Tzocomá*, 5 Av, beyond *Hotel Pasqual Abaj*, delicious snacks, lunch for about US$5.50, the owner is an artist whose paintings are displayed. *Comedor Isabel*, 5 Calle 4-16, good. No meals anywhere under US$2.50.

Exchange Banco del Ejército, very slow, but nowhere else changes TCs, beware queues on market days, also open Sats. *Mayan Inn* will exchange cash, *Santo Tomás* cheques and cash at holiday times.

Post Chichicargo, by *Pensión Girón*, T 561056, sends packages abroad and will insure the contents.

Buses Veloz Quiché direct from/to the capital, US$1.60 (Zona 4 Terminal), half hourly service, 0500-1800, 3½ hrs. The slower Reina de Utatlán bus from the capital, 4-5 hrs (Zona 4 Terminal) costs only US$1.50, several daily. 4 a day to **Solalá** and several to **Panajachel**, direct or via Los Encuentros, prices and schedules vary according to type of service. For **Antigua**, change at Chimaltenango until 1730, after that at San Lucas Sacatepéquez until 2000 (or taxi from Chimaltenango, US$5). To **Huehuetenango**, via Los Encuentros, US$1.75. 2 weekly buses Chichicastenango-**Nebaj**, US$1, may have to change at Sacapulas, otherwise take a bus to **Santa Cruz del Quiché** (half-hourly, ½ hr journey, paved road, also lots of trucks on market day, US$0.40) and change there. Beware of overcharging on buses in the Panajachel/Chichicastenango area.

The Quiché Region 19 km N by road from Chichicastenango is **Santa Cruz del Quiché**, a quaint, friendly town at 2,000m, colourful market on Sun and Thur. There are few tourists here and prices are consequently reasonable. Good selection of local cloth. Quiché's speciality is palm hats, which are made and worn in the area, best quality and prices from shop facing the bus terminal. Population 7,750. Remains 3 km away of palaces of former Quiché capital, **Gumarcaj**, sometimes spelt **K'umarkaaj** and known also as Utatlán, destroyed by Spaniards; the ruins consist of adobe mounds, their chief attraction being the setting. They can be reached on foot (from the bus station, walk W along 10 Calle to the Y junction: take the righthand, uphill fork) open 0700-1800, entry US$0.60. There are two subterranean burial chambers (take a torch, there are unexpected drops) still used by the Indians for worship; small but interesting museum at the entrance (closed early 1994). *Fiestas*: about 14-20 August (but varies around Assumption), 3 May. Serious earthquake damage.

Hotels are reluctant to open doors late at night. **F** *Hospedaje Hermano Pedro*, friendly, clean, private shower, close to bus terminal so arrive early; **F** *Posada Calle Real*, 2 Av, 7-36, parking, hot shower, clean, friendly, rec; **F** *San Pascual*, 7 C, 0-43, T 551107, occasional hot showers, clean, quiet, locked parking; **F** *La Cascada*, friendly, clean; **G** *Centroamérica*, without bath, very basic; **G** *Pensión Santa Clara*, hot water, plus US$0.50 for good meals; **G** *Tropical*, 1 Av y 9 C. Basic accommodation near bus terminal.

Restaurants *La Samaritana*, near bus terminal, clean, friendly; *Maya Quiché* on main square, mixed reports; *Pic Nic*, 2 Av, 6-45, reasonable prices; *Café Kail* on main square, good ice cream, cakes, also main dishes; *Musicafé* good food, reasonable; good *comedor* 2 blocks N of NE corner of main square, clean, cheap, friendly, pretty wooden tables. Many are dirty.

Thermal baths at Pachitac, 4 km away, and beside the market building.

Electric Current 220 volts.

Cinema *Astor*, 3 Av y 6 C.

Exchange Banco de Guatemala, 3 C y 2 Av; Banco G y T, 6 Calle y 3 Av.

Post Office on 3 C, Zona 5; **Guatel**, on 1 Av, Zona 5.

Buses Terminal at 10 C y 1 Av Reina de Utatlán from **Guatemala City**, Zona 4 bus terminal, 0600-1600, 4-5 hrs (US$1.60), via Los Encuentros and Chichicastenango. ½ hr from **Chichicastenango**, US$0.30, every ½ hr from *Pensión Chigüilá*. To **Nebaj**, 2 a day 0800 and 0900, US$1.20, 4-5 hrs; a rough but breathtaking trip, arrive in good time to get a window seat (may leave early if full). At 0930, 1130 and 1330 to Uspantán, 5 hrs, US$1.25, ride on top for good view. Bus to **Joyabaj**, 0930 daily, US$0.50, 1½ hrs 0300 bus Uspantán to **Cobán** and **San Pedro Carchá**, about 5 hrs, the best part is done in darkness. If going to **Momostenango** for the market, take the bus at 0400 as the 0800 one arrives too late (6 hr journey). It is possible to get to **Huehuetenango** in a day via Sacapulas (0930 bus), then truck from bridge to Aguacatan (1¼ hrs), bus from there 1430 to Huehuetenango.

There is a paved road E from Quiché to (8 km) **Santo Tomás Chiché**, a picturesque village with a fine rarely-visited Indian Sat market (*fiesta*, 21-28 December). Buses and vans (US$0.25) run from Quiché. (There is also a road to this village from Chichicastenango. Although it is a short-cut, it is rough and now virtually impassable in any vehicle. It makes a good 3 to 4 hr walk however.)

On 32 km from Chiche is **Zacualpa**, where beautiful woollen bags are woven. There is an unnamed *pensión* near the square; on the square itself is a private house which has cheap rooms and meals. (Mosquito coils are a must.) Market: Sun, Thur. Church with remarkably fine façade. Two shops opposite each other on the road into town sell weavings, good prices. On another 11 km is **Joyabaj**, where women weave fascinating *huipiles*; **F** *Pensión Mejía*, near the church, basic but clean. This was a stopping place on the old route from Mexico to Antigua. During *fiesta* week (the second in August) Joyabaj has a *palo volador*—two men dangle from a 20m pole while the ropes they are attached to unravel to the ground. The villages of San Pedro and San Juan Sacatepéquez (**see p 462**) can be reached from Joyabaj by a dry-season road suitable only for strong vehicles. The scenery en route is spectacular (Joyita bus, Guatemala City 3-4 Av, 7-9 C, Zona 4, to Joyabaj, US$1.50).

A poor road goes N from Quiché, 48 km, to **Sacapulas**, 1,220m, at the foot of the Cuchumatanes mountains. Bus ride from Quiché to Sacapulas recommended, fabulous views on switchback road. Several a day, one leaves at 0930, very crowded, US$1, 3 hrs. Try to persuade them to let you ride on the roof, you will see much more! Return buses, Sacapulas-Quiché appear all to be in the early hours. Bus to Huehuetenango via Aguacatán (see below), at 0500, 4½ hrs, road can be closed in rainy season. Remains of bridge over Río Negro built by Las Casas. Primitive salt extraction. Market under large ceiba trees on Thur and Sun. There is a *pensión*, **G** *Comedor Gloris*, near the bridge which is a basic, cheap flea circus, with poor meals, US$0.65, best avoided, and another in the orange-painted house above the river (no reports); *Tienda Bartolomé* nearby, better (also, clean rooms, G, rec, municipal parking lot nearby); *Comedor Central* near the market. Colonial church with surprising treasures inside, built 1554. There are hot springs along the S bank of the river a few hundred metres E of the bridge, which are rec for a hot bath. They are shallow, dug out depressions along the bank and a small bucket (a *guacal* or a *palangana*) is rec to assist in bathing.

The road E to Cobán from Sacapulas is one of the most beautiful, if rough, mountain roads in all Guatemala, with magnificent scenery in the narrow valleys. Truck to Cobán, 5 daily am, US$1.25, 5 hrs, if lucky, usually much longer. There is no direct bus to Cobán; instead, take one of the three Quiché-Uspantán buses (passing Sacapulas at about 1230, 1400, 1600), or a truck, to **Uspantán**, *fiesta* 6-10 May. Stay the night at the **G** *Hospedaje El Viajero* (3 blocks E of Plaza, basic, clean, pleasant, informative about the area), or **G** *Galindo*, clean, friendly, good meals available, rec (*Comedor Kevin* is good, serves vegetables), then take early morning bus (0300-0400, you can spend the night on the bus before it leaves, also 0900—riding on top recommended) or hitch-hike to Cobán. (Truck Uspantán-San Cristóbal Verapaz, US$1.25.) Buses to Quiché at 0200, 0300, 2200. A morning bus starts at 0200 in Quiché, with a change at **Cunén** (*fiesta* 5-7 February, with dancing with silver deer masks, especially interesting at night; nowhere to stay unless you have a tent; *Tienda y Comedor Rech Kanah María*, next to church, good; no food after 2000 anywhere). The road W of Sacapulas, through Aguacatán, to Huehuetenango is also beautiful, but tough on the driver who has little time to admire the scenery.

It is a 5-hr walk from Uspantán S to Chimul, the birthplace of Rigoberta Menchú, the Nobel Peace Prize winner in 1992. The village was virtually erased during the 1980s, but settlement is coming to life again. You can get a lift on market day in the afternoon, but not all the way.

Branching off this road, about 13 km N of Sacapulas, is a spectacular road to the village of Nebaj (see below). It is easy enough to get by truck to Nebaj (US$0.50) and there are buses from Quiché. It is not so easy to get to the other two villages of the Ixil Triangle, **Chajul** and **San Juan de Cotzal** (a new road has been built between the two), but the 0500 bus from Quiché and Sacapulas to Nebaj on Sun seems to continue to both. Chajul has a *pensión*, near the post office, basic, clean, G; also a small *comedor*. Cotzal also has a *pensión*. The village's fiesta is 21-24 June, culminating in the day of St John the Baptist on 24 June. There is a conquistador dance and it is very colourful. The local women's headwear has huge pom poms. Nebaj to Cotzal is a beautiful 4-hr walk. There are no formal lodging or restaurant facilities in other small villages and it is very difficult to specify what transport facilities are in fact available in this area as trucks and the occasional pick-up or commercial van (probably the best bet—ask, especially in *Las Tres Hermanas*, Nebaj) are affected by road and weather conditions. For this reason, be prepared to have to spend the night in villages. Chajul has a pilgrimage to Christ of Golgotha on the second Friday in Lent, beginning the Wednesday before (the image is escorted by 'Romans' in blue police uniforms!) Chajul has market Tues and Fri. A 1½-hr walk up the river between Chajul and Nebaj, look for an attractive waterfall. In Cotzal the market is on Sat. Look out for the attractive local *huipiles*.

On the main square of **Nebaj** is the Casa de la Cultura selling handicrafts from the town and the surrounding area, bargaining possible. *Huipiles* may be bought from María Santiago Chel (central market) or Juana Marcos Solís (Cantón Simacol), who gives weaving lessons from 1 day to 6 months. The local costume is colourful and very beautiful; the *corte* (skirt) is bright red and the *huipil* is of a geometric design in red, purple, green and yellow. The women also wear a headdress with pom poms on it. Visitors are asked by young women to visit their homes to see (and buy) 'típicas', weavings (prices are usually better than in the market, but the sellers can be very persistent); boys meet all incoming buses and will guide you to a *hospedaje*. This village has very good Sun and Thur markets. Nebaj has a *fiesta* on 15 Aug. There are magnificent walks from Nebaj along the river or in the surrounding hills. The views of the Cuchumatanes mountains are spectacular.

Accommodation and Food G *Ixil Hotel*, basic but perhaps a bit more upmarket than the others, clean, pleasant and comfortable, big rooms, good cheap meals for guests, just before entering town. Alternatively you can get a room in a private house for slightly less. **G** *Hospedaje Esperanza*, very friendly, clean, hot shower extra, owner's daughter gives weaving lessons, US$7/day; **G** *Las Clavellinas*, nice, basic, without bath, rec; **G** *Las Tres Hermanas*, friendly, full of character, popular with foreigners, wood-fired hot water, basic, some beds very hard, good food available for about US$0.50. 2 other *pensiones*. *Comedor de Olimpia Irene Moreno*, 1 block SE from square, painted blue-green, good food, plenty of vegetables, nicknamed 'binliner' for its pink plastic wall and ceiling coverings, full of character; *Comedor Las Delicias*, across from the Parque Central, limited menu but OK. *Los Boxboles* a *comedor* at the home of the weaver Juana Marcos Solís (see above) in Cantón Simacol, head towards Chajul from the plaza on Av 15 de Septiembre, turn right at the pila on Salida Chajul, take first left and her house is up on the left, excellent *tamalitos*, *boxboles* (leaves with *masa* spread on them, rolled tightly, boiled and served with a *salsa* and fresh orange juice) and other local dishes, rec. There is also an army camp.

The headquarters of the Shawcross Aid Programme is in Nebaj (see **Volunteer Work** in **Information for Visitors**); the house is 50m from the Post Office.

Buses to Quiché and Guatemala City all leave early am or late at night. From Nebaj, bus to Sacapulas and Quiché 0100, 0400, 0500 (coming from Cotzal), and on Sun 0800, 2½ hrs to Sacapulas (US$0.60), a further 1½ to Quiché (service times unreliable). You can travel to Cobán in a day by getting a truck or pick-up from outside the village or earliest bus to Sacapulas, get off at junction to Cunén and hitch or catch a bus from there.

There is good walking W of Nebaj, and the roads are better in this direction than to Chajul and Cotzal since there are a number of 'model villages' resettled by the government. These include **Acul** (follow the road down from *Comedor de Olimpia* towards the cemetery, than go up a long hill and down the other side to Acul, 2 hrs there, 2½ back by road); there is a good cheese farm 1 km before the village, whose late Italian owner was making Swiss cheese for 50 years (the cheese is for sale); *Tzalbal*, 2½ hrs walking; *Salquil Grande*, 26 km NW of Nebaj (several hours walk); *La Pista*, where the airstrip is. None has accommodation or restaurants; apart from the rare bus, there is no public transport, only pick-ups; ask for advice at *Las Tres Hermanas*. **Las Violetas**, 15 mins walk from the centre of Nebaj, is a squatters' village where people who have come down from the mountains live when they arrive in Nebaj. To a waterfall take the road to Chajul and after 20 mins take the left fork to follow the river; another 40 mins brings you to a pretty waterfall; lovely scenery. A guide is Jacinto (has a notebook of testimonials); he charges US$2 for a morning's walking.

WESTERN GUATEMALA (6)

Yet more market towns and villages, with characteristic weaving or other crafts, can be found on the routes through western Guatemala. The volcanic chain is also still in evidence. In the cool highlands,

WESTERN GUATEMALA (6) 505

Quezaltenango is a good centre for reaching Indian villages, or for heading to Mexico, including a descent to the Pacific lowlands. Another good centre is Huehuetenango, on the highland route to Mexico. Also from Huehuetenango you can go to the Indian village and weaving centre of Todos Santos Cuchumatán, or head E to Aguacatán and the scenic road to Quiché.

The stretch of Pan-American Highway between Los Encuentros and San Cristóbal Totonicapán runs past **Nahualá**, at 2,470m, an Indian village where *metates*, or stones on which maize is ground to make *tortillas*, are made. The inhabitants wear distinctive costumes, and are considered by other Indians to be somewhat hostile. Good church. Market on Thursdays and Sundays (this is the time to visit), at which finely embroidered cuffs and collars are sold, also very popular *huipiles*, but check the colours, many run. No accommodation except perhaps with Indian families at a small cost. *Fiesta* (Santa Catalina) on 25 November. Remember the Indians do not like to be photographed. Population 1,370.

There is another all-weather road a little to the N and 16 km longer, from Los Encuentros to San Cristóbal Totonicapán. In 40 km it reaches Totonicapán. The route Chichicastenango-Quiché-Totonicapán takes a day by car or motorcycle, but is well worth taking. No buses.

Totonicapán, 14½ km E of Cuatro Caminos (see below), is the capital of its Department, at 2,500m. Population 52,000, almost all Indian. There are sulphur baths, but they are dirty and crowded. Market (mind out for pickpockets) considered by Guatemalans to be one of the cheapest, and certainly very colourful, on Tues (small), and Sat (the main market noted for ceramics and cloth); annual fair 26-30 September; *fiestas* on 29 September and 25 July. *Chuimekená* cooperative is at 9 Av between C 1 and 2, Zona Palín, fine variety of handicrafts and woven cloth.

Hotels: **G** *El Centro*, 7 C, 7-33, Zona 4; **F** pp *Hospedaje San Miguel*, 3 C, 7-49, Zona 1, T 661452, clean, comfortable, hot water, prices treble on market day.

Restaurants *Antojitos Chuimelcaná*, 4 C, 9 y 10 Av, smart, good light meals and snacks; *Comedor Lety*, near *Hospedaje San Miguel*, excellent; *Comedor Brenda*, 8 Av, 6 y 7 C, also good.

Exchange Banco de Guatemala, 7 Av y 5 C, Zona 1.

Buses Frequent buses to **Quezaltenango** along a paved road (fine scenery), US$0.35. Bus to **Los Encuentros**, US$1.50.

San Cristóbal Totonicapán, 1 km from the **Cuatro Caminos** road junction (Pan-American Highway, with the roads to Quezaltenango, Totonicapán, Los Encuentros and Huehuetenango; **D** *Nuevo Hotel Reforma*, a/c, parking and **E** *Pensión Reforma*, a/c, parking, restaurant, in Barrio La Reforma, F/T 661438) has a huge church, built by Franciscan friars, of which the roof has recently been renovated. The silver-plated altars and screens, all hand-hammered, are worth seeing. Noted for textiles (and *huipiles* in particular) sold all over Guatemala. Also well known for ceramics. Market, Sunday, on the other side of the river from the church (only 2 blocks away), spreading along many streets. Annual fair, 20-26 July. Altitude 2,340m, population 3,186. Bus service to Quezaltenango.

Excursion Two km W of the Cuatro Caminos junction a road runs N to San Francisco El Alto (3 km) and Momostenango (19 km). *San Francisco El Alto*, at 2,640m (also reached by a new paved road 5 km W of Cuatro Caminos, at Km 151), stands in the mountain cold, above the great valley in which lie Totonicapán, San Cristóbal and Quezaltenango. Church of metropolitan magnificence, notice the double-headed, Hapsburg eagle. Visit the roof on market days for a fine view of activities and surroundings. Crammed market on Friday; Indians buying woollen blankets for resale throughout country, and fascinating cattle market. An excellent place for buying woven and embroidered textiles of good quality, but beware of pickpockets. Colourful New Year's Day celebrations. It is a pleasant walk from San Francisco down to the valley floor, then along the river to San Cristóbal. Frequent buses to Quezaltenango and Totonicapán, about 1 hr to either. Close by in the mountains to the W is San Andrés Xequl, see under Quezaltenango **Excursions**.

Hotel F *Vista Hermosa*, 3 Av, 2-22, T 661030, no showers, fleas. Good *comedor* opposite. **G** *Hospedaje Central San Francisco de Asís* on main street near market. Good restaurant, *Dixie*.

Momostenango, at 2,220m, is the chief blanket-weaving centre. Indians can be seen beating the blankets on stones to shrink them. The Feast of the Uajxaquip Vats (pronounced 'washakip') is celebrated by 30,000 Indians every 260 days by the ancient Mayan calendar. Frequent masked dances also. Momostenango means 'place of the altars', and there are many on the outskirts but they are not worth looking for; there is, however, a hilltop image of a Mayan god, similar to the one outside Chichicastenango. There are said to be 300 medicine-men practising in the town; their insignia of office is a little bag containing beans and quartz crystals. Outside town are three sets of *riscos*: eroded columns of sandstone with embedded quartz particles, which are worth visiting. The most striking are the least accessible, in the hills to the N of the town. The town is quiet except on Wed and Sun, the market days (the latter being larger, and interesting for weaving; also try Tienda Manuel del Jesús Agancel, 1 Av, 1-50, Zona 4 for good bargains, especially blankets and carpets; on non-market days, ask for weavers' houses). It has a spring-fed swimming pool; also a sulphur bath (5 in all) at Pala Grande, 4 km NW of Momostenango (take the road first towards Santa Ana); the water is black, but worth experiencing, take soap. Bus service from Cuatro Caminos (US$0.35) and Quezaltenango, US$0.45.

Accommodation G *Hospedaje Paclom*, on main street, clean, pretty inner courtyard, water mornings only, no showers, friendly but watch out for overcharging, cheap meals; **G** *Hospedaje Roxane*, bad. avoid. *Comedor Tonia*, friendly, cheap. Bottled water is impossible to find.

At San Cristóbal the old and the new routes of the Pan-American Highway, which joined at Los Encuentros, part again. The new route to the Mexican border at Ciudad Cuauhtémoc goes NW, by-passing Huehuetenango before entering the Selegua canyon stretch, known as El Tapón, now in very good condition.

The old route, running W to Tapachula, in Mexico, reaches, 5 km from San Cristóbal, the small *ladino* town of *Salcajá*, where jaspé skirt material has been woven since 1861, well worth a visit. Yarn is tied and dyed, then untied and warps stretched around telephone poles along the road or along the riverside. Many small home weavers will sell the lengths—5 or 8 *varas*—depending on whether the skirt is to be wrapped or pleated. The finest, of imported English yarn, cost US$40. The Artexco cooperative is *San Luis*, Calle Capitán Juan de León y Cardona, Zona 2. Market, Tues, mostly fruit and vegetables; it is early, as in all country towns. The church of San Jacinto behind the market is 16th century and also worth a visit. The taxi rate is US$2.50-3 per hour. Several minibuses a day from new commercial centre, 10 Av and 8 C. There are two hotels in town; **F** *Salcajá*, 3 Av final, Zona 1, restaurant; **E** *La Mansión de Don Hilario*, 3 Av, 3-21, Zona 2, T 616101, next door to *Cafesama* restaurant, which is good. Excellent unnamed bakery on third street up the hill parallel to main street where buses pass in town centre.

Quezaltenango (commonly known as Xela), 14½ km SW of Cuatro Caminos, over 125,000 people, is the most important city in western Guatemala. Altitude 2,335m, and climate decidedly cool and damp (particularly November to April, and there is no heating anywhere). Set among a group of high mountains and volcanoes, one of which, Santiaguito, the lower cone of Santa María (which can be easily climbed), destroyed the city in 1902 and is still active sometimes. A modern city, but with narrow colonial-looking streets and a magnificent plaza (between 11 and 12 Av and 4 and 7 Calle). Especially interesting is the stately but quaint Teatro Municipal (14 Av and 1 C). There is a modern gothic-style church, the Sagrado Corazón, on the Parque Juárez near the market; other churches include San Juan de Dios on 14 Av and La Transfiguración, from which there is a good view. The cathedral is modern with a 17th-century façade. Festivals 30 March-5 April, 12-18 Sept and Holy Week (very interesting). The Museo de Historia Natural on the S side of the Parque Central, open Mon-Fri, 0900-1800, Sat 0800-1600 (closed in December) has a delightful collection of historical documents, precolumbian pottery, stuffed birds, and many other items. There is also the Museo de Arte, 12 Av y 7 C, interesting collection of contemporary Guatemalan art with special exhibitions. A good centre for buses to all parts of the Indian highlands. Airfield. (All addresses given are in Zona 1, unless otherwise stated.)

Hotels At Easter, 12-18 September and Christmas, rooms need to be booked well in advance. **A** *Pensión Bonifaz*, 4 C, 10-50, T 612279, good restaurant (really not a *pensión* but an excellent hotel), clean, comfortable, US cable TV in all rooms, central heating but lower rooms are warmer than upper rooms, quiet, lounge with fireplace (good for taking afternoon coffee and cakes); **A** *Villa Real Plaza*, 4 C, 12-22, T 614045, dignified colonial building nicely converted, restaurant has good vegetarian food; **E** *Los Alpes*, Diagonal 3, 31-04, Zona 3, T 635721, Swiss-owned, private bath, rec; **B** *Del Campo*, a Best Western lookalike, Km 224 Carretera a Cantel, T 612064, at city limits (4 km) at turn-off to Retalhuleu, good meals (*El Trigal*, European and Chinese), rec; **B** *Modelo*, 14 Av 'A', 2-31, Zona 1, T 612715, friendly staff, good restaurant (4 course meal US$3) and early breakfast; **D** *Anexo Hotel Modelo*, 14 Av 'A', 3-22, T 612606, good value; **D** *Centroamérica Inn*, Boulevard Minerva 14-09, Zona 3, T 4901; **D** *Gran Hotel Americano*, 14 Av, 3-47, T 612118, 'tourists' pay more than 'travellers' (so look like a traveller!), good, friendly, restaurant, breakfast rec, TV; **D-E** *Río Azul*, 2 C, 12-15, T 630654, all rooms with bath, clean, comfortable, friendly, good location, rec; *Arturos*, 14 Av y 3 C, nice atmosphere, friendly, food good; **E** *Casa del Viajero*, 8 Av, 9-17, T 614594, with bath, hot water, limited but good restaurant, English-speaking manager, parking (US$0.30 extra), has fax but charges US$10 for one page to USA; **E** *Casa Kaehler*, 13 Av, 3-33, T 612091, very nice, clean but not much hot water, some rooms very cold; **E** *Casa Suiza*, 14 Av A, 2-36, T 630242, with bath, breakfast US$1.50, pleasant; **E** *Kiktem-Ja*, 13 Av, 7-18, T 614304, good location, Colonial style rooms, all with bath, open fires, car parking inside gates, rec; **E** guest house of **Elena Herzog**, also known as *International House*, 11 C, 13A-41, T 6764, with and without fireplace, shared hot showers, laundry, cooking facilities, drinking water, patios, cable TV, book exchange, clean, highly rec (Sra Herzog is director of Inglés Ya language school and hires native-speakers as teachers, US$1.50/hr, min 2 months); **E** *Pensión Andina*, 8 Av, 6-07, Zona 1, T 611012, hot water all day, friendly, clean, restaurant, good value; **E** *Pensión Altense*, 9 C, 8-48, T 612811, with bath (cheaper without), new part rec, friendly, hot water extra, restaurant, parking; **F** *El Aguila*, 12 Av y 3 C, friendly, hot water extra; **F** *Pensión Hariana*, 12 Av y 2 C, clean and friendly; **F** *Radar 99*, 13 Av near C 4, with bath and hot water (advise the previous night for the morning), cheaper without bath, friendly, will arrange parking in guarded car park opposite (Q3); **F** *El Rincón de los Antojitos*, 15 Av, 4-59, near the Post Office, see **Restaurants** below, bed and breakfast, cable TV, long stays have use of kitchen, English, French and Spanish spoken; **G** *Pensión El Quijote*, 8 Av A, 7-25, hot water, clean; **G** *Pensión Emperador*, 15 C y 1 Av, clean, no hot water. **G** *Pensión Nicolás*, Av 12, 3-16, very basic, hot shower in early am, friendly, sunny patio, parking; **G** *Quetzalteca*, 12 Av y 3C, basic, clean, cold at night, icy water if there is any; **G** *Regia*, 9 Av y 10 C, narrow rooms, basic. **NB** All cheap hotels charge per person.

Restaurants *Kopetin*, 14 Av, 3-31, friendly, good, meat and seafood dishes, about US$5.50 per meal; *Maruc*, 23 Av A-16, good, medium-priced, barbecued meat, dancing, rec; *Royal París*, 16 Av, 3-05, Zona 3, Parque Benito Juárez, small but reasonably priced, good food, excellent choice, inc vegetarian, cheap snacks and soups, main course US$4-6, chocolate crêpes, nice atmosphere, French owner, rec; *El Rincón de los Antojitos*, 15 Av y 5 C, French café (French/Guatemalan owned, Thierry y María Antonieta Roquet), French, vegetarian and local cuisine, good food, US$3-4 main course, see also **Travel Agents** and **Cultural Institutions** below; *La Gondola*, 10 Av, 5 y 6 C, Italian, good and inexpensive, popular, pleasant, rec; *Shanghai*, 4 C, 12-22, Chinese, reasonable prices; *Pizza Ricca*, 14 Av, 2-42,

QUEZALTENANGO

MAC-46

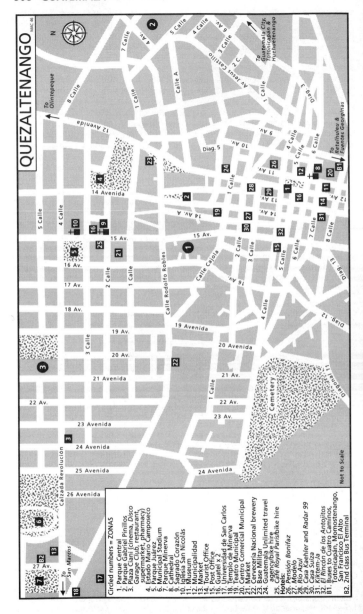

Circled numbers = ZONAS

1. Parque Central Pirillos
2. Parque Gabriel Pinillos
3. Plaza Ciani (cinema, *Disco Garage Club*, restaurant, supermarket, pharmacy)
4. Estado Mario Camposeco
5. Parque Juárez
6. Minerva Municipal Stadium
7. Parque Minerva
8. Cathedral
9. Sagrado Corazón
10. Iglesia San Nicolás
11. Municipalidad
12. Museum
13. Market
14. Tourist Office
15. Post Office
16. Guatel x 2
17. Universidad de San Carlos
18. Templo de Minerva
19. Teatro Municipal
20. Centro Comercial Municipal
21. Market
22. Cervecería Nacional brewery
23. Base Militar
24. guatemala unlimited travel agency
25. *Café Royal París*/bike hire

Hotels:
26. *Pensión Bonifaz*
27. *Modelo*
28. *Río Azul*
29. *Casa Gaehler and Radar 99*
30. *Casa Suiza*
31. *Kiktem-Ja*
32. *El Rincón de los Antojitos*
B1. Buses to Cuatro Caminos, Totonicapán, Momostenango, San Francisco El Alto
B2. 2nd class Bus Terminal

good; best pizzas at *Pizza Bambino*, 14 Av y 4 C, Zona 3, good prices; *Arturo's*, 14 Av 'A', 03-9, good for meat; *Casa Grande*, 4 C, 16-29, Zona 3, good but expensive. Steakhouses: *La Rueda*, 100m from Templo Minerva, Zona 3, expensive; *Pocholo's*, 7 Av, 10-17, Zona 5, international and Spanish; *Panchoy*, 0 Calle 8-81, Zona 9, expensive. *Comedor Rosalinda*, Av 14, C5, cheap, good, friendly; *Albamar*, 4 C entre 12 y 13 Av, Zona 3 and other locations, good meals; *El Deli Crepe*, 14 Av, 1C, good tacos, reasonable prices; *Ut'z Hua*, Av 12 y C 3, typical food, very good, filling, inexpensive but look out for hidden extras; *El Chaparral*, 1 C y 14 Av, Zona 3, for good grills, good atmosphere; *Café Bavaria*, 5 C, 12-50, nice atmosphere, good cheap meals and excellent pies and coffee; *Café Berna*, 16 Av, 3-35, Zona 3, excellent sandwiches, cheesecake, open until 2000. *Salón Tecún*, Edificio Pasaje Enríquez, on plaza, bar, local food, video bar. The *comedor* opp Galgos office is rec for good, filling breakfast before a journey. *Super Antojitos Tiky*, 9C, 11 05, super *licuados*. *Santa Ana*, 8 Av, 8 C, beer US$0.30, guaranteed interaction with inebriated locals. *Xelapan*, several locations, good cakes and bread, inc wholemeal.

Shopping *Artexco*, the National Federation of Artisans' Cooperatives, a long way from centre, guided tour but shop is very small and the business seems to cater mostly for wholesale. For local items better to try the markets of which there are 4: main market at **Templo de Minerva** at Western edge of town (take local bus, US$0.04), has craft section; at the SE corner of **Parque Centro América** (central park) is a shopping centre with craft stalls on the upper levels, food, clothes, etc below; another market at 2 C y 16 Av, Zona 3, S of Parque Benito Juárez. *Típica Chivita*, Centro Comercial Municipal, 2nd level, makes up locally produced woollen blankets into jackets. *Xekijel*, just off plaza, same side of road as tourist office, T 4734, very good for textile lengths. Every first Sunday of the month, there is an *artesanía* market in central park, with a marimba band playing in the morning. Of the markets around Quetzaltenango, the more interesting are at Zunil, San Andrés Xequl and San Francisco el Alto. For food shopping, *Mont Blanc* supermarket is good, a couple of blocks N of Galgos bus terminal; also *El País*, 4 C y 19 Av, Zona 3.

Cinemas *Cadore*, 13 Av y 7 C, *Roma*, 14 Av 'A' and Calle 'A'; from US$0.15. *Alpino*, Plaza Ciani, 24 Av y 4 C, Zona 3.

Exchange Many banks on the central plaza. **Banco de Guatemala**, 12 Av, 5-12, Zona 1, on W side, Mon-Thur 0830-1400, Fri to 1430, Sat 0830-1400. **Banco Inmobiliario**, NW corner; many banks are open 0900-1800 and on Sat am.

Spanish Language Schools There are many schools, most of which offer individual tuition, accommodation with families, extra-curricular activities and excursions. Mayan languages are also offered by some. Several schools fund community development projects and students are invited to participate with voluntary work. Prices start from US$100/week inc accommodation but rise in June-Aug to US$120-150. The following have been rec by students: **English Club and International Language School**, 3 Calle, 15-16, Zona 1. **Projecto Lingüístico Quezalteco de Español**, 5 C, 2-40, Zona 1, T/F 063 1061, see also under Todos Santos Cuchumatán for US and European offices; **SAB Spanish Center**, 1 C, 12-35, Zona 1, T 2042. For information also write to National Registration Center for Study Abroad, 823 N 2nd St, PO Box 1393, Milwaukee W1, 53201, USA. **Casa Xelahú de Español**, 9 C, 11-26, Zona 1, T/F 9612628, USA contact: 1022 St Paul Ave, St Paul MN 55116, T/F (612) 690-9471. **Spanish School Juan Sisay**, 15 Av, 8-38, Zona 1, Apartado Postal 392, USA contact 3465 Cedar Valley Ct, Smyrna, GA 30080, T (404) 436-6283. **Instituto Central America (ICA)**, 1 Calle 16-93, Zona 1, T/F 631871, in USA: RR Box 101, Stanton, Nebraska, 68779 T 402-439-2943. **Centro de Estudios de Español Pop Wuj**, 1 C, 17-72, 5 C, 2-40, Zona 1, T 618286; **Desarrollo del Pueblo**, Diagonal 12, 6-28, Zona 1, Apartado Postal 41, T/F 961-4624, or 18 Av, 0-33, Zona 3 (director's house), in UK, Hannah Roberts, 48 Thorncliffe Rd, Oxford OX2 7BB, T (0865) 52653;**Ulew Tinimit**, 14 Av 'A', 8-38, Zona 3, PO Box 346, T 614886; **Academia Latinoamericana Mayense** (ALM) 15 Av 6-75, Zona 1, PO Box 375 and 376, T 961 2707; **Projecto Lingüístico de Santa María**, 14 Av 'A', 1-26, Zona 1, Apartado Postal 230, T 961 2570, F 961 8281; **Ututlan**, 12 Av, 4-32, Zona 1, PO Box 239, T 630446; **Centro del Lenguaje América Latina** 19 Av, 3-63, Zona 3, T 6416. **Minerva Spanish School**, 24 Av, 4-39, Zona 3. **Guatemalensis**, 19 Av, 2-41, Zona 1.

Cultural Institutions Alianza Francesa de Quezaltenango, 14 Av 'A', A-80, Zona 1, T 614076, runs French courses, many cultural events (exhibitions, films on Thur evening, lectures, etc). For information contact Thierry Roquet at *El Rincón de los Antojitos* restaurant.

Consulate Mexican, 9 Av 6-19, Zona 1, T 612547, Mon-Fri 0900-1230, 1400-1600, take photocopies of passport and some nationalities have to show copy of international credit card.

Health Dr Oscar R de León at the hospital is an English speaking doctor, 9 C, 10-41, Zona 1, T 4414.

Laundry *Minimax*, Av 14, No C-47, 0730-1930, US$2.15, wash and dry.

Communications Post and Telegraph Office, 15 Av and 4 Calle, Telephone (Guatel) 13 Av between 6 and 7 C, Zona 1, and 15 Av and 3 Calle, Zona 3, near Mercado La Democracia. The Tourist Service Centre on Calle Rodolfo Robles 17-23 will send a fax cheaper than Guatel, eg US$10 per min to UK compared with US$22 per sheet at Guatel; you can also receive phone calls here. Also *Salón Tecún*, Edificio Pasaje Enríquez on the plaza, interlinked with *Maya Communications* offices in Antigua and Panajachel. T/F 502-9-0612832.

Insurance Granai and Townson motoring insurance from Seguros Occidental behind Banco del Café, which is on main square.

Travel Agents *SAAB Agencia de Viajes*, 1 C, 12-35, Zona 1, T 612042/6402. Thierry Roquet at *El Rincón de los Antojitos* restaurant arranges trips to volcanoes, hot springs, markets, etc. For rock climbing contact Luis and Miguel Morales, 4 Calle D, 3-67, Zona 1, T 631411.

Tourist Office 7 C, 11-35, Zona 1, SW corner of the Plaza, Mon-Fri, 0900-1200, 1430-1700, T 614931. Helpful. Free maps of city. Ask here for the Club de Andinismo for information on mountain climbing in the area.

Bicycle Hire *Café Royal Paris* on 16 Av opp Parque Juárez (16 Av, 3-4 C) hires mountain bikes at US$6/day or US$20/week, plus US$100 deposit. Better, more expensive bikes at *Guatemala Unlimited* travel agency, 12 Av, 11 C, Zona 1, T/F 616043, US$6/day, US$30/week, deposit required.

Mechanic Taller Enderezad, corner of 8a Av and 3a C, Zona 1, rec for car repairs.

Buses Rutas Lima, 11 Av, 3-68, Zona 1 and 2 C, 6-32, Zona 2, T 614134 and 612033 (best), 4 a day to **Guatemala City** (US$2.50, 3½ hrs). The 0800 bus has connections to Chichicastenango, Panajachel (US$2.50, 2½ hrs) and Sololá (US$1.50, 2½ hrs). Galgos, C Rodolfo Robles 17-43, T 2248, Zona 3, 1st class buses to Guatemala City, 8 a day from 0530-2100 (US$3, 4 hrs, will carry bicycles); Marquensita twice a day, US$2.50 (office in the capital 21 C, 1-56, Zona 1). Líneas Americanas to Guatemala City 2 a day from 7 Av, 3-33 Zona 2, T 4587. For **Antigua**, change at Chimaltenango (Galgos, US$3 to Chimaltenango 0800, 1000, Rutas Lima 0715, 1415). To **Huehuetenango** 0500 and 1530, US$1. From Quetzaltenango you can get to three border crossings: La Mesilla via Huehuetenango (if you cannot get a regular bus catch a chicken bus from behind the market, no 13 on map, plenty of them and not too crowded early in the morning); Talismán bridge and Tecún Umán (frequent buses from there to Tapachula), buses run all day from Miverva terminal, but you will probably have to change buses in Malacatán. To **San Pedro** (see p 515) at 1200. Regular buses to **Cuatro Caminos** US$0.75 (where buses for Guatemala City and Huehuetenango stop on the highway; bus Guatemala City-Cuatro Caminos, US$1.65), **Totonicapán**, 1 hr (US$0.35), **San Francisco El Alto** (US$0.35) and **Momostenango** (0600, US$0.45). Also many second class buses to many parts of the country from Zona 3 market by Parque Minerva (13 Av y 4 C'A'), eg Transportes Velásquez to **Huehuetenango**, US$0.65; to **Malacatán**, 5 hrs, US$2; to **Los Encuentros**, US$2; to **Chichicastenango**, US$0.65, 1200, 2 hrs; to **Zunil**, US$0.30, 40 mins; also to **La Mesilla** at 0800. Bus to town from 2nd class terminal, No 3 from just below Templo de Minerva.

Excursions Many places of interest around on roads N to Huehuetenango, W to San Marcos and Mexico, S to Ocós and Champerico. Six km SE is *Almolonga*, which is noted for its fine 16th-century church (may be locked) and beautiful costumes, especially skirts, which are hard to buy. There is also an interesting vegetable market, market days Wed and Sat. *Fiesta* 26-29 June. Good swimming pool (entrance, US$0.25). About 1 km further on are the thermal baths of Cirilo Flores (US$0.50 for large pool, US$1 to soak for an hour, hot, soothing water but heavily used— frequently cleaned) and El Recreo (entrance, US$0.30); bus from Quetzaltenango, US$0.15. The Fuentes Georginas hot springs, 15 km from Quetzaltenango, are mentioned under Zunil (**p 517**), bus to Zunil then pickup truck. Take picnic or barbecue equipment, but it might be best to avoid Sundays when the Guatemalans descend on the springs. There are also hot steam baths at Los Vahos, reached by a dirt road to the right (3 km) on the outskirts of town on the road to Almolonga; a taxi will take you there and back with a one-hour wait for US$1.50. El Baúl, a hill to the E, may be reached by winding road, or direct trail to the top where there is a cross (visible from the city), monument to Tecún Umán. To reach the *Santa María volcano* (3,772m) take bus to Llano del Piñal from Central bus station (every 30 mins or when full from the Shell station on Av 9; last bus back from Llano del Piñal leaves at 1830). Get off at cross roads and follow dirt road until it sweeps up to the right, where you should take the footpath on left (marked with paint for some distance); bear right at the saddle where another path comes in from left—look carefully, it is easily missed. A rough 4½ hr climb (1,500m – take plenty of water) but worth it for the superb views of the Pacific and to watch the still active crater, *Santiaguito* (2,488m), on the Pacific side. Do not attempt to climb this cone, several people were killed in 1990 when overtaken by an eruption. There are frequent clouds of poisonous gas. The volcano can also be reached from Retalhuleu (**see p 518**) by bus to Palajunoz, from where it is also a 4½-hr climb. It is possible to camp at the summit, but cold and windy. Early morning is the best time for views, and the dawn can be 'magic'. Santa María is popular with picnickers on Sun. You can arrange a guide in Llano del Piñal for about US$6 (eg Alfonso, who lives in the last house on the right before the road turns upward on to the foot of Santa María). There is a good view from the *Siete Orejas volcano* (inactive, 3,370m) 10 km NW of Santa María.

According to folklore, at *Olintepeque*, an Indian town 6 km N from Quezaltenango (on a road parallel to the main road), the greatest battle of the conquest was fought, and Alvarado slew King Tecún Umán in single combat. Its river is still known as Xequizel, the river of blood. Market, Tues; *fiestas*, June 20-25, August 29 (beware of theft). The local idol, San Pascual Baillón, has its own little church. Frequent buses from Quezaltenango. A further 8 km to the NE is *San Andrés Xequl*, a small village in beautiful surroundings and a very colourful church with extraordinary figurines. Rituals can be observed at the Altar 'Maya'. The direct road climbs 18 km to San Carlos Sija, at 2,642m, with wide views. The Spanish strain is still noticeable amongst the inhabitants, most of whom are tall and fair. A climb through conifers for another 10 km to *Cumbre del Aire*, with grand views behind of volcanoes, and ahead of Cuchumatanes mountains. Another 25 km to the junction with the Pan-American Highway.

From Cuatro Caminos the Pan-American Highway climbs for several km before dropping down past the *ladino* town of Malacatancito (48 km) and swinging NW through the **Selegua (El Tapón) gap** to Mexico.

A 6½ km spur from this road leads to **Huehuetenango**, a mining centre in farming country, with Indians from remote mountain fastnesses coming in for the daily market, and particularly Wed. Fair, 12-18 July. Racecourse. Population, 39,000; altitude, 1,905m. The Honorary Mexican Consul at the *Farmacia del Cid* (5 Av and 4 C) will provide you with a Mexican visa or tourist card for US$1; Huehuetenango is the last town before the La Mesilla border post, on the Pan-American Highway into Mexico. It is also a good town for the serious Spanish language student: there is very little English spoken here, and good language schools.

Hotels C *Centro Turístico Pino Montano*, at Km 259 on the Pan-American Highway, 2 km past the fork to Huehuetenango on the way to La Mesilla, a bit run down, pool, a/c, restaurant, parking, T 641637; **C** *Los Cuchumatanes*, about 3 km out of town, Zona 7, T 641951, good restaurant, clean swimming pool (known as Brasilia), good value; **C** *El Prado*, at entrance to town, T 641622, clean, new; **E** *Río Lindo*, 3 Av, 0-20, Zona 1, T 642641, 3 blocks from Zócalo, shower, hot water (but beware poor electrical installation), small rooms, clean, nice; **D** *Zaculeu*, 5 Av, 1-14, Zona 1, T 641086, attractive hotel, with charming lounge, cable TV, restaurant (varying reports); **E** *Mary*, 2 C, 3-52, Zona 1, T 641569, with bath, cheaper without, clean, safe; **E** *Todos Santos Inn*, 2 C, 6-74, Zona 1, T 641241, shared bath, hot water, inc breakfast, helpful, clean, rec; **F** *Auto Hotel Vásquez*, 2 C, 6-67, T 641338, 2 blocks W of Plaza, with bath, clean; **F** *Maya*, 3 Av, 3-55, with bath, tepid water, safe, basic; **E** *Pensión Astoria*, 4 Av, 1-45, T 641197, cafetería serves breakfast; **E** *Gran Hotel Shinula*, 4 C, 2-3 Av, T 641225, clean bright rooms, bath, restaurant; **F** *Del Centro*, 6 Av between 4 C and 5 C, with bath, cheaper without, clean, good value; **F** *Hospedaje Huehueteco*, 2 C between 2-1 Av, close to market, basic but clean, small single rooms, larger doubles with bath, no electricity 0700-1800; **G** *Centroamericana*, 1 Av, 4-85. **G** *Central*, 5 Av, 1-33, communal baths, meals available, washing facilities, dark and depressing, but cheap, good lunches; **G** *Hospedaje El Viajero*, 2 C, 5-20, Zona 1, basic but friendly. There are a number of cheap *pensiones* on 1 Av, by the market, including **G** *Pensión San Ramón*, near 1 Av, basic, dirty toilets, friendly, convenient for bus stations; **G** *Tikal*, (reasonably clean); **G** *San Antonio*, very cheap, unpleasant toilets, good hot showers for US$0.50, also charge for cold showers; next door, **G** *Tikal 2*, friendly, bed bugs, hot shower extra. **NB** The cheap *hospedajes* (F and under) are not rec for single women.

Camping at Zaculeu ruins, or further on the same road at the riverside, unofficial, no facilities.

Restaurants All hotel restaurants are open to the public. *Las Bouganvillas*, on the Plaza, large, popular; *Las Brasas*, 4 Av, corner of 2 C, steak house and Chinese dishes, rec; *Rincón Hogareña*, 6 Av, A, 7-21, pizzas, meat dishes; *La Fonda de Don Juan*, 2 C, 5-35, Italian,

HUEHUETENANGO MAC 47

1. Plaza
2. Cathedral
3. Mercado Municipal
4. Post Office
5. Guatel
6. Mexican Consul / Farmacía del Cid
7. Transport to Zaculeu
8. Bus to Chiantla

Hotels:
9. Zaculeu
10. Mary
11. Auto Hotel Vásquez
12. Maya and transport to Zaculeu
13. Pensión Astoria
14. Hospedaje el Viajero
15. del Centro & Rincón Hogareña

To Chiantla & Todos Santos Cuchumatán

To Zaculeu

To Panamerican Highway & Guatemala City

0   100
metres

excellent sandwiches, big choice of desserts, *licuados*, avoid pizzas, reasonable prices; *Los Pollos*, 3 C, 5 y 6 Av, full chicken meal US$3, also takeaway. There are numerous cheap *comedores* near the market, but check for hygiene. *El Edén*, 2 km down road to Chiantla, new, good food; *Jardín*, 6 Av y 4 C, Zona 1, meat dishes, good pancakes and milkshakes, rec; *Cafetería Las Palmeras*, 5 Av, 4 C, dirty, not rec; *Pizza Hogareña*, 6 Av between 4C and 5C, rec, popular, always full; *Rico Mac Pollo*, 3 Av, for chicken; *Le Kaf*, 6 C, 6-40, Western-style, new, varied menu, live music at weekends, rec; *Doña Estercita's*, 6 Av, 2-6, coffee, licuados and pastries, rec; *Ebony*, 2 C near market, cheap but poor service, particularly if your Spanish is not perfect. The *panadería* opp Guatel office has excellent and cheap breakfasts. Good *taco* stand on corner opp bus station.

Shopping Artesanías y Antigüedades Ixquil, 5 Av, 1-56, good selection of *huipiles* from local villages, reasonable prices, rec.

Exchange Several local banks, some open Sat am. All change TCs, but no bank changes pesos. Try also the *Farmacia del Cid* for good rates for pesos.

Spanish Language Schools Most operate in the summer months only (see notes on schools in Antigua and Quezaltenango). Casa Xelajú, Aptdo Postal 302, 6 C, 7-42, Zona 1. Fundación XXIII, 6 Av, 6-126, Zona 1, T 641478. Instituto El Portal, 1 C, 1-64, Zona 3; Rodrigo Morales (at Sastrería La Elegancia), 9 Av, 6-55, Zona 1, private classes, rec. Instituto Zaculeu de Español, 4 C, 9-25, Zona 1, Spanish Academy Xinabajul, 6 Av, 0-69, Zona 1, T 1518. Private teacher, Abesaida Guevara de López, 3 C Poniente, 7-14, Zona 1, US$50 per week, rec. Information on schools is posted in several restaurants: *Pizza Hogareña, El Jardín, La Fonda* and at the Post Office.

Post and Phones Guatel and Post Office are on 2 C across the street from *Hotel Mary*.

Buses There is a new bus terminal on SW outskirts of town about 2 km from the centre. Yellow urban buses shuttle between 'Terminal' and 'Centro'. To Guatemala City (about 5 hrs): US$3.75. Los Halcones, 7 Av, 3-62, Zona 1, 0700, 1400 in each direction, reliable; Rápidos Zaculeu, 3 Av, 5-25, 0600 and 1500, good service; El Cóndor, 5 a day. To Zaculeu, Los Flamingos, S side of market, 0445. To La Mesilla: (2 hrs), frequent buses, US$1; Los Verdes, 1 Av, 1-34, 0500 and 1330; Osiris, 1 Av y 3 C, 0430, 1030, 1230; López, 4 C, 2-39, 0630. El

Cóndor, office opposite *Hotel Zaculeu*, 0600, 1000, 1300, 1500. To **Cuatro Caminos**, US$1; to **Los Encuentros**, for Lake Atitlán and Chichicastenango, US$2.50; also, direct to **Chichicastenango**, Rutas García, 0300 and 1100, via Sacapulas and Santa Cruz del Quiché, others including Rutas Zaculeu to **Sacapulas**, US$0.75; to **Cobán** every other day at 0400, Sr Castro's bus (better to take 1100 bus to Sacapulas and continue next day); to **Nentón**, **Cuilco** and other outlying villages, enquire on 1 Av near market. Beware of touts at the bus station who tell you, as you arrive from the border, that the last bus to wherever you want to go is about to leave; it's probably not true. Also, buy your tickets to where the bus takes you, eg Cuatro Caminos, Los Encuentros, not to your final destination if a change of buses is involved.

Car Insurance for Mexico and Guatemala can be arranged at Granai & Townson, next door to Mexican Consulate (see above).

Ruins of **Zaculeu**, old capital of the Mam tribe, pyramids, a ball court and a few other structures, completely reconstructed, concrete stepped forms, devoid of any ornamentation (museum), disappointing, 5 km NW on top of a rise ringed by river and *barrancas* (admission US$0.60, open 0800-1800). Yellow Alex bus runs at 1030, 1330 and 1530 as long as at least 5 people are going (fare US$0.20) and minibuses (US$0.25) to the ruins from *Hotel Maya*. It is possible to walk to the ruins in about 60 mins.

The views are fine on the road which runs between Huehuetenango and Sacapulas. **Aguacatán** at 1,670m is 26 km E of Huehuetenango, 36 km from Sacapulas (**G** *Pensión La Paz*; **G** *Hospedaje Aguacatán*, 2 blocks E of market and 1 N). Aguacatán has an interesting market on Sun (beginning Sat night) and Thur (excellent peanuts). The women wear beautiful costumes and head-dresses.

The source of the Río San Juan is about 2 km down the Calle Principal N of the centre of Aguacatán, then 3 km down a signposted turnoff. There is a 2 km walking route, turn left up a dirt road by the evangelist Templo Buenas Nuevas, and straight to the 'fuente'. There is no admission charge to the park, which is a delightful place for a freezing cold swim. It is surrounded by onion and garlic fields. Take a picnic, only soft drinks available nearby. Camping is permitted. Los Verdes, 1 Av, 2-34, Huehuetenango, has buses to Aguacatán at 1300 (last return bus at 1500), US$0.50, and buses for **Sacapulas**, Quiché, Nebaj and Cobán pass through the village. There are jeeps, Huehuetenango-Aguacatán. Taxi Huehuetenango-Aguacatán US$15 for a 3-hr trip including source of Río San Juan. Zaculeu, 1 Av, 2-53, to Sacapulas, 1400, 2 hrs, US$1 (truck at 1630, arrives 2000, US$1), and from the same place Alegres Mañanitas has a bus to Quiché at 0415. Bus to Chichicastenango from Aguacatán 0400, very crowded, or take a truck. The Campo Alegre company has buses to Nebaj from the *Hospedaje San José*, 1 Av and 4 C'A', and buses for Cobán leave from the same area.

Chiantla, 5 km N of Huehuetenango, has a great pilgrimage to the silver Virgin of La Candelaria on 28 January to 2 February. The stable is set behind glass, upstairs; ask the priest's permission to take photos. Another *fiesta* on 8 September and interesting processions in Holy Week. The church is well worth a visit. Good walking in the neighbourhood. Daily market, largest on Sun. Buses leave regularly from 1 Av and 1 Calle. Road runs N 117 km to **San Mateo Ixtatán**, at 2,530m, in the Cuchumatanes mountains. The *huipiles* made there are unique and are much cheaper than in Huehuetenango. Market, Sun and Thur. The road passes through San Juan Ixcoy, **Soloma** (watch out for young pickpockets in plaza and market; **D-E** *Nuevo Hotel Río Lindo*, with bath, hot water, parking, rec; *Mansión Kathy*, run down; *Hospedaje San Ignacio*; **G** *Hospedaje San Juan*, charge for hot shower, secure parking; and **Santa Eulalia** (**G** *Hospedaje El Cisne*). San Mateo itself (**G** *Pensión El Aguilar*, very basic, no showers, bring own sheets or sleeping bag) is a colourful town, with an interesting old church and black salt mines nearby. There are some impressive ruins on the outskirts of the town. The European Community has an office here. First bus from Huehuetenango to San Juan Ixcoy, Soloma, Santa Eulalia, San Mateo Ixtatán (US$2) and Barillas leaves at 0200, very crowded, be early and get your name high up on the list as passengers are called in order. The bus returns to

Huehuetenango from San Mateo (at least 5 hrs) at 0200, 0300, 0700, 1100 and 1330, but it is advised to take two days over the trip. Solomerita buses (1 Av and 2 C) run as far as Soloma, at 0500 and 1300. 5 km beyond the turn off to Todos Santos Cuchumatán (see below) the road becomes rough, narrow and steep.

After San Mateo the road runs 27 km E to **Barillas** (several cheap *pensiones*, **G** *Terraza*, rec: a fine scenic route. Some 13 km N of Chiantla is a viewpoint with magnificent views over mountain and valley.

The village of **Todos Santos Cuchumatán** is very interesting but can be cold (2,481m). Some of Guatemala's best weaving is done there, and fine *huipiles* may be bought in the cooperative on the main street (cash and TCs exchanged) and direct from the makers. There are also embroidered cuffs and collars for men's shirts, and colourful crocheted bags made by the men. There is an Artexco cooperative, *Estrella de Occidente*. A fair selection of old woven items can be bought from a small house behind the church. The Sat-Sun market is fascinating (best Sat); also Wed. *Fiesta*: 1 Nov, characterized by a horse race in which riders race between two points, having a drink at each turn until they fall off. A museum (US$1 entrance) in the main square has a collection of antiques, farm tools and (poorly) stuffed animals. The attendant is pleased to explain everything. Proceeds go to the city park fund. A Spanish Language School, Proyecto Lingüístico de Español, is one block from the Parque Central (June-Aug, US$125, Sept-May, US$100), food rather basic; you can also learn Mam, the local dialect; one of the teachers, Benito, offers dinner and sauna for US$5 for 2 at his home, he also plays chess. The school is part of La Hermandad Educativa non-profit language study organization with a schcol in Quezaltenango and offices in the USA (PO Box 205-337, Sunset Park, NY 11220-0006, T (718) 965 8522, F (718) 965 4643) and Europe (c/o R Bjordal, Johs Bjordalsv 8, 6400 Molde, Norway, T (072) 51376, F (072) 54050).

Hotels and Food G *Hospedaje Tres Olguitas*, very basic, hot showers US$0.40, good cheap meals; **F** *Hospedaje La Paz*, fleas and cold, enclosed parking, shared showers; *Katy* is one of two cheap *comedores*, but it has limited selection, poor service and indifferent food; *comedor* also in market; new in 1993, *Pancho's Café* at entrance to town, rec; rooms for rent, F, from Santiaga Mendoza Pablo, owner of *Tienda Ruinas de Tecumanchua*, 2 houses up from *Comedor Katy*, new extension, can use family's hot showers and sauna (US$1), called *chu* in Mam. Santiaga's sister-in-law, Nicolasa Jerónimo Ramírez, owns the *Tienda Maribe* further up the hill and rents rooms, G. Both women make and sell *típicas* and give weaving lessons, US$1/hr: other families offer basic accommodation.

Transport Bus from Huehuetenango at 0300 (very cold) and 1130 (Vásquez bus leaves 1300, arrives 1600), 3-4 hrs, US$1, crowded on Mon and Fri (return at 0400-0600, 1130 and 1300, arrive early for a seat, best views from roof). The drive is spectacular, ascending to 3,290m (approximately), but much of the land has been overgrazed and there is much soil erosion.

From Todos Santos, one can walk to **San Juan Atitán**, 5 hrs (more interesting costumes; Artexco cooperative *Atiteca*, markets Thur and Sun) and from there the highway, 1 day's walk. Also, walk to San Martín (3 hrs), or **Santiago Chimaltenango** (7 hrs, stay in school, ask at Municipalidad; the Artexco cooperative here is *Flor de Pascua*), then to San Pedro Necta, and on to the Pan-American Highway for bus back to Huehuetenango.

The road from Todos Santos continues NW through Concepción Huista (where the women wear towels as shawls) to **Jacaltenango** (bus from Todos Santos at 1600, bus to Huehuetenango at 0230 and 0300, may be others, also pick-ups). In this area Jacalteco is spoken; the *feria titular* is 28 January to 2 February, with a firework jamboree (mostly at ground and eye level) and a community dance. Much pride is taken in marimba playing, eg at football matches. The hat maker in Canton Pilar supplies the hats for Todos Santos, he welcomes viewers and will make a hat to your specifications (but if you want a typical Todos Santos leather *cincho*, you must get it there). The town is, as yet, well off the tourist trail. (Thanks to Will Paine, Maidstone, for this information). Apparently a bus goes from Todos Santos to **Buenavista** (NW) near the Mexican border, 4 hrs there, 4 hrs back, passing through highlands and tropical lowlands; it leaves 0700, but it's not known if this is only on market days. **NB** Remember the warning on violence in this region.

The Pan-American Highway runs W from Huehuetenanango to *La Mesilla*, the Guatemalan border post, and on 3.7 km to Ciudad Cuauhtémoc (not a town, despite its name, just a few buildings), the Mexican border point, a very good, interesting and beautiful route. Rooms at Ciudad Cuauhtémoc and La Mesilla (both very basic); best to avoid having to stay at either, by leaving Huehuetenango early. Coming into Guatemala, the peso-quetzal rate is better than the dollar-quetzal rate (don't change dollars until Huehuetenango or, better still, Guatemala City). Going the other way, there are better exchange rates in Mexico than at La Mesilla. There is a tourist office (Inguat) in the Guatemalan immigration building. The Guatemalan authorities charge Q5-20 exit tax. Outside the hours of 0800-1200, 1400-1800, an extra US$0.50 is charged. A US$0.20 'bridge tax' (!) may also be demanded. See p 519 on bribery at borders; see also **Road Travel** in **Information for Visitors** on driving to Mexico. Mexican visas are obtainable at the border, but better at *Farmacia El Cid* in Huehuetenango, for US$1, which saves time at the border. From Ciudad Cuauhtémoc, Cristóbal Colón and Transportes Tuxtla buses go to Comitán and San Cristóbal de Las Casas. There are 'taxis', US$1 pp, between the border posts during the day; Mexican officials charge exorbitant fees for transport between the border posts, bargain hard.

At the first gas station, 7 km from La Mesilla, is **E** *Hotel Reposo La Gasolinera*, with hot shower, cheaper without, clean, good breakfast in restaurant (other meals, US$1.75, poor), rec, ample parking; in La Democracia, 14 km from La Mesilla, is an unsigned *mesón*, 1 block N of the market, basic, clean, G.

Buses from La Mesilla to Huehuetenango US$1.50-1.85 (first class—foreigners tend to be overcharged). Express buses run by El Cóndor go to Guatemala City (US$5, 6 hrs). From Guatemala City, 19 C, 2-01, Zona 1, at 0400, 0900, 1000 and 1100. Change at Los Encuentros for Lake Atitlán and Chichicastenango, and at Chimaltenango or San Lucas for Antigua. When changing buses at the border, note that Mexican buses are more spacious for luggage; the Guatemalan ones often put large bags on the roof, so keep valuables, breakables, etc in your hand luggage. Also be prepared to push for a seat.

Quezaltenango W to Mexico Fifteen km to *San Juan Ostuncalco*, a pleasant, prosperous town, at 2,530m, noted for good weekly market on Sun and beautiful sashes worn by men. *Fiesta*, Virgen de la Candelaria, 2 Feb. See below for road S to Pacific town of Ocós. The road, which is paved, then switchbacks 37 km down valleys and over pine-clad mountains to a plateau looking over the valley in which are San Pedro and San Marcos, also known as La Unión. *San Marcos*, at 2,350m, is 1 km or so beyond San Pedro. *San Pedro* (full name San Pedro Sacatepéquez, same name as the town near Guatemala City) has a huge market Thur. Its Sun market is less interesting. There is an interesting Palacio Municipal (known as the Palacio Maya) built in 1926, with a wooden clocktower. The Indian women wear golden-purple skirts. *Tajumulco* volcano, 4,220m (the highest in Central America), can be reached by taking the road from San Marcos to San Sebastián; after the latter, several km on is the summit of a pass at which a junction to the right goes to Tacana, and to the left is the start of the ascent of Tajumulco, about 5 hrs' climb. Once you have reached the ridge on Tajumulco, turn right along the top of it; there are two peaks, the higher is on the right. The one on the left is used for shamanistic rituals; people are not very friendly, so do not climb alone. The last bus back from Tajumulco village leaves about 1500 so you need to start out from San Marcos very early, 0200 bus rec, very slow road, 20 km takes 2 hrs, no accommodation available on the way. *Tacana* volcano may be climbed from Sibinal village. About 15 km W of San Marcos the road begins its descent from 2,500m to the lowlands. In 53 km to *Malacatán* it drops to 366m. This was one of the toughest stretches in Central America, but now the surface is paved. It is a tiring ride with continuous bends, but the scenery is attractive.

Hotels At **San Juan Ostuncalco**: **F** *Ciprés Inn*, 6 Av, 1-29, T 616174, clean, hot water, good atmosphere, TV, good restaurant, traditional blue wooden building, converted private house (1992), modern bathrooms, highly rec; **F** *El Embajador*, 7 Calle, 1 Av, good views; *Ricafé* for burgers and sandwiches, aquarium. At **San Marcos**: E/F *Maya*, negotiate price, shower, hot water; **E** *Pérez*, 9 C, 2-25, T 601007, with good dining room, meals US$2. At **San Pedro**: **G** *Bagod*, fallen on hard times, noisy; **G** *Bethalonia*, 3 blocks N of main square; **G** *El Valle*, simple but clean; *Pensión Victoria*, 4C and 9 Av, basic but clean, rooms around a central courtyard, pleasant owner. Restaurants: *La Cueva de Los Faraones*, 5 C, 1-11, a real Italian menu, chef Sr Franco Manzini, moderate prices, rec; *Brasilia*, 7 Av, 4-19, excellent typical breakfast for US$0.85. At **Malacatán**: **F** *América*, lunch, US$1, good; **E** *La Estancia*, 3 C, 3-43, T 769382; **G** *Hospedaje Rodríguez*, good; **G** *Hospedaje La Predilecta*; **G** *Hospedaje Santa Emilia*; **F** *Pensión Santa Lucía*, 5 C, 5-25, Zona 1, T 769415.

The international bridge over the Suchiate river at **Talismán** into Mexico is 18 km W of Malacatán. Beyond the bridge the road goes on to Tapachula.

There is a Mexican consular service at the border, and at Malacatán (closed after 1300). Travelling by bus to Mexico is quicker from Quezaltenango than from San Marcos. Most traffic seems to go via Coatepeque and not via San Marcos; the former road is longer but is reported very good. From Quezaltenango, there are frequent buses to Talismán via San Marcos or Coatepeque, and probably more via Coatepeque to Ciudad Tecún Umán; buses from Xela marked 'Talismán' usually involve a change in Malacatán, 40 mins from border (US$0.30 by bus from shelter at back of Malacatán bus station). From San Pedro, frequent local buses from 0430 to 1630 to Malacatán, from where colectivos, often crowded, will get you to the border where you have a 200m walk through Guatemalan and Mexican immigration and a similar colectivo service to Tapachula for US$1. Or take bus from Quezaltenango to Retalhuleu, 1½ hrs, US$0.55, then another to the border, 2 hrs, US$1.85. From the border to Quezaltenango, it is best to go via Retalhuleu (take Galgos bus from the border, but you can go by bus to Malacatán, then bus (or taxi US$5) to San Marcos, 1½ hrs, lovely scenery, walk up hill to Parque Central, ask for Greyhound bus stop or catch a van, US$0.70 pp plus US$0.70 for bags on top, to Quezaltenango). Beware of overcharging on buses from the border to Quezaltenango. Bus Talismán-Guatemala City, US$4, Galgos 7 a day (1330 and 2000 direct from the capital), 5 hrs because of checkpoints. Guatemala City-Mexico City in one day is possible if you start early enough and allow plenty of time for the border crossing. **NB** We have received reports of robbery at knife point in the toilets at immigration, day or night.

NB If entering Guatemala by car, especially a rented car, be prepared for hours of red tape, miscellaneous charges, vehicle fumigation and frustration. See **Road Travel** in **Information for Visitors**.

Quezaltenango to Ocós After San Juan Ostuncalco (see above) S for 1½ km to **Concepción Chiquirichapa**, one of the wealthiest villages in the country. It has a small market early every Thursday morning. 5½ km to **San Martín Sacatepéquez** (sometimes known as Chile Verde; this village appears in Miguel Angel Asturias' *Mulata de Tal*), in a windy, cold gash in the mountains. *Huipiles* and shirts from the cottage up behind the church. Accommodation next door to the Centro de Salud (ask at the Centro), US$0.50. Food in *comedor* opposite church, US$0.20. Indians speak a dialect of Mam not understood by other Maya tribes, having been separated from them during the Quiché invasion of the Guatemalan highlands. The men wear very striking costumes. Market, Sunday. *Fiesta*, 11 Nov (lasts 5 days). Ceremonies of initiation held on 2 May at nearby **Laguna Chicabal**, in the crater of a volcano. The walk to the lake from San Martín takes about 2 hrs, ask any campesino for the path to Laguna Chicabal. It is possible to camp at the lake. The last bus to Quezaltenango leaves at 1900. Road descends to lowlands. From Colomba a road branches S (28 km) to Retalhuleu: the road to Ocós runs 21 km W from Colomba to **Coatepeque**, at 700m, with a population of 13,657; one of the richest coffee zones in the country; also maize, sugar-cane and bananas, and cattle. Fair, 10-15 March.

Hotels at Coatepeque: **E** *Beachli*, 6 C, 5-35, T 751483; **E** *Europa*, 6 C, 4-01, T 751396; **F** *Residencial*, 0 Av, 11-49, Zona 2, T 752018; **D** *Villa Real*, 6 C, 6-57, T 751939; **C** *Virginia*, at Km 220, T 751801; **F** *Posada Santander*, 6 C, 6-43. Bus from Quezaltenango, US$0.40 (buses to/from the capital as for Talismán).

Both railway and paved Pacific Highway go to **Tecún Umán**, 34 km W, on the Mexican frontier, separated by the Suchiate river from the Mexican town of Suchiate. This is an alternative crossing point to the Talismán bridge and many buses run to it from Guatemala. It is quite a quick border crossing. Buses run from the Mexican side of the border to Tapachula, $\frac{1}{2}$ hr, cheap (beware of overcharging). Be warned, however, that you have to walk across a very long bridge (toll, US$0.20) over the river between the two border posts. For a small fee, boys will help you with your luggage. Banks in Tecún Umán will only change US dollars, change Mexican pesos on the street. (Banco de Guatemala at 1 Av entre 4 y 5 C, Zona 2). After crossing the bridge and going through customs, turn left at the first corner, buses are three blocks along. The bus to the capital costs US$4, run by Forteleza, 4 direct buses daily, 5 hrs, frequent slower buses via Retalhuleu and Mazatenango. Colectivo from Coatepeque, US$0.50. Trains to Guatemala City, Wed and Sun, depart 0600, arrive 1800, US$1.40. Road N to Malacatán for international road bridge into Mexico. Population 4,250. Hotels: **E** *Maxcel*, 3 Av, 1 C, Zona 2; **F** *Lourdes*, 1 Av A, Zona 1.

Ocós, a small port now closed to shipping, is served by a 22-km road S from Tecún Umán. Across the river from Ocós is **Tilapa**, a small resort; buses from Coatepeque and ferries from Ocós (**G** *Pensión Teddy*, friendly). The swimming is good, but both here and at Ocós there are sharks, so stay close to the shore.

Quezaltenango to Champerico, via Retalhuleu: a 53-km link between the old Pan-American Highway and Pacific Highway, paved all the way. A toll (Quezaltenango-Retalhuleu, US$0.25) is collected. The first town (11 km) is **Cantel**, which has the largest textile factory in the country. There are three Artexco cooperatives: *Ixchel*, at Xecán; *Monja Blanca*, Barrio Centenario Antiguo; *Copavic*, a cooperative of glassblowers. Market, Sunday; *fiestas*, 15 August and a passion play at Easter.

Nine km from Quezaltenango is **Zunil**, picturesquely located in the canyon of Río Samalá. Market, Mon, Fri, small and colourful but drowned if two busloads of tourists come in (beware pickpockets); *fiesta*, 25 November, and a very colourful Holy Week. On the Sat there is a very slow procession through the village, followed by a performance of Christ's life in the square outside the church (fascinating to watch the crowd's enjoyment), lots of comedy. No market that Mon when the inhabitants go to the cemetery and pray for their dead. Striking church, inside and out. The local sacred idol is San Simón, described by a traveller as a life size dummy, dressed in ski wear: hat, scarf, gloves and sunglasses; the statue is moved from time to time to different houses and dressed differently, eg black suit and wide-brimmed hat, and complete with cigar; enquire locally for the present location. Behind the church is a cooperative (*Santa Ana*) which sells beautiful *huipiles*, and shirt and skirt materials. Zunil mountain, rises to 3,542m to the SE of the town. On its slopes are the thermal baths of **Fuentes Georginas**, entrance US$1, closed Mon for cleaning; **E** *Turicentro Fuentes Georginas*, bungalows with 2 double beds, cold shower, fireplace with wood, no electricity after 2100, candles provided, fair restaurant, beware overcharging, barbecue grills for guests' use near baths, in attractive surroundings. The Fuentes' temperature and water level have been reduced as a result of a geothermal energy project nearby and are now only lukewarm. There are steam vents in the slopes above the Fuentes, worth a 45-min hike up the hill. The path is in good condition, but keep left to avoid a cul-de-sac. Fuentes Georginas can be reached either by walking the 8 km, uphill (300m ascent; take right fork after 4 km, robbery reported 1993) to S of Zunil, by pickup truck, or hitch a ride. Alternatively, take the bus from Quezaltenango to Mazatenango, but get out at the sign to Fuentes Georginas, or ask for advice in Zunil. The springs are 13 km from Almolonga (**see p 510**).

The road descends through Santa María de Jesús (large hydro-electric station) to **San Felipe**, at 760m, 35 km from Zunil. Tropical jungle fruits. Spur line to Mulua, on Guatemalan Railways. Beyond, 3 km, is San Martín, with a branch road to Mazatenango. The thermal baths of Aguas Amargas are also on Zunil mountain, below Fuentes Georginas; they are reached by a road E before Santa María de Jesús is reached. **NB** The main road by-passes San Felipe, which has a one-way road system (delays of up to 1½ hrs if you go through the town).

Mazatenango, 18 km from San Martín, is the chief town of the Costa Grande zone, but it is not especially attractive and rather dirty. Altitude 380m, population 37,850. Chitalón airfield 3 km away. The Pacific Highway passes through. Road paved to Quezaltenango. There is a huge festival in the last week of Feb, when hotels are very full and double their prices. Beware of children carrying (and throwing) bags of flour. There is a cinema.

Hotels D *Hotel Alba*, 7 C, 0-26, Zona 2, T 720264, OK; **F** *Sarah*, by railway station, with bath; **E** *La Gran Tasca*, 7 Av, No 10, T 720316; **E** *Roma*, 3 C, 5-30, T 720139; **F** *Recreo*, Av La Libertad 8-27, Zona 1, T 720435, friendly family, close to main square; **G** *Costa Rica*; **G** *Jumay*; **G** *Pensión Mejía*, without bath. **Motel** *Texas*.

Exchange Banco de Guatemala, 7 C, 3-18, Zona 1.

Buses leave frequently from Esso station to **Guatemala City**, US$1.50; to the border at Tecún Umán US$1.50.

At *Cuyotenango*, 7 km W of Mazatenango, a dirt road goes 65 km down to the coast, at *El Tulate*. There is a white sand bar with a lagoon behind.

SW 11 km from San Martín is ***Retalhuleu***, at 240m, a town of 42,000 people on the Pacific Highway and on Guatemalan Railways to the border with Mexico. It serves a large number of coffee and sugar estates. *Fiesta*, 6-12 Dec.

Hotels *Astor*, 5 C, 4-60, Zona 1, T 710475; **E** *Modelo*, 5 C, 4-53, T 710256, rec; **B** *Posada de Don José*, 5 C, 3-67, T 710180, good food; **G** *Pacífico*, opp Mercado San Nicolás. **Motel B** *La Colonia* (swimming pool), 1½ km to the N at Km 178, T 710054, is good, good food, rec.

Exchange Banco de Guatemala, 6 Av, 6-18, Zona 1.

Trains to the capital on Wed, Fri and Sun at 0900.

NB Retalhuleu is normally referred to as 'Reu', both in conversation and on bus signs.

Champerico, 43 km SW of Retalhuleu on a paved road, once the third most important port in the country, is little used now. Population 4,500. Good beach, though the sand is black and there is a strong undercurrent; good fishing. There is a municipal fresh water swimming pool US$0.50.

Hotels D *Posada del Mar*, on outskirts of town, Km 222, T 717104; **G** *Martita*, Av Coatepeque between 2-3 C, without private bath, restaurant; **F** *Miramar*, 2 C, Av Coatepeque, T 717231, nice restaurant with dark wood bar, Spanish owners, good; **G** *Hospedaje Recinos*, and *Hospedaje Buenos Aires*, are both very basic.

Post Office two blocks behind *Hotel Martita*, in direction of port.

Buses Last bus to **Quezaltenango** departs at 1700. Every 30 mins to **Retalhuleu**. Direct bus to **Guatemala City**, 0300 and 0600, 4-5 hrs.

INFORMATION FOR VISITORS

Documents Necessary, a passport and a tourist card, or a visa. Countries which do *not* need a visa or tourist card, according to Inguat, March 1994: all Central American countries, Western European countries (except UK and Eire), Israel, Japan and Argentina. UK, USA, Canada, Eire, Australia, Iceland and Mexico citizens, when entering by air, are issued with a tourist card on arrival at the airport; if entering overland they need a visa, which must be obtained in advance. Others require an obligatory visa, which is valid for 30 days, US$10, one passport photo required, must be used within 30 days. Many Eastern European, Asian and African countries need a visa with prior authorization, which takes 3-4 weeks. Check carefully in advance with consulates, airlines, travel agencies etc, experiences vary. Tourist cards, which cost US$5, are valid for 30 days from day of issue, then 30 days from entry into Guatemala. However, if you intend to stay longer than 30 days, it is worth asking on entering if they will grant a tourist card or visa authority for a longer period. Children under 13 do not require a tourist card provided they are included on their parents' document. Tourist cards must be renewed in Guatemala City after 30 days (visas also after 30 days or on expiry) at the Migración office, on 41 Calle 17-36, Zona 8, T 714670, F 714678, open weekdays 0800-1630. This office extends visas and renews tourist cards on application (before noon) for 30 days at a time (up to 90 days maximum), this takes one day, usually two (but you will have to insist in any event), costs US$10, fingerprints and photograph required, and you may not be given the full 90 days. To stay more than 6 months, seek permission at the Immigration Department in Guatemala City. You may need stamped paper (*papel sellado*). Avoid Fridays, get there early. Diplomatic passport holders go to the Ministerio de Relaciones Exteriores in the National Palace, Zona 1. Multiple entry visas for tourist purposes only are free for US citizens and are valid for five years (very useful if travelling back and forth between neighbouring countries). Business visas cost US$10. Two photographs and a letter from the company (in duplicate) required. If experiencing obstruction in renewing a visa, it is easier to leave the country for 3 days and then come back.

Although not officially required, some airlines may not allow you to board a flight to Guatemala without an outward ticket (eg SAM in Colombia).

Apart from the visa or tourist card charge, there should be no other entry fees if you are travelling by public transport; see note on **Taxes** below. For cars, see under **Road Travel**. If entering overland it is most advisable to have obtained a visa in advance (fewer hassles).

Identification must always be carried while you are in Guatemala for police and military checks.

Taxes There is a 17% ticket tax, single or return, on all international tickets sold in Guatemala. A stamp tax of 2% is payable on single, return, baggage tickets and exchange vouchers issued in Guatemala and paid for in or out of the country. Hence it is usually cheaper to buy air tickets outside the country. A US$5 tourism tax is levied on all tickets sold in Guatemala to Guatemalan residents for travel abroad. There is also a Q50/US$10 airport and departure tax (expected to be doubled by law in Mid-1994), and a Q5/US$1 (officially) tourist tax at all borders, charged on leaving overland. Entry tax is Q5 at land borders. An additional US$0.50 is charged outside official working hours (0800-1200, 1400-1800—borders are open 24 hrs). These taxes vary from one border crossing to another, from one official to another, entry or departure, to as much as Q25 (entry from Ahuachapán, El Salvador), or as little as Q5 coming by land from Belize. One correspondent from Finland was charged Q5 at Tecún Umán, Q10 at El Florido because it was Sat, but nothing at Melchor de Mencos, even though it was also Sat. Bribery is rife at border crossings, whether you are entering with a car or on foot. Always ask for a receipt and, if you have time and the language ability, do not give in to corrupt officials.

By Air From Europe: KLM flies from Amsterdam via Mexico City, Iberia flies from Barcelona and Madrid via Miami, with connecting flights from other European cities. Alternatively, fly British Airways, to Mexico City (3 a week) and connect with United Airlines, or fly British Airways, Lufthansa, Air France, Alitalia, Aeroflot, Virgin Atlantic, Continental or Delta to Miami and connect with daily flights to Guatemala City with Aviateca, United and American.

From the USA: American (Austin, Texas; Dallas/Ft Worth; Miami; New York; Orlando), Continental (Boston; Chicago; Dallas; Houston; Las Vegas; Los Angeles; New York; San Antonio, Texas; San Francisco; Washington DC), Aviateca (Chicago; Houston; Los Angeles; Miami; New Orleans), United (Los Angeles; Miami; San Diego; San Francisco), Lacsa (Los Angeles; New York; San Francisco), Taca (Los

Angeles; New York; Washington DC). From Canada: connections are made through Los Angeles, Miami or Dallas.

Carriers from Central America/Caribbean: from San Salvador: Taca, Aviateca, Aero Nica, Copa. From Tegucigalpa: Taca. From San Pedro Sula: Lacsa, Taca (via San Salvador). From Mexico: Aviateca, Mexicana, United, Lacsa. From Cancún: Lacsa, Aviateca. From Mérida: Aviateca. From Belize: Taca (via San Salvador), Aviateca. From Managua: Copa, Nica, Aviateca, Taca. From San José: Aviateca, Lacsa, SAM, Copa, Mexicana, United, Nica. From Panama: Copa, Aviateca, Nica, Taca (via San Salvador), Lacsa (via San José). See **Introduction and Hints**, p 13, for regional airpasses. From San Andrés: SAM. Carriers from South America: Ladeco, SAM from Bogotá; Ladeco from Iquique and Santiago, Chile; SAM from San Andrés; flight connections through Panama, San José or Miami. **NB** You will have to have an outward ticket from Colombia to be allowed a visa (though worth checking with Colombian embassy first); round trip tickets Guatemala-Colombia are stamped 'Refundable only in Guatemala', but it is possible either to sell the return part on San Andrés island—at a discount—or to change it to an alternative destination. There are no direct flights to Peru or Ecuador; connections via Panama or Colombia. From the Caribbean: Copa from Santo Domingo and San Juan; Copa from Kingston, Jamaica, and Port au Prince via Panama. Round-trips Miami-Guatemala are good value, and useful if one does not want to visit other Central American countries. MCOs are not sold in Guatemala.

There are flights to Flores from Belize City with Aviateca, TropicAir and Mexicana; from Cancún with Aviateca and Mexicana; from Guatemala City with Aviateca, connecting with flights from Chicago, Los Angeles, Managua, Mexico City, Miami, San José and San Salvador.

Customs You are allowed to take in, free of duty, personal effects and articles for your own use, 2 bottles of spirit and 80 cigarettes or 100 grams of tobacco. Once every 6 months you can take in, free, dutiable items worth US$100. Temporary visitors can take in any amount in quetzales or foreign currencies; they may not, however, take out more than they brought in. The local equivalent of US$100 per person may be reconverted into US dollars on departure at the airport, provided a ticket for immediate departure is shown.

Road Travel Tourists can get an entry permit from the customs to take their cars into Guatemala for 30 days for Q30, more if it is an 'extraordinary time', ie out of hours, public holidays etc. However border officials might try to charge you more (up to Q65). Demand a written receipt or resist if one is not given. The permit is renewable at the Aduana, 10 C, 13-92, Zona 1, or 12 floor of Edif Financiero, 8 Av y 20 C, Zona 1 (this can take several days). Your passport must contain a visa for the period requested. There is an exit tax for cars of Q10 (to return driving permit) plus Q5 (quarantine) and to take a car across the Mexico-Guatemala border costs US$5.50. There is also a charge of US$2.50 when the tyres are fumigated on entry. Motorcycle entry permit costs the same as a car, better to pay in quetzales if you can. Spare tyres for cars and motorcycles must be listed in the vehicle entry permit, otherwise they are liable to confiscation. It is better not to import and sell foreign cars in Guatemala as import taxes are very high. We understand you can air freight a motorcycle and maybe a car to Colombia from Guatemala without too much hassle. Check with SAM office in Guatemala City.

The paved roads are generally quite good, but can be poor in places; the dirt roads are often very bad. There has, however, been a general deterioration in the state of the busiest roads in 1993-4 owing to strikes and a lack of funds for maintenance. High clearance is essential on many roads and 4WD useful. Identification should be carried at all times. There are frequent transit police stops, especially near borders. Stopping is compulsory: if driving your own vehicle, watch out for the 'ALTO' sign. When driving, keep at least 200m in front of, or behind, army vehicles; their drivers are concerned about attacks on military personnel.

Police may impound your licence if you are stopped for an infraction which can take some time to redeem. To avoid this if your papers are in order, a tip of say US$3.50-9, depending on circumstances, will help. If your papers are not in order, a larger tip may be necessary. Another suggestion is to take one or more International Driving Licences as well as your national licence. Tourists involved in traffic accidents will have to pay whether the guilty party or not. If someone is injured or killed, the foreigner will have to pay all damages. Car insurance can be arranged at **Granai & Townson**, 7 Av, 1-82, Zona 4, Guatemala City, T 61361 and at their offices in Quezaltenango and Huehuetenango, US$30-40 depending on length of stay, etc, 1994 prices: for Guatemala only. Also La Ceiba SA, 7 Av, 7-07, Zona 4, Edificio El Patio, oficina 210, T 313528/342178, F 316247. Sanborns in the USA (see **Automobiles**, Mexico **Information for Visitors**), provides insurance for Guatemala only if you buy Mexico cover through them.

Gasoline costs US$1.30 'normal', US$1.40 'premium' for the US gallon. Limited amounts of unleaded is available in major cities and along the Pan-American Highway but not in the countryside. Diesel costs US$1.10 a gallon. If coming in from Mexico fill up before you enter. All Japanese motorbike parts and accessories are available at decent prices in Guatemala, better than anywhere else in Central America.

Hired cars may not always be taken into neighbouring countries (none is allowed into Mexico); rental companies that do allow their vehicles to cross borders charge US$7-10 for the permits and paperwork. Credit cards or cash are accepted for car rental.

Border crossings from Mexico to Western Guatemala: **Tecún Umán/Ciudad Hidalgo** is the main truckers' crossing. It is very busy and should be avoided at all costs by car (hitch hikers, on the other hand, are sure to find a long-distance lift here). **Talismán** is more geared to private cars; there are the usual hordes of helpers to guide you through the procedures, for a fee. **La Mesilla** is the simplest for private cars and you can do your own paperwork with ease. Note, though, that if entering Mexico at La Mesilla without all the necessary documents here, you will be sent to Tapachula as the Mexican side does not have the full facilities. Guatemalan officials will let you cross to check that you will be allowed into Mexico before you officially leave Guatemala. Apart from this problem, any of the three crossings is straightforward going from Guatemala to Mexico (with thanks to Francesca Pagnacco, Exeter.)

Most **buses** are in a poor state of repair and breakdowns can be expected; they are always overloaded. Although recent government legislation has reduced problems of overcrowding, it is still difficult to get on buses in mid route. The correct fare should be posted up; if not, ask your neighbours. Many long distance buses leave very early in the morning. Try to arrange your passage the previous day and arrive in good time to get a seat. Make sure you can get out of your hotel/*pensión*. In the smaller towns, you will probably be woken up by the horns of arriving and departing buses. A fare increase for urban and interurban buses was announced in mid-1994, but no date was given. Estimates are for 20% up. This is a sensitive political issue and public order may be affected. At Easter there are few buses on Good Friday or the Saturday but they run again on Easter Sunday.

On several popular tourist routes, eg airport-Antigua, Antigua-Panajachel, there are minibuses, comfortable, overpriced, not as much fun as regular buses but convenient. They can be booked through hotels and travel agencies and will usually pick you up from your hotel.

Note Many long names on bus destination boards are abbreviated: Guate = Guatemala City, Chichi = Chichicastenango, Xela = Xelajú = Quezaltenango, Toto = Totonicapán, etc. Buses in the W and N are called *camionetas*. Regarding pronunciation, 'X' is pronounced 'sh' in Guatemala, as in Yucatán.

Railways The railways operate from Atlantic to Pacific and to the Mexican border. Service is neither luxurious nor reliable but very cheap and less crowded than buses.

Cycling Shirley Hudson (Mosier, Oregon) writes: The scenery is gorgeous, the people friendly and colourful. The hills are steep, steep, steep and sometimes long. The Pan-American Highway is OK from Guatemala City W; it has a shoulder and traffic is not very heavy. S from Guatemala City has no shoulder and heavier traffic. Cycling is hard, but enjoyable. Buses are frequent and easy to load a bicycle on the roof; many buses do so, charging about ⅔ of the passenger fare. On the road, buses are a hazard for cyclists, Guatemala City is particularly dangerous.

Hitchhiking is comparatively easy, but increasingly risky, especially for single women, also beware of theft of luggage, especially in trucks. The best place to try for a lift is at a bridge or on a road out of town; be there no later than 0600, but 0500 is better as it is when truck drivers start their journey. Trucks usually charge US$1-1.50 for a lift, per day. It may be worth asking around the trucks the night before if anyone is going your way. The only way to retrieve 'lost' luggage is by telling the police the vehicle registration number.

Walkers If walking in the Quiché, Huehuetenango or Totonicapán regions, it is wise to check on conditions before setting out. The authorities may be reluctant to let you venture into outlying areas, although a letter of permission from the army or civil defence in the main town is not obligatory.

Hotels The tourist institute Inguat publishes a list of maximum prices for single, double and triple occupancy of almost 300 hotels throughout the country in all price ranges. They will deal with complaints about overcharging if you can produce bills etc. Room rates should be posted in all registered hotels. Hotel rooms are subject to 7% sales tax and 10% tourism tax. Most budget hotels do not supply toilet paper, soap or towels. Busiest seasons, when hotels in main tourist centres are heavily booked, are Easter, December and the European summer holiday (July-August).

Food and Drink Traditional Central American/Mexican food such as tortillas, tamales, tostadas, etc are found everywhere. Tacos are less spicy than in Mexico. *Chiles rellenos* are a speciality in Guatemala, chiles stuffed with meat and vegetables which may be *picante* (spicy) or *no picante*. *Churrasco*, charcoal-grilled steak, is often accompanied by *chirmol*, a sauce of tomato, onion and mint. *Guacamole* (avocado mashed with onion and spices) is also excellent. Local dishes include *pepián* (thick meat stew with vegetables) in Antigua, *patín* (tomato-based sauce served with *pescaditos*, ie small fish from Lake Atitlán, wrapped in leaves), *sesina* (beef marinated in lemon and bitter orange) from the same region.

Desserts include *mole* (plantain and chocolate), *torrejas* (sweet bread soaked in egg and panela or honey) and *buñuelos* (similar to profiteroles) served with hot cinnamon syrup.

For breakfast try *mosh* (oats cooked with milk and cinnamon), fried plantain with cream, black beans in various forms. *Pan dulce* (sweet bread), in fact bread in general, and local cheese are recommended. Try *borracho* (cake soaked in rum).

Local beers are good (Monte Carlo and Cabra, which are better than Gallo, and Moza, a dark beer); bottled, carbonated soft drinks (*gaseosas*) are safest, milk should be pasteurised. Cold, freshly made *refrescos* and ice creams are delicious made of many varieties of local fruits, *licuados* are fruit juices with milk or water, but the standard of hygiene varies, take care. Water should be filtered or bottled 'Salvavidas' (although bottled water may not always be available).

Tipping Hotel staff: bell boys, US$0.25 for light luggage, US$0.50 for heavy. Chamber maids at discretion. Restaurants: 10%, minimum US$0.25. Taxi drivers: none. Airport porters: US$0.25 per piece of luggage. Cloakroom attendants and cinema usherettes are not tipped.

Guatemalan children are becoming persistent in asking for money in some tourist areas. It may be better to pass on items like soap, shampoo, sewing kits picked up from hotels.

Shopping Woven goods are normally cheapest bought in the town of origin, or possibly even cheaper at big markets held nearby. Try to avoid middlemen and buy direct from the weaver or from a member-cooperative of Artexco, to be found in all main towns. You won't do better anywhere else in Central America. Guatemalan coffee is highly recommended, although the best is exported; that sold locally is not vacuum-packed.

Kerosene is called 'Gas corriente', and is good quality, US$0.80 per US gallon; sold only in gas stations.

Film is very expensive, and film for transparencies is hard to find (it is available at 9 Calle, 6-88, Zona 1, Guatemala City, US$15 for 36 exposures, also in large cities like Antigua, Xela, Cobán, Kodak 36 exp US$10, Agfa 36 exp US$6).

Security Conditions in the northern departments of Huehuetenango, Quiché, Alta Verapaz and El Petén, in Chimaltenango, San Marcos and S of Lake Atitlán should be checked prior to travelling because of sporadic guerrilla and military activities. This applies particularly if you intend to travel at night. In some parts of the country you may be subject to military or police checks. Chichicastenango and Tikal, however, are safe. Local people are reluctant to discuss politics with strangers; it is best not to raise the subject. Do not necessarily be alarmed by 'gunfire' which is much more likely to be fireworks etc, a national pastime, especially early in the morning.

Robberies and assaults on tourists are becoming more common (1993-94). Single women should be especially careful, but tourist groups are not immune and some excursion companies take necessary precautions. Specific warnings are given in the text, but visitors are advised to seek up-to-date local advice on places to avoid at the earliest opportunity.

Health Guatemala is healthy enough if precautions are taken about drinking-water, milk, uncooked vegetables and peeled fruits; carelessness on this point is likely to lead to amoebic dysentery, which is endemic. Water sterilization tablets cannot be bought in Guatemala. In Guatemala City the Bella Aurora, and Centro Médico hospitals are good. Herrera Llerandi is a good private hospital. Most small towns have clinics. At the public hospitals you may have an examination for a nominal fee, but drugs are expensive. There is an immunization centre at Centro de Salud No 1, 9 C, 2-64, Zona 1, Guatemala City (no yellow fever vaccinations). In the high places avoid excessive exertion. If going to the Maya sites and the jungle areas, prophylaxis against malaria is strongly advised; there may also be a yellow fever risk. Cholera has been reported since 1991 and you should be particularly careful buying uncooked food in market *comedores* where good hygiene may be doubtful.

Clothing Trousers are OK for women. It is illegal to bring in, or wear, military-style clothing and equipment; such items will be confiscated.

Hours of Business Business and commercial offices are open from 0800-1200, and 1400-1800 except Saturdays. Shops: 0900-1300, 1500-1900, but many am only on Saturday. Banks in Guatemala City: 0900-1500. In the interior banks tend to open earlier in the morning and close for lunch, and be open later. In the main tourist towns, some banks are open 7 days a week. Government offices open 0700-1530.

British Business Travellers should read 'Hints to Exporters: Guatemala', obtainable from DTI Export Publications, PO Box 55, Stratford-upon-Avon, Warwickshire, CV37 9GE.

Public Holidays 1 January; Holy Week (4 days); 1 May: Labour Day; 30 June; 15 August (Guatemala City only); 15 September: Independence Day; 12 October: Discovery of America; 20 October: Revolution Day; 1 November: All Saints; 24 Dec: Christmas Eve: from noon; 25 Dec: Christmas Day; 31 Dec (from noon).

12 October and Christmas Eve are not business holidays. During Holy Week, bus fares may be doubled.

Although specific dates are given for *fiestas* there is often about a week of jollification beforehand.

Time Guatemalan time is 6 hrs behind GMT; 5 hrs during Summer Time, which was first introduced in 1976 after the earthquake and has been used intermittently since. Check carefully when you arrive.

Currency The unit is the *quetzal*, divided into 100 centavos. There are coins of 25, 10, 5 and 1 centavos. The paper currency is for 50 centavos and 1, 5, 10, 20, 50 and 100 quetzales. If you have money sent to Guatemala, you will only be given half in US dollars. In January 1985, the Banco de Guatemala authorized the establishment of exchange houses, effectively legalizing the black market. The black market disappeared in November 1989 when the exchange rate was freed. Miami airport is sometimes a good place to buy quetzales at favourable rates. **Warning**: Torn notes are not always accepted, so avoid accepting them yourself if possible. There is often a shortage of small change, but when you arrive in Guatemala and change money, especially at weekends, insist on being given some small notes to pay hotel bills, transport, etc. Banks usually charge about 2% per transaction to advance quetzales on Visa card or other, and you will probably get a less favourable rate of exchange. ATMs for the withdrawal of cash are available for Visa and Mastercard/Cirrus (3 branches of Credomatic, *Hotel Santo Tomás* Chichicastenango, and *Hotel Petén*). Visa assistance, T 099-0115.

Weights and Measures The metric system is obligatory on all Customs documents: specific duties are levied on the basis of weight, usually gross kilograms. United States measures are widely used in commerce; most foodstuffs are sold by the pound. The metric tonne of 1,000 kg is generally used; so is the US gallon. Old Spanish measures are often used; eg *vara* (32.9 inches), *caballería* (111.51 acres), *manzana* (1.727 acres), *arroba* (25 lbs), and *quintal* (101.43 lbs). Altitudes of towns are often measured in feet.

Electric Current Generally 110 volts AC, 60 cycles, but for variations see under individual towns.

Posts and Telecommunications Airmail to Europe takes 6-12 days (letters cost 60 centavos for first 5 grammes, 15 centavos for each additional 5 g, max weight, 2 kg). Airmail parcel service to the US is reliable (4-14 days); 2-3 months by boat (if operating). Parcels sent abroad must be checked before being wrapped for sending; take unsealed package, tape and string to office 119 at the Central Post Office between 0800 and 1530. Parcels by air to Europe cost about US$16/kg; a good service. Note, though, that parcels over 2 kg may only be sent abroad from Guatemala City (except 5 kg of books from Antigua); in all other cities, packets under 2 kg must be sent registered abroad. (See in the text for alternative services to the Post Office for sending packets abroad.) Mail from Mexico is specially slow. **NB** The Lista de Correos charges US$0.03 per letter received. Correos y Telégrafos, 7 Av y 12 C, Zona 1; Guatel next door. Also, no letters may be included in parcels: they will be removed. **NB also** Postal services have been disrupted by strikes and indecision by the authorities. At the time of publication both internal and external mail were virtually non-existent. Try to use the good phone and fax systems for communication.

Urgent telegrams are charged double the ordinary rate. Telephone calls to other countries can be made at any time; to Europe, these are slightly cheaper between 1900 and 0700. The cost of overseas calls will fluctuate according to the current exchange rate, but are generally expensive, USA US$2/min, Canada US$3.50, Europe US$6-7.50 (1994). Collect calls may be made from public phones in Guatemala City, Antigua, Quezaltenango (possibly elsewhere) only to Central America, Mexico, USA (including Alaska—dial 190 for the operator), Canada (198), Italy (193), Spain (191), Sweden and Japan. Collect calls cannot be made to the UK;

To use AT&T USADirect® Service from Guatemala dial **190** from telephones throughout Guatemala City and neighboring cities. Coin deposit is required from public telephones. Service to Alaska not available If you require assistance, please call the AT&T office in Guatemala City at **2-334-211**.

AT&T USADirect® Service.

from a private phone you can call for one minute and ask the person at the other end to phone back (at Guatel you have to pay for a minimum of 3 mins). All telephone services and the international cable service are in the hands of Guatel, but local telegrams are dealt with at the post office. Remember there are very few public telephones outside the main towns. Fax: sending a fax from a public place is expensive, a minimum of 3 mins is charged, plus a surcharge (eg US$28-30 to Europe).

Press   The main newspapers are *Prensa Libre* and *El Gráfico* in the morning; *La Hora* in the afternoon (best). *Siglo Veintuno* is a good new newspaper, started in 1989. *Tinamit* is a left-wing weekly, on Thur. Weekly magazine *La Crónica* is worth reading, rec. There are several free booklets and newsletters aimed at the tourist: *The Classifieds*, produced in Antigua weekly, carries advertisements, lodgings, tours and excursions, covering Antigua, Panajachel, Xela, Río Dulce and Guatemala City; *Guía Turística* covers Antigua, Atitlán, Tikal and Copán.

Information   Instituto Guatemalteco de Turismo (Inguat), 7 Av 1-17, Zona 4, Guatemala, provides bus timetables, hotel and camping lists and road maps. Tourist information is provided at the Mexican border for those entering Guatemala. Inguat also has an office in Paris, France. Recommended reading: Paul Glassman's *Guatemala Guide* (Passport Press), and *Guatemala for You* by Barbara Balchin de Koose (Piedra Santa, Guatemala City). *I, Rigoberta Menchú*, by Rigoberta Menchú; *Inside Guatemala* by Tom Barry (The Inter-Hemispheric Education Resource Center, Albuquerque, distributed in UK by Latin American Bureau, London). Maps include Belize as Guatemalan territory. Roads marked in the Petén are inaccurate.

In the UK, information on Guatemala and the Maya of Guatemala, Mexico, Belize and Honduras can be found at The Guatemalan Indian Centre, 94A Wandsworth Bridge Road, London SW6 27F, T 071-371 5291, library, video archive, textile collection and travel advice. Open Wed, Thur, Sat 1000-1800; closed January and August.

Volunteer Work   If you would be interested to volunteer to help in local children's homes, write to: Casa Guatemala, 14 C, 10-63, Zona 1, Guatemala City, or Casa Alianza, Apartado Postal 400, Antigua, Guatemala. The Permanent Commission on Refugees is at 6 Av, 3-23, Zona 1, Oficina 301, Guatemala City (T/F 517549). They sometimes require assistants to help with returning refugees from Mexico; you pay your own way. Several language schools in Quezaltenango and Huehuetenango fund community development projects and seek volunteers from among their students.

For information on Guatemala we are grateful to Lic Hans Gehlert Mata (Iguat, Guatemala City), Peter Pollard (who travelled in Guatemala, April 1994), Donald T Lee (Antigua) and the following travellers: Allyn van Alstyne (Montara, CA, USA), Janet Arnold (Melbourne, Australia), Simon Attewell (Loughborough, Leicestershire), Susanne Baader (Bremen, Germany), Jack Bailey & Diana Musacchio (Santa Barbara, CA, USA), Sheila Barron (Mexico City), Efrat Barber (Rishon Le Zion, Israel), Harald Bauder (Detroit, MI, USA), David Beasley & Liz Brooks (Horsham, West Sussex), Massimo Bietti (Rome, Italy), Diego Bittel (Visp, Switzerland), Erich Blum (Ruemlang, Switzerland), Sybille Böhme (Kahl/Main, Germany), Debra Brender (Davis, CA, USA), Sulay Burns (Nashville, Tennessee), Suzanne Carter (Basingstoke, Hants), Suzanne Morgan Carry (Vancouver, Canada), & Lindsay Kenyon (Canada), Jon Chambers (Moreton-in-Marsh, Gloucestershire), & Marianne Mller (Denmark), Louis Chavance (Las Vegas, USA), Nadia Christinet (Geneva, Switzerland), Jay Connerley (Fremont NE, USA), Augustus L Cyphers (Athens, West Virginia, USA), Joe Docherty (Bath, UK), Frank Dux (Passau, Germany), Kim Edgin (Springfield, TN, USA), Lene Eilrich (Ribe, Denmark), Ariane Fàssler (Wettswil, Switzerland), Matthias Fehrenbach (Immenstaad, Germany), Joy Hale & Derek Fess (Columbus, Ohio), Karin Fischli & Veli Hermann (Reichenburg, Switzerland), Ann Frechette & Jean Luc Massicotte for Charles Huot (Montréal), Darrel Freeman (Lancaster, PA, USA), P D Gadd & R del Tufo (London N1), Kelly Gallagher-Mackay (Toronto), & Ruth Mack (Ottumwa, Iowa), Alessandra Gavirati (Arese, Italy), Karl Gebert (San Antonio, Texas), Julio Gonzalez (Saint-Bonnet près Riom, France), J Roy Goodall (Belize City), Mark B Gordon (Houston, Texas), Martin Gottwald (Vienna, Austria), Thomas Gregid (Zurich, Switzerland), Kathy Griffiths (Melbourne, Victoria), Heidi Gürtler (Friedrichshafen, Germany), Sarah Hammond (Blackpool), Pasi Hannonen (Jy vä Skylä, Finland), Susy Happ & Susan Fitch (Oregon, USA), Patrick Hasenböhler & Claudia Jung (Zürich, Switzerland), Sally & Mike Hayden (Cheltenham, Glos), Norman Higginson (Redondo Beach, CA), Markus Hohl (London W11), Psiche Hughes (London, NW1), Bente Iren Jakobsen (Oslo, Norway), Ken Jones (Victoria, BC, Canada), Daniel Kaiser (Triesen, Liechtenstein), Noel, Nenagh & Zoë Kemp (Lindisfarne, Australia), Oliver Kirbach (Berlin, Germany), Amy Klein (Roseville, MN, USA), Dr Jürgen Koch

(Leonburg, Germany), Ronna Koharst (Plymouth, MN, USA), Christoph Künzi (Zurich, Switzerland), Christopher Kwasizur (La Cañaada, CA, USA), Kris Larson (Seattle, WA, USA), Michelle Mason (Brightwalton Green, Berkshire), Miss E M McLeod (London NW6), Demetris Michael (Dear Park, Victoria, Australia), Rob Minnee (Lisse, The Netherlands), Claudia Modrow & Massimo Godenzi (Bergheim, Germany), Dr William R C Munro (Stanley, Perth), Matthias Müth (Oftersheim, Germany), Paul Myatt (Hitchin, Herfordshire), Pat Neate (Massachusetts), Andrea Neumann, F Stehlik & A Mikula (Vienna, Austria), Bill & Michelle Osment (London), Tom Owens (Denver, Colorado), Francesca Pagnacco (Exeter, Devon), for a very helpful contribution, Patrick & Tina (Aachen, Germany), Antoine Pecard (Paris), Lisa Pollitt (Newcastle, UK), Warren Post (Santa Rosa de Copán, Honduras), Nigel & Maggie Potter (San José, Honduras), Helmut Quitt (Rosenheim, Germany), Angelika Rätz (Duisburg, Germany), Helle Regine Hansen (Denmark), (Sandy), Alexandra Reid (Leichhardt, NSW, Australia), Sebastian Retzlaff (Berlin), Tanya Reynolds (Northfield, MN, USA), Claudio Rivero (Buenos Aires), Paul S Robinson (Wellington, Shropshire), Dr Robert Rosen Jacobson (Amsterdam), Frank & Christine Ruiz (Brossard, Quebec), Erica Schultz (Ulricehamm, Sweden), Johannes Schmeer (Munich, Germany), Florian Schulz & Chris Schindler (Berlin), Jan & Truus van Ingen Schenau (Amsterdam), Joel Schiavoni (Durango, Colorado), Adrian van Schie (New Zealand), Rolf Schmitz (Bern, Switzerland), Nina Schramm (Sheringham, Norfolk), Mary Nicoll & Charlie Schreiber (London NW5), Mark Schuringa (Amsterdam, Holland), Harald Schwender & Birgitte Hächer (Sandhausen, Germany), Peter Selley (London SW11), Katrin Sickert (Krefeld, Germany), Eveline Sievi (Zurich, Switzerland), Mark Simmermann (Mayetta, Kansas), Cheryl Sortwell (Neuhausen, Switzerland), Dennis Speakman (Cambridge), Stefan Cotting (Nevenegg, Switzerland), Bärbel Strauch (Heidelberg, Germany), Jennifer Suthrell (Oxford), Jan Svoboda (Vancouver, BC, Canada), K W Tarr (Fruit Heights, WT, USA), Karin Taraschewski (Plüderhausen, Germany), Trevor Toone (Burnaby, BC, Canada), Dan Toporoski (San Diego, CA), Suzanne Elise Tourville (St Louis, MO, USA), Christopher J S Tuppen (Southampton), Bill Vallis (Surbiton, Surrey), Edwin van der Werf & Harold Bierens (Holland), Anke & Herman Van Weeghel (Wychen, The Netherlands), Benderoth Vitus (Hadamar), Andy Walter (Swindon, Wiltshire), Kathleen Wilder (Portland, OR, USA), Sheila Wilson (Stoke Poges, Slough), Florian Wüllen Kemper (Bad Salzujlen, Germany) and Sarah Wyles (Christchurch, New Zealand).

WILL YOU HELP US?

We do all we can to get our facts right in the MEXICO & CENTRAL AMERICAN HANDBOOK. Each section is thoroughly revised each year, but the territory is vast and our eyes cannot be everywhere. We are always pleased to hear about your travels; do write to us in as much detail as possible. In return we will send you information about our special guidebook offer.

TRADE & TRAVEL
Handbooks

Write to The Editor, Mexico & Central American Handbook, Trade & Travel, 6 Riverside Court, Lower Bristol Road, Bath BA2 3DZ. England

BELIZE

INTRODUCTION

BELIZE, formerly known as British Honduras, borders on Mexico and Guatemala, and has a land area of about 8,867 square miles, including numerous small islands. Its greatest length (N-S) is 174 miles and its greatest width (E-W) is 68 miles. Forests occupy some 65% of the area.

The coastlands are low and swampy with much mangrove, many salt and fresh water lagoons and some sandy beaches. In the N the land is low and flat, but in the SW there is a heavily forested mountain massif with a general elevation of between 2,000 and 3,000 ft. In the eastern part are the Maya Mountains, not yet wholly explored, and the Cockscomb Range which rises to a height of 3,675 ft at Victoria Peak. To the W are some 250 square miles of the Mountain Pine Ridge, with large open spaces and some of the best scenery in the country.

From 10 to 40 miles off the coast an almost continuous, 150-mile line of reefs and cayes (meaning islands, pronounced 'keys') provides shelter from the Caribbean and forms the longest coral reef in the Western Hemisphere (the fifth-longest barrier reef in the world). Most of the cayes are quite tiny, but some have been developed as tourist resorts. Many have beautiful sandy beaches with clear, clean water, where swimming and diving are excellent. (However, on the windward side of inhabited islands, domestic sewage is washed back on to the beaches, and some beaches are affected by tar.)

The most fertile areas of the country are in the northern foothills of the Maya Mountains: citrus fruit is grown in the Stann Creek valley, while in the valley of the Mopan, or upper Belize river, cattle raising and mixed farming are successful. The northern area of the country has long proved suitable for sugar cane production. In the S bananas and mangoes are cultivated. The lower valley of the Belize river is a rice-growing area as well as being used for mixed farming and citrus cultivation.

Climate Shade temperature is not often over 90°F (32°C) on the coast, even in the hotter months of February to May (the 'dry season', but see below). Inland, in the W, day temperatures can exceed 100°F (38°C), but the nights are cooler. Between November and February there are cold spells during which the

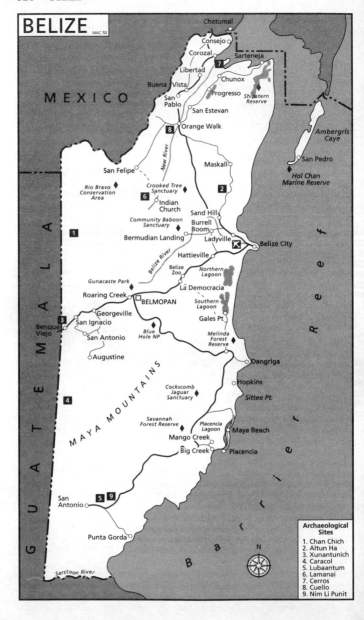

BELIZE MAC 50

Chetumal
Consejo
Corozal
Sarteneja
Libertad
7
Chunox
Buena Vista
Progresso
San Pablo
Shipstern Reserve
San Estevan
Orange Walk
8
Maskall
Ambergris Caye
San Pedro
Hol Chan Marine Reserve
San Felipe
Rio Bravo Conservation Area
Crooked Tree Sanctuary
6
Indian Church
Sand Hill
Community Baboon Sanctuary
Burrell Boom
1
Bermudian Landing
Ladyville
Belize City
Hattieville
Northern Lagoon
Gunacaste Park
Belize Zoo
Roaring Creek
La Democracia
BELMOPAN
Southern Lagoon
Georgeville
Gales Pt
San Ignacio
3
Blue Hole NP
Benque Viejo
San Antonio
Melinda Forest Reserve
Augustine
Dangriga
4
Hopkins
Sittee Pt.
Cockscomb Jaguar Sanctuary
Savannah Forest Reserve
Placencia Lagoon
Maya Beach
Mango Creek
Big Creek
Placencia
5 **9**
San Antonio
Punta Gorda
Sarstoon River

MEXICO
GUATEMALA
Belize River
New River
MAYA MOUNTAINS
Reef
Barrier

Archaeological Sites
1. Chan Chich
2. Altun Ha
3. Xunantunich
4. Caracol
5. Lubaantum
6. Lamanai
7. Cerros
8. Cuello
9. Nim Li Punit

N

temperature at Belize City may fall to 55°F (13°C). Humidity is normally high, making it 'sticky' most of the time in the lowlands.

There are sharp annual variations of rainfall—there is even an occasional drought—but the average at Belize City is 65 inches, with about 50 inches in the N and a great increase to 170 inches in the S. Generally, the driest months are April and May; in June and July there are heavy showers followed by blue skies; September and October tend to be overcast and there are lots of insects. Hurricanes can threaten the country from June to November, but there have been only 4 in the past thirty years. An efficient warning system has been established and there are hurricane shelters in most towns and large villages. Hurricane Preparedness instructions are issued annually.

History Throughout the country, especially in the forests of the centre and S, are many ruins of the Classic Maya Period, which flourished here and in neighbouring Guatemala from the 4th to the 9th century and then somewhat mysteriously emigrated to Yucatán. It has been estimated that the population then was ten times what it is now.

The first settlers were English with their black slaves from Jamaica who came about 1640 to cut logwood, then the source of textile dyes. The British Government made no claim to the territory but tried to secure the protection of the wood-cutters by treaties with Spain. Even after 1798, when a strong Spanish force was decisively beaten off at St George's Caye, the British Government still failed to claim the territory, though the settlers maintained that it had now become British by conquest.

When they achieved independence from Spain in 1821, both Guatemala and Mexico laid claim to sovereignty over Belize as successors to Spain, but these claims were rejected by Britain. Long before 1821, in defiance of Spain, the British settlers had established themselves as far S as the river Sarstoon, the present southern boundary. Independent Guatemala claimed that these settlers were trespassing and that Belize was a province of the new republic. By the middle of the 19th century Guatemalan fears of an attack by the United States led to a *rapprochement* with Britain. In 1859, a Convention was signed by which Guatemala recognized the boundaries of Belize while, by Article 7, the United Kingdom undertook to contribute to the cost of a road from Guatemala City to the sea 'near the settlement of Belize'; an undertaking which was never carried out.

Heartened by what it considered a final solution of the dispute, Great Britain declared Belize, still officially a settlement, a Colony in 1862, and a Crown Colony 9 years later. Mexico, by treaty, renounced any claims it had on Belize in 1893, but Guatemala, which never ratified the 1859 agreement, renewed its claims periodically.

Belize became independent on 21 September 1981, following a United Nations declaration to that effect. Guatemala refused to recognize the independent state, but in 1986, President Cerezo of Guatemala announced an intention to drop his country's claim to Belize. A British military force was maintained in Belize from independence until 1993, when the British government announced that the defence of Belize would be handed over to the government on 1 January 1994 and that it would reduce the 1,200-strong garrison to about 100 soldiers who would organize jungle warfare training facilities. Belize was admitted into the OAS in 1991 following negotiations between Belize, Guatemala and Britain. As part of Guatemala's recognition of Belize as an independent nation (ratified by Congress in 1992) Britain will recompense Guatemala by providing financial and technical assistance to construct road, pipeline and port facilities that will guarantee Guatemala access to the Atlantic. In Belize there will be a referendum to decide whether to accept the proposed Maritime Areas Bill which will delimit Belize's southern maritime borders in such a manner as to allow

Guatemala uncontested and secure access to the high seas.

Mr George Price, of the People's United Party, who had been reelected continuously as Prime Minister since internal self-government was instituted in 1964, was defeated by Mr Manuel Esquivel, of the United Democratic Party (UDP), in general elections held in December 1984 (the first since independence), but was returned as Prime Minister in 1989. The National Alliance for Belizean Rights (NABR) was created in 1992 by a defector from the UDP. General elections were held early, in 1993, and contrary to forecasts, the PUP was defeated. The UDP, in alliance with the NABR, won 16 of the 29 seats, many by a very narrow margin, and Mr Esquivel took office as Prime Minister with the additional portfolios of Finance and Defence. In the months following the elections, a corruption scandal rocked Belizean politics. Several PUP members, including the former Foreign Minister were arrested on charges of offering bribes to 2 UDP members of the House of Representatives to persuade them to cross the floor.

The People In the 1991 census, the population was estimated at 190,790; subsequent estimates for 1992 put the figure at 196,000. About 40% of them are of mixed ancestry, the so-called Creoles, a term widely used in the Caribbean. They predominate in Belize City and along the coast, and on the navigable rivers. 33% of the population are mestizo; 10% are Indians, mostly Mayas, who predominate in the N between the Hondo and New rivers and in the extreme S and W. About 8% of the population are Garifuna (Black Caribs), descendants of the Black Caribs deported from St Vincent in 1797; they have a distinct language, and can be found in the villages and towns along the southern coast. They are good linguists, many speaking Mayan languages as well as Spanish and 'Creole' English. They also brought their culture and customs from the West Indies, including religious practices and ceremonies, for example Yankanu (John Canoe) dancing at Christmas time. The remainder are of unmixed European ancestry (the majority Mennonites, who speak a German dialect, and are friendly and helpful) and a rapidly growing group of North Americans. The Mennonites fall into 2 groups, generally speaking: the most rigorous, in the Shipyard area on The New River, and the more 'integrated' in the W, Cayo district, who produce much of Belize's poultry, dairy goods and corn. The newest Mennonite settlements are E of Progresso Lagoon in the NE. There are also East Indian and Chinese immigrants.

English is the official language, although about 75% speak mostly 'Creole' English. Spanish is the mother tongue for about 15%. About 30% are bilingual, and 10% trilingual (see above). Spanish is widely spoken in the northern and western areas. Free elementary education is available to all, and all the towns have secondary schools.

The Economy Belize's central problem is how to become self-sufficient in food: imports of food are still some 25% of the total imports. Necessity is forcing the people to grow food for themselves and this is gathering pace. One difficulty is that the territory is seriously under-populated and much skilled labour emigrates. Three immigrant Mennonite communities have already increased farm production, and new legislation provides for the development of lands not utilized by private landowners.

Agriculture is still the most important sector of the Belizean economy, employing more than half the population, and bringing in 65% of the country's total foreign exchange earnings. The main export crops, in order of importance, are sugar, citrus and bananas. Maize, beans, cocoa and rice are grown, and attempts are also being made to increase the cattle herd. Poultry, eggs and honey production grew significantly during the 1980s.

Timber is extracted during the first 6 months of the year. Forest products were for a long time the country's most important export, but their relative importance has fallen. The government has reduced incentives for logging, while encouraging

---

BELIZE : FACT FILE

Geographic
Land area   22,965 sq km
  forested   44.4%
  pastures   2.1%
  cultivated   2.5%

Demographic
Population (1992)   196,000
  annual growth rate (1987-92)   2.5%
  urban   51.6%
  rural   48.4%
  density   8.5 per sq km
Religious affiliation
  Roman Catholic   62.0%
  Protestant   30.6%
Birth rate per 1,000 (1990)   38.1
              (world av 26.4)
Death rate per 1,000 (1990)   5.0
              (world av 9.2)

Education and Health
Life expectancy at birth (1991),
  male   67 years
  female   72 years
Infant mortality rate
  per 1,000 live births (1991)   35
Physicians (1990)   1 per 1,543 persons
Hospital beds   1 per 309 persons
Calorie intake as %
  of FAO requirement   118%
Population age 25 and over
  with no formal schooling   10.7%
Literacy (over 15)   93%

Economic
GNP (1990 market prices)   US$373mn
GNP per capita   US$1,970
Public external debt (1990)US$142.8mn
Tourism receipts (1990)   US$91mn
Inflation
  (annual av 1987-92)   3.5%

Radio   1 per 1.9 persons
Television   1 per 16 persons
Telephone   1 per 12 persons

Employment
Population economically active
  (1983-84)   47,325
Unemployment rate   na
% of labour force in
  agriculture   27.6
  mining   0.2
  manufacturing   8.9
  construction   4.2
Military forces   665
Source *Encyclopaedia Britannica.*

---

the establishment of a veneer plant to increase the domestic value added in wood product exports. Fish products (eg shrimp and conch) are exported, though some of the traditional grounds have been overfished and restrictions necessary for conservation are enforced.

There is also some light industry and manufacturing (dominated by sugar refining and citrus processing) now contributes about 15% of gdp. The value of clothing exports has risen to 11% of total exports, making garments the third most important export item after sugar and orange concentrate. Oil was discovered, near the Mexican border, in 1981; the search for oil is being intensified.

With the emergence of ecotourism and natural history-based travel as a major expansion market within the travel industry, the Belize government is encouraging the development of tourism facilities and services. Tourism in Belize is the second largest foreign revenue earner, behind agriculture. There are now 269 hotels, with 3,020 rooms available, an increase of 650 rooms between October 1990 and October 1991. The Belize Tourist Board estimates a figure of over 200,000 tourists visiting Belize a year.

The slowing down of economic growth at the beginning of the 1980s was attributable to decline in the sugar industry and pressures on Belize's international accounts. Prudent financial policies in the mid-1980s led to the elimination of external debt arrears and the increase of foreign exchange reserves. In 1988-92 gdp grew at an average of nearly 9% a year, while interest payments due fell from 4.7% of exports of goods and non-factor services in 1985 to 2.0% in 1992.

Government Belize is a constitutional monarchy; the British monarch is the chief of state, represented by a Governor-General, who is a Belizean. The head of government is the Prime Minister. There is a National Assembly, with a House of Representatives of 28 members (not including the Speaker) elected by universal adult suffrage, and a Senate of 8: 5 appointed by the advice of the Prime Minister, 2 on the advice of the Leader of the Opposition, 1 by the Governor-General after consultation. General elections are held at intervals of not more than 5 years.

Communications   Formerly the only means of inland communication were the rivers, with sea links between the coastal towns and settlements. The Belize river can be navigated by light motor boats, with enclosed propellers, to near the Guatemalan border in most seasons of the year, but this route is no longer used commercially because of the many rapids. The Hondo River and the New River are both navigable for small boats for 100 miles or so. Although boats continue to serve the sugar industry in the N, the use of waterborne transport is much diminished.

Some 1,865 miles of roads, of which 13% are paved, connect the 8 towns and many villages in the country. There are road links with Chetumal, the Mexican border town, and the Guatemalan border town of Melchor de Mencos.

The road system has been upgraded in the interests of tourism. There are no railways in Belize.

Nature Conservation   has become a high priority, with nature reserves sponsored by the Belize Audubon Society, the Government and various international agencies. 'Nature tourism' is Belize's fastest growing industry. By 1992 18 national parks and reserves had been established, including: Half Moon Caye, Cockscomb Basin Wildlife Sanctuary (the world's only jaguar reserve), Crooked Tree Wildlife Sanctuary (swamp forests and lagoons with wildfowl), Community Baboon Sanctuary, Blue Hole National Park, Guanacaste Park, Society Hall Nature Reserve (a research area with Maya presence), Bladen Nature Reserve (watershed and primary forest), Hol Chan Marine Reserve (reef eco-system), Rio Bravo Conservation Area (managed by the Programme for Belize, 1 King Street, Belize City, T 02-75616/7, or John Burton, Old Mission Hall, Sibton Green, Saxmundham, Suffolk, IP17 2JY), the Shipstern Nature Reserve (butterfly breeding, forest, lagoons, mammals and birds: contact PO Box 1694, Belize City, T 08-22149 via BCL Radio phone, or International Tropical Conservation Foundation, Box 31, CH-2074 Marin-Ne, Switzerland). Five Blue Lakes National Park, based on an unusually deep karst lagoon in the far S near Guatemala was designated in April 1991. On 8 December 1991 the government created 3 new forest reserves and national parks: the Vaca Forest Reserve (52,000 acres), Chiquibul National Park (containing the Maya ruins of Caracol, 265,894 acres), both in Cayo District, and Laughing Bird Caye National Park (off Placencia). The first 8 listed are managed by the Belize Audubon Society, 29 Regent Street, Belize City (PO Box 1001), T 02-77369/78239. Glovers Reef was declared a marine reserve in 1993.

Belize Enterprise for Sustained Technology (BEST) is a non-profit organization committed to the sustainable development of Belize's disadvantaged communities and community-based ecotourism, eg Gales Point and Hopkins Village; PO Box 35, Forest Drive, Belmopan, T 08-23043, F 08-22563.

NB   A wildlife protection Act was introduced in 1982, which forbids the sale, exchange or dealings in wildlife, or parts thereof, for profit; the import, export, hunting or collection of wildlife is not allowed without a permit; only those doing scientific research or for educational purposes are eligible for exporting or collecting permits. Also prohibited are removing or exporting black coral, picking orchids, exporting turtle or turtle products, and spear fishing in certain areas or while wearing scuba gear.

Bird watchers are recommended to take Petersen's *Field Guide to Mexican Birds*.

Fishing   The rivers abound with tarpon and snook. The sea provides game fish such as sailfish, marlin, wahoo, barracuda and tuna. On the flats, the most exciting fish for light tackle—the bonefish—are found in great abundance. Seasons are given below. In addition to the restrictions on turtle and coral extraction noted above under **Nature Conservation**, the following regulations apply: no person may take, buy or sell crawfish (lobster) between 15 March and 14 July, shrimp from 15 April to 14 August, or conch between 1 July and 30 September.

Fishing seasons: Billfish: blue marlin, all year (best Nov-March); white marlin, Nov-May; sailfish, March-May. Oceanic: yellowfin tuna, all year; blackfin tuna, all year; bonito, all year; wahoo, Nov-Feb; sharks, all year. Reef: kingfish, March-June; barracuda, all year; jackfish, all year; mackerel, all year; grouper, all year; snapper, all year; permit, all year; bonefish, Nov-April; tarpon, June-Aug. River: tarpon, Feb-Aug; snook, Feb-Aug; snapper, year round.

Operators In Belize City: **Blackline Marine**, PO Box 332, Mile 2, Western Highway, T 44155, F 31975; **Sea Masters Company Ltd**, PO Box 59, 1 33185, F 026-2028; **Caribbean Charter Services**, PO Box 752, Mile 5, Northern Highway, T 45814 (have guarded car and boat park), fishing, diving and sightseeing trips to the Cayes. **Belize River Lodge**, PO Box 459, T 025-2002, F 025-2298, excellent reputation.

Diving The shores are protected by the longest barrier reef in the Western Hemisphere. Old wrecks and other underwater treasures are protected by law and cannot be removed. Spear fishing, as a sport, is discouraged in the interests of conservation. The beautiful coral formation is a great attraction for scuba diving, with canyons, coves, overhangs, ledges and walls. There are endless possibilities for underwater photography: schools of fishes amid the hard and soft coral, sponges and fans. Boats can only be hired for diving, fishing or sightseeing if they are licensed for the specific purpose by the government. This is intended to ensure that tourists travel on safe, reliable vessels and also to prevent the proliferation of self-appointed guides. Try to see that the boat which is taking you to see the reef does not damage this attraction by dropping its anchor on, or in any other way destroying, the coral. The coral reefs around the northerly, most touristy cayes are dying. There are decreasing numbers of small fishes as a necessary part of the coral lifecycle in more easily accessible reefs, including the underwater parks.

BELMOPAN AND BELIZE CITY

Belmopan, the capital, suffers from being created for political rather than economic reasons, and apart from some interesting buildings, it has little to offer the visitor. The real centre of the country remains Belize City which, while typical of the main cities of Central America—considerable historical interest, all the main services, good communications to everywhere else, and a certain amount of street crime, is quite Caribbean in appearance.

Belmopan is the capital; the seat of government was moved there from Belize City in August 1970. It is 50 miles inland to the W, near the junction of the Western Highway and the Hummingbird Highway to Dangriga (Stann Creek Town)—very scenic. It has a National Assembly building (which is open to the public), 2 blocks of government offices (which are copies of Mayan architecture), police headquarters, a public works department, a hospital, over 700 houses for civil servants, a non-governmental residential district to encourage expansion, and a market. It was projected to have a population of 40,000, so far there are only 5,256 (1990). Many government workers still commute from Belize City. The Department of Archaeology in the government plaza has a vault containing specimens of the country's artefacts, as there is no museum to house them. Guided tours are offered on Mon, Wed and Fri 1330-1430 only (a 2-day prior appointment is necessary, T 08-22106). Visits are free, but donations are encouraged to help preserve the country's treasures. The city can be seen in less than an hour (break Belize City-San Ignacio bus journey, storing luggage safely at Batty Bus or Novelo terminal—but see below). A recent addition is the civic centre. The Western Highway from Belize City is now good (1 hrs drive), continuing to San Ignacio, and there is an airfield (for charter services only).

Belmopan telephone numbers are prefaced with 08 (8 from outside Belize).

Hotels and Restaurants A-L *Belmopan Convention Hotel*, 2 Bliss Parade, T 22130 (opp bus stop and market), a/c, hot water, swimming pool, restaurant, bars; **B** *Bull Frog Hotel*, 23/25 Half Moon Avenue, T 22111, a/c, good, reasonably priced, good restaurant, laundry (these 2 are a 15-min walk E of the market through the Parliament complex); **B** *Circle A Lodgings*, 35/37 Half Moon Avenue, T 22296, with bath, a/c and fans available, despite sign, friendly, breakfast is extra, dinner also served, laundry US$1.90, noisy restaurant next door; **C** *El Rey Inn*, 23 Moho Street, T 23438, big room with fan, hot and cold water, basic, clean, friendly, restaurant, laundry on request, central. There are 3 restaurants (*Caladium*, next to market, limited fare, moderately priced, small portions, and *Bullfrog* and *El Rey* , see above); there is a *comedor* at the back of the market, which is very clean. Local food is sold by vendors, 2 stands in front sell ice cream (closed Sat and Sun), fruit and vegetable market open daily, limited produce available Sun. Shops close 1200-1400. No cafés open Sun.

Note Belmopan has been described as 'a disaster for the budget traveller'; also, taxi drivers tend to overcharge.

Buses To **San Ignacio**, 45-60 mins, US$1.12 frequent service by Batty and Novelo from 0730-1700. To **Belize City**, 60 mins, US$1.50 frequent service by Batty, Z line and others. To **Dangriga**, **Mango Creek** and **Punta Gorda**, see under those towns. To **Orange Walk** and **Corozal** take an early bus to Belize City and change. Novelo's bus terminus will store luggage, but note that on Sunday it closes at 1500.

Exchange Barclays Bank International (0800-1300, Mon-Fri, and 1500-1800 Fri). Visa transactions, no commission (but see under Belize City, below).

British High Commission, 34/36 Halfmoon Ave, Embassy Square (PO Box 91, T 22146/7, F 22761). Officially 'visits' Belize City, 11 Marks Street, T 45108, Mon, 0900-1100. **El Salvador**, 2 Ave Rio Grande, visa on the spot valid 1 month for 90-day stay, 1 photo, US$38 cash, better to get it in Guatemala, maps available, (PO Box 215, T/F 23404); **Costa Rica**, 2 Sapodilla St, T 22725, F 22731; **Panama**, 79 Unity Blvd, T 22714 (Embassy, for Consulate see Belize City); **Venezuelan Consul General**, 18/20 Unity Blvd, T 22384.

Excursions Nearby are Belize Zoo and Guanacaste Park both well worth a visit (as Belmopan's accommodation is so expensive it may be better to take an early bus to either from Belize City rather than go from the capital). See under **Western Belize**, below.

Belize City is the old capital and chief town. Most of the houses are built of wood, often of charming design, with galvanized iron roofs; they stand for the most part on piles about 7 feet above the ground, which is often swampy and flooded. Ground-floor rooms are used as kitchens, or for storage. A sewerage system has been installed, and the water is reported safe to drink, though bottled water may be a wise precaution. Note the vast water butts outside many houses, with pipes leading to the domestic supply. Humidity is high, but the summer heat is tempered by the NE trades. The population, 43,621, is just under a quarter of the total population, with the African strain predominating.

Haulover Creek divides the city; the swing bridge across the river is opened at 1730 daily to let boats pass. Among the commonest craft are sandlighters, whose lateen sails can be seen off Belize City. Three canals further divide the city. The main commercial area is either side of the swing bridge, although most of the shops are on the S side, many being located on Regent and Albert streets. The area around Central Park is always busy, but it is no distance to Southern Foreshore with its views of the rivermouth, harbour and out to sea. At the southern end of Regent Street, the Anglican Cathedral and Government House nearby are interesting; both were built in the early 19th century. In the days before the foundation of the Crown Colony the kings of the Mosquito Coast were crowned in the Cathedral. In the Cathedral, note the 19th century memorial plaques which give a harrowing account of early death from 'country fever' (yellow fever) and other tropical diseases.

On the N side of the swing bridge, turn left up North Front Street for some of the cheaper hotels and the A and R Station, from which most boats leave for the Cayes. Turn right for the Post Office, Tourist Office and roads which lead to Marine Parade (also with sea views). At the junction of Cork Street at Marine Parade is the *Fort George Hotel* whose new Club Wing, a copper-coloured glass tower, is

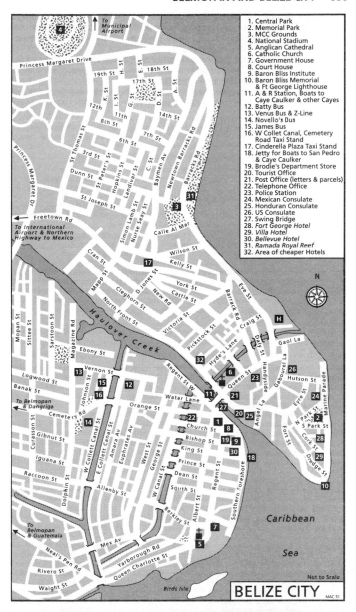

1. Central Park
2. Memorial Park
3. MCC Grounds
4. National Stadium
5. Anglican Cathedral
6. Catholic Church
7. Government House
8. Court House
9. Baron Bliss Institute
10. Baron Bliss Memorial
    & Ft George Lighthouse
11. A & R Station, Boats to
    Caye Caulker & other Cayes
12. Batty Bus
13. Venus Bus & Z-Line
14. Novello's Bus
15. James Bus
16. W Collet Canal, Cemetery
    Road Taxi Stand
17. Cinderella Plaza Taxi Stand
18. Jetty for Boats to San Pedro
    & Caye Caulker
19. Brodie's Department Store
20. Tourist Office
21. Post Office (letters & parcels)
22. Telephone Office
23. Police Station
24. Mexican Consulate
25. Honduran Consulate
26. US Consulate
27. Swing Bridge
28. Fort George Hotel
29. Villa Hotel
30. Bellevue Hotel
31. Ramada Royal Reef
32. Area of cheaper Hotels

To Municipal Airport

Princess Margaret Drive

19th St
18th St
17th St
H. St
E. St
12th
K. St
I. St
G. St
D. St
A. St
11th
8th St
7th St
6th St
St Thomas St
3rd St
Baymen Av
Newtown Barracks Rd
St Peter's St
Hopkins St
Dunn St
Landivar St
Barracks Rd
St Joseph St

Princess Margaret Dr

Freetown Rd
To International
Airport & Northern
Highway to Mexico

Simon Lamb St
Nurse Seay St
C. St
B. St

Calle Al Mar

Cran St

Wilson St
Kelly St
York St
Castle St
New Rd
Cleghorn St
D Jones St
Mapp St

North Front St

Haulover Creek

Mopan St
Sittee St
Sarstoon St
Magazine Rd
Ebony St
Vernon St
Johnson St
Logwood St
Banak St
To Belmopan
& Dangriga

Pickstock St
Barrack Rd
Eve St
Craig St
Gaol La
Daly St
Hyde's Lane

Handyside
Gabourel La
Hutson St

Victoria St
Regent St W

Water Lane

Orange St

Cemetery Rd
Curasson St
Gibnut St
Iguana St
Raccoon St
Dolphin St

W Collett Canal St
E Collett Canal St
Amara Av
Euphrates Av
West St
George St
W Canal St

Church St
Bishop St
King St
Prince St
Dean St
South St
Albert St
Regent St
Berkley St
Southern Foreshore

Allenby St

Mex Av
Neal's Pen Rd
Yarborough Rd
Queen Charlotte Rd
Rivero St
Waight St
Birds Isle

To Belmopan
& Guatemala

Caribbean

Sea

N

Queen St
Angel La
Fort St
N Park St
S Park St
Eyre St
Cork St
Dredge St
Marine Parade

Not to Scale

BELIZE CITY

MAC 51

a considerable landmark. Memorial Park on Marine Parade has a small obelisk, 2 cannon, concrete benches, and is peppered with the holes of landcrabs. The small park by the Fort George Lighthouse has a children's play area and is a popular meeting place.

Coming in by sea, after passing the barrier reef, Belize City is approached by a narrow, tortuous channel. This and the chain of mangrove cayes give shelter to what would otherwise be an open roadstead.

Belize is the nearest adequate port to the State of Quintana Roo (Mexico), and re-exports mahogany from that area. It also handles substantial container traffic for Yucatán.

Note Hurricane Hattie swept a 10-ft tidal wave into the town on 31 October 1961, and caused much damage and loss of life. Hattieville, 16 miles from Belize City on the road to Cayo, originally a temporary settlement for the homeless after the hurricane, still has from 2,000 to 3,000 people. In 1978, Hurricane Greta caused extensive damage.

Warning Cars should only be left in guarded carparks (such as Budget Store in N Front St, US$5 a night; cars can enter at any time—no sleeping in parked vehicles allowed—but can only be collected between 0800-1630). For a tip, the security officer at the *Ramada* will look after your car for a few days while you go to the Cayes.

Watch out for conmen, some in uniform, who would like to disappear with your money. Do not trust the many self-appointed 'guides' who also sell hotel rooms, boat trips to the Cayes, drugs, etc. Local advice is not even to say 'no'; just shake your head and wag your finger if approached by a stranger. Street money changers are not to be trusted either. Recent government measures have increased the security presence in downtown areas. It is still wise to avoid small, narrow side streets and stick to major thoroughfares, although even on main streets you can be victim to unprovoked and violent threats and racial abuse. A common sense attitude is needed and a careful watch on your possessions is recommended. Travel by taxi (cheap) is advisable particularly at night and in the rain but you can get mugged even in broad daylight. Areas which are best avoided at night (because they are frequented by crack users) are near Pinks and Bride's Alleys opp Tourist Office, on the Southern Foreshore and the area bounded by the Southside Canal, Haulover Creek and Collet Canal (where the bus stations are). No jewellery or watches should be worn.

The whole city closes down on Sunday except for a few shops open on Sunday morning, eg Brodies in the centre of town. Banks and many shops are closed on Wednesday afternoons.

Unless otherwise indicated, preface Belize City phone numbers with 02 (2 from outside Belize).

Hotels All hotels are subject to 6% government tax (on room rate only). **L-A+** *Radisson Fort George Hotel*, 2 Marine Parade (PO Box 321, T 77400, F 73820), in 2 wings (Club Wing and Colonial Section), each with excellent rooms, a/c, helpful staff, reservations should be made, safe parking, good restaurant, good pool (non-residents who use pool for US$10), rec. **L-L+** *Ramada Royal Reef and Marina*, Newtown Barracks (PO Box 1248), T 32670, F 32660, on sea front (but not central), a/c, good food and service in restaurant and bar (a/c with sea views, expensive), pool; **L** *Holiday Inn Villa*, 13 Cork St, T 32800, F 30276, a/c, TV, good restaurant (local and Lebanese), excellent rooftop bar with views of cayes and harbour, pool, nice gardens. **A+-L** *Belize Biltmore Plaza*, Mile 3 Northern Highway, T 32302, F 32962, comfortable rooms, a/c, restaurant (nice atmosphere, a/c, good selection), excellent English pub-style bar (but karaoke in bar most evenings), pool, conference facilities, a long way from town (US$3.50 or more by taxi); **A+-L** *Bellevue*, 5 Southern Foreshore (T 77051, F 73253), a/c, private bath, good laundry service, restaurant (nice atmosphere, good lunches with live music, steaks), leafy courtyard pool, nice bar with live music Fri and Sat nights, good entertainment, rec; **A-A+** *Chateau Caribbean*, 6 Marine Parade, by *Fort George* (T 30800, F 30900), a/c, with good bar, restaurant (excellent Chinese and seafood, sea view, good service) and discotheque, parking, rec. **A+-A** *Belize International* , at Ladyville, 9 miles on Northern Highway, T 52150 or 44001, 1½ miles from airport, tennis court, restaurant and bar; **A** *Alicia's Guest House*, corner Dean St and Chapel Lane, T 75082, with a/c, some with fan, fruit and tea/coffee included, owner Anselmo Ortiz (Alicia, his daughter) friendly and helpful; **A** *Bakadeer Inn*, 74 Cleghorn Street, T 31286, F 31963, private bath, breakfast US$4, a/c, TV, fridge, friendly, rec; **B** *Bliss*, 1 Water Lane (T 72552), with bath and a/c, cheaper with fan, good value; **B** *El Centro*, 4 Bishop St, T 72413, a/c, restaurant, good value; **B** *Mopan*, 55 Regent Street, T 77351, with bath, breakfast, a/c, in historic house, has restaurant and bar (owners Tom and Jean Shaw), nice but pricey, helpful with information, transport arrangements; **B** *Royal Orchid*, 153 New Rd and Douglas Jones St, T 32783, F 32789, a/c, with bar, restaurant, laundry service, Chinese, not central; **B** *The City and the*

Sea Belize Guest House, 2 Hutson St, T and F 77569, a/c or fan, with or without bath, check rooms first as some are not as good as others, colonial house on sea front, nice balcony, helpful owner. **B** *Four Fort Street* (address as name, T 30116, F 78808), 6 rooms, all with 4-poster beds and shared bath, charming, excellent restaurant, rec.

C *Glenthorne Manor*, 27 Barrack Rd. (T 44212), with or without bath, colonial-style, getting run down, meals available, rec; **C** *Colton House Guest House*, T 30451, F 44666, 9 Cork Street; **C** *Orchidia*, Regent St, clean, safe; **D** *Annis Louise*, 3 Freetown Rd, T 44670, shared bath, fan; **D** *Belize River Lodge*, Ladyville, PO Box 459 Belize City, T 52002, F 52298, 10 mins from airport on Belize River, excellent accommodation, food and fishing (from lodge or cruises), also scuba facilities, numerous packages. **D** *Eyre Street Guest House*, 7 Eyre St T 77724, fans, restaurant, good breakfast, ask for Anthony here if you want a local guide, building work under way, mixed reports. **D** *Isabel Guest House*, 3 Albert St, above Matus Store, PO Box 362, T 73139, 3 double rooms, 1 huge triple room, quiet, private shower, clean, friendly, safe, Spanish spoken, highly rec.

D *Sea Side Guest House*, 3 Prince Street, T 78339, F in bunk room, comfortable, quiet, very popular, very helpful American owners, German spoken, 6 rooms, breakfast only (good), will store luggage, repeatedly rec; **D** *Freddie's*, 86 Eve St, T 44396, with shower and toilet, fan, hot water, clean, very nice, secure, very small; **D** *Golden Dragon*, 29 Queen St, T 72817, with bath and a/c, cheaper rooms with bath and fan, cheaper without bath (but still overpriced), hot water, clean but noisy, beside cinema, has restaurant; **D** *Golden Star Guest House*, 114 New Rd, T 45271, fan, clean, shower, simple, facilities leave something to be desired, not very friendly. **D** *Venus*, Magazine Rd, T 77390, at Venus Bus Station; C with a/c, rooms without a/c have ceiling fans, and are quieter and lighter, private bath, clean, safe.

D *North Front Street Guest House*, T 77595, 1 block N of Post Office, 15 mins walk from Batty bus station, 124 North Front St, F pp in dormitory, no hot water, fan, book exchange, TV, friendly, laundry, mice, French spoken, good information, keep windows closed at night and be sure to lock your door; **D** *Bell's Hotel*, 140 North Front St, T 31083, or F pp, owner Richard Clarke-Bell has a boat and can provide transport to the Cayes.

E *Bon Aventure*, 122 North Front St, T 44248, F in dormitory, purified water available, a bit run down, but Hong Kong Chinese owners helpful, Spanish spoken, laundry service, good meals at reasonable prices, a few rooms rented by 'working girls'; opposite are *Mira Rio*, 59 North Front St, similar prices, fan, toilet, clean, covered verandah overlooking Haulover Creek, Spanish spoken, rec, and *Riverside*, T 32397, 61 North Front St, Chinese run, same prices; **E** *Han's Guest House*, 53 Queen St, little or no English spoken by Chinese owners, basic, noisy, mice; **E** *Marin Travel Lodge*, 6 Craig St, T 45166, good, fans, shared hot showers, clean, safe, laundry facilities, regretfully keep unhappy coati on short chain; **E** *Riverview*, 25 Regent St West, T 73392, basic; **E** *Simon Quan's 'Luxury' Hotel*, 24-26 Queen St, T 45793, with fan, and D, private shower, hot water, a/c, filthy, unattractive building.

Camping No tent sites. Camping on the beaches, in forest reserves, or in any other public place is not allowed. **NB** Butane gas in trailer/coleman stove size storage bottles is available in Belize.

Restaurants It can be difficult to find places to eat between 1500 and 1800. See also Hotels above. *Golden Dragon*, Queen St, good, reasonably priced, rec for Chinese food; *Four Fort Street* (at that address), near Memorial Park, nice atmosphere, sit out on the verandah, desserts a speciality, rec, also has 6 rooms (see above); *Macy's*, 18 Bishop Street (T 73419), rec for well-prepared local game, Creole cooking, different fixed menu daily, charming host; *Barracks Restaurant and Bar*, 136 Barrack Rd, excellent value, much frequented by expatriate community and Belizeans alike, Chinese and Far Eastern cuisine; *Grill*, 164 Newtown Barracks (a short taxi ride from major hotels), English owner Richard Price, considered by many as best restaurant in the city, varied menu, T 45020; *DIT's*, 50 King St, good, cheap; *GG's Café and Patio*, 2-3 King St, popular for lunches, about US$5 for a main dish, good quality, good service, George Godfrey well informed host, rec; *King's*, St Thomas St, good value; *Big Daddy's*, in Pickstock St burned down in 1991 but has reappeared on Church St in front of TBL office, good cheap food, also vegetarian. *Pearl's*, Handyside St, Italian and pizza, good value, friendly host Bill (ex-Placencia), no bar; *Marlin*, 11 Regent St West, overlooking Belize River, T 73913, varied menu, good seafood.

Caribbean, 36 Regent St, Creole and Chinese, rec; *New Chon Saan*, 55 Euphrates Av, T 72709, best Chinese in town, pleasant atmosphere (taxi ride), take away; *Hong Kong*, 50 Queen St, Chinese, reasonably priced; *Canton*, New Rd, large portions, good, cheap; *China Garden*, 46 Regent St, lunch specials; *Shek Kei*, 80 Freetown Rd, Chinese, good; *Ding Ho*, North Front St, good Chinese, try their 'special' dishes; other Chinese (fair): *Yin Kee*, 64 Freetown Rd, *Taiwan*, 93 Cemetery Rd. *Krischna Fast Food*, Queen St, near police station, very good Indian food, very cheap, order 2 hrs in advance (only 2 tables). *Pop 'n' Taco*, Regent Street, good sweet and sour chicken, cheap, friendly service; *Edward Quan Fried Chicken*,

New Rd, take away, good. *H & L Burgers*, 4 locations; *Playboy*, 11 King St, good sandwiches; *Pizza House*, King St, closed Mon, large pizzas, inexpensive, good also for juices and shakes. *Blue Bird*, Albert St, cheap fruit juices; specialities, modest, clean, reasonable; *Babb's*, Queen and Eve Sts, good pastries, meat pies, juices, friendly.

Bars Best and safest bars are found at major hotels, *Paddle Lounge* at the *Fort George*, *Lighthouse Lookout Lounge* at the *Holiday Inn Villa*, *Biltmore Plaza*, *Bellevue* and *Four Fort Street*. If you want a little local charm *Lindbergh's Landing*, 164A Newtown Road (next to *Grill*) is fun, open air with sea view. Lots of bars some with juke boxes and poolrooms. *Privateer*, Mile 4$\frac{1}{2}$ on Northern Highway, on seafront, expensive drinks but you can sit outside. Try the local drink, anise and peppermint, known as 'A and P'; also the powerful 'Old Belizeno' rum. The local beer, Belikin, is good, as is the 'stout', strong and free of gas. Guinness is also served, but is expensive.

Clubs and Discos *Hard Rock Café*, 35 Queen Street/Handyside, T 32041, best atmosphere in town, laid back, discriminating door policy, frequented by Belizeans, young, affluent and foreigners, call taxi before leaving; *Riverview Café*, North Front St, bar and disco, admission charged, taped music; *The Big Apple*, same street, live music at weekends, good. *The Louisville Democratic Bar*, psychedelic decor, lively and amusing, good loud music, best Fri-Sun, rec.

Shopping Handicrafts, woodcarvings, straw items, are all good buys. The Belize Chamber of Commerce has opened a Belize crafts sales room on Fort St, opp *Four Fort Street* restaurant, to be a showcase and promote the efforts of crafts people from all over Belize, come here first. *Admiral Burnaby's Coffee Shop*, Regent St, combination art gallery, book and craft shop, serving also coffee and juices; *Nile*, 49 Eve St, Middle East. *The Holy Redeemer Book Centre*, North Front St, close to bridge and Catholic church, very good, has secondhand books and back issues of US magazines, front of shop sells T-shirts and souvenirs. *Belize Bookshop*, Regent St (opp *Mopan Hotel*), ask at counter for 'racy' British greetings cards. *Angelus Press*, 10 Queen Street, excellent selection of stationery supplies, books, cards, etc *Go Tees*, 23 Regent St, T 74082, excellent selection of T-shirts (printed on premises), arts and crafts from Belize, Guatemala and Mexico: jewellery, silver, wood carvings, clothes, paintings, etc; also has a branch at Belize Zoo, good zoo T-shirts and cuddly animals. Zericote (or Xericote) wood carvings can be bought in Belize City, for example at *Brodies Department Store* (Central Park end of Regent St), which also sells postcards, the *Fort George Hotel*, the small gift shop at *Four Fort Street*, or from Egbert Peyrefitte, 11a Cemetery Road. Such wood carvings are the best buy, but to find a carver rather than buy the tourist fare in shops, ask a taxi driver. (At the Art Centre, near Government House, the wood sculpture of Charles Gabb, who introduced carving into Belize, can be seen.) Wood carvers sell their work in front of the *Fort George* and *Holiday Inn Villa* hotels. A new craft centre at the southern end of the swing bridge, on the site of the old market, should be open by 1993. The market is by the junction of North Front St and Fort St. *Ro-Macs*, 27 Albert St, excellent supermarket including wide selection of imported foods and wines.

Taxis have green licence plates (drivers must also have identification card); within Belize, US$2.50 for 1 person; for 2 or more passengers, US$1.75 pp. International Airport to Belize centre, US$15; municipal airport to centre, US$7.50. (Note, if you check several hotels, you may be charged for each ride.) There is a taxi stand on Central Park, opposite Barclays, another on the corner of Collet Canal Street and Cemetery Road. Outside Belize City, US$1.75 per mile, regardless of number of passengers. Belize City to the resorts in Cayo District approx US$100-125, 1-4 people (ask for Edgar August or Martin at *Radisson Fort George* desk, they are reliable and can do guided tours around Belize). Best to ask price of the ride before setting off. No meters, so beware of overcharging and make sure fare is quoted in BZ$. No tips necessary. If you have a complaint, take the licence plate and report to the Taxi Union.

Car Hire Only 1 car rental company will release registration papers to enable cars to enter Guatemala or Mexico (Crystal–see below). Without obtaining them at the time of hire it is impossible to take hire cars across national frontiers. It is best to take a scheduled tour to Tikal or Flores in Guatemala, if intending to return to Belize, because the road is in a poor state and because entry through military checkpoints is quicker.

Car hire cost is high in Belize owing to heavy wear and tear on the vehicles. You can expect to pay between US$65 for a Suzuki Samuri to US$125 for an Isuzu Trooper per day. Cautious driving is advised in Belize as road conditions, while improving steadily, are generally poor except for the Northern and Western Highways and there is no street lighting in rural areas. When driving in the Mountain Pine Ridge area it is prudent to check carefully on road conditions at the entry gate; good maps are essential. Emory King's *Drivers Guide to Belize* is helpful when driving to the more remote areas.

Budget PO Box 863, 771 Bella Vista (near International Airport, can pick up and drop off car at airport, office almost opposite *Biltmore Plaza Hotel*), T 32435, good service, well-maintained vehicles, good deals (Suzukis and Isuzu Troopers); **Crystal**, Mile 1.5 Northern Highway, T 31600, Jay Crofton, cheapest deals in town, but not always most reliable, wide selection of vehicles inc 30-seater bus, will release insurance papers for car entry to Guatemala and Mexico (speak to Jay about his scheme to drive imported vehicles from Houston to Belize); **Pancho's**, 5747 Lizarraga Av, T 44554; **National**, International Airport, T 31586 (Cherokee Chiefs); **Avis**, at *Fort George Hotel*, T 78637, largest fleet, well-maintained, Daihatsus and Isuzu Troopers. **Smith & Sons**, 125 Cemetery Road, T 73779 (less reliable than in the past); **Gilly's**, 31 Regent St, T 77613; **Lewis**, 23 Cemetery Rd, T 74461. CDW ranges from US$10 to US$20 per day.

Bike Hire Trailbikes, minibikes, scooters, bicycles and camping gear can be hired from Bike Belize at the *Bakadeer Inn*, 74 Cleghorn St, T 33855, F 31963, from US$5 for 1/2 day for a bicycle to US$240/week for a trailbike.

Exchange All banks have facilities to arrange cash advance on Visa card. If you want US dollars against a credit card or travellers' cheques, you will be sent to get permission from the Central Bank, 2 Bishop St, US$200 maximum in cash, the remainder in cheques—alternatively you may show proof that you are leaving the country; 3% commission is charged. The **Belize Bank** is particularly efficient and modern, US$0.50 commission on Amex cheques; also **Barclays Bank International**, with some country branches, slightly better rates, 2% commission. **Atlantic Bank**, 6 Albert St, or 16 New Road, quick efficient service, smaller queues than Belize Bank or Barclays. **Bank of Nova Scotia**. Banking hours: 0800-1300 Mon-Thur, 0800-1300, 1500-1800 Fri. It is easy to have money telexed to Belize City. Guatemalan quetzales are very easy to obtain at the borders, less easy in Belize City. American Express at Global Travel, 41 Albert Street (T 77185/77363/4). Money changers at Batty Bus terminal just before departure of bus to Chetumal (the only place to change Mexican pesos except at the border). Some shops change without commission.

Cultural Institutions Baron Bliss Institute, public library, temporary exhibitions; has 1 Stela and 2 large discs on display. Audubon Society: see under Nature Conservation in the Introduction.

Places of Worship There are an Anglican Cathedral, a Catholic Cathedral, a Methodist and a Presbyterian church. The Baptist Church is on Queen St.

Cinemas Two, Palace and Majestic, films and prices change according to popularity. Majestic stages sporting events from time to time.

Consulates See also under Belmopan. **Mexico**, 20 Park St, T 30193/4 (open 0900-1300, Mon-Fri, documents returned 1530-1630; if going to Mexico and requiring a visa, get it here, not at the border, tourist card given on the spot, note that long queues are normal, arrive early, get visa the afternoon before departure; **Honduras**, 91 North Front St, T 45889; **El Salvador**, 120 New Road, T 44318; **Costa Rica**, 8-18th St, T 44796; **Panama Consulate**, 5481 Princess Margaret Drive, T 44940. **Guatemala**, 6A Saint Matthew St, near municipal airstrip, T 33150, open 0900-1300, advisable to obtain visas or tourist cards here rather than leave it till you reach the border; **Jamaica**, 26 Corner Hyde's Lane and New Road, T 45926, F 23312.

USA, 29 Gabourel Lane, T 77161/2, consulate is on Hutson St, round corner from embassy's entrance on Gabourel Lane, consulate open 0800-1000 for visitor visas, library 0830-1200, 1330-1630 Mon-Fri, but am only on Wed; **Canada**, c/o Vogue Ltd, Corner Queen & North Front St (PO Box 216, T 45773/45769); **Belgium**, Marcelo Ltd, Queen St, T 45769; **The Netherlands**, 14 Central American Blvd, T 75936; **France**, 10 Queen St, T 45777; **German Honorary Consul**, 2 Cork St, T 77316; **Denmark**, 13 Southern Foreshore, T 72172; **Norway**, 1 King St, T 77031, F 77062; **Sweden**, 13 Queen St, T 77234; **Italy**, 18 Albert St, T 78449; **Israel**, 4 Albert and Bishop St, T 73991/73150, F 30750.

Laundry Carry's, 41 Hyde Lane, Mon-Sat 0800-1730.

Post Office Letters, Queen St and N Front St, 0800-1200 and 1300-1700 (1630 Fri); parcels, beside main Post Office. Letters held for 1 month. Beautiful stamps sold.

International Telecommunications Telegraph, telephone, telex services, Belizean Telecommunications Ltd, No 1 Church Street just off Central Park, 0800-2100, 0800-1200 on Sun. Also public fax service and booths for credit card and charge calls to USA, UK.

Tourist Information Belize Tourist Bureau, 83 North Front Street, Belize, PO Box 325, T 77213/73255, F 77490 (open 0800-1200, 1300-1700 Mon-Thur, and till 1630 Fri), provides complete bus schedule with a map of Belize City, as well as list of hotels and their prices. Also has *Mexico and Central American Handbook* for sale and a list of recommended taxi guides and tour operators, and free publications on the country and its Maya ruins, practical and informative. Excellent maps of the country for US$3 (postage extra). The Tourist Office at the airport will check prices and availability of hotel rooms. **Belize Tourism Industry Association** (private sector body for hotels, tour companies, etc), 99 Albert St, T 75717, F 78710, brochures and information on all members throughout Belize. Enquire for all details of all Belize tour operators. Suggested reading is *Hey Dad, this is Belize*, by Emory King, a collection of anecdotes, or more seriously, *Warlords and Maize Men, a guide to the Mayan Sites of Belize*, Association for Belize Archaeology, available in bookshops. Maps (US$3), books on Belizean fauna etc available at Angelus Press, Queen St. Above the Post office is the Survey Office selling maps, 2-sheet, 1:250,000 US$10, dated, or more basic map US$2 (open Mon-Thur 0830-1200, 1300-1600, but 1530 on Fri).

Caribbean Charter Services, Mile 5 North Highway, PO Box 752. Belize City, T 30404, F 33711, is a tourist information centre and agency for airline flight tickets, boat charters, inland resorts and other facilities, Bulletin Board Service, owned by Ms Ruha'mah Stadtlander.

Tours *S and L Guided Tours*, 91 North Front St, T 77593, F 77594, recommended group travel (minimum 4 persons for most tours, 2 persons to Tikal); *Native Guide Systems*, 1 Water Lane, T 75819, F 74007, PO Box 1045, individual and group tours. A great many others both inside and outside Belize; Tourist Bureau has a full list. If booking tours in Belize from abroad it is advisable to check prices and services offered with a reputable tour operator in Belize first.

Transport There are bus services to the main towns. To Chetumal (see Mexico, **Yucatán Peninsula, Section 10**), several daily each way between 0400 and 1800 (there is an express Batty Bus at 1400 stopping at Orange Walk and Corozal only), US$5, 3-4 hrs (up to 5 including crossing), with 2 companies: Batty Bus, 54 East Collet Canal, T 72025, and Venus, Magazine Rd, T 73354. Do not take a bus from Chetumal which will arrive in Belize City after dark. Batty Bus to **Belmopan** and **San Ignacio**, 4 hrs, US$4.50, Mon-Sat frequent 0600 to 1900, Sun C 530 to 1700. The 0600, 0630 and 1015 buses connect at the border with services to Flores, Guatemala. To San Ignacio, Benque Viejo and the Guatemalan border via Belmopan, Novelo's, West Collet Canal, T 77372, US$1.40 to Belmopan, US$3 to Benque, US$2.50 to San Ignacio, hourly Mon-Sat, 1100 to 1800 (to 1600 on Sun). To **Flores, Guatemala**, minibuses leave the Shell Station on Front Street at 0500, make reservation the previous day. To **Dangriga**, via Belmopan and the Hummingbird Highway. Z-line (T 73937), from Venus bus station, daily, 0800, 1000, 1100, 1500, 1600, plus Mon 0600, US$9.50 to Dangriga; James Bus Line, Pound Yard Bridge (Collet Canal), unreliable, slow, 9-12 hrs, US$9.50, to **Punta Gorda** via Dangriga and Mango Creek, daily 0800 and 1500. Within the city the fare is US$0.50. Take a taxi to town from the bus stations at night; in the day, however, since it is not far from the bus terminals to the centre, or to the boat dock for the Cayes, don't be given the run-around by taxi drivers.

Airport There is a 10-mile tarmac road to the Phillip SW Goldson International Airport; modern check-in facilities, toilets, restaurant, viewing deck and duty-free shop, a/c. No facilities on Arrivals side. Taxi fare US$15; make sure your taxi is legitimate. Any bus going up the Northern Highway passes the airport junction (US$0.75), then 1½ mile walk.

There is a municipal airstrip for local flights, 15 mins out of town, taxi, US$7.50, no bus service. Services to San Pedro, Caye Chapel, Caye Caulker with Tropic Air, Island Air and Maya Air, flights every hour 0700 to 1630, US$35 municipal to San Pedro return, US$30 municipal to Caye Chapel return and US$30 to Caye Caulker return. Flights to and from the islands can be taken from the International Airport and companies link their flights to meet or leave international departures; add approx US$10 each way to the price to/from municipal airport.

Services also to Corozal (Tropic Air), 30 mins, US$39. To Big Creek (Placencia) US$42; Dangriga, US$25; Punta Gorda, US$62 with Maya Air and Tropic Air, 5 flights daily from 0700, last return flight 1705 (one way fares).

Airline Offices Local: Tropic Air, Belize City T 02-45671, San Pedro 026-2012/2117/2029, F 026-2338; Island Air, Belize City T 02-31140, International airport 025-2219, San Pedro 026-2435/2484, F 026-2192; Maya Air, 6 Fort St, Belize City T 02-72312, municipal airport 02-44234/44032, International 025-2336, San Pedro 026-2611, F 02-30585.

Taca (Belize Global Travel), 41 Albert St (T 02-77363/77185, F 75213), International T 025-2163, F 025-2453, also British Airways, T 77363; International 025-2060/2458. American, Valencia Building, T 02-32522/3/4 and Continental Airlines, 32 Albert St, T 02-78309/78463/78223, International 025-2263/2488. Aerovias, in *Mopan Hotel*, 55 Regent St, T 02-75383/ 75445/6, F 75383, for Flores/Guatemala; Belize Trans Air, T 02-77666, for Miami.

Shipping The only boat to Guatemala goes from Punta Gorda. Obtain all necessary exit stamps and visas before sailing. To Puerto Cortés, Honduras, US$360, 2-4 days, for 8 people. For Dangriga and Punta Gorda boats must be chartered. Ask for Elwood Fairweather, T 72866, or through the *Sea Side Guest House*. For boats to the Cayes and other places in Belize, see under destinations.

At Ladyville, on the other side of the Northern Highway from the turning to the airport, the Secretariat for Mundo Maya is being built at Bella Vista. This will be the headquarters for all the countries involved in this regional tourism promotion.

THE NORTHERN CAYES

The Cayes off the coast are most attractive, relaxing, slow and very 'Caribbean'. An excellent place for all forms of diving and sea fishing.

The Cayes are popular destinations, especially from February to May and in August. Ask around (for example, the skippers of the boats to Caye Caulker or Chapel) for information on staying with families on the smaller, lesser populated cayes.

There are 212 square miles of cayes. **St George's Caye**, 9 miles NE of Belize, was once the capital and was the scene of the battle in 1798 which established British possession. The larger ones are Turneffe Island and Ambergris and Caulker Cayes. Fishermen live on some cayes, coconuts are grown on others, but many are uninhabited swamps. The smaller cayes do not have much shade, so be careful if you go bathing on them. Sandflies infest some cayes (eg Caulker), the sandfly season is December to beginning of February; mosquito season June, July, sometimes October.

Travel by boat to and between the islands is becoming increasingly regulated and the new licensing requirements will probably drive the cheaper boats out of business. In general, it is easier to arrange travel between the islands once there, than from Belize City. All authorized boats leave from Jan's Shell Station (A and R) on North Front Street, or, especially for San Pedro, from the boat dock on Southern Foreshore outside *Bellevue Hotel*. **Care** Do not pay for your trip until you are on the boat, or better, on arrival. Cargo boats are no longer allowed to carry passengers, too many have capsized with tourists on board, causing loss of life.

On **St George's Caye**: **A-A+** *Cottage Colony*, PO Box 428, Belize City, T 02-77051, F 02-73253, colonial-style cabañas with dive facilities, price varies according to season, easy access from Belize City *St George's Island Cottages*, PO Box 625, Belize City, 6 rooms. Boat fare is US$15, day trips are possible.

Caye Chapel is free of sandflies and mosquitoes and there are several beaches, cleaned daily. 40 mins by boat from Belize City. The *Pyramid Island Resort* owns the island (A price range, credit cards not accepted); it has an excellent beach and dive courses (PADI). Be careful if you hire a boat for a day to visit Caye Chapel: the boatmen enjoy the bar on the island and your return journey can be unreasonably exciting. Also, there are very few fish now round this caye. There is a landing strip used by local airlines.

On **Long Caye** is a guesthouse, C full board, superb food and value, clean, very friendly. The island is quiet, relaxing, with bird watching, snorkelling, fishing, but weekends can be busy when the fishermen drop by for a drink and chat. If the hotel is full, ask Bob and he may make room for you somewhere. Boat from Jan's Shell Station US$7.50.

Small caye resorts within easy reach of Belize City: *Moonlight Shadows Lodge*, **Middle Long Caye**, T 08-22587, still in early stages of development. *Ricardo's Beach Huts*, Blue Field Range (59 North Front St, PO Box 55, Belize City, T 02-44970), recommended, charming and knowledgeable host, rustic, authentic fish camp feel, overnight camps to Rendez-vous Caye, English Caye and Sargeants Caye can be arranged with Ricardo, excellent food, snorkelling. *Spanish Bay*

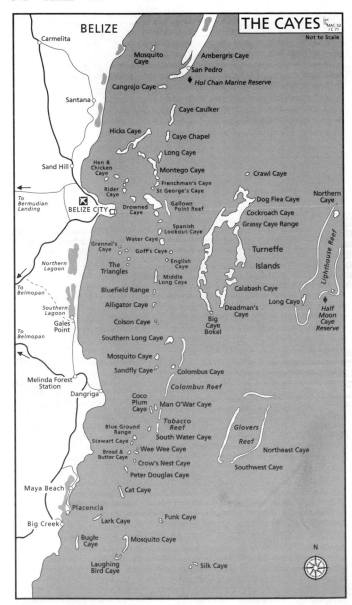

THE CAYES

IWC
MAC 52
/C 71

Not to Scale

BELIZE

Carmelita

Mosquito
Caye

Ambergris Caye

San Pedro

Hol Chan Marine Reserve

Cangrejo Caye

Santana

Caye Caulker

Hicks Caye

Caye Chapel

Long Caye

Sand Hill

Hen &
Chicken
Caye

Montego Caye

Crawl Caye

Frenchman's Caye

Rider
Caye

St George's Caye

Dog Flea Caye

Northern
Caye

BELIZE CITY

Drowned
Caye

Gallows
Point Reef

Cockroach Caye

Grassy Caye Range

To
Bermudian
Landing

Spanish
Lookout Caye

Lighthouse Reef

Water Caye

Grennel's
Caye

Goff's Caye

Turneffe
Islands

Northern
Lagoon

The
Triangles

English
Caye

To
Belmopan

Middle
Long Caye

Calabash Caye

Long Caye

Southern
Lagoon

Bluefield Range

Alligator Caye

Half
Moon
Caye
Reserve

Deadman's
Caye

Gales
Point

Colson Caye

Big
Caye
Bokel

To
Belmopan

Southern Long Caye

Mosquito Caye

Melinda Forest
Station

Sandfly Caye

Colombus Caye

Colombus Reef

Dangriga

Coco
Plum
Caye

Man O'War Caye

Tobacco
Reef

Glovers
Reef

Blue Ground
Range

South Water Caye

Stewart Caye

Northeast Caye

Bread &
Butter Caye

Wee Wee Caye

Crow's Nest Caye

Southwest Caye

Peter Douglas Caye

Maya Beach

Cat Caye

Placencia

Lark Caye

Funk Caye

Big Creek

Bugle
Caye

Mosquito Caye

Laughing
Bird Caye

Silk Caye

N

Resort, PO Box 35, Belize City, T 02-77288, also in early stages of development, dive facilities. *The Wave*, Gallows Point Caye (9 Regent St, Belize City, T 02-73054), 6 rooms, water sports facilities and diving.

Ambergris Caye   This island (pronounced Am*ber*gris), with its town of **San Pedro**, pop 1,527, has grown rapidly over the last couple of years, with 50 hotels and guest houses registered on the island. Buildings are still restricted to no more than 3 storeys in height and the many wooden structures retain an authentic village atmosphere. It should be noted that, although sand is in abundance, there are few excellent beach areas around San Pedro town. The emphasis is on snorkelling on the nearby barrier reef and Hol Chan Marine Park, as well as the fine scuba diving, sailing, fishing and board sailing. In fact it can be dangerous to swim near San Pedro as there have been serious accidents with boats. A short distance to the N and S of San Pedro lie miles of deserted beach front, where picnic barbecues are popular for day-tripping snorkellers and birders who have visited nearby small cayes hoping to glimpse flamingoes or scarlet ibis. The British Ordnance Survey has published a Tourist Map of Ambergris Caye, scale 1:50,000, with a plan of **San Pedro**, 1:5,000.

Accommodation   **L-A+** *Ramon's Village Resort*, San Pedro Village, T 026-2071/2213, F 2214, or USA 601-649-1990, F 601-425-2411 (PO Drawer 4407, Laurel, MS 39441), agree on which currency you are paying in, 61 rooms, a diving and beach resort, all meals and all diving, highly rec even for non-divers (fishing, swimming, boating, snorkelling), very efficient, comfortable rooms, pool with beach club atmosphere; **L** *Belize Yacht Club*, San Pedro town, PO Box 1, T 026-2005/2060, F 026-2331, all rooms are suites with fully-furnished kitchens, pool, docking facilities. **A+** *Sun Breeze*, San Pedro Town, T 026-2347/2191/2345, F 026-2346, near airport, Mexican style building, a/c, comfortable, all facilities, excellent restaurant, good dive shop, rec; **A+-A** *Paradise Resort Hotel*, San Pedro, T 026-2083, F 026-2232, wide selection of rooms and villas, good location, villas better value, cheaper summer rates, all water sports; **A+-B** *Coral Beach*, San Pedro, T 026-2013, F 026-2001, central location, slightly run down but good local feel and excellent water sports facilities inc dive boat charter, tours for fishing and scuba available; **A+** *San Pedro Holiday Hotel*, PO Box 1140, Belize City, T 026-2014/2103, F 026-2295, 16 rooms in good central location, fun atmosphere with good facilities, reasonable value; **A** *Spindrift Hotel*, San Pedro, T 026-2018, F 026-2251, 24 rooms, 4 apartments, unattractive block but central location, good bar and restaurant, popular meeting place, trips up the Belize River, a/c, comfortable; **A+** *Rock's Inn Apartments*, San Pedro Town, T 026-2326, F 026-2358, good value and service.

Just outside San Pedro: **L** *El Pescador*, on Punta Azul beach 3 miles N, PO Box 793, Belize City, T and F 026-2398, access by boat, specialist fishing lodge with good reputation, a/c, good food and service; **L** *Journey's End*, PO Box 13, San Pedro, T 026-2173, F 026-2028, 4.5 miles N, excellent resort facilities including diving, resort club theme; **L** *Captain Morgan's Retreat*, 3 miles N of town, T 026-2567, F 026-2616, access by boat, thatched roofed cabañas with private facilities, pool, dock, secluded, rec; **A+-L** *Victoria House*, PO Box 22, San Pedro, T 026-2067/2240, F 026-2429, inc meals, 1 mile from town, 3 different types of room, excellent facilities, good dive shop and water sports, windsurfing US$15/hr, highly rec; **A-L** *Royal Palm*, PO Box 18, San Pedro, T 026-2148/2244, F 026-2329, good location near *Victoria House*, 12 new villas with pool and full facilities just completed; **A** *House of the Rising Sun*, T 026-2336/2505, F 026-2349, nice location, reasonable rooms and value.

Other, cheaper hotels: **A** *San Pedrano*, San Pedro, T 026-2054/2093, clean and good value; **B** *Conch Shell Inn*, facing sea, some rooms with kitchenette, T 026-2062; **B** *Hide Away Lodge*, PO Box 484, Belize City, T 026-2141/2269, good value but a bit run down; **A** *Lily's*, rooms with sea view, fan, clean, T 026-2059; **B** *Rubie's*, San Pedro Town on the beach, fan, private bath, good views, beach cabaña, central, rec as best value in town, T 026-2063/2434; **B** *Martha's Hotel* (D in low season), PO Box 27, San Pedro, T 026-2054, F 026-2589, good value, rec; *La Joya del Caribe*, San Pedro T 026-2050/2385, F 026-2316, nice location just out of town, rec; **B** *Casa Blanca*, San Pedro town, T 026-2630; **B** *Pirate's Lantern*, in town, T 026-2146; **C** *Thomas*, airy rooms, fan, bath (tub, not shower), drinking water, clean, friendly; **E** *Milo's*, T 026-2033, comfortable, clean, hot water; *Seven Seas*, T 026-2382/2137. At Coral Beach, the Forman, Gómez, Gónzalez and Paz families provide rooms and meals for US$9 each. At Sea Breeze, the Paz and Núñez families offer the same accommodation at the same price.

Restaurants   The *San Pedro Grill* is a good place to meet other travellers and swap information on boats, etc. Other eating places are: *Elvi's Kitchen*, popular, newly upmarket; 1 block N is *Ambergris Delight*, pleasant, inexpensive, clean; 1 block S of *Elvi's* is *Marinos*, excellent food, good prices, popular with locals, erratic service; *Lily's Restaurant*, best seafood in town, friendly, good breakfast; *Jade Garden Restaurant*, Chinese, sweet and sour everything, drinks expensive; *The Hut*, Mexican, friendly; *Estel's* on the beach, good food and '40s-'50s music.

In the same building complex as the *Spindrift* is the *Pier Restaurant*, very Mexican, dinners from US$10, also a branch of the Atlantic Bank, a post office and a chemist. *Big Daddy's Disco*, rec. For entertainment, try 'Chicken Drop' at *Sea Breeze Hotel*, you bet US$1 on which square the chicken may leave its droppings on.

Diving Instruction to PADI open water widely available, from US$400 at Coral Beach to US$350 at Amigos del Mar, opp *Lily's*; freelance instructor Lynne Stevens can be contacted through *Marinos* restaurant.

Vehicle Rental Golf carts US$10/hour, make sure battery is fully charged before hiring; gives quick access to southern, quieter end. Bicycles US$5/hour, try negotiating for long-term rates, good way to get around.

Transport Several flights daily to and from Belize City municipal airport with Tropic, Island and Maya Air, prices under Belize City. Universal Travel at San Pedro airfield helpful. They can arrange charter flights to Corozal, with a request stop at Sarteneja (for the Shipstern Butterfly Farm **see p 551**). More interesting than going by air are the boats from Shell station, Belize City, US$10-15, non-stop. From Southern Foreshore jetty boats leave for San Pedro Mon-Fri 1600, return 0700, Sat 1300, return 0800, none on Sun, US$10, 1½ hrs. *Triple J* boat leaves from N end of swing bridge, daily round trip to Caye Caulker and San Pedro leaving Belize City 0900, return 1500, to San Pedro US$10 one way, US$17.50 return, fast, dependable, rec. Boats, irregular, between Ambergris and Caye Caulker, no set fare. Remember, pay on arrival. Bikes can be rented for US$2/hour. One cannot in practice walk N along the beach from San Pedro to Xcalak, Mexico.

Just S of Ambergris Caye, and not far from Caye Caulker, is the **Hol Chan Marine Park**, an underwater natural park. Divided into 3 zones, zone A is the reef, where fishing is prohibited. Entry US$1.50. Zone B is the seagrass beds, where fishing can only be done with a special licence; the Boca Ciega blue hole is here. Zone C is mangroves where fishing also requires a licence. Only certified scuba divers may dive in the reserve. Contact the Reserve Manager in San Pedro for further information. Several boatmen in San Pedro offer snorkelling trips to the park, US$15 (not including entry fee), 2 hrs. You can see shark, manta ray, many other fish and coral; a highly recommended trip. Fish feeding is prohibited. Only very experienced snorkellers should attempt to swim in the cutting between the reef and the open sea; seek advice on the tides.

Caye Caulker A lobster-fishing island, which used to be relatively unspoilt, but the number of tourists is now increasing. The houses are of wood, the majority built on stilts. It has been allowed to run down and the main landing jetty has been closed. Some services are reported to have deteriorated, and theft and unpleasantness from some mainlanders who go to the caye with tourists; on the other hand the islanders are friendly. The atmosphere seems to be much more relaxed out of the high tourist season; nevertheless, women should take care if alone at night. There are no beaches as the coast is largely mangrove forest, but you can swim at the channel ('cutting' or 'split', formed by a recent hurricane) or off one of the many piers. A reef museum has opened with enlarged photos of reef fish, free for school parties, tourists are asked for a US$2 donation to help expansion. There are only 2 vehicles on the island, one of which is used solely to transport Belikin beer. Sandflies are ferocious in season (Dec-Feb), take trousers and a good repellent. Make sure you fix prices before going on trips or hiring equipment, and clarify whether you are talking US$ or BZ$. Do not pay the night before. One trickster is known as 'Jimmy the Worm'.

A walk S along the shore takes you to the new airstrip, a gash across the island, and to mangroves where the rare Black Catbird (*Melanoptila glabirostris*) can be seen and its sweet song heard. In this area there are lots of mosquitoes. A campaign to make the Black Catbird's habitat and the associated reef a Nature Reserve (called Siwa-Ban, after the catbird's Maya name) can be contacted at *Hiriarco Giftshop* (Ellen McCrea, near *Tropical Paradise*), or 143 Anderson, San Francisco, California.

Hotels The cheapest end of town is the S, but it is a long way from the 'cutting' for swimming or snorkelling. A map which can be bought on arrival lists virtually everything on the island. Camping on the beach is forbidden. **B** *Rainbow Hotel*, on the beach, T 022-2123, 10 small bungalows, with shower, rooms also, C, hot water. Beach houses can also be rented for US$50-150 a month. **B** *Tropical Paradise*, T 022-2124, F 022-2225 (PO Box 1206 Belize City), cabins, rooms C, restaurant (see below), good excursions; **B** *CB's*, further S than *Tropical Paradise*, T 022-2176, with bath, clean 12 beds, no advance bookings, good, small beds, restaurant; **C** *Reef* or *Martínez Hotel*, T 022-2196, small rooms, smelly recycled shower water, basic, but reasonable for the caye; **C** *Shirley's Guest House*, T 022-2145, S end of village, very relaxing, rec; **C** *Jiminez's Cabins*, delightful self-contained huts, friendly staff; **D** *Marin*, T 022-44307 (also private hut) with bath, clean, helpful, rec (the proprietor, John Marin, will take you out for a snorkelling trip on the reef); **D** *Vega's Far Inn* rents 7 rooms, all doubles, T 022-2142, with ceiling fan and fresh linen, flush toilets and showers (limited hot water) shared with camping ground, which is guarded, has drinking water, hot water, clean toilets, barbecue, can rent out camping gear (camping costs US$6 pp, overpriced); **D** *Anchorage Hotel*, near *Ignacio's*, basic, large cabañas with cold showers but no fan, discounts for stays of over 4 days, pleasant atmosphere, friendly family, breakfast and drinks served under shade on the beach.

D-E *Mira Mar*, T 022-44307, 2nd floor rooms best, clean showers, rec, bargain if staying longer, helpful owner Melvin Badillo, he owns liquor store, his family runs a pastry shop and grocery store; **D** *Deisy's*, T 022-2150, with shower, toilet and fan, reductions for longer stays, cheaper rooms downstairs, cash TCs, rooms with communal bathroom not good value, cold water only; **E** *Edith's*, per bed in room (whether occupied or not), good; **E** *Hideaway*, round corner from *Deisy's*, clean, quiet, shared toilets and shower (cold, unpotable water), rec; **E** *Ignacio Beach Cabins*, T 022-2212, (PO Box 1169, Belize City), small huts or hammocks just outside town, for double room, D for a hut for 3-4, rec, camping space US$6, plus US$1 for luggage store, toilet and shower facilities in private cabins only, cheap lobster tails and free coconuts (Ignacio runs reef trips and he has equipment; he is principally a lobster fisherman); **E** *Riva's Guest House*, T 022-2127, basic accommodation; their reef trips in an attractive schooner are the longest; snorkelling equipment hire, US$2.50; **E** *Sandy Lane Hotel*, T 022-2217, 1 block back from main street, bungalow-type accommodation, clean, shared toilet and hot showers, run by Rico and Elma Novelo, rec; **E-D** *Tom's Hotel*, T 022-2102, with shared bath and fan, up to C in cabin with 3 beds, basic, clean, cold water, long walk from beach, laundry service US$5, safe deposit, barbecue. Tom's boat trips go to various destinations, including Hol Chan and coral gardens, and to Belize City. In all accommodation take precautions against theft.

Restaurants *Rodriguez* for dinner at 1800 onwards for US$3.50, US$5 for lobster, very good (limited accommodation available). *Melvin's*, excellent lobster meals (opp *Riva's*); *Tropical Paradise* for excellent seafood, slightly more expensive than others (also the only place selling ice cream); *The Sandbox*, run by American couple, one of the Caye's social centres. Cakes and pastries can be bought at houses displaying the sign, rec are *Deisy's*, *Jessie's* (open 0830-1300, 1500-1700, behind *Riva's*), and a very good one near the telephone exchange office; *Glenda's*, near *Hotel Marin*, try the delicious lobster, or chicken 'Burritos', chicken, vegetables, chile and sauce wrapped in a tortilla for US$0.50, also good breakfast with cinnamon rolls, closed evenings; also good for 'Burritos', *Claudette*, next to Fishermen's Wharf, US$1.25, delicious. *Pinx Diner*, good value breakfasts, lunches and dinners, good waffles, rec; *Marin's*, good seafood in evening at reasonable prices; *Syd's* home cooking, big portions. Many private houses serve food. Buy lobster or fish from the cooperative and cook up at the barbecue on the beach; beer is sold by the crate at the wholesaler on the dock by the generator; ice for sale at *Tropical Paradise*.

Services There are at least 4 small 'markets' on the island where a variety of food can be bought; prices are 20-50% higher than the mainland. Better to buy food in Belize City beforehand, but rates for changing cash and TCs are reasonable; there is a bank and many places for exchange including the Post Office. Gift shops will charge a commission.

International telephone and fax connections available on Caye Caulker (telephone exchange is open till 1600; Fax number at telephone exchange is 501-22-2239). The island also boasts 2 book swaps, including *Seaing is Belizing* (see also under **Sailing** below) and Belize Diving Service. Bookstore on opposite side of island to ferries has many different magazines, including *Time* and *Newsweek*. Dolphin Bay is a helpful travel agency on the island.

Transport Boats leave from behind A & R Shell Station on North Front Street (see above), for Caye Caulker, at 0630, then from 0900 until afternoon daily (US$6-7.50 pp, US$5 on 'sunrise boat', payable only on arrival at Caye Caulker—otherwise you'll be swindled, even if you buy tickets in advance it does not guarantee you a place on the boat), 45 mins one way (boats depend on weather and number of passengers—can be 'exciting' if it's rough), return boats from 0630 till pm (if booked in advance at some places, inc *Edith's Hotel*, US$6). You can sometimes catch a boat as late as 1600, but do not rely on it. Jerry Pacheco's *Blue Wave* (rec as fast and good, also snorkelling trips), Emilio Novelo's *Ocean Star* (good, cheaper than others) and 'Chocolate's' *Soledad* are the currently authorized boats, but there are many others (including *Rainbow Runner*, 0830 from Belize City via Caye Chapel, boat in good condition, 2 motors, *Good Grief*, mixed reports, and *C Train*). Boats from San Pedro en route to Belize City 0700-0800, US$7.50. Incidentally, 'Chocolate' is white, over 50 yrs old and has a white moustache. Anyone else introducing himself as Chocolate is an imposter! *Triple J* (see above, San Pedro) boat, rec, US$6 one way, US$11 round trip, daily service.

The airstrip has been newly constructed; all 3 airlines fly every 30 mins most of the day to and from San Pedro and/or Belize City, flight details under Belize City. Flying is rec if you have a connection to make.

You can rent golf carts, US$5/hr, popular, the locals rent them to take the family for a drive.

Reef trips (see also above, under Hotels), US$7.50-12.50 each (sometimes less) for 3-7 hrs as long as there are 4 or more in a group. It is almost impossible to arrange boat trips the evening before; just wander down the main street at 1000, ask around for names of boat men, and you can not fail. Hol Chan gets very crowded and the earlier you get there the better. Try to ascertain that the boat operator is reliable. We have received reports of theft of valuables left on board while snorkelling and even of swimmers being left in the water while the boat man went off to pick up another group. Protect against sunburn on reef trips, even while snorkelling. Mervin, a local man, is reliable for snorkelling trips, he will also take you to Belize City. Try 'Bongo' for yacht trips to the reefs, 'first mate' Donna (a Canadian) will guide first time snorkellers. Another is Ignacio; also Gamoosa and his wife Tina, who may spend all day with you on the reef and then sometimes invites you to his house to eat the fish and lobster you have caught, prepared deliciously by his wife; she also offers a healthy breakfast of banana, yoghurt, granola and honey for US$2.50. Also recommended is Alfonso Rosardo, a Mexican, reef trips for up to 6 people, 5-6 hrs, sometimes offers meals at his house afterwards. Also recommended is Lawrence (next to *Riva's Guest House*), Obdulio Lulu (a man) at *Tom's Hotel* goes to Hol Chan and San Pedro for a full day (if he catches a barracuda on the return, he will barbecue it at the hotel for US$0.75), Raoul and Charles, also from *Tom's Hotel*, US$12.50; also Harrison (ask around for him, rec). Lobster fishing and diving for conch is also possible. 'Island Sun', near the 'cutting', local husband and American wife, very conscientious; day tours to reef, plus snorkel hire (1000-1400); day tour to San Pedro and Hol Chan, plus snorkel hire, plus entry fee for reserve, rec. Snorkel Equipment Rental and Pastries Shop, do tour, rental gear, on same route 1015-1630, boat has sunshade. Capt Jim Novelo, of *Sunrise* boat, does daily trips to Hol Chan and San Pedro, 1000-1600, and snorkelling excursions to the Turneffe Islands, Half Moon Caye and Blue Hole, 0630-1700, every Tues, December-April, July-August, or on request, T 022-2195, F 022-2239. A sailing boat also goes to Hol Chan, but the trip takes a long time, leaving only a short while for snorkelling, departs 1000, US$12 for a day. Mask, snorkel and fins for US$2.50, cheapest (for instance at the post office, or *Sammie's Pastry Shop*). Benji, owner of a small sailboat and Joe Joe, his Rasta captain, will take you to Placenica or the Cayes, fun.

Wind-surfing equipment hire from Orlando, US$10/hr, poor quality, bring your own or go to San Pedro. **Canoes** for hire from Salvador, at painted house behind *Marin's* restaurant, US$10 a day. Go **fishing** with Rolly Rosardo, 4 hrs, US$45, up to 5 people, equipment, fresh bait and instruction provided. **Diving** Frank and Janie Bounting of Belize Diving Service (PO Box 667, T 44307, ext 143 mainland side, past the football pitch) charge US$55 for 2 scuba dives, day and night, good equipment, good value; they also offer a 4-day PADI certificate course for US$300, rec, also 2 and 3-day trips to Lighthouse Reef on the *Reef Roamer*, highly rec; the 3-day trip comprises 7 dives, including the Blue Hole, a visit to a bird reserve, good food and crew, US$290. Frenchie's Diving Service, T 022-2234, charges US$330 for a 4-day PADI course, friendly and effective, 2-tank dive US$60, also advanced PADI instruction. For **sailing** charters, Jim and Dorothy Beveridge, 'Seaing is Belizing', who also run scuba trips to Goff's Caye Park and the Turneffe Islands (5-10 days). They arrange slide shows of the reefs and the Jaguar Reserve (Cockscomb) at 2000, from time to time, US$2, excellent photography, personally narrated (they, too, have a book exchange); PO Box 374, Belize City, T 022-2189. Ask Chocolate for all-day trips to the manatee reserve in the S of Belize, about US$25 pp for a group of at least 8. There is a sailing school, charging US$30 for a 5-hr, solo beginner's course. It may be possible to hire a boat for 6-8 people to Chetumal. There are also boats leaving for Placencia and Honduras from Caye Caulker, but be sure to get exit stamps and other documentation in Belize City first if going to Honduras.

English Caye, 12 miles off Belize City, is beautiful, with no facilities; take a day trip only. It is part of the reef so you can snorkel right off the beach. Sunrise Travel, Belize City, T 72051/32670, can help arrange a trip, book in advance, US$15.

The **Turneffe Islands** are one of Belize's 3 atolls. On **Big Caye Bokel** is *Turneffe Islands Lodge*, PO Box 480, Belize City, which can accommodate 16 guests for week-long fishing and scuba packages. *Turneffe Flats*, 56 Eve St, Belize City, T 02 45634, in a lovely location, also offers week-long packages, for fishing and scuba; it can take 12 guests, but is soon to expand. *Blackbird Caye Resort*, 81 West Collet Canal St, Belize City, T 02-77670, F 02-73092, is a new, ecologically-oriented resort on this 4,000 acre island used by the Oceanic Society and is a potential site for a Biosphere Reserve 2 underwater project. Reservations in the USA, T (713) 658-1142, F (713) 658-0379. Diving or fishing packages available, no bar, take your own alcohol.

Lighthouse Reef is the outermost of the 3 N-S reef systems off Belize, some 45 miles to the E of Belize City. There are 2 cayes of interest, Half Moon Caye (on which the lighthouse stands) and 12 miles to the N, the caye in which Blue Hole is found. **Half Moon Caye** is the site of the **Red-Footed Booby Sanctuary**, a national reserve. Besides the booby, which is unusual in that almost all the individuals have the white colour phase (normally they are dull brown), magnificent frigate birds nest on the island. The seabirds nest on the western side, which has dense vegetation (the eastern side is covered mainly in coconut palms). Of the 98 other bird species recorded on Half Moon Caye, 77 are migrants. Iguana, the wish willy (smaller than the iguana) and the *anolis allisoni* lizard inhabit the caye, and hawksbill and loggerhead turtles lay their eggs on the beaches. The Belize Audubon Society, 29 Regent Street, maintains the sanctuary; there is a lookout tower and trail. The lighthouse on the caye gives fine views of the reef. Around sunset you can watch the boobies from the lookout as they return from fishing. They land beside their waiting mates at the rate of about 50 a minute. They seem totally unbothered by humans.

There are no facilities; take all food, drink and fuel. On arrival you must register with the warden near the lighthouse (the warden will provide maps and tell you where you can camp).

In Lighthouse Reef is the *Blue Hole*, an almost circular sinkhole, 1,000 ft across and with depths exceeding 400 feet. It was studied by Jacques Cousteau in 1984. Stalagmites and stalactites can be found in the underwater cave. Scuba diving is outstanding at Lighthouse Reef, including 2 walls which descend almost vertically from 30-40 feet to several thousand.

Bobby takes passengers by sailing boat from Caye Caulker to Half Moon Caye and the Blue Hole for US$25 pp including food (bring your own tent and sleeping bag). To charter a motor boat in Belize City costs about US$50 pp if 10 people are going (6 hr journey). Bill Hinkis, in San Pedro Town, Ambergris Caye, offers 3-day sailing cruises to Lighthouse Reef for US$150 (you provide food, ice and fuel). Bill and his boat *Yanira* can be found beside the lagoon off Back Street, just N of the football field. Out Island Divers, San Pedro, do various 2-3 day trips. Other sailing vessels charge US$150-250 per day. Speed boats charge US$190 pp for a day-trip inc lunch and 3 dives, rec. The main dive in the Blue Hole is very deep, at least 130 ft (almost 50m). Check your own qualifications as the dive operator probably will not. It is well worth doing if you are qualified. Keep an eye on your computer or dive charts if doing subsequent dives.

For southern cayes, see under **Southern Belize**.

NORTHERN BELIZE

North Belize is notable for its agricultural productivity, sugar, fruit, market gardening, providing much of Belize's food. There are some notable wildlife sanctuaries and nature reserves, and a fair share of the country's countless Maya sites, many recently found and yet to be fully explored.

Two main roads penetrate the country from Belize City: one to the N and other to the W. The Northern Highway is very patched up as it leaves Belize City until it divides into the New Alignment, which is well paved to the Mexican border, and the Old Northern Highway (narrow, paved, in reasonable condition). Fifteen miles out of Belize City there is a turning left to **Bermudian Landing** (12 miles on a rough road from the turn off), once a transfer point for timber floated down the Belize river and now a small Creole village. Here there is a local wild life museum and the **Community Baboon Sanctuary** nearby, with black howler monkeys. Trails have been made in and around the reserve, which encompasses 8 villages, all of whose inhabitants collaborate to protect the howlers' habitat. Check with the Sanctuary warden if you wish to visit. Boats can be hired from the warden for river trips to see monkeys and birds. Booklet (US$3, excellent) from the Audubon Society, 29 Regent Street, Belize City. A guided walk costs US$6 pp. The warden will also arrange accommodation locally, T 44405. Many freelance guides seek business from arriving vehicles, but it is better to get a licensed guide from the visitor's centre. At Burrell Boom Cutoff, just before the Belize River bridge on the road to Bermudian Landing, is *Little Eden* (Fred and Sally Cuckow, T/F 028-2052, PO Box 1317, Belize City), 2 bedrooms, B, bed and breakfast, weekly rates available, camping possible, ceramics made and sold; at Bermudian Landing new cabañas have been built by John Estefan of the tour company, Jungle Drift (PO Box 1442, Belize City, T 02-32842, F 02-78160), river tours rec; canoe rentals in Burrell Boom for trips on Belize River to see birds, howler monkeys, manatee, hicatee. Bus from Belize City about midday, return 1700. A day trip is very difficult by public transport so it is best to stay the night.

The Northern Highway continues to **Sand Hill** where a dusty 3 mile road turns off to the NW to the **Crooked Tree Lagoons and Wildlife Sanctuary**, set up in 1984, an exceptionally rich area for birds. The mango and cashew trees in the village of Crooked Tree are said to be 100 years old. Birdwatching is best in the early morning, but the only bus from Belize City (Jex) leaves 1035, arriving at 1230, so for a day trip take an early Corozal bus, get off at the main road (about 1¼ hrs from Belize City) and walk or hitch to the Sanctuary. Lots of birds can be seen on the walk, especially near the lagoon. Glenn Crawford is a very good guide. It is easy to get a lift, and someone is usually willing to take visitors back to the main road for a small charge. Entry is free but you must register at the visitor's centre, drinks are on sale, but take food. Cabins may be rented at US$33 for a night, up to 4 people. There is a helpful, friendly warden, Steve, who will let you sleep on the porch of the visitors' centre. Camping and cheap rooms (house of Rev Rhayburn, E, rec, meals available) can also be arranged if you ask. **B** *Paradise Inn*, run by the Crawfords, is well maintained and friendly, better than some of the other lodges, T 02-52535, F 02-52534, boat trips, fishing, horse riding and tours available. **A** *Bird's Eye View Lodge*, T 02-32040 (manager Verna Samuels; in USA T New York 718-845-0749), also bunk accommodation, US$10, camping US$5, meals available, boat trips, horseriding, canoe rental, nature tours with licensed guide. Ask for information at the Audubon Society (address above).

N of Sand Hill the road forks, the quicker route heading direct to Orange Walk, the older road looping N then NW.

The Maya remains of **Altun Ha**, 31 miles N of Belize City and 2 miles off the old Northern Highway, are worth a visit, entrance US$1.50 (insect repellent necessary); they are open 0900-1700. Since there is so little transport on this road, hitching is not rec, best to go in a private vehicle or a tour group. Vehicles leave Belize City for **Maskall** village, 8 miles N of Altun Ha, several days a week, but same-day return is not possible. Camping is not permitted at the site and there is no accommodation in nearby villages. Tourist Board booklets on the ruins are out of print now. The site consists of 2 central plazas surrounded by thirteen partially excavated pyramids and temples. What the visitor sees now is composite, not how the site would have been at any one time in the past. Nearby is a large reservoir, now called Rockstone Road ('Altun Ha' is a rough translation of the modern name). The largest piece of worked Maya jade ever found, a head of the Sun God Kinich Ahau weighing $9\frac{1}{2}$ pounds, was found here, in the main temple (B-4) in 1968. It is now in a bank vault in Belize City.

Beyond Maskall is **A+ Maruba Resort** (T 03-22199), a hotel, restaurant and spa, all rooms different, some a/c, German spoken, good birdwatching, including storks in the nearby swamp; has caged animals and birds.

The New Alignment runs to (66 miles) Orange Walk, centre of a district where about 17,000 Creoles, Mennonites and Maya Indians get their living from timber, sugar planting and general agriculture.

The population of **Orange Walk**, a bustling agricultural centre and the country's second city, is 10,410. A toll bridge (US$0.40) now spans the New River a few miles S of the town at Tower Hill. Spanish is the predominant language. It is a centre for refugees from other parts of Central America, although Mennonites from the surrounding colonies also use it as their marketing and supply town. There are some pleasant wooden buildings on the streets leading off Queen Victoria Avenue, which is the main road through town. The clock tower, town hall and Park, on this street at the heart of the city, is where the Belize City-Mexico border buses stop. Also on this street, which is dusty in dry weather, are some concrete buildings such as 'Big Pink', otherwise known as *Mi Amor Hotel*, Chinese restaurants, shoe shops, electrical goods sellers and purveyors of reggae music. The other public buildings are beside the football pitch, while the Catholic cathedral and school are towards the river from the Park (take Church St out of the Park). The only battle fought on Belizean soil took place here, during the Yucatecan Race Wars (1840-1860s); the Maya leader, Marcus Canul was shot in the fighting.

Hotels and Restaurants C *Victoria*, 40 Belize Rd (Main St), T 03-22518, a/c, shower, hot water, parking, quite comfortable, pool; **D** *Camie's Hotel and Restaurant*, on Park at Queen Victoria Avenue, T 03-22661, with bath and fan, hot rooms, spartan but OK, offstreet parking; **C** *Chula Vista Hotel*, Trial Farm, T 03-22227, at gas station (closed) just N of town, safe, clean, helpful owner, but overpriced. **D** *Mi Amor*, 19 Belize-Corozal road, T 03-22031, with shared bath, **C** with bath and fan, **B** with a/c, restaurant; **E** *Jane's*, 2 Baker's St, T 22473 (extension on Market Lane), large house in pleasant location; **E** *La Nueva Ola*, 73 Otro Benque Rd, T 03-22104.

The majority of restaurants in town are Chinese, eg *Hong Kong II*, next to *Mi Amor*, *Golden Gate*, Baker's St, Chinese specialities, cheap. *Julie's*, nr police station, good, inexpensive creole cooking; similarly at *Juanita's*, 8 Santa Ana St (take road beside Shell station), open 0600 for breakfast and all meals. Most restaurants and bars are open on Sun. Many bars have prostitutes, but not *San Martín*. About $1\frac{1}{2}$ miles from the centre is *The Diner*, good meals for US$3, very friendly, taxi US$4 or walk.

Exchange Scotia Bank on Park; Bank of Belize on Main Street (down Park St from Park, turn left); same hours as Belize City (**see p 539**). Shell Station will change TCs.

Bus All Chetumal buses pass Orange Walk Town (hourly); Belize-Orange Walk, US$1.75.

A road heads W from Orange Walk, then turns S, parallel first to the Mexican border, then the Guatemalan (where it becomes unmade). Along this road are several archaeological sites: **Cuello** is 4 miles W on San Antonio road, behind

Cuello Distillery (ask there for permission to visit); taxi about US$3.50. Site dates back to 2600 BC; although it has yielded important discoveries in the study of Maya and pre-Maya cultures, there is little for the layman to appreciate and no facilities for visitors. At **Yo Creek**, the road divides, N to San Antonio, and S, through miles of cane fields and tiny farming settlements parallel to the Mexican border as far as **San Felipe** (20 miles—via San Lazaro, Trinidad and August Pine Ridge). At San Felipe, a branch leads SE to Indian Church (35 miles from Orange Walk, 1 hr driving on improved, white marl road, passable all year, 4WD needed when wet).

Lamanai, one of Belize's largest sites, stretches along the W side of New River Lagoon 22 miles by river S of Orange Walk. While the earliest buildings were erected about 700 BC, culminating in the completion of the 112-feet-high major temple, N10-43, about 100 BC (the tallest known preclassic, Maya structure), there is evidence the site was occupied from 1500 BC. With the Spanish and British sites mentioned below, and the present day refugee village nearby, Lamanai has a very long history. The Maya site has been partially cleared, but covers a large area so a guide is recommended. The views from temple N10-43, dedicated to Chac, are superb; look for the Yin-Yang-like symbol below the throne on one of the other main temples, which also has a 4-metre tall mask overlooking its plaza. Visitors can wander freely along narrow trails and climb the stairways. At nearby **Indian Church** a Spanish mission was built over one of the Maya temples in 1580; the British established a sugar mill here last century; remains of both buildings can still be seen. Note the huge flywheel engulfed by a strangler fig. The archaeological reserve is jungle again and howler monkeys can be seen (with luck) in the trees. There are many birds, and mosquitoes in the wet season, but the best way to see birds is to reach Lamanai by boat. The earlier you go the better. Boats can be hired in Orange Walk, Shipyard or Guinea Grass (US$100 for 6). Herminio and Antonio Novelo run boat trips from Orange Walk (T 03-22293, F 03-22201, PO Box 95, 20 Lovers Lane), 5 passengers per boat, 1½-2 hrs to Lamanai. If staying in Orange Walk, leave after a 0600 breakfast; if coming from Belize City, take the 0600 Batty Express to be in Orange Walk by 0700, you return from Lamanai in time to take a pm bus back to Belize City. Accommodation at Indian Church: **A+ Lamanai Outpost Lodge**, opened 1992 by Colin and Ellen Howells, T/F 23-3578, a short walk from Lamanai ruins, overlooking New River Lagoon, package deals available, day tours, 28ft pontoon boat, canoes, thatched wooden cabins with bath and fan, hot water, electricity, restaurant, still expanding.

West of San Felipe is Blue Creek (10 miles), largest of the trim Mennonite settlements clustered as far W as Neustadt. Many of the inhabitants of these close-knit villages arrived in 1959—members of a Canadian colony which had migrated to Chihuahua to escape encroaching modernity; they preserve their Low German dialect, are exempt from military service, and their industry now supplies the country with most of its poultry, eggs and vegetables. A large area to the S along the **Rio Bravo** has been set aside as a conservation area (see **Nature Conservation** in the Introduction). A bad road can be followed 35 miles S to Gallon Jug, where **Chan Chich**, a jungle tourism lodge, has been built around a small Maya ruin; recommended, PO Box 37, Belize City, T 02-75634, F 02-75635 (flights to Chan Chich can be chartered). A better road has recently been cut S to San José, from where seasonal tracks lead E to Hill Bank and S to the Belize River and San Ignacio; travel in this region is strictly a dry weather affair.

From Orange Walk a road crosses New River and runs 6 miles NE to **San Estevan**. San Estevan can also be reached either by a poor road going N from Carmelita (the junction of the Old and New Alignments of the Northern Highway, 7 miles S of Orange Walk), or by a road heading SE from the Northern Highway between San José and San Pablo. These 2 towns, some 10 miles N of Orange Walk, merge into one another; the turning, unsigned on the right is before San Pablo proper. Drive 4 miles on a rough road through sugar cane field to a T-junction; turn right and after 3 miles you come to a hand-cranked ferry across the New River (fare anything from nothing to US$1.50, operates 0600-2200). If going to Progresso and Sarteneja, after the ferry turn left up the hill to the police station, where the road bears right. Follow this road straight through San Estevan. The Maya ruins near San Estevan have reportedly been 'flattened' to a large extent and are not very impressive. 10 miles from San Estevan is a road junction: straight on is **Progresso**, a village picturesquely located on the lagoon of the same name. The right turn, signposted, runs off to the Mennonite village of Little Belize and continues (in poor condition) to **Chunox**, a village with many Maya houses of pole construction. In the dry season it is possible to drive from Chunox to the Maya site of Cerros (see below).

The main road continues E, in improved state, over swampy land to **Sarteneja** (40 miles from Orange Walk; 1 hrs drive, only impassable in the very wet), a small fishing and boat-building settlement founded by Yucatán refugees in 19th century. There are many remains of an extensive Maya city scattered throughout the village. You can stay at *Diani's*, on the seashore, D, restaurant. Houses can be rented for longer stays. The main catch is lobster and conch. On Easter Sunday there is a regatta, with all types of boat racing, dancing and music; very popular. There is also windsurfing. Sarteneja can be reached by boat from Corozal in $^{1}/_{2}$ hr, but only private charters, so very expensive (compared with 3 hrs by road). Bus from Belize City daily, around noon, through Orange Walk; return bus 0330.

Three miles before Sarteneja is the visitors' centre for the **Shipstern Nature Reserve**, which covers 9,000 ha of this NE tip of Belize. Hardwood forests, saline lagoon systems and wide belts of savannah shelter a wide range of mammals (all the fauna found elsewhere in Belize, except monkeys), reptiles and 200 species of birds. Of the mammals you are most likely to see coatis and foxes. Also, there are mounds of Maya houses and fields everywhere. The remotest forest, S of the lagoon, is not accessible to short-term visitors. There is a botanical trail leading into the forest with trees labelled with Latin and local Yucatec Maya names; a booklet is available. At the visitor's centre is the Butterfly Breeding Centre, where pupae are bred for sale to European butterfly houses; 200 species can be seen in the reserve. Entry free, guided tours 1-4 people US$12.50, 5-8 US$2.50 pp, open daily 0900-1200, 1300-1600 except Christmas and Easter. (Choose a sunny day for a visit if possible; on dull days the butterflies hide themselves in the foliage.) In the wet season, mosquito repellent is essential. There is no accommodation at the reserve other than for research students; stay either at *Diani's* in Sarteneja, or in Orange Walk (a day trip by private car is possible).

One mile from the Northern Highway, in San José and San Pablo, is the archaeological site of **Nohmul**, a ceremonial centre whose main acropolis dominates the surrounding cane fields (the name means 'Great Mound'). Permission to visit the site must be obtained from Sr Estevan Itzab, whose house is opposite the water tower.

The Northern Highway continues to **Corozal** (96 miles from Belize City, population 7,268), formerly the centre of the sugar industry. It is a mixture of modern concrete commercial buildings and Caribbean clapboard seafront houses on stilts. Much of the old town was destroyed by Hurricane Janet in 1955. Like Orange Walk Town it is economically depressed because the local sugar factory has been closed; there has been a greater dependence on marijuana as a result. Corozal is much the safer place. It is open to the sea with a pleasant waterfront where the market is held, but no beach.

Hotels and Restaurants Two motels: **C** *Caribbean Motel and Trailer Park*, South End (PO Box 55, T 04-22045), basic, restaurant with great cheeseburgers; **A/B** *Tony's*, South End also,

T 04-22055, F 04-22829, C with a/c, clean, comfortable units in landscaped grounds, rec, but restaurant overpriced. **D** *Nestor's*, 123, 5th Av South (T 04-22354), with bath and fan, OK but basic, refrescos available, good food but noisy; **E** *Capri*, 14 Fourth Ave, on the seafront, T 04-22042, somewhat run down; **E** *Maya*, South End, T 04-22082, hot water, quieter than *Nestor's* but food not as good, plain meal US$5. Other restaurants: *Club Campesino*, decent bar, good fried chicken after 1800; *Skytop*, 5th Av South, friendly, good food, excellent breakfast, rec, good view from roof; *Border*, 6th Av South, friendly Chinese, good food, cheap; *Rexo*, North 5th St, Chinese; also Chinese: *Bumpers* (rec); *King of Kings*; *Hong Kong*.

Camping *Caribbean Motel and Trailer Park*, see above, camping possible but not very safe (US$2 pp), shaded sites, good restaurant, beach.

Exchange Barclays Bank International, Bank of Nova Scotia, open same hours as Belize City (**see p 539**).

Air Maya Airways, 2 flights daily to San Pedro (Ambergris Caye), and on to Belize City, 0800 and 1530 (not Sunday). Airstrip 3m S, taxi US$1.50.

Buses There are 15 buses a day from Belize to **Corozal** by Venus Bus, Magazine Road, and Batty Bus, 54 East Collet Canal, 3½-5 hrs, US$3.75. Both continue to Chetumal where there is a new bus terminal on the outskirts of town; because of the frequency, there is no need to take a colectivo to the Mexican border unless travelling at unusual hours (US$2.50). The increased frequency of buses to Chetumal and the number of money changers cater for Belizeans shopping cheaply in Mexico—very popular, book early. For those coming from Mexico who are more interested in Tikal than Belize, it is possible to make the journey border to border in a day, with a change of bus, to Novelo's, in Belize City. Timetables change frequently, so check at the time of travel. There are also tourist minibuses which avoid Belize City. Fishermen return to Sartaneja from Corozal pm, you can bargain for a ride.

6 miles NE of Corozal, to the right of the road to Chetumal, is **4 Miles Lagoon**, about ¼ mile off the road (buses will drop you there). Clean swimming, better than Corozal bay, some food and drinks available; it is often crowded at weekends.

A road leads 7 miles NE to **Consejo**, a seaside fishing village on Chetumal Bay; taxi about US$10. **C** *Adventure Inn*, no meals, rising to L full board, T 04-2187 (US res: 813-346-1997), low-key pleasant resort in Consejo Shores residential development, 15 well-equipped cottages, many facilities, airport pickup arranged (no public transport), bar and restaurant open from 0700, archaeological trips arranged. **D-E** *Kelly's Hotel*, No 1 Consejo Shores, only 2 rooms, basic but clean and quiet, no phone contact.

Across the bay to the S of Corozal stand the mounds of **Cerros**, once an active Maya trading port whose central area was reached by canal. Some of the site is flooded but 1 pyramid, 21m high with stucco masks on its walls, has been partially excavated. Boat from Corozal, walk around bay (boat needed to cross mouth of the New River) or dry-season vehicular trail from Progresso and Chunox (see above). More easily accessible are the ruins of **Santa Rita**, only a mile out on the Northern Highway, opposite the Coca Cola plant; once a powerful and cosmopolitan city, and still occupied when the Spaniards arrived in Belize, the site's post-classic murals and buildings have long been destroyed; only 50-foot-tall Structure 7 remains standing.

8 miles N beyond Corozal is the Mexican frontier, where a bridge across the Río Hondo connects with Chetumal, 7 miles into Mexico. Border crossing formalities are relatively relaxed, and open 24 hrs a day. Exit tax from Belize, US$0.50. Driving time, Belize-frontier, 3 hrs, Belize City-Chetumal, 4-5 hrs including the border stop. (Taxi, US$4 Corozal-border, US$16.50 Corozal-Chetumal, bus, Belize City-Chetumal US$5). From Chetumal to Belize City Venus Bus runs hourly between 0400 and 1000, Batty Bus runs at 1100, 1400 (express), 1600 and 1830. The buses operate as local buses until they hit the Northern Highway, then they speed up. Mexican tourist cards for 30 days are available at the border; to be safe, get one at the Mexican Consulate in Belize City. If entering Belize for only a few days, you can ask the Mexican officials to save your tourist card for you (but don't depend on it). If you want to return with a new tourist card for a full 30 days you must get it in Belize City. The Belizean Consulate in Chetumal is at Av Alvaro Obregón 232-1. If driving into Belize, third party insurance is obligatory,

available from the building opposite the immigration post. It is possible to buy pesos at the border with either US, Canadian or Belizean dollars (outside office hours, try the shops; rates at the border are on a par with those in the Yucatán). If coming from Mexico it is best to get rid of pesos at the border. Bargain for good rates of exchange at the border (there is a small bank near customs, so compare rates), better here than with money changers in Orange Walk Town or Corozal.

WESTERN BELIZE

W Belize, from Belmopan to the Guatemalan border, has some spectacular natural sights, exciting rivers and, in the Mountain Pine Ridge area, some of the best limestone scenery in Central America, notably waterfalls and caves. There are many Maya sites.

The Western Highway leaves Belize City past the cemetery, where burial vaults stand elevated above the boggy ground, and runs through palmetto scrub and savannah landscapes created by l9th century timber cutting. At Mile 16 is Hattieville (see above) from which an all-weather road runs N to **Burrell Boom** (Texaco station) and the Northern Highway, a convenient bypass for motorists wishing to avoid Belize City. The Highway roughly parallels the Sibun River, once a major trading artery where mahogany logs were floated down to the coast in the rainy season; the placename 'Boom' recalls spots where chains were stretched across rivers to catch the logs.

The small but excellent **Belize Zoo**, moved in 1992 to a new location close to its old site at Mile 28.5; it is open daily 0900-1600, US$5. Wonderful collection of local species (originally gathered for a wildlife film), lovingly cared-for and displayed in wire-mesh enclosures amid native trees and shady vegetation, including jaguar and smaller cats, pacas (called 'gibnuts' in Belize), snakes, monkeys, parrots, crocodile, tapir ('mountain cow'), peccary ('wari') and much more. Rec, even for those who hate zoos. Get there early to avoid coach parties' arrival. Tours by enthusiastic guides; T-shirts and postcards sold for fundraising. Nearest restaurant 3 miles away, only cold drinks sold at the zoo.

The highway gently climbs toward the foothills of the Maya Mountains through stands of Caribbean pine. Look out for the foothill known as the 'Sleeping Giant', seen in profile S of the highway when heading W. About 5 miles beyond the Zoo a new track runs SE to **Gales Point**, a charming fishing village of 300 on a peninsula at the S end of Manatee Lagoon, 15 miles N of Dangriga. The villagers are keen to preserve their natural resources and there are a lot of the endangered manatee and hawksbill turtles. Boat tours of the lagoon are rec. Turn off the highway at **La Democracia** (signed Manatee Road) and head E, then SE, around Cumberland Hill, to join the Gales Point-Melinda road about 3 miles S of Gales Point (La Democracia to the junction 23.2 miles). At **Melinda Forest Station** turnoff it is signed Belize New Road. The government plans in time to upgrade the road as a short cut to Dangriga, bypassing Belmopan; at present it is suitable only for sturdy vehicles, although from Gales Point to Dangriga it is good. (**L Manatee Lodge**, resort fishing camp, about US$l,000 for 7-day all-inclusive package; T 77593, US res: T 800- 782-7238). The Gales Point Bed and Breakfast Association arranges basic accommodation, E, no indoor plumbing, meals available, contact Hortence Welch on arrival. Day and overnight excursions of a wide variety, from US$30 per boat holding 6-8 people, contact Kevin Andrewin of Manatee Tour Guides Association on arrival. Community phone, T 05-22087, ask for Alice or Josephine. Gales Point can be reached by inland waterways from Belize City. Boats leave Belize (Bolton Bridge) at 1000 Wed and Sat for Gales Point US$10, return Wed, Fri, 0400. There is also a bus at 0600 from Belize (Pound Yard Bridge) Mon, Wed, Fri and Sat, US$3.

At Mile 31.5 is the **Monkey Bay Wildlife Sanctuary**, sponsored by the Belize Center for Environmental Studies (PO Box 666, Belize City, T 02-45545) and Rainforest Action Information Network (RAIN, PO Box 4418, Seattle, Washington 98104, T 206-324-7163). It contains 1,070 acres of tropical forest and savannah between the Highway and the Sibun River ('no monkeys and no bay, but lots of natural beauty, hospitality and peace'—Darrell Hutchinson, Olds, Canada). Birds are abundant and there is a good chance of seeing mammals. Pedro, the caretaker, can be hired for guided tours of the trails. You can camp for US$5, swim in a river, showers available, take meals with family for US$4 (it is planned to provide sleeping accommodation and cooking facilites in the future). Nearby at mile 33 is **JB's**, a bar and restaurant 'in the middle of nowhere', a popular stopping place decorated with the insignia of the British soldiers who have passed through.

47 miles from Belize City, a minor road runs 2 miles N to **Banana Bank Ranch**, resort accommodation, B with meals, horseriding, birding, river trips, etc, American- owned, Caroline and John Carr (T 08-22677, PO Box 48, Belmopan). A mile further on is the highway junction for Belmopan and Dangriga. At the confluence of the Belize River and Roaring Creek here is the 50-acre **Guanacaste Park**, a national park protecting a parcel of rainforest and a huge 100-year-old guanacaste (tubroos) tree, which shelters a wide collection of epiphytes including orchids. Many mammals (jaguarundi, kinkajou, agouti, etc) and up to 100 species of birds may be seen from the 3 miles of nature trails cut along the river. This is a particularly attractive swimming and picnicking spot at which to break the journey to Guatemala. It has a visitors' centre, where luggage can be left. Take an early morning bus from Belize City, see the park in a couple of hours, then pick up a bus going to San Ignacio or Dangriga.

Soon after the junction is **Roaring Creek** (pop, 1,000), once a thriving town but now rather overshadowed by the nearby capital. Six miles beyond the turning to the capital is **Warrie Head Ranch and Lodge**, Teakettle Village, T 02-77185 (PO Box 244, Belize City), a working farm offering accommodation. The Highway now becomes narrower and curves through increasingly lush countryside. At Mile 62 is **C Caesar's Place**, camping US$2.50 pp with showers and bathroom facilities, restaurant and bar, good general store, swimming, musicians welcome to play with 'in-house' group, T 092-2341 (PO Box 48, San Ignacio, under same ownership as *Black Rock*—see below). The important but unimpressive **Baking Pot** archaeological site is just beyond the bridge over Barton Creek (Mile 64); 2 more miles brings us to **Georgeville** (another Mennonite community; try the ice cream and cheese), from where a gravel road runs S into the Mountain Pine Ridge Forest Reserve (see below). The highway passes the turnoff at Norland for **Spanish Lookout**, a Mennonite settlement area 6 miles N; ask in San Ignacio if you are interested in visiting this area. Climbing up a forested valley the road reaches Santa Elena, linked by the substantial Hawkesworth suspension bridge to its twin city of San Ignacio. (At the bridge is Belize's first set of traffic lights; the bridge is only 1 vehicle's width.)

72 miles from Belize City and ten miles from the border, **San Ignacio** (locally called Cayo) is the capital of Cayo District and western Belize's largest town (pop about 7,990 inc Santa Elena), a bustling agricultural centre serving the citrus, cattle and peanut farms of the area, and a good base for excursions into the Mountain Pine Ridge. It stands amid attractive wooded hills at 200-500 feet, with a good climate, and is a nice town to rest in after Guatemala.

Hotels In centre of town: Up the hill, as you turn left on the San Ignacio side of the suspension bridge, is **A+-B** *San Ignacio*, 18 Buena Vista St, T 092-2034/2125, F 092-2134, on road to Benque Viejo, with bath, a/c or fan, hot water, clean, helpful staff, swimming pool, excellent restaurant, highly rec, bar opens at 1000; **C** *Venus*, 29 Burns Av, with bath, E without, fan, clean, quiet, rec; **D** *Belmoral*, 12 Burns Av, T 092-2024, with shower, or F per bed without, hot water, fan, a bit noisy (clean and friendly); **D** *Jaguar*, 19 Burns Av (Nazim Juan), without

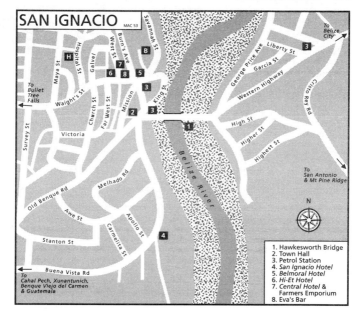

SAN IGNACIO MAP 53

To Belize City

Liberty St

Savannah St

Burn's Ave

West St

Hospital St

Maya St

Galvez St

Church St

Far West St

Mission Rd

King St

George Price Ave

Garcia St

Western Highway

Cristo Rey Rd

To Bullet Tree Falls

Waight's St

High St

Higher St

Highest St

Survey Rd

Victoria

Melhado Rd

Belize River

To San Antonio & Mt Pine Ridge

Old Benque Rd

Awe St

Apollo St

Carmelita St

N

Stanton St

Buena Vista Rd

To Cahal Pech, Xunantunich, Benque Viejo del Carmen & Guatemala

1. Hawkesworth Bridge
2. Town Hall
3. Petrol Station
4. San Ignacio Hotel
5. Belmoral Hotel
6. Hi-Et Hotel
7. Central Hotel & Farmers Emporium
8. Eva's Bar

bath, fan, good restaurant, bar, very helpful with tourist information, rec; **D** *Martha's Guest House*, 10 West St, T 092-2276, inc breakfast, friendly, clean, kitchen facilities, the family also runs August Laundromat; **E-D** *Piache*, 18 Buena Vista Rd, around the bend in the road from *San Ignacio* (PO Box 54, T 092-2032/2109) with or without bath, cold water, basic, bar in pm; **E** *Central*, 24 Burns Av, T 092-2253, clean, secure, fans, shared hot showers, book exchange, friendly, verandah with hammocks, rec, no restaurant but breakfast and packed lunches possible, excellent value; **E** *Hi-Et*, 12 West St, T 092-2828, noisy, fans, low partition walls, family run, clothes washing permitted, no meals; **F** Mrs Espat's, up the hill from *Hi-Et*, rooms next door to small shop and house; **E** *Imperial*, 22 Burns Av, basic, noisy, shared bath, dirty.

Camping *Mida's*, 1 km from town, near river, go down Burns Av, turn right down unpaved road after wooden church, after 200 yards turn left, campground is 300 yards on right, US$15 per car and 2 people inc electricity, cabins available at US$20, hot showers, electricity, water, restaurant, English owner, Mike, and his Belizean wife, Maria, very helpful, also organize trips to Tikal. 1 km further is *Cosmos* camping, US$5, washing and cooking facilities, tent renting, American-owned, rec.

Restaurants Doña Elvira Espat serves good meals at her house (inc breakfast), advance notice required, good, friendly with a wealth of local information (no sign, corner of Galvez Street and Bullet Tree Road). *Maxim's*, Bullet Tree Rd and Far West St, Chinese, cheap, very good food, noisy TV at the bar; *Serendip*, 27 Burns Av, good food and good value, Sri Lankan owners; *Early Bird*, between Burns and West St, cheap local food, open every day, lots of peace corps volunteers eat there. Highly informative is Bob at *Eva's Bar*, 22 Burns Av, T 092-2267, good, helpful, local dishes, bike rental, tours (see below). *Farmers Emporium*, 24 Burns Av, a shop selling wholewheat bread, raisins, juices, fresh milk and cheese, also handicrafts. *Belbrit*, 30 Burns Av, good breakfast and service, clean. *Roots*, vegetarian, near square, good. Fruit and vegetable market every Sat am. Note that all shops and businesses close 1700-1900.

On a hill, with TV station, beside the road to Benque Viejo before the edge of town is *Cahal Pech* tavern, good cheap drinks and meals, with music and dancing at weekends, the place to be, live bands are broadcast on TV and radio all over Belize, good views. On a hill across the track from the tavern is Cahal Pech archaeological site (see below). The *Blue*

Angel on Burns Av is popular with the younger crowd, very dark, fun, live bands, dancing, small admission charge.

Exchange Belize Bank offers full service, TCs, Visa and Mastercard cash advances; Atlantic Bank, Burns Av also does cash advances. Changers in the town square give better rates of exchange for dollars cash and travellers' cheques than you can get at the border with Guatemala. The best place to change dollars into quetzales is in Guatemala.

Post Office Above the police station, reliable parcel service.

Tours Local taxis which offer tours of Mountain Pine Ridge in the wet season probably won't get very far; also, taking a tour to Xunantunich is not really necessary. Canoe trips up the Macal River are well worthwhile. They take about 3 hrs upstream, half that on return, guides point out iguanas in the trees and bats asleep on the rock walls. Ask at *Eva's Bar* (T 092-2267) for information on canoe trips with Toni, bird and wildlife watching, visiting medicinal plant research farm (US$5 extra), small rapids, etc, 0830-1600, good value; or with Luis for good value tours of Mountain Pine Ridge; or with Chris Heckert, a German, who will take you to the Maya ruins at Caracol, about 30 miles (as the crow flies), S through the jungle (group of 8, US$300); or with Bob, who does jungle river trips, US$30 for 2 people in a canoe, all-day tour, highly rec. Bob is very helpful and will organize tours for you but you may end up with an indifferent guide, make sure you tell him exactly what you want. Hiring a canoe to go upstream without a guide is not rec unless you are highly proficient as there are class 2 rapids 1 hr from San Ignacio. *Red Rooster Bar*, US-run, has mountain bike hire, white water rafting trips, also hire out solo inflatable canoe, US$20 inc lunch.

Bus To **Belize City**: Batty Bus departs 1300, 1400, 1500 and 1600; early morning buses from the border stop at the bridge in front of the police station, later morning trips go from Benque Viejo at parking area behind Burns Avenue, US$2.50, 3½ hrs. A 1000 or 1100 bus will connect with the 1500 bus to Chetumal. Novelo, starts at 0400 and runs on the hour until about 1200. Taxi to Guatemalan border, about US$5 (colectivo US$3), to Xunantunich US$20, to Belize City US$75, to Tikal US$100. Minibuses also run to Tikal, US$75 for 7-8 people, making a day trip possible. Ask taxi drivers for information.

A short walk from San Ignacio (400m from *Hotel San Ignacio*) is **Cahal Pech**, a Maya site and nature reserve on a wooded hill overlooking the town. A small part of the centre is under reconstruction (the new work looks very bright). A museum is being built on site. Admission US$1.50. The man who sells tickets will lend you a guidebook written by some of the archaeologists who worked on the site; it is now out of print so must be returned. At nearby Tipu are the remains of one of the few old Spanish mission churches established in Belize. 4 miles W on a good road is Bullet Tree Falls on the western branch of the Belize River, here in its upper course known as the Macal River; a pleasant cascade amid relaxing surroundings. About 10 miles S, above the river and adjacent to the Chaa Creek Cottages at Ix Chel Farm (see below), is the unusual **Panti Trail**, established as a place for study and preservation of native medicinal plants by Dr Rosita Arvigo, an American disciple of Mayan healer Eligio Panti of San Antonio in the Mountain Pine Ridge. From the turn off on the Benque road it is a pleasant 4-mile walk to Ix Chel; lifts are often possible. The plants are labelled in 4 languages. Visits can be arranged by calling 08-23180; self-guided tour with field guide, US$5 pp, guided tours with local guide, US$7.50 pp, group tours with the director by arrangement (Belizeans free). Dr Arvigo sells selections of herbs (the jungle salve, US$5, has been found effective against mosquito bites) and a book on medicinal plants used by the Maya (US$8, US$2 postage and packing, from General Delivery, San Ignacio, Cayo District).

The British Army's Holdfast camp is about 12 miles from the border.

San Ignacio is on the eastern branch of the Old, or Belize River, known as the Macal, navigable almost to the Guatemalan frontier. The river journey of 121 miles from Belize, broken by many rapids, needs considerable ingenuity to negotiate the numerous 'runs'.

Other Places to Stay Nearby W of San Ignacio: **A+ Chaa Creek Cottages**, on the Macal River, 5 miles upstream from San Ignacio, inc breakfast, lunch US$9, dinner US$16.50, discounts June-Oct, set on a working farm in pleasant countryside, highly rec. Electricity in the restaurant/bar area only; cabins have oil lamps. You can swim or canoe in the river. Trips on the river, to Xunantunich, to Tikal, to Mountain Pine Ridge, to Caracol, nature walks, horse riding and jungle safaris organized by Chaa Creek Inland Expeditions; also joint vacations arranged with *Rum Point Inn*, Placencia. Latest project is blue morpho butterfly breeding centre. If coming by road, turn off the Benque road at Chial, 6 miles from San Ignacio; hotel will collect you by boat from San Ignacio (US$25 for 4), or from international airport (US$125); reservations PO Box 53, San Ignacio, T 092-2037, F 092-2501, or hotel office at 56 Burns Av, San Ignacio.

Nabitunich Cottages (Rudi and Margaret Juan), turn off the Benque road 1½ miles beyond Chial, offers spectacular views of Xunantunich and another, unexcavated Maya ruin, jungle trails, excellent birdwatching, horse riding, canoeing; T 093-2309, F 093-2096 or c/o Benque Viejo Post Office, Cayo. Room rates from **B** for d without meals to **A** full board. You may camp here, US$0.25.

A+ *duPlooys'*, turn left on the road to Benque on same road for Chaa Creek, then follow signs (including 1 steep hill), on the Macal River, T 092-3180, F 092-2057, including all meals in jungle lodge, A in hotel room, hot water showers, all day coffee and tea, bar with deck overlooking trees and river, a small jungle area on the 20-acre property, trips arranged to many local activities and sites. Run by Ken and Judy du Plooy formerly of Charleston, S Carolina. Good food, rec.

A *Windy Hill Cottages*, on Graceland Ranch 2 miles W off highway, bed and breakfast, T 092 2055, 14 cottage units, all d with bath, dining room, pool, nature trails, horse riding, river trips etc.

D *Parrot Nest*, run by Fred, near village of Bullet Tree Falls, 3 miles from San Ignacio (taxi US$5), small but comfortable tree houses in beautiful grounds by the river, breakfast and dinner inc, canoeing, birdwatching, horse riding available.

A *Black Rock*, on the Macal River, 20 mins walk from the end of the road from which turnings lead to *Chaa Creek* and *du Plooys'*, 'eco' resort with accommodation in tents under thatched roofs, solar-powered electricity and hot water, restaurant, hiking, riding, canoeing, birdwatching, excursions, without meals; Caesar Sherrard, PO Box 48, San Ignacio, Cayo, T 092-2341, F 092-3449 (see also *Caesar's Place*, above).

E of San Ignacio: **B-A** *Maya Mountain Lodge* (Bart and Suzi Mickler), ¾ mile from San Ignacio at 9 Cristo Rey Road (taxi from town US$2.50, bus US$0.25), welcoming, special weekly and monthly rates and for families, also discounts on lodging (50%) and food (20%) to backpackers with Trade & Travel Publications' *Handbooks*, T 092-2164, F 092-2029 (The Farm Store), PO Box 46, San Ignacio, laundry, postal service, self-guided nature trail. Swimming, hiking, riding, canoeing, fishing can be arranged. Explore Belize Tours in the region and beyond; also 'Parrot's Perch' social and educational area with resident naturalist and ornithologist. Edgar is a good taxi driver/guide.

Mountain Equestrian Trails, Mile 8, Mtn Pine Ridge Rd (from Georgeville), Central Farm PO, Cayo District, F 082-3235, T 082-3188 for reservations, 082-2149 for office, and 092-2197 for transport (Mr Parham), offers ½-day, full-day and 4-day adventure tours on horseback in western Belize, 'Turf' and 'Turf and Surf' packages, and other expeditions; bird watching tours start on the owners' verandah; accommodation in 4 *cabañas* doubles with bath, no electricity, hot water, mosquito nets, good food in *cantina*; highly rec (owners Jim and Marguerite Bevis, in conjunction with neighbouring landowners, have set up a biosphere reserve, incorporating nearby Salvadorean refugees).

Blancaneaux Lodge, Mountain Pine Ridge Rd, Central Farm, PO Box B, Cayo District, T/F 092-3878, once the mountain retreat of Francis Ford Coppola and his family, now villas and cabañas, full amenities, overlooking river, private air strip.

At **Xunantunich** ('Maiden of the Rock'), now freed from heavy bush, there are Classic Maya remains in beautiful surroundings; the heart of the city was 3 plazas aligned on a N-S axis, lined with many temples, the remains of a ball court, and surmounted by the 'Castillo'; at 130-ft this was thought to be the highest man made structure in Belize until recent measurement of the Sky Palace at Caracol; the impressive view takes in jungle, the lowlands of the Petén and the blue flanks of the Maya Mountains. Maya graffiti can still be seen on the wall of Structure A-16; friezes on the Castillo, some restored in modern plaster, represent astronomical symbols. Extensive excavations took place in 1959-60 but only limited restoration work has been undertaken. A leaflet on the area is available from the Archaeological Dept for US$0.15. About 1½ miles further N are the ruins of Actuncan, probably a satellite of Xunantunich; both sites show evidence of earthquake damage.

To reach Xunantunich hitch, or take a 0800-0830, or 0900-0930 bus from San Ignacio towards the border to the village of San José Succotz (7 miles, US$0.75), where a hand-operated ferry takes visitors and their cars across the Mopan River (0800-1700, free weekdays, US$0.50 at weekends); there is then a 20 mins walk uphill on dirt road (even motorcyclists may find the track impossible after rain). Xunantunich is open 0800-1700, entry US$1.50, no facilities for visitors, but very helpful guides at the site, bring own refreshments; beware of robbery on the road up to the ruins, government employees accompany visitors up the hill (try hitching back to the ferry with tourists travelling by car). You can swim in the river after visiting the ruins. Return buses to San Ignacio pass at about lunchtime. Just E of the ferry, Magaña's Art Centre and the Xunantunich Women's Group sell locally made crafts and clothing in a shop on a street off the highway. Opposite the ferry, a 1½ mile walk brings you to *Rancho de los Amigos*, a farm run by Americans Edward and Virginia Jenkins, T 093-2483 where you can stay in rural surroundings, C pp inc 2 home-cooked meals, vegetarian available, open air dining room built on the side of a Mayan temple, cabins, bucket showers, quiet, peaceful, also herbal healing and acupuncture, will pick you up at Xunantunich bus stop on highway.

San José Succotz is a large Yucatec Maya village below Xunantunich where Spanish is the first language and a few inhabitants preserve the old Maya customs of their ancestral village (San José in the Petén); the colourful fiestas of St Joseph and the Holy Cross are celebrated on 19 March and 3 May respectively each year. There is a Guatemalan Consulate on the Western Highway, opp the Xununtunich ferry.

Mountain Pine Ridge is a Forest Reserve (59,000 ha) covering the NW portion of the Maya Mountains. The undulating country is well-watered and covered in largely undisturbed temperate pine and gallery forest; in the valleys are lush hardwood forests filled with orchids, bromeliads and butterflies. The enjoyable river scenery, high waterfalls, numerous limestone caves and shady picnic sites attract about 50 visitors per day during the dry season—a popular excursion despite the rough roads. Two reasonable roads lead into the reserve: from Georgeville to the N and up from Santa Elena via Cristo Rey; these meet at **San Antonio**, a Mopan Maya village with many thatched-roof houses and the nearby Pacbitun archaeological site (where stelae and musical instruments have been unearthed). At San Antonio, the García Sisters have their workshop, museum and shop where they sell carvings in local slate; this is a regular stop on tours to the Mountain Pine Ridge. A donation of US$0.50 is requested; US$12.50 is charged to take photos of the sisters at work. The main forest road meanders along rocky spurs, from which unexpected and often breathtaking views emerge of jungle far below and streams plunging hundreds of feet over red-rock canyons; a lookout point has been provided to view the impressive **Hidden Valley Falls**, said to be over 1,000 ft high (often shrouded in fog October-January); on a clear day it is said you can see Belmopan from the viewpoint. On many heights stand forestry observation towers: bushfires are a constant threat in the dry season. 18 miles into the reserve the road crosses the **Río On**. Here, where the river tumbles in inviting pools over huge granite boulders, is one of Belize's most beautiful picnic and swimming spots. The rocks can be slippery and, in the wet season, bathing is not possible.

Five miles further is **Augustine** (also called Douglas D'Silva, or **Douglas Forest Station**), the main forest station (pop 170) where there is a shop, accommodation in 2 houses (bookable through the Forestry Dept in Belmopan) and a camping ground, US$1, no mattresses (see rangers for all information on the area). Keep your receipt, a guard checks it on the way out of Mountain Pine Ridge. A mile beyond Augustine is a cluster of caves in rich rainforest; the entrance to the **Rio Frio Cave** (in fact a tunnel) is over 65-ft high; many spectacular rock formations and sandy beaches where the river flows out. Trees in the parking area and along the Cuevas Gemelas nature trail, which starts 1 hr from the Rio Frio cave, are labelled. A beautiful excursion; highly rec. In the Mountain Pine Ridge note the frequent changes of colour of the soil and look out for the fascinating insect life. If lucky you may see deer.

Forestry roads continue S further into the mountains, reaching San Luis (6 miles), the only other inhabited camp in the area (pop 100, post office, sawmill and forest station), and continuing on over the granite uplands of the Vaca Plateau into the Chiquibul Forest Reserve (186,000 ha). About 20 miles SSW of Augustine is **Caracol**, a rediscovered Maya city; the area is now a National Monument Reservation. Caracol was established about 300 BC and continued well into the Late Classic period; glyphs record a victorious war against Tikal. Why Caracol was built in such a poorly-watered region is not known, but Maya engineers showed great ingenuity in constructing reservoirs and terracing the fields. The Sky Palace ('Caana') pyramid climbs 138 ft above the site, which is being excavated by members of the University of Central Florida. Excavations take place February-May but there are year-round caretakers who will show you around. The site is not open to wander around although charging and entry times are being considered. Throughout this largely unknown region are vast cave systems stretching W into Guatemala, but there are absolutely no facilities and none of the caves is open to the casual traveller. The only months in which a trip to Caracol can be quaranteed are April and May. A number of places in San Ignacio, and Mountain Equestrian Trails (see above), offer horseback tours to Caracol, US$185.

Mountain Pine Ridge has no public transport. Apart from tours, hiring your own vehicle or a taxi is the only alternative. The private pick-ups which go into San Ignacio from Augustine are usually packed, so hitching is impossible. Taxis charge US$88 for 5 people. Roads are passable but rough between January and May, but after June they are marginal and are impossible in the wet (September-November); essential to seek local advice at this time. The 4 forest reserves which cover the Maya Mountains are the responsibility of the Forestry Department, who have only about 20 rangers to patrol 400,000 ha of heavily-forested land. A hunting ban prohibits the carrying of firearms. Legislation, however, allows for controlled logging; all attempts to have some areas declared National Parks or biosphere reserves have so far been unsuccessful.

NB At the driest time of year, normally February to May, ie when the Mountain Pine Ridge is reasonably accessible, there is an ever-present danger of fire. Open fires are strictly prohibited and you are asked to be as careful as possible.

Nine miles up-river from San Ignacio is **Benque Viejo del Carmen**, near the Guatemalan frontier (road is now sealed). Population, 3,312, many of whom are Maya Mopan Indians. There are police and military barracks near the border. Visas and tourist cards must be obtained in Belize City. There is virtually no difference in the rates for buying quetzales from money changers on either side of the border. Lots of money changers at the border give excellent rates and will also change TCs at official BZ$/US$ rate with no commission. If entering here and going on to the Cayes, where commission is at least 2%, you might as well take advantage. If going to Tikal, change what money you think you will need at Banco de Guatemala at the border, where you will get a much better rate than anywhere in the Petén.

Hotels and Restaurants **E** *Hospedaje Roxy*, 70 Joseph St, basic. **E** *Hotel Maya*, 11 George St, T 093-2116, and **E** *Okis*, George St, T 093-2006, opposite the bus station, are the least bad. (The hotels on the Guatemalan side are much cheaper than Belize so if on a tight budget try to cross the border even late in the afternoon. From Benque to the border is a 20 mins walk—1.6 km) Meals at *Riverside Restaurant*, on main square; *Restaurant Los Angeles*, Church St; *Hawaii*, on main street, rec; or at one of picturesque huts.

Transport Novelo's run many daily buses from Belize City to **Benque Viejo**, US$3; frequent buses from San Ignacio to Benque Viejo, taxi US$10, or colectivo from central square, US$2 (or US$2 to Melchor de Mencos in Guatemala, 30 mins). To **Guatemala** from Benque Viejo by taxi, US$1.50 or US$0.50 by colectivo. Free passage of border only weekdays (or if your stay in Belize was 24 hrs or less), 0800-1200 and 1400-1700; at other times a fee is charged (US$1). On far side someone will carry the luggage to **Melchor de Mencos** (hotels, and money change possible—see **Guatemala, Section 3, El Petén**), where there is a landing strip (flights to Flores). There is also a road (very rough) on to Santa Elena, for Flores (a bus leaves the border for Flores at 1330, US$2, or several daily buses from Melchor de Mencos, 3½ hrs, US$2, leave Belize City at 0600, 0630 or 1015 to make a connection to Flores); unless you take a tourist minibus, US$10, it is only possible to get to Tikal by bus by asking the driver of the border-Flores bus to let you off at the road junction (El Cruce), where you can get a connecting bus to Tikal (**see same section of Guatemala chapter**). See that section also, under **Flores Travel Agents** for direct minibus services between Flores/Santa Elena and Belize City.

SOUTHERN BELIZE AND THE SOUTHERN CAYES

Southern Belize is the remotest part of the country, sparsely populated but with many Indian settlements akin to those across the border in Guatemala. Maya ruins abound and nature reserves are increasing in numbers. Roads are poor, not helped by the wetter climate. However, access to the attractive coast is improving.

The narrow Hummingbird Highway branches off the Western Highway 48 miles W of Belize City, passes Belmopan and branches 52 miles SE to Dangriga. Its surface is well-paved for the 12 miles to Caves Branch. The next section of Highway was being repaired and widened in 1993. It climbs through rich tropical hardwood forest until reaching Mile 13, where a track leads off to *St Herman's Cave*; the path passes through shady ferns until descending in steps to the cave entrance. You can walk for more than a mile underground: torch and spare batteries essential.

Two miles further on is the *Blue Hole National Park*, an azure blue swimming hole fringed with vines and ferns, fed by a stream which comes from St Herman's Cave and re-enters another 100 feet away. A sign on the roadway warns visitors against thieves; lock your car and leave someone on guard if possible when swimming. An armed guard and more wardens have been hired to prevent further theft and assaults.

There is a rest area and snack bar at Mile 21 and several *tiendas* thereafter for snacks and drinks, but otherwise few other stopping places. The peaks of the mountains continue to dominate the S side of the highway until about Mile 30, when the valley of the Stann Creek begins to widen out into Belize's most productive agricultural area. Large citrus groves stretch along the highway: grapefruit, bananas and Valencia oranges, which are processed into canned juices and concentrates at centres like Pomona (Mile 40). The drive to Dangriga from Belmopan can take from 2-2$\frac{1}{2}$ hrs, depending on road conditions.

Palacios Mountain Retreat, Augustus Palacio, St Martha, Hummingbird Highway, Cayo District, between Belmopan and Danriga, good for relaxing, *cabañas* US$5 pp, friendly, helpful, family atmosphere, safe, good local food; swimming in river, tours to waterfall in forest, caves and lagoon; beware sandflies.

Dangriga, chief town of the Stann Creek District, has a population of 6,838, largely Black Caribs (Garifunas—always ask before taking photographs). It is on the seashore, with the usual Belizean aspect of wooden houses elevated on piles, and is a cheerful and busily commercial place. Water and electricity can be in short supply. The 2 rivers which meet the sea here—North Stann Creek and Havana Creek—are alive with flotillas of boats and enthusiastic fishermen. There are several gas stations, a cinema, a good hospital and an airfield with regular flights. Mosquitoes and sand flies can be a nuisance on the narrow, dirty beach. Dangriga (until recently called Stann Creek) means 'standing waters' in Garifuna.

Local Holiday 18-19 Nov, Garifuna, or Settlement Day, re-enacting the landing of the Black Caribs in 1823, fleeing a failed rebellion in Honduras. Dancing all night and next day; very popular. All transport to Dangriga is booked up a week in advance and hotel rooms impossible to find. Private homes rent rooms, though. At this time, boats from Puerto Barrios to Punta Gorda (see below) tend to be full, but launches take passengers for US$10 pp.

Hotels A *Pelican Beach*, outside town (PO Box 14), on the beach N of town, T 05-22044, F 05-22570, L, with private bath and a/c, restaurant expensive, in need of investment (taxi from town US$2.50, or 15 mins walk from North Stann Creek). **A** *Bonefish*, Mahogany Street, T 05-22165, on seafront on outskirts of town, a/c, colour TV with US cable, hot water, takes Visa, good, refurbished 1993. **C** *Pal's Guest House*, 10 new units on beach, 868A Magoon Street, Dangriga, T (05) 22095, Dangriga Dive Centre, T (05) 23262, runs from here. **D** *Hub Guest House*, 573 South Riverside, T 05-22397, F 05-22813, with private bath, S end of bridge over Stann Creek, meals, helpful; **D** *Riverside*, 5 Commerce St, T 05-22168, F 05-22296, not always clean, good restaurant; **E** *Cameleon*, 119 Commerce St, T 05-22008, shared cold shower, fans, cramped but reasonably safe and friendly. **D** *Rio Mar*, 977 Southern Foreshore, friendly, good, music piped into all rooms, you will hear your neighbour's even if yours is turned off; **D** *Sofie's Hotel & Restaurant*, Chatuye St, unimpressive but pleasant; **E** *Tropical*, 115 Commerce Street; **E** *Catalina*, 37 Cedar St, T 05-22390, very small, dirty but friendly, store luggage. Also you can stay in private homes (basic), eg Miss Caroline's. There is a cooperative which runs a place to pitch a tent or sling a hammock. Unfurnished houses are rented out for US$20-30 a month.

Restaurants *Ten Kitchen*, next to Z-line bus office, good. At Mile 25.5 on the Hummingbird Highway, N of Dangriga, is *Hummingbird Café*, owned by Canadians Ron and Louise Lines, PO Box 120, Belmopan; excellent meals and very helpful. *Starlight* near *Cameleon*, towards bridge, Chinese, cheapish, good; *Ritchie's Dinette*, creole and Spanish food, cheap, simple, large portions, rec; *Sunrise*, similar; *Ricky's*, good reasonable local food; *Burger King* do good breakfasts.

Entertainment Listen for local music 'Punta Rock', a unique Garifuna/African based Carib sound, now popular throughout Belize. *Local Motion Disco*, next to *Cameleon*, open weekends, Punta rock, reggae, live music. A local band, the Turtles, maintain a Punta museum in town. Studios can be visited. Homemade instruments are a Garifuna speciality, especially drums.

Exchange Bank of Nova Scotia; Barclays Bank International; Belize Bank. Same hours as Belize City. (See p 539.)

Travel Agent The Treasure House at 64 Commerce St, T 05-22578, is very helpful. Run by Diane.

Bus from Belize City, Z Line, Magazine Street, several daily from 0700, plus 0600 Mon, returning daily from 0500, Sun at 0900, 1000, 1500, US$5, 4½ hrs (buy ticket in advance to reserve seat—the bus stops at the Blue Hole National Park); truck, US$1.25. Three buses daily to **Punta Gorda**, 1200, 1230 and 1930, 4-5 hrs, US$4.25 (very crowded), stops at Independence, near Mango Creek. Bus to **Placencia** Mon, Wed, Fri, Sat 1430, US$3.50, to **Belmopan** US$2.50, to **Gales Point**, 1200 Mon, Wed, Fri, Sat; to **Hopkins**, 1400 daily.

Air Maya Airways flies from Belize City 3 daily (continuing to Independence and Punta Gorda), US$25. Tickets at office on Commerce St, or at *Pelican Beach Hotel*.

Boats Boats leave irregularly, but roughly once a week, from Dangriga for Puerto Cortés (Honduras), ask around the bridge; US$25. Departures depend on passenger load (8 minimum) and the weather. 3-4 hrs in a long canoe with 2 powerful outboard motors. 'Flies across the waves' claims 1 boatman! The captain will arrange all exit formalities; no departure tax. You can hire a boat for around US$25 pp in a party to Belize City, enquire locally.

On **South Water Caye** are *Blue Marlin Lodge*, PO Box 21, Dangriga, T 05-22243, F 05-22296, an excellent dive lodge offering various packages; small sandy island with snorkelling off the beach; good accommodation and food. *Leslie Cottages*, 2 rooms, US contact T 800-548-5843 or 508-655-1461. *Coral Cay Conservation Ltd–Belize 90/95* (CCC), a UK-based reef ecology research group is also based on South Water Caye; contact 154 Clapham Park Road, London, SW4 7DE, T 071-498 6248, F 071-498 8447. CCC is undertaking a 5-year survey of the reef on behalf of the Belizean government in order to develop a management plan for protecting the barrier reef.

Volunteers usually spend from 1 to 3 months (or longer) working a 12-hr day, 5 days a week; 2 survey dives a day, with leisure diving on Thur evenings and Sat. Every fourth weekend is a free long weekend. Accommodation is basic in communal dormitories, and food is Youth Hostel style and quality, but South Water Caye is a tropical Paradise, a few minutes swim from the reef, white sand and palm-fringed. All inclusive costs from the UK at £1725 for 1 month, £2678 for 2 months and £3296 for 3 months. This is no holiday, you have to work hard, if you consider privileged diving hard work, but is a wonderful way of spending part of a year off. There is nothing to stop you spending time on the project then starting your Central or South American travels afterwards. Not much use contacting on spec in Belize as everything tends to be pre-arranged, but can be contacted by radio link via *Pelican Beach Resort* in Dangriga on 05-22044 (with thanks to Neil McAllister).

Tobacco Caye 1 hr by speedboat from Dangriga (US$12.50), this tiny island, quite heavily populated, has lots of local flavour and fishing camp charm. It is becoming a little commercialized, but still has an authentic feel. It sits right on the reef; you can snorkel from the beach although there are no large schools of fish. No sandflies on the beach; snorkelling equipment for rent. Boats go daily, enquire at *The Hub* or *Rio Mar* restaurants, Dangriga,

Captain Buck or Anthony charge US$12-15 pp. *Reefs End Lodge*, PO Box 10, Dangriga, basic, small rooms, excellent host and food, boat transfer on request from Dangriga; *Island Camps*, PO Box 174 (51 Regent St, Belize City, T 02-72109), owner Mark Bradley will pick up guests in Dangriga, neat, spacious campground, meals on request, reef excursions, friendly; **D** *Ellwood Fairweather and Friends*, friendly, good seafood, tax not inc, check the bill, 'not very serious'. Several families on the island take guests; accommodation very basic and grubby, 3 meals are usually provided. A dive camp is scheduled to open on Tobacco Caye, in the meanwhile tank dives can be taken from nearby *Blue Marlin Lodge* on South Water Caye. There is no electricity on the island.

The Southern Highway connects Dangriga with Punta Gorda in the S. It is unpaved: rough and dusty in the dry season, muddy in the wet. Public transport is limited and may be suspended after heavy rain. Hitching possible, but little traffic. Six miles inland from Dangriga the road branches from the Hummingbird Highway and heads S through mixed tropical forests and palmettos and pines along the fringes of the Maya Mountains. 15 miles from Dangriga a minor road forks off 4 miles E to the Garifuna fishing village of **Hopkins**, with the **D-E** *Sandy Beach Lodge*, T 05-22023, a women's cooperative, run by 10 women who work in shifts, arrive before 1900 or they will have gone home, 9 beachside rooms and large restaurant, 20-min walk S of village, quiet, safe, friendly, clean. At N end of village, **D-E** *Caribbean View*. Restaurant *Over The Waves* has good food. Watch out for sandflies when the weather is calm. The villagers throw household slops into the sea and garbage on the beach. Bus from Dangriga, Mon, Wed, Fri, Sat, 1200.

4 miles further on, the Southern Highway crosses the Sittee River at the small village of **Kendal** (ruins nearby); 1 mile beyond (20 miles from Dangriga) is the new village of **Maya Centre**, from where a bad 7-mile track winds W through Cabbage Haul Gap to the **Cockscomb Basin Wildlife Sanctuary** (41,457 ha), the world's first jaguar sanctuary. This was created out of the Cockscomb Basin Forest Reserve in 1986 to protect the country's highest recorded density of jaguars (*Panthera onca*) and their smaller cousins, the puma ('red tiger'), the endangered ocelot, the diurnal jaguarundi, and the exquisite margay. Many other mammals share the heavily-forested reserve, including coatis, collared peccaries, agoutis, anteaters, Baird's tapirs, and tayras (a small weasel-like animal). There are Red-eyed Tree Frogs, boas, iguanas and fer-de-lances, and over 290 species of birds, including King Vultures and Great Curassows. Park HQ is at the former settlement of Quam Bank (whose milpa-farming inhabitants founded Maya Centre outside the reserve); here there is a visitors' centre, picnic area and camping area (US$1.50); there are several 6-person basic cabins for rent (US$8 pp) with cooking facilities. Potable water is available, also toilets, but you must bring your own food, other drinks, matches, torch, sheet sleeping bag, eating utensils and mosquito repellent; nearest shop is at Maya Centre. 3 miles of jungle trails spread out from the visitors' centre, but walkers are unlikely to see any of the big cats. You will see birds, frogs, lizards and snakes. Longer hikes can be planned with the staff; it is an arduous 2-3 day climb to Victoria Peak (3,675 ft) and should not be undertaken casually. The Sanctuary is a good place for relaxing, listening to birds, showering under waterfalls, etc. This unique reserve is sponsored by the government, the Audubon Society, the World Wildlife Fund and private firms like the Jaguar car company; donations are very welcome. Before a visit travellers should contact the Belize Audubon Society, 29 Regent St, Belize City, T 02-77369, Dangriga T 05-22044 (*Pelican Beach Hotel*), or write to Ernesto Saqui, PO Box 90, Dangriga. Transport can be booked at the time of reservation, otherwise it is a 6-mile, uphill walk from Maya Centre to the reserve. Z-Line bus goes from Dangriga to Maya Centre at 1200, 40 mins, US$1.50, and others; return bus at 0900 to Dangriga (allow 2 hrs for the walk down to Maya Centre). If walking, leave all unneeded gear in Dangriga in view of the uphill stretch from Maya Centre; note also that radio communication is not always perfect and may lead

to problems of accommodation. A taxi from Dangriga will cost about US$50, it is not difficult to hitch back. The rainy season here extends from June to January.

Turning E towards the Caribbean just before Kendal a road leads down the Sittee River to **Sittee River Village** and **Possum Point** Biological Station, with a 16-room hotel, restaurant, D; also **C** Sittee River Lodge, T 05-22006; **F** Glover's Atoll Guest House, T 08-22505, 5 rooms, on river bank, restaurant, camping, jungle river trips, run by Lomont-Cabral family and starting point for boat to their Glover's Atoll Resort (see below); **B** Bocatura Bank, T (also) 05-22006, cottages, restaurant.

Glover's Reef, about 45 miles offshore , is an atoll with beautiful diving and a Marine Reserve since 1993. Manta Reef Resort, Glover's Reef Atoll, PO Box 215, 3 Eyre St, Belize City, T 02-31895/32767, F 02-32764; 9 individual cabins with full facilities, In perfect desert island setting, 1 week packages available only, reservations essential; excellent diving and fishing, good food, highly rec (E6 photo lab available). On 15-acre **Long Cay** is Glover's Atoll Resort (Gilbert, Marsha-Jo and Madeleine Lomont and Becky and Breeze Cabral, PO Box 563, Belize City, T 08-23505/22149, F 08-23505/23235, no reservations needed) with cabins for 2, US$55 pp a week, discounts for longer stays, with cooking facilities, cold shower, rainwater for drinking, basic groceries, meals available at advance notice. On 9-acre **North East Cay** there are unfurnished cabins with wood burning stoves, US$15/night. Camping on either island US$30 pp a week. The resort also comprises Lomont Caye and Cabral Caye, both of 1 acre and within swimming distance. Boats for hire, with or without guide, also canoes, rowboats, windsurfer; snorkel and scuba rental, tank of air US$12; 4-day NAUI certification course US$250. Contact the Lomonts in advance to obtain a full breakdown of all services and costs. To get there take any bus for Punta Gorda, Placencia or Hopkins-Sittee River or 0800 Z-Line bus from Venus terminal in Belize City (US$8); ask the driver to stop 1½ miles past the Sittee River road (about 5 hrs) at Kendal Village G & G Cool Spot. For US$10 (share the fare) a truck takes you to Glover's Atoll Guest House at Sittee River Village (see above). At 0800 Sunday a boat leaves for the Reef 5 hrs, US$20 pp one way, returns Saturday. At other times, charter a boat (skiff or sailing boat, US$200 one way, up to 8 people, diesel sloop US$350, up to 30 people).

Further down the Southern Highway watch for the sign for **Maya Beach**. 9 miles leads to Riversdale, then down a spit of land to Maya Beach. **A** Tropical Lodge, T 06-22077, full board, camping, hot showers, own dock and diving facilities, run by Ted and Peggy Williams, remote, good place to relax, or enjoy the Caribbean US reservations T 813-639-5717; **A+** Singing Sands Inn, T/F 06-22243, run by Bruce Larkin and Sally Steeds, 6 thatched cabins with bathrooms, hot water, fans, ocean view, snorkelling in front of the resort at False Cay, diving instruction with Sally, windsurfing, canoe and mountain bike hire, fishing, tours arranged, restaurant and bar on the beach. The road continues S to Seine Bight, **L** Rum Point Inn, T/F 06-22017 (in USA T 504-465 0769, F 464 0325), full board, Cabañas, owned by an American entomologist, good food. Visit the **Kulcha Shack** restaurant, gift shop, bar with dancing, run by Dewey, promoting Garifuna culture and traditions. 5 miles further is Placencia.

Placencia (also spelt Placentia), is a little resort 30 miles S of Dangriga, at the end of a long spit of land reached by bus (leaves Dangriga pm 4 times a week, 1½ hrs, US$3.50, returns at 0600, connects with 0900 bus to Belize City). There are no streets, just a concrete footpath and wooden houses under the palms. Electricity and lighting on the main path have been installed. The atmosphere has been described as good, with lots of Jamaican music and lots of substances to make it tolerable for over 1 hrs listening. Maya Airways fly 3 times a day Belize City-Dangriga-Placencia-Big Creek (dugout Placencia-Big Creek arranged at Sonny's; flight tickets are sold at Placencia's post office), about US$45 one way. **Big Creek**, on the mainland opposite Placencia, is 3 miles from Mango Creek (see below). A mail boat leaves Placencia for Big Creek Mon, Wed and Fri 1400, which, with transfer from Big Creek to Independence where the buses between Punta Gorda and Belize City stop, costs US$5. Dug out hire Placencia–Big Creek US$15 per boat; many people take passengers across from the Punta Gorda bus, boats leave 5 mins walk N of Big Creek bus stop.

Hotels (note that rooms may be hard to find in pm, eg after arrival of the bus from Dangriga) **C** Paradise Vacation Resort, full board or single meals available, clean, creole cooking, run by Dalton Eiley and Jim Lee; they offer reef fishing, snorkelling, excursions to the jungle, Pine Ridge, Mayan ruins and into the mountains. If arriving by air at Big Creek, first contact Hubert

Eiley, T 06-23118 who will arrange for a boat to take you to Placencia; **A** *Cove Resort*, PO Box 007, Placencia, T 06-22024; **A** *Ranguana Lodge*, T 06-23112, wooden cabins on the ocean, very clean; **E** *Ran's Travel Lodge*, T 06-22027, shared shower, toilet, friendly, fresh coconut bread baked next door (1000-1100). **D** *Conrad and Lydia's Rooms*, 5 double rooms with shared toilet and shower, situated on a quiet part of the beach, with excellent breakfast, good other meals, rec, Conrad is a boat owner, aks for his prices; *Kitty's Place*, T 06-22027, beach apartment B, weekly rates cheaper, rooms D with hot showers; **E** *Lucille's Rooms*, run by Lucille and her family, clean rooms, good beds, fans, good value, meals by arrangement; **E** *Julia's Budget Hotel*, no private bath, central, friendly, reliable wakeup call for bus. Mrs Leslie at the Post Office rents houses D (4-6 people, fridge and cooker); she also has hammock space for 3, G (noisy); Mr Clive rents 2 houses, F pp per day, also camping; George Cabral has a 2-bed apartment to rent in town T 06-23130. Camping on the beach or under the coconut palms. Ask at *Jennie's Restaurant*, or T 06-23148 for lodgings at **D** *Seaspray* with bath, **F** without, 5 new rooms added in 1992, very nice, good value, bar.

Restaurants, etc *The Galley*, good fish and shellfish (depending on the day's catch), try the seaweed punch, information on fishing and snorkelling, rec; *Flamboyant Restaurant and Bar*, a bit of cool luxury and excellent food. *Tentacles*, thatch roof, good food, pricey; *Jamie's*, typical food, good; *Ed's*, 20m behind *Lydia's* on sandy road out of town, pleasant, good value, great specials, bacon for breakfast; *King Fisher's*, on beach, open sided hall with thatched roof, seafood, tour arrangements; *Sonny's Resort Restaurant*, excellent fish and seafood; *Daisy's*, has good, homemade ice cream; *Omar's Fast Food* (misleading name), fish, meat, burgers. At least 5 shops (fresh fruit and vegetables supplied to *The Market* once a week, mostly sold out the same day), a video-cassette movie theatre, 4 bars (*Cosy's* is rec, disco every night, good hamburgers), the fishing cooperative, open Mon-Sat, am, sells fish cheaply, and supplies the town's electricity.

There is a police station. The people are very friendly and excursions can be made to the coral reef, 16 km off-shore (US$75-100 for 6 people). The only telephone for public use is at the Post Office (good source of information on boats). Nearest bank in Mango Creek (Bank of Nova Scotia) open Fri only 0900-1200, but shops and market change travellers' cheques. Visa extensions obtainable in Mango Creek.

Mango Creek is a banana exporting port, 30 miles (40 by road) S of Dangriga. Bus Belize City-Mango Creek, Southern Transport, James Bus Service, from Pound Yard Bridge, daily 0800 and 1500, US$8.50; bus Mango Creek-Belmopan, US$6.50. There is an airport at *Independence*, nearby.

Hotels and Restaurants B *Bill Bird Lodge*, at Mango Creek/Independence Airport, a/c, pool, good restaurant, T 06-22084; **C** *Hello I Hotel* (at Independence) run by Antonio Zabaneh at the shop where the Z-Line bus stops, clean, comfortable, helpful; **D** *Ursella's Guest House*, 6 rooms. Hotel above **F** *People's Restaurant*, clean, basic, ask to borrow a fan and lamp, at night you can listen to 'the sounds of the whole Belizean Zoo on the wooden floor, walls and ceiling', shower is a bucket of water in a cabin, 'don't use too much soap or you'll have to go back to the house for a refill; restaurant basic also' (Harry Balthussen); food better at the white house with green shutters behind it (book 2 hrs in advance if possible). *Goyo's Inn/Restaurant*, family-owned, good food, Independence.

Boats Motorized canoe from Mango Creek to Puerto Cortés, Honduras, irregular; ask Antonio Zabaneh at his store, T 06-22011, who knows when boats will arrive, US$50 one way, 7-9 hrs (rubber protective sheeting is provided—hang on to it, usually not enough to go round, nor lifejackets—but you will still get wet unless wearing waterproofs, or just a swimming costume on hot days; it can be dangerous in rough weather). Remember to get an exit stamp, preferably in Belize City, but normally obtainable at the police station in Mango Creek, not Placencia (the US$10 departure tax demanded here is not official). The *Christmas Bird* sailing boat leaves from Glover's Reef, (see above) on Sunday, returns on Friday. Boats from Mango Creek to Placencia cost about US$15, ask at Antonio Zabaneh's store or at *People's Restaurant*, or hitch a lift for US$5 with locals on shopping trip. About 15 mins-1 hr depending on the boat, the weather, the locals' timetable, and can be very wet.

The turnoff from the Southern Highway for Mango Creek, Independence and Big Creek (accommodation at *Toucan Inn*, B, a/c, private bath, restaurant) comes 15 miles after the Riverside turnoff, running 4 miles E through the **Savannah Forest Reserve** to the swampy coast opp Placencia. The Highway itself continues through forest and limestone outcrops, as the foothills of the mountains press in on the W About 38 miles beyond the junction, $10\frac{1}{2}$ miles N of the T-junction for Punta Gorda, $\frac{1}{2}$ mile N E of the road, is the **Nim Li Punit** archaeological site;

unrestored, partially cleared, Nim Li Punit ('Big Hat') was only discovered in 1974; a score of stelae,15-20 ft tall, were unearthed, dated 700-800 AD. A ball court, several groups of buildings and plazas, only southernmost group open to visitors. Signed trail from the highway.

A short distance beyond, the highway passes **Big Falls**, where there are hot springs; here you can swim, camp or sling a hammock, but first seek permission of the landowner (Mr Peter Alaman, who runs the general store on the highway). This is a popular weekend picnicking spot and a pleasant place to break the dusty (or muddy) journey S. 4 miles from Big Falls, the Highway reaches a T-junction (Shell station), the road to San Antonio branches right (W), the main road turns sharp left and runs down through another forest reserve for 14 miles to Punta Gorda.

Punta Gorda, pop 2,585, capital of Toledo District, is the last town of any size in Belize, a marketing centre and fishing port with a varied ethnic makeup: Creoles, Kekchi, Mopan, Chinese, East Indians, etc, descendants of the many races brought here over the years as labourers in ill-fated settlement attempts. At **Toledo**, 3 miles N, can be seen the remains of the sugar cane settlement founded by Confederacy refugees after the Civil War. Rainfall in this region is exceptionally heavy, over 170 inches annually, and the vegetation suitably luxuriant. The coast, about 100 feet above sea level, is fringed with coconut palms. Punta Gorda is a pleasant, breezy, quiet place; the seafront is clean and enjoyable but swimming is not rec. The Voice of America has a tall antenna complex on the edge of town; there is a substantial British army presence. On Front Street is a pretty park with a new clock tower, civic centre and post office/government office (with dark verandahs and a pole on which a signal beacon is raised each evening), but most of the (little) activity takes place around the pier.

Hotels C-A *Mira Mar*, 35 Front St, T 07-2033 (PO Box 2), overpriced, fishing on local rivers arranged, noisy disco, restaurant not rec; **C** *St Charles Inn*, 23 King St, T 07-2149/2197, with or without bath, spacious rooms, fan, good; **D** *Pallavi*, 19 Main St, T 07-2117, small, tidy, balcony, clean, friendly; **E** *Sea Breeze*, 6 Front St, restaurant, bar, cold showers, good bakery next door; **D** *Nature's Way Guest House*, 65 Front Street, T 07-2119 (PO Box 75), clean, good breakfast, will arrange ecologically-aware tours, fishing, sailing, has van, camping gear and trimaran for rent, rec; **D** *Goyo's*, facing clocktower, new, clean, cable TV, restaurant, good chicken, rice and beans; **E** *Mahung's Hotel*, corner North and Main St, T 07-2044, cockroaches, reasonable; **F** *Wahima*, 11 Front St, on waterfront, small rooms, primitive, but clean and safe, owner is local school teacher, friendly and informative, new rooms under construction (will be D). You can flag down the 0500 bus to Belize in front of *Wahima* or *Pallavi*—buy ticket the night before. It is hard to find accommodation late at night.

Restaurants *Kowloon*, 35 Main Middle St, good food; *Shaiba Tropical*, Front St, slow service; *Lucette's Kitchen*, Main St next to Texaco, friendly, good, cheap meals and breakfast. Bakery selling excellent 'sticky buns' near *Wahima*.

Exchange *Belize Bank*, at one end of the park (a/c, a cool haven), will change excess BZ$ for US$ on production of passport and ticket out of the country. They do not change Quetzales nor accept Visa card. You can change BZ$ for Quetzales at the Customs in Punta Gorda and Puerto Barrios, but don't expect a good rate.

Information Toledo Visitors Information Center, PO Box 73, T 07-22470, Alfredo and Yvonne Villoria; information on travel, tours, guiding, accommodation with Indian families, message service, book exchange, for the whole of Toledo district, free.

Bus from Belize, 9-12 hrs, US$10, Z-Line, Mon to Sat 0700, 0800 and 1500, Sun 1000 and 1500, ticket can be bought day before, beautiful but rough ride; returns 0500 and 1000, also James Bus Service, slower, unreliable times. To Mango Creek, US$3.50, 2½ hrs. To **Dangriga**, Z-Line daily at 0500. To **San Antonio** 3 buses daily, buses also to **San Pedro Colombia**. Buses are usually delayed in the wet season.

Air Daily flights to Big Creek, Dangriga, Belize City and if requested to International airport. Tickets at Bob Pennell's hardware store on Main St. Advance reservations essential.

Ferry to Guatemala The ferry to **Puerto Barrios** leaves Tues and Fri at 1400, 3 hrs BZ$10.75 (US$5.40) or Q21.40 (US$4.30), ticket must be purchased from the office of the Agencia de

Líneas Marítimas Tomás de Castillo, which opens at 1400 the day before departure (ie Mon and Thur). The office is half a block N of the clocktower on Middle Main Street in the same building as the Tienda Indita-Maya. Alternatively, tickets can be bought from Carlos Godoy, Agente Empresa Portuaria Punta Gorda (T 07-22065), the day before, or as early as 0830 on the day of travel; tickets can be reserved by phone, even from overseas. You must have a visa or tourist card for Guatemala (unless you are a Guatemalan citizen). You cannot obtain these in Punta Gorda, only in Belize City. Immigration Office is at the wharf, opens 1300 to 1400 on the day of sailing. If the ferry is not running the day you wish to travel, or is full, small boats are available. There are also boats to Livingston, charging Q50 pp (US$10). Beware however of unsafe, unseaworthy craft. The weather can be treacherous, and you and your luggage will certainly get wet.

Neil McAllister writes: An interesting alternative from Punta Gorda is to stay in Indian villages. A number of schemes exist, most are exploitative. One is run by villagers as a non-competitive co-operative. San Miguel, San José, Laguna, and Santa Cruz are isolated villages beyond Dump towards San Ignacio. Barranco is a Garifuna village S of Punta Gorda, accessible by boat. These have joined together and have developed a visitor scheme which benefits the villages. Each village has built a well appointed guest house, simple, but clean, with sheets, towels, mosquito nets, oil lamps, ablutions block, and total of 8 bunks in 2 4-bunk rooms. Visitors stay here, but eat in the villagers' houses on strict rotation, so each household gains equal income and only has to put up with intruding foreigners for short periods. They have their privacy, and so do you.

Villages at present have no electricity, but this due to arrive in 1993. Village children and many men speak English. Many expressed fears for what the arrival of power (and television) will do to their culture, and are keen to protect their heritage. Dancing and music were previously banned by the Church, but the Indians have re-learned old dances from elderly villagers and are buying and learning instruments to put on evening entertainments. Home-made excursions are arranged, these vary from 4-hr trek through local forest, looking at medicinal plants, and explaining agriculture (very interesting) as well as seeing very out-of-the-way sights like caves and creeks (take boots, even in dry season). The village tour could be skipped, as it is easy to walk around and chat to people, although by doing this freelance, you deprive the 'guide' of income.

This experience does not come cheap: 1 night for 2 people, with a forest tour and 2 meals came to almost US$50 but all profits go direct to the villages, with no outsiders as middlemen. All villagers share equally in the venture, so there is no resentment, or pressure from competing households, and gross profits from the Guest House are ploughed back into the villages infrastructure, schools etc. The scheme is co-ordinated by Chet at *Nature's Way Guest House*, who donates assistance and booking facilities for the scheme. You have to arrange your own transport, which can be problematic (buses run from Punta Gorda once a day for schoolkids), or a vehicle can be hired. Hitching not recommended, as some villages are remote, and may have 1 car a day visiting.

There is a road inland to 2 villages in the foothills of the Maya Mountains; ***San Antonio*** (21 miles), founded by refugees from San Luis in Guatemala in the late 19th century. Nearby there are Maya ruins of mainly scientific interest (**E** *Bol's Hilltop Hotel*, meals extra, clean; *Hotel Indita Bonita*, with *comedor*, good, clean; picturesque accommodation at *Tacho's*, G; may be allowed use of an army hut); medical centre here. About 3 miles along the road to San Antonio is a branch to ***San Pedro Columbia***, a Kekchi village. (Kekchi is a sub-tribe of Maya speaking a distinct language.) The Maya and Kekchi women wear picturesque costumes, including Guatemalan huipiles. There are many religious celebrations, at their most intense (mixed with general gaiety) on San Luis Rey day (5 August). There is a place to stay, run by Hawaiians. You can buy drinks and get breakfast at the large, yellow stone house. ***Blue Creek***, beyond San Antonio, is another attractive Indian village with a marked trail to Blue Creek caves through forest and along rock strewn creeks. Good swimming nearby.

Transport Bus from Punta Gorda, or pick-up vans for hire in Dangriga, or get a ride in a truck from the market or rice co-operative's mill in Punta Gorda (one leaves early pm); alternatively, go to the road junction, known as Dump, where the northern branch goes to Independence/Mango Creek, the other to San Antonio, 6 miles, either hitch or walk. Transport daily from San Antonio to **Punta Gorda** at 0500, 0530 punctually, also, reportedly, 1230, 1300, 1330; if going to **Dangriga**, take the 0500, get out at Dump to catch 0530 Z-line bus going N. Hire a dugout canoe for a trip up the river for US$2.50.

Beyond San Antonio, a dirt road leads to **Santa Cruz** and **Pueblo Viejo**, both attractive villages.

Beyond San Pedro, continuing left around the church, then right and downhill to the new concrete bridge, then left for a mile, is the trail to the Maya remains of **Lubaantun** ('Fallen Stones'), the major ceremonial site of southern Belize. It was last excavated by a Cambridge University team in 1970 and found to date from the 8th-9th centuries, late in the Maya culture and therefore unique. A series of terraced plazas surrounded by temples and palaces ascend along a ridge from S to N; the buildings were constructed with unusual precision and some of the original lime- mortar facings can still be discerned. Excavation revealed some interesting material: whistle figurines, iron pyrite mirrors, obsidian knives, conch shells from Wild Cane Caye, etc. The site is little-visited and, according to latest reports, is fast reverting to jungle. Opening hours are 0800-1700 daily; a caretaker will point out things of interest. Refreshments should be taken; there are no facilities on site except perhaps some dubious local food at a hut nearby. This whole region is a network of hilltop sites, mostly unexcavated and unrecognizable to the layman. Close to the border is one of the most interesting cities—**Pusilhá**—which is only accessible by boat. Many stelae were found here dating from 573 to 731 AD; carvings are similar to those at Quiriguá, Guatemala. Rare features are a walled-in ball court and the abutments remaining from a bridge which once spanned the Moho River. Swimming in the rivers is safe and refreshing. There are plenty of logging trails and hunters' tracks penetrating the southern faces of the Maya Mountains, but if hiking in the forest do not go alone.

Agricultural 'roads' push down to the southern border with Guatemala along the Sarstoon (Sarstún) River but there is little permanent settlement. At **Barranco**, the only coastal hamlet S of Punta Gorda, American Bob ('Willow') Jacobs offers a room with meals, D, in his seaside house—very much an 'away-from-it-all' experience. He visits Punta Gorda every few days (a bad track leads to Barranco through Blue Creek and San Lucas), where information can be had at *Nature's Way* or the *Isabela*.

INFORMATION FOR VISITORS

Documents All nationalities need passports, as well as sufficient funds and, officially, an onward ticket. Visas are usually not required from nationals of all the countries of EC, some Commonwealth countries, eg Australia, New Zealand, most Caribbean states (citizens of India, Austria and Switzerland do need a visa), USA, Canada, Leichtenstein, Mexico, Norway, Finland, Panama, Sweden, Turkey, Uruguay, Venezuela. There is a Belizean Consulate in Chetumal, Mexico, at Av Alvaro Obregón 232-1, T 24908, US$25. Visas may not be purchased at the border. Free transit visas are available at borders (for 24 hrs). It is possible that a visa may not be required if you have an onward ticket, but check all details at a Consulate before arriving at the border. Those going to other countries after leaving Belize should get any necessary visas in their home country. Visitors are initially granted 30 days' stay in Belize; this may be extended every 30 days for US$12.50 up to 6 months at the Immigration Office, 115 Barrack Rd, Belize City. At the end of 6 months, visitors must leave the country for at least 24 hrs. Visitors must not engage in any type of employment, paid or unpaid, without first securing a work permit from the Department of Labour; if caught, the penalty for both the employer and the employee is severe. Travellers should note that the border guards seem to have complete power to refuse entry to people whose looks they do not like. There have also been reports that tourists carrying less than US$30 for each day of intended stay have been refused entry. Cyclists should get a passport stamp to indicate an 'imported' bicycle.

GLOBAL TRAVEL CLUB

Beautiful
BELIZE

THE BEST KEPT SECRET
IN THE CARIBBEAN

Majestic Mountains, Tropical Rainforests,
Ancient Mayan Ruins & Pyramids,
1,000 Palm-fringed Coral Islands on the 2nd
largest Barrier Reef in the World.
For a holiday in Paradise
Phone: 0268 541732 (24 hrs) Fax: 0268 542275
or write to:
ANN MILES, GLOBAL TRAVEL CLUB
1 KILNSHAW, BASILDON, ESSEX SS16 6LE

Tailor-made itineraries to individual requirements and
fabulous small group tours escorted by expert guides.
Tours to neighbouring countries, Mexico, Guatemala and
Honduras also arranged. Diving holiday specialists.

 Latin American
Travel Association

 Belize Tourism
Industry Assoc.

Departure tax of US$12 on leaving from the international airport, but not for transit passengers who have spent less than 24 hrs in the country. There is also a security screening charge of US$1.25.

How to get there There is no regular sea passenger service (but see under Belize City and Punta Gorda). There is a first-class airport, 10 miles from Belize, served by American, Sahsa and Taca International from Miami. Flights from London (Virgin and British Airways), Frankfurt (Lufthansa), Toronto (Delta and Air Canada), Montreal (Air Canada), and several US cities connect with the daily Taca flight from Miami. Other US points served direct: New Orleans (Taca), Dallas, Chicago, Detroit, Cleveland and Denver (Continental), Houston (Continental, Taca), New York (Continental and American) and Los Angeles (Taca). Also daily flights to San Pedro Sula (Taca), San Salvador, San José, and Panama (all Taca). Flights to Flores (Guatemala), with Aviateca, TropicAir and AeroCaribe, to Guatemala City (Taca, Aviateca). In 1993 the Mexican airline, Bonanza, began a Mon/Wed/Fri service, Mérida-Belize via Chetumal, 0700-0925, US$100 one way.

Customs Clothing and articles for personal use are allowed in without payment of duty, but a deposit may be required to cover the duty payable on typewriters, dictaphones, cameras and radios. The duty, if claimed, is refunded when the visitor leaves the country. Import allowances are: 200 cigarettes or $1/2$ lb of tobacco; 20 fluid ozs of alcohol; 1 bottle of perfume. Visitors can take in an unspecified amount of other currencies (charges were brought in 1993 against 2 people who brought in an excessive amount of US dollars, later dropped, maximum amount may now be set). No fruit or vegetables may be brought into Belize; searches are very thorough. Firearms may be imported only with prior arrangements. Pets must have proof of rabies inoculations and a vet's certificate of good health. CB radios are held by customs until a licence is obtained from Belize Communications Ltd.

Sellers of cars must pay duty (if the buyer pays it, he may be able to bargain with the customs official), but prices are quite good particularly in Orange Walk (ask taxi drivers in Belize City). Also, O Perez & Sons, 59 West Canal St, Belize City may be able to help.

Internal Transport Maya Airways flies daily to each of the main towns (see under Belize City) and offers charter rates to all local airstrips of which there are 25; only twin-engined planes are used and their safety record is good. Tropic Air flies to San Pedro, Caye Chapel and Corozal. 5 other companies have charters from Belize City to outlying districts. (Belize Aero Company, T 02-44021; Cari Bee Air Service, flies mainly to the Cayes, also scheduled service to San Pedro, indifferent service but no major problems, T 02-44253; Javier Flying Services, T 02-45332; National Charters, T 02-45332; Island Air Service, flies mainly to the Cayes, also scheduled service to San Pedro, indifferent service but no major problems, T 02-31140/ 026-2435).

Public transport between the main towns is by colectivo or bus, and trucks also carry passengers to many isolated destinations, although they are no longer allowed to carry passengers to places served by buses. Enquire at market place in Belize City. By law, buses are not allowed to carry standing passengers; some companies are stricter than others. Most buses are ex-US school buses, small seats, limited legroom. There are a few ex-Greyhounds. All bus companies sell seats in advance. Most buses have no luggage compartments so bags which do not fit on the luggage rack are stacked at the back of the bus. Get a seat at the back to keep an eye on your gear; rough handling is more of a threat than theft. Hitch hiking is very difficult as there is little traffic.

Motoring Motorists should carry their own driving licence and certificate of vehicle ownership. Third party insurance is mandatory, and can be purchased at any border (US$25 a week). There may be no one to collect it after 1900 or on Sundays. Valid International Driving Licences are accepted in place of Belize driving permits. Fuel costs US$4.50 for a US gallon. There is no unleaded gasoline in Belize.

Traffic drives on the right. When making a left turn, it is the driver's responsibility to ensure clearance of both oncoming traffic and vehicles behind; generally, drivers pull over to the far right, allow traffic from behind to pass, then make the left turn. Many accidents are caused by failure to observe this procedure. All major roads have been, or are being, improved.

For details of **Car Hire**, see under Belize City.

Food   Seafood is abundant, fresh and reasonably cheap; beef is plentiful. Presentation varies: vegetables are not always served with a meat course. For the cheapest meals, order rice. It will come with beans and (as often as not) banana or plantain, or chicken, vegetables or even a blending of beef with coconut milk. Better restaurants have a selection of Mexican dishes; there are also many Chinese restaurants, not always good and sometimes overpriced. Belikin beer is the cheapest, many brands of local rum available. The local liqueur is called *nanche*, made from crabou fruit; it is very sweet. All imported food and drink is expensive. Rainwater is commonly served as drinking water. See **Fishing, p 533,** with regard to the closed season for certain seafoods: do not order these items during these periods unless you are certain they have been legally caught.

Health   Those taking common precautions find the climate pleasant and healthy. Malaria was reportedly under control, but once again precautions against the disease are essential. Also use mosquito repellent. Dengue fever exists in Belize. Inoculation against yellow fever and tetanus is advisable but not obligatory. No case of either has been reported in years. Out-patients' medical attention is free of charge. Myo' On Clinic Ltd, Belize City (central, off Queen St) has been recommended, but it charges for its services. Also recommended is Dr Lizama, Handyside St, consultation US$17.50.

Security   Apart from taking certain precautions in Belize City, the visitor should feel at no personal risk anywhere in Belize. The authorities are keen to prevent the illegal use of drugs. The penalties for possession of marijuana are 6 months in prison or a US$3,000 fine, minimum.

Tipping In restaurants, 10% of the bill; porters in hotels US$2; chambermaids US$0.50/day. Taxi drivers are not tipped.

Clothing The business dress for men is a short-sleeved cotton or poplin shirt or *guayabera* (ties not often worn) and trousers of some tropical weight material. Formal wear may include ties and jackets, but long-sleeved embroidered *guayaberas* are commoner. Women should not wear shorts in the cities and towns; acceptable only on the cayes and at resorts.

Hours of Business Retail shops are open 0800-1200, 1300-1600 and Fri 1900-2100, with a half day from 1200 on Wed. Small shops open additionally most late afternoons and evenings, and some on Sundays 0800-1000. Government and commercial office hrs are 0800-1200 and 1300-1600 Mon to Fri.

Public Holidays 1 January: New Year's Day; 9 March: Baron Bliss Day; Good Friday and Saturday; Easter Monday; 21 April: Queen's birthday; 1 May: Labour Day; 24 May: Commonwealth Day; 10 Sept: St George's Caye Day; 21 Sept: Belize Independence Day; 12 Oct: Pan American Day (Corozal and Orange Walk); 19 Nov: Garifuna Settlement Day; 25 December: Christmas Day; 26 December: Boxing Day.

Warning Most services throughout the country close down Good Friday to Easter Monday: banks close at 1130 on the Thursday, buses run limited services Holy Saturday to Easter Monday, and boats to the Cayes are available. St George's Caye Day celebrations in September start 2 or 3 days in advance and require a lot of energy.

Official time is 6 hrs behind GMT.

The **monetary unit** is the Belizean dollar, stabilized at BZ$2=US$1. Currency notes (Monetary Authority of Belize) are issued in the denominations of 100, 50, 20, 10, 5, 2 and 1 dollars, and coinage of 1 dollar, 50, 25, 10, 5 and 1 cent is in use. Notes marked Government of Belize, or Government of British Honduras, are only redeemable at a bank; all notes should be marked Central Bank of Belize. The American expressions Quarter (25c), Dime (10c) and Nickel (5c) are common, although 25c is sometimes referred to as a shilling. US dollars are accepted in many places. Belize Bank gives cash on Visa and Mastercard (but see under **Exchange**, Belize City, above). Good rates for Mexican pesos in Belize. Best rates of exchange at the borders.

The **Cost of Living** is high because of the heavy reliance on imports and extra duties. This applies especially to food, car hire, driving. In addition, licences are required to provide many services, which involve payment. Budget travellers also find exploring the interior difficult because public transport is limited and car hire is beyond the means of many.

Weights and measures Imperial and US standard weights and measures. The US gallon is used for gasoline and motor oil.

Electricity 110/220 volts single phase, 60 cycles for domestic supply. Some hotels use 12 volt generators.

Telephone and Cable There is a direct-dialling system between the major towns and to Mexico and USA. Local calls cost US$0.25 for 3 mins, US$0.12 for each extra minute within the city, US$0.15-0.55 depending on zone. Belize Telecommunications Ltd, Church St, Belize City, open 0800-2100 Mon-Sat, 0800-1200 Sun and holidays, has an international telephone, telegraph and telex service. To make an international call from Belize costs far less than from neighbouring countries. US$12 for 3 min to UK and Europe, US$3 for each extra minute (a deposit of US$15 required on all international calls); US$6.40 to USA, US$1.60 for each extra minute; US$16 for 3 mins elsewhere, US$4 for each extra minute. Collect calls to USA, Canada, Australia and UK only. International telex US$1.60 per minute to USA, US$3 to Europe, US$4 elsewhere; telegram US$0.16 per word to USA, US$0.30 to Europe, US$0.40 elsewhere. AT&T's USA Direct, UK Direct, Hong Kong Direct must have AT&T card and ID. Fax US$4.80 minimum plus US$2.50 service charge.

Belize Communications, Belmopan (Rick and Sue Simpson), is a telephone and fax service used by many establishments not yet reached by direct phone line: T 08-23180, F 08-23235. Those on the service, who will be contacted by Belize Communications by radio, include the US Embassy, CARE, Maya Airlines, Guanacaste Park, The Blue Hole, Coxcomb, Shipstern Nature Reserve, Chaa Creek, Ix Chel Farm, Mountain Equestrian Trails, Maya Mountain Lodge, duPlooy's, Banana Bank Ranch, Warrie Head, Belize Audubon Society.

Airmail Postage to UK 4-5 days. US$0.38 for a letter, US$0.20 for a postcard; US$0.30 for a letter to USA, US$0.15 for a post card; US$0.30 postcard, US$0.50 letter to Australia, takes 4-6 weeks. Parcels: US$3.50 per half-kilo to Europe, US$0.38 per half-kilo to USA. The service to Europe and USA has been praised, but sea mail is not reliable. Belize postage stamps are very attractive. Mail may be sent to any local post office, c/o General Delivery.

Press Belize: *Belize Times* (PUP supported), in total opposition to *People's Pulse* (UPD supported), *Reporter* (weekly); *Amandala*; monthlies *Belize Today*, and *Belize Review*; bi-monthly *Belize Currents*.

Belize First, published 5 times a year in the USA, has articles on travel, life, news and history in the country: Equator Travel Publications Inc, 280 Beaverdam Road, Candler, NC 28715, USA, F (704) 667-1717 (US$27 a year in Belize, USA, Canada, Mexico, US$37 elsewhere).

Language English is the official language, but Spanish is widely spoken. Belize Broadcasting Network (BBN) devotes about 40 per cent of its air-time to the Spanish language. A Low German dialect is spoken by the Mennonite settlers, and Mayan languages and Garifuna are spoken by ethnic groups.

Representation Overseas Canada, 112 Kent Street, Suite 2005, Place de Ville, Tower B, Ottawa, Ontario, K1P 5P2, T 613 232-7389, F 613 232-5804; **UK**, High Commission, Harcourt House, 19A Camden Sq, London W1M 9AD, T 071 499-9728; F 071 491-4139; **USA**, 415 Seventh Avenue, New York, NY 10001, T 800 624-0686, F 212 695-3018.

To use AT&T USADirect® Service from Belize dial **555** from designated calling centers throughout Belize City and from major hotels.

AT&T USADirect® Service.

Tourist Information The Belize Tourist Board, as well as its office in Belize City (83 North Front Street, T 02-77213/73255, F 02-77490), also has offices in the **USA**, 15 Penn Plaza, 415 Seventh Avenue, 18th floor, New York, NY 10001, T 800-624-0686, 212-268-8798, F 212-695-3018; **Canada**, Belize High Commission, 273 Patricia Avenue, Ottawa, K1Y V6C, T 613-722-7187; **Germany**, Belize Tourist Board/WICRG, Lomenstr-28, 2000 Hamburg 70, T 49-40-695-8846, F 49-40-380-0051; **UK**, c/o Belize High Commission (See **Representation Overseas** above).

For information on Belize we are grateful to the following travellers: Janet Arnold (Melbourne, Australia), Wilhelm Baumeister (Hannover, Germany), David Beasley & Liz Brooks (Horsham, West Sussex), Alexander Beck (Altessing, Germany), Sybille Böhme (Kahl/Main, Germany), Sarah & Philippe Bonay (Auterine, France), Frank Dux (Passau, Germany), Matthias Fehrenbach (Immenstaad, Germany), Karin Fischli & Veli Hermann (Reichenburg, Switzerland), Ann Frechette & Jean Luc Massicotte for Charles Huot (Montréal), Fränzi Gäggel (Glahfelden, Switzerland), J Roy Goodall (Belize City), Thomas Gredig (Zurich, Switzerland), Pasi Hannonen (Jy vä Skylä, Finland), Noel, Nenagh & Zoë Kemp (Lindisfarne, Australia), Iruin Mitchell (Lyle, WA, USA), Claudia Modrow & Massimo Godenzi (Bergheim, Germany), Dr Martin Mowforth (Tavistock, Devon), Marlies Ostermann (Hüven, Germany), Patrick & Tina (Aachen, Germany), Jo Protéro (Bath), Helmut Quitt (Rosenheim, Germany), Sebastian Retzlaff (Berlin), Claudio Rivero (Buenos Aires), Dr Robert Rosen Jacobson (Amsterdam), Frank & Christine Ruiz (Brossard, Quebec), Johannes Schmeer (Munich, Germany), Jan & Truus van Ingen Schenau (Amsterdam), Adrian van Schie (New Zealand), Mary Nicoll & Charlie Schreiber (London NW5), Harald Schwender & Birgitte Hächer (Sandhausen, Germany), Peter Selley (London SW11), Suzanne Elise Tourville (St Louis, MO, USA), Benderoth Vitus (Hadamar), Andy Walter (Swindon, Wiltshire), Sheila Wilson (Stoke Poges, Slough) and Dirk Zeiler (Giessen, Germany).

WILL YOU HELP US?

We do all we can to get our facts right in the MEXICO & CENTRAL AMERICAN HANDBOOK. Each section is thoroughly revised each year, but the territory is vast and our eyes cannot be everywhere. We are always pleased to hear about your travels; do write to us in as much detail as possible. In return we will send you information about our special guidebook offer.

TRADE & TRAVEL *Handbooks*

Write to The Editor, Mexico & Central American Handbook, Trade & Travel, 6 Riverside Court, Lower Bristol Road, Bath BA2 3DZ. England

EL SALVADOR

INTRODUCTION

El Salvador is the smallest, most densely populated and most integrated of the Central American republics. Its intermont basins are a good deal lower than those of Guatemala, rising to little more than 600m at the capital, San Salvador. Across this upland and surmounting it run 2 more or less parallel rows of volcanoes, 14 of which are over 900m. The highest are Santa Ana (2,365m), San Vicente (2,182m), San Miguel (2,129m), and San Salvador (1,893m). One important result of this volcanic activity is that the highlands are covered with a deep layer of ash and lava which forms a porous soil ideal for coffee planting.

The total area of El Salvador is 21,041 sq km. Guatemala is to the W, Honduras to the N and E, and the Pacific coastline to the S is approximately 321 km long.

Lowlands lie to the N and S of the high backbone. In the S, on the Pacific coast, the lowlands of Guatemala are confined to just E of Acajutla; beyond are lava promontories till we reach another 30-km belt of lowlands where the 325 km long Río Lempa flows into the sea. The northern lowlands are in the wide depression along the course of the Río Lempa, buttressed S by the highlands of El Salvador and N by the basalt cliffs edging the highlands of Honduras. The highest point in El Salvador, Cerro El Pital (2,730m) is part of the mountain range bordering on Honduras. After 160 km the Lempa cuts through the southern uplands to reach the Pacific; the depression is prolonged SE till it reaches the Gulf of Fonseca.

El Salvador is located on the SW coast of the Central American Isthmus on the Pacific Ocean. As the only country in the region lacking access to the Caribbean Sea it does not posses the flora associated with that particular coastal zone. El Salvador nevertheless has a wide variety of colourful, tropical vegetation; for example over 200 species of orchid grow all over the country. As a result of excessive forest cutting and therefore the destruction of their habitats, many of the animals (such as jaguars and crested eagles) once found in the highlands of the country have diminished at an alarming rate. In response to this problem several nature reserves have been set up in areas where flora and fauna can be found in their most unspoilt states. Among these nature reserves are the Cerro Verde, Deininger Park, El Imposible Woods, El Tocatal Lagoon and the Montecristo Cloud Forest.

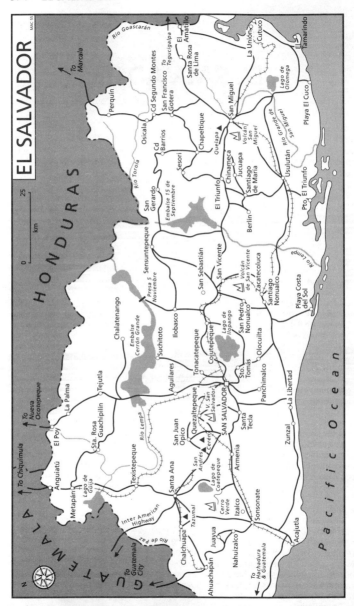

EL SALVADOR

Climate El Salvador is fortunate in that its temperatures are not excessively high. Along the coast and in the lowlands it is certainly hot and humid, but the average for San Salvador is 28°C with a range of only about 3°. March, April and May are the hottest months; December, January and February the coolest. There is one rainy season, from May to October, with April and November being transitional periods; there are only light rains for the rest of the year: the average is about 1,830 mm. Occasionally, in September or October, there is a spell of continuously rainy weather, the *temporal*, which may last from 2 or 3 days to as many weeks. The pleasantest months are from November to January. From time to time the water shortage can become acute.

History When Spanish expeditions arrived in El Salvador from Guatemala and Nicaragua, they found it relatively densely populated by several Indian groups, of whom the most populous were the Pipiles. By 1550, the Spaniards had occupied the country, many living in existing Indian villages and towns. The settlers cultivated cocoa in the volcanic highlands and balsam along the coast, and introduced cattle to roam the grasslands freely. Towards the end of the sixteenth century, indigo became the big export crop: production was controlled by the Spaniards, and Indians provided the workforce, many suffering illness as a result. A period of regional turmoil accompanied El Salvador's declaration of independence from the newly-autonomous political body of Central America in 1839: Indian attempts to regain their traditional land rights were put down by force.

Coffee emerged as an important cash crop in the second half of the nineteenth century, bringing with it improvements in transport facilities and the final abolition of Indian communal lands.

The land question was a fundamental cause of the peasant uprising of 1932, which was brutally crushed by the dictator General Maximiliano Hernández Martínez. Following his overthrow in 1944, the military did not relinquish power: a series of military coups kept them in control, and they protected the interests of the landowning oligarchy.

The most recent military coup, in October 1979, led to the formation of a civilian-military junta which promised far-reaching reforms. When the reforms were not carried out, the opposition unified forming a broad coalition, the Frente Democrático Revolucionario, which adopted a military wing, the Farabundo Marti National Liberation Front (FMLN) in 1980. Later the same year, the Christian Democrat, Ing José Napoleón Duarte was named as President of the Junta. At about the same time, political tension reached the proportions of civil war.

Duarte was elected to the post of President in 1984, following a short administration headed by Dr Alvaro Magaña. Duarte's periods of power were characterized by a partly-successful attempt at land reform, the nationalization of foreign trade and the banking system, and violence. In addition to deaths in combat, 40,000 civilians were killed between 1979 and 1984, mostly by right-wing death squads. Among the casualties was Archbishop Oscar Romero, who was shot while saying mass in March 1980. Nothing came of meetings between Duarte's government and the FMLN, aimed at seeking a peace agreement.

The war continued in stalemate until 1989, by which time an estimated 70,000 had been killed. The Christian Democrats' inability to end the war, reverse the economic decline or rebuild after the 1986 earthquake, combined with their reputation for corruption, caused a resurgence of support for the right-wing National Republican Alliance (ARENA). An FMLN offer to participate in presidential elections, dependent on certain conditions, was not accepted, and the ARENA candidate, Lic Alfredo Cristiani, won the presidency comfortably in March 1989, taking office in June.

Peace talks again failed to produce results, and in November 1989, the FMLN guerrillas staged their most ambitious offensive ever, which paralysed the capital and caused a violent backlash from government forces. FMLN-government negotiations resumed with UN mediation following the offensive, but the 2 sides could not reach agreement about the purging of the Armed Forces, which had become the most wealthy institution in the country after 10 years of US support.

Although El Salvador's most left-wing political party, the Unión Democrática Nacionalista, agreed to participate in municipal elections in 1991, the FMLN remained outside the electoral process, and the civil war continued unresolved. Talks were held in Venezuela and Mexico after initial agreement was reached in April on reforms to the electoral and judicial systems, but further progress was stalled over the restructuring of the armed forces and disarming the guerrillas. There were hopes that human rights would improve after the establishment in June 1991 of a UN Security Council human rights observer commission (ONUSAL), charged with verifying compliance with the human rights agreement signed by the Government and the FMLN in Geneva in April 1990. Offices were opened in San Salvador and the departments of San Miguel, San Vicente, Morazán and Chalatenango. Finally, after considerable UN assistance, the FMLN and the Government signed a peace accord in New York in January 1992 and a formal ceasefire began in February. A detailed schedule throughout 1992 was established to demobilize the FMLN, dismantle 5 armed forces elite battalions and initiate land requests by ex-combatants from both sides. The demobilization process was reported as completed, after 2 months extension, in December 1992 formally concluding the civil war. The US agreed at this point to 'forgive' a substantial portion of the US$2bn international debt of El Salvador. In March 1993, the United Nations Truth Commission published its investigation of human rights abuses during the civil war. Five days later, the legislature approved a general amnesty for all those involved in criminal activities in the war. This included those named in the Truth Commission report. The Cristiani government was slow to implement not only the constitutional reforms proposed by the Truth Commission, but also the process of land reform and the establishment of the National Civilian Police. The president, shortly before the end of his term, denied UN criticisms to this effect.

Presidential and congressional elections on 20 March 1994 failed to give an outright majority to any presidential candidate. The 2 main contenders, Armando Calderón Sol of Arena and Rubén Zamora, of a coalition of the FMLN, Democratic Convergence and the National Revolutionary Movement, faced a run-off election on 24 April. Calderón Sol won 70% of the vote, but it was feared that a smooth transition of power might be jeopardized by voting irregularities alleged in the first round.

The People The population is far more homogeneous than that of Guatemala. The reason for this is that El Salvador lay comparatively isolated from the main stream of conquest, and had no precious metals to act as magnets for the Spaniards. The small number of Spanish settlers intermarried with those Indians who survived the plagues brought from Europe, to form a group of mestizos. There were only about half a million people as late as 1879. With the introduction of coffee, the population grew quickly and the new prosperity fertilized the whole economy, but internal pressure of population has led to the occupation of all the available land. Several hundred thousand Salvadorans have emigrated to neighbouring republics because of the shortage of land and the concentration of land ownership, and more lately because of the civil war.

Of the total population, 5,460,000 in 1992, some 20% are regarded as ethnic Indians, although the traditional Indian culture has almost completely vanished. Other estimates put the percentage of pure Indians as low as 5%. The Lenca and the Pipil, the 2 surviving indigenous groups, are predominantly peasant farmers. Less than 5% are of unmixed white ancestry, the rest are mestizos.

El Salvador : Fact File

Geographic

Land area	21,041 sq km
forested	5.0%
pastures	29.4%
cultivated	35.4%

Demographic

Population (1992)	5,460,000
annual growth rate (1987-92)	1.6%
urban	44.4%
rural	55.6%
density	259.5 per sq km
Religious affiliation	
Roman Catholic	91.8%
Birth rate per 1,000 (1991)	34.0
	(world av 26.4)
Death rate per 1,000 (1991)	7.0
	(world av 9.2)

Education and Health

Life expectancy at birth,	
male	63 years
female	68 years
Infant mortality rate	
per 1,000 live births (1991)	47.0
Physicians (1991)	1 per 1,322 persons
Hospital beds	1 per 973 persons
Calorie intake as %	
of FAO requirement	94%
Population age 25 and over	
with no formal schooling	30.2%
Literate males (over 15)	76.2%
Literate females (over 15)	70.0%

Economic

GNP (1990 market prices)	US$5,767mn
GNP per capita	US$1,100
Public external debt (1990)	US$1,758mn
Tourism receipts (1990)	US$70mn
Inflation	
(annual av 1986-91)	20.1%
Radio	1 per 2.8 persons
Television	1 per 11 persons
Telephone	1 per 42 persons

Employment

Population economically active (1990)	
	982,802
Unemployment rate	10.0%
% of labour force in	
agriculture	8.1
mining	0.1
manufacturing	21.7
construction	6.5
Military forces	49,700

Source *Encyclopaedia Britannica*

With a population of 256 to the sq km, El Salvador is the most densely populated country on the American mainland. Health and sanitation outside the capital and some of the main towns leave much to be desired, and progress was very limited in the 1980s and early 1990s because of the violence.

The Economy Agriculture is the dominant sector of the economy, accounting for three quarters of export earnings. Coffee, sugar and cotton are the most important crops, but attempts have been made at diversification and now soya, sesame, vegetables, tropical flowers and ornamental plants are being promoted as foreign exchange earners. Shrimp farming investment has risen and shrimp is now an important export item. Land ownership has been unevenly distributed with a few wealthy families owning most of the land, while the majority of agricultural workers merely lived at subsistence level; this led to serious political and social instability despite attempts at agrarian reform by successive governments, including a determined one involving cooperatives in 1980. The ARENA Government put an end to the formation of cooperatives and encouraged existing cooperatives to divide into individual farms. In 1992 the Government and the FMLN agreed a Land Transfer Programme (PTT) designed to distribute 166,000 hectares of land to about 48,000 Salvadoreans at a cost of US$143mn. Problems with implementation of the plan and acquisition of land led to delays and many potential beneficiaries had still not received land by March 1994.

With the expansion of the industrial sector in the 1960s and 1970s, there was a rapid growth in the middle and industrial working classes. The most important industries are food processing and petroleum products: others include textiles, pharmaceuticals, shoes, furniture, chemicals and fertilizers, cosmetics, construction materials, cement (and asbestos cement), drink processing, rubber goods. Maquila factories have grown rapidly in recent years, particularly garment assemblers, providing an estimated 20,000 jobs in 1992. Exports of manufactured goods, mostly to other Central American countries, account for some 24% of foreign exchange earnings.

There are small deposits of various minerals: gold, silver, copper, iron ore, sulphur, mercury, lead, zinc, salt and lime, but only limited amounts of gold, silver and limestone are produced. There is a gold and silver mine at San Cristóbal in the Department of Morazán. In 1975 a geothermal power plant came into operation at Ahuachapán, with capacity of 30 mw. The plant was expanded by 60 mw in 1978. Hydraulic resources are also being exploited as a means of generating power and saving oil import costs, but the intention of closing thermal plants has been thwarted by the poor condition of the infrastructure and disruption by guerrilla attacks. Electricity has been rationed since 1991, first as a result of extensive sabotage, then as a result of a lack of rain to fill the hydroelectricity lakes.

The country's agricultural and industrial production, and consequently its exporting capability, have been severely curtailed by political unrest. In 1986 further economic and social damage was caused by an earthquake; damage to housing and government property alone was estimated at US$311mn, while the total, including destruction and disruption of businesses was put at US$2bn. El Salvador was heavily dependent upon aid from the USA to finance its budget. Total US assistance was estimated at over US$4bn in the 1980s. In 1989 the new government outlined a national rescue plan to provide jobs, food and low cost housing to those most in need but it was not fully implemented. Efforts were also made to put order into public finances, reduce inflation and encourage exports, but the initial effect was to increase inflation, unemployment and poverty. However, the lack of foreign exchange reserves remained a serious constraint and El Salvador was declared ineligible for World Bank lending after arrears exceeded limits.

By 1990 progress was becoming evident as inflation eased, gdp grew slightly and the fiscal deficit was reduced. The privatization of banks and other state-run enterprises got under way, the trade deficit was lowered by an 18% increase in exports, private savings rose and so did foreign exchange reserves. International creditors praised the Government's economic stabilization efforts; in February 1991 the IMF signed a US$50mn standby agreement while the World Bank and the InterAmerican Development Bank were expected to lend US$100mn each during the year. Improvement in economic indicators continued in 1991 and a second stage of the World Bank structural adjustment loan was initiated. Nevertheless, it was expected that real progress would take some time and alleviation of poverty (some two-thirds of the population are classified as living in extreme poverty) and unemployment would be slow (official estimates put the unemployment rate at 10%, under-employment 29%; unofficial estimates are much higher – unemployment was forecast to rise as ex-combatants sought jobs). Remittances from Salvadorans resident abroad (about US$800mn a year) were expected to dry up as they came home, but in 1993 these funds accounted for some 12% of gdp. The Consultative Group for El Salvador (22 donor countries and 15 international and regional organizations) agreed in 1992 to provide about US$800mn to support the National Reconstruction Plan (PNR), a 5-year, US$1.4bn project to alleviate poverty and consolidate peace. During the first year US$500mn was disbursed but, after an evaluation in 1993, it was agreed that the balance should support the next 3 years' programmes. Nevertheless, foreign aid and loans in 1993 helped to boost private investment and stabilize the colón against the US dollar. Other positive factors in 1993 were growth in construction and services (10% and 12% respectively) as rebuilding and rehabilitation of infrastructure after the civil war progressed, overall gdp growth of 5% (against 4.7% in 1992) and a fall in inflation from 20.2% to 13%.

Government Legislative power is vested in a unicameral Legislative Assembly, which has 84 seats and is elected for a 3-year term. The head of state and government is the president, who holds office for 5 years. The country is divided into 14 departments.

Communications There are 602 km of railway but no long-distance passenger services. In 1989 the road length was 12,495 km, of which 14% was paved.

Education and Religion 30% of the population aged over 10 have no formal schooling. Education is free if given by the government, and nominally obligatory. There are 43 universities, 3 national and the others private or church-affiliated. There is also a National School of Agriculture. The most famous are the government-financed Universidad Nacional and the Jesuit-run Universidad Centroamericana (UCA). Roman Catholicism is the prevailing religion.

Note For comments on travel within El Salvador, see the **Note** after **Documents** in the **Information for Visitors**.

SAN SALVADOR AND ENVIRONS

A city which has suffered from natural and man-made disasters from which it has not had the ability to recover. Probably not a place to stay for long, but the best point to start from to see the many attractions of El Salvador.

San Salvador, the capital, is in an intermont basin on the Río Acelhuate, at 680m, with a ring of mountains round it. The valley is known as 'Valle de las Hamacas' because of its frequent seismic activity. The population of the central city is 478,000, but when outlying suburbs are included, estimates rise to 1.5 million. It was founded in 1525, but not where it now stands. The city was destroyed by an earthquake in 1854, so the present capital is a modern city, most of its architecture conditioned by its liability to seismic shocks. However, in the earthquake of 10 October 1986, many buildings collapsed; over 1,000 people died. A great amount of reconstruction has been carried out, but much remains to be done, especially underground. The city centre is still in bad condition, and many people have not yet returned to proper housing. The climate is semi-tropical and healthy, the water-supply relatively pure. Days are often hot, especially in the dry season, but the temperature drops in the late afternoon and nights are usually pleasantly mild. Since it is in a hollow, the city has a very bad smog problem, caused mainly by traffic pollution.

Four broad streets meet at the centre: Av Cuscatlán and its continuation Av España run S to N, Calle Delgado and its continuation Calle Arce from E to W. This principle is retained throughout: all the *avenidas* run N to S and the *calles* E to W. The even-numbered *avenidas* are E of the central *avenidas*, odd numbers W; N of the central *calles*, they are dubbed Norte, S of the central *calles* Sur. The even-numbered *calles* are S of the 2 central *calles*, the odd numbers N. E of the central *avenidas* they are dubbed Oriente, W of the central *avenidas* Poniente. Although it sounds complicated, this system is really very straightforward, and can be grasped quickly.

A number of important buildings are near the main intersection. On the E side of Av Cuscatlán is the Plaza Barrios, the heart of the city. A fine equestrian statue looks W towards the renaissance-style Palacio Nacional (1904-11). To the N is the new cathedral, which was left unfinished for several years after Archbishop Romero suspended its construction (to use the money to alleviate poverty): work was resumed in 1990. To the E of the Plaza Barrios, on Calle Delgado, is the Teatro Nacional (the interior has been magnificently restored). If we walk along 2a Calle

Av. España
Av. Cuscatlán
Diplomáticos
28
1A Av. Norte
1A Av. Sur
27
C 15 de sept.
Av. 29 de Agosto
To Planes de Renderos
13A Av. Norte
Parque Infantil
3A Calle Poniente
1A Calle Poniente
Calle Arce
C. Rubén Darío
4A Calle Poniente
Gerardo Barrios
Cementerio
Cementerio General
17A Av. Sur
Calle Madrid
Overlap with 56R
25A Av. Norte
25A Av. Sur
32
Roosevelt
17
33 Av. N.
33 Av. Sur
To Autopista Norte
18
Arenal Tutunichapa
41 Av. N.
Sexta Décima C. poniente
Ferrocarril
Cementerio
El Bermejo
43 Av. Sur
30
Blvd. los Héroes
19
49 Av. Norte
49A Av. Sur
57A Av. Norte
Boulevard Venezuela
B2
1A Calle Poniente
Alameda
El Progreso
Av. Olímpica
El Bermejo
San Antonio
Escalón
N
73A Av. N.
C. Nueva 1
C. Loma Linda
Antigua Calle del Ferrocarril
29
C. La Reforma
25
21
24
Av. Las Magnolias
C. Las Palmas
Autopista Sur
79A Av. Norte
79 Av. Sur
23
9A C Poniente
Calle la Mascota
Av. La Capilla
31
22
Av. La Revolución
26
87A Av. Norte
Blvd. Hipódromo
89A Av. Norte
Carretera Panamericana
Av. Los Almendros
Circunvalación
To Nueva San Salvador
To Nueva San Salvador, Santa Ana & Guatemala

MAC 56L   **Not to Scale**

SAN SALVADOR
Centre & West

Centre East
1. Plaza Barrios
2. Palacio Nacional
3. Cathedral
4. Teatro Nacional
5. Parque Libertad
6. Church of El Rosario
7. La Merced
8. Plaza Morazán
9. Parque Bolívar
10. Church of El Sagrado Corazón de Jesús
11. Director General of Police
12. Centro de Gobierno / Immigration / Post office / Antel
13. Central Market
14. Mercado Modelo
15. Instituto Salvadoreño de Turismo
16. Plaza Hula Hula

Centre West
17. Parque Cuscatlán
18. Metrocentro
19. National Stadium
20. Monumento al Salvador del Mundo
21. Plaza Beethoven
22. *Hotel Presidente*
23. Museo Nacional David J. Guzmán
24. Feria Internacional
25. Baseball Stadium
26. *Hotel El Salvador*
27. Zoo
28. Casa Presidencial
29. Estado Mayor de la Fuerza Armada
30. *Hotel Camino Real*
31. *Hotel Terraza*
32. Hospital Rosales
B2. Terminal de Occidente

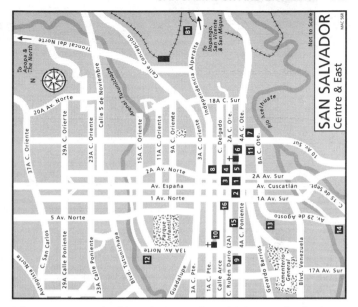

Oriente we come on the right to the Parque Libertad: in its centre is a flamboyant monument to Liberty looking E towards the rebuilt church of El Rosario where José Matías Delgado, father of the independence movement, lies buried. The Palacio Arquiepiscopal is next door. Not far away to the SE (on 10a Av Sur) is another rebuilt church, La Merced, from whose bell-tower went out Father Delgado's tocsin call to independence in 1811.

Across Calle Delgado, opposite the theatre, is Plaza Morazán, with a monument to General Morazán. Calle Arce runs W to the Hospital Rosales, in its own gardens. SW of the Hospital, along Av Roosevelt, is the Estadio Nacional. On the way to the Hospital, if you turn S opposite the great church of El Sagrado Corazón de Jesus, you come after 1 block to the Parque Bolívar, with the national printing office to the S and the Department of Health to the N.

NB The city centre is considered unsafe after dark. In general robberies, particularly on crowded city buses, have increased of late: pickpocketing and bag-slashing are common. Women are advised not to wear expensive jewellery on the street. See also **Note** after **Documents** in Information for Visitors.

Festivals At the edge of the city (to the N along Avenida España and W along 9a Calle Poniente) is the Campo de Marte, a large and popular park where the Palacio de Deportes has been built, and through which runs the Avenida Juan Pablo II. During Holy Week, and the fortnight preceding 6 August, is held the *Fiesta of the Saviour* ('El Salvador'). As a climax colourful floats wind up the Campo de Marte. On 5 August, an ancient image of the Saviour is borne before a large procession: there are church services on the 6th, Feast of the Transfiguration. On 12 December, Day of the Indian, there are processions honouring the Virgin of Guadalupe in El Salvador (take bus 101 to the Basílica de Guadalupe, on the edge of the city on the Carretera a Santa Tecla, to see colourful processions.)

Hotels Prices are without meals unless otherwise stated. Hotel tax 10%.
A+ *Camino Real*, Blvd de los Héroes, T 79-3888, F 23-5660 (a Westin hotel), completely renovated, formal atmosphere (popular with business visitors, used to

expense-accounts—beware overcharging); **A+** *Hotel El Salvador* (formerly *Sheraton*), T 79-0177, F 23-2901, 11 C Poniente y 89 Av Norte on the slopes of the volcano on the outskirts, outdoor pool, partly renovated, very pleasant, friendly. **A+** *Presidente*, T 98-2044, F 23-4912, Av La Revolución, San Benito, pool, garden, very pleasant, good buffets some nights, excellent service but expensive; **A** *Terraza*, T 79-0083, F 23-3223, 85 Av Sur and Calle Padre Aguilar; **A** *Alameda*, T 79-0299, F 79-3011, 43a Av Sur and Alameda Roosevelt; **B** *Novo Apart Hotel*, T 79-0099, 61 Av N 4617 (in cul-de-sac), rooms with bath and kitchen, mini swimming pool, garden, pleasant; **A** *Ramada Inn*, T 79-1820, F 79-1889, 85 Av Sur and Paseo General Escalón; **A** *Siesta*, T 79-0377, F 24-6575, on Autopista Sur, off Pan-American Highway, W of the city, very friendly, good restaurant; **B** *Ritz Continental*, T 22-0033, 7a Av Sur 219, pool, a/c, big rooms, quiet, good restaurant, charm of a somewhat run down luxury hotel; **B** *Austria*, T 24-0791, 1a Calle Poniente 3843 (between 73 and 75 Av), small, quiet, family atmosphere, English and German-speaking owner, price includes coffee and toast, helpful, convenient, rec; **B** *Internacional Puerto Bus*, Alameda Juan Pablo II y 19 Av Norte, at international bus terminal, T 21-1000, F 22-2138, a/c, TV, etc.

D *American Guest House*, T 71-0224, 17 Av N y 1a C Poniente 953, friendly, helpful; **C** *Happy House*, Av Sisimiles 2951, Col Miramonte, T 26-6866 (turn left at *Camino Real* and go uphill 200m), good; **C** *Casa Grande*, Calle Los Sisimiles y Av Bernal, Col Miramonte, T 74-7450; **D** *Phoenix*, 17 Av Norte 119, T 711269; **D** *Family Guest Home*, T 22-1202, 1a C Poniente Bis 925, safe, clean, friendly, expensive meals available; **D** *Florida Guest House*, T 26-1858, Pasaje Los Almendros 115, off Blvd de los Héroes, all rooms with bath, proprietor speaks English, good value, very clean, highly rec (near *Camino Real*: popular with journalists); **E** *Imperial*, T 22-4920, Calle Concepción 659, serves reasonable meals and has car park, more expensive with toilet and shower, rec; 3 doors along Concepción is **F-G** *Emperador*, friendly, good value, clean, laundry facilities on roof, rec. **F** *San Carlos*, T 22-8975, Calle Concepción 121, with bath, early morning call, cold drinks available, good; **E** *Casa de Huéspedes Clementina*, Avda Morazán 34 y Washington, T 255962, restaurant, clean, bulletin board; **E** *Centro*, 9 Av Sur 410, T 71-5045, TV, phone, friendly, washing facilities, clean, safe, rec; **E** *Ximena's Guest House*, T 26-9268, Calle San Salvador 202-A, Colonia Centroamérica, a bit cheaper without bath, 6 rooms, also has 2 apartments for longer stays, US$100 and US$120 a month, clean, pleasant, conveniently located, but not easy to find (take the little pathway down to Blvd Los Héroes); **E** *Custodio*, T 22-5503, 10 Av Sur 109, basic, clean, safe, and friendly; **E** *Hospedaje Izalco*, T 22-2616, Calle Concepción 666; **E** *Nuevo Panamericano*, 8 Av Sur 113, T 22-2959, with cold shower, safe, closes early (but knock on the door), meals from US$2 and parking space, rec; **E** *León*, T 22-0951, Calle Delgado 621, friendly, poor water supply, safe, parking; **E** *Pensión Rex*, 10 Av N 213, quiet, safe, run by Sra Rosalinda, rec; **E** *Yucatán*, Calle Concepción, shared bath, safe, with parking; **F** *Hospedaje El Turista*, 1C y 12 Av N 210, fan, clean, quiet, does laundry.

Restaurants Many close between 2000 and 2100.
On the Paseo General Escalón: *Siete Mares*, very good seafood; *Diligencia* (at 83 Av Sur, for good steaks) and *El Bodegón* (at 77 Av Norte, Spanish style —proprietor Spanish), both excellent; *La Mar* (seafoods), *Betos* (Italian—also *Hola/Betos*, Av Pasco y Calle Lamatepec, behind *Camino Real Hotel*). *La Pampa Argentina*, highly rec for steaks, popular; *Asia* moderately-priced Chinese; *Quecos*, Mexican, good variety; *La Carnitas de Don Carlos*, good beef, reasonable prices, less pretentious and costly than similar places; *La Fonda del Sol*, No 4920, opp Villas Españolas shopping centre, Italian, popular with business set, good value, highly rec; *Pip's Carymar* (also in Santa Tecla—good, cheap typical food), *Rancho Alegre* (good choice of food, relatively cheap, travellers' meeting place—also at Metrosur, S of Metrocentro, and *tacos* and *pupusas* at Redondel Masferrer (good view over the city, lively atmosphere, mariachis).

Restaurants in the Zona Rosa, Blvd Hipódromo, are generally very good, but expensive. These include: *Marcelino's*; *Mediterranée*, No 131 (good *ceviche*); *La Ola*, very good meals and moderately priced; *Chili's*; *Paradise*, for steak and lobster, excellent food and service, another branch on Blvd de los Héroes (all popular); *Basilea/Schaffer's*, restaurant and excellent cakes (from *Shaw's Bakery* next door), nice garden atmosphere. *Dynasty*, known for best Chinese food in city, but not cheap.

Others include: *Texas Meats*, Calle La Mascota, good for steaks; *Doña Mercedes*, Metrocentro, Blvd de Los Héroes, is another good steakhouse; *München*, Av Roosevelt, German; opp is *China Palace*, No 2731, excellent value (oldest Chinese restaurant in San Salvador); *Dallas*, nr Zona Rosa, good steaks and seafood, exaggerated service, prices from moderate to expensive; *El Arbol de Dios*, inside art gallery in Av La Mascota in the Escalón, international, secluded, can be dear; *Señor Tenedor*, Av Olímpica, opp Ciné Deluxe, 0900-2200, nearest thing to an American deli, good value, breakfast buffet, good choice of salads and sandwiches; *Felipe's*, off Blvd de Los Héroes, popular Mexican, good value;

Madeira, la C Poniente, Col Escalón, international, pleasant atmosphere, expensive. *Pupusería Margot*, opp Estado Mayor on the road to Santa Tecla, good; *Rosal*, 93 Av Norte y Calle El Mirador, near *Hotel El Salvador*, Italian, good; *Spaghetería*, opp Salvador del Mundo, generous portions of good quality pasta at reasonable prices; *Pizza Capri*, Italian-owned, behind *Hotel Camino Real*. Good chicken and *pupusas* at *Pollo Real*, 1 C Poniente y 69 Av Norte.

Vegetarian restaurants: *La Zanahoria*, Calle Arce 1144; *Govinda's*, 51 Av Norte 147, Col Flor Blanca, T 23-2468, take bus 44 (a bit hard to find, but worth it); *Kalpataru*, Av Masferrer 127, 100m N of Redondel Masferrer, nice atmosphere; *El Tao*, 21 Av Norte, Calles 27 y 29 Poniente, and Centro de Gobierno, 19 Calle Poniente, and 19a Av Norte, Col Layco.

Branches of fast-food restaurants may be found in many parts of town: *Pizza Hut*, *MacDonalds* and *Biggest* (hamburgers), *Wendy*, on Paseo Escalón, *Pollo Campero* (fried chicken), *Mr Donut* (pastries, sandwiches, soups, salad, fresh juice) at Metrocentro Paseo Escalón, and elsewhere, *Pops* and *Vips* (ice cream parlours), several outlets throughout town, rec.

Cafés There are numerous *cafeterías* serving cheap traditional meals such as *tamales*, *pupusas*, *frijoles*, rice with vegetables, etc. Often these places can be found around the major hotels, catering for guests who find the hotel meals overpriced. *Café Don Alberto*, Calle Arce and 15 Av Sur, good and cheap; *Actoteatro*, 1 Calle Poniente (between 15 and 13 Av N), good atmosphere, patio, music, good buffet lunch, cheap, central, rec; *Café de Don Pedro*, Roosevelt y Alameda, next to Esso filling station, good range of food, mariachi groups, open all night; *Café Teatro*, attached to the Teatro Nacional, serves very good lunches, good value (see also **Night Clubs** below). Good, cheap *comedores* in Occidente bus terminal. *Victoria*, bakery, good for pastries. Food markets in various parts of the city have stalls selling cheap food. Gourmet and delicatessen fare at *Señor Tenedor*, Plaza Jardín, Av Olímpica 3544, good but expensive sandwiches. **Coffee shops** *Shaw's* (good coffee and 'sinful' chocolates), Paseo Escalón 1 block W of Plaza Beethoven, and at Metrocentro.

Bars *El Malibú*, Blvd de los Héroes, many local and imported beers, tasty snacks, good latin and rock music, very friendly and lively atmosphere; *Las Antorchitas*, next to *El Malibú*, good local orchestra with a dance floor, French and English spoken, cover charge US$1.20; *La Luna*, Calle Berlín 228, off Blvd de los Héroes, Urb Buenos Aires 3, T 25-4987, good mixture of music, different themes each night, matched well by mixed arty clientèle, reasonably-priced drinks and snacks. See also **Night Clubs**, below.

Clubs *Club Salvadoreño* admits foreigners, owns a fine Country Club on Lago Ilopango called Corinto (with a golf course), and has a seaside branch at Km 43 on the coast road, near La Libertad, much frequented during the dry season, November to April. The *Automobile Club of El Salvador* has a chalet for bathing at La Libertad. See also *Atami Beach Club* under La Libertad, **Excursions**. *British Club* (Paseo Escalón 4714, T 23-6004) has British newspapers, an English language library, darts (on Wed), snooker and a small swimming pool (temporary visitor's cards if introduced by a member). *El Centro Español*, off the Paseo Escalón, is open to non-members, has 2 pools (one for children), tennis courts, weight training room and aerobics salon. The *Country Club Campestre* (Paseo Escalón), admits foreigners with cards only. *Club Náutico*, at the Estero de Jaltepeque, famous for its boat races across the mud flats at low tide.

Shopping *Mercado Cuartel*, crafts market, 8 Av Norte, 1a C Oriente, a few blocks E of the Teatro Nacional. Towels (Hilasal brand) may be bought here with various Maya designs. Crafts may also be bought at the *Mercado Nacional de Artesanías*, opposite the Estado Mayor on the road to Santa Tecla, at prices similar to the Mercado Cuartel. A large shopping precinct with adequate parking is on the Boulevard de los Héroes, NW of the city centre: it is called *Metrocentro*; it contains 2 of best known department stores, *Siman* and *Swartz*, together with boutiques, gift shops and a small supermarket. It is accompanied by another shopping complex, *Metrosur*, to the S, which has fewer shops. Another shopping centre, *Villas Españolas*, has opened on the Paseo Escalón, 1 block S of the Redondel Masferrer; it is rather more exclusive, with expensive boutiques, several impressive furniture stores, and a minimarket specializing in tinned food from around the world. There is another called *Feria Rosa* opposite the Foreign Ministry on the road to Santa Tecla (Pan-American Highway), which is by no means fully occupied. Paseo Escalón has a wide variety of boutiques and gift shops in all price ranges. Prices in shopping centres are much higher than in the centre of town or crafts markets. There are also some exclusive shops in the Zona Rosa. *El Sol* and *Europa* are 2 major supermarkets in Plaza Beethoven, Paseo General Escalón and Av 75 Nte. Towels can also be bought in the centre at *Hula Hula*, 2 blocks E of the Cathedral, where there are also street traders. Visa and Mastercard are increasingly accepted in shops.

Bookshops At the Universidad de El Salvador (UES) and the Universidad Centroamericana (UCA). *Cervantes*, 9a Av Sur 114 in the Centre and Edificio El Paseo No 3, Paseo Escalón. *Bautista* (T 22-2457), 10 Calle Poniente 124, good. *Cultura Católica*, opp Teatro Nacional. *El Arabe* (T 22-3922) Av España 101. *Clásicos Roxil* (T 28-1212), 6 Av Sur 1-6, Santa Tecla. Regular book fairs at the Teatro Nacional. Some English books at *Librería Cultural Salvadoreña* (T 24-5443) in Metrosur. Others at *Librería Quixaje*, Calle Arce, and a few at *Shaw's* chocolate shop. American magazines and secondhand books at *La Revista*, Hipódromo 235, Zona Rosa, large selection. Magazines and newspapers in English can be bought at leading hotels (eg *Miami Herald* at *Hotel Presidente*, 1 day old, US$2.25).

Hairdressing *Pino di Roma*, Colonia San Benito, for ladies, high standards, latest styles, US$10 cut, shampoo and blow-dry.

Local buses US$0.07 for normal services (all blue and white), US$0.10 after 1800; US$0.12-0.15 for special services (red and white, and some better quality blue and white.)

Taxis Plenty (all yellow), none has a meter, ask fare before getting in. Fares: from centre to outskirts or *Hotel El Salvador* US$2.50; shorter runs no more than $3.50. Drivers will try to charge more after dark or in the rain. More expensive taxis may be hired from: Acontaxis (T 22-3361, 22-3268, 22-3294), Acosat (T 25-4015), Dos Pinos (T 21-1285, 21-1286, 22-2321), Acomet (T 25-9114, 25-9576). Taxis Acacya specializes in services to the airport (T San Salvador: 71-4937, 71-4938, Airport: 39-9271, 39-9282.)

Car Hire Rentals from **Avis**, 43a Av Sur 137 (T 23-6321, 23-7268), International Airport and leading hotels; **Budget**, 85 Av Sur 220 (T San Salvador 23-5677, 24-2802, Airport 39-9186, 39-9187); **Hertz**, Calle Los Andes behind *Hotel Camino Real* (T San Salvador 26-8099, Airport 39-9481); **Dollar**, Alameda Roosevelt 2119 (T 24-4385); **Imosa**, Edif Kent, local No 3 Blvd de los Héroes (T 24-6082, 24-1416, 22-2458, 22-4624); **Rentautos**, 29 C Poniente and 7 Av Norte (T 25-3685, 74-2331, 25-0073).

Night Clubs All leading hotels have their own night club. Cover charge is usually ¢10/US$1.20. *Mario's* on Blvd Hipódromo, Zona Rosa, with good live music; *Memories*, Paseo General Escalón; *My Place*, Paseo General Escalón and 83 Av Norte. *Café Teatro*, by National Theatre, Tues-Sat, jazz on Tues, various music other nights; *La Luna*, C Berlín 228, Urb Buenos Aires 3, 2 blocks from Blvd de Los Héroes, see under *Bars*, above; *Las Puertas*, Paseo Gen Escalón, live music and art exhibitions; *Malibu*, end of Blvd de Los Héroes y C San Antonio Abad, see under *Bars*, above; *Quinto Sol*, 1a C Poniente y 15 Av Norte, Tues 1000-2000, Wed-Sat 0900-2400, dance to music by Banda Tepeuani, food US$1-3; *Tabu Bar Club*, final C Gabriela Mistral No 721, nr Ciné Variedades, mainly Latin music, some rock, small bar/restaurant serving good traditional food, live music Thur-Sat after 2100, closed Sun and Mon, no cover charge; *Sur*, Calle Las Rosas y Av Central 25, T 26-3968, for Jamaican music, jazz and blues, also *Cine Club Zorba*; *Villa Fiesta*, Blvd de Los Héroes, restaurant/bar, Mon-Wed Latin music (Grupo Fiesta), Thur Rumba Seis, Fri-Sat Latin music with guest bands.

Entertainments Many Cinemas, including: *Presidente*, near *Hotel Presidente* in Col San Benito; *Colonial*, Col La Sultana, near entrance to the UCA; *Variedades*, Calle San Antonio Abad; *Beethoven*, Plaza Beethoven, Paseo Escalón. Best quality cinemas cost US$2, films in English with Spanish subtitles. Alliance Française arranges film seasons, T 23-8084. Ballet and plays at the Teatro Nacional de Bellas Artes, and music or plays at the Teatro Cámera. Folk music in *Café Teatro*, in the Teatro Nacional.

Sports Bowling at Bolerama Jardín and Club Salvadoreño. Soccer is played on Sun and Thur according to programme at the Cuscatlán and Flor Blanca Stadiums. Motor racing at new El Jabalí autodrome on lava fields near Quetzaltepeque. Basketball, tennis, international swimming, fishing, target shooting, wrestling, boxing and boat and sailing boat races, but in private clubs only.

Museums **Museo Nacional David J Guzmán**, opposite Feria Internacional on Av de la Revolución, has a small but good archaeological exhibition. Open Tues-Sun. 0900-1200 and 1400-1700. **Museo de Historia Nacional**, end of Calle Los Víveros, Col Nicaragua, Wed-Sun 0930-1630.

Exchange Since the colón now floats, exchange has been liberalized and simplified. Banks generally accept dollars and TCs, but *casas de cambio* give better rates. There are *casas de cambio* throughout the city, offering prices that differ by no more than a few centavos. The black market still exists along the S of the Parque Infantil, and concentrated around the Central Post Office in Centro de Gobierno (assaults are not frequent). Quetzales and lempiras may sometimes be changed there (quetzales are also changed at the Occidente bus terminal where international buses leave for Guatemala.) Dollars may be bought freely at *casas de cambio* and on the black market, with little variation in price. Accounts in dollars may be opened at

Citibank, Edificio SISA, 2nd floor near El Salvador de Mundo. **Credomatic**, for obtaining funds with either Visa or Mastercard, Edificio Cidema, Alameda Roosevelt and Calle 51, offers a poor rate and charges commission. In emergency, for Visa International or Mastercard, T 24-5100; American Express, loss or theft, T 23-0177. Banks open 0900-1300, 1330-1600, *casas de cambio* open longer hours.

Spanish Language School Escuela de Idiomas Salvador Miranda, PO Box 3274, Correo Centro de Gobierno, T 22-1352, US$125 per week including board. Cihuatan Spanish Language Institute (Ximena's), Calle San Salvador 202-B, San Salvador, Col Centro América (near *Hotel Camino Real*), T (503) 26-9268, René or Lisa Carmona, F (503) 79-4580 c/o Donald Lee – Antel; rates are US$125 per week including board at *Ximena's Guesthouse* in the city or nearby farm, *Lisa's Inn*, 17 km from the capital between Apopa and Guazapa (buses San Salvador-Chalatenango stop at the farm).

Library The library of the UCA, Universidad Centro Americana José S Cañas, Autopista Sur, the road to the airport, is said to be the most complete collection in the capital.

Embassies **Guatemalan**, 15 Av Norte 135 y Calle Arce (0900-1200), T 22-2903/ 71-2225, visas issued within 24 hrs; **Honduran**, 7 C Poniente y 83 Av Norte No 4326, Colonia Escalón, T 98-0524; **Nicaraguan**, 89a Ave. N and 9a Calle Pte No 4612, T 24-6662; **Belizean**, Condominio Médico, local 34, 3rd floor, Blvd Tutunichapa, Urb la Esperanza, T 25-8499; **Mexican**, Paseo General Escalón 3832 (T 98-1176/98-1074/98-1079); **Panamanian**, 21 Ave Las Bugambilias Col San Francisco, T 98-0773; **Costa Rican**, Edificio Centroamericano, 3rd floor, Alameda Roosevelt 3107, T 79-0303.

US, Final Estación Antigua, Antiguo Cuscutlán, Unit 3116, T 78-4444, F 78-6011; **British**, Edif Inter Inversiones, Paseo General Escalón 4828, PO Box 1591, T 98-1763, has British newspapers (also Honorary Consul 71-1050); **German**, 3a C Poniente 3832, Col Escalón (T 23-6140); **French**, 1a C Poniente 3178 y 73 Av Norte, Col Escalón (T 23-8186); **Swiss**, Honorary Consul only: T 24-3940/23-2080.

Immigration Department In the Ministry of Interior Building, Centro de Gobierno, T 21-2111, open Mon-Fri 0800-1600. They will consider sympathetically extending tourist visas, but be prepared with photos and plenty of patience.

Complaints Director General of Police, 6a Calle Oriente, T 71-4422.

Post Office Central Post Office at the Centro de Gobierno with EMS, super-fast service: branches at Almacenes Siman (Centro), Librería Hispanoamérica, Centro Comercial Gigante (Col Escalón), Metrocentro, with EMS, CASA on la Plaza Suiza, Mercado Local No 3, Mercado Modelo, 1st floor above PHL stationer on Plaza Morazán. Open Mon-Fri 0730-1700, Sat 0730-1700. Lista de Correos, Mon-Fri 0800-1200, 1430-1700.

Telephones Antel at the Centro de Gobierno.

Places of Worship **Anglican Centre (St John's Episcopal Church)**, 63 Av Sur and Av Olímpica, services on Sun, 0900 in English, 1000 in Spanish; **American Union Church**, Calle 4, off Calle La Mascota, has services in English on Sun at 0930, and also has a gift shop (local crafts and textiles) and an English paperback library (both open Wed and Sat). **Synagogue**, Colonia San Benito.

International Industrial Fair, held in November, every 2 years (even dates) in the International Fair buildings, Calle a Santa Tecla, turnoff for Colonia San Benito (near *Hotel Presidente*). Site is also used for other functions such as the August fair.

Tourist Office Instituto Salvadoreño de Turismo (ISTU), Calle Rubén Darío 619, T 22-8000/3241 (Mon-Fri 0800-1600, Sat 0800-1200, closed Sun). They will advise on the security situation in the country. They give away several leaflets about services in the country, and a map of the country and city, also 'Advice to Tour Guides,' a rec booklet. The office is very helpful. The tourist office at the international airport is open 0800-1630 all year round except 25 Dec and 1 Jan, T 39-9454, 39-9464. Texaco and Esso also sell good **maps** at their respective service stations. The best maps of the city and country (US$3 and $2 respectively) are available from the **Instituto Geográfico Nacional**, Av Juan Bertis No 79, Ciudad Delgado.

Conventions facilities, including organized tours for delegates, may be arranged by the Salvadoran Conventions Bureau, *Hotel Presidente* rooms 274-276, T 24-0819/24-0536/24-0508.

Tourist Agents Numerous, including: *El Salvador Travel Service*, Centro Comercial La Mascota, Local No 1, T 23-0177; *Avia*, 1a Calle Pte y 73 Av Norte, Col Escalón, T 24-0122/24-2770; *Alpha Travel Agency*, Alameda Roosevelt y 55 Av Sur No 2827, Edif Carolina, T 24-6928/23-1652; *Travel and Tours*, 73 Av Norte No 136, local 2, T 23-6558/23-6650; *Maya*, Av Olímpica No 3008, Edif HMH, Frente a Centro Comercial

Gigante, T 24-2570/24-3316. For day tours or short trips phone Donald Lee (503) 26-9268, F 79-4580, or Lorena Díaz T (503) 84-1117, San Salvador. List of approved tourist agents available from the Instituto Salvadoreño de Turismo.

Airport The new international airport at Comalapa is 44 km from San Salvador near Costa del Sol beach, reached by a 4-line highway. Acacya minibus to airport, from 3 C Pte y 19 Av Norte (T San Salvador 71-4937/71-4938, Airport 39-9271/39-9282), 0600, 0700, 1200, 1500 (be there 15 mins before), US$2 one-way. (Leave from airport when full, on right as you go out.) The prices in the gift-shops at the airport are exorbitant; there is a post office, a bank (normal banking hours), and a tourist office.

Taca provide all necessary meals, transport and accommodation for those making stop-overs on their flights, making no charge but using whichever of the major hotels is convenient at the time. Taca, T 23-2244.

The old airport is at Ilopango, 13 km away. It is primarily used by the air force. However, small planes fly from Ilopango to San Miguel (30 mins, good), Usulután, Santa Rosa de Lima, San Francisco Gotera and La Unión; tickets from the civilian traffic offices (TAES, Taxis Aéreos El Salvador, T 27-0120—in San Miguel T Sra de Domínguez 61-3954 —, or Gutiérrez Flying Service). No regular internal air lines but charter flights are easily arranged.

Rail A daily passenger service runs from San Salvador to Apopa (except Sun), US$0.10. Other services only exist in very inaccessible parts of El Salvador, taking campesinos from one coffee plantation to another. There are no tourist services.

Long Distance Buses Domestic services go from Terminal de Occidente, off Blvd Venezuela, T 23-3784 (take city buses 4, 27 or 34) and Terminal de Oriente, end of Av Peralta in Centro Urb Lourdes (take city buses 7, 33, 34 or 29), very clean and well-organized. Routes and fares are given under destinations.

International services: **To Guatemala**: Many buses a day to Guatemala City (5 hrs) from new terminal (1992) 'Puerto Bus' at the end of Av San Antonio Abad, Av Juan Pablo II, in W of city, T 22-2158/3224, F 22-2138; you can walk there from city centre (scary), or take city bus 29; the terminal has a *casa de cambio* (open daily) and a hotel, **C** range. Melva (T 24-2953), comfortable and fast, 9 a day between 0530 and 1400 (be at terminal half hour before departure, US$5.50); Tica Bus, address below (T 22-4808), 0600, US$8; Centroamérica (T 24-4258) 0600—home pick-up at 0530, US$7; Taca (T 24-3236), 15 a day; also Pezzarossi and others. Inter Tours/Quality, Condominio Balam Quitzé, Paseo Escalón y 89 Av, T 79-4166, F 23-7616, runs a daily service at 0615 from *Hotel Siesta*, 0630 *Hotel Presidente* to Guatemala City for US$40 return (US$64 inc hotel), luxury service, with a/c, film, drinks and meals. Confort Line charges the same fare, departing daily from *Hotel El Salvador* at 0800 and 1400 (single fare US$22).

To Tegucigalpa: Tica Bus from Calle Concepción 121, *Hotel San Carlos*, T 22-8975, or Tica Bus T 22-4808, 0500, US$15. Buses to Tegucigalpa also with Cruceros del Golfo from 'Puerto Bus', 0600 and 1300, US$15. Tica Bus to Managua (US$35), San José (US$50), and Panama (US$75). All via Tegucigalpa. Alternatively take local services to El Amatillo or to Santa Rosa, 4 hrs, US$1.25, 4 a day then Ruta 346 to El Amatillo, 30 min US$0.25, last bus to the border 1730.

A good **sightseeing tour** of from 2 to 3 hrs by car is along Av Cuscatlán, past the Zoo (which though small, is quiet and attractive—open Wed-Sun 0930-1630) and the Casa Presidencial and up to the new residential district in the mountain range of **Planes de Renderos**. This place is crowned by the beautiful Parque Balboa (good view of city from El Mirador at foot of Park). Parque Balboa is a Turicentro, with cycle paths, playground, gardens, etc, open daily 0800-1800. From the park a scenic road runs to the summit of **Cerro Chulo**, from which the view, seen through the Puerta del Diablo (Devil's Door), is even better. The Door consists of 2 enormous vertical rocks which frame a magnificent view of the San Vicente volcano. At the foot of Cerro Chulo is Panchimalco (see below). There are local buses to Parque Balboa (12, US$0.20 and 17 from eastern side of Mercado Central), and to Puerta del Diablo (No 12 marked 'Mil Cumbres') about every hour. There are reports that mugging is increasingly common at Cerro Chulo; it is unsafe to make the trip alone. The Teleférico on the hill overlooking the city and Lago de Ilopango has good views, cafeterias and a children's funfair. Reached by 9 bus from centre, US$1.60. Open Fri, Sat, Sun only, 0900-1900.

Excursions can be made by road to Panchimalco and Lago de Ilopango; to the crater of San Salvador volcano (see under Santa Tecla, below); and to the volcano of Izalco (1,910m) and the near-by park of Atecosol, and Cerro Verde (**see Sonsonate, p 589**); to the garden park of Ichanmichen (**see Zacatecoluca, p 599**); to Lago de Coatepeque (lunch at *Hotel del Lago*) and to Cerro Verde in 90 mins. Bus 495 from the Terminal del Occidente goes to Costa del Sol, a developing seaside resort (**see p 600**). Sihuatehuacán and the pyramid of Tazumal (p 593) The Instituto Salvadoreño de Turismo organizes a whole series of excursions by bus on Sunday to many destinations outside San Salvador. They last the full day and leave from Plaza Libertad at 0700. The trips are very popular so arrive at 0600. Prices start at US$1.50; for information T 22-8000, ext 214-238, Departamento de Turismo Interno.

The Mountaineering Club of the University of San Salvador sponsors day hikes every Sunday morning. Transportation from downtown San Salvador is provided. See local papers on Saturdays for details. The club is extremely friendly and the excursions are strongly recommended.

Panchimalco is 14½ km S by a paved road. Around it live the Pancho Indians, descendants of the original Pipil tribes; a few have retained more or less their old traditions and dress. Streets of low adobe houses thread their way among huge boulders at the foot of Cerro Chulo. A very fine baroque colonial church has splendid woodcarvings in the interior and a bell incised with the cypher and titles of the Holy Roman Emperor Charles V, and the cemetery is said to be colourful (the church was reported closed in late 1993). An ancient ceiba tree shades the market place (disappointing market). Bus 17 from Mercado Central at 12 Calle Poniente, San Salvador, every 45 min, US$0.30, 1½ hrs, or minibus from near Mercado Central, very crowded but quicker (30 mins), and cheaper (US$0.24).

Lago de Ilopango A 4-lane highway, the Boulevard del Ejército, runs E for 14½ km from San Salvador to Ilopango airport, quite near Lago de Ilopango, 15 km by 8, in the crater of an old volcano, well worth a visit. Pre-Conquest Indians used to propitiate the harvest gods by drowning 4 virgins here each year. There are a number lakeside cafés and bathing clubs, some of which hire dug-outs by the hour. *Hotel Vista del Lago*, 3 km from Apulo turn off on Highway, is on a hill top. Private chalets make access to the lake difficult, except at clubs and the Turicentro Apulo. Bus 15, marked Apulo, runs from the bus stop on Parque Hula Hula to the lake (via the airport), 70 mins, US$0.30. Entrance to the Turicentro camping site costs US$0.40; bungalow US$4; parking US$0.40; plenty of hammock hanging opportunities; showers and swimming facilities, all rather dirty. The water is reported to be polluted in parts near the shore and it is busy at weekends.

Santa Tecla, also known as Nueva San Salvador, 13 km W of the capital by the Pan-American Highway, is 240m higher and much cooler, in a coffee-growing district. Population, 63,400. (**D** *Hotel Monte Verde*, on the main road, T 28-1263; **E** *Hospedaje San Antonio*, 4 Av Poniente, 2 blocks S of Plaza, and a **F** *Hospedaje*, no name, Calle Daniel Hernández y 6 Av, 3 blocks from Parque San Martín, white door, good, safe, will store luggage. *Restaurant La Tortuga Feliz*, 4 C Poniente 1-5, marimba music, garden, pleasant setting, good local food.) The huge crater of **San Salvador volcano** (known as **Boquerón** by the locals)—1½ km wide and 543m deep—can be reached from Santa Tecla, road starts 1 block E of Plaza Central, going due N (very rough). Bus (101) leaves 3 Av Norte, near the junction with Calle Rubén Darío, San Salvador, every 10 mins for Santa Tecla (US$0.12). There is a bus (103) from there to Boquerón hourly, last one back at 1500 (US$0.30) and from there you must walk the last 1½ km to the crater. A walk clockwise round the crater takes about 2 hrs; the first half is easy, the second half rough (the path was used by soldiers and guerrillas). Take care, a tourist fell from the ridge in 1991. The views are magnificent, if somewhat spoilt by TV and radio towers and litter. The inner slopes of the crater are covered with trees, and at the bottom is a smaller cone left by the eruption of 1917. The path down into the crater starts at the westernmost of a row of antennae studding the rim, 45 mins down (don'T miss the turn straight down after 10 mins at an inconspicuous junction with a big, upright slab of rock 20m below), 1 hr up. There are a number of army checkpoints on the way to the summit. A machete can be helpful. A road further N leads also to San Salvador volcano, also known at **El Picacho**, through extensive coffee plantations. This makes an excellent climb from the Escalón suburb of San Salvador, in the early morning preferably, taking about 3-4 hrs return trip. Santa Tecla has a training school for factory technicians, set up with British funds and technical help.

At *Los Chorros*, in a natural gorge 6 km NW of Santa Tecla, there is a beautiful landscaping of 4 pools below some waterfalls. The first pool is shallow, and bathers can stand under the cascades, but there is good swimming in the other 3. Entry, US$0.40. Car park fee: US$0.40. There is a trailer park at Los Chorros, with restaurant and showers and a hotel **D** *Monte Sinai*, T 26-6623. Bus 79 from 11 Av Sur y Calle Rubén Darío in San Salvador.

Just before Santa Tecla is reached, a branch road turns S for 24 km to *La Libertad*, 32 km from San Salvador, now only a fishing port. Population 22,800. It is also a popular seaside resort during the dry season, with good fishing and surf bathing (El Zunzal beach is the surfers' favourite, see below). Watch out for undercurrents and sharks. The beaches are black volcanic sand (which can be very hot); they are dirty but the surf is magnificent (watch your belongings). Surf season is Nov-April. There are also swimming pools, admission US$0.15. (The Automobile Club and the Club Salvadoreño have beach chalets.) Bus 102 from San Salvador leaves from 4 Calle Poniente, between 13 and 15 Av Sur, 1 hr, US$0.20. Bus from Santa Tecla, US$0.10.

The Costa del Bálsamo (the Balsam Coast), between La Libertad and Acajutla (see below), is now rather a myth, but on the steep slopes of the departments of Sonsonate and La Libertad, scattered balsam trees are still tapped. The pain-relieving balsam, once a large export, has almost disappeared. Bus along the coast to Sonsonate at 0600 and 1300, about 4 hrs.

Hotels B *El Malecón de Don Lito*, T 35-3201 (also **B** *La Posada de Don Lito*, T 35-3166); at Playa Conchalío, both **C** *Conchalío*, T 35-3194, large, nice, and *Los Arcos*, T 35-3490, safe, quiet, with pool, garden and restaurant; **E** *Nuevo Amanecer*, 1 C Poniente No 24-1, safe, clean, rec; **E** *Posada Familiar*, basic, shared bath; **F** *Pensión Amor y Paz*, very basic, friendly, but overpriced; **E** *Rik*, opposite *Punta Roca* restaurant, clean, friendly; **F** *Puerto Bello*, on the main avenue, with bath, clean, small rooms. **F** *Bar Gringo* on the beach front lets rooms, so does the *Miramar* restaurant (F, negotiable). **Motel** *Siboney*, nearby, good. 4 km W of Libertad are the **D** *Cabañas Don Chepe*.

Restaurant Food is good in the town, especially at *Punta Roca* (American-owned, by Don Bobby), try the shrimp soup, and *Altamar* for seafood. *Sagrado Corazón de Jesus*, 1 Av Norte, good value, large helpings, try their *pupusas de queso*. *Pupusería*, specializes in snacks, rec. *Los Mariscos*, good, reasonable prices, popular, closed Mons. *The Fisherman's Club*, excellent seafood, expensive, bar, swimming pool, tennis court, private beach, entry fee US$2. Cheap restaurants near the pier; also cheap food in the market. Good value restaurants at Playa Obispo, 1½ km from town towards San Diego.

Car repairs Good workshop on 7 Av Sur, Francisco is helpful, good quality work, you can sleep in vehicle while the job is done.

Excursions To the large village of *Jicalapa*, on high rockland above the sea, for its magnificent festival on St Ursula's day (21 October). 8 km to the W is *Zunzal*, which has superb surf (**E** *Hospedaje El Pacífico*, 1 km towards La Libertad, surfers' hotel; **G** pp *Hospedaje Surfers-In*, very basic but friendly, run by Marta who serves meals; bus 80, from La Libertad). 15 km away is the *Atami Beach Club*, Carretera Litoral, Km 49.5, T 23-7698/9000, with pool, private beach, restaurant, 2 bars, gardens, a beautiful place; tourists may enter for US$2, and stay the night for US$11, food (prices are reasonable). At Km 42 is *El Bosque Club*, T 35-3011, closes 1800, day cabins only. 17 km W of La Libertad is Turicentro Bocana, Playa El Zonte; accommodation at Ranch House with kitchen, pool, *cabaña* sleeping 5 adults, US$40/day, US$200/week, swimming, surfing; transport is provided by the owner, Oscar López, T (503) 28-9976, Santa Tecla, or fax Donald Lee (503) 79-4580 for reservations. Bus to San Diego beach (from road parallel to La Libertad beach), US$1, ½ hourly, nice but deserted (*Río Mar Club*, T 22-7879, San Salvador). To the **Salto y Cueva Los Mangos**: walk along the 2 km trail almost opposite *Motel Siboney* to a 60m waterfall; a little further downstream is the Salto San Antonio (50m), best reached by bus 287 from La Libertad to San Antonio quarry (just before San Diego beach), then walking 1 km upstream. Generally the coast road to Acajutla is very scenic with rocky bays, tunnels and remote black sand beaches for bathing, but take great care with the sea which can be dangerous.

WESTERN EL SALVADOR

Some very interesting natural features and beautiful countryside. The trip to Cerro Verde and Izalco is a 'must'. Santa Ana is an important coffee-growing centre and the city is worth a visit.

The route from the capital S to La Libertad has already been given. A paved road connects San Salvador with Sonsonate and the port of Acajutla. The road goes W through Santa Tecla (**see p 587**) to Sonsonate, and then S to the port. 6 km W of Santa Tecla on the main road is Los Chorros (see under Santa Tecla); 3½ km beyond, the Pan-American Highway (good) runs NW past Lago de Coatepeque to Santa Ana. There are 4 roads which cross into Guatemala, through La Hachadura (see under Sonsonate), San Cristóbal (or the Pan-American Highway), Las Chinamas (see under Santa Ana) and Anguiatú (beyond Metapán).

Acajutla, Salvador's main port serving the western and central areas, is 85 km from San Salvador (bus 207 from Occidente terminal, US$2.80), or 252 from Sonsonate US$0.30, 58 km from Santa Ana (it is 8 km S of the Coastal Highway). It handles about 40% of the coffee exports and is a popular seaside resort during the summer (good surfing, though beaches have reportedly become dirty). It is not an attractive town. Population: 36,000.

Hotels and Restaurants E *California*, run down; F *El Greco*; F *Brisas del Mar*; *Lara* by beach, with bath and fan, clean, car parking; G *Pensión Gato Negro*, opposite Belinda store, run by Japanese couple, with good restaurant, varied food, generous portions, meals US$1 to US$1.50. There are 2 motels, D, on the outskirts of town. *Pizza y Restaurante Perla del Mar* serves good shakes and food at reasonable prices.

The nearby beaches (NW of Acajutla) at Metalio (safe for camping) and Barra de Santiago are rec. Also rec is Salinitas, scenic, peaceful but too many rocks for safe bathing; a modern tourist complex here contains cabins, restaurants, gardens, pool, and a zoo. Los Cóbanos (S of Acajutla) is dirty, expensive and unsafe; 2 hotels here: **D** Sol y Mar, T 51-0137, weekends only; **E** Mar de Plata, 17 cabins.

Sonsonate (altitude 225m), 19 km N on the road to the capital (64 km) produces sugar, tobacco, rice, tropical fruits, hides and balsam. An important market is held each Sun. Sonsonate is in the chief cattle-raising region. Population: 60,900. It was founded in 1552. The beautiful El Pilar church is strongly reminiscent of the church of El Pilar in San Vicente. The Cathedral has many of the cupolas (the largest covered with white porcelain) which serve as a protection against earthquakes. The old church of San Antonio del Monte, just outside the city, draws pilgrims from afar. The market outside the church is quite well-organized and is good for leather items. Capital to Sonsonate by bus 205, US$0.50, 90 mins, very frequent. In the northern outskirts of the city there is a waterfall on the Sensunapán river. Legend has it that an Indian princess drowned there, and on the anniversary of her death a gold casket appears below the falls.

Hotels D *Sonsonate*, 6 Av Norte with Calle Obispo Marroquín, with a/c, meals available; **E** *Castro*, 3 blocks from Parque, with bath, good, safe, friendly, some rooms with bed and hammock; **E** *El Brasil*, 4 Av Norte, basic, clean and friendly; **E** *Hospedaje Veracruz*, Av Rafael Campo, T 51-0616, very noisy, unfriendly, not rec; **E** *Orbe*, 14 C Oriente, T 51-1416, parking, good restaurant; **F** *Hospedaje Blue River*, with bath, large, clean rooms; **G** *Florida*, beside bus terminal, basic, manager speaks English; also near bus station, **F** *Pensión Oriente*, not bad.

Restaurants *Milkbar; Comedor Santa Cecilia; Via del Mar; Hilay; El Rancho*.

Roads N to Santa Ana, 39 km a beautiful journey through high, cool coffee country, with volcanoes in view; NW to Ahuachapán (**see p 593**), 40 km, frequent buses from Sonsonate, US$0.50, 2 hrs (road paved from Ahuachapán through Apaneca and passes through some spectacular scenery); S and W to the Guatemalan frontier point of *La Hachadura* at the bridge over the Río Paz (**G** *Hotel El Viajero*, fans, safe, clean, good value; some shops and a filling station). Border crossing is straightforward, but if in a private vehicle requires a lot of paperwork (about 2 hrs). Exit tax US$0.60 per person. Bus 498 from Terminal de Occidente, San Salvador, US$0.75, and No 503 from Ahuachapan, by market, US$0.65, 1 hr.

At the foot of Izalco volcano, 8 km from Sonsonate, is the town of **Izalco** (population 43,000), which has resulted from the gradual merging of the *ladino* village of Dolores Izalco and the Indian village of Asunción Izalco (**G** pp *Hospedaje San Rafael*, on the Central Park, very basic, no shower, but safe and friendly). Festivals, 15 to 15 August and during the Feast of St John the Baptist from 17 to 24 June. Near Izalco, on the slopes, is the spacious swimming pool of Atecozol, in the middle of a beautiful park with a restaurant (Turicentro, admission US$0.40, parking US$0.40, bungalow US$3). The park is shaded by huge mahogany trees, palms, aromatic balsam trees and *amates*. There is a battlemented tower; a monument to Tlaloc, god of rain; another to Atlacatl, the Indian who, on this spot, shot the arrow which lamed the *conquistador* Pedro de Alvarado; and a statue to the toad found jumping on the spot where water was found. Izalco village and Izalco volcano are not directly connected by road. A paved road branches off the highway 14 km from the turning for Izalco village (about 22 km from Sonsonate, bus 53-C, US$0.10) and goes up towards Lago de Coatepeque (see below); when you reach the summit, a paved road branches round the S end of the lake for **Cerro Verde** with its fine views from the side of the Izalco crater. Bungalows (US$3) and car park (US$0.40) at 1,980m overlook the crater (entry US$0.40). The camping is good, ask the warden if you need basics for preparing meals. Camping is free, although permission must be obtained first from the Departamento de Bienestar, Ministerio de Trabajo in San Bartolo on the outskirts of San Salvador. To climb Izalco: a path leads off the road (signposted) just below the car park on Cerro Verde. In 20-30 mins descend to the saddle between Cerro Verde and Izalco, then 1-1½ hrs up (rather steep, but manageable). A spectacular view from the top. For a quick descent, find a rivulet of soft volcanic sand and half-slide, half-walk down in 15 mins, then 45 mins to 1 hr back up the saddle. This 'cinder running' needs care, strong shoes and a thought for those below. You are probably also aiding erosion. Cerro Verde can be very busy at weekends.

The fine **A-B** *Hotel Montaña* (T 71-2434, F 22-1208, or reserve through Instituto Salvadoreño de Turismo in San Salvador) at the top of Cerro Verde was originally built so that the international set could watch Izalco in eruption; unfortunately, the eruptions stopped just as the hotel was completed. Room prices vary according to day of the week and view. Good food is provided at fairly reasonable prices, US$1 to enter hotel and US$1 for parking, very comfy rooms with views of Izalco volcano, forest and Lago Coatepeque, for and huge fireplaces; relaxing. There is a bus (No 248) from Santa Ana to a junction 14 km from the top of Cerro Verde (US$1): 3 buses daily going up, first at 0600, last bus down at 1700. From Sonsonate to the turn-off for Cerro Verde costs US$0.30; from there it is easy to hitch a lift at weekends.

The road to Cerro Verde has fine views of Lago de Coatepeque; ¾ of the way to Cerro Verde, a track branches off to the right to Finca San Blas (also can be reached on foot from Cerro Verde car park, 20 mins). From there it is a 1½ hr walk straight up the very impressive **Santa Ana volcano**. There are 4 craters inside one another; the newest crater has a lake and fuming columns of sulphur clouds. You can walk around the edge and down on to the ledge formed by the third crater (beware of the fumes). The main, unpaved road goes on to the lakeshore.

In the Sonsonate district are a number of waterfalls and other sites of natural beauty: to the W, near the village of **Santo Domingo de Guzmán** (bus 246 from Sonsonate) are the falls of El Escuco, Tepechapa and La Quebrada, all within walking distance of Santo Domingo and each other. To the E, a few kms off the main road to San Salvador is **Caluco** which has a colonial church and a ruined Dominican church, bus 432 from Sonsonate. On the main road is the Atecozol Turicentro, see above. Some 8 km further E near the railway are Las Victorias Falls, with 2 caves above the falls, the meeting of hot and cold streams at Los Encuentros to form the Shuteca/Aguas Calientes river, and La Chapina pool and springs. Bus 219 goes to Cuisnahuat, from where it is 2 km S to the Río Apancoyo, or 4 km N to **Peñón El Escalón** (covered in balsam trees) and El Istucal Cave, at the foot of the Escalón hill, where Indian rites are celebrated in November.

Between Sonsonate and Ahuachapán (see below) is the Indian village of **Nahuizalco**. The older women still wear the *refajo* (a doubled length of cloth of tie-dyed threads worn over a wrap-round skirt), and various crafts are still carried on, although use of the Indian language is dying out. (Bus 53 from Sonsonate, US$0.10). Beyond is **Jayúa**, with Los Chorros de la Calera 2 km N (bus 205 from Sonsonate), *Hotel El Típico*. From **San Pedro Puxtla** (bus 246) you can visit the Tequendama Falls on the Sihuapán river. (Details on these and other sites from the Instituto Salvadoreño de Turismo.)

The Pan-American Highway runs through Santa Tecla to Santa Ana. A new dual carriageway road parallels the old Pan-American Highway, bypassing Santa Ana; toll: US$0.40. (Keep your ticket if turning off to Coatepeque, as it serves for the return.) The road, with turnoffs for Sonsonate and Ahuachapán, carries on to San Cristóbal on the Guatemalan frontier.

There is an excavated archaeological site at **San Andrés**, half-way between Santa Tecla and Coatepeque on the estate of the same name. (Its full name is La Campana de San Andrés.) It is 32 km W of San Salvador (bus 201 from Terminal de Occidente, US$0.50), but not very impressive. Exhibits from it and from Tazumal are at the National Museum. 11 km off to the right (N) from San Andrés is **San Juan Opico**, on the road to which is a Maya settlement, recently found, named Joya de **Cerén**. Apparently it was buried by the ash from the nearby Laguna Caldera volcano about 600 AD. The site is open to visitors, permits can be obtained from the COPREFA office on Carretera Panamericana in San Salvador (or the guards may let you in anyway). Bus from San Salvador No 108, Terminal de Occidente, to San Juan.

Some 13 km short of Santa Ana a short branch road leads (left) to **Lago de Coatepeque**, a favourite weekend resort with good sailing and fishing near the foot of the Santa Ana volcano. The surroundings are exceptionally beautiful. (Bus 201 from San Salvador to Santa Ana, where one changes to a 220 (hourly) for the lake, US$0.40, or take a bus from San Salvador to El Congo on Pan-American Highway, US$1, then bus 220 'El Lago' to the lake, US$0.20; Confort bus from Guatemala City will stop at El Congo if requested.) Cerro Verde is easily reached in 90 mins by good roads through impressive scenery.

Tourists are put up free in cabins with mattresses and showers at Balneario Los Obreros (a resort for workers). When you reach the lake shore from the rim of the crater follow the road a little. Permission to stay must be obtained from the Departamento de Bienestar, Ministerio de Trabajo, in San Bartolo on the outskirts of San Salvador. Restaurant and supervised swimming. Otherwise, the water is difficult to reach because of the number of weekend homes.

Hotels C *Del Lago*, T 46-9511 (try the crab soup), pool, good beds, beautiful lakeside view; **C** *Torremolinos*, T 46-9437, pool, good rooms, friendly (*Comedor Janet* opposite is good); **D** *Amacuilco*, 300m from Antel, Mauricio Gutiérrez, good personal service, 3 rooms, art gallery, all meals available, pool, good view, rec, tours arranged from US$20 per day (US$100 d per week inc breakfast and dinner; in Santa Ana, contact through *Almacén Amacuilco*, Av Independencia Sur 11 b, 1 block from *Pollo Campero*, T 41-0608, Amita Gutiérrez, or fax c/o Donald Lee (503) 79-4580); **E** *Lido*, **F** *Costa Azul*, very basic.

Santa Ana, 55 km from San Salvador and capital of its Department, is the second largest city in the country (bus 201 from Terminal del Occidente, San Salvador, US$0.50). The intermont basin in which it lies at 776m on the NE slopes of Santa

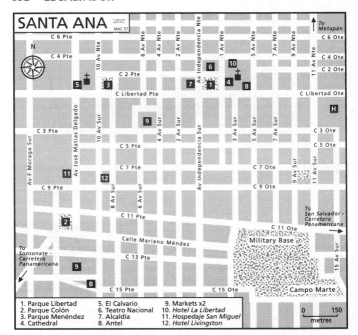

SANTA ANA *LAM COST Santa Ana* *MAC 57*

To Metapán

1. Parque Libertad
2. Parque Colón
3. Parque Menéndez
4. Cathedral
5. El Calvario
6. Teatro Nacional
7. Alcaldía
8. Antel
9. Markets x2
10. *Hotel La Libertad*
11. *Hospedaje San Miguel*
12. *Hotel Livingston*

0 — 150 metres

Ana volcano is exceptionally fertile. Coffee is the great crop, with sugar-cane a good second. The city is the business centre of western El Salvador. There are some fine buildings, particularly the classical theatre, the neo-gothic cathedral, and several other churches, especially El Calvario, in colonial style. Population: 208,322.

Hotels **E** *Internacional-Inn*, 25 C Poniente y 10 Av Sur, with bath, T 40-0810, TV, not the most conventional of hotels; **E** *La Libertad*, near cathedral, T 41-2358, with bath, friendly, clean, helpful, safe car park across the street US$2 for 24 hrs; **E** *Roosevelt*, 8 Av, rooms with bath and cold water, choose between noisy monkeys at the front, cockroaches in back rooms, meals available when full, free parking; **E** *Viajero*, 6 Av, 2 blocks N of main plaza, clean, friendly; *Venecia*, 11 C Poniente between 14 and 16 Av Sur, T 41-1534; **E** *Colonial*, 8 Av Norte 2, clean, helpful, good breakfasts for less than US$1, a little noisy, not recommended for single women; **E** *Hospedaje Carao*, Av José Matías Delgado, with bath, basic, quite clean; **E** *Hospedaje San Miguel*, Av J Matías Delgado 26, T 41-3465, basic, clean, car park; **E** *Pensión Lux*, on Parque Colón, Av JM Delgado No 57, T 40-3383, large rooms; **E** *Pensión Monterrey*, 10 Av Sur, 9-11, T 41-2738, without bathroom; **F** *Hospedaje El Santaneco*, without bath, basic, voracious cockroaches, on same street; **F** *Livingston*, 10 Av Sur, 29, T 41-1801, with bath, cheap and clean; **F** 3 *hospedajes* S of Parque Colón.

Restaurants *Kiyomi*, 4 Av Sur between 3 and 5C, good food and service, clean, reasonable prices; *Las Canoas*, 2 blocks from cathedral, gourmet meals at fair prices; *Talitunel*, 5 Av Sur, 1 C Oriente, vegetarian. *Pupusería Memita*, 25 C Pte, rec for fresh *pupusas* made to order. It is cheaper and usually good value to eat in *comedores*, or at the market in front of the cathedral. Everything closes at about 1900.

Exchange Local banks. Open 0830-1200, 1430-1700. Black market around the banks (called Wall Street by the locals!).

The border with Guatemala is 30 km along the paved Pan-American Highway from Santa

Ana at **San Cristóbal** (**F** *Hotel El Paso*, basic, friendly). The border is open from 0600 to 2000. There are frequent buses from Santa Ana. The fastest road link from San Salvador to Guatemala City is via the Santa Ana bypass, then to Ahuachapán and on to the border at **Las Chinamas**—tourist office here. This is a very busy crossing, patience required. Buses (Melva) leave daily at 0540 from the *Pensión Lux* on the E side of Parque Colón for Guatemala City, US$3, 5½ hrs including border stops. Also Inter Futuro Express, Transportes Centroamérica, and Mermex, US$5, unreliable. Alternatively there are local buses to the border for US$0.35; they leave from the market. Bus 406 from the capital (Terminal del Occidente), goes direct to the frontier at Las Chinamas (US$0.70).

Excursions To Lago de Coatepeque, 19 km (220 bus to *Hotel del Lago* US$0.40). **Chalchuapa**, 16 km from Santa Ana, on the road to Ahuachapán, population 34,865, is at 640m. President Barrios of Guatemala was killed in battle here in 1885, when trying to reunite Central America by force. There is some good colonial-style domestic building; the church of Santiago is particularly striking. See the small but picturesque lake; the very interesting church, almost the only one in El Salvador which shows strong indigenous influences, and the **Tazumal** ruin next to the cemetery in Chalchuapa, built about AD 980 by the Pipil Indians but with its 14-step pyramid now, alas, restored in concrete. The site has been occupied since 5000 BC and in the simple museum are the artefacts found in the mud under the lake. There are very interesting bowls used for burning incense, intricately decorated with animal designs. The ruin, which is open 0900-1200 and 1300-1730, closed on Mondays, is free of entry and only 5 mins walk from the main road. Near the ruins is a souvenir shop (selling copies) run by Elena Vides, T 44-0803, on the main road. Bus (No 236) from Santa Ana, 20 mins, US$0.20. On the W of the town is the El Trapiche swimming pool. Bus 51 or 50 goes to **Turicentro Sihuatehuacán**, on city outskirts; US$0.40 admission to pools, café, park, etc, same price for parking, but run down.

Hotel at Chalchuapa: **E** *Gloria*, Av 2 de Abril, T 44-0131.

Guatemalan consul in Chalchuapa, Av Club de Leones Norte, between Primero and Calle Ramón Flores—unmarked blue house, knock for attention.

Ahuachapán, capital of its Department, is 35 km from Santa Ana, at 785m. Population, 63,500. It is a quiet town with low and simple houses, but an important distribution centre. Coffee is the great product. Like many places in the area, it draws the mineral water for its bath-house from some hot springs near the falls of Malacatiupán, nearby. Power is from the falls of Atehuezián on the Río Molino, which cascade prettily down the mountain-side. See also the *ausoles*—geysers of boiling mud with plumes of steam and strong whiffs of sulphur, which have been harnessed to produce electric power. A road runs NW through the treeless Llano del Espino, with its small lake, and across the Río Paz into Guatemala. This crossing, Valle Nuevo/El Oratorio, is quite straightforward. Ahuachapán is 116 km from the capital by bus 202 from San Salvador (US$0.55). Buses to the border, US$0.30.

The *ausoles* are interesting—an area of ground which is warm to the touch. They are used for generating electricity; only the smallest remains uncovered by drums and pipes. One can take a bus from Ahuachapán to El Barro, take a taxi or walk the 5 km to the area. Permission to visit the power station can be obtained from the barracks on the hill overlooking the town as the site is guarded by the Army.

Hotels and Restaurants In our **E** range or below: *San José*, by market, with bath, clean, friendly, parking; *Astoria*; **F** *Hospedaje Granada*, 3 blocks down from plaza by market, shared bath, clean, friendly; *La Ahuachapaneca* guest house; *El Gran Rancho*; *Hospedaje Casa Blanca*, Av 2 Norte, clean, good; *Hospedaje Milagro*, clean, basic, near bus station; *Hospedaje San Juan*. One can get good meals at *Restaurant El Paseo*, *Restaurant Tanya* and *El Parador*. Good and inexpensive meals at *Mixta's Restaurante*; *Pastelería María*, good cakes and biscuits.

Between Ahuachapán and Sonsonate are 2 small lakes, **Laguna Verde** and **Apaneca**, whose crater-like walls are profusely covered in tropical forest, in the Cordillera de Apaneca, part of the narrow highland belt running SE of Ahuachapán; they are popular with tourists. It is possible to swim in the former, but the latter is too shallow and reedy. Local buses run some distance away, leaving one with a fairly long walk. Laguna Verde can also be reached by road via Cantón Tulapa, from a turn off on the CA-8 road E of Apaneca. S of here is the Cascada del Río Cauta (take bus 216 from Ahuachapán towards Jujutla, alight 3 km after the turn-off to Apaneca, then walk along trail for 300m). 9 km W of Ahuachapán near the village of *Los Toles* are the Tehuasilla falls, where the El Molino river falls 75m.

Metapán (32 km N of Santa Ana) is about 10 km NE of Lago de Güija. Its colonial baroque cathedral is one of the very few to have survived in the country. The altarpieces have some very good silver work (the silver is from local mines) and the façade is splendid. Lots of easy walks with good views towards Lago de Metapán and further on Lago de Güija. There are many lime kilns and a huge cement plant. Population: 51,800. Bus from Santa Ana No 235, US$0.55.

Hotels F *Ferrocarril*; F *Gallo de Oro*; F *Hospedaje Central*, with bath. Restaurant *Rincón del Pelon*, best in town, helpful, friendly.

A mountain track from Metapán gives access to *Montecristo National Nature Reserve*, El Salvador's last remaining cloud forest. There is an abundance of protected wildlife; permits to visit have to be obtained in San Salvador (and are not given during the breeding season, thought to be Feb to May). This now forms part of El Trifinio, or the International Biosphere 'La Fraternidad', administered jointly by Guatemala, Honduras and El Salvador. Near the top of Cerro Montecristo (2,418m), which is the point where the 3 frontiers meet, there is an orchid garden, with over 100 species (best time to see them in flower is early Spring), an apple orchard and a camping ground in the forest. A 4-wheel drive vehicle is essential to get there; allow 2 hrs from Metapán. For information and permission to visit, contact the Centro de Recursos Naturales (CENREN), Cantón El Matazano, Soyapango, T 770622.

If planning to walk in the hills near Metapán, seek local advice and do not walk alone.

A good paved road runs from Metapán to the Guatemalan frontier.

Lago de Güija, on the Guatemalan border, 16 km by 8, is very beautiful and dotted with small islands, but it is not easy to reach. A new dam at the lake's outlet generates electricity for the western part of the country. It is possible to walk round parts of the lake, but there is no proper track and fences reach down to the water's edge. Boat trip to Isla Tipa, once a sacred Maya site, may be arranged through *Amacuilco Guest House* at Lago de Coatepeque. The border with Guatemala passes through the lake so there is the chance that you may have to account for your presence there. Bus 235 from Santa Ana, US$0.45.

From *Texistepeque*, 17 km N of Santa Ana on the road to Metapán, a railway runs eastwards along the S bank of the Río Lempa to Aguilares on Troncal del Norte (San Salvador—Cerrón Grande reservoir—El Poy, on the border with Honduras, see next section). A passenger service of sorts operates, every day except Sunday, leaving Texistepeque at 1000 approximately, arriving 1345. Passengers are carried free in open boxcars and the train stops at villages along the way for 1 min only. Train from Aguilares leaves at 0800 (with thanks to Will Paine, Maidstone, Kent).

NORTHERN EL SALVADOR

The route from San Salvador to Western Honduras passes through the delightful handicraft centre of La Palma.

There was much guerrilla and counter-insurgency activity in the northern areas, but there is now freedom of movement. The Troncal del Norte (Ruta CA4) is paved throughout, and runs due N through Apopa (junction with a good road to Quezaltepeque) and *Aguilares* (see above) to the western extremity of the Cerrón Grande reservoir. A branch to the right skirts the northern side of the reservoir to Chalatenango, capital of the department of the same name. *Chalatenango* (altitude 450m), 55 km from San Salvador, was a delightful little town with an annual fair and *fiesta* on 24 June. Now, unfortunately, it is dominated by the military presence. (Bus 125 from Oriente terminal, San Salvador, US$0.60.)

Population, 30,000. It is the centre of an important region of traditional livestock farms. Good market. 2 *hospedajes*: **F** *El Nuevo Amanecer*, good views of the Cathedral from the 2nd floor; one unnamed, **F**.

Do not walk in the countryside: areas off the main road may be mined. Local residents usually (but not always) know which places are safe.

The main road continues N through Tejutla to *La Palma* (81 km from San Salvador, altitude 1,100m; municipal pop 14,770). **F-G** pp *Hotel La Palma*, no reports as yet; there is also an awful *hospedaje* next to the pharmacy, **G**, very dirty and in need of repair. A charming village set in pine clad mountains, and well worth a visit. It is famous for its local crafts, particularly the brightly-painted wood carvings and hand-embroidered tapestries. Also produced are handicrafts in clay, metal, cane and seeds. There are a number of workshops in La Palma where the craftsmen can be seen at work and purchases made. (The products are also sold in San Salvador, but are much more expensive, *Artesanías La Palma*, Av Sisimiles 2911, Col Miramonte, T 26-9948.) *Fiesta*: 20-28 February, Dulce Nombre de María. Buses run from San Salvador, Terminal de Oriente, to La Palma (No 119, US$0.60, 3 hrs).

The road continues N to the frontier at *El Poy*, for western Honduras (at least 5 buses a day, last one at 1600—No 119, US$1—from Terminal de Oriente in San Salvador, frequent military checks, 3-4 hrs in all). 2 km before El Poy is **E** *Hotel Cayahuanca*, clean, friendly, restaurant a bit expensive. Travellers' cheques exchanged at El Poy. Enquire in San Salvador about requirements for this border crossing.

EASTERN EL SALVADOR

An agricultural zone, the N of which was fiercely disputed between the army and guerrillas. Among the attractions are lakes, volcanoes, beaches and the towns of the Lempa Valley.

E to La Unión/Cutuco There are 2 roads to the port of La Unión/Cutuco on the Gulf of Fonseca: (i) the Pan-American Highway, 185 km mostly in bad condition, through Cojutepeque, San Vicente and San Miguel; (ii) the Coastal Highway, also paved, running through Santo Tomás, Olocuilta, Zacatecoluca, and Usulután. The roads were frequently cut by guerrilla action against bridges; most rivers are now crossed by Bailey bridges or dry fords.

By Pan-American Highway Some 5 km from the capital a dry-weather highway branches N to Tonocatepeque and *Suchitoto*, on the southern shore of the Embalse **Cerrón Grande**. Suchitoto is an attractive small town with an interesting church. Try the local *tortillas* filled with meat and beans. **F** *Hospedaje San Rafael*, showers, basic, friendly. Boat trips go to lakeside villages associated with the FMLN in the recent civil war.

Tonocatepeque, 13 km from the capital, is an attractive small town on the high plateau, in an agricultural setting but with a small textile industry. There has been some archaeological exploration of the town's original site, 5 km away.

There was much guerrilla and counter-insurgency activity in this northern area: visitors are still advised to take care. A road runs E from Suchitoto to Ilobasco (see below), through the disputed territory, passing Cinquera, whose villagers returned home in February 1991 after 6 years displacement, and Tejutepeque.

Continuing along the Pan-American Highway: a short branch road (about 2 km beyond the airport) leads off right to the W shores of Lago de Ilopango. The first town on the Pan-American Highway is *Cojutepeque*, capital of Cuscatlán Department, 34 km from San Salvador, reached by bus 113 from Oriente terminal in San Salvador, US$0.55; buses leave from here on the corner of the plaza 2 blocks from the main plaza. Population 31,300. Lago de Ilopango is to the SW. Good weekly market. The town is famous for cigars, smoked sausages and tongues, and its annual fair on 29 August has fruits and sweets, saddlery, leather goods, pottery and headwear on sale from neighbouring villages, and sisal hammocks, ropes, bags and hats from the small factories of Cacaopera (Dept of Morazán).

Hotels E *Motel Edén*, with shower. E *Hospedaje Viajero*, 1 block E of *Turista* (also hourly rentals); E *Turista*, 5 C Oriente 130, warning of extra charges. *Comedor Toyita*, good value.

Cerro de las Pavas, a conical hill near Cojutepeque, dominates **Lago de Ilopango** and gives splendid views of wide valleys and tall mountains. Its shrine of Our Lady of Fátima draws many pilgrims.

Excursion From **San Rafael Cedros**, 6 km E of Cojutepeque, a 16-km paved road N to Ilobasco has a branch road E to Sensuntepeque at about Km 13. **Ilobasco** has 48,100 people, many of them workers in clay; its decorated pottery is now mass-produced and has lost much of its charm. The area around, devoted to cattle, coffee, sugar and indigo, is exceptionally beautiful. Annual fair: 29 September. An all-weather road leads from Ilobasco to the great dam and hydroelectric station of Cinco de Noviembre at the Chorrera del Guayabo, on the Río Lempa. Bus 111 from Terminal de Oriente US$0.50. Another road with fine views leads to the Cerrón Grande dam and hydroelectric plant; good excursion by bus or truck. Permission is given in normal times to enter the dam area and one can climb the hill with the Antel repeater on top for a view of the whole lake created by the dam. The whole Lempa valley is a security zone.

Sensuntepeque, 35 km E of Ilobasco, is a pleasant town at 900m, in the hills S of the Lempa valley. It is the capital of Cabañas Department, once a great source of indigo. There are some interesting ceremonies during its fair on 4 December, the day of its patroness, Santa Bárbara. It can be reached from the Pan-American Highway from near San Vicente. Population: 45,000.

Hotels E *Hospedaje Jandy*; E *Hospedaje Oriental*.

Infrastructure in the Department of Cabañas E of Sesuntepeque to **Ciudad Barrios** is in atrocious disrepair because of the war. There is often no electricity, little water, no bus services and appalling roads. The conventional way E is to head back to the Pan-American Highway by bus and continue to San Miguel. It is possible, however, to alight at Dolores (no accommodation), take a truck at dawn to the Río Lempa, cross in a small boat to San Juan ('struggling to stay inhabited, graffiti spattered, reeks of war'), then walk 3 hrs to **San Gerardo** ('little better') from where one bus at 1100 goes daily to Ciudad Barrios (Will Paine). Before visiting this area check in advance on conditions.

4 km from the turning to Ilobasco, further S along the Pan-American Highway at **San Domingo** (Km 44 from San Salvador) an unpaved road leads in 5 km to **San Sebastián** where colourfully patterned hammocks and bedspreads are made. You can watch them being woven on complex looms of wood and string, and can buy from the loom. The 110 bus from the Oriente terminal runs from San Salvador to San Sebastián (US$0.50). There are also buses from Cojutepeque.

San Vicente, 61 km from the capital, is a little SE of the Highway on the Río Alcahuapa, at the foot of the double-peaked **San Vicente volcano** (or **Chinchontepec**), with very fine views of the Jiboa valley as it is approached. Population: 56,800. Its pride and gem is El Pilar (1762-69), most original church in the country. It was here that the **Indian chief, Anastasio Aquino**, took the crown from the statue of San José and crowned himself King of the Nonualcos during the Indian rebellion of 1833. In its main square is the *tempesque* tree under which the city's foundation charter was drawn up. San Vicente has a lovely setting and is a peaceful place to spend a night or two. Bus 116 from Oriente terminal, San Salvador, US$0.40. You have to take 2 buses to get to San Miguel (see below), first to the Pan-American Highway (a few km), then another on to San Miguel, US$1.30 total. Carnival day: 1 November. Exchange at Banco Hipotecario.

Hotels E *Central Park*, on Parque Central, good, clean, fan, cafe downstairs; **E** *Pensión Vicentina*. Better is **E** *Casa Romero*, which is after the bridge at the corner of the first turning on the right, no sign, clean, rec, good meals but not cheap, free parking available. **E** *Hospedaje Rivoly*, good food. **F** *Casa de Huéspedes El Turista*, with bath, some rooms with hammocks, family run, friendly; **F** *Casa de Huéspedes Germán y Marlon*, 1 block from plaza, shared bath, 1 bed and 1 hammock in each room, very clean and friendly. **F** *Hospedaje Viajero*, OK. *Vips* restaurant to the right of *Central Park Hotel*.

Excursions 2 km E of the town is the Balneario **Amapulapa**, one of a number of Turicentro recreational centres developed by the National Tourist Board. There are 3 pools at different levels in a wooded setting. US$0.40 entry and US$0.40 parking charges. Reached by bus 172 from San Vicente. **Laguna de Apastepeque**, near San Vicente off the Pan-American Highway, is small but picturesque. The Turicentro at the lake costs US$0.40 to enter and to park.

The Highway (in reasonable condition after San Vicente) used to cross the Río Lempa by the 411m-long Cuscatlán suspension bridge (destroyed by guerrillas in 1983). It now crosses an emergency bridge.

10 km S of the Pan-American Highway is *Berlín*, known for its quality coffee plantations. *Hotel Berlines* and *Villa Hermosa*, both E.

From Berlín there is a road round the N of Volcán de Tecapa to Santiago de María. Half way is Alegría from which you can visit the *Laguna de Alegría* in the crater of the volcano, fed by both hot and cold springs. The lake level is low during the day but rises at 1600 each afternoon.

San Miguel, 136 km from San Salvador, capital of its Department, founded in 1530 at the foot of the volcanoes of **San Miguel** (**Chaparrastique**—which erupted in 1976, and **Chinameca**). It has some very pleasant squares and a bare 18th century cathedral. Some silver and gold are mined. It is an important distributing centre. The arid climate all year round makes the region ideal for growing maize, beans, cotton and sisal. Population, about 250,000. Bus 301 from Oriente terminal, San Salvador (US$1.60, every $\frac{1}{2}$ hr from 0500 to 1630). Fiesta of the Virgen de la Paz: 3rd Saturday in November. The Turicentro of Altos de la Cueva is 1 km N; take town bus 60, admission, car parking US$0.40; swimming pools, gardens, restaurants, sports facilities, bungalows for rent US$3; busy at weekends. A popular spot is El Copulín, whose warm waters are said to be medicinal; the waters run from a cave with walls of pumice stone, which gives the place an air of mystery. There is a charming church with statues and fountains in its gardens about 16 km away at Chinameca.

Hotels Very few in centre, most on the entrance roads: **B** *Trópico Inn*, Av Roosevelt, T 61-1288, clean, comfortable, reasonable restaurant, swimming pool, garden; **C** *Motel Milián*, Panamericana Km 136, T 61-1970 (pool), good value, rec, good food; **D** *China House*, Panamericana Km 137, T 61-0568, clean, friendly; **E** *Central*, 4 Av Sur, No 607; **E** *Santa Rosa*, 8 Av Norte y 6C, good; **E** *Hispanoamericano*, 6A Av Norte y 8 C Oriente, T 61-1202, with toilet and shower, air-conditioned (cheaper in older rooms without a/c, rec); **F** *Hospedaje Argueta*, 4C Oriente y 6-8 Av, price per person; **F** *Pension Lux*, 4 C Oriente, 6 Av Oriente, reasonable. Plenty of cheap places near the bus station, eg **F** *Migueleña*, 4 C Oriente No 610, very basic but good value, clean, large rooms, towels, bath, fan.

Restaurants *La Puerta del Sol*, 3 Av Sur, 4 C Poniente, good variety; *El Gran Tejano*, 4 C Poniente near cathedral, great steaks; *Chetino's Pizzería*, 5 C Poniente, near Centro Médico; *Bati Club Carlitos*, 12 Av Norte. There is a *Pollo Campero* and a *Burger King* for fast food lovers. Try *bocadillos de totopostes*, maize balls with either chilli or cheese; also *tustacos*, which are like small tortillas with sugar or honey. Both are delicious and traditional in San Miguel.

Exchange Local banks. Open: 0830-1200, 1430-1800. **Banco Cuscatlán** will change TCs, but you must produce receipt of purchase. **Casa de Cambio Lego**, 2 C Poniente, overlooking market, cashes TCs into dollars, 2% commission.

Airline TACA, Condominio San Benito, opp *Hotel Trópico Inn*, Av Roosevelt, T 61-1477.

From San Miguel a good paved road runs S to the Pacific Highway. Go S along it for 12 km, where a dirt road leads to Playa El Cuco (**see p 600**). Bus 320 from San Miguel, US$1. The climate in this area is good. A mainly paved, reasonable road goes to San Jorge and Usulután: leave the Pan-American Highway 5 km W of San Miguel. The road goes through hills and coffee plantations with superb views of San Miguel volcano. The volcano can be climbed from **Placita** on the road to San Jorge, about 4 hrs up. Ask at Placita for information, a guide costs about US$5. To the N are the Indian ruins of **Quelapa** (bus 99, US$0.50), but there is not much to see.

There are frequent buses from San Miguel to the Honduran border at El Amatillo, US$1.

San Francisco Gotera, the capital of Morazán Department, can be reached from the Oriente terminal in San Salvador, or from San Miguel (bus 328). Foreigners are not usually allowed beyond here on Route 7 to the Honduran border. 2 places to stay: F *Hospedaje San Francisco*, Av Morazán 29, T 64-0066, nice garden and hammocks; *Motel Arco Iris*, next door. Beyond San Francisco, the road runs to Jocaitique (there is a bus) from where an unpaved road climbs into the mountains through pine forests to Sabanetas, near the Honduran border. Accommodation at both Jocaitique and Sabanetas.

22 km NE of San Francisco is **Corinto** with 2 rock overhangs which show faint evidence of precolumbian wall paintings. They are 20 mins N of the village on foot, just E of the path to the Cantón Coretito. For Corinto take bus 327 from San Miguel, US$1. Enquire if it is possible to visit.

8 km N of San Francisco Gotera is **Ciudad Segundo Montes**, a group of villages housing 8,500 repatriated Salvadoran refugees (the community is named after one of the 6 Jesuit priests murdered in November 1989). If you would like to visit this welcoming, energetic place, ask for the Ciudad Segundo Montes (CSM) office in San Salvador, or in San Francisco Gotera (T 64-0033). When you get to CSM, ask to be let off at San Luis and go to the Oficina de Recepción. You will put up in a communal dormitory; meals in *comedores* cost US$1; there is a bath house (spring-fed showers). Free tours of the community are given and there is beautiful hiking. From CSM it is possible to continue by bus or truck to **Perquín**, which was the guerrilla's 'Capital'. Note, though, that you should be able to speak Spanish, that transport back to CSM or San Miguel may be difficult in the afternoons (it's a 3-hr walk). This was the scene of much military activity. War damage is still clearly visible around the town, but all is now peaceful. There is a very interesting museum, entrance US$1. Bus San Miguel-Perquín, No 332B, US$1.50.

It is another 42 km from San Miguel to the port of La Unión/Cutuco. Before it gets there the Pan-American Highway turns N for the Goascarán bridge to Honduras. At the border, **El Amatillo**, there are 2 basic *hospedajes*, F *Anita*, with *comedor*, and *Dos Hermanos*. Duty free shops tend to be cheaper than those in El Amatillo, Honduras. The border closes 1700 (see also Honduras, **From Tegucigalpa to the Pacific**). Bus San Miguel-El Amatillo, No 330, US$1. Beware of helpers who offer to guide you through officialdom (although Chevo has been recommended). Some will gather all kinds of stamps for your documents, and then charge for them. One visitor travelling by foot, later noticed he had paid a tax for importing a car into Honduras! Car searches are thorough. There are plenty of money changers, accepting all Central American currencies and TCs, but beware of short-changing on Nicaraguan and Costa Rican currencies.

To save time when travelling eastwards, take the Ruta Militar NE through (34 km) Santa Rosa de Lima to the Goascarán bridge on the border with Honduras, 56 km, at El Amatillo.

Santa Rosa de Lima (27,300 people) is a charming little place with a wonderful colonial church, set in the hills. There are gold and silver mines. Don'T miss the excellent *sopa de apretadores* (soup of crayfish to some, crab to others, the best in El Salvador) at lunchtime, 1000-1600, near the town centre— made by La Pema on Calle Lario and Calle 4 Oriente, everyone knows the place. Banco de Comercio will change TCs, also Servicambio near the church. Popular market on Wed, many Hondurans come to shop. The FMLN office here has details about the Codelum project, a refugee camp in Monte Barrios, very interesting. Buses to the Honduran border half-hourly, US$0.40. Direct buses also to San Salvador, No 306, US$2.10 from 0400 until 1400.

Hotels and eating places All accommodation **F**: *Hospedaje Gómez*, basic, hammocks, fan, clean; *Hospedaje Mundial*, nr market, rooms OK, with fan, basic, friendly, lots of parking space; *Hotel Recreo*, 2 blocks from town centre, friendly, fan, clean; *Hotel Florida*, Ruta Militar, helpful, fairly clean, basic, 3 parking spaces (arrive early). *Hotel y Comedor El Tejano*, behind main church, serves good standard meals, friendly. Many *comedores*, most popular is *Chayito*, 'buffet', US$0.25 per ingredient, on Ruta Militar, and *Comedor Leyla*, next to bus stop, is good. Unnamed *comedor* on the Pan-American Highway, good and cheap.

La Unión/Cutuco, on the Gulf of Fonseca, has a population of 43,000. The port handles half the country's trade. The whole coast is a military zone.

Hotels **E** *Centroamérica*, T 64-4029, with fan, more with a/c, noisy; **E** *San Carlos*, opposite railway station, good meals available; **F** *Hospedaje El Dorado*, 1 block from plaza, shared bath, nice rooms with fan, some with bath, very clean, rec; opposite *Hospedaje Annex Santa Marta*, a bit further away from square is **E** *San Francisco*, friendly, some rooms with hammocks, noisy, but OK. **F** *Hospedaje Annex Santa Marta*, with shower and fan, not bad; **F** *Miramar*, good; *Hospedaje Santa Rosa*.

Restaurant *La Patia*, for fish; *Comedores Gallego* and *Rosita* rec. *Comedor Tere*, Av General Menéndez 2.2, fairly good; *Amanacer Marino*, beautiful view of the bay. Bottled water is impossible to find.

Exchange at *Cafetín Brisas del Mar*, 3 Av Norte y 3 Calle Oriente. **Banco Agrícola Comercial** for US$ cash and TCs. Black market sometimes in centre.

Customs 3 Av Norte 3.9; **Immigration** at 3 Calle Oriente 2.8.

Ferry There is no longer a ferry to Puntarenas (Costa Rica). It may be possible to take a cargo boat to Costa Rica; ask the captains in Cutuco. Outboards cross daily from La Unión to Potosí (Nicaragua), weather permitting. You must get your exit permission in La Unión. Make arrangements 1 day ahead, and check at customs office. There is reportedly a boat to Honduras, but it is easier to go by land.

Buses Terminal is at 3 Calle Poniente (block 3); to San Salvador, No 304, US$2, 4 hrs, many daily, direct or via San Miguel, one passes the harbour at 0300. (No 320 to San Miguel US$0.80). Bus to Honduran border at El Amatillo, No 353, US$1.65.

Excursions To *Conchagua* to see one of the few old colonial churches in the country (good bus service, No 382, US$0.10); Conchagua volcano (1,243m) can also be climbed and is a hard walk, particularly near the top where stout clothing is useful against the vegetation. About 4 hrs up and 2 hrs down. You will be rewarded by superb views over San Miguel volcano to the W and the Gulf of Fonseca which is bordered by El Salvador, Honduras and Nicaragua (where the Cosigüina volcano is prominent) to the E. One can take an early morning boat to the Salvadorean islands in the Gulf of Fonseca. These include Isla Zacatillo (about 1 hr), Isla Conchagüita and the largest *Isla Meanguera* (about 4 km by 7 km) which takes about 2½ hrs. Meanguera has attractive small secluded beaches with good bathing, eg Marahual, fringed with palm trees. You must obtain permission and may have to leave your passport. The customs will check your luggage. Take your own provisions, although there is excellent seafood, lobster, shark steaks, etc, available from fishermen. There are no official *hospedajes*, but locals will allow you to camp and may offer a room (better to arrange in La Unión before you arrive). Launches leave La Unión between 0900 and 1200, back very early, 0300-0400, cost US$3. Also you can reach El Tamarindo on the mainland coast (see below) from La Unión, bus 383, US$0.50. Also from La Unión, the ruins of Los Llanitos can be visited.

By Coastal Highway This is the second road route, running through the southern cotton lands. It begins on a 4-lane motorway to Comalapa airport. The first place of any importance after leaving the capital (is 13 km) *Santo Tomás*. There are Indian ruins at *Cushululitán*, a short distance N.

Beyond, a new road to the E, rising to 1,000m, runs S of Lago de Ilopango to join the Pan-American Highway beyond Cojutepeque.

10 km on from Santo Tomás is *Olocuilta*, an old town with a colourful market on Sunday under a great tree. Good church. (Both Santo Tomás and Olocuilta can be reached by bus 133 from San Salvador.)

From the airport, the road becomes a 2-lane toll-road, going E across the Río Jiboa to *Zacatecoluca*, capital of La Paz Department (altitude 201m) 56 km from San Salvador by road and 19 km S of San Vicente. Bus 133 from Occidente terminal, San Salvador. José Simeón Cañas, who abolished slavery in Central America, was born here. Population, 81,000.

Hotels **D** *El Litoral*, on the main road Km 56; **E** *Hospedaje Viroleño*; **F** *Hospedajes América* and *Popular* clean; **F** *Hospedaje Primavera*, clean, friendly, fan. *Comedor Margoth* (beware high charging).

Near the town is the garden park and Turicentro of *Ichanmichen* ('the place of the little fish'). It is crossed by canals and decorated with pools: there is, in fact, an attractive swimming pool. It is very hot but there is plenty of shade. Admission and car parking each US$0.40, bungalow rental US$3; take bus 92 from Zacatecoluca.

Between Olocuilta and Zacatecoluca, a road branches N to the small towns of **San Pedro Nonualco** and **Santa María Ostuma** (with an interesting colonial church and a famous *fiesta* on 2 February); both are worth visiting, but not easy to get to. Bus 135 from Terminal del Occidente goes to San Pedro. If you get off this bus at the turn off to San Sebastián Arriba, you can walk to the **Peñón del Tacuazín** (or del Indio Aquino), 480m above sea level, which is 4$\frac{1}{2}$ km N of Santiago Nonualco. A cave at its summit was used as a refuge by Anastasio Aquino (**see p 596**), before his execution in April 1833.

A branch road to the S before Zacatecoluca leads to the Playa **Costa del Sol** on the Pacific, being developed as a tourist resort. You can rent huts in the Turicentro for US$3 for the day, or US$6 for 24 hrs, admission and car parking US$0.40 each. Vehicle camping possible on the beach. There are extensive black sand beaches and some luxury hotels: **L** *Tesoro Beach*, T 34-0600, F 23-2891, apartment style rooms, swimming pool, 9-hole golf course; **A** *Izalco Cabaña Club*, T 23-6764, F 24-0363, 30 rooms, pool, seafood a speciality. Take bus 495 from Terminal del Occidente, San Salvador. Cheaper accommodation can be found 1 km E on the next beach, Los Blancos.

Both road and railway cross the wide Río Lempa by the Puente de Oro (Golden Bridge) at **San Marcos**. (The road bridge has been destroyed; cars use the railway bridge.) Off the main road near here is **La Nueva Esperanza** where there is a community that has returned from Nicaragua, dormitories to sleep and a good place to go and help if you have a few days to spare. 20 km beyond the bridge, a branch road (right) leads to tiny **Puerto El Triunfo** on the Bahía de Jiquilisco, with a large shrimp-freezing plant (**E** *Hotel/Restaurant Jardín*). About 110 km from the capital is **Usulután**, capital of its Department (90m above sea level). Population, 69,000. Bus 302 from San Salvador, US$1.40.

Hotels *Hotel and Restaurant España*, on main square, T 62-0378, rec, nice patio, bar and discotheque. **E** *Motel Usulután*; **E** *Central*; **E** *Florida*.

A road branches NE from Usulután, some 45 km to San Miguel (**see p 597**). On this road is **Laguna El Jocotal**, a national nature reserve supported by the World Wildlife Fund, which can be visited by arrangement with the warden. It has an abundance of birds and snakes.

The Coastal Highway goes direct from Usulután to La Unión/Cutuco.

12 km from junction for San Miguel there is a turn to the right leading in 7 km to **Playa El Cuco**, a popular beach with several places to stay (F), near the bus station (buses to San Miguel). **E** *Hotel Cucolindo*, 1 km along the coast, cabin for 4, basic, cold water, mosquitos; *Hotel Posada*, cold showers, parking US$6; **G** pp *Hotel El Rancho*, hammocks only, in cane shacks, basic, friendly, shower from bucket drawn from well; **E** *Hotel Palmera*, with or without bath, impersonal and no direct beach access; **E** *Los Leones Marinos*, T 61-2870, with bath, clean and tidy (cases of malaria have been reported from El Cuco, and locals warn against walking along beach after sunset). Nearby is the **B** *Trópico Club*, T 61-1288, with several cabins, run by the *Trópico Inn* in San Miguel which can provide information. Another popular beach, **El Tamarindo**, is reached by another right turn off the road to La Unión, *cabañas* for rent (**C** *Las Tunas*), and basic *pensión*. In Tamarindo you can stay at the Workers' Recreational Centre, but first obtain a permit from the Ministry of Labour in San Salvador. Boat from El Tamarindo across the bay leads to a short cut to La Unión.

INFORMATION FOR VISITORS

Documents   A passport is necessary for nationals of all countries. Citizens of most countries require a visa; those that do not need visas are: Germany, Austria, Belgium, Spain, UK, Italy, Switzerland, Luxemburg, Denmark, Finland, Ireland, Liechtenstein, Norway, Sweden, The Netherlands, Japan, Israel, Guatemala, Honduras, Costa Rica, Argentina, Panama, Chile, Mexico, Nicaragua and Colombia. This is subject to change, and we do recommend that you apply in your own country. Visas cost US$30, though this can vary, and the waiting-time for issue depends on the country where the application is made: they can take up to a week in countries neighbouring El Salvador. Visas are not available at borders. If authorization from El Salvador is required, allow 14 days for an application to be processed. A photocopy of flight tickets is necessary, as well as a photograph. For citizens of the USA and Israel, visas are free, but a letter of clearance from the police and an employer may be required. Maximum validity of a visa is 90 days. Immigration officers at Salvadoran land borders and the airport have absolute discretion to determine the permitted length of a traveller's stay: they can grant a maximum of 30 days, but permits for only 3 days are not unknown. Permits can be renewed for up to 30 days at the Immigration Department, in the Ministry of the Interior building, Centro de Gobierno, San Salvador, next to the ANTEL office, at a cost of 12.50 colones.

Border formalities tend to be relatively brief, although thorough searches are common. There is an exit tax of about US$0.60. There may be restrictions on entry for Cuban citizens.

Journalists must register on arrival with the Secretaría Nacional de Comunicaciones (SENCO), T 71-0058, office near the Casa Presidencial.
   Travellers doing business directly in the country should get a business visa. Applications should be accompanied by a company letter and a photograph. It is easier if supply or client companies within the country make the necessary arrangements. Business travellers are sometimes assessed for income tax during their stay.

Note   At the time of going to press, the peace accord signed in early 1992 was holding, but the legacy of many years of civil war is still visible in certain areas. In addition, poverty abounds. In the main, tourists are made very welcome, and the military are comparatively low profile.
   Peace has left many ex-combatants armed but unemployed, which has resulted in cases of robbery at gunpoint, especially of people in cars. Do not drive alone, even better drive in groups of cars. Do not drive up close to army vehicles. Carry your embassy's phone number with you, just in case. Do not stop for lone gunmen dressed in military-looking uniforms. The new Policia Civil is still under training, but efforts are being made to combat an increase in serious crime. Visitors to San Salvador should be most vigilant and should seek advice on where is not safe outside the city. Despite these warnings, we have received many letters from correspondents who have had trouble-free visits to El Salvador.
   Foreigners are prohibited from participating in politics by Salvadoran law and we suggest you keep away from the subject. If you wish to travel to parts of the N of the country where the FMLN strongholds were, you will be free to do so. We understand no permissions are now needed, but ask about it before you go. It is wise not to camp out. Be prepared for police checks and possibly body searches on buses (the officers are polite, if respected.)
   Life starts early in the day in El Salvador, and ends early, a legacy of the frequent curfews during the troubles; few people to be seen on the streets after 2000, and everything, including street lights, is closed by 2100.
   You are strongly advised to register with your embassy if staying for more than just a few days. The British consulate advises on local legal procedures, lawyers, English-speaking doctors, help with money transfers and with contacting banks or relatives, and will make local hospital visits. The consulate cannot give free legal advice, supply money or obtain employment or accommodation. The services it does provide are only for those who have registered. Other consulates may provide the same services, but you should find out in advance what your own country's diplomatic procedures are.

Taxes There is a 10% tax on international air tickets bought in El Salvador, and a 5-colón boarding tax. There is also an airport tax of US$13 if staying more than 6 hrs. MCO tickets can be bought.

How to get there From London: to Miami with American, Continental, British Airways or Virgin Atlantic, thence to San Salvador with American, Continental, United, Iberia (twice a week) or Taca. Other connecting cities with flights to San Salvador are: Chicago (Continental via Houston, Aviateca via Guatemala City, United via Miami), Dallas (Continental), Houston (Continental, Taca), New Orleans (Aviateca, Taca), Los Angeles (Continental, United, Taca, Lacsa, Aviateca), San Francisco (Taca direct), New York (Taca via Washington and Guatemala, Continental via Houston), Washington (Continental via Houston, Taca). Taca flies to all Central American capitals, and also to San Pedro Sula and Mexico City (also served by Lacsa and United). Copa flies to the other Central American capitals, except Belize City and Tegucigalpa. Lacsa flies to San José and Copa to Panama, with connection twice a week to Kingston (Jamaica). Nica flies to Managua, Guatemala City, San José and Panama. From Europe, San Salvador can be reached from Madrid with Iberia (twice a week, change planes in Miami), or with Taca connecting flights from Guatemala City, to which Iberia and KLM fly (3 times a week each). Alternatively, go to Miami and connect from there. Connections for South America through San José or Panama.

Customs All personal luggage is allowed in free. Also allowed: 1kg of tobacco products, or 100 cigars or 600 cigarettes, and 2 bottles of liquor. The first US$100 on imported articles is tax exempt. There are no restrictions on the import of foreign currency; up to the amount imported and declared may be exported. The import and export of local currency is limited to 200 colones, although at land borders you may bring in more. All animal products are prohibited from importation, with the exception of boned, sterilized and hermetically sealed meat products. Fruits are inspected carefully and destroyed if necessary. Hide, skins and woollen goods will be fumigated against disease. Animals must be free of parasites, fully inoculated and have a veterinary certificate and import permit.

Internal Transport Bus services are good and cover most areas, although buses themselves are sometimes crowded and their drivers are not always very careful. Hitchhiking is comparatively easy. Passenger rail services exist on one short route out of the capital and in some rural areas (most inaccessible).

Motoring At the border, after producing a driving licence and proof of ownership, you are given a permit costing 100 colones to stay for 30 days by the Customs Office and Police Department. This can be extended at the Dirección General de la Renta Aduanas in San Bartolo, to the E of San Salvador. In any case, the formalities for bringing in a car involve considerable paperwork. There is a 7-colón charge for tyre-fumigation and a car inspection charge of about US$1, although these are not always carried out. There may also be a 2-colón quarantine charge, a 5-colón transit fee for cars, and possibly a local municipality tax adding up to a total of over 20 colones. It is best to pay any charges at the cashier's office only. Insurance is not compulsory in El Salvador, but you should arrange cover. A good map, both of republic and of capital, can be obtained from Texaco or Esso, or from the Tourist Institute. Petrol costs US$1.74 (super) per US gallon, US$1.55 (regular) and diesel costs US$0.90. Roads are generally good throughout the country.

Food Try *pupusas*—stuffed *tortillas* made of corn or ricemeal, in several varieties (including *chicharrón*—pork; *queso*—cheese; *revueltas*, typical, tasty and cheap); also *garobo* (iguana) and *cusuco* (tatou—armadillo). They are sold at many street stalls, and are better there than at restaurants, but beware stomach infection. On Sat and Sun nights people congregate in *pupuserías*. *Pavo* (turkey) is common and good, as are the red beans (*frijoles*). Coffee makes an excellent souvenir and is good value.

Tipping At hotels and restaurants: 10%, but 15% for small bills. Nothing for taxi-drivers except when hired for the day; airport porters, 'boinas rojas', US$1 per bag; haircut US$0.20, not obligatory.

Health The gastro-enteric diseases are most common. Visitors should take care over what they eat during the first few weeks, and should drink *agua cristal* (bottled water). Specifics against malaria should be taken if a night is spent on the coast, especially in the E of the country. Cases of dengue have been reported, even in the capital city. The San Salvador milk supply is good, and piped water is relatively pure.

Business is active all year round, except in August, which is the holiday season. Christmas and Easter periods should also be avoided by businessmen. Business is centralized in the capital, but it is as well to visit Santa Ana and San Miguel.

'Hints to Exporters: El Salvador' can be obtained from Dept of Trade, DTI Export Publications, PO Box 55, Stratford-upon-Avon, Warwickshire, CV37 9GE. For information about investment and export, see 'El Salvador is Your Best Buy,' from FUSADES, Boulevard Santa Elena, Urbanización Santa Elena, Antiguo Cuscatlán, La Libertad, El Salvador (off the road to Santa Tecla—Pan American Highway—to SW of the capital) T 24-3975/5636/1224 or 98-0243/0241.

Hours of business 0800-1200 and 1400-1730 Mon to Fri; 0800-1200 Sat. Banks in San Salvador 0900-1300, 1330-1600 Mon to Fri; different hours for other towns given in text. Government offices: 0800-1600 Mon to Fri.

Public holidays The usual ones are 1 January, Holy Week (3 days, government 10 days), 1 May, 10 May, Corpus Christi (half day), 5-6 August, 15 September, 12 October, 2 and 5 November (half day), 24 December (half-day) and Christmas Day. Government offices are also closed on religious holidays. Little business in Easter Week, the first week of August, and the Christmas-New Year period. Banks are closed for balance 29, 30 June and 30, 31 December.

Look in the newspapers for details of regional fiestas, rodeos, etc. There are many artesan fairs, eg at San Sebastián and San Vicente, which are worth a visit but which go largely unnoticed in the capital.

Time in El Salvador is 6 hrs behind GMT.

Currency The unit is the colón (¢), divided into 100 centavos. Banknotes of 5, 10, 25, 50 and 100 colones are used, and there are nickel coins for 1 colón, and for fractional amounts. The colón is often called a peso. Black market trading is done in the street, but *casas de cambio* may give better rates. Either is preferable to the border, where rates may be low and cheating is common. Credit card payments are subject to 5% commission and are charged at the official rate. **NB** Change all colones before entering Guatemala or Honduras, where they may only be changed at international bus terminals at unfavourable rates.

Warning Prices in El Salvador are sometimes quoted in US dollars. Make sure which currency is being used.

The **metric system** of weights and measures is used alongside certain local units such as the *vara* (836 mm, 32.9 inches), *manzana* (7,000 sq m, or 1.67 acres), the *libra* (0.454 kilogramme, about 1 English pound), and the *quintal* of 100 libras. Some US weights and measures are also used. US gallons are used for gasoline and quarts for oil.

Electric Current 110 volts, 60 cycles, AC (plugs are American, 2 flat pin style). Supply is far from stable; mains supply alarm clocks will not work and important electrical equipment should have surge protectors.

Posts and Telecommunications Air mail to and from Europe can take up to 1 month, but normally about 15 days, US$0.35; from the USA, 1 week. The correct address for any letter to the capital is 'San Salvador, El Salvador, Central America'. The main post office is at the Centro de Gobierno.

The charge for a local telephone call is 0.10 centavos for 3 mins. A private call or telex to Europe costs US$22 for the first 3 mins, then US$5.50 for each additional minute (if made from private telephones or the state telecommunications company, ANTEL, which has offices in the Centre, in the Centro de Gobierno and in Metrocentro, among other places.) Calls made from hotels are more expensive. Direct dialling is available to Europe, 3 mins, minimum, USA (US$2 per minute) and other parts of the world. No collect calls to Europe, except to Spain. For long-distance calls within El Salvador, T 110 for enquiries; international long-distance 119; US Sprint operator 191; MCI operator 195.

To use AT&T USADirect® Service from El Salvador dial **190** from any telephone. Coin deposit is required from all public telephones. If you require assistance, please call the AT&T office in San Salvador at **981-166.**

AT&T USADirect® Service.

Radio Inc communicates with all parts of the world through local stations. Public telex at ANTEL. British business travellers can use the telex system at the Embassy.

Press In San Salvador: *Diario de Hoy* and *La Prensa Gráfica* (both right wing) every morning, including Sunday. *El Mundo* and *Diario Latino* in the afternoons, except Sunday. New is *La Noticia*, popular. There are provincial newspapers in Santa Ana, San Miguel and elsewhere. Weekly bilingual newspaper (English and Spanish, right wing), *El Salvador News Gazette*, available from most hotels which take foreigners. US newspapers and magazines available at leading hotels.

There are 80 radio stations: one is government owned, one belongs to the armed forces, 7 to the FMLN and several are owned by churches. There are 4 commercial television stations, all with national coverage, and one government-run station with 2 channels.

Representation Overseas UK, 5 Great James St, London WC1N 3DA, T 071-430 2141, F 071-430 0484.

Local Information can be got from the Instituto Salvadoreño de Turismo (ISTU), Calle Rubén Darío 619, San Salvador. The Tourist Institute provides a small map of the country with the main beaches and the 13 'Turicentros' marked on it.

Language Spanish, but English is widely understood in business circles. Spanish should be used for letters, catalogues etc.

We are grateful to Huw Clough and Kate Hennessy for updating this chapter and to the following travellers: Simon Attewell (Loughborough, Leicestershire) Alexander Beck (Altessing, Germany), Calvin Blattner (Los Angeles, CA, USA) Jay Connerley (Fremont NE, USA) Frank Dux (Passau, Germany), Joy Hale & Derek Fess (Columbus, Ohio) Ann Frechette & Jean Luc Massicotte for Charles Huot (Montréal), J Roy Goodall (Belize City) Pasi Hannonen (Jy vä Skylä, Finland) Norman Higginson (Redondo Beach, CA) Markus Hohl (London W11) Noel, Nenagh & Zoë Kemp (Lindisfarne, Australia), Christoph Künzi (Zurich, Switzerland) Helmut Lüder (Potomac, MD, USA) Rob Minnee (Lisse, The Netherlands) Claudia Modrow & Massimo Godenzi (Bergheim, Germany) Monica Müller (Blonay) & Klaus Högle (Marin, Switzerland) Claudio Rivero (Buenos Aires) Nadine Rocamora (Lattes, France) Mark Schuringa (Amsterdam, Holland) Harald Schwender & Birgitte Hächer (Sandhausen, Germany) Stefan Cotting (Nevenegg, Switzerland), Bärbel Strauch (Heidelberg, Germany) John W Underwood (Bellevue, Washington, USA) and Reto Wildschek (Kloten, Switzerland).

WILL YOU HELP US?

We do all we can to get our facts right in the MEXICO & CENTRAL AMERICAN HANDBOOK. Each section is thoroughly revised each year, but the territory is vast and our eyes cannot be everywhere. We are always pleased to hear about your travels; do write to us in as much detail as possible. In return we will send you information about our special guidebook offer.

TRADE & TRAVEL *Handbooks*

Write to The Editor, Mexico & Central American Handbook, Trade & Travel, 6 Riverside Court, Lower Bristol Road, Bath BA2 3DZ. England

HONDURAS

INTRODUCTION

HONDURAS is larger than all the other Central American republics except Nicaragua, but has a smaller population than El Salvador, less than a fifth its size. Bordered by Nicaragua, Guatemala, and El Salvador, it has a narrow Pacific coastal strip, 124 km long, on the Gulf of Fonseca, but its northern coast on the Caribbean is some 640 km long.

Much of the country is mountainous: a rough plateau covered with volcanic ash and lava in the S, rising to peaks such as Cerro de las Minas in the Celaque range (2,849m), but with some intermont basins at between 900 and 1,800m. The volcanic detritus disappears to the N, revealing saw-toothed ranges which approach the coast at an angle; the one in the extreme NW, along the border with Guatemala, disappears under the sea and shows itself again in the Bay Islands. At most places in the N there is only a narrow shelf of lowland between the sea and the sharp upthrust of the mountains, but along two rivers—the Aguán in the NE, and the Ulúa in the NW—long fingers of marshy lowland stretch inland between the ranges. The Ulúa lowland is particularly important; it is about 40 km wide and stretches southwards for 100 km. From its southern limit a deep gash continues across the highland to the Gulf of Fonseca, on the Pacific. The distance between the Caribbean and the Pacific along this trough is 280 km; the altitude at the divide between the Río Comayagua, running into the Ulúa and the Caribbean, and the streams flowing into the Pacific, is only 950m. In this trough lies Comayagua, the old colonial capital. The lowlands along the Gulf of Fonseca are narrower than they are along the Caribbean; there is no major thrust inland

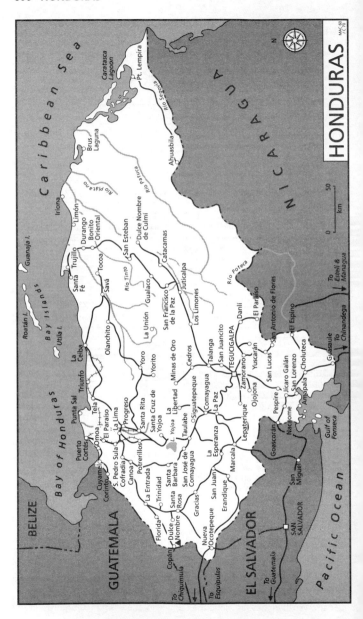

HONDURAS

MAC 60 /C 70

Caribbean Sea

BELIZE

GUATEMALA

EL SALVADOR

NICARAGUA

Pacific Ocean

Gulf of Fonseca

Bay of Honduras

Bay Islands

Guanaja I.

Roatán I.

Utila I.

Carataska Lagoon

Pt. Lempira

Brus Laguna

Ahuasbila

Río Segovia

Río Patuca

Río Plátano

Río Poteca

Iriona

Limón

Trujillo

Santa Fé

Tocoa

Savá

Durango Bonito Oriental

San Esteban

Dulce Nombre de Culmí

Catacamas

Río Tinto

Gualaco

La Unión

San Francisco de la Paz

Juticalpa

Los Limones

Olanchito

Yoro

Yorito

Minas de Oro

Cedros

Talanga

San Juancito

TEGUCIGALPA

Danlí

El Paraíso

San Antonio de Flores

To Estelí & Managua

El Espino

To Chinandega

La Ceiba

Triunfo

Tela

La Lima

Progreso

El Paraíso

Tenoa

Santa Rita

Santa Cruz de Yojoa

La Libertad

Siguatepeque

Comayagua

La Paz

Zamorano

San Lucas

Yuscarán

Jícaro Galán

San Lorenzo

Amapala

Guasaule

To Chinandega

Choluteca

Puerto Cortés

Corinto

Cuyamel

Canoa

S. Pedro Sula

Cofradia

Potrerillos

La Entrada

Trinidad

Santa Bárbara

San José de Comayagua

L. Yojoa

Taulabe

La Esperanza

Lepaterique

Ojojona

Pespire

Nacaome

Goascorán

San Miguel

Florida

Dulce Nombre

Copán

Nueva Ocotepeque

Santa Rosa

Gracias

San Juan

Erandique

Marcala

Punta Sal

Punta Caxinas

To Chiquimula

To Esquipulas

To Guatemala

SAN SALVADOR

Río Platano

N

0   50
km

as along the Ulúa.

The prevailing winds are from the E, and the Caribbean coast has a high rainfall and is covered with deep tropical forest. The intermont basins, the valleys, and the slopes sheltered from the prevailing winds bear oak and pine down to as low as 600m. Timber is almost the only fuel available. In the drier areas, N and S of Tegucigalpa, there are extensive treeless savannas.

The Spaniards, arriving in the early 16th century, found groups of Indians of the Maya and other cultures. Pushing E from Guatemala City they came upon silver in the SE, and in 1578 founded Tegucigalpa near the mines. The yield was comparatively poor, but enough to attract a thin stream of immigrants. Settlement during the ensuing century was mostly along the trail from Guatemala City: at Gracias, La Esperanza, Comayagua and the department of Santa Bárbara, where the largest white population is found. Gradually these settlements spread over the S and W, and this, with the N coast, is where the bulk of the population lives today. The Spaniards and their descendants ignored the northern littoral and the Ulúa lowlands, but during the 19th century US companies, depending largely on black workers from the British West Indies and Belize, developed the northern lowlands as a great banana-growing area. Today the largest concentration of population per square kilometre is in the Department of Cortés, which extends northwards from Lago Yojoa towards the Caribbean; it includes the major portion of the river basins of Ulúa and Chamelecón, also known as the Sula valley: the most important agricultural area in the country, with San Pedro Sula as its commercial centre and Puerto Cortés as its seaport. The Atlantic littoral consumes two-thirds of the country's imports, and ships the bananas which are the country's major export.

Even today, land under some form of cultivation is only 16% of the total, while meadows and pastures make up 23% of total land use; 31% of Honduras is forest. Rugged terrain makes large areas unsuitable for any kind of agriculture. Nevertheless, there are undeveloped agricultural potentials in the flat and almost unpopulated lands of the coastal plain E of Tela to Trujillo and Puerto Castilla, in the Aguán valley southward and in the region NE of Juticalpa. The area further to the NE, known as the Mosquitia plain, is largely unexploited and little is known of its potential.

Climate Rain is frequent on the Caribbean littoral during the whole year; the heaviest occurs from September to February inclusive. In Tegucigalpa the dry season is normally from November to April inclusive. The coolest months are December and January, but this is when heavy rains fall on the North Coast, which may impede travel. The driest months for this area are April and May, though very hot.

History For Honduras' early history, see the introductory chapter to Central America. Honduras was largely neglected by Spain and its colonists, who concentrated on their trading partners further N or S. The resulting disparity in levels of development between Honduras and its regional neighbours caused problems after independence in 1821. Harsh partisan battles among provincial leaders resulted in the collapse of the Central American Federation in 1838. The national hero, General Francisco Morazán was a leader in unsuccessful attempts to maintain the Federation and the restoration of Central American unity was the main aim of foreign policy until 1922.

Honduras has had a succession of military and civilian rulers and there have been 300 internal rebellions, civil wars and changes of government since independence, most of them in the 20th century. Political instability in the past led to a lack of investment in economic infrastructure and sociopolitical integration, making Honduras one of the poorest countries in the Western Hemisphere. It earned its nickname of the 'Banana Republic' in the first part of the 20th century following the founding of a company in 1899 by the Vaccaro brothers of New Orleans which eventually became the Standard Fruit Company and which was to make bananas the major export crop of Honduras. The United Fruit Company of Boston was also founded in 1899 and in 1929 was merged with the Cuyamel Fruit Company of Samuel Zemurray, who controlled the largest fruit interests in Honduras. United Fruit (UFCo), known as El Pulpo (the octopus), emerged as a major political influence in the region with strong links with several dictatorships.

The 1929 Great Depression caused great hardship in the export-oriented economies of the region and in Honduras it brought the rise of another authoritarian régime. Tiburcio Cariás Andino was elected in 1932 but through his ties with foreign companies and other neighbouring dictators he was able to hold on to power until renewed turbulence began in 1948 and he voluntarily withdrew from power in 1949. The two political parties, the Liberals and the Nationals, came under the control of provincial military leaders and after two more authoritarian Nationalist governments and a general strike in 1954 by radical labour unions on the North Coast, young military reformists staged a palace coup in 1955. They installed a provisional junta and allowed elections for a constituent assembly in 1957. The assembly was led by the Liberal Party, which appointed Dr Ramón Villeda Morales as President, and transformed itself into a national legislature for six years. A newly created military academy graduated its first class in 1960 and the armed forces began to professionalize its leadership in conjunction with the civilian economic establishment. Conservative officers, nervous of a Cuban-style revolution, preempted elections in 1963 in a bloody coup which deposed Dr Villeda, exiled Liberal Party members and took control of the national police, which they organized into special security forces.

In 1969, Honduras and El Salvador were drawn into a bizarre episode known as the 'Football War", which took its name from its origin in a disputed decision in the third qualifying round of the World Cup. Its root cause, however, was the social tension aroused by migrating workers from overcrowded El Salvador to Honduras. In 13 days, 2,000 people were killed before a ceasefire was arranged by the Organization of American States. A peace treaty was not signed, though, until 1980, and the dispute provoked Honduras to withdraw from the Central American Common Market (CACM), which helped to hasten its demise.

The armed forces, led chiefly by General López Arellano and his protegés in the National Party, dominated government until 1982. López initiated land reform, but despite liberal policies, his régime was brought down in the mid-1970s by corruption scandals involving misuse of hurricane aid funds and bribes from the United Brands Company. His successors increased the size and power of the security forces and created the largest air force in Central America, while slowly preparing for a return to civilian rule. A constituent assembly was elected in 1980 and general elections held in 1981. A constitution was promulgated in 1982 and President Roberto Suazo Córdoba, of the Liberal Party, assumed power. During this period, Honduras cooperated closely with the USA on political and military issues, particularly in moves to isolate Nicaragua's left wing government, and became host to some 12,000 right wing Nicaraguan contra rebels. It was less willing to take a similar stand against the FMLN left wing guerrillas in El Salvador for fear of renewing border tensions. In 1986 the first peaceful transfer of power between civilian presidents for 30 years took place when José Azcona del Hoyo (Liberal) won the elections. Close relations with the USA were maintained in the 1980s, Honduras had the largest Peace Corps Mission in the world, non-governmental and international voluntary agencies proliferated and the government became increasingly dependent upon US aid to finance its budget.

In 1989, general elections were won by the right wing Rafael Leonardo Callejas Romero of the National Party, which won a 14-seat majority in the National Assembly. Under the terms of the Central American Peace Plan, the contra forces were demobilized and disarmed by June 1990. The Honduran armed forces have come under greater pressure for reform as a result of US and domestic criticism of human rights abuses. An Ad Hoc Commission, set up by President Callejas, published a report in April 1993 recommending a series of institutional reforms in the judiciary and security services, including the resolution by the Supreme Court of all cases of jurisdictional conflict between civilian and military courts. This and other measures led to some, but not complete improvement in the respect for human rights. In the campaign leading up to the 1993 general elections, the Liberal candidate, Carlos Roberto Reina Idiáquez, promised a 'moral revolution' if he won. His targets were human rights abuse, government corruption and partisan state institutions. He also pledged to provide every citizen 'techo, trabajo, tierra y tortilla' (roof, work, land and food), arguing for a more socially-conscious face to the economic adjustment programme inaugurated by President Callejas. Reina duly won the elections with a 53.4% majority over his National Party rival, Oswaldo Ramos Soto. In the National Assembly the Liberals won 71 seats, the Nationals 55 and the Innovation and Unity Party (Pinu) 2. The Liberals also won 60% of elections for town mayors throughout the country. President Reina took office on 27 January 1994.

Population There are few pure Indians (an estimated 7% of the total population), and fewer of pure Spanish and other European ancestry. The two largest concentrations of Indians are 1) from Santa Rosa de Copán westwards to the border with Guatemala; the Chortis in the departments of Lempira, Intibucá and, above all, the Lencas in the highlands of La Paz. 2) There are about 45,000 Miskito Indians who live on the Caribbean coast, as well as several communities of Garifunas (black Caribs). The population is 90% *mestizo*. Some 53% are peasants or agricultural labourers, with a relatively low standard of living. It was estimated in 1993 that 40% of Hondurans are unemployed and that 68-80% of the population live below the poverty line.

The Economy Honduras has traditionally been the poorest economy in Central America with one of the lowest income rates per head in all Latin America although the war in Nicaragua depressed income levels there below even those of Honduras (see Economic Indicators at the end of the book). The distribution of land continues to be a pressing problem, with an estimated 170,000 farming families lacking sufficient land for subsistence agriculture. New legislation in 1992 was designed to encourage private enterprise, making it easier to sell land and prompting large landholdings, leaving campesinos with only small parcels of land. Unemployment is about 40% of the working population, owing to low investment, and poor harvests and labour disputes in the agricultural sector. After decades of low inflation when the currency was fixed, the 1990s have been a severe shock to the population and real incomes have fallen sharply as the effects of economic liberalization have been felt.

Over half of the population lives by the land: coffee, bananas and shrimp are the main export crops and Honduras is the world's fourth largest exporter of bananas. Cotton, once important, is now far less so. Tobacco, maize, beans, rice and sugar are grown mostly for domestic use but small quantities are sometimes exported. Cattle raising is important and exports of both meat and livestock are growing. Timber is a major export; controversy over the development of forestry reserves in the Department of Olancho has laid the future expansion of the industry open to doubt.

Honduras has considerable reserves of silver, gold, lead, zinc, tin, iron, copper, coal and antimony, but only lead and zinc and small quantities of gold and silver are mined and exported. Considerable offshore exploration for petroleum is in progress. There is an oil refinery at Puerto Cortés and exports of petroleum derivatives are becoming significant. The US$600mn hydroelectric scheme at El

HONDURAS : FACT FILE

Geographic
Land area	112,088 sq km
forested	29.9%
pastures	22.8%
cultivated	16.2%

Demographic
Population (1992)	4,996,000
annual growth rate (1987-92)	3.3%
urban	41.1%
rural	58.9%
density	44.6 per sq km
Religious affiliation	
Roman Catholic	85.0%
Birth rate per 1,000 (1991)	39.0
	(world av 26.4)
Death rate per 1,000 (1991)	8.0
	(world av 9.2)

Education and Health
Life expectancy at birth,	
male	63 years
female	67 years
Infant mortality rate	
per 1,000 live births (1991)	48.0
Physicians (1990)	1 per 1,586 persons
Hospital beds	1 per 818 persons
Calorie intake as %	
of FAO requirement	99%
Population age 25 and over	
with no formal schooling	33.4%
Literate males (over 15)	75.5%
Literate females (over 15)	70.6%

Economic
GNP (1990 market prices)	US$3,023mn
GNP per capita	US$590
Public external debt (1990)	US$2,992mn
Tourism receipts (1990)	US$29mn
Inflation (annual av 1986-91)	14.2%
Radio	1 per 2.6 persons
Television	1 per 24 persons
Telephone	1 per 46 persons

Employment
Population economically active (1991)	1,523,300
Unemployment rate (1990)	40%
% of labour force in	
agriculture	46.1
mining	0.3
manufacturing	11.8
construction	5.8
Military forces	17,500

Source *Encyclopaedia Britannica*

Cajón was constructed to reduce the country's oil bill.

Local industries are small, turning out a wide range of consumer goods, besides being engaged in the processing of timber and agricultural products. The more important products are furniture, textiles, footwear, chemicals, cement and rubber. Maquila industries have grown rapidly, with exports rising from US$42mn in 1987 to US$365mn in 1992, over a third of total exports. Most are in clothing, but there are others processing wood and a variety of goods, employing about 38,000 people on higher wages than elsewhere in the country.

Honduras' total external debt amounts to some US$3.6bn, nearly four times merchandise exports. From 1982 the government held negotiations to reschedule its debt with commercial banks but failed to sign any agreement. Arrears mounted and in 1989 the negotiating committee disbanded to allow banks individually to recover their debts as best they could. In 1990 a new economic package was introduced with emergency spending cuts and revenue raising measures designed to reduce the fiscal deficit. The lempira was allowed to float freely against the US dollar in a legalization of the black market rate where the currency had been trading at L4=US$1 compared with the official rate since 1926 of L2=US$1. There are now several rates covering trade and tourism. President Callejas thereby attempted a rapprochement with the international financial community; Honduras had previously been declared ineligible to borrow from the IMF, the World Bank and the Inter- American Development Bank, while US aid had been cut by 30%. Negotiations with the multilateral agencies led to the clearing of arrears and new loans to support the economic programme. In 1991 the USA forgave US$435mn of the US$600mn debt owed by Honduras. At the same time, the private foreign debt was reduced from

US$225mn to US$80mn through debt conversions and privatizations of state enterprises. The effect of structural adjustment measures on the population, however, were not favourable: unemployment rose, inflation soared and poverty grew, causing considerable social problems. By 1992 inflation was down to 8.8% and gdp rose by 4.6% although structural adjustment remained unpopular. Inflation rose to 13.7% in 1993 and gdp growth declined to 3.7%. In 1994, the new President's intention of honouring the international and domestic financial commitments undertaken by his predecessor, while adding a 'human face' to the programme, would present a major challenge to the new administration. Not only had the foreign debt risen and targets not been met in the last year of Callejas' term, but also the foreign lending institutions' loss of confidence in Honduras would make it difficult for Reina to fund social programmes.

Government Honduras is a multi party republic. The Legislature consists of a single 128-seat Chamber. Deputies are elected by a proportional vote. Executive authority rests with a President, directly elected for 4 years. No President may serve two terms in succession. The National Assembly elects members of the Supreme Court, which, together with the Court of Appeal, Justices of the Peace and lesser tribunals, constitute the judiciary. The Constitution was revised by a Constituent Assembly elected in April 1980. The country is divided into 18 departments, each with an administrative centre.

Communications The railways are in the N. In 1993 the Tela Railroad Company closed its entire operation along the Atlantic coast, while the Ferrocarril Nacional de Honduras downgraded its one remaining passenger service between San Pedro Sula and Puerto Cortés to a daily ferrobus.

A light aeroplane is the only way of getting to large areas of the country, but the road system has improved rapidly in recent years. Total road length is now 18,629 km, of which 12% are paved. The main paved roads are the Northern Highway linking Tegucigalpa, San Pedro Sula and Puerto Cortés; the road W from Puerto Cortés along the North Coast, through Omoa, to the Guatemalan frontier; the highway from Tegucigalpa to Olancho, passing through Juticalpa and Catacamas; the Pan- American Highway in the SW between El Salvador and Nicaragua, and the Southern Highway which runs to it from Tegucigalpa; the North Coast Highway joining San Pedro Sula with Progreso, Tela and La Ceiba, and on to Trujillo (Progreso- Tela stretch being paved); from Progreso a paved road runs S through Santa Rita de Yoro to join the San Pedro Sula-Tegucigalpa highway 44 km S of San Pedro; the Western Highway linking San Pedro Sula with Santa Rosa de Copán, Nueva Ocotepeque and the Guatemalan and Salvadorean frontiers, with a branch from La Entrada to Copán ruins; the road from Santa Rosa de Copán to Gracias is also paved; the Carretera de Santa Bárbara and on to the Western Highway (Carretera del Occidente), from Lago Yojoa to Santa Bárbara, and the stretch from La Paz to Marcala in the Department of La Paz; the road linking Choluteca on the Pan-American Highway with the Nicaraguan frontier at Guasaule; the Eastern Highway linking Tegucigalpa, Danlí, El Paraíso and Las Manos (Nicaraguan frontier); the road from Tegucigalpa to Santa Lucía and Valle de Angeles; some of the road along the island of Roatán. Travel is still by foot and mule in many areas. Tegucigalpa, La Ceiba, San Pedro Sula and Roatán all have international airports. More details in the text below.

Religion and Education Education is compulsory, but not all the rural children go to school. 34% of the population over the age of 25 have no formal schooling. The National University is based in Tegucigalpa though it also has departments in San Pedro Sula and La Ceiba. Also in Tegucigalpa is the Universidad José Cecilio del Valle, the Universidad Católica and the Universidad Tecnológica Centro Americana; there is also the Universidad de San Pedro Sula. The majority of the population is Catholic, but there is complete freedom of religion.

National Parks The National Parks office, Conama, is next to the Instituto Nacional Agrario, chaotic but friendly, a good source of information. The Asociación Hondureña de Ecología, ¹/₂ block N of Farmacia Tegucigalpa, Parque Finlay (near *Hotel Granada)*, street has no sign, but the house has AHE plaque, T 32-38-62/ 32-18-00, has drawn up a list of over 70 natural reserves in Honduras which it hopes will be developed as national parks or reserves, and 56 plant, animal, bird and aquatic species in danger. Its book *Areas silvestres de Honduras* gives all details (US$7.50). It publishes *Ecosistemas terrestres de Honduras* (US$3.50) and *Mamíferos silvestres de Honduras* (US$6); *Aves de Honduras*. There are offices elsewhere in the country, see text. Cohdefor, the national forestry agency is also much involved with the parks, they have an office at 10 Av 4 C NO, San Pedro Sula, T 53-49-59. The parks system has been in existence legally since a congressional decree was passed in 1987. Natural Reserves continue to be established, several on the Caribbean coast in 1992/3 and all support and interest is most welcome. Parks in existence are La Tigra, outside Tegucigalpa (see p 620), and the Biosphere of the Río Plátano (see p 663). Under development since 1987 are Monte Celaque, (see p 652), Cusuco (see p 642), Punta Sal (see p 624) and Pico Bonito (p 627—these parks will have visitors' centres, hiking trails and primitive camping), and the following have been designated national parks by the government: Montecristo-Trifinio (see p 649), Cerro Azul (Copán), Santa Bárbara (see p 644), Azul Meámbar (Cortés and Comayagua, see p 649), Pico Pijol (Yoro, see p 625), Montaña de Yoro, Agalta (Olancho—p 662) and Montaña Comayagua (see p 655). Wildlife Refuges covered in the text are Punto Izopo (p 624), Cuero y Salado (p 628), Las Trancas (p 652) and La Muralla-Los Higuerales (p 661). For information on protected areas in the Bay Islands, see p 631. Some of these sites have Peace Corps Volunteers, who would be a good source of information.

NB Electricity rationing is in force in Honduras, until January 1995 at least. The main reasons are increased demand, the effect of deforestation on the rivers feeding El Cajón hydroelectric scheme and the failure to purchase neighbouring countries' excess power.

TEGUCIGALPA

The capital and nearby exursions to old mining settlements in the forested mountains: a great contrast between the functional modern city and some of the oldest villages in the country.

Tegucigalpa, the capital, a city of over 800,000 inhabitants, stands in an intermont basin at between 950 and 1,100m above sea level. It was founded as a mining camp in 1578: the miners found their first gold where the N end of the Soberanía bridge now is. The name means 'silver hill' in the original Indian tongue. It did not become the capital until 1880. On three sides it is surrounded by sharp, high peaks. It comprises two former towns: Comayagüela and Tegucigalpa built at the foot and up the slopes of El Picacho. A steeply banked river, the Choluteca, divides the two towns, now united administratively as the Distrito Central. Tegucigalpa has not been subjected to any disaster by fire or earthquake, being off the main earthquake fault line, so retains many traditional features. Many of the stuccoed houses, with a single heavily barred entrance leading to a central patio, are attractively coloured. However, the old low skyline of the city has now been punctuated by several modern tall buildings.

Its altitude gives it a reliable climate: temperate during the rainy season from May to November; warm, with cool nights, in March and April, and cool and dry, with very cool nights, in December to February. The annual mean temperature is about 74°F (23°C).

The Carretera del Sur (Southern Highway), which brings in travellers from the S and from Toncontín Airport, 6¹/₂ km from Plaza Morazán, runs through Comayagüela into Tegucigalpa. It goes past the obelisk set up to commemorate a hundred years of Central American independence, and the Escuela Nacional de Bellas Artes, with a decorated Mayan corridor and temporary exhibitions of contemporary paintings and crafts.

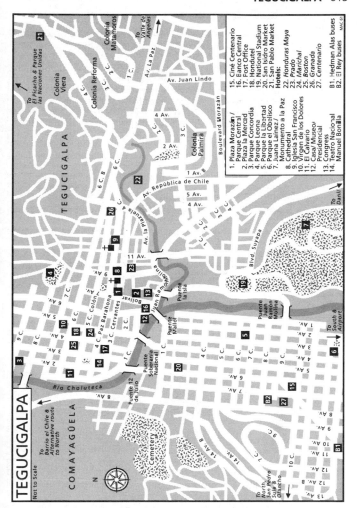

1. Plaza Morazán /
   Parque Central
2. Parque la Merced
3. Parque Concordia
4. Parque Leona
5. Parque la Libertad
6. Parque el Obelisco
7. Juana Laínez
   Monumento a la Paz
8. Cathedral
9. Iglesia San Francisco
10. Virgen de los Dolores
11. El Calvario
12. Casa/ Museo
    Presidencial
13. Correos
14. Teatro Nacional
    Manuel Bonilla

15. Ciné Centenario
16. Banco Central
17. Post Office
18. Hondutel
19. National Stadium
20. San Isidro Market
21. San Pablo Market
    Hotels:
22. *Honduras Maya*
23. *Prado*
24. *Marichal*
25. *Boston*
26. *Granada*
27. *Centenario*

B1. Hedman Alas buses
B2. El Rey buses

Crossing the river from Comayagüela by the colonial Mallol bridge, on the left is the old Casa Presidencial (1919, now the Museo Presidencial—the new one is a modern building on Blvd de las Fuerzas Aramadas). Calle Bolívar runs through the area containing the Congress building and the former site of the University, founded in 1847. The site is now the Paraninfo Universitario, where cultural events are held. Calle Bolívar leads to the main square, Plaza Morazán (commonly known as Parque Central). On the eastern side of the square are the Palacio del Distrito Central, and the domed and double-towered Cathedral built in the late 18th century. See the beautiful gilt colonial altarpiece, the fine examples of Spanish colonial art, the cloisters and, in Holy Week, the ceremony of the Descent from the Cross.

Av Paz Barahona, running through the northern side of the square, is a key avenue. On it to the E is the church of San Francisco, with its clangorous bells, and (on 3a Calle, called Av Cervantes) the old Spanish Mint (1770), now the national printing works. If, from Plaza Morazán, we go along Av Paz Barahona westwards towards the river, by turning right along 4 Av we come to the 18th century church of Virgen de los Dolores. Two blocks N and 3 blocks W of the church is Parque Concordia with good copies of Maya sculpture and temples.

Back on Av Paz Barahona and further W are the Teatro Nacional Manuel Bonilla, with a rather grand interior (1915) and, across the square, the beautiful old church of El Calvario. Built in elegant colonial style, El Calvario's roof is supported by 14 pillars. It contains images of the Virgen de la Soledad, San Juan and the archangels San Miguel and San Rafael. On Easter Friday processions start and end here. Crossing the bridge of 12 de Julio (quite near the theatre) one can visit Comayagüela's market of San Isidro.

In Colonia Palmira, Tegucigalpa, is the Boulevard Morazán, with shopping and business complexes, banks, restaurants, cafeterias, bars, etc. You can get a fine view of the city from the Monumento a La Paz on Juana Laínez hill, near the Estadio Nacional (National Stadium), open till 1700.

One is always conscious, in Tegucigalpa, of the summit of El Picacho looming up to the N (at the top is a zoo of mostly indigenous animals, open Thurs-Sun, US$0.25). From Plaza Morazán go up Calle 7a and the Calle de la Leona to Parque La Leona, a handsome small park with a railed walk overlooking the city. Higher still is the reservoir in El Picacho, also known as the United Nations Park, which can be reached by a special bus from the number 9 bus stop, behind Los Dolores church (in front of Farmacia Santa Bárbara), Sun only, US$0.15; camping is allowed here.

NB Generally speaking, Tegucigalpa is cleaner and safer (especially at night) than Comayagüela. If you have anything stolen, report it to Dirección General de Investigación Nacional, DIN, $1/2$ block N of Los Dolores church.

Hotels in Tegucigalpa: A+ *Honduras Maya*, Av República de Chile, Colonia Palmira, T 32-31-91, F 32-76-29, rooms and apartments, casino, swimming pool US$3.50, bars (the main bar is relaxed and you get appetizers with every alcoholic drink, US TV channels), cafeterias (*Black Jack's Snack Bar*, *Cafeteria 2000*), restaurant (*El Candelero*), conference hall and convention facilities for 1,000, view over the city (only from uppermost rooms); **A** *Plaza San Martín*, on Plaza San Martín (near *Honduras Maya*), Colonia Palmira, T 32-82-67, F 31-13-66, good cafeteria, nice bar, great views of the city from the top terrace; **A** *Suites La Aurora*, Apart-Hotel, Av Luis Bográn 1519, Colonia Tepeyac, T 32-98-91, F 32-01-88, rooms with kitchenette, cable TV, excellent restaurant, swimming pool, helpful staff; **B** *Alameda*, Blvd Suyapa (some distance from centre), T 32-68-74, F 32-69-32, comfortable, pool, restaurant *Le Chalet* (T 32-69-20). At El Hatillo, on the hill N of Tegucigalpa is the comfortable mountain inn *Gloriales*, beautiful setting and fine views of La Tigra forest, T 22-4950, lovely rooms, fine cuisine, reservations essential. Downtown: **A** *Plaza*, on Av Paz Barahona, in front of Post Office (T 37-21-11, F 37-21-19), good, *Papagayo* restaurant good for breakfast and set lunch; **A** *La Ronda*, 6 Av, 11 C, 5 blocks from cathedral (T 37-81-51/55, F 37-14-54), a/c, TV, cafeteria (*Rondalla*) and night club, completely renovated; **A-B** *Prado*, Av Cervantes, 7 y 8 Av, T 37-01-21, F 37-14-54, *La Posada* restaurant; **B** *Istmania*, 5 Av, 7 and 8 C (T 37-16-38/39, F 37-14-46) near Church of Los Dolores, *Versalles* restaurant; **C** *Hotel MacArthur*, 8C, 4 y 5 Av, T 37-56-09, F 38-02-94, a/c, TV, private bath, cheaper without a/c; **D** *Excelsior*, Av Cervantes 1515, T 37-26-38, hot showers (hot water unpredictable), large comfortable rooms, laundry facilities, quiet at the back, garden (with cabins), mixed reports, overnight car parking nearby 1800-0700; **D-E** *Imperio Maya*, 7 Av, 1225, good, reasonably-priced restaurant; **E** *Marichal*, 5 Av, 5 C (T 37-00-69) (ask for a back room), noisy, clean, centrally located; **E** *Don Tito*, 3 Av, 7-8 C, clean, comfortable, hot water; **E** *Krystal*, 200m NW of Parque Central, TV, a/c, parking, restaurant for 1,000, roof top bar with good view; **E** *Granada*, Av Gutemberg 1401, Barrio Guanacaste (hot water on 2nd floor only), good, clean, safe, TV lounge, table tennis, T 37-23-81, annex $1\frac{1}{2}$ blocks uphill, turn right at sign for Cinés Tauro and Aries, also **E** (but a bit more than old building), better beds, hot water in all rooms, safe parking, both can be noisy from passing traffic, but rec, popular with Peace Corps; **E** *Fortuna*, 5 Av, near Los Dolores church, with or without bath; there are several other cheap hotels in this area; **E** *Iberia*, Peatonal Los Dolores, hot showers, clean, noisy, friendly, T 37-92-67, no meals; **E** *Nuevo Boston*, Av Jérez No 321, T 37-94-11, hot water, central, repeatedly rec, good value, no credit cards, rooms on street side noisy, friendly, stores luggage; **E** *Punta del Este*, Av La Paz 2408, 8 blocks from Honduras Maya, clean, generally quiet; **F** pp, 5 rooms for 4 people each above *Café Allegro* (see **Restaurants** below), run similar to a youth hostel, shared accommodation, shared bathrooms, comfortable, very clean, best value, cable TV room, popular with Peace Corps, very international, changes money, possible work available in exchange for room and board, please contact Jorge.

Comayagüela is convenient for buses to the N and W and there are many cheap *pensiones* and rooms. It is noisier and dirtier than Tegucigalpa, and many establishments are unsuitable for travellers. If you are carrying luggage, take a taxi. **E** *San Pedro*, 9 C, 6 Av, with bath, **F** without or with private cold shower, popular, restaurant; **D/E** *Real de Oro*, Av Cabañas, 11 and 12 C, clean, friendly; **C-D** *Centenario*, 6 Av, 9-10 C, T 37-10-50, safe parking, rec; **D-E** *Palace*, 8-9 Av, 12 C, T 37-66-60, new; **E** *Condesa Inn*, 7 Av, 12 C, clean, a/c, TV, cafeteria, very friendly, a bargain, rec; **E** *Ismary*, 4-5 Av, 5 C, T 38-13-93, with bath, new; **E** *Renieri*, 10 C, 3-4 Av, T 37-24-30; **F/E** *Hotel Richard No 1*, 4 C, 6 and 7 Av, 'laundry' on roof; **F** *Colonial*, 6a y 7a Av, 6 C, No 617, T 375785, price per person with bath, hot water, clean, good value, restaurant next door; **F** *Teleño*, 7 Av, clean, friendly; **G** *Hotelito Latino*, 6 Av, 8 C, friendly, safe, cafeteria, clean; **G** *Lisboa*, 7 C, 4-5 Av, small rooms, OK.

A 7% sales tax is added to hotel bills.

Restaurants A meal in a good restaurant costs between US$5-9; for hotel restaurants, see above. Most places are closed on Sundays. **International food:** *El Arriero*, Av República de Chile, near *Honduras Maya*, good steaks and seafood, expensive; *El Novillero*, Av Rep de Chile, charbroiled steaks; *Alondra*, Av República de Chile on E side of *Honduras Maya*, fine, expensive; *Marbella*, 6 C, 3-4 Av, central, good for breakfast. *El Trapiche*, Blvd Suyapa, opp National University, colonial ranch atmosphere, good steaks, expensive, rec. **Seafood:** *Hungry Fisherman*, Av República de Chile 209, Col Palmira, good, salad bar included in price. **Italian:** *Café Allegro*, Av República de Chile 360, Colonia Palmira, T 32-81-22, very good coffee and pastas, magazines to read, international atmosphere, changes money, owner Jorge provides good information on diving, national parks, forests, etc, welcoming, warmly rec (*Mexico and Central American/South American Handbook* sold here—jazz bar, *Il Piano Roto*, TV room, souvenirs room with Honduran ceramics and handicrafts and 22 bunk beds to rent—see above); near Av Rep de Chile, Col Palmira. Pizzerias: *Tito*, Blvd Morazán, Col Palmira. **Spanish:** *Rincón Español*, Blvd Morazán. *Waldschenke* (*Posada del Bosque*), Cerro El Trigo, El Hatillo, Tegucigalpa, 2½ km from church to the right, Swiss run, open Sat and Sun. **Latin American:** *Taco Loco*, Blvd Morazán, Mexican fast food; *José y Pepe's*, Av República de Panamá, excellent steaks, good service, rec; *Gauchos*, Av de La Paz, near US Embassy, very good *lomito al trozo*. **Chinese:** *China Food*, 2 blocks before the easternmost bridges on Blvd Morazán, ½ block to the right, the best Chinese in town, good value; on same road No 2001 is *China Town Palace*, T 32-82-55, delicious meals, excellent value; *On-Lock*, Blvd Morazán, good; *Pekín*, 3 C, No 525, Barrio San Rafael, 1 block from *Hotel Maya*; *Mei-Mei*, Pasaje Midence Soto, central, rec; *Ley-Hsen*, Pasaje Fiallos Soto. There are several other Chinese restaurants in 4 Av in centre, enormous helpings at reasonable prices. **Meat:** *El Patio 2*, Blvd Morazán, excellent traditional food and kebabs, good service and atmosphere, good value for the hungry, rec; *Jack's Steak House*, same street, also burgers and American style sandwiches; *Jimmy West*, Col Paseo República de Argentina, Casa 322, barbecue, good, affordable, dinners include assortment of relishes and salad; *Bar Mediterráneo*, city centre, delicious goat meat, and cheap set meals; *Duncan Maya*, opp central *Pizza Hut*, good and cheap.

2 *Burger Huts*, one N of Parque La Merced, in the centre and one on Blvd Morazán. *Pizza Huts*: one near Parque Central (with good salad bar), one on Blvd Morazán, one on Av Juan Pablo II, near the new Ministry of Foreign Affairs building (other restaurants on this avenue). *'Stacolosal*, 5 C, 4 Av, is a good cheap eating place, classical music and friendly owner, open 0700-1900. *Super Donuts*, Peatonal, Blvd Morazán, good for filling breakfasts (not just doughnuts!), popular with locals; *Café y Librería Paradiso*, Av Paz Barahona, and Calle Las Damas, good library, paintings, prints and photos to enjoy, newspapers and magazines on sale, good meeting place; *Don Pepe's Terraza*, near Bancahsa, downtown, cheap, noisy orchestra but typical Honduran atmosphere, rec. *Al Natural*, Calle Hipolito Matute y Av Miguel Cervantes, some vegetarian, some meat dishes, huge fresh fruit juices, antiques, caged birds, nice garden atmosphere. *Dunkin Donuts*, several outlets. *Basilio's*, *repostería y panadería*, Calle Peatonal off Plaza Morazán, good cakes, breads and pastries; *Pastelería Francesa*, opp French embassy, rec; *Salman's* bakeries, several outlets in the centre, good bread and pastries; *Brik Brak*, Calle Peatonal just off the Parque Central, open 24 hrs, rec.

Markets Mercado Colón or San Isidro, 6 Avenida at 1 Calle, Comayagüela, many things for sale, fascinating but filthy, do not buy food here. Saturday is busiest day. Mercado de Artesanías, 3 Av, 15 C next to Parque El Soldado, good value. Good supermarkets: Sucasa, in Blvd Morazón, Más x Menos, in Av de la Paz.

Souvenir Shops *Candú*, opp *Hotel Maya*, and in Av República de Chile; *Carmen Honduras Quality Art and Handicrafts*, 1½ blocks S of *Hotel Maya* on Av República de Chile, 338, *Café Allegro* (see above). Also in Valle de Angeles, see **Excursions**. *El Mundo Maya*, Calle Adolfo Zuniga 1114, T 22-29-46, art gallery, souvenir shop and tourist information, also changes US dollars, cash and TCs, run by Alejandro Villela Franco, open Mon-Fri 0900-1830, Sat 0900-1600.

Bookshops *Book Village*, Centro Comercial Los Castaños, Blvd Morazán, English books, both new and secondhand, for sale or exchange (small fee for exchange), wide selection of US magazines. *Librería Paradiso* (see under café listing above). For books in Spanish on Honduras and Central America, *Editorial Guaymuras*, Av Miguel Cervantes 1055. Good book and news stand, and maps in *Hotel Honduras Maya*. Secondhand bookstalls in Mercado San Isidro (6 Av y 2 Calle, Comayagüela), good value. Book exchange in TV room at *Café Allegro*, see above. There is an English weekly called *Honduras This Week*.

Pharmacy *Farmacia Rosna*, in pedestrian mall off Parque Central, T 370605, English spoken, rec; *Regis Palmira*, Ed Ciicsa, Av República de Panamá, Col Palmira; *El Castaño*, Blvd Morazán.

Car Rentals Avis, T 32-00-88 or 33-95-48, *Hotel Honduras Maya* and airport; **Toyota**, Col El Prado, T 33-40-04; **Molinari**, T 37-53-35 or 33-13-07, la Av Comayagüela No 1002, *Honduras Maya* and airport; **Budget**, T 32-68-32 or 33-51-70, *Honduras Maya* and airport; **National**, T 33-26-53 or 33-49-62, Colonia El Prado, *Honduras Maya* and airport.

Car Repairs Metal Mecánica, 1 block S of Av de los Próceres, Colonia Lara. Volkswagen dealer near Parque Concordia, good for repairs.

Taxis About US$1 pp (no reduction for sharing, but bargaining possible); more after 2200, but cheaper (US$0.25) on designated routes eg Miraflores to centre.

Local buses Cost US$0.05, stops are official but unmarked.

Cinemas Plaza 1, 2 3, and 4 in Centro Comercial Plaza Miraflores; Regis, Real and Opera at Centro Comercial Centroamérica, Blvd Miraflores (all have good US films). In city centre, double cinemas Lido Palace, and Variedades. Tauro and Aries, Av Gutemberg, Barrio Guanacaste opposite *Hotel Granada*. Tickets cost US$1.

Entertainment In front of the National University is a *peña*, where people dance and sing. On Av República de Chile: bars *Hungry Fisherman*, *Café Allegro*; *Backstreet Pub*, Av Rep de Uruguay in Colonia Tepeyac, bar/disco, good atmosphere, no cover except when live music. Boulevard Morazán has plenty of choice in night life including *Taco Taco*, a nice bar, sometimes with live Mariachi music; next door *Tequila*, a popular drinking place only open at weekends; *Cocteles*, the in-place in Tegucigalpa for dancing, and *Holiday*, Caribbean music, rec. Blvd Juan Pablo II has discos with various types of music. On Parque del Valle there is a disco called *Black and White*, popular with locals.

Museums Museo Nacional Villa Roy, in home of a former President, has an exhibition of archaeological finds and an interesting display of present-day indigenous cultures in Honduras. A section on the history of the country from independence is being developed. It is situated on a hilltop 1 block above the beautiful Parque Concordia on Calle Morelos 3A (entry US$1, open 0830-1530, closed Mon and Tues). In the Edificio del Banco central, 12 C entre 5 y 6 Av, Comayagüela, is the **Pinacoteca Arturo H Medrano**, with a collection of approximately 500 works by 5 Honduran artists and, in the same building, the **Museo Numismático**, with a collection of coins and banknotes from Honduras and around the world.

Exchange All banks have several branches throughout the city; we list the main offices. **Lloyds Bank**, Av Ramón E Cruz, off Blvd Morazán and Av de la Paz, take any San Felipe bus (Rivera y Cía), get out above US Embassy, walk back, turn left and bank is 300m on right. Open 0900-1500; closed Sat. **Banco Atlántida**, 5 C in front of Plaza Morazán; **Banco de Honduras (Citibank)**, Blvd Suyapa; **Banco de Ahorro Hondureño**, 5 C in front of Plaza Morazán; **Banco Ficensa**, Blvd Morazán, does Visa advances. All accept TCs, and cash TCs. Visa cash advances and TCs, **Credomatic de Honduras**, Blvd Morazán. Visa advances in lempiras at branches of **Futuro** and **Banco Occidente**. **Mundirama Travel Agency**, Edif Ciicsa, Av Rep de Panamá, Colonia Palmira, T 32-39-09, American Express agents, sells and cashes Amex TCs etc, also travel service. Banks are allowed to trade at the current market rate—see **Currency** in **Information for Visitors**—but there is a street market along the Calle Peatonal off the Parque Central, opp the Post Office and elsewhere.

Institutes Alliance Française, Colonia Lomas del Guijarro, cultural events Fri pm, French films Tues 1930, T 53-11-78; **Centro Cultural Alemán**, 8 Av, Calle La Fuente, German newspapers to read, cultural events, T 37-15-55; **Instituto Hondureño de Cultura Interamericana** (IHCI), Calle Real de Comayagüela has an English library and cultural events, T 37-75-39.

Embassies **El Salvador**, Colonia San Carlos No 205, one block from Blvd Morazán, T 32-13-44, friendly; **Guatemala**, Calle Arturo López Rodenzo 2421, T 32-15-80, Colonia Lomas de Tepeyac, 2 blocks below the Nicaraguan Embassy, Mon-Fri, 0900-1300, take photo, visa given on the spot, US$10; **Nicaragua**, Colonia Lomas del Tepeyac (T 32-64-71/32-90-25), 0800-1200, US$25, visa issued same day, but can take up to 2 days; has to be used within 4 weeks of issue; for Guatemalan and Nicaraguan embassies, take Alameda bus from street behind Congress building (from Parque Merced descend towards river, but don'T cross bridge, instead turn left behind Congress and ask for bus stop on right-hand side), alight before Planificación de Familia and climb street on left beside Planificación: 250m up on right is Guatemalan Embassy; can also be reached with a very steep climb from Av Juan Lindo by the *gasolinera* on corner of Av La Paz below the US Embassy. **Costa Rica**, Residencial El Triángulo, T 32-17-68, bus to Lomas del Guijarro to last stop, then walk up on your left for 300m; **Mexico**, 3 Av, 2 C, No 1277, Col Palmira, beginning of Av de la Paz, T 32-64-71, opens 0900, visa takes 24 hrs. **Panama** (T 31-54-41) and **Colombia**, T 32-97-09 (Embassy 32-51-31), both in Ed Palmira, opp *Honduras Maya*. **Belize Consulate**, in *Hotel Honduras Maya*, Ricardo Vinelli consul, T 32-31-91.

Argentina, Col Rubén Darío 308, T 32-33-76; **Brazil**, Av República de Argentina, Col Palmira, T 32-20-21; **Chile**, Ed Interamericana, piso 6, Blvd Morazán, T 31-37-03; **Ecuador**, Av Juan Lindo 122, Col Palmira, T 32-29-80; **Peru**, Calle Rubén Darío 1902, Col Alameda, T 31-52-61; **Uruguay**, Ed Palmira, piso 4, T 31-53-84; **Venezuela**, 1 Calle 642, Col Palmira, T 32-18-86.

USA, Av La Paz (0800-1700, Mon-Fri, take any bus from N side of Parque Central in direction 'San Felipe", T 32-31-20); **Canada**, Ed Comercial Los Castaños, piso 6, Blvd Morazán, T 31-45-45. **Japan**, Colonia San Carlos, entre C 4 y 5, 2 blocks off Blvd Morazán and Av de la Paz, T 32-68-29, behind Los Castaños Shopping Mall.

UK, Ed Palmira, 3rd floor, opp *Hotel Honduras Maya* (Apartado Postal 290, T 32-54-29); **Germany**, Ed Paysen, 3rd floor, Blvd Morazán, T 32-31-61. **France**, Av Juan Lindo 416, Colonia Palmira, T 32-18-00. **Spain**, Col Matamoros 801, T 32-65-89, nr Av de la Paz and US Embassy; **Israel**, Ed Palmira, 5th floor, T 32-51-76, opp *Hotel Maya*; **Italy**, Av Principal 2602, Col Reforma, T 38-33-91; **Netherlands**, Av Juan Manuel Gálvez, Col Alameda, next to Festival; **Norway**, Av Juan Lindo, Col Las Minitas; **Switzerland**, consul at Oficina de Cosude (Cooperación Suiza al Desarrollo), Ed Galerías, Blvd Morazán, T 32-96-92/32-62-39. **Finnish Consulate**, Av de los Próceres, T 31-13-22; **Swedish Consulate**, Col Miraflores, Av Principal 27-58, T 32-49-35; **Czech Consul**, Santa Lucía nr football field.

To get to Colonia Palmira where most Embassies are, take buses marked 'San Miguel' and 'Lomas' Take 'San Felipe' bus from Rivera y Coy, 3 mins walk from Parque Central for the following consulates: USA, Mexico, Venezuela and El Salvador.

Immigration Dirección General de Migración, at top of Calle Jérez, above *Hotel Ronda*, Tegucigalpa.

Hospitals Private hospitals: Hospital y Clínica Viera, 5 C, 11 y 12 Av, Tegucigalpa, T 37-71-36; Hospital la Policlínica SA 3 Av, 7 y 8 Calles, Comayagüela, T 37-35-03; Centro Médico Hondureño, 3 Av, 3 C, Barrio La Granja, Comayagüela, T 33-60-28. **Dentist** Dr Roberto Ayala, Ed Europa, Av Ramón Ernesto Cruz, above Lloyds Bank, T 31-04-04, speaks English.

Laundry *Lavandería Maya*, 1 block off Blvd Morazán, 0700-1900, Mon-Sat. *Mi Lavandería*, opp *Repostería Calle Real*, 3 Calle, 2 Av, Comayagüela, T 37-65-73, Mon-Sat 0800-1800, Sun and holidays 0800-1700, rec. *Lavandería Super Jet*, Av Guthemberg, about 300m E of *Hotel Granada*, rec.

Churches Episcopal Anglican (Col Florencia, take Suyapa bus) and Union Church, Colonia Lomas del Guijarro, with services in English. Catholic mass in English at the chapel of Instituto San Francisco at 1000 every Sunday.

Peace Corps Edificio Ciicsa, on Av República de Chile, up hill past *Hotel Honduras Maya*. The volunteers are a good source of information.

Post Office Av Miguel de Cervantes y Calle Morelos, 4 blocks from Parque Central. *Lista de Correos* (Poste Restante) mail held for 1 month. Mail boxes in main supermarkets. Books should be packed separately from clothes etc when sending packages.

Telecommunications Hondutel, 5 C and 4 Av, has several direct AT&T lines to USA, no waiting. Phone, fax and telegrams; open 24 hrs.

Tour Operators *Trek Honduras*, Ed Midence Soto 217, downtown, tours of the city, Bay Islands, Copán, San Pedro Sula, Valle de Angeles and Santa Lucía. *Mundirama*, see **Exchange** above. *Explore Honduras Tour Service*, Ed Med'cast, 2nd level, Blvd Morazán, T 39-16-94, F 36-10-03, Copán and Bay Islands; *La Moskitia Ecoaventuras*, PO Box 3577, Tegucigalpa, T/F 37-93-98, for trips to Mosquitia; *Centro Americana de Turismo*, Western side of Blvd Morazán before the bridges, Tegucigalpa, specializing in Honduras; *Gloria Tours* across from N side of Parque Central in Casa Colonial, information centre and tour operator.

Tourist Office Instituto Hondureno de Turismo, Ed Europa, Av Ramón E Cruz y Calle Principal Clínicas Médicas, 3rd floor, above Lloyds Bank, Col San Carlos, T 22-40-02, F 38-21-02, also at Toncontín airport. Open 0730-1530, provides lists of hotels and sells posters, postcards (cheaper than elsewhere) and slides. Information on cultural events around the country from Teatro Manuel Bonilla, better than at regional tourist offices. Also, a tourist booth in the Parque Central. For information on **National Parks**, see p 612. The best maps of the country are produced by the **Instituto Geográfico Nacional** and may be bought from the Institute on production of passport and map request, typed, in triplicate (it is a long process, involving a trip to the Treasury): open weekdays 0730-1530. There are maps of the departments and a 1:50,000 series of which a few sheets are available. A map of the Republic is much more easily available at the shop under the *Hotel Honduras Maya*. Some hotels sell these for double the price, but no paperwork. Various shops sell the tourist map and guide published by Editorial Honduras Turística (1989), which has received mixed reports, US$2.30. A good map is the *Mapa Turístico de Honduras* with a guide, US$2.20 from souvenir shops.

Motorists Motorists leaving Tegucigalpa for San Pedro Sula or Olancho can avoid the congestion of Comayagüela market by driving N down to Barrio Abajo, crossing the river to Barrio El Chile and taking the motorway up the mountainside, to turn right to Olancho, or left to rejoin the northern outlet to San Pedro Sula (at the second intersection, turn right for the old, winding route, go straight on for the new, fast route). A peripheral highway is being built around the city.

Airport Toncontín, 6½ km from the centre, opens at 0530. Check-in at least 2 hrs before departure; snacks, souvenir shop. Buses to airport from Comayagüela, Loarque Rutas No 1 and No 11, on 4a Av between 6 and 7 C, or opp Ciné Palace in downtown Tegucigalpa; into town US$0.05, 20 mins from left-hand side outside the airport; yellow cabs, US$3; smaller colectivo taxis, US$1.

Airlines For national flights: Isleña airlines fly to La Ceiba, Mosquitia and the Bay islands; flights from Tegucigalpa twice a day; T Toncontín airport 33-11-30. **Taca International**, Blvd Morazán, T 31-24-83 or airport 33-57-56; **Lacsa**, Ed Jarros, Blvd Morazán, T 31-15-25; **Iberia**, Ed Palmira, opp *Honduras Maya*, T 31-52-53, also **American** in this building, T 32-13-47 (airport 33-96-80); **KLM**, Ed Ciicsa, Av República de Chile y Av Rep de Panamá, Col Palmira, T 32-64-10; **Lufthansa**, Edificio Leaitz, nr airport.

Buses To **San Pedro Sula** on Northern Highway; 4 hrs (6 companies including Sáenz, Centro Comercial Perisur, Blvd Unión Europea, T 33-30-10, El Rey, Av 6, Calle 9, Comayagüela, comfy, Hedmán Alas, 13-14 C, 11 Av, Comayagüela, T 37-71-43, 7 a day, and Norteños, T 37-07-06), all charge US$2.50, except Hedmán Alas, US$4, excellent; first bus leaves at 0530, then 9 more at intervals to 1730. Saenz and Hedmán Alas both have a luxury service to San Pedro Sula, both US$8.90, Saenz at 0600, 1000, 1400, 1800, Hedmán Alas at 0545, 1130 and 1645, with a/c, film, snacks and refreshments, 3 hrs 15 mins. To **Tela** and **La Ceiba** Traliasa, C 12, Av 9-10, Comayagüela, at 0600 and 0900, US$4.50 (to Tela), US$5 to La Ceiba. Mi Esperanza, Av 6, Calle 23 or 26, Comayagüela, to **Choluteca**, 4 hrs, US$1.90, 0400 onwards. To **Trujillo** direct 9 hrs, US$6.20, 0500 and 1200. To **Santa Rosa de Copán**, Sultana, from Comayagüela, 0345, US$3. To **La Esperanza**, Empresa Joelito, 4 Calle, No 834, Comayagüela, 8 hrs, US$2.60. To **Comayagua**, US$1.20, Transportes Catrachos, Comayagüela, every 45 mins, 1½-2 hrs. For **Danlí** and **El Paraíso**, for the Nicaraguan border at Las Manos, see under those towns in **East of Tegucigalpa**.

For travellers leaving Tegucigalpa, take the Tiloarque bus in Av Máximo Jérez, by Cine Palace, and alight in Comayagüela at Cine Centenario (Av 6a) for nearby Empresa Aurora buses (**for Olancho**) and El Rey buses (for San Pedro Sula or **Olancho**); 3 blocks NW is Cine Lux, near which are Empresas Unidas and Maribel for **Siguatepeque**, US$1.25 (to town centre, US$0.50 cheaper but 1 hr slower than San Pedro Sula buses which drop you on the main road, a US$0.50 taxi ride from Siguatepeque). By the Mamachepa market is the Norteños bus line for San Pedro Sula; also nearby are buses for **Nacaome** and **El Amatillo** frontier with El Salvador. Tiloarque bus continues to Mi Esperanza bus terminal (for Choluteca and Nicaraguan frontier—see below). Take a 'Carrizal' or 'Santa Fe' bus from Tegucigalpa for the hill ascending Belén (9a C) for Hedmán Alas buses to San Pedro Sula and for Comayagua buses (to town centre, cheaper but slower than main line buses to San Pedro Sula which drop passengers on main road, a taxi ride away from the centre).

International Buses Tica Bus to Managua (US$20), San José (US$35), San Salvador (US$15), Guatemala City (US$24) and Panama daily, early morning departures, from 7 Av, 17 C, Comayagüela. Alternatively to **Nicaragua**, take bus to San Marcos de Colón, then taxi or local bus to El Espino on border. To San Marcos, 4 a day from 0730, and direct to frontier at 0400, US$2.50, 5 hrs (0730 is the latest one that will get you into Nicaragua the same day). To **San Salvador**, King Quality first class service with stewardess, refreshments, video, a/c, leaves from *Hotel Alameda*, Blvd Suyapa, 0715, T 39-11-85/86/87; Cruceros del Golfo, Barrio Guacerique, Blvd Comunidad Económica Europea, Comayagüela, T 33-74-15, US$13.70, at 0600 and 1300, 6 hrs travelling, 1 hr at border, connections to Guatemala and Mexico; direct bus to border at El Amatillo, US$2.50, 3 hrs, several daily; alternatively from San Pedro Sula via Nueva Ocotepeque and El Poy. To **Guatemala**, go to San Pedro Sula and take either Impala or Congolón to Nueva Ocotepeque and the frontier at Agua Caliente, or take the route via Copán (see p 646).

Excursions NE of Tegucigalpa is **Suyapa**, a village with a big church which attracts pilgrims to its wooden figure of the Virgin, a tiny image about 8 cm high set into the altar. Take a bus to the University or to Suyapa from 'La Isla", one block NW of the city stadium. Visits to the Agricultural School at Zamorano, and sight-seeing tours of Tegucigalpa and Comayagüela are arranged by several tour operators. It is about a ½ hr drive to **Valle de Angeles**, 6,635 people, 1,310m on a plain below Monte San Juan, of which Cerro El Picacho, 2,270m, is the highest point, and Cerro La Tigra. It is surrounded by pine forests and the climate stays cool the year round. There are old mines, many walks possible in the forests, picnic areas, swimming pool, crowded on Sundays, **D** *Hotel y Restaurante Posada del Angel*, rec, moderate prices; *Restaurant Papagayo* for typical dishes; *Comedor La Abejita*; several others (bank: Banco del Occidente). Hospital de los Adventistas, in the valley, a modern clinic, sells vegetables and handicrafts; there are many handicraft shops in town, good for leather goods, items in wood, hats, etc. A visit to the pavilion of arts and crafts organized by the national Asociación de Artesanías is recommended. 3 km before the town is *Cerámicas Ucles* which has a wide variety of ceramics. Continue to San Juan de Flores (also called Cantarranas) and San Juancito, an old mining town. From here you can climb the La Tigra cloud forest (see next page) and even walk along the top before descending to El Hatillo and then to Tegucigalpa. (Bus to Valle de Angeles hourly on the hour, US$0.40, leaves from Av Rep Dominicana, take a Colonia 21 de Octubre bus from Parque Central to Mercado San Pablo in Barrio El Manchen, 10 mins; to San Juan de Flores 1000, 1230, 1530.)

On the way to Valle de Angeles take a right turn off to visit the quaint old mining village of **Santa Lucía** (4,230 people, alt 1,400-1,600m), perched precariously on a steep mountainside overlooking the wide valley with Tegucigalpa below. The town has a beautiful colonial church with a Christ given by King Philip II of Spain in 1592; there is a festival in the 2nd and 3rd weeks of January. There is a charming legend of the Black Christ which the authorities ordered to be taken down to Tegucigalpa when Santa Lucía lost its former importance as a mining centre. Every step it was carried away from Santa Lucía it became heavier. When impossible to carry it further, they turned round and by the time they were back to Santa Lucía, it was as light as a feather. One small *comedor* next to the plaza/terrace of the municipality, but on Sunday there is more food available on the streets; also Czech restaurant *Miluška* serving Czech and Honduran food, rec. The town is lively with parties on Saturday night. There are souvenir shops in the town, including *Cerámicas Ucles* (as above) just past the lagoon, 2nd street on left, and another ceramics shop at the entrance on your right. There are good walks up the mountain on various trails; fine views of Tegucigalpa from above. Bus to Santa Lucía from Mercado San Pablo, hourly service, US$0.30, past the statue of Simón Bolívar by the Esso station, Av de los Próceres, Tegucigalpa.

Delightful walk down old mule trail across pine-clad ridges to the city (1½ hrs). From Santa Lucía, walk up the mountain for beautiful views of Tegucigalpa and the mountains. A good circuit is to descend E from the mountain towards San Juan del Rancho through lovely landscapes on a good dirt road, then connect with the paved road to El Zamorano. From there continue either to El Zamorano, or return to Tegucigalpa (see below for opposite direction).

There are bracing climbs to the heights of Picacho in the *La Tigra* National Park rain forest. Sunday morning early is a good time but weekdays are quieter. Single hikers should keep to the road, there have been robberies on the short cuts. There are two approach routes: go to El Piligüin, from where you can start hiking, or to *Gloriales Inn*, in direction Corralitos. To **San Juancito** (G *Hospedaje Don Jacinto*; simple meals in the village at the Post Office, very good), above which is the National Park (a stiff, 1-hr uphill walk to El Rosario visitor centre, park offices and 6 trails ranging from 30 mins to 8 hrs, bring insect repellent); a few quetzal birds survive here; do not leave paths when walking as there are precipitous drops; highest point El Picacho, 2,270m and a spectacular 100m waterfall (Cascada de la Gloria) which falls on a vast igneous rock. There is accommodation on a first come, first served basis (no problem on weekdays, can be cold at night), at El Rosario, bring your own food; there are many bunkbeds in separate rooms, water, electricity, minimum contribution of US$1.50, payable at visitors' centre. Meals can be had at the house of Señora Amalia Elvir, before El Rosario. The association which promotes La Tigra is called Amitigra.

Bus leaves from San Pablo market, Tegucigalpa, from 1000, 1½ hrs, on Sat and Sun bus at 0800, US$0.75 for San Juancito; passes turn-off to Santa Lucía and goes through Valle de Angeles. Alternatively, from behind Los Dolores church in Tegucigalpa you can take a bus to Jutiapa at 1300; it passes through beautiful scenery by El Hatillo and other communities. It is 24 km from Tegucigalpa to the Jutiapa entrance to the park. Then hike to the visitors' centre of La Tigra (10 km). A recommended hike is the Sendero La Esperanza, which leads to the road; turn right then take the Sendero Bosque Nublado on your left. The whole circuit takes about 1 hr 20 mins.

From Parque Herrera buses throughout the day go to the village of **Piligüin**; a delightful 40-min walk down the pineclad mountainside leads to El Chimbo (meals at *pulpería* or shop—ask anyone the way), then take bus either to Valle de Angeles or Tegucigalpa.

At Km 17 on Zamorano road (at the summit of the range overlooking Suyapa church) take dirt road left to TV tower. From here a delightful 2-hr walk over forested ridges leads to Santa Lucía. At Km 24 on Zamorano road, climb the highest peak through the Uyuca rain forest, information from Escuela Agrícola Panamericana in the Valle del Zamorano, or from their office in the Edificio Glasso, T 33-27-17, in Tegucigalpa. The school has rooms for visitors. On the NW flank of Uyuca is the picturesque village of Tatumbla.

A 1-hr drive, 24 km from Tegucigalpa, is *Ojojona* (1,400m), another quaint old village (6,670 people); turn right down Southern Highway. The village's pottery is interesting (but selection reported to be poor). There is a small museum. The Galería de Arte, open 0900-1500, is owned by the noted landscape painter Carlos Garay. *Fiesta* 18-20 Jan. There are 2 well preserved colonial churches in Ojojona (notice the fine paintings), plus two more in nearby Santa Ana which is passed on the way from Tegucigalpa. Ojojona is completely unspoiled; F *Posada Joxone*, comfortable; *comedor*. Bus every 15-30 mins from Calle 4, Av 6, Comayagüela, near San Isidro market, US$0.40, 1 hr. From same location, buses go to **Lepaterique** ("place of the jaguar"), another colonial village, over an hour's drive through rugged, forested terrain. Distant view of Pacific on fine days from heights above village.

North of Tegucigalpa

Taking the Olancho road, one comes to **Talanga** with post office and Hondutel near the market on the main road. From the Parque Central an unpaved road S leads to Cantarranas (19 km), San Francisco (18 km), where the road becomes paved, and Ojo de Agua (a further 17 km) on the Tegucigalpa-Danlí road. Just beyond Talanga, an unpaved road turns N to Minas de Oro, 66 km. After 41 km, take the small road to your left; at Km 58 is the turn off to Esquías (8 km away). The last part of the road to Minas de Oro is in poor condition, high clearance recommended.

Cedros, one of Honduras' earliest settlements, dates from Pedro de Alvarado's mining operations of 1536. It is an outstanding colonial mining town, with cobbled streets, perched high on an eminence, amid forests. The festival of El Señor del Buen Fin takes place in the first two weeks of January. A daily bus from Comayagüela to Minas de Oro passes Cedros.

Minas de Oro, on a forested tableland at about 1,060m, is a centre for walking in attractive hill country, 4-hrs bus ride with Transportes Victoria, 10 Av 11 C Barrio Belén, Comayagüela at 1300, returning from Minas de Oro at 0400 daily (US$1.90). It is a picturesque old mining town (pop 6,000). Several *pensiones*, incl **G** *Hotelito Girón* and *Los Pinares* (meals US$1); *Comedor El Rodeo*, or eat at Doña Gloria's house, good, large helpings, US$0.80. There is a fine view from Cerro Grande which overlooks the town, and a more interesting hike up Cerro El Piñón about 3 km N towards Victoria (poor road Minas de Oro to Victoria 18 km, on to Yorito with connections to San Pedro Sula and the North Coast, no buses). To the W of Minas de Oro it is 3 km to Malcotal and a further 4 km to Minas de San Antonio both surrounded by hills, mostly stripped of trees (high clearance vehicle, 4WD in wet, recommended between Minas de Oro and San Antonio). There is a fine 2-hr forested walk over to *Esquías* (good comedor, *Tita's*, accommodation available in private houses, ask at *Tita's*) with a fine church with one of the most fascinating colonial façades in Honduras, extravagant palm motifs, floating angels and, at the apex, a bishop with hands outstretched in blessing. There is a monument in the plaza to a local hero, the American Harold Brosious, 1881-1950, who arrived in Malcotal in 1908 to prospect for gold. He founded a school there (closed since his death in 1950), for the children of local illiterate peasants. As Brosious' fame as a teacher spread, pupils arrived from throughout Honduras and neighbouring countries. Daily bus services Esquías-Tegucigalpa and Esquías-Comayagua.

10 km E of Minas de Oro is San José del Potrero beyond which is *Sulaco*. Above Sulaco is the Montaña de la Flor region where there are settlements of Xicaque Indians. They are also to be found in the lowlands around Victoria where they sell their handicrafts.

THE NORTH COAST

Honduras' Caribbean coast has a mixture of banana-exporting ports, historic towns (in particular Trujillo), beach resorts, and Garifuna villages. There is Pico Bonito national park, other wildlife refuges, and the overland 'Jungle Trail' to Guatemala.

Puerto Cortés, at the mouth of the Ulúa river, is 58 km by road and rail from San Pedro Sula, 333 from Tegucigalpa, and only two days' voyage from New Orleans. About half of Honduran trade passes through it. The climate is hot, tempered by sea breezes; many beautiful palm-fringed beaches nearby; rainfall, 2,921 mm. It has a small oil refinery, and a free zone. Population 65,000. The Central Park contains many fine trees with a huge Indian poplar in the centre providing an extensive canopy. The tree was planted as a sapling in 1941. Festival, in August, including 'Noche Veneciana' on 3rd Saturday.

Hotels B *Playa*, 4 km W at Cienaguita, T 55-11-05, F 55-22-87, hotel complex, directly on beach, local TV, good fish dishes in restaurant; **B** *Costa Azul*, Playa El Faro, T 55-22-60, F 55-22-62, restaurant, disco-bar, billiards, ping-pong, horse riding, volley ball; **B** *International Mr Ggeerr*, 9 Calle, 2 Av E, T 55-04-44, F 55-07-50, hot water, a/c, bar, video, satellite TV, rec; **B** *Hotel-restaurante Costa Mar*, Playas de la Coca Cola, T 55-15-39/55-13-67, new, pleasant. **E** *Tuek-San*, on the central park, large rooms, cold water, good restaurant, clean, period charm but a bit run down. **F** *Colón*, 3 Av O, clean, safe, basic; **F** *Formosa*, with bath, good value, friendly Chinese owners. Other hotels in the **F** range: *Las Vegas*, *La Cascada* and *Puntarenas* in the docklands area.

Restaurants *Café Viena*, on Parque, good, reasonable, but check the prices when you order, excellent coffee; *Chun Wah*, 2 Av, 8 Calle E, good, big *comidas* but noisy and uncomfortable; *A La Porra*, on corner of Parque, good, music; *Reynold's Place*, 1 block towards central park from pier, good, inexpensive; *Café Kalúa*, 2 Av, 6 Calle E, good international menu, a/c, reasonable prices; *Pub El Centro*, 5 Calle, 2 Av near Parque Central, open till 0200, a/c, pleasant atmosphere, bar and light meals, reasonable prices, rec; *El Torito*, 3 Av, 9 Calle E, good steaks; *La Roca*, Av Ferrocarril; *Playa*, in Cienaguita; *Príncipe Maya* on road to Omoa.

Shops There are two souvenir shops in the customs house at the entrance to the National Port Authority, which sell hand-embroidered clothes. The market in the town centre is quite interesting.

Exchange Lloyds Bank, 2a Av y 3a Calle; Banco Atlántida, Banffaa and other local banks. Banco de Comercio cashes TCs. Banco de Occidente, Calle Principal; Bancahsa, 2 Av, 2 Calle. Open 0800-1130, 1330-1600; Sats 0800-1100. El Puesto de Tenis, near plaza, behind the market, changes money and TCs.

Protestant Church Anglican/Episcopal.

Travel Agencies *Bahía Travel/Maya Rent-a-Car*, 3 Av, 3 Calle. Also *Cortés* and *Trans Mundo*.

Rail The train passenger service was suspended in 1993 but a daily ferrobus was introduced on the line to **San Pedro Sula**, 1.067m gauge. Timetables change—check if you wish to travel.

Road To San Pedro Sula and Potrerillos and on to the capital. Bus service hourly to San Pedro Sula, US$0.75, 45 mins, Citul and Impala lines.

Shipping A *goleta* (canoe) leaves Pueblo Nuevo, Puerto Cortés, for Mango Creek, Belize, US$50, 7 hrs, no fixed schedule; can be dangerous in rough weather. Remember to get your exit stamp. The Immigration Office is on 3 Av, 5 C (it is not noted for its efficiency—exit stamps cost US$2.50-US$5, depending on the official). If entering Puerto Cortés by boat, go to Immigration immediately. Passports are sometimes collected at the dock and you must go later to Immigration to get them; US$1 entry fee, make sure that you have the stamp. This is the only official payment; if asked for more, demand a receipt. There are occasional boats to the Bay Islands, but none scheduled, 7 hrs, US$7.50. It is possible to visit the harbour on Sun morning, ask at the gate.

Excursions W to *Tulián*, along the bay, for picnics and very good freshwater bathing. Minibuses departing from the Esso petrol station in the centre (US$0.35 each way) ply along the tropical shoreline past Tulián W to the 'laid-back' village of *Omoa* (or 3-hr walk—15 km from Puerto Cortés), with its 18th century castle, Fortaleza de San Fernando, now being renovated. There is a Visitors' Centre and a small interesting museum (a popular site, admission, US$1.80). At Omoa you can stay at **F** *Hospedaje Champa Julieta*, on beach, friendly, fan, basic; also on the beach is *Don Pedrito's Hospedaje*, clean, quiet and fair prices; on the road to the beach is *Hospedaje Puerto Grande*, but rooms are boxlike and sanitation unspeakable. **G** *Hospedaje El Centro* is in the centre of the village. The alternatives are going back to Puerto Cortés or going back 3 km to Chivana, where there is **B** *Acantilados del Caribe* (*Caribbean Cliff Marine Club*), on the road to Omoa, restaurant, good food, bar, discotheque, supermarket, beach, speed boats, nice atmosphere. Near Omoa are waterfalls (Los Chorros) and good hiking in attractive scenery both along the coast and inland. Restaurants include *El Delfin*, *Pancho*, *Champa Julieta*, *Wahoo*, good seafood and *El Botín del Suizo*, run by the popular Ulrich and his wife, excellent seafood.

There is a paved road through Omoa, continuing to the Guatemalan border at Corinto, but the road stops there and there is no way through by car to Puerto Barrios. The road should be completed 'in a few years".

For a crossing on foot from Guatemala to Honduras, see the description of the 'Jungle Trail' in **Guatemala, Section 2**. A summary of accounts we have received on the trip from Honduras to Guatemala is as follows: Before leaving for the frontier, obtain your exit stamp from the Oficina de Migración in Puerto Cortés (see under Puerto Cortés, **Shipping**). Buses leave Puerto Cortés for Omoa and *Corinto* on the frontier every hour or so (Línea Costeños, Ruta 3 or 4). From Corinto there is a 2-3 hrs walk to the Guatemalan frontier post at El Cinchado on the Río Motagua. There are many birds through the forest, waterways to cross and to avoid. You will have to ask frequently if you are on the right trail or, better, engage a guide as far as the river. Thereafter, negotiate a river crossing. Make your way along the river bank to Finca Chinoq to the light railway and hitch a lift if possible for the 15 km to Entre Ríos. Start early, this is not a route to be caught on overnight or in bad weather.

An alternative route recommended by Harald Bauder from Detroit, is to catch the 0600 bus from Puerto Cortés market to a damaged bridge a few km before Cuyamel. Walk over the bridge and catch another bus to the crossing to Cuyamelito. From here it is a 2 hr walk to Cuyamelito where a dug out takes you through the swamps to the border, US$1.50, no controls. Another boat on the Guatemalan side leaves you at a bus stop by a banana plantation where you have to wait for a bus to Puerto Barrios. The whole trip takes 7 hrs but may take longer if it is raining hard.

A compass could be useful. Beware of snakes, wear high factor sun cream, wear strong boots if possible, especially in the rainy season, take plenty of water (buy some from the villagers if you run out) and keep your arms covered if you can stand it as the mosquitoes are plentiful.

Buses from Puerto Cortés go E to beaches of coconut palms at **Travesía**, Baja Mar, etc, which are beautiful, and unspoilt. Café at Travesía, and at Baja Mar. The best stretch of beach is between the two villages, but the width of sand is narrow even at low tide. Just before Travesía the **E-F** *Hotel/Restaurant Fronteras del Caribe*, has good bathing facilities. The black fishing communities are very friendly. Beware of sunburn, and mosquitoes at dusk.

Tours from Puerto Cortés to La Lima to visit the banana plantations, trips to Copán to visit the Maya ruins and tourist parties at the Ustaris Hacienda can be arranged with travel agents.

Tela, some 50 km to the E, is reached from San Pedro Sula (bus service via El Progreso). Tela used to be an important banana port before the pier was partly destroyed by fire. It is pleasantly laid out, with a sandy beach. Tela Viejo is the original city; Tela Nuevo is the residential area built for the executives of the American banana and farming company which established itself in the city. Old and new Tela are joined by two bridges. There is a pleasant walk along the beach E to Ensenada (a café and not much else) and Triunfo, or W to San Juan (see **Excursions**). Population 67,890. *Fiesta*: San Antonio in June.

Hotels B *Villas Telamar*, T 48-21-96, F 48-29-84, a complex of wooden bungalows, set on a palm-fringed beach, price for rooms, villas from A, restaurant, bar, golf club, swimming pool, mixed reports, check your bill, bicycle and house rentals arranged; **C** *Presidente*, on central park, T 48-28-21, good restaurant and pleasant bar; **C-E** *Playas del Paradise*, in a palm grove about 3 km W of Tela, beside magnificent beach, cabins, insecure, good place for contact with Garifuna, highly rec, to be upgraded into a luxury resort by mid-1995; **C** *Sherwood*, T 48-24-16, on waterfront, a/c, TV, hot water, small stuffy rooms, balconies, price negotiable; **D-E** *Nuevo Puerto Rico*, on the waterfront, lovely situation but exposed in June-Dec wet season, a/c, small rooms, good restaurant especially seafood; **D** *Tela*, 9 Calle, 3-4 Av NE, T 48-21-50, clean, airy, fans, with restaurant; **E** *Atlántico*, 11 Calle, 6 Av NE (with a/c, F without, both on western end of beach), not good value, deteriorating; **E** *Caribe*, next to Shell, with bath, friendly, clean, a/c; **F** *Robert*, 9 Calle, 6 Av NE, basic, G with shared bathroom, will do laundry, noisy, close to bus station; **F** *Marazul*, 11 Calle, 5 Av NE, with fan and bath; **F** *Playa*, 11 Calle, 3-4 Av NE, basic, bedbugs, but pleasant and peaceful; **F** *Preluna*, 9 Calle, 7-8 Av NE, delightful clapboard building, restaurant, quiet; **F** *Bertha's*, 8 Calle, 9 Av NE, near bus terminal, cheap, excellent value; **F** *Minihotel La Posada del Sol*, 4 blocks into town from beach. Out of town, 3 km on highway to La Ceiba, *El Retiro*, set back from the road by a small river, attractive setting. **G** *Boarding House Sara*, 11 Calle, 6 Av behind the restaurant *Tiburón Playa*, clean, basic, with bath, or without, has 3 good cabins priced according to number of occupants, popular with backpackers, friendly; **G** *Liberia*, Av Honduras, basic, friendly, none too clean. Plenty of cheap *hospedajes* near railway station, eg **G** *Valencia*, shared bath, mixed reports (on R-hand side of tracks as you arrive); also **G** *Sinai*, friendly, clean. During Easter week, the town is packed; room rates double and advance booking is essential.

Camping Possible, but not safely, on beach.

Restaurant The best eating in Tela is in the hotel restaurants. *Luces del Norte*, of Doña Mercedes, 11 Calle, 2 Av NE, towards beach from Parque Central, delicious seafood and good typical breakfasts, very popular, also English book exchange; *Slim Jim's Spaghetti Bar*, beside *Hotel Puerto Rico*, nice location, sea views, English book exchange; *César's*, on the beach, serves good food; also *Sherwood's*, attractive, not such good food as *César's*, but popular, slow service allows you to enjoy the view from the terrace. *Los Angeles*, 9 Calle, 2 Av, NE, Chinese, run by Hong Kong owners, large helpings, good. *Tuti* bar, 9 Calle NO near Parque Central, excellent fruit drinks and good lunch specials, closed Sun; *OLA*, a block further down the road serves good, inexpensive meals; *Pizzería El Bambino*, 1/2 block from main street, Tela Vieja; *Los Pinchos* (typical, rec), and *Maribú* (fancy), both on main street, Tela Nueva. *Tiburón Playero*, on eastern beach, good for a drink and watching the sea, food not so good. Across the bridge in Tela West (or Tela Nueva) are many bars and cafeterías—a selection: *Oso Polar* (nice patio), *MacDonalds* (not the international chain), *Don Moncho*.

Exchange Banco Atlántida, Bancahsa, Banadesa. Casa de Cambio La Teleña, 4 Av, 9 Calle NE for $ cash and TCs. Exchange dealers on street outside Post Office.

Laundry *El Centro*, ½ block from main street in Tela Viejo, US$2 wash and dry.

Hondutel and Post Office both on 4 Av NE.

Protestant Church Anglican.

Tourist Offices **Centro de Visitantes**, 9 Calle, 2-3 Av NE, useful information on National Parks and Refuges, operated by members of the Peace Corps. There is an unnamed travel agent on main street for airline arrangements.

Buses Cati or Tupsa lines from San Pedro Sula to **El Progreso** (US$0.45) where you must change to go on to **Tela** (3 hrs in all) and **La Ceiba** (last bus at 1900). Bus from Tela to El Progreso every 30 mins, US$0.95; to La Ceiba, 2½ hrs, US$1. Direct to Tegucigalpa, Traliasa, 1 a day from *Hotel Los Arcos*, US$4.50, same bus to La Ceiba (this service avoids San Pedro Sula).

Excursions Jardín Botánico at *Lancetilla* (established 1926), 5 km inland; open Tues-Fri, 0730-1530; Sat, Sun and holidays 0830-1600, admission US$0.20. The garden was founded as a plant research station by United Fruit Co but has been run by Cohdefor since 1975. It has fruit trees from every continent, the most extensive collection of Asiatic fruit trees in the Western Hemisphere, orchid garden, plantations of mahogany and teak alongside a 1,200-hectare virgin tropical rainforest with over 160 species of birds and wildlife. Guided tours rec. *Hospedaje* (**E** *Turicentro Lancetilla*, T 48-20-07, a/c) and *comedor*, full at weekends, and camping facilities. Either take employees' bus from town centre at 0700, or local bus to the main road turn-off, 4 km from the botanical gardens. Alternatively take a taxi from Tela. Ask for a good guided tour at the Cohdefor office. Over 1,000 varieties of plants and over 200 bird species have been identified. Be warned, there are many mosquitoes.

Local buses and trucks from the corner just E of the market go E to the Black Carib village of *Triunfo*, site of the first Spanish settlement on the mainland, in a beautiful bay, in which a sea battle between Cristóbal de Olid and Francisco de las Casas (2 of Cortés' lieutenants) was fought in 1524. Bus to Triunfo, US$0.40 (about 5 km, if no return bus, walk to main road where buses pass). Cheap houses for rent in Triunfo. A recommended day trip is by bus to Triunfo, lunch on seafood there, then walk back to Tela, if you have sturdy shoes on (the stretch of beach towards the headland is rugged but rewarding). Otherwise, take the easier route inland to Ensenada, then along the beach to Tela. Beyond Triunfo is an interesting coastal area including the cape, *Punta Izopo* and the mouth of the Río Leán. This and the immediate hinterland was declared a National Wildlife Refuge in 1992. For information contact Prolansate, T 48-20-35 or the Tourist Office noted above.

The area W of Tela is being developed for tourism, a new bridge has been built and the road upgraded. New hotels and other facilities will be available soon. The Carib villages of **Tornabé** and **San Juan** (4 km W of *Villas Telamar*), are worth a visit, beautiful food (fish cooked in coconut oil). In Tornabé (taxi US$3) there are 8 bungalows for rent at **A** *The Last Resort*, with breakfast, run by Swiss Werni Eckert, who also organizes tours. A great place to relax, full board available, good restaurant. Further NW, along palm-fringed beaches and blue lagoons, is *Punta Sal*, a lovely place. To get there you need a motor boat or take a bus to Tornabé and hitch a ride 12 km on to Miami and walk the remaining 10 km along the beach. Alternatively, take a motorized *cayuco* from Tela to *Río Tinto* beyond Punta Sal, and explore from there. This area is now a National Park, contact the Asociación de Ecología, Calle de Comercio, Tela, T 48-2035, or Apartado Postal 32, for information. There are plans to extend significantly the national parks in this area and at the same time develop them for tourism. The composite park would be named Parque Nacional de Tornasal and may involve relocating some of the Garifuna villages.

There is a small hotel in Río Tinto, two *comedores* and accommodation is also available in private houses. From Río Tinto it is possible to walk W along the beach to Puerto Cortés; it is about 20 km from Río Tinto to Baja Mar (4-5 hrs' walk), from where buses run to Puerto Cortés. This would be quicker than taking buses Tela-Progreso-San Pedro Sula-Puerto Cortés. *Cayucos* arrive in Tela early am for shopping, returning to Río Tinto between 1000 and 1200, very good value.

El Progreso, on the Río Ulúa, an important but unattractive agricultural and commercial centre (no longer just a banana town) is less than an hour's drive on the paved highway SE of San Pedro Sula en route to Tela. Population about

106,550. Local *fiesta*: La Virgen de Las Mercedes, third week of September. Visit the Santa Isabel handicraft centre, where women are taught wood carving.

Hotel D *Gran Hotel Las Vegas*, 2 Av, 11 Calle N, smart, a/c, good restaurant called *La Copa Dorada*; **D** *Municipal*, 1 Av, 7-8 Calle N, with a/c and bath, clean. **E** *Plaza Victoria*, 2 Av, 5-6 Calle S, opp Migración, pool, good; **F** *Emperador*, 2 Av, 4-5 Calle S, 8 blocks W of bus terminal, attractive, with bath, G without; **F** *Honduras*, price pp, with bath, run down, meals US$1.25; **F** *La Casa Blanca*, 4 Calle, 2 Av N, traditional white and yellow clapboard house with covered balcony, quiet.

Restaurants *Elite*, 1 Av, 4-5 Calle N, mixed reports; *Mr Kike* (pronounced Keekeh) on the ground floor of the *Hotel Municipal* building, a/c, good; *Red Dragon Pub*, 4 Calle, 1-2 Av N, owned by an Englishman, Steve, good source of local information, good bar and restaurant; *Tarro*, on San Pedro Sula road just before bridge, good but not cheap.

Exchange Bancahsa, Banco Atlántida, Banco del Comercio, Banco Sogerín, Banadesa, Banffaa, Banco de Occidente, Ficensa, Bamer.

Travel Agent *Agencia de Viajes El Progreso*, 2 Av 3-4 Calle N, T 66-41-01.

5 km S of El Progreso is the Santuario Señor de Esquipulas in the village of Arena Blanca where there is a festival on 13 January in honour of the Black Christ of Esquipulas. The temple has baroque and modern architecture, with trees and gardens.

The highway is paved 25 km S of El Progreso to Santa Rita; if you continue towards the San Pedro Sula-Tegucigalpa highway, you avoid San Pedro Sula when travelling from the N Coast to the capital. The highway is also paved from Santa Rita to Yoro. (**See also p 649.**) 10 km S of El Progreso on the paved highway to Yoro or Santa Rita, at the village of Las Minas, is El Chorro (1 km off the highway), a charming waterfall and natural swimming pool. A rugged hike can be made into the mountains and on to El Negrito from here.

Parque Nacional Pico Pijol can be reached from Morazán, Yoro, a town 41 km from Progreso (bus from Progreso or Santa Rita). In Morazán are *Hospedaje El Corazón Sagrado*, several restaurants and a disco. The lower slopes of Pico Pijol have been heavily farmed, but the top is primary cloud forest. The trail to the summit (2,282m) starts at Nueva Esperanza village (bus from Morazán, ask for the Parque Central); ask for the correct trail. The first day is tough, the second tougher: the first is all uphill with no shade, the second requires a lot of clearing with a machete. At the summit is a tree with a guest register. Take a compass and a topographical map. Also in the park is the waterfall at Las Piratas; take a bus from Morazán to Los Murillos and then walk to El Ocotillo. Ask for Las Piratas. Further up the river are some beautiful, deep pools.

La Ceiba, 100 km E of Tela, is known as 'Ceibita La Bella". The capital of Atlántida Department, pop 80,160, it stands on the narrow coastal plain between the Caribbean and the rugged Nombre de Dios mountain range, crowned by the spectacular Pico Bonito (2,435m—see below). It was once the country's busiest port but trade has now passed to Puerto Cortés and Puerto Castilla. There is still some activity mainly to serve the Bay Islands; La Ceiba is the usual starting point for visits to the Bay Islands. The climate is hot, but tempered by sea winds. The main square is well worth walking around; it has white statues of various famous Hondurans including Lempira and two ponds with turtles and alligators basking in the sun. There are some white sand beaches and good river bathing (eg Venado, 3 km up the Río Cangrejal) nearby, but the beaches near the dock are not rec (for details see under **Excursions** below). There is a Garífuna community by the beach at the end of Calle 1E. The festival of San Isidro, La Ceiba's patron saint, is on 15 May. The celebrations continue for 2 weeks, ending 28 May, the highlight being the international carnival on the third Saturday in May, when La Ceiba dons party dress and dances all night to the Afro-Caribbean rhythms of the country's Garífuna bands.

Hotels B *Gran Hotel París*, Parque Central, T/F 43-23-91, some rooms cheaper, a/c, faded, unfriendly, cafetería (*Le Petit Café*), swimming pool (open to non-residents for US$2), parking; **B-C** *La Quinta*, exit, carretera La Ceiba-Tela, opp Club de Golf, T 43-02-23, F 43-02-26, restaurant, laundry, cable TV, swimming pool; **C** *Colonial*, Av 14 de Julio, entre 6a y 7a Calle, T 43-19-53, F 43-19-55, the best, a/c, sauna, jacuzzi, cable TV, rooftop bar, restaurant with varied menu, nice atmosphere, tours available; **C** *Partenon Beach* (Greek-owned, family apartments), swimming pool, restaurant, T 43-04-04, F 43-04-34;

LA CEIBA MAC 64

Not to Scale

Caribbean Sea

Av. Valle
Av. Cabañas
Av. Morazán
Av. Colón
Av. La República
Av. San Isidro
Av. Atlántida
Av. 14 de Julio
Av. Ramón Rosa
Av. La Bastilla

N

1 Calle
4 Calle
5 Calle
6 Calle
7 Calle
8 Calle
9 Calle
10 Calle

To Bus Station & West

To East

Boulevard 15 de Septiembre

1. Parque Central and tourist kiosk
2. Cathedral
3. Parque Manuel Bonilla
4. Post Office & Telephones
5. Customs
6. Municipal Library
7. Municipal Market
8. Cinema
9. Quay
10. TACA
11. Isleña, Sosa, & Cambio C.A.
12. Lafitte Travel Agency
13. Fundación Cuero y Salado-Fucsa
14. Hotels Ceiba & Iberia
15. Hotel Príncipe
16. Hotel El Paso & cheap Hotels
17. Hotel Colonial
18. Gran Hotel París
19. Hotel Italia

C *Ceiba*, Av San Isidro, 5 C, T 43-27-37, with fan or a/c and bath, restaurant and bar, uncomfortable, but good breakfast; next door from *Ceiba* is **D** *Iberia*, T 43-04-01, a/c, clean, comfortable, ample hot water, good value; **D** *Italia*, four doors from the *Colonial*, on Av 14 de Julio, T 43-01-50, clean, a/c, good restaurant with reasonable prices, parking in interior courtyard; one block down from the *Iberia* is **E** *El Caribe*, with bath, friendly, clean. **D** *San Carlos*, also near *Iberia*, rooms are clean with fan, colourful cafetería, and its own bakery, where Bay Islanders assemble Tuesday mornings for boat trip to Utila.

There are several hotels on Av 14 de Julio: **E** *Florencia*, clean, bath, rec; **F** *Royal* and *Real* (at corner of 6 C); between Avs 14 de Julio and San Isidro, all on same street as *El Caribe*: **F** *Tropical*, Av Atlántida between 4 and 5 Calle, restaurant, new, clean, good value, rec; **E** *Ligeros*, same street; **E** *Príncipe*, 7 Calle between Av 14 de Julio and Av San Isidro, central, with bath, and a/c, cheaper with fan, cheaper still without, clean, washing facilities on roof; **F** *La Isla*, 4 Calle between 11 and 12 Av, with bath, nice rooms, fans. **G** *Tropical*, central, near market, clean. Many cheap hotels on Av La República, beside railway line leading from central plaza to pier, eg *Arias*, *Los Angeles* (clean), *Ligeros* and *Grenada* on which we have received mixed reports. This area can be unsafe at night. **Camping** at the airport for US$0.20. You may sleep in your vehicle but no tent camping. Hotel at airport entrance **F** *El Cique*, basic but convenient.

Restaurants *Ricardo's*, Av 14 de Julio, very good seafood, garden setting and a/c tables, rec; *Deportivo*, Blvd Las Américas, 9 Calle, Av 14 de Julio, large Chinese menu, seafood, churrasco, rec; *La Carreta*, 4 C, 2 Av E, Barrio Potrerito (near Parque Manuel Bonilla), good value, charcoal-broiled meat, rec; *Toto's*, Av San Isidro, one block S of main square, good pizzería; *Las Dos Fronteras*, Av San Isidro, 12 Calle, good Mexican food; *Cafetería Mi Delicia*, Av San Isidro, 11 Calle, good food at low prices, plentiful breakfasts at US$1.25, family atmosphere but be patient!; *Cric-Cric Burger*, Av 14 de Julio, 3 Calle, facing attractive Parque Bonilla good fast food, rec; *Pizzería Italiana*, 1 block from main square on Av La República, good, pleasant atmosphere, clean; *Pizza Hut*, on main square, very good salad bar, US$2 as much as you can eat; *La Cabana*, opp *Hotel Partenon*, good seafood, pleasant atmosphere, live music on Sat. *Co Bel*, excellent set lunches, rec. *Paty's*, Av 14 de Julio between 6 and 7 Calle, excellent juices, milkshakes, wheatgerm, cereals, donuts, etc, purified water, clean, rec. Opposite is an excellent pastry shop. There are 2 good fish restaurants, *El Pescado* and *Brisas de la Naturaleza* at end of Calle IE. Numerous small, cheap eating places, including *La Combra*, open 24 hrs, good for breakfast before early morning bus. *Helados Castillo*, Plaza del Sol, Av San Isidro and Casino Atlántida, best ice cream in town.

Car Rental Molinari in *Hotel París* on Parque Central, a new office in *Hotel Ceiba*, and **Aries Rent-a-Car** in *Hotel Iberia* (César Quesada, the owner, can assist in all types of travel arrangements, T 43-05-24).

Cinema Av 14 de Julio y 8 Calle.

Discotheques *Leonardo's*; *D'Lido*; *Black and White*, popular; *Santé's* and *Ocean Club*, nicer, reasonable prices.

Exchange Bancahsa, 9 C, Av San Isidro and **Bancomer**, Parque Central, both cash TCs. Open 0830-1130, 1330-1600; Sats 0800-1200. Better rates for US$ cash from *cambistas* in the lounges of the bigger hotels. **Supermercado Los Almendros**, 1 block S and 2 blocks E of *Hotel Los Angeles*, changes TCs, good rates, open Sun.

Medical Hospital: Vincente D'Antoni, Av Morazán, T 43-22-64, private, competent, well equipped. Private room and doctor's fees about US$40 per day for in-patients. **Doctor**: Dr Gerardo Meradiaga, Edif Rodríguez García, Ap No 4, Blvd 15 de Septiembre, general practitioner, speaks English.

Non-Catholic Churches Anglican, Methodist, Mennonite, Evangelist and Jehovah's Witnesses, among others.

Post Office Av Morazán, 13 Calle O and 2 Av, 5 and 6 Calle E. **Hondutel**, for international telephone calls is also at 2 Av, 5 and 6 Calle E.

Travel Agents *Cambio CA* (see under San Pedro Sula **Travel Agents**), T 43-09-33; *EuroHonduras*, Ed Hospital Centro Médico con entrada por Calle de la Playa, T/F 43-09-33, local tours, good value, information, German and some English spoken, highly rec; *Hondutours*, 9 Calle, Av 14 de Julio, T 43-04-57; *Laffitte*, Av San Isidro between 5 and 6 Calles, T 43-01-15, helpful and informative, T 43-01-15/6; *Trans Mundo*, at *Hotel Paris* (also *La Ceiba Ecotours*, T 43-23-91) T 43-28-20; *Sea Safaris*, Ocean Club, 14 de Julio, Calle 1, PO Box 601, T/F 504 432272, offer trips to the Hog Islands, as well as a book exchange, US$0.80 and Travellers' Message Desk; *Atlántida*, Blvd 15 de Septiembre y Av La República, T 43-03-37; *Caribbean Travel Agency*, Av San Isidro, Edif Hermanos Kawas, T 43-13-60/1, F 43-13-60, helpful, British owners. Contact Anne Creighton at *Caribbean Travel* for information on Ríos Honduras (affiliate of Rocky Mountain Outdoor Center, Howard, Colorado, USA), which operates out of La Ceiba Nov-Feb offering white-water rafting; daily trips on the Río Cangrejal, spectacular, reservations one day in advance.

Tourist Office is a kiosk in the Parque Central with good information and maps.

Buses Taxi from centre to bus terminal, which is a little way W of town (follow Boulevard 15 de Septiembre), costs US$0.40 pp, or there are buses from Parque Central. Most buses leave from here. Traliasa bus service to **Tegucigalpa** via Tela US$5, avoiding San Pedro Sula (US$1 to Tela, 2 hrs); also hourly service to **San Pedro Sula**, US$2 (3-4 hrs). To **Trujillo**, 3 hrs *directo*, 4 hrs *local*, every 1½ hrs or so, US$3; to **Olanchito**, US$1, 3 hrs; also regular buses to Sonaguera, Tocoa, Balfate, Isletas, San Esteban and other regional locations.

Airport Golosón, 9.7 kms out of town, with direct jet services to Grand Cayman, Miami, Houston and New Orleans as well as internal destinations: Tegucigalpa, Roatán and San Pedro Sula. For full details of flights to Bay Islands, see next section. To Puerto Lempira, Isleña (Ed Hermanos Kawas, T 43-01-79, airport T 43-23-26), and to other local destinations, including Tegucigalpa, Utila and the other Bay Islands. Sosa flies daily to the Bay Islands from La Ceiba, and to Puerto Lempira and Brus Laguna on Tues, Thur and Sat (T 43-13-99). Taxi to town US$2.15 per passenger or walk 200m to the main road and share for US$0.50 with other passengers, also buses from bus station near *Cric Cric Burger* at end 3 Av, US$0.15.

The *Pico Bonito* national park (674 sq km) is the largest of the 11 new parks designated in 1987. It has deep tropical hardwood forests which shelter, among other things, jaguars and three species of monkey, deep canyons and tumbling streams and waterfalls (including Las Gemelas which fall vertically some 200m). Development of the park by CURLA (Centro Universitario Regional del Litoral Atlántico) continues under the supervision of Cohdefor, the forestry office. CURLA has a *campamento* with accommodation under construction for visiting scientists, but you can camp. The camp is 5 km and 1½ hrs walk on a good path from Armenia Bonito to the W of La Ceiba, frequent buses from SW corner of main square on Av La República (in front of the Texaco petrol station) by the Ruta 1 de Mayo urban bus, 1 hr. Visitors can take the path to the Río Bonito with some spectacular river scenery. Swimming possible in deep rock pools. A route is being created around the foothills and there are a few interesting trails in the forest. Guide recommended: Oscar Zelaya, a forest inspector appointed by CURLA, who can be contacted in Armenia Bonito. Pico Bonito itself (2,433m) has been climbed infrequently, it takes at least nine days. The preferred route is along the Río Bonito, starting 10 km from La Ceiba, and from there up a ridge which climbs all the way to the summit. Expertise in rock climbing is not necessary, but several steep pitches do require a rope for safety; good physical condition is a necessity. Poisonous snakes, including the fer-de-lance (*barba amarilla*) will probably be encountered en route.

For further information on the Park contact Cohdefor at their local office 6 km out of town along the Carretera La Ceiba-Tela, T 43-10-33, where the project director is Sr Allan Herrera. Maps are being prepared by CURLA but not yet available. Take care if you enter the forest: tracks are not yet developed, a compass is advisable.

Excursions Jutiapa, a town with a pleasant colonial church. Contact United Brands office in La Ceiba (on main square) to visit a local pineapple plantation. Two interesting Garífuna villages near La Ceiba are **Corozal** (with beach Playas de Sambrano, and *Hotel Villa Rhina*, with pool and restaurant near the town cliff from the main road) and *Sambo Creek* (also beach and simple hotel-restaurant *Hermanos Avila*). White sand beaches in and near La Ceiba include: Playa Miramar (dirty, not rec), La Barra (better), Perú (across the Río Cangrejal, better still, quiet except weekends, deserted tourist complex, restaurant, access by road to Tocoa, 10 km, then signposted side road 1½ km, or along the beach 6 km from La Ceiba), La Encenada (close to Corozal). The beaches near the fishing villages of Río Esteban and Balfate are very special and are near Cayos Cochinos (Hog Islands) where the snorkelling and diving is spectacular. Near the towns of Esparta and El Porvenir thousands of crabs come out of the sea in July and August and travel long distances inland. Cataraca El Bejuco, 7 km along the old dirt road to Olanchito (11 km from La Ceiba): follow a path signposted to Balneario Los Lobos to the waterfall about 1 km up the river through the jungle. Good swimming from a pebbly beach where the river broadens. 20 km down the old road to Olanchito is Yaruca, reached by bus; good views of Pico Bonita. **Eco-Zona Río María**, 5 km along the Trujillo highway, signposted path up to the foothills of the Cordillera Nombre de Dios, a beautiful walk through the lush countryside of a protected area. Just beyond Río María is Balneario Los Chorros (signposted) a series of small waterfalls through giant boulders into a deep rock pool. Great for swimming. Refreshments nearby. Another bathing place, Agua Azul with restaurant is a short distance away.

37 km W of La Ceiba between the Cuero and Salado rivers, near the coast, is the **Cuero y Salado Wildlife Reserve**, which has a great variety of flora and fauna, with a large population of local and migratory birds. It extends for 13,225 hectares of swamp and forest.

The reserve is managed by the Fundación Cuero y Salado—Refugio de Vida Silvestre, Fucsa, Edif Reyes, 2 piso, No 5, Av San Isidro (behind Carrion's Dept Store), La Ceiba, T/F (504) 43-03-29, Apartado Postal 674, which was formed in 1987. Travel agencies in La Ceiba run tours there, but Fucsa arranges visits and owns the only accommodation in the reserve. Before going to the Reserve, check with Fucsa in La Ceiba. A charge of about US$10 is made to enter the reserve, plus US$5 pp for accommodation, dinner and breakfast. Guides/boatmen charge about US$20. To get there independently, take a bus to La Unión (about every 2 hrs from La Ceiba terminus, US$0.30, 1½ hrs), an interesting journey through pineapple fields. At La Unión, a few houses around the road junction and railhead, take a *burra*, a flat-bed railcar propelled by two men with poles (a great way to see the countryside) to the community on the banks of the Río Salado (9 km, 1 hr, US$8). Here is Fucsa's administration centre, with photos, charts, maps, radio and a 2-room visitors house, sleeping 4 in basic bunks, electricity from 1800-2100. The refuge is becoming increasingly popular, so book lodging in advance. Meals are served by Doña Estela Cáceres (refried beans, egg, tortillas, etc) in her main family room, with pigs, chickens and children wandering in and out.

Nilmo, a knowledgeable biologist who acts as a guide, takes morning and evening boat trips for those staying overnight, either through the canal dug by Standard Fruit, parallel to the beach, between the palms and the mangroves, or down a tributary of the Salado. The morning is the best time for views of the Pico Bonito national park, for birdlife and for howler monkeys. Also in the reserve are spider and capuchin monkeys, iguanas, jaguar, tapirs, crocodiles, manatee, eagles, and vultures. The beach along the edge of the reserve is 28 km long, with a strip of the sea also protected by Fucsa. Fishing is possible, and camping at Salado Barra but you need a permit for both. There are extensive coconut groves along the coast owned by Standard Fruit Co. Although it is possible to go to the Salado and hire a villager and his boat, a qualified guide will show you much more.

To return to La Unión, it is a 2-hr walk along the railway, little shade; then, either wait for a La Ceiba bus, or ask for the short cut through grapefruit groves, 20 mins, which leads to the main La Ceiba-Tela road on which there are many more buses back to town, 20 mins, US$0.40.

A paved road runs from La Ceiba to Trujillo (see below). At Savá, the La Ceiba-Trujillo road meets the new, scenic gravel road which heads NE from Yoro, through Olanchito, continuing to Trujillo.

Olanchito, a prosperous but hot town (called La Ciudad Cívica) is in the Agúan valley in the hills to the SE of La Ceiba. From La Ceiba, motorists can only reach Olanchito via Savá. However, after about 33 km on the La Ceiba-Savá road, a 16 km track (with severe landslides and river crossings) leads to a 5 km dirt road to Olanchito. There is also an old dirt road up the Río Cangrejal to Yaruco, which connects with the Yoro-Olanchito road 8 km W of Olanchito (we have no reports on its condition beyond Yaruca). The town was founded, according to tradition, by a few stragglers who escaped from the destruction of Olancho el Viejo, between Juticalpa and Catacamas, then a wealthy town. They brought with them the crown made of hides which the image of the Virgin still wears in the church of Olanchito. Population: 12,200. Festival: 2nd week of September, Semana Cívica. There is a natural bathing spot, Balneario El Higueral.

Hotels E *Valle Aguán y Chabelito*, 1 block N of Parque Central, price per person with a/c, F with fan, all rooms with cable TV, best in town, with best restaurant; **F** *Colonial*, Calle del Presidio, basic.

Restaurants *Wendy's*, expensive but good; *Comedor Doña Luisa* in front of Radio Station and 3 blocks S of Park; *Bar/restaurant Uchapa*, *La Gavilla*, *Helados Castillo*.

Exchange El Ahorro Hondureño; Sogerín; Atlántida. Importadora Rosita has better exchange rates.

Bus From **La Ceiba**, 2½ hrs, US$1 via Jutiapa and Savá (Cotol 7 times a day; Cotrail); to **Trujillo**, 3 hrs, US$3.75 via Savá and Tocoa (Cotol).

Between Savá and Trujillo is the rapidly-growing town of **Tocoa**, the sixth largest in Honduras, also in the Aguán valley. The Catholic church is the modern design of a Peace Corps Volunteer.

Hotels *La Esperanza*, T 44-33-71; *Victoria*, T 44-30-31, both in Barrio El Centro; *Ho Chi Minh*, T 44-38-04. **Restaurants** *Rigo*, Barrio El Centro, good Italian food and pizzas; *Gran Vía*, on E side of park.

Cinema Ciné Maya.

Exchange Banadesa, Bancahsa, Banco Atlántida, Banco Sogerín.

Trujillo, 90 km to the E again, was a port and former capital. The population is 45,000, including a rapidly expanding North American community. This quiet town with a pleasant atmosphere was founded in 1525 (the oldest in Honduras) by Juan de Medina; Hernán Cortés arrived there after his famous march overland from Yucatán in pursuit of his usurping lieutenant, Olid. It was near here that William Walker (see under Nicaragua) was shot in 1860 (a commemorative stone marks the spot in the rear garden of the hospital, 1 block E of the Parque Central); the old cemetery where he is buried is interesting, giving an idea of where early residents came from. Fortaleza Santa Bárbara, a ruined Spanish fortress overlooking the Bay, is worth a visit. Most of the relics found there have been moved to the museum of Rufino Galán (see below).

Local holiday: San Juan Bautista in June, with participation from surrounding Garífuna (Black Carib) settlements.

Hotels B *Christopher Columbus Beach Resort*, T 44-43-95, F 44-49-71, a/c, cable TV, swimming pool, restaurant, water sports; **B** *Villa Brinkley* (known locally as Miss Peggy's) T 44-44-44, F 44-40-45, on the mountain overlooking the bay, swimming pool, good view, run down, mixed reports (in USA T 412-791-2273, Rd 3, Parker, PA16049); **C-D** *Colonial*, T 44-46-10, with bath, near plaza, restaurant (*El Bucanero*, see below), a/c, safe and clean, recently refurbished; **E** *Trujillo*, up the hill from the market, fan, clean sheets daily, rooms with shower and toilet; good value, rec, but ask for a room away from factory; **F** *Central*, shared bath, nice rooms with balcony, basic, no water during the day; **F** *Emperador*, with bath and fan, small but comfortable rooms, friendly, helpful, rec; **F** *Catracho*, 2 blocks SW of Parque Central, basic, clean, wooden cabins facing a garden. *Colón*, top of the hill above the market, clean, good value. A huge tourist development, by Isleña airline, **B** *Trujillo Bay Resort*, is now complete at airstrip, 25 a/c rooms with cable TV, inc continental breakfast, laundry. In the village of Silin, nr Trujillo, is **B** *Resort y Spa Agua Caliente Silin*, T 44-42-47, F 44-42-48, cabañas with cable TV, pool, thermal waters, private beach, restaurant, massage given by Pech Indian, Lastenia Hernández, very relaxing.

Restaurants *El Bucanero*, on main plaza, a/c, video, good *desayuno típico* for US$1.50; *Galaxia*, one block W of plaza, good seafood at reasonable prices, popular with locals; *Granada*, in the centre, good Garífuna dishes and standard meals, great *sopa de camarones*, rec, breakfasts and snacks, also bar. Excellent, cheap seafood at *Menudo*, a shack on the beach which has live Garífuna music Fri and Sat, entry US$1; another shack, *La China*, is good; in town *Nice and Ease*, sells ice cream and cakes; nearby is *Pantry*, Garifuna cooking and standard menu, cheap pizzas, but extremely slow service, a/c; *Truxillo Paradise*, uphill from *Pantry*, attractive garden setting, bar and restaurant, rec; *Bar-Restaurant Bahía*, American-owned, on the beach by the landing strip; *La Taberna*, just W of Parque Central, open early and late, cheap breakfast and lunch; *pan de coco*, delicious, is baked almost daily. 'Punta' band and dancing at the *Cristales*. *Arca de Alianza* in Barrio Cristales, standard food.

Nightclub *Black and White*, Barrio Cristales, weekends only, Punta music, lively atmosphere.

Shopping *Glenny's Super Tienda*, Mr Glenny speaks English.

Exchange Banco Atlántida on Parque Central.

Travel Agents *Turtle Tours* at *Hotel Village Brinkley* (address above) run trips to Río Plátano, 6 days, 5 nights US$380, also to beaches, jungle hikes, etc. *Cambio CA*, Barrio Conventillo, T 44-40-45 (see under San Pedro Sula **Travel Agents**).

Transport The town can be reached by bus from San Pedro Sula, Tela and La Ceiba by a paved road through Savá, Tocoa and Corocito. From La Ceiba it is 3 hrs by direct bus, 4 hrs by *local*. 3 direct buses in early am from Trujillo, buses every 1½ hrs, US$3. Bus from **Tegucigalpa** (Comayagüela) with Cotraipbal, 7 Av between 11 and 12C, 0500 and 1200, US$6.20, 9 hrs return 0400 and 0900. Public transport also to San Esteban and Juticalpa (from plaza at 0400 arriving 1130, US$5.20—**see p 661**). There are no scheduled flights to Trujillo though small aircraft can use the local airstrip and aircraft can be chartered. Flights to La Ceiba with Isleña may soon be introduced (1994). Cargo boats leave irregularly for ports in Mosquitia, the Bay Islands and Honduran ports to the W. Enquire at the jetty.

Good beaches are on the peninsula and around the Bay. Take a bus from near the Parque Central towards Puerto Castilla and ask the driver to let you off at the path about 1 km beyond the bridge over the lagoon. The other beaches around Puerto Castilla are separated by mangroves, are littered and have sandflies. Other sandy beaches can be reached by taking any bus from the Parque Central, or walking, 1½ km, to the side road leading to the landing strip and *Bar-Restaurant Bahía*; the white sand stretches for many km northwards.

20 mins walk from Trujillo plaza (follow on road beyond *Hotel Trujillo*) is the **Museo y Piscina Rufino Galán Cáceres** which has a swimming pool filled from the Río Cristales with changing rooms and picnic facilities. Close-by, the wreckage of a US C-80 aircraft which crashed in 1985 forms part of Sr Galán's museum; inside the museum is more information and memorabilia about the accident. The rest of the collection is a mass of curios, but with some very interesting objects as well as many archaeological finds. Entry US$0.50, including swim.

There are interesting villages of Black Caribs (Garifuna) W of Trujillo. **Santa Fe**, 10 km W of Trujillo (US$0.50 by bus), is a friendly place with several good Garifuna restaurants eg *Comedor Caballero* and *Las Brisas de Santa Fe*, on the endless white sandy beach. Further on are Guadalupe and San Antonio. It is recommended to take a bus to Santa Fe and then walk back to Trujillo along the beach (10 km), taking plenty of water and sun block. This stretch of beach is outstanding. At **Puerto Castilla** there is a meat-packing station and active shrimping centre. Puerto Castilla is one of the main ports of the Honduran Caribbean coast, mainly containerized traffic with exports including bananas, grapefruit and palm oil. There is a naval base and helicopter station. Near the village, a large crucifix marks the spot where Columbus reputedly conducted the first mass on American soil in 1502. One reasonable restaurant, *Los Amigos*.

Guaymoreto lagoon, has a bird island (Isla de Pájaros) and monkeys. To visit, either arrange a trip with an agency, or take a bus from Trujillo towards Puerto Castilla, alight just after the bridge which crosses the lagoon, then walk away from the lagoon for about 200m to a dirt track on the left. Follow this and cross a low bridge and on the left is the house of a man who rents dugout canoes for US$1. The Isla de los Pájaros is about 3 km up the lagoon, a bit too far for a dugout. There are no roads, paths or facilities in the area which will soon be declared a protected Wildlife Refuge.

To the S, and E to the Río Segovia, lies a huge territory of jungled swamps and mountains lived in by a few Indians and timber men (see p 662).

THE BAY ISLANDS

Warm Caribbean waters with excellent diving, white sand beaches, tropical sunsets are some of the attractions. The culture is very un-Latin American: English is widely spoken and there are still Black Carib descendants of those deported from St Vincent in 1797.

The **Hog Islands** (**Cayos Cochinos**), with lovely primeval hardwood forests, are 17 km NE of La Ceiba (two small islands and thirteen palm-fringed cays): privately owned with reserved accommodation at Cayos del Sol. On the Isla de Cochino Grande is a dive resort; very beautiful. The owner of the largest island, Bobby Griffith, permits camping, especially if you can give him a news magazine or two. Also see under *Sea Safaris* (Travel Agents in La Ceiba). Take a bus from the La Ceiba bus terminal on the western outskirts to Nueva Armenia (US$2), then try to hitch on a dugout, or charter one (about US$10). See also **Diving** under Utila.

The **Bay Islands** (Islas de la Bahía) lie in an arc which curves NE away from a point 32 km N of La Ceiba. The three main islands are Utila, Roatán, and Guanaja. At the eastern end of Roatán are three small ones: Morat, Santa Elena, and Barbareta; there are other islets and 52 cays. Their total population is 30,000. The main industry is fishing, mostly shellfish, with fleets based at French Harbour. Boat-building is a dying industry. Apart from fish, trade is mostly in coconuts, bananas and plantains. There are English-speaking blacks who constitute the majority of the population, particularly on Roatán. Utila has a population which is about half black and half white, the latter of British stock descended mainly from settlers from Grand Cayman who arrived in 1830. Latin Hondurans have been moving to the islands from the mainland in recent years. Columbus anchored here in 1502, on his fourth voyage. In the 18th century the islands were bases for English, French and Dutch buccaneers. They were in British hands for over a century but were finally ceded to Honduras in 1859. The government schools teach in Spanish, and the population is bi-lingual. The islands are very beautiful, but beware of the strong sun (the locals bathe in T-shirts) and sand gnats and other insects, especially away from the resorts.

The underwater environment is rich and extensive; reefs surround the islands, often within swimming distance of the shore. Caves and caverns are a common feature, with a wide variety of sponges and the best collection of pillar coral in the Caribbean. Several parts have been proposed as marine reserves by the Asociación Hondureña de Ecología: the Santuario Marino de Utila, Parque Nacional Marino Barbareta and Santuario Marino West End (both on Roatán) and Parque Nacional Marino Guanaja. The Bay Islands have their own conservation

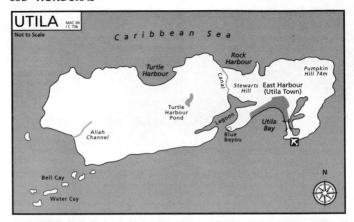

association (see under Roatán, below). We strongly recommend snorkellers and divers not to touch or stand on the coral reefs; any contact, even the turbulence from a fin, will kill the delicate organisms. The islands are a major diving centre.

Utila (41 sq km, population 1,515) is only 32 km from La Ceiba and is low lying, with only two hills, Pumpkin, and the smaller Stewarts with an aerial. The latter is nearer the main town, which is known locally as East Harbour. There are caves to which you can hike, one of them being reputed locally to have been a hideout for Henry Morgan. There is some evidence of Paya Indian culture. You can hike to Pumpkin Hill (45 mins beyond *Bucket of Blood Bar*, on E side of the island) where there are some fresh water caves and a beach nearby (watch out for sharp coral), with a bar open in season. It can be very muddy after rain. It is also possible to walk on a forested, jungle-like road to the northern part of the island (40 mins); nice views and beach but it is rocky so wear sandals. Utila is the cheapest and least developed of the islands to visit; there are no big resorts, but rather simpler dwellings where you can rent rooms. Sunbathing and swimming are not particularly good, but there is a swimming hole near the airport. At the left-hand end of the airstrip (from the town) is one of the best places for coral and quantity of fish. Snorkelling and diving equipment for hire. Snorkelling gear costs US$3 per day. Going rate for 2 dives is US$30, shop around for the best price (see below).

A 20-min motorboat ride from East Harbour are the Cays, a chain of small islands populated by fisherfolk off the SW coast of Utila. On the main Cay, a few families live; they are very friendly to foreigners, but there is nowhere to put a tent. 3 islands further out is Water Cay, one of the few places where you can camp, sling a hammock or, in emergency, sleep in, or under, the house of the caretaker; take food and fresh water. The caretaker collects a US$1 pp fee for landing. There are no facilities, but children sell cheap *pasteles de carne*. It is a coconut island with 'white holes' (sandy areas with wonderful hot bathing in the afternoon) and some of the most beautiful underwater reefs in the world. The best snorkelling is off the S shore, a short walk from the beach, shallow water all around. To hire a *dory* (big motorized canoe) costs US$30 for up to eight; many boatmen go and will collect you in the evening, rec.

Hotels on Utila The best hotel on the island is **A** *Utila Lodge*, T 45-31-43, usually booked through US agent T (904) 588-4131, an all-wooden building with decks and balconies, harbour view, a/c, 8 rooms, clean and modern, run by Americans Shirley and Tom, meals only when they have guests; **D** *Harbour View*, a few 100m past the bank on the left, clean, fans, bathrooms clean, no hot water, restaurant downstairs, owner takes guests to Water Cay for diving or snorkelling; **E** *Trudy's*, T 45-31-95, 5 mins from airport, with and without bath, clean, comfortable, good breakfast and evening meals (but very expensive), rec; **F** *Laguna del Mar*, opposite *Trudy's*, T 45-31-03, terrace, clean, fans, mosquito nets, diving offered with Underwater Vision (see below); **E** *Spencer*, Main St, T 45-31-62. *Palm Villa*, cabins at US$15 for 4, cooking facilities, good value, run by Willis Bodden; *Bay View*, 100m from *Utila Lodge*, with bath, spotlessly clean, private pier, great location with sea views, family run, highly rec; **F** *Blue Bayou*, 25 mins out of town, 1 hr walk from airfield, opposite end from airport, a beautiful spot for diving off the reef, may be closed out of season, snacks and drinks available, restaurant only in high season, hammocks on the porch in the day, breeze usually keeps the mosquitoes away, bike rental US$2/day (take torch for night-time riding), rents canoes; **F** *Coopers Inn*, very clean and friendly, rec; **F** *Cross Creek* (see also **Diving** below), clean rooms, basic bathrooms, house rental US$40 for 2, US$45 for 3 and US$50 for 4; **F** *Monkey Tail Inn*, noisy, wooden building, you may share your room with bats, cooking facilities, water all the time (beyond the *Bucket of Blood Bar*); **E** *Sea Side*, on Sand Beach Road, new, pleasant, clean, private pier and garden, helpful owner. Cheap and basic rooms at **F** *Blueberry Hill* (run by Norma and Will, very friendly, clothes washing facilities), opposite *Bucket of Blood*, and *Dolores*; plenty of other houses and rooms for rent.

Restaurants *Mis Delicias*, small, go early, good fish, good breakfasts, but slow service and not that clean; *Tropical Sunset and Bar*, pleasant atmosphere, good food and cheap drinks; *Orma's*, simple but good food in nice little thatched bar overlooking the harbour; *Mermaid's Corner Souvenir Shoppe* has good pastries when open; *Sea Side Inn* (see above under **Hotels**) offers good food; *Comedor El Teleño*, good food, good breakfasts, meeting point; *Nolan's Place*, run by Dorothy, popular with locals, good food; *Selly's*, up the hill beyond *Bucket of Blood*, the best food, popular with travellers, cable TV; *Underground*, on Main Street, Caribbean style food, pleasant, good value. *Utila* for ice cream, lemonade and food. Good yogurt at Henderson's store. *Green Ribbon* store has cakes and sandwiches to order.

Bars *Bucket of Blood*, owned by Mr Woods, a mine of information on the history of Utila and the Cays; on same side of road is *Tompsons*, good breakfasts; *The Lost Soles* (sic), *07* and *Casino* are lively (Sat night), as is *Captain Roy's*, next to the airport. *Bahía del Mar*, bar with pier, swimming. *Sea Breaker*, on waterfront behind *Orma's*.

Electricity goes off between 2400 and 0600.

On dry days and when there is no breeze sandflies are most active. Coconut oil or Avon 'Skin-so-Soft' helps to ward them off; they get stuck in your skin. Take insect repellent.

Arts and Crafts Günther Kordovsky is a painter and sculptor with a gallery at his house (up the hill, near *Selly's* restaurant), good map of Utila, paintings, cards, wood carving; another sculptor is Bill Green, ask for him at *Casino Bar*.

Services There is a bank for changing dollars (Bancahsa) and you can get cash against a Visa card, but not Mastercard. Dollars are accepted on the island. There is a post office and a Hondutel office near *Utila Lodge*. There is a paved road through the town and a 60m concrete pier.

Churches 7th Day Adventist, Baptist, Church of God, Mormon, Methodist (with a charming wooden church built in 1870).

Information Shelby McNab, who runs Robinson Crusoe Tours, is president of the local branch of the Bay Islands Conservation Association, about which he is most happy to talk (Troy Bodden, see below, is vice-president). He also takes visitors on half-day tours around the island (US$10 pp) explaining his theory that Daniel Defoe based his famous book on Robinson Crusoe on Utila (not Alexander Selkirk off Chile), fascinating. He also runs Gables Health Club, keep-fit, weight machines, steam bath and massages.

Diving All 8 schools offer similar prices and include accommodation. If planning to do a diving course, take a passport-sized photograph with you for the PADI certificate. **NB** It may be difficult to pay by credit card. *Bay Islands Divers* give instruction to PADI certification level; prices start at US$145 for individually structured courses. *Cross Creek*, run by Ronald Janssen, T 45-31-34, F 45-32-34, scuba trips for beginners and certified divers, US$30 for 2 dives in one day, free accommodation for that day; 4-day beginner course (PADI, open water), 4 nights' accommodation, US$175; advanced open water, 2 days, 5 dives US$150; rescue and dive master, 3 weeks, US$750; snorkel equipment (mask, snorkel and fins) US$2.50, 2-3 instructors, new equipment. Gunter Kordovsky teaches a range of PADI courses, including instructor training, with 26 years' diving experience on Utila, at his dive school, T 45-31-13/31-30, based at Sea Side Inn, also video and photographic services (and arts and crafts, see above). *Utila Watersports*, excellent equipment, popular with travellers (but pay in dollars), run by Troy Bodden, who also owns Bell Cay, a tiny immaculately-kept cay next to Water Cay (2 houses, fully self-contained, usually booked by groups, up to 14 people, US$50 per day pp, bookings through Caribbean Travel Agency in La Ceiba, T 43-13-60/1), Troy also hires out snorkel equipment and takes boat trips and one of his scuba instructors, Chris Watto, has been highly rec, he has an underwater video camera and you can have your dives transferred onto VHS to take home, US$35 for each video. Also recommended is Chris Phillips from the Utila Dive Centre, who is patient with beginners and speaks English, PADI certificates, dive trips. Linda Geraci of **Underwater Vision** is rec, English speaking, good equipment and good ratio of students/instructors. **Sea-Eye** (Danish run) also rec, Peder is a thorough instructor and equipment is good.

Transport Isleña and Sosa fly from **La Ceiba** for US$9 one way. Flights leave at 0600, 1500 and 1600, 15 mins. Fare to Tegucigalpa US$25. Check all flight times in advance, flight information and ticket sales at *Salon 07*. Sosa in La Ceiba T 43-13-99, Isleña T 43-01-97 (downtown) 43-23-26 (airport). Always reserve flights and make onward reservations in advance. There are no flights to the other islands. Local transport between airport and hotels.

Boats *MV Starfish* goes from Utila to the new harbour in **La Ceiba** Mon 0400 returning from La Ceiba Tues 1200, US$4.50 each way (information from *Green Ribbon* store). There are irregular boats to **Puerto Cortés**, times posted in main street, 7 hrs, US$7.50, ask at public dock. Fishing boats from La Ceiba charge US$10 to Utila.

Boats from Utila to Roatán can be chartered for about US$70; with enough passengers this can work out cheaper than flying back to La Ceiba and out to Roatán. Occasional freight boats, eg *Utila Tom*, take passengers from Utila to Roatán. It's a 3-hr journey between the two islands and you and your possessions are liable to get soaked.

It is a few hours' sail to **Roatán**, the largest of the islands (127 sq km, population 10,245). It has a paved road running from West End to just beyond French Harbour, continuing unpaved to Oak Ridge, Punta Gorda and Wilkes Point; there are other, unmade roads. Renting a car or scooter gives access to many places that public transport does not reach. The capital of the department, **Coxen Hole**, or Roatán City is on the south-western shore. Besides being the seat of the local government, it has immigration, customs and the law courts. Port Royal, towards the eastern end of the island, and famous in the annals of buccaneering, is now just a community of private houses with no public facilities (see below). Archaeologists have been busy on the islands but their findings are very confusing.

From Coxen Hole to Sandy Bay, with the Sandy Bay Marine Reserve and the Carambola Botanical Gardens, is a 2-hr walk, or a US$1 bus ride, hourly 0600-1700 (taxi drivers may try to charge US$12; it should only be US$2 from the airport). The Marine Reserve, which protects coral reef ecosystems, is managed by Bay Islands Conservation Association (see **Information** below). For details on Carambola contact Bill or Irma Brady, T 45-11-17 (open 0700-1700 daily, guided tours or nature trails). The gardens were begun in 1985 and contain many flowering plants, ferns and varieties of trees; a 20-min walk from the garden goes to the top of Monte Carambola past the Iguana Wall, a breeding ground for iguanas and parrots. West End, a further 5 mins by road beyond Sandy Bay, is a quiet community near the W tip of the island. There are several good

CROSS CREEK DIVERS & UTILA DIVE CENTRE
LEARN TO DIVE

- P.A.D.I. certifications + dive trips
- Dive manuals in 8 languages
- Fully outfitted dive shop (Authorised DACOR scuba Equipment dealer).

- Fully licensed instructors (OWSI 54664 & OWSI 39223)
- Full line of Nikon underwater cameras/lenses/video and own foto development lab.

BEST PRICES OF THE WESTERN HEMISPHERE

- Course prices from $125 (4 days) ■ Free rooms available if you take the course

Ask for: Ronald Janssen or Chris Phillips

Telephone: (504) 453134, Fax: (504) 453234 Islands de Bahia, Utila, Honduras, Central America

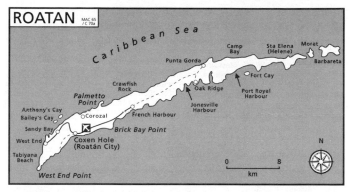

restaurants as well as hotels with bungalows and rooms to rent. You can take a small motor boat from *Foster and Vivian's Restaurant* for a 10-min ride to West Bay (US$1). West Bay is a beautiful, clean, unspoilt beach with excellent snorkelling at the far end; there are a couple of jetties where you can escape the sandflies which lurk in the powdery white sand (coconut oil, or Avon 'Skin-so-Soft' oil is good protection against sandflies, sold in Coxen Hole supermarket). Take your own food and drinks, and insect repellent, because there are no facilities there. It is a stiff walk from Coxen Hole over the hills (3 hrs) to West End, or take the bus on the paved road for US$1, 20 mins, they run until 1700.

There are many minibuses which wait on Calle Principal in Coxen Hole, going to points E and W; they usually leave on the hour or half-hour. Mi Esperanza has a service every 30 mins to French Harbour and Oak Ridge (US$1.50). French Harbour, with its shrimping and lobster fleet, is the main fishing port of Roatán. There are two seafood packing plants: Mariscos Agua Azul and Mariscos Hybour. The road passes *Coleman's (Midway) Bakery*, where you can buy freshly-baked products.

The main road goes across the mountain ridge to Wilkes Point with side roads to Jonesville, Punta Gorda and Oak Ridge. Taking a bus on this route is the best way to see the island's hilly interior, with beautiful views from coast to coast. **Jonesville** is known for its mangrove canal, which is best reached by hiring a taxi boat in Oak Ridge. In **Punta Gorda** on the North Coast, the oldest established community on Roatán, Black Caribs retain their own language, music, dance, food, crafts and religion. Carib Week, 8-12 April, is a good time to experience their customs. Bus from Coxen's Hole costs US$1. There are also boat tours which include Punta Gorda (information from Kiwi woman at 2nd hand bookstore in West End). **Oak Ridge**, situated on a cay (US$0.40 crossing in a dory from the bus stop), is built around a deep inlet. It is a charming little fishing port, with rows of dwellings on stilts built on the water's edge (bus Coxen Hole-Oak Ridge, 1 hr, US$1.60). You can hire a taxi boat to show you round. As well as its hotels, there is a grocery store and a couple of good restaurants.

Hire a boat for an hour's sail up the coast to **Port Royal**; old British gun emplacements on Fort Cay, 1 km off-shore. No bus from Port Royal to Oak Ridge, and it's a tough 3-hr walk. The Port Royal Park and Wildlife Refuge is the largest highland reserve on Roatán, protecting pines and endemic species of flora and fauna. At present it lacks facilities or management and is relatively inaccessible (contact Bay Islands Conservation Association for information). Note the Black Carib village of Punta Gorda on the North Coast (probably the first non-Indian settlement on the islands). Beaches excellent; the best is said to be Camp Bay on the North Coast at the eastern end (road sometimes too muddy to get there by land). Roatán is expensive, twice as dear as the mainland.

Hotels and Restaurants on Roatán At West End, **A** *Lost Paradise*, T 45-13-06, F 45-13-88, full board only, delicious meals (open to non-residents, book in advance), snorkelling equipment, transport back to airport, dollars exchange; **A** *Sunrise Resort*, T 45-12-65, dive shop, offers packages with diving, full board etc, laundry, good value; **B** *Coconut Tree Hotel and Restaurant* (owner Vince), private cabins (3 double beds), hot water, fan, fridge, clean, friendly; **B** *Seagrape Plantation*, T 45-14-28, cabins, family atmosphere, friendly; **C** *Keifitos Plantation Resort*, bungalows on private beach, beautiful setting, friendly owners, rec; **C** *Half Moon Bay Cabins*, T 45-10-80/13-82, F 45-12-13, bungalows and cabins with bath, restaurant with excellent seafood (same owner as *Coral* at Coxen Hole); **C** *Roberts-Hill*, T 45-11-76, with bath and fan, more basic rooms with shared bath E, meals, snorkelling, etc, friendly, good value, mosquitoes; **C** *Seaside Cottages*, individual cabins, pleasant owner Rudy, coffee shop with excellent cookies and breakfasts, T 45-12-05; **F** *Jimmy's Lodge*, hammocks, very friendly, cheap meals, snorkelling gear and horseriding available, it is very cheap to string a hammock here, but very exposed and tin roof not waterproof, you'll be bitten by sandflies, hosepipe as a shower; **F** *Mario's Rooms*, friendly, on beach, water; **F** *Stass' Place*, cheap rooms. *Sam's*, at far end, near *Jimmy's*, very cheap, but hot rooms, no water, popular with travellers, cheap food. Other rooms for rent, about US$5, some rather dingy.

Places to eat at West End: *Foster and Vivian's Restaurant* is on the beach, good atmosphere and seafood, not cheap, built over the water, no sandflies, owned by Foster Diaz, his wife Vivian is the cook (they are Texans and jointly own a duplex on the beach, enquire at the restaurant, or to the other partner Robert Beels in Mount Dora, Florida, T 904-383-7424). *Sea View Restaurant*, go early since it's small and often runs out of food, large portions, home cooking, band dances on Fridays; *Luna's Bay Café*, good for breakfast, downstairs at *Lucy's Minimart* for basic foodstuffs; *Bite on the Beach*, open Tues-Sun, daily menu, 5 mins from beach, excellent fresh seafood at reasonable prices, run by Dian and Gene, formerly backpackers. *Rudy's*, has good pancakes and cookies for breakfast; next door is *Bamboo Hut*, breakfasts and snacks, film shows in evenings, US$1. Try the coconut bread which can be bought from the local women. There is a good gift shop, *Joanna's* next to *Roberts-Hill*, with some good quality products. At Gibson Bight, on the road to West End, are *Alexander's Cabins*, T 45-15-01.

At **Sandy Bay**: **A+** *Anthony's Key Resort*, T 45-10-03/13-27, F 45-13-27 (US$75 full board), glorious situation, accommodation in small wooden cabins, launch and diving facilities (US$20, US$40 non-residents, the owner, Julio Galindo, is very serious about helping the environment and local community, the resort's own cay, Bailey's, has a small wildlife reserve (parrots, cockatoo, toucan, monkeys, agoutis, turtles), it has a museum of some archaeological and colonial history, natural history laboratory, A-V lecture hall (entry for non-guests US$2); it also has a dolphin enclosure in a natural pool, guests can swim with the dolphins for US$45, non-guests US$50; **A** pp *Oceanside Inn*, T (504) 45-15-52, F 45-15-32, full board, clean, comfortable, friendly owners Joseph and Jenny, nice deck with view of bay, superb restaurant, diving packages offered, highly rec. *Quinn's*, reasonable.

At **French Harbour**: **A** *Coco View Resort*, T 45-10-11; **B** *French Harbour Yacht Club*, T 45-14-78, F 45-14-59, cable TV in every room, reasonable rates, good food (especially lunch), friendly; **C-A** *Buccaneer*, T 45-10-32, F 45-12-89 (Tegucigalpa T 36-90-03, F 36-98-00, San Pedro Sula T 52-62-42, F 52-62-39), 3-day, 2-night packages, US$195 pp, good food, rec; **A-L** *Fantasy Island Beach Resort*, T 45-11-28/45-12-22, F 45-12-68, 80 a/c rooms, on a 15-acre cay, 3-day, 2-night packages US$390, pool, diving and many other watersports, mixed reports; **E-D** *Coral Reef*; **E** *Britos*, with fan, very good value; **E** *Hotelito*, sometimes no water, in the village; **E** *Isabel*, comfortable, restaurant, free transport to airport; **E** *Dixon's Plaza*, past the *Buccaneer*, good; *Romeo's Restaurant*, T 45-15-18, good for seafood. *Celebrations*, is a good a/c nightclub, entrance US$1.50, drinks expensive, with restaurant and marina, open evenings, T 45-15-44.

At **Brick Bay**: **A** *Caribbean Sailing Club*, modern hotel, with breakfast; **C** *Romeo's Resort Dive and Yacht Club*, T 45-11-27, F 45-15-94, dedicated dive resort, good.

At **Oak Ridge**: **L** *Reef House Resort*, T 45-21-42/22-97, F 45-21-42, in USA (512) 681-2888, 1-800- 328-8897, F (512) 341-7942, inc meals, various packages, including diving, offered, wooden cabins with seaview balconies, seaside bar, private natural pool, good snorkelling from the shore, manager Carlos Acosta. **E** *San José Hotel*, with bath (2 rooms), cheaper without (3 rooms), clean, pleasant, good value, good food, English-speaking owner, Louise Solórzano. There is a *pizzería* and, next door, a supermarket.

At **Port Royal**: **L** *Roatán Lodge*, accommodation in cabins, hosts Brian and Lisa Blancher provide scuba diving and snorkelling expeditions; **A** *Camp Bay Resort*; *Miss Merlee's Guest House*.

At **Coxen Hole: C** *Airport View* (D without bath or a/c), T 45-10-74; *Cay View*, Calle Principal, T 45-12-02, F 45-11-79, a/c, phone, laundry, restaurant, bar, fishing, diving; **E** *Coral*, T 45-10-80, owner Dr Jackeline Bush, shared bath, clean, comfortable, Peace Corps favourite; **E** *El Paso*, T 45-10-59, next door, shared bath, restaurant (not cheap). Many of the cheaper hotels have water shortages.

Comedor Ray Monty, very cheap, set meal US$1.50 but avoid the meat, fish good; *Burger Hut*, opp *Hotel Coral*, clean, good, chicken and fish, not expensive; *Hungry Diver*, pizzas and expensive seafood. *El Punto*, bar with one basic dish, very cheap. *HB Warren*, large well-stocked supermarket with cafetería, mainly lunch and snacks, open 0700-1800. *Hibiscus Sweet Shop*, homemade fruit pies, cakes and biscuits. There is also good food at *DJ's Bar & Grill*, on Osgood Cay a few minutes by free water taxi from wharf.

There are other, cheaper, places to stay, for example, Miss Effie's (near **Anthony's Key Resort**) and houses to let (at West End, Half Moon Bay, or Punta Gorda).

At Coxen Hole are a post office, tourist information, *VIPs* duty free shop, groceries and several souvenir shops.

Discotheques 2 informal ones which come alive about midnight, *Paraguas* and *Harbour View*. They play mostly reggae, salsa, *punta* and some rock.

Banks Banco Atlántida and Bancahsa in Coxen Hole and French Harbour; also **Banco Sogerín** and **Banffaa**. Bancahsa in Oak Ridge, T 45-22-10, Mastercard for cash advances. No banks in West End, but TCs will be changed at *Bamboo Hut*.

Car Rental National, *Hotel Fantasy Island*, T 45-11-28; **Amigo** at the airport. **Tokio Motorbike Rental**, attached to *Chino's* at West End, US$21 pp per day.

Information Bay Islands Conservation Association, Edif Cooper, Calle Principal, Coxen Hole, T 45-14-24, Charles George; Farley Smith, an American volunteer, is extremely helpful. There is a tourist information office at the airport, T 45-15-59. Excellent map of the island at about 1:50,000 supplied by Antonio E Rosales, T 45-15-59. *Coconut Telegraph* is the local magazine, every 2 months, plenty of information and articles.

Travel Agents *Bay Islands Tour and Travel Center*, in Coxen Hole and French Harbour. *Tropical Travel*, in *Hotel Cay View*, T 45-11-46; *Columbia Tours*, Barrio El Centro, T 45-11-60.

Diving West End: *Tyll Sass*, T 45-13-14 or in USA (813) 593-1259, one-tank dive US$20, windsurfing US$4 per hour, resort courses in both sports and charters available; *Seagrape* in West End does PADI courses for US$150; *Roatán Divers*, Half Moon Bay, T 45-12-65, Tino and Alejo Monterrosa, many years experience, US$20 a dive; *Ocean Divers*, diving and snorkel hire, mask, snorkel and fin rental US$5 per day. French Harbour: John Davis, Green House on pier below Yachting Club, US$300 for 4 days (less pp for groups); Off the Wall Divers, at **French Harbour Yacht Club**. See also above under **Hotels and Restaurants**. The most popular dive sites have permanent mooring buoys; most dive shops hold briefings on diving in the Reserve to minimize ecological damage.

Ambulance and Decompression Chamber 'Cornerstone", at entrance to *Anthony's Key Resort*, Sandy Bay, T 45-15-15.

Excursions In glass-bottomed boat of Dennis, at *Foster and Vivian's Restaurant*, West End, to Hottest Sparrow Bay, for example, beyond *Anthony's Key Resort*, where the boat anchors for snorkelling, about US$4 pp in a group of 16, 4½ hrs. He also takes charters and cruises all along the coast. Horseriding available with Sharky, find him by Brewsters Place (restaurant in West End), 2-3 hr rides to Flowers Bay, US$10, experienced riders only.

Barbareta Beach Club on Barbareta Island; excellent diving, but expensive. The adjacent Pigeon Cays are ideal for snorkelling, shallow scuba, picnics. There are stone artefacts on the island, and you can hike in the hills to caves which may have been inhabited by Paya Indians. The island was once owned by the descendants of Henry Morgan. The island, plus its neighbours Santa Elena and Morat, are part of the proposed Barbareta National Marine Park.

Transport Take a plane to Coxen Hole (airport is 20 mins walk from town, taxi US$1.50) and launch up coast to French Harbour and Oak Ridge. Isleña and Taca fly from **La Ceiba** several times a day, US$16 one way (fewer on Sunday); flights also to and from **Tegucigalpa** and **San Pedro Sula**, frequency varies according to season. These flights are reported to be chaotic at times, US$22. From the USA, Taca flies on Sat from **Houston** via San Pedro Sula, on Sunday from **Miami**, and on Friday from **New Orleans**; Taca/Isleña connection from Miami via San Pedro Sula, daily in season, Sosa fly from La Ceiba to Roatán 0700 and 1300 Mon-Sat, continuing to **Guanaja** (US$15 one way) about 10 mins after arrival in Roatán. Roatán airport takes jets. Airlines: Taca, Edificio Shop and Save, Coxen Hole, T 45-12-36, at airport

T 45-13-87; Isleña, airport T 45-10-88.

Boats go irregularly from Puerto Cortés to Roatán, US$5 plus US$0.50 dock charge for tourists. Boats occasionally from the new harbour 5 km E of La Ceiba, US$20; on Roatán, enquire at the wharf for boats to La Ceiba. Fishing boats to **La Ceiba** for US$10 pp.

Columbus called **Guanaja**, the easternmost of the group, the Island of Pines, and the tree is still abundant. The island was declared a forest reserve in 1961, and is now designated a national marine park also. Good (but sweaty) clambering on the island gives splendid views of the jungle and the sea. Several attractive waterfalls. The locals call the island Bonacca. Much of Guanaja town, covering a small cay off the coast, is built on stilts above sea water, hence its nick-name: the 'Venice of Honduras". The island's population is about 4,000, its area 56 sq km. Bathing is made somewhat unpleasant by the many sandflies. These and mosquitos cannot be escaped on the island, all the beaches are infected (coconut oil will help to ward off sandflies and doubles as sun protection). The cays are better, including Guanaja town. South West Cay is specially recommended.

Hotels A-L *Bayman Bay Club* (beautiful location, T 45-41-79) and **A-L** *Posada del Sol* (on an outlying cay, T 45-43-11), both with launch trips, diving gear for rent, fitness studio, first class; **A** *Club Guanaja Este*, full board, many aquatic activities, and horseriding and hiking, reservations and information PO Box 40541, Cincinnati, Ohio 45240 or travel agents. **C** *Alexander*, T 45-43-26, or US$100 in 3-bed, 3-bathroom apartment. **C** *El Rosario*, T 45-42-40, with bath and a/c. **D-C** *Miller* (cheaper without a/c or bath), TV, restaurant, T 45-43-27; **E-D** *Harry Carter*, ask for a fan, all the a/c is broken down, clean however. *Casa Sobre El Mar*, on Bound Cay, T 45-42-69 (31-05-95 in Tegucigalpa), offers all-inclusive packages. *Day Inn*, hotel and restaurant.

Restaurants *Harbour Light*, through *Mountain View* discotheque, good food reasonably priced for the island; *The Nest*, T 45-42-90, good eating in the evening; *Glenda's*, good standard meals for under US$1, small sandwiches.

Banks Bancahsa, Banco Atlántida.

Sailing and Diving *SV Railovy*, T (504) 45-41-35, F (504) 45-42-74, is a 40 foot yacht running local cruises and excursion packages; also sailing, diving and snorkelling services, and PADI courses. Ask for Hans on VHF radio channel 70.

Transport An airport on Bonacca Island, boat to **Guanaja**, US$1; Isleña has flights daily except Sun from La Ceiba leaving at 1430, 30 mins, US$20 each way. Flights from San Pedro Sula leave at 1500, US$62 return. Other non-scheduled flights available.

The *Suyapa* sails between Guanaja, La Ceiba and Puerto Cortés. The *Miss Sheila* also does the same run and goes on to George Town (Grand Cayman). Cable Doly Zapata, Guanaja, for monthly sailing dates to Grand Cayman (US$75 one way). Irregular sailings from Guanaja to Trujillo, twice a week, 5 hrs, US$10. Irregular but frequent sailings in lobster boats for next to nothing to Puerto Lempira in Caratasco Lagoon, Mosquitia, or more likely, only as far as the Río Plátano (see p 663).

SAN PEDRO SULA

San Pedro Sula, 58 km S of Puerto Cortés by road and railway, 265 km from Tegucigalpa (60-150m above sea level), the second largest city in Honduras, is a centre for the banana, coffee, sugar and timber trades, a focal distributing point for northern and western Honduras with good road links, and the most industrialized centre in the country. Its business community is mainly of Arab origin. It is considered the fastest growing city between Mexico and Colombia. The population is 500,000.

The city was founded by Pedro de Alvarado on 27 June 1536. The large neo-colonial-style cathedral, started in 1949, was completed many years later. San Pedro Sula is situated in the lush and fertile valley of the Ulúa (Sula) river, beneath the forested slopes of the Merendón mountains and, though pleasant in the cooler season from November to February, reaches very high temperatures in the rest of the year with considerable humidity levels.

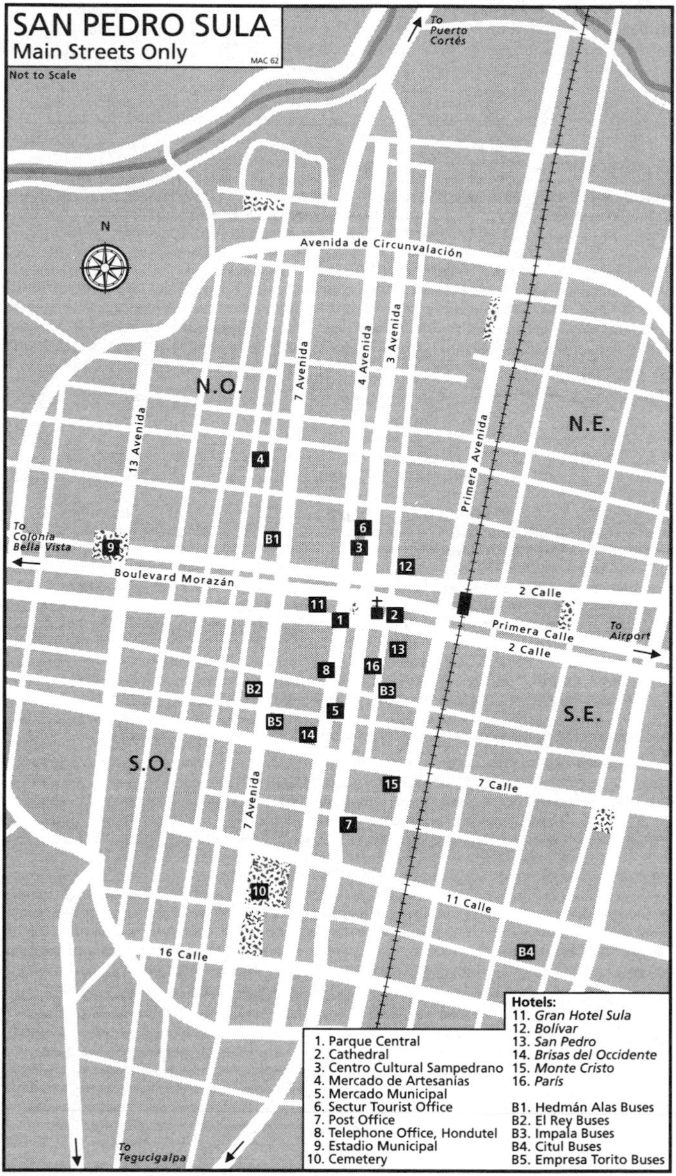

SAN PEDRO SULA
Main Streets Only
MAC 62
Not to Scale

To Puerto Cortés

N

Avenida de Circunvalación

13 Avenida

7 Avenida

4 Avenida

3 Avenida

Primera Avenida

N.O.

N.E.

To Colonia Bella Vista

Boulevard Morazán

2 Calle

To Airport

Primera Calle

2 Calle

S.E.

7 Avenida

S.O.

7 Calle

11 Calle

16 Calle

To Tegucigalpa

Hotels:
11. *Gran Hotel Sula*
12. *Bolívar*
13. *San Pedro*
14. *Brisas del Occidente*
15. *Monte Cristo*
16. *París*

1. Parque Central
2. Cathedral
3. Centro Cultural Sampedrano
4. Mercado de Artesanías
5. Mercado Municipal
6. Sectur Tourist Office
7. Post Office
8. Telephone Office, Hondutel
9. Estadio Municipal
10. Cemetery

B1. Hedmán Alas Buses
B2. El Rey Buses
B3. Impala Buses
B4. Citul Buses
B5. Empresa Torito Buses

The higher and cooler suburb of Bella Vista with its fine views over the city affords relief from the intense heat of the town centre. The cafeteria and foyer swimming pool of *Hotel Sula* provide a cool haven for visitors. The city's main festival, Feria Juniana, is in the last days of June.

A highway is being constructed between San Pedro Sula and Puerto Cortés, completion expected 1995. In the meantime, traffic is slow especially near the construction area.

The city is divided into four quadrants: noreste (northeast—NE), noroeste (north-west—NO), sudeste (southeast—SE) and sudoeste (southwest—SO), where most of the hotels are located.

Hotels A+ *Gran Hotel Sula* (the best), 1 C, 3 and 4 Av, T 52-99-91, F 57-70-00, pool, restaurant (upstairs, very good, reasonably priced) and café (for authentic American breakfast, view of pool), also good, 24-hr service; **A** *Copant*l *Sula*, modern, in Col Los Arcos, T 53-09-00, F 57-38-90, free bus to city centre, Telex IT5584; **C** *Ambassador*, 5a y 7a Calles SO, T 57-68-24, F 57-58-60; **C** *Internacional Palace*, 3a Calle, 8 Av SO, Barrio El Benque, T 57-79-22, F 52-28-38, a/c; **C** *Gran Conquistador*, 7 y 8 Av, 2 Calle SO, opp Cine Tropicana, T 52-76-05; **C** *Terraza*, with a/c, E without, dining room rather dark and grimy, friendly staff, 6 Av, 4-5 Calle SO, T 53-31-08; **C-D** *Bolívar*, 2a C, 2 Av, NO, T 53-32-24, F 52-48-23, cabins beside pool, with a/c, good and reasonably priced restaurant, rec; **D** *San Pedro*, 3 C, and 2 Av, SO, with bath and overhead fan, also rooms with fan, E, popular, clean, good value, inexpensive café with good snacks; **D** *Palmira*, 6 Calle entre 6 y 7 Av SO, No 32, T 53-36-74/57-65-22, clean, convenient, large parking area, good value; (there are 2 *Palmiras* in same street; they and the *Brisas*, are nr Av Los Leones, not the best area late at night); **D-E** *Calle Real*, 6 Av, 7 C, SE, T 57-46-04, above Centro Comercial Medina, a/c for fan; **D-E** *Colombia*, 3 Calle, 5-6 Av SO, with a/c, E without; **E** *Colombia Annex*, a few blocks away, without bath, run down, pricey; **E-D** *Manhattan*, 7 Av 3-4 C, SO with a/c; **E** *El Nilo*, 3 C y 2 Av SO, nice rooms; **E** *Brazilia*, 7 C y 2 Av SE, a/c, cheaper with fan, bath, cold water, clean, helpful, cold drinks for sale, guarded car park round corner at Texaco station (US$1), nearby *Boarding House Castro*, C 6 between 2 and 3 Av SE 'a colourful affair' offers 'amplio parqueo"; **F** *Brisas del Occidente*, a 5-storey building on Av 5, with fan (F without bath), ask for room with window, laundry facilities, friendly, rec (do not confuse with nearby *Brisas de Copán*, a dive which rents rooms by the hour); **F** *Moderno*, 7 Av, 5-6 C, opp Empresa el Rey buses, very basic; **F** *Siesta*, 2 Av SE, 7 C (T 52-26-50), cheaper without bath, clean, safe, rec, but noisy; **F** *Ceibeño*, close to bus station, T 57-85-62, dirty bathrooms; **F** *Monte Cristo*, 2 Av 7 C SE, clean, fan, safe. **F** *París*, 3 Av, 3 C SO, near *El Nilo* and bus station for Puerto Cortés, shared bath, poor water supply, clean but noisy; **F** *San Juan*, 6 C, 6 Av SO, modern building, noisy, clean, helpful, good value. Cheap hotels between bus terminals and downtown market, eg **G** *Hospedaje Faro*, 2 blocks from bus station, clean, friendly, fan, own bath. 5 km S, on the road to Tegucigalpa, is *Tropical*, strictly hourly rentals (just over US$1 per hour), hot water, a/c, upmarket, very private rooms but only internal locks on doors, locking garages.

Restaurants *La Espuela*, Av Circunvalación, 5-6 C, NO, good grilled meats, rec; *Don Udo's*, Blvd Los Próceres, restaurant and café-bar; *Madrid* on Plaza, good, rec; *Italia*, 7 Av 1 Calle NO, good lasagne, inexpensive, good; *Vicente*, 7 Av, 1-2 Calle NO, elegant, a/c, extensive Italian menu, good bar/wines, rec; *Copa de Oro*, 2 Av, 2-3 C, SO, extensive Chinese and western menu, a/c, pleasant, rec; *Sim Kon*, 5 C Av Circunvalación, Chinese; *Nápoli*, centre of town, Italian, reasonable; *Toto's Pizza*, Ed Samara, Blvd Morazán; *La Gondola*, 15 Av, 7-8 Calles SO, Barrio Suyapa; *Las Tejas*, 9 Calle, 16-17 Av, Av Circunvalación; *Pat's Steak House*, 5a Calle, 17 Av No 22, Av Circunvalación SO; *José y Pepe's*, Av Circunvalación SO, top end of 6 Calle, Mexican, smart, friendly; *La Estancia*, 2 C, 9-10 Av NO, Uruguayan; *Pinchos Palace*, is a bar-restaurant behind *Gran Hotel Sula*, expatriot hang-out, good atmosphere; *Cafetería Mayan Way*, 6 Av, 4-5 Calle SO, very clean, good typical breakfast and set meal, cheap, closed Sun, English spoken; *Popeye's Chicken and Biscuits*, in front of Cervecería Hondureña on road to Puerto Cortés; *Pizza Hut* at W end of Blvd Morazán and in the city centre; *Taos*, Blvd El Norte, good ice cream.

Shopping Large artesan market, Mercado Guamilito Artesanía, 6 blocks NW of Central Park, typical Honduran handicrafts at good prices (bargain). *Candu Original*, 5 Av 1-2 C SO, excellent selection of arts and crafts; *José Lino Chávez*, C Peatonal No 7, mahogany woodcraft and leatherwork. *The Book Store*, 3 Av, 2 C SE for good selection of Latin American and English books.

Car Rentals American, 3a Av, 3-4 Calle NO (T 52-76-26), *Hotel Copant*l and airport (T 56-23-37); Avis, 1 C, 8 y 9 Av, T 53-09-55; Blitz, *Hotel Sula* and airport (T 52-2405 or 56-24-71); Budget, airport T 56-24-67; Maya, 3a Av NO, 7-8 Calle and airport (T 52-26-70 or 68-24-63); Molinari, *Hotel Sula* and airport (T 53-26-39 or 56-24-63); Toyota, 4a Av, 2-3

Calles NO, T 57-26-44.

Taxis Ask the price first and bargain if necessary (US$0.80 per journey within city).

Car Repairs Invanal, 13 C between 5 and 6 Av NE, T 52-70-83, excellent service from Sr Víctor Mora.

Discotheques *Henry's, Confettis,* and *Baccus,* all on Av Circunvalación NO; *Cocodril,* Parque Central. **Shows** *Boleros,* Zona Viva, *peña artística,* live music on Fri and Sat, bar and restaurant.

Museum Museo de Antropología e Historia, 3a Av NO, with displays of the cultures that once inhabited the Ulúa valley, up to Spanish colonization, and, on the first floor, local history since colonization; open Tues-Sun 1000-1700.

Exhibitions Expocentro, Av Junior, off Blvd to Puerto Cortés, temporary exhibitions, conferences and fairs.

Theatre The Círculo Teatral Sampedrano puts on plays at the Centro Cultural Sampedrano, 3 Calle 4 C NO, which also has an art gallery and an English and Spanish library. There are several air-conditioned cinemas.

Exchange Lloyds Bank at 4a Av SO 26, between 3a and 4a Calle; **Banco de Honduras (Citibank); Banco de Ahorro Hondureño,** has a beautiful mural in its head office, 5 Av, 4 Calle SO Bancahsa, 5 Av, SO, No 46, changes TCs; **Banco Continental,** 3a Av, 3-5 Calle SO No 7; **Banffaa, Banco de Occidente,** 6a Av, 2-3 Calles SO; **Bancomer,** 4 C 3-4 Av NO; **Bahncafe,** 1C, 1 Av SE and all other local banks. Open 0830-1500, closed Sat except Bancomer and Bahncafe, open Mon-Fri 0900-1900, Sat 0900-1200. Rates are better in some shops; they will also accept TCs. Good rates at *Multicambios,* 6 Av, 2-3 C NO, exchange house worth checking out and at *Lempira Cambios,* 4 C and 3 Av SO. A host of dealers buy dollars in Parque Central and the pedestrian mall.

Consulates Belize, Sr Roberto Canahuati, 2 Av, 7 Calle 102, Colonia Bella Vista, T 52-61-91. **Guatemalan,** 8 C, 5-6 Av No 38. **British,** Terminales Cortés, Aptdo 298, T 53-26-00. **French,** Av 12 No 30, T 53-09-53.

Cultural Institutions Centro Cultural Sampedrano, 3a Calle, 4a Av NO No 20, T 53-39-11, library, cultural events and 8 plays per year. **Alianza Francesa,** on 8a Avenida, number not known, has a library, French films on Wed, and cultural events on Fri.

Churches Episcopal Church, round corner from Sports Stadium, English service, Sun, 1000. High Mass on Suns, 1030, at Orthodox church at Río Piedras is picturesque and colourful.

Dentist Clínicas Dentales Especializadas, Ed María Antonia, 3a Calle entre 8 y 9 Av NO, apartamento L-1, Barrio Guamilito, T 58-04-64.

Laundry *Lavandería Almich,* 9-10 Av, 5 Calle SO No 29, Barrio El Benque; *Excelsior,* 14-15 Av Blvd Morazán; *Rodgers,* 4a Calle, 15-16 Av SO, No 114. *Lava Facil,* 7 Av, 5 Calle, US$1.50 per load.

Post Office 3 Av SO between 9-10 C.

Telephone, Telex and Cables from Hondutel, 4a Calle SO No 25.

Tourist Office Sectur, Edificio Inmosa, 4C, NO, 3-4 Av, T 52-30-23/95, and at airport, road maps US$2.25 but no other maps.

Travel Agents *Cambio CA,* Edificio Copal, 2 piso, 1 Calle 5-6 Av Centro, T 52-72-74, F 52-05-23, PO Box 2666, tours to all the most interesting ecological sites in Honduras including Mosquitia, professional guides, German and English spoken, equipment, rec; *Super Viajes,* 7a Av, SO, 2-3 Calles, T 53-46-16; *Alas,* 3a Calle, 4-5 Avs, SO No 25, T 53-10-20; *Cramer Tours,* 4a Av SO No 2, T 53-26-74, tour operators; *Honduras Travel,* 4a Av SO No 10, T 53-32-59; *Mundirama Travel Service,* Ed Martínez Valenzuela, next to Banco Banffaa, T 52-34-00, American Express agents; *Transmundo de Sula,* 6a Av, SO No 15, Apdo 410, T 53-47-52, F 53-11-40, rec; several others.

Airport 17 km from city centre, US$5 pp by taxi, but bargain hard; US$1 by colectivo. Buses do not go to the airport terminal itself; you have to walk the final 1½ km from the La Lima road (bus to this point, US$0.30). Flights to Tegucigalpa (35 mins, US$12), La Ceiba and to Roatán. Direct flights every day to Belize, Guatemala, New Orleans, Miami, Houston, New York, San José (Costa Rica) and San Salvador. Several flights a week (frequency varies according to the time of year) to Cancún, Mexico City, Madrid, San Francisco, Panama City and Los Angeles.
  Airlines: **Lacsa,** 8a Av, 1-2 Av SO, Ed Romar, T 52-68-88; **American,** Ed Firenze, Barrio Los Andes, 16 Av, 1-2 Calles, T 58-05-24; **Continental,** 1 C, 3 y 4 Av NO, T 57-41-41, airport T 57-47-40. COPA, 10a Av, 1 y 2 C SO, T 52-08-83, airport T 56-25-18.

Buses To **Tegucigalpa**, 4-4½ hrs, 250 km by paved road. Main bus services with comfortable coaches and terminals in the town centre are Hedmán Alas, 7-8 Av NO, 3 C, Casa 51, T 53-13-61, 7 per day 0630 to 1730 4 hrs (US$4), which is the best, and Transportes Sáenz (Av 9 y 10, C 9 SO), El Rey, Av 7, Calle 5 y 6, Transportes Norteños (all US$2.50), last bus at 1900. Both Hedmán Alas and Saenz (from Terminal Saenz, *Hotel Copantl Sula*, T 53-18-29) have luxury services to the capital, US$8.90. The road to **Puerto Cortés** is paved; a pleasant 1-hr journey down the lush river valley. Buses run N to Puerto Cortés (Empresa Impala, 2 Av, 4-5 C, several each hour, or Citul, US$0.75), to **Omoa** (Calle 3 E from 0600), E to **La Lima**, **El Progreso** (US$0.60), **Tela** and **La Ceiba** (Tupsa, 2 Av N, 1-2 Calle, hourly on the hour, US$2.70, 2½-3 hrs) with a change of bus in El Progreso. To La Ceiba also with Catisa, leave from near *Siesta Hotel*, US$2. Buses run S to **Lago Yojoa** and Tegucigalpa, and SW to **Santa Rosa** and then through the Department of Ocotepeque with its magnificent mountain scenery to the **Guatemalan border** (US$3.40 to the border by bus). Transportes Impala, 2 Av, 4-5 Calle SO No 23, has 6 buses every other day to **Nueva Ocotepeque** and **Agua Caliente** on the Guatemalan border (first at 0330, last 1500), on alternate days Congolón runs this route, terminal US$0.75 from centre; Empresa Torito and Transportes Copanecos go to **Santa Rosa de Copán** every 30 mins from 0445 to 1715 US$1.80 (6 y 7 Avs, between Calles 8 and 9, T 54-19-54/53-49-30, and 6 C, 4-5 Av SO, respectively, latter's terminal US$0.75 taxi ride from centre). Take these buses to La Entrada, 2 hrs, US$1.10, for connection to **Copán**. Journey some 3-4 hrs. Road paved all the way. There is one direct bus to Copán at 1300 leaving in front of *Hotel Palmira*.

Motoring If coming from the S, and wishing to avoid the city centre when heading for La Lima or El Progreso, follow signs to the airport.

Train Ferrobus to Puerto Cortés US$0.30. All other rail services were suspended in 1993.

Excursions One can take a taxi up the mountain behind the city for US$2-2.50; good view, and interesting vegetation on the way up. Lake Ticamaya, near Choloma, is worth visiting between June and December. The head office of the former United Brands subsidiary is at *La Lima* (45,000 inhabitants), 15 km to the E by road (bus frequent, US$0.25), where the banana estate and processing plants can be seen. It is possible to visit a Chiquita banana plantation with permission from the headquarters (private car needed). There is a club (golf, tennis, swimming) which takes members from outside; branches of local banks. **D** *Hotel La Lima*, central, a/c, phone, cable TV, cafeteria, restaurant; *Restaurante Los Marinos*, opp Supermercado Manuel Bonilla, live Caribbean music twice a week; *Cafetería Jacky's*, Lima Vieja, next to Hondutel, shrimp, beef, chicken, soups, etc; a cheap place to eat is *Golosinas Cristy* (from US$0.70). A little to the E, near the Ulúa river, is Travesía (not the Travesía near Puerto Cortés, see under **The North Coast**, Puerto Cortés), where Mayan pottery remains have been found, but no ruins as such.

Twenty km W of San Pedro Sula, the cloud forest national park of **Cusuco** is managed by Fundación Ecologista HRPF, 3 Av, 9-10 Calle NO, Barrio Las Acacias, San Pedro Sula, T 53-33-97. Also contact Cohdefor, 10 Av, 4 C NW, Barrio Guamilito, San Pedro Sula, T 53-49-59/29-29, or Cambio CA, who run tours. In the 1950s this area was exploited for lumber but was declared a protected area in 1959 when the Venezuelan ecologist, Geraldo Budowski reported that the pine trees here were the highest in Central America. Cutting was stopped and the lumber company abandoned the site. The area includes tropical rainforest and cloud forest with all the associated flora and fauna. It includes Cerro Jilinco, 2,242m and Cerro San Ildefonso 2,228m, the highest points within 25 km of the Caribbean coast of Central America. HRPF produces a bird checklist. There are 4 trails, ranging from 30 mins to 2 days. They use old logging roads, traversing forested ridges with good views. There is a visitors' centre with kitchen, bathroom, shower and beds; take your own food. Camping is possible. Access by dirt road from Cofradía, on the road to Santa Rosa de Copán, then to Buenos Aires: 2 hrs by car from San Pedro Sula, 4WD recommended; bus San Pedro Sula-Cofradía, 1 hr, US$0.15, from same street as *Hotel Brisas del Occidente*, 4 blocks down; pick-up Cofradía-Buenos Aires 1½ hrs, US$1.75, best on Mon at 1400; the park is 5 km from Buenos Aires.

COPAN AND WESTERN HONDURAS

Honduras' major Maya attraction is close to the Guatemalan border; it is a lovely site, with a pleasant town nearby. This whole area has many interesting towns and villages, most in delightful hilly surroundings, often producing handicrafts.

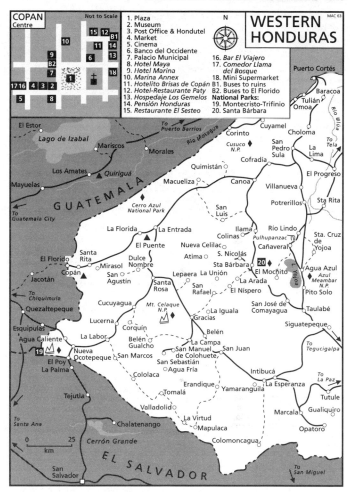

COPAN Centre — Not to Scale

1. Plaza
2. Museum
3. Post Office & Hondutel
4. Market
5. Cinema
6. Banco del Occidente
7. Palacio Municipal
8. Hotel Maya
9. Hotel Marina
10. Marina Annex
11. Hotelito Brisas de Copán
12. Hotel-Restaurante Paty
13. Hospedaje Los Gemelos
14. Pensión Honduras
15. Restaurante El Sesteo
16. Bar El Viajero
17. Comedor Llama del Bosque
18. Mini Supermarket

B1. Buses to ruins
B2. Buses to El Florido

National Parks:
19. Montecristo-Trifinio
20. Santa Bárbara

WESTERN HONDURAS MAC 63

The Western Highway runs from San Pedro Sula SW along the Río Chamelecón to Canoa (58 km, from where there is a paved road S to Santa Bárbara, a further 53 km) and Santa Rosa de Copán; it goes on to the border with Guatemala and El Salvador. **Santa Bárbara** (23,000 inhabitants; altitude 290m) is 32 km W of Lago Yojoa, 221 km from Tegucigalpa, in hot lowlands. Panama hats and other goods of *junco* palm are made in this, one of the nicest main towns in Honduras. It is surrounded by high mountains (eg Cerro Guatemalilla), hills, forests and rivers. The majority of the population is white or fair-skinned and the people are very lively. Santa Bárbara is a good base for visiting the villages in the department of the same name (see below). In the vicinity the ruined colonial city of **Tencoa** has recently been rediscovered. The paved road goes on to join the Northern Highway S of Lago Yojoa.

Hotels D *Boarding House Moderno*, Barrio Arriba, T 64-22-03, with hot shower, rec; **F** *Herrera*, *Santa Marta*, both on La Independencia; *Gran Hotel Colonial*, 1½ blocks from Parque Central, T 64-26-65, fans in all rooms; **F** *Hospedaje Rodríguez*, with bath, rec; **F** *Ruth*, Calle La Libertad, and *Hotel Santa Lucía*.

Restaurants *El Maxim*, Av La Independencia, Barrio El Centro; *Doña Ana*, opp Red Cross, no sign, but best place to eat, although you are only served if and when the owners want. *Doña Mirna*, 1 block N of the park, good pastries and local food.

Cinema Galaxia.

Exchange Banco Atlántida, Bancafé, Banco Sogerín, Banadesa.

Bus to **Tegucigalpa**, 0700 and 1400 daily, weekends 0900, US$3, 4½ hrs with Transportes Junqueños (passing near remote villages in beautiful mountain scenery); from **San Pedro Sula**, 2 hrs, US$1.90, 7 a day between 0500 and 1630.

Between Santa Bárbara and Lago Yojoa is the **Parque Nacional de Santa Bárbara** which contains the country's second highest peak, Montaña de Santa Bárbara, 2,744m. The rock is principally limestone with many subterranean caves (see also below). There is little touristic development as yet, although a visitors' centre is under construction in the village of Sauce and a guide can be found in Los Andes, a village above Peña Blanca and Las Vegas. A few trails exist; best time to visit is the dry season, January-June. For more information contact Asociación Ecológica Corazón Verde, Apartado 28, Santa Bárbara, or Cohdefor in Santa Bárbara.

The Department of Santa Bárbara is called the 'Cuna de los Artesanos", with over 10,000 manufacturers of handicrafts. The main products come from the small *junco* palm, for example fine hats, baskets, etc. The principal towns for *junco* items are *La Arada*, 25 mins from Santa Bárbara on the road to San Nicolas (see below), then branching off S, and Ceguaca, on a side road off the road to Tegucigalpa. Hats and baskets are made in Nueva Celilac (also below). *Mezcal* is used to make carpets, rugs, hammocks, etc, it is easy to find in towns such as *Ilama* (pop 7,000) on the road to San Pedro Sula, with one of the best small colonial churches in Honduras (no accommodation). *Tule* is used to make *petates* (rugs) and purses.

In the Department of Santa Bárbara is an area known as **El Resumidero**, in which are the Quezapaya mountain, and six others over 1,400m, and a number of caves (Pencaligüe, Los Platanares, El Quiscamote, and others). From Santa Bárbara, go to El Níspero and thence to El Quiscamote; or go to San Vicente Centenario (thermal springs nearby), and on to San Nicolás, Atima, Berlín, and La Unión, all of which have thermal waters, fossils, petrified wood and evidence of volcanic activity.

San Nicolás is 20 km from Santa Bárbara on a paved road; it was founded on 20 February 1840 after the disappearance of Viejo Celilac, near Cerro Capire. In the centre of town is the big tree called 'Anacahuite' (in Lenca, place of reunion), planted in 1927. There is a nice Catholic church; other points of interest, La Peña, Las Cuevas del Masical (a local guide will take you to the caves for a fee), Quebrada Arriba and El Violín. You can drive to the ruined church of Viejo Celilac and on to Nueva Celilac, high on the mountain, a pleasant little town with a Via Crucis procession on Good Friday.

North of Santa Bárbara is **Colinas**, reached by bus from San Pedro Sula (from near Av Los Leones). The village is picturesque, with a basic *pension* (G), near the church; excellent set meals from *Chinita* near the gas station. Climb the mountain with El Gringo Guillermo (Bill Walton) to Laguna Colorada, US$3 (a long drive through coffee *fincas*); he plans to build tourist cabins.

The road from San Pedro Sula towards Guatemala runs SW through Sula (*Hotel Comedor Sula*, looks OK) to La Entrada (115 km from San Pedro), where it forks left for Santa Rosa (see below) and right for an attractive 60 km road through deep green scenery to Copán. The regular bus is recommended rather than the dangerous minibus service. The road is paved throughout but is not in the best condition.

La Entrada is a hot, dusty town. (*Hotel San Carlos*, just before road to San Pedro Sula, T 98-50-38, a/c, cable TV, bar, restaurant, excellent value; **E** *Hotel Central*, with 2 beds, **F** with 1, either with bath, fans, cold water, OK; **F** *Hospedaje Copaneco*, 1 Av No 228; *Hospedajes Alexandra, Mejía; Hotel Tegucigalpa;* **F** *Hospedaje María*, clean, good, limited food also; eat in the market or at the bus station, or at **Comedor Isis**, excellent. Plenty of other good restaurants.) There is a small archaeological museum on main street next to Banco Atlántida (US$0.50). This bank won'T cash travellers' cheques, but Banco Sogerín will.

El Puente archaeological site is reached by taking a turn-off to the left, 1.5 km from La Entrada on the Copán road. It is at the confluence of the Chamelecón and Chinamito rivers and is thought to have been a regional centre between 600 and 900 AD. There are several structures, including a 12m high pyramid; there are also stelae. The visitors' centre has a *cafetería* and a souvenir shop.

A few km beyond La Entrada is the small town of La Florida (24,100 inhabitants, primitive accommodation). The owner of the gas station here will advise archaeologists about the many Maya ruins between La Florida and Copán. There are a number of hilltop stelae between the border and Copán. At Jihua, 3 km to the left from Km 4 from La Entrada, is a restored colonial church.

The magnificent Maya ruins of **Copán** are 395 km by road from Tegucigalpa or 172 from San Pedro Sula, and 1 km from the pleasant village, called Copán Ruinas (population 22,185). There is a signposted path beside the road from the village of Copán to the ruins, passing two stelae en route (1 km, no need to take a minibus). It is advisable to get to the ruins (open 0800-1600) as early as possible, or late in the day (though it takes a full day to see them properly). If you go early you may meet the tame spider monkey, Pancho, who comes over to the main gate before it opens to be fed by the guards. He likes a hug and may return the compliment by searching your hair for whatever may be lurking there (he sometimes comes out during the day, too). Several scarlet macaws are also apparently tame. There is a cafeteria by the entrance to the ruins, and also a shop. Guided tours available all year (recommended). There is a tourist office in the Parque Arqueológico, next to the shop, with local and country maps, and a Spanish/English guide book for the ruins, which is rather generalized. Luggage can be left for no charge (clean toilets here, too). Entry to ruins US$5, open 0800-1600, admission valid for 2 days includes the museum on the town square (same hours, good explanations in Spanish of the Maya empire and stelae) and Las Sepulturas (see below). It is a good idea to visit the museum before the ruins. Photographs of the excavation work and a maquette of the site are located in a small exhibition room at the ruins' Visitors' Centre.

When Stephens and Catherwood examined the ruins in 1839, they were engulfed in jungle. In the 1930s the Carnegie Institute cleared the ground and rebuilt the Great Stairway, and since then they have been maintained by the Government. Some of the most complex carvings are found on the 21 stelae, or 3m columns of stones on which the passage of time was originally believed to be recorded, and which are still in their original sites among the buildings. Under many of the stelae is a vault; some have been excavated. The stelae are deeply incised and carved with faces, figures and animals. They are royal portraits with inscriptions recording deeds and lineage of those portrayed as well as dates of birth, marriage(s) and death. (Some of the finest examples of sculpture in the round from Copán are now in the British Museum or at Boston.) Ball courts were revealed during excavation, and one of them has been fully restored. The Hieroglyphic Stairway leads up a pyramid; the upper level supported a temple. Its other sides are still under excavation. The Stairway is covered for protection, but a good view can be gained from the foot and there is access to the top via the adjacent plaza. Much fascinating excavation work is in progress, stacks of labelled carved stones under shelters, and the site looks like becoming even more interesting as new buildings are revealed. The most atmospheric buildings are those still half-buried under roots and soil. A huge museum and sculpture park should be completed in 1995 to house the newly excavated carvings.

The last stela was set up in Copán between AD 800 and 820, after less than five centuries of civilized existence. The nearby river has been diverted to prevent it encroaching on the site when in flood. 1 km from the town (in the opposite direction from the main ruins) is an area called Las Sepulturas, a residential area where ceramics dating back to 1000 BC have been found. A tomb from the site is on display in the museum. Also near the ruins is a nature trail (called Sendero Natural, open until 1700) through the jungle to the minor ball court; take mosquito repellent if you intend to stand still. The trail takes 30 mins. After 1600 is the best time to see animals on the Sendero Natural, open until 1700. Useful recent books are: *Scribes, Warriors and Kings: City of Copán*, by William and Barbara Fash (1991), and *History Carved in Stone, a guide to Copán* by William Fash and Ricardo Agarcía (1992), published locally and available at the site. (See also general account of Maya history in the Introduction to this book.)

How to get there There are regular buses (Copanecos, Impala or Torito lines) from San Pedro Sula to La Entrada, US$1.50 (2 hrs); from La Entrada to Copán, US$1.50 by bus (2 hrs), from 0600 hourly (or when full) till 1600, stops at entrance to ruins. For minibus from village to La Entrada, see below. If going by bus from San Pedro Sula, and returning, it is impossible to see Copán in one day. But if going on to Guatemala, one can take the 0445 San Pedro-La Entrada bus, 0600 La Entrada-Copán, arriving 0800, then the 1300 bus from Copán to the border; minibus Copán-border or vice-versa, leave when full, first at 0710 outside *Paty* US$1.90, 1 hr, but not on Sundays. This is met by a bus to Chiquimula at 0830. Etumi bus (beware of overcharging) from San Pedro Sula direct to Copán, at 1030 and 1300, 5-6 hrs. Direct bus also from 6 Av S O y 7 C S O, at 1100 daily, US$1.90, 5-6 hrs. Return to San Pedro Sula direct at 0400, 0500 and 1500 from bottom of hill opposite football pitch, by *Hotels Paty* and *Honduras*. 3 early am buses from Copán to Santa Rosa, 4 hrs, US$1.90. Buses to La Entrada for connecting buses going N or S, US$1.50, 2 hrs, longer in the rain, last bus at 1630. To return to San Pedro Sula, minibuses will take you to La Entrada (every 40 mins 0500-1800) with connections to San Pedro Sula.

Copán can also be reached by road from Guatemala City. The Honduran immigration office is at the border; one can get exit stamps there. For the most direct route from Guatemala, **see Section 2, Guatemala City to the Caribbean.**

To enter (or return to) Guatemala an alternative route is via Santa Rosa de Copán and Nueva Ocotepeque (see below and under **Guatemala, Section 2** for transit into Guatemala).

Exit tax from Guatemala is officially Q5. If you are leaving Honduras make sure to get your passport stamped at the police check point just outside Copán on the road to the border. The nearest Guatemalan consulate is in San Pedro Sula, so if you need a visa, you must get one there.

Hotels in Copán: **A/C** *Marina*, on the Plaza, T 98-30-70, F 98-30-72 (or T 39-09-56 in Tegucigalpa), swimming pool, sauna, restaurant, large rooms with TV, very friendly, nice atmosphere; **B** *Madrugada*, at end of the 1st street to the left after the bridge by the river, colonial, nice; **D** *Popul Nah*, on SW corner of Plaza, fan, hot shower, safe parking, very clean, hospitable, rec; **D** *Maya*, corner of main square with bath, restaurant, clean, airy rooms, nice patio garden with parrot, balcony on some upstairs rooms, water unreliable, staff surly; **F** *Hospedaje Los Gemelos*, without bath, clean, fans, good value, use of kitchen on request, pleasant patio, rec; **F** pp *Hotelito Brisas de Copán*, without bath, quiet, rec, limited parking; **F** *Hotelito Peña*, clean, friendly, showers, ask for fan; **F** *Hotel Paty*, friendly, under the same ownership as one of the minibus companies, has 10 clean rooms, price per person without bath, no hot water, E in newer rooms with bath, no hot water, parking; **F** *Pensión Honduras*, food available, nice patio, clean, friendly, good, parking; *Paty* and *Honduras* are noisy from buses after 0400; **G** *Hotelito Copán*, clean, friendly, safe, limited parking. Free camping by the Texaco station next to the ruins, no facilities.

Restaurants *Restaurant El Sesteo*, opposite *Brisas de Copán*, breakfast, reasonable. *Comedor Izabel* near the plaza, good, cheap; *Comedor San José*, good food, friendly; *La Llama del Bosque*, 2 blocks W of central Plaza, pleasant, reasonable food, touristy, expensive (check prices on bill carefully). *Tunkul*, proprietors Honduran/American, good kitchen, happy hour 1800-2000, always loud music, helpful, rec.

Services Phone calls can be made from the office of Hondutel 0700 to 2100. A telex service is also available but unreliable. Post office next to museum; stamps also sold at corner shop opposite.

There is a cinema (films at 1930, daily except Tues and Wed), which leaves much to be desired. Horses for hire near the square, US$10 per hour (but look around and bargain). You will probably be approached with offers of horse and bicycle hire: either is a good way of getting to nearby caves and hot springs (best in dry season).

Travellers' cheques may be changed at the Banco de Occidente (0830-1200, 1400-1600, Mon-Fri, 0800-1100 Sat, very crowded on Sat). Guatemalan currency is rarely accepted at Copán; it is possible to change quetzales near where buses leave for the border. Change dollars at the better hotels.

There is a Texaco filling station at Copán.

Go Native Tours, T (504) 57-62-15, same number for *Ixbalanque* language school one-to-one teaching, US$125/week with room and board with local family, 4 hrs classes a day.

Santa Rosa de Copán, 153 km by road from San Pedro Sula, is the centre of a rich agricultural and cattle-raising area. Altitude 1,160m, pop 28,865, the town is set in some of the best scenery in Honduras; the weather is remarkably fine. Much maize and tobacco is grown in the area. Cigar factory near the *Hotel Elvir* sometimes arranges tours; large selection of cigars for sale. Santa Rosa is a colonial town with cobbled streets. The central plaza and church are perched on a hilltop. It holds a festival to Santa Rosa de Lima from 21 to 31 August. The Tobacco Queen is crowned at the end of the week. The water is also good here, you can buy cheap, purified drinking water from Copán Bottling Plant, 4 Av SE, 3 C SE, take container.

Hotels D *Elvir* (the best), Calle Real Centenario SO, 2 Av SO, safe, clean, quiet, all rooms have own bath, TV, hot water, drinking water, good meals in cafeteria or restaurant; D *Mayaland*, opp bus station on Carretera Internacional, price per person, parking, restaurant, but noisy and hostile management; D *El Rey*, also opp bus terminal, price per person, rooms with bath, check door locks, restaurant, parking; E *Copán*, 3 Av NE y 4 C NE, with bath, F without, cell-like rooms but clean; E *Rosario*, 3 Av NE No 139, with bath, F without; E *Continental*, 2 C NO y 2-3 Av, on second floor, clean, with bath, friendly management. F *Hospedaje Calle Real*, Real Centenario y 6 Av NE, clean, quiet, friendly, sometimes water failures; G *Hospedaje Maya*, 1 C NE y 3-4 Av, friendly, noisy, not too clean, car park; F *Hospedaje Santa Eduvigis*, 2 Av NO y 1 C NO, good beds, with reasonable restaurant next door; E *Hotel Maya* (not to be confused with *Hospedaje Maya*, see above), 1 C NO y 3 Av NO.

Restaurants *Flamingo*, 1 Av SE, off main square, relatively expensive but good pasta and chop suey, popular with locals; *Las Haciendas*, 1 Av SE, varied menu, filling *comida corriente*, rec; *Hamburguesas Marbella*, 1/2 block W of Parque Central, despite its name serves good Honduran and Mexican dishes, good value; *Miraflores* in Col Miraflores; *El Rodeo*, 1 Av SE, good menu, nice atmosphere (if you don'T mind animal skins on the walls). There is a good *comedor* at the bus terminal, *Merendera El Campesino*.

Discotheques *Tiffany's* and *Disco Classic*, both near centre.

Exchange Banco de Occidente (best exchange rates) and Atlántida, both on main plaza. Banadesa, Calle Real. Bancahsa (fast service), Calle Centenario (Occidente and Bancahsa change TCs).

Dentist Dr Ricardo Reyes, Barrio Santa Teresa, T 62-00-07.

Bus from Santa Rosa to Tegucigalpa (lovely scenery, lush pine forests, colonial villages) leaves at 0400 from main square, US$3, 7-8 hrs. 6 buses daily to Gracias from 0730, 2 hrs, US$1.50 (road paved). To San Pedro Sula, US$1.80, 4 hrs every 30 mins (Empresa Torito, and Transportes Copanecos), bus to La Entrada, 1 hr, US$0.50. To Copán Ruinas, 4 hrs for 100 km on good road, US$1.90, several direct daily, but you may have to change at La Entrada (eg Etumi at 1100 and 1230). S to Nueva Ocotepeque (US$1.50, 3 hrs). Local 'El Urbano' bus to centre from bus station (on Carretera Internacional, 2 km below town, opp *Hotel Mayaland*), US$0.35, goes all around the houses; taxi US$0.50. If coming from the Guatemalan border at Nueva Ocotepeque, the bus will stop at the end of town near Av Centenario (main street). The stretch of road between La Entrada and Nueva Ocotepeque is being resurfaced, so expect delays to and from Santa Rosa (1993-94).

Excursions There are buses from Santa Rosa W to the small town of **Dulce Nombre de Copán** (US$0.55). There are rooms available next to the Hondutel office. Hardy hikers can continue W through forested mountains to stay at the primitive village of **San Agustín** (take hammock or sleeping bag), continuing next day through Mirasol to emerge a few kms from Copán ruins at **Santa Rita**, about 7-8 hrs walking. From Santa Rosa there is a 2-hr, 0630 and 0730, US$1 bus ride to **Lepaera** (a few hundred inhabitants, very basic *hospedaje*, G, opp market and *comedores*, the best one adjoins the market) perched on a lovely mountainside (also reached from Gracias). One can scale the peak (Cerro Puca, 2,234m, stiff climb, start early am for day trip) or descend on foot by an old mule trail heading back to Santa Rosa, crossing the river on a swingbridge (*hamaca*), then hitch-hiking.

Numerous daily buses go through Cucuyagua and **San Pedro de Copán**, an attractive village and an entry point into the Parque Nacional Celaque, to **Corquín**, altitude 850m (US$0.75, 2 hrs), 2 good *pensiones*, one with a charming garden. From here take a bus, twice a day or a rough, dusty, 1½-hr ride in a pick-up truck (US$0.75) to **Belén Gualcho**, 1,500m up in mountains, a good base to explore the surrounding mountains and valleys, especially N towards Monte Celaque. Belén Gualcho is perched on a mountainside, with two colonial churches, one architecturally fine with three domes and a fine colonnaded façade with twin bell towers, the other rustic. There is an interesting Sunday market. **G** *Hotelito El Carmen* (2 blocks E down from the church in the plaza), pleasant, clean, good views, rec; **F** *Pensión René*, primitive; one other simple *pension* (cheap meals); electricity goes off at 2130 so take a torch and candle. Films are shown every evening at 1930, ask anyone, US$0.10. *Comedor Mery*, 1 block NW of plaza, good food in a welcoming family atmosphere; 2 more *comedores* on S side of plaza and E side on corner with store.

A steep descent E from Belén by mule trail leads in 5 hrs to **San Manuel de Colohuete** (altitude 1,500m), with a magnificent colonial church whose façade is sculpted with figures of saints. There is an equally fine colonial church 30 mins by 4WD vehicle to the SW at **San Sebastián Colosuca**. The village is at 1,550m, with a mild climate (*hospedaje* with 4 rooms); one other; or try Don Rubilio; food at Doña Clementina García or Doña Alicia Molina). The *feria de San Sebastián* is on 20 Jan. No alcohol may be sold in the village and there are no soldiers here. An hour's walk away is the Cueva del Diablo; 6 km away is Cerro El Alto with a lagoon at the top. From San Sebastián, a mule trail goes via the heights of Agua Fría to reach the route near the frontier at Tomalá.

Alternatively, one can walk 5 hrs E from San Manuel to **La Campa** (very nice colonial church); for non-walkers there is a daily bus San Manuel-La Campa-Gracias. There is a *hospedaje* in La Campa, ask at Hondutel. Red pottery is made there.

There are buses from Santa Rosa to Mapulaca and villages bordering El Salvador. Mapulaca is also accessible from Erandique (**see p 653**).

From San Pedro Sula there are regular buses via Santa Rosa S to **Nueva Ocotepeque** (6 hrs, US$3.40); road is well paved. From Nueva Ocotepeque, buses to San Pedro Sula stop at La Entrada (US$1.70), first at 0030, for connections to Copán. There are splendid mountain views. Colectivos to El Poy on the El Salvadorean border, US$0.50, buses, US$0.20, and several buses daily from El Poy to San Salvador. You can cross into Guatemala at Atulapa, just after Agua Caliente (tourist office here, one *hospedaje*, bargain). There are several buses a day from San Pedro Sula to Agua Caliente, first at 0300 (eg Congolón, Impala; US$3.50, 6-7 hrs; money changers get on the bus between Nueva Ocotepeque and the border, very good rates for US dollars cash—there are 3 banks in Nueva Ocotepeque, none accepts El Salvadorean colones). In Nueva Ocotepeque is a Salvadorean consul near Parque Central, where visas for El Salvador can be obtained, and an immigration office. Minibuses go to Esquipulas (US$0.25), from where bigger buses run to Guatemala City. You can get into El Salvador via Esquipulas, Guatemala (see Guatemala, Section 2, **Guatemala City to the Caribbean**). The nearest Guatemalan consul is in San Pedro Sula; get a visa there, as it is no longer possible at the border. There is an old colonial church, La Vieja (or La Antigua) between Nueva Ocotepeque and the border; it is in the village of Antigua Ocotepeque, founded in the 1540s, but destroyed by a flood from Cerro El Pital in 1934. The Museo Ocotepecano de Ciencias Naturales, in the Governor's office, Parque Central, Mon-Fri 0800-1600, free, has information on the natural history of the Department.

Hotels in Nueva Ocotepeque E-G *San Antonio*, 1 Calle, 3 Av, small rooms but OK; **F** *Hotel y Comedor Congolón*, also bus agency, shared bath, very noisy in am; **F** *Gran*, with bath, cold water, pleasant, clean, single beds only, about ¼ km from town at the junction of the roads for El Salvador (S) and Guatemala (W) nearby, at Sinuapa. **G** *Hotelito San Juan*, pleasant and cheap; **G** *Ocotepeque* (by Transportes Impala), clean but noisy); restaurant *La Cabaña*.

National Parks The **Guisayote Biological Reserve** protects 35 square km of cloud forest, about 50% virgin, reached from the Carretera Occidental. Access is from El Portillo. There are trails and good hiking. El Portillo to El Sillón, the park's southern entrance, 3-5 hrs. Twice daily *busita* from El Sillón to Ocotepque. **El Pital**, 3 km E of Nueva Ocotepeque, but 2 km vertically above the town, 2,730m; the third highest point in Honduras with several square km of cloud forest. The park has not been developed for tourism.

The **Montecristo National Park** forms part of the Trifinio/La Fraternidad project, administered jointly by Honduras, Guatemala and El Salvador. The park is quite remote from the Honduran side, 2-3 days to the summit, but there are easy-to-follow trails. Access is best from Metapán in El Salvador. From the lookout point at the peak you can see about 90% of El Salvador and 20% of Honduras on a clear day. The natural resources office, for information, is opp Texaco, 2 blocks from *Hotel y Comedor Congolón*. Also go to the Museo for information, see above. Raymond J Sabella of the US Peace Corps has written a very thorough description of the natural and historical attractions of the Department, including hikes, waterfalls and caves.

SAN PEDRO SULA TO TEGUCIGALPA

On or near the country's main road route are Lago Yojoa and the former capital of Comayagua, but the section deals mainly with the towns and villages in the forested mountains and coffee zone W of the road. Some of these places have a colonial history, some are Lenca Indian communities.

The paved Northern Highway, possibly the best road in Central America, runs S from San Pedro. At Km 46 there is a paved road leading E through banana plantations to Santa Rita, thence either E to Yoro, or N to Progreso and Tela, thus enabling travellers between Tegucigalpa and the North Coast greatly to shorten their route by avoiding San Pedro Sula. An unpaved road right, at Caracol, leads up to Ojo de Agua (a pretty bathing spot), then on to El Mochito, Honduras' most important mining centre. (A bus from 2 Av in San Pedro Sula goes to Las Vegas-El Mochito mine where there is a cheap *pensión* (F) and walks along the W side of Lago Yojoa. This same turnoff at Caracol, marked 'Río Lindo", also leads to Peña Blanca (bus to Santa Bárbara via Mochito 0600), on the N side of Lago Yojoa, and to the Pulhapanzak waterfall, with some unexcavated ceremonial mounds adjacent.

The waterfall at **Pulhapanzak** is on the Río Lindo; by car it's a 1$\frac{1}{2}$ hr drive from San Pedro, longer by bus. Take a Mochito bus from San Pedro Sula (hourly 0500-1700) and alight at the sign to the falls, US$0.95. Alternatively stay on the bus to Cañaveral (take identification because there is a power plant here), and walk back along the Río Lindo, 3-4 hrs past interesting rock formations and small falls. The waterfall (42m) is beautiful in, or just after the rainy season, and in sunshine there is a rainbow at the falls. There is a picnic area and a small *cafetería*, but the site does get crowded at weekends and holidays; there is a small admission charge (US$0.20). The caretaker allows camping for a tip, rec. Leave early for this trip. Return buses leave only up to mid afternoon.

10 km N of the lake is the turn off for the village of **Santa Cruz de Yojoa**, and at 24 km is the **El Cajón** hydroelectric project (to visit the dam, apply at least 10 days in advance by phone—22-21-77, or in writing to Oficina de Relaciones Públicas de la ENEE, 1 Av, Ed Valle-Aguiluz, Comayagüela, DC). El Cajón hydroelectric dam (226m high) has formed a 94 square km lake, which lies between the departments of Cortés, Yoro and Comayagua. The dam is 22 km from Santa Cruz de Yojoa.

It is a climb of some 37 km from the hot lowlands to **Lago Yojoa** (81 km S of San Pedro Sula), 635m high, 22$\frac{1}{2}$ km long and 10 km wide, splendidly set among mountains. To the W rise the Montañas de Santa Bárbara; to the E the **Montaña Cerro Azul-Meámbar National Park**. Pumas, jaguars and other animals can be seen in the forests and pine-clad slopes. It also has a great many waterfalls. To get to any of the entry points (Meámbar, Jardines, Bacadia, Monte Verde or San Isidro), 4WD is necessary. For more information, contact Proyecto Humuya, Atrás Iglesia Betel, 21 de Agosto (T 73-24-26) Siguatepeque, or Proyecto de Desarrollo Río Yure, San Isidro, Cortés, Apartado 1149, Tegucigalpa. On the northern shore of Lago Yojoa a paved road skirts the lake for 12 km and a further 4 km (unpaved) to Pulhapanzak. The Northern Highway follows the eastern margin to the lake's southern tip at *Pito Solo*, where sailing boats and motor boats can be hired. (Bus to lake from San Pedro Sula, US$1, 1½ hrs; bus from Lake to Tegucigalpa with Hedmán-Alas, US$3, 3-5 hrs, 185 km).

Accommodation A *Brisas del Lago*, reopened 1993, overpriced; **C-D** *Motel Agua Azul* (at N end of lake), T 52-71-25, cabins for 2 or more persons, meals for non-residents; facilities for swimming, fishing, horseriding and boating, rec; **C** *Restaurante Los Remos* has cabins and camping facilities at Pito Solo, at the southern end of the lake, and rooms in E range, not too clean, beautiful setting, good food, nice for breakfasts, no beach but swimming pool (not always full), boat trips, parking US$3. *Only Bass*, 500m from *Motel Agua Azul* serves fresh fish from lake. *Comedores* on the road beside the lake serve the fish that is caught there (*Restaurant Marigoth*, rec) and roadside stalls near Peña Blanca sell fruit. Buses between Tegucigalpa and San Pedro stop to let passengers off at *Los Remos*, and at Peña Blanca, 5 km from the turning for *Agua Azul*. At Peña Blanca on N side of Lake are **G** *Hotel Manolito*, clean, and *Comedor El Cruce*, very good home cooking.

16 km S of the lake about 1 km S of *Los Remos* is the turnoff NW of a paved road to Santa Bárbara (**see p 643**). 1 km S of *Taulabé* uphill on the highway S are the caves of Taulabé, with stalactites and bats (illuminated and with guides, open daily). The road now ascends an enormous forested escarpment of the continental divide to reach cool, forested highlands around Siguatepeque.

Siguatepeque (32 km beyond Pito Solo, pop 39,165, altitude 1,150m) is a town with a cool climate. It is the site of the Escuela Nacional de Ciencias Forestales (which is worth a visit) and, being exactly half-way between Tegucigalpa and San Pedro Sula (128 km), a collection point for the produce of Intibucá, Comayagua and Lempira departments. The Cerro and Bosque de Calanterique, behind the Evangelical Hospital, is ¾ hr's walk from town centre. The Parque Central is pleasant, shaded by tall trees with the church of San Pablo on the N side and the cinema, *Hotel Versalles* and *Boarding House Central* on the E side; Hondutel and the Post Office are on the S side.

Hotels and Restaurants **E** *Hotel Internacional Gómez*, 3 Av SE, the main street, T 73-21-26, with bath, cheaper without, clean, use of kitchen on request, parking; **E** *Boarding House Central*, T 73-21-08, simple, but very good value, beware of the dog which bites; **F** *Versalles*, on the park; both have restaurants; **F** *Mi Hotel*, 1 km from highway on road into town, with bath, parking, restaurant.

China Palace, Chinese and international; *Pizzería Venezia*, good, also serves good sandwiches and fruit drinks; *Pollos Kike*, next door, pleasant setting for fried chicken addicts; *Juanci's*, also on main street, American-style hamburgers, good steaks and snacks, open until 2300; *Bicos*, SW corner of Parque Central, nice snack bar/patisserie; *Supermercado Food* has a good snack bar inside; *Cafetería Colonial*, 4 Av SE (just behind the church), good pastries and coffee, outside seating; on the Northern Highway there are several restaurants, best are *Nuevo* and *Antiguo Bethania*, quite a long way out of town, good, abundant, inexpensive meals.

Shopping A good leatherworker is Celestino Alberto Díaz, Barrio San Antonio, Casa 53, 2A Calle NE, 6A Av NE. One block N of Celestino's is a good shoemaker, leather shoes made for US$25.

Exchange Bancahsa, Banco Atlántida, Banco de Occidente, Banco Sogerin.

Bus to **San Pedro Sula**, from the town centre about 6 a day, US$1.35; **Tegucigalpa** with Empresas Unidas or Maribel, US$1.50, 3 hrs. Alternatively take a taxi, US$0.30, 2 km to the highway intersection and catch a Tegucigalpa-San Pedro Sula bus which passes every 30 mins; to **Comayagua**, Transpinares, US$0.50, 45 mins; to **La Esperanza** buses leave from the beginning of the road to La Esperanza, about 3 km along the N highway (by the side of the Texaco petrol station), first departure 0530, several daily, taxi from town centre US$0.50.

From Siguatepeque, an excellent all-weather road goes through lovely forested mountainous country, SW via Jesús de Otoro (two basic *hospedajes* and Balneario San Juan de Quelala, US$0.30 entry, *cafetería* and picnic sites) to **La Esperanza** (98 km). Capital of Intibucá Department, at 1,485m, this old colonial town is set in a pleasant valley. It has an attractive church in front of the park. There is a grotto carved out of the mountainside W of the town centre, a site of religious festivals. Good views. Market: Sun, at which Lenca Indians from nearby villages sell wares and food but no handicrafts. Nearby is **Yaramanguila**, an Indian village. The area is excellent for walking in forested hills, with lakes and waterfalls. In Dec-Jan it is very cold.

Hotels and Restaurants in La Esperanza There are simple but pleasant *pensiones*, eg **E** *Hotel Solis*, 1 block E of market, bath and hot water, restaurant, rec; **F** *El Rey*, in Barrio La Morera, clean, friendly; **F** *Hotel Mina*, good beds, clean, unfriendly, 1 block S of market, food available; **F** *Hotel y Comedor San Antonio*; **F** *La Esperanza*, basic, clean, friendly, good meals; **F** *Rosario*, basic, on road to Siguatepeque; **F** *San Cristóbal*; **F** *San José*, 4 Av Gen Vásquez No C-0005; **F** *San José*, in same building as Farmacia La Esperanza, 2 blocks S of Plaza. *Restaurant Magus*, 1 block E of Plaza, 'good food in a formica video bar atmosphere"; *Café El Ecológico*, corner of Parque Central, home-made cakes and pastries, fruit drinks, delicious home-made jams.

Banks Banco de Occidente and Banadesa.

Bus from La Esperanza to **Tegucigalpa** several daily (Cobramil, also to San Pedro Sula, and Joelito, 4 hrs, US$2.60), to **Siguatepeque** 0700, 0900, last at 1000, US$1.20, 2 hrs; bus, La Esperanza, Siguatepeque, Comayagua at 0600; buses also go from La Esperanza to the Salvadorean border; bus stops by market. Several minibuses daily to Yaramanguila. Daily minibus service to San Juan, dep between 1100-1200, very crowded; for Erandique, alight at Erandique turn off, 1 km before San Juan and wait for truck to pass (*comedor* plus basic *hospedaje* at intersection). Road from La Esperanza to San Juan winds through beautiful mountain pine forests, but slow going over mostly rough and stony surface.

An unpaved road of 35 km, bus 2 hrs at 1230 (but check), US$0.75, runs from La Esperanza SE to **Marcala** (1,300m, pop 10,770), Department of La Paz (a paved road goes to La Paz). The Marcala region is one of the finest coffee-producing areas of Honduras. Visit 'Comarca' at the entrance to town to get a good idea of how coffee is processed. *Fiesta* in honour of San Miguel Arcángel, last week of September. No immigration office.

Hotels E *Medina* the most comfortable, clean, modern with bath; **F** *Margoth*, very good value; **G** *Hotel-Comedor Rosita* at end of main street, opp *Darwin*; **G** *Hospedaje Edgar*, main street, beginning of town, clean, basic; **G** *Ideal*; **G** *Hospedaje Jairo*, with bath, 2 blocks E of main square.

    Restaurant *El Mirador*, on entering town, good, nice views from verandah; *Darwin*, on main street in centre, cheap breakfasts from 0700, rec; *Jarito*, opp market entrance, good; *Café Express*, beside Esso, good breakfast and *comida corrida*, rec. **Discotheque** *Geminis*.

Buses To Tegucigalpa 0500 and 1000 daily via La Paz, 4 hrs (bus from Tegucigalpa at 0800 and 1400, Empresa Lila, 4-5 Av, 7 C, No 418 Comayagüela, opp Hispano cinema); bus to La Paz only, 0800, 2 hrs, US$0.50; several minibuses a day, 1½ hrs, US$1. Bus also from Comayagua. Pick-up truck to **San José** at around 1000 from market, ask for drivers, Don Santos, Torencio, or Gustavo. Bus to **La Esperanza** at 0830, otherwise hitching possible, going rate US$0.80.

During the hotter months, March to May for example, a cooler climate can be found in the highlands of La Paz, pleasant temperatures during the day and cold (depending on altitude) at night. Marcala is a good base from which to visit Yarula, Santa Elena, Opatoro, San José and Guajiquiro, but transport to these places is erratic (see p 655). In the immediate vicinity of Marcala is **Balneario El Manzanal**, 3 km on the road to La Esperanza; it has a restaurant, 2 swimming pools and a boating lake, open Sat and Sun only.

    There are caves nearby on Musula mountain, the Cueva de las Animas in Guamizales and Cueva de El Gigante and El León near La Estanzuela with a high waterfall close by. Other waterfalls are El Chiflador, 67m high, Las Golondrinas,

La Chorrera and Santa Rosita. Transport goes to La Florida where there is good walking to village of *Opatoro* and climbing Cerro Guajiquiro. Between Opatoro and Guajiquiro is the **Reserva Las Trancas**, a heavily-forested mountain where quetzales have been seen.

Yarula and *Santa Elena* are 2 tiny municipalities, the latter about 40 km from Marcala, with beautiful views (bus Marcala-Santa Elena 1230 returns 0500 next day, 2 hrs 45 mins, enquire at Gámez bus office opp market; truck daily 0830 returns from Santa Elena at 1300). Sometimes meals are available at *comedores* in Yarula and Santa Elena. The dirt road from Marcala gradually deteriorates, the last 20 km being terrible; high clearance essential, 4WD rec. In **La Cueva Pintada**, S of Santa Elena, there are precolumbian cave paintings ("pinturas rupestres") of snakes, men and dogs; ask for a guide in Santa Elena. Ask also in this village about the 'Danza de los Negritos", performed at the annual fiesta of Santiago, 24-25 March, in front of the church. A special performance may be organized, the dancers wearing their old, wooden masks, if suitable payment is offered.

S of Marcala, the road crosses into El Salvador, but there is no border crossing.

NW from La Esperanza a very bad road runs to Gracias (see below) and then a paved road on to Santa Rosa de Copán (see above). There are a number of settlements including *San Juan del Caite* (40 km—two *hospedajes*, *Lempira* and *Sánchez*, two restaurants nearby, helpful people and Peace Corps workers). This is the turn-off for Erandique. The largest town on this road is *Gracias* (pop 19,380, altitude 765m). It is one of the oldest and most historic settlements in the country, dominated by the highest mountains in Honduras, Montañas de Celaque. There are 3 colonial churches, San Sebastián, Las Mercedes, San Marcos (a fourth, Santa Lucía, is 2½ km SW of Gracias), and a restored fort, with two fine Spanish cannon, on a hill in the outskirts. The fort, El Castillo San Cristóbal, has been well restored, and at the foot of the northern ramparts is the tomb of Juan Lindo, President of Honduras 1847-1852, who introduced free education through a system of state schools. Some 5 km from Gracias swim in hot, communal thermal pools in the forest, Balneario Las Aguas Termales (1 hr by a path, 1 hr 20 mins by the road, ask anyone, entry US$0.20, rec). Good place to barbeque.

Gracias was the centre from which Francisco de Montejo, thrice Governor of Honduras, put down the great Indian revolt of 1537-38. Alonzo de Cáceres, his lieutenant, besieging Lempira the Indian leader in his impregnable mountain-top fortress at Cerquín, finally lured him out under a flag of truce, ambushed him and treacherously killed him. When the Audiencia de los Confines was formed in 1544 Gracias became for a time the administrative centre of Central America.

18 km away is La Campa (**see p 648**). From Gracias buses go through coffee plantations to San Rafael (makeshift accommodation) from where one can hitch to El Níspero (*pensión*) and catch a bus to Santa Bárbara. Also on the road to San Rafael, a short detour leads to La Iguala, a tiny village attractively set between 2 rivers, magnificent colonial church. Irregular transport from/to Gracias.

It takes at least a whole day to climb from Gracias to the summit of *Monte Celaque* (2,849m, the highest point in Honduras). The trail begins from behind the visitors' centre of the Celaque National Park which is 8 km (2 hrs' walk) from Gracias. The first 5½ km can be driven in a standard car, the rest only with 4-wheel drive. At the centre there are 7 beds, shower and cooking facilities, US$1, drinks available, well-maintained. Behind the centre is a trail going down to the river where a crystal clear pool and waterfall make for wonderful bathing. There is a warden living nearby, but contact Cohdefor in Gracias, just off the square, before leaving for full information. There are a number of international volunteers working on the project. Division Chief Enrique is exceedingly helpful and friendly. There is a trail all the way to the summit (trees are marked with ribbons) which takes 6 hrs: the first 3 hrs are easy to a small hut, the rest of the way is steep.

There are 2 camping sites, with water, at about 2,000m and 2,500m. Don'T forget warm clothing, and given the dense forest and possibility of heavy cloud, a compass is recommended for safety. Also, beware of snakes. There are plans to extend the trail westward from the summit to Belén Gualcho, and to create a nature trail near the visitors' centre. Quetzales have been seen near the summit.

Hotels in Gracias **E** *Iris*, 3 blocks S of Plaza, 1 block W, opp San Sebastián church, best; **F** *Erick*, with bath, comfortable beds and shop, same street as bus office, rec; **G** *Herrera*, shared bath, noisy, basic; **G** *Hospedaje Corazón de Jesús*, on main street by market, clean, OK; **G** *Hospedaje El Milagro*, N side of market, basic.

Restaurants *La Fonda*, 2 blocks S of Parque Central, good food, good value, attractively decorated, rec; *El Señorial*, main street, simple meals and snacks, once house of Dr Juan Lindo; *Comedor Graciano* and *Pollo Gracianito* on main street. *Lenca*, good food, cheap, good information, books, videos, Dutch owner, next to Parque Central. *Guancasto*, on Parque Central, good atmosphere; *Rancho de Lily*, 4 blocks SW of Parque, good value. *Casita del Pastel*, good cakes, *tacos* etc and juices. For breakfast, *comedores* near the market.

Exchange Banco de Occidente.

Hondutel and Post Office 1 block S of Parque Central.

Buses To La Esperanza take the daily 0430 truck (sometimes leaves early) to San Juan del Caite, get off at El Crucero checkpoint (3 hrs), 1 km from San Juan, then hitch (police at the checkpoint will help), or rides can be taken on pick-up trucks for US$1.50 (dep early am from S end of main street on highway). The road is appalling and can be impassable during rainy season. There is also a bus service from Gracias to **Santa Rosa de Copán**, US$1.50, 6 times a day, 2 hrs (**see p 647**); beautiful journey through majestic scenery, the road is now paved (1994). Daily bus service to Lepaera 1400, 1½ hrs, US$0.85; daily bus to San Manuel de Colohuete via La Campa, 1400. Cotral bus ticket office is 1 block N of Parque Central.

SW from Gracias, up in the Celaque mountains is Belén Gualcho (again, **see p 648**). Also on the way are Corquín, San Pedro de Copán and Cucuyagua on the highway between Santa Rosa and Nueva Ocotepeque. The river flowing by Cucuyagua is very attractive, OK for swimming, and there is good camping on the banks.

Alban Johnson of Sandy Bay, Tasmania, and Jorge Valle-Aguiluz write: Roughly half way between Gracias and La Esperanza is San Juan del Caite (see above), from where a road runs 26 km S to **Erandique**. Set high in pine-clad mountains not far from the border with El Salvador, Erandique is a friendly town, and very beautiful. Lempira was born nearby, and was killed a few km away. The third weekend in January is the local *fiesta* of San Sebastián. Best time to visit is at the weekend. Market days are Fri and Sun. Each of the three *barrios* has a nice colonial church. There is one basic *hospedaje*, G, in the main street and one simple *comedor* down a side street; no electricity, torch essential. For the visitor there are lakes, rivers, waterfalls, springs and bathing ponds; you need to ask around. Nearby is **San Antonio** where fine opals (not cut gems, but stones encased in rock) are mined and may be purchased. The many hamlets in the surrounding mountains are reached by roads that have been resurfaced or recently built. The landscapes are magnificent. There are no buses to Erandique, most people go by truck from Gracias or La Esperanza (US$1.70, Erandique-Gracias, US$2.55, Erandique-San Juan-La Esperanza, change trucks at San Juan intersection, very dusty). Trucks leave Erandique 0700 daily, but sometimes earlier, and sometimes a second one leaves around 0800 for Gracias, otherwise be prepared for a long wait for a pick-up.

There are several roads radiating from Erandique, including one to **Mapulaca** and the frontier with El Salvador (no migración or aduana or bridge here, at the Río Lempa), a road to San Andrés and another to Piraera (all passable with a car).

32 km beyond Siguatepeque the Northern Highway dips into the rich Comayagua plain, part of the gap in the mountains which stretches from the Ulúa lowlands to the Gulf of Fonseca. In this plain lies

Comayagua, a colonial town of 59,535 people at about 550m, 1½ hrs' drive

(93.5 km) N from the capital. It was founded on 7 December 1537 as Villa Santa María de Comayagua, on the site of an Indian village by Alonzo de Cáceres. On 3 September 1543, it was designated the Seat of the Audiencia de los Confines by King Felipe II of Spain. President Marco Aurelio Soto transferred the capital to Tegucigalpa in 1880. There are several old colonial buildings: the former University, the first in Central America, founded in 1632, closed in 1842 (it was located in the Casa Cural, Bishop's Palace, where the bishops have lived since 1558); the churches of La Merced (1550-58) and La Caridad (1730); San Francisco (1574); San Sebastián (1575). San Juan de Dios (1590, destroyed by earthquake in 1750), the church where the Inquisition sat, is now the site of the Santa Teresa Hospital. El Carmen was built in 1785. The most interesting building is the Cathedral in the Central Park, with its square plain tower and its decorated façade with sculpted figures of the saints, which contains some of the finest examples of colonial art in Honduras (closed 1300-1500). The clock in the tower was originally made over 800 years ago in Spain; it was given to Comayagua by Felipe II in 1582. At first it was in La Merced when that was the Cathedral, but moved to the new Cathedral in 1715. There are two colonial plazas shaded by trees and shrubs. A stone portal and a portion of the façade of Casa Real (the viceroy's residence) survives. It was built 1739-41, but was damaged by an earthquake in 1750 and destroyed by tremors in 1856. The army still uses a quaint old fortress built when Comayagua was the capital. There is a lively market area.

There are two museums nearby: the ecclesiastical museum, ½ block N of Cathedral (daily 0930-1200, 1400-1700, US$0.60) and the Museo de Arqueología (housed in the former Palacio de Gobernación, 1 block S of Cathedral at the corner of 6 C and 1 Av NO, open Wed-Fri 0800-1600, Sat, Sun 0900-1200, 1300-1600, US$1.70). The latter is small scale but fascinating, with six rooms each devoted to a different period. Much of the collection comes from digs in the El Cajón region, 47 km N of Comayagua, before the area was flooded for the hydroelectricity project.

The US military base at Palmerola, 8 km from Comayagua, was designated a commercial national and international airport in 1993, to operate initially as a cargo export/import facility and later to take passenger traffic.

Hotels **D** *Nora y Max*, Calle Central y 3 Av E, T 72-12-10, a/c, cheaper rooms also, all with bath, hot water, car park, restaurant; **E** *Emperador*, Calle Central y 4 Av SO, T 72-03-32, good, a/c, cable TV, cheaper with fan; **E** *Imperial*, 3 Av SO, Barrio Torondón, opp *Nora y Max*, with bath and fan, attractive, parking; **E** *América Inc*, 1 Av NO y 2 C NO, a/c, hot water, private bath, TV, cheaper with fan; **E** *Motel Puma*, off the same Boulevard, garage parking, hot water, with bath (catering for short-stay clientèle). **E** *Quan*, 8 C NO, 3 y 4 Av, excellent, with private bath, popular; **E** *Quan Annex*. **F** *Boulevard*, small, clean, economic, dark rooms; **F** *Honduras*, 2 Av NO, 1 C, clean, friendly, some rooms with bath; **F** *Luxemburgo*, 4 Av NO y 2 C, reasonable, but no keys to the doors. **G** *Libertad*, on Parque Central, much choice of room size, clean, good restaurant two doors away. Plenty of places at **G** pp, eg *Hospedajes Tióluis* and Miramar, 1 C NO y 1 Av NO, *Hospedajes Galaxia* and *Primavera* 2 C NO y 1 Av NO by Texaco station on Panamericana by bus stop, *Hospedaje Terminal*, 2 C NO y 3 Av NO, all basic, not very clean but cheap.

Camping possible 2 km N of town, beside the stream; beware of mosquitoes.

Restaurants Parque Central is surrounded by restaurants and fast food establishments. *Hein Wong* on Parque Central, Chinese and international food, good, a/c, reasonable prices; *Flipper*, 1 Av NO y 6 C, ice cream, tacos, etc; *Juanis Burger Shop*, 1 Av NO, 5 C, near SW corner of Parque Central; *Pájaro Rojo* and *Disco La Fonda del Recuerdo*, 4 Av NO y 1 C, food good; *Palmeras*, S side of Parque Central, good breakfasts, open 0800; some food in the market. *Garfield's Pizzería*, E side of Parque Central beside Cathedral, good vegetarian pizza; *Fruty Tacos*, 4 C NO, just off SW corner of Parque Central, good snacks and licuados. In the Centro Turístico Comayagua is a restaurant, bar, disco, and swimming pool; good for cooling off and relaxing; Calle del Estadio Hispano, Barrio Arriba.

Cinema Valladolid.

Car Rental *Amigo*, on the road to Tegucigalpa and San Pedro Sula, T 72-03-71.

Exchange Banco Atlántida, Banco de Occidente, Bancahsa, Bancahorro, Banco Sogerín, Banhcafe, Ficensa, Banadesa.

Dentist Dr José de Jesús Berlioz, next to Colegio León Alvarado, T 72-00-54.

Immigration Migración is at 6 C NO, 1 Av, good place to get visas renewed, friendly.

Travel Agencies *Cramer Tours* in Pasaje Arias; *Rolando Barahona*, Avenida Central.

Bus To Tegucigalpa, US$1.20, every 45 mins, 2 hrs; to **Siguatepeque**, US$0.40 with Transpinares. To **San Pedro Sula**, US$1.80, 3 hrs, either catch a bus on the highway (very crowded) or go to Siguatepeque and change buses there.

Excursion To the coffee town of *La Libertad* (hourly bus, 2 hrs, US$0.75), several *hospedajes* and *comedores*; a friendly place. Before La Libertad is *Jamalteca* (1½ hrs by bus US$0.50), from where it is a 40-min walk to a large, deep pool into which drops a 10m waterfall surrounded by lush vegetation. Here you can swim, picnic or camp, but it is on private property and a pass must be obtained from the owner (ask at Supermercado Carol in Comayagua). Best to avoid weekends, when the owners' friends are there.

The **Parque Nacional Montaña de Comayagua** is only 13 km from Comayagua, reached from the villages of San José de la Mora (4WD necessary) or San Jerónimo and Río Negro (usually passable in 2-wheel drive). No tourist facilities exist yet, but a new office, Fundación Ecosimco, was due to open in Comayagua in 1994 (next to Cine Valladolid). The mountain, 2,407m, has about 6,000 ha of cloud forest and is a major watershed for the area.

A paved road runs S of Comayagua to *La Paz*, capital of its Department in the western part of the Comayagua valley. Population: 19,900 (altitude 690m). From the new church of the Virgen del Perpetuo Socorro, on the hill, there is a fine view of the town, the US military base, and the Comayagua Valley. The town has all paved roads, a soccer stadium and many public services thanks to ex-president Córdoba who lives there. A short road runs E from La Paz to Villa San Antonio on the highway to Tegucigalpa. 5 km from La Paz is *Ajuterique*, which has a fine colonial church, worth a visit. Bus from Comayagua, Cotrapal (opp Iglesia La Merced), every hour from 0600, US$0.30, passing Ajuterique and Lejamaní; frequent minibus Comayagua-La Paz, 25 mins, US$0.50. Lila bus from the capital, from opp Hispano cinema in Comayagüela. Colectivo taxi from main N-S highway to La Paz, US$2. In La Paz all buses leave from Boulevard crossroads, look for the statue of the soldier. Minibus to Marcala, 3 daily, 0530, 0630, 0800, 1½ hrs, US$1.

Hotels in La Paz: all **F**: *Pensión San Francisco* (quite nice); *Ali* (5 rooms, bath, hot water), eat at *Ali's Restaurant* food and lodging excellent. *Rico Lunch*, near church, good and friendly.

Exchange Bancahsa, Banco Atlántida, Banadesa.

A paved road runs SW from La Paz to Marcala (**see p 651**, frequent minibuses 2 hrs, US$1). 2 km off this road lies *San Pedro de Tutule*, the marketplace for the Indians of **Guajiquiro** (one of the few pure Indian communities in Honduras); altitude 1,400m. Market: Sun morning and Thur. (**G** *Hospedaje Valestia*, good, basic, *comedor* opposite.) From San Pedro de Tutule you can go to Guajiquiro (altitude 2,035m) and the village of *San José* (altitude 2,000m), another Lenca Indian community 1 hr 15 mins up into the mountains. The scenery is superb. In *San José*, a sleepy village, the women make rustic ceramics. (Small *hospedaje* recently opened, run by British couple, Nayo and Margarita, basic, with meals). Good hill walking. Following this road you can make a detour to Opatoro, or keep straight ahead to complete the circuit to Marcala (20 km from San José).

At the southern end of the Comayagua valley the Northern Highway ascends another forested mountainous escarpment. After about 5 km climb a track leading off to the left (ask for directions), with about half-an-hour's climb on foot to a tableland and natural fortress of *Tenampua* where Indians put up their last resistance to the *conquistadores*, even after the death of Lempira. It has an interesting wall and entrance portal.

The road continues its ascent through lovely forested heights to Zambrano (altitude 1,460m) and **Parque Aurora**, midway between Comayagua and Tegucigalpa, about 50 km from the capital. It has a small zoo and picnic area among pine-covered hills, a lake with rowing boats (hire US$1 per hour), a snack bar and lovely scenery. Good birdwatching. This spot would be perfect for camping and for caravans, which need to avoid the narrow streets and congestion of Tegucigalpa (camping US$0.50 pp, admission US$0.75, food supplies nearby). The road then descends to the vast intermont basin of *Támara*. ½ km SW of the toll station near the Balneario San Francisco is *Hotel Posada/Posada Don Willy*, F with bath (electric shower), clean, quiet, fan, excellent value. A turning right at Támara village leads to San Matías waterfall, another delightful area for walking in cool forested mountains. There is another entry to San Matías when the road S has once more climbed about 9 km NE of the capital.

FROM TEGUCIGALPA TO THE PACIFIC

From the capital to the Gulf of Fonseca, with volcanic islands and Honduras' Pacific ports, San Lorenzo and Amapala. Also, the Pan-American Highway routes to El Salvador and Nicaragua, the latter through the hot plain of Choluteca.

A paved road runs S from the capital through fine scenery. Just off the highway is Sabanagrande, with an interesting colonial church (1809, Nuestra Señora del Rosario 'Apa Kun Ka", the place of water for washing); *fiesta* La Virgen de Candelaria, 1-11 February. Further S is **Pespire**, a picturesque colonial village with a beautiful church, San Francisco, with triple domes. Pespire produces small, delicious mangoes. At **Jícaro Galán** (92 km) the road joins the Pan-American Highway, which in one direction heads W through **Nacaome**, where there is a colonial church (5 *hospedajes*; **F** *Intercontinental* in centre, basic but friendly; **G** *Suyapa*, basic, cheap), to the border with El Salvador at **Goascarán**. The road crosses the Santa Clara bridge here. A temporary pass can be purchased in Honduras for US$1.50 for a visit to the Salvadorean village of El Amatillo for an hour or so (many Hondurans cross to purchase household goods and clothes; towels are the best buy. El Amatillo appears to be on both sides of the border. Bus Tegucigalpa-El Amatillo, US$1.90, 4 hrs). This border is very relaxed, with good rates of exchange with money changers. Border closes 1700 (two cheap *hospedajes, San Andrés* and *Los Arcos* on the Honduran side).

There are hotels of a sort at Goascarán (pop 2,190), Nacaome (pop 4,475). At Jícaro Galán (pop 3,000) is *Oasis Colonial* (T 81-22-20), hotel, restaurant and pool, and an unnamed, basic guesthouse. Restaurants at all these places.

In the other direction from Jícaro Galán, the Pan-American Highway goes S to the Pacific coast (46 km) at **San Lorenzo**, on the shores of the Gulf of Fonseca (21,025 people), a dirty town. The climate on the Pacific littoral is very hot.

Hotels The only good modern hotel is the **D** *Miramar* at San Lorenzo, 26 rooms, 4 a/c, good restaurant, overpriced, in rough area, best not to walk there. Also **E** *Paramount*, and **E/F** *Perla del Pacífico*, fan, bath, charming, new block, rec. *Restaurant-Bar Henecán*, on Parque Central, a/c, good food and service, not cheap but worth it, rec. *Restaurant and Disco Don Paco*, main street.

Banks In San Lorenzo: **Bancahorro** and **Banco Atlántida** (no exchange); Chinese grocery gives good rates for US$ cash.

Frequent service of small *busitos* from Tegucigalpa to San Lorenzo (US$1) and to Choluteca (US$1.50).

The Pacific port of **Amapala** (pop 7,925), on Isla del Tigre, has been replaced by Puerto de Henecán in San Lorenzo, reached by a 3.5 km road which leaves the Pan-American Highway on the eastern edge of San Lorenzo. The Isla del Tigre is yet another place reputed to be the hiding-place of pirate treasure. In the 16th century it was visited by a number of adventurers, such as Sir Francis Drake. Amapala was capital of Honduras for a brief period in 1876, when Marco Aurelio Soto was president. Amapala has a naval base, but otherwise it is 'a charming, decaying backwater". Fishermen will take you—but not by motor launch— to San Lorenzo for a small fee: the trip takes half a day. It is possible to charter boats to La Unión in El Salvador. The deep-sea fishing in the gulf is good. *Hotel Playa Blanca*, exclusive, tiny private beach; **G** *Pensión Internacional* on the harbour, very basic, otherwise only local accommodation of low standard; ask for Doña Marianita, who rents the first floor of her house, F; *Al Mar*, above Playa Grande, fan, scorpions, lovely view of mountains and sunset. Bancahorro on Parque Central; several clean *comedores* in the new Mercado Municipal; *Restaurant-Bar Miramar* by the harbour, overlooking the sea, pleasant, good meals when the fish catch is brought in. Swimming at Playa Grande, black sand, 40 mins walk from Amapala. The 1,000m volcano-like hill on the island has a road to the summit, where there is a US army unit and a DEA contingent. You can walk round the island in half a day.

A 31 km road leaves the Pan-American Highway 2 km W of San Lorenzo, signed to Coyolito. It passes through scrub and mangrove swamps before crossing a causeway to a hilly island, around which it winds to the jetty at **Coyolito** (no *hospedajes* but a *comedor* and *refrescarías*). Motorized launches sail between Coyolito and Ampala, US$0.35 pp when launch is full (about 10 passengers), about US$4 to hire a launch (but you will probably have to pay for the return as well). First boat leaves Amapala at 0700 to connect with first Coyolito-San Lorenzo bus at 0800; next bus from Coyolito at 0900.

The Pan-American Highway runs SE from San Lorenzo past Choluteca and San Marcos de Colón to the Nicaraguan border at El Espino, on the Río Negro. The Pan-American Highway's total length in Honduras is 151 km: 40 km Goascarán-Jícaro Galán, 111 km Jícaro Galán-El Espino.

Choluteca, 34 km from San Lorenzo in the plain of Choluteca, has a population of 87,889, expanding rapidly. Coffee, cotton and cattle are the local industries. The town was one of the earliest foundations in Honduras (1535) and has still a colonial centre. The church of La Merced (1643) is being renovated and will be reconsecrated before the end of the 1990s. The Casa de la Cultura and Biblioteca Municipal are in the colonial house of José Cecilio del Valle on the corner of the Parque Central. The social centre of San José Obrero is at 3 Calle SO; handicrafts can be bought there. Look out for carved wood, especially chairs. A fine steel suspension bridge crosses the broad river at the entrance into Choluteca from the N (it was built in 1937). The local feast day, of the Virgen de la Concepción, 8 December begins a week of festivities, followed by the Festival del Sur, 'Ferisur", which attracts many visitors from Tegucigalpa. The climate is very hot; there is much poverty here.

Hotels C *La Fuente*, Carretera Panamericana, past the bridge, T 82-02-53/63, F 82-02-73, with bath, rec, swimming pool, a/c, meals, souvenir shop; one block away is **D** *Imperio Maya*, T 82-35-25, F 82-29-00, a/c, restaurant, bar, pool; opp is *Restaurant Conquistador*, a bit pricey, but changes money for customers; **D/E** *Pierre*, Av Valle y C Williams, T 82-06-76, with bath (ants in the taps), a/c or fan, TV, free protected parking, cafetería has good but expensive breakfasts, very central, credit cards accepted, rec; **D** *Camino Real*, road to Guasaule, T 82-06-10, F 82-28-60, swimming pool, good steaks in restaurant, rec; **F** *Lisboa*, 3 Calle NO, in the centre, just W of market, T 82-03-55, some with bath, pleasant patio, rec, laundry facilities, clean; **E** *Pacífico*, near Mi Esperanza terminal, outside the city, clean, quiet, safe parking, water supply 'algal", breakfast US$1.50; **F** *Rosita*, with bath, G without, very basic, friendly, modest *comedor*; **F** *Colonial*, main street in centre, clean; *Tomalag*, moderately priced with bath and fan; **F** *Hibueras*, with bath and fan, clean, purified water, *comedor* attached, good value, Av Bojorque; **F** *San Carlos*, with shower, fan, very clean, pleasant, Paz Barahona 757, Barrio El Centro; *Hotel Brazabola*, Barrio Cabañas.

Restaurants *El Conquistador*, on Panamericana, opp *La Fuente*, steaks etc, outdoor seating, good; *Palace Imperial*, around corner on Boulvard, Chinese, a/c, inexpensive, good; *Alondra*, Parque Central, old colonial house, open Fri-Sun only; *Comedor Central*, opp side of Parque, *comida corriente* daily specials, *licuados*, sandwiches, good for breakfast. Local specialities are the drinks *posole* and *horchata de morro*.

Shopping and Services Mercado Municipal, 7 Av SO, 3 Calle SO, on outskirts. Post Office (0800-1700, 0800-1200 on Sat, US$0.15 per letter for poste restante; telephone collect calls to Spain, Italy, USA only). **Banco de Honduras, Banco Atlántida, Banco de Occidente** (Blvd Choluteca) and other local banks (open 0800-1630, and on Sat 0830-1130 or 1200). Travel agency Trans Mundo. The Texaco service station is just before the bridge.

The **El Salvadorean Consulate** is to S of town, fast and friendly, open 0800-1500 daily.

Bus to El Espino (Nicaraguan border) from Choluteca, US$1.15, 1 hr, first at 0700, last at 1400. Also frequent minibuses to El Amatillo (El Salvador border) via San Lorenzo. Buses to Choluteca from Tegucigalpa with Mi Esperanza, Bonanza and El Dandy; Bonanza continue to San Marcos and depart Tegucigalpa hourly from 0530, 4 hrs to Choluteca, US$1.90. The municipal bus terminal is about 10 blocks from the new municipal market, about 8 blocks from Cathedral/Parque Central; Mi Esperanza has its own terminal 1 block from municipal terminal. Taxis will wait at the border post as you go through the formalities and then take you into Nicaragua.

An hour's drive from Choluteca over a paved road (deteriorates after Punta Ratón turn-off) leads to **Cedeño** beach, rough accommodation, eg **F** *Miramar*, reasonable, very noisy, loud music; *Cintia*; *Dunia*; all on beach; basic *hospedaje* on main street. Many restaurants on beach, some open only at weekends; *El Tiburón* is popular; *El Ranchito*; and others. A lovely though primitive spot, with clean sand stretching for miles and thundering surf; avoid public holiday and weekend crowds. Take a good insect repellent. Spectacular views and sunsets over the Gulf of Fonseca S to Nicaragua and W to El Salvador, with the volcanic islands in the bay. The turning for Cedeño is 13 km W of Choluteca. Hourly bus from Choluteca, US$0.60 (1 hr). A turn off leads from the Choluteca- Cedeño road to Ratón beach, much more pleasant than Cedeño, bus from Choluteca 1130, returns next morning.

Beyond Choluteca is a long climb to *San Marcos de Colón*, 915m in the hills (a clean, tidy town of 9,570 people). 3 *pensiones* in San Marcos: **E** *Colonial*, friendly, clean; **F** *Hotelito Mi Esperanza*, one block W of Banco Atlántida, near the bus terminal, 17 rooms, nice, friendly; **F** *Hospedaje Flores*, friendly, clean, cell-like rooms, washing facilities, breakfast and typical dinner, good, exchange. Restaurant: *Pollos Bonanza*, near main square, clean, good food, not just chicken dishes. Buses from Choluteca throughout the day, US$0.75, 1½ hrs; buses from Tegucigalpa, Mi Esperanza, 6 Av 23 or 26 C, Comayagüela and Bonanza, 5 a day from 0530, US$2, 5 hrs.

6 km beyond San Marcos the road enters Nicaragua at *El Espino* (altitude 890m); immigration is 100m from the border. Taxis/minibuses run from Choluteca and San Marcos to the border. Border closes between 1600 and 0800 (open till 1630 on the Nicaraguan side). Beware of taxis offering to take you to the border arriving after 1600. From the border to Tegucigalpa, there is a direct bus through Choluteca, with Empresa Mi Esperanza, 4 hrs. Exchange is easy at the border for dollars, córdobas, Costa Rican colones, Salvadorean colones, but the rate for buying córdobas is better on the Nicaraguan side. Border formalities can be tedious at El Espino.

There is an alternative road from Choluteca to Nicaragua through *El Triunfo* to the border at the bridge over the Río Guasaule. The bridge was washed away by floods in 1982 and was closed until 1991 when a temporary bridge was opened. A permanent bridge is being constructed (1993-94). Bus Choluteca-Guasaule US$0.50, 1½ hrs. A through route to Chinandega is now possible, but several rivers have to be forded. Check conditions in wet season. Note that the Nicaraguan border closes 1200-1330 (and is 1 hr ahead of Honduras).

EAST OF TEGUCIGALPA

The alternative route to Nicaragua, through Danlí and Las Manos: off this road is a detour to old mining centres in the hills.

A good paved road runs E from Tegucigalpa to Danlí, 121 km away, in the Department of El Paraíso. Some 40 km along, in the Zamorano valley (**see p 619**), is the Escuela Agrícola Panamericana run for all students of the Americas with US help; it has a fine collection of tropical flowers. At **Zamorano** turn off up a narrow winding road for about 5 km to the picturesque old mining village of **San Antonio de Oriente**, much favoured by Honduran painters such as Velásquez (it has a beautiful church). Direct bus from Tegucigalpa at 0630, return trip 0400, US$1.75.

Huw Clough and Kate Hennessy describe the hike to San Antonio del Oriente: Take a bus to Zamorano (see below under Danlí **Buses**, but from outside the right side of the Jacaleapa market as you look at it, almost hourly, 40 mins). At Zamorano the bus will drop you off a few 100m before the road junction to San Antonio, from where a small path on the left goes through some trees for 10 mins before joining the main dirt road. From here on up it is a winding, rocky route through tall, thin pine woods, rising quickly for an impressive view of the broad, flat valley. After about 40 mins the main road turns sharply to the right, while a smaller track continues in roughly the same direction along the left-hand slope of a mountain. If you go to the right this leads to San Antonio del Oriente after a fairly long climb for an hour. If it is sunny, the path is dusty and glaring and there is little shade in the middle of the day. But reaching the village is a fine reward: red-tiled roofs and white plastered walls clinging to the hillside, with a very quaint little church overlooking the valley. There is one *pulpería* at this very peaceful, unspoilt village From here, a steep, 15-min climb over the ridge leads to San Antonio del Occidente, an even simpler, smaller village (also with one tiny *pulpería*). A much shorter (about 30 mins) walk from San Antonio del Occidente down the other side of the mountain comes back to the junction mentioned above. The hike can be done in reverse, which is probably easier. It is little problem to hitch back to Tegucigalpa.

From Zamorano, a road goes to **Güinope** (**G** *Merlin*, with bath, clean, good value; *Comedor Lilian*, down side street; snack bar next to bus office on Parque Central). A pretty, white, dusty town with a church (1820) whose façade is charming. The town is famed for its oranges and jam; try the orange wine 'La Trilla", matured in oak barrels, US$2.50 per bottle. Good walking in the area. *Fiesta*, Festival de la Naranja, at the end of March. Bus from Tegucigalpa, mercado Jacaleapa, first at 0730, from Güinope at 0515, frequent service. Some buses to Güinope continue S to San Lucas and San Antonio de Flores.

15 km further E, a paved road branches S to **Yuscarán**, in rolling pine-land country at 1,070m (**F** *Hotel Carol*, 6 modern rooms with bath and hot water, annex to owner's fine colonial house, safe, family atmosphere, good value; *Cafetería Colonial*, opp Banco de Occidente, which changes cash and TCs, excellent *desayuno típico* and *comida corrida*). Population, 9,270. The climate here is semi-tropical. Yuscarán was an important mining centre in colonial days and is a picturesque, typically Spanish colonial village, with cobbled streets and houses on a steep hillside. Ask to see the museum near the town plaza, you have to ask around to find the person who has the key, antiques and photographs displayed in a restored mansion which belonged to a mining family. The Yuscarán distilleries, one in the centre, the other on the outskirts, are considered by many to produce the best *aguardiente* in Honduras (tours possible). Cardomom plantations are being developed here. The Montserrat mountain which looms over Yuscarán is riddled with mines. The old Guavias mine is close to Yuscarán, some 4 km along the road to Agua Fría. About 10 km further along this road, a narrow, winding road climbs steeply through pine woods to the summit of *Pico Montserrat* (1,891m), with fine views all around. The summit of Montserrat is the **Reserva Biológica de Yuscarán**. Frequent buses to Zamorano and Tegucigalpa; from the capital buses leave from Mercado Jacaleapa. For information, ask anyone

in the Parque Central in Yuscarán.

Danlí (pop 30,000, 102 km from Tegucigalpa), a pleasant town at an altitude of 760m, is noted for sugar and coffee production, a large meat-packing company (Orinsa), and is a centre of the tobacco industry. There are 4 cigar factories; visit the Honduras-América SA factory (right-hand side of Ciné Aladino) and purchase export quality cigars at good prices (open Mon-Fri, 0800-1200, 1300-1700, Sat 0800-1200), or Placencia Tabacos, on the road to Tegucigalpa to see cigar-making. Museo de Cabildo in the town hall on the Parque Central has a 'funky collection of ancient bric-à-brac, presided over by an elderly curator who is a mine of information about the town and its history' (free). Its *fiesta* lasts all of the 3rd week of August (Fiesta del Maíz, with cultural and sporting events, all-night street party on the Saturday); it is very crowded with people from Tegucigalpa. One road continues from Danlí to Santa María (several buses daily), crossing a mountain range with panoramic views. Another poor road (but being paved in 1993) goes S 18 km to ***El Paraíso*** (124 km from the capital; pop 27,291), from which a connecting paved road, 12 km, links with the Nicaraguan road network at Las Manos/Ocotal. El Paraíso is a picturesque town in an area producing coffee, bananas and rice. This is the best of the three routes from Tegucigalpa to the Nicaraguan border. The border is open 0800-1600, exchange sometimes runs out of córdobas.

Hotels at Danlí Centro Turístico Granada with **C/D** *Gran Hotel Granada*, T 93-24-99, F 93-27-74, bar, restaurant and swimming pool, locals pay half price of non-nationals, rec; **F** *Apólo*, El Canal, next to Shell station, with bath, clean, basic; **E** *La Esperanza*, Gabriela Mistral, next to Esso station, bath, hot water, fan (more with a/c), TV, drinking water, friendly, good car parking; **F** *Danlí*, Calle El Canal, opp *Apólo*, without bath, good; **F** *Las Vegas*, next to bus terminal, noisy, restaurant, washing facilities, parking; **F** *Regis*, 3 blocks N of Plaza Central, with bath, car park, basic; **F** *Hospedaje San Jorge*, 1 block from *La Esperanza*, shared bath, basic, clean, friendly; **F** *Xalli*, Barrio Pueblo Nuevo, 4 blocks from bus terminal, with bath, cheap, basic; **F** *Eben Ezer*, 3½ blocks N of Shell station, T 93-26-35, basic, hot showers.

Restaurants *Pepylus*, very good food at reasonable prices; *Rancho Típico* nr *Hotel Danlí*, excellent; *Pizzería Picolino*, 2 blocks SW of Parque Central, good pizzas, pleasant atmosphere; *McBeth's*, snackbar, good ice cream. *Nan-kin 2*, Chinese. *Rodeo*, good food and service. *El Gaucho* and *España*, in the centre of town, are good.

Hotels at El Paraíso **E-F** *5a Av Hotel y Restaurant*, with bath, hot water, parking, restaurant specializes in Mexican-American food; **F** *Florida*; **F** *Lendy's*, clean, friendly, prepares food; **F** *Recreo*, neither recommended, lacking most basic facilities. There are others, but better stay in Danlí, 18 km away by road. **Restaurant** *Comedor Edith*, on a small square on main road, after Parque Central towards border, US$0.85 for a meal.

Exchange in both towns, Bancahsa, Banco Atlántida, Banadesa, Bancahorro, Banhcafé, Banco Sogerín.

Dentist in Danlí: Dr Juan Castillo, Barrio El Centro, T 93-20-83.

Buses To Danlí, US$1.20, from Blvd Miraflores near Mercado Jacaleapa (from left hand side of market as you face it), Colonia Kennedy, Tegucigalpa, hourly, 2 hrs, arrive 1½ hrs before you intend to leave, long slow queues for tickets (take 'Kennedy' bus from Calle La Isla near the football stadium in central Tegucigalpa, or taxi, US$1.20, to Mercado Jacaleapa); minibuses run from Danlí terminal to El Paraíso, frequent (0600 to 1740), US$0.40, 30 mins, don'T believe taxi drivers who say there are no minibuses. Emtra Oriente, Av 6, C 6-7, runs 4 times a day to El Paraíso, 2½ hrs, US$1.50; irregular buses from El Paraíso to Las Manos, US$0.30, 30 mins, or taxi US$4, many people willing to share, 15 mins bumpy ride.

From Danlí to the N is Cerro San Cristóbal and the beautiful Lago San Julián; to the S Piedra de Apagüizto.

NORTH-EAST OF TEGUCIGALPA

Through the agricultural and cattle lands of Olancho a road runs to Trujillo on the Caribbean coast. Reachable only by air or sea is Honduras' Mosquitia coast with rivers and swamps, coastal lagoons,

tropical forests and very few people.

The Carretera de Olancho runs from the capital to the Río Guayape, 143 km. By the river crossing at **Los Limones** is an unpaved road N to **La Unión**, through beautiful forests and lush green countryside. One unnamed *hospedaje* in La Unión (no electricity in town). 14 km N is the **Refugio de Vida Silvestre La Muralla-Los Higuerales**, where quetzales can be seen in March-May in the cloud forest. The refuge comprises the three peaks of La Muralla, 1,981m, Las Parras, 2,064m and Los Higuerales, 1,985m. Park entrance fee US$1. Cohdefor has a campamento, F (T 22-10-27 for prior arrangements), or there is accommodation for 1-2 at the visitor's centre. Buses from Comayaguela to La Unión, daily, take 4 hrs. (If driving from San Pedro Sula, take the road E through Yoro and Mangulile; from La Ceiba, take the Savá-Olanchito road and turn S 13 km before Olanchito.)

The main road continues another 50 km from Los Limones to **Juticalpa** (capital of Olancho department), at 420m above sea-level in a rich agricultural area, herding cattle and growing cereals and sugar-cane. Population 74,000. Airfield. There is a paved road NE through the cattle land of Catacamas, continuing to just beyond Dulce Nombre de Culmi. The road from Juticalpa to Trujillo on the coast is described on the next page.

Hotels at Juticalpa D *Antúñez*, 1 Calle NO y 1 Av NO, a block W of Parque Central, T 95-2250, with bath, E without, friendly, clean, also annex in same street (E without bath); **E** *El Paso*, 1 Av NE y 6 C No, 6 blocks S of Parque, T 95-2311, quiet, clean, bath, fan, rec; **E** *Las Vegas*, 1 Av NE, T 95-2700, central, ½ block N of Parque, cafetería, clean, friendly; **F** *Regis*, 1 Calle NO, good value; **F** *Familiar*, 1 Calle NO between Parque and Antúñez, with bath, clean, basic but rec; **F** *Hotelito Granada*, 5 mins from bus station on left side of main road to town centre, basic but rooms are large and clean; **G** *Juticalpa*, clean, basic, shared showers, friendly owner.

Restaurants *El Centro*, 2 Calle NO, *Dino's Pizzeria* on Parque Central; *Asia*, Chinese food, also on Parque Central; *La Galera*, 2 Av NE, specializes in *pinchos*; *Casa Blanca*, 1 Calle SE, quite smart with a good cheap menu; *El Rancho*, 2 Av NE specializes in meat dishes, wide menu, pleasant; *Comedor Any*, 1a Av, NO, good value, friendly; *El Tablado*, 1 Av NE entre 3 y 4 Calles NO, good fish, bar.

Exchange Local banks: **Bancahsa** (the only one that will change TCs, with insistence), **Banco Atlántida, Bancahorro, Banco de los Trabajadores, Banco de Occidente, Banco Sogerín.**

Telephones Hondutel on main street, 1 block from Parque Central.

Post Office 2 blocks from bus station, hard to find.

Bus station is on 1 Av NE, 1 km SE of Parque Central, taxis US$0.50. Hourly to **Tegucigalpa** from 0330 to 1800, see below; bus to **San Esteban** from opp Aurora bus terminal at 0800, 6 hrs, US$2.25. Bus to **Trujillo** dep 0400, 9 hrs, US$5.20. Bus to **Tocoa** at 0500.

Catacamas, 210 km from Tegucigalpa, is in the Río Guayape valley, altitude 400m, at the foot of the Agalta Mountains in the Department of Olancho. It is an agricultural and cattle-raising district with the National School of Agriculture (ENA) in town, and El Sembrador school, which offers room and board. The Río Guayape (named after an Indian dress, *guayapis*) is famous for the gold nuggets found in it. During the hot months, the banks near the bridge are a popular bathing place, at Paso del Burro on the way to San Pedro Catacamas. From February to May you can taste the *vino de coyol*, extracted from a palm (a hole is made at the top of the trunk and the sap which flows out is drunk neat). With sugar added it becomes alcoholic (*chicha*), so strong it is called *patada de burro* (mule kick). *Fiesta* St Francis of Assisi, 4 October. Near Catacamas is the Río Talgua with interesting caves; worth a visit.

Hotels All **F** *Central*, in Barrio El Centro; *Juan Carlos*, rec, good restaurant, Barrio José Trinidad Cábanas; *Catacamas*, Blvd Las Acacias; *La Colina*; *Rápalo*, Barrio San Sebastián.

Restaurants *Ice and Chicken's*, Calle del Comercio; *La Cascada*, good food; *El Rodeo*; *Los Castaños*. One **discotheque**, *Tacumaca*.

Banks Bancahsa, Barrio El Centro; Banhcafé, W side of park; branches of 4 other local banks.

Bus Tegucigalpa to Juticalpa/Catacamas, Empresa Aurora, 8 C 615, Av Morazán, hourly 0400-1700, 2½ hrs US$2 to Juticalpa, 3½ hrs US$2.75 to Catacamas. Bus Catacamas-**Dulce Nombre de Culmí** (see below), 3 hrs, US$1.35, several daily.

Excursion Hiking to El Boquerón. Stop off at the main road near Punuare and walk up Río Olancho, which has nice limestone cliffs and a pretty river canyon. Through much of the canyon the stream flows underground. Hiking in the mountains behind Catacamas is very beautiful. From Murmullo there are trails to coffee farms.

Beyond Catacamas, a rough road continues NE up the Río Tinto valley to **Dulce Nombre de Culmí**, *Hospedaje Tania*, G, very basic, on the main street, several *comedores* on the main square. Some 34 km further on is Paya where the road becomes a mule track but in 3-4 days in the dry season a route can be made over the divide (Cerro de Will) and down the Río Paulaya to Mosquitia (see next section). Local police say that there is a path in the dry season from Dulce Nombre to San Esteban (about 30 km).

The bus service from Juticalpa to Trujillo (see p 629), leaves at 1200, 8 hrs, US$2, usually packed; it goes via **San Francisco de la Paz** and **San Esteban** (*Hotel San Esteban*, G, very friendly, clean; 3 nice *comedores* nearby); it passes through interesting scenery. Petrol filling stations at both towns.

The route by road from Tegucigalpa to Trujillo is 403 km via Talanga, San Diego (restaurant *El Arriero*), Los Limones and Juticalpa (it is not recommended to drive this road at night, holdups reported). After Juticalpa, take the turn off, where the paved road ends, to San Francisco de la Paz. Beyond San Francisco is **Gualaco**, which has an interesting colonial church; from here to San Esteban you pass Agalta mountain and some of the highest points in Honduras, and the waterfalls on the Babilonia river.

After San Esteban the road continues to **Bonito Oriental** (via El Carbón, a mahogany collection point with Paya Indian communities in the vicinity). There are two hotels here. The final 38 km from Bonito Oriental to Trujillo are paved, through Corocito. There are many dirt roads between San Francisco and Trujillo. If driving, ask directions if in any doubt. Fuel is available in each big village, but there is none between San Francisco and Bonito Oriental (90 km).

Between the roads Juticalpa-Gualaco-San Esteban and Juticalpa-Catacamas-Dulce Nombre de Culmí lies the cloudforest of the **Parque Nacional Sierra de Agalta**, extending over 1,200 ha and reaching a height of 2,354m at Monte de Babilonia. Several different ecosystems have been found with a wide variety of fauna and flora: 200 species of birds have been identified so far. There are several points of entry. Contact Cohdefor in Juticalpa, Culmí, Gualaco, San Esteban or Catacamas for information on access, maps, guides, mules, lodging etc. There is no infrastructure in the park, but a base camp is being built. A good trail leads to La Picucha mountain, the highest in E Honduras (2,354m); access strictly on foot, hiking time 2 days. From Gualaco you can hike in 4-5 days up Mt Babilonia (spectacular views over Olancho and Mosquitia); from La Venta you can visit the double waterfall of the Río Babilonia, another track from the E side skirts the flank of Montaña de Malacate.

Mosquitia is the name given to the region in the far NE of the country, which is forested, swampy and almost uninhabited, but well worth visiting. The western boundary of Mosquitia is Cabo Camarón near Plaplaya and the mouth of the Río Sico. Apart from the one road that stretches 100 km from Puerto Lempira to Leymus and a further 100 km to Ahuasbila, both on the Río Coco, there are no roads in the Honduran Mosquitia.

How to Get There By plane from **Tegucigalpa**: Setco flies Tues and Thur to Mocorón and Puerto Lempira, US$64 one way, US$120 return, T 33-17-11/2; agent in Mocorón is Charly (who also has a restaurant), and in Puerto Lempira the wife of Federico, the local mechanic. Alas de Socorro fly on Tues to Ahuas, and other days if they happen to have a flight there; T 33-70-25. This company charters planes for US$565, but it is cheaper to go as a passenger, one way to Ahuas US$60.

From **La Ceiba**, by plane: Sosa lands in Brus Laguna and Puerto Lempira three times a week; US$40-45, T 43-13-99 (La Ceiba). Isleña has daily (ex Sun) Puerto Lempira flights at similar prices, T 41-01-79/43-23-54.

Coastal vessels leave irregularly from La Ceiba to Brus Laguna and Puerto Lempira and back (2-3 day journey), carrying passengers and cargo. Information is available from the Mopawi office in La Ceiba, near the pier and the railway track, or at the pier itself. Essential equipment: torch.

La Moskitia Ecoaventuras, PO Box 3577, Tegucigalpa, T/F 37-93-98, specializes in tours and expeditions in Mosquitia.

Transport inside Mosquitia Many places can only be reached by plane, boat or on foot. SAMi flies to various villages from Puerto Lempira, for example Ahuas, Brus Laguna, Belén. There are expensive express flights to places like Auka, Raya, Kaukira. Alas de Socorro operates from Ahuas to collect sick people from villages to take them to Ahuas hospital, contact the Moravian church (in Puerto Lempira Reverend Stanley Goff, otherwise local pastors will help).

At **Puerto Lempira** on the large Caratasca Lagoon are **D** *Gran Hotel Flores*, some rooms with bath, rec; *Villas Caratascas*, new, huts with bath, restaurant, disco, prices not yet established; **F** *Pensión Moderno* (good, friendly, electricity 1800-2230), and inferior **F** *Pensión Santa Teresita*. Restaurants: *La Moquitia*, Centro Comercial Segovia in main street, breakfasts and cheap fish; *Glorieta*, left of landing bridge, fish, lagoon breezes; *Delmy*, 3 blocks N of main street, chicken and other dishes, noisy; *Doña Aida*, N side of main road to landing bridge, fresh orange juice; *Quinto Patio*, good breakfasts. Discoteca *Hampu*, by landing bridge. Banco Nacional de Desarrollo Agrícola changes dollars at poor rates, bad reputation. In Puerto Lempira is the main office of Mopawi, an organization promoting development of Mosquitia; write to Apdo 2175, Tegucigalpa, T 32-64-74. The airstrip is only 5 mins walk from town.

Regular *tuk-tuks* (motorized canoes) cross the lagoon to Kaukira, US$1.20 (a nice place, but no hotels or anything), Yagurabila and Palkaka. The *tuk-tuks* leave Kaukira daily, except Sun, at 0500, returning during the morning. In the afternoon the lagoon is usually too rough to cross.

Inland from Puerto Lempira are **Mocorón**; a pick up is supposed to leave around 0800 most days (*Charly's* restaurant—see above—rooms available F pp) and Rus Rus which may be visited with difficulty (in terms of getting transport, any vehicle will give a lift); a beautiful, quiet village (accommodation at Friends of America hospital's house; meals from *Capi's* next door, ask Friends about transport out).

It is a 15-min scenic flight above Caratasca Lagoon and grassy, pine-covered savannas to **Ahuas**, 1 hr's walk from the Patuca River (fabled for gold). There is a hospital here. **F** *Hospedaje y Comedor Suyapa*, basic, no electricity, meals, US$1.25; mosquito repellent and coils absolutely essential here. Irregular *cayucos* sail down to **Brus Laguna** (Brewer's Lagoon) for US$2.50, at one mouth of the Patuca River, or US$12.50 (15-mins) scenic flight in the mission plane. The airstrip is 4 km from village, take a lift for US$1. George Goff rents rooms (good but basic, limited electricity, G) and his wife Elga cooks tasty meals for US$1, he speaks English and will also help with mission-plane flights. Behind his house is a *hospedaje* being built by the 'Medio-Francés', Colindre (who speaks English, German, French, 'Scandinavian' and Spanish); he operates tours on the Brus Lagoon and Río Plátano (can pick up people in La Ceiba if requested). Food and lodging only to those on tour with him. Write to him: Sr Colindre, Brus Laguna, Gracias a Dios, Honduras. Meals generally to be ordered in advance, try *Hospedaje Cruz* or Doña Norma, Doña Aurora or Doña Gladys. There is a disco at the riverside to the left of the bridge. Plague of mosquitoes for all but 5 months of the year (winter and spring). Two tiny hilly islands near the entrance to the wide lagoon were hideouts where pirates once lurked. It is better to fly direct from Ahuas via Brus and the mouth of the Plátano River to mosquito-free **Cocobila** (Belén), picturesquely situated on a sandspit between the ocean and huge, sweetwater Ibans Lagoon. Excellent meals (US$1.25) with Miss Erlinda; ask at the Mopawi office about accommodation. Boats go to **Plaplaya** at the mouth of the Río Negro or Sico (bad mosquitoes and 'niguas' which burrow into the soles of your feet), or walk the distance in over 2 hrs along the beach. Malaria is endemic in this area; take anti-malaria precautions. Room and meals with Doña Evritt de Woods at Plaplaya. Boats to La Ceiba, or up the Río Sico to Sico. Plátano village at the mouth of the Río Plátano can be reached by lobster boat from Guanaja or by the supply ships from La Ceiba to Brus Laguna (in all cases *cayucos* take passengers from ship to shore); Plátano-Brus Laguna, 1½ hrs, US$2.50, Plátano-La Ceiba, US$17.50.

The **Río Plátano Preserve** was established by the UN and the Honduran government in 1980 to protect the outstanding natural and cultural resources of the Río Plátano valley and environs. The tropical jungles that still cloak the landscape here shelter a number of endangered birds, mammals, and fish, among them scarlet macaws and harpy eagles, jaguars and tapirs, and the cuyamel, a prized food fish going extinct throughout Honduras. In addition, there are a number of archaeological sites about which little is known, and the fabled lost White City of the Maya is said to be hidden somewhere in the thick jungles of the Plátano headwaters.

Miskito and Paya (who call themselves 'Pech") Indians living along the lower Plátano cultivate yuca, bananas, rice, corn, and beans, as well as hunting and fishing. The upper (southern) portion of the Plátano watershed was virgin jungle until quite recently, but is being quickly populated by *mestizo* immigrants from the poverty-stricken S of Honduras. These new residents are cutting down the forest to plant crops, hunting wildlife mercilessly, and using homemade dynamite in a very destructive form of fishing. Given the pressure the Preserve is under, it is recommended to visit it sooner rather than later.

To get there, you can fly or take one of the boats that periodically leave from La Ceiba and Trujillo to either Palacios, Cocobila/Belén or Barra Río Plátano, the main villages in the vicinity of the river mouth. Expect to pay perhaps US$25 for passage from Ceiba. A boat from Palacios to Cocobila/Belén cost US$3 pp, US$20 for the whole boat. From Belén to the Biosphere headquarters in Kuri it is a 45 min walk or 10 min ride (US$2). The staff and locals are friendly and the staff or the teacher (of the few who can speak Spanish) can probably put you up for the night. They can also help you contract with a *tuk-tuk* (motorized dug-out canoe) to carry you upriver as far as **Las Marías**, the Miskito-Pech village that is the limit of upstream settlement. The cost is about US$100 one way, regardless of the number of passengers (up to 6) and takes 10 hrs (3-4 downstream). The journey upstream, although beautiful, can become very tedious and painful on the back and backside. Birdwatching can provide diversion; there are 3 species of toucan, tanagers, herons, kingfishers, vultures, hawk eagles, oropendolas. If lucky you may see crocodiles or iguanas.

Once in Las Marías, it is possible to contract villagers for trips upstream in a *pipante*. This is a shallow dugout canoe manoeuvered with poles called *palancas* and paddles (*canaletes*): remarkably graceful. Each *pipante* can carry up to two passengers and their gear, plus three villagers who pole it upstream. The cost per day to rent *pipante* and crew is about US$12.50 per passenger (negotiable). It is also possible to take an excursion into the forest for 4, or 8 hrs. The walk (or run, it's taken very briskly) is an interesting way to see neotropical jungle, but do not expect to see much wildlife. High prices are charged for everything in Las Marías, but remember that it is their only source of income. On your return, use the radio in Kuri to call Palacios for a boat to fetch you in Belén and don'T forget to reserve a flight out of Palacios if you need one. On any trip take drinking water, or water purifiers, food, insect repellent, sun protection for boat journeys and camping gear.

The rainy season is from June-December: it is harder to advance upriver then.

Palacios, situated in the next lagoon W of Plaplaya has few mosquitoes; cannons are relics of an old English fort. Room for US$2.50 with Felix Marmol (information on boats to lagoons) and meals for US$1. A 7-room *hospedaje* has been built by Trek de Honduras, accommodation for 14 guests, electricity, filtered water, restaurant, 5-day tours (including fishing expeditions) arranged out of La Ceiba; T 38-19-44/5, Trek de Honduras, or USA 1-800-654-9915, Trek International. Alternatively, the local teacher may let you sleep at the school. There are daily flights to Palacios from La Ceiba with Isleña/Sosa, US$25 one way. Two boats, the *Margarita* and the *Sheena Dee* sail irregularly from La Ceiba to Palacios.

One can also cross the lagoon by *cayuco* (US$0.50) from Palacios to the Black Carib village of Batalla, from which it is 112 km W along beach to Limón (see below). Trips down the Río Plátano are possible, boats very expensive and have to be arranged through Felix Marmol. Trips can go as far as Las Marías (see above).

One can take a picturesque *cayuco* trip from Plaplaya and from Palacios up the Río Sico for US$50 for a hired trip or about US$6 if you can get a lift on a cargo *cayuco* to **Sico** village (contact Mr Carlos Mejía who speaks perfect English and has basic rooms to rent, G, his wife Ofelia sells meals for US$1, also possible food and meals with David Jones). At Sico the remains of a railway built in the late 1920s by a banana company can be seen, including the pillars of a bridge over the river. This was abandoned after disastrous floods in the 1930s. There is no public electricity or piped water in Sico but 2 schools, a health centre and alligators in the river. A strenuous 32 km walk from Sico may be made (only in dry months from March to May) up forested Río Paulaya Valley to stay with Mundo Jones, whose father mined gold here for 60 years and on eventually to Dulce Nombre de Culmí (see above). For notes on Nicaraguan Mosquitia, **see Nicaragua, The Caribbean Coast**.

The beach route out of Mosquitia from Palacios/Batalla is gruelling, past *morenales*, or Black Carib villages (honest, friendly) of Tocoamacho (meals available, boats to Palacios, Reverend Donald Grable is a godsend to benighted travellers), Sangrelaya (2 rooms available, G, a woman opposite cooks meals, Catholic mission, ask Max to take you to Tocoamacho by canoe, fix price first, nice trip down river but make sure you don'T go out into the sea), Iriona Siraboya (dry weather walk from here across forested mountain to Sico River, and downriver to Sico village) and Cusuna. From Cusuna it is a short distance to **Punto de Piedra** (*pensión*, G) from where you can get a boat to Sangrelaya (see above). From Punto de Piedra there is a track over to the Río Sico (which at this point is quite close to the coast) at Los Fales and a road of sorts to **Icoteya** further up river but also on the Río Sico. From Icoteya the Río Sico is navigable downstream to Sico village past the farms of Los Fales, Los Naranjos, Los Andes etc. Here and there they occasionally wash for gold. *Cayucos* can be hired, though expensive.

It is also possible to go on foot/horseback along the river from Sico to Los Fales, known locally as the 'Camino Real'.

From Icoteya there are two buses daily to Tocoa through Limoncito (for Limón on the coast) and Francia. In dry weather the bus coming from Tocoa terminates at Punto de Piedra; so far the road on to Iriona is suitable for pick-ups, but no buses run on it. Alternatively, you can walk along the beach from Punto de Piedra around the beautiful forested headland of Farellones to Limón, but it is about 40 'interminable' kilometres. There are buses from La Ceiba to Limoncito and Limón. At **Limón** there is a fine, clean beach, with lovely swimming; accommodation is available at *Hospedaje Martínez* (also serves meals) and there is a friendly *comedor*, *Bar-Restaurant Kerolyn*. This is a Spanish-speaking Garífuna community. 2 buses a day Trujillo-Limón, first at 0830, continuing to Punto de Piedra and Cusuna; from Limón, several buses daily to Tocoa and La Ceiba. The road between Cusuna and Bonito Oriental is good, all-weather, as is the 3 km side road to Limón.

INFORMATION FOR VISITORS

Documents A visa is not required, nor tourist card, for nationals of all West European countries, USA, Canada, Australia, New Zealand, or Japan. Citizens of other countries need either a tourist card which can be bought from Honduran consulates for US$2-3, occasionally less, or a visa, and they should enquire at a Honduran consulate in advance to see which they need. The price of a visa seems to vary per nationality, and according to where bought. It is imperative to check entry requirements in advance at a consulate. 2-day transit visas costing US$5, for any travellers it seems, are given at the El Florido border for visiting Copán, but you must leave at the same point and your right of return to Guatemala is not guaranteed, especially if your Guatemalan visa is valid for one journey only.

Officials at land borders and airports generally allow only 30 days for visitors, regardless of arrangements made prior to arrival, although some travellers have reported 90 day permits given in airport immigrations. Make sure border officials fill in your entry papers correctly and in accordance with your wishes. Extensions of 30 days are easy to obtain (up to a maximum of 6 months' stay, cost US$5). There are immigration offices for extensions at Tela, La Ceiba, San Pedro Sula, Santa Rosa de Copán, Siguatepeque, La Paz and Comayagua, and all are more helpful than the Tegucigalpa office. A valid International Certificate of Vaccination against smallpox is required only from visitors coming from the Indian subcontinent, Indonesia and the countries of southern Africa. A ticket out of the country is necessary for air travellers (if coming from USA, you won'T be allowed on the plane without one); onward tickets must be bought outside the country. (It is not impossible to cash in the return half of the ticket in Honduras, but there is no guarantee and plenty of time is needed.) Proof of adequate funds is normally asked for at land borders. According to the Honduran Consulate in London, there is neither an entry nor an exit tax at land borders. Nevertheless, almost without exception, travellers are charged about US$2 on entry and exit. If officials make a charge for entry or exit, ask for a receipt. Do not attempt to enter Honduras at an unmanned border crossing; when it is discovered that you have no entry stamp you will either be fined US$60, or escorted to the border and you have to pay the guard's food and lodging (you may be able to defray some of this cost by spending a night in jail). It is advisable always to carry means of identification, since spot-checks have increased.

On entering with a car (from El Salvador at least), customs give a 30-day permit for the vehicle, but transit police only give 8 days entry. This must be renewed in Tegucigalpa (anywhere else authorization is valid for only one department). Charges for motorists appear to be: on entry, US$14 in total for a vehicle with 2 passengers, including provisional permission from the police to drive in Honduras, US$1 (official minimum) for car papers, fumigation and baggage inspection; on exit, US$2.30 in total. These charges are changing all the time and differ significantly from one border post to another. They are also substantially increased on Sat, Sun and holidays and by bribery. You can be fined if you do not have two reflecting triangles and a fire extinguisher in your car. Be prepared for hassle from police and military, both of whom have road check points, especially near towns, watch out for stop signs ("Alto Repórtese"), but only stop if signalled to do so. Keep cameras and valuables hidden while driving. If unfair fines are demanded, ask to be taken to the police office. If you don'T get a receipt, don'T pay. Bicycles are regarded as vehicles but are not officially subject to entrance taxes. No fresh food is allowed to cross the border. On leaving with a vehicle there are so many checks that it pays to hire a guide to steer you to the correct officials in the correct order (US$1 for the guide). There is a certain amount of bribery at border crossings.

Taxes There is an airport tax and hospital tax of 3% on all tickets sold for domestic journeys, and a 10% tax on airline tickets for international journeys. There is an airport departure tax of US$18 and a customs tax of 20 lempiras (neither charged if in transit less than 9 hrs). Note that the border offices close at 1700, not 1800 as in most other countries; there is an extra fee charged after that time.

How to get there There are no direct flights to Tegucigalpa from Europe, but connecting flights can be made via Guatemala (with KLM or Iberia) or Miami, then American Airlines, or Taca. To Tegucigalpa from New Orleans with Lacsa, or with Continental (via Houston); from Houston, besides Continental, Taca flies daily via San Salvador. Iberia flies to San Pedro Sula via Miami from Madrid twice a week. Lacsa flies to San Pedro Sula from New York (also Continental and American), New Orleans, Los Angeles, Cancún and Mexico City. Taca and American fly direct Miami-San Pedro Sula. Taca and Lacsa fly from Tegucigalpa to all Central American capitals; Lacsa and Aero Costa Rica fly to San José from San Pedro Sula direct; Taca also flies to Mexico City. Copa flies from Panama City and Mexico City to San Pedro Sula. Connections with Curaçao are made at Guatemala City (KLM/Taca).

Customs There are no Customs duties on personal effects; 200 cigarettes or 100 cigars, or $\frac{1}{2}$ kg of tobacco, and 2 quarts of spirit are allowed in free.

Internal Flights There are airstrips in the larger and smaller towns. Sosa, SAMi and Isleña have daily services between Tegucigalpa, San Pedro Sula, La Ceiba, and the Caribbean coastal towns and islands.

Internal Land Transport Buses tend to start early in the day; however, some night buses run between major urban centres. Try to avoid bus journeys after dark as there are many more accidents, mostly owing to the appalling road conditions. Hitchhiking is relatively easy. If hiring a car, make sure it has the correct papers, and emergency triangles which are required by law. The main arteries are in excellent condition, but off the main roads standards decline rapidly. Children fill in holes with grit in the hope of receiving a tip. **NB** There are frequent police searches on entry or exit from towns and villages. Be alert if there are policemen around—they will try to spot an infraction of the laws to collect a fine, eg parking on the wrong side of the road, stopping with your wheels beyond the line at a 'Stop' sign. Petrol costs about US$0.90 'regular", US$1.15 'premium' per US gallon. Unleaded petrol is not available (1994). Diesel costs US$0.70.

Food Cheapest meals are the *comida corriente* or (sometimes better prepared and dearer) the *comida típica*; these usually contain some of the following: beans, rice, meat, avocado, egg, cabbage salad, cheese, *plátanos*, potatoes or yucca, and always tortillas. Pork is not rec as pigs are often raised on highly insanitary swill. *Carne asada* is charcoal roasted and served with grated cabbage between tortillas is good, though rarely sanitarily prepared. *Tajadas* are crisp, fried *plátano* chips topped with grated cabbage and sometimes meat; *nacatamales* are ground, dry maize mixed with meat and seasoning, boiled in banana leaves. *Baleadas* are soft flour tortillas filled with beans and various combinations of butter, egg, cheese and cabbage. *Pupusas* are thick corn tortillas filled with chicharrón (pork sausage), or cheese, served as snacks with beer. *Tapado* is a stew with meat or fish (especially on the North Coast), plantain, yucca and coconut milk. *Pinchos* are meat, poultry, or shrimp kebabs. *Sopa de mondongo* (tripe soup) is very common.

Cheap fish is best found on the beaches at Trujillo and Cedeño and on the shores of Lago Yojoa. While on the North Coast, look for *pan de coco* (coconut bread) made by *garifuna* (Black Carib) women and *sopa de camarones* prepared with coconut milk and lemon juice.

Drinks Soft drinks are called *refrescos*, or *frescos* (the name also given to fresh fruit blended with water, beware as drinking water is unsafe, see **Health** below); *licuados* are fruit blended with milk. Bottled drinking water is reported to be difficult to find in Honduras. Fresh orange juice, unsweetened, is available in paper cartons everywhere. *Horchata* is *morro* seeds, rice water and cinnamon. Coffee is thick and sweet. There are 5 main brands of beer, Port Royal Export, Imperial, Polar, Nacional and Salvavidas (more malty than the other 4).

Tipping Normally 10% of bill.

Shopping The best articles are those in wood: straw baskets, hats, etc, are also highly rec. Leather is cheaper than in El Salvador and Nicaragua, but not as cheap as in Colombia. The coffee is good. Note that film is expensive, but Konica film can be bought for US$4 to US$5 for 36 exposures, eg at Laboratorio Villatoro, stores in major towns. For bulk purchases (say 50 rolls) try their head office on Calle Peatonal, Jardín de Italia, Tegucigalpa.

Health Dysentery and stomach parasites are common and malaria is endemic in coastal regions, where a prophylactic regime should be undertaken and mosquito nets carried. Inoculate against typhoid and tetanus. Cholera is on the increase, so eating on the street or at market stalls can no longer be recommended. Drinking water is definitely not safe; drink bottled water, if you can find it. Otherwise boil or sterilize water. Salads and raw vegetables must be sterilized under personal supervision. There are hospitals at Tegucigalpa and all the larger towns. Excellent ointments for curing the all-too-prevalent tropical skin complaints are Scabisan (Mexican) and Betnovate (Glaxo).

Hours of Business Mon to Fri: 0900-1200; 1400-1800 Sat: 0800-1200, and some open in the afternoon. Banks in Tegucigalpa 0900-1500; 0800-1100 only along the N coast on Sat. In San Pedro Sula and along the N coast most places open and close half an hour earlier in the morning and afternoon than in Tegucigalpa. Post Offices: Mon-Fri 0700-2000, Sat 0800-1200.

Clothing Western; suits optional for most businessmen, on the North Coast, which is much hotter and damper, dress is less formal. Laundering is undertaken by most hotels.

British business travellers planning a visit should get a copy of 'Hints to Exporters: Honduras", on application to DTI Export Publications, PO Box 55, Stratford-upon-Avon, Warwickshire, CV37 9GE.

Public Holidays Most of the feast days of the Roman Catholic religion and also 1 January: New Year's Day; 14 April: Day of the Americas; Holy Week: Thurs, Fri, and Sat, before Easter Sunday; 1 May: Labour Day; 15 September: Independence Day; 3 October: Francisco Morazán; 12 October: Columbus' arrival in America; 21 October: Army Day.

Official Time 6 hrs behind GMT.

Currency The unit is a lempira. It is divided into 100 centavos. There are nickel coins of 5, 10, 20, and 50 centavos. Bank notes are for 1, 2, 5, 10, 20, 50 and 100 lempiras. Any amount of any currency can be taken in or out.

Note With the floating of the lempira against the dollar in 1990, Honduras has become a much cheaper country for visitors travelling with US dollars, but the floating of the currency and inflation have caused prices to rise sharply. Money may be changed at the free rate in banks, but a street market offers rates which are usually higher than the official rate.

Credit Cards Mastercard and Visa are accepted in major hotels and most restaurants in cities and larger towns. Cash advances from Credomatic, Blvd Morazán, Tegucigalpa, and branches of Bancahsa, Ficensa and Futuro throughout the country. Cash advances using Mastercard costs US$10 in banks. Mastercard/Cirrus ATMs at branches of Credomatic, Banco de Occidente or Ficensa at 11 locations, including Tegucigalpa, La Ceiba, Puerto Cortés, Roatán, San Pedro Sula and Tela.

Weights and Measures The metric system of weights is official and should be used, but the *libra* (pound) is still often used for meat, fish etc. Land is measured in *varas* (838 mm) and *manzanas* (0.7 hectare).

Electric Current generally 110 volts but, increasingly, 220 volts is being installed. US-type flat-pin plugs.

Air Mail takes 4 to 7 days to Europe and the same for New York. Airmail costs 85 centavos for a letter to N America (1 lempira to Europe), 60 centavos for a postcard (80 centavos to Europe); aerograms (not easy to find), 75 centavos. Parcels, US$11 up to 2 kg to Europe by air; no air mail over 2 kg: sea mail to Europe US$3 up to 5 kg, US$4.50 up to 10 kg, takes 6-10 months.

Telephones Hondutel provides international telephone, fax and telex services from stations at Tegucigalpa, San Pedro Sula, Puerto Cortés, Tela, La Ceiba, Comayagua, Siguatepeque, Copán (Ruinas), Santa Rosa de Copán, Danlí, Choluteca, Juticalpa, La Paz, La Lima, El Progreso, Valle de Angeles, El Paraíso, Catacamas and Marcala.

Telephone service between Honduras and Europe costs about US$30 for a 5-min call; calls to USA L22 for 3 mins. Collect calls to N America, Central America and Europe (not possible to Israel) can be made from Hondutel office in Tegucigalpa. Fax to Europe costs US$5 for one page.

Representation Overseas **Belgium**, Avenue des Gaulois 3, 1040 Brussels, T 322 734-0000, F 322 735-2626; **Canada**, 151 Slater Street, Suite 300, Ottawa, Ontario K1P 5H3, T 613 233-8900, F 613 232-0193; **France**, 8 Rue Crevaux, 75116 Paris, T 4755-8645, F 4755-8648; **Germany**, Uberstrasse-1, 5300 Bonn 2, T 228-356394, F 228-351981; **Italy**, Via Boezio No 45, 2do Piso, 00192 Roma, T 396 687-6051, F 396 687-6051; **Japan**, 38 Kowa Bldg, 8F No 802, 12-24 Nishi Azabu 4, Chome Minato Ku, Tokyo 106, T 03 3409-1150, F 03 3409-0305; **Netherlands**, Johan Van Oldenbarneveltlaan 85, 2582 NK Den Haag, T 703-540-152, F 703-504-183; **Switzerland**, 6 Route de Meyrin 1202, Geneva, T 022 734-6916, F 022 734-1608; **Spain**, Calle Rosario Pino 6, Cuarto Piso Letra A, Madrid 28020, T 341 579-0251, F 341 572-1319; **USA**, 3007 Tilden Street, Pod 4M, Washington, DC 20008, T 202 966-7702, F 202 966-9751.

Media The principal **newspapers** in Tegucigalpa are *El Heraldo*, *La Tribuna* and *El Periódico*. In San Pedro Sula: *El Tiempo* and *La Prensa* (circulation about 45,000). All five newspapers are owned by politicians.

There are 6 television channels and 167 broadcasting stations. Cable TV is available in every large town.

Language Spanish, but English is spoken in the N, in the Bay Islands, by West Indian settlers on the Caribbean coast, and is understood in most of the big business houses. Trade literature and correspondence should be in Spanish.

We are most grateful to Huw Clough and Kate Hennessy for updating this chapter. Thanks also to Jorge Valle-Aguiluz (Tegucigalpa), for a very important contribution and to Robert Millar; also to the following travellers: Simon Attewell (Loughborough, Leicestershire), Susanne Baader (Bremen, Germany), Jack Bailey & Diana Musacchio (Santa Barbara, CA, USA), Frank Bakker & Nike Darley (Amsterdam), Harald Bauder (Detroit, MI, USA), David Beasley & Liz Brooks (Horsham, West Sussex), Alexander Beck (Altessing, Germany), Erich Blum (Ruemlang, Switzerland), Sybille Böhme (Kahl/Main, Germany), Sarah & Philippe Bonay (Auterine, France), Debra Brender (Davis, CA, USA), Michael Carter (Stratford, Ontario, Canada), Frank Dux (Passau, Germany), Antje E (Leipzig), Lene Eilrich (Ribe, Denmark), Ernst

To use AT&T USADirect® Service from Honduras dial **123** from any telephone. Coin deposit is required from public telephones.

AT&T USADirect® Service.

A Erbe (El Paso, Texas), Ariane Fàssler (Wettswil, Switzerland), Joy Hale & Derek Fess (Columbus, Ohio), Richard N Frank (Clearwater, FL, USA), Ann Frechette & Jean Luc Massicotte for Charles Huot (Montréal), Darrel Freeman (Lancaster, PA, USA), Fränzi Gäggel (Glahfelden, Switzerland), Robert L Gaynor (Dearborn, MI, USA), Julio Gonzalez (Saint-Bonnet près Riom, France), Mark B Gordon (Houston, Texas), Heidi Gürtler (Friedrichshafen, Germany), Pasi Hannonen (Jy vä Skylä, Finland), Sally & Mike Hayden (Cheltenham, Glos), Markus Hohl (London W11), Mathew Hunter (Anna-Maria, FL, USA), Ken Jones (Victoria, BC, Canada), Daniel Kaiser (Triesen, Liechtenstein), Noel, Nenagh & Zoë Kemp (Lindisfarne, Australia), Oliver Kirbach (Berlin, Germany), Christoph Künzi (Zurich, Switzerland), Monika Langner (Trujillo, Honduras), Helmut Lüder (Potomac, MD, USA), Stefan Malmgren (Malmö, Sweden), Joseph Marchner (Neubiberg, Germany), Michelle Mason (Brightwalton Green, Berkshire), Mechthild Mench (Tegucigalpa), Rob Minnee (Lisse, The Netherlands), Claudia Modrow & Massimo Godenzi (Bergheim, Germany), Monica Müller (Blonay), & Klaus Högle (Marin, Switzerland), J Michael Nehrbass (Portland, OR, USA), Antoine Pecard (Paris), Lisa Pollitt (Newcastle, UK), Warren Post (Santa Rosa de Copán, Honduras), Nigel & Maggie Potter (San José, Honduras), Helmut Quitt (Rosenheim, Germany), Claudio Rivero (Buenos Aires), Roh (Switzerland), Hans-Joachim Rösel (Granada, Nicaragua), Frank & Christine Ruiz (Brossard, Quebec), Adrian van Schie (New Zealand), Mark Schuringa (Amsterdam, Holland), Harald Schwender & Birgitte Hächer (Sandhausen, Germany), Mark Simmermann (Mayetta, Kansas), Gaylord E Smith (Prunedale, CA), Cheryl Sortwell (Neuhausen, Switzerland), Stefan Cotting (Nevenegg, Switzerland), Gregor Stöcting (Berlin), Bärbel Strauch (Heidelberg, Germany), George Tanber (Anniston, Alabama), Bill Vallis (Surbiton, Surrey), Edwin van der Werf & Harold Bierens (Holland), Anke & Herman Van Weeghel (Wychen, The Netherlands), Benderoth Vitus (Hadamar), Simon Watson Taylor (Goa), Sheila Wilson (Stoke Poges, Slough), Florian Wüllen Kemper (Bad Salzujlen, Germany), Sarah Wyles (Christchurch, New Zealand).

WILL YOU HELP US?

We do all we can to get our facts right in the MEXICO & CENTRAL AMERICAN HANDBOOK. Each section is thoroughly revised each year, but the territory is vast and our eyes cannot be everywhere. We are always pleased to hear about your travels; do write to us in as much detail as possible. In return we will send you information about our special guidebook offer.

 **TRADE & TRAVEL** *Handbooks*

Write to The Editor, Mexico & Central American Handbook, Trade & Travel, 6 Riverside Court, Lower Bristol Road, Bath BA2 3DZ. England

NICARAGUA

INTRODUCTION

NICARAGUA, the same size as England and Wales, is the largest Central American republic. It has 541 km of coast on the Caribbean and 352 km on the Pacific. Costa Rica is to the S, Honduras to the N. Only 8% of the whole country, out of a possible 28%, is in economic use.

There are three well-marked regions. (1) A large triangular-shaped central mountain land whose apex rests almost on the southern border with Costa Rica; the prevailing moisture-laden NE winds drench its eastern slopes, which are deeply forested with oak and pine on the drier, cooler heights. (2) A wide belt of eastern lowland through which a number of rivers flow from the mountains into the Atlantic. (3) The belt of lowland which runs from the Gulf of Fonseca, on the Pacific, to the Costa Rican border S of Lake Nicaragua. Out of it, to the E, rise the lava cliffs of the mountains to a height of from 1,500 to 2,100m. Peninsulas of high land jut out here and there into the lowland, which is from 65 to 80 km wide along the Pacific.

In this plain are two large sheets of water. The capital, Managua, is on the shores of Lake Managua, 52 km long, 15 to 25 wide, and 39m above sea-level. The Río Tipitapa drains it into Lake Nicaragua, 148 km long, about 55 km at its widest, and 32m above the sea; Granada is on its shores. Launches ply on the Río San Juan which drains it into the Caribbean.

Through the Pacific lowland runs a row of volcanoes. The northernmost is the truncated zone of Cosegüina, overlooking the Gulf of Fonseca; then the smoking San Cristóbal, the highest of them all; a number of smaller volcanoes, of which Cerro Negro was built up during its last eruption in 1971; and the famous Momotombo, which normally smokes a little and now has a geothermal power station at its foot. Around Managua, even in the city centre, there are small craters, but none is active. Further S is the twin cone of Masaya/Santiago, which stopped smoking in late 1986. In Lake Nicaragua is the beautiful Concepción, the second highest, on the Isla de Ometepe, on which also stands the extinct Las Maderas. The volcanic chain continues NW into El Salvador and to the S into Costa Rica. The volcanic ash makes rich soil for crops.

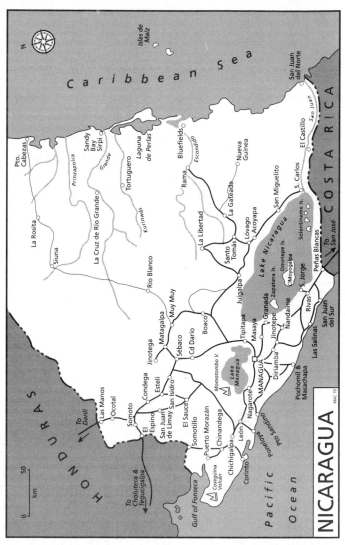

Climate The wet, warm winds off the Caribbean pour heavy rain on the Atlantic coastal zone, especially in the southern basin of the San Juan river, with more than 6m annually. While the dry season on the Atlantic coast is only short and not wholly dry, the Pacific dry season, or summer (November to April), becomes very dusty, especially when the winds begin to blow in February. There is a wide range of climates. According to altitude, average annual temperatures vary between 15°C and 35°C. Mid-day temperatures at Managua range from 30° to 36°C, but readings of 38° are not uncommon from March to May, or of 40° in January and February in the W. It can get quite cold, especially after rain, in the Caribbean lowlands. Maximum daily humidity ranges from 90% to 100%.

History The Spanish *conquistadores* reached the lowland from Panama as early as 1519. On the south-western shores of Lake Nicaragua they found an area comparatively densely settled by peaceful Indians, who lavished gold ornaments on them. Five years later another expedition founded colonies at Granada and León, but the flow of gold soon stopped and most of the Spaniards moved elsewhere. In 1570 both colonies were put under the jurisdiction of Guatemala. The local administrative centre was not rich Granada, with its profitable crops of sugar, cocoa, and indigo, but impoverished León, then barely able to subsist on its crops of maize, beans and rice. This reversal of the Spanish policy of choosing the most successful settlement as capital was due to the ease with which León could be reached from the Pacific. In 1858 Managua was chosen as a new capital as a compromise, following violent rivalry between Granada and León.

For more on Nicaragua's early history, see the introductory chapter to Central America. The country became an independent state in 1838. The famous (or infamous) filibustering expedition of William Walker is often referred to in the text. William Walker (1824-1860) was born in Nashville, Tennessee, graduated at the University in 1838, studied medicine at Edinburgh and Heidelberg, was granted his MD in 1843, and then studied law and was called to the bar. On 5 October 1853, he sailed with a filibustering force to conquer Mexican territory, declared Lower California and Sonora an independent republic and was then driven out. In May 1855, with 56 followers armed with a new type of rifle, he sailed for Nicaragua, where Liberal Party leaders had invited him to help them in their struggle against the Conservatives. In October he seized a steamer on Lake Nicaragua belonging to the Accessory Transit Company, an American corporation controlled by Cornelius Vanderbilt. He was then able to surprise and capture Granada and make himself master of Nicaragua as Commander of the Forces. Two officials decided to use him to get control of the Transit Company; it was seized and handed over to his friends. A new Government was formed and in June 1856 Walker was elected President. On 22 September, to gain support from the southern states in America he suspended the Nicaraguan laws against slavery. His Government was formally recognized by the US that year. A coalition of Central American states, backed by Cornelius Vanderbilt, fought against him, but he was able to hold his own until May 1857, when he surrendered to the US Navy to avoid capture. In November 1857, he sailed from Mobile with another expedition, but soon after landing near Greytown, Nicaragua, he was arrested and returned to the US. In 1860 he sailed again from Mobile and landed in Honduras. There he was taken prisoner by Captain Salmon, of the British Navy, and handed over to the Honduran authorities, who tried and executed him on 12 September 1860. Walker's own book, *The War in Nicaragua*, is a fascinating document.

In 1909, US Marines assisted Nicaraguan Conservative leaders in an uprising to overthrow the Liberal president, José Santos Zelaya. In 1911 the United States pledged help in securing a loan to be guaranteed through the control of Nicaraguan customs by an American board. In 1912 the United States sent marines into Nicaragua to enforce the control. Apart from short intervals, they stayed there until 1933. During the last five years of occupation, nationalists under General Augusto César Sandino waged relentless guerrilla war against the US Marines. American forces were finally withdrawn in 1933, when President Franklin Roosevelt announced the 'Good Neighbour' policy, pledging non-intervention. An American-trained force, the Nicaraguan National Guard, was left behind, commanded by Anastasio Somoza García. Somoza's men assassinated General Sandino in February 1934 and Somoza himself took over the presidency in 1936. From 1932, with brief intervals, Nicaraguan affairs were dominated by General Anastasio Somoza until he was assassinated in 1956. His two sons both served a presidential term and the younger, Gen Anastasio Somoza Debayle, dominated the country from 1963 until his deposition in 1979; he was later assassinated in Paraguay.

The 1978-79 revolution against the Somoza Government by the Sandinista guerrilla organization (loosely allied to a broad opposition movement) resulted in extensive damage and many casualties (estimated at over 30,000) in certain parts of the country, especially in Managua, Estelí, León, Masaya, Chinandega and Corinto. After heavy fighting General Somoza resigned on 17 July 1979 and the Government was taken over by a Junta representing the Sandinista guerrillas and their civilian allies. Real power was exercised by nine Sandinista *comandantes* whose chief short-term aim was reconstruction. A 47-member Council of State formally came into being in May 1980; supporters of the Frente Sandinista de Liberación Nacional had a majority. Elections were held on 4 November 1984 for an augmented National Constituent Assembly with 96 seats; the Sandinista Liberation Front won 61 seats, and Daniel Ortega Saavedra, who had headed the Junta, was elected president. The Democratic Conservatives won 14 seats, the Independent Liberals 9 seats and the Popular Social Christians 6 (the Socialists, Communists and Marxists/Leninists won 2 seats each). The failure of the Sandinista Government to meet the demands of a right-wing grouping, the Democratic Coordinating Board (CDN), led to this coalition boycotting the elections and to the US administration condemning the poll as a 'sham'.

Despite substantial official and private US support, anti-Sandinista guerrillas (the 'contras') could boast no significant success in their war against the Government. In 1988, the Sandinistas and the contras met for the first time to discuss the implementation of the Central American Peace Plan drawn up by President Oscar Arias Sánchez of Costa Rica, and signed in August 1987. To comply with the Plan, the Nicaraguan Government made a number of political concessions. By 1989 the contras, lacking funds and with diminished numbers, following a stream of desertions, appeared to be a spent force; some participated in general elections held on 25 February 1990. The Sandinista Government brought major improvements in health and education, but the demands of the war against the contras and a complete US trade embargo did great damage to the economy as a whole. The electorate's desire for a higher standard of living was reflected in the outcome of the elections, when the US-supported candidate of the free market National Opposition Union (UNO), Sra Violeta Chamorro, won 55.2% of the vote, compared with 40.8% for President Ortega. The 14-party alliance, UNO, won 52 seats in the National Assembly, the FSLN 38 and the Social Christian Party one seat. Sra Chamorro, widow of the proprietor of *La Prensa*, who was murdered by General Somoza's forces in 1978, took office on 25 April 1990. The USA was under considerable pressure to provide substantial aid for the alliance it created and promoted, but of the US$300mn promised for 1990 by the US Congress, only half had been distributed by May 1991. President Chamorro's refusal to dismiss the Sandinista, General Humberto Ortega, from his post as head of the armed forces (EPS), and to drop the Nicaraguan case against the USA at the International Court of Justice, were said to be hindrances to more rapid disbursement. (The Court in The Hague found the USA guilty in 1986 of crimes against Nicaragua in mining its harbours.)

The lack of foreign financial assistance prevented any quick rebuilding of the economy. The Government's scant resources did not permit it to give the disarmed contra forces the land and services that had been promised to them. Demilitarized Sandinistas and landless peasants also pressed for land in 1991, with a consequent rise in tension. Factions of the two groups rearmed, to be known as recontras and recompas; there were many bloody conflicts. Divisions within the UNO coalition, particularly between supporters of President Chamorro and those of vice-president Virgilio Godoy, added to the country's difficulties. Austerity measures introduced in early 1991, including a devaluation of the new córdoba oro, strained the relationship between the administration, Sandinista politicians and the National Workers' Front (FNT), the so-called 'concertación', a pact which the private sector refused to sign. Pacts signed in January 1992 between Government, recontras and recompas failed to stop occasional heavy fighting over the next 2 years.

Throughout 1993, the UNO boycotted the National Assembly because of major disagreements with the Chamorro administration, both its policies and its ministers. The UNO coalition began to fragment as new allegiances were forged between political groupings. At the same time, differences between factions of the FSLN widened, basically between the reforming group led by Sergio Ramírez and the Forum for the Revolutionary Left of Daniel Ortega. The position of Ortega's brother, Humberto, as head of the army remained a bone of contention. In 1993 President Chamorro said that Humberto Ortega would be replaced in 1994, to FSLN disgust but to US and recontra approval, yet she confirmed his post in early 1994, only for Ortega to announce his retirement in mid-year. Despite these uncertainties, the National Assembly returned to full operation in 1994 as all parties resumed their seats. UNO decided to press for constitutional change to solve Nicaragua's deep-seated political problems. A series of bilateral meetings between previously entrenched parties and ceasefires announced by the EPS and the main recontra group, FN 3-80 (Northern Front 3-80) contributed to a disarmament accord proposed by archbishop Miguel Obando y Bravo between the Government and FN 3-80. It was hoped that the plan would lead to the peace and reconciliation that Chamorro had campaigned for, but which had eluded her, since becoming president. The plan's success rests heavily on the Government being able to implement lasting economic and social programmes to integrate former combattants into civilian life. To this end, not only significant foreign aid, but also a loosening of the international financial community's conditions on loans, was required. In late 1993, President Chamorro signed a number of financing deals with foreign Governments, but assistance from the USA was both limited and tied to human rights and other demands. In early 1994, approaches to the IMF and World Bank raised hopes for credits worth US$250mn.

The People Population density is low: 34.3 persons to the square km, compared with El Salvador's 260. An odd feature for a country so slightly industrialized is that almost two thirds of its people live in towns and urban population growth is 4.6% a year. Nine in ten of the people of Nicaragua live and work in the lowland between the Pacific and the western shores of Lake Nicaragua, the south-western shore of Lake Managua, and the south-western sides of the row of volcanoes. It is only of late years that settlers have taken to coffee-growing and cattle-rearing in the highlands at Matagalpa and Jinotega. Elsewhere the highlands, save for an occasional mining camp, are very thinly settled.

The densely forested eastern lowlands fronting the Caribbean were neglected, because of the heavy rainfall and their consequent unhealthiness, until the British settled several colonies of Jamaicans in the 18th century at Bluefields and San Juan del Norte (Greytown). But early this century the United Fruit Company of America (now United Brands) opened banana plantations inland from Puerto Cabezas, worked by blacks from Jamaica. Other companies followed suit along the coast, but the bananas were later attacked by Panama disease and exports today are small. Along the Mosquito coast there are still English-speaking communities of African, or mixed African and indigenous, descent. Besides the *mestizo* intermixtures of Spanish and Indian (77%), there are pure blacks (9%),

NICARAGUA : FACT FILE

Geographic

Land area	130,682 sq km
forested	28.5%
pastures	45.5%
cultivated	10.7%

Demographic

Population (1992)	4,131,000
annual growth rate (1987-92)	3.4%
urban	59.8%
rural	40.2%
density	34.3 per sq km
Religious affiliation	
Roman Catholic	90.7%
Birth rate per 1,000 (1991)	37.0
(world av 26.4)	
Death rate per 1,000 (1991)	7.0
(world av 9.2)	

Education and Health

Life expectancy at birth,	
male	60 years
female	65 years
Infant mortality rate	
per 1,000 live births (1991)	60.0
Physicians (1988)	1 per 2,024 persons
Hospital beds	1 per 761 persons
Calorie intake as %	
of FAO requirement	110%
Population age 25 and over	
with no formal schooling	53.9%
Literacy (over 15)	74.0%

Economic

GNP (1988 market prices)	US$1,661mn
GNP per capita	US$460
Public external debt (1990)	US$7,920mn
Tourism receipts (1990)	US$12mn
Inflation (annual av 1988-91)	6,350%
Radio	1 per 4.5 persons
Television	1 per 19 persons
Telephone	1 per 82 persons

Employment

Population economically active (1991)	
	1,386,300
Unemployment rate (1992)	60.0%
% of labour force in	
agriculture	32.4
mining	0.3
manufacturing	8.0
construction	1.5
Military forces	14,700

Source Encyclopaedia Britannica

pure Indians (4%), and mixtures of the two (mostly along the Atlantic coast). A small proportion is of unmixed Spanish and European descent. For a brief survey of the people of eastern Nicaragua, see the introductory paragraphs of **The Caribbean Coast**.

The Economy Nicaragua's economy showed a fairly stable average annual growth rate over the two decades up to 1977, despite sharp fluctuations from year to year as agricultural production and world commodity prices varied. The economy is based on agriculture, principal export items being cotton, coffee, sugar, beef, seafood and bananas. The Government encouraged a diversification of exports, and exports of tobacco and other agricultural products gained in importance. At present agriculture constitutes 30% of gdp and is responsible for by far the largest proportion of exports. Land reform was actively undertaken by the Sandinistas. In the 1970s substantial industrialization developed, mainly through foreign investment. Main industries are food processing (sugar, meat, shrimps), textiles, wood, chemical and mineral products. There are few mineral resources in Nicaragua; although gold, copper and silver are mined, they are of little importance to the overall economy.

Since the late 1970s gdp has fallen, starting with a decline of 29% in 1979. In 1981-90 it fell by an annual average of 2.4%, with only one year of positive growth. In the same period per capita income fell by an average of 5.6% a year. The collapse was caused by guerrilla insurgency, the US trade embargo, fluctuations in Central American Common Market trade, floods, drought and changing commodity prices. Growth has usually been led by agriculture when weather, international prices and political conditions have been favourable.

Inflation, which had been traditionally low, has been a problem since the 1972 earthquake; it rose to 84% in 1979 as a result of the civil war, moderating to an average of 30% in

1980-84. As an effect of insurgency requiring heavy budget spending on defence and other difficulties, the rate shot up to an estimated 750% in 1986, 1,200% in 1987 and 24,000% in 1988, while the public sector deficit rose to 27% of gnp. In 1988 a new currency was introduced as part of an anti-inflation package which realigned prices of the dollar and basic goods, but neither this nor subsequent economic packages succeeded in eliminating inflation. Nicaragua is dependent upon foreign aid, which averaged US$600mn a year in 1980-89, of which the USSR is believed to have granted nearly half. The EEC and Canada were the other major donors. There have been no new investment projects for several years. Nicaragua's foreign debt, including arrears, amounts to some US$10.9bn, but reduced foreign exchange earnings in the mid-1980s (partly because of the US blockade) made it impossible for the Government to service the debt.

In 1990 the US-supported Government of Pres Violeta Chamorro took office amid great optimism that the economy could be revived on the back of renewed trade with the USA. Trade sanctions were lifted and the US Congress was asked to provide US$300mn in aid immediately, to be followed by a further US$200mn. Other countries were also asked for US$100mn. These funds were to be used to resume debt service to the IMF and multilateral development agencies, for economic restructuring, for agricultural, oil and medical supplies, to rebuild bridges, schools, roads and hospitals and repatriate and resettle the contra rebel forces and other refugees. However by mid-1991 disbursements had been insufficient to help the administration out of its extremely straightened circumstances. Emergency measures, including the introduction of another new currency, the córdoba oro, failed to stabilize the economy. With the old and new currencies in circulation side-by-side, a shortfall in foreign aid and a consequent lack of economic progress, confidence in each currency collapsed. By 1992, however, progress was apparent in some areas as slow growth resumed (0.8%) and inflation fell to only 3.9%; the trend was reversed in 1993 owing to deep austerity and political instability. Gdp fell by 0.1% and inflation rose to 28.3%; gdp per capita declined, for the tenth year running, by 4.6%. After many coffee and cotton growers failed to sow their crops because of violence and lack of credit in 1992-93, the agricultural sector's decline continued in 1993. 4,000 coffee producers marched on Managua in February 1994 to demand improved credit terms and financial support. Manufacturing also continued in recession in 1993 and unemployment levels were about 60% of the economically active population. In the light of this economic crisis, President Chamorro urged foreign aid donors to treat Nicaragua as a special case and not demand severe structural adjustment conditions. Nevertheless, several organizations, internal and foreign, were highly critical of many of her Government's policies. Since Nicaragua is highly dependent on foreign aid, a priority is to secure financial assistance which is sufficient to meet local demands and which does not flow out immediately to service the massive foreign debt.

Government A new Constitution was approved by the 92-member National Constituent Assembly in 1986 and signed into effect on 9 January 1987. Legislative power is vested in a unicameral, directly elected National Assembly of 92 representatives, each with an alternate representative, with a six-year term. In addition, unelected presidential and vice presidential candidates become representatives and alternates respectively if they receive a certain percentage of the votes. Executive power is vested in the President, assisted by a Vice President and an appointed Cabinet. The Presidential term is six years.

Ports and Communications The main Pacific ports are Corinto, San Juan del Sur and Puerto Sandino. The two main Atlantic ports are Puerto Cabezas and Bluefields. The **roads** have been greatly extended and improved. The Pan-American Highway from the Honduran border to the borders of Costa Rica

(384 km), is paved the whole way and so is the shorter international road to the Honduran frontier via Chinandega; the road between Managua and Rama (for Bluefields) is paved, but is not in good condition. There are now 14,997 km of road, 1,650 paved and 1,300 km all-weather. Until 1 January 1994, there was one operational **railway**, the Ferrocarril del Pacífico, 349 km long, single track, with a gauge of 1.067m. On that date all railway services were suspended and the tracks were being torn up. See also **Internal Transport** in **Information for Visitors**.

Religion and Education Roman Catholicism is the prevailing religion, but there are Episcopal, Baptist, Methodist and other Protestant churches. Illiteracy has been reduced by a determined Government campaign. Higher education at the Universidad Nacional Autónoma de Nicaragua at León, with 3 faculties at Managua, and the private Jesuit Universidad Centroamericana (UCA) at Managua is good (with strong Sandinista links). There are two, separate Universidades Nacionales Autónomas de Nicaragua (UNAN).

MANAGUA

Managua, the nation's capital and commercial centre since 1858, is on the southern shores of Lake Managua (Lago Xolotlán), at an altitude of between 40 and 150mn. It is 45 km from the Pacific, but 148 km from the main port, Corinto, though a new port, Puerto Sandino (formerly Puerto Somoza), is only 70 km away. Managua was destroyed by earthquake in March 1931, and part of it swept by fire five years later; it was completely rebuilt as an up-to-date capital and commercial city (population 850,000) but the centre was again completely destroyed, apart from a few modern buildings, by another earthquake in December 1972. There was further severe damage during the Revolution of 1978-79.

The Sandinista Government decided that the old centre should be rebuilt, adding parks and recreational facilities, but shortage of funds prevented much progress. The UNO Government subsequently announced similar proposals, including a Parque de la Paz for central Managua; it is anticipated that this project will take years to complete. Present-day Managua has no centre as such, but rather consists of a series of commercial developments in what used to be the outskirts of the old city. No street names are in evidence, and the overall effect can be disconcerting.

The principal commercial areas of Managua are now situated on the Masaya road and the two bypass roads S of the city. These centres contain a variety of shops, cinemas and discotheques.

In the old centre of Managua, one can still see examples of colonial architecture in the Palacio de los Héroes de la Revolución (previously the Palacio Nacional) and the Cathedral. The Cathedral is open, although its interior is in ruins, and its exterior cracked. In 1992 the Government was reported to be trying to raise the funds to restore and reroof it. These buildings are situated on the Parque Central and provide a striking contrast with the modern Teatro Rubén Darío on the lake shore (good plays and musical events, entry US$1.50 to US$3.50 depending on show; also Sala Experimental) and the Banco de América building in the background. A new Cathedral has been inaugurated (1993) 500m S of the Laguna de Tiscapa. It was designed by an Italian architect with an Arabic-style exterior, but an unimpressive interior. Access, for pedestrians only, is from the Metrocentro junction. The Iglesia Santa María de los Angeles, Barro Riguero, was the initial setting for the 'misa revolucionaria' a Catholic/secular mass, interesting wall paintings. The mass is now celebrated only on special occasions and not necessarily at this church.

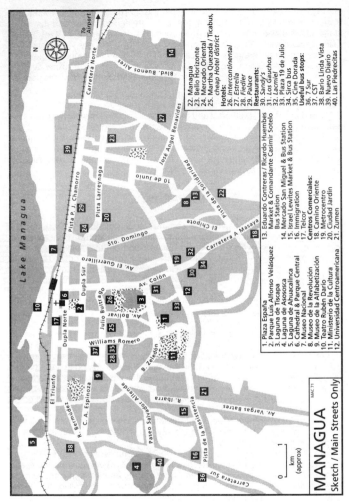

Hotels:
22. Managua
23. Bello Horizonte
24. Mercado Oriental
25. Martha Quezada / Ticabus, *cheap Hotel district*
26. *Intercontinental*
27. *Estrella*
28. *Fiedler*
29. *Palace*

Restaurants:
30. *Sandy's*
31. *Los Gauchos*
32. *Lacmiel*
33. *Plaza 19 de Julio*
34. *Sirca bus*
35. *Cine Dorada*

Useful bus stops:
36. 7 Sur
37. CST
38. Barrio Linda Vista
39. Nuevo Diario
40. Las Piedrecitas

1. Plaza España
2. Parque Luis Alfonso Velásquez
3. Laguna de Tiscapa
4. Laguna de Asososca
5. Laguna de Ahukalinca
6. Cathedral & Parque Central
7. Museo Nacional
8. Museo de la Revolución
9. Museo de la Alfabetización
10. Teatro Rubén Darío
11. Ministerio de la Cultura
12. Universidad Centroamericana
13. Eduardo Contreras / Ricardo Huembes Market & Comandante Casimir Sotelo Bus Station
14. Mercado San Miguel & Bus Station
15. Israel Lewites Market & Bus Station
16. Immigration
17. Telcor

Centros Comerciales:
18. Camino Oriente
19. Metrocentro
20. Ciudad Jardín
21. Zumen

MANAGUA
Sketch / Main Streets Only

km (approx)
0   1

NAC 71

A significant landmark is the *Hotel Intercontinental*, designed a little like a Maya pyramid, which is about a dozen blocks S of the Cathedral (not too far to walk). Its entrance is on Av Bolívar and in front of it an area of open land separates it from Calle Julio Buitrago. The Bolívar-Buitrago junction is on a number of important bus routes. To the W of the hotel is the Barrio Martha Quezada. This district, which also has a number of good eating places, is where many gringos congregate and is known as 'gringolandia'; the barrio is a mixture of quite well-to-do housing side by side with very poor dwellings. S again is Plaza España, with banks, airline offices, etc, and, nearby, exchange houses. Plaza España is reached either by continuing over the hill above the *Intercontinental* and branching right at the big junction, or by going S on Williams Romero, the Avenida at the W edge of Barrio Martha Quezada (bus 118).

One suggested route into the Barrio Martha Quezada: from the *Intercontinental* take the street 1 block S of the Buitrago/Bolívar junction (ie the street on which traffic leaves the barrio). Pass *Bar/Restaurant Fanny* and *Hotel Magut*. At Ciné Cabrera, a couple of blocks further on, turn left; on the left is an unnamed *comedor* (1½ blocks from the cinema), then the *Cipitío* restaurant (2½ blocks). Beyond *Cipitío* is a Y-junction; turn right for *Tres Laureles*, *Norma* and *El Colibrí* hotels. About 1½ blocks past *Colibrí* is the Avenida Williams Romero; turn left for Plaza España. At the junction of Buitrago and Williams Romero is the Centro Sandino de Trabajadores, CST.

Directions are given according to landmarks; in place of cardinal points, the following are used: Al Lago (N), Arriba (E), Al Sur (S), Abajo (W). (This applies to the whole country, even where there are street names or numbers, Nicaraguans give direction by landmarks).

Warning Pickpocketing is common in the markets and on buses (don't stand near the exit; take care if you are pushed repeatedly). The bus routes to avoid are 105, 110, 112, 114, 116, 117, 118, 119; take a taxi in preference. Thieves tend to be smartly dressed, work in groups and carry knives.

Fiesta Santo Domingo is the patron saint of Managua. His festival is held at El Malecón from 1 to 10 August: church ceremonies, horse racing, bull-fights, cock-fights, a lively carnival; proceeds to the General Hospital. 1 August (half day) and 10 August are local holidays.

Hotels Until recently, hotel bills had to be paid in US dollars, now invariably córdobas oro are accepted. 15% tax is added. Several hotels have been built along the highway that bypasses the old part of the city. Try to choose a central hotel (ie near *Intercontinental* or Plaza España) since transport to the outskirts is so difficult. There are, however, 2 good hotels close to the airport, **A+** *Camino Real*, Apartado Postal C118, T 31410, 2 km from terminal, shuttle bus to the airport free, no English spoken, restaurant, live music; and **A** *Las Mercedes*, T 32121/9, good food, but expensive, charming open-air restaurant, pleasant hotel but service generally slow, opp airport (4 mins walk), 3 swimming pools, beware mosquitoes after dark, tennis court, barber shop, all rooms have cable TV, a/c, bath, fridge, phone, local phone calls can be made here when airport office is shut. There is regular water rationing and most hotels do not have large enough water tanks. The Government stipulates a small additional charge for rooms with a telephone (whether used or not).

A+ *Intercontinental*, 101 Octava Calle SO, T (505-2) 23531/9, F 25208, PO Box 3278, service poor, sauna, use of swimming pool for non-residents on Sunday, US$3, bookshop, handicraft shop, buffet, breakfast and lunch (see below), Visa cards accepted, if wishing to take photographs in vicinity, check what is permissible as there is a large military area above and behind the hotel; **A** *Estrella*, Pista de la Solidaridad, a/c, swimming pool, with breakfast, long way from centre, book in advance as it's very popular; at Km 3.5 on Carretera Sur is **B** *Hotel D'Lido*, + 10%, use of swimming pool by non-residents, US$1; at Km 8.5 on Carretera Sur is **B** *Hotel Restaurante Cesar*, Swiss-run, garden, safe, very good food, garage, swimming pool for children; **B** *Las Cabañas*, nr Plaza 19 de Julio, good, helpful, with pool and decent restaurant next door; **B** *Ticomo* at Km 81/2, Carretera Sur, has parking facilities, rents apartments, a/c, with maid service and kitchenette, breakfast extra, good for longer stay; **C** *Casa de Fiedler*, 8a Calle Sur-Oeste 1320 (W of Barrio Martha Quezada – from CST 2 blocks S and 2 blocks W), with bath and a/c or fan, comfortable, soft mattresses, clean, friendly, cold Victoria beer sold, good breakfasts; **C** *Casa San Juan*, Calle Esperanza 560, shared bath and private bath, clean, owner's family sleeps in, safe, excellent breakfasts for US$3; **C** *Palace*, Av Pedro A Flores, with a/c and bath (cheaper without a/c), cold shower, toilet paper on request, run down, no restaurant, helpful, TV lounge, quiet, 'free' city tour will cost you US$10-15; **D** *Colón*, near Sirca bus terminal and road to Masaya, with bath and fan, a bit run down, secure, clean, good restaurant.

Many hotels W of *Intercontinental Hotel* in the Barrio Martha Quezada and nr the Cine Dorado (replaced by a restaurant, of same name, still ask for 'Cine Dorado'). To get from *Intercontinental Hotel* to the Cine Dorado, walk W for 10 mins to a main N-S road, Cine Dorado is just S. Most hotels here have very thin walls and are therefore noisy. **C** *Magut*, 1 block W of *Intercontinental*, on same street as Ciné Cabrera, *La Fragata* restaurant (opp is *Bar/Restaurant Fanny*). **D** *Tres Laureles*, a few blocks from *Intercontinental* (see above), with bath, fan, clean, filtered water, laundry facilities, only 3 rooms, English spoken, quiet, friendly, rec; **D** *Hospedaje Quintana*, from Ticabus, 1 block N, then ½ a block W, rooms with fan, shared shower (cold), laundry, clean, good value, family-run, rec for longer stays. **E** *Jardín de Italia*, W of *Hotel Intercontinental*, 3 blocks E and 1/2 block N of Cine Dorado, with bath, new; **E** *Pensión Norma*, on same street as *Tres Laureles*, shared rooms, basic, friendly, popular (excellent pancakes, breakfast, lunch on nearest corner to this *pensión*); **E** *Casa de Huéspedes Santos*, on street leading to *Intercontinental Hotel* in Barrio Martha Quezada, shared rooms, basic, spacious courtyard with hammocks, friendly, serves meals; **E** *Hospedaje Meza* one block away on same street (T 22046), very basic, TV, friendly, popular. Many others in same area, eg *Azul* (blue doors, no sign), E of Lewites terminal; nearby is **F** *El Portal*, shower, friendly, clean, cheap; **F** *Hospedaje Solidaridad*, 2 blocks S from Cine Dorado, with breakfast, dormitories, bar, workshop for wheelchair invalids. **F** *Hospedaje Carlos* 2 blocks W of Cine Dorado, good value, clean, good *comedor* on opposite corner; **F** *Hospedaje Meléndez*, near *Comedor Sara*, use of kitchen, no privacy.

Other accommodation in our **E** range or below: *Hospedaje Oriental*, nr Mercado Oriental, clean; *Royal*, near railway station, shared shower and toilet, nice family, always full (though often guests not obvious); *Sultana* (basic) noisy, by the Tica Bus Station, handy if you have an early bus otherwise noisy from 0500, if full, staff will arrange for you to stay at *Mi Siesta* on the other side of town (D with bath and a/c, E no a/c), good, friendly, laundry facilities; **F** *El Molinito*, one street from Tica bus station, basic, quiet, clean, safe luggage store, rec.

Camping 181/2 km from the centre, W of Managua on Route 12, 21/2 km after the junction with Ruta 2.

Restaurants The *Hotel Intercontinental* serves enormous breakfasts (0600-1100) for US$8 (plus 15% tax and service charge), and an excellent lunch between 1200 and 1500, US$12 for as much as you want, open to non-residents (best to dress smartly). Bill is made out in US dollars, major credit cards accepted.

In the *Intercontinental*/Plaza España/Barrio Martha Quezada area: *Antojitos*, opp *Intercontinental*, Mexican, a bit overpriced, interesting photos of Managua pre-earthquake, good food and good portions, and garden (open at 1200); a good piano bar next door; *Costa Brava*, N of Plaza España, excellent seafood; opp German Embassy, 200m N of Plaza España is *Bavaria Haus*, German and European specialities, German beer, food and service highly rec, only Spanish spoken, open Mon-Sat 1100-2300. Also near Plaza España, *Plaza*, moderate prices, open-air setting, food and service OK, Earl Grey tea, nice ice cream, casata, Australian owner and Thai cook. *La Terraza*, 300m N of Plaza España, good; *Taco's*, Av Williams Romero on corner with and opp road to *Tres Laureles*, *tacos* and natural *refrescos*. 2 good *sorbeterías* on the street N of Plaza España. *La Panadería de Plaza España*, with *Rapi-Lunch* stall outside, on main road S opp Plaza España. *Comedor Sara*, cheap, popular with gringos; good curries, vegetarian dishes, other cheap *comedores* in the area. Near *Comedor Sara* is *Cipitío*, Salvadorean, good food, reasonable prices, nice atmosphere; *Eskimo* ice cream, W of *Intercontinental* and 2 opp Cine Dorado (you can eat at the factory at Km 3 on Carretera Sur). Cine Dorada is now *Restaurant El Dorado*. 2 blocks 'a la montaña' from *Casa de Huéspedes Santos* is an unnamed café with white plastic tables which serves excellent breakfasts, also lunch, closed in evening; and a stall (ask for Doña Pilar), halt a block E from the *Santos*, and one block S, excellent value food, filling and delicious for about US$2. Uphill from *Intercontinental*, at a junction on the right, *Amatl Libro Café*, drinks, snacks, magazines, books, postcards, maps, photocopier, a few handicrafts.

On Carretera a Masaya: *La Carreta* (Km 12), rec; *Sacuanjoche* (Km 8), international cuisine; *Lacmiel* (Km 4.5), good value, a/c, real ice cream; *Los Gauchos*, steaks; *Nerja*, on the highway a few 100m from the bypass, good; *La Marseillaise*, Colonia Los Robles, French, excellent. *Sandy's* is the bad local version of MacDonalds, one on Carretera a Masaya, door Km 5, and 2 other branches. Vegetarian: *Soya Restaurant*, just off the Carretera on Pista de la Resistencia; *Licuado Ananda*, just E of Estatua Montoya, open for breakfast and lunch. On Carretera Sur, Km 81/2, *César*, specializes in European food and Swiss desserts; at Km 61/2 is *The Lobster's Inn*, very good seafood but beware of overcharging and additions to your bill (report any sharp practices to the police).

Other recommendations: Cheap meals at Mercado Huembes, but look to see what you're getting first. *Mirador Tiscapa*, overlooking Laguna Tiscapa, good food, slow service, live music 2000-2400 (0200 Sat, closed Wed); health food bakery near Tiscapa (E from *Intercontinental*, turn R at drycleaners, after 2 blocks turn L, bread sales at 1100, get ticket at 1000, max 4 loaves pp). In Camino Oriente entertainment centre, *El Ternero* and *La Fonda* (also has a *Sandy's*—see above, cinemas, discos and bowling alley). Opp Metrocentro is *El Cartel*, local dishes; *Rincón Criollo* on Plaza Julio Martínez, similar. If you can find it, try the local fish, *guapote*, excellent eating. Cheap places close by 2100.

Shopping Some handicrafts (goldwork, embroidery, etc) are available in the Centro Comercial Managua; good general shopping here and at Mercado Huembes (also called

Eduardo Contreras), both on Pista de la Solidaridad (buses 110 or 119). The Mercado Huembes and the Mercado Oriental both have a wide selection of handicrafts. At the Mercado Oriental you can get just about anything, on the black market. Good shopping also at Metrocentro, Pista de la Resistencia. Best bookshops at the Centro Sandinista de Trabajadores, Ho Chi Minh Way, and in the Centro Antonio Valdivieso, Calle José Martí, near *Mirador Tiscapa* (also sells records), and at the Centro Comercial Managua; see *Amatl Libro Café* above. Many bookshops sell maps; postcards, badges, stickers and other touristy items. Most ordinary shops are in private houses without signs. Almacenes Internacionales (formerly Dollartienda, and Diplotienda), opp *Los Gauchos* restaurant on Carretera a Masaya, offers Western-style goods, take your passport, accepts dollars and travellers' cheques if to value of purchase. There is an a/c supermarket on Plaza España.

Local Transport Bus service in Managua is cheap and as good as can be expected under the circumstances. US$0.13 approximately. Buses can be very full, though not always so. City buses run every 10 mins 0530-1800, every 15 mins 1800-2200, when last services begin their routes; buses are frequent but it is difficult to fathom their routes. Beware of pickpockets on the crowded urban buses particularly those on tourist routes (see **Warning** above). The principal bus routes are: 101 from Las Brisas, passing CST, *Intercontinental Hotel*, Mercado Oriental, then on to Mercados San Miguel and Mayoreo; 103 from 7 Sur to Mercado Lewites, Plaza 19 de Julio, Metrocentro, Mercado San Miguel and Villa Libertad; 109 from Teatro Darío to the Bolívar/Buitrago junction just before *Intercontinental*, turns E, then SE to Casimir Sotelo bus station/Mercado Huembes; 110 runs from 7 Sur to Villa San Jacinto passing en route Mercado Lewites, Plaza 19 de Julio, Metrocentro, Mercado Huembes/Casimir Sotelo bus station and Mercado San Miguel; 113 from Ciudad Sandino, Las Piedrecitas, CST, *Intercontinental*, to Mercado Oriental; 116 runs E-W below *Intercontinental*, on Buitrago, also passing CST; 118 takes a similar route but turns S on Williams Romero to Plaza España, thence to Israel Lewites bus station; 119 runs from Plaza España to Casimir Sotelo bus station via Plaza 19 de Julio; 123 runs from Mercado Lewites via 7 Sur and Linda Vista to Telcor Sur (near Palacio Nacional), and Nuevo Diario. A map from the Tourist Office (poor), and a couple of days riding the buses will help you orient yourself.

Taxis can be flagged down along the street. They also cruise the bus stations looking for arriving passengers, but it is cheaper to get a taxi on the street nearby. There is a taxi stand just below *Hotel Magut*, W of *Intercontinental*. Taxis are the best method of transport for foreigners in Managua; bargain the fare before entering (fares range from US$0.40-US$1.50). One pays per zone.

Car Hire Hertz, Avis and **Budget. Targa** at the airport (T 31176) and *Hotel Intercontinental* (T 24875). Rates are US$45 per day plus US$0.25 per km not including tax and insurance—credit cards accepted; special weekend rates available. Given the poor public transport and the decentralized layout of Managua, renting a car is often the best way to get around. Alternatively hire a taxi for journeys out of Managua, about US$10/hr from an office opp *Hotel Intercontinental* (opens 0930).

Renault Garage Km 6 Carretera Norte, in front of Coca Cola; efficient spare parts service.

Entertainment Discotheques: *Lobo Jack*, the largest disco in Central America, *La Nueva Managua*, *Frisco Disco*, *Casa Blanca*, *Pantera Rosa*. 2 discos, cinemas, restaurants in Camino Oriente centre (bus 119 or 117). Live music is offered at *La Vista*, *Torre Blanca*, *Tiffany's Saloon* and *El Arroyito*, Plaza 19 de Julio, Pista de la Resistencia opp Universidad Centroamericana, two live bands, crowded, festive, great dancing. *La Cabaña* in the *Intercontinel* and the *Piano Bar* across the street, the latter is a cultural experience. Jazz club at *Cafetería de la ASTC* in El Carmen, from 2000, inexpensive, good food. **Ballet** Ballet Tepenahuatl, folkloric dances in the ruins of the *Gran Hotel*.

Cinemas Most films in English with Spanish sub-titles (US$0.50). Cinemateca, on Av Bolívar (behind Cine González), Government theatre with good programmes (only US$0.20 on Sun am).

Sport Baseball—between Plaza de España and Plaza 19 de Julio on Sun mornings (the national game), a good seat US$0.20. Also there are basketball, cockfighting and bullfighting (but no kill), swimming, sailing, tennis, golf.

Museums The **Museo Nacional** is near the lakeshore, to the E of the railway station, disappointing, little on display and poor labelling (closed Sun). **Museo de la Alfabetización** (closed Mon) near Parque Las Palmas in W section of city commemorates the Sandinista Government's literacy programme. **Museo de Artes Contemporáneos**, opposite the Post Office, features Latin American art donated from all over the continent, open Wed-Sun, 1400-1700, free. **Centro Cultural Ruinas del Gran Hotel**, near Palacio Nacional, permanent display of 'revolutionary' art and visiting exhibitions; small cafeteria (expect to have to deposit your bag at the door).

Exchange Banco Central de Nicaragua, Km 7, Carretera del Sur (not for exchange). **Banco Nicaragüense del Interior y Comercio** at Plaza España changes bank notes only. *Casas de cambio; Buro Internacional de Cambio*, 0830-1200, 1300-1600, 250m S of traffic lights by Plaza España, for US$ cash and TCs (also Mexican and other Central American currencies, but at very poor rates); *Multicambio SA* opp Plaza España on same road; behind Ed Oscar Pérez Cazar at Km 4.5 on road to Masaya, takes Master Card, open 0900-1200, 1400-1600; at terminal for Granada buses, several in Ciudad Jardín; much quicker than banks (ask taxi drivers). It is advisable to change money in Managua as it is difficult elsewhere, though getting easier. Córdoba cash advances on Visa, Master Card at Cred-o-matic, Camino Oriente on Carretera a Masaya. Many public places, like more expensive restaurants, will change money at the official rate (see also **Currency** in Information for Visitors). Dollars cash can be changed on the street: first ask in a bank for the current exchange rate, then ask the *coyotes*, the illegal moneychangers on the street. Those on Avenida Batahola, W of Mercado Lewites, and at Mercado Oriental offer good rates; those near *Hotel Intercontinental* offer low rates and try to cheat. Always take great care; always check the rate first, ask for large denomination notes (*coyotes* try to confuse gringos with small bills) and leave the scene as quickly as possible.

Cultural Institutions Lending library, Casa Ben Linder, 3 blocks S 1½ blocks E of Estatua Monseñor Lezcano, also good book exchange, T 66-4373. Alianza Francesa, near Mexican Embassy, films on Fri evenings, friendly.

Spanish Classes and thorough introduction to Nicaragua: Casa Nicaragüense de Español, Km 11.5 Carretera Sur; accommodation with families. Universidad Centroamericana has Spanish courses which are cheaper, but with larger classes.

Embassies **Panamanian** Consulate, from *Lacmiel* restaurant on Carreta a Masaya turn left and then the 4th street on right, it is 200m on the left, T 670154, F 74223, open 0800-1300, visa on the spot, valid 3 months for a 30-day stay, US$10, maps and information on the Canal; **Costa Rican**, Pista Benjamín Zeledón, nr Plaza España, 1 block to the S. **Honduran** Consulate, Carretera del Sur, Km 15, Colonia Barcelona, open Mon-Fri, 0800-1400 (bus 118 from *Hotel Intercontinental*), Embassy, Planes de Altamira 29, T 670182, F 670184; **Guatemalan**, just after Km 11 on Masaya road, visa US$10, fast service, 0900-1200 only. **Mexican**, from *Lacmiel* on Carreta a Masaya take the 2nd street on the left and it's at the first cross roads on your right, T 5886, F 784923. **Venezuelan**, about 1 km closer to city on same road (Km 10.5, T 675308, F 678327).

USA, Km 41/2 Carretera del Sur (T 666-010, F 663865); **Canadian Consul**, 208 C del Triunfo, Fuente Plazoleta Telcor Central, T 24541.

British, El Reparto, 'Los Robles', Primera Etapa, Entrada Principal de la Carretera a Masaya, Cuarta Casa a la mano derecha, T 780014, F 784083, Telex 2166, Apdo Aéreo 169, it is located on a R-turn at the Telsat shop, off Carretera a Masaya; **French**, Km 12 Carretera del Sur, T 26210, F 62057; **Dutch**, del Terraza 1 cuadra al norte, 1 cuadre al oeste, Apartado 3534, T(010-505-2) 666175, F 660364; **Swiss**, c/o Cruz Corena SA, Km 6.5 Carretera Norte entrada de la Tona, Apartado postal 166, T 492671; **Swedish**, from Plaza España, 1 block W (Abajo), 2 blocks to the Lake, 1/2 block W (Abajo), Apartado Postal 2307, T 60085; **Danish** Cosulate General, Iglesia del Carmen, 2 cuadros al Oeste No 1610, T 23189; **German**, 200m N of Plaza España (towards lake), T 663917/8, open Mon-Fri 0900-1200; **Italian**, Km 15 Carretera al Sur, T 666486, F 663987.

Immigration Pista de la Resistencia, approx 1 km from Km 7 Carretera del Sur, open till 1400. Buses 118 and 110.

Customs Km 5 Carretera del Norte, bus No 108.

Health Hospitals are generally crowded and queues very long. Recommended is Hospital Alemán-Nicaragüense HNA, from Siemens on Km 6 of Carretera Norte, 3 blocks S, operated with German aid, mostly Nicaraguan staff, make an appointment by phone in advance. Private clinics are an alternative, eg Policlínica Nicaragüense, consultation US$30. Dr César Zepeda Monterrey speaks English, American-trained. Medicines are in short supply, take your own if possible.

General Post Office 3 blocks W of Palacio Nacional and Cathedral, 0700-1600 (closed Sat pm). Separate entrance and exit. Wide selection of beautiful stamps. Poste Restante (l ista de Correos) keeps mail for 1 month.

Telecommunications Telcor, same building as Post Office. Mercado Roberto Huembes (Eduardo Contreras), on bus route 110 from *Hotel Intercontinental*, open 0700-2230. The Telcor office in Barrio Altamira (take taxi) sells and excellent phone directory for US$6 which is also the best tourist guide.

Tourist Information Inturismo, 1 block W of *Hotel Intercontinental*, enter by side door, Apdo postal 122, T 22498/27423, F 25314. Standard information available, including on all types of transport in the country. Maps of Managua (almost up-to-date), with insets of León and Granada and whole country on reverse, US$4. Inturismo will help with finding accommodation with families, with full board. Post cards for sale at Tourist Office, Ministry of Culture, Mercado Huembes and *Intercontinental Hotel* (more expensive); also at Tarjetas Gordión and at bookshops. **Turnica**, Av 11 SO, 300m, 2 mins from Plaza España, T 661387/660406, sells maps of Managua and of the country. It offers tours of Managua, US$15 pp, Masaya, US$30 pp, Granada, US$40 pp, Matagalpa and León, US$50 pp each, in all cases minimum 2 people.

Travel Agents *Central American Tours*, T 41356, new in 1993, economical tours for individual travellers, ask for an English speaking guide if you need one.

Airlines Around Plaza España: Nica (international and internal flight information, T 663136), Aeroflot, Iberia, KLM (300m E), Lufthansa, Continental (next to Multicambio); in Colonia Los Robles (Carretera a Masaya), Copa, Taca, Cubana (E of Plaza 19 de Julio, turn right on road opp *Restaurant Lacmiel*, T 73976). La Costeña (for the Atlantic coast), T 631228. Foreigners may pay in dollars or córdobas for internal flight tickets, but dollars only for international tickets.

Airport César Augusto Sandino, 12 km E of city, near the lake. Take any bus marked 'Tipitapa' from Mercado Huembes, Mercado San Miguel or Mercado Oriental (near Victoria brewery), US$0.16. Alternatively take a taxi for no more than US$5. Be early for international flights since formalities are slow and thorough and can take 2 hrs. X-ray machines reported safe for film. Two duty free shops, café, toilets through immigration; some departing passengers (eg on Aviateca and Nica flights) are offered free coffee, juice and a *pastel* in the departure hall. Internal flights to eg Bluefields and the Corn Islands are given in the text below. You are not allowed to stay overnight in the airport.

Rail All rail services were suspended on 31 December 1993. The ruins of the station are 5 blocks E of the old Cathedral.

Buses The Comandante Casimir Sotelo bus station by the Mercado Roberto Huembes (Mercado Eduardo Contreras), on Pista de la Solidaridad (see map), is for Rivas, Granada, Masaya, Estelí, Somoto, Matagalpa, etc, and all destinations in the N. Take bus 109, which starts from Parque Central and runs below the *Hotel Intercontinental*, or bus 119. Bus to **Granada**, Ruta 4, 0540-2020, every 20 mins, US$0.80, 1 hr 15 mins. To **Somoto**, 0700 and 1400 via Estelí, 5 hrs 10 mins, US$2.40. To **Ocotal**, 0845 and 1615, 4 hrs 50 mins, US$3.35. For full details, see under destinations. For **León**, **Corinto** and **Pacific Coast** and **Chinandega**, the terminal is beside Mercado Israel Lewites, Pista de la Resistencia, on SW side of city. To get from the first bus station to the second, take bus 110, or take bus 109, then change at *Intercontinental* to bus 118. It is probably simpler to take a taxi, US$3. Buses to **Boaco**, **Juigalpa** and **Rama** leave from the Terminal Atlántico at Mercado San Miguel, on Pista José Angel Benavides, in the E of the city. Buses tend to be very full; children scramble on board first, grab seats and 'sell' them to passengers. Possible (and safer) to sit on your luggage than put it on the roof. You may have to pay extra for your baggage.

International Buses Look in *El Nuevo Diario* Sección 2, 'Servicios', for buses running to San Salvador, Tegucigalpa, Guatemala City and Mexico. Ticabus to San José daily at 0500, US$50 single, 12 hrs; also to Tegucigalpa (0600, US$20), San Salvador (US$35) and Guatemala City (US$45), terminal is in Barrio Martha Quezada (Cine Dorado, 2 cuadras arriba, W of *Hotel Intercontinental*, T 22094/23031). Sirca Express leaves 0600 Mon, Wed, Fri and Sat to San José, US$30, 10 hrs (inc 1 hr minimum at border, you can stop anywhere in Costa Rica, but same price); Sirca office and terminal Puente Los Robles, Km 4.5 Carretera a Masaya, T 73833. A cheaper way of travelling to San José is to take a bus Managua-Rivas, then colectivo to border and another between the border posts, then take local bus to San José; takes 15 hrs altogether. International buses are always booked-up many days in advance and tickets will not be sold until all passport/visa documentation is complete. **NB** If arriving in Managua with Ticabus beware touts who try to take you to hotels; their commission will be added to your hotel bill.

Excursions There are several volcanic-crater lakes in the environs of Managua, some of which have become centres of residential development and also have swimming, boating, fishing and picnicking facilities for the public. Among the more attractive of these lakes is **Laguna de Xiloá**, situated about 16 km from Managua just off the new road to León. At Xiloá there is a private aquatic club

(El Náutico); small restaurants and hotels; boats can be rented; bathing possible on the narrow beach (with caves, recent reports of locals drowned). On Sat and Sun, the only days when buses run, Xiloá gets very crowded, but it is quiet during the week, when you must walk there. You can camp there. Take bus 113 to Las Piedrecitas for bus to Xiloá (US$0.35); admission US$1.60 for cars, US$0.30 for pedestrians. Other lakes within a 45-min drive of Managua are the Laguna de Apoyo and Laguna de Masaya (**see p 696** and **695**), situated respectively at Kms 35 and 15 on the Masaya road.

The **Huellas de Acahualinca** are Managua's only site of archaeological interest. These are prehistoric (6,000 year old) animal and human footprints which have been preserved in tufa, located close to the old centre of town, near the lakeshore at the end of the S Highway. Bus No 102 passes the site, on which there is also a small museum which exhibits a variety of prehistoric artefacts. Entry US$2.

A 10-km drive down Carretera Sur—this is the Pan-American Highway— through the residential section of Las Piedrecitas passes the US Ambassador's residence to **Laguna de Asososca**, another small lake (the city's reservoir) in the wooded crater of an old volcano. Piedrecitas Park is to one side of the lake: there is a beautiful 3½-km ride, playgrounds for children, a café, and splendid view of Lake Managua, two smaller lakes—Asososca and Xiloá—and of Momotombo volcano. Beyond again is the little **Laguna de Nejapa** (medicinal waters). The Pan-American Highway to Costa Rica passes through **Casa Colorada** (hotel), 26 km from Managua, at 900m, with commanding views of both the Pacific and of Lake Managua, and a delightful climate (but no trees because of poisonous gases from Santiago volcano, **see p 695**).

Boats can be hired on the shores of **Lake Managua** for visiting the still-smoking Momotombo and the shore villages (**see also p 690**). A fine drive skirts the shores of the lake. Do not swim in Lake Managua as it is polluted in places.

Beaches There are several beaches on the Pacific coast, about an hour's drive from Managua. The nearest are **Pochomil** and **Masachapa** (54 km from Managua, side by side, half hourly bus service from terminal in Israel Lewites market) and **Casares** (69 km from Managua, dirty, thorns on beach; 2 restaurants). A few km from Casares is **La Boquita**, visited by turtles from Aug to Nov. Otherwise La Boquita beach is to be avoided, frequent muggings and no tap water supplies for most of 1991. Because of their proximity to the capital, these are very popular during the season (Jan-April) and tend to be somewhat crowded. Out of season, except at weekends, Pochomil is deserted (don't sleep on the beach, mosquitoes will eat you alive); it is clean and being developed as a tourist centre with hotels and restaurants. Only hotel at present, **B** Baja Mar, with a/c, **C** without, basic, not worth the money. Masachapa is cheaper but dirtier; hotels on beach, **F** (but **Terraza** not rec); **D** Hotel Summer on the main street to the beach, restaurant, fair; **F** Hotel Rex, very very basic. Very slow bus journey from Managua. Near Pochomil and Masachapa is the **Montelimar** resort, built by the Sandinistas, now owned by Spain's Barceló group. It is expensive and becoming popular with package tours. It has a broad, unspoilt sandy beach ideal for bathing and surfing; 202 apartments in bungalows, a/c, minibar, cable TV, bathroom; 'largest swimming pool in Central America', 2 smaller ones, fine restaurant, several bars, disco, fitness centre, shops, laundry, tennis, casino. The nearest public transport is 3 km away at Masachapa, taxi from Managua US$30 (70 km), or hire a car. Reservations T Managua 284132/33/37/45, F 284146.

A visit to the broad, sandy **El Velero** beach (turn off at Km 60 on the old road to León and then follow signs) is recommended despite the US$3.50 entrance charge and poor road. All facilities controlled by the INSSBI, for the benefit of state employees, and at weekends is fully booked for weeks in advance. You may be able to rent a cabin (**E** for 2) in the week, pay extra for sheet and pillows. You can eat in the restaurant (Pirata Cojo, not cheap), at the INSSBI cafeteria (bring your own utensils, buy meal ticket in advance, or take your own food). However, the beach itself is beautiful, and the sea is ideal for both surfing and swimming. **El Tránsito** is a beautiful, undeveloped Pacific beach; bus from Managua at 1200 (from Terminal Lewites), return at 0600 or 0700. Good cheap meals from Sra Pérez on the beach (possible accommodation); Restaurant Yolanda; beach flats for 4-6 people normally available mid-week at N end (Centro Vacacional de Trabajadores, good value).

MANAGUA TO HONDURAS

There are three border crossings to Honduras, the Pan-American Highway gives access to each. After leaving Lake Managua, the road goes through hilly country, with various types of agriculture, mining and pines. A detour through Matagalpa and Jinotega enters good walking country. Estelí, a major centre, has, like many other places, evidence of Revolution damage.

The Pan-American Highway runs from Managua to Honduras (214 km) and is paved the whole way. Also paved is the branch road to Matagalpa and Jinotega. The border crossings with Honduras on the Pan-American Highway is through Somoto to El Espino (see below).

The first stretch of 21 km to Tipitapa is along the southern edge of Lake Managua. **Tipitapa**, to the SE of the lake about $2\frac{1}{2}$ km away from the shore, on the other side of the Highway, was a tourist resort with hot sulphur baths and a casino. This is now in ruins though you can still swim in the baths. There is a colourful market, and a *fiesta* of El Señor de Esquipulas on 13-16 January. Swimming in El Trapice park, US$0.50.

Hotel E *Aguas Calientes*, with shower, filthy, cold water, fan, no sheets, not rec.

Restaurant *Salón Silvia*, unpretentious. Slightly cheaper, but good, is the a/c restaurant attached to the thermal baths. *Entre Ríos*, helpful, looks like the best in town.

Bus from **Managu**, Terminal Atlántico (minibus), US$0.30. Bus to **Estelí**, US$1.40. Bus to **Masaya**, US$0.35, change there for Granada.

The Pan-American Highway goes N through Tipitapa to Sébaco, 105 km. Fourteen km before reaching Sébaco is **Ciudad Darío** (off the main road, turning N of town, is not signposted), where the poet Rubén Darío was born; you can see the house, which is maintained as a museum. There is no hotel in Ciudad Darío, but in **Sébaco** there is *Motel Valle*, on the Highway 1 km towards Ciudad Darío, with restaurant. E of the Highway is **Esquipula**, 100 km from Managua, $2\frac{1}{2}$ hrs by bus, a good place for hiking, fishing, riding; **F** *Hotel Oscar Morales*, clean, shower, friendly.

From Sébaco a 24-km branch road leads (right) to **Matagalpa** at 678m, in the best walking country in Nicaragua, population 70,000. Matagalpa has an old church, but it is about the only colonial style building left; the town has developed rapidly in recent years. It was badly damaged in the Revolution, but is undergoing reconstruction, retaining much of its original character. The birthplace of Carlos Fonseca is now a museum, 1 block E of the more southerly of the 2 main squares; in the northerly square (with the Cathedral) is a Galería de los Héroes y Mártires. The Centro Popular de la Cultura, with murals on the outside, is $2\frac{1}{2}$ blocks N, 4 blocks E from the NE corner of the Cathedral plaza. The town has a very erratic water supply. There is a small zoo in the northern suburbs along the river. The main occupation is coffee planting and there are cattle ranges; the chief industry is the Nestlé powdered-milk plant. A 32-km road runs from Matagalpa to the Tuma valley. 24 September, Día de La Merced, is a local holiday.

Hotels Many places shut their doors by 2200-2300. **C** *Selva Negra*, at 1,200m, 10 km on road to Jinotega, cabins, B, more comfortable, good, as is the expensive restaurant (reserve in advance at weekends by telegram), good starting point for walks in jungle, ask hotel for free map; **D** *Ideal*, with bath, **E** without, better rooms are upstairs, beware overcharging, good but expensive restaurant, disco on Sat; **E** *Bermúdez*, E of NE corner of the southerly plaza, with bath, reasonably clean, good car parking, not very helpful, no meals; $\frac{1}{2}$ block W is **E** *Hospedaje Matagalpa*, wtih bath, clean, light and airy; **E** *Soza*, opp river, basic; **F** *Hospedaje Colonial*, on main plaza, basic; on the other side of the square **F** *Hospedaje Plaza*, clean, small and bright rooms, quiet, no sign, basic, inexpensive.

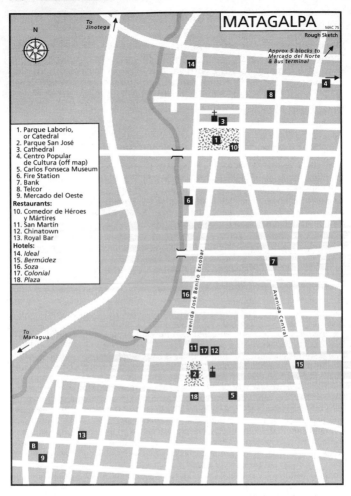

MATAGALPA MAC 75
Rough Sketch

N

To Jinotega

Approx 5 blocks to Mercado del Norte & Bus terminal

1. Parque Laborio, or Catedral
2. Parque San José
3. Cathedral
4. Centro Popular de Cultura (off map)
5. Carlos Fonseca Museum
6. Fire Station
7. Bank
8. Telcor
9. Mercado del Oeste
Restaurants:
10. Comedor de Héroes y Mártires
11. San Martín
12. Chinatown
13. Royal Bar
Hotels:
14. *Ideal*
15. *Bermúdez*
16. *Soza*
17. *Colonial*
18. *Plaza*

Avenida José Benito Escobar

Avenida Central

To Managua

Restaurants *Comedor San Martín*, main street, good breakfasts; *Comedor de Héroes y Mártires Anónimos* in park near church (built with assistance from Tilburg, Neth), rec; *Comedor Vicky*, S of cathedral, good breakfast and lunch (closed pm); *Sorbetería*, 1 block E of square with Fonseca quotes, on a corner, rec; *Chinatown*, Chinese, on plaza, next to *Hospedaje Colonial*, good and cheap; *Lanchería Marcia*, opp fire station, excellent value lunch; *Los Pinchitos Morenos*, near the centre, good and cheap. *Pizzas Don Diego*, opp cinema.

Shopping Mercado del Norte, close to northern highway (filthy); Mercado del Oeste, unfriendly *comedor*, swarms of flies and mosquitoes, is 2 blocks W of *Royal Bar*. Bookshop: Fundación Manolo Morales, 1 block N, ½ block E of plaza, Spanish editions of international literature and stamps. Look for fine black pottery made in a local cooperative.

Exchange Banco Nacional de Desarrollo. Moneychangers near the Cathedral offer 'interesting' rates.

Buses Terminal Sur, by Mercado del Oeste for Managua, Estelí amd Jinotega: every half hour to/from **Managua**, 127 km, take 3 hrs, US$1.65. To **Jinotega**, from Terminal del Sur, US$1, 17 a day; to **Estelí**, frequent, US$1. Terminal Norte, by Mercado del Norte, is for all other destinations. Taxi between terminals US$0.50. 1 bus a day to **León**, 0600, US$3 (luggage US$1); check which terminal in advance.

There is a badly deteriorated 34-km highway from Matagalpa to **Jinotega** (altitude 1,004m), which is served by buses from Managua (4 a day each way, US$3.35, buy ticket 2 hrs in advance) and Matagalpa. Population 20,000; famous images in church. The Somoza jail has been converted into a youth centre. (Hotels: **F** *Hospedaje Carlos*, 2 blocks from bus station, basic; *Rosa*, near main square. Restaurant *El Tico*, near bus terminal, beware overcharging. Several banks near main square.) There is a beautiful hike from behind the cemetery to the cross above the city, 90 mins round trip, a steep climb. Excellent coffee grown here and in Matagalpa. Road (18 km) to El Tuma power station; another to Estelí, through La Concordia, unpaved, picturesque, but very little transport from La Concordia to Estelí.

From Jinotega an 80-km, unpaved road goes to the main highway at Condega, 51 km from the Honduran border (see below). This road passes through **San Rafael del Norte** (**F** *Hospedaje Rocío*, shared bath, reasonable, good food; **E** *Hospedaje Aura*, basic, dirty). There are some good murals in the local church, and a chapel on the hill behind, at Tepeyak, built as a spiritual retreat; very interesting recent history, involved in Sandinista struggle. Trucks from Jinotega market to San Rafael del Norte at 0700, 0800 and 0900, thereafter regular buses; trucks to Estelí at 0700, US$1, 3 hrs. The road passes through another picturesque village, **Yalí**.

The 134-km section from Sébaco (see above) to the border at El Espino is through sharp hills with steep climbs and descents, but reasonably well banked and smooth.

A reasonable road leads off the Pan-American Highway 10 km N of Sébaco, near **San Isidro**, to join the Pacific Highway near León (110 km). This is an attractive alternative route to Managua through the Chinandega cotton growing area, past the spectacular chain of volcanoes running W from Lake Managua, and through León. (Bus Estelí-San Isidro, US$0.50, San Isidro-León, 3-4 hrs, US$2). On this road, 12 km N of the intersection with the Chinandega-León road, is **San Jacinto**; 200m to the W of the road is a field of steaming, bubbling mud holes (approach carefully, the ground may give and scald your legs).

The Pan-American Highway goes through **Estelí** (606m), a rapidly developing departmental capital of about 20,000 people (heavily damaged during the Revolution of 1978-79). It is the site of prehistoric carved stone figures (in park in front of tourist information office, also has a nice playground). Worth visiting are the Casa de Cultura (fiestas, meetings, exhibitions), Galería de los Héroes y Mártires next door, opp fire station (mementoes and photographs of those killed defending the Revolution, sad but interesting, wonderful paintings on the outside walls), small café adjoining in which you are encouraged to have a drink as a way of contributing to the museum. For the Salvadorean cooperative, take Av Bolívar/Calle Principal from Cathedral Plaza towards bus station—some crafts, café with posters all over the walls, good. The Ministry of Health Information Centre, on Gran Vía Bolívar, 4 blocks from Plaza, is involved with projects to revive traditional medicine and healing; it offers advice on a wide range of herbal remedies. Also ask at the Reforma Agraria Office (above Banco de América) if you wish to see any local farming cooperatives. The Amnlae women's centre has social and educational projects which are interesting to visit and which may welcome volunteers. Tourist information off Calle Principal beyond hospital, to S of main plaza. Cinema on S side of main plaza.

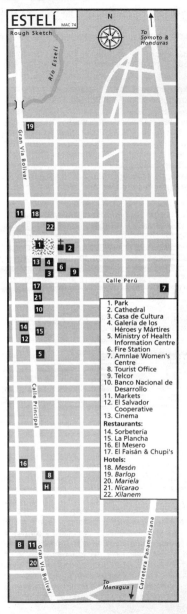

ESTELÍ MAC 74
Rough Sketch

1. Park
2. Cathedral
3. Casa de Cultura
4. Galería de los Héroes y Mártires
5. Ministry of Health Information Centre
6. Fire Station
7. Amnlae Women's Centre
8. Tourist Office
9. Telcor
10. Banco Nacional de Desarrollo
11. Markets
12. El Salvador Cooperative
13. Cinema

Restaurants:
14. Sorbetería
15. La Plancha
16. El Mesero
17. El Faisán & Chupi's

Hotels:
18. Mesón
19. Barlop
20. Mariela
21. Nicarao
22. Xilanem

Hotels D *Mesón*, Av Bolívar, 1 block N of Cathedral and plaza, with shower, fan, clean, restaurant, changes TCs, rec; **E** *Barlop*, 5 blocks N of main square, 12 rooms, 6 of which good, 6 basic, former have showers, T (071) 2486, good, friendly; **F** *Mariela*, behind bus station, clean, safe, washing facilities, very small rooms, parking inside gates, basic; **E** *Nicarao*, 1½ blocks S of main square, Av Bolívar/Calle Principal, with shower (cheaper without), good restaurant, good service, leafy patio, closes at 2200, rec; **E-D** *Nahuali* good, pricey, without bath, but good food (dinner US$6-9); **F** *Bolívar*, unmarked, 2 blocks S on Calle Principal from *Restaurant La Plancha*; **F** *Galo*, Nicaragua y Central; **F** *Hospedaje El Chepito*, next to bus station, clean, friendly, ; **F** *Juárez*, near bus station, very basic, filthy, noisy, parking inside gates; **F** *La Florida*, very basic, not rec, but safe parking; **F** *Xilanem*, one block N of main square, clean, noisy.

Restaurant Opp *Sorbetería Estelí*, is *La Plancha*; *China Garden*, on main square, good; *El Mesero*, on street which joins Av Bolívar at hospital, opp an open field (from Texaco 1 'abajo', 'al Norte'), popular and very good despite appearance. *Chupi's* ice cream, in *El Faisán* restaurant on Av Bolívar (latter promotes use of soya); about 3 blocks N of park on same street *Panadería España*, good but pricey. 50m W of main square is *Dona Pizza*, good pizza, large vegetarian is about US$9.

Shopping 2 small markets, one N, one S of Cathedral Plaza. Dollartienda.

Exchange Banco Nacional de Desarrollo. *Agencia de Viajes Tisey* in *Hotel Mesón* changes TCs at the official rate; many street changers, for cash only, on Av Bolívar.

Language School Cenac, Centro Nicaragüense de Aprendizaje Cultura, Casa Blanca Sevilla, de la Oficina de Dr Briones 1 cuadra al Oeste, Barro Orlando Ochoa, Estelí, Apartado No 29 (or de los Bancos 1 cuadra al Sur, ½ Cuadra al Este), 4 week programmes learning Spanish, living with a family, travelling to countryside, meetings and seminars, from US$600 to US$800. Also teaches English to Nicaraguans and others and welcomes volunteer tutors.

Buses Leave from the market S of central plaza; walk down Av Bolívar/Calle Principal, 20 mins, or take a *camioneta*. To/from **Managua**, US$1.60, 3 hrs 35 mins, half-hourly service. For **León**, take any bus going on the main road E towards Managua and change at San Isidro, 30 mins, US$0.50; from here buses wait by the roadside to continue S to León (see above). There is a daily minibus to **León** at 0645 (0545 Mon); and another bus at 1510, US$2. For Honduras change at Somoto (bus leaves Estelí 1030 and 1730, US$0.70, 2 hrs, and shuttle service from there, 45 mins, US$0.40) or Ocotal (buses at 1140 and 1910).

Bathing near Estelí at Puente La Sirena, 200m off the road to Condega, or Salta Estanzuela, 5 km S of Estelí, a waterfall of 25m, with a deep pool at the bottom, surrounded by trees and flowers (inc orchids—only worth it in the rainy season), at least 5 km off the Managua road, four-wheel drive recommended. Take the dirt road, starting 1/2 km S of Estelí on Pan-American Highway, through San Nicolás. Since there are no signs, it is worth hiring a guide.

A very poor but spectacular gravel road from Estelí runs to El Sauce, 45 km (**see** p 693); after 20 km an equally rough road branches N to Achuapa. N of **Achuapa**, an unmade road continues through **San Juan de Limay** (one *hospedaje*), an *artesanía*, and marble town, and **Pueblo Nuevo** (2 basic *hospedajes*), near which is an archaeological site. From here the road goes on to join the Pan-American Highway a few km E of Somoto. The Inturismo map shows a road running from San Juan de Limay to San José de Cusmapa (5,073 inhabitants, 1,500m) and La Sabana (meals at shop on right on Parque Central when coming from Somoto), continuing to the Highway just W of Somoto. There is no road between San Juan de Limay and San José de Cusmapa.

The Highway then goes to **Condega** (5,000 people; **F** pp *Hotel Primavera*, nothing special, but plumbing works) and to **Somoto** (15,000 people), centre of pitch-pine industry, thence to **El Espino** (20 km), 5 km from Honduran border at La Playa. The Nicaraguan passport control and customs are at El Espino in the ruined customs house, 100m from the Honduran border. Minibuses run between Somoto and the border (US$0.40, plus US$0.40 per bag), and 2 buses daily between Somoto and Estelí, 0600 and 1415 (US$0.80); Somoto-Managua, 5 hrs 35 mins, US$2.40 plus extra for luggage, same buses as for Estelí. The Nicaraguan side opens from 0900-1300 and 1400-1700. Note that there is no public transport back to Somoto after 1600 and nowhere to stay in El Espino. Nicaragua is 1 hr ahead of Honduras. (There is a food bar on the Nicaraguan side but several cafés on the Honduran side.) Motorists leaving Nicaragua should enquire in Somoto if an exit permit has to be obtained there, or in El Espino. This applies to cyclists as well.

Hotels in Somoto F *Baghal*, clean, friendly, helpful, rec; **F** *Internacional*, 1 block from central plaza, clean and basic; **F** *Panamericano*, on main square, but new section being built will be more expensive, landlord helpful, speaks English, rec. **G** *Pensión Marina*, shared shower, bargain. **Restaurant**: *Victoria*, serves good food; *Chinatlan*, good.

Just before reaching Somoto a road leads off from Yalagüina right (18 km) to **Ocotal**, a clean, cool, whitewashed town of 60,000 people at 600m on a sandy plain (well worth a visit). The Shell petrol station here changes US$ cash. It is near the Honduran border, to which a road runs N (bus marked Las Manos), wonderful scenery. Money changers operate only on the Honduran side, offering rates a little better than the Nicaraguan black market, although sometimes no córdobas are available. Inturismo sells its map for US$4 (not worth the price). There is a pleasant hotel near the border, 8 km N of Ocotal, called **Las Colinas**, pool, safe car park, bar, information. Close by, at **San Albino**, there are many gold mines and gold is washed in the Río Coco (bus only from Ciudad Sandino—formerly Jícaro, 50 km from Ocotal). Friendly, helpful Tourist Office 2 blocks from main square, opposite the market. The bus station is on the highway, 1 km from town centre, 15-20 mins walk from Parque Central. Bus (or truck) Ocotal-Somoto, US$0.40; Estelí-Ocotal, US$1.25, 2 hrs, beautiful views; Ocotal-Managua, 0900 and 1530, US$3.35. Beware of taking a taxi from Ocotal to the border, drivers often try to rip you off.

Hotels at Ocotal D *Frontera*, not too clean, but better than others, pool, cold water only from 0500 to 0900; **F** *El Portal*, reasonable, rec; **F** *El Castillo*, basic, quiet; *Segovia*, 1 block N of plaza on Calle Central, cheap, basic, OK; **F** *Pensión Centroamericana*, not as dirty as most others, but unfriendly; **F** *Pensión Wilson*, good, friendly. For eating, *Restaurant La Cabaña*; *El Deportivo*, excellent value *comida corriente*, friendly; *Brasilia*, very good, ask for directions; *Café Capri* is best for *refrescos*.

Exchange Banco Nicaragüense del Interior y Comercio and Banco Banic (near the plaza) will change TCs.

The Las Manos/Ocotal crossing is quite straightforward and, being high up, is quite cool. Entering by car here you will receive help from the truckers crossing here. Go first to Migración (US$2), then Tránsito (US$20), then Fumigación (US$1). Finally, queue up at Aduana to get your car papers. This takes over an hour and, rather than standing in line, go to Aduana first of all to get your number in the queue (shout at the clerks until they give you one), then check periodically how the queue is progressing. You will save all of 10 mins (Francesca Pagnacco, Exeter).

MANAGUA TO CORINTO

The route from the capital through Pacific lowlands to the Gulf of Fonseca runs beside a chain of volcanoes, from Momotombo on Lake Managua to Cosigüina overlooking the Gulf. The city of León has been deeply involved in Nicaragua's history since colonial times. On the Pacific coast are the beaches at Poneloya and the major port of Corinto.

The first city of note along the highway is León, 88 km from Managua. The Pacific Highway between Managua and Corinto (140 km) follows the shore of Lake Managua and goes on to Chinandega; it has been continued to Corinto and to the Honduran border. The old, paved road to León crosses the Sierra de Managua, offering fine views of the lake (it is no longer than the Pacific Highway, but is in good condition).

About 60 km down the new road to León lies the village of *La Paz Centro* (road to here paved; **F** *Hospedaje El Caminante*, close to Highway, basic, friendly, cheap; much handmade pottery here, good range and very cheap, ask to see the potters' ovens and production of bricks; try the local speciality *quesillo*, cream cheese served ready-to-eat in plastic bags, all along the highway). Frequent bus service from Managua, Terminal Lewites, every $\frac{1}{2}$ hr. It is from here that one can gain access to the volcano **Momotombo**, which dominates the Managua skyline from the W. It is also possible to camp on the lakeside here in full view of the volcano.

One now has to have a permit from Empresa Nacional de Luz y Fuerza in Managua to climb Momotombo from the S; they have built a geothermal power station on the volcano's slopes; alternatively ask police in León Viejo for a permit (very difficult to get). We understand no permit is required to climb the volcano from the N.

At the volcano's foot lies **León Viejo**, which was destroyed by earthquake on 31 December 1609 and is now being excavated. It was in the Cathedral here that Pedrarias and his wife were buried (see **Early, Post-Conquest History** in Introduction to Central America). The ruins can be reached by boat from Managua. Near the large volcano is a smaller one, Momotombito.

León, with a population of 130,000, was founded by Hernández de Córdoba in 1524 at León Viejo, 32 km from its present site. The city moved to its present site in 1610. It was the capital from its foundation until Managua replaced it in 1858; it is still the 'intellectual' capital, with a university (founded 1804), religious colleges, the largest cathedral in Central America, and several colonial churches. It is said that Managua became the capital, although at the time it was only an Indian settlement, because it was half-way between violently Liberal León and equally violently Conservative Granada.

The city has a traditional air, its colonial charm unmatched elsewhere in

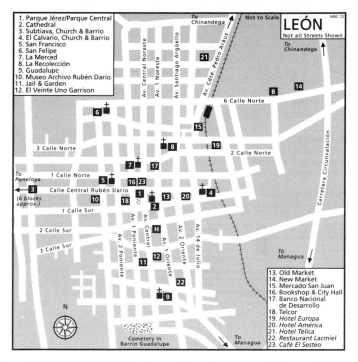

1. Parque Jérez/Parque Central
2. Cathedral
3. Subtiava, Church & Barrio
4. El Calvario, Church & Barrio
5. San Francisco
6. San Felipe
7. La Merced
8. La Recolección
9. Guadalupe
10. Museo Archivo Rubén Darío
11. Jail & Garden
12. El Veinte Uno Garrison

13. Old Market
14. New Market
15. Mercado San Juan
16. Bookshop & City Hall
17. Banco Nacional de Desarrollo
18. Telcor
19. *Hotel Europa*
20. *Hotel América*
21. *Hotel Telica*
22. *Restaurant Lacmiel*
23. *Café El Sesteo*

LEÓN
MAC 72
Not all Streets Shown
Not to Scale

Nicaragua: narrow streets, roofs tiled in red, low adobe houses and time-worn buildings everywhere. The old Plaza de Armas, in front of the Cathedral, is now Parque Jérez, but is usually referred to as Parque Central; it contains a statue of General Jérez, a mid-19th century Liberal leader. Next to the park is an interesting mural covering the history from precolumbian times to the Sandinista revolution, completed in 1990.

The Cathedral, begun in 1746 and not completed for 100 years, is an enormous building. It has a famous shrine, 145 cm high, covered by white topazes from India given by Philip II of Spain, which is kept in a safe in the vestry, and the bishop holds the key; a very fine ivory Christ; the consecrated Altar of Sacrifices and the Choir of Córdoba; the great Christ of Esquipulas, a colonial work in bronze whose cross is of very fine silver; and statues of the 12 Apostles. At the foot of one of these statues is the tomb of Rubén Darío, the 19th-century Nicaraguan poet, and one of the greatest in Latin America, guarded by a sorrowing lion.

The western end of the city is the oldest, and here is the oldest of all the churches: the parish church of Subtiava (1530) where Las Casas, the Apostle of the Indies, preached on several occasions. It has a fine façade, the best colonial altar in the country and an interesting representation of the sun ('El Sol') revered by the Indians. The church has been beautifully reconstructed. The roof was rebuilt, under the supervision of the 'Cocusión 500 años'. Near the Subtiava church are a small town museum (entrance free) and the ruins of the parish church of Vera Cruz, now crumbling. Also in the suburb of Subtiava is the Casa de Cultura with interesting murals. Other churches well worth visiting include El Calvario (beautifully decorated ceiling), La Recolección (fine façade), La Merced, San Felipe, Zaragoza, San Francisco and El Laborío. There is a pleasant walk S across the bridge, past the church of Guadalupe, to the cemetery. The house of Rubén Darío, the famous 'Four Corners' in Calle Rubén Darío, is now the Museo-Archivo Rubén Darío; it has an interesting collection of personal possessions and library with a wide range of books of poetry in Spanish, English and French. Darío died in 1916 in another house in the NW sector marked with a plaque. A plaque also marks the spot in the centre of the city where the first President Somoza was assassinated in 1956 by poet Rigoberto López Pérez.

León was the centre of heavy fighting during the 1978-79 Revolution; much of the damage has still to be repaired (a public works programme was promised in 1988), but there are also many monuments from that time in the city (descriptions of León's fight against the Somoza régime can be found in *Fire from the Mountain: The Making of a Sandinista* by Omar Cabezas). Visitors can see El Fortín, the ruined last stronghold of the Somocista national guard (a commemorative march goes there each July, from the Cathedral, go W about 10 blocks, then S, best in early am, great views of town and several volcanoes); El Veinte Uno, the national guard's 21st garrison, also ruined, with the jail around the corner converted into a garden (3 blocks S of cathedral); statue of Luisa Amanda Espinoza, the first woman member of the FSLN to die (in 1970), after whom the women's organization (AMNLAE) is named (7-8 blocks N of market behind Cathedral, in Barrio San Felipe); 2 blocks W of La Merced church is the Centro Popular de la Cultura (frequent exhibitions and events). In the blocks N of the Cathedral is a commemorative park with portraits of Sandino, Carlos Fonseca and Jérez.

Festivals and Local Holidays The Holy Week ceremonies are outstanding, as are the festivities on 7 December, Día de la Concepción, much singing, dancing, fireworks, and festive crowds. 20 June (Liberation by Sandinistas), 24 September, 1 November (All Saints' Day).

Hotels **D** *Europa*, 2 blocks S of railway station, best, with bath and a/c, cheaper without bath, but with fan, comfortable patios with bar and shade, mice, restaurant expensive, limited parking inside, guard will watch vehicles parked on street; **E** *América*, Av Santiago Argüello, 2 blocks E of central market, with bath and fan, clean, good value, slow service, cold drinks, convenient location, also secure garage nearby; **F** *Hospedaje Primavera*, 5 blocks N, and 1½ blocks E of railway station, not very clean, basic. **F** *Telica*, with shower, noisy, cockroaches, not rec, good breakfast, 4 blocks N of railway station. **E** *Restaurante Pilar*, Av Comandante, 3 blocks from old railway station, has one room with 3 beds, own bathroom, clean, owner speaks English. Several cheap *pensiones* near the railway station, including **G** *Tecotal*, good breakfast.

Restaurants *El Filete*, 4 blocks N of Parque Jérez, good for all types of seafood, friendly, pricey; *Jorón*, very good steaks, expensive, friendly service, from Parque Central 1 block W, 2 blocks N; *Pollo Loco*, Calle 1 Norte, rec; *Los Angeles* and *Dragón de Oro* (Chinese), ½ block N of Parque Jérez. Gringo café; *El Sesteo*, on plaza; *La Casa Vieja*, 1½ blocks N of San Francisco church, pleasant bar, good quality snacks, good value, highly rec; *El Barcito*, NW of Parque Central, popular, soft drinks, milk shakes, slow service; *Central*, Calle 4 Norte, good *comida corriente*; *Marisquería Solmar*, 1 block from main square, good seafood but expensive; *Metropolitano*, 1 block W of Post Office, good steaks. *La Cueva del León*, seafood and steaks (usually poor), two blocks N of Parque Jérez, slow service, dirty; *Capricornio*, nr Central University, good *comida corriente*, interesting atmosphere; good value *comida corriente* at *Comedores Emu* (nr La Recolección church, opp *Solmar*, US$2, good value) and *La Cucaracha* (1 block S of *Hotel América* on opp side of street, no sign); *Sacuanjoche*, Calle Darío opp Museo Archivo Darío, expensive but good steaks, good service; *Lacmiel*, 5 blocks S of Cathedral, good food, live music, open air, rec; *Los Pescaditos*, nr Subtiava church, excellent for fish at reasonable prices, rec. Excellent ice cream parlour, *Chupi's*, 1 block N of central square. *Soda Metro*, US style fast food, US$2 buys a tasty lunch; *Libro-Café La Casona de Colón*, Calle 1 Norte 307, esquina de los Bancos, 150 metros al este, T 5573, café-cum-museum, coffee, cocktails, Nicaraguan meals (indoors or outdoors), many artefacts of Nicaraguan history, owner speaks English. *El Rincón Azul*, Calle Central Rubén Darío, about 1½ blocks E of Parque Jérez, an excellent bar, very cheap, also a local art gallery, evenings only, rec. *Casa Popular de Cultura*, 1 block N of plaza central, 2½ blocks abajo, good inexpensive dinners, nice atmosphere, find out what's going on. *Centro Decorativo* on main square, large airy bar with roof-top roller skating rink, good views. On the Carretera Circunvalación, *Caña Brava*, good, try their 'pollo deshuesado' (boneless chicken).

Shopping The old market (dirty) is in the centre, and the new market is at the bus terminal, 5-6 blocks E of railway station. Also Mercado San Juan, not touristy, good local atmosphere. Good supermarket on Calle 1 Norte, by *Pollo Loco* and Banco Nacional de Desarrollo. Good bookshop next to city hall at Parque Jérez. Dollartienda.

Cinemas 3 in centre, eg González on corner of main square diagonally opp Cathedral. 2 discotheques at weekends, one is *The Tunnel*.

Exchange Supercambio, 1 block from cathedral, open 0800-1230, 1400-1730 Mon-Fri, 0800-1130 Sat, will change TCs at poor rates, banks will not change TCs.

Post Office and Telephones Telcor, Parque Central, opposite Cathedral. Phone calls abroad possible. Small Telcor office on Darío, on road to Subtiava, about 10 blocks from main plaza, open till 2200.

Buses From bus station at new market: **Managua**-León, Route 12, 1 hr 50 mins, US$1, every 30 mins, US$1.70 express, frequent but check if it goes to the León bus terminal or the Shell station on the Managua highway. Colectivo, US$5. Bus to **Chinandega** (US$0.50) and **Corinto** half-hourly between 0530 and 1830. For Estelí, daily express minibus at 1500, or take a bus to **San Isidro** (every 30 mins), 3 hrs, US$2, hourly service, then catch a bus going N from Managua or Matagalpa. To **Matagalpa** direct, 1 per day at 1400, US$2.80, but cheaper to take a bus to San Isidro and catch one of the many buses there from Estelí to Matagalpa, US$0.80. To border with Honduras take a bus from the market to Chinandega, and from there another bus to Somotillo, about 200m walk to border (possible to change córdobas on the bus but better rate for US dollars at Tegucigalpa). The Tica Bus to El Salvador stops at the Shell Station on the Managua side of town sometime between 0630 and 0730 daily. Pick-up from bus terminal to centre US$0.20.

Bus every 30 mins to *El Sauce*, 72 km, 3-4 hrs, where there is a large 19th century church, and a riotous fair in February (F *Hospedaje Diana*, clean, basic; *Viajero*, noisy, fan, friendly, good food; *Restaurant Mi Rancho* and others) via *Malpaisillo* (unnamed *hospedaje* at village entrance, 4 rooms, basic, F). Buses from El Sauce: to León, frequent, 3 hrs, US$1.40; to Honduran border 0500 daily, 3 hrs, US$1.60. 4 daily trucks between El Sauce and Estelí, on a very rough road.

Note On 9 April 1992, Cerro Negro, a volcano 28 km NE of León erupted, depositing vast quantities of volcanic ash and sand on the municipality of León and surrounding areas. Many people were made homeless and there was much damage as roofs collapsed under the weight of ash.

There is a road (20 km) to the sandy Pacific beach at *Poneloya* (main beach can have large waves, strong currents, extremely dangerous). (F *Hotel Lacayo*, basic, unfriendly, meals, beware of insects at night, bring coils; *Restaurante Cáceres, La Peña del Tigre*, good but expensive fish restaurant down the road, huge portions, friendly, open air, nice views—it is near a tall rock on the beach where bathing is dangerous and prohibited.) The place is pretty run down and all the houses of wealthy León families are locked up. It only comes alive during Semana Santa, at which time it gets crowded. Camping possible on the beach. Take bus 101 from León's Terminal Interurbana, or the central market W to the bus stop near Subtiava church on Calle Darío, then walk 3 mins to Terminal Poneloya, from where a small bus leaves every hour or so for Las Peñitas (US$0.45) at the S end of Poneloya beach (swimming much safer here; several small restaurants). Taxi from León costs around US$6.

Chinandega, one of the hottest and driest towns in Nicaragua, is about 35 km beyond León. Population 37,000. This is one of the main cotton-growing districts, and also grows bananas and sugar cane. Horse-drawn cabs for hire. Local holiday: 26 July.

Hotels Cosigüina, in city centre, just S of Banco Nacional, expensive, a/c, cable TV; **E** *Glomar* (shower extra), safe, may be closed Sun pm, owner (Filio) will change dollars, but mistrusts foreigners, his son is friendly, good food, cold beer; **F** *Hospedaje Aguirre*. **F** *Pensión Cortés*, S of Parque Central, basic. **F** *Salón Carlos*, with breakfast, shared shower, helpful; **G** *Chinandega*, nearby, basic, fan, shared bath, decent; **G** *Pensión Urbina*, basic.

Restaurants *Corona de Oro*, Chinese, 1½ blocks E of Parque Central, T 351, expensive; *Central Palace*, same street; *Caprax Pizza*, one block E of Parque Central.

Exchange Banco Nacional de Desarrollo.

Post Office and Telephones in new Telcor building opp *Caprax Pizza*.

Buses From **Managua**, by road, 3 hrs, US$2.15. From Chinandega, buses leave from near the new market at SE edge of town for **Corinto**, **León**, **Managua** and **Somotillo**. From **León**, 1 hr by bus, US$0.50. Buses for **Potosí**, **El Viejo** and **Puerto Morazán** leave from the Mercadito at NW of town. A local bus connects Terminal, Mercado and Mercadito.

Not far away, near **Chichigalpa**, is Ingenio San Antonio, the largest sugar mill in Nicaragua, with a railway between the town and the mill (6 km, 7 trains a day each way, passengers taken, US$0.10). On the edge of Chichigalpa itself is the Flor de Caña distillery; on leaving you will recognize the picture on all the labels, a palm-shaded railway leading towards Chichigalpa with volcanoes in the background. Telcor in Chichigalpa: from Texaco on the main road take 2nd street on left, then 1st on right, open 0800-1200, 1400-1700.

A road runs NE to Puerto Morazán. This passes through the village of El Viejo (US$0.20 by bus from Chinandega, 5 km) where there is an old church. (Restaurant: *El Retoño*, on main street, N of market; bars close to market.) Puerto Morazán (hotel), 26 km from Chinandega (buses, 8 a day, 1½ hrs, US$0.40), is a poor, muddy village with reed huts on a navigable river running into the Gulf of Fonseca. From Chinandega there are 4 buses a day to **Potosí**, at least 3 hrs, US$1. *Comedor Adela*, 24-hr service, cheap. You can sling your hammock at the *comedor* 150m past immigration for US$0.50. Ask Héctor for permission to stay in the fishing cooperative. The fishermen are very friendly. The passenger ferry from Potosí to La Unión (El Salvador) has been suspended, but there is an open boat from La Unión ad hoc. Ask around.

It is a 4-hr hike to the cone of **Cosigüina** volcano. On 23 January 1835, one of the biggest eruptions in history blew off most of the cone, reducing it from 3,000m to its present height of 870m. There are beautiful views from the cone over the islands belonging to Honduras and El Salvador. There is plenty of wildlife in the area, including poisonous snakes, so take a machete. The path is overgrown and very difficult to follow, you may need a guide. There are pleasant black sand beaches; the sea, although the colour of *café con leche*, is clean. In the centre of the village are warm thermal springs in which the population relaxes each afternoon.

From Chinandega a paved road, badly in need of repair in its middle section in 1994, goes to the Honduran border at **Somotillo**, on the Río Guasaule, where it is continued by a better road to Choluteca, Honduras. The Tica Bus now uses this route to Honduras. The border crossing is reported as very slow, exit tax US$2. The distance between border posts is ½ km. There are no colectivos, so you must walk or hitch a lift. Buses run every ½ hr from the border to Chinandega.

Jiquilillo beach, 42 km from Chinandega, is reached by a mostly-paved road branching off the El Viejo-Potosí road. It lies on a long peninsula; small restaurants (eg *Fany*) and lodgings.

Corinto, 21 km from Chinandega, is the main port of entry, and the only port at which vessels of any considerable size can berth. About 60% of the country's commerce passes through it. The town itself is on a sandy island, Punto Icaco, connected with the mainland by long railway and road bridges. There are beautiful old wooden buildings with verandahs, especially by the port. (Entry to the port is barred to all except those with a permit.) Population: 30,000. On the Corinto-Chinandega road is Paseo Cavallo beach (*Restaurante Buen Vecino*). The sea is treacherous, people drown here every year.

Hotel G *Hospedaje Luvy*, fan, dirty bathrooms, 2 blocks from plaza. **Restaurants** *Meléndez*, on main square, good but pricey; *El Imperial*, evenings only; cheapest meals in market, but not rec.

MANAGUA TO GRANADA

From Lake Managua to Lake Nicaragua, with more volcanoes in view: Santiago is near Masaya, a centre for handicrafts in a tobacco-growing zone; Mombacho is near Granada, a richly historical city; Concepción is a perfect cone rising out of Isla Ometepe, one of a number of islands that can be visited by boat on Lake Nicaragua.

The main route is by a 61 km paved road with a fast bus service through Masaya.

Santiago Volcano The entrance to **Volcán Masaya National Park** is at Km 23. Father Francisco de Bobadilla planted a cross on the summit of Masaya in the 16th century to exorcise the 'Boca del Infierno'; the cross visible today commemorates the event. Many Spanish chroniclers visited the crater, including Oviedo in 1529 and Blas de Castillo in 1538, who descended into it in search of gold! Volcán Nindiri last erupted in 1670, Volcán Masaya burst forth in 1772 and again in 1852, forming the Santiago crater between the two peaks; this in turn erupted in 1932, 1946, 1959 and 1965 before collapsing in 1985 and the resulting pall of sulphurous smoke made the soil in a broad belt to the Pacific uncultivable. 90 years ago German engineers Schomberg and Scharfenberg, attempting to produce sulphuric acid from the volcano's emissions, drilled into a unexpected 400m-wide lava tube, resulting in explosions and landslides; no-one has attempted anything similar since! Remains of these old installations can still be seen; consult the *guardabosques* for information.

Volcán Masaya was the first of the country's national parks (1975), 54 square km. Visitor's Centre 1.5 km in from entrance (called the *Centro de Interpretación Ambiental*). Shortly after is a beautiful area with toilets, picnic facilities and barbeques (*asadores*) for the use of visitors, and a fine but expensive restaurant (next door is a good science museum, entrance US$0.15). From here a short path leads up to Cerro El Comalito, good views of Mombacho, the lakes and the extraordinary volcanic landscapes of the Park; longer trails continue to Lake Masaya and San Fernando crater. Because of the potential danger involved, visits to the fumaroles at Comalito require special authorization from rangers, who warn that they may have to place this area off-limits if visitors are injured touching or throwing the surrounding rocks. The paved road (20-25 kph speed limit) continues S across the 1670 lava flow to the twin crests of Masaya and Nindiri, which actually consist of 5 craters (Santiago—still emitting sulphurous gases, San Fernando, San Juan, Nindiri and San Pedro). There is parking and a recreation area here. Park rangers will escort groups of no more than 5 down a path leading to several lava caverns, visitors are not allowed to touch the fragile walls or roofs of these caves. Park guides and *guardabosques* are very knowledgeable about the area's history and early indigenous inhabitants. The park is a wonderful excursion but take something to drink, a hat and robust footware if planning much walking. Drivers have to pay US$3 in córdobas (more for camper vans etc) to get their vehicles in; pedestrians US$0.25 (bus passengers alight at Km 23 on the Managua-Masaya route). The Park is open 0900-1700, Tues-Fri, and until 1900 on Sat and Sun.

Masaya (population 70,000), 29 km SE of Managua, is the centre of a rich agricultural area growing tobacco. Small **Laguna de Masaya** (at the foot of Masaya volcano, water too polluted for swimming), and Santiago volcano are near the town. Interesting Indian handicrafts and a gorgeous *fiesta* on 30 September, for its patron, San Jerónimo (Indian dances and local costumes). Another important pilgrimage is 16 March, the Virgen de Masaya and the Cristo de Milagros of Nindirí (see below) are taken down to the lake, whose waters are blessed. The ceremony leaves the church at 1500. The market is reportedly commercialized now, but the selection and quality are good. There is a new Centro de Artesanías (closed Sun), near the hospital and overlooking Laguna de Masaya, but the choice is not as wide as the market. Masaya is also the centre for Nicaraguan rocking chairs (but to send them home you have to go to the post office in Managua and this will probably cost twice the price of the chair). The Cooperativo Teófilo Alemán has a good selection at around US$35. The best place for Indian craft work is ***Monimbo*** (visit the church of Magdalena here), and 15 mins from Masaya is ***Villa Nindirí***, which has a rich museum and an old church with some even older images. There are horse-drawn carriages, some very pretty and well-kept. Statue of Sandino. The town suffered severely in the Revolution of 1978-79. Visit the Museo de Héroes y Mártires. Another museum is that of Camilo Ortega, which has interesting exhibits on recent history; 45 min walk from central plaza, ask directions.

Hotels **C** *Motel Cailagua* (Km 29.5, Carretera a Granada), about 2 km from Masaya, with bath and a/c, D with bath and fan, large rooms, clean, good, very friendly, meals available (but breakfast only by arrangement), reasonably priced, parking inside gates, rec. **C** *Motel El Nido*, expensive, not too good. **E** *Regis*, Sergio Delgado (main street), shared bath, being modernised in 1993, fan, breakfast (other meals if ordered), helpful owner, rec; **F** *Rex*, dark, dirty, can be obstructive, near the church; *pensiones* are hard to find, and dirty when you've found them.

Restaurants *Chema*, Arturo Velazques, one block from the *Hotel Regis*, no sign (except *Nueva Bar*), very good food, service and value; *Alegría*, nr main square, good, not expensive, good pizzas; *El Arabe* at station; *Mini 16*, W end of town, nr hospital. *Pochil*, near park, good food, ask for vegetarian dishes. *Cafetín Verdí*, in central park, good atmosphere, snacks, ice cream. *Panadería Corozán de Oro*, 2-3 blocks towards highway from the church, excellent cheese bread (*pan de queso*), US$0.50 a loaf.

Exchange Banco Nacional de Desarrollo, and street changer around market and plaza.

Doctor Dr Freddy Cárdenas Ortega, near bus terminal, recommended gynaecologist.

Tourist Office On main highway in the block between the 2 main roads into Masaya; helpful, mostly Spanish spoken, but some English 'if you look baffled'.

Buses Depart from the terminal near the market. To **Managua** every 15 mins, US$0.40; to **Granada** every 20 mins, US$0.60, to **Jinotepe** via Niquinohomo, Masatepe, San Marcos and Diriamba every 20 mins. There is also a bus service to **Tisma**.

Excursions Just outside Masaya, on the road from Managua, is an old fortress, Coyotepe, also called La Fortillera. It was once a torture centre, and is now deserted, eerie 'with a Marie Celeste feel to it' (take a torch), or offer a volunteer US$1-2 to show you around. Near the Masaya Lake, S of the town there are caves with prehistoric figures on the walls; ask around for a guide.

To **Niquinohomo**, Sandino's birthplace: the house where Sandino lived from the age of 12 with his father and his father's family is a museum, open Sunday 0900-1300, Tues-Sat 0900-1200, 1400-1700. The house is opposite the church in the main square.

James N Maas writes: Take a bus from Masaya (or Granada) to **San Juan de Oriente**, a colonial village with an interesting school of pottery (products are for sale). It is a short walk to neighbouring Catarina, and a 1 km walk uphill to El Mirador, with a wonderful view of **Laguna de Apoyo** (very clean, quiet during week but busy at weekends—swimming, drinking, drowning—entrance fee US$0.20; get out of bus at Km 38 on Managua-Granada road, walk 1½ hrs or hitch—easy at weekends), Granada and Volcán Mombacho in the distance. Return by bus.

Another 19 km by road is **Granada**, on Lake Nicaragua. It is the third city of the republic, with a population of 45,200, and was founded by Hernández de Córdoba in 1524 at the foot of Mombacho volcano. The rich city was three times attacked by British and French pirates coming up the San Juan and Escalante rivers, and much of old Granada was burnt by filibuster William Walker in 1856, but it still has many beautiful buildings and has faithfully preserved its Castilian traditions.

The centre of the city, some distance from the lake, is the Parque Central, with many trees and food stalls in its park, civic buildings, the *Hotel Alhambra* and the Cathedral around its edge. The Cathedral, rebuilt in neo-classical style, is simpler in design and ornamentation than the church of La Merced, which was built in 1781-3, half-destroyed in the civil wars of 1854 and restored in 1862. Its interior is painted in pastel shades, predominantly green and blue. Continuing away from the centre, beyond La Merced, is the church of Jalteva (or Xalteva), which faces a pleasant park with formal ponds. Not far from Jalteva is La Pólvora church. If one heads towards the Managua bus terminal from Jalteva, the Hospital is passed. Built in 1886, it is now in very poor shape. The chapel of María Auxiliadora, where

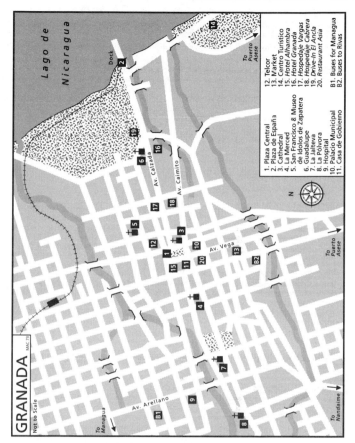

GRANADA
MAC 73
Not to Scale

Lago de Nicaragua

To Puerto Asese

To Puerto Asese

To Managua

To Nandaime

To Rivas

Av. Calzada
Av. Caimito
Av. Vega
Av. Arellano

1. Plaza Central
2. Plaza de España
3. Cathedral
4. La Merced
5. San Francisco & Museo de Idolos de Zapatera
6. Guadalupe
7. La Jalteva
8. La Pólvora
9. Hospital
10. Palacio Municipal
11. Casa de Gobierno
12. Telcor
13. Market
14. Centro Turístico
15. Hotel Alhambra
16. Hotel Granada
17. Hospedaje Vargas
18. Hospedaje Cabrera
19. Drive-In El Ancla
20. Restaurant Asia
B1. Buses for Managua
B2. Buses to Rivas

Las Casas, Apostle of the Indies, often preached, is hung with Indian lace and needlework (church open to public at 1600). From the Parque Central, in the opposite direction to La Merced, is the fortress-church of San Francisco. Next door is the Instituto Nacional del Oriente, originally a convent (1524), then a Spanish garrison, William Walker's garrison, a university and lastly an institute. Now it is just a museum in the midst of ruined, deserted classrooms; the cloister surrounds about 3 dozen tall palms. Reconstruction has begun, but much work has to be done. The museum houses 28 sculptures from Isla Zapatera in the lake. They date from AD800-1200, note especially the double sculptures of standing or seated figures bearing huge animal masks, or doubles, on their heads and shoulders ('El Lagarto', 'La Tortuga', jaguars, etc). The museum is open 0800-1200, 1330-1700; US$0.60 entrance. Horse-drawn cabs are for hire (bargain over the price—horses in very poor condition), there are many oxcarts and a fine cemetery.

A road runs from the Parque central to Plaza España by the dock on the lake; the church of Guadalupe is on this road. From Plaza España it is a short distance to the Complejo Turístico, a large area with restaurants and bars (see below), paths and benches. The lake beach is popular, but dirty; marimba bands stroll the beach and play a song for you for a small charge.

Fiestas Holy Week: Assumption of the Virgin, 14-30 August; and Christmas (masked and costumed mummers).

Warning A conman operates in Granada, often near the tourist complex. He claims he is a Miskito Indian who was a political prisoner, he has just escaped and is now heading for Costa Rica. He also gives you the address of his mother, a refugee in Germany. His story is not true: do not give him money to finance his 'escape'.

Hotels A *Alhambra*, Parque Central, T 2035, pleasant, comfortable rooms with bath, large restaurant serves good food, often has good, live music, parked cars guarded by nightwatchman. **B** *Granada*, Calle La Calzada (opp Guadalupe church), luxury, swimming pool, a/c, restaurant for all meals, café, disco, bar, very good, T 2974. **E** *Hospedaje Cabrera*, Calle La Calzada, D in the one room with bath, clean, with fan, filtered drinking water, family run, nice garden, pleasant; opposite is **E** *Pensión Vargas*, Calle La Calzada, basic, 'shower' (tap and bucket), mixed reports. These three hotels are on the road from the main square to the wharf. **F** *Hospedaje Esfinge*, opposite market, even with private shower, friendly, clean, safe. **G** pp at rooms behind restaurant *China Nica* on Calle Calzada, very basic, take mosquito coil, shower is a tap and bucket. There is a shortage of hotels and restaurants in Granada (do not arrive after 2100 at the latest).

Restaurants *Drive Inn El Ancla*, opp *Hotel Granada*, clean, good; *Coffee Shop*, next to *Hospedaje Cabrera*, breakfasts, lunch from 1200; *Eskimo's*, opposite *Hospedaje Cabrera*, good ice cream; between *El Ancla* and *Eskimo's* is a cheap, good chicken place; *China Nica*, between *Hotel Cabrera* and the Cathedral, good traditional food, reasonable prices; *Interamericano*, road to Masaya next to Esso, clean, dear. *El Otro*, Plaza Central, coffee shop with meals; cheap food at the friendly *Cafe Astoria*, near plaza central; *Chupi's Ice Cream Parlour*. Good breakfasts at the market.

In the Complejo Turístico, see above, there are restaurants and bars of all types, they tend to be expensive (lively Fri and Sat at night); walking from the gate they include: *La Vista*, *Rincón Criollo* (with boat trips, see below), *Rancho Colomer*, *Omotepe*, *Restaurante Disco El Pingüino*, *Bahía*, *Carolina* (with fiestas on Sun); lots of loud juke boxes; *Cacibolca* restaurant on Isla Cacibolca is reached by launch.

Shopping Market (large green building in the centre) is dark and packed; lots of stalls on the streets outside, also horse cab rank and taxis. Dollartienda near *Hotel Alhambra*.

Exchange Banco Nacional de Desarrollo; Banco Nicaragüense de Comercio e Industria. Neither will change TCs nor will they advance cash on Visa or Amex. Only change cash dollars on the street.

Post Office, telephones Telcor in moorish building on Parque Central, left of Cathedral.

Buses leave from an area 200m beyond the market, except those going to/from Managua, which leave from a 'fenced lot uptown' (see map); buses to the capital every 20 mins. Many fast minibuses to **Managua**, US$0.80, 1 hr (these do not stop in Masaya). Another bus service from the capital leaves from **La Piñata**, opp Universidad Centroamericana (UCA) every 2 hrs after 1000, US$1, no a/c but seat guaranteed. Bus to **Masaya**, US$0.60, 15 mins. Bus to **Nandaime**, every 20 mins, US$0.25. To **Rivas** hourly between 0600 and 1800 (timings erratic), 1½ hrs, US$2. It's often quicker to take a bus to Nandaime and then another on from there. Sirca Bus from Granada to **San José** Mon, Wed, Fri 0730, from corner 1 block from plaza on road to market, US$15, worth booking ahead, office is at Sr Cabezas, **Camas y Colchones Sant Ana**, 1½ blocks from plaza on road to market. Tica from Granada to San José.

Lake Nicaragua, the 'Gran Lago de Nicaragua' or Lago Cacibolca, 148 km long by 55 at its widest, is a fresh-water lake abounding in salt-water fish, which swim up the San Juan river from the sea and later return. It is said to include sharks, though none have been seen for some years; some say because Somoza had them fished out. Terrapins can be seen sunning themselves on the rocks and there are many interesting birds. There are about 310 small islands, Las Isletas (most of them inhabited), with different and unusual vegetation. They can be visited either by hired boats or motor launches, from the Complejo Turístico (see above), eg from *Rincón Criollo*, T 4317, at US$17 per hour for the whole boat, or from the restaurant at the end of the road beyond the Complejo Turístico, US$50 per hour for 6 in a motor launch, or US$10 per hour for 2 in a rowing boat. On Sunday at 1400 a boat makes a round trip to the islands, returning in the evening, US$3.30, take a picnic and drinks (those sold are expensive). Ask around for other boats. There is plenty of lakeside birdlife to see. Alternatively, take the morning bus from Granada to **Puerto Asese**, 3 km further S, a tranquil town at the base of the Asese peninsula at the head of the Ensenada de Asese. (Pleasant **Restaurante Asese**, T 2269, on the lake, good value, fish specialities.) Boats can be hired. Trips to various lake destinations (Zapatera, El Muerto, the Solentiname islands, Río San Juan) can be arranged in the yacht *Pacífico*, up to 15 people on day trips, 8 for overnight voyages, lunch included, rec for a group (information and reservations T Granada 4305/2269).

The largest island, **Ometepe** (population 20,000), has two volcanoes, one of them, **Concepción**, a perfect cone rising to 1,610m. There are two villages on the island: **Moyogalpa** (population 4,500) and **Alta Gracia**, which are connected by bus (1 hr US$0.60). Moyogalpa is more attractive than Alta Gracia. In Moyogalpa there is a Banco Nacional del Desarrollo and a shop which changes money (sign above door, lousy rates). There is a new tourist office, up the hill from the harbour, which offers good information, tours, horseriding, bus timetables, etc. Write to: Fundación Entre Volcanes, de la Gasolinera Esso 1 C y ½ al Sur, Moyogalpa, Ometepe, Nicaragua. Cockfights in Moyogalpa on Sunday afternoons. Ask for the birdwatching place about 3 km from Alta Gracia; birds fly in the late afternoon to nest on offshore islands. There is also Charco Verde lagoon and a waterfall worth visiting. One can stroll to the base of Volcán Concepción for good views of the lake and the company of many birds and howler monkeys (*congos*). To climb the volcano you need permission from the police who will give information on paths. Leave from Cuatro Cuadros, 2 km from Alta Gracia, and make for a cinder gully between forested slopes and a lava flow. There are several fincas on the lower part of the volcano. The ascent takes about 5 hrs (take water). Alpine vegetation, the crater radiating heat and the howler monkeys are attractions. Very steep near summit. You can get a guide by asking near the pier, worthwhile as visibility is often restricted by clouds, and it is easy to get lost, especially in the final stages. Eduardo Ortiz and his son, José, of Cuatro Cuadros, will also guide.

Accommodation Alta Gracia has several *hospedajes* of varying quality—take your own toilet paper: eg **F** *Castillo*, friendly, good food, owner Ramón Castillo, is 'an uncappable fount of information' and can organize trips to rock carvings on the volcano, US$3 for a guide. In Moyogalpa, **E** *Ometepl*, on main street from dock, bath, fan, clean, small but comfortable rooms, service and food disappointing, car hire; **F** *Pensión Aly*, opp Esso, friendly, clean, uncomfortable beds but good food, helpful and **F** *Pensión Moyogalpa*, the first place you'll see from the landing, very noisy, cheap, food OK, large portions; **F** pp *Asyl*, close to jetty, with restaurant; **F** *El Pirata*, on the E side of town.

Launches sail from Granada to Alta Gracia, continuing to San Carlos (see below); leave Granada Mon and Thur, 1430 and 1530. 4½ hrs to Alta Gracia, US$1, 8 hrs Alta Gracia-San Carlos, US$1.30 (Granada-San Carlos US$2.05). Boats arrive in San Carlos at 0500 and 0630 (passengers stay on board till daylight) and return on Tues and Fri. Everything left on deck will get wet; as it can be very crowded, a good spot for sleeping is on the cabin roof. There is also a boat Granada-Alta Gracia on Sat at 1200, returning Sun 1000. Ticket office in Granada is at the dock.

Moyogalpa can be reached from **San Jorge** on the lake's SW shore; 3 boats a day (1000, 1100, 1200, 1630, 1800, returning 0600, 0700, 0800, 1330 and 1700—on Sun the 1000, 1100 and 1200 from San Jorge don't sail, but there is one at 1145; no boats at 0600 or 1700 from Moyogalpa on Sun), US$0.70, 1¼ hrs. **F** *Hotel El Galeón*, opp ferry dock, friendly, very basic, mosquitoes and **F** *Hotel Nicarao*, left off the Rivas-San Jorge road, basic meals, friendly. Meals are not easy to come by in San Jorge. From San Jorge a road runs through Rivas (bus service every 10 mins, US$0.30, 30 mins) to the port of San Juan del Sur. The Río San Juan, running through deep jungles, drains the lake from the eastern end into the Caribbean at San Juan del Norte. Launches ply down the river irregularly from the lakeside town of **San Carlos** (15-20,000 people) at the SE corner of the Lake. Much of the town was destroyed by fire in 1984, but some rebuilding has been done. See under Alta Gracia above for boat schedules. The slower boats stop at San Miguelito (pop 8,000, one primitive *pensión*). (Buses out of San Carlos do not run on Sunday; there are buses to Granada and Managua (not weekends), US$6 approx; on Monday there is a truck at 0600 to Santo Tomás, change in Lóvago for buses to Managua. San Carlos-Lóvago US$2, 5 hrs, a tough ride, Lóvago-Tipitapa US$2, 3 hrs. Bus Granada-San Miguelito, Mon, Tues, Wed, Thurs 0830 from the pier, 8 hrs); bus San Carlos-Acoyapa, US$2.30, 'hellish' road for first 4 hrs.

At San Carlos are the ruins of a fortress built for defence against pirates (**F** *hospedaje* on main square, basic; *Restaurante Río San Juan*, good meals, rooms for rent, G, dirty, noisy; also *San Carlos* and 2 more basic *pensiones*; several *comedores*; exchange at Banco Nacional de Desarrollo). Some 4½ hrs down river, boat US$2, Tues and Fri 1000, returning Mon and Thur (9 hrs back) are the ruins of another Spanish fort, **Castillo Viejo** (**F** *Hospedaje Aurora*, basic, serves food; **D** *Albergue Turística*, new, shared bath, Telcor will instal an international phone link). It is now possible to take a boat from San Carlos down to the mouth of the Río San Juan to San Juan del Norte, but there are no regular sailings (**see p 707**).

Boats also run from San Carlos to the **Solentiname Islands** in the Lake. Hotels: *Hotel Isla Solentiname*, on San Fernando island, safe, acceptable but basic (you wash in the lake), cost including meals C; and a second hotel, E, neat and comfortable rooms, on Mancarrón island, the largest, which has a library and an interesting church. Ernesto Cardenal (the poet and former Minister of Culture) lived and worked here. The islands are home to many renowned primitive painters and are pleasant to hike around.

About 40 km S of San Carlos, on the Río Frío, is Los Chiles, over the border in Costa Rica (**see Section 3, The Central Northwest**). Despite information to the contrary from Inturismo in Managua, foreigners are now allowed to cross into Costa Rica from San Carlos, though Costa Rican immigration officers can be difficult. Exit stamps must be obtained from immigration in San Carlos (closed Sat and Sun). Check with the police in advance for the latest position. 5 launches a week San Carlos-Los Chiles. Border is open Mon-Fri 0800-1600 only. **See p 709**. **NB** The entire Nicaragua/Costa Rica border along the San Juan river is ill-defined and the subject of inter-governmental debate.

Warning The lake is dirty in some places, so swim in it with care. Swimming is possible in nearby **Laguna de Apoyo** (see p 696).

There is a proposal to create a national park, Sí-a-paz (Yes to Peace), which will stretch from the southern shore of Lake Nicaragua to the Caribbean coast along the Río San Juan. It will include the Solentiname islands and the Costa Rican side of the river, linking with the Caño Negro and Bara del Colorado Wildlife Refuges in Costa Rica.

MANAGUA TO COSTA RICA

The Pan-American Highway to the Costa Rican border passes through agricultural land, with branches inland to Granada and to the Pacific coast. A useful stopping place is Rivas: from here to the border, Lake Nicaragua and Volcán Concepción are to be seen. For sunsets, go to San Juan del Sur.

The Pan-American Highway, in good condition, has bus services all the way to San José de Costa Rica (148 km). The road runs into the Sierra de Managua, reaching 900m at Casa Colorada, 26 km from Managua. Further on, at El

Crucero, a paved branch road goes through the Sierra S to the Pacific bathing beaches of Pochomil and Masachapa (**see p 684**). The Highway continues through the beautiful scenery of the Sierras to **Diriamba**, 42 km from Managua, at 760m, in a coffee-growing district. Population 26,500. Hotel: *Diriangén*, F with bath. Good fish at restaurant *2 de Junio*. Its great *fiesta* is on 20 January. There is a 32-km dirt road direct to Masachapa (no buses). 5 km N of Diriamba a paved road branches off the highway to Managua and runs E through San Marcos, Masatepe and Niquinohomo to Catarina and Masaya.

Five km beyond Diriamba is **Jinotepe**, capital of the coffee-growing district of Carazo, joined also by railway with Diriamba and Masaya. It has a fine neo-classical church with modern stained glass windows from Irún, in Spain. The *fiesta* in honour of St James the Greater is on 24-26 July. 5 July is celebrated here as 'liberation day'. Altitude 760m; population 17,600; **D** *Hotel Escuela Jinotepe*, modern, 3-storey building 1 block N and 1 block W of Parque Central, comfortable, with bath and fan, dance floor, fine restaurant, good service; **F** *Hospedaje San Carlos*, no sign, ask around for it. *Pizza Danny's* is very good, 50m N of municipal building (try their *especial*, small but delicious, US$7). Banco Nacional de Desarrollo for exchange; black market for dollars in Parque Central. Buses for Managua leave from the terminal in the NE corner of town, every 20 mins, US$0.70; to Nandaime every 30 mins, US$0.35; to Diriamba-Masaya every 20 mins.

From **Nandaime**, 21 km from Jinotepe, altitude 130m, a paved road runs N to Granada (bus US$0.50). Nandaime has two interesting churches, El Calvario and La Parroquia (1859-72). The annual *fiesta* is 24-27 July, with masked dancers. Unnamed *hospedaje*, E. About 45 km beyond Nandaime (US$0.40 by bus) is **Rivas**, a town of 21,000 people. The Costa Rican national hero, the drummer Juan Santamaría, sacrificed his life here in 1856 when setting fire to a building captured by the filibuster William Walker and his men. On the town's Parque Central is a lovely old church (in need of repair). In the dome of the Basilica, see the fresco of the sea battle against the ships of Protestantism and Communism. The parque has some old, arcaded buildings on one side, but also some new buildings. Rivas is a good stopping place (rather than Managua) if in transit by land through Nicaragua. The bus station, adjacent to the market is on the NW edge of town about 8 blocks from the main highway. The road from the lake port of San Jorge joins this road at Rivas; 11 km beyond Rivas, at La Virgen on the shore of Lake Nicaragua, it branches S to San Juan del Sur.

Hotels **D** *Nicaragua* (or *Nicarao*), 2 blocks W of Parque Central, near cinema (3 blocks S and 2 E from bus terminal), with a/c, cheaper with fan, comfortable, slow service, shower, cold water, best in town, clean, well-equipped, good restaurant; **E** *Pensión Primavera*, basic; **F** *El Coco*, on Pan-American Highway near where bus from frontier stops, basic, small rooms, shower, interesting bar, *comedor* with vegetarian food, nice garden; *Hospedaje El Mesón*, basic; **F** *Hospedaje Delicia*, on main Managua-border road, basic and dirty, friendly; several on Highway, **E** *Hospedaje Lidia*, near Texaco, clean, noisy, family-run. (At the Texaco station, Lenín, who speaks English, is very helpful.) *Restaurant Chop Suey*, in the arcade in Parque Central; *Rinconcito Salvadoreño*, in the middle of the Parque Central, open air, charming. *Comedor Lucy*, on street leaving Parque Central at corner opp Banco de Nicaragua, *'comidas corrientes y vegetarianos'*; *Soda*, 1 block W of Parque then turn left from cinema; *Restaurant El Ranchito*, near *Hotel El Coco*, friendly, serves delicious chicken and *churrasco*.

Exchange Banco Nacional de Desarrollo. You may have to persuade them to cash TCs. Black market near market.

Telecommunications Telcor is 3 blocks S of Parque Central, or 7 blocks S and 3 blocks E from bus terminal.

Buses to the frontier Sapoá/Peñas Blancas: every hour or so: 0500 and 0700 good for connections for buses to San José (US$0.80, 1 hr) (taxis available, about US$15 from bus terminal, add US$2 from town centre, or a place in a colectivo, US$3), or try to get on the Sirca bus which stops at the Sirca office about 0800, Mon, Wed, Fri and Sat (NB Tica bus stops in Rivas, but only to let people off). Trucks on this section are generous with hitchhikers and are useful for continuing through the gap between customs and beyond. Bus to **Managua**, from 0500 (last one 1700), 2½ hrs, US$1.40; taxi, US$40. Several daily buses to **Granada**, US$3; it may be quicker to go via Nandaime. Irregular bus to **San Jorge** on Lake Nicaragua, US$0.60 (taxi to San Jorge, US$2).

A few km before Rivas, coming from Nandaime, is a road to the left to Potosí, a quiet village with *Comedor Soda Helen*, one block from the Parque Central; meals are available in the evening if you request them.

Between Nandaime and Rivas are various turnings S which lead eventually to the Pacific coast (all are rough, high clearance better than 4WD). Ask for Las Salinas, and from there go to **Astillero**, which has a fishing cooperative. Camping is safe and you can buy fish from the coop. 5 km further by truck from Astillero (leaves very early) is **Chococente**, at which is an Irena office, a Government-sponsored turtle sanctuary. The Irena wardens protect newly-hatched turtles and help them make it to the sea (a magnificent sight during November and December). Unfortunately, new-laid turtle eggs are considered to have aphrodisiac properties and are used as a dietary supplement by the locals. Irena is virtually powerless to prevent egg theft; do not get involved since threats against the officers have been made (international smuggling rings handle the trade in stolen eggs). The Irena personnel are friendly and helpful; ask for Doña Felipa, the cook and 'surrogate mother of the team' (with thanks to Francesca Pagnacco, Exeter, for this information.) Bring a tent or hammock and food if you plan to stay at Chococente. To get there you have to wade through a river.

San Juan del Sur is 28 km from Rivas (regular minibus from market, crowded, 45 mins, US$0.60), 93 km from Granada. There are roads from Managua (a 2½ hr drive, direct bus costs US$1.80) and Granada. Population 4,750. It has a beautiful bay with a sandy beach and some rocky caves reached by walking round the point opposite the harbour. Best beaches are Playa del Coco and Playa del Tamarindo, 15 km away on the poor road to Ostional; and Marsella, 5 km N of San Juan. (Watch out for sting rays at low tide.) Sunsets here have to be seen to be believed. Check tides with officials at the Customs Office, who will give permission to park motor-caravans and trailers on the wharves if you ask them nicely.

These vehicles may also be parked on Marsella beach: coming S, turn right on entering San Juan, by shrimp-packing plant.

Hotels B *Barlovento*, Government-owned on hill above town with excellent views, poor service and restaurant, tax free shop (US$ only) for toiletries, radios etc. **D** *Estrella*, on Pacific, with meals, balconies overlooking the sea, partitioned walls, take mosquito net, toilet facilities outside, rooms must be shared as they fill up, 'popular with hippies'; **E** *Buengusto*, opposite, very basic but very friendly, helpful, good fish restaurant, near beach. On same street as *Estrella* is **D** *Casa Internacional Joxi*, T 0466-348, friendly, clean (apart from a few cockroaches), a/c, bath, Danish run, sailing trips on the boat 'Pelican Eyes' can be arranged here; **E** *Casa Quebec*, near market, good, generous restaurant, Canadian run, rec; *Irazú*, one block from beach, some rooms with bath, very run down; **F** pp *Hospedaje Casa No 28*, 40m from beach, near minibus stop for Rivas, shared showers, mosquitos (ask owner for coils), kitchen and laundry facilities, clean; **F** *Gallo de Oro*, ½ km N of town, very basic but friendly and cheapest around.

Restaurants *Salón Siria*, good; *Soya*, vegetarian and meat dishes, fruit, *refrescos*, *chorizo de soya*, cheap and friendly; good *panadería* one block from beach. Good cafés along the beach for breakfast and drinks; the beach front restaurants all serve good fish. Lobster and prawns are specialities. Breakfast and lunch in market; *Comedor Angelita* serves very good fish dishes. Food in the evening from a stall in street running W from the market; *Lago Azul*, good fish restaurant at N end of bay beyond the river; *Rancho Miravalle*, good for fish.

Exchange Banco Nacional de Desarrollo.

Laundry Near *Soya Restaurant* (ask there) hand wash, line dry.

Post Office 2 blocks S along the front from *Hotel Estrella*.

The road reaches the Costa Rican boundary at Peñas Blancas, 37 km beyond Rivas (no gasoline for sale between border and Rivas; no hotels at the border). It is easy and better value to exchange money on the Costa Rican side of the border, which is closed from 1200-1300 and 1800-0900. Nicaraguan side closes 1200-1300 and 1600-0900 (note that Nicaragua is 1 hr ahead of Costa Rica). There is a duty free shop at the Nicaraguan side of the border. It is $3\frac{1}{2}$ – 4 hrs by bus to Managua, $5\frac{1}{2}$ to San José, but through journeys can be longer because of slow border formalities (last bus to Liberia, 1330). When the Tica or Sirca bus passes through, the queues are long and you can waste a lot of time; if not on a Tica or Sirca bus, arrive at border before 0900 to miss the queues. You will have to queue at three booths to obtain the necessary clearances, insist on keeping your place and on being told where to go next. Minibuses run the 4 km from the Nicaraguan border offices at **Sapoá** to the Costa Rican border posts frequently, waiting till they are full, US$0.75, plus US$0.15 per bag, otherwise you must walk or hitch. This border presents no problems for motorists, but remember that it is compulsory to buy insurance in Costa Rica (see **Motoring** in Costa Rica—**Information for Visitors**).

Entering Nicaragua: show your passport as you cross the border then take the minibus to Sapoá for entry formalities. Go to Migración and first fill in a *tarjeta de embarque*, then pay US$2 immigration tax. Queue up to have your passport stamped; you must give an address in Nicaragua (if you don't have one, just mention a hotel, or the official will put one down for you). Go to customs; after your bags have been checked, retain the small ticket for the release of your bags. Go to the exit gate (bag carriers charge about US$1.75 to take your luggage in a trolley); hand in your customs ticket, show passport with *tarjeta de embarque* and receipt for immigration tax. Finally, hope that there is transport to Rivas or Managua; buses stop early so if you have missed one you will have to take a taxi (US$15 to Rivas).

Entering by car: pay immigration tax (US$2) plus 5 córdobas, then queue up to have your car papers typed out at Ingreso Vehículo (make sure you are not given a 72-hr transit permit); next to this desk is where you pay the charge to have your vehicle checked (córdobas accepted, depending on number of passengers). Go to Información and wait for an official to come out to check your car. Finally go to Tránsito to pay US$20 for the car permit. **NB** All taxes to be paid on the Nicaraguan side of the border can be paid in córdobas.

THE CARIBBEAN COAST

Nicaragua's eastern tropical lowlands are very different from the rest of the country: there is heavy rainfall between May and December; the economy is based on timber, fishing and mining. The people are mostly Miskito Indians, but with much African influence. English is widely spoken. To reach the Caribbean port of Bluefields, from where you can go to the Corn Islands, you either have to fly or take the famous 'Bluefields Express' down river.

The area, together with about half the coastal area of Honduras, was never colonized by Spain. From 1687 to 1894 it was a British Protectorate known as the Miskito kingdom. It was populated then, as now, by Miskito Indians, whose numbers are estimated at 75,000. There are two other Indian groups, the Sumu (5,000) and the Rama, of whom only a few hundred remain, near Bluefields. Also near Bluefields are a number of Garifuna communities. Today's strong African influence has its roots in the black labourers brought in by the British to work the plantations and in Jamaican immigration. The Afro-Nicaraguan people call themselves creoles (*criollos*). The largest number of inhabitants of this zone are Spanish-speaking *mestizos*. The Sandinista revolution, like most other political developments in the Spanish-speaking part of Nicaragua, was met with mistrust. Although the first Sandinista junta recognized the indigenous peoples' rights to organize themselves and choose their own leaders, many of the programmes initiated in the region failed to encompass the social, agricultural and cultural traditions of eastern Nicaragua. Relations deteriorated and many Indians engaged in fighting for self-determination. About half the Miskito population fled as refugees to Honduras, but most returned after 1985 when a greater understanding grew between the Sandinista Government and the people of the

E Coast. The Autonomous Atlantic Region was given the status of a self-governing region in 1987; it is divided into Región Autonomista Atlántico Norte (RAAN) and Región Autonomista Atlántico Sur (RAAS).

In late February 1994, elections for the Atlantic coastal autonomous regional councils were held. The party to win most votes in the North and South was the Liberals, with the Sandinistas second in each case. The poor showing of both government and FSLN was a mark of the discontent felt in rural areas, especially the Atlantic coast and central mountain regions.

Note In Nicaragua, the Caribbean coast is almost always referred to as the Atlantic coast.

At *San Benito*, 35 km from Managua on the Pan American Highway going N, the Atlantic Highway branches E, paved all the way to Rama on the Río Escondido, or Bluefields River. Shortly after Teustepe, a paved road goes NE to Boaco. A turn-off, unpaved, goes to *Santa Lucía*, a village inside a crater, with a women's handicraft shop. There is also a cooperative here with an organic farming programme (information from Unag in Matagalpa). *Casa de Soya*, good food, friendly owners, single room for rent, basic, F. Good views from nearby mountains. 2 trucks a day from Boaco, US$1, one bus a day to/from Managua. *Boaco* (15,000 people) has a nice square with good views of the surrounding countryside. **E** *Hotel Sobalvarro*, on the square, is good; **G** *Hotel Boaco*, at the entrance to the town, basic. Its specialities are white cheese and cream. From Boaco, unpaved roads go N to Muy Muy and Matagalpa, and S to Comoapa (4,000 people). Bus Managua-Boaco every 45 mins from Mercado San Miguel, US$1.50.

The Atlantic Highway continues through *Juigalpa* (30,000 people; 139 km from Managua, buses every $^1/_2$ hr, US$2, 4 hrs). Here is one of the best museums in Nicaragua, with a collection of idols resembling those at San Agustín, Colombia. Small zoo in the valley below town. The bus terminal is in the town centre near the market, up the hill.

Lodging at **D** *Hotel La Quinta*, T 081-2485, on main road at the eastend of town, a/c or fan, bath, clean, friendly, restaurant has good food and a fine view of surrounding mountains; **F** *Hospedaje Central*, basic and noisy; *Hospedaje Angelita* the same; the hospedaje in *Comedor San Martín* is unfriendly; better is *Presillas* (Km 269), unnamed, beside *Comedor González*; all F pp.

A gravel road goes to La Libertad, a goldmining town at 600m (4,000 people, *hospedaje*), and on to Santo Domingo. From Juigalpa a road goes direct to the shore of Lake Nicaragua at Puerto Díaz. From here pick-ups will go to the monastery of San Juan de las Aguas for about US$1.20 pp if 4 passengers (Pedro Córtez rec, Oswaldo Melón not so). The guide will show you the path through swamps to the monastery (2-3 km) which was founded in 1689. It's a little neglected, but has several wooden statues. The monks are very friendly and will let you stay the night if you ask. Take your own food and leave a donation. Ask to see the cave/tunnel complex that was used when the monks hid from besieging Indians (Vincent van Es, Enschede, Netherlands).

25 km S of Juigalpa an unpaved road turns off to *Acoyapa* (7 km, 5,000 people, *hospedaje*), El Morrito, San Miguelito and San Carlos on Lake Nicaragua (see p 700).

The main road goes S to *Santo Tomás* (10,000 people, several *hospedajes*) and smaller villages (including La Gateada, turn-off to Nuevo Güinea, centre of cacao production), to *Cara de Mono* (*hospedaje*), on the Río Mico, and finally to *Rama* (pop 12,000), 290 km from Managua. The town was badly hit by Hurricane Joan in October 1988 when the river rose 16m above normal height. It is now poor and dirty. *Hospedaje Ramada Inn* seems to be the best; *Hotels Amy* and *Johanna* both E, neither has showers, *Amy* cleaner and quieter, near main jetty. Good cheap food at *Comedor Torres*. Bus Juigalpa to Rama every $^1/_2$ hr 0430 to 1430, $4^1/_2$ hrs, US$2.50, terrible road even though paved.

From Managua to Bluefields Take a bus from Mercado San Miguel (Terminal Atlántico), Managua to Rama along the paved road (in poor condition), 7-8 hrs, leaves 2300, Mon, Wed, Fri to connect with boat to Bluefields at 1130, Tues, Thur, Sat (check days—bus US$5.85, boat US$5, combined ticket US$10.85, buy ticket at reservation office at the terminal, preferably one day in advance). Food and soft drinks are sold on the ferry. Trip downriver takes 6 hrs. Fast boats, *pangas*, can be hired for US$12-15 Rama—Bluefields, taking 1½ hrs, or hitch on a fishing boat. Return from Bluefields: boat at 0530 Tues, Thur, Sat, bus to Managua 1030 (combined tickets available, ticket office at Encab, nr dock). There is also one boat each way on Sunday dep Rama 1130, dep Bluefields 0530. Or take your car and park it in the compound at the Chinaman's store at Rama (opposite *Hotel Amy*) for US$0.50 a day.

On the 'Bluefields Express', some two hundred people, assorted animals and goods crowd the deck. The journey passes through the sparsely populated eastern half of Nicaragua. The river is wide and fast flowing, passing land that is mostly cultivated, with the occasional poor farmer's dwelling. After the devastation of Hurricane Joan in 1988, some reconstruction has taken place although much of the population has not returned from the capital.

Bluefields, the most important of Nicaragua's 3 Caribbean ports, gets its name from the Dutch pirate Abraham Blaauwveld. It stands on a lagoon behind the bluff at the mouth of the Bluefields river (Río Escondido), which is navigable as far as Rama (96 km). In May there is a week-long local festival, Mayo-Ya!, with elements of the British Maypole tradition and local music, poetry and dancing. *Fiesta*, 30 September for San Jerónimo. Bananas, cabinet woods, frozen fish, shrimps and lobsters were the main exports until the hurricane in 1988 (see below). Population 17,700.

Tragically, in October 1988, Hurricane Joan detroyed virtually all of Bluefields, but the rebirth is well underway. Information on the region can be found at the Cidca office. Local bands practice above the Ivan Dixon Cultural Centre, beside the library. There are several bars, a couple of reggae clubs, *comedores* and restaurants (2 with a/c), and a Dollartienda. Prices are about the same as in Managua, but the atmosphere has become tense and grasping (1994), with many 'guides' offering their services and leading visitors to buy things at inflated prices.

Hotels B *South Atlantic*, near central square, next to Telcor, run by Fanny and Hubert Chambers (native language English), with bath, safe, a/c, cable TV, fridge, clean, friendly, excellent food; **D** *Caribbean*, bath, a/c, near centre of town, good cook (Angela), friendly, rec; **C** *Costa Sur*, per person, **E** *El Dorado*, may offer floor space to late arrivals; **E** *Hollywood*, has its own well and generator; **E** *Marda Maus*, one of the nicer places in its price range with bath and fan, dark, not too clean, no restaurant, soft drinks available, near market. **F** *Cuento*, showers, intermittant water. *Café Central*, good value meals, provides accommodation, has colour TV. Everywhere can be full if you arrive late, or are last off the ferry.

Flights The airport is a long way from the city centre; either walk 30 mins or take a taxi jeep that waits by the runway. Between Managua and Bluefields, Nica and La Costeña, US$45 one way, US$90 return plus US$1.50 departure tax. Nica at 0640 daily, return 0930; La Costeña up to 3 flights daily, depending on the weather (Nica and one of La Costeña's flights continue to the Corn Islands). La Costeña also flies twice weekly Bluefields-Puerto Cabezas, US$55 each way. Managua offices of both airlines are in the domestic terminal at the airport. Bring passport, it is sometimes asked for in the departure lounge. There is a customs check on return to Managua.

Boats El Bluff is a small island with a village harbour, some oil tanks and a small, dirty beach. It is accessible by *panga* (speedboat) from the wharf at the market. When the *panga* is full, pay your fare, no more than US$1.60.

From the main wharf small boats leave irregularly for villages on the coast and Laguna de Perlas, such as Tasbapounie (*hospedaje* run by Mr Leonard Richard Brent); food may be scarce in all settlements. A boat leaves most days around 0600 to **Laguna de Perlas** (Pearl Lagoon) 80 km N of Bluefields 3-6 hrs, US$5. The lagoon itself is some 50 km long with mostly Creole villages round its shores, eg Pearl Lagoon, Haulover, Brown Bank, La Fe, Orinoco, Mashall Point and San Vicente. Raitipura and Kakabila are Indian villages. At the village of Pearl Lagoon there is a hostel, *Miss Ingrid's*, very friendly, stay with the entertaining family. Larger vessels may be available for transport to Puerto Cabezas, but there is no transport S of Bluefields.

On outlying areas of the Región Autonomista Atlántico Sur, Cindy Gersony of Sarasota,

Florida, writes: **Río Kurinwás** area: It might occasionally be possible to get a boat to the town of **Tortuguero** (also called Nuevo Amanecer) on the Kurinwás River. The Kurinwás is a fascinating, largely uninhabited jungle area, where it is possible to see monkeys and much other wildlife. Significantly upriver is Tortuguero (about a 6-hr speedboat ride from Bluefields, several days by regular boat), a *mestizo* town of about 1,000. It will really give you a taste of the frontier.

Río Grande area: The Río Grande is the next river N of the Kurinwás, connected to the Pearl Lagoon by the Top-Lock Canal. At its mouth are five interesting villages: the four Miskito communities of Kara, Karawala, Sandy Bay Sirpi, and Walpa, and the Creole village of La Barra. **Sandy Bay Sirpi** is situated on both the river and the Caribbean, and has a nice beach. Travelling upriver, the Río Grande is a noticeable contrast to the Río Kurinwás; it is much more settled, dotted with farms and cattle grazing. Quite a bit upriver (also about a 6-hr speedboat ride from Bluefields, several days by regular boat), the traveller will come to the *mestizo* town of **La Cruz de Río Grande**. Population about 1,700, it was founded about 1922 by Chinese traders to serve workers from a banana plantation (now defunct) further upriver. La Cruz has a very pretty church, and there are resident expatriate (US) priests of the Capuchin order in the town. The adventurous can walk between La Cruz and Tortuguero: each way takes about 10 hrs in the dry season, 12 in the rainy.

Provisions For travel to the Atlantic Coast, a traveller should bring a mosquito net, sleeping bag, mosquito spray, flashlight, toilet paper, rain jacket, Zip-lock bags (to store toilet paper, film, cameras, etc), and sunscreen. (If not venturing beyond Bluefields or Puerto Cabezas, you may not need more than protection against the sun, rain and mosquitoes, although these are not as voracious as they are outside the large towns.) For travel inland to the rural areas, the traveller should add water, water purification tablets, more anti-mosquito protection, and carry his/her own food (such as rice, potatoes, dried soup packets, tomatoes, coffee, canned food). You should have no trouble finding someone to cook for you for a nominal fee (such as US$1 per person) or for trade (items such as sugar, inexpensive watches, tapes, etc). Ask for the village leader or pastor (either Catholic or Moravian) if you need a place to stay for the night; usually one can stay in the chapel, school, or someone's house. Do not leave your things unattended. It should be stressed that nowhere in the country are the mosquitos and other insects so voracious as in the southern Atlantic coast region; you must take particular care, and as dusk approaches, it would be wise to put on long pants and socks, and wear long sleeves. The mosquitos are particularly vicious at this time.

Corn Islands (*Islas del Maíz*), in the Caribbean opposite Bluefields, are two small beautiful islands fringed with white coral and slender coconut trees, though sadly many on the larger island were blown down by the 1988 hurricane. The smaller island escaped serious damage; it can be visited by boat from the larger island, but there are no facilities for the tourist. The larger is a popular Nicaraguan holiday resort; its surfing and bathing facilities make it ideal for tourists (best months March and April). Everything is naturally more expensive than on the mainland. For fishing (barracuda, etc), contact Ernie Jenkie (about US$5/hour). It is possible to dive off the Corn Islands although the equipment 'looks like leftovers from World War II'. The reef is good, however, and dives are very cheap. If you climb the mountain, wear long trousers, as there are many ticks. The language of the islands is English. The islanders are very friendly but petty thievery has been reported, even clothes stolen off a washing line. The local coconut oil industry has been devastated by Hurricane Joan, but lobsters provide much prosperity.

Passenger-carrying cargo boats leave Bluefields for the Corn Islands from the docks of Copesnica, N of town, around a small bay and past the ruined church. The water around Bluefields is dirty, muddy brown, soon becoming a clear, sparkling blue. There is usually a boat from Bluefields, via El Bluff, on Wed at 0900, 8 hrs, but there is no guarantee. Boats back to Bluefields leave from Will Bowers Wharf on Thurs; tickets available in advance from nearby office, US$4.50 one way. It is possible to hitch a lift on a fishing boat, enquire at Inpesca at the port; also N to Puerto Cabezas or S to San Juan del Norte. There is an irregular boat service to and from Jamaica. Nica and La Costeña fly daily from Managua and Bluefields to the Corn Islands, Nica schedule as for Bluefields, US$60 from Managua, US$40 from Bluefields one way, plus US$1.50 departure tax; the same advice on passport and customs applies as under Bluefields. Air services are suspended from time to time because of the poor state of the runway on Isla del Maíz. Book well in advance and book return immediately on arrival.

Hotels and Restaurants There are 4 hotels: *Hospedaje Miramar* is rec, serves meals; *Hospedaje Playa Coco*, also serves meals; **F** pp *Brisas del Mar*, with restaurant; one other; one can find rooms for about US$2 (rec is Miss Florence's house, called *Casa Blanca*, even though it is blue, E, at Playa Coco). The chief problem in all the hotels is rats, which may not be dangerous, but neither are they pleasant. *Comedor Blackstone*; *Mini Café*; ice cream parlour; several bars and reggae clubs. Ask around for where meals are available; the restaurants serve mainly chicken and chop suey, but in private houses you can find much better fare. Try banana porridge and sorrel drink (red, and ginger-flavoured). There is a severe shortage of food, water and most drinks (except rum). Main market area is near Will Bowers Wharf. Dollars are widely used and there is a dollartienda. Since the price of everything is generally high and there is no bank, take the cash you need with you.

The best beach for swimming is Long Beach on Long Bay; walk across the island from Playa Coco.

San Juan del Norte on the Costa Rican border was destroyed in the civil war, but is now being rebuilt a short distance up-river. No hotels, *pensiones* or restaurants, but the very friendly people will look after you. Check in San Carlos on Lake Nicaragua with ANCUR for boats, irregular sailings, 12 hrs or more to San Juan, up to 48 hrs return trip. You need to take your own food and a hammock is recommended. No permits are now needed.

From San Juan you can cross to Costa Rica and Barra del Colorado. Try for a boat or a canoe, or a combination with walking. Ask at a National Guard post for a letter to present to Immigration in San José.

Puerto Cabezas is the capital of the RAAN, the northern Atlantic Coast autonomous region, and it has a distinctly different atmosphere from Bluefields; it is principally a large Miskito village. A town of about 30,000 residents, Puerto Cabezas can offer an excellent introduction to the Miskito part of the country. There are significant minorities of *mestizos* (referred to on the Coast as *españoles* or the Spanish) and Creoles, many of whom came to 'Port' by way of Las Minas (see below). Spanish is a second language for most residents, although most speak it well (at least those who live in Puerto itself); many speak at least some English, and for some, it is their native language. The local name for Puerto Cabezas is Bilwi, although the name is of Sumo origin. The Miskitos conquered the Sumos to obtain the town sometime in the last century. There are no restrictions on travel to Puerto Cabezas, nor to the surrounding region, although it is occasionally necessary to go through police checkpoints.

From the airport, it is possible to get a taxi that will charge US$1 to any point in Puerto (it is also possible to walk, the distance to the centre of town is about 2-3 km). There are two main roads, the only paved streets, which run parallel to each other and to the sea. At the southern end of the town (the airport is at the northern end) is the port area; a walk along the pier at sunset is highly recommended. The main market occupies the central part of town.

Accommodation and Food *Hospedaje*: **E** *Cayos Miskitos*, 2 blocks E of the plaza, new, good, comfortable rooms with bath, clean, friendly, breakfast by arrangement in advance only; **E** *El Viajante*, also new and clean, central, very friendly, basic wooden rooms with fan, singles only, shared baths, *comedor* serves good breakfast to its guests. **Restaurants**: The three best restaurants are the *Atlántico*, *Jumbo*, which serves Chinese food and is close to the sea, and *Pizzería Mercedita*, near the harbour, very good, expensive, rec, wide liquor selection, good service. *El Zaire*, popular, with TV, food and service disappointing. There are also numerous *comedores*. Prices are much higher than elsewhere in Nicaragua because everything has to be brought in by air.

Hospital A new hospital was inaugurated in February 1993. It is located on the outskirts of Puerto, on the road leading out of town.

Beaches There is a beach in the town limits, but it is reputed to be dirty. A clean, and lovely, beach, Poza Verde, can be found several kilometres N of town: it has white sand, calm water and sandflies. Take the road out of town for about 15 mins and turn right on the track marked

SW Tuapi (*SW* stands for *switch*); follow it for a few kilometers to the sea. You can also walk 6 km along the beach from Puerto Cabezas, or take a taxi (US$30 for 3 hrs, with bargaining, the track is very bad).

Flights Two airlines currently offer flights from Managua: Nica, the national airline, and La Costeña each flies daily in small (20 seats) planes. Price is US$55 one way with Nica, US$57.85 with La Costeña, plus US$1.50 departure tax. In addition, La Costeña flies twice weekly from Bluefields, US$55 each way, daily to Waspám on the Río Coco, US$30, and to the towns of Las Minas, US$40 each way. Round trip tickets can be purchased and are honoured; the Managua offices of both airlines are in the domestic terminal of the airport. Bring your passport: there are 'immigration' checks by the police in Puerto, and sometimes in the waiting lounge in Managua; also, there is a customs check when returning from the Coast by air to Managua.

Transport It is not possible to rent a vehicle or bicycle in Puerto, but arrangements for a car and driver can be made with a taxi driver or others (ask a taxi or at your *hospedaje*). Public bus service is available between Puerto and Waspám (see below) and from Matagalpa (14 hrs). Furthermore, Puerto is connected by road to Managua; however, this 559-km trip should only be attempted in the dry season (early January to mid-May) in a 4-wheel drive vehicle. With luck, it will take only 2-3 days (the road, almost all of it unpaved, is not bad from Managua to Siuna, but becomes very difficult after that); do not drive at night. **NB** If you drive back from Puerto to Managua, take the road out of town and make a left turn at the sign, *SW Wawa*.

Excursions outside Puerto The road from Puerto to Waspám, on the Coco River, has been mostly rehabilitated; during the dry season, the 130-km trip takes about 3 hrs by 4-wheel drive vehicle, several hours longer by public bus (leaves Puerto 0700, returns from Waspám 1200). The bus can be boarded at several points in Puerto along the road leading out of town, cost is US$5 to go to Waspám. This trip will take you through the pine forests, red earth, and plains N of Puerto towards the Coca River (the border with Honduras), and you will pass through two Miskito villages, Sisin and Santa Marta.

Waspám and the Coco River The Coco River (called the *Wangki* in Miskito) is the heart of Miskito country and there are numerous Miskito villages along the river, stretching as far inland as northern Jinotega Department all the way to the Caribbean. Waspám (Spanish spelling Waspán), a town of about 2,500 people, is often referred to as 'the capital of the Río Coco'. A recommended place to eat is the *Comedor La Bondad* (a delicious meal of chicken, rice, beans, tomatoes, and a soft drink costs US$4). Waspám also has *hospedajes* and other *comedores*, as well as guest houses run by international organizations and local voluntary agencies.

A project has been working to repair the roads and bridges connecting the villages of the river, and it is now possible to go by vehicle as far as Kum, in one direction, and Leimus, in the other. An irregular boat service travels upriver from Waspám to San Carlos. Flights to Managua with La Costeña via the mining towns, US$60 one way; from Puerto Cabezas US$30.

Provisions The same information as under *Bluefields* applies here; along the river it can sometimes get chilly at night; bring a sweater or jacket.

A few words of Miskito *Tingki* - Thank you; *Tingki-pali* - Thank you very much; *Nakis-ma* - How are you; *Apu* - There isn't any (*no hay*); *sirpi*- little. Most numbers are the same as English as are the words 'Christmas', 'trouser', and 'book'.

Las Minas This area comprises the gold mining towns of Siuna, La Rosita, and Bonanza, and is part of the RAAN (Northern Atlantic Coast Autonomous Region), but is significantly inland from the Coast. Las Minas is a somewhat depressed region since the demise of the mines (Bonanza has the only working mine of the three towns, although Siuna's still employs some people), but the atmosphere is very much frontierish. **Siuna** is the largest town, and all three are predominatly *mestizo*, with a Creole minority; the surrounding rural areas have a significant Sumo population as well as some Miskitos. La Costeña (T Managua 631228), flies from the capital to Siuna and Bonanza Mon-Sat (US$48 one way to Siuna, US$57 to La Rosita and Bonanza); flights also from Puerto Cabezas, US$40 one way.

There are two relatively good road links from Managua, one through Matagalpa and Waslala, the other through Boaco, Muy Muy, Matiguás, and Río Blanco; the 330-km drive is very scenic (and takes about 7 hrs by 4-wheel drive vehicle in the dry season); however, check on the security situation before starting out. There are also bus links. *La Rosita* is 70 km E of Siuna, and it is also possible to drive on through to Puerto Cabezas, although the road is in very poor shape. Do not drive after dark.

Hotels and Restaurants E *Hotel Hilton*, in Siuna, is clean; another *hospedaje* is **E** *Cayopinto Hotel*; a recommended place to eat is either of the two *comedores* called *Despuque*, one in the market, and the other on a hill near the baseball stadium and airstrip. In **Rosita**, a recommended place to eat is *Comedor Jassy*, near the entrance of town on the Siuna side; there is an *hospedaje*, **E**, no name, near the market (noisy, but basically clean).

We are deeply grateful to Cindy Gersony of Sarasota, Florida, for new information on the Región Autonomista Atlántico Norte.

In the S of Región Autonomista Atlántica Sur is **San Juan del Norte/Greytown**, a quiet, undeveloped town which can be reached either down the Río San Juan or from Barra del Colorado in Costa Rica. There is a police station, school, small restaurant serving beans and rice, a small grocery store and accommodation for US$5 (clean, friendly, fruit in the back garden, good value, ask for the Aguilar family). 150 people live here, mostly from fishing; no cars, only boats. Excellent for wildlife excursions; no nightlife. Use Costa Rican colones in town and all along the Río San Juan. The only safe bathing is in the Laguna Azul, although it is possible in the river, where there are alligators and sharks, and the sea, also sharks and can be rough.

Transport An irregular boat goes to Bluefields, possibly once a week. 3-4 boats a week upriver to San Carlos, one to two days depending on the height of the river; an interesting trip but the sun is very hot. There are small settlements on the Costa Rican bank, but the first part of the Nicaraguan side is a park. Halfway is Boca de San Carlos where a meal and beer is available on the Costa Rican side; boats generally stop here for the night. Further upriver is Castillo, 6 hrs from San Carlos.

Warnings When locals go into the jungle around Greytown they are armed. The entire Caribbean coastal area is a narcotics zone, with drugs being landed from San Andrés.

Border formalities: when leaving Costa Rica, get an exit stamp; there is no emigration in Barra del Colorado. Nor is there immigration in Greytown; you must go to Bluefields or some point on the Río San Juan. Do not wait until San Carlos, even if the police say that it is OK to do so. Underestimating the likely problems over entry stamps may land you up in jail. The whole area of the Río San Juan is a restricted area so you must find out as soon as possible, on either side of the border, exactly what requirements are and where to get them.

We thank Lars Bo Nielsen (Arhus, Denmark) for the above information.

INFORMATION FOR VISITORS

Documents Visitors must have a passport with 6 months validity (at least), an onward ticket and proof of US$500 (or equivalent in córdobas) in cash or cheques for a stay of more than a week in the country. **NB** credit cards are becoming gradually more widely used in Nicaragua, so may be accepted instead of cash. No visa is required by nationals of Guatemala, El Salvador, Honduras, Chile, Bolivia, Argentina, USA, Belgium, Denmark, Finland, Greece, Hungary, Ireland, Liechtenstein, Luxembourg, Netherlands, Norway, Spain, Sweden, Switzerland or the United Kingdom for a 90-day stay. **NB** Visa rules are changing frequently, check before you travel. Citizens of all other countries need a visa, which can be bought before arriving at the border, is valid for arrival within 30 days, and for a stay of up to 30 days, it costs US$25 (£18); 2 passport photographs are required. It was reported in late 1992 that a full 30-day visa can be bought at the border.

It is best to get your visa in advance. Visas take less than 2 hrs to process in the embassies in Guatemala City and Tegucigalpa, but have been known to take 48 hrs elsehwere. When consultation with Managua is required (the countries to which this applies are Libya, Cuba, the People's Republic of China and Hong Kong) it takes longer. Extensions can be obtained at the Dirección de Migración y Extranjería in Managua: arrive at the office before 0830. From the small office on the righthand side you must obtain the *formulario* (3 córdobas). Then queue at the *caja* in the large hall to pay US$25 or 150 córdobas for your extension. This can take hours. In the meantime you can complete forms. With the receipt of payment you queue at the window on the right. With luck you will receive the extension stamp for midday; at any event you should get it the same day. Germans can obtain visas from Konsulat Nicaragua, Konstantinstr 41, 53179 Bonn. Send SAE with DM70 (cheques honoured), 2 photos and the complicated application form and allow 10 days for delivery. Commercial travellers should carry a document from their form accrediting them as such. An air ticket can be cashed if not used, especially if issued by a large company, but bus tickets are sometimes difficult to encash. It is reported, however, that the Nicaraguan Embassy in a neighbouring country is empowered to authorize entry without the outward ticket, if the traveller has enough money to buy the ticket. Also, if you have a visa to visit another Central American country, you are unlikely to be asked to show an outward ticket (this applies to all Central American countries: be two visas ahead!).

The cost of entry is US$3.50 (possibly paid in córdobas), but US$7 at weekends, but take care if you exchange money or expect change. Exit tax is US$2 in dollars cash, US$4 on Sat and Sun, and US$1 in córdobas. If in the slightest doubt about charges, insist on being given a receipt and go to the Immigration Department in Managua to verify the charge. Motorists and motorcyclists must pay US$20 in cash on arrival at the border (bicyclists pay US$2, and up to US$9 at weekends, though this tends to vary from one customs post to the next). One cyclist suggested typing out a phoney 'cycle ownership' document to help at border crossings. Also there are charges of US$1 for fumigation and US$2 for immigration (double at weekends). A doctor's certificate, preferably in English and Spanish stating the driver is allergic, can avoid fumigation inside the vehicle. Do not lose the receipts, they have to be produced when you leave; without them you will have to pay again. Vehicles not cleared by 1630 are held at customs overnight. Up to 4 hrs of formalities are possible when entering Nicaragua with a vehicle. Also, the last transport into Nicaragua (to Somoto) leaves at 1600; the same applies crossing from Costa Rica, the last public transport to Managua or Rivas may leave even earlier than 1700. There is nowhere to stay at either border. Make sure you get all the correct stamps on arrival, or you will encounter all sorts of problems once inside the country.

Taxes All passengers have to pay a sales tax of US$5 on all tickets issued in and paid for in Nicaragua; a transport tax of 1% on all tickets issued in Nicaragua to any destination; and an airport tax of US$12, payable in US dollars, on all departing passengers.

Air Services From London: British Airways, Virgin Atlantic, American Airlines, Continental or Delta to Miami and connect to American, Nica, Central American Airlines, Lacsa, Iberia, or Taca via San Salvador. Continental flies from Houston 4 times a week. From other US cities: Chicago with Aviateca (change in Guatemala City); Los Angeles and San Francisco, Continental (change in Houston), Aviateca; New York, Continental via Houston. Nica flies daily to Guatemala City, San José, San Salvador and Panama City; Taca flies to Tegucigalpa daily; Copa flies to Guatemala City, San José, San Salvador and Panama. From Europe, with Iberia to Managua Thur and Sun from Madrid via Miami (connections from other European cities). Aeroflot flies on Wed from Moscow via Shannon and Havana. All flight tickets purchased by non-residents must be paid in US dollars.

Customs   Duty-free import of ¹/₂ kg of tobacco products, 3 litres of alcoholic drinks and 1 large bottle (or 3 small bottles) of perfume is permitted.

Internal Transport   Hitchhiking is widely accepted, but not easy because so many people do it and there is little traffic—offer to pay ('pedir un ride'). Local buses are the cheapest in Central America, but are extremely crowded owing to a lack of vehicles and fuel. Baggage that is loaded on to the roof or in the luggage compartment is charged for, usually at half the rate for passengers.

Information on all Nicaragua's transport services can be found in *Nicaragua Timetable*, published twice a year in Spanish, English and German by Mathias Hock Services, Grazer Weg 38, D-60599 Frankfurt, Germany, Fax +49-69655710, US$7 per issue. We acknowledge our debt here to this publication.

Motoring   Low octane gasoline costs US$2 a US gallon, super, US$2.20; diesel, US$1.20. For costs on entry, see above under **Documents**. For motorcyclists, the wearing of crash helmets is compulsory. Service stations close at 1700-1800. Beware when driving at night, the national shortage of spare parts means that many cars have no lights. Your car may be broken into if unattended and not in secure shape. In general, major roads are in good shape.

Food   15% tax is added to all restaurant bills. Note the Government-owned *Colectivo de Soja* which encourages the use of soya as an alternative source of protein; vegetarian restaurants of this chain are in Masaya, Managua, Granada, San Juan del Sur and Estelí. Some Nicaraguan 'pizzas' are not much like the real thing, and the coffee can be terrible.

Tipping   in Nicaragua: 10% of bill in hotels and restaurants (many restaurants add 10% service); US$0.50 per bag for porters; no tip for taxi drivers.

Security   Visitors to Nicaragua must carry their passports (or a photocopy) with them at all times. There are police checkpoints on roads and in outlying districts; the police search for firearms. Border officials do not like army-type clothing on travellers, and may confiscate green or khaki rucksacks (backpacks), parkas, canteens. They usually inspect all luggage thoroughly on entering and leaving Nicaragua. Do not photograph any military personnel or installations.

Pickpocketing and bagslashing has increased greatly in Managua, especially in crowded places, and on buses throughout the country. Apart from Managua at night, most places are generally safe. Reports of robberies and assaults in Northern Nicaragua in 1993 indicate that care should be taken in this area, enquire about conditions before going, especially if proposing to leave the beaten track.

The political upheavals have produced much dislocation of all services. Be prepared for transport difficulties. Take essential personal items with you and a torch plus batteries. Keep out of politics which is still (1994) a highly-charged subject.

Health   Take the usual tropical precautions about food and drink. Tap water is not recommended for drinking generally and avoid uncooked vegetables and peeled fruit. Intestinal parasites abound; if requiring treatment, take a stool sample to a Government laboratory before going to a doctor. Malaria risk exists especially in the wet season; take regular prophylaxis. Medicines are in very short supply and you are strongly advised to bring anything you may need with you. Treatment in Centros de Salud, medical laboratories and dispensaries is free, though we have reports that visitors may have to pay. You may also be able to get prescribed medicines free. Private dentists are better-equipped than those in the national health service (but no better trained).

Clothing   Dress is informal; business men often shed jackets and wear sports shirts, but shorts are never worn. The wearing of trousers is perfectly OK for women. The dry season runs from December to May, and the wettest months are usually June and October. Best time for a business visit: from March to June, but December and January are the pleasantest months.

Hours of Business   0800-1200, 1430-1730 or 1800. Banks: 0830-1200, 1400-1600, but 0830-1130 on Sat. Government offices are not normally open on Sat in Managua, or in the afternoon anywhere.

Much detailed commercial information is given in 'Hints to Exporters: Nicaragua', obtainable on application to the DTI Export Publications, PO Box 55, Stratford-upon-Avon, Warwickshire, CV37 9GE.

Public Holidays   1 January: New Year's Day. March or April: Thursday of Holy Week and Good Friday. 1 May: Labour Day. 19 July: Revolution of 1979. 14 September: Battle of San Jacinto. 15 September: Independence Day. 2 November: All Souls' Day (Día de los Muertos). 7 and 8 December: Immaculate Conception (Purísima). 25 December: Christmas Day.

Businesses, shops and restaurants all close for most of Holy Week; many companies also close down during the Christmas-New Year period. Holidays which fall on a Sunday are taken the following Monday. Local holidays are given under the towns.

Standard Time   Five hours behind GMT; at beginning of 1992 Nicaragua introduced daylight saving, putting itself 1 hr ahead of Mexico and the rest of Central America, but in the same time zone as Panama. Many people refer to 'old time' and 'new time'.

Currency   The unit is the córdoba oro (C$), divided into 100 centavos. It was introduced in July, 1990, at a par with the US dollar. The córdoba oro was devalued to 5 = US$1 in March 1991 and the old córdoba was withdrawn from circulation on 30 April 1991; a further devaluation in January 1993 set the dollar at 6 córdobas oro, to be followed by continuous mini-devaluations. The black market rate at the end of March 1994 was 6.50 córdobas oro = US$1 (compared with an official rate of 6.35). Notes in circulation are for $\frac{1}{2}$, 1, 5, 10, 20, 50 and 100 córdobas oro. Try to avoid obtaining the larger notes, as no-one every has enough change (but see **Exchange** under Managua). A decree, passed on 22 March 1991, permitted private banks to operate (the financial system was nationalized in 1979). The import and export of foreign and local currencies are unrestricted. Visa and Mastercard are accepted in nearly all restaurants and hotels, and in many shops. This applies to a lesser extent to Amex, Cred-o-Matic and Diners Club. Don't rely exclusively on credit cards.

Changing TCs is difficult outside Managua; while the situation is improving, it is best to carry US dollar notes and sufficient local currency away from the bigger towns.

Cost of living   In 1993/94 Nicaragua was a relatively expensive country as far as hotel accommodation was concerned, but public transport was fairly cheap. For food, as a rough guide, a *comida corrida* costs about US$2-2.50 (meals in restaurants US$6-10, breakfasts US$3-4); a beer US$0.60-1, a coke US$0.30-50 (depending on the establishment) and a newspaper US$0.33.

Weights and Measures   The metric system is official, but in domestic trade local terms are in use; for example, the *medio*, which equals a peck (2 dry gallons), and the *fanega*, of 24 *medios*. These are not used in foreign trade. The principal local weight is the *arroba*=25 lb and the *quintal* of 101.417 English lb. Random variety of other measures in use include US gallon for petrol, US quart and pint for liquids; *vara* (33 ins) for short distances and the lb for certain weights.

Voltage   110 volts AC, 60 cycles.

Postal Services   Airmail to Europe takes 2-4 weeks (letter rate US$0.80, 5 córdobas); from Europe 7-10 days.

Telegraph and Telephone   lines are owned by the Government (Telcor). Automatic national and international telephone calls are possible from any private or public phone. Quality is now of the highest international standard. Card phones were due to be introduced in 1994. There are wireless transmitting stations at Managua, Bluefields and Cabo Gracias a Dios, and private stations at Puerto Cabezas, El Gallo, and Río Grande.

Telephone   International or national calls can be made at any Telcor office, open 0700-2200. All phone calls can be paid for in córdobas. Rates in early 1994 were: US$10 for 3 mins to USA, US$11.50 to Europe. You may have to wait a long time for a line, except for early in the morning on weekdays. You have to say in advance how long you want to talk for. Collect calls to the USA are easy ('a pagarse allá'), also possible to Europe. International Fax service is available in all major cities, US$4.50 per page to Eruope. See under Managua **Telecommunications** for Telcor's excellent telephone directory.

Representation Overseas **Belgium**, 55 Avenue de Wolvendael, 1180 Brussels, T 02 375-6500, F 02 375-7188; **Canada**, 170 Laurier Avenue West, Ottawa, Ontario KIP 5V5, T 613 234 9361-2, F 613 238-7666; **France**, 8 Rue de Sfax, 75016, Paris, T 1 4500-4102, F 1 4500-9681; **Mexico**, Payo de Rivera 120, Lomas de Chapultepec, CP 11000, T 540 5625-6, F 520-6960; **Sweden**, Sandhamnasgatan 40, 6TR, 11528 Stockholm, T 8 667-1857, F 8 662-4160; **UK**, 8 Gloucester Road, London, SW7 4PP, T 071 584-4365, F 071 823-8790; **USA**, 61 Broadway, Suite 2528-29, New York, N.Y. 1006, T 212 344-4491, F 212 344-4428.

Press Managua: *La Prensa* (pro-Government), *El Nuevo Diario*. *La Barricada*, official organ of the Sandinista Front. León: *El Centroamericano*. *La Gaceta* is the official gazette. *Ya Veremos*, monthly, covering international subjects. *Revista Conservadora* is the best monthly magazine. Other magazines: *Semana Cómica*, weekly satirical. *Envío* (monthly, English and Spanish editions, Jesuit); *Pensamiento Propio* (current affairs, monthly); *Análisis*, economic journal; *Soberanía* (Nicaraguan affairs, Spanish/English bilingual). *El Pez y la Serpiente* is a monthly magazine devoted to the arts, poetry and literature.

Sports Baseball is the national game, more important than soccer, and the best building in many towns is the baseball stadium. The season runs from November to the end of April.

Working in Nicaragua Volunteer work in Nicaragua is not as common after the 1990 elections as it was during the Sandinista years. Foreigners now work in environmental brigades supporting the FSLN, construction projects, agricultural cooperatives and environmental organizations. Certain skills are in demand, as elsewhere in the developing world; to discover the current situation, contact non-governmental organizations in your home country, (eg Nicaraguan Network, 1247 E Sreet, SE, Washington, DC 20003, T (202) 544-9355, F 544-9360, or PO Box 4496, Fresno, CA 93744, T (209) 226-0477, in the USA, twin town/sister-city organizations and national solidarity campaigns (NSC/ENN Brigades, 129 Seven Sisters Road, London N7 7QG, T 071-272 9619; Dutch Nicaragua Komitee, Aptdo Postal 1922, Managua).

We are grateful to Huw Clough and Kate Hennessy for doing the updating; to Mathias Hock for a complete review of the chapter, to Kevin Healey for additional notes and to the following travellers: Alexander Beck (Altessing, Germany), Massimo Bietti (Rome, Italy), Diego Bittel (Visp, Switzerland), Michael Carter (Stratford, Ontario, Canada), Nadia Christinet (Geneva, Switzerland), Jay Connerley (Fremont NE, USA), Frank Dux (Passau, Germany), Lene Eilrich (Ribe, Denmark), Ernst A Erbe (El Paso, Texas), Joy Hale & Derek Fess (Columbus, Ohio), Darrel Freeman (Lancaster, PA, USA), Cynthia Gersony (Sarasota, FL, USA), Julio Gonzalez (Saint-Bonnet près Riom, France), Pasi Hannonen (Jyövä Skylä, Finland), Sally & Mike Hayden (Cheltenham, Glos), Penny Jones (Barva, Heredia, Costa Rica), Daniel Kaiser (Triesen, Liechtenstein), Noel, Nenagh & Zoë Kemp (Lindisfarne, Australia), Martin Kopp (Stuttgart, Germany), Christoph Künzi (Zurich, Switzerland), Johannes Latsch (Bad Homburg var der Höhe, Germany), Frank Löwen (Rosengarten, Germany), Helmut Lüder (Potomac, MD, USA), Stefan Malmgren (Malmö, Sweden), Dr Martin Mowforth (Tavistock, Devon), Monica Müller (Blonay) & Klaus Högle (Marin, Switzerland), Dr William R C Munro (Stanley, Perth), Helmut Quitt (Rosenheim, Germany), Mike Rhodes (Fresno, CA, USA), Claudio Rivero (Buenos Aires), Mark Schuringa (Amsterdam, Holland), Harald Schwender & Birgitte Hächer (Sandhausen, Germany), Stefan Cotting (Nevenegg, Switzerland), Bill Vallis (Surbiton, Surrey), Vincent Van Es (Enschede, Holland), Benderoth Vitus (Hadamar) and Reto Wildschek (Kloten, Switzerland).

To use AT&T USADirect® Service from Nicaragua dial **174** from any phone. Some public telephones may require a card for dial tone. If you require assistance, please call the AT&T office in Managua at **66-8626**.

AT&T USADirect® Service.

COSTA RICA

INTRODUCTION

COSTA RICA is the smallest but two—El Salvador and Belize—of the Central American republics. Only Panama and Belize have fewer inhabitants, but it is known throughout Latin America as the continent's purest democracy. In November 1989, Costa Rica celebrated its centenary of democracy. The Army was abolished in 1949, though it should be stressed that there is a very efficient-looking khaki-clad Civil Guard. Costa Rica has the highest standard of living in Central America, the second lowest birth rate (after Panama) and the greatest degree of economic and social advance.

Costa Rica lies between Nicaragua and Panama, with coastlines on both the Caribbean (212 km) and the Pacific (1,016 km). The distance between sea and sea is from 119 to 282 km. A low, thin line of hills between Lake Nicaragua and the Pacific is prolonged into northern Costa Rica with several volcanoes (including the active volcano, Arenal), broadening and rising into high and rugged mountains and volcanoes in the centre and S. The highest peak, Chirripó Grande, SE of the capital, reaches 3,820m. Within these highlands are certain structural depressions; one of them, the Meseta Central, is of paramount importance. To the SW this basin is rimmed by the comb of the Cordillera; at the foot of its slopes, inside the basin, are the present capital, San José, and the old capital, Cartago. NE of these cities about 30 km away, four volcano cones rise from a massive common pedestal. From NW to SE these are Poás (2,704m), Barva (2,906m), Irazú (3,432m), and Turrialba (3,339m). Irazú and Poás are intermittently active. Between the Cordillera and the volcanoes is the Meseta Central: an area of 5,200 square km at an altitude of between 900 and 1,800m, where two-thirds of the

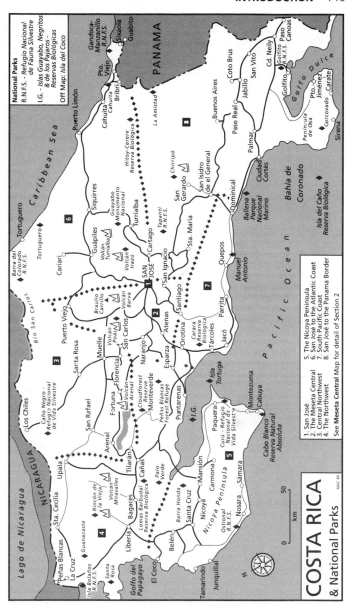

COSTA RICA
& National Parks

National Parks
R.N.F.S. - Refugio Nacional
de Fauna Silvestre
I.G. - Islas Guayabo, Negritos
& de los Pájaros -
Reservas Biológicas
Off Map: Isla del Coco

1. San José
2. The Meseta Central
3. Central Northwest
4. The Northwest

5. The Nicoya Peninsula
6. San José to the Atlantic Coast
7. South Pacific Coast
8. San José to the Panama Border

See Meseta Central Map for detail of Section 2

population live. The northeastern part of the basin is drained by the Reventazón through turbulent gorges into the Caribbean; the Río Grande drains the western part of it into the Pacific.

There are lowlands on both coasts. The Nicaraguan lowland along the Río San Juan is continued into Costa Rica, wide and sparsely inhabited as far as Puerto Limón. A great deal of this land, particularly near the coast, is swampy; SE of Puerto Limón the swamps continue as far as Panama in a narrow belt of lowland between sea and mountain.

The Gulf of Nicoya, on the Pacific side, thrusts some 65 km inland; its waters separate the mountains of the mainland from the 900m high mountains of the narrow Nicoya Peninsula. From a little to the S of the mouth of the Río Grande de Tárcoles, a lowland savanna stretches NW past the port of Puntarenas and along the whole northeastern shore of the Gulf towards Nicaragua.

Below the Río Grande the savanna is pinched out by mountains, but there are other banana-growing lowlands to the S. Small quantities of African palm and cacao are now being grown in these lowlands. In the far S there are swampy lowlands again at the base of the Peninsula of Osa and between the Golfo Dulce and the borders of Panama. Here there are 12,000 hectares planted to bananas. The Río General which flows into the Río Grande de Térraba, runs through a southern structural depression almost as large as the Meseta Central.

Climate Altitude, as elsewhere in Central America, determines the climate, but the *tierra templada* and the *tierra fría* start at about 300m lower on the Pacific than on the Atlantic side. The Pacific side is the drier, with patches of savanna among the deciduous forest; the Atlantic side has heavy rainfall— 300 days a year of it—and is covered far up the slopes with tropical forest: about a quarter of Costa Rica is forested (half forested in 1950).

The climate varies from the heat and humidity of the Caribbean and Atlantic lowlands to warm temperate on the Meseta Central and chilly temperate at the greater heights. On the Cordillera Talamanca, the average temperature is below 16C. There are dry and wet seasons: the dry runs from December to April, the wet from May to November, when the rainfall in the Meseta Central averages 1,950 mm and roads are often bogged down. The hottest months are March and April. Between December and April is the best time to visit.

History During his last voyage in September 1502, Columbus landed on the shores of what is now Costa Rica. Rumours of vast gold treasures (which never materialized) led to the name of Costa Rica (the Rich Coast). The Spaniards settled in the Meseta Central, where there were some thousands of sedentary Indian farmers (whose numbers were soon greatly diminished by the diseases brought by the settlers). Cartago was founded in 1563 by Juan Vásquez de Coronado, but there was no expansion until 145 years later, when a small number left Cartago for the valleys of Aserrí and Escazú. They founded Heredia in 1717, and San José in 1737. Alajuela, not far from San José, was founded in 1782. The settlers were growing in numbers (many farmers emigrated from northern Spain) but were still poor and raising subsistence crops only. Independence from Spain was declared in 1821 whereupon Costa Rica, with the rest of Central America, immediately became part of Mexico. This led to a civil war, during which, two years later, the capital was moved from Cartago to San José. After independence, the government sought anxiously for some product which could be exported and taxed for revenue. It was found in coffee, introduced from Cuba in 1808, which Costa Rica was the first of the Central American countries to grow. The Government offered free land to coffee growers, thus building up a peasant landowning class. In 1825 there was a trickle of exports, carried on mule-back to the ports. By 1846 there were ox-cart roads to Puntarenas. By 1850 there was a large flow of coffee to overseas markets: it was greatly increased by the opening of a railway from San José and Cartago to Puerto Limón along the valley of the Reventazón in 1890.

From 1850, coffee prosperity began to affect the country profoundly: the birth rate grew, land for coffee was free, and the peasant settlements started spreading, first down the Río Reventazón as far as Turrialba; then up the slopes of the volcanoes, then down the new railway from San José to the old Pacific port of Puntarenas.

Bananas were first introduced in 1878; Costa Rica was the first Central American republic to grow them and is now the second largest exporter in the world. Labour was brought in from Jamaica to clear the forest and work the plantations. The industry grew and in 1913, the peak year, the Caribbean coastlands provided 11 million bunches for export, but the spread of disease lowered the exports progressively. The United Fruit Company then turned its attentions to the Pacific litoral especially in the S around the port of Golfito. However, although some of the Caribbean plantations were turned over to cacao, *abacá* (Manilla hemp) and African palm, the region has regained its ascendancy over the Pacific litoral as a banana producer (the Standard Fruit Company is an important redeveloper of the region).

Costa Rica's long tradition of democracy begain in 1889 and has continued to the present day with only a few lapses. In 1917 the elected president Alfredo González, was ousted by Federico Tinoco, who held power until 1919, when a counter revolution and subsequent elections brought Julio Acosta to the presidency. Democratic and orderly government followed until the campaign of 1948 when violent protests and a general strike surrounded disputed results. A month of fighting broke out after the Legislative Assembly annulled the elections, leading to the abolition of the constitution and a junta being installed, led by José Figueres Ferrer. In 1949 a constituent assembly drew up a new constitution and abolished the army. The junta stepped down and Otilio Ulate Blanco, one of the candidates of the previous year, was inaugurated. In 1952, Figueres, a socialist, founded the Partido de Liberación Nacional (PLN), and was elected President in 1953. He dominated politics for the next two decades, serving as President in 1953-58 and 1970-74. The PLN introduced social welfare programmes and nationalization policies, while the intervening conservative governments encouraged private enterprise. The PLN was again in power from 1974-78 (Daniel Oduber Quirós) 1982-86 (Luis Alberto Monge) and 1986-90 (Oscar Arias Sánchez).

President Arias drew up proposals for a peace pact in Central America and concentrated greatly on foreign policy initiatives. Efforts were made to expel Nicaraguan contras resident in Costa Rica and the country's official proclamation of neutrality, made in 1983, was reinforced. The Central American Peace Plan, signed by the five Central American presidents in Guatemala in 1987, earned Arias the Nobel Peace Prize, although progress in implementing its recommendations was slow.

In the 1990 general elections, Rafael Angel Calderón Fournier, a conservative lawyer and candidate for the Social Christian Unity Party (PUSC), won a narrow victory with 51% of the vote, over the candidate of the PLN. Calderón, the son of a former president who was one of the candidates in the 1948 disputed elections, had previously stood for election in 1982 and 1986. The President's popularity slumped as the effects of his economic policies were felt on people's living standards, while his Government was brought into disrepute by allegations of corruption and links with narcotraffickers. In the February 1994 elections another former president's son was elected by a narrow margin. José María Figueres, 39, of the PLN, won 49.6% of the vote, 2.2 points ahead of his PUSC rival. During the rather dirty campaign both candidates were implicated in corruption scandals but the election was won on economic policies. Figueres argued against neo-liberal policies, claiming he would renegotiate agreements

COSTA RICA : FACT FILE

Geographic

Land area	51,100 sq km
forested	32.1%
pastures	45.4%
cultivated	10.4%

Demographic

Population (1992)	3,161,000
annual growth rate (1987-92)	2.5%
urban	54.0%
rural	46.0%
density	61.9 per sq km
Religious affiliation	
Roman Catholic	88.5%
Birth rate per 1,000 (1990)	27.4
	(world av 26.4)
Death rate per 1,000 (1990)	3.8
	(world av 9.2)

Education and Health

Life expectancy at birth,	
male	72.9 years
female	77.6 years
Infant mortality rate	
per 1,000 live births (1989)	15.3
Physicians (1989)	1 per 798 persons
Hospital beds	1 per 454 persons
Calorie intake as %	
of FAO requirement	125%
Population age 25 and over	
with no formal schooling	8.3%
Literate males (over 15)	92.6%
Literate females (over 15)	93.1%

Economic

GNP (1990 market prices)	US$5,342mn
GNP per capita	US$1,910
Public external debt (1990)	US$2,832mn
Tourism receipts (1990)	US$275mn
Inflation	
(annual av 1986-91)	20.3%
Radio	1 per 12 persons
Television	1 per 5.1 persons
Telephone	1 per 7.0 persons

Employment

Population economically active (1990)	
	1,108,440
Unemployment rate	5.5%
% of labour force in	
agriculture	24.4
mining	0.2
manufacturing	17.4
construction	6.4
Military and Police forces	7,500

Source *Encyclopaedia Britannica*

with the IMF and the World Bank, but he was expected to have little room for manoeuvre given the difficulties of maintaining the welfare state and economic growth. In the Legislature, the PLN won 29 seats and the PUSC 25, while smaller parties won the remaining seats.

The People In all provinces save Limón over 98% are whites and *mestizos* but in Limón 33.2% are blacks and 3.1% indigenous Indians, of whom only 5,000 survive in the whole country. There are three groups, the Bribri (3,500), Boruca (1,000) and Guatuso. Although officially protected, the living conditions of the indigenous Indians are very poor. In 1992 Costa Rica became the first Central American country to ratify the International Labour Oranganization treaty on indigenous populations and tribes. However, even in Limón the percentage of blacks is falling: it was 57.1 in 1927. Many of them speak Jamaican English as their native tongue. Much of the Caribbean coastland, more especially in the N, remains unoccupied. On the Pacific coastlands a white minority owns the land on the *hacienda* system rejected in the uplands. About 46% of the people are *mestizos*. The population has risen sharply in the mountainous Peninsula of Nicoya, which is an important source of coffee, maize, rice and beans.

Contact with the rural population is easy: the people are friendly and enjoy talking. (The national adjective, *costarricense*, is rather a mouthful: the universal short form is 'tico/a'.)

The Economy The country's economy is based on the export of coffee, bananas, meat, sugar and cocoa. The Meseta Central with its volcanic soil is the coffee-growing area: here too are grown the staple crops: beans, maize, potatoes and sugar cane, and the dairy farming is both efficient and lucrative. Diversification of exports has been successful, with non-traditional crops now accounting for 58% of revenues. Coffee exports have fallen as prices have declined and producers have turned to other crops. Costa Rica remains the second largest banana exporter in the world, but the industry is threatened by new European quotas. The country's timber industry is very small and its resources have yet to be commercially utilized although deforestation has occurred at an alarming rate.

High growth in the industrial sector has led to considerable economic diversification, and manufacturing accounts for about 19% of gdp, compared with 16% in the case of agriculture. Industry is largely concerned with food processing but there is also some production of chemicals (including fertilizers—also exported), plastics, tyres, etc. Current major industrial projects include aluminium processing, a petrochemical plant at Moín, and a tuna-fish processing plant at Golfito.

There are small deposits of manganese, mercury, gold and silver, but only the last two are worked. Deposits of iron ore are estimated at 400 million tons and sulphur deposits at 11 million tons. Considerable bauxite deposits have been found but have not yet been developed. In 1980, the Arenal hydroelectric plant was opened and there are projects to develop the Corobicí and other hydroelectric complexes. The port of Caldera on the Pacific coast has been improved and manufacturing for export is being encouraged. Oil companies are interested in offshore concessions in the Pacific. There is an oil refinery at Puerto Limón.

Tourism is now a major industry and is the main source of foreign exchange revenue generating around US$500mn in 1993, from 700,000 tourists. The construction of hotels has soared and although most new businesses are small-scale eco-lodges of less than 50 rooms, the Government has allowed foreign investors to build some huge resorts for mass tourism in a controversial reversal of previous policy. Land prices have soared, driven up by foreign, mainly US, purchasers.

Despite several IMF-supported austerity programmes, the Costa Rican economy still suffers from large public sector deficits, partly because of a high level of government spending on social welfare. The country amassed a large foreign debt, which including accumulated arrears, amounted in 1989 to US$5bn and was one of the highest per capita in the developing world. In the late 1980s, Costa Rica turned to the IMF and the World Bank for help in adjusting its economy and was one of the first countries to take advantage of a US-sponsored, debt reduction proposal. An agreement was negotiated with commercial bank creditors in 1989-90, to be supported by funds from official creditors. The economic programme was hugely unpopular as spending cuts in health, social security and education increased poverty and unemployment, leading to strikes and protests. By end-1991 total debt had fallen to less than US$4bn. In 1991-92 economic growth picked up, inflation declined and unemployment fell. Many new jobs were created in tourism, with 54 new hotels being built in 1992. In 1993 a third structural adjustment loan was negotiated with the IMF against considerable local opposition. The new government is under pressure to reduce poverty (22% of the population) while maintaining the 6.5% gdp growth rate recorded in 1993 (7.8% in 1992), the low inflation rate (9.5% in 1993) and foreign exchange reserves of around US$1bn.

Government Legislative power is vested in a Legislative Assembly of 57 deputies, elected by proportional representation for four years. Executive authority is in the hands of the President, elected for the same term by popular vote. Men and women over 18 have the right to vote. Voting is secret, direct and free. Judicial power is exercised by the Supreme Court of Justice.

Communications Costa Rica has a total of 35,556 km of roads of which 15% are paved. The Pan-American Highway runs the length of the country, from the Nicaraguan to the Panamanian borders. A new highway has been built from Orotina to Caldera, a new port on the Gulf of Nicoya which has replaced

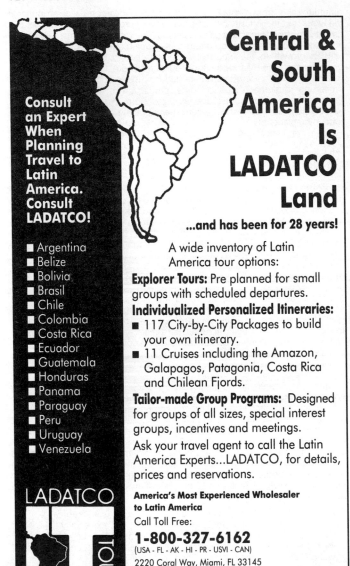

Consult an Expert When Planning Travel to Latin America. Consult LADATCO!

- Argentina
- Belize
- Bolivia
- Brasil
- Chile
- Colombia
- Costa Rica
- Ecuador
- Guatemala
- Honduras
- Panama
- Paraguay
- Peru
- Uruguay
- Venezuela

Central & South America Is LADATCO Land

...and has been for 28 years!

A wide inventory of Latin America tour options:

Explorer Tours: Pre planned for small groups with scheduled departures.

Individualized Personalized Itineraries:
- 117 City-by-City Packages to build your own itinerary.
- 11 Cruises including the Amazon, Galapagos, Patagonia, Costa Rica and Chilean Fjords.

Tailor-made Group Programs: Designed for groups of all sizes, special interest groups, incentives and meetings.

Ask your travel agent to call the Latin America Experts...LADATCO, for details, prices and reservations.

America's Most Experienced Wholesaler to Latin America

Call Toll Free:

1-800-327-6162
(USA - FL - AK - HI - PR - USVI - CAN)

2220 Coral Way, Miami, FL 33145
Miami: (305) 854-8422
Fax: (305) 285-0504

LADATCO TOURS

Puntarenas as the principal Pacific port, and another has been completed from San José via Guápiles and Siquirres to Puerto Limón. Also a new road has been built to improve access to the Pacific beaches, from Playas de Jacó to Quepos and Ciudad Cortés, the paving of which was completed in 1993. All 4-lane roads into San José are toll roads (US$0.35).

There used to be 1,286 km of railways, all of 1.067m gauge. These are now closed, except for a limited section of track running through the E of San José for commuter passengers, and plantation lines near the Caribbean coast. Unfortunately the spectacular line from San José to Puerto Limón suffered major damage from landslides in 1991. Some portions may be reactivated in the future, mainly for tourists.

Religion and Education Roman Catholicism is the official religion and about 85% of the population are Roman Catholic, the remainder being mostly Protestant. Educational standards are high: only 8.3% of the economically active population over the age of 25 have no formal schooling. Consequently literacy is high.

National Parks Tourists particularly enjoy the many well-kept and well-guarded national parks and nature reserves which protect some samples of the extraordinarily varied Costa Rican ecosystems. Some of the last patches of dry tropical forest, for instance, can be found in the Santa Rosa National Park, and other parks protect the unique cloud forest.

The **Servicio de Parques Nacionales** (SPN, Av 8, Calle 25, open Mon-Fri, 0800-1600, write in advance to Apartado 10094, or T 233-4070, 233-4246, 233-4118) in San José, issues permits if necessary. Most permits can be obtained at park entrances. All the parks are marked in the excellent Instituto Geográfico maps, which can be purchased at various places. To contact park personnel by radio link or make reservations, T 233-4160, but good Spanish is a help. If you want to work as a volunteer in the parks, contact Stanley Arquedas of the SPN, mornings only. The daily park entry fee for all National Parks is only US$1.50 and a campaign is now being mounted to increase the fee (approval from the Legislative Assembly is required) and use part of the funds for park preservation. Pressure of visitor numbers (250,000 in 1991 compared with 50,000 to parks in 1986) has caused problems with conservation, particularly in the popular Cabo Blanco Reserve, Carara and Manuel Antonio.

Bird watchers and butterfly lovers have long flocked to Costa Rica to see some of the 850 or so species of birds (the whole of the United States counts only about 800 species) and untold varieties of butterflies. All of these can best be seen in the parks, together with monkeys, deer, coyotes, armadillos, anteaters, turtles, coatimundis, raccoons, snakes, wild pigs, and, more rarely, wild cats and tapirs. Bird lists, with a breakdown by park, can be purchased in San José from the Organization for Tropical Studies which is 4½ blocks W of Colegio Lincoln, in front of the Bodega del Banco Central. Take the Florida or Llorente bus from Calle 2. You can also get plant and butterfly lists from them, and other valuable natural history information as well. Good field guides are Petersen, *Birds of Mexico and Central America* and *Birds of North America*; Stiles/Skutch, *Guide to the Birds of Costa Rica*; Ridgely, *Birds of Panama*; Golden Guide, *Birds of North America*; Daniel H Janzen, *Costa Rican Natural History*; Philip J de Vries, *Butterflies of Costa Rica*.

Nature guides can be found at The Bookshop in San José, and there is also available an illustrated book, *The National Parks of Costa Rica*, by Mario A Boza (1986), which gives a good impression of what the different parks are like.

Although the National Parks and other privately owned reserves are a main tourist attraction, many are in remote areas and not easy to get to on public transport; buses or coaches that do go tend to stay for a short time only. There is a growing tendency for tour companies to dominate the National Park 'market' to the exclusion of other public transport. For those on tight budgets, try making up a party with others and sharing taxis or hiring a car. Descriptions of the individual parks, and how to get there, will be found in the text.

The Audubon Society holds an Eco-Tourism Seminar on Wednesdays at 1830 at the Friends' Peace Center, Calle 15 Av 8 corner, San José. A National Park slide show with 164 slides on the National Park system, with a period for questions and answers, is held on Mon, Wed, Sat, at 1000-1130 at Cine Variedades, Calle 5, Av 1-Central, 50m N of Plaza de la Cultura, US$3.

A debate over development of tourism in Costa Rica raged in 1993-94 with the Government in favour of developing mass tourism along the beaches of Nicoya and Guanacaste Provinces. Ecotourism lobbyists argued hotly that small scale tourism was more beneficial for conservation purposes, supported by many tour agents, who pointed out that at present, ecotourists spend an average of 15 days in the country, spending freely on local services, while holidaymakers to resorts average 5 days and spend almost nothing. One particular project at Tambor sparked heated criticism, when Barceló the Spanish developers of a 400-room hotel on the beach, infringed several laws and regulations (see **Tambor, p 759**). The incident severely tarnished Costa Rica's ecotourism reputation. Growth of hotels has been spectacular in the 1990s and although most have been of less than 50 rooms, there are plans for several large resorts along the beaches, which, like Tambor, would damage habitats and the ecology.

Watersports The rivers of Costa Rica have proved to be highly popular for **white water rafting**, kayaking and canoeing, both for the thrill of the rapids and the wildlife interest of the quieter sections. The seven most commonly run rivers are the Reventazón, Pacuaré, Corobicí, Pascua, Peralta, Sarapiquí and El General. You can do a day-trip but to reach the big class IV rapids you usually have to take 2-3 days. The Reventazón is perhaps the most accessible but the Pacuaré has been recommended as a more beautiful experience. The Corobicí is slow and popular with bird watchers. Ríos Tropicales (see **San José Travel Agencies, p 734**) has been recommended for its guides and its equipment. Offshore, **snorkelling** and **scuba diving** are offered by several hotels, but you have to pick your spot carefully. Anywhere near a river will suffer from poor visibility and the coral reef has died in many places because of agricultural pollutants washed downstream. Generally, on the Caribbean side you can see wrecks and coral reefs, particularly in the SE towards the Panamanian border, while on the Pacific side you see large pelagics and sportsfish. Liveaboard dive boats head for the islands of Caño and Isla del Coco. Divers are not permitted in National Parks or reserves, nor within 500m of the protected sea turtle zone north of Tortuguero National Park. **Windsurfing** is good along the Pacific coast and on Lake Arenal, particularly the W end. Lots of hotels have equipment for hire and operators in San José will know where the best conditions prevail at any time. Be careful of obstacles in the water along rocky coastlines and near river mouths. **Surfing** is also popular off the Pacific beaches, attracting professionals who follow storm surges along the coast. **Sport fishing** is done off either coast and at different times of the year. Snook and tarpon are caught in the Caribbean, the largest snook being found in Sept and Oct, mostly N of Limón (where there are several fishing lodges), but also towards Panama. In the Pacific bill fishing is well-developed.

SAN JOSE (1)

San José, (pop 294,167, metropolitan area 1,040,000), stands in a broad, fertile valley at an altitude of 1,150m, which produces coffee and sugar-cane. It was founded in 1737 but frequent earthquakes have destroyed most of the colonial buildings and the modern replacements are not very inspiring. The climate is excellent, though the evenings can be chilly. The lowest and highest temperatures run from 15 to 26°C. Slight earthquake shocks are frequent. Rainy season: May to Nov. Other months are dry.

Streets cross one another at right-angles. Avenidas run E-W; the Calles N-S.

The three main streets are Av Central, Av 2 and the intersecting Calle Central: the business centre is here. The best shops are along Av Central. Avenidas to the N of Av Central are given odd numbers; those to the S even numbers. Calles to the W of Calle Central are even-numbered; those to the E odd-numbered. The Instituto Costarricense de Turismo has an excellent map of the city, marking all the important sights and business houses. **NB** Few buildings have numbers, so find out the nearest cross-street when getting directions (200m means 2 blocks)

It is best not to take a car into San José between 0700 and 2000; traffic is very heavy although new traffic laws have freed up the flow. Watch out for no parking zones or you will get towed away. Many of the narrow streets are heavily polluted with exhaust fumes. Seven blocks of the Av Central, from Banco Central running E to Plaza de la Cultura, are closed to traffic. Many people prefer to stay in the suburbs or in Heredia to escape the pollution.

Sightseeing Many of the most interesting public buildings are near the intersection of Avenida Central and Calle Central. The Teatro Nacional (1897)—marble staircases, statuary, frescoes and foyer decorated in gold with Venetian plate mirrors—is just off Av Central, on Calle 3. It has a good coffee bar. Nearby is Plaza de la Cultura, Av Central, C 3/5. The Palacio Nacional (Av Central, Calle 15) is where the Legislative Assembly meets; any visitor can attend the debates, sessions start normally at 1600. Along Calle Central is Parque Central, with a bandstand in the middle among trees (bands play at 1100 on each second Sun of the month). To the E of the park is the Cathedral; to the N are the Raventos and Palace theatres, interesting; to the S are the Rex Theatre and a branch of the Banco Nacional. N of Av Central, on Calle 2, is the Unión Club, the principal social centre of the country. Opposite it is the General Post and Telegraph Office. The Museo Nacional, with a good collection of precolumbian antiquities, is in the reconstructed Vista Buena barracks, E along Av Central. Facing it is the new Plaza de la Democracia, constructed to mark the November 1989 centenary of Costa Rican democracy. Two blocks N of the Museo Nacional is Parque Nacional, with a grandiloquent bronze monument representing the five Central American republics ousting the filibuster William Walker (see Nicaraguan chapter) and the abolition of slavery in Central America. There is also a statue donated by the Sandinista Government of Nicaragua to the people of Costa Rica. To the N of the park is the Biblioteca Nacional.

Still further N is Parque Bolívar, now turned into a recreation area, small charge for entry, with zoo (sloths in the trees). Along Av 3, to the W of Parque Nacional, are the four gardens of the remodelled Parque Morazán, with another bandstand at the centre. A little to the NE, Parque España—cool, quiet, and intimate—has for neighbours the Casa Amarilla (Yellow House), seat of the Ministry of Foreign Affairs, and the Edificio Metálico, which houses several of the main schools. In the park opposite the church of La Merced is a huge carved granite ball brought from the archaeological site at Palmar Norte.

The attractive Paseo Colón continues the Av Central W to the former La Sabana airport (now developed as a sports centre, which is worth visiting) with a colonial-style building with frescoes of Costa Rican life in the Salón Dorado, see **Museo de Arte Costarricense** under **Museums** below. Further W is La Sabana, which has the Estadio Nacional, seating 20,000 spectators at (mainly) football matches, basketball, volleyball and tennis courts, a running track, lake and swimming pool.

Local Holiday 28 to 31 December. Festivities last from 18 December to 5 January, with dances, horse shows and much confetti-throwing in the crowded streets. The annual El Tope horse parade starts at noon on 26 Dec and travels along the principal avenues of San José. A carnival starts next day at about 1700 in the same area. Fairs, firework displays and bull running (anyone can take part!) at El Zapote, frequent buses from the centre. Also parades during Easter week in the streets.

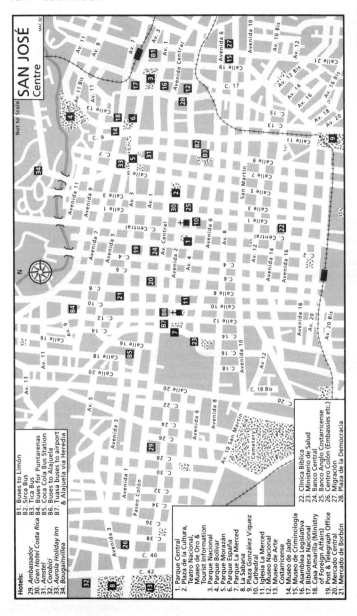

SAN JOSÉ
Centre

Not to scale

MAC 82

Hotels:
29. Ambassador
30. Gran Hotel Costa Rica
31. Amstel
32. Corobicí
33. Aurola Holiday Inn
34. Bougainvillea

B1. Buses to Limón
B2. Sirca Bus
B3. Tica Bus
B4. Buses for Puntarenas
B5. Coca Cola Bus Station
B6. Buses to Alajuela
B7. Juan Santamaría Airport & Alajuela via Heredia

1. Parque Central
2. Plaza de la Cultura, Teatro Nacional, Museo de Oro & Tourist Information
3. Parque Nacional
4. Parque Bolívar
5. Parque Morazán
6. Parque España
7. Parque La Merced
8. La Sabana
9. Plaza González Víquez
10. Cathedral
11. Iglesia La Merced
12. Museo Nacional
13. Museo de Arte Costarricense
14. Museo de Jade
15. Museo de Criminología
16. Asamblea Legislativa
17. Biblioteca Nacional
18. Casa Amarilla (Ministry of Foreign Affairs)
19. Post & Telegraph Office
20. Mercado Central
21. Mercado de Borbón
22. Clínica Bíblica
23. Ministerio de Salud
24. Banco Central
25. Banco Anglo Costarricense
26. Centro Colón (Embassies etc.)
27. Migración
28. Plaza de la Democracia

Warning Pickpockets, grab and run thieves, and muggings are on the increase in San José, especially in the centre, in the market, at the Coca Cola bus station, in the Barrios of Cuba, Cristo Rey, México, 15 de Setiembre and León XIII. Keep away from these areas at night and on Sunday, when few people are around. Also be careful on buses. A special tourism police force is being set up which will work with the San José municipal police to help protect tourists from theft. The US embassy has produced a booklet *Helpful Hints For United States Citizens In Costa Rica*, available at the *Tico Times* office, some hotels and the US embassy. You must carry your passport (or a photocopy) with you at all times and make sure your papers are in order.

Hotels 10% sales tax plus 3% tourism tax are added to the basic price. A deposit is recommended at the more expensive hotels, especially in the high season, Dec-April, to guarantee reservations. If you arrive late at night, even a guaranteed reservation may not be honoured. In the **L** price range (stars in brackets), are the *Herradura Resort and Convention Center* (4), near the airport, Japanese-owned, *Sakura* Japanese restaurant, pool, T 239-0033, F 239-2292; *Aurola Holiday Inn* (4), C 5, Av 5, pool, T 233-7233, F 255-1036, casino, good view of city, go to 16th floor and walk up emergency stairs; *Cariari* (4), near airport, T 239-0022, F 239-2803, pool, tennis, golf, described as a 'Florida resort motel in Costa Rica'. *Corobicí* (3), Sabana Norte, T 232-8122, F 231-5834, Japanese-owned, same chain as *Cariari*, 215 new rooms to be built, casino, conference facilities, pool and fitness centre, efficiency and service of front desk has been criticized; *Tara Resort Hotel*, San Antonio de Escazú, T 228-6992, F 228-9651, beautiful mansion, inc breakfast and transport, suites, conference facilities, rec restaurant, pool, beautiful views, climb nearby Pico Blanco mountain. 5-star huge *Camino Real* due to open in 1994 in Guachipelín de Ecazú.

In the **A+** range are *Balmoral* (3), C 7, Av Central, T 222-5022, F 221-7826, café/restaurant slow service, opp *Torremolinos* (3), C 40, Av 5 bis, T 222-5266, F 255-3167, LanChile office, bar, restaurant, pool, sauna, 200m from Sabana, near Yoahan commercial centre, free transport into town; *Hotel del Rey*, Av 1, C 9, on busy corner in restored pink and white building, looks like iced cake, nice single, double, triple rooms, standard or deluxe, suites, children under 12 free, walls a bit thin, restaurant, casino, Apdo 6241-1000, T 221-7272, 257-3130, F 221-0096; *San José Palacio*, near airport, T 220-2034, F 231-1990, part of the Barceló chain, all rooms a/c, fridge, cable TV, 1 executive floor, 5 normal floors, pool, spa, squash, tennis, sauna, casino, convention centre, café, piano bar, restaurant, but out of town and few shops etc nearby; *Irazú* (3), La Uruca, next to San José 2000 shopping centre, T 232-4811, F 232-3159, rooms without a/c, children under 12 free, casino, conference facilities, pool, tennis, sauna, rec, transport downtown, hotel will organize excursions and visits, mixed reports. *Villa Tournon* (3), Barrio Tournon, T 233-6622, F 22-5211, attractive, excellent service, pool, rooms facing the street are noisy from traffic; *Ambassador* (3), C 26, P Colón, T 221-8155, F 255-3396, modern, casino, bar, restaurant, coffee shop, cable TV, phone in rooms, travel agency, restaurants and cinemas opp, front rooms noisy from traffic, back rooms fine, nice suite; *L'Ambiance* (4), C 13, Av 9, T 222-6702, F 223-0481, US-owned, elegant 19th century restored mansion, antique furnishings, only 7 rooms, 20-seat restaurant rec, book in advance, bar, patio, very pleasant, no credit cards, front doors locked at 2300; *Gran Hotel Costa Rica* (3), C 3, Av 2, T 221-4000, F 221-3501, all right for one night stopover but service criticized (1993), dirty dining room, although food adequate, breakfast from 0400, buffet US$7, English-speaking staff, casino, noisy; *D' Raya Vida*, bed and breakfast villa run by Debbi McMurray-Long, near Hospital Calderón Guardia, inc airport transfers, 4 double rooms, children by prior arrangement, meals available, wonderful garden, T 223-4168, F 223-4157.

Those in the **A** range include *Ara Macao*, Barrio California, 50m S of Pizza Hut, 5 mins from centre, T 233-2742, inc breakfast, small, quiet; *Casa Verde de Amon*, 100m E of Invu Barrio Amon, T/F 233-0969, small, deluxe, close to 200, jade museum, markets; *Presidente* (3), C 7, Av Central, T 222-3022, F 221-1205; *Europa* (3), C Central, Av 3, T 222-1222, F 221-3976, pleasant, comfortable rooms, cable TV, pool, central, good for business visitors, suites available, prior reservation rec, rooms on street side can be noisy, good restaurant; *Edelweiss*, Av 9, C 13-15, 100m E of Condovac offices, T 221-9702, F 222-1241, English, German and Spanish spoken, Austrian and German cuisine, clean, comfortable, native hardwood furniture and carved doors, pleasant courtyard bar, helpful, friendly, rec; *Bougainvillea Santo Domingo* (3), 20 mins drive from the centre, near International airport, a few mins walk from El Pueblo (see **Shopping**); *Amstel Morazán* (3), C 7, Av 1, T 222-4622, F 223-3329, conflicting reports on both food and service, book in advance, rooms vary, highly rec by some; *Amstel Escazú*, T 228-1764, opened 1993, 14 rooms, 2 suites, pool, *Amstel Amon* opened 1993 in Barrio Amon (no sign), very helpful, clean, 75 rooms, plus suites. *Petit Victoria*, C 26, 50m from Paseo Colón, T 233-1812, F 233-1938, bath, minibar, cable TV, kitchen, convenient, breakfast included, but overpriced; *Royal Dutch*, C 4, Av Central-2, T 222-1066, F 233-2927, 2-star, suites, restaurant, rec; *Santo Tomás*, Av 7, C 3-5,

T 255-0448, F 222-3950, central, US owner demands full payment in advance but will not refund if you cut short your stay, noisy; *Villa Escazú Bed and Breakfast*, 1 km SW of Escazú, near bus route, 4 rooms with private or shared bathroom, large gardens and patio, T/F 228-9566, ask for Inéz or Mary Ann; *Tennis Club*, Sábana Sur, Apartado 4964, T 232-1266, F 232-3867, 2-star, 20 mins from centre, a/c, shower, TV, swimming pool, tennis courts, snack bar, restaurant, rec; *Grano de Oro*, C 30, Av 2, T 255-3322, F 221-2782, converted 19th century mansion, tasteful, good value; *Dunn Inn*, Barrio Amón, C 5, Av 11, Apdo 6241-1000, T 222-3232/3426, F 221-4596, inc breakfast and local phone calls; *Diana's Inn*, C 5, Av 3, Parque Morazán, near *Holiday Inn*, an old building formerly used by the president, now restored, inc breakfast and taxes, discounts available, a/c, TV, hot water, noisy, luggage storage, safety box, T 223-6542, F 233-0495. 25 mins from San José, nr Rancho Redondo, is *Hacienda San Miguel*, T 229-1094, F 221-3871, inc breakfast, restaurant, pool, horseriding, jacuzzi, steam bath, magnificent views, continental divide passes through property, Pacific and Caribbean slope birds to be seen. *Don Carlos* (3), C 9, Av 7, T 221-6707, F 255-0828, inc bath and breakfast, 15 rooms, clean, comfortable, convenient but most rooms are extremely noisy and you cannot guarantee a quiet room even if requested with advance reservation (one night deposit to require reservation, no credit cards), US$1 bag storage, US$10 to change reservation, unfriendly desk staff.

B hotels are *Royal Garden* (3), C Central, Av 2, T 257-0023, F 257-1517, central, casino, Chinese restaurant, Dim Sum for breakfast; *Doral*, C 6-8, Av, T 233-5069, F 233-4827, bath, TV, central, clean, helpful staff, soft mattresses, a bit noisy, restaurant; *D'Galahi* (2), behind University of Costa Rica, San Pedro, pool, nice rooms and apartments, T 234-1743; *La Gema*, Av 12, C 9-11, T 257-2524, F 222-1074, bath, TV, pleasant, friendly; *La Gran Vía* (2), C 3, Av Central, T 222-7737, F 222-7205, comfortable, not noisy, helpful, good value; *Plaza* (1), C 2, Av Central, T 222-5533, F 222-2614, TV, phone, bar, restaurant; *Galilea*, Av Central, C 13, T 233-6925, friendly, hot showers, back rooms quiet, rooms on C 3 have nice view of Plaza Democracia and Museo Nacional, run by Dutch lady, English and German also spoken; *Casa Verde/Victorian Inn*, C 7, Av 9, No 910, T 223-0969, renovated old house, private atmosphere, owner Carl Evan Stanley helpful, good breakfast, deluxe suite available A+; *Pico Blanco Inn* (1), San Antonio de Escazú, T 228-1908, F 228-4812, all rooms with balconies and views of Central Valley, several cottages, English owner, restaurant with English pub—Costa Rican flavour, rec; *Garden Court*, Av 7, C 6-8, T 220-1441, F 232-3159, bath, TV, a/c, inc breakfast, pool, sauna, parking; *Tres Arcos*, Av 10, C 37-39, no 3773, Los Yoses, T 225-0271, Canadian-owned, close to restaurants, buses, nice area, inc breakfast; *Park*, C 2, Av 4, T 221-6944, clean with bar. **B-C** *Aranjuez*, C 19, Av 11-13, T 223-3559, F 223-3528, shared or private bathroom, splendid breakfast, free coffee all day, friendly English speaking staff, clean, well-kept, nice gardens, bag store, rec, Apdo 457-2070.

C hotels include *Alameda* (1), C 12, Av Central, T 223-6333, F 222-9673, 5 mins from buses going to the Pacific, hot water, most rooms noisy, inside rooms quieter but no windows, staff friendly, English spoken, beds uncomfortable; *Cacts*, Av 3 bis, C 28-30, near *Pizza Hut Paseo Colón*, safe, good service, breakfast included, friendly, rec; *Capital*, Av 3-5, C 4, T 221-8497, remodelled, cable TV, bath, fan; *Brunelles's* bed and breakfast, T 235-1561, Bo Fletcher, Tibas, pick-up available; *Talamanca* (1), C 8, Av 2, T 233-5033, F 233-5420, small rooms, good breakfast, try their rum punch; *Bonaire*, Escazú, English-speaking bed and breakfast, nice, friendly, T 228-0866; *Bienvenido*, C 10, Av 1-3, very clean, hot shower, near centre; *Belmondo*, C 20, Av 9, T 222-9624, 20 refurbished rooms, clean, inc breakfast; *Linda Vista Lodge Bed and Breakfast*, Escazú, cosy rooms, spectacular views; *Mr Tucker's Inn*, Los Yoses, T 253-7911 (in Canada 905-562-5591), inc breakfast, some rooms with bath, comfortable, rec, Mr Tucker has microbus for airport transfers, day trips, etc; *Ritz*, C Central, Av 8, T 222-4103, F 222-8849, with bath and hot water, helpful, Swiss-run, German and English spoken, friendly, free coffee, good breakfast, 2nd-hand book exchange, clothes washing facilities, rec. This is linked to **D-E** *Pensión Centro Continental*, same address, T 233-1731, hot water, clean, friendly, laundry, helpful, coffee available, no meals except for breakfast, rec.

D *Cocori*, C 16, Av 3, T 233-0081/233-2188, with bath, hot water, by bus to Peñas Blancas, parking; **D** *Berlín*, Av 8, C 2, clean, safe, quiet, fans, central; **D** *Johnson*, C 8, Av Central, T 223-7633, friendly, clean, restaurant and bar, good value, popular with Peace Corps and cockroaches, rec; **D** *Centroamericano*, Av 2, C 6-8, private bath, clean small rooms, very helpful, will arrange accommodation in other towns, free shuttle (Mon-Fri) to airport, laundry facilities, rec; *Pensión de la Cuesta*, Av 1, C 11-15, T 255-2896, 4 rooms with shared bath, inc breakfast; **D-E** *Generaleño*, Av 2 entre C 8 y 10, with bath, cold water, good value; **E** *Aurora*, Av 4, C 8, with bath, F without, good value, hot shower, nylon sheets and plastic mattress covers—sweaty, very noisy nightclub nearby (till 0500), rooms on 2nd floor are the least noisy, mixed reports, *Soda Aladino* next door is very good. **E** *Bellavista*, Av Central, C 19/21, T 223-0095, friendly and helpful, with bath, clean, opposite *Dennies* restaurant;

E *Boston*, C Central, Av 8, T 221-0563, with or without bath, good, very friendly, but noisy; **E** *Napoleón*, C 6, Av 3-5, T 221-0694, bath, friendly, small rooms, run down; **E** *Roma*, C 14, Av Central and 1, T 223-2179, uphill from Alajuela bus station, clean, safe, good value but windowless rooms, stores luggage. **E** *Marlyn*, C 4, Av 7-9, hot showers, safe, parking for motorcycles; **F** *Gran Imperial*, C 8, Av 1 and Central, big rooms, clean, hot showers, sinks for laundry, restaurant with good prices, several recs, 1993, best to reserve, locked luggage store, T 222-7899; **F** *Rialto*, Av 5, C 2, 1 block from Correos, shared bath, very clean, hot water, safe, friendly, rec; **F** *Nuevo Rialto*, Av 1, C 6-8, popular but leave valuables with office; **F** *Residencial Balboa*, Av 10, C 6, safe, cold shower, thin walls, basic, cheap.

Pensiones are: **E** *Americana*, C 2, Av 2, without bath, clean, large rooms, friendly, luggage store, laundry facilities, rec; **F** *Araica*, Av 2 No 1125, T 222-5233, without bath, clean, dark, thin walls, friendly; **E** *Asia*, C 11 No 63N (between Avs Central and 1), T 223-3893, clean, friendly, but paper-thin walls, lots of noise from rapid turnover, hot showers, Chinese-run, English spoken; **E** *Astoria*, Av 7, No 749, T 221-2174, but rooms vary, cockroaches, hot showers, uncomfortable beds, thin walls, noisy; **E** *Boruca*, C 14, Av 1/3, Coca Cola market, T 223-0016, without bath, hot water, laundry service, popular with Peace Corps; *Morazán*, Av 3, C 11-15, near Parque Morazán, big rooms, pleasant Guatemalan owners; **E** *Moreno*, C 12, Av 6-8, T 221-7136, with bath; **E** *Superfamiliar*, Av 2, C 9-11, shared bath; **E** *Musoc*, C 16, Av 3/5, T 222-9437, with or without private bath, very clean, hot water, luggage stored, friendly, near to (and somewhat noisy because of) bus stations, but rec; **E** *Reforma Hilton*, C 11, No 105, with bath, T 221-9705, restaurant; **D** *San José*, C 14 and Av 5, with shower, clean, friendly, near bus station; **F** *Otoya*, C Central, Av 5-7, clean, friendly, rec; **E** *América*, Av 7, C 4, clean, large rooms, good value; **F** *Corobicí*, Av 1, between C 10 and 12, cold shared showers, run down, like a men's boarding house; **F** *Managua*, C 8, Av 1/3, small rooms, basic, hard beds, some short term activity, cold shared showers, clean and cheap, safe, helpful, will wash clothes, rec; **F** *Pensión Familiar* (also called *Hotel Delca*), Av 6, C 6-8, bath, clean, good value, also rented hourly; **F** *Pensión Palmas*, Av 6 nr National Museum, basic, friendly, stores luggage.

Near Tica Bus terminal are: **E** *Avenida Segunda*, Av 2, C 9-11, price varies, friendly, stores luggage, shared hot showers; **F** *Salamanca*, Av 2, C 9-11, cold water, adequate; **F** *Tica Linda*, Av 2, No 553 (unsigned), friendly, noisy, some beds uncomfortable, redecorated, fairly clean, little privacy, cheap laundry, good information, good place to receive international phone calls, 'gringo' place, often full, next door is the *Esmeralda Mariachi Palace*, Av 2, C 5-7, large restaurant/bar with live bands playing requests, which operates all night except Sunday. There are several hotels in F range near the various markets, such as the *España*, Av 3/5, C 8, run by a Spanish family; *Comerciante* annex, C 10, Av 3/5, quite clean, and *Valencia*, C 8, Av 1, T 221-3347, cheap but very basic. Cheaper hotels usually have only wooden partitions for walls, so they are noisy. Also, they often rent only by the hour. **NB** Hotels in the red light district, C 6, Avs 1-5, near Mercado Central, charge on average US$10 with toilet and shower for a night. **NB also** It is difficult to find cheap hotels with parking. There are a couple of cheap *parqueos* on C 9 between Avs 1 and 3 with cheap hotels in the vicinity.

Toruma Youth Hostel, the only official YHA member in Costa Rica, T 224-4085, Av Central, C 31-33, 95 beds, restaurant, clean, hot water not always available, crowded but safe, lockable compartments in each room, F pp inc breakfast, more expensive for those who do not hold International Student Identity Card or YHA membership; music, free for guests, on Fri and Sat nights; a good place for meeting other travellers to arrange group travel. You can leave bags there safely for US$0.50/day. Youth hostel information: Recaj, PO Box 10227, 1000 San José. Discounts at affiliated hotels and lodges (see text) are available if reservations are made through Recaj.

Bed and Breakfast For B-and-B accommodation in San José and Costa Rica contact *Costa Rica Bed and Breakfast Group*, c/o Debbi McMurray, Apdo 493-1000, San José, or at *D'Raya Vida*, T 223-4168, F 223-4157; also Pat Bliss, *Park Place*, Escazú, T/F 228-9200. They have 50 inns and hotels in their directory. Rec is **B** *La Casa de los Gardner*, PO Box 1028-1200, Pavas, in the suburb of Rohrmoser, convenient for airport, clean, US run.

Apartotels (with kitchen etc) can be cheaper for longer stays, weekly or monthly rates. *Apartamentos Scotland*, C 27, Av 1, C weekly or monthly for furnished apartments, T 223-0833. **A** *Apartotel Los Yoses*, T 225-0033, Los Yoses, passably clean, comfortable beds, fridge and stove functional, tiny pool, attractive and secure area with supermarket, laundromat and restaurants nearby.

Trailer Park *Belén*, in San Antonio de Belén, 2 km W of intersection at Cariari and San Antonio, 5 km from airport, turn off Highway 1 on to Route 111, turn R at soccer field then first L for 1 km, T 239-0421, F 239-1316, US$6.50/day, American-owned, shade, hot showers, laundry, friendly, rec, good bus service to San José. **Camping** 16 km E of San José near Tres Ríos, 1 km S of Pan-American Highway, turn off signed to Istaru Campo Escuela, first *finca* on the right is *Para Las Orejas*, where you can camp, bathrooms available, T/F 279-9752, back-packing Spanish goats for hikers, goats milk.

Restaurants In 1994 a meal in an upmarket restaurant cost US$20-25. Apart from the hotels, the best ones are the *Bastille*, French type (limited choice), on Paseo Colón; *Ile de France*, C 7, Av Central and 2 (T 222-4241), good French chef; next door is *La Hacienda Steak House*, expensive but good; *La Tranquera* (parking space) on the highway to Cartago at Curridabat, 6-8 km E of San José, serves good steaks and other foods (orchestra for dancing at weekends); *La Estancia* in El Pueblo, typical Costa Rican steak house, be sure to use the garlic sauce, rec; *Los Ranchos* Steak House, Sabana Norte near *Hotel Corobicí*, reliable, good food. On N side of old La Sabana airport on Av 3 and about C 50 are two good restaurants, *El Chicote* (country-style; good grills) and *El Molino*. *Los Anonos*, in Escazú area, grills; also *Il Tula*, very good, same area; *El Chalet Suizo*, Av 1, C 5-7 (T 222-3118), good food and service, international. *La Flecha*, Centro Colón Building, Paseo Colón, superb; *Lobster Inn*, Paseo Colón, C 24, T 223-8594, seafood, large choice, expensive; *La Cocina de Lana*, El Pueblo, seafood, excellent menu, upmarket, pricey; *La Casa de los Mariscos*, Los Yoses; *Italiano*, Carretera a Sabanilla, 1 block N of Av Central; *Machu Picchu*, C 32, Av 1-3, good, rec; *Goya*, Av 1, C 5/7, Spanish food. *Casa de España*, in Bank of America, C 1, good lunches; *Masia de Triquell*, Av 2, Calle 38/40, Barra 1, T 221-5073, Catalan, warmly rec; *Tomy's Ribs*, Av 6, C 11-13, good barbecued beef and pork; *Los Lechones*, Av 6, C 11 and 13, good food, live music Fri and Sat, reasonable prices; *Antojitos*, on Paseo Colón and in Centro Comercial Cocorí (road to suburb of San Pedro), serves excellent Mexican food at moderate prices; *La Perla*, C Central y Av 2, 24 hr, adequate, friendly staff; *El Balcón de Europa*, Av Central y C1, many recs, great atmosphere, popular, good, especially the cheeses; *Pizzería Finisterre*, next door, similar menu, good pizzas, rec, but cheaper if slightly less posh; *Pizza Metro*, Av 2, C 5 y 7, good Italian, small and cosy, not cheap, rec; *San Remo*, Av 3-5, C 2, also Italian, local food too, friendly service, good value, frequently rec (closed Sun); *La Esmeralda*, Av 2, C 7, reasonably priced, clean, live Costa Rican music in the evenings, rec.

Chinese: *Kuang Chaou* on C 11 between Av Central and Av 2; *Kiam Kon*, C Central and Av Central-2, good, large helpings; *Kaw Wah*, Av 2, C 5-7, rec; *Wing On*, Av 7, C 13-15, good, cheap; *Fortuna*, Av 6, C 2-4; *Lung Mun* on Av 1, between C 5 and 7, reasonably priced. Also rec, *Fu Lu Su*, C 7, Av 2, Chinese, Korean, very good; *Tin Hao*, Av 10, C 4, T 221-1163, good; and *Kam King*, Av 10, C 19-21: *Jardín Jade*, Av 4, C 4-6, good value; *Corona de Oro*, Av 3, round the corner from the Post Office, good and cheap.

Vegetarian: *La Mazorca*, in San Pedro, near University of Costa Rica (Rodrigo Facio site), vegetarian and health foods; *Macrobiótica*, C 11, Av 6-8, health shop selling good bread; *Shakti*, Av 8, C 13, excellent; *Don Sol*, Av 7b No 1347, excellent 3 course lunch US$1.60, run by integral yoga society (open only for lunch); *La Nutrisoda*, Edif Las Arcadas, open 1100 to 1800, homemade natural ice cream; *Naturama 1*, Av 1, opp Omni building, cheap; *Vishnu*, Av 1, C 1-3, good quality, cheap and good *plato del día*, try their soya cheese sandwiches and ice cream, sells good wholemeal bread, also on Calle 14, Av 2, open daily, 0800-2000; *El Edén*, Av 5, C Central, same food and prices as *Vishnu*; *Laxmi*, Av 8, C 8.

Pollo Obay, Av 10, 6 C, good fried chicken; *Pollo Tico*, Av 1 C 10-12, variety of meals with good dishes around US$1, popular, open 24 hrs; *La Fánega*, in San Pedro, for excellent hamburgers, folk music some nights; *Orléans*, also in San Pedro, serves crêpes; *Churrería Manolo*, Av Central, C Central and 2 (new restaurant upstairs), and another branch on Av Central, good sandwiches and hot chocolate; *Pizza Hut*, several branches, open Sun, good value pasta and salad, popular, queues to get in, rec; *José Taco*, Av 1, C 3-5, Mexican fast food, *plato del día* US$1.50; *Pastel de Pollo*, C 2, Av 6-8, excellent pies; *Comedor* beneath 'Dorado' sign, C 8, Av 4-6, very cheap; *Las Condes*, Av Central/1, C 11, inexpensive; *Lido Bar*, C 2, Av 3, for *casado*. *Soda Magaly*, Av Central, C 23, nr Youth Hostel, good, cheap; *Soda Coliseo*, Av 3, C 10-12, next to Alajuela bus station, rec; *Soda Poás*, Av 7, C 3-5, good value; *Soda Amon*, C 7, Av 7-9, good, cheap *casados*; *Salón París*, Av 3, C 1/3, rec; *Soda Nini*, Av 3, C 2-4, cheap; *La Geishita*, C Central, Av 14, cheap *casado*; *Soda La Casita*, Av 1, C Central, clean, breakfast US$1.25; *Soda Maly*, Av 4, C 2-4, Chinese and tico, good; *Soda Puntarenas*, C 12, Av 7-9, good for light meals and breakfast, open 0500-2200, useful for buses to Puntarenas and Puerto Viejo de Sarapiquí which leave from there; *The Sandwich*, good all-night soda, 1 block N of Ticabus station.

Restaurants are expensive in San José, they add on 23% tax and service to the bill (*sodas* do not). *Autoservicios* do not charge tax and service and represent best value; they also sell beer. Eg *Corona de Oro*, Av 3, C 2-4 (next to *Nini*) excellent, and *Kings*, Av 1, C 1-3, opp Cini Omni. Food bars in restaurants in the Mercado Central (C 6/8) are good for breakfast and lunch, but none of them is open in the evening, high standards of sanitation. Try *Soda Flor de Costa Rica*, entrada Noroeste, pabellón de las flores, very good and cheap meals, very clean, open 0700-1800, T 221-7881. At lunchtime cheaper restaurants offer a set meal called a *casado*,

US$1.50-2.50, which is good value; eg in the snack bars in the *Galería* complex, Av Central-2, C 5-7. Try *Chicharronera Nacional*, Av 1, C 10/12, very popular, or *Popular*, Av 3, C 6/8, good *casado*; *El Merendero*, Av 6, C 0-2, cheap local food, popular with Ticos.

Ice cream, confectionery, etc: *Helados Rena*, C 8, Av Central, excellent; also *Helados Boni*, C Central, Av 6-8, home-made ice cream; *Pops*, near Banco Central, and other outlets, for ice cream (excellent); also for ice cream *Mönpik*, Av Central, C Central and other outlets in San José, great ice cream. *Spoon*, Av Central, C 5-7, good coffee and pastries, gives 10% ISTC discount; *Fudge*, Centro Comercial Los Lagos, Escazú, coffee and pastries; *Heladería Italiano*, excellent ice cream; *El ABC*, Av Central between Calles 11 and 9, self-service, good, clean, cheap. *La Selecta* bakeries rec; *Le Croissant*, Av Central, C 33, good French bakery. *Café del Teatro*, in foyer of National Theatre, reasonably priced, belle époque interior, popular meeting place for poets and writers, pleasant for a snack. At the bus station women sell *panbon* and delicious coconut pies.

Bars Good places to have a drink include *Key Largo*, Av 3 C 7, three bars, live music, popular and *El Cuartel de la Boca del Monte*, Av 1, C 21-23, live music, popular, rec, '60s atmosphere, entrance US$5.40 but worth it. The *Lido Bar* opp the Post Office has good beer and offers *bocas*.

Shopping Market on Av Central, Calles 6/8, open 0630-1800 (Sun 0630-1200), good leather suitcases and wood. Mercado Borbón, Avs 3/5, Calles 8/10, fruit and vegetables in abundance. At weekends there is a handicraft market on the Plaza de la Cultura with goods from Guatemala to Ecuador, inc hammocks and clothing. More and more *artesanía* shops are opening, eg *Mercanapi* (a cooperative, cheaper than most, C 11, Av 1) and *Mercado Nacional de Artesanía* (C 11, Av 4), and others on Av Central, C 1 and 3. *La Casona*, a market of small *artesanía* shops, Av Central-1, C Central, is interesting, lots of little stalls. For jade, try *Brazil Gems*, Parque Morazán. In Moravia (8 km from centre) *El Caballo Blanco*, T 235-6797, workshops alongside, and *HHH* are good for leather work. The leather rocking chairs (which dismantle for export) found in some *artesanía* shops are sometimes cheaper in Sarchí. *Amir Galería de Arte*, Av Central, Calle 1 y 3, Edif Galería Nacional for local paintings. One traveller asked them to hold a painting until he returned to Europe, he forwarded the funds and received the item promptly. Coffee is good value and has an excellent flavour (although the best quality is exported). *Automercados* are good supermarkets in several locations (eg C 3, Av 3). *Cocina de Leña* in El Pueblo, is a recommended restaurant, T 255-1360, and *Rías Bajas*, seafood, T 221-7123. Generally, shopping is cheaper in the centre than in the suburbs. At the international airport on the second floor, above Continental airlines ticket counter, you can buy cut orchids which are approved by the USDA and Canadian Department of Agriculture, T 487-7086.

El Pueblo, near the *Bougainvillea Santo Domingo Hotel*, is an area of shops, bars, restaurants and discos, recently built in a traditional 'pueblo' style.

Bookshops *The Bookshop*, Av 1, Calle 1 and 3 (T 221-6847), good selection of English language books (double US prices); buys secondhand books, but no exchange, very good range, some English. *Universal*, Av Central, Calles Central and 1, T 222-4038, for Spanish books and maps. *Lehmann*, Av Central and C 3, F 233-6270, maps (large-scale topo maps not always in stock), Spanish, a few English and German books and magazines; *Librería Italiana/Francesa*, C 3, Av Central/1, English, French, Italian books, German magazines; *Staufer*, nr Centro Cultural, Los Yoses, also in Centro Comercial San José 2000 and Plaza del Sol shopping mall in Curridabat, English and German books; *Book Traders*, Av 1, C 3-5, T 255-0508, over *Pizza Hut* in the Omni building, open Mon-Sat, 0900-1900, buy (at 1/4 face value) and sell (at 1/2 marked price) English, French, German and Spanish used books; a book exchange, no name, Av 6, C 3-5, has large choice of Spanish books and a few in English; *Casey's*, C Central between Av 7 and 9, second-hand books and book exchange (1 new for 2 old), English only, mostly romances (future uncertain after Casey's death in 1993); *Gambit*, C 37, Av Central, used books, English, French, German. *Kiosko La Catedral*, opp Parque Central, sells American magazines, newspapers from several countries, inc Financial Times, books, postcards and gifts.

Photography 1 hr colour processing available at all IFSA (Kodak) branches, poor reports received. Fuji processing in 1 hr at Universal stores. Minor camera repairs undertaken. Camera repairs, Taller de Equipos Fotográficos, 120m E of kiosk Parque Morazán, Av 3, C 3-5, 2nd floor, T 223-1146 (Canon authorized workshop). Film prices are well above those of Europe. Video Camera Rentals, Av 7, behind *Aurola Holiday Inn*, T 257-0232, US$29/day, US$168/week for Panasonic 'Palmcorders'. **Warning** The X-ray machine at Juan Santamaría airport is not filmsafe, regardless of what the airport security guards try to make you believe.

Buses Bus fares in San José: large buses: US$0.10, small: US$0.15 from the centre outwards.

Hand baggage in reasonable quantities is not charged, but no trunks of any kind are taken. A cheap tour of San José can be made on the bus marked 'periférico' from Paseo Colón in front of the Cine Colón, a 45-min circle of the city. A smaller circle is made by the 'Sabana/cementerio' bus, pick it up at the Parque Morazán.

Taxis Minimum fare US$0.60 for first km, US$0.26 additional km (US$30 outside San José), 20% extra 2200-0500. Waiting time US$2.20 per hour. To order a taxi, T 254-5847, 235-9966. Taxis are red and should have electronic meters (called 'Marías'). However, disputes with the Government over prices mean that they are often not used. Agree a fare beforehand; short journeys in the city are around US$1, bargain if you feel the price is too high. For journeys over 12 km price should be negotiated between driver and passenger. One reader answered a classified advert in the *Tico Times* and hired a car and driver for a day for US$55 (1993) inc fuel. It was 'an ageing station wagon with probably no insurance, but still well worth the price.

Car Rentals Check your vehicle carefully as the rental company will try to claim for the smallest of 'damages'. International driver's licence and credit card generally required (**see also p 789**). Insurance costs US$10-15 per day extra; deductible is between US$300 and US$1,000 depending on company, some will charge extra to waive deductible, eg Budget, US$2.50 a day; basic prices: smallest car US$48 per day inc insurance and unlimited mileage or US$298 per week; jeep costs US$66 per day, US$408 per week, inc insurance and unlimited mileage. Cash deposits or credit card charges range from US$600 to US$1,000, so check you have sufficient credit. **Budget**, C 30, Paseo Colón, T 223-3284, open Mon-Sat, 0800-1800, Sun, 0800-1600, also at international airport, T 441-4444, open Mon-Sun, 0600-2100, and at *Hotel Cariari*; **Avis**, Sabana Norte (T 232-9922); **Dollar**, C Central, Av 9 (T 233-3339); **Hertz**, C 38, Paseo Colón; **National**, C 36, Av 7 (T 233-4044), easy to get on to autopista for Alajuela; and many local ones (**Elegante**, C 10 Av 13-15, T 221-0066, has branches throughout the country, rec). Various companies at airport, including **Ada**, T 441-1260, **Santos**, T 441-3044, **Hertz**, T 441-0097. You can often obtain lower rentals by making reservations before arrival with the major companies. Insurance will not cover broken windscreens (unless you are involved in an accident), driving on unsurfaced roads or damaged tyres. If you have an accident always call the traffic police and rental car company. Licence plates will automatically be removed. Do not move your car until the police arrive. Never bribe traffic police, ask them to issue a ticket. Some traffic police will tell you to return to San José, or another place, trying to get you to bribe them to avoid interrupting your trip. Always report any demands for money to the tourism authorities. Never leave anything in a hired car, always use car parks in San José, never leave your car on the street, even in daylight. Car parking costs US$0.75 for the first hour, US$0.60 each subsequent hour, worth it when so many cars are broken into. Regular reports of robbery in the National Parks.

Motorcycle rental from **Heat Renta Moto**, Edificio Ofomeco, 7th floor, 2 Av, 11 y 13 C, T 221-6671, F 221-3786, with offices in other tourist centres, for motorcycles, scooters, mountain motorbikes, US$30-35/day, US$5-7/hour. Deposit US$500. **Rent-a-Moto La Aventura**, C 8, Av 10, T 222-0055, F 223-2759, US$35/day Honday XL250R, inc insurance, helmet and free mileage. **Moto Rental SA**, Thilo Pfleiderer, T 232-7850, Suzuki Enduro for US$200 pw unlimited mileage, deposit US$500 or credit card. An Enduro is best for seeing all the country. Keep clear of taxis and buses who will pay no attention to you. Wearing a helmet is obligatory, renters provide simple ones without front glass. You will need strong dark glasses. The paved roads offer frequent surprises, deep holes, rivers and landslides over the road, planks of bridges in a rotten state. You need good rainwear even in the dry season. However you have increased mobility and speed on dirt roads and riding is very enjoyable outside the San José area due to low traffic (**see also Motoring, p 788**).

Night Clubs *Grill La Orquidea* at the *Hotel Balmoral*; *Les Moustaches* in Centro Colón, Paseo Colón, C 38, expensive. Many restaurants and bars with varying styles of music at El Pueblo centre on road to San Francisco (take 'Calle Blancos' bus from C 1, Av 5-7, alight 500m after river); also 3 discos here, *Cocoloco*, *Infinito* (US$2.90, not crowded) and *La Plaza* (very luxurious, US$2.90, great discothèque). Discos in the centre: *Kamakiri*, on the way to Tibas; *Top One* (US rock music); *La Rueda* (for the over 30's). Other ni:ce, less expensive dance spots downtown: *El Túnel del Tiempo*, *Talamanca* and *Disco Salsa 54* (do not wear shorts, they will not let you in). *La Torre*, C 7 between Av Central and Av 1, popular gay disco. Also *Montecarlo*, corner of C 2 and Av 4 (Parque Central). *El Cuartel de la Boca del Monte*, see under **Bars**. Night spots W of Calle 8 are in the red light district. Some hotels have **casinos** with Black Jack and a sort of roulette shooting an arrow on a revolving wheel. No entrance fee, no formal dress required. Some night spots do not appreciate long haired men. You can buy chips with colones or dollars from the croupier and once you start to play, the drinks and cigarettes are free. The casino at the *Gran Hotel Costa Rica* has been recommended.

Theatres All are closed on Monday. Teatro Nacional, Av 2, C 3/5 (reopened 1993 after restoration; rec for the productions, the architecture and the bar/café), US$1.15 for guided tour, behind it is La Plaza de la Cultura, a large complex. Teatro Carpa, outdoor, alternative; plays, films, C 9, opp Parque Morazán. Teatro Tiempo (also called Sala Arlequín), C 13 between Av 2 and Central. Compañía Nacional de Teatro. Teatro Melico Salazar on Parque Central for popular, folkloric shows every Tues, T 221-4952. Teatro del Angel, Av Central, between C 13 and 15. 3 modern dance companies. All good.

Cinemas Many excellent modern cinemas showing latest releases. Sala Garbo, Av 2, C 28. Prices, US$2.50-US$3. See *La Nación* for films and times. **See also under National Parks, p 721.**

Swimming Pools The best is at Ojo de Agua, 5 mins from the airport, 15 mins from San José. It is open until 1700; direct bus from Parque Carrillo, Av 2, C 20-22, US$0.25 or take bus to Alajuela via San Antonio de Belén. There is also a pool in La Sabana (at W end of Paseo Colón), entrance US$3, open 1200-1400, about 2 km from the city centre. Open air pool at Plaza González Víquez (SE section of city).

Museums Museo Nacional, Calle 17, Av Central and 2, very interesting, archaeology, anthropology, national history, some gold, ex-President Arias' Nobel Peace Prize, open Tues-Sun, 0830-1630; replicas of precolumbian jewellery may be bought at reasonable prices (entrance, US$0.75, ISIC holders and children free). **Museo de Oro** in the Plaza de la Cultura complex with art museums adjoining the Teatro Nacional, Av Central, C 3/5, excellent, entrance free, open Fri-Sun 1000-1700, free 1½-hr bilingual guided tour available (get ticket in advance, deposit all bags at entrance); **Museo de Arte Costarricense** at the end of Paseo Colón, Calle 42, in La Sabana park in the old airport building (Tues-Sun 1000-1700, free), small but interesting display of paintings and sculptures. In the INS building, Av 7, C 9-11, is the **Museo de Jade** on the 11th floor (Mon-Thur, 0900-1500), with jade carvings, pottery, sculpture etc, interesting, a 'must', and a beautiful view over the city. **Museo de Ciencias Naturales**, Colegio La Salle, Mon-Fri, 0800-1500, Sat, 0800-1200; US$0.30 (in the grounds of the Ministry of Agriculture; take 'Estadio Sabana' bus from Av 2, C 2-Central to the gate). **Museo de Entomología**, in basement of School of Music building of the University of Costa Rica in San Pedro. Mon-Fri 1300-1700, to check times T 225-5555, extension 318, many beautiful insects, only museum of its kind in Central America. **Museo de Criminología**, 2nd floor, Supreme Court Building, Av 6, C 17-19, Mon Wed and Fri 1300-1600, small but very interesting, 'pretty grisly'; **Museo Postal, Telegráfico y Filatélico**, 2nd floor main Post Office, Mon-Fri, 0800-1600 (closed for reorganization 1992); **Museo Histórico Imprenta Nacional**, La Uruca, open Mon-Fri 1000-1500. **Museo Nacional de la Carreta y el Campesino**, oxcart museum located in Salitral de Desamparados, display in typical old Costa Rican house of *campesino* life, open Tues-Sun, 0800-1600.

Zoo There is a small zoo in Parque Simón Bolívar (Av 11, just E of C 7). Entrance US$0.60, open 0830-1530, Tues-Fri, 0900-1600, Sat. Go down C 11 about 3 blocks from Av 7; not very satisfactory. Poor conditions and small cages for cats and other mammals. Cages badly labelled or without labels, many empty. **Serpentarium**, Av 1, C 9-11, worth a visit especially if you are going to the National Parks or the jungle. Entrance US$1.50. Good variety of snakes and other reptiles but some not well cared for. Staff helpful if you speak Spanish. **Mundo Sumergido Aquarium**, San Francisco de Ríos (400m E, 200m N of Y-shaped roundabout to San Francisco), Mon-Sat 1000-2000.

Exchange Opening times: Mon-Fri, 0900-1500. **Banco Nacional**, head office, Av 3, C 2-4, branch at Plaza de la Cultura open until 1200 on Sats, accepts Visa credit cards; **Banco de Costa Rica**, Av Central, C 4, changes TCs for colones and for dollars, but must present a ticket out of Costa Rica—take passport. **Banco de San José**, C Central, Av 3-5. Money can be sent through Banco de San José or Banco de Costa Rica at 4% commission. **Banco Anglo Costarricense**, Av 2 near Teatro Nacional, very good service for TCs. For money transfers it charges US$10, cheaper than most. Credit card holders can obtain cash advances from Banco de San José (Visa, Mastercard) and Credomatic Los Yoses (Mastercard ATM) and Banco Popular y Desarrollo (Visa ATM); minimum cash advance: US$50 equivalent. **Banco Crédito Agrícola de Cartago**, 9 branches, also makes advances on Visa, no limits. **Banco Metropolitano**, C Central, Av 2, charges 0.49% commission on currency exchange. **NB** Apart from Credomatic and Banco Popular y Desarrollo, local cash machines accept local credit cards only, not international credit cards. Since August 1986, banks may charge whatever commission they please on foreign exchange transactions and other services: shop around for the best deal. Dollars are available at banks (not at Banco de Costa Rica, Banco de San José or Banco Crédito Agrícola de Cartago) but a commission is payable when cashing any cheque and there is a maximum limit of US$50-worth (in some cases, much paperwork and at least 1-hr wait involved; you have to show your ticket out of the country and the dollars can only be obtained when you are leaving; in others, it's straightforward, no paperwork or onward ticket required, eg **Banco Anglo Costarricense, Banco Banex**, Av 1, C 1, 2% commission, minimum US$10). The best exchange rates for Amex TCs can be found at American Express (see **Travel Agencies** below). **Banco Mercantil**, Av 1, C Central-2, has safe deposit lockers for US$15/month. A legal 'parallel' market has existed since February 1992, the centre for which is the corner of Av 2, C 2, also all around the **Banco Central** (beware fake notes), up to 10% better rates, will even accept TCs. Take all the usual precautions. Try the 'Helicopter Office', Ed Schyfter, C 2, between Av 1 and Av Central, 2nd floor; there is another office in the same corridor which changes cheques at a poorer rate. Most hotels will change dollars (cash or TCs) into colones, but only for guests; hotels cannot sell dollars, however.

Libraries Centro Cultural Costarricense Norteamericano (C 37, Av 1-5, Los Yoses, good films, plays, art exhibitions and English-language library), University of Costa Rica (in San Pedro suburb), and National Library (opp Parque Nacional; has art and photography exhibitions), all entry free. Alianza Franco Costarricense, Av 7, C 5, French newspapers, French films every Wed evening, friendly.

Language Schools The number of schools has increased rapidly and only those which have been rec by travellers in 1993-94 are included here. Generally, schools offer tuition in groups of 2-5 over 2-4 weeks. Lectures, films, outings and social occasions are usually included and accommodation with families is encouraged. Many schools are linked to the university and can offer credits towards a US course. Rates, inc lodging, are around US$1,000 a month. **Instituto Universal de Idiomas**, Av 2, C 9, T 257-0441, stresses conversational Spanish. **Costa Rican Language Academy**, Av Central, C 25-27, Apartado 336-2070 Sabanilla, Montes de Oca, T 233-8938, 233-8914, F 233-8670, run by Aída Chávez, offers Latin American music and dancing as well as language study and accommodation with local families. **Academia Latinoamericana de Español**, Aptdo 1280, 2050 San Pedro, Montes de Oca, T 224-9917, F 225-8125, rec. The **British Institute (Instituto Británico)** in Los Yoses, teaches English and Spanish, T 225-0256, F 253-1894, Apartado 8184, 1000 San José. **Intensa**, C 33, Av 5-7, Barrio Escalante, PO Box 8110-1000, T 224-6353, 225-6009, F 225-6167. **Instituto de Lenguaje Pura Vida**, in USA T (714) 534-0125, F 534-1201, airport pick-up, 5 days', 7 days' accommodation with local family, 2 meals a day, cultural activities, US$320. Also rec, but no address or phone number given, is *Progresa*, one of the cheapest, very good classes up to 4, or individual tuition.

Embassies and Consulates Nicaraguan, Av Central, Calles C 25-27, opp *Pizza Hut*, T 222-2373, 233-3479, 233-8747, Mon-Fri, 0830-1200, US$25, dollars only, passport photo, 24-hr wait for visa (in some cases, 2 weeks, apply elsewhere); **Panamanian**, La Granja, de San Pedro, del Antiguo Higuerón 600m Sur (T 225-3401, 225-0667), none further S. The Consulate is three blocks S, 1 W, tough about onward ticket, open 0800-1300. You need a photograph. Visa costs US$10 cash and takes 24 hrs. If they tell you to come back after 1300 to collect your visa, be there at 1245; **Honduran**, Del Itan, 300 Este y 200 Norte, T 234-9502; **Salvadorean**, Los Yoses, de Pulpería la Luz, 300m Sur, 50m Este (Final Av 10), T 225-3861, receives documents 0900-1300, returns them 1430-1500 (take 3 photos, photocopy of first 3 passport pages, tickets into/out of El Salvador and US$30 for visa); **Guatemalan**, Embassy and Consulate, carretera a Pavas from Sabana Oeste 250m from *Restaurante Regio*, take bus to Pavas from Coca Cola bus station. Open Mon-Fri, 0900-1300 (T 231-6645/54), visa given on the spot, US$10 in some cases (dollars only—see Guatemala **Information for Visitors**); **Mexican**, Consulate, Av 7, C 13-15, T 222-5528, 221-4448, Mon-Fri 0830-1200 to receive

COSTA RICAN LANGUAGE ACADEMY

- **Located near the center of San José, COSTA RICA**
- **Costa Rican owned and operated**
- **Private or group classes (6 students maximum)**
- **Homestays and free airport transportation (24hrs.)**
- **ALL INCLUDED: Afternoon Latin Dance, Costa Rican Cooking and Latin Music classes.**

Ask for a brochure in English, French, German, Italian and Japanese.

Costa Rican Language Academy, P.O. Box 336-2070, San José, Costa Rica.
Tel: (506) 233-8938, 233-8914, 221-1624 Fax: (506) 233-8670.

documents, returns them 1500-1600. **Belizean**, Rohrmoser, 25m Oeste, 75m Sur de Plaza Mayor, T 232-6637, 231-7766.

Argentine, Av 6, C 21-25, T 221-6869; **Bolivian**, C 19 and 21, Av 2, T 233-6244; **Brazilian**, C 20-22, Av 2, T 233-1544, 233-1092; **Colombian**, Barrio la California, C 29, Av 1, T 221-0725 (Mon-Fri 0900-1200) issues free tourist cards for Colombia, but onward ticket must be shown and sometimes 2 photos provided; **Ecuadorean**, Sabana Sur, Colegio Médicos 100m E, 125m SW, T 232-1503, 231-1899, open Mon-Fri 0800-1100, 1200-1400; **Peruvian**, Los Yoses, 200m Sur, 50m Oeste del Automercado, T 225-9145; **Uruguayan**, Los Yoses, Av 14, C 35-37, T 253-2755; **Chilean**, Los Yoses, 50m Este, 225m Oeste del Automercado, T 224-4243; **Venezuelan**, Los Yoses, de la 5 ta, entrada, 100m S, 50m W, consulate open Mon-Fri 0900-1230, T 225-5813, 225-8810, visa issued same day, US$30, helpful.

US, Consulate and Embassy (T 220-3939, 0800-1630 Mon-Fri, T 220-3127 after hours and weekends) in the western suburb of Pavas, opp Centro Comercial, open Mon-Fri, 0800-1630 (0800-1000 only for visa applications). Catch a ruta 14 bus to Pavas Zona 1 from Av 1 and Calle 18. **Canadian**, Av Central, C 3, Cronos Building, 6th floor, reception on ground floor, Aptdo 10303 (T 255-3522); **Japanese**, Rohrmoser, de la Nunciatura 400m Oeste y 100m Norte, T 232-1255; **South Korean**, Rohrmoser, 200m Oeste y 100m Sur Entrada Boulevard de Rohrmoser, T 220-3141. **Israeli** C 2, Av 2-4, Edif Parque Central, 5th floor, T 221-6444, 221-6011.

British, Centro Colón, 11th floor, end of Paseo Colón with C 38 (Apartado 815-1007), T 221-5566; **German**, Rohrmoser, 200m Norte y 75m Este de la casa de Oscar Arias, T 232-5533, open Mon-Fri, 0900-1200; **Swiss**, Paseo Colón, Centro Colón, 4th floor, Calles 34/36, T 221-4829, open Mon-Fri, 0900-1200; **French**, Curridabat, 200m S, 25m W of Indoor Club, T 225-0733; **Belgian**, C 35-37, Av 3, T 225-6633; **Dutch**, Los Yoses, Av 8, C 35-37, Aptdo 10285, Mon-Fri 0900-1200, T 234-0949; **Italian**, Los Yoses, C 33-35, Av 10, T 234-2326; **Spanish**, Paseo Colón, C 32, T 222-1933; **Danish**, 11th floor, Centro Colón, T 257-2695/6; **Finnish**, Centro Colón Building, 9th floor, Paseo Colón, T 257-0210; **Norwegian**, Centro Colón, 10th floor, T 257-1414; **Austrian**, C 36-38, Av 4, Edif Nagel, T 255-3007; **Swedish**, La Uruca, de la Fábrica Pozuelo, 100m al Este, T 232-8549.

Immigration   On the airport highway, opp Hospital México; you need to go here for exit visas, extensions, etc. If they are busy, you could queue all day. To get there, take bus 10 or 10A Uruca, marked 'Mexico', then cross over highway at the bridge and walk 200m along highway. Better to find a travel agent who can obtain what you need for a fee, say US$5. Make sure you get a receipt if you give up your passport.

Emergency Phone Numbers   Police, T 117, Fire, T 118.

Judiciary   Thefts should be reported in San José to Recepción de Denuncias, Organismo de Investigación Judicial, Calle 19, Av 6-8.

Places of Worship   Protestant, in English: The Good Shepherd, Sun 0830, Av 4, C 3-5 (Anglican); Union Church, Moravia, services 1000; free bus service from downtown hotels; times and locations given in Friday *Tico Times*. International Baptist Church, in San Pedro, 150m N from Banco Anglo Costarricense corner, on San Pedro or Periférico bus route, English services at 0900 on Sun, Spanish services 1800, Sunday school at 1100, nursery provided, Chinese services at 1100 on Sun. Bible study on Tues, T 259-8743 for information. Escazú Christian Fellowship (Country Day School campus), Sun 1800, T 228-2754; Victory Christian Centre (from Hermanos Monge Gas Station, 200m S, 100m E, 200m S, Santa Ana, free shuttle bus, T 282-7720, Sun 1000. Roman Catholic services in English at *Herradura* Hotel, 1600 every Sun. Centro de los Amigos para la Paz, Quaker, English books, US periodicals, information, T 221-0302.

Post Office   Av 1 and 3, C 2, open for sale of stamps Mon-Fri, 0700-2400, Sat 0800-1200 (outside these hours stamps may be bought from the lottery seller who sits under the big tree opposite the Post Office entrance). Stamp vending machine in main post office. Post office charges 20 colones for receiving letters (*Lista de Correos*, open 0800-1700). Give yourself plenty of time when visiting the Post Office, do not leave it until the last minute.

Telephone and Cable Services   Internal telegrams from main post office. Cable abroad from Compañía Radiográfica Internacional de Costa Rica, Av 5, C 1, 0730-1000. ICE, Instituto Costarricense de Electricidad, Av 2, C 1, has a fax service, US$3.30 a minute to Europe; to receive, US$0.25 on F 506-257-2272/3, also phone calls here, friendly service. Fax service at International Telecommunications Av 2 C1, about US$2 per page to USA, or try hotels. Collect telephone calls can be made from any public telephone. For MCI call USA, dial 162, Sprint Express, dial 163 to make collect calls to the USA. Italia Directo, dial 169 for Italy; Canada Direct, dial 161 for collect calls to Canada. English speaking operators are available. See also under **Information for Visitors**.

Hospitals and Inoculations Social Security Hospitals have good reputations (free to social security members, few members of staff speak English), free ambulance service run by volunteers: Dr Calderón Guardia (T 222-4133), San Juan de Dios (T 222-0166), México (T 232-6122). The Clínica Bíblica C 1, Av 14, 24-hr pharmacy (T 223-6422) and Americana (C Central-1, Av 14 (T 222-1010) have been rec; both offer 24-hr emergency service at reasonable charges and have staff who speak English; better than the large hospitals, where queues are long. Bíblica will arrange TB vaccinations, prepares Spanish summaries of treatment, medication, etc, accepts credit cards, and has addresses for emergencies it cannot handle. Yellow fever inoculation, Ministerio de Salud (Av 4, C 16), Departamento de Enfermedades Epidémicos, Dr Rodrígo Jiménez Monge, or at his private clinic, C 5, Av 4, T 221-6658. Free malaria pills also from Ministerio de Salud, from information desk in office to left of ministry. Although the Ministerio de Salud does not have a stock of gamma globulin (Hepatitis A), they will inject it free if you buy it in a pharmacy. Dermatologist: Dr Elias Bonilla Dib, C Central, Av 7-9, T 221-2025. Red Cross Ambulance, T 221-5818.

Dentist Clínica Dental Dr Francisco Cordero Guilarte, T 232-3645, Sabana Oeste, opposite Colegio La Salle. Take bus marked Sabana Estadio. Dra Fresia Hidalgo, Uned Building, San Pedro, 1400-1800, English spoken, reasonable prices, rec (T 234-2840). Dr Otto J Ramírez Gonález, C 14, Av Central, Noreste Hospital San Juan de Dios, Edificio Maro, T 233-4576, speaks only Spanish. Fernando Baldioceda and Silvia Oreamuno, 225m N of Paseo Colón on the street which intersects at the Toyota dealership: both speak English; Alfonso Villalobos Aguilar, Edif Herdocía, 2nd floor, Av 3, C 2-4, T 222-5709.

Laundromat Washing and dry cleaning at Centro Comercial San José 2000, 0730-2000, US$3.75 for large load. **Sixaola**, branches throughout San José, US$3.50 a load, 2-hr dry cleaning available, expensive. **Doña Anna**, Av 20, C 13 (off Plaza González Víquez), cheap and fast. **Martinizing**, US franchise, at Curridabat, Sabana Norte and Escazú, rec. **Lava-matic Doña Anna**, C 13, Av 16, US$3.50 wash and dry.

Travel Agencies *Swiss Travel Service*, in *Hotel Corobicí*, T 231-4055, PO Box 7-1970, F 231-3030, with branches in *Hotels Sheraton, Irazú, Cariari, Amstel* and *Balmoral*, large agency, good guides, much cruise business, warmly rec. *Viajes Alrededor del Mundo*, T 223-6011, at the *Holiday Inn*, Eduardo Ureña is rec for finding cheap flights to South America. *Tam Travel Corporation*, four branches, one in *San José Palacio Hotel*, open 7 days a week, PO Box 1864, 24-hr answering service T 222-2642/2732, F 221-6465; *LA Tours*, PO Box 492-1007, Centro Colón, T 221-4501, F 224-5828, Kathia Vargas extremely helpful in rearranging flights and reservations; *Aviatica*, C1, Av 1, T 222-7461, helpful for airline tickets; *American Express*, clients' mail, Banco de San José, Apartado 5445, 1000 San José,; financial transactions, Banco de San José/Credomatic, C Central, Ave 3-5, T 223-3644/257-1792.

Aventuras Naturales, Av Central, C 33-35, T 225-3939, offers white water rafting. *Trópico Saragundi Speciality Tours*, T 255-0011, for bungee jumping (see also below, **Excursions**). Those specializing in naturalist tours include: *Costa Rica Expeditions*, Av 3, C Central/2, upmarket wildlife adventures including white water rafting (US$89 for 1-day trip on Río Pacuare, inc lunch and transport, good) etc (PO Box 6941), T 257-0766/222-0333, F 257-1665, staffed 365 days a year, 0530-2100, also answering service, highly rec, good range of postcards in their souvenir shop next door; *Ríos Tropicales*, Paseo Colón, next to Mercedes Benz, PO Box 472, 1200 San José, T 233-6455, F 255-4354, rec for whitewater rafting and kayaking, good selection and careful to assess your abilities; heavy rains may result in cancellations, so you need flexibility in your plans, good food, excellent guides. *Costa Rica Sun Tours* 'Eco-Center' offers reservations and Sansa ticketing for adventure or nature lovers, regular departures for Arenal, Monteverde, Corcovado, Tortuguero and Manuel Antonio, Av 7, C 3-5, T 255-2011, F 255-3529. Tours can often be arranged at very short notice, warmly rec. *Typical Tours*, 2nd and 3rd floors of Las Arcadas, next to the *Gran Hotel Costa Rica*, PO Box 623-1007, T 233-8486 24 hrs, F 233-8474, city tours, volcano tours, nature reserves, rafting, cruising. *Braun Eco Tourism*, Av 8-10, C Central (in *Hotel Ritz*), T 233-1731, F 222-8849, basic but beautiful tours to out of the way places, rec, but tour guides need to improve their biology. *Exotur*, T 227-5169, F 227-2180, Nella Fiorentini, very helpful, rec.

Day tours to the Gulf of Nicoya with transport from San José include: luxury yacht cruise on the *Fantasia* (T 255-0791) to Tortuga island, Wed, Sat, Sun, from San José US$65 inc lunch; Calypso Island Cruise Wed, Fri, Sun, US$69 inc lunch, T 233-3617; Bay Island Cruises to Tortuga Island (T 231-2898); Blue Sea Cruises, T 233-7274, to Tortuga Island; *Cruceros del Sur*, T 220-1679, F 220-2103, PO Box 1198-1200, Pavas, San José, offers cruises to Curú Wildlife Refuge and Tortuga Island, US$79. Costa Sol Cruises, Wed, Fri, Sat, Sun, US$70 inc breakfast and lunch, visits beach near Tambor; Seaventures Yacht, 2-night packages, floating hotel visits Cabo Blanco Nature Reserve in Gulf of Nicoya (T 220-0722). **NB** It is much cheaper to take tours aimed at the local rather than the tourist market.

Tourist Office *Instituto Costarricense de Turismo*, information office: below Plaza de la Cultura, C 5, Av Central/2, T 223-4481, 223-1733, ext 277, and 222-1090, F 223-4476 (Mon-Fri 0900-1700, 0900-1300 Sat, closed Sun). Also at Juan Santamaría airport (very helpful, will check hotels for you) and borders. Head office (for administrative purposes only) is at Av 4, C 3/5 (open at 0900). Excellent service. Road maps of Costa Rica, San José and the metropolitan area and public transport timetables available. Infotur computerized hotel reservation and information system at Av 10, C 3, T 223-4481, check whether there is a commission (reports of 20%) before making a booking. **Otec, youth and student travel office** and cheap lodgings, extremely helpful, C 3, Av 1-3, Edif Victoria, 2nd floor, T 222-0866, for ISTC and FIYTO members (has discount booklet for shops, hotels, restaurants; Otec Tours, Edif Ferenez, C 3 Av 1-3, T 255-0554, their buses tend to be rather crowded. The *Instituto Geográfico*, Av 20, C 9-11 at Ministry of Public Works and Transport, supplies very good topographical maps for walkers (which can easily be bought at Librerías Universal and Lehmann). *American Express* office has good, free maps of San José. New up-to-date maps are available at most bookstores. Recommended on the city is a map published by Jitan, US$3.

Airports The Juan Santamaría international airport is at El Coco, 16 km from San José by motorway (5 km from Alajuela). Airport information, 24 hrs, T 441-0744. Bus from Av 2, C 10-12, or Av 2, C 12-14, every 10 mins from 0500-2100, US$0.50, or by Alajuela bus via the motorway from C 14, Av 5-7. Taxi to and from airport, US$11 (can be less if ordered in advance); Sansa runs its own bus service to the airport. Taxis run all night from the main square to the airport and for early flights, you can reserve a taxi from any San José hotel the night before. All taxi companies run a 24-hour service. Bank at the airport open 0800-1600; at other times try car rental desks, the restaurant cash desk or money changers at the entrance. X-ray machines reported unsafe for film. Light aircraft use the Tobias Bolaños airport at Pavas, about 5 km W of San José.

Airlines Addresses (and telephone numbers) of major airlines: **Copa**, Av 5, C 1 (223-7033); **SAM**, Av 7, C5-7 (233-3066); **Lacsa**, Av 5, C 1 (231-0033); **Sansa**, Paseo Colón, C 24 (221-9414, see also below); **Taca**, Av 3, C 40 (222-1790); **Mexicana**, Av 5, C 38 (222-1711), Mexican Tourist Card available here; **Varig**, Av 5, C 3-5 (257-0094); **Viasa**, Av 5, C 1 (223-3411); **Servivensa**, 2nd floor Centro Colón building, Paseo Colón, C 38-40 (257-1441); **TWA**, C 1, Av Central-1 (222-1332); **Continental**, Oficentro La Virgen No 2, 200m S, 300m E and 50m N of American Embassy, Pavas (296-4911); **British Airways**, C 32, between Paseo Colón and Av 2 (223-5648); **Iberia**, Paseo Colón, C 40 (221-3311); **KLM**, Sabana Sur, behind Contraloría General Building (220-4112); **Lufthansa**, Av 7-9, C 5 (221-7444); **Air France**, Av 1, C 4-6 (222-8811); **Swiss Air**, Av 1-3 C Central (221-6613). **Singapore Airlines**, Av 1, C 3-5 (255-3555). **Lloyd Aéreo Boliviano**, Av 2, C 2-4, upstairs, T 255-1530; **American**, opposite *Hotel Corobicí*, Sabana Este (257-1266); **Aviateca**, Av 3, C 40, (233-8390); **Lan Chile**, *Hotel Torremolinos* (257-0280); **Ladeco**, Av 5, C 1 (233-0632); **Alitalia**, Av Central/2, C 1, (222-6009); **Aeroperú**, Av 5, C 1-3, (223-7033); **LTU International Airways** (German charter airline), C 1-3, Av 9, T 257-2990; **Condor Airlines** (German charter airline), C 5, Av 7-9, T 221-7444; **Aero Costa Rica** (to Miami and Orlando), 200m N of Fuente de la Hispanidad, San Pedro (253-4753); **United Airlines**, Sabana Sur, behind Contraloría General building, T 220-4844 (at airport); **Korean Air**, Edif Alde, 2nd floor, Av Central-1, C 1 (222-1332); **Travelair**, T 232-7883, 220-3054, F 220-0413.

Internal Flights Sansa and Travelair operate internal flights throughout the country (the latter is more expensive) from Juan Santamaría airport. Sansa check-in is at office on Paseo Colón at C 24 one hour before departure (free bus to and from airport). Check schedules on 221-9414 or 233-3258, F 255-2176. Sansa airport office T 441-8035/1401. If you made reservations before arriving in Costa Rica, confirm and collect tickets as soon as possible after arrival. Book ahead, especially for the beaches. In February and March, planes can be fully booked 3 weeks ahead. On all internal scheduled and charter flights there is a baggage allowance of 12 kg/25 lb.

Sansa or Travelair flights operate daily (latter not Sun) to **Barra del Colorado**, Wed and Sun to **Carrillo**, **Golfito**, Mon-Sat (Travelair, also Sun), **Quepos** several flights daily, **Coto 47**, Mon-Sat, **Palmar Sur**, daily, Travelair, Sansa Mon, Wed, Fri), **Tamarindo** twice daily, (Travelair, Sansa Mon, Wed, Fri), **Sámara**, Sansa as for Tamarindo, similarly **Nosara** (Travelair, Wed, Sun), **Limón**, Mon, Wed, Fri (Travelair), **Tambor**, 2 daily (Travelair), **Tortuguero**, Mon-Sat (Travelair), **Liberia**, Wed, Sun (Travelair). **Sansa Vacaciones**, T 221-9414, offer 1-3 night packages including flight and accommodation at Manuel Antonio, Sámara, Nosara and Tamarindo. **Hustler Tours** offer San José-Quepos daily flights from Tobias Bolaños airport at Pavas, W of San José, T 237-5400/4900; Quepos, T 777-0505. **Travelair** also flies from Pavas Tobías Bolanos airport.

Railway Services During 1990-91 passenger services W to Puntarenas and E to Limón were

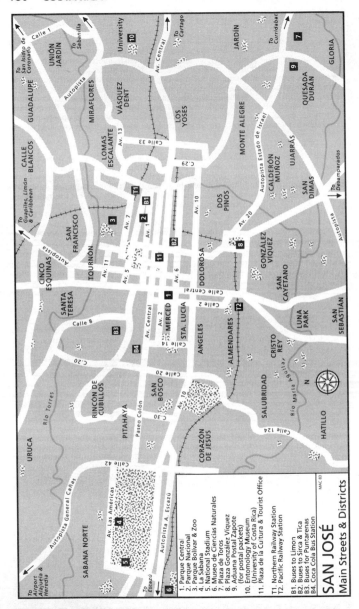

To San Isidro de
San Isidro de
Coronado

To Sabanilla

University

10

Av. Central

To Cartago

JARDÍN

To Curridabat

7

GLORIA

UNIÓN
JARDÍN

GUADALUPE

Autopista

MIRAFLORES

VÁSQUEZ
DENT

LOS
YOSES

Av. 13

Calle 33

MONTE ALEGRE

Autopista Estado de Israel

QUESADA
DURÁN

9

CALDERÓN
MUÑOZ

SAN
DIMAS

UJARRÁS

To Desamparados

Autopista

CALLE
BLANCOS

LOMAS
ESCALANTE

C.29

Av. 10

DOS
PINOS

Av. 20

GONZÁLEZ
VÍQUEZ

To Guápiles, Limón
& Caribbean

SAN
FRANCISCO

T1

B1

3

Av. 7

2

Av. 1

B2

8

SAN
CAYETANO

Autopista

CINCO
ESQUINAS

TOURNÓN

11

Av. 5

Av. 6

DOLOROSA

Calle Central

SAN
SEBASTIÁN

SANTA
TERESA

Calle 8

Av. Central

Av. 2

1
MERCED

STA. LUCIA

Calle 2

Calle Central

12

LUNA
PARK

Río Torres

B3

B4

Av. Central

Calle 14

ANGELES

ALMENDARES

CRISTO
REY

SALUBRIDAD

SAN
BOSCO

Calle 20

C.20

Paseo Colón

C.30

A. 10

Río María Aguilar

Calle 124

N

RINCÓN DE
CUBILLOS

PITAHAYA

CORAZÓN
DE JESÚS

HATILLO

URUCA

Río Torres

Av. Las Américas

4

5

Autopista General Cañas

SABANA NORTE

Calle 42

Autopista A. Escazú

To
Escazú

6

To Limón

To
Airport
Alajuela &
Heredia

MAC 83

1. Parque Central
2. Parque Nacional
3. Parque Bolívar & Zoo
4. La Sabana
5. National Stadium
6. Museo de Ciencias Naturales
7. Plaza de Toros
8. Plaza González, Víquez
9. Aduana Postal Zapote
   (for postal packets)
10. Entomology Museum
    (University of Costa Rica)
11. Plaza de la Cultura & Tourist Office

T1. Northern Railway Station
T2. Pacific Railway Station

B1. Buses to Limón
B2. Buses to Sirca & Tica
B3. Buses for Puntarenas
B4. Coca Cola Bus Station

SAN JOSÉ
Main Streets & Districts

terminated. The main station of the Ferrocarril Eléctrico al Pacífico to the Pacific ports of Puntarenas and Caldera is in the extreme S of the city C 2, Av 20, T 226-0011 (take bus marked Paso Ancho). There is a new urban line which uses part of the old Atlantic track and the San José-Limón station which runs from San Pedro (University of Costa Rica) through the city and on an extension to Heredia. Leaves San Pedro 0545, 1200, 1715 weekdays, 1000, 1200 Sun; returns from Heredia 0630, 1300, 1800 weekdays, 1045, 1300 Sun, 30 mins, US$0.30. Also a Pavas-San José Intertren commuter service. *Tam Tours*, see **Travel Agencies** above, runs a tourist train into the banana plantations, transport to and from the train by a/c coach through the Braulio Carrillo National Park, US$70. The journey on the Northern Railway to **Limón** used to be one of the most beautiful railway journeys anywhere but in 1990 service was suspended after a 250-metre section of track in the Chiz area was covered by a landslide. From the continental divide near Cartago the line followed the narrow, wooded Reventazón valley down past Turrialba and Siquirres. The 40 km of line in the lowlands near Limón cost 4,000 lives during building in the 1870s, mostly from yellow fever. The last 16 km into Limón ran along the seashore, amid groves of coconut palms. See under Limón for lowland services.

Buses There are services to most towns, see text for details of times, prices etc. Up to date timetables can be obtained from the Instituto Costarricense de Turismo (Infotur), Av 10 Calle 3 No 868, T 223-4481. **Cartago**, every 10 mins, 0500-1900, then every 30 mins until 2400, and every hour 2400-0500, buses depart Av 18, C 5. **Puntarenas** every 15 mins, 0400-2100, 2 hrs, C 12, Av 7-9. **Heredia**, every 10 mins, C 4, Av 5-7. Minibuses from Av 6, C 14. **Alajuela** (including airport and immigration office), 30 mins Av 2, Calle 12-14 every 10 mins, 0530-1900, every 40 mins 1900-2400; every hour 2400-0530 from C 2, Av 2; to Sarchí, change at Alajuela, they depart every ½ hr, express bus to Sarchí from C 16, Av 1-3, 1215 and 1730, return 0530, 0615, 1345; to Poás Volcano, from C 12, Av 2/4, Sun and holidays 0830, return 1430, T 222-5325, or change at Alajuela's central park where bus leaves, Sun only. **Quepos**, from near Coca Cola bus station, Calle 16, Av 1-3, 0500, 1100, 1400, return 0430, 1030, 1500, 3½ hrs. Direct bus to **Manuel Antonio**, 0600, 1200, 1800, return 0600, 1200, 1700, 4 hrs, from Coca Cola station, T 223-5567. Many buses for nearby towns and others to the W of San José leave from the main Coca Cola bus station or the streets nearby (eg: *Santa Ana, Escazú, Acosta, Puriscal, Santa María Dota, San Marcos, San Ramón*). **Escazú** minibuses from Av 6, Calle 14; buses from front of Coca Cola terminal. **San Isidro de El General**, two companies, Musoc and Tuasur, both on C 16, Av 1-3, frequent service. **Liberia, Nicoya, Sta Cruz, Cañas** buses, Empresa Alfaro, Coca Cola bus station office at C 14-16, Av 5; Pulmitan de Liberia on C 14, Av 1-3, of Coca Cola terminal, 8 a day to Liberia between 0700 and 2000, same company to Coco Beach. To the beaches on Nicoya peninsula express buses daily: to Tamarindo from C 14, Av 3/5, Alfaro Co, T 222-2750 or from C 20, Av 3, Tralapa Co, T 221-7202; to Coco from C 14, Av 1/3, T 222-1650; to Junquillal from C 20, Av 3, T 221-7202; to Hermosa from C 12, Av 5-7, Empresa Esquivel, T 666-1249; to Samara via Nicoya from C 14, Av 3-5, T 685-5352, 222-2750. **Grecia**, bus Calle 6, Av 5-7. **San Carlos** bus every hour 0500-1930 from Coca Cola terminal. **Guápiles**, Calle 12, Av 7-9, every 30 mins 0530-1900. **Monteverde** express bus Mon-Thurs 1430, Sat 0630, from C 14, Av 9-11 or take Puntarenas bus and change. **Turrialba**, hourly, 0500-2200, 1½ hrs, from C 13, Av 6, US$1. **Siquirres**, Av Ctl, Calle 11-13. **Limón**, hourly service, 0500-1900, 2½ hrs, good views, leaving on time, you may buy ticket the day before, Calle 19-21, Av 3 Transportes Unidos/ Coop Limón, T 223-7811. **Paso Canoas** (Panamanian border), 5 daily, **Golfito**, 3 daily, 8 hrs, **Ciudad Neily** (Zona Sur) buses, Tracopa, Calle 2-4, Av 18 (T 223-7685, 221-4214). **Puerto Viejo de Sarapiquí** and **Río Frío**, several daily via Horquetas from C 1-Central, Av 11. Direct to **Sixaola** (via Puerto Limón, Cahuita and Bribri), C1 Central, Av 11, 5 hrs. **Jacó Beach** from Coca Cola terminal, 2 express buses 0715, 1530, 2½ hrs, and 3 indirect buses, Transp Morales, T 223-1109. **La Cruz, Peñas Blancas**, from C 14, Av 3, at *Hotel Cocorí* (on corner opp Coca Cola market, CNT (office open 0700-1600 daily), buses run from 0400, take this bus if going to Nicaragua and if international buses are fully booked, cheaper but takes longer; from same location buses to **Upala**. **San Vito de Coto Brus**, Tracopa or Alfaro from C 14-16, Av 5.

Minibuses run on most routes to nearby towns offering better service, never crowded like the regular buses. Fares about US$0.20-0.25, always count your change. Beware of theft, which is common around buses.

International Buses It is important to check how far in advance you must book tickets for international buses; in Dec-Jan, buses are often booked 2 weeks ahead, while at other times of the year outside holiday seasons, there is no need to book at all. Sirca (C 7 between Avs 6 and 8, 2nd building from corner, on 2nd floor, open Mon-Sat 0600-1800, T 222-5541, 223-1464) runs a scheduled service along the Pan-American Highway from San José to **Peñas Blancas**, on the Nicaraguan frontier, and on to **Managua** (US$30), dep 0500 (Wed, Fri, Sun; schedules appear to change frequently), about 13 hrs, reports of unreliability with this company (book on Fri for following week). Ticabus terminal is at C 9-11, Av 4 (T 221-8954), office open Mon-Sat 0600-1800, book before Sat for Mon buses. It is here that all refund claims have to be made (have to be collected in person). Ticabus to **Managua**, US$50 (and on to Guatemala, US$61 overnight Managua and El Salvador, US$50, in each case departs 0600) leaves at 0700, Mon, Wed, Fri, Sat buses not a/c. Ticabus can also be taken from Managua to Tegucigalpa. The Ticabus journey from San José to **Panama City** leaves at 2200 daily, US$25 (book at least 3 days in advance). To get a Panamanian tourist card one must buy a return ticket. Tracopa, opposite Pacific railway station on C 2-4, Av 18, open 0700-1800 (T 221-4214, 223-7685), goes as far as **David**, US$7 (buses daily at 0730 and 1100 sometimes, 9 hrs); book in advance. They are modern, comfortable buses, although there is not much room for long legs, but they have the advantage of covering a scenic journey in daylight. A bus to **Changuinola** via the Sixaola-Guabito border post leaves San José at 1000 daily, from a parking place a short distance from the *Hotel Cocorí*, C 14, Av 5-7, T 556-1432 Bernardo Fumero for information, best to arrive 1 hr before departure; the bus takes the splendidly scenic, fast new road through the Braulio Carrillo National Park to Guápiles and Siquirres and is the quickest route to **Limón**. The journey from San José to Changuinola takes 8 hrs.

Excursions San José is a good centre for excursions into the beautiful Meseta Central. The excursions to the Orosí valley and volcano of Irazú are given under Cartago. Poás volcano (described on **p 740**) can be visited from Alajuela. Enquire first about the likely weather when planning a visit to Poás or Irazú. To reach Barva take a bus to San José de la Montaña (**see p 764**). A road runs NE of San José to (11 km) San Isidro de Coronado, a popular summer resort (bus from Terminal Coronado, Av 7, C Central and 1). Those interested in medical research can visit the Instituto Clodomiro Picado snake farm, open Mon-Fri 0800-1600 (snake feeding, Fri only 1330-1600), take Dulce Nombre de Coronado bus from C3, Av 5-7, 30 mins, or San Antonio Coronado bus to end of line and walk 200m downhill. They also sell snake-bite serum. The road goes on through fine countryside to Las Nubes (32 km), a country village which commands a great view of Irazú. San Antonio de Escazú hosts the National Oxcart Drivers' Day (Dia del Boyero) festival, the second weekend in March, with festivities culminating on the Sunday in a colourful oxcart parade from the school to the centre, accompanied by typical *payasos*. Open air dancing in the evening to a marimba.

Just outside **La Guácima**, 35 mins W of San José, 20 mins S of Alajuela, is the Butterfly Farm, dedicated to rearing and exporting over 60 species of butterfly, open daily, 0930-1630, US$10 adults (Costa Ricans US$4), US$6 students, US$2 children under 12. T 438-0115. The farm is believed to be the second largest in the world (the largest is in Taiwan). It was created by Joris Brinckerhoff, a former Peace Corp volunteer, and his wife in 1990. Latest reports say it is very commercialized with no literature to take away, although guides are most informative. Bus for La Guácima Mon-Sat from Av 1, C 20-22, 1100 and 1400, return 1500 and 1900, 1 hr, US$0.40, at last stop walk 300m from school S to butterfly sign (also minibuses, US$5). From Alajuela take bus marked 'La Guácima abajo', 0900, 1100, 1300, 40 mins, returns 1145, 1345, 1545, 1745. Another butterfly farm is **Spirogyra**, 100m E, 150m S of Centro Comercial El Pueblo (nr *Hotel Villa Tournon*), open daily except Tues, 0900-1600, printed guide in English, last guided tour 1530, US$2-4 depending on nationality, T 222-2937, take 'Calle Blancos' bus from C3 and Av 5 to El Pueblo.

Bungee Jumping: after Rafael Iglesias Bridge (Río Colorado), continue on Pan-American Highway 1½ km, turn right at *Salón Los Alfaro*, down track to Puente Colorado. Tropical Bungee operate 0800-1400 Sat and Sun; available weekdays for groups of 5 or more, US$45 first jump, T 233-6455; full moon and water dips on request. ASP Eurobungy, Wed, Sat, Sun departing San José 0900, US$55 first jump, US$27 second, inc transport and lunch, reservations T 255-0011. Geoventuras Bike Tours run tours from San José, Tues, Thur, and Sat, 0800, return about 1700, US$85 inc lunch, T 221-2053.

THE MESETA CENTRAL (2)

Hilly and fertile, the temperate climate makes this a major coffee growing area. Fairly heavily populated, with picturesque and prosperous towns, each with a unique church, built in the shadow of volcanoes.

The Pan-American Highway runs initially through the Meseta Central from San José to the Nicaraguan border, 332 km, completely paved and good From San José it leads past the airport, bypassing Alajuela and a number of smaller towns mentioned below, to San Ramón before descending to Esparza on the coastal plain.

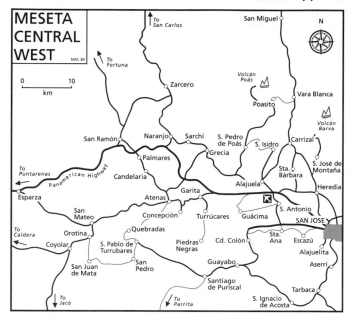

A paved road and a railway run from the capital to the two other main towns of the Meseta: Heredia and Alajuela.

Heredia, capital of its province, 10 km from San José, is a great coffee and cattle centre. Altitude 1,137m, population 30,000. The town is mostly new and only the main square has a colonial atmosphere in its architecture. The main church was built in 1797. There is a statue to the poet Aquileo Echeverría (1866-1909). The School of Marine Biology at the Universidad Nacional campus has a Museo Zoological Marina, check opening times. One of the largest coffee 'beneficios' is La Meseta; the bus from Heredia to Santa Bárbara will drop you at the gate and you can ask for a guided tour. There is also a coffee tour from San José to Café Britt's coffee farm near Barva de Heredia where you can see the processing factory, tasting room and multimedia presentation of the story of coffee, US$5, tours in low season at 1100, T 238-4618 for details. (Take 'Barva' bus from 200m N of main square to stop after 'El Castillo'.) Heredia is a convenient and pleasant place to stay, away from the pollution of San José but close to the capital and the airport, with good public transport.

Hotels L *Rosa Blanca Country Inn*, de luxe suites, restaurant and bar for guests only, 1.6 km from Santa Bárbara de Heredia, change of management 1993, Apdo Postal 41-30-09, T 269-9392, F 269-9555; **A+** *Bougainvillea de Santo Domingo*, inc breakfast, excellent service, pool, rec, T 240-8822, F 240-8484, spectacular mountain setting, free shuttle bus to San José; **A-B** *Apartotel Vargas*, 8 large, well-furnished apartments with cooking facilities, hot water, laundry facilities, TV, enclosed patio with garage and nightwatchman, English speaking staff, Sr Vargas will collect you from airport, rec, 800m N of Colegio Santa Cecilia and San Francisco Church, Apartado 510-3000, Heredia, T 237-8526, 238-1810, F 260-4698; **B** *La Posada de la Montaña Bed and Breakfast* at San Isidro de Heredia, T 268-8096 (USA T (417) 637-2066) inc breakfast, 2 nights min, some rooms with kitchenette, suites, airport or San José pickup; **B** *Zurqui Lodge Bed and Breakfast*, just off Limón highway at San Luís de Santo Domingo, 5 mins from entrance to Braulio Carrillo National Park, 6 rooms with private or shared bathroom, inc breakfast, T 235-2403. **E** *Herediana*, Calle 6, friendly, safe parking, restaurant; **F** *Colonial*, C4-6, Av 4, clean, friendly, parking for motorcycles in restaurant; **F** *El Parqueo*, C 4, Av 6-8, opp central market, friendly; **F** *El Verano*, C4, Av 6, clean and friendly.

Restaurants *La Nueva Floresta*, S side of main square, Chinese, balcony, large portions, good value, rec; pastry shop, *Pastelería Snoopy*, ½ block W of main square, good.

Buses from the terminal on the main square for San José, US$0.35, frequent service.

Train Mon-Fri, 0545, 1200, 1715 from San Pedro University, returns 0630, 1300, 1800. On Sun 1000, 1200 to Heredia return 1045, 1300. You can take this train from the Atlantic station, San José.

Above Heredia is the historic town of **Barva**, on the slope of the Barva volcano. At Barva the Huetar Gallery is recommended for arts, crafts and delicious food. Beyond Barva is Santa Bárbara, good seafood at the *Banco de los 'Mariscos* on the N side of the central plaza.

Alajuela (pop 41,390), 13 km beyond Heredia (5 km from Juan Santamaría international airport), capital of its province, stands at 952m, and is a midsummer resort for people from the capital. It is famous for its flowers and its market days (Sat market is good value for food); an interesting craft cooperative produces pictures in relief metalwork; the unusual church of La Agonía in the E part of town has murals done from life. The national hero, Juan Santamaría, the drummer who fired the building at Rivas (Nicaragua) in which Walker's filibusters were entrenched in 1856, is commemorated by a monument. The Museo Histórico Juan Santamaría (Tues-Sun 1000-1700) tells the story of this war, confusingly. Alajuela Souvenir and Gift Center next door. Just outside the town is the Ojo de Agua swimming pool (good restaurant) in beautiful surroundings: a popular bathing and boating resort. Entrance, US$0.75 pp, plus US$0.80 per vehicle. The gushing spring which feeds the pool also supplies water for Puntarenas. At Río Segunda de Alajuela there is an experimental bird breeding farm; contact owners, Richard and Margo Frisius (T 441-2658), to arrange a visit. Bus San José-Alajuela US$0.40. To Sarchí US$0.50, 1 hr.

Hotels C *Alajuela*, C 2, Av Central and 2 (T 441-1241), new rooms with TV and phone, C with shower, clean, friendly, free coffee, the only one appropriate for women travellers (best to book in advance). **F** *El Americano*, at Turrucares (T 487-7192), with bath; **F** *El Real*, C 8, Av 1-Central, not rec, short stay only, opp bus terminal; **F** *Moderno*, same street but other side of railway, 'modern' is an overstatement, but basic and clean. **G** *Chico*, hourly rentals till 2100, but cheapest, price per person.

Near Carrizal (on the road to San Miguel), which can be reached by bus from Alajuela, is a Bed and Breakfast run by John and Henny Dekker, from Holland; they have 2 large, bright, clean rooms with separate entrance, **D** pp, lovely gardens, wonderful view over central valley, warmly rec, for US$50 plus fuel, John Dekker will drive you anywhere in his 4WD, T 288-3662, F 442-1404, 150m Noroeste Esquina Los Pérez, Carrizal de Alajuela.

Restaurants *El Cencerro*, on Parque Central, good meat, especially steaks, good service, nice view over park from the terrace; *Pizza Hut*, central; *La Jarra*, near Alajuela hotel, good cheap meals in pleasant surroundings; *La Sirenita*, nothing special but OK.

Excursion From Alajuela two paved roads run to 2,708-metre volcano **Poás** (57 km by road from San José either through San Pedro de Poás and Fraijanas, or along the road to San Miguel, turning to Poás at the restaurant on the bend in the road just before you get to Vara Blanca. In the National Park of Poás (5,317 hectares), the still-smoking volcano is set in beautiful tropical forest. The crater is 1½ km across (said to be the second largest in the world). The lake in the main crater, shown on postcards, no longer exists owing to geological changes. In another area geysers may throw steam 600m or so. Just before the viewing point there is a path off the road leading to a still, forest-fringed lake in another crater, 30 mins return. Another path is an alternative route back to the Visitors' Centre, 30 mins walk. Clouds often hang low over the crater after 1000 permitting little to be seen. Entrance to Park, US$1.50 for adults, children free. The Park gates are open 0800-1530 daily, but if you wish to get in earlier you can leave your car/taxi at the gates and walk the 3 km up the hill. The main crater is 1 km along a road from the car park. There is a visitors' centre by the car park, with explanations of the recent changes in the structure, and a good café next door, and toilets further along the road to the crater. The volcano can be reached by car from San José. Typical tour prices from San José US$25 for Poás volcano tour in morning, or the volcano and Sarchí US$30. A taxi for 6 hrs with a side trip will cost about US$37. Make sure you arrive at the volcano before the clouds. It is difficult to get to Poás by public transport mid-week. On Sunday and public holidays there is a regular excursion bus from the main square of Alajuela right up to the crater, leaving at 0900, connecting with 0830 bus from San José (from C 12, Av 2-4); be there early for a seat, if full before 0900 the bus will leave, although extra buses run if necessary, the area gets very crowded, US$3 return, T 237-2449 or 222-5325 for information. The bus waits at the top with ample time to see everything (clouds permitting), returning at 1400-1430. Daily bus Alajuela-Poasito 1200 (US$1). From **Poasito** hitch a lift as it is a 10 km walk. Other options include taking a 1600 bus from Alajuela to **San Pedro de Poás**, hitch/taxi to Poasito and stay overnight there, hiking or hitching up the mountain next morning; taking a 0500 bus from Alajuela to Poasito which arrives 2 hrs before the Park gates open. If you get stuck in Poás ask the Peace Corps volunteer for help in finding somewhere to sleep. The volcano is very crowded on Sun, go in the week if possible. The park has abundant birdlife and has the only true dwarf cloudforest in Costa Rica. Trails are well marked.

Hotels You cannot camp in the Park but there are several places advertising cabins on the road up to Poás; take food and water. **A** *Albergue Ecológico La Providencia*, nr Poás NP (2 km from green entrance gate to volcano, unpaved road), private reserve, horse-riding tour US$25-30 inc lunch, T 231-7884. At the Alajuela, La Garita, San Pedro de Poás fork is **B** *Orquideas Inn*, T 433-9346, F 433-9740, 12 rooms with bath, 4 rooms shared bath, pick up from airport, pool. **A** *Río Real*, La Garita, T/F 487-7022, inc breakfast, pool, restaurant, bar. At San Pedro de Poás there is an interesting bar, *La Vía*, with cheap food, free snacks and good music. Further on look for **A** *El Cortijo* farm, also known as *Poás Volcano Lodge*, 200m from Vara Blanca junction on road to Poasito, sign on gate broken, difficult to spot in cloud, rough farm track 1 km to house, English-owned, inc breakfast, dinner available if only a few guests, good wholesome food, rooms in converted outbuildings with bath, or in farmhouse with shared bath, some rooms cheaper, good walking, 25 mins to volcano by car, 1½ hrs from San José, T/F 441-9102, PO Box 5723-1000, San José, or in UK T 071-586 3538. **D** *Country Club Monte del Mago*, about 40 km away at Carrillo de Poás (T 661-2410), with bath, swimming pool, restaurant, sometimes no food or water. **Campsite** Trailer park nearby, with hookups: the *Inca*.

From **Vara Blanca** the road continues N round the E side of the volcano through Cinchona and Cariblanco (voluntary toll/lottery US$0.20 for road construction). The road is twisty, winding through lush forest, waterfalls down to the lowlands at **San Miguel**. Here the road splits, leading either NE to Puerto Viejo de Sarapiquí (see below) or NW to **Venecia** (3½ hrs, US$2.50 by bus from San José); one hotel, F, clean, friendly. Nearby is **Ciudad Cutris**, precolumbian tumuli (a good road goes to within 2 km of Cutris, from there walk or take 4-wheel drive vehicle; get a permit to visit from the local *finca* owner). W of Venecia is Aguas Zarcas, another road junction. Just beyond, on the road to San Carlos, is **El Tucán Country Club**, **A**, pleasant, hot springs of iron and sulphur, swimming pool; jacuzzi, mini golf, small zoo, horse riding, Italian restaurant, T 460-1822, F 460-1692, from here it is only 8 km to San Carlos (**see p 744**).

10 km NE of San Miguel is **La Virgen**, where *Rancho Leona* is located near the Río Sarapiquí. Good for kayaking, T 710-6312 for 2-night packages, US$75, equipment and guides included, very basic accommodation and expensive but good home cooked dishes at the ranch and nightly frog concerts. Take the Río Frío bus from San José and ask to get off at *Rancho Leona*, the 1600 bus goes through the Braulio Carrillo National Park and ends at *Rancho Leona*, 3½ hrs. At Chilamate, 15 km further on, is the **B** pp *Albergue Ecológico Islas del Río*, inc meals, 5 rooms with private bathroom, 3 rooms with shared bathroom, Río Sarapiquí trips arranged, T 233-0366 in San José, 710-6898 Lodge (affiliated to the Youth Hostel network). **Puerto Viejo de Sarapiquí** is 10 km beyond Chilamate and was once an important port on the Río Sarapiquí. Launches can be taken via the Río Colorado to the Canales de Tortuguero and from there it is reported to be a cargo boat once a week to Barra del Colorado (no facilities, bring own food, hammock, sleeping bag) (**see p 769-771**), and on to Moín, about 10 km by road from Puerto Limón. There is good fishing on the Río Sarapiquí. (**A** *El Bambú*, opp park, T 766-6005, F 766-6132, in centre, new, bath, fan, TV, inc breakfast, very nice; **D** *Mi Lindo Sarapiquí* by Park, new with 6 rooms with bath, fan, hot water, restaurant, T 766-6281; **F** *Cabinas Monteverde*, T 766-6236, with bath, but reported dirty; Hotels *El Antiguo* (T 766-6205) and *Santa Marta*, both **G**; *pensiones Las Brisas* and *González*, both **F**, latter above hardware store (ferretería), not signed, *Pip's* restaurant, good.) There is a bus service from San José, C 1-Central, Av 11, US$2.50, via Río Frío, several daily. Buses from Puerto Viejo to Río Frío and San Carlos. Nearby is **A** *Selva Verde Lodge*: on 600 acres of virgin rainforest reserve, 49 double rooms, 5 bungalows for 4, caters mainly for tour

groups, independent travellers in 1993 found it unfriendly and felt unwanted, T 710-6459 (Lodge), T 220-1712 (San José reservations), extensive library, evening lectures by biologists, excellent for birdwatchers and naturalists with extensive trail system, rafting, canoeing and riding through property; tours with biologists organized. It is next to the Sarapiquí Conservation Learning Center, community library and resource centre for environmental protection. Also in the neighbourhood is the Organization for Tropical Studies station at La Selva Biological Station on the Río Sarapiquí. To visit, phone in advance to book San José OTS office, T 240-6696 or 240-5033. Visitors are provided with maps of the superb primary rain forest. There are different styles of accommodation, including dormitories; rates in 1993 were US$17 day entry, enter at 0700 or earlier, very good jungle walks, lots of animals to see; overnight rates reduced for a senior researcher, student researcher (letter of introduction required and prior arrangement). book well in advance. High rates for tourists help to support the scientists. Try to avoid the rainy season. To get there by car, take Route 9 from San José, park at the suspension bridge then walk. Across the river from the OTS station is the **B** *Sarapiquí Ecolodge*, 4 rooms, shared bathroom, price pp inc meals, E without food, riding, birdwatching, river trips, T 235-9280. Buses run from Puerto Viejo. The river flows into the San Juan, which forms the northern border of Costa Rica. River trips on the Sarapiquí and on the Río Sucio are beautiful (US$15 for 2 hrs); contact William Rojas in Puerto Viejo (T 766-6260) for trips on the Río Sarapiquí or to Barra del Colorado and Tortuguero (good prices). Near La Selva Biological Station is **B** *El Gavilán Lodge*, inc meals, 10 rooms private bath, 10 rooms shared bath, special group and student/reseacher rates, T 234-9507, F 253-6556, day trips and overnight trips from San José. **The Oro Verde Station** is located where the Río Sarapiquí flows into the Río San Juan with over 1,900 hectares (almost 100% forest), 1½-hr boat ride from Puerto Viejo, US $30 pp, accommodation in A range with meals, beautiful setting, quiet, excellent food, good place to unwind, T San José 223-6613, F 223-7479, Braun Eco Tourism (see above, **Travel Agents**) do 3-day all-inclusive packages, rec. 17 km S of Puerto Viejo, near *Las Horquetas de Sarapiquí* is *Rara Avis*, rustic lodges in a 1,500 acre forest reserve owned by ecologist Amos Bien. **L** *Waterfall Lodge*, inc meals, private bath, **A** *Albergue El Plástico*, rustic with shared bath, min 2 nights, book well in advance. This admirable experiment in educating visitors about rainforest conservation takes small groups, led by biologists. You must be prepared for rough and muddy trails. T 253-0844. (Affiliated to the Youth Hostel network). The road from the Limón Highway to Puerto Viejo is now paved, the turn off is near Santa Clara, 14 km W of Guápiles, it bypasses Río Frío and goes via Las Horquetas.

The road from Alajuela to San Carlos (**see p 744**) passes through several of the Meseta Central towns, with good paved roads to others. Much of this region is devoted to coffee growing and the hills are covered with green coffee bushes, interspersed with other plants for shade, often shrouded in cloud and rain. 18 km NW from Alajuela, *Grecia* is in a major pineapple-growing area and has an interesting church, made entirely of metal to replace a wooden one. The Museo Regional de Grecia is in the Centro de Cultura, check opening times. Hotels: *Cabaña Los Cipreses*, D per cabin; *Complejo Trailer y Cabinas Los Trapiches*; *Pensión Quirós*, G with bath. A few km further is *Sarchí*, where you can visit the factory that produces the traditional painted ox-carts, which are almost a national emblem. The three main *artesanías* are together, either side of the road and selling hand-made furniture, cowhide rocking chairs and wooden products as well as the ox-carts, which come in all sizes. Look out for the bus shelters, painted in the style of the carts. The pink church in Sarchí is especially attractive at sunset. Travel agents in San José charge US$20 or more, often combining Sarchí with a trip to Poás volcano. Express bus from San José, C 16, Av 1-3, 1215 and 1730 daily, returning 0530, 0615, 1345. Tuansa buses every 30 mins, 0500-2200 from Alajuela bus station. There is nowhere to stay in Sarchí. The road continues on through Naranjo (Roberto Kopper offers balloon tours, about 30 mins, 1,000 feet, T 450-0318) to *Zarcero*, notable for its topiary. There are frequent bus services from San José/Alajuela through Naranjo to San Carlos (Ciudad Quesada) and buses stop in Zarcero in the main square, which is the highlight of the place. The bushes are clipped into the shapes of arches leading up to the white church with twin towers, animals, people dancing, a helicopter, baskets—many designs like Henry Moore sculptures, also a small grotto. The interior of the church is entirely of wood, even the pillars, painted cream and pale grey with patterns in blue, brown, green and pink; cartouches, emblems and paintings. *Soda/Restaurant El Jardín*, on first floor, overlooks the square with good view of topiary, local lunches and breakfasts. The town is also known for cheese and fruit preserves.

Just after Llano Bonito, before reaching Zarcero, a turning left goes to **San Ramón**, 76 km from San José. A clean town with an attractive Central Park. Street market Saturday mornings. The Museo de San Ramón, Frente de Parque, open Tues-Fri, 1300-1700, records the history and culture of the local community. **E** *Hotel Nuevo Jardín*, with bath, hot water; **F** *El Viajero*, basic, clean, communal bathroom, TV in lounge; **F** *Washington*, dirty, unfriendly, not rec. *Restaurant Tropical*. Excellent ice cream parlour near the NW corner of the Park. There are local families who offer rooms and board, try Sra Miriam Bamfi, T 445-6331 or Sra María del Carmen Ulate, T 445-6007, Spanish speaking only. Buses leave from the Central Park to San José and the surrounding towns and villages. Good walking for example to the NW, take the bus to La Paz and get off at the bridge over the River Barranca. Also you can visit the coffee processing plant (in season) at the Cooperativa de Café in San Ramón. 7 km beyond San Ramón is **Palmares** (one hotel), which has a pretty central park with lovely tall trees, in which are said to be 5 sloths (the editors failed to verify this in the pouring rain). Eight paths radiate from the bandstand. On the side of the park opposite the stone church is the municipal market.

After Palmares you can either pick up the Pan-American Highway, or continue S to **Atenas**, which is on the road from San José to San Mateo, leading on to Esparza and the Pacific coast. This road to the coast is well-used and in good condition. The church and main square in Atenas lie on an earthquake fault. There is a Library on the square, which also serves as the office for the bus company, Cooptransatenas, T 446-5767. Many daily buses to San José, either direct or via Alajuela, US$0.60. Local speciality, *toronja rellena*, a sweet filled grapefruit. Atenas is reputed to have the best climate in the world, with stable temperatures of between 17 and 32°C the year round (plus rain of course).

Hotel B *Villa Los Malinches*, inc breakfast, private bathroom, special weekly/monthly rates, T 446-5019.

Driving from Atenas towards Alajuela, you pass *Fiesta de la Maíz* soda/restaurant by a green church on the side of the road, where they sell only products made of maize, you can try spoonfuls before you buy. Open weekends only, very busy, a stopping place for weekenders on their way to Jacó Beach. Nearby is the Enchanted Forest, popular with children. Also the Zoológica de Aves, known as Zooave, between Atenas and Alajuela in **La Garita de Alajuela**, Canadian owner, about 450 birds, toucans, parrots, black swans, eagles, pleasant, open 0900-1700, US$5.15. **A** *Chatelle Country Resort*, T 487-7095, 6 rooms with bath, some rooms with kitchenette, TV, spacious, comfortable beds, beautiful gardens, good restaurant, pool, weekly/monthly rates, airport pickup available at no extra charge. The area is quiet and agricultural with fields of sugar cane and cattle pastures; pleasant walking to places of interest. Opposite the *Chatelle Country Resort* is an orchid nursery with a marvellous variety of blooms, run as a hobby by an enthusiastic English-speaking optometrist, who will give you a guided tour for US$3.50.

10 km S of San José is **Aserrí**, a village with a beautiful white church, where on Fri and Sat evenings, street bands play from 2000, followed by marimbas. Extremely popular among locals, the dancing is fabulous. *Chicharrones* and *tortillas* to eat, plus liquor. Further along the same road is *Mirador Ram Luna*, a restaurant with a fine panoramic view. At the end of the black-top road is **San Ignacio de Acosta**, again with a good church containing life-size Nativity figures. The unpaved road continues to **Santiago de Puriscal**, which was the epicentre

for many earthquakes in 1990, the church is now closed as a result. Excellent views from the town and the road. From here it is possible to take a dirt road to the Pacific coast, joining the coastal road near Parrita (**see p 775**). Alternatively, take the road to *San Pablo de Turrubares* (a soccer field, a church, a soda and a bar), from where you can either head W for Orotina, via an unpaved road through San Pedro and San Juan de Mata, or for Atenas via Quebradas, then E to Escobal, next stop on railway, then 4-wheel drive necessary to Atenas.

A road has been built from San José W to Ciudad Colón, which will eventually pass San Pedro de Turrubares going to Orotina, with the aim of replacing the Pan-American Highway to the coast.

THE CENTRAL NORTHWEST (3)

The northern lowlands stretching to the Nicaraguan border. In the eastern foothills of the Cordillera de Tilarán is Lago Arenal, beneath the highly active Volcán Arenal. The rivers provide fine opportunities for seeing wildlife.

San Carlos, also known as *Ciudad Quesada*, lies 48 km from the Pan-American Highway and can be reached by a road which branches off the highway near Naranjo. At the foot of the mountains it is the main town of the lowland cattle and farming region and is a hub of communications. The market (*centro comercial*) is near the Parque Central. It is very clean and there are serveral places to eat. There is a large, efficient Social Security Hospital on the N side of town on the road to Florencia, better to come here for first aid treatment rather than to local village doctors. Direct bus from Coca Cola bus station, San José, 3 hrs, hourly, US$1.50. From San Carlos buses go NW to Tilarán via Fortuna and Arenal (0600 and 1500), other buses go to Fortuna through El Tanque (5 daily), San Rafael de Guatuso and Upala, N to Los Chiles, NE to towns on the Río San Carlos and Río Sarapiquí, including Puerto Viejo de Sarapiquí, and E to the Río Frío district.

Accommodation E *Balneario Carlos*, T 460-1822, cottages with cooking facilities, with bath, swimming pool; **E** *Conquistador*, with bath; **E** *El Retiro*, T 460-0403, with bath, clean and comfortable, but noisy; **E** *La Central*, T 460-0301, with bath, restaurant;   *Lily, Cristal* (not rec); *Diana, Ugalde, París, Los Fernandos*, all **F**; **G** *La Terminal*.

From San Carlos a paved road runs NW to *Florencia* (service station). At a junction the route to the N leads 13 km to *Muelle San Carlos* (**A+** *Country Club Tilajari Hotel Resort*, T/F 460-1083, 48 luxurious rooms, 4 suites, tennis, 3 pools, sauna, bar and restaurant, horses, boat trips and other excursions organized, 29 km to Arenal, rec) and on a further 74 km through flat land where orange plantations have replaced forest, to *Los Chiles* near the Nicaraguan border (bus from San José 5-8 hrs). Cheap accommodation (F range) and restaurants. From here you can arrange boat/fishing trips up the slow-moving Río Frío, through dense tropical vegetation into the **Caño Negro** Wildlife Refuge and Caño Negro Lake, to see alligators, turtles, monkeys, a wide variety of birdlife, fish and fauna. See under **San Carlos** and **San Juan del Sur/Greytown** for details on the Río San Juan border.

The road running W from the junction in Florencia (paved, good) leads to *Fortuna*, from where you can explore the Arenal region. There are daily buses at 0615, 0840, 1130, from San José, C 16, Av 1-3, via San Carlos, US$3.30, 5 buses a day from San Carlos, 1 hr. Two buses a day to Tilarán, 0800 (connecting bus Tilarán-Puntarenas 1300) and 1600 US$2, 3 hrs. **E** *pp Albergue Burío*, inc continental breakfast, private bath, T 479-9076, F 479-9010, 8 rooms with bath, try to get an inside cabin, others noisy, Arenal volcano trips, fishing arranged, affiliated to the Youth Hostel network; **B-C** *Cabinas San Bosco*, all rooms with private bath, quiet, signs on main road, clean, friendly, rec; **D** *Las Colindas*, private bath, pleasant; **F** pp *La Central*, quiet, cold showers, friendly, restaurant not cheap, laundry service, you may put up a tent on the lawn for US$1.50, T 479-9004 (phone this number to be put in contact with Gabino Hidalgo Solís, who runs a tourist information office on the main square, he also acts as a guide to the area, including Volcán Arenal, by night, US$6.50, horse riding to the waterfalls, US$14 day trip, bring own lunch); **F** pp *Cabina Las Tejas*, private bath, bike rental, tours to Arenal and hot springs, US$7; **F** *Fortuna*, basic, shared bath or D with private bath, next to bus station, very clean, friendly, good food, good value tours; **F** *Centro Recreación Volcán Arenal*, 50m S of church, private accommodation, simple rooms, breakfast, owned by local dentist. *Restaurant El Jardín*, good food. *Choza de Laurel*, behind the church, self-service US$1.50-4.50, typical food, friendly; *Rancho Cascada*, on corner of Parque with high conical thatched roof, good; *La Vaca Muca*, a bit out of the village on the way to Tabacón. Public phone with international access.

About 6 km from Fortuna are the Río Fortuna Waterfalls, up a pleasant road through yuca and papaya plantations. You can drive but 4WD is necessary, or you can hire a horse for the day at around US$14. From Fortuna the road travels around the base of the 1,633m volcano *Arenal* to the man-made **Lago Arenal** and hydroelectric dam. The volcano has been continuously active since July 1968, when an eruption killed 78 people and destroyed a village. It is a classic cone shape and although the side facing Fortuna is green, the side facing the lake is grey and barren, with lava flows clearly visible. There have been no major eruptions since 1968, but there are three active craters and several fumaroles which spew out red hot lava and steam. The activity is particularly impressive at night, accompanied by rumbles, crashes and intermittent roars (rather like someone moving furniture upstairs) to wake you up. (In January 1994 there was no visible activity from the volcano; it is not known if this was temporary.) On no account try to walk up the volcano beyond the level of the vegetation; some of those who have tried have not returned alive. However there is good hiking on the lower slopes from Fortuna. There are many chalets and tourist facilities round the attractive lake, but not many people. Bathing in the warm water from quiet shady beaches is possible.

Accommodation 10 km from Fortuna is *Balneario Tabacón*, a thermal pool with bar/restaurant, recommended for swimming after dark when you can see the lava coming down the volcano, a spectacular sight, not to be missed (but see above). The water is hot and stimulating: there are a number of pools at descending heights and different temperatures, waterslides, a waterfall to sit under, etc. The food is good and the fruit drinks thirst quenching. The entrance fee seems to vary and is reported cheaper both after 0500 and after 1800. The resort was remodelled in 1993 to reopen in 1994 as a luxury resort. Buses from San Carlos en route to Tilarán daily, return transport to Fortuna at 2200. 4 km after El Tabacón a left turn on to a gravel road (sign 1 km Parqueo) leads eventually to the **A** *Arenal Observatory Lodge* (PO Box 1195, 1250 Escazú, Costa Rica, T 255-3418, F 255-4410 (Costa Rica Sun Tours) or T 255-2011 (Eco-Center), 4WD recommended along this 9-km stretch as you have to ford a river (taxi-jeep from Fortuna, US$12). The Observatory was built in 1987 as a research station and now has basic cabins with bunk beds and bath, a dining room/lodge, 14 rooms, double, or triple, private bathroom, hot water showers, price per person, inc taxes and meals, depending on size of group, children under 3 free, 3-10 half price; one-day tour from San José US$69; spectacular views of volcano across valley of Río Agua Caliente and of Lake Arenal, good walking and bird watching in the area, fishing with guide on the lake US$95 pp. Also offers trips to Caño Negro with experienced naturalist, and hiking to Monteverde. On the N side of the lake about 2 km off the paved road from Fortuna (4WD required) is the more comfortable **A+** *Arenal Lodge*, meals extra, good food, 5 rooms with bath, 6 junior suites, front 10 units have fine views (but Unit 1 has trees in front), cheaper new rooms, smaller, at back, T 228-2588, F 228-2798, expensive breakfast, viewing deck, fishing trips arranged on the lake. Newly built (1992) is the **C** *Mirador Los Lagos*, T 695-5169, cabins, excellent food and spectacular views of the volcano over the lake with a campsite. About 4 km from Fortuna on the road to Lake Arenal, turn at sign on left side of the road 'Bienvenidos a Junglas y Senderos Los Lagos'. Site is 2 km uphill, good facilities, G pp, hot showers, tours to hot springs at night.

There are several tour agencies offering night tours to Arenal volcano and thermal baths, US$7.50. *Celin's*, in front of *Hotel Fortuna*, is rec, runs day and night tours to the volcano, inc boat on the lake and baths, US$18. The entry fee to the baths may not be included in your tour price, check. You leave Fortuna at about 1815 and return by 2200. If you are visiting in the rainy season you will not see much as the volcano is obscured by clouds and rain. However, if you can hire a taxi for a trip at about 0400-0500, the sky is often clearer then.

The S side of the lake is very difficult to drive, with many fords; it is possible to get a boat from the dam across the lake to Río Chiquito then hike to Monteverde.

There is a road round the N of the lake, mostly paved, which leads to Tilarán. If driving yourself, you can get from Fortuna to Monteverde via Tilarán in a day, but set out in good time to avoid driving after dark. The lakeside road is frequently impassable because of fallen bridges and landslides (check before setting out), and the last 10 km just before Arenal village are rough although passable with high clearance vehicles all year. Works are expected in 1994 to repair the damage. An alternative route is to take the road from Fortuna to *San Rafael de Guatuso*, which runs parallel but further N. There is a 'voluntary' toll of US$1 between Jicarito and San Rafael for reconstruction work on this road. You can come back to the lake either by turning off before San Rafael through Venado (where there are caves), or from San Rafael itself, where there are a couple of basic hotels. Both roads are unpaved and very slow, 20 kph maximum speed in a car, but go through lovely countryside with beautiful views, especially when you approach the lake.

3 km from Colonia Río Celeste near San Rafael de Guatuso is the **B** *Magil Forest Lodge*, set in 800 acres on the foothills of the 1,916m volcano **Tenorio**. The *Lodge*, inc meals, has 10 rooms with private bath. If you continue along the road from San Rafael NW towards the Nicaraguan border you come to **Upala** (airport) and Caño Negro. There is now a direct bus from San José to Upala (from Av 5, C 14 at 1445, 4 hrs, US$2.80), where there are the *Hotel Rigo*, *Hotel Upala*, T 470-0169, *Pensión Isabella*, **F** *Pensión Buena Vista*, basic, food available. Nearby is **A+** *Los Ceibos Lodge*, B without meals, T 228-0054, private reserve, riding US$6/hr, tours to Caño Negro, Río Celeste and Volcán Tenorio.

The San Rafael-Arenal road joins the lakeside road just N of **Arenal** town; no signs if driving from Arenal to San Rafael, it is just a track. If you turn left about 4 km out of San Rafael before the river, 4WD necessary, you come to the Guatuso Indian villages of Tonjibe, Margarita and El Sol. Arenal is a pleasant little town, 20 km along the lake from the volcano, with wonderful views. 4 km E of the town is Arenal Botanical Gardens (T 695-5266 ext 273, F 695-5387), opened in 1993, hours 0900-1600 (closed Oct), US$3.50, with many flowers, birds, butterflies, a delightful place (still under development). There are frequent buses to Tilarán, a branch of the Banco Nacional and accommodation: **C** *Hotel-Restaurant Lajas*, excellent food, good service; *Cabinas Rodríguez*; **B** *Chalet Nicolás*, bed and breakfast, run by retired Americans, friendly, rec, 2 km from the centre towards Tilarán. *Pizzería e Ristorante Tramonti*, T 695-5266, ext 282, for Italian cuisine. There is also a campsite on Lago Cote, N of Lake Arenal. The **A** *Lago Cote Eco-Lodge*, is popular with birdwatchers, rooms in main building with shared bathrooms rather grim, or brighter cabins with private bath and newer furniture, family-style meals, bar, pool table, games, lots of tours, watch out for snakes on roads and paths, T 221-4209 in San José.

From Arenal, the lakeside road is good, paved, with fine views, 25 km to Tilarán. Several places rent fishing tackle, but if you want a boat, guide and full package try Rainbow Bass Fishing Safaris, run by Dave Myers, US$200 a day for 2 anglers, fishing licence US$30 for 2 months, PO Box 7758-1000, San José, T 229-2550, 222-834, F 235-7662. Luis Diego Murillo, T 695-5008, operates sightseeing tours around the lake and the volcano. The Tilawa Windsurfing Center is on the W side of the lake, which is the best side for windsurfing; mornings are best, particularly

Dec-Jan, equipment for rent.

Tilarán is a modern town, with some hotels: **B** *The Spot Tourist Center*, Tilarán, 16 rooms with bath, restaurant, fishing, horses, day trips, T 695-5711, F 695-5579. **F** *Grecia*, with shower, cheaper without, clean, friendly; **F** *Cabinas Mary*, T 695-5470, with bath, small pleasant rooms upstairs rec; **B** *Cabinas Naralit*, T 695-5393, S of church, clean, new buildings; **E** *Surf* (Youth Hostel), small, clean, very friendly; **F** *Cabinas Central*, T 695-5363, with shared bath (more with), noisy, and **D** *Cabinas El Sueño*, T 695-5347, rooms around central patio, hot water, quiet, friendly, rec; **E** *Lago Lindo Lodge*, same street as *El Sueño*, comfortable, bright and friendly. Other hotels in the area: **C** *Hotel Puerto San Luis Lake Resort*, 15 rooms with private bathroom, refrigerator, TV and fan, restaurant, boat rentals, fishing equipment, windsurf boards, trips to Arenal volcano and lake, T 695-5950; **B** *Rock River Lodge* on the road skirting the lake, 6 rooms with bathroom, restaurant, T 222-4547. The office of the *Albergue La Casona del Lago* (affiliated to the Youth Hostel network), on the left hand corner (with public phone) of first main junction as you come into town from the lake, has windsurfing equipment, very helpful. Tourist office ½ block from plaza, on right side of church. Cata Tours have a branch office in Tilarán, T 695-5953, offering several excursions and pickup from Cañas-Libreria area hotels. Direct bus from San José, 4 daily, 4 hrs, from C 14, Av 9-11, T 222-3854, and 5 daily buses from Cañas. Two daily buses to Arenal, buses through to San Carlos via Fortuna. Daily bus to Santa Elena (for Monteverde), 1230, 3 hrs. Tilarán-Puntarenas 0600, 1300, 3 hrs, US$3. If you get the 1230 bus Tilarán-Liberia you can get from there to the Nicaraguan border before it closes.

To get to Monteverde (2-3 hrs, 4-wheel drive rec), go through the town until you come to a T-junction opposite a green house, go left and follow paved road to Quebrada Grande. As you enter Quebrada Grande, take the unpaved road to the left before the church, it is very rough. At Dos de Tilarán is a sign—30 km to Monteverde—follow this road to Cabeceras. There the road forks, take either the left, longer route via Nubes, or right, down dale and uphill, both poor, to Santa Elena (9 km) and thence to Monteverde.

THE NORTHWEST (4)

The route of the Pan-American Highway passes near the cloud forest of Monteverde in the Cordillera de Tilarán, the marshes of the Palo Verde National Park, the active Volcán Rincón and the dry tropical forest of the Santa Rosa National Park on the Pacific coast as it crosses the great cattle haciendas of Guanacaste.

The Pan-American Highway from San José descends from the Meseta Central to *Esparza*, an attractive town with **E** *Hotel Castanuelas*, T 635-5105, a/c, quiet, cooler alternative to Puntarenas; **F** pp *Pensión Córdoba*, clean and modern.

The stretch of the Highway between San Ramón and Esparza (34 km) includes the sharp fall of 800m from the Meseta Central. (Beware of fog on this stretch if driving or cycling.) Beyond Esparza there is the *Bar/Restaurant Mirador Enis*, a popular stopping place for tour buses et al, service station opposite, fruit stalls nearby, before a left turn at Barranca for Puntarenas, 15 km.

Puntarenas (population 50,000) is on a 5-km spit of land thrusting out into Nicoya Gulf and enclosing the Estero lagoon. It is hot (mean temperature 27°C), the beaches are dirty, and are crowded on Suns. There is a public swimming pool on the end of the point (US$1 entrance), very hot. Good surfing off the headland. Across the gulf are the mountains of the Nicoya Peninsula. In the gulf are several islands, the Islas Negritos, to which there are passenger launches. The chief products around Puntarenas are bananas, rice, cattle, and coconuts. Puntarenas is being replaced as the country's main Pacific port by Caldera.

Festival *Fiesta de la Virgen del Mar*, Saturday closest to 16 July, carnival and regatta of decorated fishing boats and yachts.

Hotels L *Fiesta*, at El Roble, 174 rooms with bath, a/c, cable TV, pool, restaurants, tennis, casino, T 663-0185, F 663-1516; **A-B** *Tioga*, Barrio El Carmen (T 661-0271), beachfront and C 17, with bath, hot water, inc continental breakfast, swimming pool, very good indeed. **C** *Colonial*, C 72-74, Av Central, a/c, swimming pool, with breakfast, T 661-1833, very friendly, comfortable, a bit run down, some distance from the centre of town; **B** *Porto Bello*, C 68 y 70, Av Central, next door, with bath, a/c, pool, quiet, clean, gardens, excellent food, helpful Italian owner, T 661-1322; *Yacht Club*, T 661-0784, at Cocal, caters for members of foreign yacht clubs. Others are **C** *Las Brisas*, on the waterfront, Paseo Los Turistas Al Final, with bath, good restaurant, swimmimg pool, T 661-2120, but reservations reported not honoured; **D** *Viking*, C 32, Av 2, new, on the beach; **B** *Villa del Roble*, by the sea 18 km E (T 663-0447), 5 rooms, quiet, charming; **C** *Chorotega*, C 3, Av 3, with bath and fan, C without, although price list disagrees with what they actually charge, clean, central (one block E of river); **C** *La Punta*, Av 2, C 6-8, T 661-0696, 1 block from car ferry, with bath, friendly, clean, hot water, restaurant, secure parking, pool, American-owned, big rooms; **D** *Cabinas Los Jorón*, C 25, 7 blocks from ferry, T 661-0467, roomy, fridge, a/c, restaurant, rec; **D** *Cabinas Orlando* at San Isidro de Puntarenas, with bath and kitchen; **D** *Río Mar Hotel* at Barranca, 15 km from Puntarenas, with bath, restaurant, good, pricey; **D** *Las Hamacas* on waterfront, T 661-0398, nice rooms but noisy. **E** *Ayo Can*, C 2, Av 1-3, a little noisy but clean; **E** *Cayuga*, Calle 4, Av Central, with shower, a/c, restaurant, dirty, run down. **E** *Gran Imperial*, 500m from station on road to town, friendly, hot water, private bath; **F** *Cabezas*, Av 1, C 2-4, with fan, cheaper without, basic, clean, very good value. **F** *Río*, Av 3, C Central/2, near market, Chinese owners, with shower, basic and noisy, but friendly. **F** *Miramar*, also near market, fan, good deal; *Cabinas Thelma*, very good, friendly (ask at Holman Bar, C 7). Many *cabinas* on Av 2. Apartments for rent from Jacob Puister, Contigua Casino, Central, 2 piso, T 661-0246, US$37 for 2 weeks. Accommodation difficult to find Dec-April, especially at weekends.

Restaurants Next to *Hotel Tioga* is *Aloha Restaurant* (pushy waiters). *Mariscos Kahite Blanco*, C 17, near launch, excellent seafood. A number of Chinese restaurants on the main street (eg *Mandarín*, good value). Good food from market stalls, eg *sopa de carne*. *Fonda Brisas del Pacífico*, near wharf, good value *casado*. *Soda Vanessa*, Av 1, clean, cheap, good breakfast for under US$1. There is a lively night life in the cheaper bars. On the beach, *Miramare*, C 17-19, good but expensive; nearby, C 19-21, is *Bierstube*, good for sandwiches, hamburgers, but beware overcharging. Rec bars: *Pier 14*, near wharf, good pizza and hamburgers made by Captain Ed from Mobile (Alabama) and his wife; *Yate Bar*, friendly, English-speaking owner (no girls at either). *El Fela* bar, opp Banco Anglo Costarricense, clean, cool, a must for women just to see the toilet decor.

Shopping and Services Market, shops and banks on Calle Central, opposite end to beach. **Banco Nacional** changes TCs, but painfully slow service; much better al **Banco Anglo Costarricense**, but for cash. **Post Office** near church on C5, beach side, hard to find. **Telecommunications**, ICE and Radiográfica.

Travel Agency *Turisol Travel Agency*, C 1, Av 3, T 661-1212. For boat excursions (sailing or motor boats) from Puntarenas call Cath Mercer T 232-1020 at ASICS tours in San José. See under San José **Travel Agents** for cruises in the Gulf & Nicoya.

Warning Thieves abound on the beach.

Transport Terminal for San José is by the beach. Buses every 15 mins 0400-2100 to San José, $2\frac{1}{2}$ hrs, US$2.65. Daily bus to Santa Elena for Monteverde, **see p 749**. Buses S to Quepos from around corner from San José terminal, 0500, 1100 and 1400 (high season) via Jacó, US$2.50, $3\frac{1}{2}$ hrs. Several daily to Liberia from 0530. Good café at bus terminal where you can await your bus. Tourist information office near main church has up to date bus timetables.

Crossing to Nicoya Peninsula see p 757.

Isla San Lucas was a prison island, but a luxury resort is now being built, expected to be finished in 1994. You may visit its beautiful beaches on Sundays. Launch leaves Puntarenas Sun 0900; returns 1500, US$1.50.

Isla Jesuita, in Gulf of Nicoya has an hotel: *Hotel Isla Jesuita*, lodge and cottages, hammocks reached by hotel's boat or public launch from Puntarenas. Package rates from San José, also arrangements can be made in the USA T 800-327-9408.

Isla Gitana, 13 km SW of Puntarenas has 2 rustic cabins, A pp inc meals, tropical paradise island, white sand beach, lots of wildlife, swimming pool, kayaking, windsurfing. The lodge can arrange speed boat transfers from Puntarenas or meet the Puntarenas-Paquera launch. Contact Linda Ruegg, T 661-2994.

On the old San José-Puntarenas railway, near the new port of Caldera, is *Mata de Limón*, which has a beach. It is on a lagoon surrounded by mangroves, peaceful. Bus from Puntarenas market every hour (marked to Caldera). Hotels: **E** *Casablanca*, C 2-4, Av 14, T 222-2921, full board available, or cabins; **E** *Manglares*, near former train stop, reasonable, good restaurant; excellent bar/restaurant next to railway booking office. S of the village (care when crossing wooden bridge at night, missing planks!) there are several basic places to stay, all basic, F, but acceptable: *Viña del Mar*, *Villas Fanny*, *Villas América*. Good fishing nearby.

To visit the Monteverde Cloud Forest Reserve, follow the Pan-American Highway NW to km 149, turning right just before the Río Lagarto. Continue for about 40 km on mostly gravel road (allow 2½ hrs) to Santa Elena. Parts of the road are quite good, but in wet weather 4-wheel drive is recommended for the rough parts. Check that your car rental agreement allows you to visit Monteverde. A 33-km shorter route is to take the Pipasa/Sardinal turn-off from the Pan-American Highway. At the park in Sardinal turn L, then go via Guacimal to the Monteverde road.

Santa Elena, 2½ km before Monteverde village, has several places to stay, and it is cheaper than staying nearer to the Reserve. Banco Nacional, open 0900-1500, will change TCs with commission. Bus from Puntarenas, daily at 1415, 2½-4 hrs, returns 0600, US$1.50—this bus arrives in time to catch a bus to Puerto Quepos for Manuel Antonio (the company has one new bus and one old bus—take the new, safer in many respects). For an alternative route to Santa Elena from Arenal, see p 745-747. Daily bus to Tilarán 0700, 3 hrs.

Accommodation B *Finca Valverdas*, 300m E of Banco Nacional, T 645-5157, with bath, nice gardens for birdwatching, bar, restaurant; **B** *Sunset Hotel*, on road to Tilarán, T 661-3558, on top of hill, nice location, friendly, clean, warm showers, good breakfast, German spoken; **C** *Montaña Arco Iris*, 100m N of Banco Nacional, with bath, restaurant, horses for rent, plenty of parking, T 645-5067, F 645-5022; under the same management is **D** *El Gran Mirador San Gerardo*, 6 km N of Santa Elena, dirt road, May-Nov you probably need a horse, cabins with bath or dormitory accommodation, restaurant, own private rain forest park for birdwatching nearby; **E** *Pensión Santa Elena*, T 661-1151, pleasant, clean, good food, vegetarians catered for, unlimited free coffee (C including 3 meals); **D** *Pensión Tucán*, T 645-5017, showers, basic, friendly management, restaurant but closed Sun lunch; **E** *Hotel La Hospedaje Guest House*, above the grocery store opp Post Office, clean, shared bathrooms, hot water; **F** *Pensión A Different Place*, clean, friendly, 5 rooms, shared bathroom, inc breakfast, beside Santa Elena Health Clinic about 300m from bus stop; **F** *Pensión Cabinas Marín*, 500m uphill past the Agricultural College, spacious rooms, friendly; **F** *Pensión Iman*, clean, friendly, electric hot shower, free transport to Monteverde for guests, riding on healthy horse, US$5/hr, food average, but good *casado*; **F** *Hospedaje el Banco*, family-run, friendly, clean, good information, English spoken, good breakfast; **F** *Pensión El Sueno (The Dream)*, very friendly, small but nice rooms, clean, run by Rafa Trejos who does horseback trips into the mountains to see quetzals, etc.

The settlement at *Monteverde* was founded by American Quakers in the 1950s; it is strung out along the road without any centre. It is essentially a group of dairy farms and a cheese factory run by a cooperative, which you can tour. Excellent cheeses of various types can be bought, also fresh milk and *cajeta* (a butterscotch spread) are sold. The Quakers have an English Library at Monteverde. The Monteverde Butterfly Garden is open daily, 0930-1600, US$5 inc guided tour, best time for a visit 1100-1300, beautifully presented large garden. They are mainly concerned with breeding and research and do not export. There is a service station, open Mon-Sat, 0700-1800, Sun 0700-1200. Casem, a cooperative gift shop, is located just outside Monteverde on the road to the Reserve next to *El Bosque* restaurant. It sells embroidered shirts, T-shirts, wooden and woven articles and baskets. From Monteverde to the Reserve is a minimum 45 mins walk uphill,

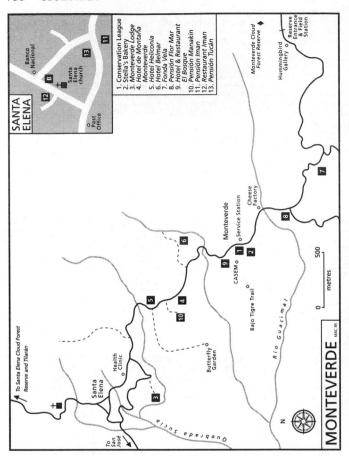

1. Conservation League
2. Stella's Bakery
3. Monteverde Lodge
4. Hotel de Montaña Monteverde
5. Hotel Heliconia
6. Hotel Belmar
7. Fonda Vela
8. Pensión Flor Mar
9. Hotel & Restaurant El Bosque
10. Pensión Manakin
11. Pensión Iman
12. Restaurant Iman
13. Pensión Tucán

SANTA ELENA

Banco Nacional

Santa Elena church

Post Office

Monteverde Cloud Forest Reserve

Monteverde

Cheese Factory

Service Station

CASEM

Bajo Tigre Trail

Hummingbird Gallery

Reserve Entrance & Field Station

Rio Guacimal

Butterfly Garden

Health Clinic

Santa Elena

To Santa Elena Cloud Forest Reserve and Tilarán

To San José

Quebrada Sucia

metres

0   500

N

MONTEVERDE

MAC 85

about 4 km, but there are lovely views looking towards the sea and the Nicoya peninsula, particularly in the evening (when you are coming down and can appreciate them). Several places rent horses; look for signs between Santa Elena and Monteverde or ask at your hotel. Rafa (Rafael) will take you on horseback for a day trip (US$20) into the forest (the horses tend to gallop without prompting).

Hotels A *El Establo*, next to *Heliconia*, T/F 645-5033, F 645-5041, San José T 225-0569, 19 carpeted rooms with private bathroom, restaurant, 120-acre farm with 50% cloud forest, own nature guide, good birdwatching, riding stables, 35 horses, family-run, transport available, very accommodating, rec; **A** *Monteverde Lodge*, T 800-633-4734 toll free in USA, T 645-5057 locally, F 645-5126, or book through Costa Rica Expeditions, T 222-0333, rec, restaurant, jacuzzi, daily slide shows 1815; **A** *Sapo Dorado*, just before *Hotel de Montaña*, 10 suites with fireplace, good but expensive restaurant open 0700-2100, T 645-5010, F 645-5180; **B** *Cloud Forest Lodge*, 300m N of *Sapo Dorado*, T 645-5058, F 645-5168, 12 rooms with bath, restaurant, beautiful views; **B** *Belmar*, T 645-5201, F 645-5135, 300m from service station, Swiss chalet-style, beautiful views of Nicoya, restaurant, good, transport from San José available; **B** *Fonda Vela*, T 645-5109, F 645-5007 (or San José T 257-1413, F 257-1416), private bathroom, cabins, suites available, nearest to Reserve, 25 mins walk, on a 35-hectare farm with forest and trail system, good birding, some camping, horses for hire, excellent restaurant (open to public), art gallery; **B** *Heliconia*, T 645-5109, F 645-5007, 100m before *Hotel de Montaña*, private bathroom, restaurant, very comfortable, excellent food, warmly rec; **B** *Hotel de Montana Monteverde*, I 645-5046, Γ 645-5320, in San José T 233-7078, F 222-6184, EP, just before service station on right, comfortable, rec, set meals, good, wholesome food, sauna, jacuzzi, horses for hire, good views of Nicoya, excellent birdwatching on 15-acre reserve, transport from San José available; **C** *Hotel Villa Verde*, 2 km before reserve, several rooms with shared bath, cabins with kitchenette, inc meals, restaurant, clean, nice, T 645-5025, F 645-5115; **C** *Pensión Flor Mar*, T 645-5009, F 645-5088, between Monteverde and Reserve, price per person, full board, or E with breakfast in dormitory, helpful, American owner, but considered expensive, poorly furnished and noisy, small area for camping; **D** *Monteverde Inn*, T 645-5156, turnoff 100m before *Hotel de Montaña*, private bathroom, full board, good mattresses; **D** *Pensión Manakin*, just before *Hotel de Montaña*, turn right, drive 75m, T 645-5080, 6 cabins with bath or F with shared bath, 10% discount for students with ID, meals available (US$3-4), clean, friendly, good food. Youth Hostel annex, E pp with breakfast, or full board, if not busy can arrange to use kitchen facilities, 800m off the main road at Cerro Plano, transport to Reserve or Santa Elena, US$2 pp. **D-B** *Hotel El Bosque*, next to restaurant of same name, 21 rooms, T 645-5158, F 645-5129, hot showers, comfortable, clean, lovely rooms with fine views, safe parking, rec. Gary Diller, an American guide, highly rec, rents rooms in his house, D, T 645-5045, late afternoon, early evening; **F** pp *Cabaña Los Pinos*, T/F 645-5005, opp *Hotel de Montaña Monteverde*, sleeps 12, hot water, English spoken, clean, secure, horse rental, run by Freddy Mejíos. *Restaurant El Bosque*, next to Casem Shop, good food, clean, open from 0630; between Gas Station and El Bosque, *La Cascada* and *Cerro Verde*; *Stella's Bakery*, next to the Conservation League office has good granola and cakes.

Transport A direct bus, Monteverde Express, runs from C 14, Av 9-11, San José (4 hrs, US$5) Mon-Thurs 1430, Sat 0630, returning Tues-Thurs 0630, Fri and Sun 1530. Be early. Check times in advance, Sat bus does not always run in low season, T 645-5159 in Monteverde, T 222-3854 in San José for information. Alternatively, get the bus to Puntarenas and change there for Santa Elena, daily service at 1415, US$2.20. Taxis available between Santa Elena and Monteverde and between Monteverde and the Reserve (hunt around for good prices). Not so easy to find a taxi for return trip, best to arrange beforehand.

The 10,500-hectare, private **Monteverde Cloud Forest Reserve** (owned and managed by the non-profit research and educational association, the Tropical Science Centre) is mainly primary cloud forest. It contains over 400 species of birds (including the resplendant quetzal, best seen between January and May, which are the dry months, especially near the start of the Nuboso trail, three-wattled bellbird and bare-necked umbrellabird), over 100 species of mammals (including monkeys, baird's tapir and six endangered cats: jaguar, jaguarundi, margay, ocelot, tigrillo and puma), reptiles, amphibians (including the golden toad, now thought to be extinct not having been seen for 5 years—1994). The reserve includes an estimated 2,500 species of plants and more than 6,000 species of insects. The best months are January to May, especially February, March and April. The entrance is at 1,500m , but the maximum altitude in the reserve is over 1,800m. Mean temperature is between 16° and 18°C and average annual rainfall is 3,000 mm. The weather changes quickly and wind and humidity often make the air feel cooler. The trails are in good condition and there are easy, short and interesting walks for those who do not want to hike all day. Trail walks take from 2 hrs to all day or more. Sendero Brillante is restricted; Camino a Peñas Blancas needs permission and a guide. The Bajo Tigre trail (US$3) takes $1\frac{1}{2}$ hrs (now closed) parking available with notice (T 661-2953) a guide can be arranged), no horses allowed on trail, takes $1\frac{1}{2}$ hrs. There is a plan to prepare a trail northwards to the Arenal volcano. Free maps of the reserve at the entrance and an excellent Nature Trail Guide. Follow the rules, sign the register, indicating where you are going in case you get lost, stay on the paths, leave nothing behind, take no fauna or flora out, no radios or tape recorders allowed.

The Reserve entrance is at the field station, 45 mins walk from the settlement at Monteverde. The total number of visitors to the Reserve at any one time has been increased from 100 to 250, but be there before 0700 to make sure of getting in during high season (hotels will book you a place for the following day). Tour buses come in from San José every day and travellers have told us there is little chance of seeing any wildlife. Entrance fee US$9 (students with ID half-price) valid for multiple entry during the day, can not be purchased in advance; 3-day pass 20% discount. Reserve office open 0700-1630 daily; the park opens at 0600 and closes at 1700. Shelter facilities throughout the Reserve cost US$3 plus key deposit of US$4, bring sleeping bag and flashlight. You can make your own meals. Dormitory-style accommodation for up to 30 people at entrance, *Albergue Reserva Biológica de Monteverde*, T 661-2655, US$20 full board only. Reservations required for all Reserve accommodation. A small shop at the office sells various checklists, postcards, slides, gifts and excellent T-shirts, the proceeds of which help towards the conservation project. Just before the Field Station is the Hummingbird Gallery, where masses of different hummingbirds can be seen darting around a glade, visiting feeding dispensers filled with sugared water, open 0930-1700. A small shop/photo gallery sells pictures and gifts. Slide shows daily at 1630 (3 times a week sometimes), US$3.70, T 661-1259 (photos by Michael and Patricia Fogden).

Natural History walks with biologist guides, every morning and afternoon, 3-4 hrs, US$12 (children half price); reserve in advance at the office or at your hotel. If you use a private (non-Reserve) guide you must pay his entrance fee. An experienced and recommended guide is Gary Diller (Apdo 10165, 1000 San José, T 645-5045); he specializes in birds, there are six others operating, of varying specialization and experience. Tomás Guindon offers a night tour in the Reserve, 1900, T 661-1008. A guide is recommended if you want to see wildlife since the untrained eye misses a lot.

Recommended equipment includes binoculars (750s—1040s), good camera with 400-1,000 ASA film, insect repellent, sweater and light rainwear. Rubber boots are a must for the longer walks, at all times of year but especially in the rainy season, and can be rented at the park office for US$0.80 or at hotels.

Donations to the Reserve can be made at the Reserve office or Tropical Science Centre (Apdo 8-3870, 100 San José, T 225-2649 or 253-3308, F 253-4963) at El Higuerón, 100m Sur y 125m Este, Barrio La Granja, San Pedro, or the Monteverde Conservation League (Apdo 10165, 1000 San José, T 661-2953), open 0830-1600, opp Monteverde service station. Donations are welcomed for purchasing additional land and for maintaining and improving the existing Reserve area. If you are interested in volunteer work, from non-skilled trail maintenance to skilled scientific assistance work, surveying, teaching or studying on a tropical biology programme, contact Polly Morrison at the Conservation League, or write to the address above. The Conservation League is working with schools in the area on education regarding conservation, forests, etc.

Adjoining the Monteverde Cloud Forest is the International Children's Rainforest (*El Bosque Eterno de los Niños*), established in 1988 after an initiative by Swedish schoolchildren to save forests. Currently at 32,000 acres, the land is bought and maintained with children's donations and the aim is to expand to include a further 14,000 acres. There are plans to bring school groups to the forest, but there are no trails open to the public so far.

Reserva Sendero Tranquilo, a private property near the Monteverde Cheese Factory arranges entrance reservations and guiding with owner David Lowther, or Julie Kraft, T 661-2754.

Monteverde Music Festival, classical and jazz concerts between Dec and March at sunset, local and foreign musicians, entry US$7, T 661-2950; schedules and transportation from hotels.

An alternative trail network is in the **Bosque de Mariano Arguedes**, 2 km SW of Santa Elena. The trails are flat and there is good birdwatching and wildlife, US$3 entrance.

1 km along the road from Santa Elena to Tilarán, a 5 km track is signposted to the **Santa Elena Cloud Forest Reserve**, managed by the Centro Ecológico Bosque Nuboso de Monteverde. It is 83% primary cloudforest and the rest 17-year-old secondary forest at an elevation of 1,700m, bordered by the Monteverde Cloud Forest Reserve and the Arenal Forest Reserve. There is an 8 km path network and several lookouts where you can see and hear the Arenal volcano. There are generally fewer visitors here than at Monteverde. The Centro Ecológico Bosque Nuboso is administered by the local community and profits go to five local schools. It was set up by the Costa Rican government in 1989 with collaboration from Canada. The rangers are very friendly and enthusiastic. There is a small information centre where rubber boots can be hired. Hand-painted T-shirts for sale. Entrance US$5, opens 0700-1600, T 661-1154 or 661-2858 for information.

43 km N of Barranca on the Pan-American Highway is the turn off for Juntas where there is an old gold mine museum, Cuatro Vientos.

47 km N of Barranca a L turn goes to the Tempisque ferry and after about 6 km a road off to the R at San Joaquín leads to the **A** pp *Hacienda Solimar Lodge*, a 3,200-acre cattle farm with over half dry tropical virgin forest bordering Palo Verde National Park near Porozal in the lower Tempisque river basin. The freshwater madrigal estuary on the property is one of the most important areas for waterbirds in Costa Rica, surrounded by gallery forest. Rec for serious birdwatchers. Reservations essential, T 237-0196 or contact Birdwatch, Apartado 6951, 1005 San José, T 228-4768, F 228-1573, 8 rooms with private or shared bathroom, inc meals, min 2 nights, transport available on request, local guide, horseriding.

67 km N of Barranca is **Cañas** (buses daily, every 2 hrs from 0630-1830 from Coca Cola terminal, San José. Hotels: **D** *Cañas*, C 2, Av 1, with bath, clean, pleasant; **E** *Gran*, with bath and fan, grubby; **E** *El Corral*, C 4, Av Central, with bath; **F** *Guillén*, C Central, Av 2; also *Luz* and others; *Restaurant Panchitos* on main square is good and inexpensive.) From there are buses to Tilarán, Nuevo Arenal, past the volcano and on to San Carlos. The turn off for Tilarán is at the filling station, no signs. For a description of this route in reverse **see p 744-747**.

Two local **tour agencies** are Safaris Corobicí (T/F 669-1091, 669-0544) and Transporte Palo Verde, F 669-0544), run by Jay Thomas Connerly and Gregg Dean, offering bird watching, boat trips down the Corobicí, no white water but lots of wildlife, and Río Bebedero to Palo Verde, bicycling and other trips. Safaris Corobicí is 4 km past Cañas on the Pan-American Highway, 25 m before the entrance to Centro Ecológico La Pacífica; Transporte Palo Verde is in *Hotel El Corral* in Cañas on the Pan-American Highway.

4 km N of Cañas is a hotel, **B** *La Pacífica*, on Pan-American Highway, T 669-0050, F 669-0555, Swiss-run, with good restaurant, cottages, cabins, pool, and rafting down the Río Bebedero to Palo Verde. There is free camping along the river. The property extends to 2,000 hectares, of which half is a cattle farm and half dry, tropical forest. You can have a free guided tour of the farm and there is an extensive library on dry, tropical forests. The restaurant *Rincón Corobicí*, next to *La Pacífica*, clean and pleasant, has a small zoo and offers rafting down Río Corobicí, T 669-0544.

On the Nicoya Peninsula, is the **Palo Verde National Park**, over 5,700 hectares of marshes with many water birds. Indeed, in the Laguna, over 50,000 birds are considered resident. Research Station, operated by OTS, T 240-5033, has accommodation facilities, ordinary visitors US$40 with meals, student researchers, US$22, senior researchers, US$32. Day visits with lunch, US$10, min 6 persons. Make advance reservations. Turn off the Pan-American Highway at **Bagaces**, half way between Cañas and Liberia, no public transport. The Palo Verde Administration offices are in Bagaces, next to service station, T 671-1062. Camping and possible lodging in park. Two ranger stations, Palo Verde and Catalina. Check roads in wet season, fantastic views from limestone cliffs.

If you turn N at Bagaces on Route 164 and drive through Guayabo to Km 30, you get to *Parador Las* **Nubes del Miravalles**, T 671-1011 ext 280, home cooking for breakfast, lunch and dinner, tent and mattress rental, horse rental, good hiking to Miravalles volcano and waterfalls, very friendly and hospitable people on working *finca*, from here you can take a boat up the Río Pizote to Lake Nicaragua.

The Pan-American Highway runs for 198 km from Cañas to the Nicaraguan border. It passes through the lowhills of **Guanacaste** Province, which includes the Peninsula of Nicoya and the lowlands at the head of the gulf. The Province, with its capital at Liberia, has a distinctive people, way of life, flora and fauna.

The smallholdings of the highlands give way here to large *haciendas* and great cattle estates. Maize, rice, cotton, beans and fruit are other products, and there is manganese at Playa Real. The rivers teem with fish; there are all kinds of wildlife in the uplands.

The people are open-handed, hospitable, fond of the pleasures of life: music, dancing (the Punto Guanacasteco has been officially declared the typical national dance), and merry-making (cattle and jollity often go together). There are many *fiestas* in January and February in the various towns and villages, which are well worth seeing. Rainfall is moderate: 1,000 to 2,000 mm a year, there is a long dry season which makes irrigation important, but the lowlands are deep in mud during the rainy season.

Liberia (pop 40,000) is a neat, clean, cattle town with a triangular, rather unattractive church in the most modern style and a small meticulous market (119 km from Esparza, 79 from Peñas Blancas). A well paved branch road leads SW into the Nicoya Peninsula. There is a tourist information centre, three blocks from the plaza, look for signs on the main road, helpful, English spoken, leave donation as the centre is not formally funded, open 0900-1800, closed Mon. Information however not always accurate. Social security hospital is quite good.

Hotels B *Boyeros*, on Pan-American Highway, T 666-0722, F 666-2529, pool, bath, restaurant; **B** *La Siesta*, Calle 4, Av 4-6, with bath, clean, swimming pool, helpful owner who speaks English; **B** *Las Espuelas*, 2 km S, expensive but good, swimming pool, round trip bus service from San José, day tour to San Antonio cattle ranch, US$60, American Express accepted (T 666-0144, F 233-1787); **B** *El Sitio*, just off highway on road to Nicoya, bath, a/c, good; **C** *Bramadero Motel*, not all rooms have bath, open air restaurant and bar but somewhat noisy, swimming pool, Guanacaste Tours located here, T 666-0306; **D** *Guanacaste* (previously *Oriental*), 4 blocks from plaza towards Pan-American Highway, 2 blocks S of bus station, friendly, clean, restaurant; **D** *Intercontinental*, new, good; **E** *La Ronda* (about 2 km S on the Highway, T 666-0417), with bath, restaurant; **D** *Liberia*, 50m from main square, with bath, **E** with shared bath, fans, clean, friendly, good information board and restaurant, noisy, rec; **E** *Motel Delfín*, 5 km N of Liberia on the Pan-American Highway, with bath, run down, large swimming pool; **F** *Pensión Golfito*, 1 block NE of square, basic, noisy, unfriendly, no fan.

Good Chinese **restaurants**: *Cantón*, *Shan Ghai*; *Hong Kong*, 1½ blocks E of church, Chinese, cheap and cheerful. *Pronto Pizzeria*, 100m E, 200m S from Parque Central, good food (not just pizzas) in a charming colonial house. On the W side of the Plaza is *Soda Las Tinajas*, which specializes in *refrescos*. *Jardín de Azúcar*, just off plaza, self service, good variety and tasty.

Puntonorte Travel Agency, T 666-0363, Frente Banco Anglo. For money exchange, ask around, eg *Restaurant Chun San*, behind the Cathedral.

Airport The Tomás Guardia International Airport at Liberia was re-opened in 1992; the new runway can handle large jets and charter flights. Flight details under San José.

Buses Bus station is outside town, 200m off Pan-American Highway, before junction to Nicoya. CNT bus Liberia-Peñas Blancas, US$1.25, first bus at 0530, several daily, usually very crowded at 0900 and 1200, 1½ hrs. Regular Pulmitan de Liberia buses Liberia- San José, 8 a day between 0430 and 2000, 4 hrs, US$2.70, you can buy the ticket the day before from the office (blue house) diagonally opp bus terminal. Liberia- Filadelfia-Santa Cruz-Nicoya, 14 a day between 0500-2030, 2 hrs, US$1.80, T 680-0111, Empresa Esquivel Liberia-Nicoya, 4 daily; to Playa Panamá and Playa Hermosa 1130 and 1900; to Playa de Coco 4 daily.

Rincón de la Vieja National Park (14,084 hectares, NE of Liberia) was created to preserve the area around the Volcán Rincón de la Vieja, including dry tropical forest and various geothermal curiosities: mudpots, hot sulphur springs, hot springs of various other kinds. The ridge of which the volcano is the highest peak can be seen from a wide area around Liberia; it is often shrouded in clouds. The area is cool at night and subjected to strong, gusty winds and violent rains; in the day it can be very hot, although always windy. These fluctuations mark all of the continental side, of which the ridge is a part. From time to time the volcano erupts, tossing rocks and lava down its slopes. To get there: a bumpy 2-hr ride from Liberia in a truck leaving at irregular hours; alternatively, inquire when the park's truck will visit Liberia; a frequent occurrence. A taxi costs US$35 from Liberia. If you take your own transport you will need four-wheel drive, although during the dry season a vehicle with high clearance is adequate. There are two ways into the park: the first one turns right off the Pan-American Highway 5 km NW of Liberia, through Curubandé and a private property (US$2.20-4 pp to cross); the second one is an unpaved road, turn off after Puente La Victoria, 25 km. Entrance

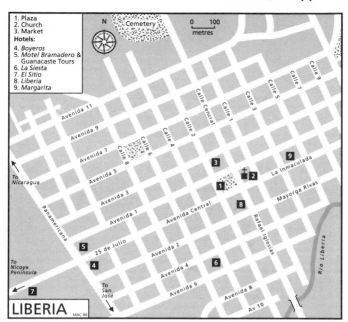

Map legend:
1. Plaza
2. Church
3. Market
Hotels:
4. Boyeros
5. Motel Bramadero & Guanacaste Tours
6. La Siesta
7. El Sitio
8. Liberia
9. Margarita

N
Cemetery
0   100
metres

Avenida 11
Avenida 9
Avenida 7
Avenida 5
Avenida 3
Avenida 1
Avenida Central
Avenida 2
25 de Julio
Avenida 4
Avenida 6
Avenida 8
Av 10

Calle Central
Calle 1
Calle 2
Calle 3
Calle 4
Calle 5
Calle 6
Calle 7
Calle 9

La Inmaculada
Mayorga Rivas
Rafael Iglesias
Río Liberia

Panamericana

To Nicaragua
To Nicoya Peninsula
To San José

LIBERIA MAC 86

US$1.50 and US$1 to stay in the shelter, or camp. Accommodation at **B** *Hacienda Lodge Guachipelin*, T 441-6545, F 442-1910, meals available, 10 rooms, naturalist guides, riding, hot springs, sulphur springs, mud pools, waterfalls: 5 km N of Liberia turn right and go 18 km on an unpaved road through Carubande to the main gate (transport from Liberia arranged, US$16 pp round trip). Also *Buena Vista Lodge*, T 695-6147, pickup arranged from Liberia. If you stay at the farm, **C** *Albergue Rincón de la Vieja*, (affiliated to the Youth Hostel network) T 666-0473, inc food, pool, call the proprietor, Alvaro Wiessel, who will pick you up in Liberia. Also packages inc transport from San José. The *Albergue* is on the edge of the Park, there are horses for rent, guides, tours. From there it is 3¼ hrs to the volcano, 30 mins to las Pailas, 45 mins to the thermal springs, Azufrales, 2¼ hrs to the Hidden Waterfalls. You can stay for free in an old, spacious, refurbished *hacienda* 2 km inside the park. Bring your own food and bedding. From the old *hacienda* you can hike to the boiling mudpots and come back in the same day; the sulphur springs are on a different trail and only 1 hr away. Lots of birds including toucans, parrots, and also howler monkeys and coatimundi. There are also lots of ticks and other biting insects. Horses can be rented from the park. The climb to the volcano requires camping near the top (need a tent), or at the warden's station, in order to ascend early in the morning before the clouds come in.

20 km N of Liberia is Costa Rica's first commercial ostrich farm, blueneck and black breeds; T 228-6646/231-5068, Javnai Menahen for information on tours.

37 km N of Liberia, about half-way to the Nicaraguan border, is the **Santa Rosa National Park** (entry US$2; camping US$2.15 pp). Together with the Murciélago Annex, which lies N of the developed park, it preserves some of the last dry tropical forests in Costa Rica, and shelters abundant and relatively easy-to-see wildlife. They are also attempting to reforest some of the cattle ranches of the area (helped by the fact that cattle have not been profitable in recent years). During the dry season, the animals depend on the water holes, and are thus easy to find (except at the end of the season when the holes dry up). Santa Rosa National Park (37,118 hectares) is easy of access from San José, as it lies W of the Pan-American Highway, about one hour N of Liberia. Any bus going to Peñas Blancas (from Liberia) on the Nicaraguan border will drop you right at the entrance at a cost of US$0.70, ½ hour. Last bus

returns to Liberia at about 1800. There is a pleasant campground at Administration, about 7 km from the entrance with giant strangler figs that shade your tent from the stupendously hot sun, and very adequate sanitary facilities, picnic tables, and so forth. There is a small *comedor* for meals and drinks near the camp ground but rec to bring some of your own supplies; a tent is useful—essential in the wet season. You can rent tents in Liberia for US$5/day with a US$100 deposit; ask at the tourist information centre. You may be able to sleep on the verandah of one of the scientists' houses. Bring a mosquito net and insect repellent. If the water is not running, ask at Administration. Take care, there are plenty of poisonous snakes. In the park is the Santa Rosa *hacienda* (*Casona*), at the start of the nature trail and close to the camp. There the patriots repelled the invasion of the filibuster Walker, who had entrenched himself in the main building. A Museo Histórico de Santa Rosa in the *casona* is open daily 0800-1630.

Michael Tesch and Leone Thiele of Cape Paterson, Australia, write 'Playa Naranjo (3 hrs' walk or more or use 4WD) and Playa Nancite (about the same distance from the entrance) are major nesting sites of Leatherback and Olive Ridley sea turtles. The main nesting season is between August and October (although stragglers are seen up to January regularly) when flotillas of up to 10,000 Ridley turtles arrive at night on the 7 km long Playa Nancite. Females clumsily lurch up the beach, scoop out a 2-foot hole, deposit and bury an average of 100 ping-pong-ball sized eggs before returning exhausted to the sea' (**see also Optional, p 761**). Playa Nancite is a restricted access beach; you need a written permit to stay there free, otherwise, US$1 per day to camp, or US$1.50 in dormitories. Permits from SPN in San José, and the Park Administration building at Santa Rosa. Make sure you have permission before going, rangers may otherwise give you a hard time. Research has been done in the Playa Nancite area on howler monkeys, coatis and the complex interrelation between the fauna and the forest. No horses are available to rent. Playa Naranjo has good camping, drinking water and a barbecue. The beach is unspoilt and quiet and very good for surfing.

The last town before the border is **La Cruz**, with a bank (terribly slow service for exchange of cash or TCs) and hotels. **F** *El Faro del Norte*, just off the Panamericana, without bath, friendly, pleasant, clean; **F** *Pensión Tica*, without bath, dark, basic, no fan, mosquitoes; **F** *Cabinas Santa Rita*, nice, clean, cheap, on main road, 200m from bus terminal; *Soda Estadio*, good, cheap; *Restaurant Mirador*, at the end of the only paved street, has superb views; *Ehecatl*, good fish and rice, also has lovely views over the bay. At nearby Ciruelas de Miramar, there is a good restaurant; *Palenque Garabito*; try their fried yucca. 16 km E of La Cruz is **A** pp *Hotel Hacienda Los Inocentes*, on slopes of volcano Orosí, inc meals, 11 rooms with bath, pool, horses, forest trails and guides, T 265-5484 or 679-9190.

W of La Cruz, on Bahía Salinas looking over to Isla Bolaños, is *La Salinas Trailer Park y Cabinas*, drinking water, showers, toilets, tennis, barbecue, fishing boats and horses to rent, 1 km beach, T 233-6912, 228-2447, 228-0690, PO Box 449-1007, San José. **Isla Bolaños** is a 25-hectare National Wildlife Refuge to protect the nesting sites of the brown pelican, frigatebird and American Oystercatcher. The island is covered with dry forest and you can only walk round the island at low tide. No camping allowed. The incoming tidal surge is very dangerous, be off the island before the tide comes in.

At **Peñas Blancas** there are a duty-free shop, two banks (the one in the main building changes TCs but closes at 1400, the one in *aduana* changes cash, closes at 1430) and a black market (several express or ordinary buses a day from/to San José 4 hrs or 5½ hrs, only the earliest from San José will get you to the border before it closes). There is a good bar and restaurant adjoining the Costa Rican immigration offices; a good free map of Costa Rica is available from the tourist office at the border (the desk opp the counter where one pays entry tax). Costa Rican entry tax: 75 colones, exit tax US$5; on leaving Costa Rica you have to go through two passport checks, trolley pullers charge US$0.50 to carry bags between these posts, a short distance. (Entering Costa Rica here you must visit the Ministry of Health post and show anti-malaria tablets, you will be given a card which you must show the doctor if you become ill. Visa stamps, US$20, are given at the border, but officials may try to send you back to Rivas.) Across the border, passports are inspected on the Nicaraguan side, then you must take the minibus to Sapoá, where entry formalities are carried out, 4 km away (US$0.65, plus US$0.15 per bag). The Costa Rican border offices are closed 1200-1300 and 1800; the Nicaraguan offices 1230-1330 and 1600 (both open 0800, but note Nicaragua is in a different time zone from Costa Rica). Crossing to Nicaragua may be a slow process; if you arrive when a Tica or Sirca bus is passing through this is especially true (at least 3 hrs). If you have no outward ticket for Costa Rica, you can buy a cheap bus ticket back to Nicaragua at the border (valid for 1 year). Entering Costa Rica by car, first pay your entrance stamp, then queue up at the immigration desk to hand in your details; opposite is the desk for car papers (at least 1000 colones). For documents and other requirements, see under **Information for visitors—Documents**.

THE NICOYA PENINSULA (5)

Fringed by white sand beaches, hilly and hot. Few towns and poor roads; a few large hotel resorts are taking over what were isolated coves; small reserves to protect wildlife and the geological formations of Barra Honda.

The Nicoya Peninsula can be reached by road via Liberia (bus Liberia-Nicoya, **see p 754**); or one can take the Pan-American Highway to a point 62 km beyond Puntarenas, at a sign to Río Tempisque ferry. After crossing on this ferry (hourly 0630-2030, car US$3.50, bicycle or motorbike US$1, pedestrians US$0.50) one can drive to Nicoya (at Mansión junction there is a good restaurant, *Tony Zecca Ristorante Il Nonno*, sandwiches and steaks, reasonable prices, menu in 6 languages, interesting international visitor's book to sign). An 800m bridge is to be built across the river 5 km N of the present ferry. A third route is to take the Salinero car ferry from Puntarenas across the Gulf of Nicoya to Playa Naranjo, US$1.15 pp, US$3.35 for motorcycle or bicycle, US$8.50 per car, 1 hr, crossings start at 0400 with 4 or 5 crossings a day, T 661-1069 for exact times. Snacks and drinks sold on the ferry. The ferry dock is about 1 km from Puntarenas bus station, local buses run between the two. Buses meet the ferry for Nicoya (through Carmona, 40 km unpaved, 30 km paved road, crowded, noisy, frequently break down, US$1.25, 2¼ hrs), Sámara (US$1.30), Coyote, Bejuco and Jicaral. A fourth route is to take the boat from Puntarenas to Paquera (1½ hrs, US$2, 0615 and 1500 does not run in bad weather, no cars, passengers only, has toilets, drinks and snacks). On arrival, get on the bus as quickly as possible (to Cóbano 2-3 hrs, US$1.25, bad road, to Montezuma US$2.60, 1½ hrs at least) pay on the bus, or get a taxi. Boat Paquera-Puntarenas at 0830 and 1730; tickets are sold only when the incoming boat has docked. In Puntarenas this boat docks in the canal N of the city centre; it is a 10-minute walk due S to the bus terminal for San José. All the beaches on the Nicoya Peninsula are accessible by road in the dry season. Most places can be reached by bus from Nicoya. There is no bus connection between Playa Naranjo and Paquera. Montezuma (popular) can be reached in 4 hrs from Puntarenas if you get the early launch.

Nicoya, on the Peninsula, is a pleasant little town distinguished by possessing the country's second-oldest church. The main square is leafy, with occasional concerts. Use the telephones on the square for international calls.

Hotels D *Curime*, with bath, restaurant; **D** *Jenny*, with bath, T 685-5050, a/c, towels and soap, TV, spotless, rec; **E** *Chorotega*, with bath (F without), very good, clean, quiet, clothes washing facilities; **E** *Las Tinajas*, near bus station, with bath, modern, clean, good value; **E/F** *Cabinas Loma Bonita*, behind hospital, T 685-5269, fans, bar, shaded parking. **F** *Ali*, dirty, avoid; **F** *La Elegancia*, with bath; **E** *Pensión Venecia*, opp old church, rec.

Restaurants A good restaurant is *Chop Suey* (Chinese); *Daniela*, breakfast, lunches, coffee, refrescos, good; *Restaurant Jade*, 1½ blocks behind church, Chinese, not rec. Opposite *Chorotega* is *Soda El Triángulo*, good juices and snacks, friendly Japanese owners.

Exchange Banks charge commission and are very slow, but the a/c is welcome; try *Soda El Triángulo*, see above.

19 km NE of Nicoya and 12 km SE of Santa Cruz, is *Guaitil*, where local artisans specialize in reproductions of indigenous Chorotegan pottery. They use the same methods used by Indians long ago, with minimal or no use of a wheel and no artificial paints. Ceramics are displayed at the local *pulpería*, or outside houses. At *San Vicente*, 2 km SE of Guaitil, local craftsmen work and sell their pottery at a new building in the centre.

Beaches on the Nicoya Peninsula There can be dangerous undertows on

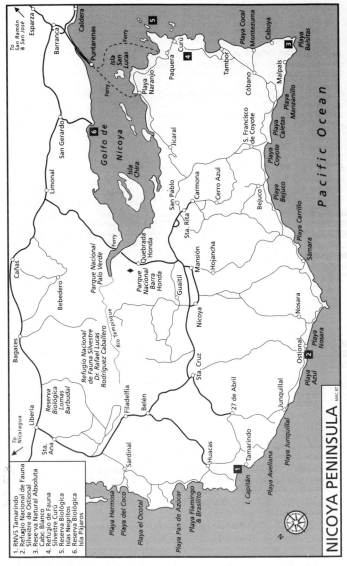

NICOYA PENINSULA MAC 87

1. RNVS Tamarindo
2. Refugio Nacional de Fauna Silvestre de Ostional
3. Rese'va Natural Absoluta Cabo Blanco
4. Refugio de Fauna Silvestre Curú
5. Reserva Biológica Islas Negritos
6. Reserva Biológica Isla Pájaros

exposed beaches; the safest bathing is from those beaches where there is a protective headland, such as at Playa Panamá in the N. Beaches are described here working round the peninsula from where the car ferry docks in the Gulf.

At **Playa Naranjo** is B *Oasis del Pacífico* (D in rainy season), a/c, bath, clean, quiet, pool, good restaurant, free transport from ferry, rec; C *El Paso*, with bath, D without, cold water, clean, pool, T 661-2610; *Disco Bar Restaurante Maquinay*, past *El Paso*, has a couple of rooms, E with shower, insects, Belgian-run, disco on Sun; several expensive eating places by the ferry landing, also a gas station.

North of Playa Tambor is the **Curu National Wildlife Refuge**. Only 84 hectares, but 5 different habitats exist here with 110 species of birds. Access is through private land, T 661-2392/6392 in advance and ask for Doña Julieta.

At **Tambor**, much of the beach has been absorbed by the large and controversial A+ *Playa Tambor Beach Resort*, inc meals, 5-star, all amenities, tennis, pool, exercise room, TV, entertainment, bus from Montezuma stops outside gate, most people arrive by plane to the airstrip or by resort bus, T 661-2039, F 661-2069, Apartado Postal 771-1150, La Uruca, San José. Built around a cattle farm by the Barceló group, of Spain, the resort is alleged to have encroached on the public beach, drained a swamp which was a wildfowl habitat and imported sand without permission from other areas along the coast, making a white sand beach where previously it was black. A second stage is planned at Punta Piedra Amarilla, with 500-ship yacht marina, villas and a total of 1,100 rooms.

Also at Tambor, E *Dos Lagartos*, T 661-1122, ext 236, cheap, clean, but also poor management. L *Tango Mar*, T 661-2798, 3 km from Tambor. The beach is beautiful: 14 km long, rolling surf, 1½ hrs on a boneshaking road from ferry; cruise ships 5 km from Puntarenas come here. On the beach, E *Hotel Hermosa Playa*, basic but clean, shared bath, restaurant. Follow signs on main road as you enter town. *Bahía Ballena Yacht Club*, 15 min walk from Tambor, friendly, free English book exchange, weekly traditional dances, good restaurant/bar, excellent place if you are looking for a crew position on a yacht June to August, many US craft here at that time. There is a shop with public phones. Good, American-owned restaurant on the jetty, best value, take torch for returning to hotel at night.

Cóbano, near Montezuma, can be reached by bus from Paquera ferry terminal, and buses for Tambor, Cóbano and Montezuma meet the launches from Puntarenas (there is an airstrip, see **Internal Flights** San José). All roads out of Cóbano, N, W and S, require 4WD. Cóbano has a petrol/gas station.

From Cóbano it is a ½-hr ride by taxi or hitch) to **Montezuma**, a very popular small village on the sea (hence noisy and not too clean). It has become very touristy and, in busy periods, hotels fill up every day, so check in early. Although it does get crowded, there are some wonderful beaches, many are rocky, with strong waves making it difficult to swim, but very scenic. There are beautiful walks along the beach, sometimes sandy, sometimes rocky, always lined with trees. There is a tourist information centre, Monte Aventuras, which is very helpful and often knows which hotel has space; ask here first before looking around (ask for Jaime or Rebeca). The centre hires bicycles, US$11/day and organizes tours, eg to Tortuga Island (1 hr away), white sand, palms, whole day with lunch and snorkelling, US$30; Sunset Cruise, US$17; 4-day, 3-night Ecotour to Curú, Arenal, Cano Negro and Barra Honda, US$180 pp inc transport, accommodation, breakfast, guides, minimum 6.

Lodging and food B *Mangoes*, 20 cabins, clean, new; C *Hotel Amor de Mar*, lovely garden, breakfast and snacks available, clean, friendly, away from town, rec; C *Restaurant El Pargo Feliz*, has cabins with bath, and serves good food in a calm atmosphere; D-B *Alfaro*, prices vary according to demand, beware overcharging, rents tents (US$7 for 2), poor facilities but clean tents and mattresses; D *Cabinas Mar y Cielo*, with restaurant, good food, popular, has cabins for up to 8; D *Casa Blanca*, 3 rooms, fans, kitchen facilities, German-owned; D *Cabinas Las Rocas*, 20 mins S of Montezuma, good but quite expensive meals, small, seashore setting, isolated; 5 km S is D *Fernando Morales Cabins*; see also Cabuya below (these 3 places usually have space when other places are full); D *Montezuma Pacific*, bath, hot water, a/c, T 661-1122 ext 200; **D** *Hermanos y Hermanas de la Madre Tierra*, 2 km from village, camping F, American-run, higher up and cooler at night than on beach, vegan food, small portions, overpriced, nice walks; *Hotel La Aurora*, run by Kenneth (German) and Angela (Costa Rican) Kock, 8 rooms with bath, fan, mosquito net, breakfast room, garden, hammocks, T/F 661 2320, also boat trips for fishing or snorkelling; **E** *Pensión Tucán*, clean, shared shower and toilet, fan, mosquito net on window; **E** *Hotel Montezuma*, T 661-2472, next to *Mar y Cielo*, F in off season, with private shower (cold) and fan, cheaper with shared bath, ask for sea view, large rooms (but some have cracked white asbestos wall covering), clean, restaurant (adds 23% tax and service), small book exchange; **E** *Lucy*, opposite *Alfaro*, without bath, sea views, friendly, follow road around the beach to the S, rec; **F** *Cabinas Karen*, price varies according to length of stay, 2 rooms in small, cosy clean cottage (no electricity) in the village, plus 3 one-room beach front cottages with outdoor kitchen in Karen's 170-acre private nature reserve, which has lots of wild monkeys etc (open only to those staying at Doña Karen's). Doña Karen, who lives 1½ km N, is Danish, speaks English, is very friendly. She and her late husband established Costa Rica's first national park; the income from renting rooms goes towards the upkeep of her nature reserve. After her death it will be a national park too. **E** *Pensión Arenas*, on the beach, run by Doña Meca, basic but OK, without bath, with fan, friendly, cool, clean, also camping, but noisy cockerels at dawn. **F** *Cabinas Jenny*. Next door to the *Cabinas Karen* there is the **Sano Banano**, a health food restaurant, good vegetarian food, large helpings, milkshakes, fresh fruit and yoghurt, owned by Dutch/Americans. At night they show movies free if you spend over US$1.50 on food or US$1.25 pp (also has cabins on beach, B). Several restaurants, eg *Tutiles Spaghetti y Pizzas*, Italian, quite pricey, at back of village; the **Soda**, by the *tienda* is good value, delicious shrimp; fruit and vegetable cars come to Montezuma.

Made in Costa Rica souvenir shop, next to *Hotel Montezuma*, is good; a percentage of the profits goes to an ecological fund, including clearing up the beach; also has book exchange.

Transport Bus Montezuma-**Paquera** daily at 0530 and 1330, tickets available in advance from tourist information centre; be at bus stop in centre in good time as the bus fills up quickly, US$2.60, 1 hr 40 mins. Bus connects with boats to Puntarenas. Taxi Montezuma-**Cóbano** US$3.50; taxi Paquera-Montezuma US$12.

Close to the village, 20 mins up the Montezuma river, is a beautiful, huge waterfall with a big, natural swimming pool (it's beyond a smaller waterfall). Intrepid walkers can carry on up to further waterfalls but it is very dangerous and fatal accidents have been reported. 6 km N of Montezuma is another waterfall with a pool right by the beach; the walk there passes Playa Cocal (huge, flat, sandy), and Playa Cocalito, where Sr Vásquez lives in a house with Cocalito written on the balcony and sells coconuts and mangoes in season. Horses for hire from the hotels, but carefully inspect that the horses are fit and not overworked, for the sake of the horses! Luis hires horses at US$2.50 pp per hour without guide for experienced riders, but is not recommended. Roger, though, is good and takes care of his horses, contact him at the little white house opposite the grocery store.

11 km from Montezuma is the **Cabo Blanco Reserve** (1,172 hectares). Marine birds include frigate birds, pelicans and redfooted boobies. There are also monkeys, anteaters, kinkajou and collared peccary. Bathing in the sea or under small waterfall. Open 0800-1600, jeep from Montezuma US$11 pp at 0700, stops for breakfast, arrives 0800, returns 1430, juice on way back (all included in price), guide US$3.65 extra (tickets sold at tourist information centre). 300m from the entrance is **F** *El Palenque*, camping, restaurant, American run, friendly, rec. 6 km from the entrance is beautiful Playa Balsitas, where there are lots of pelicans and howler monkeys. At **Cabuya**, 2 km from Cabo Blanco Reserve is **C** *Cabinas y Restaurante El Ancla de Oro* (also some at E), cabins with shared bathroom, seafood restaurant, filling breakfasts, owned by Alex Villalobos, T 661-1122 ext 201, horses US$20/day with local guide, transport from Parquera launch available. The sea here can be dirty and polluted. Just before Cabuya is **La Conchita**, with 2 rooms. A road goes beyond Cabuya to the attractive little village of Mal País on the W coast of the peninsula. The coast here is virtually unspoilt with long white beaches, creeks and natural pools, just a few facilities, including a camping place.

The beach at **Sámara**, 37 km from Nicoya, is recommended as probably the safest major bathing beach in Costa Rica. The litter problem is being tackled with litter bins, warning signs, refuse collection and bottle banks on Playa Carrillo. Bus from Nicoya, US$1.15, 2 hrs, once daily (bad road, poor bus). Express bus to San José daily at 0400; from San José, C 14, Av 3-5, at 1200, T 222-2750. It is not possible to go S from Sámara along the coast to Montezuma, except in 4 WD vehicle; not enough traffic for hitching. Sansa operates flights Mon, Wed and Fri from San José; Travelair to Playa Carrillo, Wed, Sun. **A+ Guanamar Beach Resort**, on hill at end of Playa Carrillo, T 220-0722, F 220-2095, beautiful view from bar, pool, satellite TV, private airstrip, horseriding, sport fishing; **A+ Las Brisas del Pacífico**, bungalows with a/c, hotel rooms with fan, A, T 680-0876, hotel part on hill, beautiful grounds, direct access to beach, pool, expensive restaurant, German-owned; **B Marbella**, also German-run, beautiful grounds, pool, good service, about 300m from beach, rec; **E Doña Marta**, on beach, with bath, not too clean, camping allowed in garden US$0.75; next door is **Camping Coco**, clean, with showers, lights in trees, good for hammocks, rec, occasionally noisy, good restaurant behind (there is another good restaurant on the beach with a fishing boat outside); **C Cabinas Bellavista**, horses for rent; **C-D Cabinas Cecilia**, excellent food; **E Cabinas Los Almendros**, on beach, restaurant, disco Sat; **E Cabinas Punto**, Sámara. Camping on the beach possible. N of Sámara is **Nosara** (one bus daily from Nicoya at 1300, US$2, 2 hrs, 31 km and 5 flights a week from San José), with 2 beaches, Guiones, which is safe for swimming, and Peladas; a colony of North Americans has formed the Nosara Association, to protect its wildlife and forests, and prevent exploitation. There is the **A Hotel Playa de Nosara** (T 680-0495), expensive restaurant; **B Rancho Suizo Lodge**, T 255-0011, Swiss-owned, bungalows, restaurant, hiking, bird-and turtle-watching; **B Villa Taype**, T 680-0763, 2 pools, tennis, restaurant, bar; **F Pensión Estancia Nosara**, and a condominium. 12 km S of Nosara is **L Hotel Villaggio La Guaria Morada**, at Punta Guiones de Garza, a luxury beach hotel (30 bungalows, Italian restaurant, club house, bars, pool, disco, T 680-0784).

N of Nosara is Playa Ostional where Olive Ridley turtles lay their eggs in July-November and where a coastal strip is now protected by the **Refugio Nacional de Fauna Silvestre de Ostional**. The turtles arrive for nesting at high tide in the last moon of the lunar cycle. The villagers are allowed to harvest the eggs in a designated area of the beach, the rest are protected and monitored. There is very basic accommodation in cabins next to the village shop in Ostional. Outside the egg laying period it is exceptionally quiet.

A number of beaches are reached by unpaved roads from the Nicoya-Liberia road. They can be reached by bus from the Liberia bus station. **Playa Junquillal** is reached by taking a bus from Liberia to Santa Cruz (on the Nicoya road), then bus at 1000 or 1415 from Guillermo Sánchez store to Paraíso (US$0.80), from where it is a 4 km walk to Playa Junquillal, or take a car from one of the cantinas. An express bus goes to San José daily at 0500, 5 hrs, returning 1400 from C 20, Av 3, T 221-7202. **A Hotel Antumalal**, with bath, pool, T 680-0506; **A Villa Serena**, with meals, T 680-0737, German owners, helpful; **B Iguanazú**, 3 km N of Playa Junquillal, 24 rooms with private bathroom, pool, T 232-1423; **E Junquillal**, cabins, nice, friendly, good food.

Another good beach is **Playa Tamarindo**, which has an airport (Sansa Mon, Wed, Fri, to San José, Travelair daily), and is served by buses from Santa Cruz, 1030, 1500. Tamarindo to Santa Cruz bus 0600, 1200, US$1. Express bus from San José daily 1600, C 20, Av 3. From San José, C 14, Av 3-5, T 222-2750, departs 0715 and 1530. There is a small, expensive, mini-market. **A+ Hotel Tamarindo Diria**, with bath, T 680-0652, excellent, full range of services, good restaurants, house parrots; **A+ El Jardín de Edén**, T 231-5221, F 231-6346, inc breakfast, 150m from beach on hill, 18 rooms with fan and a/c, jacuzzi, 2 pools, 2 apartments; **A** *Pueblo Dorado*, T 222-5741, 22 rooms, a/c, pool; **D** *Cabinas Marielos*, with bath, clean, use of kitchen; **C** *Pozo Azul*, cabins, E in low season with bargaining, cooking facilities, clean, good, swimming pool; **D** *Cabinas Zullymar*, rec, friendly bats, and **E** *Dolis*, basic (camping nearby, a cheap place to sling a hammock or rent a tent but thefts reported). **Restaurants: Fiesta del Mar**, large thatched open barn, good food, good value; *Stellas*, very good, try dorado with mango cream. *Johan's Bakery*, good breakfasts from 0600, exceptional pastries and pizzas; *Coconut Café*, pizzas, pastries and best fish on beach. The beaches go on for many km. **A+-B** *Hotel Las Tortugas*, is at *Playa Grande*, N of Playa Tamarindo and surrounded by the **Tamarindo Wildlife Refuge**, 11 rooms with bathroom, pool, restaurant, meals included, T 680-0496, giant leatherback turtle nesting ground November-March.

At **Playa Flamingo** (white sand and aggressively developed) are **L** *The Presidential Suites*, (T 680-0620-0444), **B** *Villas Flamingo*, T 680-0960; **A** *Centro Vacacional Playa Bahía Flamingo*, T 680-0976; **L** *Club Flamingo*, T 233-8056; *Flamingo Beach Condo Rentals* and **L** *Club Playa Flamingo*, T 680-0620. The *Flamingo Beach* operates bus service to San José Mon, Wed, Fri, Sun, dep San José 0800, Flamingo 1400. At **Playa Potrero** (black sand): **D** *Hotel Potrero*, T 680-0669; bus from Santa Cruz at 1030 and 1430. **Playa Conchal**, a beautiful 3 km beach full of shells, recently bought by Spanish interests and due to have huge resort built on it, starting 1994. **Playa Brasilito**, several hotels/cabinas along the road: **D** *Al Odisea*, *cabinas*, hot water, helpful owner, Marc, T 654-4125, *Bar Marisquería* attached, excellent food, reasonable prices, fresh juices rec. **Playa Pan de Azúcar**: **A** *Hotel Sugar Beach*, T 654-4242, 10 rooms, 6 with a/c, 50m from beach, fishing trips and horseriding available, 7 km N of Playa Flamingo. **Playa Ocotal**: a particularly nice beach, good diving facilities, **L** *Hotel El Ocotal*, T 670-0230.

Popular (but noisy) is **Playa del Coco** in an attractive islet-scattered bay hemmed in by rocky headlands, the best beaches are to the S; to reach it one should leave the bus at Comunidad. There are bars, restaurants and one or two motels along the sandy beach; all activities concentrate on the beach and fishing. Snorkelling and diving are nothing special. **D** *Cabinas Chalé*; **B** *Flor de Itabo*, T 670-0011/0292, F 670-0003, a/c rooms, 5 bungalows, good restaurant and bar with really cold beer, pool, horse-riding, excursions, specialists in big-game fishing; **E** *Casino Playa del Coco*, with bath and cockroaches; **D** *Luna Tica*, T 670-0127, also has a dormitory (friendly, clean), both usually full at weekends. Bus to San José 0915, return 1000, C 14, Av 1-3, T 222-1650, also 5 buses daily from Liberia 0530-1815 (Arata company). At **Playa Hermosa** is **B** *Playa Hermosa Cabinas*, run by an American couple, T 670-0136, clean, good reasonably-priced food; also cheaper cabins (F pp); **E** *Cabinas Vallejos*; 3 small restaurants on the beach. **A+** *Condovac La Costa*, T 670-0267, luxury bungalows, a/c, more expensive are the suites with kitchenettes, TV, a/c, lots of hot water, arranges scuba-diving etc, good beach access, good restaurants and bars; **B** *Condo hotel Costa Alegre*, T 670-0218; **L** *Complejo Turístico Los Corales*, T 670-0255; cheaper places at the other end of the beach. Walking either to the left or the right you can find isolated beaches with crystal-clear water. Express bus to San José daily 0500; from San José, C 12, Av 5-7, at 1530; also buses from Liberia, empresa Esquivel, 1130, 1900, return 0500, 1600. Bus leaves you some 500m from accommodation.

At **Playa de Panamá** is **D** *Los Bananos*, cabins, restaurant and bar, with bath, friendly, English spoken, good hiking, swimming, horseriding can be arranged, rec (address is Apdo 137, Liberia, Guanacaste); **D** *Cabinas Vallejo*, with bath; camping possible on beach; *Jardín del Mar* with good facilities, restaurant, tents for hire; a few basic fish restaurants, one *pulpería*—a peaceful place. Buy food inland in *Santa Cruz*, NW of Nicoya. Santa Cruz is known as Costa Rica's National Folklore City because of its colourful *fiestas*, dancing and regional food. January is the month for the *fiesta* dedicated to Santo Cristo de Esquipulas. Much of the town was damaged by fire in February 1993. Hotels in Santa Cruz: **D** *Palenque Diria*, bath, restaurant; **F** *Posada Tu Casa*. *La Tortillera* is an excellent place to eat. Bus San José-Santa Cruz, 5 daily, 5 hrs, US$2.80, C 20, Av 1-3; bus Santa Cruz-Tamarindo, two a day, US$1, also to Playa Flamingo and nearby beaches; Santa Cruz-Nicoya, US$0.35; taxi Santa Cruz-Nicoya US$10.50 for 2 people.

Barra Honda National Park Small park in the N of the Nicoya Peninsula (2,295 hectares). No permit required, entry US$1.50. Created to protect some caves (in particular Terciopelo) on a *mesa* and small remainders of dry tropical forest at the *mesa's* foot. First go to Nicoya, there are several buses a day to Quebrada Honda (first bus 1030, last bus returns for Nicoya 1630, giving you only 2 hrs in the Park), a settlement one hour's walk away, from the park, or get a lift. The park office is there at Barra Honda, at the foot of the *mesa*, and there are two different trails to the top; two hour's hiking. Also noteworthy are the *cascadas*, bizarre limestone fountains built by sedimentation on a seasonal riverbed. You'll need a guide to get here, as the trails are hopelessly muddled by cowpaths; arrange in advance for the visit to the cave. A full visit requires harnesses, ropes and guides, US$33 for 3 guides, US$11 pp for equipment. Avoid coming in the rainy season (May to November), but the dry season is exceedingly hot in the open fields. Bring your own food from Nicoya. Turinsa operates a Sat tour from San José to the Barra Honda caves, T 221-9185, US$90 inc breakfast and lunch. Las Delicias Ecotourism Project, owned and operated by local community at park entrance, T 685-5580, 3 bungalows, comfortable accommodation, camping, F, Costa Rican meals at reasonable prices, guided tours available.

FROM SAN JOSE TO THE ATLANTIC COAST (6)

Initially dominated by active volcanoes and mountainous rain forest, the land falls away to the flat Caribbean lowlands, sparsely populated, with major tropical rain forest national parks at Tortuguero and Barra del Colorado, where canals and rivers are the means of communication.

There are two routes from San José to Puerto Limón on the Atlantic coast. The main road goes over the Cordillera Central through the Braulio Carrillo National Park down to Guápiles and Siquirres. This new road is prone to fog and can be dangerous. The old road follows the route of the railway to Cartago, S of Irazú volcano to Turrialba and Siquirres.

Braulio Carrillo National Park This large park was created to protect the high rain forest N of San José from the impact of the new San José-Guápiles-Puerto Limón highway. It extends for 44,099 hectares with five different types of forest (entry US$1.50). Wildlife includes many species of birds, jaguar, ocelot and Baird's tapir. Various travel agencies offer naturalist tours, approx US$65 from San José. San José to Guápiles and Puerto Limón buses go through the park. There are three main centres, two are on the highway: Zurquí as you enter from San José with services, a visitor centre and trails, Carillo, 2 km inside the park from the bridge over the Rio Sucio at the Guápiles end where trails include the 'Sendero Botella' in the rain forest (information at the Ranger Station), with waterfall en route. The views down the Río Patria canyon are impressive. Bird watchers will also get their fill. The park also includes **Barva Volcano**, 2,906m. The latter is only accessible from Heredia, there is no entrance from the new highway; take a bus to **San José de la Montaña** (hotels with beautiful views across the Meseta Central: **A** *El Pórtico*, T 237-6022, cosy, clean, pool, sauna, good food, rec; **D** *Cabinas Montaña Cypresal*, T 237-4466, **D** *Cabinas Las Ardillas*, T 237-6022, all with bath; **A** *Hotel Chalet Tirol*, 3 km N of *Castillo Country Club*, bath, beautiful views, T 267-7070, tours to *Dundee Ranch Hotel* at Cascajal) from there it is 4 hrs' walk to Sacramento (**B** *Volcán Barva Lodge*, one cabin with kitchen sleeps 4, more cabins being built, T 228-3197), but some buses (about 4 a day) continue towards Sacramento halving the walk time (otherwise walk, hitchhike, or arrange a ride with the park director). Taxi Heredia-Sacramento, US$7. Ranger station and camping site nearby, from which 3 km of easy climb to the top. Good views; no permit needed here. Jungle Trails (T 255-3486) offers day trips from San José to Barva Volcano. Easter Week is a good choice. The park is widely known among (illegal) birdcatchers. Be careful when leaving your car, regular reports of theft from rental cars.

Guápiles, 1 hr from San José, is the centre of the Río Frío banana region. Standard Fruit have built about 75 km of railway lines on from Guápiles

Hotels E *Keng Wa* and **E** *As de Oro* (with bath); all **F**: *Hugo Sánchez Cheng*, *Cariari* and *Alfaro* (with bath, above noisy bar); *Hospedaje Guápiles*, good, T 710-6179. Before reaching Guápiles, 800m off the highway at the Río Corinto is *Morpho Lodge*, opened 1993, good for hiking, river swimming, cooking facilities.

The new highway runs alongside a railway to **Guácimo**, and on to **Siquirres**, a clean, friendly town and junction for roads and railways. Hotels (all **E**) include *Wilson*, *Cocal*, *Idamar*, *Las Brisbas* and *Vidal*. Also *Cabinas Pacaya*, on the main road. Buses leave San José (Calle 12, Av 7-9) every 45 mins.

Cartago, 22½ km from San José on a toll road (US$0.15), stands at 1,439m at the foot of the Irazú volcanic peak and is encircled by mountains. It was founded in 1563 and was the capital until 1823. It has a population of only 30,000, though the neighbourhood is densely populated. Earthquakes destroyed it in 1841 and 1910, and it has been severely shaken on other occasions. That is why there are no old buildings, though some have been rebuilt in colonial style.

The most interesting church is the Basilica, rebuilt 1926 in Byzantine style, of Nuestra Señora de Los Angeles, the Patroness of Costa Rica; it houses La Negrita, under 15 cm high, an Indian image of the Virgin which draws pilgrims from all over Central America because of great healing powers attributed to it. The feast day is 2 August, when the image is carried in procession to other churches in Cartago and there are celebrations throughout Costa Rica. In the Basilica is an extraordinary collection of very finely-made silver and gold images, no larger than 3 cm high, of various parts of the human anatomy, presumably offered in the hope of being healed. Worth seeing is the old parish church (La Parroquia), ruined by the 1910 earthquake and now converted into a delightful garden retreat with flowers, fish and humming birds. There is an impressive procession on Good Friday.

Hotels E *Casa Blanca* in Barrio Asís, 2 km from centre, easy walk, not very clean, no sheets, hot water, clean towels, noisy all night; **F** *Pensión El Brumoso*, C 5, Av 6-8, very dirty; **F** *Vanecia*, cold water, are among the very few NOT in the red light district; **E** *Hospedaje Familiar*, C 3, just N of the railway line, box rooms, reasonable. **F** *Familiar Las Arcadas*, at railway station, (rents rooms hourly late into the night). **F** *Pensión La Provincia*, safer than most.

Restaurants *Salón París*, very good food; *City Garden*, Av 4, C 2-4; *Puerta del Sol*, in front of the Basilica. *Pizza Hut*, opp La Parroquia ruins. *Auto 88*, E of public market, meal US$2-3, cafeteria style, beer drinking room adjoining dining room. Restaurants, among other places, are closed on the Thursday and Friday of Holy Week, so take your own food.

Shopping Bookshop at *Librería Cartago*, C 1, Av 2-4. There is a market facing the train station. The main **post office** is at C 1, Av 2-4, near the park. **Exchange** Banco Fincomer changes TCs quickly with 1% commission.

Buses Facing the Museo Nacional between Av 1 and 3 and buses leave for **San José** as soon as they are full, (every 10 mins or so throughout the day).

Excursions Best is by a road (40 km, paved) to the crater of **Irazú** (3,432m). Irazú crater is a half-mile cube dug out of the earth, and all around is desolate grey sand, with little wildlife other than the ubiquitous Volcano Junco, a bird like a dunnock, and the few plants which survive in this desert. The phrase 'it's like the surface of the moon' describes Irazú quite well.

National Park rules forbid visitors to walk around the crater: on the tourist track on the N side is a 'Prohibido pasar' sign, which can be passed only at your own risk, there are some very dangerous drops, and the rim is cracking (we advise obeying the rules). There is an easier walk on the southerly side, which ends before the high crest; J Douglas Porteous of the University of Victoria, BC, writes: 'Stupendous views: you look down on mountain tops, clouds, light aircraft. Wear good shoes and a hat, the sun is strong. Those with sensitive skins should consider face cream if the sulphur fumes are heavy. By 1300 (sometimes by even 0900 or 1000) clouds have enveloped the lower peaks and are beginning to close in on Irazú; time to eat your picnic on the far side of the crater before returning to the tourist side.'

Mike Marlowe, of Blacksburg, Virginia, writes: 'In the afternoon the mountain top is buried in fog and mist or drizzle, but the ride up in the mist can be magical, for the mountainside is half-displaced in time. There are new jeeps and tractors, but the herds of cattle are small, the fields are quilt-work, handcarts and oxcarts are to be seen under the fretworked porches of well-kept frame houses. The land is fertile, the pace is slow, the air is clean. It is a very attractive mixture of old and new. Irazú is a strange mountain, well worth the ride up.'

Entrance to Irazú in season, US$1.50, open 0800-1600, out of season free. There is a small museum. A yellow 'school' bus run by Buses Metropoli SA T 272-0651, runs from San José Sat, Sun and holidays, 0800 from *Gran Hotel Costa Rica*, stops at Cartago ruins 0830 to pick up more passengers, returns 1300 with lunch stop at Restaurant *Linda Vista* (whose every internal surface is covered with business cards, bank notes, etc), US$4. A public bus leaves 0730 on Sat from the same place, Av 2, C3, in front of the hotel. Taxi from Cartago is US$24 return (it is very difficult to get taxis to return for you in the morning if you have stayed at the crater overnight). Beware of theft from hired cars. Overnight parking US$3. Since it can be difficult to find a hotel in Cartago that is not rented hourly (and therefore very expensive for a full night) it may be easier to take one of the guided tours leaving from San José, about US$25; tours to Irazú and Orosi valley US$28-30. Horse riding tour, 5½ hrs inc lunch, transport from San José, T 255-2011, US$70. The clouds come down early, obscuring the view, but if you can get there early (no entrance gate) it is wonderful to see the sun shining on the mountain and the clouds in the valley. It is possible to get a bus from Cartago to Tierra Blanca and hitch a ride in a pick-up truck. Alternatively you can take a bus from Cartago to Sanatorio. Ask the driver at the crossroads just outside the village. From there you walk to the summit. 16 km; on the way up are the **D** *Hotel Montana* (not very helpful, no keys to rooms), **F** *Hotel Gestoria Irazú*, T 253-0827, and 10 km further on, the *Bar-Restaurant Linda Vista*, the highest restaurant in Central America at about 3,000m. 1½ km from the crater a road leads to Laguna Verde; the road is paved, but steep beyond the Laguna. If driving from San José, take the road signed 'Plantel MOPT Cartago, 3 kms', just after Río Taras, which goes directly to Irazú, avoiding Cartago. The walk down, on a dirt road through Pinchas, is also rec. On Sat and Mon a bus goes from Cartago to San Juan, 12 km from the summit (0630 and 1300); **E** *Hotel Gran Irazú*, comfortable, clean.

Aguas Calientes is 4 km SE of Cartago and 90m lower. Its *balneario* (warm water swimming pool) is a good place for picnics. 4 km from Cartago on the road to Paraíso is the **Jardín Lankester orchid garden** (run by the University of Costa Rica), 10 mins' walk from the main road (ask bus driver to let you out at Campo Ayala—Cartago-Paraíso bus, departs every 30 mins from S side of central park in Cartago), taxi from Cartago, US$3; the best display is in April. Although off the beaten track, the gardens are definitely worth a visit; open 0800-1500, entry with guided 1-hour tour at 30 mins past each hour, US$2.15. 1 km further on is Parque Doña Ana (La Expresión), a lake with picnic area, basketball courts, exercise track and bird watching, open 0900-1700, US$0.50. Get off bus at Cementario in Paraíso and walk 1 km S. At Paraíso, *Restaurant Continental* is recommended.

Ujarrás (ruins of a colonial church and village) is 6$^1/_2$ km E of Cartago by a road which goes from Paraíso through a beautiful valley to the small town of *Orosi*, in the enchanting Orosi valley, down which flows the tumultuous Reventazón (**C** *Hotel Río*, T 533-3128, two pools, and *Restaurant Río Palomo*). Bus from Cartago, every 90 mins, more frequent at weekends, US$0.15. Here are magnificent views of the valley, a 17th century mission with colonial treasures (closed on Mondays), and just outside the town two *balnearios* (bathing, US$1.60) and restaurants serving good meals at fair prices. The *miradores* of Ujarrás and Orosi both offer excellent views of the Reventazón valley. There are buses from Cartago to all these places. A beautiful one-day drive from Cartago is to Orosi, then to Ujarrás, and on to *Cachí* where there is a dam with artificial lake (very popular with residents of San José, Charrarra buses from 1 block N of Cartago ruins, several daily). The Charrarra tourist complex, with a good campsite, good restaurant, swimming pool, boat rides on the Orosi river and walks, can be reached by direct bus on Sun, otherwise $^1/_2$-hr walk from Ujarrás.

12 km beyond Orosi is the **Tapanti Wildlife Refuge** (Refugio Nacional de Fauna Silvestre Tapantí, run by the Forest Service), on the headwaters of the Reventazón. It is a 4,700 hectare reserve of mainly cloud forest and pre-montaine humid forest with 211 species of birds recorded, including the quetzal which nests in late spring and can be found on the western slopes near the entry point. Jaguar and ocelot are found in the reserve as well as monkeys, orchids and ferns. There are picnic areas, a nature centre with slide shows (ask to see them) and good swimming in the dry season (Nov-June), and trout fishing (1 April to 31 October). Open daily 0800-1600, US$0.10. From June to Nov-Dec it rains every afternoon. To get there take 0600 bus from Cartago to Orosi which goes to Puricil by 0700, then walk (5 km), or take any other Cartago-Orosi bus to Río Macho and walk 9 km to the refuge, or take a taxi from Orosi (ask for Julio who, for US$7 round trip, will take 6 passengers). The *Kiri Lodge* is 1$^1/_2$ km from the entrance, or the guards may let you camp on or near the parking lot at the entrance.

The **Turrialba volcano** may be visited from Cartago by a bus to the village of Pacayas, where horses may be hired to take you to the top (fine view and a guesthouse).

Turrialba (57 km from San José, 40,000 people, altitude 625m), on the old railway between Cartago and Puerto Limón, has the Centro Agronómico Tropical de Investigación y Enseñanza (CATIE) and many fine coffee farms. CATIE covers more than 2,000 acres of this ecologically diverse zone, has one of the largest tropical fruit collections in the world and houses an important library on tropical agriculture; visitors welcome. The railway runs down to Limón on a narrow ledge poised between mountains on the left and the river on the right but no longer operates. Buses run from San José every hour 0500-2200 from C 13, Av 6-8.

Hotels SE of Turrialba beyond La Suiza is **A+** *Albergue de Montaña Rancho Naturalista*, price per person inc meals, with bath, gourmet meal, horse riding, guided tours, transfers from San José and airport, 10 rooms, reservations essential—write PO Box 364-1002 San José, T 267-7138, 7-14 night programmes organized for birdwatchers and naturalists. 14 km from Turrialba, 2 km before La Suiza, 1 km from main road at Hacienda Atirro, **A+** *Hotel Casa Turire*, 12 luxury rooms with bath, 4 suites, cable TV, phone, restaurant, 4-hole golf course, virgin rainforest, trails, horses, pool, jacuzzi, no children under 16, T 531-1111, **F** 531-1075. **C** *Wagelia*, Entrada de Turrialba (T 556-1596), with bath, 18 rooms, some a/c, restaurant, best, Annex just outside town, beautiful gardens, pool, bar, highly rec; **F** *Albergue La Calzada*; **F** *Central*, with restaurant, no bath, clean and comfortable; **F** *Interamericano*, with bath, clean, popular, parking (all opp railway station); **F** *Pensión Primavera*, 1 block away, nearby is *Restaurant Nuevo Hong Kong*, reasonable prices.

Many whitewater rafting companies are based in Turrialba, offering trips to the Reventazón and Pacuare rivers. By contacting the guides in Turrialba (all foreigners, go to the *pizzería* on the main square) you can save about 30% on a trip booked in San José (Phil Coleman rec 1993, knowledgeable, US$40-50). The rafting is excellent; the Pascua section of the Reventazón can be class 5 at rainy times. Pacuare is more beautiful (and more expensive).

From Turrialba you can get to the village of **Moravia del Chirripó**, where guides and horses can be hired for an excursion into the jungled, trackless area of the Talamanca Indians, where there are legends of lost goldfields (bus from Turrialba takes 4 hrs, only certain in dry season; in wet season go to Gran d'Oro, from where it's one hr walk—no accommodation in Moravia, stay put at *pulpería* in Gran d'Oro). About 19 km N of Turrialba, near **Guayabo**, an Indian ceremonial centre has been excavated and there are clear signs of its paved streets and stone-lined water-channels. Archaeological site, 217 hectares, 4 km from town of Guayabo, open daily 0800-1500, local guide required, US$1.50 admission. This area is now a National Monument, and the site dates from the period AD 1000 to 1400. There are buses 1000, return 1500 (check times, if you miss it is quite difficult to hitch as there is little traffic) from Turrialba (US$0.45) to Guayabo (**E Albergue y Restaurant La Calzada**, T 556-0465, best to make a reservation) from where it is a 1½ hour walk to the site. If you cannot get a bus all the way to Guayabo, several buses each day pass the turn-off to Guayabo, the town is a 2-hr walk uphill (taxi US$10, easy to hitch back). On Sun there is a bus from the main bus station in Turrialba, 0900 to the Monuments, return 1700. It is possible to camp at the park (water and toilets, but no food); entry US$1. Further along this road (1½ hrs' drive) is Santa Cruz, from which the Turrialba volcano can be reached. Bus from Cartago to Turrialba, 1 hr, US$0.60, runs until about 2200. Costa Rica Expeditions and other tour operators offer day trips to Guayabo for about US$65 pp (min 4 persons).

Going NE from Turrialba, the main road follows the Río Reventazón down to Siquirres (**see p 764**). On this road is Parones with **D Albergue Mirador Pochotel**, T 556-0111.

Puerto Limón (pop 49,600), on a palm-fringed shore backed by mountains, is the country's most important port. It was built on the site of an ancient Indian village, Cariari, where Columbus landed on his fourth and last voyage. It is very humid and it rains nearly every day. Much of the population is black but there is also a large Chinese contingent, involved mainly in restaurants, food stores and hotels; they even have their own part of the cemetery. The seafront promenade and the Parque Vargas next to it are popular places for social gatherings, especially in the evening. In Parque Vargas is a botanical display, a shrine to sailors and fishermen and a bandstand. In 1993/94 the park was reported in bad condition and the Hoffman's two-toed sloths which live in its trees were not easily seen. The Museo Etnohistórico de Limón, C 2, Av 1-2, open Mon-Thur, 1400-1700, features material relating to Columbus' arrival in Limón. The nightlife is good, particularly for Caribbean music and dancing. Fiesta: in October, very crowded and expensive. Some 2.8 million bunches of bananas are exported each year. New docks were recently completed.

Warning Beware of theft at night, and remember it is a port as well as a tourist town; there are a lot of drunks roaming the streets.

Hotels In Puerto Limón: **A** *Maribu Caribe*, T 58-45-43, bungalow accommodation, swimming pool; **C** *Acón*, C 3, Av 3, T 758-1010, with bath, a/c, clean, safe, good restaurant, popular discotheque *Aquarius*; **D** *King*, Av 2, next to PO on main square, with bath and fan, very clean; **E** *Caribe*, C 1-3, Av 2, T 758-0138; **E** *Hotel Los Angeles*, Av 3, C 4-5, T 758-2068; **E** *Lincoln*, Av 5, Calle 2-3, with bath, fan, damp, cockroaches, rats, dirty and run down, not rec; **E** *Miami*, C 4-5, Av 2, T 758-0490, back rooms quieter, a/c, Chinese food in restaurant; **D** *Park*, C 1-2, Av 3, T 758-3476, sea facing rooms quiet and cool, rooms not clean but restaurant good; **E** *Palace*, near market, small, basic, plants, chairs on balcony; **F** *Fung*, without bath, dirty, poorly maintained, by market, modern; **F** *Hong Kong*, on main street, clean but noisy; **F** *Linda Vista*, Parque Vargas, basic, friendly, noisy. **E** *Ng*, C 3, Av 5,

PUERTO LIMÓN MAC 88

↑ To Portete & Moín

0   150
metres

Avenida 8

Avenida 7

Avenida 6

Avenida 5

Avenida 4

Avenida 3

Avenida 2

Avenida 1

Calle 3

Calle 4

Calle 5

Calle 6

Calle 7

Calle 9

Calle 1

Calle 2

Paseo Juan Santamaría

To San José ←

To Airport & Cahuita ↓

Breakwater

Muelle Nacional

N

1. Parque Vargas
2. Market & Plaza
3. Gobernación
4. Museo Etnohistórico
5. Customs
6. Swimming pool
7. Radio Casino
8. Baseball Park

Hotels:

9. Acón
10. Miami
11. Los Angeles
12. Park
13. Costa Rica

B1. Bus to San José
B2. Bus to Cahuita

7   B2   12   3   1   9   13   11   2   B1   4   10   8   5   6

T 758-2134, cheaper rooms without bath, fan extra charge, basic, untidy, friendly, laundry; **F** *Paraíso*, Av 4, C 4, shared bath, clean, noisy, friendly, basic but good value; *Pensión Dorita*, C 3-4, Av 4, fairly clean, friendly, basic, reported no blacks accommodated, close to bus stop for Cahuita; **F** *Pensión El Sauce*, one block from main square, rats; **F** *Pensión Hotel Costa Rica*, 1½ blocks E of central park, small rooms, noisy; **F** *Venus*, Av 5 near Lincoln, beach view, rats, spiders, beds 'like medical plank beds', avoid; **G** *Balmoral*, near market, basic; **G** *Pensión Los Angeles*, Calle 6-7, Av 7, with bath, cheap, noisy, mosquitoes, probably of ill repute; **G** *Pensión El Cano*, next to *Pensión Los Angeles*, fan, friendly, clean, share showers, OK. There are several hotels in the C 3, Av 1-3, area where San José buses arrive, eg *Río*, *Cariari*, *Palmeras*, all E.

In nearby Portete: **A** *Matama*, Playa Bonita, T 758-1123/4200, F 758-4499, recently refurbished, bath, a/c, restaurant, tennis, pool, boats for rent to Tortuguero; **C** *Cabinas Getsemaní*, cabins, bath, a/c, restaurant, pleasant (T 758-1123).

Restaurants A place to eat is harder to find than a nightclub. Several Chinese restaurants. *Park Hotel*, C 1-2, Av 3, does good meals, US$2.25; *Restaurant La Chucheca* serves good *comidas* and breakfast. *Springfield*, serves good, Caribbean-style meals, rec, also has disco; *La Hacienda*, for steaks, cheap. *Soda/Restaurant Mares*, on market square, good food; *Soda/Restaurant Roxie*, opp hospital, some way out of town, good value *casado*. *Doña Toda*, good, near market; *Harbour Restaurant*, good value meal of the day. *Mönpik* for good ice cream (the biggest supermarket in town); *Milk Bar La Negra Mendoza* at the central market has good milk shakes and snacks. *Casados* in market in the day, outside it at night, good, cheap food. Cheap food at the corners of the Central Park and at *Familia Torres*, Av 5, ½ block from *Hotel Ng*, very good value. *Diplo's Bar*, cheap Limón food, try the soup.

Swimming Japdeva, the harbour authority, has a 25-metre pool open to the public for a small fee in the harbour area.

Exchange Banco Nacional de Costa Rica, and also Banco Anglo Costarricense (open Sat am) next to Limón-San José bus terminal.

Post Office opp central market. There is a branch of ICE at Av 2 C 5-6 for international telephone calls. **Cables** Radiográfica maintain offices in Limón.

Protestant Church Baptist, with services in English.

Hospital Social Security Hospital.

Rail Trains to San José were suspended in 1990 because of track damage, but passenger services operate to **Valle de Estrella**, Mon-Fri 0400 and 1500, 1½ hrs, US$1.50, and to Finca 10 Río Frío.

Buses Town bus service is irregular and crowded. Service to **San José** with Coop Limón, T 223-7811 and Transportes Unidos del Atlántico, every hour on the hour between 0500-1900; leave from the street between central plaza and Parque Vargas (ignore the old signs for the departure point), US$2.90, 3-4 hrs. To **Cartago**, US$2. Bus to **Cahuita** 0500, 1000, 1300, 1600, US$0.80, 45 mins, continues to Puerto Viejo and Sixaola. To **Manzanillo** at 0600, 1400, returning 0900, 1630, 2 hrs, US$1.50.

Flights Travelair from the capital, see under San José. Keep luggage to a minimum or you will be charged for excess baggage.

Moín, 6½ km N of Puerto Limón, has docks for tankers, container and ro-ro ships, and is also the departure point for barges to Barra del Colorado (8 hrs). Moín has a pleasant beach, buses run every 40 mins from 0600-1740, ½ hr, US$0.10. Boats run from Moín to Tortuguero (see below) and may be hired at the dockside. Go early for a good bargain. Accommodation is difficult and not recommended, best to stay in Limón.

Note A severe earthquake struck the Caribbean coast of Costa Rica and Panama in April 1991. Many buildings were damaged or destroyed. Most bridges have been repaired, the permanent bridge across the Río Estrella has now been rebuilt, and roads to the Panamanian border are open. Because the land was raised by the earthquake, the Tortuguero canals (see below) around Matina dried up. Japdeva have started dredging work but boats for Tortuguero river now also depart from Hamburgo de Siquirres on the Río Reventazón. Boats still run from Barra del Colorado to Tortuguero.

The Atlantic Coast The Río San Juan forms the border between Costa Rica and Nicaragua; the frontier is not in mid-river but on the Costa Rican bank. English is spoken widely along the coast. Between Puerto Limón and the Río San Juan is a long stretch of coastline with various settlements linked by a canal system which follows the coast.

Tortuguero is a 18,947-hectare National Park protecting the Atlantic green turtle egg-laying grounds and the Caribbean lowland rain forest inland. The turtles lay their eggs at night from June to August (the eggs start hatching in the second week of September), but before going to watch, contact the National Park administration (they have some basic but good guide books of the area for sale), or the scientists at Casa Verde (very helpful), Km 0.6, for instructions, otherwise you may disturb the protected turtles (take a torch if going at night). Unfortunately people still eat turtle eggs and meat, even though they are protected. It is depressing to see the nests robbed by morning. No permission is needed to enter the park, but to visit the turtles you must pay US$1.50 park entrance fee and US$2 each for a guide, no matter how many you are. Guides will let you watch one turtle laying eggs, although you may have to wait an hour; be patient. Do not swim at Tortuguero because of the sharks.

A regular boat leaves Moín or Siquirres for Tortuguero twice a week. Tickets sold once boat is under way. You can bargain at Moín for a boat to take you to Tortuguero and bring you back 3-4 days later, at around US$50-60 provided a party of 6 can be arranged. *Viajes Laura*, T 758-2410, highly rec, daily service, open return US$50 if phoned direct, more through travel agencies, pick up from hotel, will store luggage, lunch provided, excellent for pointing out wildlife on the way. It is also possible to take a bus from Siquirres to Freeman (unpaved road), a Del Monte banana plantation, from where unscheduled boats go to Tortuguero; ask around at the bank of the Río Pacuare, or call the public phone office in

Tortuguero (T 710-6716, open 0730-2000) and ask for Johnny Velázquez to come and pick you up, US$57, maximum 4 passengers, 4 hrs. Sometimes heavy rains block the canals, preventing passage there or back. Contact Willis Rankin (Apartado 1055, Limón, T 758-1686) an excellent captain who will negotiate rampaging rivers. All river boats for the major lodges (see below) leave from Hamburgo or Freeman. If excursion boats have a spare seat you may be allowed on. Generally it is getting more difficult to 'do it yourself', but it is still possible, ask around the boat owners in Moín. Official tours and tourist guides with accommodation included are now normal, typical cost is US$180 for four day trip, all inclusive. A 2-day, 1-night trip from Puerto Limón with basic accommodation, turtle watching trip and transport (no food) costs about US$65 pp, T 225-6220. A road is under construction from Guápiles. You can take a bus from Guápiles to Cariari on the Río Tortuguero and take a boat from there, 9½ hrs, US$15 return, to Tortuguero, or a boat from Puerto Viejo de Sarapiquí to Barra del Colorado and from there to Tortuguero (see below). Flights from San José, see **Internal Flights, p 735**.

Accommodation   At the Southern end of the Park is **Parismina**, where you can stay at the **L** *Tarpon Lodge*, T 235-7766, including meals, boat and guide; there is also a cheap *pensión*, F, basic, fan, bargain. Further N is the settlement of Tortuguero itself. There are several hotels: *Río Parismina Lodge*, T 222-6633 (USA toll free 800-338-5688, F 512-829-3770), new, luxury, fishing packages from US$999; **L** *Tortuga Lodge*, price per person inc meals, T 257-0766, F 257-1665, comfortable accommodation, but rooms 1-6 are dark and lack fresh air, excellent food (owner Costa Rican Expeditions, packages available from San José, better value than staying there independently when you will be charged extra for everything, 2 min boat ride from village, US$8); **A+** *Ilan Ilan*, price per person inc meals, T 255-2031, clean, basic, cold showers, friendly, English-speaking owner; **A+** *Jungla Lodge*, price per person inc meals, T 233-0155, F 222-0568, 3-day, 2-night package tours with transport from San José; **A** *Mawamba Lodge*, T 222-5463, 223-7490, F 255-4039, price per person inc meals, comfortable, fans, restaurant, canal and egg-laying turtles in front of property; **C** *Sabina's Cabañas*, somewhat overpriced but clean, small, basic rooms, but next to beach, some cabinas with separate bathroom. **D** *Cabinas Tortuguero Tatane*; *Hotel Mayscar*, Nicaraguan-owned, fans, safe, cheap food. N of Tortuguero is *Samay Laguna*, opened 1993, T 223-0867, PO Box 12767-1000, San José, tours offered, transport by seaplane possible, no travellers' reports yet.

6 km N of Tortuguero is the Caño Palma Biological Station, administered by the Canadian Organization for Tropical Education and Rainforest Conservation (in Canada T (416) 683-2116), basic rooms, B pp, inc meals, pickup from Sansa flights to Barra del Colorado can be arranged; a good place for serious naturalists or just for unwinding, accommodation for up to 16 in wooden cabin, fresh water well for drinking and washing. Don't dally on arrival if you want cheap accommodation. You can sometimes camp at the National Park office for US$2.50.

Restaurants   Good food is limited: *Miss Junie's* with Mona Lisa painting (order meals in advance, lodging expected to be available late 1993); the *Pancana Restaurant*, owned by Jacob and Edna Dases, good hospitality, homemade bread, good information on turtles and canoe hire; *El Dolar*, Tortuguero, good food, gift shop opposite; *Tío Leo's*. Saturday night is dancing night, happy, enjoyable, great dancing, but a notorious surplus of men. Disco near *Sabina's Cabinas*.

Tours   The main tours are *Mawamba Boats*, T 222-5463, 223-7490, F 255-4039, min 2 people, 3 days/2 nights, US$219 pp, daily, private launch so you can stop en route, with launch tour of National Park included, accommodation at *Mawamba Lodge*, PO Box 10050 San José, you can return to San José by charter flight (US$344 pp) or take the Río San Juan-Río Sarapiquí trip from Puerto Viejo de Sarapiquí (5 hrs, US$347 pp based on 2 people); then bus back to San José or stay at *Selva Verde Lodge*; *Miss Caribe* and *Miss America* boats, T 233-0155 operate Tues, Fri, Sun, 2-night 3-day packages using *Jungla Lodge*; *Colorado Prince* boat, 3 day/2 night package, Tues, Fri, Sun US$200, using *Ilan Ilan Lodge*, T 255-3031. Parismina Tarpon Rancho (PO Box 10560-1000, San José, F 222-1760) offers tours of Tortuguero, Braulio Carrillo National Park and fishing trips. OTEC (see p 735) runs 3-day, 2-night tours for US$180, with small student discount, a trip to see the turtles in July-September costs extra. Park rangers are friendly and make trips into the jungle waterways; particularly recommended for viewing tropical rain forest wildlife (birds, alligators, tapirs, jaguars, ocelots, peccaries, anteaters, manatees, sloths, monkeys, gars); their trips are quite short, about US$2 pp for 3-4 hr trip. You can hire a canoe and guide for about US$3 per hour pp, minimum 4, excellent way to see wildlife including crocodiles, ask for Damma. Johnny Velázquez (see above) does tours, US$3.55 pp per hour for tours of canals in a motor boat, US$30/hour in fishing boat on the sea, maximum 2, gear and bait included, US$10/hour night tour. Alberto does canoe tours: US$2.25/hr pp if he goes with you, or US$1.25 if you go alone, he lives next to *Hotel Mayscar*. Rubén, who lives in the last house before you get to the National Park office, sign on pathway, is rec for 4 hr tour at dusk and in the dark. Chico lives behind *Sabina's Cabinas*, US$2/hr, rec as local guide and will take you anywhere in his motor boat. Rafael, a biologist, is recommended, speaks Spanish and English (his wife speaks French), lives 1/2 km behind Park Rangers' office, ask rangers for directions, he also rents canoes. There are several boats for rent from Tortuguero, ask at the *pulpería*. Take insect repellent against the ferocious mosquitoes, ticks and chiggers.

The canals pass many small settlements, and for many of them the barge is their only means of communication. The canals are part artificial, part natural; they were originally narrow lagoons running parallel to the sea, separated from it by 3/4 km of land. Now all the lagoons are linked, and it is possible to sail as far as **Barra del Colorado**, in the extreme NE of Costa Rica, 25 km beyond Tortuguero. The town is divided by the river, the main part being on the northern bank. There is a plan to link the Parque Nacional Tortuguero with the Refugio Nacional de Fauna Silvestre Barra del Colorado into a continuous National Park area. The area is world famous for fishing. Boat from Barra to Tortuguero takes 5 hrs and costs US$28.50. A motorized canoe can take 8 people and costs up to US$50, 2 hrs. Try and arrive in a group as boats are infrequent.

Hotels and Flights There is a luxury hotel lodge operated by Swiss Travel Service; **A** *Hotel Pesca Casa Mar*, with bath (T 441-2820); **A** *Silver King Lodge*, T 288-0849 (toll free in USA 1-800-847-3474), price pp, deluxe sports fishing hotel, 5-night packages inc flights, fishing, meals, rooms with bath, fan, hot water (price does not include fishing); **C** *Río Colorado Lodge*, price per person inc 3 meals and fishing with guide, reservations rec, T 232-4063; **C** *Isla de Pesca*, with bath (T 232-8219); *Cabinas New Tropical Tarpon* with bath (T 227-0473); **C** *Tarponland Lodge*, cabins, run by Guillermo Cunningham, very knowledgeable and helpful, T 710-6917. If you have a tent you may be able to camp at *Soda La Fiesta*. Lots of mosquitoes. Flight San José-Barra del Colorado with Sansa and Travelair, see under **Internal Flights**, San José.

Once across the Río Colorado (which in fact is the S arm of the Río San Juan delta), you can walk to Nicaragua (see under Nicaragua, San Juan del Norte) along the beach, take food and water. Consult the Guardia Civil before setting out anywhere, they are very helpful and knowledgeable. There is much to see in this unspoilt region though transport, mostly by boat, is costly, typically US$30 for a half day. There are several fishermen who will take you up the coast on their way to fish in Nicaraguan waters, US$20-30. You can go by irregular boat from Barra up the Río Colorado, Río San Juan and Río Sarapiquí to Puerto Viejo, about 5-6 hrs. A small boat for 4 without roof costs US$150 (or US$50 pp), a larger boat for 6 with roof (rec) costs US$185 for 4; you see caimans, turtles and lots of birds. There are several border checkpoints. Another alternative to going S along the coast to Puerto Limón is by bus from the river bank opposite Isla Buena Vista 25 km up the Río Colorado, daily except Sundays, leaves 0600, by dirt track to Cariari and then to Guápiles. Interesting trip through rainforest and then banana plantations. Throughout this area police are on the lookout for drugs traffickers. Expect to have your luggage searched thoroughly.

Southward from Limón, the road is paved to **Penshurst**. Here the road (and railway) branches to Valle de Estrella, a large Standard Fruit banana plantation; camping is easy in the hills and there are plenty of rivers for swimming. Small buses leave Limón (C 4, Av 6) for Valle de Estrella/Pandora, 7 a day from 0500, at 2-hourly intervals, last at 1800, 1 1/2 hrs (returning from Pandora at similar times).

From Penshurst it is 11 1/2 km to **Cahuita**; this stretch of the road is paved to the edge of Cahuita. There is a bus service direct from San José (Av 11, C 1-Central), 0600, 1330 and 1530, T 221-0524, 4 hrs, US$5.60, return 0630, 0930, 1630, and from Puerto Limón, in front of Radio Casino (0500, 1000, 1300, 1600, return 0600, 1000, 1200, 1730, US$0.80, 45 mins, T 758-1572), both continuing on paved road to Bribri, two basic *residencias*, and on to Sixaola on the Panamanian border (US$1, 2 hrs). Taxi Puerto Limón—Cahuita, US$20. The **Cahuita National Park** has a narrow strip of beach (1,068 hectares) and a coral reef off shore (600 hectares), sadly badly damaged by agricultural chemicals etc from the rivers. An old Spanish wrecked ship may be seen, although the water can be very cloudy at times (both can be reached without a boat; take snorkelling equipment, but the undercurrent is strong and take care not to bump into the reef). There is a black sand beach to the N, take hammock, good swimming, beautiful. The Park extends from Cahuita town to Puerto Vargas further SE. Best access to the Park is from Puerto Vargas where there are the Park headquarters, a nature trail, camping facilities, toilets, take drinking water (take the bus to Km 5, then turn left at the sign; the road from the Cahuita-Bribri road to Puerto Vargas is muddy; take a torch if walking it after dark). Entry charge to the Park US$1.50. The length of the beach can be walked in 2 hrs, passing endless coconut palms and interesting tropical forest, through which there is also a path, including fording the shallow Río Perezoso, which is brown with tannin. It is hot and humid, but a wide range of fauna can be seen, including howler monkeys, white face monkeys, coatimundis, snakes, butterflies and hermit crabs. Over 500 species of fish inhabit the surrounding waters. Reef tours avilable. No permission is necessary from SNP to enter the Park. Best to visit during the week when it is quieter.

The bus drops you at the crossing of the 2 main roads in Cahuita. **C** pp *Hotel Jaguar Cahuita*, 800m N of Cahuita centre, easy walk to National Park, 17-acre property with nature trails, 22 beach front rooms with private bathroom, inc breakfast and dinner, good value, T 758-1515 ext 238, San José T 226-3775. There are other new developments in this area. On the street parallel to the sea, towards the Park entrance are **E** *Hotel Vaz Cabañas*, friendly, cold shower, some fans, quite clean, rec, good restaurant, safe parking, T 758-1515 ext 218, and **C** *Hotel Cahuita*, renovated, nice hotel, pool, T 758-1515 ext 238 (opp is *Sol y Mar*, rec). **E-D** *Cabinas Surf Side*, for cabin on beach with bathroom, T 758-1515 ext 246 English spoken, clean, good value, rec, get there early to get a room. A little road from the bus stop goes straight to the seafront, passing **D** *Cabinas Palmer*, T 758-1515, ext 243), clean, good, friendly and helpful, but noisy; carry on to the sea, and on left is **C** *Jenny's Cabinas* (same phone, but ext 256), clothes washing area, balconies with view, Canadian owned, bath, fan, breakfast available, running water, close to the sea but surrounding area dirty, overpriced; **F** pp *Bar Hannia*, very friendly Jamaican owner, on main street, English speaking, good place for a beer, his wife also has nice cabins available. On the road from Limón to Cahuita, Km 22, is **C** *Club Campestre Cahuita*, with bath, fans, swimming pool, T 255-6176, isolated and difficult to get to Cahuita National Park from here. For cheaper rooms, walk 15 mins N to **Playa Negra**: **E** *Cabinas Vito*, clean, quiet, cabins sleep 2-3, good value; **C** *Cabinas Iguana*, Swiss-owned, cabins or houses to rent, with kitchen, fan, mosquito netting, balcony, clean, nice location, rec; **D** *Cabinas Sol y Mar*, clean, pleasant with bath and fan, quiet, close to beach, mosquitoes; **F** *Cabinas Grant* (*Cabinas Bello Horizonte*), good water service, Señorita Letty Grant (North American, also has *artesanía* shop), blue house on right of track to Black Beach, rents rooms (F) and *cabañas*, clean, nice, friendly, beautiful setting, garden and birds, good value; **B** *Atlántida Lodge*, next to football ground, nice gardens, inc tax and breakfast (rec), T 758-1515 ext 213, with bath, cold water, fan, mosquito screen, pleasant, free safe parking for cars and motorcycles (also known as Canadian Jean's (French) rec); **E** *Cabinas Black Beach*, clean and well situated, bar, you may camp here for US$1; **E** *Brigitte's*, friendly, quiet, Swiss run, restaurant, good for wildlife, sloth shelters from rain on verandah at night, rec. At the end of Black Beach, 300m on left side, **F** *Rootsman Paradise*, *cabinas*, café, juice bar, boutique, quiet, friendly, good service. There are also empty rooms to let, so take a hammock or sleeping bag, horses to rent (US$3.50/hour). Camping: at *Vishnu's*, clean, cold showers, great breakfasts, vehicle US$6 per night. Also in the park (see above).

If the catch is good many restaurants have lobster at reasonable prices. *Típico*, good; *Restaurant Vishnu*, vegetarian dishes, excellent breakfasts. *Miss Edith's*, delicious Caribbean food, nice people, good value, no alcohol licence, take your own, many recommendations for breakfast and dinner, though don't expect quick service; *Deni*, in centre of town, original décor inc driftwood and birds' nests, reggae music, go to look but very mixed reports about food and service; *Sol y Mar*, good value, open 0730-1200, 1630-2000, need to arrive early and wait at least 45 mins for food, red snapper and volcano potato especially good, US$5, also good breakfasts, try cheese, egg and tomato sandwich, US$2, ask for Chepe who speaks English and is fun to talk to, also has cabins, see above; *Vista del Mar*, facing entrance to

Park, good fish dishes; *La Fiesta Italiana*, good food, nice atmosphere; *Soda Kukula*, great breakfast, fresh bread, German owner; *Cabinas Algebra* on the Black Beach has a good restaurant and the bar on Black Beach is away from the crowds, rec. *Salón Vaz*, lively at weekends with reggae music and Rastas, popular with travellers and locals, main gathering point, safe for lone women.

On public holidays Cahuita is very crowded, expensive and difficult to get a room; the remainder of the year it is a favourite resort of backpackers (don't bathe or sun-bathe naked). Money exchange is difficult except occasionally for cash dollars (Cahuita Tours changes US$ and TCs). Take plenty of colones from Limón. Several places accept credit cards. Tony Mora runs glass-bottomed boats over the coral reef. Also horses can be hired, but ensure they are in good shape. Bicycles can be hired for about US$7/day and you can cycle to Puerto Viejo and the Panamanian border through some beautiful scenery. The National Park services have warned against muggings in the park at night, if walking the path take a torch. There have also been some rapes. Some of the jungle has been cleared for safety. Also beware of theft on the beach, and drug pushers who may be undercover police.

The beaches at **Puerto Viejo (Limón)**, 19 km SE of Cahuita (bus from San José—en route to Sixaola—$4^{1}/_{2}$ hrs, US$3, $^{1}/_{2}$ hr from Cahuita, US$0.45), are also worth a visit (be alert for thieves). They are quiet during the week, busy at weekends, good surfing. Note that water can be scarce in Puerto Viejo. There is a public telephone in the Chinaman store in Puerto Viejo, the only one in the area. You need to bring towels, insect repellent and a torch. There is a small, English book exchange, ask for directions. It is possible to walk along the beach from Puerto Viejo to Cahuita in one day (22 km, 5 hrs) but not recommended. There is a channel to cross (Home Creek) and reports of tourists being robbed.

Hotels A *El Pizote Lodge*, cabin with bath, **B**, room with shared bath, T 229-1428 or 758-1938; **D** *Pura Vida*, Swiss run, friendly, very clean, hammocks, rec; **C** *Maritza*, in cabins, with bath, clean, highly rec, **D**, shared bathroom, clean, friendly, English spoken, a map in the bar shows all the hotels and *cabinas* in the area; **F** *Kiskadee*, small jungle lodge with two dormitories, kitchen available, American-run, about 200m from football field, from where it is signposted, rec, take torch and rubber boots; **F** *Cabinas Manuel León*, with bath, T 758-0854; **D** *Cabinas Chimuri*, N edge of town, thatched huts with balconies from which you can observe the wildlife, horseriding; good breakfasts at **E** *Hotel Puerto Viejo*, nice balconies, rec, Mexican food, popular with surfers; **D** *Cabinas Jacaranda*; **F** *Cabinas Salsa Brava*, popular with surfers; **D** *Escape Caribeño Bungalows*, 500m along road to Punta Ura, German management, communal kitchen, free morning coffee, well-furnished cottages with TV, fully equipped; *Cabinas Black Sands*, a bamboo, laurel wood and thatch cabin of Bri-Bri Indian design T 556-1132.

Restaurants café *Pizzería Coral*, good breakfasts, good main meals, not cheap, rec; *Garden Restaurant*, serves excellent breakfasts, rec; *El Parquecito*, facing sea, nice breezy atmosphere, specializes in fish and seafood (evenings only); *Green Garden*, clean, nice pastries, food from Trinidad, Californian style, very expensive; *Johnny's Place*, Chinese food, large portions, specialities of the day rec; *Soda Tamara*, open 0600-2100, local good quality homemade snacks. *Stanford's Disco*, lively nightlife; *Bambú*, nearby, good food; *Bar Sandborn*, rec for an evening beer. *Taberna Popo*, lively bar-disco, live music some nights, Carib and rock.

There are a number of popular beaches SE along the road from Puerto Viejo. At about 4 km is **Playa Cocles** which has some of the best surfing on this coast. **D** *Cabinas Surf Point*; **F** *Cabinas y Soda Garibaldi*. 2 km further on is *Playa Chiquita* with many places to stay including **A** *Hotel Punta Cocles*, rec, 40 nice cabins, a/c, pool, forest trails, car rentals, boat trips, guides, horse riding, mountain bikes, transport from San José available, T San José 224-3926, F 234-0014. **A** *Playa Chiquita Lodge*, 11 rooms with private bathroom, French restaurant and bar, 500m from beach, naturalist guides available, T 233-6613, F 223-7479; **D** *Tío Lou Cabins*, T 227-3517; **A+** *Villas del Caribe*, 2 floor apartments with kitchen, living room, bath, T 233-2200; **E** *Cabinas Dasa*; **E** *Cabinas Maracú*; *Miraflores Lodge and Restaurant*, T 233-5127, F 233-5390, 10 rooms, a/c, breakfast inc, beautiful gardens, lots of wildlife, English and French spoken, boating tours to Monkey point. Beyond this is Punta Uva with *Selvin Cabins* and restaurant, *Walaba Travellers Hostel*, with rooms and dormitory accommodation and a delightful *Restaurant Naturales*, excellent food on a hill overlooking the beach. Another 5 km to Manzanillo, **A** *Hotel Las Palmas*, cabins, 60 ocean-view rooms, pool, snorkelling, rainforest, tours, transport from San José, Wed, Fri, Sun, US$30 return, US$20 one way, T/F 255-3939; **E** *Cabinas/Restaurant Maxi*, followed by white sand beaches and rocky headlands to Punta Mona and the **Gandoca-Manzanillo Wildlife Refuge**.

Take road from Cahuita to Hotel Creek where one road (dirt) goes to Puerto Viejo and another (paved) to **Bribri**, one of the villages at the foot of the Talamanca range, which has been declared an Indian Reserve. Halfway between Hotel Creek and Puerto Viejo is *Violeta's Pulpería*. From Limón, Aerovías Talamaqueñas Indígenas fly cheaply to Amubri in the Reserve (there is a *Casa de Huéspedes* run by nuns in Amubri). Villages such as Bribri, Chase, Bratsi, Shiroles and San José Cabécar can be reached by bus from Cahuita. (For a good introduction to the Talamanca mountains, read *Mamita Yunai* by Fallas, or *What Happen* by Palmer.)

Continuing S from Bribri is **Sixaola**, on the border with Panama. 3 hotels just before the bridge: **E** *Cabinas Sánchez*, with bath, **F** *Central*, Chinese run with good restaurant, and **F** *Pensión Doris*. There are no banks in Sixaola, but it may be possible to change money in one of the shops before the bridge, eg. *Soda Central*, but rates, especially to the US dollar are very poor. A narrow-gauge railway runs to Almirante (Panama) from Guabito, on the Panamanian side (shops will accept colones. Care: shops in Changuinola and beyond do not accept colones. Remember to advance watches by 1 hr on entering Panama (border open 0700-1700 Costa Rican time). If crossing to Panama take the earliest bus possible to Sixaola (see Panama, **The North-Eastern Caribbean Coast**). Direct Sixaola-San José bus, Autotransportes Mepe, 5 hrs, US$5.45 (T 221-0524), 0500, 0800, 1430, return 0600, 1330, 1530 daily; also 3 a day to Puerto Limón via Cahuita 2½ hrs. It is cheaper to take the bus from Sixaola to Puerto Limón then another from Limón to San José rather than the through service.

The local greeting in this area is 'OK?'. This means, 'good morning, how are you', 'I'm not going to attack you', 'can I help you?' If you don't want a chat, simply answer 'all right'.

THE SOUTH PACIFIC COAST (7)

At the foot of the cordillera, the narrow lowlands are cattle ranches or planted to African palm. Beaches, particularly those in the Manuel Antonio National Park, are a major attraction.

From Esparza on the Pan-American Highway a road runs SE to San Mateo (from where a road runs NE to Atenas—see Meseta Central section) and **Orotina**. Orotina excursion: Finca Los Angeles, T 224-5828, offers one-day nature tour on horseback US$65 through the mountains to the beach. W of Orotina the road forks, NW to the port of Caldera, SW to the Pacific Coast at Tárcoles. Along the Caldera road is Cascajal, where the **A+** *Dundee Ranch Hotel*, a working ranch, has 11 rooms with private bathroom, a/c, pool and restaurant, T 428-8776. **A** *Hacienda Doña Marta* is a 260-ha working ranch and dairy farm with 6 cabinas, pool, bar and restaurant for guests, horseriding, next to Carara Biological Reserve, see below, reservations and information from *Finca Rosa Blanca Country Inn*, PO Box 23, Santa Bárbara de Heredia, T 269-9392, F 269-9555. The coastal road continues through Jacó, Quepos, Playa Dominical and thence inland to San Isidro de El General. The road is paved as far as Parrita (after Jacó) and is generally good with few pot holes. Thereafter it is a good, but dusty, gravel road (difficult for motorbikes because of loose gravel), paved in villages, until Paquita, just before Quepos. Here the road deteriorates and paving is poor. After Quepos the road is still unpaved to Dominical, a hard ride, and although from Dominical the road inland through Barú to San Isidro is paved, landslides can make this section hazardous. Check the state of the roads and bridges before setting out to San Isidro if driving yourself and do not assume that if the buses are getting through, cars can too. High clearance is needed if a bridge is down. In the dry season motorists can do a round trip in a day starting from San José.

Between Orotina and Jacó, just after the Río Tárcoles bridge (where scarlet macaws may be seen flying out of the forest into the sunset just before dusk, 1700-1730), is the **Carara Biological Reserve**, 4,700 hectares with abundant wildlife—scarlet macaws (best seen around 0630 or 1700), whitefaced monkeys, coatimundis and crocodiles. Open 0800-1600, entrance US$2 for foreigners, US$0.50 for Costa Ricans. There is a 30-40 minute circular path starting by the office, approximately 1,300m; trails have been improved with funds from British Embassy. San José travel agencies offer tours.

A *Hotel Villa Lapas*, next to the reserve (from Río Tarcolitos, turn left and go 500m), reservations T 239-4104, hotel T 288-1611, with bath, pool, good restaurant, good birdwatching, riding, guided tours to Carara, rec, animals come close to the hotel at night.
At **Playa Tárcoles**, E *Cabinas La Guaria*, bath; C *Cabinas Carara*, basic, 16 cabins with bath, small, simple restaurant, pool, superb birdwatching at mouth of Río Tárcoles about 5 km along this road, T 661-0455. 3 km from Tárcoles is *El Tico*, a good seafood restaurant.
A+A- *Tarcol Lodge*, on S bank of mouth of Río Tárcoles, high tide surrounds lodge on 3 sides, low tide uncovers mud flats attracting thousands of birds, packages inc transport, meals and tours, 5 bedrooms, 2 bathrooms, Apdo 364-1002, San José, T/F 267-7138, same management as *Albergue de Montaña Rancho Naturalista*, near Turrialba.
Further S is **Punta Leona** with **B** *Punta Leona Hotel and Club*, bungalows with bath, a/c, T 231-3131, F 232-3074.

15 km from Carara is **Jacó** Beach, a large stretch of sandy beach, rather noisy and commercial, popular with surfers and weekenders from San José. Be careful of the rip tides all along this coast. Bus from Coca Cola bus station, San José, 0715 and 1530 daily, returning 0500, 1500, 2½-3 hrs, US$1.60. Indirect buses also at 0730, 1030, 1530. An Americana VIP Coach Service runs Mon, Wed, Fri, Sun, luxury Greyhound bus, US$45 return, T 222-8134.

Accommodation and Food A+ *Hotel Villas Jacó Princess*, villas with kitchenette, a/c, T 643-3064, F 643-3010; **A+** *Hacienda Lilipoza*, T 643-3062, F 643-3158, 4-star, spacious, pool, Swiss restaurant; **A** *Jacó Fiesta*, T 643-3147, F 643-3148, bath, cable TV, phone, refrigerator, rooms hold 4/5 people, 4 pools, tennis, restaurant, highly rec, English, German, French spoken; **A** *Paraíso del Sol*, T 643-3250, two types of room, pool and children's pool, rec; **A+** *Jacó Beach*, T 643-3064, F 643-3246 (or San José 220-1725), a/c, TV, minibar, hot water, tennis, volley ball, restaurant and coffee shop, helpful staff, good service, but neither very clean nor good value; **A** *Copacabana*, Apartado 15, Jacó, T/F 643-3131, Canadian-owned, on beach, attractive, clean, tours and sporting activities arranged, rooms quiet, fans, hot showers, suites for 4 with kitchenettes available, pool, bar with TV and live music, boutique, restaurant, car rentals, credit cards accepted, rec; **B** *Cabinas Tanyeri*, T 442-0977, modern, attractive landscaping, pool, excellent value for groups; **B** *Club de Mar*, T 643-3194, bath, fans, S end of beach; **D** *Cabinas Heredia*, with bath, and **D** *Cabinas Las Brisas*, T 643-3087, attractive grounds, on beach, but run down; other hotels and many *cabinas*, including **C** *Cabinas Las Palmas*, with bath and fan, cold water, clean; **C** *Coral*, T 643-3067, on beach S of town, 2 pools, hammocks, German owned, restaurant, warmly rec; **D** *El Jardín*, with bath, pool; **E** *Antonio*; **E** *Bohío*, near beach, private bath, cold water, fan, swimming pool; *Camping El Hicaco* and *Restaurant Los Hicacos* both down same access to the beach.

From Jacó the road runs along the coast giving lovely views of the ocean, several turnoffs to beaches along the way, including **Esterillos Este** (**A** *Hotel El Delfín*, T 771-1640, swimming pool, all rooms with breezy balcony, secluded, clean, rec, good restaurant, considered by many one of the most delightful beach hotels in Costa Rica; other *cabinas*) and **Playa Palma**, near Parrita (**F** *Hotel El Nopal*, and **E** *Hotel Memo*, with bath). After Parrita the gravel road travels through palm plantations and the landscape is flat, becoming rather tedious after a few kilometres of palm trees. Many of the plantation villages along the way are worth seeing for their two-storey, balconied houses laid out around a central football pitch.

Puerto Quepos, built by United Brands as a banana exporting port is now run down. The banana plantations were overwhelmed by Panama disease in the early 1950s and have been replaced by 8,200 hectares of African Palm for oil.

Mechanization was cut back when it was realized that tractors were damaging the roots of the palm trees and now oxen or mules pull carts along the rows, while tractors pulling several wagons load up at the ends of the rows. S of Quepos the coast has been developed for tourism, with numerous hotels built along the beach, and Quepos is now important as a transport hub. It is also cheaper to stay here than on the beach and there are more bars and shops. The Post Office is on the walkway by the football pitch, open 0800-1700. The municipal market is at the bus station, buy fruit and bread here as the Super Mas supermarket is not well stocked. There is a good laundry near the football pitch. Immigration is on the same street as the Banco de Costa Rica, one of the three banks in town. Visa card is the preferred credit card in this area, Mastercard can attract a 6% added commission. Police T 777-0196. *La Buena Nota*, souvenir shop, also sells some English language newspapers etc, a good place to seek local information, run by Anita Myketuk and Donald Milton, who has initiated a lifesaving programme and publicity on rip tides, T 777-0345.

Accommodation and Food Difficult to find accommodation on Sats, Dec-April and when local schools are on holiday. **A** *Kamuk*, central, T 777-0379, shower, TV, ocean view, bar, restaurant, a/c; **D** *El Parque*, T 777-0063, on waterfront road, friendly, clean, good value, private bath, fan; **D** *Viña del Mar*, T 777-0070, with bath, fan, restaurant; **E** *Luna*, fleas, dirty, not rec; **E** *Linda Vista*, good, will wash clothes for you and **E** *Majestic*, cheap, noisy, shared bath, are on the same street as Banco de Costa Rica; **F** *Hospedaje La Macha*, with fan, basic, noisy, little privacy, next to Post Office and soccer field behind bus station. On the road which leads to Manuel Antonio but still in town are **C** *Hotel Quepos*, T 777-0274, with bath, D without, simple, rec; **C** *Cabinas Mar-Su* in Boca Vieja district, no signs, about 300m before bridge entering town, large, clean, comfortable cabins, fan, bathroom, a/c extra, car park; **C** *Cabinas Mary* by football pitch behind bus station, clean, OK; **B-D** *Ceciliano* T 777-0245 with bath, family run, quiet, small rooms, hot; **D** *Mavio*, with bath, rec. **D** *Itzamaná*, cross bridge on way out of Quepos, turn half left at telephone box, continue past stop sign and along dog-leg in road, follow road to left where it peters out, hotel about 30m back on right, bath, cold water, clean, fan, friendly, good value, free bus to Manuel Antonio. The best restaurants are further along the coast towards Manuel Antonio. In town is the *Iris* restaurant and *Arco Iris* discotheque both T 777-0449; *Isabel*, good breakfast choice, bulletin board, helpful staff, good food; *Restaurant El Turista* has good, cheap fruit juices; *El Gran Escape*, central, good food, good value, rec; *Soda Nido* and *Restaurant Ana*, cheap casados; *Soda Nahomi*, good sandwiches, near park, next to laundry, *Lavanderías de Costa Rica*; *Soda El Kiosko* on seafront, near *Hotel Kamuk*, good juices, fish dishes, international cuisine, popular; *Pizza Gabriel*, beware overcharging; *George's American Bar and Grill*, on road to Manuel Antonio, one block from sea, on corner, breakfast, lunch, dinner, popular with travellers and English-speaking residents, T 777-0186.

Transport There are four direct buses a day from the capital, book a day in advance, 3 hrs, US$3.15; a local bus, US$3.50, takes 6½-7 hrs, leaving the main road at Parrita to wind its way through the mountains and rural settlements, crowded, uncomfortable, you could walk faster at times. From **Quepos** there are buses NW along the coast to **Puntarenas**, 3½ hrs, 0430, 1030, and 1500, US$2.10. Two daily buses via Dominical to **San Isidro de El General**, 0700 and 1330, 3½ hrs, connections can be made there to get to the Panamanian border. There are daily flights from San José, with Sansa and Travelair, see **Internal Flights** under San José. Book in advance. In Quepos the Sansa office is under *Hotel Quepos*, T 777-0161. Hustler Tours also run flights. Blue Marlin shop, with tours, information, next to *Hotel Quepos*. Taxis congregate at the junction of the coastal road and the park, by the road to Manuel Antonio. Minibuses meet flights at the airport. **Motorbike Hire** Pico Rent-a-Bike, opposite *Hotel Malinche* 200m from beach, T 777-0125, several models from US$25 per day. See also information at *Restaurant Isabel*.

7 km S of Quepos along a paved road is **Manuel Antonio National Park**, 683 hectares of swamps and beaches with a rich variety of fauna and flora. Plenty of birds, snakes, lizards, monkeys and sloths can be seen. The forest grows right down to three beautiful, but often crowded beaches: Espadilla Sur, Manuel Antonio and Puerto Escondido, and iguanas and white-faced monkeys often come down on to the sand. Hiking is good in the park. A 45-min trail, steep in places, runs round the Punta Catedral between Espadilla Sur and Manuel Antonio

beaches. The walk to Puerto Escondido, where there is a blow hole, takes about 50 mins. The map sold at the entrance shows a walk up to a *mirador*, which has good views of the coastline, worth taking. The entrance to the park is reached by crossing a tidal river (plastic shoes recommended – it is sometimes very high), open 0700-1600, US$1.50 for foreigners, US$0.50 for Costa Ricans, children under 10 free. Early and late are the best times to see the wildlife. Breakfast and other meals available from stalls just before the river, where cars can be parked and minded for US$1 by the stallholders. Basic toilets and picnic tables by the beaches, cold water showers at Manuel Antonio and Espadillas Sur beaches. Keep clear of the manzanilla trees and do not eat their poisonous apples. You are not supposed to feed the monkeys but people do, which means that they can be a nuisance, congregating around picnic tables expecting to be fed and rummaging through bags if given the chance. Leave no litter and take nothing out of the park, not even sea shells. Overdevelopment outside the park and overuse within has led to problems of how to manage the park with inadequate funds. In 1992 the National Park Service (SPN) threatened to close it and a number of tour operators removed it from their itineraries. The beaches in the park are safer than those outside, but rip tides are dangerous all along the coast. Look for local safety literature. Beaches slope steeply and the force of the waves can be too strong for children. Watch out for logs and other debris in the water. Sea Kayaking, T 777-0574, Ríos Tropicales, 50m N of Manuel Antonio School, one-day or multi-day tours, inc transport, equipment and professional guides, Kelly and John have been rec.

Accommodation and Food There are hotels all along the road from Quepos to Manuel Antonio, many shut in the low season. In high season, best to book ahead. Nearest the park is **D** *Hotel Manuel Antonio*, T 777-0290, restaurant, good breakfast, rec, and **D** *Bar y cabinas Manuel Antonio*, without bath in house behind beach, **F** in small rooms at the back, dirty, smelly, which you will share with ants, cockroaches, crabs etc or D-C for nicer cabin with bath on beach, gets damp in rainy season. On a side road just before the park is **F** *Costa Linda*, 6-bedded rooms, with cooking facilities, fan, water shortage, T 777-0304, dirty, mosquitoes, watch out for racoons raiding the outdoor kitchen in the night, good breakfasts, dinner rather pricey; **A** *Hotel Villabosque*, 50m from beach, 150m from National Park, 10 rooms with a/c, private bathroom, inc breakfast, T/F 777-0401. **B** *Cabinas Espadilla*, T 777-0416, fan (not very effective), water shortages, clean, 10 mins walk from beach; **D-B** *Vela Bar*, T 777-0413, Apt 13 Quepos, large rooms with bath, fans, safes, very good restaurant, fishing and other trips, also has a fully-equipped house to rent; further along is *Soda El Grano de Oro*, basic rooms at back, see Betty. Heading towards Quepos, on the main road, is *Bar del Mar*, T 777-0543, which rents surfboards, sells drinks and light meals and has a collection of English novels to read in the bar. Just off the road 25m further on, in a small lay-by, are the restaurants *Mar y Sombra*, T 777-0003, good *casado especial* and jumbo shrimps and *Amor y Mar*, T 777-0510, a souvenir shop, **D** *Caycosta* and *Cabinas Ramírez*, T 777-0510 and 777-0003, with bath, food and bar, friendly (although women have remarked on feeling uncomfortable with the male employees), hammocks and camping free, guests can help with cooking in exchange; **C** *Cabinas Los Almendos*, private bath, fan, clean, quiet, T 777-0225.

Proceeding along the main road towards Quepos, you come to *Cabinas Pisces*, T 777-0294/0046, and **A+** *Karahé*, T 777-0170, F 777-0152, inc breakfast, cabins on a steep hillside with lovely view sleep 3/4, rec, fridge, bath, a/c or fan, good restaurant, swimming pool across the road, access to beach, can walk to park along the beach; **A** *Costa Verde*, near beach, apartments for 2-3 people, with kitchenette and bath, 2-bedroom villas available, T 777-0584, F 777-0560, well-appointed, rec; **B-D** *La Arboleda*, T 777-0414, cabins on hillside leading down to beach sleep 2/3, bath, fan, good rec. Uruguayan restaurant, 8 hectare wood, beware snakes, crabs and monkeys in the yard at night; **L** *Hotel El Salto*, T 777-0130, F 441-2938, PO Box 119, Quepos, MAP in cabins with bath sleeping up to 4, inc taxes and eco-tour of own Reserve with water falls, 4 km of trails, horses, lovely peaceful setting on hill, open air restaurant and bar, gardens, pool; **L** *Makanda by the Sea*, T 777-0442, 1 km from main road, 6 villas and studios; back on main road; **A** *Hotel Casablanca*, T 777-0377, smart, new, lovely view, German-owned, friendly, all facilities, pool, rec, on corner of road to **L+** *Hotel Mariposa*, T 777-0355, also fine position, villas 800 feet above beach, inc breakfast, dinner, taxes and service, no credit cards, no guests under 15, bar, mixed reports about restaurant (book in advance), pool (US$1 for non-residents); **A+** *Los Mogotes*, T 777-0582, inc breakfast, 8 rooms, pool and restaurant; **A+** *Villas Nicolás*, T 777-0538, 10 rooms, 10 suites with kitchenette, pool; **A** *Byblos*, T 777-0411, low season, L high season MAP, all in bungalows, sleep 1-4, French restaurant, pool, cruise in *Byblos I* boat 0800-1500, US$50 pp inc drink and sandwiches; nearby are the cabins of John and Mavis Beisanz, T 249-1507, also expensive but very good; further on same side road, **A** *Divisamar*, T 777-0371, low season, A+ high season, pool, restaurant, a/c; *Barba Roja* restaurant, popular, not cheap, grilled tuna good, art gallery and gift shop, boat charter T 777-0424; **A** *Villa Oso*, T 777-0233, spectacular sea views; off the main road away from the sea, **B** *El Lirio*, T 777-0404, low season, A+ high season inc breakfast and taxes, small, very comfortable; almost opposite, *Ríos Tropicales* (see San José **Travel Agencies**) offers sea kayaking, mountain biking and tours; close to Quepos, **C** *Plinio*, T 777-0055, low season, B high season, on hillside, 13 rooms, restaurant, bar, rec; *Cabinas Pedro Miguel*, opposite, T 777-0035. **B** *El Mirador del Pacífico*, 8 rooms, bath and fan, German-owned, T/F 777-0119, location not known. Take a torch when walking on roads at night; there are snakes, some poisonous. Take all precautions against mosquitoes, even in daytime.

The exact location of the following is unknown: **A** *Eclipse*, Apartado 11-6350, Quepós, T/F 777-0408, Costa Rican/French run, Mediterranean feel, pool, very helpful, rec; *La Brise* restaurant, nearby towards the beach, elegant breakfast, worth the money. **A-B** Carol Christiansen runs a 4-room guest house, 10 mins walk N of main intersection.

Transport There are 3-4 buses a day (depending on season) am, midday and pm, direct from San José, 4 hrs, US$5. Tickets are sold on main road between the few sodas, get them in advance, bus gets crowded in Quepos. The Americana VIP coach service operates Mon, Wed, Fri, Sun, to San José, US$55 round trip, T 222-8134. A regular bus service runs six times a day (roughly hourly in high season) from beside **Quepos** market, starting at 0545, last bus back at 1700, US$0.35. Taxi from Quepos, shared, US$0.65 pp. Minibuses meet flights from San José to the airport at Quepos (see above), but fare high: US$2.25.

30 km SE from Quepos along the unpaved coastal road ('carretera Costanera') is Playa Matapalo, a huge, beautiful sandy beach recommended for surfing and relaxing. Accommodation is available, including *Bar y Cabinas El Coquito del Pacífico*, C, comfortable new cabins with bath, palm gardens, good breakfast, Swiss owned, rec (T Braun Ecoturismo in San José T 233-1731, F 222-8849). 12 km further is **Dominical**, at the mouth of the Río Barú, where the road turns inland to San Isidro de El General (bus Quepos-Dominical 0700, 1330). This road is very steep and has many unpaved sections, from a few metres to a few kilometres. **C** *Willis Cabañas*, restaurant opposite; **D-C** *Albergue Willdale*, T 771-1903/0866, fan and bath, bikes, boat trips, fishing and horses available; **E-D** *Cabinas El Coco*, with or without bath, negotiate price, reported dirty, unfriendly, noisy; **E** *Cabinas Roca Verde*, friendly, fan, restaurant, rec; **E** *Cabinas Costa Brava*, S of the village, restaurant, basic but friendly. 4 km S is Punta Dominical (no transport); **D** *Cabinas Punta Dominical*, T 771-0866, restaurant, fishing, riding, good value for seekers of solitude. **B** pp *Finca Brian y Milena*, near Dominical, 400m above ocean, T 771-1903 (leave message), cabins with bath, inc meals, forest, waterfall, horses. Last bus from San Isidro to Dominical 1500. 18 km S of Dominical is the village of **Uvita**, where there is camping, **F** *El Chaman*, German owner, very friendly, nice beach, isolated. The road S from Uvita has been paved as far as Ciudad Cortés, and access to the beaches of Playa Ballena and Playa Bahía is getting easier with consequent development of the area and the construction of *cabinas*. You can hire boats to take you out to Isla Ballena, part of **Ballena National Marine Park**, wonderful views looking back to the mainland. Be careful of the surf, do not attempt to swim ashore on to the island.

SAN JOSE TO THE PANAMA BORDER (8)

Through the mountains, past El Chirripó, the highest peak, dropping down along the valley of the Río de El General to the tropical lowlands of the Pacific coast and the Panama border.

The Pan-American Highway to the Panama border runs 352 km from San José (frequent rockslides during rainy season), first to Cartago (toll road, US$0.10), and southwards over the mountains between Cartago and San Isidro de El General (124 km). This is a spectacular journey. The climate is ideal for orchids. At Cartago begins the ascent of Cerro Buena Vista, a climb of 1,830m to the continental divide at 3,490m; this is the highest spot on the Highway (with an interesting *páramo* ecosystem). Those unaccustomed to high altitude should beware of mountain sickness brought on by a too rapid ascent—see **Health Information**. For 16 km it follows the crest of the Talamanca ridge, with views, on clear days, of the Pacific 50 km away, and even of the Atlantic, over 80 km away.

About 50 km from San José, a side road leads off the Pan-American Highway to the peaceful and very pleasant mountain villages of **Santa María de Dota** (E *Hotel Santa María*, with bath; F *Hotel Marieuse*, without bath, T 541-1176, very friendly, run by an elderly lady, Doña Elsie) and **San Marcos de Tarrazú** (Hotels: F *Marilú*, restaurant; E *Continental*, with bath; F *Zacateca*, with bath). Santa María is quiet, and beautifully situated; it is in a good area for walking, and 8 km away is a small lake where many waterbirds nest. Nearby is **San Gerardo de Dota**; C pp *Cabinas Chacón*, inc meals, good cabins, simple meals, T 771-1732, good chance of seeing quetzales on the property (short trail map available), and there is trout fishing in the Río Savegre. From Santa María one can hike (10 hrs) to the Pacific coast of the Puerto Quepos district, or go by road (3 hrs in a 4-wheel drive vehicle).

At Km 58 is **Genesis II** at Cerro de la Muerte, 100-acre cloudforest reserve at 2,360m, rooms with shared bath, for birders and naturalists, advance reservation necessary, messages T 225-0271, transportation available from San José. There is also a student volunteer programme: write to Steve and Paula Friedman, Apartado 10303, 1000 San José (conditions are basic, the climate can be cold and damp and rooms are heated with kerosene heaters but the plant and animal life make it a worthwhile stopover; ascertain precisely in advance what you will be expected to do, what food you will receive and how much time you will spend in the reserve, to avoid disappointment). At Km 62 on the Pan-American Highway is the **A** *Albergue de Montaña Tapantí*, also called *Tapantí Mountain Lodge*, Spanish-owned, 6 bungalows, beautiful location, 1 hr to San José, one-night packages inc transport and guided trips available, T 233-0133. At Km 70: *Finca El Mirador Los Quetzales*, 43 ha forest property at 2,400m, Eddie Serano or one of his sons will show visitors quetzales and other endemic species of the highlands, US$7 pp; you can also fish for your own trout (price according to weight); cabin under construction. At Km 71 is another *Finca Quetzal*. Km 78: *Casa Refugio de Ojo de Agua*, a historic pioneer home with picnic tables in front of the house. S of the highest point (at Km 95, 3,335m, temperatures below zero at night) is **E** *Hotel Georgina*, basic, clean, friendly, good food, ask owners for directions for a good walk to see quetzales. The road then drops down into **San Isidro de El General**, 702m above sea-level in a fertile valley in the centre of a coffee and cattle district. The town is growing fast. The **Museo Regional de Pérez Zeledón** is in the old marketplace, open Mon-Fri, 0800-1200, 1300-1630.

Hotels and Restaurants C *Del Sur*, T 771-0233, 10 km S of town, with bath, comfortable, swimming pool, tennis, good restaurant; E *Amaneli*, with restaurant E *Hotel Chirripó*, S side of Parque Central, shared bath, near bus office, small rooms, clean, very good restaurant, free covered parking, good; E *Manhattan*, with bath; F *El Jardín*, (good value), and good restaurant (especially the breakfast); F *Hotel Balboa* in the centre, bath; E *Iguazu*, modern; *Astoria*, not rec. *Restaurant Wu Fu* is good, *Hong Kong*, across the park from *Hotel Chirripó*, reasonable prices; *Restaurant El Tenedor*, good food, not expensive, friendly, big pizzas. *Soda Mönpik*, good hamburgers, *batidos*, ice cream, N side of Parque Central; *Panadería El Tío Marcos*, S side of Parque, very good bakery; *Café del Teatro*, small snack bar, helpful owner is planning to open a tourist office; paintings for sale and plays in Spanish every month or so. Ask in advance for early (0400) breakfast if climbing Chirripó.

Transport bus terminal at Av 6, C Central/2 at the back of the new market and adjacent streets. To and from **San José**, hourly service, US$3, 3 hr. However, Tracopa buses coming from San José, going S go from Calle 3/Pan-American Highway, behind church, to **Paso Canoas**, 0830-1545, 1930 (direct), 2100; **David** (Panama) direct, 1000 and 1500; **Golfito** direct at 1800. Waiting room but no reservations or tickets sold.

From San Isidro de El General one can go to the highest mountain in Costa Rica, Cerro El Chirripó (3,820m) in the middle of the **Chirripó National Park** (50,150 hectares), including the highest peaks of Costa Rica and a considerable portion of cloud forest (entry US$1.50). Splendid views from the mountaintops; interesting alpine environment on the high plateau, with lakes of glacial origin and very diverse flora and fauna. The Chirripó National Park and the neighbouring **La Amistad International Park** (193,929 hectares), established in 1982, extend along the Cordillera de Talamanca to the Panamanian border and comprise the largest area of virgin forest in the country with the greatest biological diversity. At Las Mellizas entrance to La Amistad Park there is a chalet lodge on a coffee plantation, **A** pp *La Amistad*, all inclusive, good hiking, excellent guide, rec rooms and food, contact owner Roberto Montero, c/o Trobical Rainbow Tours, T 233-8228, F 255-4636, San José.

At San Isidro de El General, get food and take the Pueblo Nuevo bus to San Gerardo de Rivas (0500 or 1400; be early; it leaves from the W side of the central plaza, but enquire carefully or you may miss it). Highly interesting trip up the Río Chirripó valley; *San Gerardo de Rivas* is situated in a cool, pleasant landscape at the confluence of two rivers. Bus at 0700 to San Isidro. Sr Francisco Elizondo Badilla and his family have a small cabin, **G** pp *Posada El Descanso*, with seven bunks, bathroom, hearty meals available, rec, phone town administrator for information on availability, T 771-0433 ext 106. Horses for rent and guide services offered. Macho Elizondo is a recommended guide who lives in San Gerardo. Along the road beyond the Rangers office, bear left over a bridge and on the left is *Posada Chirripó*, owned by Francisco the local 'champion' climber, a good place to stay. You can stay at the small hotel opposite the football pitch called **G** *Soda y Cabinas Chirripó*, hot shower, clean, basic, friendly, restaurant. You can camp at or near the park office, in San Gerardo near the bus stop. Check in first and pay US$0.30. Horses can be rented. There is a hot spring 1 km from San Gerardo. If you wish to climb the mountains, obtain a permit from the SPN office in San José (see National Parks in Introduction). Start in the early morning for the 8- to 10-hr hike, US$1.40 entry for each day spent in the Park, plus US$2.90 shelter fee per night, max 40 persons in park at any one time. Pay at the Park office in San Gerardo. The first shelter, where the horses will take you, is barely adequate and located in a windy spot; the second, 40 min away, is better built, larger, and more convenient for reaching Cerro Chirripó the next morning before the clouds come in. There are 2 huts 1½ hrs from the top at 3,400m where there normally is a park ranger. Stay in the yellow one, toilet, shower. Hang up food or the mice will get it. Bring your own gas stove, which can be hired from *Posada El Descanso* or the shop near *Cabinas Chirripó*. Two other peaks can be reached from these huts, Crestones, 45 mins, and Ventisqueres, 1½ hrs. Plan for at least two nights on the mountain, and bring warm sleeping bags and clothing. It can be hot in the daytime, though. In the rainy season trails up the plateau are uncomfortably slippery and muddy, and fog obscures the views. These are stiff walks, but no technical climbing is called for. Time your descent to catch the 1530 bus to San Isidro.

Also, in this central area of Costa Rica, there are many rivers running NE to the Caribbean that are good for white water rafting, especially July to December eg Pacuare, Chirripó and Reventazón. Enquire at Costa Rica Expeditions, Calle Central, Av 3, San José (see also under **Turrialba**, p 767 and San José **Travel Agencies**).

At Km 197 (from San José) is **Buenos Aires**, with F *Cabinas Mary*, 500m from centre, quiet clean, F *Cabinas La Redonda Familiares*, close to the Pan-American Highway and a unnamed *cabinas* across from the bus station (with or without bath, clean, good value); next door is **Soda Refresquería El Parque**, good *casados*; *Flor de la Sabana*, good restaurant, good value. The section of the highway running alongside the Río Grande de Térraba is prone to landslides which can cut it off for days. At **Palmar Norte** (Km 257) are E cabin F room *Hotel y Cabinas Casa Amarilla*, with fan, rooms at back quieter, rooms over restaurant noisy but cheaper; also **Quebrada**, noisy and basic, *El Puente Hotel y Restaurante*, and *Xinia*. From here a paved road leads to Ciudad Cortés and from there you can follow a new road along the coast NW to Dominical (**see p 778**). At **Palmar Sur** (gas station), 99 km from the Panamanian border, a banana plantation has stone spheres, $1\frac{1}{2}$m in diameter and accurate within 5 mm, which can also be seen in other places in Costa Rica. They are of precolumbian Indian manufacture, but their use is a matter of conjecture; among recent theories are that they were made to represent the planets of the solar system, or that they were border markers. Flights with Sansa and Travelair San José-Palmar Sur, see **Internal Flights**, San José. 6 buses a day from San José to Palmar Norte, 5 hrs, C 2-4, Av 18, Tracopa.

Near the border is the town of **San Vito**, built by Italian immigrants among denuded hills; it is a prosperous but undistinguished town. E *Hotel Pitier*, $\frac{1}{2}$ km out of town on road to Sabalito, new, clean, with bath; *Las Mirlas* in same location and price range but more attractive; and D *El Ceibo*, in new part with bath and hot water, E in old part, T 773-3025, good restaurant. There are also two good Italian restaurants in San Vito, *Lilianas* and *Mama Mías*, genuine Italian cuisine, reasonable prices. Hotels also in the nearby village of Cañas Gordas. At **Las Cruces** there are the **Wilson Botanical Gardens**, T 773-3278, owned by the Organization for Tropical Studies, 6 km from San Vito. It consists of 145 hectares of tropical plants, orchids, other epiphytes, and tropical trees, entrance US$4.50, good self guide booklet for the principal trail US$2.20. Many birdwatchers come here. It is possible to spend the night here if you arrange first with the Organization of Tropical Studies in San José, T 240-6696 (cost around US$55 a night with food, senior researchers US$32, day visits with lunch US$12. Direct buses San José to San Vito, 4 daily, 9 hrs, C 14, Av 5; alternative route, not all paved, via Ciudad Neily (see below); from San Vito to Las Cruces at 0530 and 0700; sit on the right to admire the wonderful scenery; return buses pass Las Cruces at 1510. The road from Paso Real to San Vito is now paved and has lovely views. There is a 2-car ferry over the Río Terraba just after the Paso Real junction (US$1.50 cars, US$0.20 bicycles); runs on demand. The road from San Vito to Ciudad Neily is paved for the first 12 km to Aguas Buenas, thereafter, despite what maps say, it is unpaved to Ciudad Neily, 19 km, steep, bumpy and rocky (it would be very difficult in a passenger car). From San Vito a paved road runs to the Panama border at Sabalito/Río Sereno, but you need a visa to be allowed to cross here (if entering Costa Rica, get a tourist card in advance).

33 km N of the border a road (26 km) branches S at Río Claro (several *pensiones*) to **Golfito**, the former banana port (fuel available at the junction on the Pan-American Highway). Many of the banana plantations have been turned over to oil palm and other crops but the port is active with container traffic and Standard Fruit have their local HQ here. Golfito is really two towns—the banana company community and the town itself—about $2\frac{1}{2}$ km apart. Golfito became a free port in 1990, has become popular with shoppers and at weekends it is difficult to get a hotel room.

Hotels A *Sierra*, near airport, a/c, pool, restaurant, overpriced; D *Costa Sur*, also near airport, good restaurant. In the 'banana town', E *Cabinas Evelyn*, with fan and bath; F *Cabinas Marlin*, small neat rooms, fan, hot water, friendly; G *Cabinas Ajilio*; F *Cabinas Wilson*; E *Cabinas Princesa del Golfo* and *Casa Blanca Lodge*, both in fine frame houses with beautiful gardens. In the 'main town' to the S, *Del Cerro*, Edif Wachong, some a/c, private bathroom, fishing boat rentals, T 775-0006; D *Costa Rica Surf*, also one cheap, single room; G *Delfina*, friendly, basic; E *Golfito*, T 775-0047, with bath, run down; C *Las Gaviotas*, with excellent restaurant on waterfront; *El Refugio*, T 775-0449; G *El Uno*, above restaurant of same name, basic, friendly.

The **Refugio Nacional de Fauna Silvestre Golfito** has been created in the steep forested hills overlooking Golfito, originally to protect Golfito's watershed. It is rich in rare and medicinal plants and has abundant fauna. There are some excellent hikes in the Refuge. It is supervised by the University of Costa Rica and they have a field office in Golfito. About 6 km (1½ hr walk) from Golfito is the **Playa de Cacao**. A taxi boat from Golfito will take you there for US$0.50, or you can drive (if it hasn't rained too heavily) along an inland road, starting at the left of the police station in Golfito, and left again a few km later. At Playa de Cacao: **C Cabinas Palmas**, 6 cabins, American-owned, friendly, clean, shower and toilet, directly on beach, T 775-0373 (leave message). Next to Cabinas Palmas, good, cheap restaurant, **Siete Mares**. At **Playa Zancudo** you can stay in cabins at **E Sol y Mar**, run by Bob and Monika Hara who speak German and English. To get there contact staff of Yacht Club at the entrance of Golfito and ask to radiophone to Zancudo, 775-0056; well recommended. **Cabinas Los Almendros**, 10 mins by boat from Golfito, cabins with bath, T 775-0515. 30 mins by boat from Golfito, at Playa Cativo, is Michael Medill's **L Rainbow Adventures**, cabinas, inc all meals, snacks, beer and soft drinks, transport, also double rooms, dining room, private beach with no other hotels, jungle tours, water sports, bordered by Corcovado National Park expansion, Apdo 63, Golfito, T/F 775-0220, in USA, 5875 NW Kaiser Rd, Portland, Oregon 97229, T 503-690-7750.

Transport Bus from **San José** 0700, 1100, 1500 daily from C 2-4, Av 18, T 221-4214 (US$5) with Tracopa, 8 hrs; from San Isidro de El General, take 0730 bus to Río Claro and wait for bus coming from Ciudad Neily. Daily flights San José-Golfito, with Sansa (not Sun) and Travelair, see **Internal Flights**, San José. Runway is all-weather, tight landing between trees; 2 km from town, taxi US$0.50. Bus Golfito-**Paso Canoas**, US$0.80 from outside *Soda Pavo*, 1¼ hrs.

S of Golfito, at **Punta Banco** is **A** *Tiskita Lodge*, T 255-3518, a 400-acre property including a fruit farm, with excellent birdwatching, 9 cabins, owned by Peter Aspinall c/o Sun Tours, Apdo 1195-1250 Escazú. Overlooks beach, cool breezes, waterfall, jungle pools, trails through virgin forest. All-inclusive package tours from San José including roundtrip air transportation. *Tiskita* can be combined with **Corcovado Tent Lodge Camp** at Carate, Osa Peninsula. Day trips offered to Sirena Ranger Station in Corcovado National Park. 500m S of Pavones near Punta Banco is **B** *Pavones Surf Camp*, inc meals, 2 cabins with bath, 6 rooms with shared bath, T 225-0786. The beach is rocky, but good surfing. A bus leaves Golfito for Pavones at 1400, and from Pavones to Golfito at 0500 3 hrs US$2.50.

At the southern end of the country is the **Osa Peninsula**. From San José there are 2 buses daily to **Puerto Jiménez** at 0600 and 1200 via San Isidro, US$7, 8 hrs, return 0500 and 1100, T 771-2550. There are also buses from San Isidro, leaving from **Soda Frutera del Sol** at 0530 and 1200 daily, next to Texaco on Pan-American Highway, US$3, returns at 0330 and 1100, 6 hrs. To reach Puerto Jiménez from the Pan-American Highway (70 km), turn right at the restaurant about 30 km S of Palmar Sur; the road is newly paved to Rincón, therafter best tackled with four-wheeled drive as a few rivers have to be forded (high clearance essential). They are working on bridges. Bus Puerto Jiménez-Ciudad Neily 0500 and 1400, 3½ hrs, US$2.50. There is a police checkpoint 47 km from the Pan-American Highway. Trucks, called 'taxis' run daily between Puerto Jiménez and La Palma (several, 1 hr, US$1.50); from the small settlement of La Palma an all-weather road goes to Rincón. There are daily flights between Puerto Jiménez and Golfito, US$20, for information T 735-5017 or 775-0607. Two boats leave from Golfito to Puerto Jiménez at 1100, US$2.50, 1½ hrs, return 0600, or you can charter a taxi boat for about US$60, up to 8 passengers. Alternatively, if you want to visit the western side of the peninsula, take taxi or bus from Palmar Norte to Sierpe (30 mins) and ask for a boat going down the river. This may take some time because boats are heavily laden with the locals' shopping. It is a 2-hr boat trip down river and across the sea to Agujitas (see below), a small village near the **Marenco** Biological Station (information, PO Box 4025, San José, T 221-1594).

Accommodation and Food in Puerto Jiménez: best is **C** *Manglares*, with bath and fan, clean, small, cold showers, café, bar, friendly, rec, T 735-5002 for reservation, Ramón can arrange tours to Corcovado, Mangrove gardens attract many species of birds; **E** *Cabinas Marcelina*, with bath, clean, friendly, nice front yard, rec; **E** *Hotel Restaurant Choza del Maglan*, cabins in garden; **F** *Cabinas Brisas del Mar*, with bath (T 735-5012); **G** pp *Pensión Quintero*, clean, good value, ask here for Fernando Quintero, who rents horses and has a boat for up to 6 passengers, good value, he is also a guide, rec. *Restaurant El Paraíso*, typical food, cheap. *Carolina's Restaurant*, highly rec for fish. 5 km from Rincón, on the road to Puerto Jiménez, at the NE side of the neck of the peninsula, is **G** pp *Projecto Boscoso*, a naturalists' camp where visitors can stay in camp beds, 3 meals US$3.65, information from Fundación Neotrópica, C 20, between Av 3 y 5, San José, T 233-0003, ask for Walter Rodríguez, who is developing ecotourism facilities.

At the tip of the Peninsula at *Cabo Matapalo*, is **A** pp *Bosque del Cabo Wilderness Lodge*, inc meals, 30 min taxi jeep ride from Puerto Jiménez; **A+** *Lapa Ríos Wilderness Resort*, T 735-5130, inc meals, 14 luxury palm-thatched bungalows on private 1,000 acre reserve (80% virgin forest, owners Karen and John Lewis), Carbonera beach, camping trips, boats can be arranged from Golfito, or drive from San José (4WD rec); the Osa Trail, to Sierpe, starts at Laspa Ríos. Plenty of deserted beaches (tide goes out a long way, sandflies at high tide). Puerto Jiménez is full of North Americans because of the gold mines near *Carate* on the Pacific coast and elsewhere on the Peninsula. Several buses a day to *Dos Brazos* to see the gold mines; ask for the road which goes uphill, beyond town, for the mines. Last bus back from Dos Brazos at 1530 (often late). Rubber boots advisable as a precaution against venomous snakes (see below).

Corcovado National Park, including the *Isla del Caño* (200 hectares), comprises 41,989 hectares. It consists largely of tropical rainforests, and includes swamps, miles of empty beaches, and some cleared areas now growing back. It is located at the western end of the Osa Peninsula, on the Pacific Ocean. If short of time and/or money, the simplest way to the park is to take the pick-up truck from outside *Carolina's Restaurant* in Puerto Jiménez to Playa Carate, Mon, Thur, Sat, usually between 0700 and 0800, 2½ hrs, US$3.65, returns same day, ask in advance about departure (one of the drivers is Cirilo Espinosa). It may be possible to book a flight with the Servicio de Parques Nacionales (SPN) in Puerto Jiménez, or take the Velsa/Sansa Charter flights which continue from Golfito-Puerto Jiménez to Carate (see above). They will also take private flights to La Sirena in the park for US$36 pp. The SPN office in Puerto Jiménez is next to the bank, 1 block parallel to the main street, daily 0730-1200, 1300-1700, T 735-5036; they will give permits for entering the park and will book accommodation at *La Sirena* in dormitories, maximum 20 people, **F** for bed (reservation essential), camping F, no reservation needed, 3 meals available. Bring mosquito netting. Another suggestion is vitamin B1 pills (called 'tiamina'). Mosquitoes detest the smell and leave you alone. There is occasional trouble between gold prospectors and the park guards. If it is dangerous for visitors you will not be allowed into those parts.

At Carate there is a dirt airstrip and a store, run by Gilberto Morales and his wife Roxana (they rent rooms, but often full of gold miners, they also have a tent for hire, but take sleeping bag). 30 mins walk W along the beach is *Corcovado Lodge*, **C** inc breakfast, with 20 walk-in tents with 2 campbeds each, in a beautiful coconut grove with hammocks overlooking the beach; to be sure of space book through Costa Rica Expeditions in San José (see under **Travel Agencies**). Clean showers and toilets; good food, take a flashlight. Behind the camp is a trail into the jungle with a wonderful view of the bay from a clearing; many birds to be seen, plus monkeys and frogs. The whole place is highly rec. If you want to continue to Panama you have to take a truck out, US$3.50, or a flight must be arranged, US$150.

5 mins walk further down the beach is *La Leona* park wardens' station and entrance to the park. To go beyond here costs US$1.50 per day, whether you are walking to La Sirena (18 km along the beach), or just visiting for the day. Lodging

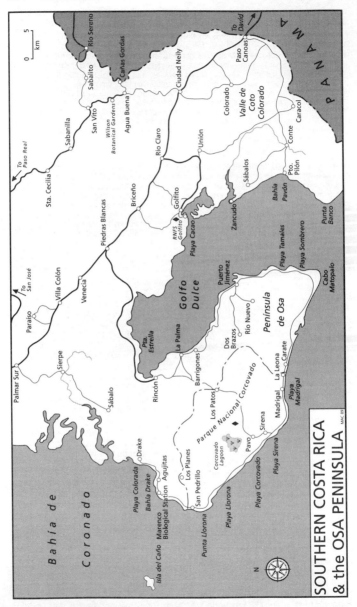

SOUTHERN COSTA RICA
& the OSA PENINSULA

is available at La Leona, F, maximum 12 people in basic rooms or camping, meals available, book in high season through SPN; horses for hire. Beyond here to the end of Playa Madrigal is another 2-2$\frac{1}{2}$ hrs walk, partly sandy, partly rocky, with some rock pools and rusty shipwrecks looking like modern art sculptures. The shore rises very steeply into the jungle which grows thickly with mangroves, almonds and coconut palms. Check with wardens about high tide so you don't get stuck. There are a couple of rivers along the beach, the first Río Madrigal, is only about 15 mins beyond La Leona (lovely and cool, clear and deep enough for swimming about 200m upstream—a good place for spotting wildlife). The best place for seeing wildlife, though, is La Sirena (about 6 hrs hiking from La Leona, mostly along the beach), where there are paths inland and the terrain is flatter and more isolated.

You can head inland from Sirena on a trail past three conveniently spaced shelters to **Los Patos** after passing several rivers full of reptiles (4 hrs). A wooden house in dilapidated condition gives protection overnight. Its balcony is a great observation point for birds especially the redheaded woodpecker. From Los Patos you can carry on to the park border, then, crisscrossing the Río Rincón to La Palma (small hostal), a settlement near the opposite side of the Peninsula (6 more hrs); from which there are several 'taxis' making the 1-hr trip to Puerto Jiménez (see above). An offshoot of this trail will lead you to a raffia swamp that rings the Corcovado Lagoon. The lagoon is only accessible by boat, but there are no regular trips. Caymans and alligators survive here, sheltered from the hunters. Horses can be rented cheaply at Sirena. Chiggers (*coloradillas*) and horseflies infest the horse pastures and can be a nuisance, similiarly, sandflies on the beaches; bring spray-on insect repellent.

From Sirena you can walk N along the coast to the shelter at **Llorona** (adequate; plenty of water—waterfalls, in fact), from which there is a trail to the interior with another shelter at the end. From Llorona you can proceed N through a forest trail and then along the beach to the station at **San Pedrillo** on the edge of the park. You can stay here, camping or under roof, and eat with the rangers, who love company. From San Pedrillo you can take the park boat (not cheap) to Isla del Caño, a lovely park outpost with 2 men. Continue N to the village of **Agujitas**, outside the park, (**B** pp *Cabinas Sir Francis Drake*, with bath, meals, T 771-2436; **B** *Playa Cocalito Lodge*, Punta Agujitas, 7 cabins, restaurant serving organically-grown fruit and vegetables, horseriding, trips to Corcovado National Park, T/F 786-6291; **D-E** *Cecilia's Lodge*, bunk beds in dormitory with shower or room in the house, full board, camping possible, Cecilia rents horses, takes you for a ride, visit to Isla del Caño or Marenco possible, will arrange return transport to Sierpe, nice landscape, friendly family, rec). Frequent trips with the park boat from San Pedrillo to Agujitas. New tourist facilities at **Bahía Drake**, close to Isla del Caño include: **A+** pp *La Paloma Jungle Lodge*, inc meals, T 239-0954, radio phone 239-2801, 6 cabins with bath, guided tours with resident biologist; **B** pp *Drake Bay Wilderness Camp*, with meals, tents available, pleasant family atmosphere, canoeing, ocean fishing, trips to Corcovado, Isla del Cano, horse riding facilities, large reductions for children, rec, T 771-2436, charter flights available; *Hotel El Caballito de Mar*, 7 rooms, owned by Rob Messenger, scuba diving trips to Isla de Cano sport fishing and jungle trips, T 231-5028. In March 1579, Sir Francis Drake careened his ship on Playa Colorada in Bahía Drake; a plaque commemorating the 400th anniversary of the event was erected in Agujitas. From Agujitas you can get a boat (road under construction) to **Sierpe** on the Río Sierpe (see above; boat from Sierpe to Bahía Drake, 1$\frac{1}{2}$ hrs, US$60 return pp); **L** pp *Río Sierpe Lodge*, inc meals, 8 rooms with bath, trips to Corcovado, Isla del Cano, diving, birdwatching. Sierpe is connected by bus with the town of Palmar Sur (flights from San José, see above) on the Pan-American Highway.

Avoid the rainy season. Bring umbrellas (not raincoats—too hot), because it will rain, unless you are hiking, in which case it is preferable to get wet. Shelters can be found here and there, so only mosquito netting is indispensable. Bring all your food if you haven't arranged otherwise; food can only be obtained at Puerto Jiménez and Agujitas in the whole peninsula, and lodging likewise. The cleared areas (mostly outside the park, or along the beach) can be devastatingly hot. Get the Instituto Geográfico maps, scale 1:50,000. Remember finally that, as in any tropical forest, you may find some unfriendly wildlife, like snakes (fer-de-lance and bushmaster snakes may attack without provocation), and herds of wild pigs. (You should find the most suitable method for keeping your feet dry and protecting your ankles; for some, rubber boots are the thing, for others light footwear which dries quickly.)

Isla del Coco is a thickly-wooded island and National Park of 24 square km, 320 km off the Peninsula of Osa on the submarine Cocos Ridge which extends some 1400 km SW to the Galápagos Islands. It has a 2-man outpost. Contact Michael Kaye of Costa Rican Expeditions for reasonably priced tours; also Otec in San José, **see p 735**. Arrangements for reaching it by chartered boat can be made in Puntarenas, after a permit has been got from the Government, or you can take a scuba diving cruise on the *Okeanos Agressor*, 10 days, two sailings a month, T 232-0572 ext 60 (in USA: PO Drawer K, Morgan City, LA 70381, T 504-385-2416, F 504-384-0817). It was at one time a refuge for pirates, who are supposed to have buried great treasure there, though none has been found by the 500 expeditions which have sought it. Treasure seekers make an initial cash payment, agree to share any treasure found with the Government, and are supervised by Costa Rican police. The offshore waters are a fisherman's paradise.

At **Ciudad Neily**, about 18 km from the border, are the **F** *Motel Rancho*, with bath; **E** *Hotel Musuco*, with bath, F without, fan, good, clean, quiet; 4 sets of *cabinas* (all E with bath) and *pensiones* in F range. 10 km from the border is the **E** *Camino Real*, with restaurant, where it is possible to camp. Here and there on the road *cantinas* sell local food. Bus Ciudad Neily to border, US$0.25. Daily bus to San José, Tracopa, from main square, US$2.70, 7 hrs (on Sunday buses from the border are full by the time they reach Ciudad Neily). The road goes (plenty of buses, 20 mins) to **Paso Canoas** (**E** *Azteca*; F *Cabinas Interamericano*, with bath and fan, very good value; **F** *Evelyn*, and **F** *El Descanso* all with bath) on the Panama border. No fruit or vegetables can be taken into Panama. At Paso Canoas shops sell luxury items brought from Panama at prices considerably lower than those of Costa Rica (eg sunglasses, stereo equipment, kitchen utensils, etc); banks either side of border close at 1600. Banco Nacional de Panamá charges 1% commission for cashing TCs. No difficulty in getting rid of surplus colones with money changers. Bus San José-Paso Canoas, US$5.25, 8 hrs, Tracopa terminal Av 18, C 2-4 at 0500, 0730, 1300, 1630, 1800, and several others, check times, not all buses go to border. Those motoring N can get insurance cover at the border for US$13 ensuring public liability and property damage. Border open 0600-1100, 1300-1700, 1800-2200. **NB** If you need a tourist card only to enter Panama, you are strongly advised to get it before the border, as Panamanian border officials often do not have them (**see Panama, Information for Visitors**). Reports vary on border requirements, some people, but not all, have been asked for an onward ticket on entering Panama. Those without a ticket have been asked how much money they have, but have not had to prove anything.

INFORMATION FOR VISITORS

Documents A passport is required. For visits of up to 90 days the following do not need visas: nationals of most Western European countries, the USA, Canada, Israel, Japan, Romania, Hungary, Poland, Argentina, Uruguay, Panama, Paraguay and South Korea. The following also do not need a visa, but visits are limited to 30 days: citizens of Australia, New Zealand, Iceland, Monaco, most East European countries, South Africa, Taiwan, Singapore, most Middle Eastern countries, most Caribbean countries and most Central and South American countries, including Brazil, Mexico, Ecuador, Guyana, Guatemala, El Salvador and Honduras. Notwithstanding this, some travellers since November 1989 report that 90 days may be allowed for nationals of some of these countries. All other nationalities need a visa, costing US$20, valid for only 30 days (this includes France, Greece, Eire, Nicaragua, Peru, Dominican Republic, CIS, India, Indonesia, Egypt, Turkey). Make absolutely sure that you get an entry stamp in your passport and insist even if border officials tell you otherwise. Failure to have a stamp can lead to numerous problems on departure. Some nationalities have to have a tourist card, US$2 on entry.

With any extension, you have to get an exit visa when you leave (*timbre de salida*, US$7) and pay a US$45 (6,500 colones) departure tax (the same as Costa Ricans or residents). Alternatively you can just get an exit permit, which is valid for one month. This involves going to Tribunales in San José to declare that you are leaving no dependants in Costa Rica. There is an emigration tax of US$2. For longer stays ask for a Prórroga de Turismo at Migración in San José. For this you need 3 passport photos, an airline or bus ticket out of the country and proof of funds (eg travellers' cheques); you can apply for an extension of 1 or 2 months, 300 colones per month. The paperwork takes three days. If you leave the country, you must wait 72 hrs before returning, but it may be cheaper and easier to do this and get a new 30-day entry. Travel agents can arrange all extension and exit formalities for a small fee.

An onward ticket (a bus ticket—which can be bought at the border immigration office or sometimes from the driver on Tica international buses—a transatlantic ticket or an MCO will sometimes do) is asked for, but can be refunded in San José with a loss of about US$3 on a US$20 ticket. Cashing in an air ticket is difficult because you may be asked to produce another ticket out of the country. Also, tourists may have to show at least US$300 in cash or travellers' cheques before being granted entry (especially if you have no onward ticket). Always carry a passport, or photocopy, for presentation at spot-checks. Failure to do so may mean imprisonment.

NB If entering from Nicaragua, you may be forced to take a blood-test for malaria at the border point, and if you are not carrying anti-malaria tablets, officials may oblige you to buy and swallow some in their presence. Some report merely being asked if they were carrying malaria tablets and no checks were made.

NB Exit taxes, by air or land, and legislation regarding visa extensions, are subject to frequent change and travellers should check these details as near to the time of travelling as possible.

Warnings Those arriving by air from Colombia can expect to have their persons and baggage carefully searched because of the rampant drug traffic in the area. In Costa Rica, particularly on the Atlantic coast, do not get involved with drugs: many dealers are undercover police agents.

There has been much illegal immigration into Costa Rica: this explains why Migración officials sometimes grill visitors in their hotels.

Taxes There is an airport departure tax of US$7.25 (980 colones) for tourists. There is an 8% tax on airline tickets purchased in the country. The exit tax at land borders is US$5.

Air Services From the USA: American Airlines flies from Miami, Dallas/Fort Worth, New York (direct and via Miami), San Francisco (direct and via Miami) and Philadelphia with connections from several other US cities via Miami. United Airlines fly from Miami daily direct to San José, New York, from Washington and from San Francisco daily via Los Angeles and Guatemala City. Continental flies from Houston, also from Boston, Chicago, Cleveland Ohio, Dallas/Fort Worth, Denver, Los Angeles, New York, San Francisco and Washington DC, all changing planes in Houston. Taca flies from Houston via Belize City and San Salvador, on its way to Panama City; from other US cities with connections in El Salvador. Lacsa flies daily from Miami direct, or via Managua; from Los Angeles via Mexico City and Guatemala City and San Pedro Sula; from New York via Cancún, Tegucigalpa and San Pedro Sula; from New Orleans via Cancún and San Pedro Sula. Taca flies from Houston via Belize City and San Salvador. Mexicana de Aviación from Mexico City and Guatemala City. Aviateca from Chicago, Guatemala City and Managua. Aero Costa Rica also has direct Miami-San José flights and regular flights from Orlando.

    From Europe: connections can be made through US cities or direct with KLM from Amsterdam via Curaçao and Aruba and with Iberia from Madrid and Barcelona via San Juan or Miami. United Airlines has flights from Frankfurt and Munich via Washington DC. Condor and LTU International Airways offer charter flights from Germany.

    From Latin America: in addition to routes mentioned above, Lacsa flies from Caracas via Barranquilla and Panama City, from Santiago, Chile, via Lima and Panama City, from Quito and Guayaquil, and from San Juan, Puerto Rico via Panama City. Varig, Ecuatoriana and Lacsa run a joint operation once a week from Rio de Janeiro via São Paulo, Guayaquil and Quito. Ladeco flies from Santiago on its way to Mexico. SAM flies from Bogotá via San Andrés and continues on to Guatemala City. Viasa flies from Caracas via Cartagena. Copa and Nica fly from Guatemala City via San Salvador and Managua, continuing on to Panama City. Copa also flies from San Juan via Santo Domingo.

Shipping Services Shipping a vehicle from Puerto Limón to Guayaquil costs US$1,500 in a container (virtually impossible to travel with your car on the ship); arrange through an Agente de Vapores (look in Yellow Pages), US$200-500 for agents' fees and 'miscellaneous charges'. A similar charge was made from Puerto Limón to Cartagena (1992). In this case, the agent was Rafael Angel Ulloa y Cia, C 3, Av 10-12, San José, T 223-7233, talk to Grace Barboza. High disembarcation charges in Colombia. For shipping information, see also **Introduction and Hints** at the beginning of the book.

Air Freight You can fly a motorcycle from San José to Bogotá, with Sansa, T 441-8035 or SAM, the latter costs about US$1,000 for 2 bikes and 2 passengers. To Quito with Varig, 2 motorcycles costs about US$600, but it is more difficult to get them out of customs.

Customs Half a kilo of manufactured tobacco and 3 litres of liquor are allowed in duty-free. Any amount of foreign or local currency may be taken in or out.

Motoring Driving in Costa Rica allows for much flexibility of travel, with certain precautions. Speed limits are low (80 kmph, 100 kmph on some roads) and there are rigorous radar speed traps, especially at the entry to towns and on the Pan-American Highway. If caught, you may have your number plate confiscated and have to pay a court fine to get it back. Do not attempt to pay an on-the-spot fine. Unpaved roads are slow going, so leave plenty of time for your trip, 20 kph may be your maximum speed. Many of the nature parks are in remote areas and 4-wheel drive may well be needed, certainly a car with high clearance is recommended; in the wet season some roads will be impassable. Check that bridges are not down. Always ask locals or bus drivers what the state of the road is before embarking on a journey, but do not assume that if the buses are running, a car can get through too. Car hire firms are not covered by tourist regulations and many complaints have been made to the authorities concerning their operations. If hiring a car, be very cautious. Most leases do not allow the use of a normal car off paved roads. Always make sure the spare tyre is in good order, as holes are frequent. You can have tyres fixed at any garage for about US$3 in half an hour. Hired cars bear special number plates and are easily identified. Be particularly careful not to leave valuables in a hired car, which is a sitting target.

Beware of policemen trying to charge on-the-spot fines. Fines in Costa Rica may only validly be paid at official stations in San José and major towns. If you pay a fine immediately, you still run the risk of getting reported and having to pay when you leave the country.

Tourists who come by car pay US$10 road tax and can keep their cars for an initial period of 90 days. This can be extended for a total period of 6 months, for about US$10 per extra month, at the Instituto Costarricense de Turismo, or at the Customs office, Av 3, C 14, if you take your passport, car entry permit, and a piece of stamped paper (*papel sellado*) obtainable at any bookshop. Cars are fumigated on entry: exterior US$2.20; interior US$1.40. It is now mandatory for foreign drivers to buy insurance stamps on entry; eg motorcycle, approx US$6 and car, US$7.50. If you want to travel on from Costa Rica without your car, you should leave it in the customs warehouse at Calle Blancos in San José. A customs agent is recommended unless you want to spend several weeks learning the system. Recommended, at a reasonable price, is Camilo Lacayo SA (Apdo 54-1300 San José, T 255-3174), located 100m W and 25m S of the Calle Blancos *Aduanas*. Boris Barrantes León is helpful and speaks English. The requisite papers are called guías: either for up to two months or up to a year (US$100 for the latter). Charges at the warehouse depend on the value of the car, eg a 1970 VW microbus valued at US$3,500 cost US$1 per day. A complete inventory of the vehicle and contents is made when leaving the car. Recovering the car is a lengthy procedure of several days. You have to visit the Central Bank to certify that you have not requested dollars for the price of the car, ie, you have not sold it. The customs agency you first dealt with should guide you through this for no extra charge. The *aduanas* will either escort you to the frontier or you can buy another three months' insurance and have the car stamped back into your passport. Insurance costs about US$18. This requires a visit to Central Customs (orange building, Av 1, Calle 14). Be sure to tell the Customs Agency that you want to reinsure the car when depositing it, doing this should save some paperwork and time. The whole operation needs time and patience. Do not expect to arrive in Costa Rica one evening and be leaving the next.

San José is the best place to get Land Rover spares. Car parts are very expensive because of high import tax. If the parts are needed for leaving the country you can order them from abroad yourself and avoid the tax but it takes time. Ask Sr Marcheno in the Aduana de Vehículos, Av 3, C 10, Spanish required. It is best not to try and sell your car here as the import tax is 70%. Main fuel stations have regular US$0.33 (45 colones) and diesel US$0.30 per litre; super gasoline (unleaded) is available but less common, US$0.36 (50 colones). Tyres without rims are confiscated and burnt by the Customs. It is illegal to ride in a car or taxi without wearing seatbelts. Motorcyclists must wear crash helmets. Spares are available for Japanese makes in San José. Also, try Oswaldo von Breymann, Av 7, Casa 27, Calle 5-7, T 21-22-74, San José, for motorcycle spares (BMW and MZ); he is a good mechanic. If you have an accident, contact Policia de Tránsito, San José T 226-8436 or 227-2189. If you intend to drive in the country for more than 3 months, you are required to apply for a Costa Rican Driver's Licence at Av 18, C 5, San José (see also **Car and Motorcycle Rental, p 730**).

Cycling John Gilchrist tells us that cycling is easier in Costa Rica than elsewhere in Central America; the asphalted roads are better, there is less heavy traffic and it is generally 'cyclist friendly'. However, paving is thin and soon deteriorates; look out for cracks and potholes, which bring traffic to a crawl. Unsurfaced roads are horrible on a bicycle. The prevailing wind is from the northeast, so if making an extensive tour, travelling in the direction of Panama-Nicaragua is slightly more favourable. Be prepared for a lot of rain. It is perfectly possible to travel light, without tent, sleeping bag or cooking equipment.

Recommended reading for all users: *Baker's The Essential Road Guide to Costs Rica*, with detailed strip maps, km by km road logs, motoring information plus San José map and Bus Guide (130 pages: Bill Baker, Apartado 1185-1011, San José, T/F 220-1415).

Hitchhiking is easy and safe by day in the week, though there is not much traffic off the main roads.

Accommodation The Costa Rica Bed & Breakfast Group includes 50 B&B inns and small hotels around the country in its membership. They can be contacted through the president, Debbi McMurray, Apdo 493-1000, San José, T 223-4168, F 223-4157.

Food *Sodas* (small restaurants) serve local food, which is worth trying. Very common is *casado*, a cheap lunch which includes rice, beans, stewed beef or fish, fried plantain and cabbage. *Olla de carne* is a soup of beef, plantain, corn, yuca, *ñampi* and *chayote* (local vegetables). *Sopa negra* is made with black beans, and comes with a poached egg in it; *picadillo* is another meat and vegetable stew. Snacks are popular: *gallos* (filled tortillas), *tortas* (containing meat and vegetables), *arreglados* (bread filled with the same) and *empanadas*. *Pan de yuca* is a speciality, available from stalls in San José centre. For breakfast, try *gallo pinto* (rice and beans) with *natilla* (a slightly sour cream). Best ice cream can be found in *Pops* shops in San José. *Schmidt* bakeries are highly rec; they also serve coffee. Also *La Selecta* bakeries. In general, eating out in Costa Rica is more expensive than elsewhere in Central America.

Drink There are many types of cold drink, made either from fresh fruit, or milk drinks with fruit (*batidos*) or cereal flour whisked with ice cubes. Drinks are often sugared well beyond North American tastes. The fruits range from the familiar to the exotic; others include *cebada* (barley flour), *pinolillo* (roasted corn), *horchata* (rice flour with cinnamon), *chan*, 'perhaps the most unusual, looking like mouldy frogspawn and tasting of penicillin' (Michael J Brisco). All these drinks cost the same as, or less than, bottled fizzy products. Excellent coffee. Local beers are Bavaria, Pilsen, Imperial and Tropical (which is low alcohol).

Tipping A 10% service charge is automatically added to restaurant and hotel bills, as well as 10% government tax. Tip porters, hairdressers and cloakroom attendants. Taxis and cinema usherettes, nil.

Shopping Best buys are wooden items, ceramics and leather handicrafts. Note that many wooden handicrafts are made of rainforest hardwoods and that deforestation is a critical problem. Coffee should have 'puro' on the packet or it may have additives.

Health Drinking water is safe in all major towns; elsewhere it should be boiled. Water purification tablets etc hard to find but Tratagua, SA, Apartado 141-2050, Montes de Oca will make up Superdor (a chlorine based product) for you, two drops for each litre of water, at a nominal cost. Intestinal disorders are prevalent in the lowlands although Chagas disease is now rare. Malaria is on the increase; malaria prophylaxis is advised for visitors to the lowlands, especially near the Nicaraguan border; in Costa Rica it is available only from the Ministerio de Salud in San José (free). Dengue fever broke out in several areas in 1993, with over 1,000 cases in Liberia. Puntarenas was also badly affected. Only a few cases were reported in San José. Uncooked foods should not be eaten. The standards of health and hygiene are among the best in Latin America. Ice cream, milk, etc are safe. See also notes on snakebite and mosquitoes under Corcovado National Park, **pp 783-786.**

Security Look after your belongings in hotels (use the safe), hired cars and on beaches. Theft is on the increase and we have received reports of violent robberies in those dangerous parts of San José mentioned in the **Warning, p 725.**

Business Hours 0800 or 0830 to 1100 or 1130 and 1300 to 1700 or 1730 (1600, government offices), Mon to Fri, and 0800 to 1100 on Sat Shops: 0800 to 1200, 1300 to 1800 Mon to Sat.

British business travellers going to Costa Rica are advised to get a copy of 'Hints to Exporters: Costa Rica' from DTI Export Publications, PO Box 55, Stratford-upon-Avon, Warwickshire, CV37 9GE.

Public Holidays 1 January: New Year's Day; 19 March: St Joseph; Easter: 3 days; 11 April: Battle of Rivas; 1 May: Labour Day; June: Corpus Christi; 29 June: St Peter and St Paul; 25 July: Guanacaste Day; 2 August: Virgin of Los Angeles; 15 August: Mothers' Day; 15 September: Independence Day; 12 October: Columbus Day; 8 December: Conception of the Virgin; 25 December: Christmas Day; 28-31 December: San José only.

NB During Holy Week, nearly everyone is on holiday. Everywhere is shut on Thur, Fri, many shops on Sat, and Sun, and most of the previous week as well (in San José and Cartago only a small percentage of businesses and services close Mon-Wed and Sat of Holy Week; almost all transport stops on Good Friday only, with limited transport on Thursday).

Standard Time is 6 hrs behind Greenwich Mean Time.

Currency The unit is the colón, sub-divided into 100 céntimos. The old coins of 5, 10, 25 and 50 céntimos and 1 and 2 colones, and notes of 5, 10 and 20 colones are being phased out. New coins in use are for 25 and 50 céntimos and 1, 2, 5, 10 and 20 colones. Public telephones now use 5, 10 and 20 colón coins (a 5 colón coin is needed to initiate a call). Paper money in use: 50, 100, 500, 1,000 and 5,000 colones. (10,000 colón notes have not yet been issued, although they are planned).

Exchange of US dollars (etc) must be effected in a bank, and for bank drafts and transfers commission may be charged (set by the banks themselves). Most tourist and first class hotels will change dollars for guests only, the same applies in restaurants and shops if you buy something. A legal parallel (street) market has existed since February 1992. It is almost impossible to exchange any other major currency in Costa Rica; only the Banco Lyon, SA, will do so (eg Barclays sterling cheques) but at very poor rates. ATMs for Visa cards can be found at 21 branches of Banco Popular y Desarrollo; cash from Mastercard/Cirrus ATMs at Credomatic in San José and Atajuela.

NB Credomatic handles all credit card billings; they will not accept a credit card charge that does not have the imprint of the borrower's card plus an original signature. This is the result of fraud, but it makes it difficult to book tours or accommodation over the phone. For card loss or theft, Amex T 233-0044, Visa T 223-2211, Mastercard T 253-2155.

For Customs the metric system of **weights and measures** is compulsory. Traders use a variety of weights and measures, including English ones and the old Spanish ones.

Electric Current 110, 60 cycles, AC (US flat-pin plugs).

Mail by sea from the UK takes from 2-3 months and 10 to 14 days by airmail. Airmail letters to Europe cost 55 colones, postcards 50 colones; to North/South America, 45 colones, postcards 40 colones; to Australia, Africa and Asia, 70 colones, postcards 60 colones. 'Expreso' letters, 55 colones extra, several days quicker to USA and N Europe. Registered mail, 60 colones extra. All parcels sent out of the country by foreigners must be taken open to the post office for clearance. *Lista de Correos* charges per letter, and will keep letters for 4 weeks. The contents of incoming parcels will be the subject of plenty of paperwork, and probably high duties. You normally have to come back the next day. There has been considerable local publicity (1992) on theft in the postal system, especially international mail.

Telephone and Cable Services Long-range radio-telephone services are run by the Instituto Costarricense de Electricidad (ICE) and by Cía Radiográfica Internacional de Costa Rica (CRI).

Local cables, though, are sent from the main post office in San José, Av 1-3, C 2. A telephone system connects San José with the country's main centres. The Government's wireless station at San José communicates with Mexico, Guatemala and El Salvador. A Radio and Telephone Ground Satellite Station was opened at Aserrí in January 1982. Direct dial from a private phone is cheaper than rates from a public phone or CRI office. Calls abroad can be made from phone booths; collect calls abroad may be made from special booths in the telephone office, Av 5, C 1, San José, or from any booth nationwide if you dial 116 for connection with the international operator. Collect calls can be made from any public phone, see p 733 for dialling codes. Phone cards from the following countries are accepted: Brazil, Canada, France, Holland, Hong Kong, Italy, Japan, S Korea, UK and USA. A minimum telephone call to the UK costs US$3 per minute, US$2.40 at weekends plus 10% VAT; to USA and Canada, US$1.60-3.80 per min, US$0.65-1.50 at night (2200-0700) and weekends, depending on to which state or province; to Australia, Africa, Asia, US$3.50-5 per minute. Public telex booth at Radiográfica SA, Av 5, C 1 (telex CR 1050); the telex must show your name and Tel no or address for them to advise you; also public Fax service, to receive, 100 colones (F +506-223-1609 or +506-233-7932); to send, US$5.50 per page to Europe (CRI; US$3.40 ICE), US$4 per page to USA.

Newspapers The best San José morning papers are *La Nación* and *La República*; new is *Al Día*. *La Prensa Libre* is a good evening paper. *Libertad*, weekly newspaper (socialist). *El Debate* is another good weekly. Three weekly news magazines are: *Rumbo* (political), *Triunfo* and *Perfil* (popular). *La Gazette* is the official government weekly paper. *Tico Times* (Fri, subscriptions Dept 717, PO Box 025216, Miami FL 33102) and *Costa Rica Today* (free in better hotels and restaurants. subscriptions Ediciones 2000 SA, Acc No 117, PO Box 025216, Miami FL 33102) in English (look in the classifieds for Spanish classes). The former is better for news and classifieds, the latter has weekly features of interest to travellers, eg hotels under US$10 in San José or railway news. *The Latin America*, US$1, has travel information, bed and breakfast places, local airline schedules, useful, Apdo 661, Alajuela, T 441-9263, F 441-0222.

Broadcasting 6 local TV stations, many MW/FM radio stations throughout the country. Local Voz de América (VOA) station. Many hotels and private homes receive one of the 4 TV stations offering direct, live, 24-hr TV from the USA (Canal 19, Supercanal, Cable Color and Master TV-channels 56, 58, 60—all US cable TV can be received in San José on the 2 cable stations).

Association football (soccer) is the **national sport** (played every Sunday at 1100, May to October, at the Saprissa Stadium). There are golf courses at San José and Puerto Limón. There is sea-bathing on both Atlantic and Pacific coasts (see text). The Meseta is good country for riding; horses can be hired by arrangement directly with owners. Most *fiestas* end with bullfighting in the squares, an innocuous but amusing set-to with no horses used. Bullfights are held in San José during the Christmas period. There is no kill and spectators are permitted to enter the ring to chase, and be chased by, the bull. For **Watersports**, see p 722.

The information offices of the **Instituto Costarricense de Turismo** are by the Plaza de la Cultura, entrance on C 5, Av Central/2, San José (T 222-1090), open 0900-1700 Mon to Fri, till 1200 on Sat and not every Sat. All tourist information is given here. Take complaints about hotel overcharging to the Instituto. There is a free weekly magazine, *The San José Gourmet*, dealing with tourism and restaurant news. For more details, see p 735.

We are most grateful to Simon Ellis (San José) and to the following travellers: Jens Arnold (Borken, Germany), Jack Bailey & Diana Musacchio (Santa Barbara, CA, USA), David Beasley & Liz Brooks (Horsham, West Sussex) Alexander Beck (Altessing, Germany), Martin Better (Uster, Switzerland), Erich Blum (Ruemlang, Switzerland) Sybille Böhme (Kahl/Rain, Germany) Walter Brehm (Daun, Germany), Ludwig M Brinckmann (Wohltorf, Germany) Peter Brunnbauer (Puerto Jiménez, Costa Rica) Jon Chambers (Moreton-in-Marsh, Gloucestershire) & Marianne Mller (Denmark) Jay Connerley (Fremont NE, USA) Daniel Daeniker (Zurich,

To use AT&T USADirect® Service from Costa Rica dial **114** from any phone. Some public telephones may require a coin deposit. If you require assistance, please call the AT&T office in San José at **257-1944**.

AT&T USADirect® Service.

Switzerland) Günther Deutinger (Saalfelden, Austria) Karl Griffith & Julie Duckworth (Preston, Lancashire) Frank Dux (Passau, Germany), Kim Edgin (Springfield, TN, USA) Lene Eilrich (Ribe, Denmark) Ariane Fàssler (Wettswil, Switzerland) Matthias Fehrenbach (Immenstaad, Germany) Joy Hale & Derek Fess (Columbus, Ohio) Vincent Fitzgerald (Miami, Florida) Richard N Frank (Clearwater, FL, USA), Ann Frechette & Jean Luc Massicotte for Charles Huot (Montréal), Darrel Freeman (Lancaster, PA, USA), Julio Gonzalez (Saint-Bonnet près Riom, France) Pasi Hannonen (Jy vä Skylä, Finland) Sally & Mike Hayden (Cheltenham, Glos), Mary Hayward (Edinburgh) Penny Jones (Barva, Heredia, Costa Rica), Ken Jones (Victoria, BC, Canada), Daniel Kaiser (Triesen, Liechtenstein), Christoph Künzi (Zurich, Switzerland) Rosemarie Langenstein (Zug, Switzerland), Johannes Latsch (Bad Homburg var der Höhe, Germany) Sandor Legrady (Trenton, NJ, USA), Gérald Lorin (Kourou, Guyane), Helmut Lüder (Potomac, MD, USA) James N Maas (Bocas del Toro, Panama), Martina Mager (Costa Rica) Trine Mette Mork (Otterburn Park, PQ, Canada) Claudia Modrow & Massimo Godenzi (Bergheim, Germany) Monica Müller (Blonay) & Klaus Högle (Marin, Switzerland) Dr William R C Munro (Stanley, Perth) Carlos G Murillo (San José) Ray Peters (Panama) Dr Oscar Puls (Newport, Gwent), D J Puls & R J Chapp (Amsterdam), Helmut Quitt (Rosenheim, Germany), Mary Ann Rabion (Milwaukee, Wisconsin, USA) Arthur Rhodes (Costa Rica) Claudio Rivero (Buenos Aires) Lisa J Robertson (North Vancouver, BC, Canada) Nadine Rocamora (Lattes, France) Bruce and Page Oberlin Rumage (Pawleys Island, USA) John Schaefer (Palo Alto, California) Nina Schramm (Sheringham, Norfolk) Mark Schuringa (Amsterdam, Holland) Harald Schwender & Birgitte Hächer (Sandhausen, Germany) Frampton Simons (Atlanta, GA, USA), Stefan Cotting (Nevenegg, Switzerland), Jan Svoboda (Vancouver, BC, Canada), Christopher J S Tuppen (Southampton), Bill Vallis (Surbiton, Surrey), Vincent Van Es (Enschede, Holland) Tom & Nancy Vineski (Pennsylvania, USA) Benderoth Vitus (Hadamar), Robert W Warner (Council Bluffs, Iowa), Simon Watson Taylor (Goa) Dirk & Laura Weisheit (Mexico City) Wayne & Florine Wentworth (Seabrook, Texas) Reto Wildschek (Kloten, Switzerland) Ilona Wittber (St Ingbert, Germany) Florian Wüllen Kemper (Bad Salzujlen, Germany) Giulio Zanetti (Ivrea, Italy).

WILL YOU HELP US?

We do all we can to get our facts right in the MEXICO & CENTRAL AMERICAN HANDBOOK. Each section is thoroughly revised each year, but the territory is vast and our eyes cannot be everywhere. We are always pleased to hear about your travels; do write to us in as much detail as possible. In return we will send you information about our special guidebook offer.

TRADE & TRAVEL *Handbooks*

Write to The Editor, Mexico & Central American Handbook, Trade & Travel, 6 Riverside Court, Lower Bristol Road, Bath BA2 3DZ. England

PANAMA

INTRODUCTION

THE S-SHAPED ISTHMUS OF PANAMA, 80 km at its narrowest and no more than 193 km at its widest, is one of the great cross-roads of the world. Its destiny has been entirely shaped by that fact. To it Panama owes its national existence, the make-up of its population and their distribution: two-fifths of the people are concentrated in the two cities which control the entry and exit of the canal. The Canal Area, formerly Zone, is being gradually incorporated into Panamanian jurisdiction; this long process began in 1964, when Panama secured the right to fly its flag in the Zone alongside that of the USA, and is due for completion, with Panamanian operation of the Canal, by 2000.

Only about a quarter of the country is inhabited and most of it is mountainous, with shelvings of lowland on both its 1,234 km of Pacific and 767 km of Atlantic coastlines. The country's axis is, in general, SW to NE, but the mountain chains do not conform to this and run NW to SE. At the border with Costa Rica there are several volcanic cones, the boldest of which is the extinct Barú, 3,383m high. The sharp-sided Cordillera de Talamanca continues SE at a general altitude of about 900m, but subsides suddenly SW of Panama City. The next range, the San Blas, rises E of Colón and runs into Colombia; its highest peaks are not more than 900m. A third range rises from the Pacific littoral in the SE; it, too, runs into Colombia and along the Pacific coast as the Serranía de Baudó.

Good fortune decreed a gap between the Talamanca and San Blas ranges in which the divide is no more than 87m high. The ranges are so placed that the gap, containing the Canal, runs from NW to SE. To reach the Pacific from the Atlantic we must travel eastwards, and at dawn the sun rises over the Pacific.

Climate Rainfall is heavy along the Caribbean coast: more than 3,800 mm a year in some places, with huge but brief downpours between April and December. Rain can be expected 365 days a year on the Caribbean coast, though.

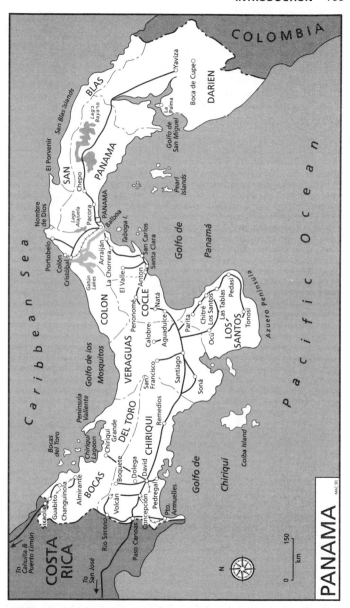

PANAMA

MAC '90

Temperature in the lowland ranges from 21°C (70°F) at night to 32°C (90°F) by day. The result is deep tropical forest along the coast and up the sides of the ranges of Panama, though little remains forested. The rain begins to shade off towards the crests of the mountains (10° to 18°C), and is much less along the Pacific, though there is no scarcity of it anywhere. At Balboa it is only 1,727 mm a year, and the tropical forest gives way to semi-deciduous trees and converted areas of savanna between the Pacific and the mountains. The wet season is called *invierno*—winter, the dry, *verano*—summer.

The rate of deforestation in Panama has accelerated in the 1980s and early 1990s. Although more of the country is forested than any other Central American republic except Belize, the loss of forest in 1990 was estimated at 220,000 acres, against felling of up to 154,000 acres per year between 1985 and 1989. Deforestation is affecting the pattern of rainfall upon which depend not only the birds (over 800 species), animals, insects and plants, but also the Panama Canal. A further threat to the Canal is silting as a result of soil erosion.

History The history of Panama is the history of its pass-route; its fate was determined on that day in 1513 when Balboa first glimpsed the Pacific (see the Introduction to the Central America section). Panama City was of paramount importance for the Spaniards: it was the focus of conquering expeditions northwards and southwards along the Pacific coasts. All trade to and from these Pacific countries passed across the isthmus.

Panama City was founded in 1519 after a trail had been discovered between it and the Caribbean. The Camino Real (the Royal Road) ran from Panama City to Nombre de Dios until it was re-routed to Portobelo. An alternative route was used later for bulkier, less valuable merchandise: a road built from Panama City to Las Cruces, now swallowed up by Gatún Lake; it ran near Gamboa on the Culebra Cut, and traces of it can still be seen. Las Cruces was on the Chagres river, which was navigable to the Caribbean, particularly during the rainy season.

Intruders were early attracted by the wealth passing over the Camino Real. Sir Francis Drake attacked Nombre de Dios, and in 1573 his men penetrated inland to Venta Cruz, further up the Chagres river on the Camino Real, plundering the town. Spain countered later attacks by building strongholds and forts to protect the route: among others San Felipe at the entrances to Portobelo and San Lorenzo at the mouth of the Chagres. Spanish galleons, loaded with treasure and escorted against attack, left Portobelo once a year. They returned with European goods which were sold at great fairs held at Portobelo, Cartagena and Veracruz. There was feverish activity for several weeks as the galleons were loaded and unloaded. It was a favourite time for attack by enemies, especially those with political as well as pecuniary motives. Perhaps the most famous was the attack by Henry Morgan in 1671. He captured the fort of San Lorenzo and pushed up the Chagres river to Las Cruces. From there he descended upon Panama City, which he looted and burnt. A month later Morgan returned to the Caribbean with 195 mules loaded with booty. Panama City was re-built on a new site, at the base of Ancón hill, and fortified. With Britain and Spain at war, attacks reached their climax in Admiral Vernon's capture of Portobelo in 1739 and the fort of San Lorenzo the next year. Spain abandoned the route in 1746 and began trading round Cape Horn. San Lorenzo was rebuilt: it is still there, tidied up and landscaped by the US Army.

A century later, streams of men were once more moving up the Chagres and down to Panama City: the forty-niners on their way to the newly discovered gold fields of California. Many perished on this 'road to hell', as it was called, and the gold rush brought into being a railway across the isthmus. The Panama Railroad from Colón (then only two streets) to Panama City took four years to build, with great loss of life. The first train was run on 26 November 1853. The railway was an enormous financial success until the re-routing of the Pacific Steam Navigation Company's ships round Cape Horn in 1867 and the opening of the first US transcontinental railroad in 1869 reduced its traffic.

Ferdinand de Lesseps, builder of the Suez Canal, arrived in Panama in 1881, and decided to build a sea-level canal along the Chagres river and the Río Grande. Work started in 1882. One of the diggers in 1886 and 1887 was the painter Gauguin, aged 39. Thirty km had been dug before the Company crashed in 1893, defeated by extravagance and tropical diseases (22,000 people died). Eventually Colombia (of which Panama was then a Department) authorized the Company to sell all its rights and properties to the United States, but the Colombian Senate rejected the treaty, and the inhabitants of Panama, encouraged by the States, declared their independence on 3 November 1903. The United States intervened and, in spite of protests by Colombia, recognized the new republic. Colombia did not accept the severance until 1921.

Before beginning the task of building the Canal the United States performed one of the greatest sanitary operations in history: the clearance from the area of the more malignant tropical diseases. The name of William Crawford Gorgas will always be associated with this, as will that of George Washington Goethals with the actual building of the Canal. On 15 August 1914, the first passage was made, by the ship *Ancón*.

The history of Panama then became that of two nations, with the Canal Zone responsible only to the President of the USA. As a result of bitter resentment, the USA ended Panama's protectorate status in 1939 with a treaty which also limited US rights of intervention. However, the disparity in living standards continued to provoke anti-US feeling, culminating in riots in 1964 and the suspension of diplomatic relations for some months. During this period, a small, commercially-oriented oligarchy dominated Panamanian politics, although presidential successions were not always smooth and peaceful.

In 1968 Dr Arnulfo Arias Madrid was elected president for the third time, having been ousted twice previously. After only ten days in office he was forcibly removed by the National Guard which installed a provisional junta. Brig General Omar Torrijos Herrera ultimately became Commander of the National Guard and principal power in the junta, dominating Panamanian politics for the next 13 years. Constitutional government was restored in 1972 after elections for a 505-member National Assembly of Community Representatives, which revised the 1946 constitution, elected Demetrio Basilio Lakas Bahas as president and vested temporary extraordinary executive powers in Gen Torrijos for six years. Torrijos' rule was characterized by his pragmatic nationalism; he carried out agrarian reform, yet satisfied business interests; he had close links with left wing movements in Cuba, El Salvador and Nicaragua, yet reached agreement with the USA to transfer sovereignty of the Canal of Panama. In 1978 elections for a new National Assembly were held and the new representatives elected Dr Arístedes Royo Sánchez as president. Gen Torrijos resigned as Chief of Government but retained the powerful post of Commander of the National Guard until his death in an air crash in 1981. There followed several years of rapid governmental changes as tension rose between presidents and National Guard leaders.

Elections were held in May 1984, resulting in a narrow (and contested) victory for the government candidate, Nicolás Ardito Barletta, who took office in October 1984 for a six-year term but was removed from office by military pressure in September 1985. He was replaced by Eric Arturo Delvalle. Sr Delvalle's attempts to reduce military influence in government, concentrated principally in the hands of General Manuel Antonio Noriega Morena, led to his own removal by General Noriega in February 1988. Manuel Solís Palma was named president in his place. Elections were held in May 1989 but the civil unrest which immediately followed led to their annulment by the military; both the ruling party and an opposition coalition had claimed an overwhelming majority of votes.

General Noriega appointed Francisco Rodríguez as provisional President in

September. However, in December, General Noriega formally assumed power as Head of State, which provoked a US military invasion (Operation Just Cause) to overthrow him. He finally surrendered on 20 December and was taken to the USA for trial on charges of drugs trafficking and other corruption offences. Guillermo Endara Galimany, who was widely believed to have won the May elections, was installed as President. The Panamanian Defence Forces were immediately remodelled into a new Public Force with a two-year limitation on the commander's term of office and compulsory retirement after 25 years' service. Over 150 senior officers were dismissed and many were arrested.

After the overthrow of General Noriega's administration, the US Senate approved a US$480mn aid package to provide liquidity and get the economy moving again. A further US$540mn aid package was requested from the USA, Japan, Taiwan and the EEC to enable Panama to help clear its US$610mn arrears with multilateral creditors and support the Panamanian banking system, but inevitably there were delays and little progress was made until 1991. The USA put Panama under considerable pressure to sign a Treaty of Mutual Legal Assistance, which would end bank secrecy and enable investigation into suspected drug traffickers' bank accounts. Aid was withheld pending agreement, with a consequent deterioration of the economy, rising unemployment, poverty and crime. Higher levels of crime and drugs trafficking led to the Government passing a law to create the Technical Judicial Police (PTJ) to pursue criminals. As economic difficulties increased, President Endara came under greater political pressure; the Christian Democratic Party (PDC) broke away from the ruling ADOC coalition in April 1991 and five ministers were removed from their posts. The Vice President, Ricardo Arias Calderón (PDC), retained his elected position, however. Charges of corruption at the highest level were made by US officials and President Endara was further weakened by allegations that his law firm had been involved with companies owned by drugs traffickers. Violence became more apparent and bomb attacks more commonplace as President Endara failed to deal with political instability, social problems and an increasingly hostile population.

Fears that violence would disrupt the 1994 elections were unfounded. In the presence of 2,000 local and international observers, polling was largely incident-free and open, receiving praise worldwide. The winner of the presidency was Enesto Pérez Balladares of the Partido Revolucionario Democrático (PRD), whose campaign harked back to the record of the party's founder, Omar Torrijos, successfully avoiding any links with its more recent leader, Noriega. In second place was Mireya Moscoso de Gruber of the Partido Arnulfista, supported by Endara, and third was the Salsa star and actor, Rubén Blades, whose party Papa Egoró won 6 seats in the legislature on its first electoral outing. Pérez Balladares, who appointed a cabinet containing members of opposition parties as well as from the PRD, gave priority in his campaign to tackling the problem of social inequality, unemployment, deteriorating education and rising crime which had characterized the end of Endara's term.

The former Canal Zone was a ribbon of territory under US control extending 8 km on either side of the Canal and including the cities of Cristóbal and Balboa. The price paid by the United States Government to Panama for construction rights was US$10mn. The French company received US$40mn for its rights and properties. US$25mn were given to Colombia in compensation for the transfer of the French company's rights. The total cost at completion was US$387mn. Panama long ago rejected the perpetuity clause of the original Canal Treaty. In April 1978 a new treaty was ratified and on 1 October 1979 the Canal Zone, now known officially as the Canal Area, was formally transferred to Panamanian sovereignty, including the ports of Cristóbal and Balboa, the Canal dry docks and the trans-isthmus railway, but the US still retains extensive military base areas. Some Panamanians feel that a US military presence should be retained in the

Canal Area and, in 1994, president-elect Pérez Balladares did not rule out the possibility that further negotiations may take place, as long as a majority of Panamanians approve. Until the final transfer of ownership in 2000 the Canal administration is in the hands of the Comisión del Canal, on which the USA retains majority representation. At the beginning of 1990, a Panamanian was appointed acting administrator of the Panama Canal in succession to an American who had held the post since 1979.

The People The population is mostly of mixed descent but there are communities of Indians, blacks and a few Asians. Most of the rural population live in the 6 provinces on the Pacific side, W of the Canal. There is only one rural population centre of any importance on the Caribbean: in Bocas del Toro, in the extreme NW. Of the sixty Indian tribes who inhabited the isthmus at the time of the Spanish conquest, only three have survived in any number: the Cunas of the San Blas Islands (50,000), the Guaymíes of the western provinces (80,000), and the Chocóes of Darién (10,000). These, and a few others, account for 6% of the total population. Only a few of the indigenous Indians can speak Spanish.

In Bocas de Toro half the population speaks Spanish, half speaks English.

Numbers of African slaves escaped from their Spanish owners during the 16th century. They set up free communities in the Darién jungles and their Spanish-speaking descendants can still be seen there and in the Pearl Islands. The majority of Panama's blacks are English-speaking British West Indians, descended from those brought in for the building of the railway in 1850, and later of the Canal. There are also a number of East Indians and Chinese who tend to cling to their own languages and customs.

The Economy Panama's economy has traditionally been founded on income derived from services rendered to incoming visitors, taking advantage of its geographical position, its banking centre, and Canal employees and US military personnel spending money in the Republic. However, this contribution is lessening proportionately as the country develops new sources of income: tourism, industry, copper, etc.

Apart from the Canal (see above), the other traditional mainstay of the Panamanian economy is agriculture, which contributes about 11% of gdp. Agrarian reform has begun, and has brought the post-1968 governments much support from tenant-farmers and squatters. 44% of the land is classified as forested, but deforestation has been occurring at an alarming rate (see above under Climate), principally because of pressures from increasing unemployment and a rising population, as people move into isolated areas. The leading agricultural export crop is bananas, three-quarters of which are produced by the transnational Chiquita Brands, which has a monopoly on marketing. Shrimp is another major export, having grown to about 14% of total earnings and competing strongly with Ecuador and Honduras for the US market. Raw sugar is also an important export item, while lesser amounts of coffee and hides and skins are sold abroad.

Recently the Government has taken a more significant role in industry and now owns sugar mills and cement plants. The main industry is food processing and there are textile and clothing concerns and chemicals, plastics and other light industries. Petroleum products are the only industrial export. The lowering of import tariffs in 1993, as a part of trade liberalization measures, contributed to a decline in manufacturing output. At the same time, the IMF has encouraged the state to privatize many of the industries it controls, but the programme has been restricted by congressional disapproval. Vast deposits of copper have been found at Cerro Colorado and if fully developed the mine could be one of the largest in the world. There is also copper at Petaquilla, Cerro Chorca and Río Pinto. Large coal deposits have been found at Río Indio. The country also has gold and silver deposits. So far

PANAMA : FACT FILE

Geographic
Land area	75,517 sq km
forested	43.9%
pastures	20.4%
cultivated	7.6%

Demographic
Population (1992)	2,515,000
annual growth rate (1987-92)	2.0%
urban	52.9%
rural	47.1%
density	33.3 per sq km
Religious affiliation	
Roman Catholic	84.0%
Birth rate per 1,000 (1991)	26.0
	(world av 26.4)
Death rate per 1,000 (1991)	
	(world av 9.2)

Education and Health
Life expectancy at birth,	
male	72.0 years
female	76.0 years
Infant mortality rate	
per 1,000 live births (1991)	21.0
Physicians (1990)	1 per 880 persons
Hospital beds	1 per 330 persons
Calorie intake as %	
of FAO requirement	110%
Population age 25 and over	
with no formal schooling	17.4%
Literate males (over 15)	88.1%
Literate females (over 15)	88.2%

Economic
GNP (1990 market prices)	US$4,414mn
GNP per capita	US$1,830
Public external debt (1990)	US$3,758mn
Tourism receipts (1990)	US$167mn
Inflation (annual av 1986-91)	5.9%
Radio	1 per 5.5 persons
Television	1 per 12 persons
Telephone	1 per 9.4 persons

Employment
Population economically active (1989)	
	820,042
Unemployment rate (1992)	28.0%
% of labour force in	
agriculture	25.4
manufacturing	9.8
construction	3.9
National Police force	11,000

Source Encyclopaedia Britannica

no oil has been discovered, but exploration is taking place.

One of the most dynamic sectors of the economy is banking. Since 1970 offshore banks have increased from 20 in number to 130 with the establishment of liberal conditions and the abolition of currency controls. In the mid-1980s, total assets amounted to over US$40bn, while deposits were around US$35bn. However, in 1987-88, political uncertainties severely affected the international banking centre. Loss of confidence led many banks to close their offices and move to other offshore centres such as the Bahamas or the Cayman Islands, the level of assets declined, and deposits fell to US$5bn by 1990. In 1990 the new government amended banking regulations to prevent money laundering and legislation to end banking secrecy was approved by the Legislative Assembly in July 1991. By 1993, the financial sector was flourishing again, boosted by the relaxation of restrictions on financial services throughout Latin America.

Following a rapid accumulation of foreign debt by the public sector in the late 1970s and early 1980s, the debt service burden became intolerable. Panama received assistance after 1983 from the IMF and the World Bank in support of its fiscal and structural adjustment programme, while commercial banks rescheduled existing loans and provided new money on easier terms. As a result of the 1988 financial crisis, Panama fell into arrears to all its creditors; consequently, capital inflows were halted; the IMF declared Panama ineligible to borrow and the World Bank cut off loan disbursements. Moreover, the US economic blockade which began in 1988 directly caused a 16% fall in gdp that year followed by a 12% fall the next. In 1990 the economy recovered slightly from its very low base, principally because of 20% increase in commercial activity in the Colón Free Zone, but delays in reaching agreements with external creditors over the repayment of US$2.7bn of arrears postponed economic recovery.

In 1992 Panama succeeded in paying US$646mn in arrears to multilateral and governmental creditors, making it eligible for new credits for the first time in four years. Until then it had relied heavily on US aid, which amounted to US$985mn since President Endara took office in 1990, of which US$451mn were donations. The adoption of neoliberal economic policies brought rising discontent as spending cuts caused job losses. Strikes and demonstrations became commonplace. Poverty increased and UN agencies estimated that nearly 55% of Panamanians lived in absolute poverty. After 1990, however, the economy showed strong growth with gdp increasing at over 5% a year. Growth was not uniform throughout the economy as sectors such as private investment and construction (especially of luxury homes in 1993) provided the main impetus. There was a consequent easing of urban unemployment in 1993, and the minimum wage, frozen for the previous 5 years, was raised by 22%. The consumer price index remained very low, growing by no more than 2.5% in any of the years between 1990 and 1993.

Government Constitutional reforms were adopted by referendum in April 1983. Legislative power is vested in a unicameral, 67-member Legislative Assembly which is elected by universal, compulsory adult suffrage for a term of five years. Executive power is held by the President, assisted by two Vice Presidents and an appointed Cabinet. Panama is divided into nine provinces and one autonomous Indian reservation. Provincial governors and mayors of towns are appointed by the central authorities.

Communications There are now about 9,690 km of roads, of which 3,100 km are paved. Road building is complicated by the extraordinary number of bridges and the large amount of grading required. The road running from Colón to Panama City is the only paved one crossing the isthmus, and the Pan-American Highway connecting Chepo and Panama City with the Costa Rican border is paved throughout.

Education Education is compulsory from the age of 6 to 15. About 93% of children attend elementary school. English is the compulsory second language in schools. There are three universities, one private.

COLON, THE CANAL AND THE ISLANDS

Landfall on the Caribbean side for the passage of the Canal is made at the twin cities of Cristóbal and Colón, the one merging into the other almost imperceptibly and both built on Manzanillo Island at the entrance of the Canal; the island has now been connected with the mainland. Colón was founded in 1852 as the terminus of the railway across the isthmus; Cristóbal came into being as the port of entry for the supplies used in building the Canal.

Cristóbal Ships usually dock at Pier No 9, 5 mins from the shops of Colón. Vehicles are always waiting at the docks for those who want to visit Colón and other places.

Colón (pop 122,500) was originally called Aspinwall, after one of the founders of the transisthmian railway. The French-influenced **Cathedral** at Calle 5 y Av Herrera has an attractive altar and good stained glass windows, open 1400-1745 daily. The *Washington Hotel*, on the seafront at the N end of the town, is the most historic structure and is worth a look. The original wooden hotel was built in 1850 for employees of the Railroad Company; President Taft ordered a new fireproof hotel be built in 1912 and the old one was later razed. Although remodelled a number of times, today's building, with its broad verandahs, waving palms, splendid chandelier, plush carpets and casino, still conjures up a past age;

the a/c cafeteria provides an excellent view of ships waiting to enter the Canal. Next door is the **Casa de Lesseps**, home of the Suez Canal's chief engineer during the 1880s. Across from the *Washington* is the Old Stone Episcopal Church, built in 1865 for the railway workers; it was then the only Protestant church in Colombia (of which Panamá was a province). Running N through the centre of Colón is the palm-lined Avenida Central, with many statues (including one of Columbus and the Indian Girl, a gift from the Empress of France); the public market is at the corner of Calle 11 but holds little of interest. Front Street (Av del Frente), facing the Bahía de Limón, has many old wooden buildings with wide verandahs. This is the main commercial street and is quite active but has lost its past splendour; the famous Bazar Francés closed in 1990, the curio shops are unnoteworthy and the railway station stands virtually deserted except for the movement of a few freight trains. Nevertheless, there is talk of declaring the whole of Colón a Free Zone, the authorities are moving to give the city new housing and employment (residential estates like 'Rainbow City' and 'Puerto Escondido' are being extended on the landward side to relocate entire neighbourhoods of slums), and the demands on Cristóbal's busy port facilities (200 million tons of cargo a year) continue to increase. It is to be hoped that if these plans are realized, Colón may become a pleasant place again.

The main reason to come to Colón is to shop at the present Zona Libre (Free Zone), the second-largest in the world, an extensive compound of international stores and warehouses established in 1949 and surrounded by a Berlin-like wall. Businessmen and tourists from all over Latin America come here to place orders for the (mostly bulk) merchandise on offer, or to arrange duty-free importation of bulk goods for re-export to neighbouring countries after packaging; commercial turnover in 1992 exceeded US$9bn. Individual items can be bought at some stores, which theoretically must be mailed out of the country or sent in-bond to Tocumen airport before you leave (allow a day for delivery and check-in 2 hrs early to pick up the goods); or you can try smuggling them out! Bargain hard for good prices, but most items are almost as competitively priced in Panama City. Several banks provide exchange facilities. A passport or official ID must be shown to gain entry to the Zone, which is open Mon-Fri 0800-1700 (a few places retail on Sat am). If with your own car, pay a minder US$1 to watch it while in the Zone, very necessary.

The 30-min beach drive around Colón's perimeter is pleasant and cool in the evening; despite the slums at the S end there are some nice homes along the E shore of the peninsula. Permission from the Port Authority security officer is required to enter the port area, where agents for all the world's great shipping lines are located in colonial Caribbean-style buildings dating from 1914. Almost lost in a forest of containers is the **Cristóbal Yacht Club** (T 41-5881), whose open-air restaurant and historically decorated bar offer very good food (seafood and Chinese); this is the place to enquire about sailing boat charters to the San Blas Islands or shorter trips aboard visiting yachts.

Warning In May 1993, a curfew was in operation in Colón from 2100-0500 for all under the age of 18. The US military cannot be on the street between 0200 and 0500. Do not go to the city alone. Mugging, even in daylight, is a real threat in both Colón and Cristóbal. We have received repeated warnings of robbery in Colón, often within 5 mins of arrival. The two main streets and some of the connecting ones are guarded by armed Panama Public Force men; you are strongly recommended not to leave their range of sight. One traveller recommends having a few dollars handy, so that 'muggers are less likely to strip you for more'.

Hotels A *Washington*, Av del Frente Final, T 41-1870, art deco style, guarded enclave, there is a small casino; **B** *Carlton*, Calle 10 y Av Meléndez, T 45-0717, is the next best hotel; *Sotelo*, Calle 10 y 11 con Av Guerrero, T 41-7702, also has a casino, same price range; **D** *Andros*, Av Herrera, between Calles 9 y 10, T 41-0477/41-7923, modern, clean, fan or a/c, bath, TV, good. These rates are without meals. **D** *Pensión Plaza*, Av Central, T 41-3216, is clean, cheap. **E** *Pensión Acrópolis*, Av Amador Guerrero y Calle 11, opp *Sotelo*, T 41-1456, shared bath.

If destitute try the Salvation Army.

Restaurants See above for *Cristóbal Yacht Club*. *VIP Club*, Front St, T 41-3563, popular with visiting businessmen and port officials; *Panamá* and *Antonio*, both cnr Av Herrera y Calle 11, unremarkable but decent. For Caribbean food: *Restaurant Teresa*, Av Amador Guerrero y Calle 12; *La Cabaña*, Av Central y Calle 8. *Hotels Washington, Carlton* and *Andros* have good restaurants. *YMCA* restaurant, Av Bolívar between Calles 11 y 12, mostly Chinese menu, comparatively expensive. Several fast food outlets, eg *KFC*, Paseo Centenario near Calle 7.

Taxis Tariffs vary but not expensive, US$57 per hour, US$50-80 per day. Car rental and taxis on Front Street facing Calle 11; most drivers speak some English and can advise on 'no-go' areas. Avis has two offices.

Cinemas Teatro Lido, across from YMCA on Bolívar, and Teatro Rex, Calle 5 and Av Central.

Clubs Golf (18 holes) at Brazos Brook Country Club. Rotary Club, weekly lunches.

Exchange Chase Manhattan Bank; Citibank; Banco Nacional de Panamá; Caja de Ahorros; Lloyds Bank agency in Colón Free Zone, at Av Santa Isabel y Calle 14, T 452177. Open 0800-1300, Mon to Fri.

Cables Intel.

Post Office In Cristóbal Administration Building, on corner of Av Bolívar and Calle 9.

Shipping a vehicle All ships leave from Coco Solo Wharf; to South America, see p 846.

Bus Service Bus station on Front Street and Calle 12. Express (a/c) and regular buses daily to **Panama City** every 20 min, hourly on Sat, no Sun service, US$1.75-2.25, about 2 hrs. Hourly to **Portobelo** daily, US$2, 1 hr.

Air Service To Paitilla domestic airport in Panama City: Former US France Field AFB has replaced Colón's old airstrip as the busy local airport, on mainland E of city, taxi under US$1 but bargain. Aeroperlas has many flights daily Mon-Fri in each direction; US$50 return. The above flights are hectic with Free Zone executives, no reservation system so allow plenty of time or plan to stay the night in Colón.

Excursions   A well-paved road branches off the Transisthmus Highway at Sabanitas, 10 km E of Colón, and runs NE along the coast for 34 km to the historic Spanish garrison port of Portobelo, founded in 1519 on the protected bay in which Columbus sought shelter in 1502. The rocky Costa Arriba is very attractive, with a number of lovely white-sand beaches (crowded at weekends). María Chiquita (14 km) has a bathing pavilion, toilets, bar and restaurant managed by the government tourist bureau; a local speciality is *saos*, Jamaican-style pig's feet cooked with lime and chillies, sold from roadside stalls. 3 km further on is Playa Langosta, also with swimming facilities, bar and restaurant. There are plenty of small restaurants along this road serving fresh seafood. A group of people can rent a coastal boat at Puerto Pilón (US$100-150 a day) for an adventurous ride to Portobelo, seas are often rough, take precautions. In Buenavista, just before entering Portobelo, a cannon marks the spot where Henry Morgan landed for his devastating 15-day sack of the town in 1668.

Portobelo ('Beautiful Port') was the northern terminus of the Camino Real, where Peruvian treasure carried on mule trains across the Isthmus from Panama City was stored in fortified warehouses until the periodic arrival of the Spanish Armada, the famed Fairs where the wealth of the New World was exchanged for goods and supplies from Europe. So much material changed hands that the 1637 Fair (described by Englishman Thomas Gage) took 30 days for the loading and unloading to be completed. In the Royal **Contaduría** or Customs House bars of gold and silver were piled up like firewood. Such riches could hardly fail to attract foreign corsairs; Portobelo was one of Francis Drake's favourite targets but also his downfall; he died here of dysentery in 1596 and was buried in a lead-lined coffin in the bay off Isla Drake. By the beginning of the 17th century several stone *castillos* (Santiago, San Gerónimo and San Fernando) had been built to protect the harbour. Attacks continued, however, until in 1740 the treasure fleets were re-routed around the Horn and the Portobelo Fairs ended. The fortifications were rebuilt after Vernon's attack in 1744 but they were no longer seriously challenged, leaving the fortresses visible today. The largest, the aptly-named 'Iron Castle', was largely dismantled during Canal construction (its stones form the breakwaters at the N entrance to the Canal), but there are many other interesting ruined fortresses, walls, rows of cannon and remains of the town's 120 houses and public buildings to be seen standing along the foreshore amid the present-day village (population 5,850). (Note that Fuerte San Lorenzo and the nearby beach of La Huerta can only be reached by boat.) The Contaduría (1630) was recently restored, with similar plans in place for the Plaza, Hospital Chapel and the Fernández House.

In **San Felipe Church** (1776) is the 17th century, cocobolo-wood statue of the Black Christ, about whose origin there are many legends. One tells of how it cured the townspeople of cholera. Another says that the life-size image was on its way to Cartagena when the ship put in to Portobelo to buy supplies; after being thwarted 5 times by contrary weather to leave port, the crew decided the statue wished to remain in Panamá, it was thrown overboard, floated ashore and was rescued by the locals. The figure's miraculous reputation is celebrated each 21 October, when purple-clad pilgrims come from all over the country and the statue is paraded through the town at 1800 on a flower- and candle-covered platform carried by 80 men (who take 3 steps forward and 2 steps back to musical accompaniment); feasting and dancing till dawn follow the solemn procession.

Other *fiestas* in the Portobelo region (eg New Year's Eve, Carnival, Patron Saint's Day 20 March) are opportunities to experience the *Congos*. Unlike the dance of the same name found elsewhere on the Caribbean coast, the *Congo* here is the name given both to the main, male participants and a slowly enfolding ritual which lasts from Epiphany (6 January) to Easter. Among the various explanations of its symbolism are elements of the people's original African religions, their capture into slavery, their conversion to Catholicism and mockery of the colonial Spaniards. Members of the audience are often 'imprisoned' in a makeshift palisade and have to pay a 'ransom' to be freed. IPAT now has an office in Portobelo (T 48-2060) and can provide guides, schedules of *Congos* and other performances, and comprehensive information about the many local points of interest, including the surrounding 4,850-ha Portobelo National Park, scuba diving sites (superb) and renting a boat to visit secluded beaches nearby.

Hotel D *Divers Haven*, friendly, US owner. **Restaurants**: *El Hostal del Rey*, corner of central park, good meals and value; a number of small *fondas* serving coconut rice with fresh shrimps, Caribbean food (spicy) with octopus or fish, or *fufú* (fish soup cooked with coconut milk and vegetables).

Buses From Colón, every hour from 0700 from the bus station on Front Street y Calle 13, 1 hr, US$2; María Chiquita, 40 min, US$0.80. Portobelo can be visited from Panama City in a day without going into Colón by taking an early bus as far as the Sabanitas turnoff (US$1) and waiting for a Colón-Portobelo service (US$1).

A narrow gravel road (being extended by the US military but 4WD rec at present, limited bus service) continues on NE from Portobelo to Isla Grande, Nombre de Dios (25 km) and Palenque. It passes through Garrote and La Guaira (**D** *Cabañas Montecarlo*, T 41-2054), from where *pangas* can be hired (US$1) at the car park to cross to **Isla Grande**, a favourite with international visitors because of its relaxed lifestyle, fishing, scuba diving and snorkelling, windsurfing and dazzling white palm-fringed beaches. The island's 300 black inhabitants make a living from fishing and coconut cultivation, and a powerful French-built lighthouse crowns the small island's northern point. There are a number of colourful African-tinged festivals held here throughout the year, particularly on 24 June, 16 July and the pre-Lenten Carnival with *Congos*.

Accommodation Popular on holidays and dry season weekends, make reservations in advance, prices often double during high season. **A** *Isla Grande*, T 64-3046, F 64-0646, bungalows scattered along an excellent sandy beach; boat, snorkel and jet ski hire, restaurant, minizoo (toucans, crocodiles, monkeys, etc), reduced tariffs on weekdays, rec; **B** *Posada Villa Ensueño*, T 68-2926/1445, good café/bar; **B** *La Cholita*, similar prices; **B** *Candy Rose*; **C** *Cabañas*

Jackson, T 41-6472, many huts/bungalows available; **C** *Posada Guayaco*. All have bars and simple restaurants, *Candy Rose* serves drinks with a special octopus cooked in coconut milk.

The beautiful, deserted mainland beaches continue as the 'road' heads E to **Nombre de Dios**. The historic town (1520) near the present village was once the thriving trading port which first hosted the famed Fairs, located at the end of the stone-paved Camino Real from the capital. By the 1550s more than half the trade between Spain and its colonies was passing through its lightly-defended harbour, but in 1594 the decision was made to move operations to the more-sheltered site of Portobelo. The Royal Road was diverted and Nombre de Dios was already dying when Drake captured and burnt it two years later, so that William Dampier could describe the site some years later as 'only a name ... everything is covered by the Jungle with no sign that it was ever populated'. Excavations have taken place, revealing the Spanish town, parts of the Camino Real, a broken cannon and other objects (most now in the National Museum). The modern village has few facilities (no hotel), but a beautiful beach can be enjoyed by those few who get this far. A *cayuco* (US$3 pp, 12 min) can be taken to Playa Damas, an unusual beach where alternating patches of red and white sand resemble a chess board; the beach is owned by an amateur ecologist who has built some rustic huts and a campsite (*Costa El Oro*, T 63-5955) on a small island here, he also offers expert guidance on local fishing and diving spots.

The track staggers on as far as Cuango, a few km E of **Palenque**, another unspoilt hamlet with a good beach where very rudimentary huts are being built for visitors. Locals eagerly await the road's eventual extension through a succession of seaside villages to the Golfo de San Blas opposite El Porvenir, the capital of the Kuna Indian's self-governed *comarca* of San Blas or 'Kuna Yala' (Kuna Earth). If a good road is built, tropical fishing villages like Miramar and Palmira, with their welcoming people, white-sand beaches, offshore reefs and crystal-clear waters will become wonderful resorts.

Although little of the Camino Real remains, its two branches from Madden Lake/Lago Alajuela across the mountains to Nombre de Dios (30 km) and Portobelo can still be hiked. The trail starts at the old manganese mining zone (Mina 1, at the end of the dirt road from Boquerón and Salamanca), where the Río Boquerón empties into Madden Lake, and follows the river up to the continental divide and the Río Nombre de Dios down the northern watershed to the coast near the present-day town. This historic trek is easy for anyone with reasonable fitness, as one can drive to entry and exit points. Guides are not really necessary, the rivers are beautiful (and carry little water in the dry season) and the jungle almost untouched; the trail is straightforward and rises only to 330m at the divide. Allow about three days for the Boquerón-Nombre de Dios trek. The trail to Portobelo branches off the above at the Río Diablo or Río Longue. After you leave the Boquerón you will need to navigate by compass. The Diablo takes the trekker higher into the divide (700m) than the Longue (the route the treasure-laden mules followed, 350m) and the terrain is more broken; both lead to the Río Cascajal (higher reaches are strewn with large boulders), which descends to the Caribbean around Cerro Brujo, the highest point in the region. There are jaguars in this forested refuge, but they are unlikely to present any danger to hikers. The Cascajal crosses the Sabanitas-Portobelo road some 5 km from the latter, a lift to town shouldn't be a problem. The Boquerón-Portobelo hike is more demanding than the other and takes about four days, a good machete is essential, solitude is guaranteed for at least two days.

From Colón the Caribbean **Costa Abajo**, stretching W of the Canal, can also be visited. The road leaves Colón through new housing developments (on the left is the modern city of Margarita) and runs 10 km SW to the Gatún Locks (see under **The Canal** below).

The N road branch at Gatún follows Limón Bay through a well-preserved forest reserve to Fort Sherman, running beside the only remaining remnants of the French Canal excavations (most of their work on the Atlantic side is now below the Lake while the Pacific excavations were incorporated into the US construction). Fort Sherman is heavily-forested military property and a guard at the gate may issue you with a pass; since it is also the US Army's Jungle and Guerrilla Warfare Training Center it is advisable not to court any unpleasant surprises by leaving the road, which is gravel and well signposted (no public transport) for the 10 km to **Fuerte San Lorenzo**. Perched on a cliff-top promontory overlooking the mouth of the Río Chagres with great views of the coast, San Lorenzo is one of the oldest and best-preserved Spanish fortifications in the Americas. Construction had began the year before Drake launched a 23-ship attack on the post (1596) and proceeded up the Chagres in an unsuccessful attempt to reach Panama City. Morgan fought a bloody 11-day battle to take the fort as a prelude to his decisive swoop on Panamá Viejo in 1671. Although new defences were then built, they were unable to prevent British Admiral Edward Vernon's successful attack in 1740 (one of Vernon's cannon with the GR monogram can still be seen). Engineer Hernández then spent seven years strengthening the garrison (1760-67), but the threat to San Lorenzo gradually receded as Spanish galleons were diverted to the Cape Horn route and the era of the freebooters approached its end. The last Royalist soldiers left the fort in 1821 as Colombia declared its independence from Spain. The earliest artillery sheds can be seen on the lower cliff level but most of the bulwarks, arched stone rooms and lines of cannon are 18th century. The site recently underwent an extensive UNESCO renovation programme and is well worth a visit. There is a picnic area and a tiny beach is accessible by a steep path down the cliff. Take insect repellent.

There is no crossing of the Chagres at San Lorenzo; to continue down the **Costa Abajo** one must return to the Gatún Dam and take the gravel road along the W side of the river, which winds its way through pristine forest to the coastal village of Piña and its kilometre-long beach. The road runs W along a steep and rocky shore punctured by many small coves to Nuevo Chagres and Palmas Bellas, quiet fishing resorts in coconut palm groves, but with few facilities. 4WD is required to continue to Río Indio and Miguel de la Borda, where the road comes to an end. The villages beyond, including historic Río Belén where one of Columbus' ships was abandoned in 1502, remain accessible only by sea.

San Blas Islands An interesting trip can be made to the San Blas archipelago, which has 365 islands ranging in size from tiny ones with a few coconut palms to islands on which hundreds of Cuna Indians live. About 50 are inhabited. The islands, off the Caribbean coast E of Colón, vary in distance from the shore from 100m to several kilometres.

The Cuna are the most sophisticated and politically organized of the country's three major groups. They run the San Blas Territory virtually on their own terms, with internal autonomy and, uniquely among Panama's Indians, send their representative to the National Assembly. They have their own language, but Spanish is widely spoken. The women wear gold nose- and ear-rings, and costumes with unique designs based on local themes, geometric patterns, stylized fauna and flora, and pictorial representations of current events or political propaganda. They are outside the Panamanian tax zone and have negotiated a treaty perpetuating their long-standing trade with small craft from Colombia. Many men work on the mainland, but live on the islands.

Photographers need plenty of small change, as set price for a Cuna to pose is US$0.25. *Molas* (decorative handsewn appliqué for blouse fronts) cost upwards of US$10 each (also obtainable in many Panama City and Colón shops).

There are about 20 airports in the San Blas Islands and province, but most are 'larger' than the islands or places on which they are built. They include: Porvenir, Carti, Río Sidra, Río Azúcar, Narganá, Corazón, Río Tigre, Playón Chico, Tupile, Tikankiki, Alligandi, Achutupu, Mamitupu, Ogobsucum, Ustupu, Mansucum,

Mulatupu, Tubuala, Caledonia, Puerto Obaldía. Two companies fly the routes from Paitilla airport, Transpasa, T 26-0932/26-0843 (a couple of 6-seater Cessnas) and Ansa, who no longer take passengers, T 26-7891/26-6881 (twin-engined Islanders). All tourists go to Porvenir and then are picked up by boat to go to a neighbouring island, about 20 mins ride. One way fares to the islands are US$25 to Porvenir and US$40 to Puerto Obaldía. All other airport fares are scaled in between (price includes a 5% sales tax). You must take your passport because every month or so a hijack attempt to Colombia is made. All flights leave between 0600 and 0630, Mon-Sat, returning 0700-0730. Sunday flights must be booked privately. You can be dropped off at any island or village and discuss your return with the pilot. It is probably not a wise idea since most of the islands may have nice-looking beaches, but no drinking water or food.

Any travel agent in Panama can book a San Blas tour. A one-night stay in Porvenir costs US$120 including food and lodging at the *Hotel Hanay Kantule* (also spelt *Anai Katule*), T 20-0746. You have to get up early for the return flight. Other hotels in the Porvenir area include **San Blas**, T 62-1606/5410, on Nalunega Island (two daily tours included in the price), and **Residencial Turístico Yeri**, T 623402; the **Hanay Kantule** charges US$55 a night, all others US$25, including food. For the *Hanay*, ask for Israel Fernández on arrival at Porvenir. One of the agents who will handle bookings is Chadwicks, see **Balboa** below. At Narganá there is a basic hotel, F, and one restaurant, *El Caprichito*, good crab dishes.

There are occasional boats to the San Blas islands from Colón, but there is no scheduled service and the trip can be rough. One ship that goes from time to time is the *Almirante*, try to find the captain, Figueres Cooper, who charges US$30 for the trip. The port captain's office at Coco Solo may have information on boat departures, T 41-5231, although most boats are 'not keen on being landed with potentially stranded gringos'. Alternatively, go to Portobelo (see above) and try for a boat from there, 9 hrs to Porvenir.

The Canal As the crow flies the distance across the isthmus is 55 km. From shore to shore the Canal is 67½ km, or 82 km (44.08 nautical miles) from deep water to deep water. It has been widened to 150m in most places. The trip normally takes 8 or 9 hrs for the 30 ships a day passing through.

10 km SW of Colón are the **Gatún Locks** *(Esclusas de Gatún)* and their neat attendant town. The observation point here (open 1000-1630) is perhaps the best spot in the Canal Area for photographing the passage of ships. (Bus from Colón to Gatún Locks US$0.25.) The most magnificent of the Canal's locks, Gatún integrates all three lock 'steps' on the Atlantic side, raising or lowering ships to the 26m level of the Lake in one operation. The flights are in duplicate to allow ships to be passed in opposite directions simultaneously. Passage of the Locks takes about 1 hr. The road forks after crossing the Lock: the left-hand branch crosses the Chagres River by bridge just downstream from the graceful Gatún Dam, which was the largest earth dam in the world when constructed in 1906. Enough water must be impounded in the reservoir during the rainy season to operate the locks throughout the 34-month dry season, since a single ship's transit can use up to 50 million gallons. (A high level reservoir, Lago Alajuela, formerly Madden Lake, feeds the lake and maintains its level.) Opposite the power plant is the **Tarpon Club** (T 43-5316/5216 - owned by the same family as the posh *Tropic Star Lodge* in Piñas), a fishing club which has a very nice restaurant, disco and bar; good place to rent boats for a cruise around the Lake. A short distance further S is an attractive lakeside picnic area and small boat launching area. The partly-paved road goes on down the lake to Escobal and Cuipo through lovely scenery (good birding); no hotels in Cuipo but plenty of buses to/from Colón (US$1.60, 2 hrs; US$0.25 to the Locks).

The largest section of the Canal is in Lago Gatún. In the lake is **Barro Colorado** island, to which the animals fled as the basin slowly filled. It is now a biological

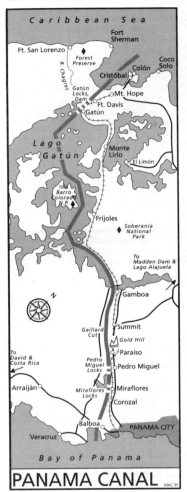

Caribbean Sea

Fort Sherman

Ft. San Lorenzo
R. Chagres
Forest Preserve
Coco Solo
Cristóbal
Colón
Gatún Locks, Dam
Mt. Hope
Ft. Davis
Gatún

Lago Gatún
Monte Lirio
El Limón

Isla Barro Colorado N.P.

Frijoles
Soberanía National Park

To Madden Dam & Lago Alajuela

Gamboa

Gaillard Cut
Summit
Gold Hill
Paraíso

To David & Costa Rica
Pedro Miguel Locks
Pedro Miguel

Arraiján
Miraflores Locks
Miraflores
Corozal

Balboa
PANAMA CITY

Veracruz

Bay of Panama

PANAMA CANAL MAC 91

reserve for scientific research. Visits can be arranged with the Smithsonian Institute in Ancón, US$22 including boat, audio-visual display and lunch; take a Gamboa Summit bus from next to Plaza 5 de Mayo (0600 and 0615) to the Dredging Division dock at Gamboa (US$0.65), from where the boat leaves. Trips go on Tuesdays and Saturdays only for 15 people. Make arrangements with the Institute in Ancón, preferably the previous week to see if a space is available (the tours are booked up many months in advance). Individuals may be able to join a tour party. The excursion is highly recommended for seeing wildlife, especially monkeys. Visitors without permits will be turned away on arrival. For longer stays, write to the Director, Smithsonian Tropical Research Institute, Box 2072, Balboa, Panamá. Administration, T 27-6022; hours 0800-1145, 1315-1515. Tours also arranged by Eco-Tours, Panama City, T 36-3575/3076, F 36-3550: Barro Colorado island is only seen from the water, but tourists walk a nature trail on the Gigante Peninsula, which is also part of the national park.

After travelling over the lake for 37 km and then through the narrow rock defile of the Gaillard or Culebra Cut for 13 km to Pedro Miguel Locks, the descent to sea-level begins. Culebra Cut can be seen from Contractor's Hill, reached by car (no buses) by turning right 3 km past the Bridge of the Americas, passing Cocoli, then turning left as signed. The first stage is a descent into **Miraflores** Lago, 16½m above sea-level. The process is completed at the Miraflores Locks, 1½ km further on. The road beyond Cocoli goes on to Posa, where there are good views of the locks, the cut and former Canal Zone buildings. Opposite Miraflores Locks is a swing bridge which only operates when traffic is heavy (eg on long weekends). The Canal channel continues to Balboa and the Pacific. An odd fact is that the mean level of the Pacific is some 20 cm higher than the Atlantic, but the disparity is not constant throughout the year. On the Atlantic side there is a normal variation of 30 cm between high and low tides, and on the Pacific of about 380 cm, rising sometimes to 640 cm. (See also Panama City **Excursions**.)

Most people are surprised by the Canal. Few foresee that the scenery is so beautiful, and it is interesting to observe the mechanics of the passage. Eco-Tours de Panamá (T and F numbers above) offer a day-long full transit through the canal on a luxury yacht for US$109. Agencia Giscomes, T 64-0111, also offers trips through the canal every 2nd and 4th Saturday of the month. Partial boat trips are also offered on the canal, through Miraflores locks as for Pedro Miguel locks. They go about twice monthly (eg Argo Tours, T 28-4348, F 28-1234, every other Saturday from pier 17, Balboa, US$40, children under 12 US$20, refreshments and snacks on sale); enquire at any travel agent. Otherwise since the Panama City-Colón train is not running, travellers should take a bus to the Miraflores Locks (open 0900-1700, best between 0600-1000 for photos and 1430-1800 for viewing only) to see shipping. The viewing gallery is free. A detailed model of the canal, formerly in the Department of Transport at Ancón, has been moved here and there is also a free slide show given throughout the day, with explanations in English. About 250m past the entrance to the Locks is a road (left) to the filtration plant and observatory, behind which is a picnic area and viewing point. Orange bus from Panama City to Miraflores Locks leaves from the bus station next to Plaza 5 de Mayo (direction Paraíso or Gamboa), 15 mins, US$0.35. Ask driver to let you off at the stop for 'Esclusas de Miraflores', from where it's a 10-min walk to the Locks. Taxi to the Locks, US$10 per hour. Another good way to see the Panama Canal area is to rent a car.

The very best way to see the Canal is by boat: it is possible to traverse the canal as a linehandler (no experience necessary) on a yacht; the journey takes two days. Note that more boats pass the canal from N to S than the other way around. Yachts are allowed into the canal on Tues and Thur only. The yacht owners need 4 line handlers. Go to the Panama Canal Yacht Club in Colón, or the Yacht Clubs in Cristóbal (downstairs from the building next to the Wharf), or in Balboa a couple of days before, and ask people hanging around the bar. The Balboa Club offers good daily lunch special. Good place to watch canal traffic. 50m right of the Club is a small white booth which has a list of boat departures for the next day; ask here if you can go to the dock and take the motor boat which shuttles out to yachts preparing for passage. Ask to speak to captains from the launch and see if they'll let you 'transit'. At Cristóbal you can approach the boats directly at their moorings. They have to book their passage through the canal 48 hrs in advance and are subject to a hefty fine if they default through lack of line handlers. However, don't expect too much, at times less than one private boat a week goes through the Canal.

Balboa The ship usually berths at Pier 18. Panama City is about $3\frac{1}{4}$ km from the docks, an average of 10 mins by taxi.

Balboa stands attractively between the Canal quays and Ancón hill, which lies between it and Panama City. It has been described as an efficient, planned, sterilized town, a typical American answer to the wilfulness and riot of the tropics.

The Canal administration building (with fine murals on the ground floor) and a few official residences are on Balboa Heights. At the foot of Balboa Heights is Balboa, with a small park, a reflecting pool and marble shaft commemorating Goethals, and a long parkway flanked with royal palms known as the Prado. At its eastern end is a theatre, a service centre building, post office and bank. Farther along Balboa Road are a large YMCA, where only male employees of the Canal Company can stay, but where all comers may eat, various churches and a Masonic temple. Beyond the Puente de las Américas is a long peninsula into the Pacific on which is **Fuerte Amador**, formerly the HQ of the Panamanian Defence Force, held by US forces since December 1989. It will be returned to Panama in 1994. To cross the causeway costs US$0.25. There are many interesting buildings in this area bearing the marks of the conflict and some attractive lawns and parkland.

Banks Citibank; Chase Manhattan Bank.

Post Office Av Balboa and El Prado. **Telecommunications** INTEL; Tropical Radio & Telegraph Co Public Telex booth.

Travel Agency: *Chadwick's*, in YMCA building, excellent, English spoken, T 52-28-63-29.

Excursions There is a launch service to **Taboga Island**, about 20 km offshore (return fare US$6). Taboga is reached in 1-1$\frac{1}{2}$ hrs from Pier 17-18 in Balboa (check the times in advance—T 64-3549 office, or 32-5395 pier); taxi Bella Vista-Pier 18, US$3-4 pp. There are 2 boats daily during the week (0830 and 1500 or 1700-Thur) and 3 boats on Sat, Sun and holidays (0830, 1130 and 1600). Return boats at 1000 and 1630 or 1830-Thur; 1000, 1430 and 1730 at weekends. From November to January there are 3 boats daily. The island is a favourite year-round resort; its pineapples and mangoes have a high reputation and its church is the second oldest in the western hemisphere (admission to beach at *Hotel Taboga*, US$6, redeemable in 'funny money' to buy food and drink, good swimming, covered picnic huts extra).

The trip out to Taboga is very interesting, passing the naval installations at the Pacific end of the Canal, the great bridge linking the Americas, tuna boats and shrimp fishers in for supplies, visiting yachts from all over the world at the Balboa Yacht Club, and the 4-km Causeway connecting Fuerte Amador on the mainland with 3 islands in the bay. Part of the route follows the channel of the Canal, with its busy traffic. Taboga itself, with a promontory rising to 488m, is carpeted with flowers at certain seasons. There are few cars in the meandering, helter-skelter streets, and only one footpath as a road.

The first Spanish settlement was in 1515, two years after Balboa's discovery of the Pacific. It was from here that Pizarro set out for Peru in 1524. For two centuries it was a stronghold of the pirates who preyed on the traffic to Panama. Because it has a deep-water, sheltered anchorage, it was during colonial times the terminal point for ships coming up the W coast of South America. El Morro, at low tide joined to Taboga, is at high tide an island; it was once owned by the Pacific Steam Navigation Company, whose ships sailed from there. For a fine view, walk through the town and up to the top of Cerro Turco, the hill with a cross at the summit (285m), to the right of the radar station (there is a shady short cut, ask locals). When surveying the view, don't miss the pelican rookery on the back side of the island; it is an easy walk down. Further S is Cerro Vigía (307m), the highest point, a 2-hr hike from the central plaza; wear ankle boots and take mosquito repellent. Another trail runs W along the N coast, about 1 hr, pleasant beaches. The southern coast of Taboga and all of neighbouring Isla Uraba are wildlife reserves; permit from Inrenare required, office near *Hotel Taboga*.

Hotels B-C *Taboga*, T 50-2122, F 23-0116, Apdo 55-0357, Paitilla, Panamá, 300m E of wharf, a/c, TV, restaurant, café; **D** *Chu*, on main street, 200m left of wharf, T 50-2036, wooden colonial style, thin walls, no bath, beautiful views, own beach, terrace restaurant serving traditional fish and chicken dishes.

It is a longer trip by launch—some 75 km—to the **Pearl Islands**, visited mostly by sea-anglers for the Pacific mackerel, red snapper, corvina, sailfish, marlin, and other species which teem in the waters around. High mountains rise from the sea, but there is a little fishing village on a shelf of land at the water's edge. There was much pearl fishing in colonial days. (Flight Paitilla airport-San Miguel, twice weekly, US$35 return.) **Contadora**, one of the smallest Pearl Islands, has become quite famous since its name became associated with a Central American peace initiative. It was also where the Shah of Iran was exiled, in a house called Puntalara, after the Iranian Revolution.

Contadora has **A** *El Galeón Hotel*, *Hotel de Villas*, T 50-4030, and the very luxurious chalet complex known as **L** *Caesar Park Contadora Resort and Casino*, nice location on beach, T 50-4033, F 50-4000, in Panama City T 69-5269, 69-4721. *Gallo Nero* restaurant, pizza and pasta, by runway; cheap café nearby, *Fonda Sagitario*, and a supermarket. Return air ticket from Paitilla, US$45 by Aeroperlas, T 69-4555 (extra flights at weekends, 15 mins, crowded). Mountain bike hire US$5/hr, by entrance to *Caesar Park*. Beautiful beaches with crystal-clear water. Good skin-diving and sailing, 3-hr boat trip. Beware the sharks. Three day package tour to Contadora, US$150 for 2, recommended. Argonaut Steamship Agency, Calle 55 No 7-82, Panama City, T 64-3459, runs launch cruises.

Ancón curves round the hill N and E and merges into Panama City. It has picturesque views of the palm-fringed shore. The following walk takes in the sights of Ancón: walk to the top of the hill in the morning for views of the city, Balboa and the Canal (conveniences and water fountain at the top – you may have to climb part of the radio tower to see anything); the entrance is on Av 4 de Julio (Av de los Mártires). Return to Av 4 de Julio and take a clockwise route around the hill, bearing right on to Balboa Road (Av Estado de Jamaica), passing YMCA, Chase Manhattan and Citibank, until you reach Stevens Circle where Cuna Indians sell *molas*. Here is the Post Office and a cafeteria. Then walk down the Prado lined with royal palms to the Goethals Memorial and up the steps to the Administration Building to see the murals of the Construction of the Canal (entrance free, identity must be shown to the guards). Follow Heights Road until it becomes Gorgas Road. You will pass the headquarters of the Smithsonian Tropical Research Institute (where applications to visit Barro Colorado Island are made) and, among trees and flowers, the Gorgas Army Community Hospital. Gorgas Road leads back to Av 4 de Julio, but look out for the sign to the **Museo de Arte Contemporáneo** (open Mon-Fri 0800-1230, 1430-1800, Sat 0800-1200), before Av 4 de Julio. 2 libraries are open to the public: that of the Smithsonian Tropical Research Institute in the Canal Area, opp Plaza 5 de Mayo, and that of the Panama Canal College, underneath the Bridge of the Americas. **NB** Take care on Ancon Hill, robberies reported in 1993.

At the foot of Ancón Hill the Instituto Nacional stands on the 4-lane Avenida 4 de Julio (Tivoli). The University City is on the Transisthmian Highway. Opposite the campus is the Social Security Hospital.

PANAMA CITY

Panama City, capital of the Republic, has a metropolitan population of over 600,000 (585,000 at 1990 census), plus 250,000 in the satellite town of San Miguelito; there are 1.1 million in the province of Panamá. It was founded on its present site in 1673 after Morgan had sacked the old town, now known as Panamá Viejo, 6½ km away by road. Most of Panama City is modern; the old quarter of the city (the Casco Viejo)—the part that Spain fortified so massively just as the era of widespread piracy was coming to an end—lies at the tip of the peninsula; both it and Panamá Viejo are being extensively restored.

Note Some of the street names have recently been changed, which may make finding your way around a little difficult. The locals are likely still to refer to the streets by their old names, so if in doubt ask. Also, few buildings display their numbers, so try to find out the nearest cross street.

Panama City is a curious blend of old Spain, American progress, and the bazaar atmosphere of the East. It has a polyglot population unrivalled in any other Latin American city. For the sober minded, the palm-shaded beaches, the islands of the Bay and the encircling hills constitute a large part of its charm. The cabarets and night life (very enterprising) are an attraction to those so inclined. The city has been expanding since 1979, with new developments along the southern end of the Canal and skyscrapers springing up around the Bahía de Panamá.

Most of the interesting sights and the budget hotels are in the Casco Viejo (the 'Old Compound', also known as the Casco Colonial or San Felipe), which occupies the narrow peninsula E of Calle 11. In 1992 local authorities began reviving some of the area's past glory by painting many of the post-colonial houses in soft pastels and their decorations and beautiful iron-clad balconies in relief; new shops and restaurants are being installed in restored buildings in an attempt to make the Casco Viejo a tourist attraction. A good starting place for a walking tour is the picturesque **Plaza Francia**, at the walled tip of the peninsula, with its red poinciana trees and obelisk topped by a cockerel (symbol of the Gallic nation), which has a document with 5,000 signatures buried beneath it. Twelve large narrative plaques (in Spanish) and many statues recall the French Canal's construction history and personalities; the work of Cuban doctor Carlos Finlay in establishing the cause of yellow fever is commemorated on one tablet. Facing the

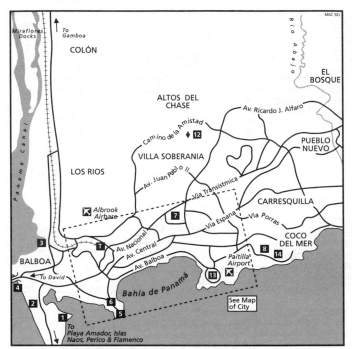

plaza is the French Embassy, housed in a pleasant early 20th century building. Built flush under the old seawalls around the plaza are *Las Bóvedas* (The Vaults), the thick-walled colonial dungeons where prisoners in tiny barred cells were immersed up to their necks during high tides. Nine 'vaults' were restored by IPAT in 1982 and converted into art galleries and a handicraft centre. The French restaurant *Las Bóvedas* occupies another two 'vaults' next to the former Palacio de Justicia (partly burned during Operation Just Cause and now housing the National Institute of Culture).

Steps lead up from the Plaza Francia to the promenade (**Paseo de Las Bóvedas**) which runs along the top of the defensive walls surrounding the peninsula on three sides. This is a popular place for an evening stroll; it is ablaze with bougainvillea and affords good views of the Bahía de Panamá, the Sierra Majé on the Panamá/Darién provincial border (on a clear day), and the fortified islands of Naos, Perico and Flamenco, linked by a causeway (**Calzada Amador**) built during Canal construction. The Calzada is used by joggers and cyclists (bikes for hire at the causeway entrance, US$1.50-2.00 per hour); it has fine views of the Puente de las Américas and ships lined up to enter the Canal. There are small charges for entry and for swimming at shark net-protected Solidaridad beach on Naos (crowded on weekends but not rec – water polluted). Flamenco is headquarters for the National Maritime Service and is closed to the public.

Two blocks NW of the Plaza (Avenida A and Calle 3) are the restored ruins of the impressive **Church and Convent of Santo Domingo** (1673, but destroyed by fires in 1737 and 1756), both with paired columns and brick inlaying on their

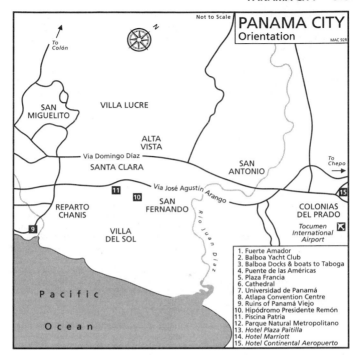

PANAMA CITY
Orientation

MAC 92R

Not to Scale

To Colón

To Chepo

SAN MIGUELITO

VILLA LUCRE

ALTA VISTA

Via Domingo Díaz

SANTA CLARA

SAN ANTONIO

Via José Agustín Arango

REPARTO CHANIS

SAN FERNANDO

COLONIAS DEL PRADO

Tocumen International Airport

VILLA DEL SOL

Río Juan Díaz

P a c i f i c

O c e a n

1. Fuerte Amador
2. Balboa Yacht Club
3. Balboa Docks & boats to Taboga
4. Puente de las Américas
5. Plaza Francia
6. Cathedral
7. Universidad de Panamá
8. Atlapa Convention Centre
9. Ruins of Panamá Viejo
10. Hipódromo Presidente Remón
11. Piscina Patria
12. Parque Natural Metropolitano
13. *Hotel Plaza Paitilla*
14. *Hotel Marriott*
15. *Hotel Continental Aeropuerto*

façades. The famous 15m-long flat arch (*arco chato*) which formed the base of the choir was built entirely of bricks and mortar with no internal support. When the great debate as to where the Canal should be built was going on, a Nicaraguan stamp showing a volcano, with all its implications of earthquakes, and the stability of this arch – a proof of no earthquakes – are said to have played a large part in determining the choice in Panama's favour. A chapel on the site has been converted into the interesting **Museo de Arte Colonial Religioso** (open Mon-Fri 0900-1600), whose treasures include a precious golden altar, a delicate snail staircase, silver relics and wooden scuptures from as far away as Lima and México, 19th century engravings of the city, and the skeleton of a woman found by archaeologists during excavation of the Church. Behind Santo Domingo, across Avenida Central, the recently-restored neoclassical **Teatro Nacional** (850-seat capacity) opened in 1908 with Verdi's *Aida* being performed in what was then considered the state of the art in acoustics. French-influenced sculptures and friezes enliven the façade, while Roberto Lewis' paintings depicting the birth of the nation adorn the theatre's dome. Dame Margot Fonteyn, a long-time resident of Panama until her death in 1991, danced at the theatre's re-inauguration, after many years of restoration, in 1974. Free entry during normal working hours after asking permission of the security guard.

Diagonally opposite the Teatro Nacional (Av B & Calle 3) is the peaceful **Plaza Bolívar**, with an equestrian statue of the Liberator surrounded by laurels brought from India. Facing the square are the faded *Hotel Colonial*, the **Church of San Felipe Neri** (interesting but open only on 26 May), and many 19th century houses still displaying roofs of red clay tiles bearing the stamp 'Marseilles 1880'. On the E side stand **San Francisco Church** (colonial but 'modified' in 1917 and modernized in 1983) and the **San Francisco Convent** (1678), largest of all the religious buildings, which was restored by Peruvian architect Leonardo Villanueva. The Bolivarian Congress of June 1826, at which Bolívar proposed a United States of South America, was held in the Chapter Room of the Convent; here also the 1904 Constitution was drafted. This northern wing was dedicated as the **Instituto Bolívar** in 1956; its wood panelling, embossed leather benches and paintings (restored in part by the government of Ecuador) may be viewed with an authorized guide from the Bolivarian Society, T 62-2947.

Another long block W of Plaza Bolívar, on the seafront (Av Alfaro) between Calles 3 y 4, is the **Palacio Presidencial**, the most impressive building in the city, built as an opulent residence in 1673 for successive colonial auditors and governors, enlarged and restored under President Belisario Porras in 1922. Graceful patios and mother-of-pearl decorated columns give a Moorish flavour, and murals by Lewis adorn the official reception salons. The President lives on the first floor; some travellers have been allowed to view the ground floor but the public is usually turned away; exterior photography is allowed. Porras introduced two white Darién herons during one of his presidential terms and a number of their descendants are always to be seen around the fountain of the Moorish patio, leading to the popular nickname of the residence: *Palacio de las Garzas* or Palace of the Herons. A few blocks W, Av Alfaro begins to curve N around the waterfront to the colourful **Central Market** (see **Shopping**, below) and the wharves where fishermen land their catches, coastal vessels anchor (a 15m tidal range allows beaching for maintenance) and cargo boats leave for Colombia (Muelle Inglés).

Two blocks S of the Presidential Palace is the heart of the old town, the **Plaza Catedral or Independencia**, with busts of the Republic's founders and surrounding public buildings. On the W is the **Cathedral** (1688-1794), its twin towers, domes and classical façade encrusted with mother-of-pearl; three of the tower bells were brought from Old Panamá Cathedral. To the right of the main altar is a subterranean passage which leads to other *conventos* and the sea. On the SW corner with Calle 7 is the neoclassical **Palacio Municipal** (City Hall), on the 1st floor of which is the **Museo de Historia de Panamá** (see **Museums**, below). The **Post Office** next door, originally built in 1875 as the Grand Hotel ('the largest edifice of that kind between San Francisco and Cape Horn' according to a contemporary newspaper), is the city's best example of French architecture. It became de Lesseps' headquarters during Canal excavations in the 1880s and was sold back to Panamá in 1912; plans are today well advanced for its conversion into a Museum of the Panama Canal. The E side of the Plaza is dominated by the **Archbishop's Palace** and the *Central Hotel* (1884), once the most luxurious in Central America (interior Palm Garden, restaurants, barber shop, 100 rooms with private baths, wooden staircase imported from New York, etc) and the centre of Panamá's social life for decades; today it is somewhat frayed but still retains echoes of its former elegance.

There are a number of other interesting religious structures within two or three blocks of the Cathedral but the most-visited is the church of **San José** (Av A y Calle 8a, one block W and S of the Plaza Catedral) with its famous Altar de Oro, a massive baroque altar carved from mahogany and veneered with gold. This was one of the few treasures saved from Henry Morgan's attack on Old Panamá in 1671 and there are different versions of how it was concealed from the buccaneers (whitewashed by the priest, covered in mud by nuns, even a remark attributed to Morgan hinting that he was not deceived!). A beautiful organ, an 18th century original pulpit with a painting by an unknown artist on its tiny roof and several smaller carved wooden altars can also be seen. Two blocks further W along Avenida Central is the church of **La Merced**, burnt in 1963 and now completely restored. It was near here that the landward gate of the fortified city stood. A block to the S down Calle 9 is **Plaza Herrera**; the French influence is evident in the Mansard windows and flower-filled cast-iron balconies of the green and light pink coloured houses and *pensiones*. Behind Plaza Herrera are the ruins of the 'Tiger's Hand Bulwark', where the defensive wall ended and the landward side moat began. The strongpoint held a 50-man military post and thirteen cannon, was demolished in 1856 as the town expanded westwards but restored again in 1983. Portions of the moat can still be detected.

From Calle 10 onwards the Avenida Central, Panama City's main commercial street, enters the 'mainland' and begins to curve NW then sweeps NE almost parallel with the shore through the whole town, changing its name to Av Central España and finally Vía España on its course NE to Tocumen Airport. At its crossing with Calle B is the small Plaza Santa Ana with a colonial church (1764), a favourite place for political meetings; the plaza has many restaurants and is a good place at which to catch buses to all parts of the city. Nearby, running towards the Central Market between Av Central and Calle B is an exotic, narrow alley called **Sal Si Puedes** – 'Get out if you can' – (also known as Carrera de Chiriquí) where crowded stalls sell everything from fruit to old books to medicinal plants; 78% of the street's residents in 1892 were Chinese merchants but the city's Chinatown *(Barrio Chino)* is now largely confined to nearby Calle Juan Mendoza and adjacent Calle B (several good Chinese restaurants). The neighbourhood is safe enough during the day (watch for pickpockets in the throng) but don't linger late at night, best to leave before 1930.

The next section of Avenida Central was recently converted into a pedestrian precinct, with trees and decorations, air-conditioned department stores, and wandering street vendors. **Plaza 5 de Mayo** (at Calle 22 Este) is another busy bus stop from which buses leave for the Canal and the airport. In the centre of the Plaza is an obelisk honouring firemen who died in a gunpowder magazine explosion on the site in May 1914. Housed in the old railway station (1913-46) here is the **Museo Antropológico Reina Torres de Araúz** (see **Museums**, below), formerly called the Museum of Panamanian Man, almost opposite the Plaza de Lesseps. This area is the southern fringe of the Caledonia district, where live the descendants of the British West Indian blacks brought in to build the railway and the Canal. Caledonia is a labyrinth of tightly-packed wooden structures, exotic and unassimilated, where whites are definitely unwelcome. Poor districts like Curundú, Hollywood and Marañón are also best avoided.

Calle 23 Este leads E from the Plaza down to the broad Avenida Balboa along the waterfront. The sprawling Santo Tomás Hospital is here (Calle 36); facing it on a semi-circular promontory jutting out from this promenade (another popular jogging stretch) is a great monument to Vasco Núñez de Balboa (1924), who stands sword and cross aloft as when he strode into the Pacific on 1 October 1513 on a white marble globe poised on the shoulders of a supporting group representing the four races of Man. A short distance up the esplanade is the US Embassy. Two more pleasant plazas, Porras and Arías, can be found behind the Santo Tomás Hospital across Av 3 Sur (Justo Arosemena). This central part of the city is known as **La Exposición** because of the international exhibition held here in 1916 to celebrate the building of the Canal. Further N, as Av Balboa begins to curve around the other end of the Bay of Panama to Punta Paitilla and the domestic airport, is Bella Vista, another main business district with some of the city's best hotels. Bordering this on the N, where Avenida España passes the Iglesia de Carmen, is the **El Cangrejo** ('the crab') restaurant and banking district, with many upmarket stores and boutiques. All these areas are evidence of Panama City's sensational growth since the post-war economic boom and the spread of the centre eastwards; the attractive residential suburb of Punta Paitilla was an empty hill where hunting was practiced as recently as the 1960s.

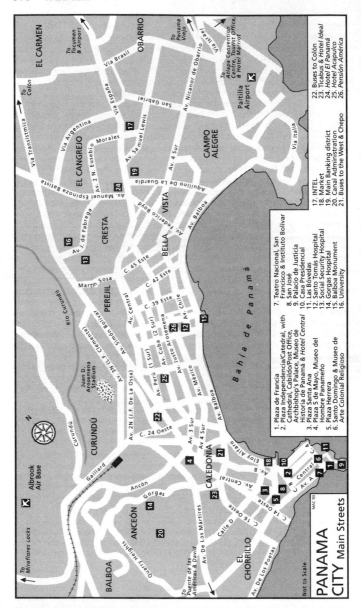

PANAMA CITY Main Streets

Not to Scale

1. Plaza de Francia
2. Plaza Independencia/Catedral, with Cathedral, Cabildo/Post Office, Archbishop's Palace, Museo de Historia de Panamá & Hotel Central
3. Plaza Santa Ana
4. Plaza 5 de Mayo, Museo del Hombre Panameño
5. Plaza Herrera
6. Santo Domingo & Museo de Arte Colonial Religioso
7. Teatro Nacional, San Francisco & Instituto Bolívar
8. San José
9. Palacio de Justicia
10. Casa Presidencial
11. Las Bóvedas
12. Santo Tomás Hospital
13. Social Security Hospital
14. Gorgas Hospital
15. Balboa Monument
16. University
17. INTEL
18. Market
19. Main Banking district
20. Canal Administration
21. Buses to the West & Chepo
22. Buses to Colón
23. Ticabus & Hotel Ideal
24. Hotel El Panamá
25. Hotel Acapulco
26. Pensión América

Claimed to be the only natural forest within the limits of a Latin American metropolitan capital, the 265-ha **Parque Natural Metropolitano** is located between Av Juan Pablo II and the Camino de la Amistad, W of El Cangrejo along the Río Curundú. Open Tue-Sun 0900-1500. As well as a *mirador* (150m) with a splendid view over the city and Canal, there are two interpretive walking trails from which tití monkeys, agoutis, coatis, white-tailed deer, sloths, turtles and up to 200 species of birds may be glimpsed (go early in am for best viewing); green iguanas sun themselves on every available branch. The Smithsonian Institution has installed a unique crane for studying the little-known fauna in the canopy of this remnant of tropical semi-deciduous lowland forest. The Visitor's Centre (T 32-5516) on Av Juan Pablo runs guided 1-hr tours and holds regular slide shows. No Inrenare permit is required for this recommended, easy excursion.

On Independence Day, 3 November, practically the whole city seems to march in a parade lasting about 3$\frac{1}{2}$ hrs, based in the old part of the city. Colourful, noisy, spectacular. Another parade takes place the following day.

Warning The same curfews apply in the Province of Panama as in Colón. Muggings are frequent. It is not advisable to walk on any streets alone after dark (ie after 1730). Most hotels and restaurants have locked doors, or armed guards in their parking lots (give them US$0.25 to look after your car). Attacks have been reported in the Casco Viejo and Panamá Viejo. Marañón (around the market), San Miguelito (on the way in from Tocumen airport) and Caledonia can be dangerous; never walk there at night and take care in daylight, too. For this reason, be careful when booking into a hotel or *pensión* between Calles 9 and 30, ie W of Plaza Herrera (where most of the cheap ones are to be found). Probably the safest area for visitors to stay is Bella Vista. Taxis are the safest way to travel around the city, and drivers will give you good advice on where not to go. Take the new taxis on the streets. It is also more expensive to take taxis from the hotels. All the same, most Panamanians are friendly and helpful.

El Chorrillo, the area W from Plaza Santa Ana to Ancón hill, was largely destroyed in Operation Just Cause; it was a dangerous area so if you wish to visit it show a genuine interest in the district's recent history. We have received recent reports of muggings here. Some rebuilding has taken place, but long-term plans are to build a new bus terminal here.

Hotels Note a 10% tax on all hotel prices. All hotels are air-conditioned.
    L *El Marriott Caesar Park*, Vía Israel and Calle 17, T 26-4077, F 26-0116, 5 mins from centre, near the sea and the Atlapa convention centre, restaurant, pool, health spa, etc; *El Panamá*, Vía España, 111 y Calle 55, T 69-5000, F 69-5990, former *Hilton*, tropical Art Deco style, vast rooms, good swimming pool, 'bags of charm'. Hotels in our **A+** range include: *Plaza Paitilla Inn* (former *Holiday Inn*), Punta Paitilla, PO Box 1807, T 69-1122, F 23-1470, weekend cheap rates available, restaurant, café, nightclub, swimming pool; *Riande Continental*, also on Vía España, T 63-9999, F 69-4559, in the business district, pool, night clubs, restaurants, but noisy till 2230 from organ music (a Wurlitzer). In our **A** range, and belonging to the same group are *Continental* are *Granada*, Av Eusebio Morales, T64-4900, F 64-0930, also with casino, pool, restaurant; *Continental Airport*, near Tocumen airport (10 mins), T20-3333, F 20-5017, a/c, good (reductions for more than one night), free transport to airport, pool, tennis, casino; *El Ejecutivo*, Calle Aquilino de la Guardia, T 64-3333, F 69-1944, pool. *Aramo*, Vía Brasil y Abel Bravo, a/c, restaurant, T 69-0174, F 69-2406.
    In our **B** range: *Caribe*, Av Perú, T 27-2525, a/c; *Europa*, Vía España y Calle 42, T 63-6369, F 63-6749, opp Teatro Bella Vista, another casino hotel, restaurants and pool, rec; *Gran Hotel Soloy*, Av Perú y Calle 30, T 27-1133, F 27-0884; *Vera Cruz*, Av Perú y Calle 4, T 27-3022, F 27-3789, without breakfast, new, clean, good, but rooms at front noisy; *Doral*, Calle Monteserín (T 62-5133), a/c, TV, cold water, rec as safe, although not in safe area, cheaper commercial rates available; *Costa Inn*, Av Perú y Calle 39, T 27-1522, F 25-1281, a/c, hot water, TV, pool, use of fridge, safe parking, rec; *Roma*, Av Justo Arosemena, T 27-3844, F 27-3711; *Gran Hotel Lux*, Av Perú, T27-1066.
    C *Acapulco*, Calle 30 Este y Av Perú, T 25-3832, a/c, clean, comfortable, TV, private bath, excellent restaurant, conveniently located, rec; **C** *California*, Vía España y Calle 43, T 63-7844, with bath, a/c, TV, restaurant (breakfast US$1.75); **C** *Centroamericano*, Av Justo Arosemena y Av Ecuador, T27-4555, very clean, good reading lights, TV; **C-D** *Dos Mares*, Calle 30 entre Perú y Cuba, T 27-6150, a/c, bath, hot water, TV, phone, rec; **C** *Riazor*, Calle 16 Oeste, near *Ideal*, Calle 17 Oeste, T 28-0777, a/c with bath, hot water, good value, cheap restaurant downstairs next to the Ticabus office, therefore well placed as you arrive late from Costa Rica on the bus. **D** *Discovery*, Av Ecuador, clean, safe parking, good value; **D** *Colón*,

Calle 12, Oeste and Calle 'B', T 28-8510, with shower (cheaper without), a/c, erratic water supply; around corner from *Soloy*; **D** *Central*, Plaza Catedral (62-8044/96), with bath, E shared bath, very spacious foyer, faded colonial charm—ie a bit run down, safe motorcycle parking, reasonably clean and friendly, rooms on plaza have balcony, you can bargain if staying more than a week, very good value; **D** *Ideal*, Calle 17 just off Av Central, T 62-2400, good location, between Plazas Santa Ana y 5 de Mayo; **D** *Las Tablas*, between Av Perú *Hotels Soloy* and *Caribe*, with bath, E without, clean, safe, quiet; **D** *Residencia Turística Volcán*, Calle 29, between Avs Perú y Cuba, T 25-5263, opp Migración, next to Museo de Ciencias Naturales, fan, a/c extra, with shower, clean.

Cheaper accommodation can be found in *pensiones*: **D** *América*, Av Justo Arosemena and Av Ecuador, T 25-1140, back rooms best to avoid street noise, communal bathrooms, short stay couples, not rec (airport bus stops outside), proprietors can arrange safe parking for vehicles at *Hotel Costa Inn*, 5-10 mins walk away; **D-E** *Colonial*, Plaza Bolívar y Calle 4, Casco Viejo, T 62-3858, with bath, some balconies overlooking plaza, faded but enjoyable; **E** *Colón*, Av Central, 30 Calle, T 28-8510, without bath, clean, but noisy in the front rooms; **E** *Panamá*, Calle 6 No 8-40, T 226490, clean; **E** *Las Palmeras*, Av Cuba between Calle 38-39, T 250811, safe, clean; **E** *Mi Posada*, Calle 12 y Av Central (Plaza Santa Ana, dangerous area), OK; many (unlisted here) on Av México; **E** *Vásquez*, Av A No 2-47, opp Santo Domingo, T 28-8453, with fan but without bath, quiet, clean, safe, friendly, nice rooms, one or two with view of ocean and sand, rec, with bath but without bath E, laundry; **E** *Rivera*, Av Calle 11 Oeste, 8-14, off Av A, pleasant and friendly, but noisy (monthly rates available); **E** *Pensión Panamericana*, Plaza Herrera, Casco Viejo, dark rooms, balcony rooms good value; **E** *Pensión Universal*, Av Central 8-16, behind Cathedral, T 28-2796, shared bath, fan; **E** *Herrera*, Plaza Herrera y Calle 9, T 28-8994, variety of prices, cheapest F, some dearer with a/c, TV and fridge, nice location, restaurant; **E** *Residencial Primavera*, Av Cuba y Calle 42, on edge of Bella Vista, 1 block E of Av España, T 25-1195, with bath and fan, quiet residential area, rec; **E** *Tropical*, Calle de San Blas No 8-18, 2½ blocks from Post Office, T 227034, clean; **F** *Santa Ana*, overlooking Plaza Santa Ana, helpful.

Apartments for rent at **A+** *Costa del Sol*, Av España y Av Federico Boyd, T 23-7111, F 23-6636, central, pool, tennis courts and spa; **A+** *Suites Ambassador*, Calle D in centre of El Cangrejo district, T 63-7274, F 64-7872, well-furnished rooms, pool, gym; **A** *Las Vegas Apartotel*, Calle 55 y Av EA Morales, T 69-0722, F 23-0047, rec; **B** *Apartotel Suites Alvear*, Vía Argentina 2, T 69-4055; **B** *Apartotel Plaza*, Av Batista in front of University campus, T 64-5033, F 64-2256; **B** *Tower House Suites*, Calle 51-36, Bella Vista, T 69-2526, F 69-2869, centre of commercial district, and others. All have kitchenette, colour and cable TV, some with pool. Daily, weekly and monthly rates are available. 'Mini-studios' without a/c for D per day.

On the way to the airport are 'love motels', *pulsa botones* (push buttons), with drive-in garages. For US$10-15 you have a nice room and shower and a few hours relaxation, even with noble intentions. If your time is up a bell rings and you have to return to your car. You wait while they count the towels, then they open the garage.

NB It may not be easy to find accommodation just before Christmas, as Central Americans tend to invade the city to do their shopping, nor during Carnival. In the higher parts of the city, water shortages are common in summer, and electricity cuts are common in late summer everywhere.

Camping The Panamanian Embassy in London advises that it is not safe for female travellers to camp in Panama. There are no official sites but it is possible to camp on some beaches or, if in great need (they agree, but don't like it much) in the Balboa Yacht Club car park. It is also possible to camp in the Hipódromo grounds (11 km E of the city, on Vía España) but there are no facilities; this is allowed if you are waiting to ship your vehicle out of the country. Also possible, by previous arrangement, at La Patria swimming pool nearby, and at the Chorrera (La Herradura) and La Siesta beaches on the Pan-American Highway. Camping Gaz is available at Ferretería Tam SA, Av B, No 54; at *Super 99* grocery stores, cheap and at the army and navy store.

Restaurants (apart from hotels). Good are: *Lesseps*, Vía España y Calle 46, La Cresta, French restaurant and bar (decorated with memorabilia of the early French thwarted effort to build the canal); *Sarti's* (Italian food), Calle Ricardo Arias 5; *Panamar*, end of Calle 50, specializes in seafood; *La Mejicanita*, Av Justo Arosemena; *Las Américas*, Calle San Miguel, Obarrio; *La Fregata*, Av Samuel Lewis, Obarrio, good food, medium priced; *Nápoli*, Calle 57, Obarrio, 1½ blocks S of Vía España, good Italian, pizzas with real Italian dough. *La Casa del Marisco* (sea food) on Av Balboa, is open-air. *Las Bóvedas*, in converted dungeons at seaward end of Casco Viejo, good French food, expensive, art galleries adjoining. In El Cangrejo, *El Cortijo*, between Eusebio A Morales and Vía Argentina on Calle D; *Tinajas*, on Calle 51, near *Ejecutivo*

Hotel, Panamanian food and entertainment, craft shop, rec. *Le Bistrot*, Centro Comercial La Florida, Calle 53, expensive.

Other restaurants include: *El Trapiche*, Vía Argentina, Panamanian food (*hojaldres* – meat filled fritters, and *mondongo* – seasoned tripe); good; *Manolo*, Vía Argentina; *Piscolabis*, Transisthmian Highway, Vista Hermosa district, local food, reasonable; *Santana*, on pedestrian area of Av Central for Panamanian specialities. *El Jorrón*, Vía Fernández de Córdoba, Vista Hermosa district, local food, reasonable; *La Tablita*, Transisthmian Highway, Los Angeles district, reasonable; *Nápoli*, Av Estudiante, corner with Calle 16, Italian, closed Tuesdays, good and cheap (but rough neighbourhood), and many other good Italian places. *El Rincón Suizo*, Calle Eusebio A Morales, charming atmosphere, Swiss; *1985*, same street, similar style; *La Cascada*, Av Balboa and Calle 25, seafood, rec, enormous helpings, open air, 'doggy bags' welcome, fake waterfall, lifesize animal décor in concrete ('OTT Disneyland'), good service, credit cards not accepted, menus in charming English to take away, highly rec; the same management runs *Las Costallitas* on Vía Argentina, same menu (which takes ½ hr to read), same reasonable prices; *El Dorado*, Calle Colombia 2, good service, excellent seafood, rec.

Vegetarian: *Mireya* Calle Ricardo Araneo and Calle Ricardo Arias, near *Continental Hotel*, good value, rec. *Mi Salud*, Calle 31 y Av México 3-30, owned by dietary specialist Carlos Raúl Moreno, open Mon-Sat 0700-1930; *Govinda's*, Calle 47, No 24, Marbella, many specialities.

Many good Oriental places. *Matsuei*, Av Eusebio A Morales A-12, Japanese, excellent, pricey; *Lung Fung*, Transisthmian Highway and Los Angeles, very popular with Chinese residents for Sat and Sun. Cantonese-style brunch, very good food and value; *Kwang Chow*, in the Sal si Puedes area of Av Balboa, sells Tsingtao beer, rec; *Gran China*, Av Balboa, between Calles 26 and 27, Chinese, good value; *Palacio Imperial*, Calle 17 near Ticabus office, Chinese, good and cheap; *Bajwa's Shamiana*, Galerías Marbella, Paitilla, T 63-8586, Indian, US$15 pp, fair. *Chipré*, Av Central y Calle 11 Oeste, rec.

Krispy, *Macdonalds*, *Frutilandia*, *Dairy Queen*, *Hardee's*, *Burger King* and *Kentucky Fried Chicken* all have their branches; *La Viña*, corner Calle 6 Oeste and Av A, behind Post Office, good, cheap; also *La Esquina*, Av A y Calle 12 Oeste; *Jimmy's*, Paseo Cincuentenario just beyond Atlapa Centre, T 26-1096, good fast food and fish, served under a thatched roof; *Niko's Café*, just off Vía España opposite Rey's Supermarket, and another at the El Dorado Shopping Centre, good meals at reasonable prices, good sandwiches, rec; *La Conquista*, Calle J, up Av Central. *La Cresta* (good food from US$1), Vía España and Calle 45. *A & P* on Avenida Central opposite the National Museum, good. *Markany*, Av Cuba y Av Ecuador, good snacks. *Casa de la Cerveza*, Via España, good bar serving beer and tapas, Spanish run; *Frutijugos* off Vía España (look for *Café Sitton* on corner) for fruit juices without sugar (very rare) and snacks, expensive. *Café Coca Cola*, Av Central and Plaza Santa Ana (no sign 1992, you must ask), pleasant, reasonably-priced; *Café Jaime*, corner of Calle 12 and Av Central, for good *chichas* (natural drinks). *Cafe Central*, Av Central, between Calle 28 and 29, Caledonia, basic and cheap food, OK. There are good pavement cafés along Av Balboa.

Shopping Duty-free imported luxuries of all kinds are an attraction for (technically only) US military personnel and shoppers at the *Zona Libre* in Colón (purchases sealed and delivered to Tocumen airport), but Panama City is a booming fashion and merchandise centre where bargains are not hard to find; anything from crystal to cashmere may often be cheaper than at point of origin. The smartest shops are along Av España in Bella Vista and El Cangrejo, but Avenida Central is cheaper and the best and most popular place for clothing (not great quality), hi-fi and photographic equipment, perfumes, curios, souvenir T-shirts and Hindu handicrafts. Colombian emeralds and pearls may also be purchased at reasonable prices from many establishments.

Traditional Panamanian *artesanía* includes: *molas* (embroidered blouse fronts made by Kuna Indians, eg Emma Vence, T 61-8009); straw, leather and ceramic items; the *pollera* circular dress, the *montuno* shirts (embroidered), the *chácara* (a popular bag or purse), the *chaquira* necklace made by Guaymí Indians, and jewellery. Indigenous Darién carvings of jungle birds and animals from wood or *tagua* nut make interesting souvenirs (from $10 up to $250 for the best, museum-quality pieces); *Colecciones*, Vía Italia in front of *Hotel Playa Paitilla Inn*, has a wide selection. Plenty of straw articles available, including baskets, bags, traditional masks and Panama hats ($150 for the best quality); try *Flory Salzman* (not cheap) on Vía Venetto near *El Panamá Hotel*, nearby *Inovación*, or *Indutípica*, Av A y Calle 8 Oeste (opp San José Church) for reproductions of precolumbian ceramics and jewellery, necklaces, Kuna *molas* from the Darién and Guaymí dresses from Bocas del Toro. The *Gran Morrison* department store chain (best-supplied is in Paitilla, also at *Hotel Continental* and on Av España near Calle 51 Este) have good-quality handicraft sections, as well as postcards and books in English. Another good selection is at *Artesanías Nacionales* in Panamá Viejo, one of several

Indian co-ops selling direct from open-air outlets, eg in the Canal Area at Balboa and along the road to Miraflores Locks at Corozal (every day if not raining). The Tourist Office has a full list of *artesanía* shops available, including those in the main hotels. *Reprosa*, Av Samuel Lewis y Calle 54 (T 69-0457) features a unique collection of precolumbian gold artefacts reproduced in sterling silver vermeil; David and Norma Dickson make excellent reproductions for sale (*Panama Guacas*, T 66-6176). Of the various commercial centres, with banking, entertainment and parking facilities, the largest is *El Dorado Mall and Shopping Centre*, in the Tumbo Muerto district at Av Ricardo Franco y Calle 71 (shops open Mon-Sat 0900-1900, Sun 1500-1900; cinema, plenty of restaurants and playgrounds). Similar are: *Plaza New York*, Calle 50, which has several travel agencies and a well-known disco; *Plaza California*, near *El Dorado*; and *Bal Harbour*, Vía Italia near Punta Paitilla (Mon-Sat 0900-1900, Sun 1100-1900); the *Balboa Mall* on Av Balboa is the newest but is closed on Sundays. The *Supermercado El Rey* at *El Dorado*, *Super 99*, *Farmacías Arrocha*, *Casa de la Carne* (expensive) and *Machetazo* (on Av Central) are said to be the best of the city's supermarkets. Army-Navy store on Central near Plaza 5 de Mayo sells camping and hiking equipment.

The *Mercado Central*, close to the docks and Presidential Palace, is the place for fresh produce (pigs, ducks, poultry, geese, etc) as well as parrots and pets; bargain hard as prices are extremely competitive. Most interesting part of the Market is the chaotic shopping area along Calle 13 and the waterfront (Terraplen), the best place to buy secondhand jungle and military supplies (eg powerful insect repellents, machetes, webbing, cooking equipment, etc) for a trek into the forested interior. The nearby fish market is clean and prices are the best in town. Another bazaar-like shopping area lines Avenida España as it passes through Caledonia beyond the Plaza 5 de Mayo; as has been said, this *barrio* is for the adventurous by day and definitely dangerous at night.

Bookshops *Librería Argosy*, Vías Argentina y España, El Cangrejo, T 23-5344, very good selection in English, Spanish and French, rec; *Gran Morrison* department stores around the city stock some books, travel guides and many magazines in English; many Spanish and English magazines also at branches of *Farmacías Arrocha, Super 99* and *Gago* supermarkets/drugstores. *National University Bookshop*, on campus between Av Manuel Espinosa Batista and Vía Simón Bolívar, T 23-3155, for excellent range of specialized books on Panamá, national authors, social sciences and history, open Mon-Fri 0800-1600, closed weekends, highly rec. (The campus *Simón Bolívar Library* has extensive Panamanian material, only for national students but visitors engaged in special research can obtain a temporary permit from the Director, Mon-Fri 0800-2000, Sat 0900-1300.) Near the University is *La Garza* bookshop, Av José de Fábrega y Calle 47, good supply of Latin American literature (Spanish only). The *Smithsonian Tropical Research Institute Public Library*, Edificio Topper, Av de los Mártires (opp National Assembly), has best English-language scientific library in Panamá, open Mon-Fri 0800-1600. International edition of the *Miami Herald* printed locally on *La Prensa's* presses, widely available at news-stands and hotels, as are leading US papers and magazines.

Photographic Foto Enodi and Foto Decor, Via Porras, Kodak slides developed in a day. Many other places for developing and equipment. In some places you will get a free film. Camera repairs at *Relojería*, watch shop, on Calle Medusin, off Av Central in Caledonia.

Local Transport Taxis have no meters; charges are according to how many 'zones' are traversed (about US$1 per zone): ask driver to show you the zone map and settle fare beforehand if you can. Note that there are large taxis (*grandes*) and cheaper small ones (*chicos*). Taxis charge US$10 per hour for a tour to Miraflores locks and the Canal Area. There are numerous small buses nicknamed *chivas* (goats), gradually being replaced. These charge US$0.05 per zone, are not very comfortable but are very colourful, and run along the major streets (eg Av Central as far as Calle 12, Av Perú and Av Justo Arosemena); all buses go to Bella Vista—the business section—except those marked Tumba Muerta or Transístmica). The number of fingers held up by the conductor indicates the fare in 5-cents, or *reales* (eg 3 fingers = 15 cents). Travel into the suburbs costs more. Yell '*parada*' to stop the bus.

Traffic System Several major downtown arteries become one-way during weekday rush hours, eg Av 4A Sur (called Calle 50 by everyone), one-way heading W 0600-0900, E 1600-1900. The Puente de las Américas can be used only to go into or out of town depending on time and day, mostly weekends; these directions are not always clearly signed.

Car Rental At the airport (Hertz—T 38-4081, Avis—T 38-4069, National—T 38-4144; also International, Budget and Dollar). Other offices in El Cangrejo: Avis, Calle 55, T 64-0722; International, Calle 55, T 64-4540; Barriga, Edif Wonaga 1 B, Calle D, T 69-0221; Gold, Calle 55, T 64-1711. Hertz, Via España 130, T 64-1729; Budget T 63-8777; Discount, T 23-6111. Rates vary from company to company and from model to model: on average they start at US$24/day for a small saloon to US$65 for 4WD jeep, free mileage, insurance

US$8/day, 5% tax, US$500 deposit (can be paid by credit card), minimum age 23, home driver's licence acceptable. In general 4WDs must be booked 5 days in advance.

Motorcycle Club Road Knights, at the Albrook Air Force base (T 86-3348), very welcoming; has repair and maintenance workshop. Reliable information on flights and ships to Colombia. Please leave a donation for the club.

Cabarets and Discotheques Hotel *El Continental*; *Josephine's*, Calle 50, El Cangrejo; *Oasis*, Vía Brasil. Recommended discos: *Bacchus*, Vía España and *Magic*, Calle 50; *Cubares*, next door; *Las Molas*, entrance to Chase Manhattan Bank, Vía España, Los Angeles district, small band, rural decor, drinks US$1.50; *Unicornio*, Calle 50 y R Arías 23 is night club with discothèque and gambling; reasonable prices, will admit foreigners for US$3 a week. *La Parrillita*, Av 11 de Octubre in Hato Pintado district, is a restaurant in a railway carriage. *El Pavo Real*, off Calle 50 Oeste in Campo Alegre, hard to find, pub selling British beer (at a price), darts board, popular with expats.

Live Music Clubs *Nottingham*, Fernández de Córdoba, Vista Hermosa, T 61-0314, live salsa at weekends, no cover charge, restaurant; *Vino's Bar*, Calle 51 y Colombia, Bella Vista, T 64-0520, live salsa at weekends, cover charge, restaurant; *Hotels Granada* and *Soloy* (*Bar Maitai*, T 27-1133) are rec for live Latin music at weekends. *Giorgio's*, 1 block S of Vía Porras. Panamanian musicians currently popular (1993) are: Bush (salsa), Pedro Altamiranda (salsa and murga mix), Solinca (female singer), Arena Blanca (salsa group), Martha Estela Paredes, Miguel Fernández, Leoni Herrera and Rubén Blades (who ran for president for the Papá Egoro party).

Theatres and Cinemas There are occasional official presentations and concerts held at the *Teatro Nacional* (folklore sessions every other Sun, check dates; monthly National Ballet performances when not on tour). The *Anayansi Theatre* in the Atlapa Convention Centre, Vía Israel, San Francisco, has a 3000-seat capacity, good acoustics, regular recitals and concerts. *Balboa Theatre* near Steven's Circle and Post Office in Balboa, with folkloric groups and jazz concerts sponsored by National Institute of Culture. *Guild Theatre* in the Canal Area at Ancón mounts amateur productions mainly in English. *La Prensa* gives full listings of cultural events. The usual a/c cinemas (US$2.50 except Balboa cinema near Steven's Circle, US$2); by law all foreign films must be subtitled in Spanish. Newspapers publish daily programming (*cartelera*). *Cine Universitario* in the National University, US$1.50 for general public, shows international festivals and classic movies, daily (not holidays) at 1700, 1900 and 2100.

Casinos More than 20, some in main hotels. State-managed and profits to charitable public institutions; most offer black jack, baccarat, poker, roulette and poker machines (*traganiqueles*). Winnings are tax-free and paid without deductions. The *National Lottery* is solemnly drawn (televised) each Wed and Sun at 1300 in Plaza de la Lotería between Avs Perú y Cuba; four-digit tickets cost US$1, 'chance' tickets, with only two digits cost US$0.25.

Bathing Piscina Patria (the Olympic pool), take San Pedro or Juan Díaz bus, US$0.15. Piscina Adán Gordon, between Av Cuba and Av Justo Arosemena, near Calle 31, 0900-1200, 1300-1700 (except weekends to 1700 only). Admission US$0.50 (take identification), but beards and long hair frowned on (women must wear bathing caps). Many beaches within 1½ hrs' drive of the city. Fort Kobbe beach (US$7.50 admission, with vouchers given for drinks and hotdogs, bus from Canal Area bus station US$0.75, ½ hr) and Naos beach (US$1, Amador bus from same station, US$0.30, then 2 km walk along causeway) have been rec; both have shark nets, but at low tide at the former you must go outside it to swim! Vera Cruz beach is not recommended as it is both dirty and dangerous (all are dangerous at night).

Golf Panama Golf Club; courses at Summit and Horoko; Coronado Beach Golf Club (open to tourists who get guest cards at Coronado office on Calle 50). Similarly at Fort Amador Golf Club tourists can play, green fees and rented clubs US$20 for the day. A spectacular view of the canal and the city.

Horse Races (pari-mutuel betting) are held Sat, Sun and holidays at the Presidente Remón track (bus to Juan Díaz, entry from US$0.50 to 2.50).

Cockfights at the Club Gallístico, Vía España y Calle 50, T 21-5652, every Sun, same bus as for race track, but get out at crossing with Calle 150.

Museums Museo Afro-Antillano, Justo Arosemena y Calle 24, one block E of Plaza 5 de Mayo, T 62-5348, illustrated history of Panamá's West Indian community and their work on the Canal, small library, Mon-Fri 1000-1530, US$0.25; **Museo de Arte Colonial Religioso** (Santo Domingo Convent, see above); **Museo Antropológico Reina Torres de Araúz**, Av Central at S side of Plaza 5 de Mayo, T 62-0415, five salons (partly looted during Operation Just Cause) exhibiting Panamanian history, anthropology and archaeology, rare collection of precolumbian gold objects and ceramics; a good introduction to Panama's early Indian cultures. Library, guided tours, ceramics workshop, book stall. Opening hours change often: Mon-Fri 1000-1430, US$0.50. (Profesora Torres de Aráuz was a renowned anthropologist and founder of the museum, died 1982.) **Museo de Historia de Panamá**, in the Palacio Municipal on Plaza Catedral (see above), T 28-6231/62-8089, the nation's history since European landfall, open Mon-Fri 0830-1530, US$0.35; **Museo de Ciencias Naturales**, Av Cuba y Calle 30, T 25-0645, good sections on geology, palaeontology, entomology and marine biology, Mon-Fri 0900-1600, US$0.35; **Museo de Arte Contemporáneo**, Av de los Mártires (Ancón), entrance on Av San Blás, T 62-8012, in former Masonic Lodge (1936), permanent exhibition of national and international modern paintings and sculptures with special exhibitions from time to time; marquetry, silkscreen and engraving workshops, library of contemporary visual art open to students, entry free but donations welcomed (privately owned), open Mon-Fri 0900-1600, Sat 0900-1200; **Museo Casa de Banco Nacional**, Av Cuba y Calle 34, T 25-0640, large numismatic and stamp collection and history of banking from the 19th century, old postal and telephone items and historic photos, not widely-known but worth a visit, open Mon-Fri 0800-1200, 1330-1600, Sat 0830-1300; **Museum of the Independence Soldier**, Paseo de las Bóvedas near the Plaza Francia, T 28-1905, small, even less well-known museum dedicated to mementos and souvenirs of Panama's independence from Colombia in 1903, interesting for the history buff, open Mon-Fri 0800-1600, US$0.25.

Exchange The **Chase Manhattan Bank** (US$0.65 commission on each cheque), Visa advances; **Citibank; Lloyds Bank**, Calle Aquilino de la Guardia y Calle 48, Bella Vista, T 63-6277, 63-8693 for foreign exchange, offers good rates for sterling (the only bank which will change sterling cash, and only if its sterling limit has not been exhausted); **Bank of America**, Av José de la Cruz Herrera, Calle 53 Este, no commission on own travellers' cheques, US$0.10 tax; **Swiss Bank Corporation**. Thomas Cook TCs only exchangeable at **Banco Sudameris** and **Algemene Bank Nederland**; Deutschmarks exchanged at **Deutsch- Südamerikanische Bank**. Panamanian banks, open 0800-1300, closed Sat, except for **Banco General** which takes American Express, Bank of America and Thomas Cook TCs (no commission, no queues, but avoid Friday pm, pay day). Also **Banco del Istmo**, Calle 50, open Mon-Fri 0800-1500, Sat 0900-1200, changes TCs. You can buy Amex TCs at **Banco Mercantil del Istmo** on Vía España (they also give cash advances on Mastercard). American Express, Torre Exterior, Av Balboa, 9th floor, Mon-Fri 0830-1600, does not exchange TCs, clients' mail only.

If travelling N remember that US dollar notes, especially smaller denominations, are useful in all Central American countries and may be difficult to obtain in the other republics.

Possible to change South American currencies (poor rates) at Panacambios, ground floor, Plaza Regency, behind *Adam's Store*, Vía España, near the Banco Nacional de Panamá and opp *Hotel El Continental* (it also has postage stamps for collectors). The US dollar is the normal circulating medium in Panama.

Alianza Francesa, Av 4 A Sur y Av Boyd, film each Wed at 2000.

Embassies and Consulates: **Costa Rican**, Calle Gilberto Ortega 7, Edif Miramar, T 64-2980 (open 0800-1330). **Nicaraguan**, Av Federico Boyd y Calle 50, T 23-0981 (0900-1300, 1500-1800). **Salvadorean**, Vía España, Edif Citibank, piso 4, T 23-3020, (0900-1300). **Guatemalan**, Calle 55, El Congrejo, Condominio Abir, piso 6, T 69-3475, open 0800-1300. **Honduran**, Av Justo Arosemena y Calle 31, Edif Tapia, piso 2, T 25-8200, (0900-1400). **Mexican**, Ed Bank of America, piso 5, Calle 50 y 53, T 63-5021 (0830-1300). **Venezuelan**, Banco Unión Building, Av Samuel Lewis, T 69-1014 (0830-1230), visa takes 24 hrs. **Colombian**, MM Icaza 12, Edif Grobman, 6th floor, PO Box 4407 (Zona 5), T 64-9266, open 0800-1300; the **Chilean** and **Ecuadorean** embassies are housed in the same building, T 23-5364 and 64-2654 respectively, neither is open in pm.

US, Av Balboa and 40, Edif Macondo, piso 3, T 27-1777, F 27-1964, PO Box 6959 (Zona 5) (0800-1700). **Canadian**, Calle MM Icaza, Ed Aeroperú, piso 5, T 64-7014 (0800-1100). **British**, Torre Swiss Bank, Calle 53, Zona 1, T 69-0866, F (507) 69-0866, Apartado 889 (0800-1200). **French**, Plaza Francia, T 28-7835 (0830-1230). **German**, Edif Bank of America, Calle 50 y 53, T 63-7733 (0900-1200). **Netherlands**, Altos de Algemene Bank, Calle MM Icaza, 4, T 64-7257 (0830- 1300, 1400-1630). **Swedish**, Vía José Agustín Arango/Juan Díaz, T 33-5883 (0900-1200, 1400-1600). **Swiss**, Av Samuel Lewis y Calle Gerardo Ortega, Ed Banco Central Cancellería, piso 4, T 64-9731, PO Box 499 (Zona 9A), open 0845-1145. **Italian**, Calle 1, Parque Lefevre 42, T 26-3111, open 0900-1200. **Danish**, Calle Ricardo Arias, Ed Ritz Plaza, piso 2, T 63-5872, open 0800- 1200, 1330-1630. **Spanish**, entre Av Cuba y Av Perú, Calle 33A, T 27-5122 (0900-1300). **Norwegian**, Av Justo Arosemena y Calle 35, T 25-8217 (0900-1300, 1400-1630). **Japanese**, Calle 50 y 61, Ed Don Camilo, T 63-6155 (0830-1200, 1400-1700). **Israeli Embassy**, Ed Grobman, Calle MM Icaza, 5th floor, PO Box 6357, T 64-8022/8257.

Customs for renewal of permits and obtaining exit papers for vehicles at Paitilla airport.

Immigration Inmigración y Naturalización, Av Cuba (2 Sur) y Calle 28E, T 25-8925; visa extensions and exit permits issued Mon-Fri 0800-1500. **Ministerio de Hacienda y Tesoro**, Calles 35 y 36, entre Avs Perú y Cuba, T 27-4879, for exit visas (*permiso de salida*), ask for a *paz yu salvo*.

Conservation Asociación de Conservación de la Naturaleza (Ancon), on Calle 50, Bella Vista (Apdo 1387, Panamá 1), near *Discoteca Magic*, T 64-1836, for comprehensive information on the country's natural attractions and environmental matters.

Hospitals The US Gorgas Army Community Hospital (see map) is only for US military personnel, except in emergency. The private clinics charge high prices; normally visitors are treated at either the Clínica San Fernando or the Clínica Paitilla (both have hospital annexes). For inoculations buy vaccine at a chemist, who will recommend a clinic; plenty in La Exposición around Parque Belisario Porras. **Dentist**: Dr Daniel Wong, Clínica Dental Marbella, Ed Alfil (Planta Baja), near Centro Comercial Marbella, T 63-8998. Dr D Lindo, T 23-8383.

Laundry *Lavamático Lavarápido*, Calle 7 Central No 7-45, $1/2$ block from Plaza Independencia, Mon-Sat 0800-2000, Sun 0900-1400, US$0.75 with hot water, US$0.60 cold, soap and drying extra. Many around Plaza Catedral; wash and dry US$2.

Worship Services in English at St John's Episcopalian, Avs 12 de Octubre y La Paz, Betania, Sun 0700; Baptist, Calle Balboa 914, La Boca, Sun 1100 and 1900; Methodist, Av Central y Calle 16 Este, Sun 0900. Kol Shearith Israel Synagogue, Av Cuba y Calle 36, services Fri 2000, Sat 1100. Baha'i Temple, Mile 8 on Transístmica Highway (Ojo de Agua district), Baha'i HQ for all of Latin America, modern, white domed, worth seeing for its architecture (open daily 1000-1800, Sun service 1000), taxi round trip for US$6 with an hour to see the temple can be arranged. Church services for various denominations are also held on the US military bases.

Post Office On Plaza Catedral in the Old Town, open Mon-Fri 0700-1745, Sat 0700-1645; 'Poste Restante' *(Entrega General)* items held for a month. Official name and zone must be included in the address: Main Post Office = 'Zona 1, Catedral'; Calle 30 E nr Av Balboa = 'Zona 5, La Exposición'; El Dorado Shopping Centre = 'Zona 6A, El Dorado'; Vía España, Bella Vista (in front of Piex store) = 'Zona 7, Bella Vista'; National University, Faculty of Humanities. Parcels sent 'poste restante' are delivered to Encomiendas Postales Transístmicas at the El Dorado Centro Comercial if there is duty to pay on the goods; if not they are delivered to the nearest post office. If asked for a tip, fiegn inability to understand! Post Office operates a courier system called EMS to most Central and South American countries, Europe, US and some Asian countries. Packages up to 20 kg: 2 to 3 days to USA (500g documents to Miami US$13); 3 to 4 days Europe US$20; Asia US$25. Also private courier services, eg *United Parcel Services*, Edificio Fina, Calle 49, El Cangrejo, $1/2$ kg to London or Paris, 34 days, US$30; *Dispatch & Federal Express*, Edificio Helga, Vía España, $1/2$ kg to Miami, 2 days, US$19. Panamá issues highly-regarded stamps; foreigners may open a 'philatelic account' and order stamps, first-day covers, commemorative issues, etc, provided a minimum $20 in account: Dirección de Filatelía, Dirección de Correos y Telégrafos, PO Box 3421, Panamá 1 (Vía España, Caledonia, in front of Don Bosco Church).

Telecommunications Intel offices (eg Edificio Avesa, Vía España; Edificio Di Lido, Calle Manuel María Icaza, near *Hotel Continental*; Edificio 843, Gavilán Road, Balboa; and at the international airport) offer excellent international telephone, telex, fax and modem (use Bell 212A type) facilities; open every day 0730-2300. Collect calls to 21 countries, dial 106. Public payphones take 5, 10, 25 and sometimes 50 cent coins. MCI and AT&T cards can be used: dial 108 for MCI or 109 for AT&T and give a/c number and password.

Travel Agency *Viajes Panamá SA*, Calle 52, Av Federico Boyd, Edif Costa del Sol, T 23-0644 or 23-0630, English spoken; *Tropic Tours*, Edif Comosa near El Panamá Hotel, well organized trips, multilingual; *Eco Tours Panama*, Ricardo J Alfaro (Tumba Muerto), Centro Comercial La Alhambra, upper level, No 6A, PO Box 465, T 36-3076, F 36-3550, 0800-1700 Mon-Sat, a wide variety of trips, from relaxing cultural excursions to the San Blas islands, to high altitude forest hikes, bilingual guides, highly rec; *Viajes Airemar*, Calle 52 y Ricardo Arias 21, T 23-5395/23-5336, highly rec for flights to South American destinations; *Viajes Marsal*, Calle 50 y Manuel M Icaza, near Banco Iberoamericano, T 23-5321/5447/9851, helpful, efficient, English spoken. *5 Continentes*, Av Principal La Alameda, Ed Plaza San Marcos, T 60-8447/9, helpful with shipping a car, rec. *Rapid Travel*, Calle 53, El Cangrejo, Ed Las Margaritas, T 64-6638, F 64-6371. *Chadwick's*, see under Balboa, above.

Tourist Bureau Information office of the Instituto Panameño de Turismo (IPAT), in the Atlapa Convention Centre, Vía Israel opp *Hotel Marriott* (0900 to 1600) issues good list of hotels, *pensiones*, motels and restaurants, and issue a free *Focus on Panama* guide (available at all major hotels, and airport); T 26-7000/26-3544, F 26-3483, ask for 'información', helpful, English spoken. *Getting to Know Panama*, by Michelle Labrut, published by Focus Publications (Apdo 6-3287, El Dorado, Panamá, RP, F 25-0466, US$12), has been recommended as very informative. Best **maps** from Instituto Geográfico Nacional Tommy Guardia (IGNTG), on Vía Simón Bolívar, opp the National University (footbridge nearby, fortunately), take Transístmica bus from Calle 12 in Santa Ana: physical map of the country in 2 sheets, US$3.50 each; Panama City map in many sheets, US$1.50 per sheet (travellers will need 3 or so). At the back of the Panama Canal Commission telephone books are good maps of the Canal Area, Panama City and Colón.

Buses Ticabus, with office by *Hotel Ideal*, Calle 17 Oeste, T 62-2084/6275, run air-conditioned buses to **San José**, daily 1000, arrives 0400, US$25 one way; also to **Managua** daily; this service now runs as far as Guatemala City (4 days, overnight in Managua and El Salvador, US$75), leaves 1100, US$87 one way. Air conditioners rarely work. (Tickets are refundable; they pay on the same day, minus 15%.) Impossible to do Panama City-San José in one day on public transport. Buses going N tend to be well booked up, so make sure you reserve a seat in advance, and never later than the night before you leave. Buses to the W of the country (and Darién) leave from a terminal, Piquera, at the corner of Av A and Av Balboa E of Av Central between Plazas 5 de Mayo and Santa Ana, partly hidden by a 13-storey block of flats. Buses to Chiriquí and Veraguas provinces are usually a/c. To **David**, U-Transchiri (separate section at Av Balboa y Calle 17 Este) hourly from 0700-1300, then 1½ hourly till 1900, express bus at 2400 (5½-6 hrs), 2 stops, usually Penenomé and Santiago, US$15, tickets sold on day of travel only. Change at David for Bocas del Toro. For other fares see destinations in text below. Buses to **Colón** leave from the station at Av Central y Calle 26 Oeste, opp San Miguel church 2 blocks N of Plaza 5 de Mayo; Ultracopa express buses every 30 min 0500-1900, US$2.20, under 2 hrs. Buses to all **Canal Area** destinations (Balboa, Miraflores, Pedro Miguel, Kobbe, etc) leave from Canal Area bus station (SACA) on Plaza 5 de Mayo. To **Kobbe Beach** by bus ½ hr.

Rail Station on Av de los Mártires, 1 km NW of Plaza 5 de Mayo, not a pleasant area at night. **NB** At the time of writing in 1994 the railway is closed, and it is not clear when (or even if) it will reopen. For information, T 52-7720.

Airport Tocumen, 27 km. Taxi fares about US$20, but you can try to bargain down, colectivo US$8 pp (if staying for only a couple of days, it is cheaper to rent a car at the airport). For about US$3 (should only be US$1.20) driver takes you by Panamá Viejo, just off the main airport road. Travellers whiling away hours at the airport can visit the delightful nearby village of Pacora, a few km off the Pan-American Highway. There is a 24-hr left-luggage office near the Avis car rental desk for US$1 per article per day (worth it, since theft in the departure lounge is common). There are duty-free shops at the airport but more expensive than those downtown.

   The national airport is at La Paitilla, on N side of Punta Paitilla, near *Hotel Marriott* and Atlapa Convention Centre. No 2 bus from Calle 40 along Av Balboa, marked 'Boca La Caja', US$0.30. For fares, see under destinations in the text. Charter flights go to many Darién outposts. Sample hourly rates for private hire: Twin Otter 20 passenger, US$630; Rodolfo Causadias of Transpasa (T 26-0842) is an experienced pilot for photographic work. There is also an active Aero-Club.

Airline Offices Copa, Av Justo Arosemena y Calle 39, T 27-5000, F 27-1952 for reservations, airport T 38-4053; **Alas Chiricanas**, Paitilla Airport, T 64-7759/6448, F 64-7190; **Ansa**, Paitilla Airport, T 26-7891, F 26-4070; **Aeroperlas**, Paitilla Airport, T 69-4555, F 23-0606; **Parsa**, Paitilla Airport, T 26-3803, F 26-3422. **Nica**, Vía España y Calle 52, Ed Ogawa, T 64-4144, F 69-4855; **Aviateca**, Suite Montecarlo p 6, T 23-2992, F 23-2993; **Lacsa**, Av Justo Arosemena 31-44, T 25-0193 for reservations, airport T 38-4116; **Taca**, Calle B, Suites Montecarlo, p. 6, El Cangrejo, T 69-6214/6066 for reservations, airport T 38-4015; **SAM**, Calle MM Icaza No 12, Edif Grobman, T 69-1222 for reservations, airport T 38-4096; **Avianca**, T 23-5225; **Ecuatoriana**, T 27-1466; **Avensa**, Calle MM Icaza, T 64-9924, F 63-9022; **American**, Calle 50, Plaza New York, T 69-6022 for reservations, airport T 38-4140, F 69-0830; **British Airways** at Lacsa (above); **Continental**, Av Balboa y Av 4, Ed No 17, T 63-9177; **United**, T 69-8555; **Iberia**, Av Balboa y Calle 45, T 27-3966 reservations, airport T 38-4163, F 27-2070; **KLM**, Urb Obarrio y Calle 53E, T 27-2759 for reservations, airport T 38-4025, F 64-6358; **Lufthansa**, Agencias Continental, Calle 50, Ed Fidanque, piso 1, T 69-1549, F 63-8641; **Cubana**, T 27-2122; **Aerolíneas Argentinas**, T 69-3815; **LAB**, T 64-1330; **LanChile**, T 26-0133; **Varig**, Calle MM Icaza, T 64-7666 for reservations, airport T 38-4501, F 63-8179.

Excursions A visit is recommended to the ruins of *Panamá Viejo*, 6½ km NE along the coast. This was the original site of Panama City, founded by Pedro Arias de Avila (often called 'Pedrarias') on 15 August 1519 as a storage point for Peruvian gold until it could be loaded onto mules and transported across the Isthmus, initially to Venta de Cruces and Fort San Lorenzo, later along the Royal Road to Nombre de Dios and Portobelo for shipment to Spain. The town became the centre of the New World, gold mines in Veraguas and Darién contributed two tons of gold a year, and many expeditions to North, Central and South America were launched from here. Panamá was recognized as a town in 1521 and granted a coat of arms. By 1570 a quarter of its 500 residents were extremely wealthy, and the town could boast a grand cathedral, a dozen religious institutions, a hospital, lavish public buildings, huge warehouses and a thriving slave market. No enemy had ever penetrated as far as 'Golden Panama', not even Francis Drake, so the shock was all the greater when Henry Morgan and his 1,200 men, after a gruelling nine-day overland trek from San Lorenzo, fell upon the town on 28 January 1671 and captured it after a 3-hr battle. They took 600 prisoners for ransom, looted for 3 weeks and took away a fortune in gold, silver and gemstones valued at £70,000, which required 165 mules to transport it back to the Caribbean. (With this Morgan bought respectability: he was knighted and appointed Governor of Jamaica, where he died in 1688.) After the attack, the population was transferred to the present-day Casco Viejo section of Panama City, which could be enclosed by walls and defended on both landward and seaward sides.

A wander among the ruins still gives an idea of the site's former glory, although many of the structures have been worn by time, fungus and the sea. The narrow King's Bridge (1620) at the N end of the town's limits is a good starting point; it marked the beginning of the three trails across the Isthmus and took seven years to build. Walking S brings the visitor to Convento de San José, where the Golden Altar originally stood (see above under Panama City); it was spared by the great fire that swept the town during Morgan's attack (which side started it is still debated). Several blocks further S is the main Plaza, where the square stone tower of the Cathedral (1535, 1580) is a prominent feature. In the immediate vicinity are the Cabildo, with imposing arches and columns, the remnants of Convento de Santo Domingo, the Bishop's Residence, and the Slave Market (or House of the Genovese), whose gaol-like structure was the hub of the American slave trade; there were about 4,000 African slaves in 1610, valued at about 300 pesos apiece! Beyond the plazas to the S, on a rocky eminence overlooking the bay, stand the Royal Houses, the administrative stronghold including the Quartermaster's House, the Court and Chancellery, the Real Audiencia and the Governor's Residence.

Further W along the Pacific strand are the dungeons, kitchens and meat market (now almost obliterated by the sea); a store and refreshment stands cluster here on the S side of the plaza, and handicrafts from the Darién are sold along the beach. Across Calle de la Carrera stands another great complex of religious convents: La Concepción (1598) and the Compañía de Jesús (1621). These too were outside the area destroyed by the 1671 fire but are today little more than rubble. Only a wall remains of the Franciscan Hospital de San Juan de Dios, once a huge structure encompassing wards, courtyards and a church. Another block W can be seen part of the Convento de San Francisco and its gardens, facing the rocky beach. 100m W is the beautiful Convento de La Merced, where Pizarro, Almagro and their men attended Mass on the morning they sailed on their final and momentous expedition to Perú; Morgan stored his plunder here until it could be counted, divided up and sent back to the Atlantic side. At the western limit of Panamá Viejo stands La Navidad Fort (1658). Its purpose was merely to defend the Matadero (Slaughterhouse) Bridge across the Río Agarroba but its 50-man garrison and half-dozen cannon were no match for the determined force of privateers; the bridge is also known as Morgan's Bridge because it was here that the attack began.

The whole area (unfenced, free entry) is attractively landscaped, with plenty of benches to rest on, and floodlit at night. Late afternoon when the sun is low is an especially nice time to visit, although at least 2 hrs should be allowed to appreciate the site fully. The main ruins are police patrolled and reasonably safe. Take care, though, between the King's Bridge and the ruins; if arriving at this N entrance by taxi, it is prudent to pause at the bridge then continue in the taxi the 1 km to San José, where the main ruins begin. Dame Margot Fonteyn, the ballerina, is buried alongside her husband Roberto Arías Guardia in the Jardín de la Paz cemetery behind Panamá Viejo; as of early 1994 her grave was still unmarked. IPAT has a handicrafts store (*Artesanía Nacional*) at the ruins, although prices are rather expensive. It also organizes free folkloric events and local dance displays on six Saturdays in the dry season (*verano*), which are worth seeing. The Tourist Office in Panama City (T 26-7000) has full schedules and can supply professional guides if required. Taxi from the centre, US$1.80; buses 1 or 2 from Vía España or Av Balboa, US$0.20. Panamá Viejo also makes a good excursion for passengers with time to kill at nearby Tocumen Airport; taxis are overpriced (US$3) but still reasonable, especially if this is all one will have the chance to see of Panamá.

See Balboa (p 809) for trips to Taboga Island and Pearl Islands. A good excursion—a 2-hr drive through picturesque jungle—is to Lago Alajuela (formerly Madden Dam, east of the Canal). The drive runs from Balboa along the Gaillard Highway and near the Canal. Beyond Fort Clayton there is a fine view of the Pedro Miguel and Miraflores locks. Beyond Pedro Miguel town a road branches off to the left to Summit (Las Cumbres), where there are experimental gardens containing tropical plants from all over the world (closed Mondays) and a good, small zoo containing native wild life. (The trip to Summit may be made by buses marked Gamboa, every 1-1$\frac{1}{2}$ hrs, from bus station next to Plaza 5 de Mayo, US$0.35, 1$\frac{1}{2}$ hr journey; the Paraíso bus will also take you to the Miraflores and Pedro Miguel locks.) The road to Lago Alajuela (37 km) crosses the Las Cruces trail (old cannon mark the spot), and beyond is deep jungle (if walking the trail, take machete and compass and arrange boat across the Chagres river at the end of the trail well in advance). A large area of rain forest between Lago Gatún and Lago Alajuela has been set aside as **Parque Nacional Soberanía** (trails for walking). The Park has an information centre at the Summit Garden. For excursion to Portobelo, **see p 803**.

The Madden Dam (Lago Alajuela) is used to generate electricity. A trip through part of the Canal by launch *Fantasía del Mar* costs US$20 for adults, US$10 for children, and lasts about 4 hrs. A trip to Lago Alajuela by taxi is only worth while if there are enough people to fill the taxi.

The return from Lago Alajuela to Panama City can be made by the Transisthmian Highway. In Las Cumbres the restaurant *La Hacienda* serves native dishes.

WEST FROM PANAMA CITY

Cross the Puente de las Américas for a Panama that is in great contrast to the cosmopolitan capital and the Canal: colonial towns, a variety of agricultural zones, traditional crafts and music, Pacific beaches and beautiful mountain landscapes with some good walking. The Pan-American Highway traverses this region en route to Costa Rica.

The Pan-American Highway runs westwards from Panama City through Concepción to the Costa Rican border (489 km), and is well graded and completely paved. The Highway begins at the **Puente de las Américas** across the Canal at the Pacific entrance. The bridge, 1,653m long and high enough to allow all ships to pass under it, has 3 lanes, a 4-lane approach from Panama City and a pedestrian pavement all the way (muggings have occurred on the bridge in broad daylight, so be careful!). Buses run to a *mirador* on the far side of the bridge from the city.

Where the road W crosses the savannas, there are open pastures and fields where clumps of beautiful trees, largely mangoes and palms, alternate with grass.

The first place you reach, 13 km from Panama City, is the small town of **Arraiján** (pop 6,600). On 21 km by 4-lane highway (toll US$0.50) is **La Chorrera** (pop 37,000); an interesting store, Artes de las Américas, has items in wood, etc. **D** *Hotel Clolysa*, safe parking; **E** *Pensión Arco Iris*, without bath, fan, clean, partial walls between rooms, hourly rentals; similar, but more expensive and 'better' looking is a *pensión* across the street and a couple of blocks towards Panama City. A branch road (right) leads 1½ km to a waterfall. On 20 km, among hills, is the old town of Capira; good food next to Shell station run by Chinese. We pass through the orange groves of Campana (where a 10-km road climbs to **Cerro Campana National Park**; no lodgings), and then twist down to Río Sajalises (bathing) and the low-level plains. Good views on the road to the summit of Cerro Campana; a few km before the village of Chicá is the big house of Richard from the USA. He appreciates visitors. On through Bejuco and Chame (turn off to Punta Chame, at the end of a peninsula, white-sand beach, a few houses, a hotel/restaurant) to the town of **San Carlos**, near the sea; good river and sea-bathing (beware jelly fish). Not many restaurants in San Carlos, but there are plenty of shops where food can be bought. Between San Carlos and Chame are two beaches: **Nueva Gorgona** (**B** *Hotel Nueva Gorgona*, with pool; **B** *Cabañas Nueva Gorgona*, cheaper, with kitchenettes, barbecue grills, pool, shade, hammocks, on the ocean, prices rise at weekend; another set of *cabañas*) the beach is about 3-4 km long, waves increase in size from west to east, and there is a well-stocked grocery store. The other is **Playa Coronado**, the most popular in Panama, even so it is rarely crowded. Minibus Panama City-San Carlos, US$3.50, San Carlos-David, US$10. Beyond San Carlos is the Río Mar beach, with **Río Mar** hotel, which has a good seafood restaurant.

5 km on a road (right) leads after a few km to a climb through fine scenery to the summit of Los Llanitos (792m), and then down 200m to a mountain-rimmed plateau (7 by 5½ km) on which is comparatively cool **El Valle**, a small summer resort direct bus from Panama City US$3.50, or US$1 from San Carlos. 4 km before El Valle is a parking spot with fine views of the village, waterfall nearby. (**B** *Hotel Campestre*, T 93-6146/21-9602, F 26-4069, lunch from US$5.95; **D** *El Greco Motel*, Calle central, T 93-6149; private houses nearby rent rooms, F with meals; accommodation hard to find at weekends.) Soapstone carvings of animals, straw birds, painted gourds, carved wood tableware, pottery and *molas* are sold in the famous Sunday market, which is very popular with Panamanians and tourists. There is also a colourful flower market. Gold coloured frogs can be seen in the area, and there are trees with square-shaped trunks, near *Hotel Campestre*. The orchid nursery has a small zoo and Panama's only petroglyphs can be seen near the town. This is one of many good walks in the vicinity (ask directions); another is to the cross in the hills to the W of town.

We leave Panamá Province at La Ermita and enter Coclé, whose large tracts of semi-arid land are used for cattle raising.

Santa Clara, with its famous beach, 115 km from Panama City, is the usual target for motorists: fishing, launches for hire, and riding (Hotels: **B** *Muu Muu*, T 28-5555; **A** *Vista Bella*, T 23-5848, per cabin, for weekend). About 13 km beyond is **Antón** (5,100 people): it has a special local type of *manjar blanco*. There is a crucifix here which is reputed to be miraculous. (**D** *Hotel Rivera*, with bath and a/c, cheaper without bath, a/c or fan, clean, Km 31, T 97-2245; across the

Pan-American Highway is *Pensión/Restaurant Panamá*; *Chung*, on Highway, moderately-priced food.) On 20 km is the capital of Coclé: **Penonomé** (pop 10,715), an old town even when the Spaniards arrived. An advanced culture here, revealed by archaeologists was overwhelmed by volcanic eruption (things found are in Museo Nacional, Panama City, also **Museo Conte de Penonomé** here, open Tues-Sat 0900-1200, 1400-1700, Sun 0900-1200, T 978490). University and Mercado de Artesanato on Highway.

Hotels C *Dos Continentes*, Av JD Arosemena, T 97-2325, with shower, a/c, restaurant; **E** *Pensión Dos Reales*, Calle Juan Vásquez, basic, mosquitos, noisy; **E** *Pensión Los Pinos*, on left of Highway to Panama City, with bath and fan (D with a/c); *Pensión Motel*; **E** *Pensión Ramírez*, with bath, Calle Juan Arosemena near church and Parque.

Just under a km N of Penonomé is Balneario Las Mendozas, on street of the same name, an excellent river pool for bathing in deep water. Further up the Río Zaratí is La Angostura, a canyon; dirt access road usually suitable for ordinary cars. NE of Penonomé is Churuquite Grande (camping possible near river); Feria de la Naranja last weekend of January. Further inland, a purpose-built lodge for walkers and ecotourists has been opened: *Posada del Cerro Viejo*, Apdo 543-9A, Chiguiri Arriba, Coclé, T 23-4553, F 69-2328; it offers guided treks on foot or mule, including through the mountains to El Valle, or across the isthmus to the Atlantic coast. The final stage being done by dugout.

In another 31 km from Penonomé, is **Natá** (pop 5,150), one of the oldest towns in Panama, if not the Americas (1520). The early colonists fought constant Indian attacks led by Urraca. The Iglesia de Santiago Apóstol (1522) is impressive, with some interesting wood carvings. It is sadly rundown now; donations gratefully received for restoration work in progress. Around the plaza are other colonial buildings. Nearby is the **Parque Arqueológico del Caño** with a small museum, some excavations (several human skeletons found in the burial site), and standing stones (entrance charge US$0.50, open Tues-Fri 0900-1600, Sat-Sun 1030-1530, closed Mon). 10 km beyond we enter the sugar area and come to **Aguadulce**, pop 14,800, a prosperous supply centre (bus from Panamá, US$6); native pottery for sale; cane fields, tomato-processing plants and *salinas* nearby. Hotels: **C** *El Interamericano*, on Pan-American Highway, T 97-4363, with bath, a/c, TV, balcony, clean rooms, swimming pool; **E** *Pensión Sarita*, pp, and others (it may be possible to sleep by the fire station). 17 km beyond Aguadulce, just after the large Santa Rosa sugar plantation, a road leads off right to the mountain spa of **Calobre** (31 km); the hot springs are, however, a good hour's drive away, on a very rough road; grand mountain scenery. (Bus Panama City-Aguadulce, US$5.)

6 km after this turnoff is the crossroads town of **Divisa**, 1 km N of the highway and 214 km from the capital. From here a major paved road branches off S into the **Azuero Peninsula**, one of the earliest parts of Panamá to be settled. Despite recent road paving in the S and E, many of the peninsula's small towns are still remote and preserve much of their 400-year-old colonial traditions, costumes and substantial white churches. After passing through **Parita** (pop 6,600), whose church dates from 1556, our road reaches (37 km) the thriving cattle centre of **Chitré** (pop 34,400), capital of Herrera Province and the best base for exploration. The Cathedral (1578) is imposing and beautifully preserved. The small **Museo de Herrera** on Calle Manuel Correa, has interesting historical exhibits, open Tue-Sat 0830-1200, 1300-1600; Sun 0900-1200, US$0.35. The town is known for its woven mats and carpets. The IPAT tourist office is in the Ministerio de Comercio e Industria building on the main road out to Los Santos; very friendly but no English spoken, details on the Peninsula's many festivals and points of interest, open Mon-Fri, 0830-1200, 1245-1630. *Fiesta de San Juan Bautista*, 24 June; the district's founding (1848) is celebrated with colourful parades and historical events each 19 October. There are some nice beaches close to Chitré served by local

buses (20 min, US$0.90); eg Playas Monagre and El Rompio and at Punta Agallito, where many migratory birds congregate and are studied at the Humboldt Ecological Station. Along the swampy coast just to the N is the 8000-ha **Sarigua National Park**, established in 1984 to preserve the distinctive tropical desert and mangrove margins of the Bahía de Parita; ancient artefacts have been unearthed within the park's boundaries; the precolombian site of Monegrillo is considered very significant but there is little for the non-specialist to appreciate.

Hotels D *El Prado*, Av Herrera 4260, opp Cathedral, T 96-4620, clean and modern, quiet, well run, a/c, parking, upstairs restaurant, rec; **D/E** *Santa Rita*, Calle M Correa y Av Herrera, T 96-4610, near main plaza, clean, large rooms, modern, cheaper rooms have fans and cold water, restaurant (currently closed for renovation); **E** *Pensión Colombia*, Calle Manuel Correa near museum (3 blocks from Plaza), T 96-1856, fans and private baths, good budget value; **E** *Pensión Central*, next to *El Prado*, with bath, very clean and friendly, excellent value, highly rec. Plenty of eating places near the Plaza and in the *mercado* (beside the Cathedral).

Transport Chitré is the transport hub of the peninsula but has no central bus terminal; most buses leave from different points around the Cathdral. To **Panama City** (250 km), regular departures by several companies, 4 hrs, US$7.25. To **Divisa**, ½ hr, US$1.30; same fare and time to **Las Tablas**. To **Tonosí**, 3 hrs, US$4.15; to **Santiago**, 1½ hrs, US$2.50. Daily **flights** (except Sun) to the capital with Chitreana de Aviación, US$27.50—these also serve Los Santos, Guararé and Las Tablas; taxi to the small airport US$1.50 (maximum).

2 km W of Chitré is **La Arena**, the centre for Panamanian native pottery. The Christmas festivities here, 22-25 December, are worth seeing, with music, dancing, bull running in the *plaza de toros* and cock fights (popular all over Panamá). Tourist agencies in Panama City can arrange whirlwind shopping tours to La Arena. Bus from Chitré; 5 min, US$0.30, taxi US$1.50; the walk takes you past an army camp and you may be asked for your documents.

Los Santos (pop 9,000), only 4 km across the Río La Villa from Chitré in Los Santos province, is an old, charming town with a fine 18th century church (San Anastácio) containing many images. The first call for Independence came from here; the interesting **Museo de la Nacionalidad** on the Plaza Bolívar is in the lovely house where the Declaration was signed on 10 November 1821, entrance charge US$0.25. (**E** *Pensión Deportiva*, no single rooms, private showers; **C** *Hotel La Villa de Los Santos*, a/c caravans, with swimming pool and good restaurant.) The 4-day Feast of Corpus Christi (40 days after Easter) is celebrated in Los Santos with one of the country's most famous and popular festivals, medieval dances, skits and costumes galore, a glorious distillation of the Peninsula's uniquely-strong Spanish roots and well worth attending. The *Feria de Azuero* is held at the end of April (variable date); 'Little Devil' (*diablito*) and other masks featuring prominently in these *fiestas* are the local handicraft speciality and may be purchased from many stalls or workshops around town (also in Parita).

The main road continues 22 km SE through agricultural country to the tiny town of **Guararé** (pop 700), notable only for its folkloric museum, the **Museo Manuel Zárate** two blocks behind the church, T 96-2535, where examples of Azuero's many traditional costumes, masks and crafts are exhibited in a turn-of-the-century house. There is also a wealth of traditional dance, music and singing contests during the annual National Festival of *La Mejorana* (24 September). Two hotels: *Eida* and *Guavaré*.

Las Tablas (6 km further, pop 22,140) is capital of Los Santos province and the Peninsula's second-largest city, 67 km from the Divisa turnoff. The central Iglesia de Santa Librada with its gold-leaf altar and majestic carvings, is one of the finest churches in this part of Panamá and is now a National Historic Monument. Lacking other outstanding points of interest (except perhaps El Pausilipo, former home of thrice-President Porras—known to Panamanians as 'the great man'—and in the process of being turned into a museum), Las Tablas is nevertheless widely-known for its *Fiesta de Santa Librada* and incorporated *Fiesta de la Pollera* (19-23 July). The *pollera* is a ruffled, intricately-embroidered off-the-shoulder dress based on colonial fashions and now the national costume of Panamá; *polleras* are made in a number of villages near Las Tablas (eg La Tiza, El Cocal, San José), the most beautiful coming from Santo Domingo (5 km E); another high-quality manufacturing centre is La Enea, a small village close to Guararé. Most towns of any size on the Peninsula have annual Carnivals (the four days before Ash Wednesday) but Las Tablas' is especially picturesque and popular with visitors; accommodation is in short supply at this time throughout the region. The lovely and unspoilt beach of El Uverito is about 10 km to the E of town but has no public transport; taxi US$4.50. A paved road also runs to the port of Mensabé.

Hotels: C *Oria*, Via Santo Domingo, T 94-6315, out of town; **D** *Piamonte*, Av Belisario Porras, T 94-6372, a/c only; **E** *Pensión Mariela*, opposite, basic, run down; **E** *Pensión Marta*; swimming pool near National Guard barracks, US$0.25, not friendly, not rec. Some eating places around the church but not a lot of variety.

Transport From Chitré, buses leave when full, 1/2 hr, US$1.20. To **Panama City**, several daily, 4 1/2 hrs, US$7; to **Santo Domingo**, 10 min, US$0.40; to **Tonosí**, 2 1/2 hrs, US$4.25. Last bus from Los Santos to Las Tablas at 1800.

South of Las Tablas Smaller, badly-paved roads fan out from Las Tablas to the beaches along the S coast and the small hill villages in the interior. A circular tour around the eastern mountain range can be done by continuing S to Pocrí and Pedasí (42 km), then W to Tonosí, all with their ancient churches and lack of spectacular sights, but typical of the Azuero Peninsula. Another 57-km paved road runs directly over the hills from Las Tablas to Tonosí, good as far as the small tropical village of Flores (no hotel). In *Pedasí*, a peaceful colonial town, the municipal library, near the church (in front of a service station) has many old volumes. Beautiful empty beaches (beware dangerous cross-currents when swimming) and crystal-clear seas are 3 km away. **E** *Pensión Moscoso*, with shower, good, friendly, only place in town, meals arranged by owner at nearby bar. Most things hereabouts, it seems, are run by the Moscoso clan, including a charming wild fowl reserve near the beach, with storks and herons. The local festival is *Patronales de San Pablo* (29 June). Buses from Las Tablas leave when full, US$2.65, 1 1/2 hrs, bumpy trip. Offshore between Pocrí and Pedasí is *Isla Iguana*, a wildlife sanctuary protecting the island's bird life, reptiles and forest; the IPAT office in Chitré can arrange a tour with knowledgeable naturalist René Chan who lives locally.

The road onwards is quite good as far as **Cañas** (no hotel), running near the Pacific coast for a short distance, with a string of lovely coves and sandy beaches accessible by rough tracks. 10 km before Cañas, a small sign points to the black-sand beach of **Playa Venado**, a surfer's paradise down a long dirt road (being improved); there are *cabañas* for rent (US$10 pp) plenty of idyllic camping spots and a small restaurant; one bus a day from Las Tablas, about 2 hrs, US$3.20. **Tonosí** has the **D** *Pensión Boamy*, with a/c, E with bath, a restaurant, gas station, chemist and a few basic shops. A branch road goes a few km further south to Cambutal; little reason to detour here as the beaches are a long way out and difficult to get to. The main inland road turns back N following the Río Tonosí, crosses a saddle between the town mountain ranges occupying the centre of the Peninsula (picturesque views of forested Cerro Quema, 950m), and arrives at **Macaracas**, another attractive but unremarkable colonial town, from where two paved roads return to Los Santos and Chitré (35 km). No direct bus Pedasí-Tonosí; Pedasí-Cañas at 1500, US$1 (returns 0700); Cañas-Tonosí one per day. Tonosí-Las Tablas, 4 a day between 0700 and 1300, US$2, 1 1/2 hrs, leave when full; a milk truck leaves Tonosí at 0700 for Chitré, via Cañas, Puerto Venado, Pedasí and Las Tablas, takes passengers, returns 1230. Hitching very difficult in this area. Bus Tonosí-Chitré via Macaracas, 4 a day before 1100, 3 hrs, US$4, mostly good, paved road.

About 45 km W of Chitré is **Ocú** (pop 2,750), another old colonial town with a gracefully curving 16th century church, whose inhabitants celebrate quite a few notable *fiestas* throughout the year with traditional dress, music, masks and dancing, eg San Sebastián the district's patron saint, costumed folklore groups, 19-24 January; the *Festival del Manito* at the Assumption (15 August); straight from medieval Spain, and well-worth witnessing, are the festivities of *Matrimonio Campesino*, *El Penitente de la Otra Vida* and *El Duelo del Tamarindo*. IPAT tourist offices (Panama City, David, Santiago, Chitré) are best informed about dates and details. Ocú is also known for its woven hats, which are cheaper than elsewhere in Panamá.

Hotel E *Posada San Sebastián*, on the plaza, fans, clean bathrooms, patio, charming.

Travel Ocú can be reached directly from the Pan-American Highway (19 km) by a paved turnoff S just past the Río Conaca bridge (11 km W of Divisa); *colectivos* run from here for US$0.80. Alternatively, a mostly gravel road runs W from Parita along the Río Parita valley, giving good views of the fertile agricultural landscapes of the northern Peninsula. Several buses a day from Chitré, 1 hr, US$1.75, and minibuses on to Panama City, US$7. For those with limited time, a representative glimpse of the countryside and villages could be had by taking a bus from Chitré to Pesé, Los Pozos or Las Minas, all in the foothills of the western range, and then another to Ocú; staying the night and taking another bus on to Santiago to return to the Panama City-David highway.

The central mountains effectively cut off the western side of the Pensinsula from the more developed eastern half. Only one road down from the Highway, a gruelling gravel/dirt ribbon which staggers from near Santiago as far S as the village of Arenas (80 km) before giving up in the face of the surrounding scrubby mountain slopes. Eastward from here the Peninsula reaches its highest point at Cerro Hoya (1,559m); no roads penetrate either to the coast or into the mountains, ensuring solitude for the **Cerro Hoya National Park**, which protects most of the SW tip.

The road from Divisa to Santiago, the next town, 37 km, runs across the Province of Veraguas, the only one which has seaboards on both oceans. It is very dry in the summer. **Santiago** (pop 32,560), capital of the Province, is well inland; one of the oldest towns in the country, in a grain-growing area (very good—and cheap—macramé bags are sold in the market here). Nearby is **San Francisco**; it has a wonderful old church with wooden images, altar pieces and pulpit. Bus from Penonomé, US$4, from Aguadulce, US$2.50; no bus to David, walk to Panamericana and stop Panama City-David bus, US$6.

Hotels in Santiago: **D** *Motel Gran David*, on Pan-American Highway, T 98-2622 a/c, TV, cheaper with black and white TV, E with fan, all rooms have bath, clean, rec, good inexpensive restaurant; **D** *Nuevo Piramidal* on Pan-Am Highway, T 98, 3123, a/c, TV, shower, clean, quiet, good pool, rec; **D** *Santiago*, Calle 2 near the Cathedral, T 98-4824, clean, with a/c, TV and shower, cheaper with shared bath, rec. *Pensiones* on Av Central: **E** *Jigoneva*, No 2038, basic, friendly; **E** *Central*, next door, basic, all rooms with shower, Chinese owner; *Continental*, next door, friendly, basic, shared bath. Swimming pool near town centre.

W of Santiago is La Mesa, with a beautiful, white colonial church. The bad road through **Soná** (43 km, pop 5,000) in a deep fertile valley to **Guabalá**, near Remedios the country's largest stock-raising centre, has been replaced by a direct paved highway from Santiago to Guabalá. This saves a couple of hours. From Guabalá to David is 92 km.

About 17 km W of Guabalá is **Las Lajas**, take turn-off at San Félix. Las Lajas has good, wide beaches (no facilities, 2 bars, costly shade for cars—shark-infested waters and strong waves, nearest accommodation in David or Santiago). To get there take a bus from David to the turn off (US$2.50), then walk 3 km to the town, from where it is 10 km to the beach (taxis only, US$5).

David (pop 102,400), capital of Chiriquí Province (pop 368,023), a hot and humid city, rich in timber, coffee, cacao, sugar, rice, bananas and cattle, is the third city of the Republic. It was founded in colonial times and has kept its traditions intact while modernizing itself. The town has a fine central plaza, Parque Cervantes, with the colonial Inglesia de San José on its W side; the bell tower was built separately as a defence against Indian attacks. Palacio Municipal, opp *Hotel Nacional* on Av and C Central. 24-hr Shell station at Av Cincuentenario y Calle C Norte; other service stations at E entrance to Pan-American Highway. International fair and *fiesta*, 19 March.

Hotels B *Fiesta*, on Pan-American Highway, T 75-5454, good pool (US$2 for non-residents); **D** *Iris* on Parque Cervantes T 75-2251, with bath and fan (a/c more), rec; **D** *Nacional*, Calle Central, T 75-2221, clean rooms, good restaurant, small gaming room; **E** *Hotel Valle de la Luna*, fine, except that it hasn't been cleaned this century, appreciated by cockroaches etc, some distance from centre; **D** *Saval*, Calle D Norte between Cincuentenario y Ave 1 Este, T 75-3543, a/c, small restaurant, clean and friendly; **E** *Pensión El Amanecer*, Av 1 Oeste entre Calles C y D Norte, T 74-3922, some a/c, small basic rooms, quiet; **E** *Pensión Clark*, Av Francisco Clark, T 74-3452, bath, N of bus terminal; **E** *Pensión Costa Rica*, Av 5 Este, Calle A Sur, with shower, D with a/c, F, in small, noisier rooms, toilet and fan, basic, clean, safe, and friendly; **E** *Pensión Fanita*, Manuel J Posa between Calles 5 and 6, price pp, with bath and a/c, cheaper without a/c, fairly clean; *Pensión y Restaurante Canton*, Calle Central, Av 4-6 Este, opp supermarket, very clean and friendly; **F** *Pensión Rocío No 2*, with shower, clean, big rooms with partition walls, restaurant. Most cheap hotels are on Av 5 Este.

Restaurants *Mariscos Daiquiri*, Av Central, Calle C Sur, fish and seafood, not cheap, but good; *Jimar*, corner of Calle C Norte and Av Bolívar, good value; *Las Brisas*, Av Obaldía, good steaks; *Las Vegas*, opposite *Hotel Nacional*, steaks and pastas; *Parrillada El Portal*, Calle A Sur, Av 5 E, good; *El Portal Valle de la Luna*, Calle A Sur, near *Pensión Costa Rica*, good food; *Restaurant Bar Bon Jour*, just outside town towards Boquete, very pleasant, steaks and pizzas good. Many around central plaza (*Parque*, *don Pedro*, *Pollo Riko*, all a/c; *Café Don Dicky*, Calle C Norte nr Av Domingo Díaz, better than it looks, Pizza House round corner. *América* in bus station, 0500-2400, others opposite and of varying quality in municipal market, Av Obaldía, nr Av 3 de Noviembre, 4 blocks N of plaza.

Entertainment Discotheque, *Metropolitan*, plays salsa. Plaza cinema, by Parque Cervantes.

Museum Museo José de Obaldía, Calle 8 Este, No 5067 y Calle A Norte, 4 blocks from Plaza, historical and art museum in house of the founder of Chiriquí province, open Tues-Sat 0900-1600, US$0.25.

Car Hire Budget, T 75-5597; **Hertz**, T 75-6828; **Mike's**, T 75-4963; **Fecar**, T 75-3246, reasonable. If wishing to rent a 4WD vehicle for Volcán Barú, do so in David.

Local Transport Urban buses US$0.20; taxis US$0.65 in city.

Exchange Citibank on Plaza, only Citibank TCs; **Banco del Istmo**, Av 2 Este between Calle B Norte and Calle Central, changes Bank of America TCs. **Banco Nacional de Panamá**, 0800-1330, changes Amex TCs, 1% commission plus US$0.10 tax per cheque. **Banco General**, one block from main plaza, changes TCs, no commission.

Costa Rican Consulate Av 2 Oeste entre Calles D y G, diagonal a la Provedora Barú, T 74-1923 (according to Panamanian Consulate in London – one report says it moved in 1992). Consul is Juan Flores Badilla.

Laundry *La Fuente*, Calle 5 Este y Calle A Sur, Mon-Sat 0800-1800, Sun 0830-1330. Laundry next to *Pensión Costa Rica*, US$2 a load, wash and dry.

Post Office Calle C Norte, 1 block from Parque Cervantes. **Telecommunications** Intel, Calle C Norte, telex and long-distance telephone.

Tourist Office On Central Plaza, Edificio Galerma, to left of church, above *Pazin* shop, 1st floor, office 4, T 75-4120, not much information, Mon-Fri 0830-1630. **Immigration Office** Calle C Sur nr Av Central, T 75-4515, Mon-Fri 0800-1530.

Bus from **Panama City**: apart from Ticabus, ordinary buses, US$11 (7 hrs), every hour from 0700 to 1300, 1½ hourly till 1900, plus express buses at midnight, 5½ hrs, US$15. All regional and long distance buses leave from the bus terminal at the end of Av 2 Este/Cincuentenario, 200m N of Av Obaldía, except that Tracopa, T 75-0585, have buses to San José, with a stop at San Isidro, at 0830 and 1230 (8 hrs to San José), US$18 both destinations, from Av 5 Este, Calle A Sur next to *Pensión Costa Rica*. Boarding buses here can be chaotic as tickets are only sold once the bus has arrived, and then people start clamouring for seats immediately. An alternative way to Panama City is to Santiago (US$7) and then to Panama City (US$7). Regular minibus to **Boquete** from bus station (US$1.20) 1 hr. Frequent 'frontera' buses to Paso Canoas, US$1.50, 1½ hrs. To **Volcán**, 2 hrs, US$2.65, half-hourly, 0700-1800; **Chiriquí Grande**, 3 hrs, US$6, 1½ hourly intervals 0630-1600.

Air Several Alas Chiricanas flights a day from Panama City, also Aeroperlas twice daily US$50 one way. Chircanas also to Bocas del Toro and Changuinola, both US$22.50 one way.

Note: If driving S, stock up with food in David: it is much cheaper than in Panama City.

Excursion A few km N of David is *Balneario Majagua*, where you can swim in a river under a waterfall; cold drinks for sale. Take a Dolega or Boquete bus and ask the driver to let you out.

A well-paved road climbs gently N from David into the cool highlands around Volcán Barú, passing (10 km) a waterfall with a swimming hole at its base, open-air restaurant/bar and space for wild camping. It passes through Dolega (swimming pool, good carnival 4 days before Ash Wednesday) before reaching (35 km) the popular mountain resort of ***Boquete*** (pop 14,400), at 1,060m, on the slopes of Chiriquí (bus costs US$1.20). It enjoys a spring-like climate the year round: the mingling of Atlantic and Pacific winds creates an atmospheric oddity called the *bajareque* (literally 'falling down'), a fine mist or moisture always in the air, which combined with the black volcanic soil, creates highly fertile conditions. Around is a beautiful panorama of coffee plantations, orange groves, strawberry fields, and gardens which grow the finest flowers and vegetables in the country. The town has many attractions: good lodging and facilities, excellent river bathing, fishing, riding, and mountain climbing, and not too expensive. The main plaza is attractive, but prettier is Parque de las Madres, with fountains, flower beds, a monument to motherhood and a children's playground. The fair ground E of the river is the site for the *Feria de las Flores y el Café*, held each year early April (the dates are variable, usually around the 11th, but it took place 14-23 January in 1994). The cemetery is worth a visit (see map). There is a panoramic view from the 'Bienvenidos a Boquete' arch at the *Coffee Bean Restaurant* (see below).

Hotels B *Panamonte*, T 70-1327/4, with bath, or **A** with kitchen, dinner costs US$13.50 and is highly rec, popular, garden boasts over 200 varieties of orchid, very attractive surroundings, run by Inga Collins (Swedish/American), horse hire US$3/hr, guides available

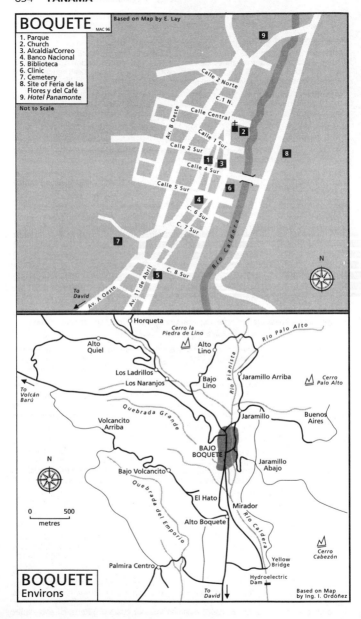

BOQUETE
MAC 96

1. Parque
2. Church
3. Alcaldía/Correo
4. Banco Nacional
5. Biblioteca
6. Clinic
7. Cemetery
8. Site of Feria de las Flores y del Café
9. *Hotel Panamonte*

Not to Scale

Based on Map by E. Lay

Calle 2 Norte
C. 1 N.
Calle Central
Av. B Oeste
Calle 1 Sur
Calle 2 Sur
Calle 4 Sur
Calle 5 Sur
C. 6 Sur
C. 7 Sur
C. 8 Sur
Av. A Oeste
Av. 11 de Abril
Río Caldera

To David

N

BOQUETE
Environs

Horqueta
Cerro la Piedra de Lino
Alto Quiel
Alto Lino
Río Palo Alto
Los Ladrillos
Los Naranjos
Bajo Lino
Jaramillo Arriba
Cerro Palo Alto
To Volcán Barú
Quebrada Grande
Volcancito Arriba
Jaramillo
Buenos Aires
BAJO BOQUETE
Bajo Volcancito
Jaramillo Abajo
Quebrada del Emporio
El Hato
Mirador
Río Caldera
Alto Boquete
Cerro Cabezón
Palmira Centro
Yellow Bridge
Hydroelectric Dam
To David

N

0   500
metres

Based on Map by Ing. I. Ordóñez

(ask about hot springs, Los Pozos de Caldera, see **Excursions** below, and Finca Lérida, see under Volcán Barú below; other excursions also available, such as the Río Monte Ecological Tour, reported expensive, ask for maps of the area). *Villa Lorena Cabañas*, US$50 per day for 4 people. Cheaper hotels: **C** *Fundadores*, T 70-1298, good restaurant; **D** *Pensión Virginia*, S side of plaza, T 70-1260, with bath, D for cheapest rooms, hot water, clean, friendly, English spoken, pretty garden, cheap restaurant downstairs, highly rec. **C** *Rebequet*, T 70-1365, excellent rooms around a garden, with bath, TV and fridge, kitchen and eating area for guests' use, popular; **D** *Pensión Marilós*, Av a Este y Calle 6 Sur, T 70-1380, opposite *Rebequet*, with bath (one room E without bath), English spoken, very clean and well run with excellent, cheap food, rec, tours also organized.

Restaurants *Coffee Bean/Grano de Café*, T 70-1624, a café on road 3 km S of town, fantastic views, good snacks, book exchange, very friendly, English-speaking owner (they have a lioness—Elsa—born in captivity, she looks very healthy). *Chinese Food*, yes that's its name, on Parque Central, cheap and good; *Pizzería Volcánica*, ½ block from main plaza, good pizzas and pasta at reasonable prices; opp is *La Conquista*, delicious trout. Plenty of cheap eating places eg *Lourdes* (outside terrace) and *Túnel* on plaza, *Rocío*, ½ block away. 45 mins walk from Boquete (past *Hotel Panamonte*) is a new restaurant *El Explorador*, beautiful location, picnic area, children's playground, hammocks etc, entrance to area, US$1, but free to restaurant (excellent local food, breakfast and dinner).

Laundry Econopronto, Av Central, 50m from church, closed Sun and lunchtimes.

Services On the main street, Av 11 de Abril, or Fundadores, are Banco Nacional (cashes TCs, as will the cooperative opp the bank on the plaza), *farmacia*, cinema, *Dejud* supermarket; on Av A Este are the post office, market and church of San Juan Bautista.

Excursions Huw Clough and Kate Hennessy write: To *Volcán Barú*, 21 km W of Boquete, the first 7 km is paved, but the rest of the track is very rough, bumpy and steep for which 4WD is necessary (there are no service stations en route). The paved road, sometimes lined with aromatic pines, goes through coffee groves, mainly tended by Guaymí indians. Shortly after the end of the paved road you come to the entrance to the national park. There is a small Inrenare (National Resources Institute) office here, not always manned, and there is also an office on the southern outskirts of town, near the Colegio Franciscano, at which it may be worth enquiring if a permit is needed. The track winds up from the office through impressive, tall cloud forest, thick with hanging creepers, lichen and bromeliads. The steep cuttings are carpeted with a glorious array of ferns and colourful flowers; many birds can be seen, including bee-sized hummingbirds and wild turkeys, also squirrels. The perfume from the flowers, especially in the wet season when there are many more blooms, is magnificent.

As the road rises, increasingly steeply, wonderful views appear, of the Boquete valley, the Río Caldera running through a steep gorge, and the misty plain beyond stretching to the sea (best seen in the early morning with the rising sun behind). About three-quarters of the way up there is a crater on the left, with a sign leading to a mirador, about a 15 min walk.

At the summit the jungle is replaced by a forest of TV and radio aerials, in fenced-off enclosures. A short path leads to a small cross and a trigonometric point, from which there are the best views all around, of dusty craters and the valley of Volcán, Bambito and Cerro Punta below. The barren, dusty slopes contrast spectacularly with the dark green forest, with wisps of mist and cloud clinging to the treetops. Sometimes horizontal rainbows can be seen in the haze, formed in the *bajareque* drizzle. There are many mini-craters around the main summit, with dwarf vegetation, lichens and orchids.

There is a makeshift campsite in a small grove of bushes on the left of the road before the final summit. From the cross there is a path down to the main crater where there is also plenty of flat ground for camping (local hikers say it is dangerous, safer in groups). There appears to be no running water. Previous campers have badly littered the camping area and the graffiti is appalling. Take back everything you bring with you. After about 1100 you will probably have the place to yourself; it is very quiet and atmospheric. The path that leads down from the cross branches right for Cerro Punta (see below).

In a suitable vehicle it takes about 3½ hrs to the top, 2½ hrs down (depending on the weather), or from the park office, 6 hrs hike up, 3 hrs down. Gonzalo Miranda and Generoso Rodríguez, neither trained guides, but both very knowledgeable and willing, take visitors to the summit, and to other sites, fix a price beforehand. T 70-1165 (Generoso's home, he speaks some English) or 70-1261, his office, or leave a message with Frank, who speaks good English, at *Pensión Marilós*. Vehicles belonging to Intel, the cable and telephone companies, often go up to the summit. They are not allowed to take passengers officially, but drivers may give you a lift if you start walking from their office in Boquete before 0800. A taxi to the end of the paved road costs US$4.

Mrs Inga Collins of *Hostal Panamonte* will give permission to visit her *Finca Lérida*, on the slopes of Barú volcano (ask at the hotel's front desk); there are many trails in the cloud forest where quetzales have been seen and bell birds heard. Entrance to the Finca costs US$1.50 pp.

Other attractions include: Café Ruiz, on the northern edge of Boquete, a small coffee factory which welcomes visitors for a free guided tour (José Ruiz speaks English), explaining the whole process from harvesting to selecting only the green beans; T 70-1392/1432. Los Ladrillos, a few km further up the Caldera valley, is a small area of basalt cliffs with octagonal fingers of rock in clusters, just like Northern Ireland's Giant's Causeway. Beyond is Horqueta, a picturesque hillside area of coffee groves, with a roadside waterfall and banks of pink impatiens; beautiful views of the south.

15 km before Boquete is a turn off E to Caldera (14 km), from where a 45-min walk leads to *Los Pozos de Caldera*, a well-known series of hot springs said to be good for rheumatism sufferers. No facilities, they are on land belonging to the Collins family (*Hotel Panamonte* in Boquete), who ask only that visitors and campers leave the area clean and litter-free. There is one bus a day from David to Caldera.

A recommended half-day walk is across the suspension bridge in Boquete, then take a righthand fork winding steeply uphill. After about ½ hr the paved road gives way to gravel; keep going to a crossroads where you take the righthand fork, heading due south. This track continues with the river on your right and sweeping hillsides to your left. Eventually you rejoin the main road, turning right along an avenue lined with pine trees. The road winds down and across a big yellow bridge by a dam. After an exposed, flat stretch you meet the main road into Boquete from David; from here it is ½ hr back to town and a well-deserved stop at the *Grano de Café*.

After David, a dirt road turns off to the left to *Las Palmas*, a pleasant orange-growing village which welcomes tourists. Just before the village is a waterfall where a single column of water falls into a pool, delightful for swimming and camping.

The Highway (fenced with posts which grow into trees if not trimmed back) and a railway go on through cattle land from David 26 km W to *La Concepción* (pop 11,900), an important agricultural shipping point also widely-known for its hand-made saddles. There are several fair hotels (eg *Rico*, Calle 2a Oeste and the Highway; and *Caribe*, Av 1a Sur), but better accommodation in David; a local *fiesta* is held at end January. Buses depart from the main plaza, every 20 mins to Volcán, David, and Paso Canoas. Calle 2a Oeste becomes the good paved road running 31 km N to *Volcán* (1,500m). Hotels: **C** *Cabañas Reina*, signed from main road, T 71-4338, self-contained units with a kitchen in lawn setting, attractive; **D** *Motel California*, on main street, T 71-4272, friendly Croatian owner speaks English, clean private baths, hot water, larger cabins for up to 7, US$45, quiet, good; **D** *Cabañas Señorial*, also on main street, T 71-4239, OK. Plenty of cheap eating places. Bus from La Concepción US$1.20, also direct buses from David.

The road divides at Volcán: one paved branch loops 48 scenic km W to *Río Sereno* on the Costa Rican frontier (**D** *Hotel Los Andes*, good), a minor international crossing post with uncertain hours and the probability that visa applications will be out-of-stock (better to arrange in advance, perhaps in David); no public transport but an easy crossing for private vehicles. The other branch (deteriorating) continues N to Bambito and Cerro Punta (22 km), following the Chiriquí Viejo river valley up the NW foothills of Volcán Barú. At tiny, windy *Bambito* is the luxurious **A** *Hotel Bambito*, indoor pool, spa, casino, conference room, good but expensive restaurant, tennis courts, horse-riding—the lot! Very good bargains can be negotiated here in the off-season. Directly opposite is the interesting Truchapan rainbow trout hatchery, good retail prices for fishing gear rental. *Cerro Punta* (2,130m), at the end of the road (buses from David, 2¼ hrs, US$3), is sometimes called 'Little Switzerland' because of its Alpine-style houses and the influence of Swiss and former-Yugoslav settlers; there is no accommodation and few facilities but the countryside, full of orchids and rainbows, is beautiful. Just beyond Cerro Punta lies the Finca Rogelio Rodríguez Argüello (only a 4-wheel drive vehicle can get to it), where Sr José will show you the haunts of the quetzal; see the quetzal also at the Finca Fernández in the **Volcán National Park**, to which there is a good asphalt road. Cerro Punta itself, in a beautiful valley devoted to vegetables and flowers, has many fine walks in the crisp mountain air. One such is a 6-8 hr hike, mostly downhill after an initial climb, to Boquete (the track is clear in places and there are a few signs showing the direction and time—ambitious—to Boquete); the last part is down the Río Caldera canyon. Don't hike alone, take a machete and sufficient provisions for 2 days in case of mishap, wear ankle boots, and notify someone before leaving and on arrival. This hike is also recommended for bird watching. Parque la Amistad is another park, 6 km from the centre of Cerro Punta (signposted at road junction), the last section to the park office for 4WD only. It has been open since 1991, with 2 trails, good for bird watching, including quetzals.

30 km from La Concepción is **Paso Canoas** on the Costa Rican border (open 0700-1200, 1400-1800, 1900-2200, Panamanian customs are open 24 hrs— remember Panama is 1 hr ahead of Costa Rica). Entering Panama is quite straightforward. For those who need tourist cards, they are sold at the tourist office near immigration for US$2, free maps of Panama available here. No other charges are made. Money changers on the Panamanian side will change colones into dollars at a good rate (the bank on the Costa Rican side sells dollars, rates slightly better than moneychangers). Regular buses run to David for US$1.50, 1½ hrs.

Chiriquí Railway, S from La Concepción to Puerto Armuelles, but no passenger trains. Passenger service Puerto Armuelles-Progreso (half away to Paso Canoas), twice a day each way, 2 hrs, US$1. There is also a 'Finca Train', 4 decrepit, converted banana trucks, leaving at 1500 for the banana *fincas*, returning, by a different route, at 1800. No charge for passengers. Minibuses also leave all day for the *fincas*. Freight service only to David and to Pedregal.

Puerto Armuelles (pop 12,975), is the port through which all the bananas grown in the area are exported. Puerto Armuelles and Almirante (Bocas del Toro) are the only ports in Panama outside the Canal area at which ocean-going vessels habitually call and anchor in deep water close inshore; there is now an oil transit pipeline across the isthmus between the two places. Bus from David, every 15 mins 0500-2000, 2½ hrs, US$3.

Hotels E *Pensión Balboa*, on waterfront, pleasant; E *Pensión Trébol*, 1 block from waterfront. Plenty of cheap eating places, eg **Enrique's**, Chinese, good; **Club Social**, on water, ask any taxi, chicken and rice dishes.

THE NORTH-WESTERN CARIBBEAN COAST

Different again, Panama's Caribbean, banana-growing region has historical links with Columbus' 4th voyage and with black slaves imported to work the plantations. Ports of varying age and activity lie on the Laguna de Chiriquí, all linked by ferry. Here is an alternative land route to Costa Rica.

Across the Cordillera from David, on the Caribbean side, is the important banana growing region which extends from **Almirante** NW across the border to Costa Rica. In the 1940-1950 period, disease virtually wiped out the business and plantations were converted to *abacá* and cacao. Resistant strains of banana were developed and have now all but replaced *abacá* and cacao. Thriving banana plantations are throughout this area on the mainland owned by Cobanat, a subsidiary of Standard Fruit (Dole Chiquita etc). Around 20 million boxes of banana are exported annually to Europe alone from Almirante, which is not a place to stay, though there are two hotels, **D/E San Francisco**, a/c or fan, small dark rooms, overpriced; **D/E Hong Kong**, with fan, or more expensive with a/c, restaurant; and a *pensión*, *Colón*, basic nice rooms, friendly owner. Banana production suffered a setback with the earthquake of 1991 (see below).

Across the bay are a number of islands, the most important of which is Isla Colón, which used to be a major banana producer, but this did not revive with the mainland plantations. Its main sources of income now are fishing and tourism, centred on **Bocas del Toro** on the SE tip of the island. Bocas del Toro deserves a visit (*Fiesta del Mar* end September/early October): peaceful, quiet, English spoken by most of the black population. The protected bay offers all forms of water sport and diving (snorkelling gear for hire at *Botel Thomas*, US$5 a day), beautiful sunrises and sunsets, and, on land, tropical birds, butterflies and wild life. Do not go to deserted stretches of beach alone. Excursions can be made to the islands of the archipelago (Bastimentos—see below, Carenero, Solarte), to Isla del Cisne, a bird sanctuary, and to the beautiful Islas Zapatillas, for beaches and fishing. At Bastimentos is a National Marine Park: on this island and on Isla Colón are turtle nesting grounds, whose protection is being improved. Colón also has a cave of long-beaked white bats, which fly out at dusk (tour, US$10). If hiring a boat, try to arrange it the day before, US$5 per hour not including petrol, 4 hrs min, can take 5 people. Note that many of the names relate to Columbus' landfall here on his fourth voyage in October 1502 (Carenero was where he careened his ships, Bastimentos where he took on supplies, etc). The area has a rich buccaneering past, too.

Between Almirante and the Costa Rica border is **Changuinola** with an airstrip and **Banco del Istmo**, open till 1500 weekdays, 1200 Sats, changes Amex TCs and cash advances on Visa and Mastercard.

50 km to the SE of Almirante is **Chiriquí Grande** which has a road connection with the rest of the country (see below) but none to Almirante. There are understood to be plans for one but nothing has been done. (See below for all **Transport** details.)

NB A devastating earthquake struck NW Panamá and SE Costa Rica on 21 April 1991. The area is now recovering (1994) and reconstruction is proceeding. An island in the bay which sank during the earthquake now shows as a patch of shallow turquoise water. **NB** also It can rain at any time in this Caribbean region. The months to avoid are December and June-August.

Hotels At Bocas del Toro: **C-D** *Botel Thomas*, on the sea, T 78-9428/9309, Apartado 5, Bocas del Toro, wooden building on stilts, with bath and fan, restaurant, bicycle, snorkel and canoe hire, good but cockroaches and thin walls; **D** *Bahía*, T 78-9211, building formerly the HQ of the United Fruit Company, marginally more expensive than the *Botel Thomas*, 'classy but bathrooms need some cleaning', nice cafeteria, laundry; **F** *Pensión Peck*, no sign, on main road, white building, excellent homely atmosphere (sadly, the owner, Miss Xenia Peck, died in 1994, but the *pensión* is as popular as before). **Restaurants** *Las Delicias*, *El Lorito*, both good, and a good Chinese, with take-away, on the main street; *Don Chico's Restaurant* does a mean *casado* for US$2; bar by public dock very active, especially at weekends.

At **Bastimentos**, rooms may be arranged through Gabriel and meals through the disco-bar.

At **Changuinola**: **D** *Changuinola*, near airport; **D** *Carol*, 100m from bus station, with bath, a/c, restaurant next door same ownership; restaurant *El Caribe*, nr airport, rec; also nightclubs (*54* best), cinema and theatre.

At **Chiriquí Grande**: **D** *Pensión Emperador*, overlooking wharf, clean, friendly, balcony; **E** *Hotel Buena Vista*, does breakfasts, friendly, shared bath, mice; **F** pp *Osiris*, fan, basic but OK, awful food; **E** *Pensión Guillerma*, both are further away from the port's 24-hr generator so may be quieter, basic, shared bath (latter has noisy bar downstairs), take a flashlight, power only from 1800-2400. **E** *Hotel Fuente*, with bath, 1 block from waterfront next to *panadería*, friendly, clean, best in town, no name, just ask. **Restaurants** *Mama Gina*, next to ferry dock, good; *Dallys* (popular, to right of wharf) and *Café*, also good.

Transport Water taxis from Almirante to Bocas del Toro daily from 0700 till 1430, except Wed, 30 mins minimum, US$3. From Almirante to Chiriquí Grande, take daily (except Mon) vehicle ferry ('Palanga') at 0800, US$40 per car, and US$3 per adult, children US$2, 5 hrs if lucky, or water taxi, frequent, 1½hrs, US$8. Ferry Chiriquí Grande-Almirante daily (except Mon), 1330, express launch daily from 0800 regularly to 1430, US$8. To Bocas del Toro by canoe with outboard motor, US$10. Bocas del Toro and Changuinola can be reached by Aeroperlas, or Alas Chiricanas, both from Paitilla Airport (US$42-47 one-way) and David. Fare Changuinola-Bocas del Toro, US$8 one way.

Roads There is a road from Changuinola to Almirante (buses every ½ hr till 2000, 30 mins, US$1). Bus to San José leaves Changuinola 1000 daily US$6, 6-7 hrs, one stop for refreshments but many police checks.

From Chiriquí Grande there is a spectacular road over the mountains, mostly paved but some rough stretches and some earthquake damage under repair, passing through virgin rain forest, the Cricamola Indian Reservation and the Fortuna hydroelectric plant, to Gualaca and finally Chiriquí on the Pan-American Highway E of David (the turn off is 10 km E of David, just after the Río Chiriquí bridge). Bus to David from Chiriquí Grande several daily, 3 hrs, US$7. Bus Panama City to Changuinola via Chiriquí Grande, ferry to Almirante, then road, departs Panama City from Calle 30 between Hotels *Dos Mares* and *Suloy* at 0500, none on Monday; leaves Changuinola from *Tropicana* restaurant opp Banco Nacional, 0645, 19 hrs, US$22.

At the continental divide (Km 56 from Pan-American Highway) there is a good restaurant, *Mary's*, buses stop here. On the southern side of the Fortuna Reserve is **Finca La Suiza**, owned by a Swiss couple, excellent for birdwatching on forest trails, very good food, comfortable accommodation with bath and hot water (rates are C for one person, D pp double, breakfast US$3.50, dinner US$8.50), contact through Mohne, Transportes Ferguson, David, F 75-0113, allowing 10 days for reservations. To get there from Gualaca: pass the sign to Los Planes (16.4 km) and the turning to Chiriquicito; 300m after this junction is the sign for the Fortuna Reserve, 1 km beyond the sign is the gate to the *Finca* on the right. There are basic rest stops with views of both oceans 20.5 and 22.5 km S of the continental divide. There is a 10m waterfall 3 km S of the divide. Going N from the continental divide to Chiriquí Grande is a cyclist's delight—good road, spectacular views, little traffic and downhill all the way.

Railways The banana railways provide links between Guabito on the Costa Rican frontier, Changuinola and Almirante. No passenger trains although passage can be negotiated with officials. Schedules and fares should be checked with the Chiriquí Land Company, T Almirante 78-8414.

To Costa Rica The bus from Changuinola to the frontier is marked 'Las Tablas'; it departs regularly from the bus station. Formalities for entry/exit for each country are performed at either end of the banana train bridge which crosses the frontier. Just a short walk over the bridge; onward ticket may not be asked for on the Costa Rican side.

Entering Panama from Costa Rica The border at Sixaola-Guabito is open 0800-1600 Panama time. If you need a visa or tourist card, best to obtain it in San José. Entry charge normally US$0.75 (receipt given) although if you already have a Visa you may not be charged, 30 days given if you already have a visa, 5 days' entry card if not, US$2 (extensions at Changuinola airport immigration, opens 0830—5 passport photos, photographer nearby charges US$7 for 6). Advance clocks 1 hr entering Panama.

No accommodation in **Guabito**; bus to Changuinola US$0.75, ½ hr (every ½ hr until 1700), or colectivo taxi, US$1.25 pp (private taxi US$10). If seeking cheap accommodation, cross border as early as possible in order to get as far as Almirante (US$1 by bus).

DARIEN AND HOW TO GET TO COLOMBIA

The Pan-American Highway ends at Yaviza; from there, if you want to cross by land to South America, it's on foot through the jungles of Darién. Alternative routes to Colombia are also given.

NB In planning your trip by land or along the coast to Colombia, remember there are strict rules on entry into Colombia and you must aim for either Turbo or Buenaventura to obtain your entry stamp. Failure to do this will almost certainly involve you in significant fines, accusations of illegal entry, or worse in Colombia. Also, do not enter Darién without first obtaining full details of which areas to avoid because of narcotics and guerrilla activities.

By Land The Pan-American Highway runs E 60 km from Panama City to the sizeable town of **Chepo**. From Chepo the Highway has been completed to Yaviza, 240 km from Panama City; it is gravel from Chepo until the last 30 km which are of earth (sometimes impassable in rainy season). 35 km E of Chepo it crosses the new Lago Bayano dam by bridge (the land to the N of the Highway as far as Cañazas is the **Reserva Indígena del Bayano**). There are no hotels or *pensiones* in Chepo, but if you are stuck there, ask at the fire station, they will be able to find a place for you. Strangers arriving in Chepo may be interrogated by police and told to return to Panama City.

Buses From Piquera bus terminal in Panama City, buses leave every 2 hrs 0630-1430 for Pacora, US$0.80, Chepo, US$1.60, Cañitas, 4 hrs, US$3.10, Arretí, 6 hrs, US$9 and Canglón, 8 hrs, US$11.20. Beyond, to Yaviza, in the dry season only, Jan-April, US$14, 10 hrs minimum.

Darién East of Chepo is Darién, almost half the area of Panama and almost undeveloped. Most villages are accessible only by air or river and on foot. At **Bahía Piñas** is the **Tropic Star Lodge**, where a luxury fishing holiday may be enjoyed on the sea and in the jungle for over US$1,000 a week. (Information from *Hotel El Panamá*.)

At the end of 1992, Panama and Colombia revealed a plan to build a road through the Darién Gap which includes environmental protection. Construction had been halted in the 1970s by a lawsuit filed by US environmental groups who feared deforestation, soil erosion, endangerment of indigenous groups and the threat of foot-and-mouth disease reaching the USA. Of course, the more people who walk the Darién Gap, the greater the pressure for building a road link. Consider, therefore, the environmental implications of crossing between Panama and Colombia just for the sake of it. The Darién Gap road linking Panama with Colombia will not be open for many years, though, so the usual way of getting to Colombia is by sea or air. It is possible to go overland: the journey is in fact more expensive than going by air, and while still challenging, the number of travellers going overland is increasing.

Notes and Cautions Anyone considering crossing the Darién Gap overland should bear in mind that the area is becoming less safe because of the activities of drug traffickers, bandits and guerrillas, mostly from Colombia, but operating both sides of the border. The New Tribes Mission, after the kidnap of 3 missionaries, has withdrawn its staff from the area and therefore one of a traveller's main sources of assistance has disappeared. Ed Culberson (see below) endorses the following advice.

1. The best time to go is in the dry months (Jan-mid April); in the wet season (from May) it is only recommended for the hardy.

2. Travel with a reliable campanion or two.

3. Talk to knowledgeable locals for the best advice. Hire at least one Indian guide, but do it through the village *corregidor*, whose involvement may add to the reliability of the guides he selects. (Budget up to US$8/day per guide and his food. Negotiate with the chief, but do not begrudge the cost.)

4. Travel light and move fast. The journey as described below takes about 7 days to Turbo.

5. Maps of the Darién area can be purchased from the Ministro de Obras Públicas, Instituto Geográfico Nacional Tommy Guardia, in Panama City (US$5, reported to contain serious mistakes). Information is also available from Asociación Nacional de Conservación de la Naturaleza, near *Discoteca Magic*, Calle 53 Bella Vista, Panamá City.

The main villages (Yaviza, Púcuro, Paya and Cristales) have electricity, radios and cassette decks, canned food is available in Yaviza, Púcuro and Paya (but no gasoline), only the Chocó Indians and the Cuna women retain traditional dress. Organized jungle tours to Cuna Indians, Chocó Indians and the Río Bayano costing from US$65 to over US$300 can be purchased through Mar Go Tours, Aptdo 473, Balboa.

The bus service from Panama City (see above) has its problems, the road is bad and may be washed out after rains. Find out before you leave how far you can get. Alternatively there is an irregular boat, about once a week. The only sleeping accommodation is the deck and there is one primitive toilet for about 120 people. The advertised travel time is 16 hrs, but it can take as much as 2 days. Another possbility is to fly to Yaviza/El Real (3 a week, US$68 return), or to La Palma (**see p 845**) and take the much shorter boat trip to Yaviza. There is only one hotel at **Yaviza** (**E** *Tres Américas*, basic, noisy, meals available but not very sanitary); there is a TB clinic run by a Canadian (who appreciates classical music and is good for up-to-date

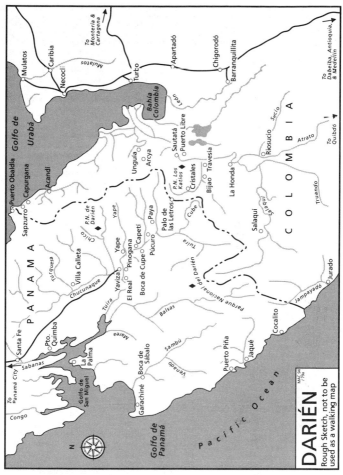

DARIÉN
Rough Sketch, not to be
used as a walking map

information), and a hospital. Crossing the river in Yaviza costs US$0.25. From Yaviza it is an easy 1-2 hr walk to **Pinogana** (small and primitive), where you have to cross the Río Tuira by dugout, US$1 pp. From Pinogana you can walk on, keeping the river to your left to Vista Alegre (3 hrs), recross the river and walk a further ½ hr to **Unión de Chocó** (some provisions and you can hammock overnight). 1 km upriver is Yape, on the tributary of the same name, then 3-4 hrs walking to Boca de Cupe. Alternatively you can go by motor dugout from Pinogana to Boca de Cupe (about US$15 pp). Or you can take a boat from Yaviza to **El Real** (US$10), where there is a very basic place to stay, **El Nazareno**, for US$6 a night. Directly opposite there is a lady who will prepare meals if given notice. From there take a motor dugout to Boca de Cupe, about US$12 pp (if possible, take a banana dugout, otherwise bargain hard on boats). There are also boats from Panama City (at the harbour by the market in the old town) to El Real for US$12 pp inc meals. Boats from El Real are not very frequent and may only go as far as Unión de Chocó or Pinogana. There are various other combinations of going on foot or by boat, prices for boat trips vary widely, so negotiate. They tend to be lower going downstream than up. It is wise to make payment always on arrival.

Stay the night at **Boca de Cupe** with a family; food and cold beer on sale here (last possibility if you are going through to Colombia); **Restaurant Nena** (blue building near landing dock) meals US$2, good information. You can go with Chocó Indians to Unión de Chocó, stay one or two days with them and share some food (they won't charge for lodging). Chocós are very friendly and shy, better not to take pictures. In Boca de Cupe get your exit stamp (though you may be told to get it at Púcuro) and keep your eye on your luggage. Lodging in Boca de Cupe for US$12.50 with Antonio (son of María who helped many hikers crossing Darién, but who died in 1989). Don Ramón will prepare meals for US$2 and let you sleep on his floor. From Boca de Cupe to Púcuro, dugout, US$20-50, to Paya (if river level high enough) US$80. We have not heard of anyone doing the section Boca de Cupe-Púcuro on foot.

Púcuro is a Cuna Indian village and it is customary to ask the chief's permission to stay (he will ask to see your passport – immigration here, if arriving from Colombia, can be very officious). The women wear colourful ornamented *molas* and gold rings through their noses. There is a small shop selling tinned meats, salted biscuits etc. Visitors usually stay in the assembly house. People show little interest in travellers there; stop with your luggage. From Púcuro you can walk through lush jungle to Paya, 6 hrs (guide costs US$20, not really necessary, do not pay in advance), which was the capital of the Cuna empire. From Púcuro to Paya there are 4 river crossings. The path is clear after the first kilometre.

In **Paya** you may be able to stay in the assembly house at the village, but it is mandatory to go 2 km away eastwards to the barracks. You can stay there, US$2.50 pp, rec (passport check, baggage search and, on entry into Panama at least, all gear is treated with a chemical which eats plastic and ruins leather—wash it off as soon as possible), and for US$2-2.50 you will get meals. The Cuna Indians in Paya are more friendly than in Púcuro. From Paya there are two routes.

First, from Paya, the next step is a 4-6 hr walk to **Palo de las Letras**, the frontier stone, where you enter Los Katios, one of Colombia's National Parks (see below). The path is not difficult, but frequently blocked up to the frontier. From there you go down until you reach the left bank of the Tulé river (in 3 hrs, no water between these points), you follow it downstream, which involves 7 crossings (at the third crossing the trail almost disappears, so walk along the river bed—if possible—to the next crossing). If any of these watercourses are dry, watch out for snakes. About ½ hr after leaving this river you cross a small creek; 45 mins further on is the abandoned camp of the Montadero, near where the Tulé and Pailón rivers meet to form the Río Cacarica. Cross the Cacarica and follow the trail to the Inderena at **Cristales** (7 hrs from Palo de las Letras). Guides Paya-Cristales (they always go in pairs), US$55. If you insist on walking beyond Montadero, a machete, compass and fishing gear (or extra food) are essential; the path is so overgrown that it is easier, when the river is low, to walk and swim down it (Cristales is on the left bank, so perhaps it would be better to stick to this side). The rangers at Cristales (friendly) may sell you food, will let you sleep at the hut, cook, and will take you, or arrange a dugout to **Bijao** (or Viajado), 2 hrs, for around US$30-40 pp. The rangers are often not there and there is no village nearby, so arrive prepared. It is possible to walk to Bijao down the right (W) bank of the Río Cacarica (heavy going). From the bend to the E of the river the path improves and it is 1 hr to Bijao. At Bijao ask for the Inderena station, where you can eat and sleep (floor space, or camp). From Bijao a motor dugout runs to **Travesía** (also called Puerto América) for US$30 pp (2-3 hrs), from where motorboats go to Turbo for US$6 to US$10 (in scheduled boat—if it stops; if not it'll cost you about US$130 to hire a boat). Once again, there is a walking route S to Limón (2 hrs) and E to La Tapa (½ hr). A cargo boat may be caught from here to Turbo (1994 price unknown). One *residencial* and a shop in Travesía. The last section from Travesía down the Atrato goes through an area full of birdlife, humming birds, kingfishers, herons, etc, and 'screamers', about the size of turkeys and believed to be unique to the Atrato valley. The river enters the Great Atrato swamp and thence to the Bahía de Colombia. Turbo is on the opposite coast.

On arrival in Turbo, you must go to the DAS office in the barracks on the water-front to get your entrance stamp. If you fail to do this, you will have to wait until Cartagena, or elsewhere, and then explain yourself in great detail to DAS and quite likely be fined. If you arrive at the weekend and the DAS is closed, make sure you obtain a letter or document from the police in Turbo that states when you arrived in Colombia. The problems with this route are mostly on the Colombian side, where route finding is difficult, the undergrowth very difficult to get through, and the terrain steep. Any rain adds greatly to the difficulties, though equally, when the water is low, boats need more pole assistance, and the cost increases. As a general guide, a party of four can cross from Yaviza to Turbo for about US$160 pp (1993).

If you are coming into Panama from Colombia by these routes, and you have difficulty in obtaining entry stamps at Púcuro or Boca de Cupe, obtain a document from an official en route stating when you arrived in Panama. This may be equally hard to get, but the missionaries may be able to give advice. Then go to the Oficina Nacional de Migración in Panama City (who may send you to the port immigration) and explain the problem. One traveller reports hearing of several arrests of travellers caught without their entry stamp. Many of these 'illegals' stay arrested for weeks. It may help to be able to prove that you have sufficient money to cover your stay in Panama.

The **Katios National Park** (**Warning**: entry by motorized vehicle is prohibited), extending in Colombia to the Panamanian border, can be visited with mules from the Inderena headquarters in Sautatá (rangers may offer free accommodation, very friendly). In the park is the Tilupo waterfall, 125m high; the water cascades down a series of rock staircases, surrounded by orchids and fantastic plants. Also in the park are the Alto de la Guillermina, a mountain behind which is a strange forest of palms called 'mil pesos', and the Ciénagas de Tumaradó, with red monkeys, waterfowl and alligators.

The second route from Paya is a strenuous hike up the Paya river valley through dense jungle (machete country) for about 16 hrs to the last point on the Paya (fill up with water), then a further 3 hrs to the continental divide where you cross into Colombia. Down through easier country (3-4 hrs) brings you to *Unguía* (accommodation, restaurants) where motor boats are available to take you down the Río Tarena, out into the Gulf of Urabá, across to Turbo. This trip should not be taken without a guide, though you may be lucky and find an Indian, or a group of Indians making the journey and willing to take you along. They will appreciate a gift when you arrive in Unguía. Hazards include blood-sucking ticks, the inevitable mosquitoes and, above all, thirst.

There are many other possible routes from Panama crossing the land frontier used by locals. Most involve river systems and are affected by water levels. There are few tracks and no reliable maps. We have heard of successful crossings using the Ríos Salaqui and Balsas, and a land route Jaqué-Jurado-Riosucio. Good guides and serious planning are essential.

Dr Richard Dawood, author of *Travellers' Health: How to Stay Healthy Abroad*, and photographer Anthony Dawton, crossed the Darien Gap at the end of the wet season (November). We are pleased to include Dr Dawood's health recommendations for such a journey: **Heat** Acclimatization to a hot climate usually takes around 3 weeks. It is more difficult in humid climates than in dry ones, since sweat cannot evaporate easily, and when high humidity persists through the night as well, the body has no respite. (In desert conditions, where the temperature falls at night, adaptation is much easier.) Requirements for salt and water increase dramatically under such conditions. We had to drink 12 litres per day to keep pace with our own fluid loss on some parts of the trip.

We were travelling under extreme conditions, but it is important to remember that the human thirst sensation is not an accurate guide to true fluid requirements. In hot countries it is always essential to drink beyond the point of thirst quenching, and to drink sufficient water to ensure that the urine is consistently pale in colour.

Salt losses also need to be replaced. Deficiency of salt, water, or both, is referred to as heat exhaustion; lethargy, fatigue, and headache are typical features, eventually leading to coma and death. Prevention is the best approach, and we used the pre-salted water regime pioneered by Colonel Jim Adam and followed by the British Army; salt is added to all fluids, one quarter of a level teaspoon (approx 1 gram) per pint—to produce a solution that is just below the taste theshold. Salt tablets, however, are poorly absorbed, irritate the stomach and may cause vomiting; plenty of pre-salted fluid should be the rule for anyone spending much time outdoors in the tropics. (Salted biscuits are recommended by Darién travellers.)

Sun Overcast conditions in the tropics can be misleading. The sun's rays can be fierce, and it is important to make sure that all exposed skin is constantly protected with a high factor sun screen—preferably waterproof for humid conditions. This was especially important while we were travelling by canoe. A hat was also essential.

Food and Water Diarrhoea can be annoying enough in a luxurious holiday resort with comfortable sanitary facilities. The inconvenience under jungle conditions would have been more than trivial, however, with the added problem of coping with further fluid loss and dehydration.

Much caution was therefore needed with food hygiene. We carried our own supplies, which we prepared carefully ourselves: rather uninspiring camping fare, such as canned tuna fish, sardines, pasta, dried soup, biscuits and dried fruit. In the villages, oranges, bananas and coconuts were available. The freshly baked bread was safe, and so would have been the rice.

We purified our water with 2% tincture of iodine carried in a small plastic dropping bottle, 4 drops to each litre—more when the water is very turbid—wait 20 mins before drinking. This method is safe and effective, and is the only suitable technique for such conditions.

(Another suggestion from Peter Ovenden is a water purifying pump based on a ceramic filter. There are several on the market, Peter used a Katadyn. It takes about a minute to purify a litre of water. When the water is cloudy, eg after rain, water pumps are less effective and harder work. Take purification tablets as back-up—Ed.) It is also worth travelling with a suitable antidiarrhoeal medication such as Arret.

Malaria Drug resistant malaria is present in the Darien area, and antimalarial medication is essential. We took Paludrine, two tablets daily, and chloroquine, two tablets weekly. Free advice on antimalarial medication for all destinations is available from the Malaria Reference Laboratory, T (071) 636 7921 in the UK. An insect repellent is also essential, and so are precautions to avoid insect bites.

Insects Beside malaria and yellow fever, other insect-borne diseases such as dengue fever and leishmaniasis may pose a risk. The old fashioned mosquito net is ideal if you have to sleep outdoors, or in a room that is not mosquito-proof. Mosquito nets for hammocks are widely available in Latin America. An insecticide spray is valuable for clearing your room of flying insects before you go to sleep, and mosquito coils that burn through the night giving off an insecticidal vapour, are also valuable.

Ticks It is said that ticks should be removed by holding a lighted cigarette close to them, and we had an opportunity to put this old remedy to the test. We duly unwrapped a pack of American duty-frees that we had preserved carefully in plastic just for such a purpose, as our Indian guides looked on in amazement, incredulous that we should use these prized items for such a lowly purpose. The British Army expedition to Darien in 1972 carried 60,000 cigarettes among its supplies, and one wonders if they were for this purpose! The cigarette method didn't work, but caused much amusement. (Further discussion with the experts indicates that the currently favoured method is to ease the tick's head gently away from the skin with tweezers.)

Columbia University advises covering the tick with a few drops of thick olive oil or mineral oil (or a few drops of kerosine or gasoline) to immobilize and suffocate the tick. Then the tick may be gently removed with a pair of tweezers—Ed.

Vaccinations A yellow fever vaccination certificate is required from all travellers arriving from infected areas, and vaccination is advised for personal protection.

Immunization against hepatitis A (see **Health Information** in the Introduction) and typhoid are strongly advised.

Attacks by dogs are relatively common: the new rabies vaccine is safe and effective, and carrying a machete for the extra purpose of discouraging animals is advised.

In addition, all travellers should be protected against tetanus, diptheria and polio.

You can get some food along the way, but take enough for at least 5 days. Do take, though, a torch/flashlight, and a bottle of rum (or similar!) for the ranger at Cristales and useful items for others who give help and information. Newspapers are of interest to missionaries etc. A compass can save your life in the remoter sections if you are without a guide–getting lost is the greatest danger according to the rangers. It is highly recommended to travel in the dry season only, when there is no mud and fewer mosquitoes. Ticks can be a problem, especially on the Colombian side. A hammock can be very useful. If you have time, bargains can be found, but as pointed out above, costs of guides and water transport are steadily increasing. Buying pesos in Panama is recommended as changing dollars when you enter Colombia will be at poor rates. You will need small denomination dollar notes on the trip.

Taking a motorcycle through Darién is not an endeavour to be undertaken lightly, and cannot be recommended. Ed Culberson (who, in 1986 after two unsuccessful attempts, was the first to accomplish the feat) writes: 'Dry season passage is comparatively easy on foot and even with a bicycle. But it simply cannot be done with a standard sized motorcycle unless helped by Indians at a heavy cost in dollars...It is a very strenuous, dangerous adventure, often underestimated by motorcyclists, some who have come to untimely ends in the jungle.' Culberson's account of his Journey (in the October 1986 issue of *Rider* and in a book, *Obsessions Die Hard*, published 1991 by Gazelle Book Services, Lancaster, England, T 0524-68765) makes harrowing reading, not least his encounter with an emotionally unstable police offical in Bijao; the 46-km 'ride' from Púcuro to Palo de las Letras took 6 days with the help of 6 Indians (at US$8 a day each). Two riders were caught in an early start of rains in 1991 and barely escaped with their machines.

Not to be outdone, crossing by bicycle has been successfully completed. David Pindar of Sale, Cheshire did the trip in February 1990. He followed the usual route from Yaviza to Cristales taking about a week. The most difficult sections were to Unión de Chocó, and over the divide between Paya and Cristales mainly owing to overgrown paths. He actually rode between Púcuro and Paya but unfortunately a tree branch got caught in the wheel, broke two spokes and bent the rear gear changer.

By Sea There are about two boats a week from Colón for San Andrés Island (**see next chapter**), from which there are connections with Cartagena; the *Johnny Walker* takes 30 hrs, but the service is very irregular and travellers have sometimes waited over a week in vain. There are (contraband) boats from Coco Solo, Colón, to the Guajira Peninsula, Colombia. 3-day journey, uncomfortable, and entirely at your own risk; captains of these boats are reluctant to carry travellers (and you may have to wait days for a sailing—the customs officials will let you sleep in the wind-shadow of their office, will watch your luggage and let you use the sanitary facilities). A passenger travelling in a contraband boat had some problems in the DAS office about getting an entrance stamp: they wanted official papers from the boat's captain showing that he brought him in. You have to bargain for your fare on these boats. Accommodation is a little primitive. Boats also leave, irregularly, from the Coco Solo wharf in Colón (minibus from Calle 12, 15 mins, US$0.30) for **Puerto Obaldía**, via the San Blas Islands. These are small boats and give a rough ride in bad weather. There are flights with Ansa (T 267891/266881) and Transpasa (T 260932/260843) at 0600-0630 from Paitilla, Panama City to Puerto Obaldía daily except Sunday for US$40 single (book well in advance). There are also flights with Aerotaxi and Saansa to Puerto Obaldía. Puerto Obaldía is a few km from the Colombian border. There are *expresos* (speedboats) from Puerto Obaldía (after clearing Customs) to Capurgana, and then another on to Acandí (**F** *Hotel Central*, clean, safe; **G** *Hotel Pilar*, safe). From Acandí you can go on to Turbo, on the Gulf of Urabá, no fixed schedule (you cannot get to Turbo in the same day; take shade and drinks and be prepared for seasickness). From Turbo, Medellín can be reached by road. Walk from Puerto Obaldía to Zapzurro, just beyond the frontier, for a dugout to Turbo, US$10, where you must get your Colombia entry stamp. It seems that most of the boats leaving Puerto Obaldía for Colombian ports are contraband boats. One traveller obtained an unnecessary visa (free) from the Colombian consul in Puerto Obaldía which proved to be useful in Colombia where soldiers and police took it to be an entry stamp.

There is a good *pensión* in Puerto Obaldía: *Residencia Cande*, nice and clean (E) which also serves very good meals for US$1.50. Book in advance for meals. Also in Puerto Obaldía are shops, Colombian consulate, Panamanian immigration, but nowhere to change travellers' cheques until well into Colombia (not Turbo); changing cash is possible. (**NB** Arriving in Puerto Obaldía you have to pass through the military control for baggage search, immigration—proof of funds and onward ticket asked for, and malaria control).

Alternatively one can get from Puerto Obaldía to Acandí on the Colombian side of the border, either by walking 9 hrs or by hiring a dugout or a launch to Capurgana (US$60), thence another launch at 0715, 1 hr, US$3. Several hotels in **Capurgana**, **E** *Almar*, T 24889, Medellín, for reservations, **B** *Calypso* also with a Medellín number for reservations, 2503921, **D** *Naútico*, **E** *Uvita*, clean, safe. There are cheaper *pensiones* and you can camp near the beach. Good snorkelling. There is a Panamanian consul in Capurgana (Roberto) who issues Panamanian visas. There are Twin Otter flights to Medellín. To walk to Capurgana takes 4 hrs, guide recommended (they charge US$10); first to go to La Miel (2 hrs), then to Zapzurro (20 mins), where there are shops and cabins for rent, then 1-1½ hrs to Capurgana. Most of the time the path follows the coast, but there are some hills to cross (which are hot—take drinking water). From Acandí a daily boat is scheduled to go at 0800 to Turbo (US$8, 3 hrs). Take pesos, if possible, to these Colombian places, the rate of exchange for dollars is poor.

On the Pacific side, there is another possible route to Colombia. Although not quick, it is relatively straightforward (spoken Spanish is essential). Take a bus from Panama (Plaza 5 de Mayo) to **Santa Fe**, which is 100 km short of Yaviza and off to the S, a rough but scenic 6-8 hrs (US$8, 3 a day, check times). In Santa Fe it is possible to camp near the national guard post (no *pensiones*). Then hitch a ride on a truck (scarce), or walk 2 hrs to the Río Sabanas at Puerto Lardo (11 km) where you must take a dugout or launch to La Palma, or hire one (US$5, 2 hrs; also reached by boat from Yaviza, US$3, 8 hrs—bank changes travellers' cheques in La Palma). **La Palma** is the capital of Darién; it has one *pensión* (friendly, English-speaking owners, F, pricey, with cooking and laundry facilities, or see if you can stay with the *guardia*). There are regular flights from Panama City to La Palma, daily at 0630 US$31, returning at 0900, to Jaqué, US$33.50 three days a week and to Yaviza, also three days a week, but check with the airline Parsa, T 26-3883/3803. They have an office at the Paitilla airport in Panama City. It is not clear if you can get a plane from La Palma to Jaque, but there are boats. *Jaqué* is on the Pacific coast, near Puerto Piña, 50 km N of the Colombian border.

Alternatively, at the Muelle Fiscal in Panama City (next to the main waterfront market, near Calle 13), ask for a passenger boat going to Jaqué. The journey takes 18 hrs, is cramped and passengers cook food themselves, but costs only US$12. Jaqué (pop 1,000) is only reached by sea or air (the airstrip is used mostly by the wealthy who come for sport fishing); there are small stores with few fruit and vegetables, a good *comedor*, one *hospedaje*, **F** *Hospedaje Chauela*, clean, basic, friendly (but it is easy to find accommodation with local families), and camping is possible anywhere on the beautiful 4 km beach. The guard post is open every day and gives exit stamps. Canoes from Jaqué go to Jurado (US$20, 4½ hrs) or Bahía Solano (US$45, 160 km, with two overnight stops) in Chocó. The first night is spent in Jurado (where the boat's captain may put you up and the local military commander may search you out of curiosity). There are flights from Jurado to Turbo, but it is possible to get 'stuck' in Jurado for several days. Bahía Solano is a deep-sea fishing resort with an airport and *residencias*. Flights from Bahía Solano go to Quibdó, connecting to Cali (with Satena), or Medellín (all flights have to be booked in advance; the town is popular with Colombian tourists). On this journey, you sail past the lush, mountainous Pacific coast of Darién and Chocó, with its beautiful coves and beaches, and you will see a great variety of marine life.

NB It is not easy to get a passage to any of the larger Colombian ports as the main shipping lines rarely take passengers. Those that do are booked up well in advance. The Agencias Panamá company, Muelle 18, Balboa, represents Delta Line and accepts passengers to Buenaventura. Anyone interested in using the Delta Line ships should book a passage before arriving in Panama. The only easy way of getting to Colombia is to fly. Copa, SAM and Lacsa fly to Medellín, Cartagena and Barranquilla.

Shipping agencies have not the authority to charge passages. Many travellers think they can travel as crew on cargo lines, but this is not possible because Panamanian law requires all crew taken on in Panama to be Panamanian nationals.

Colombia officially demands an exit ticket from the country. If you travel by air the tickets should be bought outside Panama and Colombia, which have taxes on all international air tickets. If you buy air tickets from IATA companies, they can be refunded. Copa tickets can be refunded in Cartagena (Calle Santos de Piedra 3466—takes 4 days), Barranquilla—2 days, Cali or Medellín. Refunds in pesos only. Copa office in Panama City, Av Justo Arosemena y Calle 39, T 27-5000.

Shipping a Vehicle from Panama to Colombia, Venezuela or Ecuador is not easy or cheap. The best advice is to shop around the agencies in Panama City or Colón to see what is available when you want to go. Both local and international lines take vehicles, and sometimes passengers, but schedules and prices are very variable. 1993 prices were on average US$750 without a container, US$1,500-1,800 in a container, eg Sudamericana de Vapores, T 29-3844, Cristóbal-Buenaventura, with container US$1,500, without US$80/cu m; Boyd Steamship Corporation, T 63-6311, Balboa-Buenaventura or Guayaquil in container US$1,700. In March 1992, a German couple shipped a VW camper for about US$1000 to Cartagena, including themselves, on a small freighter with the help of steamship agent Captain Newball, Edif Los Cristales, 3 Piso, Calle 38 y Av Cuba, Panama City. On the same route Central American Lines sail once a week, agent in Panama, T Colón 412880, Panama City 361036. An American couple shipped their 4WD Toyota from Colón to Cartagena for US$700 in 1993 with Geminís Shipping Co SA, Apdo Postal No 3016, Zona Libre de Colón, Rep de Panamá, T 41-6269/41-6959, F 41-6571. Mr Ricardo Gil was helpful and reliable. If sending luggage separately, make enquiries at Tocumen airport. Tampa, T 38-4439, charged US$70/kg Panama-Cali in 1993.

One alternative is to try to ship on one of the small freighters that occasionally depart from Coco Solo Wharf in Colón for Turbo in Colombia, which allow you to travel with your car. Obviously there is a considerable element of risk involved (suspect cargo, crews and seaworthiness), though the financial cost is not very great, about US$500.

Once you have a bill of lading, have it stamped by a Colombian consulate. Note that the Colombian consul in Colón will only stamp a bill of lading if the carrier is going to Cartagena or Barranquilla. The consulate also provides tourist cards. They require proof, in the form of a letter from your Embassy (or the Embassy representing your country in Panama) that you do not intend to sell the car in Colombia, though this requirement is usually dispensed with. Then go to the customs office in Panama City (Calle 80 and 55) to have the vehicle cleared for export. After that the vehicle details must be removed from your passport at the customs office at the port of departure. In Colón the customs office is behind the post office; in Cristóbal, at the entrance to the port on your left. The utmost patience is needed for this operation as regulations change frequently, so do not expect it to be the work of a few minutes.

Some small freighters go only to intermediate ports such as San Andrés, and it is then necessary to get another freighter to Cartagena. Navieras Mitchell ship cars regularly to San Andrés and Barranquilla. Office at Coco Solo Wharf, T 416942. You may have to wait up to a week in San Andrés to make the onward connection. From Colón to San Andrés takes 2 days and from San Andrés to Cartagena takes 3 days. There are two boats plying regularly between Colón (Pier 3) and San Andrés that are big enough for vans, but there is no schedule; they leave when they finish loading. There are also two regular boats between San Andrés and Cartagena; each stays in port about 15 days, but it can be longer. Shipping companies on San Andrés know that they have a monopoly, so take care when dealing with them and do not believe all they tell you.

Customs formalities at the Colombian end will take 1-3 days to clear (customs officials do not work at weekends). Make sure the visa you get from the Colombian consulate in Colón is *not* a 15 day non-extendable transit visa, but a regular tourist visa, because it is difficult to get an extension of the original visa. Clearance from the Colombian consul at the Panamanian port of embarkation may reduce the bureaucracy when you arrive in Colombia, but it will cost you US$10. In Colombia you have to pay US$15 per cu m for handling, as well as other document charges. An agent can reduce the aggravation but neither the waiting time, nor the cost (they charge US$55-70 per day). Get as much help as possible inside the port; outside they only want your money, in Buenaventura at least. It is understood that Cartagena is much more efficient (and therefore less expensive) as far as paperwork is concerned. Apparently the delays and redtape at either end of the passage to Colombia may be reduced if you have a *Carnet de Passages*. The Carnet will exempt you from the bond of 10% of the vehicle's value.

TNE (Transportes Navieros Ecuatorianos, T 69-2022) ship vehicles to Guayaquil for US$770 in container (1993 price), leaves Thurs, 4 days; agent in Cristóbal, Agencia Continental SA, T 45-1818. Do not ship or fly your vehicle to Ecuador without the *Carnet de Passages*, or you may be held up for up to two weeks at customs, and only allowed to continue to Peru with a police escort! Seek advice on paperwork from the Ecuadorean consul in Panama. Barwil (T Panama City 63-7755, Colón 41-5533) will ship vehicles to Arica, Chile, US$470 for a Chevrolet Sprint, US$685 for a jeep, container used, rec, 1993 prices.

It is also possible to ship a vehicle to **Venezuela**, from Cristóbal usually to La Guaira, but Puerto Cabello is possible. 1993 price: Cia Transatlántica España, T 69-6300, US$1,700 in container to La Guaira. Also Barwil Agencies, T 63-7755 (see above), US$400 without container. Also Vencaribe (a Venezuelan line), agent in Cristóbal: Associated Steamship, T 52-12-58 (Panamá), 45-04-61 (Cristóbal). There are several agencies in Colón/Cristóbal across the street from the Chase Manhattan Bank and next door to the YMCA building. Formalities before leaving can be completed through a travel agency—recommended is Continental Travel Agency, at the *Hotel Continental*, T 63-61-62—Rosina Wong was very helpful.

Warning The contents of your vehicle are shipped at your own risk—generally considered to be a high one! Anything loose, tools, seat belts, etc, is liable to disappear, or to be swapped for an inferior replacement (eg spare tyre). One reader who escaped theft had chained two padlocked, wooden boxes to the car seats.

Air-freighting a Vehicle Most people ship their vehicles from Panama to South America by sea but some find air-freighting much more convenient. Generally it is faster and avoids many of the unpleasant customs hassles, but is more expensive. Prices vary considerably. The major carriers (Avianca, Ecuatoriana), if they permit it on a regular commercial flight, tend to charge more than the cargo lines and independents. In 1994, TLN's rate to anywhere in Colombia for a vehicle was US$1,600, while Challenge Air Cargo (T 26-7161) charged US$1,700. Prices and availability change from month to month depending on the demand by regular commercial shippers. You are generally not allowed to accompany the vehicle. For Copa Cargo, T 384414, Tocumen airport, talk to Otto Littman. Varig will ship vehicles to Brazil (Rio), Buenos Aires or Santiago de Chile for US$6,000 (1994 price). Taking a motorcycle from Panama to Colombia can only be done on a cargo flight. In 1994 CAC carried motorcycles between Panama and Colombia; approx US$150 for a 200 kg bike, pallet system, good service, bargaining may be possible for a smaller bike or for several bikes. Drain oil and gasoline, and remove battery before loading; the bike goes in with just an inch to spare so you must expect a scratch or two. Insist on loading the bike yourself. Having bought your passenger ticket, and checked bike in at the carrier's office, go to customs in Paitilla airport (**see p 823**) with your entry permit and freight papers, and pay US$4.20 to have stamp cancelled in passport. You may have to take your airweighbill to the Colombian Consulate for stamping 3 hrs before flight time. Allow 2 days in Panama. Retrieving the bike in Colombia, although costing very little (US$10 approx.), will take from 0900 to 1630 for paperwork (or up to 2 days if there are any peculiarities in your documents).

INFORMATION FOR VISITORS

Documents Visitors must have a passport, together with a tourist card (issued for 30 days and renewable for another 60 in the Immigration Office, Panama City, see below) or a visa (issued for 30 days, extendable to 90 days in Panama). Tourist cards are available at borders, from Panamanian consulates, Ticabus or airlines. To enter Panama you must have an onward flight ticket, travel agent confirmation of same, or, if entering by land, sufficient funds to cover your stay (US$550; US$300 may be asked for if you have an onward ticket). 'Sufficient funds' do not have to be in cash; credit cards and travellers' cheques accepted. One traveller reported that he was forced to buy a bus ticket from David to San José, US$10, which he was unable to get refunded. At Puerto Obaldía (Darién), both an onward ticket and funds are asked for. Once in Panama, you cannot get a refund for an onward flight ticket unless you have another exit ticket. Copa tickets can be refunded at any office in any country (in the currency of that country). **Customs at Paso Canoas**, at the border with Costa Rica, have been known to run out of tourist cards. If not entering Panama at the main entry points (Tocumen airport, Paso Canoas), expect more complicated arrangements.

Neither visas nor tourist cards are required by nationals of Austria, Costa Rica, Finland, Germany, Honduras, Spain, Switzerland and the UK.

Citizens of the following countries need a visa which is free: USA, the Netherlands, Norway, Denmark, Colombia and Mexico. Before visiting Panama it is advisable to enquire at a Panamanian consulate whether you need a visa stamped in your passport, or whether a tourist card will suffice. Citizens of the United States, for example, may buy a tourist card at a border for US$5 instead of a visa. A visa costing the local equivalent of £10 (US$10 in Central American capitals) must be obtained by citizens of Australia, New Zealand, Canada, Japan, France, Italy, Sweden, Israel, El Salvador, Dominican Republic. Visas for citizens of many African, Eastern European and Asian countries require authorization from Panama, which takes 3 days (this includes Hong Kong, India, Poland, the former Soviet republics, and also Cuba and South Africa).

30-day tourist cards can be renewed for another 60 days; requirements are 2 passport photos, a ticket out of the country, a letter explaining why you wish to extend your stay, proof of sufficient funds may be asked for. Obtainable from Departamento de Inmigración y Naturalización; an exit permit will also be necessary from Ministerio de Hacienda y Tesoro. Addresses of both offices are given under Panama City.

Taxes An airport tax of US$20 has to be paid by all passengers (cash only). There is a 5.5% tax on air tickets purchased in Panama.

Air Services From London: British Airways, American, Delta, Continental or Virgin Atlantic to Miami, then by American, United, Copa, or LAB to Panama City. From elsewhere in North America: New York City, Continental via Houston, or American or United, change planes in Miami; from Los Angeles, Aviateca (4 stops), Continental (via Houston), American (via Miami) or Lacsa (via San José); from San Francisco, Taca and Continental; from Houston, Continental, Taca. From Mexico, Aeroperú, Copa, or connections with Lacsa via San José, Taca via San Salvador, or American via Miami. From Central America, Copa, Lacsa (to San José, to connect with its Central American network and Los Angeles/Mexico/Miami/New Orleans/ San Juan-Puerto Rico routes), Taca (including to Belize) and Nica. There are no direct flights to Tegucigalpa, only Lacsa with connection in San José or Taca in San Salvador, but Copa flies direct to San Pedro Sula. Copa also flies to Kingston and Santo Domingo. From South America, Lacsa (Barranquilla, Caracas, Lima, Santiago de Chile), Copa (Barranquilla, Bogotá, Cartagena, Cali, Medellín, Quito, Guayaquil). Note that one-way tickets are not available from Colombia to Panama, on SAM, or Copa, but a refund on an unused return portion is possible, less 17% taxes, on SAM. To Bogotá direct with Avianca and Copa, be at airport very early because it can leave before time; also to Cali with Avianca. To Guayaquil, Continental (also to Quito), Aerolíneas Argentinas and AeroPerú. Cubana flies direct to Havana on Thursday, from Havana on Wednesday. Other carriers are Avianca, Servivensa, Lloyd Aéreo Boliviano, SAM, Aerolíneas Argentinas, AeroPerú. From Europe, Iberia (Madrid via Santo Domingo), KLM (from

Amsterdam via Curaçao), Aeroflot from Moscow and Shannon.

Customs Even if you only change planes in Panama you must have the necessary papers for the airport officials. Cameras, binoculars, etc, 500 cigarettes or 500 grams of tobacco and 3 bottles of alcoholic drinks for personal use are taken in free. The Panamanian Customs are strict; drugs without a doctor's prescription and books deemed 'subversive' are confiscated. In the latter case, a student's or teacher's card helps. **Note**: Passengers leaving Panama by land are *not* entitled to any duty-free goods, which are delivered only to ships and aircraft.

Internal Air Services There are local flights to most parts of Panama by the national airlines Ansa, Aeroperlas, Alas Chiricanas, Parsa, Aerotaxi and others. On all internal flights passengers must carry a passport and declare the weight of their luggage.

Roads Speed limit on the Inter-American Highway is 90 kmph (but 60 is more realistic when planning the day's drive); the toll stretch (US$0.60) between Chame and Panama City has a 100 kmph limit. Observe 40 kmph speed zones in villages. Most streets have no lighting, many hotel signs are unlit, etc, so try to be at your destination before dusk (about 1830 Jan, 1800 July). Right turn against a red light is legal in cities if no vehicles are approaching from the left. If charged with a traffic violation, you should receive a document stipulating the infraction; fines to be paid to Dirección Nacional de Tránsito y Transporte Terrestre (Departamento de Infracciones Menores, Panama City, T 62-5687). In general, Panamanian highway police are helpful and approachable, but some Spanish is an advantage.

Motoring Coming in by road from Costa Rica, passengers and vehicle (car or motorcycle) are given 30 days at the frontier. US$1 is payable for fumigation, US$3 for minibus. Exit calls for 4 papers which cost US$4.20 (obtainable, as are extensions for entry permits, from Customs in Paitilla airport). Taking a car with Panamanian plates to Costa Rica requires a lot of paperwork, eg proof of ownership, proof that the vehicle has not been stolen, etc. A travel agency eg Chadwick's in Balboa, will arrange this for you, for US$30. Rental cars are not allowed out of the country; they are marked by special license plates. Super grade gasoline costs US$1.80 per gallon, low octane US$1.72 and diesel US$1.25. For motorcyclists, note that a crash helmet must be worn. **Note** that you may not take dogs into Panama by car, though they may be flown or shipped in if they have general health and rabies certificates; dogs and cats now have to spend 40 days in quarantine after entry.

Note It used to be virtually impossible for a tourist to sell a car in Panama unless he /she can show (with help from the Consulate) that he/she needed the money for a fare home. A recent report (4/93) suggests that the whole procedure is now a lot easier. The vendor needs a document stating that the car has been sold, obtainable from a notary/lawyer. Taxes have to be paid by the buyer and if the title of the car is still in the seller's name, the buyer needs a similar document to be able to arrange all the paperwork at the Aduana/Customs. You have to authorize the buyer to pay the taxes for you by means of this document. A helpful address, both for finding potential buyers, and for the paperwork, is: Fernie and Co Shipping Agency, Sr Pérez, Panama City, English spoken. Another helpful office with English-speaking staff is in the same building as the Diablo Height supermarket (in the street across the railway from the main entry of Albrook air base), which deals with license plates, transfer of titles. A great many US service personnel use this facility. There is a bulletin board outside.

What to Eat Best hors d'oeuvre is *carimañola*, cooked mashed yuca wrapped round a savoury filling of chopped seasoned fried pork and fried a golden brown. The traditional stew, *sancocho*, made from chicken, yuca, dasheen, cut-up corn on the cob, plantain, potatoes, onions, flavoured with salt, pepper and coriander. *Ropa vieja*, shredded beef mixed with fried onions, garlic, tomatoes and green peppers and served with white rice, baked plantain or fried yuca. *Sopa borracha*, a rich sponge cake soaked in rum and garnished with raisins and prunes marinated in sherry. Panama is famous for its seafood: lobsters, corvina, shrimp, tuna, etc. Piquant *ceviche* is usually corvina or white fish seasoned with tiny red and yellow peppers, thin slices of onion and marinated in lemon juice; it is served very cold and has a bite. *Arroz con coco y tití* is rice with coconut and tiny dried shrimp. Plain coconut rice is also delicious. For low budget try *comida corriente* or *del día* (US$1.50 or so). Corn (maize) is eaten in various forms, depending on season, eg *tamales* (or *bollos*), made of corn meal mash filled with cooked chicken or pork, olives and prunes; or *empanadas*, toothsome meat pies fried crisp. Plantain, used as a vegetable, appears in various forms. A fine dessert is made from green plantain flour served with coconut cream. Other desserts are *arroz con cacao*, chocolate rice pudding; *buñuelos de viento*, a puffy fritter served with syrup; *sopa de gloria*, sponge cake soaked in cooked cream mixture with rum added; *guanábana* ice cream is made from sweet ripe soursop.

Tipping at hotels, restaurants: 10% of bill. Porters, 15 cents per item, but US$1 would be expected for assistance at the airport. Cloakroom, 25 cents. Hairdressers, 25 cents. Cinema usherettes, nothing. Taxi drivers don't expect tips; rates should be arranged before the trip.

Health No particular precautions are necessary. Water in Panama City and Colón is safe to drink. Yellow fever vaccination is recommended before visiting Darién. Malaria prophylaxis for that area is highly recommended. It is currently very difficult to obtain chloroquine in Panama; stock up before arrival. In fact, stock up with all medicines, they are very costly in Panama. Tampons (with applicator only) are available in Panama City at the same price as in UK. Hospital treatment is also expensive; insurance underwritten by a US company would be of great help.

Clothing Light weight tropical type clothes for men, light cotton or linen dresses for women, for whom the wearing of trousers is quite OK. The dry season, January-April, is the pleasantest time. Heavy rainfall sometimes in October and November.

Hours of Business Government departments, 0800-1200, 1230-1630 (Mon to Fri). Banks: open and close at different times, but are usually open all morning, but not on Sat. Shops and most private enterprises: 0700 or 0800-1200 and 1400-1800 or 1900 every day, including Sat.

Business interests are concentrated in Panama City and Colón.

British business travellers are advised to get 'Hints to Exporters: Panama' on application to DTI Export Publications, PO Box 55, Stratford-upon-Avon, Warwickshire, CV37 9GE.

Public Holidays 1 Jan: New Year's Day; 9 Jan: National Mourning; Shrove Tuesday: Carnival. Good Friday; 1 May: Labour Day (Republic); 15 Aug: Panama City only (O); 11 Oct: National Revolution Day; 1 Nov: National Anthem Day (O); 2 Nov: All Souls (O); 3 Nov: Independence Day; 4 Nov: Flag Day (O); 5 Nov: Independence Day (Colón only); 10 Nov: First Call of Independence; 28 Nov: Independence from Spain; 8 Dec: Mothers' Day; 25 Dec: Christmas Day.

O=Official holiday, when banks and government offices close. On the rest—national holidays—business offices close too. Many others are added at short notice.

School holidays are Dec-March when holiday areas are busy; make reservations in advance.

Festivals and music The *fiestas* in the towns are well worth seeing. That of Panama City at Carnival time, held on the four days before Ash Wednesday, is the best. During carnival women who can afford it wear the *pollera* dress, with its 'infinity of diminutive gathers and its sweeping skirt finely embroidered', a shawl folded across the shoulders, satin slippers, tinkling pearl hair ornaments in spirited shapes and colours. The men wear a *montuno* outfit: native straw hats, embroidered blouses and trousers sometimes to below the knee only, and carry the *chácara*, or small purse.

At the Holy Week ceremonies at Villa de Los Santos the farces and acrobatics of the big devils—with their debates and trials in which the main devil accuses and an angel defends the soul—the dance of the 'dirty little devils' and the dancing drama of the Montezumas are all notable. The ceremonies at Pesé (near Chitré) are famous all over Panama. For other festivals in this region, see under the **Azuero Peninsula**. At Portobelo, near Colón, there is a procession of little boats in the canals of the city. See under Portobelo for the *Congos*.

There are, too, the folk-tunes and dances. The music is cheerful, combining the rhythms of Africa with the melodic tones and dance-steps of Andalusia, to which certain characteristics of the Indian pentatonic scale have been added. The *tamborito* is the national dance. Couples dance separately and the song— which is sung by the women only, just as the song part of the *mejorana* or *socavón* is exclusively for male voices—is accompanied by the clapping of the audience and three kinds of regional drums. The *mejorana* is danced to the music of native guitars and in the interior are often heard the laments known as the *gallo* (rooster), *gallina* (hen), *zapatero* (shoemaker), or *mesano*. Two other dances commonly seen at *fiestas* are the *punto*, with its promenades and foot tapping, and the *cumbia*, of African origin, in which the dancers carry lighted candles and strut high.

The Guaymí Indians of Chiriquí province meet around 12 February to transact tribal business, hold feasts and choose mates by tossing balsa logs at one another; those unhurt in this contest, known as Las Balserías, are allowed to select the most desirable women.

Official time: GMT minus 5 hrs.

Currency Panama is one of the few countries in the world which issues no paper money; US banknotes are used exclusively, being called balboas instead of dollars. **Note**: There is great concern over counterfeit money in Panama; many establishments will not accept bills over US$20, some US$10. Change large denomination bills in hotels, as US$50 and US$100 notes are very difficult to change. There are 'silver' coins of 50c (called a *peso*), 25c, 10c, nickel of 5c (called a *real*) and copper of 1c. All the 'silver' money is used interchangeably with US currency; each coin is the same size and material as the US coin of equivalent value. You can take in or out any amount of foreign or Panamanian currency. Visa ATMs are available at branches of Telered (T 001-800-111-0016 if card is lost or stolen). Mastercard/Cirrus ATMs are available at 24 locations, in branches of Chase Manhattan and Banco del Istmo.

Living is costly, although food is much the same price as in Costa Rica. Military personnel buy their supplies at low prices in special stores. These facilities are not available to tourists. The annual average increase in consumer prices fluctuates in line with US trends.

Weights and Measures Both metric and the US system are used.

Electricity In modern homes and hotels, 220 volts. Otherwise 110 volt 3 phase, 60 cycles AC.

Foreign Postage Great care should be taken to address all mail as 'Republic of Panama' or 'RP', otherwise it is returned to sender. Air mail takes 3-10 days, sea mail 3-5 weeks from Britain. Rates (examples) for air mail (up to 15 grams) are as follows: Central, North and South America and Caribbean, 30c; Europe, 37c up to 10 grams, 5c for every extra 5 grams; Africa, Asia, Oceania, 44c; all air letters require an extra 2c stamp. Parcels to Europe can only be sent from the post office in the El Dorado shopping centre in Panama City (bus from Calle 12 to Tumba Muerta).

Post offices, marked with blue and yellow signs, are the only places permitted to sell stamps.

Telecommunications The radio station at Gatún is open to commercial traffic; such messages are handled through the Government telegraph offices. The telegraph and cable companies are given under the towns in which they operate. **Telex** is available at the airport, the cable companies and many hotels. Rate for a 3-min call to Britain is US$14.40, and US$4.80 for each minute more. **Telephone** calls can be made between the UK and Panama any time, day or night. Collect calls are possible. Minimum charge for 3 min call: US$10 station to station, but person to person, US$16 on weekdays, US$12 on Sun plus tax of US$1 on

To use AT&T USADirect® Service from Panama dial **109** from any phone. In the canal zone dial **281-0109**. If you require assistance, please call the AT&T office in Panama City at **63-5377**.

AT&T USADirect® Service.

852 PANAMA

each call. To the USA the charge is US$4 for 3 mins. Phone to Australia costs US$16 for 3 mins (US$13 on Sunday).

Inter-continental contact by satellite is laid on by the Pan-American Earth Satellite Station. The local company is Intercomsa.

Press *La Prensa* is the major local daily newspaper, others are *La Estrella de Panamá*, *La República*, *El Panamá América*, *Crítica Libre* and *El Siglo*. *Colón News* (weekly—Spanish and English). The imported *Miami Herald* and *USA Today* are widely available.

Language Spanish (hard to understand), but English is widely understood.

Tourist Information See under Panama City for address of IPAT, Instituto Panameño de Turismo. In USA: Laura Haayen, 1110 Brickell Ave, Suite 103, Miami, FL 33131, T (305) 579-2001, F 579-0910.

We are most grateful to Huw Clough and Kate Hennessy for updating the chapter, to Kevin Healey (Melbourne) for much new information on Panamá City and Colón, to Sean Hignett (Edinburgh) for a very useful contribution, to Ed Culberson (Palm Bay, Florida) for new information on Darién, and to the following travellers: Jack Bailey & Diana Musacchio (Santa Barbara, CA, USA), Sybille Böhme (Kahl/Rain, Germany), Ludwig M Brinckmann (Wohltorf, Germany), Ed Culberson (Palm Bay, FL, USA), Günther Deutinger (Saalfelden, Austria), Karl Griffith & Julie Duckworth (Preston, Lancashire), Frank Dux (Passau, Germany), Richard N Frank (Clearwater, FL, USA), Darrel Freeman (Lancaster, PA, USA), Edmund F Giesbert (Beverly Hills, California), Julio Gonzalez (Saint-Bonnet près Riom, France), Sally & Mike Hayden (Cheltenham, Glos), Sean Hignett (Edinburgh), a very interesting contribution, Toni Jöhr (Berne, Switzerland), Noel, Nenagh & Zoë Kemp (Lindisfarne, Australia), Johannes Latsch (Bad Homburg var der Höhe, Germany), Arthur V Lindo (Panama City), Gérald Lorin (Kourou, Guyane), Helmut Lüder (Potomac, MD, USA), James N Maas (Bocas del Toro, Panama), Thomas Meiberg (New York), Charles D Moody (Austin, Texas), Don Nafzigu (Kamloops, BC, Canada), Malcolm Parkes (Halesowen, West Midlands), Ray Peters (Panama), Dr Oscar Puls (Newport, Gwent), Claudio Rivero (Buenos Aires), Mark Schuringa (Amsterdam, Holland), Fredy Stadlin (Zug, Switzerland), Vincent Van Es (Enschede, Holland), Benderoth Vitus (Hadamar), C A Walker (San José, Costa Rica), Reto Wildschek (Kloten, Switzerland).

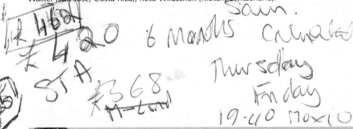

WILL YOU HELP US?

We do all we can to get our facts right in the MEXICO & CENTRAL AMERICAN HANDBOOK. Each section is thoroughly revised each year, but the territory is vast and our eyes cannot be everywhere. We are always pleased to hear about your travels; do write to us in as much detail as possible. In return we will send you information about our special guidebook offer.

 **TRADE & TRAVEL** *Handbooks*

Write to The Editor, Mexico & Central American Handbook, Trade & Travel, 6 Riverside Court, Lower Bristol Road, Bath BA2 3DZ. England

tonights
last 6m
pm £522.50   6 wks
£60.50
p.l.m

SAN ANDRES AND PROVIDENCIA, COLOMBIA

Since the Colombian island of San Andrés is a popular stop-over point between Central America and mainland South America, we give a description of the island and neighbouring Providencia here.

COLOMBIA'S Caribbean islands of the San Andrés and Providencia archipelago are 480 km N of the South American coast, 400 km SW of Jamaica, and 180 km E of Nicaragua. This proximity has led Nicaragua to claim them from Colombia in the past. They are small and attractive, but very expensive by South American standards. Nevertheless, with their surrounding islets and cays, they are a popular holiday and shopping resort. Colombia itself encompasses a number of distinct regions, the most marked difference being between the sober peoples of the Andean highlands (in which the capital, Bogotá, is built) and the more light-hearted *costeños*, or people of the coast. The islands belong in the latter category, but, owing to their location, have more in common with the Caribbean's history of piracy, planters and their slaves than with Colombia's rich imperial past. The original inhabitants, mostly black, speak some English, but the population has swollen with unrestricted immigration from Colombia. There are also Chinese and Middle Eastern communities. The population in 1992 was about 41,580.

History and Economy Before the European explorers and pirates came upon the islands, Miskito fisherman from Central America are known to have visited them. The date of European discovery is subject to controversy; some say Columbus found them in 1502, others that Alonso de Ojedo's landing in 1510 was the first. The earliest mention is on a 1527 map. Although the Spaniards were uninterested in them, European navies and pirates recognized the group's strategic importance. The first permanent settlement, called Henrietta, was not set up until 1629, by English puritans. The first slaves were introduced in 1633, to extract timber and plant cotton, but in that century, pirates held sway. Henry Morgan had his headquarters at San Andrés; the artificial Aury channel between Providencia and Santa Catalina is named after another pirate of that time. Although more planters arrived in the eighteenth century from Jamaica, England agreed in 1786 that the islands should be included in the Dominions of Spain. In 1822 they became Colombian possessions. After the abolition of slavery in 1837, coconut production replaced cotton and remained the mainstay of the economy until disease ruined the trade in the 1920s. In 1953, San Andrés was declared a freeport, introducing its present activities of tourism and commerce.

The main problem is deteriorating water and electricity supplies (in most hotels the water is salty). Being a customs-free zone, San Andrés is very crowded with Colombian shoppers looking for foreign-made bargains. Although alcoholic drinks are cheap, essential goods are extremely costly, and electronic goods are more expensive than in the UK.

Festivals 20 July: independence celebrations on San Andrés with various events. Providencia holds its carnival in June.

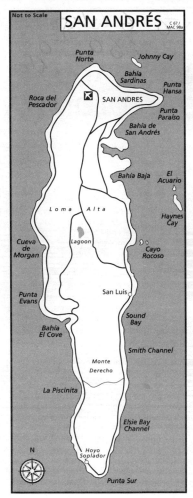

SAN ANDRÉS C 67 /
MAC 98a

Not to Scale

Punta Norte
Johnny Cay
Bahía Sardinas
Punta Hansa
Roca del Pescador
SAN ANDRES
Punta Paraíso
Bahía de San Andrés
Bahía Baja
El Acuario
Loma Alta
Haynes Cay
Cueva de Morgan
Lagoon
Cayo Rocoso
Punta Evans
San Luis
Sound Bay
Bahía El Cove
Smith Channel
Monte Derecho
La Piscinita
Elsie Bay Channel
N
Hoyo Soplador
Punta Sur

San Andrés

San Andrés is of coral, some 11 km long, rising at its highest to 104m. The town, commercial centre, major hotel sector and airport are at the northern end. A picturesque road circles the island. Places to see, besides the beautiful cays and beaches on the eastern side, are the Hoyo Soplador (South End), a geyser-like hole through which the sea spouts into the air most surprisingly when the wind is in the right direction. The W side is less spoilt, but there are no beaches on this side. Instead there is The Cove, the island's deepest anchorage, and Morgan's Cave (Cueva de Morgan, reputed hiding place for the pirate's treasure) which is penetrated by the sea through an underwater passage. At The Cove, the road either continues round the coast, or crosses the centre of the island back to town over La Loma, on which is a Baptist Church, built in 1847.

Hotels NB Some hotels raise their prices by 20-30% on 15 December. *Bahía Marina*, road to San Luis Km 5, T 23539, luxury resort; **A+** *Aquarium*, Av Colombia 1-19, T 23120, F 26174, all suites; **A+** *Casablanca*, Av Colombia y Costa Rica, T 25950, central, food; **A+** *Casa Dorada*, Av Las Américas, T 24008, salt water washing, reasonable food; *Decamerón*, road to San Luis Km 15, book through *Decamerón Cartagena*, T 655-4400, F 653-738, all-inclusive resort, pool, a/c, TV, good restaurant, rec; **A+** *Royal Abacoa*, Av Colombia No 2-41, good restaurant, T 24043; **A+** *Cacique Toné*, Av Colombia, No 5-02, T 24251, deluxe, air conditioning, pool, on sea-front.

A *Tiuna*, Av Colombia No 3-59, T 23235, a/c, swimming pool. New expensive hotel, *Mary Land*, nr airport and beach (no details, 1993); **B** *Abacoa*, Av Colombia, T 4133/4, with bath and a/c; **A** *Bahía Sardinas*, Av Colombia No 4-24, T 23793, across the street from the beach, a/c, TV, fridge, good service, comfortable, clean, no swimming pool; **B** *Capri*, Av Costa Rica No 1A-64, T 24315, with bath and a/c, good value; **A** *El Isleño* Av de la Playa 3-59, T 23990, F 23126, 2 blocks from airport, in palm grove, good sea views; **B** *Nueva Aurora*, Av de las Américas No 3-46, T 23811, fan and private bath, pool, restaurant; **A** *El Dorado*, Av Colombia No 1A-25, T 24057, a/c, restaurant, casino, swimming pool; **D** *Coliseo*, Av Colombia No 1-59, T 23330, friendly, noisy, good restaurant; **A** *Verde Mar*, Av 20 de Julio, T 25525, quiet and friendly, a/c, rec. **C** *Mediterráneo*, Av Los Libertadores, T 26722, clean, friendly, poor water supply.

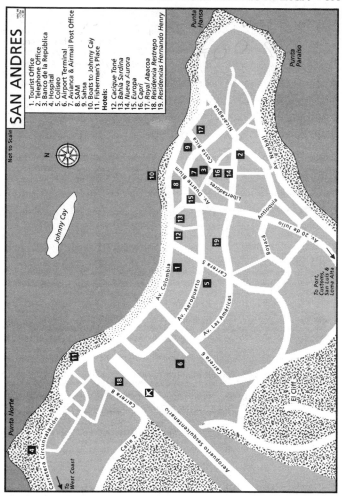

SAN ANDRES

Not to Scale

1. Tourist Office
2. Telephone Office
3. Banco de la República
4. Hospital
5. Coliseo
6. Airport Terminal
7. Avianca & Airmail Post Office
8. SAM
9. Sahsa
10. Boats to Johnny Cay
11. Fisherman's Place

Hotels:
12. Cacique Toné
13. Bahía Serdina
14. Nueva Aurora
15. Europa
16. Capri
17. Royal Abacoa
18. Residencia Restrepo
19. Residencias Hernando Henry

D *Residencias Hernando Henry*, Av de las Américas 4-84, T 26416, restaurant, fan, clean, good value, often full, on road from airport; *Residencia Restrepo*, 'gringo hotel', Av 8 near airport, noisy ('share a room with a Boeing 727'—till midnight), much cheaper than others, F, or less for a hammock in the porch, but you get what you pay for, the accommodation is in a poor state and the grounds are a junkyard, not rec. On the way to *Restrepo* you pass a good food shop, breakfast, juices, snacks. Campsite at South End said to be dirty and mosquito-ridden.

Restaurants *Oasis* (good), Av Colombia No 4-09; *Popular*, on Av Bogotá, good square meal; *El Pimentón*, Av de las Américas, good *menú*, cheap; *El Zaguán de los Arrieros*, Av 20 de Julio (50m after cinema), good food and value; *Bahía*, good food; *Fonda Antioqueña Nos 1 and 2*, on Av Colombia near the main beach, and Av Colombia at Av Nicaragua, best value for fish; *Sea Food House*, Av 20 de Julio, at Parque Bolívar, good cooking, not expensive, second floor terrace; excellent fruit juices at *Jugolandia*, Calle 20 de Julio; *Jugosito*, Av Colombia, 1½ blocks from tourist office towards centre, cheap meals; *Nueva China*, next to *Restrepo*, reasonable Chinese. *Fisherman's Place*, in the fishing cooperative at N end of main beach, very good, simple. Fish meals for US$2.50 can be bought at San Luis beach.

Island Travel Buses cover the eastern side of the island all day (15 mins intervals), US$0.25 (more at night and on holidays). A 'tourist train' (suitably converted tractor and carriages) tours the island in 3 hrs for US$3. Taxis round the island, US$8; to airport, US$3.50; in town, US$0.60; colectivo to airport, US$0.50.

Boat transport: Cooperativa de Lancheros, opposite *Hotel Abacoa*.

Vehicle Rental Bicycles are a popular way of getting around on the island and are easy to hire, eg opposite *El Dorado Hotel*—usually in poor condition, choose your own bike and check all parts thoroughly (US$1.10 per hour, US$6 per day); motorbikes also easy to hire, US$3.50 per hour. Cars can be hired for US$15 for 2 hrs, with US$6 for every extra hour.

Culture San Andrés and Providencia are famous in Colombia for their music, whose styles include the local form of calypso, soca, reggae and church music. A number of good local groups perform on the islands and in Colombia. Concerts are held at the Old Coliseum (every Saturday at 2100 in the high season); the Green Moon Festival is held in May. There is a cultural centre at Punta Hansa in San Andrés town (T 25518).

Exchange Banco Industrial Colombiano, Av Costa Rica; Banco de Bogotá will advance pesos on a Visa card. Aerodisco shop at airport will change dollars cash anytime at rates slightly worse than banks, or try the Photo Shop on Av Costa Rica. Many shops will change US$ cash; it is impossible to change travellers' cheques at weekends. (Airport employees will exchange US$ cash at a poor rate.)

Tourist Information Avenida Colombia No 5-117, English spoken, maps.

Marine Life and Watersports Diving off San Andrés is very good; depth varies from 10 to 100 feet, visibility from 30 to 100 feet. There are 3 types of site: walls of sea-weed and minor coral reefs, large groups of different types of coral, and underwater plateaux with much marine life. 70% of the insular platform is divable. Names of some of the sites are: The Pyramid, Big Channel, Carabela Blue, Blue Hole, Blowing Hole, The Cove and Small Mountain/La Montañita.

Diving trips to the reef cost US$60 with Pedro Montoya at Aquarium diving shop, Punta Hansa, T 26649; also Buzos del Caribe, Centro Comercial Dann, T 23712; both offer diving courses and equipment hire.

For the less-adventurous, take a morning boat (20 mins, none in the afternoon) to the so-called Aquarium (US$3 return), off Haynes Key, where, using a mask and wearing sandals as protection against sea-urchins, you can see colourful fish. Snorkelling equipment can be hired on San Andrés for US$4-5, but it is better and cheaper on the shore than on the island.

Pedalos can be rented for US$4 per hour. Windsurfing and sunfish sailing rental and lessons are available from Bar Boat, road to San Luis (opposite the naval base), 1000-1800 daily (also has floating bar, English and German spoken), and Windsurf Spot, *Hotel Isleño*, T 23990; water-skiing at Water Spot, *Hotel Aquarium*, T 23117, and Jet Sky. From Tominos Marina there are boat trips around the island. Bay trips for 2 hrs cost US$8.75, for 4 hrs US$17.50, including 3 free rum-and-cokes.

Beaches and Cays Boats go in the morning from San Andrés to Johnny Key with a white beach and parties all day Sunday (US$3 return, you can go in one boat and return in another). Apart from those already mentioned, other cays and islets in the archipelago are Bolívar, Albuquerque, Algodón/Cotton (included in the Sunrise Park development in San Andrés), Rocky, the Grunt, Serrana, Serranilla and Quitasueño.

On San Andrés the beaches are in town and on the eastern coast (some of the most populated ones have been reported dirty). Perhaps the best is at San Luis and Bahía Sonora/Sound Bay.

Providencia

Providencia, commonly called Old Providence (3,000 inhabitants), 80 km back to the N-NE from San Andrés, is 7 km long and is more mountainous than San Andrés, rising to 610m. There are waterfalls, and the land drops steeply into the sea in places. Superb views can be had by climbing from Casabaja/Bottom House or Aguamansa/Smooth Water to the peak. There are relics of the fortifications

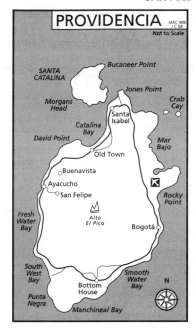

built on the island during its disputed ownership. Horse riding is available, and boat trips can be made to neighbouring islands such as **Santa Catalina** (an old pirate lair separated from Providencia by a channel cut for their better defence), and to the NE, Cayo Cangrejo/Crab Cay (beautiful swimming and snorkelling) and Cayos Hermanos/Brothers Cay. Trips from 1000-1500 cost about US$7 pp. On the W side of Santa Catalina is a rock formation called Morgan's Head; seen from the side it looks like a man's profile.

On Providencia the 3 main beaches are Bahía Manzanillo/ Manchincal Bay, the largest, most attractive and least developed, Bahía del Suroeste/ South West Bay and Bahía Agua Dulce/ Freshwater Bay, all in the SW.

Like San Andrés, it is an expensive island. There is no bank, best to take sufficient pesos with you, exchange rates from shops and hotels are poor. Alternatively, use credit cards. The sea food is good, water and fresh milk are generally a problem. English is widely spoken. Day tours are arranged by the Providencia office in San Andrés, costing US$30 inclusive. SAM fly from San Andrés, US$35, 25 mins, up to 5 times a day, bookable only in San Andrés. (Return flight has to be confirmed at the airport, where there is a tourist office.) Boat trips from San Andrés take 8 hrs, but are not regular.

Hotels Most of the accommodation is at Freshwater (Playa Agua Dulce): **B** *Cabañas El Recreo* (Captain Brian's, T 48010), **A+** *Cabañas El Paraíso* (T 26330, a/c, TV, fridge; **B** *Cabañas Aguadulce Miss Elma's* recommended for cheap food; also *Morgan's Bar* for fish meals and a good breakfast. On Santa Catalina is the German-owned *Cabañas Santa Catalina*, friendly, use of small kitchen. Several houses take in guests. Camping is possible at Freshwater Bay. Truck drivers who provide transport on the island may be able to advise on accommodation.

Cartagena and Barranquilla

Mention should be made here of the 2 Caribbean cities on the mainland to which access is made from San Andrés, Cartagena and Barranquilla.

Cartagena, old and steeped in history, is one of the most interesting towns in South America, and should not be missed if you are taking this route. As well as the historical sites, Cartagena also has a popular beach resort at Bocagrande, a 10-mins bus ride from the city centre. Cartagena de Indias, to give it its full name, was founded on 13 January, 1533, as one of the storage points for merchandise sent out from Spain and for treasure collected from the Americas to be sent back to Spain. A series of forts protecting the approaches from the sea, and the formidable walls built around the city, made it almost impregnable. All the same, it was challenged again and again by enemies. Sir Francis Drake, with

1,300 men, broke in successfully in 1586. The Frenchmen Baron de Pointis and Ducasse, with 10,000 men, sacked the city in 1697. But the strongest attack of all, by Sir Edward Vernon with 27,000 men and 3,000 pieces of artillery, failed in 1741 after besieging the city for 56 days. It was defended by the 1-eyed, 1-armed, 1-legged hero Blas de Lezo.

A full description of the city, with its churches, forts, colonial streets and other attractions, is given in *The South American Handbook*.

Barranquilla (also described in detail in *The South American Handbook*) is Colombia's fourth city, with almost 2 million people. It is a modern, industrial sea and river port on the W bank of the Magdalena, one of the country's main waterways. The 4-day Carnival in February is undoubtedly the best in Colombia.

INFORMATION FOR VISITORS

Documents A passport is always necessary; an onward ticket is officially necessary, but is not always asked for at land borders. Visitors are sometimes asked to prove that they have US$20 for each day of their stay (US$10 for students). You are given 90 days permission to stay on entry. Extensions (*salvoconducto*) for 15-day periods can be applied for at the DAS office in any major city up to a maximum of 6 months (including the first 90 days). Application must be made within 3 weeks of the expiry of the first 90 days and 2 weeks are needed for authorization from the Ministerio de Relaciones Exteriores in Bogotá. The 30-day extension runs from the day authorization is received by the DAS office (so if you apply on the last of your 90 days you could get 30 days more). Leaving the country and re-entering to get a new permit is not always allowed. To visit Colombia as a tourist, nationals of only China, Taiwan and Haiti need a visa (this information was correct according to the Colombian consulate in London, May 1994). You must check regulations before leaving your home country. Visas are issued only by Colombian consulates. When a visa is required you must be prepared to show 3 photographs, police clearance and medical certificates, an application form (£11 or equivalent), as well as a passport (allow 48 hrs). Various business and temporary visas are needed for foreigners who have to reside in Colombia for a length of time. Fees range from £54 (or equivalent) for a student visa, £90 for a business visa, to £131 for a working visa. You may find that your onward ticket, which you must show before you can obtain a visa, is stamped 'non-refundable'. If you do not receive an entry card when flying in, the information desk will issue one, and restamp your passport for free. Note that to leave Colombia you must get an exit stamp from the DAS (security police). They often do not have offices at the small frontier towns, so try to get your stamp in a main city, and save time.

NB It is highly recommended that you have your passport photocopied, and witnessed by a notary. This is a valid substitute (although some travellers report difficulties with this variant) and your passport can then be put into safe-keeping. Also, photocopy your travellers' cheques, airline ticket and any other essential documents. For more information, check with your consulate.

How To Get There By Air San Andrés is a popular stopover on the routes from Central America to Colombia. By changing planes in San Andrés you can save money on flight fares. SAM flies to Guatemala City, Panama City and San José, Costa Rica, Aero Costa Rica also flies to San José. Note that Panama, Costa Rica and Honduras all require onward tickets which cannot be bought on San Andrés, but can be in Cartagena. SAM office in San Andrés town will not issue one way tickets to Central America (although the airport office is reported to do so). You buy a return and the SAM office on the mainland will refund once you show an onward ticket. The refund (less 15%) may not be immediate. Avianca and SAM have flights to most major Colombian cities: SAM to Barranquilla, Bogotá, Bucaramanga, Cali, Cartagena, Cúcuta, Medellín; Avianca to Bogotá with connections to many other cities; Aces flies to Bogotá and Medellín; Intercontinental de Aviación to Cali and Medellín; Aerorepública to Cali. With SAM you can arrange a stop-over in Cartagena, which is good value; the onward flight from Cartagena to Bogotá, Cali and Medellín does not cost much more than the bus fare and saves a lot of time.

Airport Information San Andrés airport is 15 mins' walk to town (taxi US$3 pp). All airline offices are in town (Avianca and SAM on Av Duarte Blum), except Aces at the airport. Improvement of the airport was undertaken in 1992/93. There is a customs tax of 15% on some items purchased if you are continuing to mainland Colombia.

On arrival all visitors have to pay an entry tax of US$15 (on it is stamped 'Welcome Home'!). There is a Colombian airport exit tax of US$18 (in cash, dollars or pesos), from which only travellers staying less than 24 hrs are exempt. When you arrive, ensure that all necessary documentation bears a stamp for your date of arrival; without it you will have to pay double the exit tax on leaving (with the correct stamp, you will only be charged half the exit tax if you have been in the country less than 60 days). Visitors staying more than 60 days have to pay an extra US$12 tax, which can only be avoided by bona-fide tourists who can produce the card given them on entry. There is a 17% tax on all international air tickets bought in Colombia for flights out of the country (7.5% on international return flights). Do not buy tickets for domestic flights to or from San Andrés island outside Colombia; they are much more expensive. When getting an onward ticket from Avianca for entry into Colombia, reserve a seat only and ask for confirmation in writing, otherwise you will pay twice as much as if purchasing the ticket inside Colombia.

Sunday flights are always heavily booked. In July and August, December and January, it is very difficult to get on flights into and out of San Andrés; book in advance if possible. If wait-listed for a flight, do not give up, most passengers get on a plane. Checking in for flights can be difficult because of queues of shoppers with their goods.

If flying from Guatemala to Colombia with SAM, via San Andrés, you have to purchase a round-trip ticket, refundable only in Guatemala. To get around this (if you are not going back to Guatemala) you will have to try to arrange a ticket swap with a traveller going in the other direction on San Andrés. There is, however, no difficulty in exchanging a round-trip ticket for a San Andrés-Colombian ticket with the airline, but you have to pay extra.

Flights To Colombia British Airways has a twice-weekly service from London to **Bogotá**, via Caracas. Airlines with services from continental Europe are Air France, Iberia, Alitalia, and Lufthansa. Avianca, the Colombian national airline, flies from Frankfurt, Paris and Madrid. Frequent services to and from the USA by Avianca, Aces, Continental and American.

Avianca flies from Miami and Newark to **Cartagena**; the same airline flies from **Barranquilla** to Miami (as does American, daily), Newark (also Continental via Houston), Aruba (also SAM) and Curaçao.

Customs Duty-free admission is granted for portable typewriters, radios, binoculars, personal and ciné cameras, but all must show use; 200 cigarettes or 50 cigars or 250 grams of tobacco or up to 250 grams of manufactured tobacco in any form, 2 bottles of liquor or wine per person.

How To Get There By Sea Cruise ships and tours go to San Andrés; there are no other, official passenger services by sea. Cargo ships are not supposed to carry passengers to the mainland, but many do. If you want to leave by sea, speak only to the ship's captain. (Any other offer of tickets on ships to/from San Andrés, or of a job on a ship, may be a con trick.) Sometimes the captain may take you for free, otherwise he will charge anything between US$10-25; the sea crossing takes 3-4 days, depending on the weather. In Cartagena, ships leave from the Embarcadero San Andrés, opposite the Plaza de la Aduana.

Car Rental National driving licences may be used by foreigners in Colombia, but must be accompanied by an official translation if in a language other than Spanish. International drivers licences are also accepted. Carry driving documents with you at all times. Even if you are paying in cash, a credit card may be asked for as proof of identity (Visa, Mastercard, American Express), in addition to passport and driver's licence (see also **credit cards, p 789**).

Hotels There is a tourist tax of 5% on rooms and an insurance charge, but no service charge, and tipping is at discretion. The Colombian tourist office has lists of authorized prices for all hotels which are usually at least a year out of date. If you are overcharged the tourist office will arrange a refund. Most hotels in Colombia charge US$1 to US$6 for extra beds for children, up to a maximum (usually) of 4 beds per room.

Food Colombia's food is very regional; it is quite difficult to buy in one area a dish you particularly liked in another. If you are economizing, ask for the *'plato del día'* or *'plato corriente'* (dish of the day). Of the Caribbean dishes, Cartagena's rice with coconut can be compared with rice *a la valenciana*; an egg *empanada*, consists of 2 layers of corn (maize) dough that open like an oyster-shell, fried with eggs in the middle, and try the *patacón*, a cake of mashed and baked plantain (green banana). *Huevos pericos*, eggs scrambled with onions and tomatoes, are a popular, cheap and nourishing snack for the impecunious—available almost anywhere. Throughout the country there is an abundance of fruits: bananas, oranges, mangoes, avocado pears, and (at least in the tropical zones) *chirimoyas, papayas*, and the delicious *pitahaya*, taken either as an appetizer or dessert and, for the wise, in moderation, because even a little of it has a laxative effect. Other fruits such as the *guayaba* (guava), *guanábana* (soursop), *maracuyá* (passion fruit), *lulo* (*naranjilla*), *mora* (blackberry) and *curuba* make delicious juices, sometimes with milk added to make a *sorbete*—satisfy yourself, though, that the milk is fresh. Fruit yoghurts are nourishing and cheap (try *Alpina* brand; *crema* style is best).

Drink *Tinto*, the national small cup of black coffee, is taken ritually at all hours. Colombian coffee is always mild. (Coffee with milk is called *café perico*; *café con leche* is a mug of milk with coffee added.) *Agua de panela* is a common beverage (hot water with unrefined sugar), also made with limes, milk, or cheese. Many acceptable brands of beer are produced. The local rum is good and cheap; ask for *ron*, not *aguardiente*, because in Colombia the latter word is used for a popular drink containing aniseed (*aguardiente anisado*).

Warning Great care should be exercised when buying imported spirits in shops. It has been reported that bottles bearing well-known labels have often been 'recycled' and contain a cheap and poor imitation of the original contents. This can be dangerous to the health, and travellers are warned to stick to beer and rum. Also note that ice is usually not made from potable water.

Tipping Hotels and restaurants 10%. Porters, cloakroom attendants, hairdressers and barbers, US$0.05-0.25. Taxi-drivers are not tipped.

Shopping Local handicrafts are made from coral and coconut. Otherwise shopping is concentrated on the duty-free items so readily available. Typical Colombian products which are good buys: emeralds, leatherwork and handworked silver.

Currency The monetary unit is the peso, divided into 100 centavos. There are coins of 5, 10, 20 and 50 pesos; there are notes of 100, 200, 500, 1,000, 2,000, 5,000 and 10,000 pesos. Large notes of over 1,000 pesos are often impossible to spend on small purchases as change is in short supply, especially in small cities, and in the morning. There is a limit of US$25,000 import of foreign currency, with the export limit set at the equivalent of the amount brought in. Travellers' cheques can in theory be exchanged in any bank, except the Banco de la República which, since June 1991, no longer undertakes exchange transactions. There are some legitimate *casas de cambio*, which are quicker to use than banks. Always check which rate of exchange is being offered. Hotels may give very poor rates of exchange, especially if you are paying in dollars, but practice varies. Owing to the quantity of counterfeit American Express travellers' cheques in circulation, travellers may experience difficulty in cashing these cheques, but the procedure is always slow, involving finger printing and photographs. A photocopy of your passport will be taken; you may have to provide your own, so take a supply. It is also very difficult, according to our correspondents, to get reimbursement for lost American Express travellers cheques. Take Thomas Cook's or a US bank's dollar traveller cheques in small denominations, but better still take a credit card (see below). Sterling travellers' cheques are practically impossible to change in Colombia.

As it is unwise to carry large quantities of cash, **credit cards** are widely used, especially Mastercard and Visa; Diner's Club is also used, while American Express is only accepted in high-priced establishments in Bogotá. Branches of Banco de Colombia and Banco Popular advance pesos against Visa, and Banco Industrial de Colombia give cash advances against Mastercard (Cajeo BIC for ATMs). In 1993-94 cash advances against credit cards gave the best rates of exchange. American Express cards are rarely accepted for cash advances.

Note In 1993-94, there were so many dollars in circulation (as a result of drugs trafficking) that it was very difficult to change dollars into pesos. Banks were reluctant to do so for anyone but account holders. The official rate of exchange was much higher than the street rate. In general, the best option was to use a Visa or Mastercard credit card.

Security Carry your passport (or photocopy) at all times.

Avoid money changers on the street who offer over-favourable rates of exchange. They often short-change you or run off with your money, pretending that the police are coming. Beware of counterfeit dollars and pesos.

Colombia is part of a major drug-smuggling route. Police and customs activities have greatly intensified and smugglers increasingly try to use innocent carriers. Travellers are warned against carrying packages for other people without checking the contents (even taking your own books, packages or gift-wrapped parcels through customs may cause problems). Penalties run up to 12 years in none too comfortable jails. Be very polite if approached by policemen. If your hotel room is raided by police looking for drugs, try, if possible, to get a witness to prevent drugs being planted on you. Colombians who offer you drugs may well be setting you up for the police, who are very active on the N coast and San Andrés island.

If someone accosts you on the street, saying he's a plain-clothes policeman or drugs officer, and asks you to go to his office, offer to go with him to the nearest policeman (the tourist police where possible) or police station. He may well be a 'confidence man' (if he doesn't ask to see your passport, he almost certainly is). These conmen usually work in pairs.

Health Emergency medical treatment is given in hospitals: if injured in a bus accident, for example, you will be covered by insurance and treatment will be free. Take water sterilizer with you, or boil the water, or use the excellent mineral waters, when travelling outside the capital. Choose your food and eating places with care everywhere. Hepatitis is common; get protection before your trip. There is some risk of malaria and yellow fever in the coastal areas; prophylaxis is advised.

Climate And Clothing Tropical clothing is needed in the hot and humid climate of the coast. Average temperature on the islands is 27-31°C.

Tourist Seasons On the Caribbean coast and San Andrés and Providencia, high season is 15 December-30 April, 15 June-31 August.

Working Hours Monday to Friday, commercial firms work 0800-1200 and from 1400-1730 or 1800. Government offices follow the same hours on the whole as the commercial firms, but generally prefer to do business with the public in the afternoon only. Embassy hours for the public are from 0900-1200 and from 1400-1700 (weekdays). Bank hours in San Andrés are 0800-1100, 1400-1500 Monday to Friday, Saturday am only. Shopping hours are 0900-1230 and 1430-1830, including Saturday.

Public Holidays Circumcision of our Lord (1 January), Epiphany* (6 January), St Joseph* (19 March), Maundy Thursday, Good Friday, Labour Day (1 May), Ascension Day*, Corpus Christi*, Sacred Heart*, SS Peter and Paul* (29 June), Independence Day (20 July), Battle of Boyacá (7 August), Assumption* (15 August), Discovery of America* (12 October), All Saints' Day* (1 November), Independence of Cartagena* (11 November), Immaculate Conception (8 December), Christmas Day (25 December).

When those marked with an asterisk do not fall on a Monday, or when they fall on a Sunday, they will be moved to the following Monday.

Time Zone Eastern Standard Time—5 hrs behind GMT.

Useful Addresses DAS (immigration authorities) are at the San Andrés airport, T 25540. (In Cartagena, DAS is just beyond Castillo San Felipe, behind the church-ask, helpful, T 664649. San Andrés Police, T 14; Red Cross, T 3333; Panamanian Consulate, Av Atlántico No 1A-60, T 26545. Other diplomatic representation in Barranquilla, Cartagena, or Bogotá.

Weights And Measures Metric; weights should always be quoted in kilograms. Litres are used for liquid measures but US gallons are standard for the petroleum industry. Linear measures are usually metric, but the inch is quite commonly used by engineers and the yard on golf courses. For land measurement the hectare and cubic metre are officially employed but the traditional measures *vara* (80 cm) and *fanegada* (1,000 square *varas*) are still in common use. Food etc is often sold in *libras* (pounds), which are equivalent to ½ kilo.

Electric Current 120 volts AC Transformer must be 110-150 volt AC, with flat-prong plugs (all of same size). Be careful with electrically heated showers.

Postal Services Send all letters by airmail. Avianca controls all airmail services and has offices in provincial cities (Catalina Building, Av Duarte Blum in San Andrés). Correspondence with UK is reported to be good. It costs US$0.35 to send a letter or postcard to the US or Europe; a 1 kg package to Europe costs US$13 by air (Avianca).

Telecommunications Systems have been automated; the larger towns are interconnected. Inter-city calls and cables must be made from Telecom offices unless you have access to a private phone (Telecom in San Andrés: Av Américas No 2A-23). Long-distance pay 'phones are located outside most Telecom offices, also at bus stations and airports. They take 50 peso coins (at San Andrés airport, advice and exchange for phone usage is available). 5 peso coins are needed for ordinary phones which also take 20 peso coins. From the larger towns it is possible to telephone to Canada, the USA, the UK, and to several of the Latin American republics. International phone charges are high about US$6 a minute to USA, US$8 to Europe, US$12 to Australia), but there is a 20% discount on Sunday. A deposit is required before the call is made which can vary between US$18 and US$36 (try bargaining it down), US$1 is charged if no reply, for person-to-person add an extra minute's charge to Canada, 2 mins' to UK; all extra minutes' conversation cost ⅓ more. The best value is to purchase a phone card and dial direct yourself. AT&T's USA Direct service can be dialled on 980-11-0010. Canada Direct is 980-19-0057; UK Direct 980-44-0057. Collect, or reversed-charge, telephone calls are only possible from private telephones; make sure the operator understands what is involved or you may be billed in any case. It is also possible that the operator, once you have got through to him/her, may not call you back. The surest way of contacting home, assuming the facilities are available at each end, is to fax your hotel phone number to home and ask them to call you.

Tourist Information In San Andrés, Corporación Nacional de Turismo (CNT), Avenida Colombia No 5-117, English spoken, maps, friendly. CNT has its headquarters at Calle 28, No 13A-59, **Bogotá** (T 284-3761); it has branches in every departmental capital and other places of interest (in **Cartagena**, Av Blas de Lezo, Ed Muelle de los Pegasos, Empresa Promotora de Turismo de Cartagena, or CNT, Calle de la Factoría, Cra 3, No 36-57; in **Barranquilla**, Carrera 54 No 75-45, T 454458). They should be visited as early as possible not only for information on accommodation and transport, but also for details on areas which are dangerous to visit.

CNT also has offices in **New York**: 140 East 57th St, T 688-0151; **Caracas**: Planta Baja 5 Av Urdaneta Ibarras a Pelota, T 561-3592/5805; **Madrid**: Calle Princesa No 17 Tercero Izquierda, T 248-5090/5690; and **Paris**: 9, Boulevard de la Madeleine, 75001 Paris, T 260-3565.

TEMPERATURE CONVERSION TABLE

°C	°F	°C	°F	°C	°F	°C	°F	°C	°F
1	34	11	52	21	70	31	88	41	106
2	36	12	54	22	72	32	90	42	108
3	38	13	56	23	74	33	92	43	109
4	39	14	57	24	75	34	93	44	111
5	41	15	59	25	77	35	95	45	113
6	43	16	61	26	79	36	97	46	115
7	45	17	63	27	81	37	99	47	117
8	46	18	64	28	82	38	100	48	118
9	48	19	66	29	84	39	102	49	120
10	50	20	68	30	86	40	104	50	122

The formula for converting °C to °F is: °C x 9 ÷ 5 + 32 = °F

CLIMATIC TABLES

The following tables have been very kindly furnished by Mr R K Headland. Each weather station is given with its altitude in metres (m). Temperatures (Centigrade) are given as averages for each month; the first line is the maximum and the second the minimum. The third line is the average number of wet days encountered in each month.

MEXICO AND CENTRAL AMERICA

	Jan	Feb	Mar	Apr	May	Jun	Jul	Aug	Sep	Oct	Nov	Dec
Acapulco, Mexico	29	31	31	31	32	32	32	32	31	31	31	31
3m	21	21	21	22	23	24	24	24	24	23	22	21
	0	0	0	0	2	9	7	7	12	6	1	0
Guatemala City	23	25	27	28	29	27	26	26	26	24	23	22
1490m	11	12	14	14	16	16	16	16	16	15	14	13
	2	2	2	5	8	20	17	16	17	13	6	2
Havana	26	27	28	29	30	31	31	32	31	29	27	26
49m	18	18	19	21	22	23	24	24	24	23	21	19
	6	4	4	4	7	10	9	10	11	11	7	6
Managua,	30	30	30	32	32	31	31	31	31	31	30	30
Nicaragua	23	24	26	28	27	26	26	25	26	24	24	24
46m	0	0	0	0	6	12	11	12	15	16	4	1
Mérida, Mexico	28	29	32	33	34	33	33	33	32	31	29	28
22m	17	17	19	21	22	23	23	23	23	22	19	18
	4	2	1	2	5	10	11	12	13	7	3	3
Mexico City	19	21	24	25	26	24	23	23	23	21	20	19
2309m	6	6	8	11	12	13	12	12	12	10	8	6
	2	1	2	6	9	14	19	18	17	8	3	2
Monterrey, Mexico	20	22	24	29	31	33	32	33	30	27	22	18
538m	9	11	14	17	20	22	22	22	21	18	13	10
	3	3	3	4	4	4	4	3	8	5	4	4
Panama City	31	31	32	32	31	30	30	31	30	30	29	30
36m	21	21	22	23	23	23	23	23	23	22	22	23
	4	2	1	6	15	16	15	15	15	16	18	12
San José, Costa Rica	24	24	26	27	27	27	26	26	27	26	25	24
1172m	14	14	15	16	16	16	16	16	16	15	15	15
	1	0	1	4	17	20	18	19	20	22	14	4
San Salvador	30	31	32	32	31	30	30	30	29	29	29	29
700m	16	16	17	19	19	19	18	18	19	18	17	16
	0	3	2	5	12	20	21	20	18	14	4	1
Tegucigalpa,	25	27	29	30	30	28	28	28	29	27	26	25
Honduras	14	14	15	16	18	19	17	17	17	17	16	15
935m	4	2	1	3	14	18	10	10	17	16	8	4

EXCHANGE RATES

COUNTRY	Exchange rate/US$
BELIZE (Belize dollar)	2.00
COSTA RICA (colón)	165.60
EL SALVADOR (colón)	8.71
GUATEMALA (quetzal)	5.71
HONDURAS (lempira)	8.60
MEXICO (Mexican peso)	3.39
NICARAGUA (córdoba oro)	6.70
PANAMA (balboa)	1.00

Exchange rates at 1 July 1994.

WEIGHTS AND MEASURES

Metric

Weight:
1 kilogram (kg) = 2,205 pounds
1 metric ton = 1.102 short tons
            = 0.984 long ton

Length:
1 millimetre (mm) = 0.03937 inch
1 metre = 3.281 feet
1 kilometre (km) = 0.621 mile

Area:
1 hectare = 2.471 acres
1 square km (km^2) = 0.386 sq mile

Capacity:
1 litre = 0.220 Imperial gallon
        = 0.264 US gallon

Volume:
1 cubic metre (m^3) = 35.31 cubic feet
                    = 1.31 cubic yards

British and US

1 pound (lb) = 454 grams
1 short ton (2,000lb) = 0.907 metric ton
1 long ton (2,240lb) = 1.016 metric tons

1 inch = 25.417 millimetres
1 foot (ft) = 0.305 metre
1 mile = 1.609 kilometres

1 acre = 0.405 hectare
1 square mile (sq mile) = 2,590 km^2

1 Imperial gallon = 4.546 litres
1 US gallon = 3.785 litres

(5 Imperial gallons are approximately equal to 6 US gallons)

1 cubic foot (cu ft) = 0.028 m^3
1 cubic yard (cu yd) = 0.765 m^3

NB The *manzana,* used in Central America, is about 0.7 hectare (1.73 acres).

INDEX TO ADVERTISERS

Airlines

Services and Telecommunications

Travel Specialists and Tour Operators

Language Schools

INDEX

The key used is as follows: Archaeological site ▲; Beach or Marine Resort ♠; Colonial City ✤; Festival (religious or otherwise) ☆; Historical site ✳; Inland Resort ✺; Market or Traditional Shopping ✿; National Park, Natural Feature, Recommended Zoological or Botanical Garden ◆; People ▢.

Index Key: Colonial City ◆; Festival ☆; Inland Resort ✳; Market ❀; Historical site ✳; People ❑; Archaeological site ▲; National Park ◆; Beach ♠.

Index Key: Colonial City ✤; Festival ☆; Inland Resort ✳; Market ✿; Historical site ✳; People
❑; Archaeological site ▲; National Park ◆; Beach ♠.

Index Key: Colonial City ✦; Festival ☆; Inland Resort ✱; Market ✿; Historical site ✱; People ❏; Archaeological site ▲; National Park ◆; Beach ♠.

Index Key: Colonial City ✛; Festival ☆; Inland Resort ✱; Market ✿; Historical site ✱; People ❑; Archaeological site ▲; National Park ◆; Beach ♠.

Index Key: Colonial City ✤; Festival ☆; Inland Resort ✳; Market ✿; Historical site ✳; People ❑; Archaeological site ▲; National Park ◆; Beach ♠.

Index Key: Colonial City ✚; Festival ☆; Inland Resort ✳; Market ✿; Historical site ✳; People □; Archaeological site ▲; National Park ◆; Beach ♠.

Index Key: Colonial City ♣; Festival ☆; Inland Resort ✳; Market ✿; Historical site ✳; People ❑; Archaeological site ▲; National Park ◆; Beach ♠.

Index Key: Colonial City ✤; Festival ☆; Inland Resort ✳; Market ✿; Historical site ✤; People ☐; Archaeological site ▲; National Park ◆; Beach ♠.

Index Key: Colonial City ✤; Festival ☆; Inland Resort ✳; Market ♖; Historical site ✳; People ❏; Archaeological site ▲; National Park ◆; Beach ♠.

Estrella Blanca

$69 9.45
   12.45

$55 Flecha Amarilla
   6.50 7.05
   11.35 18.50
   Estrella Blanca $69
   9.45 12.45 18.15

TNS   Omnibus de Mexico
   6.15   4.30 5.01pm

Index Key: Colonial City ♣; Festival ☆; Inland Resort ✳; Market ✿; Historical site ❋; People ❏; Archaeological site ▲; National Park ◆; Beach ♠.

INDEX TO TOWN AND REGIONAL MAPS

TRADE & TRAVEL
Handbooks

1995

Award-winning guidebooks for all independently minded travellers. This annually updated series of impeccable accuracy and authority now covers over 120 countries, dependencies and dominions from Latin America and the Caribbean across the globe to Africa, India and Southeast Asia.

Practical, pocket sized and excellent value - **Handbooks** take you further.

South American Handbook

Mexico & Central American Handbook

Caribbean Islands Handbook

India Handbook (formerly *South Asian Handbook*)

Thailand & Burma Handbook

Vietnam, Laos & Cambodia Handbook

Indonesia, Malaysia & Singapore Handbook

North African Handbook
includes Andalucía (Moorish southern Spain)

East African Handbook
includes Zanzibar, Madagascar and the Seychelles

Write for our latest catalogue
Trade & Travel, 6 Riverside Court, Lower Bristol Road, Bath BA2 3DZ, England.
Tel 01225 469141   Fax 01225 469461

"More information - less blah!"

TRADE & TRAVEL
Handbooks

1995 VIETNAM LAOS & CAMBODIA HANDBOOK

1995 SOUTH AMERICAN HANDBOOK 71st EDITION

1995 CARIBBEAN ISLANDS HANDBOOK With Bermuda and the Bahamas

1995 INDIA HANDBOOK With Bhutan, Sri Lanka and the Maldives

1995 EAST AFRICAN HANDBOOK With Mauritius, Madagascar, Seychelles

NEW

ALSO IN THE SERIES

MEXICO & CENTRAL AMERICAN HANDBOOK
·
INDONESIA, MALAYSIA & SINGAPORE HANDBOOK
·
THAILAND & BURMA HANDBOOK
·
NORTH AFRICAN HANDBOOK

THE ANNUAL GUIDEBOOK SERIES FOR ALL TRAVELLERS

Write to us for more details.

"Superb – you don't need anything else!"